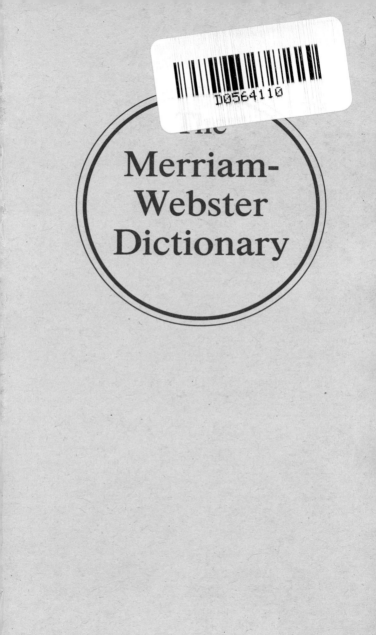

The
Merriam-
Webster
Dictionary

The Merriam-Webster Dictionary

Merriam-Webster, Incorporated
Springfield, Massachusetts

A GENUINE MERRIAM-WEBSTER

The name *Webster* alone is no guarantee of excellence. It is used by a number of publishers and may serve mainly to mislead an unwary buyer.

Merriam-Webster™ is the name you should look for when you consider the purchase of dictionaries or other fine reference books. It carries the reputation of a company that has been publishing since 1831 and is your assurance of quality and authority.

PREFACE

This new edition of *The Merriam-Webster Dictionary* is the seventh in a line of Merriam-Webster paperback dictionaries which began in 1947. It is based on and preserves the best aspects of preceding editions, but it now includes the most important recent vocabulary that was added to *Merriam-Webster's Collegiate Dictionary, Eleventh Edition* over the past decade. Throughout the dictionary, over 8,000 usage examples, including 1,000 that are newly added for this edition, illustrate meanings and help to clarify definitions. All the new material has been based on examples of actual use found in the Merriam-Webster citation files and in edited texts online.

The nearly 65,000 entries and more than 75,000 definitions in this dictionary give coverage to the most frequently used words in the language. The heart of the dictionary is the A-Z vocabulary section, where readers will find information about meaning, spelling, pronunciation, etymology, and synonyms. This section is followed by others that users have long found useful: the section Foreign Words and Phrases covers words and phrases from other languages that often occur in English texts but have not become part of the English vocabulary; the section Biographical Names identifies individuals from history and contemporary culture, as well as biblical, legendary, and mythological characters; the section Geographical Names identifies places of importance in the United States and the world, along with current population figures.

The Merriam-Webster Dictionary has been created by a company that has been publishing dictionaries for more than 150 years and continues to maintain an in-house staff of experienced lexicographers. For this edition, the primary editing of the main A-Z vocabulary section and the Foreign Words and Phrases was done by Senior Editor James G. Lowe. Daniel J. Hopkins edited the Geographical Names, and Michael G. Belanger edited the Biographical Names. Specialist editors included Adrienne M. Scholz for cross-reference, Joshua S. Guenter for pronunciation, James L. Rader for etymology, and Joan I. Narmontas for life science. Data entry and data-file processing were handled by Daniel B. Brandon. Susan L. Brady acted as production editor, guiding the book through its typesetting stages, assisted by Emily A. Vezina. Proofreaders included Tasha Martino Bigelow, Serenity H. Carr, Ilya A. Davidovich, Allison M. DeJordy, Joanne M. Despres, Benjamin T. Korzec, Maria A.

Sansalone, Neil S. Serven, Mark A. Stevens, Paul S. Wood, and Judy Yeh, as well as some of the other editors mentioned above. All the editors join in the hope that users will find *The Merriam-Webster Dictionary* to be a concise, handy, and reliable guide to the English language of today.

EXPLANATORY NOTES

The dictionary contains so much information, that it is necessary to condense much of it to accommodate the limitations of the printed page. This section provides information on the conventions used throughout the dictionary, from the styling of entries and pronunciation to how we present information on usage and meaning. An understanding of the information contained in these notes will make the dictionary both easier and more rewarding to use.

ENTRIES

A boldface letter or a combination of such letters, including punctuation marks and diacritics where needed, that is set flush with the left-hand margin of each column of type is a main entry. The main entry may consist of letters set solid, of letters joined by a hyphen or a diagonal, or of letters separated by one or more spaces:

> alone . . . *adj*
> avant–garde . . . *n*
> and/or . . . *conj*
> assembly language *n*
> av·a·lanche . . . *n*

The material in lightface type that follows each main entry on the same line and on succeeding indented lines presents information about the main entry.

The main entries follow one another in alphabetical order letter by letter: *bill of attainder* follows *billion; Day of Atonement* follows *daylight saving time*. Those containing an Arabic numeral are alphabetized as if the numeral were spelled out: *4-H* comes between *fourfold* and *Four Hundred; 3-D* comes between *three* and *three-dimensional*. Those that often begin with the abbreviation *St.* in common usage have the abbreviation spelled out: *Saint Valentine's Day*. Main entries that begin with *Mc* are alphabetized just as they are spelled.

A pair of guide words is printed at the top of each page. These indicate that the entries falling alphabetically between the words at the top of the outer column of each page are found on that page.

The guide words are the first and last main entries printed on the page:

archway • armadillo

When one main entry has exactly the same written form as another, the two are distinguished by superscript numerals preceding each word:

> [1]melt . . . *vb*
> [2]melt *n*
> [1]pine . . . *n*
> [2]pine *vb*

Full words come before parts of words made up of the same letters; solid compounds come before hyphenated compounds; hyphenated compounds come before open compounds; and lowercase entries come before those with an initial capital:

²**super** *n*
super- . . . *prefix*
run·down . . . *n*
run–down . . . *adj*
run down *vb*
dutch . . . *adv*
Dutch . . . *n*

The centered dots within entry words indicate division points at which a hyphen may be put at the end of a line of print or writing. Thus the noun *cap·puc·ci·no* may be ended on one line and continued on the next in this manner:

> *cap-*
>
> *puccino*
>
> > *cappuc-*
> >
> > *cino*
> >
> > > *cappucci-*
> > >
> > > *no*

Centered dots are not shown after a single initial letter or before a single terminal letter because typesetters seldom cut off a single letter:

abyss . . . *n*
flighty . . . *adj*
idea . . . *n*

Nor are they usually shown at the second and succeeding homographs unless they differ among themselves:

¹**sig·nal** . . : *n*
²**signal** *vb*
³**signal** *adj*
but
¹**min·ute** . . . *n*
²**mi·nute** . . . *adj*

There are acceptable alternative end-of-line divisions just as there are acceptable variant spellings and pronunciations, but no more than one division is shown for any entry in this dictionary.

A double hyphen at the end of a line in this dictionary (as in the definition at **cod**) stands for a hyphen that is retained when the word is written as a unit on one line. This kind of fixed hyphen is always represented in boldface words in this dictionary with an en dash, longer than an ordinary hyphen.

When a main entry is followed by the word *or* and another spelling, the two spellings are equal variants. Both are standard, and either one may be used according to personal inclination:

ocher *or* **ochre**

If two variants joined by *or* are out of alphabetical order, they remain equal variants. The one printed first is, however, slightly more common than the second:

¹**plow** *or* **plough**

When another spelling is joined to the main entry by the word *also*, the spelling after *also* is a secondary variant and occurs less frequently than the first:

ab·sinthe *also* **ab·sinth**

Secondary variants belong to standard usage and may be used according to personal inclination. Once the word *also* is used to signal a secondary variant, all following secondary variants are joined by *or*:

²**wool·ly** *also* **wool·ie** *or* **wooly**

Variants whose spelling puts them alphabetically more than a column away from the main entry are entered at their own alphabetical places as well as at the applicable main entry:

²**gage** *var of* GAUGE
. . .
¹**gauge** *also* **gage**
²**gauge** *also* **gage**

Variants having a usage label appear only at their own alphabetical places:

me·tre . . . *chiefly Brit var of* METER

To show all the stylings that are found for English compounds would require space that can be better used for other information. So this dictionary limits itself to a single styling for a compound:

peace·mak·er
pell–mell
boom box

When a compound is widely used and one styling predominates, that styling is shown. When a compound is uncommon or when the evidence indicates that two or three stylings are approximately equal in frequency, the styling shown is based on the comparison of other similar compounds.

A main entry may be followed by one or more derivatives or by a homograph with a different functional label. These are run-on entries. Each is introduced by a long dash and each has a functional label. They are not defined, however, since their meanings are readily understood from the meaning of the root word:

fear·less . . . *adj* . . . — **fear·less·ly**
adv — **fear·less·ness** *n*
hic·cup . . . *n* . . . — **hiccup** *vb*

A main entry may be followed by one or more phrases containing the entry word or an inflected form of it. These are also run-on entries. Each is introduced by a long dash but there is no functional label. They are, however, defined, since their meanings are more than the sum of the meanings of their elements:

¹set . . . *vb* . . . — **set sail** : . . .

¹hand . . . *n* . . . — **at hand** : . . .

Defined phrases of this sort are run on at the entry defining the first major word in the phrase. When there are variants, however, the run-on appears at the entry defining the first major invariable word in the phrase:

¹seed . . . *n* . . . — **go to seed** *or* **run to seed 1** : . . .

Boldface words that appear within parentheses (as **co·ca** at **co·caine** and **jet engine** and **jet propulsion** at **jet– propelled**) are run-in entries.

Attention is called to the definition of *vocabulary entry* on page 810. The term *dictionary entry* includes all vocabulary entries as well as all boldface entries in the back sections headed "Foreign Words & Phrases," "Biographical Names," and "Geographical Names."

PRONUNCIATION

The matter between a pair of reversed slashes \ \ following the entry word indicates the pronunciation. The symbols used are explained in the chart at the end of this section.

A hyphen is used in the pronunciation to show syllabic division. These hyphens sometimes coincide with the centered dots in the entry word that indicate end-of-line division:

ab·sen·tee \ˌab-sən-ˈtē\

Sometimes they do not:

met·ric \ˈme-trik\

A high-set mark ˈ indicates major (primary) stress or accent; a low-set mark ˌ indicates minor (secondary) stress or accent:

heart·beat \ˈhärt-ˌbēt\

The stress mark stands at the beginning of the syllable that receives the stress.

A syllable with neither a high-set mark nor a low-set mark is unstressed:

¹struc·ture \ˈstrək-chər\

The presence of variant pronunciations indicates that not all educated speakers pronounce words the same way. A second-place variant is not to be regarded as less acceptable than the pronunciation that is given first. It may, in fact, be used by as many educated speakers as the first variant, but the requirements of the printed page are such that one must precede the other:

apri·cot \ˈa-prə-ˌkät, ˈā-\
fore·head \ˈfȯr-əd, ˈfȯr-ˌhed\

Symbols enclosed by parentheses represent elements that are present in the pronunciation of some speakers but are absent from the pronunciation of other speakers, or elements that are present in some but absent from other utterances of the same speaker:

¹om·ni·bus \ˈäm-ni-(ˌ)bəs\
ad·di·tion·al \ə-ˈdi-sh(ə-)nəl\

Thus, the above parentheses indicate that some people say \ˈäm-ni-ˌbəs\ and others say \ˈäm-ni-bəs\; some \ə-ˈdi-shə-nəl\, others \ə-ˈdi-shnəl\.

When a main entry has less than a full pronunciation, the missing part is to be supplied from a pronunciation in a preceding entry or within the same pair of reversed slashes:

> **cham·pi·on·ship** \-ˌship\
> **pa·la·ver** \pə-ˈla-vər, -ˈlä-\

The pronunciation of the first three syllables of *championship* is found at the main entry *champion*. The hyphens before and after \ˈlä\ in the pronunciation of *palaver* indicate that both the first and the last parts of the pronunciation are to be taken from the immediately preceding pronunciation.

In general, no pronunciation is indicated for open compounds consisting of two or more English words that have own-place entry:

> **witch doctor** *n*

Only the first entry in a sequence of numbered homographs is given a pronunciation if their pronunciations are the same:

> **¹re·ward** \ri-ˈwȯrd\ *vb*
> **²reward** *n*

The absent but implied pronunciation of derivatives and compounds run on after a main entry is a combination of the pronunciation at the main entry and the pronunciation of the other element as given at its alphabetical place in the vocabulary:

> **— quick·ness** *n*
> **— hold with**

Thus, the pronunciation of *quickness* is the sum of the pronunciations given at *quick* and *-ness;* that of *hold with*, the sum of the pronunciations of the two elements that make up the phrase.

FUNCTIONAL LABELS

An italic label indicating a part of speech or another functional classification follows the pronunciation or, if no pronunciation is given, the main entry. The eight traditional parts of speech are indicated as follows:

> **bold** ... *adj*
> **forth·with** ... *adv*
> **¹but** ... *conj*
> **ge·sund·heit** ... *interj*
> **bo·le·ro** ... *n*
> **²un·der** ... *prep*
> **¹it** ... *pron*
> **slap** ... *vb*

Other italicized labels used to indicate functional classifications that are not traditional parts of speech include:

> **AT** *abbr*
> **self-** *comb form*
> **un-** ... *prefix*
> **-ial** *adj suffix*
> **²-ly** *adv suffix*
> **²-er** ... *n suffix*
> **-ize** *vb suffix*
> **Fe** *symbol*
> **may** ... *verbal auxiliary*

Functional labels are sometimes combined:

> **afloat** ... *adj or adv*

INFLECTED FORMS

NOUNS

The plurals of nouns are shown in this dictionary when suffixation brings about a change of final *-y* to *-i-*, when the noun ends in a consonant plus *-o* or in *-ey*, when the noun ends in *-oo*, when the noun has an irregular plural or an uninflected plural or a foreign plural, when the noun is a compound that pluralizes any element but the last, when a final consonant is doubled, when the noun has variant plurals, and when it is believed that the dictionary user might have reasonable doubts about the spelling of the plural or when the plural is spelled in a way contrary to what is expected:

²spy *n, pl* **spies**
si·lo . . . *n, pl* **silos**
val·ley . . . *n, pl* **valleys**
²shampoo *n, pl* **shampoos**
mouse . . . *n, pl* **mice**
moose . . . *n, pl* **moose**
cri·te·ri·on . . . *n, pl* **-ria**
son–in–law . . . *n, pl* **sons–in–law**
¹quiz . . . *n, pl* **quiz·zes**
¹fish . . . *n, pl* **fish** *or* **fish·es**
pi . . . *n, pl* **pis**
³dry *n, pl* **drys**

Cutback inflected forms are used when
the noun has three or more syllables:

ame·ni·ty . . . *n, pl* **-ties**

The plurals of nouns are usually not
shown when the base word is unchanged
by suffixation, when the noun is a compound whose second element is readily
recognizable as a regular free form entered at its own place, or when the noun
is unlikely to occur in the plural:

night . . . *n*
fore·foot . . . *n*
mo·nog·a·my . . . *n*

Nouns that are plural in form and that
are regularly construed as plural are
labeled *n pl*:

munch·ies . . . *n pl*

Nouns that are plural in form but that
are not always construed as plurals are
appropriately labeled:

lo·gis·tics . . . *n sing or pl*

VERBS

The principal parts of verbs are shown
in this dictionary when suffixation
brings about a doubling of a final consonant or an elision of a final *-e* or a
change of final *-y* to *-i-*, when final *-c*
changes to *-ck* in suffixation, when
the verb ends in *-ey*, when the inflection is irregular, when there are variant inflected forms, and when it is
believed that the dictionary user
might have reasonable doubts about
the spelling of an inflected form or
when the inflected form is spelled in a
way contrary to what is expected:

²snag *vb* **snagged; snag·ging**
¹move . . . *vb* **moved; mov·ing**
¹cry . . . *vb* **cried; cry·ing**
¹frol·ic . . . *vb* **frol·icked; frol·ick·ing**
¹sur·vey . . . *vb* **sur·veyed; sur-**
    vey·ing
¹drive . . . *vb* **drove . . . driv·en . . .**
    driv·ing
²bus *vb* **bused** *or* **bussed; bus·ing**
    or **bus·sing**
²visa *vb* **vi·saed . . . vi·sa·ing**
²chagrin *vb* **cha·grined . . . cha-**
    grin·ing

The principal parts of a regularly inflected verb are shown when it is desirable to indicate the pronunciation
of one of the inflected forms:

learn . . . *vb* **learned** \'lərnd, 'lərnt\;
    learn·ing

¹al·ter \'ȯl-tər\ *vb* **al·tered; al·ter-**
    ing \-t(ə-)riŋ\

Cutback inflected forms are usually
used when the verb has three or more
syllables, when it is a two-syllable
word that ends in *-l* and has variant
spellings, and when it is a compound
whose second element is readily recognized as an irregular verb:

elim·i·nate . . . *vb* **-nat·ed; -nat·ing**
²quarrel *vb* **-reled** *or* **-relled; -rel-**
    ing *or* **-rel·ling**
¹re·take . . . *vb* **-took . . . -tak·en . . .**
    -tak·ing

The principal parts of verbs are usually not shown when the base word is
unchanged by suffixation or when the
verb is a compound whose second
element is readily recognizable as a
regular free form entered at its own
place:

¹jump . . . *vb*
pre·judge . . . *vb*

Another inflected form of English
verbs is the third person singular of
the present tense, which is regularly
formed by the addition of *-s* or *-es* to
the base form of the verb. This inflected form is not shown except at a
handful of entries (as *have* and *do*) for
which it is in some way unusual.

ADJECTIVES & ADVERBS

The comparative and superlative forms of adjectives and adverbs are shown in this dictionary when suffixation brings about a doubling of a final consonant or an elision of a final -e or a change of final -y to -i-, when the word ends in -ey, when the inflection is irregular, and when there are variant inflected forms:

> ¹red . . . *adj* red·der; red·dest
> ¹tame . . . *adj* tam·er; tam·est
> ¹kind·ly . . . *adj* kind·li·er; -est
> hors·ey *also* horsy . . . *adj* hors·i·er; -est
> ¹good . . . *adj* bet·ter . . . best
> ¹far . . . *adv* far·ther . . . *or* fur·ther . . . far·thest *or* fur·thest

The superlative forms of adjectives and adverbs of two or more syllables are usually cut back:

> ³fancy *adj* fan·ci·er; -est
> ¹ear·ly . . . *adv* ear·li·er; -est

The comparative and superlative forms of regularly inflected adjectives and adverbs are shown when it is desirable to indicate the pronunciation of the inflected forms:

> ¹young \'yəŋ\ *adj* youn·ger \'yəŋ-gər\; youn·gest \'yəŋ-gəst\

The inclusion of inflected forms in -er and -est at adjective and adverb entries means nothing more about the use of *more* and *most* with these adjectives and adverbs than that their comparative and superlative degrees may be expressed in either way: *lazier* or *more lazy; laziest* or *most lazy*.

At a few adjective entries only the superlative form is shown:

> ²mere *adj, superlative* mer·est

The absence of the comparative form indicates that there is no evidence of its use.

The comparative and superlative forms of adjectives and adverbs are usually not shown when the base word is unchanged by suffixation, when the inflected forms of the word are identical with those of a preceding homograph, or when the word is a compound whose second element is readily recognizable as a regular free form entered at its own place:

> ¹near . . . *adv*
> ³good *adv*
> un·wor·thy . . . *adj*

Inflected forms are not shown at undefined run-ons.

CAPITALIZATION

Most entries in this dictionary begin with a lowercase letter. A few of these have an italicized label *often cap*, which indicates that the word is as likely to be capitalized as not and that it is as acceptable with an uppercase initial as it is with one in lowercase. Some entries begin with an uppercase letter, which indicates that the word is usually capitalized. The absence of an initial capital or of an *often cap* label indicates that the word is not ordinarily capitalized:

> salm·on . . . *n*
> gar·gan·tuan . . . *adj, often cap*
> Mo·hawk . . . *n*

The capitalization of entries that are open or hyphenated compounds is similarly indicated by the form of the entry or by an italicized label:

> dry goods . . . *n pl*
> french fry *n, often cap 1st F*
> un—Amer·i·can . . . *adj*
> Par·kin·son's disease . . . *n*
> lazy Su·san . . . *n*
> Jack Frost *n*

A word that is capitalized in some senses and lowercase in others shows variations from the form of the main entry by the use of italicized labels at the appropriate senses:

> Trin·i·ty . . . *n* . . . 2 *not cap*
> To·ry . . . *n* . . . 3 *often not cap*
> ti·tan . . . *n* 1 *cap*
> re·nais·sance . . . *n* . . . 1 *cap* . . . 2 *often cap*

ETYMOLOGY

This dictionary gives the etymologies for a number of the vocabulary entries. These etymologies are inside square brackets preceding the definition. Meanings given in roman type within these brackets are not definitions of the entry, but are meanings of the Middle English, Old English, or non-English words within the brackets.

The etymology gives the language from which words borrowed into English have come. It also gives the form of the word in that language or a representation of the word in our alphabet if the form in that language differs from that in English:

> **phi·lo·den·dron** . . . [NL, fr. Gk, neut. of *philodendros* loving trees . . .]
> **¹sav·age** . . . [ME, fr. AF *salvage, savage,* fr. LL *salvaticus,* alter.

of L *silvaticus* of the woods, wild . . .]

An etymology beginning with the name of a language (including ME or OE) and not giving the foreign (or Middle English or Old English) form indicates that this form is the same as the form of the entry word:

> **le·gume** . . . [F]
> **¹jour·ney** . . . [ME, fr. OF . . .]

An etymology beginning with the name of a language (including ME or OE) and not giving the foreign (or Middle English or Old English) meaning indicates that this meaning is the same as the meaning expressed in the first definition in the entry:

> **ug·ly** . . . *adj* . . . [ME, fr. ON *uggligr* . . .] **1** : FRIGHTFUL, DIRE

USAGE

Three types of status labels are used in this dictionary—temporal, regional, and stylistic—to signal that a word or a sense of a word is not part of the standard vocabulary of English.

The temporal label *obs* for "obsolete" means that there is no evidence of use since 1755:

> **³post** *n 1 obs*

The label *obs* is a comment on the word being defined. When a thing, as distinguished from the word used to designate it, is obsolete, appropriate orientation is usually given in the definition:

> **cat·a·pult** . . . *n* **1** : an ancient military machine for hurling missiles

The temporal label *archaic* means that a word or sense once in common use is found today only sporadically or in special contexts:

> **¹mete** . . . *vb* . . . **1** *archaic*
> **¹thou** . . . *pron, archaic*

A word or sense limited in use to a specific region of the U.S. has an appropriate label. The adverb *chiefly*

precedes a label when the word has some currency outside the specified region, and a double label is used to indicate considerable currency in each of two specific regions:

> **²wash** *n* . . . **8** *West*
> **do·gie** . . . *n, chiefly West*
> **crul·ler** . . . *n* . . . **2** *Northern & Midland*

Words current in all regions of the U.S. have no label.

A word or sense limited in use to one of the other countries of the English-speaking world has an appropriate regional label:

> **chem·ist** . . . *n* . . . **2** *Brit*
> **loch** . . . *n, Scot*
> **²wireless** *n* . . . **2** *chiefly Brit*

The label *dial* for "dialect" indicates that the pattern of use of a word or sense is too complex for summary labeling: it usually includes several regional varieties of American English or of American and British English:

> **²mind** *vb* **1** *chiefly dial*

The stylistic label *slang* is used with words or senses that are especially appropriate in contexts of extreme informality:

    ³can . . . *vb* . . . 2 *slang*
    ²grand *n* . . . *slang*

There is no satisfactory objective test for slang, especially with reference to a word out of context. No word, in fact, is invariably slang, and many standard words can be given slang applications.

The stylistic labels *offensive* and *disparaging* are used for those words or senses that in common use are intended to hurt or that are likely to give offense even when they are used without such an intent:

    dumb . . . *adj* 1 *often offensive*
    half–breed . . . *n, often disparaging*

Definitions are sometimes followed by verbal illustrations that show a typical use of the word in context. These illustrations are enclosed in angle brackets, and the word being illustrated is usually replaced by a lightface swung dash. The swung dash stands for the boldface entry word, and it may be followed by an italicized suffix:

    ¹jump . . . *vb* . . . 5 . . . ⟨~ town⟩
    all–around . . . *adj* 1 . . . ⟨best ~ performance⟩
    ¹can·on . . . *n* . . . 3 . . . ⟨the ~s of good taste⟩
    en·joy . . . *vb* . . . 2 . . . ⟨~ed the concert⟩

The swung dash is not used when the form of the boldface entry word is changed in suffixation, and it is not used for open compounds:

    ²deal *vb* . . . 2 . . . ⟨*dealt* him a blow⟩
    drum up *vb* 1 . . . ⟨*drum up* business⟩

Definitions are sometimes followed by usage notes that give supplementary information about such matters as idiom, syntax, and semantic relationship. A usage note is introduced by a lightface dash:

    ²cry *n* . . . 5 . . . — usu. used in the phrase *a far cry*
    ²drum *vb* . . . 4 . . . — usu. used with *out*
    ¹jaw . . . *n* . . . 2 . . . — usu. used in pl.
    ¹ada·gio . . . *adv or adj* . . . — used as a direction in music
    hajji . . . *n* . . . — often used as a title

Sometimes a usage note is used in place of a definition. Some function words (as conjunctions and prepositions) have chiefly grammatical meaning and little or no lexical meaning; most interjections express feelings but are otherwise untranslatable into lexical meaning; and some other words (as honorific titles) are more amenable to comment than to definition:

    or . . . *conj* — used as a function word to indicate an alternative
    ¹at . . . *prep* 1 — used to indicate a point in time or space
    auf Wie·der·seh·en . . . *interj* . . . — used to express farewell
    sir . . . *n* . . . 2 — used as a usu. respectful form of address

SENSE DIVISION

A boldface colon is used in this dictionary to introduce a definition:

    equine . . . *adj* . . . : of or relating to the horse

It is also used to separate two or more definitions of a single sense:

    no·ti·fy . . . *vb* . . . 1 : to give notice of : report the occurrence of

Boldface Arabic numerals separate the senses of a word that has more than one sense:

    add . . . *vb* 1 : to join to something else so as to increase in number or amount 2 : to say further . . . 3 : to combine (numbers) into one sum

A particular semantic relationship between senses is sometimes suggested by the use of one of the two italic sense dividers *esp* or *also*.

The sense divider *esp* (for *especially*) is used to introduce the most common meaning included in the more general preceding definition:

crys·tal . . . *n* . . . 2 : something resembling crystal (as in transparency); *esp* : a clear colorless glass of superior quality

The sense divider *also* is used to introduce a meaning related to the preceding sense by an easily understood extension of that sense:

chi·na . . . *n* : porcelain ware; *also* : domestic pottery in general

The order of senses is historical: the sense known to have been first used in English is entered first. This is not to be taken to mean, however, that each sense of a multisense word developed from the immediately preceding sense. It is altogether possible that sense 1 of a word has given rise to sense 2 and sense 2 to sense 3, but frequently sense 2 and sense 3 may have developed independently of one another from sense 1.

When an italicized label follows a boldface numeral, the label applies only to that specific numbered sense. It does not apply to any other boldface numbered senses:

craft . . . *n* . . . 3 *pl usu* craft
¹fa·ther . . . *n* . . . 2 *cap* . . . 5 *often cap*
dul·ci·mer . . . *n* . . . 2 *or* dul·ci·more \-ˌmȯr\
²lift *n* . . . 5 *chiefly Brit*

At *craft* the *pl* label applies to sense 3 but to none of the other numbered senses. At *father* the *cap* label applies only to sense 2 and the *often cap* label only to sense 5. At *dulcimer* the variant spelling and pronunciation apply only to sense 2, and the *chiefly Brit* label at *lift* applies only to sense 5.

CROSS-REFERENCE

Four different kinds of cross-references are used in this dictionary: directional, synonymous, cognate, and inflectional. In each instance the cross-reference is readily recognized by the lightface small capitals in which it is printed.

A cross-reference following a lightface dash and beginning with *see* is a directional cross-reference. It directs the dictionary user to look elsewhere for further information:

eu·ro . . . *n* . . . — see MONEY table

A cross-reference following a boldface colon is a synonymous cross-reference. It may stand alone as the only definition for an entry or for a sense of an entry; it may follow an analytical definition; it may be one of two or more synonymous cross-references separated by commas:

pa·pa . . . *n* : FATHER
¹par·tic·u·lar . . . *adj* . . . 4 : attentive to details : PRECISE
²main *adj* 1 : CHIEF, PRINCIPAL
¹fig·ure . . . *n* . . . 6 : SHAPE, FORM, OUTLINE

A synonymous cross-reference indicates that an entry, a definition at the entry, or a specific sense at the entry cross-referred to can be substituted as a definition for the entry or the sense in which the cross-reference appears.

A cross-reference following an italic *var of* ("variant of") is a cognate cross-reference:

pick·a·back . . . *var of* PIGGYBACK

Occasionally a cognate cross-reference has a limiting label preceding *var of* as an indication that the variant is not standard American English:

aero·plane . . . *chiefly Brit var of* AIRPLANE

A cross-reference following an italic label that identifies an entry as an inflected form (as of a noun or verb) is an inflectional cross-reference:

calves *pl of* CALF
woven *past part of* WEAVE

Inflectional cross-references appear only when the inflected form falls at least a column away from the entry cross-referred to.

SYNONYMS

A bold italic *Synonyms* preceded by a small black diamond figure near the end of an entry introduces words that are synonymous with the word being defined:

    alone . . . *adj* . . . ♦ *Synonyms* LONE-LY, LONESOME, LONE, SOLITARY

Synonyms are not definitions although they may often be substituted for each other in context.

COMBINING FORMS, PREFIXES, & SUFFIXES

An entry that begins or ends with a hyphen is a word element that forms part of an English compound:

    -wise . . . *adv comb form* . . . ⟨slant-*wise*⟩
    ex- . . . *prefix* . . . **2** . . . ⟨*ex*-president⟩
    -let *n suffix* **1** . . . ⟨book*let*⟩

Combining forms, prefixes, and suffixes are entered in this dictionary for two reasons: to make understandable the meaning of many undefined run-ons and to make recognizable the meaningful elements of words that are not entered in the dictionary.

LISTS OF UNDEFINED WORDS

Many words that begin with the prefixes or combining forms *anti-, in-, non-, over-, re-, self-, semi-, sub-, super-,* and *un-* are self-explanatory combinations of the prefix or combining form and a word entered elsewhere in the dictionary, and they are listed undefined at the bottom of the page or spread on which they would normally appear if defined.

ABBREVIATIONS & SYMBOLS

Abbreviations and symbols for chemical elements are included as main entries in the vocabulary:

    RSVP *abbr* . . . please reply
    Ca *symbol* calcium

Abbreviations have been normalized to one form. In practice, however, there is considerable variation in the use of periods and in capitalization (as *vhf, v.h.f., VHF,* and *V.H.F.* for the entry **VHF**), and stylings other than those given in this dictionary are often acceptable.

ABBREVIATIONS IN THIS WORK

ab	about	*masc*	masculine
abbr	abbreviation	*MD*	Middle Dutch
abl	ablative	*ME*	Middle English
acc	accusative	*MexSp*	Mexican Spanish
A.D.	anno Domini	*MF*	Middle French
adj	adjective	*MGk*	Middle Greek
adv	adverb	*mi*	miles
alter	alteration	*ML*	Medieval Latin
Am, Amer	American	*modif*	modification
AmerF	American French	*MS*	manuscript
AmerInd	American Indian	*Mt*	Mount
AmerSp	American Spanish	*n*	noun
Ar	Arabic	*neut*	neuter
Aram	Aramaic	*NewEng*	New England
B.C.	before Christ	*NGk*	New Greek
Brit	British	*NHeb*	New Hebrew
C	Celsius	*NL*	New Latin
ca	circa	*No*	North
Calif	California	*Norw*	Norwegian
Canad	Canadian	*n pl*	noun plural
CanF	Canadian French	*obs*	obsolete
cap	capital, capitalized	*OE*	Old English
Celt	Celtic	*OF*	Old French
cen	central	*OIt*	Old Italian
cent	century	*ON*	Old Norse
Chin	Chinese	*OPer*	Old Persian
comb	combining	*orig*	originally
compar	comparative	*part*	participle
conj	conjunction	*Per*	Persian
D	Dutch	*perh*	perhaps
Dan	Danish	*Pg*	Portuguese
dat	dative	*pl*	plural
deriv	derivative	*Pol*	Polish
dial	dialect	*pp*	past participle
dim	diminutive	*prep*	preposition
E	English	*pres*	present, president
Egypt	Egyptian	*prob*	probably
Eng	English	*pron*	pronoun, pronunciation
esp	especially	*prp*	present participle
est	estimated	*pseud*	pseudonym
F	Fahrenheit, French	*r*	reigned
fem	feminine	*Russ*	Russian
fl	flourished	*Sc*	Scotch, Scots
fr	from	*Scand*	Scandinavian
ft	feet	*ScGael*	Scottish Gaelic
G, Ger	German	*Scot*	Scottish
Gk	Greek	*sing*	singular
Gmc	Germanic	*Skt*	Sanskrit
Heb	Hebrew	*Slav*	Slavic
Hung	Hungarian	*So*	South
Icel	Icelandic	*Sp, Span*	Spanish
imit	imitative	*St*	Saint
imper	imperative	*superl*	superlative
interj	interjection	*Sw*	Swedish
Ir	Irish	*syn*	synonym, synonymy
irreg	irregular	*trans*	translation
It, Ital	Italian	*Turk*	Turkish
Jp	Japanese	*US*	United States
K	Kelvin	*USSR*	Union of Soviet Socialist Republics
km	kilometers		
L	Latin	*usu*	usually
LaF	Louisiana French	*var*	variant
LG	Low German	*vb*	verb
LGk	Late Greek	*vi*	verb intransitive
LHeb	Late Hebrew	*VL*	Vulgar Latin
lit	literally	*vt*	verb transitive
LL	Late Latin	*W*	Welsh
m	meters		

PRONUNCIATION SYMBOLS

ə   abut, collect, suppose

ˈə, ˌə   humdrum

ᵊ   (in ᵊl, ᵊn) battle, cotton; (in lᵊ, mᵊ, rᵊ) French table, prisme, titre

ər   operation, further

a   map, patch

ā   day, fate

ä   bother, cot, father

är   car, heart

au̇   now, out

b   baby, rib

ch   chin, catch

d   did, adder

e   set, red

er   bare, fair

ē   beat, easy

f   fifty, cuff

g   go, big

h   hat, ahead

hw   whale

i   tip, banish

ir   near, deer

ī   site, buy

j   job, edge

k   kin, cook

k̠   German Bach, Scots loch

l   lily, cool

m   murmur, dim

n   nine, own

ⁿ   indicates that a preceding vowel is pronounced through both nose and mouth, as in French bon \bōⁿ\

ŋ   sing, singer, finger, ink

ō   bone, hollow

ȯ   saw

ȯr   boar, port

œ   French bœuf, feu, German Hölle, Höhle

ȯi   toy

p   pepper, lip

r   rarity

s   source, less

sh   shy, mission

t   tie, attack

th   thin, ether

t̲h̲   then, either

ü   boot, few \ˈfyü\

u̇   put, pure \ˈpyu̇r\

u̇r   boor, tour

œ̄   French rue, German füllen, fühlen

v   vivid, give

w   we, away

y   yard, cue \ˈkyü\

ʸ   indicates that a preceding \l\, \n\, or \w\ is modified by having the tongue approximate the position for \y\, as in French digne \dēnʸ\

z   zone, raise

zh   vision, pleasure

\   slant line used in pairs to mark the beginning and end of a transcription: \ˈpen\

ˈ   mark at the beginning of a syllable that has primary (strongest) stress: \ˈshə-fəl-ˌbȯrd\

ˌ   mark at the beginning of a syllable that has secondary (next-strongest) stress: \ˈshə-fəl-ˌbȯrd\

-      mark of a syllable division in pronunciations (the mark of end-of-line division in boldface entries is a centered dot ·)

( )   indicate that what is symbolized between sometimes occurs and sometimes does not occur in the pronunciation of the word: **bakery** \ˈbā-k(ə-)rē\ = \ˈbā-kə-rē, ˈbā-krē\

A

¹**a** \'ā\ *n, pl* **a's** *or* **as** \'āz\ *often cap* **1** : the 1st letter of the English alphabet **2** : a grade rating a student's work as superior

²**a** \ə, (')ā\ *indefinite article* : ONE, SOME — used to indicate an unspecified or unidentified individual ⟨there's ∼ man outside⟩

³**a** *abbr, often cap* **1** absent **2** acre **3** alto **4** answer **5** are **6** area

AA *abbr* **1** Alcoholics Anonymous **2** antiaircraft **3** associate in arts

AAA *abbr* American Automobile Association

A and M *abbr* agricultural and mechanical

A and R *abbr* artists and repertory

aard·vark \'ärd-,värk\ *n* [obs. Afrikaans, fr. Afrikaans *aard* earth + *vark* pig] : a large burrowing African mammal that feeds on ants and termites with its long sticky tongue

¹**ab** \'ab\ *n* : an abdominal muscle

²**ab** *abbr* about

AB *abbr* **1** able-bodied seaman **2** airman basic **3** [NL *artium baccalaureus*] bachelor of arts

ABA *abbr* American Bar Association

aback \ə-'bak\ *adv* : by surprise ⟨taken ∼⟩

aba·cus \'a-bə-kəs,\ *n, pl* **aba·ci** \-,sī, -,kē\ *or* **aba·cus·es** : an instrument for making calculations by sliding counters along rods or grooves

¹**abaft** \ə-'baft\ *prep* : to the rear of

²**abaft** *adv* : toward or at the stern : AFT

ab·a·lo·ne \,a-bə-'lō-nē, 'a-bə-,\ *n* : any of a genus of large edible sea mollusks with a flattened slightly spiral shell with holes along the edge

¹**aban·don** \ə-'ban-dən\ *vb* [ME *abandounen*, fr. AF *abanduner*, fr. (*mettre*) *a bandun* to hand over, put in someone's control] : to give up completely : FORSAKE, DESERT — **aban·don·ment** *n*

²**abandon** *n* : a thorough yielding to natural impulses; *esp* : EXUBERANCE

aban·doned \ə-'ban-dənd\ *adj* : morally unrestrained ♦ *Synonyms* PROFLIGATE, DISSOLUTE, REPROBATE

abase \ə-'bās\ *vb* **abased**; **abas·ing** : HUMBLE, DEGRADE — **abase·ment** *n*

abash \ə-'bash\ *vb* : to destroy the composure of : EMBARRASS — **abash·ment** *n*

abate \ə-'bāt\ *vb* **abat·ed**; **abat·ing** **1** : to put an end to ⟨∼ a nuisance⟩ **2** : to decrease in amount, number, or degree

abate·ment \ə-'bāt-mənt\ *n* **1** : DECREASE **2** : an amount abated; *esp* : a deduction from a tax

ab·at·toir \'a-bə-,twär\ *n* [F] : SLAUGHTERHOUSE

ab·ba·cy \'a-bə-sē\ *n, pl* **-cies** : the office or term of office of an abbot or abbess

ab·bé \a-'bā, 'a-,\ *n* : a member of the French secular clergy — used as a title

ab·bess \'a-bəs\ *n* : the superior of a convent for nuns

ab·bey \'a-bē\ *n, pl* **abbeys** **1** : MONASTERY **2** : CONVENT **3** : an abbey church

ab·bot \'a-bət\ *n* [ME *abbod*, fr. OE, fr. LL *abbat-, abbas*, fr. LGk *abbas*, fr. Aramaic *abbā* father] : the superior of a monastery for men

abbr *abbr* abbreviation

ab·bre·vi·ate \ə-'brē-vē-,āt\ *vb* **-at·ed**; **-at·ing** : SHORTEN, CURTAIL; *esp* : to reduce to an abbreviation

ab·bre·vi·a·tion \ə-,brē-vē-'ā-shən\ *n* **1** : the act or result of abbreviating **2** : a shortened form of a word or phrase used for brevity esp. in writing

¹**ABC** \,ā-(,)bē-'sē\ *n, pl* **ABC's** *or* **ABCs** \-'sēz\ **1** : ALPHABET — usu. used in pl. **2** : RUDIMENTS — usu. used in pl.

²**ABC** *abbr* American Broadcasting Company

Ab·di·as \ab-'dī-əs\ *n* : OBADIAH

ab·di·cate \'ab-di-,kāt\ *vb* **-cat·ed**; **-cat·ing** : to give up (as a throne) formally — **ab·di·ca·tion** \,ab-di-'kā-shən\ *n*

ab·do·men \'ab-də-mən, ab-'dō-\ *n* **1** : the cavity in or area of the body between the chest and the pelvis **2** : the part of the body posterior to the thorax in an arthropod — **ab·dom·i·nal** \ab-'dä-mə-nᵊl\ *adj* — **ab·dom·i·nal·ly** *adv*

ab·duct \ab-'dəkt\ *vb* : to take away (a person) by force : KIDNAP — **ab·duc·tion** \-'dək-shən\ *n* — **ab·duc·tor** \-tər\ *n*

abeam \ə-'bēm\ *adv or adj* : on a line at right angles to a ship's keel

abed \ə-'bed\ *adv or adj* : in bed

Abe·na·ki \,a-bə-'nä-kē\ *also* **Ab·na·ki** \ab-'nä-kē\ *n, pl* **Abenaki** *or* **Abenakis** *also* **Abnaki** *or* **Abnakis** : a member of a group of American Indian peoples of northern New England and southern Quebec

ab·er·ra·tion \,a-bə-'rā-shən\ *n* **1** : deviation esp. from a moral standard or normal state **2** : failure of a mirror or lens to produce exact point-to-point correspondence between an object and its image **3** : unsoundness of mind : DERANGEMENT — **ab·er·rant** \a-'ber-ənt\ *adj*

abet \ə-'bet\ *vb* **abet·ted**; **abet·ting** [ME *abetten*, fr. AF *abeter*, fr. *beter* to bait] **1** : INCITE, ENCOURAGE **2** : to assist or support in the achievement of a purpose ⟨∼ a fugitive⟩ — **abet·tor** *or* **abet·ter** \-'be-tər\ *n*

abey·ance \ə-'bā-əns\ *n* : a condition of suspended activity — **abey·ant** \-ənt\ *adj*

ab·hor \ab-'hȯr, ab-\ *vb* **ab·horred**; **ab·hor·ring** [ME *abhorren*, fr. L *abhorrēre*, fr. *ab-* + *horrēre* to shudder] : LOATHE, DETEST — **ab·hor·rence** \-əns\ *n*

ab·hor·rent \-ənt\ *adj* : LOATHSOME, DETESTABLE ⟨∼ crimes⟩

abide \ə-'bīd\ *vb* **abode** \-'bōd\ *or* **abid·ed**; **abid·ing** **1** : BEAR, ENDURE **2** : DWELL, REMAIN, LAST — **abide by** : to conform to or acquiesce to ⟨*abide by* the law⟩

abil·i·ty \ə-'bi-lə-tē\ *n, pl* **-ties** : the quality of being able : POWER, SKILL

-ability *also* **-ibility** *n suffix* : capacity, fitness, or tendency to act or be acted on in a (specified) way 〈flamm*ability*〉

ab·ject \'ab-ˌjekt, ab-'jekt\ *adj* : low in spirit, hope, or state 〈~ poverty〉 — **ab·jec·tion** \ab-'jek-shən\ *n* — **ab·ject·ly** *adv* — **ab·ject·ness** *n*

ab·jure \ab-'jür\ *vb* **ab·jured; ab·jur·ing** 1 : to renounce solemnly : RECANT 2 : to abstain from — **ab·ju·ra·tion** \ˌab-jə-'rā-shən\ *n*

abl *abbr* ablative

ab·late \a-'blāt\ *vb* **ab·lat·ed; ab·lat·ing** : to remove or become removed esp. by cutting, abrading, or vaporizing

ab·la·tion \a-'blā-shən\ *n* 1 : surgical cutting and removal 2 : loss of a part (as the outside of a nose cone) by melting or vaporization

ab·la·tive \'ab-lə-tiv\ *adj* : of, relating to, or constituting a grammatical case (as in Latin) expressing typically the relation of separation and source — **ablative** *n*

ablaze \ə-'blāz\ *adj or adv* : being on fire : BLAZING

able \'ā-bəl\ *adj* **abler** \-b(ə-)lər\; **ablest** \-b(ə-)ləst\ [ME, fr. AF, fr. L *habilis* apt, fr. *habēre* to hold, possess] 1 : having sufficient power, skill, or resources to accomplish an object 2 : marked by skill or efficiency — **ably** \-blē\ *adv*

-able *also* **-ible** *adj suffix* 1 : capable of, fit for, or worthy of (being so acted upon or toward) 〈break*able*〉 〈collect*ible*〉 2 : tending, given, or liable to 〈knowledge*able*〉 〈perish*able*〉

able–bod·ied \ˌā-bəl-'bä-dēd\ *adj* : having a sound strong body

abloom \ə-'blüm\ *adj* : BLOOMING

ab·lu·tion \ə-'blü-shən, a-\ *n* : the washing of one's body or part of it

ABM \ˌā-(ˌ)bē-'em\ *n, pl* **ABM's** *or* **ABMs** : ANTIBALLISTIC MISSILE

Abnaki *var of* ABENAKI

ab·ne·gate \'ab-ni-ˌgāt\ *vb* **-gat·ed; -gat·ing** 1 : DENY, RENOUNCE 2 : SURRENDER, RELINQUISH 〈~ her powers〉 — **ab·ne·ga·tion** \ˌab-ni-'gā-shən\ *n*

ab·nor·mal \ab-'nȯr-məl\ *adj* : deviating from the normal or average — **ab·nor·mal·i·ty** \ˌab-nȯr-'ma-lə-tē\ *n* — **ab·nor·mal·ly** *adv*

¹aboard \ə-'bȯrd\ *adv* 1 : ALONGSIDE 2 : on, onto, or within a car, ship, or aircraft 3 : in or into a group or association 〈welcome new workers ~〉

²aboard *prep* : ON, ONTO, WITHIN

abode \ə-'bōd\ *n* 1 : STAY, SOJOURN 2 : HOME, RESIDENCE

abol·ish \ə-'bä-lish\ *vb* : to do away with : ANNUL 〈~ slavery〉 — **ab·o·li·tion** \ˌa-bə-'li-shən\ *n*

ab·o·li·tion·ism \ˌa-bə-'li-shə-ˌni-zəm\ *n* : advocacy of the abolition of slavery — **ab·o·li·tion·ist** \-'li-sh(ə-)nist\ *n or adj*

A–bomb \'ā-ˌbäm\ *n* : ATOMIC BOMB — **A–bomb** *vb*

abom·i·na·ble \ə-'bä-mə-nə-bəl\ *adj* : causing disgust or hatred : DETESTABLE

abominable snow·man \-'snō-mən, -ˌman\ *n, often cap A&S* : a mysterious creature with human or apelike characteristics reported to exist in the high Himalayas

abom·i·nate \ə-'bä-mə-ˌnāt\ *vb* **-nat·ed; -nat·ing** [L *abominari*, lit., to deprecate as an ill omen, fr. *ab-* away + *omen* omen] : to hate or loathe intensely

abom·i·na·tion \ə-ˌbä-mə-'nā-shən\ *n* 1 : something abominable 2 : extreme disgust or hatred : LOATHING

ab·orig·i·nal \ˌa-bə-'ri-jə-nəl\ *adj* : ORIGINAL, INDIGENOUS, PRIMITIVE

ab·orig·i·ne \ˌa-bə-'ri-jə-nē\ *n* : a member of the original race of inhabitants of a region : NATIVE

aborn·ing \ə-'bȯr-niŋ\ *adv* : while being born or produced

¹abort \ə-'bȯrt\ *vb* 1 : to cause or undergo abortion 2 : to terminate prematurely 〈~ a spaceflight〉 — **abor·tive** \-'bȯr-tiv\ *adj*

²abort *n* : the premature termination of a mission or of a procedure relating to an aircraft or spacecraft

abor·tion \ə-'bȯr-shən\ *n* : the spontaneous or induced termination of a pregnancy after, accompanied by, resulting in, or closely followed by the death of the embryo or fetus

abor·tion·ist \-sh(ə-)nist\ *n* : one who induces abortions

abound \ə-'baund\ *vb* 1 : to be plentiful : TEEM 2 : to be fully supplied

¹about \ə-'baut\ *adv* 1 : reasonably close to; *also* : on the verge of 〈~ to join the army〉 2 : on all sides 3 : NEARBY

²about *prep* 1 : on every side of 2 : near to 3 : CONCERNING

about–face \-'fās\ *n* : a reversal of direction or attitude — **about–face** *vb*

¹above \ə-'bəv\ *adv* 1 : in the sky; *also* : in or to heaven 2 : in or to a higher place; *also* : higher on the same page or on a preceding page

²above *prep* 1 : in or to a higher place than : OVER 〈storm clouds ~ the bay〉 2 : superior to 〈he thought her far ~ him〉 3 : more than : EXCEEDING 4 : as distinct from 〈~ the noise〉

above–board \-ˌbȯrd\ *adv or adj* : without concealment or deception : OPENLY

abp *abbr* archbishop

abr *abbr* abridged; abridgment

ab·ra·ca·dab·ra \ˌa-brə-kə-'da-brə\ *n* 1 : a magical charm or incantation against calamity 2 : GIBBERISH

abrade \ə-'brād\ *vb* **abrad·ed; abrad·ing** 1 : to wear away by friction 2 : to wear down in spirit : IRRITATE — **abra·sion** \-'brā-zhən\ *n*

¹abra·sive \ə-'brā-siv\ *n* : a substance (as pumice) for abrading, smoothing, or polishing

²abrasive *adj* : tending to abrade : causing irritation 〈~ relationships〉 — **abra·sive·ly** *adv* — **abra·sive·ness** *n*

abreast \ə-'brest\ *adv or adj* 1 : side by side 2 : up to a standard or level esp. of knowledge 〈kept ~ of the news〉

abridge \ə-'brij\ vb **abridged; abridging** [ME *abregen*, fr. AF *abreger*, fr. LL *abbreviare*, fr. L *ad* to + *brevis* short] : to lessen in length or extent : SHORTEN — **abridg·ment** or **abridge·ment** n

abroad \ə-'brȯd\ adv or adj 1 : over a wide area 2 : away from one's home 3 : outside one's country

ab·ro·gate \'a-brə-ˌgāt\ vb **-gat·ed; -gating** : ANNUL, REVOKE — **ab·ro·ga·tion** \ˌa-brə-'gā-shən\ n

abrupt \ə-'brəpt\ adj 1 : broken or as if broken off 2 : SUDDEN, HASTY ⟨an ∼ turn⟩ 3 : so quick as to seem rude ⟨an ∼ reply⟩ 4 : DISCONNECTED 5 : STEEP — **abrupt·ly** adv

abs abbr absolute

ab·scess \'ab-ˌses\ n, pl **ab·scess·es** [L *abscessus*, lit., act of going away, fr. *abscedere* to go away, fr. *abs-, ab-* away + *cedere* to go] : a localized collection of pus surrounded by inflamed tissue — **ab·scessed** \-ˌsest\ adj

ab·scis·sa \ab-'si-sə\ n, pl **abscissas** also **ab·scis·sae** \-'si-(ˌ)sē\ : the horizontal coordinate of a point in a plane coordinate system obtained by measuring parallel to the x-axis

ab·scis·sion \ab-'si-zhən\ n 1 : the act or process of cutting off 2 : the natural separation of flowers, fruits, or leaves from plants — **ab·scise** \ab-'sīz\ vb

ab·scond \ab-'skänd\ vb : to depart secretly and hide oneself

ab·sence \'ab-səns\ n 1 : the state or time of being absent 2 : WANT, LACK 3 : INATTENTION ⟨∼ of mind⟩

¹**ab·sent** \'ab-sənt\ adj 1 : not present 2 : LACKING 3 : INATTENTIVE

²**ab·sent** \ab-'sent\ vb : to keep (oneself) away

³**ab·sent** \'ab-sənt\ prep : in the absence of : WITHOUT

ab·sen·tee \ˌab-sən-'tē\ n : one that is absent or keeps away

absentee ballot n : a ballot submitted (as by mail) in advance of an election by a voter who is unable to be present at the polls

ab·sen·tee·ism \ˌab-sən-'tē-ˌi-zəm\ n : chronic absence (as from work or school)

ab·sent-mind·ed \ˌab-sənt-'mīn-dəd\ adj : unaware of one's surroundings or actions : INATTENTIVE — **ab·sent-mind·ed·ly** adv — **ab·sent-mind·ed·ness** n

ab·sinthe also **ab·sinth** \'ab-ˌsinth\ n [F] : a liqueur flavored esp. with wormwood and anise

ab·so·lute \'ab-sə-ˌlüt, ˌab-sə-'lüt\ adj 1 : free from imperfection or mixture 2 : free from control, restriction, or qualification ⟨∼ power⟩ 3 : lacking grammatical connection with any other word in a sentence ⟨∼ construction⟩ 4 : POSITIVE ⟨∼ proof⟩ 5 : relating to the fundamental units of length, mass, and time 6 : FUNDAMENTAL, ULTIMATE ⟨∼ knowledge⟩ — **ab·so·lute·ly** adv

absolute pitch n 1 : the position of a tone in a standard scale independently determined by its rate of vibration 2

: the ability to sing a note asked for or to name a note heard

absolute value n : a nonnegative number equal to a given real number with any negative sign removed

absolute zero n : a theoretical temperature marked by a complete absence of heat and motion and equivalent to exactly -273.15°C or -459.67°F

ab·so·lu·tion \ˌab-sə-'lü-shən\ n : the act of absolving; *esp* : a remission of sins pronounced by a priest in the sacrament of reconciliation

ab·so·lut·ism \'ab-sə-ˌlü-ˌti-zəm\ n 1 : the theory that a ruler or government should have unlimited power 2 : government by an absolute ruler or authority

ab·solve \əb-'zälv, -'sälv\ vb **ab·solved; ab·solv·ing** : to set free from an obligation or the consequences of guilt

ab·sorb \əb-'sȯrb, -'zȯrb\ vb 1 : to take in and make part of an existent whole 2 : to suck up or take in in the manner of a sponge 3 : to engage (one's attention) : ENGROSS 4 : to receive without recoil or echo ⟨a ceiling that ∼s sound⟩ 5 : ASSUME, BEAR ⟨∼ all costs⟩ 6 : to transform (radiant energy) into a different form esp. with a resulting rise in temperature — **ab·sorb·ing** adj — **ab·sorb·ing·ly** adv

ab·sor·bent also **ab·sor·bant** \əb-'sȯr-bənt, -'zȯr-\ adj : able to absorb ⟨∼ cotton⟩ — **ab·sor·ben·cy** \-bən-sē\ n — **absorbent** also **absorbant** n

ab·sorp·tion \əb-'sȯrp-shən, -'zȯrp-\ n 1 : a process of absorbing or being absorbed 2 : concentration of attention ⟨∼ in his work⟩ — **ab·sorp·tive** \-tiv\ adj

ab·stain \ab-'stān\ vb : to refrain from an action or practice — **ab·stain·er** n — **ab·sten·tion** \-'sten-chən\ n

ab·ste·mi·ous \ab-'stē-mē-əs\ adj : sparing in use of food or drink : TEMPERATE — **ab·ste·mi·ous·ly** adv — **ab·ste·mi·ous·ness** n

ab·sti·nence \'ab-stə-nəns\ n : voluntary refraining esp. from eating certain foods, drinking liquor, or engaging in sexual intercourse — **ab·sti·nent** \-nənt\ adj

abstr abbr abstract

¹**ab·stract** \ab-'strakt, 'ab-ˌstrakt\ adj 1 : considered apart from a particular instance 2 : expressing a quality apart from an object ⟨*whiteness* is an ∼ word⟩ 3 : having only intrinsic form with little or no pictorial representation ⟨∼ painting⟩ — **ab·stract·ly** adv — **ab·stract·ness** n

²**ab·stract** \'ab-ˌstrakt; 2 also ab-'strakt\ n 1 : a written summary 2 : an abstract thing or state

³**ab·stract** \ab-'strakt, 'ab-ˌstrakt; 2 usu 'ab-ˌstrakt\ vb 1 : REMOVE, SEPARATE 2 : to make an abstract of : SUMMARIZE 3 : to draw away the attention of 4 : STEAL — **ab·stract·ed·ly** \ab-'strak-təd-lē, 'ab-ˌstrak-\ adv

abstract expressionism n : art that expresses the artist's attitudes and emotions through abstract forms — **abstract expressionist** n

ab·strac·tion \ab-'strak-shən\ n 1 : the act of abstracting : the state of being abstracted 2 : an abstract idea 3 : an abstract work of art

ab·struse \ab-'strüs\ adj : hard to understand : RECONDITE — **ab·struse·ly** adv — **ab·struse·ness** n

ab·surd \əb-'sərd, -'zərd\ adj [MF absurde, fr. L absurdus, fr. ab- from + surdus deaf, stupid] : RIDICULOUS, UNREASONABLE — **ab·sur·di·ty** \-'sər-də-tē, -'zər-\ n — **ab·surd·ly** adv

abun·dant \ə-'bən-dənt\ adj [ME, fr. AF, fr. L abundant-, abundans, prp. of abundare to abound, fr. ab- from + unda wave] : more than enough : amply sufficient ♦ Synonyms COPIOUS, PLENTIFUL, AMPLE, BOUNTIFUL — **abun·dance** \-dəns\ n — **abun·dant·ly** adv

¹**abuse** \ə-'byüs\ n 1 : a corrupt practice 2 : MISUSE ⟨drug ∼⟩ 3 : coarse and insulting speech ⟨verbal ∼⟩ 4 : MISTREATMENT ⟨child ∼⟩

²**abuse** \ə-'byüz\ vb **abused; abus·ing** 1 : to put to a wrong use : MISUSE 2 : to use excessively ⟨∼ alcohol⟩ 3 : MISTREAT 4 : to attack in words : REVILE — **abus·er** n — **abu·sive** \-'byü-siv\ adj — **abu·sive·ly** adv — **abu·sive·ness** n

abut \ə-'bət\ vb **abut·ted; abut·ting** : to touch along a border : border on

abut·ment \ə-'bət-mənt\ n : the part of a structure (as a bridge) that supports weight or withstands lateral pressure

abut·ter \ə-'bə-tər\ n : one that abuts; esp : the owner of a contiguous property

abuzz \ə-'bəz\ adj : filled or resounding with activity or excitement ⟨an office ∼ with rumors⟩

abys·mal \ə-'biz-məl\ adj 1 : immeasurably deep : BOTTOMLESS 2 : absolutely wretched ⟨∼ living conditions of the poor⟩ — **abys·mal·ly** adv

abyss \ə-'bis\ n 1 : the bottomless pit in old accounts of the universe 2 : an immeasurable depth

abys·sal \ə-'bi-səl\ adj : of or relating to the bottom waters of the ocean depths

ac abbr account

-ac n suffix : one affected with ⟨hypochondriac⟩

Ac symbol actinium

AC abbr 1 air-conditioning 2 alternating current 3 [L ante Christum] before Christ 4 [L ante cibum] before meals 5 area code

aca·cia \ə-'kā-shə\ n : any of a genus of leguminous trees or shrubs with round white or yellow flower clusters and often feathery leaves

acad abbr academic; academy

ac·a·deme \'a-kə-ˌdēm, ˌa-kə-'\ n : SCHOOL; also : academic environment

¹**ac·a·dem·ic** \ˌa-kə-'de-mik\ n : a person who is academic in background, outlook, or methods

²**academic** adj 1 : of, relating to, or associated with schools or colleges 2 : literary or general rather than technical 3 : theoretical rather than practical — **ac·a·dem·i·cal·ly** \-mi-k(ə-)lē\ adv

ac·a·de·mi·cian \ˌa-kə-də-'mi-shən, ə-ˌka-də-\ n 1 : a member of a society of scholars or artists 2 : ACADEMIC

ac·a·dem·i·cism \ˌa-kə-'de-mə-ˌsi-zəm\ also **acad·e·mism** \ə-'ka-də-ˌmi-zəm\ n 1 : a formal academic quality 2 : purely speculative thinking

acad·e·my \ə-'ka-də-mē\ n, pl **-mies** [Gk Akadēmeia, school of philosophy founded by Plato, fr. Akadēmeia, gymnasium where Plato taught, fr. Akadēmos Greek mythological hero] 1 : a school above the elementary level; esp : a private high school 2 : a society of scholars or artists

acan·thus \ə-'kan-thəs\ n, pl **acanthus** 1 : any of a genus of prickly herbs of the Mediterranean region 2 : an ornamentation (as on a column) representing the leaves of the acanthus

a cap·pel·la also **a ca·pel·la** \ˌä-kə-'pe-lə\ adv or adj [It a cappella in chapel style] : without instrumental accompaniment

acc abbr accusative

ac·cede \ak-'sēd\ vb **ac·ced·ed; ac·ced·ing** 1 : to become a party to an agreement 2 : to express approval 3 : to enter upon an office ♦ Synonyms AGREE, ACQUIESCE, ASSENT, CONSENT, SUBSCRIBE

ac·cel·er·ate \ik-'se-lə-ˌrāt, ak-\ vb **-at·ed; -at·ing** 1 : to bring about earlier 2 : to speed up : QUICKEN — **ac·cel·er·a·tion** \-ˌse-lə-'rā-shən\ n

ac·cel·er·a·tor \ik-'se-lə-ˌrā-tər, ak-\ n 1 : one that accelerates 2 : a pedal for controlling the speed of a motor-vehicle engine 3 : an apparatus for imparting high velocities to charged particles

ac·cel·er·om·e·ter \ik-ˌse-lə-'rä-mə-tər, ak-\ n : an instrument for measuring acceleration or vibrations

¹**ac·cent** \'ak-ˌsent, ak-'sent\ vb : to give stress to : EMPHASIZE

²**ac·cent** \'ak-ˌsent\ n 1 : prominence given to one syllable of a word esp. by stress 2 : a distinctive manner of pronunciation ⟨a foreign ∼⟩ 3 : a mark (as ´, `, ˆ) over a vowel used usu. to indicate a difference in pronunciation from a vowel not so marked — **ac·cen·tu·al** \ak-'sen-chə-wəl\ adj

ac·cen·tu·ate \ak-'sen-chə-ˌwāt\ vb **-at·ed; -at·ing** : STRESS, EMPHASIZE — **ac·cen·tu·a·tion** \-ˌsen-chə-'wā-shən\ n

ac·cept \ik-'sept, ak-\ vb 1 : to receive willingly 2 : to agree to 3 : to assume an obligation to pay

ac·cept·able \ik-'sep-tə-bəl, ak-\ adj : capable or worthy of being accepted — **ac·cept·abil·i·ty** \ik-ˌsep-tə-'bi-lə-tē, ak-\ n

ac·cep·tance \ik-'sep-təns, ak-\ n 1 : the act of accepting 2 : the state of being accepted or acceptable 3 : an accepted bill of exchange

ac·cep·ta·tion \ˌak-ˌsep-'tā-shən\ n : the generally understood meaning of a word

¹**ac·cess** \'ak-ˌses\ n 1 : capacity to enter or approach 2 : a way of approach : ENTRANCE

²**access** *vb* : to get at : gain access to

ac·ces·si·ble \ik-ˈse-sə-bəl, ak-, ek-\ *adj* **1** : capable of being reached ⟨~ by train⟩ **2** : capable of being used or seen ⟨~ archives⟩ **3** : capable of being understood ⟨an ~ film⟩ — **ac·ces·si·bil·i·ty** \-ˌse-sə-ˈbi-lə-tē\ *n*

ac·ces·sion \ik-ˈse-shən, ak-\ *n* **1** : increase by something added **2** : something added **3** : the act of coming to a high office or position

ac·ces·so·ry *also* **ac·ces·sa·ry** \ik-ˈse-sə-rē, ak-\ *n, pl* **-ries** **1** : a person who though not present abets or assists in the commission of an offense **2** : something helpful but not essential ♦ *Synonyms* APPURTENANCE, ADJUNCT, APPENDAGE, APPENDIX — **accessory** *adj*

ac·ci·dent \ˈak-sə-dənt\ *n* **1** : an event occurring by chance or unintentionally **2** : CHANCE ⟨met by ~⟩ **3** : a nonessential property

¹**ac·ci·den·tal** \ˌak-sə-ˈden-tᵊl\ *adj* **1** : happening unexpectedly or by chance **2** : happening without intent or through carelessness ♦ *Synonyms* CASUAL, FORTUITOUS, INCIDENTAL, CHANCE — **ac·ci·den·tal·ly** \-ˈden-tᵊl-ē\ *also* **ac·ci·dent·ly** \-ˈdent-lē\ *adv*

²**accidental** *n* : a musical note foreign to a key indicated by a signature

ac·claim \ə-ˈklām\ *vb* **1** : to give strong approval or praise to **2** : to declare by acclamation ♦ *Synonyms* EXTOL, LAUD, COMMEND, HAIL — **acclaim** *n*

ac·cla·ma·tion \ˌa-klə-ˈmā-shən\ *n* **1** : loud eager applause **2** : an overwhelming affirmative vote by shouting or applause rather than by ballot

ac·cli·mate \ˈa-klə-ˌmāt, ə-ˈklī-mət\ *vb* **-mat·ed; -mat·ing** : to accustom or become accustomed to a new climate or situation — **ac·cli·ma·tion** \ˌa-klə-ˈmā-shən, -ˌklī-\ *n*

ac·cli·ma·tise *Brit var of* ACCLIMATIZE

ac·cli·ma·tize \ə-ˈklī-mə-ˌtīz\ *vb* **-tized; -tiz·ing** : ACCLIMATE — **ac·cli·ma·ti·za·tion** \-ˌklī-mə-tə-ˈzā-shən\ *n*

ac·cliv·i·ty \ə-ˈkli-və-tē\ *n, pl* **-ties** : an ascending slope

ac·co·lade \ˈa-kə-ˌlād\ *n* [F, fr. *accoler* to embrace, ultim. fr. L *ad-* to + *collum* neck] : an expression of praise : AWARD

ac·com·mo·date \ə-ˈkä-mə-ˌdāt\ *vb* **-dat·ed; -dat·ing** **1** : to make fit or suitable : ADAPT, ADJUST **2** : HARMONIZE, RECONCILE **3** : to provide with something needed **4** : to hold without crowding **5** : to undergo visual accommodation

ac·com·mo·dat·ing *adj* : OBLIGING

ac·com·mo·da·tion \ə-ˌkä-mə-ˈdā-shən\ *n* **1** : something supplied to satisfy a need; *esp* : LODGINGS — usu. used in pl. **2** : the act of accommodating : ADJUSTMENT **3** : the automatic adjustment of the eye for seeing at different distances

ac·com·pa·ni·ment \ə-ˈkəm-pə-nē-mənt, -ˈkəmp-nē-\ *n* : something that accompanies another; *esp* : subordinate music to support a principal voice or instrument

ac·com·pa·ny \-nē\ *vb* **-nied; -ny·ing** **1** : to go or occur with : ATTEND **2** : to play

an accompaniment for — **ac·com·pa·nist** \-nist\ *n*

ac·com·plice \ə-ˈkäm-pləs, -ˈkəm-\ *n* : an associate in wrongdoing

ac·com·plish \ə-ˈkäm-plish, -ˈkəm-\ *vb* : to bring to completion ♦ *Synonyms* ACHIEVE, EFFECT, EXECUTE, PERFORM — **ac·com·plish·er** *n*

ac·com·plished \-plisht\ *adj* **1** : EXPERT, SKILLED ⟨an ~ pianist⟩ **2** : established beyond doubt ⟨an ~ fact⟩

ac·com·plish·ment \ə-ˈkäm-plish-mənt, -ˈkəm-\ *n* **1** : COMPLETION **2** : something completed or effected **3** : an acquired excellence or skill

¹**ac·cord** \ə-ˈkord\ *vb* [ME, fr. AF *acorder,* fr. VL **accordare,* fr. L *ad-* to + *cord-, cor* heart] **1** : GRANT, CONCEDE **2** : AGREE, HARMONIZE ⟨his interpretation does not ~ with the facts⟩ — **ac·cor·dant** \-ˈkor-dᵊnt\ *adj*

²**accord** *n* **1** : AGREEMENT, HARMONY **2** : willingness to act ⟨gave of their own ~⟩

ac·cor·dance \ə-ˈkor-dᵊns\ *n* **1** : ACCORD **2** : the act of granting

ac·cord·ing·ly \ə-ˈkor-diŋ-lē\ *adv* **1** : in accordance **2** : CONSEQUENTLY, SO

according to *prep* **1** : in conformity with ⟨paid *according to* ability⟩ **2** : as stated or attested by ⟨*according to* you⟩

¹**ac·cor·di·on** \ə-ˈkor-dē-ən\ *n* [G *Akkordion,* fr. *Akkord* chord] : a portable keyboard instrument with a bellows and reeds — **ac·cor·di·on·ist** \-ə-nist\ *n*

²**accordion** *adj* : folding like the bellows of an accordion ⟨~ pleats⟩

ac·cost \ə-ˈkost\ *vb* [MF *accoster,* ultim. fr. L *ad-* to + *costa* rib, side] : to approach and speak to esp. aggressively

¹**ac·count** \ə-ˈkaunt\ *n* **1** : a statement of business transactions **2** : a formal business arrangement for regular dealings or services **3** : a statement of reasons, causes, or motives **4** : VALUE, IMPORTANCE ⟨his opinion is of little ~⟩ **5** : a sum of money deposited in a bank and subject to withdrawal by the depositor — **on account of** : BECAUSE OF — **on no account** : under no circumstances — **on one's own account** : on one's own behalf

²**account** *vb* **1** : CONSIDER ⟨I ~ him lucky⟩ **2** : to give an explanation ⟨~ for the money you spent⟩ — used with *for*

ac·count·able \ə-ˈkaun-tə-bəl\ *adj* **1** : ANSWERABLE, RESPONSIBLE **2** : EXPLICABLE — **ac·count·abil·i·ty** \-ˌkaun-tə-ˈbi-lə-tē\ *n*

ac·coun·tant \ə-ˈkaun-tᵊnt\ *n* : a person skilled in accounting — **ac·coun·tan·cy** \-tᵊn-sē\ *n*

account executive *n* : a business executive in charge of a client's account

ac·count·ing \ə-ˈkaun-tiŋ\ *n* : the art or system of keeping and analyzing financial records

ac·cou·tre *or* **ac·cou·ter** \ə-ˈkü-tər\ *vb* **-tred** *or* **-tered; -tring** *or* **-ter·ing** \-ˈkü-t(ə-)riŋ\ : EQUIP, OUTFIT ⟨the knights were *accoutred* for battle⟩

ac·cou·tre·ment *or* **ac·cou·ter·ment**

\ə-'kü-trə-mənt, -'kü-tər-\ n [F] **1** : an accessory item — usu. used in pl. **2** : an identifying characteristic

ac·cred·it \ə-'kre-dət\ vb **1** : to endorse or approve officially **2** : CREDIT — **ac·cred·i·ta·tion** \-,kre-də-'tā-shən\ n

ac·cre·tion \ə-'krē-shən\ n **1** : growth or enlargement esp. by addition from without **2** : a product of accretion

accretion disk n : a disk of usu. gaseous matter surrounding and gradually accumulating onto a massive celestial object

ac·crue \ə-'krü\ vb **ac·crued; ac·cru·ing 1** : to come by way of increase **2** : to be added by periodic growth — **ac·cru·al** \-əl\ n

acct abbr account; accountant

ac·cul·tur·a·tion \ə-,kəl-chə-'rā-shən\ n : cultural modification of an individual or group by borrowing and adapting traits from another culture

ac·cu·mu·late \ə-'kyü-myə-,lāt\ vb **-lat·ed; -lat·ing** [L accumulare, fr. ad- to + cumulare to heap up] : to heap or pile up ♦ **Synonyms** AMASS, GATHER, COLLECT, STOCKPILE — **ac·cu·mu·la·tion** \-,kyü-myə-'lā-shən\ n — **ac·cu·mu·la·tive** \-'kyü-myə-lə-tiv\ adj — **ac·cu·mu·la·tor** \-'kyü-myə-,lā-tər\ n

ac·cu·rate \'a-kyə-rət\ adj : free from error : EXACT, PRECISE — **ac·cu·ra·cy** \-rə-sē\ n — **ac·cu·rate·ly** adv — **ac·cu·rate·ness** n

ac·cursed \ə-'kərst, -'kər-səd\ or **ac·curst** \ə-'kərst\ adj **1** : being under a curse **2** : DAMNABLE, EXECRABLE

ac·cus·al \ə-'kyü-zəl\ n : ACCUSATION

ac·cu·sa·tive \ə-'kyü-zə-tiv\ adj : of, relating to, or being a grammatical case marking the direct object of a verb or the object of a preposition — **accusative** n

ac·cu·sa·to·ry \ə-'kyü-zə-,tòr-ē\ adj : expressing accusation ⟨an ~ tone⟩

ac·cuse \ə-'kyüz\ vb **ac·cused; ac·cus·ing** : to charge with an offense : BLAME — **ac·cu·sa·tion** \,a-kyə-'zā-shən\ n — **ac·cus·er** n

ac·cused \ə-'kyüzd\ n, pl **accused** : the defendant in a criminal case

ac·cus·tom \ə-'kəs-təm\ vb : to make familiar through use or experience

ac·cus·tomed \ə-'kəs-təmd\ adj : USUAL, CUSTOMARY ⟨with ~ grace⟩; also : being in the habit ⟨~ed to winning⟩

¹ace \'ās\ n [ME as a die face marked with one spot, fr. AF, fr. L, unit, a copper coin] **1** : a playing card bearing a single large pip in its center **2** : a point (as in tennis) won on a serve that goes untouched **3** : a golf score of one stroke on a hole **4** : a combat pilot who has downed five or more enemy planes **5** : one that excels **6** : the best pitcher on a baseball team

²ace vb **aced; ac·ing 1** : to score an ace against (an opponent) or on (a golf hole) **2** : to defeat decisively **3** : to perform extremely well in or on ⟨aced the quiz⟩

³ace adj : of first rank or quality

ACE in·hib·i·tor \'ā-,sē-'ē-in-'hi-bə-tər, 'ās-\ n : any of a group of drugs that lower blood pressure by relaxing the arteries

acer·bic \ə-'sər-bik, a-\ adj : acid in temper, mood, or tone ⟨~ wit⟩

acer·bi·ty \ə-'sər-bə-tē\ n, pl **-ties** : SOURNESS, BITTERNESS

acet·amin·o·phen \ə-,sē-tə-'mi-nə-fən\ n : a crystalline compound used in chemical synthesis and in medicine to relieve pain and fever

ac·e·tate \'a-sə-,tāt\ n **1** : a salt or ester of acetic acid **2** : a textile fiber made from cellulose and acetic acid; also : a fabric or plastic made of this fiber

acetic acid \ə-'sē-tik-\ n : a colorless pungent liquid acid that is the chief acid of vinegar and is used esp. in making chemical compounds

ac·e·tone \'a-sə-,tōn\ n : a volatile flammable fragrant liquid compound used in making other chemical compounds and as a solvent

ace·tyl·cho·line \ə-,sē-tᵊl-'kō-,lēn\ n : a compound that is released at nerve endings of the autonomic nervous system and is active in the transmission of nerve impulses

acet·y·lene \ə-'se-tᵊl-ən, -tᵊl-,ēn\ n : a colorless flammable gas used as a fuel (as in welding and soldering)

acetyl·sal·i·cyl·ic acid \ə-'sē-tᵊl,sa-lə-,si-lik-\ n : ASPIRIN 1

ache \'āk\ vb **ached; ach·ing 1** : to suffer a usu. dull persistent pain ⟨an aching back⟩ **2** : LONG, YEARN ⟨aching to go home⟩ — **ache** n — **ach·ing·ly** \'ā-kiŋ-lē\ adv

achieve \ə-'chēv\ vb **achieved; achiev·ing** [ME acheven, fr. AF achever to finish, fr. a- to (fr. L ad-) + chef end, head, fr. L caput] : to gain by work or effort ♦ **Synonyms** ACCOMPLISH, ATTAIN, REALIZE — **achiev·able** \-'chē-və-bəl\ adj — **achieve·ment** n — **achiev·er** n

Achil·les' heel \ə-,ki-lēz-\ n [fr. the story that the Greek warrior Achilles was vulnerable only in the heel] : a vulnerable point

Achil·les tendon \ə-,ki-lēz-\ n : the tendon joining the muscles in the calf of the leg to the bone of the heel

ach·ro·mat·ic \,a-krə-'ma-tik\ adj : giving an image almost free from extraneous colors ⟨~ lens⟩

achy \'ā-kē\ adj **ach·i·er; ach·i·est** : afflicted with aches — **ach·i·ness** n

¹ac·id \'a-səd\ adj **1** : sour or biting to the taste; also : sharp or sour in manner **2** : of or relating to an acid — **acid·i·ty** \ə-'si-də-tē\ n — **acid·ly** adv

²acid n **1** : a sour substance **2** : a usu. water-soluble chemical compound that has a sour taste, reacts with a base to form a salt, and reddens litmus **3** : LSD — **ac·id·ic** \a-'si-dik\ adj

acid·i·fy \ə-'si-də-,fī\ vb **-fied; -fy·ing 1** : to make or become acid **2** : to change into an acid — **acid·i·fi·ca·tion** \-,si-də-fə-'kā-shən\ n

ac·i·do·sis \,a-sə-'dō-səs\ n, pl **-do·ses** \-,sēz\ : an abnormal state of reduced alkalinity of the blood and body tissues

acid precipitation *n* : precipitation with above normal acidity that is caused esp. by atmospheric pollutants

acid rain *n* : acid precipitation in the form of rain

acid test *n* : a severe or crucial test

ac·id·u·lous \ə-'si-jə-ləs\ *adj* : somewhat acid or harsh in taste or manner

ack *abbr* acknowledge; acknowledgment

ac·knowl·edge \ik-'nä-lij, ak-\ *vb* **-edged; -edg·ing** 1 : to recognize the rights or authority of 2 : to admit as true 3 : to express thanks for; *also* : to report receipt of ⟨~ a letter⟩ 4 : to recognize as valid — **ac·knowl·edg·ment** *or* **ac·knowl·edge·ment** *n*

ACL \ā-sē-'el\ *n* : ANTERIOR CRUCIATE LIGAMENT

ACLU *abbr* American Civil Liberties Union

ac·me \'ak-mē\ *n* [Gk *akmē*] : the highest point

ac·ne \'ak-nē\ *n* [Gk *aknē*, MS var. of *akmē*, lit., point] : a skin disorder marked by inflammation of skin glands and hair follicles and by pimple formation esp. on the face

ac·o·lyte \'a-kə-,līt\ *n* 1 : one who assists a member of the clergy in a liturgical service 2 : FOLLOWER

ac·o·nite \'a-kə-,nīt\ *n* 1 : MONKSHOOD 2 : the dried root of a common Eurasian monkshood used formerly as a drug

acorn \'ā-,kȯrn, -kərn\ *n* : the nut of the oak

acorn squash *n* : an acorn-shaped dark green winter squash with a ridged surface and yellow to orange flesh

acous·tic \ə-'kü-stik\ *or* **acous·ti·cal** \-sti-kəl\ *adj* 1 : of or relating to the sense or organs of hearing, to sound, or to the science of sounds 2 : deadening sound ⟨~ tile⟩ 3 : operated by or utilizing sound waves 4 : having a sound that is not electronically modified ⟨~ guitar⟩ — **acous·ti·cal·ly** \-k(ə-)lē\ *adv*

acous·tics \ə-'kü-stiks\ *n sing or pl* 1 : the science of sound 2 : the qualities in a room that make it easy or hard for a person in it to hear distinctly

ac·quaint \ə-'kwānt\ *vb* [ME, ultim. fr. L *ad-* + *cognoscere* to know] 1 : to cause to know personally 2 : INFORM

ac·quain·tance \ə-'kwān-t°ns\ *n* 1 : personal knowledge 2 : a person with whom one is acquainted — **ac·quain·tance·ship** *n*

acquaintance rape *n* : rape committed by someone known to the victim

ac·qui·esce \,a-kwē-'es\ *vb* **-esced; -esc·ing** : to accept, comply, or submit without open opposition ♦ *Synonyms* CONSENT, AGREE, ASSENT, ACCEDE — **ac·qui·es·cence** \-'e-s°ns\ *n* — **ac·qui·es·cent** \-s°nt\ *adj* — **ac·qui·es·cent·ly** *adv*

ac·quire \ə-'kwī(-ə)r\ *vb* **ac·quired; ac·quir·ing** : to gain possession of : GET — **ac·quir·able** \-'kwī-rə-bəl\ *adj*

acquired *adj* 1 : gained by or as a result of effort or experience 2 : caused by environmental forces and not passed from parent to offspring in the genes ⟨~ characteristics⟩

acquired immune deficiency syndrome *n* : AIDS

acquired immunodeficiency syndrome *n* : AIDS

ac·quire·ment \ə-'kwī(-ə)r-mənt\ *n* 1 : ATTAINMENT, ACCOMPLISHMENT 2 : the act of acquiring

ac·qui·si·tion \,a-kwə-'zi-shən\ *n* 1 : ACQUIREMENT 2 : something acquired

ac·quis·i·tive \ə-'kwi-zə-tiv\ *adj* : eager to acquire : GREEDY — **ac·quis·i·tive·ly** *adv* — **ac·quis·i·tive·ness** *n*

ac·quit \ə-'kwit\ *vb* **ac·quit·ted; ac·quit·ting** 1 : to pronounce not guilty 2 : to conduct (oneself) usu. satisfactorily — **ac·quit·tal** \-'kwi-t°l\ *n*

acre \'ā-kər\ *n* 1 *pl* : LANDS, ESTATE 2 — see WEIGHT table

acre·age \'ā-k(ə-)rij\ *n* : area in acres

ac·rid \'a-krəd\ *adj* 1 : sharp and biting in taste or odor 2 : deeply bitter : CAUSTIC — **ac·rid·i·ty** \a-'kri-də-tē\ *n* — **ac·rid·ly** *adv* — **ac·rid·ness** *n*

ac·ri·mo·ny \'a-krə-,mō-nē\ *n, pl* **-nies** : harsh or biting sharpness of language or feeling — **ac·ri·mo·ni·ous** \,a-krə-'mō-nē-əs\ *adj* — **ac·ri·mo·ni·ous·ly** *adv* — **ac·ri·mo·ni·ous·ness** *n*

ac·ro·bat \'a-krə-,bat\ *n* [F *acrobate*, fr. Gk *akrobatēs*, fr. *akros* topmost + *bainein* to go] : a performer of gymnastic feats — **ac·ro·bat·ic** \,a-krə-'ba-tik\ *adj* — **ac·ro·bat·i·cal·ly** \-ti-k(ə-)lē\ *adv*

ac·ro·bat·ics \,a-krə-'ba-tiks\ *n sing or pl* : the performance of an acrobat

ac·ro·nym \'a-krə-,nim\ *n* : a word (as *radar*) or abbreviation (as *FBI*) formed from the initial letter or letters of each of the successive parts or major parts of a compound term

ac·ro·pho·bia \,a-krə-'fō-bē-ə\ *n* : abnormal dread of being in a high place : fear of heights

acrop·o·lis \ə-'krä-pə-ləs\ *n* [Gk *akropolis*, fr. *akros* topmost + *polis* city] : the upper fortified part of an ancient Greek city

¹across \ə-'krȯs\ *adv* 1 : to or on the opposite side 2 : so as to be understandable ⟨get the point ~⟩

²across *prep* 1 : to or on the opposite side of ⟨ran ~ the street⟩ 2 : on so as to cross or pass at an angle ⟨a log ~ the road⟩

across–the–board *adj* 1 : placed to win if a competitor wins, places, or shows ⟨an ~ bet⟩ 2 : including all classes or categories ⟨an ~ wage increase⟩

acros·tic \ə-'krȯs-tik\ *n* : a composition usu. in verse in which the initial or final letters of the lines taken in order form a word or phrase — **acrostic** *adj*

acryl·ic \ə-'kri-lik\ *n* 1 : ACRYLIC RESIN 2 : a paint in which the vehicle is acrylic resin 3 : a quick-drying synthetic textile fiber

acrylic resin *n* : a glassy thermoplastic used for cast and molded parts or as coatings and adhesives

¹act \'akt\ *n* 1 : a thing done : DEED 2 : STATUTE, DECREE 3 : a main division of a play; *also* : an item on a variety program

4 : an instance of insincere behavior : PRETENSE

²**act** *vb* **1** : to perform by action esp. on the stage; *also* : FEIGN, SIMULATE, PRETEND **2** : to take action **3** : to conduct oneself : BEHAVE **4** : to perform a specified function **5** : to produce an effect

³**act** *abbr* **1** active **2** actual

ACT *abbr* Australian Capital Territory

actg *abbr* acting

ACTH \ˌā-ˌ)sē-(ˌ)tē-ˈāch\ *n* : a protein hormone of the pituitary gland that stimulates the adrenal cortex

act•ing \ˈak-tiŋ\ *adj* : doing duty temporarily or for another ⟨∼ president⟩

ac•tin•i•um \ak-ˈti-nē-əm\ *n* : a radioactive metallic chemical element

ac•tion \ˈak-shən\ *n* **1** : a legal proceeding **2** : the manner or method of performing **3** : ACTIVITY **4** : ACT, DEED **5** : the accomplishment of a thing usu. over a period of time, in stages, or with the possibility of repetition **6** *pl* : CONDUCT **7** : COMBAT, BATTLE **8** : the events of a literary plot **9** : an operating mechanism ⟨the ∼ of a gun⟩; *also* : the way it operates ⟨stiff ∼⟩

ac•tion•able \ˈak-sh(ə-)nə-bəl\ *adj* : affording ground for an action or suit at law — **ac•tion•ably** \-blē\ *adv*

ac•ti•vate \ˈak-tə-ˌvāt\ *vb* **-vat•ed; -vat•ing 1** : to spur into action; *also* : to make active, reactive, or radioactive **2** : to treat (as carbon) so as to improve adsorptive properties **3** : to set up (a military unit) formally; *also* : to call to active duty — **ac•ti•va•tion** \ak-tə-ˈvā-shən\ *n* — **ac•ti•va•tor** \ˈak-tə-ˌvā-tər\ *n*

ac•tive \ˈak-tiv\ *adj* **1** : causing or involving action or change **2** : asserting that the grammatical subject performs the action represented by the verb ⟨∼ voice⟩ **3** : BRISK, LIVELY **4** : erupting or likely to erupt ⟨∼ volcano⟩ **5** : presently in operation or use **6** : tending to progress or to cause degeneration ⟨∼ tuberculosis⟩ — **active** *n* — **ac•tive•ly** *adv* — **ac•tive•ness** *n*

ac•tive-ma•trix \ˈak-tiv-ˌmā-triks\ *adj* : of, relating to, or being an LCD in which each pixel is individually controlled

ac•tive•wear \ˈak-tiv-ˌwer\ *n* : clothing designed for recreation or informal wear

ac•tiv•ism \ˈak-ti-ˌvi-zəm\ *n* : a doctrine or practice that emphasizes vigorous action for political ends — **ac•tiv•ist** \-vist\ *n or adj*

ac•tiv•i•ty \ak-ˈti-və-tē\ *n, pl* **-ties 1** : the quality or state of being active **2** : forceful or energetic action **3** : an occupation in which one is engaged

ac•tor \ˈak-tər\ *n* : a person who acts in a play or motion picture

ac•tress \ˈak-trəs\ *n* : a woman who is an actor

Acts \ˈakts\ *or* **Acts of the Apostles** *n* — see BIBLE table

ac•tu•al \ˈak-chə-wəl, -shə-\ *adj* : really existing : REAL — **ac•tu•al•i•ty** \ˌak-chə-ˈwa-lə-tē, -shə-\ *n* — **ac•tu•al•i•za•tion** \ˌak-chə-wə-lə-ˈzā-shən, -shə-\ *n* — **ac•tu•al•ize** \ˈak-chə-wə-ˌlīz, -shə-\ *vb*

ac•tu•al•ly \ˈak-chə-wə-lē, -shə-\ *adv* : in fact or in truth : REALLY

ac•tu•ary \ˈak-chə-ˌwer-ē, -shə-\ *n, pl* **-ar•ies** : a person who calculates insurance risks and premiums — **ac•tu•ar•i•al** \ˌak-chə-ˈwer-ē-əl, -shə-\ *adj*

ac•tu•ate \ˈak-chə-ˌwāt\ *vb* **-at•ed; -at•ing 1** : to put into action **2** : to move to action — **ac•tu•a•tion** \ˌak-chə-ˈwā-shən, -shə-\ *n* — **ac•tu•a•tor** \ˈak-chə-ˌwā-tər, -shə-\ *n*

act up *vb* **1** : MISBEHAVE **2** : to function improperly

acu•ity \ə-ˈkyü-ə-tē\ *n, pl* **-ities** : keenness of perception

acu•men \ə-ˈkyü-mən\ *n* : mental keenness and penetration ♦ *Synonyms* DISCERNMENT, INSIGHT, PERCIPIENCE, PERSPICACITY

acu•pres•sure \ˈa-kyù-ˌpre-shər\ *n* : a finger massage of those points on the body stimulated in acupuncture

acu•punc•ture \-ˌpəŋk-chər\ *n* : an orig. Chinese practice of inserting thin needles through the skin at specific points esp. to cure disease or relieve pain — **acu•punc•tur•ist** \ˌa-kyù-ˈpəŋk-chə-rist\ *n*

acute \ə-ˈkyüt\ *adj* **acut•er; acut•est** [ME, fr. L *acutus*, pp. of *acuere* to sharpen, fr. *acus* needle] **1** : SHARP, POINTED **2** : containing less than 90 degrees ⟨an ∼ angle⟩ **3** : sharply perceptive; *esp* : mentally keen **4** : SEVERE ⟨∼ distress⟩; *also* : having a sudden onset, sharp rise, and short duration ⟨∼ inflammation⟩ **5** : of, marked by, or being an accent mark having the form ´ — **acute•ly** *adv* — **acute•ness** *n*

acy•clo•vir \(ˌ)ā-ˈsī-klō-ˌvir\ *n* : a drug used esp. to treat the genital form of herpes simplex

ad \ˈad\ *n* : ADVERTISEMENT

AD *abbr* **1** after date **2** [L *anno Domini*] in the year of our Lord — often printed in small capitals and often punctuated **3** assistant director **4** athletic director

ad•age \ˈa-dij\ *n* : an old familiar saying : PROVERB, MAXIM

ada•gio \ə-ˈdä-j(ē-)ō, -zh(ē-)ō\ *adv or adj* [It] : at a slow tempo — used as a direction in music

²**adagio** *n, pl* **-gios 1** : an adagio movement **2** : a ballet duet or trio displaying feats of lifting and balancing

¹**ad•a•mant** \ˈa-də-mənt, -ˌmant\ *n* [ME, fr. AF, fr. L *adamant-, adamas* hardest metal, diamond, fr. Gk] : a stone believed to be impenetrably hard — **ad•a•man•tine** \ˌa-də-ˈman-ˌtēn, -ˌtīn\ *adj*

²**adamant** *adj* : very determined : INFLEXIBLE, UNYIELDING — **ad•a•man•cy** \ˈa-də-mən-sē\ *n* — **ad•a•mant•ly** *adv*

Ad•am's apple \ˈa-dəmz-\ *n* : the projection in front of the neck formed by the largest cartilage of the larynx

adapt \ə-ˈdapt\ *vb* **1** : to make suitable or fit (as for a new use or to a different situation) **2** : to adjust to environmental conditions ♦ *Synonyms* ADJUST, ACCOMMODATE, CONFORM — **adapt•abil•i•ty**

\ə-ˌdap-tə-'bi-lə-tē\ *n* — **adapt·able** *adj* — **ad·ap·ta·tion** \ˌa-ˌdap-'tā-shən\ *n* — **ad·ap·ta·tion·al** \-sh(ə-)nəl\ *adj* — **adap·tive** \ə-'dap-tiv\ *adj* — **ad·ap·tiv·i·ty** \ˌa-ˌdap-'ti-və-tē\ *n*

adapt·er *also* **adap·tor** \ə-'dap-tər\ *n* **1** : one that adapts **2** : a device for connecting two dissimilar parts of an apparatus **3** : an attachment for adapting apparatus for uses not orig. intended

adaptive optics *n sing or pl* : a telescopic system that improves image resolution by compensating for distortions from atmospheric turbulence

ADC *abbr* **1** aide-de-camp **2** Aid to Dependent Children

add \'ad\ *vb* **1** : to join to something else so as to increase in number or amount **2** : to say further ⟨let me ~ this⟩ **3** : to combine (numbers) into one sum

ADD *abbr* attention deficit disorder

ad·dend \'a-ˌdend\ *n* : a number to be added to another

ad·den·dum \ə-'den-dəm\ *n, pl* **-da** \-də\ [L] : something added; *esp* : a supplement to a book

1ad·der \'a-dər\ *n* [ME, alter. (by false division of *a naddre*) of *naddre*, fr. OE *nǣddre*] **1** : a poisonous European viper or a related snake **2** : any of various harmless No. American snakes (as the hognose snake)

2add·er \'a-dər\ *n* : one that adds; *esp* : a device that performs addition

1ad·dict \ə-'dikt\ *vb* **1** : to devote or surrender (oneself) to something habitually or excessively **2** : to cause addiction to a substance in (as a person) — **ad·dic·tive** \-'dik-tiv\ *adj*

2ad·dict \'a-(ˌ)dikt\ *n* : one who is addicted esp. to a substance

ad·dic·tion \ə-'dik-shən\ *n* **1** : the quality or state of being addicted **2** : compulsive need for and use of a habit-forming substance (as heroin, nicotine, or alcohol) characterized by well-defined physiological symptoms upon withdrawal; *also* : persistent compulsive use of a substance known by the user to be harmful

ad·di·tion \ə-'di-shən\ *n* **1** : the act or process of adding; *also* : something added **2** : the operation of combining numbers to obtain their sum ♦ *Synonyms* ACCRETION, INCREMENT, ACCESSION, AUGMENTATION

ad·di·tion·al \ə-'di-sh(ə-)nəl\ *adj* : coming by way of addition : ADDED, EXTRA

ad·di·tion·al·ly \ə-'di-sh(ə-)nə-lē\ *adv* : in or by way of addition : FURTHERMORE

1ad·di·tive \'a-də-tiv\ *adj* **1** : of, relating to, or characterized by addition **2** : produced by addition — **ad·di·tiv·i·ty** \ˌa-də-'ti-və-tē\ *n*

2additive *n* : a substance added to another in small quantities to effect a desired change in properties ⟨food ~s⟩

ad·dle \'a-dᵊl\ *vb* **ad·dled; ad·dling 1** : to throw into confusion : MUDDLE **2** : to become rotten ⟨*addled* eggs⟩

addn *abbr* addition

addnl *abbr* additional

add–on \'ad-ˌón, -ˌän\ *n* : something (as a

feature or accessory) added esp. as an enhancement

1ad·dress \ə-'dres\ *vb* **1** : to direct the attention of (oneself) **2** : to direct one's remarks to : deliver an address to **3** : to mark directions for delivery on **4** : to identify (as a memory location) by an address

2ad·dress \ə-'dres, 'a-ˌdres\ *n* **1** : skillful management **2** : a formal speech : LECTURE **3** : the place where a person or organization may be communicated with **4** : the directions for delivery placed on mail; *also* : the designation of a computer account from which one can send or receive e-mail **5** : a location (as in a computer's memory) where particular data is stored; *also* : URL

ad·dress·ee \ˌa-ˌdre-'sē, ə-ˌdre-'sē\ *n* : one to whom something is addressed

ad·duce \ə-'düs, -'dyüs\ *vb* **ad·duced; ad·duc·ing** : to offer as argument, reason, or proof ♦ *Synonyms* ADVANCE, ALLEGE, CITE, SUBMIT — **ad·duc·er** *n*

-ade *n suffix* **1** : act : action ⟨block*ade*⟩ **2** : product; *esp* : sweet drink ⟨lim*ade*⟩

ad·e·nine \'a-də-ˌnēn\ *n* : a purine base that codes genetic information in the molecular chain of DNA and RNA

ad·e·noid \'a-də-ˌnòid, 'ad-ˌnòid\ *n* : an enlarged mass of tissue near the opening of the nose into the throat — usu. used in pl. — **adenoid** *or* **ad·e·noi·dal** \ˌa-də-ˌnòi-dᵊl\ *adj*

aden·o·sine tri·phos·phate \ə-'de-nə-ˌsēn-trī-'fäs-ˌfāt\ *n* : ATP

ad·e·no·vi·rus \ˌa-dᵊn-ō-'vī-rəs\ *n* : any of a family of viruses causing infections of the respiratory tract, conjunctiva, and gastrointestinal tract

1ad·ept \'a-ˌdept\ *n* : EXPERT

2adept \ə-'dept\ *adj* : highly skilled : EXPERT — **adept·ly** *adv* — **adept·ness** *n*

ad·e·quate \'a-di-kwət\ *adj* : equal to or sufficient for a specific requirement — **ad·e·qua·cy** \-kwə-sē\ *n* — **ad·e·quate·ly** *adv* — **ad·e·quate·ness** *n*

ad·here \ad-'hir\ *vb* **ad·hered; ad·her·ing 1** : to give support : maintain loyalty **2** : to stick fast : CLING — **ad·her·ence** \-'hir-əns\ *n* — **ad·her·ent** \-ənt\ *adj or n*

ad·he·sion \ad-'hē-zhən\ *n* **1** : the act or state of adhering **2** : the union of bodily tissues abnormally grown together after inflammation; *also* : the newly formed uniting tissue **3** : the molecular attraction between the surfaces of bodies in contact

1ad·he·sive \-'hē-siv, -ziv\ *adj* **1** : tending to adhere : STICKY **2** : prepared for adhering

2adhesive *n* : an adhesive substance

adhesive tape *n* : tape coated on one side with an adhesive mixture; *esp* : one used for covering wounds

1ad hoc \'ad-'häk, -'hōk\ *adv* [L, for this] : for the case at hand apart from other applications

2ad hoc *adj* : concerned with or formed for a particular purpose ⟨an *ad hoc* committee⟩ ⟨*ad hoc* solutions⟩

adi·a·bat·ic \ˌa-dē-ə-'ba-tik\ *adj* : occurring

without loss or gain of heat — **adi·a·bat·i·cal·ly** \-ti-k(ə-)lē\ adv

adieu \ə-'dü, -'dyü\ n, pl **adieus** or **adieux** \ə-'düz, -'dyüz, -'dyüz\ : FAREWELL — often used interjectionally

ad in·fi·ni·tum \ˌad-ˌin-fə-'nī-təm\ adv or adj : without end or limit

ad in·ter·im \ad-'in-tə-rəm, -ˌrim\ adv adj : for the intervening time — **ad interim** adj

adi·os \ˌa-dē-'ōs, ˌä-\ interj [Sp adiós, lit., to God] — used to express farewell

ad·i·pose \'a-də-ˌpōs\ adj : of or relating to animal fat : FATTY

adj abbr **1** adjective **2** adjutant

ad·ja·cent \ə-'jā-sᵊnt\ adj : situated near or next ◆ **Synonyms** ADJOINING, CONTIGUOUS, ABUTTING, JUXTAPOSED, CONTERMINOUS — **ad·ja·cent·ly** adv

ad·jec·tive \'a-jik-tiv\ n : a word that typically serves as a modifier of a noun — **ad·jec·ti·val** \ˌa-jik-'tī-vəl\ adj — **ad·jec·ti·val·ly** adv

ad·join \ə-'jȯin\ vb : to be situated next to

ad·join·ing adj : touching or bounding at a point or line ⟨∼ rooms⟩

ad·journ \ə-'jərn\ vb **1** : to suspend indefinitely or until a stated time **2** : to transfer to another place — **ad·journment** n

ad·judge \ə-'jəj\ vb **ad·judged; ad·judging 1** : JUDGE, ADJUDICATE **2** : to hold or pronounce to be : DEEM **3** : to award by judicial decision

ad·ju·di·cate \ə-'jü-di-ˌkāt\ vb **-cat·ed; -cat·ing** : to settle judicially — **ad·ju·di·ca·tion** \ə-ˌjü-di-'kā-shən\ n

ad·junct \'a-ˌjəŋkt\ n : something joined or added to another but not essentially a part of it ◆ **Synonyms** APPENDAGE, APPURTENANCE, ACCESSORY, APPENDIX — **adjunct** adj

ad·jure \ə-'jur\ vb **ad·jured; ad·jur·ing** : to command solemnly : urge earnestly ◆ **Synonyms** BEG, BESEECH, IMPLORE — **ad·ju·ra·tion** \ˌa-jə-'rā-shən\ n

ad·just \ə-'jəst\ vb **1** : to bring to agreement : SETTLE **2** : to cause to conform : ADAPT, FIT **3** : REGULATE ⟨∼ a watch⟩ — **ad·just·able** adj — **ad·just·er** also **ad·jus·tor** \ə-'jəs-tər\ n — **ad·just·ment** \ə-'jəst-mənt\ n

ad·ju·tant \'a-jə-tənt\ n : one who assists; esp : an officer who assists a commanding officer by handling correspondence and keeping records

ad·ju·vant \'a-jə-vənt\ n : one that helps or facilitates; esp : something that enhances the effectiveness of medical treatment — **adjuvant** adj

¹**ad-lib** \'ad-'lib\ vb **ad-libbed; ad-libbing** : IMPROVISE — **ad-lib** n

²**ad-lib** adj : spoken, composed, or performed without preparation

ad lib \'ad-'lib\ adv [NL ad libitum] **1** : at one's pleasure **2** : without limit

adm abbr administration; administrative

ADM abbr admiral

ad·man \'ad-ˌman\ n : one who writes, solicits, or places advertisements

admin abbr administration; administrative

ad·min·is·ter \əd-'mi-nə-stər\ vb **1** : MANAGE, SUPERINTEND **2** : to mete out : DISPENSE ⟨∼ punishment⟩ **3** : to give ritually or remedially ⟨∼ quinine for malaria⟩ **4** : to perform the office of administrator — **ad·min·is·tra·ble** \-strə-bəl\ adj — **ad·min·is·trant** \-strənt\ n

ad·min·is·tra·tion \əd-ˌmi-nə-'strā-shən\ n **1** : the act or process of administering **2** : MANAGEMENT **3** : the officials directing the government of a country **4** : the term of office of an administrative officer or body — **ad·min·is·tra·tive** \əd-'mi-nə-ˌstrā-tiv\ adj — **ad·min·is·tra·tive·ly** adv

ad·min·is·tra·tor \əd-'mi-nə-ˌstrā-tər\ n : one that administers; esp : one who settles an intestate estate

ad·mi·ra·ble \'ad-m(ə-)rə-bəl\ adj : worthy of admiration : EXCELLENT — **ad·mi·ra·bil·i·ty** \ˌad-m(ə-)rə-'bi-lə-tē\ n — **ad·mi·ra·ble·ness** n — **ad·mi·ra·bly** \-blē\ adv

ad·mi·ral \'ad-m(ə-)rəl\ n [ME, ultim. fr. Ar amīr-al- commander of the (as in amīr-al-baḥr commander of the sea)] : a commissioned officer in the navy ranking next below a fleet admiral

ad·mi·ral·ty \'ad-m(ə-)rəl-tē\ n **1** cap : a British government department formerly having authority over naval affairs **2** : the court having jurisdiction over questions of maritime law

ad·mire \əd-'mī(-ə)r\ vb **ad·mired; ad·mir·ing** [MF admirer, fr. L admirari, fr. ad- to + mirari to wonder] : to regard with high esteem — **ad·mi·ra·tion** \ˌad-mə-'rā-shən\ n — **ad·mir·er** n — **ad·mir·ing·ly** \-'mī-riŋ-lē\ adv

ad·mis·si·ble \əd-'mi-sə-bəl\ adj : that can be or is worthy to be admitted or allowed : ALLOWABLE ⟨∼ evidence⟩ — **ad·mis·si·bil·i·ty** \-ˌmi-sə-'bi-lə-tē\ n

ad·mis·sion \əd-'mi-shən\ n **1** : the act of admitting **2** : the privilege of being admitted **3** : a fee paid for admission **4** : the granting of an argument **5** : the acknowledgment of a fact

ad·mit \əd-'mit\ vb **ad·mit·ted; ad·mit·ting 1** : PERMIT, ALLOW **2** : to recognize as genuine or valid **3** : to allow to enter ⟨admitted to the club⟩ **4** : to accept into a hospital as an inpatient

ad·mit·tance \əd-'mi-tᵊns\ n : the act or process of admitting : permission to enter

ad·mit·ted·ly \əd-'mi-təd-lē\ adv **1** : as has been or must be admitted **2** : it must be admitted

ad·mix \ad-'miks\ vb : to mix in

ad·mix·ture \ad-'miks-chər\ n **1** : something added in mixing **2** : MIXTURE

ad·mon·ish \əd-'mä-nish\ vb : to warn gently : reprove with a warning ◆ **Synonyms** CHIDE, REPROACH, REBUKE, REPRIMAND, REPROVE — **ad·mon·ish·er** n — **ad·mon·ish·ing·ly** adv — **ad·mon·ish·ment** n — **ad·mo·ni·tion** \ˌad-mə-'ni-shən\ n — **ad·mon·i·to·ry** \əd-'mä-nə-ˌtȯr-ē\ adj

ad nau·se·am \ad-'nȯ-zē-əm\ adv [L] : to a sickening or excessive degree

ado \ə-'dü\ *n* **1** : heightened fuss or concern **2** : TROUBLE

ado·be \ə-'dō-bē\ *n* **1** : sun-dried brick; *also* : clay for making such bricks **2** : a structure made of adobe bricks

ad·o·les·cence \ˌa-də-'le-sᵊns\ *n* : the process or period of growth between childhood and maturity — **ad·o·les·cent** \-sᵊnt\ *adj or n*

adopt \ə-'däpt\ *vb* **1** : to take (a child of other parents) as one's own child **2** : to take up and practice as one's own **3** : to accept formally and put into effect — **adopt·able** \-'däp-tə-bəl\ *adj* — **adopter** *n* — **adop·tion** \-'däp-shən\ *n*

adop·tive \ə-'däp-tiv\ *adj* : made or acquired by adoption ⟨the ∼ father⟩ — **adop·tive·ly** *adv*

ador·able \ə-'dór-ə-bəl\ *adj* **1** : worthy of adoration **2** : extremely charming ⟨an ∼ child⟩ — **ador·able·ness** *n* — **adorably** \-blē\ *adv*

adore \ə-'dór\ *vb* **adored; ador·ing** [ME *adouren*, fr. AF *aurer, adourer*, fr. L *adorare*, fr. *ad-* to + *orare* to speak, pray] **1** : WORSHIP **2** : to regard with loving admiration ⟨∼s his wife⟩ **3** : to be extremely fond of ⟨∼s pecan pie⟩ — **ado·ra·tion** \ˌa-də-'rā-shən\ *n*

adorn \ə-'dórn\ *vb* : to enhance the appearance of esp. with ornaments ⟨blouses ∼ed with sequins⟩ — **adorn·ment** *n*

ad·re·nal \ə-'drē-nᵊl\ *adj* : of, relating to, or being a pair of endocrine organs (**adrenal glands**) that are located near the kidneys and produce several hormones and esp. epinephrine

adren·a·line \ə-'dre-nə-lən\ *n* : EPINEPHRINE

adrift \ə-'drift\ *adv or adj* **1** : afloat without motive power or moorings **2** : without guidance or purpose

adroit \ə-'dróit\ *adj* [F, fr. OF, fr. *a-* to + *droit* right] **1** : dexterous with one's hands **2** : SHREWD, RESOURCEFUL ♦ **Synonyms** CANNY, CLEVER, CUNNING, INGENIOUS — **adroit·ly** *adv* — **adroit·ness** *n*

ad·sorb \ad-'sórb, -'zórb\ *vb* : to take up (as molecules of gases) and hold on the surface of a solid or liquid — **ad·sorption** \-'sórp-shən, -'zórp-\ *n*

ad·u·la·tion \ˌa-jə-'lā-shən\ *n* : excessive admiration or flattery — **ad·u·late** \'a-jə-ˌlāt\ *vb* — **ad·u·la·tor** \-ˌlā-tər\ *n* — **ad·u·la·to·ry** \-lə-ˌtór-ē\ *adj*

¹adult \ə-'dəlt, 'a-ˌ\ *adj* [L *adultus*, pp. of *adolescere* to grow up, fr. *ad-* to + *alescere* to grow] : fully developed and mature — **adult·hood** *n*

²adult *n* : one that is adult; *esp* : a human being after an age (as 18) specified by law

adul·ter·ant \ə-'dəl-tə-rənt\ *n* : something used to adulterate another

adul·ter·ate \ə-'dəl-tə-ˌrāt\ *vb* **-at·ed; -at·ing** [L *adulterare*, fr. *ad-* to + *alter* other] : to make impure by mixing in a foreign or inferior substance — **adul·ter·a·tion** \-ˌdəl-tə-'rā-shən\ *n*

adul·tery \ə-'dəl-t(ə-)rē\ *n, pl* **-ter·ies** : sexual unfaithfulness of a married person — **adul·ter·er** \-tər-ər\ *n* — **adul-**

ter·ess \-t(ə-)rəs\ *also* **adul·tress** \-trəs\ *n* — **adul·ter·ous** \-t(ə-)rəs\ *adj*

ad·um·brate \'a-dəm-ˌbrāt\ *vb* **-brat·ed; -brat·ing 1** : to foreshadow vaguely : INTIMATE **2** : to suggest or disclose partially **3** : SHADE, OBSCURE — **ad·um·bra·tion** \ˌa-dəm-'brā-shən\ *n*

adv *abbr* **1** adverb **2** advertisement

ad va·lo·rem \ˌad-və-'lór-əm\ *adj* [L, according to the value] : imposed at a percentage of the value ⟨an *ad valorem* tax⟩

¹ad·vance \əd-'vans\ *vb* **ad·vanced; ad·vanc·ing 1** : to assist the progress of ⟨∼ a cause⟩ **2** : to bring or move forward ⟨∼ a pawn⟩ **3** : to promote in rank **4** : to make earlier in time **5** : PROPOSE **6** : LEND **7** : to raise in rate : INCREASE — **ad·vance·ment** *n*

²advance *n* **1** : a forward movement **2** : IMPROVEMENT **3** : a rise esp. in price or value **4** : OFFER — **in advance** : BEFOREHAND

³advance *adj* : made, sent, or furnished ahead of time ⟨∼ payment⟩

ad·van·tage \əd-'van-tij\ *n* **1** : superiority of position **2** : BENEFIT, GAIN **3** : the 1st point won in tennis after deuce — **ad·van·ta·geous** \ˌad-ˌvan-'tā-jəs\ *adj* — **ad·van·ta·geous·ly** *adv*

ad·vent \'ad-ˌvent\ *n* **1** *cap* : a penitential period beginning four Sundays before Christmas **2** *cap* : the coming of Christ **3** : a coming into being or use

ad·ven·ti·tious \ˌad-vən-'ti-shəs\ *adj* **1** : ACCIDENTAL, INCIDENTAL **2** : arising or occurring sporadically or in other than the usual location ⟨∼ buds⟩ — **ad·ven·ti·tious·ly** *adv*

¹ad·ven·ture \əd-'ven-chər\ *n* **1** : a risky undertaking **2** : a remarkable and exciting experience — **ad·ven·tur·ous** \-ch(ə-)rəs\ *adj*

²adventure *vb* **-ven·tured; -ven·tur·ing** \-'ven-ch(ə-)riŋ\ **1** : RISK, HAZARD ⟨∼ their capital in foreign trade⟩ **2** : to engage in adventure

ad·ven·tur·er \əd-'ven-ch(ə-)rər\ *n* **1** : a person who engages in new and risky undertakings **2** : a person who follows a military career for adventure or profit **3** : a person who tries to gain wealth by questionable means

ad·ven·ture·some \əd-'ven-chər-səm\ *adj* : inclined to take risks

ad·ven·tur·ess \əd-'ven-ch(ə-)rəs\ *n* : a female adventurer

ad·verb \'ad-ˌvərb\ *n* : a word that typically serves as a modifier of a verb, an adjective, or another adverb — **ad·ver·bi·al** \ad-'vər-bē-əl\ *adj* — **ad·ver·bi·al·ly** *adv*

¹ad·ver·sary \'ad-vər-ˌser-ē\ *n, pl* **-sar·ies** : FOE

²adversary *adj* : involving antagonistic parties or interests

ad·verse \ad-'vərs, 'ad-ˌvərs\ *adj* **1** : acting against or in a contrary direction ⟨∼ winds⟩ **2** : UNFAVORABLE ⟨∼ criticism⟩ — **ad·verse·ly** *adv*

ad·ver·si·ty \ad-'vər-sə-tē\ *n, pl* **-ties** : serious difficulty : MISFORTUNE

ad·vert \ad-'vərt\ *vb* : REFER ⟨∼ to a previous remark⟩

ad·ver·tise \'ad-vər-ˌtīz\ *vb* **-tised; -tising 1** : INFORM, NOTIFY **2** : to call public attention to esp. in order to sell — **ad·ver·tis·er** *n*

ad·ver·tise·ment \ˌad-vər-'tīz-mənt; əd-'vər-təs-mənt\ *n* **1** : the act of advertising **2** : a public notice intended to advertise something

ad·ver·tis·ing \'ad-vər-ˌtī-ziŋ\ *n* : the business of preparing advertisements

ad·vice \əd-'vīs\ *n* **1** : recommendation with regard to a course of action : COUNSEL **2** : INFORMATION, REPORT

ad·vis·able \əd-'vī-zə-bəl\ *adj* : proper to be done : EXPEDIENT ⟨∼ to stay fit⟩ — **ad·vis·abil·i·ty** \-ˌvī-zə-'bi-lə-tē\ *n*

ad·vise \əd-'vīz\ *vb* **advised; ad·vis·ing 1** : to give advice to : COUNSEL **2** : INFORM, NOTIFY **3** : CONSULT, CONFER ⟨∼ with your friends⟩ — **ad·vis·er** *also* **ad·vi·sor** \-'vī-zər\ *n*

ad·vised \əd-'vīzd\ *adj* : thought out : CONSIDERED ⟨well-*advised*⟩ — **ad·vis·ed·ly** \-'vī-zəd-lē\ *adv*

ad·vise·ment \əd-'vīz-mənt\ *n* **1** : careful consideration ⟨take the matter under ∼⟩ **2** : the act of advising

ad·vi·so·ry \əd-'vī-zə-rē\ *adj* **1** : having or exercising power to advise **2** : containing or giving advice

¹ad·vo·cate \'ad-və-kət, -ˌkāt\ *n* [ultim. fr. L *advocare* to summon, fr. *ad-* to + *vocare* to call] **1** : one who pleads another's cause **2** : one who argues or pleads for a cause or proposal — **ad·vo·ca·cy** \-və-kə-sē\ *n*

²ad·vo·cate \-ˌkāt\ *vb* **-cat·ed; -cat·ing** : to plead in favor of — **ad·vo·ca·tion** \ˌad-və-'kā-shən\ *n*

advt *abbr* advertisement

adze *also* **adz** \'adz\ *n* : a tool with a curved blade set at right angles to the handle that is used in shaping wood

AEC *abbr* Atomic Energy Commission

ae·gis \'ē-jəs\ *n* **1** : SHIELD, PROTECTION ⟨under the ∼ of the constitution⟩ **2** : PATRONAGE, SPONSORSHIP ⟨under the ∼ of the museum⟩

ae·o·li·an harp \ē-'ō-lē-ən-\ *n* : a box with strings that produce musical sounds when the wind blows on them

ae·on *or* **eon** \'ē-ən, -ˌän\ *n* : an indefinitely long time : AGE

aer·ate \'er-ˌāt\ *vb* **aer·at·ed; aer·at·ing 1** : to supply, impregnate, or combine with a gas and esp. air **2** : to supply (blood) with oxygen by respiration — **aer·a·tion** \ˌer-'ā-shən\ *n* — **aer·a·tor** \'er-ˌā-tər\ *n*

¹ae·ri·al \'er-ē-əl\ *adj* **1** : inhabiting, occurring in, or done in the air **2** : AIRY **3** : of or relating to aircraft

²aer·i·al \'er-ē-əl\ *n* : ANTENNA 2

ae·ri·al·ist \'er-ē-ə-list\ *n* : a performer of feats above the ground esp. on a trapeze

ae·rie \'er-ē, 'ir-ē\ *n* : a highly placed nest (as of an eagle)

aer·o·bat·ics \ˌer-ə-'ba-tiks\ *n sing or pl* : spectacular flying feats and maneuvers

aer·o·bic \ˌer-'rō-bik\ *adj* **1** : living or active only in the presence of oxygen ⟨∼ bacteria⟩ **2** : involving or increasing oxygen consumption; *also* : of or relating to aerobics — **aer·o·bi·cal·ly** \-bi-k(ə-)lē\ *adv*

aer·o·bics \-biks\ *n sing or pl* : strenuous exercises that produce a marked temporary increase in respiration and heart rate; *also* : a system of physical conditioning involving these

aero·drome \'er-ə-ˌdrōm\ *n, chiefly Brit* : AIRPORT

aero·dy·nam·ics \ˌer-ō-dī-'na-miks\ *n* : the science dealing with the forces acting on bodies in motion in a gas (as air) — **aero·dy·nam·ic** \-mik\ *also* **aero·dy·nam·i·cal** \-mi-kəl\ *adj* — **aero·dy·nam·i·cal·ly** \-mi-k(ə-)lē\ *adv*

aero·naut \'er-ə-ˌnȯt\ *n* [F *aéronaute*, ultim. fr. Gk *aēr* air + *nautēs* sailor] : one who operates or travels in an airship or balloon

aero·nau·tics \ˌer-ə-'nȯ-tiks\ *n* : the science of aircraft operation — **aero·nau·ti·cal** \-ti-kəl\ *also* **aero·nau·tic** \-tik\ *adj*

aero·pho·bia \ˌer-ō-'fō-bē-ə\ *n* : fear or strong dislike of flying

aero·plane \'er-ə-ˌplān\ *chiefly Brit var of* AIRPLANE

aero·sol \'er-ə-ˌsäl, -ˌsȯl\ *n* **1** : a suspension of fine solid or liquid particles in a gas; *also, pl* : the particles themselves **2** : a substance (as an insecticide) dispensed from a pressurized container as an aerosol

aero·space \'er-ō-ˌspās\ *n* : the earth's atmosphere and the space beyond — **aerospace** *adj*

aery \'er-ē\ *adj* **aer·i·er; -est** : having an aerial quality : ETHEREAL ⟨∼ visions⟩

aes·thete *also* **es·thete** \'es-ˌthēt\ *n* : a person having or affecting sensitivity to beauty esp. in art

aes·thet·ic *also* **es·thet·ic** \es-'the-tik\ *adj* **1** : of or relating to aesthetics : ARTISTIC **2** : appreciative of the beautiful — **aes·thet·i·cal·ly** *also* **es·thet·i·cal·ly** \-ti-k(ə-)lē\ *adv*

aes·thet·ics *also* **es·thet·ics** \-tiks\ *n* : a branch of philosophy dealing with the nature, creation, and appreciation of beauty

ae·ti·ol·o·gy *chiefly Brit var of* ETIOLOGY

AF *abbr* **1** air force **2** audio frequency

¹afar \ə-'fär\ *adv* : from, at, or to a great distance

²afar *n* : a great distance

AFB *abbr* air force base

AFC *abbr* **1** American Football Conference **2** automatic frequency control

AFDC *abbr* Aid to Families with Dependent Children

af·fa·ble \'a-fə-bəl\ *adj* : courteous and agreeable in conversation — **af·fa·bil·i·ty** \ˌa-fə-'bi-lə-tē\ *n* — **af·fa·bly** \'a-fə-blē\ *adv*

af·fair \ə-'fer\ *n* [ME *afere*, fr. AF fr. *afaire*, fr. *a faire* to do] **1** : something that relates to or involves one : CONCERN **2** : a romantic or sexual attachment of limited duration

¹**af·fect** \ə-ˈfekt, a-\ *vb* **1** : to be fond of using or wearing **2** : to pretend that an attitude or behavior is genuine

²**affect** *vb* : to produce an effect on : INFLUENCE

³**af·fect** \ˈa-ˌfekt\ *n* : EMOTION; *also* : an observable display of emotion ⟨an expressionless ~⟩

af·fec·ta·tion \ˌa-ˌfek-ˈtā-shən\ *n* : an attitude or behavior that is assumed by a person but not genuinely felt

af·fect·ed \a-ˈfek-təd\ *adj* **1** : given to or marked by affectation **2** : artificially assumed to impress others — **af·fect·ed·ly** *adv*

af·fect·ing \a-ˈfek-tiŋ\ *adj* : arousing pity, sympathy, or sorrow ⟨an ~ story⟩ — **af·fect·ing·ly** *adv*

af·fec·tion \a-ˈfek-shən\ *n* : tender attachment — **af·fec·tion·ate** \-sh(ə-)nət\ *adj* — **af·fec·tion·ate·ly** *adv*

af·fec·tive \a-ˈfek-tiv\ *adj* : relating to, influencing, or expressing an emotion or feeling : EMOTIONAL ⟨an ~ disorder⟩

af·fer·ent \ˈa-fə-rənt, -ˌfer-ənt\ *adj* : bearing or conducting inward toward a more central part and esp. a nerve center (as the central nervous system)

af·fi·ance \ə-ˈfī-əns\ *vb* **-anced; -anc·ing** : to promise oneself or another in marriage

af·fi·da·vit \ˌa-fə-ˈdā-vət\ *n* [ML, he has made an oath] : a sworn statement in writing

¹**af·fil·i·ate** \ə-ˈfi-lē-ˌāt\ *vb* **-at·ed; -at·ing** : to associate as a member or branch — **af·fil·i·a·tion** \-ˌfi-lē-ˈā-shən\ *n*

²**af·fil·i·ate** \ə-ˈfi-lē-ət\ *n* : an affiliated person or organization

af·fin·i·ty \ə-ˈfi-nə-tē\ *n, pl* **-ties 1** : KINSHIP, RELATIONSHIP **2** : attractive force : ATTRACTION, SYMPATHY

affinity card *n* : a credit card issued in affiliation with an organization (as a charity or an airline) the use of which benefits the organization or possessor of the card

af·firm \ə-ˈfərm\ *vb* **1** : CONFIRM **2** : to assert positively **3** : to make a solemn and formal declaration or assertion in place of an oath ♦ *Synonyms* AVER, AVOW, AVOUCH, DECLARE, ASSERT — **af·fir·ma·tion** \ˌa-fər-ˈmā-shən\ *n*

¹**af·fir·ma·tive** \ə-ˈfər-mə-tiv\ *adj* : asserting that the fact is so : POSITIVE

²**affirmative** *n* **1** : an expression of affirmation or assent **2** : the side that upholds the proposition stated in a debate

affirmative action *n* : an active effort to improve the employment or educational opportunities of members of minority groups and women

¹**af·fix** \ə-ˈfiks\ *vb* : ATTACH, ADD

²**af·fix** \ˈa-ˌfiks\ *n* : one or more sounds or letters attached to the beginning or end of a word that produce a derivative word or an inflectional form

af·fla·tus \ə-ˈflā-təs\ *n* : divine inspiration

af·flict \ə-ˈflikt\ *vb* : to cause pain and distress to ♦ *Synonyms* RACK, TRY, TORMENT, TORTURE — **af·flic·tion** \-ˈflik-shən\ *n*

af·flic·tive \ə-ˈflik-tiv\ *adj* : causing affliction : DISTRESSING ⟨~ emotions⟩ — **af·flic·tive·ly** *adv*

af·flu·ence \ˈa-ˌflü-ən(t)s, a-ˈflü-\ *n* : abundant supply; *also* : WEALTH, RICHES — **af·flu·ent** \-ənt\ *adj*

af·ford \ə-ˈfȯrd\ *vb* **1** : to manage to bear or bear the cost of without serious harm or loss **2** : PROVIDE, FURNISH ⟨the roof ~ed a fine view⟩

af·for·es·ta·tion \a-ˌfȯr-ə-ˈstā-shən\ *n* : the act or process of establishing a forest — **af·for·est** \a-ˈfȯr-əst, -ˈfär-\ *vb*

af·fray \ə-ˈfrā\ *n* : FIGHT, FRAY

af·fright \ə-ˈfrīt\ *vb, archaic* : FRIGHTEN, ALARM — **affright** *n*

af·front \ə-ˈfrənt\ *vb* **1** : INSULT **2** : CONFRONT ⟨~ death⟩ — **affront** *n*

af·ghan \ˈaf-ˌgan\ *n* **1** *cap* : a native or inhabitant of Afghanistan **2** : a blanket or shawl of colored wool knitted or crocheted in sections — **Afghan** *or* **Af·ghani** \af-ˈga-nē, -ˈgä-\ *adj*

Afghan hound *n* : any of a breed of tall slim swift hunting dogs with a coat of silky thick hair and a long silky top-knot

af·ghani \af-ˈga-nē\ *n* — see MONEY table

afi·cio·na·do \ə-ˌfi-sh(ē-)ə-ˈnä-dō, -sē-ə-\ *n, pl* **-dos** [Sp, fr. pp. of *aficionar* to inspire affection] : DEVOTEE, FAN

afield \ə-ˈfēld\ *adv or adj* **1** : to, in, or on the field **2** : away from home **3** : out of the way : ASTRAY

afire \ə-ˈfī(-ə)r\ *adj or adv* : being on fire : BURNING

AFL *abbr* American Football League

aflame \ə-ˈflām\ *adj or adv* : FLAMING

AFL–CIO *abbr* American Federation of Labor and Congress of Industrial Organizations

afloat \ə-ˈflōt\ *adj or adv* **1** : borne on or as if on the water **2** : CIRCULATING ⟨rumors were ~⟩ **3** : ADRIFT

aflut·ter \ə-ˈflə-tər\ *adj* **1** : FLUTTERING **2** : nervously excited ⟨~ at the news⟩

afoot \ə-ˈfu̇t\ *adv or adj* **1** : on foot **2** : in action : in progress

afore·men·tioned \ə-ˈfȯr-ˈmen-chənd\ *adj* : mentioned previously

afore·said \-ˌsed\ *adj* : said or named before

afore·thought \-ˌthȯt\ *adj* : planned beforehand : PREMEDITATED ⟨with malice ~⟩

a for·ti·o·ri \ˌä-ˌfȯr-tē-ˈȯr-ē\ *adv* [NL, lit., from the stronger (argument)] : with even greater reason

afoul of \ə-ˈfau̇l-əv\ *prep* **1** : in or into conflict with **2** : in or into collision or entanglement with

Afr *abbr* Africa; African

afraid \ə-ˈfrād\ *adj* **1** : FRIGHTENED, FEARFUL **2** : filled with concern or regret ⟨~ I won't be able to go⟩

A–frame \ˈā-ˌfrām\ *n* : a building having triangular front and rear walls with the roof reaching to the ground

afresh \ə-ˈfresh\ *adv* : ANEW, AGAIN

Af·ri·can \ˈa-fri-kən\ *n* **1** : a native or inhabitant of Africa **2** : a person of African ancestry — **African** *adj*

Af·ri·can–Amer·i·can \-ə-'mer-ə-kən\ *n* : an American of African and esp. of black African descent — **African–American** *adj*

Af·ri·can·ized bee \'a-frə-kə-ˌnīzd-\ *n* : a highly aggressive hybrid honeybee accidentally produced from Brazilian and African stocks that has spread from So. America into Mexico and the southern U.S.

Africanized honeybee *n* : AFRICANIZED BEE

African violet *n* : a tropical African plant widely grown indoors for its velvety fleshy leaves and showy purple, pink, or white flowers

Af·ri·kaans \ˌa-fri-'käns\ *n* : a language developed from 17th century Dutch that is one of the official languages of the Republic of So. Africa

Af·ro \'a-(ˌ)frō\ *n, pl* **Afros** : a hairstyle of tight curls in a full evenly rounded shape

Af·ro–Amer·i·can \ˌa-frō-ə-'mer-ə-kən\ *n* : AFRICAN-AMERICAN — **Afro–American** *adj*

aft \'aft\ *adv* : near, toward, or in the stern of a ship or the tail of an aircraft

AFT *abbr* American Federation of Teachers

¹**af·ter** \'af-tər\ *adv* : AFTERWARD, SUBSEQUENTLY

²**after** *prep* **1** : behind in place **2** : later than ⟨~ dinner⟩ **3** : in pursuit or search of ⟨he's ~ your job⟩

³**after** *conj* : following the time when ⟨we will come ~ we make plans⟩

⁴**after** *adj* **1** : LATER ⟨in ~ years⟩ **2** : located toward the rear

af·ter·birth \'af-tər-ˌbərth\ *n* : the placenta and membranes of the fetus that are expelled after childbirth

af·ter·burn·er \-ˌbər-nər\ *n* : a device incorporated in the tail pipe of a turbojet engine for injecting fuel into the hot exhaust gases and burning it to provide extra thrust

af·ter·care \-ˌker\ *n* : the care, nursing, or treatment of a convalescent patient

af·ter·deck \-ˌdek\ *n* : the rear half of the deck of a ship

af·ter·ef·fect \-ə-ˌfekt\ *n* : an effect that follows its cause after an interval

af·ter·glow \-ˌglō\ *n* : a glow remaining where a light has disappeared

af·ter·im·age \-ˌim-ij\ *n* : a usu. visual sensation continuing after the stimulus causing it has ended

af·ter·life \-ˌlīf\ *n* : an existence after death

af·ter·math \-ˌmath\ *n* **1** : a secondgrowth crop esp. of hay **2** : CONSEQUENCES, EFFECTS ♦ *Synonyms* AFTEREFFECT, UPSHOT, RESULT, OUTCOME

af·ter·noon \ˌaf-tər-'nün\ *n* : the time between noon and evening

af·ter·shave \'af-tər-ˌshāv\ *n* : a usu. scented lotion for the face after shaving

af·ter·taste \-ˌtāst\ *n* : a sensation (as of flavor) continuing after the stimulus causing it has ended

af·ter–tax \'af-tər-'taks\ *adj* : remaining after payment of taxes and esp. of income tax ⟨an ~ profit⟩

af·ter·thought \-ˌthȯt\ *n* : an idea occurring later

af·ter·ward \-wərd\ *or* **af·ter·wards** \-wərdz\ *adv* : at a later time

Ag *symbol* [L *argentum*] silver

AG *abbr* **1** adjutant general **2** attorney general

again \ə-'gen, -'gin\ *adv* **1** : once more : ANEW ⟨come see us ~⟩ **2** : on the other hand ⟨we may, and ~ we may not⟩ **3** : in addition : BESIDES

against \ə-'genst\ *prep* **1** : in opposition to **2** : directly opposite to : FACING **3** : as defense from **4** : so as to touch or strike ⟨threw him ~ the wall⟩; *also* : TOUCHING

aga·pe \ä-'gä-pā, 'ä-gə-ˌpā\ *n* [LL, fr. Gk *agapē*, lit., love] : unselfish unconditional love for another

agape \ə-'gāp\ *adj or adv* : having the mouth open in wonder or surprise : GAPING

agar \'ä-ˌgär\ *n* **1** : a jellylike substance extracted from a red alga and used esp. as a gelling and stabilizing agent in foods **2** : a culture medium containing agar

agar–agar \ˌä-ˌgär-'ä-ˌgär\ *n* : AGAR

ag·ate \'a-gət\ *n* **1** : a striped or clouded quartz **2** : a playing marble of agate or of glass

aga·ve \ə-'gä-vē\ *n* : any of a genus of spiny-leaved plants (as a century plant) related to the amaryllis

agcy *abbr* agency

¹**age** \'āj\ *n* **1** : the length of time during which a being or thing has lived or existed **2** : the time of life at which some particular qualification is achieved; *esp* : MAJORITY **3** : the latter part of life **4** : a long time **5** : a period in history

²**age** *vb* **aged; ag·ing** *or* **age·ing 1** : to grow old or cause to grow old **2** : to become or cause to become mature or mellow

-age *n suffix* **1** : aggregate : collection ⟨track*age*⟩ **2** : action : process ⟨haul*age*⟩ **3** : cumulative result of ⟨break*age*⟩ **4** : rate of ⟨dos*age*⟩ **5** : house or place of ⟨orphan*age*⟩ **6** : state : rank ⟨vassal*age*⟩ **7** : fee : charge ⟨post*age*⟩

aged \'ā-jəd *for 1;* 'ājd *for 2*\ *adj* **1** : of advanced age **2** : having attained a specified age ⟨a man ~ 40 years⟩

age·ism \'ā-ˌji-zəm\ *n* : discrimination against persons of a particular age and esp. the elderly — **age·ist** \-jist\ *n*

age·less \'āj-ləs\ *adj* **1** : not growing old or showing the effects of age **2** : TIMELESS, ETERNAL ⟨~ truths⟩

agen·cy \'ā-jən-sē\ *n, pl* **-cies 1** : one through which something is accomplished : INSTRUMENTALITY **2** : the office or function of an agent **3** : an establishment doing business for another **4** : an administrative division (as of a government) ♦ *Synonyms* MEANS, MEDIUM, VEHICLE

agen·da \ə-'jen-də\ *n* : a list of things to be done : PROGRAM

agent \'ā-jənt\ *n* **1** : one that acts **2**

: MEANS, INSTRUMENT **3** : a person acting or doing business for another **4** : a computer program designed to automate certain tasks (as gathering information online) ♦ *Synonyms* ATTORNEY, DEPUTY, PROXY, DELEGATE

Agent Orange *n* : an herbicide widely used in the Vietnam War that is composed of 2,4-D and 2,4,5-T and contains a toxic contaminant

agent pro·vo·ca·teur \'ä-ˌzhäⁿ-prō-ˌvä-kə-'tər, 'ä-jənt-\ *n, pl* **agents provoca·teurs** \'ä-ˌzhäⁿ-prō-ˌväk-ə-'tər, 'ä-jənts-prō-\ [F] : a person hired to infiltrate a group and incite its members to illegal action

age of consent : the age at which one is legally competent to give consent esp. to marriage or to sexual intercourse

age–old \'āj-'ōld\ *adj* : having existed for ages : ANCIENT

ag·er·a·tum \ˌa-jə-'rā-təm\ *n, pl* **-tum** *also* **-tums** : any of a genus of tropical American plants that are related to the daisies and have small showy heads of usu. blue or white flowers

age spots *n pl* : benign flat spots of dark pigmentation on the skin occurring esp. among older people

Ag·ge·us \a-'gē-əs\ *n* : HAGGAI

¹**ag·glom·er·ate** \ə-'glä-mə-ˌrāt\ *vb* **-at·ed; -at·ing** [L *agglomerare* to heap up, join, fr. *ad-* to + *glomer-, glomus* ball] : to gather into a mass : CLUSTER — **ag·glom·er·a·tion** \-ˌglä-mə-'rā-shən\ *n*

²**ag·glom·er·ate** \-rət\ *n* : rock composed of volcanic fragments

ag·glu·ti·nate \ə-'glü-tᵊn-ˌāt\ *vb* **-nat·ed; -nat·ing 1** : to cause to adhere : gather into a group or mass **2** : to cause (as red blood cells or bacteria) to collect into clumps — **ag·glu·ti·na·tion** \-ˌglü-tᵊn-'ā-shən\ *n*

ag·gran·dise *Brit var of* AGGRANDIZE

ag·gran·dize \ə-'gran-ˌdīz, 'a-grən-\ *vb* **-dized; -diz·ing** : to make great or greater ⟨~ an estate⟩ — **ag·gran·dize·ment** \ə-'gran-dəz-mənt, -ˌdīz-; ˌa-grən-'dīz-\ *n*

ag·gra·vate \'a-grə-ˌvāt\ *vb* **-vat·ed; -vat·ing 1** : to make more severe : INTENSIFY **2** : IRRITATE — **ag·gra·va·tion** \ˌa-grə-'vā-shən\ *n*

¹**ag·gre·gate** \'a-gri-gət\ *adj* : formed by the gathering of units into one mass

²**ag·gre·gate** \-ˌgāt\ *vb* **-gat·ed; -gat·ing** : to collect into one mass

³**ag·gre·gate** \-gət\ *n* : a mass or body of units or parts somewhat loosely associated with one another; *also* : the whole amount

ag·gre·ga·tion \ˌa-gri-'gā-shən\ *n* **1** : a group, body, or mass composed of many distinct parts **2** : the collecting of units or parts into a mass or whole

ag·gres·sion \ə-'gre-shən\ *n* **1** : an unprovoked attack **2** : the practice of making attacks **3** : hostile, injurious, or destructive behavior or outlook esp. when caused by frustration — **ag·gres·sor** \-'gre-sər\ *n*

ag·gres·sive \ə-'gre-siv\ *adj* **1** : tending toward or exhibiting aggression; *esp*

: marked by combative readiness **2** : marked by driving energy or initiative : ENTERPRISING **3** : more intensive or comprehensive esp. in dosage or extent — **ag·gres·sive·ly** *adv* — **ag·gres·sive·ness** *n*

ag·grieve \ə-'grēv\ *vb* **ag·grieved; ag·griev·ing 1** : to cause grief to **2** : to inflict injury on : WRONG

ag·gro \'a-ˌgrō\ *adj* : aggressive or aggressively daring in style or manner ⟨~ music⟩ ⟨~ surfing⟩

aghast \ə-'gast\ *adj* : struck with amazement or horror

ag·ile \'a-jəl\ *adj* : able to move quickly and easily — **ag·ile·ly** *adv* — **agil·i·ty** \ə-'ji-lə-tē\ *n*

ag·i·ta \'a-jə-tə\ *n* [southern It dial. pron. of It *acido*, lit., heartburn, acid] : a feeling of agitation or anxiety

ag·i·tate \'a-jə-ˌtāt\ *vb* **-tat·ed; -tat·ing 1** : to move with an irregular rapid motion **2** : to stir up : EXCITE **3** : to discuss earnestly **4** : to attempt to arouse public feeling — **ag·i·ta·tion** \ˌa-jə-'tā-shən\ *n* — **ag·i·ta·tor** \'a-jə-ˌtā-tər\ *n*

ag·it·prop \'a-jət-ˌpräp\ *n* [Russ] : political propaganda promulgated esp. through the arts

agleam \ə-'glēm\ *adj* : GLEAMING ⟨eyes ~ with tears⟩

aglit·ter \ə-'gli-tər\ *adj* : GLITTERING

aglow \ə-'glō\ *adj* : GLOWING

ag·nos·tic \ag-'näs-tik\ *adj* [Gk *agnōstos* unknown, unknowable, fr. *a-* un- + *gnōstos* known] : of or relating to the belief that the existence of any ultimate reality (as God) is unknown and prob. unknowable — **agnostic** *n* — **ag·nos·ti·cism** \-'näs-tə-ˌsi-zəm\ *n*

ago \ə-'gō\ *adj or adv* : earlier than the present time ⟨10 years ~⟩

agog \ə-'gäg\ *adj* [MF *en gogues* in mirth] : full of excitement : EAGER

a–go–go \ä-'gō-ˌgō\ *adj* ⟨*Whisky à Gogo*, café and disco in Paris, France, fr. F *à gogo* galore⟩ : GO-GO

ag·o·nise *Brit var of* AGONIZE

ag·o·nize \'a-gə-ˌnīz\ *vb* **-nized; -niz·ing** : to suffer or cause to suffer agony — **ag·o·niz·ing·ly** *adv*

ag·o·ny \'a-gə-nē\ *n, pl* **-nies** [ME *agonie*, fr. L *agonia*, fr. Gk *agōnia* struggle, anguish, fr. *agōn* gathering, contest for a prize] : extreme pain of mind or body ♦ *Synonyms* SUFFERING, DISTRESS, MISERY

ago·ra \ˌä-gə-'rä\ *n, pl* **ago·rot** \-'rōt\ — see *shekel* at MONEY table

ag·o·ra·pho·bia \ˌa-gə-rə-'fō-bē-ə\ *n* : abnormal fear of being in a helpless, embarrassing, or inescapable situation characterized esp. by avoidance of open or public places — **ag·o·ra·pho·bic** \-'fō-bik, -'fä-\ *adj or n*

agr *abbr* agricultural; agriculture

agrar·i·an \ə-'grer-ē-ən\ *adj* **1** : of or relating to land or its ownership ⟨~ reforms⟩ **2** : of or relating to farmers or farming interests — **agrarian** *n* — **agrar·i·an·ism** *n*

agree \ə-'grē\ *vb* **agreed; agree·ing 1**

: ADMIT, CONCEDE ⟨~s that he was wrong⟩ **2** : to be similar : CORRESPOND ⟨both copies ~⟩ **3** : to express agreement or approval **4** : to be in harmony **5** : to settle by common consent **6** : to be fitting or healthful : SUIT ⟨this climate ~s with her⟩

agree·able \ə-ˈgrē-ə-bəl\ *adj* **1** : PLEASING, PLEASANT ⟨an ~ fragrance⟩ **2** : ready to consent ⟨I'm ~ to their proposal⟩ **3** : being in harmony : CONSONANT — **agree·able·ness** *n* — **agree·ably** \-blē\ *adv*

agree·ment \ə-ˈgrē-mənt\ *n* **1** : harmony of opinion or action **2** : mutual understanding or arrangement; *also* : a document containing such an arrangement

ag·ri·busi·ness \ˈa-grə-ˌbiz-nəs, -nəz\ *n* : an industry engaged in the manufacture and sale of farm equipment and supplies and in the production, processing, storage, and sale of farm commodities

agric *abbr* agricultural; agriculture

ag·ri·cul·ture \ˈa-gri-ˌkəl-chər\ *n* : FARMING, HUSBANDRY — **ag·ri·cul·tur·al** \ˌa-gri-ˈkəl-ch(ə-)rəl\ *adj* — **ag·ri·cul·tur·ist** \-ch(ə-)rist\ *or* **ag·ri·cul·tur·al·ist** \-ch(ə-)rə-list\ *n*

agron·o·my \ə-ˈgrä-nə-mē\ *n* : a branch of agriculture that deals with the raising of crops and the care of the soil — **agro·nom·ic** \ˌa-grə-ˈnä-mik\ *adj* — **agron·o·mist** \ə-ˈgrä-nə-mist\ *n*

aground \ə-ˈgrau̇nd\ *adv or adj* : on or onto the bottom or shore ⟨ran ~⟩

agt *abbr* agent

ague \ˈā-gyü\ *n* : a fever (as malaria) with recurrent chills and sweating

ahead \ə-ˈhed\ *adv or adj* **1** : in or toward the front **2** : into or for the future ⟨plan ~⟩ **3** : in or toward a more advantageous position

ahead of *prep* **1** : in front or advance of **2** : in excess of : ABOVE

ahoy \ə-ˈhȯi\ *interj* — used in hailing ⟨ship ~⟩

AI *abbr* artificial intelligence

¹aid \ˈād\ *vb* : to provide with what is useful in achieving an end : ASSIST

²aid *n* **1** : ASSISTANCE **2** : ASSISTANT

AID *abbr* Agency for International Development

aide \ˈād\ *n* : a person who acts as an assistant; *esp* : a military officer assisting a superior

aide–de–camp \ˌād-di-ˈkamp, -ˈkäⁿ\ *n, pl* **aides–de–camp** \ˌādz-di-\ [F] : AIDE

AIDS \ˈādz\ *n* [*a*cquired *i*mmunodeficiency *s*yndrome] : a serious disease of the human immune system that is characterized by severe reduction in the numbers of helper T cells and increased vulnerability to life-threatening illnesses and that is caused by infection with HIV commonly transmitted in infected blood esp. during illicit intravenous drug use and in bodily secretions (as semen) during sexual intercourse

AIDS–related complex *n* : a group of symptoms (as fever, weight loss, and lymphadenopathy) that is associated with the presence of antibodies to HIV and is

followed by the development of AIDS in a certain proportion of cases

AIDS virus *n* : HIV

ai·grette \ā-ˈgret, ˈā-ˌ\ *n* [F, plume, egret] : a plume or decorative tuft for the head

ail \ˈāl\ *vb* **1** : to be the matter with : TROUBLE **2** : to be unwell

ai·lan·thus \ā-ˈlan-thəs\ *n* : any of a genus of Asian trees or shrubs with pinnate leaves and ill-scented greenish flowers; *esp* : TREE OF HEAVEN

ai·le·ron \ˈā-lə-ˌrän\ *n* : a movable part of an airplane wing used in banking

ail·ment \ˈāl-mənt\ *n* : a bodily disorder

¹aim \ˈām\ *vb* [ME, fr. AF *aesmer & esmer*; AF *aesmer*, fr. *a-* to (fr. L *ad-*) + *esmer* to estimate, fr. L *aestimare*] **1** : to point a weapon at an object **2** : to direct one's efforts : ASPIRE **3** : to direct to or toward a specified object or goal

²aim *n* **1** : the pointing of a weapon at an object **2** : the ability to hit a target **3** : OBJECT, PURPOSE ⟨my ~ is to win⟩ — **aim·less** \-ləs\ *adj* — **aim·less·ly** *adv* — **aim·less·ness** *n*

AIM *abbr* American Indian Movement

ain't \ˈānt\ **1** : are not **2** : is not **3** : am not — though disapproved by many and more common in less educated speech, used in both speech and writing to catch attention and to gain emphasis

Ai·nu \ˈī-nü\ *n, pl* **Ainu** *or* **Ainus** **1** : a member of an indigenous people of northern Japan **2** : the language of the Ainu people

¹air \ˈer\ *n* **1** : the gaseous mixture surrounding the earth **2** : a light breeze **3** : MELODY, TUNE **4** : the outward appearance of a person or thing : MANNER **5** : an artificial manner **6** : COMPRESSED AIR ⟨~ sprayer⟩ **7** : AIRCRAFT ⟨traveled by ~⟩ **8** : AVIATION ⟨~ safety⟩ **9** : the medium of transmission of radio waves; *also* : RADIO, TELEVISION

²air *vb* **1** : to expose to the air ⟨~ clothes⟩ **2** : to expose to public view **3** : to broadcast on radio or television

air bag *n* : a bag designed to inflate automatically to protect automobile occupants in case of collision

air·boat \ˈer-ˌbōt\ *n* : a shallow-draft boat driven by an airplane propeller

air·borne \-ˌbȯrn\ *adj* : done or being in the air

air brake *n* **1** : a brake operated by a piston driven by compressed air **2** : a surface projected into the airflow to lower an airplane's speed

air·brush \ˈer-ˌbrəsh\ *n* : a device for applying a fine spray (as of paint) by compressed air — **airbrush** *vb*

air con·di·tion·er \ˌer-kən-ˈdi-sh(ə-)nər\ *n* : an apparatus for filtering air and controlling its humidity and temperature — **air–con·di·tion** \-ˈdi-shən\ *vb*

air·craft \ˈer-ˌkraft\ *n, pl* **aircraft** : a vehicle for traveling through the air

aircraft carrier *n* : a warship with a deck on which airplanes can be launched and landed

air·drop \ˈer-ˌdräp\ *n* : delivery of cargo

or personnel by parachute from an airplane in flight — **air-drop** *vb*

Aire-dale terrier \'er-ˌdāl-\ *n* : any of a breed of large terriers with a hard wiry coat

air-fare \'er-ˌfer\ *n* : fare for travel by airplane

air-field \-ˌfēld\ *n* : AIRPORT

air-flow \-ˌflō\ *n* : the motion of air relative to a body in it

air-foil \-ˌfȯi(-ə)l\ *n* : an airplane surface designed to produce reaction forces from the air through which it moves

air force *n* : the military organization of a nation for air warfare

air-frame \'er-ˌfrām\ *n* : the structure of an aircraft, rocket, or missile without the power plant; *also* : AIRCRAFT

air-freight \-ˈfrāt\ *n* : freight transport by aircraft in volume; *also* : the charge for this service

air gun *n* **1** : a gun operated by compressed air **2** : a hand tool that works by compressed air; *esp* : AIRBRUSH

air-head \'er-ˌhed\ *n* : a mindless or stupid person

air lane *n* : AIRWAY 1

air-lift \'er-ˌlift\ *n* : transportation (as of supplies or passengers) by aircraft — **air-lift** *vb*

air-line \-ˌlīn\ *n* : a transportation system using airplanes

air-lin-er \-ˌlī-nər\ *n* : a large passenger airplane operated by an airline

air lock *n* : an airtight chamber separating areas of different pressure

air-mail \'er-ˌmāl\ *n* : the system of transporting mail by aircraft; *also* : mail so transported — **airmail** *vb*

air-man \-mən\ *n* **1** : AVIATOR, PILOT **2** : an enlisted person in the air force ranking next below an airman first class

airman basic *n* : an enlisted person of the lowest rank in the air force

airman first class *n* : an enlisted person in the air force ranking next below a senior airman

air mass *n* : a large horizontally homogeneous body of air

air-mo-bile \'er-ˌmō-bəl, -ˌbēl\ *adj* : of, relating to, or being a military unit whose members are transported to combat areas usu. by helicopter

air-plane \-ˌplān\ *n* : a powered heavier-than-air aircraft that has fixed wings from which it derives lift

air-play \-ˌplā\ *n* : the playing of a musical recording on the air by a radio station

air pocket *n* : a condition of the atmosphere (as a local downdraft) that causes an airplane to drop suddenly

air police *n* : the military police of an air force

air-port \'er-ˌpȯrt\ *n* : a place from which aircraft operate that usu. has paved runways and a terminal

air rage *n* : an airline passenger's uncontrolled anger that is usu. expressed in aggressive or violent behavior

air raid *n* : an attack by armed airplanes on a surface target

air-ship \'er-ˌship\ *n* : a lighter-than-air

aircraft having propulsion and steering systems

air-sick \-ˌsik\ *adj* : affected with motion sickness associated with flying — **air-sick-ness** *n*

air-space \-ˌspās\ *n* : the space above a nation and under its jurisdiction

air-speed \-ˌspēd\ *n* : the speed of an object (as an airplane) with relation to the surrounding air

air-strip \-ˌstrip\ *n* : a runway without normal airport facilities

air-tight \'er-ˈtīt\ *adj* **1** : so tightly sealed that no air can enter or escape **2** : leaving no opening for attack

air–to–air *adj* : launched from one airplane in flight at another; *also* : involving aircraft in flight

air-waves \'er-ˌwāvz\ *n pl* : AIR 9

air-way \-ˌwā\ *n* **1** : a regular route for airplanes **2** : AIRLINE

air-wor-thy \-ˌwər-thē\ *adj* : fit for operation in the air ⟨an ~ plane⟩ — **air-wor-thi-ness** *n*

airy \'er-ē\ *adj* **air-i-er; -est 1** : LOFTY ⟨~ perches⟩ **2** : lacking in reality : EMPTY **3** : DELICATE **4** : BREEZY

aisle \'ī(-ə)l\ *n* [ME *ile*, fr. AF *ele*, lit., wing, fr. L *ala*] **1** : the side of a church nave separated by piers from the nave proper **2** : a passage between sections of seats

ajar \ə-ˈjär\ *adj or adv* : partly open

AK *abbr* Alaska

aka *abbr* also known as

AKC *abbr* American Kennel Club

akim-bo \ə-ˈkim-bō\ *adj or adv* : having the hand on the hip and the elbow turned outward

akin \ə-ˈkin\ *adj* **1** : related by blood **2** : similar in kind

Al *symbol* aluminum

AL *abbr* **1** Alabama **2** American League **3** American Legion

¹-al *adj suffix* : of, relating to, or characterized by ⟨direction*al*⟩

²-al *n suffix* : action : process ⟨rehears*al*⟩

Ala *abbr* Alabama

al-a-bas-ter \'a-lə-ˌbas-tər\ *n* **1** : a compact fine-textured usu. white and translucent gypsum often carved into objects (as vases) **2** : a hard translucent calcite

à la carte \ˌä-lə-ˈkärt, ˌa-\ *adv or adj* [F] : with a separate price for each item on the menu

alac-ri-ty \ə-ˈla-krə-tē\ *n* : cheerful readiness : BRISKNESS

à la mode \ˌä-lə-ˈmōd, ˌä-\ *adj* [F, according to the fashion] **1** : FASHIONABLE, STYLISH **2** : topped with ice cream

¹alarm \ə-ˈlärm\ *also* **ala-rum** \ə-ˈlär-əm, -ˈler-\ *n* [ME *alarme*, fr. MF, fr. OIt *all'arme*, lit., to arms] **1** : a warning signal or device **2** : the terror caused by sudden danger

²alarm *also* **alarum** *vb* **1** : to warn of danger **2** : FRIGHTEN

alarm-ist \ə-ˈlär-mist\ *n* : a person who alarms others esp. needlessly

alas \ə-ˈlas\ *interj* — used to express unhappiness, pity, or concern

al-ba-core \'al-bə-ˌkȯr\ *n, pl* **-core** *or*

-cores : a large tuna that is a source of canned tuna

Al·ba·nian \al-'bā-nē-ən\ *n* : a native or inhabitant of Albania

al·ba·tross \'al-bə-ˌtrós, -ˌträs\ *n, pl* **-tross** *or* **-tross·es** : any of a family of large web-footed seabirds

al·be·do \al-'bē-(ˌ)dō\ *n, pl* **-dos** : the fraction of incident radiation that is reflected by a body or surface

al·be·it \ól-'bē-ət, al-\ *conj* : even though : ALTHOUGH

al·bi·no \al-'bī-nō\ *n, pl* **-nos** : a person or animal lacking coloring matter in the skin, hair, and eyes — **al·bi·nism** \'al-bə-ˌni-zəm\ *n*

al·bum \'al-bəm\ *n* **1** : a book with blank pages used for making a collection (as of stamps or photographs) **2** : one or more recordings (as on tape or disk) produced as a single unit

al·bu·men \al-'byü-mən\ *n* **1** : the white of an egg **2** : ALBUMIN

al·bu·min \al-'byü-mən\ *n* : any of numerous water-soluble proteins of blood, milk, egg white, and plant and animal tissues

al·bu·min·ous \al-'byü-mə-nəs\ *adj* : containing or resembling albumen or albumin

al·bu·ter·ol \al-'byü-tə-ˌról, -ˌról\ *n* : a drug used as an aerosol or in tablet form to treat asthma

alc *abbr* alcohol

al·cal·de \al-'käl-dē\ *n* : the chief administrative and judicial officer of a Spanish or Spanish-American town

al·ca·zar \al-'kä-zər, -'ka-\ *n* [Sp *alcázar*, fr. Ar *al-qasr* the castle] : a Spanish fortress or palace

al·che·my \'al-kə-mē\ *n* : medieval chemistry chiefly concerned with efforts to turn base metals into gold — **al·che·mist** \-kə-mist\ *n*

al·co·hol \'al-kə-ˌhól\ *n* [NL, fr. ML, powdered antimony, fr. Sp, fr. Ar *al-kuḥul* the powdered antimony] **1** : a colorless flammable liquid that is the intoxicating agent in fermented and distilled liquors **2** : any of various carbon compounds similar to alcohol **3** : beverages containing alcohol

¹**al·co·hol·ic** \ˌal-kə-'hó-lik, -'hä-\ *adj* **1** : of, relating to, caused by, or containing alcohol **2** : affected with alcoholism — **al·co·hol·i·cal·ly** \-li-k(ə-)lē\ *adv*

²**alcoholic** *n* : a person affected with alcoholism

al·co·hol·ism \'al-kə-ˌhó-ˌli-zəm\ *n* : continued excessive and usu. uncontrollable use of alcoholic drinks; *also* : a complex chronic psychological and nutritional disorder associated with such use

al·cove \'al-ˌkōv\ *n* **1** : a nook or small recess opening off a larger room **2** : a niche or arched opening (as in a wall)

ald *abbr* alderman

al·der \'ól-dər\ *n* : any of a genus of trees or shrubs related to the birches and growing in wet areas

al·der·man \'ól-dər-mən\ *n* : a member of a city legislative body

ale \'āl\ *n* : an alcoholic beverage brewed from malt and hops that is usu. more bitter than beer

ale·a·tor·ic \ˌā-lē-ə-'tór-ik\ *adj* : characterized by chance or random elements ⟨~ music⟩

ale·a·to·ry \'ā-lē-ə-ˌtór-ē\ *adj* : ALEATORIC

alee \ə-'lē\ *adv* : on or toward the lee

ale·house \'āl-ˌhaùs\ *n* : a place where ale is sold to be drunk on the premises

¹**alert** \ə-'lərt\ *adj* [It *all'erta*, lit., on the ascent] **1** : watchful against danger **2** : quick to perceive and act — **alert·ly** *adv* — **alert·ness** *n*

²**alert** *n* **1** : ALARM 1 **2** : the period during which an alert is in effect

³**alert** *vb* **1** : WARN **2** : to make aware of

Aleut \ˌa-lē-'üt, ə-'lüt\ *n* **1** : a member of a people of the Aleutian and Shumagin islands and the western part of Alaska Peninsula **2** : the language of the Aleuts

ale·wife \'āl-ˌwīf\ *n, pl* **ale·wives** \-ˌwīvz\ : a food fish related to the herring that is abundant esp. along the Atlantic coast

Al·ex·an·dri·an \ˌa-lig-'zan-drē-ən\ *adj* **1** : HELLENISTIC **2** : of or relating to Alexander the Great

al·ex·an·drine \-'zan-drən\ *n, often cap* : a line of six iambic feet

al·fal·fa \al-'fal-fə\ *n* : a leguminous plant widely grown for hay and forage

al·fres·co \al-'fres-kō\ *adj or adv* [It] : taking place in the open air

alg *abbr* algebra

al·ga \'al-gə\ *n, pl* **al·gae** \'al-(ˌ)jē\ : any of a group of lower plants having chlorophyll but no vascular system and including seaweeds and related freshwater plants — **al·gal** \-gəl\ *adj*

al·ge·bra \'al-jə-brə\ *n* [ML, fr. Ar *al-jabr*] : a generalization of arithmetic in which letters representing numbers are combined according to the rules of arithmetic — **al·ge·bra·ic** \ˌal-jə-'brā-ik\ *adj* — **al·ge·bra·i·cal·ly** \-'brā-ə-k(ə-)lē\ *adv*

Al·gon·qui·an \al-'gän-kwē-ən, -'gän-\ *or* **Al·gon·quin** \-kwən\ *n* **1** *usu* Algonquin : a member of an American Indian people of the Ottawa River valley **2** *usu* Algonquian : a family of American Indian languages of eastern and central No. America

al·go·rithm \'al-gə-ˌri-thəm\ *n* : a procedure for solving a problem esp. in mathematics or computing — **al·go·rith·mic** \ˌal-gə-'rith-mik\ *adj* — **al·go·rith·mi·cal·ly** \-mi-k(ə-)lē\ *adv*

¹**ali·as** \'ā-lē-əs, 'āl-yəs\ *adv* [L, otherwise, fr. *alius* other] : otherwise called

²**alias** *n* : an assumed name

¹**al·i·bi** \'a-lə-ˌbī\ *n* [L, elsewhere, fr. *alius* other] **1** : a plea offered by an accused person of not having been at the scene of an offense **2** : an excuse (as for failure)

²**alibi** *vb* **-bied; -bi·ing** **1** : to furnish an excuse for **2** : to offer an excuse

¹**ali·as** \'ā-lē-əs, 'āl-yəs\ *adv* [L, otherwise, fr. *alius* other] : otherwise called

alien *n* **1** : a foreign-born resident who has not been naturalized **2** : EXTRATERRESTRIAL

alien·able \'āl-yə-nə-bəl, 'ā-lē-ə-nə-\ *adj*
: transferable to the ownership of another ⟨~ property⟩

alien·ate \'ā-lē-ə-,nāt, 'āl-yə-\ *vb* **-at·ed;**
-at·ing 1 : to make hostile : ESTRANGE **2**
: to transfer (property) to another —
alien·ation \,ā-lē-ə-'nā-shən, ,āl-yə-\ *n*

alien·ist \'ā-lē-ə-nist, 'āl-yə-\ *n* : PSYCHIATRIST

¹**alight** \ə-'līt\ *vb* **alight·ed** *also* **alit** \ə-'lit\;
alight·ing 1 : to get down (as from a vehicle) **2** : to come to rest from the air
♦ *Synonyms* SETTLE, LAND, PERCH

²**alight** *adj* : lighted up

align *also* **aline** \ə-'līn\ *vb* **1** : to bring into line **2** : to array on the side of or against a cause — **align·er** *n* — **alignment** *also* **aline·ment** *n*

¹**alike** \ə-'līk\ *adv* : EQUALLY ⟨denounced by teachers and students ~⟩

²**alike** *adj* : LIKE ⟨~ in their beliefs⟩
♦ *Synonyms* AKIN, ANALOGOUS, SIMILAR, COMPARABLE

al·i·ment \'a-lə-mənt\ *n* : NOURISHMENT **1** — **aliment** *vb*

al·i·men·ta·ry \,a-lə-'men-t(ə-)rē\ *adj* : of, relating to, or functioning in nourishment or nutrition

alimentary canal *n* : the tube that extends from the mouth to the anus and functions in the digestion and absorption of food and the elimination of residues

al·i·mo·ny \'a-lə-,mō-nē\ *n, pl* **-nies** [L *alimonia* sustenance, fr. *alere* to nourish] : an allowance made to one spouse by the other for support pending or after legal separation or divorce

A–line \'ā-,līn\ *adj* : having a flared bottom and a close-fitting top ⟨an ~ skirt⟩

alive \ə-'līv\ *adj* **1** : having life **2** : being in force or operation **3** : SENSITIVE ⟨~ to the danger⟩ **4** : ALERT, BRISK **5** : ANIMATED ⟨streets ~ with traffic⟩ — **alive·ness** *n*

alk *abbr* alkaline

al·ka·li \'al-kə-,lī\ *n, pl* **-lies** *or* **-lis 1** : a substance (as a hydroxide) that has a bitter taste and neutralizes acids **2** : a mixture of salts in the soil of some dry regions in such amount as to make ordinary farming impossible — **al·ka·line** \-kə-lən, -,līn\ *adj* — **al·ka·lin·i·ty** \,al-kə-'li-nə-tē\ *n*

al·ka·loid \'al-kə-,lȯid\ *n* : any of various usu. basic and bitter organic compounds found esp. in seed plants

al·kane \'al-,kān\ *n* : a hydrocarbon in which each carbon atom is bonded to 4 other atoms

al·kyd \'al-kəd\ *n* : any of numerous synthetic resins used esp. for protective coatings and paint

¹**all** \'ȯl\ *adj* **1** : the whole of ⟨sat up ~ night⟩ **2** : every member of **3** : EVERY ⟨~ manner of problems⟩ **4** : any whatever ⟨beyond ~ doubt⟩ **5** : nothing but ⟨~ ears⟩ **6** : being more than one person or thing ⟨who ~ is coming⟩

²**all** *adv* **1** : WHOLLY ⟨sat ~ alone⟩ **2** : selected as the best — used in combination ⟨*all*-state champs⟩ **3** : so much ⟨~ the

better for it⟩ **4** : for each side ⟨the score is two ~⟩

³**all** *pron sing or pl* **1** : the whole number, quantity, or amount ⟨~ of it is gone⟩ **2** : EVERYBODY, EVERYTHING ⟨~ are members⟩ ⟨that is ~⟩

⁴**all** *n* : the whole of one's resources ⟨gave his ~⟩

Al·lah \'ä-lə, 'a-; 'ä-,lä, ä-'lä\ *n* [Ar *allāh*] : GOD 1 — used in Islam

all along *adv* : all the time ⟨knew it *all along*⟩

all–Amer·i·can \,ȯl-ə-'mer-ə-kən\ *adj* **1** : selected as the best in the U.S. **2** : composed wholly of American elements **3** : typical of the U.S. — **all–American** *n*

all–around \,ȯl-ə-'raúnd\ *adj* **1** : considered in all aspects ⟨best ~ performance⟩ **2** : competent in many fields : VERSATILE ⟨an ~ athlete⟩

al·lay \ə-'lā\ *vb* **1** : ALLEVIATE **2** : CALM
♦ *Synonyms* LIGHTEN, RELIEVE, EASE, ASSUAGE

all clear *n* : a signal that a danger has passed

al·lege \ə-'lej\ *vb* **al·leged; al·leg·ing 1**
: to assert without proof **2** : to offer as a reason — **al·le·ga·tion** \,a-li-'gā-shən\ *n*
— **al·leged** \ə-'lejd, -'le-jəd\ *adj* — **al·leg·ed·ly** \ə-'le-jəd-lē\ *adv*

al·le·giance \ə-'lē-jəns\ *n* **1** : loyalty owed by a citizen to a government **2** : loyalty to a person or cause

al·le·go·ry \'a-lə-,gȯr-ē\ *n, pl* **-ries** : the expression through symbolism of truths or generalizations about human experience — **al·le·gor·i·cal** \,a-lə-'gȯr-i-kəl\ *adj* — **al·le·gor·i·cal·ly** \-k(ə-)lē\ *adv*

¹**al·le·gro** \ə-'le-grō, -'lā-\ *n, pl* **-gros** : an allegro movement

²**allegro** *adv or adj* [It, merry] : at a brisk lively tempo — used as a direction in music

al·lele \ə-'lēl\ *n* : any of the alternative forms of a gene that may occur at a given site on a chromosome — **al·le·lic** \-'lē-lik, -'le-\ *adj*

al·le·lu·ia \,a-lə-'lü-yə\ *interj* : HALLELUJAH

Al·len wrench \'a-lən-\ *n* [*Allen* Manufacturing Company, Hartford, Conn.] : an L-shaped hexagonal metal bar of which either end fits the socket of a screw or bolt

al·ler·gen \'a-lər-jən\ *n* : something that causes allergy — **al·ler·gen·ic** \,a-lər-'je-nik\ *adj*

al·ler·gist \'a-lər-jist\ *n* : a specialist in allergies

al·ler·gy \'a-lər-jē\ *n, pl* **-gies** [G *Allergie*, fr. Gk *allos* other + *ergon* work] : exaggerated or abnormal reaction (as by sneezing) to substances or situations harmless to most people — **al·ler·gic** \ə-'lər-jik\ *adj*

al·le·vi·ate \ə-'lē-vē-,āt\ *vb* **-at·ed; -at·ing**
: RELIEVE, LESSEN ⟨~ pain⟩ ♦ *Synonyms* LIGHTEN, MITIGATE, ALLAY — **al·le·vi·a·tion** \ə-,lē-vē-'ā-shən\ *n*

al·ley \'a-lē\ *n, pl* **alleys 1** : a garden or park walk **2** : a place for bowling **3** : a narrow passageway esp. between buildings

al·ley–oop \ˌa-lē-ˈyüp\ *n* : a basketball play in which a player catches a pass above the basket and immediately dunks the ball

al·ley·way \ˈa-lē-ˌwā\ *n* : ALLEY 3

all–fired \ˈol-ˌfī(-ə)rd\ *adv* : EXTREMELY, EXCESSIVELY ⟨~ stubborn⟩

All·hal·lows \ol-ˈha-lōz\ *n, pl* **Allhallows** : ALL SAINTS' DAY

all hours *n pl* : a very late time ⟨stayed up until *all hours*⟩

al·li·ance \ə-ˈlī-əns\ *n* : a union to promote common interests ♦ *Synonyms* LEAGUE, COALITION, CONFEDERACY, FEDERATION

al·li·ga·tor \ˈa-lə-ˌgā-tər\ *n* [Sp *el lagarto* the lizard] : either of two large short-legged reptiles resembling crocodiles but having a shorter and broader snout

alligator pear *n* : AVOCADO

al·lit·er·ate \ə-ˈli-tə-ˌrāt\ *vb* **-at·ed; -at·ing** **1** : to form an alliteration **2** : to arrange so as to make alliteration

al·lit·er·a·tion \ə-ˌli-tə-ˈrā-shən\ *n* : the repetition of initial sounds in adjacent words or syllables — **al·lit·er·a·tive** \-ˈli-tə-ˌrā-tiv\ *adj*

al·lo·cate \ˈa-lə-ˌkāt\ *vb* **-cat·ed; -cat·ing** : ALLOT, ASSIGN — **al·lo·ca·tion** \ˌa-lə-ˈkā-shən\ *n*

al·lot \ə-ˈlät\ *vb* **al·lot·ted; al·lot·ting** : to distribute as a share ♦ *Synonyms* ASSIGN, APPORTION, ALLOCATE — **al·lot·ment** *n*

all–out \ˈol-ˈaut\ *adj* : made with maximum effort

¹all over *adv* : EVERYWHERE

²all over *prep* **1** : in eagerly affectionate, attentive, or aggressive pursuit **2** : in or into a state marked by excessive criticism

al·low \ə-ˈlau\ *vb* **1** : to assign as a share ⟨~ time for rest⟩ **2** : to count as a deduction **3** : to make allowance ⟨~ for expansion⟩ **4** : ADMIT, CONCEDE ⟨~ed that the situation was serious⟩ **5** : PERMIT ⟨~s the dog to roam⟩ — **al·low·able** *adj*

al·low·ance \-əns\ *n* **1** : an allotted share **2** : money given regularly for expenses **3** : a taking into account of extenuating circumstances

al·loy \ˈa-ˌloi, ə-ˈloi\ *n* **1** : a substance composed of metals melted together **2** : an admixture that lessens value — **alloy** \ə-ˈloi, ˈa-ˌloi\ *vb*

all right *adv* **1** — used interjectionally esp. to express agreement or resignation or to indicate the resumption of a discussion ⟨*all right*, let's go⟩ **2** : beyond doubt **3** : SATISFACTORILY ⟨does *all right* in school⟩ — **all right** *adj*

All Saints' Day *n* : a Christian feast on November 1 in honor of all the saints

All Souls' Day *n* : a day of prayer observed by some Christian churches on November 2 for the souls of the faithful departed

all·spice \ˈol-ˌspīs\ *n* : the berry of a West Indian tree related to the European myr-tle; *also* : the mildly pungent and aromatic spice made from it

all–star \ˈol-ˌstär\ *n* : a member of a team of star performers — **all–star** *adj*

all–ter·rain vehicle *n* : a small motor vehicle with three or four wheels for use on a wide range of terrain

all told *adv* : with everything or everyone counted ⟨expecting eight guests *all told*⟩

al·lude \ə-ˈlüd\ *vb* **al·lud·ed; al·lud·ing** [L *alludere*, lit., to play with] : to refer indirectly — **al·lu·sion** \-ˈlü-zhən\ *n* — **al·lu·sive** \-ˈlü-siv\ *adj* — **al·lu·sive·ly** *adv* — **al·lu·sive·ness** *n*

al·lure \ə-ˈlur\ *vb* **al·lured; al·lur·ing** : to attract by something desirable — **allure** *n* — **al·lur·ing·ly** *adv*

al·lu·vi·um \ə-ˈlü-vē-əm\ *n, pl* **-vi·ums** or **-via** \-vē-ə\ : soil material (as clay) deposited by running water — **al·lu·vi·al** \-vē-əl\ *adj or n*

all–wheel \ˈol-ˌwēl\ *adj* : acting independently on or by means of all four wheels of a vehicle

al·ly \ə-ˈlī, ˈa-ˌlī\ *vb* **al·lied; al·ly·ing** : to enter into an alliance — **al·ly** \ˈa-ˌlī, ə-ˈlī\ *n*

-ally *adv suffix* : ²-LY ⟨specific*ally*⟩

al·ma ma·ter \ˌal-mə-ˈmä-tər\ *n* [L, fostering mother] **1** : an educational institute that one has attended **2** : the song or hymn of an alma mater

al·ma·nac \ˈol-mə-ˌnak, ˈal-\ *n* **1** : a publication esp. of astronomical and meteorological data **2** : a usu. annual publication of miscellaneous information

al·man·dite \ˈal-mən-ˌdīt\ *n* : a deep red garnet

al·mighty \ol-ˈmī-tē\ *adj* **1** *often cap* : having absolute power over all ⟨*Almighty* God⟩ **2** : relatively unlimited in power — **al·might·i·ness** *n*

Almighty *n* : GOD 1

al·mond \ˈä-mənd, ˈa-; ˈal-\ *n* : a small tree related to the peach; *also* : the edible nutlike kernel of its fruit

al·mo·ner \ˈal-mə-nər, ˈä-mə-\ *n* : a person who distributes alms

al·most \ˈol-ˌmōst, ol-ˈmōst\ *adv* : very nearly but not exactly

alms \ˈämz, ˈälmz\ *n, pl* **alms** [ME *almesse, almes,* fr. OE *ælmesse, ælms,* fr. L *eleemosyna* alms, fr. Gk *eleēmosynē* pity, alms, fr. *eleēmōn* merciful, fr. *eleos* pity] : something given freely to relieve the poor

alms·house \-ˌhaus\ *n* : POORHOUSE

al·oe \ˈa-lō\ *n* **1** : any of a large genus of succulent chiefly southern African plants related to the lilies **2** *pl* : the dried juice of the leaves of an aloe used esp. formerly as a laxative

aloe vera \-ˈver-ə, -ˈvir-\ *n* : an aloe with leaves that yield a jellylike emollient extract used esp. in cosmetics; *also* : this extract

aloft \ə-ˈloft\ *adv* **1** : high in the air **2** : in flight

alo·ha \ə-ˈlō-ə, ä-ˈlō-hä\ *interj* [Hawaiian] — used to greet or bid farewell

alone \ə-ˈlōn\ *adj* **1** : separated from others **2** : not including anyone or anything else : ONLY ⟨she ∼ knows why⟩ ◆ **Syn-onyms** LONELY, LONESOME, LONE, SOLITARY — **alone** *adv*

¹**along** \ə-ˈlȯŋ\ *prep* **1** : in a line matching the direction of ⟨sail ∼ the coast⟩ **2** : at a point on or during ⟨stopped ∼ the way⟩

²**along** *adv* **1** : FORWARD, ON ⟨move ∼⟩ **2** : as a companion ⟨bring her ∼⟩ **3** : at an advanced point ⟨plans are far ∼⟩

along·shore \ə-ˈlȯŋ-ˈshȯr\ *adv or adj* : along the shore or coast ⟨walked ∼⟩

¹**along·side** \-ˌsīd\ *adv* : along or by the side

²**alongside** *prep* **1** : along or by the side of **2** : in association with

alongside of *prep* : ALONGSIDE

aloof \ə-ˈlüf\ *adj* : removed or distant physically or emotionally — **aloof·ly** *adv* — **aloof·ness** *n*

al·o·pe·cia \ˌa-lə-ˈpē-sh(ē-)ə\ *n* : BALD-NESS

aloud \ə-ˈlau̇d\ *adv* : with the speaking voice ⟨read ∼⟩

alp \ˈalp\ *n* : a high rugged mountain

al·paca \al-ˈpa-kə\ *n* : a domesticated mammal esp. of Peru that is prob. descended from the vicuña; *also* : its woolly hair or a thin cloth made from this hair

al·pha \ˈal-fə\ *n* **1** : the 1st letter of the Greek alphabet — A or α **2** : something first : BEGINNING

al·pha·bet \ˈal-fə-ˌbet\ *n* : the set of letters or characters used in writing a language

al·pha·bet·i·cal \ˌal-fə-ˈbe-ti-kəl\ *or* **al·pha·bet·ic** \-ˈbe-tik\ *adj* **1** : arranged in the order of the letters of the alphabet **2** : of or employing an alphabet — **al·pha·bet·i·cal·ly** \-ti-k(ə-)lē\ *adv*

al·pha·bet·ize \ˈal-fə-bə-ˌtīz\ *vb* **-ized; -iz·ing** : to arrange in alphabetical order — **al·pha·bet·iz·er** *n*

al·pha·nu·mer·ic \ˌal-fə-nü-ˈmer-ik, -nyü-\ *adj* : consisting of letters and numbers and often other symbols ⟨an ∼ code⟩; *also* : being a character in an alphanumeric system

alpha particle *n* : a positively charged particle identical with the nucleus of a helium atom that is ejected at high speed in certain radioactive transformations

alpha rhythm *n* : ALPHA WAVE

alpha wave *n* : an electrical rhythm of the brain often associated with a state of wakeful relaxation

Al·pine \ˈal-ˌpīn\ *adj* **1** : relating to, located in, or resembling the Alps **2** *often not cap* : of, relating to, or growing on upland slopes above timberline **3** : of or relating to competitive ski events consisting of slalom and downhill racing

al·ready \ȯl-ˈre-dē\ *adv* : by this time : PREVIOUSLY

al·right \ȯl-ˈrīt\ *adv* : ALL RIGHT

al·so \ˈȯl-sō\ *adv* : in addition : TOO

al·so–ran \-ˌran\ *n* **1** : a horse or dog that finishes out of the money in a race **2** : a contestant that does not win

alt *abbr* **1** alternate **2** altitude

Alta *abbr* Alberta

al·tar \ˈȯl-tər\ *n* **1** : a structure on which sacrifices are offered or incense is burned **2** : a table used as a center of ritual or worship

altar server *n* : a boy or girl who assists the celebrant at a church service

¹**al·ter** \ˈȯl-tər\ *vb* **al·tered; al·ter·ing** \-t(ə-)riŋ\ **1** : to make or become different **2** : CASTRATE, SPAY — **al·ter·able** \ˈȯl-tə-rə-bəl\ *adj* — **al·ter·a·tion** \ˌȯl-tə-ˈrā-shən\ *n*

²**alter** *abbr* alteration

al·ter·ca·tion \ˌȯl-tər-ˈkā-shən\ *n* : a noisy or angry dispute

alter ego \ˌȯl-tər-ˈē-gō\ *n* [L, lit., second I] : a second self; *esp* : a trusted friend

al·ter·i·ty \ȯl-ˈter-ə-tē\ *n* : the quality or state of being radically alien to the conscious self or a particular cultural orientation

¹**al·ter·nate** \ˈȯl-tər-nət, ˈal-\ *adj* **1** : arranged or succeeding by turns **2** : every other **3** : being an alternative ⟨an ∼ route⟩ — **al·ter·nate·ly** *adv*

²**al·ter·nate** \-ˌnāt\ *vb* **-nat·ed; -nat·ing** : to occur or cause to occur by turns — **al·ter·na·tion** \ˌȯl-tər-ˈnā-shən, ˌal-\ *n*

³**alternate** *n* : SUBSTITUTE

alternating current *n* : an electric current that reverses its direction at regular intervals

al·ter·na·tive \ȯl-ˈtər-nə-tiv, al-\ *adj* **1** : offering a choice ⟨several ∼ plans⟩ **2** : different from the usual or conventional — **alternative** *n*

alternative medicine *n* : any of various systems of healing (as homeopathy) not typically practiced in conventional Western medicine

al·ter·na·tor \ˈȯl-tər-ˌnā-tər, ˈal-\ *n* : an electric generator for producing alternating current

al·though *also* **al·tho** \ȯl-ˈt͟hō\ *conj* : in spite of the fact that : even though

al·tim·e·ter \al-ˈti-mə-tər, ˈal-tə-ˌmē-tər\ *n* : an instrument for measuring altitude

al·ti·tude \ˈal-tə-ˌtüd, -ˌtyüd\ *n* **1** : angular distance above the horizon **2** : vertical distance : HEIGHT **3** : the perpendicular distance in a geometric figure from the vertex to the base, from the vertex of an angle to the side opposite, or from the base to a parallel side or face

al·to \ˈal-tō\ *n, pl* **altos** [It, lit., high, fr. L *altus*] : the lower female voice part in a 4-part chorus; *also* : a singer having this voice or part

¹**al·to·geth·er** \ˌȯl-tə-ˈge-t͟hər\ *adv* **1** : WHOLLY ⟨stopped raining ∼⟩ **2** : in all ⟨spent $100 ∼⟩ **3** : on the whole ⟨∼ their efforts were successful⟩

²**altogether** *n* : NUDE ⟨posed in the ∼⟩

al·tru·ism \ˈal-trü-ˌi-zəm\ *n* [F *altruisme*, fr. *autrui* other people, fr. OF, oblique case form of *autre* other, fr. L *alter*] : unselfish interest in the welfare of others — **al·tru·ist** \-ist\ *n* — **al·tru·is·tic** \ˌal-trü-ˈis-tik\ *adj* — **al·tru·is·ti·cal·ly** \-ti-k(ə-)lē\ *adv*

al·um \ˈa-ləm\ *n* : either of two colorless crystalline aluminum-containing compounds used esp. as an emetic or as an astringent and styptic

alu·mi·na \ə-ˈlü-mə-nə\ n : the oxide of aluminum occurring in nature as corundum and in bauxite

al·u·min·i·um \ˌal-yə-ˈmi-nē-əm\ n, chiefly Brit : ALUMINUM

alu·mi·nize \ə-ˈlü-mə-ˌnīz\ vb **-nized; -niz·ing** : to treat with aluminum

alu·mi·num \ə-ˈlü-mə-nəm\ n : a silver-white malleable ductile light metallic element that is the most abundant metal in the earth's crust

aluminum oxide n : ALUMINA

alum·na \ə-ˈləm-nə\ n, pl **-nae** \-(ˌ)nē\ : a woman graduate or former student of a college or school

alum·nus \ə-ˈləm-nəs\ n, pl **-ni** \-ˌnī\ [L, foster son, pupil, fr. alere to nourish] : a graduate or former student of a college or school

al·ways \ˈȯl-wēz, -wəz, -(ˌ)wāz\ adv **1** : at all times : INVARIABLY **2** : FOREVER

Alz·hei·mer's disease \ˈälts-ˌhī-mərz-, ˈalts-\ n : a degenerative brain disease of unknown cause that is characterized esp. by progressive mental deterioration and memory loss

am pres 1st sing of BE

¹Am abbr America; American

²Am symbol americium

¹AM \ˈā-ˌem\ n : a broadcasting system using amplitude modulation; also : a radio receiver for broadcasts made by such a system

²AM abbr **1** ante meridiem — often not cap. and often punctuated **2** [NL artium magister] master of arts

AMA abbr American Medical Association

amah \ˈä-(ˌ)mä\ n : a female servant in eastern Asia; esp : a Chinese nurse

amain \ə-ˈmān\ adv, archaic : with full force or speed

amal·gam \ə-ˈmal-gəm\ n **1** : an alloy of mercury with another metal used in making dental cements **2** : a mixture of different elements

amal·gam·ate \ə-ˈmal-gə-ˌmāt\ vb **-at·ed; -at·ing** : to unite or merge into one body — **amal·gam·ation** \-ˌmal-gə-ˈmā-shən\ n

aman·u·en·sis \ə-ˌman-yə-ˈwen-səs\ n, pl **-en·ses** \-ˌsēz\ : one employed to write from dictation or to copy what another has written : SECRETARY

am·a·ranth \ˈa-mə-ˌranth\ n **1** : any of a large genus of coarse herbs sometimes grown for their showy flowers **2** : a flower that never fades

am·a·ran·thine \ˌa-mə-ˈran-thən, -ˌthīn\ adj **1** : relating to or resembling an amaranth **2** : UNDYING

am·a·ryl·lis \ˌa-mə-ˈri-ləs\ n : any of various plants related to the lilies; esp : an autumn-flowering South African bulbous herb widely grown for its large showy red to whitish flowers

amass \ə-ˈmas\ vb : ACCUMULATE

am·a·teur \ˈa-mə-(ˌ)tər, -ˌtür, -ˌtyür, -ˌchür, -chər\ n [F, fr. L amator lover, fr. amare to love] **1** : a person who engages in a pursuit for pleasure and not as a profession **2** : a person who is not expert — **am·a·teur·ish** \ˌa-mə-ˈtər-ish, -ˈtür-, -ˈtyür-, -ˈchür-, -ˈchər-\ adj — **am·a·teur·ism** \ˈa-mə-(ˌ)tər-i-zəm, -ˌtür-, -ˌtyür-, -ˌchür-, -ˌchər-\ n

am·a·tive \ˈa-mə-tiv\ adj : indicative of love : AMOROUS — **am·a·tive·ly** adv — **am·a·tive·ness** n

am·a·to·ry \ˈa-mə-ˌtȯr-ē\ adj : of or expressing sexual love

amaze \ə-ˈmāz\ vb amazed; amaz·ing : to fill with wonder : ASTOUND ♦ **Synonyms** ASTONISH, SURPRISE, DUMBFOUND — **amaze·ment** n — **amaz·ing·ly** adv

am·a·zon \ˈa-mə-ˌzän, -zən\ n **1** cap : a member of a race of female warriors of Greek mythology **2** : a tall strong often masculine woman — **am·a·zo·ni·an** \ˌa-mə-ˈzō-nē-ən\ adj, often cap

amb abbr ambassador

am·bas·sa·dor \am-ˈba-sə-dər\ n : a representative esp. of a government — **am·bas·sa·do·ri·al** \ˌba-sə-ˈdȯr-ē-əl\ adj — **am·bas·sa·dor·ship** n

am·ber \ˈam-bər\ n : a yellowish or brownish fossil resin used esp. for ornamental objects; also : the color of this resin

am·ber·gris \ˈam-bər-ˌgris, -ˌgrēs\ n : a waxy substance from the sperm whale used in making perfumes

am·bi·dex·trous \ˌam-bi-ˈdek-strəs\ adj : using both hands with equal ease — **am·bi·dex·trous·ly** adv

am·bi·ence or **am·bi·ance** \ˈam-bē-əns, äⁿ-ˈbyäⁿs\ n : a pervading atmosphere

¹am·bi·ent \ˈam-bē-ənt\ adj : existing on all sides

²ambient : music intended to serve as an unobtrusive accompaniment to other activities

am·big·u·ous \am-ˈbi-gyə-wəs\ adj : capable of being understood in more than one way — **am·bi·gu·i·ty** \ˌam-bə-ˈgyü-ə-tē\ n — **am·big·u·ous·ly** adv

am·bi·tion \am-ˈbi-shən\ n [ME, fr. MF or L; MF, fr. L ambition-, ambitio, lit., act of soliciting for votes, fr. ambire to go around] : eager desire for success or power

am·bi·tious \-shəs\ adj : characterized by ambition — **am·bi·tious·ly** adv — **am·bi·tious·ness** n

am·biv·a·lence \am-ˈbi-və-ləns\ n : simultaneous attraction toward and repulsion from a person, object, or action — **am·biv·a·lent** \-lənt\ adj

¹am·ble \ˈam-bəl\ vb am·bled; am·bling \-b(ə-)liŋ\ : to go at an amble

²amble n : an easy gait esp. of a horse

am·bro·sia \am-ˈbrō-zh(ē-)ə\ n : the food of the Greek and Roman gods — **am·bro·sial** \-zh(ē-)əl\ adj

am·bu·lance \ˈam-byə-ləns\ n : a vehicle equipped for carrying the injured or sick

am·bu·lant \ˈam-byə-lənt\ adj : AMBULATORY

¹am·bu·la·to·ry \ˈam-byə-lə-ˌtȯr-ē\ adj **1** : of, relating to, or adapted to walking **2** : able to move or walk about

²ambulatory n, pl **-ries** : a sheltered place (as in a cloister) for walking

am·bus·cade \ˈam-bə-ˌskād\ n : AMBUSH

am·bush \'am-ˌbúsh\ *n* : a trap in which concealed persons wait to attack by surprise — **ambush** *vb*

amdt *abbr* amendment

ameba, ameboid *var of* AMOEBA, AMOEBOID

ame·lio·rate \ə-'mēl-yə-ˌrāt\ *vb* **-rat·ed; -rat·ing** : to make or grow better : IMPROVE — **ame·lio·ra·tion** \-ˌmēl-yə-'rā-shən\ *n*

amen \(ˌ)ä-'men, (ˌ)ä-\ *interj* — used esp. at the end of prayers to affirm or express approval

ame·na·ble \ə-'mē-nə-bəl, -'me-\ *adj* **1** : ANSWERABLE ⟨~ to the law⟩ **2** : agreeable to something asked for

amend \ə-'mend\ *vb* **1** : to change for the better : IMPROVE **2** : to alter formally in phraseology — **amend·able** \-'men-də-bəl\ *adj*

amend·ment \ə-'mend-mənt\ *n* **1** : correction of faults **2** : the process of amending a parliamentary motion or a constitution; *also* : the alteration so proposed or made

amends \ə-'mendz\ *n sing or pl* : compensation for injury or loss

ame·ni·ty \ə-'me-nə-tē, -'mē-\ *n, pl* **-ties** **1** : AGREEABLENESS **2** : a gesture observed in social relationships **3** : something that serves as a comfort or convenience

Amer *abbr* America; American

amerce \ə-'mərs\ *vb* **amerced; amercing 1** : to penalize by a fine determined by the court **2** : PUNISH — **amercement** *n*

Amer·i·ca·na \ə-ˌmer-ə-'ka-nə, -'kä-\ *n pl* : materials concerning or characteristic of America, its civilization, or its culture

American Indian *n* : a member of any of the aboriginal peoples of No. and So. America except the Eskimos

Amer·i·can·ism \ə-'mer-ə-kə-ˌni-zəm\ *n* **1** : a characteristic feature of English as used in the U.S. **2** : attachment or loyalty to the traditions, interests, or ideals of the U.S. **3** : a custom or trait peculiar to the U.S. or to Americans

Amer·i·can·ize \ə-'mer-ə-kə-ˌnīz\ *vb* : to make or become American — **Amer·i·can·i·za·tion** \ə-ˌmer-ə-kə-nə-'zā-shən\ *n*

Amer·i·can·ness \ə-'mer-ə-kən-nəs\ *n* : the quality or state of being American

American plan *n* : a hotel plan whereby the daily rates cover the cost of room and three meals

American Sign Language *n* : a sign language for the deaf in which meaning is conveyed by a system of hand gestures and placement

amer·i·ci·um \ˌam-ə-'rish-ē-əm, -'ris-\ *n* : a radioactive metallic chemical element produced artificially from plutonium

AmerInd *abbr* American Indian

Am·er·in·di·an \ˌa-mə-'rin-dē-ən\ *n* : AMERICAN INDIAN — **Amerindian** *adj*

am·e·thyst \'a-mə-thəst\ *n* [ME *amatiste*, fr. AF & L; AF, fr. L *amethystus*, fr. Gk *amethystos*, lit., remedy against drunkenness, fr. *a-* not + *methyein* to be drunk, fr.

methy wine] : a gemstone consisting of clear purple or bluish-violet quartz

ami·a·ble \'ā-mē-ə-bəl\ *adj* **1** : AGREEABLE ⟨an ~ comedy⟩ **2** : having a friendly and sociable disposition — **ami·a·bil·i·ty** \ˌā-mē-ə-'bi-lə-tē\ *n* — **ami·a·ble·ness** *n* — **ami·a·bly** \-mē-ə-blē\ *adv*

am·i·ca·ble \'a-mi-kə-bəl\ *adj* : FRIENDLY, PEACEABLE ⟨an ~ settlement of differences⟩ — **am·i·ca·bil·i·ty** \ˌa-mi-kə-'bi-lə-tē\ *n* — **am·i·ca·bly** \'a-mi-kə-blē\ *adv*

amid \ə-'mid\ *or* **amidst** \-'midst\ *prep* : in or into the middle of : AMONG

amid·ships \ə-'mid-ˌships\ *adv* : in or near the middle of a ship

ami·no acid \ə-'mē-nō-\ *n* : any of numerous nitrogen-containing acids that include some which are used by cells to build proteins

amir *var of* EMIR

¹**amiss** \ə-'mis\ *adv* **1** : WRONGLY **2** : ASTRAY ⟨something had gone ~⟩ **3** : IMPERFECTLY

²**amiss** *adj* **1** : WRONG **2** : out of place

am·i·ty \'a-mə-tē\ *n, pl* **-ties** : FRIENDSHIP; *esp* : friendly relations between nations

am·me·ter \'a-ˌmē-tər\ *n* : an instrument for measuring electric current esp. in amperes

am·mo \'a-mō\ *n* : AMMUNITION

am·mo·nia \ə-'mō-nyə\ *n* [NL, fr. L *sal ammoniacus* sal ammoniac (ammonium chloride), lit., salt of Ammon, fr. Gk *mōniakos* of Ammon, fr. *Ammōn* Ammon, an Egyptian god near one of whose temples it was extracted] **1** : a colorless gaseous compound of nitrogen and hydrogen used in refrigeration and in the making of fertilizers and explosives **2** : a solution (**ammonia water**) of ammonia in water

am·mo·ni·um \ə-'mō-nē-əm\ *n* : an ion or chemical group derived from ammonia by combination with hydrogen

ammonium chloride *n* : a white crystalline volatile salt used in batteries and as an expectorant

am·mu·ni·tion \ˌam-yə-'ni-shən\ *n* **1** : projectiles fired from guns **2** : explosive items used in war **3** : material for use in attack or defense

Amn *abbr* airman

am·ne·sia \am-'nē-zhə\ *n* **1** : abnormal loss of memory **2** : the selective overlooking of events or acts not favorable to one's purpose — **am·ne·si·ac** \-zhē-ˌak, -zē-\ *or* **am·ne·sic** \-zik, -sik\ *adj or n*

am·nes·ty \'am-nə-stē\ *n, pl* **-ties** : an act granting a pardon to a group of individuals — **amnesty** *vb*

am·nio·cen·te·sis \ˌam-nē-ō-ˌsen-'tē-səs\ *n, pl* **-te·ses** \-ˌsēz\ : the surgical insertion of a hollow needle through the abdominal wall and uterus of a pregnant female esp. to obtain fluid used to check the fetus for chromosomal abnormality and to determine sex

am·ni·ot·ic fluid \ˌam-nē-'ä-tik-\ *n* : the

watery fluid in which the embryo or fetus is immersed

amoe·ba also **ame·ba** \ə-'mē-bə\ n, pl **-bas** or **-bae** \-(,)bē\ : any of various tiny one-celled protozoans that lack permanent cell organs and occur esp. in water and soil — **amoe·bic** \-bik\ adj

amoe·boid also **ame·boid** \-,bȯid\ adj : resembling an amoeba esp. in moving or readily changing shape

amok \ə-'mək, -'mäk\ or **amuck** \-'mək\ adv : in a violent, frenzied, or uncontrolled manner ⟨run ∼⟩

among \ə-'məŋ\ also **amongst** \-'məŋst\ prep **1** : in or through the midst of **2** : in the number, class, or company of **3** : in shares to each of **4** : by common action of

amon·til·la·do \ə-,män-tə-'lä-dō\ n, pl **-dos** [Sp] : a medium dry sherry

amor·al \ā-'mȯr-əl\ adj **1** : neither moral nor immoral; esp : being outside the sphere to which moral judgments apply **2** : lacking moral sensibility — **amor·al·ly** adv

am·o·rous \'a-mə-rəs\ adj **1** : inclined to love **2** : being in love **3** : of or indicative of love — **am·o·rous·ly** adv — **am·o·rous·ness** n

amor·phous \ə-'mȯr-fəs\ adj **1** : SHAPELESS, FORMLESS **2** : not crystallized

am·or·tize \'a-mər-,tīz, ə-'mȯr-\ vb **-tized; -tiz·ing** : to extinguish (as a mortgage) usu. by payment on the principal at the time of each periodic interest payment — **amor·ti·za·tion** \,a-mər-tə-'zā-shən, ə-,mȯr-\ n

Amos \'ā-məs\ — see BIBLE table

¹amount \ə-'maunt\ vb **1** : to be equivalent **2** : to reach a total : add up

²amount n **1** : the total number or quantity **2** : a principal sum plus the interest on it

amour \ə-'mur, ä-, a-\ n **1** : a love affair esp. when illicit **2** : LOVER

amour pro·pre \,a-,mur-'prȯpr², ,ä-, -'prȯpr²\ n [F] : SELF-ESTEEM

¹amp \'amp\ n **1** : AMPERE **2** : AMPLIFIER; also : a unit consisting of an electronic amplifier and a loudspeaker

²amp vb : EXCITE, ENERGIZE ⟨tried to ∼ up the crowd⟩

am·per·age \'am-p(ə-)rij\ n : the strength of a current of electricity expressed in amperes

am·pere \'am-,pir\ n : a unit of electric current equivalent to a steady current produced by one volt applied across a resistance of one ohm

am·per·sand \'am-pər-,sand\ n [alter. of and per se and, spoken form of the phrase & per se and, lit., (the character) & by itself (stands for the word) and] : a character & used for the word and

am·phet·amine \am-'fe-tə-,mēn, -mən\ n : a compound or one of its derivatives that stimulates the central nervous system and is used esp. to treat hyperactive children and to suppress appetite

am·phib·i·an \am-'fi-bē-ən\ n **1** : an amphibious organism; esp : any of a class of vertebrate animals (as frogs and salamanders) intermediate between fishes and reptiles **2** : an airplane that can land on and take off from either land or water

am·phib·i·ous \am-'fi-bē-əs\ adj [Gk amphibios, lit., living a double life, fr. amphi- + bios mode of life] **1** : able to live both on land and in water **2** : adapted for both land and water **3** : made by joint action of land, sea, and air forces invading from the sea; also : trained for such action

am·phi·bole \'am-fə-,bōl\ n : any of a group of rock-forming minerals of similar crystal structure

am·phi·the·ater \'am-fə-,thē-ə-tər\ n **1** : an oval or circular structure with rising tiers of seats around an arena **2** : a very large auditorium

am·pho·ra \'am-fə-rə\ n, pl **-rae** \-,rē\ or **-ras** : an ancient Greek jar or vase with two handles that rise almost to the level of the mouth

am·ple \'am-pəl\ adj **am·pler** \-plər\; **am·plest** \-pləst\ **1** : LARGE, CAPACIOUS **2** : enough to satisfy : ABUNDANT — **am·ply** \-plē\ adv

am·pli·fy \'am-plə-,fī\ vb **-fied; -fy·ing 1** : to expand by extended treatment **2** : to increase in magnitude or strength; esp : to make louder — **am·pli·fi·ca·tion** \,am-plə-fə-'kā-shən\ n — **am·pli·fi·er** \'am-plə-,fī(-ə)r\ n

am·pli·tude \-,tüd, -,tyüd\ n **1** : ample extent : FULLNESS **2** : the extent of a vibratory movement (as of a pendulum) **3** : the height or depth of an oscillation (as of an alternating current or a radio wave) compared to its average value

amplitude modulation n : modulation of the amplitude of a radio carrier wave in accordance with the strength of the signal; also : a broadcasting system using such modulation

am·poule or **am·pule** also **am·pul** \'am-,pyül, -pül\ n : a small sealed bulbous glass vessel used to hold a solution for hypodermic injection

am·pu·tate \'am-pyə-,tāt\ vb **-tat·ed; -tat·ing** : to cut off ⟨∼ a leg⟩ — **am·pu·ta·tion** \,am-pyə-'tā-shən\ n

am·pu·tee \,am-pyə-'tē\ n : one who has had a limb amputated

AMSLAN abbr American Sign Language

amt abbr amount

amuck var of AMOK

am·u·let \'am-yə-lət\ n : an ornament worn as a charm against evil

amuse \ə-'myüz\ vb **amused; amus·ing** : to entertain in a light or playful manner : DIVERT — **amuse·ment** n — **amus·ing** adj — **amus·ing·ly** adv

amusement park n : a commercially operated park having various devices (as a roller coaster) for entertainment and booths for selling refreshments

AM·VETS \'am-,vets\ abbr American Veterans (of World War II)

am·y·lase \'a-mə-,lās, -,lāz\ n : any of several enzymes that accelerate the breakdown of starch and glycogen

an \ən, (')an\ indefinite article : A — used

before words beginning with a vowel sound

¹-an *or* **-ian** *also* **-ean** *n suffix* **1** : one that belongs to ⟨Americ*an*⟩ ⟨crustac*ean*⟩ **2** : one skilled in or specializing in ⟨phonetic*ian*⟩

²-an *or* **-ian** *also* **-ean** *adj suffix* **1** : of or belonging to ⟨Americ*an*⟩ **2** : characteristic of : resembling ⟨Mozart*ean*⟩

AN *abbr* airman (Navy)

an·a·bol·ic steroid \ˌa-nə-ˈbä-lik-\ *n* : any of a group of synthetic steroid hormones sometimes abused by athletes in training to increase the size and strength of their muscles

anach·ro·nism \ə-ˈna-krə-ˌni-zəm\ *n* **1** : the error of placing a person or thing in the wrong period **2** : one that is chronologically out of place — **anach·ro·nis·tic** \ə-ˌna-krə-ˈnis-tik\ *adj* — **anach·ro·nous** \-ˈna-krə-nəs\ *adj*

an·a·con·da \ˌa-nə-ˈkän-də\ *n* : a large So. American snake that suffocates and kills its prey by constriction

anad·ro·mous \ə-ˈna-drə-məs\ *adj* : ascending rivers from the sea for breeding ⟨shad are ~⟩

anae·mia, anae·mic *chiefly Brit var of* ANEMIA, ANEMIC

an·aer·obe \ˈa-nə-ˌrōb\ *n* : an anaerobic organism

an·aer·o·bic \ˌa-nə-ˈrō-bik\ *adj* : living, active, occurring, or existing in the absence of free oxygen

an·aes·the·sia, an·aes·thet·ic *chiefly Brit var of* ANESTHESIA, ANESTHETIC

ana·gram \ˈa-nə-ˌgram\ *n* : a word or phrase made by transposing the letters of another word or phrase

¹anal \ˈā-nᵊl\ *adj* **1** : of, relating to, situated near, or involving the anus **2** : of, relating to, or characterized by the stage of psychosexual development in psychoanalytic theory during which one is concerned esp. with feces **3** : of, relating to, or characterized by personality traits (as frugality and neatness) considered typical of fixation at the anal stage of development — **anal·ly** *adv*

²anal *abbr* **1** analogy **2** analysis; analytic

an·al·ge·sia \ˌa-nᵊl-ˈjē-zhə\ *n* : insensibility to pain — **an·al·ge·sic** \-ˈjē-zik, -sik\ *adj*

an·al·ge·sic \-ˈjē-zik, -sik\ *n* : an agent for producing analgesia

analog computer *n* : a computer that operates with numbers represented by directly measurable quantities (as voltages)

anal·o·gous \ə-ˈna-lə-gəs\ *adj* : similar in one or more respects — **anal·o·gous·ly** *adv*

an·a·logue *or* **an·a·log** \ˈa-nə-ˌlóg, -ˌlag\ *n* **1** : something that is analogous to something else **2** : an organ similar in function to one of another animal or plant but different in structure or origin

anal·o·gy \ə-ˈna-lə-jē\ *n, pl* **-gies** **1** : inference that if two or more things agree in some respects they will probably agree in others **2** : a likeness in one or more ways between things otherwise unlike —

an·a·log·i·cal \ˌa-nə-ˈlä-ji-kəl\ *adj* — **an·a·log·i·cal·ly** \-k(ə-)lē\ *adv*

anal–re·ten·tive \ˈā-nᵊl-ri-ˈten-tiv\ *adj* : ANAL 3

an·a·lyse *chiefly Brit var of* ANALYZE

anal·y·sis \ə-ˈna-lə-səs\ *n, pl* **-y·ses** \-ˌsēz\ [NL, fr. Gk, fr. *analyein* to break up, fr. *ana-* up + *lyein* to loosen] **1** : separation of a thing into the parts or elements of which it is composed **2** : an examination of a thing to determine its parts or elements; *also* : a statement showing the results of such an examination **3** : PSYCHOANALYSIS — **an·a·lyst** \ˈa-nə-list\ *n* — **an·a·lyt·ic** \ˌa-nə-ˈli-tik\ *or* **an·a·lyt·i·cal** \-ti-kəl\ *adj* — **an·a·lyt·i·cal·ly** *adv*

an·a·lyte \ˈa-nə-ˌlīt\ *n* : a chemical substance that is the subject of chemical analysis

an·a·lyze \ˈa-nə-ˌlīz\ *vb* **-lyzed; -lyz·ing** : to make an analysis of

an·a·pest \ˈa-nə-ˌpest\ *n* : a metrical foot of two unaccented syllables followed by one accented syllable — **an·a·pes·tic** \ˌa-nə-ˈpes-tik\ *adj or n*

an·ar·chism \ˈa-nər-ˌki-zəm\ *n* : the theory that all government is undesirable — **an·ar·chist** \-kist\ *n or adj* — **an·ar·chis·tic** \ˌa-nər-ˈkis-tik\ *adj*

an·ar·chy \ˈa-nər-kē\ *n* **1** : a social structure without government or law and order **2** : utter confusion — **an·ar·chic** \a-ˈnär-kik\ *adj* — **an·ar·chi·cal·ly** \-ki-k(ə-)lē\ *adv*

anas·to·mo·sis \ə-ˌnas-tə-ˈmō-səs\ *n, pl* **-mo·ses** \-ˌsēz\ **1** : the union of parts or branches (as of blood vessels) **2** : NETWORK

anat *abbr* anatomical; anatomy

anath·e·ma \ə-ˈna-thə-mə\ *n* **1** : a solemn curse **2** : a person or thing accursed; *also* : one intensely disliked

anath·e·ma·tize \-ˌtīz\ *vb* **-tized; -tiz·ing** : to pronounce an anathema against : CURSE

anat·o·mise *Brit var of* ANATOMIZE

anat·o·mize \ə-ˈna-tə-ˌmīz\ *vb* **-mized; -miz·ing** : to dissect so as to examine the structure and parts; *also* : ANALYZE

anat·o·my \ə-ˈna-tə-mē\ *n, pl* **-mies** [LL *anatomia* dissection, fr. Gk *anatomē*, fr. *anatemnein* to dissect, fr. *ana-* up + *temnein* to cut] **1** : a branch of science dealing with the structure of organisms **2** : structural makeup esp. of an organism or any of its parts **3** : a separating into parts for detailed study : ANALYSIS — **an·a·tom·i·cal** \ˌa-nə-ˈtä-mi-kəl\ *or* **an·a·tom·ic** \-mik\ *adj* — **an·a·tom·i·cal·ly** \-mi-k(ə-)lē\ *adv* — **anat·o·mist** \ə-ˈna-tə-mist\ *n*

anc *abbr* ancient

-ance *n suffix* **1** : action or process ⟨futher*ance*⟩ : instance of an action or process ⟨perform*ance*⟩ **2** : quality or state : instance of a quality or state ⟨protuber*ance*⟩ **3** : amount or degree ⟨conduct*ance*⟩

an·ces·tor \ˈan-ˌses-tər\ *n* [ME *ancestre*, fr. AF, fr. L *antecessor* predecessor, fr. *antecedere* to go before, fr. *ante-* before +

cedere to go] : one from whom an individual is descended

an·ces·tress \'an-,ses-trəs\ *n* : a female ancestor

an·ces·try \'an-,ses-trē\ *n* **1** : line of descent : LINEAGE **2** : ANCESTORS — **an·ces·tral** \an-'ses-trəl\ *adj*

an·cho \'än-chō\ *n, pl* **anchos** : a poblano chili pepper esp. when mature and dried to a reddish black

¹**an·chor** \'aŋ-kər\ *n* **1** : a heavy metal device attached to a ship that catches hold of the bottom and holds the ship in place **2** : something that serves to hold an object firmly **3** : ANCHORPERSON **4** : a large store that attracts customers and other businesses to a shopping mall

²**anchor** *vb* : to hold or become held in place by or as if by an anchor

an·chor·age \'aŋ-k(ə-)rij\ *n* : a place suitable for ships to anchor

an·cho·rite \'aŋ-kə-,rīt\ *n* : HERMIT

an·chor·man \'aŋ-kər-,man\ *n* **1** : the member of a team who competes last **2** : an anchorperson who is a man

an·chor·per·son \-,pər-sən\ *n* : a broadcaster who reads the news and introduces the reports of other broadcasters

an·chor·wom·an \-,wu̇-mən\ *n* **1** : a woman who competes last **2** : an anchorperson who is a woman

an·cho·vy \'an-,chō-vē, an-'chō-\ *n, pl* **-vies** *or* **-vy** : any of a family of small herringlike fishes often used as food

an·cien ré·gime \ä⁼s-yaⁿ-rā-'zhēm\ *n* **1** : the political and social system of France before the Revolution of 1789 **2** : a system no longer prevailing

¹**an·cient** \'ān-shənt\ *adj* **1** : having existed for many years ⟨∼ customs⟩ **2** : belonging to times long past; *esp* : belonging to the period before the Middle Ages

²**ancient** *n* **1** : an aged person **2** *pl* : the peoples of ancient Greece and Rome; *esp* : the classical authors of Greece and Rome

an·cil·lary \'an-sə-,ler-ē\ *adj* **1** : SUBORDINATE, SUBSIDIARY ⟨a factory's ∼ plants⟩ **2** : AUXILIARY, SUPPLEMENTARY ⟨∼ evidence⟩ — **ancillary** *n*

-ancy *n suffix* : quality or state ⟨flamboyancy⟩

and \ənd, (')and\ *conj* **1** — used to indicate connection or addition esp. of items within the same class or type or to join words or phrases of the same grammatical rank or function **2** — used to join one finite verb to another so that together they are equivalent to an infinitive of purpose ⟨come ∼ see me⟩

¹**an·dan·te** \än-'dän-,tā, -tē\ *adv or adj* [It, lit., going, prp. of *andare* to go] : moderately slow — used as a direction in music

²**andante** *n* : an andante movement

and·iron \'an-,dī(-ə)rn\ *n* : one of a pair of metal supports for firewood in a fireplace

and/or \'and-'o̊r\ *conj* — used to indicate that either *and* or *or* may apply ⟨men ∼ women means men *and* women or men *or* women⟩

an·dro·gen \'an-drə-jən\ *n* : a male sex hormone (as testosterone)

an·drog·y·nous \an-'drä-jə-nəs\ *adj* **1** : having the characteristics of both male and female **2** : suitable for either sex ⟨∼ clothing⟩ — **an·drog·y·ny** \-nē\ *n*

an·droid \'an-,dro̊id\ *n* : a mobile robot usu. with a human form

an·ec·dot·al \,a-nik-'dōt-ᵊl\ *adj* **1** : relating to or consisting of anecdotes **2** : based on reports of an unscientific nature — **an·ec·dot·al·ly** *adv*

an·ec·dote \'an-ik-,dōt\ *n, pl* **-dotes** *also* **-dota** \,a-nik-'dō-tə\ [F, fr. Gk *anekdota* unpublished items, fr. *a-* not + *ekdidonai* to publish] : a brief story of an interesting, amusing, or biographical incident

ane·mia \ə-'nē-mē-ə\ *n* **1** : a condition in which blood is deficient in quantity, in red blood cells, or in hemoglobin and which is marked by pallor, weakness, and irregular heart action **2** : lack of vitality — **ane·mic** \ə-'nē-mik\ *adj*

an·e·mom·e·ter \,a-nə-'mä-mə-tər\ *n* : an instrument for measuring the force or speed of the wind

anem·o·ne \ə-'ne-mə-nē\ *n* : any of a large genus of herbs related to the buttercups that have showy flowers without petals but with conspicuous often colored sepals

anent \ə-'nent\ *prep* : CONCERNING

an·es·the·sia \,a-nəs-'thē-zhə\ *n* : loss of bodily sensation

an·es·the·si·ol·o·gy \-,thē-zē-'ä-lə-jē\ *n* : a branch of medical science dealing with anesthesia and anesthetics — **an·es·the·si·ol·o·gist** \-jist\ *n*

¹**an·es·thet·ic** \,a-nəs-'the-tik\ *adj* : of, relating to, or capable of producing anesthesia

²**anesthetic** *n* : an agent that produces anesthesia

anes·the·tist \ə-'nes-thə-tist\ *n* : one who administers anesthetics

anes·the·tize \ə-'nes-thə-,tīz\ *vb* **-tized**; **-tiz·ing** : to subject to anesthesia

an·eu·rysm *also* **an·eu·rism** \'an-yə-,ri-zəm\ *n* : an abnormal blood-filled bulge of a blood vessel

anew \ə-'nü, -'nyü\ *adv* **1** : over again ⟨begin ∼⟩ **2** : in a new form ⟨this film tells the story ∼⟩

an·gel \'ān-jəl\ *n* [ME, fr. OE *engel* & AF *angele*, both fr. L *angelus*, fr. Gk *angelos*, lit., messenger] **1** : a spiritual being superior to man **2** : an attendant spirit **3** : a winged figure of human form in art **4** : MESSENGER, HARBINGER ⟨∼ of death⟩ **5** : a person held to resemble an angel **6** : a financial backer — **an·gel·ic** \an-'je-lik\ *or* **an·gel·i·cal** \-li-kəl\ *adj* — **an·gel·i·cal·ly** \-k(ə-)lē\ *adv*

an·gel·fish \'ān-jəl-,fish\ *n* : any of several brightly colored tropical fishes that are flattened from side to side

an·gel·i·ca \an-'je-li-kə\ *n* : a biennial herb related to the carrot whose roots and fruit furnish a flavoring oil

¹**an·ger** \'aŋ-gər\ *vb* : to make angry

²**anger** *n* [ME, affliction, anger, fr. ON *angr* grief] : a strong feeling of displea-

sure ♦ *Synonyms* WRATH, IRE, RAGE, FURY, INDIGNATION

an·gi·na \an-ʹjī-nə\ *n* : a disorder (as of the heart) marked by attacks of intense pain; *esp* : ANGINA PECTORIS — **an·gi·nal** \an-ʹjī-nᵊl\ *adj*

angina pec·to·ris \-ʹpek-t(ə-)rəs\ *n* : a heart disease marked by brief attacks of sharp chest pain caused by deficient oxygenation of heart muscles

an·gio·gen·e·sis \an-jē-ō-ʹje-nə-səs\ *n* : the formation of blood vessels — **an·gio·gen·ic** \-ʹje-nik\ *adj*

an·gio·gram \ʹan-jē-ə-,gram\ *n* : a radiograph made by angiography

an·gi·og·ra·phy \an-jē-ʹä-grə-fē\ *n* : the use of radiography to make blood vessels visible after injection of a substance opaque to radiation

an·gio·plas·ty \ʹan-jē-ə-,plas-tē\ *n* : surgical repair of a blood vessel esp. by using an inflatable catheter to unblock arteries clogged by atherosclerotic deposits

an·gio·sperm \-,spərm\ *n* : FLOWERING PLANT

¹an·gle \ʹan-gəl\ *n* 1 : a sharp projecting corner 2 : the figure formed by the meeting of two lines in a point 3 : a point of view 4 : a special technique or plan : GIMMICK — **an·gled** *adj*

²angle *vb* **an·gled; an·gling** \-g(ə-)liŋ\ : to turn, move, or direct at an angle

³angle *vb* **an·gled; an·gling** \-g(ə-)liŋ\ : to fish with a hook and line — **an·gler** \-glər\ *n* — **an·gling** \-gliŋ\ *n*

an·gle·worm \ʹan-gəl-,wərm\ *n* : EARTHWORM

An·gli·can \ʹan-gli-kən\ *adj* 1 : of or relating to the established episcopal Church of England 2 : of or relating to England or the English nation — **Anglican** *n* — **An·gli·can·ism** \-kə-,ni-zəm\ *n*

an·gli·cize \ʹan-glə-,sīz\ *vb* **-cized; -cizing** *often cap* 1 : to make English (as in habits, speech, character, or outlook) 2 : to borrow (a foreign word or phrase) into English without changing form or spelling and sometimes without changing pronunciation — **an·gli·ci·za·tion** \an-glə-sə-ʹzā-shən\ *n, often cap*

An·glo \ʹan-glō\ *n, pl* **Anglos** : a non-Hispanic white inhabitant of the U.S.; *esp* : one of English origin and descent

An·glo·cen·tric \,an-glō-ʹsen-trik\ *adj* : centered on or favoring England or things English

An·glo–French \,an-glō-ʹfrench\ *n* : the French language used in medieval England

An·glo·phile \ʹan-glə-,fī(-ə)l\ *also* **An·glo·phil** \-,fil\ *n* : one who greatly admires England and things English

An·glo·phobe \ʹan-glə-,fōb\ *n* : one who is averse to England and things English

An·glo–Sax·on \,an-glō-ʹsak-sən\ *n* 1 : a member of any of the Germanic peoples who invaded England in the 5th century A.D. 2 : a member of the English people 3 : Old English — **Anglo–Saxon** *adj*

an·go·ra \an-ʹgōr-ə, an-\ *n* 1 : yarn or cloth made from the hair of an Angora goat or rabbit 2 *cap* : any of a breed of cats, goats, or rabbits with a long silky coat

an·gry \ʹan-grē\ *adj* **an·gri·er; -est** : feeling or showing anger ♦ *Synonyms* ENRAGED, WRATHFUL, IRATE, INDIGNANT, MAD — **an·gri·ly** \-grə-lē\ *adv*

angst \ʹänst\ *n* [G] : a feeling of anxiety

ang·strom \ʹan-strəm\ *n* : a unit of length equal to one ten-billionth of a meter

an·guish \ʹan-gwish\ *n* : extreme pain or distress esp. of mind — **an·guished** \-gwisht\ *adj*

an·gu·lar \ʹan-gyə-lər\ *adj* 1 : sharp-cornered 2 : having one or more angles 3 : being thin and bony — **an·gu·lar·i·ty** \an-gyə-ʹler-ə-tē\ *n*

An·gus \ʹan-gəs\ *n* : any of a breed of usu. black hornless beef cattle originating in Scotland

an·hy·drous \an-ʹhī-drəs\ *adj* : free from water

an·i·line \ʹa-nᵊl-ən\ *n* : an oily poisonous liquid used in making dyes, medicines, and explosives

an·i·mad·vert \,a-nə-,mad-ʹvərt\ *vb* : to remark critically : express censure — **an·i·mad·ver·sion** \-ʹvər-zhən\ *n*

¹an·i·mal \ʹa-nə-məl\ *n* 1 : any of a kingdom of living things typically differing from plants in capacity for active movement, in rapid response to stimulation, and in lack of cellulose cell walls 2 : a lower animal as distinguished from human beings; *also* : MAMMAL

²animal *adj* 1 : of, relating to, or derived from animals 2 : of or relating to the physical as distinguished from the mental or spiritual ♦ *Synonyms* CARNAL, FLESHLY, SENSUAL

an·i·mal·cule \,a-nə-ʹmal-kyül\ *n* : a tiny animal usu. invisible to the naked eye

¹an·i·mate \ʹa-nə-mət\ *adj* : having life

²an·i·mate \-,māt\ *vb* **-mat·ed; -mat·ing** 1 : to impart life to 2 : to give spirit and vigor to 3 : to make appear to move (⟨~ a cartoon for motion pictures⟩ — **an·i·mat·ed** *adj* — **an·i·mat·ed·ly** *adv*

an·i·ma·tion \,a-nə-ʹmā-shən\ *n* 1 : VIVACITY, LIVELINESS 2 : a motion picture made from a series of drawings simulating motions by means of slight progressive changes

an·i·ma·tron·ic \,a-nə-mə-ʹträ-nik\ *adj* : of, relating to, or being an electrically animated mechanical figure (as a puppet)

an·i·mism \ʹa-nə-,mi-zəm\ *n* : attribution of conscious life to objects in and phenomena of nature or to inanimate objects — **an·i·mist** \-mist\ *n* — **an·i·mis·tic** \,a-nə-ʹmis-tik\ *adj*

an·i·mos·i·ty \,a-nə-ʹmä-sə-tē\ *n, pl* **-ties** : ILL WILL, RESENTMENT

an·i·mus \ʹa-nə-məs\ *n* : deep-seated resentment and hostility

an·ion \ʹa-,nī-ən, -,nī-,än\ *n* : a negatively charged ion

an·ise \ʹa-nəs\ *n* : an herb related to the carrot with aromatic seeds (aniseed \-,sēd\) used in flavoring

an·is·ette \,a-nə-ʹset, -ʹzet\ *n* [F] : a usu. colorless sweet liqueur flavored with aniseed

ankh \'äŋk\ *n* : a cross having a loop for its upper vertical arm and serving esp. in ancient Egypt as an emblem of life

an·kle \'aŋ-kəl\ *n* : the joint or region between the foot and the leg

an·kle·bone \'aŋ-kəl-ˌbōn\ *n* : the bone that in human beings bears the weight of the body and with the tibia and fibula forms the ankle joint

an·klet \'aŋ-klət\ *n* 1 : something (as an ornament) worn around the ankle 2 : a short sock reaching slightly above the ankle

ann *abbr* 1 annals 2 annual

an·nals \'a-nºlz\ *n pl* 1 : a record of events in chronological order 2 : historical records — **an·nal·ist** \-nºl-ist\ *n*

an·neal \ə-'nēl\ *vb* 1 : to make (as glass or steel) less brittle by heating and then cooling 2 : STRENGTHEN, TOUGHEN

¹an·nex \ə-'neks, 'a-ˌneks\ *vb* 1 : to attach as an addition 2 : to incorporate (as a territory) within a political domain — **an·nex·a·tion** \ˌa-ˌnek-'sā-shən\ *n*

²an·nex \'a-ˌneks, -niks\ *n* : a subsidiary or supplementary structure

an·nexe *chiefly Brit var of* ANNEX

an·ni·hi·late \ə-'nī-ə-ˌlāt\ *vb* **-lat·ed; -lat·ing** : to destroy completely — **an·ni·hi·la·tion** \-ˌnī-ə-'lā-shən\ *n*

an·ni·ver·sa·ry \ˌa-nə-'vər-sə-rē\ *n, pl* **-ries** : the annual return of the date of a notable event and esp. a wedding

an·no Do·mi·ni \ˌa-nō-'dä-mə-nē, -'dō-, -ˌnī\ *adv, often cap A* [ML, in the year of the Lord] — used to indicate that a time division falls within the Christian era

an·no·tate \'a-nə-ˌtāt\ *vb* **-tat·ed; -tat·ing** : to furnish with notes — **an·no·ta·tion** \ˌa-nə-'tā-shən\ *n* — **an·no·ta·tor** \'a-nə-ˌtā-tər\ *n*

an·nounce \ə-'naůns\ *vb* **an·nounced; an·nounc·ing** 1 : to make known publicly 2 : to give notice of the arrival or presence of — **an·nounce·ment** *n*

an·nounc·er \ə-'naůn-sər\ *n* : a person who introduces radio or television programs, makes commercial announcements, or gives station identification

an·noy \ə-'nói\ *vb* : to disturb or irritate esp. by repeated acts : VEX ♦ **Synonyms** IRK, BOTHER, PESTER, TEASE, HARASS — **an·noy·ing·ly** *adv*

an·noy·ance \ə-'nói-əns\ *n* 1 : the act of annoying 2 : the state of being annoyed 3 : NUISANCE ⟨the delay was a minor ~⟩

¹an·nu·al \'an-yə-wəl\ *adj* 1 : covering the period of a year ⟨~ rainfall⟩ 2 : occurring once a year : YEARLY 3 : completing the life cycle in one growing season ⟨~ plants⟩ — **an·nu·al·ly** *adv*

²annual *n* 1 : a publication appearing once a year 2 : an annual plant

annual ring *n* : the layer of wood produced by a single year's growth of a woody plant

an·nu·i·tant \ə-'nü-ə-tənt, -'nyü-\ *n* : a beneficiary of an annuity

an·nu·i·ty \ə-'nü-ə-tē, -'nyü-\ *n, pl* **-ities** : an amount payable annually; *also* : the right to receive such a payment

an·nul \ə-'nəl\ *vb* **an·nulled; an·nul·ling** : to make legally void — **an·nul·ment** *n*

an·nu·lar \'an-yə-lər\ *adj* : ring-shaped

an·nun·ci·ate \ə-'nən-sē-ˌāt\ *vb* **-at·ed; -at·ing** : ANNOUNCE

an·nun·ci·a·tion \ə-ˌnən-sē-'ā-shən\ *n* 1 *cap* : March 25 observed as a church festival commemorating the announcement of the Incarnation 2 : ANNOUNCEMENT

an·nun·ci·a·tor \ə-'nən-sē-ˌā-tər\ *n* : one that annunciates; *specif* : a usu. electrically controlled signal board or indicator

an·ode \'a-ˌnōd\ *n* 1 : the positive electrode of an electrolytic cell 2 : the negative terminal of a battery 3 : the electron-collecting electrode of an electron tube — **an·od·ic** \a-'nä-dik\ *also* **an·od·al** \-'nō-dºl\ *adj*

an·od·ize \'a-nə-ˌdīz\ *vb* **-ized; -iz·ing** : to subject (a metal) to electrolytic action as the anode of a cell in order to coat with a protective or decorative film

an·o·dyne \'a-nə-ˌdīn\ *n* : something that relieves pain : a soothing agent

anoint \ə-'nóint\ *vb* 1 : to apply oil to esp. as a sacred rite 2 : CONSECRATE — **anoint·ment** *n*

anom·a·lous \ə-'nä-mə-ləs\ *adj* : deviating from a general rule : ABNORMAL

anom·a·ly \ə-'nä-mə-lē\ *n, pl* **-lies** : something anomalous : IRREGULARITY

¹anon \ə-'nän\ *adv* : SOON

²anon *abbr* anonymous; anonymously

anon·y·mous \ə-'nä-nə-məs\ *adj* : of unknown or undeclared origin or authorship — **an·o·nym·i·ty** \ˌa-nə-'ni-mə-tē\ *n* — **anon·y·mous·ly** *adv*

anoph·e·les \ə-'nä-fə-ˌlēz\ *n* [NL, genus name, fr. Gk *anōphelēs* useless, fr. *a-* not + *ophelos* advantage, help] : any of a genus of mosquitoes that includes all mosquitoes which transmit malaria to human beings

an·o·rec·tic \ˌa-nə-'rek-tik\ *adj* : ANOREXIC — **anorectic** *n*

an·orex·ia \ˌa-nə-'rek-sē-ə\ *n* 1 : loss of appetite esp. when prolonged 2 : ANOREXIA NERVOSA

anorexia ner·vo·sa \-ˌnər-'vō-sə\ *n* : a serious disorder in eating behavior marked esp. by a pathological fear of weight gain leading to faulty eating patterns, malnutrition, and usu. excessive weight loss

an·orex·ic \ˌa-nə-'rek-sik\ *adj* 1 : lacking or causing loss of appetite 2 : affected with or as if with anorexia nervosa — **anorexic** *n*

¹an·oth·er \ə-'nə-thər\ *adj* 1 : some other ⟨do it ~ time⟩ 2 : being one in addition : one more ⟨~ piece of pie⟩

²another *pron* 1 : an additional one : one more 2 : one that is different from the first or present one

ans *abbr* answer

¹an·swer \'an-sər\ *n* 1 : something spoken or written in reply to a question 2 : a solution of a problem

²answer *vb* 1 : to speak or write in reply to 2 : to be responsible 3 : to be adequate — **an·swer·er** *n*

an·swer·able \'an-sə-rə-bəl\ *adj* 1 : subject to taking blame or responsibility 2 : capable of being refuted

answering machine *n* : a machine that receives telephone calls by playing a recorded message and usu. by recording messages from callers

answering service *n* : a commercial service that answers telephone calls for its clients

¹ant \'ant\ *n* : any of a family of small social insects related to the bees and living in communities usu. in earth or wood

²ant *abbr* antonym

Ant *abbr* Antarctica

ant— see ANTI-

¹-ant *n suffix* 1 : one that performs or promotes (a specified action) ⟨cool*ant*⟩ 2 : thing that is acted upon (in a specified manner) ⟨inhal*ant*⟩

²-ant *adj suffix* 1 : performing (a specified action) or being (in a specified condition) ⟨propell*ant*⟩ 2 : promoting (a specified action or process) ⟨expector*ant*⟩

ant·ac·id \ant-'a-səd\ *n* : an agent that counteracts acidity — **antacid** *adj*

an·tag·o·nism \an-'ta-gə-ˌni-zəm\ *n* 1 : active opposition or hostility 2 : opposition in physiological action — **an·tag·o·nis·tic** \-ˌta-gə-'nis-tik\ *adj*

an·tag·o·nist \-nist\ *n* : ADVERSARY, OPPONENT

an·tag·o·nize \an-'ta-gə-ˌnīz\ *vb* **-nized; -niz·ing** : to provoke the hostility of

ant·arc·tic \ant-'ärk-tik, -'är-tik\ *adj, often cap* : of or relating to the south pole or the region near it

antarctic circle *n, often cap A&C* : the parallel of latitude that is approximately 66½ degrees south of the equator

¹an·te \'an-tē\ *n* : a poker stake put up before the deal to build the pot; *also* : an amount paid : PRICE

²ante *vb* **an·ted; an·te·ing** 1 : to put up (an ante) 2 : PAY

ant·eat·er \'ant-ˌē-tər\ *n* : any of several mammals (as an aardvark) that feed mostly on ants or termites

an·te·bel·lum \ˌan-ti-'be-ləm\ *adj* : existing before a war; *esp* : existing before the U.S. Civil War of 1861-65

an·te·ced·ent \ˌan-tə-'sē-dᵊnt\ *n* 1 : a noun, pronoun, phrase, or clause referred to by a personal or relative pronoun 2 : a preceding event or cause 3 *pl* : the unspecified conditions of one's earlier life 4 *pl* : ANCESTORS — **antecedent** *adj*

an·te·cham·ber \'an-ti-ˌchām-bər\ *n* : ANTEROOM

an·te·date \'an-ti-ˌdāt\ *vb* 1 : to date (a paper) as of an earlier day than that on which the actual writing or signing is done 2 : to precede in time

an·te·di·lu·vi·an \ˌan-ti-də-'lü-vē-ən, -dī-\ *adj* 1 : of the period before the biblical flood 2 : ANTIQUATED, OUT-OF-DATE

an·te·lope \'an-tə-ˌlōp\ *n, pl* **-lope** *or* **-lopes** [ME, fabulous heraldic beast, prob. fr. MF *antelop* savage animal with sawlike horns, fr. ML *anthalopus*, fr. LGk *antholops*] 1 : any of various deerlike ruminant mammals that chiefly inhabit Africa and have a slender build and horns extending upward and backward 2 : PRONGHORN

an·te me·ri·di·em \ˌan-ti-mə-'ri-dē-əm\ *adj* [L] : being before noon

an·ten·na \an-'te-nə\ *n, pl* **-nae** \-(ˌ)nē\ *or* **-nas** [ML, fr. L, sail yard] 1 : one of the long slender paired segmented sensory organs on the head of an arthropod (as an insect or crab) 2 *pl usu* **-nas** : a metallic device (as a rod or wire) for sending out or receiving radio waves

an·te·pe·nult \ˌan-ti-'pē-ˌnəlt\ *also* **an·te·pen·ul·ti·ma** \-ˌpi-'nəl-tə-mə\ *n* : the 3d syllable of a word counting from the end — **an·te·pen·ul·ti·mate** \-ˌpi-'nəl-tə-mət\ *adj or n*

an·te·ri·or \an-'tir-ē-ər\ *adj* 1 : situated before or toward the front 2 : situated near or nearer to the head 3 : coming before in time ♦ **Synonyms** PRECEDING, PREVIOUS, PRIOR, ANTECEDENT

anterior cruciate ligament *n* : a cross-shaped ligament of the knee that connects the tibia and femur

an·te·room \'an-ti-ˌrüm, -ˌrüm\ *n* : a room forming the entrance to another and often used as a waiting room

an·them \'an-thəm\ *n* 1 : a sacred vocal composition 2 : a song or hymn of praise or gladness

an·ther \'an-thər\ *n* : the part of a stamen of a seed plant that produces and contains pollen

ant·hill \'ant-ˌhil\ *n* : a mound thrown up by ants or termites in digging their nest

an·thol·o·gy \an-'thä-lə-jē\ *n, pl* **-gies** [NL *anthologia* collection of epigrams, fr. MGk, fr. Gk, flower gathering, fr. *anthos* flower + *logia* collecting, fr. *legein* to gather] : a collection of literary selections — **an·thol·o·gist** \-jist\ *n* — **an·thol·o·gize** \-ˌjīz\ *vb*

an·thra·cite \'an-thrə-ˌsīt\ *n* : a hard glossy coal that burns without much smoke

an·thrax \'an-ˌthraks\ *n* : an infectious and usu. fatal bacterial disease of warm-blooded animals (as cattle and sheep) that is transmissible to humans; *also* : a bacterium causing anthrax

an·thro·po·cen·tric \ˌan-thrə-pə-'sen-trik\ *adj* : interpreting or regarding the world in terms of human values and experiences

an·thro·poid \'an-thrə-ˌpȯid\ *n* 1 : any of several large tailless apes (as a gorilla) 2 : a person resembling an ape — **anthropoid** *adj*

an·thro·pol·o·gy \ˌan-thrə-'pä-lə-jē\ *n* : the science of human beings and esp. of their physical characteristics, their origin and ancestry, their environment and social relations, and their culture — **an·thro·po·log·i·cal** \-pə-'lä-ji-kəl\ *adj* — **an·thro·pol·o·gist** \-'pä-lə-jist\ *n*

an·thro·po·mor·phism \ˌan-thrə-pə-'mȯr-ˌfi-zəm\ *n* : an interpretation of what is not human or personal in terms of human or personal characteristics

: HUMANIZATION — **an·thro·po·mor·phic** \-fik\ *adj*

an·ti \'an-,tī, -tē\ *n, pl* **antis** : one who is opposed

anti- \an-ti, -tē, -,tī\ *or* **ant-** *or* **anth-** *prefix* **1** : opposite in kind, position, or action **2** : opposing : hostile toward **3** : counteractive **4** : preventive of : curative of

an·ti·abor·tion \,an-tē-ə-'bȯr-shən, ,an-,tī-\ *adj* : opposed to abortion — **an·ti·abor·tion·ist** \-shə-nist\ *n*

an·ti·bal·lis·tic missile \,an-ti-bə-'lis-tik-, ,an-,tī-\ *n* : a missile for intercepting and destroying ballistic missiles

an·ti·bi·ot·ic \-bī-'ä-tik, -bē-\ *n* : a substance produced by or derived by chemical alteration of a substance produced by a microorganism (as a fungus or bacterium) that in dilute solution inhibits or kills another microorganism — **antibiotic** *adj*

an·ti·body \'an-ti-,bä-dē\ *n* : any of a large number of proteins of high molecular weight produced normally by a specialized B cells after stimulation by an antigen and acting specifically against the antigen in an immune response

¹an·tic \'an-tik\ *n* [It *antico* ancient thing or person, fr. *antico* ancient, fr. L *antiquus*] : an often wildly playful or funny act or action

²antic *adj* **1** *archaic* : GROTESQUE **2** : PLAYFUL

an·ti·can·cer \,an-ti-'kan-sər, ,an-,tī-\ *adj* : used against or tending to arrest or prevent cancer ⟨∼ drugs⟩

An·ti·christ \'an-ti-,krīst\ *n* **1** : one who denies or opposes Christ **2** : a false Christ

an·tic·i·pate \an-'ti-sə-,pāt\ *vb* **-pat·ed; -pat·ing 1** : to foresee and provide for beforehand ⟨∼s problems⟩ **2** : to look forward to — **an·tic·i·pa·tion** \-,ti-sə-'pā-shən\ *n* — **an·tic·i·pa·to·ry** \-'ti-sə-pə-,tȯr-ē\ *adj*

an·ti·cli·max \,an-ti-'klī-,maks\ *n* : something (as the ending of a story) that is strikingly less important or dramatic than expected — **an·ti·cli·mac·tic** \-klī-'mak-tik\ *adj*

an·ti·cline \'an-ti-,klīn\ *n* : an arch of layers of rock in the earth's crust

an·ti·co·ag·u·lant \,an-ti-kō-'a-gyə-lənt\ *n* : a substance that hinders the clotting of blood — **anticoagulant** *adj*

an·ti·cy·clone \,an-ti-'sī-,klōn\ *n* : a system of winds that rotates about a center of high atmospheric pressure — **an·ti·cy·clon·ic** \-sī-'klä-nik\ *adj*

an·ti·de·pres·sant \,an-ti-di-'pres-³nt, ,an-,tī-\ *n* : a drug used to relieve psychic depression — **antidepressant** *adj*

an·ti·dote \'an-ti-,dōt\ *n* : a remedy to counteract the effects of poison

an·ti·drug \'an-,tī-,drəg\ *adj* : acting against or opposing illicit drugs

an·ti·fer·til·i·ty \,an-ti-fər-'ti-lə-tē\ *adj* : tending to reduce or destroy fertility : CONTRACEPTIVE ⟨∼ agents⟩

an·ti·freeze \'an-ti-,frēz\ *n* : a substance added to a liquid to lower its freezing temperature

an·ti·fun·gal \,an-ti-'fəŋ-gəl, ,an,-tī-\ *n* : FUNGICIDE — **antifungal** *adj*

an·ti·gen \'an-ti-jən\ *n* : any substance (as a toxin) foreign to the body that induces an immune response — **an·ti·gen·ic** \,an-ti-'je-nik\ *adj* — **an·ti·ge·nic·i·ty** \-jə-'ni-sə-tē\ *n*

an·ti·grav·i·ty \,an-ti-'gra-və-tē, ,an,-tī-\ *adj* : reducing or canceling the effect of gravity

an·ti·he·ro \'an-ti-,hē-rō, 'an-,tī-\ *n* : a protagonist who is notably lacking in heroic qualities (as courage)

an·ti·his·ta·mine \,an-ti-'his-tə-,mēn, ,an-,tī-, -mən\ *n* : any of various drugs used in treating allergies and colds — **antihistamine** *adj*

an·ti·hy·per·ten·sive \-,hī-pər-'ten-siv\ *n* : a substance that is effective against high blood pressure — **antihypertensive** *adj*

an·ti·in·flam·ma·to·ry \-in-'fla-mə-,tōr-ē\ *adj* : counteracting inflammation — **anti—inflammatory** *n*

an·ti·in·tel·lec·tu·al \-,in-tə-'lek-chə-wəl\ *adj* : opposing or hostile to intellectuals or to an intellectual view or approach

an·ti·lock \'an-ti-,läk, 'an-,tī-\ *adj* : being a braking system designed to prevent the wheels from locking

an·ti·log·a·rithm \,an-ti-'lȯ-gə-,ri-thəm, ,an-,tī-, -'lä-\ *n* : the number corresponding to a given logarithm ⟨if the logarithm in base x of a equals b then the antilogarithm in base x of b equals a⟩

an·ti·ma·cas·sar \,an-ti-mə-'ka-sər\ *n* : a cover to protect the back or arms of furniture

an·ti·mat·ter \'an-ti-,ma-tər, 'an-,tī-\ *n* : matter composed of antiparticles

an·ti·mo·ny \'an-tə-,mō-nē\ *n* : a brittle silvery white metallic chemical element used esp. in alloys

an·ti·neu·tron \,an-ti-'nü-,trän, ,an-,tī-, -'nyü-\ *n* : the antiparticle of the neutron

an·ti·no·mi·an \,an-ti-'nō-mē-ən\ *n* : one who denies the validity of moral laws

an·tin·o·my \an-'ti-nə-mē\ *n, pl* **-mies** : a contradiction between two seemingly true statements

an·ti·nov·el \'an-ti-,nä-vəl, 'an-,tī-\ *n* : a work of fiction that lacks all or most of the traditional features of the novel

an·ti·nu·cle·ar \,an-ti-'nü-klē-ər, -'nyü-\ *adj* : opposing the use or production of nuclear power

antiaging	antibacterial	anticommunist	anti-imperialism
anti-AIDS	anticapitalist	antidemocratic	anti-imperialist
antiaircraft	anti-Catholic	antidiscrimination	antiknock
antialcohol	anticholesterol	antiestablishment	antilabor
anti-American	anticlerical	antifascist	antimalarial
antianxiety	anticolonial	antigovernment	antimicrobial
antiapartheid	anticommunism	anti-HIV	antinausea

an·ti·ox·i·dant \,an-tē-'äk-sə-dənt, ,an-,tī-\ *n* : a substance that inhibits oxidation — **antioxidant** *adj*

an·ti·par·ti·cle \'an-ti-,pär-ti-kəl, 'an-,tī-\ *n* : a subatomic particle identical to another subatomic particle in mass but opposite to it in electric and magnetic properties

an·ti·pas·to \,an-ti-'pas-tō, ,än-ti-'päs-\ *n, pl* **-ti** \-(,)tē\ : any of various typically Italian hors d'oeuvres

an·tip·a·thy \an-'ti-pə-thē\ *n, pl* **-thies** **1** : settled aversion or dislike **2** : an object of aversion — **an·ti·pa·thet·ic** \,an-ti-pə-'the-tik\ *adj*

an·ti·per·son·nel \,an-ti-,pər-sə-'nel, ,an-,tī-\ *adj* : designed for use against military personnel ⟨∼ mine⟩

an·ti·per·spi·rant \-'pər-spə-rənt\ *n* : a preparation used to reduce perspiration

an·tiph·o·nal \an-'ti-fə-n^əl\ *adj* : performed by two alternating groups — **an·tiph·o·nal·ly** *adv*

an·ti·pode \'an-tə-,pōd\ *n, pl* **an·tip·o·des** \an-'ti-pə-,dēz\ [ME *antipodes*, pl., persons dwelling at opposite points on the globe, fr. L, fr. Gk, fr. pl. of *antipod-, antipous* with feet opposite, fr. *anti-* against + *pod-, pous* foot] : the parts of the earth diametrically opposite — usu. used in pl. — **an·tip·o·dal** \an-'ti-pə-d^əl\ *adj* — **an·tip·o·de·an** \(,)an-,ti-pə-'dē-ən\ *adj*

an·ti·pol·lu·tion \,an-ti-pə-'lü-shən\ *adj* : designed to prevent, reduce, or eliminate pollution ⟨∼ laws⟩

an·ti·pope \'an-ti-,pōp\ *n* : one elected or claiming to be pope in opposition to the pope canonically chosen

an·ti·pro·ton \,an-ti-'prō-,tän\ *n* : the antiparticle of the proton

an·ti·psy·chot·ic \,an-tē-sī-'kä-tik\ *adj* : any of the powerful tranquilizers used to treat psychosis — **antipsychotic** *adj*

an·ti·quar·i·an \,an-tə-'kwer-ē-ən\ *adj* **1** : of or relating to antiquities **2** : dealing in old books — **antiquarian** *n* — **an·ti·quar·i·an·ism** *n*

an·ti·quary \'an-tə-,kwer-ē\ *n, pl* **-quar·ies** : a person who collects or studies antiquities

an·ti·quat·ed \'an-tə-,kwā-təd\ *adj* : OUT-OF-DATE, OLD-FASHIONED

¹an·tique \an-'tēk\ *n* : an object made in a bygone period

²antique *adj* **1** : belonging to antiquity **2** : OLD-FASHIONED **3** : of a bygone style or period

³antique *vb* **-tiqued; -tiqu·ing** **1** : to finish or refinish in antique style : give an appearance of age to **2** : to shop around for antiques — **an·tiqu·er** *n*

an·tiq·ui·ty \an-'ti-kwə-tē\ *n, pl* **-ties** **1** : ancient times **2** : great age **3** *pl* : relics of ancient times **4** *pl* : matters relating to ancient culture

an·ti·re·tro·vi·ral \,an-tē-'re-trō-,vī-rəl, ,an-,tī-\ *adj* : effective against retroviruses ⟨∼ drugs⟩ — **antiretroviral** *n*

antis *pl of* ANTI

an·ti·Sem·i·tism \,an-ti-'se-mə-,ti-zəm, ,an-,tī-\ *n* : hostility toward Jews as a religious or social minority — **an·ti–Sem·ite** \-'se-,mīt\ *n* — **an·ti–Sem·it·ic** \-sə-'mi-tik\ *adj*

an·ti·sep·tic \,an-tə-'sep-tik\ *adj* **1** : killing or checking the growth of germs that cause decay or infection **2** : scrupulously clean : ASEPTIC **3** : coldly impersonal ⟨an ∼ greeting⟩ — **antiseptic** *n* — **an·ti·sep·ti·cal·ly** *adv*

an·ti·se·rum \'an-ti-,sir-əm, 'an-,tī-\ *n* : a serum containing antibodies

an·ti·so·cial \,an-ti-'sō-shəl\ *adj* **1** : disliking the society of others **2** : contrary or hostile to the well-being of society ⟨crime is ∼⟩; *esp* : deviating sharply from the social norm — **an·ti·so·cial·ly** *adv*

an·tith·e·sis \an-'ti-thə-səs\ *n, pl* **-e·ses** \-,sēz\ **1** : the opposition or contrast of ideas **2** : the direct opposite

an·ti·thet·i·cal \,an-tə-'the-ti-kəl\ *also* **an·ti·thet·ic** \-tik\ *adj* : constituting or marked by antithesis — **an·ti·thet·i·cal·ly** \-ti-k(ə-)lē\ *adv*

an·ti·tox·in \,an-ti-'täk-sən\ *n* : an antibody that is able to neutralize a particular toxin or disease-causing agent; *also* : an antiserum containing an antitoxin

an·ti·trust \,an-ti-'trəst\ *adj* : of or relating to legislation against trusts; *also* : consisting of laws to protect trade and commerce from unlawful restraints and monopolies or unfair business practices

an·ti·ven·in \-'ve-nən\ *n* : an antitoxin to a venom; *also* : a serum containing such antitoxin

ant·ler \'ant-lər\ *n* [ME *auntelere*, fr. AF *antiler*, fr. VL **anteocularis* located before the eye, fr. L *ante-* before + *oculus* eye] : one of the paired deciduous solid bone processes on the head of a deer; *also* : a branch of this — **ant·lered** \-lərd\ *adj*

ant lion *n* : any of various insects having a long-jawed larva that digs a conical pit in which it lies in wait for insects (as ants) on which it feeds

an·to·nym \'an-tə-,nim\ *n* : a word of opposite meaning

ant·sy \'ant-sē\ *adj* **1** : RESTLESS, IMPATIENT ⟨∼ children⟩ **2** : APPREHENSIVE ⟨∼ investors⟩

anus \'ā-nəs\ *n* [L] : the lower or posterior opening of the alimentary canal

an·vil \'an-vəl\ *n* **1** : a heavy iron block on which metal is shaped **2** : INCUS

anx·i·ety \aŋ-'zī-ə-tē\ *n, pl* **-et·ies** **1** : painful uneasiness of mind usu. over an anticipated ill **2** : abnormal apprehension and fear often accompanied by physiological signs (as sweating and increased pulse), by doubt about the nature and reality of the threat itself, and by self-doubt

anx·ious \'aŋk-shəs\ *adj* **1** : uneasy in mind : WORRIED ⟨∼ parents⟩ **2** : ear-

---

antipoverty	antistatic	antitank	antiviral
antislavery	antisubmarine	antitumor	antiwar
antispasmodic			

nestly wishing : EAGER ⟨∼ to leave⟩ — **anx·ious·ly** *adv*

¹**any** \'e-nē\ *adj* **1** : one chosen at random **2** : of whatever number or quantity

²**any** *pron* **1** : any one or ones ⟨take ∼ of the books you like⟩ **2** : any amount ⟨∼ of the money not used is to be returned⟩

³**any** *adv* : to any extent or degree : AT ALL ⟨could not walk ∼ farther⟩

any·body \-,bä-dē, -bə-\ *pron* : ANYONE

any·how \-,haủ\ *adv* **1** : in any way **2** : NEVERTHELESS; *also* : in any case

any·more \,e-nē-'mόr\ *adv* **1** : any longer ⟨won't bother you ∼⟩ **2** : at the present time

any·one \'e-nē-(,)wən\ *pron* : any person

any·place \-,plās\ *adv* : ANYWHERE 1

any·thing \-,thiŋ\ *pron* : any thing whatever

any·time \'e-nē-,tīm\ *adv* : at any time whatever

any·way \-,wā\ *adv* : ANYHOW

any·where \-,hwer\ *adv* **1** : in or to any place **2** : to any extent ⟨not ∼ near done⟩

any·wise \-,wīz\ *adv* : in any way whatever

A-OK \,ā-ō-'kā\ *adv or adj* : very definitely OK

A1 \'ā-'wən\ *adj* : of the finest quality

aor·ta \ā-'όr-tə\ *n, pl* **-tas** *or* **-tae** \-tē\ : the main artery that carries blood from the heart — **aor·tic** \-tik\ *adj*

ap *abbr* **1** apostle **2** apothecaries'

AP *abbr* **1** American plan **2** Associated Press

apace \ə-'pās\ *adv* : SWIFTLY

Apache \ə-'pa-chē\ *n, pl* **Apache** *or* **Apach·es** \-'pa-chēz, -'pa-shəz\ : a member of an American Indian people of the southwestern U.S.; *also* : any of the languages of the Apache people — **Apach·e·an** \ə-'pa-chē-ən\ *adj or n*

apanage *var of* APPANAGE

apart \ə-'pärt\ *adv* **1** : separately in place or time **2** : ASIDE **3** : in two or more parts : to pieces

apart·heid \ə-'pär-,tāt, -,tīt\ *n* [Afrikaans] : a policy of racial segregation formerly practiced in the Republic of So. Africa

apart·ment \ə-'pärt-mənt\ *n* : a room or set of rooms occupied as a dwelling; *also* : a building divided into individual dwelling units

ap·a·thy \'a-pə-thē\ *n* **1** : lack of emotion **2** : lack of interest : INDIFFERENCE — **ap·a·thet·ic** \,a-pə-'the-tik\ *adj* — **ap·a·thet·i·cal·ly** \-ti-k(ə-)lē\ *adv*

ap·a·tite \'a-pə-,tīt\ *n* : any of a group of minerals that are phosphates of calcium and occur esp. in phosphate rock and in bones and teeth

apato·sau·rus \ə-,pa-tə-'sόr-əs\ *n* : BRONTOSAURUS

APB *abbr* all points bulletin

¹**ape** \'āp\ *n* **1** : any of the larger tailless primates (as a baboon or gorilla); *also* : MONKEY **2** : MIMIC, IMITATOR; *also* : a large uncouth person

²**ape** *vb* **aped; ap·ing** : IMITATE, MIMIC

ape–man \'āp-,man\ *n* : a primate inter-

mediate in character between Homo sapiens and the higher apes

aper·çu \,a-pər-'sü\ *n, pl* **aperçus** \-'süz\ : an immediate impression; *esp* : INSIGHT

aper·i·tif \ä-,per-ə-'tēf\ *n* : an alcoholic drink taken as an appetizer

ap·er·ture \'a-pər-,chủr, -chər\ *n* : OPENING, HOLE

apex \'ā-,peks\ *n, pl* **apex·es** *or* **api·ces** \'ā-pə-,sēz, 'a-\ : the highest point : PEAK

apha·sia \ə-'fā-zh(ē-)ə\ *n* : loss or impairment of the power to use or comprehend words — **apha·sic** \-zik\ *adj or n*

aph·elion \a-'fēl-yən\ *n, pl* **-elia** \-yə\ [NL, fr. *apo-* away from + Gk *hēlios* sun] : the point in an object's orbit most distant from the sun

aphid \'ā-fəd\ *n* : any of numerous small insects that suck the juices of plants

aphis \'ā-fəs, 'a-\ *n, pl* **aphi·des** \-fə-,dēz\ : APHID

aph·o·rism \'a-fə-,ri-zəm\ *n* : a short saying stating a general truth : MAXIM — **aph·o·ris·tic** \,a-fə-'ris-tik\ *adj*

aph·ro·di·si·ac \,a-frə-'di-zē-,ak, -'dē-zē-\ *n* : an agent that excites sexual desire — **aphrodisiac** *adj*

api·ary \'ā-pē-,er-ē\ *n, pl* **-ar·ies** : a place where bees are kept — **api·a·rist** \-pē-ə-rist\ *n*

api·cal \'ā-pi-kəl, 'a-\ *adj* : of, relating to, or situated at an apex — **api·cal·ly** \-k(ə-)lē\ *adv*

apiece \ə-'pēs\ *adv* : for each one

aplen·ty \ə-'plen-tē\ *adj* : being in plenty or abundance

aplomb \ə-'pläm, -'pləm\ *n* [F, lit., perpendicularity, fr. MF, fr. *a plomb*, lit., according to the plummet] : complete composure or self-assurance

APO *abbr* army post office

Apoc *abbr* **1** Apocalypse **2** Apocrypha

apoc·a·lypse \ə-'pä-kə-,lips\ *n* **1** : a writing prophesying a cataclysm in which evil forces are destroyed **2** *cap* — see BIBLE table — **apoc·a·lyp·tic** \-,pä-kə-'lip-tik\ *also* **apoc·a·lyp·ti·cal** \-ti-kəl\ *adj*

Apoc·ry·pha \ə-'pä-krə-fə\ *n* **1** *not cap* : writings of dubious authenticity **2** : books included in the Septuagint and Vulgate but excluded from the Jewish and Protestant canons of the Old Testament — see BIBLE table **3** : early Christian writings not included in the New Testament

apoc·ry·phal \-fəl\ *adj* **1** : not canonical : SPURIOUS **2** *often cap* : of or resembling the Apocrypha — **apoc·ry·phal·ly** *adv* — **apoc·ry·phal·ness** *n*

apo·gee \'a-pə-(,)jē\ *n* [F *apogée*, fr. NL *apogaeum*, fr. Gk *apogaion*, fr. *apo* away from + *gē*, *gaia* earth] : the point at which an orbiting object is farthest from the body being orbited

apo·lit·i·cal \,ā-pə-'li-ti-kəl\ *adj* **1** : having an aversion for or no interest in political affairs **2** : having no political significance — **apo·lit·i·cal·ly** \-k(ə-)lē\ *adv*

apol·o·get·ic \ə-,pä-lə-'je-tik\ *adj* : expressing apology — **apol·o·get·i·cal·ly** \-ti-k(ə-)lē\ *adv*

ap·o·lo·gia \,a-pə-'lō-j(ē-)ə\ *n* : APOLOGY;

esp : an argument in support or justification

apol·o·gise *Brit var of* APOLOGIZE

apol·o·gize \ə-'päl-ə-ˌjīz\ *vb* **-gized; -giz·ing** : to make an apology : express regret — **apol·o·gist** \-jist\ *n*

apol·o·gy \ə-'päl-ə-jē\ *n, pl* **-gies** 1 : a formal justification : DEFENSE 2 : an expression of regret for a wrong

ap·o·plexy \'a-pə-ˌplek-sē\ *n* : STROKE 3 — **ap·o·plec·tic** \ˌa-pə-'plek-tik\ *adj*

ap·o·pto·sis \ˌa-pəp-'tō-səs, -pə-'tō-\ *n, pl* **-pto·ses** \-ˌsēz\ : a genetically directed process of cell self-destruction

aport \ə-'pòrt\ *adv* : on or toward the left side of a ship

apos·ta·sy \ə-'päs-tə-sē\ *n, pl* **-sies** : a renunciation or abandonment of a former loyalty (as to a religion) — **apos·tate** \ə-'päs-ˌtāt, -tət\ *adj or n*

a pos·te·ri·o·ri \ˌä-pō-ˌstir-ē-'òr-ē\ *adj* [L, lit., from the latter] : relating to or derived by reasoning from observed facts — **a posteriori** *adv*

apos·tle \ə-'päs-əl\ *n* 1 : one of the group composed of Jesus' 12 original disciples and Paul 2 : the first prominent missionary to a region or group 3 : a person who initiates or first advocates a great reform — **apos·tle·ship** *n*

ap·os·tol·ic \ˌa-pə-'stä-lik\ *adj* 1 : of or relating to an apostle or to the New Testament apostles 2 : of or relating to a succession of spiritual authority from the apostles 3 : PAPAL ⟨~ authority⟩

¹**apos·tro·phe** \ə-'päs-trə-(ˌ)fē\ *n* : the rhetorical addressing of a usu. absent person or a usu. personified thing (as in "O grave, where is thy victory?")

²**apostrophe** *n* : a punctuation mark ' used esp. to indicate the possessive case or the omission of a letter or figure

apos·tro·phise *Brit var of* APOSTROPHIZE

apos·tro·phize \ə-'päs-trə-ˌfīz\ *vb* **-phized; -phiz·ing** : to address as if present or capable of understanding

apothecaries' weight *n* : a system of weights based on the troy pound and ounce and used chiefly by pharmacists — see WEIGHT table

apoth·e·cary \ə-'pä-thə-ˌker-ē\ *n, pl* **-car·ies** [ME *apothecarie*, fr. ML *apothecarius*, fr. LL, shopkeeper, fr. L *apotheca* storehouse, fr. Gk *apothēkē*, fr. *apotithenai* to put away] : DRUGGIST

ap·o·thegm \'a-pə-ˌthem\ *n* : APHORISM

apo·the·o·sis \ə-ˌpä-thē-'ō-səs, ˌa-pə-'thē-ə-səs\ *n, pl* **-o·ses** \-ˌsēz\ 1 : DEIFICATION 2 : the perfect example

¹**app** \'ap\ *n* : APPLICATION 6

²**app** *abbr* 1 apparatus 2 appendix

ap·pall *also* **ap·pal** \ə-'pòl\ *vb* **ap·palled; ap·pall·ing** : to overcome with horror : DISMAY

Ap·pa·loo·sa \ˌa-pə-'lü-sə\ *n* : any of a breed of saddle horses developed in western No. America and usu. having a white or solid-colored coat with small spots

ap·pa·nage *also* **ap·a·nage** \'a-pə-nij\ *n* 1 : provision (as a grant of land) made by a sovereign or legislative body for dependent members of the royal family 2 : a rightful adjunct

ap·pa·ra·tus \ˌa-pə-'ra-təs, -'rā-\ *n, pl* **-tus·es** *or* **-tus** [L] 1 : a set of materials or equipment for a particular use 2 : a complex machine or device : MECHANISM 3 : the organization of a political party or underground movement

¹**ap·par·el** \ə-'per-əl\ *vb* **-eled** *or* **-elled; -el·ing** *or* **-el·ling** 1 : CLOTHE 2 : ADORN

²**apparel** *n* : CLOTHING, DRESS

ap·par·ent \ə-'per-ənt\ *adj* 1 : open to view : VISIBLE 2 : EVIDENT, OBVIOUS 3 : appearing as real or true : SEEMING

ap·par·ent·ly \-lē\ *adv* : it seems apparent

ap·pa·ri·tion \ˌa-pə-'ri-shən\ *n* : a supernatural appearance : GHOST

ap·peal \ə-'pēl\ *vb* 1 : to take steps to have (a case) reheard in a higher court 2 : to plead for help, corroboration, or decision 3 : to arouse a sympathetic response — **appeal** *n*

ap·pear \ə-'pir\ *vb* 1 : to become visible 2 : to come formally before an authority 3 : SEEM 4 : to become evident 5 : to come before the public

ap·pear·ance \ə-'pir-əns\ *n* 1 : outward aspect : LOOK 2 : the act of appearing 3 : PHENOMENON

ap·pease \ə-'pēz\ *vb* **ap·peased; ap·peas·ing** 1 : to cause to subside : ALLAY 2 : PACIFY, CONCILIATE; *esp* : to buy off by concessions — **ap·pease·ment** *n* — **ap·peas·able** \-'pē-zə-bəl\ *adj*

ap·pel·lant \ə-'pe-lənt\ *n* : one who appeals esp. from a judicial decision

ap·pel·late \ə-'pe-lət\ *adj* : having power to review decisions of a lower court

ap·pel·la·tion \ˌa-pə-'lā-shən\ *n* : NAME, DESIGNATION

ap·pel·lee \ˌa-pə-'lē\ *n* : one against whom an appeal is taken

ap·pend \ə-'pend\ *vb* : to attach esp. as something additional : AFFIX

ap·pend·age \ə-'pen-dij\ *n* 1 : something appended to a principal or greater thing 2 : a projecting part (as an antenna) of an animal or plant body; *esp* : an arm, leg, or similar part ♦ *Synonyms* ACCESSORY, ADJUNCT, APPENDIX, APPURTENANCE

ap·pen·dec·to·my \ˌa-pən-'dek-tə-mē\ *n, pl* **-mies** : surgical removal of the intestinal appendix

ap·pen·di·ci·tis \ə-ˌpen-də-'sī-təs\ *n* : inflammation of the intestinal appendix

ap·pen·dix \ə-'pen-diks\ *n, pl* **-dix·es** *or* **-di·ces** \-də-ˌsēz\ [L] 1 : supplementary matter added at the end of a book 2 : a narrow blind tube usu. about three or four inches long that extends from the cecum in the lower right-hand part of the abdomen

ap·per·tain \ˌa-pər-'tān\ *vb* : to belong as a rightful part or privilege

ap·pe·tis·er, ap·pe·tis·ing *Brit var of* APPETIZER, APPETIZING

ap·pe·tite \'a-pə-ˌtīt\ *n* [ME *apetit*, fr. AF, fr. L *appetitus*, fr. *appetere* to strive after, fr. *ad-* to + *petere* to go to] 1 : natural desire for satisfying some want or need esp. for food 2 : TASTE, PREFERENCE ⟨an ~ for adventure⟩

ap·pe·tiz·er \'a-pə-ˌtī-zər\ *n* : a food or drink taken just before or with a meal to stimulate the appetite

ap·pe·tiz·ing \-ziŋ\ *adj* : tempting to the appetite — **ap·pe·tiz·ing·ly** *adv*

appl *abbr* applied

ap·plaud \ə-'plȯd\ *vb* : to show approval esp. by clapping

ap·plause \ə-'plȯz\ *n* : approval publicly expressed (as by clapping)

ap·ple \'a-pəl\ *n* : a rounded fruit with firm white flesh and a seedy core; *also* : a tree that bears this fruit

ap·ple·jack \-ˌjak\ *n* : a liquor distilled from fermented cider

ap·plet \'a-plət\ *n* : a short computer program esp. for performing a simple specific task

ap·pli·ance \ə-'plī-əns\ *n* 1 : INSTRUMENT, DEVICE 2 : a piece of household equipment (as a stove or toaster) operated by gas or electricity

ap·pli·ca·ble \'a-pli-kə-bəl, ə-'pli-kə-\ *adj* : capable of being applied : RELEVANT — **ap·pli·ca·bil·i·ty** \ˌa-pli-kə-'bi-lə-tē, ə-ˌpli-kə-\ *n*

ap·pli·cant \'a-pli-kənt\ *n* : one who applies ⟨a job ∼⟩

ap·pli·ca·tion \ˌa-plə-'kā-shən\ *n* 1 : the act of applying 2 : assiduous attention 3 : REQUEST; *also* : a form used in making a request 4 : something placed or spread on a surface 5 : capacity for use 6 : a program (as a word processor) that performs one of a computer's major tasks

ap·pli·ca·tor \'a-plə-ˌkā-tər\ *n* : a device for applying a substance (as medicine or polish)

ap·plied \ə-'plīd\ *adj* : put to practical use ⟨∼ art⟩

ap·pli·qué \ˌa-plə-'kā\ *n* [F] : a fabric decoration cut out and fastened to a larger piece of material — **appliqué** *vb*

ap·ply \ə-'plī\ *vb* **ap·plied; ap·ply·ing** 1 : to put to practical use 2 : to place in contact : put or spread on a surface 3 : to employ with close attention 4 : to have reference or connection 5 : to submit a request

ap·point \ə-'pȯint\ *vb* 1 : to fix or set officially ⟨∼ a day for trial⟩ 2 : to name officially 3 : to fit out : EQUIP

ap·poin·tee \ə-ˌpȯin-'tē, ˌa-\ *n* : a person appointed

ap·point·ive \ə-'pȯin-tiv\ *adj* : subject to appointment

ap·point·ment \ə-'pȯint-mənt\ *n* 1 : the act of appointing 2 : an arrangement for a meeting 3 *pl* : FURNISHINGS, EQUIPMENT 4 : a nonelective office or position

ap·por·tion \ə-'pȯr-shən\ *vb* : to distribute proportionately : ALLOT — **ap·por·tion·ment** *n*

ap·po·site \'a-pə-zət\ *adj* : APPROPRIATE, RELEVANT ⟨an ∼ quotation⟩ — **ap·po·site·ly** *adv* — **ap·po·site·ness** *n*

ap·po·si·tion \ˌa-pə-'zi-shən\ *n* : a grammatical construction in which a noun or pronoun is followed by another that has the same referent (as *the poet* and *Burns* in "a biography of the poet Burns")

ap·pos·i·tive \ə-'pä-zə-tiv, a-\ *adj* : of, relating to, or standing in grammatical apposition — **appositive** *n*

ap·praise \ə-'prāz\ *vb* **ap·praised; ap·prais·ing** : to set a value on — **ap·prais·al** \-'prā-zəl\ *n* — **ap·prais·er** *n*

ap·pre·cia·ble \ə-'prē-shə-bəl\ *adj* : large enough to be recognized and measured — **ap·pre·cia·bly** *adv*

ap·pre·ci·ate \ə-'prē-shē-ˌāt\ *vb* **-at·ed; -at·ing** 1 : to value justly 2 : to be aware of 3 : to be grateful for 4 : to increase in value — **ap·pre·ci·a·tion** \-ˌprē-shē-'ā-shən\ *n*

ap·pre·cia·tive \ə-'prē-shə-tiv, -shē-ˌāt-\ *adj* : having or showing appreciation — **ap·pre·cia·tive·ly** *adv*

ap·pre·hend \ˌa-pri-'hend\ *vb* 1 : ARREST 2 : to become aware of 3 : to look forward to with dread 4 : UNDERSTAND — **ap·pre·hen·sion** \-'hen-chən\ *n*

ap·pre·hen·sive \-'hen-siv\ *adj* : viewing the future with anxiety — **ap·pre·hen·sive·ly** *adv* — **ap·pre·hen·sive·ness** *n*

¹ap·pren·tice \ə-'pren-təs\ *n* 1 : a person learning a craft under a skilled worker 2 : BEGINNER — **ap·pren·tice·ship** *n*

²apprentice *vb* **-ticed; -tic·ing** : to bind or set at work as an apprentice

ap·prise \ə-'prīz\ *vb* **ap·prised; ap·pris·ing** : INFORM ⟨*apprised* him of his rights⟩

ap·proach \ə-'prōch\ *vb* 1 : to move nearer to ⟨∼ the bench⟩ 2 : to be almost the same as 3 : to make advances to esp. for the purpose of creating a desired result 4 : to take preliminary steps toward ⟨∼ the subject carefully⟩ — **approach** *n* — **ap·proach·able** *adj*

ap·pro·ba·tion \ˌa-prə-'bā-shən\ *n* : APPROVAL

¹ap·pro·pri·ate \ə-'prō-prē-ˌāt\ *vb* **-at·ed; -at·ing** 1 : to take possession of 2 : to set apart for a particular use

²ap·pro·pri·ate \ə-'prō-prē-ət\ *adj* : fitted to a purpose or use : SUITABLE ♦ *Synonyms* PROPER, FIT, APT, BEFITTING — **ap·pro·pri·ate·ly** *adv* — **ap·pro·pri·ate·ness** *n*

ap·pro·pri·a·tion \ə-ˌprō-prē-'ā-shən\ *n* : something (as money) set aside by formal action for a specific use

ap·prov·al \ə-'prü-vəl\ *n* : an act of approving — **on approval** : subject to a prospective buyer's acceptance or refusal

ap·prove \ə-'prüv\ *vb* **ap·proved; ap·prov·ing** 1 : to have or express a favorable opinion of 2 : to accept as satisfactory : RATIFY ⟨∼ the treaty⟩

approx *abbr* approximate; approximately

¹ap·prox·i·mate \ə-'präk-sə-mət\ *adj* : nearly correct or exact ⟨an ∼ count⟩ — **ap·prox·i·mate·ly** *adv*

²ap·prox·i·mate \-ˌmāt\ *vb* **-mat·ed; -mat·ing** : to come or bring near or close — **ap·prox·i·ma·tion** \ə-ˌpräk-sə-'mā-shən\ *n*

appt *abbr* appoint; appointed; appointment

ap·pur·te·nance \ə-'pərt-nəns, -'pər-tə-nəns\ *n* : something that belongs to or goes with another thing ♦ *Synonyms* ACCESSORY, ADJUNCT, APPENDAGE, AP-

PENDIX — **ap·pur·te·nant** \ə-ˈpərt-nənt, -ˈpər-tə-nənt\ adj

Apr abbr April

APR abbr annual percentage rate

apri·cot \ˈa-prə-ˌkät, ˈā-\ n [alter. of earlier abrecock, ultim. fr. Ar al-birqūq, ultim. fr. L (persicum) praecox, lit., early-ripening (peach)] : an oval orange-colored fruit resembling the related peach and plum in flavor; also : a tree bearing apricots

April \ˈā-prəl\ n [ME, fr. AF & L; AF avrill, fr. L Aprilis] : the 4th month of the year

a pri·o·ri \ˌä-prē-ˈór-ē\ adj [L, from the former] 1 : characterized by or derived by reasoning from self-evident propositions 2 : independent of experience — **a priori** adv

apron \ˈā-prən\ n [ME, alter. (fr. misdivision of a napron) of napron, fr. MF naperon, dim. of nape cloth, modif. of L mappa napkin] 1 : a garment tied over the front of the body to protect the clothes 2 : a paved area for parking or handling airplanes — **aproned** adj

¹**ap·ro·pos** \ˌa-prə-ˈpō, ˈa-prə-ˌpō\ adv [F à propos, lit., to the purpose] 1 : OPPORTUNELY 2 : in passing : INCIDENTALLY

²**apropos** adj : being to the point

apropos of prep : with regard to

apse \ˈaps\ n : a projecting usu. semicircular and vaulted part of a building (as a church)

¹**apt** \ˈapt\ adj 1 : well adapted : SUITABLE 2 : having an habitual tendency : LIKELY 3 : quick to learn — **apt·ly** adv — **apt·ness** \ˈapt-nəs\ n

²**apt** abbr 1 apartment 2 aptitude

ap·ti·tude \ˈap-tə-ˌtüd, -ˌtyüd\ n 1 : natural ability : TALENT 2 : capacity for learning 3 : APPROPRIATENESS

aqua \ˈa-kwə, ˈä-\ n : a light greenish blue color

aqua·cul·ture \ˈa-kwə-ˌkəl-chər, ˈä-\ n : the cultivation of aquatic organisms (as fish or shellfish) for human use esp. as food — **aqua·cul·tur·ist** \-chə-rist\ n

aqua·ma·rine \ˌa-kwə-mə-ˈrēn, ˌä-\ n 1 : a bluish green gem 2 : a pale blue to light greenish blue

aqua·naut \ˈa-kwə-ˌnót, ˈä-\ n : a person who lives in an underwater shelter for an extended period

aqua·plane \-ˌplān\ n : a board towed behind a motorboat and ridden by a person standing on it — **aquaplane** vb

aqua re·gia \ˌa-kwə-ˈrē-j(ē-)ə\ n [NL, lit., royal water] : a mixture of nitric and hydrochloric acids that dissolves gold or platinum

aquar·i·um \ə-ˈkwer-ē-əm\ n, pl -**i·ums** or -**ia** \-ē-ə\ 1 : a container (as a glass tank) in which living aquatic animals or plants are kept 2 : a place where aquatic animals and plants are kept and shown

Aquar·i·us \ə-ˈkwer-ē-əs\ n [L, lit., water carrier] 1 : a zodiacal constellation between Capricorn and Pisces usu. pictured as a man pouring water 2 : the 11th sign of the zodiac in astrology; also : one born under this sign

¹**aquat·ic** \ə-ˈkwä-tik, -ˈkwa-\ adj 1 : growing or living in or frequenting water 2 : performed in or on water

²**aquatic** n : an aquatic animal or plant

aqua·vit \ˈä-kwə-ˌvēt\ n : a clear liquor flavored with caraway seeds

aqua vi·tae \ˌa-kwə-ˈvī-tē, ˌä-\ n [ME, fr. ML, lit., water of life] : a strong alcoholic liquor (as brandy)

aq·ue·duct \ˈa-kwə-ˌdəkt\ n 1 : a conduit for carrying running water 2 : a structure carrying a canal over a river or hollow 3 : a passage in a bodily part

aque·ous \ˈā-kwē-əs, ˈa-\ adj 1 : WATERY 2 : made of, by, or with water

aqueous humor n : a clear fluid occupying the space between the lens and the cornea of the eye

aqui·fer \ˈa-kwə-fər, ˈä-\ n : a water-bearing stratum of permeable rock, sand, or gravel

aq·ui·line \ˈa-kwə-ˌlīn, -lən\ adj 1 : of or resembling an eagle 2 : hooked like an eagle's beak ⟨an ∼ nose⟩

ar abbr arrival; arrive

Ar symbol argon

AR abbr Arkansas

-**ar** adj suffix : of or relating to ⟨molecular⟩ : being ⟨spectacular⟩ : resembling ⟨oracular⟩

Ar·ab \ˈa-rəb\ n 1 : a member of a Semitic people of the Arabian peninsula in southwestern Asia 2 : a member of an Arabic-speaking people — **Arab** adj — **Ara·bi·an** \ə-ˈrā-bē-ən\ adj or n

ar·a·besque \ˌa-rə-ˈbesk\ n : a design of interlacing lines forming figures of flowers, foliage, and sometimes animals — **arabesque** adj

¹**Ar·a·bic** \ˈa-rə-bik\ n : a Semitic language of southwestern Asia and northern Africa

²**Arabic** adj 1 : of or relating to the Arabs, Arabic, or the Arabian peninsula in southwestern Asia 2 : expressed in or making use of Arabic numerals

Arabic numeral n : any of the number symbols 0, 1, 2, 3, 4, 5, 6, 7, 8, 9

ar·a·ble \ˈa-rə-bəl\ adj : fit for or used for the growing of crops ⟨∼ land⟩

arach·nid \ə-ˈrak-nəd\ n : any of a class of usu. 8-legged arthropods comprising the spiders, scorpions, mites, and ticks — **arachnid** adj

Ar·a·ma·ic \ˌa-rə-ˈmā-ik\ n : an ancient Semitic language

ar·a·mid \ˈa-rə-məd, -ˌmid\ n : any of several light but very strong heat-resistant synthetic materials used esp. in textiles and plastics

Arap·a·ho or **Arap·a·hoe** \ə-ˈra-pə-ˌhō\ n, pl -**ho** or -**hos** or -**hoe** or -**hoes** : a member of an American Indian people of the western U.S.

ar·bi·ter \ˈär-bə-tər\ n : one having power to decide : JUDGE

ar·bi·trage \ˈär-bə-ˌträzh\ n [F, fr. MF, arbitration] : the purchase and sale of the same or equivalent securities in different markets in order to profit from price discrepancies

ar·bi·tra·geur \ˌär-bə-(ˌ)trä-ˈzhər\ or **ar·bi-**

trag·er \'är-bə-ˌträ-zhər\ *n* : one who practices arbitrage

ar·bi·tra·ment \är-'bi-trə-mənt\ *n* **1** : the act of deciding a dispute **2** : the judgment given by an arbitrator

ar·bi·trary \'är-bə-ˌtrer-ē\ *adj* **1** : AUTOCRATIC, DESPOTIC **2** : determined by will or caprice : selected at random — **ar·bi·trari·ly** \ˌär-bə-'trer-ə-lē\ *adv* — **ar·bi·trari·ness** \'är-bə-ˌtrer-ē-nəs\ *n*

ar·bi·trate \'är-bə-ˌträt\ *vb* **-trat·ed; -trat·ing** **1** : to act as arbitrator **2** : to act on as arbitrator **3** : to submit for decision to an arbitrator — **ar·bi·tra·tion** \ˌär-bə-'trā-shən\ *n*

ar·bi·tra·tor \'är-bə-ˌträ-tər\ *n* : one chosen to settle differences between two parties in a controversy

ar·bor \'är-bər\ *n* [ME *erber, herber* garden, fr. AF, fr. *herbe* herb, grass] : a shelter formed of or covered with vines or branches

ar·bo·re·al \är-'bȯr-ē-əl\ *adj* **1** : of, relating to, or resembling a tree **2** : living in trees ⟨∼ monkeys⟩

ar·bo·re·tum \ˌär-bə-'rē-təm\ *n, pl* **-re·tums** *or* **-re·ta** \-tə\ [L, plantation of trees, fr. *arbor* tree] : a place where trees and plants are grown for scientific and educational purposes

ar·bor·vi·tae \ˌär-bər-'vī-tē\ *n* : any of various evergreen trees and shrubs with scalelike leaves that are related to the cypresses

ar·bour *chiefly Brit var of* ARBOR

ar·bu·tus \är-'byü-təs\ *n* : TRAILING ARBUTUS

¹arc \'ärk\ *n* **1** : a sustained luminous discharge of electricity (as between two electrodes) **2** : a continuous portion of a curved line (as part of the circumference of a circle)

²arc *vb* **arced** \'ärkt\; **arc·ing** \'är-kiŋ\ : to form an electric arc

ARC *abbr* **1** AIDS-related complex **2** American Red Cross

ar·cade \är-'kād\ *n* **1** : an arched or covered passageway; *esp* : one lined with shops **2** : a row of arches with their supporting columns **3** : an amusement center having coin-operated games

ar·cane \är-'kān\ *adj* : SECRET, MYSTERIOUS

¹arch \'ärch\ *n* **1** : a curved structure spanning an opening (as a door) **2** : something resembling an arch **3** : ARCHWAY

²arch *vb* **1** : to cover with an arch **2** : to form or bend into an arch

³arch *adj* **1** : CHIEF, EMINENT ⟨my ∼ enemy⟩ **2** : ROGUISH, MISCHIEVOUS; *also* : deliberately playful or impudent ⟨∼ comments⟩ — **arch·ly** *adv* — **arch·ness** *n*

⁴arch *abbr* architect; architectural; architecture

ar·chae·ol·o·gy *or* **ar·che·ol·o·gy** \ˌär-kē-'ä-lə-jē\ *n* : the study of past human life as revealed by relics left by ancient peoples — **ar·chae·o·log·i·cal** \-ə-'lä-ji-kəl\ *adj* — **ar·chae·ol·o·gist** \-'ä-lə-jist\ *n*

ar·cha·ic \är-'kā-ik\ *adj* **1** : having the characteristics of the language of the past and surviving chiefly in specialized uses ⟨∼ words⟩ **2** : belonging to an earlier time : ANTIQUATED — **ar·cha·i·cal·ly** \-i-k(ə-)lē\ *adv*

arch·an·gel \'är-ˌkān-jəl\ *n* : a chief angel

arch·bish·op \ärch-'bi-shəp\ *n* : a bishop of high rank

arch·bish·op·ric \-shə-(ˌ)prik\ *n* : the jurisdiction or office of an archbishop

arch·con·ser·va·tive \(ˌ)ärch-kən-'sər-və-tiv\ *n* : an extreme conservative — **archconservative** *adj*

arch·dea·con \-'dē-kən\ *n* : a church official who assists a diocesan bishop in ceremonial or administrative functions

arch·di·o·cese \-'dī-ə-səs, -ˌsēz\ *n* : the diocese of an archbishop

arch·duke \-'dük, -'dyük\ *n* **1** : a sovereign prince **2** : a prince of the imperial family of Austria

Ar·che·an \är-'kē-ən\ *adj* : of, relating to, or being the earliest eon of geologic history — **Archean** *n*

arch·en·e·my \ˌärch-'e-nə-mē\ *n, pl* **-mies** : a principal enemy

Ar·cheo·zo·ic \ˌär-kē-ə-'zō-ik\ *adj* : ARCHEAN — **Archeozoic** *n*

ar·chery \'är-chə-rē\ *n* : the art or practice of shooting with bow and arrows — **ar·cher** \'är-chər\ *n*

ar·che·type \'är-ki-ˌtīp\ *n* : the original pattern or model of all things of the same type — **ar·che·typ·al** \ˌär-kə-'tī-pəl\ *adj*

arch·fiend \ˌärch-'fēnd\ *n* : a chief fiend; *esp* : SATAN

ar·chi·epis·co·pal \ˌär-kē-ə-'pis-kə-pəl\ *adj* : of or relating to an archbishop

ar·chi·man·drite \ˌär-kə-'man-ˌdrīt\ *n* : a dignitary in an Eastern church ranking below a bishop

ar·chi·pel·a·go \ˌär-kə-'pe-lə-ˌgō, ˌär-chə-\ *n, pl* **-goes** *or* **-gos** : a group of islands

ar·chi·tect \'är-kə-ˌtekt\ *n* **1** : a person who plans buildings and oversees their construction **2** : a person who designs and guides a plan or undertaking

ar·chi·tec·ture \'är-kə-ˌtek-chər\ *n* **1** : the art or science of planning and building structures **2** : a method or style of building **3** : the manner in which the elements (as of a design) or components (of a computer) are arranged or organized — **ar·chi·tec·tur·al** \ˌär-kə-'tek-chə-rəl, -'tek-shrəl\ *adj* — **ar·chi·tec·tur·al·ly** *adv*

ar·chi·trave \'är-kə-ˌtrāv\ *n* : the supporting horizontal member just above the columns in a building in the classical style of architecture

ar·chive \'är-ˌkīv\ *n* **1** : a place for keeping public records; *also* : public records — often used in pl. **2** : a repository esp. of information

ar·chi·vist \'är-kə-vist, -ˌkī-\ *n* : a person in charge of archives

ar·chon \'är-ˌkän, -kən\ *n* : a chief magistrate of ancient Athens

arch·ri·val \ˌärch-'rī-vəl\ *n* : a principal rival

arch·way \'ärch-ˌwā\ *n* : a passageway under an arch; *also* : an arch over a passage

arc lamp *n* : a gas-filled electric lamp that produces light when a current arcs between incandescent electrodes

¹**arc·tic** \'ärk-tik, 'är-tik\ *adj* [ME *artik*, fr. L *arcticus*, fr. Gk *arktikos*, fr. *arktos* bear, Ursa Major, north] **1** *often cap* : of or relating to the north pole or the region near it **2** : FRIGID

²**arc·tic** \'ärk-tik, 'är-tik\ *n* : a rubber overshoe that reaches to the ankle or above

arctic circle *n, often cap A&C* : the parallel of latitude that is approximately 66½ degrees north of the equator

-ard *also* **-art** *n suffix* : one that is characterized by performing some action, possessing some quality, or being associated with some thing esp. conspicuously or excessively ⟨braggart⟩ ⟨dullard⟩

ar·dent \'är-dᵊnt\ *adj* **1** : characterized by warmth of feeling : PASSIONATE **2** : FIERY, HOT ⟨an ∼ sun⟩ **3** : GLOWING ⟨∼ eyes⟩ — **ar·dent·ly** *adv*

ar·dor \'är-dər\ *n* **1** : warmth of feeling : ZEAL **2** : sexual excitement

ar·dour *chiefly Brit var of* ARDOR

ar·du·ous \'är-jə-wəs, -dyü-wəs\ *adj* : DIFFICULT, LABORIOUS — **ar·du·ous·ly** *adv* — **ar·du·ous·ness** *n*

¹**are** *pres 2d sing or pres pl of* BE

²**are** \'er\ *n* — see METRIC SYSTEM table

ar·ea \'er-ē-ə\ *n* **1** : a flat surface or space **2** : the amount of surface included (as within the lines of a geometric figure) **3** : range or extent of some thing or concept : FIELD **4** : REGION

area code *n* : a usu. 3-digit number that identifies each telephone service area in a country (as the U.S. or Canada)

are·na \ə-'rē-nə\ *n* [L *harena, arena* sand, sandy place] **1** : an enclosed area used for public entertainment **2** : a sphere of activity or competition

ar·gen·tite \'är-jən-ˌtīt\ *n* : a dark gray or black mineral of metallic luster that is an important ore of silver

ar·gon \'är-ˌgän\ *n* [Gk, neut. of *argos* idle, lazy, fr. *a-* not + *ergon* work; fr. its relative inertness] : a colorless odorless gaseous chemical element found in the air and used for filling electric lamps

ar·go·sy \'är-gə-sē\ *n, pl* **-sies** **1** : a large merchant ship **2** : FLEET

ar·got \'är-gət, -ˌgō\ *n* : the language of a particular group or class

ar·gu·able \'är-gyü-ə-bəl\ *adj* : open to argument, dispute, or question

ar·gu·ably \'är-gyü-(ə-)blē\ *adv* : as may be argued or shown by argument

ar·gue \'är-gyü\ *vb* **ar·gued; ar·gu·ing 1** : to give reasons for or against something **2** : to contend in words : DISPUTE ⟨*argued* about money⟩ **3** : DEBATE **4** : to persuade by giving reasons

ar·gu·ment \'är-gyə-mənt\ *n* **1** : a reason offered in proof **2** : discourse intended to persuade **3** : QUARREL

ar·gu·men·ta·tion \ˌär-gyə-mən-'tā-shən\ *n* : the art of formal discussion

ar·gu·men·ta·tive \ˌär-gyə-'men-tə-tiv\ *adj* : inclined to argue

ar·gyle *also* **ar·gyll** \'är-ˌgī(-ə)l\ *n, often cap* : a geometric knitting pattern of varicolored diamonds on a single background color; *also* : a sock knit in this pattern

aria \'är-ē-ə\ *n* : an accompanied elaborate vocal solo forming part of a larger work

ari·a·ry \ˌä-rē-'ä-rē\ *n, plural* **ariary** — see MONEY table

ar·id \'a-rəd\ *adj* : very dry; *esp* : having insufficient rainfall to support agriculture — **arid·i·ty** \ə-'ri-də-tē\ *n*

Ar·i·es \'er-ˌēz, -ē-ˌēz\ *n* [L, lit., ram] **1** : a zodiacal constellation between Pisces and Taurus pictured as a ram **2** : the 1st sign of the zodiac in astrology; *also* : one born under this sign

aright \ə-'rīt\ *adv* : RIGHT, CORRECTLY

arise \ə-'rīz\ *vb* **arose** \-'rōz\; **aris·en** \-'ri-z²n\; **aris·ing** \-'rī-ziŋ\ **1** : to get up **2** : ORIGINATE **3** : ASCEND ♦ *Synonyms* RISE, DERIVE, SPRING, ISSUE

ar·is·toc·ra·cy \ˌa-rə-'stä-krə-sē\ *n, pl* **-cies** **1** : government by a noble or privileged class; *also* : a state so governed **2** : the governing class of an aristocracy **3** : UPPER CLASS — **aris·to·crat** \ə-'ris-tə-ˌkrat\ *n* — **aris·to·crat·ic** \ə-ˌris-tə-'kra-tik\ *adj*

arith *abbr* arithmetic; arithmetical

arith·me·tic \ə-'rith-mə-ˌtik\ *n* **1** : a branch of mathematics that deals with computations usu. with nonnegative real numbers **2** : COMPUTATION, CALCULATION — **ar·ith·met·ic** \ˌer-ith-'me-tik\ *or* **ar·ith·met·i·cal** \-ti-kəl\ *adj* — **ar·ith·met·i·cal·ly** \-ti-k(ə-)lē\ *adv* — **arith·me·ti·cian** \ə-ˌrith-mə-'ti-shən\ *n*

arithmetic mean *n* : the sum of a set of numbers divided by the number of numbers in the set

Ariz *abbr* Arizona

ark \'ärk\ *n* **1** : a boat held to resemble that of Noah's at the time of the Flood **2** : the sacred chest in a synagogue representing to Hebrews the presence of God; *also* : the repository for the scrolls of the Torah

Ark *abbr* Arkansas

¹**arm** \'ärm\ *n* [ME, fr. OE *earm*] **1** : a human upper limb and esp. the part between the shoulder and wrist; *also* : a corresponding limb of a 2-footed vertebrate **2** : something resembling an arm in shape or position ⟨an ∼ of a chair⟩ ⟨the eight ∼s of an octopus⟩ **3** : POWER, MIGHT ⟨the ∼ of the law⟩ — **armed** \'ärmd\ *adj* — **arm·less** *adj*

²**arm** *vb* [ME, fr. AF *armer*, fr. L *armare*, fr. *arma* weapons, tools] : to furnish with weapons

³**arm** *n* **1** : WEAPON **2** : a branch of the military forces **3** *pl* : the hereditary heraldic devices of a family

ar·ma·da \är-'mä-də, -'mā-\ *n* : a fleet of warships

ar·ma·dil·lo \ˌär-mə-'di-lō\ *n, pl* **-los** [Sp, fr. dim. of *armado* armed one] : any of several small burrowing mammals with the head and body protected by an armor of bony plates

Ar·ma·ged·don \,är-mə-'ge-dᵊn\ n : a final conclusive battle between the forces of good and evil; *also* : the site or time of this

ar·ma·ment \'är-mə-mənt\ n 1 : military strength 2 : arms and equipment (as of a tank or combat unit) 3 : the process of preparing for war

ar·ma·ture \'är-mə-,chùr, -chər\ n 1 : a protective covering or structure (as the spines of a cactus) 2 : the rotating part of an electric generator or motor; *also* : the movable part in an electromagnetic device (as a loudspeaker)

arm·chair \'ärm-,cher\ n : a chair with armrests

armed forces n pl : the combined military, naval, and air forces of a nation

Ar·me·nian \är-'mē-nē-ən\ n 1 : a native or inhabitant of Armenia 2 : the Indo-European language of the Armenians

arm·ful \'ärm-,fùl\ n, pl **armfuls** or **arms·ful** \'ärmz-,fùl\ : as much as the arm or arms can hold

arm·hole \'ärm-,hōl\ n : an opening for the arm in a garment

ar·mi·stice \'är-mə-stəs\ n : temporary suspension of hostilities by mutual agreement : TRUCE

arm·let \'ärm-lət\ n : a band worn around the upper arm

ar·mor \'är-mər\ n 1 : protective covering 2 : armored forces and vehicles — **ar·mored** \-mərd\ adj

ar·mor·er \'är-mər-ər\ n 1 : a person who makes arms and armor 2 : a person who services firearms

ar·mo·ri·al \är-'mòr-ē-əl\ adj : of or bearing heraldic arms

ar·mory \'är-mə-rē\ n, pl **ar·mor·ies** 1 : a place where arms are stored 2 : a factory where arms are made

ar·mour, ar·moury chiefly Brit var of AR-MOR, ARMORY

arm·pit \'ärm-,pit\ n : the hollow under the junction of the arm and shoulder

arm·rest \-,rest\ n : a support for the arm

ar·my \'är-mē\ n, pl **armies** 1 : a body of men organized for war 2 often cap : the complete military organization of a country for land warfare 3 : a great number 4 : a body of persons organized to advance a cause

army ant n : any of various nomadic social ants

ar·my·worm \'är-mē-,wərm\ n : any of numerous moths whose larvae move about destroying crops

aro·ma \ə-'rō-mə\ n : a usu. pleasing odor : FRAGRANCE — **ar·o·mat·ic** \,ar-ə-'ma-tik\ adj

aro·ma·ther·a·py \ə-,rō-mə-'ther-ə-pē\ n : massage with a preparation of fragrant oils extracted from herbs, flowers, and fruits

arose past of ARISE

¹**around** \ə-'raùnd\ adv 1 : in a circle or in circumference ⟨a tree five feet ∼⟩ 2 : in or along a circuit ⟨the road goes ∼ by the lake⟩ 3 : on all sides ⟨nothing for miles ∼⟩ 4 : NEARBY ⟨wait ∼ awhile⟩ 5 : from one place to another ⟨travels ∼ on business⟩ 6 : in an opposite direction ⟨turn ∼⟩ 7 — used with some verbs to indicate continued action ⟨joking ∼⟩ 8 : APPROXIMATELY ⟨cost ∼ $5⟩

²**around** prep 1 : SURROUNDING ⟨trees ∼ the house⟩ 2 : to or on another side of ⟨∼ the corner⟩ 3 : NEAR ⟨stayed right ∼ home⟩ 4 : along the circuit of ⟨go ∼ the world⟩

arouse \ə-'raùz\ vb **aroused; arous·ing** 1 : to awaken from sleep 2 : to stir up — **arous·al** \-'raù-zəl\ n

ar·peg·gio \är-'pe-jē-,ō, -'pe-jō\ n, pl **-gios** [It fr. arpeggiare to play on the harp, fr. arpa harp] : a chord whose notes are performed in succession and not simultaneously

arr abbr 1 arranged 2 arrival; arrive

ar·raign \ə-'rān\ vb 1 : to call before a court to answer to an indictment 2 : to accuse of wrong or imperfection — **ar·raign·ment** n

ar·range \ə-'rānj\ vb **ar·ranged; ar·rang·ing** 1 : to put in order 2 : PLAN ⟨∼ an interview⟩ 3 : to adapt (a musical composition) to voices or instruments other than those for which it was orig. written 4 : to come to an agreement about : SETTLE ⟨∼ a business deal⟩ — **ar·range·ment** n — **ar·rang·er** n

ar·rant \'a-rənt\ adj : being notoriously without moderation : EXTREME

ar·ras \'a-rəs\ n, pl **arras** 1 : TAPESTRY 2 : a wall hanging or screen of tapestry

¹**ar·ray** \ə-'rā\ vb 1 : to dress esp. splendidly 2 : to arrange in order (as in an array)

²**array** n 1 : a regular arrangement 2 : rich apparel 3 : a large or varied group

ar·rears \ə-'rirz\ n pl 1 : a state of being behind in the discharge of obligations ⟨in ∼ with the rent⟩ 2 : overdue debts

¹**ar·rest** \ə-'rest\ vb 1 : STOP, CHECK 2 : to take into legal custody

²**arrest** n 1 : the act of stopping; *also* : the state of being stopped 2 : the taking into custody by legal authority

ar·rhyth·mia \ā-'rith-mē-ə\ n : an alteration of the heartbeat's rhythm

ar·riv·al \ə-'rī-vəl\ n 1 : the act of arriving 2 : one that arrives

ar·rive \ə-'rīv\ vb **ar·rived; ar·riv·ing** 1 : to reach a destination 2 : to make an appearance ⟨the guests have arrived⟩ 3 : to attain success

ar·ro·gant \'er-ə-gənt\ adj : offensively exaggerating one's own importance — **ar·ro·gance** \-gəns\ n — **ar·ro·gant·ly** adv

ar·ro·gate \-,gāt\ vb **-gat·ed; -gat·ing** : to claim or seize without justification as one's right — **ar·ro·ga·tion** \,ar-ə-'gā-shən\ n

ar·row \'er-ō\ n 1 : a missile shot from a bow and usu. having a slender shaft, a pointed head, and feathers at the butt 2 : a pointed mark used to indicate direction

ar·row·head \'er-ō-,hed\ *n* : the pointed end of an arrow

ar·row·root \-,rüt, -,rùt\ *n* : an edible starch from the roots of any of several tropical American plants; *also* : a plant yielding arrowroot

ar·royo \ə-'rói-ə, -ō\ *n, pl* **-royos** [Sp] **1** : a watercourse in a dry region **2** : a water-carved gully or channel

ar·se·nal \'ärs-nəl, 'är-sə-nəl\ *n* [ultim. fr. Ar *ṣinā'a* house of manufacture] **1** : a place for making and storing arms and military equipment **2** : STORE, REPERTOIRE ⟨an ∼ of tools⟩

ar·se·nic \'ärs-nik, 'är-sə-nik\ *n* **1** : a solid brittle poisonous chemical element of grayish metallic luster **2** : a very poisonous oxygen compound of arsenic used in making insecticides

ar·son \'är-s°n\ *n* : the willful or malicious burning of property — **ar·son·ist** \-ist\ *n*

¹art \'ärt\ *n* **1** : skill acquired by experience or study **2** : a branch of learning; *esp* : one of the humanities **3** : an occupation requiring knowledge or skill **4** : the use of skill and imagination in the production of things of beauty; *also* : works so produced **5** : ARTFULNESS

²art *adj* : produced as an artistic effort ⟨an ∼ film⟩

³art *abbr* **1** article **2** artificial **3** artillery **-art** — see -ARD

ar·te·fact *chiefly Brit var of* ARTIFACT

ar·te·ri·al \är-'tir-ē-əl\ *adj* **1** : of or relating to an artery; *also* : relating to or being the oxygenated blood found in most arteries **2** : of, relating to, or being a route for through traffic

ar·te·ri·ole \är-'tir-ē-,ōl\ *n* : any of the small terminal branches of an artery that ends in capillaries — **ar·te·ri·o·lar** \-,tir-ē-'ō-lər\ *adj*

ar·te·rio·scle·ro·sis \är-,tir-ē-ō-sklə-'rō-səs\ *n* : a chronic disease in which arterial walls are abnormally thickened and hardened — **ar·te·rio·scle·rot·ic** \-'rä-tik\ *adj or n*

ar·tery \'är-tə-rē\ *n, pl* **-ter·ies** **1** : one of the tubular vessels that carry blood from the heart **2** : a main channel of transportation or communication

ar·te·sian well \är-'tē-zhən-\ *n* : a well from which the water flows to the surface by natural pressure; *also* : a deep well

art·ful \'ärt-fəl\ *adj* **1** : performed with, showing, or using art or skill **2** : CRAFTY — **art·ful·ly** *adv* — **art·ful·ness** *n*

ar·thri·tis \är-'thrī-təs\ *n, pl* **-thri·ti·des** \-'thri-tə-,dēz\ : inflammation of the joints — **ar·thrit·ic** \-'thri-tik\ *adj or n*

ar·thro·pod \'är-thrə-,päd\ *n* : any of a phylum of invertebrate animals comprising those (as insects, spiders, or crabs) with segmented bodies and jointed limbs — **arthropod** *adj*

ar·thros·co·py \är-'thräs-kə-pē\ *n, pl* **-pies** : visual examination of the interior of a joint (as the knee) with a special surgical instrument; *also* : surgery on a joint using arthroscopy — **ar·thro·scope** \'är-

thrə-,skōp\ *n* — **ar·thro·scop·ic** \,är-thrə-'skä-pik\ *adj*

ar·ti·choke \'är-tə-,chōk\ *n* [It dial. *articiocco*, ultim. fr. Ar *al-khurshūf*] : a tall thistlelike herb related to the daisies; *also* : its edible flower head

ar·ti·cle \'är-ti-kəl\ *n* [ME, fr. AF, fr. L *articulus* joint, division, dim. of *artus* joint, limb] **1** : a distinct part of a written document **2** : a nonfictional prose composition forming a independent part of a publication **3** : a word (as *an, the*) used with a noun to limit or give definiteness to its application **4** : a member of a class of things; *esp* : COMMODITY

ar·tic·u·lar \är-'ti-kyə-lər\ *adj* : of or relating to a joint ⟨∼ cartilage⟩

¹ar·tic·u·late \är-'ti-kyə-lət\ *adj* **1** : divided into meaningful parts : INTELLIGIBLE **2** : able to speak; *also* : expressing oneself readily and effectively ⟨an ∼ orator⟩ **3** : JOINTED — **ar·tic·u·late·ly** *adv* — **ar·tic·u·late·ness** *n*

²ar·tic·u·late \-,lāt\ *vb* **-lat·ed; -lat·ing** **1** : to utter distinctly **2** : to unite by or as if by joints — **ar·tic·u·la·tion** \-,ti-kyə-'lā-shən\ *n*

ar·ti·fact \'är-tə-,fakt\ *n* : something made or modified by humans usu. for a purpose; *esp* : an object remaining from another time or culture ⟨prehistoric ∼s⟩

ar·ti·fice \'är-tə-fəs\ *n* **1** : TRICK; *also* : TRICKERY **2** : an ingenious device; *also* : INGENUITY

ar·ti·fi·cer \är-'ti-fə-sər, 'är-tə-fə-sər\ *n* : a skilled worker

ar·ti·fi·cial \,är-tə-'fi-shəl\ *adj* **1** : produced by art rather than nature; *also* : made by humans to imitate nature **2** : not genuine : FEIGNED — **ar·ti·fi·ci·al·i·ty** \-,fi-shē-'a-lə-tē\ *n* — **ar·ti·fi·cial·ly** *adv* — **ar·ti·fi·cial·ness** *n*

artificial insemination *n* : introduction of semen into the uterus or oviduct by other than natural means

artificial intelligence *n* : the capability of a machine and esp. a computer to imitate intelligent human behavior

artificial respiration *n* : the rhythmic forcing of air into and out of the lungs of a person whose breathing has stopped

ar·til·lery \är-'ti-lə-rē\ *n, pl* **-ler·ies** **1** : crew-served mounted firearms (as guns) **2** : a branch of the army armed with artillery — **ar·til·ler·ist** \-rist\ *n*

ar·ti·san \'är-tə-zən, -sən\ *n* : a worker who practices a trade or handicraft

art·ist \'är-tist\ *n* **1** : one who practices an art; *esp* : one who creates objects of beauty **2** : ARTISTE

ar·tiste \är-'tēst\ *n* : a skilled public performer

ar·tis·tic \är-'tis-tik\ *adj* : showing taste and skill — **ar·tis·ti·cal·ly** \-ti-k(ə-)lē\ *adv*

art·ist·ry \'är-tə-strē\ *n* : artistic quality or ability

art·less \'ärt-ləs\ *adj* **1** : lacking art or skill **2** : free from artificiality : NATURAL

3 : free from guile : SINCERE — **art·less·ly** *adv* — **art·less·ness** *n*

art nou·veau \\,är-nü-'vō, ,ärt-\\ *n, often cap A&N* [F, lit., new art] : a late 19th century design style characterized by sinuous lines and leaf-shaped forms

art·work \\'ärt-,wərk\\ *n* : an artistic production or work

arty \\'är-tē\\ *adj* **art·i·er; -est** : showily or pretentiously artistic — **art·i·ly** \\'är-tə-lē\\ *adv* — **art·i·ness** *n*

aru·gu·la \\ə-'rü-gə-lə\\ *n* : a yellowish-flowered herb related to the mustards with edible leaves used esp. in salads

ar·um \\'a-rəm\\ *n* : any of a family of plants (as the jack-in-the-pulpit or a skunk cabbage) with flowers in a fleshy enclosed spathe

ARV *abbr* American Revised Version

¹**-ary** *n suffix* : thing or person belonging to or connected with ⟨function*ary*⟩

²**-ary** *adj suffix* : of, relating to, or connected with ⟨budget*ary*⟩

Ary·an \\'a-rē-ən, 'er-ē-; 'är-yən\\ *adj* **1** : INDO-EUROPEAN **2** : NORDIC — **Aryan** *n*

¹**as** \\əz, (,)az\\ *adv* **1** : to the same degree or amount : EQUALLY ⟨∼ green as grass⟩ **2** : for instance ⟨various trees, ∼ oak or pine⟩ **3** : when considered in a specified relation ⟨my opinion ∼ distinguished from his⟩

²**as** *conj* **1** : in the same amount or degree in which ⟨green ∼ grass⟩ **2** : in the same way that ⟨farmed ∼ his father before him had farmed⟩ **3** : WHILE, WHEN ⟨spoke to me ∼ I was leaving⟩ **4** : THOUGH ⟨improbable ∼ it seems⟩ **5** : SINCE, BECAUSE ⟨∼ I'm not wanted, I'll go⟩ **6** : that the result is ⟨so guilty ∼ to leave no doubt⟩

³**as** *pron* **1** : THAT — used after *same* or *such* ⟨it's the same price ∼ before⟩ **2** : a fact that ⟨he's rich, ∼ you know⟩

⁴**as** *prep* : in the capacity or character of ⟨this will serve ∼ a substitute⟩

As *symbol* arsenic

AS *abbr* **1** American Samoa **2** Anglo-Saxon **3** associate in science

asa·fet·i·da *or* **asa·foe·ti·da** \\,a-sə-'fe-tə-dē, -'fē-\\ *n* : an ill-smelling plant gum formerly used in medicine

ASAP *abbr* as soon as possible

as·bes·tos \\as-'bes-təs, az-\\ *n* : a noncombustible grayish mineral that occurs in fibrous form and has been used as a fireproof material

as·cend \\ə-'send\\ *vb* **1** : to move upward : MOUNT, CLIMB **2** : to succeed to : OCCUPY ⟨he ∼ed the throne⟩

as·cen·dan·cy *also* **as·cen·den·cy** \\ə-'sen-dən-sē\\ *n* : controlling influence : DOMINATION

¹**as·cen·dant** *also* **as·cen·dent** \\ə-'sen-dənt\\ *n* : a dominant position

²**ascendant** *also* **ascendent** *adj* **1** : moving upward **2** : DOMINANT

as·cen·sion \\ə-'sen-chən\\ *n* : the act or process of ascending

Ascension Day *n* : the Thursday 40 days after Easter observed in commemoration of Christ's ascension into heaven

as·cent \\ə-'sent\\ *n* **1** : the act of mounting upward : CLIMB **2** : degree of upward slope

as·cer·tain \\,a-sər-'tān\\ *vb* : to learn with certainty — **as·cer·tain·able** *adj*

as·cet·ic \\ə-'se-tik\\ *adj* : practicing self-denial esp. for spiritual reasons : AUSTERE — **ascetic** *n* — **as·cet·i·cism** \\'-'se-tə-,si-zəm\\ *n*

ASCII \\'as-kē\\ *n* [*A*merican *S*tandard *C*ode for *I*nformation *I*nterchange] : a computer code for representing alphanumeric information

ascor·bic acid \\ə-'skor-bik-\\ *n* : VITAMIN C

as·cot \\'as-kət, -,kät\\ *n* [*Ascot* Heath, racetrack near Ascot, England] : a broad neck scarf that is looped under the chin

as·cribe \\ə-'skrīb\\ *vb* **as·cribed; as·crib·ing** : to refer to a supposed cause, source, or author : ATTRIBUTE — **as·crib·able** *adj* — **as·crip·tion** \\-'skrip-shən\\ *n*

asep·tic \\ā-'sep-tik\\ *adj* : free or freed from disease-causing germs

asex·u·al \\ā-'sek-shə-wəl\\ *adj* **1** : lacking sex or functional sex organs **2** : occurring or formed without the production and union of two kinds of gametes ⟨∼ reproduction⟩ **3** : devoid of sexuality — **asex·u·al·ly** *adv*

as for *prep* : with regard to : CONCERNING ⟨*as for* the others, they were late⟩

¹**ash** \\'ash\\ *n* **1** : any of a genus of trees related to the olive and having winged seeds and bark with grooves and ridges **2** : the tough elastic wood of an ash

²**ash** *n* **1** : the solid matter left when material is burned **2** : fine mineral particles from a volcano **3** *pl* : the remains of the dead human body after cremation or disintegration

ashamed \\ə-'shāmd\\ *adj* **1** : feeling shame **2** : restrained by anticipation of shame ⟨∼ to say anything⟩ — **ashamed·ly** \\-'shā-məd-lē\\ *adv*

ash·en \\'a-shən\\ *adj* : resembling ashes (as in color); *esp* : deadly pale

ash·lar \\'ash-lər\\ *n* : hewn or squared stone; *also* : masonry of such stone

ashore \\ə-'shòr\\ *adv* : on or to the shore

as how *conj* : THAT ⟨allowed *as how* she was glad to be here⟩

ash·ram \\'äsh-rəm\\ *n* : a religious retreat esp. of a Hindu sage

ash·tray \\'ash-,trā\\ *n* : a receptacle for tobacco ashes

Ash Wednesday *n* : the 1st day of Lent

ashy \\'a-shē\\ *adj* **ash·i·er; -est** : ASHEN

Asian \\'ā-zhən\\ *adj* : of, relating to, or characteristic of the continent of Asia or its people — **Asian** *n*

¹**aside** \\ə-'sīd\\ *adv* **1** : to or toward one side **2** : out of the way : AWAY ⟨putting ∼ savings⟩

²**aside** *n* : an actor's words heard by the audience but supposedly not by other characters on stage

aside from *prep* **1** : BESIDES ⟨*aside from* being pretty, she's intelligent⟩ **2** : with the exception of ⟨*aside from* one D his grades are excellent⟩

as if *conj* **1** : as it would be if ⟨it's *as if*

nothing had changed⟩ 2 : as one would if ⟨he acts *as if* he'd never been away⟩ 3 : THAT ⟨it seems *as if* nothing ever happens around here⟩

as·i·nine \'a-sə-ˌnīn\ *adj* [L *asininus*, fr. *asinus* ass] : STUPID, FOOLISH — **as·i·nin·i·ty** \ˌa-sə-'ni-nə-tē\ *n*

ask \'ask\ *vb* asked \'askt\; **ask·ing** 1 : to call on for an answer ⟨she ~ed him about his trip⟩ 2 : UTTER ⟨~ a question⟩ 3 : to make a request of ⟨~ him for help⟩ 4 : to make a request for ⟨~ help of her⟩ 5 : to set as a price ⟨~ed $800 for the car⟩ 6 : INVITE

askance \ə-'skans\ *adv* 1 : with a side glance 2 : with distrust

askew \ə-'skyü\ *adv or adj* : out of line : AWRY

ASL *abbr* American Sign Language

¹**aslant** \ə-'slant\ *adv or adj* : in a slanting direction

²**aslant** *prep* : over or across in a slanting direction

asleep \ə-'slēp\ *adv or adj* 1 : in or into a state of sleep 2 : DEAD 3 : NUMB 4 : INACTIVE

as long as *conj* 1 : provided that ⟨do as you like *as long as* you get home on time⟩ 2 : INASMUCH AS, SINCE ⟨*as long as* you're up, turn on the light⟩

aso·cial \(ˌ)ā-'sō-shəl\ *adj* : ANTISOCIAL

as of *prep* : AT, DURING, FROM, ON ⟨takes effect *as of* July 1⟩

asp \'asp\ *n* : a small poisonous African snake

as·par·a·gus \ə-'sper-ə-gəs\ *n* : a tall branching perennial herb related to the lilies; *also* : its edible young stalks

as·par·tame \'as-pər-ˌtām, ə-'spär-\ *n* : a crystalline low-calorie sweetener

ASPCA *abbr* American Society for the Prevention of Cruelty to Animals

as·pect \'as-ˌpekt\ *n* 1 : a position facing a particular direction 2 : APPEARANCE, LOOK 3 : PHASE

as·pen \'as-pən\ *n* : any of several poplars with leaves that flutter in the slightest breeze

as per \'az-ˌpər\ *prep* : in accordance with ⟨*as per* instructions⟩

as·per·i·ty \a-'sper-ə-tē\ *n, pl* **-ties** 1 : ROUGHNESS 2 : harshness of temper

as·per·sion \ə-'spər-zhən\ *n* : a slanderous or defamatory remark

as·phalt \'as-ˌfȯlt\ *also* **as·phal·tum** \as-'fȯl-təm\ *n* : a dark substance found in natural beds or obtained as a residue in petroleum refining and used esp. in paving streets

asphalt jungle *n* : a big city or a specified part of a big city

as·pho·del \'as-fə-ˌdel\ *n* : any of several Old World herbs related to the lilies and bearing flowers in long erect spikes

as·phyx·ia \as-'fik-sē-ə\ *n* : a lack of oxygen or excess of carbon dioxide in the body that results in unconsciousness and often death and is usu. caused by interruption of breathing

as·phyx·i·ate \-ē-ˌāt\ *vb* **-at·ed; -at·ing** : SUFFOCATE — **as·phyx·i·a·tion** \-ˌfik-sē-'ā-shən\ *n*

as·pic \'as-ˌpik\ *n* [F, lit., asp] : a savory meat jelly

as·pi·rant \'as-pə-rənt, ə-'spī-rənt\ *n* : one who aspires ⟨a presidential ~⟩ ♦ **Synonyms** CANDIDATE, SEEKER

¹**as·pi·rate** \'as-pə-rət\ *n* 1 : an independent sound \h\ or a character (as the letter *h*) representing it 2 : a consonant having aspiration as its final component

²**as·pi·rate** \'as-pə-ˌrāt\ *vb* **-rat·ed; -rat·ing** : to draw, remove, or take up or into by suction

as·pi·ra·tion \ˌas-pə-'rā-shən\ *n* 1 : the pronunciation or addition of an aspirate; *also* : the aspirate or its symbol 2 : a drawing of something in, out, up, or through by or as if by suction 3 : a strong desire to achieve something noble; *also* : an object of this desire

as·pire \ə-'spī-(ə)r\ *vb* **as·pired; as·pir·ing** 1 : to seek to attain or accomplish a particular goal 2 : to rise aloft

as·pi·rin \'as-p(ə-)rən\ *n, pl* **aspirin** *or* **aspirins** 1 : a white crystalline drug used to relieve pain and fever 2 : a tablet of aspirin

as regards *also* **as respects** *prep* : in regard to : with respect to

ass \'as\ *n* 1 : any of several long-eared mammals smaller than the related horses; *esp* : one of Africa ancestral to the donkey 2 : a stupid person

as·sail \ə-'sāl\ *vb* : to attack violently — **as·sail·able** \-ə-bəl\ *adj*

as·sas·sin \ə-'sa-sᵊn\ *n* [ML *assassinus*, fr. Ar *ḥashshāshīn*, pl. of *ḥashshāsh* worthless person, lit., hashish-user, fr. *ḥashīsh* hashish] : a murderer esp. for hire or fanatical reasons

as·sas·si·nate \ə-'sa-sə-ˌnāt\ *vb* **-nat·ed; -nat·ing** : to murder by sudden or secret attack — **as·sas·si·na·tion** \-ˌsa-sə-'nā-shən\ *n*

as·sault \ə-'sȯlt\ *n* 1 : a violent attack 2 : an unlawful attempt or threat to do harm to another — **assault** *vb* — **as·sault·ive** \ə-'sȯl-tiv\ *adj*

assault rifle *n* : a military automatic rifle with a large-capacity magazine

¹**as·say** \'a-ˌsā, a-'sā\ *n* : analysis to determine the quantity of one or more components present in a sample (as of an ore or drug)

²**as·say** \a-'sā, 'a-ˌsā\ *vb* 1 : TRY, ATTEMPT 2 : to subject (as an ore or drug) to an assay 3 : JUDGE 3

as·sem·blage \ə-'sem-blij, *3 & 4 also* ˌas-ˌäm-'bläzh\ *n* 1 : a collection of persons or things : GATHERING 2 : the act of assembling 3 : an artistic composition made from scraps, junk, and odds and ends 4 : the art of making assemblages

as·sem·ble \ə-'sem-bəl\ *vb* **-bled; -bling** 1 : to collect into one place : CONGREGATE 2 : to fit together the parts of 3 : to meet together : CONVENE

as·sem·bly \ə-'sem-blē\ *n, pl* **-blies** 1 : a gathering of persons : MEETING 2 *cap* : a legislative body; *esp* : the lower house of a legislature 3 : a signal for troops to assemble 4 : the fitting together of parts (as of a machine)

assembly language • aster

42

as·sem·bly language *n* : a computer language consisting of mnemonic codes corresponding to machine-language instructions

as·sem·bly–line \ə-'sem-blē-,līn\ *adj* : made by or as if by an assembly line; *esp* : lacking originality or creativity

assembly line *n* : an arrangement of machines, equipment, and workers in which work passes from operation to operation in a direct line

as·sem·bly·man \ə-'sem-blē-mən\ *n* : a member of a legislative assembly

as·sem·bly·wom·an \-,wu̇-mən\ *n* : a woman who is a member of a legislative assembly

as·sent \ə-'sent\ *vb* : AGREE, CONCUR — **assent** *n*

as·sert \ə-'sərt\ *vb* **1** : to state positively **2** : to demonstrate the existence of ♦ **Synonyms** DECLARE, AFFIRM, PROTEST, AVOW, CLAIM — **as·ser·tive** \-'sər-tiv\ *adj* — **as·ser·tive·ly** *adv* — **as·ser·tive·ness** *n*

as·ser·tion \ə-'sər-shən\ *n* : a positive statement

as·sess \ə-'ses\ *vb* **1** : to fix the rate or amount of **2** : to impose (as a tax) at a specified rate **3** : to evaluate for taxation — **as·sess·ment** *n* — **as·ses·sor** \-'se-sər\ *n*

as·set \'a-,set\ *n* **1** *pl* : the entire property of a person or company that may be used to pay debts **2** : ADVANTAGE, RESOURCE ⟨my wit is my chief ∼⟩

as·sev·er·ate \ə-'se-və-,rāt\ *vb* **-at·ed; -at·ing** : to assert earnestly — **as·sev·er·a·tion** \-,se-və-'rā-shən\ *n*

as·sid·u·ous \ə-'si-jə-wəs\ *adj* : steadily attentive : DILIGENT — **as·si·du·i·ty** \,a-sə-'dü-ə-tē, -'dyü-\ *n* — **as·sid·u·ous·ly** *adv* — **as·sid·u·ous·ness** *n*

as·sign \ə-'sīn\ *vb* **1** : to transfer (property) to another **2** : to appoint to or as a duty ⟨∼ a lesson⟩ **3** : FIX, SPECIFY ⟨∼ a limit⟩ **4** : ASCRIBE ⟨∼ a reason⟩ — **as·sign·able** *adj*

as·sig·na·tion \,a-sig-'nā-shən\ *n* : an appointment for a meeting; *esp* : TRYST

assigned risk *n* : a poor risk (as an accident-prone motorist) that an insurance company is forced to insure by state law

as·sign·ment \ə-'sīn-mənt\ *n* **1** : the act of assigning **2** : something assigned

as·sim·i·late \ə-'si-mə-,lāt\ *vb* **-lat·ed; -lat·ing** **1** : to take up and absorb as nourishment; *also* : to absorb into a cultural tradition **2** : COMPREHEND **3** : to make or become similar — **as·sim·i·la·tion** \-,si-mə-'lā-shən\ *n*

¹**as·sist** \ə-'sist\ *vb* : HELP, AID ⟨∼ed the injured⟩ — **as·sis·tance** \-'sis-təns\ *n*

²**assist** *n* **1** : an act of assistance **2** : the action of a player who enables a teammate to make a putout (as in baseball) or score a goal (as in hockey or basketball)

as·sis·tant \ə-'sis-tənt\ *n* : a person who assists : HELPER

as·sist·ed living \ə-'sis-təd-\ *n* : a system of housing and limited care for senior citizens who need assistance with daily activities but do not require care in a nursing home

as·sis·tive \ə-'sis-tiv\ *adj* : providing aid or assistance ⟨∼ technology⟩

as·size \ə-'sīz\ *n* [ME *assise*, fr. AF, session, legal action, fr. *asseer, asseoir* to seat, fr. VL **assedēre*, fr. L *assidēre* to sit beside] **1** : a judicial inquest **2** *pl* : the former regular sessions of superior courts in English counties

assn *abbr* association

assoc *abbr* associate; associated; association

¹**as·so·ci·ate** \ə-'sō-shē-,āt, -sē-\ *vb* **-at·ed; -at·ing** **1** : to join in companionship or partnership **2** : to connect in thought

²**as·so·ci·ate** \-shē-ət, -sē-; -shət\ *n* **1** : a fellow worker : PARTNER **2** : COMPANION **3** *often cap* : a degree conferred esp. by a junior college ⟨∼ in arts⟩ — **associate** *adj*

as·so·ci·a·tion \ə-,sō-shē-'ā-shən, -sē-\ *n* **1** : the act of associating **2** : an organization of persons : SOCIETY

as·so·cia·tive \ə-'sō-shē-,ā-tiv, -sē-; -shə-tiv\ *adj* **1** : of, relating to, or involved in association esp. of ideas or images **2** : of, having, or being the property of producing the same mathematical value regardless of how an expression's elements are grouped as long as their order is the same

as·so·nance \'a-sə-nəns\ *n* : repetition of vowels esp. as an alternative to rhyme in verse — **as·so·nant** \-nənt\ *adj or n*

as soon as *conj* : immediately at or shortly after the time that ⟨we'll start *as soon as* they arrive⟩

as·sort \ə-'sȯrt\ *vb* **1** : to distribute into like groups : CLASSIFY **2** : HARMONIZE

as·sort·ed \-'sȯr-təd\ *adj* : consisting of various kinds

as·sort·ment \-'sȯrt-mənt\ *n* : a collection of assorted things or persons

asst *abbr* assistant

as·suage \ə-'swāj\ *vb* **as·suaged; as·suag·ing** **1** : to make (as pain or grief) less : EASE **2** : SATISFY ♦ **Synonyms** ALLEVIATE, RELIEVE, LIGHTEN, MITIGATE

as·sume \ə-'süm\ *vb* **as·sumed; as·sum·ing** **1** : to take upon oneself **2** : to pretend to have or be **3** : to take as granted or true though not proved

as·sump·tion \ə-'səmp-shən\ *n* **1** : the taking up of a person into heaven **2** *cap* : August 15 observed in commemoration of the Assumption of the Virgin Mary **3** : a taking upon oneself **4** : PRETENSION **5** : SUPPOSITION

as·sur·ance \ə-'shur-əns\ *n* **1** : PLEDGE **2** *chiefly Brit* : INSURANCE **3** : SECURITY **4** : SELF-CONFIDENCE; *also* : AUDACITY

as·sure \ə-'shur\ *vb* **as·sured; as·sur·ing** **1** : INSURE **2** : to give confidence to **3** : to state confidently to **4** : to make certain the coming or attainment of

as·sured \ə-'shurd\ *n, pl* **assured** *or* **as·sureds** : INSURED

as·ta·tine \'as-tə-,tēn\ *n* : an unstable radioactive chemical element

as·ter \'as-tər\ *n* : any of various mostly fall-blooming leafy-stemmed composite herbs with daisylike purple, white, pink, or yellow flower heads

as·ter·isk \'as-tə-ˌrisk\ n [L asteriscus, fr. Gk asteriskos, lit., little star, dim. of astēr star] : a character * used as a reference mark or as an indication of the omission of letters or words

astern \ə-'stərn\ adv or adj 1 : in, at, or toward the stern 2 : BACKWARD

as·ter·oid \'as-tə-ˌrȯid\ n : any of the numerous small celestial bodies found esp. between Mars and Jupiter

asth·ma \'az-mə\ n : a chronic lung disorder marked by recurrent episodes of labored breathing, a feeling of tightness in the chest, and coughing — **asth·mat·ic** \az-'ma-tik\ adj or n

as though conj : AS IF

astig·ma·tism \ə-'stig-mə-ˌti-zəm\ n : a defect in a lens or an eye causing improper focusing and blurred vision — **as·tig·mat·ic** \ˌas-tig-'ma-tik\ adj

astir \ə-'stər\ adj 1 : being in action : MOVING 2 : being out of bed

as to prep 1 : ABOUT, CONCERNING ⟨uncertain as to what went on⟩ 2 : ACCORDING TO ⟨graded as to size⟩

as·ton·ish \ə-'stä-nish\ vb : to strike with sudden and usu. great wonder : AMAZE — **as·ton·ish·ing·ly** adv — **as·ton·ish·ment** n

as·tound \ə-'staund\ vb : to fill with bewilderment or wonder — **as·tound·ing·ly** adv

¹**astrad·dle** \ə-'stra-d³l\ adv : on or above and extending onto both sides

²**astraddle** prep : ASTRIDE

as·tra·khan \'as-trə-kən, -ˌkan\ n, often cap 1 : karakul of Russian origin 2 : a cloth with a usu. wool, curled, and looped pile resembling karakul

as·tral \'as-trəl\ adj : of, relating to, or coming from the stars

astray \ə-'strā\ adv or adj 1 : off the right path or route 2 : into error

¹**astride** \ə-'strīd\ adv 1 : with one leg on each side 2 : with legs apart

²**astride** prep : with one leg on each side of

¹**as·trin·gent** \ə-'strin-jənt\ adj : able or tending to shrink body tissues — **as·trin·gen·cy** \-jən-sē\ n

²**astringent** n : an astringent agent or substance

astrol abbr astrologer; astrology

as·tro·labe \'as-trə-ˌlāb\ n : an instrument formerly used for observing the positions of celestial bodies

as·trol·o·gy \ə-'strä-lə-jē\ n : divination based on the supposed influence of the stars upon human events — **as·trol·o·ger** \-jər\ n — **as·tro·log·i·cal** \ˌas-trə-'lä-ji-kəl\ adj — **as·tro·log·i·cal·ly** \-kə-lē\ adv

astron abbr astronomer; astronomy

as·tro·naut \'as-trə-ˌnȯt\ n : a traveler in a spacecraft

as·tro·nau·tics \ˌas-trə-'nȯ-tiks\ n : the science of the construction and operation of spacecraft — **as·tro·nau·tic** \-tik\ or **as·tro·nau·ti·cal** \-ti-kəl\ adj

as·tro·nom·i·cal \ˌas-trə-'nä-mi-kəl\ also **as·tro·nom·ic** \-mik\ adj 1 : of or relating to astronomy 2 : extremely large ⟨an ~ amount of money⟩

astronomical unit n : a unit of length used in astronomy equal to the mean distance of the earth from the sun or about 93 million miles (150 million kilometers)

as·tron·o·my \ə-'strä-nə-mē\ n, pl -mies : the science of objects and matter beyond the earth's atmosphere — **as·tron·o·mer** \-mər\ n

as·tro·phys·ics \ˌas-trə-'fi-ziks\ n : astronomy dealing esp. with the physical properties and dynamic processes of celestial objects — **as·tro·phys·i·cal** \-zi-kəl\ adj — **as·tro·phys·i·cist** \-'fi-zə-sist\ n

as·tute \ə-'stüt, -'styüt, a-\ adj [L astutus, fr. astus craft] : shrewdly discerning; also : WILY ⟨an ~ lawyer⟩ — **as·tute·ly** adv — **as·tute·ness** n

asun·der \ə-'sən-dər\ adv or adj 1 : into separate pieces ⟨torn ~⟩ 2 : separated in position from each other

ASV abbr American Standard Version

¹**as well as** conj : and in addition : and moreover ⟨brave as well as loyal⟩

²**as well as** prep : in addition to : BESIDES ⟨the coach, as well as the team, is ready⟩

asy·lum \ə-'sī-ləm\ n [ME, fr. L, fr. Gk asylon, neut. of asylos inviolable, fr. a- not + sylon right of seizure] 1 : a place of refuge 2 : protection given to esp. political fugitives 3 : an institution for the care of the needy or sick and esp. of the insane

asym·met·ri·cal \ˌā-sə-'me-tri-kəl\ or **asym·met·ric** \-trik\ adj : not symmetrical — **asym·met·ri·cal·ly** \-tri-kə-lē\ adv — **asym·me·try** \(ˌ)ā-'si-mə-trē\ n

asymp·tom·at·ic \ˌā-ˌsimp-tə-'ma-tik\ adj : presenting no symptoms of disease ⟨an ~ infection⟩

as·ymp·tote \'a-səmp-ˌtōt\ n : a straight line that is approached ever more closely by a curve that never coincides with it — **as·ymp·tot·ic** \ˌa-səmp-'tä-tik\ adj — **as·ymp·tot·i·cal·ly** \-ti-k(ə-)lē\ adv

¹**at** \ət, (')at\ prep 1 — used to indicate a point in time or space ⟨be here ~ 3 o'clock⟩ 2 — used to indicate a goal ⟨swung ~ the ball⟩ 3 — used to indicate position or condition ⟨~ rest⟩ 4 — used to indicate means, cause, or manner ⟨sold ~ auction⟩

²**at** also **att** \'ät\ n, pl **at** also **att** — see kip at MONEY table

At symbol astatine

AT abbr automatic transmission

at all adv : in any way : in any circumstances ⟨not ~ all likely⟩

at·a·vism \'a-tə-ˌvi-zəm\ n : appearance in an individual of a character typical of an ancestral form; also : such an individual or character — **at·a·vis·tic** \ˌa-tə-'vis-tik\ adj

atax·ia \ə-'tak-sē-ə\ n : an inability to coordinate muscular movements

ate past of EAT

¹**-ate** n suffix 1 : one acted upon (in a specified way) ⟨distillate⟩ 2 : chemical

compound or complex derived from a (specified) compound or element ⟨acetate⟩

²-ate *n suffix* **1** : office : function : rank : group of persons holding a (specified) office or rank ⟨episcopate⟩ **2** : state : dominion : jurisdiction ⟨emirate⟩

³-ate *adj suffix* **1** : acted on (in a specified way) : being in a (specified) state ⟨temperate⟩ ⟨degenerate⟩ **2** : marked by having ⟨vertebrate⟩

⁴-ate *vb suffix* : cause to be modified or affected by ⟨pollinate⟩ : cause to become ⟨activate⟩ : furnish with ⟨aerate⟩

ate·lier \ˌa-tᵊl-ˈyā\ *n* **1** : an artist's or designer's studio **2** : WORKSHOP

athe·ist \ˈā-thē-ist\ *n* : one who denies the existence of God — athe·ism \-ˌi-zəm\ *n* — athe·is·tic \ˌā-thē-ˈis-tik\ *adj*

ath·e·nae·um *or* ath·e·ne·um \ˌa-thə-ˈnē-əm\ *n* : LIBRARY 1

ath·ero·scle·ro·sis \ˌa-thə-rō-sklə-ˈrō-səs\ *n* : arteriosclerosis characterized by the deposition of fatty substances in and the hardening of the inner layer of the arteries — ath·ero·scle·rot·ic \-ˈrä-tik\ *adj*

athirst \ə-ˈthərst\ *adj* **1** *archaic* : THIRSTY **2** : EAGER, LONGING

ath·lete \ˈath-ˌlēt\ *n* [ME, fr. L *athleta*, fr. Gk *athlētēs*, fr. *athlein* to contend for a prize, fr. *athlon* prize, contest] : a person who is trained to compete in athletics

athlete's foot *n* : ringworm of the feet

ath·let·ic \ath-ˈle-tik\ *adj* **1** : of or relating to athletes or athletics **2** : VIGOROUS, ACTIVE **3** : STURDY, MUSCULAR — ath·let·i·cal·ly \-ti-kə-lē\ *adv* — ath·let·i·cism \-tə-ˌsi-zəm\ *n*

ath·let·ics \ath-ˈle-tiks\ *n sing or pl* : exercises and games requiring physical skill, strength, and endurance

athletic supporter *n* : an elastic pouch used to support the male genitals and worn esp. during athletic activity

¹athwart \ə-ˈthwȯrt\ *prep* **1** : ACROSS **2** : in opposition to

²athwart *adv* : obliquely across

atilt \ə-ˈtilt\ *adv or adj* **1** : in a tilted position **2** : with lance in hand

-ation *n suffix* **1** : action or process ⟨flirtation⟩ : something connected with an action or process ⟨discoloration⟩

Atl *abbr* Atlantic

at-large \ˈat-ˈlärj\ *adj* : of or being a political representative who is elected to serve an entire area rather than one of its subdivisions

at·las \ˈat-ləs\ *n* : a book of maps

atm *abbr* atmosphere; atmospheric

ATM *n* : a computerized electronic machine that performs basic banking functions

at·mo·sphere \ˈat-mə-ˌsfir\ *n* **1** : the gaseous envelope of a celestial body; *esp* : the mass of air surrounding the earth **2** : a surrounding influence **3** : a unit of pressure equal to the pressure of air at sea level or about 14.7 pounds per square inch (10 newtons per square centimeter) **4** : an intriguing or singular tone, effect, or appeal — at·mo·spher·ic \ˌat-mə-

ˈsfir-ik, -ˈsfer-\ *adj* — at·mo·spher·i·cal·ly \-i-k(ə-)lē\ *adv*

at·mo·spher·ics \ˌat-mə-ˈsfir-iks, -ˈsfer-\ *n pl* : radio noise from atmospheric electrical phenomena

atoll \ˈa-ˌtȯl, -ˌtäl, ˈā-\ *n* : a coral island consisting of a reef surrounding a lagoon

at·om \ˈa-təm\ *n* [ME, fr. L *atomus*, fr. Gk *atomos*, fr. *atomos* indivisible, fr. *a-* not + *temnein* to cut] **1** : a tiny particle : BIT **2** : the smallest particle of a chemical element that can exist alone or in combination

atom·ic \ə-ˈtä-mik\ *adj* **1** : of or relating to atoms; *also* : NUCLEAR 2 ⟨∼ energy⟩ **2** : extremely small

atomic bomb *n* : a very destructive bomb utilizing the energy released by splitting the atom

atomic clock *n* : a very precise clock regulated by the natural vibration of atoms or molecules (as of cesium)

atomic number *n* : the number of protons in the nucleus of an element

atomic weight *n* : the mass of one atom of an element

at·om·ise, at·om·is·er *Brit var of* ATOMIZE, ATOMIZER

at·om·ize \ˈa-tə-ˌmīz\ *vb* -ized; -iz·ing : to reduce to minute particles

at·om·iz·er \ˈa-tə-ˌmī-zər\ *n* : a device for dispensing a liquid (as perfume) as a mist

atom smasher *n* : ACCELERATOR 3

aton·al \ā-ˈtō-nᵊl\ *adj* : marked by avoidance of traditional musical tonality — ato·nal·i·ty \ˌā-tō-ˈna-lə-tē\ *n* — aton·al·ly \ā-ˈtō-nə-lē\ *adv*

atone \ə-ˈtōn\ *vb* atoned; aton·ing **1** : to make amends **2** : EXPIATE ⟨∼ for sins⟩

atone·ment \ə-ˈtōn-mənt\ *n* **1** : the reconciliation of God and mankind through the death of Jesus Christ **2** : reparation for an offense : SATISFACTION

¹atop \ə-ˈtäp\ *adv or adj* : on, to, or at the top

²atop *prep* : on top of

ATP \ˌā-ˌtē-ˈpē\ *n* [adenosine *tri*phosphate] : a compound that occurs widely in living tissue and supplies energy for many cellular processes by undergoing enzymatic hydrolysis

atri·um \ˈā-trē-əm\ *n, pl* atria \-trē-ə\ *also* atri·ums **1** : the central room of a Roman house; *also* : an open patio or court in the center of a building (as a hotel) **2** : an anatomical cavity or passage; *esp* : one of the chambers of the heart that receives blood from the veins — atri·al \-əl\ *adj*

atro·cious \ə-ˈtrō-shəs\ *adj* **1** : savagely brutal, cruel, or wicked **2** : very bad : ABOMINABLE — atro·cious·ly *adv* — atro·cious·ness *n*

atroc·i·ty \ə-ˈträ-sə-tē\ *n, pl* -ties **1** : ATROCIOUSNESS **2** : an atrocious act or object ⟨the *atrocities* of war⟩

at·ro·phy \ˈa-trə-fē\ *n, pl* -phies : decrease in size or wasting away of a bodily part or tissue — atrophy *vb*

at·ro·pine \'a-trə-ˌpēn\ *n* : a drug from belladonna and related plants used esp. to relieve spasms and to dilate the pupil of the eye

¹**att** *var of* AT

²**att** *abbr* **1** attached **2** attention **3** attorney

at·tach \ə-'tach\ *vb* **1** : to seize legally in order to force payment of a debt **2** : to bind by personal ties **3** : FASTEN, CONNECT **4** : to be fastened or connected

at·ta·ché \ˌa-tə-'shā, ˌa-ˌta-, ə-ˌta-\ *n* [F] : a technical expert on the diplomatic staff of an ambassador

at·ta·ché case \ˌa-tə-'shā-, ˌa-tə-'shā-\ *n* : a small thin suitcase used esp. for carrying business papers; *also* : BRIEFCASE

at·tach·ment \ə-'tach-mənt\ *n* **1** : legal seizure of property **2** : connection by ties of affection and regard **3** : a device attached to a machine or implement **4** : a connection by which one thing is attached to another

¹**at·tack** \ə-'tak\ *vb* **1** : to set upon with force or words : ASSAIL, ASSAULT **2** : to set to work on

²**attack** *n* **1** : an offensive action **2** : a fit of sickness **3** : a scoring action in a game

³**attack** *adj* : designed, planned, or used for a military attack

at·tain \ə-'tān\ *vb* **1** : ACHIEVE, ACCOMPLISH **2** : to arrive at : REACH — **at·tain·abil·i·ty** \-ˌtā-nə-'bi-lə-tē\ *n* — **at·tain·able** *adj*

at·tain·der \ə-'tān-dər\ *n* : extinction of the civil rights of a person upon sentence of death or outlawry

at·tain·ment \ə-'tān-mənt\ *n* **1** : the act of attaining **2** : ACCOMPLISHMENT

at·tar \'a-tər\ *n* [Pers *'aṭir* perfumed, fr. Ar, fr. *'iṭr* perfume] : a fragrant floral oil

at·tempt \ə-'tempt\ *vb* : to make an effort toward : TRY — **attempt** *n*

at·tend \ə-'tend\ *vb* **1** : to look after : TEND **2** : to be present with **3** : to be present at **4** : to apply oneself **5** : to pay attention **6** : to direct one's attention

at·ten·dance \ə-'ten-dəns\ *n* **1** : the act or fact of attending **2** : the number of persons present; *also* : the number of times a person attends

¹**at·ten·dant** \ə-'ten-dənt\ *n* : one that attends another to render a service

²**attendant** *adj* : ACCOMPANYING ⟨∼ circumstances⟩

at·ten·tion \ə-'ten-chən\ *n* **1** : the act or state of applying the mind to an object **2** : CONSIDERATION **3** : an act of courtesy **4** : a position of readiness assumed on command by a soldier — **at·ten·tive** \-'ten-tiv\ *adj* — **at·ten·tive·ly** *adv* — **at·ten·tive·ness** *n*

attention deficit disorder *n* : a behavioral syndrome esp. of children that is marked by hyperactivity, impulsive behavior, and inattention

attention–deficit/hyperactivity disorder *n* : ATTENTION DEFICIT DISORDER

attention span *n* : the length of time during which one is able to concentrate or remain interested

at·ten·u·ate \ə-'ten-yə-ˌwāt\ *vb* -**at·ed**; -**at·ing** **1** : to make or become thin **2** : WEAKEN ⟨sorrows ∼ with time⟩ — **attenuate** \-wət\ *adj* — **at·ten·u·a·tion** \-ˌten-yə-'wā-shən\ *n*

at·test \ə-'test\ *vb* **1** : to certify as genuine by signing as a witness **2** : MANIFEST ⟨her record ∼s her integrity⟩ **3** : TESTIFY ⟨∼ to a belief⟩ — **at·tes·ta·tion** \ˌa-ˌtes-'tā-shən\ *n*

at·tic \'a-tik\ *n* : the space or room in a building immediately below the roof

¹**at·tire** \ə-'tī(-ə)r\ *vb* **at·tired**; **at·tir·ing** : to put garments on : DRESS, ARRAY

²**attire** *n* : DRESS, CLOTHES

at·ti·tude \'a-tə-ˌtüd, -ˌtyüd\ *n* **1** : POSTURE **2** : a mental position or feeling with regard to a fact or state **3** : the position of something in relation to something else **4** : a negative or hostile state of mind **5** : a cocky or arrogant manner

at·ti·tu·di·nise *Brit var of* ATTITUDINIZE

at·ti·tu·di·nize \ˌa-tə-'tü-də-ˌnīz, -'tyü-\ *vb* -**nized**; -**niz·ing** : to assume an affected mental attitude : POSE

attn *abbr* attention

at·tor·ney \ə-'tər-nē\ *n, pl* -**neys** : a legal agent qualified to act for persons in legal proceedings

attorney general *n, pl* **attorneys general** *or* **attorney generals** : the chief legal representative and adviser of a nation or state

at·tract \ə-'trakt\ *vb* **1** : to draw to or toward oneself : cause to approach **2** : to draw by emotional or aesthetic appeal ♦ *Synonyms* CHARM, FASCINATE, ALLURE, CAPTIVATE, ENCHANT — **at·trac·tive** \-'trak-tiv\ *adj* — **at·trac·tive·ly** *adv* — **at·trac·tive·ness** *n*

at·trac·tant \ə-'trak-tənt\ *n* : a substance (as a pheromone) that attracts specific animals (as insects)

at·trac·tion \ə-'trak-shən\ *n* **1** : the act or power of attracting; *esp* : personal charm **2** : an attractive quality, object, or feature **3** : a force tending to draw particles together

attrib *abbr* attributive

¹**at·tri·bute** \'a-trə-ˌbyüt\ *n* **1** : an inherent characteristic **2** : a word ascribing a quality; *esp* : ADJECTIVE

²**at·trib·ute** \ə-'tri-ˌbyüt, -byət\ *vb* -**ut·ed**; -**ut·ing** **1** : to explain as to cause or origin ⟨∼ the illness to fatigue⟩ **2** : to regard as a characteristic ♦ *Synonyms* ASCRIBE, CREDIT, CHARGE, IMPUTE — **at·trib·ut·able** *adj* — **at·tri·bu·tion** \ˌa-trə-'byü-shən\ *n*

at·trib·u·tive \ə-'tri-byə-tiv\ *adj* : joined directly to a modified noun without a linking verb ⟨*red* in *red hair* is an ∼ adjective⟩ — **attributive** *n* — **at·trib·u·tive·ly** *adv*

at·tri·tion \ə-'tri-shən\ *n* **1** : the act of wearing away by or as if by rubbing **2** : a reduction in numbers as a result of resignation, retirement, or death

at·tune \ə-'tün, -'tyün\ *vb* : to bring into harmony : TUNE — **at·tune·ment** *n*

atty *abbr* attorney

ATV \ˌā-ˌtē-'vē\ *n* : ALL-TERRAIN VEHICLE

atyp·i·cal \ā-'ti-pi-kəl\ *adj* : not typical : IRREGULAR — **atyp·i·cal·ly** \-k(ə-)lē\ *adv*

Au *symbol* [L *aurum*] gold

au·burn \'ȯ-bərn\ *adj* : reddish brown — **auburn** *n*

au cou·rant \ˌȯ-kü-'räⁿ\ *adj* [F, lit., in the current] : UP-TO-DATE, STYLISH

¹auc·tion \'ȯk-shən\ *n* [L *auction-, auctio,* fr. *augēre* to increase] : public sale of property to the highest bidder

²auction *vb* **auc·tioned; auc·tion·ing** \-shə-niŋ\ : to sell at auction

auc·tion·eer \ˌȯk-shə-'nir\ *n* : an agent who conducts an auction

aud *abbr* audit; auditor

au·da·cious \ȯ-'dā-shəs\ *adj* **1** : DARING, BOLD **2** : INSOLENT — **au·da·cious·ly** *adv* — **au·da·cious·ness** *n* — **au·dac·i·ty** \-'da-sə-tē\ *n*

¹au·di·ble \'ȯ-də-bəl\ *adj* : capable of being heard — **au·di·bil·i·ty** \ˌȯ-də-'bi-lə-tē\ *n* — **au·di·bly** \'ȯ-də-blē\ *adv*

²audible *n* : a play called at the line of scrimmage — **audible** *vb*

au·di·ence \'ȯ-dē-əns\ *n* **1** : a formal interview **2** : an opportunity of being heard **3** : an assembly of listeners or spectators

¹au·dio \'ȯ-dē-ˌō\ *adj* **1** : of or relating to frequencies (as of radio waves) corresponding to those of audible sound waves **2** : of or relating to sound or its reproduction and esp. high-fidelity sound reproduction **3** : relating to or used in the transmission or reception of sound

²audio *n* **1** : the transmission, reception, or reproduction of sound **2** : the section of television or motion-picture equipment that deals with sound

au·di·ol·o·gy \ˌȯ-dē-'ä-lə-jē\ *n* : a branch of science dealing with hearing and esp. with the treatment of individuals having trouble with hearing — **au·di·o·log·i·cal** \-ə-'lä-ji-kəl\ *adj* — **au·di·ol·o·gist** \-'ä-lə-jist\ *n*

au·dio·phile \'ȯ-dē-ō-ˌfī(-ə)l\ *n* : one who is enthusiastic about high-fidelity sound reproduction

au·dio·tape \'ȯ-dē-ō-ˌtāp\ *n* : a tape recording of sound

au·dio·vi·su·al \ˌȯ-dē-ō-'vi-zhə-wəl\ *adj* : of, relating to, or making use of both hearing and sight

au·dio·vi·su·als \-wəlz\ *n pl* : audiovisual teaching materials (as videotapes)

¹au·dit \'ȯ-dət\ *n* : a formal examination and verification of financial accounts

²audit *vb* **1** : to perform an audit on or for **2** : to attend (a course) without expecting full credit

¹au·di·tion \ȯ-'di-shən\ *n* **1** : HEARING **2** : a trial performance to appraise an entertainer's merits

²audition *vb* **-tioned; -tion·ing** \-'di-shə-niŋ\ : to give an audition to; *also* : to give a trial performance

au·di·tor \'ȯ-də-tər\ *n* **1** : LISTENER **2** : a person who audits

au·di·to·ri·um \ˌȯ-də-'tȯr-ē-əm\ *n, pl* **-ri·ums** *or* **-ria** \-rē-ə\ **1** : the part of a public building where an audience sits **2** : a hall or building used for public gatherings

au·di·to·ry \'ȯ-də-ˌtȯr-ē\ *adj* : of or relating to hearing or to the sense or organs of hearing ⟨∼ stimuli⟩

auditory tube *n* : EUSTACHIAN TUBE

auf Wie·der·seh·en \aúf-'vē-dər-ˌzān\ *interj* [G] — used to express farewell

Aug *abbr* August

au·ger \'ȯ-gər\ *n* : a tool for boring

aught \'ȯt, 'ät\ *n* : ZERO, CIPHER

aug·ment \ȯg-'ment\ *vb* : ENLARGE, INCREASE — **aug·men·ta·tion** \ˌȯg-mən-'tā-shən\ *n*

au gra·tin \ō-'gra-tᵊn, ȯ-, -'grä-\ *adj* [F, lit., with the burnt scrapings from the pan] : covered with bread crumbs or grated cheese and browned

¹au·gur \'ȯ-gər\ *n* : DIVINER, SOOTHSAYER

²augur *vb* **1** : to foretell esp. from omens **2** : to give promise of ⟨the decision doesn't ∼ well⟩

au·gu·ry \'ȯ-gyə-rē, -gə-\ *n, pl* **-ries** **1** : divination from omens **2** : OMEN, PORTENT

au·gust \ȯ-'gəst\ *adj* : marked by majestic dignity or grandeur — **au·gust·ly** *adv* — **au·gust·ness** *n*

Au·gust \'ȯ-gəst\ *n* [ME, fr. OE, fr. L *Augustus,* fr. *Augustus* Caesar] : the 8th month of the year

au jus \ō-'zhü, -'zhüs, -'jüs; ō-zhœ\ *adj* [F] : served in the juice obtained from roasting

auk \'ȯk\ *n* : any of several stocky black-and-white diving seabirds that breed in colder parts of the northern hemisphere

auld \'ȯl, 'ȯld, 'äl, 'äld\ *adj, chiefly Scot* : OLD

aunt \'ant, 'änt\ *n* **1** : the sister of one's father or mother **2** : the wife of one's uncle

aunt·ie \'an-tē, 'än-\ *n* : AUNT

au pair \ō-'per\ *n* [F, on even terms] : a usu. young foreign person who does domestic work for a family in return for room and board and to learn the family's language

au·ra \'ȯr-ə\ *n* **1** : a distinctive atmosphere surrounding a given source **2** : a luminous radiation

au·ral \'ȯr-əl\ *adj* : of or relating to the ear or to the sense of hearing

aurar *pl of* EYRIR

au·re·ole \'ȯr-ē-ˌōl\ *or* **au·re·o·la** \ȯ-'rē-ə-lə\ *n* : HALO, NIMBUS

au re·voir \ˌō-rə-'vwär\ *n* [F, lit., till seeing again] : GOOD-BYE

au·ri·cle \'ȯr-i-kəl\ *n* : an atrium of the heart

au·ric·u·lar \ȯ-'ri-kyə-lər\ *adj* **1** : told privately ⟨∼ confession⟩ **2** : known or recognized by the sense of hearing

au·ro·ra \ə-'rȯr-ə\ *n, pl* **auroras** *or* **au·ro·rae** \-(ˌ)ē\ : a luminous phenomenon of streamers or arches of light appearing in the upper atmosphere esp. of a planet's polar regions — **au·ro·ral** \-əl\ *adj*

aurora aus·tra·lis \-ȯ-'strā-ləs\ *n* : an aurora that occurs in earth's southern hemisphere

au·ro·ra bo·re·al·is \-ˌbȯr-ē-ˈa-ləs\ n : an aurora that occurs in earth's northern hemisphere

AUS abbr Army of the United States

aus·pice \ˈo-spəs\ n, pl **aus·pic·es** \-spə-səz, -ˌsēz\ [L auspicium, fr. auspic-, auspex diviner by birds, fr. avis bird + specere to look, look at] 1 : observation of birds by an augur 2 pl : kindly patronage and protection 3 : a prophetic sign or omen

aus·pi·cious \ȯ-ˈspi-shəs\ adj 1 : promising success : PROPITIOUS 2 : FORTUNATE, PROSPEROUS ⟨an ~ year⟩ — **aus·pi·cious·ly** adv — **aus·pi·cious·ness** n

aus·tere \ȯ-ˈstir\ adj 1 : STERN, SEVERE, STRICT ⟨~ Puritans⟩ 2 : markedly simple ⟨an ~ lifestyle⟩ 3 : UNADORNED ⟨~ furnishings⟩ — **aus·tere·ly** adv — **aus·ter·i·ty** \-ˈster-ə-tē\ n

aus·tral \ˈȯs-trəl\ adj : SOUTHERN

Aus·tro·ne·sian \ˌȯs-trə-ˈnē-zhən\ adj : of, relating to, or constituting a family of languages spoken in the area extending from Madagascar eastward through the Malay Peninsula to Hawaii and Easter Island

auth abbr 1 authentic 2 author 3 authorized

au·then·tic \ə-ˈthen-tik, ȯ-\ adj : GENUINE, REAL — **au·then·ti·cal·ly** \-ti-k(ə-)lē\ adv — **au·then·tic·i·ty** \-ˌthen-ˈti-sə-tē\ n

au·then·ti·cate \ə-ˈthen-ti-ˌkāt, ȯ-\ vb **-cat·ed; -cat·ing** : to prove genuine — **au·then·ti·ca·tion** \-ˌthen-ti-ˈkā-shən\ n

au·thor \ˈo-thər\ n [ME auctour, fr. AF auctor, autor, fr. L auctor originator, author, fr. augēre to increase] 1 : one that originates or creates 2 : one that writes or composes a literary work

au·thor·ess \ˈo-thə-rəs\ n : a woman author

au·tho·ri·sa·tion, au·tho·rise Brit var of AUTHORIZATION, AUTHORIZE

au·thor·i·tar·i·an \ȯ-ˌthär-ə-ˈter-ē-ən, ə-, -ˌthȯr-\ adj 1 : characterized by or favoring the principle of blind obedience to authority 2 : characterized by or favoring concentration of political power in an authority not responsible to the people — **authoritarian** n

au·thor·i·ta·tive \ə-ˈthär-ə-ˌtā-tiv, ȯ-, -ˈthȯr-\ adj : supported by, proceeding from, or being an authority — **au·thor·i·ta·tive·ly** adv — **au·thor·i·ta·tive·ness** n

au·thor·i·ty \ə-ˈthär-ə-tē, ȯ-, -ˈthȯr-\ n, pl **-ties** 1 : a citation used in support of a statement or in defense of an action; also : the source of such a citation 2 : one appealed to as an expert 3 : power to influence thought or behavior 4 : freedom granted : RIGHT 5 : persons in command; esp : GOVERNMENT 6 : convincing force

au·tho·rize \ˈo-thə-ˌrīz\ vb **-rized; -riz·ing** 1 : SANCTION ⟨custom authorized by time⟩ 2 : to give legal power to — **au·tho·ri·za·tion** \ˌo-thə-rə-ˈzā-shən\ n

au·thor·ship \ˈo-thər-ˌship\ n 1 : the state of being an author 2 : the source of a piece of writing, music, or art

au·tism \ˈo-ˌti-zəm\ n : a disorder that appears by age three and is characterized esp. by impaired ability to communicate with others and form normal social relationships and by repetitive patterns of behavior — **au·tis·tic** \ȯ-ˈtis-tik\ adj

¹**au·to** \ˈo-tō\ n, pl **autos** : AUTOMOBILE

²**auto** abbr automatic

au·to·bahn \ˈo-tō-ˌbän, ˈau̇-\ n : a German, Swiss, or Austrian expressway

au·to·bi·og·ra·phy \ˌo-tə-bī-ˈä-grə-fē\ n : the biography of a person narrated by that person — **au·to·bi·og·ra·pher** \-fər\ n — **au·to·bi·o·graph·i·cal** \-ˌbī-ə-ˈgra-fi-kəl\ adj — **au·to·bi·o·graph·i·cal·ly** \-k(ə-)lē\ adv

au·toch·tho·nous \ȯ-ˈtäk-thə-nəs\ adj : INDIGENOUS, NATIVE ⟨an ~ people⟩

au·to·clave \ˈo-tō-ˌklāv\ n : an apparatus (as for sterilizing) using superheated high-pressure steam

au·toc·ra·cy \ȯ-ˈtä-krə-sē\ n, pl **-cies** : government by one person having unlimited power — **au·to·crat** \ˈo-tə-ˌkrat\ n — **au·to·crat·ic** \ˌo-tə-ˈkra-tik\ adj — **au·to·crat·i·cal·ly** \-ti-k(ə-)lē\ adv

au·to·ex·po·sure \ˌo-tō-ik-ˈspō-zhər\ n : a camera system that automatically adjusts the exposure according to ambient light

¹**au·to·graph** \ˈo-tə-ˌgraf\ n 1 : an original manuscript 2 : a person's signature written by hand

²**autograph** vb : to write one's signature on

au·to·im·mune \ˌo-tō-i-ˈmyün\ adj : of, relating to, or caused by antibodies or lymphocytes that attack molecules, cells, or tissues of the organism producing them ⟨~ diseases⟩ — **au·to·im·mu·ni·ty** \-i-ˈmyü-nə-tē\ n

au·to·mate \ˈo-tə-ˌmāt\ vb **-mat·ed; -mat·ing** 1 : to operate automatically using mechanical or electronic devices 2 : to convert to automatic operation — **au·to·ma·tion** \ˌo-tə-ˈmā-shən\ n

automated teller machine n : ATM

¹**au·to·mat·ic** \ˌo-tə-ˈma-tik\ adj 1 : INVOLUNTARY 2 : made so that certain parts act in a desired manner at the proper time : SELF-ACTING ⟨an ~ transmission⟩ — **au·to·mat·i·cal·ly** \-ti-k(ə-)lē\ adv

²**automatic** n : an automatic device; esp : an automatic firearm

automatic teller n : ATM

automatic teller machine n : ATM

au·tom·a·ton \ȯ-ˈtä-mə-tən, -ˌtän\ n, pl **-atons** or **-a·ta** \-tə, -ˌtä\ 1 : an automatic machine; esp : ROBOT 2 : an individual who acts mechanically

au·to·mo·bile \ˈo-tə-mō-ˌbēl, ˌo-tə-mə-ˈbēl\ n : a usu. 4-wheeled automotive vehicle for passenger transportation

au·to·mo·tive \ˌo-tə-ˈmō-tiv\ adj 1 : of or relating to automobiles, trucks, or buses 2 : SELF-PROPELLED

au·to·nom·ic nervous system \ˌo-tə-ˈnä-mik-\ n : a part of the vertebrate nervous system that governs involuntary actions and that consists of the sympathetic nervous system and the parasympathetic nervous system

au·ton·o·mous \ȯ-'tä-nə-məs\ *adj* : having the right or power of self-government — **au·ton·o·mous·ly** *adv* — **au·ton·o·my** \-mē\ *n*

au·top·sy \'ȯ-,täp-sē, 'ȯ-təp-\ *n, pl* **-sies** [Gk *autopsia* act of seeing with one's own eyes, fr. *autos* self + *opsis* sight] : examination of a dead body usu. with dissection sufficient to determine the cause of death or extent of change produced by disease — **autopsy** *vb*

au·tumn \'ȯ-təm\ *n* : the season between summer and winter — **au·tum·nal** \ȯ-'təm-nəl\ *adj*

aux *abbr* auxiliary

¹aux·il·ia·ry \ȯg-'zil-yə-rē, -'zi-lə-rē\ *adj* 1 : providing help 2 : functioning in a subsidiary capacity 3 : accompanying a verb form to express person, number, mood, or tense ⟨~ verbs⟩

²auxiliary *n, pl* **-ries** 1 : an auxiliary person, group, or device 2 : an auxiliary verb

aux·in \'ȯk-sən\ *n* : a plant hormone that stimulates growth in length

av *abbr* 1 avenue 2 average 3 avoirdupois

AV *abbr* 1 ad valorem 2 audiovisual 3 Authorized Version

¹avail \ə-'vāl\ *vb* : to be of use or advantage : HELP, BENEFIT

²avail *n* : USE ⟨effort was of no ~⟩

avail·able \ə-'vā-lə-bəl\ *adj* 1 : USABLE ⟨~ resources⟩ 2 : ACCESSIBLE ⟨~ in any drugstore⟩ — **avail·abil·i·ty** \-,vā-lə-'bi-lə-tē\ *n*

av·a·lanche \'a-və-,lanch\ *n* : a mass of snow, ice, earth, or rock sliding down a mountainside

avant-garde \,ä-,vän-'gärd, -,vänt-\ *n* [F, vanguard] : those esp. in the arts who create or apply new or experimental ideas and techniques — **avant-garde** *adj*

av·a·rice \'a-və-rəs\ *n* : excessive desire for wealth : GREED — **av·a·ri·cious** \,a-və-'ri-shəs\ *adj*

avast \ə-'vast\ *vb imper* — a nautical command to stop or cease

av·a·tar \'a-və-,tär\ *n* [Skt *avatāra* descent] : INCARNATION

avaunt \ə-'vȯnt\ *adv* : AWAY, HENCE

avdp *abbr* avoirdupois

ave *abbr* avenue

Ave Ma·ria \,ä-,vä-mə-'rē-ə\ *n* : HAIL MARY 1

avenge \ə-'venj\ *vb* **avenged; aveng·ing** : to take vengeance for — **aveng·er** *n*

av·e·nue \'a-və-,nü, -,nyü\ *n* 1 : a way or route to a place or goal : PATH 2 : a broad street

aver \ə-'vər\ *vb* **averred; aver·ring** : ALLEGE, ASSERT; *also* : DECLARE

¹av·er·age \'a-və-rij, 'a-vrij\ *n* [earlier, proportionally distributed charge for damage at sea, modif. of MF *avarie* damage to ship or cargo, fr. It *avaria*, fr. Ar *ʿawārīyah* damaged merchandise] 1 : ARITHMETIC MEAN 2 : a ratio of suc-

cessful tries to total tries esp. in athletics ⟨batting ~ of .303⟩

²average *adj* 1 : equaling or approximating an arithmetic mean 2 : being about midway between extremes 3 : not out of the ordinary : COMMON

³average *vb* **av·er·aged; av·er·ag·ing** 1 : to be at or come to an average 2 : to be, do, or get usually 3 : to find the average of

averse \ə-'vərs\ *adj* : having an active feeling of dislike or reluctance ⟨~ to exercise⟩

aver·sion \ə-'vər-zhən\ *n* 1 : a feeling of repugnance for something with a desire to avoid it 2 : something decidedly disliked

avert \ə-'vərt\ *vb* 1 : to turn aside or away ⟨~ the eyes⟩ 2 : to ward off

avg *abbr* average

avi·an \'ā-vē-ən\ *adj* [L *avis* bird] : of, relating to, or derived from birds

avi·ary \'ā-vē-,er-ē\ *n, pl* **-ar·ies** : a place for keeping birds confined

avi·a·tion \,ā-vē-'ā-shən, ,a-\ *n* 1 : the operation of heavier-than-air aircraft 2 : aircraft manufacture, development, and design

avi·a·tor \'ā-vē-,ā-tər, 'a-\ *n* : an airplane pilot

avi·a·trix \,ā-vē-'ā-triks, ,a-\ *n, pl* **-trix·es** \-triks-səz\ *or* **-tri·ces** \-trə-,sēz\ : a woman airplane pilot

av·id \'a-vəd\ *adj* 1 : craving eagerly : GREEDY 2 : enthusiastic in pursuit of an interest — **avid·i·ty** \ə-'vi-də-tē, a-\ *n* — **av·id·ly** *adv* — **av·id·ness** *n*

avi·on·ics \,ā-vē-'ä-niks, ,a-\ *n pl* : electronics designed for use in aerospace vehicles — **avi·on·ic** \-nik\ *adj*

avo \'a-(,)vü\ *n, pl* **avos** — see pataca at MONEY table

av·o·ca·do \,a-və-'kä-dō, ,ä-\ *n, pl* **-dos** *also* **-does** [modif. of Sp *aguacate*, fr. Nahuatl *āhuacatl*, avocado, testicle] : a pulpy green- to purple-skinned nutty-flavored fruit of a tropical American tree; *also* : this tree

av·o·ca·tion \,a-və-'kā-shən\ *n* : HOBBY

av·o·cet \'a-və-,set\ *n* : any of several long-legged shorebirds with webbed feet and slender upward-curving bills

avoid \ə-'vȯid\ *vb* 1 : to keep away from : SHUN 2 : to prevent the occurrence of 3 : to refrain from — **avoid·able** *adj* — **avoid·ably** *adv* — **avoid·ance** \ə-'vȯi-dəns\ *n*

avoir·du·pois \,a-vər-də-'pȯiz\ *n* [ME *avoir de pois* goods sold by weight, fr. AF, lit., goods of weight] 1 : AVOIRDUPOIS WEIGHT 2 : WEIGHT, HEAVINESS; *esp* : personal weight

avoirdupois weight *n* : a system of weights based on a pound of 16 ounces and an ounce of 16 drams (28 grams) — see WEIGHT table

avouch \ə-'vauch\ *vb* 1 : to declare positively : AVER 2 : to vouch for

avow \ə-'vau\ *vb* : to declare openly — **avow·al** \-'vaú-(ə)l\ *n*

avun·cu·lar \ə-'vən-kyə-lər\ *adj* : of, relating to, or resembling an uncle

await \ə-'wāt\ vb : to wait for : EXPECT

¹**awake** \ə-'wāk\ vb **awoke** \-'wōk\ also **awaked** \-'wākt\; **awo·ken** \-'wō-kən\ or **awaked** also **awoke; awak·ing** : to bring back to consciousness : wake up

²**awake** adj : not asleep; also : ALERT

awak·en \ə-'wā-kən\ vb **awak·ened; awak·en·ing** \-'wā-kə-niŋ\ : AWAKE

¹**award** \ə-'word\ vb 1 : to give by judicial decision ⟨~ damages⟩ 2 : to give in recognition of merit or achievement

²**award** n 1 : a final decision : JUDGMENT 2 : something awarded : PRIZE

aware \ə-'wer\ adj : having perception or knowledge : CONSCIOUS, INFORMED — **aware·ness** n

awash \ə-'wosh, -'wäsh\ adj 1 : washed by waves or tide 2 : AFLOAT 3 : FLOODED ⟨the street was ~ after the storm⟩

¹**away** \ə-'wā\ adv 1 : from this or that place ⟨go ~⟩ 2 : out of the way 3 : in another direction ⟨turn ~⟩ 4 : out of existence ⟨fade ~⟩ 5 : from one's possession ⟨give ~⟩ 6 : without interruption ⟨chatter ~⟩ 7 : at a distance in space or time ⟨far ~⟩ ⟨~ back in 1910⟩

²**away** adj 1 : ABSENT 2 : distant in space or time ⟨a lake 10 miles ~⟩

¹**awe** \'o\ n 1 : profound and reverent dread of the supernatural 2 : respectful fear inspired by authority

²**awe** vb **awed; aw·ing** : to inspire with awe

aweigh \ə-'wā\ adj : just clear of the bottom ⟨anchors ~⟩

awe·some \'o-səm\ adj 1 : expressive of awe ⟨~ tribute⟩ 2 : inspiring awe

awe·struck \-ˌstrək\ also **awe·strick·en** \-ˌstri-kən\ adj : filled with awe

aw·ful \'o-fəl\ adj 1 : inspiring awe 2 : extremely disagreeable 3 : very great ⟨an ~ lot of money⟩ — **aw·ful·ly** adv

awhile \ə-'hwīl\ adv : for a while

awhirl \ə-'hwərl\ adj : being in a whirl

awk·ward \'o-kwərd\ adj 1 : CLUMSY ⟨~ with needle and thread⟩ 2 : UNGRACEFUL ⟨~ writing⟩ 3 : difficult to explain : EMBARRASSING 4 : difficult to deal with — **awk·ward·ly** adv — **awk·ward·ness** n

awl \'ol\ n : a pointed instrument for making small holes

aw·ning \'o-niŋ\ n : a rooflike cover (as of canvas) extended over or in front of a place as a shelter

AWOL \'ā-ˌwol, ˌā-ˌdə-bəl-yü-ˌō-'el\ n : a person who is absent without leave — **AWOL** adj or adv

awry \ə-'rī\ adv or adj 1 : ASKEW ⟨with hair ~⟩ 2 : AMISS ⟨their plans went ~⟩

ax or **axe** \'aks\ n : a chopping or cutting tool with an edged head fitted parallel to a handle

ax·i·al \'ak-sē-əl\ adj 1 : of, relating to, or functioning as an axis 2 : situated around, in the direction of, on, or along an axis — **ax·i·al·ly** adv

ax·i·om \'ak-sē-əm\ n [L axioma, fr. Gk axiōma, lit., something worthy, fr. axioun to think worthy, fr. axios worth, worthy] 1 : a statement generally accepted as true : MAXIM 2 : a proposition regarded as a self-evident truth — **ax·i·om·at·ic** \ˌak-sē-ə-'ma-tik\ adj — **ax·i·om·at·i·cal·ly** \-ti-k(ə-)lē\ adv

ax·is \'ak-səs\ n, pl **ax·es** \-ˌsēz\ 1 : a straight line around which a body rotates 2 : a straight line or structure with respect to which a body or figure is symmetrical 3 : one of the reference lines of a system of coordinates 4 : an alliance between major powers

ax·le \'ak-səl\ n : a shaft on which a wheel revolves

ax·on \'ak-ˌsän\ n : the long thin usu. unbranched part of a nerve cell that usu. conducts impulses away from the cell body

ayah \'ī-ə\ n [Hindi & Urdu āyā, fr. Pg aia, fr. L avia grandmother] : a nurse or maid native to India

aya·tol·lah \ˌī-ə-'tō-lə\ n [Pers āyatollāh, lit., sign of God, fr. Ar aya sign, miracle + allāh God] : an Islamic religious leader — used as a title of respect

¹**aye** also **ay** \'ā\ adv : ALWAYS, EVER

²**aye** also **ay** \'ī\ adv : YES

³**aye** also **ay** \'ī\ n, pl **ayes** : an affirmative vote

AZ abbr Arizona

aza·lea \ə-'zāl-yə\ n : any of numerous rhododendrons with funnel-shaped blossoms and usu. deciduous leaves

azi·do·thy·mi·dine \ə-ˌzi-dō-'thī-mə-ˌdēn\ n : AZT

az·i·muth \'a-zə-məth\ n : horizontal direction expressed as an angular distance from a fixed point

AZT \ˌā-(ˌ)zē-'tē\ n : an antiviral drug used to treat AIDS

Az·tec \'az-ˌtek\ n : a member of a Nahuatl-speaking people that founded the Mexican empire and were conquered by Hernan Cortes in 1519 — **Az·tec·an** adj

azure \'a-zhər\ n : the blue of the clear sky — **azure** adj

¹b \'bē\ *n, pl* **b's** *or* **bs** \'bēz\ *often cap* **1** : the 2d letter of the English alphabet **2** : a grade rating a student's work as good

²b *abbr, often cap* **1** bachelor **2** bass **3** bishop **4** book **5** born

B *symbol* boron

Ba *symbol* barium

BA *abbr* **1** bachelor of arts **2** batting average

bab·ble \'ba-bəl\ *vb* **bab·bled; bab·bling 1** : to talk enthusiastically or excessively **2** : to utter meaningless sounds — **babble** *n* — **bab·bler** \-b(ə-)lər\ *n*

babe \'bāb\ *n* **1** : BABY **2** *slang* : GIRL, WOMAN

ba·bel \'bā-bəl, 'ba-\ *n, often cap* [fr. the Tower of *Babel*, Gen 11:4–9] : a place or scene of noise and confusion; *also* : a confused sound ♦ *Synonyms* HUBBUB, RACKET, DIN, UPROAR, CLAMOR

ba·boon \ba-'bün\ *n* [ME *babewin*, fr. MF *babouin*, fr. *baboue* grimace] : any of several large apes of Asia and Africa with doglike muzzles

ba·bush·ka \bə-'büsh-kə, -'bush-\ *n* [Russ, grandmother, dim. of *baba* old woman] : a kerchief for the head

¹ba·by \'bā-bē\ *n, pl* **babies 1** : a very young child : INFANT **2** : the youngest or smallest of a group **3** : a childish person — **baby** *adj* — **ba·by·hood** *n* — **ba·by·ish** *adj*

²baby *vb* **ba·bied; ba·by·ing** : to tend or treat often with excessive care

baby boom *n* : a marked rise in birthrate — **baby boom·er** \-'bü-mər\ *n*

baby's breath *n* : any of a genus of herbs that are related to the pinks and have small delicate flowers

ba·by·sit \'bā-bē-,sit\ *vb* **-sat** \-,sat\; **-sitting** : to care for children usu. during a short absence of the parents — **ba·by·sit·ter** *n*

bac·ca·lau·re·ate \,ba-kə-'lȯr-ē-ət\ *n* **1** : the degree of bachelor conferred by colleges and universities **2** : a sermon delivered to a graduating class

bac·ca·rat \,bä-kə-'rä, ,ba-\ *n* : a card game in which three hands are dealt and players may be either or both hands against the dealer's

bac·cha·nal \'ba-kə-nᵊl, ,ba-kə-'nal, ,bä-kə-'näl\ *n* **1** : ORGY **2** : REVELER

bac·cha·na·lia \,ba-kə-'näl-yə\ *n, pl* **bacchanalia** : a drunken orgy — **bac·cha·na·lian** \-'näl-yən\ *adj or n*

bach·e·lor \'bach-lər, 'ba-chə-lər\ *n* **1** : a person who has received the usu. lowest degree conferred by a 4-year college **2** : an unmarried man — **bach·e·lor·hood** *n*

bach·e·lor·ette \,bach-lə-'ret, ,ba-chə-\ *n* : a young unmarried woman

bachelor's button *n* : a European plant related to the daisies and having usu. blue, pink, or white flower heads

ba·cil·lus \bə-'si-ləs\ *n, pl* **-li** \-,lī\ [NL, fr. ML, small staff, dim. of L *baculus* staff] : any of a genus of rod-shaped bacteria; *also* : a disease-producing bacterium — **bac·il·lary** \'ba-sə-,ler-ē\ *adj*

¹back \'bak\ *n* **1** : the rear or dorsal part of the human body; *also* : the corresponding part of a lower animal **2** : the part or surface opposite the front **3** : a player in the backfield in football — **back·less** \-ləs\ *adj*

²back *adv* **1** : to, toward, or at the rear **2** : AGO **3** : so as to be restrained or delayed **4** : to, toward, or in a former place or state **5** : in return or reply

³back *adj* **1** : located at or in the back; *also* : REMOTE **2** : OVERDUE ⟨∼ rent⟩ **3** : moving or operating backward **4** : not current ⟨∼ issues of a magazine⟩

⁴back *vb* **1** : SUPPORT, UPHOLD **2** : to go or cause to go backward or in reverse **3** : to furnish with a back : form the back of — **back·er** *n*

back·ache \'bak-,āk\ *n* : a pain in the lower back

back–bench·er \-'ben-chər\ *n* : a rank-and-file member of a British legislature

back·bite \-,bīt\ *vb* **-bit** \-,bit\; **-bit·ten** \-,bi-tᵊn\; **-bit·ing** : to say mean or spiteful things about someone who is absent — **back·bit·er** *n*

back·board \-,bȯrd\ *n* : a board placed at or serving as the back of something

back·bone \-,bōn\ *n* **1** : the bony column in the back of a vertebrate that is the chief support of the trunk and consists of a jointed series of vertebrae enclosing and protecting the spinal cord **2** : firm resolute character **3** : the primary high-speed hardware and transmission lines of a telecommunication network

back·drop \'bak-,dräp\ *n* : a painted cloth hung across the rear of a stage

back·field \-,fēld\ *n* : the football players whose positions are behind the line

¹back·fire \-,fī-(ə)r\ *n* : a loud noise caused by the improperly timed explosion of fuel in the cylinder of an internal combustion engine

²backfire *vb* **1** : to make or undergo a backfire **2** : to have a result opposite to what was intended

back·flip \-,flip\ *n* : a backward somersault esp. in the air

back·gam·mon \'bak-,ga-mən\ *n* : a game played with pieces on a double board in which the moves are determined by throwing dice

back·ground \'bak-,graünd\ *n* **1** : the scenery behind something **2** : the setting within which something takes place; *also* : the sum of a person's experience, training, and understanding

back·hand \'bak-,hand\ *n* : a stroke (as in tennis) made with the back of the hand turned in the direction of movement; *also* : the side on which such a stroke is made — **back·hand** *vb*

back·hand·ed \'bak-ˌhan-dəd\ *adj* **1** : IN-DIRECT, DEVIOUS; *esp* : SARCASTIC ⟨a ∼ compliment⟩ **2** : using or made with a backhand ⟨a ∼ catch⟩

back·hoe \'bak-ˌhō\ *n* : an excavating machine having a bucket that is drawn toward the machine

back·ing \'ba-kiŋ\ *n* **1** : something forming a back **2** : SUPPORT, AID ⟨needed financial ∼⟩; *also* : a body of supporters

back·lash \'bak-ˌlash\ *n* **1** : a sudden violent backward movement or reaction **2** : a strong adverse reaction

¹back·log \-ˌlȯg, -ˌläg\ *n* **1** : a large log at the back of a hearth fire **2** : an accumulation of tasks unperformed or materials not processed

²backlog *vb* : to accumulate in reserve

back of *prep* : BEHIND

back order *n* : a business order yet to be fulfilled because stock is unavailable — **back–order** *vb*

back out *vb* : to withdraw esp. from a commitment or contest

¹back·pack \'bak-ˌpak\ *n* : a camping pack supported by an aluminum frame and carried on the back

²backpack *vb* : to hike with a backpack — **back·pack·er** *n*

back·ped·al \'bak-ˌpe-dᵊl\ *vb* : RETREAT

back·rest \-ˌrest\ *n* : a rest for the back

back·side \-ˌsīd\ *n* : BUTTOCKS

back·slap \-ˌslap\ *vb* : to display excessive cordiality — **back·slap·per** *n*

back·slide \-ˌslīd\ *vb* **-slid** \-ˌslid\; **-slid** *or* **-slid·den** \-ˌsli-dᵊn\; **-slid·ing** \-ˌslī-diŋ\ : to lapse morally or in religious practice — **back·slid·er** *n*

back·space \-ˌspās\ *vb* : to move back a space in a text with the press of a key — **backspace** *n*

back·spin \-ˌspin\ *n* : a backward rotary motion of a ball

¹back·stage \'bak-ˌstāj\ *adj* **1** : relating to or occurring in the area behind a stage **2** : of or relating to the private lives of theater people **3** : of or relating to the inner working or operation

²back·stage \'bak-ˈstāj\ *adv* **1** : in or to a backstage area **2** : SECRETLY ⟨worked ∼ to gain support⟩

back·stairs \-ˌsterz\ *adj* : SECRET, FURTIVE; *also* : SORDID, SCANDALOUS

¹back·stop \-ˌstäp\ *n* : something serving as a stop behind something else; *esp* : a screen or fence to keep a ball from leaving the field of play

²backstop *vb* **1** : SUPPORT **2** : to serve as a backstop to

back·story \-ˌstȯr-ē\ *n* : a story that tells what led up to the main story or plot (as of a film)

back·stretch \'bak-ˈstrech\ *n* : the side opposite the homestretch on a racecourse

back·stroke \-ˌstrōk\ *n* : a swimming stroke executed on the back — **back·strok·er** \-ˌstrō-kər\ *n*

back talk *n* : impudent, insolent, or argumentative replies

back·track \'bak-ˌtrak\ *vb* **1** : to retrace one's course **2** : to reverse a position or stand

back·up \-ˌəp\ *n* **1** : one that serves as a substitute or alternative **2** : a copy of computer data — **back up** *vb*

¹back·ward \'bak-wərd\ *or* **back·wards** \-wərdz\ *adv* **1** : toward the back **2** : with the back foremost ⟨ride ∼⟩ **3** : in a reverse or contrary direction or way ⟨count ∼⟩ **4** : toward the past; *also* : toward a worse state

²backward *adj* **1** : directed, turned, or done backward **2** : DIFFIDENT, SHY **3** : slow in development or learning — **back·ward·ly** *adv* — **back·ward·ness** *n*

back·wash \'bak-ˌwȯsh, -ˌwäsh\ *n* : a backward flow or movement (as of water or air) produced by a propelling force (as the motion of oars)

back·wa·ter \-ˌwȯ-tər, -ˌwä-\ *n* **1** : water held or turned back in its course **2** : an isolated or backward place or condition

back·woods \-ˈwu̇dz\ *n pl* **1** : wooded or partly cleared areas far from cities **2** : a remote or isolated place

ba·con \'bā-kən\ *n* : salted and smoked meat from the sides or back of a pig

bacteria *pl of* BACTERIUM

bac·te·ri·cid·al \bak-ˌtir-ə-ˈsī-dᵊl\ *adj* : destroying bacteria — **bac·te·ri·cide** \-ˈtir-ə-ˌsīd\ *n*

bac·te·ri·ol·o·gy \bak-ˌtir-ē-ˈä-lə-jē\ *n* **1** : a science dealing with bacteria **2** : bacterial life and phenomena — **bac·te·ri·o·log·ic** \-ə-ˈlä-jik\ *or* **bac·te·ri·o·log·i·cal** \-ə-ˈlä-ji-kəl\ *adj* — **bac·te·ri·ol·o·gist** \-ˈä-lə-jist\ *n*

bac·te·rio·phage \bak-ˈtir-ē-ə-ˌfāj\ *n* : any of various viruses that attack specific bacteria

bac·te·ri·um \bak-ˈtir-ē-əm\ *n, pl* **-ria** \-ē-ə\ [NL, fr. Gk *baktērion* staff] : any of a group of single-celled microorganisms including some that cause disease and others that are valued esp. for their chemical effects (as fermentation) — **bac·te·ri·al** \-ē-əl\ *adj*

bad \'bad\ *adj* **worse** \'wərs\; **worst** \'wərst\ **1** : below standard : POOR; *also* : UNFAVORABLE ⟨a ∼ report⟩ **2** : SPOILED, DECAYED **3** : WICKED; *also* : not well-behaved : NAUGHTY **4** : DISAGREEABLE ⟨a ∼ taste⟩; *also* : HARMFUL **5** : DEFECTIVE, FAULTY ⟨∼ wiring⟩; *also* : not valid ⟨a ∼ check⟩ **6** : UNWELL, ILL **7** : SORRY, REGRETFUL ⟨feels ∼ about forgetting to call⟩ ♦ *Synonyms* EVIL, WRONG, IMMORAL, INIQUITOUS — **bad·ly** *adv* — **bad·ness** *n*

bade *past and past part of* BID

badge \'baj\ *n* : a device or token usu. worn as a sign of status

¹bad·ger \'ba-jər\ *n* : any of several sturdy burrowing mammals with long claws on their forefeet

²badger *vb* : to harass or annoy persistently

ba·di·nage \ˌba-də-ˈnäzh\ *n* [F] : playful talk back and forth : BANTER

bad·land \'bad-ˌland\ *n* : a region marked by intricate erosional sculpturing and scanty vegetation — usu. used in pl.

bad·min·ton \'bad-₁mi-t°n, -₁min-t°n\ *n* : a court game played with light rackets and a shuttlecock volleyed over a net

bad–mouth \'bad-₁maủth\ *vb* : to criticize severely

Bae·de·ker \'bā-di-kər, 'be-\ *n* : GUIDEBOOK

¹**baf·fle** \'ba-fəl\ *vb* **baf·fled; baf·fling** \-fə-liŋ\ *: FRUSTRATE, THWART, FOIL; also : PERPLEX* — **baf·fle·ment** *n*

²**baffle** *n* : a device (as a wall or screen) to deflect, check, or regulate flow (as of liquid or sound) — **baf·fled** \'ba-fəld\ *adj*

¹**bag** \'bag\ *n* **1** : a flexible usu. closable container (as for storing or carrying) **2** : something that bulges and sags like a bag ⟨~s under the eyes⟩

²**bag** *vb* **bagged; bag·ging 1** : DISTEND, BULGE **2** : to put in a bag **3** : to get possession of; *esp* : to take in hunting ♦ *Synonyms* TRAP, SNARE, CATCH, CAPTURE, COLLAR

ba·gasse \bə-'gas\ *n* [F] : plant residue (as of sugarcane) left after a product (as juice) has been extracted

bag·a·telle \₁ba-gə-'tel\ *n* [F] : TRIFLE 1

ba·gel \'bā-gəl\ *n* [Yiddish *beygl*] : a firm doughnut-shaped roll usu. made by boiling and then baking

bag·gage \'ba-gij\ *n* **1** : the traveling bags and personal belongings of a traveler : LUGGAGE **2** : intangible things that get in the way ⟨emotional ~⟩

bag·gies \'ba-gēz\ *n pl* : baggy pants or shorts

bag·gy \'ba-gē\ *adj* **bag·gi·er; -est** : puffed out or hanging like a bag ⟨a ~ sweater⟩ — **bag·gi·ly** \-gə-lē\ *adv* — **bag·gi·ness** \-gē-nəs\ *n*

bag·man \'bag-mən\ *n* : a person who collects or distributes illicitly gained money on behalf of another

ba·gnio \'ban-yō\ *n, pl* **bagnios** [It *bagno*, lit., public bath] : BROTHEL

bag of waters : a double-walled fluid-filled sac that encloses and protects the fetus in the womb and that breaks releasing its fluid during the process of birth

bag·pipe \'bag-₁pīp\ *n* : a musical wind instrument consisting of a bag, a tube with valves, and sounding pipes — often used in pl. — **bag·pip·er** \-₁pī-pər\ *n*

ba·guette \ba-'get\ *n* [F, lit., rod] **1** : a gem having the shape of a narrow rectangle; *also* : the shape itself **2** : a long thin loaf of French bread

baht \'bät\ *n, pl* **baht** *also* **bahts** — see MONEY table

¹**bail** \'bāl\ *n* : a container for ladling water out of a boat

²**bail** *vb* : to dip and throw out water from a boat — **bail·er** *n*

³**bail** *n* : security given to guarantee a prisoner's appearance when legally required; *also* : one giving such security or the release secured

⁴**bail** *vb* : to release under bail; *also* : to procure the release of by giving bail — **bail·able** \'bā-lə-bəl\ *adj*

⁵**bail** *n* : the arched handle (as of a pail or kettle)

bai·liff \'bā-ləf\ *n* **1** : an aide of a British sheriff who serves writs and makes arrests; *also* : a minor officer of a U.S. court **2** : an estate or farm manager esp. in Britain : STEWARD

bai·li·wick \'bā-li-₁wik\ *n* : one's special province or domain ♦ *Synonyms* TERRITORY, FIELD, SPHERE

bail·out \'bā-₁laủt\ *n* : a rescue from financial distress

bairn \'bern\ *n, chiefly Scot* : CHILD

¹**bait** \'bāt\ *vb* **1** : to persecute by continued attacks **2** : to harass with dogs usu. for sport ⟨~ a bear⟩ **3** : to furnish (as a hook) with bait **4** : ALLURE, ENTICE **5** : to give food and drink to (as an animal) ♦ *Synonyms* BADGER, HECKLE, HOUND

²**bait** *n* **1** : a lure for catching animals (as fish) **2** : LURE, TEMPTATION ♦ *Synonyms* SNARE, TRAP, DECOY, COME-ON, ENTICEMENT

bait·fish \'bāt-₁fish\ *n* : a small fish that attracts and is a food source for a larger fish; *also* : a fish used for bait

bai·za \'bī-(₁)zä\ *n, pl* **baiza** *or* **baizas** — see *rial* at MONEY table

baize \'bāz\ *n* : a coarse feltlike fabric

¹**bake** \'bāk\ *vb* **baked; bak·ing 1** : to cook or become cooked in dry heat esp. in an oven **2** : to dry and harden by heat ⟨~ bricks⟩ — **bak·er** *n*

²**bake** *n* : a social gathering featuring baked food

baker's dozen *n* : THIRTEEN

bak·ery \'bā-k(ə-)rē\ *n, pl* **-er·ies** : a place for baking or selling baked goods

bake sale *n* : a fund-raising event at which usu. homemade foods are sold

bake·shop \'bāk-₁shäp\ *n* : BAKERY

bake·ware \-₁wer\ *n* : dishes used for baking and serving food

baking powder *n* : a powder that consists of a carbonate, an acid, and a starch and that makes the dough rise in baking cakes and biscuits

baking soda *n* : SODIUM BICARBONATE

bak·sheesh \'bak-₁shēsh\ *n* : payment (as a tip or bribe) to expedite service

bal *abbr* balance

bal·a·lai·ka \₁ba-lə-'lī-kə\ *n* [Russ] : a triangular 3-stringed instrument of Russian origin played by plucking or strumming

¹**bal·ance** \'ba-ləns\ *n* [ME, fr. AF, fr. VL *bilancia*, fr. LL *bilanc-, bilanx* having two scalepans, fr. L *bi* two + *lanc-, lanx* plate] **1** : a weighing device : SCALE **2** : a weight, force, or influence counteracting the effect of another **3** : an oscillating wheel used to regulate a timepiece **4** : a state of equilibrium **5** : REMAINDER, REST; *esp* : an amount in excess esp. on the credit side of an account — **bal·anced** \-lənst\ *adj*

²**balance** *vb* **bal·anced; bal·anc·ing 1** : to compute the balance of an account **2** : to arrange so that one set of elements equals another; *also* : to equal or equalize in weight, number, or proportions **3** : WEIGH **4** : to bring or come to a state or position of balance; *also* : to bring into harmony or proportion

bal·boa \bal-'bō-ə\ *n* — see MONEY table

bal·brig·gan \bal-ˈbri-gən\ *n* : a knitted cotton fabric used esp. for underwear

bal·co·ny \ˈbal-kə-nē\ *n, pl* **-nies** **1** : a platform projecting from the side of a building and enclosed by a railing **2** : a gallery inside a building

bald \ˈbȯld\ *adj* **1** : lacking a natural or usual covering (as of hair) **2** : UNADORNED, PLAIN ⟨the ~ truth⟩ ♦ **Synonyms** BARE, BARREN, NAKED, NUDE — **bald·ly** *adv* — **bald·ness** *n*

bal·da·chin \ˈbȯl-də-kən, ˈbal-\ *or* **bal·dachi·no** \ˌbal-də-ˈkē-nō\ *n, pl* **-chins** *or* **-chinos** : a canopylike structure over an altar

bald cypress *n* : either of two coniferous trees of southern U.S. swamps; *also* : their hard red wood

bald eagle *n* : a large brown eagle of No. America that when mature has white head and neck feathers and a white tail

bal·der·dash \ˈbȯl-dər-ˌdash\ *n* : NONSENSE

bald·ing \ˈbȯl-diŋ\ *adj* : becoming bald

bal·dric \ˈbȯl-drik\ *n* : a belt worn over the shoulder to carry a sword or bugle

¹bale \ˈbāl\ *n* : a large or closely packed bundle

²bale *vb* **baled**; **bal·ing** : to pack in a bale — **bal·er** *n*

ba·leen \bə-ˈlēn\ *n* : a horny substance attached in plates to the upper jaw of some large whales (**baleen whales**)

bale·ful \ˈbāl-fəl\ *adj* : DEADLY, HARMFUL; *also* : OMINOUS ♦ **Synonyms** SINISTER, MALEFIC, MALEFICENT, MALIGN

¹balk \ˈbȯk\ *n* **1** : HINDRANCE, CHECK, SETBACK **2** : an illegal motion of the pitcher in baseball while in position

²balk *vb* **1** : BLOCK, THWART **2** : to stop short and refuse to go on **3** : to commit a balk in sports ♦ **Synonyms** FRUSTRATE, BAFFLE, FOIL, THWART — **balky** \ˈbȯ-kē\ *adj*

¹ball \ˈbȯl\ *n* **1** : a rounded body or mass (as an object used in a game or as a missile); *also* : a roundish protuberant part of the body ⟨the ~ of the foot⟩ **2** : a game played with a ball **3** : a pitched baseball that misses the strike zone and is not swung at by the batter **4** : a hit or thrown ball in various games ⟨foul ~⟩ — **on the ball** : COMPETENT, KNOWLEDGEABLE, ALERT

²ball *vb* : to form into a ball

³ball *n* : a large formal dance

bal·lad \ˈba-ləd\ *n* **1** : a narrative poem of strongly marked rhythm suitable for singing **2** : a simple song : AIR **3** : a slow romantic song

bal·lad·eer \ˌba-lə-ˈdir\ *n* : a singer of ballads

¹bal·last \ˈba-ləst\ *n* **1** : heavy material used to stabilize a ship or control a balloon's ascent **2** : crushed stone laid in a railroad bed or used in making concrete

²ballast *vb* : to provide with ballast ♦ **Synonyms** BALANCE, STABILIZE, STEADY

ball bearing *n* : a bearing in which the revolving part turns upon steel balls that roll easily in a groove; *also* : one of the balls in such a bearing

ball·car·ri·er \ˈbȯl-ˌker-ē-ər\ *n* : the football player carrying the ball in an offensive play

ball·er \ˈbȯ-lər\ *n* : an implement for shaping food into a ball ⟨melon ~⟩

bal·le·ri·na \ˌba-lə-ˈrē-nə\ *n* : a female ballet dancer

bal·let \ˈba-ˌlā, ba-ˈlā\ *n* **1** : dancing in which fixed poses and steps are combined with light flowing movements often to convey a story; *also* : a theatrical art form using ballet dancing **2** : a company of ballet dancers

bal·let·o·mane \ba-ˈle-tə-ˌmān\ *n* : a devotee of ballet

bal·lis·tic missile \bə-ˈlis-tik-\ *n* : a missile that is guided during ascent and that falls freely during descent

bal·lis·tics \-tiks\ *n sing or pl* **1** : the science of the motion of projectiles (as bullets) in flight **2** : the flight characteristics of a projectile — **ballistic** *adj*

ball of fire : an unusually energetic person

¹bal·loon \bə-ˈlün\ *n* **1** : a bag filled with gas or heated air so as to rise and float in the atmosphere usu. carrying a suspended load **2** : an inflatable bag used as a toy or decoration — **bal·loon·ist** *n*

²balloon *vb* **1** : to swell or puff out **2** : to travel in a balloon **3** : to increase rapidly

¹bal·lot \ˈba-lət\ *n* [It *ballotta* small ball used in secret voting, fr. It dial., dim. of *balla* ball] **1** : a piece of paper used to cast a vote **2** : the action or a system of voting; *also* : the right to vote

²ballot *vb* : to decide by ballot : VOTE

ball·park \ˈbȯl-ˌpärk\ *n* : a park in which ball games are played

²ballpark *adj* : approximately correct ⟨~ estimate⟩

ball·point \ˈbȯl-ˌpȯint\ *n* : a pen whose writing point is a small rotating metal ball that inks itself from an inner container

ball·room \ˈbȯl-ˌrüm, -ˌrum\ *n* : a large room for dances

ballroom dance *n* : any of various dances (as the tango, two-step, and waltz) in which couples perform set moves

bal·ly·hoo \ˈba-lē-ˌhü\ *n, pl* **-hoos** : extravagant statements and claims made for publicity — **ballyhoo** *vb*

balm \ˈbäm, ˈbälm\ *n* **1** : a fragrant healing or soothing lotion or ointment **2** : any of several spicy fragrant herbs of the mint family **3** : something that comforts or soothes

balmy \ˈbä-mē, ˈbäl-\ *adj* **balm·i·er; -est** **1** : gently soothing : MILD **2** : FOOLISH, ABSURD ♦ **Synonyms** SOFT, BLAND, MILD, GENTLE — **balm·i·ness** *n*

ba·lo·ney \bə-ˈlō-nē\ *n* : NONSENSE

bal·sa \ˈbȯl-sə\ *n* : the extremely light strong wood of a tropical American tree; *also* : the tree

bal·sam \ˈbȯl-səm\ *n* **1** : a fragrant aromatic and usu. resinous substance oozing from various plants; *also* : a preparation containing or smelling like balsam **2** : a balsam-yielding tree (as balsam fir) **3** : a common garden ornamental plant — **bal·sam·ic** \bȯl-ˈsa-mik\ *adj*

balsam fir *n* : a resinous No. American evergreen tree that is widely used for pulpwood and as a Christmas tree

balsamic vinegar *n* : an aged Italian vinegar made from white grapes

Balt \'bȯlt\ *n* : a native or inhabitant of Lithuania, Latvia, or Estonia

Bal·ti·more oriole \'bȯl-tə-ˌmȯr-\ *n* : a common American oriole in which the male is brightly colored with orange, black, and white

bal·us·ter \'ba-lə-stər\ *n* [F *balustre*, fr. It *balaustro*, fr. *balaustra* wild pomegranate flower, fr. L *balaustium*; fr. its shape] : an upright support for a rail (as of a staircase)

bal·us·trade \'ba-lə-ˌstrād\ *n* : a row of balusters topped by a rail

bam·boo \bam-'bü\ *n, pl* **bamboos** : any of various woody mostly tall tropical grasses including some with strong hollow stems used for building, furniture, or utensils

bamboo curtain *n, often cap B&C* : a political, military, and ideological barrier in eastern Asia

bam·boo·zle \bam-'bü-zəl\ *vb* **-boo·zled; -boo·zling** : TRICK, HOODWINK

¹**ban** \'ban\ *vb* **banned; ban·ning** : PROHIBIT, FORBID

²**ban** *n* **1** : CURSE **2** : a legal or formal prohibition ⟨a ∼ on beef imports⟩

³**ban** \'bän\ *n, pl* **ba·ni** \'bä-nē\ — see *leu* at MONEY table

ba·nal \bə-'näl, -'nal; 'bā-nᵊl\ *adj* [F] : COMMONPLACE, TRITE ⟨∼ remarks⟩ — **ba·nal·i·ty** \bā-'na-lə-tē\ *n*

ba·nana \bə-'na-nə\ *n* : a treelike tropical plant bearing thick clusters of yellow or reddish finger-shaped fruit; *also* : this fruit

¹**band** \'band\ *n* **1** : something that binds, ties, or goes around **2** : a strip or stripe that can be distinguished (as by color or texture) from nearby ones **3** : a range of wavelengths (as in radio)

²**band** *vb* **1** : to tie up, finish, or enclose with a band **2** : to gather together or unite esp. for some common end — **band·er** *n*

³**band** *n* : a group of persons, animals, or things; *esp* : a group of musicians organized for playing together

¹**ban·dage** \'ban-dij\ *n* : a strip of material used esp. in dressing wounds

²**bandage** *vb* **ban·daged; ban·dag·ing** : to dress or cover with a bandage

Band–Aid \'ban-ˌdād\ *adj* : offering, making use of, or serving as a temporary or expedient remedy or solution

ban·dan·na *or* **ban·dana** \ban-'da-nə\ *n* : a large colored figured handkerchief

B and B *abbr* bed-and-breakfast

band·box \'band-ˌbäks\ *n* : a usu. cylindrical box for carrying clothing

band·ed \'ban-dəd\ *adj* : having or marked with bands

ban·de·role *or* **ban·de·rol** \'ban-də-ˌrōl\ *n* : a long narrow forked flag or streamer

ban·dit \'ban-dət\ *n* [It *bandito*, fr. *bandire* to banish] **1** *pl also* **ban·dit·ti** \ban-'di-tē\ : an outlaw who lives by plunder;

esp : a member of a band of marauders **2** : ROBBER — **ban·dit·ry** \'ban-də-trē\ *n*

ban·do·lier *or* **ban·do·leer** \ˌban-də-'lir\ *n* : a belt slung over the shoulder esp. to carry ammunition

band saw *n* : a saw in the form of an endless steel belt running over pulleys

band·stand \'band-ˌstand\ *n* : a usu. roofed platform on which a band or orchestra performs outdoors

b and w *abbr* black and white

band·wag·on \'band-ˌwa-gən\ *n* **1** : a wagon carrying musicians in a parade **2** : a movement that attracts growing support ⟨a political ∼⟩

band·width \-ˌwidth\ *n* : the capacity for data transfer of an electronic communication system

¹**ban·dy** \'ban-dē\ *vb* **ban·died; ban·dy·ing 1** : to exchange (as blows or quips) esp. in rapid succession **2** : to use in a glib or offhand way

²**bandy** *adj* : curved outward ⟨∼ legs⟩

bane \'bān\ *n* **1** : POISON **2** : WOE, HARM; *also* : a source of this — **bane·ful** *adj*

¹**bang** \'baŋ\ *vb* **1** : BUMP ⟨fell and ∼ed his knee⟩ **2** : to strike, thrust, or move usu. with a loud noise

²**bang** *n* **1** : a resounding blow **2** : a sudden loud noise

³**bang** *adv* : DIRECTLY, RIGHT ⟨ran ∼ up against more trouble⟩

⁴**bang** *n* : a fringe of hair cut short (as across the forehead) — usu. used in pl.

⁵**bang** *vb* : to cut (as hair) to produce bangs

ban·gle \'baŋ-gəl\ *n* **1** : BRACELET **2** : a loose-hanging ornament

bang–up \'baŋ-ˌəp\ *adj* : FIRST-RATE, EXCELLENT ⟨a ∼ job⟩

bani *pl of* ³BAN

ban·ish \'ba-nish\ *vb* **1** : to require by authority to leave a country **2** : to drive out : EXPEL ♦ **Synonyms** EXILE, OSTRACIZE, DEPORT, RELEGATE — **ban·ish·ment** *n*

ban·is·ter \'ba-nə-stər\ *n* **1** : a handrail with its supporting posts **2** : HANDRAIL **3** : BALUSTER

ban·jo \'ban-jō\ *n, pl* **banjos** *also* **banjoes** : a musical instrument with a long neck, a drumlike body, and usu. five strings — **ban·jo·ist** \-ist\ *n*

¹**bank** \'baŋk\ *n* **1** : a piled-up mass (as of cloud or earth) **2** : an undersea elevation **3** : rising ground bordering a lake, river, or sea **4** : the sideways slope of a surface along a curve or of a vehicle as it rounds a curve

²**bank** *vb* **1** : to form a bank about **2** : to cover (as a fire) with fuel to keep inactive **3** : to build (a curve) with the roadbed or track inclined laterally upward from the inside edge **4** : to pile or heap in a bank; *also* : to arrange in a tier **5** : to incline (an airplane) in turning

³**bank** *n* [ME, fr. MF or It; MF *banque*, fr. It *banca*, lit., bench, of Gmc origin] **1** : an establishment concerned esp. with the custody, loan, exchange, or issue of money, the extension of credit, and the transmission of funds **2** : a stock of or a

place for holding something in reserve ⟨a blood ∼⟩

⁴bank *vb* **1** : to conduct the business of a bank **2** : to deposit money or have an account in a bank — **bank·er** *n* — **bank·ing** *n*

⁵bank *n* : a group of objects arranged close together (as in a row or tier) ⟨a ∼ of file drawers⟩

bank·book \'baŋk-ˌbŭk\ *n* : the depositor's book in which a bank records deposits and withdrawals

bank·card \-ˌkärd\ *n* : a card (as a credit card or an ATM card) issued by a bank

bank·note \-ˌnōt\ *n* : a promissory note issued by a bank and circulating as money

bank·roll \-ˌrōl\ *n* : supply of money : FUNDS

¹bank·rupt \'baŋk-(ˌ)rəpt\ *n* [modif. of MF *banqueroute* bankruptcy, fr. It *bancarotta*, fr. *banca* bank + *rotta* broken] : an insolvent person; *esp* : one whose property is turned over by court action to a trustee to be handled for the benefit of his creditors — **bankrupt** *vb*

²bankrupt *adj* **1** : reduced to financial ruin; *esp* : legally declared a bankrupt **2** : wholly lacking in or deprived of some essential ⟨morally ∼⟩ — **bank·rupt·cy** \'baŋk-(ˌ)rəpt-sē\ *n*

¹ban·ner \'ba-nər\ *n* **1** : a piece of cloth attached to a staff and used by a leader as his standard **2** : FLAG **3** : an advertisement that runs usu. across the top of a Web page

²banner *adj* : distinguished from all others esp. in excellence ⟨a ∼ year⟩

ban·nock \'ba-nək\ *n* : a flat oatmeal or barley cake usu. cooked on a griddle

banns \'banz\ *n pl* : public announcement esp. in church of a proposed marriage

ban·quet \'baŋ-kwət\ *n* [MF, fr. It *banchetto*, fr. dim. of *banca* bench] : a ceremonial dinner — **banquet** *vb*

ban·quette \baŋ-'ket\ *n* : a long upholstered bench esp. along a wall

ban·shee \'ban-shē\ *n* [Ir *bean sídhe* & ScGael *bean sìth*, lit., woman of fairyland] : a female spirit in Gaelic folklore whose wailing warns a family that one of them will soon die

ban·tam \'ban-təm\ *n* **1** : any of numerous small domestic fowls that are often miniatures of standard breeds **2** : a small but pugnacious person

¹ban·ter \'ban-tər\ *vb* : to speak to in a witty and teasing manner

²banter *n* : good-natured witty joking

Ban·tu \'ban-ˌtü\ *n, pl* **Bantu** or **Bantus** **1** : a group of languages spoken in central and southern Africa **2** : a member of a group of African peoples who speak Bantu

ban·yan \'ban-yən\ *n* : a large tropical Asian tree whose aerial roots grow downward to the ground and from new trunks

ban·zai \bän-'zī\ *n* : a Japanese cheer or cry of triumph

bao·bab \'baù-ˌbab, 'bä-ə-\ *n* : a tropical African tree with short swollen trunk and sour edible fruits resembling gourds

bap·tism \'bap-ˌti-zəm\ *n* **1** : a Christian sacrament signifying spiritual rebirth and symbolized by the ritual use of water **2** : an act of baptizing — **bap·tis·mal** \bap-'tiz-məl\ *adj*

baptismal name *n* : GIVEN NAME

Bap·tist \'bap-tist\ *n* : a member of any of several Protestant denominations emphasizing baptism by immersion of believers only

bap·tis·tery or **bap·tis·try** \'bap-tə-strē\ *n, pl* **-ter·ies** or **-tries** : a place esp. in a church used for baptism

bap·tize \bap-'tīz, 'bap-ˌtīz\ *vb* **bap·tized**; **bap·tiz·ing** [ME, fr. AF *baptiser*, fr. L *baptizare*, fr. Gk *baptizein* to dip, baptize, fr. *baptein* to dip] **1** : to administer baptism to; *also* : CHRISTEN **2** : to purify esp. by an ordeal

¹bar \'bär\ *n* **1** : a long narrow piece of material (as wood or metal) used esp. for a lever, fastening, or support **2** : BARRIER, OBSTACLE **3** : the railing in a law court at which prisoners are stationed; *also* : the legal profession or the whole body of lawyers **4** : a stripe, band, or line much longer than wide **5** : a counter at which food or esp. drink is served; *also* : BARROOM **6** : a vertical line across the musical staff

²bar *vb* **barred**; **bar·ring** **1** : to fasten, confine, or obstruct with or as if with a bar or bars **2** : to mark with bars : STRIPE **3** : to shut up or keep out : EXCLUDE **4** : FORBID, PREVENT

³bar *prep* : EXCEPT ⟨the most popular actor, ∼ none⟩

⁴bar *abbr* barometer; barometric

Bar *abbr* Baruch

barb \'bärb\ *n* **1** : a sharp projection extending backward (as from the point of an arrow) **2** : a biting critical remark — **barbed** \'bärbd\ *adj* — **barb·less** \'bärb-ləs\ *adj*

bar·bar·ian \bär-'ber-ē-ən\ *adj* **1** : of, relating to, or being a land, culture, or people alien to another's **2** : lacking refinement, learning, or artistic or literary culture — **barbarian** *n* — **bar·bar·i·an·ism** \-ē-ə-ˌni-zəm\ *n*

bar·bar·ic \bär-'ber-ik\ *adj* **1** : BARBARIAN ⟨∼ tribes⟩ **2** : marked by a lack of restraint : WILD ⟨∼ attacks⟩ **3** : PRIMITIVE, UNSOPHISTICATED

bar·ba·rism \'bär-bə-ˌri-zəm\ *n* **1** : the social condition of barbarians; *also* : the use or display of barbarian or barbarous acts, attitudes, or ideas **2** : a word or expression that offends standards of correctness or purity

bar·ba·rous \'bär-bə-rəs\ *adj* **1** : lacking culture or refinement **2** : using linguistic barbarisms **3** : mercilessly harsh or cruel — **bar·bar·i·ty** \bär-'ber-ə-tē\ *n* — **bar·ba·rous·ly** *adv* — **bar·ba·rous·ness** *n*

¹bar·be·cue \'bär-bi-ˌkyü\ *vb* **-cued**; **-cu·ing** **1** : to cook on a rack or revolving spit over or before a source of heat **2** : to cook in a highly seasoned vinegar sauce

²**barbecue** *n* : a social gathering at which barbecued food is served

bar·bell \'bär-ˌbel\ *n* : a bar with adjustable weights attached to each end used for exercise and in weight-lifting competition

bar·ber \'bär-bər\ *n* [ME, fr. AF *barbour*, fr. *barbe* beard, fr. L *barba*] : one whose business is cutting and dressing hair and shaving and trimming beards

bar·ber·ry \'bär-ˌber-ē\ *n* : any of a genus of spiny shrubs bearing yellow flowers and oblong red berries

bar·bi·tu·rate \bär-'bi-chə-rət\ *n* : any of various compounds (as a salt or ester) formed from an organic acid (**bar·bi·tu·ric acid** \ˌbär-bə-'tür-ik-, -'tyür-\) : *esp* : one used as a sedative or hypnotic

bar·ca·role *or* **bar·ca·rolle** \'bär-kə-ˌrōl\ *n* : a Venetian boat song characterized by a beat suggesting a rowing rhythm; *also* : a piece of music imitating this

bar chart *n* : BAR GRAPH

bar code *n* : a set of printed and variously spaced bars and sometimes numerals that is designed to be scanned to provide information about the object it labels — **bar–cod·ed** \'bär-ˌkō-dəd\ *adj* — **bar coding** *n*

bard \'bärd\ *n* : POET

¹**bare** \'ber\ *adj* **bar·er; bar·est 1** : NAKED **2** : UNCONCEALED, EXPOSED **3** : EMPTY ⟨the cupboard was ∼⟩ **4** : leaving nothing to spare : MERE **5** : PLAIN, UNADORNED ⟨the ∼ facts⟩ ♦ *Synonyms* NUDE, BALD — **bare·ness** *n*

²**bare** *vb* **bared; bar·ing** : to make or lay bare : UNCOVER

bare·back \-ˌbak\ *or* **bare·backed** \-'bakt\ *adv or adj* : without a saddle

bare·faced \-'fāst\ *adj* **1** : having the face uncovered; *esp* : BEARDLESS **2** : not concealed : OPEN ⟨a ∼ lie⟩ — **bare·faced·ly** \-'fā-səd-lē, -'fāst-lē\ *adv*

bare·foot \-ˌfut\ *or* **bare·foot·ed** \-'fu-təd\ *adv or adj* : with bare feet

bare–hand·ed \-'han-dəd\ *adv or adj* **1** : without gloves **2** : without tools or weapons ⟨∼ fighting⟩

bare·head·ed \-'he-dəd\ *adv or adj* : without a hat

bare·ly \'ber-lē\ *adv* **1** : PLAINLY, MEAGERLY ⟨a ∼ furnished room⟩ **2** : by a narrow margin : only just ⟨∼ enough money⟩

bar·fly \'bär-ˌflī\ *n* : a drinker who frequents bars

¹**bar·gain** \'bär-gən\ *n* **1** : AGREEMENT **2** : an advantageous purchase **3** : a transaction, situation, or event regarded in the light of its results

²**bargain** *vb* **1** : to negotiate over the terms of an agreement; *also* : to come to terms **2** : BARTER

bar·gain–base·ment \'bär-gən-'bās-mənt\ *adj* : markedly inexpensive

¹**barge** \'bärj\ *n* **1** : a broad flat-bottomed boat usu. moved by towing **2** : a motorboat supplied to a flagship (as for an admiral) **3** : a ceremonial boat elegantly furnished — **barge·man** \-mən\ *n*

²**barge** *vb* **barged; barg·ing 1** : to carry by barge **2** : to move or thrust oneself clumsily or rudely

bar graph *n* : a graphic technique for comparing amounts by rectangles whose lengths are proportional to the amounts they represent

ba·ris·ta \bə-'rēs-tə\ *n* : a person who makes and serves coffee to the public

bari·tone \'ber-ə-ˌtōn\ *n* [F *baryton* or It *baritono*, fr. Gk *barytonos* deep sounding, fr. *barys* heavy + *tonos* tone] : a male voice between bass and tenor; *also* : a man with such a voice

bar·i·um \'ber-ē-əm\ *n* : a silver-white metallic chemical element that occurs only in combination

¹**bark** \'bärk\ *vb* **1** : to make the short loud cry of a dog **2** : to speak or utter in a curt loud tone : SNAP

²**bark** *n* : the sound made by a barking dog

³**bark** *n* : the tough corky outer covering of a woody stem or root

⁴**bark** *vb* **1** : to strip the bark from **2** : to rub the skin from : ABRADE

⁵**bark** *n* : a ship of three or more masts with the aft mast fore-and-aft rigged and the others square-rigged

bar·keep \'bär-ˌkēp\ *also* **bar·keep·er** \-ˌkē-pər\ *n* : BARTENDER

bark·er \'bär-kər\ *n* : a person who stands at the entrance esp. to a show and tries to attract customers to it

bar·ley \'bär-lē\ *n* : a cereal grass with seeds used as food and in making malt liquors; *also* : its seed

bar mitz·vah \bär-'mits-və\ *n, often cap B&M* [Heb *bar miṣwāh*, lit., son of the (divine) law] **1** : a Jewish boy who at about 13 years of age assumes religious responsibilities **2** : the ceremony recognizing a boy as a bar mitzvah

barn \'bärn\ *n* [ME *bern*, fr. OE *bereærn*, fr. *bere* barley + *ærn* house, store] : a building used esp. for storing hay and grain and often for housing livestock or farm equipment

bar·na·cle \'bär-ni-kəl\ *n* : any of numerous small marine crustaceans free-swimming when young but permanently fixed (as to rocks, whales, or ships) when adult

barn·storm \'bärn-ˌstȯrm\ *vb* : to travel through the country making brief stops to entertain (as with shows or flying stunts) or to campaign for political office

barn·yard \-ˌyärd\ *n* : a usu. fenced area adjoining a barn

baro·graph \'ber-ə-ˌgraf\ *n* : a recording barometer

ba·rom·e·ter \bə-'räm-ə-tər\ *n* : an instrument for measuring atmospheric pressure — **baro·met·ric** \ˌbar-ə-'me-trik\ *adj*

bar·on \'ber-ən\ *n* : a member of the lowest grade of the British peerage — **ba·ro·ni·al** \bə-'rō-nē-əl\ *adj* — **bar·ony** \'ber-ə-nē\ *n*

bar·on·age \'ber-ə-nij\ *n* : PEERAGE

bar·on·ess \'ber-ə-nəs\ *n* **1** : the wife or widow of a baron **2** : a woman holding a baronial title in her own right

bar·on·et \'ber-ə-nət\ *n* : a man holding a

rank of honor below a baron but above a knight — **bar·on·et·cy** \-sē\ n

ba·roque \bə-'rōk, -'räk\ adj : marked by the use of complex forms, bold ornamentation, and the juxtapositioning of contrasting elements

ba·rouche \bə-'rüsh\ n [G Barutsche, fr. It biroccio, ultim. fr. LL birotus two-wheeled, fr. L bi- two + rota wheel] : a 4-wheeled carriage with a high driver's seat in front and a folding top

bar·racks \'ber-əks\ n sing or pl : a building or group of buildings for lodging soldiers

bar·ra·cu·da \ber-ə-'kü-də\ n, pl -da or -das : any of several large slender predaceous sea fishes including some used for food

bar·rage \bə-'räzh, -'räj\ n : a heavy concentration of fire (as of artillery)

barred \'bärd\ adj : STRIPED

¹**bar·rel** \'ber-əl\ n 1 : a round bulging cask with flat ends of equal diameter 2 : the amount contained in a barrel 3 : a cylindrical or tubular part ⟨gun ∼⟩ — **bar·reled** \-əld\ adj

²**barrel** vb **-reled** or **-relled**; **-rel·ing** or **-rel·ling** 1 : to pack in a barrel 2 : to travel at high speed

bar·rel·head \-,hed\ n : the flat end of a barrel — **on the barrelhead** : asking for or granting no credit ⟨paid cash on the barrelhead⟩

barrel roll n : an airplane maneuver in which a complete revolution about the longitudinal axis is made

¹**bar·ren** \'ber-ən\ adj 1 : STERILE, UNFRUITFUL 2 : unproductive of results ⟨a ∼ scheme⟩ 3 : lacking interest or charm 4 : lacking inspiration or ideas — **bar·ren·ness** \-nəs\ n

²**barren** n : a tract of barren land

bar·rette \bä-'ret, bə-\ n : a clasp or bar for holding the hair in place

¹**bar·ri·cade** \'ber-ə-,kād, ,ber-ə-'kād\ vb **-cad·ed; -cad·ing** : to block, obstruct, or fortify with a barricade

²**barricade** n [F, fr. MF, fr. barriquer to barricade, fr. barrique barrel] 1 : a hastily thrown-up obstruction or fortification 2 : BARRIER, OBSTACLE

bar·ri·er \'ber-ē-ər\ n : something that separates, demarcates, or serves as a barricade ⟨racial ∼s⟩

barrier island n : a long broad sandy island lying parallel to a shore

barrier reef n : a coral reef roughly parallel to a shore and separated from it usu. by a lagoon

bar·ring \'bär-iŋ\ prep : excluding by exception : EXCEPTING

bar·rio \'bär-ē-,ō, 'ber-\ n, pl **-ri·os** 1 : a district of a city or town in a Spanish-speaking country 2 : a Spanish-speaking quarter in a U.S. city

bar·ris·ter \'ber-ə-stər\ n : a British counselor admitted to plead in the higher courts

bar·room \'bär-,rüm, -,rum\ n : a room or establishment whose main feature is a bar for the sale of liquor

¹**bar·row** \'ber-ō\ n : a large burial mound of earth and stones

²**barrow** n 1 : WHEELBARROW 2 : a cart with a boxlike body and two shafts for pushing it

Bart abbr baronet

bar·tend·er \'bär-,ten-dər\ n : a person who serves liquor at a bar

bar·ter \'bär-tər\ vb : to trade by exchange of goods — **barter** n — **bar·ter·er** n

Ba·ruch \'bär-,ük, bə-'rük\ n — see BIBLE table

bas·al \'bā-səl\ adj 1 : situated at or forming the base 2 : BASIC

basal metabolism n : the turnover of energy in a fasting and resting organism using energy solely to maintain vital cellular activity, respiration, and circulation as measured by the rate at which heat is given off

ba·salt \bə-'sȯlt, 'bā-,sȯlt\ n : a dark fine-grained igneous rock — **ba·sal·tic** \bə-'sȯl-tik\ adj

¹**base** \'bās\ n, pl **bas·es** \'bā-səz\ 1 : BOTTOM, FOUNDATION 2 : a side or face on which a geometrical figure stands; also : the length of a base 3 : a main ingredient or fundamental part 4 : the point of beginning an act or operation 5 : a place on which a force depends for supplies 6 : a number (as 5 in 5⁷) that is raised to a power; esp : a number that when raised to a power equal to the logarithm of a number yields the number itself ⟨the logarithm of 100 to ∼ 10 is 2 since 10² = 100⟩ 7 : the number of units in a given digit's place of a number system that is required to give the numeral 1 in the next higher place ⟨the decimal system uses a ∼ of 10⟩; also : such a system using an indicated base ⟨convert from ∼ 10 to ∼ 2⟩ 8 : any of the four stations at the corners of a baseball diamond 9 : a chemical compound (as lime or ammonia) that reacts with an acid to form a salt, has a bitter taste, and turns litmus blue ♦ **Synonyms** BASIS, GROUND, GROUNDWORK, FOOTING, FOUNDATION — **base·less** adj

²**base** vb **based; bas·ing** 1 : to form or serve as a base for 2 : ESTABLISH

³**base** adj 1 : of low value and inferior quality : DEBASED, ALLOYED 2 : CONTEMPTIBLE, IGNOBLE ⟨∼ motives⟩ 3 : MENIAL, DEGRADING ♦ **Synonyms** LOW, VILE, DESPICABLE, WRETCHED — **base·ly** adv — **base·ness** n

base·ball \'bās-,bȯl\ n : a game played with a bat and ball by two teams on a field with four bases arranged in a diamond; also : the ball used in this game

baseball cap n : a cap of the kind worn by baseball players that has a rounded crown and a long visor

base·board \-,bȯrd\ n : a line of boards or molding covering the joint of a wall and the adjoining floor

base·born \-'bȯrn\ adj 1 : MEAN, IGNOBLE 2 : of humble birth 3 : of illegitimate birth

base exchange • bastinado

base exchange *n* : a post exchange at a naval or air force base

base hit *n* : a hit in baseball that enables the batter to reach base safely with no error made and no base runner forced out

BASE jumping \'bās-\ *n* [building, antenna, span, earth] : the activity of parachuting from a high structure or cliff

base·line \'bās-ˌlīn\ *n* **1** : a line serving as a basis esp. to calculate or locate something **2** : the area within which a baseball player must keep when running between bases

base·ment \-mənt\ *n* **1** : the part of a building that is wholly or partly below ground level **2** : the lowest or fundamental part of something

base on balls *n* : an advance to first base given to a baseball player who receives four balls

base runner *n* : a baseball player who is on base or is attempting to reach a base

¹bash \'bash\ *vb* **1** : to strike violently : HIT **2** : to smash by a blow **3** : to attack physically or verbally

²bash *n* **1** : a heavy blow **2** : a festive social gathering : PARTY

bash·ful \'bash-fəl\ *adj* : inclined to shrink from public attention — **bash·ful·ly** \-fə-lē\ *adv* — **bash·ful·ness** *n*

ba·sic \'bā-sik\ *adj* **1** : of, relating to, or forming the base or essence : FUNDAMENTAL **2** : concerned with fundamental scientific principles : not applied **3** : of, relating to, or having the character of a chemical base ♦ *Synonyms* UNDERLYING, BASAL, PRIMARY — **ba·sic·i·ty** \bā-'si-sə-tē\ *n*

BA·SIC \'bā-sik\ *n* [*Beginner's All-purpose Symbolic Instruction Code*] : a simplified language for programming a computer

ba·si·cal·ly \'bā-si-k(ə-)lē\ *adv* **1** : at a basic level **2** : for the most part **3** : in a basic manner

ba·sil \'bā-zəl, 'ba-, -səl\ *n* : any of several mints with fragrant leaves used in cooking; *also* : the leaves

ba·sil·i·ca \bə-'si-li-kə, -'zi-\ *n* [L, fr. Gk *basilikē*, fr. fem. of *basilikos* royal, fr. *basileus* king] **1** : an early Christian church building consisting of nave and aisles with clerestory and apse **2** : a Roman Catholic church given ceremonial privileges

bas·i·lisk \'ba-sə-ˌlisk, 'ba-zə-\ *n* [ME, fr. L *basiliscus*, fr. Gk *basiliskos*, fr. dim. of *basileus* king] : a legendary reptile with fatal breath and glance

ba·sin \'bā-sᵊn\ *n* **1** : an open usu. circular vessel with sloping sides for holding liquid (as water) **2** : a hollow or enclosed place containing water; *also* : the region drained by a river

ba·sis \'bā-səs\ *n, pl* **ba·ses** \-ˌsēz\ **1** : FOUNDATION, BASE **2** : a fundamental principle

bask \'bask\ *vb* **1** : to expose oneself to comfortable heat **2** : to enjoy something warmly comforting 〈~*ing* in his friends' admiration〉

bas·ket \'bas-kət\ *n* : a container made of woven material (as twigs or grasses); *also* : any of various lightweight usu. wood containers — **bas·ket·ful** *n*

bas·ket·ball \-ˌbȯl\ *n* : a game played on a court by two teams who try to throw an inflated ball through a raised goal; *also* : the ball used in this game — **bas·ket·ball·er** \-ˌbȯ-lər\ *n*

basket case *n* **1** : a person who has all four limbs amputated **2** : a person who is mentally incapacitated or worn out (as from nervous tension)

basket weave *n* : a textile weave resembling the checkered pattern of a plaited basket

bas·ma·ti rice \ˌbäz-'mä-tē-\ *n* : an aromatic long-grain rice originating in southern Asia

bas mitzvah *var of* BAT MITZVAH

Basque \'bask\ *n* **1** : a member of a people inhabiting a region bordering on the Bay of Biscay in northern Spain and southwestern France **2** : the language of the Basque people — **Basque** *adj*

bas-re·lief \ˌbä-ri-'lēf\ *n* [F] : a sculpture in relief with the design raised very slightly from the background

¹bass \'bas\ *n, pl* **bass** *or* **bass·es** : any of numerous sport and food bony fishes (as a striped bass)

²bass \'bās\ *adj* : of low pitch

³bass \'bās\ *n* **1** : a deep sound or tone **2** : the lower half of the musical pitch range **3** : the lowest part in a 4-part chorus; *also* : a singer having this voice or part

bas·set hound \'ba-sət-\ *n* : any of an old breed of short-legged hunting dogs of French origin having long ears and a short smooth coat

bas·si·net \ˌba-sə-'net\ *n* : a baby's bed that resembles a basket and often has a hood over one end

bas·so \'ba-sō, 'bä-\ *n, pl* **bassos** *or* **bas·si** \'bä-ˌsē\ [It] : a bass singer

bas·soon \bə-'sün\ *n* : a musical wind instrument lower in pitch than the oboe

bass·wood \'bas-ˌwu̇d\ *n* : any of several New World lindens or their wood

bast \'bast\ *n* : BAST FIBER

¹bas·tard \'bas-tərd\ *n* **1** : an illegitimate child **2** : an offensive or disagreeable person

²bastard *adj* **1** : ILLEGITIMATE **2** : of an inferior or nontypical kind, size, or form; *also* : SPURIOUS — **bas·tardy** *n*

bas·tard·ise *Brit var of* BASTARDIZE

bas·tard·ize \'bas-tər-ˌdīz\ *vb* **-ized; -iz·ing** : to reduce from a higher to a lower state : DEBASE

¹baste \'bāst\ *vb* **bast·ed; bast·ing** : to sew with long stitches so as to keep temporarily in place

²baste \'bāst\ *vb* **bast·ed; bast·ing** : to moisten (as meat) at intervals with liquid while cooking

bast fiber *n* : a strong woody plant fiber obtained chiefly from phloem and used esp. in making ropes

bas·ti·na·do \ˌbas-tə-'nā-dō, -'nä-\ *or* **bas·ti·nade** \ˌbas-tə-'nād, -'näd\ *n, pl* **-na·does** *or* **-nades 1** : a blow or beating esp. with a stick **2** : a punishment consisting of beating the soles of the feet

bas·tion \'bas-chən\ *n* : a projecting part of a fortification; *also* : a fortified position

¹bat \'bat\ *n* **1** : a stout stick : CLUB **2** : a sharp blow **3** : an implement (as of wood) used to hit a ball (as in baseball) **4** : a turn at batting — usu. used in the phrase *at bat*

²bat *vb* **bat·ted; bat·ting** : to hit with or as if with a bat

³bat *n* : any of an order of night-flying mammals with forelimbs modified to form wings

⁴bat *vb* **bat·ted; bat·ting** : WINK, BLINK

batch \'bach\ *n* **1** : a quantity (as of bread) baked at one time **2** : a quantity of material for use at one time or produced at one operation

bate \'bāt\ *vb* **bat·ed; bat·ing** : MODERATE, REDUCE ⟨*he bated* his breath⟩

bath \'bath, 'bäth\ *n, pl* **baths** \'bathz, 'baths, 'bäthz, 'bäths\ **1** : a washing of the body **2** : water for washing the body **3** : a liquid in which objects are immersed so that it can act on them **4** : BATHROOM **5** : a financial loss ⟨took a ∼ in the market⟩

bathe \'bāth\ *vb* **bathed; bath·ing** **1** : to wash in liquid and esp. water; *also* : to apply water or a medicated liquid to ⟨*bathed* her eyes⟩ **2** : to take a bath; *also* : to take a swim **3** : to wash along, over, or against so as to wet **4** : to suffuse with or as if with light — **bath·er** *n*

bath·house \'bath-,haůs, 'bäth-\ *n* **1** : a building equipped for bathing **2** : a building containing dressing rooms for bathers

bathing suit *n* : SWIMSUIT

ba·thos \'bā-,thäs\ *n* [Gk, lit., depth] **1** : the sudden appearance of the commonplace in otherwise elevated matter or style **2** : insincere or overdone pathos — **ba·thet·ic** \bə-'the-tik\ *adj*

bath·robe \'bath-,rōb, 'bäth-\ *n* : a loose often absorbent robe worn before and after bathing or as a dressing gown

bath·room \-,rüm, -,rům\ *n* : a room containing a bathtub or shower and usu. a sink and toilet

bath·tub \-,təb\ *n* : a usu. fixed tub for bathing

ba·tik \bə-'tēk, 'ba-tik\ *n* [Javanese *baṭik*] **1** : an Indonesian method of handprinting textiles by coating with wax the parts not to be dyed; *also* : a design so executed **2** : a fabric printed by batik

ba·tiste \bə-'tēst\ *n* : a fine sheer fabric of plain weave

bat·man \'bat-mən\ *n* : an orderly of a British military officer

bat mitz·vah \bät-'mits-və\ *also* **bas mitz·vah** \bäs-\ *n, often cap B&M* [Heb *bath miṣwāh*, lit., daughter of the (divine) law] **1** : a Jewish girl who at 12 or more years of age assumes religious responsibilities **2** : the ceremony recognizing a girl as a bat mitzvah

stick with which the leader directs an orchestra or band

bats·man \'bats-mən\ *n* : a batter esp. in cricket

bat·tal·ion \bə-'tal-yən\ *n* **1** : a large body of troops organized to act together : ARMY **2** : a military unit composed of a headquarters and two or more units (as companies)

¹bat·ten \'ba-tᵊn\ *vb* **1** : to grow or make fat **2** : THRIVE

²batten *n* : a strip of wood used esp. to seal or strengthen a joint

³batten *vb* : to fasten with or as if with battens

¹bat·ter \'ba-tər\ *vb* : to beat or damage with repeated blows

²batter *n* : a soft mixture (as for cake) basically of flour and liquid

³batter *n* : one that bats; *esp* : the player whose turn it is to bat

battering ram *n* **1** : an ancient military machine for battering down walls **2** : a heavy metal bar with handles used to batter down doors

bat·tery \'ba-tə-rē\ *n, pl* **-ter·ies** **1** : BEATING; *esp* : unlawful beating or use of force on a person **2** : a grouping of artillery pieces for tactical purposes; *also* : the guns of a warship **3** : a group of electric cells for furnishing electric current; *also* : a single electric cell ⟨a flashlight ∼⟩ **4** : a number of similar items grouped or used as a unit ⟨a ∼ of tests⟩ **5** : the pitcher and catcher of a baseball team

bat·ting \'ba-tiŋ\ *n* : layers or sheets of cotton or wool (as for lining quilts)

batting cage *n* : a screen around the back and sides of the home plate area to stop baseballs during practice

¹bat·tle \'ba-tᵊl\ *n* [ME *batel*, fr. AF *bataille* battle, battalion, fr. LL *battalia* combat, alter. of *battualia* fencing exercises, fr. L *battuere* to beat] : a general military engagement; *also* : an extended contest or controversy

²battle *vb* **bat·tled; bat·tling** : to engage in battle : CONTEND, FIGHT

bat·tle–ax *or* **battle–axe** \'ba-tᵊl-,aks\ *n* **1** : a long-handled ax formerly used as a weapon **2** : a quarrelsome domineering woman

battle fatigue *n* : COMBAT FATIGUE

bat·tle·field \'ba-tᵊl-,fēld\ *n* : a place where a battle is fought

bat·tle·ment \-mənt\ *n* : a decorative or defensive parapet on top of a wall

bat·tle·ship \-,ship\ *n* : a warship of the most heavily armed and armored class

bat·tle·wag·on \-,wa-gən\ *n* : BATTLESHIP

bat·ty \'ba-tē\ *adj* **bat·ti·er; -est** : CRAZY, FOOLISH

bau·ble \'bȯ-bəl\ *n* : TRINKET

baud \'bȯd, *Brit* 'bōd\ *n, pl* **baud** *also* **bauds** : a unit of data transmission speed

baulk *chiefly Brit var of* BALK

baux·ite \'bȯk-,sīt\ *n* : a clayey mixture that is the chief ore of aluminum

bawd \'bȯd\ *n* **1** : MADAM 2 **2** : PROSTITUTE

bawdy \'bȯ-dē\ adj **bawd·i·er; -est** : OB-SCENE, LEWD — **bawd·i·ly** \'bȯ-də-lē\ adv — **bawd·i·ness** \-dē-nəs\ n

¹**bawl** \'bȯl\ vb : to cry or cry out loudly; also : to scold harshly

²**bawl** n : a long loud cry : BELLOW

¹**bay** \'bā\ adj : reddish brown

²**bay** n 1 : a bay-colored animal 2 : a red-dish brown color

³**bay** n 1 : a section or compartment of a building or vehicle 2 : a compartment projecting outward from the wall of a building and containing a window (**bay window**)

⁴**bay** vb : to bark with deep long tones

⁵**bay** n 1 : the position of one unable to escape and forced to face danger 2 : a baying of dogs

⁶**bay** n : an inlet of a body of water (as the sea) usu. smaller than a gulf

⁷**bay** n : LAUREL; also : a shrub or tree re-sembling the laurel

bay·ber·ry \'bā-,ber-ē\ n : a hardy decidu-ous shrub of coastal eastern No. America bearing small hard berries coated with a white wax used for candles; also : its fruit

bay leaf n : the dried leaf of the European laurel used in cooking

¹**bay·o·net** \'bā-ə-nət, ,bā-ə-'net\ n : a dag-gerlike weapon made to fit on the muzzle end of a rifle

²**bayonet** vb **-net·ed** also **-net·ted; -net·ing** also **-net·ting** : to use or stab with a bayonet

bay·ou \'bī-yü, -ō\ n [Louisiana French, fr. Choctaw bayuk] : a marshy or sluggish body of water

bay rum n : a fragrant liquid used esp. as a cologne or after-shave lotion

ba·zaar \bə-'zär\ n 1 : a group of shops : MARKETPLACE 2 : a fair for the sale of articles usu. for charity

ba·zoo·ka \bə-'zü-kə\ n [bazooka (a crude musical instrument made of pipes and a funnel)] : a weapon consisting of a tube that launches an explosive rocket able to pierce armor

¹**BB** \'bē-(,)bē\ n : a small round shot pellet

²**BB** abbr base on balls

BBB abbr Better Business Bureau

BBC abbr British Broadcasting Corpora-tion

bbl abbr barrel; barrels

BC abbr 1 before Christ — often printed in small capitals and often punctuated 2 British Columbia

B cell n [bone-marrow-derived cell] : any of the lymphocytes that secrete antibod-ies when mature

B complex n : VITAMIN B COMPLEX

bd abbr 1 board 2 bound

bdl or **bdle** abbr bundle

bdrm abbr bedroom

be \'bē\ vb, past 1st & 3d sing **was** \'wəz, 'wäz\; 2d sing **were** \'wər\; pl **were**; past subjunctive **were**; past part **been** \'bin\; pres part **be·ing** \'bē-iŋ\; pres 1st sing **am** \əm, 'am\; 2d sing **are** \ər, 'är\; 3d sing **is** \'iz, əz\; pl **are**; pres subjunctive **be** 1 : to equal in meaning or symbolically (God is love); also : to have a specified qualifica-tion or relationship (leaves are green)

(this fish is a trout) 2 : to have objective existence (I think, therefore I am); also : to have or occupy a particular place (here is your pen) 3 : to take place : OC-CUR (the meeting is tonight) 4 — used with the past participle of transitive verbs as a passive voice auxiliary (the door was opened) 5 — used as the auxiliary of the present participle in expressing continu-ous action (he is sleeping) 6 — used as an auxiliary with the past participle of some intransitive verbs to form archaic perfect tenses 7 — used as an auxiliary with to and the infinitive to express futu-rity, prearrangement, or obligation (you are to come when called)

Be symbol beryllium

¹**beach** \'bēch\ n : a sandy or gravelly part of the shore of an ocean or lake

²**beach** vb : to run or drive ashore

beach buggy n : DUNE BUGGY

beach·comb·er \'bēch-,kō-mər\ n : a person who searches along a shore for something of use or value

beach·head \'bēch-,hed\ n : a small area on an enemy-held shore occupied in the initial stages of an invasion

bea·con \'bē-kən\ n 1 : a signal fire 2 : a guiding or warning signal (as a light-house) 3 : a radio transmitter emitting signals for guidance of aircraft

¹**bead** \'bēd\ n [ME bede prayer, prayer bead, fr. OE bed, gebed prayer] 1 pl : a series of prayers and meditations made with a rosary 2 : a small piece of mate-rial pierced for threading on a line (as in a rosary) 3 : a small globular body 4 : a narrow projecting rim or band — **bead·ing** n — **beady** adj

²**bead** vb : to form into a bead

bea·dle \'bēd-ᵊl\ n : a usu. English parish officer whose duties include keeping or-der in church

bea·gle \'bē-gəl\ n : a small short-legged smooth-coated hound

beak \'bēk\ n : the bill of a bird and esp. of a bird of prey; also : a pointed project-ing part — **beaked** \'bēkt\ adj

bea·ker \'bē-kər\ n 1 : a large wide-mouthed drinking cup 2 : a wide-mouthed thin-walled laboratory vessel

¹**beam** \'bēm\ n 1 : a large long piece of timber or metal 2 : the bar of a balance from which the scales hang 3 : the breadth of a ship at its widest part 4 : a ray or shaft of light 5 : a collection of nearly parallel rays (as X-rays) or parti-cles (as electrons) 6 : a constant radio signal transmitted for the guidance of pi-lots; also : the course indicated by this signal

²**beam** vb 1 : to send out light 2 : BROAD-CAST 3 : to transmit (data) electronically 4 : to smile with joy

¹**bean** \'bēn\ n : the edible seed borne in pods by some leguminous plants; also : a plant or a pod bearing beans

²**bean** vb : to strike on the head with an object

bean·bag \'bēn-,bag\ n : a cloth bag par-tially filled typically with dried beans and used as a toy

bean·ball \'bēn-ˌból\ *n* : a pitch thrown at a batter's head

bean curd *n* : TOFU

bean·ie \'bē-nē\ *n* : a small round tight-fitting skullcap

beano \'bē-nō\ *n, pl* **beanos** : BINGO

¹bear \'ber\ *n, pl* **bears 1** *or pl* **bear** : any of a family of large heavy mammals with shaggy hair and small tails **2** : a gruff or sullen person **3** : one who sells (as securities) in expectation of a price decline — **bear·ish** *adj*

²bear *vb* **bore** \'bór\; **borne** \'bórn\ *also* **born** \'bórn\; **bear·ing 1** : CARRY **2** : to be equipped with **3** : to give as testimony ⟨∼ witness to the facts of the case⟩ **4** : to give birth to; *also* : PRODUCE, YIELD ⟨a tree that ∼s regularly⟩ **5** : ENDURE, SUSTAIN ⟨∼ pain⟩ ⟨bore the weight on piles⟩; *also* : to exert pressure or influence **6** : to go in an indicated direction ⟨∼ to the right⟩ — **bear·able** *adj* — **bear·er** *n*

¹beard \'bird\ *n* **1** : the hair that grows on the face of a man **2** : a growth of bristly hairs (as on a goat's chin) — **beard·ed** \'bir-dəd\ *adj* — **beard·less** *adj*

²beard *vb* : to confront boldly

bearing *n* **1** : manner of carrying oneself : COMPORTMENT **2** : a supporting object, purpose, or point **3** : a machine part in which another part (as an axle or pin) turns **4** : an emblem in a coat of arms **5** : the position or direction of one point with respect to another or to the compass; *also* : a determination of position **6** *pl* : comprehension of one's situation **7** : connection with or influence on something; *also* : SIGNIFICANCE

bear market *n* : a market in which securities or commodities are persistently declining in value

bear·skin \'ber-ˌskin\ *n* : an article (as a hat) made of the skin of a bear

beast \'bēst\ *n* **1** : ANIMAL 1; *esp* : a 4-footed mammal **2** : a contemptible person

¹beast·ly \'bēst-lē\ *adj* **beast·li·er; -est 1** : BESTIAL **2** : ABOMINABLE, DISAGREEABLE — **beast·li·ness** \-nəs\ *n*

²beastly *adv* : VERY ⟨a ∼ cold day⟩

¹beat \'bēt\ *vb* **beat; beat·en** \'bē-t⁰n\ *or* **beat; beat·ing 1** : to strike repeatedly : TREAD **2** : to affect or alter by beating ⟨∼ metal into sheets⟩ **3** : to sound (as an alarm) on a drum **4** : OVERCOME ⟨∼ his opponent⟩; *also* : SURPASS ⟨a meal hard to ∼⟩ **5** : to act or arrive before ⟨∼ his brother home⟩ **6** : THROB — **beat·er** *n*

²beat *n* **1** : a single stroke or blow esp. of a series; *also* : PULSATION **2** : a rhythmic stress in poetry or music or the rhythmic effect of these **3** : a regularly traversed course

³beat *adj* **1** : EXHAUSTED **2** : of or relating to beatniks

⁴beat *n* : BEATNIK

be·atif·ic \ˌbē-ə-'ti-fik\ *adj* : giving or indicative of great joy or bliss

be·at·i·fy \bē-'a-tə-ˌfī\ *vb* **-fied; -fy·ing 1** : to make supremely happy **2** : to declare to have attained the blessedness of heav-

en and authorize the title "Blessed" for — **be·at·i·fi·ca·tion** \-ˌa-tə-fə-'kā-shən\ *n*

be·at·i·tude \bē-'a-tə-ˌtüd, -ˌtyüd\ *n* **1** : a state of utmost bliss **2** : any of the declarations made in the Sermon on the Mount (Mt 5:3–12) beginning "Blessed are"

beat·nik \'bēt-nik\ *n* : a usu. young and artistic person who rejects the mores of established society

beau \'bō\ *n, pl* **beaux** \'bōz\ *or* **beaus** [F, fr. *beau* beautiful, fr. L *bellus* pretty] **1** : a man of fashion : DANDY **2** : SUITOR, LOVER

beau geste \bō-'zhest\ *n, pl* **beaux gestes** *or* **beau gestes** \bō-'zhest\ [F] : a graceful or magnanimous gesture

beau ide·al \ˌbō-ī-'dē(-ə)l\ *n, pl* **beau ideals** [F] : the perfect type or model

Beau·jo·lais \ˌbō-zhō-'lā\ *n* : a light fruity red wine

beau monde \bō-'mänd, -'mōⁿd\ *n, pl* **beau mondes** \-'mänz, -'mändz\ *or* **beaux mondes** \bō-'mōⁿd\ [F] : the world of high society and fashion

beau·te·ous \'byü-tē-əs\ *adj* : BEAUTIFUL — **beau·te·ous·ly** *adv*

beau·ti·cian \byü-'ti-shən\ *n* : COSMETOLOGIST

beau·ti·ful \'byü-ti-fəl\ *adj* : characterized by beauty : LOVELY ♦ *Synonyms* PRETTY, FAIR, COMELY — **beau·ti·ful·ly** \-f(ə-)lē\ *adv*

beautiful people *n pl, often cap B&P* : wealthy or famous people whose lifestyle is usu. expensive and well-publicized

beau·ti·fy \'byü-tə-ˌfī\ *vb* **-fied; -fy·ing** : to make more beautiful — **beau·ti·fi·ca·tion** \ˌbyü-tə-fə-'kā-shən\ *n* — **beau·ti·fi·er** *n*

beau·ty \'byü-tē\ *n, pl* **beauties** : qualities that give pleasure to the senses or exalt the mind : LOVELINESS; *also* : something having such qualities

beauty shop *n* : an establishment where hairdressing, facials, and manicures are done

beaux arts \bō-'zär\ *n pl* [F] : FINE ARTS

bea·ver \'bē-vər\ *n, pl* **beavers** : a large fur-bearing herbivorous rodent that builds dams and underwater houses of mud and sticks; *also* : its fur

be·calm \bi-'käm, -'kälm\ *vb* : to keep (as a ship) motionless by lack of wind

be·cause \bi-'kóz, -'kəz\ *conj* : for the reason that ⟨ran away ∼ they were afraid⟩

because of *prep* : by reason of

beck \'bek\ *n* : a beckoning gesture; *also* : SUMMONS

beck·on \'be-kən\ *vb* : to summon or signal esp. by a nod or gesture; *also* : ATTRACT

be·cloud \bi-'klaúd\ *vb* : OBSCURE

be·come \bi-'kəm\ *vb* **-came** \-'kām\; **-come; -com·ing 1** : to come to be ⟨∼ tired⟩ **2** : to suit or be suitable to ⟨her dress ∼s her⟩

becoming *adj* : SUITABLE, FIT; *also* : ATTRACTIVE — **be·com·ing·ly** *adv*

¹bed \'bed\ *n* **1** : an article of furniture to

sleep on **2** : a plot of ground prepared for plants **3** : FOUNDATION, BOTTOM ⟨the ocean ∼⟩ **4** : LAYER, STRATUM ⟨a ∼ of rice⟩

²**bed** vb **bed·ded; bed·ding 1** : to put or go to bed **2** : to fix in a foundation — EMBED **3** : to plant in beds **4** : to lay or lie flat or in layers

bed–and–breakfast n : an establishment offering lodging and breakfast

be·daub \bi-'dȯb\ vb : SMEAR

be·daz·zle \bi-'da-zəl\ vb : to confuse by or as if by a strong light; also : FASCINATE — **be·daz·zle·ment** n

bed·bug \'bed-,bəg\ n : a wingless bloodsucking bug infesting houses and esp. beds

bed·clothes \'bed-,klōthz\ n pl : materials for making up a bed

bed·ding \'be-diŋ\ n **1** : BEDCLOTHES **2** : FOUNDATION ⟨straw ∼⟩

be·deck \bi-'dek\ vb : ADORN

be·dev·il \bi-'de-vəl\ vb **1** : HARASS, TORMENT **2** : CONFUSE, MUDDLE

be·dew \bi-'dü, -'dyü\ vb : to wet with or as if with dew

bed·fast \'bed-,fast\ adj : BEDRIDDEN

bed·fel·low \-,fe-lō\ n **1** : one sharing the bed of another **2** : a close associate : ALLY ⟨politics makes strange ∼s⟩

be·di·zen \bi-'dī-z³n, -'di-\ vb : to dress or adorn with showy or vulgar finery

bed·lam \'bed-ləm\ n [Bedlam, popular name for the Hospital of St. Mary of Bethlehem, London, an insane asylum, fr. ME Bedlem Bethlehem] **1** often cap : an insane asylum **2** : a scene of uproar and confusion ⟨∼ in the court⟩

bed·ou·in also **bed·u·in** \'be-də-wən\ n, pl **bedouin** or **bedouins** also **beduin** or **beduins** often cap [ME Bedoyne, fr. MF bedoïn, fr. Ar badawī desert dweller] : a nomadic Arab of the Arabian, Syrian, or northern African deserts

bed·pan \'bed-,pan\ n : a shallow vessel used by a bedridden person for urination or defecation

bed·post \-,pōst\ n : the post of a bed

be·drag·gled \bi-'dra-gəld\ adj : soiled and disordered as if by being drenched

bed·rid·den \'bed-,ri-d³n\ adj : kept in bed by illness or weakness

¹**bed·rock** \-'räk\ n : the solid rock underlying surface materials (as soil)

²**bedrock** adj : solidly fundamental, basic, or reliable ⟨traditional ∼ values⟩

bed·roll \'bed-,rōl\ n : bedding rolled up for carrying

bed·room \-,rüm, -,rùm\ n : a room containing a bed and used esp. for sleeping

bed·side \-,sīd\ n : the place beside a bed esp. of a sick or dying person

bed·sore \-,sȯr\ n : an ulceration of tissue deprived of adequate blood supply by prolonged pressure

bed·spread \-,spred\ n : a usu. ornamental cloth cover for a bed

bed·stead \-,sted\ n : the framework of a bed

bed·time \-,tīm\ n : time for going to bed

bed–wet·ting \-,we-tiŋ\ n : involuntary

discharge of urine esp. in bed during sleep — **bed–wet·ter** n

¹**bee** \'bē\ n : any of numerous 4-winged insects (as honeybees or bumblebees) that feed on nectar and pollen and that sometimes produce honey or have a painful sting

²**bee** n : a gathering of people for a specific purpose ⟨a quilting ∼⟩

beech \'bēch\ n, pl **beech·es** or **beech** : any of a genus of hardwood trees with smooth gray bark and small sweet triangular nuts; also : its wood — **beech·en** \'bē-chən\ adj

beech·nut \'bēch-,nət\ n : the nut of a beech

¹**beef** \'bēf\ n, pl **beefs** \'bēfs\ or **beeves** \'bēvz\ **1** : the flesh of a steer, cow, or bull; also : the dressed carcass of a beef animal **2** : a steer, cow, or bull esp. when fattened for food **3** : MUSCLE, BRAWN **4** pl beefs : COMPLAINT

²**beef** vb **1** : STRENGTHEN — usu. used with up ⟨∼ed up security⟩ **2** : COMPLAIN

beef·eat·er \'bē-,fē-tər\ n : a yeoman of the guard of an English monarch

beef·steak \-,stāk\ n : a slice of beef suitable for broiling or frying

beefy \'bē-fē\ adj **beef·i·er; -est** : THICKSET, BRAWNY ⟨a ∼ wrestler⟩

bee·hive \'bē-,hīv\ n : HIVE 1, HIVE 3

bee·keep·er \-,kē-pər\ n : a person who raises bees — **bee·keep·ing** n

bee·line \-,līn\ n : a straight direct course

been past part of BE

beep·er \'bē-pər\ n : PAGER; esp : one that beeps

beer \'bir\ n : an alcoholic beverage brewed from malt and hops — **beery** adj

beer belly n : POTBELLY

bees·wax \'bēz-,waks\ n : WAX 1

beet \'bēt\ n : a garden plant with edible leaves and a thick sweet root used as a vegetable, as a source of sugar, or as forage; also : its root

¹**bee·tle** \'bē-t³l\ n : any of an order of insects having four wings of which the stiff outer pair covers the membranous inner pair when not in flight

²**beetle** vb **bee·tled; bee·tling** : to jut out : PROJECT

be·fall \bi-'fȯl\ vb **-fell** \-'fel\; **-fall·en** \-'fȯ-lən\ : to happen to : OCCUR

be·fit \bi-'fit\ vb : to be suitable to

be·fog \bi-'fȯg, -'fäg\ vb : OBSCURE; also : CONFUSE ⟨drink befogged his senses⟩

¹**be·fore** \bi-'fȯr\ adv or adj **1** : in front **2** : EARLIER

²**before** prep **1** : in front of ⟨stood ∼ him⟩ **2** : earlier than ⟨got there ∼ me⟩ **3** : in a more important category than ⟨put quality ∼ quantity⟩

³**before** conj **1** : earlier than the time that ⟨he got here ∼ I did⟩ **2** : more willingly than ⟨she'd starve ∼ she'd steal⟩

be·fore·hand \bi-'fȯr-,hand\ adv or adj : in advance

be·foul \bi-'faù(-ə)l\ vb : SOIL

be·friend \bi-'frend\ vb : to act as friend to

be·fud·dle \bi-'fə-dᵊl\ vb : MUDDLE, CONFUSE

beg \'beg\ vb **begged; beg·ging 1** : to ask as a charity; also : ENTREAT **2** : EVADE; also : assume as established, settled, or proved ⟨∼ the question⟩

be·get \bi-'get\ vb **-got** \-'gät\; **-got·ten** \-'gä-tᵊn\ or **-got; -get·ting** : to become the father of : SIRE

¹**beg·gar** \'be-gər\ n : one that begs; esp : a person who begs as a way of life

²**beggar** vb : IMPOVERISH

beg·gar·ly \'be-gər-lē\ adj **1** : contemptibly mean or inadequate **2** : marked by unrelieved poverty ⟨a ∼ life⟩

beg·gary \'be-gə-rē\ n : extreme poverty

be·gin \bi-'gin\ vb **be·gan** \-'gan\; **be·gun** \-'gən\; **be·gin·ning 1** : to do the first part of an action : COMMENCE **2** : to come into being : ARISE; also : FOUND ⟨he began the movement⟩ **3** : ORIGINATE, INVENT — **be·gin·ner** n

beg off vb : to ask to be excused from something

be·gone \bi-'gón\ vb : to go away : DEPART — used esp. in the imperative

be·go·nia \bi-'gō-nyə\ n : any of a genus of tropical herbs widely grown for their showy leaves and waxy flowers

be·grime \bi-'grīm\ vb **be·grimed; be·grim·ing** : to make dirty

be·grudge \bi-'grəj\ vb **1** : to give or concede reluctantly **2** : to be reluctant to grant or allow — **be·grudg·ing·ly** \-'grə-jiŋ-lē\ adv

be·guile \-'gī(-ə)l\ vb **be·guiled; be·guil·ing 1** : DECEIVE **2** : to while away ⟨beguiled sorrow with music⟩ **3** : to engage the interest of by guile

be·guine \bi-'gēn\ n [AmerF béguine, fr. F béguin flirtation] : a vigorous popular dance of the islands of Saint Lucia and Martinique

be·gum \'bā-gəm, 'bē-\ n : a Muslim woman of high rank

be·half \bi-'haf, -'häf\ n : BENEFIT, SUPPORT, DEFENSE ⟨argued in their ∼⟩

be·have \bi-'hāv\ vb **be·haved; be·hav·ing 1** : to bear, comport, or conduct oneself in a particular and esp. a proper way **2** : to act, function, or react in a particular way

be·hav·ior \bi-'hā-vyər\ n : way of behaving; esp : personal conduct — **be·hav·ior·al** \-vyə-rəl\ adj — **be·hav·ior·al·ly** \-rə-lē\ adv

be·hav·ior·ism \bi-'hā-vyə-ˌri-zəm\ n : a school of psychology concerned with the objective evidence of behavior without reference to conscious experience

be·hav·ior·ist \-vyə-rist\ n **1** : a person who supports behaviorism **2** : a person who studies behavior

be·hav·iour, be·hav·iour·ism chiefly Brit var of BEHAVIOR, BEHAVIORISM

be·head \bi-'hed\ vb : to cut off the head of

be·he·moth \bi-'hē-məth, 'bē-ə-ˌmäth\ n : a huge powerful animal described in Job 40:15–24; also : something of monstrous size or power

be·hest \bi-'hest\ n **1** : COMMAND **2** : an urgent prompting

¹**be·hind** \bi-'hīnd\ adv or adj **1** : BACK, BACKWARD ⟨look ∼⟩ **2** : LATE, SLOW

²**behind** prep **1** : in or to a place or situation in back of or to the rear of ⟨look ∼ you⟩ ⟨the staff stayed ∼ the troops⟩ **2** : inferior to (as in rank) : BELOW ⟨three games ∼ the first-place team⟩ **3** : in support of : SUPPORTING ⟨we're ∼ you all the way⟩

be·hind·hand \bi-'hīnd-ˌhand\ adj : being in arrears ♦ **Synonyms** TARDY, LATE, OVERDUE, BELATED

be·hold \bi-'hōld\ vb **-held** \-'held\; **-hold·ing 1** : to have in sight : SEE **2** — used imperatively to direct the attention ♦ **Synonyms** VIEW, OBSERVE, NOTICE, ESPY — **be·hold·er** n

be·hold·en \bi-'hōl-dən\ adj : OBLIGATED, INDEBTED

be·hoove \bi-'hüv\ vb **be·hooved; be·hoov·ing** : to be necessary, proper, or advantageous for

be·hove chiefly Brit var of BEHOOVE

beige \'bāzh\ n : a pale dull yellowish brown — **beige** adj

be·ing \'bē-iŋ\ n **1** : EXISTENCE; also : LIFE **2** : the qualities or constitution of an existent thing **3** : a living thing; esp : PERSON

be·la·bor \bi-'lā-bər\ vb : to assail (as with words) tiresomely or at length

be·la·bour chiefly Brit var of BELABOR

be·lat·ed \bi-'lā-təd\ adj : DELAYED, LATE ⟨∼ birthday wishes⟩

be·lay \bi-'lā\ vb **1** : to wind (a rope) around a pin or cleat in order to hold secure **2** : QUIT, STOP — used in the imperative

belch \'belch\ vb **1** : to expel (gas) from the stomach through the mouth **2** : to gush forth ⟨a volcano ∼ing lava⟩ — **belch** n

bel·dam or **bel·dame** \'bel-dəm\ n [ME beldam grandmother, fr. AF bel beautiful + ME dam lady, mother] : an old woman

be·lea·guer \bi-'lē-gər\ vb **1** : BESIEGE **2** : HARASS ⟨∼ed parents⟩

bel·fry \'bel-frē\ n, pl **belfries** : a tower for a bell (as on a church); also : the part of the tower in which the bell hangs

Belg abbr Belgian; Belgium

Bel·gian \'bel-jən\ n : the blanched shoot of chicory

Belgian waffle n : a waffle having large depressions and usu. topped with fruit and whipped cream

be·lie \bi-'lī\ vb **-lied; -ly·ing 1** : MISREPRESENT **2** : to show (something) to be false **3** : to run counter to

be·lief \bə-'lēf\ n **1** : CONFIDENCE, TRUST **2** : something (as a tenet or creed) believed ♦ **Synonyms** CONVICTION, OPINION, PERSUASION, SENTIMENT

be·lieve \bə-'lēv\ vb **be·lieved; be·liev·ing 1** : to have religious convictions **2** : to have a firm conviction about something : accept as true **3** : to hold as an opinion : SUPPOSE — **be·liev·able** \-'lē-və-bəl\ adj — **be·liev·ably** \-blē\ adv — **be·liev·er** n

be·like \bi-ˈlīk\ *adv, archaic* : PROBABLY

be·lit·tle \bi-ˈli-t⁰l\ *vb* **-lit·tled; -lit·tling** : to make seem little or less; *also* : DISPARAGE ⟨*belittled* his opponent⟩

¹**bell** \ˈbel\ *n* **1** : a hollow metallic device that makes a ringing sound when struck **2** : the sounding or stroke of a bell (as on shipboard to tell the time); *also* : time so indicated **3** : something with the flared form of a typical bell

²**bell** *vb* : to provide with a bell

bel·la·don·na \ˌbe-lə-ˈdä-nə\ *n* [It, lit., beautiful lady] : a medicinal extract (as atropine) from a poisonous European herb related to the potato; *also* : this herb

bell–bot·toms \ˈbel-ˈbä-təmz\ *n pl* : pants with wide flaring bottoms — **bell–bottom** *adj*

bell·boy \ˈbel-ˌbȯi\ *n* : BELLHOP

belle \ˈbel\ *n* : an attractive and popular girl or woman

belles let·tres \bel-ˈletr⁰\ *n pl* [F] : literature that is an end in itself and not practical or purely informative — **bel·le·tris·tic** \ˌbe-lə-ˈtris-tik\ *adj*

bell·hop \ˈbel-ˌhäp\ *n* : a hotel or club employee who takes guests to rooms, carries luggage, and runs errands

bel·li·cose \ˈbe-li-ˌkōs\ *adj* : WARLIKE, PUGNACIOUS ♦ *Synonyms* BELLIGERENT, QUARRELSOME, COMBATIVE, CONTENTIOUS — **bel·li·cos·i·ty** \ˌbe-li-ˈkä-sə-tē\ *n*

bel·lig·er·en·cy \bə-ˈli-jə-rən-sē\ *n* **1** : the status of a nation engaged in war **2** : BELLIGERENCE, TRUCULENCE

bel·lig·er·ent \-rənt\ *adj* **1** : waging war **2** : aggressively self-assertive ♦ *Synonyms* BELLICOSE, PUGNACIOUS, COMBATIVE, CONTENTIOUS, WARLIKE — **bel·lig·er·ence** \-rəns\ *n* — **belligerent** *n* — **bel·lig·er·ent·ly** *adv*

bel·low \ˈbe-lō\ *vb* **1** : to make the deep hollow sound characteristic of a bull **2** : to shout in a deep voice — **bellow** *n*

bel·lows \-lōz, -ləz\ *n sing or pl* : a closed device with sides that can be spread apart and then pressed together to draw in air and expel it through a tube

bell·weth·er \ˈbel-ˈwe-thər, -ˌwe-\ *n* : one that takes the lead or initiative; *also* : an indicator of trends

¹**bel·ly** \ˈbe-lē\ *n, pl* **bellies** [ME *bely* bellows, belly, fr. OE *belg* bag, skin] **1** : ABDOMEN 1; *also* : POTBELLY **2** : the underpart of an animal's body

²**belly** *vb* **bel·lied; bel·ly·ing** : BULGE

¹**bel·ly·ache** \ˈbe-lē-ˌāk\ *n* : pain in the abdomen : STOMACHACHE

²**bellyache** *vb* : COMPLAIN

belly button *n* : the human navel

belly dance *n* : a usu. solo dance emphasizing movement of the belly — **belly dance** *vb* — **belly dancer** *n*

belly laugh *n* : a deep hearty laugh

be·long \bi-ˈlȯŋ\ *vb* **1** : to be suitable or appropriate; *also* : to be properly situated ⟨shoes ~ in the closet⟩ **2** : to be the property ⟨this ~s to me⟩; *also* : to be attached (as through birth or membership) ⟨~ to a club⟩ **3** : to form an attribute or part ⟨this wheel ~s to the cart⟩ **4** : to be

classified ⟨whales ~ among the mammals⟩

be·long·ings \-ˈlȯŋ-iŋz\ *n pl* : GOODS, EFFECTS, POSSESSIONS

be·loved \bi-ˈləvd, -ˈlə-vəd\ *adj* : dearly loved — **beloved** *n*

¹**be·low** \bi-ˈlō\ *adv* **1** : in or to a lower place or rank **2** : on earth **3** : in hell

²**below** *prep* **1** : lower than ⟨~ sea level⟩ **2** : inferior to (as in rank)

be·low·decks \bi-ˌlō-ˈdeks, -ˈlō-ˌdeks\ *adv* : inside the superstructure of a boat or down to a lower deck

¹**belt** \ˈbelt\ *n* **1** : a strip (as of leather) worn about the waist **2** : a flexible continuous band to communicate motion or convey material **3** : a region marked by some distinctive feature; *esp* : one suited to a particular crop

²**belt** *vb* **1** : to encircle or secure with a belt **2** : to beat with or as if with a belt **3** : to mark with an encircling band **4** : to sing loudly

³**belt** *n* **1** : a jarring blow : WHACK **2** : DRINK ⟨a ~ of whiskey⟩

belt·er \ˈbel-tər\ *n* : a singer with a powerful voice

belt–tightening *n* : a reduction in spending

belt·way \ˈbelt-ˌwā\ *n* : a highway around a city

be·lu·ga \bə-ˈlü-gə\ *n* [Russ] **1** : a large white sturgeon of the Black Sea, Caspian Sea, and their tributaries that is a source of caviar; *also* : caviar from beluga roe **2** : a whale of arctic and subarctic waters that is white when mature

bel·ve·dere \ˈbel-və-ˌdir\ *n* [It, lit., beautiful view] : a structure (as a summerhouse) designed to command a view

be·mire \bi-ˈmī(-ə)r\ *vb* : to cover or soil with or sink in mire

be·moan \bi-ˈmōn\ *vb* : LAMENT, DEPLORE ♦ *Synonyms* BEWAIL, GRIEVE, MOAN, WEEP

be·muse \bi-ˈmyüz\ *vb* : BEWILDER, CONFUSE

¹**bench** \ˈbench\ *n* **1** : a long seat for two or more persons **2** : the seat of a judge in court; *also* : the office or dignity of a judge **3** : COURT; *also* : JUDGES **4** : a table for holding work and tools ⟨a carpenter's ~⟩

²**bench** \ˈbench\ *vb* **1** : to furnish with benches **2** : to seat on a bench **3** : to remove from or keep out of a game

¹**bench·mark** \ˈbench-ˌmärk\ *n usu* **bench mark** : a mark on a permanent object serving as an elevation reference in topographical surveys **2** : a point of reference for measurement; *also* : STANDARD

²**benchmark** *vb* : to study (as a competitor's business practices) in order to improve one's own performance

bench press *n* : an exercise in which a weight is raised by a person lying on a bench — **bench–press** *vb*

bench warrant *n* : a warrant issued by a presiding judge or by a court against a person guilty of contempt or indicted for a crime

¹**bend** \'bend\ *vb* **bent** \'bent\; **bend·ing**
1 : to draw (as a bow) taut **2** : to curve or
cause a change of shape in ⟨~ a bar⟩ **3**
: to make fast : SECURE **4** : DEFLECT **5**
: to turn in a certain direction ⟨*bent* his
steps toward town⟩ **6** : APPLY ⟨*bent*
themselves to the task⟩ **7** : SUBDUE **8**
: to curve downward **9** : YIELD, SUBMIT
²**bend** *n* **1** : an act or process of bending **2**
: something bent; *esp* : CURVE **3** *pl* : a
painful and sometimes fatal disorder
caused by release of gas bubbles in the
tissues upon too rapid decrease in air
pressure after a stay in a compressed atmosphere
³**bend** *n* : a knot by which a rope is fastened (as to another rope)
bend·er \'ben-dər\ *n* : SPREE ⟨hungover
after a weekend ~⟩
¹**be·neath** \bi-'nēth\ *adv* : BELOW ⟨the
mountains and the town ~⟩ ♦ **Syn-**
onyms UNDER, UNDERNEATH
²**beneath** *prep* **1** : BELOW, UNDER ⟨stood
~ a tree⟩ **2** : unworthy of ⟨considered
such behavior ~ her⟩ **3** : concealed by
⟨a warm heart ~ a gruff manner⟩
bene·dic·tion \ˌbe-nə-'dik-shən\ *n* : the
invocation of a blessing esp. at the close
of a public worship service
ben·e·fac·tion \-'fak-shən\ *n* : a charitable donation ♦ **Synonyms** CONTRIBU-
TION, ALMS, BENEFICENCE, OFFERING
ben·e·fac·tor \'ben-ə-ˌfak-tər\ *n* : one
that confers a benefit and esp. a benefaction
ben·e·fac·tress \-ˌfak-trəs\ *n* : a woman
who is a benefactor
ben·e·fice \'be-nə-fəs\ *n* : an ecclesiastical office to which the revenue from an
endowment is attached
be·nef·i·cence \bə-'ne-fə-səns\ *n* **1** : be-
neficent quality **2** : BENEFACTION
be·nef·i·cent \-sənt\ *adj* : doing or producing good (as by acts of kindness or
charity); *also* : BENEFICIAL
ben·e·fi·cial \ˌbe-nə-'fi-shəl\ *adj* : being
of benefit or help : HELPFUL ♦ **Syn-**
onyms ADVANTAGEOUS, PROFITABLE,
FAVORABLE, PROPITIOUS — **ben·e·fi-**
cial·ly *adv*
ben·e·fi·cia·ry \ˌbe-nə-'fi-shē-ˌer-ē, -'fi-
shə-rē\ *n, pl* **-ries** : one that receives a
benefit (as the income of a trust or the
proceeds of an insurance)
¹**ben·e·fit** \'be-nə-ˌfit\ *n* **1** : ADVANTAGE
⟨the ~s of exercise⟩ **2** : useful aid
: HELP; *also* : material aid or service provided or due (as in sickness or unemployment) as a right in addition to regular pay
3 : a performance or event to raise funds
²**benefit** *vb* **-fit·ed** \-ˌfi-təd\ *also* **-fit·ted;**
-fit·ing *also* **-fit·ting 1** : to be useful or
profitable to **2** : to receive benefit
be·nev·o·lence \bə-'ne-və-ləns\ *n*
1 : charitable nature **2** : an act of kindness
: CHARITY — **be·nev·o·lent** \-lənt\ *adj*
— **be·nev·o·lent·ly** *adv*
be·night·ed \bi-'nī-təd\ *adj* **1** : overtaken
by darkness or night **2** : living in ignorance
be·nign \bi-'nīn\ *adj* [ME *benigne,* fr. AF,
fr. L *benignus*] **1** : of a gentle disposition;

also : showing kindness **2** : of a mild
kind; *esp* : not malignant ⟨~ tumors⟩
♦ **Synonyms** BENIGNANT, KIND, KIND-
LY, GOOD-HEARTED — **be·nig·ni·ty**
\-'nig-nə-tē\ *n* — **be·nign·ly** *adv*
be·nig·nant \-'nig-nənt\ *adj* : BENIGN **1**
♦ **Synonyms** KIND, KINDLY, GOOD-
HEARTED
ben·i·son \'be-nə-sən, -zən\ *n* : BLESSING,
BENEDICTION
¹**bent** \'bent\ *n* **1** : strong inclination or
interest; *also* : TALENT **2** : power of endurance ♦ **Synonyms** TALENT, APTI-
TUDE, GIFT, FLAIR, KNACK, GENIUS
²**bent** *adj* **1** : changed by bending
: CROOKED ⟨~ branches⟩ **2** : strongly
inclined : DETERMINED ⟨~ on going⟩
bent grass *n* : any of a genus of stiff velvety grasses used esp. for lawns and pastures
ben·thic \'ben-thik\ *adj* : of, relating to,
or occurring at the bottom of a body of
water
ben·ton·ite \'ben-tə-ˌnīt\ *n* : an absorptive clay used esp. as a filler (as in paper)
bent·wood \'bent-ˌwùd\ *adj* : made of
wood bent into shape ⟨a ~ rocker⟩
be·numb \bi-'nəm\ *vb* **1** : DULL, DEADEN
2 : to make numb esp. by cold
ben·zene \'ben-ˌzēn\ *n* : a colorless volatile flammable liquid hydrocarbon used
in organic synthesis and as a solvent —
ben·ze·noid \-zə-ˌnóid\ *adj or n*
ben·zine \'ben-ˌzēn\ *n* : any of various
flammable petroleum distillates used as
solvents or as motor fuels
ben·zo·ate \'ben-zə-ˌwāt\ *n* : a salt or ester of benzoic acid
ben·zo·ic acid \ben-'zō-ik-\ *n* : a white
crystalline acid used as a preservative
and antiseptic and in synthesizing chemicals
ben·zo·in \'ben-zə-wən, -ˌzòin\ *n* : a balsamic resin from trees of southern Asia
used esp. in medicine and perfumes
be·queath \bi-'kwēth, -'kwēth\ *vb* [ME
bequethen, fr. OE *becwethan,* fr. *be-* +
cwethan to say] **1** : to leave by will **2** : to
hand down
be·quest \bi-'kwest\ *n* **1** : the action of
bequeathing **2** : something bequeathed
: LEGACY
be·rate \-'rāt\ *vb* : to scold harshly
Ber·ber \'bər-bər\ *n* : a member of any of
various peoples living in northern Africa
west of Tripoli
ber·ceuse \ber-'sœz, -'süz\ *n, pl* **ber-**
ceuses *same or* -'sü-zəz\ [F, fr. *bercer* to
rock] **1** : LULLABY **2** : a musical composition that resembles a lullaby
¹**be·reaved** \bi-'rēvd\ *adj* : suffering the
death of a loved one ⟨her ~ parents⟩ —
be·reave·ment *n*
²**bereaved** *n, pl* **bereaved** : one who is bereaved
be·reft \-'reft\ *adj* **1** : deprived of or lacking something — usu. used with *of* **2**
: BEREAVED ⟨a ~ mother⟩
be·ret \bə-'rā\ *n* : a round soft cap with
no visor
berg \'bərg\ *n* : ICEBERG
beri·beri \ˌber-ē-'ber-ē\ *n* : a deficiency

disease marked by weakness, wasting, and nerve damage and caused by lack of thiamine

berke·li·um \'bər-klē-əm\ n : an artificially produced radioactive chemical element

berm \'bərm\ n : a narrow shelf or path at the top or bottom of a slope; also : a mound or bank of earth

Bermuda grass n : a creeping grass often used for lawns and pastures

Ber·mu·das \bər-'myü-dəz\ n pl : BERMUDA SHORTS

Bermuda shorts n pl : knee-length walking shorts

ber·ry \'ber-ē\ n, pl berries 1 : a small pulpy fruit (as a strawberry) 2 : a simple fruit (as a grape, tomato, or cucumber) with the wall of the ripened ovary thick and pulpy 3 : the dry seed of some plants (as coffee)

ber·serk \bər-'sərk, -'zərk\ adj [ON berserkr warrior frenzied in battle, prob. fr. ber- bear + serkr shirt] : FRENZIED, CRAZED ⟨∼ behavior⟩ — **berserk** adv

berth \'bərth\ n 1 : adequate distance esp. for a ship to maneuver 2 : the place where a ship is anchored or a vehicle rests 3 : ACCOMMODATIONS 4 : JOB, POSITION ♦ **Synonyms** POST, SITUATION, OFFICE, APPOINTMENT

²berth vb 1 : to bring or come into a berth 2 : to allot a berth to

ber·yl \'ber-əl\ n : a hard silicate mineral occurring as colorless hexagonal crystals when pure

be·ryl·li·um \bə-'ri-lē-əm\ n : a light strong metallic chemical element used as a hardener in alloys

be·seech \bi-'sēch\ vb -sought \-'sòt\ or -seeched; -seech·ing : to beg urgently : ENTREAT ♦ **Synonyms** IMPLORE, PLEAD, SUPPLICATE, IMPORTUNE

be·seem \bi-'sēm\ vb, archaic : BEFIT

be·set \-'set\ vb -set; -set·ting 1 : TROUBLE, HARASS ⟨the ills that ∼ humanity⟩ 2 : ASSAIL ⟨∼ by wild dogs⟩; also : SURROUND

be·set·ting adj : persistently present

¹be·side \bi-'sīd\ prep 1 : by the side of ⟨sit ∼ me⟩ 2 : BESIDES 3 : not relevant to ⟨∼ the point⟩

²beside adv, archaic : BESIDES

¹be·sides \bi-'sīdz\ prep 1 : other than ⟨no one ∼ us⟩ 2 : together with

²besides adv 1 : as well : ALSO 2 : MOREOVER

be·siege \bi-'sēj\ vb : to lay siege to; also : to press with requests — **be·sieg·er** n

be·smear \-'smir\ vb : SMEAR

be·smirch \-'smərch\ vb : SMIRCH, SOIL

be·som \'bē-zəm\ n : BROOM

be·sot \-'sät\ vb be·sot·ted; be·sot·ting 1 : INFATUATE ⟨besotted lovers⟩ 2 : to make dull esp. by drinking

be·spat·ter \-'spa-tər\ vb : SPATTER

be·speak \bi-'spēk\ vb -spoke \-'spōk\; -spo·ken \-'spō-kən\; -speak·ing 1 : PREARRANGE 2 : ADDRESS 3 : REQUEST 4 : INDICATE, SIGNIFY ⟨her new album ∼s her talent⟩ 5 : FORETELL

be·sprin·kle \-'spriŋ-kəl\ vb : SPRINKLE

¹best \'best\ adj, superlative of GOOD 1 : excelling all others 2 : most productive (as of good or satisfaction) ⟨the ∼ thing to do⟩ 3 : LARGEST, MOST

²best adv, superlative of WELL 1 : in the best way 2 : MOST

³best n : something that is best

⁴best vb : to get the better of : OUTDO

bes·tial \'bes-chəl\ adj 1 : of or relating to beasts 2 : resembling a beast esp. in brutality or lack of intelligence

bes·ti·al·i·ty \,bes-chē-'a-lə-tē, ,bēs-\ n, -ties 1 : the condition or status of a lower animal 2 : display or gratification of bestial traits or impulses 3 : sexual relations between a human being and a lower animal

bes·ti·ary \'bes-chē-ˌer-ē\ n, pl -ar·ies : a medieval allegorical or moralizing work on the appearance and habits of animals

be·stir \bi-'stər\ vb : to rouse to action

best man n : the principal groomsman at a wedding

be·stow \bi-'stō\ vb 1 : PUT, PLACE, STOW 2 : to present as a gift — **be·stow·al** n — **be·stow·er** n

be·stride \bi-'strīd\ vb -strode \-'strōd\; -strid·den \-'stri-dᵊn\; -strid·ing : to ride, sit, or stand astride

¹bet \'bet\ n 1 : something that is wagered, risked, or pledged usu. between two parties on the outcome of a contest; also : the making of such a bet 2 : OPTION ⟨the back road is your best ∼⟩

²bet vb bet also bet·ted; bet·ting 1 : to stake on the outcome of an issue or a contest ⟨∼ $2 on the race⟩ 2 : to make a bet with 3 : to lay a bet

³bet abbr between

be·ta \'bā-tə\ n 1 : the 2d letter of the Greek alphabet — B or β 2 : a nearly complete form of a new product (as software)

beta–block·er \-ˌblä-kər\ n : any of a group of drugs that decrease the rate and force of heart contractions and lower high blood pressure

be·ta–car·o·tene \-'ker-ə-ˌtēn\ n : an isomer of carotene found in dark green and dark yellow vegetables and fruits

be·take \bi-'tāk\ vb -took \-'tuk\; -tak·en \-'tā-kən\; -tak·ing : to cause (oneself) to go

beta particle n : a high-speed electron; esp : one emitted by a radioactive nucleus

beta ray n 1 : BETA PARTICLE 2 : a stream of beta particles

beta test n : a field test of the beta version of a product esp. by outside testers and prior to commercial release — **beta test** vb

be·tel \'bē-tᵊl\ n : a climbing pepper of southern Asia whose leaves are chewed together with lime and betel nut as a stimulant

betel nut n : the astringent seed of an Asian palm that is chewed with betel leaves

bête noire \ˌbet-'nwär, ˌbāt-\ n, pl **bêtes noires** \same or -'nwärz\ [F, lit., black beast] : a person or thing strongly disliked or avoided

beth·el \'be-thəl\ n [Heb *bēth'ēl* house of God] : a place of worship esp. for seamen

be·tide \bi-'tīd\ vb : to happen to

be·times \bi-'tīmz\ adv : in good time : EARLY ♦ *Synonyms* SOON, SEASONABLY, TIMELY

be·to·ken \bi-'tō-kən\ vb 1 : PRESAGE 2 : to give evidence of ♦ *Synonyms* INDICATE, ATTEST, BESPEAK, TESTIFY

be·tray \bi-'trā\ vb 1 : to lead astray; *esp* : SEDUCE 2 : to deliver to an enemy 3 : ABANDON 4 : to prove unfaithful to 5 : to reveal unintentionally; *also* : SHOW, INDICATE ♦ *Synonyms* MISLEAD, DELUDE, DECEIVE, BEGUILE — **be·tray·al** n — **be·tray·er** n

be·troth \bi-'trōth, -'trȯth\ vb : to promise to marry — **be·troth·al** n

be·trothed n : the person to whom one is betrothed

¹**bet·ter** \'be-tər\ adj, comparative of GOOD 1 : greater than half 2 : improved in health 3 : more attractive, favorable, or commendable 4 : more advantageous or effective ⟨a ~ solution⟩ 5 : improved in accuracy or performance

²**better** vb 1 : to make or become better 2 : SURPASS, EXCEL

³**better** adv, comparative of WELL 1 : in a superior manner 2 : to a higher or greater degree; *also* : MORE

⁴**better** n 1 : something better; *also* : a superior esp. in merit or rank 2 : ADVANTAGE ⟨got the ~ of his opponent⟩

⁵**better** verbal auxiliary : had better ⟨you ~ hurry⟩

better half n : SPOUSE

bet·ter·ment \'be-tər-mənt\ n : IMPROVEMENT

bet·tor or **bet·ter** \'be-tər\ n : one that bets

¹**be·tween** \bi-'twēn\ prep 1 : by the common action of ⟨earned $10,000 ~ the two of them⟩ 2 : in the interval separating ⟨an alley ~ two buildings⟩; *also* : in intermediate relation to 3 : in point of comparison of ⟨choose ~ two cars⟩

²**between** adv : in an intervening space or interval

be·twixt \bi-'twikst\ adv or prep : BETWEEN

¹**bev·el** \'be-vəl\ n 1 : a device for adjusting the slant of the surfaces of a piece of work 2 : the angle or slant that one surface or line makes with another when not at right angles

²**bevel** vb -eled or -elled; -el·ing or -el·ling 1 : to cut or shape to a bevel 2 : INCLINE, SLANT

bev·er·age \'bev-rij\ n : a drinkable liquid

bevy \'be-vē\ n, pl **bev·ies** 1 : a large group or collection 2 : a group of animals and esp. quail

be·wail \bi-'wāl\ vb : LAMENT ♦ *Synonyms* DEPLORE, BEMOAN, GRIEVE, MOAN, WEEP

be·ware \-'wer\ vb : to be on one's guard : be wary of

be·wil·der \bi-'wil-dər\ vb : PERPLEX, CONFUSE ♦ *Synonyms* MYSTIFY, DISTRACT, PUZZLE — **be·wil·der·ment** n

be·witch \-'wich\ vb 1 : to affect by witchcraft 2 : CHARM, FASCINATE ♦ *Synonyms* ENCHANT, ATTRACT, CAPTIVATE — **be·witch·ment** n

bey \'bā\ n 1 : a former Turkish provincial governor 2 : the former native ruler of Tunis or Tunisia

¹**be·yond** \bē-'änd\ adv 1 : FARTHER ⟨extends to the river and ~⟩ 2 : BESIDES

²**beyond** prep 1 : on or to the farther side of 2 : out of the reach or sphere of 3 : BESIDES

be·zel \'bē-zəl, 'be-\ n 1 : a rim that holds a transparent covering (as on a watch) 2 : the faceted part of a cut gem that rises above the setting

bf abbr boldface

BFF abbr best friends forever

BG or **B Gen** abbr brigadier general

Bh symbol bohrium

bhang \'baŋ\ n [Hindi *bhāṅg*] : HEMP; *also* : a mildly intoxicating preparation made from hemp leaves

Bi symbol bismuth

BIA abbr Bureau of Indian Affairs

bi·an·nu·al \(ˌ)bī-'an-yə-wəl\ adj : occurring twice a year — **bi·an·nu·al·ly** adv

¹**bi·as** \'bī-əs\ n 1 : a line diagonal to the grain of a fabric 2 : PREJUDICE, BENT

²**bias** adv : on the bias : DIAGONALLY

³**bias** vb **bi·ased** or **bi·assed**; **bi·as·ing** or **bi·as·sing** : PREJUDICE

bi·ath·lon \bī-'ath-lən, -ˌlän\ n : a composite athletic contest consisting of cross-country skiing and target shooting with a rifle

¹**bib** \'bib\ n : a cloth or plastic shield tied under the chin to protect the clothes while eating

²**bib** abbr Bible; biblical

bi·be·lot \'bē-bə-ˌlō\ n, pl **bibelots** \same or -ˌlōz\ : a small household ornament or decorative object

bi·ble \'bī-bəl\ n [ME, fr. OF, fr. ML *biblia*, fr. Gk, pl. of *biblion* book, dim. of *byblos* papyrus, book, fr. *Byblos*, ancient Phoenician city from which papyrus was exported] 1 cap : the sacred scriptures of Christians comprising the Old and New Testaments 2 cap : the sacred scriptures of Judaism; *also* : those of some other religion 3 : a publication that is considered authoritative for its subject — **bib·li·cal** \'bi-bli-kəl\ adj

☞ the BIBLE table is on page 68

bib·li·og·ra·phy \ˌbi-blē-'ä-grə-fē\ n, pl **-phies** 1 : the history or description of writings or publications 2 : a list of writings (as on a subject or of an author) — **bib·li·og·ra·pher** \-fər\ n — **bib·li·o·graph·ic** \-ə-'gra-fik\ also **bib·li·o·graph·i·cal** \-fi-kəl\ adj

bib·lio·phile \'bi-blē-ə-ˌfī(-ə)l\ n : a lover of books

bib·u·lous \'bi-byə-ləs\ adj 1 : highly absorbent 2 : fond of alcoholic beverages

bi·cam·er·al \'bī-'ka-mə-rəl\ adj : having or consisting of two legislative branches

bicarb \(ˌ)bī-'kärb, 'bī-ˌ\ n : SODIUM BICARBONATE

bi·car·bon·ate \(ˌ)bī-'kär-bə-ˌnāt, -nət\ n : an acid carbonate

BOOKS OF THE BIBLE

JEWISH SCRIPTURE

LAW	PROPHETS		WRITINGS
Genesis	Joshua	Obadiah	Psalms
Exodus	Judges	Jonah	Proverbs
Leviticus	1 & 2 Samuel	Micah	Job
Numbers	1 & 2 Kings	Nahum	Song of Songs
Deuteronomy	Isaiah	Habakkuk	Ruth
	Jeremiah	Zephaniah	Lamentations
	Ezekiel	Haggai	Ecclesiastes
	Hosea	Zechariah	Esther
	Joel	Malachi	Daniel
	Amos		Ezra
			Nehemiah
			1 & 2 Chronicles

CHRISTIAN CANON—OLD TESTAMENT

ROMAN CATHOLIC	PROTESTANT	ROMAN CATHOLIC	PROTESTANT
Genesis	Genesis	Wisdom	
Exodus	Exodus	Sirach	
Leviticus	Leviticus	Isaiah	Isaiah
Numbers	Numbers	Jeremiah	Jeremiah
Deuteronomy	Deuteronomy	Lamentations	Lamentations
Joshua	Joshua	Baruch	
Judges	Judges	Ezekiel	Ezekiel
Ruth	Ruth	Daniel	Daniel
1 & 2 Samuel	1 & 2 Samuel	Hosea	Hosea
1 & 2 Kings	1 & 2 Kings	Joel	Joel
1 & 2 Chronicles	1 & 2 Chronicles	Amos	Amos
Ezra	Ezra	Obadiah	Obadiah
Nehemiah	Nehemiah	Jonah	Jonah
Tobit		Micah	Micah
Judith		Nahum	Nahum
Esther	Esther	Habakkuk	Habakkuk
Job	Job	Zephaniah	Zephaniah
Psalms	Psalms	Haggai	Haggai
Proverbs	Proverbs	Zechariah	Zechariah
Ecclesiastes	Ecclesiastes	Malachi	Malachi
Song of Songs	Song of Solomon	1 & 2 Maccabees	

PROTESTANT APOCRYPHA

1 & 2 Esdras	Baruch
Tobit	Prayer of Azariah and the Song of the Three Holy Children
Judith	
Additions to Esther	Susanna
Wisdom of Solomon	Bel and the Dragon
Ecclesiasticus or the Wisdom of Jesus Son of Sirach	The Prayer of Manasses
	1 & 2 Maccabees

CHRISTIAN CANON—NEW TESTAMENT

Matthew	Ephesians	James
Mark	Philippians	1 & 2 Peter
Luke	Colossians	1, 2, 3 John
John	1 & 2 Thessalonians	Jude
Acts of the Apostles	1 & 2 Timothy	Revelation *or*
Romans	Titus	Apocalypse
1 & 2 Corinthians	Philemon	
Galatians	Hebrews	

bicarbonate of soda : SODIUM BICARBONATE

bi·cen·te·na·ry \ˌbī-sen-ˈte-nə-rē, bī-ˈsen-t³n-ˌer-ē\ n : BICENTENNIAL — **bicentenary** adj

bi·cen·ten·ni·al \ˌbī-sen-ˈte-nē-əl\ n : a 200th anniversary or its celebration — **bicentennial** adj

bi·ceps \ˈbī-ˌseps\ n, pl **biceps** also **biceps·es** [NL, fr. L, two-headed, fr. bi-two + caput head] : a muscle (as in the front of the upper arm) having two points of origin

¹**bick·er** \ˈbi-kər\ n : ALTERCATION

²**bicker** vb : to engage in a petty quarrel

bi·coast·al \bī-ˈkōs-t³l\ adj : living or working on both the east and west coasts of the U.S.

bi·con·cave \ˌbī-(ˌ)kän-ˈkāv, (ˌ)bī-ˈkän-ˌkāv\ adj : concave on both sides

bi·con·vex \ˌbī-(ˌ)kän-ˈveks, (ˌ)bī-ˈkän-ˌveks\ adj : convex on both sides

bi·cus·pid \bī-ˈkəs-pəd\ n : PREMOLAR

¹**bi·cy·cle** \ˈbī-ˌsi-kəl\ n : a light 2-wheeled vehicle with a saddle, pedals, and handlebars for steering

²**bicycle** vb **-cy·cled; -cy·cling** \-ˌsi-k(ə-)liŋ, -ˌsī-\ : to ride a bicycle — **bi·cy·cler** \-k(ə-)lər\ n — **bi·cy·clist** \-k(ə-)list\ n

¹**bid** \ˈbid\ vb **bade** \ˈbad, ˈbād\ or **bid; bid·den** \ˈbi-d³n\ or **bid** also **bade; bid·ding** 1 : COMMAND, ORDER 2 : INVITE 3 : to give expression to ⟨bade a tearful farewell⟩ 4 : to make a bid : OFFER — **bid·der** n

²**bid** n 1 : the act of one who bids; also : an offer for something 2 : INVITATION 3 : an announcement in a card game of what a player proposes to accomplish 4 : an attempt to win or gain ⟨a ~ for mayor⟩

bid·da·ble \ˈbi-də-bəl\ adj 1 : OBEDIENT, DOCILE 2 : capable of being bid

bid·dy \ˈbi-dē\ n, pl **biddies** : HEN; also : a young chicken

bide \ˈbīd\ vb **bode** \ˈbōd\ or **bid·ed; bid·ed; bid·ing** 1 : to wait for 2 : WAIT, TARRY 3 : DWELL

bi·det \bi-ˈdā\ n : a bathroom fixture used esp. for bathing the external genitals and the anal region

bi·di·rec·tion·al \ˌbī-də-ˈrek-sh(ə-)nəl\ adj : involving, moving, or taking place in two usu. opposite directions — **bi·di·rec·tion·al·ly** adv

bi·en·ni·al \bī-ˈe-nē-əl\ adj 1 : taking place once in two years 2 : lasting two years 3 : producing leaves the first year and fruiting and dying the second year — **biennial** n — **bi·en·ni·al·ly** adv

bi·en·ni·um \bī-ˈe-nē-əm\ n, pl **-niums** or **-nia** \-ə\ [L, fr. bi- two + annus year] : a period of two years

bier \ˈbir\ n : a stand bearing a coffin or corpse

bi·fo·cal \ˈbī-ˌfō-kəl\ adj : having two focal lengths

bifocals \-kəlz\ n pl : eyeglasses with lenses that have one part that corrects for near vision and one for distant vision

bi·fold \ˈbī-ˌfōld\ adj : designed to fold twice ⟨~ doors⟩

bi·fur·cate \ˈbī-fər-ˌkāt, bī-ˈfər-\ vb **-cat·ed; -cat·ing** : to divide into two branches or parts — **bi·fur·ca·tion** \ˌbī-fər-ˈkā-shən\ n

big \ˈbig\ adj **big·ger; big·gest** 1 : large in size, amount, or scope 2 : PREGNANT; also : SWELLING 3 : IMPORTANT, IMPOSING 4 : NOBLE, GENEROUS 5 : POPULAR — **big·ness** n — **big on** : strongly favoring or liking

big·a·my \ˈbi-gə-mē\ n : the act of marrying one person while still legally married to another — **big·a·mist** \-mist\ n — **big·a·mous** \-məs\ adj

big bang theory n : a theory in astronomy: the universe originated in an explosion (**big bang**) from a single point of nearly infinite energy density

big brother n 1 : an older brother 2 : a man who befriends a delinquent or friendless boy 3 cap both Bs : the leader of an authoritarian state or movement

big cheese n : ³BOSS

big crunch n : a hypothetical event in which all matter in the universe collapses to a single point of nearly infinite density

Big Dipper n : the seven principal stars of Ursa Major in a form resembling a dipper

big·foot \ˈbig-ˌfu̇t\ n : SASQUATCH

big·horn sheep \ˈbig-ˌhȯrn\ n : a wild sheep of mountainous western No. America

bight \ˈbīt\ n 1 : a curve in a coast; also : the bay formed by such a curve 2 : a slack part in a rope

big-name \ˈbig-ˈnām\ adj : widely popular ⟨a ~ performer⟩ — **big name** n

big·ot \ˈbi-gət\ n : one who regards or treats members of a group with hatred and intolerance ◆ Synonyms FANATIC, ENTHUSIAST, ZEALOT — **big·ot·ed** \-gə-təd\ adj — **big·ot·ry** \-trē\ n

big screen n : the motion picture medium as contrasted to television

big shot \ˈbig-ˌshät\ n : an important person

big time n 1 : a high-paying vaudeville circuit requiring only two performances a day 2 : the top rank of an activity or enterprise — **big-tim·er** n

big top n 1 : the main tent of a circus 2 : CIRCUS

big·wig \ˈbig-ˌwig\ n : BIG SHOT

bike \ˈbīk\ n 1 : BICYCLE 2 : MOTORCYCLE

bik·er n : MOTORCYCLIST; esp : one who is a member of an organized gang

bike·way \ˈbīk-ˌwā\ n : a thoroughfare for bicycles

bi·ki·ni \bə-ˈkē-nē\ n [F, fr. Bikini, atoll in the Marshall Islands] : a woman's brief 2-piece bathing suit

bi·lat·er·al \bī-ˈla-tə-rəl\ adj 1 : having or involving two sides 2 : affecting reciprocally two sides or parties — **bi·lat·er·al·ism** \-tə-rə-ˌli-zəm\ n — **bi·lat·er·al·ly** adv

bile \ˈbī(-ə)l\ n 1 : a bitter greenish fluid secreted by the liver that aids in the digestion of fats 2 : an ill-humored mood

bilge \ˈbilj\ n 1 : the part of a ship that

lies between the bottom and the point where the sides go straight up **2** : stale or worthless remarks or ideas

bi·lin·gual \bī-'liŋ-gwəl\ *adj* : expressed in, knowing, or using two languages

bil·ious \'bil-yəs\ *adj* **1** : marked by or suffering from disordered liver function **2** : IRRITABLE, ILL-TEMPERED ⟨a ~ disposition⟩ — **bil·ious·ness** *n*

bilk \'bilk\ *vb* : CHEAT, SWINDLE

¹bill \'bil\ *n* : the jaws of a bird together with their horny covering; *also* : a mouthpart (as of a turtle) resembling these — **billed** \'bild\ *adj*

²bill *vb* : to caress fondly

³bill *n* **1** : an itemized statement of particulars; *also* : INVOICE **2** : a written document or note **3** : a printed advertisement (as a poster) announcing an event **4** : a draft of a law presented to a legislature for enactment **5** : a written statement of a legal wrong suffered or of some breach of law **6** : a piece of paper money

⁴bill *vb* **1** : to enter in or prepare a bill; *also* : to submit a bill or account to **2** : to advertise by bills or posters

bill·board \-,bȯrd\ *n* : a flat surface on which advertising bills are posted

¹bil·let \'bil-ət\ *n* **1** : an order requiring a person to provide lodging for a soldier; *also* : quarters assigned by or as if by such an order **2** : POSITION, APPOINTMENT

²billet *vb* : to assign lodging to by billet

bil·let–doux \,bil-ā-'dü\ *n, pl* **billets–doux** *same or* -'düz\ [F *billet doux*, lit., sweet letter] : a love letter

bill·fold \'bil-,fōld\ *n* : WALLET

bil·liards \'bil-yərdz\ *n* : any of several games played on an oblong table by driving balls against each other or into pockets with a cue

bil·lings·gate \'bi-liŋz-,gāt, *Brit usu* -git\ *n* [*Billingsgate*, old gate and fish market, London, England] : coarsely abusive language

bil·lion \'bil-yən\ *n* **1** : a thousand millions **2** *Brit* : a million millions — **billion** *adj* — **bil·lionth** \-yənth\ *adj or n*

bill of attainder : a legislative act that imposes punishment without a trial

bill of health : a usu. favorable report following an examination

bill of sale : a legal document transferring ownership of goods

¹bil·low \'bi-lō\ *n* **1** : WAVE; *esp* : a great wave **2** : a rolling mass (as of fog or flame) like a great wave — **bil·lowy** \'bi-lə-wē\ *adj*

²billow *vb* : to rise and roll in waves; *also* : to swell out ⟨~ing sails⟩

bil·ly \'bi-lē\ *n, pl* **billies** : BILLY CLUB

billy club *n* : a heavy usu. wooden club; *esp* : a police officer's club

bil·ly goat \'bi-lē-\ *n* : a male goat

bi·met·al \'bī-,me-tᵊl\ *adj* : BIMETALLIC — **bimetal** *n*

bi·me·tal·lic \,bī-mə-'ta-lik\ *adj* : made of two different metals — often used of devices having a bonded expansive part — **bimetallic** *n*

bi·met·al·lism \bī-'me-tᵊl-,i-zəm\ *n* : the

use of two metals at fixed ratios to form a standard of value for a monetary system

¹bi·month·ly \bī-'mənth-lē\ *adj* **1** : occurring every two months **2** : occurring twice a month : SEMIMONTHLY — **bimonthly** *adv*

²bimonthly *n* : a bimonthly publication

bin \'bin\ *n* : a box, crib, or enclosure used for storage

bi·na·ry \'bī-nə-rē, -,ner-ē\ *adj* **1** : consisting of two things or parts **2** : relating to, being, or belonging to a system of numbers having 2 as its base ⟨the ~ digits 0 and 1⟩ **3** : involving a choice between or condition of two alternatives only (as on-off, yes-no) — **binary** *n*

binary star *n* : a system of two stars revolving around each other

binary system *n* : BINARY STAR

bin·au·ral \bī-'nȯr-əl\ *adj* : of or relating to sound reproduction involving the use of two separated microphones and two transmission channels to achieve a stereophonic effect

bind \'bīnd\ *vb* **bound** \'baȯnd\; **binding 1** : TIE; *also* : to restrain as if by tying **2** : to put under an obligation; *also* : to constrain with legal authority **3** : BANDAGE **4** : to unite into a mass **5** : to compel as if by a pledge ⟨a handshake ~s the deal⟩ **6** : to strengthen or decorate with a band **7** : to fasten together and enclose in a cover ⟨~ books⟩ **8** : to exert a tying, restraining, or compelling effect — **binder** *n*

bind·ing \'bīn-diŋ\ *n* : something (as a ski fastening, a cover, or an edging fabric) used to bind

bin·dle \'bin-dᵊl\ *n* : a bundle of clothes or bedding

¹binge \'binj\ *n* **1** : SPREE **2** : an act of excessive consumption (as of food)

²binge *vb* **binged**; **binge·ing** *or* **bing·ing** : to go on a binge — **bing·er** *n*

bin·go \'biŋ-gō\ *n, pl* **bingos** : a game of chance played with cards having numbered squares corresponding to numbered balls drawn at random and won by covering five squares in a row

bin·na·cle \'bi-ni-kəl\ *n* [alter. of ME *bitakle*, fr. Pg or Sp; Pg *bitácola* & Sp *bitácula*, fr. L *habitaculum* dwelling place, fr. *habitare* to inhabit] : a container holding a ship's compass

¹bin·oc·u·lar \bī-'nä-kyə-lər, bə-\ *adj* : of, relating to, or adapted to the use of both eyes — **bin·oc·u·lar·ly** *adv*

²bin·oc·u·lar \bə-'nä-kyə-lər, bī-\ *n* **1** : a binocular optical instrument (as a microscope) **2** : a hand-held optical instrument composed of two telescopes and a focusing device — usu. used in pl.

bi·no·mi·al \bī-'nō-mē-əl\ *n* **1** : a mathematical expression consisting of two terms connected by the sign plus (+) or minus (−) **2** : a biological species name consisting of two terms — **binomial** *adj*

bio·chem·is·try \,bī-ō-'ke-mə-strē\ *n* : chemistry that deals with the chemical compounds and processes occurring in living things — **bio·chem·i·cal** \-mi-kəl\

adj or n — **bio·chem·i·cal·ly** \-k(ə-)lē\ *adv* — **bio·chem·ist** \-'mist\ *n*

bio·de·grad·able \-di-'grā-də-bəl\ *adj* : capable of being broken down esp. into innocuous products by the actions of living things (as microorganisms) ⟨a ~ detergent⟩ — **bio·de·grad·abil·i·ty** \-,grā-də-'bi-lə-tē\ *n* — **bio·deg·ra·da·tion** \-,de-grə-'dā-shən\ *n* — **bio·de·grade** \-di-'grād\ *vb*

bio·di·ver·si·ty \-də-'vər-sə-tē, -dī-\ *n* : biological diversity in an environment as indicated by numbers of different species of plants and animals

bio·en·gi·neer·ing \-,en-jə-'nir-iŋ\ *n* **1** : the application of engineering principles to medicine and biology **2** : GENETIC ENGINEERING

bio·eth·ics \-'e-thiks\ *n* : the ethics of biological research and its applications esp. in medicine — **bio·eth·i·cal** \-'e-thi-kəl\ *adj* — **bio·eth·i·cist** \-'e-thə-sist\ *n*

bio·feed·back \-'fēd-,bak\ *n* : the technique of making unconscious or involuntary bodily processes (as heartbeats or brain waves) perceptible to the senses (as by use of an oscilloscope) in order to manipulate them by conscious mental control

biog *abbr* biographer; biographical; biography

bio·ge·og·ra·phy \,bī-ō-jē-'ä-grə-fē\ *n* : a science that deals with the geographical distribution of plants and animals — **bio·ge·og·ra·pher** *n*

bi·og·ra·phy \bī-'ä-grə-fē, bē-\ *n, pl* **-phies** : a written history of a person's life; *also* : such writings in general — **bi·og·ra·pher** *n* — **bio·graph·i·cal** \,bī-ə-'gra-fi-kəl\ *also* **bio·graph·ic** \-fik\ *adj*

bio·in·for·mat·ics \,bī-ō-in-fər-'ma-tiks\ *n* : the storage, classification, and analysis of biological information using computers

biol *abbr* biologic; biological; biologist; biology

bi·o·log·i·cal \,bī-ə-'lä-ji-kəl\ *also* **bi·o·log·ic** \-jik\ *adj* **1** : of, relating to, or produced by biology or life and living processes **2** : connected by direct genetic relationship rather than by adoption or marriage ⟨her ~ father⟩ — **bi·o·log·i·cal·ly** \-ji-k(ə-)lē\ *adv*

biological clock *n* : an inherent timing mechanism in a living system that is inferred to exist in order to explain the timing of various physiological and behavioral states and processes

biological warfare *n* : warfare in which harmful living organisms (**biological weapons**) are used against an enemy esp. to cause large-scale death or disease

bi·ol·o·gy \bī-'ä-lə-jē\ *n* [G *Biologie,* fr. Gk *bios* mode of life + *logos* word, discourse] **1** : a science that deals with living beings and life processes **2** : the life processes of an organism or group — **bi·ol·o·gist** \bī-'ä-lə-jist\ *n*

bio·mass \'bī-ō-,mas\ *n* **1** : the amount of living matter (as in a unit area) **2** : plant materials and animal waste used esp. as fuel

bio·med·i·cal \,bī-ō-'me-di-kəl\ *adj* : of, relating to, or involving biological, medical, and physical science

bi·on·ic \bī-'ä-nik\ *adj* : having normal biological capability or performance enhanced by or as if by electronic or mechanical devices

bio·phys·ics \,bī-ō-'fi-ziks\ *n* : a branch of science concerned with the application of physical principles and methods to biological problems — **bio·phys·i·cal** \-zi-kəl\ *adj* — **bio·phys·i·cist** \-'fi-zə-sist\ *n*

bio·pic \'bī-ō-,pik\ *n* : a biographical movie

bi·op·sy \'bī-,äp-sē\ *n, pl* **-sies** : the removal of tissue, cells, or fluids from the living body for examination

bio·rhythm \'bī-ō-,ri-thəm\ *n* : an innately determined rhythmic biological process (as sleep); *also* : the internal mechanism controlling such a process

bio·sci·ence \-'sī-əns\ *n* : BIOLOGY 1; *also* : LIFE SCIENCE

bio·sphere \'bī-ə-,sfir\ *n* **1** : the part of the world in which life can exist **2** : living organisms together with their environment

bio·tech \'bī-ō-,tek\ *n* : BIOTECHNOLOGY

bio·tech·nol·o·gy \,bī-ō-tek-'nä-lə-jē\ *n* : the manipulation (as through genetic engineering) of living organisms to produce useful products; *also* : biological science so applied

bio·ter·ror·ism \-'ter-ər-,i-zəm\ *n* : terrorism involving the use of biological weapons — **bio·ter·ror·ist** \-ist\ *adj or n*

bi·ot·ic \bī-'ä-tik\ *adj* : of, relating to, or caused by living organisms

bi·o·tin \'bī-ə-tən\ *n* : a vitamin of the vitamin B complex found esp. in yeast, liver, and egg yolk and active in growth promotion

bi·o·tite \'bī-ə-,tīt\ *n* : a dark mica containing iron, magnesium, potassium, and aluminum

bi·par·ti·san \bī-'pär-tə-zən\ *adj* : marked by or involving cooperation, agreement, and compromise between two major political parties — **bi·par·ti·san·ship** \-,ship\ *n*

bi·par·tite \bī-'pär-,tīt\ *adj* **1** : being in two parts **2** : shared by two ⟨~ treaty⟩

bi·ped \'bī-,ped\ *n* : a 2-footed animal — **bi·ped·al** \(,)bī-'pe-d°l\ *adj*

bi·plane \'bī-,plān\ *n* : an aircraft with two wings placed one above the other

bi·po·lar \bī-'pō-lər\ *adj* : having or involving the use of two poles — **bi·po·lar·i·ty** \,bī-pō-'ler-ə-tē\ *n*

bipolar disorder *n* : any of several psychological disorders of mood characterized usu. by alternating episodes of depression and mania

bi·ra·cial \bī-'rā-shəl\ *adj* : of, relating to, or involving members of two races

¹**birch** \'bərch\ *n* **1** : any of a genus of mostly short-lived deciduous shrubs and trees with membranous outer bark and pale close-grained wood; *also* : this wood **2** : a birch rod or bundle of twigs for flogging — **birch** *or* **birch·en** \'bər-chən\ *adj*

²**birch** *vb* : WHIP, FLOG

¹bird \\'bərd\ *n* : any of a class of warm=
blooded egg-laying vertebrates having
the body feathered and the forelimbs
modified to form wings

²bird *vb* : to observe or identify wild birds
in their native habitat — **bird·er** *n*

bird·bath \\'bərd-ˌbath, -ˌbäth\ *n* : a usu.
ornamental basin set up for birds to
bathe in

bird·house \-ˌhau̇s\ *n* : an artificial nest-
ing place for birds; *also* : AVIARY

bird·ie \\'bər-dē\ *n* : a score of one under
par on a hole in golf

bird·lime \-ˌlīm\ *n* : a sticky substance
smeared on twigs to snare small birds

bird of paradise : any of numerous brilliantly colored plumed birds of the New
Guinea area

bird of prey : a carnivorous bird that
feeds wholly or chiefly on carrion or on
meat taken by hunting

bird·seed \\'bərd-ˌsēd\ *n* : a mixture of
small seeds (as of hemp or millet) used
for feeding birds

bird's-eye \\'bərdz-ˌī\ *adj* **1** : marked
with spots resembling birds' eyes ⟨~
maple⟩ **2** : seen from above as if by a
flying bird ⟨~ view⟩; *also* : CURSORY

bi·ret·ta \bə-'re-tə\ *n* : a square cap with
three ridges on top worn esp. by Roman
Catholic clergymen

birr \\'bir, 'bər\ *n, pl* **birr** — see MONEY
table

¹birth \\'bərth\ *n* **1** : the act or fact of being
born or of bringing forth young **2** : LIN-
EAGE, DESCENT **3** : ORIGIN, BEGINNING
— **birth** *vb*

²birth *adj* : BIOLOGICAL 2 ⟨~ parents⟩

birth canal *n* : the channel formed by the
cervix, vagina, and vulva through which
the fetus passes during birth

birth control *n* : control of the number of
children born esp. by preventing or lessening the frequency of conception

birth·day \\'bərth-ˌdā\ *n* : the day or anniversary of one's birth

birth defect *n* : a physical or biochemical
defect present at birth and inherited or
environmentally induced

birth·mark \\'bərth-ˌmärk\ *n* : an unusual
mark or blemish on the skin at birth

birth·place \-ˌplās\ *n* : place of birth or
origin

birth·rate \-ˌrāt\ *n* : the number of births
per number of individuals in a given area
or group during a given time

birth·right \-ˌrīt\ *n* : a right, privilege, or
possession to which one is entitled by
birth ♦ **Synonyms** LEGACY, PATRIMO-
NY, HERITAGE, INHERITANCE

birth·stone \-ˌstōn\ *n* : a gemstone associated symbolically with the month of
one's birth

bis·cuit \\'bis-kət\ *n* [ME *bisquite*, fr. AF
besquit, fr. (*pain*) *besquit* twice-cooked
bread] **1** : a crisp flat cake; *esp*, *Brit*
: CRACKER 2 **2** : a small quick bread
made from dough that has been rolled
and cut or dropped from a spoon

bi·sect \\'bī-ˌsekt\ *vb* : to divide into two
usu. equal parts; *also* : CROSS, INTERSECT

— **bi·sec·tion** \\'bī-ˌsek-shən\ *n* — **bi-
sec·tor** \-tər\ *n*

bi·sex·u·al \bī-'sek-shə-wəl\ *adj* **1** : possessing characters of or having sexual
desire for both sexes **2** : of, relating to, or
involving both sexes — **bisexual** *n* — **bi-
sex·u·al·i·ty** \ˌbī-ˌsek-shə-'wal-ə-tē\ *n*

bish·op \\'bi-shəp\ *n* [ME *bisshop*, fr. OE
bisceop, fr. LL *episcopus*, fr. Gk *episkop-
os*, lit., overseer, fr. *epi-* on, over + *skept-
esthai* to look] **1** : a member of the clergy
ranking above a priest and typically governing a diocese **2** : any of various Protestant church officials who superintend
other clergy **3** : a chess piece that can
move diagonally across any number of
adjoining unoccupied squares

bish·op·ric \\'bi-shə-prik\ *n* **1** : DIOCESE
2 : the office of bishop

bis·muth \\'biz-məth\ *n* : a heavy brittle
grayish white metallic chemical element
used in alloys and medicine

bi·son \\'bī-sᵊn, -zᵊn\ *n, pl* **bison** : BUF-
FALO 2

bisque \\'bisk\ *n* : a thick cream soup

bis·tro \\'bēs-trō, 'bis-\ *n, pl* **bistros** [F]
1 : a small or unpretentious restaurant **2**
: BAR; *also* : NIGHTCLUB

¹bit \\'bit\ *n* **1** : the biting or cutting edge
or part of a tool **2** : the part of a bridle
that is placed in a horse's mouth

²bit *n* **1** : a morsel of food; *also* : a small
piece or quantity of something **2** : a
small coin; *also* : a unit of value equal to
12½ cents **3** : something small or trivial
4 : an indefinite usu. small degree or extent ⟨a ~ tired⟩

³bit *n* [*bi*nary digi*t*] : a unit of computer
information equivalent to the result of a
choice between two alternatives; *also* : its
physical representation

¹bitch \\'bich\ *n* **1** : a female canine; *esp* : a
female dog **2** : a malicious, spiteful, or
overbearing woman

²bitch *vb* : COMPLAIN

¹bite \\'bīt\ *vb* **bit** \\'bit\; **bit·ten** \\'bi-tᵊn\
also **bit**; **bit·ing** \\'bī-tiŋ\ **1** : to grip with
teeth or jaws; *also* : to wound or sting
with or as if with fangs **2** : to cut or
pierce with or as if with an edged instrument **3** : to cause to smart or sting **4**
: CORRODE **5** : to take bait

²bite *n* **1** : the act or manner of biting **2**
: FOOD **3** : a wound made by biting; *also*
: a penetrating effect

bite–size \\'bīt-ˌsīz\ *adj* **1** : of a size that
can be eaten in one bite **2** : being or
made small or brief esp. so as to be easily
manageable

biting *adj* : SHARP, CUTTING

bit·map \\'bit-ˌmap\ *n* : an array of binary
data representing a bitmapped image or
display

bit·mapped \\'bit-ˌmapt\ *adj* : of, relating
to, or being a digital image or display for
which an array of binary data specifies
the value of each pixel

bit·ter \\'bi-tər\ *adj* **1** : being or inducing
the one of the basic taste sensations that
is acrid, astringent, or disagreeable and is
suggestive of hops **2** : marked by intensity or severity (as of distress or hatred)

3 : extremely harsh or cruel — **bit·ter·ly** *adv* — **bit·ter·ness** *n*

bit·tern \'bi-tərn\ *n* : any of various small or medium-sized herons

bit·ters \'bi-tərz\ *n sing or pl* : a usu. alcoholic solution of bitter and often aromatic plant products used in mixing drinks and as a mild tonic

¹**bit·ter·sweet** \'bi-tər-ˌswēt\ *n* **1** : a poisonous nightshade with purple flowers and reddish berries **2** : a woody vine with yellow capsules that open when ripe to show scarlet seed covers

²**bittersweet** *adj* : being at once both bitter and sweet

bi·tu·mi·nous coal \bə-'tü-mə-nəs-, bī-, -'tyü-\ *n* : a coal that when heated yields considerable volatile waste matter

bi·valve \'bī-ˌvalv\ *n* : any of a class of mollusks (as clams or scallops) of two separate parts that open and shut — **bivalve** *adj*

¹**biv·ouac** \'bi-və-ˌwak\ *n* [F, fr. LG *biwacht*, fr. *bi* at + *wacht* guard] : a temporary encampment or shelter

²**bivouac** *vb* **-ouacked; -ouack·ing** : to form a bivouac : CAMP

¹**bi·week·ly** \ˌbī-'wē-klē\ *adj* **1** : occurring twice a week **2** : occurring every two weeks : FORTNIGHTLY — **biweekly** *adv*

²**biweekly** *n* : a biweekly publication

bi·year·ly \-'yir-lē\ *adj* **1** : BIANNUAL **2** : BIENNIAL

bi·zarre \bə-'zär\ *adj* : ODD, ECCENTRIC, FANTASTIC ⟨∼ costumes⟩ — **bi·zarre·ly** *adv*

bi·zar·ro \bə-'zär-ō\ *adj* : characterized by a bizarre, fantastic, or unconventional approach ⟨∼ horror movies⟩

bk *abbr* **1** bank **2** book

Bk *symbol* berkelium

bkg *abbr* banking

bkgd *abbr* background

bks *abbr* barracks

bkt *abbr* **1** basket **2** bracket

bl *abbr* **1** bale **2** barrel **3** blue

blab \'blab\ *vb* **blabbed; blab·bing** : TATTLE, GOSSIP

¹**black** \'blak\ *adj* **1** : of the color black; *also* : very dark **2** : SWARTHY **3** : of or relating to various groups of dark-skinned people **4** : of or relating to the African-American people or their culture **5** : SOILED, DIRTY **6** : lacking light ⟨a ∼ night⟩ **7** : WICKED, EVIL ⟨∼ magic⟩ **8** : DISMAL, GLOOMY ⟨a ∼ outlook⟩ **9** : SULLEN ⟨a ∼ mood⟩ — **black·ish** *adj* — **black·ly** *adv* — **black·ness** *n*

²**black** *n* **1** : a black pigment or dye; *also* : something (as clothing) that is black **2** : the characteristic color of soot or coal **3** : a person of a dark-skinned race **4** : AFRICAN-AMERICAN

³**black** *vb* : BLACKEN

black·a·moor \'bla-kə-ˌmúr\ *n* : a dark-skinned person

black–and–blue \ˌbla-kən-'blü\ *adj* : darkly discolored from blood effused by bruising

black–and–white \ˌbla-kən-'hwīt\ *n* : SQUAD CAR

black·ball \'blak-ˌból\ *vb* **1** : to vote against; *esp* : to exclude from membership by casting a negative vote **2** : OSTRACIZE — **black·ball** *n*

black bass *n* : any of several freshwater sunfishes native to eastern and central No. America

black bear *n* : a usu. black-furred bear of No. American forests

¹**black belt** \'blak-ˌbelt\ *n, often cap both Bs* : an area densely populated by blacks

²**black belt** \-'belt\ *n* : one who holds the rating of expert (as in judo or karate); *also* : the rating itself

black·ber·ry \-ˌber-ē\ *n* : the usu. black or purple juicy but seedy edible fruit of various brambles; *also* : a plant bearing this fruit

black·bird \-ˌbərd\ *n* : any of various birds (as the red-winged blackbird) of which the male is largely or wholly black

black·board \-ˌbórd\ *n* : a smooth usu. dark surface used for writing or drawing on with chalk

black·body \-'bä-dē\ *n* : a body or surface that completely absorbs incident radiation with no reflection

black box *n* **1** : a usu. complicated electronic device whose components and workings are unknown or mysterious to the user **2** : a device used in aircraft to record cockpit conversations and flight data

black death *n* : an epidemic of bacterial plague and esp. bubonic plague that spread rapidly in Europe and Asia in the 14th century

black·en \'bla-kən\ *vb* **black·ened; black·en·ing 1** : to make or become black **2** : DEFAME, SULLY ⟨∼ed her reputation⟩

black·ened *adj* : coated with spices and quickly seared in a very hot skillet ⟨∼ swordfish⟩

black eye *n* : a discoloration of the skin around the eye from bruising

black–eyed Su·san \ˌblak-ˌīd-'sü-z°n\ *n* : a coarse No. American plant that is related to the daisies and has deep yellow to orange flower heads with dark conical centers

Black·foot \'blak-ˌfút\ *n, pl* **Black·feet** *or* **Blackfoot** : a member of an American Indian people of Montana, Alberta, and Saskatchewan

black·guard \'bla-gərd, -ˌgärd\ *n* : SCOUNDREL, RASCAL

black·head \'blak-ˌhed\ *n* : a small usu. dark oily mass plugging the outlet of a skin gland

black hole *n* : a celestial object with a gravitational field so strong that light cannot escape from it

black·ing \'bla-kiŋ\ *n* : a substance applied to something to make it black

¹**black·jack** \'blak-ˌjak\ *n* **1** : a leather-covered club with a flexible handle **2** : a card game in which the object is to be dealt cards having a higher count than the dealer but not exceeding 21

²**blackjack** *vb* : to hit with or as if with a blackjack

black light *n* : invisible ultraviolet light

black·list \'blak-,list\ *n* : a list of persons who are disapproved of and are to be punished or boycotted — **blacklist** *vb*

black·mail \'blak-,māl\ *n* : extortion by threats esp. of public exposure; *also* : something so extorted — **blackmail** *vb* — **black·mail·er** *n*

black market *n* : illicit trade in goods; *also* : a place where such trade is carried on

Black Mass *n* : a travesty of the Christian Mass ascribed to worshipers of Satan

Black Muslim *n* : a member of a chiefly black group that professes Islamic religious belief

black nationalist *n, often cap B&N* : a member of a group of militant blacks who advocate separatism from whites and the formation of self-governing black communities — **black nationalism** *n, often cap B&N*

black–on–black *adj* : involving a black person against another black person ⟨∼ crime⟩

black·out \'blak-,aut\ *n* 1 : a period of darkness due to electrical power failure 2 : a transitory loss or dulling of vision or consciousness 3 : the prohibition or restriction of the telecasting of a sports event — **black out** *vb*

black pepper *n* : a spice that consists of the dried berry of a pepper plant ground with the black husk still on

black power *n* : the mobilization of the political and economic power of black Americans esp. to compel respect for their rights and improve their condition

black sheep *n* : a member of a group who is disreputable or not regarded favorably

black·smith \'blak-,smith\ *n* : a smith who forges iron — **black·smith·ing** *n*

black·strap molasses \'blak-,strap-\ *n* : a thick dark molasses obtained from successive processing of raw sugar

black·thorn \-,thȯrn\ *n* : a European thorny plum

black–tie \'blak-'tī\ *adj* : characterized by or requiring semiformal evening clothes consisting of a usu. black tie and tuxedo for men and a formal dress for women

black·top \'blak-,täp\ *n* : a dark tarry material (as asphalt) used esp. for surfacing roads — **blacktop** *vb*

black widow *n* : a venomous New World spider having the female black with an hourglass-shaped red mark on the underside of the abdomen

blad·der \'bla-dər\ *n* : a sac in which liquid or gas is stored; *esp* : one in a vertebrate into which urine passes from the kidneys

¹**blade** \'blād\ *n* 1 : a leaf of a plant and esp. of a grass; *also* : the flat part of a leaf as distinguished from its stalk 2 : something (as the flat part of an oar or an arm of a propeller) resembling the blade of a leaf 3 : the cutting part of an instrument or tool 4 : SWORD; *also* : SWORDSMAN 5 : a dashing fellow ⟨a gay ∼⟩ 6 : the runner of an ice skate — **blad·ed** \'blā-dəd\ *adj*

²**blade** *vb* **blad·ed; blad·ing** : to skate on in-line skates — **blad·er** \'blā-dər\ *n*

blain \'blān\ *n* : an inflammatory swelling or sore

¹**blame** \'blām\ *vb* **blamed; blam·ing** [ME, fr. AF *blamer, blasmer,* fr. L *blasphemare* to blaspheme, fr. Gk *blasphēmein*] 1 : to find fault with 2 : to hold responsible or responsible for ♦ *Synonyms* CENSURE, DENOUNCE, CONDEMN, CRITICIZE — **blam·able** *adj*

²**blame** *n* 1 : CENSURE, REPROOF 2 : responsibility for fault or error ♦ *Synonyms* GUILT, FAULT, CULPABILITY, ONUS — **blame·less** *adj* — **blame·lessly** *adv* — **blame·less·ness** *n*

blame·wor·thy \-,wȯr-thē\ *adj* : deserving blame — **blame·wor·thi·ness** *n*

blanch \'blanch\ *vb* : to make or become white or pale ⟨fear ∼*ed* her cheeks⟩

blanc·mange \blə-'mänj, -'mä[n]zh\ *n* : a dessert made from gelatin or a starchy substance and milk usu. sweetened and flavored

bland \'bland\ *adj* 1 : smooth in manner : SUAVE ⟨a ∼ smile⟩ 2 : gently soothing ⟨a ∼ diet⟩; *also* : INSIPID ♦ *Synonyms* GENTLE, MILD, SOFT, BALMY — **bland·ly** *adv* — **bland·ness** *n*

blan·dish·ment \'blan-dish-mənt\ *n* : flattering or coaxing speech or action : CAJOLERY

¹**blank** \'blaŋk\ *adj* 1 : showing or causing an appearance of dazed dismay; *also* : EXPRESSIONLESS 2 : free from writing or marks; *also* : having spaces to be filled in 3 : DULL, EMPTY ⟨∼ moments⟩ 4 : ABSOLUTE, DOWNRIGHT ⟨a ∼ refusal⟩ 5 : not shaped in final form — **blank·ly** *adv* — **blank·ness** *n*

²**blank** *n* 1 : an empty space 2 : a form with spaces for the entry of data 3 : an unfinished form (as of a key) 4 : a cartridge with propellant and a seal but no projectile

³**blank** *vb* 1 : to cover or close up : OBSCURE 2 : to keep from scoring

blank check *n* 1 : a signed check with the amount unspecified 2 : complete freedom of action

¹**blan·ket** \'blaŋ-kət\ *n* 1 : a heavy woven often woolen covering 2 : a covering layer ⟨a ∼ of snow⟩

²**blanket** *vb* : to cover with a blanket

³**blanket** *adj* : covering a group or class ⟨∼ insurance⟩; *also* : applicable in all instances ⟨∼ rules⟩

blank verse *n* : unrhymed iambic pentameter

blare \'bler\ *vb* **blared; blar·ing** : to sound loud and harsh; *also* : to proclaim loudly — **blare** *n*

blar·ney \'blär-nē\ *n* [*Blarney stone,* a stone in Blarney Castle, near Cork, Ireland, held to bestow skill in flattery on those who kiss it] : skillful flattery : BLANDISHMENT

bla·sé \blä-'zā\ *adj* [F] : apathetic to pleasure or excitement as a result of excessive indulgence; *also* : SOPHISTICATED

blas·pheme \blas-'fēm, 'blas-,\ *vb* **blasphemed; blas·phem·ing** 1 : to speak of or address with irreverence **2** : to utter blasphemy — **blas·phem·er** n

blas·phe·my \'blas-fə-mē\ n, pl **-mies 1** : the act of expressing lack of reverence for God **2** : irreverence toward something considered sacred — **blas·phe·mous** \-məs\ adj

¹blast \'blast\ n **1** : a violent gust of wind; also : its effect **2** : sound made by a wind instrument **3** : a current of air forced at high pressure through a hole in a furnace (**blast furnace**) **4** : a sudden withering esp. of plants : BLIGHT **5** : EXPLOSION; also : the shock wave of an explosion

²blast vb : to shatter by or as if by an explosive

blast off vb : TAKE OFF **4** — used esp. of rocket-propelled vehicles — **blast·off** \'blast-,ȯf\ n

bla·tant \'blā-tᵊnt\ adj : offensively obtrusive : vulgarly showy ♦ **Synonyms** VOCIFEROUS, BOISTEROUS, CLAMOROUS, OBSTREPEROUS — **bla·tan·cy** \-tᵊn-sē\ n — **bla·tant·ly** adv

blath·er \'bla-thər\ vb : to talk foolishly at length — **blather** n

blath·er·skite \'bla-thər-,skīt\ n : a person who blathers

¹blaze \'blāz\ n **1** : FIRE **2** : intense direct light accompanied by heat **3** : something (as a dazzling display or sudden outburst) suggesting fire ⟨a ∼ of autumn leaves⟩ ♦ **Synonyms** GLARE, GLOW, FLAME

²blaze vb **blazed; blaz·ing 1** : to burn brightly; also : to flare up **2** : to be conspicuously bright : GLITTER

³blaze vb **blazed; blaz·ing** : to make public or conspicuous

⁴blaze n **1** : a usu. white stripe on the face of an animal **2** : a trail marker; esp : one made on a tree

⁵blaze vb **blazed; blaz·ing** : to mark (as a tree or trail) with blazes

blaze orange n : a very bright orange used in clothing for visibility

blaz·er \'blā-zər\ n : a sports jacket often with notched collar and pockets that are stitched on

¹bla·zon \'blā-zᵊn\ n **1** : COAT OF ARMS **2** : ostentatious display

²blazon vb **1** : to publish widely : PROCLAIM **2** : DECK, ADORN

bldg abbr building

bldr abbr builder

¹bleach \'blēch\ vb : to WHITEN, BLANCH

²bleach n : a preparation used in bleaching

bleach·ers \'blē-chərz\ n sing or pl : a usu. uncovered stand of tiered seats for spectators

bleak \'blēk\ adj **1** : desolately barren and often windswept **2** : lacking warm or cheering qualities ⟨the future looks ∼⟩ — **bleak·ly** adv — **bleak·ness** n

blear \'blir\ adj : dim with water or tears ⟨∼ eyes⟩

bleary \'blir-ē\ adj **1** : dull or dimmed esp. from fatigue or sleep **2** : poorly outlined or defined ⟨a ∼ view⟩

bleat \'blēt\ n : the cry of a sheep or goat or a sound like it — **bleat** vb

bleed \'blēd\ vb **bled** \'bled\; **bleed·ing**

1 : to lose or shed blood **2** : to be wounded; also : to feel pain or distress **3** : to flow or ooze from a wounded surface; also : to draw fluid from ⟨∼ a tire⟩ **4** : to extort money from

bleed·er \'blē-dər\ n : one that bleeds; esp : HEMOPHILIAC

bleeding heart n **1** : a garden plant related to the poppies that has usu. deep pink or white drooping heart-shaped flowers **2** : a person who shows extravagant sympathy esp. for an object of alleged persecution

¹blem·ish \'ble-mish\ vb : to spoil by a flaw : MAR

²blemish n : a noticeable flaw

¹blench \'blench\ vb [ME, to deceive, blench, fr. OE blencan to deceive] : FLINCH, QUAIL ♦ **Synonyms** SHRINK, RECOIL, WINCE, START

²blench vb : to grow or make pale

¹blend \'blend\ vb **blend·ed; blend·ing 1** : to mix thoroughly **2** : to prepare (as coffee) by mixing different varieties **3** : to combine into an integrated whole **4** : HARMONIZE ♦ **Synonyms** FUSE, MERGE, MINGLE, COALESCE — **blend·er** n

²blend n : a product of blending ♦ **Synonyms** COMPOUND, COMPOSITE, ALLOY, MIXTURE

blended family n : a family that includes children of a previous marriage of one spouse or both

bless \'bles\ vb **blessed** \'blest\ also **blest** \'blest\; **bless·ing** [ME, fr. OE blētsian, fr. blōd blood; fr. the use of blood in consecration] **1** : to consecrate by religious rite or word **2** : to sanctify with the sign of the cross **3** : to invoke divine care for **4** : PRAISE, GLORIFY **5** : to confer happiness upon

bless·ed \'ble-səd\ also **blest** \'blest\ adj **1** : HOLY **2** : BEATIFIED **3** : DELIGHTFUL ⟨∼ relief from the heat⟩ — **bless·ed·ly** adv — **bless·ed·ness** n

bless·ing \'ble-siŋ\ n **1** : the act or words of one who blesses; also : APPROVAL **2** : a thing conducive to happiness ⟨count your ∼s⟩ **3** : grace said at a meal

blew past of BLOW

¹blight \'blīt\ n **1** : a plant disease or injury marked esp. by withering and death of parts; also : an organism causing blight **2** : an impairing or frustrating influence; also : a deteriorated condition ⟨urban ∼⟩

²blight vb : to affect with or suffer from blight

blimp \'blimp\ n : an airship that maintains its form by pressure of contained gas

¹blind \'blīnd\ adj **1** : lacking or grossly deficient in ability to see; also : intended for blind persons **2** : not based on reason, evidence, or knowledge ⟨∼ faith⟩ **3** : not intelligently controlled or directed ⟨∼ chance⟩ **4** : performed solely by using aircraft instruments ⟨a ∼ landing⟩ **5** : hard to discern or make out : HIDDEN ⟨a ∼ seam⟩ **6** : lacking an opening or outlet ⟨a ∼ alley⟩ — **blind·ly** adv — **blind·ness** \'blīnd-nəs\ n

²**blind** vb 1 : to make blind 2 : DAZZLE 3 : DARKEN; also : HIDE

³**blind** n 1 : something (as a shutter) to hinder vision or keep out light 2 : a place of concealment 3 : SUBTERFUGE

blind date n : a date between persons who have not previously met; also : either of these persons

blind·er \'blīn-dər\ n : either of two flaps on a horse's bridle to prevent it from seeing to the side

blind·fold \'blīnd-ˌfōld\ vb : to cover the eyes of with or as if with a bandage — **blindfold** n

¹**blink** \'bliŋk\ vb 1 : WINK 2 : TWINKLE 3 : EVADE, IGNORE 4 : YIELD, GIVE IN

²**blink** n 1 : GLIMMER, SPARKLE 2 : a usu. involuntary shutting and opening of the eye

blink·er \'bliŋ-kər\ n : a blinking light used as a signal

blin·tze \'blint-sə\ or **blintz** \'blints\ n [Yiddish blintse] : a thin rolled pancake with a filling usu. of cream cheese

blip \'blip\ n 1 : a spot on a radar screen 2 : ABERRATION 1

bliss \'blis\ n : complete happiness : JOY ♦ **Synonyms** BEATITUDE, BLESSEDNESS — **bliss·ful** \-fəl\ adj — **bliss·ful·ly** adv

¹**blis·ter** \'blis-tər\ n 1 : a raised area of skin containing watery fluid; also : an agent that causes blisters 2 : something (as a raised spot in paint) suggesting a blister 3 : a disease of plants marked by large raised patches on the leaves

²**blister** vb : to develop a blister; also : to cause blisters

blithe \'blīth, 'blith\ adj **blith·er; blith·est** : happily lighthearted ♦ **Synonyms** MERRY, JOVIAL, JOLLY, JOCUND — **blithe·ly** adv — **blithe·some** \-səm\ adj

blitz \'blits\ n 1 : an intensive series of air raids 2 : a fast intensive campaign 3 : a rush of the passer by the defensive linebackers in football — **blitz** vb

blitz·krieg \-ˌkrēg\ n [G, fr. Blitz lightning + Krieg war] : a sudden violent enemy attack

bliz·zard \'bli-zərd\ n : a long severe snowstorm

blk abbr 1 black 2 block

bloat \'blōt\ vb : to swell by or as if by filling with water or air

blob \'bläb\ n : a small lump or drop of a thick consistency

bloc \'bläk\ n [F, lit., block] : a combination of individuals or groups (as nations) working for a common purpose

¹**block** \'bläk\ n 1 : a solid piece of substantial material (as wood or stone) 2 : HINDRANCE, OBSTRUCTION; also : interruption of normal function of body or mind ⟨heart ∼⟩ 3 : a frame enclosing one or more pulleys and having a hook or strap by which it may be attached 4 : a piece of material with a hand-cut design on its surface from which copies are to be made 5 : a large building divided into separate units (as apartments or offices) 6 : a row of houses or shops 7 : a city

square; also : the distance along one of the sides of such a square 8 : a quantity of things considered as a unit ⟨a ∼ of seats⟩

²**block** vb 1 : OBSTRUCT, CHECK 2 : to outline roughly ⟨∼ out a design⟩ 3 : to provide or support with a block ♦ **Synonyms** BAR, IMPEDE, HINDER, OBSTRUCT — **block·er** n

block·ade \blä-'kād\ n : the isolation of a place usu. by troops or ships — **blockade** vb — **block·ad·er** n

block·age \'blä-kij\ n : an act or instance of obstructing : the state of being blocked

block·bust·er \'bläk-ˌbəs-tər\ n : one that is very large, successful, expensive, or extravagant ⟨a ∼ movie⟩

block·head \'bläk-ˌhed\ n : DOLT, DUNCE

block·house \-ˌhaủs\ n : a small strong building used as a shelter (as from enemy fire) or observation post

blog \'blȯg, 'bläg\ n [short for Weblog] : a website containing one's reflections, opinions, and comments; also : the contents of such a site — **blog** vb — **blog·ger** n

¹**blond** or **blonde** \'bländ\ adj : fair in complexion; also : of a light or bleached color ⟨∼ mahogany⟩ — **blond·ish** \'blän-dish\ adj

²**blond** or **blonde** n : a person having blond hair

blood \'bləd\ n 1 : a usu. red liquid that circulates in the heart, arteries, and veins of animals 2 : LIFEBLOOD; also : LIFE 3 : LINEAGE, STOCK 4 : KINSHIP; also : KINDRED 5 : the taking of life 6 : TEMPER, PASSION 7 : DANDY 1 — **blood·less** adj — **bloody** adj

blood·bath \'bləd-ˌbath, -ˌbäth\ n : MASSACRE

blood count n : the determination of the number of blood cells in a specific volume of blood; also : the number of cells so determined

blood·cur·dling \'bləd-kərd-liŋ, -ˌkər-dᵊl-iŋ\ adj : arousing fright or horror

blood·ed \'blə-dəd\ adj 1 : having blood of a specified kind ⟨warm-blooded animals⟩ 2 : entirely or largely purebred ⟨∼ horses⟩

blood group n : one of the classes into which human beings can be separated by the presence or absence in their blood of specific antigens

blood·hound \'bləd-ˌhaủnd\ n : any of a breed of large powerful hounds with long drooping ears, a wrinkled face, and keen sense of smell

blood·let·ting \-ˌle-tiŋ\ n 1 : PHLEBOTOMY 2 : BLOODSHED

blood·line \-ˌlīn\ n : a sequence of direct ancestors esp. in a pedigree

blood·lust \-ˌləst\ n : desire for bloodshed

blood·mo·bile \-mō-ˌbēl\ n : a motor vehicle equipped for collecting blood from donors

blood poisoning n : invasion of the bloodstream by virulent microorganisms from a focus of infection accompanied esp. by chills, fever, and prostration

blood pressure *n* : pressure of the blood on the walls of blood vessels and esp. arteries

blood·root \'blǝd-ˌrüt, -ˌrút\ *n* : a plant related to the poppy that has a red root and sap, a solitary leaf, and a white flower in early spring

blood·shed \-ˌshed\ *n* : wounding or taking of life : CARNAGE, SLAUGHTER

blood·shot \-ˌshät\ *adj* : inflamed to redness ⟨~ eyes⟩

blood·stain \-ˌstān\ *n* : a discoloration caused by blood — **blood·stained** \-ˌstānd\ *adj*

blood·stone \-ˌstōn\ *n* : a green quartz sprinkled with red spots

blood·stream \-ˌstrēm\ *n* : the flowing blood in a circulatory system

blood·suck·er \-ˌsǝ-kǝr\ *n* : an animal that sucks blood; *esp* : LEECH — **blood·suck·ing** *adj*

blood test *n* : a test of the blood (as to detect disease-causing agents)

blood thinner *n* : a drug used to prevent the clotting of blood

blood·thirsty \'blǝd-ˌthǝr-stē\ *adj* : eager to shed blood — **blood·thirst·i·ly** \-ˌthǝr-stǝ-lē\ *adv* — **blood·thirst·i·ness** \-stē-nǝs\ *n*

blood type *n* : BLOOD GROUP — **blood–typ·ing** *n*

blood vessel *n* : a vessel (as a vein or artery) in which blood circulates in the body

Bloody Mary \-'mer-ē\ *n, pl* **Bloody Marys** : a drink made essentially of vodka and tomato juice

¹**bloom** \'blüm\ *n* **1** : FLOWER 1; *also* : flowers or amount of flowers (as of a plant) **2** : the period or state of flowering **3** : a state or time of beauty and vigor **4** : a powdery coating esp. on fruits and leaves **5** : rosy color; *also* : an appearance of freshness or health — **bloomy** *adj*

²**bloom** *vb* **1** : to produce or yield flowers **2** : MATURE **3** : to glow esp. with healthy color ♦ *Synonyms* FLOWER, BLOSSOM

bloo·mers \'blü-mǝrz\ *n pl* [Amelia *Bloomer* †1894 Am. reformer] : a woman's garment of short loose pants gathered at the knee

bloop·er \'blü-pǝr\ *n* **1** : a fly ball hit barely beyond a baseball infield **2** : an embarrassing public blunder

¹**blos·som** \'blä-sǝm\ *n* **1** : the flower of a plant **2** : the period or state of flowering

²**blossom** *vb* : FLOWER, BLOOM

¹**blot** \'blät\ *n* **1** : SPOT, STAIN ⟨ink ~s⟩ **2** : BLEMISH ♦ *Synonyms* STIGMA, BRAND, SLUR

²**blot** *vb* **blot·ted; blot·ting 1** : SPOT, STAIN **2** : OBSCURE, ECLIPSE ⟨~ out the sun⟩ **3** *obs* : MAR; *esp* : DISGRACE **4** : to dry or remove with or as if with an absorbing material **5** : to make a blot

blotch \'bläch\ *n* : a usu. large and irregular spot or mark (as of ink or color) — **blotch** *vb* — **blotchy** *adj*

blot·ter \'blä-tǝr\ *n* **1** : a piece of blotting paper **2** : a book for preliminary records (as of sales or arrests)

blot·ting paper *n* : a spongy paper used to absorb ink

blouse \'blaús, 'blaúz\ *n* **1** : a loose outer garment like a smock **2** : a usu. loose garment reaching from the neck to about the waist

¹**blow** \'blō\ *vb* **blew** \'blü\; **blown** \'blōn\; **blow·ing 1** : to be in motion; *esp* : to move forcibly ⟨the wind *blew*⟩ **2** : to send forth a current of gas (as air) **3** : to act on with a current of gas or vapor; *esp* : to drive with such a current **4** : to clear with a current of air **5** : to sound or cause to sound ⟨~ a horn⟩ **6** : PANT, GASP; *also* : to expel moist air in breathing ⟨the whale *blew*⟩ **7** : BOAST; *also* : BLUSTER **8** : ERUPT, EXPLODE **9** : MELT — used of an electrical fuse **10** : to shape or form by blown or injected air ⟨~ glass⟩ **11** : to shatter or destroy by or as if by explosion **12** : to make breathless by exertion **13** : to spend recklessly **14** : BOTCH ⟨*blew* her lines⟩ — **blow·er** *n*

²**blow** *n* **1** : a usu. strong blowing of air : GALE **2** : BOASTING, BRAG **3** : an act or instance of blowing

³**blow** *vb* **blew** \'blü\; **blown** \'blōn\; **blow·ing** : FLOWER, BLOOM

⁴**blow** *n* **1** : a forcible stroke ⟨a ~ to the head⟩ **2** : COMBAT ⟨come to ~s⟩ **3** : a severe and usu. unexpected calamity

blow–by–blow *adj* : minutely detailed ⟨~ account⟩

blow–dry \-ˌdrī\ *vb* : to dry and usu. style hair with a blow dryer

blow–dryer \-ˌdrī(-ǝ)r\ *n* : a hand-held hair dryer

blow·fly \'blō-ˌflī\ *n* : any of a family of dipteran flies (as a bluebottle) that deposit their eggs or maggots on meat or in wounds

blow·gun \-ˌgǝn\ *n* : a tube from which an arrow or a dart may be shot by the force of the breath

blow·out \'blō-ˌaút\ *n* **1** : a bursting of something (as a tire) because of pressure of the contents (as air) **2** : a depression created by the wind in sand or soil

blow·sy *also* **blow·zy** \'blaú-zē\ *adj* : DISHEVELED, SLOVENLY

blow·torch \'blō-ˌtórch\ *n* : a small portable burner whose flame is made hotter by a blast of air or oxygen

blow–up \'blō-ˌǝp\ *n* **1** : EXPLOSION **2** : an outburst of temper **3** : a photographic enlargement

blowy \'blō-ē\ *adj* : WINDY

BLT \ˌbē-ˌel-'tē\ *n* : a bacon, lettuce, and tomato sandwich

¹**blub·ber** \'blǝ-bǝr\ *vb* : to cry noisily

²**blubber** *n* **1** : the fat of large sea mammals (as whales) **2** : a noisy crying

¹**blud·geon** \'blǝ-jǝn\ *n* : a short often loaded club

²**bludgeon** *vb* : to strike with or as if with a bludgeon

¹**blue** \'blü\ *adj* **blu·er; blu·est** [ME, fr. AF *blef, blew,* of Gmc origin] **1** : of the color blue; *also* : BLUISH **2** : MELANCHOLY; *also* : DEPRESSING **3** : PURITANICAL **4** : INDECENT **5** : tending to support

Democratic candidates ⟨∼ states⟩ — **blue·ness** n

²blue n **1** : a color between green and violet in the spectrum : the color of the clear daytime sky **2** : something (as clothing or the sky) that is blue

blue baby n : a baby with bluish skin due to faulty circulation caused by a heart defect

blue·bell \-ˌbel\ n : any of various plants with blue bell-shaped flowers

blue·ber·ry \ˈblü-ˌber-ē, -bə-rē\ n : the edible blue or blackish berry of various shrubs of the heath family; *also* : one of these shrubs

blue·bird \-ˌbərd\ n : any of three small No. American thrushes that are blue above and reddish-brown or pale blue below

blue·bon·net \ˈblü-ˌbä-nət\ n : either of two low-growing annual lupines of Texas with silky foliage and blue flowers

blue·bot·tle \ˈblü-ˌbä-t⁰l\ n : any of several blowflies with iridescent blue bodies or abdomens

blue cheese n : cheese having veins of greenish-blue mold

blue–col·lar \ˈblü-ˈkä-lər\ adj : of, relating to, or being the class of workers whose duties call for work clothes

blue·fish \-ˌfish\ n : a marine sport and food fish that is bluish above and silvery below

blue·grass \-ˌgras\ n **1** : KENTUCKY BLUEGRASS **2** : country music played on stringed instruments having free improvisation and close harmonies

blue jay \-ˌjä\ n : a crested bright blue No. American jay

blue jeans n pl : pants usu. made of blue denim

blue·nose \ˈblü-ˌnōz\ n : a person who advocates a rigorous moral code

blue·point \-ˌpȯint\ n : a small oyster typically from the south shore of Long Island, New York

blue·print \-ˌprint\ n **1** : a photographic print in white on a blue ground used esp. for copying mechanical drawings and architects' plans **2** : a detailed plan of action — **blueprint** vb

blues \ˈblüz\ n pl **1** : MELANCHOLY **2** : music in a style marked by recurrent minor intervals and melancholy lyrics

blue screen n : a technique in which a subject is filmed in front of a blue background so as to allow the creation of a composite with other footage

blue·stock·ing \ˈblü-ˌstä-kiŋ\ n : a woman having intellectual interests

blu·et \ˈblü-ət\ n : a low No. American herb with dainty bluish flowers

blue whale n : a very large baleen whale that may reach a weight of 150 tons (135 metric tons) and a length of 100 feet (30 meters)

¹bluff \ˈbləf\ adj **1** : having a broad flattened front **2** : rising steeply with a broad flat front **3** : OUTSPOKEN, FRANK ♦ *Synonyms* ABRUPT, BLUNT, BRUSQUE, CURT, GRUFF

²bluff n : a high steep bank : CLIFF

³bluff vb : to frighten or deceive by pretense or a mere show of strength

⁴bluff n : an act or instance of bluffing; *also* : one who bluffs

blu·ing or **blue·ing** \ˈblü-iŋ\ n : a preparation used in laundering to counteract yellowing of white fabrics

blu·ish \ˈblü-ish\ adj : somewhat blue

¹blun·der \ˈblən-dər\ vb **1** : to move clumsily or unsteadily **2** : to make a stupid or needless mistake

²blunder n : an avoidable and usu. serious mistake

blun·der·buss \ˈblən-dər-ˌbəs\ n [obs. D donderbus, fr. D donder thunder + obs. D bus gun] : an obsolete short-barreled firearm with a flaring muzzle

¹blunt \ˈblənt\ adj **1** : not sharp : DULL **2** : lacking in tact : BLUFF ⟨∼ criticism⟩ ♦ *Synonyms* BRUSQUE, CURT, GRUFF, ABRUPT, CRUSTY — **blunt·ly** adv — **blunt·ness** n

²blunt vb : to make or become dull

¹blur \ˈblər\ n **1** : a smear or stain that obscures **2** : something vaguely perceived; *esp* : something moving too quickly to be clearly perceived — **blur·ry** \-ē\ adj

²blur vb **blurred**; **blur·ring** : DIM, CLOUD, OBSCURE ⟨blurred vision⟩

blurb \ˈblərb\ n : a short publicity notice (as on a book jacket)

blurt \ˈblərt\ vb : to utter suddenly and impulsively

blush \ˈbləsh\ n **1** : a reddening of the face (as from modesty or confusion) : FLUSH **2** : a cosmetic used to tint the face pink — **blush** vb — **blush·ful** adj

blus·ter \ˈbləs-tər\ vb **1** : to blow in stormy noisy gusts **2** : to talk or act with noisy swaggering threats — **bluster** n — **blus·tery** \-tə-rē\ adj

blvd abbr boulevard

B lymphocyte n : B CELL

BM abbr bowel movement

B movie n : a cheaply produced motion picture

BO abbr **1** best offer **2** body odor **3** box office **4** branch office

boa \ˈbō-ə\ n **1** : a large snake (as the **boa con·stric·tor** \-kən-ˈstrik-tər\ or the related anaconda) that suffocates and kills its prey by constriction **2** : a fluffy scarf usu. of fur or feathers

boar \ˈbȯr\ n : a male swine; *also* : WILD BOAR

¹board \ˈbȯrd\ n **1** : the side of a ship **2** : a thin flat length of sawed lumber; *also* : material (as cardboard) or a piece of material formed as a thin flat firm sheet **3** pl : STAGE 1 **4** : a table spread with a meal; *also* : daily meals esp. when furnished for pay **5** : a table at which a council or magistrates sit **6** : a group or association of persons organized for a special responsibility (as the management of a business or institution); *also* : an organized commercial exchange **7** : a sheet of insulating material carrying circuit elements and inserted in an electronic device **8** : BULLETIN BOARD

²board vb **1** : to go or put aboard ⟨∼ a

boat⟩ **2 :** to cover with boards **3 :** to provide or be provided with meals and often lodging — **board·er** n

board game n : a game of strategy (as checkers or chess) played by moving pieces on a board

board·ing·house \'bȯr-diŋ-ˌhaủs\ n : a house at which persons are boarded

board·walk \'bȯrd-ˌwȯk\ n : a promenade (as of planking) along a beach

boast \'bōst\ vb **1 :** to praise oneself **2 :** to mention or assert with excessive pride **3 :** to prize as a possession; *also* : HAVE ⟨the house ∼s a fireplace⟩ — **boast** n — **boast·ful** \-fəl\ adj — **boast·ful·ly** adv

boat \'bōt\ n : a small vessel for travel on water; *also* : SHIP — **boat** vb

boat·er \'bō-tər\ n **1 :** one that travels in a boat **2 :** a stiff straw hat

boat·man \'bōt-mən\ n : a man who operates, works on, or deals in boats

boat people n pl : refugees fleeing by boat

boat·swain or **bo·sun** \'bō-sᵊn\ n : a subordinate officer of a ship in charge of the hull and related equipment

¹**bob** \'bäb\ vb **bobbed; bob·bing 1 :** to move up and down jerkily or repeatedly **2 :** to emerge, arise, or appear suddenly or unexpectedly

²**bob** n : a bobbing movement

³**bob** n **1 :** a knob, knot, twist, or curl esp. of ribbons, yarn, or hair **2 :** a short haircut of a woman or child **3 :** FLOAT **2 4 :** a weight hanging from a line

⁴**bob** vb **bobbed; bob·bing :** to cut hair in a bob

⁵**bob** n, pl **bob** slang Brit : SHILLING

bob·bin \'bä-bən\ n : a cylinder or spindle for holding or dispensing thread (as in a sewing machine)

bob·ble \'bä-bəl\ vb **bob·bled; bob·bling 1 :** to move up and down quickly or repeatedly **2 :** FUMBLE ⟨the catcher *bobbled* the ball⟩ — **bobble** n

bob·by \'bä-bē\ n, pl **bobbies** [*Bobby*, nickname for Sir *Robert* Peel, who organized the London police force] Brit : a police officer

bobby pin n : a flat wire hairpin with prongs that press close together

bob·cat \'bäb-ˌkat\ n : a small usu. rusty-colored No. American lynx

bob·o·link \'bä-bə-ˌliŋk\ n : an American migratory songbird related to the meadowlarks

bob·sled \'bäb-ˌsled\ n **1 :** a short sled usu. used as one of a joined pair **2 :** a racing sled with two pairs of runners, a steering wheel, and a hand brake — **bob·sled** vb

bob·white \(ˌ)bäb-ˈhwīt\ n : any of a genus of quail; *esp* : a popular game bird of eastern and central No. America

boc·cie or **boc·ci** or **boc·ce** \'bä-chē\ n : Italian lawn bowling played on a long narrow court

bock \'bäk\ n : a strong dark beer usu. sold in early spring

bod \'bäd\ n : BODY

¹**bode** \'bōd\ vb **bod·ed; bod·ing :** to indicate by signs : PRESAGE

²**bode** past of BIDE

bo·de·ga \bō-ˈdā-gə\ n [Sp, fr. L *apotheca* storehouse] : a usu. small store specializing in Hispanic groceries

bod·ice \'bä-dəs\ n [alter. of *bodies*, pl. of *body*] : the usu. close-fitting part of a dress above the waist

bodi·less \'bä-di-ləs\ adj : lacking a body or material form

¹**bodi·ly** \'bä-dᵊl-ē\ adj : of or relating to the body ⟨∼ contact⟩ ⟨∼ organs⟩

²**bodily** adv **1 :** in the flesh **2 :** as a whole ⟨lifted the crate up ∼⟩

bod·kin \'bäd-kən\ n **1 :** DAGGER **2 :** a pointed implement for punching holes in cloth **3 :** a blunt needle for drawing tape or ribbon through a loop or hem

body \'bä-dē\ n, pl **bod·ies 1 :** the physical whole of a living or dead organism; *also* : the trunk or main mass of an organism as distinguished from its appendages **2 :** a human being : PERSON **3 :** the main part of something **4 :** a mass of matter distinct from other masses **5 :** GROUP ⟨the student ∼⟩ **6 :** VISCOSITY, FIRMNESS **7 :** richness of flavor — used esp. of wines — **bod·ied** \'bä-dēd\ adj

body·build·ing \'bä-dē-ˌbil-diŋ\ n : the developing of the body through exercise and diet — **body·build·er** \-dər\ n

body English n : bodily motions made in a usu. unconscious effort to influence the movement of a propelled object (as a ball)

body·guard \'bä-dē-ˌgärd\ n : a personal guard; *also* : RETINUE

body language n : movements (as with the hands) or posture used as a means of communication

body stocking n : a sheer close-fitting one-piece garment for the torso that often has sleeves and legs

body·work \'bä-dē-ˌwərk\ n : the making or repairing of vehicle bodies

Boer \'bȯr, 'bủr\ n [D, lit., farmer] : a South African of Dutch or Huguenot descent

¹**bog** \'bäg, 'bȯg\ n : wet, spongy, poorly drained, and usu. acid ground — **bog·gy** adj

²**bog** vb **bogged; bog·ging :** to sink into or as if into a bog

bo·gey also **bo·gie** or **bo·gy** \'bủ-gē, 'bō- for 1; 'bō- for 2\ n, pl **bogeys** also **bo·gies 1 :** SPECTER, HOBGOBLIN; *also* : a source of fear or annoyance **2 :** a score of one over par on a hole in golf

bo·gey·man \'bủ-gē-ˌman, 'bō-, 'bủ-\ n : an imaginary monster used in threatening children

bog·gle \'bä-gəl\ vb **bog·gled; bog·gling :** to overwhelm or be overwhelmed with fright or amazement

bo·gus \'bō-gəs\ adj : SPURIOUS, SHAM

Bo·he·mi·an \bō-ˈhē-mē-ən\ n **1 :** a native or inhabitant of Bohemia **2** often not cap : VAGABOND, WANDERER **3** often not cap : a person (as a writer or artist) living an unconventional life — **bohemian** adj, often cap

bohrium • bond

bohr·i·um \ˈbȯr-ē-əm\ n : an artificially produced radioactive chemical element

¹boil \ˈbȯi(-ə)l\ n : an inflamed swelling on the skin containing pus

²boil vb **1** : to heat or become heated to a temperature (**boiling point**) at which vapor is formed and rises in bubbles ⟨water ~s and changes to steam⟩; also : to act on or be acted on by a boiling liquid ⟨~ eggs⟩ **2** : to be in a state of seething agitation

³boil n **1** : the act or state of boiling **2** : a boiled dish (as of seafood) **3** : a gathering where boiled food is served

boil·er \ˈbȯi-lər\ n **1** : a container in which something is boiled **2** : a strong vessel used in making steam **3** : a tank holding hot water

boil·er·mak·er \ˈbȯi-lər-ˌmā-kər\ n : whiskey with a beer chaser

bois·ter·ous \ˈbȯi-st(ə-)rəs\ adj : noisily turbulent or exuberant — **bois·ter·ous·ly** adv

bok choy \ˈbäk-ˈchȯi\ n : a Chinese vegetable related to the mustards that forms a loose head of green leaves with long thick white stalks

bo·la \ˈbō-lə\ or **bo·las** \-ləs\ n, pl **bolas** \-ləz\ also **bo·las·es** [AmerSp bolas, fr. Sp bola ball] : a cord with weights attached to the ends for hurling at and entangling an animal

bold \ˈbōld\ adj **1** : COURAGEOUS, INTREPID **2** : IMPUDENT **3** : STEEP ⟨~ cliffs⟩ **4** : ADVENTUROUS, FREE ⟨a ~ thinker⟩ ♦ **Synonyms** DAUNTLESS, BRAVE, VALIANT — **bold·ly** adv — **bold·ness** \ˈbōld-nəs\ n

bold·face \ˈbōld-ˌfās\ n : a heavy-faced type; also : printing in boldface — **bold·faced** \-ˈfāst\ adj

bole \ˈbōl\ n : the trunk of a tree

bo·le·ro \bə-ˈler-ō\ n, pl **-ros 1** : a Spanish dance or its music **2** : a short loose jacket open at the front

bo·li·var \bə-ˈlē-ˌvär, ˈbä-lə-vər\ n, pl **-vares** \bä-lə-ˈvär-ˌās, ˌbō-\ or **-vars** — see MONEY table

Bo·liv·i·an \bə-ˈli-vē-ən\ n : a native or inhabitant of Bolivia — **Bolivian** adj

bo·li·vi·a·no \bə-ˌli-vē-ˈä-(ˌ)nō\ n, pl **-nos** — see MONEY table

boll \ˈbōl\ n : a seed pod (as of cotton)

boll weevil n : a small usu. grayish or brown weevil that infests the cotton plant both as a larva and as an adult

boll·worm \ˈbōl-ˌwərm\ n : any of several moths and esp. the corn earworm whose larvae feed on cotton bolls

bo·lo·gna \bə-ˈlō-nē\ n [short for Bologna sausage, fr. Bologna, Italy] : a large smoked sausage of beef, veal, and pork

Bol·she·vik \ˈbōl-shə-ˌvik\ n, pl **Bolsheviks** also **Bol·she·vi·ki** \ˌbōl-shə-ˈvi-kē\ [Russ bol'shevik, fr. bol'shiĭ larger] **1** : a member of the party that seized power in Russia in the revolution of November 1917 **2** : COMMUNIST — **Bolshevik** adj

bol·she·vism \ˈbōl-shə-ˌvi-zəm\ n, often cap : the doctrine or program of the Bolsheviks advocating violent overthrow of capitalism

¹bol·ster \ˈbōl-stər\ n : a long pillow or cushion

²bolster vb : to support with or as if with a bolster; also : REINFORCE

¹bolt \ˈbōlt\ n **1** : a missile (as an arrow) for a crossbow or catapult **2** : a flash of lightning : THUNDERBOLT **3** : a sliding bar used to fasten a door **4** : a roll of cloth or wallpaper of specified length **5** : a rod with a head at one end and a screw thread at the other used with a nut to fasten objects together **6** : a metal cylinder that drives the cartridge into the chamber of a firearm

²bolt vb **1** : to move suddenly (as in fright or hurry) : START, DASH **2** : to break away (as from association) ⟨~ from a political platform⟩ **3** : to produce seed prematurely **4** : to secure or fasten with a bolt **5** : to swallow hastily or without chewing

³bolt n : an act of bolting

bo·lus \ˈbō-ləs\ n, pl **bo·lus·es 1** : a large pill **2** : a soft mass of chewed food

¹bomb \ˈbäm\ n **1** : a fused explosive device designed to detonate under specified conditions (as impact) **2** : an aerosol or foam dispenser (as of insecticide or hair spray) : SPRAY CAN **3** : FAILURE, FLOP **4** : a long pass, shot, or hit

²bomb vb **1** : to attack with bombs **2** : FAIL ⟨~ed at the audition⟩

bom·bard \bäm-ˈbärd\ vb **1** : to attack esp. with artillery or bombers **2** : to assail persistently **3** : to subject to the impact of rapidly moving particles (as electrons) — **bom·bard·ment** n

bom·bar·dier \ˌbäm-bər-ˈdir\ n : a bomber-crew member who releases the bombs

bom·bast \ˈbäm-ˌbast\ n [ME, cotton padding, fr. MF bombace, fr. ML bombax cotton, alter. of L bombyx silkworm, silk, fr. Gk] : pretentious wordy speech or writing — **bom·bas·tic** \bäm-ˈbas-tik\ adj — **bom·bas·ti·cal·ly** \-ti-k(ə-)lē\ adv

bom·ba·zine \ˌbäm-bə-ˈzēn\ n **1** : a twilled fabric with silk warp and worsted filling **2** : a silk fabric in twill weave dyed black

bomb·er \ˈbä-mər\ n : one that bombs; esp : an airplane for dropping bombs

bomb·proof \ˈbäm-ˌprüf\ adj : safe against the explosive force of bombs

bomb·shell \ˈbäm-ˌshel\ n **1** : BOMB 1 **2** : one that stuns, amazes, or completely upsets

bona fide \ˈbō-nə-ˌfīd, ˈbä-; ˌbō-nə-ˈfī-dē, -də\ adj [L, in good faith] **1** : made in good faith ⟨a bona fide agreement⟩ **2** : GENUINE, REAL ⟨a bona fide bargain⟩

bo·nan·za \bə-ˈnan-zə\ n [Sp, lit., calm sea, fr. ML bonacia, alter. of L malacia, fr. Gk malakia, lit., softness, fr. malakos soft] **1** : something yielding a rich return **2** : a spectacular event

bon·bon \ˈbän-ˌbän\ n : a candy with a creamy center and a soft covering (as of chocolate)

bond \ˈbänd\ n **1** : FETTER **2** : a binding or uniting force or tie ⟨~s of friendship⟩ **3** : an agreement or obligation often made binding by a pledge of money or goods **4** : a person who acts as surety for another **5** : an interest-bearing certificate of public or private indebtedness **6** : the state of goods subject to supervision pending payment of taxes or duties due

²**bond** vb **1** : to assure payment of duties or taxes on (goods) by giving a bond **2** : to insure against losses caused by the acts of ⟨~ a bank teller⟩ **3** : to make or become firmly united as if by bonds ⟨~ iron to copper⟩ **4** : to form a close relationship ⟨~ed with her stepmother⟩

bond·age \'bän-dij\ n : SLAVERY, SERVITUDE

bond·hold·er \'bänd-ˌhōl-dər\ n : one that owns a government or corporation bond

bond·ing \'bän-diŋ\ n **1** : the formation of a close personal relationship esp. through frequent or constant association **2** : the attaching of a material (as porcelain) to a tooth surface esp. for cosmetic purposes

bond·man \'bänd-mən\ n : SLAVE, SERF

¹**bonds·man** \'bändz-mən\ n : SURETY 3

²**bondsman** var of BONDMAN

bond·wom·an \'bänd-ˌwu̇-mən\ n : a female slave or serf

¹**bone** \'bōn\ n **1** : a hard largely calcareous tissue forming most of the skeleton of a vertebrate animal; also : one of the pieces of bone making up a vertebrate skeleton **2** : a hard animal substance (as ivory or baleen) similar to true bone **3** : something made of bone — **bone·less** adj — **bony** also **bon·ey** \'bō-nē\ adj

²**bone** vb **boned; bon·ing** : to free from bones ⟨~ a chicken⟩

bone black n : the black carbon residue from calcined bones used esp. as a pigment

bone marrow n : MARROW

bone·meal \'bōn-ˌmēl\ n : crushed or ground bone used esp. as fertilizer or feed

bon·er \'bō-nər\ n : a stupid and ridiculous blunder

bone up vb **1** : CRAM 3 **2** : to refresh one's memory ⟨boned up on the speech before giving it⟩

bon·fire \'bän-ˌfī(-ə)r\ n [ME bonefire a fire of bones, fr. bon bone + fire] : a large fire built in the open air

bon·go \'bäŋ-gō\ n, pl **bongos** also **bongoes** [AmerSp bongó] : one of a pair of small tuned drums played with the hands

bon·ho·mie \ˌbä-nə-'mē\ n [F bonhomie, fr. bonhomme good-natured man, fr. bon good + homme man] : good-natured easy friendliness

bo·ni·to \bə-'nē-tō\ n, pl **-tos** or **-to** : any of several medium-sized tunas

bon mot \bōⁿ-'mō\ n, pl **bons mots** \same\ or **bon mots** \same\ [F, lit., good word] : a clever remark

bon·net \'bä-nət\ n : a covering (as a cap) for the head; esp : a hat for a woman or infant tied under the chin

bon·ny \'bä-nē\ adj **bon·ni·er; -est** chiefly Brit : ATTRACTIVE, FAIR; also : FINE, EXCELLENT

bon·sai \bōn-'sī, 'bän-ˌ\ n, pl **bonsai** [Jp]

: a potted plant (as a tree) dwarfed and trained to an artistic shape; also : the art of growing such a plant

bo·nus \'bō-nəs\ n : something in addition to what is expected

bon vi·vant \ˌbän-vē-'vänt, ˌbōⁿ-vē-'väⁿ\ n, pl **bons vivants** \ˌbän-vē-'vänts, ˌbōⁿ-vē-'väⁿ\ or **bon vivants** \same\ [F, lit., good liver] : a person having cultivated, refined, and sociable tastes esp. in food and drink

bon voy·age \ˌbōⁿ-ˌvȯi-'äzh, ˌbän-; ˌbōⁿ-ˌvwä-'yäzh\ n : FAREWELL — often used as an interjection

bony fish n : any of a class of fishes (as eels or sturgeons) with a bony rather than a cartilaginous skeleton

bonze \'bänz\ n : a Buddhist monk

boo \'bü\ n, pl **boos** : a shout of disapproval or contempt — **boo** vb

boo·by \'bü-bē\ n, pl **boobies** : an awkward foolish person : DOPE

booby hatch n : a psychiatric hospital

booby prize n : an award for the poorest performance in a contest

booby trap n : a trap for the unwary; esp : a concealed explosive device set to go off when some harmless-looking object is touched — **booby–trap** vb

boo·dle \'bü-dᵊl\ n **1** : bribe money **2** : a large amount of money

¹**book** \'bu̇k\ n **1** : a set of sheets bound into a volume **2** : a long written or printed narrative or record **3** : a major division of a work of a long literary work **4** cap : BIBLE — **in one's book** : in one's own opinion

²**book** vb **1** : to engage, reserve, or schedule by or as if by writing in a book ⟨~ seats on a plane⟩ **2** : to enter charges against in a police register

book·case \-ˌkās\ n : a piece of furniture consisting of shelves to hold books

book·end \-ˌend\ n : a support to hold up a row of books

book·ie \'bu̇-kē\ n : BOOKMAKER

book·ish \'bu̇-kish\ adj **1** : fond of books and reading **2** : inclined to rely unduly on book knowledge

book·keep·er \'bu̇k-ˌkē-pər\ n : a person who records the accounts or transactions of a business — **book·keep·ing** n

book·let \'bu̇k-lət\ n : PAMPHLET

book·mak·er \'bu̇k-ˌmā-kər\ n : a person who determines odds and receives and pays off bets — **book·mak·ing** n

book·mark \-ˌmärk\ or **book·mark·er** \-ˌmär-kər\ n **1** : a marker for finding a place in a book **2** : a shortcut to a previously viewed location (as a website) on a computer — **bookmark** vb

book·mo·bile \'bu̇k-mō-ˌbēl\ n : a truck that serves as a traveling library

book·plate \'bu̇k-ˌplāt\ n : a label pasted in a book to show who owns it

book·sell·er \'bu̇k-ˌse-lər\ n : one that sells books; esp : the proprietor of a bookstore

book·shelf \-ˌshelf\ n : a shelf for books

book·worm \'bu̇k-ˌwərm\ n : a person unusually devoted to reading and study

¹**boom** \'büm\ vb **1** : to make a deep hollow sound : RESOUND **2** : to grow or

cause to grow rapidly esp. in number, value, esteem, or importance

²**boom** n 1 : a booming sound or cry 2 : a rapid expansion or increase esp. of economic activity

³**boom** n [D, tree, beam] 1 : a long spar used to extend the bottom of a sail 2 : a line of floating timbers used to obstruct passage or catch floating objects 3 : a beam projecting from the upright pole of a derrick to support or guide the object lifted 4 : a long usu. horizontal supporting arm (as for a microphone)

boom box n : a large portable radio and often tape or CD player

boo·mer·ang \ˈbü-mə-ˌraŋ\ n [Dharuk (an Australian aboriginal language) *bumarin*] : a bent or angular club that can be so thrown as to return near the starting point

boom·ing \ˈbü-miŋ\ adj 1 : making a loud deep sound ⟨a ~ voice⟩ 2 : powerfully executed ⟨hit a ~ serve⟩

¹**boon** \ˈbün\ n [ME bone prayer, request, the favor requested, fr. ON bōn request] : BENEFIT, BLESSING ♦ Synonyms FAVOR, GIFT, LARGESS, PRESENT

²**boon** adj [ME bon, fr. AF, good] : CONVIVIAL ⟨a ~ companion⟩

boon·docks \ˈbün-ˌdäks\ n pl [Tagalog (language of the Philippines) bundok mountain] 1 : rough country filled with dense brush 2 : a rural area

boon·dog·gle \ˈbün-ˌdä-gəl, -ˌdȯ-\ n : a useless or wasteful project or activity

boor \ˈbu̇r\ n 1 : YOKEL 2 : a rude or insensitive person ♦ Synonyms CHURL, LOUT, CLOWN, CLODHOPPER — **boor·ish** adj

boost \ˈbüst\ vb 1 : to push up from below 2 : INCREASE, RAISE ⟨~ prices⟩ 3 : AID, PROMOTE ⟨voted a bonus to ~ morale⟩ — **boost** n — **boost·er** n

¹**boot** \ˈbüt\ n, chiefly dial : something to equalize a trade — **to boot** : BESIDES

²**boot** vb, archaic : AVAIL, PROFIT

³**boot** n 1 : a covering for the foot and leg 2 : a protective sheath (as of a flower) 3 Brit : an automobile trunk 4 : KICK; also : a discharge from employment 5 : a navy or marine corps trainee

⁴**boot** vb 1 : KICK 2 : to eject or discharge summarily 3 : to load or become loaded into a computer from a disk 4 : to start or become ready for use esp. by booting a program ⟨~ up the computer⟩

boot·black \ˈbüt-ˌblak\ n : a person who shines shoes

boot camp n 1 : a navy or marine corps training camp 2 : a facility with a rigorous disciplinary program for young offenders

boo·tee or **boo·tie** \ˈbü-tē\ n : an infant's knitted or crocheted sock

booth \ˈbüth\ n, pl **booths** \ˈbüthz, ˈbüths\ 1 : a small enclosed stall (as at a fair) 2 : a small enclosure giving privacy for a person ⟨voting ~⟩ ⟨telephone ~⟩ 3 : a restaurant accommodation having a table between backed benches

boot·leg \ˈbüt-ˌleg\ vb : to make, transport, or sell (as liquor) illegally — **bootleg** adj or n — **boot·leg·ger** n

boot·less \ˈbüt-ləs\ adj : USELESS ⟨their efforts were ~⟩ ♦ Synonyms FUTILE, VAIN, ABORTIVE, FRUITLESS — **boot·less·ly** adv — **boot·less·ness** n

¹**boo·ty** \ˈbü-tē\ n, pl **booties** : PLUNDER, SPOIL

²**booty** also **boo·tie** \ˈbü-tē\ n, pl **booties** slang : BUTTOCKS

¹**booze** \ˈbüz\ vb **boozed**; **booz·ing** : to drink liquor to excess — **booz·er** n

²**booze** n : intoxicating liquor — **boozy** adj

bop \ˈbäp\ vb **bopped**; **bop·ping** : HIT, SOCK — **bop** n

BOQ abbr bachelor officers' quarters

bor abbr borough

bo·rate \ˈbȯr-ˌāt\ n : a salt or ester of boric acid

bo·rax \ˈbȯr-ˌaks\ n : a crystalline borate of sodium that occurs as a mineral and is used as a flux and cleanser

bor·del·lo \bȯr-ˈde-lō\ n, pl **-los** [It] : BROTHEL

¹**bor·der** \ˈbȯr-dər\ n 1 : EDGE, MARGIN 2 : BOUNDARY, FRONTIER ♦ Synonyms RIM, BRIM, BRINK, FRINGE, PERIMETER

²**border** vb **bor·dered**; **bor·der·ing** 1 : to put a border on 2 : ADJOIN 3 : VERGE

border collie n, often cap B : any of a British breed of medium-sized longhaired sheepdogs

bor·der·land \ˈbȯr-dər-ˌland\ n 1 : territory at or near a border 2 : an outlying or intermediate region often not clearly defined

bor·der·line \-ˌlīn\ adj : being in an intermediate position or state; esp : not quite up to what is standard or expected ⟨~ intelligence⟩

¹**bore** \ˈbȯr\ vb **bored**; **bor·ing** 1 : to make a hole in with or as if with a drill 2 : to make (as a well) by boring or digging away material ♦ Synonyms PERFORATE, DRILL, PRICK, PUNCTURE — **bor·er** n

²**bore** n 1 : a hole made by or as if by boring 2 : a cylindrical cavity 3 : the diameter of a hole or tube; esp : the interior diameter of a gun barrel or engine cylinder

³**bore** past of BEAR

⁴**bore** n : a tidal flood with a high abrupt front

⁵**bore** n : one that causes boredom

⁶**bore** vb **bored**; **bor·ing** : to weary with tedious dullness

bo·re·al \ˈbȯr-ē-əl\ adj : of, relating to, or located in northern regions

bore·dom \ˈbȯr-dəm\ n : the condition of being bored

bo·ric acid \ˈbȯr-ik-\ n : a white crystalline weak acid that contains boron and is used esp. as an antiseptic

born \ˈbȯrn\ adj 1 : brought into life by birth 2 : NATIVE ⟨American-born⟩ 3 : having special natural abilities or character from birth ⟨a ~ leader⟩

born-again adj : having experienced a revival of a personal faith or conviction ⟨a ~ believer⟩ ⟨a ~ liberal⟩

borne *past part of* BEAR

bo·ron \'bȯr-ˌän\ *n* : a chemical element that occurs in nature only in combination (as in borax)

bor·ough \'bər-ō\ *n* [ME *burgh*, fr. OE *burg* fortified town] **1** : a British town that sends one or more members to Parliament; *also* : an incorporated British urban area **2** : an incorporated town or village in some U.S. states; *also* : any of the five political divisions of New York City **3** : a civil division of the state of Alaska corresponding to a county in most other states

bor·row \'bär-ō\ *vb* **1** : to take or receive (something) temporarily and with intent to return ⟨~ed my car⟩ **2** : to take into possession or use from another source : DERIVE, APPROPRIATE ⟨~ a metaphor⟩

borscht \'bȯrsht\ *or* **borsch** \'bȯrsh\ *n* [Yiddish *borsht* & Ukrainian & Russ *borshch*] : a soup made mainly from beets

bosh \'bäsh\ *n* [Turk *boş* empty] : foolish talk or action : NONSENSE

bosky \'bäs-kē\ *adj* : covered with trees or shrubs

¹bos·om \'bu̇-zəm, 'bü-\ *n* **1** : the front of the human chest; *esp* : the female breasts **2** : the seat of secret thoughts and feelings **3** : the part of a garment covering the breast — **bos·omed** \-zəmd\ *adj*

²bosom *adj* : CLOSE, INTIMATE

¹boss \'bäs, 'bȯs\ *n* : a knoblike ornament : STUD

²boss *vb* : to ornament with bosses

³boss \'bȯs\ *n* **1** : one (as a foreman or manager) exercising control or supervision **2** : a politician who controls votes or dictates policies — **bossy** *adj*

⁴boss \'bȯs\ *vb* : to act as or in the manner of a boss

bosun *var of* BOATSWAIN

bot *abbr* **1** botanical; botanist; botany **2** robot

bot·a·ny \'bä-tə-nē, 'bät-nē\ *n, pl* **-nies 1** : a branch of biology dealing with plants and plant life **2** : plant life (as of a given region); *also* : the biology of a plant or plant group — **bo·tan·i·cal** \bə-'ta-ni-kəl\ *adj or n* — **bo·tan·i·cal·ly** \-kə-lē\ *adv* — **bot·a·nist** *n* — **bot·a·nize** \'bät-ə-ˌnīz\ *vb*

botch \'bäch\ *vb* : to foul up hopelessly : BUNGLE — **botch** *n*

¹both \'bōth\ *pron* : both ones : the one as well as the other

²both *conj* — used as a function word to indicate and stress the inclusion of each of two or more things specified by coordinated words, phrases, or clauses ⟨~ New York and London⟩

³both *adj* : being the two : including the one and the other ⟨went to ~ museums⟩

both·er \'bä-thər\ *vb* : PESTER, TROUBLE ⟨was ~ed by bees⟩ **2** : to concern oneself : make an effort ⟨didn't ~ asking⟩ ♦ **Synonyms** VEX, ANNOY, IRK, PROVOKE — **bother** *n* — **both·er·some** \-səm\ *adj*

¹bot·tle \'bä-t³l\ *n* **1** : a container (as of glass) with a narrow neck and usu. no handles **2** : the quantity held by a bottle **3** : intoxicating liquor

²bottle *vb* **bot·tled; bot·tling 1** : to confine as if in a bottle : RESTRAIN ⟨*bottled* up his anger⟩ **2** : to put into a bottle

bot·tle·neck \'bä-t³l-ˌnek\ *n* **1** : a narrow passage or point of congestion **2** : something that obstructs or impedes

¹bot·tom \'bä-təm\ *n* **1** : an under or supporting surface; *also* : BUTTOCKS **2** : the surface on which a body of water lies **3** : the lowest part or place; *also* : an inferior position ⟨start at the ~⟩ **4** : BOTTOMLAND **5** : BASIS, SOURCE ⟨get to the ~ of this mystery⟩ **6** : a quark with a charge of -⅓ and a measured energy of approximately 5 billion electron volts — **bottom** *adj* — **bot·tom·less** *adj*

²bottom *vb* **1** : to furnish with a bottom **2** : to reach the bottom **3** : to reach a point where a decline is halted or reversed — usu. used with *out*

bot·tom·land \'bä-təm-ˌland\ *n* : low land along a river

bottom line *n* **1** : the essential point : CRUX **2** : the final result : OUTCOME

bot·u·lism \'bä-chə-ˌli-zəm\ *n* : an acute paralytic disease caused by a bacterial toxin (**bot·u·li·num toxin** \ˌbä-chə-'lī-nəm-\) esp. in tainted food

bou·doir \'bü-ˌdwär, 'bu̇-, ˌbü-', ˌbu̇-'\ *n* [F, fr. *bouder* to pout] : a woman's dressing room or bedroom

bouf·fant \bü-'fänt, 'bü-ˌfänt\ *adj* [F] : puffed out ⟨~ hairdos⟩

bough \'bau̇\ *n* : a usu. large or main branch of a tree

bought *past and past part of* BUY

bouil·la·baisse \ˌbü-yə-'bäs\ *n* [F] : a highly seasoned fish stew made with at least two kinds of fish

bouil·lon \'bu̇-ˌyän; 'bu̇l-ˌyän, -yən\ *n* : a clear soup made usu. from beef

boul·der *also* **bowl·der** \'bōl-dər\ *n* : a large detached rounded or worn mass of rock — **boul·dered** \-dərd\ *adj*

bou·le·vard \'bu̇-lə-ˌvärd, 'bü-\ *n* [F, modif. of MD *bolwerc* bulwark] : a broad often landscaped thoroughfare

bounce \'bau̇ns\ *vb* **bounced; bounc·ing 1** : to cause to rebound ⟨~ a ball⟩ **2** : to rebound after striking **3** : to issue (a check) from an account with insufficient funds — **bounce** *n* — **bouncy** \'bau̇n-sē\ *adj*

bounc·er \'bau̇n-sər\ *n* : a person employed in a public place to remove disorderly persons

¹bound \'bau̇nd\ *adj* : intending to go ⟨homeward ~⟩

²bound *n* : LIMIT, BOUNDARY — **bound·less** *adj* — **bound·less·ness** *n*

³bound *vb* **1** : to set limits to **2** : to form the boundary of **3** : to name the boundaries of

⁴bound *past and past part of* BIND

⁵bound *adj* **1** : constrained by or as if by bonds : CONFINED, OBLIGED ⟨was duty ~ to help⟩ **2** : enclosed in a binding or cover **3** : RESOLVED, DETERMINED; *also* : SURE

⁶**bound** n **1** : LEAP, JUMP **2** : REBOUND, BOUNCE

⁷**bound** vb : SPRING, BOUNCE

bound·ary \'baún-drē\ n, pl **-aries** : something that marks or fixes a limit or extent (as of territory) ♦ Synonyms BORDER, FRONTIER, MARCH

bound·en \'baún-dən\ adj : BINDING ⟨our ~ duty⟩

boun·te·ous \'baún-tē-əs\ adj **1** : GENEROUS **2** : ABUNDANT — **boun·te·ous·ly** adv — **boun·te·ous·ness** n

boun·ti·ful \'baún-ti-fəl\ adj **1** : giving freely **2** : PLENTIFUL — **boun·ti·ful·ly** adv — **boun·ti·ful·ness** n

boun·ty \'baún-tē\ n, pl **bounties** [ME bounte goodness, fr. AF bunté, fr. L bonitas, fr. bonus good] **1** : GENEROSITY **2** : something given liberally **3** : a reward, premium, or subsidy given usu. for doing something

bou·quet \bō-'kā, bü-\ n [F, fr. MF, thicket, bunch of flowers, fr. OF (dial. of Normandy and Picardy) bosquet thicket, fr. bosc forest] **1** : flowers picked and fastened together in a bunch **2** : a distinctive aroma (as of wine) ♦ Synonyms SCENT, FRAGRANCE, PERFUME, REDOLENCE

bour·bon \'bər-bən\ n : a whiskey distilled from a corn mash

bour·geois \'búrzh-,wä, búrzh-'wä\ n, pl **bourgeois** \same or -,wäz, -'wäz\ [MF, fr. OF burgeis townsman, fr. burc, borg town, fr. L burgus fortified place, of Gmc origin] : a middle-class person — **bourgeois** adj

bour·geoi·sie \,búrzh-,wä-'zē\ n : a social order dominated by bourgeois

bourne also **bourn** \'bórn, 'búrn\ n **1** : BOUNDARY; also : DESTINATION

bourse \'búrs\ n : a European stock exchange

bout \'baút\ n **1** : CONTEST, MATCH **2** : OUTBREAK, ATTACK ⟨a ~ of measles⟩

bou·tique \bü-'tēk\ n : a small fashionable specialty shop

bou·ton·niere \,bü-t°n-'iər\ n : a flower or bouquet worn in a buttonhole

¹**bo·vine** \'bō-,vīn, -,vēn\ adj **1** : of or relating to bovines **2** : having qualities (as placidity or dullness) characteristic of oxen or cows

²**bovine** n : any of a group of mammals including oxen, buffalo, and their close relatives

bovine spon·gi·form encephalopathy \-'spən-ji-,fórm-\ n : MAD COW DISEASE

¹**bow** \'baú\ vb **1** : SUBMIT, YIELD **2** : to bend the head or body (as in submission, courtesy, or assent) **3** : DEBUT ⟨the play ~s next month⟩

²**bow** n : an act or posture of bowing

³**bow** \'bō\ n **1** : BEND, ARCH; esp : RAINBOW **2** : a weapon for shooting arrows; also : ARCHER **3** : a knot formed by doubling a line into two or more loops **4** : a wooden rod strung with horsehairs for playing an instrument of the violin family

⁴**bow** \'bō\ vb **1** : BEND, CURVE **2** : to play (an instrument) with a bow

⁵**bow** \'baú\ n : the forward part of a ship — **bow** adj

bowd·ler·ise Brit var of BOWDLERIZE

bowd·ler·ize \'bōd-lə-,rīz, 'baúd-\ vb **-ized; -iz·ing** : to expurgate by omitting parts considered vulgar

bow·el \'baú(-ə)l\ n **1** : INTESTINE; also : one of the divisions of the intestine — usu. used in pl. **2** pl : the inmost parts ⟨the ~s of the earth⟩

bow·er \'baú(-ə)r\ n : a shelter of boughs or vines : ARBOR

¹**bowl** \'bōl\ n **1** : a concave vessel used to hold liquids **2** : a drinking vessel **3** : a bowl-shaped part or structure — **bowl·ful** \-,fúl\ n

²**bowl** n **1** : a ball for rolling on a level surface in bowling **2** : a cast of the ball in bowling

³**bowl** vb **1** : to play a game of bowling; also : to roll a ball in bowling **2** : to travel (as in a vehicle) rapidly and smoothly **3** : to strike or knock down with a moving object

bowlder var of BOULDER

bow-legged \'bō-,le-gəd\ adj : having legs that bow outward at or below the knee — **bow-leg** \-,leg\ n

¹**bowl·er** \'bō-lər\ n : a person who bowls

²**bowl·er** \'bō-lər\ n : DERBY 3

bow·line \'bō-lən, -,līn\ n : a knot used to form a loop that neither slips nor jams

bowl·ing \'bō-liŋ\ n : any of various games in which balls are rolled on a green or alley at an object or a group of objects

bow·man \'bō-mən\ n : ARCHER

bow·sprit \'baú-,sprit\ n : a spar projecting forward from the prow of a ship

bow·string \'bō-,striŋ\ n : the cord connecting the two ends of a shooting bow

¹**box** \'bäks\ n, pl **box** or **box·es** : an evergreen shrub or small tree used esp. for hedges

²**box** n **1** : a rigid typically rectangular receptacle often with a cover; also : the quantity held by a box **2** : a small compartment (as for a group of theater patrons); also : a boxlike receptacle or division **3** : a usu. rectangular space demarcated for a particular purpose ⟨the batter's ~⟩ **4** : a difficult situation : PREDICAMENT — **boxy** \'bäk-sē\ adj

³**box** vb : to enclose in or as if in a box

⁴**box** n : a punch or slap esp. on the ear

⁵**box** vb **1** : to strike with the hand **2** : to engage in boxing with

box·car \'bäks-,kär\ n : a roofed freight car usu. with sliding doors in the sides

box cutter n : a small cutting tool with a retractable razor blade

¹**box·er** \'bäk-sər\ n **1** : a person who engages in boxing **2** pl : BOXER SHORTS

²**boxer** n : any of a German breed of compact medium-sized dogs with a short usu. fawn or brindled coat

boxer shorts n pl : men's loose-fitting shorts worn as underwear

box·ing \'bäk-siŋ\ n : the sport of fighting with the fists

box office n : an office (as in a theater) where admission tickets are sold

box turtle *n* : any of several No. American land turtles able to withdraw completely into their shell

box·wood \'bäks-,wùd\ *n* : the tough hard wood of the box; *also* : a box tree or shrub

boy \'bòi\ *n* **1** : a male child : YOUTH **2** : SON — **boy·hood** \-,hùd\ *n* — **boy·ish** *adj* — **boy·ish·ly** *adv* — **boy·ish·ness** *n*

boy·cott \'bòi-,kät\ *vb* [Charles C. Boycott †1897 Eng. land agent in Ireland who was ostracized for refusing to reduce rents] : to refrain from having any dealings with — **boycott** *n*

boy·friend \'bòi-,frend\ *n* **1** : a male friend **2** : a frequent or regular male companion in a romantic relationship

Boy Scout *n* : a member of any of various national scouting programs (as the Boy Scouts of America)

boy·sen·ber·ry \'bòi-z°n-,ber-ē, 'bòis-\ *n* : a large reddish-black fruit with a raspberry flavor; *also* : the hybrid bramble bearing it developed by crossing blackberries and raspberries

bo·zo \'bō-,zō\ *n, pl* **bozos** : a foolish or incompetent person

bp *abbr* **1** bishop **2** birthplace

BP *abbr* **1** batting practice **2** blood pressure **3** boiling point

bpl *abbr* birthplace

BPOE *abbr* Benevolent and Protective Order of Elks

br *abbr* **1** branch **2** brass **3** brown

¹Br *abbr* Britain; British

²Br *symbol* bromine

BR *abbr* bedroom

bra \'brä\ *n* : BRASSIERE

¹brace \'brās\ *vb* **braced; brac·ing 1** *archaic* : to make fast : BIND **2** : to tighten preparatory to use; *also* : to get ready for : prepare oneself **3** : INVIGORATE **4** : to furnish or support with a brace; *also* : STRENGTHEN **5** : to set firmly **6** : to gain courage or confidence

²brace *n, pl* **brac·es 1** *or pl* **brace** : two of a kind ⟨a ∼ of dogs⟩ **2** : a crank-shaped device for turning a bit **3** : something (as a tie, prop, or clamp) that distributes, directs, or resists pressure or weight **4** *pl* : SUSPENDERS **5** : an appliance for supporting a body part (as the shoulders) **6** *pl* : a dental appliance used to exert pressure to straighten misaligned teeth **7** : one of two marks { } used to connect words or items to be considered together

brace·let \'brā-slət\ *n* [ME, fr. MF, dim. of *bras* arm, fr. L *bracchium*, fr. Gk *brachiōn*] : an ornamental band or chain worn around the wrist

bra·ce·ro \brä-'ser-ō\ *n, pl* **-ros** : a Mexican laborer admitted to the U.S. esp. for seasonal farm work

brack·en \'bra-kən\ *n* : a large coarse fern; *also* : a growth of such ferns

¹brack·et \'bra-kət\ *n* **1** : a projecting framework or arm designed to support weight; *also* : a shelf on such framework **2** : one of a pair of punctuation marks [ ] used esp. to enclose interpolated matter **3** : a continuous section of a series; *esp* : one of a graded series of income groups

²bracket *vb* **1** : to furnish or fasten with brackets **2** : to place within brackets; *also* : to separate or group with or as if with brackets

brack·ish \'bra-kish\ *adj* : somewhat salty — **brack·ish·ness** *n*

bract \'brakt\ *n* : an often modified leaf on or at the base of a flower stalk

brad \'brad\ *n* : a slender nail with a small head

brae \'brā\ *n, chiefly Scot* : a hillside esp. along a river

brag \'brag\ *vb* **bragged; brag·ging** : to talk or assert boastfully — **brag** *n* — **brag·ger** *n*

brag·ga·do·cio \,bra-gə-'dō-shē-,ō, -sē-, -chē-\ *n, pl* **-cios 1** : BRAGGART, BOASTER **2** : empty boasting **3** : arrogant pretension : COCKINESS

brag·gart \'bra-gərt\ *n* : one who brags

Brah·man *or* **Brah·min** \'brä-mən *for 1;* 'brä-, 'brä-, 'bra- *for 2* *n* **1** : a Hindu of the highest caste traditionally assigned to the priesthood **2** : any of a breed of large vigorous humped cattle developed in the southern U.S. from Indian stock **3** *usu* **Brahmin** : a person of high social standing and cultivated intellect and taste

Brah·man·ism \'brä-mə-,ni-zəm\ *n* : orthodox Hinduism

¹braid \'brād\ *vb* **1** : to form (strands) into a braid : PLAIT; *also* : to make from braids **2** : to ornament with braid

²braid *n* **1** : a length of braided hair **2** : a cord or ribbon of three or more interwoven strands; *esp* : a narrow ornamental one

braille \'brāl\ *n, often cap* : a system of writing for the blind that uses characters made up of raised dots

¹brain \'brān\ *n* **1** : the part of the vertebrate central nervous system enclosed in the skull and continuous with the spinal cord that is composed of neurons and supporting structures and is the center of thought and nervous system control; *also* : a centralized mass of nerve tissue in an invertebrate **2** : INTELLECT, INTELLIGENCE — often used in pl. — **brained** \'brānd\ *adj* — **brain·less** *adj* — **brainy** *adj*

²brain *vb* **1** : to kill by smashing the skull **2** : to hit on the head

brain·child \'brān-,chī(-ə)ld\ *n* : a product of one's creative imagination

brain death *n* : final cessation of activity in the central nervous system esp. as indicated by a flat electroencephalogram — **brain–dead** \-,ded\ *adj*

brain drain *n* : the departure of educated or professional people from one country, sector, or field to another usu. for better pay or living conditions

brain·storm \-,stòrm\ *n* : a sudden inspiration or idea — **brainstorm** *vb*

brain·teas·er \-,tē-zər\ *n* : a challenging puzzle

brain·wash·ing \'brān-,wò-shiŋ, -,wä-\ *n* **1** : a forcible indoctrination to induce someone to give up basic political, social, or religious beliefs and attitudes and to accept contrasting regimented ideas **2**

: persuasion by propaganda or salesmanship — **brain·wash** *vb*

brain wave *n* **1** : BRAINSTORM **2** : rhythmic fluctuations of voltage between parts of the brain; *also* : a current produced by brain waves

braise \'brāz\ *vb* **braised; brais·ing** : to cook slowly in fat and little moisture in a closed pot

¹brake \'brāk\ *n* : a common bracken fern

²brake *n* : rough or wet land heavily overgrown (as with thickets or reeds)

³brake *n* : a device for slowing or stopping motion esp. by friction — **brake·less** *adj*

⁴brake *vb* **braked; brak·ing** **1** : to slow or stop by or as if by a brake **2** : to apply a brake

brake·man \'brāk-mən\ *n* : a train crew member who inspects the train and assists the conductor

bram·ble \'bram-bəl\ *n* : any of a large genus of prickly shrubs (as a blackberry) related to the roses; *also* : any rough prickly shrub or vine — **bram·bly** \-b(ə-)lē\ *adj*

bran \'bran\ *n* : the edible broken husks of cereal grain sifted from flour or meal

¹branch \'branch\ *n* [ME, fr. AF *branche*, fr. LL *branca* paw] **1** : a natural subdivision (as a bough or twig) of a plant stem **2** : a division (as of an antler or a river) related to a whole like a plant branch to its stem **3** : a discrete element of a complex system ⟨the executive ∼⟩; *esp* : a division of a family descended from one ancestor — **branched** \'brancht\ *adj*

²branch *vb* **1** : to develop branches **2** : DIVERGE **3** : to extend activities ⟨the business is ∼ing out⟩

¹brand \'brand\ *n* **1** : a piece of charred or burning wood **2** : a mark made (as by burning) usu. to identify; *also* : a mark of disgrace : STIGMA **3** : a class of goods identified as the product of a particular firm or producer **4** : a distinctive kind ⟨my own ∼ of humor⟩

²brand *vb* **1** : to mark with a brand **2** : STIGMATIZE ⟨was ∼ed a traitor⟩

bran·dish \'bran-dish\ *vb* : to shake or wave menacingly ⟨∼ a knife⟩ ♦ *Synonyms* FLOURISH, FLASH, FLAUNT

brand–new \'bran-'nü, -'nyü\ *adj* : conspicuously new and unused

bran·dy \'bran-dē\ *n, pl* **brandies** [short for *brandywine*, fr. D *brandewijn*, fr. MD *brantwijn*, fr. *brant* distilled + *wijn* wine] : a liquor distilled from wine or fermented fruit juice — **brandy** *vb*

brash \'brash\ *adj* **1** : IMPETUOUS, AUDACIOUS **2** : aggressively self-assertive — **brash·ly** *adv* — **brash·ness** *n*

brass \'bras\ *n* **1** : an alloy of copper and zinc; *also* : an object of brass **2** : brazen self-assurance **3** : persons of high rank (as in the military) — **brassy** *adj*

bras·siere \brə-'zir\ *n* : a woman's close-fitting undergarment designed to support the breasts

brat \'brat\ *n* : an ill-behaved child — **brat·ti·ness** *n* — **brat·ty** *adj*

bra·va·do \brə-'vä-dō\ *n, pl* **-does** or

-dos **1** : blustering swaggering conduct **2** : a show of bravery

¹brave \'brāv\ *adj* **brav·er; brav·est** [MF, fr. It & Sp *bravo* courageous, wild, prob. fr. L *barbarus* barbarous] **1** : showing courage **2** : EXCELLENT, SPLENDID ♦ *Synonyms* BOLD, INTREPID, COURAGEOUS, VALIANT — **brave·ly** *adv*

²brave *vb* **braved; brav·ing** : to face or endure bravely

³brave *n* : an American Indian warrior

brav·ery \'brā-və-rē\ *n, pl* **-er·ies** : COURAGE

bra·vo \'brä-vō\ *n, pl* **bravos** : a shout of approval — often used as an interjection in applauding

bra·vu·ra \brə-'vyúr-ə, -'vúr-\ *n* **1** : a florid brilliant musical style **2** : self-assured brilliant performance — **bravura** *adj*

brawl \'brȯl\ *n* : a noisy quarrel ♦ *Synonyms* FRACAS, ROW, RUMPUS, SCRAP, FRAY, MELEE — **brawl** *vb* — **brawl·er** *n*

brawn \'brȯn\ *n* **1** : strong muscles; *also* : muscular strength — **brawn·i·ness** *n* — **brawny** *adj*

bray \'brā\ *n* : the characteristic harsh cry of a donkey — **bray** *vb*

braze \'brāz\ *vb* **brazed; braz·ing** : to solder with an alloy (as brass) that melts at a lower temperature than the metals being joined — **braz·er** *n*

¹bra·zen \'brā-z⁰n\ *adj* **1** : made of brass **2** : sounding harsh and loud **3** : of the color of brass **4** : marked by contemptuous boldness ⟨a ∼ rebuff⟩ — **bra·zen·ly** *adv* — **bra·zen·ness** *n*

²brazen *vb* : to face boldly or defiantly

¹bra·zier \'brā-zhər\ *n* : a worker in brass

²brazier *n* **1** : a vessel holding burning coals (as for heating) **2** : a device on which food is grilled

Bra·zil nut \brə-'zil-\ *n* : a triangular oily edible nut borne in large capsules by a tall So. American tree; *also* : the tree

¹breach \'brēch\ *n* **1** : a breaking of a law, obligation, tie (as of friendship), or standard (as of conduct) **2** : an interruption or opening made by or as if by breaking through ♦ *Synonyms* VIOLATION, TRANSGRESSION, INFRINGEMENT, TRESPASS

²breach *vb* **1** : to make a breach in ⟨the army ∼ed the castle wall⟩ **2** : to leap out of water ⟨whales ∼ing⟩

¹bread \'bred\ *n* **1** : baked food made basically of flour or meal **2** : FOOD

²bread *vb* : to cover with bread crumbs

bread·bas·ket \'bred-ˌbas-kət\ *n* : a major cereal-producing region

bread·fruit \-ˌfrüt\ *n* : a round usu. seedless fruit resembling bread in color and texture when baked; *also* : a tall tropical tree related to the mulberry and bearing breadfruit

bread·stuff \-ˌstəf\ *n* : GRAIN, FLOUR

breadth \'bredth, 'bretth\ *n* **1** : WIDTH **2** : comprehensive quality : SCOPE ⟨her ∼ of knowledge⟩

bread·win·ner \'bred-ˌwi-nər\ *n* : a member of a family whose wages supply its livelihood

¹**break** \'brāk\ *vb* **broke** \'brōk\; **bro·ken** \'brō-kən\; **break·ing** 1 : to separate into parts usu. suddenly or violently; *also* : to render inoperable ⟨*broke* his watch⟩ 2 : TRANSGRESS ⟨~ a law⟩ 3 : to force a way into, out of, or through 4 : to disrupt the order or unity of ⟨~ ranks⟩ ⟨~ up a gang⟩; *also* : to bring to submission or helplessness 5 : EXCEED, SURPASS ⟨~ a record⟩ 6 : RUIN 7 : to make known ⟨~ the bad news⟩ 8 : HALT, INTERRUPT; *also* : to act or change abruptly (as a course or activity) 9 : to come esp. suddenly into being or notice ⟨as day ~s⟩ 10 : to fail under stress 11 : HAPPEN, DEVELOP ⟨report news as it ~s⟩ — **break·able** *adj or n* — **break into** 1 : to begin with a sudden throwing off of restraint ⟨*broke into* tears⟩ 2 : to make entry or entrance into ⟨*break into* show business⟩

²**break** *n* 1 : an act of breaking 2 : a result of breaking; *esp* : an interruption of continuity ⟨coffee ~⟩ ⟨a ~ for the commercial⟩ 3 : a stroke of luck

break·age \'brā-kij\ *n* 1 : loss due to things broken 2 : the action of breaking 3 : articles or amount broken

break·down \'brāk-,daùn\ *n* 1 : functional failure; *esp* : a physical, mental, or nervous collapse 2 : DISINTEGRATION 3 : DECOMPOSITION 4 : ANALYSIS, CLASSIFICATION — **break down** *vb*

break·er \'brā-kər\ *n* 1 : one that breaks 2 : a wave that breaks into foam (as against the shore)

break·fast \'brek-fəst\ *n* : the first meal of the day — **breakfast** *vb*

break in *vb* 1 : to enter a building by force 2 : INTERRUPT; *also* : INTRUDE 3 : TRAIN ⟨*break in* new employees⟩ — **break–in** \'brāk-,in\ *n*

break·neck \'brāk-'nek\ *adj* : very fast or dangerous ⟨~ speed⟩

break out *vb* 1 : to develop or erupt suddenly or with force 2 : to develop a skin rash

break·through \'brāk-,thrü\ *n* 1 : an act or instance of breaking through an obstruction or defensive line 2 : a sudden advance in knowledge or technique ⟨a scientific ~⟩

break·up \-,əp\ *n* 1 : DISSOLUTION 2 : a division into smaller units — **break up** *vb*

break·wa·ter \'brāk-,wò-tər, -,wä-\ *n* : a structure protecting a harbor or beach from the force of waves

bream \'brim, 'brēm\ *n, pl* **bream** *or* **breams** : any of various small freshwater sunfishes

breast \'brest\ *n* 1 : either of the pair of mammary glands extending from the front of the chest esp. in pubescent and adult human females 2 : the front part of the body between the neck and the abdomen 3 : the seat of emotion and thought

breast·bone \'brest-,bōn\ *n* : STERNUM

breast–feed \-,fēd\ *vb* : to feed (a baby) from a mother's breast

breast·plate \-,plāt\ *n* : a metal plate of armor for the breast

breast·stroke \-,strōk\ *n* : a swimming stroke executed by extending both arms forward and then sweeping them back with palms out while kicking backward and outward with both legs

breast·work \-,wərk\ *n* : a temporary fortification

breath \'breth\ *n* 1 : the act or power of breathing 2 : a slight breeze 3 : air inhaled or exhaled in breathing 4 : spoken sound 5 : SPIRIT — **breath·less** *adj* — **breath·less·ly** *adv* — **breath·less·ness** *n* — **breathy** \'bre-thē\ *adj*

breathe \'brēth\ *vb* **breathed**; **breath·ing** 1 : to inhale and exhale 2 : LIVE 3 : to halt for rest 4 : to utter softly or secretly — **breath·able** *adj*

breath·er \'brē-thər\ *n* 1 : one that breathes 2 : a short rest

breath·tak·ing \'breth-,tā-kiŋ\ *adj* 1 : making one out of breath 2 : EXCITING, THRILLING ⟨~ beauty⟩ — **breath·tak·ing·ly** *adv*

brec·cia \'bre-chē-ə, -chə\ *n* : a rock composed of sharp fragments held in fine-grained material

breech \'brēch\ *n* 1 *pl \usu* 'bri-chəz\ : pants ending near the knee 2 : BUTTOCKS, RUMP 3 : the part of a firearm at the rear of the barrel

¹**breed** \'brēd\ *vb* **bred** \'bred\; **breed·ing** 1 : BEGET; *also* : ORIGINATE 2 : to propagate sexually; *also* : MATE 3 : BRING UP, NURTURE 4 : to produce (fissionable material) from material that is not fissionable ◆ **Synonyms** GENERATE, REPRODUCE, PROCREATE, PROPAGATE — **breed·er** *n*

²**breed** *n* 1 : a strain of similar and presumably related plants or animals usu. developed in domestication 2 : KIND, SORT, CLASS

breeding *n* 1 : ANCESTRY 2 : training in polite social interaction 3 : sexual propagation of plants or animals

¹**breeze** \'brēz\ *n* 1 : a light wind 2 : CINCH, SNAP — **breeze·less** *adj*

²**breeze** *vb* **breezed**; **breez·ing** : to progress quickly and easily

breeze·way \'brēz-,wā\ *n* : a roofed open passage connecting two buildings (as a house and garage)

breezy \'brē-zē\ *adj* 1 : swept by breezes 2 : briskly informal ⟨~ prose⟩ — **breez·i·ly** \'brē-zə-lē\ *adv* — **breez·i·ness** \-zē-nəs\ *n*

breth·ren \'breth-rən, 'bre-thə-; 'brethərn\ *pl of* BROTHER — used esp. in formal or solemn address

Brethren *n pl* : members of one of several Protestant denominations originating chiefly in a German religious movement and stressing personal religious experience

bre·via·ry \'brē-vyə-rē, -vē-,er-ē\ *n, pl* **-ries** *often cap* : a book of prayers, hymns, psalms, and readings used by Roman Catholic priests

brev·i·ty \'bre-və-tē\ *n, pl* **-ties** 1 : shortness or conciseness of expression 2 : shortness of duration

brew \'brü\ *vb* 1 : to prepare (as beer) by

steeping, boiling, and fermenting 2 : to prepare (as tea) by steeping in hot water — **brew** *n* — **brew·er** *n* — **brew·ery** \'brü-ə-rē, 'brü(-ə)r-ē\ *n*

¹**bri·ar** *also* **bri·er** \'brī-ər\ *n* : a plant (as a bramble or rose) with a thorny or prickly usu. woody stem; *also* : a mass or twig of these — **bri·ary** \'brī-ə-rē\ *adj*

²**briar** *n* : a tobacco pipe made from the root or stem of a European heath

¹**bribe** \'brīb\ *n* [ME, morsel given to a beggar, bribe, fr. AF, morsel] : something (as money or a favor) given or promised to a person to influence conduct

²**bribe** *vb* **bribed; brib·ing** : to influence by offering a bribe — **brib·able** *adj* — **brib·er** *n* — **brib·ery** \'brī-bə-rē\ *n*

bric-a-brac \'bri-kə-ˌbrak\ *n pl* [F] : small ornamental articles

¹**brick** \'brik\ *n* : a block molded from moist clay and hardened by heat used esp. for building

²**brick** *vb* : to close, cover, or pave with bricks

brick·bat \'brik-ˌbat\ *n* 1 : a piece of a hard material (as a brick) esp. when thrown as a missile 2 : an uncomplimentary remark

brick·lay·er \'brik-ˌlā-ər\ *n* : a person who builds or paves with bricks — **brick·lay·ing** *n*

¹**brid·al** \'brī-d°l\ *n* [ME *bridale*, fr. OE *brȳdealu*, fr. *brȳd* bride + *ealu* ale] : MARRIAGE, WEDDING

²**bridal** *adj* : of or relating to a bride or a wedding

bride \'brīd\ *n* : a woman just married or about to be married

bride·groom \'brīd-ˌgrüm, -ˌgrùm\ *n* : a man just married or about to be married

brides·maid \'brīdz-ˌmād\ *n* : a woman who attends a bride at her wedding

¹**bridge** \'brij\ *n* 1 : a structure built over a depression or obstacle for use as a passageway 2 : something (as the upper part of the nose) resembling a bridge in form or function 3 : a curved piece raising the strings of a musical instrument 4 : the forward part of a ship's superstructure from which it is navigated 5 : an artificial replacement for missing teeth

²**bridge** *vb* **bridged; bridg·ing** : to build a bridge over — **bridge·able** *adj*

³**bridge** *n* : a card game for four players developed from whist

bridge·head \-ˌhed\ *n* : an advanced position seized in enemy territory

bridge·work \-ˌwərk\ *n* : dental bridges

¹**bri·dle** \'brī-d°l\ *n* 1 : headgear with which a horse is controlled 2 : CURB, RESTRAINT

²**bridle** *vb* **bri·dled; bri·dling** 1 : to put a bridle on; *also* : to restrain with or as if with a bridle 2 : to show hostility or scorn usu. by tossing the head

Brie \'brē\ *n* : a soft cheese with a whitish rind and a pale yellow interior

¹**brief** \'brēf\ *adj* 1 : short in duration or extent 2 : CONCISE; *also* : CURT — **brief·ly** *adv* — **brief·ness** *n*

²**brief** *n* 1 : a concise statement or document; *esp* : one summarizing a law cli-

ent's case or a legal argument 2 *pl* : short snug underpants

³**brief** *vb* : to give final instructions or essential information to

brief·case \'brēf-ˌkās\ *n* : a flat flexible case for carrying papers

brier *var of* BRIAR

¹**brig** \'brig\ *n* : a 2-masted square-rigged sailing ship

²**brig** *n* : the place of confinement for offenders on a naval ship

³**brig** *abbr* brigade

bri·gade \bri-'gād\ *n* 1 : a military unit composed of a headquarters, one or more units of infantry or armored forces, and supporting units 2 : a group organized for a particular purpose (as fire fighting)

brig·a·dier general \ˌbri-gə-ˌdir-\ *n* : a commissioned officer (as in the army) ranking next below a major general

brig·and \'bri-gənd\ *n* : BANDIT — **brig·and·age** \-gən-dij\ *n*

brig·an·tine \'bri-gən-ˌtēn\ *n* : a 2-masted square-rigged ship with a fore-and-aft mainsail

Brig Gen *abbr* brigadier general

bright \'brīt\ *adj* 1 : SHINING, RADIANT 2 : ILLUSTRIOUS, GLORIOUS 3 : INTELLIGENT, CLEVER; *also* : LIVELY, CHEERFUL ⟨a ~ smile⟩ ♦ **Synonyms** BRILLIANT, LUSTROUS, BEAMING — **bright** *adv* — **bright·ly** *adv* — **bright·ness** *n*

bright·en \'brī-t°n\ *vb* : to make or become bright or brighter ⟨the good news ~ed her mood⟩ — **bright·en·er** *n*

¹**bril·liant** \'bril-yənt\ *adj* [F *brillant*, prp. of *briller* to shine, fr. It *brillare*] 1 : very bright 2 : STRIKING, DISTINCTIVE 3 : very intelligent ⟨a ~ idea⟩ ♦ **Synonyms** RADIANT, LUSTROUS, BEAMING, LUCID, BRIGHT, LAMBENT — **bril·liance** \-yəns\ *n* — **bril·lian·cy** \-yən-sē\ *n* — **bril·liant·ly** *adv*

²**brilliant** *n* : a gem cut in a particular form with many facets

¹**brim** \'brim\ *n* : EDGE, RIM ♦ **Synonyms** BRINK, BORDER, VERGE, FRINGE — **brim·less** *adj*

²**brim** *vb* **brimmed; brim·ming** : to be or become full often to overflowing

brim·ful \-'fúl\ *adj* : full to the brim

brim·stone \'brim-ˌstōn\ *n* : SULFUR

brin·dled \'brin-d°ld\ *adj* : having dark streaks or flecks on a gray or tawny ground ⟨a ~ Great Dane⟩

brine \'brīn\ *n* 1 : water saturated with salt 2 : OCEAN — **brin·i·ness** *n* — **briny** \'brī-nē\ *adj*

bring \'brin\ *vb* **brought** \'brót\; **bring·ing** \'brin-in\ 1 : to cause to come with one 2 : INDUCE, PERSUADE, LEAD 3 : PRODUCE, EFFECT 4 : to sell for ⟨~ a good price⟩ — **bring·er** *n*

bring about *vb* : to cause to take place

bring up *vb* 1 : to give a parent's fostering care to 2 : to come or bring to a sudden halt 3 : to call to notice

brink \'brink\ *n* 1 : an edge at the top of a steep place 2 : the point of onset

brio \'brē-ō\ *n* : VIVACITY, SPIRIT

bri·quette *or* **bri·quet** \bri-'ket\ *n* : a

compacted often brick-shaped mass of fine material ⟨a charcoal ∼⟩

bris also **briss** \'bris\ n : the Jewish rite of circumcision

brisk \'brisk\ adj 1 : ALERT, LIVELY 2 : INVIGORATING ⟨∼ weather⟩ 3 : highly active ⟨a ∼ business⟩ ♦ *Synonyms* AGILE, SPRY, NIMBLE — **brisk·ly** adv — **brisk·ness** n

bris·ket \'bris-kət\ n : the breast or lower chest of a quadruped; also : a cut of beef from the brisket

bris·ling \'briz-liŋ, 'bris-\ n : SPRAT 1

¹**bris·tle** \'bri-səl\ n : a short stiff coarse hair — **bris·tle·like** \'bri-səl-,līk\ adj — **bris·tly** adj

²**bristle** vb **bris·tled; bris·tling** 1 : to stand stiffly erect 2 : to show angry defiance ⟨bristled at the charges⟩ 3 : to appear as if covered with bristles

Brit abbr Britain; British

Bri·tan·nic \bri-'ta-nik\ adj : BRITISH

britch·es \'bri-chəz\ n pl : BREECHES, TROUSERS

Brit·ish \'bri-tish\ n pl : the people of Great Britain or the Commonwealth — **British** adj — **Brit·ish·ness** n

British thermal unit n : the quantity of heat needed to raise the temperature of one pound of water one degree Fahrenheit

Brit·on \'bri-tᵊn\ n 1 : a member of a people inhabiting Britain before the Anglo-Saxon invasion 2 : a native or inhabitant of Great Britain

brit·tle \'bri-tᵊl\ adj **brit·tler; brit·tlest** : easily broken : FRAGILE ♦ *Synonyms* CRISP, CRUMBLY, FRIABLE — **brit·tle·ness** n

bro \'brō\ n, pl **bros** 1 : BROTHER 1 2 : SOUL BROTHER

¹**broach** \'brōch\ n : a pointed tool

²**broach** vb 1 : to pierce (as a cask) in order to draw the contents 2 : to open up (a subject) for discussion

broad \'brōd\ adj 1 : WIDE 2 : SPACIOUS ⟨the ∼ plains⟩ 3 : CLEAR, OPEN ⟨∼ daylight⟩ 4 : OBVIOUS ⟨a ∼ hint⟩ 5 : COARSE, CRUDE ⟨∼ stories⟩ 6 : tolerant in outlook 7 : GENERAL ⟨a ∼ rule⟩ 8 : dealing with essential points — **broad·ly** adv — **broad·ness** n

broad·band \'brōd-,band\ n : a system of high-speed telecommunication in which a frequency range is divided into multiple independent channels for simultaneous transmission of signals

¹**broad·cast** \'brōd-,kast\ vb **broadcast** also **broad·cast·ed; broad·cast·ing** 1 : to scatter or sow broadcast 2 : to make widely known 3 : to transmit a broadcast — **broad·cast·er** n

²**broadcast** adv : to or over a wide area

³**broadcast** n 1 : the transmission of sound or images by radio or television 2 : a single radio or television program

broad·cloth \-,klȯth\ n 1 : a smooth dense woolen cloth 2 : a fine soft cloth of cotton, silk, or synthetic fiber

broad·en \'brȯ-dᵊn\ vb : WIDEN

broad·loom \-,lüm\ adj : woven on a wide loom esp. in a solid color

broad–mind·ed \-'mīn-dəd\ adj : tolerant of varied opinions — **broad–mind·ed·ly** adv — **broad–mind·ed·ness** n

¹**broad·side** \-,sīd\ n 1 : a sheet of paper printed usu. on one side (as an advertisement) 2 : all of the guns on one side of a ship; also : their simultaneous firing 3 : a volley of abuse or denunciation

²**broadside** adv 1 : with one side forward : SIDEWAYS 2 : from the side ⟨the car was hit ∼⟩

broad–spectrum adj : effective against a wide range of organisms ⟨∼ antibiotics⟩

broad·sword \'brȯd-,sȯrd\ n : a broad-bladed sword

broad·tail \-,tāl\ n : a karakul esp. with flat and wavy fur

bro·cade \brō-'kād\ n : a usu. silk fabric with a raised design

broc·co·li \'brä-kə-lē\ n [It, pl. of *broccolo* flowering top of a cabbage, dim. of *brocco* small nail, sprout, fr. L *broccus* projecting] : the stems and immature usu. green or purple flower heads of either of two garden vegetable plants closely related to the cabbage; also : either of the plants

bro·chette \brō-'shet\ n : SKEWER

bro·chure \brō-'shu̇r\ n [F, fr. *brocher* to sew, fr. MF, to prick, fr. OF *brochier*, fr. *broche* pointed tool] : PAMPHLET, BOOKLET

bro·gan \'brō-gən, brō-'gan\ n : a heavy shoe

brogue \'brōg\ n : a dialect or regional pronunciation; esp : an Irish accent

broil \'brȯi(-ə)l\ vb : to cook by exposure to radiant heat : GRILL — **broil** n

broil·er \'brȯi-lər\ n 1 : a utensil for broiling 2 : a young chicken fit for broiling

broil·ing \'brȯi-(ə)-liŋ\ adj : extremely hot ⟨a ∼ sun⟩

¹**broke** \'brōk\ past of BREAK

²**broke** adj : PENNILESS

¹**bro·ken** \'brō-kən\ past part of BREAK

²**broken** adj 1 : SHATTERED ⟨∼ glass⟩ 2 : having gaps or breaks : INTERRUPTED, DISRUPTED 3 : SUBDUED, CRUSHED ⟨a ∼ spirit⟩ 4 : BANKRUPT 5 : imperfectly spoken ⟨∼ English⟩ — **bro·ken·ly** adv

bro·ken–heart·ed \,brō-kən-'här-təd\ adj : overcome by grief or despair

bro·ker \'brō-kər\ n : an agent who negotiates contracts of purchase and sale — **broker** vb

bro·ker·age \'brō-kə-rij\ n 1 : the business of a broker 2 : the fee or commission charged by a broker

bro·mance \'brō-,man(t)s\ n [blend of *bro* and *romance*] : a close nonsexual friendship between men — **bro·man·tic** \brō-'man-tik\ adj

bro·me·li·ad \brō-'mē-lē-,ad\ n : any of several tropical American ornamental plants related to the pineapple that usu. grow on trees

bro·mide \'brō-,mīd\ n : a compound of bromine and another element or chemical group including some (as potassium bromide) used as sedatives

bromidic • bruit

bro·mid·ic \brō-'mi-dik\ *adj* : TRITE, UN-ORIGINAL

bro·mine \'brō-ˌmēn\ *n* [F *brome* bromine, fr. Gk *brōmos* stink] : a deep red liquid corrosive chemical element that gives off an irritating vapor

bronc \'bräŋk\ *n* : an unbroken or partly broken range horse of western No. America; *also* : MUSTANG

bron·chi·al \'bräŋ-kē-əl\ *adj* : of, relating to, or affecting the bronchi or their branches

bron·chi·tis \brän-'kī-təs, bräŋ-\ *n* : inflammation of the bronchi and their branches — **bron·chit·ic** \-'ki-tik\ *adj*

bron·chus \'bräŋ-kəs\ *n, pl* **bron·chi** \'bräŋ-ˌkī, -ˌkē\ : either of the main divisions of the trachea each leading to a lung

bron·co \'bräŋ-kō\ *n, pl* **broncos** [Mex-Sp, fr. Sp, rough, wild] : BRONC

bron·to·sau·rus \ˌbrän-tə-'sȯr-əs\ *also* **bron·to·saur** \'brän-tə-ˌsȯr\ *n* [NL, fr. Gk *brontē* thunder + *sauros* lizard] : any of a genus of large 4-footed sauropod dinosaurs of the Jurassic

Bronx cheer \'bräŋks-\ *n* : RASPBERRY 2

¹bronze \'bränz\ *vb* **bronzed; bronz·ing** : to give the appearance of bronze to

²bronze *n* **1** : an alloy of copper and tin and sometimes other elements; *also* : something made of bronze **2** : a yellowish brown color — **bronzy** \'brän-zē\ *adj*

brooch \'brōch, 'brüch\ *n* : an ornamental clasp or pin

¹brood \'brüd\ *n* : a family of young animals or children and esp. of birds

²brood *adj* : kept for breeding ⟨a ∼ mare⟩

³brood *vb* **1** : to sit on eggs to hatch them; *also* : to shelter (hatched young) with the wings **2** : to think anxiously or gloomily about something — **brood·ing·ly** *adv*

brood·er \'brü-dər\ *n* **1** : one that broods **2** : a heated structure for raising young birds

¹brook \'brùk\ *n* : a small natural stream

²brook *vb* : TOLERATE, BEAR ⟨would ∼ no interference with his plan⟩

brook·let \'brù-klət\ *n* : a small brook

brook trout *n* : a common speckled coldwater char of No. America

broom \'brüm, 'brùm\ *n* **1** : any of several shrubs of the legume family with long slender branches and usu. yellow flowers **2** : an implement with a long handle (**broom·stick** \-ˌstik\) used for sweeping

broth \'brȯth\ *n, pl* **broths** \'brȯths, 'brȯthz\ **1** : liquid in which meat or sometimes vegetable food has been cooked **2** : a fluid culture medium

broth·el \'brä-thəl, 'brȯ-\ *n* : a house of prostitution

broth·er \'brə-thər\ *n, pl* **brothers** *also* **breth·ren** \'breth-rən, 'bre-thə-; 'bre-thərn\ **1** : a male having one or both parents in common with another individual **2** : a man who is a religious but not a priest **3** : KINSMAN; *also* : SOUL BROTHER — **broth·er·li·ness** \-lē-nəs\ *n* — **broth·er·ly** *adj*

broth·er·hood \'brə-thər-ˌhùd\ *n* **1** : the state of being brothers or a brother **2** : ASSOCIATION, FRATERNITY **3** : the whole body of persons in a business or profession ⟨the medical ∼⟩

broth·er–in–law \'brə-thə-rən-ˌlȯ, 'brə-thərn-ˌlȯ\ *n, pl* **brothers–in–law** \'brə-thər-zən-\ : the brother of one's spouse; *also* : the husband of one's sister or of one's spouse's sister

brougham \'brü(-ə)m, 'brō(-ə)m\ *n* : a light closed horse-drawn carriage with the driver outside in front

brought *past and past part of* BRING

brou·ha·ha \'brü-ˌhä-ˌhä\ *n* : HUBBUB, UPROAR

brow \'braù\ *n* **1** : the eyebrow or the ridge on which it grows; *also* : FOREHEAD **2** : the projecting upper part of a steep place

brow·beat \'braù-ˌbēt\ *vb* **-beat; -beaten** \-ˌbē-tᵊn\ *or* **-beat; -beat·ing** : to intimidate by sternness or arrogance

¹brown \'braùn\ *adj* : of the color brown; *also* : of dark or tanned complexion

²brown *n* : a color like that of coffee or chocolate that is a blend of red and yellow darkened by black — **brown·ish** *adj*

³brown *vb* : to make or become brown

brown bag·ging \-'ba-giŋ\ *n* : the practice of carrying one's lunch usu. in a brown bag — **brown bag·ger** *n*

brown bear *n* : any of various large typically brown-furred bears including the grizzly bear

brown·ie \'braù-nē\ *n* **1** : a legendary cheerful elf who performs good deeds at night **2** *cap* : a member of a program of the Girl Scouts for girls in the first through third grades **3** : a small square or rectangle of chocolate cake

brown·nose \'braùn-ˌnōz\ *vb* : to ingratiate oneself with — **brownnose** *n*

brown·out \'braù-ˌnaùt\ *n* : a period of reduced voltage of electricity caused esp. by high demand and resulting in reduced illumination

brown rice *n* : hulled but unpolished rice that retains most of the bran layers

brown·stone \'braùn-ˌstōn\ *n* : a dwelling faced with reddish-brown sandstone

¹browse \'braùz\ *vb* **browsed; brows·ing** **1** : to feed on browse; *also* : GRAZE **2** : to read or look over something in a casual way **3** : to access (a network) with a browser

²browse *n* : tender shoots, twigs, and leaves fit for food for cattle

brows·er \'braù-zər\ *n* : a computer program for accessing sites or information on a network (as the World Wide Web)

bru·in \'brü-ən\ *n* : BEAR

¹bruise \'brüz\ *vb* **bruised; bruis·ing** **1** : to inflict a bruise on; *also* : to become bruised **2** : to break down (as leaves or berries) by pounding

²bruise *n* : a surface injury to flesh : CONTUSION

bruis·er \'brü-zər\ *n* : a big husky man

bruit \'brüt\ *vb* : to make widely known by common report ⟨word of his dismissal was ∼ed about⟩

brunch \'brənch\ *n* : a meal that combines a late breakfast and an early lunch

bru·net *or* **bru·nette** \brü-'net\ *adj* [F *brunet*, masc., *brunette*, fem., brownish, fr. OF, fr. *brun* brown, of Gmc origin] : having brown or black hair and usu. a relatively dark complexion — **brunet** *or* **brunette** *n*

brunt \'brənt\ *n* : the main shock, force, or stress esp. of an attack; *also* : the greater burden

bru·schet·ta \brü-'she-tə, -'ske-\ *n* : an appetizer of grilled bread with toppings

¹**brush** \'brəsh\ *n* **1** : BRUSHWOOD **2** : scrub vegetation or land covered with it

²**brush** *n* **1** : a device composed of bristles set in a handle and used esp. for cleaning or painting **2** : a bushy tail (as of a fox) **3** : an electrical conductor that makes contact between a stationary and a moving part (as of a motor) **4** : a quick light touch in passing

³**brush** *vb* **1** : to treat (as in cleaning or painting) with a brush **2** : to remove with or as if with a brush; *also* : to dismiss in an offhand manner **3** : to touch gently in passing

⁴**brush** *n* : SKIRMISH ⟨a ~ with the law⟩
♦ **Synonyms** ENCOUNTER, RUN-IN

brush fire *n* **1** : a fire involving low-growing plants **2** : a minor conflict or crisis

brush-off \'brəsh-ˌȯf\ *n* : a curt offhand dismissal

brush up *vb* : to renew one's skill

brush·wood \'brəsh-ˌwu̇d\ *n* **1** : small branches of wood esp. when cut **2** : a thicket of shrubs and small trees

brusque \'brəsk\ *adj* [F *brusque*, fr. It *brusco*, fr. ML *bruscus* a plant with stiff twigs used for brooms] : CURT, BLUNT, ABRUPT ⟨a ~ answer⟩ ♦ **Synonyms** GRUFF, BLUFF, CRUSTY, SHORT — **brusque·ly** *adv*

brus·sels sprout \'brəs-əlz-\ *n, often cap B* : one of the edible green heads borne on the stalk of a plant closely related to the cabbage; *also, pl* : this plant

bru·tal \'brü-t³l\ *adj* **1** : befitting a brute : UNFEELING, CRUEL **2** : HARSH, SEVERE ⟨~ weather⟩ **3** : unpleasantly accurate ⟨a ~ depiction of war⟩ — **bru·tal·i·ty** \brü-'ta-lə-tē\ *n* — **bru·tal·ly** *adv*

bru·tal·ise *Brit var of* BRUTALIZE

bru·tal·ize \'brü-t³l-ˌīz\ *vb* **-ized; -iz·ing** **1** : to make brutal **2** : to treat brutally

¹**brute** \'brüt\ *adj* [ME, fr. MF *brut* rough, fr. L *brutus* brutish, lit., heavy] **1** : of or relating to beasts **2** : BRUTAL **3** : UNREASONING; *also* : purely physical ⟨~ strength⟩

²**brute** *n* **1** : BEAST 1 **2** : a brutal person

brut·ish \'brü-tish\ *adj* **1** : BRUTE 1 2 **2** : strongly sensual; *also* : showing little intelligence

BS *abbr* bachelor of science
BSA *abbr* Boy Scouts of America
bskt *abbr* basket
Bt *abbr* baronet
btry *abbr* battery
Btu *abbr* British thermal unit
bu *abbr* bushel

¹**bub·ble** \'bə-bəl\ *n* **1** : a globule of gas in a liquid **2** : a thin film of liquid filled with gas **3** : something lacking firmness or solidity — **bub·bly** *adj*

²**bubble** *vb* **bub·bled; bub·bling** : to form, rise in, or give off bubbles

bub·kes \'bəp-kəs, 'bu̇p-\ *n pl* [Yiddish] : the least amount ⟨didn't win ~⟩

bu·bo \'bü-bō, 'byü-\ *n, pl* **buboes** : an inflammatory swelling of a lymph gland

bu·bon·ic plague \bü-'bä-nik-, byü-\ *n* : plague caused by a bacterium transmitted to human beings by flea bites and marked esp. by chills and fever and by buboes usu. in the groin

buc·ca·neer \ˌbə-kə-'nir\ *n* : PIRATE

¹**buck** \'bək\ *n, pl* **bucks** 1 *or pl* **buck** : a male animal (as a deer or antelope) **2** : DANDY **3** : DOLLAR

²**buck** *vb* **1** : to spring with an arching leap ⟨a ~ing horse⟩ **2** : to charge against something; *also* : to strive for advancement sometimes without regard to ethical behavior

buck·board \-ˌbȯrd\ *n* : a 4-wheeled horse-drawn wagon with a floor of long springy boards

buck·et \'bə-kət\ *n* **1** : PAIL **2** : an object resembling a bucket in collecting, scooping, or carrying something ⟨a tractor's ~⟩ — **buck·et·ful** *n*

bucket list *n* [from *kick the bucket* (to die)] : a list of things one has not done before but wants to do before dying

bucket seat *n* : a low separate seat for one person (as in an automobile)

buck·eye \'bə-ˌkī\ *n* : any of various trees or shrubs related to the horse chestnut; *also* : the large nutlike seed of such a shrub or tree

buck fever *n* : nervous excitement of an inexperienced hunter at the sight of game

¹**buck·le** \'bə-kəl\ *n* : a clasp (as on a belt) for two loose ends

²**buckle** *vb* **buck·led; buck·ling** **1** : to fasten with a buckle **2** : to apply oneself with vigor **3** : to crumple up : BEND, COLLAPSE

³**buckle** *n* : BEND, FOLD, KINK

buck·ler \'bə-klər\ *n* : SHIELD

buck·ram \'bə-krəm\ *n* : a coarse stiff cloth used esp. for binding books

buck·saw \'bək-ˌsȯ\ *n* : a saw set in a usu. H-shaped frame for sawing wood

buck·shot \'bək-ˌshät\ *n* : lead shot that is from .24 to .33 inch (about 6.1 to 8.4 millimeters) in diameter

buck·skin \-ˌskin\ *n* **1** : the skin of a buck **2** : a soft usu. suede-finished leather — **buckskin** *adj*

buck·tooth \-'tüth\ *n* : a large protruding front tooth — **buck–toothed** \-'tütht\ *adj*

buck·wheat \-ˌhwēt\ *n* : either of two plants grown for their triangular seeds which are used as a cereal grain; *also* : these seeds

bu·col·ic \byü-'kä-lik\ *adj* [L *bucolicus*, fr. Gk *boukolikos*, fr. *boukolos* cowherd] : PASTORAL, RURAL ⟨~ countryside⟩

¹**bud** \'bəd\ *n* **1** : an undeveloped plant shoot (as of a leaf or a flower); *also* : a

partly opened flower **2** : an asexual reproductive structure that detaches from the parent and forms a new individual **3** : something not yet fully developed 〈nipped in the ∼〉

²bud *vb* **bud·ded; bud·ding 1** : to form or put forth buds; *also* : to reproduce by asexual buds **2** : to be or develop like a bud **3** : to reproduce a desired variety (as of peach) by inserting a bud in a plant of a different variety

Bud·dhism \'bü-ˌdi-zəm, 'bù-\ *n* : a religion of eastern and central Asia growing out of the teachings of Gautama Buddha — **Bud·dhist** \'bü-dist, 'bù-\ *n or adj*

bud·dy \'bə-dē\ *n, pl* **buddies 1** : COMPANION; *also* : FRIEND **2** : FELLOW

budge \'bəj\ *vb* **budged; budg·ing** : MOVE, SHIFT; *also* : YIELD

bud·ger·i·gar \'bə-jə-rē-ˌgar\ *n* : a small brightly colored Australian parrot often kept as a pet

¹bud·get \'bə-jət\ *n* [ME *bowgette*, fr. MF *bougette*, dim. of *bouge* leather bag, fr. L *bulga*] **1** : STOCK, SUPPLY **2** : a financial report containing estimates of income and expenses; *also* : a plan for coordinating income and expenses **3** : the amount of money available for a particular use — **bud·get·ary** \'bə-jə-ˌter-ē\ *adj*

²budget *vb* **1** : to allow for in a budget **2** : to draw up a budget

³budget *adj* : INEXPENSIVE

bud·gie \'bə-jē\ *n* : BUDGERIGAR

¹buff \'bəf\ *n* **1** : a yellow to orange yellow color **2** : FAN, ENTHUSIAST

²buff *adj* : of the color buff

³buff *vb* : POLISH, SHINE

buf·fa·lo \'bə-fə-ˌlō\ *n, pl* **-lo** *or* **-loes** *also* **-los 1** : WATER BUFFALO **2** : a large shaggy-maned No. American wild bovine mammal that has short horns and heavy forequarters with a large muscular hump

buffalo soldier *n* : an African-American soldier serving in the western U.S. after the Civil War

¹buf·fer \'bə-fər\ *n* : something or someone that protects or shields (as from physical damage or a financial blow)

²buffer *n* : one that buffs

¹buf·fet \'bə-fət\ *n* : BLOW, SLAP

²buffet *vb* **1** : to strike with the hand; *also* : to pound repeatedly **2** : to struggle against or on ♦ **Synonyms** BEAT, BATTER, DRUB, PUMMEL, THRASH

³buf·fet \(ˌ)bə-ˈfā, bü-\ *n* **1** : SIDEBOARD **2** : a counter for refreshments; *also* : a meal at which people serve themselves informally

buff leather *n* : a strong supple oil-tanned leather

buf·foon \(ˌ)bə-ˈfün\ *n* [MF *bouffon*, fr. It *buffone*] : CLOWN **2** — **buf·foon·ery** \-ˈfü-nə-rē\ *n* — **buf·foon·ish** \-ˈfü-nish\ *adj*

¹bug \'bəg\ *n* **1** : an insect or other creeping or crawling invertebrate animal; *esp* : an insect pest (as the cockroach or bedbug **2** : any of an order of insects with sucking mouthparts and incomplete metamorphosis that includes many plant pests **3** : an unexpected flaw or imperfec-

tion 〈a ∼ in a computer program〉 **4** : a disease-producing germ; *also* : a disease caused by it **5** : a concealed listening device — **bug·gy** \'bə-gē\ *adj*

²bug *vb* **bugged; bug·ging 1** : BOTHER, ANNOY **2** : to plant a concealed microphone in

³bug *vb* **bugged; bug·ging** *of the eyes* : PROTRUDE, BULGE

bug·a·boo \'bə-gə-ˌbü\ *n, pl* **-boos** : BOGEY 1

bug·bear \'bəg-ˌber\ *n* : BOGEY 1; *also* : a source of dread

bug·gy \'bə-gē\ *n, pl* **buggies** : a light horse-drawn carriage; *also* : a carriage for a baby

bu·gle \'byü-gəl\ *n* [ME, buffalo, instrument made of buffalo horn, bugle, fr. AF, fr. L *buculus*, dim. of *bos* head of cattle] : a valveless brass instrument resembling a trumpet and used esp. for military calls — **bu·gler** *n*

bug out *vb* **1** : to flee in panic **2** : to depart in a hurry

¹build \'bild\ *vb* **built** \'bilt\; **build·ing 1** : to form or have formed by ordering and uniting materials 〈∼ a house〉; *also* : to bring into being or develop **2** : to produce or create gradually 〈∼ an argument on facts〉 **3** : INCREASE, ENLARGE; *also* : ENHANCE **4** : to engage in building — **build·er** *n*

²build *n* : form or mode of structure; *esp* : PHYSIQUE

build·ing \'bil-diŋ\ *n* **1** : a usu. roofed and walled structure (as a house) for permanent use **2** : the art or business of constructing buildings

build-up \'bild-ˌəp\ *n* : the act or process of building up; *also* : something produced by this

built-in \'bilt-ˈin\ *adj* **1** : forming an integral part of a structure **2** : INHERENT

bulb \'bəlb\ *n* **1** : an underground resting stage of a plant (as a lily or an onion) consisting of a short stem base bearing one or more buds enclosed in overlapping leaves; *also* : a fleshy plant structure (as a tuber) resembling a bulb **2** : a plant having or growing from a bulb **3** : a rounded more or less bulb-shaped object or part (as for an electric lamp) — **bul·bous** \'bəl-bəs\ *adj*

¹bulge \'bəlj\ *vb* **bulged; bulg·ing** : to become or cause to become protuberant

²bulge *n* : a swelling projecting part

bu·li·mia \bü-ˈlē-mē-ə, byü-, -ˈli-\ *n* **1** : an abnormal and constant craving for food **2** : a serious eating disorder chiefly of females that is characterized by compulsive overeating usu. followed by self-induced vomiting or laxative or diuretic abuse — **bu·lim·ic** \-ˈlē-mik, -ˈli-\ *adj or n*

¹bulk \'bəlk\ *n* **1** : MAGNITUDE, VOLUME **2** : material that forms a mass in the intestine; *esp* : FIBER 2 **3** : a large mass **4** : the major portion

²bulk *vb* **1** : to cause to swell or bulge **2** : to appear as a factor : LOOM

bulk·head \'bəlk-ˌhed\ *n* **1** : a partition separating compartments **2** : a structure built to cover a shaft or a cellar stairway

bulky \'bəl-kē\ *adj* **bulk·i·er; -est** : having bulky; *esp* : being large and unwieldy

¹**bull** \'bul\ *n* **1** : a male bovine animal; *also* : a usu. adult male of various large animals (as the moose, elephant, or whale) **2** : one who buys securities or commodities in expectation of a price increase — **bull·ish** *adj*

²**bull** *adj* **1** : of, relating to, or suggestive of a bull : MALE **2** : large of its kind ⟨a ~ lathe⟩

³**bull** *n* [ME *bulle,* fr. ML *bulla,* fr. L, bubble, amulet] **1** : a papal letter **2** : DECREE

⁴**bull** *n, slang* : NONSENSE

⁵**bull** *abbr* bulletin

¹**bull·dog** \'bul-,dog\ *n* : any of a breed of compact muscular short-haired dogs of English origin

²**bulldog** *vb* : to throw (a steer) by seizing the horns and twisting the neck

bull·doze \-,dōz\ *vb* **1** : to move, clear, or level with a tractor-driven machine (**bull·doz·er**) having a broad blade for pushing **2** : to force as if by using a bulldozer

bul·let \'bu̇-lət\ *n* [MF *boulette* small ball & *boulet* missile, dims. of *boule* ball, fr. L *bulla* bubble] : a missile to be shot from a firearm

bul·le·tin \'bu̇-lə-tᵊn\ *n* **1** : a brief public report intended for immediate release on a matter of public interest **2** : a periodical publication (as of a college)

bulletin board *n* **1** : a board for posting notices **2** : a public forum on a computer network in which users write or read messages or download files

bul·let·proof \'bu̇-lət-,prüf\ *adj* **1** : impenetrable to bullets **2** : not subject to correction, alteration, or modification **3** : INVINCIBLE

bull·fight \'bul-,fīt\ *n* : a spectacle in which people ceremonially fight with and usu. kill bulls in an arena — **bull·fight·er** *n*

bull·frog \-,frog, -,fräg\ *n* : a large deep-voiced frog

bull·head \-,hed\ *n* : any of several common large-headed freshwater catfishes of the U.S.

bull·head·ed \-'he-dəd\ *adj* : stupidly stubborn : HEADSTRONG

bul·lion \'bul-yən\ *n* : gold or silver esp. in bars or ingots

bull market *n* : a market in which securities or commodities are persistently rising in value

bull·ock \'bu̇-lək\ *n* : a young bull; *also* : STEER

bull pen *n* : a place on a baseball field where pitchers warm up; *also* : the relief pitchers of a baseball team

bull session *n* : an informal discussion

bull's-eye \'bu̇lz-,ī\ *n, pl* **bull's-eyes** : the center of a target; *also* : a shot that hits the bull's-eye

¹**bul·ly** \'bu̇-lē\ *n, pl* **bullies** : a person habitually cruel to others who are weaker

²**bully** *adj* : EXCELLENT, FIRST-RATE — often used interjectionally ⟨~ for you⟩

³**bully** *vb* **bul·lied; bul·ly·ing** : to behave as a bully toward : DOMINEER ♦ **Syn-**

onyms BROWBEAT, INTIMIDATE, HECTOR

bul·rush \'bul-,rəsh\ *n* : any of several large rushes or sedges of wetlands

bul·wark \'bul-(,)wərk, -,wȯrk; 'bəl-(,)wərk\ *n* **1** : a wall-like defensive structure **2** : a strong support or protection

¹**bum** \'bəm\ *adj* **1** : of poor quality ⟨~ advice⟩ **2** : disabled by damage or injury ⟨a ~ knee⟩

²**bum** *vb* **bummed; bum·ming** **1** : to spend time unemployed and wandering; *also* : LOAF **2** : to obtain by begging

³**bum** *n* **1** : LOAFER **2** : one whose time is devoted to a recreational activity ⟨a ski ~⟩ **3** : TRAMP 1

bum·ble \'bəm-bəl\ *vb* **bum·bled; bum·bling** **1** : to speak in a stuttering and faltering manner **2** : to proceed unsteadily **3** : BUNGLE

bum·ble·bee \'bəm-bəl-,bē\ *n* : any of numerous large hairy social bees

bum·mer \'bə-mər\ *n* **1** : an unpleasant experience **2** : FAILURE

¹**bump** \'bəmp\ *n* **1** : a local bulge; *esp* : a swelling of tissue **2** : a sudden forceful blow or impact — **bumpy** *adj*

²**bump** *vb* **1** : to strike or knock forcibly; *also* : to move by or as if by bumping **2** : to collide with

¹**bum·per** \'bəm-pər\ *n* **1** : a cup or glass filled to the brim **2** : something unusually large — **bumper** *adj*

²**bump·er** \'bəm-pər\ *n* : a device for absorbing shock or preventing damage; *esp* : a usu. metal bar at either end of an automobile

bump·kin \'bəmp-kən\ *n* : an awkward and unsophisticated country person

bump·tious \'bəmp-shəs\ *adj* : obtusely and often noisily self-assertive

bun \'bən\ *n* : a sweet or plain round roll

¹**bunch** \'bənch\ *n* **1** : SWELLING **2** : CLUSTER, GROUP — **bunchy** *adj*

²**bunch** *vb* : to form into a group or bunch

bun·co *or* **bun·ko** \'bəŋ-kō\ *n, pl* **buncos** *or* **bunkos** : a swindling scheme — **bunco** *vb*

¹**bun·dle** \'bən-dᵊl\ *n* **1** : several items bunched and fastened together; *also* : something wrapped for carrying **2** : a considerable amount : LOT **3** : a small band of mostly parallel nerve or muscle fibers **4** : a package offering related products or services at a single price

²**bundle** *vb* **bun·dled; bun·dling** : to gather or tie in a bundle

bundling *n* : a former custom of a courting couple's occupying the same bed without undressing

bung \'bəŋ\ *n* : the stopper in the bunghole of a cask

bun·ga·low \'bəŋ-gə-,lō\ *n* [Hindi & Urdu *banglā,* lit., (house) in the Bengal style] : a one-storied house with a low-pitched roof

bun·gee cord \'bən-jē-\ *n* : a long elastic cord used esp. as a fastening or shock-absorbing device

bungee jump *vb* : to jump from a height while attached to a bungee cord — **bungee jumper** *n*

bung·hole \'bəŋ-ˌhōl\ n : a hole for emptying or filling a cask

bun·gle \'bəŋ-gəl\ vb **bun·gled; bun·gling** : to do badly : BOTCH — **bungle** n — **bun·gler** n

bun·ion \'bən-yən\ n : an inflamed swelling of the first joint of the big toe

¹**bunk** \'bəŋk\ n : BED; esp : a built-in bed that is often one of a tier

²**bunk** n : BUNKUM, NONSENSE

bunk bed n : one of two single beds usu. placed one above the other

bun·ker \'bəŋ-kər\ n 1 : a bin or compartment for storage (as for coal on a ship) 2 : a protective embankment or dugout 3 : a sand trap or embankment constituting a hazard on a golf course

bun·kum or **bun·combe** \'bəŋ-kəm\ n [Buncombe County, N.C.; fr. a remark made by its congressman, who defended an irrelevant speech by claiming that he was speaking to Buncombe] : insincere or foolish talk

bun·ny \'bə-nē\ n, pl **-nies** : RABBIT

bunny slope n : a gentle incline used by novice skiers

Bun·sen burner \'bən-sən-\ n : a gas burner usu. consisting of a straight tube with air holes at the bottom

¹**bunt** \'bənt\ vb 1 : BUTT 2 : to push or tap a baseball lightly without swinging the bat

²**bunt** n : an act or instance of bunting; also : a bunted ball

¹**bun·ting** \'bən-tiŋ\ n : any of numerous small stout-billed finches

²**bunting** n : a thin fabric used esp. for flags; also : FLAGS

¹**buoy** \'bü-ē, 'bȯi\ n 1 : a floating object anchored in water to mark something (as a channel) 2 : a float consisting of a ring of buoyant material to support a person who has fallen into the water

²**buoy** vb 1 : to mark by a buoy 2 : to keep afloat 3 : to raise the spirits of

buoy·an·cy \'bȯi-ən-sē, 'bü-yən-\ n 1 : the tendency of a body to float or rise when submerged in a fluid 2 : the power of a fluid to exert an upward force on a body placed in it 3 : resilience of spirit — **buoy·ant** \-ənt, -yənt\ adj

¹**bur** var of BURR

²**bur** abbr bureau

burbs \'bərbz\ n pl : SUBURBS

¹**bur·den** \'bər-dⁿn\ n 1 : LOAD; also : CARE, RESPONSIBILITY 2 : something oppressive : ENCUMBRANCE ⟨the tax ∼⟩ 3 : CARGO; also : capacity for cargo

²**burden** vb : LOAD, OPPRESS ⟨∼ed with guilt⟩ — **bur·den·some** \-səm\ adj

³**burden** n 1 : REFRAIN, CHORUS 2 : a main theme or idea : GIST

bur·dock \'bər-ˌdäk\ n : any of a genus of coarse composite herbs with globe-shaped flower heads surrounded by prickly bracts

bu·reau \'byu̇r-ō\ n, pl **bureaus** also **bureaux** \-ōz\ [F, desk, cloth covering for desks, fr. OF burel woolen cloth, ultim. fr. L burra shaggy cloth] 1 : a chest of drawers 2 : an administrative unit (as of a government department) 3 : a branch

of a publication or wire service in an important news center

bu·reau·cra·cy \byu̇-'rä-krə-sē\ n, pl **-cies** 1 : a body of appointive government officials 2 : government marked by specialization of functions under fixed rules and a hierarchy of authority; also : an unwieldy administrative system burdened with excessive complexity and lack of flexibility — **bu·reau·crat** \'byu̇r-ə-ˌkrat\ n — **bu·reau·crat·ic** \ˌbyu̇r-ə-'kra-tik\ adj

bur·geon \'bər-jən\ vb : to put forth fresh growth (as from buds) : grow vigorously : FLOURISH

burgh \'bər-ō\ n : a Scottish town

bur·gher \'bər-gər\ n 1 : TOWNSMAN 2 : a prosperous solid citizen

bur·glary \'bər-glə-rē\ n, pl **-glar·ies** : forcible entry into a building esp. at night with the intent to commit a crime (as theft) — **bur·glar** \-glər\ n — **bur·glar·ize** \'bər-glə-ˌrīz\ vb

bur·gle \'bər-gəl\ vb **bur·gled; bur·gling** : to commit burglary on

bur·go·mas·ter \'bər-gə-ˌmas-tər\ n : the chief magistrate of a town in some European countries

bur·gun·dy \'bər-gən-dē\ n, pl **-dies** often cap 1 : a red or white table wine from the Burgundy region of France 2 : a blended red wine

buri·al \'ber-ē-əl\ n : the act or process of burying

bur·ka or **bur·qa** \'bu̇r-kə\ n : a loose garment that covers the face and body and is worn in public by certain Muslim women

burl \'bərl\ n : a hard woody often flattened hemispherical outgrowth on a tree

bur·lap \'bər-ˌlap\ n : a coarse fabric usu. of jute or hemp used esp. for bags

¹**bur·lesque** \(ˌ)bər-'lesk\ n [burlesque, adj., comic, droll, fr. F, fr. It burlesco, fr. burla joke, fr. Sp] 1 : a witty or derisive literary or dramatic imitative work 2 : broadly humorous theatrical entertainment consisting of several items (as songs, skits, or dances)

²**burlesque** vb **bur·lesqued; bur·lesqu·ing** : to make ludicrous by burlesque
♦ **Synonyms** CARICATURE, PARODY, TRAVESTY

bur·ly \'bər-lē\ adj **bur·li·er; -est** : strongly and heavily built : HUSKY
♦ **Synonyms** MUSCULAR, BRAWNY, BEEFY, HEFTY

¹**burn** \'bərn\ vb **burned** \'bərnd, 'bərnt\ or **burnt** \'bərnt\; **burn·ing** 1 : to be on fire 2 : to feel or look as if on fire 3 : to alter or become altered by or as if by the action of fire or heat 4 : to use as fuel ⟨∼ coal⟩; also : to destroy by fire ⟨∼ trash⟩ 5 : to cause or make by fire ⟨∼ a hole⟩; also : to affect as if by heat 6 : to record digital data or music on (an optical disk) using a laser ⟨∼ a CD⟩

²**burn** n : an injury or effect produced by or as if by burning

burn·er \'bər-nər\ n : the part of a fuel-burning or heat-producing device where the flame or heat is produced

bur·nish \'bər-nish\ vb : to make shiny

esp. by rubbing : POLISH — **bur·nish·er**
n — **bur·nish·ing** *adj or n*
bur·noose *or* **bur·nous** \(ˌ)bər-ˈnüs\ *n* : a
hooded cloak worn esp. by Arabs
burn·out \ˈbərn-ˌau̇t\ *n* **1** : the cessation
of operation of a jet or rocket engine **2**
: exhaustion of one's physical or emotional strength; *also* : a person suffering
from burnout
burp \ˈbərp\ *n* : an act of belching —
burp *vb*
burp gun *vb* : a small submachine gun
burr \ˈbər\ *n* **1** *usu* **bur** : a rough or prickly envelope of a fruit; *also* : a plant that
bears burs **2** : roughness left in cutting or
shaping metal **3** : a trilled \r\ as used by
some speakers in northern England and
Scotland **4** : WHIR — **bur·ry** *adj*
bur·ri·to \bə-ˈrē-tō\ *n* [AmerSp, fr. Sp, little donkey, dim. of *burro*] : a flour tortilla
rolled around a filling and baked
bur·ro \ˈbər-ō, ˈbu̇r-\ *n, pl* **burros** [Sp] : a
usu. small donkey
¹bur·row \ˈbər-ō\ *n* : a hole in the ground
made by an animal (as a rabbit)
²burrow *vb* **1** : to form by tunneling; *also*
: to make a burrow **2** : to progress by or
as if by digging — **bur·row·er** *n*
bur·sar \ˈbər-sər\ *n* : a treasurer esp. of a
college
bur·si·tis \(ˌ)bər-ˈsī-təs\ *n* : inflammation
of the serous sac (**bur·sa** \ˈbər-sə\) of a
joint (as the elbow or shoulder)
¹burst \ˈbərst\ *vb* **burst** *or* **burst·ed;**
burst·ing **1** : to fly apart or into pieces
2 : to show one's feelings suddenly; *also*
: PLUNGE ⟨~ into song⟩ **3** : to enter or
emerge suddenly : SPRING **4** : to be filled
to the breaking point
²burst *n* **1** : a sudden outbreak : SPURT **2**
: EXPLOSION **3** : result of bursting
bury \ˈber-ē\ *vb* **bur·ied; bury·ing 1** : to
deposit in the earth; *also* : to inter with
funeral ceremonies **2** : CONCEAL, HIDE
3 : SUBMERGE, ENGROSS — usu. used
with *in* ⟨*buried* himself in work⟩
¹bus \ˈbəs\ *n, pl* **bus·es** *also* **bus·ses**
[short for *omnibus*, fr. F, fr. L, for all, dat.
pl. of *omnis* all] : a large motor vehicle
for carrying passengers
²bus *vb* **bused** *or* **bussed; bus·ing** *or*
bus·sing **1** : to travel or transport by
bus **2** : to work as a busboy
³bus *abbr* business
bus·boy \ˈbəs-ˌbȯi\ *n* : a waiter's helper
bus·by \ˈbəz-bē\ *n, pl* **busbies** : a military full-dress fur hat
bush \ˈbu̇sh\ *n* **1** : SHRUB **2** : rough un-
cleared country **3** : a thick tuft ⟨a ~ of
hair⟩ — **bushy** *adj*
bushed \ˈbu̇sht\ *adj* : TIRED, EXHAUSTED
bush·el \ˈbu̇-shəl\ *n* — see WEIGHT table
bush·ing \ˈbu̇-shiŋ\ *n* : a usu. removable
cylindrical lining for an opening of a mechanical part to limit the size of the opening, resist wear, or serve as a guide
bush·mas·ter \ˈbu̇sh-ˌmas-tər\ *n* : a large
venomous pit viper of Central and So.
America
bush·whack \-ˌhwak\ *vb* **1** : AMBUSH **2**
: to clear a path through esp. by chopping

down bushes and branches — **bush-**
whack·er *n*
busi·ness \ˈbiz-nəs, -nəz\ *n* **1** : OCCUPA-
TION; *also* : TASK, MISSION **2** : a commercial or industrial enterprise; *also*
: TRADE ⟨~ is good⟩ **3** : AFFAIR, MAT-
TER **4** : personal concern
busi·ness·man \-ˌman\ *n* : a man engaged in business esp. as an executive
busi·ness·per·son \-ˌpər-sᵊn\ *n* : a businessman or businesswoman
busi·ness·wom·an \-ˌwu̇-mən\ *n* : a
woman engaged in business esp. as an executive
bus·kin \ˈbəs-kən\ *n* **1** : a laced boot
reaching halfway to the knee **2** : tragic
drama
buss \ˈbəs\ *n* : KISS — **buss** *vb*
¹bust \ˈbəst\ *n* [F *buste*, fr. It *busto*, fr. L
bustum tomb] **1** : sculpture representing
the upper part of the human figure **2**
: the part of the human torso between the
neck and the waist; *esp* : the breasts of a
woman
²bust *vb* **bust·ed** *also* **bust; bust·ing 1**
: BREAK, SMASH; *also* : BURST **2** : to ruin
financially **3** : TAME **4** : DEMOTE **5** *slang*
: ARREST; *also* : RAID
³bust *n* **1** : a drinking session **2** : a complete failure : FLOP **3** : a business depression **4** : PUNCH, SOCK **5** *slang* : a police
raid; *also* : ARREST
¹bus·tle \ˈbə-səl\ *vb* **bus·tled; bus·tling**
: to move or work in a brisk busy manner
²bustle *n* : briskly energetic activity
³bustle *n* : a pad or frame worn to support
the fullness at the back of a woman's
skirt
¹busy \ˈbi-zē\ *adj* **busi·er; -est 1** : engaged in action : not idle **2** : being in use
⟨~ telephones⟩ **3** : full of activity ⟨~
streets⟩ **4** : full of distracting detail ⟨a ~
design⟩ — **busi·ly** \ˈbi-zə-lē\ *adv*
²busy *vb* **bus·ied; busy·ing** : to make or
keep busy : OCCUPY
busy·body \ˈbi-zē-ˌbä-dē\ *n* : MEDDLER
busy·work \-ˌwərk\ *n* : work that appears
productive but only keeps one occupied
¹but \ˈbət\ *conj* **1** : except for the fact
⟨would have protested ~ that he was
afraid⟩ **2** : THAT ⟨there's no doubt ~ he
won⟩ **3** : without the certainty that ⟨nev-
er rains ~ it pours⟩ **4** : on the contrary
⟨not one, ~ two job offers⟩ **5** : YET
⟨poor ~ proud⟩ **6** : with the exception
of ⟨none ~ the strongest attempt will⟩
²but *prep* : other than : EXCEPT ⟨this letter
is nothing ~ an insult⟩; *also* : with the
exception of ⟨no one here ~ me⟩
bu·tane \ˈbyü-ˌtān\ *n* : either of two gaseous hydrocarbons used as a fuel
butch \ˈbu̇ch\ *adj* : notably masculine in
appearance or manner
¹butch·er \ˈbu̇-chər\ *n* [ME *bocher*, fr. AF,
fr. *buc* he-goat] **1** : one who slaughters
animals or dresses their flesh; *also* : a
dealer in meat **2** : one that kills brutally
or needlessly **3** : one that botches —
butch·ery \-chə-rē\ *n*
²butcher *vb* : to slaughter and dress for
meat ⟨~ hogs⟩ **2** : to kill barbarously **3**

: BOTCH ⟨the band ∼ed my favorite song⟩

but·ler \'bət-lər\ *n* [ME *buteler,* fr. AF *butiller,* † fr. OF *botele* bottle] : the chief male servant of a household

¹butt \'bət\ *vb* : to strike with the head or horns

²butt *n* : a blow or thrust with the head or horns

³butt *n* : a large cask

⁴butt *n* **1** : TARGET **2** : an object of abuse or ridicule ⟨the ∼ of everyone's jokes⟩

⁵butt *n* **1** : BUTTOCKS **2** : a large, thicker, or bottom end of something

⁶butt *vb* **1** : ABUT — used with *on* or *against* **2** : to place or join edge to edge without overlapping

butte \'byüt\ *n* : an isolated steep hill

¹but·ter \'bət-ər\ *n* [ME, fr. OE *butere,* fr. L *butyrum* butter, fr. Gk *boutyron,* fr. *bous* cow + *tyros* cheese] **1** : a solid edible emulsion of fat obtained from cream by churning **2** : a substance resembling butter — **but·tery** *adj*

²butter *vb* : to spread with or as if with butter ⟨∼ed toast⟩

but·ter–and–eggs \ˌbə-tər-ᵊn-'egz\ *n sing or pl* : a common perennial herb related to the snapdragon that has showy yellow and orange flowers

butter bean *n* **1** : LIMA BEAN **2** : WAX BEAN **3** : a green shell bean

but·ter·cream \'bə-tər-ˌkrēm\ *n* : a sweet butter-based mixture used esp. as a filling or frosting

but·ter·cup \'bə-tər-ˌkəp\ *n* : any of a genus of herbs having usu. yellow flowers with five petals and sepals

but·ter·fat \-ˌfat\ *n* : the natural fat of milk and chief constituent of butter

but·ter·fin·gered \-ˌfiŋ-gərd\ *adj* : likely to let things fall or slip through the fingers — **but·ter·fin·gers** \-gərz\ *n sing or pl*

but·ter·fly \-ˌflī\ *n* : any of a group of slender day-flying insects with broad often brightly-colored wings

but·ter·milk \-ˌmilk\ *n* : the liquid remaining after butter is churned

but·ter·nut \-ˌnət\ *n* : the sweet egg-shaped nut of an American tree related to the walnut; *also* : this tree

butternut squash *n* : a smooth buff-colored cylindrical winter squash

but·ter·scotch \-ˌskäch\ *n* : a candy made from brown sugar, corn syrup, and water; *also* : the flavor of such candy

but·tock \'bə-tək\ *n* **1** : the back of a hip that forms one of the fleshy parts on which a person sits **2** *pl* : the seat of the body : RUMP

¹but·ton \'bə-tᵊn\ *n* **1** : a small knob secured to an article (as of clothing) and used as a fastener by passing it through a buttonhole or loop **2** : something that resembles a button **3** : PUSH BUTTON **4** : a hidden sensitivity that can be manipulated to produce a desired response **5** : a usu. box-shaped computer icon that initiates a software function

²button *vb* : to close or fasten with or as if with buttons

¹but·ton·hole \'bə-tᵊn-ˌhōl\ *n* : a slit or loop for a button to pass through

²buttonhole *vb* : to detain in conversation by or as if by holding on to the outer garments of

¹but·tress \'bə-trəs\ *n* [ME *butres,* fr. AF *(arche) boteraz* thrusting (arch), ultim. fr. *buter* to thrust] **1** : a projecting structure to support a wall **2** : PROP, SUPPORT

²buttress *vb* : PROP, SUPPORT

bu·tut \bü-'tüt\ *n, pl* **bututs** *or* **butut** — see *dalasi* at MONEY table

bux·om \'bək-səm\ *adj* : healthily plump; *esp* : full-bosomed

¹buy \'bī\ *vb* **bought** \'bȯt\; **buy·ing 1** : to obtain for a price : PURCHASE; *also* : BRIBE **2** : to accept as true — **buy·er** *n*

²buy *n* **1** : PURCHASE 1, 2 **2** : an exceptional value : BARGAIN

buzz \'bəz\ *vb* **1** : to make a buzz **2** : to fly fast and close to

²buzz *n* **1** : a low humming sound **2** : RUMOR, GOSSIP

buz·zard \'bə-zərd\ *n* : any of various usu. large birds of prey and esp. the turkey vulture

buzz·er \'bə-zər\ *n* : a device that signals with a buzzing sound

buzz saw *n* : CIRCULAR SAW

buzz·word \'bəz-ˌwərd\ *n* : a voguish word or phrase often from technical jargon

BVM *abbr* Blessed Virgin Mary

BWI *abbr* British West Indies

bx *abbr* box

BX *abbr* base exchange

¹by \'bī, bə\ *prep* **1** : NEAR ⟨stood ∼ the window⟩ **2** : through or through the medium of **:** VIA ⟨left ∼ the door⟩ **3** : PAST ⟨drove ∼ the house⟩ **4** : DURING, AT ⟨studied ∼ night⟩ **5** : no later than ⟨get here ∼ 3 p.m.⟩ **6** : through the means or direct agency of ⟨∼ force⟩ **7** : in conformity with; *also* : ACCORDING TO ⟨did it ∼ the book⟩ **8** : with respect to ⟨a doctor ∼ profession⟩ **9** : to the amount or extent of ⟨won ∼ a nose⟩ **10** — used to express relationship in multiplication, in division, and in measurements ⟨divide *a* ∼ *b*⟩ ⟨multiply ∼ 6⟩ ⟨15 feet ∼ 20 feet⟩

²by \'bī\ *adv* **1** : near at hand; *also* : IN ⟨stop ∼⟩ **2** : PAST ⟨saw him go ∼⟩ **3** : ASIDE, APART ⟨put some money ∼⟩

bye \'bī\ *n* : a position of a participant in a tournament who advances to the next round without playing

by–elec·tion *also* **bye–election** \'bī-ə-ˌlek-shən\ *n* : a special election held between regular elections in order to fill a vacancy

by·gone \'bī-ˌgȯn\ *adj* : gone by : PAST — **bygone** *n*

by·law *also* **bye·law** \'bī-ˌlȯ\ *n* : a rule adopted by an organization for managing its internal affairs

by–line \'bī-ˌlīn\ *n* : a line at the beginning of a news story or magazine article giving the writer's name

BYO *abbr* bring your own

BYOB *abbr* bring your own beer; bring your own booze; bring your own bottle

¹by·pass \'bī-ˌpas\ *n* : a passage to one

side or around a blocked or congested area; *also* : a surgical procedure establishing this ⟨a coronary ∿⟩

²by·pass *vb* : to avoid by means of a bypass

by·path \-,path, -,päth\ *n* : BYWAY

by·play \'bī-,plā\ *n* : action engaged in on the side (as of a stage) while the main action proceeds

by–prod·uct \-,prä-(,)dəkt\ *n* : a sometimes unexpected product or result produced in addition to the main product or result

by·stand·er \-,stan-dər\ *n* : one present but not participating ♦ *Synonyms* ON-

LOOKER, WITNESS, SPECTATOR, EYEWITNESS

byte \'bīt\ *n* : a unit of computer information consisting of a group of 8 bits

by·way \'bī-,wā\ *n* **1** : a little-traveled side road **2** : a secondary aspect

by·word \-,wərd\ *n* **1** : PROVERB **2** : one that is noteworthy or notorious

Byz·an·tine \'biz-ᵊn-,tēn, 'bī-, -,tīn; bə-'zan-, bī-\ *adj* **1** : of, relating to, or characteristic of the ancient city of Byzantium or the Byzantine Empire **2** *often not cap* : intricately involved and often devious

¹c \'sē\ *n, pl* **c's** *or* **cs** \'sēz\ *often cap* **1** : the 3d letter of the English alphabet **2** *slang* : a sum of $100 **3** : a grade rating a student's work as fair

²c *abbr, often cap* **1** calorie **2** carat **3** Celsius **4** cent **5** centigrade **6** centimeter **7** century **8** chapter **9** circa **10** cocaine **11** copyright

C *symbol* carbon

ca *abbr* circa

Ca *symbol* calcium

CA *abbr* **1** California **2** chartered accountant **3** chief accountant **4** chronological age

cab \'kab\ *n* **1** : a light closed horse-drawn carriage **2** : TAXICAB **3** : the covered compartment for the engineer and controls of a locomotive; *also* : a similar compartment (as on a truck) — **cab** *vb*

CAB *abbr* Civil Aeronautics Board

ca·bal \kə-'bäl, -'bal\ *n* [F *cabale*, fr. ML *cabbala* cabala, fr. Heb *qabbālāh*, lit., received (lore)] **1** : a secret group of plotters or political conspirators **2** : CLUB, GROUP ⟨a ∿ of artists⟩

cabala *var of* KABBALAH

ca·bana \kə-'ban-yə, -'ba-nə\ *n* : a shelter at a beach or swimming pool

cab·a·ret \,ka-bə-'rā\ *n* : NIGHTCLUB

cab·bage \'ka-bij\ *n* [ME *caboche*, fr. MF dial., lit., head, noggin] : a vegetable related to the mustard with a dense head of leaves

cab·bie *or* **cab·by** \'ka-bē\ *n, pl* **cabbies** : a driver of a cab

cab·er·net sau·vi·gnon \,ka-bər-'nā-sō-vē-'nyōⁿ\ *n* : a dry red wine made from a single variety of black grape

cab·in \'ka-bən\ *n* **1** : a private room on a ship; *also* : a compartment below deck on a boat for passengers or crew **2** : an aircraft or spacecraft compartment for passengers, crew, or cargo **3** : a small simple one-story house

cabin boy *n* : a boy working as a servant on a ship

cabin class *n* : a class of accommodations on a passenger ship superior to tourist class and inferior to first class

cabin cruiser *n* : CRUISER 3

cab·i·net \'kab-nit\ *n* **1** : a case or cupboard for holding or displaying articles **2** : the advisory council of a head of state (as a president or sovereign)

cab·i·net·mak·er \-,mā-kər\ *n* : a woodworker who makes fine furniture — **cab·i·net·mak·ing** *n*

cab·i·net·work \-,wərk\ *n* : the finished work of a cabinetmaker

¹ca·ble \'kā-bəl\ *n* **1** : a very strong rope, wire, or chain **2** : a bundle of insulated wires usu. twisted around a central core **3** : CABLEGRAM **4** : CABLE TELEVISION

²cable *vb* **ca·bled; ca·bling** : to telegraph by cable

cable car *n* : a vehicle moved by an endless cable

ca·ble·cast \'kā-bəl-,kast\ *n* : a cable television transmission — **cablecast** *vb*

ca·ble·gram \'kā-bəl-,gram\ *n* : a message sent by a submarine telegraph cable

cable modem *n* : a modem for connecting a computer to a network over a cable television line

cable television *n* : a system of television reception in which signals from distant stations are sent by cable to the receivers of paying subscribers

ca·bo·chon \'ka-bə-,shän\ *n* : a gem or bead cut in convex form and highly polished but not given facets; *also* : this style of cutting — **cabochon** *adv*

ca·boose \kə-'büs\ *n* : a car usu. at the rear of a freight train for the use of the train crew and railroad workers

cab·ri·o·let \,ka-brē-ə-'lā\ *n* [F] **1** : a light 2-wheeled one-horse carriage **2** : a convertible coupe

cab·stand \'kab-,stand\ *n* : a place where cabs wait for passengers

ca·cao \kə-'kaü, -'kā-ō\ *n, pl* **cacaos** [Sp, fr. Nahuatl *cacahuatl*] : a So. American tree whose seeds (**cacao beans**) are the source of cocoa and chocolate; *also* : its dried fatty seeds

cac·cia·to·re \,kä-chə-'tòr-ē\ *adj* [It] : cooked with tomatoes and herbs ⟨chicken ∿⟩

cache \'kash\ n [F] : a hiding place esp. for preserving provisions; *also* : something hidden or stored in a cache — **cache** vb

ca·chet \ka-'shā\ n [F] 1 : a seal used esp. as a mark of official approval 2 : a feature or quality conferring prestige; *also* : PRESTIGE 3 : a design, inscription, or advertisement printed or stamped on mail

cack·le \'ka-kəl\ vb **cack·led; cack·ling** 1 : to make the sharp broken cry characteristic of a hen 2 : to laugh or chatter noisily — **cackle** n — **cack·ler** n

ca·coph·o·ny \ka-'kä-fə-nē\ n, pl **-nies** : harsh or discordant sound — **ca·coph·o·nous** \-nəs\ adj

cac·tus \'kak-təs\ n, pl **cac·ti** \-ˌtī\ or **cac·tus·es** also **cactus** : any of a large family of drought-resistant flowering plants with succulent stems and with leaves replaced by scales or prickles

cad \'kad\ n : a man who deliberately disregards another's feelings — **cad·dish** \'ka-dish\ adj — **cad·dish·ly** adv — **cad·dish·ness** n

ca·dav·er \kə-'da-vər\ n : a dead body

ca·dav·er·ous \kə-'da-və-rəs\ adj : suggesting a corpse esp. in gauntness or pallor ♦ *Synonyms* WASTED, EMACIATED, GAUNT — **ca·dav·er·ous·ly** adv

cad·die or **cad·dy** \'ka-dē\ n, pl **caddies** [Sc, errand boy, modif. of F *cadet* military cadet] : a person who assists a golfer esp. by carrying the clubs — **caddie** or **caddy** vb

cad·dy \'ka-dē\ n, pl **caddies** [Malay *kati* a unit of weight] : a small box, can, or chest; *esp* : one to keep tea in

ca·dence \'kād-ᵊns\ n : the measure or beat of a rhythmical flow : RHYTHM — **ca·denced** \-ᵊnst\ adj

ca·den·za \kə-'den-zə\ n [It] : a brilliant sometimes improvised passage usu. toward the close of a musical composition

ca·det \kə-'det\ n [F, fr. Occitan (Gascony) *capdet* chief, fr. L *capitellum*, fr. L *caput* head] 1 : a younger son or brother 2 : a student in a service academy

Ca·dette \kə-'det\ n : a member of a Girl Scout program for girls in sixth through ninth grades

cadge \'kaj\ vb **cadged; cadg·ing** : SPONGE, BEG ⟨~ a free meal⟩ — **cadg·er** n

cad·mi·um \'kad-mē-əm\ n : a bluish-white metallic chemical element used esp. in protective platings

cad·re \'ka-ˌdrä, 'kä-, -drē\ n [F] 1 : FRAMEWORK 2 : a central unit esp. of trained personnel able to assume control and train others 3 : a group of indoctrinated leaders active in promoting the interests of a revolutionary party

ca·du·ceus \kə-'dü-sē-əs, -'dyü-, -shəs\ n, pl **-cei** \-sē-ˌī\ [L] 1 : the staff of a herald; *esp* : a representation of a staff with two entwined snakes and two wings at the top 2 : an insignia bearing a caduceus and symbolizing a physician

cae·cum var of CECUM

Cae·sar \'sē-zər\ n 1 : any of the Roman emperors succeeding Augustus Caesar — used as a title 2 *often not cap* : a powerful ruler : AUTOCRAT, DICTATOR; *also* : the civil or temporal power

caesarean also **caesarian** var of CESAREAN

cae·si·um *chiefly Brit var of* CESIUM

cae·su·ra \si-'zhùr-ə\ n, pl **-suras** or **-surae** \-'zhùr-(ˌ)ē\ : a break in the flow of sound usu. in the middle of a line of verse

ca·fé \ka-'fā\ n [F, lit., coffee] 1 : RESTAURANT 2 : BARROOM 3 : NIGHTCLUB

ca·fé au lait \(ˌ)ka-ˌfā-ō-'lā\ n : coffee with hot milk in about equal parts

caf·e·te·ria \ˌka-fə-'tir-ē-ə\ n [AmerSp *cafetería* coffeehouse] : a restaurant in which the customers serve themselves or are served at a counter

caf·fein·at·ed \'ka-fə-ˌnā-təd\ adj 1 : stimulated by or as if by caffeine 2 : containing caffeine

caf·feine \ka-'fēn, 'ka-ˌfēn\ n : a stimulating alkaloid found esp. in coffee and tea

caf·fe lat·te \ˌkä-fā-'lä-tā\ n [It] : espresso mixed with hot or steamed milk

caf·tan \kaf-'tan, 'kaf-ˌtan\ n [Russ *kaftan*, fr. Turk, fr. Pers *qaftān*] : an ankle-length garment with long sleeves worn in countries of the eastern Mediterranean

¹**cage** \'kāj\ n 1 : an openwork enclosure for confining an animal 2 : something resembling a cage

²**cage** vb **caged; cag·ing** : to put or keep in or as if in a cage

ca·gey also **ca·gy** \'kā-jē\ adj **ca·gi·er; -est** : wary of being trapped or deceived : SHREWD ⟨a ~ dealer⟩ — **ca·gi·ly** \-jə-lē\ adv — **ca·gi·ness** \-jē-nəs\ n

CAGS *abbr* Certificate of Advanced Graduate Study

ca·hoot \kə-'hüt\ n : PARTNERSHIP, LEAGUE — usu. used in pl. ⟨officials in ~s with the underworld⟩

cai·man also **cayman** \'kā-mən; kā-'man, kī-\ n : any of several Central and So. American reptiles closely related to alligators and crocodiles

cairn \'karn\ n : a heap of stones serving as a memorial or a landmark

cais·son \'kā-ˌsän, 'kās-ᵊn\ n 1 : a usu. 2-wheeled vehicle for artillery ammunition 2 : a watertight chamber used in underwater construction work or as a foundation

caisson disease n : ²BEND 3

cai·tiff \'kā-təf\ adj [ME *caitif*, fr. AF *caitif*, *chaitif* wretched, despicable, fr. L *captivus* captive] : being base, cowardly, or despicable — **caitiff** n

ca·jole \kə-'jōl\ vb **ca·joled; ca·jol·ing** [F *cajoler*] : to persuade or coax esp. with flattery or false promises — **ca·jole·ment** n — **ca·jol·ery** \-'jō-lə-rē\ n

Ca·jun \'kā-jən\ n : a Louisianian descended from French-speaking immigrants from Acadia (Nova Scotia) — **Cajun** adj

¹**cake** \'kāk\ n 1 : a baked or fried bread-like food usu. in a small flat shape 2 : a sweet baked food made from batter or dough usu. containing flour, sugar, shortening, and a leaven (as baking powder) 3

: a hardened or compacted substance ⟨a ~ of soap⟩ 4 : something easily done ⟨the quiz was ~⟩
²cake vb caked; cak·ing 1 : ENCRUST 2 : to form or harden into a cake
cake·walk \'kāk-,wȯk\ n 1 : a stage dance typically involving a high prance with backward tilt 2 : a one-sided contest or an easy task
cal abbr 1 calendar 2 caliber
Cal abbr 1 California 2 calorie
cal·a·bash \'ka-lə-,bash\ n : the fruit of a gourd; also : a utensil made from its hard shell
cal·a·boose \'ka-lə-,büs\ n [Sp calabozo dungeon] : JAIL
ca·la·di·um \kə-'lā-dē-əm\ n : any of a genus of tropical American ornamental plants related to the arums
cal·a·mari \,ka-lə-'mär-ē\ n [It] : squid used as food
cal·a·mine \'ka-lə-,mīn\ n : a lotion of oxides of zinc and iron
ca·lam·i·ty \kə-'la-mə-tē\ n, pl -ties 1 : great distress or misfortune 2 : an event causing great harm or loss and affliction : DISASTER ⟨an economic ~⟩ — ca·lam·i·tous \-təs\ adj — ca·lam·i·tous·ly adv — ca·lam·i·tous·ness n
calc abbr calculate; calculated
cal·car·e·ous \kal-'kar-ē-əs\ adj : resembling calcium carbonate in hardness; also : containing calcium or calcium carbonate
cal·cif·er·ous \kal-'si-fə-rəs\ adj : producing or containing calcium carbonate
cal·ci·fy \'kal-sə-,fī\ vb -fied; -fy·ing : to make or become calcareous — cal·ci·fi·ca·tion \,kal-sə-fə-'kā-shən\ n
cal·ci·mine \'kal-sə-,mīn\ n : a thin water paint used esp. on plastered surfaces — calcimine vb
cal·cine \'kal-'sīn\ vb cal·cined; cal·cin·ing : to heat to a high temperature but without fusing to drive off volatile matter and often to reduce to powder — cal·ci·na·tion \,kal-sə-'nā-shən\ n
cal·cite \'kal-,sīt\ n : a crystalline mineral consisting of calcium carbonate — cal·cit·ic \kal-'si-tik\ adj
cal·ci·um \'kal-sē-əm\ n : a silver-white soft metallic chemical element occurring only in combination
calcium carbonate n : a substance found in nature as limestone and marble and in plant ashes, bones, and shells
cal·cu·late \'kal-kyə-,lāt\ vb -lat·ed; -lat·ing [L calculare, fr. calculus pebble (used in reckoning)] 1 : to determine by mathematical processes : COMPUTE 2 : to reckon by exercise of practical judgment : ESTIMATE 3 : to design or adapt for a purpose 4 : COUNT, RELY — cal·cu·la·ble \-lə-bəl\ adj — cal·cu·la·tor \-,lā-tər\ n
cal·cu·lat·ed \-,lā-təd\ adj 1 : undertaken after estimating the chance of success or failure ⟨a ~ risk⟩ 2 : planned purposefully : DELIBERATE ⟨a ~ strategy⟩
cal·cu·lat·ing \-,lā-tiŋ\ adj : marked by shrewd consideration esp. of self-interest — cal·cu·lat·ing·ly adv

cal·cu·la·tion \,kal-kyə-'lā-shən\ n 1 : the process or an act of calculating 2 : the result of an act of calculating 3 : studied care; also : cold heartless planning to promote self-interest
cal·cu·lus \'kal-kyə-ləs\ n, pl -li \-,lī\ also -lus·es [L, pebble (used in reckoning)] 1 : a method of computation or calculation in a special notation (as of logic) 2 : a branch of mathematics concerned with the rate of change of functions and with methods of finding lengths, areas, and volumes 3 : a concretion usu. of mineral salts esp. in hollow organs or ducts
cal·de·ra \kal-'der-ə, kȯl-, -'dir-\ n [Sp, lit., cauldron] : a large crater usu. formed by the collapse of a volcanic cone
cal·dron var of CAULDRON
¹cal·en·dar \'ka-lən-dər\ n 1 : an arrangement of time into days, weeks, months, and years; also : a sheet or folder containing such an arrangement for a period 2 : an orderly list
²calendar vb : to enter in a calendar
¹cal·en·der \'ka-lən-dər\ vb : to press (as cloth or paper) between rollers or plates so as to make smooth or glossy or to thin into sheets
²calender n : a machine for calendering
ca·lends \'ka-ləndz, 'kā-\ n sing or pl : the first day of the ancient Roman month
ca·len·du·la \kə-'len-jə-lə\ n : any of a genus of yellow-flowered herbs related to the daisies
¹calf \'kaf, 'kȧf\ n, pl calves \'kavz, 'kȧvz\ 1 : the young of the domestic cow; also : the young of various large mammals (as the elephant or whale) 2 : CALFSKIN
²calf n, pl calves \'kavz, 'kȧvz\ : the fleshy back of the leg below the knee
calf·skin \'kaf-,skin, 'kȧf-\ n : leather made of the skin of a calf
cal·i·ber or cal·i·bre \'ka-lə-bər\ n [MF calibre, fr. It calibro, fr. Ar qālib shoemaker's last] 1 : degree of mental capacity, excellence, or importance 2 : the diameter of a projectile 3 : the diameter of the bore of a gun
cal·i·brate \'ka-lə-,brāt\ vb -brat·ed; -brat·ing : to adjust precisely
cal·i·bra·tion \,ka-lə-'brā-shən\ n : a set of graduated marks indicating values or positions — usu. used in pl.
cal·i·co \'ka-li-,kō\ n, pl -coes or -cos 1 : printed cotton fabric 2 : a mottled or spotted animal — calico adj
Calif abbr California
Cal·i·for·nia poppy \,ka-lə-'fȯr-nyə-\ n : a widely cultivated herb with usu. yellow or orange flowers that is related to the poppies
cal·i·for·ni·um \,ka-lə-'fȯr-nē-əm\ n : an artificially prepared radioactive chemical element
cal·i·per \'ka-lə-pər\ n 1 : any of various instruments having two arms, legs, or jaws used esp. to measure diameter or thickness — usu. used in pl. 2 : a device for pressing a frictional material against the sides of a rotating wheel or disk
ca·liph \'kā-ləf, 'ka-\ n : a successor of

Muhammad as head of Islam — used as a title — **ca·liph·ate** \-lə-ˌfāt, -fət\ n

cal·is·then·ics \ˌka-ləs-'the-niks\ n sing or pl [Gk kalos beautiful + sthenos strength] : bodily exercises usu. done without apparatus — **cal·is·then·ic** adj

calk \'kȯk\ var of CAULK

¹call \'kȯl\ vb **1** : SHOUT, CRY; also : to utter a characteristic note or cry **2** : to utter in a loud clear voice 〈~ed out my name〉 **3** : to announce authoritatively **4** : SUMMON 〈was ~ed to testify〉 **5** : to make a request or demand 〈~ for an investigation〉 **6** : to halt (as a baseball game) because of unsuitable conditions **7** : to demand payment of (a loan); also : to demand surrender of (as a bond) for redemption **8** : to get or try to get in communication by telephone **9** : to make a brief visit **10** : to speak of or address by name : give a name to **11** : to estimate or consider for practical purposes 〈~ it ten miles〉 **12** : to temporarily transfer control of computer processing to (as a subroutine or procedure) — **call·er** n

²call n **1** : SHOUT **2** : the cry of an animal (as a bird) **3** : a request or a command to come or assemble : INVITATION, SUMMONS **4** : DEMAND, CLAIM; also : REQUEST **5** : a brief usu. formal visit **6** : an act of calling on the telephone **7** : DECISION 〈a tough ~〉 **8** : a temporary transfer of control of computer processing to a particular set of instructions

cal·la lily \'ka-lə-\ n : a plant related to the arums and grown for its large white lilylike bract that surrounds a fleshy spike of small yellow flowers

call·back \'kȯl-ˌbak\ n : a calling back; esp : RECALL 5

call·board \-ˌbȯrd\ n : a board for posting notices (as of rehearsal calls)

call down vb : REPRIMAND

call girl n : a prostitute with whom appointments are made by phone

cal·lig·ra·phy \kə-'li-grə-fē\ n : artistic or elegant handwriting; also : the art of producing such writing — **cal·lig·ra·pher** \-fər\ n — **cal·li·graph·ic** \ˌka-lə-'graf-ik\ adj

call-in \'kȯl-ˌin\ adj : allowing listeners to engage in broadcast telephone conversations 〈a ~ show〉

call in vb **1** : to order to return or be returned **2** : to summon to one's aid **3** : to report by telephone

call·ing \'kȯ-liŋ\ n **1** : a strong inner impulse toward a particular course of action **2** : the activity in which one customarily engages as an occupation

cal·li·ope \kə-'lī-ə-(ˌ)pē, 'ka-lē-ˌōp\ n [fr. Calliope, chief of the Muses, fr. L, fr. Gk Kalliopē] : a keyboard musical instrument similar to an organ and made up of a series of whistles

cal·li·per chiefly Brit var of CALIPER

call number n : a combination of characters assigned to a library book to indicate its place on a shelf

call off vb : CANCEL 〈called off the trip〉

cal·los·i·ty \ka-'lä-sə-tē\ n, pl -ties **1** : the quality or state of being callous **2** : CALLUS 1

¹cal·lous \'ka-ləs\ adj **1** : being thickened and hardened 〈~ skin〉 **2** : feeling no emotion or sympathy — **cal·lous·ly** adv — **cal·lous·ness** n

²callous vb : to make callous

cal·low \'ka-lō\ adj [ME calu bald, fr. OE] : lacking adult sophistication 〈a ~ youth〉 — **cal·low·ness** n

call-up \'kȯ-ˌləp\ n : an order to report for active military service

call up vb : to summon for active military duty

cal·lus \'ka-ləs\ n **1** : a callous area on skin or bark **2** : tissue that is converted into bone in the healing of a bone fracture — **callus** vb

call-waiting n : a telephone service by which during a call in progress an incoming call is signaled (as by a click)

¹calm \'käm, 'kälm\ n **1** : a period or a condition free from storms, high winds, or rough water **2** : complete or almost complete absence of wind **3** : a state of tranquillity

²calm vb : to make or become calm

³calm adj : marked by calm : STILL, UNRUFFLED — **calm·ly** adv — **calm·ness** n

cal·o·mel \'ka-lə-məl, -ˌmel\ n : a chloride of mercury used esp. as a fungicide

ca·lor·ic \kə-'lȯr-ik\ adj **1** : of or relating to heat **2** : of, relating to, or containing calories — **ca·lor·i·cal·ly** \-i-k(ə-)lē\ adv

cal·o·rie also **cal·o·ry** \'ka-lə-rē\ n, pl -ries : a unit for measuring heat; esp : one for measuring the value of foods for producing heat and energy in the human body equivalent to the amount of heat required to raise the temperature of one kilogram of water one degree Celsius

cal·o·rim·e·ter \ˌka-lə-'ri-mə-tər\ n : an apparatus for measuring quantities of heat — **cal·o·rim·e·try** \-trē\ n

cal·u·met \'kal-yə-ˌmet, -mət\ n : an American Indian ceremonial pipe

ca·lum·ni·ate \kə-'ləm-nē-ˌāt\ vb -at·ed; -at·ing : to make false and malicious statements about ♦ Synonyms DEFAME, MALIGN, LIBEL, SLANDER, TRADUCE — **ca·lum·ni·a·tion** \-ˌləm-nē-'ā-shən\ n — **ca·lum·ni·a·tor** \-'ləm-nē-ˌā-tər\ n

cal·um·ny \'ka-ləm-nē\ n, pl -nies : false and malicious accusation — **ca·lum·ni·ous** \kə-'ləm-nē-əs\ adj

calve \'kav, 'käv\ vb calved; calv·ing : to give birth to a calf

calves pl of CALF

Cal·vin·ism \'kal-və-ˌni-zəm\ n : the theological system of John Calvin and his followers — **Cal·vin·ist** \-nist\ n or adj — **Cal·vin·is·tic** \ˌkal-və-'nis-tik\ adj

ca·lyp·so \kə-'lip-sō\ n, pl -sos : a style of music originating in the British West Indies and having lyrics that usu. satirize local personalities and events

ca·lyx \'kā-liks, 'ka-\ n, pl ca·lyx·es or ca·ly·ces \'kā-lə-ˌsēz, 'ka-\ : the usu. green or leaflike outer part of a flower consisting of sepals

cal·zo·ne \kal-ˈzōn, -ˈzō-nē\ *n* : a baked or fried turnover of pizza dough stuffed with cheese and various fillings

¹cam \ˈkam\ *n* : a rotating or sliding piece in a mechanical linkage by which rotary motion is transformed into linear motion or vice versa

²cam *n* : CAMERA

ca·ma·ra·de·rie \ˌkäm-ˈrä-də-rē, ˌkam-, -ˈra-\ *n* [F] : friendly feeling and goodwill among comrades

cam·bi·um \ˈkam-bē-əm\ *n, pl* **-bi·ums** *or* **-bia** \-bē-ə\ : a thin cellular layer between xylem and phloem of most higher plants from which new tissues develop — **cam·bi·al** \-əl\ *adj*

Cam·bri·an \ˈkam-brē-ən, ˈkäm-\ *adj* : of, relating to, or being the earliest period of the Paleozoic era — **Cambrian** *n*

cam·bric \ˈkām-brik\ *n* : a fine thin white linen or cotton fabric

cam·cord·er \ˈkam-ˌkȯr-dər\ *n* : a small portable combined camera and VCR

came *past of* COME

cam·el \ˈka-məl\ *n* : either of two large hoofed cud-chewing mammals used esp. in desert regions of Asia and Africa for carrying and riding

camel hair *also* **camel's hair** *n* **1** : the hair of a camel or a substitute for it **2** : cloth made of camel hair or of camel hair and wool

ca·mel·lia \kə-ˈmēl-yə\ *n* : any of a genus of shrubs and trees related to the tea plant and grown in warm regions and greenhouses for their showy roselike flowers

Cam·em·bert \ˈka-məm-ˌber\ *n* : a soft cheese with a grayish rind and yellow interior

cam·eo \ˈka-mē-ˌō\ *n, pl* **-eos** **1** : a gem carved in relief; *also* : a small medallion with a profiled head in relief **2** : a brief appearance esp. by a well-known actor in a play or movie

cam·era \ˈkam-rə, ˈka-mər-ə\ *n* : a device with a lightproof chamber fitted with a lens through which the image of an object is projected onto a surface for recording (as on film) or for conversion into electrical signals (as for television broadcast) — **cam·era·man** \-ˌman, -mən\ *n* — **cam·era·wom·an** *n*

cam·i·sole \ˈka-mə-ˌsōl\ *n* : a short sleeveless garment for women

camomile *var of* CHAMOMILE

cam·ou·flage \ˈka-mə-ˌfläzh, -ˌfläj\ *n* [F] **1** : the disguising of military equipment with paint, nets, or foliage; *also* : the disguise itself **2** : deceptive behavior — **camouflage** *vb*

¹camp \ˈkamp\ *n* **1** : a place where tents or buildings are erected for usu. temporary shelter **2** : a collection of tents or other shelters **3** : a program offering recreational activities (as boating and hiking) for a limited time ⟨summer ∼⟩ **4** : a body of persons encamped **5** : a training session for athletes outside of the regular season — **camp·ground** \-ˌgrau̇nd\ *n* — **camp·site** \-ˌsīt\ *n*

²camp *vb* **1** : to make or occupy a camp **2** : to live in a camp or outdoors

³camp *n* **1** : exaggerated effeminate mannerisms **2** : something so outrageous, inappropriate, or theatrical as to be considered amusing — **camp** *adj* — **camp·i·ly** \ˈkam-pə-lē\ *adv* — **camp·i·ness** \-pē-nəs\ *n* — **campy** \-pē\ *adj*

⁴camp *vb* : to engage in camp : exhibit the qualities of camp

cam·paign \kam-ˈpān\ *n* **1** : a series of military operations forming one distinct stage in a war **2** : a series of activities designed to bring about a particular result ⟨advertising ∼⟩ — **campaign** *vb* — **cam·paign·er** *n*

cam·pa·ni·le \ˌkam-pə-ˈnē-lē\ *n, pl* **-ni·les** *or* **-ni·li** \-ˈnē-lē\ : a usu. freestanding bell tower

cam·pa·nol·o·gy \ˌkam-pə-ˈnä-lə-jē\ *n* : the art of bell ringing — **cam·pa·nol·o·gist** \-jist\ *n*

camp·er \ˈkam-pər\ *n* **1** : one who camps **2** : a portable dwelling (as a specially equipped vehicle) for use during casual travel and camping

Camp Fire Girl *n* : a member of a national organization of girls from ages 5 to 18

camp follower *n* **1** : a civilian (as a prostitute) who follows a military unit to attend or exploit its personnel **2** : a follower of a group who is not an adherent; *esp* : a politician who joins a movement solely for personal gain

cam·phor \ˈkam-fər\ *n* : a gummy volatile aromatic compound obtained from an evergreen Asian tree (**camphor tree**) and used esp. in medicine

camp meeting *n* : a series of evangelistic meetings usu. held outdoors

camp·o·ree \ˌkam-pə-ˈrē\ *n* : a gathering of Boy Scouts or Girl Scouts from a given geographic area

cam·pus \ˈkam-pəs\ *n* [L, plain] : the grounds and buildings of a college or school; *also* : grounds resembling a campus ⟨hospital ∼⟩

cam·shaft \ˈkam-ˌshaft\ *n* : a shaft to which a cam is fastened

¹can \kən, ˈkan\ *vb, past* **could** \kəd, ˈku̇d\; *pres sing & pl* **can** **1** : be able to **2** : may perhaps ⟨∼ he still be alive⟩ **3** : be permitted by conscience or feeling to ⟨you ∼ hardly blame her⟩ **4** : have permission to ⟨you ∼ go now⟩

²can \ˈkan\ *n* **1** : a usu. cylindrical container or receptacle ⟨garbage ∼⟩ ⟨coffee ∼⟩ **2** : JAIL **3** : TOILET

³can \ˈkan\ *vb* **canned; can·ning** **1** : to put in a can : preserve by sealing in airtight cans or jars **2** *slang* : to discharge from employment **3** *slang* : to put a stop or an end to — **can·ner** *n*

Can *or* **Canad** *abbr* Canada; Canadian

Can·a·da goose \ˈka-nə-də-\ *n* : a common wild goose of No. America

ca·naille \kə-ˈnī, -ˈnāl\ *n* [F, fr. It *canaglia*, fr. *cane* dog] : RABBLE, RIFFRAFF

ca·nal \kə-ˈnal\ *n* **1** : a tubular passage in the body : DUCT **2** : an artificial waterway (as for boats or irrigation)

can·a·lize \'kan-ᵊl-ᵢīz\ *vb* **-lized; -liz·ing** **1** : to provide with a canal or make into or like a channel **2** : to provide with an outlet; *esp* : to direct into preferred channels — **ca·nal·i·za·tion** \ˌkan-ᵊl-ə-'zā-shən\ *n*

can·a·pé \'ka-nə-pē, -ˌpā\ *n* [F, lit., sofa, fr. ML *canopeum, canapeum* mosquito net] : a piece of bread or toast or a cracker topped with a savory food

ca·nard \kə-'närd\ *n* : a false or unfounded report, story or belief

ca·nary \kə-'ner-ē\ *n, pl* **ca·nar·ies** [fr. the *Canary* islands] **1** : a usu. sweet wine similar to Madeira **2** : a usu. yellow or greenish finch often kept in a cage as a pet

ca·nas·ta \kə-'nas-tə\ *n* [Sp, lit., basket] : rummy played with two full decks of cards plus four jokers

canc *abbr* canceled

can·can \'kan-ˌkan\ *n* : a woman's dance of French origin characterized by high kicking

¹**can·cel** \'kan-səl\ *vb* **-celed** *or* **-celled; -cel·ing** *or* **-cel·ling** [ME *cancellen,* fr. AF *canceller, chanceller,* fr. LL *cancellare,* fr. L, to make like a lattice, fr. *cancelli* lattice] **1** : to destroy the force or validity of : ANNUL **2** : to match in force or effect : OFFSET **3** : to cross out : DELETE **4** : to remove (a common divisor) from a numerator and denominator; *also* : to remove (equivalents) on opposite sides of an equation or account **5** : to mark (a postage stamp or check) so that it cannot be reused **6** : to neutralize each other's strength or effect — **can·cel·la·tion** \ˌkan-sə-'lā-shən\ *n* — **can·cel·er** *or* **can·cel·ler** *n*

²**cancel** *n* **1** : CANCELLATION **2** : a deleted part

can·cer \'kan-sər\ *n* [L, lit., crab] **1** *cap* : a zodiacal constellation between Gemini and Leo usu. pictured as a crab **2** *cap* : the 4th sign of the zodiac in astrology; *also* : one born under this sign **3** : a malignant tumor that tends to spread in the body; *also* : an abnormal state marked by such tumors **4** : a malignant evil that spreads destructively — **can·cer·ous** \-sə-rəs\ *adj* — **can·cer·ous·ly** *adv*

can·de·la·bra \ˌkan-də-'lä-brə, -'la-\ *n* : an ornamental branched candlestick or lamp with several lights

can·de·la·brum \-brəm\ *n, pl* **-bra** *also* **-brums** : CANDELABRA

can·did \'kan-dəd\ *adj* **1** : FRANK, STRAIGHTFORWARD ⟨a ~ critique⟩ **2** : relating to photography of subjects acting naturally or spontaneously without being posed — **can·did·ly** *adv* — **can·did·ness** *n*

can·di·da·cy \'kan-də-də-sē\ *n, pl* **-cies** : the state of being a candidate

can·di·date \'kan-də-ˌdāt, 'kan-nə-, -dət\ *n* [L *candidatus,* fr. *candidatus* clothed in white, fr. *candidus* white; fr. the white toga worn by office seekers in ancient Rome] : one who seeks or is proposed for an office, honor, or membership ⟨a ~ for governor⟩

can·di·da·ture \'kan-də-də-ˌchùr, 'ka-nə-\ *n, chiefly Brit* : CANDIDACY

can·died \'kan-dēd\ *adj* : preserved in or encrusted with sugar

¹**can·dle** \'kan-dᵊl\ *n* : a usu. slender mass of tallow or wax molded around a wick that is burned to give light

²**candle** *vb* **can·dled; can·dling** : to examine (as eggs) by holding between the eye and a light — **can·dler** *n*

can·dle·light \'kan-dᵊl-ˌlīt\ *n* **1** : the light of a candle; *also* : any soft artificial light **2** : the time when candles are lit : TWILIGHT

can·dle·lit \-ˌlit\ *adj* : illuminated by candlelight ⟨a ~ dinner⟩

Can·dle·mas \'kan-dᵊl-məs\ *n* : February 2 observed as a church festival in commemoration of the presentation of Christ in the temple

can·dle·stick \-ˌstik\ *n* : a holder with a socket for a candle

can·dle·wick \-ˌwik\ *n* : a soft cotton yarn; *also* : embroidery made with this yarn usu. in tufts

can·dor \'kan-dər\ *n* : FRANKNESS, OUTSPOKENNESS

can·dour *chiefly Brit var of* CANDOR

C and W *abbr* country and western

¹**can·dy** \'kan-dē\ *n, pl* **candies** [ME *sugre candy,* fr. MF *sucre candi,* fr. OF *sucre* sugar + Ar *qandī* candied, fr. *qand* crystallized sugar] **1** : a confection made from sugar often with flavoring and filling **2** : something that appeals in a light or frivolous way

²**candy** *vb* **can·died; can·dy·ing** : to encrust in sugar often by cooking in a syrup

candy strip·er \-'strī-pər\ *n* : a teenage volunteer worker at a hospital

¹**cane** \'kān\ *n* **1** : a slender hollow or pithy stem (as of a reed or bramble) **2** : a tall woody grass or reed (as sugarcane or sorghum) **3** : a walking stick; *also* : a rod for flogging

²**cane** *vb* **caned; can·ing** **1** : to beat with a cane **2** : to weave or make with cane — **can·er** *n*

cane·brake \'kān-ˌbrāk\ *n* : a thicket of cane

¹**ca·nine** \'kā-ˌnīn\ *n* **1** : a pointed tooth between the outer incisor and the first premolar **2** : a canine mammal (as a domestic dog)

²**canine** *adj* [L *caninus,* fr. *canis* dog] : of or relating to dogs or to the family to which they belong

can·is·ter \'ka-nə-stər\ *n* : an often cylindrical container

can·ker \'kaŋ-kər\ *n* : a spreading sore that eats into tissue — **can·ker·ous** \-kə-rəs\ *adj*

can·ker·worm \-ˌwərm\ *n* : either of two moths and esp. their larvae that are pests of fruit and shade trees

can·na \'ka-nə\ *n* : any of a genus of tropical herbs with large leaves and racemes of bright-colored flowers

can·na·bis \'ka-nə-bəs\ *n* : any of the psychoactive preparations (as marijuana) or chemicals (as THC) derived from hemp; *also* : HEMP

canned \'kand\ *adj* : prepared in standardized form for general use or wide distribution ⟨∼ music⟩

can·nery \'ka-nə-rē\ *n, pl* **-ner·ies** : a factory for the canning of foods

can·ni·bal \'ka-nə-bəl\ *n* [NL *Canibalis* a member of a Caribbean Indian people, fr. Sp *Caníbal*] : one that eats the flesh of its own kind — **can·ni·bal·ism** \-bə-,li-zəm\ *n* — **can·ni·bal·is·tic** \-bə-'lis-tik\ *adj*

can·ni·bal·ise *Brit var of* CANNIBALIZE

can·ni·bal·ize \'ka-nə-bə-,līz\ *vb* **-ized; -iz·ing** **1** : to take usable parts from (as an inoperative machine) to construct or repair another machine **2** : to practice cannibalism

can·non \'ka-nən\ *n, pl* **cannons** *or* **cannon** [ME *canon*, fr. AF, fr. It *cannone*, lit., large tube, fr. *canna* reed, tube, fr. L, cane, reed] : a large heavy gun; *esp* : one mounted on a carriage

can·non·ade \,ka-nə-'nād\ *n* : a heavy fire of artillery — **cannonade** *vb*

can·non·ball \'ka-nən-,bȯl\ *n* : a usu. round solid missile for a cannon

can·non·eer \,ka-nə-'nir\ *n* : an artillery gunner

can·not \'ka-,nät; kə-'nät\ : can not — **cannot but** : to be unable to do otherwise than ⟨we *cannot* but wonder why⟩

can·nu·la \'kan-yə-lə\ *n, pl* **-las** *or* **-lae** \-,lē\ : a small tube for insertion into a body cavity or into a duct or vessel

can·ny \'ka-nē\ *adj* **can·ni·er; -est** : PRUDENT, SHREWD — **can·ni·ly** \'kan-ᵊl-ē\ *adv* — **can·ni·ness** \'ka-nē-nəs\ *n*

ca·noe \kə-'nü\ *n* : a light narrow boat with sharp ends and curved sides that is usu. propelled by paddles — **canoe** *vb* — **ca·noe·ist** *n*

ca·no·la \kə-'nō-lə\ *n* : a rape plant producing seeds that are low in a toxic acid and yield an edible oil (**canola oil**) high in monounsaturated fatty acids; *also* : this oil

¹can·on \'ka-nən\ *n* **1** : a regulation decreed by a church council; *also* : a provision of canon law **2** : an official or authoritative list (as of works of literature) **3** : an accepted principle ⟨the ∼s of good taste⟩

²canon *n* : a member of the clergy on the staff of a cathedral

ca·non·i·cal \kə-'nä-ni-kəl\ *adj* **1** : of, relating to, or forming a canon **2** : conforming to a general rule or acceptable procedure : ORTHODOX **3** : of or relating to a canon of a cathedral — **ca·non·i·cal·ly** \-k(ə-)lē\ *adv*

can·on·ize \'ka-nə-,nīz\ *vb* **can·on·ized** \-,nīzd\; **can·on·iz·ing** **1** : to declare (a deceased person) an officially recognized saint **2** : GLORIFY, EXALT — **can·on·i·za·tion** \,ka-nə-nə-'zā-shən\ *n*

canon law *n* : the law governing a church

can·o·py \'ka-nə-pē\ *n, pl* **-pies** [ME *canope*, fr. ML *canopeum* mosquito net, fr. L *conopeum*, fr. Gk *kōnōpion*, fr. *kōnōps* mosquito] **1** : an overhanging cover, shelter, or shade **2** : the uppermost spreading layer of a forest **3** : a transparent cover for an airplane cockpit

4 : the fabric part of a parachute — **canopy** *vb*

¹cant \'kant\ *vb* : to give a slant to

²cant *n* **1** : an oblique or slanting surface **2** : TILT, SLANT

³cant *vb* **1** : to beg in a whining manner **2** : to talk hypocritically

⁴cant *n* **1** : the special idiom of a profession or trade : JARGON **2** : insincere speech; *esp* : insincerely pious words or statements

Cant *abbr* Canticle of Canticles

can·ta·bi·le \kän-'tä-bə-,lā\ *adv or adj* [It] : in a singing manner — used as a direction in music

can·ta·loupe *also* **can·ta·loup** \'kant-ᵊl-,ōp\ *n* : MUSKMELON; *esp* : one with orange flesh and rough skin

can·tan·ker·ous \kan-'taŋ-kə-rəs\ *adj* : difficult to deal with : ILL-NATURED ⟨a ∼ mule⟩ — **can·tan·ker·ous·ly** *adv* — **can·tan·ker·ous·ness** *n*

can·ta·ta \kən-'tä-tə\ *n* [It] : a choral composition usu. sung to instrumental accompaniment

can·teen \kan-'tēn\ *n* [F *cantine* bottle case, canteen (store), fr. It *cantina* wine cellar] **1** : a flask for carrying liquids **2** : a place of recreation and entertainment for military personnel **3** : a small cafeteria or counter at which snacks are served

can·ter \'kan-tər\ *n* : a horse's 3-beat gait resembling but smoother and slower than a gallop — **canter** *vb*

Can·ter·bury bell \'kant-ər-,ber-ē-\ *n* : any of several plants related to the bluebell that are cultivated for their showy flowers

can·ti·cle \'kan-ti-kəl\ *n* : SONG; *esp* : any of several liturgical songs taken from the Bible

Canticle of Canticles *n* : SONG OF SONGS

¹can·ti·le·ver \'kant-ᵊl-,ē-vər\ *n* : a projecting beam or structure supported only at one end; *also* : either of a pair of such structures projecting toward each other so that when joined they form a bridge

²cantilever *vb* **1** : to support by a cantilever ⟨a ∼ed shelf⟩ **2** : to build as a cantilever **3** : to project as a cantilever

can·tle \'kant-ᵊl\ *n* : the upwardly projecting rear part of a saddle

can·to \'kan-,tō\ *n, pl* **cantos** [It, fr. L *cantus* song] : one of the major divisions of a long poem

can·ton \'kant-ᵊn, 'kan-,tän\ *n* : a small territorial division of a country; *esp* : one of the political divisions of Switzerland — **can·ton·al** \'kant-ᵊn-əl, kan-'tän-ᵊl\ *adj*

can·ton·ment \kan-'tōn-mənt, -'tän-\ *n* : usu. temporary quarters for troops

can·tor \'kan-tər\ *n* **1** : a choir leader **2** : a synagogue official who sings liturgical music and leads the congregation in prayer

can·vas *also* **can·vass** \'kan-vəs\ *n* **1** : a strong cloth formerly much used for making tents and sails **2** : a set of sails **3** : a group of tents **4** : a piece of cloth prepared as a surface for a painting; *also* : a painting on this surface **5** : the canvas-covered floor of a boxing or wrestling ring

can·vas·back \'kan-vəs-ˌbak\ *n* : a No. American wild duck with red head and gray back

¹can·vass *also* **can·vas** \'kan-vəs\ *vb* **canvassed; can·vass·ing** : to go through (a district) or to (persons) to solicit votes or orders for goods or to determine public opinion or sentiment — **can·vass·er** *n*

²canvass *n* : an act or instance of canvassing

can·yon \'kan-yən\ *n* : a deep narrow valley with high steep sides

¹cap \'kap\ *n* **1** : a covering for the head esp. with a visor and no brim; *also* : something resembling such a covering esp. on a tip, knob or end ⟨a bottle ∼⟩ **2** : a container holding an explosive charge (as for a toy gun) **3** : an upper limit ⟨as on expenditures⟩

²cap *vb* **capped; cap·ping 1** : to provide or protect with a cap **2** : to form a cap over : CROWN ⟨snow-*capped* mountains⟩ **3** : OUTDO, SURPASS **4** : to bring to a conclusion ⟨∼ off dinner with coffee⟩

³cap *abbr* **1** capacity **2** capital **3** capitalize; capitalized

CAP *abbr* Civil Air Patrol

ca·pa·ble \'kā-pə-bəl\ *adj* : having ability, capacity, or power to do something : ABLE, COMPETENT — **ca·pa·bil·i·ty** \ˌkā-pə-'bi-lə-tē\ *n* — **ca·pa·bly** *adv*

ca·pa·cious \kə-'pā-shəs\ *adj* : able to contain much — **ca·pa·cious·ly** *adv* — **ca·pa·cious·ness** *n*

ca·pac·i·tance \kə-'pa-sə-təns\ *n* : the property of an electric nonconductor that permits the storage of energy

ca·pac·i·tor \kə-'pa-sə-tər\ *n* : an electronic circuit device for temporary storage of electrical energy

¹ca·pac·i·ty \kə-'pa-sə-tē\ *n, pl* **-ties 1** : legal qualification or fitness ⟨∼ to stand trial⟩ **2** : the ability to contain, receive, or accommodate ⟨seating ∼⟩ **3** : the maximum amount or number that can be contained — see METRIC SYSTEM table, WEIGHT table **4** : ABILITY **5** : position or character assigned or assumed

²capacity *adj* : equaling maximum capacity ⟨a ∼ crowd⟩

cap–a–pie *or* **cap–à–pie** \ˌka-pə-'pē\ *adv* [MF] : from head to foot : at all points

ca·par·i·son \kə-'par-ə-sən\ *n* **1** : an ornamental covering for a horse **2** : TRAPPINGS, ADORNMENT — **caparison** *vb*

¹cape \'kāp\ *n* **1** : a point of land jutting out into water **2** *often cap* : CAPE COD COTTAGE

²cape *n* : a sleeveless garment hanging from the neck over the shoulders — **caped** *adj*

Cape Cod cottage \'kāp-'käd-\ *n* : a compact rectangular dwelling of one or one-and-a-half stories usu. with a steep gable roof

¹ca·per \'kā-pər\ *n* : the greenish flower bud or young berry of a Mediterranean shrub pickled for use as a relish; *also* : this shrub

²caper *vb* **ca·pered; ca·per·ing** : to leap about in a playful manner

³caper *n* **1** : a frolicsome leap **2** : a capricious escapade **3** : an illegal or questionable act

cape·skin \'kāp-ˌskin\ *n* : a light flexible leather made from sheepskins

cap·ful \'kap-ˌfu̇l\ *n, pl* **cap·fuls** *also* **caps·ful** \-ˌkaps-\ : as much as a cap will hold

cap·il·lar·i·ty \ˌka-pə-'lar-ə-tē\ *n, pl* **-ties** : the action by which the surface of a liquid where it is in contact with a solid (as in a slender tube) is raised or lowered depending on the relative attraction of the molecules of the liquid for each other and for those of the solid

¹cap·il·lary \'ka-pə-ˌler-ē\ *adj* **1** : resembling a hair **2** : having a very small bore ⟨∼ tube⟩ **3** : of or relating to capillaries or to capillarity

²capillary *n, pl* **-lar·ies** : any of the tiny thin-walled blood vessels that carry blood between the smallest arteries and their corresponding veins

¹cap·i·tal \'ka-pət-ᵊl\ *n* : the top part or piece of an architectural column

²capital *adj* **1** : conforming to the series A, B, C rather than a, b, c ⟨∼ letters⟩ ⟨∼ G⟩ **2** : punishable by death ⟨a ∼ crime⟩ **3** : most serious ⟨a ∼ error⟩ **4** : first in importance or position : CHIEF; *also* : being the seat of government ⟨the ∼ city⟩ **5** : of or relating to capital ⟨∼ expenditures⟩; *esp* : relating to or being assets that add to the long-term net worth of a corporation **6** : FIRST-RATE, EXCELLENT

³capital *n* **1** : accumulated wealth esp. as used to produce more wealth **2** : the total face value of shares of stock issued by a company **3** : persons holding capital **4** : ADVANTAGE, GAIN **5** : a letter larger than the ordinary small letter and often different in form **6** : the capital city of a state, province or country; *also* : a city preeminent in some activity ⟨the fashion ∼⟩

capital gain *n* : the increase in value of an asset (as stock or real estate) between the time it is bought and the time it is sold

capital goods *n pl* : machinery, tools, factories, and commodities used in the production of goods

cap·i·tal·ise *Brit var of* CAPITALIZE

cap·i·tal·ism \'ka-pət-ᵊl-ˌi-zəm\ *n* : an economic system characterized by private or corporate ownership of capital goods and by prices, production, and distribution of goods that are determined mainly by competition in a free market

¹cap·i·tal·ist \-ist\ *n* **1** : a person who has capital esp. invested in business **2** : a person of great wealth : PLUTOCRAT **3** : a believer in capitalism

²capitalist *or* **cap·i·tal·is·tic** \ˌka-pət-ᵊl-'is-tik\ *adj* **1** : owning capital **2** : practicing or advocating capitalism **3** : marked by capitalism — **cap·i·tal·is·ti·cal·ly** \-ti-k(ə-)lē\ *adv*

cap·i·tal·iza·tion \ˌka-pət-ᵊl-ə-'zā-shən\ *n* **1** : the act or process of capitalizing **2**

: the total amount of money used as capital in a business

cap·i·tal·ize \'ka-pət-ᵊl-ˌīz\ *vb* **-ized; -izing 1 :** to write or print with an initial capital or in capitals **2 :** to convert into or use as capital **3 :** to supply capital for **4 :** to gain by turning something to advantage : PROFIT

cap·i·tal·ly \'ka-pət-ᵊl-ē\ *adv* : ADMIRABLY, EXCELLENTLY

cap·i·ta·tion \ˌka-pə-'tā-shən\ *n* : a direct uniform tax levied on each person

cap·i·tol \'ka-pət-ᵊl\ *n* : the building in which a legislature holds its sessions

ca·pit·u·late \kə-'pi-chə-ˌlāt\ *vb* **-lated; -lating 1 :** to surrender esp. on conditions agreed upon **2 :** to cease resisting : ACQUIESCE ♦ *Synonyms* SUBMIT, YIELD, SUCCUMB, CAVE, DEFER — **ca·pit·u·la·tion** \-ˌpi-chə-'lā-shən\ *n*

cap·let \'ka-plət\ *n* : a capsule-shaped medicinal tablet

ca·pon \'kā-ˌpän, -pən\ *n* : a castrated male chicken

cap·puc·ci·no \ˌka-pə-'chē-nō, ˌkä-\ *n* [It, lit., Capuchin; fr. the likeness of its color to that of a Capuchin's habit] : espresso mixed with foamy hot milk or cream and often flavored with cinnamon

ca·pric·cio \kə-'prē-chē-ˌō, -chō\ *n, pl* **-cios** [It, lit., whim, prank] : an instrumental piece in free form usu. lively in tempo and brilliant in style

ca·price \kə-'prēs\ *n* [F, fr. It *capriccio*] **1 :** a sudden whim or fancy **2 :** an inclination to do things impulsively **3 :** CAPRICCIO — **ca·pri·cious** \-'pri-shəs\ *adj* — **ca·pri·cious·ly** *adv* — **ca·pri·cious·ness** *n*

Cap·ri·corn \'ka-pri-ˌkȯrn\ *n* **1 :** a zodiacal constellation between Sagittarius and Aquarius usu. pictured as a goat **2 :** the 10th sign of the zodiac in astrology; *also* : one born under this sign

cap·ri·ole \'ka-prē-ˌōl\ *n* : ³CAPER 1; *also* : an upward leap of a horse with a backward kick at the height of the leap — **capriole** *vb*

caps *abbr* **1** capitals **2** capsule

cap·sa·i·cin \kap-'sā-ə-sən\ *n* : a colorless compound found in various capsicums that gives hot peppers their hotness

cap·si·cum \'kap-si-kəm\ *n* : PEPPER 2

cap·size \'kap-ˌsīz, kap-'sīz\ *vb* **capsized; cap·siz·ing :** UPSET, OVERTURN

cap·stan \'kap-stən, -ˌstan\ *n* **1 :** a machine for moving or raising heavy weights that consists of a vertical drum which can be rotated and around which cable is turned **2 :** a rotating shaft that drives recorder tape

cap·su·lar \'kap-sə-lər\ *adj* : of, relating to, or resembling a capsule

cap·su·lat·ed \-ˌlā-təd\ *adj* : enclosed in a capsule

¹**cap·sule** \'kap-səl, -sül\ *n* **1 :** a membrane or sac enclosing a body part (as of a joint) **2 :** a case bearing spores or seeds **3 :** a shell usu. of gelatin that is used for packaging something (as a drug); *also* : such a shell together with its contents **4**

: a small pressurized compartment or vehicle (as for space flight)

²**capsule** *adj* **1 :** very brief ⟨a ∼ biography⟩ **2 :** very compact ⟨a ∼ camera⟩

Capt *abbr* captain

¹**cap·tain** \'kap-tən\ *n* **1 :** a commander of a body of troops **2 :** a commissioned officer in the army, air force, or marine corps ranking next below a major **3 :** an officer in charge of a ship **4 :** a commissioned officer in the navy ranking next below a rear admiral or a commodore **5** : a leader of a side or team **6 :** a dominant figure — **cap·tain·cy** *n*

²**captain** *vb* : to be captain of : LEAD

cap·tion \'kap-shən\ *n* **1 :** a heading esp. of an article or document : TITLE **2 :** the explanatory matter accompanying an illustration **3 :** a motion-picture subtitle — **cap·tion** *vb*

cap·tious \'kap-shəs\ *adj* : marked by an inclination to find fault — **cap·tious·ly** *adv* — **cap·tious·ness** *n*

cap·ti·vate \'kap-tə-ˌvāt\ *vb* **-vat·ed; -vating :** to attract and hold irresistibly by some special charm or art — **cap·ti·va·tion** \ˌkap-tə-'vā-shən\ *n* — **cap·ti·va·tor** \'kap-tə-ˌvā-tər\ *n*

cap·tive \'kap-tiv\ *adj* **1 :** made prisoner esp. in war **2 :** kept within bounds : CONFINED **3 :** held under control — **captive** *n* — **cap·tiv·i·ty** \kap-'ti-və-tē\ *n*

cap·tor \'kap-tər\ *n* : one that captures

¹**cap·ture** \'kap-chər\ *n* **1 :** the act of capturing **2 :** one that has been captured

²**capture** *vb* **cap·tured; cap·tur·ing 1 :** to take captive : WIN, GAIN ⟨∼ the crown⟩ **2 :** to preserve in a relatively permanent form ⟨∼ the moment on film⟩

Ca·pu·chin \'ka-pyə-shən\ *n* : a member of an austere branch of the order of St. Francis of Assisi engaged in missionary work and preaching

car \'kär\ *n* **1 :** a vehicle moving on wheels **2 :** the compartment of an elevator **3 :** the part of a balloon or airship that carries passengers or equipment

car·a·cole \'kar-ə-ˌkōl\ *n* : a half turn to right or left executed by a mounted horse — **caracole** *vb*

car·a·cul \'kar-ə-ˌkəl\ *n* : the pelt of a karakul lamb after the curl begins to loosen

ca·rafe \kə-'raf, -'räf\ *n* **1 :** a bottle with a flaring lip used esp. to hold wine **2 :** a usu. glass pitcher for pouring coffee

car·am·bo·la \ˌkar-əm-'bō-lə\ *n* **1 :** a 5-angled green to yellow edible tropical fruit of star-shaped cross section **2 :** a tropical Asian tree widely cultivated for carambolas

car·a·mel \'kar-ə-məl, 'kär-məl\ *n* **1 :** an amorphous substance obtained by heating sugar and used for flavoring and coloring **2 :** a firm chewy candy

car·a·pace \'kar-ə-ˌpās\ *n* : a protective case or shell on the back of some animals (as turtles or crabs)

¹**carat** *var of* KARAT

²**car·at** \'kar-ət\ *n* : a unit of weight for precious stones equal to 200 milligrams

car·a·van \'kar-ə-ˌvan\ *n* **1 :** a group of

travelers journeying together through desert or hostile regions **2** : a group of vehicles traveling in a file

car·a·van·sa·ry \ˌkar-ə-ˈvan-sə-rē\ *or* **car·a·van·se·rai** \-sə-ˌrī\ *n, pl* **-ries** *or* **-rais** *or* **-rai** [Pers *kārvānsarāī*, fr. *kārvān* caravan + *sarāī* palace, inn] **1** : an inn in eastern countries where caravans rest at night **2** : HOTEL, INN

car·a·vel \ˈkar-ə-ˌvel\ *n* : a small 15th and 16th century ship with a broad bow, high narrow poop, and usu. three masts

car·a·way \ˈkar-ə-ˌwā\ *n* : an aromatic herb related to the carrot with fruits (**caraway seed**) used in seasoning and medicine; *also* : its fruit

car·bide \ˈkär-ˌbīd\ *n* : a compound of carbon with another element

car·bine \ˈkär-ˌbēn, -ˌbīn\ *n* : a short-barreled lightweight rifle

car·bo·hy·drate \ˌkär-bō-ˈhī-ˌdrāt, -drət\ *n* : any of various compounds composed of carbon, hydrogen, and oxygen (as sugars and starches)

car·bol·ic acid \ˌkär-ˈbä-lik-\ *n* : PHENOL

car·bon \ˈkär-bən\ *n* **1** : a nonmetallic chemical element occurring in nature esp. as diamond and graphite and as a constituent of coal, petroleum, and limestone **2** : a sheet of carbon paper; *also* : CARBON COPY 1 — **car·bon·less** \-ləs\ *adj*

car·bo·na·ceous \ˌkär-bə-ˈnā-shəs\ *adj* : relating to, containing, or composed of carbon

¹car·bon·ate \ˈkär-bə-ˌnāt, -nət\ *n* : a salt or ester of carbonic acid

²car·bon·ate \-ˌnāt\ *vb* **-at·ed; -at·ing** : to combine or infuse with carbon dioxide ⟨*carbonated* beverages⟩ — **car·bon·ation** \ˌkär-bə-ˈnā-shən\ *n*

carbon black *n* : any of various black substances consisting chiefly of carbon and used esp. as pigments

carbon copy *n* **1** : a copy made by carbon paper **2** : DUPLICATE

carbon dating *n* : the determination of the age of old material (as an archaeological specimen) by its content of carbon 14

carbon dioxide *n* : a heavy colorless gas that does not support combustion and is formed in animal respiration and in the combustion and decomposition of organic substances

carbon footprint *n* : the amount of carbon dioxide emitted by something in a given period

carbon 14 *n* : a heavy radioactive form of carbon used esp. in dating old materials (as archaeological specimens)

car·bon·ic acid \kär-ˈbä-nik-\ *n* : a weak acid that decomposes readily into water and carbon dioxide

car·bon·if·er·ous \ˌkär-bə-ˈni-fə-rəs\ *adj* **1** : producing or containing carbon or coal **2** *cap* : of, relating to, or being the period of the Paleozoic era between the Devonian and the Permian — **Carboniferous** *n*

carbon monoxide *n* : a colorless odorless very poisonous gas formed by the incomplete burning of carbon

carbon paper *n* : a thin paper coated with a pigment and used for making copies

carbon tet·ra·chlo·ride \-ˌte-trə-ˈklōr-ˌīd\ *n* : a colorless nonflammable toxic liquid used esp. as a solvent

carbon 12 *n* : the most abundant isotope of carbon having a nucleus of 6 protons and 6 neutrons and used as a standard for measurements of atomic weight

car·boy \ˈkär-ˌbȯi\ *n* [Pers *qarāba*, fr. Ar *qarrāba* demijohn] : a large container for liquids

car·bun·cle \ˈkär-ˌbəŋ-kəl\ *n* : a painful inflammation of the skin and underlying tissue that discharges pus from several openings

car·bu·re·tor \ˈkär-bə-ˌrā-tər, -byə-\ *n* : an apparatus for premixing vaporized fuel and air and supplying the mixture to an internal combustion engine

car·bu·ret·tor *also* **car·bu·ret·ter** \ˌkär-byə-ˈre-tər, ˈkär-byə-ˌ\ *chiefly Brit var of* CARBURETOR

car·case *Brit var of* CARCASS

car·cass \ˈkär-kəs\ *n* : a dead body; *esp* : one of an animal dressed for food

car·cin·o·gen \kär-ˈsi-nə-jən\ *n* : a substance or agent causing cancer — **car·ci·no·gen·ic** \ˌkärs-ᵊn-ō-ˈje-nik\ *adj* — **car·ci·no·ge·nic·i·ty** \-jə-ˈni-sə-tē\ *n*

car·ci·no·ma \ˌkärs-ᵊn-ˈō-mə\ *n, pl* **-mas** *also* **-ma·ta** \-tə\ : a malignant tumor of epithelial origin — **car·ci·no·ma·tous** \-təs\ *adj*

¹card \ˈkärd\ *vb* : to comb with a card : cleanse and untangle before spinning ⟨~*ed* cotton⟩ — **card·er** *n*

²card *n* : an instrument for combing fibers (as wool or cotton)

³card *n* **1** : PLAYING CARD **2** *pl* : a game played with playing cards; *also* : card playing **3** : an emotional issue used to one's advantage (as in a political campaign) **4** : a usu. clownishly amusing person : WAG **5** : a flat stiff usu. small piece of paper, cardboard, or plastic often bearing pictures or information **6** : PROGRAM; *esp* : a sports program — **in the cards** : INEVITABLE

⁴card *vb* **1** : to list or schedule on a card **2** : SCORE **3** : to ask for identification (as at a bar)

⁵card *abbr* cardinal

car·da·mom \ˈkär-də-məm\ *n* : the aromatic capsular fruit of an Indian herb related to the ginger whose seeds are used as a spice or condiment and in medicine; *also* : this plant

card·board \ˈkärd-ˌbȯrd\ *n* : a material thicker than paper and made from cellulose fiber

card–car·ry·ing \ˈkärd-ˌkar-ē-iŋ\ *adj* : being a regularly enrolled member of an organization (as a political party)

card catalog *n* : a catalog (as of books) in which the entries are arranged systematically on cards

car·di·ac \ˈkär-dē-ˌak\ *adj* [L *cardiacus*, fr. Gk *kardiakos*, fr. *kardia* heart] **1** : of, relating to, or located near the heart **2** : of, relating to, or affected with heart disease ⟨∼ patients⟩

car·di·gan \'kär-di-gən\ n : a sweater or jacket usu. without a collar and with a full-length opening in the front

¹car·di·nal \'kärd-nəl, 'kär-dᵊn-əl\ n **1** : an ecclesiastical official of the Roman Catholic Church ranking next below the pope **2** : a crested No. American finch that is nearly completely red in the male

²cardinal adj [ME, fr. LL cardinalis, fr. L serving as a hinge, fr. cardo hinge] **1** : of basic importance : CHIEF, MAIN, PRIMARY ⟨a ∼ principle⟩ **2** : very serious ⟨a ∼ sin⟩ — **car·di·nal·ly** adv

car·di·nal·ate \'kärd-nə-lət, -'kär-dᵊn-ə-let, -ˌlāt\ n : the office, rank, or dignity of a cardinal

cardinal flower n : a No. American plant that bears a spike of brilliant red flowers

cardinal number n : a number (as 1, 5, 82, 357) that is used in simple counting and answers the question "how many?" — compare ORDINAL NUMBER

cardinal point n : one of the four principal compass points north, south, east, and west

car·dio \'kär-dē-ō\ adj : CARDIOVASCULAR 2

car·di·ol·o·gy \ˌkär-dē-'ä-lə-jē\ n : the study of the heart and its action and diseases — **car·di·ol·o·gist** \-jist\ n

car·dio·pul·mo·nary   resuscitation \ˌkär-dē-ō-'pùl-mə-ˌner-ē-\ n : a procedure to restore normal breathing after cardiac arrest that includes the clearance of air passages to the lungs, mouth-to-mouth method of artificial respiration, and heart massage by the exertion of pressure on the chest

car·dio·vas·cu·lar \-'-vas-kyə-lər\ adj **1** : of or relating to the heart and blood vessels **2** : causing a temporary increase in heart rate ⟨a ∼ workout⟩

card·sharp \-ˌshärp\ or **card·sharp·er** \'kärd-ˌshär-pər\ n : a cheater at cards

¹care \'ker\ n **1** : a disquieted state of uncertainty and responsibility : ANXIETY **2** : watchful attention : HEED **3** : CHARGE, SUPERVISION ⟨under a doctor's ∼⟩ **4** : a person or thing that is an object of anxiety or solicitude

²care vb **cared; car·ing 1** : to feel anxiety **2** : to feel interest **3** : to give care **4** : to have a liking, fondness, taste, or inclination **5** : to be concerned about ⟨∼ what happens⟩

CARE abbr Cooperative for American Relief to Everywhere

ca·reen \kə-'rēn\ vb **1** : to put (a ship or boat) on a beach esp. in order to clean or repair its hull **2** : to sway from side to side **3** : CAREER

¹ca·reer \kə-'rir\ n [MF carrière, fr. Old Occitan carriera street, fr. ML carrarius road for vehicles, fr. L carrus car] **1** : COURSE, PASSAGE; also : speed in a course ⟨ran at full ∼⟩ **2** : an occupation or profession followed as a life's work

²career vb : to go at top speed esp. in a headlong manner

care·free \'ker-ˌfrē\ adj : free from care or worry

care·ful \-fəl\ adj **care·ful·ler; care·ful·lest 1** : using or taking care : VIGILANT **2** : marked by solicitude, caution, or prudence — **care·ful·ly** adv — **care·ful·ness** n

care·giv·er \-ˌgi-vər\ n : a person who provides direct care (as for children, elderly people, or the chronically ill)

care·less \-ləs\ adj **1** : free from care : UNTROUBLED **2** : UNCONCERNED, INDIFFERENT ⟨∼ of the consequences⟩ **3** : not taking care **4** : not showing or receiving care — **care·less·ly** adv — **care·less·ness** n

care package n : a package of useful or pleasurable items given as a gift to another

¹ca·ress \kə-'res\ vb : to touch or stroke tenderly or lovingly — **ca·ress·er** n

²caress n : a tender or loving touch or embrace

car·et \'ker-ət\ n [L, there is lacking, fr. carēre to lack, be without] : a mark ^ used to indicate the place where something is to be inserted

care·tak·er \'ker-ˌtā-kər\ n **1** : one in charge usu. as occupant in place of an absent owner **2** : one temporarily fulfilling the functions of an office

care·worn \-ˌwórn\ adj : showing the effects of grief or anxiety

car·fare \'kär-ˌfer\ n : passenger fare (as on a streetcar or bus)

car·go \'kär-gō\ n, pl **cargoes** or **cargos** : the goods carried in a ship, airplane, or vehicle : FREIGHT

Ca·rib·be·an \ˌker-ə-'bē-ən, kə-'ri-bē-ən\ adj : of or relating to the eastern and southern West Indies or the Caribbean Sea

car·i·bou \'ker-ə-ˌbü\ n, pl **caribou** or **caribous** : a large circumpolar gregarious deer of northern taiga and tundra that usu. has large branched antlers usu. in both sexes — used esp. for one of the New World

car·i·ca·ture \'ker-i-kə-ˌchùr\ n **1** : distorted representation to produce a ridiculous effect **2** : a representation esp. in literature or art having the qualities of caricature — **caricature** vb — **car·i·ca·tur·ist** \-ist\ n

car·ies \'ker-ēz\ n, pl **caries** : tooth decay

car·il·lon \'ker-ə-ˌlän\ n : a set of tuned bells sounded by hammers controlled from a keyboard

car·i·ous \'ker-ē-əs\ adj : affected with caries

car·jack·ing \'kär-ja-kiŋ\ n : the theft of an automobile by force or intimidation — **car·jack·er** n

car·load \'kär-ˌlōd\ n : a load that fills a car

car·mi·na·tive \kär-'mi-nə-tiv\ adj : expelling gas from the stomach or intestines — **carminative** n

car·mine \'kär-mən, -ˌmīn\ n : a vivid red

car·nage \'kär-nij\ n : great destruction of life : SLAUGHTER

carnal • carry

car·nal \'kär-n°l\ *adj* [ME, fr. LL *carnalis,* fr. L *carn-, caro* flesh] **1** : of or relating to the body **2** : relating to or given to sensual pleasures and appetites — **car·nal·i·ty** \kär-'nal-ə-tē\ *n* — **car·nal·ly** *adv*

car·na·tion \kär-'nā-shən\ *n* : a cultivated pink of any of numerous usu. double-flowered varieties derived from an Old World species

car·nau·ba wax \kär-'nò-bə-, -'naù-; ˌkär-nə-'ü-bə-\ *n* : a brittle yellowish wax from a Brazilian palm that is used esp. in polishes

car·ne·lian \kär-'nēl-yən\ *n* : a hard red chalcedony used as a gem

car·ni·val \'kär-nə-vəl\ *n* [It *carnevale,* alter. of *carnelevare,* lit., removal of meat] **1** : a festival of merrymaking just before Lent **2** : a boisterous merrymaking **3** : a traveling enterprise offering amusements **4** : an organized program of entertainment

car·ni·val·esque \ˌkär-nə-və-'lesk\ *adj* : suggestive of a carnival

car·niv·o·ra \kär-'ni-və-rə\ *n pl* : carnivorous mammals

car·ni·vore \'kär-nə-ˌvòr\ *n* : a flesh-eating animal; *esp* : any of an order of mammals (as dogs, cats, bears, minks, and seals) feeding mostly on animal flesh

car·niv·o·rous \kär-'ni-və-rəs\ *adj* **1** : feeding on animal tissues **2** : of or relating to the carnivores — **car·niv·o·rous·ly** *adv* — **car·niv·o·rous·ness** *n*

car·ny *or* **car·ney** *or* **car·nie** \'kär-nē\ *n, pl* **carnies** *or* **carneys** **1** : CARNIVAL 3 **2** : one who works with a carnival

car·ol \'ker-əl\ *n* : a song of joy or devotion — **carol** *vb* — **car·ol·er** *or* **car·ol·ler** *n*

car·om \'ker-əm\ *n* **1** : a shot in billiards in which the cue ball strikes two other balls **2** : a rebounding esp. at an angle — **carom** *vb*

car·o·tene \'ker-ə-ˌtēn\ *n* : any of several orange to red pigments (as beta-carotene) formed esp. in plants and used as a source of vitamin A

ca·rot·en·oid \kə-'rä-tə-ˌnòid\ *n* : any of various usu. yellow to red pigments (as carotenes) found widely in plants and animals

ca·rot·id \kə-'rä-təd\ *adj* : of, relating to, or being the chief artery or pair of arteries that pass up the neck and supply the head — **carotid** *n*

ca·rous·al \kə-'raù-zəl\ *n* : CAROUSE

ca·rouse \kə-'raùz\ *n* [MF *carrousse,* fr. *carous,* adv., all out (in *boire carous* to empty the cup), fr. G *garaus*] : a drunken revel — **carouse** *vb* — **ca·rous·er** *n*

car·ou·sel *also* **car·rou·sel** \ˌker-ə-'sel, 'kar-ə-ˌsel\ *n* **1** : MERRY-GO-ROUND **2** : a circular conveyor ⟨a baggage ∼⟩

¹carp \'kärp\ *vb* : to find fault : CAVIL, COMPLAIN — **carp** *n* — **carp·er** *n*

²carp *n, pl* **carp** *or* **carps** : a large variable Asian freshwater fish of sluggish waters often raised for food

¹car·pal \'kär-pəl\ *adj* : of or relating to the wrist or the bones of the wrist

²carpal *n* : a carpal element or bone

carpal tunnel syndrome *n* : a condition characterized esp. by weakness, pain, and disturbances of sensation (as numbness) in the hand and fingers and caused by compression of a nerve in the wrist

car·pe di·em \ˌkär-pe-'dē-ˌem, -'dī-\ *n* [L, lit., pluck the day] : enjoyment of the present without concern for the future

car·pel \'kär-pəl\ *n* : one of the highly modified leaves that together form the ovary of a flower of a seed plant

car·pen·ter \'kär-pən-tər\ *n* : one who builds or repairs wooden structures — **carpenter** *vb* — **car·pen·try** \-trē\ *n*

car·pet \'kär-pət\ *n* : a heavy fabric used as a floor covering — **carpet** *vb*

car·pet·bag \-ˌbag\ *n* : a traveling bag common in the 19th century

car·pet·bag·ger \-ˌba-gər\ *n* : a Northerner in the South after the American Civil War usu. seeking private gain under the reconstruction governments

car·pet·ing \'kär-pə-tiŋ\ *n* : material for carpets; *also* : CARPETS

car pool *n* : an arrangement in which a group of people commute together by car; *also* : a group having this arrangement — **car·pool** \-ˌpül\ *vb*

car·port \'kär-ˌpòrt\ *n* : an open-sided automobile shelter

car·pus \'kär-pəs\ *n* : the wrist or its bones

car·ra·geen·an *or* **car·ra·geen·in** \ˌker-ə-'gē-nən\ *n* : a colloid extracted esp. from a dark purple branching seaweed and used in foods esp. to stabilize and thicken them

car·rel \'ker-əl\ *n* : a table often partitioned or enclosed for individual study in a library

car·riage \'ker-ij\ *n* **1** : the act of carrying **2** : manner of holding the body **3** : a wheeled vehicle **4** *Brit* : a railway passenger coach **5** : a movable part of a machine for supporting some other moving part ⟨a typewriter ∼⟩

carriage trade *n* : trade from well-to-do or upper-class people

car·ri·er \'ker-ē-ər\ *n* **1** : one that carries **2** : a person or organization in the transportation business **3** : AIRCRAFT CARRIER **4** : one whose system carries the causative agents of a disease but who is immune to the disease **5** : an individual having a gene for a trait or condition that is not expressed outwardly **6** : an electromagnetic wave whose amplitude or frequency is varied in order to convey a radio or television signal

carrier pigeon *n* : a pigeon used esp. to carry messages

car·ri·on \'ker-ē-ən\ *n* : dead and decaying flesh

car·rot \'ker-ət\ *n* : the elongated usu. orange root of a common garden plant that is eaten as a vegetable; *also* : this plant

carrousel *var of* CAROUSEL

¹car·ry \'ka-rē, 'ker-ē\ *vb* **car·ried; car·ry·ing** [ME *carien,* fr. AF *carier,* fr. *carre* vehicle, fr. L *carrus*] **1** : to move while supporting : TRANSPORT, CONVEY, TAKE **2** : to influence by mental or emotional appeal **3** : to get possession or control of : CAPTURE, WIN **4** : to transfer from one place (as a column) to another ⟨~ a number in adding⟩ **5** : to have or wear on one's person; *also* : to bear within one **6** : INVOLVE, IMPLY **7** : to hold or bear (oneself) in a specified way **8** : to keep in stock for sale **9** : to sustain the weight or burden of : SUPPORT **10** : to prolong in space, time, or degree **11** : to keep on one's books as a debtor **12** : to succeed in (an election) **13** : to win adoption (as in a legislature) **14** : PUBLISH, PRINT **15** : to reach or penetrate to a distance ⟨voices ~ well over water⟩

²**carry** *n* **1** : the range of a gun or projectile or of a struck or thrown ball **2** : PORTAGE **3** : an act or method of carrying ⟨fireman's ~⟩

car·ry·all \-ˌȯl\ *n* : a capacious bag or case

carry away *vb* : to arouse to a high and often excessive degree of emotion

carrying charge *n* : a charge added to the price of merchandise sold on the installment plan

car·ry-on \-ˌȯn, -ˌän\ *n* : a piece of luggage suitable for being carried aboard an airplane by a passenger — **carry-on** *adj*

carry on *vb* **1** : CONDUCT, MANAGE **2** : to behave in a foolish, excited, or improper manner **3** : to continue in spite of hindrance or discouragement

carry out *vb* **1** : to bring to a successful conclusion **2** : to put into execution

car·sick \ˈkär-ˌsik\ *adj* : affected with motion sickness esp. in an automobile — **car sickness** *n*

¹**cart** \ˈkärt\ *n* **1** : a heavy 2-wheeled wagon **2** : a small wheeled vehicle

²**cart** *vb* : to convey in or as if in a cart — **cart·er** *n*

cart·age \ˈkär-tij\ *n* : the act of or rate charged for carting

carte blanche \ˈkärt-ˈblänsh\ *n, pl* **cartes blanches** *same or* -ˈblän-shəz\ [F, lit., blank document] : full discretionary power

car·tel \kär-ˈtel\ *n* : a combination of independent business enterprises designed to limit competition ◆ *Synonyms* POOL, SYNDICATE, MONOPOLY, TRUST

car·ti·lage \ˈkär-tə-lij\ *n* : a usu. translucent somewhat elastic tissue that composes most of the skeleton of young vertebrate embryos and later is mostly converted to bone in higher vertebrates — **car·ti·lag·i·nous** \ˌkär-tə-ˈla-jə-nəs\ *adj*

cartilaginous fish *n* : any of a class of fishes (as a shark or ray) having the skeleton wholly or largely composed of cartilage

car·tog·ra·phy \kär-ˈtä-grə-fē\ *n* : the making of maps — **car·tog·ra·pher** *n* — **car·to·graph·ic** \ˌkär-tə-ˈgra-fik\ *adj*

car·ton \ˈkär-tᵊn\ *n* : a cardboard box or container

car·toon \kär-ˈtün\ *n* **1** : a preparatory sketch (as for a painting) **2** : a drawing intended as humor, caricature, or satire **3** : COMIC STRIP — **cartoon** *vb* — **cartoon·ist** *n*

car·tridge \ˈkär-trij\ *n* **1** : a tube containing a complete charge for a firearm **2** : a container of material for insertion into an apparatus **3** : a small case containing a phonograph needle and transducer that is attached to a tonearm **4** : a case containing a magnetic tape or disk **5** : a case for holding integrated circuits containing a computer program

cart·wheel \ˈkärt-ˌhwēl\ *n* **1** : a large coin (as a silver dollar) **2** : a lateral handspring with arms and legs extended

carve \ˈkärv\ *vb* **carved; carv·ing** **1** : to cut with care or precision : shape by cutting **2** : to cut into pieces or slices **3** : to slice and serve meat at table — **carv·er** *n*

cary·at·id \ˌker-ē-ˈa-təd\ *n, pl* **-ids** *or* **-i·des** \-ˈa-tə-ˌdēz\ : a sculptured draped female figure used as an architectural column

CAS *abbr* certificate of advanced study

ca·sa·ba \kə-ˈsä-bə\ *n* : any of several muskmelons with a yellow rind and sweet flesh

¹**cas·cade** \kas-ˈkād\ *n* **1** : a steep usu. small waterfall **2** : something arranged in a series or succession of stages so that each stage derives from or acts upon the product of the preceding

²**cas·cade** *vb* **cas·cad·ed; cas·cad·ing** : to fall, pass, or connect in or as if in a cascade ⟨water *cascaded* over the rocks⟩

cas·cara \ka-ˈska-rə\ *n* : the dried bark of a small Pacific coastal tree of the U.S. and southern Canada used as a laxative; *also* : this tree

¹**case** \ˈkās\ *n* [ME *cas*, fr. AF, fr. L *casus* fall, chance, fr. *cadere* to fall] **1** : a particular instance or situation **2** : an inflectional form of a noun, pronoun, or adjective indicating its grammatical relation to other words; *also* : such a relation whether indicated by inflection or not **3** : what actually exists or happens : FACT **4** : a suit or action in law : CAUSE **5** : a convincing argument **6** : an instance of disease or injury; *also* : PATIENT **7** : INSTANCE, EXAMPLE — **in case** : as a precaution — **in case of** : in the event of

²**case** *n* [ME *cas*, fr. AF *case, chase*, fr. L *capsa*] **1** : a box or container for holding something; *also* : a box with its contents **2** : an outer covering **3** : a divided tray for holding printing type **4** : CASING 2

³**case** *vb* **cased; cas·ing** **1** : to enclose in or cover with a case **2** : to inspect esp. with intent to rob

ca·sein \ˈkā-ˌsēn, kā-ˈ\ *n* : any of several phosphorus-containing proteins occurring in or produced from milk

case·ment \ˈkās-mənt\ *n* : a window that opens like a door

case·work \-ˌwərk\ *n* : social work that involves the individual person or family — **case·work·er** *n*

¹**cash** \ˈkash\ *n* [MF or It; MF *casse* money box, fr. It *cassa*, fr. L *capsa* chest, case] **1** : ready money **2** : money or its equivalent paid at the time of purchase or delivery

²**cash** *vb* : to pay or obtain cash for

ca·shew \ˈka-shü, kə-ˈshü\ *n* : an edible

kidney-shaped nut of a tropical American tree related to the sumacs; *also* : the tree

¹ca·shier \ka-ˈshir\ *vb* : to dismiss from service; *esp* : to dismiss in disgrace

²cash·ier \ka-ˈshir\ *n* **1** : a bank official responsible for moneys received and paid out **2** : a person who receives and records payments

cashier's check *n* : a check drawn by a bank upon its own funds and signed by its cashier

cash in *vb* **1** : to convert into cash ⟨*cash in* bonds⟩ **2** : to settle accounts and withdraw from a gambling game or business deal **3** : to obtain financial profit or advantage

cash·less \ˈkash-ləs\ *adj* : relying on monetary transactions that use electronic means rather than cash

cash·mere \ˈkazh-ˌmir, ˈkash-\ *n* : fine wool from the undercoat of an Indian goat (**cashmere goat**) or a yarn spun of this; *also* : a soft twilled fabric orig. woven from this yarn

cash out *vb* : to convert noncash assets into cash

cash register *n* : a business machine that usu. has a money drawer, indicates each sale, and records the money received

cash–strapped \ˈkash-ˌstrapt\ *adj* : lacking sufficient money

cas·ing \ˈkā-siŋ\ *n* **1** : something that encases **2** : the frame of a door or window

ca·si·no \kə-ˈsē-nō\ *n, pl* **-nos** [It, fr. *casa* house] **1** : a building or room for social amusements; *esp* : one used for gambling **2** *also* **cas·si·no** : a card game in which players win cards by matching those on the table

cask \ˈkask\ *n* : a barrel-shaped container usu. for liquids; *also* : the quantity held by such a container

cas·ket \ˈkas-kət\ *n* **1** : a small box (as for jewels) **2** : COFFIN

casque \ˈkask\ *n* : HELMET

cas·sa·va \kə-ˈsä-və\ *n* : any of several tropical spurges with rootstocks yielding a nutritious starch from which tapioca is prepared; *also* : the rootstock or this starch

cas·se·role \ˈkas-ə-ˌrōl\ *n* **1** : a dish in which food may be baked and served **2** : food cooked and served in a casserole

cas·sette *also* **ca·sette** \kə-ˈset\ *n* **1** : a lightproof container for photographic plates or film **2** : a plastic case containing magnetic tape

cas·sia \ˈka-shə\ *n* **1** : a dried coarse cinnamon bark **2** : any of a genus of leguminous herbs, shrubs, and trees of warm regions including several which yield senna

cas·sit·er·ite \kə-ˈsi-tə-ˌrīt\ *n* : a dark mineral that is the chief tin ore

cas·sock \ˈka-sək\ *n* : an ankle-length garment worn esp. by Roman Catholic and Anglican clergy

cas·so·wary \ˈka-sə-ˌwer-ē\ *n, pl* **-war·ies** : any of a genus of large flightless birds closely related to the emu

¹cast \ˈkast\ *vb* **cast; cast·ing** **1** : THROW,

FLING **2** : DIRECT ⟨~ a glance⟩ **3** : to deposit (a ballot) formally **4** : to throw off, out, or away : DISCARD, SHED **5** : COMPUTE; *esp* : to add up **6** : to assign the parts of (a play) to actors; *also* : to assign to a role or part **7** : to shape (a substance) by pouring in liquid or plastic form into a mold and letting harden without pressure **8** : to make (as a knot or stitch) by looping or catching up

²cast *n* **1** : THROW, FLING **2** : a throw of dice **3** : the set of actors in a dramatic production **4** : something formed in or as if in a mold; *also* : a rigid surgical casing (as for protecting and supporting a fractured bone) **5** : TINGE, HUE **6** : APPEARANCE, LOOK ⟨features of delicate ~⟩ **7** : something thrown out or off, shed, or expelled ⟨worm ~s⟩

cas·ta·net \ˌkas-tə-ˈnet\ *n* [Sp *castañeta*, fr. *castaña* chestnut, fr. L *castanea*] : a rhythm instrument consisting of two small wooden, ivory, or plastic shells held in the hand and clicked together

cast·away \ˈkas-tə-ˌwā\ *adj* **1** : thrown away : REJECTED **2** : cast adrift or ashore as a survivor of a shipwreck — **castaway** *n*

caste \ˈkast\ *n* [Pg *casta*, lit., race, lineage, fr. fem. of *casto* pure, chaste, fr. L *castus*] **1** : one of the hereditary social classes in Hinduism **2** : a division of a society based on wealth, inherited rank, or occupation **3** : social position : PRESTIGE **4** : a system of rigid social stratification

cas·tel·lat·ed \ˈkas-tə-ˌlā-təd\ *adj* : having battlements like a castle

cast·er \ˈkas-tər\ *n* **1** *or* **cas·tor** : a small container to hold salt or pepper at the table **2** : a small wheel that turns freely and is used to support and move furniture, trucks, and equipment

cas·ti·gate \ˈkas-tə-ˌgāt\ *vb* **-gat·ed; -gat·ing** : to punish or criticize severely — **cas·ti·ga·tion** \ˌkas-tə-ˈgā-shən\ *n* — **cas·ti·ga·tor** \ˈkas-tə-ˌgā-tər\ *n*

cast·ing \ˈkas-tiŋ\ *n* **1** : CAST 7 **2** : something cast in a mold

casting vote *n* : a deciding vote cast by a presiding officer to break a tie

cast iron *n* : a hard brittle alloy of iron, carbon, and silicon cast in a mold

cas·tle \ˈka-səl\ *n* **1** : a large fortified building or set of buildings **2** : a large or imposing house **3** : ³ROOK

castle in the air : an impracticable project

cast–off \ˈkast-ˌof\ *adj* : thrown away or aside — **cast·off** *n*

cas·tor oil \ˈkas-tər-\ *n* : a thick yellowish oil extracted from the poisonous seeds of an herb (**castor–oil plant**) and used as a lubricant and purgative

cas·trate \ˈkas-ˌtrāt\ *vb* **cas·trat·ed; cas·trat·ing** : to deprive of sex glands and esp. testes — **cas·tra·tion** \kas-ˈtrā-shən\ *n* — **cas·tra·tor** \-ər\ *n*

ca·su·al \ˈka-zhə-wəl\ *adj* **1** : resulting from or occurring by chance **2** : OCCASIONAL, INCIDENTAL ⟨~ employment⟩ **3** : OFFHAND, NONCHALANT ⟨a ~ approach to cooking⟩ **4** : designed for informal use ⟨∼ clothing⟩ — **ca·su·al·ly** *adv* — **ca·su·al·ness** *n*

ca·su·al·ty \'ka-zhəl-tē, 'ka-zhə-wəl-\ *n, pl* **-ties 1** : serious or fatal accident **2** : a military person lost through death, injury, sickness, or capture or through being missing in action **3** : a person or thing injured, lost, or destroyed

ca·su·ist·ry \'ka-zhə-wə-strē\ *n, pl* **-ries** : specious argument : RATIONALIZATION — **ca·su·ist** \-wist\ *n* — **ca·su·is·tic** \ˌka-zhə-'wis-tik\ *or* **ca·su·is·ti·cal** \-ti-kəl\ *adj*

ca·sus bel·li \ˌkä-səs-'be-ˌlē, ˌkä-səs-'be-ˌlī\ *n, pl* **ca·sus belli** \ˌkä-ˌsüs-, ˌkä-\ [NL, occasion of war] : a cause or pretext for a declaration of war

¹cat \'kat\ *n* **1** : a carnivorous mammal long domesticated as a pet and for catching rats and mice **2** : any of a family of animals (as the lion, lynx, or leopard) including the domestic cat **3** : a malicious woman **4** : GUY

²cat *abbr* catalog

ca·tab·o·lism \kə-'ta-bə-ˌli-zəm\ *n* : destructive metabolism involving the release of energy and resulting in the breakdown of complex materials — **cat·a·bol·ic** \ˌka-tə-'bä-lik\ *adj*

cat·a·clysm \'ka-tə-ˌkli-zəm\ *n* : a violent change or upheaval — **cat·a·clys·mal** \ˌka-tə-'kliz-məl\ *or* **cat·a·clys·mic** \-'kliz-mik\ *adj*

cat·a·comb \'ka-tə-ˌkōm\ *n* : an underground burial place with galleries and recesses for tombs

cat·a·falque \'ka-tə-ˌfalk, -ˌfolk, -ˌfòk\ *n* : an ornamental structure sometimes used in solemn funerals to hold the body

cat·a·lep·sy \'ka-tə-ˌlep-sē\ *n, pl* **-sies** : a trancelike state characterized esp. by loss of voluntary motion — **cat·a·lep·tic** \ˌka-tə-'lep-tik\ *adj or n*

¹cat·a·log *or* **cat·a·logue** \'ka-tə-ˌlȯg\ *n* **1** : LIST, REGISTER **2** : a systematic list of items with descriptive details; *also* : a book containing such a list

²catalog *or* **catalogue** *vb* **-loged** *or* **-logued; -log·ing** *or* **-logu·ing 1** : to make a catalog of **2** : to enter in a catalog — **cat·a·log·er** *or* **cat·a·logu·er** *n*

ca·tal·pa \kə-'tal-pə\ *n* : any of a genus of broad-leaved trees with showy flowers and long slim pods

ca·tal·y·sis \kə-'ta-lə-səs\ *n, pl* **-y·ses** \-ˌsēz\ : a change and esp. increase in the rate of a chemical reaction brought about by a substance (**cat·a·lyst** \'ka-tə-list\) that is itself unchanged at the end of the reaction — **cat·a·lyt·ic** \ˌka-tə-'li-tik\ *adj* — **cat·a·lyt·i·cal·ly** \-ti-k(ə-)lē\ *adv*

catalytic converter *n* : an automobile exhaust-system component in which a catalyst changes harmful gases into mostly harmless products

cat·a·lyze \'ka-tə-ˌlīz\ *vb* **-lyzed; -lyz·ing** : to bring about the catalysis of (a chemical reaction)

cat·a·ma·ran \ˌka-tə-mə-'ran\ *n* [Tamil (a language of southern India) *kaṭṭumaram*,

fr. *kaṭṭu* to tie + *maram* tree] : a boat with twin hulls

cat·a·mount \'ka-tə-ˌmaùnt\ *n* : COUGAR; *also* : LYNX

cat·a·pult \'ka-tə-ˌpəlt, -ˌpùlt\ *n* **1** : an ancient military machine for hurling missiles **2** : a device for launching an airplane (as from an aircraft carrier) — **catapult** *vb*

cat·a·ract \'ka-tə-ˌrakt\ *n* **1** : a cloudiness of the lens of the eye obstructing vision **2** : a large waterfall; *also* : steep rapids in a river

ca·tarrh \kə-'tär\ *n* : inflammation of a mucous membrane esp. of the nose and throat — **ca·tarrh·al** \-əl\ *adj*

ca·tas·tro·phe \kə-'tas-trə-(ˌ)fē\ *n* [Gk *katastrophē*, fr. *katastrephein* to overturn, fr. *kata-* down + *strephein* to turn] **1** : a great disaster or misfortune **2** : utter failure — **cat·a·stroph·ic** \ˌka-tə-'strä-fik\ *adj* — **cat·a·stroph·i·cal·ly** \-fi-k(ə-)lē\ *adv*

cat·a·ton·ic \ˌka-tə-'tä-nik\ *adj* : of, relating to, or marked by schizophrenia characterized esp. by stupor, negativism, rigidity, purposeless excitement, and bizarre posturing — **catatonic** *n*

cat·bird \'kat-ˌbərd\ *n* : an American songbird with a catlike mewing call

cat·boat \'kat-ˌbōt\ *n* : a single-masted sailboat with a single large sail extended by a long boom

cat·call \-ˌkȯl\ *n* : a loud cry made esp. to express disapproval — **catcall** *vb*

¹catch \'kach, 'kech\ *vb* **caught** \'kȯt\; **catch·ing** [ME *cacchen*, fr. AF *cacher*, *chacher*, *chacer* to hunt, ultim. fr. L *captare* to chase] **1** : to capture esp. after pursuit **2** : TRAP **3** : to discover unexpectedly ⟨*caught* in the act⟩ **4** : to become suddenly aware of **5** : to take hold of : SNATCH ⟨∼ at a straw⟩ **6** : INTERCEPT **7** : to get entangled **8** : to become affected with or by ⟨∼ fire⟩ ⟨∼ cold⟩ **9** : to seize and hold firmly; *also* : FASTEN **10** : OVERTAKE **11** : to be in time for ⟨∼ a train⟩ **12** : to take in and retain **13** : to look at or listen to ⟨∼ a TV show⟩

²catch *n* **1** : something caught : the act of catching; *also* : a game consisting of throwing and catching a ball **3** : something that catches or checks or holds immovable ⟨a door ∼⟩ **4** : one worth catching esp. as a mate **5** : FRAGMENT, SNATCH **6** : a concealed difficulty or complication

catch·all \'kach-ˌȯl, 'kech-\ *n* : something to hold a variety of odds and ends

catch–as–catch–can *adj* : using any means available

catch·er \'kach-ər, 'ke-\ *n* : one that catches; *esp* : a player positioned behind home plate in baseball

catch·ing *adj* **1** : INFECTIOUS, CONTAGIOUS **2** : ALLURING, CATCHY

catch·ment \'kach-mənt, 'kech-\ *n* **1** : something that catches water **2** : the action of catching water

catch on *vb* **1** : UNDERSTAND **2** : to become popular

catch·pen·ny \'kach-ˌpe-nē, 'kech-\ *adj* : using sensationalism or cheapness for appeal ⟨a ~ newspaper⟩

catch-phrase \-ˌfrāz\ *n* : a word or expression frequently used to represent or characterize a person, group, idea, or point of view

catch–22 \-ˌtwen-tē-'tü\ *n, pl* **catch–22's** *or* **catch–22s** *often cap C* [fr. *Catch-22*, a paradoxical rule found in the novel *Catch-22* (1961) by Joseph Heller] **a** : a problematic situation for which the only solution is denied by a circumstance inherent in the problem or by a rule; *also* : the circumstance or rule that denies a solution

catchup *var of* KETCHUP

catch up *vb* : to travel or work fast enough to overtake or complete

catch·word \'kach-ˌwərd, 'kech-\ *n* **1** : GUIDE WORD **2** : CATCHPHRASE

catchy \'ka-chē, 'ke-\ *adj* **catch·i·er; -est** **1** : likely to catch the interest or attention **2** : TRICKY ⟨a ~ question⟩

cat·e·chism \'ka-tə-ˌki-zəm\ *n* : a summary or test (as of religious doctrine) usu. in the form of questions and answers — **cat·e·chist** \-ˌkist\ *n* — **cat·e·chize** \-ˌkīz\ *vb*

cat·e·chu·men \ˌka-tə-'kyü-mən\ *n* : a religious convert receiving training before baptism

cat·e·gor·i·cal \ˌka-tə-'gȯr-i-kəl\ *adj* **1** : ABSOLUTE, UNQUALIFIED ⟨a ~ denial⟩ **2** : of, relating to, or constituting a category — **cat·e·gor·i·cal·ly** \-i-k(ə-)lē\ *adv*

cat·e·go·rise *Brit var of* CATEGORIZE

cat·e·go·rize \'ka-ti-gə-ˌrīz\ *vb* **-rized; -riz·ing** : to put into a category : CLASSIFY — **cat·e·go·ri·za·tion** \ˌka-ti-gə-rə-'zā-shən\ *n*

cat·e·go·ry \'ka-tə-ˌgȯr-ē\ *n, pl* **-ries** : a division used in classification; *also* : CLASS, GROUP, KIND

ca·ter \'kā-tər\ *vb* [obs. *cater* buyer of provisions, fr. ME *catour*, short for *acatour*, fr. AF, fr. *acater, achater* to buy] **1** : to provide a supply of food **2** : to supply what is wanted — **ca·ter·er** *n*

catercorner *or* **cater–cornered** *var of* KITTY-CORNER

cat·er·pil·lar \'ka-tər-ˌpi-lər\ *n* [ME *catyrpel*, fr. OF *catepelose*, lit., hairy cat] : a wormlike often hairy insect larva esp. of a butterfly or moth

cat·er·waul \'ka-tər-ˌwȯl\ *vb* : to make a harsh cry — **caterwaul** *n*

cat·fish \'kat-ˌfish\ *n* : any of an order of chiefly freshwater stout-bodied fishes with slender tactile processes around the mouth

cat·gut \-ˌgət\ *n* : a tough cord made usu. from sheep intestines

ca·thar·sis \kə-'thär-səs\ *n, pl* **ca·thar·ses** \-ˌsēz\ **1** : an act of purging or purification **2** : elimination of a complex by bringing it to consciousness and affording it expression

¹ca·thar·tic \kə-'thär-tik\ *adj* : of, relating to, or producing catharsis

²cathartic *n* : PURGATIVE

ca·the·dral \kə-'thē-drəl\ *n* : the principal church of a diocese

cath·e·ter \'ka-thə-tər\ *n* : a tube for insertion into a bodily passage or cavity usu. for injecting or drawing off material or for keeping a passage open

cath·e·ter·i·za·tion \ˌka-thə-tə-rə-'zā-shən\ *n* : the use of or introduction of a catheter — **cath·e·ter·ize** \'ka-thə-tə-ˌrīz\ *vb*

cath·ode \'ka-ˌthōd\ *n* **1** : the negative electrode of an electrolytic cell **2** : the positive terminal of a battery **3** : the electron-emitting electrode of an electron tube — **cath·od·al** \ˌka-ˌthō-d²l\ *adj* — **ca·thod·ic** \ka-'thä-dik\ *adj*

cathode–ray tube *n* : a vacuum tube in which a beam of electrons is projected on a phosphor-coated screen to produce a luminous spot

cath·o·lic \'kath-lik, 'ka-thə-\ *adj* [ME *catholik* relating to the church universal, ultim. fr. Gk *katholikos* universal, general, fr. *katholou* in general] **1** *cap* : of or relating to Catholics and esp. Roman Catholics **2** : GENERAL, UNIVERSAL

Cath·o·lic \'kath-lik, 'ka-thə-\ *n* : a member of a church claiming historical continuity from the ancient undivided Christian church; *esp* : a member of the Roman Catholic Church — **Ca·thol·i·cism** \kə-'thä-lə-ˌsi-zəm\ *n*

cath·o·lic·i·ty \ˌka-thə-'li-sə-tē\ *n, pl* **-ties** **1** *cap* : the character of being in conformity with a Catholic church **2** : liberality of sentiments or views **3** : comprehensive range

cat·ion \'kat-ˌī-ən\ *n* : the ion in an electrolyte that migrates to the cathode; *also* : a positively charged ion

cat·kin \'kat-kən\ *n* : a long flower cluster (as of a willow) bearing crowded scaly and prominent bracts

cat·like \-ˌlīk\ *adj* : resembling a cat or its behavior; *esp* : STEALTHY

cat·nap \-ˌnap\ *n* : a very short light nap — **catnap** *vb*

cat·nip \-ˌnip\ *n* : an aromatic mint that is esp. attractive to cats

cat–o'–nine–tails \ˌka-tə-'nīn-ˌtālz\ *n, pl* **cat–o'–nine–tails** : a whip made of usu. nine knotted cords fastened to a handle

CAT scan \'kat-\ *n* [*computerized axial tomography*] : an image made by computed tomography

CAT scanner *n* : a medical instrument consisting of integrated X-ray and computing equipment that is used to make CAT scans

cat's cradle *n* : a game played with a string looped on the fingers in such a way as to resemble a small cradle

cat's-eye \'kats-ˌī\ *n, pl* **cat's-eyes** : any of various iridescent gems

cat's-paw \-ˌpȯ\ *n, pl* **cat's-paws** : a person used by another as a tool

cat·suit \'kat-ˌsüt\ *n* : a close-fitting one-piece garment that covers the torso and the legs

catsup *var of* KETCHUP

cat·tail \'kat-ˌtāl\ *n* : any of a genus of tall

113   cattle • cavitation

reedlike marsh plants with furry brown spikes of tiny flowers

cat·tle \'ka-t³l\ *n pl* : LIVESTOCK; *esp* : domestic bovines (as cows, bulls, or calves) — **cat·tle·man** \-mən, -ˌman\ *n*

cat·ty \'ka-tē\ *adj* **cat·ti·er; -est** : slyly spiteful ⟨~ comments⟩ — **cat·ti·ly** \'ka-tə-lē\ *adv* — **cat·ti·ness** *n*

catty–corner *or* **catty–cornered** *var of* KITTY-CORNER

CATV *abbr* community antenna television

cat·walk \'kat-ˌwȯk\ *n* : a narrow walk (as along a bridge)

Cau·ca·sian \kȯ-'kā-zhən\ *adj* : of or relating to the white race of humankind — **Caucasian** *n* — **Cau·ca·soid** \'kȯ-kə-ˌsȯid\ *adj or n*

cau·cus \'kȯ-kəs\ *n* : a meeting of a group of persons belonging to the same political party or faction usu. to decide upon policies and candidates — **caucus** *vb*

cau·dal \'kȯ-d³l\ *adj* : of, relating to, or located near the tail or the hind end of the body — **cau·dal·ly** *adv*

cau·di·llo \kau̇-'thē-(ˌ)yō, -'thēl-\ *n, pl* **-llos** : a Spanish or Latin-American military dictator

caught \'kȯt\ *past and past part of* CATCH

caul \'kȯl\ *n* : the inner fetal membrane of higher vertebrates esp. when covering the head at birth

caul·dron \'kȯl-drən\ *n* : a large kettle

cau·li·flow·er \'kȯ-li-ˌflau̇-(ə)r\ *n* [It *cavolfiore*, fr. *cavolo* cabbage + *fiore* flower] : a garden plant closely related to cabbage and grown for its compact edible head of undeveloped flowers; *also* : this head used as a vegetable

cauliflower ear *n* : an ear deformed from injury and excessive growth of scar tissue

¹**caulk** *or* **calk** \'kȯk\ *vb* [ME, fr. AF *cauker, calcher* to trample, fr. L *calcare*, fr. *calx* heel] : to stop up and make tight against leakage (as a boat or its seams) — **caulk·er** *n*

²**caulk** *or* **calk** *also* **caulk·ing** *or* **calk·ing** *n* : material used to caulk

caus·al \'kȯ-zəl\ *adj* 1 : expressing or indicating cause 2 : relating to or acting as a cause — **cau·sal·i·ty** \kȯ-'za-lə-tē\ *n* — **caus·al·ly** *adv*

cau·sa·tion \kȯ-'zā-shən\ *n* 1 : the act or process of causing 2 : the means by which an effect is produced

¹**cause** \'kȯz\ *n* 1 : REASON, MOTIVE 2 : something that brings about a result; *esp* : a person or thing that is the agent of bringing something about 3 : a suit or action in court : CASE 4 : a question or matter to be decided 5 : a principle or movement earnestly supported — **cause·less** *adj*

²**cause** *vb* **caused; caus·ing** : to be the cause or occasion of — **caus·a·tive** \'kȯ-zə-tiv\ *adj* — **caus·er** *n*

cause cé·lè·bre \ˌkȯz-sā-'lebr³, ˌkȯz-\ *n, pl* **causes célèbres** *same*\ [F, lit., celebrated case] 1 : a legal case that excites widespread interest 2 : a notorious person, thing, incident, or episode

cau·se·rie \ˌkȯz-'rē, ˌkȯ-zə-\ *n* [F] 1 : an informal conversation : CHAT 2 : a short informal essay

cause·way \'kȯz-ˌwā\ *n* : a raised way or road across wet ground or water

¹**caus·tic** \'kȯ-stik\ *adj* 1 : CORROSIVE 2 : SHARP, INCISIVE ⟨~ wit⟩

²**caustic** *n* : a substance that burns or destroys organic tissue by chemical action 2 : SODIUM HYDROXIDE

cau·ter·ize \'kȯ-tə-ˌrīz\ *vb* **-ized; -iz·ing** : to burn or sear usu. to prevent infection or bleeding — **cau·ter·i·za·tion** \ˌkȯ-tə-rə-'zā-shən\ *n*

¹**cau·tion** \'kȯ-shən\ *n* 1 : ADMONITION, WARNING 2 : prudent forethought to minimize risk 3 : one that astonishes — **cau·tion·ary** \-shə-ˌner-ē\ *adj*

²**caution** *vb* : to advise caution to

cau·tious \'kȯ-shəs\ *adj* : marked by or given to caution : CAREFUL — **cau·tious·ly** *adv* — **cau·tious·ness** *n*

cav *abbr* 1 cavalry 2 cavity

cav·al·cade \ˌka-vəl-'kād\ *n* 1 : a procession of riders or carriages; *also* : a procession of vehicles 2 : a dramatic sequence or procession ⟨a ~ of films⟩

¹**cav·a·lier** \ˌka-və-'lir\ *n* [MF, fr. It *cavaliere*, fr. Old Occitan *cavalier*, fr. LL *caballarius* horseman, fr. L *caballus* horse] 1 : a mounted soldier : KNIGHT 2 *cap* : an adherent of Charles I of England 3 : GALLANT

²**cavalier** *adj* 1 : DEBONAIR 2 : DISDAINFUL, HAUGHTY ⟨a ~ attitude toward money⟩ — **cav·a·lier·ly** *adv*

cav·al·ry \'ka-vəl-rē\ *n, pl* **-ries** : troops mounted on horseback or moving in motor vehicles — **cav·al·ry·man** \-mən, -ˌman\ *n*

cave \'kāv\ *n* : a natural underground chamber open to the surface

²**cave** *vb* **caved; cav·ing** 1 : to collapse or cause to collapse 2 : to cease to resist : SUBMIT — usu. used with *in*

ca·ve·at \'ka-vē-ˌät, -ˌat; 'kä-vē-ˌät\ *n* [L, let him beware] : WARNING

caveat emp·tor \-'emp-tər, -ˌtȯr\ *n* [NL, let the buyer beware] : a principle in commerce: without a warranty the buyer takes a risk

cave–in \'kā-ˌvin\ *n* 1 : the action of caving in 2 : a place where earth has caved in

cave·man \'kāv-ˌman\ *n* 1 : a cave dweller esp. of the Stone Age 2 : a man who acts in a rough or crude manner

cav·ern \'ka-vərn\ *n* : CAVE; *esp* : one of large or unknown size — **cav·ern·ous** *adj* — **cav·ern·ous·ly** *adv*

cav·i·ar *also* **cav·i·are** \'ka-vē-ˌär, 'kä-\ *n* : the salted roe of a large fish (as sturgeon) used as an appetizer

cav·il \'ka-vəl\ *vb* **-iled** *or* **-illed; -il·ing** *or* **-il·ling** : to make frivolous objections or raise trivial objections to — **cavil** *n* — **cav·il·er** *or* **cav·il·ler** *n*

cav·ing \'kā-viŋ\ *n* : the sport of exploring caves : SPELUNKING

cav·i·ta·tion \ˌka-və-'tā-shən\ *n* : the formation of partial vacuums in a liquid by a swiftly moving solid body (as a propeller) or by high-intensity sound waves

cav·i·ty \'ka-və-tē\ *n, pl* **-ties** **1** : an unfilled space within a mass : a hollow place **2** : an area of decay in a tooth

ca·vort \kə-'vȯrt\ *vb* : PRANCE, CAPER

ca·vy \'kā-vē\ *n, pl* **cavies** : GUINEA PIG 1

caw \'kȯ\ *vb* : to utter the harsh call of the crow or a similar cry — **caw** *n*

cay \'kē, 'kā\ *n* : ²KEY

cay·enne pepper \kī-'en-, kā-\ *n* : a condiment consisting of ground dried fruits or seeds of a hot pepper

cayman *var of* CAIMAN

Ca·yu·ga \kā-'ü-gə, kī-\ *n, pl* **Cayuga** or **Cayugas** : a member of an American Indian people of New York

Cay·use \'kī-,yüs, kī-'\ *n* **1** *pl* **Cayuse** or **Cayuses** : a member of an American Indian people of Oregon and Washington **2** *pl* **cayuses**, *not cap*, *West* : a native range horse

Cb *symbol* columbium

CB \'sē-'bē\ *n* : CITIZENS BAND; *also* : the radio set used for citizens-band communications

CBC *abbr* Canadian Broadcasting Corporation

CBD *abbr* cash before delivery

CBS *abbr* Columbia Broadcasting System

CBW *abbr* chemical and biological warfare

cc *abbr* cubic centimeter

CC *abbr* **1** carbon copy **2** community college **3** country club

CCD \,sē-,sē-'dē\ *n* : CHARGE-COUPLED DEVICE

CCTV *abbr* closed-circuit television

CCU *abbr* **1** cardiac care unit **2** coronary care unit **3** critical care unit

ccw *abbr* counterclockwise

cd *abbr* cord

Cd *symbol* cadmium

¹CD \'sē-'dē\ *n* : CERTIFICATE OF DEPOSIT

²CD *n* : a small optical disk usu. containing recorded music or computer data; *also* : the content of a CD

³CD *abbr* Civil Defense

CDR *abbr* commander

CD–ROM \,sē-,dē-'räm\ *n* : a CD containing computer data that cannot be altered

CDT *abbr* central daylight (saving) time

Ce *symbol* cerium

CE *abbr* **1** chemical engineer **2** civil engineer **3** Corps of Engineers

cease \'sēs\ *vb* **ceased; ceas·ing** : to come or bring to an end : STOP

cease–fire \'sēs-'fī(-ə)r\ *n* : a suspension of active hostilities

cease·less \'sēs-ləs\ *adj* : being without pause or stop : CONTINUOUS — **cease·less·ly** *adv* — **cease·less·ness** *n*

ce·cum *also* **cae·cum** \'sē-kəm\ *n, pl* **ce·ca** \-kə\ : the blind pouch at the beginning of the large intestine into which the small intestine opens — **ce·cal** *also* **cae·cal** \-kəl\ *adj*

ce·dar \'sē-dər\ *n* : any of numerous coniferous trees (as a juniper) noted for their fragrant durable wood; *also* : this wood

cede \'sēd\ *vb* **ced·ed; ced·ing** **1** : to

yield or give up esp. by treaty **2** : ASSIGN, TRANSFER — **ced·er** *n*

ce·di \'sā-dē\ *n* — see MONEY table

ce·dil·la \si-'dil-lə\ *n* : a mark placed under the letter *c* (as ç) to show that the *c* is to be pronounced like *s*

ceil·ing \'sē-liŋ\ *n* **1** : the overhead inside lining of a room **2** : the height above the ground of the base of the lowest layer of clouds when over half of the sky is obscured **3** : the greatest height at which an airplane can operate efficiently **4** : a prescribed upper limit ⟨price ∼⟩

cel·an·dine \'se-lən-,dīn, -,dēn\ *n* : a yellow-flowered herb related to the poppies

cel·e·brant \'se-lə-brənt\ *n* : one who celebrates; *esp* : a priest officiating at the Eucharist

cel·e·brate \'se-lə-,brāt\ *vb* **-brat·ed; -brat·ing** **1** : to perform (as a sacrament) with appropriate rites **2** : to honor (as a holiday) by solemn ceremonies or by refraining from ordinary business **3** : to observe a notable occasion with festivities **4** : EXTOL — **cel·e·bra·tion** \,se-lə-'brā-shən\ *n* — **cel·e·bra·tor** \'se-lə-brā-tər\ *n* — **cel·e·bra·to·ry** \-brə-,tȯr-ē, ,se-lə-'brā-tə-rē\ *adj*

celebrated *adj* : widely known and often referred to ⟨a ∼ author⟩ ♦ **Synonyms** DISTINGUISHED, RENOWNED, NOTED, FAMOUS, ILLUSTRIOUS, NOTORIOUS

ce·leb·ri·ty \sə-'le-brə-tē\ *n, pl* **-ties** **1** : the state of being celebrated : RENOWN **2** : a celebrated person

ce·ler·i·ty \sə-'ler-ə-tē\ *n* : SPEED, RAPIDITY

cel·ery \'se-lə-rē\ *n, pl* **-er·ies** : a European herb related to the carrot and widely grown for the crisp edible stems of its leaves

celery cabbage *n* : CHINESE CABBAGE 2

ce·les·ta \sə-'les-tə\ *or* **ce·leste** \sə-'lest\ *n* : a keyboard instrument with hammers that strike steel plates

ce·les·tial \sə-'les-chəl\ *adj* **1** : HEAVENLY, DIVINE **2** : of or relating to the sky ⟨∼ bodies⟩ — **ce·les·tial·ly** *adv*

celestial navigation *n* : navigation by observation of the positions of stars

celestial sphere *n* : an imaginary sphere of infinite radius against which the celestial bodies appear to be projected

cel·i·ba·cy \'se-lə-bə-sē\ *n* **1** : the state of being unmarried; *esp* : abstention by vow from marriage **2** : abstention from sexual intercourse

cel·i·bate \'se-lə-bət\ *n* : one who lives in celibacy — **celibate** *adj*

cell \'sel\ *n* **1** : a small room (as in a convent or prison) usu. for one person; *also* : a small compartment, cavity, or bounded space **2** : a tiny mass of protoplasm that usu. contains a nucleus, is enclosed by a membrane, and forms the smallest structural unit of living matter capable of functioning independently **3** : a container holding an electrolyte either for generating electricity or for use in electrolysis **4** : a single unit in a device for converting radiant energy into electrical energy — **celled** \'seld\ adj

cel·lar \'se-lər\ n 1 : BASEMENT 1 2 : the lowest place in the standings (as in an athletic league) 3 : a stock of wines

cel·lar·ette or **cel·lar·et** \se-lə-'ret\ n : a case or cabinet for a few bottles of wine or liquor

cell body n : the nucleus-containing central part of a neuron exclusive of its processes

cel·lo \'che-lō\ n, pl **cellos** : a bass member of the violin family tuned an octave below the viola — **cel·list** \-list\ n

cel·lo·phane \'se-lə-ˌfān\ n : a thin transparent material made from cellulose and used as a wrapping

cell phone n : a portable cordless telephone for use in a cellular system

cel·lu·lar \'sel-yə-lər\ adj 1 : of, relating to, or consisting of cells (~ proteins) 2 : of, relating to, or being a radiotelephone system in which a geographical area is divided into small sections each served by a transmitter of limited range

cel·lu·lite \'sel-yə-ˌlīt\ n : deposits of lumpy fat within connective tissue (as in the thighs, hips, and buttocks)

cel·lu·lose \'sel-yə-ˌlōs\ n : a complex carbohydrate of the cell walls of plants used esp. in making paper or rayon — **cel·lu·los·ic** \ˌsel-yə-'lō-sik\ adj or n

Cel·si·us \'sel-sē-əs\ adj : relating to or having a scale for measuring temperature on which the interval between the triple point and the boiling point of water is divided into 99.99 degrees with 0.01° being the triple point and 100.00° the boiling point; also : CENTIGRADE

Celt \'kelt, 'selt\ n : a member of any of a group of peoples (as the Irish or Welsh) of western Europe — **Celt·ic** adj

cem·ba·lo \'chem-bə-ˌlō\ n, pl **-ba·li** \-ˌlē\ or **-balos** [It] : HARPSICHORD

¹ce·ment \si-'ment\ n 1 : CONCRETE; also : a powder that is produced from a burned mixture chiefly of clay and limestone and that is used in mortar and concrete 2 : a binding element or agency 3 : CEMENTUM; also : a substance for filling cavities in teeth

²cement vb 1 : to unite by or as if by cement 2 : to cover with concrete — **cement·er** n

ce·men·tum \si-'men-təm\ n : a specialized external bony layer covering the dentin of the part of a tooth normally within the gum

cem·e·tery \'se-mə-ˌter-ē\ n, pl **-ter·ies** [ME cimitery, fr. AF cimiterie, fr. LL coemeterium, fr. Gk koimētērion sleeping chamber, burial place, fr. koiman to put to sleep] : a burial ground : GRAVEYARD

cen·o·bite \'se-nə-ˌbīt\ n : a member of a religious group living together in a monastic community — **cen·o·bit·ic** \ˌse-nə-'bi-tik\ adj

ceno·taph \'se-nə-ˌtaf\ n [F cénotaphe, fr. L cenotaphium, fr. Gk kenotaphion, fr. kenos empty + taphos tomb] : a tomb or a monument erected in honor of a person whose body is elsewhere

Ce·no·zo·ic \ˌsē-nə-'zō-ik, ˌse-\ adj : of, relating to, or being the era of geologic history that extends from about 65 million years ago to the present — **Cenozoic** n

cen·ser \'sen-sər\ n : a vessel for burning incense (as in a religious ritual)

¹cen·sor \'sen-sər\ n 1 : a person who inspects printed matter or motion pictures with power to suppress anything objectionable 2 : one of two early Roman magistrates whose duties included taking the census — **cen·so·ri·al** \sen-'sȯr-ē-əl\ adj

²censor vb : to subject to censorship

cen·so·ri·ous \sen-'sȯr-ē-əs\ adj : marked by or given to censure : CRITICAL — **cen·so·ri·ous·ly** adv — **cen·so·ri·ous·ness** n

cen·sor·ship \'sen-sər-ˌship\ n 1 : the action of a censor esp. in stopping the transmission or publication of matter considered objectionable 2 : the office of a Roman censor

¹cen·sure \'sen-chər\ n 1 : the act of blaming or condemning sternly 2 : an official reprimand

²censure vb **cen·sured**; **cen·sur·ing** : to find fault with and criticize as blameworthy — **cen·sur·able** adj — **cen·sur·er** n

cen·sus \'sen-səs\ n 1 : a periodic governmental count of population 2 : COUNT, TALLY — **census** vb

¹cent \'sent\ n [F, hundred, fr. L centum] 1 — see birr, dollar, euro, leone, lilangeni, nakfa, rand, rupee, shilling at MONEY table 2 : a coin, token, or note representing one cent 3 : a monetary unit formerly used in Suriname (¹⁄₁₀₀ gulden), Malta (¹⁄₁₀₀ lira), and Cyprus (¹⁄₁₀₀ pound)

²cent abbr 1 centigrade 2 central 3 century

cen·tas \'sen-ˌtäs\ n, pl **cen·tai** \-ˌtī\ or **cen·tu** \-ˌtü\ : a monetary unit equal to ¹⁄₁₀₀ litas formerly used in Lithuania

cen·taur \'sen-ˌtȯr\ n : any of a race of creatures in Greek mythology half man and half horse

¹cen·ta·vo \sen-'tä-(ˌ)vō\ n, pl **-vos** 1 — see boliviano, cordoba, lempira, peso, quetzal at MONEY table 2 : a monetary unit equal to ¹⁄₁₀₀ sucre formerly used in Ecuador

²cen·ta·vo \-'tä-(ˌ)vü, -(ˌ)vō\ n, pl **-vos** 1 — see escudo, metical, real at MONEY table 2 : a former monetary unit equal to ¹⁄₁₀₀ Portuguese escudo

cen·te·nar·i·an \ˌsen-tə-'ner-ē-ən\ n : a person who is 100 or more years old

cen·te·nary \sen-'te-nə-rē, 'sen-tə-ˌner-ē\ n, pl **-ries** : CENTENNIAL — **centenary** adj

cen·ten·ni·al \sen-'te-nē-əl\ n : a 100th anniversary or its celebration — **centennial** adj

¹cen·ter \'sen-tər\ n 1 : the point that is equally distant from all points on the circumference of a circle or surface of a sphere; also : MIDDLE 1 2 : the point about which an activity concentrates or from which something originates 3 : a region of concentrated population 4 : a middle part **5** *often cap* : political figures holding moderate views esp. between those of conservatives and liberals **6** : a player occupying a middle position (as in football or basketball)

²**center** *vb* **1** : to place or fix at or around a center or central area **2** : to give a central focus or basis : CONCENTRATE **3** : to have a center : FOCUS

cen·ter·board \'sen-tər-,bȯrd\ *n* : a retractable keel used esp. in sailboats

cen·ter·piece \-,pēs\ *n* **1** : an object in a central position; *esp* : an adornment in the center of a table **2** : one that is of central importance or interest in a larger whole ⟨tax reform was the ∼ of his speech⟩

cen·tes·i·mal \sen-'te-sə-məl\ *adj* : marked by or relating to division into hundredths

¹**cen·tes·i·mo** \chen-'te-zə-,mō\ *n, pl* **-mi** \-(,)mē\ : a former monetary unit equal to ¹/₁₀₀ Italian lira

²**cen·tes·i·mo** \sen-'te-sə-,mō\ *n, pl* **-mos** — see *balboa, peso* at MONEY table

cen·ti·grade \'sen-tə-,grād, 'sän-\ *adj* : relating to, conforming to, or having a thermometer scale on which the interval between the freezing and boiling points of water is divided into 100 degrees with 0° representing the freezing point and 100° the boiling point ⟨10° ∼⟩ — compare CELSIUS

cen·ti·gram \-,gram\ *n* — see METRIC SYSTEM table

cen·ti·li·ter \'sen-ti-,lē-tər\ *n* — see METRIC SYSTEM table

cen·time \'sän-,tēm\ *n* **1** : a former monetary unit of any of several countries (as Belgium, France, and Luxembourg) equal to ¹/₁₀₀ franc **2** — see *dinar, dirham, franc, gourde* at MONEY table

cen·ti·me·ter \'sen-tə-,mē-tər, 'sän-\ *n* — see METRIC SYSTEM table

centimeter–gram–second *adj* : of, relating to, or being a system of units based on the centimeter as the unit of length, the gram as the unit of mass, and the second as the unit of time

cen·ti·mo \'sen-tə-,mō\ *n, pl* **-mos** **1** — see *bolivar, colón, dobra, guarani, sol* at MONEY table **2** : a former monetary unit equal to ¹/₁₀₀ peseta

cen·ti·pede \'sen-tə-,pēd\ *n* [L *centipeda,* fr. *centum* hundred + *pes* foot] : any of a class of long flattened segmented arthropods with one pair of legs on each segment except the first which has a pair of poison fangs

¹**cen·tral** \'sen-trəl\ *adj* **1** : constituting a center **2** : ESSENTIAL, PRINCIPAL ⟨the novel's ∼ character⟩ **3** : situated at, in, or near the center **4** : centrally placed and superseding separate units ⟨∼ heating⟩ — **cen·tral·ly** *adv*

²**central** *n* : a central controlling office

cen·tral·ise *Brit var of* CENTRALIZE

cen·tral·ize \'sen-trə-,līz\ *vb* **-ized; -iz·ing** : to bring to a central point or under central control — **cen·tral·i·za·tion** \,sen-trə-lə-'zā-shən\ *n* — **cen·tral·iz·er** \'sen-trə-,lī-zər\ *n*

central nervous system *n* : the part of the nervous system which integrates nervous function and activity and which in vertebrates consists of the brain and spinal cord

cen·tre *chiefly Brit var of* CENTER

cen·trif·u·gal \sen-'tri-fyə-gəl, -fi-\ *adj* [NL *centrifugus,* fr. *centr-* center + L *fugere* to flee] **1** : proceeding or acting in a direction away from a center or axis **2** : using or acting by centrifugal force

centrifugal force *n* : the apparent force felt by an object moving in a curved path and acting outward from a center of rotation

cen·tri·fuge \'sen-trə-,fyüj\ *n* : a machine using centrifugal force (as for separating substances of different densities or for removing moisture)

cen·trip·e·tal \sen-'tri-pə-t²l\ *adj* [NL *centripetus,* fr. *centr-* center + L *petere* to seek] : proceeding or acting in a direction toward a center or axis

centripetal force *n* : the force needed to keep an object revolving about a point moving in a circular path

cen·trist \'sen-trist\ *n* **1** *often cap* : a member of a center party **2** : one who holds moderate views

cen·tu·ri·on \sen-'tùr-ē-ən, -'tyùr-\ *n* : an officer commanding a Roman century

cen·tu·ry \'sen-chə-rē\ *n, pl* **-ries** **1** : a subdivision of a Roman legion **2** : a group or sequence of 100 like things **3** : a period of 100 years

century plant *n* : a Mexican agave maturing and flowering only once in many years and then dying

CEO \,sē-(,)ē-'ō\ *n* : the executive with the chief decision-making authority in an organization or business

ce·phal·ic \sə-'fa-lik\ *adj* **1** : of or relating to the head **2** : directed toward or situated on or in or near the head

ce·ram·ic \sə-'ra-mik\ *n* **1** *pl* : the art or process of making articles from a nonmetallic mineral (as clay) by firing **2** : a product produced by ceramics — **ceramic** *adj*

ce·ra·mist \sə-'ra-mist\ *or* **ce·ram·i·cist** \sə-'ra-mə-sist\ *n* : one who engages in ceramics

¹**ce·re·al** \'sir-ē-əl\ *adj* [L *cerealis,* fr. *Ceres,* the Roman goddess of agriculture] : relating to grain or to the plants that produce it; *also* : made of grain

²**cereal** *n* **1** : a grass (as wheat) yielding grain suitable for food; *also* : its grain **2** : a food and esp. a breakfast food prepared from the grain of a cereal

cer·e·bel·lum \,ser-ə-'be-ləm\ *n, pl* **-bel·lums** *or* **-bel·la** \-lə\ [ML, fr. L, dim. of *cerebrum* brain] : a part of the brain that projects over the medulla and is concerned esp. with coordination of muscular action and with bodily balance — **cer·e·bel·lar** \-lər\ *adj*

ce·re·bral \sə-'rē-brəl, 'ser-ə-\ *adj* **1** : of or relating to the brain, intellect, or cerebrum **2** : appealing to or involving the intellect — **ce·re·bral·ly** *adv*

cerebral cortex *n* : the surface layer of

gray matter of the cerebrum that functions chiefly in coordination of sensory and motor information

cerebral palsy n : a disorder caused by brain damage usu. before, during, or shortly after birth and marked esp. by defective muscle control

cer·e·brate \'ser-ə-ˌbrāt\ vb **-brat·ed; -brat·ing** : THINK — **cer·e·bra·tion** \ˌser-ə-'brā-shən\ n

ce·re·brum \sə-'rē-brəm, 'ser-ə-\ n, pl **-brums** or **-bra** \-brə\ [L, brain] : the enlarged front and upper part of the brain that contains the higher nervous centers

cere·ment \'ser-ə-mənt, 'sir-mənt\ n : a shroud for the dead

¹cer·e·mo·ni·al \ˌser-ə-'mō-nē-əl\ adj : of, relating to, or forming a ceremony; also : stressing careful attention to form and detail — **cer·e·mo·ni·al·ly** adv

²ceremonial n : a ceremonial act or system : RITUAL, FORM

cer·e·mo·ni·ous \ˌser-ə-'mō-nē-əs\ adj 1 : devoted to forms and ceremony 2 : CEREMONIAL 3 : according to formal usage or procedure 4 : marked by ceremony — **cer·e·mo·ni·ous·ly** adv — **cer·e·mo·ni·ous·ness** n

cer·e·mo·ny \'ser-ə-ˌmō-nē\ n, pl **-nies** 1 : a formal act or series of acts prescribed by law, ritual, or convention 2 : a conventional act of politeness 3 : a mere outward form with no deeper significance 4 : FORMALITY

ce·re·us \'sir-ē-əs\ n : any of various cacti of the western U.S. and tropical America

ce·rise \sə-'rēs\ n [F, lit., cherry] : a moderate red color

ce·ri·um \'sir-ē-əm\ n : a malleable metallic chemical element used esp. in alloys

cer·met \'sər-ˌmet\ n : a strong alloy of a heat-resistant compound and a metal used esp. for turbine blades

cert abbr certificate; certification; certified; certify

¹cer·tain \'sər-t²n\ adj 1 : FIXED, SETTLED 2 : of a specific but unspecified character ⟨~ people in authority⟩ 3 : DEPENDABLE, RELIABLE 4 : INDISPUTABLE, UNDENIABLE ⟨it is ~ that we exist⟩ 5 : assured in mind or action ⟨I am ~ that they are right⟩ — **cer·tain·ly** adv

²certain pron : certain ones

cer·tain·ty \-tē\ n, pl **-ties** 1 : something that is certain 2 : the quality or state of being certain

cer·tif·i·cate \sər-'ti-fi-kət\ n 1 : a document testifying to the truth of a fact 2 : a document testifying that one has fulfilled certain requirements (as of a course) 3 : a document giving evidence of ownership or debt ⟨a stock ~⟩

certificate of deposit : a money-market bond redeemable without penalty only on maturity

cer·ti·fi·ca·tion \ˌsər-tə-fə-'kā-shən\ n 1 : the act of certifying : the state of being certified 2 : a certified statement

certified mail n : first class mail for which proof of delivery may be secured but no indemnity value is claimed

certified public accountant n : an ac-

countant who has met the requirements of a state law and has been granted a certificate

cer·ti·fy \'sər-tə-ˌfī\ vb **-fied; -fy·ing** 1 : VERIFY, CONFIRM 2 : to endorse officially 3 : to guarantee (a bank check) as good by a statement to that effect stamped on its face 4 : to recognize as having met specific qualifications within a field ⟨certified teachers⟩ ♦ **Synonyms** ACCREDIT, APPROVE, SANCTION, ENDORSE — **cer·ti·fi·able** \-ə-bəl\ adj — **cer·ti·fi·ably** \-blē\ adv — **cer·ti·fi·er** n

cer·ti·tude \'sər-tə-ˌtüd, -ˌtyüd\ n : the state of being or feeling certain

ce·ru·le·an \sə-'rü-lē-ən\ adj : AZURE

ce·ru·men \sə-'rü-mən\ n : EARWAX

cer·vi·cal \'sər-vi-kəl\ adj : of or relating to a neck or cervix

cervical cap n : a contraceptive device in the form of a thimble-shaped molded cap that fits snugly over the uterine cervix and blocks sperm from entering the uterus

cer·vix \'sər-viks\ n, pl **cer·vi·ces** \-və-ˌsēz\ or **cer·vix·es** 1 : NECK; esp : the back part of the neck 2 : a constricted portion of an organ or part; esp : the narrow outer end of the uterus

ce·sar·e·an or **cae·sar·e·an** also **ce·sar·i·an** or **cae·sar·i·an** \si-'zer-ē-ən\ n, often cap : CESAREAN SECTION — **cesarean** or **caesarean** also **cesarian** or **caesarian** adj

cesarean section also **caesarean section** n, often cap C [fr. the legendary association of such a delivery with the Roman cognomen Caesar] : surgical incision of the walls of the abdomen and uterus for delivery of offspring

ce·si·um \'sē-zē-əm\ n : a silver-white soft ductile chemical element

ces·sa·tion \se-'sā-shən\ n : a temporary or final ceasing (as of action)

ces·sion \'se-shən\ n : a yielding (as of rights) to another

cess·pool \'ses-ˌpül\ n 1 : an underground pit or tank for receiving household sewage 2 : a filthy or corrupt situation

ce·ta·cean \si-'tā-shən\ n : any of an order of aquatic mostly marine mammals that includes whales, porpoises, dolphins, and related forms — **cetacean** adj

cf abbr [L confer] compare

Cf symbol californium

CF abbr cystic fibrosis

CFC abbr chlorofluorocarbon

CFL abbr compact fluorescent lamp; compact fluorescent light bulb

CFO abbr chief financial officer

cg abbr centigram

CG abbr 1 coast guard 2 commanding general

cgs abbr centimeter-gram-second

ch abbr 1 chain 2 champion 3 chapter 4 church

CH abbr 1 clearinghouse 2 courthouse 3 customhouse

Cha·blis \sha-'blē, shə-, shä-; 'sha-ˌblē\ n, pl **Cha·blis** \-'blēz, -(ˌ)blēz\ 1 : a dry sharp white Burgundy wine **2** : a white California wine

cha–cha \'chä-ˌchä\ *n* : a fast rhythmic ballroom dance of Latin American origin

chafe \'chāf\ *vb* **chafed; chaf·ing 1** : IRRITATE, VEX **2** : FRET **3** : to warm by rubbing **4** : to rub so as to wear away; *also* : to make sore by rubbing

cha·fer \'chā-fər\ *n* : any of various scarab beetles

¹chaff \'chaf\ *n* **1** : debris (as husks) separated from grain in threshing **2** : something comparatively worthless — **chaffy** *adj*

²chaff *n* : light jesting talk : BANTER

³chaff *vb* : to tease good-naturedly

chaf·fer \'cha-fər\ *vb* : BARGAIN, HAGGLE — **chaf·fer·er** *n*

chaf·finch \'cha-ˌfinch\ *n* : a common European finch with a cheerful song

chaf·ing dish \'chā-fiŋ-\ *n* : a utensil for cooking food at the table

¹cha·grin \shə-'grin\ *n* : mental uneasiness or annoyance caused by failure, disappointment, or humiliation

²chagrin *vb* **cha·grined** \-'grind\; **cha·grin·ing** : to cause to feel chagrin

¹chain \'chān\ *n* [ME *cheyne*, fr. AF *chaene*, fr. L *catena*] **1** : a flexible series of connected links : a chainlike surveying instrument; *also* : a unit of length equal to 66 feet (about 20 meters) **3** *pl* : BONDS, FETTERS **4** : a series of things linked together ⟨mountain ∼s⟩; *also* : a group of usu. identical enterprises with a single owner ⟨fast-food ∼s⟩ ♦ **Synonyms** TRAIN, STRING, SEQUENCE, SUCCESSION, SERIES

²chain *vb* : to fasten, bind, or connect with a chain; *also* : FETTER

chain gang *n* : a gang of convicts chained together

chain letter *n* : a letter sent to several persons with a request that each send copies to an equal number of persons

chain mail *n* : flexible armor of interlocking metal rings

chain reaction *n* **1** : a series of events in which each event initiates the succeeding one **2** : a chemical or nuclear reaction yielding products that cause further reactions of the same kind

chain saw *n* : a portable power saw that has teeth linked together to form an endless chain — **chain-saw** \'chān-ˌsȯ\ *vb*

chain–smoke \'chān-'smōk\ *vb* : to smoke esp. cigarettes continuously

¹chair \'cher\ *n* [ME *chaiere*, fr. AF, fr. L *cathedra*, fr. Gk *kathedra*, fr. *kata-* down + *hedra* seat] **1** : a seat with a back for one person **2** : ELECTRIC CHAIR **3** : an official seat; *also* : an office or position of authority or dignity **4** : CHAIRMAN

²chair *vb* : to act as chairman of

chair·lift \'cher-ˌlift\ *n* : a motor-driven conveyor for skiers consisting of seats hung from a moving cable

chair·man \-mən\ *n* : the presiding officer of a meeting, committee, or event — **chair·man·ship** *n*

chair·per·son \-ˌpər-sən\ *n* : CHAIRMAN

chair·wom·an \-ˌwu̇-mən\ *n* : a woman who serves as chairman

chaise \'shāz\ *n* : a 2-wheeled horse-drawn carriage with a folding top

chaise longue \'shāz-'lȯŋ\ *n, pl* **chaise longues** *same or* -'lȯŋz\ [F, lit., long chair] : a long reclining chair

chaise lounge \-'lau̇nj\ *n* : CHAISE LONGUE

chal·ced·o·ny \kal-'se-dᵊn-ē\ *n, pl* **-nies** : a translucent quartz of various colors

chal·co·py·rite \ˌkal-kə-'pī-ˌrīt\ *n* : a yellow mineral constituting an important copper ore

cha·let \sha-'lā\ *n* **1** : a herdsman's cabin in the Swiss mountains **2** : a building in the style of a Swiss cottage with a wide roof overhang

chal·ice \'cha-ləs\ *n* : a drinking cup; *esp* : the eucharistic cup

¹chalk \'chȯk\ *n* **1** : a soft limestone **2** : chalk or chalky material esp. when used as a crayon — **chalky** *adj*

²chalk *vb* **1** : to rub or mark with chalk **2** : to record with or as if with chalk — usu. used with *up*

chalk·board \'chȯk-ˌbȯrd\ *n* : BLACKBOARD

chalk up *vb* **1** : ASCRIBE, CREDIT **2** : ATTAIN, ACHIEVE ⟨*chalk up* a victory⟩

¹chal·lenge \'cha-lənj\ *vb* **chal·lenged; chal·leng·ing** [ME *chalengen* to accuse, fr. AF *chalenger*, fr. L *calumniari* to accuse falsely, fr. *calumnia* calumny] **1** : to order to halt and prove identity **2** : to take exception to : DISPUTE ⟨∼ a ruling⟩ **3** : to issue an invitation to compete ⟨*challenged* me to another game⟩ **4** : to stimulate by presenting difficulties ⟨a job that ∼s her⟩ — **chal·leng·er** *n*

²challenge *n* **1** : a summons to a duel **2** : an invitation to compete in a sport **3** : a calling into question **4** : an exception taken to a juror **5** : a sentry's command to halt and prove identity **6** : a stimulating or interesting task or problem

challenged *adj* : presented with difficulties (as by a disability)

chal·lis \'sha-lē\ *n, pl* **chal·lises** \-lēz\ : a lightweight clothing fabric of wool, cotton, or synthetic yarns

cham·ber \'chām-bər\ *n* **1** : ROOM; *esp* : BEDROOM **2** : an enclosed space or cavity **3** : a hall for meetings of a legislative body **4** : a judge's consultation room — usu. used in pl. **5** : a legislative or judicial body; *also* : a council for a business purpose **6** : the part of a firearm that holds the cartridge or powder charge during firing — **cham·bered** \-bərd\ *adj*

cham·ber·lain \'chām-bər-lən\ *n* **1** : a chief officer in the household of a king or nobleman **2** : TREASURER

cham·ber·maid \-ˌmād\ *n* : a maid who takes care of bedrooms

chamber music *n* : music intended for performance by a few musicians before a small audience

chamber of commerce : an association of businesspeople for promoting commercial and industrial interests in the community

cham·bray \'sham-ˌbrā\ *n* : a lightweight clothing fabric of white and colored threads

cha·me·leon \kə-'mēl-yən\ *n* [ME *camelion*, fr. MF, fr. L *chamaeleon*, fr. Gk *chamaileōn*, fr. *chamai* on the ground + *leōn* lion] : a small lizard whose skin changes color esp. according to its surroundings

¹cham·fer \'cham-fər\ *vb* 1 : to cut a furrow in (as a column) : GROOVE 2 : to make a chamfer on : BEVEL

²chamfer *n* : a beveled edge

cham·ois \'sha-mē\ *n, pl* **cham·ois** *same or* -mēz\ 1 : a small goatlike ruminant mammal of Europe and the Caucasus region of Russia 2 *also* **cham·my** \'sha-mē\ : a soft leather made esp. from the skin of the sheep or goat 3 : a cotton fabric made in imitation of chamois leather

cham·o·mile *or* **cam·o·mile** \'ka-mə-ˌmī(-ə)l, -ˌmēl\ *n* : any of a genus of strong-scented herbs related to the daisies and having flower heads that yield a bitter substance used esp. in tonics and teas

¹champ \'champ, 'chämp\ *vb* 1 : to chew noisily 2 : to show impatience of delay or restraint

²champ \'champ\ *n* : CHAMPION

cham·pagne \sham-'pān\ *n* : a white effervescent wine

¹cham·pi·on \'cham-pē-ən\ *n* 1 : a militant advocate or defender 2 : one that wins first prize or place in a contest 3 : one that is acknowledged to be better than all others

²champion *vb* : to protect or fight for as a champion ♦ *Synonyms* BACK, ADVOCATE, UPHOLD, SUPPORT

cham·pi·on·ship \-ˌship\ *n* 1 : the position or title of a champion 2 : the act of championing : DEFENSE 3 : a contest held to determine a champion

¹chance \'chans\ *n* 1 : something that happens without apparent cause 2 : the unpredictable element in existence : LUCK, FORTUNE 3 : OPPORTUNITY 4 : the likelihood of a particular outcome in an uncertain situation : PROBABILITY 5 : RISK 6 : a raffle ticket — **chance** *adj* — **by chance** : in the haphazard course of events

²chance *vb* **chanced; chanc·ing** 1 : to take place by chance : HAPPEN 2 : to come casually and unexpectedly — used with *upon* 3 : to leave to chance 4 : to accept the risk of

chan·cel \'chan-səl\ *n* : the part of a church including the altar and choir

chan·cel·lery *or* **chan·cel·lory** \'chan-sə-lə-rē\ *n, pl* **-ler·ies** *or* **-lor·ies** 1 : the position or office of a chancellor 2 : the building or room where a chancellor works 3 : the office or staff of an embassy or consulate

chan·cel·lor \'chan-sə-lər\ *n* 1 : a high state official in various countries 2 : the head of a university 3 : a judge in the equity court in various states of the U.S. 4 : the chief minister of state in some European countries — **chan·cel·lor·ship** *n*

chan·cery \'chan-sə-rē\ *n, pl* **-cer·ies** 1 : a record office for public or diplomatic archives 2 : any of various courts of equity in the U.S. and Britain 3 : a chancellor's court or office 4 : the office of an embassy 5 : the business office of a diocese

chan·cre \'shaŋ-kər\ *n* [F, fr. OF, fr. L *cancer*] : a primary sore or ulcer at the site of entry of an infective agent (as of syphilis)

chan·croid \'shaŋ-ˌkrȯid\ *n* : a sexually transmitted disease caused by a bacterium and characterized by chancres that differ from those of syphilis in lacking hardened margins

chancy \'chan-sē\ *adj* **chanc·i·er; -est** 1 *Scot* : AUSPICIOUS 2 : RISKY

chan·de·lier \ˌshan-də-'lir\ *n* : a branched lighting fixture suspended from a ceiling

chan·dler \'chand-lər\ *n* [ME *chandeler* a maker or seller of candles, fr. AF, fr. *chandele* candle, fr. L *candela*] : a dealer in provisions and supplies of a specified kind ⟨ship's ∼⟩ — **chan·dlery** *n*

¹change \'chānj\ *vb* **changed; chang·ing** 1 : to make or become different : ALTER 2 : to replace with another 3 : to give or receive an equivalent sum in notes or coins of usu. smaller denominations or of another currency 4 : to put fresh clothes or covering on ⟨∼ a bed⟩ 5 : to put on different clothes 6 : EXCHANGE — **change·able** *adj* — **chang·er** *n*

²change *n* 1 : the act, process, or result of changing 2 : a fresh set of clothes 3 : money given in exchange for other money of higher denomination 4 : money returned when a payment exceeds the sum due 5 : coins esp. of small denominations — **change·ful** *adj*

change·ling \'chānj-liŋ\ *n* : a child secretly exchanged for another in infancy

change of life : MENOPAUSE

change·over \'chānj-ˌō-vər\ *n* : CONVERSION, TRANSITION

change ringing *n* : the art or practice of ringing a set of tuned bells in continually varying order

¹chan·nel \'cha-nᵊl\ *n* 1 : the bed of a stream 2 : the deeper part of a waterway 3 : STRAIT 4 : a means of passage or transmission 5 : a range of frequencies of sufficient width for a single radio or television transmission 6 : a usu. tubular enclosed passage : CONDUIT 7 : a long gutter, groove, or furrow

²channel *vb* **-neled** *or* **-nelled; -neling** *or* **-nel·ling** 1 : to make a channel in 2 : to direct into or through a channel

chan·nel·ize \'cha-nə-ˌlīz\ *vb* **-ized; -iz·ing** : CHANNEL — **chan·nel·i·za·tion** \ˌcha-nə-lə-'zā-shən\ *n*

chan·son \shäⁿ-'sōⁿ\ *n, pl* **chan·sons** *same or* -'sōⁿz\ : SONG; *esp* : a cabaret song

¹chant \'chant\ *vb* 1 : SING; *esp* : to sing a chant 2 : to utter or recite in the manner of a chant 3 : to celebrate or praise in song — **chant·er** *n*

²chant *n* 1 : a repetitive melody in which several words are sung to one tone

: SONG; *esp* : a liturgical melody **2** : a manner of singing or speaking in musical monotones

chan·te·relle \,shan-tə-'rel\ *n* : a fragrant edible mushroom

chan·teuse \shäⁿ-'tərz, shan-'tüz\ *n, pl* **chan·teuses** *same or* -'tər-zəz, -'tü-zəz\ [F] : a woman who is a concert or night-club singer

chan·tey *or* **chan·ty** \'shan-tē, 'chan-\ *n, pl* **chanteys** *or* **chanties** : a song sung by sailors in rhythm with their work

chan·ti·cleer \,chan-tə-'klir, ,shan-\ *n* : ROOSTER

Chanukah *var of* HANUKKAH

cha·os \'kā-,äs\ *n* **1** *often cap* : the confused unorganized state existing before the creation of distinct forms **2** : the inherent unpredictability in the behavior of a complex natural system (as the atmosphere or the beating heart) **3** : complete disorder ♦ *Synonyms* CONFUSION, JUMBLE, SNARL, MUDDLE, DISARRAY — **cha·ot·ic** \kā-'ä-tik\ *adj* — **cha·ot·i·cal·ly** \-ti-k(ə-)lē\ *adv*

chaos theory *n* : a branch of mathematical and physical theory concerned with chaotic systems

¹**chap** \'chap\ *vb* **chapped; chap·ping** : to dry and crack open usu. from wind and cold ⟨*chapped* lips⟩

²**chap** *n* : a jaw with its fleshy covering — usu. used in pl.

³**chap** *n, chiefly Brit* : FELLOW

⁴**chap** *abbr* chapter

chap·ar·ral \,sha-pə-'ral\ *n* **1** : a dense impenetrable thicket of shrubs or dwarf trees **2** : an ecological community esp. of southern California composed of shrubby plants

chap·book \'chap-,bùk\ *n* : a small book of ballads, tales, or tracts

cha·peau \sha-'pō\ *n, pl* **cha·peaus** \-'pōz\ *or* **cha·peaux** \-'pō, -'pōz\ [MF] : HAT

cha·pel \'cha-pəl\ *n* [ME, fr. AF *chapele,* fr. ML *cappella,* fr. LL *cappa* cloak; fr. the cloak of St. Martin of Tours preserved as a sacred relic in a chapel built for that purpose] **1** : a private or subordinate place of worship **2** : an assembly at an educational institution usu. including devotional exercises **3** : a place of worship used by a Christian group other than an established church

¹**chap·er·one** *or* **chap·er·on** \'sha-pə-,rōn\ *n* [F *chaperon,* lit., hood, fr. MF, head covering, fr. *chape* cape, fr. LL *cappa*] **1** : a person (as a matron) who accompanies young unmarried women in public for propriety **2** : an older person who accompanies young people at a social gathering to ensure proper behavior

²**chaperone** *or* **chaperon** *vb* **-oned; -oning 1** : ESCORT, GUIDE **2** : to act as a chaperone to or for ⟨∼ a dance⟩ ⟨∼ teenagers⟩ — **chap·er·on·age** \-,rō-nij\ *n*

chap·fall·en \'chap-,fò-lən, 'chäp-\ *adj* **1** : having the lower jaw hanging loosely **2** : DEJECTED, DEPRESSED

chap·lain \'cha-plən\ *n* **1** : a member of the clergy officially attached to a special group (as the army) **2** : a person chosen to conduct religious exercises (as for a club) — **chap·lain·cy** \-sē\ *n*

chap·let \'cha-plət\ *n* **1** : a wreath for the head **2** : a string of beads : NECKLACE

chap·man \'chap-mən\ *n, Brit* : an itinerant dealer : PEDDLER

chaps \'shaps, 'chaps\ *n pl* [MexSp *chaparreras*] : leather leggings resembling pants without a seat that are worn esp. by western ranch hands

chap·ter \'chap-tər\ *n* **1** : a main division of a book **2** : a body of canons (as of a cathedral) **3** : a local branch of a society or fraternity

¹**char** \'chär\ *n, pl* **char** *or* **chars** : any of a genus of trouts (as the common brook trout) with small scales

²**char** *vb* **charred; char·ring 1** : to burn or become burned to charcoal **2** : SCORCH

³**char** *vb* **charred; char·ring** : to work as a cleaning woman

char·ac·ter \'ker-ik-tər\ *n* [ME *caracter,* fr. L *character* mark, distinctive quality, fr. Gk *charaktēr,* fr. *charassein* to scratch, engrave] **1** : a graphic symbol (as a letter) used in writing or printing **2** : a symbol that represents information; *also* : a representation of such a character that may be accepted by a computer **3** : a distinguishing feature : ATTRIBUTE **4** : the complex of mental and ethical traits marking a person or a group **5** : a person marked by conspicuous often peculiar traits **6** : one of the persons in a novel or play **7** : REPUTATION ⟨an attack on his ∼⟩ **8** : moral excellence

¹**char·ac·ter·is·tic** \,ker-ik-tə-'ris-tik\ *n* : a distinguishing trait, quality, or property

²**characteristic** *adj* : serving to mark individual character ♦ *Synonyms* INDIVIDUAL, PECULIAR, DISTINCTIVE — **char·ac·ter·is·ti·cal·ly** \-ti-k(ə-)lē\ *adv*

char·ac·ter·ize \'ker-ik-tə-,rīz\ *vb* **-ized; -iz·ing 1** : to describe the character of **2** : to be characteristic of — **char·ac·ter·i·za·tion** \,ker-ik-tə-rə-'zā-shən\ *n*

cha·rades \shə-'rādz\ *n sing or pl* : a game in which some of the players try to guess a word or phrase from the actions of another player who may not speak

char·coal \'chär-,kōl\ *n* **1** : a porous carbon prepared from vegetable or animal substances **2** : a piece of fine charcoal used in drawing; *also* : a drawing made with charcoal

chard \'chärd\ *n* : SWISS CHARD

char·don·nay \,shar-d°n-'ä\ *n, often cap* [F] : a dry white wine made from a single variety of white grape

¹**charge** \'chärj\ *n* **1** : a quantity (as of fuel or ammunition) required to fill something to capacity **2** : a store or accumulation of force **3** : an excess or deficiency of electrons in a body **4** : THRILL, KICK **5** : a task or duty imposed **6** : CARE, RESPONSIBILITY **7** : one given into another's care **8** : instructions from a judge to a jury **9** : COST, EXPENSE, PRICE; *also*

: a debit to an account **10** : ACCUSATION, INDICTMENT **11** : ATTACK, ASSAULT
²**charge** *vb* charged; charg·ing **1** : to load or fill to capacity **2** : to give an electric charge to; *also* : to restore the activity of (a storage battery) by means of an electric current **3** : to impose a task or responsibility on **4** : COMMAND, ORDER **5** : ACCUSE **6** : to rush against : rush forward in assault **7** : to make liable for payment; *also* : to record a debt or liability against **8** : to fix as a price — **charge·able** *adj*
charge–coupled device *n* : a semiconductor device used esp. as an optical sensor
char·gé d'af·faires \shär-ˌzhä-də-ˈfer\ *n, pl* **chargés d'affaires** \-ˌzhä-, -ˌzhäz-\ [F] : a diplomat who substitutes for an ambassador or minister
¹**char·ger** \ˈchär-jər\ *n* : a large platter
²**charg·er** *n* **1** : a device or a worker that charges something **2** : WARHORSE 1
char·i·ot \ˈcher-ē-ət\ *n* : a 2-wheeled horse-drawn carriage of ancient times used esp. in war and in races — **char·i·o·teer** \ˌcher-ē-ə-ˈtir\ *n*
cha·ris·ma \kə-ˈriz-mə\ *n* : a personal quality of leadership arousing popular loyalty or enthusiasm — **char·is·mat·ic** \ˌkar-əz-ˈma-tik\ *adj*
char·i·ta·ble \ˈcher-ə-tə-bəl\ *adj* **1** : liberal in giving to needy people **2** : merciful or lenient in judging others ♦ **Synonyms** BENEVOLENT, PHILANTHROPIC, ALTRUISTIC, HUMANITARIAN — **char·i·ta·ble·ness** *n* — **char·i·ta·bly** \-blē\ *adv*
char·i·ty \ˈcher-ə-tē\ *n, pl* **-ties 1** : goodwill toward or love of humanity **2** : an act or feeling of generosity **3** : the giving of aid to the poor; *also* : ALMS **4** : an institution engaged in relief of the poor **5** : leniency in judging others ♦ **Synonyms** MERCY, CLEMENCY, LENITY
char·la·tan \ˈshär-lə-tən\ *n* : a person making usu. showy pretenses to knowledge or ability : FRAUD, FAKER
Charles·ton \ˈchärl-stən\ *n* : a lively dance in which the knees are swung in and out and the heels are turned sharply outward on each step
char·ley horse \ˈchär-lē-ˌhȯrs\ *n* : a muscular pain, cramping, or stiffness from a strain or bruise
¹**charm** \ˈchärm\ *n* [ME *charme*, fr. AF, fr. L *carmen* song, fr. *canere* to sing] **1** : a practice or expression believed to have magic power **2** : something worn about the person to ward off evil or bring good fortune : AMULET **3** : a trait that fascinates or allures **4** : physical grace or attraction **5** : a small ornament worn on a bracelet or chain **6** : a quark with a charge of +⅔ and a measured energy of approximately 1.5 billion electron volts
²**charm** *vb* **1** : to affect by or as if by a magic spell **2** : to protect by or as if by charms **3** : FASCINATE, ENCHANT ♦ **Synonyms** ALLURE, CAPTIVATE, BEWITCH, ATTRACT — **charm·er** *n*
charmed \ˈchärmd\ *adj* : extremely lucky or prosperous ⟨a ~ life⟩

charm·ing \ˈchär-miŋ\ *adj* : PLEASING, DELIGHTFUL — **charm·ing·ly** *adv*
char·nel house \ˈchär-nᵊl-\ *n* : a building or chamber in which bones or bodies are deposited
¹**chart** \ˈchärt\ *n* **1** : MAP **2** : a sheet giving information in the form of a table, list, or diagram; *also* : GRAPH
²**chart** *vb* **1** : PLAN ⟨~ a course⟩ **2** : to make a chart of **3** : CHRONICLE ⟨~ed his adventures⟩
¹**char·ter** \ˈchär-tər\ *n* **1** : an official document granting rights or privileges (as to a colony, town, or college) from a sovereign or a governing body **2** : CONSTITUTION **3** : a written instrument from a society creating a branch **4** : a mercantile lease of a ship
²**charter** *vb* **1** : to grant a charter to **2** *Brit* : CERTIFY ⟨~ed engineer⟩ **3** : to hire, rent, or lease for temporary use ⟨~ a bus⟩ — **char·ter·er** *n*
charter member *n* : an original member of an organization
char·treuse \shär-ˈtrüz, -ˈtrüs\ *n* : a brilliant yellow green
char·wom·an \ˈchär-ˌwu̇-mən\ *n* : a cleaning woman esp. in large buildings
chary \ˈcher-ē\ *adj* **char·i·er; -est** [ME, sorrowful, dear, fr. OE *cearig* sorrowful, fr. *caru* sorrow] **1** : CAUTIOUS, CIRCUMSPECT **2** : SPARING — **char·i·ly** \-ə-lē\ *adv*
¹**chase** \ˈchās\ *n* **1** : PURSUIT; *also* : HUNTING **2** : QUARRY **3** : a tract of unenclosed land used as a game preserve
²**chase** *vb* chased; chas·ing **1** : to follow rapidly : PURSUE **2** : HUNT **3** : to seek out ⟨chasing down clues⟩ **4** : to cause to depart or flee : drive away **5** : RUSH, HASTEN
³**chase** *vb* chased; chas·ing : to decorate (a metal surface) by embossing or engraving
⁴**chase** *n* : FURROW, GROOVE
chas·er \ˈchā-sər\ *n* **1** : one that chases **2** : a mild drink (as beer) taken after hard liquor
chasm \ˈka-zəm\ *n* : GORGE 2
chas·sis \ˈcha-sē, ˈsha-sē\ *n, pl* **chas·sis** \-sēz\ : the supporting frame of a structure (as an automobile or television set)
chaste \ˈchāst\ *adj* chast·er; chast·est **1** : innocent of unlawful sexual intercourse : VIRTUOUS, PURE **2** : CELIBATE **3** : pure in thought : MODEST **4** : severe or simple in design — **chaste·ly** *adv* — **chaste·ness** *n*
chas·ten \ˈchā-sᵊn\ *vb* : to correct through punishment or suffering : DISCIPLINE; *also* : PURIFY — **chas·ten·er** *n*
chas·tise \chas-ˈtīz\ *vb* **chas·tised; chas·tis·ing** [ME *chastisen*, alter. of *chasten*] **1** : to punish esp. bodily **2** : to censure severely : CASTIGATE — **chas·tise·ment** \-mənt, ˈchas-təz-\ *n*
chas·ti·ty \ˈchas-tə-tē\ *n* : the quality or state of being chaste; *esp* : sexual purity
cha·su·ble \ˈcha-zə-bəl, -sə-\ *n* : the outer vestment of the priest at mass
chat \ˈchat\ *n* **1** : light familiar informal

talk **2** : online discussion in a chat room — **chat** *vb*

châ·teau \sha-'tō\ *n, pl* **châ·teaus** \-'tōz\ *or* **châ·teaux** \-'tō, -'tōz\ [F, fr. OF *chastel*, fr. L *castellum* castle, dim. of *castra* camp] **1** : a feudal castle in France **2** : a large country house **3** : a French vineyard estate

chat·e·laine \'shat-ə-'lān\ *n* **1** : the mistress of a chateau **2** : a clasp or hook for a watch, purse, or keys

chat room *n* : a real-time online interactive discussion group

chat·tel \'chat-ᵊl\ *n* **1** : an item of tangible property other than real estate **2** : SLAVE, BONDMAN

chat·ter \'cha-tər\ *vb* **1** : to utter speechlike but meaningless sounds **2** : to talk idly, incessantly, or fast **3** : to click repeatedly or uncontrollably — **chatter** *n* — **chat·ter·er** *n*

chat·ter·box \'cha-tər-,bäks\ *n* : one who talks incessantly

chat·ty \'cha-tē\ *adj* **chat·ti·er; -est** : TALKATIVE **2** : having qualities of light informal conversation — **chat·ti·ly** \-tə-lē\ *adv* — **chat·ti·ness** \-tē-nəs\ *n*

¹**chauf·feur** \'shō-fər, shō-'fər\ *n* [F, lit., stoker, fr. *chauffer* to heat] : a person employed to drive an automobile

²**chauffeur** *vb* **1** : to do the work of a chauffeur **2** : to transport in the manner of a chauffeur ⟨~ed the kids to school⟩

chaunt *var of* CHANT

chau·vin·ism \'shō-və-,ni-zəm\ *n* [F *chauvinisme*, fr. Nicolas *Chauvin*, fictional soldier of excessive patriotism and devotion to Napoleon] **1** : excessive or blind patriotism **2** : an attitude of superiority toward members of the opposite sex — **chau·vin·ist** \-nist\ *n or adj* — **chau·vin·is·tic** \,shō-və-'nis-tik\ *adj* — **chau·vin·is·ti·cal·ly** \-ti-k(ə-)lē\ *adv*

cheap \'chēp\ *adj* **1** : INEXPENSIVE **2** : costing little effort to obtain ⟨~ tickets⟩ **3** : worth little : SHODDY, TAWDRY ⟨~ workmanship⟩ **4** : worthy of scorn **5** : STINGY — **cheap** *adv* — **cheap·ly** *adv* — **cheap·ness** *n*

cheap·en \'chē-pən\ *vb* **1** : to make or become cheap or cheaper in price or value **2** : to make tawdry

cheap·skate \'chēp-,skāt\ *n* : a miserly or stingy person; *esp* : one who tries to avoid paying a fair share of costs

¹**cheat** \'chēt\ *vb* **1** : to deprive of something through fraud or deceit ⟨~ed workers of their pay⟩ **2** : to practice fraud or trickery **3** : to violate rules dishonestly ⟨~ at cards⟩ **4** : to be sexually unfaithful — **cheat·er** *n*

²**cheat** *n* **1** : the act of deceiving : FRAUD, DECEPTION **2** : one that cheats : a dishonest person

¹**check** \'chek\ *n* **1** : exposure of a chess king to an attack **2** : a sudden stoppage of progress **3** : a sudden pause or break **4** : something that stops or restrains **5** : a standard for testing or evaluation **6** : EXAMINATION, INVESTIGATION **7** : the act of testing or verifying **8** : a written order to a bank to pay money **9** : a ticket or token showing ownership or identity **10**

: a slip indicating an amount due **11** : a pattern in squares; *also* : a fabric in such a pattern **12** : a mark typically ✓ placed beside an item to show that it has been noted **13** : CRACK, SPLIT

²**check** *vb* **1** : to put (a chess king) in check **2** : to slow down or stop : BRAKE **3** : to restrain the action or force of : CURB **4** : to compare with a source, original, or authority : VERIFY **5** : to inspect or test for satisfactory condition **6** : to mark with a check as examined **7** : to consign for shipment for one holding a passenger ticket **8** : to mark into squares **9** : to leave or accept for safekeeping in a checkroom **10** : to prove to be consistent or truthful **11** : CRACK, SPLIT

check·book \'chek-,bùk\ *n* : a book containing blank checks

¹**check·er** \'che-kər\ *n* : a piece in the game of checkers

²**checker** *vb* **1** : to variegate with different colors or shades **2** : to vary with contrasting elements ⟨a ~ed career⟩ **3** : to mark into squares

³**checker** *n* : one that checks; *esp* : an employee who checks out purchases in a store

check·er·ber·ry \'che-kər-,ber-ē\ *n* : WINTERGREEN 1; *also* : the spicy red fruit of this plant

check·er·board \-,bórd\ *n* : a board of 64 squares of alternate colors used in various games

check·ered \'che-kərd\ *adj* : marked by inconsistent fortune or recurring problems ⟨his ~ past⟩

check·ers \'che-kərz\ *n* : a checkerboard game for 2 players each with 12 pieces

check in *vb* : to report one's presence or arrival (as at a hotel)

check·list \'chek-,list\ *n* : a list of things to be checked or done; *also* : a comprehensive list

check·mate \'chek-,māt\ *vb* [ME *chekmaten*, fr. *chekmate*, interj. used to announce checkmate, fr. AF *eschec mat*, fr. Ar *shāh māt*, fr. Pers, lit., the king is left unable to escape] **1** : to thwart completely : DEFEAT, FRUSTRATE **2** : to attack (an opponent's king) in chess so that escape is impossible — **checkmate** *n*

check·off \'chek-,óf\ *n* : the deduction of union dues from a worker's paycheck by the employer

check·out \'chek-,aùt\ *n* **1** : the action or an instance of checking out **2** : a counter at which checking out is done **3** : the process of examining and testing something as to readiness for intended use

check out *vb* **1** : to settle one's account (as at a hotel) and leave **2** : to total or have totaled the cost of purchases in a store and to make or receive payment for them

check·point \'chek-,póint\ *n* : a point at which a check is performed

check·room \-,rüm, -,rúm\ *n* : a room at which baggage, parcels, or clothing is left for safekeeping

checks and balances *n pl* : a system allowing each branch of a government to restrict the actions of another branch (as by a veto)

check·up \'chek-,əp\ n : EXAMINATION; esp : a general physical examination

ched·dar \'che-dər\ n, often cap : a hard mild to sharp white or yellow cheese of smooth texture

cheek \'chēk\ n 1 : the fleshy side part of the face 2 : IMPUDENCE, BOLDNESS, AUDACITY 3 : BUTTOCK 1 — **cheeked** \'chēkt\ adj

cheek·bone \'chēk-,bōn\ n : the bone or bony ridge below the eye

cheeky \'chē-kē\ adj **cheek·i·er; -est** : IMPUDENT, SAUCY — **cheek·i·ly** \-kə-lē\ adv — **cheek·i·ness** \-kē-nəs\ n

cheep \'chēp\ vb : to utter faint shrill sounds : PEEP — **cheep** n

¹**cheer** \'chir\ n [ME chere face, cheer, fr. AF, face, fr. ML cara, prob. fr. Gk kara head, face] 1 : state of mind or mood : SPIRIT 2 : ANIMATION, GAIETY 3 : hospitable entertainment : WELCOME 4 : food and drink for a feast 5 : something that gladdens 6 : a shout of applause or encouragement

²**cheer** vb 1 : to give hope or courage to : COMFORT 2 : to make glad 3 : to urge on esp. by shouts 4 : to applaud with shouts 5 : to grow or be cheerful — usu. used with up — **cheer·er** n

cheer·ful \'chir-fəl\ adj 1 : having or showing good spirits 2 : conducive to good spirits : pleasant and bright — **cheer·ful·ly** adv — **cheer·ful·ness** n

cheer·lead·er \'chir-,lē-dər\ n : a person who directs organized cheering esp. at a sports event — **cheer·lead·ing** n

cheer·less \'chir-ləs\ adj : BLEAK, DISPIRITING ⟨a ~ office⟩ — **cheer·less·ly** adv — **cheer·less·ness** n

cheery \'chir-ē\ adj **cheer·i·er; -est** : CHEERFUL ⟨~ music⟩ — **cheer·i·ly** \-ə-lē\ adv — **cheer·i·ness** \-ē-nəs\ n

cheese \'chēz\ n : the curd of milk usu. pressed into cakes and cured for use as food

cheese·burg·er \-,bər-gər\ n : a hamburger topped with cheese

cheese·cake \-,kāk\ n 1 : a dessert consisting of a creamy filling usu. containing cheese baked in a shell 2 : photographs of shapely scantily clad women

cheese·cloth \-,klȯth\ n : a lightweight coarse cotton gauze

cheese·par·ing \-,per-iŋ\ n : miserly economizing — **cheeseparing** adj

cheese·steak \-,stāk\ n : a sandwich of thinly sliced beef topped with melted cheese

cheesy \'chē-zē\ adj **chees·i·er; -est** 1 : resembling, suggesting, or containing cheese 2 : CHEAP 3 ⟨~ motels⟩

chee·tah \'chē-tə\ n [Hindi cītā leopard, fr. Skt citraka, fr. citra bright, variegated] : a large long-legged swift-moving spotted cat of Africa and formerly Asia

chef \'shef\ n : COOK; esp : one who manages a kitchen (as of a restaurant)

chef d'oeu·vre \shā-'dœvrᵊ\ n, pl **chefs d'oeuvre** \same\ : MASTERPIECE

chem abbr chemical; chemist; chemistry

¹**chem·i·cal** \'ke-mi-kəl\ adj 1 : of, relating to, used in, or produced by chemistry ⟨~ reactions⟩ 2 : acting or operated or produced by chemicals — **chem·i·cal·ly** \-k(ə-)lē\ adv

²**chemical** n 1 : a substance obtained by a chemical process or producing a chemical effect 2 : DRUG

chemical engineering n : engineering dealing with the industrial application of chemistry — **chemical engineer** n

chemical warfare n : warfare using incendiary mixtures, smokes, or irritant, burning, or asphyxiating gases

chemical weapon n : a weapon used in chemical warfare

che·mise \shə-'mēz\ n 1 : a woman's one-piece undergarment 2 : a loose straight-hanging dress

chem·ist \'ke-mist\ n 1 : one trained in chemistry 2 Brit : PHARMACIST

chem·is·try \'ke-mə-strē\ n, pl **-tries** 1 : the science that deals with the composition, structure, and properties of substances and of the changes they undergo 2 : chemical composition or properties ⟨the ~ of gasoline⟩ 3 : a strong mutual attraction; also : harmonious interaction among people (as on a team)

che·mo \'kē-mō\ n : CHEMOTHERAPY

che·mo·ther·a·py \,kē-mō-'ther-ə-pē\ n : the use of chemicals in the treatment or control of disease — **che·mo·ther·a·peu·tic** \-,ther-ə-'pyü-tik\ adj

che·nille \shə-'nēl\ n [F, lit., caterpillar, fr. OF, fr. L canicula, dim. of canis dog] : a fabric with a deep fuzzy pile often used for bedspreads and rugs

cheque chiefly Brit var of ¹CHECK 7

che·quer chiefly Brit var of CHECKER

cher·ish \'cher-ish\ vb 1 : to hold dear : treat with care and affection 2 : to keep deeply in mind ⟨~ a memory⟩ — **cher·ish·able** adj — **cher·ish·er** n

Cher·o·kee \'cher-ə-(,)kē\ n, pl **Cherokee** or **Cherokees** : a member of an American Indian people orig. of Tennessee and No. Carolina; also : their language

che·root \shə-'rüt\ n : a cigar cut square at both ends

cher·ry \'cher-ē\ n, pl **cherries** [ME chery, fr. AF cherise, cirice (taken as a plural), fr. LL ceresia, fr. L cerasus cherry tree, fr. Gk kerasos] 1 : the small fleshy pale yellow to deep blackish red fruit of a tree related to the roses; also : the tree or its wood 2 : a moderate red

chert \'chərt, 'chat\ n : a rock resembling flint and consisting essentially of fine crystalline quartz and fibrous chalcedony — **cherty** adj

cher·ub \'cher-əb\ n 1 pl **cher·u·bim** \'cher-ə-,bim\ : an angel of the 2d highest rank 2 pl **cherubs** : a chubby rosy person — **che·ru·bic** \chə-'rü-bik\ adj

chess \'ches\ n : a game for 2 played on a chessboard with each player having 16 pieces — **chess·man** \-,man, -mən\ n

chess·board \'ches-,bȯrd\ n : a checkerboard used in the game of chess

chest \'chest\ n 1 : a box, case, or boxlike receptacle for storage or shipping **2** : the part of the body enclosed by the ribs and sternum — **chest·ed** \'ches-təd\ *adj* — **chest·ful** \'chest-,fûl\ *n*

ches·ter·field \'ches-tər-,fēld\ *n* : an overcoat with a velvet collar

chest·nut \'ches-(,)nət\ *n* **1** : the edible nut of any of a genus of trees related to the beeches and oaks; *also* : this tree or its wood **2** : a grayish to reddish brown **3** : an old joke or story

chet·rum \'che-trəm\ *n, pl* **chetrums** or **chetrum** — see *ngultrum* at MONEY table

che·val glass \shə-'val-\ *n* : a full-length mirror that may be tilted in a frame

che·va·lier \,she-və-'lir, shə-'val-,yā\ *n* : a member of one of various orders of knighthood or of merit

chev·i·ot \'she-vē-ət\ *n, often cap* **1** : a twilled fabric with a rough nap **2** : a sturdy soft-finished cotton fabric

chev·ron \'she-vrən\ *n* : a sleeve badge of one or more V-shaped or inverted V-shaped stripes worn to indicate rank or service (as in the armed forces)

¹**chew** \'chü\ *vb* : to crush or grind with the teeth — **chew·able** *adj* — **chew·er** *n* — **chewy** \'chü-ē\ *adj* — **chew on** : to think about : PONDER ⟨*chew on* the proposals⟩ — **chew the fat** : to make conversation : CHAT

²**chew** *n* **1** : an act of chewing **2** : something for chewing

Chey·enne \shī-'an, -'en\ *n, pl* **Cheyenne** or **Cheyennes** [AmerF, fr. Dakota *šahíyena*] : a member of an American Indian people of the western plains of the U.S.; *also* : their language

chg *abbr* **1** change **2** charge

chi \'kī\ *n* : the 22d letter of the Greek alphabet — X or χ

Chi·an·ti \kē-'än-tē, -'an-\ *n* : a dry usu. red wine

chiar·oscu·ro \kē-,är-ə-'skúr-ō, -'skyúr-\ *n, pl* **-ros** [It, fr. *chiaro* clear, light + *oscuro* obscure, dark] **1** : pictorial representation in terms of light and shade without regard to color **2** : the arrangement or treatment of light and dark parts in a pictorial work of art

¹**chic** \'shēk\ *n* : STYLISHNESS

²**chic** *adj* : cleverly stylish : SMART; *also* : currently fashionable

Chi·ca·na \chi-'kä-nə also shi-\ *n* : an American woman or girl of Mexican descent — **Chicana** *adj*

chi·cane \shi-'kän\ *n* : CHICANERY

chi·ca·nery \-'kä-nə-rē\ *n, pl* **-ner·ies** : TRICKERY, DECEPTION

Chi·ca·no \chi-'kä-nō\ *n, pl* **-nos** : a usu. male American of Mexican descent — **Chicano** *adj*

chi·chi \'shē-(,)shē, 'chē-(,)chē\ *adj* [F] **1** : SHOWY, FRILLY **2** : ARTY, PRECIOUS ⟨~ poetry⟩ **3** : CHIC ⟨~ nightclubs⟩ — **chichi** *n*

chick \'chik\ *n* **1** : a young chicken; *also* : a young bird **2** *slang* : GIRL, WOMAN

chick·a·dee \'chi-kə-(,)dē\ *n* : any of several small grayish American birds with black or brown caps

Chick·a·saw \'chi-kə-,só\ *n, pl* **Chicka-**

saw or **Chickasaws** : a member of an American Indian people of Mississippi and Alabama

¹**chick·en** \'chi-kən\ *n* **1** : a common domestic fowl esp. when young; *also* : its flesh used as food **2** : COWARD

²**chicken** *adj* **1** : COWARDLY **2** *slang* : insistent on petty esp. military discipline

chicken feed *n, slang* : an insignificant sum of money

chick·en·heart·ed \,chi-kən-'här-təd\ *adj* : TIMID, COWARDLY

chicken out *vb* : to lose one's courage

chicken pox *n* : an acute contagious viral disease esp. of children characterized by a low fever and blisters

chicken wire *n* : a light wire netting of hexagonal mesh

chick·pea \'chik-,pē\ *n* : an Asian herb of the legume family cultivated for its short pods with one or two edible seeds; *also* : its seed

chick·weed \'chik-,wēd\ *n* : any of several low-growing small-leaved weeds related to the pinks

chi·cle \'chi-kəl\ *n* : a gum from the latex of a tropical tree used as the chief ingredient of chewing gum

chic·o·ry \'chi-kə-rē\ *n, pl* **-ries** : a usu. blue-flowered herb related to the daisies and grown for its root and for use in salads; *also* : its dried ground root used to flavor or adulterate coffee

chide \'chīd\ *vb* **chid** \'chid\ or **chid·ed** \'chī-dəd\; **chid** or **chid·den** \'chid-³n\ or **chided; chid·ing** : to speak disapprovingly to ♦ **Synonyms** REPROACH, REPROVE, REPRIMAND, ADMONISH, SCOLD, REBUKE

¹**chief** \'chēf\ *adj* **1** : highest in rank ⟨the ~ executive⟩ **2** : most important ⟨the ~ complaint⟩ ♦ **Synonyms** PRINCIPAL, MAIN, LEADING, MAJOR — **chief·ly** *adv*

²**chief** *n* **1** : the leader of a body or organization : HEAD **2** : the principal or most valuable part — **chief·dom** *n*

chief master sergeant *n* : a noncommissioned officer of the highest rank in the air force

chief of staff 1 : the ranking officer of a staff in the armed forces **2** : the ranking office of the army or air force

chief of state : the formal head of a national state as distinguished from the head of the government

chief petty officer *n* : an enlisted person in the navy ranking next below a senior chief petty officer

chief·tain \'chēf-tən\ *n* : a chief esp. of a band, tribe, or clan — **chief·tain·cy** \-sē\ *n* — **chief·tain·ship** *n*

chief warrant officer *n* : a warrant officer of senior rank

chif·fon \shi-'fän, 'shi-,\ *n* [F, lit., rag, fr. *chiffe* old rag] : a sheer fabric esp. of silk

chif·fo·nier \,shi-fə-'nir\ *n* : a high narrow chest of drawers

chig·ger \'chi-gər\ *n* : a bloodsucking larval mite that causes intense itching

chi·gnon \'shēn-,yän\ *n* [F, fr. MF *chaignon* chain, collar, nape] : a knot of hair worn at the back of the head

Chi·hua·hua \chə-'wä-,wä\ n : any of a breed of very small large-eared dogs that originated in Mexico

chil·blain \'chil-,blān\ n : a sore or inflamed swelling (as on the feet or hands) caused by exposure to cold

child \'chī(-ə)ld\ n, pl **chil·dren** \'chil-drən\ 1 : an unborn or recently born person 2 : a young person between the periods of infancy and youth 3 : a male or female offspring : SON, DAUGHTER 4 : one strongly influenced by another or by a place or state of affairs — **child·ish** adj — **child·ish·ly** adv — **child·ish·ness** n — **child·less** adj — **child·less·ness** n — **child·like** adj

child·bear·ing \'chīld-,ber-iŋ\ n : CHILD-BIRTH — **childbearing** adj

child·birth \-,bərth\ n : the act or process of giving birth to offspring

child·hood \-,hud\ n : the state or time of being a child

¹**child·proof** \-,prüf\ adj 1 : made to prevent opening or use by children ⟨~ lighters⟩ 2 : made safe for children

²**childproof** vb : to make childproof ⟨~ a house⟩

child's play n : a simple task or act

chili also **chile** or **chil·li** \'chi-lē\ n, pl **chil·ies** also **chil·es** or **chilis** or **chil·lies** 1 : any of various pungent peppers related to the tomato 2 : a thick sauce of meat and chilis 3 : CHILI CON CARNE

chili con car·ne \,chi-lē-kän-'kär-nē\ n [AmerSp chile con carne chili with meat] : a spiced stew of ground beef and chilies or chili powder usu. with beans

chili powder n : a seasoning made of ground chilis and other spices

chili sauce n : a spiced tomato sauce usu. made with red and green peppers

¹**chill** \'chil\ n 1 : a feeling of coldness accompanied by shivering 2 : moderate coldness 3 : a check to enthusiasm or warmth of feeling

²**chill** adj 1 : moderately cold 2 : COLD, RAW 3 : DISTANT, FORMAL ⟨a ~ reception⟩ 4 : DEPRESSING, DISPIRITING

³**chill** vb 1 : to make or become cold or chilly 2 : to make cool esp. without freezing 3 : RELAX — **chill·er** n

chill·ing \'chi-liŋ\ adj : gravely disturbing or frightening ⟨a ~ scene⟩

chilly \'chi-lē\ adj **chill·i·er**; **-est** 1 : noticeably cold 2 : unpleasantly affected by cold 3 : lacking warmth of feeling ⟨a ~ reception⟩ — **chill·i·ness** n

chimaera chiefly Brit var of CHIMERA

¹**chime** \'chīm\ n 1 : a set of bells musically tuned 2 : the sound of a set of bells — usu. used in pl. 3 : a musical sound suggesting bells

²**chime** vb **chimed**; **chim·ing** 1 : to make bell-like sounds 2 : to indicate (as the time of day) by chiming 3 : to be or act in accord : be in harmony

chime in vb : to break into or join in a conversation

chi·me·ra \kī-'mir-ə, kə-\ n [L chimaera, fr. Gk chimaira she-goat, chimera] 1 : an imaginary monster made up of incongru-

ous parts 2 : an illusion or fabrication of the mind; esp : an impossible dream

chi·me·ri·cal \ki-'mer-i-kəl\ also **chi·me·ric** \-ik\ adj 1 : FANTASTIC, IMAGINARY 2 : inclined to fantastic schemes

chim·ney \'chim-nē\ n, pl **chimneys** 1 : a vertical structure extending above the roof of a building for carrying off smoke 2 : a glass tube around a lamp flame

chimp \'chimp\ n : CHIMPANZEE

chim·pan·zee \,chim-,pan-'zē, chim-'pan-zē\ n : an African ape related to the much larger gorilla

¹**chin** \'chin\ n : the part of the face below the lower lip including the prominence of the lower jaw — **chin·less** adj

²**chin** vb **chinned**; **chin·ning** : to raise (oneself) while hanging by the hands until the chin is level with the support

chi·na \'chī-nə\ n : porcelain ware; also : domestic pottery in general

Chi·na·town \-,taun\ n : the Chinese quarter of a city

chinch bug \'chinch-\ n : a small black and white bug destructive to cereal grasses

chin·chil·la \chin-'chi-lə\ n 1 : either of two small So. American rodents with soft pearl-gray fur; also : this fur 2 : a heavy long-napped woolen cloth

chine \'chīn\ n : BACKBONE, SPINE; also : a cut of meat including all or part of the backbone

Chi·nese \chī-'nēz, -'nēs\ n, pl **Chinese** 1 : a native or inhabitant of China 2 : any of a group of related languages of China — **Chinese** adj

Chinese cabbage n 1 : BOK CHOY 2 : an Asian garden plant related to the cabbage and widely grown in the U.S. for its tight elongate cylindrical heads of pale green to cream-colored leaves

Chinese checkers n : a game in which each player in turn transfers a set of marbles from a home point to the opposite point of a pitted 6-pointed star

Chinese gooseberry n : a subtropical vine that bears kiwifruit; also : KIWI-FRUIT

Chinese lantern n : a collapsible translucent cover for a light

¹**chink** \'chiŋk\ n : a small crack or fissure

²**chink** vb : to fill the chinks of : stop up

³**chink** n : a slight sharp metallic sound

⁴**chink** vb : to make a slight sharp metallic sound

chi·no \'chē-nō\ n, pl **chinos** 1 : a usu. khaki cotton twill 2 pl : an article of clothing made of chino

Chi·nook \shə-'nuk, chə-, -'nük\ n, pl **Chinook** or **Chinooks** : a member of an American Indian people of Oregon

chintz \'chints\ n : a usu. glazed printed cotton cloth

chintzy \'chint-sē\ adj **chintz·i·er**; **-est** 1 : decorated with or as if with chintz 2 : GAUDY, CHEAP ⟨a ~ low-budget film⟩ 3 : STINGY — **chintz·i·ness** n

chin–up \'chin-,əp\ n : the act of chinning oneself

¹**chip** \'chip\ n 1 : a small usu. thin and flat piece (as of wood) cut or broken off

2 : a thin crisp morsel of food 3 : a counter used in games (as poker) 4 *pl, slang* : MONEY 5 : a flaw left after a chip is broken off 6 : INTEGRATED CIRCUIT 7 : a very small slice of silicon containing electronic circuits — **chip off the old block** : a child that resembles his or her parent

²**chip** *vb* **chipped; chip·ping** 1 : to cut or break chips from 2 : to break off in small pieces at the edges 3 : to play a chip shot **chip in** *vb* : CONTRIBUTE

chip·munk \'chip-ˌməŋk\ *n* [earlier *chitmunk*, prob. fr. Ojibwa *ačitamoʼnʔ*] red squirrel] : any of a genus of small striped No. American and Asian rodents closely related to the squirrels and marmots

chi·pot·le \chə-'pōt-lā\ *n* : a smoked and usu. dried jalapeño pepper

chipped beef \'chipt-\ *n* : smoked dried beef sliced thin

¹**chip·per** \'chi-pər\ *n* : one that chips

²**chipper** *adj* : LIVELY, CHEERFUL

Chip·pe·wa \'chi-pə-ˌwȯ, -ˌwä, -ˌwā, -wə\ *n, pl* **Chippewa** *or* **Chippewas** : OJIBWA

chip shot *n* : a short usu. low shot to the green in golf

chi·rog·ra·phy \kī-'rä-grə-fē\ *n* : HANDWRITING, PENMANSHIP — **chi·ro·graph·ic** \ˌkī-rə-'gra-fik\ *adj*

chi·rop·o·dy \kə-'rä-pə-dē, shə-\ *n* : PODIATRY — **chi·rop·o·dist** \-dist\ *n*

chi·ro·prac·tic \'kī-rə-ˌprak-tik\ *n* : a system of therapy based esp. on manipulation of body structures — **chi·ro·prac·tor** \-tər\ *n*

chirp \'chərp\ *n* : a short sharp sound characteristic of a small bird or cricket — **chirp** *vb* — **chirpy** \'chər-pē\ *adj*

¹**chis·el** \'chi-zəl\ *n* : a metal tool with a sharpened edge at one end used to chip, carve, or cut into a solid material (as wood or stone)

²**chisel** *vb* **-eled** *or* **-elled; -el·ing** *or* **-el·ling** 1 : to work with or as if with a chisel 2 : to obtain by shrewd often unfair methods; *also* : CHEAT — **chis·el·er** *n*

¹**chit** \'chit\ *n* [ME *chitte* kitten, cub] 1 : CHILD 2 : a pert young woman

²**chit** *n* [Hindi *ciṭṭhī* letter, note] : a signed voucher for a small debt

chit·chat \'chit-ˌchat\ *n* : casual or trifling conversation — **chitchat** *vb*

chi·tin \'kī-tᵊn\ *n* : a sugar polymer that forms part of the hard outer integument esp. of insects — **chi·tin·ous** *adj*

chit·ter·lings *or* **chit·lins** \'chit-lənz\ *n pl* : the intestines of hogs esp. when prepared as food

chi·val·ric \shə-'val-rik\ *adj* : relating to chivalry : CHIVALROUS

chiv·al·rous \'shi-vəl-rəs\ *adj* 1 : of or relating to chivalry 2 : marked by honor, courtesy, and generosity 3 : marked by especial courtesy to women — **chiv·al·rous·ly** *adv* — **chiv·al·rous·ness** *n*

chiv·al·ry \'shi-vəl-rē\ *n, pl* **-ries** 1 : mounted men-at-arms 2 : the system or practices of knighthood 3 : the spirit or character of the ideal knight

chive \'chīv\ *n* : an herb related to the onion that has slender leaves used for flavoring; *also* : its leaves

chla·myd·ia \klə-'mi-dē-ə\ *n, pl* **-i·ae** \-dē-ˌē\ 1 : any of a genus of bacteria that cause various diseases of the eye and urogenital tract 2 : a disease or infection caused by chlamydiae

chlo·ral hydrate \'klȯr-əl-\ *n* : a white crystalline compound used as a hypnotic and sedative

chlor·dane \'klȯr-ˌdān\ *n* : a highly chlorinated persistent insecticide

chlo·ride \'klȯr-ˌīd\ *n* : a compound of chlorine with another element or group

chlo·ri·nate \'klȯr-ə-ˌnāt\ *vb* **-nat·ed; -nat·ing** : to treat or combine with chlorine or a chlorine compound — **chlo·ri·na·tion** \ˌklȯr-ə-'nā-shən\ *n* — **chlo·ri·na·tor** \'klȯr-ə-ˌnā-tər\ *n*

chlo·rine \'klȯr-ˌēn\ *n* : a nonmetallic chemical element that is found alone as a strong-smelling greenish-yellow irritating gas and is used as a bleach, oxidizing agent, and disinfectant

chlorine monoxide *n* : a reactive radical that plays a major role in stratospheric ozone depletion

chlo·rite \'klȯr-ˌīt\ *n* : a usu. green mineral found with and resembling mica

chlo·ro·flu·o·ro·car·bon \ˌklȯr-ə-'flȯr-ə-ˌkär-bən, -'flu̇r-\ *n* : any of several gaseous compounds that contain carbon, chlorine, fluorine, and sometimes hydrogen and are used esp. as solvents, refrigerants, and aerosol propellants

¹**chlo·ro·form** \'klȯr-ə-ˌfȯrm\ *n* : a colorless heavy fluid with etherlike odor used as a solvent

²**chloroform** *vb* : to treat with chloroform to produce anesthesia or death

chlo·ro·phyll \-ˌfil\ *n* : the green coloring matter of plants that functions in photosynthesis

chlo·ro·plast \'klȯr-ə-ˌplast\ *n* : a cytoplasmic organelle that contains chlorophyll and is the site of photosynthesis

chm *abbr* chairman

chock \'chäk\ *n* : a wedge for steadying something or for blocking the movement of a wheel — **chock** *vb*

chock·a·block \'chä-kə-ˌbläk\ *adj* : very full : CROWDED

chock-full \'chək-'fu̇l, 'chäk-\ *adj* : full to the limit : CRAMMED

choc·o·late \'chä-k(ə-)lət, 'chȯ-\ *n* [Sp, fr. Nahuatl *chocolātl*] 1 : a food prepared from ground roasted cacao beans; *also* : a drink prepared from this 2 : a candy made of or with a coating of chocolate 3 : a dark brown color — **choc·o·laty** *or* **choc·o·lat·ey** \-k(ə-)lə-tē\ *adj*

Choc·taw \'chäk-ˌtȯ\ *n, pl* **Choctaw** *or* **Choctaws** : a member of an American Indian people of Mississippi, Alabama, and Louisiana; *also* : their language

¹**choice** \'chȯis\ *n* 1 : the act of choosing : SELECTION 2 : the power or opportunity of choosing : OPTION 3 : the best part 4 : a person or thing selected 5 : a variety offered for selection

²**choice** *adj* **choic·er; choic·est** 1 : wor-

thy of being chosen **2** : selected with care **3** : of high quality

choir \'kwī(-ə)r\ *n* **1** : an organized company of singers (as in a church service) **2** : the part of a church occupied by the singers or by the clergy

choir·boy \'kwī-(-ə)r-ˌbȯi\ *n* : a boy member of a choir

choir·mas·ter \-ˌmas-tər\ *n* : the director of a choir (as in a church)

¹choke \'chōk\ *vb* **choked; chok·ing** **1** : to hinder breathing (as by obstructing the trachea) : STRANGLE **2** : to check the growth or action of **3** : CLOG, OBSTRUCT **4** : to enrich the fuel mixture of (a motor) by restricting the carburetor air intake **5** : to perform badly in a critical situation

²choke *n* **1** : the act of choking **2** : a narrowing in size toward the muzzle in the bore of a gun **3** : a valve for choking a gasoline engine

choke hold *n* **1** : a hold that involves strong choking pressure **2** : absolute control

chok·er \'chō-kər\ *n* : something (as a necklace) worn tightly around the neck

cho·ler \'kä-lər, 'kō-\ *n* : a tendency toward anger : IRASCIBILITY

chol·era \'kä-lə-rə\ *n* : any of several bacterial diseases usu. marked by severe vomiting and dysentery

cho·ler·ic \'kä-lə-rik, kə-'ler-ik\ *adj* **1** : IRASCIBLE **2** : ANGRY, IRATE

cho·les·ter·ol \kə-'les-tə-ˌrȯl\ *n* : a physiologically important waxy steroid alcohol found in animal tissues and in high concentrations implicated as a cause of arteriosclerosis

chomp \'chämp, 'chȯmp\ *vb* : to chew or bite on something heavily

chon \'chän\ *n, pl* **chon** — see *won* at MONEY table

choose \'chüz\ *vb* **chose** \'chōz\; **cho·sen** \'chō-z³n\; **choos·ing** \'chü-ziŋ\ **1** : to select esp. after consideration **2** : DECIDE **3** : to have a preference for — **choos·er** *n*

choosy *or* **choos·ey** \'chü-zē\ *adj* **choos·i·er; -est** : very particular in making choices

¹chop \'chäp\ *vb* **chopped; chop·ping** **1** : to cut by repeated blows **2** : to cut into small pieces : MINCE **3** : to strike (a ball) with a short quick downward stroke

²chop *n* **1** : a sharp downward blow or stroke **2** : a small cut of meat often including part of a rib **3** : a short abrupt motion (as of a wave)

³chop *n* **1** : an official seal or stamp **2** : a mark on goods to indicate quality or kind; *also* : QUALITY, GRADE

chop·house \'chäp-ˌhaus\ *n* : RESTAURANT

chop·per \'chä-pər\ *n* **1** : one that chops **2** *pl, slang* : TEETH **3** : HELICOPTER

chop·pi·ness \'chä-pē-nəs\ *n* : the quality or state of being choppy

¹chop·py \'chä-pē\ *adj* **chop·pi·er; -est** **1** : rough with small waves ⟨a ~ sea⟩ **2** : JERKY, DISCONNECTED ⟨short ~ sentences⟩ — **chop·pi·ly** \-pə-lē\ *adv*

²choppy *adj* **chop·pi·er; -est** : CHANGEABLE, VARIABLE ⟨a ~ wind⟩

chops \'chäps\ *n pl* **1** : the fleshy covering of the jaws **2** : expertise in a particular field or activity ⟨acting ~⟩

chop·stick \'chäp-ˌstik\ *n* : one of a pair of sticks used chiefly in Asian countries for lifting food to the mouth

chop su·ey \chäp-'sü-ē\ *n, pl* **chop su·eys** : a dish made of vegetables (as bean sprouts, bamboo shoots, water chestnuts, onions, mushrooms) and meat or fish and served with rice

cho·ral \'kōr-əl\ *adj* : of, relating to, or sung by a choir or chorus or in chorus — **cho·ral·ly** *adv*

cho·rale \kə-'ral, -'räl\ *n* **1** : a hymn or psalm sung in church; *also* : a harmonization of a traditional melody **2** : CHORUS, CHOIR

¹chord \'kȯrd\ *n* [alter. of ME *cord,* short for *accord*] : three or more musical tones sounded simultaneously

²chord *n* **1** : CORD 2 **2** : a straight line joining two points on a curve

chore \'chȯr\ *n* [ME *char* turn, piece of work, fr. OE *chierr*] **1** *pl* : the daily light work of a household or farm **2** : a routine task or job **3** : a difficult or disagreeable task

cho·rea \kə-'rē-ə\ *n* : any of various nervous disorders marked by spasmodic uncontrolled movements

cho·re·og·ra·phy \ˌkȯr-ē-'ä-grə-fē\ *n, pl* **-phies** : the art of composing and arranging dances and esp. ballets — **cho·re·ograph** \'kȯr-ē-ə-ˌgraf\ *vb* — **cho·re·og·ra·pher** \ˌkȯr-ē-'ä-grə-fər\ *n* — **cho·re·o·graph·ic** \ˌkȯr-ē-ə-'gra-fik\ *adj* — **cho·re·o·graph·i·cal·ly** \-fi-k(ə-)lē\ *adv*

cho·ris·ter \'kȯr-ə-stər\ *n* : a singer in a choir

chor·tle \'chȯr-t³l\ *vb* **chor·tled; chor·tling** : to laugh or chuckle esp. in satisfaction or exultation — **chortle** *n*

¹cho·rus \'kōr-əs\ *n* **1** : an organized company of singers : CHOIR **2** : a group of dancers and singers (as in a musical comedy) **3** : a part of a song repeated at intervals **4** : a composition to be sung by a chorus; *also* : group singing **5** : sounds uttered by a number of persons or animals together ⟨a ~ of boos⟩

²chorus *vb* : to sing or utter in chorus

chose *past of* CHOOSE

cho·sen \'chō-z³n\ *adj* : selected or marked for special favor or privilege

chou·croute \shü-'krüt\ *n* **1** : SAUERKRAUT **2** *or* **choucroute gar·nie** \-gär-'nē\ : sauerkraut cooked and served with meat

¹chow \'chau\ *n* : FOOD

²chow *vb* : EAT — often used with *down*

³chow *n* : CHOW CHOW

chow-chow \'chau-ˌchau\ *n* : chopped mixed pickles in mustard sauce

chow chow \'chau-ˌchau\ *n* : any of a breed of thick-coated muscular dogs of Chinese origin with a blue-black tongue and a short tail curled close to the back

chow·der \'chau-dər\ *n* : a soup or stew

made from seafood or vegetables and containing milk or tomatoes

chow mein \'chaù-'mān\ *n* : a seasoned stew of shredded or diced meat, mushrooms, and vegetables that is usu. served with fried noodles

chrism \'kri-zəm\ *n* : consecrated oil used esp. in baptism, confirmation, and ordination

Christ \'krīst\ *n* [ME *Crist*, fr. OE, fr. L *Christus*, fr. Gk *Christos*, lit., anointed] : Jesus esp. as the Messiah — **Christ-like** *adj* — **Christ-ly** *adj*

chris-ten \'kri-s°n\ *vb* **1** : BAPTIZE **2** : to name at baptism **3** : to name or dedicate (as a ship) by a ceremony suggestive of baptism — **chris-ten-ing** *n*

Chris-ten-dom \'kri-s°n-dəm\ *n* **1** : CHRISTIANITY **2** : the part of the world in which Christianity prevails

¹**Chris-tian** \'kris-chən\ *n* : an adherent of Christianity

²**Christian** *adj* **1** : of or relating to Christianity **2** : based on or conforming with Christianity **3** : of or relating to a Christian **4** : professing Christianity

Chris-ti-an-i-ty \,kris-chē-'a-nə-tē\ *n* : the religion derived from Jesus Christ, based on the Bible as sacred scripture, and professed by Christians

Chris-tian-ize \'kris-chə-,nīz\ *vb* **-ized; -iz-ing** : to make Christian

Christian name *n* : GIVEN NAME

Christian Science *n* : a religion and system of healing founded by Mary Baker Eddy and taught by the Church of Christ, Scientist — **Christian Scientist** *n*

chris-tie *or* **chris-ty** \'kris-tē\ *n, pl* **chris-ties** : a skiing turn made by shifting body weight forward and skidding into a turn with parallel skis

Christ-mas \'kris-məs\ *n* : December 25 celebrated as a church festival in commemoration of the birth of Christ and observed as a legal holiday

Christmas club *n* : a savings account in which regular deposits are made to provide money for Christmas shopping

Christ-mas-tide \'kris-məs-,tīd\ *n* : the season of Christmas

chro-mat-ic \krō-'ma-tik\ *adj* **1** : of or relating to color **2** : proceeding by half steps of the musical scale — **chro-mat-i-cism** \-tə-,si-zəm\ *n*

chro-mato-graph \krō-'ma-tə-,graf\ *n* : an instrument used in chromatography

chro-ma-tog-ra-phy \,krō-mə-'tä-grə-fē\ *n* : the separation of a complex mixture into its component compounds as a result of the different rates at which the compounds travel through or over a stationary substance due to differing affinities for the substance — **chro-mato-graph-ic** \krō-,ma-tə-'gra-fik\ *adj* — **chro-mato-graph-i-cal-ly** \-fi-k(ə-)lē\ *adv*

chrome \'krōm\ *n* **1** : CHROMIUM **2** : a chromium pigment **3** : something plated with an alloy of chromium

chro-mi-um \'krō-mē-əm\ *n* : a bluish white metallic element used esp. in alloys and chrome plating

chro-mo-some \'krō-mə-,sōm, -,zōm\ *n* [G *Chromosom*, fr. Gk *chrōma* color, pigment + *sōma* body] : any of the rod-shaped or threadlike DNA-containing structures of cellular organisms that contain most or all of the genes of the organism — **chro-mo-som-al** \,krō-mə-'sō-məl, -'zō-\ *adj*

chro-mo-sphere \'krō-mə-,sfir\ *n* : the lower part of a star's atmosphere

chron *abbr* **1** chronicle **2** chronological; chronology

Chron *abbr* Chronicles

chron-ic \'krä-nik\ *adj* : marked by long duration or frequent recurrence ⟨a ~ disease⟩; *also* : HABITUAL ⟨a ~ grumbler⟩ — **chron-i-cal-ly** \-ni-k(ə-)lē\ *adv*

chronic fatigue syndrome *n* : a disorder of unknown cause that is characterized by persistent profound fatigue

¹**chron-i-cle** \'krä-ni-kəl\ *n* : HISTORY, NARRATIVE

²**chronicle** *vb* **-cled; -cling** : to record in or as if in a chronicle — **chron-i-cler** *n*

Chronicles *n* — see BIBLE table

chro-no-graph \'krä-nə-,graf\ *n* : an instrument for measuring and recording time intervals with accuracy — **chro-no-graph-ic** \,krä-nə-'gra-fik\ *adj* — **chro-nog-ra-phy** \krə-'nä-grə-fē\ *n*

chro-nol-o-gy \krə-'nä-lə-jē\ *n, pl* **-gies** **1** : the science that deals with measuring time and dating events **2** : a chronological list or table **3** : arrangement of events in the order of their occurrence — **chron-o-log-i-cal** \,krän-°l-'ä-ji-kəl\ *adj* — **chron-o-log-i-cal-ly** \-k(ə-)lē\ *adv* — **chro-nol-o-gist** \krə-'nä-lə-jist\ *n*

chro-nom-e-ter \krə-'nä-mə-tər\ *n* : a very accurate timepiece

chrys-a-lid \'kri-sə-ləd\ *n* : CHRYSALIS

chrys-a-lis \'kri-sə-ləs\ *n, pl* **chry-sal-i-des** \kri-'sa-lə-,dēz\ *or* **chrys-a-lis-es** : an insect pupa in a firm case without a cocoon

chry-san-the-mum \kri-'san-thə-məm\ *n* [L, fr. Gk *chrysanthemon*, fr. *chrysos* gold + *anthemon* flower] : any of various plants related to the daisies including some grown for their showy brightly colored flowers or for medicinal products or insecticides; *also* : a flower of a chrysanthemum

chub \'chəb\ *n, pl* **chub** *or* **chubs** : any of various small freshwater fishes related to the carp

chub-by \'chə-bē\ *adj* **chub-bi-er; -est** : PLUMP ⟨a ~ child⟩ — **chub-bi-ness** *n*

¹**chuck** \'chək\ *vb* **1** : to give a pat or tap **2** : TOSS **3** : DISCARD; *also* : EJECT **4** : to have done with ⟨~ed his job⟩

²**chuck** *n* **1** : a light pat under the chin **2** : TOSS

³**chuck** *n* **1** : a cut of beef including most of the neck and the parts around the shoulder blade and the first three ribs **2** : a device for holding work or a tool in a machine (as a lathe)

chuck-hole \'chək-,hōl\ *n* : POTHOLE

chuck-le \'chə-kəl\ *vb* **chuck-led; chuck-ling** : to laugh in a quiet hardly audible manner — **chuckle** *n*

chuck wagon n : a wagon equipped with a stove and food supplies

¹chug \'chəg\ n : a dull explosive sound made by or as if by a laboring engine

²chug vb **chugged; chug·ging** : to move or go with chugs

chuk·ka \'chə-kə\ n : a usu. ankle-length leather boot

chuk·ker \'chə-kər\ also **chuk·ka** \'chə-kə\ n : a playing period of a polo game

¹chum \'chəm\ n : a close friend

²chum vb **chummed; chum·ming 1** : to room together **2** : to be a close friend

chum·my \'chə-mē\ adj **chum·mi·er; -est** : quite friendly — **chum·mi·ly** \-mə-lē\ adv — **chum·mi·ness** \-mē-nəs\ n

chump \'chəmp\ n : FOOL, BLOCKHEAD

chunk \'chəŋk\ n **1** : a short thick piece ⟨a ~ of meat⟩ **2** : a sizable amount

chunky \'chəŋ-kē\ adj **chunk·i·er; -est 1** : STOCKY **2** : containing chunks

church \'chərch\ n [ME chirche, fr. OE cirice, ultim. fr. LGk kyriakon, fr. Gk. neut. of kyriakos of the lord, fr. kyrios lord, master] **1** : a building esp. for Christian public worship **2** often cap : the whole body of Christians **3** : DENOMINATION **4** : CONGREGATION **5** : public divine worship

church·go·er \'chərch-ˌgō-ər\ n : one who habitually attends church — **church·go·ing** adj or n

church·less \'chərch-ləs\ adj : not affiliated with a church

church·man \'chərch-mən\ n **1** : CLERGYMAN **2** : a member of a church

church·war·den \'chərch-ˌwȯr-dᵊn\ n : WARDEN 5

church·yard \-ˌyärd\ n : a yard that belongs to a church and is often used as a burial ground

churl \'chərl\ n **1** : a medieval peasant **2** : RUSTIC **3** : a rude ill-bred person — **churl·ish** adj — **churl·ish·ly** adv — **churl·ish·ness** n

¹churn \'chərn\ n : a container in which milk or cream is agitated in making butter

²churn vb **1** : to stir in a churn; also : to make (butter) by such stirring **2** : to shake around violently

churn out vb : to produce mechanically or in large quantity

chute \'shüt\ n **1** : an inclined surface, trough, or passage down or through which something may pass ⟨a coal ~⟩ ⟨a mail ~⟩ **2** : PARACHUTE

chut·ney \'chət-nē\ n, pl **chutneys** : a thick sauce containing fruits, vinegar, sugar, and spices

chutz·pah \'hu̇t-spə, 'ku̇t-, -(ˌ)spä\ n : supreme self-confidence

CIA abbr Central Intelligence Agency

cía abbr [Sp compañía] company

cia·bat·ta \chə-'bä-tə\ n [It, lit., slipper] : a flat bread with a moist interior and a crispy crust

ciao \'chau̇\ interj — used to express greeting or farewell

ci·ca·da \sə-'kā-də\ n : any of a family of stout-bodied insects related to the aphids

and having wide blunt heads and large transparent wings

ci·ca·trix \'si-kə-ˌtriks\ n, pl **ci·ca·tri·ces** \ˌsi-kə-'trī-ˌsēz\ [L] : a scar resulting from formation and contraction of fibrous tissue in a wound

ci·ce·ro·ne \ˌsi-sə-'rō-nē, ˌchē-chə-\ n, pl **-ni** \-(ˌ)nē\ : a guide who conducts sightseers

CID abbr Criminal Investigation Department

ci·der \'sī-dər\ n : juice pressed from fruit (as apples) and used as a beverage, vinegar, or flavoring

cie abbr [F compagnie] company

ci·gar \si-'gär\ n [Sp cigarro] : a roll of tobacco for smoking

cig·a·rette \ˌsi-gə-'ret, 'si-gə-ˌret\ n [F, dim. of cigare cigar] : a slender roll of cut tobacco enclosed in paper for smoking

cig·a·ril·lo \ˌsi-gə-'ri-lō, -'rē-ō\ n, pl **-los** [Sp] **1** : a very small cigar **2** : a cigarette wrapped in tobacco rather than paper

ci·lan·tro \si-'län-trō, -'lan-\ n : leaves of coriander used as a flavoring or garnish; also : the coriander plant

cil·i·ate \'si-lē-ˌāt\ n : any of a group of protozoans characterized by cilia

cil·i·um \'si-lē-əm\ n, pl **cil·ia** \-lē-ə\ **1** : a minute short hairlike process; esp : one of a cell **2** : EYELASH

C in C abbr commander in chief

cinch \'sinch\ n **1** : a girth for a pack or saddle **2** : a sure or an easy thing — **cinch** vb

cin·cho·na \siŋ-'kō-nə\ n : any of a genus of So. American trees related to the madder; also : the bitter quinine-containing bark of a cinchona

cinc·ture \'siŋk-chər\ n : BELT, SASH

cin·der \'sin-dər\ n **1** : SLAG **2** pl : ASHES **3** : a hot piece of partly burned wood or coal **4** : a fragment of lava from an erupting volcano — **cin·dery** adj

cinder block n : a building block made of cement and coal cinders

cin·e·ma \'si-nə-mə\ n **1** : a motion-picture theater **2** : MOVIES — **cin·e·mat·ic** \ˌsi-nə-'ma-tik\ adj

cin·e·ma·theque \ˌsi-nə-mə-'tek\ n : a small movie house specializing in avant-garde films

cin·e·ma·tog·ra·phy \ˌsi-nə-mə-'tä-grə-fē\ n : motion-picture photography — **cin·e·ma·tog·ra·pher** n — **cin·e·mat·o·graph·ic** \-ˌma-tə-'gra-fik\ adj

cine·phile \'si-nə-ˌfi(-ə)l\ n : a lover of motion pictures

cin·e·plex \'si-nə-ˌpleks\ n : a complex that houses several movie theaters

cin·er·ar·i·um \ˌsi-nə-'rer-ē-əm\ n, pl **-ia** \-ē-ə\ : a place to receive the ashes of the cremated dead — **cin·er·ary** \'si-nə-ˌrer-ē\ adj

cin·na·bar \'si-nə-ˌbär\ n **1** : a red mineral that is the only important ore of mercury **2** : a deep vivid red

cin·na·mon \'si-nə-mən\ n : a spice prepared from the highly aromatic bark of any of several Asian trees related to the true laurel; also : a tree that yields cinnamon

cinque·foil \'siŋk-ˌfȯi(-ə)l, 'saŋk-\ *n* : any of a genus of plants related to the roses with leaves having five lobes

¹**ci·pher** \'sī-fər\ *n* [ME, fr. ML *cifra*, fr. Ar *ṣifr* empty, zero] **1** : ZERO, NAUGHT **2** : a method of secret writing

²**cipher** *vb* : to compute arithmetically

cir *or* **circ** *abbr* circular

cir·ca \'sər-kə\ *prep* : ABOUT ⟨~ 1600⟩

cir·ca·di·an \sər-'kā-dē-ən\ *adj* : being, having, characterized by, or occurring in approximately 24-hour intervals (as of biological activity)

¹**cir·cle** \'sər-kəl\ *n* **1** : a closed curve every point of which is equally distant from a fixed point within it **2** : something circular **3** : an area of action or influence **4** : CYCLE **5** : a group bound by a common tie ⟨sewing ~⟩

²**circle** *vb* **cir·cled; cir·cling 1** : to enclose in a circle **2** : to move or revolve around; *also* : to move in a circle

cir·clet \'sər-klət\ *n* : a small circle; *esp* : a circular ornament

cir·cuit \'sər-kət\ *n* **1** : a boundary around an enclosed space **2** : a course around a periphery **3** : a regular tour (as by a judge) around an assigned territory **4** : the complete path of an electric current; *also* : an assemblage of electronic components **5** : LEAGUE; *also* : a chain of theaters

circuit board *n* : BOARD 7

circuit breaker *n* : a switch that automatically interrupts the current of an overloaded circuit

circuit court *n* : a court that sits at two or more places within one judicial district

cir·cu·i·tous \ˌsər-'kyü-ə-təs\ *adj* : having a circular or winding course ⟨a ~ route⟩ **2** : not being forthright or direct in language or action ⟨a ~ explanation⟩

cir·cuit·ry \'sər-kə-trē\ *n, pl* **-ries** : the plan or the components of an electric circuit

cir·cu·ity \ˌsər-'kyü-ə-tē\ *n, pl* **-ities** : INDIRECTION

¹**cir·cu·lar** \'sər-kyə-lər\ *adj* **1** : having the form of a circle : ROUND **2** : moving in or around a circle **3** : CIRCUITOUS **4** : intended for circulation ⟨a ~ letter⟩ — **cir·cu·lar·i·ty** \ˌsər-kyə-'ler-ə-tē\ *n*

²**circular** *n* : a paper (as a leaflet) intended for wide distribution

cir·cu·lar·ise *Brit var of* CIRCULARIZE

cir·cu·lar·ize \'sər-kyə-lə-ˌrīz\ *vb* **-ized; -iz·ing 1** : to send circulars to **2** : to poll by questionnaire **3** : to make circular

circular saw *n* : a power saw with a round cutting blade

cir·cu·late \'sər-kyə-ˌlāt\ *vb* **-lat·ed; -lat·ing 1** : to move or cause to move in a circle, circuit, or orbit **2** : to pass from place to place or from person to person — **cir·cu·la·tion** \ˌsər-kyə-'lā-shən\ *n*

cir·cu·la·to·ry \'sər-kyə-lə-ˌtȯr-ē\ *adj* : of or relating to circulation or the circulatory system

circulatory system *n* : the system of blood, blood vessels, lymphatic vessels, and heart concerned with the circulation of the blood and lymph

cir·cum·am·bu·late \ˌsər-kəm-'am-byə-ˌlāt\ *vb* **-lat·ed; -lat·ing** : to circle on foot esp. as part of a ritual

cir·cum·cise \'sər-kəm-ˌsīz\ *vb* **-cised; -cis·ing** [ME, fr. L *circumcisus*, pp. of *circumcidere*, lit., to cut around, fr. *circum* around + *caedere* to cut] : to cut off the foreskin of — **cir·cum·ci·sion** \ˌsər-kəm-'si-zhən\ *n*

cir·cum·fer·ence \sər-'kəm-f(ə-)rəns\ *n* **1** : the perimeter of a circle **2** : the external boundary or surface of a figure or object

cir·cum·flex \'sər-kəm-ˌfleks\ *n* : the mark ^ over a vowel

cir·cum·lo·cu·tion \ˌsər-kəm-lō-'kyü-shən\ *n* : the use of unnecessary words in expressing an idea

cir·cum·lu·nar \-'lü-nər\ *adj* : revolving about or surrounding the moon

cir·cum·nav·i·gate \-'na-və-ˌgāt\ *vb* : to go completely around (as the earth) esp. by water — **cir·cum·nav·i·ga·tion** \-ˌna-və-'gā-shən\ *n*

cir·cum·po·lar \-'pō-lər\ *adj* **1** : continually visible above the horizon ⟨a ~ star⟩ **2** : surrounding or found near a pole of the earth ⟨a ~ current⟩

cir·cum·scribe \'sər-kəm-ˌskrīb\ *vb* **1** : to constrict the range or activity of **2** : to draw a line around — **cir·cum·scrip·tion** \ˌsər-kəm-'skrip-shən\ *n*

cir·cum·spect \'sər-kəm-ˌspekt\ *adj* : careful to consider all circumstances and consequences : PRUDENT — **cir·cum·spec·tion** \ˌsər-kəm-'spek-shən\ *n*

cir·cum·stance \'sər-kəm-ˌstans\ *n* **1** : a fact or event that must be considered along with another fact or event **2** : surrounding conditions **3** : CHANCE, FATE **4** *pl* : situation with regard to wealth **5** : CEREMONY ⟨pomp and ~⟩

cir·cum·stan·tial \ˌsər-kəm-'stan-chəl\ *adj* **1** : consisting of or depending on circumstances **2** : INCIDENTAL **3** : containing full details — **cir·cum·stan·tial·ly** *adv*

cir·cum·vent \ˌsər-kəm-'vent\ *vb* : to check or defeat esp. by stratagem — **cir·cum·ven·tion** \-'vent-shən\ *n*

cir·cus \'sər-kəs\ *n* **1** : a usu. traveling show that features feats of physical skill, wild animal acts, and performances by clowns **2** : a circus performance; *also* : the equipment, livestock, and personnel of a circus

cirque \'sərk\ *n* : a deep steep-walled mountain basin formerly the blunt end of a valley

cir·rho·sis \sə-'rō-səs\ *n, pl* **-rho·ses** \-ˌsēz\ [NL, fr. Gk *kirrhos* orange-colored] : fibrosis of the liver — **cir·rhot·ic** \-'rä-tik\ *adj or n*

cir·rus \'sir-əs\ *n, pl* **cir·ri** \'sir-ˌī\ : a wispy white cloud usu. of minute ice crystals at high altitudes

cis·lu·nar \(ˌ)sis-'lü-nər\ *adj* : lying between the earth and the moon or the moon's orbit

cis·sy *Brit var of* SISSY

cis·tern \'sis-tərn\ *n* : an often underground tank for storing water

cit *abbr* **1** citation; cited **2** citizen

cit·a·del \'si-tə-dəl, -,del\ *n* **1** : a fortress commanding a city **2** : STRONGHOLD

ci·ta·tion \sī-'tā-shən\ *n* **1** : an official summons to appear (as before a court) **2** : QUOTATION **3** : a formal statement of the achievements of a person; *also* : a specific reference in a military dispatch to meritorious performance of duty

cite \'sīt\ *vb* **cit·ed; cit·ing 1** : to summon to appear before a court **2** : QUOTE **3** : to refer to esp. in commendation or praise

cit·i·fied \'si-ti-,fīd\ *adj* : of, relating to, or characterized by an urban style of living

cit·i·zen \'si-tə-zən\ *n* **1** : an inhabitant of a city or town **2** : a person who owes allegiance to a government and is entitled to its protection — **cit·i·zen·ship** *n*

cit·i·zen·ry \-rē\ *n, pl* **-ries** : a whole body of citizens

citizens band *n* : a range of radio frequencies set aside for private radio communications

cit·ric acid \'si-trik-\ *n* : a sour organic acid obtained from lemon and lime juices or by fermentation of sugars and used chiefly as a flavoring

cit·ron \'si-trən\ *n* **1** : the oval lemonlike fruit of a citrus tree; *also* : the tree **2** : a small hard-fleshed watermelon used esp. in pickles and preserves

cit·ro·nel·la \,si-trə-'ne-lə\ *n* : a lemon-scented oil obtained from a fragrant grass of southern Asia and used in perfumes and as an insect repellent

cit·rus \'si-trəs\ *n, pl* **citrus** *or* **cit·rus·es** : any of a genus of often thorny evergreen trees or shrubs grown in warm regions for their fruits (as the orange, lemon, lime, and grapefruit); *also* : the fruit

city \'si-tē\ *n, pl* **cit·ies** [ME *citie* large or small town, fr. AF *cité*, fr. ML *civitas*, fr. L, citizenship, state, city of Rome, fr. *civis* citizen] **1** : an inhabited place larger or more important than a town **2** : a municipality in the U.S. governed under a charter granted by the state; *also* : an incorporated municipal unit of the highest class in Canada

city manager *n* : an official employed by an elected council to direct the administration of a city government

city-state \'si-tē-,stāt\ *n* : an autonomous state consisting of a city and surrounding territory

civ *abbr* **1** civil; civilian **2** civilization

civ·et \'si-vət\ *n* : a yellowish strong-smelling substance obtained from a cat-like Old World mammal (**civet cat**) and used in making perfumes

civ·ic \'si-vik\ *adj* : of or relating to a city, citizenship, or civil affairs

civ·ics \-viks\ *n* : a social science dealing with the rights and duties of citizens

civ·il \'si-vəl\ *adj* **1** : of or relating to citizens or to the state as a political body **2** : COURTEOUS, POLITE **3** : of or relating to legal proceedings in connection with private rights and obligations ⟨the ~ code⟩ **4** : of or relating to the general population : not military or ecclesiastical

civil defense *n* : protective measures and emergency relief activities conducted by civilians in case of enemy attack or natural disaster

civil disobedience *n* : refusal to obey governmental commands esp. as a nonviolent means of protest

civil engineer *n* : an engineer whose training or occupation is in the design and construction esp. of public works (as roads or harbors) — **civil engineering** *n*

ci·vil·ian \sə-'vil-yən\ *n* : a person not on active duty in a military, police, or firefighting force

civ·i·li·sa·tion, civ·i·lise *chiefly Brit var of* CIVILIZATION, CIVILIZE

ci·vil·i·ty \sə-'vi-lə-tē\ *n, pl* **-ties 1** : POLITENESS, COURTESY **2** : a polite act or expression

civ·i·li·za·tion \,si-və-lə-'zā-shən\ *n* **1** : a relatively high level of cultural and technological development **2** : the culture characteristic of a time or place — **civ·i·li·za·tion·al** \-shə-nºl\ *adj*

civ·i·lize \'si-və-,līz\ *vb* **-lized; -liz·ing 1** : to raise from a primitive state to an advanced and ordered stage of cultural development **2** : REFINE — **civ·i·lized** *adj*

civil liberty *n* : freedom from arbitrary governmental interference specifically by denial of governmental power — usu. used in pl.

civ·il·ly \'si-vəl-lē\ *adv* **1** : in terms of civil rights, matters, or law ⟨~ dead⟩ **2** : in a civil manner : POLITELY

civil rights *n pl* : the nonpolitical rights of a citizen; *esp* : those guaranteed by the 13th and 14th amendments to the Constitution and by acts of Congress

civil servant *n* : a member of a civil service

civil service *n* : the administrative service of a government

civil war *n* : a war between opposing groups of citizens of the same country

civ·vies \'si-vēz\ *n pl* : civilian clothes as distinguished from a military uniform

CJ *abbr* chief justice

ck *abbr* **1** cask **2** check

cl *abbr* **1** centiliter **2** class

Cl *symbol* chlorine

¹**clack** \'klak\ *vb* **1** : CHATTER, PRATTLE **2** : to make or cause to make a clatter

²**clack** *n* **1** : rapid continuous talk : CHATTER **2** : a sound of clacking ⟨the ~ of a typewriter⟩

clad \'klad\ *adj* **1** : CLOTHED, COVERED **2** : being or consisting of coins made of outer layers of one metal bonded to a core of a different metal

¹**claim** \'klām\ *vb* [ME, fr. AF *claimer*, *clamer*, fr. L *clamare* to cry out, shout] **1** : to ask for as one's own; *also* : to take as the rightful owner **2** : to call for : REQUIRE **3** : to state as a fact : MAINTAIN

²**claim** *n* **1** : a demand for something due ⟨an insurance ~⟩ **2** : a right to something usu. in another's possession **3** : an assertion open to challenge **4** : something claimed (as a tract of land)

claim·ant \'klā-mənt\ *n* : a person making a claim

clair·voy·ant \klar-'vȯi-ənt\ *adj* [F, fr. *clair* clear + *voyant* seeing] **1** : able to see beyond the range of ordinary perception **2** : having the power of discerning objects not present to the senses — **clair·voy·ance** \-əns\ *n* — **clairvoyant** *n*

clam \'klam\ *n* **1** : any of numerous bivalve mollusks including many that are edible **2** : DOLLAR

clam·bake \-,bāk\ *n* : a party or gathering (as at the seashore) at which food is cooked usu. on heated rocks covered by seaweed

clam·ber \'klam-bər\ *vb* : to climb awkwardly — **clam·ber·er** *n*

clam·my \'kla-mē\ *adj* **clam·mi·er; -est** : being damp, soft, sticky, and usu. cool — **clam·mi·ness** *n*

clam·or \'kla-mər\ *n* **1** : a noisy shouting **2** : a loud continuous noise **3** : insistent public expression (as of support or protest) — **clamor** *vb* — **clam·or·ous** *adj*

clam·our *chiefly Brit var of* CLAMOR

¹clamp \'klamp\ *n* : a device that holds or presses parts together firmly

²clamp *vb* : to fasten with or as if with a clamp

clamp down *vb* : to impose restrictions : become repressive — **clamp·down** \'klamp-,daun\ *n*

clam·shell \'klam-,shel\ *n* **1** : the shell of a clam **2** : a bucket or grapnel (as on a dredge) having two hinged jaws

clam up *vb* : to become silent

clan \'klan\ *n* [ME, fr. ScGael *clann* offspring, clan, fr. Old Irish *cland* plant, offspring, fr. L *planta* plant] : a group (as in the Scottish Highlands) made up of households whose heads claim descent from a common ancestor — **clan·nish** *adj* — **clan·nish·ness** *n*

clan·des·tine \klan-'des-tən\ *adj* : held in or conducted with secrecy

clang \'klaŋ\ *n* : a loud metallic ringing sound — **clang** *vb*

clan·gor \'klaŋ-ər, -gər\ *n* : a resounding clang or medley of clangs

clan·gour *chiefly Brit var of* CLANGOR

clank \'klaŋk\ *n* : a sharp brief metallic ringing sound — **clank** *vb*

¹clap \'klap\ *vb* **clapped; clap·ping 1** : to strike noisily **2** : APPLAUD

²clap *n* **1** : a loud noisy crash **2** : the noise made by clapping the hands

³clap *n* : GONORRHEA

clap·board \'kla-bərd, -,bȯrd; 'klap-,bȯrd\ *n* : a narrow board thicker at one edge than the other used for siding — **clap·board** *vb*

clap·per \'kla-pər\ *n* : one that claps; *esp* : the tongue of a bell

clap·trap \'klap-,trap\ *n* : pretentious nonsense

claque \'klak\ *n* [F, fr. *claquer* to clap] **1** : a group hired to applaud at a performance **2** : a group of sycophants

clar·et \'kler-ət\ *n* [ME, fr. AF (*vin*) *claret* clear wine] : a dry red wine

clar·i·fy \'kler-ə-,fī\ *vb* **-fied; -fy·ing** : to make or become clear — **clar·i·fi·ca·tion** \,kler-ə-fə-'kā-shən\ *n*

clar·i·net \,kler-ə-'net\ *n* : a single-reed woodwind instrument in the form of a cylindrical tube with a moderately flaring end — **clar·i·net·ist** *or* **clar·i·net·tist** \-'ne-tist\ *n*

clar·i·on \'kler-ē-ən\ *adj* : brilliantly clear ⟨a ∼ call⟩

clar·i·ty \'kler-ə-tē\ *n* : CLEARNESS

¹clash \'klash\ *vb* **1** : to make or cause to make a clash **2** : CONFLICT, COLLIDE

²clash *n* **1** : a noisy usu. metallic sound of collision **2** : a hostile encounter **3** : a sharp conflict ⟨a ∼ of opinions⟩

clasp \'klasp\ *n* **1** : a device (as a hook) for holding objects or parts together **2** : EMBRACE, GRASP — **clasp** *vb*

¹class \'klas\ *n* [F *classe*, fr. L *classis* group called to military service, fleet, class] **1** : a group of students meeting regularly in a course; *also* : a group graduating together **2** : a course of instruction; *also* : the period when such a course is taught **3** : social rank; *also* : high quality **4** : a group of the same general status or nature; *esp* : a major category in biological classification that is above the order and below the phylum **5** : a division or rating based on grade or quality — **class·less** *adj*

²class *vb* : CLASSIFY

class action *n* : a legal action undertaken in behalf of the plaintiffs and all others having an identical interest in the alleged wrong

¹clas·sic \'kla-sik\ *adj* **1** : serving as a standard of excellence ⟨a ∼ novel⟩; *also* : TRADITIONAL **2** : CLASSICAL **2 3** : notable esp. as the best example ⟨his winning goal was ∼⟩ **4** : AUTHENTIC ⟨a ∼ folk dance⟩

²classic *n* **1** : a work of enduring excellence and esp. of ancient Greece and Rome; *also* : its author **2** : a traditional event ⟨a football ∼⟩

clas·si·cal \'kla-si-kəl\ *adj* **1** : CLASSIC **2** : of or relating to the ancient Greek and Roman classics **3** : of or relating to a form or system of primary significance before modern times ⟨∼ economics⟩ **4** : concerned with a general study of the arts and sciences — **clas·si·cal·ly** \-k(ə-)lē\ *adv*

clas·si·cism \'kla-sə-,si-zəm\ *n* **1** : the principles or style of the literature or art of ancient Greece and Rome **2** : adherence to traditional standards believed to be universally valid — **clas·si·cist** \-sist\ *n*

clas·si·fied \'kla-sə-,fīd\ *adj* : withheld from general circulation for reasons of national security

clas·si·fieds \-,fīdz\ *n pl* : advertisements grouped by subject

clas·si·fy \'kla-sə-,fī\ *vb* **-fied; -fy·ing** : to arrange in or assign to classes — **clas·si·fi·able** *adj* — **clas·si·fi·ca·tion** \,kla-sə-fə-'kā-shən\ *n* — **clas·si·fi·er** *n*

class·mate \'klas-,māt\ *n* : a member of the same class (as in a college)

class·room \-,rüm, -,rum\ *n* : a place where classes meet

classy \'kla-sē\ *adj* **class·i·er; -est** : EL-

EGANT, STYLISH ⟨a ~ clientele⟩ — **class·i·ness** n

clat·ter \'kla-tər\ n : a rattling sound ⟨the ~ of dishes⟩ — **clatter** vb

clause \'klȯz\ n **1** : a group of words having its own subject and predicate but forming only part of a compound or complex sentence **2** : a separate part of an article or document

claus·tro·pho·bia \ˌklȯ-strə-'fō-bē-ə\ n : abnormal dread of being in closed or narrow spaces — **claus·tro·pho·bic** \-bik\ adj

clav·i·chord \'kla-və-ˌkȯrd\ n : an early keyboard instrument in use before the piano

clav·i·cle \'kla-vi-kəl\ n [F clavicule, fr. NL clavicula, fr. L, dim. of L clavis key] : COLLARBONE

cla·vier \klə-'vir; 'kla-vē-ər\ n **1** : the keyboard of a musical instrument **2** : an early keyboard instrument

¹claw \'klȯ\ n **1** : a sharp usu. curved nail on the toe of an animal **2** : a sharp curved process (as on the foot of an insect); also : a pincerlike organ at the end of a limb of some arthropods (as a lobster) — **clawed** \'klȯd\ adj

²claw vb : to rake, seize, or dig with or as if with claws

clay \'klā\ n **1** : an earthy material that is plastic when moist but hard when fired and is used in making pottery; also : finely divided soil consisting largely of such clay **2** : EARTH, MUD **3** : a plastic substance used for modeling **4** : the mortal human body — **clay·ey** \'klā-ē\ adj

clay·more \'klā-ˌmȯr\ n : a large 2-edged sword formerly used by Scottish Highlanders

clay pigeon n : a saucer-shaped target thrown from a trap in trapshooting

¹clean \'klēn\ adj **1** : free from dirt, disease, or pollution ⟨~ air⟩ **2** : PURE ⟨the ~ thrill of one's first flight⟩; also : HONORABLE **3** : THOROUGH ⟨made a ~ sweep⟩ **4** : TRIM ⟨a ~ edge⟩ ⟨a ship with ~ lines⟩; also : EVEN **5** : habitually neat — **clean** adv — **clean·ly** \'klēn-lē\ adv — **clean·ness** \'klēn-nəs\ n

²clean vb : to make or become clean — **clean·able** \'klē-nə-bəl\ adj — **clean·er** n

clean–cut \'klēn-'kət\ adj **1** : cut so that the surface or edge is smooth and even **2** : sharply defined or outlined **3** : giving an effect of wholesomeness

clean·ly \'klen-lē\ adj **clean·li·er; -est 1** : careful to keep clean **2** : habitually kept clean — **clean·li·ness** n

clean room \'klēn-ˌrüm, -ˌrúm\ n : an uncontaminated room maintained for the manufacture or assembly of objects (as precision parts)

cleanse \'klenz\ vb **cleansed; cleans·ing** : to make clean — **cleans·er** n

¹clean·up \'klēn-ˌəp\ n **1** : an act or instance of cleaning **2** : a very large profit

²cleanup adj : being 4th in the batting order of a baseball team — **cleanup** adv

clean up vb : to make a spectacular business profit

¹clear \'klir\ adj [ME clere, fr. AF cler, fr. L clarus] **1** : BRIGHT, LUMINOUS; also : UNTROUBLED, SERENE **2** : CLOUDLESS **3** : CLEAN, PURE; also : TRANSPARENT **4** : easily heard, seen, or understood **5** : capable of sharp discernment; also : free from doubt **6** : INNOCENT ⟨a ~ conscience⟩ **7** : free from restriction, obstruction, or entanglement — **clear** adv — **clear·ness** n

²clear vb **1** : to make or become clear **2** : to go away : DISPERSE **3** : to free from accusation or blame; also : to certify as trustworthy **4** : to free from obstruction **5** : SETTLE ⟨~ a debt⟩ **7** : NET ⟨~ed a profit⟩ **8** : to get free from obstruction **6** : REMOVE ⟨~ed the snow off the driveway⟩ **9** : to jump or go by without touching; also : PASS ⟨the bill ~ed the legislature⟩

³clear n : a clear space or part

clear·ance \'klir-əns\ n **1** : an act or process of clearing **2** : the distance by which one object clears another **3** : AUTHORIZATION

clear–cut \'klir-'kət\ adj **1** : sharply outlined **2** : DEFINITE, UNEQUIVOCAL ⟨a ~ victory⟩

clear–cut·ting \-ˌkə-tiŋ\ n : removal of all the trees in a stand of timber — **clear-cut** \-ˌkət\ vb

clear·head·ed \-'he-dəd\ adj : having a clear understanding : PERCEPTIVE

clear·ing \'klir-iŋ\ n **1** : a tract of land cleared of wood and brush **2** : the passage of checks and claims through a clearinghouse

clear·ing·house \-ˌhaús\ n : an institution maintained by banks for making an exchange of checks and claims held by each bank against other banks; also : an informal channel for information or assistance

clear·ly \'klir-lē\ adv **1** : in a clear manner **2** : it is clear

cleat \'klēt\ n : a piece of wood or metal fastened on or projecting from something to give strength, provide a grip, or prevent slipping

cleav·age \'klē-vij\ n **1** : a splitting apart : SPLIT **2** : the depression between a woman's breasts esp. when exposed by a low-cut dress

¹cleave \'klēv\ vb **cleaved** \'klēvd\ or **clove** \'klōv\; **cleaved; cleav·ing** : ADHERE, CLING ⟨the child cleaved to her mother⟩

²cleave vb **cleaved** \'klēvd\ also **cleft** \'kleft\ or **clove** \'klōv\; **cleaved** also **cleft** or **clo·ven** \'klō-vən\; **cleav·ing 1** : to divide by force : split asunder ⟨~ logs⟩ **2** : DIVIDE

cleav·er \'klē-vər\ n : a heavy chopping knife for cutting meat

clef \'klef\ n : a sign placed on the staff in music to show what pitch is represented by each line and space

cleft \'kleft\ n : FISSURE, CRACK

cleft lip n : a birth defect in which the upper lip is vertically split

cleft palate n : a split in the roof of the mouth that appears as a birth defect

clem·a·tis \'kle-mə-təs; kli-'ma-təs\ *n* : any of a genus of vines or herbs related to the buttercups that have showy usu. white or purple flowers

clem·en·cy \'kle-mən-sē\ *n, pl* **-cies** 1 : disposition to be merciful 2 : mildness of weather

clem·ent \'kle-mənt\ *adj* 1 : MERCIFUL, LENIENT ⟨a ~ judge⟩ 2 : TEMPERATE, MILD ⟨~ weather for this time of year⟩

clem·en·tine \'kle-mən-ˌtēn\ *n* : a small citrus fruit that is probably a hybrid between a tangerine and an orange

clench \'klench\ *vb* 1 : CLINCH 1 2 : to hold fast 3 : to set or close tightly

clere·sto·ry \'klir-ˌstōr-ē\ *n* : an outside wall of a room or building that rises above an adjoining roof and contains windows

cler·gy \'klər-jē\ *n* : a body of religious officials authorized to conduct services

cler·gy·man \-mən\ *n* : a member of the clergy

cler·gy·per·son \-ˌpər-sᵊn\ *n* : a member of the clergy

cler·ic \'kler-ik\ *n* : a member of the clergy

cler·i·cal \'kler-i-kəl\ *adj* 1 : of or relating to the clergy ⟨~ vestments⟩ 2 : of or relating to a clerk

cler·i·cal·ism \'kler-i-kə-ˌli-zəm\ *n* : a policy of maintaining or increasing the power of a religious hierarchy

clerk \'klərk, *Brit* 'klärk\ *n* 1 : CLERIC 2 : an official responsible for correspondence, records, and accounts; *also* : a person employed to perform general office work 3 : a store salesperson — **clerk** *vb* — **clerk·ship** *n*

clev·er \'kle-vər\ *adj* 1 : showing skill or resourcefulness 2 : marked by wit or ingenuity — **clev·er·ly** *adv* — **clev·er·ness** *n*

clev·is \'kle-vəs\ *n* : a U-shaped shackle used for fastening

¹**clew** \'klü\ *n* 1 : CLUE 2 : a metal loop on a lower corner of a sail

²**clew** *vb* : to haul (a sail) up or down by ropes through the clews

cli·ché \kli-'shā\ *n* [F] : a trite phrase or expression — **cli·chéd** \-'shād\ *adj*

¹**click** \'klik\ *vb* 1 : to make or cause to make a click 2 : to fit or work together smoothly 3 : to select or make a selection on a computer by pressing a button on a control device (as a mouse) — **click·able** \'kli-kə-bəl\ *adj*

²**click** *n* 1 : a slight sharp noise 2 : an instance of clicking ⟨a mouse ~⟩

click·er \'kli-kər\ *n* : REMOTE CONTROL 2

cli·ent \'klī-ənt\ *n* 1 : DEPENDENT 2 : a person who engages the professional services of another; *also* : PATRON, CUSTOMER 3 : a computer in a network that uses the services (as access to files) provided by a server

cli·en·tele \ˌklī-ən-'tel, ˌklē-\ *n* : a body of clients and esp. customers

cliff \'klif\ *n* : a high steep face of rock, earth, or ice

cliff-hang·er \-ˌhaŋ-ər\ *n* 1 : an adventure serial or melodrama usu. presented in installments each of which ends in suspense 2 : a contest whose outcome is in doubt up to the very end

cli·mac·ter·ic \klī-'mak-tə-rik\ *n* 1 : a major turning point or critical stage 2 : MENOPAUSE; *also* : a corresponding period in the male

cli·mate \'klī-mət\ *n* [ME *climat,* fr. MF, fr. LL *clima,* fr. Gk *klima* inclination, latitude, climate, fr. *klinein* to lean] 1 : a region having specific climatic conditions 2 : the average weather conditions at a place over a period of years 3 : the prevailing set of conditions (as temperature and humidity) indoors 4 : a prevailing atmosphere or environment ⟨the ~ of opinion⟩ — **cli·mat·ic** \klī-'ma-tik\ *adj* — **cli·mat·i·cal·ly** \-ti-k(ə-)lē\ *adv*

cli·ma·tol·o·gy \ˌklī-mə-'tä-lə-jē\ *n* : the science that deals with climates — **cli·ma·to·log·i·cal** \-mə-tə-'lä-ji-kəl\ *adj* — **cli·ma·to·log·i·cal·ly** \-k(ə-)lē\ *adv* — **cli·ma·tol·o·gist** \-mə-'tä-lə-jist\ *n*

¹**cli·max** \'klī-ˌmaks\ *n* [L, fr. Gk *klimax,* lit., ladder, fr. Gk *klinein* to lean] 1 : a series of ideas or statements so arranged that they increase in force and power from the first to the last; *also* : the last member of such a series 2 : the highest point ⟨the ~ of her career⟩ 3 : ORGASM — **cli·mac·tic** \klī-'mak-tik\ *adj*

²**climax** *vb* : to come or bring to a climax

¹**climb** \'klīm\ *vb* 1 : to rise to a higher point 2 : to go up or down esp. by use of hands and feet; *also* : to ascend in growing — **climb·er** *n*

²**climb** *n* 1 : a place where climbing is necessary 2 : the act of climbing : ascent by climbing

clime \'klīm\ *n* : CLIMATE ⟨warmer ~s⟩

¹**clinch** \'klinch\ *vb* 1 : to turn over or flatten the end of something sticking out ⟨~ a nail⟩; *also* : to fasten by clinching 2 : to make final : SETTLE ⟨~ a deal⟩ 3 : to hold a boxing opponent 4 : to hold fast or firmly

²**clinch** *n* 1 : a fastening by means of a clinched nail, rivet, or bolt 2 : an act or instance of clinching in boxing

clinch·er \'klin-chər\ *n* : one that clinches; *esp* : a decisive fact, argument, act, or remark

cling \'kliŋ\ *vb* **clung** \'kləŋ\; **cling·ing** 1 : to adhere as if glued; *also* : to hold or hold on tightly 2 : to have a strong emotional attachment — **clingy** \'kliŋ-ē\ *adj*

cling·stone \'kliŋ-ˌstōn\ *n* : any of various fruits (as some peaches) whose flesh adheres strongly to the pit

clin·ic \'kli-nik\ *n* 1 : a medical class in which patients are examined and discussed 2 : a group meeting for teaching a certain skill and working on individual problems ⟨a reading ~⟩ 3 : a facility (as of a hospital) for diagnosis and treatment of outpatients

clin·i·cal \'kli-ni-kəl\ *adj* 1 : of, relating to, or typical of a clinic; *esp* : involving direct observation of the patient ⟨~ studies⟩ 2 : scientifically dispassionate — **clin·i·cal·ly** \-k(ə-)lē\ *adv*

cli·ni·cian \kli-'ni-shən\ *n* : a person qualified in the clinical practice of medicine, psychiatry, or psychology as distinguished from one specializing in laboratory or research techniques or in theory

¹**clink** \'kliŋk\ *vb* : to make or cause to make a sharp short metallic sound

²**clink** *n* : a clinking sound

clin·ker \'kliŋ-kər\ *n* : stony matter fused together : SLAG

¹**clip** \'klip\ *vb* **clipped; clip·ping** : to fasten with a clip

²**clip** *n* **1** : a device that grips, clasps, or hooks **2** : a cartridge holder for a rifle

³**clip** *vb* **clipped; clip·ping 1** : to cut or cut off with shears ⟨*clipped* a recipe from the magazine⟩ **2** : CURTAIL, DIMINISH **3** : HIT, PUNCH **4** : to illegally block (an opponent) in football

⁴**clip** *n* **1** : a 2-bladed instrument for cutting esp. the nails **2** : a sharp blow **3** : a rapid pace ⟨the train moved at a good ∼⟩

clip art *n* : ready-made usu. copyright-free illustrations

clip·board \'klip-,bȯrd\ *n* **1** : a small writing board with a spring clip at the top for holding papers **2** : a section of computer memory that temporarily stores data esp. to facilitate its movement or duplication

clip joint *n, slang* : an establishment (as a nightclub) that makes a practice of defrauding its customers

clip·per \'kli-pər\ *n* **1** : an implement for clipping esp. the hair or nails — usu. used in pl. **2** : a fast sailing ship

clip·ping \'kli-piŋ\ *n* : a piece clipped from something (as a newspaper)

clique \'klēk, 'klik\ *n* [F] : a small exclusive group of people : COTERIE ⟨high school ∼s⟩ — **cliqu·ey** \'klē-kē, 'kli-\ *adj* — **cliqu·ish** \-kish\ *adj*

cli·to·ris \'kli-tə-rəs\ *n, pl* **cli·to·ris·es** : a small erectile organ at the anterior or ventral part of the vulva homologous to the penis — **cli·to·ral** \-rəl\ *adj*

clk *abbr* clerk

clo *abbr* clothing

¹**cloak** \'klōk\ *n* **1** : a loose outer garment **2** : something that conceals

²**cloak** *vb* : to cover or hide with a cloak

cloak-and-dagger *adj* : involving or suggestive of espionage

clob·ber \'klä-bər\ *vb* **1** : to pound mercilessly; *also* : to hit with force : SMASH **2** : to defeat overwhelmingly

cloche \'klōsh\ *n* [F, lit., bell] : a woman's small close-fitting hat

¹**clock** \'kläk\ *n* : a timepiece not intended to be carried on the person

²**clock** *vb* **1** : to time (a person or a performance) by a timing device **2** : to register (as speed) on a mechanical recording device — **clock·er** *n*

³**clock** *n* : an ornamental figure on a stocking or sock

clock·wise \'kläk-,wīz\ *adv* : in the direction in which the hands of a clock move — **clockwise** *adj*

clock·work \-,wərk\ *n* **1** : the machinery that runs a mechanical device (as a clock

or toy) **2** : the precision or regularity associated with a clock

clod \'kläd\ *n* **1** : a lump esp. of earth or clay **2** : a dull or insensitive person

clod·hop·per \-,hä-pər\ *n* **1** : an uncouth rustic **2** : a large heavy shoe

¹**clog** \'kläg\ *n* **1** : a weight attached esp. to an animal to impede motion **2** : a thick-soled shoe

²**clog** *vb* **clogged; clog·ging 1** : to impede with a clog : HINDER **2** : to obstruct passage through **3** : to become filled with extraneous matter

cloi·son·né \,klȯi-zə-'nā\ *adj* : a colored decoration made of enamels poured into the divided areas in a design outlined with wire or metal strips

¹**clois·ter** \'klȯi-stər\ *n* [ME *cloistre*, fr. AF, fr. ML *claustrum*, fr. L, bar, bolt, fr. *claudere* to close] **1** : a monastic establishment **2** : a covered usu. colonnaded passage on the side of a court — **clois·tral** \-strəl\ *adj*

²**cloister** *vb* : to shut away from the world

clone \'klōn\ *n* [Gk *klōn* twig, slip] **1** : the collection of genetically identical cells or organisms produced asexually from a single ancestral cell or organism; *also* : an individual grown from a single cell and genetically identical to it ⟨a sheep ∼⟩ **2** : a group of replicas of a biological molecule (as DNA) **3** : one that appears to be a copy of an original form — **clon·al** \'klōn-ᵊl\ *adj* — **clone** *vb*

clop \'kläp\ *n* : a sound made by or as if by a hoof or wooden shoe against pavement — **clop** *vb*

¹**close** \'klōz\ *vb* **closed; clos·ing 1** : to bar passage through : SHUT **2** : to suspend the operations (as of a school) **3** : END, TERMINATE **4** : to bring together the parts or edges of; *also* : to fill up **5** : GRAPPLE ⟨∼ with the enemy⟩ **6** : to enter into an agreement — **clos·able** *or* **close·able** *adj*

²**close** \'klōz\ *n* : CONCLUSION, END

³**close** \'klōs\ *adj* **clos·er; clos·est 1** : having no openings **2** : narrowly restricting or restricted **3** : limited to a privileged class **4** : SECLUDED; *also* : SECRETIVE **5** : RIGOROUS ⟨keep ∼ watch⟩ **6** : SULTRY, STUFFY **7** : STINGY **8** : having little space between items or units **9** : fitting tightly; *also* : SHORT ⟨∼ haircut⟩ **10** : NEAR ⟨at ∼ range⟩ **11** : INTIMATE ⟨∼ friends⟩ **12** : ACCURATE **13** : decided by a narrow margin ⟨a ∼ game⟩ — **close** *adv* — **close·ly** *adv* — **close·ness** *n*

closed-circuit \'klōzd-'sər-kət\ *adj* : used in, shown on, or being a television installation in which the signal is transmitted by wire to a limited number of receivers

closed shop *n* : an establishment having only members of a labor union on the payroll

close·fist·ed \'klōz-'fis-təd, 'klōs-\ *adj* : STINGY

close-knit \'klōs-'nit\ *adj* : closely bound together by social, cultural, or political ties

close·mouthed \'klōz-'mauthd, 'klōs-'mauṭht\ *adj* : cautious or reticent in speaking

close·out \'klōz-,aut\ *n* : a sale of a business's entire stock at low prices

close out *vb* **1** : to dispose of by a closeout **2** : to dispose of a business : SELL OUT

clos·er \'klō-zər\ *n* : one that closes; *esp* : a relief pitcher who specializes in finishing games

¹**clos·et** \'klä-zət, 'klȯ-\ *n* **1** : a small room for privacy **2** : a small compartment for household utensils or clothing **3** : a state or condition of secrecy ⟨came out of the ∼⟩

²**closet** *vb* : to take into a private room for an interview

close–up \'klōs-,əp\ *n* **1** : a photograph or movie shot taken at close range **2** : an intimate view or examination

clo·sure \'klō-zhər\ *n* **1** : an act of closing : the condition of being closed **2** : something that closes **3** : CLOTURE

clot \'klät\ *n* : a mass formed by a portion of liquid (as blood) thickening and sticking together — **clot** *vb*

cloth \'klȯth\ *n, pl* **cloths** \'klȯthz, 'klȯths\ **1** : a pliable fabric made usu. by weaving or knitting natural or synthetic fibers and filaments **2** : TABLECLOTH **3** : distinctive dress of the clergy; *also* : CLERGY

clothe \'klōth\ *vb* **clothed** *or* **clad** \'klad\; **cloth·ing 1** : DRESS; *also* : to provide with clothes **2** : to express by suitably significant language ⟨policies *clothed* in rhetoric⟩

clothes \'klōthz, 'klōz\ *n pl* **1** : CLOTHING **2** : BEDCLOTHES

clothes·horse \-,hȯrs\ *n* **1** : a frame on which to hang clothes **2** : a conspicuously dressy person

¹**clothes·line** \-,līn\ *n* : a rope or cord on which clothes are hung to dry

²**clothesline** *vb* : to knock down by catching by the neck with one's outstretched arm

clothes moth *n* : any of several small pale moths whose larvae eat wool, fur, and feathers

clothes·pin \'klōthz-,pin, 'klōz-\ *n* : a device for fastening clothes on a line

clothes·press \-,pres\ *n* : a receptacle for clothes

cloth·ier \'klōth-yər, 'klō-thē-ər\ *n* : a maker or seller of clothing

cloth·ing \'klō-thiŋ\ *n* : garments in general

clo·ture \'klō-chər\ *n* : the closing or limitation (as by calling for a vote) of debate in a legislative body

¹**cloud** \'klaud\ *n* [ME, rock, cloud, fr. OE *clūd*] **1** : a visible mass of particles of condensed vapor (as water or ice) suspended in the atmosphere **2** : a usu. visible mass of minute airborne particles; *also* : a mass of obscuring matter in interstellar space **3** : CROWD, SWARM ⟨a ∼ of mosquitoes⟩ **4** : something having a dark or threatening aspect ⟨a ∼ of suspicion⟩ **5** : something that obscures or blemishes

⟨a ∼ of ambiguity⟩ — **cloud·i·ness** \'klau̇-dē-nəs\ *n* — **cloud·less** *adj* — **cloudy** *adj*

²**cloud** *vb* **1** : to darken or hide with or as if with a cloud **2** : OBSCURE ⟨∼ed in mystery⟩ **3** : TAINT, SULLY ⟨a ∼ed reputation⟩

cloud·burst \-,bərst\ *n* : a sudden heavy rainfall

cloud·let \-lət\ *n* : a small cloud

cloud nine *n* : a feeling of extreme well-being or elation — usu. used with *on*

¹**clout** \'klaut\ *n* **1** : a blow esp. with the hand **2** : PULL, INFLUENCE

²**clout** *vb* : to hit forcefully

¹**clove** \'klōv\ *n* : one of the small bulbs that grows at the base of the scales of a large bulb ⟨a ∼ of garlic⟩

²**clove** *past of* CLEAVE

³**clove** *n* [ME *clowe*, fr. AF *clou* (*de girofle*), lit., nail of clove, fr. L *clavus* nail] : the dried flower bud of a tropical tree used esp. as a spice

clo·ven \'klō-vən\ *past part of* CLEAVE

cloven foot *n* : CLOVEN HOOF — **clo·ven–foot·ed** \-'fu̇-təd\ *adj*

cloven hoof *n* : a foot (as of a sheep) with the front part divided into two parts — **cloven–hoofed** \-'hu̇ft, -'hu̇vd\ *adj*

clo·ver \'klō-vər\ *n* : any of a genus of leguminous herbs with usu. 3-parted leaves and dense flower heads

clo·ver·leaf \-,lēf\ *n, pl* **cloverleafs** \-,lēfs\ *or* **clo·ver·leaves** \-,lēvz\ : an interchange between two major highways that from above resembles a 4-leaf clover

¹**clown** \'klau̇n\ *n* **1** : BOOR **2** : a fool or comedian in an entertainment (as a circus) **3** : a person given to joking and buffoonery — **clown·ish** *adj* — **clown·ish·ly** *adv* — **clown·ish·ness** *n*

²**clown** *vb* : to act like a clown

cloy \'klȯi\ *vb* : to disgust or nauseate with excess of something orig. pleasing — **cloy·ing·ly** *adv*

clr *abbr* clear

¹**club** \'kləb\ *n* **1** : a heavy wooden stick or staff used as a weapon; *also* : BAT **2** : any of a suit of playing cards marked with a black figure resembling a clover leaf **3** : a group of persons associated for a common purpose; *also* : the meeting place of such a group **4** : CLUB SANDWICH

²**club** *vb* **clubbed**; **club·bing 1** : to strike with a club **2** : to unite or combine for a common cause **3** : to patronize nightclubs

club·foot \'kləb-'fu̇t\ *n* : a misshapen foot twisted out of position from birth; *also* : this deformed condition — **club·foot·ed** \-'fu̇-təd\ *adj*

club·house \'kləb-,hau̇s\ *n* **1** : a house occupied by a club **2** : locker rooms used by an athletic team **3** : a building at a golf course with locker rooms and usu. a pro shop and a restaurant

club sandwich *n* : a sandwich of three slices of bread with two layers of meat (as turkey) and lettuce, tomato, and mayonnaise

club soda *n* : SODA WATER

cluck \'klək\ *n* : the call of a hen esp. to her chicks — **cluck** *vb*

¹**clue** \'klü\ *n* 1 : something that guides through an intricate procedure or maze; *esp* : a piece of evidence leading to the solution of a problem 2 : IDEA, NOTION ⟨has no ∼ what he's doing⟩

²**clue** *vb* **clued; clu·ing** *or* **clu·ing** : to provide with a clue; *also* : to give information to ⟨∼ me in⟩

¹**clump** \'kləmp\ *n* 1 : a group of things clustered together 2 : a heavy tramping sound

²**clump** *vb* : to tread clumsily and noisily

clum·sy \'kləm-zē\ *adj* **clum·si·er; -est** 1 : lacking dexterity, nimbleness, or grace 2 : not tactful or subtle ⟨a ∼ attempt at a joke⟩ — **clum·si·ly** \-zə-lē\ *adv* — **clum·si·ness** \-zē-nəs\ *n*

clung *past and past part of* CLING

clunk·er \'kləŋ-kər\ *n* 1 : a dilapidated automobile 2 : a notable failure

¹**clus·ter** \'kləs-tər\ *n* : GROUP, BUNCH

²**cluster** *vb* : to grow or gather in a cluster

¹**clutch** \'kləch\ *vb* : to grasp with or as if with the hand

²**clutch** *n* 1 : the claws or a hand in the act of grasping; *also* : CONTROL, POWER 2 : a device for gripping an object 3 : a coupling used to connect and disconnect a driving and a driven part of a mechanism; *also* : a lever or pedal operating such a coupling 4 : a crucial situation

³**clutch** *adj* : made, done, or successful in a crucial situation

⁴**clutch** *n* 1 : a nest or batch of eggs; *also* : a brood of chicks 2 : GROUP, BUNCH

¹**clut·ter** \'klə-tər\ *vb* : to fill or cover with a disorderly scattering of things

²**clutter** *n* : a crowded mass

cm *abbr* centimeter

Cm *symbol* curium

CM *abbr* [Commonwealth of the Northern Mariana Islands] Northern Mariana Islands

cmdr *abbr* commander

cml *abbr* commercial

CMSgt *abbr* chief master sergeant

Cn *symbol* copernicium

CNO *abbr* chief of naval operations

CNS *abbr* central nervous system

co *abbr* 1 company 2 county

Co *symbol* cobalt

CO *abbr* 1 Colorado 2 commanding officer 3 conscientious objector

c/o *abbr* care of

¹**coach** \'kōch\ *n* [MF *coche*, ultim. fr. Hung *kocsi (szekér)*, lit., (wagon) of Kocs (town in Hungary)] 1 : a large closed 4-wheeled carriage with an elevated outside front seat for the driver 2 : a railroad passenger car esp. for day travel 3 : BUS 4 : a private tutor; *also* : one who instructs or trains ⟨an acting ∼⟩ ⟨a soccer ∼⟩

²**coach** *vb* : to instruct, direct, or prompt as a coach

coach·man \-mən\ *n* : a man who drives a coach or carriage

co·ad·ju·tor \ˌkō-ə-'jü-tər, kō-'a-jə-tər\ *n* : ASSISTANT; *esp* : an assistant bishop having the right of succession

co·ag·u·lant \kō-'a-gyə-lənt\ *n* : something that produces coagulation

co·ag·u·late \-ˌlāt\ *vb* **-lat·ed; -lat·ing** : CLOT — **co·ag·u·la·tion** \kō-ˌa-gyə-'lā-shən\ *n*

¹**coal** \'kōl\ *n* 1 : EMBER 2 : a black solid combustible mineral used as fuel

²**coal** *vb* 1 : to supply with coal 2 : to take in coal

co·a·lesce \ˌkō-ə-'les\ *vb* **co·a·lesced; co·a·lesc·ing** : to grow together; *also* : FUSE ♦ *Synonyms* MERGE, BLEND, MINGLE, MIX — **co·a·les·cence** \-'ns\ *n*

coal·field \'kōl-ˌfēld\ *n* : a region rich in coal deposits

coal gas *n* : gas from coal; *esp* : gas distilled from bituminous coal and used for heating

co·a·li·tion \ˌkō-ə-'li-shən\ *n* : UNION; *esp* : a temporary union for a common purpose — **co·a·li·tion·ist** *n*

coal oil *n* : KEROSENE

coal tar *n* : tar distilled from bituminous coal and used in dyes and drugs

co·an·chor \'kō-'aŋ-kər\ *n* : a newscaster who shares the duties of head broadcaster

coarse \'kórs\ *adj* **coars·er; coars·est** 1 : of ordinary or inferior quality 2 : composed of large parts or particles ⟨∼ sand⟩ 3 : CRUDE ⟨∼ manners⟩ 4 : ROUGH, HARSH — **coarse·ly** *adv* — **coarse·ness** *n*

coars·en \'kór-sⁿn\ *vb* : to make or become coarse

¹**coast** \'kōst\ *n* [ME *cost*, fr. AF *coste*, fr. L *costa* rib, side] 1 : SEASHORE 2 : a slide down a slope 3 : the immediate area of view — used in the phrase *the coast is clear* — **coast·al** *adj*

²**coast** *vb* 1 : to sail along the shore 2 : to move (as downhill on a sled) without effort

coast·er *n* 1 : one that coasts 2 : a shallow container or a plate or mat to protect a surface

coaster brake *n* : a brake in the hub of the rear wheel of a bicycle

coast guard *n* : a military force employed in guarding or patrolling a coast — **coast·guards·man** \'kōst-ˌgärdz-mən\ *n*

coast·line \'kōst-ˌlīn\ *n* : the outline or shape of a coast

¹**coat** \'kōt\ *n* 1 : an outer garment for the upper part of the body 2 : an external growth (as of fur or feathers) on an animal 3 : a covering layer ⟨a ∼ of paint⟩ — **coat·ed** \'kō-təd\ *adj*

²**coat** *vb* : to cover usu. with a finishing or protective coat

coat·ing \'kō-tiŋ\ *n* : COAT, COVERING

coat of arms : the heraldic bearings (as of a person) usu. depicted on an escutcheon

coat of mail : a garment of metal scales or rings worn as armor

co·au·thor \'kō-'ò-thər\ *n* : a joint or associate author — **coauthor** *vb*

coax \'kōks\ *vb* : WHEEDLE; *also* : to gain by gentle urging or flattery

co·ax·i·al \'kō-'ak-sē-əl\ *adj* : having co-incident axes — **co·ax·i·al·ly** *adv*

coaxial cable *n* : a cable that consists of a tube of electrically conducting material surrounding a central conductor

cob \'käb\ *n* **1** : a male swan **2** : CORN-COB **3** : a short-legged stocky horse

co·balt \'kō-‚bȯlt\ *n* [G *Kobalt*, alter. of *Kobold*, lit., goblin; fr. its occurrence in silver ore, believed to be due to goblins] : a tough shiny silver-white magnetic metallic chemical element found with iron and nickel

cob·ble \'kä-bəl\ *vb* **cob·bled; cob·bling** : to make or put together roughly or hastily ⟨~ together a solution⟩

cob·bler \'kä-blər\ *n* **1** : a mender or maker of shoes **2** : a deep-dish fruit pie with a thick crust

cob·ble·stone \'kä-bəl-‚stōn\ *n* : a naturally rounded stone larger than a pebble and smaller than a boulder

co·bra \'kō-brə\ *n* [Pg *cobra (de capello)*, lit., hooded snake] : any of several venomous snakes of Asia and Africa that when excited expand the skin of the neck into a broad hood

cob·web \'käb-‚web\ *n* [ME *coppeweb*, fr. *coppe* spider, fr. OE ātor*coppe*] **1** : SPIDERWEB; *also* : a thread spun by a spider or insect larva **2** : something flimsy or entangling — **cob·web·by** \-‚we-bē\ *adj*

co·caine \kō-'kān, 'kō-‚kān\ *n* : a drug obtained from the leaves of a So. American shrub (**co·ca** \'kō-kə\) that can result in severe psychological dependence and is sometimes used in medicine as a local anesthetic and illegally as a stimulant of the central nervous system

coc·cus \'kä-kəs\ *n, pl* **coc·ci** \'käk-‚sī\ : a spherical bacterium

coc·cyx \'käk-siks\ *n, pl* **coc·cy·ges** \'käk-sə-‚jēz\ *also* **coc·cyx·es** \'käk-sik-səz\ : the end of the spinal column beyond the sacrum esp. in humans

co·chi·neal \'kä-chə-‚nēl\ *n* : a red dye made from the dried bodies of females of a tropical American insect (**cochineal insect**)

co·chlea \'kō-klē-ə, 'kä-\ *n, pl* **co·chle·as** *or* **co·chle·ae** \-klē-‚ē, -‚ī\ : the usu. spiral part of the inner ear containing nerve endings which carry information about sound to the brain — **co·chle·ar** \-klē-ər\ *adj*

¹**cock** \'käk\ *n* **1** : the adult male of a bird and esp. of the common domestic chicken **2** : VALVE, FAUCET **3** : LEADER **4** : the hammer of a firearm; *also* : the position of the hammer when ready for firing

²**cock** *vb* **1** : to draw back the hammer of a firearm **2** : to set or draw back in readiness for some action ⟨~ your arm to throw⟩ **3** : to turn or tilt usu. to one side ⟨~ one's head⟩

³**cock** *n* : a small pile (as of hay)

cock·ade \kä-'kād\ *n* : an ornament worn on the hat as a badge

cock·a·tiel \‚kä-kə-'tēl\ *n* : a small crested gray parrot often kept as a cage bird

cock·a·too \'kä-kə-‚tü\ *n, pl* **-toos** [D *kaketoe*, fr. Malay *kakatua*] : any of various

large noisy crested parrots chiefly of Australia

cock·a·trice \'kä-kə-trəs, -‚trīs\ *n* : a legendary serpent with a deadly glance

cock-crow \'käk-‚krō\ *n* : DAWN

cocked hat \'käkt-\ *n* : a hat with the brim turned up on two or three sides

cock·er·el \'kä-kə-rəl\ *n* : a young male domestic chicken

cock·er spaniel \'kä-kər-\ *n* [*cocking* woodcock hunting] : any of a breed of small spaniels with long ears, square muzzle, and silky coat

cock·eyed \'kä-'kīd\ *adj* **1** : turned or tilted to one side **2** : slightly crazy : FOOLISH

cock·fight \'käk-‚fīt\ *n* : a contest of gamecocks usu. fitted with metal spurs

¹**cock·le** \'kä-kəl\ *n* : any of several weedy plants related to the pinks

²**cockle** *n* : a bivalve mollusk with a heart-shaped shell

cock·le·shell \-‚shel\ *n* **1** : the shell of a cockle **2** : a light flimsy boat

cock·ney \'käk-nē\ *n, pl* **cockneys** : a native of London and esp. of the East End of London; *also* : the dialect of a cockney

cock·pit \'käk-‚pit\ *n* **1** : a pit for cockfights **2** : a space or compartment in a vehicle from which it is steered, piloted, or driven

cock·roach \'käk-‚rōch\ *n* [Sp *cucaracha*] : any of an order or suborder of active nocturnal insects including some which infest houses and ships

cock·sure \'käk-'shu̇r\ *adj* **1** : perfectly sure : CERTAIN **2** : COCKY

cock·tail \'käk-‚tāl\ *n* **1** : an iced drink made of liquor and flavoring ingredients **2** : an appetizer (as tomato juice) served as a first course of a meal

cocky \'kä-kē\ *adj* **cock·i·er; -est** : marked by overconfidence : PERT, CONCEITED — **cock·i·ly** \-kə-lē\ *adv* — **cock·i·ness** \-kē-nəs\ *n*

co·coa \'kō-kō\ *n* **1** : CACAO **2** : chocolate deprived of some of its fat and powdered; *also* : a drink made of this heated with water or milk

cocoa butter *n* : a pale vegetable fat obtained from cacao beans

co·co·nut \'kō-kə-(‚)nət\ *n* : a large edible hard-shelled fruit produced by a tall tropical palm (**coconut palm**)

co·coon \kə-'kün\ *n* **1** : a case usu. of silk formed by some insect larvae for protection during the pupal stage **2** : something that offers protection or isolation

cod \'käd\ *n, pl* **cod** *also* **cods** : a bottom-dwelling bony fish of the North Atlantic that is an important food fish; *also* : a related fish of the Pacific Ocean

COD *abbr* **1** cash on delivery **2** collect on delivery

co·da \'kō-də\ *n* : a closing section in a musical composition that is formally distinct from the main structure

cod·dle \'kä-dᵊl\ *vb* **cod·dled; cod·dling** **1** : to cook slowly in water below the boiling point **2** : PAMPER

¹**code** \'kōd\ *n* [ME, fr. MF, fr. L *caudex, codex* trunk of a tree, document formed orig. from wooden tablets] **1** : a systematic statement of a body of law **2** : a system of principles or rules ⟨moral ∼⟩ **3** : a system of signals **4** : a system of symbols (as in secret communication) with special meanings **5** : GENETIC CODE

²**code** *vb* **cod·ed; cod·ing** : to put into the form or symbols of a code

co·deine \'kō-ˌdēn\ *n* : a narcotic drug obtained from opium and used esp. as an analgesic and cough suppressant

co·dex \'kō-ˌdeks\ *n, pl* **co·di·ces** \'kō-də-ˌsēz, 'kä-\ : a manuscript book (as of the Scriptures or classics)

cod·fish \'käd-ˌfish\ *n* : COD

cod·ger \'kä-jər\ *n* : an odd or cranky and usu. elderly fellow

cod·i·cil \'kä-də-səl, -ˌsil\ *n* : a legal instrument modifying an earlier will

cod·i·fy \'kä-də-ˌfī, 'kō-\ *vb* **-fied; -fy·ing** : to arrange in a systematic form — **cod·i·fi·ca·tion** \ˌkä-də-fə-'kā-shən, ˌkō-\ *n*

co·ed \'kō-ˌed\ *n* : a female student in a coeducational institution — **coed** *adj*

co·ed·u·ca·tion \ˌkō-ˌe-jə-'kā-shən\ *n* : the education of male and female students at the same institution — **co·ed·u·ca·tion·al** \-shə-nəl\ *adj* — **co·ed·u·ca·tion·al·ly** *adv*

co·ef·fi·cient \ˌkō-ə-'fi-shənt\ *n* **1** : a constant factor as distinguished from a variable in a mathematical term **2** : a number that serves as a measure of some property (as of a substance, device, or process)

coe·len·ter·ate \si-'len-tə-ˌrāt, -rət\ *n* : any of a phylum of radially symmetrical invertebrate animals including the corals, sea anemones, and jellyfishes

co·equal \kō-'ē-kwəl\ *adj* : equal with another — **coequal** *n* — **co·equal·i·ty** \ˌkō-ē-'kwä-lə-tē\ *n* — **co·equal·ly** *adv*

co·erce \kō-'ərs\ *vb* **co·erced; co·erc·ing** **1** : RESTRAIN, REPRESS **2** : COMPEL **3** : ENFORCE — **co·er·cion** \-'ər-zhən, -shən\ *n* — **co·er·cive** \-'ər-siv\ *adj*

co·e·val \kō-'ē-vəl\ *adj* : of the same age — **coeval** *n*

co·ex·ist \ˌkō-ig-'zist\ *vb* **1** : to exist together or at the same time **2** : to live in peace with each other — **co·ex·is·tence** \-'zis-təns\ *n*

co·ex·ten·sive \ˌkō-ik-'sten-siv\ *adj* : having the same scope or extent in space or time

C of C *abbr* Chamber of Commerce

cof·fee \'kó-fē\ *n* [It & Turk; It *caffè*, fr. Turk *kahve*, fr. Ar *qahwa*] : a drink made from the roasted and ground seeds of a fruit of a tropical shrub or tree; *also* : these seeds (**coffee beans**) or a plant producing them

cof·fee·house \-ˌhaús\ *n* : a place where refreshments (as coffee) are sold

coffee klatch \-ˌklach\ *n* : KAFFEE= KLATSCH

cof·fee·pot \-ˌpät\ *n* : a pot for brewing or serving coffee

coffee shop *n* : a small restaurant

coffee table *n* : a low table customarily placed in front of a sofa

cof·fer \'kó-fər\ *n* : a chest or box used esp. for valuables

cof·fer·dam \-ˌdam\ *n* : a watertight enclosure from which water is pumped to expose the bottom of a body of water and permit construction

cof·fin \'kó-fən\ *n* : a box or chest for burying a corpse

C of S *abbr* chief of staff

¹**cog** \'käg\ *n* : a tooth on the rim of a wheel or gear — **cogged** \'kägd\ *adj*

²**cog** *abbr* cognate

co·gen·er·a·tion \ˌkō-je-nə-'rā-shən\ *n* : the simultaneous generation of electricity and heat from the same fuel

co·gent \'kō-jənt\ *adj* : having power to compel or constrain : CONVINCING ⟨a ∼ argument⟩ — **co·gen·cy** \-jən-sē\ *n*

cog·i·tate \'kä-jə-ˌtāt\ *vb* **-tat·ed; -tat·ing** : THINK, PONDER ⟨*cogitated* about his future⟩ — **cog·i·ta·tion** \ˌkä-jə-'tā-shən\ *n* — **cog·i·ta·tive** \'kä-jə-ˌtā-tiv\ *adj*

co·gnac \'kōn-ˌyak\ *n* : a French brandy

cog·nate \'käg-ˌnāt\ *adj* **1** : of the same or similar nature **2** : RELATED; *esp* : related by descent from the same ancestral language — **cognate** *n*

cog·ni·tive \'käg-nə-tiv\ *adj* : of, relating to, or being conscious intellectual activity (as thinking, remembering, reasoning, or using language) — **cog·ni·tion** \käg-'ni-shən\ *n* — **cog·ni·tive·ly** *adv*

cog·ni·zance \'käg-nə-zəns\ *n* **1** : apprehension by the mind : AWARENESS ⟨had no ∼ of the crime⟩ **2** : NOTICE, HEED — **cog·ni·zant** \'käg-nə-zənt\ *adj*

cog·no·men \käg-'nō-mən, 'käg-nə-\ *n, pl* **cognomens** *or* **cog·no·mi·na** \käg-'nä-mə-nə, -'nō-\ : NAME; *esp* : NICKNAME

co·gno·scen·te \ˌkän-yə-'shen-tē, ˌkän-\ *n, pl* **-scen·ti** \-tē\ [obs. It] : CONNOISSEUR

cog·wheel \'käg-ˌhwēl\ *n* : a wheel with cogs or teeth

co·hab·it \kō-'ha-bət\ *vb* : to live together as a couple — **co·hab·i·ta·tion** \-ˌha-bə-'tā-shən\ *n*

co·here \kō-'hir\ *vb* **co·hered; co·her·ing** : to stick together

co·her·ent \kō-'hir-ənt\ *adj* **1** : having the quality of cohering **2** : logically consistent ⟨a ∼ explanation⟩ — **co·her·ence** \-əns\ *n* — **co·her·ent·ly** *adv*

co·he·sion \kō-'hē-zhən\ *n* **1** : a sticking together **2** : molecular attraction by which the particles of a body are united — **co·he·sive** \-siv\ *adj* — **co·he·sive·ly** *adv* — **co·he·sive·ness** *n*

co·ho \'kō-ˌhō\ *n, pl* **cohos** *or* **coho** : a rather small Pacific salmon with light= colored flesh

co·hort \'kō-ˌhórt\ *n* **1** : a group of warriors or followers **2** : COMPANION, ACCOMPLICE

coif \'kóif; 2 usu 'kwäf\ *n* **1** : a close-fitting hat **2** : COIFFURE

coif·feur \kwä-'fər\ *n* [F] : HAIRDRESSER

coif·feuse \kwä-'fərz, -'fəz, -'füz, -'fyüz\ *n* : a female hairdresser

coif·fure \kwä-'fyür\ *n* : a manner of arranging the hair

¹**coil** \'kȯi(-ə)l\ *vb* : to wind in a spiral shape

²**coil** *n* : a series of rings or loops (as of coiled rope, wire, or pipe) : RING, LOOP

¹**coin** \'kȯin\ *n* [ME, wedge, corner, image on a coin, fr. AF *coing*, fr. L *cuneus* wedge] **1** : a piece of metal issued by government authority as money **2** : metal money

²**coin** *vb* **1** : to make (a coin) esp. by stamping : MINT **2** : CREATE, INVENT ⟨~ a phrase⟩ — **coin·er** *n*

coin·age \'kȯi-nij\ *n* **1** : the act or process of coining **2** : COINS

co·in·cide \ˌkō-ən-'sīd, 'kō-ən-ˌsīd\ *vb* **-cid·ed; -cid·ing 1** : to occupy the same place in space or time **2** : to correspond or agree exactly

co·in·ci·dence \kō-'in-sə-dəns\ *n* **1** : exact agreement **2** : occurrence together apparently without reason; *also* : an event that so occurs

co·in·ci·dent \-sə-dənt\ *adj* **1** : of similar nature **2** : occupying the same space or time — **co·in·ci·den·tal** \kō-ˌin-sə-'den-t°l\ *adj*

co·i·tus \'kō-ə-təs\ *n* [L, fr. *coire* to come together] : SEXUAL INTERCOURSE **1** — **co·i·tal** \-t°l\ *adj*

¹**coke** \'kōk\ *n* : a hard gray porous fuel made by heating soft coal to drive off most of its volatile material

²**coke** *n* : COCAINE

¹**col** *abbr* **1** colonial; colony **2** column

²**col** *or* **coll** *abbr* **1** collect, collected, collection **2** college, collegiate

Col *abbr* **1** colonel **2** Colorado **3** Colossians

COL *abbr* **1** colonel **2** cost of living

co·la \'kō-lə\ *n* : a carbonated soft drink usu. containing sugar, caffeine, caramel, and special flavoring

col·an·der \'kə-lon-dər, 'kä-\ *n* : a perforated utensil for draining food

¹**cold** \'kōld\ *adj* **1** : having a low or decidedly subnormal temperature **2** : lacking warmth of feeling **3** : suffering or uncomfortable from lack of warmth — **cold·ly** *adv* — **cold·ness** *n* — **in cold blood** : with premeditation : DELIBERATELY ⟨murdered her *in cold blood*⟩

²**cold** *n* **1** : a condition marked by low temperature; *also* : cold weather **2** : a chilly feeling **3** : a bodily disorder popularly associated with chilling; *esp* : COMMON COLD

³**cold** *adv* **1** : TOTALLY, FINALLY ⟨stopped them ~⟩ **2** : without notice or preparation ⟨performed the song ~⟩

cold–blood·ed \'kōld-'blə-dəd\ *adj* **1** : lacking normal human feelings **2** : having a body temperature not internally regulated but close to that of the environment **3** : sensitive to cold

cold cuts *n pl* : sliced assorted cold cooked meats

cold feet *n pl* : doubt or fear that prevents action

cold front *n* : an advancing edge of a cold air mass

cold shoulder *n* : cold or unsympathetic behavior — **cold–shoul·der** *vb*

cold sore *n* : a group of fluid-filled blisters appearing in or about the mouth in the oral form of herpes simplex

cold sweat *n* : concurrent perspiration and chill usu. associated with fear, pain, or shock

cold turkey *n* : abrupt complete cessation of the use of an addictive drug

²**cold turkey** *adv* **1** : without a period of adjustment **2** : without preparation

cold war *n* : a conflict characterized by the use of means short of sustained overt military action

cole·slaw \'kōl-ˌslȯ\ *n* [D *koolsla*, fr. *kool* cabbage + *sla* salad] : a salad made of raw cabbage

col·ic \'kä-lik\ *n* **1** : sharp sudden abdominal pain **2** : a condition marked by recurrent episodes of crying and irritability in an otherwise healthy infant — **col·icky** \'kä-li-kē\ *adj*

col·i·se·um \ˌkä-lə-'sē-əm\ *n* : a large structure esp. for athletic contests

co·li·tis \kō-'lī-təs\ *n* : inflammation of the colon

col·lab·o·rate \kə-'la-bə-ˌrāt\ *vb* **-rat·ed; -rat·ing 1** : to work jointly with others (as in writing a book) **2** : to cooperate with an enemy force occupying one's country — **col·lab·o·ra·tion** \-ˌla-bə-'rā-shən\ *n* — **col·lab·o·ra·tive** \-'la-bə-ˌrā-tiv, -b(ə-)rə-\ *adj* — **col·lab·o·ra·tor** \-'la-bə-ˌrā-tər\ *n*

col·lage \kə-'läzh\ *n* [F, lit., gluing] : an artistic composition of fragments (as of printed matter) pasted on a surface; *also* : a work that combines various elements into a cohesive whole

col·la·gen \'kä-lə-jən\ *n* : any of a group of fibrous proteins widely found in vertebrate connective tissue

¹**col·lapse** \kə-'laps\ *vb* **col·lapsed; col·laps·ing 1** : to shrink together abruptly **2** : DISINTEGRATE; *also* : to fall in : give way **3** : to break down physically or mentally; *esp* : to fall helpless or unconscious **4** : to fold down compactly — **col·laps·ible** *adj*

²**collapse** *n* : BREAKDOWN

¹**col·lar** \'kä-lər\ *n* **1** : a band, strip, or chain worn around the neck or the neckline of a garment **2** : something resembling a collar — **col·lar·less** *adj*

²**collar** *vb* : to seize by the collar; *also* : ARREST, GRAB ⟨~ a fugitive⟩

col·lar·bone \-ˌbōn\ *n* : the bone of the shoulder that joins the breastbone and the shoulder blade

col·lard \'kä-lərd\ *n* : a stalked smooth-leaved kale — usu. used in pl.

col·late \kə-'lāt; 'kä-ˌlāt, 'kō-\ *vb* **col·lat·ed; col·lat·ing 1** : to compare (as two texts) carefully and critically **2** : to assemble in proper order

¹**col·lat·er·al** \kə-'la-tə-rəl\ *adj* **1** : associated but of secondary importance **2** : descended from the same ancestors but not in the same line **3** : PARALLEL **4** : of, relating to, or being collateral used as security; *also* : secured by collateral

²**collateral** *n* : property (as stocks) used as security for the repayment of a loan

col·la·tion \kä-'lā-shən, kō-\ n 1 : a light meal 2 : the act, process, or result of collating

col·league \'kä-,lēg\ n : an associate esp. in a profession

¹**col·lect** \'kä-likt, -,lekt\ n : a short prayer comprising an invocation, petition, and conclusion

²**col·lect** \kə-'lekt\ vb 1 : to bring or come together into one body or place : GATHER 2 : to accumulate (as coins) as a hobby 3 : to gain control of ⟨~ his thoughts⟩ 4 : to receive payment of — **col·lect·ible** or **col·lect·able** adj or n — **col·lec·tor** \-'lek-tər\ n

³**col·lect** \kə-'lekt\ adv or adj : to be paid for by the receiver

col·lect·ed \kə-'lek-təd\ adj 1 : gathered together ⟨his ~ poems⟩ 2 : SELF-POSSESSED, CALM

col·lec·tion \kə-'lek-shən\ n 1 : the act or process of collecting ⟨garbage ~⟩ 2 : something collected ⟨a stamp ~⟩ 3 : GROUP, AGGREGATE

¹**col·lec·tive** \kə-'lek-tiv\ adj 1 : of, relating to, or denoting a group of individuals considered as a whole 2 : involving all members of a group as distinct from its individuals ⟨~ action⟩ 3 : shared or assumed by all members of the group ⟨a ~ groan⟩ — **col·lec·tive·ly** adv

²**collective** n 1 : GROUP 2 : a cooperative unit or organization

collective bargaining n : negotiation between an employer and a labor union

col·lec·tiv·ise chiefly Brit var of COLLECTIVIZE

col·lec·tiv·ism \kə-'lek-ti-,vi-zəm\ n : a political or economic theory advocating collective control esp. over production and distribution

col·lec·tiv·ize \-,vīz\ vb **-ized; -iz·ing** : to organize under collective control — **col·lec·tiv·i·za·tion** \-,lek-ti-və-'zā-shən\ n

col·leen \kä-'lēn, 'kä-,lēn\ n : an Irish girl

col·lege \'kä-lij\ n [ME, endowed body of clergy or scholars, fr. AF, fr. L collegium society, fr. collega colleague, fr. com- with + legare to depute] 1 : a building used for an educational or religious purpose 2 : an institution of higher learning or division of a university granting a bachelor's degree; also : an institution offering instruction esp. in a vocational or technical field ⟨barber ~⟩ 3 : an organized body of persons having common interests or duties ⟨~ of cardinals⟩ — **col·le·giate** \kə-'lē-jət\ adj

col·le·gi·al·i·ty \kə-,lē-jē-'a-lə-tē\ n : the relationship of colleagues

col·le·gian \kə-'lē-jən\ n : a college student or recent college graduate

col·le·gi·um \kə-'lē-gē-əm, -'lā-\ n, pl **-gia** \-gē-ə\ or **-giums** : a group in which each member has approximately equal power

col·lide \kə-'līd\ vb **col·lid·ed; col·lid·ing** 1 : to come together with solid impact 2 : to come into conflict : CLASH

col·lid·er \kə-'lī-dər\ n : a particle accelerator in which two beams of particles are made to collide

col·lie \'kä-lē\ n : any of a breed of large

dogs developed in Scotland for herding sheep that occur in rough-coated and smooth-coated varieties

col·lier \'käl-yər\ n 1 : a coal miner 2 : a ship for carrying coal

col·liery \'käl-yə-rē\ n, pl **-lier·ies** : a coal mine and its associated buildings

col·li·mate \'kä-lə-,māt\ vb **-mat·ed; -mat·ing** : to make (as light rays) parallel

col·li·sion \kə-'li-zhən\ n : an act or instance of colliding

col·lo·ca·tion \,kä-lə-'kā-shən\ n : the act or result of placing or arranging together; esp : a noticeable arrangement or conjoining of linguistic elements (as words)

col·loid \'kä-,lȯid\ n : a substance in the form of submicroscopic particles that when in solution or suspension do not settle out; also : such a substance together with the medium in which it is dispersed — **col·loi·dal** \kə-'lȯi-d°l\ adj

colloq abbr colloquial

col·lo·qui·al \kə-'lō-kwē-əl\ adj : of, relating to, or characteristic of conversation and esp. of familiar and informal conversation

col·lo·qui·al·ism \-'lō-kwē-ə-,li-zəm\ n : a colloquial expression

col·lo·qui·um \kə-'lō-kwē-əm\ n, pl **-quiums** or **-quia** \-ə\ : CONFERENCE, SEMINAR

col·lo·quy \'kä-lə-kwē\ n, pl **-quies** : a usu. formal conversation or conference

col·lu·sion \kə-'lü-zhən\ n : secret agreement or cooperation for an illegal or deceitful purpose — **col·lu·sive** \-siv\ adj

Colo abbr Colorado

co·logne \kə-'lōn\ n [Cologne, Germany] : a perfumed liquid — **co·logned** \-'lōnd\ adj

Co·lom·bi·an \kə-'ləm-bē-ən\ n : a native or inhabitant of Colombia — **Colombian** adj

¹**co·lon** \'kō-lən\ n, pl **colons** or **co·la** \-lə\ : the part of the large intestine extending from the cecum to the rectum — **co·lon·ic** \kō-'lä-nik\ adj

²**colon** n, pl **colons** : a punctuation mark : used esp. to direct attention to following matter (as a list)

co·lón also **co·lone** \kə-'lōn\ n, pl **co·lo·nes** \-'lō-,näs\ — see MONEY table

col·o·nel \'kər-n°l\ n [alter. of coronel, fr. MF, fr. It colonnello column of soldiers, colonel, ultim. fr. L columna column] : a commissioned officer (as in the army) ranking next below a brigadier general

¹**co·lo·nial** \kə-'lō-nē-əl\ adj 1 : of, relating to, or characteristic of a colony; also : possessing or composed of colonies 2 often cap : of or relating to the original 13 colonies forming the U.S.

²**colonial** n 1 : a member or inhabitant of a colony 2 : a house built in the style of the American colonial period

co·lo·nial·ism \-ə-,li-zəm\ n : control by one power over a dependent area or people; also : a policy advocating or based on such control — **co·lo·nial·ist** \-list\ n or adj

col·o·nise Brit var of COLONIZE

col·o·nist \'kä-lə-nist\ n 1 : COLONIAL 2

: one that colonizes or settles in a new country

col·o·nize \'kä-lə-ˌnīz\ vb **-nized; -niz·ing** 1 : to establish a colony in or on 2 : SETTLE — **col·o·ni·za·tion** \ˌkä-lə-nə-'zā-shən\ n — **col·o·niz·er** n

col·on·nade \ˌkä-lə-'nād\ n : an evenly spaced row of columns usu. supporting the base of a roof structure

co·lo·nos·co·py \ˌkō-lə-'näs-kə-pē\ n, pl **-pies** : endoscopic examination of the colon — **co·lon·o·scope** \kō-'lä-nə-ˌskōp\ n

col·o·ny \'kä-lə-nē\ n, pl **-nies** 1 : a body of people living in a new territory; also : the territory inhabited by these people 2 : a localized population of organisms ⟨a ∼ of bees⟩ 3 : a group with common interests situated in close association ⟨a writers' ∼⟩; also : the area occupied by such a group

col·o·phon \'kä-lə-fən, -ˌfän\ n 1 : an inscription placed at the end of a book with facts relative to its production 2 : an identifying mark used by a printer or publisher

¹col·or \'kə-lər\ n 1 : a phenomenon of light (as red or blue) or visual perception that enables one to differentiate otherwise identical objects; also : a hue as contrasted with black, white, or gray 2 : APPEARANCE 3 : complexion tint 4 pl : FLAG; also : military service ⟨a call to the ∼s⟩ 5 : VIVIDNESS, INTEREST — **col·or·ful** adj — **col·or·less** adj

²color vb 1 : to give color to; also : to change the color of 2 : BLUSH

Col·o·ra·do potato beetle \ˌkä-lə-'ra-dō-, -'rä-\ n : a black-and-yellow striped beetle that feeds on the leaves of the potato

col·or·ation \ˌkə-lə-'rā-shən\ n : use or arrangement of colors

col·or·a·tu·ra \ˌkä-lə-rə-'tùr-ə, -'tyùr-\ n 1 : elaborate ornamentation in vocal music 2 : a soprano specializing in coloratura

col·or-blind \'kə-lər-ˌblīnd\ adj 1 : partially or totally unable to distinguish one or more chromatic colors 2 : not influenced by differences of race — **color blindness** n

co·lo·rec·tal \ˌkō-lō-'rek-t⁸l\ adj : relating to or affecting the colon and rectum ⟨∼ cancer⟩

col·ored \'kə-lərd\ adj 1 : having color 2 : SLANTED, BIASED

col·or·fast \'kə-lər-ˌfast\ adj : having color that does not fade or run — **col·or·fast·ness** n

col·or·ize \'kə-lə-ˌrīz\ vb **-ized; -iz·ing** : to add color to by means of a computer — **col·or·i·za·tion** \ˌkə-lə-rə-'zā-shən\ n

co·los·sal \kə-'lä-səl\ adj : of very great size or degree ⟨a ∼ feat⟩

Co·los·sians \kə-'lä-shənz\ n — see BIBLE table

co·los·sus \kə-'lä-səs\ n, pl **co·los·si** \-ˌsī\ [L] : a gigantic statue; also : something of immense size or power

col·our chiefly Brit var of COLOR

col·por·teur \'käl-ˌpòr-tər\ n [F] : a peddler of religious books

colt \'kōlt\ n : FOAL; also : a young male horse, ass, or zebra — **colt·ish** adj

col·um·bine \'kä-ləm-ˌbīn\ n [ME, fr. AF, fr. ML columbina, fr. L, fem. of columbinus dovelike, fr. columba dove] : any of a genus of plants with showy spurred flowers that are related to the buttercups

co·lum·bi·um \kə-'ləm-bē-əm\ n : NIOBIUM

Columbus Day \kə-'ləm-bəs-\ n : the 2d Monday in October or formerly October 12 observed as a legal holiday in many states in commemoration of the landing of Columbus in the Bahamas in 1492

col·umn \'kä-ləm\ n 1 : one of two or more vertical sections of a printed page; also : one in a usu. regular series of articles (as in a newspaper) 2 : a supporting pillar; esp : one consisting of a usu. round shaft, a capital, and a base 3 : something resembling a column ⟨a ∼ of water⟩ 4 : a long row (as of soldiers) 5 : a statistical category tracked vertically (as on a spreadsheet) — **col·um·nar** \kə-'ləm-nər\ adj

col·um·nist \'kä-ləm-nist\ n : a person who writes a newspaper or magazine column

com abbr 1 comedy; comic 2 comma 3 commercial organization

co·ma \'kō-mə\ n : a state of deep unconsciousness caused by disease, injury, or poison — **co·ma·tose** \'kō-mə-ˌtōs, 'kä-\ adj

Co·man·che \kə-'man-chē\ n, pl Comanche or Comanches : a member of an American Indian people ranging from Wyoming and Nebraska south into New Mexico and Texas

¹comb \'kōm\ n 1 : a toothed instrument for arranging the hair or for separating and cleaning textile fibers 2 : a fleshy crest on the head of a fowl 3 : HONEYCOMB

²comb vb 1 : to pass a comb through 2 : to search through systematically

³comb abbr combination; combining

com·bat \kəm-'bat, 'käm-ˌbat\ vb **-bat·ed** or **-bat·ted; -bat·ing** or **-bat·ting** 1 : FIGHT, CONTEND 2 : to struggle against : OPPOSE — **com·bat** \'käm-ˌbat\ n — **com·bat·ant** \kəm-'ba-t⁸nt, 'käm-bə-tənt\ n — **com·bat·ive** \kəm-'ba-tiv\ adj

combat fatigue n : a traumatic psychological reaction occurring under wartime conditions (as combat) that cause intense stress

comb·er \'kō-mər\ n 1 : one that combs 2 : a long curling wave of the sea

com·bi·na·tion \ˌkäm-bə-'nā-shən\ n 1 : a result or product of combining 2 : a sequence of letters or numbers chosen in setting a lock 3 : the act or process of combining; also : the quality or state of being combined

¹com·bine \kəm-'bīn\ vb **com·bined; com·bin·ing** : to become one : UNITE

²com·bine \'käm-ˌbīn\ n 1 : a combination esp. of business or political interests

2 : a machine that harvests and threshes grain while moving over a field

comb·ings \\'kō-miŋz\\ *n pl* : loose hairs or fibers removed by a comb

combining form *n* : a linguistic form that occurs only in compounds or derivatives

com·bo \\'käm-bō\\ *n, pl* **combos** : a small jazz or dance band

comb-over \\'kōm-ˌō-vər\\ *n* : a hairstyle in which hair from the side of the head is combed over a bald spot

com·bus·ti·ble \\kəm-'bəs-tə-bəl\\ *adj* **1** : capable of being burned **2** : easily excited — **com·bus·ti·bil·i·ty** \\-ˌbəs-tə-'bi-lə-tē\\ *n* — **combustible** *n*

com·bus·tion \\kəm-'bəs-chən\\ *n* **1** : an act or instance of burning **2** : slow oxidation (as in the animal body)

comdg *abbr* commanding

comdr *abbr* commander

comdt *abbr* commandant

come \\'kəm\\ *vb* **came** \\'kām\\; **come; com·ing** \\'kə-miŋ\\ **1** : APPROACH **2** : ARRIVE **3** : to reach the point of being or becoming ⟨∼ to a boil⟩ **4** : AMOUNT ⟨the bill *came* to $10⟩ **5** : to take place **6** : ORIGINATE, ARISE ⟨wine ∼s from grapes⟩ **7** : to be available ⟨∼s in three sizes⟩ **8** : REACH, EXTEND ⟨grass that ∼s to our knees⟩ — **come across 1** : to make a specified impression ⟨*came across* as rude⟩ **2** : to find esp. by chance ⟨*came across* an intriguing story⟩ — **come clean** : CONFESS — **come into** : ACQUIRE, ACHIEVE — **come of age** : MATURE — **come to grips with** : to meet or deal with frankly — **come to pass** : HAPPEN — **come to terms** : to reach an agreement

come·back \\'kəm-ˌbak\\ *n* **1** : RETORT **2** : a return to a former position or condition — **come back** *vb*

co·me·di·an \\kə-'mē-dē-ən\\ *n* **1** : an actor in comedy **2** : a comic person; *esp* : an entertainer specializing in comedy

co·me·di·enne \\-ˌmē-dē-'en\\ *n* : a woman who is a comedian

come·down \\'kəm-ˌdaůn\\ *n* : a descent in rank or dignity

com·e·dy \\'kä-mə-dē\\ *n, pl* **-dies** [ME, narrative that ends happily, fr. ML *comoedia*, fr. L, play with a happy ending, fr. Gk *kōmōidia*, fr. *kōmos* revel + *aeidein* to sing] **1** : a light amusing play with a happy ending **2** : a literary work treating a comic theme or written in a comic style **3** : humorous entertainment — **co·me·dic** \\kə-'mē-dik\\ *adj*

come·ly \\'kəm-lē\\ *adj* **come·li·er; -est** : ATTRACTIVE, HANDSOME — **come·li·ness** *n*

come off *vb* **1** : APPEAR, SEEM ⟨*comes off* as crass⟩ **2** : SUCCEED **3** : to have recently ended ⟨is *coming off* surgery⟩

come-on \\'kə-ˌmȯn, -ˌmän\\ *n* : INDUCEMENT, LURE

come out *vb* **1** : to come into public view **2** : to declare oneself **3** : TURN OUT **6** ⟨everything *came out* all right⟩ — **come out with** : SAY **1**

com·er \\'kə-mər\\ *n* **1** : one that comes ⟨all ∼s⟩ **2** : a promising beginner

¹co·mes·ti·ble \\kə-'mes-tə-bəl\\ *adj* : EDIBLE

²comestible *n* : FOOD — usu. used in pl.

com·et \\'kä-mət\\ *n* [ME *comete*, fr. OE *cometa*, fr. L, fr. Gk *komētēs*, lit., long-haired, fr. *komē* hair] : a small bright celestial body that develops a long tail when near the sun

come to *vb* : to regain consciousness

come·up·pance \\kə-'mə-pəns\\ *n* : a deserved rebuke or penalty

com·fit \\'kəm-fət\\ *n* : a candied fruit or nut

¹com·fort \\'kəm-fərt\\ *vb* **1** : to give strength and hope to **2** : CONSOLE

²comfort *n* **1** : CONSOLATION **2** : freedom from pain, trouble, or anxiety; *also* : something that gives such freedom

com·fort·able \\'kəm-fər-tə-bəl, 'kəmf-tər-\\ *adj* **1** : providing comfort or security **2** : feeling at ease — **com·fort·ably** \\-blē\\ *adv*

com·fort·er \\'kəm-fər-tər\\ *n* **1** : one that comforts **2** : QUILT

com·frey \\'kəm-frē\\ *n, pl* **comfreys** : any of a genus of perennial herbs that have coarse hairy leaves and are often used in herbal remedies

com·fy \\'kəm-fē\\ *adj* : COMFORTABLE

¹com·ic \\'kä-mik\\ *adj* **1** : relating to comedy or comic strips **2** : provoking laughter or amusement ♦ *Synonyms* LAUGHABLE, FUNNY, FARCICAL — **com·i·cal** *adj*

²comic *n* **1** : COMEDIAN **2** *pl* : the part of a newspaper devoted to comic strips

comic book *n* : a magazine containing sequences of comic strips

comic strip *n* : a group of cartoons in narrative sequence

coming *adj* **1** : APPROACHING, NEXT **2** : gaining importance ⟨the ∼ trend⟩

co·mi·ty \\'kä-mə-tē, 'kō-\\ *n, pl* **-ties** : friendly civility : COURTESY

coml *abbr* commercial

comm *abbr* **1** command; commander **2** commerce; commercial **3** commission; commissioner **4** committee **5** common **6** commonwealth

com·ma \\'kä-mə\\ *n* : a punctuation mark , used esp. as a mark of separation within the sentence

¹com·mand \\kə-'mand\\ *vb* **1** : to direct authoritatively : ORDER **2** : DOMINATE, CONTROL, GOVERN **3** : to overlook from a strategic position

²command *n* **1** : an order given **2** : ability to control : MASTERY **3** : the act of commanding **4** : a signal that actuates a device (as a computer); *also* : the activation of a device by means of a signal **5** : a body of troops under a commander; *also* : an area or position that one commands **6** : a position of highest authority

com·man·dant \\'kä-mən-ˌdant, -ˌdänt\\ *n* : an officer in command

com·man·deer \\ˌkä-mən-'dir\\ *vb* : to take possession of by force

com·mand·er \\kə-'man-dər\\ *n* **1** : LEADER, CHIEF; *esp* : an officer commanding an army or subdivision of an army **2** : a

commander in chief • common

144

commissioned officer in the navy ranking next below a captain

commander in chief : the supreme commander of the armed forces

com·mand·ment \kə-ˈmand-mənt\ n : COMMAND, ORDER; esp : any of the Ten Commandments

command module n : a space vehicle module designed to carry the crew and reentry equipment

com·man·do \kə-ˈman-dō\ n, pl **-dos** or **-does** : a member of a military unit trained for surprise raids

command sergeant major n : a noncommissioned officer in the army ranking above a sergeant major

com·mem·o·rate \kə-ˈme-mə-ˌrāt\ vb **-rat·ed; -rat·ing** 1 : to call or recall to mind 2 : to serve as a memorial of — **com·mem·o·ra·tion** \-ˌme-mə-ˈrā-shən\ n

com·mem·o·ra·tive \kə-ˈmem-rə-tiv, -ˈme-mə-ˌrā-tiv\ adj : intended to commemorate an event ⟨a ∼ stamp⟩

com·mence \kə-ˈmens\ vb **com·menced; com·menc·ing** : BEGIN, START ⟨∼ the festivities⟩

com·mence·ment \-mənt\ n 1 : the act or time of a beginning 2 : the graduation exercises of a school or college

com·mend \kə-ˈmend\ vb 1 : to commit to one's care 2 : RECOMMEND 3 : PRAISE — **com·mend·able** \-ˈmen-də-bəl\ adj — **com·mend·ably** \-blē\ adv — **com·men·da·tion** \ˌkä-mən-ˈdā-shən, -ˌmen-\ n — **com·mend·er** n

com·men·su·ra·ble \kə-ˈmen-sə-rə-bəl\ adj : having a common measure or a common divisor

com·men·su·rate \kə-ˈmen-sə-rət, -ˈmen-chə-\ adj : equal in measure or extent; also : PROPORTIONAL, CORRESPONDING ⟨a job ∼ with her abilities⟩

com·ment \ˈkä-ˌment\ n 1 : an expression of opinion 2 : an explanatory, illustrative, or critical note or observation : REMARK — **comment** vb

com·men·tary \ˈkä-mən-ˌter-ē\ n, pl **-tar·ies** : a systematic series of comments

com·men·ta·tor \-ˌtā-tər\ n : one who comments; esp : a person who discusses news events on radio or television

com·merce \ˈkä-(ˌ)mərs\ n : the buying and selling of commodities : TRADE

¹**com·mer·cial** \kə-ˈmər-shəl\ adj : having to do with commerce; also : designed for profit or for mass appeal — **com·mer·cial·ly** adv

²**commercial** n : an advertisement broadcast on radio or television

com·mer·cial·ise Brit var of COMMERCIALIZE

com·mer·cial·ism \kə-ˈmər-shə-ˌli-zəm\ n 1 : a spirit, method, or practice characteristic of business 2 : excessive emphasis on profit

com·mer·cial·ize \-ˌlīz\ vb **-ized; -iz·ing** 1 : to manage on a business basis for profit 2 : to exploit for profit

com·mi·na·tion \ˌkä-mə-ˈnā-shən\ n : DENUNCIATION — **com·mi·na·to·ry** \ˈkä-mə-nə-ˌtȯr-ē\ adj

com·min·gle \kə-ˈmiŋ-gəl\ vb : MINGLE, BLEND

com·mis·er·ate \kə-ˈmi-zə-ˌrāt\ vb **-at·ed; -at·ing** : to feel or express pity : SYMPATHIZE — **com·mis·er·a·tion** \-ˌmi-zə-ˈrā-shən\ n

com·mis·sar \ˈkä-mə-ˌsär\ n [Russ komissar] : a Communist party official

com·mis·sar·i·at \ˌkä-mə-ˈser-ē-ət\ n 1 : a system for supplying troops with food 2 : a department headed by a commissar

com·mis·sary \ˈkä-mə-ˌser-ē\ n, pl **-sar·ies** : a store for equipment and provisions esp. for military personnel

¹**com·mis·sion** \kə-ˈmi-shən\ n 1 : a warrant granting certain powers and imposing certain duties 2 : a certificate conferring military rank and authority 3 : authority to act as agent for another; also : something to be done by an agent 4 : a body of persons charged with performing a duty 5 : the doing of some act ⟨∼ of a crime⟩; also : the thing done 6 : the allowance made to an agent for transacting business for another

²**commission** vb 1 : to give a commission to 2 : to order to be made ⟨∼ a portrait⟩ 3 : to put (a ship) into a state of readiness for service

commissioned officer n : an officer of the armed forces holding rank by a commission from the president

com·mis·sion·er \kə-ˈmi-shə-nər\ n 1 : a member of a commission 2 : an official in charge of a department of public service ⟨a police ∼⟩ 3 : the administrative head of a professional sport — **com·mis·sion·er·ship** n

com·mit \kə-ˈmit\ vb **com·mit·ted; com·mit·ting** 1 : to put into charge or trust : ENTRUST 2 : to put in a prison or mental institution : TRANSFER, CONSIGN 3 : to carry into action : PERPETRATE ⟨∼ a crime⟩ 5 : to pledge or assign to some particular course or use — **com·mit·ment** n — **com·mit·tal** n

com·mit·tee \kə-ˈmi-tē\ n : a body of persons selected to consider and act or report on some matter — **com·mit·tee·man** \-mən\ n — **com·mit·tee·wom·an** \-ˌwu̇-mən\ n

commo abbr commodore

com·mode \kə-ˈmōd\ n [F, fr. commode, adj., suitable, convenient, fr. L commodus, fr. com- with + modus measure] 1 : a movable washstand with cupboard below 2 : TOILET 3

com·mo·di·ous \kə-ˈmō-dē-əs\ adj : comfortably spacious : ROOMY

com·mod·i·ty \kə-ˈmä-də-tē\ n, pl **-ties** 1 : a product of agriculture or mining 2 : an article of commerce 3 : something useful or valued ⟨that valuable ∼ patience⟩

com·mo·dore \ˈkä-mə-ˌdȯr\ n 1 : a commissioned officer in the navy ranking next below a rear admiral 2 : an officer commanding a group of merchant ships 3 : the chief officer of a yacht club

¹**com·mon** \ˈkä-mən\ adj 1 : belonging to or serving the community : PUBLIC 2 : shared by a number in a group 3 : wide-

ly or generally known, found, or observed : FAMILIAR 〈~ knowledge〉 **4** : VERNACULAR 3 〈~ names of plants〉 **5** : not above the average esp. in social status ♦ **Synonyms** UNIVERSAL, GENERAL, GENERIC — **com·mon·ly** adv

²common n 1 pl : the common people **2** pl : a dining hall **3** pl, cap : the lower house of the British and Canadian parliaments **4** : a piece of land subject to common use — **in common** : shared together

com·mon·al·ty \'kä-mə-nəl-tē\ n, pl **-ties** : the common people

common cold n : a contagious respiratory disease caused by a virus and characterized by a sore, swollen, and inflamed nose and throat, usu. by much mucus, and by coughing and sneezing

common denominator n **1** : a common multiple of the denominators of a group of fractions **2** : a common trait or theme

common divisor n : a number or expression that divides two or more numbers or expressions without remainder

com·mon·er \'kä-mə-nər\ n : one of the common people : a person having no rank of nobility

common fraction n : a fraction (as ½ or ¾) in which the numerator and denominator are both integers and are separated by a horizontal or slanted line

common law n : a group of legal practices and traditions based on judges' decisions and social customs and usu. having the same force as laws passed by legislative bodies

common logarithm n : a logarithm whose base is 10

common market n : an economic association formed to remove trade barriers among members

common multiple n : a multiple of each of two or more numbers or expressions

¹com·mon·place \'kä-mən-ˌplās\ n : something that is ordinary or trite

²commonplace adj : ORDINARY

common sense n : ordinary good sense and judgment — **com·mon·sen·si·cal** \'kä-mən-'sen-si-kəl\ adj

com·mon·weal \'kä-mən-ˌwēl\ n **1** archaic : COMMONWEALTH **2** : the general welfare

com·mon·wealth \-ˌwelth\ n **1** : the body of people politically organized into a state **2** : STATE; also : an association or federation of autonomous states

com·mo·tion \kə-'mō-shən\ n **1** : DISTURBANCE, UPRISING **2** : AGITATION

com·mu·nal \kə-'myü-nᵊl, 'käm-yə-nᵊl\ adj **1** : of or relating to a commune or community **2** : marked by collective ownership and use of property **3** : shared or used in common

¹com·mune \kə-'myün\ vb **com·muned; com·mun·ing** : to communicate intimately 〈~ with nature〉

²com·mune \'käm-ˌyün; kə-'myün\ n **1** : the smallest administrative district in some European countries **2** : a community organized on a communal basis

com·mu·ni·ca·ble \kə-'myü-ni-kə-bəl\ adj : capable of being communicated 〈~ diseases〉 — **com·mu·ni·ca·bil·i·ty** \-ˌmyü-ni-kə-'bi-lə-tē\ n

com·mu·ni·cant \-'myü-ni-kənt\ n **1** : a church member entitled to receive Communion **2** : one that communicates; esp : INFORMANT

com·mu·ni·cate \kə-'myü-nə-ˌkāt\ vb **-cat·ed; -cat·ing 1** : to make known **2** : to pass from one to another : TRANSMIT **3** : to receive Communion **4** : to be in communication **5** : JOIN, CONNECT — **com·mu·ni·ca·tor** \-ˌkā-tər\ n

com·mu·ni·ca·tion \kə-ˌmyü-nə-'kā-shən\ n **1** : an act of transmitting **2** : MESSAGE **3** : exchange of information or opinions **4** : a means of communicating — **com·mu·ni·ca·tive** \-'myü-nə-ˌkā-tiv, -ni-kə-tiv\ adj

com·mu·nion \kə-'myü-nyən\ n **1** : a sharing of something with others **2** cap : a Christian sacrament in which bread and wine are consumed as the substance or symbols of Christ's body and blood in commemoration of the death of Christ **3** : intimate fellowship or rapport **4** : a body of Christians having a common faith and discipline 〈the Anglican ~〉

com·mu·ni·qué \kə-'myü-nə-ˌkā, -ˌmyü-nə-'kā\ n : BULLETIN 1

com·mu·nism \'käm-yə-ˌni-zəm\ n **1** : social organization in which goods are held in common **2** : a theory of social organization advocating common ownership of means of production and a distribution of products of industry based on need **3** cap : a political doctrine based on revolutionary Marxist socialism that was the official ideology of the U.S.S.R. and some other countries; also : a system of government in which one party controls state-owned means of production — **com·mu·nist** \-nist\ n or adj, often cap — **com·mu·nis·tic** \ˌkäm-yə-'nis-tik\ adj, often cap

com·mu·ni·ty \kə-'myü-nə-tē\ n, pl **-ties 1** : a body of people living in the same place under the same laws; also : a natural population of plants and animals that interact ecologically and live in one place (as a pond) **2** : society at large **3** : joint ownership 〈~ of goods〉 **4** : SIMILARITY, LIKENESS 〈~ of interests〉

community college n : a 2-year government-supported college that offers an associate degree

community property n : property held jointly by husband and wife

com·mu·ta·tion \ˌkäm-yə-'tā-shən\ n : substitution of one form of payment or penalty for another

com·mu·ta·tive \'käm-yə-ˌtā-tiv, kə-'myü-tə-\ adj : of, having, or being the property that the result obtained using a mathematical operation on any two elements of a set does not differ with the order in which the elements are used 〈a x b = b x a because multiplication is ~〉 — **com·mu·ta·tiv·i·ty** \kə-ˌmyü-tə-'ti-və-tē, ˌkäm-yə-tə-\ n

com·mu·ta·tor \'käm-yə-ˌtā-tər\ n : a device (as on a generator or motor) for changing the direction of electric current

¹**com·mute** \kə-'myüt\ *vb* **com·mut·ed; com·mut·ing** **1** : EXCHANGE **2** : to revoke (a sentence) and impose a milder penalty **3** : to travel back and forth regularly — **com·mut·er** *n*

²**commute** *n* : a trip made in commuting

comp *abbr* **1** comparative; compare **2** compensation **3** compiled; compiler **4** composition; compositor **5** compound **6** comprehensive **7** comptroller

¹**com·pact** \kəm-'pakt, 'käm-ˌpakt\ *adj* **1** : SOLID, DENSE **2** : BRIEF, SUCCINCT **3** : occupying a small volume by efficient use of space ⟨~ camera⟩ — **com·pact·ly** *adv* — **com·pact·ness** *n*

²**compact** *vb* : to pack together — COMPRESS — **com·pac·tor** \kəm-'pak-tər, 'käm-ˌpak-\ *n*

³**com·pact** \'käm-ˌpakt\ *n* **1** : a small case for cosmetics **2** : a small automobile

⁴**com·pact** \'käm-ˌpakt\ *n* : AGREEMENT, COVENANT

compact disc \'käm-ˌpakt-\ *n* : CD

com·pa·dre \kəm-'pä-drā\ *n* : a close friend : BUDDY

¹**com·pan·ion** \kəm-'pan-yən\ *n* [ME *companoun*, fr. AF *cumpaing, cumpaignun*, fr. LL *companion-, companio*, fr. L *com-* together + *panis* bread] **1** : an intimate friend or associate : COMRADE **2** : one that is closely connected with something similar **3** : a celestial body that appears close to another but that may not be associated with it in space — **com·pan·ion·able** *adj* — **com·pan·ion·ship** *n*

²**companion** *n* : COMPANIONWAY

com·pan·ion·way \-ˌwā\ *n* : a ship's stairway from one deck to another

com·pa·ny \'kəm-pə-nē\ *n, pl* **-nies** **1** : association with others : FELLOWSHIP; *also* : COMPANIONS **2** : GUESTS **3** : a group of persons or things **4** : an infantry unit consisting of two or more platoons and normally commanded by a captain **5** : a group of musical or dramatic performers **6** : the officers and crew of a ship **7** : an association of persons for carrying on a business ♦ **Synonyms** PARTY, BAND, TROOP, TROUPE, CORPS, OUTFIT

com·pa·ra·ble \'käm-pə-rə-bəl, -prə-\ *adj* : capable of being compared ⟨singers of ~ talent⟩ ♦ **Synonyms** PARALLEL, SIMILAR, LIKE, ALIKE, CORRESPONDING — **com·pa·ra·bil·i·ty** \ˌkäm-pə-rə-'bi-lə-tē\ *n*

¹**com·par·a·tive** \kəm-'per-ə-tiv\ *adj* **1** : of, relating to, or constituting the degree of grammatical comparison that denotes increase in quality, quantity, or relation **2** : RELATIVE ⟨a ~ stranger⟩ — **com·par·a·tive·ly** *adv*

²**comparative** *n* : the comparative degree or form in a language

¹**com·pare** \kəm-'per\ *vb* **com·pared; com·par·ing** **1** : to represent as similar : LIKEN **2** : to examine for likenesses and differences **3** : to inflect or modify (an adjective or adverb) according to the degrees of comparison

²**compare** *n* : the possibility of comparing ⟨beauty beyond ~⟩

com·par·i·son \kəm-'per-ə-sən\ *n* **1** : the act of comparing **2** : change in the form of an adjective or adverb to show different levels of quality, quantity, or relation

com·part·ment \kəm-'pärt-mənt\ *n* **1** : a separate division **2** : a section of an enclosed space : ROOM

com·part·men·tal·ise *Brit var of* COMPARTMENTALIZE

com·part·men·tal·ize \kəm-ˌpärt-'men-t⁹l-ˌīz\ *vb* **-ized; -iz·ing** : to separate into compartments

¹**com·pass** \'kəm-pəs, 'käm-\ *vb* [ME, fr. AF *cumpasser* to measure, fr. VL **compassare* to pace off, fr. L *com-* + *passus* pace] **1** : CONTRIVE, PLOT **2** : ENCIRCLE, ENCOMPASS **3** : BRING ABOUT, ACHIEVE

²**compass** *n* **1** : BOUNDARY, CIRCUMFERENCE **2** : an enclosed space **3** : RANGE, SCOPE **4** : a device for determining direction by means of a magnetic needle swinging freely and pointing to the magnetic north; *also* : a nonmagnetic device that indicates direction **5** : an instrument for drawing circles or transferring measurements consisting of two legs joined by a pivot

com·pas·sion \kəm-'pa-shən\ *n* : sympathetic feeling : PITY, MERCY — **com·pas·sion·ate** \-shə-nət\ *adj* — **com·pas·sion·ate·ly** *adv*

com·pat·i·ble \kəm-'pa-tə-bəl\ *adj* : able to exist or act together harmoniously ⟨~ colors⟩ ⟨~ drugs⟩ ♦ **Synonyms** CONSONANT, CONGENIAL, SYMPATHETIC — **com·pat·i·bil·i·ty** \-ˌpa-tə-'bi-lə-tē\ *n*

com·pa·tri·ot \kəm-'pā-trē-ət, -ˌät\ *n* : a fellow countryman

com·peer \'käm-ˌpir\ *n* : EQUAL, PEER

com·pel \kəm-'pel\ *vb* **com·pelled; com·pel·ling** : to drive or urge with force

com·pen·di·ous \kəm-'pen-dē-əs\ *adj* : concise and comprehensive; *also* : COMPREHENSIVE ⟨a ~ almanac⟩

com·pen·di·um \kəm-'pen-dē-əm\ *n, pl* **-di·ums** *or* **-dia** \-ə\ **1** : a brief summary of a larger work or of a field of knowledge **2** : COLLECTION

com·pen·sate \'käm-pən-ˌsāt\ *vb* **-sat·ed; -sat·ing** **1** : to be equivalent to : make up for **2** : PAY, REMUNERATE ♦ **Synonyms** BALANCE, OFFSET, COUNTERBALANCE, COUNTERPOISE — **com·pen·sa·tion** \ˌkäm-pən-'sā-shən\ *n* — **com·pen·sa·to·ry** \kəm-'pen-sə-ˌtȯr-ē\ *adj*

com·pete \kəm-'pēt\ *vb* **com·pet·ed; com·pet·ing** : CONTEND, VIE ⟨~ for the title⟩ ⟨~ for customers⟩

com·pe·tence \'käm-pə-təns\ *n* **1** : adequate means for subsistence **2** : FITNESS, ABILITY ⟨trusted his doctor's ~⟩

com·pe·ten·cy \-tən-sē\ *n, pl* **-cies** : COMPETENCE

com·pe·tent \-tənt\ *adj* : CAPABLE, FIT, QUALIFIED ⟨a ~ mechanic⟩ ⟨a ~ juror⟩

com·pe·ti·tion \ˌkäm-pə-'ti-shən\ *n* **1** : the act of competing : RIVALRY **2** : CONTEST, MATCH; *also* : one's competiors — **com·pet·i·tive** \kəm-'pe-tə-tiv\ *adj* — **com·pet·i·tive·ly** *adv* — **com·pet·i·tive·ness** *n*

com·pet·i·tor \kəm-'pe-tə-tər\ *n* : one that competes : RIVAL

com·pile \kəm-'pī(-ə)l\ *vb* **com·piled; com·pil·ing** [ME, fr. AF *compiler*, fr. L *compilare* to plunder] **1** : to compose out of materials from other documents **2** : to collect and edit into a volume **3** : to translate (a computer program) with a compiler **4** : to build up gradually ⟨∼ a record of four wins and two losses⟩ — **com·pi·la·tion** \ˌkäm-pə-'lā-shən\ *n*

com·pil·er \kəm-'pī-lər\ *n* **1** : one that compiles **2** : a computer program that translates any program correctly written in a specific programming language into machine language

com·pla·cence \kəm-'plā-sᵊns\ *n* : COM·PLACENCY — **com·pla·cent** \-sᵊnt\ *adj* — **com·pla·cent·ly** *adv*

com·pla·cen·cy \-sᵊn-sē\ *n, pl* **-cies** : SATISFACTION; *esp* : SELF-SATISFACTION

com·plain \kəm-'plān\ *vb* **1** : to express grief, pain, or discontent **2** : to make a formal accusation — **com·plain·ant** *n* — **com·plain·er** *n*

com·plaint \kəm-'plānt\ *n* **1** : expression of grief, pain, or dissatisfaction **2** : a bodily ailment or disease **3** : a formal accusation against a person

com·plai·sance \kəm-'plā-sᵊns, ˌkäm-plā-'zans\ *n* [F] : disposition to please — **com·plai·sant** \-sᵊnt, -'zant\ *adj* — **com·plai·sant·ly** *adv*

com·pleat \kəm-'plēt\ *adj* : PROFICIENT

com·plect·ed \kəm-'plek-təd\ *adj* : having a specified facial complexion ⟨dark-complected⟩

¹com·ple·ment \'käm-plə-mənt\ *n* **1** : something that fills up or completes; *also* : the full quantity, number, or amount that makes a thing complete **2** : an added word by which a predicate is made complete **3** : a group of proteins in blood that combines with antibodies to destroy antigens — **com·ple·men·ta·ry** \ˌkäm-plə-'men-t(ə-)rē\ *adj*

²com·ple·ment \-ˌment\ *vb* : to be complementary to : fill out

complementary medicine *n* : ALTERNATIVE MEDICINE

¹com·plete \kəm-'plēt\ *adj* **com·plet·er; -est** **1** : having all parts or elements **2** : brought to an end **3** : fully carried out; *also* : ABSOLUTE **2** ⟨∼ silence⟩ — **com·plete·ly** *adv* — **com·plete·ness** *n* — **com·ple·tion** \-'plē-shən\ *n*

²complete *vb* **com·plet·ed; com·plet·ing** **1** : FINISH, CONCLUDE **2** : to make whole or perfect ⟨the hat ∼s the outfit⟩

com·plet·ist \kəm-'plē-tist\ *n* : one who wants to make something (as a collection) complete

¹com·plex \'käm-ˌpleks\ *n* **1** : a whole made up of or involving intricately inter-related elements **2** : a group of repressed desires and memories that exert a dominating influence on one's personality and behavior ⟨a guilt ∼⟩

²com·plex \käm-'pleks, 'käm-ˌpleks\ *adj*

1 : composed of two or more parts **2** : consisting of a main clause and one or more subordinate clauses ⟨∼ sentence⟩ **3** : hard to separate, analyze, or solve — **com·plex·i·ty** \käm-'plek-sə-tē\ *n* — **com·plex·ly** *adv*

complex fraction *n* : a fraction with a fraction or mixed number in the numerator or denominator or both

com·plex·ion \kəm-'plek-shən\ *n* **1** : the hue or appearance of the skin esp. of the face **2** : overall appearance — **com·plex·ioned** \-shənd\ *adj*

complex number *n* : a number of the form $a + b \sqrt{-1}$ where *a* and *b* are real numbers

com·pli·ance \kəm-'plī-əns\ *n* **1** : the act of complying to a demand or proposal **2** : a disposition to yield — **com·pli·ant** \-ənt\ *adj*

com·pli·cate \'käm-plə-ˌkāt\ *vb* **-cat·ed; -cat·ing** : to make or become complex or intricate

com·pli·cat·ed \'käm-plə-ˌkā-təd\ *adj* **1** : consisting of parts intricately combined **2** : difficult to analyze, understand, or explain ⟨a ∼ issue⟩ — **com·pli·cat·ed·ly** *adv*

com·pli·ca·tion \ˌkäm-plə-'kā-shən\ *n* : the quality or state of being complicated; *also* : a complex feature **2** : a disease or condition that develops during and affects the course of a primary disease or condition

com·plic·i·ty \kəm-'pli-sə-tē\ *n, pl* **-ties** : the state of being an accomplice

¹com·pli·ment \'käm-plə-mənt\ *n* **1** : an expression of approval or admiration; *esp* : a flattering remark **2** *pl* : best wishes : REGARDS

²com·pli·ment \-ˌment\ *vb* : to pay a compliment to

com·pli·men·ta·ry \ˌkäm-plə-'men-t(ə-)rē\ *adj* **1** : containing or expressing a compliment **2** : given free as a courtesy ⟨∼ ticket⟩

com·ply \kəm-'plī\ *vb* **com·plied; com·ply·ing** : CONFORM, YIELD

¹com·po·nent \kəm-'pō-nənt, 'käm-ˌpō-\ *n* : a component part ♦ **Synonyms** IN·GREDIENT, ELEMENT, FACTOR, CONSTITUENT

²component *adj* : serving to form a part of : CONSTITUENT

com·port \kəm-'pōrt\ *vb* **1** : AGREE, ACCORD ⟨actions that ∼ with policy⟩ **2** : CONDUCT ⟨∼ oneself with dignity⟩ ♦ **Synonyms** BEHAVE, ACQUIT, DEPORT — **com·port·ment** *n*

com·pose \kəm-'pōz\ *vb* **com·posed; com·pos·ing** **1** : to form by putting together : FASHION **2** : to produce (as pages of type) by composition **3** : ADJUST, ARRANGE **4** : CALM, QUIET ⟨∼ yourself before acting⟩ **5** : to practice composition ⟨∼ music⟩ — **com·pos·er** *n*

¹com·pos·ite \käm-'pä-zət\ *adj* **1** : made up of distinct parts or elements **2** : of, relating to, or being a large family of flowering plants (as a daisy or aster) that bear many small flowers united into compact heads resembling single flowers

²**composite** n **1** : something composite **2** : a plant of the composite family ♦ *Synonyms* BLEND, COMPOUND, MIXTURE, AMALGAMATION

com·po·si·tion \ˌkäm-pə-'zi-shən\ n **1** : the act or process of composing; *esp* : arrangement esp. in artistic form **2** : the arrangement or production of type for printing **3** : general makeup **4** : a product of mixing various elements or ingredients **5** : a literary, musical, or artistic product; *esp* : ESSAY

com·po·si·tion·ist \-'zi-shə-nist\ n : a teacher of writing

com·pos·i·tor \kəm-'pä-zə-tər\ n : one who sets type

com·post \'käm-ˌpōst\ n : a fertilizing material consisting largely of decayed organic matter — **compost** vb

com·po·sure \kəm-'pō-zhər\ n : CALMNESS, SELF-POSSESSION

com·pote \'käm-ˌpōt\ n **1** : fruits cooked in syrup **2** : a bowl (as of glass) usu. with a base and stem for serving esp. fruit or compote

¹**com·pound** \käm-'paùnd, 'käm-ˌ\ vb [ME *compounen*, fr. AF **cumpundre*, fr. L *componere*, fr. *com-* together + *ponere* to put] **1** : COMBINE **2** : to form by combining parts ⟨∼ a medicine⟩ **3** : SETTLE ⟨∼ a dispute⟩; *also* : to refrain from prosecuting (an offense) in return for a consideration **4** : to increase (as interest) by an amount that can itself vary; *also* : to add to

²**com·pound** \'käm-ˌpaùnd\ adj **1** : made up of individual parts **2** : composed of united similar parts esp. of a kind usu. independent ⟨a ∼ plant ovary⟩ **3** : formed by the combination of two or more otherwise independent elements ⟨∼ sentence⟩

³**com·pound** \'käm-ˌpaùnd\ n **1** : a word consisting of parts that are words **2** : something formed from a union of elements or parts; *esp* : a distinct substance formed by the union of two or more chemical elements ♦ *Synonyms* MIXTURE, COMPOSITE, BLEND, ADMIXTURE, ALLOY

⁴**com·pound** \'käm-ˌpaùnd\ n [by folk etymology fr. Malay *kampung* group of buildings, village] : an enclosure containing buildings

compound interest n : interest computed on the sum of an original principal and accrued interest

com·pre·hend \ˌkäm-pri-'hend\ vb **1** : UNDERSTAND **2** : INCLUDE — **com·pre·hen·si·ble** \-'hen-sə-bəl\ adj — **com·pre·hen·sion** \-'hen-chən\ n

com·pre·hen·sive \ˌkäm-pri-'hen-siv\ adj : covering completely or broadly ⟨∼ insurance⟩ — **com·pre·hen·sive·ly** adv — **com·pre·hen·sive·ness** n

¹**com·press** \kəm-'pres\ vb **1** : to squeeze together **2** : to reduce in size as if by squeezing ♦ *Synonyms* CONSTRICT, CONTRACT, SHRINK — **com·pres·sor** \-'pre-sər\ n

²**com·press** \'käm-ˌpres\ n : a folded pad or cloth used to press upon a body part

compressed air n : air under pressure greater than that of the atmosphere

com·pres·sion \kəm-'pre-shən\ n **1** : the act or process of compressing **2** : the process of compressing the fuel mixture in an internal combustion engine **3** : conversion (as of data) in order to reduce the space occupied or the bandwidth required

com·prise \kəm-'prīz\ vb **com·prised**; **com·pris·ing 1** : INCLUDE, CONTAIN **2** : to be made up of ⟨the play ∼s three acts⟩ **3** : COMPOSE, CONSTITUTE

¹**com·pro·mise** \'käm-prə-ˌmīz\ n : a settlement of differences reached by mutual concessions

²**compromise** vb **-mised; -mis·ing 1** : to settle by compromise **2** : to expose to suspicion or loss of reputation

comp·trol·ler \kən-'trō-lər, 'kämp-ˌtrō-\ n : an official who audits and supervises expenditures and accounts

com·pul·sion \kəm-'pəl-shən\ n **1** : an act of compelling **2** : a force that compels **3** : an irresistible persistent impulse to perform an act ♦ *Synonyms* CONSTRAINT, FORCE, VIOLENCE, DURESS — **com·pul·sive** \-siv\ adj — **com·pul·sive·ly** adv — **com·pul·so·ry** \-sə-rē\ adj

com·punc·tion \kəm-'pəŋk-shən\ n : anxiety arising from guilt : REMORSE

com·pute \kəm-'pyüt\ vb **com·put·ed; com·put·ing** : CALCULATE, RECKON — **com·pu·ta·tion** \ˌkäm-pyù-'tā-shən\ n — **com·pu·ta·tion·al** adj

computed tomography n : radiography in which a three-dimensional image of a body structure is constructed by computer from a series of plane cross-sectional images made along an axis

com·put·er \kəm-'pyü-tər\ n : a programmable electronic device that can store, retrieve, and process data

com·put·er·ise *chiefly Brit var of* COMPUTERIZE

com·put·er·ize \kəm-'pyü-tə-ˌrīz\ vb **-ized; -iz·ing 1** : to carry out, control, or produce by means of a computer **2** : to provide with computers **3** : to store in a computer; *also* : put into a form that a computer can use — **com·put·er·i·za·tion** \-ˌpyü-tə-rə-'zā-shən\ n

computerized axial tomography n : COMPUTED TOMOGRAPHY

com·rade \'käm-ˌrad\ n [MF *camarade* group sleeping in one room, roommate, companion, fr. Sp *camarada*, fr. *cámara* room, fr. LL *camera*] : COMPANION, ASSOCIATE — **com·rade·ly** adj — **com·rade·ship** n

¹**con** \'kän\ vb **conned; con·ning 1** : MEMORIZE **2** : STUDY

²**con** adv : in opposition : AGAINST

³**con** n : an opposing argument, person, or position ⟨pros and ∼s⟩

⁴**con** vb **conned; con·ning 1** : SWINDLE **2** : PERSUADE, CAJOLE

⁵**con** n : CONVICT

conc abbr concentrated

con·cat·e·nate \kän-'ka-tə-ˌnāt\ vb **-nat·ed; -nat·ing** : to link together in a series

chain — con·cat·e·na·tion \(,)kän-
a-tə-'nā-shən\ n

¹con·cave \kän-'kāv, 'kän-,\ adj : curved
or rounded inward like the inside of a
bowl — con·cav·i·ty \kän-'ka-və-tē\ n

con·ceal \kən-'sēl\ vb : to place out of
sight : HIDE ⟨~ evidence⟩ — con·ceal·
er n — con·ceal·ment n

con·cede \kən-'sēd\ vb con·ced·ed;
con·ced·ing 1 : to admit to be true 2
: GRANT, YIELD ♦ Synonyms ALLOW,
ACKNOWLEDGE, AVOW, CONFESS

con·ceit \kən-'sēt\ n 1 : excessively high
opinion of one's self or ability : VANITY 2
: an elaborate or strained metaphor —
con·ceit·ed adj — con·ceit·ed·ly adv —
con·ceit·ed·ness n

con·ceive \kən-'sēv\ vb con·ceived;
con·ceiv·ing 1 : to become pregnant or
pregnant with ⟨~ a child⟩ 2 : to form an
idea of : THINK, IMAGINE ⟨~ a plan⟩ —
con·ceiv·able \-'sē-və-bəl\ adj — con·
ceiv·ably \-blē\ adv

con·cel·e·brant \kən-'se-lə-brənt\ n : one
that jointly participates in celebrating the
Eucharist

¹con·cen·trate \'kän-sən-,trāt\ vb -trat·
ed; -trat·ing 1 : to gather into one body,
mass, or force 2 : to make less dilute 3
: to fix one's powers, efforts, or attentions

²concentrate n : something concentrated

con·cen·tra·tion \,kän-sən-'trā-shən\ n 1
: the act or process of concentrating : the
state of being concentrated; esp : direction of attention on a single object 2
: the amount of a component in a given
area or volume

concentration camp n : a camp where
persons (as prisoners of war or political
prisoners) are confined

con·cen·tric \kän-'sen-trik\ adj 1 : having a common center ⟨~ circles⟩ 2 : CO-
AXIAL

¹con·cept \'kän-,sept\ n : THOUGHT, NO-
TION, IDEA — con·cep·tu·al \kən-'sep-
chə-wəl\ adj — con·cep·tu·al·ly adv

²concept adj 1 : organized around a main
idea or theme ⟨a ~ album⟩ 2 : created
to illustrate a concept ⟨a ~ car⟩

con·cep·tion \kən-'sep-shən\ n 1 : the
process of conceiving or being conceived
2 : the power to form or understand ideas
or concepts 3 : IDEA, CONCEPT 4 : the
originating of something

con·cep·tu·al·ise Brit var of CONCEPTU-
ALIZE

con·cep·tu·al·ize \-'sep-chə-wə-,līz\ vb
-ized; -iz·ing : to form a conception of

¹con·cern \kən-'sərn\ vb 1 : to relate to 2
: to be the business of : INVOLVE 3 : EN-
GAGE, OCCUPY

²concern n 1 : INTEREST, ANXIETY 2
: AFFAIR, MATTER 3 : a business organi-
zation ♦ Synonyms CARE, WORRY, DIS-
QUIET, UNEASE

con·cerned \-'sərnd\ adj 1 : ANXIOUS,
UNEASY ⟨~ for their safety⟩ 2 : IN-
VOLVED ⟨is ~ed with films⟩

con·cern·ing \-'sər-niŋ\ prep : relating to
: REGARDING ⟨news ~ his business⟩

con·cern·ment \kən-'sərn-mənt\ n 1

: something in which one is concerned 2
: IMPORTANCE, CONSEQUENCE

¹con·cert \'kän-(,)sərt\ n 1 : agreement in
a plan or design 2 : a public performance
(as of music)

²con·cert \kən-'sərt\ vb : to plan together

con·cert·ed \kən-'sər-təd\ adj : mutually
agreed on; also : performed in unison

con·cer·ti·na \,kän-sər-'tē-nə\ n : an instrument of the accordion family

concertina wire n : a coiled wire with
sharp points for use as an obstacle

con·cert·mas·ter \'kän-sərt-,mas-tər\ or
con·cert·meis·ter \-,mī-stər\ n : the
leader of the first violins of an orchestra
and assistant to the conductor

con·cer·to \kən-'cher-tō\ n, pl -ti \-(,)tē\
or -tos [It] : a piece for one or more solo
instruments and orchestra in three movements

con·ces·sion \kən-'se-shən\ n 1 : an act
of conceding or yielding 2 : something
yielded 3 : a grant by a government of
land or of a right to use it 4 : a grant of
a portion of premises for some specific
purpose; also : the activities or enterprise
carried on — con·ces·sion·ary \-'se-
shə-,ner-ē\ adj

con·ces·sion·aire \kən-,se-shə-'ner\ n
: one that owns or operates a concession

conch \'käŋk, 'känch\ n, pl conchs
\'käŋks\ or conch·es \'kän-chəz\ : a
large spiral-shelled marine gastropod
mollusk; also : its shell

con·cierge \kōⁿ-'syerzh\ n, pl con·cierg·
es \same or -'syer-zhəz\ [F] 1 : a resident
in an apartment building who performs
services for the tenants 2 : a usu. multi-
lingual hotel staff member who usu.
handles mail and reservations

con·cil·i·ate \kən-'si-lē-,āt\ vb -at·ed; -at·
ing 1 : to bring into agreement : RECON-
CILE 2 : to gain the goodwill of — con·
cil·i·a·tion \-,si-lē-'ā-shən\ n — con·cil·i·a·
tor \-'si-lē-,ā-tər\ n — con·cil·ia·to·ry
\-'si-lē-ə-,tōr-ē\ adj

con·cise \kən-'sīs\ adj : expressing much
in few words : BRIEF ⟨a ~ history⟩ —
con·cise·ly adv — con·cise·ness n

con·clave \'kän-,klāv\ n [ME, fr. ML, fr.
L, room that can be locked, fr. com- together + clavis key] : a private gathering;
also : CONVENTION

con·clude \kən-'klüd\ vb con·clud·ed;
con·clud·ing 1 : to bring to a close
: END 2 : DECIDE, JUDGE 3 : to bring
about as a result ♦ Synonyms CLOSE,
FINISH, TERMINATE, COMPLETE, HALT

con·clu·sion \kən-'klü-zhən\ n 1 : the
logical consequence of a reasoning process 2 : TERMINATION, END 3 : OUT-
COME, RESULT — con·clu·sive \-siv\ adj
— con·clu·sive·ly adv — con·clu·sive·
ness n

con·coct \kən-'käkt, kän-\ vb 1 : to prepare by combining raw materials 2 : DE-
VISE — con·coc·tion \-'käk-shən\ n

con·com·i·tant \-'kä-mə-tənt\ adj : AC-
COMPANYING, ATTENDING — concomi-
tant n

con·cord \'kän-,kȯrd, 'käŋ-\ n : AGREE-
MENT, HARMONY

con·cor·dance \kən-'kȯr-dᵊns\ n 1 : an alphabetical index of words in a book or in an author's works with the passages in which they occur 2 : AGREEMENT, COVENANT

con·cor·dant \-dᵊnt\ adj : HARMONIOUS, AGREEING

con·cor·dat \kən-'kȯr-ˌdat\ n : CONCORDANCE 2

con·course \'kän-ˌkȯrs\ n 1 : a spontaneous coming together : GATHERING 2 : an open space or hall (as in a bus terminal) where crowds gather

¹**con·crete** \kän-'krēt, 'kän-ˌkrēt\ adj 1 : naming a real thing or class of things : not abstract 2 : not theoretical : ACTUAL 3 : made of or relating to concrete

²**con·crete** \'kän-ˌkrēt, kän-'krēt\ vb con·cret·ed; con·cret·ing 1 : SOLIDIFY 2 : to cover with concrete

³**con·crete** \'kän-ˌkrēt, kän-'krēt\ n : a hard building material made by mixing cement, sand, and gravel with water

con·cre·tion \kän-'krē-shən\ n : a hard mass esp. when formed abnormally in the body

con·cu·bine \'käŋ-kyù-ˌbīn\ n [ME, fr. AF, fr. L concubina, fr. com- with + cubare to lie] : a woman who is not legally a wife but lives with a man and sometimes has a recognized position in his household; also : MISTRESS — **con·cu·bi·nage** \kän-'kyü-bə-nij\ n

con·cu·pis·cence \kän-'kyü-pə-səns\ n : ardent sexual desire : LUST

con·cur \kən-'kər\ vb con·curred; con·cur·ring 1 : to act together 2 : AGREE 3 : COINCIDE ♦ Synonyms UNITE, COMBINE, COOPERATE, BAND, JOIN

con·cur·rence \-'kər-əns\ n 1 : agreement in action or opinion 2 : occurrence together : CONJUNCTION

con·cur·rent \-'kər-ənt\ adj 1 : happening or operating at the same time 2 : joint and equal in authority

con·cus·sion \kən-'kə-shən\ n 1 : a hard blow or collision; also : bodily injury (as to the brain) resulting from a sudden jar 2 : AGITATION, SHAKING

con·demn \kən-'dem\ vb 1 : to declare to be wrong 2 : to convict of guilt 3 : to sentence judicially 4 : to pronounce unfit for use ⟨~ a building⟩ 5 : to declare forfeited or taken for public use ♦ Synonyms DENOUNCE, CENSURE, BLAME, CRITICIZE, REPREHEND — **con·dem·na·tion** \ˌkän-ˌdem-'nā-shən\ n — **con·dem·na·to·ry** \kən-'dem-nə-ˌtȯr-ē\ adj

con·den·sate \'kän-dən-ˌsāt, kən-'den-\ n : a product of condensation

con·dense \kən-'dens\ vb con·densed; con·dens·ing 1 : to make or become more compact or dense : CONCENTRATE 2 : to change from vapor to liquid ♦ Synonyms CONTRACT, SHRINK, COMPRESS, CONSTRICT — **con·den·sa·tion** \ˌkän-den-'sā-shən\ n

con·dens·er \kən-'den-sər\ n 1 : one that condenses 2 : CAPACITOR

con·de·scend \ˌkän-di-'send\ vb : to assume an air of superiority — **con·de-**

scend·ing·ly \-'sen-diŋ-lē\ adv — **de·scen·sion** \-'sen-chən\ n

con·dign \kən-'dīn, 'kän-ˌdīn\ adj : DESERVED, APPROPRIATE ⟨~ punishmen..⟩

con·di·ment \'kän-də-mənt\ n : some..thing used to make food savory; esp : a pungent seasoning (as pepper)

¹**con·di·tion** \kən-'di-shən\ n 1 : something essential to the occurrence of some other thing 2 : state of being 3 : social status 4 pl : state of affairs : CIRCUMSTANCES 5 : a bodily state in which something is wrong ⟨a heart ~⟩ 6 : a state of health, fitness, or working order ⟨in good ~⟩

²**condition** vb 1 : to put into proper condition for action or use 2 : to adapt, modify, or mold to respond in a particular way 3 : to modify so that an act or response previously associated with one stimulus becomes associated with another

con·di·tion·al \kən-'di-shə-nəl\ adj : containing, implying, or depending on a condition — **con·di·tion·al·ly** adv

con·di·tioned \-'di-shənd\ adj : determined or established by conditioning

con·di·tion·er \-'di-shə-nər\ n : a preparation used to improve the condition of hair

con·do \'kän-ˌdō\ n : CONDOMINIUM 3

con·dole \kən-'dōl\ vb con·doled; con·dol·ing : to express sympathetic sorrow — **con·do·lence** \kən-'dō-ləns\ n

con·dom \'kän-dəm, 'kən-\ n : a usu. rubber sheath worn over the penis (as to prevent pregnancy or venereal infection during sexual intercourse)

con·do·min·i·um \ˌkän-də-'mi-nē-əm\ n, pl -ums 1 : joint sovereignty (as by two or more nations) 2 : a politically dependent territory under condominium 3 : individual ownership of a unit (as an apartment) in a multiunit structure; also : a unit so owned

con·done \kən-'dōn\ vb con·doned; con·don·ing : to overlook or forgive esp. by treating (an offense) as harmless or trivial ♦ Synonyms EXCUSE, PARDON, FORGIVE, REMIT — **con·do·na·tion** \ˌkän-dō-'nā-shən\ n

con·dor \'kän-dər, -ˌdȯr\ n [Sp cóndor, fr. Quechua kuntur] : a very large American vulture of the high Andes; also : a related nearly extinct vulture of southern California now resident only in captivity

con·duce \kən-'düs, -'dyüs\ vb con·duced; con·duc·ing : to lead or contribute to a particular result — **con·du·cive** adj

¹**con·duct** \'kän-(ˌ)dəkt\ n 1 : MANAGEMENT, DIRECTION 2 : BEHAVIOR

²**con·duct** \kən-'dəkt\ vb 1 : GUIDE, ESCORT 2 : MANAGE, DIRECT 3 : to act as a medium for conveying or transmitting 4 : BEHAVE — **con·duc·tion** \-'dək-shən\ n

con·duc·tance \kən-'dək-təns\ n : the readiness with which a conductor transmits an electric current

con·duc·tive \kən-'dək-tiv\ adj : having the power to conduct (as heat or electricity) — **con·duc·tiv·i·ty** \ˌkän-ˌdək-'ti-və-tē\ n

con·duc·tor \kən-'dək-tər\ n 1 : one that conducts; esp : a material that permits an electric current to flow easily 2 : a collector of fares in a public conveyance 3 : the leader of a musical ensemble

con·duit \'kän-,dü-ət, ,dyü-, -dwət\ n 1 : a channel for conveying fluid 2 : a tube or trough for protecting electric wires or cables 3 : a means of transmitting or distributing

con·dyle \'kän-,dī(-ə)l, -dᵊl\ n : an articular prominence of a bone — **con·dy·lar** \-də-lər\ adj

cone \'kōn\ n 1 : the scaly usu. ovate fruit of trees of most conifers usu. a solid figure formed by rotating a right triangle about one of its legs 2 : a solid figure that slopes evenly to a point from a usu. circular base 4 : any of the conical light-sensitive receptor cells of the retina that function in color vision 5 : something shaped like a cone

cone-flow·er \'kōn-,flau̇(-ə)r\ n : any of several composite plants having cone-shaped flower disks

Con·es·to·ga wagon \,kä-nə-'stō-gə-\ n : a broad-wheeled covered wagon used esp. for transporting freight across the prairies

co·ney or **co·ny** \'kō-nē\ n, pl **coneys** or **conies** 1 : RABBIT; also : its fur 2 : PIKA

conf abbr 1 conference 2 confidential

con·fab \'kän-,fab, kən-'fab\ n : CONFABULATION 1

con·fab·u·la·tion \kən-,fab-yə-'lā-shən\ n 1 : CHAT; also : CONFERENCE 2 : a filling in of gaps in memory by fabrication — **con·fab·u·late** \-'fa-byə-,lāt\ vb

con·fec·tion \kən-'fek-shən\ n 1 : something put together from varied material 2 : a fancy dish or sweet; also : CANDY — **con·fect** \kən-'fekt\ vb

con·fec·tion·er \-sh(ə-)nər\ n : a maker of or dealer in confections

con·fec·tion·ery \-shə-,ner-ē\ n, pl **-er·ies** 1 : sweet foods 2 : a confectioner's place of business

Confed abbr Confederate

¹**con·fed·er·ate** \kən-'fe-də-rət\ adj 1 : united in a league : ALLIED 2 cap : of or relating to the Confederacy

²**confederate** n 1 : ALLY, ACCOMPLICE 2 cap : an adherent of the Confederacy

³**con·fed·er·ate** \-'fe-də-,rāt\ vb **-at·ed; -at·ing** : to unite in a confederacy

con·fed·er·a·tion \kən-,fe-də-'rā-shən\ n 1 : an act of confederating : ALLIANCE 2 : LEAGUE

con·fer \kən-'fər\ vb **con·ferred; con·fer·ring** 1 : GRANT, BESTOW ⟨~ an award⟩ 2 : to exchange views : CONSULT — **con·fer·ee** \,kän-fə-'rē\ n

con·fer·ence \'kän-f(ə-)rəns\ n 1 : an interchange of views; also : a meeting for this purpose 2 : an association of athletic teams

con·fer·enc·ing \'kän-f(ə-)rən-siŋ\ n : the holding of conferences esp. by means of electronic devices

con·fess \kən-'fes\ vb 1 : to acknowledge or disclose one's misdeed, fault, or sin 2 : to acknowledge one's sins to God or to a priest 3 : to receive the confession of (a penitent) ♦ **Synonyms** ADMIT, OWN, AVOW, CONCEDE, GRANT

con·fessed·ly \-'fe-səd-lē\ adv : by confession : ADMITTEDLY

con·fes·sion \-'fe-shən\ n 1 : an act of confessing (as in the sacrament of penance) 2 : an acknowledgment of guilt 3 : a formal statement of religious beliefs 4 : a religious body having a common creed — **con·fes·sion·al** adj

con·fes·sion·al \-'fe-shə-nəl\ n : a place where a priest hears confessions

con·fes·sor \kən-'fe-sər\ n 1 : one that confesses 2 : a priest who hears confessions

con·fet·ti \kən-'fe-tē\ n [It, pl. of confetto sweetmeat, fr. ML confectum, fr. L, neut. of confectus, pp. of conficere to prepare] : bits of colored paper or ribbon for throwing (as at weddings)

con·fi·dant \'kän-fə-,dänt, -,dant\ n : one to whom secrets are confided

con·fi·dante \-,dänt, -,dant\ n : CONFIDANT; esp : one who is a woman

con·fide \kən-'fīd\ vb **con·fid·ed; con·fid·ing** 1 : to have or show faith : TRUST ⟨~ in a friend⟩ 2 : to tell confidentially ⟨~ a secret⟩ 3 : ENTRUST

¹**con·fi·dence** \'kän-fə-dəns\ n 1 : TRUST, RELIANCE 2 : SELF-ASSURANCE, BOLDNESS 3 : a state of trust or intimacy 4 : SECRET 2 — **con·fi·dent** \-dənt\ adj — **con·fi·dent·ly** adv

²**confidence** adj : of or relating to swindling by false promises ⟨a ~ game⟩

con·fi·den·tial \,kän-fə-'den-shəl\ adj 1 : SECRET, PRIVATE ⟨~ information⟩ 2 : entrusted with confidences ⟨~ clerk⟩ — **con·fi·den·ti·al·i·ty** \-,den-shē-'a-lə-tē\ n — **con·fi·den·tial·ly** \-'den-shə-lē\ adv

con·fig·u·ra·tion \kən-,fi-gyə-'rā-shən\ n : structural arrangement of parts : SHAPE

con·fig·ure \kən-'fi-gyər\ vb **-ured; -ur·ing** : to set up for operation esp. in a particular way

con·fine \kən-'fīn\ vb **con·fined; con·fin·ing** 1 : to hold within a location; also : IMPRISON 2 : to keep within limits ⟨will ~ my remarks to one subject⟩ — **con·fine·ment** n — **con·fin·er** n

con·fines \'kän-,fīnz\ n pl : BOUNDS, BORDERS

con·firm \kən-'fərm\ vb 1 : to give approval to : RATIFY 2 : to make firm or firmer 3 : to administer the rite of confirmation to 4 : VERIFY, CORROBORATE — **con·fir·ma·to·ry** \-'fər-mə-,tōr-ē\ adj

con·fir·ma·tion \,kän-fər-'mā-shən\ n 1 : a religious ceremony admitting a person to full membership in a church or synagogue; also : an act of ratifying or corroborating; also : PROOF

con·fis·cate \'kän-fə-,skāt\ vb **-cat·ed; -cat·ing** [L confiscare, fr. com- with + fiscus treasury] : to take possession of by or as if by public authority — **con·fis·ca·tion** \ˌkän-fə-ˈskā-shən\ n — **con·fis·ca·to·ry** \kən-ˈfis-kə-ˌtōr-ē\ adj

con·fit \kōn-ˈfē\ n : a garnish of fruit or vegetables cooked in a seasoned liquid

con·fla·gra·tion \ˌkän-flə-ˈgrā-shən\ n : FIRE; esp : a large disastrous fire

¹**con·flict** \ˈkän-ˌflikt\ n 1 : WAR 2 : a clash between hostile or opposing elements, ideas, or forces

²**con·flict** \kən-ˈflikt\ vb : to show opposition or irreconcilability : CLASH

con·flu·ence \ˈkän-ˌflü-əns, kən-ˈflü-\ n 1 : a coming together at one point 2 : the meeting or place of meeting of two or more streams — **con·flu·ent** \-ənt\ adj

con·flux \ˈkän-ˌfləks\ n : CONFLUENCE

con·form \kən-ˈfórm\ vb 1 : to be similar or identical; also : AGREE 2 : to obey customs or standards; also : COMPLY ⟨~ to regulations⟩ — **con·form·able** adj — **con·form·ist** \-ˈfór-mist\ adj

con·for·mance \kən-ˈfór-məns\ n : CONFORMITY

con·for·ma·tion \ˌkän-fòr-ˈmā-shən\ n : a forming into a whole by arranging parts

con·for·mi·ty \kən-ˈfór-mə-tē\ n, pl **-ties** 1 : HARMONY, AGREEMENT 2 : COMPLIANCE, OBEDIENCE

con·found \kən-ˈfaủnd, kän-\ vb 1 : to throw into disorder or confusion 2 : CONFUSE 2 ♦ *Synonyms* BEWILDER, PUZZLE, PERPLEX, BEFOG

con·fra·ter·ni·ty \ˌkän-frə-ˈtər-nə-tē\ n : a society devoted esp. to a religious or charitable cause

con·frere \ˈkän-ˌfrer, ˈkōⁿ-\ n : COLLEAGUE, COMRADE

con·front \kən-ˈfrənt\ vb 1 : to face esp. in challenge : OPPOSE; also : to deal unflinchingly with ⟨~ed the issue⟩ 2 : to cause to face or meet — **con·fron·ta·tion** \ˌkän-frən-ˈtā-shən\ n — **con·fron·ta·tion·al** \-shə-nᵊl\ adj

Con·fu·cian \kən-ˈfyü-shən\ adj : of or relating to the Chinese philosopher Confucius or his teachings — **Con·fu·cian·ism** \-shə-ˌni-zəm\ n

con·fuse \kən-ˈfyüz\ vb con·fused; con·fus·ing 1 : to make mentally unclear or uncertain; also : to disturb the composure of 2 : to mix up : JUMBLE ♦ *Synonyms* MUDDLE, BEFUDDLE, ADDLE, FLUSTER — **con·fused·ly** \-ˈfyü-zəd-lē\ adv — **con·fus·ing·ly** \-ˈfyü-ziŋ-lē\ adv

con·fu·sion \-ˈfyü-zhən\ n 1 : an act or instance of confusing 2 : the quality or state of being confused

con·fute \kən-ˈfyüt\ vb con·fut·ed; con·fut·ing : to overwhelm by argument : REFUTE ⟨~ a proposition⟩ — **con·fu·ta·tion** \ˌkän-fyü-ˈtā-shən\ n

cong abbr congress; congressional

con·ga \ˈkäŋ-gə\ n : a Cuban dance of African origin performed by a group usu. in single file

con·geal \kən-ˈjēl\ vb 1 : FREEZE 2 : to make or become hard or thick

con·gee \ˈkän-jē\ n : porridge made from rice

con·ge·ner \ˈkän-jə-nər\ n : one related to another; esp : a plant or animal of the same taxonomic genus as another — **con·ge·ner·ic** \ˌkän-jə-ˈner-ik\ adj

con·ge·nial \kən-ˈjē-nyəl\ adj 1 : KINDRED, SYMPATHETIC ⟨~ companions⟩ 2 : suited to one's taste or nature : AGREEABLE — **con·ge·ni·al·i·ty** \-ˌjē-nē-ˈa-lə-tē\ n — **con·ge·nial·ly** adv

con·gen·i·tal \kən-ˈje-nə-tᵊl\ adj : existing or dating from birth ⟨~ deafness⟩ ♦ *Synonyms* INBORN, INNATE, NATURAL

con·ger eel \ˈkän-gər-\ n : a large edible marine eel of the Atlantic

con·ge·ries \ˈkän-jə-(ˌ)rēz\ n, pl **congeries** : AGGREGATION, COLLECTION

con·gest \kən-ˈjest\ vb 1 : to cause excessive fullness of the blood vessels of (as a lung) 2 : to obstruct by overcrowding — **con·ges·tion** \-ˈjes-chən\ n — **con·ges·tive** \-ˈjes-tiv\ adj

congestive heart failure n : heart failure in which the heart is unable to keep enough blood circulating in the tissues or is unable to pump out the blood returned to it by the veins

¹**con·glom·er·ate** \kən-ˈglä-mə-rət\ adj [L conglomerare to roll together, fr. com- together + glomerare to wind into a ball, fr. glomer-, glomus ball] : made up of parts from various sources

²**con·glom·er·ate** \-ˌrāt\ vb **-at·ed; -at·ing** : to form into a mass — **con·glom·er·a·tion** \-ˌglä-mə-ˈrā-shən\ n

³**con·glom·er·ate** \-rət\ n 1 : a mass formed of fragments from various sources; esp : a rock composed of fragments varying from pebbles to boulders held together by a cementing material 2 : a widely diversified corporation

con·grat·u·late \kən-ˈgra-chə-ˌlāt\ vb **-lat·ed; -lat·ing** : to express sympathetic pleasure to on account of success or good fortune : FELICITATE — **con·grat·u·la·tion** \-ˌgra-chə-ˈlā-shən\ n — **con·grat·u·la·to·ry** \-ˈgra-chə-lə-ˌtōr-ē\ adj

con·gre·gate \ˈkäŋ-gri-ˌgāt\ vb **-gat·ed; -gat·ing** [ME, fr. L congregatus, pp. of congregare, fr. com- together + greg-, grex flock] : ASSEMBLE

con·gre·ga·tion \ˌkäŋ-gri-ˈgā-shən\ n 1 : an assembly of persons met esp. for worship; also : a group that habitually so meets 2 : a religious community or order 3 : the act or an instance of congregating

con·gre·ga·tion·al \-shə-nəl\ adj 1 : of or relating to a congregation 2 cap : observing the faith and practice of certain Protestant churches which recognize the independence of each congregation in church matters — **con·gre·ga·tion·al·ism** \-nə-ˌli-zəm\ n, often cap — **con·gre·ga·tion·al·ist** \-list\ n, often cap

con·gress \ˈkäŋ-grəs\ n 1 : an assembly esp. of delegates for discussion and usu. action on some question 2 : the body of senators and representatives constituting a nation's legislature — **con·gres·sio·nal** \kən-ˈgre-shə-nəl\ adj

con·gress·man \ˈkäŋ-grəs-mən\ n : a member of a congress

con·gress·wom·an \-ˌwủ-mən\ n : a woman who is a member of a congress

con·gru·ence \kən-'grü-əns, 'käŋ-grü-\ *n* : the quality of agreeing or coinciding : CONGRUITY — **con·gru·ent** \kən-'grü-ənt, 'käŋ-grü-\ *adj*

con·gru·en·cy \-sē\ *n, pl* **-cies** : CONGRUENCE

con·gru·ity \kän-'grü-ə-tē\ *n, pl* **-ities** : correspondence between things — **gru·ous** \'käŋ-grü-əs\ *adj*

con·ic \'kä-nik\ *adj* 1 : of or relating to a cone 2 : CONICAL

con·i·cal \'kä-ni-kəl\ *adj* : resembling a cone esp. in shape

co·ni·fer \'kä-nə-fər, 'kō-\ *n* : any of an order of shrubs or trees (as the pines) that usu. are evergreen and bear cones — **co·nif·er·ous** \kō-'ni-fə-rəs\ *adj*

conj *abbr* conjunction

con·jec·ture \kən-'jek-chər\ *n* : GUESS, SURMISE — **con·jec·tur·al** \-chə-rəl\ *adj* — **conjecture** *vb*

con·join \kən-'jȯin\ *vb* : to join together — **con·joint** \-'jȯint\ *adj*

con·ju·gal \'kän-ji-gəl\ *adj* : of or relating to marriage : MATRIMONIAL

¹**con·ju·gate** \'kän-ji-gət, -jə-ˌgāt\ *adj* 1 : united esp. in pairs : COUPLED 2 : of kindred origin and meaning ⟨*sing* and *song* are ~⟩ — **con·ju·gate·ly** *adv*

²**con·ju·gate** \-jə-ˌgāt\ *vb* **-gat·ed; -gat·ing** 1 : INFLECT ⟨~ a verb⟩ 2 : to join together : COUPLE

con·ju·ga·tion \ˌkän-jə-'gā-shən\ *n* 1 : an arrangement of the inflectional forms of a verb 2 : the act of conjugating : the state of being conjugated

con·junct \kän-'jəŋkt\ *adj* : JOINED, UNITED

con·junc·tion \kən-'jəŋk-shən\ *n* 1 : COMBINATION 2 : occurrence at the same time 3 : a word that joins together sentences, clauses, phrases, or words

con·junc·ti·va \ˌkän-ˌjəŋk-'tī-və\ *n, pl* **-vas** *or* **-vae** \-(ˌ)vē\ : the mucous membrane lining the inner surface of the eyelids and continuing over the forepart of the eyeball

con·junc·tive \kən-'jəŋk-tiv\ *adj* 1 : CONNECTIVE 2 : CONJUNCT ⟨the ~ operation of different factors⟩ 3 : being or functioning like a conjunction

con·junc·ti·vi·tis \kən-ˌjəŋk-ti-'vī-təs\ *n* : inflammation of the conjunctiva

con·junc·ture \kən-'jəŋk-chər\ *n* 1 : CONJUNCTION, UNION 2 : JUNCTURE 3

con·jun·to \kōn-'hün-tō\ *n* : Mexican-American music influenced by the music of German immigrants to Texas

con·jure \'kän-jər, 'kən- *for 1, 2;* kən-'jur *for 3*\ *vb* **con·jured; con·jur·ing** 1 : to implore earnestly or solemnly 2 : to practice magic; *esp* : to summon (as a devil) by sorcery 3 : to practice sleight of hand — **con·ju·ra·tion** \ˌkän-jə-'rā-shən, ˌkən-\ *n* — **con·jur·er** *or* **con·ju·ror** \'kän-jər-ər, 'kən-\ *n*

conk \'käŋk\ *vb* : BREAK DOWN; *esp* : STALL ⟨the motor ~ed out⟩

Conn *abbr* Connecticut

con·nect \kə-'nekt\ *vb* 1 : JOIN, LINK 2 : to associate in one's mind 3 : to establish a communications connection ⟨~ to

the Internet⟩ — **con·nect·able** *adj* — **con·nec·tor** *n*

con·nec·tion \kə-'nek-shən\ *n* 1 : JUNCTION, UNION 2 : logical relationship : COHERENCE; *esp* : relation of a word to other words in a sentence 3 : family relationship 4 : BOND, LINK 5 : a person related by blood or marriage 6 : relationship in social affairs or in business 7 : an association of persons; *esp* : a religious denomination 8 : a means of communication or transport ⟨a telephone ~⟩

¹**con·nec·tive** \kə-'nek-tiv\ *adj* : serving to connect — **con·nec·tiv·i·ty** \ˌkä-ˌnek-'ti-və-tē\ *n*

²**connective** *n* : a word (as a conjunction) that connects words or word groups

connective tissue *n* : a tissue (as bone or cartilage) that forms a supporting framework for the body or its parts

con·nex·ion *chiefly Brit var of* CONNECTION

con·ning tower \'kä-niŋ-\ *n* : a raised structure on the deck of a submarine

con·nip·tion \kə-'nip-shən\ *n* : a fit of rage, hysteria, or alarm

con·nive \kə-'nīv\ *vb* **con·nived; con·niv·ing** [F or L; F *conniver*, fr. L *conivēre* to close the eyes, connive] 1 : to pretend ignorance of something one ought to oppose as wrong 2 : to cooperate secretly : give secret aid — **con·niv·ance** *n* — **con·niv·er** *n*

con·nois·seur \ˌkä-nə-'sər\ *n* : a critical judge in matters of art or taste

con·no·ta·tion \ˌkä-nə-'tā-shən\ *n* : a meaning in addition to or apart from the thing explicitly named or described by a word

con·no·ta·tive \'kä-nə-ˌtā-tiv, kə-'nō-tə-\ *adj* 1 : connoting or tending to connote 2 : relating to connotation

con·note \kə-'nōt\ *vb* **con·not·ed; con·not·ing** : to suggest or mean as a connotation

con·nu·bi·al \kə-'nü-bē-əl, -'nyü-\ *adj* : of or relating to marriage : CONJUGAL

con·quer \'käŋ-kər\ *vb* 1 : to gain by force of arms : WIN 2 : to get the better of : OVERCOME ♦ *Synonyms* DEFEAT, SUBJUGATE, SUBDUE, OVERTHROW, VANQUISH — **con·quer·or** \-ər\ *n*

con·quest \'kän-ˌkwest, 'käŋ-\ *n* 1 : an act of conquering : VICTORY 2 : something conquered

con·quis·ta·dor \kȯn-'kēs-tə-ˌdȯr, kän-'kwis-\ *n, pl* **-do·res** \-ˌkēs-tə-'dȯr-ēz, -ˌkwis-\ *or* **-dors** : CONQUEROR; *esp* : a leader in the Spanish conquest of the Americas in the 16th century

cons *abbr* consonant

con·san·guin·i·ty \ˌkän-ˌsan-'gwi-nə-tē, -ˌsaŋ-\ *n, pl* **-ties** : blood relationship — **con·san·guin·e·ous** \-nē-əs\ *adj*

con·science \'kän-chəns\ *n* : consciousness of the moral right and wrong of one's own acts or motives — **con·science·less** *adj*

con·sci·en·tious \ˌkän-chē-'en-chəs\ *adj* : guided by one's own sense of right and wrong ♦ *Synonyms* SCRUPULOUS,

HONORABLE, HONEST, UPRIGHT, JUST —
con·sci·en·tious·ly *adv*

conscientious objector *n* : a person who refuses to serve in the armed forces or to bear arms on moral or religious grounds

¹**con·scious** \ˈkän-chəs\ *adj* 1 : AWARE 2 : known or felt by one's inner self 3 : mentally awake or alert : not asleep or unconscious 4 : done with awareness or purpose ⟨a ~ decision⟩ — **con·scious·ly** *adv* — **con·scious·ness** *n*

²**conscious** *n* : the upper level of mental life of which a person is aware : CONSCIOUSNESS

con·script \kən-ˈskript\ *vb* : to enroll by compulsion for military or naval service — **conscript** \ˈkän-ˌskript\ *n* — **con·scrip·tion** \kən-ˈskrip-shən\ *n*

con·se·crate \ˈkän-sə-ˌkrāt\ *vb* **-crat·ed; -crat·ing** [ME, fr. L *consecratus*, pp. of *consecrare*, fr. *com-* together + *sacrare* to set aside as sacred, fr. *sacer* sacred] 1 : to induct (as a bishop) into an office with a religious rite 2 : to make or declare sacred ⟨~ a church⟩ 3 : to devote solemnly to a purpose — **con·se·cra·tion** \ˌkän-sə-ˈkrā-shən\ *n*

con·sec·u·tive \kən-ˈse-kyə-tiv\ *adj* : following in regular order : SUCCESSIVE — **con·sec·u·tive·ly** *adv*

con·sen·su·al \kən-ˈsen-chə-wəl\ *adj* : involving or based on mutual consent

con·sen·sus \kən-ˈsen-səs\ *n* 1 : agreement in opinion, testimony, or belief 2 : collective opinion

¹**con·sent** \kən-ˈsent\ *vb* : to give assent or approval ⟨~ed to the marriage⟩

²**consent** *n* : approval or acceptance of something done or proposed by another

con·se·quence \ˈkän-sə-ˌkwens\ *n* 1 : RESULT 2 : IMPORTANCE ♦ *Synonyms* EFFECT, OUTCOME, AFTERMATH, UPSHOT

con·se·quent \-kwənt, -ˌkwent\ *adj* : following as a result or effect

con·se·quen·tial \ˌkän-sə-ˈkwen-chəl\ *adj* 1 : having significant consequences 2 : showing self-importance

con·se·quent·ly \ˈkän-sə-ˌkwent-lē, -kwənt-\ *adv* : as a result : ACCORDINGLY

con·ser·van·cy \kən-ˈsər-vən-sē\ *n, pl* **-cies** : an organization or area designated to conserve natural resources

con·ser·va·tion \ˌkän-sər-ˈvā-shən\ *n* : PRESERVATION; *esp* : planned management of natural resources

con·ser·va·tion·ist \-shə-nist\ *n* : a person who advocates conservation esp. of natural resources

con·ser·va·tism \kən-ˈsər-və-ˌti-zəm\ *n* : disposition to keep to established ways : opposition to change

¹**con·ser·va·tive** \kən-ˈsər-və-tiv\ *adj* 1 : PRESERVATIVE 2 : disposed to maintain existing views, conditions, or institutions 3 : MODERATE, CAUTIOUS ⟨a ~ investment⟩ — **con·ser·va·tive·ly** *adv*

²**conservative** *n* : a person who is conservative esp. in politics

con·ser·va·tor \kən-ˈsər-və-tər, ˈkän-sər-ˌvā-\ *n* 1 : PROTECTOR, GUARDIAN 2

: one named by a court to protect the interests of an incompetent (as a child)

con·ser·va·to·ry \kən-ˈsər-və-ˌtōr-ē\ *n, pl* **-ries** 1 : GREENHOUSE 2 : a place of instruction in one of the fine arts (as music)

¹**con·serve** \kən-ˈsərv\ *vb* **con·served; con·serv·ing** : to keep from losing or wasting : PRESERVE ⟨~ energy⟩

²**con·serve** \ˈkän-ˌsərv\ *n* 1 : CONFECTION 2; *esp* : a candied fruit 2 : PRESERVE; *esp* : one prepared from a mixture of fruits

con·sid·er \kən-ˈsi-dər\ *vb* [ME, fr. AF *considerer*, fr. L *considerare* to observe, think about, fr. *com-* together + *sider-, sidus* heavenly body] 1 : THINK, PONDER 2 : HEED, REGARD 3 : JUDGE, BELIEVE — **con·sid·ered** *adj*

con·sid·er·able \-ˈsi-dər-ə-bəl, -ˈsi-drə-bəl\ *adj* 1 : IMPORTANT 2 : large in extent, amount, or degree — **con·sid·er·ably** \-blē\ *adv*

con·sid·er·ate \kən-ˈsi-də-rət\ *adj* : observant of the rights and feelings of others ♦ *Synonyms* THOUGHTFUL, ATTENTIVE

con·sid·er·ation \kən-ˌsi-də-ˈrā-shən\ *n* 1 : careful thought : DELIBERATION 2 : a matter taken into account 3 : thoughtful attention 4 : JUDGMENT, OPINION 5 : RECOMPENSE

con·sid·er·ing \-ˈsi-d(ə-)riŋ\ *prep* : in view of : taking into account ⟨did well ~ his limitations⟩

con·sign \kən-ˈsīn\ *vb* 1 : ENTRUST, COMMIT 2 : to deliver formally 3 : to send (goods) to an agent for sale — **con·sign·ee** \ˌkän-sə-ˈnē, -ˌsī-; kən-ˌsī-\ *n* — **con·sign·or** \ˌkän-sə-ˈnȯr, -ˌsī-; kən-ˌsī-\ *n*

con·sign·ment \kən-ˈsīn-mənt\ *n* : something consigned esp. in a single shipment

con·sil·ience \kən-ˈsil-yəns\ *n* : the linking together of principles from different disciplines when forming a comprehensive theory

con·sist \kən-ˈsist\ *vb* 1 : to be inherent : LIE — usu. used with *in* 2 : to be composed or made up — usu. used with *of*

con·sis·tence \kən-ˈsis-təns\ *n* : CONSISTENCY

con·sis·ten·cy \-tən-sē\ *n, pl* **-cies** 1 : COHESIVENESS, FIRMNESS 2 : agreement or harmony in parts or of different things 3 : UNIFORMITY ⟨~ of behavior⟩ — **con·sis·tent** \-tənt\ *adj* — **con·sis·tent·ly** *adv*

con·sis·to·ry \kən-ˈsis-tə-rē\ *n, pl* **-ries** : a solemn assembly (as of Roman Catholic cardinals)

consol *abbr* consolidated

¹**con·sole** \ˈkän-ˌsōl\ *n* [F] 1 : the desklike part of an organ at which the organist sits 2 : the combination of displays and controls of a device or system 3 : a cabinet for a radio or television set resting directly on the floor 4 : a small storage cabinet between bucket seats in an automobile

²**con·sole** \kən-ˈsōl\ *vb* **con·soled; con·sol·ing** : to soothe the grief of : COMFORT, SOLACE — **con·so·la·tion** \ˌkän-

sə-ˈlä-shən\ n — con·so·la·to·ry \kən-ˈsō-lə-ˌtōr-ē, -ˈsä-\ adj

con·sol·i·date \kən-ˈsä-lə-ˌdāt\ vb -dat·ed; -dat·ing 1 : to unite or become united into one whole : COMBINE 2 : to make firm or secure 3 : to form into a compact mass — con·sol·i·da·tion \-ˌsä-lə-ˈdā-shən\ n — con·sol·i·da·tor \-ˈsä-lə-ˌdā-tər\ n

con·som·mé \ˌkän-sə-ˈmā\ n [F] : a clear soup made from well-seasoned stock

con·so·nance \ˈkän-sə-nəns\ n 1 : AGREEMENT, HARMONY 2 : repetition of consonants esp. as an alternative to rhyme in verse

¹con·so·nant \-nənt\ adj : having consonance, harmony, or agreement ♦ **Synonyms** CONSISTENT, COMPATIBLE, CONGRUOUS, CONGENIAL, SYMPATHETIC — con·so·nant·ly adv

²consonant n : a speech sound (as \p\, \g\, \n\, \l\, \s\, \r\) characterized by constriction or closure at one or more points in the breath channel 2 : a letter other than a, e, i, o, and u — con·so·nan·tal \ˌkän-sə-ˈnan-tᵊl\ adj

¹con·sort \ˈkän-ˌsȯrt\ n 1 : a ship accompanying another 2 : SPOUSE, MATE

²con·sort \kən-ˈsȯrt\ vb 1 : to keep company 2 : ACCORD, HARMONIZE

con·sor·tium \kən-ˈsȯr-shəm; -shē-əm, -tē-\ n, pl -sor·tia \-shə-; -shē-ə, -tē-\ [L, fellowship] : an agreement or combination (as of companies) formed to undertake a large enterprise

con·spec·tus \kən-ˈspek-təs\ n 1 : a brief survey or summary 2 : SUMMARY

con·spic·u·ous \kən-ˈspi-kyə-wəs\ adj : attracting attention : PROMINENT, STRIKING ♦ **Synonyms** NOTICEABLE, REMARKABLE, OUTSTANDING — con·spic·u·ous·ly adv

con·spir·a·cy \kən-ˈspir-ə-sē\ n, pl -cies : an agreement among conspirators : PLOT

con·spir·a·tor \kən-ˈspir-ə-tər\ n : one who conspires — con·spir·a·to·ri·al \-ˌspir-ə-ˈtȯr-ē-əl\ adj

con·spire \kən-ˈspī(-ə)r\ vb conspired; con·spir·ing [ME, fr. AF conspirer, fr. L conspirare to be in harmony, conspire, fr. com- together + spirare to breathe] : to plan secretly an unlawful act : PLOT

const abbr 1 constant 2 constitution; constitutional

con·sta·ble \ˈkän-stə-bəl, ˈkən-\ n [ME conestable, fr. AF, fr. LL comes stabuli, lit., officer of the stable] : a public officer responsible for keeping the peace

con·stab·u·lary \kən-ˈsta-byə-ˌler-ē\ n, pl -lar·ies 1 : the police of a particular district or country 2 : a police force organized like the military

con·stan·cy \ˈkän-stən-sē\ n, pl -cies 1 : firmness of mind 2 : STABILITY

¹con·stant \ˈkän-stənt\ adj 1 : STEADFAST, FAITHFUL ⟨~ friends⟩ 2 : FIXED, UNCHANGING ⟨a ~ flow⟩ 3 : continually recurring : REGULAR ⟨a ~ annoyance⟩ — con·stant·ly adv

²constant n : something unchanging

con·stel·la·tion \ˌkän-stə-ˈlā-shən\ n 1

: any of 88 groups of stars forming patterns 2 : a group of usu. related persons, qualities, or things

con·ster·na·tion \ˌkän-stər-ˈnā-shən\ n : amazed dismay and confusion

con·sti·pa·tion \ˌkän-stə-ˈpā-shən\ n : abnormally difficult or infrequent bowel movements — con·sti·pate \ˈkän-stə-ˌpāt\ vb

con·stit·u·en·cy \kən-ˈsti-chə-wən-sē\ n, pl -cies : a body of constituents; also : an electoral district

¹con·stit·u·ent \-wənt\ n 1 : a person entitled to vote for a representative for a district 2 : a component part

²constituent adj 1 : COMPONENT ⟨~ parts⟩ 2 : having power to create a government or frame or amend a constitution

con·sti·tute \ˈkän-stə-ˌtüt, -ˌtyüt\ vb -tut·ed; -tut·ing 1 : to appoint to an office or duty 2 : SET UP, ESTABLISH ⟨~ a law⟩ 3 : MAKE UP, COMPOSE

con·sti·tu·tion \ˌkän-stə-ˈtü-shən, -ˈtyü-\ n 1 : an established law or custom 2 : the physical makeup of the individual 3 : the structure, composition, or makeup of something ⟨~ of the sun⟩ 4 : the basic law in a politically organized body; also : a document containing such law

¹con·sti·tu·tion·al \-shə-nəl\ adj 1 : of or relating to the constitution of body or mind 2 : being in accord with the constitution of a state or society; also : of or relating to such a constitution — con·sti·tu·tion·al·ly adv

²constitutional n : an exercise (as a walk) taken for one's health

con·sti·tu·tion·al·i·ty \-ˌtü-shə-ˈna-lə-tē, -ˌtyü-\ n : the quality or state of being constitutional

con·sti·tu·tive \ˈkän-stə-ˌtü-tiv, -ˌtyü-; kən-ˈsti-chə-tiv\ adj 1 : CONSTRUCTIVE 2 : CONSTITUENT, ESSENTIAL

constr abbr construction

con·strain \kən-ˈstrān\ vb 1 : COMPEL, FORCE 2 : CONFINE 3 : RESTRAIN

con·straint \-ˈstrānt\ n 1 : COMPULSION; also : RESTRAINT 2 : repression of one's natural feelings

con·strict \kən-ˈstrikt\ vb : to draw together : SQUEEZE — con·stric·tion \-ˈstrik-shən\ n — con·stric·tive \-ˈstrik-tiv\ adj

con·stric·tor \kən-ˈstrik-tər\ n : a snake that coils around and compresses its prey

con·struct \kən-ˈstrəkt\ vb : BUILD, MAKE — con·struc·tor \-ˈstrək-tər\ n

con·struc·tion \kən-ˈstrək-shən\ n 1 : INTERPRETATION 2 : the art, process, or manner of building; also : something built, created, or established : STRUCTURE 3 : syntactical arrangement of words in a sentence — con·struc·tive \-tiv\ adj

con·struc·tion·ist \-shə-nist\ n : a person who construes a legal document (as the U.S. Constitution) in a specific way ⟨a strict ~⟩

con·strue \kən-ˈstrü\ vb con·strued; con·stru·ing 1 : to analyze the mutual relations of words in a sentence; also

: TRANSLATE 2 : EXPLAIN, INTERPRET ⟨*construed* the act as hostile⟩ — **con·stru·able** *adj* — **con·stru·al** \-'strü-əl\ *n*

con·sub·stan·ti·a·tion \ˌkän-səb-ˌstan-chē-'ā-shən\ *n* : the actual substantial presence and combination of the body and blood of Christ with the eucharistic bread and wine

con·sul \'kän-səl\ *n* 1 : a chief magistrate of the Roman republic 2 : a government official who resides in a foreign country to care for the commercial interests of the appointing government's citizens — **con·sul·ar** \-sə-lər\ *adj* — **con·sul·ate** \-lət\ *n* — **con·sul·ship** *n*

con·sult \kən-'səlt\ *vb* 1 : to ask the advice or opinion of 2 : CONFER — **con·sul·tant** \-'səl-t°nt\ *n* — **con·sul·ta·tion** \ˌkän-səl-'tā-shən\ *n*

con·sume \kən-'süm\ *vb* **con·sumed**; **con·sum·ing** 1 : DESTROY ⟨*consumed* by fire⟩ 2 : to spend wastefully 3 : to eat up : DEVOUR 4 : to absorb the attention of : ENGROSS ⟨*consumed* with jealousy⟩ 5 : to utilize as a customer — **con·sum·able** *adj* — **con·sum·er** *n*

con·sum·er·ism \kən-'sü-mə-ˌri-zəm\ *n* : the promotion of consumers' interests (as against false advertising)

consumer price index *n* : an index measuring the change in the cost of widely purchased goods and services from the cost in some base period

¹**con·sum·mate** \'kän-sə-mət, kən-'sə\ *adj* : PERFECT ⟨a ~ team player⟩ ♦ *Synonyms* FINISHED, ACCOMPLISHED

²**con·sum·mate** \'kän-sə-ˌmāt\ *vb* **-mat·ed**; **-mat·ing** : to make complete : FINISH, ACHIEVE — **con·sum·ma·tion** \ˌkän-sə-'mā-shən\ *n*

con·sump·tion \kən-'səmp-shən\ *n* 1 : progressive bodily wasting away; *also* : TUBERCULOSIS 2 : the act of consuming or using up 3 : the use of economic goods

¹**con·sump·tive** \-'səmp-tiv\ *adj* 1 : tending to consume 2 : relating to or affected with consumption

²**consumptive** *n* : a person who has consumption

cont *abbr* 1 containing 2 contents 3 continent; continental 4 continued 5 control

¹**con·tact** \'kän-ˌtakt\ *n* 1 : a touching or meeting of bodies 2 : ASSOCIATION, RELATIONSHIP; *also* : CONNECTION, COMMUNICATION 3 : a person serving as a go-between or source of information 4 : CONTACT LENS

²**contact** *vb* 1 : to come or bring into contact : TOUCH 2 : to get in communication with ⟨~ed his lawyer⟩

contact lens *n* : a thin lens fitting over the cornea usu. to correct vision

con·ta·gion \kən-'tā-jən\ *n* [ME, fr. L *contagio*, fr. *contingere* to have contact with, pollute, fr. *com-* together + *tangere* to touch] 1 : a contagious disease; *also* : the transmission of such a disease 2 : a disease-producing agent (as a virus) 3 : transmission of an influence on the mind or emotions

con·ta·gious \-jəs\ *adj* 1 : able to be passed by contact between individuals ⟨colds are ~⟩ ⟨~ disease⟩; *also* : capable of passing on a contagious disease 2 : communicated or transmitted like a contagious disease; *esp* : exciting similar emotion or conduct in others

con·tain \kən-'tān\ *vb* 1 : RESTRAIN 2 : to have within : HOLD 3 : COMPRISE, INCLUDE — **con·tain·able** \-'tā-nə-bəl\ *adj* — **con·tain·ment** \-'tān-mənt\ *n*

con·tain·er \kən-'tā-nər\ *n* : RECEPTACLE

con·tam·i·nant \kən-'ta-mə-nənt\ *n* : something that contaminates

con·tam·i·nate \kən-'ta-mə-ˌnāt\ *vb* **-nat·ed**; **-nat·ing** : to soil, stain, or infect by contact or association — **con·tam·i·na·tion** \-ˌta-mə-'nā-shən\ *n*

contd *abbr* continued

con·temn \kən-'tem\ *vb* : to view or treat with contempt : DESPISE

con·tem·plate \'kän-təm-ˌplāt\ *vb* **-plat·ed**; **-plat·ing** [L *contemplari*, fr. *com-* with + *templum* space marked out for observation of auguries] 1 : to view or consider with continued attention 2 : INTEND — **con·tem·pla·tion** \ˌkän-təm-'plā-shən\ *n* — **con·tem·pla·tive** \kən-'tem-plə-tiv, 'kän-təm-ˌplā-\ *adj*

con·tem·po·ra·ne·ous \kən-ˌtem-pə-'rā-nē-əs\ *adj* : CONTEMPORARY 1

con·tem·po·rary \kən-'tem-pə-ˌrer-ē\ *adj* 1 : occurring or existing at the same time 2 : marked by characteristics of the present period — **contemporary** *n*

con·tempt \kən-'tempt\ *n* 1 : the act of despising : the state of mind of one who despises 2 : the state of being despised 3 : disobedience to or open disrespect of a court or legislature

con·tempt·ible \kən-'temp-tə-bəl\ *adj* : deserving contempt : DESPICABLE — **con·tempt·ibly** \-blē\ *adv*

con·temp·tu·ous \-'temp-chə-wəs\ *adj* : feeling or expressing contempt — **con·temp·tu·ous·ly** *adv*

con·tend \kən-'tend\ *vb* 1 : to strive against rivals or difficulties 2 : ARGUE 3 : MAINTAIN, ASSERT — **con·tend·er** *n*

¹**con·tent** \kən-'tent\ *adj* : SATISFIED

²**content** *vb* : SATISFY; *esp* : to limit (oneself) in requirements or actions

³**content** *n* : CONTENTMENT ⟨ate to his heart's ~⟩

⁴**con·tent** \'kän-ˌtent\ *n* 1 : something contained ⟨~s of a room⟩ 2 : subject matter or topics treated (as in a book) 3 : material (as text or music) offered by a website 4 : MEANING, SIGNIFICANCE 5 : the amount of material contained

con·tent·ed \kən-'ten-təd\ *adj* : SATISFIED — **con·tent·ed·ly** *adv* — **con·tent·ed·ness** *n*

con·ten·tion \kən-'ten-chən\ *n* 1 : CONTEST, STRIFE 2 : an idea or point for which a person argues — **con·ten·tious** \-chəs\ *adj* — **con·ten·tious·ly** *adv*

con·tent·ment \kən-'tent-mənt\ *n* : ease of mind : SATISFACTION

con·ter·mi·nous \kän-'tər-mə-nəs\ *adj* : having the same or a common boundary — **con·ter·mi·nous·ly** *adv*

¹con·test \kən-'test\ vb 1 : to engage in a struggle or competition : COMPETE, VIE 2 : CHALLENGE, DISPUTE ⟨~ the accusations⟩ — con·tes·tant \-'tes-tənt\ n

²con·test \'kän-,test\ n : STRUGGLE, COMPETITION

con·text \'kän-,tekst\ n [ME, fr. L contextus connection of words, coherence, fr. contexere to weave together] : the parts of a discourse that surround a word or passage and help to explain its meaning; also : the circumstances surrounding an act or event ⟨the ~ of the war⟩ — con·tex·tu·al·ly adv

con·tig·u·ous \kən-'ti-gyə-wəs\ adj : being in contact : TOUCHING ⟨the 48 ~ states⟩; also : NEXT, ADJOINING — con·ti·gu·i·ty \,kän-tə-'gyü-ə-tē\ n

con·ti·nence \'kän-tə-nəns\ n 1 : SELF-RESTRAINT; esp : a refraining from sexual intercourse 2 : the ability to retain urine or feces voluntarily

¹con·ti·nent \'kän-tə-nənt\ adj : exercising continence

²continent n 1 : any of the great divisions of land on the globe 2 cap : the continent of Europe

¹con·ti·nen·tal \,kän-tə-'nen-tᵊl\ adj 1 : of or relating to a continent; esp, often cap : of or relating to the continent of Europe 2 often cap : of or relating to the colonies later forming the U.S. 3 : of or relating to cuisine based on classical European cooking

²continental n 1 often cap : a soldier in the Continental army 2 : EUROPEAN

continental drift n : a slow movement of the continents over a fluid layer deep within the earth

continental shelf n : a shallow submarine plain forming a border to a continent

continental slope n : a comparatively steep slope from a continental shelf to the ocean floor

con·tin·gen·cy \kən-'tin-jən-sē\ n, pl -cies : a chance or possible event

¹con·tin·gent \-jənt\ adj 1 : liable but not certain to happen : POSSIBLE 2 : happening by chance : not planned 3 : dependent on something that may or may not occur 4 : CONDITIONAL ♦ Synonyms ACCIDENTAL, CASUAL, INCIDENTAL, ODD

²contingent n : a quota (as of troops) supplied from an area or group

con·tin·u·al \kən-'tin-yə-wəl\ adj 1 : CONTINUOUS, UNBROKEN 2 : steadily recurring — con·tin·u·al·ly adv

con·tin·u·ance \-yə-wəns\ n 1 : unbroken succession 2 : the extent of continuing : DURATION 3 : adjournment of legal proceedings

con·tin·u·a·tion \kən-,tin-yə-'wā-shən\ n 1 : extension or prolongation of a state or activity 2 : resumption after an interruption; also : something that carries on after a pause or break

con·tin·ue \kən-'tin-yü\ vb -tin·ued; -tinu·ing 1 : to maintain without interruption 2 : ENDURE, LAST ⟨the tradition ~s⟩ 3 : to remain in a place or condition ⟨~ at this job⟩ 4 : to resume (as a story)

after an intermission 5 : EXTEND ⟨~ a subscription⟩; also : to persist in ⟨will ~ to remind you⟩ 6 : to allow to remain 7 : to keep (a legal case) on the calendar or undecided

con·ti·nu·i·ty \,kän-tə-'nü-ə-tē, -'nyü-\ n, pl -ties 1 : the state of being continuous 2 : something (as a film script) that has or provides continuity

con·tin·u·ous \kən-'tin-yə-wəs\ adj : continuing without interruption — con·tin·u·ous·ly adv

con·tin·u·um \-yə-wəm\ n, pl -ua \-yə-wə\ also -u·ums : something that is the same throughout or consists of a series of variations or of a sequence of things in regular order

con·tort \kən-'tȯrt\ vb : to twist out of shape ⟨a ~ed face⟩ ⟨~ the truth⟩ — con·tor·tion \-'tȯr-shən\ n

con·tor·tion·ist \-'tȯr-shə-nist\ n : an acrobat able to twist the body into unusual postures

con·tour \'kän-,tu̇r\ n [F, fr. It contorno fr. contornare to round off, fr. ML, to turn around, fr. L com- together + tornare to turn on a lathe, fr. tornus lathe] 1 : OUTLINE 2 : SHAPE, FORM — often used in pl. ⟨the ~s of a statue⟩

contr abbr contract; contraction

con·tra·band \'kän-trə-,band\ n : goods legally prohibited in trade; also : smuggled goods

con·tra·cep·tion \,kän-trə-'sep-shən\ n : intentional prevention of conception and pregnancy — con·tra·cep·tive \-'sep-tiv\ adj or n

¹con·tract \'kän-,trakt\ n 1 : a binding agreement; also : a document stating its terms 2 : an undertaking to win a specified number of tricks in bridge — con·tract adj — con·trac·tu·al \kən-'trak-chə-wəl\ adj — con·trac·tu·al·ly adv

²con·tract \kən-'trakt, 2 usu 'kän-,trakt\ vb 1 : to become affected with ⟨~ a disease⟩ 2 : to establish or undertake by contract 3 : SHRINK, LESSEN; esp : to draw together esp. so as to shorten ⟨~ a muscle⟩ 4 : to shorten (a word) by omitting letters or sounds in the middle — con·tract·ible \kən-'trak-tə-bəl, 'kän-\ adj — con·trac·tion \kən-'trak-shən\ n — con·trac·tor \'kän-,trak-tər, kən-'trak-\ n

con·trac·tile \kən-'trak-tᵊl\ adj : able to contract — con·trac·til·i·ty \,kän-,trak-'ti-lə-tē\ n

con·tra·dict \,kän-trə-'dikt\ vb : to assert the contrary of : deny the truth of ⟨~ a rumor⟩ — con·tra·dic·tion \-'dik-shən\ n — con·tra·dic·to·ry \-'dik-tə-rē\ adj

con·tra·dis·tinc·tion \,kän-trə-dis-'tiŋk-shən\ n : distinction by contrast

con·trail \'kän-,trāl\ n : a streak of condensed water vapor created by an airplane or rocket at high altitudes

con·tra·in·di·cate \,kän-trə-'in-də-,kāt\ vb : to make (a treatment or procedure) inadvisable — con·tra·in·di·ca·tion \-,in-də-'kā-shən\ n

con·tral·to \kən-'tral-tō\ n, pl -tos : the

lowest female voice; *also* : a singer having such a voice

con·trap·tion \kən-ˈtrap-shən\ *n* : CONTRIVANCE, DEVICE

con·tra·pun·tal \ˌkän-trə-ˈpən-tᵊl\ *adj* : of or relating to counterpoint

con·tra·ri·ety \ˌkän-trə-ˈrī-ə-tē\ *n, pl* **-eties** : the state of being contrary : DISAGREEMENT, INCONSISTENCY

con·trari·wise \ˈkän-ˌtrer-ē-ˌwīz, kän-ˈtrer-\ *adv* **1** : on the contrary **2** : VICE VERSA

con·trary \ˈkän-ˌtrer-ē; *4 often* kən-ˈtrer-ē\ *adj* **1** : opposite in nature or position **2** : COUNTER, OPPOSED **3** : UNFAVORABLE — used of wind or weather **4** : unwilling to accept control or advice — **con·trar·i·an** \kən-ˈtrer-ē-ən, kän-\ *n or adj* — **con·trari·ly** \ˈkän-ˌtrer-ə-lē, kən-ˈtrer-\ *adv* — **con·trary** *n is* ˈkän-ˌtrer-ē, *adv is like adj*\ *n or adv*

¹con·trast \kən-ˈtrast\ *vb* [F *contraster,* fr. MF, to oppose, resist, fr. VL **contrastare,* fr. L *contra-* against + *stare* to stand] **1** : to show differences when compared **2** : to compare in such a way as to show differences

²con·trast \ˈkän-ˌtrast\ *n* **1** : diversity of adjacent parts in color, emotion, tone, or brightness ⟨the ~ of a photograph⟩ **2** : unlikeness as shown when things are compared : DIFFERENCE

con·tra·vene \ˌkän-trə-ˈvēn\ *vb* **-vened;** **-ven·ing 1** : to go or act contrary to ⟨~ a law⟩ **2** : CONTRADICT ⟨~ a claim⟩

con·tre·temps \ˈkän-trə-ˌtäⁿ, kōⁿ-trə-ˈtäⁿ\ *n, pl* **con·tre·temps** \-ˌtäⁿ, -ˌtäⁿz\ [F] : an inopportune or embarrassing occurrence

contrib *abbr* contribution; contributor

con·trib·ute \kən-ˈtri-byət\ *vb* **-ut·ed;** **-ut·ing** : to give along with others (as to a fund); *also* : HELP, ASSIST — **con·tri·bu·tion** \ˌkän-trə-ˈbyü-shən\ *n* — **con·trib·u·tor** \kən-ˈtri-byə-tər\ *n* — **con·trib·u·to·ry** \-byə-ˌtòr-ē\ *adj*

con·trite \ˈkän-ˌtrīt, kən-ˈtrīt\ *adj* : PENITENT, REPENTANT — **con·trite·ly** *adv* — **con·tri·tion** \kən-ˈtri-shən\ *n*

con·triv·ance \kən-ˈtrī-vəns\ *n* **1** : a mechanical device **2** : SCHEME, PLAN

con·trive \kən-ˈtrīv\ *vb* **con·trived; con·triv·ing 1** : PLAN, DEVISE **2** : FRAME, MAKE **3** : to bring about with difficulty — **con·triv·er** *n*

con·trived \-ˈtrīvd\ *adj* : lacking in natural quality ⟨a ~ plot⟩

¹con·trol \kən-ˈtrōl\ *vb* **con·trolled; con·trol·ling** [ME *countrollen* to verify, fr. AF *countrerouler,* fr. *countreroule* copy of an account, audit, fr. ML *contrarotulus,* fr. L *contra* against + ML *rotulus* roll] **1** : to exercise restraining or directing influence over : REGULATE **2** : DOMINATE, RULE — **con·trol·la·ble** \-ˈtrō-lə-bəl\ *adj*

²control *n* **1** : power to direct or regulate **2** : RESERVE, RESTRAINT **3** : a device for regulating a mechanism

con·trol·ler \kən-ˈtrō-lər, ˈkän-ˌtrō-lər\ *n* **1** : COMPTROLLER **2** : a person or thing that controls ⟨an air traffic ~⟩ ⟨a game ~⟩

con·tro·ver·sy \ˈkän-trə-ˌvər-sē\ *n, pl* **-sies** : a clash of opposing views : DISPUTE — **con·tro·ver·sial** \ˌkän-trə-ˌvər-shəl, -sē-əl\ *adj*

con·tro·vert \ˈkän-trə-ˌvərt, ˌkän-trə-ˈvərt\ *vb* : DENY, CONTRADICT ⟨~ an allegation⟩ — **con·tro·vert·ible** *adj*

con·tu·ma·cious \ˌkän-tü-ˈmā-shəs, -tyü-\ *adj* : stubbornly disobedient

♦ **Synonyms** REBELLIOUS, INSUBORDINATE, SEDITIOUS — **con·tu·ma·cy** \kän-ˈtü-mə-sē, -ˈtyü-; ˈkän-tyə-\ *n* — **con·tu·ma·cious·ly** *adv*

con·tu·me·ly \kän-ˈtü-mə-lē, -ˈtyü-; ˈkän-tə-ˌmē-lē, -tyə-\ *n, pl* **-lies** : contemptuous treatment : INSULT

con·tu·sion \kən-ˈtü-zhən, -ˈtyü-\ *n* : BRUISE — **con·tuse** \-ˈtüz, -ˈtyüz\ *vb*

co·nun·drum \kə-ˈnən-drəm\ *n* : RIDDLE

conv *abbr* **1** convention **2** convertible

con·va·lesce \ˌkän-və-ˈles\ *vb* **-lesced;** **-lesc·ing** : to recover health gradually — **con·va·les·cence** \-ˈle-sᵊns\ *n* — **con·va·les·cent** \-sᵊnt\ *adj or n*

con·vec·tion \kən-ˈvek-shən\ *n* : circulatory motion in a fluid due to warmer portions rising and cooler denser portions sinking; *also* : the transfer of heat by such motion — **con·vec·tion·al** \-shə-nəl\ *adj* — **con·vec·tive** \-ˈvek-tiv\ *adj*

convection oven *n* : an oven with a fan that circulates hot air uniformly and continuously around the food

con·vene \kən-ˈvēn\ *vb* **con·vened; con·ven·ing** : ASSEMBLE, MEET

con·ve·nience \kən-ˈvē-nyəns\ *n* **1** : SUITABLENESS **2** : a laborsaving device **3** : a suitable time ⟨at your ~⟩ **4** : personal comfort : EASE

convenience store *n* : a small market that is open long hours

con·ve·nient \-nyənt\ *adj* **1** : suited to personal comfort or ease **2** : placed near at hand — **con·ve·nient·ly** *adv*

con·vent \ˈkän-vənt, -ˌvent\ *n* [ME *covent,* fr. AF, fr. ML *conventus,* fr. L, assembly, fr. *convenire* to come together] : a local community or house of a religious order esp. of nuns — **con·ven·tu·al** \kän-ˈven-chə-wəl\ *adj*

con·ven·ti·cle \kən-ˈven-ti-kəl\ *n* : MEETING; *esp* : a secret meeting for worship

con·ven·tion \kən-ˈven-chən\ *n* **1** : an agreement esp. between states on a matter of common concern **2** : MEETING, ASSEMBLY **3** : an assembly of persons convened for some purpose **4** : generally accepted custom, practice, or belief

con·ven·tion·al \-chə-nəl\ *adj* **1** : sanctioned by general custom **2** : COMMONPLACE, ORDINARY — **con·ven·tion·al·i·ty** \-ˌven-chə-ˈna-lə-tē\ *n* — **con·ven·tion·al·ize** \-ˈven-chə-nə-ˌlīz\ *vb* — **con·ven·tion·al·ly** *adv*

con·verge \kən-ˈvərj\ *vb* **con·verged; con·verg·ing** : to approach one common center or single point ⟨*converging* paths⟩ — **con·ver·gence** \kən-ˈvər-jəns\ *n* — **con·ver·gent** \-jənt\ *adj*

con·ver·sant \kən-ˈvər-sᵊnt\ *adj* : having knowledge and experience — used with *with*

con·ver·sa·tion \ˌkän-vər-ˈsā-shən\ n : an informal talking together — **con·ver·sa·tion·al** \-shə-nᵊl\ adj — **con·ver·sa·tion·al·ly** adv

con·ver·sa·tion·al·ist \-shə-nᵊl-ist\ n : a person who converses a great deal or who excels in conversation

¹**con·verse** \ˈkän-ˌvərs\ n : CONVERSATION

²**con·verse** \kən-ˈvərs\ vb **con·versed; con·vers·ing** : to engage in conversation

³**con·verse** \ˈkän-ˌvərs\ n : a statement related to another statement by having its hypothesis and conclusion or its subject and predicate reversed or interchanged

⁴**con·verse** \kən-ˈvərs, ˈkän-ˌvərs\ adj : reversed in order or relation — **con·verse·ly** adv

con·ver·sion \kən-ˈvər-zhən\ n   1 : a change in nature or form   2 : an experience associated with a decisive adoption of religion

¹**con·vert** \kən-ˈvərt\ vb   1 : to turn from one belief or party to another   2 : TRANSFORM, CHANGE   3 : MISAPPROPRIATE   4 : EXCHANGE — **con·vert·er** or **con·ver·tor** \-ˈvər-tər\ n

²**con·vert** \ˈkän-ˌvərt\ n : a person who has undergone religious conversion

¹**con·vert·ible** \kən-ˈvər-tə-bəl\ adj : capable of being converted

²**convertible** n : an automobile with a top that may be lowered or removed

con·vex \kän-ˈveks, ˈkän-ˌveks\ adj : curved or rounded outward like the exterior of a sphere or circle — **con·vex·i·ty** \kän-ˈvek-sə-tē\ n

con·vey \kən-ˈvā\ vb   1 : CARRY, TRANSPORT ⟨a river ~ing logs⟩   2 : TRANSFER, COMMUNICATE ⟨~ a message⟩ — **con·vey·or** also **con·vey·er** \-ər\ n

con·vey·ance \-ˈvā-əns\ n   1 : the act of conveying   2 : a legal paper transferring ownership of property   3 : VEHICLE

¹**con·vict** \kən-ˈvikt\ vb : to prove or find guilty

²**con·vict** \ˈkän-ˌvikt\ n : a person serving a prison sentence

con·vic·tion \kən-ˈvik-shən\ n   1 : the act of convicting esp. in a court   2 : the state of being convinced : BELIEF

con·vince \kən-ˈvins\ vb **con·vinced; con·vinc·ing** : to bring (as by argument) to belief or action — **con·vinc·ing** adj — **con·vinc·ing·ly** adv

con·viv·ial \kən-ˈvi-vē-əl\ adj [LL convivialis, fr. L convivium banquet, fr. com- together + vivere to live] : enjoying companionship and the pleasures of feasting and drinking : JOVIAL, FESTIVE ⟨a ~ gathering⟩ — **con·viv·i·al·i·ty** \-ˌvi-vē-ˈa-lə-tē\ n — **con·viv·ial·ly** adv

con·vo·ca·tion \ˌkän-və-ˈkā-shən\ n   1 : a ceremonial assembly (as of the clergy)   2 : the act of convoking

con·voke \kən-ˈvōk\ vb **con·voked; con·vok·ing** : to call together to a meeting ⟨convoked a meeting of the delegates⟩

con·vo·lut·ed \ˈkän-və-ˌlü-təd\ adj   1 : folded in curved or tortuous windings   2 : INVOLVED, INTRICATE ⟨~ logic⟩

con·vo·lu·tion \ˌkän-və-ˈlü-shən\ n : a tortuous or winding structure; esp : one of the ridges of the brain

¹**con·voy** \ˈkän-ˌvȯi, kən-ˈvȯi\ vb : to accompany for protection

²**con·voy** \ˈkän-ˌvȯi\ n   1 : one that convoys; esp : a protective escort (as for ships)   2 : the act of convoying   3 : a group of moving vehicles

con·vulse \kən-ˈvəls\ vb **con·vulsed; con·vuls·ing** : to agitate violently

con·vul·sion \kən-ˈvəl-shən\ n   1 : an abnormal and violent involuntary contraction or series of contractions of muscle   2 : a violent disturbance — **con·vul·sive** \-siv\ adj — **con·vul·sive·ly** adv

cony var of CONEY

coo \ˈkü\ n : a soft low sound made by doves or pigeons; also : a sound like this — **coo** vb

COO abbr chief operating officer

¹**cook** \ˈkȯok\ n : a person who prepares food for eating

²**cook** vb   1 : to prepare food for eating   2 : to subject to heat or fire   3 : CONCOCT, FABRICATE — usu. used with up ⟨~ up a scheme⟩ — **cook·er** n — **cook·ware** \-ˌwer\ n

cook·book \-ˌbu̇k\ n : a book of cooking directions and recipes

cook·ery \ˈku̇-kə-rē\ n, pl -**er·ies** : the art or practice of cooking

cook·ie or **cooky** \ˈku̇-kē\ n, pl **cook·ies** [D koekje, dim. of koek cake]   1 : a small sweet flat cake   2 cookie : a file containing information about a website user created and read by a website server and stored on the user's computer

cookie–cutter adj : marked by a lack of originality or distinction ⟨~ malls⟩

cook·out \ˈku̇k-ˌau̇t\ n : an outing at which a meal is cooked and served in the open

¹**cool** \ˈkül\ adj   1 : moderately cold   2 : not excited : CALM   3 : not friendly   4 : IMPUDENT   5 : protecting from heat   6 slang : very good   7 slang : FASHIONABLE

♦ **Synonyms** UNFLAPPABLE, COMPOSED, COLLECTED, UNRUFFLED, NONCHALANT — **cool·ly** adv — **cool·ness** n

²**cool** vb : to make or become cool

³**cool** n   1 : a cool time or place   2 : INDIFFERENCE; also : SELF-ASSURANCE, COMPOSURE ⟨kept his ~⟩

cool·ant \ˈkü-lənt\ n : a usu. fluid cooling agent

cool·er \ˈkü-lər\ n   1 : a container for keeping food or drink cool   2 : JAIL, PRISON   3 : a tall iced drink

coo·lie \ˈkü-lē\ n [Hindi & Urdu qulī] : an unskilled laborer usu. in or from the Far East

coon \ˈkün\ n : RACCOON

coon·hound \-ˌhau̇nd\ n : a sporting dog trained to hunt raccoons

coon·skin \-ˌskin\ n : the pelt of a raccoon; also : something (as a cap) made of this

¹**coop** \ˈküp, ˈku̇p\ n : a small enclosure or building usu. for poultry

²**coop** vb : to confine in or as if in a coop — usu. used with up

co–op \ˈkō-ˌäp\ n : COOPERATIVE

coo·per \'kü-pər, 'kú-\ n : one who makes or repairs barrels or casks — **cooper** vb — **coo·per·age** \-pə-rij\ n

co·op·er·ate \kō-'ä-pə-ṛāt\ vb : to act jointly or in compliance with others — **co·op·er·a·tion** \-ṛä-pə-'rä-shən\ n — **co·op·er·a·tor** \-'ä-pə-ṛä-tər\ n

¹**co·op·er·a·tive** \kō-'ä-prə-tiv, -'ä-pə-ṛā-\ adj 1 : willing to work with others 2 : of or relating to an association formed to enable its members to buy or sell to better advantage by eliminating middlemen's profits

²**cooperative** n : a cooperative association

co–opt \kō-'äpt\ vb 1 : to choose or elect as a colleague 2 : ABSORB, ASSIMILATE; also : TAKE OVER ⟨a style ∼ed by advertisers⟩

¹**co·or·di·nate** \kō-'ȯr-də-nət\ adj 1 : equal in rank or order 2 : of equal rank in a compound sentence ⟨∼ clause⟩ 3 : joining words or word groups of the same rank — **co·or·di·nate·ly** adv

²**co·or·di·nate** \-'ȯr-də-ṇāt\ vb -nat·ed; -nat·ing 1 : to make or become coordinate ⟨∼ our schedules⟩ 2 : to work or act together harmoniously ⟨a coordinated wardrobe⟩ — **co·or·di·na·tion** \-ȯr-də-'nä-shən\ n — **co·or·di·na·tor** \-'ȯr-də-'nä-tər\ n

³**co·or·di·nate** \-'ȯr-də-nət\ n 1 : one of a set of numbers used in specifying the location of a point on a surface or in space 2 pl : articles (as of clothing) designed to be used together and to attain their effect through pleasing contrast

coot \'küt\ n 1 : a dark-colored ducklike bird related to the rails 2 : any of several No. American sea ducks 3 : a harmless simple person

coo·tie \'kü-tē\ n : a body louse

¹**cop** \'käp\ n : POLICE OFFICER

²**cop** vb 1 slang : STEAL ⟨∼ a glance⟩ 2 slang : ADMIT — used with to ⟨∼ to the charges⟩ 3 : ADOPT ⟨∼ an attitude⟩

co–pay \'kō-'pā\ n : CO-PAYMENT

co–pay·ment \'kō-,pā-mənt, ,kō-'\ n : a fixed fee required of a patient by a health insurer (as an HMO) at the time of each outpatient service or filling of a prescription

¹**cope** \'kōp\ n : a long cloaklike ecclesiastical vestment

²**cope** vb coped; cop·ing : to struggle to overcome problems or difficulties ⟨∼ with tragedy⟩

co·per·nic·i·um \,kō-pər-'ni-sē-əm\ n [NL, fr. Nikolaus Copernicus] : a short-lived artificially produced radioactive element

copi·er \'kä-pē-ər\ n : one that copies; esp : a machine for making copies

co·pi·lot \'kō-,pī-lət\ n : an assistant pilot of an aircraft or spacecraft

cop·ing \'kō-piŋ\ n : the top layer of a wall

co·pi·ous \'kō-pē-əs\ adj : LAVISH, ABUNDANT ⟨a ∼ harvest⟩ — **co·pi·ous·ly** adv — **co·pi·ous·ness** n

cop–out \'käp-,aút\ n : an excuse for copping out; also : an act of copping out

cop out vb : to back out (as of an unwanted responsibility)

cop·per \'kä-pər\ n 1 : a malleable reddish metallic chemical element that is one of the best conductors of heat and electricity 2 : a coin or token made of copper — **cop·pery** adj

cop·per·head \'kä-pər-,hed\ n : a largely coppery brown pit viper esp. of the eastern and central U.S.

cop·pice \'kä-pəs\ n : THICKET

co·pra \'kō-prə\ n : dried coconut meat yielding coconut oil

copse \'käps\ n : THICKET

cop·ter \'käp-tər\ n : HELICOPTER

cop·u·la \'kä-pyə-lə\ n : LINKING VERB — **cop·u·la·tive** \-lə-tiv, -,lā-\ adj

cop·u·late \'kä-pyə-,lāt\ vb -lat·ed; -lat·ing : to engage in sexual intercourse — **cop·u·la·tion** \,kä-pyə-'lā-shən\ n — **cop·u·la·to·ry** \'kä-pyə-lə-,tȯr-ē\ adj

¹**copy** \'kä-pē\ n, pl cop·ies 1 : an imitation or reproduction of an original work 2 : material to be set in type 3 : DUPLICATE ♦ **Synonyms** DUPLICATE, REPRODUCTION, FACSIMILE, REPLICA

²**copy** vb cop·ied; copy·ing 1 : to make a copy of 2 : IMITATE — **copy·ist** n

copy·book \'kä-pē-,búk\ n : a book formerly used to teach handwriting containing examples to be copied

copy·boy \-,bȯi\ n : a person who carries copy and runs errands (as in a newspaper office)

copy·cat \-,kat\ n : a slavish imitator

copy·desk \-,desk\ n : the desk at which newspaper copy is edited

copy editor n : one who edits or prepares copy (as headlines) esp. for a newspaper

copy·read·er \-,rē-dər\ n : COPY EDITOR

¹**copy·right** \-,rīt\ n : the sole right to reproduce, publish, sell, or distribute a literary or artistic work

²**copyright** vb : to secure a copyright on

copy·writ·er \'kä-pē-,rī-tər\ n : a writer of advertising copy

co·quet or **co·quette** \kō-'ket\ vb co·quet·ted; co·quet·ting : FLIRT — **co·quet·ry** \'kō-kə-trē, kō-'ke-trē\ n

co·quette \kō-'ket\ n [F, fem. of coquet, flirtatious man, dim. of coq cock] : FLIRT — **co·quett·ish** adj

cor abbr corner

Cor abbr Corinthians

cor·a·cle \'kȯr-ə-kəl\ n [W corwgl] : a boat made of a frame covered usu. with hide or tarpaulin

cor·al \'kȯr-əl\ n 1 : a stony or horny material that forms the skeleton of colonies of tiny sea polyps and includes a red form used in jewelry; also : a coral-forming polyp or polyp colony 2 : a deep pink color — **coral** adj

coral snake n : any of several venomous chiefly tropical New World snakes brilliantly banded in red, black, and yellow or white

cor·bel \'kȯr-bəl\ n : a bracket-shaped architectural member that projects from a wall and supports a weight

¹**cord** \'kȯrd\ n 1 : a usu. heavy string consisting of several strands woven or twisted together 2 : a long slender anatomical structure (as a tendon or nerve) 3 : a

small flexible insulated electrical cable used to connect an appliance with a receptacle **4** : a cubic measure used esp. for firewood and equal to a stack 4×4×8 feet **5** : a rib or ridge on cloth

²**cord** vb **1** : to tie or furnish with a cord **2** : to pile (wood) in cords

cord·age \ˈkȯr-dij\ n : ROPES, CORDS; esp : ropes in the rigging of a ship

¹**cor·dial** \ˈkȯr-jəl\ adj [ME, fr. ML cordialis, fr. L cord-, cor heart] : warmly receptive or welcoming — HEARTFELT, HEARTY — **cor·di·al·i·ty** \ˌkȯr-jē-ˈa-lə-tē, kȯr-ˈja-\ n — **cor·dial·ly** adv

²**cordial** n **1** : a stimulating medicine or drink **2** : LIQUEUR

cor·dil·le·ra \ˌkȯr-dəl-ˈyer-ə, -də-ˈler-\ n [Sp] : a series of parallel mountain ranges

cord·less \ˈkȯrd-ləs\ adj : having no cord; esp : powered by a battery ⟨a ~ phone⟩ — **cordless** n

cór·do·ba \ˈkȯr-də-bə, -və\ n — see MONEY table

cor·don \ˈkȯr-dᵊn\ n **1** : an ornamental cord or ribbon **2** : an encircling line (as of troops or police) — cordon vb

cor·do·van \ˈkȯr-də-vən\ n : a soft fine-grained leather

cor·du·roy \ˈkȯr-də-ˌrȯi\ n, pl -roys **1** : a heavy ribbed fabric; also, pl : pants of this material

cord·wain·er \ˈkȯrd-ˌwā-nər\ n : SHOEMAKER

¹**core** \ˈkȯr\ n **1** : the central usu. inedible part of some fruits (as the apple); also : an inmost part of something **2** : GIST, ESSENCE

²**core** vb cored; cor·ing : to take out the core of — **cor·er** n

CORE \ˈkȯr\ abbr Congress of Racial Equality

co·re·op·sis \ˌkȯr-ē-ˈäp-səs\ n, pl coreopsis : any of a genus of widely cultivated composite herbs with showy often yellow flower heads

co·re·spon·dent \ˌkō-ri-ˈspän-dənt\ n : a person named as guilty of adultery with the defendant in a divorce suit

co·ri·an·der \ˈkȯr-ē-ˌan-dər\ n : an herb related to the carrot; also : its aromatic dried fruit used as a flavoring

Cor·in·thi·ans \kə-ˈrin-thē-ənz\ n — see BIBLE table

¹**cork** \ˈkȯrk\ n **1** : the tough elastic bark of a European oak (**cork oak**) used esp. for stoppers and insulation; also : a stopper of this **2** : a tissue of a woody plant making up most of the bark — **corky** adj

²**cork** vb : to furnish with or stop up with cork or a cork ⟨~ a bottle⟩

cork·screw \ˈkȯrk-ˌskrü\ n : a device for drawing corks from bottles

corm \ˈkȯrm\ n : a solid bulblike underground part of a stem (as of the crocus or gladiolus)

cor·mo·rant \ˈkȯr-mə-rənt, -ˌrant\ n [ME cormeraunt, fr. MF cormorant, fr. OF cormareng, fr. corp raven + marenc of the sea, fr. L marinus] : any of various dark-colored water birds with a long neck, hooked bill, and distensible throat pouch

¹**corn** \ˈkȯrn\ n **1** Brit : the seeds of a cereal grass and esp. of the chief cereal crop of a region (as wheat in Britain); also : a cereal grass **2 a** : a tall widely cultivated cereal grass grown for its large ears of starchy seeds **b** : the typically yellow or whitish seeds of corn used esp. as a food **c** : an ear of corn

²**corn** vb : to salt (as beef) in brine and preservatives

³**corn** n : a local hardening and thickening of skin (as on a toe)

corn·ball \ˈkȯrn-ˌbȯl\ n : an unsophisticated person; also : something corny

cornball adj : CORNY ⟨~ humor⟩

corn bread n : bread made with cornmeal

corn·cob \-ˌkäb\ n : the woody core on which the kernels of corn are arranged

corn·crib \-ˌkrib\ n : a crib for storing ears of corn

cor·nea \ˈkȯr-nē-ə\ n : the transparent part of the coat of the eyeball covering the iris and the pupil — **cor·ne·al** adj

corn ear·worm \-ˈir-ˌwərm\ n : a moth whose larva is destructive esp. to corn

¹**cor·ner** \ˈkȯr-nər\ n [ME, fr. AF cornere, fr. corne horn, corner, fr. L cornu horn, point] **1** : the point or angle formed by the meeting of lines, edges, or sides **2** : the place where two streets come together **3** : a quiet secluded place **4** : a position from which retreat or escape is impossible **5** : control of enough of the available supply (as of a commodity) to permit manipulation of the price — **cornered** adj — **around the corner** : IMMINENT ⟨has a birthday just around the corner⟩

²**corner** vb **1** : to drive into a corner **2** : to get a corner on ⟨~ the wheat market⟩ **3** : to turn a corner

cor·ner·stone \ˈkȯr-nər-ˌstōn\ n **1** : a stone forming part of a corner in a wall; esp : such a stone laid at a formal ceremony **2** : something of basic importance

cor·net \kȯr-ˈnet\ n : a brass band instrument resembling the trumpet

corn flour n, Brit : CORNSTARCH

corn·flow·er \ˈkȯrn-ˌflau̇(-ə)r\ n : BACHELOR'S BUTTON

cor·nice \ˈkȯr-nəs\ n : the horizontal projecting part crowning the wall of a building

corn·meal \ˈkȯrn-ˌmēl\ n : meal ground from corn

corn·row \-ˌrō\ n : a section of hair braided flat to the scalp in rows — **cornrow** vb

corn·stalk \-ˌstȯk\ n : a stalk of corn

corn·starch \-ˌstärch\ n : a starch made from corn and used in cookery as a thickening agent

corn syrup n : a sweet syrup obtained from cornstarch

cor·nu·co·pia \ˌkȯr-nə-ˈkō-pē-ə, -nyə-\ n [LL, fr. L cornu copiae horn of plenty] **1** : a horn-shaped container filled with fruits and grain emblematic of abundance **2** : ABUNDANCE

corny \ˈkȯr-nē\ adj corn·i·er; -est : tiresomely simple or sentimental

co·rol·la \kə-ˈrä-lə, -ˈrō-\ n : the petals of a flower

cor·ol·lary \'kȯr-ə-ˌler-ē\ n, pl **-lar·ies** 1 : a deduction from a proposition already proved true 2 : CONSEQUENCE, RESULT

co·ro·na \kə-'rō-nə\ n 1 : a colored circle often seen around and close to a luminous body (as the sun or moon) 2 : the outermost part of the atmosphere of a star (as the sun) — **co·ro·nal** \'kȯr-ə-nᵊl, kə-'rō-\ adj

cor·o·nal \'kȯr-ə-nᵊl\ n : a circlet for the head

¹cor·o·nary \'kȯr-ə-ˌner-ē\ adj : of or relating to the heart or its blood vessels

²coronary n, pl **-nar·ies** 1 : a coronary blood vessel 2 : CORONARY THROMBOSIS; also : HEART ATTACK

coronary thrombosis n : the blocking by a thrombus of one of the arteries supplying the heart tissues

cor·o·na·tion \ˌkȯr-ə-'nā-shən\ n : the act or ceremony of crowning a monarch

cor·o·ner \'kȯr-ə-nər\ n [ME, an officer of the crown, fr. AF, fr. corone crown, fr. L corona] : a public official who investigates causes of deaths possibly not due to natural causes

cor·o·net \ˌkȯr-ə-'net\ n 1 : a small crown 2 : an ornamental band worn around the temples

corp abbr 1 corporal 2 corporation

¹cor·po·ral \'kȯr-p(ə-)rəl\ adj : of or relating to the body ⟨~ punishment⟩

²corporal n : a noncommissioned officer (as in the army) ranking next below a sergeant

cor·po·rate \'kȯr-p(ə-)rət\ adj 1 : INCORPORATED; also : belonging to an incorporated body 2 : of or relating to large-scale business ⟨~ mergers⟩ 3 : combined into one body

cor·po·ra·tion \ˌkȯr-pə-'rā-shən\ n : the municipal authorities of a town or city 2 : a legal creation authorized to act with the rights and liabilities of a person; also : COMPANY

cor·po·rat·ize \'kȯr-pə-rə-ˌtīz\ vb **-ized; -iz·ing** : to subject to corporate control ⟨~ education⟩

cor·po·re·al \kȯr-'pȯr-ē-əl\ adj 1 : PHYSICAL, MATERIAL 2 archaic : BODILY — **cor·po·re·al·i·ty** \-ˌpȯr-ē-a-lə-tē\ n — **cor·po·re·al·ly** adv

corps \'kȯr\ n, pl **corps** \'kȯrz\ [F, fr. OF cors, fr. L corpus body] 1 : an organized subdivision of a country's military forces 2 : a group acting under common direction

corpse \'kȯrps\ n : a dead body

corps·man \'kȯr-mən, 'kȯrz-\ n : an enlisted person trained to give first aid

cor·pu·lence \'kȯr-pyə-ləns\ n : excessive fatness : OBESITY

cor·pu·lent \-lənt\ adj : OBESE

cor·pus \'kȯr-pəs\ n, pl **cor·po·ra** \-pə-rə\ [ME, fr. L] 1 : BODY; esp : CORPSE 2 : a body of writings or works

cor·pus·cle \'kȯr-pə-səl, -ˌpə-\ n 1 : a minute particle 2 : a living cell (as in blood or cartilage) not aggregated into continuous tissues — **cor·pus·cu·lar** \kȯr-'pəs-kyə-lər\ adj

cor·pus de·lic·ti \ˌkȯr-pəs-di-'lik-ˌtī, -tē\ n, pl **corpora delicti** [NL, lit., body of the crime] 1 : the substantial fact proving that a crime has been committed 2 : the body of a victim of murder

corr abbr 1 correct; corrected; correction 2 correspondence; correspondent; corresponding

cor·ral \kə-'ral\ n [Sp] : an enclosure for confining or capturing animals; also : an enclosure of wagons for defending a camp — **corral** vb

¹cor·rect \kə-'rekt\ vb 1 : to make right ⟨~ an error⟩ 2 : REPROVE, CHASTISE ⟨~ed the child⟩ — **cor·rect·able** \-'rek-tə-bəl\ adj — **cor·rec·tion** \-'rek-shən\ n — **cor·rec·tion·al** \-'rek-sh(ə-)nəl\ adj — **cor·rec·tive** \-'rek-tiv\ adj

²correct adj 1 : conforming to a conventional standard ⟨~ behavior⟩ 2 : agreeing with fact or truth ⟨a ~ answer⟩ 3 : conforming to the standards of a specific ideology ⟨environmentally ~⟩ — **cor·rect·ly** adv — **cor·rect·ness** n

cor·re·late \'kȯr-ə-ˌlāt\ vb **-lat·ed; -lat·ing** : to connect in a systematic way : establish the mutual relations of — **cor·re·late** \-lət, -ˌlāt\ n — **cor·re·la·tion** \ˌkȯr-ə-'lā-shən\ n

cor·rel·a·tive \kə-'re-lə-tiv\ adj 1 : reciprocally related 2 : regularly used together (as either and or) — **correlative** n — **cor·rel·a·tive·ly** adv

cor·re·spond \ˌkȯr-ə-'spänd\ vb 1 : to be in agreement : SUIT, MATCH 2 : to communicate by letter — **cor·re·spond·ing·ly** adv

cor·re·spon·dence \-'spän-dəns\ n 1 : agreement between particular things 2 : communication by letters; also : the letters exchanged

¹cor·re·spon·dent \-dənt\ adj 1 : SIMILAR 2 : FITTING, CONFORMING

²correspondent n 1 : something that corresponds 2 : a person with whom one communicates by letter 3 : a person employed to contribute news regularly from a place ⟨a war ~⟩

cor·ri·dor \'kȯr-ə-dər, -ˌdȯr\ n 1 : a passageway into which compartments or rooms open (as in a hotel or school) 2 : a narrow strip of land esp. through foreign-held territory 3 : a densely populated strip of land including two or more major cities 4 : an area identified by a common characteristic or purpose ⟨a ~ of liberalism⟩

cor·ri·gen·dum \ˌkȯr-ə-'jen-dəm\ n, pl **-da** \-də\ [L] : an error in a printed work discovered after printing and shown with its correction on a separate sheet

cor·ri·gi·ble \'kȯr-ə-jə-bəl\ adj : CORRECTABLE

cor·rob·o·rate \kə-'rä-bə-ˌrāt\ vb **-rat·ed; -rat·ing** [L corroborare, fr. robur strength] : to support with evidence : CONFIRM — **cor·rob·o·ra·tion** \-ˌrä-bə-'rā-shən\ n — **cor·rob·o·ra·tive** \-'rä-bə-ˌrā-tiv, -'rä-bə-rə-\ adj — **cor·rob·o·ra·to·ry** \-'rä-bə-rə-ˌtȯr-ē\ adj

cor·rode \kə-'rōd\ vb **cor·rod·ed; cor·rod·ing** : to wear or be worn away gradually (as by chemical action) — **cor·ro-**

sion \-'rō-zhən\ *n* — **cor·ro·sive** \-'rō-siv\ *adj or n*

cor·ru·gate \'kȯr-ə-ˌgāt\ *vb* **-gat·ed; -gat·ing** : to form into wrinkles or ridges and grooves — **cor·ru·gat·ed** *adj* — **cor·ru·ga·tion** \ˌkȯr-ə-'gā-shən\ *n*

¹**cor·rupt** \kə-'rəpt\ *vb* **1** : to make evil : DEPRAVE; *esp* : BRIBE **2** : ROT, SPOIL — **cor·rupt·ible** *adj* — **cor·rup·tion** \-'rəp-shən\ *n*

²**corrupt** *adj* : morally degenerate; *also* : characterized by improper conduct ⟨∼ officials⟩

cor·sage \kȯr-'säzh, -'säj\ *n* [F, bust, bodice, fr. OF, bust, fr. *cors* body, fr. L *corpus*] **1** : the waist or bodice of a dress **2** : a bouquet to be worn or carried

cor·sair \'kȯr-ˌser\ *n* : PIRATE

cor·set \'kȯr-sət\ *n* : a stiffened undergarment worn for support or to give shape to the waist and hips

cor·tege *also* **cor·tège** \kȯr-'tezh, 'kȯr-ˌtezh\ *n* [F] : PROCESSION; *esp* : a funeral procession

cor·tex \'kȯr-ˌteks\ *n, pl* **cor·ti·ces** \'kȯr-tə-ˌsēz\ *or* **cor·tex·es** : an outer or covering layer of an organism or one of its parts ⟨the adrenal ∼⟩ ⟨∼ of a plant stem⟩; *esp* : CEREBRAL CORTEX — **cor·ti·cal** \'kȯr-ti-kəl\ *adj*

cor·ti·co·ste·roid \ˌkȯr-ti-kō-'stir-ˌȯid, -'ster-\ *n* : any of various steroids made in the adrenal cortex and used medically as anti-inflammatory agents

cor·ti·sone \'kȯr-tə-ˌsōn, -ˌzōn\ *n* : a corticosteroid used esp. in treating rheumatoid arthritis

co·run·dum \kə-'rən-dəm\ *n* : a very hard aluminum-containing mineral used as an abrasive or as a gem

cor·us·cate \'kȯr-ə-ˌskāt\ *vb* **-cat·ed; -cat·ing** : FLASH, SPARKLE — **cor·us·ca·tion** \ˌkȯr-ə-'skā-shən\ *n*

cor·vette \kȯr-'vet\ *n* **1** : a naval sailing ship smaller than a frigate **2** : an armed escort ship smaller than a destroyer

co·ry·za \kə-'rī-zə\ *n* : an inflammatory disorder of the upper respiratory tract; *esp* : COMMON COLD

cos *abbr* cosine

COS *abbr* **1** cash on shipment **2** chief of staff

co·sig·na·to·ry \kō-'sig-nə-ˌtȯr-ē\ *n* : a joint signer

co·sign·er \'kō-ˌsī-nər\ *n* : COSIGNATORY; *esp* : a joint signer of a promissory note

co·sine \'kō-ˌsīn\ *n* : the trigonometric function that is the ratio between the side next to an acute angle in a right triangle and the hypotenuse

¹**cos·met·ic** \käz-'me-tik\ *adj* [Gk *kosmētikos* skilled in adornment, fr. *kosmein* to arrange, adorn, fr. *kosmos* order, ornament, universe] **1** : intended to beautify the hair or complexion **2** : correcting physical defects esp. to improve appearance ⟨∼ dentistry⟩ **3** : SUPERFICIAL ⟨∼ changes⟩ — **cos·met·i·cal·ly** \-ti-k(ə-)lē\ *adv*

²**cosmetic** *n* : a cosmetic preparation

cos·me·tol·o·gist \ˌkäz-mə-'tä-lə-jist\ *n*

: one who gives beauty treatments — **cos·me·tol·o·gy** \-jē\ *n*

cos·mic \'käz-mik\ *also* **cos·mi·cal** \-mi-kəl\ *adj* **1** : of or relating to the cosmos **2** : VAST, GRAND **3** : of or relating to spiritual or metaphysical ideas ⟨a ∼ thinker⟩ — **cos·mi·cal·ly** *adv*

cosmic ray *n* : a stream of very penetrating atomic nuclei that enter the earth's atmosphere from outer space

cos·mog·o·ny \käz-'mä-gə-nē\ *n, pl* **-nies** : the origin or creation of the world or universe

cos·mol·o·gy \-'mä-lə-jē\ *n, pl* **-gies** : a branch of astronomy dealing with the origin and structure of the universe — **cos·mo·log·i·cal** \ˌkäz-mə-'lä-ji-kəl\ *adj* — **cos·mol·o·gist** \käz-'mä-lə-jist\ *n*

cos·mo·naut \'käz-mə-ˌnȯt\ *n* : a Soviet or Russian astronaut

cos·mo·pol·i·tan \ˌkäz-mə-'pä-lə-tən\ *adj* : belonging to all the world : not local

♦ **Synonyms** UNIVERSAL, GLOBAL, CATHOLIC — **cosmopolitan** *n*

cos·mos \'käz-məs, 1 *also* -ˌmōs, -ˌmäs\ *n* **1** : UNIVERSE **2** : a tall garden herb related to the daisies

co·spon·sor \'kō-ˌspän-sər, -'spän-\ *n* : a joint sponsor — **cosponsor** *vb*

Cos·sack \'kä-ˌsak, -sək\ *n* [Pol & Ukrainian *kozak*, of Turkic origin] : a member of one of several autonomous communities drawn from various ethnic groups in southern Russia; *also* : a mounted soldier from one of these communities

¹**cost** \'kȯst\ *n* **1** : the amount paid or charged for something : PRICE **2** : the loss or penalty incurred in gaining something **3** *pl* : expenses incurred in a lawsuit — **at all costs** : regardless of consequences ⟨win *at all costs*⟩

²**cost** *vb* **cost; cost·ing** **1** : to require a specified amount in payment **2** : to cause to pay, suffer, or lose

co-star \'kō-ˌstär\ *n* : one of two leading players in a motion picture or play — **co-star** *vb*

cos·tive \'käs-tiv\ *adj* : affected with or causing constipation

cost·ly \'kȯst-lē\ *adj* **cost·li·er; -est** **1** : of great cost or value ⟨∼ gems⟩ **2** : done at great expense or sacrifice ⟨a ∼ error⟩ ♦ **Synonyms** DEAR, VALUABLE, EXPENSIVE — **cost·li·ness** *n*

cos·tume \'käs-ˌtüm, -ˌtyüm\ *n* [F, fr. It, custom, dress, fr. L *consuetudo* custom] **1** : the style of attire characteristic of a period or country **2** : a special or fancy dress ⟨Halloween ∼s⟩ — **cos·tum·er** \'käs-ˌtü-mər, -ˌtyü-\ *n*

costume jewelry *n* : inexpensive jewelry

cosy *chiefly Brit var of* COZY

¹**cot** \'kät\ *n* : a small house : COTTAGE

²**cot** *n* : a small often collapsible bed

cote \'kōt, 'kät\ *n* : a small shed or coop (as for sheep or doves)

co·te·rie \'kō-tə-ˌrē, ˌkō-tə-'rē\ *n* [F] : an intimate often exclusive group of persons with a common interest

co·ter·mi·nous \ˌkō-'tər-mə-nəs\ *adj* : having the same scope or duration

co·til·lion \kō-'til-yən, kə-\ n : a formal ball

cot·tage \'kä-tij\ n : a small house — **cot·tag·er** n

cottage cheese n : a soft uncured cheese made from soured skim milk

cot·tar *or* **cot·ter** \'kä-tər\ n : a peasant or farm laborer occupying a cottage and often a small holding

cotter pin n : a metal strip bent into a pin whose ends can be spread apart after insertion through a hole or slot

cot·ton \'kä-tᵊn\ n [ME coton, fr. AF cotun, fr. Ar quṭun] **1** : a soft fibrous usu. white substance composed of hairs attached to the seeds of various tropical plants related to the mallow; also : this plant **2** : thread or cloth made of cotton — **cot·tony** adj

cotton candy n : a candy made of spun sugar

cot·ton·mouth \'kä-tᵊn-ˌmauth\ n : WATER MOCCASIN

cot·ton·seed n : the seed of the cotton plant yielding a protein-rich meal and a fatty oil (**cottonseed oil**) used esp. in cooking

cot·ton·tail \-ˌtāl\ n : a No. American rabbit with a white-tufted tail

cot·ton·wood \-ˌwud\ n : a poplar having seeds with cottony hairs

cot·y·le·don \ˌkä-tə-'lē-dᵊn\ n : the first leaf or one of the first pair or whorl of leaves developed by a seed plant

¹couch \'kauch\ vb **1** : to lie or place on a couch **2** : to phrase in a specified manner ⟨proposals ~ed in jargon⟩

²couch n : a piece of furniture (as a bed or sofa) that one can sit or lie on

couch·ant \'kau-chənt\ adj : lying down with the head raised ⟨coat of arms with lion ~⟩

couch potato n : one who spends a great deal of time watching television

cou·gar \'kü-gər\ n, pl **cougars** also **cougar** [F couguar, fr. NL cuguacuarana, modif. of Tupi (a Brazilian Indian language) stwasuarána, fr. stwásu deer + -ran resembling] : a large powerful tawny brown wild American cat

cough \'kof\ vb : to force air from the lungs with short sharp noises; also : to expel by coughing — **cough** n

could \kəd, 'kud\ past of CAN — used as an auxiliary in the past or as a polite or less forceful alternative to can in the present

cou·lee \'kü-lē\ n **1** : a small stream **2** : a dry streambed **3** : GULLY

cou·lomb \'kü-ˌläm, -ˌlōm\ n : a unit of electric charge equal to the electricity transferred by a current of one ampere in one second

coun·cil \'kaun-səl\ n **1** : ASSEMBLY, MEETING **2** : an official body of lawmakers ⟨city ~⟩ — **coun·cil·lor** or **coun·cil·or** \-sə-lər\ n — **coun·cil·man** \-səl-mən\ n — **coun·cil·wom·an** \-ˌwu-mən\ n

¹coun·sel \'kaun-səl\ n **1** : ADVICE **2** : a plan of action **3** : deliberation together **4** pl **counsel** : LAWYER

²counsel vb **-seled** or **-selled; -sel·ing** or **-sel·ling 1** : ADVISE **2** : CONSULT

coun·sel·or or **coun·sel·lor** \'kaun-sə-lər\ n **1** : ADVISER **2** : LAWYER **3** : one who has supervisory duties at a summer camp

¹count \'kaunt\ vb [ME, fr. AF cunter, counter, fr. L computare, fr. com- with + putare to consider] **1** : to name or indicate one by one in order to find the total number **2** : to recite numbers in order **3** : CONSIDER, ACCOUNT **4** : RELY ⟨you can ~ on me⟩ **5** : to be of value or account ⟨~s toward your grade⟩ — **count·able** adj

²count n **1** : the act of counting; also : the total obtained by counting **2** : a particular charge in an indictment or legal declaration ⟨two ~s of murder⟩

³count n [ME, fr. AF cunte, fr. LL comes, fr. L, companion, one of the imperial court, fr. com- with + ire to go] : a European nobleman whose rank corresponds to that of a British earl

count·down \'kaunt-ˌdaun\ n : a backward counting in fixed units (as seconds) to indicate the time remaining before an event (as the launching of a rocket) — **count down** vb

¹coun·te·nance \'kaun-tᵊn-əns\ n **1** : the human face **2** : FAVOR, APPROVAL

²countenance vb **-nanced; -nanc·ing** : SANCTION, TOLERATE

¹count·er \'kaun-tər\ n **1** : a piece (as of metal or plastic) used in reckoning or in games **2** : a level surface over which business is transacted, food is served, or work is conducted

²count·er n : a device for recording a number or amount

³coun·ter vb : to act in opposition to

⁴coun·ter adv : in an opposite direction : CONTRARY

⁵coun·ter n **1** : OPPOSITE, CONTRARY **2** : an answering or offsetting force or blow

⁶coun·ter adj : CONTRARY, OPPOSITE

coun·ter·act \ˌkaun-tər-'akt\ vb : to lessen the force of : OFFSET — **coun·ter·ac·tive** \-'ak-tiv\ adj

coun·ter·at·tack \'kaun-tər-ə-ˌtak\ n : an attack made to oppose an enemy's attack — **counterattack** vb

¹coun·ter·bal·ance \'kaun-tər-ˌba-ləns\ n : a weight or influence that balances another

²counterbalance \ˌkaun-tər-'ba-ləns\ vb : to oppose with equal weight or influence

coun·ter·claim \'kaun-tər-ˌklām\ n : an opposing claim esp. in law

coun·ter·clock·wise \ˌkaun-tər-'kläk-ˌwiz\ adv : in a direction opposite to that in which the hands of a clock rotate — **counterclockwise** adj

coun·ter·cul·ture \'kaun-tər-ˌkəl-chər\ n : a culture with values and mores that run counter to those of established society

coun·ter·es·pi·o·nage \ˌkaun-tər-'es-pē-ə-ˌnäzh, -nij\ n : activities intended to discover and defeat enemy espionage

¹coun·ter·feit \'kaün-tər-ˌfit\ adj : SHAM, SPURIOUS; also ♦ FORGED ⟨~ money⟩

²counterfeit vb 1 : to copy or imitate in order to deceive 2 : PRETEND, FEIGN — coun·ter·feit·er n

³counterfeit n : something counterfeit : FORGERY ♦ Synonyms FRAUD, SHAM, FAKE, IMPOSTURE, DECEIT, DECEPTION

coun·ter·in·sur·gen·cy \ˌkaün-tər-in-ˈsər-jən-sē\ n : military activity designed to deal with insurgents

coun·ter·in·tel·li·gence \-in-ˈte-lə-jəns\ n : organized activities of an intelligence service designed to counter the activities of an enemy's intelligence service

coun·ter·in·tu·i·tive \-in-ˈtü-ə-tiv, -ˈtyü-\ adj : contrary to what would intuitively be expected

count·er·man \'kaün-tər-ˌman, -mən\ n : one who tends a counter

coun·ter·mand \'kaünt-ər-ˌmand\ vb : to withdraw (an order already given) by a contrary order

coun·ter·mea·sure \-ˌme-zhər\ n : an action or device designed to counter another

coun·ter·of·fen·sive \-ə-ˌfen-siv\ n : a large-scale counterattack

coun·ter·pane \-ˌpān\ n : BEDSPREAD

coun·ter·part \-ˌpärt\ n : a person or thing very closely like or corresponding to another person or thing

coun·ter·point \-ˌpóint\ n : music in which one melody is accompanied by one or more other melodies all woven into a harmonious whole

coun·ter·poise \-ˌpóiz\ n : COUNTERBAL-ANCE

coun·ter·rev·o·lu·tion \ˌkaün-tər-ˌre-və-ˈlü-shən\ n : a revolution opposed to a current or earlier one — coun·ter·rev·o·lu·tion·ary \-shə-ˌner-ē\ adj or n

coun·ter·sign \'kaün-tər-ˌsīn\ n 1 : a confirmatory signature added to a writing already signed by another person 2 : a military secret signal that must be given by a person who wishes to pass a guard — countersign vb

coun·ter·sink \-ˌsiŋk\ vb -sunk \-ˌsəŋk\; -sink·ing 1 : to form a funnel-shaped enlargement at the outer end of a drilled hole 2 : to set the head of (as a screw) at or below the surface — countersink n

coun·ter·spy \-ˌspī\ n : a spy engaged in counterespionage

coun·ter·ten·or \-ˌte-nər\ n : a tenor with an unusually high range

coun·ter·vail \ˌkaün-tər-ˈvāl\ vb : COUNTERACT

coun·ter·weight \'kaün-tər-ˌwāt\ n : COUNTERBALANCE

count·ess \'kaün-təs\ n 1 : the wife or widow of a count or an earl 2 : a woman holding the rank of a count or an earl in her own right

count·ing·house \'kaün-tiŋ-ˌhaüs\ n : a building or office for keeping books and conducting business

count·less \'kaünt-ləs\ adj : INNUMERABLE

coun·tri·fied also coun·try·fied \'kən-tri-ˌfīd\ adj 1 : RURAL, RUSTIC 2 : UNSO-PHISTICATED 3 : played or sung in the manner of country music

¹coun·try \'kən-trē\ n, pl countries [ME contree, fr. AF cuntree, contré, fr. ML contrata, fr. L contra against, on the opposite side] 1 : REGION, DISTRICT 2 : FATHERLAND 3 : a nation or its territory 4 : rural regions as opposed to towns and cities 5 : COUNTRY MUSIC

²country adj 1 : RURAL 2 : of or relating to country music ⟨a ~ singer⟩

country and western n : COUNTRY MUSIC

country club n : a suburban club for social life and recreation; esp : one having a golf course — country-club adj

coun·try·dance \'kən-trē-ˌdans\ n : an English dance in which partners face each other esp. in rows

coun·try·man \'kən-trē-mən, 2 often -ˌman\ n 1 : an inhabitant of a specified country 2 : COMPATRIOT 3 : one raised or living in the country : RUSTIC

country music n : music derived from or imitating the folk style of the southern U.S. or of the Western cowboy

coun·try·side \'kən-trē-ˌsīd\ n : a rural area or its people

coun·ty \'kaün-tē\ n, pl counties 1 : the domain of a count 2 : a territorial division of a country or state for purposes of local government

coup \'kü\ n, pl coups \'küz\ [F, blow, stroke] 1 : a brilliant sudden stroke or stratagem 2 : COUP D'ÉTAT

coup de grace \ˌkü-də-ˈgräs\ n, pl coups de grace \same⟩ [F coup de grâce, lit., stroke of mercy] : DEATHBLOW; also : a final decisive stroke or event

coup d'état \ˌkü-dā-ˈtä\ n, pl coups d'état \same or -ˈtäz\ [F, lit., stroke of state] : a sudden violent overthrow of a government by a small group

cou·pé or coupe \kü-ˈpā, 2 often 'küp\ [F coupé, fr. couper to cut] 1 : a closed horse-drawn carriage for two persons inside with an outside seat for the driver 2 usu coupe : a 2-door automobile with an enclosed body

¹cou·ple \'kə-pəl\ n 1 : two persons married, engaged, or otherwise romantically paired 2 : PAIR 3 : BOND, TIE 4 : an indefinite small number : FEW ⟨a ~ of days ago⟩

²couple vb cou·pled; cou·pling : to link together

cou·plet \'kə-plət\ n : two successive rhyming lines of verse

cou·pling \'kə-pliŋ (usual for 2), -pə-liŋ\ n 1 : CONNECTION 2 : a device for connecting two parts or things

cou·pon \'kü-ˌpän, 'kyü-\ n 1 : a statement attached to a bond showing interest due and designed to be cut off and presented for payment 2 : a form surrendered in order to obtain an article, service, or accommodation 3 : a printed document or slip used to submit orders or inquiries or to obtain a discount on merchandise or services

cour·age \'kər-ij\ n : ability to conquer fear or despair : BRAVERY, VALOR —

cou·ra·geous \kə-ˈrā-jəs\ *adj* — **cou·ra·geous·ly** *adv*

cou·ri·er \ˈku̇r-ē-ər, ˈkər-ē-\ *n* : one who bears messages or information esp. for the diplomatic or military services

¹course \ˈkȯrs\ *n* **1** : PROGRESS, PASSAGE; *also* : direction of progress **2** : the ground or path over which something moves **3** : method of procedure : CONDUCT, BE-HAVIOR **4** : an ordered series of acts or proceedings : sequence of events **5** : a series of instruction periods dealing with a subject **6** : the series of studies leading to graduation from a school or college **7** : the part of a meal served at one time — **of course** : as might be expected

²course *vb* **coursed; cours·ing 1** : to hunt with dogs **2** : to run or go speedily

cours·er \ˈkȯr-sər\ *n* : a swift or spirited horse

¹court \ˈkȯrt\ *n* [ME, fr. AF, fr. L *cohort-, cohors* enclosure, group, retinue, cohort] **1** : the residence of a sovereign or similar dignitary **2** : a sovereign's formal assembly of officials and advisers as a governing power **3** : an assembly of the retinue of a sovereign **4** : an open space enclosed by a building or buildings **5** : a space walled or marked off for playing a game (as tennis or basketball) **6** : the place where justice is administered; *also* : a judicial body or a meeting of a judicial body **7** : attention intended to win favor

²court *vb* **1** : to try to gain the favor of **2** : WOO **3** : ATTRACT, TEMPT

cour·te·ous \ˈkər-tē-əs\ *adj* : marked by respect for others : CIVIL, POLITE — **cour·te·ous·ly** *adv*

cour·te·san \ˈkȯr-tə-zən, -ˌzan\ *n* : PROSTITUTE

cour·te·sy \ˈkər-tə-sē\ *n, pl* **-sies 1** : courteous behavior : POLITENESS **2** : a favor courteously performed

court·house \ˈkȯrt-ˌhau̇s\ *n* : a building in which courts of law are held or county offices are located

court·ier \ˈkȯr-tē-ər\ *n* : a person in attendance at a royal court

court·ly \ˈkȯrt-lē\ *adj* **court·li·er; -est** : REFINED, ELEGANT, POLITE ♦ *Synonyms* GALLANT, GRACIOUS — **court·li·ness** *n*

court–mar·tial \ˈkȯrt-ˌmär-shəl\ *n, pl* **courts–martial** : a military or naval court for trial of offenses against military or naval law; *also* : a trial by this court — **court–martial** *vb*

court·room \-ˌrüm, -ˌru̇m\ *n* : a room in which a court of law is held

court·ship \-ˌship\ *n* : the act of courting : WOOING

court·yard \-ˌyärd\ *n* : an enclosure next to a building

cous·cous \ˈküs-ˌküs\ *n* : a No. African dish of steamed semolina usu. served with meat or vegetables; *also* : the semolina itself

cous·in \ˈkə-zən\ *n* [ME *cosin,* fr. AF, fr. L *consobrinus,* fr. *com-* with + *sobrinus* second cousin, fr. *soror* sister] : a child of one's uncle or aunt

cou·ture \kü-ˈtu̇r, -ˈtu̇r\ *n* [F] : the business of designing fashionable custom-made women's clothing; *also* : the designers and establishments engaged in this business

cou·tu·ri·er \kü-ˈtu̇r-ē-ər, -ē-ˌā\ *n* [F, dressmaker] : the owner of an establishment engaged in couture

cove \ˈkōv\ *n* : a small sheltered inlet or bay

co·ven \ˈkə-vən\ *n* : an assembly or band of witches

cov·e·nant \ˈkə-və-nənt\ *n* : a formal binding agreement : COMPACT — **cov·e·nant** \-nənt, -ˌnant\ *vb*

¹cov·er \ˈkə-vər\ *vb* **1** : to bring or hold within range of a firearm **2** : PROTECT, GUARD ⟨∼ed by insurance⟩ ⟨∼ third base⟩ **3** : HIDE, CONCEAL ⟨∼ up a crime⟩ **4** : to place something over or upon **5** : INCLUDE, COMPRISE **6** : to have as one's field of activity ⟨one salesman ∼s the state⟩ **7** : to buy (stocks) in order to have them for delivery on a previous short sale

²cover *n* **1** : something that protects or shelters **2** : LID, TOP **3** : CASE, BINDING **4** : TABLECLOTH **5** : a cloth used on a bed **6** : SCREEN, DISGUISE **7** : an envelope or wrapper for mail

cov·er·age \ˈkə-və-rij\ *n* **1** : the act or fact of covering **2** : the total group covered : SCOPE

cov·er·all \ˈkə-vər-ˌȯl\ *n* : a one-piece outer garment worn to protect one's clothes — usu. used in pl.

cover charge *n* : a charge made by a restaurant or nightclub in addition to the charge for food and drink

cover crop *n* : a crop planted to prevent soil erosion and to provide humus

cov·er·let \ˈkə-vər-lət\ *n* : BEDSPREAD

¹co·vert \ˈkō-ˌvərt, ˈkə-vərt\ *adj* **1** : HIDDEN, SECRET ⟨a ∼ operation⟩ **2** : SHELTERED — **co·vert·ly** *adv*

²co·vert \ˈkə-vərt, ˈkō-\ *n* **1** : a secret or sheltered place; *esp* : a thicket sheltering game **2** : a feather covering the bases of the quills of the wings and tail of a bird

cover–up \ˈkə-vər-ˌəp\ *n* **1** : a device for masking or concealing **2** : a usu. concerted effort to keep an illegal or unethical act or situation from being made public

cov·et \ˈkə-vət\ *vb* : to desire enviously (what belongs to another) — **cov·et·ous** *adj* — **cov·et·ous·ness** *n*

cov·ey \ˈkə-vē\ *n, pl* **coveys** [ME, fr. AF *covee* sitting (of a hen), fr. *cover* to sit on, brood over, fr. L *cubare* to lie] **1** : a bird with her brood of young **2** : a small flock (as of quail) **3** : GROUP 1

¹cow \ˈkau̇\ *n* **1** : the mature female of cattle or of an animal (as the moose, elephant, or whale) of which the male is called *bull* **2** : any domestic bovine animal irrespective of sex or age

²cow *vb* : INTIMIDATE, DAUNT, OVERAWE

cow·ard \ˈkau̇-(ə)rd\ *n* [ME, fr. AF *cuard,* fr. *cue, coe* tail, fr. L *cauda*] : one who lacks courage or shows shameful fear or timidity — **coward** *adj* — **cow·ard·ice** \ˈkau̇-ər-dəs\ *n* — **cow·ard·ly** *adv or adj*

cow·bird \'kaù-ˌbərd\ *n* : a small No. American blackbird that lays its eggs in the nests of other birds

cow·boy \-ˌbòi\ *n* : one (as a mounted ranch hand) who tends cattle or horses

cow·er \'kaù-(ə)r\ *vb* : to shrink or crouch down from fear or cold : QUAIL

cow·girl \'kaù-ˌgərl\ *n* : a girl or woman who tends cattle or horses

cow·hand \'kaù-ˌhand\ *n* : COWBOY

cow·herd \-ˌhərd\ *n* : one who tends cows

cow·hide \-ˌhīd\ *n* **1** : the hide of a cow; *also* : leather made from it **2** : a coarse whip of braided rawhide

cowl \'kaù-(ə)l\ *n* : a monk's hood

cow·lick \'kaù-ˌlik\ *n* : a turned-up tuft of hair that resists control

cowl·ing \'kaù-liŋ\ *n* : a usu. metal covering for the engine or another part of an airplane

cow·man \'kaù-mən, -ˌman\ *n* : COWBOY; *also* : a cattle owner or rancher

co·work·er \'kō-ˌwər-kər\ *n* : a fellow worker

cow·poke \'kaù-ˌpōk\ *n* : COWBOY

cow pony *n* : a strong and agile horse trained for herding cattle

cow·pox \'kaù-ˌpäks\ *n* : a mild disease of the cow that when communicated to humans protects against smallpox

cow·punch·er \-ˌpən-chər\ *n* : COWBOY

cow·slip \'kaù-ˌslip\ *n* **1** : a yellow-flowered European primrose **2** : MARSH MARIGOLD

cox·comb \'käks-ˌkōm\ *n* : a conceited foolish person : FOP

cox·swain \'käk-sən, -ˌswän\ *n* : the steersman of a ship's boat or a racing shell

coy \'kòi\ *adj* [ME, quiet, shy, fr. AF *quei, quoi, koi* quiet, fr. L *quietus*] **1** : BASHFUL, SHY **2** : marked by artful playfulness : COQUETTISH — **coy·ly** *adv* — **coy·ness** *n*

coy·ote \'kī-ˌōt, kī-'ō-tē\ *n, pl* **coyotes** *or* **coyote** : a mammal of No. America smaller than the related wolves

coy·pu \'kòi-pü\ *n* : NUTRIA 2

coz·en \'kə-z⁰n\ *vb* : CHEAT, DEFRAUD — **coz·en·age** \-ij\ *n* — **coz·en·er** *n*

¹co·zy \'kō-zē\ *adj* **co·zi·er; -est** : SNUG, COMFORTABLE ⟨a ∼ cabin⟩ — **co·zi·ly** \-zə-lē\ *adv* — **co·zi·ness** \-zē-nəs\ *n*

²cozy *n, pl* **co·zies** : a padded covering for a vessel (as a teapot) to keep the contents hot

cp *abbr* **1** compare **2** coupon

CP *abbr* **1** cerebral palsy **2** chemically pure **3** command post **4** communist party

CPA *abbr* certified public accountant

CPB *abbr* Corporation for Public Broadcasting

cpd *abbr* compound

CPI *abbr* consumer price index

Cpl *abbr* corporal

CPO *abbr* chief petty officer

CPOM *abbr* master chief petty officer

CPOS *abbr* senior chief petty officer

CPR *abbr* cardiopulmonary resuscitation

CPT *abbr* captain

CPU \ˌsē-ˌpē-'yü\ *n* [central *processing*

unit] : the part of a computer that performs its basic operations, manages its components, and exchanges data with memory or peripherals

CQ *abbr* charge of quarters

cr *abbr* credit; creditor

Cr *symbol* chromium

¹crab \'krab\ *n, pl* **crabs** *also* **crab** : any of various crustaceans with a short broad shell and small abdomen

²crab *n* : an ill-natured person

³crab *vb* **crabbed; crab·bing** : COMPLAIN, GROUSE

crab apple *n* : a small often highly colored sour apple; *also* : a tree that produces crab apples

crab·bed \'kra-bəd\ *adj* **1** : MOROSE, PEEVISH ⟨a ∼ view of human nature⟩ **2** : CRAMPED, IRREGULAR ⟨∼ handwriting⟩

crab·by \'kra-bē\ *adj* **crab·bi·er; -est** : CROSS, ILL-NATURED

crab·grass \'krab-ˌgras\ *n* : a weedy grass with creeping or sprawling stems that root freely at the nodes

crab louse *n* : a louse infesting the pubic region in humans

¹crack \'krak\ *vb* **1** : to break with a sharp sudden sound **2** : to break with or without completely separating into parts **3** : to fail in tone or become harsh ⟨her voice ∼ed⟩ **4** : to subject (as a petroleum oil) to heat for breaking down into lighter products (as gasoline)

²crack *n* **1** : a sudden sharp noise **2** : a witty or sharp remark **3** : a narrow break or opening : FISSURE **4** : a sharp blow **5** : ATTEMPT, TRY **6** : a potent form of cocaine in small chips used illicitly for smoking

³crack *adj* : extremely proficient

crack·down \'krak-ˌdaùn\ *n* : an act or instance of taking positive disciplinary action ⟨a ∼ on gambling⟩ — **crack down** *vb*

crack·er \'kra-kər\ *n* **1** : FIRECRACKER **2** : a dry thin crispy baked bread product made of flour and water

crack·er·jack \-ˌjak\ *adj* : EXCELLENT, GREAT ⟨a ∼ salesperson⟩ — **crackerjack** *n*

crack·le \'kra-kəl\ *vb* **crack·led; crack·ling** **1** : to make small sharp snapping noises **2** : to develop fine cracks in a surface — **crackle** *n* — **crack·ly** \-k(ə-)lē\ *adj*

crack·pot \'krak-ˌpät\ *n* : an eccentric person

crack-up \'krak-ˌəp\ *n* : CRASH, WRECK; *also* : BREAKDOWN

crack up *vb* **1** : PRAISE ⟨isn't all it's *cracked up* to be⟩ **2** : to laugh or cause to laugh out loud **3** : to crash a vehicle

¹cra·dle \'krā-d⁰l\ *n* **1** : a baby's bed or cot **2** : a framework or support (as for a telephone receiver) **3** : INFANCY ⟨from ∼ to the grave⟩ **4** : a place of origin

²cradle *vb* **cra·dled; cra·dling** **1** : to place in or as if in a cradle **2** : SHELTER, REAR

craft \'kraft\ *n* **1** : ART, SKILL; *also* : an occupation requiring special skill **2**

: CUNNING, GUILE ⟨used ~ to close the deal⟩ **3** *pl usu* **craft** : a boat esp. of small size; *also* : AIRCRAFT, SPACECRAFT

crafts·man \'krafts-mən\ *n* : a skilled artisan — **crafts·man·ship** *n*

crafty \'kraf-tē\ *adj* **craft·i·er; -est** : CUNNING, DECEITFUL, SUBTLE — **craft·i·ly** \-tə-lē\ *adv* — **craft·i·ness** \-tē-nəs\ *n*

crag \'krag\ *n* : a steep rugged cliff or rock — **crag·gy** *adj*

cram \'kram\ *vb* **crammed; cram·ming 1** : to pack in tight : JAM **2** : to eat greedily **3** : to study rapidly under pressure for an examination

¹**cramp** \'kramp\ *n* **1** : a sudden painful contraction of muscle **2** : sharp abdominal pain — usu. used in pl.

²**cramp** *vb* **1** : to affect with a cramp or cramps **2** : to restrain from free action : HAMPER

cran·ber·ry \'kran-,ber-ē, -bə-rē\ *n* : the red acid berry of any of several trailing plants related to the heaths; *also* : one of these plants

¹**crane** \'krān\ *n* **1** : any of a family of tall wading birds related to the rails; *also* : any of several herons **2** : a machine for lifting and carrying heavy objects

²**crane** *vb* **craned; cran·ing** : to stretch one's neck to see better

crane fly *n* : any of a family of long-legged slender dipteran flies that resemble large mosquitoes but do not bite

cranial nerve *n* : any of the nerves that arise in pairs from the lower surface of the brain and pass through openings in the skull to the periphery of the body

cra·ni·um \'krā-nē-əm\ *n, pl* **-ni·ums** or **-nia** \-ə\ : SKULL; *esp* : the part enclosing the brain — **cra·ni·al** \-əl\ *adj*

¹**crank** \'krank\ *n* **1** : a bent part of an axle or shaft or an arm at right angles to the end of a shaft by which circular motion is imparted to or received from it **2** : an eccentric person **3** : a bad-tempered person : GROUCH

²**crank** *vb* : to start or operate by or as if by turning a crank

crank·case \'krank-,kās\ *n* : the housing of a crankshaft

crank out *vb* : to produce in a mechanical manner

crank·shaft \'krank-,shaft\ *n* : a shaft turning or driven by a crank

cranky \'kran-kē\ *adj* **crank·i·er; -est 1** : IRRITABLE **2** : operating uncertainly or imperfectly ⟨a ~ old tractor⟩

cran·ny \'kra-nē\ *n, pl* **crannies** : CREVICE, CHINK

craps \'kraps\ *n* : a gambling game played with two dice

crap·shoot·er \'krap-,shü-tər\ *n* : a person who plays craps

¹**crash** \'krash\ *vb* **1** : to break noisily : SMASH **2** : to damage an airplane in landing **3** : to enter or attend without invitation or without paying ⟨~ a party⟩ **4** : to suffer a sudden major failure usu. with loss of data ⟨my computer ~ed⟩

²**crash** *n* **1** : a loud sound (as of things smashing) **2** : an instance of crashing ⟨a plane ~⟩; *also* : COLLISION **3** : a sudden failure (as of a business)

³**crash** *adj* : marked by concentrated effort over the shortest possible time ⟨a ~ diet⟩

⁴**crash** *n* : coarse linen fabric used for towels and draperies

crash–land \'krash-'land\ *vb* : to land an aircraft or spacecraft under emergency conditions usu. with damage to the craft — **crash landing** *n*

crass \'kras\ *adj* : GROSS, INSENSITIVE ⟨~ ignorance⟩ — **crass·ly** *adv* — **crass·ness** *n*

crate \'krāt\ *n* : a container often of wooden slats — **crate** *vb*

cra·ter \'krā-tər\ *n* [L, mixing bowl, crater, fr. Gk *kratēr*, fr. *kerannynai* to mix] **1** : the depression around the opening of a volcano **2** : a depression formed by the impact of a meteorite or by the explosion of a bomb or shell

cra·vat \krə-'vat\ *n* : NECKTIE

crave \'krāv\ *vb* **craved; crav·ing 1** : to ask for earnestly : BEG **2** : to long for : DESIRE

cra·ven \'krā-vən\ *adj* : COWARDLY — **craven** *n* — **cra·ven·ly** *adv*

crav·ing \'krā-vin\ *n* : an urgent or abnormal desire

craw·fish \'kro-,fish\ *n* **1** : CRAYFISH 1 **2** : SPINY LOBSTER

¹**crawl** \'krol\ *vb* **1** : to move slowly by drawing the body along the ground **2** : to advance feebly, cautiously, or slowly **3** : to be swarming with or feel as if swarming with creeping things ⟨a place ~ing with ants⟩ ⟨her flesh ~ed⟩

²**crawl** *n* **1** : a very slow pace **2** : a prone speed swimming stroke

cray·fish \'krā-,fish\ *n* **1** : any of numerous freshwater crustaceans usu. much smaller than the related lobsters **2** : SPINY LOBSTER

cray·on \'krā-,än, -ən\ *n* : a stick of chalk or wax used for writing, drawing, or coloring; *also* : a drawing made with such material — **crayon** *vb*

¹**craze** \'krāz\ *vb* **crazed; craz·ing** [ME *crasen* to crush, craze, of Scand origin] : to make or become insane

²**craze** *n* : FAD, MANIA

cra·zy \'krā-zē\ *adj* **cra·zi·er; -est 1** : mentally disordered : INSANE **2** : wildly impractical ⟨a ~ plan⟩; *also* : ERRATIC ⟨~ drivers⟩ — **cra·zi·ly** \-zə-lē\ *adv* — **cra·zi·ness** \-zē-nəs\ *n*

CRC *abbr* Civil Rights Commission

creak \'krēk\ *vb* : to make a prolonged squeaking or grating sound — **creak** *n* — **creaky** *adj*

¹**cream** \'krēm\ *n* **1** : the yellowish fat-rich part of milk **2** : a thick smooth sauce, confection, or cosmetic **3** : the choicest part **4** : a pale yellow color — **creamy** *adj*

²**cream** *vb* **1** : to prepare with a cream sauce **2** : to beat or blend into creamy consistency **3** : to defeat decisively

cream cheese *n* : a cheese made from whole milk enriched with cream

cream·ery \'krē-mə-rē\ *n, pl* **-er·ies** : an

establishment where butter and cheese are made or milk and cream are prepared for sale

crease \'krēs\ n : a mark or line made by or as if by folding — **crease** vb

cre·ate \krē-'āt\ vb **cre·at·ed; cre·at·ing** : to bring into being : cause to exist : MAKE, PRODUCE — **cre·a·tive** \-'ā-tiv\ adj — **cre·a·tive·ness** n — **cre·a·tiv·i·ty** \ˌkrē-(ˌ)ā-'ti-və-tē\ n

cre·a·tion \krē-'ā-shən\ n 1 : the act of creating or producing ⟨∼ of the world⟩ 2 : something that is created 3 : all created things : WORLD

cre·a·tion·ism \krē-'ā-shə-ˌni-zəm\ n : a doctrine or theory holding that matter, the various forms of life, and the world were created by God out of nothing — **cre·a·tion·ist** \-nist\ n or adj

cre·a·tor \krē-'ā-tər\ n 1 : one that creates : MAKER, AUTHOR 2 cap : GOD 1

crea·ture \'krē-chər\ n : a lower animal; also : a human being

crèche \'kresh\ n [F, manger, crib, fr. OF creche, of Gmc origin] : a representation of the Nativity scene

cre·dence \'krē-dᵊns\ n : mental acceptance as true or real

cre·den·tial \kri-'den-chəl\ n : something that gives a basis for credit or confidence

cre·den·za \kri-'den-zə\ n [It, lit., belief, confidence] : a sideboard, buffet, or bookcase usu. without legs

cred·i·ble \'kre-də-bəl\ adj : TRUSTWORTHY, BELIEVABLE — **cred·i·bil·i·ty** \ˌkre-də-'bi-lə-tē\ n — **cred·i·bly** \'kre-də-blē\ adv

¹**cred·it** \'kre-dət\ n [MF, fr. It credito, fr. L creditum something entrusted to another, loan, fr. credere to believe, entrust] 1 : the balance (as in a bank) in a person's favor 2 : time given for payment for goods sold on trust 3 : an accounting entry of payment received 4 : BELIEF, FAITH 5 : financial trustworthiness 6 : ESTEEM 7 : a source of honor or distinction 8 : a unit of academic work

²**credit** vb 1 : BELIEVE 2 : to give credit to ⟨the players all —ed their coach⟩

cred·it·able \'kre-də-tə-bəl\ adj : worthy of esteem or praise ⟨did a ∼ job⟩ — **cred·it·ably** \-blē\ adv

credit card n : a card authorizing purchases on credit

cred·i·tor \'kre-də-tər\ n : a person to whom money is owed

cre·do \'krē-dō, 'krā-\ n, pl **credos** [ME, fr. L, I believe] : CREED

cred·u·lous \'kre-jə-ləs\ adj : inclined to believe esp. on slight evidence — **cre·du·li·ty** \kri-'dü-lə-tē, -'dyü-\ n — **cred·u·lous·ly** adv

Cree \'krē\ n, pl **Cree** or **Crees** : a member of an American Indian people of Canada

creed \'krēd\ n [ME crede, fr. OE crēda, fr. L credo I believe, first word of the Apostles' and Nicene Creeds] : a statement of the essential beliefs of a religious faith

creek \'krēk, 'krik\ n 1 chiefly Brit : a small inlet 2 : a stream smaller than a river and larger than a brook

Creek \'krēk\ n : a member of an American Indian people of Alabama, Georgia, and Florida

creel \'krēl\ n : a wicker basket esp. for carrying fish

creep \'krēp\ vb **crept** \'krept\; **creep·ing** 1 : CRAWL 2 : to feel as though insects were crawling on the skin 3 : to spread or grow over a surface like ivy — **creep** n — **creep·er** n

creep·ing \'krē-piŋ\ adj : developing or advancing by imperceptible degrees

creepy \'krē-pē\ adj **creep·i·er; -est** : having or producing a nervous shivery fear

cre·mate \'krē-ˌmāt\ vb **cre·mat·ed; cre·mat·ing** : to reduce (a dead body) to ashes with fire — **cre·ma·tion** \kri-'mā-shən\ n

cre·ma·to·ry \'krē-mə-ˌtȯr-ē, 'krē-\ n, pl **-ries** : a furnace for cremating; also : a structure containing such a furnace

crème or **creme** \'krem, 'krēm\ n, pl **crèmes** or **cremes** \same or 'kremz, 'krēmz\ [F, lit., cream] : a sweet liqueur

cren·el·lat·ed or **cren·el·at·ed** \'kre-nə-lā-təd\ adj : having battlements — **cren·el·la·tion** \ˌkre-nə-'lā-shən\ n

Cre·ole \'krē-ˌōl\ n 1 : a descendant of early French or Spanish settlers of the U.S. Gulf states preserving their speech and culture; also : a person of mixed French or Spanish and black descent speaking a dialect of French or Spanish 2 not cap : a language that has evolved from a pidgin but serves as the native language of a speech community

cre·o·sote \'krē-ə-ˌsōt\ n : an oily liquid obtained by distillation of coal tar and used in preserving wood

crepe or **crêpe** \'krāp\ n : a light crinkled fabric of any of various fibers

crêpe su·zette \ˌkrāp-sü-'zet\ n, pl **crêpes suzette** \same or 'krāps-\ or **crêpe suzettes** \-sü-'zets\ often cap S : a thin folded or rolled pancake in a hot orange-butter sauce that is sprinkled with a liqueur and set ablaze for serving

cre·pus·cu·lar \kri-'pəs-kyə-lər\ adj 1 : of, relating to, or resembling twilight 2 : occurring or active during twilight ⟨∼ insects⟩

cre·scen·do \krə-'shen-dō\ adv or adj [It] : increasing in loudness — used as a direction in music — **crescendo** n

cres·cent \'kre-sᵊnt\ n [ME cressant, fr. AF fr. prp. of crestre to grow, increase, fr. L crescere] : the moon at any stage between new moon and first quarter and between last quarter and new moon; also : something shaped like the figure of the crescent moon with a convex and a concave edge — **cres·cen·tic** \kre-'sen-tik\ adj

cress \'kres\ n : any of several salad plants related to the mustards

¹**crest** \'krest\ n 1 : a tuft or process on the head of an animal (as a bird) 2 : a heraldic device 3 : an upper part, edge,

or limit ⟨the ∼ of a hill⟩ — **crest·ed** \'kres-təd\ adj — **crest·less** adj

²crest vb **1** : CROWN **2** : to reach the crest of **3** : to rise to a crest

crest·fall·en \'krest-ˌfȯ-lən\ adj : DISPIRITED, DEJECTED

Cre·ta·ceous \kri-'tā-shəs\ adj : of, relating to, or being the latest period of the Mesozoic era marked by great increase in flowering plants, diversification of mammals, and extinction of the dinosaurs — **Cretaceous** n

cre·tin \'krē-tᵊn\ n [F crétin, fr. F dial. cretin, lit., wretch, innocent victim, fr. L christianus Christian] **1** : one affected with cretinism **2** : a stupid person

cre·tin·ism \-ˌi-zəm\ n : a usu. congenital abnormal condition characterized by physical stunting and mental retardation

cre·tonne \'krē-ˌtän\ n : a strong unglazed cotton cloth for curtains and upholstery

cre·vasse \kri-'vas\ n : a deep fissure esp. in a glacier

crev·ice \'kre-vəs\ n : a narrow fissure

¹crew \'krü\ chiefly Brit past of CROW

²crew n [ME crue, fr. MF, a reinforcement, lit., increase, fr. croistre to grow, fr. L crescere] **1** : a body of people trained to work together for certain purposes **2** : a group of people who operate a ship, train, aircraft, or spacecraft **3** : the rowers and coxswain of a racing shell; also : the sport of rowing engaged in by a crew — **crew·man** \-mən\ n

crew cut n : a very short bristly haircut

crew·el \'krü-əl\ n : slackly twisted worsted yarn used for embroidery — **crew·el·work** \-ˌwərk\ n

¹crib \'krib\ n **1** : a manger for feeding animals **2** : a child's bedstead with high sides **3** : a building or bin for storage (as of grain) **4** : something used for cheating in an exam

²crib vb **cribbed; crib·bing 1** : to put in a crib **2** : STEAL, PLAGIARIZE — **crib·ber** n

crib·bage \'kri-bij\ n : a card game usu. played by two players and scored on a board (**cribbage board**)

crib death n : SUDDEN INFANT DEATH SYNDROME

crick \'krik\ n : a painful spasm of muscles (as of the neck)

¹crick·et \'kri-kət\ n [ME criket, fr. AF, of imit. origin] : any of a family of leaping insects related to the grasshoppers and noted for the chirping noises of the male

²cricket n [MF criquet goal stake in a bowling game] : a game played with a bat and ball by two teams on a field centering upon two wickets each defended by a batsman

cri·er \'krī-(ə)r\ n : one who calls out proclamations and announcements

crime \'krīm\ n : a serious offense against the public law

¹crim·i·nal \'kri-mə-nᵊl\ adj **1** : involving or being a crime **2** : relating to crime or its punishment — **crim·i·nal·i·ty** \ˌkri-mə-'na-lə-tē\ n — **crim·i·nal·ly** adv

²criminal n : one who has committed a crime

crim·i·nol·o·gy \ˌkri-mə-'nä-lə-jē\ n : the scientific study of crime and criminals — **crim·i·no·log·i·cal** \-mə-nə-'lä-ji-kəl\ adj — **crim·i·nol·o·gist** \ˌkri-mə-'nä-lə-jist\ n

¹crimp \'krimp\ vb : to cause to become crinkled, wavy, or bent

²crimp n : something (as a curl in hair) produced by or as if by crimping

crim·son \'krim-zən\ n : a deep purplish red color — **crimson** adj

cringe \'krinj\ vb **cringed; cring·ing** : to shrink in fear : WINCE, COWER

crin·kle \'kriŋ-kəl\ vb **crin·kled; crin·kling** : to form many short bends or curves; also : WRINKLE — **crinkle** n — **crin·kly** \-kə-lē\ adj

crin·o·line \'kri-nə-lən\ n **1** : an open-weave cloth used for stiffening and lining **2** : a full stiff skirt or underskirt made of crinoline

¹crip·ple \'kri-pəl\ n : one that is disabled or deficient in a specified manner ⟨a social ∼⟩

²cripple vb **crip·pled; crip·pling 1** : to make lame **2** : to make useless or imperfect — **crip·pler** \'kri-p(ə-)lər\ n

cri·sis \'krī-səs\ n, pl **cri·ses** \-ˌsēz\ [ME, fr. L, fr. Gk krisis, lit., decision, fr. krinein to decide] **1** : the turning point for better or worse in an acute disease or fever **2** : a decisive or critical moment

crisp \'krisp\ adj **1** : CURLY, WAVY **2** : BRITTLE ⟨a ∼ potato chip⟩ **3** : FIRM, FRESH ⟨∼ lettuce⟩ **4** : being sharp and clear ⟨a ∼ photo⟩ **5** : LIVELY, SPARKLING **6** : FROSTY, SNAPPY; also : INVIGORATING — **crisp** vb — **crisp·ly** adv — **crisp·ness** n — **crispy** adj

¹criss·cross \'kris-ˌkrȯs\ vb **1** : to mark with crossed lines **2** : to go or pass back and forth

²crisscross adj : marked or characterized by crisscrossing — **crisscross** adv

³crisscross n : a pattern formed by crossed lines

crit abbr critical; criticism

cri·te·ri·on \krī-'tir-ē-ən\ n, pl **-ria** \-ē-ə\ : a standard on which a judgment may be based

crit·ic \'kri-tik\ n **1** : a person who judges literary or artistic works **2** : one inclined to find fault

crit·i·cal \'kri-ti-kəl\ adj **1** : being or relating to a condition or disease involving danger of death ⟨∼ care⟩ **2** : being a crisis **3** : inclined to criticize **4** : relating to criticism or critics **5** : requiring careful judgment ⟨∼ thinking⟩ — **crit·i·cal·ly** \-k(ə-)lē\ adv

crit·i·cise Brit var of CRITICIZE

crit·i·cism \'kri-tə-ˌsi-zəm\ n **1** : the act of criticizing; esp : CENSURE **2** : a judgment or review **3** : the art of judging works of literature or art

crit·i·cize \'kri-tə-ˌsīz\ vb **-cized; -ciz·ing 1** : to judge as a critic : EVALUATE **2** : to find fault : express criticism ◆ **Synonyms** BLAME, CENSURE, CONDEMN

cri·tique \krə-'tēk\ *n* : a critical estimate or discussion

crit·ter \'kri-tər\ *n* : CREATURE

croak \'krōk\ *n* : a hoarse harsh cry (as of a frog) — **croak** *vb*

croak·er \'krō-kər\ *n* **1** : an animal that croaks **2** : a fish that produces croaking or grunting noises

Croat \'krō-ˌat\ *n* : CROATIAN

Cro·atian \krō-'ā-shən\ *n* **1** : a native or inhabitant of Croatia **2** : a Slavic language spoken by Croatians — **Croatian** *adj*

cro·chet \krō-'shā\ *n* : needlework done with a single thread and hooked needle — **crochet** *vb*

crock \'kräk\ *n* : a thick earthenware pot or jar

crock·ery \'krä-kə-rē\ *n* : EARTHENWARE

croc·o·dile \'krä-kə-ˌdī(-ə)l\ *n* [ME & L; ME *cocodrille*, fr. AF, fr. ML *cocodrillus*, alter. of L *crocodilus*, fr. Gk *krokodilos* lizard, crocodile, fr. *krokē* shingle, pebble + *drillos* worm] : any of several thick-skinned long-bodied carnivorous reptiles of tropical and subtropical waters

cro·cus \'krō-kəs\ *n*, *pl* **cro·cus·es** *also* **crocus** *or* **cro·ci** \-ˌkī\ : any of a large genus of low herbs related to the irises and having brightly colored flowers borne singly in early spring

Crohn's disease \'krōnz\ *n* : a chronic inflammatory disease of the gastrointestinal tract and esp. the ileum

crois·sant \krȯ-'sänt, krwä-'säⁿ\ *n*, *pl* **croissants** *same or* -'sänts, -'säⁿz\ : a rich crescent-shaped roll

Cro–Ma·gnon \krō-'mag-nən, -'man-yən\ *n* : a hominid of a tall erect race known from skeletal remains found in southern France and usu. classified as the same species as present-day humans — **Cro-Magnon** *adj*

crone \'krōn\ *n* : HAG

cro·ny \'krō-nē\ *n*, *pl* **cronies** : a close friend esp. of long standing

¹crook \'krȯk\ *vb* : to curve or bend sharply

²crook *n* **1** : a bent or curved implement **2** : a bent or curved part; *also* : BEND, CURVE **3** : SWINDLER, THIEF

crook·ed \'krȯ-kəd\ *adj* **1** : having a crook : BENT, CURVED **2** : DISHONEST — **crook·ed·ly** *adv* — **crook·ed·ness** *n*

croon \'krün\ *vb* : to sing or hum in a gentle murmuring voice — **croon·er** *n*

¹crop \'kräp\ *n* **1** : the handle of a whip; *also* : a short riding whip **2** : a pouch in the throat of many birds and insects where food is received **3** : something (as a plant product) that can be harvested; *also* : the yield at harvest

²crop *vb* **cropped; crop·ping 1** : to remove the tips of : cut off short; *also* : TRIM **2** : to feed on by cropping **3** : to devote (land) to crops **4** : to appear unexpectedly ⟨new problems have *cropped* up⟩

crop duster *n* : a person who uses an airplane to spray crops with insecticidal dusts; *also* : an airplane so used

crop·land \-ˌland\ *n* : land devoted to the production of plant crops

crop·per \'krä-pər\ *n* : a raiser of crops; *esp* : SHARECROPPER

cro·quet \krō-'kā\ *n* : a game in which mallets are used to drive wooden balls through a series of wickets set out on a lawn

cro·quette \krō-'ket\ *n* [F] : a small often rounded mass of minced meat, fish, or vegetables fried in deep fat

cro·sier *or* **cro·zier** \'krō-zhər\ *n* : a staff carried by bishops and abbots

¹cross \'krȯs\ *n* **1** : a structure consisting of an upright beam and a crossbar used esp. by the ancient Romans for execution **2** : a figure of the cross on which Christ was crucified used as a Christian symbol **3** : a hybridizing of unlike individuals or strains; *also* : a product of this **4** : a punch delivered with a circular motion over an opponent's lead

²cross *vb* **1** : to lie or place across; *also* : INTERSECT **2** : to cancel by marking a cross on or by lining through **3** : THWART, OBSTRUCT **4** : to go or extend across : TRAVERSE **5** : HYBRIDIZE **6** : to meet and pass on the way ⟨our letters ~*ed* in the mail⟩

³cross *adj* **1** : lying across **2** : CONTRARY, OPPOSED **3** : marked by bad temper **4** : HYBRID — **cross·ly** *adv*

cross·bar \'krȯs-ˌbär\ *n* : a transverse bar or piece

cross·bow \-ˌbō\ *n* : a short bow mounted crosswise at the end of a wooden stock that shoots short arrows

cross·breed \'krȯs-ˌbrēd, -'brēd\ *vb* **-bred** \-'bred\; **-breed·ing** : HYBRIDIZE

cross–coun·try \-'kən-trē\ *adj* **1** : extending or moving across a country **2** : proceeding over the countryside (as fields and woods) and not by roads **3** : of or relating to racing or skiing over the countryside instead of over a track or run — **cross–country** *adv*

cross·cur·rent \-'kər-ənt\ *n* **1** : a current running counter to another **2** : a conflicting tendency — usu. used in pl.

¹cross·cut \-ˌkət\ *vb* : to cut or saw crosswise esp. of the grain of wood

²crosscut *adj* **1** : made or used for crosscutting ⟨a ~ saw⟩ **2** : cut across the grain

³crosscut *n* : something that cuts through transversely

cross–ex·am·ine \ˌkrō-sig-'za-mən\ *vb* : to examine with questions to check the answers to previous questions — **cross-ex·am·i·na·tion** \-ˌza-mə-'nā-shən\ *n* — **cross–ex·am·in·er** *n*

cross–eyed \'krȯ-ˌsīd\ *adj* : having one or both eyes turned inward toward the nose

cross–fer·til·i·za·tion \ˌfər-tə-lə-'zā-shən\ *n* **1** : fertilization between sex cells produced by separate individuals or sometimes by individuals of different kinds; *also* : CROSS-POLLINATION **2** : a broadening or productive interchange (as between cultures) — **cross–fer·til·ize** \-'fərt-ə-ˌlīz\ *vb*

cross fire n 1 : crossing lines of fire in combat 2 : rapid or angry interchange

cross·hair \'krȯs-ˌher\ n : a fine wire or thread in the eyepiece of an optical instrument used as a reference line

cross·hatch \'krȯs-ˌhach\ vb : to mark with two series of parallel lines that intersect — **cross·hatch·ing** n

cross·ing \'krȯ-siŋ\ n 1 : a place or structure for crossing something (as a river) 2 : a point of intersection (as of a street and a railroad track)

cross·over \'krȯs-ˌō-vər\ n 1 : CROSSING 2 : a member of a political party who votes in the primary of the other party 3 : a broadening of the popular appeal of an artist (as a musician) by a change in the artist's style, genre, or medium 4 : an instance of breaking into another category

cross over vb : to achieve broader popularity by a change of medium or style

cross·piece \'krȯs-ˌpēs\ n : a horizontal member

cross·pol·li·na·tion \ˌkrȯs-ˌpä-lə-'nā-shən\ n : transfer of pollen from one flower to the stigma of another — **cross·pol·li·nate** \'krȯs-'pä-lə-ˌnāt\ vb

cross·pur·pose \'krȯs-'pər-pəs\ n : a purpose contrary to another purpose ⟨working at ∼s⟩

cross·ques·tion \-'kwes-chən\ vb : CROSS-EXAMINE — **cross·question** n

cross·re·fer \ˌkrȯs-ri-'fər\ vb : to refer by a notation or direction from one place to another (as in a book or list) — **cross·ref·er·ence** \'krȯs-'re-frəns\ n

cross·road \'krȯs-ˌrōd\ n 1 : a road that crosses a main road or runs between main roads 2 : a place where roads meet — usu. used in pl. 3 : a crucial point where a decision must be made — usu. used in pl.

cross section n 1 : a section cut across something; also : a representation made by or as if by such cutting 2 : a number of persons or things selected from a group that show the general nature of the whole group — **cross·sec·tion·al** adj

cross·walk \'krȯs-ˌwȯk\ n : a marked path for pedestrians crossing a street

cross·ways \-ˌwāz\ adv : CROSSWISE

cross·wind \-ˌwind\ n : a wind not parallel to a course (as of an airplane)

cross·wise \-ˌwīz\ adv : so as to cross something : ACROSS — **crosswise** adj

cross·word \'krȯs-ˌwərd\ n : a puzzle in which words are put into a pattern of numbered squares in answer to clues

cros·ti·ni \krȯ-'stē-nē\ n pl : small slices of toasted bread served with a topping

crotch \'kräch\ n : an angle or area formed by the parting of two legs, branches, or members

crotch·et \'krä-chət\ n : an odd notion : WHIM — **crotch·ety** adj

crouch \'kraůch\ vb 1 : to stoop or bend low 2 : CRINGE, COWER — **crouch** n

croup \'krüp\ n : laryngitis esp. of infants marked by a hoarse ringing cough and difficult breathing — **croupy** adj

crou·pi·er \'krü-pē-ər, -pē-ˌā\ n [F, lit.,

rider on the rump of a horse, fr. *croupe* rump] : an employee of a gambling casino who collects and pays bets at a gaming table

crou·ton \'krü-ˌtän\ n [F *croûton*, dim. of *croûte* crust] : a small cube of bread toasted or fried crisp

¹**crow** \'krō\ n 1 : any of various large glossy black birds related to the jays 2 cap : a member of an American Indian people of a region in Montana and Wyoming; also : the language of the Crow people

²**crow** vb 1 : to make the loud shrill sound characteristic of the cock 2 : to utter a sound expressive of pleasure 3 : EXULT, GLOAT; also : BRAG, BOAST

³**crow** n : the cry of the cock

crow·bar \'krō-ˌbär\ n : a metal bar usu. wedge-shaped at the end for use as a pry or lever

¹**crowd** \'kraůd\ vb 1 : to press close 2 : to collect in numbers : THRONG 3 : CRAM, STUFF ⟨a box ∼ed with toys⟩

²**crowd** n : a large number of people gathered together at random : THRONG

¹**crown** \'kraůn\ n 1 : a mark of victory or honor; esp : the title of a champion in a sport 2 : a royal headdress 3 : the top of the head; also : the part of a hat that covers the top of the head 4 : the highest part (as of a tree or tooth) 5 often cap : sovereign power; also : MONARCH 6 — : a formerly used British silver coin — **crowned** \'kraůnd\ adj

²**crown** vb 1 : to place a crown on 2 : HONOR 3 : TOP, SURMOUNT 4 : to fit (a tooth) with an artificial crown

crown vetch n : a Eurasian leguminous herb with umbels of pink-and-white flowers and sharp-angled pods

crow's-foot \'krōz-ˌfůt\ n, pl **crow's-feet** \-ˌfēt\ : any of the wrinkles around the outer corners of the eyes — usu. used in pl.

crow's nest n : a partly enclosed platform high on a ship's mast for use as a lookout

crozier var of CROSIER

¹**CRT** \ˌsē-(ˌ)är-'tē\ n, pl **CRTs** or **CRT's** : CATHODE-RAY TUBE; also : a display device incorporating a cathode-ray tube

²**CRT** abbr carrier route

cru·cial \'krü-shəl\ adj 1 : DECISIVE ⟨a ∼ step⟩; also : IMPORTANT, SIGNIFICANT ⟨a ∼ question⟩

cru·ci·ate \'krü-shē-ˌāt\ adj : CRUCIFORM

cru·ci·ble \'krü-sə-bəl\ n : a heat-resistant container in which material can be subjected to great heat

cru·ci·fix \'krü-sə-ˌfiks\ n : a representation of Christ on the cross

cru·ci·fix·ion \ˌkrü-sə-'fik-shən\ n 1 cap : the crucifying of Christ 2 : the act of crucifying

cru·ci·form \'krü-sə-ˌfȯrm\ adj : shaped like a cross

cru·ci·fy \'krü-sə-ˌfī\ vb **-fied; -fy·ing** 1 : to put to death by nailing or binding the hands and feet to a cross 2 : MORTIFY 1 3 : TORTURE, PERSECUTE

¹**crude** \'krüd\ adj **crud·er; crud·est** 1

: not refined : RAW ⟨~ oil⟩ ⟨~ statistics⟩ 2 : lacking grace, taste, tact, or polish : RUDE — **crude·ly** adv — **crude·ness** n — **cru·di·ty** \'krü-də-tē\ n

²**crude** n : unrefined petroleum

cru·el \'krü-əl\ adj **cru·el·er** or **cru·el·ler; cru·el·est** or **cru·el·lest** [ME, fr. AF, fr. L crudelis, fr. crudus crude] : causing pain and suffering to others : MERCILESS — **cru·el·ly** adv — **cru·el·ty** \-tē\ n

cru·et \'krü-ət\ n : a small usu. glass bottle for vinegar, oil, or sauce

cruise \'krüz\ vb **cruised; cruis·ing** [D kruisen to make a cross, cruise] 1 : to sail about touching at a series of ports 2 : to travel for enjoyment 3 : to travel about the streets at random 4 : to travel at the most efficient operating speed ⟨the cruising speed of an airplane⟩ 5 : SURF 2 — **cruise** n

cruis·er \'krü-zər\ n 1 : SQUAD CAR 2 : a large fast moderately armored and gunned warship 3 : a motorboat equipped for living aboard

cruis·er·weight \-,wāt\ n : a boxer weighing no more than 190 pounds

crul·ler \'krə-lər\ n 1 : a small sweet cake in the form of a twisted strip fried in deep fat 2 Northern & Midland : an unraised doughnut

¹**crumb** \'krəm\ n : a small fragment

²**crumb** vb 1 : to break into crumbs 2 : to cover with crumbs

crum·ble \'krəm-bəl\ vb **crum·bled; crum·bling** : to break into small pieces : DISINTEGRATE — **crum·bly** adj

crum·my also **crumby** \'krə-mē\ adj **crum·mi·er** also **crumb·i·er; -est** : very poor or inferior : LOUSY

crum·pet \'krəm-pət\ n : a small round unsweetened bread cooked on a griddle

crum·ple \'krəm-pəl\ vb **crum·pled; crum·pling** 1 : to crush together : RUMPLE 2 : COLLAPSE

¹**crunch** \'krənch\ vb 1 : to chew with a grinding noise; also : to grind or press with a crushing noise

²**crunch** n 1 : an act of or a sound made by crunching 2 : a tight or critical situation — **crunchy** adj

cru·sade \krü-'sād\ n 1 cap : any of the expeditions in the 11th, 12th, and 13th centuries undertaken by Christian countries to take the Holy Land from the Muslims 2 : a reforming enterprise undertaken with zeal — **crusade** vb — **cru·sad·er** n

cruse \'krüz, 'krüs\ n : a jar for water or oil

¹**crush** \'krəsh\ vb 1 : to squeeze out of shape 2 : HUG, EMBRACE 3 : to grind or pound to small bits 4 : OVERWHELM, SUPPRESS

²**crush** n 1 : an act of crushing 2 : a violent crowding 3 : INFATUATION

crust \'krəst\ n 1 : the outside part of bread; also : a piece of old dry bread 2 : the cover of a pie 3 : a hard or brittle surface layer — **crust·al** adj

crus·ta·cean \,krəs-'tā-shən\ n : any of a large class of mostly aquatic arthropods

(as lobsters or crabs) having a firm crustlike shell — **crustacean** adj

crusty \'krəs-tē\ adj **crust·i·er; -est** 1 : having or being a crust 2 : CROSS, GRUMPY

crutch \'krəch\ n : a supporting device; esp : a support fitting under the armpit for use by the disabled in walking

crux \'krəks, 'krùks\ n, pl **crux·es** [L, cross, torture] 1 : a puzzling or difficult problem 2 : a crucial point

¹**cry** \'krī\ vb **cried; cry·ing** 1 : to call out : SHOUT 2 : to proclaim publicly : ADVERTISE 3 : WEEP

²**cry** n, pl **cries** 1 : a loud outcry 2 : APPEAL, ENTREATY 3 : a fit of weeping 4 : the characteristic sound uttered by an animal 5 : DISTANCE — usu. used in the phrase a far cry

cry·ba·by \'krī-,bā-bē\ n : one who cries easily or often

cryo·gen·ic \,krī-ə-'je-nik\ adj : of or relating to the production of very low temperatures; also : involving the use of a very low temperature — **cryo·gen·i·cal·ly** \-ni-k(ə-)lē\ adv

cryo·gen·ics \-niks\ n : a branch of physics that relates to the production and effects of very low temperatures

cryo·lite \'krī-ə-,līt\ n : a usu. white mineral formerly used in making aluminum

crypt \'kript\ n : a chamber wholly or partly underground

cryp·tic \'krip-tik\ adj : meant to be puzzling or mysterious ⟨~ messages⟩

cryp·to·gram \'krip-tə-,gram\ n : a communication in cipher or code

cryp·tog·ra·phy \krip-'tä-grə-fē\ n : the coding and decoding of secret messages — **cryp·tog·ra·pher** \-fər\ n

cryp·to·sys·tem \,krip-tō-'sis-təm\ n : a method for coding and decoding messages

crys·tal \'kris-t²l\ n [ME cristal, fr. AF, fr. L crystallum, fr. Gk krystallos ice, crystal] 1 : transparent quartz 2 : something resembling crystal (as in transparency); esp : a clear colorless glass of superior quality 3 : a body that is formed by solidification of a substance and has a regular repeating arrangement of atoms and often of external plane faces ⟨a salt ~⟩ 4 : the transparent cover of a watch dial

crystal clear adj : perfectly or transparently clear

crys·tal·line \'kris-tə-lən\ adj 1 : made of or resembling crystal 2 : very clear or sparkling

crys·tal·lise Brit var of CRYSTALLIZE

crys·tal·lize \'kris-tə-,līz\ vb **-lized; -liz·ing** 1 : to assume or cause to assume a crystalline form 2 : to take or cause to take a definite form ⟨publicity can ~ public opinion⟩ — **crys·tal·li·za·tion** \,kris-tə-lə-'zā-shən\ n

crys·tal·log·ra·phy \,kris-tə-'lä-grə-fē\ n : the science dealing with the forms and structures of crystals — **crys·tal·log·ra·pher** n

cs abbr case; cases

Cs symbol cesium

CS abbr 1 civil service 2 county seat

CSA *abbr* Confederate States of America

C–section \'sē-,sek-shən\ *n* : CESAREAN SECTION

CSM *abbr* command sergeant major

CST *abbr* central standard time

ct *abbr* **1** carat **2** cent **3** count **4** county **5** court

CT *abbr* **1** central time **2** Connecticut

ctn *abbr* carton

ctr *abbr* **1** center **2** counter

CT scan \'sē-'tē-\ *n* : CAT SCAN

cu *abbr* cubic

Cu *symbol* [L *cuprum*] copper

cub \'kəb\ *n* : a young individual of some animals (as a fox, bear, or lion)

Cu·ban sandwich \'kyü-bən-\ *n* : a usu. grilled and pressed sandwich served on a long split roll

cub·by·hole \'kə-bē-,hōl\ *n* : a snug place (as for storing things)

¹cube \'kyüb\ *n* **1** : a solid having 6 equal square sides **2** : the result of raising a number to the third power ⟨the ∼ of 3 is 27⟩

²cube *vb* **cubed; cub·ing 1** : to raise to the third power **2** : to form into a cube **3** : to cut into cubes

cube root *n* : a number whose cube is a given number

cu·bic \'kyü-bik\ *also* **cu·bi·cal** *adj* **1** : having the form of a cube **2** : being the volume of a cube whose edge is a specified unit **3** : having length, width, and height

cu·bi·cle \'kyü-bi-kəl\ *n* : a small separate space (as for sleeping, studying, or working)

cubic measure *n* : a unit (as cubic inch) for measuring volume — see METRIC SYSTEM table, WEIGHT table

cubic zir·co·nia \-,zər-'kō-nē-ə\ *also* **cubic zirconium** \-əm\ *n* : a synthetic gemstone resembling a diamond made from an oxide of zirconium

cub·ism \'kyü-,bi-zəm\ *n* : a style of art characterized by the abstraction of natural forms into fragmented geometric shapes — **cub·ist** \-bist\ *n or adj*

cu·bit \'kyü-bət\ *n* : an ancient unit of length equal to about 18 inches (46 centimeters)

Cub Scout *n* : a member of the program of the Boy Scouts for boys in the first through fifth grades in school

cuck·old \'kə-kəld, 'kú-\ *n* : a man whose wife is unfaithful — **cuckold** *vb*

¹cuck·oo \'kü-kü, 'kú-\ *n, pl* **cuckoos** : a largely grayish brown European bird that lays its eggs in the nests of other birds for them to hatch

²cuckoo *adj* : SILLY, FOOLISH

cu·cum·ber \'kyü-(,)kəm-bər\ *n* : the long fleshy many-seeded fruit of a vine of the gourd family that is grown as a garden vegetable; *also* : this vine

cud \'kəd\ *n* : food brought up into the mouth by some animals (as cows) from the rumen to be chewed again

cud·dle \'kə-dʰl\ *vb* **cud·dled; cud·dling** : to lie close : SNUGGLE

cud·gel \'kə-jəl\ *n* : a short heavy club — **cudgel** *vb*

¹cue \'kyü\ *n* **1** : a word, phrase, or action in a play serving as a signal for the next actor to speak or act **2** : HINT — **cue** *vb*

²cue *n* : a tapered rod for striking the balls in billiards or pool

cue ball *n* : the ball a player strikes with a cue in billiards or pool

¹cuff \'kəf\ *n* **1** : a part (as of a sleeve or glove) encircling the wrist **2** : the folded hem of a trouser leg

²cuff *vb* : to strike esp. with the open hand : SLAP

³cuff *n* : a blow with the hand esp. when open

cui·sine \kwi-'zēn\ *n* : style of cooking; *also* : the food prepared

cuke \'kyük\ *n* : CUCUMBER

cul–de–sac \,kəl-di-'sak, ,kúl-\ *n, pl* **culs–de–sac** *same or* ,kəlz-, ,külz-\ *also* **cul–de–sacs** \,kəl-də-'saks, ,kúl-\ [F, lit., bottom of the bag] : a street or passage closed at one end

cu·li·nary \'kə-lə-,ner-ē, 'kyü-\ *adj* : of or relating to the kitchen or cookery

¹cull \'kəl\ *vb* : to pick out from a group

²cull *n* : something rejected from a group or lot as worthless or inferior

cul·mi·nate \'kəl-mə-,nāt\ *vb* **-nat·ed; -nat·ing** : to reach the highest point — **cul·mi·na·tion** \,kəl-mə-'nā-shən\ *n*

cu·lotte \'kü-,lät, ,kyü-, kü-,lät, kyü-\ *n* [F, breeches, fr. dim. of *cul* backside] : a divided skirt; *also* : a garment having a divided skirt — often used in pl.

cul·pa·ble \'kəl-pə-bəl\ *adj* : deserving blame — **cul·pa·bil·i·ty** \,kəl-pə-'bi-lə-tē\ *n*

cul·prit \'kəl-prət\ *n* [AF *cul.* (abbr. of *culpable* guilty) + *prest, prit* ready (i.e., to prove it), fr. L *praestus*] : one accused or guilty of a crime

cult \'kəlt\ *n* **1** : formal religious veneration **2** : a religious system; *also* : its adherents **3** : faddish devotion; *also* : a group of persons showing such devotion — **cult·ish** \'kəl-tish\ *adj* — **cult·ist** \-tist\ *n*

cul·ti·va·ble \'kəl-tə-və-bəl\ *adj* : capable of being cultivated

cul·ti·var \'kəl-tə-,vär, -ver\ *n* : a plant variety originating and persisting under cultivation

cul·ti·vate \'kəl-tə-,vāt\ *vb* **-vat·ed; -vat·ing 1** : to prepare for the raising of crops **2** : to foster the growth of by tilling or by labor and care ⟨∼ vegetables⟩ **3** : REFINE, IMPROVE ⟨∼ the mind⟩ **4** : ENCOURAGE, FURTHER ⟨∼ the arts⟩ **5** : to seek the friendship of — **cul·ti·va·tion** \,kəl-tə-'vā-shən\ *n* — **cul·ti·va·tor** \'kəl-tə-,vā-tər\ *n*

cul·ture \'kəl-chər\ *n* **1** : TILLAGE, CULTIVATION **2** : the act of developing by education and training **3** : refinement or intellectual and artistic taste **4** : the customary beliefs, social forms, and material traits of a racial, religious, or social group — **cul·tur·al** \'kəl-chə-rəl\ *adj* — **cul·tur·al·ly** *adv* — **cul·tured** \-chərd\ *adj*

cul·vert \'kəl-vərt\ *n* : a drain crossing under a road or railroad

cum *abbr* cumulative

cum·ber \'kəm-bər\ *vb* : to weigh down : BURDEN, HINDER

cum·ber·some \'kəm-bər-səm\ *adj* : hard to handle or manage because of size or weight — **cum·ber·some·ly** *adv*

cum·brous \'kəm-brəs\ *adj* : CUMBERSOME — **cum·brous·ly** *adv* — **cum·brous·ness** *n*

cum·in \'kə-mən, 'kyü-\ *n* : the seedlike fruit of a small annual herb related to the carrot that is used as a spice; *also* : this herb

cum·mer·bund \'kə-mər-,bənd, 'kəm-bər-\ *n* [Hindi & Urdu *kamarband*, fr. Pers, fr. *kamar* waist + *band* band] : a broad sash worn as a waistband

cu·mu·la·tive \'kyü-myə-lə-tiv, -,lā-\ *adj* : increasing in force or value by successive additions

cu·mu·lo·nim·bus \,kyü-myə-lō-'nim-bəs\ *n* : an anvil-shaped cumulus cloud extending to great heights

cu·mu·lus \'kyü-myə-ləs\ *n, pl* **-li** \-,lī, -,lē\ : a dense puffy cloud having a flat base and rounded outlines

cu·ne·i·form \kyü-'nē-ə-,form\ *adj* 1 : wedge-shaped 2 : composed of wedge-shaped characters

cun·ni·lin·gus \,kə-ni-'liŋ-gəs\ *also* **cun·ni·linc·tus** \-'liŋk-təs\ *n* : oral stimulation of the vulva or clitoris

¹**cun·ning** \'kə-niŋ\ *adj* 1 : SKILLFUL, DEXTEROUS 2 : marked by wiliness and trickery ⟨~ schemes⟩ 3 : CUTE ⟨a ~ kitten⟩ — **cun·ning·ly** *adv*

²**cunning** *n* 1 : SKILL 2 : SLYNESS

¹**cup** \'kəp\ *n* 1 : a small bowl-shaped drinking vessel 2 : the contents of a cup 3 : the consecrated wine of the Communion 4 : something resembling a cup : a small bowl or hollow 5 : a half pint — **cup·ful** *n* — **cup·like** \-,līk\ *adj*

²**cup** *vb* **cupped; cup·ping** : to curve into the shape of a cup

cup·board \'kə-bərd\ *n* : a small closet with shelves for food or dishes

cup·cake \'kəp-,kāk\ *n* : a small cake baked in a cuplike mold

cu·pid \'kyü-pəd\ *n* : a winged naked figure of an infant often with a bow and arrow that represents the god Cupid

cu·pid·i·ty \kyü-'pi-də-tē\ *n, pl* **-ties** : excessive desire for money

cu·po·la \'kyü-pə-lə, -,lō\ *n* : a small structure on top of a roof or building

¹**cur** \'kər\ *n* : a mongrel dog

²**cur** *abbr* 1 currency 2 current

cu·rate \'kyür-ət\ *n* 1 : a member of the clergy who is in charge of a parish 2 : a member of the clergy who assists a rector or vicar — **cu·ra·cy** \-ə-sē\ *n*

cu·ra·tive \-ə-tiv\ *adj* : relating to or used in the cure of diseases ⟨~ therapy⟩ ⟨~ powers⟩ — **curative** *n*

cu·ra·tor \'kyür-,ā-tər, kyü-'rā-tər\ *n* : CUSTODIAN; *esp* : one in charge of a place of exhibit (as a museum or zoo)

¹**curb** \'kərb\ *n* 1 : a bit that exerts pressure on a horse's jaws 2 : CHECK, RESTRAINT 3 : a raised edging (as of stone or concrete) along a paved street

²**curb** *vb* : to hold in or back : RESTRAIN

curb·ing \'kər-biŋ\ *n* 1 : the material for a curb 2 : CURB

curd \'kərd\ *n* : the thick protein-rich part of coagulated milk

cur·dle \'kər-dᵊl\ *vb* **cur·dled; cur·dling** : to form curds; *also* : SPOIL, SOUR

¹**cure** \'kyür\ *n* 1 : spiritual care 2 : recovery or relief from disease 3 : a curative agent : REMEDY 4 : a course or period of treatment

²**cure** *vb* **cured; cur·ing** 1 : to restore to health : HEAL, REMEDY; *also* : to become cured 2 : to process for storage or use ⟨~ bacon⟩ — **cur·able** *adj*

cu·ré \kyü-'rā\ *n* [F] : a parish priest

cure–all \'kyür-,ol\ *n* : a remedy for all ills : PANACEA

cu·ret·tage \,kyür-ə-'täzh\ *n* : a surgical scraping or cleaning of a body part (as the uterus)

cur·few \'kər-,fyü\ *n* [ME, fr. AF *covrefeu*, signal given to bank the hearth fire, curfew, fr. *coverir* to cover + *fu, feu* fire, fr. L *focus* hearth] : a regulation that specified persons (as children) be off the streets at a set hour of the evening; *also* : the sounding of a signal (as a bell) at this hour

cu·ria \'kyür-ē-ə, 'kúr-\ *n, pl* **cu·ri·ae** \'kyür-ē-,ē, 'kúr-ē-,ī\ *often cap* : the body of congregations, tribunals, and offices through which the pope governs the Roman Catholic Church

cu·rie \'kyür-ē\ *n* : a unit of radioactivity equal to 37 billion disintegrations per second

cu·rio \'kyür-ē-,ō\ *n, pl* **cu·ri·os** : an object or article valued because it is strange or rare

cu·ri·ous \'kyür-ē-əs\ *adj* 1 : having a desire to investigate and learn 2 : STRANGE, UNUSUAL, ODD ⟨a ~ coincidence⟩ — **cu·ri·os·i·ty** \,kyür-ē-'ä-sə-tē\ *n* — **cu·ri·ous·ness** *n*

cu·ri·ous·ly *adv* 1 : in a curious manner 2 : as is curious

cu·ri·um \'kyür-ē-əm\ *n* : a metallic radioactive element produced artificially

¹**curl** \'kərl\ *vb* 1 : to form into ringlets 2 : CURVE, COIL — **curl·er** *n*

²**curl** *n* 1 : a lock of hair that coils : RINGLET 2 : something having a spiral or twisted form — **curly** *adj*

cur·lew \'kər-lü, 'kərl-yü\ *n, pl* **curlews** *or* **curlew** : any of various long-legged brownish birds that have a down-curved bill and are related to the sandpipers and snipes

curli·cue \'kər-li-,kyü\ *n* : a fancifully curved or spiral figure

cur·rant \'kər-ənt\ *n* 1 : a small seedless raisin 2 : the acid berry of various shrubs related to the gooseberry; *also* : this plant

cur·ren·cy \'kər-ən-sē\ *n, pl* **-cies** 1 : general use or acceptance 2 : something that is in circulation as a medium of exchange : MONEY

¹**cur·rent** \'kər-ənt\ *adj* 1 : occurring in or belonging to the present ⟨the ~ crisis⟩ 2 : used as a medium of exchange 3 : generally accepted or practiced

²**current** *n* **1** : the part of a body of fluid moving continuously in a certain direction; *also* : the swiftest part of a stream **2** : a flow of electric charge; *also* : the rate of such flow

cur·ric·u·lum \kə-'ri-kyə-ləm\ *n, pl* **-la** \-lə\ *also* **-lums** [L, running, course, fr. *currere* to run] : the courses offered by an educational institution

¹**cur·ry** \'kər-ē\ *vb* **cur·ried; cur·ry·ing** **1** : to clean the coat of (a horse) with a currycomb **2** : to treat (tanned leather) esp. by incorporating oil or grease — **curry favor** : to seek to gain favor by flattery or attention

²**cur·ry** *n, pl* **cur·ries** : a powder of pungent spices used in cooking; *also* : a food seasoned with curry

cur·ry·comb \-ˌkōm\ *n* : a comb used esp. to curry horses — **currycomb** *vb*

¹**curse** \'kərs\ *n* **1** : a prayer for harm to come upon one **2** : something that is cursed **3** : evil or misfortune coming as if in response to a curse

²**curse** *vb* **cursed; curs·ing** **1** : to call on divine power to send injury upon **2** : BLASPHEME **3** : AFFLICT ♦ *Synonyms* EXECRATE, DAMN, ANATHEMATIZE, OBJURGATE

cur·sive \'kər-siv\ *adj* : written with the strokes of the letters joined together and the angles rounded

cur·sor \'kər-sər\ *n* : a visual cue (as a pointer) on a computer screen that indicates position (as for data entry)

cur·so·ry \'kər-sə-rē\ *adj* : rapidly and often superficially done : HASTY ⟨a ∼ reading of the report⟩ — **cur·so·ri·ly** \-rə-lē\ *adv*

curt \'kərt\ *adj* : rudely short or abrupt — **curt·ly** *adv* — **curt·ness** *n*

cur·tail \(ˌ)kər-'tāl\ *vb* : to cut off the end of : SHORTEN — **cur·tail·ment** *n*

cur·tain \'kər-tᵊn\ *n* **1** : a hanging screen that can be drawn back esp. at a window **2** : the screen between the stage and auditorium of a theater — **curtain** *vb*

curt·sy *also* **curt·sey** \'kərt-sē\ *n, pl* **curt·sies** *or* **curtseys** : a courteous bow made by women chiefly by bending the knees — **curtsy** *also* **curtsey** *vb*

cur·va·ceous *also* **cur·va·cious** \ˌkər-'vā-shəs\ *adj* : having curves suggestive of a well-proportioned feminine figure

cur·va·ture \'kər-və-ˌchùr\ *n* : a measure or amount of curving : BEND

¹**curve** \'kərv\ *vb* **curved; curv·ing** : to bend from a straight line or course

²**curve** *n* **1** : a line esp. when curved **2** : something that bends or curves without angles ⟨a ∼ in the road⟩ **3** : a baseball pitch thrown so that it swerves esp. downward and to one side

cur·vet \(ˌ)kər-'vet\ *n* : a prancing leap of a horse — **curvet** *vb*

¹**cush·ion** \'kù-shən\ *n* [ME *cusshin*, fr. AF *cussin, quissin,* fr. VL **coxinus,* fr. L *coxa* hip] **1** : a soft pillow or pad to rest on or against **2** : the springy pad inside the rim of a billiard table **3** : something soft that prevents discomfort or protects against injury

²**cushion** *vb* **1** : to provide (as a seat) with a cushion **2** : to soften or lessen the force or shock of

cusp \'kəsp\ *n* : a pointed end or part (as of a tooth)

cus·pid \'kəs-pəd\ *n* : a canine tooth

cus·pi·dor \'kəs-pə-ˌdòr\ *n* : SPITTOON

cus·tard \'kəs-tərd\ *n* : a sweetened cooked mixture of milk and eggs

cus·to·di·al \ˌkəs-'tō-dē-əl\ *adj* : marked by watching and protecting rather than seeking to cure ⟨∼ care⟩

cus·to·di·an \ˌkəs-'tō-dē-ən\ *n* : one who has custody (as of a building)

cus·to·dy \'kəs-tə-dē\ *n, pl* **-dies** : immediate charge and control

¹**cus·tom** \'kəs-təm\ *n* **1** : habitual course of action : recognized usage **2** *pl* : taxes levied on imports **3** : business patronage

²**custom** *adj* **1** : made to personal order **2** : doing work only on order

cus·tom·ary \'kəs-tə-ˌmer-ē\ *adj* **1** : based on or established by custom **2** : commonly practiced or observed : HABITUAL — **cus·tom·ar·i·ly** *adv*

cus·tom—built \ˌkəs-təm-'bilt\ *adj* : built to individual order

cus·tom·er \'kəs-tə-mər\ *n* : BUYER, PURCHASER; *esp* : a regular or frequent buyer

cus·tom·house \'kəs-təm-ˌhaùs\ *n* : the building where customs are paid

cus·tom·ise *Brit var of* CUSTOMIZE

cus·tom·ize \'kəs-tə-ˌmīz\ *vb* **-ized; -iz·ing** : to build, fit, or alter according to individual specifications

cus·tom—made \ˌkəs-təm-'mād\ *adj* : made to individual order

¹**cut** \'kət\ *vb* **cut; cut·ting** **1** : to penetrate or divide with a sharp edge : CLEAVE, GASH; *also* : to experience the growth of (a tooth) through the gum **2** : to hurt the feelings of **3** : to strike sharply **4** : SHORTEN, REDUCE **5** : to remove by severing or paring **6** : INTERSECT, CROSS **7** : to divide into parts **8** : to go quickly or change direction abruptly **9** : to cause to stop

²**cut** *n* **1** : something made by cutting : GASH, CLEFT **2** : SHARE **3** : a segment or section of a meat carcass **4** : an excavated channel or roadway **5** : BAND 4 **6** : a sharp stroke or blow **7** : REDUCTION ⟨a ∼ in wages⟩ **8** : the shape or manner in which a thing is cut

cut—and—dried \ˌkət-ᵊn-'drīd\ *also* **cut—and—dry** \-'drī\ *adj* : according to a plan, set procedure, or formula

cu·ta·ne·ous \kyü-'tā-nē-əs\ *adj* : of, relating to, or affecting the skin

cut·back \'kət-ˌbak\ *n* **1** : something cut back **2** : REDUCTION

cute \'kyüt\ *adj* **cut·er; cut·est** [short for *acute*] **1** : CLEVER, SHREWD **2** : daintily attractive : PRETTY

cu·ti·cle \'kyü-ti-kəl\ *n* **1** : an outer layer (as of skin or a leaf) **2** : dead or horny epidermis esp. around a fingernail — **cu·tic·u·lar** \kyü-'ti-kyə-lər\ *adj*

cut in *vb* **1** : to thrust oneself between others **2** : to interrupt a dancing couple and take one as one's partner

cut·lass \'kət-ləs\ n : a short heavy curved sword

cut·ler \'kət-lər\ n [ME, fr. AF *cuteler*, fr. LL *cultellarius*, fr. L *cultellus* knife] : one who makes, deals in, or repairs cutlery

cut·lery \'kət-lə-rē\ n : edged or cutting tools; *esp* : implements for cutting and eating food

cut·let \'kət-lət\ n : a slice of meat (as veal) for broiling or frying

cut·off \'kət-ˌȯf\ n 1 : the channel formed when a stream cuts through the neck of an oxbow; *also* : SHORTCUT 2 : a device for cutting off 3 *pl* : shorts orig. made from jeans with the legs cut off at the knees or higher

cut·out \'kət-ˌaůt\ n : something cut out or prepared for cutting out from something else

cut out *vb* 1 : to determine or assign through necessity ⟨had her work *cut out* for her⟩ 2 : DISCONNECT 3 : to cease operating ⟨the engine *cut out*⟩ 4 : ELIMINATE ⟨*cut out* unnecessary expense⟩

cut–rate \'kət-'rāt\ *adj* : relating to or dealing in goods sold at reduced rates

cut·ter \'kə-tər\ n 1 : a tool or a machine for cutting 2 : a ship's boat for carrying stores and passengers 3 : a small armed vessel in government service 4 : a light sleigh

¹**cut·throat** \'kət-ˌthrōt\ n : MURDERER

²**cutthroat** *adj* 1 : MURDEROUS, CRUEL 2 : RUTHLESS ⟨~ competition⟩

cutthroat trout n : a large American trout with a red mark under the jaw

¹**cut·ting** \'kə-tiŋ\ n : a piece of a plant able to grow into a new plant

²**cutting** *adj* 1 : SHARP, EDGED 2 : marked by piercing cold 3 : likely to hurt the feelings : SARCASTIC ⟨a ~ remark⟩

cut·tle·fish \'kə-t⁰l-ˌfish\ n : any of various marine mollusks having eight arms and two usu. longer tentacles and an internal shell (**cut·tle·bone** \-ˌbōn\) composed of calcium compounds

cut–up \'kət-ˌəp\ n : a person who clowns or acts boisterously — **cut up** *vb*

cut·worm \-ˌwərm\ n : any of various smooth-bodied moth larvae that feed on plants at night

cw *abbr* clockwise

CWO *abbr* 1 cash with order 2 chief warrant officer

cwt *abbr* hundredweight

-cy \sē\ n *suffix* 1 : action : practice ⟨mendicancy⟩ 2 : rank : office ⟨chaplaincy⟩ 3 : body : class ⟨constituency⟩ 4 : state : quality ⟨accuracy⟩

cy·an \'sī-ˌan, -ən\ n : a greenish blue color

cy·a·nide \'sī-ə-ˌnīd, -nəd\ n : a poisonous compound of carbon and nitrogen with another element (as potassium)

cy·ber \'sī-bər\ *adj* : of, relating to, or involving computers or computer networks

cyber- *comb form* : computer : computer network

cy·ber·bul·ly·ing \'sī-bər-ˌbů-lē-iŋ, -ˌbə-\ n : the electronic posting of mean-spirited messages about a person

cy·ber·ca·fe \'sī-bər-ka-ˌfā\ n : a small restaurant offering use of computers with Internet access

cy·ber·net·ics \ˌsī-bər-'ne-tiks\ n : the science of communication and control theory that is concerned esp. with the comparative study of automatic control systems — **cy·ber·net·ic** *adj*

cy·ber·punk \'sī-bər-ˌpəŋk\ n 1 : science fiction dealing with computer-dominated future societies 2 : HACKER 3

cy·ber·sex \'sī-bər-ˌseks\ n 1 : online sex-oriented conversations 2 : sex-oriented material available on a computer

cy·ber·space \'sī-bər-ˌspās\ n : the online world of the Internet

cy·ber·ter·ror·ism \-ˌter-ər-ˌi-zəm\ n : terrorist activities intended to damage or disrupt computer systems

cy·cla·men \'sī-klə-mən\ n : any of a genus of plants related to the primroses and having showy nodding flowers

¹**cy·cle** \'sī-kəl\ n 1 : a period of time occupied by a series of events that repeat themselves regularly and in the same order 2 : a recurring round of operations or events 3 : one complete occurrence of a periodic process (as a vibration or current alternation) 4 : a circular or spiral arrangement 5 : a long period of time : AGE 6 : BICYCLE 7 : MOTORCYCLE — **cy·clic** \'sī-klik, 'sī-\ *or* **cy·cli·cal** \klik-kəl\ *adj* — **cy·cli·cal·ly** \-k(ə-)lē\ *also* **cyclic·ly** *adv*

²**cy·cle** \'sī-kəl\ *vb* **cy·cled; cy·cling** : to ride a cycle — **cy·clist** \'sī-klist, -kə-list\ n

cy·clone \'sī-ˌklōn\ n 1 : a storm or system of winds that rotates about a center of low atmospheric pressure and advances at 20 to 30 miles (about 30 to 50 kilometers) an hour 2 : TORNADO — **cy·clon·ic** \sī-'klä-nik\ *adj*

cy·clo·pe·dia *also* **cy·clo·pae·dia** \ˌsī-klə-'pē-dē-ə\ n : ENCYCLOPEDIA

cy·clo·tron \'sī-klə-ˌträn\ n : a device for giving high speed to charged particles by magnetic and electric fields

cy·der *Brit var of* CIDER

cyg·net \'sig-nət\ n : a young swan

cyl *abbr* cylinder

cyl·in·der \'si-lən-dər\ n : the solid figure formed by turning a rectangle about one side as an axis; *also* : a body or space of this form ⟨an engine ~⟩ ⟨a bullet in the ~ of a revolver⟩ — **cy·lin·dri·cal** \sə-'lin-dri-kəl\ *adj*

cym·bal \'sim-bəl\ n : a concave brass plate that produces a brilliant clashing sound

cyn·ic \'si-nik\ n : one who attributes all actions to selfish motives — **cyn·i·cal** \-ni-kəl\ *adj* — **cyn·i·cal·ly** \-k(ə-)lē\ *adv* — **cyn·i·cism** \-nə-ˌsi-zəm\ n

cy·no·sure \'sī-nə-ˌshůr, 'si-\ n [MF & L; MF, fr. L, Ursa Minor, guide, fr. L *cynosura* Ursa Minor, fr. Gk *kynosoura*, fr. *kynos oura*, lit., dog's tail] : a center of attraction

CYO *abbr* Catholic Youth Organization

cy·pher *chiefly Brit var of* CIPHER

cy·press \'sī-prəs\ n 1 : any of a genus of scaly-leaved evergreen trees and shrubs 2 : BALD CYPRESS 3 : the wood of a cypress

cyst \'sist\ n : an abnormal closed bodily sac usu. containing liquid — **cys·tic** \'sis-tik\ adj

cystic fibrosis n : a common hereditary disease marked esp. by deficiency of pancreatic enzymes, by respiratory symptoms, and by excessive loss of salt in the sweat

cy·tol·o·gy \sī-'tä-lə-jē\ n : a branch of biology dealing with cells — **cy·to·log·i·cal** \,sī-tə-'lä-ji-kəl\ or **cy·to·log·ic** \-jik\ adj — **cy·tol·o·gist** \sī-'tä-lə-jist\ n

cy·to·plasm \'sī-tə-,pla-zəm\ n : the protoplasm of a cell that lies external to the nucleus — **cy·to·plas·mic** \,sī-tə-'plaz-mik\ adj

cy·to·sine \'sī-tə-,sēn\ n : a chemical base that is a pyrimidine coding genetic information in DNA and RNA

CZ abbr 1 Canal Zone 2 cubic zirconia

czar also **tsar** or **tzar** \'zär, 'tsär\ n [NL, fr. Russ tsar'; ultim. fr. L Caesar Caesar] : the ruler of Russia until 1917; also : one having great authority — **czar·ist** also **tsar·ist** or **tzarist** \-ist\ n or adj

cza·ri·na \zä-'rē-nə\ n : the wife of a czar

Czech \'chek\ n 1 : a native or inhabitant of Czechoslovakia or the Czech Republic 2 : the language of the Czechs — **Czech** adj

¹**d** \'dē\ n, pl **d's** or **ds** \'dēz\ often cap 1 : the 4th letter of the English alphabet 2 : a grade rating a student's work as poor 3 : DEFENSE

²**d** abbr, often cap 1 date 2 daughter 3 day 4 dead 5 deceased 6 degree 7 Democrat 8 [L denarius, denarii] penny; pence 9 depart; departure 10 diameter

D symbol deuterium

DA abbr 1 deposit account 2 district attorney 3 don't answer

¹**dab** \'dab\ n 1 : a sudden blow or thrust : POKE; also : PECK 2 : a gentle touch or stroke : PAT

²**dab** vb **dabbed; dab·bing** 1 : to strike or touch gently : PAT 2 : to apply lightly or irregularly : DAUB — **dab·ber** n

³**dab** n 1 : DAUB 2 : a small amount

dab·ble \'da-bəl\ vb **dab·bled; dab·bling** 1 : to wet by splashing : SPATTER 2 : to paddle or play in or as if in water 3 : to work or involve oneself without serious effort — **dab·bler** n

da ca·po \dä-'kä-(,)pō\ adv or adj [It] : from the beginning — used as a direction in music to repeat

dace \'dās\ n, pl **dace** : any of various small No. American freshwater fishes related to the carp

da·cha \'dä-chə\ n [Russ] : a Russian country house

dachs·hund \'däks-,hunt\ n [G, fr. Dachs badger + Hund dog] : any of a breed of long-bodied short-legged dogs of German origin

dac·tyl \'dak-t³l\ n [ME dactile, fr. L dactylus, fr. Gk daktylos, lit., finger; fr. the fact that the three syllables have the first one longest like the joints of the finger] : a metrical foot of one accented syllable followed by two unaccented syllables — **dac·tyl·ic** \dak-'ti-lik\ adj or n

dad \'dad\ n : FATHER 1

Da·da \'dä-(,)dä\ n : a movement in art and literature based on deliberate irrationality and negation of traditional artistic values — **da·da·ism** \-,i-zəm\ n, often cap — **da·da·ist** \-,ist\ n or adj, often cap

dad·dy \'da-dē\ n, pl **daddies** : FATHER 1

dad·dy long·legs \,da-dē-'lȯn-,legz\ n, pl **daddy longlegs** : any of an order of arachnids resembling the true spiders but having small rounded bodies and long slender legs

daemon var of DEMON

daf·fo·dil \'da-fə-,dil\ n : any of various bulbous herbs with usu. large flowers having a trumpetlike center

daf·fy \'da-fē\ adj **daf·fi·er; -est** : DAFT

daft \'daft\ adj : FOOLISH; also : INSANE — **daft·ness** n

dag abbr dekagram

dag·ger \'da-gər\ n 1 : a sharp pointed knife for stabbing 2 : a character † used as a reference mark or to indicate a death date

da·guerre·o·type \də-'ger-(ē-)ə-,tīp\ n : an early photograph produced on a silver or a silver-covered copper plate

dahl·ia \'dal-yə, 'däl-\ n : any of a genus of tuberous herbs related to the daisies and having showy flowers

¹**dai·ly** \'dā-lē\ adj 1 : occurring, done, or used every day or every weekday 2 : of or relating to every day ⟨~ visitors⟩ 3 : computed in terms of one day ⟨~ wages⟩ ♦ **Synonyms** DIURNAL, QUOTIDIAN — **dai·li·ness** \-lē-nəs\ n — **daily** adv

²**daily** n, pl **dailies** : a newspaper published every weekday

daily double n : a system of betting on races in which the bettor must pick the winners of two stipulated races in order to win

¹**dain·ty** \'dān-tē\ n, pl **dainties** [ME deinte high esteem, delight, fr. AF deinté, fr. L dignitas dignity, worth] : something delicious or pleasing to the taste : DELICACY

²**dainty** adj **dain·ti·er; -est** 1 : pleasing to the taste 2 : delicately pretty 3 : having or showing delicate taste; also : FASTIDIOUS ♦ **Synonyms** CHOICE, DELICATE, EXQUISITE, RARE, RECHERCHÉ — **dain·ti·ly** \-tǝ-lē\ adv — **dain·ti·ness** \-tē-nəs\ n

dai·qui·ri \'da-kə-rē, 'dī-\ n [Daiquirí, Cuba] : a cocktail made usu. of rum, lime juice, and sugar

dairy \'der-ē\ *n, pl* **dair·ies** [ME *deyerie,* fr. *deye* dairymaid, fr. OE *dǣge* kneader of bread] **1** : CREAMERY **2** : a farm specializing in milk production

dairy·ing \'der-ē-iŋ\ *n* : the business of operating a dairy

dairy·maid \-ˌmād\ *n* : a woman employed in a dairy

dairy·man \-mən, -ˌman\ *n* : a person who operates a dairy farm or works in a dairy

da·is \'dā-əs\ *n* : a raised platform usu. above the floor of a hall or large room

dai·sy \'dā-zē\ *n, pl* **daisies** [ME *dayeseye,* fr. OE *dægesēage,* fr. *dæg* day + *ēage* eye] : any of numerous composite plants having flower heads in which the marginal flowers resemble petals

dai·sy–chain \-ˌchān\ *vb* : to link (as computer components) together in series — **daisy chain** *n*

daisy wheel *n* : a disk with spokes bearing type that serves as the printing element of an electric typewriter or printer; *also* : a printer that uses such a disk

Da·ko·ta \də-'kō-tə\ *n, pl* **Dakotas** *also* **Dakota** : a member of an American Indian people of the northern Mississippi valley; *also* : their language

dal *abbr* dekaliter

da·la·si \dä-'lä-sē\ *n, pl* **dalasi** *or* **dalasis** — see MONEY table

dale \'dāl\ *n* : VALLEY

dal·ly \'da-lē\ *vb* **dal·lied; dal·ly·ing 1** : to act playfully; *esp* : to play amorously **2** : to waste time **3** : LINGER, DAWDLE ◆ **Synonyms** FLIRT, COQUET, TOY, TRIFLE — **dal·li·ance** \-lē-əns\ *n*

dal·ma·tian \dal-'mā-shən\ *n, often cap* : any of a breed of medium-sized dogs having a white short-haired coat with many black or brown spots

¹dam \'dam\ *n* : the female parent of an animal and esp. of a domestic animal

²dam *n* : a barrier (as across a stream) to stop the flow of water — **dam** *vb*

³dam *abbr* dekameter

¹dam·age \'da-mij\ *n* **1** : loss or harm due to injury to persons, property, or reputation **2** *pl* : compensation in money imposed by law for loss or injury ⟨bring a suit for ~s⟩

²damage *vb* **dam·aged; dam·ag·ing** : to cause damage to ⟨~ the furniture⟩

dam·a·scene \'da-mə-ˌsēn\ *vb* **-scened; -scen·ing** : to ornament (as iron or steel) with wavy patterns or with inlaid work of precious metals

dam·ask \'da-məsk\ *n* **1** : a firm lustrous reversible figured fabric used for household linen **2** : a tough steel having decorative wavy lines

dame \'dām\ *n* **1** : a woman of rank, station, or authority **2** : an elderly woman **3** : WOMAN

damn \'dam\ *vb* [ME *dampnen,* fr. AF *dampner,* fr. L *damnare,* fr. *damnum* damage, loss, fine] **1** : to condemn esp. to hell **2** : CURSE — **damned** *adj*

dam·na·ble \'dam-nə-bəl\ *adj* **1** : liable to or deserving punishment **2** : DETEST-ABLE ⟨~ weather⟩ — **dam·na·bly** \-blē\ *adv*

dam·na·tion \dam-'nā-shən\ *n* **1** : the act of damning **2** : the state of being damned

¹damp \'damp\ *n* **1** : a noxious gas **2** : MOISTURE

²damp *vb* : DAMPEN

³damp *adj* : MOIST — **damp·ness** *n*

damp·en \'dam-pən\ *vb* **1** : to check or diminish in activity or vigor ⟨~ enthusiasm⟩ **2** : to make or become damp ⟨~ a sponge⟩

damp·er \'dam-pər\ *n* **1** : a dulling or deadening influence ⟨put a ~ on the party⟩ **2** : one that damps; *esp* : a valve or movable plate (as in the flue of a stove, furnace, or fireplace) to regulate the draft

dam·sel \'dam-zəl\ *n* : MAIDEN, GIRL

dam·sel·fly \-ˌflī\ *n* : any of a group of insects that are closely related to the dragonflies but fold their wings above the body when at rest

dam·son \'dam-zən\ *n* : a plum with acid purple fruit; *also* : its fruit

Dan *abbr* Daniel

¹dance \'dans\ *vb* **danced; danc·ing 1** : to glide, step, or move through a set series of movements usu. to music **2** : to move quickly and up and down or about **3** : to perform or take part in as a dancer — **danc·er** *n*

²dance *n* **1** : an act or instance of dancing **2** : a social gathering for dancing **3** : a piece of music (as a waltz) by which dancing may be guided **4** : the art of dancing

D & C *n* [*dilation and curettage*] : a surgical procedure that involves stretching the cervix and scraping the inside walls of the uterus (as to test for cancer or to perform an abortion)

dan·de·li·on \'dan-də-ˌlī-ən, -dē-\ *n* [ME *dendelyoun,* fr. AF *dent de lion,* lit., lion's tooth] : any of a genus of common yellow-flowered composite herbs

dan·der \'dan-dər\ *n* : ANGER, TEMPER

dan·di·fy \'dan-di-ˌfī\ *vb* **-fied; -fy·ing** : to cause to resemble a dandy

dan·dle \'dan-dᵊl\ *vb* **dan·dled; dan·dling** : to move up and down in one's arms or on one's knee in affectionate play ◆ **Synonyms** CARESS, FONDLE, LOVE, PET

dan·druff \'dan-drəf\ *n* : scaly white or grayish flakes of dead skin cells that come off the scalp — **dan·druffy** \-drə-fē\ *adj*

¹dan·dy \'dan-dē\ *n, pl* **dandies 1** : a man unduly attentive to personal appearance **2** : something excellent in its class ◆ **Synonyms** FOP, COXCOMB, POPINJAY

²dandy *adj* **dan·di·er; -est** : very good : FIRST-RATE

Dane \'dān\ *n* **1** : a native or inhabitant of Denmark **2** : GREAT DANE

dan·ger \'dān-jər\ *n* [ME *daunger* control, resistance, peril, fr. AF *dangier,* fr. VL **dominiarium,* fr. L *dominium* ownership] **1** : exposure or liability to injury, harm, or evil **2** : something that may cause injury or harm ♦ *Synonyms* PER-IL, HAZARD, RISK, JEOPARDY

dan·ger·ous \'dān-jə-rəs\ *adj* 1 : HAZ-ARDOUS, PERILOUS ⟨a ~ slope⟩ 2 : able or likely to inflict injury ⟨a ~ man⟩ — **dan·ger·ous·ly** *adv*

dan·gle \'daŋ-gəl\ *vb* **dan·gled; dan·gling** 1 : to hang loosely esp. with a swinging motion : SWING 2 : to be a hanger-on or dependent 3 : to be left without proper grammatical connection in a sentence ⟨a *dangling* participle⟩ 4 : to keep hanging uncertainly 5 : to offer as an inducement

Dan·iel \'dan-yəl\ *n* — see BIBLE table

Dan·ish \'dā-nish\ *n* : the language of the Danes — **Danish** *adj*

Danish pastry *n* : a pastry made of a rich yeast-raised dough

dank \'daŋk\ *adj* : disagreeably wet or moist : DAMP — **dank·ness** *n*

dan·seuse \däⁿ-'sərz, -'səz; dän-'süz\ *n* [F] : a female ballet dancer

dap·per \'da-pər\ *adj* 1 : SPRUCE, TRIM 2 : being alert and lively in movement and manners : JAUNTY

dap·ple \'da-pəl\ *vb* **dap·pled; dap·pling** : to mark with different-colored spots

DAR *abbr* Daughters of the American Revolution

¹**dare** \'der\ *vb* **dared; dar·ing** 1 : to have sufficient courage : be bold enough to 2 : CHALLENGE ⟨*dared* him to jump⟩ 3 : to confront boldly

²**dare** *n* : an act or instance of daring : CHALLENGE

dare·dev·il \-ˌde-vəl\ *n* : a recklessly bold person — **daredevil** *adj*

dar·ing \'der-iŋ\ *n* : venturesome boldness — **daring** *adj* — **dar·ing·ly** *adv*

¹**dark** \'därk\ *adj* 1 : being without light or without much light 2 : not light in color ⟨a ~ suit⟩ 3 : GLOOMY ⟨a ~ outlook⟩ 4 *often cap* : being a period of stagnation or decline ⟨the *Dark* Ages⟩ 5 : SECRETIVE ⟨~ dealings⟩ ♦ *Synonyms* DIM, DUSKY, MURKY, TENEBROUS — **dark·ly** *adv* — **dark·ness** *n*

²**dark** *n* 1 : absence of light : DARKNESS; *esp* : NIGHT 2 : a dark or deep color — **in the dark** 1 : in secrecy 2 : in ignorance ⟨kept *in the dark* about the plans⟩

dark·en \'där-kən\ *vb* 1 : to make or grow dark or darker 2 : DIM 3 : BESMIRCH, TARNISH 4 : to make or become gloomy or forbidding

dark horse *n* : a contestant or a political figure whose abilities and chances as a contender are not known

dark·ling \'där-kliŋ\ *adj* 1 : DARK ⟨a ~ plain⟩ 2 : MYSTERIOUS

dark·room \'därk-ˌrüm, -ˌru̇m\ *n* : a light-proof room in which photographic materials are processed

¹**dar·ling** \'där-liŋ\ *n* 1 : a dearly loved person 2 : FAVORITE

²**darling** *adj* 1 : dearly loved : FAVORITE 2 : very pleasing : CHARMING

darm·stadt·i·um \ˌdärm-'sta-tē-əm\ *n* : a short-lived radioactive chemical element produced artificially

¹**darn** \'därn\ *vb* : to mend with interlacing stitches — **darn·er** *n*

²**darn** *or* **darned** \'därnd\ *adv* : VERY, EXTREMELY ⟨a ~ good job⟩

darning needle *n* 1 : a needle for darning 2 : DRAGONFLY

¹**dart** \'därt\ *n* 1 : a small missile with a point on one end and feathers on the other; *also, pl* : a game in which darts are thrown at a target 2 : something causing a sudden pain 3 : a stitched tapering fold in a garment 4 : a quick movement

²**dart** *vb* 1 : to throw with a sudden movement 2 : to thrust or move suddenly or rapidly ⟨~ed across the street⟩ 3 : to shoot with a dart containing a usu. tranquilizing drug

dart·er \'där-tər\ *n* : any of numerous small No. American freshwater fishes related to the perches

Dar·win·ism \'där-wə-ˌni-zəm\ *n* : a theory explaining the origin and continued existence of new species of plants and animals by means of natural selection acting on chance variations — **Dar·win·ist** \-nist\ *n or adj*

¹**dash** \'dash\ *vb* 1 : SMASH 2 : to knock, hurl, or thrust violently 3 : SPLASH, SPATTER 4 : RUIN 5 : DEPRESS, SADDEN 6 : to perform or finish hastily ⟨~ off a letter⟩ 7 : to move with sudden speed ⟨~ed down the hall⟩

²**dash** *n* 1 : a sudden burst or splash 2 : a stroke of a pen 3 : a punctuation mark — that is used esp. to indicate a break in the thought or structure of a sentence 4 : a small addition ⟨a ~ of salt⟩ 5 : flashy showiness 6 : animation in style and action 7 : a sudden rush or attempt ⟨made a ~ for the door⟩ 8 : a short foot race 9 : DASHBOARD

dash·board \-ˌbȯrd\ *n* : a panel in an automobile or aircraft below the windshield usu. containing dials and controls

dash·er \'da-shər\ *n* : a device (as in a churn) for agitating something

da·shi·ki \də-'shē-kē\ *also* **dai·shi·ki** \dī-\ *n* [modif. of Yoruba (an African language) *dàṣíkí*] : a usu. brightly colored loose-fitting pullover garment

dash·ing \'da-shiŋ\ *adj* 1 : marked by vigorous action 2 : marked by smartness esp. in dress and manners ♦ *Synonyms* STYLISH, CHIC, FASHIONABLE, MODISH, SMART, SWANK

das·tard \'das-tərd\ *n* 1 : COWARD 2 : a person who acts treacherously — **das·tard·ly** *adj*

dat *abbr* dative

da·ta \'dā-tə, 'da-, 'dä-\ *n sing or pl* [L, pl. of *datum*] : factual information (as measurements or statistics) used as a basis for reasoning, discussion, or calculation

da·ta·base \-ˌbās\ *n* : a usu. large collection of data organized esp. for rapid search and retrieval (as by a computer) — **database** *vb*

data processing *n* : the action or process of supplying a computer with information and having the computer use it to produce a desired result

¹**date** \'dāt\ *n* [ME, fr. AF, ultim. fr. L *dac-*

tylus, fr. Gk *daktylos,* lit., finger] : the oblong edible fruit of a tall palm; *also* : this palm

²**date** *n* [ME, fr. AF, fr. LL *data,* fr. *data* (as in *datu Romae* given at Rome), fem. of L *datus,* pp. of *dare* to give] **1** : the day, month, or year of an event **2** : a statement giving the time of execution or making (as of a coin or check) **3** : the period to which something belongs **4** : APPOINTMENT; *esp* : a social engagement between two persons that often has a romantic character **5** : a person with whom one has a usu. romantic date — **to date** : up to the present moment

³**date** *vb* **dat·ed; dat·ing 1** : to record the date of or on **2** : to determine, mark, or reveal the date, age, or period of **3** : to go on a date or dates with ⟨*~ed* her for a year⟩ **4** : ORIGINATE ⟨*~s* from ancient times⟩ **5** : EXTEND ⟨*dating* back to childhood⟩ **6** : to show qualities typical of a past period

dat·ed \ˈdā-təd\ *adj* **1** : provided with a date **2** : OLD-FASHIONED ⟨a *~* custom⟩
♦ *Synonyms* ANTIQUATED, ARCHAIC, OLD HAT, OUTDATED, OUTMODED, PASSÉ

date·less \ˈdāt-ləs\ *adj* **1** : ENDLESS **2** : having no date **3** : too ancient to be dated **4** : TIMELESS

date·line \ˈdāt-ˌlīn\ *n* : a line in a publication giving the date and place of composition or issue — **dateline** *vb*

date rape *n* : rape committed by the victim's date

da·tive \ˈdā-tiv\ *adj* : of, relating to, or constituting a grammatical case marking typically the indirect object of a verb — **dative** *n*

da·tum \ˈdā-təm, ˈda-, ˈdä-\ *n, pl* **da·ta** \-tə\ *or* **datums** : a single piece of data : FACT

dau *abbr* daughter

¹**daub** \ˈdȯb\ *vb* **1** : to cover with soft adhesive matter **2** : SMEAR, SMUDGE **3** : to paint crudely — **daub·er** *n*

²**daub** *n* **1** : something daubed on : SMEAR **2** : a crude picture

daugh·ter \ˈdȯ-tər\ *n* **1** : a female offspring esp. of human beings **2** : a female adopted child **3** : a human female descendant — **daughter** *adj* — **daugh·ter·less** \-ləs\ *adj*

daugh·ter–in–law \ˈdȯ-tə-rən-ˌlȯ\ *n, pl* **daugh·ters–in–law** \-tər-zən-\ : the wife of one's son

daunt \ˈdȯnt\ *vb* [ME, fr. AF *danter, daunter,* fr. L *domitare* to tame] : to lessen the courage of : INTIMIDATE, OVERWHELM

daunt·ing \ˈdȯn-tiŋ\ *adj* : tending to overwhelm or intimidate ⟨a *~* task⟩

daunt·less \-ləs\ *adj* **1** : FEARLESS, UNDAUNTED ♦ *Synonyms* BRAVE, BOLD, COURAGEOUS, LIONHEARTED — **daunt·less·ly** *adv*

dau·phin \ˈdȯ-fən\ *n, often cap* : the eldest son of a king of France

DAV *abbr* Disabled American Veterans

dav·en·port \ˈda-vən-ˌpȯrt\ *n* : a large upholstered sofa

da·vit \ˈdā-vət, ˈda-\ *n* : a small crane on a

ship used in pairs esp. to raise or lower boats

daw·dle \ˈdȯ-dᵊl\ *vb* **daw·dled; daw·dling 1** : to spend time wastefully or idly **2** : LOITER — **daw·dler** *n*

¹**dawn** \ˈdȯn\ *vb* **1** : to begin to grow light as the sun rises **2** : to begin to appear or develop **3** : to begin to be understood ⟨the solution *~ed* on him⟩

²**dawn** *n* **1** : the first appearance of light in the morning **2** : a first appearance : BEGINNING ⟨the *~* of a new era⟩

day \ˈdā\ *n* **1** : the period of light between one night and the next; *also* : DAYLIGHT, DAYTIME **2** : the period of rotation of a planet (as earth) or a moon on its axis **3** : a period of 24 hours beginning at midnight **4** : a specified day or date ⟨wedding *~*⟩ **5** : a specified time or period : AGE ⟨in olden *~s*⟩ **6** : the conflict or contention of the day **7** : the time set apart by usage or law for work ⟨the 8-hour *~*⟩

day·bed \ˈdā-ˌbed\ *n* : a couch that can be converted into a bed

day·book \-ˌbu̇k\ *n* : DIARY, JOURNAL

day·break \-ˌbrāk\ *n* : DAWN

day care *n* : supervision of and care for children or disabled adults provided during the day; *also* : a program offering day care

day·dream \ˈdā-ˌdrēm\ *n* : a pleasant reverie — **daydream** *vb*

day·light \ˈdā-ˌlīt\ *n* **1** : the light of day **2** : DAYTIME **3** : DAWN **4** : understanding of something that has been obscure **5** *pl* : CONSCIOUSNESS; *also* : WITS **6** : a perceptible space, gap, or difference

daylight saving time *n* : time usu. one hour ahead of standard time

Day of Atonement *n* : YOM KIPPUR

day school *n* : a private school without boarding facilities

day student *n* : a student who attends regular classes at a college or preparatory school but does not live there

day·time \ˈdā-ˌtīm\ *n* : the period of daylight

daze \ˈdāz\ *vb* **dazed; daz·ing 1** : to stupefy esp. by a blow **2** : DAZZLE — **daze** *n* — **da·zed·ly** \ˈdā-zəd-lē\ *adv*

daz·zle \ˈda-zəl\ *vb* **daz·zled; daz·zling 1** : to overpower with light **2** : to impress greatly or confound with brilliance ⟨*dazzled* by her wit⟩ — **dazzle** *n*

dB *abbr* decibel

Db *symbol* dubnium

d/b/a *abbr* doing business as

dbl *or* **dble** *abbr* double

DC *abbr* **1** [It *da capo*] from the beginning **2** direct current **3** District of Columbia **4** doctor of chiropractic

DD *abbr* **1** days after date **2** demand draft **3** dishonorable discharge **4** doctor of divinity

D–day *n* [*D,* abbr. for *day*] : a day set for launching an operation (as an invasion)

DDS *abbr* doctor of dental surgery

DDT \ˌdē-(ˌ)dē-ˈtē\ *n* : a persistent insecticide poisonous to many higher animals

DE *abbr* Delaware

dea·con \'dē-kən\ n [ME dekene, fr. OE dēacon, fr. LL diaconus, fr. Gk diakonos, lit., servant] : a subordinate officer in a Christian church

dea·con·ess \'dē-kə-nəs\ n : a woman chosen to assist in the church ministry

de·ac·ti·vate \dē-'ak-tə-ˌvāt\ vb : to make inactive or ineffective

1dead \'ded\ adj **1** : LIFELESS **2** : DEATHLIKE, DEADLY ⟨in a ~ faint⟩ **3** : NUMB **4** : very tired **5** : UNRESPONSIVE **6** : EXTINGUISHED ⟨~ coals⟩ **7** : INANIMATE, INERT **8** : no longer active or functioning ⟨a ~ battery⟩ **9** : lacking power, significance, or effect ⟨a ~ custom⟩ **10** : OBSOLETE ⟨a ~ language⟩ **11** : lacking in gaiety or animation ⟨a ~ party⟩ **12** : QUIET, IDLE, UNPRODUCTIVE ⟨a ~ capital⟩ **13** : lacking elasticity ⟨a ~ tennis ball⟩ **14** : not circulating : STAGNANT ⟨~ air⟩ **15** : lacking warmth, vigor, or taste ⟨~ wine⟩ **16** : absolutely uniform ⟨~ level⟩ **17** : UNERRING, EXACT ⟨a ~ shot⟩ **18** : ABRUPT ⟨a ~ stop⟩ **19** : COMPLETE ⟨a ~ loss⟩

2dead n, pl **dead** **1** : one that is dead — usu. used collectively ⟨the living and the ~⟩ **2** : the time of greatest quiet ⟨the ~ of the night⟩

3dead adv **1** : UTTERLY ⟨~ right⟩ **2** : in a sudden and complete manner ⟨stopped ~⟩ **3** : DIRECTLY ⟨~ ahead⟩

dead·beat \-ˌbēt\ n : a person who persistently fails to pay personal debts or expenses

dead duck n : GONER

dead·en \'de-d²n\ vb **1** : to impair in vigor or sensation : BLUNT ⟨~ pain⟩ **2** : to lessen the luster or spirit of **3** : to make (as a wall) soundproof

dead end n **1** : an end (as of a street) without an exit **2** : a position, situation, or course of action that leads to nothing further — **dead-end** \ˌded-'end\ adj

dead heat n : a contest in which two or more contestants tie (as by crossing the finish line simultaneously)

dead horse n : an exhausted topic or issue

dead letter n **1** : something that has lost its force or authority without being formally abolished **2** : a letter that cannot be delivered or returned

dead·line \'ded-ˌlīn\ n : a date or time before which something must be done

dead·lock \'ded-ˌläk\ n **1** : a stoppage of action because neither faction in a struggle will give in **2** : a tie score — **deadlock** vb

1dead·ly \'ded-lē\ adj **dead·li·er; -est** **1** : likely to cause or capable of causing death **2** : HOSTILE, IMPLACABLE **3** : very accurate : UNERRING **4** : tending to deprive of force or vitality ⟨a ~ habit⟩ **5** : suggestive of death **6** : very great : EXTREME — **dead·li·ness** n

2deadly adv **1** : suggesting death ⟨~ pale⟩ **2** : EXTREMELY ⟨~ dull⟩

deadly sin n : one of seven sins of pride, covetousness, lust, anger, gluttony, envy, and sloth held to be fatal to spiritual progress

dead meat n : one that is doomed

1dead·pan \'ded-ˌpan\ adj : marked by an impassive manner or expression ⟨~ humor⟩ — **deadpan** vb — **deadpan** adv

2deadpan n : a completely expressionless face

dead reckoning n : the determination of the position of a ship or aircraft solely from the record of the direction and distance of its course

dead·weight \'ded-'wāt\ n **1** : the unrelieved weight of an inert mass **2** : a ship's load including the weight of cargo, fuel, crew, and passengers

dead·wood \-ˌwůd\ n **1** : wood dead on the tree **2** : useless personnel or material

deaf \'def\ adj **1** : unable to hear **2** : unwilling to hear or listen ⟨~ to all suggestions⟩ — **deaf·ness** n

deaf·en \'de-fən\ vb : to make deaf

1deal \'dēl\ n **1** : a usu. large or indefinite quantity or degree ⟨a great ~ of support⟩ **2** : the act or right of distributing cards to players in a card game; also : HAND

2deal vb **dealt** \'delt\; **deal·ing** **1** : DISTRIBUTE; esp : to distribute playing cards to players in a game **2** : ADMINISTER, DELIVER ⟨dealt him a blow⟩ **3** : to concern itself : TREAT ⟨the book ~s with crime⟩ **4** : to take action in regard to something ⟨~ with offenders⟩ **5** : TRADE; also : to sell or distribute something as a business ⟨~ in used cars⟩ **6** : to reach a state of acceptance ⟨~s with her child's death⟩ — **deal·er** n

3deal n **1** : BARGAINING, NEGOTIATION **2** : TRANSACTION; esp : an agreement by contract **3** : treatment received ⟨a raw ~⟩ **4** : an often secret agreement or arrangement for mutual advantage **5** : BARGAIN

4deal n : wood or a board of fir or pine

deal·er·ship \'dē-lər-ˌship\ n : an authorized sales agency ⟨an auto ~⟩

deal·ing \'dē-lin\ n **1** : a way of acting or of doing business **2** pl : friendly or business transactions

dean \'dēn\ n [ME deen, fr. AF deien, fr. LL decanus, lit., chief of ten, fr. Gk dekanos, fr. deka ten] **1** : a clergyman who is head of a group of canons or of joint pastors of a church **2** : the head of a division, faculty, college, or school of a university **3** : a college or secondary school administrator in charge of counseling and disciplining students **4** : DOYEN ⟨the ~ of a diplomatic corps⟩ — **dean·ship** n

dean·ery \'dē-nə-rē\ n, pl **-er·ies** : the office, jurisdiction, or official residence of a clerical dean

1dear \'dir\ adj **1** : highly valued : PRECIOUS **2** : AFFECTIONATE, FOND **3** : EXPENSIVE **4** : HEARTFELT — **dear·ly** adv — **dear·ness** n

2dear n : a loved one : DARLING

Dear John \-'jän\ n : a letter (as to a soldier) in which a woman breaks off a marital or romantic relationship

dearth \'dərth\ n **1** : SCARCITY, FAMINE

2 : an inadequate supply : LACK ⟨a ~ of jobs⟩
death \'deth\ *n* **1** : the end of life **2** : the cause of loss of life **3** : a cause of ruin **4** : the state of being dead **5** : DESTRUCTION, EXTINCTION **6** : SLAUGHTER — **death·like** *adj*
death·bed \-,bed\ *n* **1** : the bed in which a person dies **2** : the last hours of life
death·blow \-,blō\ *n* : a destructive or killing stroke or event
death grip *n* : an extremely tight grip or hold
death·less \-ləs\ *adj* : IMMORTAL, IMPERISHABLE ⟨~ fame⟩
death·ly \-lē\ *adj* **1** : FATAL **2** : of, relating to, or suggestive of death ⟨a ~ pallor⟩ — **deathly** *adv*
death rattle *n* : a sound produced by air passing through mucus in the lungs and air passages of a dying person
death's–head \'deths-,hed\ *n* : a human skull emblematic of death
death·watch \'deth-,wäch\ *n* : a vigil kept over the dead or dying
deb \'deb\ *n* : DEBUTANTE
de·ba·cle \di-'bä-kəl, -'ba-\ *also* **dé·bâcle** *same or* -'bäk\ *n* [F *débâcle*] : DISASTER, FAILURE, ROUT ⟨stock market ~⟩
de·bar \di-'bär\ *vb* : to bar from having or doing something : PRECLUDE
de·bark \di-'bärk\ *vb* : DISEMBARK — **de·bar·ka·tion** \,dē-,bär-'kā-shən\ *n*
de·base \di-'bās\ *vb* : to lower in character, quality, or value ♦ *Synonyms* DEGRADE, CORRUPT, DEPRAVE — **de·base·ment** *n*
de·bate \di-'bāt\ *vb* **de·bat·ed; de·bat·ing** **1** : to discuss a question by considering opposed arguments **2** : to take part in a debate — **de·bat·able** *adj* — **debate** *n* — **de·bat·er** *n*
de·bauch \di-'bóch\ *vb* : SEDUCE, CORRUPT ♦ *Synonyms* DEBASE, DEMORALIZE, DEPRAVE, PERVERT — **de·bauch·ery** \-'bó-chə-rē\ *n*
de·ben·ture \di-'ben-chər\ *n* : BOND; *esp* : one secured by the general credit of the issuer rather than a lien on particular assets
de·bil·i·tate \di-'bi-lə-,tāt\ *vb* **-tat·ed; -tat·ing** : to impair the health or strength of ♦ *Synonyms* WEAKEN, DISABLE, ENFEEBLE, UNDERMINE
de·bil·i·ty \di-'bi-lə-tē\ *n, pl* **-ties** : an infirm or weakened state
¹**deb·it** \'de-bət\ *vb* : to enter as a debit : charge with or as a debit
²**debit** *n* **1** : an entry in an account showing money paid out or owed **2** : DISADVANTAGE, SHORTCOMING
debit card *n* : a card by which money may be withdrawn or the cost of purchases paid directly from the holder's bank account
deb·o·nair \,de-bə-'ner\ *adj* [ME *debonere*, fr. AF *deboneire*, fr. *de bon aire* of good family or nature] : SUAVE, URBANE; *also* : LIGHTHEARTED
de·bouch \di-'baùch, -'büsh\ *vb* [F *dé-*

boucher, fr. *dé-* out of + *bouche* mouth] : to come out into an open area : EMERGE
de·brief \di-'brēf\ *vb* **1** : to question (as a pilot back from a mission) in order to obtain useful information **2** : to review carefully upon completion
de·bris \də-'brē, dā-; 'dā-,brē\ *n, pl* **debris** \-'brēz, -,brēz\ **1** : the remains of something broken down or destroyed **2** : an accumulation of rock fragments **3** : RUBBISH
debt \'det\ *n* **1** : SIN, TRESPASS **2** : something owed : OBLIGATION **3** : a condition of owing
debt·or \'de-tər\ *n* **1** : one guilty of neglect or violation of duty **2** : one that owes a debt
de·bug \(,)dē-'bəg\ *vb* : to eliminate errors in ⟨~ a computer program⟩
de·bunk \dē-'bəŋk\ *vb* : to expose sham or falseness of ⟨~ a legend⟩
¹**de·but** \'dā-,byü, dā-'byü\ *n* **1** : a first appearance **2** : a formal entrance into society
²**debut** *vb* : to make a debut; *also* : INTRODUCE
deb·u·tante \'de-byù-,tänt\ *n* : a young woman making her formal entrance into society
dec *abbr* **1** deceased **2** decrease
Dec *abbr* December
de·cade \'de-,kād, de-'kād\ *n* : a period of 10 years
dec·a·dence \'de-kə-dəns, di-'kā-d°ns\ *n* : DETERIORATION, DECLINE — **dec·a·dent** \'de-kə-dənt, di-'kā-d°nt\ *adj or n*
de·caf \'dē-,kaf\ *n* : decaffeinated coffee
de·caf·fein·at·ed \(,)dē-'ka-fə-nā-təd\ *adj* : having the caffeine removed ⟨~ coffee⟩
deca·gon \'de-kə-,gän\ *n* : a plane polygon of 10 angles and 10 sides
de·cal \'dē-,kal\ *n* : a picture, design, or label made to be transferred (as to glass) from specially prepared paper
de·cal·co·ma·nia \di-,kal-kə-'mā-nē-ə\ *n* [F *décalcomanie*, fr. *décalquer* to copy by tracing (fr. *calquer* to trace, fr. It *calcare*, lit., to tread, fr. L) + *manie* mania, fr. LL *mania*] : the process of making decals; *also* : DECAL
Deca·logue \'de-kə-,lóg\ *n* : TEN COMMANDMENTS
de·camp \di-'kamp\ *vb* **1** : to break up a camp **2** : to depart suddenly ♦ *Synonyms* ESCAPE, ABSCOND, FLEE
de·cant \di-'kant\ *vb* : to pour (as wine) from one vessel into another
de·cant·er \di-'kan-tər\ *n* : an ornamental glass bottle for serving wine
de·cap·i·tate \di-'ka-pə-,tāt\ *vb* **-tat·ed; -tat·ing** : BEHEAD — **de·cap·i·ta·tion** \-,ka-pə-'tā-shən\ *n* — **de·cap·i·ta·tor** \-'ka-pə-,tā-tər\ *n*
deca·syl·lab·ic \,de-kə-sə-'la-bik\ *adj* : having or composed of verses having 10 syllables — **decasyllabic** *n*
de·cath·lon \di-'kath-lən, -,län\ *n* : a 10-event athletic contest
de·cay \di-'kā\ *vb* **1** : to decline from a sound or prosperous condition ⟨a ~*ing* town⟩ **2** : to cause or undergo decompo-

sition ⟨radium ∼s slowly⟩; *esp* : to break down while spoiling : ROT ⟨∼*ing* teeth⟩ — **decay** *n*

decd *abbr* deceased

de·cease \di-'sēs\ *n* : DEATH

¹de·ceased \-'sēst\ *adj* : no longer living; *esp* : recently dead

²deceased *n, pl* **deceased** : a dead person

de·ce·dent \di-'sē-d³nt\ *n* : a deceased person

de·ceit \di-'sēt\ *n* 1 : DECEPTION 2 : TRICK 3 : DECEITFULNESS ♦ *Synonyms* DISSIMULATION, DUPLICITY, GUILE

de·ceit·ful \-fəl\ *adj* : practicing or tending to practice deceit 2 : MISLEADING, DECEPTIVE ⟨a ∼ answer⟩ — **de·ceit·ful·ly** *adv* — **de·ceit·ful·ness** *n*

de·ceive \di-'sēv\ *vb* **de·ceived; de·ceiv·ing** 1 : to cause to believe an untruth 2 : to use or practice deceit ♦ *Synonyms* BEGUILE, BETRAY, DELUDE, MISLEAD — **de·ceiv·er** *n*

de·cel·er·ate \dē-'se-lə-ˌrāt\ *vb* **-at·ed; -at·ing** : to slow down

De·cem·ber \di-'sem-bər\ *n* [ME *Decembre*, fr. OE or AF, both fr. L *December* (tenth month), fr. *decem* ten] : the 12th month of the year

de·cen·cy \'dē-s³n-sē\ *n, pl* **-cies** 1 : PROPRIETY 2 : conformity to standards of taste, propriety, or quality 3 : standard of propriety — usu. used in pl.

de·cen·ni·al \di-'se-nē-əl\ *adj* 1 : consisting of 10 years 2 : happening every 10 years ⟨∼ census⟩

de·cent \'dē-s³nt\ *adj* 1 : conforming to standards of propriety, good taste, or morality 2 : modestly clothed 3 : free from immodesty or obscenity 4 : ADEQUATE ⟨∼ housing⟩ — **de·cent·ly** *adv*

de·cen·tral·i·za·tion \dē-ˌsen-trə-lə-'zā-shən\ *n* 1 : the distribution of powers from a central authority to regional and local authorities 2 : the redistribution of population and industry from urban centers to outlying areas — **de·cen·tral·ize** \-'sen-trə-ˌlīz\ *vb*

de·cep·tion \di-'sep-shən\ *n* 1 : the act of deceiving 2 : the fact or condition of being deceived 3 : FRAUD, TRICK — **de·cep·tive** \-'sep-tiv\ *adj* — **de·cep·tive·ly** *adv* — **de·cep·tive·ness** *n*

deci·bel \'de-sə-ˌbel, -bəl\ *n* : a unit for measuring the relative loudness of sounds

de·cide \di-'sīd\ *vb* **de·cid·ed; de·cid·ing** [ME, fr. AF & L; AF *decider*, fr. L *decidere*, lit., to cut off, fr. *de-* off + *caedere* to cut] 1 : make a final choice or judgment 2 : to bring to a definitive end ⟨one blow *decided* the fight⟩ 3 : to induce to come to a choice

de·cid·ed \di-'sī-dəd\ *adj* 1 : UNQUESTIONABLE ⟨a ∼ advantage⟩ 2 : FIRM, DETERMINED — **de·cid·ed·ly** *adv*

de·cid·u·ous \di-'si-jə-wəs\ *adj* 1 : falling off or out usu. at the end of a period of growth or function ⟨∼ leaves⟩ ⟨a ∼ tooth⟩ 2 : having deciduous parts ⟨∼ trees⟩

deci·gram \'de-sə-ˌgram\ *n* — see METRIC SYSTEM table

deci·li·ter \-ˌlē-tər\ *n* — see METRIC SYSTEM table

¹dec·i·mal \'de-sə-məl\ *adj* : based on the number 10 : reckoning by tens

²decimal *n* : any number expressed in base 10; *esp* : DECIMAL FRACTION

decimal fraction *n* : a fraction or mixed number in which the denominator is a power of 10 and that is usu. expressed with a decimal point ⟨the *decimal fraction* .25 is equivalent to the common fraction $\frac{25}{100}$⟩

decimal place *n* : the position of a digit as counted to the right of the decimal point in a decimal fraction

decimal point *n* : a period, centered dot, or in some countries a comma at the left of a decimal fraction (as .678) less than one or between a whole number and a decimal fraction in a mixed number (as 3.678)

dec·i·mate \'de-sə-ˌmāt\ *vb* **-mat·ed; -mat·ing** 1 : to take or destroy the 10th part of 2 : to cause great destruction or harm to ⟨factories *decimated* by fire⟩

dec·i·me·ter \'de-sə-ˌmē-tər\ *n* — see METRIC SYSTEM table

de·ci·pher \di-'sī-fər\ *vb* 1 : DECODE 2 : to make out the meaning of despite indistinctness — **de·ci·pher·able** *adj*

de·ci·sion \di-'si-zhən\ *n* 1 : the act or result of deciding 2 : promptness and firmness in deciding : DETERMINATION

de·ci·sive \-'sī-siv\ *adj* 1 : having the power to decide ⟨the ∼ vote⟩ 2 : RESOLUTE, DETERMINED 3 : CONCLUSIVE ⟨a ∼ victory⟩ — **de·ci·sive·ly** *adv* — **de·ci·sive·ness** *n*

¹deck \'dek\ *n* 1 : a floorlike platform of a ship; *also* : something resembling the deck of a ship 2 : a pack of playing cards

²deck *vb* 1 : ARRAY ⟨men ∼*ed* out in suits⟩ 2 : DECORATE 3 : to furnish with a deck 4 : KNOCK DOWN, FLOOR

deck·hand \'dek-ˌhand\ *n* : a sailor who performs manual duties

de·claim \di-'klām\ *vb* : to speak or deliver in the manner of a formal speech ⟨an actor ∼*ing* his lines⟩ — **dec·la·ma·tion** \ˌde-klə-'mā-shən\ *n* — **de·clam·a·to·ry** \di-'kla-mə-ˌtōr-ē\ *adj*

de·clar·a·tive \di-'kler-ə-tiv\ *adj* : making a declaration ⟨∼ sentence⟩

de·clare \di-'kler\ *vb* **de·clared; de·clar·ing** 1 : to make known formally, officially, or explicitly : ANNOUNCE ⟨∼ war⟩ 2 : to state emphatically : AFFIRM 3 : to make a full statement of ♦ *Synonyms* BLAZON, BROADCAST, PROCLAIM, PUBLISH — **dec·la·ra·tion** \ˌde-klə-'rā-shən\ *n* — **de·clar·a·to·ry** \di-'kler-ə-ˌtōr-ē\ *adj* — **de·clar·er** *n*

de·clas·si·fy \dē-'kla-sə-ˌfī\ *vb* : to remove the security classification of ⟨∼ documents⟩ — **de·clas·si·fi·ca·tion** \-ˌkla-sə-fə-'kā-shən\ *n*

de·clen·sion \di-'klen-chən\ *n* 1 : the inflectional forms of a noun, pronoun, or adjective 2 : DECLINE, DETERIORATION 3 : DESCENT, SLOPE

¹de·cline \di-'klīn\ *vb* **de·clined; de·clin·ing** 1 : to slope downward : DESCEND 2

: DROOP **3** : RECEDE ⟨morale *declined*⟩ **4** : WANE **5** : to withhold consent; *also* : REFUSE, REJECT ⟨∼ an invitation⟩ ⟨∼ to answer⟩ **6** : INFLECT 2 ⟨∼ a noun⟩ — **de·clin·able** *adj* — **dec·li·na·tion** \ˌde-klə-ˈnā-shən\ *n*

²**decline** *n* **1** : a gradual sinking and wasting away **2** : a change to a lower state or level **3** : the time when something is approaching its end ⟨an empire in ∼⟩ **4** : a descending slope

de·cliv·i·ty \di-ˈkli-və-tē\ *n, pl* **-ties** : a steep downward slope

de·code \dē-ˈkōd\ *vb* : to convert (a coded message) into ordinary language — **de·cod·er** *n*

dé·col·le·tage \dā-ˌkä-lə-ˈtäzh\ *n* : the low-cut neckline of a dress

dé·col·le·té \dā-ˌkäl-ˈtā\ *adj* [F] **1** : wearing a strapless or low-necked gown **2** : having a low-cut neckline

de·com·mis·sion \ˌdē-kə-ˈmi-shən\ *vb* : to remove from service

de·com·pose \ˌdē-kəm-ˈpōz\ *vb* **1** : to separate into constituent parts **2** : to break down in decay : ROT — **de·com·po·si·tion** \dē-ˌkäm-pə-ˈzi-shən\ *n*

de·com·press \ˌdē-kəm-ˈpres\ *vb* : to release from pressure or compression — **de·com·pres·sion** \-ˈpre-shən\ *n*

decompression sickness *n* : ²BEND 3

de·con·ges·tant \ˌdē-kən-ˈjes-tənt\ *n* : an agent that relieves congestion (as of mucous membranes)

de·con·struc·tion \ˌdē-kən-ˈstrək-shən\ *n* : the analysis of something (as language or literature) by the separation and individual examination of its basic elements — **de·con·struct** \-ˈstrəkt\ *vb*

de·con·tam·i·nate \ˌdē-kən-ˈta-mə-ˌnāt\ *vb* : to rid of contamination (as radioactive material) — **de·con·tam·i·na·tion** \-ˌta-mə-ˈnā-shən\ *n*

de·con·trol \ˌdē-kən-ˈtrōl\ *vb* : to end control of ⟨∼ prices⟩ — **decontrol** *n*

de·cor *or* **dé·cor** \dā-ˈkȯr, ˈdā-ˌkȯr\ *n* : DECORATION; *esp* : the style and layout of interior furnishings

dec·o·rate \ˈde-kə-ˌrāt\ *vb* **-rat·ed; -rat·ing** **1** : to furnish with something ornamental ⟨∼ a room⟩ **2** : to award a mark of honor (as a medal) to ⟨*decorated* soldiers⟩ ♦ **Synonyms** ADORN, BEAUTIFY, BEDECK, GARNISH, ORNAMENT

dec·o·ra·tion \ˌde-kə-ˈrā-shən\ *n* **1** : the act or process of decorating **2** : ORNAMENT **3** : a badge of honor

dec·o·ra·tive \ˈde-kə-rə-tiv\ *adj* : ORNAMENTAL

dec·o·ra·tor \ˈde-kə-ˌrā-tər\ *n* : one that decorates; *esp* : a person who designs or executes interiors and their furnishings

dec·o·rous \ˈde-kə-rəs, di-ˈkȯr-əs\ *adj* : PROPER, SEEMLY, CORRECT

de·co·rum \di-ˈkȯr-əm\ *n* [L] **1** : conformity to accepted standards of conduct **2** : ORDERLINESS, PROPRIETY

¹**de·coy** \ˈdē-ˌkȯi, di-ˈkȯi\ *n* [prob. fr. D *de kooi*, lit., the cage] **1** : something that lures or entices; *esp* : an artificial bird used to attract live birds within shot **2**

: something used to draw attention away from another

²**de·coy** \di-ˈkȯi, ˈdē-ˌkȯi\ *vb* : to lure by or as if by a decoy : ENTICE

¹**de·crease** \di-ˈkrēs\ *vb* **de·creased; de·creas·ing** : to grow or cause to grow less : DIMINISH

²**de·crease** \ˈdē-ˌkrēs\ *n* **1** : the process of decreasing **2** : REDUCTION

¹**de·cree** \di-ˈkrē\ *n* **1** : ORDER, EDICT **2** : a judicial decision

²**decree** *vb* **de·creed; de·cree·ing** **1** : COMMAND **2** : to determine or order judicially ♦ **Synonyms** DICTATE, ORDAIN, PRESCRIBE

dec·re·ment \ˈde-krə-mənt\ *n* **1** : gradual decrease **2** : the quantity lost by diminution or waste

de·crep·it \di-ˈkre-pət\ *adj* : broken down with age : WORN-OUT — **de·crep·i·tude** \-pə-ˌtüd, -ˌtyüd\ *n*

de·cre·scen·do \ˌdā-krə-ˈshen-dō\ *adv or adj* : with a decrease in volume — used as a direction in music

de·crim·i·nal·ize \dē-ˈkri-mə-nə-ˌlīz\ *vb* : to remove or reduce the criminal status of

de·cry \di-ˈkrī\ *vb* : to express strong disapproval of ⟨∼ welfare policies⟩

ded·i·cate \ˈde-di-ˌkāt\ *vb* **-cat·ed; -cat·ing** **1** : to devote to the worship of a divine being esp. with sacred rites **2** : to set apart for a definite purpose **3** : to inscribe or address as a compliment ⟨∼ a novel⟩ — **ded·i·ca·tion** \ˌde-di-ˈkā-shən\ *n* — **ded·i·ca·tor** \ˈde-di-ˌkā-tər\ *n* — **ded·i·ca·to·ry** \-kə-ˌtȯr-ē\ *adj*

de·duce \di-ˈdüs, -ˈdyüs\ *vb* **de·duced; de·duc·ing** **1** : to derive by reasoning : INFER **2** : to trace the course of — **de·duc·ible** *adj*

de·duct \di-ˈdəkt\ *vb* : SUBTRACT — **de·duct·ible** *adj*

de·duc·tion \di-ˈdək-shən\ *n* **1** : SUBTRACTION **2** : something that is or may be subtracted **3** : the deriving of a conclusion by reasoning : the conclusion so reached — **de·duc·tive** \-ˈdək-tiv\ *adj* — **de·duc·tive·ly** *adv*

¹**deed** \ˈdēd\ *n* **1** : something done **2** : FEAT, EXPLOIT **3** : a document containing some legal transfer, bargain, or contract

²**deed** *vb* : to convey or transfer by deed

dee·jay \ˈdē-ˌjā\ *n* : DISC JOCKEY

deem \ˈdēm\ *vb* : THINK, JUDGE ♦ **Synonyms** CONSIDER, ACCOUNT, RECKON, REGARD, VIEW

de—em·pha·size \dē-ˈem-fə-ˌsīz\ *vb* : to reduce in relative importance; *also* : to attach little importance to — **de·em·pha·sis** \-səs\ *n*

¹**deep** \ˈdēp\ *adj* **1** : extending far down, back, within, or outward ⟨a ∼ well⟩ **2** : having a specified extension downward or backward ⟨3 feet ∼⟩ **3** : difficult to understand; *also* : MYSTERIOUS, OBSCURE ⟨a ∼ dark secret⟩ **4** : WISE **5** : ENGROSSED, INVOLVED ⟨∼ in thought⟩ **6** : INTENSE, PROFOUND ⟨∼ sleep⟩ **7** : dark and rich in color ⟨a ∼ red⟩ **8** : having a low musical pitch or range ⟨a

∼ voice⟩ **9** : situated well within **10** : covered, enclosed, or filled often to a specified degree — **deep·ly** *adv*

²**deep** *adv* **1** : DEEPLY **2** : far on : LATE ⟨∼ in the night⟩

³**deep** *n* **1** : an extremely deep place or part; *esp* : OCEAN **2** : the middle or most intense part ⟨the ∼ of winter⟩

deep·en \'dē-pən\ *vb* : to make or become deep or deeper

deep–freeze \'dēp-'frēz\ *vb* **-froze** \-'frōz\; **-fro·zen** \-'frō-z³n\ : QUICK-FREEZE

deep–fry *vb* : to cook in enough oil to cover the food being fried

deep pocket *n* **1** : one having substantial financial resources **2** *pl* : substantial financial resources

deep–root·ed \'dēp-'rü-təd, -'rü-\ *adj* : deeply implanted or established

deep–sea \'dēp-'sē\ *adj* : of, relating to, or occurring in the deeper parts of the sea ⟨∼ fishing⟩

deep–seat·ed \'dēp-'sē-təd\ *adj* **1** : situated far below the surface **2** : firmly established ⟨∼ convictions⟩

deer \'dir\ *n, pl* **deer** [ME, deer, animal, fr. OE *dēor* beast] : any of numerous ruminant mammals with cloven hoofs and usu. antlers esp. in the males

deer·fly \-ˌflī\ *n* : any of numerous small horseflies

deer·skin \-ˌskin\ *n* : leather made from the skin of a deer; *also* : a garment of such leather

deer tick *n* : a tick that transmits the bacterium causing Lyme disease

de–es·ca·late \dē-'es-kə-ˌlāt\ *vb* : to decrease in extent, volume, or scope : LIMIT — **de–es·ca·la·tion** \-ˌes-kə-'lā-shən\ *n*

deet \'dēt\ *n, often all cap* : a colorless oily liquid insect and tick repellent

¹**def** \'def\ *adj* **def·fer; def·fest** *slang* : very good : COOL

²**def** *abbr* **1** defendant **2** definite **3** definition

de·face \di-'fās\ *vb* : to destroy or mar the face or surface of ⟨∼ a desk⟩ — **de·face·ment** *n* — **de·fac·er** *n*

de fac·to \di-'fak-tō, dā-\ *adj or adv* **1** : existing though not formally recognized ⟨a *de facto* recession⟩ **2** : actually exercising power ⟨*de facto* government⟩

de·fal·ca·tion \ˌdē-ˌfal-'kā-shən, -ˌfȯl-; ˌde-fal-\ *n* : EMBEZZLEMENT

de·fame \di-'fām\ *vb* **de·famed; de·fam·ing** : to injure or destroy the reputation of by libel or slander ♦ *Synonyms* CALUMNIATE, DENIGRATE, LIBEL, MALIGN, SLANDER, VILIFY — **def·a·ma·tion** \ˌde-fə-'mā-shən\ *n* — **de·fam·a·to·ry** \di-'fa-mə-ˌtȯr-ē\ *adj*

de·fault \di-'fȯlt\ *n* **1** : failure to do something required by duty or law; *also* : failure to appear for a legal proceeding **2** : failure to compete in or to finish an appointed contest ⟨lose a race by ∼⟩ **3** : a choice made without active consideration due to lack of viable alternatives **4** : a selection made automatically by a computer in the absence of a choice by the user — **default** *vb* — **de·fault·er** *n*

¹**de·feat** \di-'fēt\ *vb* **1** : FRUSTRATE, NULLIFY **2** : to win victory over : BEAT — **de·feat·able** \-'fē-tə-bəl\ *adj*

²**defeat** *n* **1** : FRUSTRATION **2** : an overthrow of an army in battle **3** : loss of a contest

de·feat·ism \-'fē-ˌti-zəm\ *n* : acceptance of or resignation to defeat — **de·feat·ist** \-tist\ *n or adj*

def·e·cate \'de-fi-ˌkāt\ *vb* **-cat·ed; -cat·ing 1** : to free from impurity or corruption **2** : to discharge feces from the bowels — **def·e·ca·tion** \ˌde-fi-'kā-shən\ *n*

¹**de·fect** \'dē-ˌfekt, di-'fekt\ *n* : BLEMISH, FAULT, IMPERFECTION

²**de·fect** \di-'fekt\ *vb* : to desert a cause, party, or nation esp. in order to espouse another — **de·fec·tion** \-'fek-shən\ *n* — **de·fec·tor** \-'fek-tər\ *n*

de·fec·tive \di-'fek-tiv\ *adj* : FAULTY, DEFICIENT — **defective** *n*

de·fence *chiefly Brit var of* DEFENSE

de·fend \di-'fend\ *vb* [ME, fr. AF *defendre*, fr. L *defendere*, fr. *de-* from + *-fendere* to strike] **1** : to repel danger or attack from ⟨∼ the fort⟩ **2** : to act as attorney for **3** : to oppose the claim of another in a lawsuit : CONTEST **4** : to maintain against opposition ⟨∼ an idea⟩ **5** : to try to retain against a challenge ⟨∼ed his title⟩ — **de·fend·er** *n*

de·fen·dant \di-'fen-dənt\ *n* : a person required to make answer in a legal action or suit

de·fense \di-'fens\ *n* **1** : the act of defending : resistance against attack **2** : means, method, or capability of defending **3** : an argument in support **4** : the answer made by the defendant in a legal action **5** : a defending party, group, or team — **de·fense·less** *adj* — **de·fen·si·ble** *adj*

defense mechanism *n* : an often unconscious mental process (as repression) that assists in reaching compromise solutions to personal problems

¹**de·fen·sive** \di-'fen-siv\ *adj* **1** : serving or intended to defend or protect **2** : of or relating to the attempt to keep an opponent from scoring (as in a game) — **de·fen·sive·ly** *adv* — **de·fen·sive·ness** *n*

²**defensive** *n* : a defensive position

¹**de·fer** \di-'fər\ *vb* **de·ferred; de·fer·ring** [ME *deferren, differren*, fr. MF *differer*, fr. L *differre* to postpone, be different] : POSTPONE, PUT OFF

²**defer** *vb* **deferred; deferring** [ME *deferren, differren*, fr. MF *deferer*, fr. LL *deferre*, fr. L, to bring down, bring, fr. *de-* down + *ferre* to carry] : to submit or yield to the opinion or wishes of another — **de·fer·ral** \-əl\ *n*

def·er·ence \'de-fər-əns\ *n* : courteous, respectful, or ingratiating regard for another's wishes ♦ *Synonyms* HONOR, HOMAGE, OBEISANCE, REVERENCE — **def·er·en·tial** \ˌde-fə-'ren-chəl\ *adj*

de·fer·ment \di-'fər-mənt\ *n* : the act of delaying; *esp* : official postponement of military service

de·fi·ance \di-'fī-əns\ *n* **1** : CHALLENGE **2** : disposition to resist or contend

de·fi·ant \-ənt\ *adj* : full of defiance : BOLD, IMPUDENT — **de·fi·ant·ly** *adv*

de·fi·bril·la·tor \dē-'fi-brə-ˌlā-tər\ *n* : an electronic device that applies an electric shock to restore the rhythm of a fibrillating heart — **de·fi·bril·late** \-ˌlāt\ *vb* — **de·fi·bril·la·tion** \-ˌfi-brə-'lā-shən\ *n*

deficiency disease *n* : a disease (as scurvy or beriberi) caused by a lack of essential dietary elements and esp. a vitamin or mineral

de·fi·cient \di-'fi-shənt\ *adj* : lacking in something necessary; *also* : not up to a normal standard — **de·fi·cien·cy** \-shən-sē\ *n*

def·i·cit \'de-fə-sət\ *n* : a deficiency in amount; *esp* : an excess of expenditures over revenue

¹**de·file** \di-'fī(-ə)l\ *vb* **de·filed; de·fil·ing** 1 : to make filthy 2 : CORRUPT 3 : to violate the chastity of 4 : to violate the sanctity of : DESECRATE 5 : DISHONOR ♦ **Synonyms** CONTAMINATE, POLLUTE, SOIL, TAINT — **de·file·ment** *n*

²**de·file** \di-'fī(-ə)l, 'dē-ˌfī(-ə)l\ *n* : a narrow passage or gorge

de·fine \di-'fīn\ *vb* **de·fined; de·fin·ing** 1 : to set or determine the meaning of ⟨∼ a word⟩ 2 : to fix or mark the limits of 3 : to clarify in outline or character — **de·fin·able** *adj* — **de·fin·er** *n*

def·i·nite \'de-fə-nət\ *adj* 1 : having distinct limits : FIXED 2 : clear in meaning 3 : typically designating an identified or immediately identifiable person or thing ⟨a ∼ article⟩ — **def·i·nite·ly** *adv* — **def·i·nite·ness** *n*

def·i·ni·tion \ˌde-fə-'ni-shən\ *n* 1 : an act of determining or settling 2 : a statement of the meaning of a word or word group; *also* : the action or process of defining 3 : the action or the power of making definite and clear : CLARITY, DISTINCTNESS

de·fin·i·tive \di-'fi-nə-tiv\ *adj* 1 : DECISIVE, CONCLUSIVE 2 : authoritative and apparently exhaustive ⟨a ∼ edition⟩ 3 : serving to define or specify precisely ⟨∼ laws⟩

de·flate \di-'flāt\ *vb* **de·flat·ed; de·flat·ing** 1 : to release air or gas from 2 : to reduce in size, importance, or effectiveness; *also* : to reduce from a state of inflation 3 : to become deflated

de·fla·tion \-'flā-shən\ *n* 1 : an act or instance of deflating : the state of being deflated 2 : reduction in the volume of available money or credit resulting in a decline of the general price level

de·flect \di-'flekt\ *vb* : to turn aside — **de·flec·tion** \-'flek-shən\ *n*

de·flo·ra·tion \ˌde-flə-'rā-shən\ *n* : rupture of the hymen

de·flow·er \dē-'flau̇(-ə)r\ *vb* : to deprive of virginity

de·fog \dē-'fȯg, -'fäg\ *vb* : to remove fog or condensed moisture from ⟨∼ a windshield⟩ — **de·fog·ger** *n*

de·fo·li·ant \dē-'fō-lē-ənt\ *n* : a chemical spray or dust used to defoliate plants

de·fo·li·ate \-ˌāt\ *vb* : to deprive of leaves esp. prematurely — **de·fo·li·a·tion** \dē-ˌfō-lē-'ā-shən\ *n* — **de·fo·li·a·tor** \dē-'fō-lē-ˌā-tər\ *n*

de·for·es·ta·tion \dē-ˌfȯr-ə-'stā-shən\ *n* : the action or process of clearing an area of forests; *also* : the state of having been cleared of forests — **de·for·est** \(ˌ)dē-'fȯr-əst, -'fär-\ *vb*

de·form \di-'fȯrm\ *vb* 1 : DISFIGURE, DEFACE 2 : to make or become misshapen or changed in shape — **de·for·ma·tion** \ˌdē-ˌfȯr-'mā-shən, ˌde-fȯr-\ *n*

de·for·mi·ty \di-'fȯr-mə-tē\ *n, pl* **-ties** 1 : the state of being deformed 2 : a physical blemish or distortion

de·fraud \di-'frȯd\ *vb* : CHEAT

de·fray \di-'frā\ *vb* : to provide for the payment of : PAY — **de·fray·al** *n*

de·frock \(ˌ)dē-'fräk\ *vb* : to deprive (as a priest) of the right to exercise the functions of office

de·frost \di-'frȯst\ *vb* 1 : to thaw out 2 : to free from ice — **de·frost·er** *n*

deft \'deft\ *adj* : quick and neat in action — **deft·ly** *adv* — **deft·ness** *n*

de·funct \di-'fəŋkt\ *adj* : DEAD, EXTINCT ⟨a ∼ language⟩

de·fuse \dē-'fyüz\ *vb* 1 : to remove the fuse from (as a bomb) 2 : to make less harmful, potent, or tense

de·fy \di-'fī\ *vb* **de·fied; de·fy·ing** [ME, to renounce faith in, challenge, fr. AF *desfier, defier*, fr. *de-* from + *fier* to entrust, ultim. fr. L *fidere* to trust] 1 : CHALLENGE, DARE 2 : to refuse boldly to obey or to yield to : DISREGARD ⟨∼ the law⟩ 3 : WITHSTAND, BAFFLE ⟨a scene that *defies* description⟩

deg *abbr* degree

de·gas \dē-'gas\ *vb* : to remove gas from

de·gen·er·a·cy \di-'je-nə-rə-sē\ *n, pl* **-cies** 1 : the state of being degenerate 2 : the process of becoming degenerate 3 : PERVERSION

¹**de·gen·er·ate** \di-'je-nə-rət\ *adj* : fallen or deteriorated from a former, higher, or normal condition — **de·gen·er·a·tion** \-ˌje-nə-'rā-shən\ *n* — **de·gen·er·a·tive** \-'je-nə-ˌrā-tiv\ *adj*

²**de·gen·er·ate** \di-'je-nə-ˌrāt\ *vb* : to undergo deterioration (as in morality, intelligence, structure, or function)

³**de·gen·er·ate** \-rət\ *n* : a degenerate person; *esp* : a sexual pervert

de·grad·able \di-'grā-də-bəl\ *adj* : capable of being chemically degraded

de·grade \di-'grād\ *vb* 1 : to reduce from a higher to a lower rank or degree 2 : DEBASE, CORRUPT 3 : DECOMPOSE — **deg·ra·da·tion** \ˌde-grə-'dā-shən\ *n*

de·gree \di-'grē\ *n* [ME, fr. AF *degré*, fr. VL **degradus*, fr. L *de-* down + *gradus* step, grade] 1 : a step in a series 2 : a rank or grade of official, ecclesiastical, or social position; *also* : the civil condition of a person 3 : the extent, intensity, or scope of something esp. as measured by a graded series 4 : one of the forms or sets of forms used in the comparison of an adjective or adverb 5 : a title conferred upon students by a college, university, or professional school on completion of a program of study 6 : a line or space of the musical staff; *also* : a note or tone of a musical scale **7** : a unit of measure for angles that is equal to an angle with its vertex at the center of a circle and its sides cutting off $\frac{1}{360}$ of the circumference; *also* : a unit of measure for arcs of a circle that is equal to the amount of arc extending $\frac{1}{360}$ of the circumference **8** : any of various units for measuring temperature

de·horn \dē-'hȯrn\ *vb* : to deprive of horns

de·hu·man·ize \dē-'hyü-mə-ˌnīz\ *vb* : to deprive of human qualities, personality, or spirit — **de·hu·man·i·za·tion** \dē-ˌhyü-mə-nə-'zā-shən\ *n*

de·hu·mid·i·fy \ˌdē-hyü-'mi-də-ˌfī\ *vb* : to remove moisture from (as the air) — **de·hu·mid·i·fi·er** *n*

de·hy·drate \dē-'hī-ˌdrāt\ *vb* : to remove water from; *also* : to lose liquid — **de·hy·dra·tion** \ˌdē-hī-'drā-shən\ *n*

de·hy·dro·ge·na·tion \ˌdē-(ˌ)hī-ˌdrä-jə-'nā-shən, -drə-\ *n* : the removal of hydrogen from a chemical compound — **de·hy·dro·ge·nate** \ˌdē-(ˌ)hī-'drä-jə-ˌnāt, dē-'hī-drə-jə-\ *vb*

de·ice \dē-'īs\ *vb* : to keep free or rid of ice ⟨∼ a plane⟩ — **de·ic·er** *n*

de·i·fy \'dē-ə-ˌfī, 'dā-\ *vb* **-fied; -fy·ing 1** : to make a god of **2** : WORSHIP, GLORIFY — **de·i·fi·ca·tion** \ˌdē-ə-fə-'kā-shən, ˌdā-\ *n*

deign \'dān\ *vb* [ME, fr. AF *deigner*, fr. L *dignare, dignari*, fr. *dignus* worthy] : CONDESCEND

de·ion·ize \dē-'ī-ə-ˌnīz\ *vb* : to remove ions from

de·ism \'dē-ˌi-zəm, 'dā-\ *n, often cap* : a system of thought advocating natural religion based on human morality and reason rather than divine revelation — **de·ist** \-ist\ *n, often cap* — **de·is·tic** \dē-'is-tik, dā-\ *adj*

de·i·ty \'dē-ə-tē, 'dā-\ *n, pl* **-ties 1** : DIVINITY **2** *cap* : GOD **3** : a god or goddess

dé·jà vu \ˌdā-ˌzhä-'vü\ *n* [F, adj., already seen] : the feeling that one has seen or heard something before

de·ject·ed \di-'jek-təd\ *adj* : low in spirits : SAD — **de·ject·ed·ly** *adv*

de·jec·tion \di-'jek-shən\ *n* : lowness of spirits

de ju·re \dē-'jȯr-ē\ *adv or adj* [ML] : by legal right

deka·gram \'de-kə-ˌgram\ *n* — see METRIC SYSTEM table

deka·li·ter \-ˌlē-tər\ *n* — see METRIC SYSTEM table

deka·me·ter \-ˌmē-tər\ *n* — see METRIC SYSTEM table

del *abbr* delegate; delegation

Del *abbr* Delaware

Del·a·ware \'de-lə-ˌwer\ *n, pl* **Delaware** *or* **Delawares** : a member of an American Indian people orig. of the Delaware valley; *also* : their language

¹de·lay \di-'lā\ *n* **1** : the act of delaying : the state of being delayed **2** : the time for which something is delayed

²delay *vb* **1** : POSTPONE, PUT OFF **2** : to stop, detain, or hinder for a time **3** : to move or act slowly

de·lec·ta·ble \di-'lek-tə-bəl\ *adj* **1** : highly pleasing : DELIGHTFUL **2** : DELICIOUS

de·lec·ta·tion \ˌdē-ˌlek-'tā-shən\ *n* : DELIGHT, PLEASURE, DIVERSION

¹del·e·gate \'de-li-gət, -ˌgāt\ *n* **1** : DEPUTY, REPRESENTATIVE **2** : a member of the lower house of the legislature of Maryland, Virginia, or West Virginia

²del·e·gate \-ˌgāt\ *vb* **-gat·ed; -gat·ing 1** : to entrust to another ⟨∼ authority⟩ **2** : to appoint as one's delegate

del·e·ga·tion \ˌde-li-'gā-shən\ *n* **1** : the act of delegating **2** : one or more persons chosen to represent others

de·le·git·i·mize \ˌdē-lə-'ji-tə-ˌmīz\ *vb* : to diminish or destroy the legitimacy, prestige, or authority of

de·lete \di-'lēt\ *vb* **de·let·ed; de·let·ing** [L *deletus*, pp. of *delēre* to wipe out, destroy] : to eliminate esp. by blotting out, cutting out, or erasing ⟨∼ a computer file⟩ — **de·le·tion** \-'lē-shən\ *n*

del·e·te·ri·ous \ˌde-lə-'tir-ē-əs\ *adj* : HARMFUL, NOXIOUS

delft \'delft\ *n* **1** : a Dutch pottery with an opaque white glaze and predominantly blue decoration **2** : glazed pottery esp. when blue and white

delft·ware \-ˌwer\ *n* : DELFT

deli \'de-lē\ *n, pl* **del·is** : DELICATESSEN

¹de·lib·er·ate \di-'li-bə-ˌrāt\ *vb* **-at·ed; -at·ing** : to consider carefully — **de·lib·er·a·tion** \-ˌli-bə-'rā-shən\ *n* — **de·lib·er·a·tive** \-'li-bə-ˌrā-tiv, -brə-tiv\ *adj* — **de·lib·er·a·tive·ly** *adv*

²de·lib·er·ate \di-'li-bə-rət, -'li-brət\ *adj* **1** : determined after careful thought **2** : done or said intentionally **3** : UNHURRIED, SLOW — **de·lib·er·ate·ly** *adv* — **de·lib·er·ate·ness** *n*

del·i·ca·cy \'de-li-kə-sē\ *n, pl* **-cies 1** : something pleasing to eat and considered rare or luxurious **2** : FINENESS, DAINTINESS; *also* : FRAILTY **3** : nicety or expressiveness of touch **4** : precise perception and discrimination : SENSITIVITY **5** : sensibility in feeling or conduct; *also* : SQUEAMISHNESS **6** : the quality or state of requiring delicate handling

del·i·cate \'de-li-kət\ *adj* **1** : pleasing to the senses of taste or smell esp. in a mild or subtle way **2** : marked by daintiness or charm : EXQUISITE **3** : FASTIDIOUS, SQUEAMISH ⟨a person of ∼ tastes⟩ **4** : easily damaged : FRAGILE; *also* : SICKLY **5** : requiring skill or tact **6** : marked by care, skill, or tact **7** : marked by minute precision : very sensitive ⟨a ∼ instrument⟩ — **del·i·cate·ly** *adv*

del·i·ca·tes·sen \ˌde-li-kə-'te-sᵊn\ *n pl* [G, pl. of *Delicatesse* delicacy, fr. F *délicatesse*] **1** : ready-to-eat food products (as cooked meats and prepared salads) **2** *sing, pl* **delicatessens** : a store where delicatessen are sold

de·li·cious \di-'li-shəs\ *adj* : affording great pleasure : DELIGHTFUL; *esp* : very pleasing to the taste or smell — **de·li·cious·ly** *adv* — **de·li·cious·ness** *n*

¹de·light \di-'līt\ *n* **1** : great pleasure or

satisfaction : JOY **2** : something that gives great pleasure — **de·light·ful** \-fəl\ *adj* — **de·light·ful·ly** *adv*

²**delight** *vb* **1** : to take great pleasure **2** : to satisfy greatly : PLEASE

de·light·ed *adj* : highly pleased : GRATIFIED — **de·light·ed·ly** *adv*

de·lim·it \di-ˈli-mət\ *vb* : to fix the limits of

de·lin·eate \di-ˈli-nē-ˌāt\ *vb* **-eat·ed; -eat·ing 1** : SKETCH, PORTRAY **2** : to picture in words : DESCRIBE — **de·lin·ea·tion** \-ˌli-nē-ˈā-shən\ *n*

de·lin·quen·cy \di-ˈliŋ-kwən-sē\ *n, pl* **-cies** : the quality or state of being delinquent

¹**de·lin·quent** \-kwənt\ *n* : a delinquent person

²**delinquent** *adj* **1** : offending by neglect or violation of duty or of law **2** : being overdue in payment

del·i·quesce \ˌde-li-ˈkwes\ *vb* **-quesced; -quesc·ing** : MELT, DISSOLVE — **del·i·ques·cent** \-ˈkwe-sᵊnt\ *adj*

de·lir·i·um \di-ˈlir-ē-əm\ *n* [L, fr. *delirare* to be crazy, lit., to leave the furrow (in plowing), fr. *de-* from + *lira* furrow] : mental disturbance marked by confusion, disordered speech, and hallucinations; *also* : frenzied excitement — **de·lir·i·ous** \-ē-əs\ *adj* — **de·lir·i·ous·ly** *adv*

delirium tre·mens \-ˈtrē-mənz, -ˈtre-\ *n* : a violent delirium with tremors that is induced by excessive and prolonged use of alcoholic liquors

de·liv·er \di-ˈli-vər\ *vb* **-ered; -er·ing 1** : to set free : SAVE **2** : CONVEY, TRANSFER ⟨∼ a letter⟩ **3** : to assist in giving birth or at the birth of; *also* : to give birth to **4** : UTTER, COMMUNICATE **5** : to send to an intended target or destination — **de·liv·er·able** \-ˈli-v(ə-)rə-bəl\ *adj* — **de·liv·er·ance** \-v(ə-)rəns\ *n* — **de·liv·er·er** *n*

de·liv·ery \di-ˈli-və-rē\ *n, pl* **-er·ies** : the act of delivering something; *also* : something delivered — **de·liv·ery·man** \-ˌman\ *n*

dell \ˈdel\ *n* : a small secluded valley

de·louse \dē-ˈlau̇s\ *vb* : to remove lice from

del·phin·i·um \del-ˈfi-nē-əm\ *n* : any of a genus of mostly perennial herbs related to the buttercups with tall branching spikes of irregular flowers

del·ta \ˈdel-tə\ *n* **1** : the 4th letter of the Greek alphabet — Δ or δ **2** : something shaped like a capital Δ; *esp* : the triangular silt-formed land at the mouth of a river — **del·ta·ic** \del-ˈtā-ik\ *adj*

del·toid \ˈdel-ˌtȯid\ *n* : a large triangular muscle that covers the shoulder joint and raises the arm laterally

de·lude \di-ˈlüd\ *vb* **de·lud·ed; de·lud·ing** : MISLEAD, DECEIVE, TRICK

¹**del·uge** \ˈdel-ˌyüj\ *n* **1** : a flooding of land by water **2** : a drenching rain **3** : a great amount or number ⟨a ∼ of mail⟩

²**deluge** *vb* **del·uged; del·ug·ing 1** : INUNDATE, FLOOD **2** : to overwhelm as if with a deluge ⟨*deluged* with e-mails⟩

de·lu·sion \di-ˈlü-zhən\ *n* : a deluding or being deluded; *esp* : a persistent false psychotic belief — **de·lu·sion·al** \-ˈlü-zhə-nᵊl\ *adj* — **de·lu·sive** \-ˈlü-siv\ *adj*

de·luxe \di-ˈlu̇ks, -ˈləks, -ˈlüks\ *adj* : notably luxurious or elegant

delve \ˈdelv\ *vb* **delved; delv·ing 1** : DIG **2** : to seek laboriously for information

dely *abbr* delivery

Dem *abbr* Democrat; Democratic

de·mag·ne·tize \dē-ˈmag-nə-ˌtīz\ *vb* : to cause to lose magnetic properties — **de·mag·ne·ti·za·tion** \ˌdē-ˌmag-nə-tə-ˈzā-shən\ *n*

dem·a·gogue *also* **dem·a·gog** \ˈde-mə-ˌgäg\ *n* [Gk *dēmagōgos*, fr. *dēmos* people + *agōgos* leading, fr. *agein* to lead] : a person who appeals to the emotions and prejudices of people esp. in order to gain political power — **dem·a·gogu·ery** \-ˌgä-gə-rē\ *n* — **dem·a·gogy** \-ˌgä-gē, -ˌgä-jē\ *n*

¹**de·mand** \di-ˈmand\ *n* **1** : an act of demanding; *also* : something claimed as due or just **2** : the ability and desire to buy goods or services; *also* : the quantity of goods wanted at a stated price **3** : a seeking or being sought after : urgent need **4** : a pressing need or requirement

²**demand** *vb* **1** : to ask for with authority : claim as due or just **2** : to ask earnestly or in the manner of a command **3** : REQUIRE, NEED ⟨a patient who ∼s constant care⟩

de·mar·cate \di-ˈmär-ˌkāt, ˈdē-ˌmär-\ *vb* **-cat·ed; -cat·ing 1** : DELIMIT **2** : to set apart : DISTINGUISH — **de·mar·ca·tion** \ˌdē-ˌmär-ˈkā-shən\ *n*

dé·marche *or* **de·marche** \dā-ˈmärsh\ *n* : a course of action : MANEUVER

¹**de·mean** \di-ˈmēn\ *vb* **de·meaned; de·mean·ing** : to behave or conduct (oneself) usu. in a proper manner

²**demean** *vb* **de·meaned; de·mean·ing** : DEGRADE, DEBASE

de·mean·or \di-ˈmē-nər\ *n* : CONDUCT, BEARING

de·mean·our *Brit var of* DEMEANOR

de·ment·ed \di-ˈmen-təd\ *adj* : MAD, INSANE — **de·ment·ed·ly** *adv*

de·men·tia \di-ˈmen-chə\ *n* **1** : deterioration of cognitive functioning (as in Alzheimer's disease) **2** : INSANITY

de·mer·it \di-ˈmer-ət\ *n* **1** : FAULT **2** : a mark placed against a person's record for some fault or offense

de·mesne \di-ˈmān, -ˈmēn\ *n* **1** : REALM **2** : manorial land actually possessed by the lord and not held by free tenants **3** : ESTATE **4** : REGION

demi·god \ˈde-mi-ˌgäd\ *n* : a mythological being with more power than a mortal but less than a god

demi·john \ˈde-mi-ˌjän\ *n* [F *dame-jeanne*, lit., Lady Jane] : a large narrow-necked bottle usu. enclosed in wickerwork

de·mil·i·ta·rize \dē-ˈmi-lə-tə-ˌrīz\ *vb* : to strip of military forces, weapons, or fortifications — **de·mil·i·tar·i·za·tion** \dē-ˌmi-lə-tə-rə-ˈzā-shən\ *n*

demi·mon·daine \ˌde-mi-ˌmän-ˈdān\ *n* : a woman of the demimonde

demi·monde \'de-mi-ˌmänd\ n [F *demi-monde*, fr. *demi-* half + *monde* world] 1 : a class of women on the fringes of respectable society supported by wealthy lovers 2 : a distinct isolated group having low reputation or prestige

de·min·er·al·ize \dē-'mi-nə-rə-ˌlīz\ vb : to remove the mineral matter from — **de·min·er·al·i·za·tion** \-ˌmi-nə-rə-lə-'zā-shən\ n

de·mise \di-'mīz\ n 1 : LEASE 2 : transfer of sovereignty to a successor ⟨∼ of the crown⟩ 3 : DEATH 4 : loss of status

demi·tasse \'de-mi-ˌtas\ n : a small cup of black coffee; *also* : the cup used to serve it

demo \'de-mō\ n, pl **dem·os** 1 : DEMONSTRATION 2 : a product used to show performance or merits to prospective buyers 3 : a recording used to show off a song or performer

de·mo·bi·lize \di-'mō-bə-ˌlīz, dē-\ vb 1 : DISBAND 2 : to discharge from military service — **de·mo·bi·li·za·tion** \di-ˌmō-bə-lə-'zā-shən, dē-\ n

de·moc·ra·cy \di-'mä-krə-sē\ n, pl **-cies** [MF *democratie*, fr. LL *democratia*, fr. Gk *dēmokratia*, fr. *dēmos* people + *kratos* strength, power] 1 : government by the people; *esp* : rule of the majority 2 : a government in which the supreme power is held by the people 3 : a political unit that has a democratic government 4 *cap* : the principles and policies of the Democratic party in the U.S. 5 : the common people esp. when constituting the source of political authority 6 : the absence of hereditary or arbitrary class distinctions or privileges

dem·o·crat \'de-mə-ˌkrat\ n 1 : one who believes in or practices democracy 2 *cap* : a member of the Democratic party of the U.S.

dem·o·crat·ic \ˌde-mə-'kra-tik\ adj 1 : of, relating to, or favoring democracy 2 *often cap* : of or relating to one of the two major political parties in the U.S. associated in modern times with policies of broad social reform and internationalism 3 : relating to or appealing to the common people ⟨∼ art⟩ 4 : not snobbish — **dem·o·crat·i·cal·ly** \-ti-k(ə-)lē\ adv

de·moc·ra·tize \di-'mä-krə-ˌtīz\ vb **-tized; -tiz·ing** : to make democratic

dé·mo·dé \ˌdā-mō-'dā\ adj [F] : no longer fashionable : OUT-OF-DATE

de·mo·graph·ics \ˌde-mə-'gra-fiks, ˌdē-\ n pl : the statistical characteristics of human populations

de·mog·ra·phy \di-'mä-grə-fē\ n : the statistical study of human populations and esp. their size and distribution and the number of births and deaths — **de·mog·ra·pher** \-fər\ n — **de·mo·graph·ic** \ˌde-mə-'gra-fik, ˌdē-\ adj — **de·mo·graph·i·cal·ly** \-fi-k(ə-)lē\ adv

dem·oi·selle \ˌdem-wə-'zel\ n [F] : a young woman

de·mol·ish \di-'mä-lish\ vb 1 : to destroy by breaking apart : RAZE 2 : SMASH 3 : to put an end to ⟨∼ a theory⟩

de·mo·li·tion \ˌde-mə-'li-shən, ˌdē-\ n : the act of demolishing; *esp* : destruction by means of explosives

de·mon or **dae·mon** \'dē-mən\ n 1 : an evil spirit : DEVIL 2 *usu daemon* : an attendant power or spirit 3 : one that has unusual drive or effectiveness ⟨a ∼ for work⟩

de·mon·e·tize \dē-'mä-nə-ˌtīz, -'mə-\ vb : to stop using as money or as a monetary standard ⟨∼ silver⟩ — **de·mon·e·ti·za·tion** \dē-ˌmä-nə-tə-'zā-shən, -ˌmə-\ n

de·mo·ni·ac \di-'mō-nē-ˌak\ *also* **de·mo·ni·a·cal** \ˌdē-mə-'nī-ə-kəl\ adj 1 : possessed or influenced by a demon 2 : DEMONIC

de·mon·ic \di-'mä-nik\ *also* **de·mon·i·cal** \-ni-kəl\ adj : DEVILISH, FIENDISH ⟨∼ cruelty⟩

de·mon·ize \'dē-mə-ˌnīz\ vb **-ized; -iz·ing** 1 : to convert into a demon 2 : to characterize or treat as evil or harmful

de·mon·ol·o·gy \ˌdē-mə-'nä-lə-jē\ n 1 : the study of demons 2 : belief in demons

de·mon·stra·ble \di-'män-strə-bəl\ adj 1 : capable of being demonstrated 2 : APPARENT, EVIDENT — **de·mon·stra·bly** \-blē\ adv

dem·on·strate \'de-mən-ˌstrāt\ vb **-strat·ed; -strat·ing** 1 : to show clearly 2 : to prove or make clear by reasoning or evidence 3 : to explain esp. with many examples 4 : to show publicly ⟨∼ a new car⟩ 5 : to make a public display ⟨∼ in protest⟩ — **dem·on·stra·tion** \ˌde-mən-'strā-shən\ n — **dem·on·stra·tor** \'de-mən-ˌstrā-tər\ n

¹**de·mon·stra·tive** \di-'män-strə-tiv\ adj 1 : demonstrating as real or true 2 : characterized by demonstration 3 : pointing out the one referred to and distinguishing it from others of the same class ⟨∼ pronoun⟩ 4 : marked by display of feeling : EFFUSIVE — **de·mon·stra·tive·ly** adv — **de·mon·stra·tive·ness** n

²**demonstrative** n : a demonstrative word and esp. a pronoun

de·mor·al·ize \di-'mȯr-ə-ˌlīz\ vb 1 : to corrupt in morals 2 : to weaken in discipline or spirit : DISORGANIZE — **de·mor·al·i·za·tion** \di-ˌmȯr-ə-lə-'zā-shən\ n

de·mote \di-'mōt\ vb **de·mot·ed; de·mot·ing** : to reduce to a lower grade or rank — **de·mo·tion** \-'mō-shən\ n

de·mot·ic \di-'mä-tik\ adj : COMMON, POPULAR ⟨∼ idiom⟩

de·mur \di-'mər\ vb **de·murred; de·mur·ring** [ME *demuren*, *demeren* to linger, fr. AF *demurer*, *demoerer*, fr. L *demorari*, fr. *morari* to linger, fr. *mora* delay] : to take exception : OBJECT — **de·mur** n

de·mure \di-'myu̇r\ adj 1 : quietly modest : DECOROUS 2 : affectedly modest, reserved, or serious : PRIM ♦ *Synonyms* SHY, BASHFUL, COY, DIFFICULT, RETIRING, UNASSERTIVE — **de·mure·ly** adv

de·mur·rer \di-'mər-ər\ n : a claim by the defendant in a legal action that the plaintiff does not have sufficient grounds to proceed

den \'den\ n 1 : LAIR 1 2 : HIDEOUT ⟨a robber's ∼⟩; *also* : a place like a hideout or a center of secret activity ⟨opium ∼⟩ ⟨a ∼ of iniquity⟩ **3** : a cozy private little room

Den *abbr* Denmark

de·nar \'de-ˌnär, 'dä-\ — see MONEY table

de·na·ture \dē-'nā-chər\ *vb* **de·na·tured**; **de·na·tur·ing** : to remove or change the natural qualities of; *esp* : to make (alcohol) unfit for drinking

den·drol·o·gy \den-'drä-lə-jē\ *n* : the study of trees — **den·drol·o·gist** \-jist\ *n*

den·gue \'deŋ-gē, -ˌgä\ *n* [Sp] : an acute infectious disease characterized by headache, severe joint pain, and rash

de·ni \'de-ˌnē, 'dä-\ *n pl* — see *denar* at MONEY table

de·ni·al \di-'nī(-ə)l\ *n* **1** : rejection of a request **2** : refusal to admit the truth of a statement or charge; *also* : assertion that something alleged is false **3** : DISAVOWAL **4** : restriction on one's own activity or desires

de·nier \'den-yər\ *n* : a unit of fineness for yarn

den·i·grate \'de-ni-ˌgrāt\ *vb* **-grat·ed**; **-grat·ing** [L *denigrare*, fr. *nigrare* to blacken, fr. *niger* black] : to cast aspersions on : DEFAME — **den·i·gra·tion** \ˌde-ni-'grā-shən\ *n*

den·im \'de-nəm\ *n* [F *(serge) de Nîmes* serge of Nîmes, France] **1** : a firm durable twilled usu. cotton fabric woven with colored warp and white filling threads **2** *pl* : overalls or pants of usu. blue denim

den·i·zen \'de-nə-zən\ *n* : INHABITANT

de·nom·i·nate \di-'nä-mə-ˌnāt\ *vb* : to give a name to : DESIGNATE

de·nom·i·na·tion \di-ˌnä-mə-'nā-shən\ *n* **1** : an act of denominating **2** : a value or size of a series of related values (as of money) **3** : NAME, DESIGNATION; *esp* : a general name for a category **4** : a religious organization uniting local congregations in a single body — **de·nom·i·na·tion·al** \-shə-nəl\ *adj*

de·nom·i·na·tor \di-'nä-mə-ˌnā-tər\ *n* : the part of a fraction that is below the line indicating division

de·no·ta·tive \'dē-nō-ˌtā-tiv, di-'nō-tə-tiv\ *adj* **1** : denoting or tending to denote **2** : relating to denotation

de·note \di-'nōt\ *vb* **1** : to mark out plainly : INDICATE **2** : to make known **3** : MEAN, NAME — **de·no·ta·tion** \ˌdē-nō-'tā-shən\ *n*

de·noue·ment \ˌdā-ˌnü-'mäⁿ\ *n* [F *dénouement*, lit., untying] : the final outcome of the dramatic complications in a literary work

de·nounce \di-'naúns\ *vb* **de·nounced**; **de·nounc·ing** **1** : to pronounce esp. publicly to be blameworthy or evil **2** : to inform against : ACCUSE **3** : to announce formally the termination of (as a treaty) — **de·nounce·ment** *n*

de no·vo \di-'nō-vō\ *adv or adj* [L] : over again : ANEW ⟨a case tried ∼⟩

dense \'dens\ *adj* **dens·er**; **dens·est** **1** : marked by compactness or crowding together of parts : THICK ⟨∼ forest⟩ ⟨a ∼ fog⟩ **2** : DULL, STUPID — **dense·ly** *adv* — **dense·ness** *n*

den·si·ty \'den-sə-tē\ *n, pl* **-ties** **1** : the quality or state of being dense **2** : the quantity of something per unit volume, unit area, or unit length

dent \'dent\ *n* **1** : a small depressed place made by a blow or by pressure **2** : an impression or weakening effect made usu. against resistance **3** : initial progress — **dent** *vb*

den·tal \'den-t²l\ *adj* : of or relating to teeth or dentistry — **den·tal·ly** *adv*

dental floss *n* : a thread used to clean between the teeth

dental hygienist *n* : a person licensed to clean and examine teeth

den·tate \'den-ˌtāt\ *adj* : having pointed projections : NOTCHED

den·ti·frice \'den-tə-frəs\ *n* [ME *dentifricie*, fr. L *dentifricium*, fr. *dent-, dens* tooth + *fricare* to rub] : a powder, paste, or liquid for cleaning the teeth

den·tin \'den-t²n\ *or* **den·tine** \'den-ˌtēn, den-'tēn\ *n* : a calcareous material like bone but harder and denser that composes the principal mass of a tooth

den·tist \'den-tist\ *n* : a person licensed in the care, treatment, and replacement of teeth — **den·tist·ry** *n*

den·ti·tion \den-'ti-shən\ *n* : the number, kind, and arrangement of teeth (as of a person or animal); *also* : TEETH

den·ture \'den-chər\ *n* : a set of teeth; *esp* : a partial or complete set of false teeth

de·nude \di-'nüd, -'nyüd\ *vb* **de·nud·ed**; **de·nud·ing** : to strip the covering from — **de·nu·da·tion** \ˌdē-nü-'dā-shən, -nyü-\ *n*

de·nun·ci·a·tion \di-ˌnən-sē-'ā-shən\ *n* : the act of denouncing; *esp* : a public condemnation — **de·nun·ci·a·to·ry** \-'nən-sē-ə-ˌtór-ē\ *adj*

de·ny \di-'nī\ *vb* **de·nied**; **de·ny·ing** **1** : to declare untrue **2** : to refuse to recognize or acknowledge : DISAVOW **3** : to refuse to grant ⟨∼ a request⟩ **4** : to reject as false ⟨∼ a theory⟩

de·o·dar \'dē-ə-ˌdär\ *n* [Hindi & Urdu *devadār, deodār*, fr. Skt *devadāru*, fr. *deva* god + *dāru* wood] : a Himalayan cedar

de·odor·ant \dē-'ō-də-rənt\ *n* : a preparation that destroys or masks unpleasant odors

de·odor·ize \dē-'ō-də-ˌrīz\ *vb* : to eliminate the offensive odor of

de·ox·i·dize \dē-'äk-sə-ˌdīz\ *vb* : to remove esp. elemental oxygen from

de·oxy·ri·bo·nu·cle·ic acid \dē-ˌäk-si-ˌrī-bō-nü-ˌklē-ik-, -nyü-\ *n* : DNA

de·oxy·ri·bose \dē-ˌäk-si-'rī-ˌbōs\ *n* : a sugar with five carbon and four oxygen atoms in each molecule that is part of DNA

dep *abbr* **1** depart; departure **2** deposit **3** deputy

de·part \di-'pärt\ *vb* **1** : to go away : go away from : LEAVE **2** : DIE **3** : to turn aside : DEVIATE

de·part·ee \di-pär-'tē\ *n* : a person who is departing or who has departed

de·part·ment \di-'pärt-mənt\ *n* **1** : a distinct sphere or category esp. of an activity or attribute **2** : a functional or territorial division (as of a government, business, or college) — **de·part·men·tal** \di-ˌpärt-ˈmen-tᵊl, ˌdē-\ *adj* — **de·part·men·tal·ly** *adv*

department store *n* : a store having separate sections for a wide variety of goods

de·par·ture \di-ˈpär-chər\ *n* **1** : the act of going away **2** : a starting out (as on a journey) **3** : DIVERGENCE ⟨a ~ from tradition⟩

de·pend \di-ˈpend\ *vb* **1** : to be determined, based, or contingent ⟨life ~s on food⟩ **2** : TRUST, RELY ⟨you can ~ on me⟩ **3** : to be dependent esp. for financial support **4** : to hang down ⟨a vine ~*ing* from a tree⟩

de·pend·able \di-ˈpen-də-bəl\ *adj* : TRUSTWORTHY, RELIABLE — **de·pend·abil·i·ty** \-ˌpen-də-ˈbi-lə-tē\ *n*

de·pen·dence *also* **de·pen·dance** \di-ˈpen-dəns\ *n* **1** : the quality or state of being dependent; *esp* : the quality or state of being influenced by or subject to another **2** : RELIANCE, TRUST **3** : something on which one relies **4** : drug addiction; *also* : HABITUATION 2

de·pen·den·cy \-dən-sē\ *n, pl* **-cies** **1** : DEPENDENCE **2** : a territory under the jurisdiction of a nation but not formally annexed by it

¹**de·pen·dent** \-dənt\ *adj* **1** : hanging down **2** : determined or conditioned by another; *also* : affected with drug dependence **3** : relying on another for support **4** : subject to another's jurisdiction **5** : SUBORDINATE 4 ⟨~ clauses⟩

²**dependent** *also* **de·pen·dant** \-dənt\ *n* : one that is dependent; *esp* : a person who relies on another for support

dependent variable *n* : a variable whose value is determined by that of one or more other variables in a function

de·pict \di-ˈpikt\ *vb* **1** : to represent by a picture **2** : to describe in words — **de·pic·tion** \-ˈpik-shən\ *n*

de·pil·a·to·ry \di-ˈpi-lə-ˌtȯr-ē\ *n, pl* **-ries** : a preparation for removing hair, wool, or bristles

de·plane \dē-ˈplān\ *vb* : to get out of an airplane

de·plete \di-ˈplēt\ *vb* **de·plet·ed; de·plet·ing** : to exhaust esp. of strength or resources — **de·ple·tion** \-ˈplē-shən\ *n*

de·plor·able \di-ˈplȯr-ə-bəl\ *adj* **1** : LAMENTABLE ⟨a ~ death⟩ **2** : WRETCHED — **de·plor·ably** *adv*

de·plore \-ˈplȯr\ *vb* **de·plored; de·plor·ing** **1** : to feel or express grief for **2** : to regret strongly **3** : to consider unfortunate or deserving of disapproval

de·ploy \di-ˈplȯi\ *vb* : to spread out (as troops or ships) in order for battle — **de·ploy·ment** \-mənt\ *n*

de·po·nent \di-ˈpō-nənt\ *n* : one who gives evidence

de·pop·u·late \dē-ˈpä-pyə-ˌlāt\ *vb* : to reduce greatly the population of — **de·pop·u·la·tion** \-ˌpä-pyə-ˈlā-shən\ *n*

de·port \di-ˈpȯrt\ *vb* **1** : CONDUCT, BEHAVE **2** : BANISH, EXILE — **de·por·ta·tion** \ˌdē-ˌpȯr-ˈtā-shən\ *n*

de·port·ment \di-ˈpȯrt-mənt\ *n* : BEHAVIOR, BEARING

de·pose \di-ˈpōz\ *vb* **de·posed; de·pos·ing** **1** : to remove from high office (as of king) **2** : to testify under oath or by affidavit

¹**de·pos·it** \di-ˈpä-zət\ *vb* **de·pos·it·ed** \-zə-təd\; **de·pos·it·ing** **1** : to place for safekeeping or as a pledge; *esp* : to put money in a bank **2** : to lay down : PLACE **3** : to let fall or sink ⟨silt ~*ed* by a flood⟩ — **de·pos·i·tor** \-zə-tər\ *n*

²**deposit** *n* **1** : the state of being deposited ⟨money on ~⟩ **2** : something placed for safekeeping; *esp* : money deposited in a bank **3** : money given as a pledge **4** : an act of depositing **5** : something laid down ⟨a ~ of silt⟩ **6** : a natural accumulation (as of a mineral)

de·po·si·tion \ˌde-pə-ˈzi-shən, ˌdē-\ *n* **1** : an act of removing from a position of authority **2** : TESTIMONY **3** : the process of depositing **4** : DEPOSIT

de·pos·i·to·ry \di-ˈpä-zə-ˌtȯr-ē\ *n, pl* **-ries** : a place where something is deposited esp. for safekeeping

de·pot *1, 2 usu* ˈde-pō, *3 usu* ˈdē-\ *n* **1** : a place for storing goods or vehicles **2** : a place where military supplies or replacements are kept or assembled **3** : a building for railroad or bus passengers

depr *abbr* depreciation

de·prave \di-ˈprāv\ *vb* **de·praved; de·prav·ing** [ME, fr. AF *depraver*, fr. L *depravare* to pervert, fr. *pravus* crooked, bad] : CORRUPT, PERVERT — **de·praved** *adj* — **de·prav·i·ty** \-ˈpra-və-tē\ *n*

dep·re·cate \ˈde-pri-ˌkāt\ *vb* **-cat·ed; -cat·ing** [L *deprecari* to avert by prayer, fr. *precari* to pray] **1** : to express disapproval of **2** : BELITTLE — **dep·re·ca·tion** \ˌde-pri-ˈkā-shən\ *n*

dep·re·ca·to·ry \ˈde-pri-kə-ˌtȯr-ē\ *adj* **1** : APOLOGETIC **2** : serving to deprecate : DISAPPROVING

de·pre·ci·ate \di-ˈprē-shē-ˌāt\ *vb* **-at·ed; -at·ing** [ME, fr. LL *depreciatus*, pp. of *depretiare*, fr. L *pretium* price] **1** : BELITTLE, DISPARAGE **2** : to lessen in price or value — **de·pre·cia·ble** \-shə-bəl\ *adj* — **de·pre·ci·a·tion** \-ˌprē-shē-ˈā-shən\ *n*

dep·re·da·tion \ˌde-prə-ˈdā-shən\ *n* : a laying waste or plundering — **dep·re·date** \ˈde-prə-ˌdāt\ *vb*

de·press \di-ˈpres\ *vb* **1** : to press down : cause to sink to a lower position **2** : to lessen the activity or force of **3** : SADDEN, DISCOURAGE **4** : to lessen in price or value — **de·pres·sor** \-ˈpre-sər\ *n*

de·pres·sant \di-ˈpre-sᵊnt\ *n* : one that depresses; *esp* : a chemical substance (as a drug) that reduces bodily functional activity — **depressant** *adj*

de·pressed \-ˈprest\ *adj* **1** : low in spirits; *also* : affected with psychological depression **2** : suffering from economic depression

de·pres·sion \di-ˈpre-shən\ *n* **1** : an act of depressing : a state of being depressed **2** : a pressing down : LOWERING **3** : a state of feeling sad **4** : a psychological disorder marked esp. by sadness, inactivity, difficulty in thinking and concentration, and feelings of dejection **5** : a depressed area or part **6** : a period of low general economic activity with widespread unemployment

¹**de·pres·sive** \di-ˈpre-siv\ *adj* **1** : tending to depress **2** : characterized or affected by psychological depression

²**depressive** *n* : a person affected with or prone to psychological depression

de·pres·sur·ize \(ˌ)dē-ˈpre-shə-ˌrīz\ *vb* : to release pressure from

dep·ri·va·tion \ˌde-prə-ˈvā-shən\ *n* **1** : an act or instance of depriving : LOSS **2** : PRIVATION 2

de·prive \di-ˈprīv\ *vb* **de·prived; de·priv·ing 1** : to take something away from **2** : to stop from having something

deprived *adj* : marked by deprivation esp. of the necessities of life

de·pro·gram \(ˌ)dē-ˈprō-ˌgram, -grəm\ *vb* : to dissuade from convictions usu. of a religious nature often by coercive means

dept *abbr* department

depth \ˈdepth\ *n, pl* **depths** \ˈdepths\ **1** : something that is deep; *esp* : the deep part of a body of water **2** : a part that is far from the outside or surface; *also* : the middle or innermost part **3** : ABYSS **4** : a profound or intense state ⟨the ~*s* of reflection⟩; *also* : the worst part ⟨during the ~*s* of the depression⟩ **5** : a reprehensibly low condition **6** : the distance from top to bottom or from front to back **7** : the quality of being deep **8** : the degree of intensity

depth charge *n* : an explosive device for use underwater esp. against submarines

dep·u·ta·tion \ˌde-pyə-ˈtā-shən\ *n* **1** : the act of appointing a deputy **2** : DELEGATION

de·pute \di-ˈpyüt\ *vb* **de·put·ed; de·put·ing** : DELEGATE

dep·u·tize \ˈde-pyə-ˌtīz\ *vb* **-tized; -tiz·ing** : to appoint or act as deputy

dep·u·ty \ˈde-pyə-tē\ *n, pl* **-ties 1** : a person appointed to act for or in place of another **2** : an assistant empowered to act as a substitute in the absence of a superior **3** : a member of a lower house of a legislative assembly

der *or* **deriv** derivation; derivative

de·rail \di-ˈrāl\ *vb* : to leave or cause to leave the rails — **de·rail·ment** *n*

de·rail·leur \di-ˈrā-lər\ *n* [F *dérailleur*] : a device for shifting gears on a bicycle by moving the chain from one set of exposed gears to another

de·range \di-ˈrānj\ *vb* **de·ranged; de·rang·ing 1** : DISARRANGE, UPSET **2** : to make insane — **de·range·ment** *n*

der·by \ˈdər-bē, *Brit* ˈdär-\ *n, pl* **derbies 1** : a horse race usu. for three-year-olds held annually **2** : a race or contest open to all **3** : a stiff felt hat with dome-shaped crown and narrow brim

de·re·cho \də-ˈrā-(ˌ)chō\ *n, pl* **-chos** [Sp, straight (contrasted with *tornado*, taken to mean "turned")] : a complex of thunderstorms with powerful winds

de·reg·u·la·tion \(ˌ)dē-ˌre-gyü-ˈlā-shən\ *n* : the act of removing restrictions or regulations — **de·reg·u·late** \-ˈre-gyü-ˌlāt\ *vb*

¹**der·e·lict** \ˈder-ə-ˌlikt\ *adj* **1** : abandoned by the owner or occupant **2** : NEGLIGENT ⟨~ in his duty⟩

²**derelict** *n* **1** : something voluntarily abandoned; *esp* : a ship abandoned on the high seas **2** : a destitute homeless social misfit : VAGRANT, BUM

der·e·lic·tion \ˌder-ə-ˈlik-shən\ *n* **1** : the act of abandoning : the state of being abandoned **2** : intentional neglect ⟨~ of duty⟩

de·ride \di-ˈrīd\ *vb* **de·rid·ed; de·rid·ing** [L *deridēre*, fr. *ridēre* to laugh] : to laugh at scornfully : RIDICULE

de ri·gueur \də-rē-ˈgər\ *adj* [F] : prescribed or required by fashion, etiquette, or custom : PROPER

de·ri·sion \də-ˈri-zhən\ *n* : RIDICULE — **de·ri·sive** \-ˈrī-siv\ *adj* — **de·ri·sive·ly** *adv* — **de·ri·sive·ness** *n* — **de·ri·so·ry** \-ˈrī-sə-rē\ *adj*

der·i·va·tion \ˌder-ə-ˈvā-shən\ *n* **1** : the formation of a word from an earlier word or root; *also* : an act of ascertaining or stating the derivation of a word **2** : ETYMOLOGY **3** : SOURCE, ORIGIN; *also* : DESCENT **4** : an act or process of deriving

de·riv·a·tive \di-ˈri-və-tiv\ *n* **1** : a word formed by derivation **2** : something derived **3** : the limit of the ratio of the change of a function's value to the change in its independent variable as the latter change approaches zero — **derivative** *adj*

de·rive \di-ˈrīv\ *vb* **de·rived; de·riv·ing** [ME, fr. AF *deriver*, fr. L *derivare*, lit., to draw off (water), fr. *de-* from + *rivus* stream] **1** : to receive or obtain from a source **2** : to obtain from a parent substance **3** : INFER, DEDUCE **4** : to trace the derivation of **5** : to come from a certain source

der·mal \ˈdər-məl\ *adj* : of or relating to the skin : CUTANEOUS

der·ma·ti·tis \ˌdər-mə-ˈtī-təs\ *n, pl* **-tit·i·des** \-ˈti-tə-ˌdēz\ *or* **-ti·tis·es** : inflammation of the skin

der·ma·tol·o·gy \-ˈtä-lə-jē\ *n* : a branch of medical science dealing with the structure, functions, and diseases of the skin — **der·ma·tol·o·gist** \-jist\ *n*

der·mis \ˈdər-məs\ *n* : the sensitive vascular inner layer of the skin

der·o·gate \ˈder-ə-ˌgāt\ *vb* **-gat·ed; -gat·ing 1** : to cause to seem inferior : DISPARAGE **2** : DETRACT — **der·o·ga·tion** \ˌder-ə-ˈgā-shən\ *n* — **de·rog·a·tive** \di-ˈrä-gə-tiv\ *adj*

de·rog·a·to·ry \di-ˈrä-gə-ˌtȯr-ē\ *adj* : intended to lower the reputation of a person or thing : DISPARAGING — **de·rog·a·to·ri·ly** \-ˌrä-gə-ˈtȯr-ə-lē\ *adv*

der·rick \ˈder-ik\ *n* [obs. *derrick* hangman, gallows, fr. *Derick*, name of 17th cent. Eng. hangman] **1** : a hoisting apparatus : CRANE **2** : a framework over a drill hole (as for oil) for supporting machinery

der·ri·ere *or* **der·ri·ère** \ˌder-ē-ˈer\ *n* : BUTTOCKS

der·ring-do \ˌder-iŋ-ˈdü\ n : DARING

der·rin·ger \ˈder-ən-jər\ n : a short-barreled pocket pistol

der·vish \ˈdər-vish\ n [Turk *derviş*, lit., beggar, fr. Pers *darvīsh*] : a member of a Muslim religious order noted for devotional exercises (as bodily movements leading to a trance)

de·sal·i·nate \dē-ˈsa-lə-ˌnāt\ vb **-nat·ed**; **-nat·ing** : DESALT — **de·sal·i·na·tion** \-ˌsa-lə-ˈnā-shən\ n

de·sal·i·nize \dē-ˈsa-lə-ˌnīz\ vb **-nized**; **-niz·ing** : DESALT — **de·sal·i·ni·za·tion** \-ˌsa-lə-nə-ˈzā-shən\ n

de·salt \dē-ˈsȯlt\ vb : to remove salt from ⟨∼ seawater⟩ — **de·salt·er** n

des·cant \ˈdes-ˌkant\ vb 1 : to sing or play part music : SING 2 : to discourse or write at length

de·scend \di-ˈsend\ vb 1 : to pass from a higher to a lower place or level : pass, move, or climb down or down along 2 : DERIVE ⟨∼ed from royalty⟩ 3 : to pass by inheritance or transmission 4 : to incline, lead, or extend downward 5 : to swoop down or appear suddenly (as in an attack)

de·scen·dant *also* **de·scen·dent** \-ˈsen-dənt\ adj 1 : DESCENDING 2 : proceeding from an ancestor or source

²**descendant** *also* **descendent** n 1 : one descended from another or from a common stock 2 : one deriving directly from a precursor or prototype

de·scent \di-ˈsent\ n 1 : ANCESTRY, BIRTH, LINEAGE 2 : the act or process of descending 3 : SLOPE 4 : a descending way (as a downgrade) 5 : a sudden hostile raid or assault 6 : a downward step (as in station or value) : DECLINE

de·scram·ble \dē-ˈskram-bəl\ vb : UNSCRAMBLE 2 ⟨∼ satellite transmissions⟩ — **de·scram·bler** \-b(ə-)lər\ n

de·scribe \di-ˈskrīb\ vb **de·scribed**; **de·scrib·ing** 1 : to represent or give an account of in words 2 : to trace the outline of — **de·scrib·able** adj

de·scrip·tion \di-ˈskrip-shən\ n 1 : an account of something; *esp* : an account that presents a picture to a person who reads or hears it 2 : KIND, SORT — **de·scrip·tive** \-ˈskrip-tiv\ adj

de·scry \di-ˈskrī\ vb **de·scried**; **de·scry·ing** 1 : to catch sight of 2 : to discover by observation or investigation

des·e·crate \ˈde-si-ˌkrāt\ vb **-crat·ed**; **-crat·ing** : PROFANE — **des·e·cra·tion** \ˌde-si-ˈkrā-shən\ n

de·seg·re·gate \dē-ˈse-gri-ˌgāt\ vb : to eliminate segregation in; *esp* : to free of any law or practice requiring isolation on the basis of race — **de·seg·re·ga·tion** \-ˌse-gri-ˈgā-shən\ n

de·sen·si·tize \dē-ˈsen-sə-ˌtīz\ vb : to make (a sensitized or hypersensitive individual) insensitive or nonreactive to a sensitizing agent — **de·sen·si·ti·za·tion** \-ˌsen-sə-tə-ˈzā-shən\ n

¹**des·ert** \ˈde-zərt\ n : dry land with few plants and little rainfall

²**des·ert** \ˈde-zərt\ adj : of, relating to, or resembling a desert; *esp* : being barren and without life ⟨a ∼ island⟩

³**de·sert** \di-ˈzərt\ n 1 : the quality or fact of deserving reward or punishment 2 : a just reward or punishment

⁴**de·sert** \di-ˈzərt\ vb 1 : to withdraw from 2 : ABANDON, FORSAKE — **de·sert·er** n — **de·ser·tion** \-ˈzər-shən\ n

de·serve \di-ˈzərv\ vb **de·served**; **de·serv·ing** : to be worthy of : MERIT — **de·serv·ing** adj

de·serv·ed·ly \-ˈzər-vəd-lē\ adv : according to merit : JUSTLY

deshabille *var of* DISHABILLE

des·ic·cate \ˈde-si-ˌkāt\ vb **-cat·ed**; **-cat·ing** : DRY, DEHYDRATE — **des·ic·ca·tion** \ˌde-si-ˈkā-shən\ n — **des·ic·ca·tor** \ˈde-si-ˌkā-tər\ n

de·sid·er·a·tum \di-ˌsi-də-ˈrä-təm, -ˌzi-, -ˈrā-\ n, pl **-ta** \-tə\ [L] : something desired as essential

¹**de·sign** \di-ˈzīn\ vb 1 : to conceive and plan out in the mind 2 : INTEND 3 : to devise for a specific function or end 4 : to make a pattern or sketch of 5 : to conceive and draw the plans for

²**design** n 1 : a particular purpose : deliberate planning 2 : a mental project or scheme : PLAN 3 : a secret project or scheme : PLOT 4 pl : aggressive or evil intent — used with on or against 5 : a preliminary sketch or plan 6 : an underlying scheme that governs functioning, developing, or unfolding : MOTIF ⟨the general ∼ of the epic⟩ 7 : the arrangement of elements or details in a product or a work of art 8 : a decorative pattern ⟨a floral ∼⟩ 9 : the art of executing designs

¹**des·ig·nate** \ˈde-zig-ˌnāt, -nət\ adj : chosen but not yet installed ⟨ambassador ∼⟩

²**des·ig·nate** \-ˌnāt\ vb **-nat·ed**; **-nat·ing** 1 : to appoint and set apart for a special purpose 2 : to mark or point out : INDICATE; *also* : SPECIFY, STIPULATE 3 : to call by a name or title — **des·ig·na·tion** \ˌde-zig-ˈnā-shən\ n

designated driver n : a person chosen to abstain from alcohol so as to transport others safely

designated hitter n : a baseball player designated at the start of the game to bat in place of the pitcher without causing the pitcher to be removed from the game

de·sign·er \di-ˈzī-nər\ n 1 : one who creates plans for a project or structure 2 : one who designs and manufactures high-fashion clothing — **designer** adj

designer drug n : a synthetic version of an illicit drug that has been chemically altered to avoid its prohibition

de·sign·ing \di-ˈzī-niŋ\ adj : CRAFTY, SCHEMING

de·sir·able \di-ˈzī-rə-bəl\ adj 1 : PLEASING, ATTRACTIVE 2 : ADVISABLE ⟨∼ legislation⟩ — **de·sir·abil·i·ty** \-ˌzī-rə-ˈbi-lə-tē\ n — **de·sir·able·ness** n — **de·sir·ably** \-ˈzī-rə-blē\ adv

¹**de·sire** \di-ˈzī(-ə)r\ vb **de·sired**; **de·sir·ing** [ME, fr. AF *desirer*, fr. L *desiderare*, fr. *sider-*, *sidus* heavenly body] 1 : to long

or hope for : exhibit or feel desire for **2**
: REQUEST
²**desire** n **1** : a strong wish : LONGING,
CRAVING **2** : sexual urge or appetite **3** : a
usu. formal request for action **4** : something desired
de·sir·ous \di-'zī(-ə)r-əs\ adj : eagerly
wishing ⟨∼ of fame⟩
de·sist \di-'zist, -'sist\ vb : to cease to proceed or act
desk \'desk\ n [ME deske, fr. ML desca,
fr. It desco table, fr. L discus dish, disc] **1**
: a table, frame, or case esp. for writing
and reading **2** : a counter, stand, or
booth at which a person performs duties
3 : a specialized division of an organization (as a newspaper) ⟨city ∼⟩
desk·top publishing \'desk-ˌtäp-\ n : the
production of printed matter by means of
a microcomputer
¹**des·o·late** \'de-sə-lət, -zə-\ adj **1** : DESERTED, ABANDONED **2** : FORSAKEN,
LONELY **3** : DILAPIDATED **4** : BARREN,
LIFELESS ⟨a ∼ landscape⟩ **5** : CHEERLESS, GLOOMY ⟨∼ memories⟩ — **des·o·late·ly** adv — **des·o·late·ness** n
²**des·o·late** \-ˌlāt\ vb -**lat·ed**; -**lat·ing** : to
make desolate : lay waste : make wretched
des·o·la·tion \ˌde-sə-'lā-shən, -zə-\ n **1**
: the action of desolating **2** : GRIEF, SADNESS **3** : LONELINESS **4** : DEVASTATION,
RUIN **5** : barren wasteland
des·oxy·ri·bo·nu·cle·ic acid \de-ˌzäk-sē-
ˈrī-bō-nü-ˌklē-ik-, -nyü-\ n : DNA
¹**de·spair** \di-'sper\ vb : to lose all hope or
confidence — **de·spair·ing** \-iŋ\ adj —
de·spair·ing·ly adv
²**despair** n **1** : utter loss of hope **2** : a
cause of hopelessness
des·patch chiefly Brit var of DISPATCH
des·per·a·do \ˌdes-pə-'rä-dō, -'rä-\ n, pl
-**does** or -**dos** : a bold or reckless criminal
des·per·ate \'des-pə-rət, -prət\ adj **1**
: being beyond or almost beyond hope
: causing despair **2** : RASH ⟨a ∼ attempt⟩
3 : extremely intense — **des·per·ate·ly**
adv — **des·per·ate·ness** n
des·per·a·tion \ˌdes-pə-'rä-shən\ n **1** : a
loss of hope and surrender to despair **2**
: a state of hopelessness leading to rashness
des·pi·ca·ble \di-'spi-kə-bəl, 'des-pi-\ adj
: deserving to be despised — **de·spi·ca·
bly** \-blē\ adv
de·spise \di-'spīz\ vb **de·spised**; **de·
spis·ing 1** : to look down on with contempt or aversion : DISDAIN, DETEST **2**
: to regard as negligible, worthless, or distasteful
de·spite \di-'spīt\ prep : in spite of
de·spoil \di-'spȯi(-ə)l\ vb : to strip of belongings, possessions, or value — **de·
spoil·er** n — **de·spoil·ment** n
de·spo·li·a·tion \di-ˌspō-lē-'ā-shən\ n
: the act of plundering : the state of being
despoiled
¹**de·spond** \di-'spänd\ vb : to become discouraged or disheartened
²**despond** n : DESPONDENCY
de·spon·den·cy \-'spän-dən-sē\ n : DE-

JECTION, HOPELESSNESS — **de·spon·
dent** \-dənt\ adj — **de·spon·dent·ly** adv
des·pot \'des-pət, -ˌpät\ n [MF despote, fr.
Gk despotēs master, lord, autocrat] **1** : a
ruler with absolute power and authority
2 : a person exercising power tyrannically — **des·pot·ic** \des-'pä-tik\ adj — **des·
po·tism** \'des-pə-ˌti-zəm\ n
des·sert \di-'zərt\ n : a course of sweet
food, fruit, or cheese served at the close
of a meal
de·stig·ma·tize \dē-'stig-mə-ˌtīz\ vb : to
remove associations of shame or disgrace
from
des·ti·na·tion \ˌdes-tə-'nā-shən\ n **1** : a
purpose for which something is destined
2 : an act of appointing, setting aside for
a purpose, or predetermining **3** : a place
to which one is journeying or to which
something is sent
des·tine \'des-tən\ vb **des·tined**; **des·tin·
ing 1** : to settle in advance **2** : to designate, assign, or dedicate in advance **3** : to
direct or set apart for a specific purpose
or place
des·ti·ny \'des-tə-nē\ n, pl -**nies 1**
: something to which a person or thing is
destined : FATE, FORTUNE **2** : a predetermined course of events
des·ti·tute \'des-tə-ˌtüt, -ˌtyüt\ adj **1**
: lacking something needed or desirable
2 : suffering extreme poverty — **des·ti·
tu·tion** \ˌdes-tə-'tü-shən, -'tyü-\ n
de·stroy \di-'strȯi\ vb **1** : to put an end to
: RUIN **2** : KILL
de·stroy·er \di-'strȯi-ər\ n **1** : one that
destroys **2** : a small speedy warship
de·struc·ti·ble \di-'strək-tə-bəl\ adj : capable of being destroyed — **de·struc·ti·
bil·i·ty** \-ˌstrək-tə-'bi-lə-tē\ n
de·struc·tion \di-'strək-shən\ n **1** : RUIN
2 : the action or process of destroying
something **3** : a destroying agency
de·struc·tive \di-'strək-tiv\ adj **1** : causing destruction : RUINOUS **2** : designed
or tending to hurt or destroy — **de·
struc·tive·ly** adv — **de·struc·tive·ness**
n
de·sue·tude \'de-swi-ˌtüd, -ˌtyüd\ n : DISUSE
des·ul·to·ry \'de-səl-ˌtȯr-ē\ adj : passing
aimlessly from one thing or subject to
another : DISCONNECTED
det abbr **1** detached; detachment **2** detail
de·tach \di-'tach\ vb **1** : to separate esp.
from a larger mass **2** : DISENGAGE,
WITHDRAW — **de·tach·able** adj
de·tached \di-'tacht\ adj **1** : not joined
or connected : SEPARATE **2** : ALOOF, IMPARTIAL ⟨a ∼ attitude⟩
de·tach·ment \di-'tach-mənt\ n **1** : SEPARATION **2** : the dispatching of a body of
troops or part of a fleet from the main
body for special service; also : the portion
so dispatched **3** : a small permanent
military unit of special composition **4**
: indifference to worldly concerns
: ALOOFNESS **5** : IMPARTIALITY
¹**de·tail** \di-'tāl, 'dē-ˌtāl\ n [F détail, fr. OF
detail slice, piece, fr. detaillier to cut in
pieces, fr. taillier to cut] **1** : a dealing
with something item by item ⟨go into

~\>; *also* : ITEM, PARTICULAR ⟨the ~s of a story⟩ 2 : selection (as of soldiers) for special duty; *also* : the persons thus selected

²**detail** *vb* 1 : to report in particulars : SPECIFY 2 : to assign to a special duty

de-tailed \di-'tāld, 'dē-ˌtāld\ *adj* : marked by abundant detail

de-tail-ing \'dē-ˌtāl-iŋ\ *n* : the meticulous cleaning and refurbishing of an automobile

de-tain \di-'tān\ *vb* 1 : to hold in or as if in custody 2 : STOP, DELAY

de-tect \di-'tekt\ *vb* : to discover the nature, existence, presence, or fact of — **de-tect-able** *adj* — **de-tec-tion** \-'tek-shən\ *n* — **de-tec-tor** \-'tek-tər\ *n*

¹**de-tec-tive** \di-'tek-tiv\ *adj* 1 : fitted or used for detection 2 : of or relating to detectives

²**detective** *n* : a person employed or engaged in detecting lawbreakers or getting information that is not readily accessible

dé-tente *or* **de-tente** \dā-'tänt\ *n* [F] : a relaxation of strained relations or tensions (as between nations)

de-ten-tion \di-'ten-chən\ *n* 1 : the act or fact of detaining : CONFINEMENT; *esp* : a period of temporary custody prior to disposition by a court 2 : a forced delay

de-ter \di-'tər\ *vb* **de-terred; de-ter-ring** [L *deterrēre*, fr. *terrēre* to frighten] 1 : to turn aside, discourage, or prevent from acting (as by fear) 2 : INHIBIT

de-ter-gent \di-'tər-jənt\ *n* : a cleansing agent; *esp* : a chemical product similar to soap in its cleaning ability

de-te-ri-o-rate \di-'tir-ē-ə-ˌrāt\ *vb* **-rat-ed; -rat-ing** : to make or become worse in quality or condition — **de-te-ri-o-ra-tion** \-ˌtir-ē-ə-'rā-shən\ *n*

de-ter-min-able \-'tər-mə-nə-bəl\ *adj* : capable of being determined; *esp* : ASCERTAINABLE

de-ter-mi-nant \-mə-nənt\ *n* 1 : something that determines or conditions 2 : GENE

de-ter-mi-nate \di-'tər-mə-nət\ *adj* 1 : having fixed limits : DEFINITE ⟨a ~ period of time⟩ 2 : definitely settled ⟨in ~ order⟩ — **de-ter-mi-nate-ness** *n*

de-ter-mi-na-tion \di-ˌtər-mə-'nā-shən\ *n* 1 : the act of coming to a decision; *also* : the decision or conclusion reached 2 : a fixing of the extent, position, or character of something 3 : accurate measurement (as of length or volume) 4 : firm or fixed purpose — **de-ter-mi-na-tive** \-'tər-mə-ˌnā-tiv, -'tər-mə-nə-tiv\ *adj*

de-ter-mine \di-'tər-mən\ *vb* **-mined; -min-ing** 1 : to fix conclusively or authoritatively 2 : to come to a decision : SETTLE, RESOLVE 3 : to fix the form or character of beforehand : ORDAIN; *also* : REGULATE 4 : to find out the limits, nature, dimensions, or scope of ⟨~ a position at sea⟩ 5 : to bring about as a result

de-ter-mined \-'tər-mənd\ *adj* 1 : firmly resolved 2 : characterized by or showing determination — **de-ter-mined-ly** \-mənd-lē, -mə-nəd-lē\ *adv* — **de-ter-mined-ness** *n*

de-ter-min-ism \di-'tər-mə-ˌni-zəm\ *n* : a doctrine that acts of the will, natural events, or social changes are determined by preceding events or natural causes — **de-ter-min-ist** \-nist\ *n or adj*

de-ter-rence \di-'tər-əns\ *n* : the inhibition of criminal behavior by fear esp. of punishment

de-ter-rent \-ənt\ *adj* 1 : serving to deter ⟨the law's ~ effect⟩ 2 : relating to deterrence — **deterrent** *n*

de-test \di-'test\ *vb* [L *detestari*, lit., to curse while calling a deity to witness, fr. *de-* from + *testari* to call to witness, fr. *testis* witness] : LOATHE, HATE — **de-test-able** *adj* — **de-tes-ta-tion** \ˌdē-ˌtes-'tā-shən\ *n*

de-throne \di-'thrōn\ *vb* : to remove from a throne : DEPOSE — **de-throne-ment** *n*

det-o-nate \'de-tᵊn-ˌāt\ *vb* **-nat-ed; -nat-ing** : to explode or cause to explode with violence — **det-o-na-tion** \ˌde-tᵊn-'ā-shən\ *n*

det-o-na-tor \'de-tᵊn-ˌā-tər\ *n* : a device for detonating an explosive

¹**de-tour** \'dē-ˌtu̇r\ *n* : an indirect way replacing part of a route

²**detour** *vb* : to go by detour

de-tox \'dē-ˌtäks, di-'täks\ *n* : detoxification from an intoxicating or addictive substance — **detox** *vb*

de-tox-i-fy \dē-'täk-sə-ˌfī\ *vb* **-fied; -fy-ing** 1 : to remove a poison or toxin or the effect of such from 2 : to free (as a drug user) from an intoxicating or addictive substance or from dependence on it — **de-tox-i-fi-ca-tion** \dē-ˌtäk-sə-fə-'kā-shən\ *n*

de-tract \di-'trakt\ *vb* 1 : to take away or diminish the value or effect of something 2 : DIVERT ⟨~s attention from the real issue⟩ — **de-trac-tion** \-'trak-shən\ *n* — **de-trac-tor** \-'trak-tər\ *n*

de-train \dē-'trān\ *vb* : to leave or cause to leave a railroad train

det-ri-ment \'de-trə-mənt\ *n* : INJURY, DAMAGE; *also* : a cause of injury or damage — **det-ri-men-tal** \ˌde-trə-'ment-ᵊl\ *adj* — **det-ri-men-tal-ly** *adv*

de-tri-tus \di-'trī-təs\ *n, pl* **de-tri-tus** : fragments resulting from disintegration (as of rocks) : DEBRIS

deuce \'düs, 'dyüs\ *n* 1 : a two in cards or dice 2 : a tie in a tennis game with both sides at 40 3 : DEVIL — used chiefly as a mild oath

Deut *abbr* Deuteronomy

deu-te-ri-um \dü-'tir-ē-əm, dyü-\ *n* : an isotope of hydrogen that has twice the mass of ordinary hydrogen

Deu-ter-on-o-my \ˌdü-tə-'rä-nə-mē, ˌdyü-\ *n* — see BIBLE table

deut-sche mark \'dȯi-chə-ˌmärk\ *n* : a former basic monetary unit of Germany

dev *abbr* deviation

de-val-ue \dē-'val-yü\ *vb* : to reduce the international exchange value of ⟨~ a currency⟩ — **de-val-u-a-tion** \-ˌval-yə-'wā-shən\ *n*

dev-as-tate \'de-və-ˌstāt\ *vb* **-tat-ed; -tat-**

ing 1 : to bring to ruin **2 :** to reduce to chaos or helplessness — **dev·as·tat·ing·ly** adv — **dev·as·ta·tion** \de-və-'stā-shən\ n

de·vel·op \di-'ve-ləp\ vb **1 :** to unfold gradually or in detail **2 :** to place (exposed photographic material) in chemicals to produce a visible image **3 :** to bring out the possibilities of **4 :** to make more available or usable ⟨~ land⟩ **5 :** to acquire gradually ⟨~ a taste for olives⟩ **6 :** to go through a natural process of growth, differentiation, or evolution **7 :** to come into being gradually — **de·vel·op·er** n — **de·vel·op·ment** n — **de·vel·op·men·tal** \-,ve-ləp-'men-tᵊl\ adj — **de·vel·op·men·tal·ly** \-tᵊl-ē\ adv

de·vi·ant \'dē-vē-ənt\ adj : deviating esp. from some accepted norm ⟨~ behavior⟩ — **de·vi·ance** \-əns\ n — **de·vi·an·cy** \-ən-sē\ n — **deviant** n

de·vi·ate \'dē-vē-,āt\ vb **-at·ed; -at·ing** [LL deviare, fr. L de- from + via way] : to turn aside from a course, standard, principle, or topic — **de·vi·ate** \-vē-ət, -vē-,āt\ n — **de·vi·a·tion** \,dē-vē-'ā-shən\ n

de·vice \di-'vīs\ n **1 :** SCHEME, STRATAGEM **2 :** a piece of equipment or a mechanism for a special purpose **3 :** DESIRE, INCLINATION ⟨left to my own ~s⟩ **4 :** an emblematic design

¹dev·il \'de-vəl\ n [ME devel, fr. OE dēofol, fr. LL diabolus, fr. Gk diabolos, lit., slanderer, fr. diaballein to throw across, slander, fr. dia- across + ballein to throw] **1** often cap : the personal supreme spirit of evil **2 :** DEMON **3 :** a wicked person **4 :** an energetic, reckless, or dashing person **5 :** FELLOW ⟨poor ~⟩ ⟨lucky ~⟩

²devil vb **-iled** or **-illed; -il·ing** or **-il·ling 1 :** to season highly ⟨~ed eggs⟩ **2 :** TEASE, ANNOY

dev·il·ish \'de-və-lish\ adj **1 :** befitting a devil : EVIL; also : MISCHIEVOUS **2 :** EXTREME ⟨in a ~ hurry⟩ — **dev·il·ish·ly** adv — **dev·il·ish·ness** n

dev·il·ment \'de-vəl-mənt, -,ment\ n : MISCHIEF

dev·il·ry \-rē\ or **dev·il·try** \-trē\ n, pl **-il·ries** or **-il·tries 1 :** action performed with the help of the devil **2 :** MISCHIEF

de·vi·ous \'dē-vē-əs\ adj **1 :** deviating from a straight line : ROUNDABOUT **2 :** ERRANT **3 :** TRICKY, CUNNING

¹de·vise \di-'vīz\ vb **de·vised; de·vis·ing** [ME, fr. AF deviser to divide, distinguish, invent, fr. VL *divisare, fr. L dividere to divide] **1 :** INVENT **2 :** PLOT **3 :** to give (real estate) by will

²devise n **1 :** a disposing of real property by will **2 :** a will or clause of a will disposing of real property **3 :** property given by will

de·vi·tal·ize \dē-'vī-tə-,līz\ vb : to deprive of life or vitality

de·void \di-'vȯid\ adj : being without : VOID ⟨a book ~ of interest⟩

de·voir \də-'vwär\ n **1 :** DUTY **2 :** a formal act of civility or respect

de·volve \di-'välv\ vb **de·volved; de·volv·ing :** to pass (as rights or responsibility) from one to another usu. by suc-

cession or transmission — **dev·o·lu·tion** \,de-və-'lü-shən, ,dē-\ n

De·vo·ni·an \di-'vō-nē-ən\ adj : of, relating to, or being the period of the Paleozoic era between the Silurian and the Mississippian — **Devonian** n

de·vote \di-'vōt\ vb **de·vot·ed; de·vot·ing 1 :** to commit to wholly or chiefly ⟨~s herself to serving the poor⟩ **2 :** to set apart for a special purpose : DEDICATE

de·vot·ed \-'vō-təd\ adj : characterized by loyalty and devotion : FAITHFUL ⟨~ fans⟩

dev·o·tee \,de-və-'tē, -'tā\ n : an ardent follower, supporter, or enthusiast

de·vo·tion \di-'vō-shən\ n **1 :** religious fervor **2 :** an act of prayer or private worship — usu. used in pl. **3 :** a religious exercise for private use **4 :** the fact or state of being dedicated and loyal ⟨~ to music⟩; also : the act of devoting — **de·vo·tion·al** \-shə-nəl\ adj

de·vour \di-'vaù(-ə)r\ vb **1 :** to eat up greedily or ravenously **2 :** WASTE, ANNIHILATE ⟨the forest was ~ed by fire⟩ **3 :** to enjoy avidly ⟨~ a book⟩ — **de·vour·er** n

de·vout \di-'vaùt\ adj **1 :** devoted to religion : PIOUS **2 :** expressing devotion or piety **3 :** EARNEST, SERIOUS ⟨a ~ baseball fan⟩ — **de·vout·ly** adv — **de·vout·ness** n

dew \'dü, 'dyü\ n : moisture that condenses on the surfaces of cool bodies at night — **dewy** adj

dew·ber·ry \'dü-,ber-ē, 'dyü-\ n : any of several sweet edible berries related to and resembling blackberries; also : a trailing bramble bearing these

dew·claw \-,klȯ\ n : a digit on the foot of a mammal that does not reach the ground; also : its claw or hoof

dew·lap \-,lap\ n : loose skin hanging under the neck of an animal

dew point n : the temperature at which the moisture in the air begins to condense

dex·ter·i·ty \dek-'ster-ə-tē\ n, pl **-ties 1 :** mental skill or quickness **2 :** readiness and grace in physical activity; esp : skill and ease in using the hands

dex·ter·ous \'dek-strəs\ adj **1 :** CLEVER **2 :** done with skillfulness **3 :** skillful and competent with the hands — **dex·ter·ous·ly** adv

dex·trose \'dek-,strōs\ n : the naturally occurring form of glucose found in plants and blood

DFC abbr Distinguished Flying Cross

dg abbr decigram

DG abbr **1** [LL Dei gratia] by the grace of God **2** director general

DH \dē-'āch\ n : DESIGNATED HITTER

dhow \'daù\ n : an Arab sailing ship usu. having a long overhang forward and a high poop

DI abbr drill instructor

dia abbr diameter

di·a·be·tes \,dī-ə-'bē-tēz, -təs\ n : an abnormal state marked by passage of excessive amounts of urine; esp : one (**diabetes**

mel·li·tus \-'me-lə-təs\) characterized by deficient insulin, by excess sugar in the blood and urine, and by thirst, hunger, and loss of weight — **di·a·bet·ic** \-'be-tik\ *adj or n*

di·a·bol·i·cal \ˌdī-ə-'bä-li-kəl\ *or* **di·a·bol·ic** \-lik\ *adj* : DEVILISH ⟨a ~ plot⟩ — **di·a·bol·i·cal·ly** \-k(ə-)lē\ *adv*

di·a·crit·ic \ˌdī-ə-'kri-tik\ *n* : a mark accompanying a letter and indicating a sound value different from that of the same letter when unmarked — **di·a·crit·i·cal** \-ti-kəl\ *adj*

di·a·dem \'dī-ə-ˌdem\ *n* : CROWN; *esp* : a royal headband

di·aer·e·sis *or* **di·er·e·sis** \dī-'er-ə-səs\ *n, pl* **-e·ses** \-ˌsēz\ : a mark ¨ placed over a vowel to show that it is pronounced in a separate syllable (as in *naïve*)

diag *abbr* 1 diagonal 2 diagram

di·ag·no·sis \ˌdī-ig-'nō-səs\ *n, pl* **-no·ses** \-ˌsēz\ : the art or act of identifying a disease from its signs and symptoms; *also* : the decision reached by diagnosis — **di·ag·nose** \'dī-ig-ˌnōs\ *vb* — **di·ag·nos·tic** \ˌdī-ig-'näs-tik\ *adj* — **di·ag·nos·ti·cian** \-ˌnäs-'ti-shən\ *n*

¹**di·ag·o·nal** \dī-'a-gə-nəl\ *adj* 1 : extending from one corner to the opposite corner in a 4-sided figure 2 : running in a slanting direction ⟨~ stripes⟩ 3 : having slanting markings or parts ⟨a ~ weave⟩ — **di·ag·o·nal·ly** *adv*

²**diagonal** *n* 1 : a diagonal line 2 : a diagonal row, pattern, or direction 3 : SLASH 3

¹**di·a·gram** \'dī-ə-ˌgram\ *n* : a design and esp. a drawing that makes something easier to understand — **di·a·gram·ma·ble** \-ˌgra-mə-bəl\ *adj* — **di·a·gram·mat·ic** \ˌdī-ə-grə-'ma-tik\ *adj* — **di·a·gram·mat·i·cal·ly** \-ti-k(ə-)lē\ *adv*

²**diagram** *vb* **-grammed** *or* **-gramed** \-ˌgramd\; **-gram·ming** *or* **-gram·ing** : to represent by a diagram

¹**di·al** \'dī(-ə)l\ *n* [ME *dyal*, fr. ML *dialis* clock wheel revolving daily, fr. L *dies* day] 1 : the face of a sundial 2 : the face of a timepiece 3 : a face with a pointer and numbers that indicate something ⟨the ~ of a gauge⟩ 4 : a device used for making electrical connections or for regulating operation (as of a radio)

²**dial** *vb* **di·aled** *or* **di·alled**; **di·al·ing** *or* **di·al·ling** 1 : to manipulate a dial so as to operate or select 2 : to make a telephone call or connection

³**dial** *abbr* dialect

di·a·lect \'dī-ə-ˌlekt\ *n* : a regional variety of a language

di·a·lec·tic \ˌdī-ə-'lek-tik\ *n* : the process or art of reasoning by discussion of conflicting ideas; *also* : the tension between opposing elements — **di·a·lec·ti·cal** \-ti-kəl\ *adj*

dialog box *n* : a window on a computer screen for choosing options or inputting information

di·a·logue \'dī-ə-ˌlòg\ *n* 1 : a conversation between two or more parties 2 : the parts of a literary or dramatic work that represent conversation

di·al·y·sis \dī-'a-lə-səs\ *n, pl* **-y·ses** \-ˌsēz\ 1 : the separation of substances from solution by means of their unequal diffusion through semipermeable membranes 2 : the medical procedure of removing blood from an artery, purifying it by dialysis, and returning it to a vein

diam *abbr* diameter

di·am·e·ter \dī-'a-mə-tər\ *n* [ME *diametre*, fr. MF, fr. L *diametros*, fr. Gk, fr. *dia-* through + *metron* measure] 1 : a straight line passing through the center of a figure or body; *esp* : one that divides a circle in half 2 : the length of a diameter

di·a·met·ric \ˌdī-ə-'me-trik\ *or* **di·a·met·ri·cal** \-tri-kəl\ *adj* 1 : of, relating to, or constituting a diameter 2 : completely opposed or opposite — **di·a·met·ri·cal·ly** \-k(ə-)lē\ *adv*

di·a·mond \'dī-mənd, 'dī-ə-\ *n* 1 : a hard brilliant mineral that consists of crystalline carbon and is used as a gem 2 : a flat figure having four equal sides, two acute angles, and two obtuse angles 3 : any of a suit of playing cards marked with a red diamond 4 : INFIELD; *also* : the entire playing field in baseball

di·a·mond·back rattlesnake \-ˌbak-\ *n* : either of two large and deadly rattlesnakes of the southern U.S.

di·an·thus \dī-'an-thəs\ *n* : ¹PINK 1

di·a·pa·son \ˌdī-ə-'pā-z°n, -s°n\ *n* 1 : the organ stop governing the flue pipes that form the primary basis of organ tone 2 : the entire range of musical tones

¹**di·a·per** \'dī-pər, 'dī-ə-\ *n* 1 : a cotton or linen fabric woven in a simple geometric pattern 2 : a garment for a baby drawn up between the legs and fastened about the waist

²**diaper** *vb* 1 : to ornament with diaper designs 2 : to put a diaper on

di·aph·a·nous \dī-'a-fə-nəs\ *adj* : of so fine a texture as to be transparent

di·a·pho·ret·ic \ˌdī-ə-fə-'re-tik\ *adj* : having the power to increase perspiration — **diaphoretic** *n*

di·a·phragm \'dī-ə-ˌfram\ *n* 1 : a sheet of muscle between the chest and abdominal cavities of a mammal 2 : a vibrating disk (as in a microphone) 3 : a cup-shaped device usu. of thin rubber fitted over the uterine cervix to act as a mechanical contraceptive barrier — **di·a·phrag·mat·ic** \ˌdī-ə-frəg-'ma-tik, -ˌfrag-\ *adj*

di·a·rist \'dī-ə-rist\ *n* : one who keeps a diary

di·a·ris·tic \ˌdī-ə-'ris-tik\ *adj* : of, relating to, or characteristic of a diary

di·ar·rhea \ˌdī-ə-'rē-ə\ *n* [ME *diaria*, fr. LL *diarrhoea*, fr. Gk *diarrhoia*, fr. *diarrhein* to flow through, fr. *dia-* through + *rhein* to flow] : abnormally frequent and watery bowel movements — **di·ar·rhe·al** \-'rē-əl\ *adj*

di·ar·rhoea *chiefly Brit var of* DIARRHEA

di·a·ry \'dī-ə-rē\ *n, pl* **-ries** : a daily record esp. of personal experiences; *also* : a book used as a diary

di·as·po·ra \dī-'as-pə-rə\ *n* 1 *cap* : the settling of scattered colonies of Jews outside Palestine after the Babylonian exile

2 *cap* : the Jews living outside Palestine or modern Israel **3** : the migration or scattering of a people away from an ancestral homeland

di·as·to·le \dī-ˈas-tə-(ˌ)lē\ *n* : the stretching of the chambers of the heart during which they fill with blood — **di·a·stol·ic** \ˌdī-ə-ˈstä-lik\ *adj*

dia·ther·my \ˈdī-ə-ˌthər-mē\ *n* : the generation of heat in tissue by electric currents for medical purposes

di·a·tom \ˈdī-ə-ˌtäm\ *n* : any of a class of planktonic one-celled or colonial algae with skeletons of silica

di·atom·ic \ˌdī-ə-ˈtä-mik\ *adj* : having two atoms in the molecule

di·a·tribe \ˈdī-ə-ˌtrīb\ *n* : biting or abusive speech or writing

di·az·e·pam \dī-ˈa-zə-ˌpam\ *n* : a tranquilizer used esp. to relieve anxiety, tension, and muscle spasms

dib·ble \ˈdi-bəl\ *n* : a pointed hand tool for making holes (as for planting bulbs) in the ground — **dibble** *vb*

¹dice \ˈdīs\ *n, pl* **dice** : DIE 1

²dice *vb* **diced; dic·ing** **1** : to cut into small cubes ⟨∼ carrots⟩ **2** : to play games with dice

di·chot·o·my \dī-ˈkä-tə-mē\ *n, pl* **-mies** : a division or the process of dividing into two esp. mutually exclusive or contradictory groups — **di·chot·o·mous** \-məs\ *adj*

dick·er \ˈdi-kər\ *vb* : BARGAIN, HAGGLE

dick·ey *or* **dicky** \ˈdi-kē\ *n, pl* **dickeys** *or* **dick·ies** : a small fabric insert worn to fill in the neckline

di·cot·y·le·don \ˌdī-ˌkä-tə-ˈlēd-ᵊn\ *n* : any of a group of seed plants having an embryo with two cotyledons — **di·cot·y·le·don·ous** *adj*

dict *abbr* dictionary

¹dic·tate \ˈdik-ˌtāt\ *vb* **dic·tat·ed; dic·tat·ing** **1** : to speak or read for a person to transcribe or for a machine to record **2** : COMMAND, ORDER — **dic·ta·tion** \dik-ˈtā-shən\ *n*

²dic·tate \ˈdik-ˌtāt\ *n* : an authoritative rule, prescription, or injunction : COMMAND ⟨the ∼s of conscience⟩

dic·ta·tor \ˈdik-ˌtā-tər\ *n* **1** : a person ruling absolutely and often brutally and oppressively **2** : one that dictates

dic·ta·to·ri·al \ˌdik-tə-ˈtȯr-ē-əl\ *adj* : of, relating to, or characteristic of a dictator or a dictatorship

dic·ta·tor·ship \dik-ˈtā-tər-ˌship, ˈdik-ˌtā-\ *n* **1** : the office of a dictator **2** : autocratic rule, control, or leadership **3** : a government or country in which absolute power is held by a dictator or a small clique

dic·tion \ˈdik-shən\ *n* **1** : choice of words esp. with regard to correctness, clearness, or effectiveness : WORDING **2** : ENUNCIATION

dic·tio·nary \ˈdik-shə-ˌner-ē\ *n, pl* **-nar·ies** : a reference book containing words usu. alphabetically arranged along with information about their forms, pronunciations, functions, etymologies, meanings, and syntactical and idiomatic uses

dic·tum \ˈdik-təm\ *n, pl* **dic·ta** \-tə\ *also* **dictums** : a noteworthy, formal, or authoritative statement or observation

did *past of* DO

di·dac·tic \dī-ˈdak-tik\ *adj* **1** : intended to instruct, inform, or teach a moral lesson **2** : making moral observations

di·do \ˈdī-dō\ *n, pl* **didoes** *or* **didos** : a mischievous act : PRANK

¹die \ˈdī\ *vb* **died; dy·ing** \ˈdī-iŋ\ [ME *dien*, fr. or akin to ON *deyja* to die] **1** : to stop living : EXPIRE **2** : to pass out of existence ⟨a *dying* race⟩ **3** : SUBSIDE **4** ⟨the wind *died* down⟩ **4** : to long keenly ⟨*dying* to go⟩ **5** : STOP ⟨the motor *died*⟩

²die \ˈdī\ *n* [ME *dee*, fr. AF *dé*] **1** *pl* **dice** \ˈdīs\ : a small cube marked on each face with one to six spots and used usu. in pairs in games and gambling **2** *pl* **dies** \ˈdīz\ : a device used to shape, finish, or impress an object

die·hard \ˈdī-ˌhärd\ *n* : one who is strongly devoted or determined — **die–hard** *adj*

dieresis *var of* DIAERESIS

die·sel \ˈdē-zəl, -səl\ *n* **1** : DIESEL ENGINE **2** : a vehicle driven by a diesel engine **3** : DIESEL FUEL

diesel engine *n* : an internal combustion engine in whose cylinders air is compressed to a temperature sufficiently high to ignite the fuel

diesel fuel *n* : a heavy mineral oil used as fuel in diesel engines

die·sel·ing \ˈdē-zə-liŋ\ *n* : the continued operation of an internal combustion engine after the ignition has been turned off

¹di·et \ˈdī-ət\ *n* [ME *diete*, fr. AF, fr. L *diaeta*, fr. Gk *diaita*, lit., manner of living, fr. *diaitasthai* to lead one's life] **1** : food and drink regularly consumed : FARE **2** : an allowance of food prescribed for a special reason (as to lose weight) — **di·e·tary** \-ə-ˌter-ē\ *adj or n*

²diet *vb* : to eat or cause to eat or drink less or according to a prescribed rule — **di·et·er** *n*

dietary supplement *n* : a product taken orally that contains ingredients (as vitamins or amino acids) intended to supplement one's diet

di·e·tet·ics \ˌdī-ə-ˈte-tiks\ *n sing or pl* : the science or art of applying the principles of nutrition to diet — **di·e·tet·ic** *adj*

di·e·ti·tian *or* **di·e·ti·cian** \ˌdī-ə-ˈti-shən\ *n* : a specialist in dietetics

dif *or* **diff** *abbr* difference

dif·fer \ˈdi-fər\ *vb* **dif·fered; dif·fer·ing** **1** : to be unlike : VARY **3** : DISAGREE

dif·fer·ence \ˈdi-frəns, ˈdi-fə-rəns\ *n* **1** : UNLIKENESS ⟨∼ in their looks⟩ **2** : distinction or discrimination in preference **3** : DISAGREEMENT; *also* : an instance or cause of disagreement ⟨unable to settle their ∼s⟩ **4** : the amount by which one number or quantity differs from another

dif·fer·ent \ˈdi-frənt, ˈdi-fə-rənt\ *adj* **1** : unlike in nature or quality **2** : DISTINCT ⟨∼ age groups⟩; *also* : VARIOUS ⟨∼ members of the club⟩ **3** : ANOTHER ⟨try a ∼ channel⟩ **4** : UNUSUAL, SPECIAL ⟨a quite ∼ style⟩ — **dif·fer·ent·ly** *adv*

¹**dif·fer·en·tial** \ˌdi-fə-'ren-chəl\ adj : showing, creating, or relating to a difference

²**differential** n 1 : the amount or degree by which things differ 2 : an arrangement of gears in an automobile that allows one wheel to turn faster than another (as in rounding curves)

differential gear n : DIFFERENTIAL 2

dif·fer·en·ti·ate \ˌdi-fə-'ren-chē-ˌāt\ vb **-at·ed; -at·ing** 1 : to make or become different 2 : to attain a specialized adult form and function during development 3 : to recognize or state the difference ⟨~ between them⟩ — **dif·fer·en·ti·a·tion** \-ˌren-chē-'ā-shən\ n

dif·fi·cult \'di-fi-(ˌ)kəlt\ adj 1 : hard to do or make ⟨a ~ climb⟩ 2 : hard to understand or deal with ⟨~ reading⟩ ⟨a ~ child⟩

dif·fi·cul·ty \-(ˌ)kəl-tē\ n, pl **-ties** [ME difficulte, fr. AF difficulté, fr. L difficilis not easy, fr. dis- not + facilis easy] 1 : difficult nature ⟨the ~ of a task⟩ 2 : DISAGREEMENT ⟨settled their differences⟩ 3 : OBSTACLE ⟨overcome difficulties⟩ 4 : TROUBLE ⟨in financial difficulties⟩

♦ Synonyms HARDSHIP, RIGOR, VICISSITUDE

dif·fi·dent \'di-fə-dənt\ adj 1 : lacking confidence 2 : RESERVED 1 — **dif·fi·dence** \-dəns\ n — **dif·fi·dent·ly** adv

dif·frac·tion \di-'frak-shən\ n : the bending or spreading of waves (as of light) esp. when passing through narrow slits

¹**dif·fuse** \di-'fyüs\ adj 1 : VERBOSE, WORDY ⟨~ writing⟩ 2 : not concentrated or localized ⟨~ light⟩

²**dif·fuse** \di-'fyüz\ vb **dif·fused; dif·fus·ing** 1 : to pour out or spread widely 2 : to undergo or cause to undergo diffusion 3 : to break up light by diffusion

dif·fu·sion \di-'fyü-zhən\ n 1 : a diffusing or a being diffused 2 : movement of particles (as of a gas) from a region of high to one of lower concentration 3 : the reflection of light from a rough surface or the passage of light through a translucent material

¹**dig** \'dig\ vb **dug** \'dəg\; **dig·ging** 1 : to turn up the soil (as with a spade) 2 : to hollow out or form by removing earth ⟨~ a hole⟩ 3 : to uncover or seek by turning up earth ⟨~ potatoes⟩ 4 : DISCOVER ⟨~ up information⟩ 5 : POKE, THRUST ⟨~ a person in the ribs⟩ 6 : to work hard 7 : UNDERSTAND, APPRECIATE; also : LIKE, ADMIRE

²**dig** n 1 : THRUST, POKE; also : a cutting remark : GIBE 2 pl : living or working accommodations

³**dig** abbr digest

¹**di·gest** \'dī-ˌjest\ n : a summary or shortened version esp. of a literary work

²**di·gest** \dī-'jest, də-\ vb 1 : to think over and arrange in the mind 2 : to convert (food) into simpler forms that can be absorbed by the body 3 : to compress into a short summary — **di·gest·ibil·i·ty** \-ˌjes-tə-'bi-lə-tē\ n — **di·gest·ible** adj — **di·ges·tion** \-'jes-chən\ n — **di·ges·tive** \-'jes-tiv\ adj

di·ges·tif \ˌdē-zhes-'tēf\ n : an alcoholic drink taken after a meal

dig in vb 1 : to take a defensive stand esp. by digging trenches 2 : to firmly set to work 3 : to begin eating

dig·it \'di-jət\ n [ME, fr. L digitus finger, toe] 1 : any of the Arabic numerals 1 to 9 and usu. the symbol 0 2 : FINGER, TOE

dig·i·tal \'di-jə-tᵊl\ adj 1 : of, relating to, or done with a finger or toe 2 : of, relating to, or using calculation by numerical methods or by discrete units 3 : relating to or employing communications signals in the form of binary digits ⟨a ~ broadcast⟩ 4 : providing a readout in numerical digits ⟨a ~ watch⟩ 5 : ELECTRONIC; also : characterized by computerized technology ⟨the ~ age⟩ — **dig·i·tal·ly** adv

digital camera n : a camera that records images as digital data instead of on film

dig·i·tal·is \ˌdi-jə-'ta-ləs\ n : a drug from the common foxglove that is a powerful heart stimulant; also : FOXGLOVE

digital versatile disc n : DVD

digital video disc n : DVD

dig·ni·fied \'dig-nə-ˌfīd\ adj : showing or expressing dignity

dig·ni·fy \-ˌfī\ vb **-fied; -fy·ing** : to give dignity, distinction, or attention to

dig·ni·tary \'dig-nə-ˌter-ē\ n, pl **-tar·ies** : a person of high position or honor

dig·ni·ty \'dig-nə-tē\ n, pl **-ties** 1 : the quality or state of being worthy, honored, or esteemed 2 : high rank, office, or position 3 : formal reserve of manner, language, or appearance

di·graph \'dī-ˌgraf\ n : a group of two successive letters whose phonetic value is a single sound (as ea in bread)

di·gress \dī-'gres, də-\ vb : to turn aside esp. from the main subject or argument — **di·gres·sion** \-'gre-shən\ n — **di·gres·sive** \-'gre-siv\ adj

Di·jon mustard \'dē-ˌzhän-, di-'zhän-\ n : a mustard made from dark mustard seeds, white wine, and spices

dike \'dīk\ n : a bank of earth constructed to control water : LEVEE

di·lap·i·dat·ed \də-'la-pə-ˌdā-təd\ adj : fallen into partial ruin or decay — **di·lap·i·da·tion** \-ˌla-pə-'dā-shən\ n

di·late \dī-'lāt, 'dī-ˌlāt\ vb **di·lat·ed; di·lat·ing** : SWELL, DISTEND, EXPAND ⟨her pupils were dilated⟩ — **dil·a·ta·tion** \ˌdi-lə-'tā-shən\ n — **di·la·tion** \dī-'lā-shən\ n

dil·a·to·ry \'di-lə-ˌtȯr-ē\ adj 1 : DELAYING 2 : TARDY, SLOW

di·lem·ma \də-'le-mə\ n 1 : a usu. undesirable or unpleasant choice; also : a situation involving such a choice 2 : PREDICAMENT

dil·et·tante \ˌdi-lə-'tänt, -'tant\ n, pl **-tantes** or **-tan·ti** \-'tän-tē, -'tan-\ [It, fr. prp. of dilettare to delight, fr. L dilectare] : a person having a superficial interest in an art or a branch of knowledge

dil·i·gent \'di-lə-jənt\ adj : characterized by steady, earnest, and energetic effort : PAINSTAKING — **dil·i·gence** \-jəns\ n — **dil·i·gent·ly** adv

dill \'dil\ *n* : an herb related to the carrot with aromatic leaves and seeds used as a seasoning and in pickles

dil·ly \'di-lē\ *n, pl* **dil·lies** : one that is remarkable or outstanding

dil·ly·dal·ly \'di-lē-,da-lē\ *vb* : to waste time by loitering or delaying

¹di·lute \dī-'lüt, də-\ *vb* **di·lut·ed; di·lut·ing** : to lessen the consistency or strength of by mixing with something else — **di·lu·tion** \-'lü-shən\ *n*

²dilute *adj* : DILUTED, WEAK

¹dim \'dim\ *adj* **dim·mer; dim·mest** 1 : LUSTERLESS, DULL ⟨~ colors⟩ 2 : not bright or distinct : OBSCURE, FAINT 3 : not seeing or understanding clearly — **dim·ly** *adv* — **dim·ness** *n*

²dim *vb* **dimmed; dim·ming** 1 : to make or become dim or lusterless 2 : to reduce the light from

³dim *abbr* 1 dimension 2 diminished 3 diminutive

dime \'dīm\ *n* [ME, tenth part, tithe, fr. AF *disme, dime,* fr. L *decima,* fr. fem. of *decimus* tenth, fr. *decem* ten] : a U.S. coin worth ¹/₁₀ dollar

di·men·sion \də-'men-chən, dī-\ *n* 1 : the physical property of length, breadth, or thickness; *also* : a measure of this 2 : EXTENT, SCOPE, PROPORTIONS — usu. used in pl. ⟨the ~s of this problem⟩ — **di·men·sion·al** \-'men-chə-nəl\ *adj* — **di·men·sion·al·i·ty** \-,men-chə-'na-lə-tē\ *n*

di·min·ish \də-'mi-nish\ *vb* 1 : to make less or cause to appear less 2 : BELITTLE 3 : DWINDLE 4 : TAPER — **dim·i·nu·tion** \,di-mə-'nü-shən, -'nyü-\ *n*

di·min·u·en·do \də-,min-yə-'wen-dō\ *adv or adj* : DECRESCENDO

¹di·min·u·tive \də-'min-yə-tiv\ *n* 1 : a diminutive word or affix ⟨the word "kitchenette" is a ~⟩ 2 : a diminutive individual

²diminutive *adj* 1 : indicating small size and sometimes the state or quality of being lovable, pitiable, or contemptible ⟨the ~ suffixes *-ette* and *-ling*⟩ 2 : extremely small : TINY

dim·i·ty \'di-mə-tē\ *n, pl* **-ties** : a thin usu. corded cotton fabric

dim·mer \'di-mər\ *n* : a device for controlling the amount of light from an electric lighting unit

di·mor·phic \(,)dī-'mȯr-fik\ *adj* : occurring in two distinct forms — **di·mor·phism** \-,fi-zəm\ *n*

¹dim·ple \'dim-pəl\ *n* : a small depression esp. in the cheek or chin

²dimple *vb* **dim·pled; dim·pling** : to form dimples (as in smiling)

din \'din\ *n* : a loud confused mixture of noises

di·nar \di-'när\ *n* 1 — see MONEY table 2 — see *rial* at MONEY table

dine \'dīn\ *vb* **dined; din·ing** [ME, fr. AF *disner, diner* to eat, have a meal, fr. VL **disjejunare* to break one's fast, ultim. fr. L *jejunus* fasting] 1 : to eat dinner 2 : to give a dinner to

din·er \'dī-nər\ *n* 1 : one that dines 2 : a railroad dining car 3 : a restaurant usu. resembling a dining car

di·nette \dī-'net\ *n* : an alcove or small room used for dining

ding \'diŋ\ *vb* : to cause minor damage to a surface — **ding** *n*

din·ghy \'diŋ-ē\ *n, pl* **dinghies** 1 : a small boat 2 : LIFE RAFT

din·gle \'diŋ-gəl\ *n* : a small wooded valley

din·go \'diŋ-gō\ *n, pl* **dingoes** : a reddish brown wild dog of Australia

din·gus \'diŋ-gəs, -əs\ *n* : DOODAD

din·gy \'din-jē\ *adj* **din·gi·er; -est** : DIRTY, UNCLEAN; *also* : SHABBY — **din·gi·ness** *n*

dink \'diŋk\ *n, often all cap* [double income, no kids] : a couple with two incomes and no children; *also* : a member of such a couple

din·ky \'diŋ-kē\ *adj* **din·ki·er; -est** : overly small ⟨a ~ apartment⟩

din·ner \'di-nər\ *n* : the main meal of the day; *also* : a formal banquet

din·ner·ware \'di-nər-,wer\ *n* : tableware other than flatware

di·no \'dī-nō\ *n, pl* **dinos** : DINOSAUR

di·no·fla·gel·late \,dī-nō-'fla-jə-lət, -,lāt\ *n* : any of an order of planktonic plant-like unicellular flagellates of which some cause red tide

di·no·saur \'dī-nə-,sȯr\ *n* [ultim. fr. Gk *deinos* terrifying + *sauros* lizard] : any of a group of extinct long-tailed Mesozoic reptiles often of huge size

dint \'dint\ *n* 1 : FORCE ⟨by ~ of sheer grit⟩ 2 : DENT

di·o·cese \'dī-ə-səs, -,sēz, -,sēs\ *n, pl* **-ces·es** \-'sə-səz, -,sē-zəz, -,sē-səz\ : the territorial jurisdiction of a bishop — **di·oc·e·san** \dī-'ä-sə-sən, ,dī-ə-'sē-z°n\ *adj or n*

di·ode \'dī-,ōd\ *n* : an electronic device with two electrodes or terminals used esp. as a rectifier

di·ox·in \dī-'äk-sən\ *n* : a persistent toxic hydrocarbon that occurs esp. as a byproduct of industrial processes and waste incineration

¹dip \'dip\ *vb* **dipped; dip·ping** 1 : to plunge temporarily or partially under the surface (as of a liquid) 2 : to thrust in a way to suggest immersion 3 : to scoop up or out : LADLE 4 : to lower and then raise quickly ⟨~ a flag in salute⟩ 5 : to drop or slope down esp. suddenly ⟨the moon *dipped* below the crest⟩ 6 : to decrease moderately and usu. temporarily ⟨prices *dipped*⟩ 7 : to reach inside or as if inside or below a surface ⟨*dipped* into their savings⟩ 8 : to delve casually into something; *esp* : to read superficially ⟨~ into a book⟩

²dip *n* 1 : an act of dipping; *esp* : a short swim 2 : inclination downward : DROP 3 : something obtained by or used in dipping 4 : a sauce or soft mixture into which food may be dipped 5 : a liquid into which something may be dipped (as for cleansing or coloring)

diph·the·ria \dif-'thir-ē-ə\ *n* : an acute contagious bacterial disease marked by fever and by coating of the air passages with a membrane that interferes with breathing

diph·thong \'dif-ˌthȯŋ, 'dip-\ n : two vowel sounds joined in one syllable to form one speech sound (as *ou* in *out*)

dip·loid \'di-ˌplȯid\ adj : having two haploid sets of chromosomes ⟨~ somatic cells⟩ — **diploid** n

di·plo·ma \də-'plō-mə\ n : an official record of graduation from or of a degree conferred by a school

di·plo·ma·cy \də-'plō-mə-sē\ n 1 : the art and practice of conducting negotiations between nations 2 : TACT

dip·lo·mat \'di-plə-ˌmat\ n : one employed or skilled in diplomacy — **dip·lo·mat·ic** \ˌdi-plə-'ma-tik\ adj

di·plo·ma·tist \də-'plō-mə-tist\ n : DIPLOMAT

dip·per \'di-pər\ n 1 : any of a genus of birds that are related to the thrushes and are skilled in diving 2 : something (as a ladle or scoop) that dips or is used for dipping 3 cap : BIG DIPPER 4 cap : LITTLE DIPPER

dip·so·ma·nia \ˌdip-sə-'mā-nē-ə\ n : an uncontrollable craving for alcoholic liquors — **dip·so·ma·ni·ac** \-nē-ˌak\ n

dip·stick \'dip-ˌstik\ n : a graduated rod for indicating depth

dip·ter·an \'dip-tə-rən\ adj : of, relating to, or being a fly (sense 2) — **dipteran** n — **dip·ter·ous** \-rəs\ adj

dir abbr 1 direction 2 director

di·ram \dē-'ram\ n — see *somoni* at MONEY table

dire \'dī(-ə)r\ adj **dir·er; dir·est** 1 : very horrible : DREADFUL ⟨~ suffering⟩ 2 : warning of disaster 3 : EXTREME ⟨~ poverty⟩

¹**di·rect** \də-'rekt, dī-\ vb 1 : ADDRESS ⟨~ a letter⟩; *also* : to impart orally : AIM ⟨~ a remark to the gallery⟩ 2 : to regulate the activities or course of : guide the supervision, organizing, or performance of 3 : to cause to turn, move, or point or to follow a certain course 4 : to point, extend, or project in a specified line or course 5 : to request or instruct with authority 6 : to show or point out the way

²**direct** adj 1 : stemming immediately from a source ⟨~ result⟩ 2 : being or passing in a straight line of descent : LINEAL ⟨~ ancestor⟩ 3 : leading from one point to another in time or space without turn or stop : STRAIGHT 4 : NATURAL, STRAIGHTFORWARD ⟨a ~ manner⟩ 5 : operating without an intervening agency or step ⟨~ action⟩ 6 : effected by the action of the people or the electorate and not by representatives ⟨~ democracy⟩ 7 : consisting of or reproducing the exact words of a speaker or writer — **direct** adv — **di·rect·ly** adv — **di·rect·ness** n

direct broadcast satellite n : a television broadcasting system in which satellite transmissions are received at the viewing location

direct current n : an electric current flowing in one direction only

direct deposit n : a method of payment in which money is transferred to the payee's account without the use of checks or cash

di·rec·tion \də-'rek-shən, dī-\ n 1 : MANAGEMENT, GUIDANCE 2 : COMMAND, ORDER, INSTRUCTION 3 : the course or line along which something moves, lies, or points 4 : TENDENCY, TREND — **di·rec·tion·al** \-shə-nəl\ adj

di·rec·tive \də-'rek-tiv, dī-\ n : something that directs and usu. impels toward an action or goal; *esp* : an order issued by a high-level body or official

direct mail n : printed matter used for soliciting business or contributions and mailed direct to individuals

di·rec·tor \də-'rek-tər, dī-\ n 1 : one that directs : MANAGER, SUPERVISOR, CONDUCTOR 2 : one of a group of persons who direct the affairs of an organized body — **di·rec·to·ri·al** \-ˌrek-'tȯr-ē-əl\ adj — **di·rec·tor·ship** n

di·rec·tor·ate \-tə-rət\ n 1 : the office or position of director 2 : a board of directors; *also* : membership on such a board 3 : an executive staff

director's cut n : a version of a motion picture that is edited according to the director's wishes

di·rec·to·ry \-tə-rē\ n, pl **-ries** 1 : an alphabetical or classified list esp. of names and addresses 2 : FOLDER 4

dire·ful \'dī(-ə)r-fəl\ adj : DREADFUL ⟨a ~ disease⟩; *also* : OMINOUS

dirge \'dərj\ n [ME *dirige*, fr. the first word of a LL antiphon, fr. L. imper. of *dirigere* to direct] : a song of lamentation; *also* : a slow mournful piece of music

dir·ham \dir-həm\ n 1 — see MONEY table 2 — see *dinar, riyal* at MONEY table

di·ri·gi·ble \'dir-ə-jə-bəl, də-'ri-jə-\ n : AIRSHIP

dirk \'dərk\ n : DAGGER 1

dirndl \'dərn-d²l\ n [short for G *Dirndlkleid*, fr. G dial. *Dirndl* girl + G *Kleid* dress] : a full skirt with a tight waistband

dirt \'dərt\ n 1 : a filthy or soiling substance (as mud, dust, or grime) 2 : loose or packed earth : SOIL 3 : moral uncleanness 4 : scandalous gossip 5 : embarrassing or incriminating information

¹**dirty** \'dər-tē\ adj **dirt·i·er; -est** 1 : SOILED, FILTHY 2 : INDECENT, SMUTTY ⟨~ jokes⟩ 3 : BASE, UNFAIR ⟨a ~ trick⟩ 4 : STORMY, FOGGY ⟨~ weather⟩ 5 : not clear in color : DULL ⟨a ~ red⟩ — **dirt·i·ness** n — **dirty** adv

²**dirty** vb **dirt·ied; dirty·ing** : to make or become dirty

dis·able \di-'sā-bəl\ vb **dis·abled; dis·abling** 1 : to disqualify legally ⟨~ to make unable to perform by or as if by illness, injury, or malfunction — **dis·abil·i·ty** \ˌdi-sə-'bi-lə-tē\ n

dis·abled adj : incapacitated by illness or injury; *also* : physically or mentally impaired

dis·abuse \ˌdi-sə-'byüz\ vb : to free from error, fallacy, or misconception

dis·ad·van·tage \ˌdi-səd-'van-tij\ n 1 : loss or damage esp. to reputation or finances 2 : an unfavorable, inferior, or prejudicial condition, quality, or circumstance — **dis·ad·van·ta·geous** \di-ˌsad-ˌvan-ˈtā-jəs, -vən-\ *adj*

dis·ad·van·taged \-tijd\ *adj* : lacking in basic resources or conditions believed necessary for an equal position in society

dis·af·fect \ˌdi-sə-ˈfekt\ *vb* : to alienate the affection or loyalty of — **dis·af·fec·tion** \-ˈfek-shən\ *n*

dis·agree \ˌdi-sə-ˈgrē\ *vb* **1** : to fail to agree **2** : to differ in opinion **3** : to cause discomfort or distress ⟨fried foods ∼ with her⟩ — **dis·agree·ment** *n*

dis·agree·able \-ə-bəl\ *adj* **1** : causing discomfort : UNPLEASANT, OFFENSIVE ⟨a ∼ odor⟩ **2** : ILL-TEMPERED, PEEVISH — **dis·agree·able·ness** *n* — **dis·agree·ably** \-blē\ *adv*

dis·al·low \ˌdi-sə-ˈlau̇\ *vb* : to refuse to admit or recognize : REJECT ⟨∼ a claim⟩ — **dis·al·low·ance** *n*

dis·ap·pear \ˌdi-sə-ˈpir\ *vb* **1** : to pass out of sight **2** : to cease to be : become lost — **dis·ap·pear·ance** *n*

dis·ap·point \ˌdi-sə-ˈpȯint\ *vb* : to fail to fulfill the expectation or hope of — **dis·ap·point·ment** *n*

dis·ap·pro·ba·tion \dis-ˌa-prə-ˈbā-shən\ *n* : DISAPPROVAL

dis·ap·prov·al \ˌdis-ə-ˈprü-vəl\ *n* : adverse judgment : CENSURE

dis·ap·prove \-ˈprüv\ *vb* **1** : CONDEMN **2** : to feel or express disapproval ⟨∼s of smoking⟩ **3** : REJECT — **dis·ap·prov·ing·ly** \-ˈprü-viŋ-lē\ *adv*

dis·arm \dis-ˈärm\ *vb* **1** : to take arms or weapons from **2** : to reduce the size and strength of the armed forces of a country **3** : to make harmless, peaceable, or friendly : win over ⟨a ∼ing smile⟩ — **dis·ar·ma·ment** \-ˈär-mə-mənt\ *n*

dis·ar·range \ˌdis-ə-ˈrānj\ *vb* : to disturb the arrangement or order of — **dis·ar·range·ment** *n*

dis·ar·ray \-ˈrā\ *n* **1** : DISORDER, CONFUSION **2** : disorderly or careless dress

dis·as·sem·ble \ˌdis-ə-ˈsem-bəl\ *vb* : to take apart

dis·as·so·ci·ate \-ˈsō-shē-ˌāt, -sē-\ *vb* : to detach from association

di·sas·ter \di-ˈzas-tər, -ˈsas-\ *n* [MF *desastre,* fr. It *disastro,* fr. *astro* star, fr. L *astrum*] : a sudden or great misfortune — **di·sas·trous** \-ˈzas-trəs\ *adj* — **di·sas·trous·ly** *adv*

dis·avow \ˌdis-ə-ˈvau̇\ *vb* : to deny responsibility for : REPUDIATE — **dis·avow·al** \-ˈvau̇-(ə)l\ *n*

dis·band \dis-ˈband\ *vb* : to break up the organization of : DISPERSE

dis·bar \dis-ˈbär\ *vb* : to expel from the legal profession — **dis·bar·ment** *n*

dis·be·lieve \ˌdis-bə-ˈlēv\ *vb* **1** : to hold not worthy of belief : not believe **2** : to withhold or reject belief — **dis·be·lief** \-ˈlēf\ *n* — **dis·be·liev·er** *n*

dis·bur·den \dis-ˈbər-dⁿn\ *vb* : to rid of a burden

dis·burse \dis-ˈbərs\ *vb* **dis·bursed; dis·burs·ing 1** : to pay out : EXPEND **2** : DISTRIBUTE — **dis·burse·ment** *n*

¹disc *var of* DISK

²disc *abbr* discount

dis·card \dis-ˈkärd, ˈdis-ˌkärd\ *vb* **1** : to let go a playing card from one's hand; *also* : to play (a card) from a suit other than a trump but different from the one led **2** : to get rid of as unwanted — **dis·card** \ˈdis-ˌkärd\ *n*

disc brake *n* : a brake that operates by the friction of a pair of plates pressing against the sides of a rotating disc

dis·cern \di-ˈsərn, -ˈzərn\ *vb* **1** : to detect with the eyes : DISTINGUISH **2** : DISCRIMINATE **3** : to come to know or recognize mentally ⟨∼ right from wrong⟩ — **dis·cern·ible** *adj* — **dis·cern·ment** *n*

dis·cern·ing *adj* : revealing insight and understanding ⟨a ∼ critic⟩

¹dis·charge \dis-ˈchärj, ˈdis-ˌchärj\ *vb* **1** : to relieve of a charge, load, or burden : UNLOAD; *esp* : to remove the electrical energy from ⟨∼ a storage battery⟩ **2** : to let or put off ⟨∼ passengers⟩ **3** : SHOOT ⟨∼ an arrow⟩ **4** : to set free ⟨∼ a prisoner⟩ **5** : to dismiss from service or employment ⟨∼ a soldier⟩ **6** : to get rid of by paying or doing ⟨∼ a debt⟩ **7** : to give forth fluid ⟨the river ∼s into the ocean⟩

²dis·charge \ˈdis-ˌchärj, dis-ˈchärj\ *n* **1** : the act of discharging, unloading, or releasing **2** : something that discharges; *esp* : a certification of release or payment **3** : a firing off (as of a gun) **4** : a flowing out (as of blood from a wound); *also* : something that is emitted ⟨a purulent ∼⟩ **5** : release or dismissal esp. from an office or employment; *also* : complete separation from military service **6** : a flow of electricity (as through a gas)

dis·ci·ple \di-ˈsī-pəl\ *n* [ultim. fr. LL *discipulus* follower of Jesus in his lifetime, fr. L, pupil] **1** : one who accepts and helps to spread the teachings of another; *also* : a convinced adherent **2** *cap* : a member of the Disciples of Christ

dis·ci·pli·nar·i·an \ˌdi-sə-plə-ˈner-ē-ən\ *n* : one who enforces order

dis·ci·plin·ary \ˈdi-sə-plə-ˌner-ē\ *adj* : of or relating to discipline; *also* : CORRECTIVE ⟨take ∼ action⟩

¹dis·ci·pline \ˈdi-sə-plən\ *n* **1** : PUNISHMENT **2** : a field of study : SUBJECT **3** : training that corrects, molds, or perfects **4** : control gained by obedience or training : orderly conduct **5** : a system of rules governing conduct

²discipline *vb* **-plined; -plin·ing 1** : PUNISH **2** : to train or develop by instruction and exercise esp. in self-control **3** : to bring under control ⟨∼ troops⟩; *also* : to impose self-control upon

disc jockey *or* **disk jockey** *n* : an announcer of a radio show of popular recorded music

dis·claim \dis-ˈklām\ *vb* : DENY, DISAVOW — **dis·claim·er** *n*

dis·close \dis-ˈklōz\ *vb* : to expose to view — **dis·clo·sure** \-ˈklō-zhər\ *n*

dis·co \ˈdis-kō\ *n, pl* **discos 1** : a nightclub for dancing to live or recorded music **2** : popular dance music characterized by hypnotic rhythm, repetitive lyrics, and electronically produced sounds

dis·col·or \dis-ˈkə-lər\ *vb* : to alter or change in hue or color esp. for the worse — **dis·col·or·ation** \-ˌkə-lə-ˈrā-shən\ *n*

dis·com·bob·u·late \ˌdis-kəm-ˈbä-byü-ˌlāt\ *vb* **-lat·ed; -lat·ing** : UPSET, CONFUSE

dis·com·fit \dis-ˈkəm-fət, *esp Southern* ˌdis-kəm-ˈfit\ *vb* : UPSET, FRUSTRATE — **dis·com·fi·ture** \dis-ˈkəm-fə-ˌchùr\ *n*

¹**dis·com·fort** \dis-ˈkəm-fərt\ *vb* : to make uncomfortable or uneasy

²**discomfort** *n* : mental or physical uneasiness

dis·com·mode \ˌdis-kə-ˈmōd\ *vb* **-mod·ed; -mod·ing** : INCONVENIENCE, TROUBLE

dis·com·pose \-kəm-ˈpōz\ *vb* **1** : to destroy the calmness or peace of **2** : DISARRANGE — **dis·com·po·sure** \-ˈpō-zhər\ *n*

dis·con·cert \ˌdis-kən-ˈsərt\ *vb* : CONFUSE, UPSET ⟨the bad news ∼*ed* her⟩

dis·con·nect \-kə-ˈnekt\ *vb* : to undo the connection of — **dis·con·nec·tion** \-ˈnek-shən\ *n*

dis·con·nect·ed *adj* : not connected; *also* : INCOHERENT — **dis·con·nect·ed·ly** *adv* — **dis·con·nect·ed·ness** *n*

dis·con·so·late \dis-ˈkän-sə-lət\ *adj* **1** : CHEERLESS **2** : hopelessly sad — **dis·con·so·late·ly** *adv*

dis·con·tent \ˌdis-kən-ˈtent\ *n* : uneasiness of mind : DISSATISFACTION — **dis·con·tent·ed** *adj*

dis·con·tin·ue \ˌdis-kən-ˈtin-yü\ *vb* **1** : to break the continuity of : cease to operate, use, or take **2** : END — **dis·con·tin·u·ance** \-yə-wəns\ *n* — **dis·con·ti·nu·i·ty** \dis-ˌkän-tə-ˈnü-ə-tē, -ˈnyü-\ *n* — **dis·con·tin·u·ous** \ˌdis-kən-ˈtin-yə-wəs\ *adj*

dis·cord \ˈdis-ˌkòrd\ *n* **1** : lack of agreement or harmony : DISSENSION, CONFLICT **2** : a harsh combination of musical sounds **3** : a harsh or unpleasant sound — **dis·cor·dant** \dis-ˈkòr-dənt\ *adj* — **dis·cor·dant·ly** *adv*

dis·co·theque *or* **discothèque** \ˈdis-kə-ˌtek\ *n* : DISCO 1

¹**dis·count** \ˈdis-ˌkaùnt\ *n* **1** : a reduction made from a regular or list price **2** : a deduction of interest in advance when lending money

²**dis·count** \ˈdis-ˌkaùnt, dis-ˈkaùnt\ *vb* **1** : to deduct from the amount of a bill, debt, or charge usu. for cash or prompt payment; *also* : to sell or offer for sale at a discount **2** : to lend money after deducting the discount ⟨∼ a note⟩ **3** : DISREGARD; *also* : MINIMIZE **4** : to make allowance for bias or exaggeration **5** : to take into account (as a future event) in present calculations — **dis·count·able** *adj* — **dis·count·er** *n*

³**dis·count** \ˈdis-ˌkaùnt\ *adj* : selling goods or services at a discount; *also* : sold at or reflecting a discount

dis·coun·te·nance \dis-ˈkaùn-tə-nənts\ *vb* **1** : EMBARRASS, DISCONCERT **2** : to look with disfavor on

dis·cour·age \dis-ˈkər-ij\ *vb* **-aged; -ag·ing 1** : to deprive of courage or confidence : DISHEARTEN **2** : to hinder by disfavoring **3** : to attempt to dissuade — **dis·cour·age·ment** *n* — **dis·cour·ag·ing·ly** *adv*

¹**dis·course** \ˈdis-ˌkòrs\ *n* [ME *discours,* fr. ML & LL *discursus;* ML, argument, fr. LL, conversation, fr. L, act of running about, fr. *discurrere* to run about, fr. *currere* to run] **1** : CONVERSATION **2** : formal and usu. extended expression of thought on a subject

²**dis·course** \dis-ˈkòrs\ *vb* **dis·coursed; dis·cours·ing 1** : to express oneself in esp. oral discourse **2** : TALK, CONVERSE

dis·cour·te·ous \(ˌ)dis-ˈkər-tē-əs\ *adj* : lacking courtesy : UNCIVIL, RUDE — **dis·cour·te·ous·ly** *adv*

dis·cour·te·sy \-ˈkər-tə-sē\ *n* : RUDENESS; *also* : a rude act

dis·cov·er \dis-ˈkə-vər\ *vb* **1** : to make known or visible **2** : to obtain sight or knowledge of for the first time; *also* : FIND OUT — **dis·cov·er·er** *n*

dis·cov·ery \dis-ˈkə-və-rē\ *n, pl* **-er·ies 1** : the act or process of discovering **2** : something discovered **3** : the disclosure usu. before a civil trial of pertinent facts or documents

¹**dis·cred·it** \(ˌ)dis-ˈkre-dət\ *vb* **1** : DISBELIEVE **2** : to cause disbelief in the accuracy or authority of **3** : DISGRACE — **dis·cred·it·able** *adj*

²**discredit** *n* **1** : loss of reputation **2** : lack or loss of belief or confidence

dis·creet \dis-ˈkrēt\ *adj* : showing good judgment; *esp* : capable of observing prudent silence — **dis·creet·ly** *adv*

dis·crep·an·cy \dis-ˈkre-pən-sē\ *n, pl* **-cies 1** : DIFFERENCE, DISAGREEMENT **2** : an instance of being discrepant

dis·crep·ant \-pənt\ *adj* [ME *discrepaunt,* fr. L *discrepans,* prp. of *discrepare* to sound discordantly, fr. *crepare* to rattle, creak] : being at variance : DISAGREEING ⟨∼ conclusions⟩

dis·crete \dis-ˈkrēt, ˈdis-ˌkrēt\ *adj* **1** : individually distinct ⟨several ∼ sections⟩ **2** : NONCONTINUOUS

dis·cre·tion \dis-ˈkre-shən\ *n* **1** : the quality of being discreet : PRUDENCE **2** : individual choice or judgment ⟨left the decision to his ∼⟩ **3** : power of free decision or latitude of choice — **dis·cre·tion·ary** *adj*

dis·crim·i·nate \dis-ˈkri-mə-ˌnāt\ *vb* **-nat·ed; -nat·ing 1** : DISTINGUISH, DIFFERENTIATE **2** : to make a difference in treatment on a basis other than individual merit — **dis·crim·i·na·tion** \-ˌkri-mə-ˈnā-shən\ *n*

dis·crim·i·nat·ing *adj* : marked by discrimination; *esp* : DISCERNING, JUDICIOUS — **dis·crim·i·nat·ing·ly** *adv*

dis·crim·i·na·to·ry \dis-ˈkri-mə-nə-ˌtòr-ē\ *adj* : marked by esp. unjust discrimination ⟨∼ treatment⟩

dis·cur·sive \dis-ˈkər-siv\ *adj* : passing from one topic to another : RAMBLING ⟨a ∼ speech⟩ — **dis·cur·sive·ly** *adv* — **dis·cur·sive·ness** *n*

dis·cus \ˈdis-kəs\ *n, pl* **dis·cus·es** : a heavy disk that is hurled for distance in a track-and-field contest

dis·cuss \di-'skəs\ vb [ME, fr. AF discusser, fr. L discussus, pp. of discutere to disperse, fr. dis- apart + quatere to shake] **1** : to argue or consider carefully by presenting the various sides **2** : to talk about — **dis·cus·sion** \-'skə-shən\ n

dis·cus·sant \di-'skə-s³nt\ n : one who takes part in a formal discussion

¹dis·dain \dis-'dān\ n : CONTEMPT, SCORN ⟨a look of ∼⟩ — **dis·dain·ful** \-fəl\ adj — **dis·dain·ful·ly** adv

²disdain vb **1** : to look on with scorn **2** : to reject or refrain from because of disdain ⟨∼ed gambling⟩

dis·ease \di-'zēz\ n : an abnormal bodily condition that impairs normal functioning and can usu. be recognized by signs and symptoms — SICKNESS — **dis·eased** \-'zēzd\ adj

dis·em·bark \di-səm-'bärk\ vb : to go or put ashore from a ship — **dis·em·bar·ka·tion** \di-,sem-,bär-'kā-shən\ n

dis·em·body \di-səm-'bä-dē\ vb : to deprive of bodily existence

dis·em·bow·el \-'bau̇(-ə)l\ vb : EVISCERATE 1 — **dis·em·bow·el·ment** n

dis·em·power \dis-im-'pau̇(-ə)r\ vb : to deprive of power, authority, or influence

dis·en·chant \dis-in-'chant\ vb : DISILLUSION — **dis·en·chant·ment** \-mənt\ n

dis·en·chant·ed \-'chan-təd\ adj : DISAPPOINTED, DISSATISFIED

dis·en·cum·ber \dis-³n-'kəm-bər\ vb : to free from something that burdens

dis·en·fran·chise \dis-in-'fran-,chīz\ vb : to deprive of a franchise, a legal right, or a privilege; esp : to deprive of the right to vote — **dis·en·fran·chise·ment** n

dis·en·gage \dis-³n-'gāj\ vb : RELEASE, EXTRICATE, DISENTANGLE ⟨∼ from a harness⟩ — **dis·en·gage·ment** n

dis·en·gaged \-'gājd\ adj : IMPARTIAL, DETACHED ⟨a ∼ observer⟩

dis·en·tan·gle \dis-in-'taŋ-gəl\ vb : to free from entanglement : UNRAVEL

dis·equi·lib·ri·um \dis-,ē-kwə-'li-brē-əm\ n : loss or lack of equilibrium

dis·es·tab·lish \dis-ə-'sta-blish\ vb : to end the establishment of; esp : to deprive of the status of an established church — **dis·es·tab·lish·ment** n

dis·es·teem \dis-ə-'stēm\ n : lack of esteem : DISFAVOR, DISREPUTE

dis·fa·vor \(,)dis-'fā-vər\ n **1** : DISAPPROVAL, DISLIKE **2** : the state or fact of being no longer favored

dis·fig·ure \dis-'fi-gyər\ vb : to spoil the appearance of ⟨disfigured by a scar⟩ — **dis·fig·ure·ment** n

dis·fran·chise \dis-'fran-,chīz\ vb : DISENFRANCHISE — **dis·fran·chise·ment** n

disfunction var of DYSFUNCTION

dis·gorge \-'gȯrj\ vb : VOMIT; also : to discharge forcefully or confusedly

¹dis·grace \di-'skrās, dis-'grās\ vb : to bring reproach or shame to

²disgrace n **1** : SHAME, DISHONOR; also : a cause of shame **2** : the condition of being out of favor : loss of respect — **dis·grace·ful** \-fəl\ adj — **dis·grace·ful·ly** adv

dis·grun·tle \dis-'grən-t³l\ vb **dis·grun-tled; dis·grun·tling** : to put in bad humor ⟨disgruntled employees⟩

¹dis·guise \dis-'gīz\ vb **dis·guised; dis·guis·ing 1** : to change the appearance of so as to conceal the identity or to resemble another **2** : HIDE, CONCEAL

²disguise n **1** : clothing put on to conceal one's identity or counterfeit another's **2** : an outward appearance that hides what something really is

¹dis·gust \dis-'gəst\ n : AVERSION, REPUGNANCE — **dis·gust·ful** \-fəl\ adj

²disgust vb : to provoke to loathing, repugnance, or aversion : be offensive to — **dis·gust·ed·ly** adv — **dis·gust·ing** \-'gəs-tiŋ\ adj — **dis·gust·ing·ly** \-'gəs-tiŋ-lē\ adv

¹dish \'dish\ n [ME, fr. OE disc plate, fr. L discus quoit, disk, dish, fr. Gk diskos, fr. dikein to throw] **1** : a vessel used for serving food **2** : the food served in a dish ⟨a ∼ of berries⟩ **3** : food prepared in a particular way **4** : something resembling a dish esp. in being shallow and concave **5** : SATELLITE DISH **6** : GOSSIP 2

²dish vb **1** : to put into a dish **2** : to make concave like a dish **3** : GOSSIP

dis·ha·bille \dis-ə-'bēl\ or **des·ha·bille** \de-\ n [F déshabillé] : the state of being dressed in a casual or careless manner

dis·har·mo·ny \(,)dis-'här-mə-nē\ n : lack of harmony — **dis·har·mo·ni·ous** \dis-(,)här-'mō-nē-əs\ adj

dish·cloth \'dish-,klȯth\ n : a cloth for washing dishes

dis·heart·en \dis-'här-t³n\ vb : DISCOURAGE, DEJECT

dished \'disht\ adj : CONCAVE

di·shev·el \di-'she-vəl\ vb -**shev·eled** or -**shev·elled; shev·el·ing** or -**shev·el·ling** [ME discheveled bareheaded, with disordered hair, fr. AF deschevelé, fr. des- apart + chevoil hair, fr. L capillus] : to throw into disorder or disarray — **di·shev·eled** or **di·shev·elled** adj — **di·shev·el·ment** \-mənt\ n

dis·hon·est \di-'sä-nəst\ adj : not honest : UNTRUSTWORTHY, DECEITFUL — **dis·hon·est·ly** adv — **dis·hon·es·ty** \-nə-stē\ n

¹dis·hon·or \dis-'ä-nər\ n **1** : lack or loss of honor **2** : SHAME, DISGRACE **3** : a cause of disgrace **4** : the act of dishonoring a negotiable instrument when presented for payment — **dis·hon·or·able** \dis-'ä-nə-rə-bəl\ adj — **dis·hon·or·ably** \-blē\ adv

²dishonor vb **1** : DISGRACE **2** : to refuse to accept or pay ⟨∼ a check⟩

dish out vb : to give freely

dish·rag \'dish-,rag\ n : DISHCLOTH

dish·wash·er \-,wȯ-shər, -,wä-\ n : a person or machine that washes dishes

dish·wa·ter \-,wȯ-tər, -,wä-\ n : water used for washing dishes

dis·il·lu·sion \dis-ə-'lü-zhən\ vb : to free from illusion — **dis·il·lu·sion·ment** n

dis·il·lu·sioned adj : DISAPPOINTED, DISSATISFIED

dis·in·cli·na·tion \dis-,in-klə-'nā-shən\ n : a preference for avoiding something : slight aversion

dis·in·cline \ˌdis-in-ˈklīn\ *vb* : to make unwilling

dis·in·clined *adj* : unwilling because of dislike or disapproval

dis·in·fect \ˌdis-in-ˈfekt\ *vb* : to cleanse of infection-causing germs — **dis·in·fec·tant** \-ˈfek-tənt\ *n* — **dis·in·fec·tion** \-ˈfek-shən\ *n*

dis·in·for·ma·tion \-ˌin-fər-ˈmā-shən\ *n* : false information deliberately and often covertly spread

dis·in·gen·u·ous \ˌdis-in-ˈjen-yə-wəs\ *adj* : lacking in candor; *also* : giving a false appearance of simple frankness

dis·in·her·it \ˌdis-in-ˈher-ət\ *vb* : to deprive of the right to inherit

dis·in·te·grate \dis-ˈin-tə-ˌgrāt\ *vb* **1** : to break or decompose into constituent parts or small particles **2** : to destroy the unity or integrity of — **dis·in·te·gra·tion** \-ˌin-tə-ˈgrā-shən\ *n*

dis·in·ter \ˌdis-in-ˈtər\ *vb* **1** : to take from the grave or tomb **2** : UNEARTH

dis·in·ter·est·ed \(ˌ)dis-ˈin-tə-rəs-təd, -ˌres-\ *adj* **1** : not interested **2** : free from selfish motive or interest : UNBIASED — **dis·in·ter·est·ed·ness** *n*

dis·join \(ˌ)dis-ˈjóin\ *vb* : SEPARATE

dis·joint \dis-ˈjóint\ *vb* : to disturb the orderly arrangement of; *also* : to separate at the joints

dis·joint·ed *adj* **1** : INCOHERENT ⟨∼ conversation⟩ **2** : separated at or as if at the joint

disk *or* **disc** \ˈdisk\ *n* **1** : something round and flat; *esp* : a flat rounded anatomical structure (as the central part of the flower head of a composite plant or a pad of cartilage between vertebrae) **2** *usu* **disc** : a phonograph record **3** : a round flat plate coated with a magnetic substance on which data for a computer is stored **4** *usu* **disc** : OPTICAL DISK

disk drive *n* : a device for accessing or storing data on a magnetic disk

dis·kette \dis-ˈket\ *n* : FLOPPY DISK

disk jockey *var of* DISC JOCKEY

¹dis·like \(ˌ)dis-ˈlīk\ *n* : a feeling of aversion or disapproval

²dislike *vb* : to regard with dislike : DISAPPROVE

dis·lo·cate \ˈdis-lō-ˌkāt, dis-ˈlō-\ *vb* **1** : to put out of place; *esp* : to displace (a bone or joint) from normal connections ⟨∼ a shoulder⟩ **2** : DISRUPT — **dis·lo·ca·tion** \ˌdis-(ˌ)lō-ˈkā-shən\ *n*

dis·lodge \(ˌ)dis-ˈläj\ *vb* : to force out of a place *esp* of rest, hiding, or defense

dis·loy·al \(ˌ)dis-ˈlói-(ə)l\ *adj* : lacking in loyalty — **dis·loy·al·ty** *n*

dis·mal \ˈdiz-məl\ *adj* [ME, fr. *dismal*, n., days marked as unlucky in medieval calendars, fr. AF, fr. ML *dies mali*, lit., evil days] **1** : showing or causing gloom or depression ⟨a ∼ performance⟩ **2** : lacking merit ⟨a ∼ performance⟩ — **dis·mal·ly** *adv*

dis·man·tle \(ˌ)dis-ˈman-tᵊl\ *vb* **-tled; -tling** **1** : to take apart **2** : to strip of furniture and equipment — **dis·man·tle·ment** *n*

dis·may \dis-ˈmā\ *vb* : to cause to lose courage or resolution from alarm or fear

: DAUNT — **dismay** *n* — **dis·may·ing·ly** *adv*

dis·mem·ber \dis-ˈmem-bər\ *vb* **1** : to cut off or separate the limbs or parts of **2** : to break up or tear into pieces — **dis·mem·ber·ment** *n*

dis·miss \dis-ˈmis\ *vb* **1** : to send away **2** : DISCHARGE 5 **3** : to put aside or out of mind **4** : to put out of judicial consideration ⟨∼ed all charges⟩ — **dis·miss·al** *n* — **dis·mis·sive** \-ˈmi-siv\ *adj* — **dis·mis·sive·ly** *adv*

dis·mount \dis-ˈmaúnt\ *vb* **1** : to get down from something (as a horse or bicycle) **2** : UNHORSE **3** : DISASSEMBLE

dis·obe·di·ence \ˌdis-ə-ˈbē-dē-əns\ *n* : neglect or refusal to obey — **dis·obe·di·ent** \-ənt\ *adj*

dis·obey \ˌdis-ə-ˈbā\ *vb* : to fail to obey : be disobedient

dis·oblige \ˌdis-ə-ˈblīj\ *vb* **1** : to go counter to the wishes of **2** : INCONVENIENCE

¹dis·or·der \dis-ˈór-dər\ *vb* **1** : to disturb the order of **2** : to disturb the regular or normal functions of

²disorder *n* **1** : lack of order : CONFUSION **2** : breach of the peace or public order : TUMULT **3** : an abnormal physical or mental condition : AILMENT

dis·or·der·ly \-lē\ *adj* **1** : offensive to public order **2** : marked by disorder ⟨a ∼ desk⟩ — **dis·or·der·li·ness** *n*

dis·or·ga·nize \dis-ˈór-gə-ˌnīz\ *vb* : to break up the regular system of : throw into disorder — **dis·or·ga·ni·za·tion** \dis-ˌór-gə-nə-ˈzā-shən\ *n*

dis·ori·ent \dis-ˈór-ē-ˌent\ *vb* : to cause to be confused or lost — **dis·ori·en·ta·tion** \dis-ˌór-ē-ən-ˈtā-shən\ *n*

dis·own \dis-ˈōn\ *vb* : REPUDIATE, RENOUNCE, DISCLAIM ⟨her parents ∼ed her⟩

dis·par·age \di-ˈsper-ij\ *vb* **-aged; -aging** [ME, to degrade by marriage below one's class, disparage, fr. AF *desparager* to marry below one's class, fr. *parage* equality, lineage, fr. *per* peer] **1** : to lower in rank or reputation : DEGRADE **2** : BELITTLE — **dis·par·age·ment** *n* — **dis·par·ag·ing·ly** *adv*

dis·pa·rate \ˈdis-pə-rət, di-ˈsper-ət\ *adj* : distinct in quality or character — **dis·par·i·ty** \di-ˈsper-ə-tē\ *n*

dis·pas·sion·ate \(ˌ)dis-ˈpa-shə-nət\ *adj* : not influenced by strong feeling : CALM, IMPARTIAL — **dis·pas·sion** \-ˈpa-shən\ *n* — **dis·pas·sion·ate·ly** *adv*

¹dis·patch \di-ˈspach\ *vb* **1** : to send off or away with promptness or speed *esp.* on official business **2** : to put to death **3** : to attend to rapidly or efficiently **4** : DEFEAT — **dis·patch·er** *n*

²dis·patch \di-ˈspach, ˈdis-ˌpach\ *n* **1** : MESSAGE **2** : a news item sent in by a correspondent to a newspaper **3** : the act of dispatching; *esp* : SHIPMENT **4** : the act of putting to death **5** : promptness and efficiency in performing a task

dis·pel \di-ˈspel\ *vb* **dis·pelled; dis·pel·ling** : to drive away by scattering : DISSIPATE ⟨∼ a rumor⟩

dis·pens·able \di-'spen-sə-bəl\ adj : capable of being dispensed with

dis·pen·sa·ry \di-'spen-sə-rē\ n, pl -ries : a place where medicine or medical or dental aid is dispensed

dis·pen·sa·tion \ˌdis-pən-'sā-shən\ n 1 : a system of rules for ordering affairs 2 : a particular arrangement or provision esp. of nature 3 : an exemption from a rule or from a vow or oath 4 : the act of dispensing 5 : something dispensed or distributed

dis·pense \di-'spens\ vb **dis·pensed; dis·pens·ing** 1 : to portion out 2 : AD-MINISTER ⟨~ justice⟩ 3 : EXEMPT 4 : to make up and give out (remedies) — **dis·pens·er** n — **dispense with** 1 : SUS-PEND 2 : to do without

dis·perse \di-'spərs\ vb **dis·persed; dis·pers·ing** : to break up and scatter about : SPREAD — **dis·per·sal** \-'spər-səl\ n — **dis·per·sion** \-'spər-zhən\ n

dis·pir·it \dis-'pir-ət\ vb : DEPRESS, DIS-COURAGE, DISHEARTEN

dis·place \dis-'plās\ vb 1 : to remove from the usual or proper place; esp : to expel or force to flee from home or native land ⟨displaced persons⟩ 2 : to move out of position ⟨water displaced by a floating object⟩ 3 : to take the place of : REPLACE

dis·place·ment \-mənt\ n 1 : the act of displacing : the state of being displaced 2 : the volume or weight of a fluid (as water) displaced by a floating body (as a ship) 3 : the difference between the initial position of an object and a later position

¹**dis·play** \di-'splā\ vb [ME, fr. AF desplaier, desploier, lit., to unfold, fr. des- un- + ploier, plier to fold, fr. L plicare] : to present to view : make evident

²**display** n 1 : a displaying of something 2 : an electronic device (as a cathode-ray tube) that gives information in visual form; also : the visual information

dis·please \ˌdis-'plēz\ vb 1 : to arouse the disapproval and dislike of 2 : to be offensive to : give displeasure

dis·plea·sure \-'ple-zhər\ n : a feeling of dislike and irritation

dis·port \di-'spōrt\ vb 1 : DIVERT, AMUSE 2 : FROLIC 3 : DISPLAY

dis·pos·able \di-'spō-zə-bəl\ adj 1 : remaining after deduction of taxes ⟨~ income⟩ 2 : designed to be used once and then thrown away ⟨~ diapers⟩ — **disposable** n

dis·pos·al \di-'spō-zəl\ n 1 : CONTROL, COMMAND 2 : an orderly arrangement 3 : a getting rid of 4 : MANAGEMENT, AD-MINISTRATION 5 : presenting or bestowing something ⟨~ of favors⟩ 6 : a device used to reduce waste matter (as by grinding)

dis·pose \di-'spōz\ vb **dis·posed; dis·pos·ing** 1 : to give a tendency to : IN-CLINE ⟨disposed to accept⟩ 2 : to put in place : ARRANGE ⟨troops disposed for withdrawal⟩ 3 : SETTLE — **dis·pos·er** n — **dispose of** 1 : to transfer to the control of another 2 : to get rid of 3 : to deal with conclusively

dis·po·si·tion \ˌdis-pə-'zi-shən\ n 1 : the act or power of disposing : DISPOSAL 2 : RELINQUISHMENT 3 : ARRANGEMENT 4 : TENDENCY, INCLINATION 5 : natural attitude toward things ⟨a cheerful ~⟩

dis·pos·sess \ˌdis-pə-'zes\ vb : to put out of possession or occupancy — **dis·pos·ses·sion** \-'ze-shən\ n

dis·praise \ˌdis-'prāz\ vb : DISPARAGE — **dispraise** n — **dis·prais·er** n

dis·pro·por·tion \ˌdis-prə-'pȯr-shən\ n : lack of proportion, symmetry, or proper relation — **dis·pro·por·tion·ate** \-shə-nət\ adj

dis·prove \ˌdis-'prüv\ vb : to prove to be false — **dis·proof** \-'prüf\ n

dis·pu·tant \di-'spyü-tᵊnt, 'dis-pyə-tənt\ n : one that is engaged in a dispute

dis·pu·ta·tion \ˌdis-pyü-'tā-shən\ n 1 : DEBATE 2 : an oral defense of an academic thesis

dis·pu·ta·tious \-shəs\ adj : inclined to dispute : ARGUMENTATIVE

¹**dis·pute** \di-'spyüt\ vb **dis·put·ed; dis·put·ing** 1 : ARGUE, DEBATE 2 : WRAN-GLE 3 : to deny the truth or rightness of 4 : to struggle against or over : OPPOSE — **dis·put·able** \di-'spyü-tə-bəl, 'dis-pyə-tə-bəl\ adj — **dis·put·er** n

²**dis·pute** n 1 : DEBATE 2 : QUARREL

dis·qual·i·fy \ˌdis-'kwä-lə-ˌfī\ vb : to make or declare unfit or not qualified — **dis·qual·i·fi·ca·tion** \-ˌkwä-lə-fə-'kā-shən\ n

¹**dis·qui·et** \ˌdis-'kwī-ət\ vb : to make uneasy or restless : DISTURB ⟨was ~ed by the news⟩ — **dis·qui·et·ing** adj

²**disquiet** n : lack of peace or tranquillity : ANXIETY

dis·qui·etude \ˌdis-'kwī-ə-ˌtüd, -ˌtyüd\ n : AGITATION, ANXIETY

dis·qui·si·tion \ˌdis-kwə-'zi-shən\ n : a formal inquiry or discussion

¹**dis·re·gard** \ˌdis-ri-'gärd\ vb : to pay no attention to : treat as unworthy of notice or regard

²**disregard** n : the act of disregarding : the state of being disregarded : NEGLECT — **dis·re·gard·ful** adj

dis·re·pair \ˌdis-ri-'per\ n : the state of being in need of repair

dis·rep·u·ta·ble \dis-'re-pyü-tə-bəl\ adj : having a bad reputation

dis·re·pute \ˌdis-ri-'pyüt\ n : lack of or decline of reputation : low esteem

dis·re·spect \ˌdis-ri-'spekt\ n : DISCOUR-TESY — **dis·re·spect·ful** adj

dis·robe \dis-'rōb\ vb : UNDRESS

dis·rupt \dis-'rəpt\ vb 1 : to break apart 2 : to throw into disorder 3 : INTERRUPT — **dis·rup·tion** \-'rəp-shən\ n — **dis·rup·tive** \-'rəp-tiv\ adj

dis·sat·is·fac·tion \di-ˌsa-təs-'fak-shən\ n : DISCONTENT

dis·sat·is·fy \di-'sa-təs-ˌfī\ vb : to fail to satisfy : DISPLEASE

dis·sect \dī-'sekt, di-\ vb 1 : to divide into parts esp. for examination and study 2 : ANALYZE — **dis·sec·tion** \-'sek-shən\ n — **dis·sec·tor** \-'sek-tər\ n

dis·sect·ed *adj* : cut deeply into narrow lobes ⟨a ~ leaf⟩

dis·sem·ble \di-'sem-bəl\ *vb* **-bled; -bling** **1** : to hide under or put on a false appearance : conceal facts, intentions, or feelings under some pretense **2** : SIMULATE — **dis·sem·bler** *n*

dis·sem·i·nate \di-'se-mə-ˌnāt\ *vb* **-nat·ed; -nat·ing** : to spread abroad as if sowing seed ⟨~ ideas⟩ — **dis·sem·i·na·tion** \-ˌse-mə-'nā-shən\ *n*

dis·sen·sion \di-'sen-chən\ *n* : disagreement in opinion : DISCORD

¹dis·sent \di-'sent\ *vb* **1** : to withhold assent **2** : to differ in opinion

²dissent *n* **1** : difference of opinion; *esp* : religious nonconformity **2** : a written statement in which a justice disagrees with the opinion of the majority

dis·sent·er \di-'sen-tər\ *n* **1** : one that dissents **2** *cap* : an English Nonconformist

dis·ser·ta·tion \ˌdi-sər-'tā-shən\ *n* : an extended usu. written treatment of a subject; *esp* : one submitted for a doctorate

dis·ser·vice \di-'sər-vəs\ *n* : INJURY, HARM, MISCHIEF

dis·sev·er \di-'se-vər\ *vb* : SEPARATE, DISUNITE

dis·si·dent \'di-sə-dənt\ *adj* [L *dissidens*, prp. of *dissidēre* to sit apart, disagree, fr. *dis-* apart + *sedēre* to sit] : disagreeing esp. with an established religious or political system, organization, or belief — **dis·si·dence** \-dəns\ *n* — **dissident** *n*

dis·sim·i·lar \di-'si-mə-lər\ *adj* : UNLIKE — **dis·sim·i·lar·i·ty** \ˌdi-ˌsi-mə-'ler-ə-tē\ *n*

dis·sim·u·late \di-'si-myə-ˌlāt\ *vb* : to hide under a false appearance : DISSEMBLE — **dis·sim·u·la·tion** \di-ˌsi-myə-'lā-shən\ *n*

dis·si·pate \'di-sə-ˌpāt\ *vb* **-pat·ed; -pat·ing** **1** : to break up and drive off : DISPERSE, SCATTER ⟨the breeze *dissipated* the fog⟩ **2** : SQUANDER **3** : to break up and vanish **4** : to be dissolute; *esp* : to drink alcoholic beverages to excess — **dis·si·pat·ed** *adj* — **dis·si·pa·tion** \ˌdi-sə-'pā-shən\ *n*

dis·so·ci·ate \di-'sō-shē-ˌāt\ *vb* **-at·ed; -at·ing** : DISCONNECT, DISUNITE — **dis·so·ci·a·tion** \di-ˌsō-shē-'ā-shən\ *n* — **dis·so·cia·tive** \di-'sō-shē-ˌā-tiv\ *adj*

dis·so·lute \'di-sə-ˌlüt\ *adj* : loose in morals or conduct — **dis·so·lute·ly** *adv* — **dis·so·lute·ness** *n*

dis·so·lu·tion \ˌdi-sə-'lü-shən\ *n* **1** : the action or process of dissolving **2** : separation of a thing into its parts **3** : DECAY; *also* : DEATH **4** : the termination or breaking up of (as an assembly)

dis·solve \di-'zälv\ *vb* **1** : to separate into component parts **2** : to pass or cause to pass into solution ⟨sugar ~s in water⟩ **3** : TERMINATE, DISPERSE ⟨~ parliament⟩ **4** : to waste or fade away ⟨his courage *dissolved*⟩ **5** : to be overcome emotionally ⟨~ in tears⟩ **6** : to resolve itself as if by dissolution

dis·so·nance \'di-sə-nəns\ *n* : DISCORD — **dis·so·nant** \-nənt\ *adj*

dis·suade \di-'swād\ *vb* **dis·suad·ed; dis·suad·ing** : to advise against a course of action : persuade or try to persuade not to do something — **dis·sua·sion** \-'swā-zhən\ *n* — **dis·sua·sive** \-'swā-siv\ *adj*

dist *abbr* **1** distance **2** district

¹dis·taff \'dis-ˌtaf\ *n, pl* **distaffs** \-ˌtafs, -ˌtavz\ [ME *distaf*, fr. OE *distæf*, fr. *dis-* bunch of flax + *stæf* stick, staff] **1** : a staff for holding the flax, tow, or wool in spinning **2** : a woman's work or domain **3** : the female branch or side of a family

²distaff *adj* **1** : MATERNAL **2** ⟨the ~ side of the family⟩ **2** : FEMALE **1** ⟨~ executives⟩

dis·tal \'dis-t²l\ *adj* **1** : situated away from the point of attachment or origin esp. on the body **2** : of, relating to, or being the surface of a tooth that is farthest from the middle of the front of the jaw — **dis·tal·ly** *adv*

¹dis·tance \'dis-təns\ *n* **1** : measure of separation in space or time **2** : EXPANSE **3** : the full length ⟨go the ~⟩ **4** : spatial remoteness **5** : COLDNESS, RESERVE **6** : DIFFERENCE, DISPARITY **7** : a distant point

²distance *vb* **dis·tanced; dis·tanc·ing** : to leave far behind : OUTSTRIP

³distance *adj* : taking place via electronic media linking instructors and students ⟨~ learning⟩

dis·tant \'dis-tənt\ *adj* **1** : separate in space : AWAY **2** : FAR-OFF ⟨a ~ galaxy⟩ **3** : far apart or behind **4** : not close in relationship ⟨a ~ cousin⟩ **5** : different in kind **6** : RESERVED, ALOOF, COLD ⟨~ politeness⟩ **7** : going a long distance ⟨~ voyages⟩ — **dis·tant·ly** *adv* — **dis·tant·ness** *n*

dis·taste \(ˌ)dis-'tāst\ *n* : DISINCLINATION, DISLIKE — **dis·taste·ful** *adj*

dis·tem·per \(ˌ)dis-'tem-pər\ *n* : a bodily disorder usu. of a domestic animal; *esp* : a contagious often fatal virus disease of dogs

dis·tend \di-'stend\ *vb* : EXPAND, SWELL — **dis·ten·si·ble** \-'sten-sə-bəl\ *adj* — **dis·ten·sion** *or* **dis·ten·tion** \-chən\ *n*

dis·tich \'dis-(ˌ)tik\ *n* : a unit of two lines of poetry

dis·till *also* **dis·til** \di-'stil\ *vb* **dis·tilled; dis·till·ing** **1** : to fall or let fall in drops **2** : to obtain or purify by distillation — **dis·till·er** *n* — **dis·till·ery** \-'sti-lə-rē\ *n*

dis·til·late \'dis-tə-ˌlāt, -lət\ *n* : a liquid product condensed from vapor during distillation

dis·til·la·tion \ˌdis-tə-'lā-shən\ *n* : the process of purifying a liquid by successive evaporation and condensation

dis·tinct \di-'stiŋkt\ *adj* **1** : SEPARATE, INDIVIDUAL ⟨a ~ cultural group⟩ **2** : presenting a clear unmistakable impression — **dis·tinct·ly** *adv* — **dis·tinct·ness** *n*

dis·tinc·tion \di-'stiŋk-shən\ *n* **1** : the distinguishing of a difference; *also* : the difference distinguished **2** : something that distinguishes **3** : special honor or recognition

dis·tinc·tive \di-'stiŋk-tiv\ *adj* **1** : serving

to distinguish ⟨the ∼ flight of the crane⟩ 2 : having or giving style or distinction — **dis·tinc·tive·ly** *adv* — **dis·tinc·tive·ness** *n*

dis·tin·guish \di-'stin-gwish\ *vb* [alter. of ME *distinguen*, fr. AF *distinguer*, fr. L *distinguere*, lit., to separate by pricking] 1 : to recognize by some mark or characteristic 2 : to hear or see clearly : DISCERN 3 : to make distinctions ⟨∼ between right and wrong⟩ 4 : to give prominence or distinction to; *also* : to take special notice of — **dis·tin·guish·able** *adj*

dis·tin·guished \-gwisht\ *adj* 1 : marked by eminence or excellence 2 : befitting an eminent person

dis·tort \di-'stórt\ *vb* 1 : to twist out of the true meaning 2 : to twist out of a natural, normal, or original shape or condition 3 : to cause to be perceived unnaturally — **dis·tor·tion** \-'stór-shən\ *n*

distr *abbr* distribute; distribution

dis·tract \di-'strakt\ *vb* 1 : to draw (the attention or mind) to a different object : DIVERT 2 : to stir up or confuse with conflicting emotions or motives — **dis·trac·tion** \-'strak-shən\ *n*

dis·trait \di-'strā\ *adj* : DISTRAUGHT 1

dis·traught \di-'strót\ *adj* 1 : agitated with doubt or mental conflict or pain 2 : INSANE

¹**dis·tress** \di-'stres\ *n* 1 : suffering of body or mind : PAIN, ANGUISH 2 : TROUBLE, MISFORTUNE 3 : a condition of danger or desperate need — **dis·tress·ful** *adj*

²**distress** *vb* 1 : to subject to great strain or difficulties 2 : UPSET

dis·tress·ed \-'strest\ *adj* : experiencing economic decline or difficulty

dis·trib·ute \di-'stri-byüt\ *vb* -ut·ed; -ut·ing 1 : to divide among several or many 2 : to spread out : SCATTER; *also* : DELIVER 3 : CLASSIFY — **dis·tri·bu·tion** \,dis-trə-'byü-shən\ *n*

dis·trib·u·tive \di-'stri-byü-tiv\ *adj* 1 : of or relating to distribution 2 : of, having, or being the property of producing the same value when an operation is carried out on a whole expression and when it is carried out on each part of an expression with the results then collected together ⟨*a(b + c) = ab + ac* because multiplication is ∼⟩ — **dis·trib·u·tive·ly** *adv*

dis·trib·u·tor \di-'stri-byü-tər\ *n* 1 : one that distributes 2 : one that markets goods 3 : a device for directing current to the spark plugs of an engine

dis·trict \'dis-(,)trikt\ *n* 1 : a fixed territorial division (as for administrative or electoral purposes) 2 : an area, region, or section with a distinguishing character

district attorney *n* : the prosecuting attorney of a judicial district

¹**dis·trust** \dis-'trəst\ *n* : a lack or absence of trust — **dis·trust·ful** \-fəl\ *adj* — **dis·trust·ful·ly** *adv*

²**distrust** *vb* : to have no trust or confidence in

dis·turb \di-'stərb\ *vb* 1 : to interfere with : INTERRUPT 2 : to alter the position

or arrangement of; *also* : to upset the natural and esp. the ecological balance of 3 : to destroy the tranquillity or composure of : make uneasy 4 : to throw into disorder 5 : INCONVENIENCE — **dis·tur·bance** \-'stər-bəns\ *n* — **dis·turb·er** *n* — **dis·turb·ing·ly** \-'stər-bin-lē\ *adv*

dis·turbed \-'stərbd\ *adj* : showing symptoms of emotional illness

dis·unite \,dis-yü-'nīt\ *vb* : DIVIDE, SEPARATE

dis·uni·ty \dis-'yü-nə-tē\ *n* : lack of unity; *esp* : DISSENSION

dis·use \-'yüs\ *n* : a cessation of use or practice

dis·used \-'yüzd\ *adj* : no longer used or occupied

¹**ditch** \'dich\ *n* : a long narrow channel or trench dug in the earth

²**ditch** *vb* 1 : to enclose with a ditch; *also* : to dig a ditch in 2 : to get rid of : DISCARD 3 : to make a forced landing of an airplane on water

dith·er \'di-thər\ *n* : a highly nervous, excited, or agitated state

dit·to \'di-tō\ *n, pl* **dittos** [It *ditto, detto*, pp. of *dire* to say, fr. L *dicere*] 1 : a thing mentioned previously or above — used to avoid repeating a word 2 : a mark " or " used as a symbol for the word *ditto*

dit·ty \'di-tē\ *n, pl* **ditties** : a short simple song

dit·zy *or* **dit·sy** \'dit-sē\ *adj* **ditz·i·er** *or* **dits·i·er; -est** : eccentrically silly, giddy, or inane

di·uret·ic \,dī-yə-'re-tik\ *adj* : tending to increase urine flow — **diuretic** *n*

di·ur·nal \dī-'ər-n°l\ *adj* 1 : DAILY ⟨a ∼ chore⟩ 2 : of, relating to, occurring, or active in the daytime ⟨∼ animals⟩

div *abbr* 1 divided 2 dividend 3 division 4 divorced

di·va \'dē-və\ *n, pl* **divas** *or* **di·ve** \-,vā\ [It, lit., goddess, fr. L, fem. of *divus* divine, god] 1 : PRIMA DONNA 2 : a usu. glamorous and successful female performer or personality

di·va·gate \'dī-və-,gāt\ *vb* -gat·ed; -gat·ing : to wander or stray from a course or subject : DIVERGE — **di·va·ga·tion** \,dī-və-'gā-shən\ *n*

di·van \'dī-,van, di-'van\ *n* : COUCH, SOFA

¹**dive** \'dīv\ *vb* **dived** \'dīvd\ *or* **dove** \'dōv\; **dived; div·ing** 1 : to plunge into water headfirst 2 : SUBMERGE 3 : to come or drop down precipitously 4 : to descend in an airplane at a steep angle 5 : to plunge into some matter or activity 6 : DART, LUNGE — **div·er** *n*

²**dive** *n* 1 : the act or an instance of diving 2 : a sharp decline 3 : a disreputable bar or place of amusement

di·verge \də-'vərj, dī-\ *vb* **di·verged; di·verg·ing** 1 : to move or extend in different directions from a common point : draw apart 2 : to differ in character, form, or opinion 3 : DEVIATE 4 : DEFLECT — **di·ver·gence** \-'vər-jəns\ *n* — **di·ver·gent** \-jənt\ *adj*

di·vers \'dī-vərz\ *adj* : VARIOUS

di·verse \dī-'vərs, də-, 'dī-,vərs\ *adj* 1

: UNLIKE **2** : composed of distinct forms or qualities — **di·verse·ly** *adv*

di·ver·si·fy \də-'vər-sə-ˌfī, dī-\ *vb* **-fied; -fy·ing** : to make different or various in form or quality — **di·ver·si·fi·ca·tion** \-ˌvər-sə-fə-'kā-shən\ *n*

di·ver·sion \də-'vər-zhən, dī-\ *n* **1** : a turning aside from a course, activity, or use : DEVIATION **2** : something that diverts or amuses : PASTIME

di·ver·si·ty \də-'vər-sə-tē, dī-\ *n, pl* **-ties** **1** : the condition of being diverse : VARIETY **2** : an instance of being diverse

di·vert \də-'vərt, dī-\ *vb* **1** : to turn from a course or purpose : DEFLECT **2** : DISTRACT **3** : ENTERTAIN, AMUSE

di·vert·ing \-'vər-tiŋ\ *adj* : providing amusement or entertainment

di·vest \dī-'vest, də-\ *vb* **1** : to deprive or dispossess esp. of property, authority, or rights **2** : to strip esp. of clothing, ornament, or equipment

¹di·vide \də-'vīd\ *vb* **di·vid·ed; di·vid·ing** **1** : SEPARATE; *also* : CLASSIFY **2** : CLEAVE, PART ⟨a ship *dividing* the waves⟩ **3** : DISTRIBUTE, APPORTION **4** : to possess or make use of in common : share in **5** : to cause to be separate, distinct, or apart from one another **6** : to separate into opposing sides or parties **7** : to mark divisions on **8** : to subject to or use in mathematical division; *also* : to be used as a divisor with respect to **9** : to branch out

²divide *n* : WATERSHED 1

div·i·dend \'di-və-ˌdend\ *n* **1** : an individual share of something distributed **2** : BONUS **3** : a number to be divided **4** : a sum or fund to be divided or distributed

di·vid·er \də-'vī-dər\ *n* **1** : one that divides (as a partition) ⟨room ∼⟩ **2** *pl* : COMPASS 5

div·i·na·tion \ˌdi-və-'nā-shən\ *n* **1** : the art or practice of using omens or magic powers to foretell the future **2** : unusual insight or intuitive perception

¹di·vine \də-'vīn\ *adj* **di·vin·er; -est** **1** : of, relating to, or being God or a god **2** : supremely good : SUPERB; *also* : HEAVENLY — **di·vine·ly** *adv*

²divine *n* **1** : CLERGYMAN **2** : THEOLOGIAN

³divine *vb* **di·vined; di·vin·ing** **1** : INFER, CONJECTURE **2** : PROPHESY **3** : DOWSE — **di·vin·er** *n*

divining rod *n* : a forked rod believed to reveal the presence of water or minerals by dipping downward when held over a vein

di·vin·i·ty \də-'vi-nə-tē\ *n, pl* **-ties** **1** : THEOLOGY **2** : the quality or state of being divine **3** : a divine being; *esp* : GOD 1

di·vis·i·ble \də-'vi-zə-bəl\ *adj* : capable of being divided ⟨9 is ∼ by 3⟩ — **di·vis·i·bil·i·ty** \-ˌvi-zə-'bi-lə-tē\ *n*

di·vi·sion \də-'vi-zhən\ *n* **1** : DISTRIBUTION, SEPARATION **2** : one of the parts or groupings into which a whole is divided **3** : DISAGREEMENT, DISUNITY **4** : something that divides or separates **5** : the mathematical operation of finding how many times one number is contained in another **6** : a large self-contained military unit **7** : an administrative or operating unit of a governmental, business, or educational organization — **di·vi·sion·al** \-'vi-zhə-nəl\ *adj*

di·vi·sive \də-'vī-siv, -'vi-ziv\ *adj* : creating disunity or dissension — **di·vi·sive·ly** *adv* — **di·vi·sive·ness** *n*

di·vi·sor \də-'vī-zər\ *n* : the number by which a dividend is divided

di·vorce \də-'vórs\ *n* **1** : an act or instance of legally dissolving a marriage **2** : SEPARATION, SEVERANCE — **divorce** *vb* — **di·vorce·ment** *n*

di·vor·cé \də-ˌvór-'sā\ *n* [F] : a divorced man

di·vor·cée \də-ˌvór-'sā, -'sē\ *n* : a divorced woman

div·ot \'di-vət\ *n* : a piece of turf dug from a golf fairway in making a stroke

di·vulge \də-'vəlj, dī-\ *vb* **di·vulged; di·vulg·ing** : REVEAL, DISCLOSE

Dix·ie·land \'dik-sē-ˌland\ *n* : jazz music in duple time played in a style developed in New Orleans

diz·zy \'di-zē\ *adj* **diz·zi·er; -est** [ME *disy*, fr. OE *dysig* stupid] **1** : FOOLISH, SILLY **2** : having a sensation of whirling : GIDDY **3** : causing or caused by giddiness — **diz·zi·ly** \-zə-lē\ *adv* — **diz·zi·ness** \-zē-nəs\ *n*

DJ *n, often not cap* : DISC JOCKEY

dk *abbr* **1** dark **2** deck **3** dock

dl *abbr* deciliter

DLitt *or* **DLit** *abbr* [NL *doctor litterarum*] doctor of letters; doctor of literature

DLO *abbr* dead letter office

dm *abbr* decimeter

DMD *abbr* [NL *dentariae medicinae doctor*] doctor of dental medicine

DMZ *abbr* demilitarized zone

dn *abbr* down

DNA \ˌdē-(ˌ)en-'ā\ *n* : any of various nucleic acids that are usu. the molecular basis of heredity and are localized esp. in cell nuclei

DNR *abbr* do not resuscitate

¹do \'dü\ *vb* **did** \'did\; **done** \'dən\; **do·ing; does** \'dəz\ **1** : to bring to pass : ACCOMPLISH **2** : ACT, BEHAVE ⟨∼ as I say⟩ **3** : to be active or busy ⟨up and ∼*ing*⟩ **4** : HAPPEN ⟨what's ∼*ing*?⟩ **5** : to be engaged in the study or practice of : work at ⟨he *does* tailoring⟩ **6** : COOK ⟨steak *done* rare⟩ **7** : to put in order ⟨as by cleaning or arranging⟩ ⟨∼ the dishes⟩ **8** : DECORATE ⟨*did* the hall in blue⟩ **9** : GET ALONG ⟨∼ well in school⟩ **10** : CARRY ON, MANAGE **11** : RENDER ⟨sleep will ∼ you good⟩ **12** : FINISH ⟨when he had *done*⟩ **13** : EXERT ⟨*did* my best⟩ **14** : PRODUCE ⟨*did* a poem⟩ **15** : to play the part of **16** : CHEAT ⟨*did* him out of his share⟩ **17** : TRAVERSE, TOUR **18** : TRAVEL **19** : to spend or serve out a period of time ⟨*did* ten years in prison⟩ **20** : SUFFICE, SUIT **21** : to be fitting or proper **22** : USE ⟨doesn't ∼ drugs⟩ **23** — used as an auxiliary verb (1) before the subject in an interrogative sentence ⟨*does* he work?⟩ and after some adverbs ⟨never *did* she say so), (2) in a negative statement ⟨I *don't* know⟩, (3) for emphasis ⟨you ∼ know⟩, and (4) as a substitute for a preceding predicate ⟨he works harder than I ∼⟩ — **do·able** \'dü-ə-bəl\ *adj* — **do away with 1** : to put an end to **2** : DESTROY, KILL — **do by** : to deal with : TREAT ⟨*did* right *by* her⟩ — **do for** *chiefly Brit* : to bring about the death or ruin of — **do the trick** : to produce a desired result

²**do** *n* **1** : AFFAIR, PARTY **2** : a command or entreaty to do something ⟨list of ∼s and don'ts⟩ **3** : HAIRSTYLE

³**do** *abbr* ditto

DOA *abbr* dead on arrival

DOB *abbr* date of birth

dob·bin \'dä-bən\ *n* [*Dobbin,* nickname for *Robert*] **1** : a farm horse **2** : a quiet plodding horse

Do·ber·man pin·scher \'dō-bər-mən-'pin-chər\, *n* : any of a German breed of short-haired medium-sized dogs

do·bra \'dō-brə\ *n* — see MONEY table

¹**doc** \'däk\ *n* : DOCTOR

²**doc** *abbr* document

do·cent \'dō-sᵊnt, dōt-'sent\ *n* [obs. G (now *Dozent*), fr. L *docens,* prp. of *docēre* to teach] : TEACHER, LECTURER; *also* : a person who leads a guided tour

doc·ile \'dä-səl\ *adj* [L *docilis,* fr. *docēre* to teach] : easily taught, led, or managed : TRACTABLE — **do·cil·i·ty** \dä-'si-lə-tē\ *n*

¹**dock** \'däk\ *n* : any of a genus of coarse weedy herbs related to buckwheat

²**dock** *vb* **1** : to cut off the end of : cut short **2** : to take away a part of : deduct from ⟨∼ a worker's wages⟩

³**dock** *n* **1** : an artificial basin to receive ships **2** : ²SLIP **3** : a wharf or platform for loading or unloading materials or for mooring a boat

⁴**dock** *vb* **1** : to bring or come into dock **2** : to join (as two spacecraft) mechanically in space

⁵**dock** *n* : the place in a court where a prisoner stands or sits during trial

dock·age \'dä-kij\ *n* : docking facilities

dock·et \'dä-kət\ *n* **1** : a formal abridged record of the proceedings in a legal action; *also* : a register of such records **2** : a list of legal causes to be tried **3** : a calendar of matters to be acted on : AGENDA **4** : a label attached to a document containing identification or directions — **docket** *vb*

dock·hand \'däk-ˌhand\ *n* : LONGSHOREMAN

dock·work·er \-ˌwər-kər\ *n* : LONGSHOREMAN

dock·yard \-ˌyärd\ *n* : SHIPYARD

¹**doc·tor** \'däk-tər\ *n* [ME *doctour* teacher, doctor, fr. AF & ML; AF, fr. ML *doctor,* fr. L, teacher, fr. *docēre* to teach] **1** : a person holding one of the highest academic degrees (as a PhD) conferred by a university **2** : a person skilled in healing arts; *esp* : one (as a physician, dentist, or veterinarian) academically and legally qualified to practice **3** : a person who restores or repairs things — **doc·tor·al** \-tə-rəl\ *adj*

²**doctor** *vb* **1** : to give medical treatment to **2** : to practice medicine **3** : REPAIR **4** : to adapt or modify for a desired end **5** : to alter deceptively

doc·tor·ate \'däk-tə-rət\ *n* : the degree, title, or rank of a doctor

doc·tri·naire \ˌdäk-trə-'ner\ *n* [F] : one who attempts to put an abstract theory into effect without regard to practical difficulties — **doctrinaire** *adj*

doc·trine \'däk-trən\ *n* **1** : something that is taught **2** : DOGMA, TENET — **doc·tri·nal** \-trə-nᵊl\ *adj*

docu·dra·ma \'dä-kyə-ˌdrä-mə, -ˌdra-\ *n* : a drama made for television, motion pictures, or theater that deals freely with historical events

doc·u·ment \'dä-kyə-mənt\ *n* **1** : a paper that furnishes information, proof, or support of something else **2** : a computer file containing information input by a computer user onto, via a word processor — **doc·u·ment** \-ˌment\ *vb* — **doc·u·men·ta·tion** \ˌdä-kyə-mən-'tā-shən\ *n* — **doc·u·ment·er** *n*

doc·u·men·ta·ry \ˌdä-kyə-'men-tə-rē\ *adj* **1** : consisting of documents; *also* : being in writing ⟨∼ proof⟩ **2** : giving a factual presentation in artistic form ⟨a ∼ movie⟩ — **documentary** *n*

DOD *abbr* Department of Defense

¹**dod·der** \'dä-dər\ *n* : any of a genus of leafless parasitic twining vines that are highly deficient in chlorophyll

²**dodder** *vb* **dod·dered; dod·der·ing 1** : to tremble or shake usu. from age **2** : to progress feebly and unsteadily

¹**dodge** \'däj\ *n* **1** : an act of evading by sudden bodily movement **2** : an artful device to evade, deceive, or trick **3** : EXPEDIENT

²**dodge** *vb* **dodged; dodg·ing 1** : to evade usu. by trickery **2** : to move suddenly aside; *also* : to avoid or evade by so doing — **dodg·er** *n*

do·do \'dō-dō\ *n, pl* **dodoes** *or* **dodos** [Pg *doudo,* fr. *doudo* silly, stupid] **1** : an extinct heavy flightless bird of the island of Mauritius related to the pigeons and larger than a turkey **2** : one hopelessly behind the times; *also* : a stupid person

doe \'dō\ *n, pl* **does** *or* **doe** : an adult female of various mammals (as a deer, rabbit, or kangaroo) of which the male is called *buck*

DOE *abbr* Department of Energy

do·er \'dü-ər\ *n* : one that does

does *pres 3d sing of* DO; *pl of* DOE

doff \'däf\ *vb* [ME, fr. *don* to do + *of* off] **1** : to take off (the hat) in greeting or as a sign of respect **2** : to rid oneself of

¹**dog** \'dȯg\ *n* **1** : a flesh-eating domestic mammal related to the wolves; *esp* : a male of this animal **2** : a worthless or contemptible person **3** : FELLOW, CHAP ⟨you lucky ∼⟩ **4** : a mechanical device for holding something **5** : uncharacteristic or affected stylishness or dignity ⟨put on the ∼⟩ **6** *pl* : RUIN ⟨gone to the ∼s⟩

²**dog** *vb* **dogged; dog·ging 1** : to hunt or track like a hound **2** : to worry as if by pursuit with dogs : PLAGUE

dog·bane \'dȯg-ˌbān\ *n* : any of a genus of mostly poisonous herbs with milky juice and often showy flowers

dog·cart \-ˌkärt\ *n* : a light one-horse carriage with two seats back to back

dog·catch·er \-ˌka-chər, -ˌke-\ *n* : a community official assigned to catch and dispose of stray dogs

dog–ear \'dȯg-ˌir\ *n* : the turned-down corner of a leaf of a book — **dog–ear** *vb* — **dog–eared** \-ˌird\ *adj*

dog·fight \'dȯg-ˌfīt\ *n* : a fight between fighter planes at close range

dog·fish \-ˌfish\ *n* : any of various small usu. bottom-dwelling sharks

dog·ged \'dȯ-gəd\ *adj* : stubbornly determined : TENACIOUS — **dog·ged·ly** *adv* — **dog·ged·ness** *n*

dog·ger·el \'dȯ-gə-rəl\ *n* : verse that is loosely styled and irregular in measure esp. for comic effect

dog·gie bag *or* **doggy bag** \'dȯ-gē-\ *n* : a container for carrying home leftover food from a restaurant meal

¹dog·gy *or* **dog·gie** \'dȯ-gē\ *n, pl* **doggies** : a small dog

²dog·gy *adj* **dog·gi·er; -est** : of or resembling a dog ⟨a ~ odor⟩

dog·house \'dȯg-ˌhau̇s\ *n* : a shelter for a dog — **in the doghouse** : in a state of disfavor

do·gie \'dō-gē\ *n, chiefly West* : a motherless calf in a range herd

dog·leg \'dȯg-ˌleg\ *n* : a sharp bend or angle (as in a road or golf fairway) — **dogleg** *vb*

dog·ma \'dȯg-mə\ *n, pl* **dogmas** *also* **dog·ma·ta** \-mə-tə\ [L, fr. Gk, fr. *dokein* to think, have an opinion] **1** : a tenet or code of tenets **2** : a doctrine or body of doctrines formally proclaimed by a church

dog·ma·tism \'dȯg-mə-ˌti-zəm\ *n* : positiveness in stating matters of opinion esp. when unwarranted or arrogant — **dog·mat·ic** \dȯg-'ma-tik\ *adj* — **dog·mat·i·cal·ly** \-ti-k(ə-)lē\ *adv*

do–good·er \'dü-ˌgu̇-dər\ *n* : an earnest often naive humanitarian or reformer

dog·tooth violet \'dȯg-ˌtüth-\ *n* : any of a genus of small spring-flowering bulbous herbs related to the lilies

dog·trot \'dȯg-ˌträt\ *n* : a gentle trot — **dogtrot** *vb*

dog·wood \'dȯg-ˌwu̇d\ *n* : any of a genus of trees and shrubs having heads of small flowers often with showy white, pink, or red bracts

doi·ly \'dȯi-lē\ *n, pl* **doilies** : a small often decorative mat

do in *vb* **1** : RUIN **2** : KILL **3** : TIRE, EXHAUST ⟨the climb *did* him *in*⟩ **4** : CHEAT

do·ings \'dü-iŋz\ *n pl* : GOINGS-ON

do–it–yourself *n* : the activity of doing or making something without professional training or help — **do–it–your·self·er** *n*

dol *abbr* dollar

dol·drums \'dōl-drəmz, 'däl-\ *n pl* **1** : a spell of listlessness or despondency **2** *often cap* : a part of the ocean near the equator known for calms **3** : a state or period of inactivity, stagnation, or slump

¹dole \'dōl\ *n* **1** : a distribution esp. of food, money, or clothing to the needy; *also* : something so distributed **2** : a grant of government funds to the unemployed

²dole *vb* **doled; dol·ing** : to give or distribute as a charity — usu. used with *out*

dole·ful \'dōl-fəl\ *adj* : full of grief : SAD — **dole·ful·ly** *adv*

dole out *vb* **1** : to give or deliver in small portions **2** : DISH OUT

doll \'däl, 'dȯl\ *n* **1** : a small figure of a human being used esp. as a child's plaything **2** : a pretty woman **3** : an attractive person — **doll·ish** \'dä-lish, 'dȯ-\ *adj*

dol·lar \'dä-lər\ *n* [Dutch or LG *daler*, fr. G *Taler*, short for *Joachimstaler*, fr. Sankt *Joachimsthal*, Bohemia, where talers were first made] **1** : any of various basic monetary units (as in the U.S. and Canada) — see MONEY table **2** : a coin, note, or token representing one dollar **3** : RINGGIT

dol·lop \'dä-ləp\ *n* **1** : LUMP, GLOB **2** : PORTION 1 — **dollop** *vb*

doll up *vb* **1** : to dress elegantly or extravagantly **2** : to make more attractive **3** : to get dolled up

dol·ly \'dä-lē\ *n, pl* **dollies** : a small cart or wheeled platform (as for a television or movie camera)

dol·men \'dōl-mən, 'däl-\ *n* : a prehistoric monument consisting of two or more upright stones supporting a horizontal stone slab

do·lo·mite \'dō-lə-ˌmīt, 'dä-\ *n* : a mineral found in broad layers as a compact limestone

do·lor \'dō-lər, 'dä-\ *n* : mental suffering or anguish : SORROW — **do·lor·ous** *adj* — **do·lor·ous·ly** *adv*

do·lour *chiefly Brit var of* DOLOR

dol·phin \'däl-fən\ *n* **1** : any of various small whales with conical teeth and an elongated beaklike snout **2** : either of two active food fishes of tropical and temperate seas

dolt \'dōlt\ *n* : a stupid person — **dolt·ish** \'dōl-tish\ *adj* — **dolt·ish·ness** *n*

dom *abbr* **1** domestic **2** dominant **3** dominion

-dom *n suffix* **1** : dignity : office ⟨duke*dom*⟩ **2** : realm : jurisdiction ⟨king*dom*⟩ **3** : state or fact of being ⟨free*dom*⟩ **4** : those having a (specified) office, occupation, interest, or character ⟨official*dom*⟩

do·main \dō-'mān\ *n* **1** : complete and absolute ownership of land **2** : land completely owned **3** : a territory over which dominion is exercised **4** : a sphere of knowledge, influence, or activity ⟨the ~ of science⟩ **5** : a subdivision of the Internet made up of computers whose URLs share a characteristic abbreviation (as *com* or *gov*)

domain name *n* : a sequence of characters (as Merriam-Webster.com) that specifies a group of online resources and forms part of its URL

dome \'dōm\ *n* **1** : a large hemispherical

roof or ceiling **2** : a structure or natural formation that resembles the dome of a building **3** : a roofed sports stadium — **dome** *vb*

¹do·mes·tic \də-'mes-tik\ *adj* **1** : living near or about human habitations **2** : TAME, DOMESTICATED **3** : relating and limited to one's own country or the country under consideration **4** : of or relating to the household or the family **5** : devoted to home duties and pleasures **6** : INDIGENOUS — **do·mes·ti·cal·ly** \-ti-k(ə-)lē\ *adv*

²domestic *n* : a household servant

do·mes·ti·cate \də-'mes-ti-ˌkāt\ *vb* **-cat·ed; -cat·ing** : to adapt to life in association with and to the use of humans — **do·mes·ti·ca·tion** \-ˌmes-ti-'kā-shən\ *n*

do·mes·tic·i·ty \ˌdō-ˌmes-'ti-sə-tē, də-\ *n, pl* **-ties 1** : the quality or state of being domestic or domesticated **2** : domestic activities or life

domestic violence *n* : the inflicting of injury by one family or household member on another

do·mi·cile \'dä-mə-ˌsī(-ə)l, 'dō-; 'dä-məsəl\ *n* : a dwelling place : HOME — **domicile** *vb* — **dom·i·cil·i·ary** \ˌdä-mə-'si-lēˌer-ē, ˌdō-\ *adj*

dom·i·nance \'dä-mə-nəns\ *n* **1** : AUTHORITY, CONTROL **2** : the property of one of a pair of alleles or traits that suppresses expression of the other when both are present

¹dom·i·nant \-nənt\ *adj* **1** : controlling or prevailing over all others **2** : overlooking from a high position **3** : exhibiting genetic dominance

²dominant *n* : a dominant gene or trait

dom·i·nate \'dä-mə-ˌnāt\ *vb* **-nat·ed; -nat·ing 1** : RULE, CONTROL **2** : to have a commanding position or controlling power over **3** : to rise high above in a position suggesting power to dominate — **dom·i·na·tor** \-ˌnā-tər\ *n*

dom·i·na·tion \ˌdä-mə-'nā-shən\ *n* **1** : supremacy or preeminence over another **2** : exercise of mastery, ruling power, or preponderant influence

dom·i·na·trix \ˌdä-mə-'nā-triks\ *n, pl* **-trices** \-'nā-trə-ˌsēz, -nə-'trī-sēz\ : a woman who dominates her sexual partner; *also* : a dominating woman

dom·i·neer \ˌdä-mə-'nir\ *vb* **1** : to rule in an arrogant manner **2** : to be overbearing

do·mi·nie *1 usu* 'dä-mə-nē, *2 usu* 'dō-\ *n* **1** *chiefly Scot* : SCHOOLMASTER **2** : CLERGYMAN

do·min·ion \də-'min-yən\ *n* **1** : DOMAIN **2** : supreme authority : SOVEREIGNTY **3** *often cap* : a self-governing nation of the Commonwealth

dom·i·no \'dä-mə-ˌnō\ *n, pl* **-noes** *or* **-nos 1** : a long loose hooded cloak usu. worn with a half mask as a masquerade costume **2** : a flat rectangular block used as a piece in a game (**dominoes**)

¹don \'dän\ *vb* **donned; don·ning** [ME, fr. *don* to do + *on*] : to put on (as clothes)

²don *n* [Sp, fr. L *dominus* lord, master] **1** : a Spanish nobleman or gentleman —

used as a title prefixed to the Christian name **2** : a head, tutor, or fellow in an English university

do·ña \'dō-nyə\ *n* : a Spanish woman of rank — used as a title prefixed to the Christian name

do·nate \'dō-ˌnāt\ *vb* **do·nat·ed; do·nat·ing 1** : to make a gift of : CONTRIBUTE **2** : to make a donation

do·na·tion \dō-'nā-shən\ *n* **1** : the making of a gift esp. to a charity **2** : a free contribution : GIFT

¹done \'dən\ *past part of* DO

²done *adj* **1** : doomed to failure, defeat, or death **2** : gone by : OVER ⟨when day is ~⟩ **3** : cooked sufficiently **4** : conformable to social convention

done deal *n* : FAIT ACCOMPLI

dong \'dȯŋ, 'däŋ\ *n* — see MONEY table

don·key \'däŋ-kē, 'dəŋ-\ *n, pl* **donkeys 1** : a sturdy and patient domestic mammal classified with the asses **2** : a stupid or obstinate person

don·ny·brook \'dä-nē-ˌbrúk\ *n, often cap* [*Donnybrook* Fair, annual Irish event known for its brawls] : an uproarious brawl

do·nor \'dō-nər\ *n* : one that gives, donates, or presents

donut *var of* DOUGHNUT

doo·dad \'dü-ˌdad\ *n* : an often small article whose common name is unknown or forgotten

doo·dle \'dü-dᵊl\ *vb* **doo·dled; doo·dling** : to draw or scribble aimlessly while occupied with something else — **doodle** *n* — **doo·dler** *n*

doom \'düm\ *n* **1** : JUDGMENT; *esp* : a judicial condemnation or sentence **2** : DESTINY **3** : RUIN, DEATH — **doom** *vb*

dooms·day \'dümz-ˌdā\ *n* : JUDGMENT DAY

door \'dȯr\ *n* **1** : a barrier by which an entry is closed and opened; *also* : a similar part of a piece of furniture **2** : DOORWAY **3** : a means of access or participation : OPPORTUNITY

door·keep·er \-ˌkē-pər\ *n* : a person who tends a door

door·knob \-ˌnäb\ *n* : a knob that when turned releases a door latch

door·man \-ˌman, -mən\ *n* : a usu. uniformed attendant at the door of a building (as a hotel)

door·mat \-ˌmat\ *n* : a mat placed before or inside a door for wiping dirt from the shoes

door·plate \-ˌplāt\ *n* : a nameplate on a door

door·step \-ˌstep\ *n* : a step or series of steps before an outer door

door·way \-ˌwā\ *n* **1** : the opening that a door closes **2** : DOOR 3

do·pa \'dō-pə\ *n* : a form of an amino acid that is used esp. in the treatment of Parkinson's disease

do·pa·mine \'dō-pə-ˌmēn\ *n* : an organic compound that occurs esp. as a neurotransmitter in the brain

¹dope \'dōp\ *n* **1** : a preparation for giving a desired quality **2** : an illicit, habit-forming, or narcotic drug; *esp* : MARI-

JUANA 3 : a stupid person 4 : INFORMATION

²**dope** vb **doped; dop·ing 1** : to treat with dope; esp : to give a narcotic to 2 : FIGURE OUT — usu. used with out 3 : to take dope — **dop·er** n

dop·ey also **dopy** \'dō-pē\ adj **dop·i·er; -est 1** : dulled by alcohol or a narcotic 2 : SLUGGISH 3 : STUPID — **dop·i·ness** n

doping n : the use of a substance or technique to illegally improve athletic performance

Dopp·ler effect \'dä-plər-\ n : a change in the frequency at which waves (as of sound) reach an observer from a source in motion with respect to the observer

do–rag \'dü-ˌrag\ n : a kerchief worn esp. to cover the hair

dork \'dȯrk\ n, slang : NERD; also : JERK 2

dorm \'dȯrm\ n : DORMITORY

dor·mant \'dȯr-mənt\ adj : INACTIVE; esp : not actively growing or functioning ⟨~ buds⟩ — **dor·man·cy** \-mən-sē\ n

dor·mer \'dȯr-mər\ n [MF dormeor dormitory, fr. L dormitorium, fr. dormire to sleep] : a window built upright in a sloping roof; also : the roofed structure containing such a window

dor·mi·to·ry \'dȯr-mə-ˌtȯr-ē\ n, pl **-ries 1** : a room for sleeping; esp : a large room containing a number of beds 2 : a residence hall providing sleeping rooms

dor·mouse \'dȯr-ˌmaůs\ n : any of numerous Old World rodents that resemble small squirrels

dor·sal \'dȯr-səl\ adj : of, relating to, or located near or on the surface of the body that in humans is the back but in most other animals is the upper surface — **dor·sal·ly** adv

do·ry \'dȯr-ē\ n, pl **dories** : a flat-bottomed boat with high flaring sides and a sharp bow

DOS abbr disk operating system

¹**dose** \'dōs\ n [ME, fr. MF, fr. LL dosis, fr. Gk, lit., act of giving, fr. didonai to give] **1** : a measured quantity (as of medicine) to be taken or administered at one time 2 : the quantity of radiation administered or absorbed — **dos·age** \'dō-sij\ n

²**dose** vb **dosed; dos·ing 1** : to give in doses 2 : to give medicine to

do·sim·e·ter \dō-'si-mə-tər\ n : a device for measuring doses of radiations (as X-rays) — **do·sim·e·try** \-mə-trē\ n

dos·sier \'dȯs-ˌyā, 'dȯ-sē-ˌā\ n [F, bundle of documents labeled on the back, dossier, fr. dos back, fr. OF, fr. L dorsum] : a file containing detailed records on a particular person or subject

¹**dot** \'dät\ n **1** : a small spot : SPECK 2 : a small round mark 3 : a precise point esp. in time ⟨be here on the ~⟩

²**dot** vb **dot·ted; dot·ting 1** : to mark with a dot ⟨~ an i⟩ 2 : to cover with or as if with dots — **dot·ter** n

DOT abbr Department of Transportation

dot·age \'dō-tij\ n : feebleness of mind esp. in old age : SENILITY

dot·ard \-tərd\ n : a person in dotage

dot–com \'dät-ˌkäm\ n : a company that

markets its products or services usu. exclusively via a website

dote \'dōt\ vb **dot·ed; dot·ing 1** : to be feebleminded esp. from old age 2 : to be lavish or excessive in one's attention, affection, or fondness ⟨doted on her niece⟩

dot matrix n : a rectangular arrangement of dots from which alphanumeric characters can be formed (as by a computer printer)

Dou·ay Version \dü-'ā-\ n : an English translation of the Vulgate used by Roman Catholics

¹**dou·ble** \'də-bəl\ adj [ME, fr. AF, fr. L duplus, fr. duo two + -plus multiplied by] **1** : TWOFOLD, DUAL ⟨serving a ~ function⟩ 2 : consisting of two members or parts 3 : being twice as great or as many 4 : folded in two 5 : having more than one whorl of petals ⟨~ roses⟩

²**double** vb **dou·bled; dou·bling 1** : to make, be, or become twice as great or as many 2 : to make a call in bridge that increases the trick values and penalties of (an opponent's bid) 3 : FOLD 4 : CLENCH 5 : to be or cause to be bent over 6 : to take the place of another 7 : to hit a double 8 : to turn sharply and suddenly; esp : to turn back on one's course

³**double** adv **1** : DOUBLY 2 : two together ⟨sleep ~⟩

⁴**double** n **1** : something twice another in size, strength, quantity, or value 2 : a base hit that enables the batter to reach second base 3 : COUNTERPART, DUPLICATE; esp : a person who closely resembles another 4 : UNDERSTUDY, SUBSTITUTE 5 : a sharp turn : REVERSAL 6 : FOLD 7 : a combined bet placed on two different contests 8 pl : a game between two pairs of players 9 : an act of doubling in a card game

double bond n : a chemical bond in which two atoms in a molecule share two pairs of electrons

double cross n : an act of betraying or cheating esp. an associate — **dou·ble-cross** \ˌdə-bəl-'krȯs\ vb — **dou·ble-cross·er** n

dou·ble–deal·ing \ˌdə-bəl-'dē-liŋ\ n : DUPLICITY — **dou·ble–deal·er** \-'dē-lər\ n — **double–dealing** adj

dou·ble–deck·er \-'de-kər\ n : something having two decks, levels, or layers — **dou·ble–deck** \-ˌdek\ or **dou·ble–decked** \-ˌdekt\ adj

dou·ble–dig·it \ˌdə-bəl-'di-jət\ adj : amounting to 10 percent or more

double down vb : to become more tenacious, zealous, or resolute

dou·ble en·ten·dre \ˌdüb-ᵊl-än-'tänd, ˌdə-bəl-, -'tänd-rᵊ\ n, pl **double entendres** \same or -'tän-drəz\ [obs. F, lit., double meaning] : a word or expression capable of two interpretations with one usu. risqué

dou·ble·head·er \ˌdə-bəl-'he-dər\ n : two games played consecutively on the same day

double helix n : a helix or spiral consisting of two strands (as of DNA) in the surface of a cylinder which coil around its axis

dou·ble–hung \ˌdə-bəl-ˈhəŋ\ *adj, of a window* : having an upper and a lower sash that can slide past each other

dou·ble–joint·ed \-ˈjȯin-təd\ *adj* : having a joint that permits an exceptional degree of freedom of motion of the parts joined ⟨a ∼ finger⟩

dou·ble–park \ˌdə-bəl-ˈpärk\ *vb* : to park a vehicle beside a row of vehicles already parked parallel to the curb

double play *n* : a play in baseball by which two players are put out

double pneumonia *n* : pneumonia affecting both lungs

double standard *n* : a set of principles that applies differently and usu. more rigorously to one group of people or circumstances than to another

dou·blet \ˈdə-blət\ *n* **1** : a man's close-fitting jacket worn in Europe esp. in the 16th century **2** : one of two similar or identical things

dou·ble take \ˈdə-bəl-ˌtāk\ *n* : a delayed reaction to a surprising or significant situation after an initial failure to notice anything unusual

dou·ble–talk \-ˌtȯk\ *n* : language that appears to be meaningful but in fact is a mixture of sense and nonsense

double up *vb* : to share accommodations designed for one

double whammy *n* : a combination of two usu. adverse forces, circumstances, or effects

dou·bloon \ˌdə-ˈblün\ *n* : a former gold coin of Spain and Spanish America

dou·bly \ˈdə-blē\ *adv* **1** : in a twofold manner **2** : to twice the degree ⟨∼ glad⟩

¹doubt \ˈdau̇t\ *vb* **1** : to be uncertain about **2** : to lack confidence in : DISTRUST **3** : to consider unlikely — **doubt·able** *adj* — **doubt·er** *n*

²doubt *n* **1** : uncertainty of belief or opinion **2** : a condition causing uncertainty, hesitation, or suspense ⟨the outcome was in ∼⟩ **3** : DISTRUST **4** : an inclination not to believe or accept

doubt·ful \ˈdau̇t-fəl\ *adj* **1** : QUESTIONABLE ⟨∼ they knew what happened⟩ **2** : UNDECIDED ⟨the outcome of the election is ∼⟩ — **doubt·ful·ly** *adv* — **doubt·ful·ness** *n*

¹doubt·less \ˈdau̇t-ləs\ *adv* **1** : without doubt **2** : PROBABLY

²doubtless *adj* : free from doubt : CERTAIN — **doubt·less·ly** *adv*

douche \ˈdüsh\ *n* [F] **1** : a jet of fluid (as water) directed against a part or into a cavity of the body; *also* : a cleansing with a douche **2** : a device for giving douches — **douche** *vb*

dough \ˈdō\ *n* **1** : a mixture that consists of flour or meal and a liquid (as milk or water) and is stiff enough to knead or roll **2** : something resembling dough esp. in consistency **3** : MONEY — **doughy** \ˈdō-ē\ *adj*

dough·boy \-ˌbȯi\ *n* : an American infantryman esp. in World War I

dough·nut *also* **do·nut** \-(ˌ)nət\ *n* : a small usu. ring-shaped cake fried in fat

dough·ty \ˈdau̇-tē\ *adj* **dough·ti·er; -est** : ABLE, VALIANT ⟨a ∼ warrior⟩

Doug·las fir \ˈdə-gləs-\ *n* : a tall evergreen timber tree of the western U.S.

dou·la \ˈdü-lə\ *n* : a woman who provides assistance to a mother before, during, and just after childbirth

do up *vb* **1** : to prepare (as by cleaning) for use **2** : to wrap up **3** : CLOTHE, DECORATE **4** : FASTEN

dour \ˈdau̇(-ə)r, ˈdur\ *adj* [ME, fr. L *durus* hard] **1** : STERN, HARSH **2** : OBSTINATE **3** : SULLEN — **dour·ly** *adv*

douse \ˈdau̇s, ˈdau̇z\ *vb* **doused; dous·ing** **1** : to plunge into water **2** : DRENCH **3** : EXTINGUISH ⟨∼ a match⟩

¹dove \ˈdəv\ *n* **1** : any of numerous pigeons; *esp* : a small wild pigeon **2** : an advocate of peace or of a peaceful policy — **dov·ish** \ˈdə-vish\ *adj*

²dove \ˈdōv\ *past of* DIVE

¹dove·tail \ˈdəv-ˌtāl\ *n* : something that resembles a dove's tail; *esp* : a flaring tenon and a mortise into which it fits tightly

²dovetail *vb* **1** : to join by means of dovetails **2** : to fit skillfully together to form a whole ⟨our plans ∼ nicely⟩

dow·a·ger \ˈdau̇-i-jər\ *n* **1** : a widow owning property or a title from her deceased husband **2** : a dignified elderly woman

dowdy \ˈdau̇-dē\ *adj* **dowd·i·er; -est** : lacking neatness and charm : SHABBY, UNTIDY; *also* : lacking smartness

dow·el \ˈdau̇(-ə)l\ *n* **1** : a pin used for fastening together two pieces of wood **2** : a round rod (as of wood) — **dowel** *vb*

¹dow·er \ˈdau̇(-ə)r\ *n* [ME *dowere*, fr. AF *dower, douaire*, fr. ML *dotarium*, fr. L *dot-, dos* gift, marriage portion] **1** : the part of a deceased husband's real estate which the law gives for life to his widow **2** : DOWRY

²dower *vb* : to supply with a dower or dowry : ENDOW

dow·itch·er \ˈdau̇-i-chər\ *n* : any of several long-billed wading birds related to the sandpipers

¹down \ˈdau̇n\ *adv* [ME *doun*, fr. OE *dūne*, short for *adūne*, of *dūne*, lit., from (the) hill] **1** : toward or in a lower physical position **2** : to a lying or sitting position **3** : toward or to the ground, floor, or bottom **4** : as a down payment ⟨paid $5 ∼⟩ **5** : on paper ⟨put ∼ what he says⟩ **6** : in a direction that is the opposite of up **7** : SOUTH **8** : to or in a lower or worse condition or status **9** : from a past time **10** : to or in a state of less activity **11** : into defeat ⟨voted the motion ∼⟩

²down *prep* : down in, on, along, or through : toward the bottom of ⟨fell ∼ a hole⟩ ⟨lives ∼ the road⟩

³down *vb* **1** : to go or cause to come down ⟨∼ed a warplane⟩ **2** : DEFEAT **3** : to cause (a football) to be out of play **4** : CONSUME **3** ⟨∼ed two beers⟩

⁴down *adj* **1** : occupying a low position; *esp* : lying on the ground **2** : directed or going downward **3** : being in a state of reduced or low activity **4** : DEPRESSED, DEJECTED **5** : SICK ⟨∼ with a cold⟩ **6** : FINISHED, DONE **7** : completely mastered ⟨got her lines ∼⟩ **8** : being on record ⟨you're ∼ for two tickets⟩

⁵**down** *n* **1** : a low or falling period (as in activity, emotional life, or fortunes) **2** : one of a series of attempts to advance a football **3** : a quark with a charge of -⅓ that is one of the constituents of the proton and neutron

⁶**down** *n* : a rolling usu. treeless upland with sparse soil — usu. used in pl.

⁷**down** *n* **1** : a covering of soft fluffy feathers; *also* : such feathers **2** : a downlike covering or material

down·beat \'daủn-ˌbēt\ *n* : the downward stroke of a conductor indicating the principally accented note of a measure of music

down·burst \-ˌbərst\ *n* : a powerful downdraft usu. associated with a thunderstorm that is a hazard for low-flying aircraft; *also* : MICROBURST

down·cast \-ˌkast\ *adj* **1** : DEJECTED **2** : directed down ⟨a ∼ glance⟩

down·draft \-ˌdraft\ *n* : a downward current of gas (as air)

down·er \'daủ-nər\ *n* **1** : a depressant drug; *esp* : BARBITURATE **2** : someone or something depressing

down·fall \'daủn-ˌfȯl\ *n* **1** : a sudden fall (as from high rank) **2** : something that causes a downfall — **down·fall·en** \-ˌfȯ-lən\ *adj*

¹**down·grade** \'daủn-ˌgrād\ *n* **1** : a downward slope (as of a road) **2** : a decline toward a worse condition

²**downgrade** *vb* : to lower in quality, value, extent, or status

down·heart·ed \-'här-təd\ *adj* : DEJECTED

¹**down·hill** \'daủn-'hil\ *adv* : toward the bottom of a hill — **downhill** \-ˌhil\ *adj*

²**down·hill** \-ˌhil\ *n* : the sport of skiing downhill usu. in a race against time

¹**down·load** \'daủn-ˌlōd\ *n* : an act or instance of downloading something; *also* : the item downloaded

²**download** *vb* : to transfer (data) from a computer to another device — **down·load·able** \-ˌlō-də-bəl\ *adj*

down payment *n* : a part of the full price paid at the time of purchase or delivery with the balance to be paid later

down·play \'daủn-ˌplā\ *vb* : DE-EMPHA-SIZE ⟨∼ed the allegations⟩

down·pour \'daủn-ˌpȯr\ *n* : a heavy rain

down·range \-'rānj\ *adv* : away from a launching site

¹**down·right** \-ˌrīt\ *adv* : THOROUGHLY

²**downright** *adj* **1** : ABSOLUTE, UTTER ⟨a ∼ lie⟩ **2** : PLAIN, BLUNT ⟨a ∼ man⟩

down·shift \-ˌshift\ *vb* : to shift an automotive vehicle into a lower gear

down·size \-ˌsīz\ *vb* : to reduce or undergo reduction in size or numbers

down·spout \-ˌspaủt\ *n* : a vertical pipe used to drain rainwater from a roof

Down syndrome \'daủn-\ *or* **Down's syndrome** \'daủnz-\ *n* : a birth defect characterized by mental retardation, slanting eyes, a broad short skull, broad hands with short fingers, and the presence of an extra chromosome

down·stage \'daủn-'stāj\ *adv or adj* : toward or at the front of a theatrical stage — **down-stage** \-ˌstāj\ *n*

down·stairs \-'sterz\ *adv* : on or to a lower floor and esp. the main or ground floor — **down·stairs** \-ˌsterz\ *adj or n*

down·stream \-'strēm\ *adv or adj* : in the direction of flow of a stream

down·stroke \-ˌstrōk\ *n* : a downward stroke

down·swing \-ˌswiŋ\ *n* **1** : a swing downward **2** : DOWNTURN

down–to–earth *adj* : PRACTICAL, REALISTIC

down·town \'daủn-ˌtaủn\ *n* : the main business district of a town or city — **downtown** \'daủn-'taủn\ *adj or adv*

down·trod·den \'daủn-'trä-d⁰n\ *adj* : suffering oppression

down·turn \-ˌtərn\ *n* : a downward turn esp. in economic activity

¹**down·ward** \'daủn-wərd\ *or* **down·wards** \-wərdz\ *adv* **1** : from a higher to a lower place or condition **2** : from an earlier time **3** : from an ancestor or predecessor

²**downward** *adj* : directed toward or situated in a lower place or condition

down·wind \'daủn-'wind\ *adv or adj* : in the direction that the wind is blowing

downy \'daủ-nē\ *adj* **down·i·er; -est** : resembling or covered with down

downy mildew *n* : any of various parasitic fungi producing whitish masses esp. on the underside of plant leaves; *also* : a plant disease caused by downy mildew

downy woodpecker *n* : a small black-and-white woodpecker of No. America

dow·ry \'daủ-(ə-)rē\ *n, pl* **dowries** [ME *dowarie,* fr. AF, alter. of *dower, douaire* dower] : the property that a woman brings to her husband in marriage

dowse \'daủz\ *vb* **dowsed; dows·ing** : to use a divining rod esp. to find water — **dows·er** *n*

dox·ol·o·gy \däk-'sä-lə-jē\ *n, pl* **-gies** : a usu. short hymn of praise to God

doy·en \'dȯi-ən, 'dwä-ˌyä⁰\ *n* : the senior or most experienced person in a group

doy·enne \dȯi-'yen, dwä-'yen\ *n* : a woman who is a doyen

doy·ley *chiefly Brit var of* DOILY

doz *abbr* dozen

doze \'dōz\ *vb* **dozed; doz·ing** : to sleep lightly — **doze** *n*

doz·en \'də-z⁰n\ *n, pl* **dozens** *or* **dozen** [ME *dozeine,* fr. AF *duzeine, dozeine,* fr. *duze* twelve, fr. L *duodecim,* fr. *duo* two + *decem* ten] : a group of twelve — **doz·enth** \-z⁰nth\ *adj*

¹**DP** \ˌdē-'pē\ *n, pl* **DP's** *or* **DPs** **1** : a displaced person **2** : DOUBLE PLAY

²**DP** *abbr* data processing

dpt *abbr* department

DPT *abbr* diphtheria-pertussis-tetanus (vaccines)

dr *abbr* **1** debtor **2** dram **3** drive **4** drum

Dr *abbr* doctor

DR *abbr* **1** dead reckoning **2** dining room

drab \'drab\ *adj* **drab·ber; drab·best** **1** : being of a light olive-brown color **2** : DULL, MONOTONOUS, CHEERLESS — **drab·ly** *adv* — **drab·ness** *n*

drach·ma \'drak-mə\ *n, pl* **drach·mas** *or* **drach·mai** \-ˌmī\ *or* **drach·mae** \-ˌ(ˌ)mē\ : the former basic monetary unit of Greece

dra·co·ni·an \drā-'kō-nē-ən, drə-\ *adj, often cap* : CRUEL; *also* : SEVERE

¹draft \'draft, 'dräft\ *n* **1** : the act of drawing or hauling **2** : the act or an instance of drinking or inhaling; *also* : the portion drunk or inhaled in one such act **3** : DOSE, POTION **4** : DELINEATION, PLAN, DESIGN; *also* : a preliminary sketch, outline, or version ⟨a rough ∼ of a speech⟩ **5** : the act of drawing (as from a cask); *also* : a portion of liquid so drawn **6** : the depth of water a ship draws esp. when loaded **7** : a system for or act of selecting persons (as for sports teams or compulsory military service); *also* : the persons so selected **8** : an order for the payment of money drawn by one person or bank on another **9** : a heavy demand : STRAIN **10** : a current of air; *also* : a device to regulate air supply (as in a stove) — **on draft** : ready to be drawn from a receptacle ⟨beer *on draft*⟩

²draft *adj* **1** : used or adapted for drawing loads ⟨∼ horses⟩ **2** : being or having been on draft ⟨∼ beer⟩

³draft *vb* **1** : to select usu. on a compulsory basis; *esp* : to conscript for military service **2** : to draw the preliminary sketch, version, or plan of **3** : COMPOSE, PREPARE **4** : to draw off or away

draft·ee \draf-'tē, ˌdräf-\ *n* : a person who is drafted

drafts·man \'draft-smən, 'dräft-\ *n* : a person who draws plans (as for buildings or machinery) — **drafts·man·ly** \-lē\ *adj*

drafty \'draf-tē, 'dräf-\ *adj* **draft·i·er; -est** : exposed to or abounding in drafts of air ⟨a ∼ room⟩

¹drag \'drag\ *n* **1** : a device pulled along under water for detecting or gathering **2** : something (as a harrow or sledge) that is dragged along over a surface **3** : the act or an instance of dragging **4** : something that hinders progress; *also* : something boring ⟨thinks school is a ∼⟩ **5** : STREET ⟨the main ∼⟩ **6** : clothing typical of one sex worn by a member of the opposite sex

²drag *vb* **dragged; drag·ging 1** : HAUL **2** : to move or proceed with slowness or difficulty ⟨*dragged* himself out of bed⟩ ⟨the lecture *dragged on*⟩ **3** : to force into or out of some situation, condition, or course of action **4** : PROTRACT ⟨∼ a story out⟩ **5** : to hang or lag behind **6** : to explore, search, or fish with a drag **7** : to trail along on the ground **8** : DRAW, PUFF ⟨∼ on a cigarette⟩ **9** : to move (items on a computer screen) esp. by using a mouse — **drag·ger** *n* — **drag one's feet** *also* **drag one's heels** : to act slowly or with hesitation

drag·net \-ˌnet\ *n* **1** : NET, TRAWL **2** : a network of planned actions for pursuing and catching ⟨a police ∼⟩

drag·o·man \'dra-gə-mən\ *n, pl* **-mans** *or* **-men** \-mən\ : an interpreter employed esp. in the Near East

drag·on \'dra-gən\ *n* [ME, fr. AF *dragun*, fr. L *dracon-, draco* serpent, dragon, fr. Gk *drakōn* serpent] : a fabulous animal usu. represented as a huge winged scaly serpent with a crested head and large claws

drag·on·fly \-ˌflī\ *n* : any of a group of large harmless 4-winged insects that hold the wings horizontal and unfolded in repose

¹dra·goon \drə-'gün, dra-\ *n* [F *dragon* dragon, dragoon, fr. MF] **1** : a heavily armed mounted soldier **2** : CAVALRYMAN

²dragoon *vb* : to force or attempt to force into submission : COERCE

drag race *n* : an acceleration contest between vehicles — **drag racer** *n*

drag·ster \'drag-stər\ *n* : a usu. high=powered vehicle used in a drag race

drag strip *n* : a site for drag races

¹drain \'drān\ *vb* **1** : to draw off or flow off gradually or completely **2** : to exhaust physically or emotionally ⟨∼ed by the work⟩ **3** : to make or become gradually dry or empty ⟨∼ a swamp⟩ **4** : to carry away the surface water of : discharge surface or surplus water **5** : EMPTY, EXHAUST ⟨∼ed our savings⟩ — **drain·er** *n*

²drain *n* **1** : a means (as a channel or sewer) of draining **2** : the act of draining **3** : a gradual outflow; *also* : something causing an outflow ⟨a ∼ on our savings⟩

drain·age \'drā-nij\ *n* **1** : the act or process of draining; *also* : something that is drained off **2** : a means for draining : DRAIN, SEWER **3** : an area drained

drain·pipe \'drān-ˌpīp\ *n* : a pipe for drainage

drake \'drāk\ *n* : a male duck

¹dram \'dram\ *n* **1** — see WEIGHT table **2** : FLUID DRAM **3** : a small drink

²dram \'dräm\ *n* — see MONEY table

dra·ma \'drä-mə, 'dra-\ *n* [LL, fr. Gk, deed, drama, fr. *dran* to do, act] **1** : a literary composition designed for theatrical presentation; *also* : a production (as a film) with a serious tone or subject **2** : dramatic art, literature, or affairs **3** : a series of events involving conflicting forces — **dra·mat·ic** \drə-'ma-tik\ *adj* — **dra·mat·i·cal·ly** \-ti-k(ə-)lē\ *adv* — **dra·ma·tist** \'dra-mə-tist, 'drä-\ *n*

dram·a·ti·sa·tion, dra·ma·tise *Brit var of* DRAMATIZATION, DRAMATIZE

dra·ma·tize \'dra-mə-ˌtīz, 'drä-\ *vb* **-tized; -tiz·ing 1** : to adapt for or be suitable for theatrical presentation **2** : to present or represent in a dramatic manner — **dram·a·ti·za·tion** \ˌdra-mə-tə-'zā-shən, ˌdrä-\ *n*

dra·me·dy \'drä-mə-ˌdē, 'dra-\ *n* : a comedy having dramatic moments

drank *past and past part of* DRINK

¹drape \'drāp\ *vb* **draped; drap·ing 1** : to cover or adorn with or as if with folds of cloth ⟨kings *draped* in robes⟩ **2** : to cause to hang or stretch out loosely or carelessly **3** : to arrange or become arranged in flowing lines or folds

²**drape** n **1** : CURTAIN **2** : arrangement in or of folds **3** : the cut or hang of clothing

drap·er \'drā-pər\ n, chiefly Brit : a dealer in cloth and sometimes in clothing and dry goods

drap·ery \'drā-pə-rē\ n, pl **-er·ies 1** Brit : DRY GOODS **2** : a decorative fabric esp. when hung loosely and in folds; also : hangings of heavy fabric used as a curtain

dras·tic \'dras-tik\ adj : HARSH, RIGOROUS, SEVERE ⟨~ punishment⟩ — **dras·ti·cal·ly** \-ti-k(ə-)lē\ adv

draught \'draft\, **draughty** \'dráf-tē\ chiefly Brit var of DRAFT, DRAFTY

draughts·man \'drafts-mən\ n, Brit : CHECKERS

draughts·man chiefly Brit var of DRAFTS-MAN

Dra·vid·i·an \drə-'vi-dē-ən\ n : a language family of south Asia that includes the major literary languages of southern India

¹**draw** \'dró\ vb **drew** \'drü\; **drawn** \'drón\; **draw·ing 1** : to cause to move toward a force exerted **2** : to cause to go in a certain direction ⟨drew him aside⟩ **3** : to move or go steadily or gradually ⟨night ~s near⟩ **4** : ATTRACT, ENTICE **5** : PROVOKE, ROUSE ⟨drew enemy fire⟩ **6** : INHALE ⟨~ a deep breath⟩ **7** : to bring or pull out ⟨drew a gun⟩ **8** : to cause to come out of a container or source ⟨~ blood⟩ ⟨~ water for a bath⟩ **9** : EVISCERATE **10** : to require (a specified depth) to float in **11** : ACCUMULATE, GAIN ⟨~ing interest⟩ **12** : to take money from a place of deposit : WITHDRAW **13** : to receive regularly ⟨~ a salary⟩ **14** : to take (cards) from a stack or the dealer **15** : to receive or take at random ⟨~ a winning number⟩ **16** : to bend (a bow) by pulling back the string **17** : WRINKLE, SHRINK **18** : to change shape by or as if by pulling or stretching ⟨a face drawn with sorrow⟩ **19** : to leave (a contest) undecided : TIE **20** : DELINEATE, SKETCH **21** : to write out in due form : DRAFT ⟨~ up a will⟩ **22** : FORMULATE ⟨~ comparisons⟩ **23** : INFER ⟨~ a conclusion⟩ **24** : to spread or elongate (metal) by hammering or by pulling through dies **25** : to produce or allow a draft or current of air ⟨the chimney ~s well⟩ **26** : to swell out in a wind ⟨all sails ~ing⟩ — **draw a blank** : to be unable to think of something — **draw the line** or **draw a line** : to fix an arbitrary boundary usu. between two things

²**draw** n **1** : the act, process, or result of drawing **2** : a lot or chance drawn at random **3** : a contest left undecided or deadlocked : TIE **4** : one that draws attention or patronage : ATTRACTION

draw·back \'dró-,bak\ n : DISADVANTAGE ⟨the ~s of rural living⟩

draw·bridge \-,brij\ n : a bridge made to be raised, lowered, or turned to permit or deny passage

draw·er \'drór, 'dró-ər\ n **1** : one that

draws **2** pl : an undergarment for the lower part of the body **3** : a sliding boxlike compartment (as in a table or desk)

draw·ing \'dró-iŋ\ n **1** : an act or instance of drawing; esp : an occasion when something is decided by drawing lots ⟨tonight's lottery ~⟩ **2** : the act or art of making a figure, plan, or sketch by means of lines : a representation made by drawing : SKETCH

drawing card n : DRAW 4

drawing room n : a formal reception room

drawl \'dról\ vb : to speak or utter slowly with vowels greatly prolonged — **drawl** n

draw on vb : APPROACH ⟨night draws on⟩

draw out vb **1** : PROLONG **2** : to cause to speak freely

draw·string \'dró-,striŋ\ n : a string, cord, or tape for use in closing a bag or controlling fullness in garments or curtains

draw up vb **1** : to prepare a draft or version of **2** : to pull oneself erect **3** : to bring or come to a stop

dray \'drā\ n : a strong low cart for carrying heavy loads

¹**dread** \'dred\ vb **1** : to fear greatly **2** : to feel extreme reluctance to meet or face

²**dread** n : great fear esp. of some harm to come

³**dread** adj **1** : causing great fear or anxiety ⟨a ~ disease⟩ **2** : inspiring awe

dread·ful \'dred-fəl\ adj **1** : inspiring dread or awe : FRIGHTENING **2** : extremely distasteful, unpleasant, or shocking ⟨a ~ accident⟩ — **dread·ful·ly** adv

dread·locks \'dred-,läks\ n pl : long braids of hair over the entire head

dread·nought \'dred-,nót\ n : BATTLESHIP

¹**dream** \'drēm\ n [ME dreem, fr. OE drēam noise, joy, and ON draumr dream] **1** : a series of thoughts, images, or emotions occurring during sleep **2** : a dreamlike vision : DAYDREAM, REVERIE **3** : something notable for its beauty, excellence, or enjoyable quality **4** : IDEAL — **dream·like** \-,līk\ adj : **dreamy** adj

²**dream** \'drēm\ vb **dreamed** \'dremt, 'drēmd\ or **dreamt** \'dremt\; **dream·ing 1** : to have a dream of **2** : to indulge in daydreams or fantasies : pass (time) in reverie or inaction **3** : IMAGINE — **dream·er** n

dream·boat \'drēm-,bōt\ n, slang : something highly desirable; esp : a very attractive person

dream·land \'drēm-,land\ n : an unreal delightful country that exists in imagination or in dreams

dream up vb : INVENT, CONCOCT

dream·world \-,wərld\ n : a world of illusion or fantasy

drear \'drir\ adj : DREARY

drea·ry \'drir-ē\ adj **drea·ri·er; -est** [ME drery, fr. OE drēorig sad, bloody, fr. drēor gore] **1** : DOLEFUL, SAD **2** : DISMAL, GLOOMY — **drea·ri·ly** \-ə-lē\ adv

¹**dredge** \'drej\ vb **dredged; dredg·ing** : to gather or search with or as if with a dredge — **dredg·er** n

²**dredge** n : a machine or barge for removing earth or silt

³**dredge** vb **dredged; dredg·ing** : to coat (food) by sprinkling (as with flour)

dregs \'dregz\ n pl **1** : SEDIMENT 1 **2** : the most undesirable part ⟨the ~ of humanity⟩

drench \'drench\ vb : to wet thoroughly

¹**dress** \'dres\ vb [ME, fr. AF *drescer* to direct, put right, fr. VL *directiare, fr. L *directus* direct] **1** : to make or set straight : ALIGN **2** : to prepare for use; *esp* : BUTCHER **3** : TRIM, EMBELLISH ⟨~ a store window⟩ **4** : to put clothes on : CLOTHE; *also* : to put on or wear formal or fancy clothes **5** : to apply dressings or medicine to ⟨~ a wound⟩ **6** : to arrange (the hair) by combing, brushing, or curling **7** : to apply fertilizer to ⟨~ a field⟩ **8** : SMOOTH, FINISH ⟨~ leather⟩

²**dress** n **1** : APPAREL, CLOTHING ⟨casual ~⟩ **2** : a garment usu. consisting of a one-piece bodice and skirt — **dress·mak·er** \-ˌmā-kər\ n — **dress·mak·ing** \-ˌmā-kiŋ\ n

³**dress** adj : suitable for a formal occasion; *also* : requiring formal dress

dres·sage \drə-'säzh\ n [F] : the execution by a trained horse of complex movements in response to barely perceptible signals from its rider

dress down vb : to scold severely

¹**dress·er** \'dre-sər\ n : a chest of drawers or bureau with a mirror

²**dresser** n : one that dresses

dress·ing \'dre-siŋ\ n **1** : the act or process of one who dresses **2** : a sauce for adding to a dish (as a salad) **3** : a seasoned mixture usu. used as stuffing **4** : material used to cover an injury (as a wound)

dressing gown n : a loose robe worn esp. while dressing or resting

dressy \'dre-sē\ adj **dress·i·er; -est 1** : showy in dress **2** : STYLISH, SMART

drew past of DRAW

¹**drib·ble** \'dri-bəl\ vb **drib·bled; drib·bling 1** : to fall or flow in drops : TRICKLE **2** : DROOL **3** : to propel by successive slight taps or bounces

²**dribble** n **1** : a small trickling stream or flow **2** : a drizzling shower **3** : the dribbling of a ball or puck

drib·let \'dri-blət\ n **1** : a trifling amount **2** : a drop of liquid

dri·er or **dry·er** \'drī-ər\ n **1** : a substance that speeds drying (as of paint or ink) **2** *usu* **dryer** : a device for drying

¹**drift** \'drift\ n **1** : the motion or course of something drifting; *also* : a gradual shift of position **2** : a mass of matter (as snow or sand) piled up esp. by wind **3** : earth, gravel, and rock deposited by a glacier **4** : a general underlying design or tendency : MEANING ⟨catch my ~⟩

²**drift** vb **1** : to float or be driven along by or as if by a current of water or air ⟨~ing logs⟩ **2** : to become piled up by wind or water ⟨~ing snow⟩

drift·er \'drif-tər\ n : a person who moves about aimlessly

drift net n : a fishing net often miles in

extent arranged to drift with the tide or current

drift·wood \'drift-ˌwu̇d\ n : wood drifted or floated by water

¹**drill** \'dril\ n **1** : a tool for boring holes **2** : the training of soldiers in marching and the handling of arms **3** : a regularly practiced exercise ⟨a shooting ~⟩

²**drill** vb **1** : to instruct and exercise by repetition **2** : to train in or practice military drill **3** : to bore with a drill ⟨~ a hole⟩ — **drill·er** n

³**drill** n **1** : a shallow furrow or trench in which seed is sown **2** : an agricultural implement for making furrows and dropping seed into them

⁴**drill** n : a firm cotton twilled fabric

drill·mas·ter \'dril-ˌmas-tər\ n : an instructor in military drill

drill press n : an upright drilling machine in which the drill is pressed to the work usu. by a hand lever

drily var of DRYLY

¹**drink** \'driŋk\ vb **drank** \'draŋk\; **drunk** \'drəŋk\ or **drank; drink·ing 1** : to swallow liquid : IMBIBE **2** : ABSORB **3** : to take in through the senses ⟨~ in the beautiful scenery⟩ **4** : to give or join in a toast **5** : to drink alcoholic beverages esp. to excess — **drink·able** adj — **drink·er** n

²**drink** n **1** : BEVERAGE; *also* : an alcoholic beverage **2** : a draft or portion of liquid **3** : excessive consumption of alcoholic beverages

¹**drip** \'drip\ vb **dripped; drip·ping 1** : to fall or let fall in drops **2** : to let fall drops of moisture or liquid ⟨a *dripping* faucet⟩ **3** : to overflow with or as if with moisture ⟨clothes *dripping* with sweat⟩ ⟨stories *dripping* with irony⟩

²**drip** n **1** : a falling in drops **2** : liquid that falls, overflows, or is extruded in drops **3** : the sound made by or as if by falling drops

¹**drive** \'drīv\ vb **drove** \'drōv\; **driv·en** \'dri-vən\; **driv·ing 1** : to urge, push, or force onward **2** : to carry through strongly ⟨~ a bargain⟩ **3** : to set or keep in motion or operation **4** : to direct the movement or course of **5** : to convey in a vehicle ⟨drove her to school⟩ **6** : to bring into a specified condition ⟨the noise ~s me crazy⟩ **7** : FORCE, COMPEL ⟨driven by hunger to steal⟩ **8** : to project, inject, or impress forcefully ⟨drove the lesson home⟩ **9** : to produce by opening a way ⟨~ a well⟩ **10** : to progress with strong momentum ⟨a driving rain⟩ **11** : to propel an object (as a golf ball) by a hard blow — **driv·er** n

²**drive** n **1** : a trip in a carriage or automobile **2** : a driving or collecting of animals ⟨a cattle ~⟩ **3** : the guiding of logs downstream to a mill **4** : the act of driving a ball; *also* : the flight of a ball **5** : DRIVEWAY **6** : a public road for driving (as in a park) **7** : the state of being hurried and under pressure **8** : an intensive campaign ⟨membership ~⟩ **9** : the apparatus by which motion is imparted to a machine **10** : an offensive or aggressive

move : a military attack **11** : NEED, LONGING ⟨the ~ to succeed⟩ **12** : dynamic quality **13** : a device for reading and writing on magnetic media (as magnetic tape or disks)

drive-in \'drī-ˌvin\ *adj* : accommodating patrons while they remain in their automobiles — **drive-in** *n*

¹**driv·el** \'dri-vəl\ *vb* **-eled** *or* **-elled; -el-ing** *or* **-el·ling 1** : DROOL, SLAVER **2** : to talk or utter stupidly, carelessly, or in an infantile way — **driv·el·er** *n*

²**drivel** *n* : NONSENSE

drive·shaft \'drīv-ˌshaft\ *n* : a shaft that transmits mechanical power

drive–through *also* **drive–thru** \'drīv-ˌthrü\ *adj* : designed for the service of patrons remaining in their automobiles — **drive–through** *also* **drive–thru** *n*

drive·way \-ˌwā\ *n* : a short private road leading from the street to a house, garage, or parking lot

¹**driz·zle** \'dri-zəl\ *n* : a fine misty rain

²**drizzle** *vb* **driz·zled; driz·zling** : to rain in very small drops

drogue \'drōg\ *n* : a small parachute for slowing down or stabilizing something (as a space capsule)

droid \'dróid\ *n* : ANDROID

droll \'drōl\ *adj* [F *drôle,* fr. *drôle* scamp, fr. MF *drolle,* fr. MD, imp] : having a humorous, whimsical, or odd quality ⟨a ~ expression⟩ — **droll·ery** \'drō-lə-rē\ *n* — **drol·ly** *adv*

drom·e·dary \'drä-mə-ˌder-ē\ *n, pl* **-dar-ies** [ME *dromedarie,* fr. MF *dromedaire,* fr. LL *dromedarius,* fr. L *dromad-, dromas,* fr. Gk, running] : CAMEL; *esp* : a domesticated one-humped camel of western Asia and northern Africa

¹**drone** \'drōn\ *n* **1** : a male honeybee **2** : one that lives on the labors of others : PARASITE **3** : an unmanned aircraft or ship guided by remote control **4** : one whose work is menial or monotonous

²**drone** *vb* **droned; dron·ing 1** : to sound with a low dull monotonous murmuring sound : speak monotonously

³**drone** *n* : a deep monotonous sound ⟨the ~ of engines⟩

drool \'drül\ *vb* **1** : to let liquid flow from the mouth **2** : to talk foolishly — **drool** *n*

droop \'drüp\ *vb* **1** : to hang or incline downward **2** : to sink gradually **3** : LANGUISH — **droop** *n* — **droopy** *adj*

¹**drop** \'dräp\ *n* **1** : the quantity of fluid that falls in one spherical mass **2** *pl* : a dose of medicine measured by drops **3** : a small quantity of drink **4** : the smallest practical unit of liquid measure **5** : something (as a pendant or a small round candy) that resembles a liquid drop **6** : FALL **7** : a decline in quantity or quality **8** : a descent by parachute **9** : the distance through which something drops **10** : a slot into which something is to be dropped **11** : something that drops or has dropped

²**drop** *vb* **dropped; drop·ping 1** : to fall or let fall in drops **2** : to let fall : LOWER ⟨~ a glove⟩ ⟨*dropped* his voice⟩ **3**

: SEND ⟨~ me a note⟩ **4** : to let go : DISMISS ⟨~ the subject⟩ **5** : MENTION ⟨~ a suggestion⟩ **6** : to knock down : cause to fall **7** : to go lower : become less ⟨prices *dropped*⟩ **8** : SPEND, LOSE ⟨~ $20⟩ ⟨*dropped* ten pounds⟩ **9** : to come or go unexpectedly or informally ⟨a friend *dropped* in⟩ **10** : to pass from one state into a less active one ⟨~ off to sleep⟩ **11** : to move downward or with a current **12** : QUIT ⟨*dropped* out of the race⟩

drop back : to move toward the rear —

drop behind : to fail to keep up

drop–down \'dräp-ˌdaún\ *adj* : PULL-DOWN

drop·kick \-'kik\ *n* : a kick made by dropping a ball to the ground and kicking it at the moment it starts to rebound — **drop–kick** *vb*

drop·let \'drä-plət\ *n* : a tiny drop

drop–off \'dräp-ˌóf\ *n* **1** : a steep or perpendicular descent **2** : a marked decline ⟨a ~ in attendance⟩ **3** : an act or instance of delivering or depositing something ⟨~ points along the route⟩

drop off *vb* : to fall asleep

drop out *vb* : to withdraw from participation or membership; *esp* : to leave school before graduation — **drop·out** \'dräp-ˌaút\ *n*

drop·per \'drä-pər\ *n* **1** : one that drops **2** : a short glass tube with a rubber bulb used to measure out liquids by drops

drop·pings *n pl* : MANURE, DUNG

drop·sy \'dräp-sē\ *n* [ME *dropesie,* short for *ydropesie,* fr. AF, fr. L *hydropisis,* fr. Gk *hydrōps,* fr. *hydōr* water] : EDEMA — **drop·si·cal** \-si-kəl\ *adj*

drop–top \'dräp-ˌtäp\ *n* : CONVERTIBLE

dross \'dräs\ *n* **1** : the scum that forms on the surface of a molten metal **2** : waste matter : REFUSE

drought \'draút\ *also* **drouth** \'draúth\ *n* : a long spell of dry weather

¹**drove** \'drōv\ *n* **1** : a group of animals driven or moving in a body **2** : a large number : CROWD — usu. used in pl. ⟨tourists arriving in ~s⟩

²**drove** *past of* DRIVE

drov·er \'drō-vər\ *n* : one who drives domestic animals usu. to market

drown \'draún\ *vb* **drowned** \'draúnd\; **drown·ing 1** : to suffocate by submersion esp. in water **2** : to become drowned **3** : to cover with water **4** : to cause to be muted (as a sound) by a loud noise **5** : OVERPOWER, OVERWHELM

drowse \'draúz\ *vb* **drowsed; drows·ing** : DOZE — **drowse** *n*

drowsy \'draú-zē\ *adj* **drows·i·er; -est 1** : ready to fall asleep **2** : making one sleepy ⟨~ music⟩ — **drows·i·ly** \-zə-lē\ *adv* — **drows·i·ness** \-zē-nəs\ *n*

drub \'drəb\ *vb* **drubbed; drub·bing 1** : to beat severely **2** : to berate critically **3** : to defeat decisively

drudge \'drəj\ *vb* **drudged; drudg·ing** : to do hard, menial, or monotonous work — **drudge** *n* — **drudg·ery** \'drə-jə-rē\ *n*

¹**drug** \'drəg\ *n* **1** : a substance used as a medicine or in making medicine **2** : a

substance (as heroin or marijuana) that can cause addiction, habituation, or a marked change in mental status

²**drug** *vb* **drugged; drug·ging** : to affect with or as if with drugs; *esp* : to stupefy with a narcotic

drug·gist \'drə-gist\ *n* : a dealer in drugs and medicines; *also* : PHARMACIST

drug·store \'drəg-ˌstòr\ *n* : a retail shop where medicines and miscellaneous articles are sold

dru·id \'drü-əd\ *n, often cap* : one of an ancient Celtic priesthood appearing in Irish, Welsh, and Christian legends as magicians and wizards

¹**drum** \'drəm\ *n* **1** : a percussion instrument usu. consisting of a hollow cylinder with a skin or plastic head stretched over one or both ends that is beaten with the hands or with a stick **2** : the sound of a drum; *also* : a similar sound **3** : a drum-shaped object (as a structure or container)

²**drum** *vb* **drummed; drum·ming 1** : to beat a drum **2** : to sound rhythmically : THROB, BEAT **3** : to summon or enlist by or as if by beating a drum ⟨*drummed* into service⟩ **4** : EXPEL — usu. used with *out* **5** : to drive or force by steady effort ⟨~ the facts into memory⟩ **6** : to strike or tap repeatedly so as to produce rhythmic sounds

drum·beat \'drəm-ˌbēt\ *n* : a stroke on a drum or its sound

drum major *n* : the leader of a marching band

drum ma·jor·ette \-ˌmā-jə-'ret\ *n* : a girl or woman who leads a marching band; *also* : a baton twirler who accompanies a marching band

drum·mer \'drə-mər\ *n* **1** : one that plays a drum **2** : a traveling salesman

drum·stick \'drəm-ˌstik\ *n* **1** : a stick for beating a drum **2** : the lower segment of a fowl's leg

drum up *vb* **1** : to bring about by persistent effort ⟨*drum up* business⟩ **2** : INVENT, ORIGINATE ⟨*drum up* a new method⟩

¹**drunk** *past part of* DRINK

²**drunk** \'drəŋk\ *adj* **1** : having the faculties impaired by alcohol ⟨~ drivers⟩ **2** : dominated by an intense feeling ⟨~ with power⟩ **3** : of, relating to, caused by, or characterized by intoxication

³**drunk** *n* **1** : a period of excessive drinking **2** : a drunken person

drunk·ard \'drəŋ-kərd\ *n* : one who is habitually drunk

drunk·en \'drəŋ-kən\ *adj* **1** : DRUNK **2** : given to habitual excessive use of alcohol **3** : of, relating to, or resulting from intoxication ⟨a ~ brawl⟩ **4** : unsteady or lurching as if from intoxication ⟨walked with a ~ shuffle⟩ — **drunk·en·ly** *adv* — **drunk·en·ness** *n*

drupe \'drüp\ *n* : a partly fleshy fruit (as a plum or cherry) having one seed enclosed in a hard inner shell

¹**dry** \'drī\ *adj* **dri·er** \'drī-ər\; **dri·est** \-əst\ **1** : free or freed from water or liquid ⟨~ fruits⟩; *also* : not being in or under water **2** : characterized by lack of water or moisture ⟨~ climate⟩ **3** : lacking freshness : STALE **4** : devoid of natural moisture; *also* : THIRSTY **5** : no longer liquid or sticky ⟨the ink is ~⟩ **6** : not giving milk ⟨a ~ cow⟩ **7** : marked by the absence of alcoholic beverages ⟨a ~ dormitory⟩ **8** : prohibiting the making or distributing of alcoholic beverages **9** : not sweet ⟨~ wine⟩ **10** : solid as opposed to liquid ⟨~ groceries⟩ **11** : containing or employing no liquid **12** : SEVERE; *also* : UNINTERESTING, WEARISOME **13** : not productive ⟨a writer's ~ spell⟩ **14** : marked by a matter-of-fact, ironic, or terse manner of expression ⟨~ humor⟩ — **dri·ly** *or* **dry·ly** *adv* — **dry·ness** *n*

²**dry** *vb* **dried; dry·ing** : to make or become dry

³**dry** *n, pl* **drys** : PROHIBITIONIST

dry·ad \'drī-əd, -ˌad\ *n* : WOOD NYMPH

dry cell *n* : a battery whose contents are not spillable

dry–clean \'drī-ˌklēn\ *vb* : to clean (fabrics) chiefly with solvents other than water — **dry cleaning** *n*

dry dock \'drī-ˌdäk\ *n* : a dock that can be kept dry during ship construction or repair

dryer *var of* DRIER

dry farm·ing *n* : farming without irrigation in areas of limited rainfall — **dry-farm** *vb* — **dry farm·er** *n*

dry goods \'drī-ˌgùdz\ *n pl* : cloth goods (as fabrics, ribbon, and ready-to-wear clothing)

dry ice *n* : solid carbon dioxide

dry measure *n* : a series of units of capacity for dry commodities — see METRIC SYSTEM table, WEIGHT table

dry rot *n* : decay of timber in which fungi consume the wood's cellulose

dry run *n* : REHEARSAL, TRIAL

dry·wall \'drī-ˌwòl\ *n* : a wallboard consisting of fiberboard, paper, or felt over a plaster core

Ds *symbol* darmstadtium

DSC *abbr* **1** Distinguished Service Cross **2** doctor of surgical chiropody

DSM *abbr* Distinguished Service Medal

DST *abbr* daylight saving time

DTP *abbr* diphtheria, tetanus, pertussis (vaccines)

d.t.'s \ˌdē-'tēz\ *n pl, often cap D&T* : DELIRIUM TREMENS

du·al \'dü-əl, 'dyü-\ *adj* **1** : TWOFOLD, DOUBLE **2** : having a double character or nature — **du·al·ism** \-ə-ˌli-zəm\ *n* — **du·al·i·ty** \dü-'a-lə-tē, dyü-\ *n*

du·ath·lon \dü-'ath-lən, -ˌlän\ *n* : a long-distance race involving running and bicycling — **du·ath·lete** *n*

¹**dub** \'dəb\ *vb* **dubbed; dub·bing 1** : to confer knighthood upon **2** : NAME, NICKNAME

²**dub** *n* : a clumsy person : DUFFER

³**dub** *vb* **dubbed; dub·bing** : to add (sound effects) to a motion picture or to a radio or television production

du·bi·ety \dü-'bī-ə-tē, dyü-\ *n, pl* **-eties 1** : UNCERTAINTY **2** : a matter of doubt

du·bi·ous \'dü-bē-əs, 'dyü-\ *adj* **1** : UN-

CERTAIN **2** : QUESTIONABLE ⟨a ~ choice⟩ **3** : feeling doubt : UNDECIDED — **du·bi·ous·ly** *adv* — **du·bi·ous·ness** *n*

dub·ni·um \'düb-nē-əm, 'dəb-\ *n* : a short-lived radioactive chemical element produced artificially

du·cal \'dü-kəl, 'dyü-\ *adj* : of or relating to a duke or dukedom

duc·at \'də-kət\ *n* : a gold coin formerly used in various European countries

duch·ess \'də-chəs\ *n* **1** : the wife or widow of a duke **2** : a woman holding the rank of duke in her own right

duchy \'də-chē\ *n, pl* **duch·ies** : the territory of a duke or duchess : DUKEDOM

¹**duck** \'dək\ *n, pl* **ducks** : any of various swimming birds related to but smaller than geese and swans

²**duck** *vb* **1** : to thrust or plunge under water **2** : to lower the head or body suddenly : BOW; *also* : DODGE **3** : to evade a duty, question, or responsibility ⟨~ the issue⟩

³**duck** *n* **1** : a durable closely woven usu. cotton fabric **2** *pl* : light clothes made of duck

duck·bill \'dək-ˌbil\ *n* : PLATYPUS

duck·ling \-liŋ\ *n* : a young duck

duck·pin \-ˌpin\ *n* **1** : a small bowling pin shorter and wider in the middle than a tenpin **2** *pl but sing in constr* : a bowling game using duckpins

duck sauce *n* : a thick sweet sauce made with fruits and seasonings and used in Chinese cuisine

duct \'dəkt\ *n* **1** : a tube or canal for conveying a bodily fluid **2** : a pipe or tube through which a fluid (as air) flows — **duct·less** *adj*

duc·tile \'dək-tᵊl\ *adj* : capable of being drawn out into wire or thread **2** : easily led : DOCILE — **duc·til·i·ty** \ˌdək-'ti-lə-tē\ *n*

ductless gland *n* : an endocrine gland

duct tape *n* : a cloth adhesive tape orig. designed for sealing certain ducts and joints — **duct–tape** *vb*

dud \'dəd\ *n* **1** *pl* : CLOTHING **2** : one that fails completely; *also* : a bomb or missile that fails to explode

dude \'düd, 'dyüd\ *n* **1** : DANDY 1 **2** : a city dweller; *esp* : an Easterner in the West **3** : FELLOW, GUY — sometimes used as an informal form of address

dude ranch *n* : a vacation resort offering activities (as horseback riding) typical of western ranches

dud·geon \'də-jən\ *n* : a fit or state of indignation ⟨in high ~⟩

¹**due** \'dü, 'dyü\ *adj* [ME, fr. AF *deu*, pp. of *dever* to owe, fr. L *debēre*] **1** : owed or owing as a debt **2** : owed or owing as a right ⟨is ~ a fair trial⟩ **3** : APPROPRIATE, FITTING ⟨with all ~ respect⟩ **4** : SUFFICIENT, ADEQUATE **5** : REGULAR, LAWFUL ⟨~ process of law⟩ **6** : ATTRIBUTABLE, ASCRIBABLE ⟨~ to negligence⟩ **7** : PAYABLE ⟨a bill ~ today⟩ **8** : SCHEDULED ⟨~ to arrive soon⟩

²**due** *n* **1** : something that rightfully belongs to one ⟨give everyone their ~⟩ **2** : DEBT **3** *pl* : FEES, CHARGES

³**due** *adv* : DIRECTLY, EXACTLY ⟨~ north⟩

du·el \'dü-əl, 'dyü-\ *n* : a combat between two persons; *esp* : one fought with weapons in front of witnesses — **duel** *vb* — **du·el·ist** \-ə-list\ *n*

du·en·de \dü-'en-dā\ *n* [Sp dial., charm, fr. Sp, ghost, goblin, fr. *duen de casa*, prob. fr. *dueño de casa* owner of a house] : the power to attract through personal magnetism and charm

du·en·na \dü-'e-nə, dyü-\ *n* **1** : an elderly woman in charge of the younger ladies in a Spanish or Portuguese family **2** : CHAPERONE

du·et \dü-'et, dyü-\ *n* : a musical composition for two performers

due to *prep* : BECAUSE OF

duf·fel bag \'də-fəl-\ *n* : a soft oblong bag for personal belongings

duf·fer \'də-fər\ *n* : an incompetent or clumsy person

dug *past and past part of* DIG

dug·out \'dəg-ˌaút\ *n* **1** : a boat made by hollowing out a log **2** : a shelter dug in the ground **3** : a low shelter facing a baseball diamond that contains the players' bench

DUI *n* : the act or crime of driving while under the influence of alcohol

duke \'dük, 'dyük\ *n* **1** : a sovereign ruler of a continental European duchy **2** : a nobleman of the highest rank; *esp* : a member of the highest grade of the British peerage **3** *slang* : FIST 1 ⟨put up your ~s⟩ — **duke·dom** *n*

dul·cet \'dəl-sət\ *adj* **1** : pleasing to the ear **2** : AGREEABLE, SOOTHING

dul·ci·mer \'dəl-sə-mər\ *n* **1** : a stringed instrument of trapezoidal shape played with light hammers held in the hands **2** *or* **dul·ci·more** \-ˌmȯr\ : an American folk instrument with three or four strings that is held on the lap and played by plucking or strumming

¹**dull** \'dəl\ *adj* **1** : mentally slow : STUPID **2** : slow in perception or sensibility **3** : LISTLESS **4** : slow in action : SLUGGISH ⟨a ~ market⟩ **5** : lacking intensity ⟨a ~ pain⟩; *also* : not resonant or ringing **6** : BLUNT **7** : lacking brilliance or luster ⟨a ~ finish⟩ **8** : low in saturation and lightness ⟨~ color⟩ **9** : CLOUDY, OVERCAST ⟨~ weather⟩ **10** : TEDIOUS, UNINTERESTING ⟨a ~ lecture⟩ — **dull·ness** *also* **dul·ness** *n* — **dul·ly** *adv*

²**dull** *vb* : to make or become dull

dull·ard \'də-lərd\ *n* : a stupid person

du·ly \'dü-lē, 'dyü-\ *adv* : in a due manner or time

dumb \'dəm\ *adj* **1** *often offensive* : lacking the power of speech **2** : SILENT **3** : STUPID — **dumb·ly** *adv*

dumb·bell \'dəm-ˌbel\ *n* **1** : a bar with weights at the end used for exercise **2** : one who is stupid

dumb down *vb* : to lower the level of intelligence or intellectual content of

dumb·found *also* **dum·found** \ˌdəm-'faúnd\ *vb* : ASTONISH, AMAZE — **dumb·found·ing·ly** \-'faún-diŋ-lē\ *adv*

dumb·wait·er \'dəm-ˌwā-tər\ *n* : a small elevator for conveying food and dishes from one floor to another

dum·my \'də-mē\ *n, pl* **dummies** **1** : a person who cannot speak; *also* : a stupid person **2** : the exposed hand in bridge played by the declarer in addition to that player's own hand; *also* : a bridge player whose hand is a dummy **3** : an imitative substitute for something; *also* : MANNE-QUIN **4** : one seeming to act alone but really acting for another **5** : a mock-up of matter to be reproduced esp. by printing

¹dump \'dəmp\ *vb* : to let fall in a pile ⟨~ laundry on the floor⟩; *also* : to get rid of carelessly ⟨~ed her boyfriend⟩

²dump *n* **1** : a place for dumping something (as refuse) **2** : a reserve supply; *also* : a place where such supplies are kept ⟨an ammunition ~⟩ **3** : a messy or objectionable place

dump·ing \'dəm-piŋ\ *n* : the selling of goods in quantity at below market price

dump·ling \'dəm-pliŋ\ *n* **1** : a small mass of boiled or steamed dough **2** : a dessert of fruit baked in biscuit dough

dumps \'dəmps\ *n pl* : a gloomy state of mind : low spirits ⟨in the ~⟩

dump truck *n* : a truck for transporting and dumping bulk material

dumpy \'dəm-pē\ *adj* **dump·i·er; -est** **1** : short and thick in build **2** : SHABBY

¹dun \'dən\ *n* : a brownish dark gray

²dun *vb* **dunned; dun·ning** **1** : to make persistent demands for payment **2** : PLAGUE, PESTER — **dun** *n*

dunce \'dəns\ *n* [John *Duns* Scotus, whose once accepted writings were ridiculed in the 16th cent.] : a slow stupid person

dun·der·head \'dən-dər-ˌhed\ *n* : DUNCE, BLOCKHEAD

dune \'dün, 'dyün\ *n* : a hill or ridge of sand piled up by the wind

dune buggy *n* : a motor vehicle with oversize tires for use on sand

¹dung \'dəŋ\ *n* : MANURE

²dung *vb* : to dress (land) with dung

dun·ga·ree \ˌdəŋ-gə-'rē\ *n* **1** : a heavy coarse cotton twill; *esp* : blue denim **2** *pl* : clothes made of blue denim

dun·geon \'dən-jən\ *n* [ME *dongeoun* fortress, prison, fr. AF *donjun*, fr. VL **domnion-, *domnio* keep, mastery, fr. L *dominus* lord] : a dark prison commonly underground

dung·hill \'dəŋ-ˌhil\ *n* : a manure pile

dunk \'dəŋk\ *vb* **1** : to dip or submerge temporarily in liquid **2** : to submerge oneself in water **3** : to shoot a basketball into the basket from above the rim

duo \'dü-(ˌ)ō, 'dyü-\ *n, pl* **du·os** **1** : DUET **2** : PAIR **3**

duo·dec·i·mal \ˌdü-ə-'de-sə-məl, ˌdyü-\ *adj* : of, relating to, or being a system of numbers with a base of 12

du·o·de·num \ˌdü-ə-'dē-nəm, ˌdyü-, dù-'ä-də-nəm, dyù-\ *n, pl* **du·o·de·na** \-'dē-nə, -də-nə\ *or* **-denums** : the first part of the small intestine extending from the stom-

ach to the jejunum — **du·o·de·nal** \-'dē-n⁹l, -də-nəl\ *adj*

dup *abbr* **1** duplex **2** duplicate

¹dupe \'düp, 'dyüp\ *n* : one who is easily deceived or cheated : FOOL

²dupe *vb* **duped; dup·ing** : to make a dupe of : DECEIVE, FOOL

du·ple \'dü-pəl, 'dyü-\ *adj* : having two beats or a multiple of two beats to the measure ⟨~ time⟩

¹du·plex \'dü-ˌpleks, 'dyü-\ *adj* : DOUBLE

²duplex *n* : something duplex; *esp* : a 2-family house

¹du·pli·cate \'dü-pli-kət, 'dyü-\ *adj* **1** : consisting of or existing in two corresponding or identical parts or examples **2** : being the same as another

²du·pli·cate \'dü-pli-ˌkāt, 'dyü-\ *vb* **-cat·ed; -cat·ing** **1** : to make double or twofold **2** : to make a copy of — **du·pli·ca·tion** \ˌdü-pli-'kā-shən, ˌdyü-\ *n*

³du·pli·cate \-kət\ *n* : a thing that exactly resembles another in appearance, pattern, or content : COPY

du·pli·ca·tor \'dü-pli-ˌkā-tər, 'dyü-\ *n* : COPIER

du·plic·i·ty \dù-'pli-sə-tē, dyü-\ *n, pl* **-ties** : the disguising of true intentions by deceptive words or action — **du·plic·i·tous** \-təs\ *adj* — **du·plic·i·tous·ly** *adv*

du·ra·ble \'dúr-ə-bəl, 'dyúr-\ *adj* : able to exist for a long time without significant deterioration ⟨~ goods⟩ — **du·ra·bil·i·ty** \ˌdúr-ə-'bi-lə-tē, ˌdyúr-\ *n*

du·rance \'dúr-əns, 'dyúr-\ *n* : restraint by or as if by physical force ⟨held in ~ vile⟩

du·ra·tion \dù-'rā-shən, dyü-\ *n* : the time during which something exists or lasts

du·ress \dù-'res, dyü-\ *n* : compulsion by threat ⟨confession made under ~⟩

dur·ing \'dúr-iŋ, 'dyúr-\ *prep* **1** : THROUGHOUT ⟨swims every day ~ the summer⟩ **2** : at some point in ⟨broke in ~ the night⟩

dusk \'dəsk\ *n* **1** : the darker part of twilight esp. at night **2** : partial darkness

dusky \'dəs-kē\ *adj* **dusk·i·er; -est** **1** : somewhat dark in color **2** : SHADOWY — **dusk·i·ly** \-kə-lē\ *adv* — **dusk·i·ness** *n*

¹dust \'dəst\ *n* **1** : fine particles of matter **2** : the particles into which something disintegrates **3** : something worthless **4** : the surface of the ground — **dust·less** *adj* — **dusty** *adj*

²dust *vb* **1** : to make free of or remove dust ⟨~ the furniture⟩ **2** : to sprinkle with fine particles ⟨popcorn ~ed with salt⟩ **3** : to sprinkle in the form of dust **4** : to defeat badly

dust bowl *n* : a region suffering from long droughts and dust storms

dust devil *n* : a small whirlwind containing sand or dust

dust·er \'dəs-tər\ *n* **1** : one that removes dust **2** : a dress-length housecoat **3** : one that scatters fine particles; *esp* : a device for applying insecticides to crops

dust·pan \'dəst-ˌpan\ *n* : a flat-ended pan for sweepings

dust storm *n* : a violent wind carrying dust across a dry region

dutch \'dəch\ *adv, often cap* : with each person paying his or her own way ⟨go ~⟩

Dutch \'dəch\ *n* **1** Dutch *pl* : the people of the Netherlands **2** : the language of the Netherlands — **Dutch** *adj* — **Dutch·man** \-mən\ *n*

Dutch elm disease *n* : a fungus disease of elms characterized by yellowing of the foliage, defoliation, and death

dutch treat *n, often cap D* : an entertainment (as a meal) for which each person pays his or her own way — **dutch treat** *adv, often cap D*

du·te·ous \'dü-tē-əs, 'dyü-\ *adj* : DUTIFUL, OBEDIENT

du·ti·able \'dü-tē-ə-bəl, 'dyü-\ *adj* : subject to a duty ⟨~ imports⟩

du·ti·ful \'dü-ti-fəl, 'dyü-\ *adj* **1** : motivated by a sense of duty ⟨a ~ son⟩ **2** : coming from or showing a sense of duty ⟨~ affection⟩ — **du·ti·ful·ly** *adv* — **du·ti·ful·ness** *n*

du·ty \'dü-tē, 'dyü-\ *n, pl* duties **1** : conduct or action required by one's occupation or position **2** : assigned service or business; *esp* : active military service **3** : a moral or legal obligation **4** : TAX **5** : the service required (as of a machine) : USE ⟨a heavy-*duty* tire⟩

DV *abbr* **1** [L *Deo volente*] God willing **2** Douay Version

DVD \,dē-,vē-'dē\ *n* [*d*igital *v*ideo *d*isk] : a high-capacity optical disk format; *also* : an optical disk using such a format

DVM *abbr* doctor of veterinary medicine

DVR \,dē-,vē-'är\ *n* [*d*igital *v*ideo *r*ecorder] : a device that records and plays back television programs

¹dwarf \'dwörf\ *n, pl* dwarfs \'dwörfs\ *also* dwarves \'dwörvz\ : one that is much below normal size — **dwarf·ish** *adj* — **dwarf·ism** \'dwör-,fi-zəm\ *n*

²dwarf *vb* **1** : to restrict the growth or development of : STUNT **2** : to cause to appear smaller ⟨*dwarfed* by comparison⟩

dwarf planet *n* : a spherical celestial body that orbits the sun but is too small to disturb other objects from its orbit

dwell \'dwel\ *vb* dwelt \'dwelt\ *or* dwelled \'dweld, 'dwelt\; dwell·ing [ME, fr. OE *dwellan* to go astray, hinder] **1** : ABIDE, REMAIN **2** : RESIDE, EXIST **3** : to keep the attention directed **4** : to write or speak insistently — used with *on* or *upon* — **dwell·er** *n*

dwell·ing \'dwe-liŋ\ *n* : RESIDENCE

DWI \,dē-,dəb-əl-(,)yü-'ī\ *n* [*d*riving *w*hile *i*ntoxicated] : DUI

dwin·dle \'dwin-d²l\ *vb* dwin·dled; dwin·dling : to make or become steadily less : DIMINISH

dwt *abbr* pennyweight

Dy *symbol* dysprosium

dyb·buk \'di-bək\ *n, pl* dyb·bu·kim \,di-bù-'kēm\ *also* dybbuks : a wandering soul believed in Jewish folklore to enter and possess a person

¹dye \'dī\ *n* **1** : color produced by dyeing **2** : material used for coloring or staining

²dye *vb* dyed; dye·ing **1** : to impart a new color to esp. by impregnating with a dye **2** : to take up or impart color in dyeing — **dy·er** \'dī(-ə)r\ *n*

dye·stuff \'dī-,stəf\ *n* : DYE 2

dying *pres part of* DIE

dyke *chiefly Brit var of* DIKE

dy·nam·ic \dī-'na-mik\ *also* **dy·nam·i·cal** \-mi-kəl\ *adj* : of or relating to physical force producing motion : ENERGETIC, FORCEFUL

¹dy·na·mite \'dī-nə-,mīt\ *n* : an explosive made of nitroglycerin absorbed in a porous material; *also* : an explosive made without nitroglycerin

²dynamite *vb* -mit·ed; -mit·ing : to blow up with dynamite

³dynamite *adj* : TERRIFIC, WONDERFUL

dy·na·mo \'dī-nə-,mō\ *n, pl* -mos **1** : an electrical generator **2** : a forceful energetic individual

dy·na·mom·e·ter \,dī-nə-'mä-mə-tər\ *n* : an instrument for measuring mechanical power (as of an engine)

dy·nas·ty \'dī-nəs-tē, -,nas-\ *n, pl* -ties **1** : a succession of rulers of the same family **2** : a powerful group or family that maintains its position for a long time — **dy·nas·tic** \dī-'nas-tik\ *adj*

dys·en·tery \'di-s²n-,ter-ē\ *n, pl* -ter·ies : a disease marked by diarrhea with blood and mucus in the feces; *also* : DIARRHEA

dys·func·tion *also* **dis·func·tion** \dis-'fəŋk-shən\ *n* **1** : impaired or abnormal functioning ⟨liver ~⟩ **2** : abnormal or unhealthy behavior within a group ⟨family ~⟩ — **dys·func·tion·al** \-shə-nəl\ *adj*

dys·lex·ia \dis-'lek-sē-ə\ *n* : a learning disability marked by difficulty in reading, writing, and spelling — **dys·lex·ic** \-sik\ *adj or n*

dys·pep·sia \dis-'pep-shə, -sē-ə\ *n* : INDIGESTION — **dys·pep·tic** \-'pep-tik\ *adj or n*

dys·pla·sia \dis-'plā-zh(ē-)ə\ *n* : abnormal growth or development

dys·pro·si·um \dis-'prō-zē-əm\ *n* : a metallic chemical element that forms highly magnetic compounds

dys·tro·phy \'dis-trə-fē\ *n, pl* -phies : a disorder involving atrophy of muscular tissue; *esp* : MUSCULAR DYSTROPHY

dz *abbr* dozen

¹e \'ē\ *n, pl* e's *or* es \'ēz\ *often cap* 1 : the 5th letter of the English alphabet 2 : the base of the system of natural logarithms having the approximate value 2.71828 3 : a grade rating a student's work as poor or failing

²e *abbr, often cap* 1 east; eastern 2 error 3 excellent

e- *comb form* : electronic ⟨*e*-commerce⟩

ea *abbr* each

¹each \'ēch\ *adj* : being one of the class named ⟨∼ player⟩

²each *pron* : every individual one

³each *adv* : APIECE ⟨cost five cents ∼⟩

each other *pron* : each of two or more in reciprocal action or relation ⟨looked at *each other*⟩

ea·ger \'ē-gər\ *adj* : marked by urgent or enthusiastic desire or interest ⟨∼ to learn⟩ ♦ *Synonyms* AVID, ANXIOUS, ARDENT, KEEN — ea·ger·ly *adv* — ea·ger·ness *n*

¹ea·gle \'ē-gəl\ *n* 1 : a large bird of prey related to the hawks 2 : a score of two under par on a hole in golf

²eagle *vb* ea·gled; ea·gling : to score an eagle on a golf hole

ea·glet \'ē-glət\ *n* : a young eagle

-ean — see -AN

E and OE *abbr* errors and omissions excepted

¹ear \'ir\ *n* 1 : the organ of hearing; *also* : the outer part of this in a vertebrate 2 : something resembling a mammal's ear in shape, position, or function 3 : an ability to understand and appreciate something heard ⟨a good ∼ for music⟩ 4 : sympathetic attention

²ear *n* : the fruiting spike of a cereal (as wheat or corn)

ear·ache \-ˌāk\ *n* : an ache or pain in the ear

ear·drum \-ˌdrəm\ *n* : a thin membrane that receives and transmits sound waves in the ear

eared \'ird\ *adj* : having ears esp. of a specified kind or number ⟨a long-*eared* dog⟩

ear·ful \'ir-ˌfùl\ *n* : a verbal outpouring (as of news, gossip, or complaint)

earl \'ərl\ *n* [ME *erl*, fr. OE *eorl* warrior, nobleman] : a member of the British peerage ranking below a marquess and above a viscount — earl·dom \-dəm\ *n*

ear·lobe \'ir-ˌlōb\ *n* : the pendent part of the ear

¹ear·ly \'ər-lē\ *adv* ear·li·er; -est : at an early time (as in a period or series)

²early *adj* ear·li·er; -est 1 : of, relating to, or occurring near the beginning 2 : ANCIENT, PRIMITIVE ⟨∼ tools⟩ 3 : occurring before the usual time ⟨an ∼ breakfast⟩; *also* : occurring in the near future

¹ear·mark \'ir-ˌmärk\ *n* : an identification mark (as on the ear of an animal); *also* : a distinguishing mark ⟨∼s of poverty⟩

²earmark *vb* 1 : to mark with an earmark 2 : to designate for a specific purpose ⟨money ∼*ed* for education⟩

ear·muff \-ˌməf\ *n* : one of a pair of ear coverings worn to protect against cold

earn \'ərn\ *vb* 1 : to receive as a return for service 2 : DESERVE, MERIT ♦ *Synonyms* GAIN, SECURE, GET, OBTAIN, ACQUIRE, WIN — earn·er *n*

earned run *n* : a run in baseball that scores without benefit of an error before the fielding team has had a chance to make the third putout of the inning

earned run average *n* : the average number of earned runs per game scored against a pitcher in baseball

¹ear·nest \'ər-nəst\ *n* : an intensely serious state of mind ⟨spoke in ∼⟩

²earnest *adj* 1 : seriously intent and sober ⟨an ∼ face⟩ ⟨an ∼ attempt⟩ 2 : GRAVE, IMPORTANT ♦ *Synonyms* SOLEMN, SEDATE, STAID — ear·nest·ly *adv* — ear·nest·ness *n*

³earnest *n* 1 : something of value given by a buyer to a seller to bind a bargain 2 : PLEDGE

earn·ings \'ər-niŋz\ *n pl* 1 : something (as wages) earned 2 : the balance of revenue after deduction of costs and expenses

ear·phone \'ir-ˌfōn\ *n* : a device that reproduces sound and is worn over or in the ear

ear·piece \-ˌpēs\ *n* : a part of an instrument which is placed against or in the ear; *esp* : EARPHONE

ear·plug \-ˌpləg\ *n* : a protective device for insertion into the opening of the ear

ear·ring \-ˌriŋ\ *n* : an ornament for the earlobe

ear·shot \-ˌshät\ *n* : range of hearing

ear·split·ting \-ˌspli-tiŋ\ *adj* : intolerably loud or shrill

earth \'ərth\ *n* 1 : SOIL, DIRT 2 : LAND, GROUND *often cap* : the planet on which we live that is 3d in order from the sun

earth·en \'ər-thən\ *adj* : made of earth or baked clay

earth·en·ware \-ˌwer\ *n* : slightly porous opaque pottery fired at low heat

earth·ling \'ərth-liŋ\ *n* : an inhabitant of the earth

earth·ly \'ərth-lē\ *adj* : having to do with the earth esp. as distinguished from heaven — earth·li·ness *n*

earth·quake \-ˌkwāk\ *n* : a shaking or trembling of a portion of the earth

earth science *n* : any of the sciences (as geology or meteorology) that deal with the earth or one of its parts

earth·shak·ing \'ərth-ˌshā-kiŋ\ *adj* : of great importance : MOMENTOUS

earth·ward \-wərd\ *also* earth·wards \-wərdz\ *adv* : toward the earth

earth·work \'ərth-ˌwərk\ *n* : an embankment or fortification of earth

earth·worm \-ˌwərm\ n : a long segmented worm found in damp soil

earthy \'ər-thē\ adj **earth·i·er; -est 1** : of, relating to, or consisting of earth; *also* : suggesting earth ⟨~ flavors⟩ **2** : PRACTICAL **4 3** : COARSE, GROSS ⟨~ humor⟩ — **earth·i·ness** n

ear·wax \'ir-ˌwaks\ n : the yellow waxy secretion from the ear

ear·wig \-ˌwig\ n : any of numerous insects with slender antennae and a pair of appendages resembling forceps at the end of the body

¹**ease** \'ēz\ n **1** : comfort of body or mind **2** : naturalness of manner **3** : freedom from difficulty or effort ♦ **Synonyms** RELAXATION, REST, REPOSE, LEISURE

²**ease** vb **eased; eas·ing 1** : to relieve from distress **2** : to lessen the pressure or tension of **3** : to make or become less difficult ⟨~ credit⟩

ea·sel \'ē-zəl\ n [Dutch *ezel*, lit., ass] : a frame for supporting something (as an artist's canvas)

¹**east** \'ēst\ adv : to or toward the east

²**east** adj **1** : situated toward or at the east ⟨an ~ window⟩ **2** : coming from the east ⟨an ~ wind⟩

³**east** n **1** : the general direction of sunrise **2** : the compass point directly opposite to west **3** cap : regions or countries east of a specified or implied point — **east·er·ly** \'ē-stər-lē\ adv or adj — **east·ward** adv or adj — **east·wards** adv

Eas·ter \'ē-stər\ n : a church feast observed on a Sunday in March or April in commemoration of Christ's resurrection

east·ern \'ē-stərn\ adj **1** often cap : of, relating to, or characteristic of a region designated East **2** cap : of, relating to, or being the Christian churches originating in the Church of the Eastern Roman Empire **3** : lying toward or coming from the east — **East·ern·er** n

easy \'ē-zē\ adj **eas·i·er; -est 1** : marked by ease ⟨an ~ life⟩; *esp* : not causing distress or difficulty ⟨~ tasks⟩ **2** : MILD, LENIENT ⟨be ~ on him⟩ **3** : GRADUAL ⟨an ~ slope⟩ **4** : LEISURELY ⟨an ~ pace⟩ **5** : free from pain, trouble, or worry **6** : COMFORTABLE ⟨an ~ chair⟩ **7** : showing ease : NATURAL ⟨an ~ manner⟩ — **eas·i·ly** \'ē-zə-lē\ adv — **eas·i·ness** \-zē-nəs\ n

easy·go·ing \ˌē-zē-'gō-iŋ\ adj : relaxed and casual in style or manner

eat \'ēt\ vb **ate** \'āt\; **eat·en** \'ēt-ᵊn\; **eat·ing 1** : to take in as food : eat food **2** : to use up : DEVOUR **3** : CORRODE — **eat·able** adj or n — **eat·er** n

eat·ery \'ē-tə-rē\ n, pl **-er·ies** : LUNCHEONETTE, RESTAURANT

eaves \'ēvz\ n pl : the overhanging lower edge of a roof

eaves·drop \'ēvz-ˌdräp\ vb : to listen secretly — **eaves·drop·per** n

¹**ebb** \'eb\ n **1** : the flowing back from shore of water brought in by the tide **2** : a point or state of decline

²**ebb** vb **1** : to recede from the flood **2** : DECLINE ⟨his fortunes ~ed⟩

EBCDIC \'eb-sə-ˌdik\ n [extended binary coded decimal interchange code] : a computer code for representing alphanumeric information

Ebo·la \ē-'bō-lə\ n : an often fatal hemorrhagic fever caused by a virus (**Ebola virus**) of African origin

¹**eb·o·ny** \'e-bə-nē\ n, pl **-nies** : a hard heavy blackish wood of various tropical trees related to the persimmon

²**ebony** adj **1** : made of or resembling ebony **2** : BLACK, DARK

e–book \'ē-ˌbúk\ n : a book in digital form for display on a computer screen or a handheld device

ebul·lient \i-'búl-yənt, -'bəl-\ adj **1** : BOILING, AGITATED **2** : EXUBERANT — **ebul·lience** \-yəns\ n

EC abbr European Community

ec·cen·tric \ik-'sen-trik\ adj **1** : deviating from a usual or accepted pattern **2** : deviating from a circular path ⟨~ orbits⟩ **3** : set with axis or support off center ⟨an ~ cam⟩; *also* : being off center ♦ **Synonyms** ERRATIC, QUEER, SINGULAR, CURIOUS, ODD — **eccentric** n — **ec·cen·tri·cal·ly** \-tri-k(ə-)lē\ adv — **ec·cen·tric·i·ty** \ˌek-ˌsen-'tri-sə-tē\ n

Eccles abbr Ecclesiastes

Ec·cle·si·as·tes \i-ˌklē-zē-'as-tēz\ n — see BIBLE table

ec·cle·si·as·tic \i-ˌklē-zē-'as-tik\ n : CLERGYMAN

ec·cle·si·as·ti·cal \-ti-kəl\ or **ec·cle·si·as·tic** \-tik\ adj : of or relating to a church esp. as an institution ⟨~ art⟩ — **ec·cle·si·as·ti·cal·ly** \-ti-k(ə-)lē\ adv

Ec·cle·si·as·ti·cus \i-ˌklē-zē-'as-ti-kəs\ n — see BIBLE table

Ecclus abbr Ecclesiasticus

ECG abbr electrocardiogram

ech·e·lon \'e-shə-ˌlän\ n [F *échelon*, lit., rung of a ladder] **1** : a steplike arrangement (as of troops or airplanes) **2** : a level (as of authority or responsibility) within an organization

ech·i·na·cea \ˌe-ki-'nā-sē-ə, -shə\ n : the dried root of three composite herbs that is used primarily in herbal remedies to boost the immune system; *also* : any of these herbs

echi·no·derm \i-'kī-nə-ˌdərm\ n : any of a phylum of marine animals (as starfishes and sea urchins) having similar body parts (as the arms of a starfish) arranged around a central axis and often having a calcium-containing outer skeleton

echo \'e-kō\ n, pl **ech·oes** also **ech·os** : repetition of a sound caused by a reflection of the sound waves; *also* : the reflection of a radar signal by an object — **echo** vb — **echo·ic** \e-'kō-ik\ adj

echo·lo·ca·tion \ˌe-kō-lō-'kā-shən\ n : a process for locating distant or invisible objects by sound waves reflected back to the sender (as a bat) from the objects

echt \'ekt\ adj [G] : TRUE, GENUINE ⟨an ~ New Yorker⟩

éclair \ā-'kler\ n [F, lit., lightning] : an oblong shell of light pastry with whipped cream or custard filling

éclat \ā-ˈklä\ *n* [F] **1** : a dazzling effect or success **2** : ACCLAIM

eclec·tic \e-ˈklek-tik\ *adj* : selecting or made up of what seems best of varied sources — **eclectic** *n* — **eclec·ti·cism** \-ˈklek-tə-ˌsi-zəm\ *n*

¹**eclipse** \i-ˈklips\ *n* **1** : the total or partial obscuring of one heavenly body by another; *also* : a passing into the shadow of a heavenly body **2** : a falling into obscurity or decline ⟨the author's fame has been in ~⟩

²**eclipse** *vb* **eclipsed; eclips·ing** : to cause an eclipse of; *also* : SURPASS

eclip·tic \i-ˈklip-tik\ *n* : the great circle of the celestial sphere that is the apparent path of the sun

ec·logue \ˈek-ˌlȯg, -ˌläg\ *n* : a pastoral poem

ECM *abbr* European Common Market

ecol *abbr* ecological; ecology

E. coli \ˌē-ˈkō-ˌlī\ *n*, *pl* **E. coli** : a rod-shaped bacterium that sometimes causes intestinal illness

ecol·o·gy \i-ˈkä-lə-jē, e-\ *n*, *pl* **-gies** [G *Ökologie*, fr. Gk *oikos* house + *logos* word] **1** : a branch of science concerned with the relationships between organisms and their environment **2** : the pattern of relations between one or more organisms and the environment — **eco·log·i·cal** \ˌē-kə-ˈlä-ji-kəl, ˌe-\ *also* **eco·log·ic** \-jik\ *adj* — **eco·log·i·cal·ly** \-ji-k(ə-)lē\ *adv* — **ecol·o·gist** \i-ˈkä-lə-jist, e-\ *n*

e–com·merce \ˈē-ˌkä-(ˌ)mərs\ *n* : commerce conducted via the Internet

econ *abbr* economics; economist; economy

eco·nom·ic \ˌe-kə-ˈnä-mik, ˌē-\ *adj* : of or relating to the production, distribution, and consumption of goods and services

eco·nom·i·cal \-ˈnä-mi-kəl\ *adj* **1** : THRIFTY **2** : operating with little waste or at a saving ♦ **Synonyms** FRUGAL, SPARING, PROVIDENT — **eco·nom·i·cal·ly** \-k(ə-)lē\ *adv*

eco·nom·ics \ˌe-kə-ˈnä-miks, ˌē-\ *n sing or pl* : a social science dealing with the production, distribution, and consumption of goods and services — **econ·o·mist** \i-ˈkä-nə-mist\ *n*

econ·o·mise *Brit var of* ECONOMIZE

econ·o·mize \i-ˈkä-nə-ˌmīz\ *vb* **-mized; -miz·ing** : to practice economy : be frugal — **econ·o·miz·er** *n*

¹**econ·o·my** \i-ˈkä-nə-mē\ *n*, *pl* **-mies** [MF *yconomie*, fr. ML *oeconomia*, fr. Gk *oikonomia*, fr. *oikonomos* household manager, fr. *oikos* house + *nemein* to manage] **1** : thrifty and efficient use of resources; *also* : an instance of this **2** : manner of arrangement or functioning : ORGANIZATION **3** : an economic system ⟨a money ~⟩

²**economy** *adj* : ECONOMICAL ⟨~ cars⟩

eco·sys·tem \ˈē-kō-ˌsis-təm, ˈe-\ *n* : the complex of an ecological community and its environment functioning as a unit in nature

eco·tour·ism \ˌē-kō-ˈtu̇r-ˌi-zəm, ˌe-\ *n* : the touring of natural habitats in a manner meant to minimize ecological impact — **eco·tour·ist** \-ˈtu̇r-ist\ *n*

ecru \ˈe-krü, ˈā-\ *n* [F *écru*, lit., unbleached] : BEIGE — **ecru** *adj*

ec·sta·sy \ˈek-stə-sē\ *n*, *pl* **-sies** **1** : extreme and usu. rapturous emotional excitement **2** *often cap* : an illicit drug with hallucinogenic properties that is chemically related to amphetamine — **ec·stat·ic** \ek-ˈsta-tik, ik-\ *adj* — **ec·stat·i·cal·ly** \-ti-k(ə-)lē\ *adv*

Ecua *abbr* Ecuador

ec·u·men·i·cal \ˌe-kyu̇-ˈme-ni-kəl\ *adj* **1** : general in extent or influence **2** : promoting or tending toward worldwide Christian unity — **ec·u·men·i·cal·ly** \-k(ə-)lē\ *adv*

ec·ze·ma \ig-ˈzē-mə, ˈeg-zə-mə, ˈek-sə-\ *n* : an itching skin inflammation with oozing and then crusted lesions — **ec·zem·a·tous** \ig-ˈze-mə-təs\ *adj*

ed *abbr* **1** edited; edition; editor **2** education

¹**-ed** *vb suffix or adj suffix* *after a vowel or* b, g, j, l, m, n, ŋ, r, th, v, z, zh; əd, id *after* d, t; t *after other sounds* **1** — used to form the past participle of regular weak verbs ⟨ended⟩ ⟨faded⟩ ⟨tried⟩ ⟨patted⟩ **2** : having : characterized by ⟨cultured⟩ ⟨2-legged⟩; *also* : having the characteristics of ⟨bigoted⟩

²**-ed** *vb suffix* — used to form the past tense of regular weak verbs ⟨judged⟩ ⟨denied⟩ ⟨dropped⟩

Edam \ˈē-dəm, -ˌdam\ *n* : a yellow Dutch pressed cheese made in balls

ed·a·ma·me \ˌe-də-ˈmä-mä\ *n* [Jp, fr. *eda* branch + *mame* beans] : immature green soybeans usu. in the pod

ed·dy \ˈe-dē\ *n*, *pl* **eddies** : WHIRLPOOL — **eddy** *vb*

edel·weiss \ˈā-dᵊl-ˌwīs, -ˌvīs\ *n* [G, fr. *edel* noble + *weiss* white] : a small perennial woolly composite herb that grows high in the Alps

ede·ma \i-ˈdē-mə\ *n* : abnormal accumulation of watery fluid in connective tissue or in a serous cavity — **edem·a·tous** \-ˈde-mə-təs\ *adj*

Eden \ˈē-dᵊn\ *n* : PARADISE 2

¹**edge** \ˈej\ *n* **1** : the cutting side of a blade **2** : SHARPNESS; *also* : FORCE, EFFECTIVENESS **3** : the line where something begins or ends; *also* : the area adjoining such an edge **4** : ADVANTAGE ⟨has an ~ on the competition⟩ — **edged** \ˈejd\ *adj*

²**edge** *vb* **edged; edg·ing** **1** : to give or form an edge **2** : to move or force gradually ⟨~ into a crowd⟩ **3** : to defeat by a small margin ⟨edged out her opponent⟩ — **edg·er** *n*

edge·wise \ˈej-ˌwīz\ *adv* : SIDEWAYS

edg·ing \ˈe-jiŋ\ *n* : something that forms an edge or border ⟨a lace ~⟩

edgy \ˈe-jē\ *adj* **edg·i·er; -est** **1** : SHARP ⟨an ~ tone⟩ **2** : TENSE, NERVOUS **3** : having a bold, provocative, or unconventional quality — **edg·i·ness** *n*

ed·i·ble \ˈe-də-bəl\ *adj* : fit or safe to be eaten — **ed·i·bil·i·ty** \ˌe-də-ˈbi-lə-tē\ *n* — **edible** *n*

edict \ˈē-ˌdikt\ *n* : ORDER, DECREE

ed·i·fi·ca·tion \ˌe-də-fə-ˈkā-shən\ *n* : instruction and improvement esp. in morality — **ed·i·fy** \ˈe-də-ˌfī\ *vb*

ed·i·fice \'e-də-fəs\ *n* : a usu. large building

ed·it \'e-dət\ *vb* 1 : to revise, assemble, or prepare for publication (as a motion picture) 2 : to direct the publication and policies of (as a newspaper) 3 : DELETE — **ed·i·tor** \'e-də-tər\ *n* — **ed·i·tor·ship** *n* — **ed·i·tress** \-trəs\ *n*

edi·tion \i-'di-shən\ *n* 1 : the form in which a text is published 2 : the total number of copies (as of a book) published at one time 3 : VERSION

¹**ed·i·to·ri·al** \₁e-də-'tȯr-ē-əl\ *adj* 1 : of or relating to an editor or editing 2 : being or resembling an editorial — **ed·i·to·ri·al·ly** *adv*

²**editorial** *n* : an article (as in a newspaper) giving the views of the editors or publishers; *also* : an expression of opinion resembling an editorial (a television ~)

ed·i·to·ri·al·ize \₁e-də-'tȯr-ē-ə-₁līz\ *vb* **-ized; -iz·ing** 1 : to express an opinion in an editorial 2 : to introduce opinions into factual reporting 3 : to express an opinion — **ed·i·to·ri·al·i·za·tion** \-₁tȯr-ē-ə-lə-'zā-shən\ *n* — **ed·i·to·ri·al·iz·er** *n*

EDP *abbr* electronic data processing

EDT *abbr* Eastern daylight (saving) time

educ *abbr* education

ed·u·ca·ble \'e-jə-kə-bəl\ *adj* : capable of being educated

ed·u·cate \'e-jə-₁kāt\ *vb* **-cat·ed; -cat·ing** [ME, to rear, fr. L *educatus*, pp. of *educare*, fr. *educere* to lead forth, draw out] 1 : to provide with schooling 2 : to develop mentally and morally; *also* : to provide with information ♦ **Synonyms** TRAIN, DISCIPLINE, SCHOOL, INSTRUCT, TEACH — **ed·u·ca·tor** \-₁kā-tər\ *n*

ed·u·ca·tion \₁e-jə-'kā-shən\ *n* 1 : the action or process of educating or being educated 2 : a field of study dealing with methods of teaching and learning — **ed·u·ca·tion·al** \-shə-nəl\ *adj* — **ed·u·ca·tion·al·ly** *adv*

educational television *n* 1 : television that provides educational programming (as for students) 2 : television (as public television) that receives support from contributions rather than from commercials

educe \i-'düs, -'dyüs\ *vb* **educed; educ·ing** 1 : ELICIT, EVOKE 2 : DEDUCE ♦ **Synonyms** EXTRACT, EVINCE, EXTORT

ed·u·tain·ment \₁e-jə-'tān-mənt\ *n* : entertainment that is designed to be educational

¹**-ee** \'ē, (₁)ē\ *n suffix* 1 : one that receives or benefits from (a specified action or thing) (grantee) (patentee) 2 : a person who does (a specified action) (escapee)

²**-ee** *n suffix* 1 : a particular esp. small kind of (bootee) 2 : one resembling or suggestive of (goatee)

EE *abbr* electrical engineer

EEC *abbr* European Economic Community

EEG *abbr* 1 electroencephalogram 2 electroencephalograph

eel \'ēl\ *n* : any of numerous snakelike bony fishes with a smooth slimy skin

EEO *abbr* equal employment opportunity

ee·rie *also* **ee·ry** \'ir-ē\ *adj* **ee·ri·er; -est** : WEIRD, UNCANNY — **ee·ri·ly** \'ir-ə-lē\ *adv*

eff *abbr* efficiency

ef·face \i-'fās, e-\ *vb* **ef·faced; ef·fac·ing** : to obliterate or obscure by or as if by rubbing out ♦ **Synonyms** ERASE, DELETE, ANNUL, CANCEL, EXPUNGE — **ef·face·able** *adj* — **ef·face·ment** *n*

¹**ef·fect** \i-'fekt\ *n* 1 : MEANING, INTENT 2 : RESULT 3 : APPEARANCE 4 : INFLUENCE 5 *pl* : GOODS, POSSESSIONS 6 : the quality or state of being operative : OPERATION ♦ **Synonyms** CONSEQUENCE, OUTCOME, UPSHOT, AFTERMATH, ISSUE

²**effect** *vb* : to cause to happen (~ repairs) (~ changes)

ef·fec·tive \i-'fek-tiv\ *adj* 1 : producing a decisive or desired effect 2 : IMPRESSIVE, STRIKING 3 : ready for service or action (~ manpower) 4 : being in effect (~ date) — **ef·fec·tive·ly** *adv* — **ef·fec·tive·ness** *n*

ef·fec·tu·al \i-'fek-chə-wəl\ *adj* : producing an intended effect : ADEQUATE — **ef·fec·tu·al·ly** *adv*

ef·fec·tu·ate \i-'fek-chə-₁wāt\ *vb* **-at·ed; -at·ing** : BRING ABOUT, EFFECT

ef·fem·i·nate \ə-'fe-mə-nət\ *adj* : marked by qualities more typical of women than men — **ef·fem·i·na·cy** \-nə-sē\ *n*

ef·fen·di \e-'fen-dē\ *n* [Turk *efendi* master, fr. ModGk *authentēs*] : a man of property, authority, or education in an eastern Mediterranean country

ef·fer·ent \'e-fə-rənt\ *adj* : bearing or conducting outward from a more central part (~ nerves)

ef·fer·vesce \₁e-fər-'ves\ *vb* **-vesced; -vesc·ing** 1 : to bubble and hiss as gas escapes 2 : to show liveliness or exhilaration — **ef·fer·ves·cence** \-'ve-s³ns\ *n* — **ef·fer·ves·cent** \-s³nt\ *adj* — **ef·fer·ves·cent·ly** *adv*

ef·fete \e-'fēt\ *adj* 1 : having lost character, vitality, or strength; *also* : DECADENT 2 : EFFEMINATE

ef·fi·ca·cious \₁e-fə-'kā-shəs\ *adj* : producing an intended effect (~ remedies) ♦ **Synonyms** EFFECTUAL, EFFECTIVE, EFFICIENT — **ef·fi·ca·cy** \'e-fi-kə-sē\ *n*

ef·fi·cient \i-'fi-shənt\ *adj* : productive of desired effects esp. without waste — **ef·fi·cien·cy** \-shən-sē\ *n* — **ef·fi·cient·ly** *adv*

ef·fi·gy \'e-fə-jē\ *n, pl* **-gies** : IMAGE; *esp* : a crude figure of a hated person

ef·flo·res·cence \₁e-flə-'re-s³ns\ *n* 1 : the period or state of flowering 2 : the action or process of developing 3 : fullness of development : FLOWERING

ef·flu·ence \'e-₁flü-əns\ *n* : something that flows out

ef·flu·ent \'e-₁flü-ənt\ *n* : something that flows out; *esp* : a fluid (as sewage) discharged as waste — **effluent** *adj*

ef·flu·vi·um \e-'flü-vē-əm\ *n, pl* **-via** \-ə\ *also* **-vi·ums** [L, outflow] 1 : a usu. unpleasant emanation 2 : a by-product usu. in the form of waste

ef·fort \'e-fərt\ *n* 1 : EXERTION, ENDEAVOR; *also* : a product of effort 2 : active or applied force — **ef·fort·less** *adj* — **ef·fort·less·ly** *adv*

ef·fron·tery \i-ˈfrən-tə-rē\ *n, pl* **-ter·ies** : shameless boldness : IMPUDENCE
♦ *Synonyms* TEMERITY, AUDACITY, BRASS, GALL, NERVE, CHUTZPAH

ef·ful·gence \i-ˈfu̇l-jəns, -ˈfəl-\ *n* : radiant splendor : BRILLIANCE ⟨the ~ of its golden age⟩ — **ef·ful·gent** \-jənt\ *adj*

ef·fu·sion \i-ˈfyü-zhən, e-\ *n* : a gushing forth; *also* : unrestrained utterance — **ef·fuse** \-ˈfyüz, e-\ *vb* — **ef·fu·sive** \i-ˈfyü-siv, e-\ *adj* — **ef·fu·sive·ly** *adv*

eft \ˈeft\ *n* : NEWT

EFT *or* **EFTS** *abbr* electronic funds transfer (system)

e.g. *abbr* [L *exempli gratia*] for example

Eg *abbr* Egypt; Egyptian

egal·i·tar·i·an·ism \i-ˌga-lə-ˈter-ē-ə-ˌni-zəm\ *n* : a belief in human equality esp. in social, political, and economic affairs — **egal·i·tar·i·an** *adj or n*

¹egg \ˈeg\ *vb* [ME, fr. ON *eggja*; akin to OE *ecg* edge] : to urge to action — usu. used with *on*

²egg *n* [ME *egge*, fr. ON *egg*; akin to OE *ǣg* egg, L *ovum*] **1** : a rounded usu. hard-shelled reproductive body esp. of birds and reptiles from which the young hatches; *also* : the egg of the common domestic chicken as an article of food **2** : a germ cell produced by a female

egg·beat·er \ˈeg-ˌbē-tər\ *n* : a hand-operated kitchen utensil for beating, stirring, or whipping

egg cell *n* : EGG 2

egg foo yong *or* **egg foo young** *or* **egg foo yung** \-ˈfü-ˈyəŋ\ : a fried egg patty

egg·head \-ˌhed\ *n* : INTELLECTUAL, HIGHBROW

egg·nog \-ˌnäg\ *n* : a drink consisting of eggs beaten with sugar, milk or cream, and often alcoholic liquor

egg·plant \-ˌplant\ *n* : the edible usu. large and dark purplish fruit of a plant related to the potato; *also* : the plant

egg roll *n* : a thin egg-dough casing filled with minced vegetables and often bits of meat and usu. deep-fried

egg·shell \ˈeg-ˌshel\ *n* : the hard exterior covering of an egg

egis *var of* AEGIS

eg·lan·tine \ˈe-glən-ˌtīn, -ˌtēn\ *n* : SWEETBRIAR

ego \ˈē-gō\ *n, pl* **egos** [L, I] **1** : the self as distinguished from others **2** : the one of the three divisions of the psyche in psychoanalytic theory that is the organized conscious mediator between the person and reality

ego·cen·tric \ˌē-gō-ˈsen-trik\ *adj* : concerned or overly concerned with the self; *esp* : SELF-CENTERED

ego·ism \ˈē-gō-ˌi-zəm\ *n* **1** : a doctrine holding self-interest to be the motive or the valid end of action **2** : excessive concern for oneself with or without exaggerated feelings of self-importance — **ego·ist** \-ist\ *n* — **ego·is·tic** \ˌē-gō-ˈis-tik\ *adj* — **ego·is·ti·cal·ly** *adv*

ego·tism \ˈē-gō-ˌti-zəm\ *n* **1** : the practice of talking about oneself too much **2** : an exaggerated sense of self-importance : CONCEIT — **ego·tist** \-tist\ *n* — **ego·tis·tic** \ˌē-gə-ˈtis-tik\ *or* **ego·tis·ti·cal** \-ti-kəl\ *adj* — **ego·tis·ti·cal·ly** *adv*

ego trip *n* : an act that enhances and satisfies one's ego

egre·gious \i-ˈgrē-jəs\ *adj* [L *egregius* outstanding, fr. *ex, e* out of + *greg-, grex* flock, herd] : notably bad : FLAGRANT ⟨~ errors⟩ — **egre·gious·ly** *adv* — **egre·gious·ness** *n*

egress \ˈē-ˌgres\ *n* : a way out : EXIT

egret \ˈē-grət, i-ˈgret\ *n* : any of various herons that bear long plumes during the breeding season

Egyp·tian \i-ˈjip-shən\ *n* **1** : a native or inhabitant of Egypt **2** : the language of the ancient Egyptians from earliest times to about the 3d century A.D. — **Egyptian** *adj*

ei·der \ˈī-dər\ *n* : any of several northern sea ducks that yield a soft down

ei·der·down \-ˌdau̇n\ *n* **1** : the down of the eider **2** : a comforter filled with eiderdown

ei·do·lon \ī-ˈdō-lən\ *n, pl* **-lons** *or* **-la** \-lə\ **1** : PHANTOM **2** : IDEAL

eight \ˈāt\ *n* **1** : one more than seven **2** : the 8th in a set or series **3** : something having eight units — **eight** *adj or pron* — **eighth** \ˈātth\ *adj or adv or n*

eight ball *n* : a black pool ball numbered 8 — **behind the eight ball** : in a highly disadvantageous position

eigh·teen \ˈāt-ˈtēn\ *n* : one more than 17 — **eighteen** *adj or pron* — **eigh·teenth** \-ˈtēnth\ *adj or n*

eighty \ˈā-tē\ *n, pl* **eight·ies** : eight times 10 — **eight·i·eth** \ˈā-tē-əth\ *adj or n* — **eighty** *adj or pron*

ein·stei·ni·um \īn-ˈstī-nē-əm\ *n* : an artificially produced radioactive element

ei·ren·ic *chiefly Brit var of* IRENIC

¹ei·ther \ˈē-thər, ˈī-\ *adj* **1** : being the one and the other of two : EACH ⟨trees on ~ side⟩ **2** : being the one or the other of two ⟨take ~ road⟩

²either *pron* : the one or the other

³either *conj* — used as a function word before the first of two or more words or word groups of which the last is preceded by *or* to indicate that they represent alternatives ⟨a statement is ~ true or false⟩

ejac·u·late \i-ˈja-kyə-ˌlāt\ *vb* **-lat·ed; -lat·ing 1** : to eject a fluid (as semen) **2** : to utter suddenly : EXCLAIM — **ejac·u·la·tion** \-ˌja-kyə-ˈlā-shən\ *n* — **ejac·u·la·to·ry** \-ˈja-kyə-lə-ˌtȯr-ē\ *adj*

eject \i-ˈjekt\ *vb* : to drive or throw out or off ♦ *Synonyms* EXPEL, OUST, EVICT, DISMISS — **ejec·tion** \-ˈjek-shən\ *n*

eke \ˈēk\ *vb* **eked; ek·ing** : to gain, supplement, or extend usu. with effort — usu. used with *out* ⟨~ out a living⟩

EKG *abbr* [G *Elektrokardiogramm*] electrocardiogram; electrocardiograph

el *abbr* elevation

¹elab·o·rate \i-ˈla-bə-rət, -ˈla-brət\ *adj* **1** : planned or carried out with great care **2** : being complex and usu. ornate — **elab·o·rate·ly** *adv* — **elab·o·rate·ness** *n*

²elab·o·rate \i-ˈla-bə-ˌrāt\ *vb* **-rat·ed; -rat-**

ing 1 : to build up from simpler ingredients **2 :** to work out in detail : develop fully — **elab·o·ra·tion** \-ˌla-bə-ˈrā-shən\ n

élan \ā-ˈläⁿ\ n [F] : ARDOR, SPIRIT

eland \ˈē-lənd, -ˌland\ n, pl **eland** also **elands** [Afrikaans] : either of two large African antelopes with spirally twisted horns in both sexes

elapse \i-ˈlaps\ vb **elapsed; elaps·ing** : to slip by : PASS

¹**elas·tic** \i-ˈlas-tik\ adj **1 :** SPRINGY **2 :** FLEXIBLE, PLIABLE ⟨an ~ bandage⟩ **3 :** ADAPTABLE ⟨an ~ plan⟩ ♦ **Synonyms** RESILIENT, SUPPLE, STRETCH — **elas·tic·i·ty** \-ˌlas-ˈti-sə-tē, ˌē-ˌlas-\ n

²**elastic** n **1 :** elastic material **2 :** a rubber band

elate \i-ˈlāt\ vb **elat·ed; elat·ing :** to fill with joy — **ela·tion** \-ˈlā-shən\ n

¹**el·bow** \ˈel-ˌbō\ n [ME elbowe, fr. OE elboga, fr. el- (akin to eln ell) + boga bow] **1 :** the joint of the arm; also : the outer curve of the bent arm **2 :** a bend or joint resembling an elbow in shape

elbow vb : to push aside with the elbow; also : to make one's way by elbowing

el·bow room \ˈel-ˌbō-ˌrüm, -ˌrüm\ n : enough space for work or operation

¹**el·der** \ˈel-dər\ n : ELDERBERRY **2**

²**elder** adj **1 :** OLDER **2 :** EARLIER, FORMER **3 :** of higher rank : SENIOR

³**elder** n **1 :** an older individual : SENIOR **2 :** one having authority by reason of age and experience **3 :** a church officer

el·der·ber·ry \ˈel-dər-ˌber-ē\ n **1 :** the edible black or red fruit of a shrub or tree related to the honeysuckle and bearing flat clusters of small white or pink flowers **2 :** a tree or shrub bearing elderberries

el·der·ly \ˈel-dər-lē\ adj **1 :** rather old; esp : past middle age **2 :** of, relating to, or characteristic of later life

el·dest \ˈel-dəst\ adj : of the greatest age

El Do·ra·do \ˌel-də-ˈrä-dō, -ˈrä-\ n [Sp, lit., the gilded one] : a place of vast riches, abundance, or opportunity

elec abbr electric; electrical; electricity

¹**elect** \i-ˈlekt\ adj **1 :** CHOSEN, SELECT **2 :** elected but not yet installed in office ⟨the president-elect⟩

²**elect** n, pl **elect 1 :** a selected person **2** pl : a select or exclusive group

³**elect** vb **1 :** to select by vote (as for office or membership) **2 :** CHOOSE, PICK

elec·tion \i-ˈlek-shən\ n **1 :** an act or process of electing **2 :** the fact of being elected

elec·tion·eer \i-ˌlek-shə-ˈnir\ vb : to work for the election of a candidate or party

¹**elec·tive** \i-ˈlek-tiv\ adj **1 :** chosen or filled by election **2 :** permitting a choice : OPTIONAL

²**elective** n : an elective course or subject of study

elec·tor \i-ˈlek-tər\ n **1 :** one qualified to vote in an election **2 :** one elected to an electoral college — **elec·tor·al** \i-ˈlek-tə-rəl\ adj

electoral college n : a body of electors who elect the president and vice president of the U.S.

elec·tor·ate \i-ˈlek-tə-rət\ n : a body of persons entitled to vote

elec·tric \i-ˈlek-trik\ adj [NL electricus produced from amber by friction, electric, fr. ML, of amber, fr. L electrum amber, fr. Gk ēlektron] **1** or **elec·tri·cal** \-tri-kəl\ : of, relating to, operated by, or produced by electricity **2 :** ELECTRIFYING, THRILLING ⟨an ~ performance⟩ — **elec·tri·cal·ly** adv

electrical storm n : THUNDERSTORM

electric chair n : a chair used to carry out the death penalty by electrocution

electric eye n : PHOTOELECTRIC CELL

elec·tri·cian \i-ˌlek-ˈtri-shən\ n : a person who installs, operates, or repairs electrical equipment

elec·tric·i·ty \i-ˌlek-ˈtri-sə-tē\ n, pl **-ties 1 :** a form of energy that occurs naturally (as in lightning) or is produced (as in a generator) and that is expressed in terms of the movement and interaction of electrons **2 :** electric current

elec·tri·fy \i-ˈlek-trə-ˌfī\ vb **-fied; -fy·ing 1 :** to charge with electricity **2 :** to equip for use of electric power **3 :** THRILL — **elec·tri·fi·ca·tion** \i-ˌlek-trə-fə-ˈkā-shən\ n

elec·tro·car·dio·gram \i-ˌlek-trō-ˈkär-dē-ə-ˌgram\ n : the tracing made by an electrocardiograph

elec·tro·car·dio·graph \-ˌgraf\ n : a device for recording the changes of electrical potential occurring during the heartbeat — **elec·tro·car·dio·graph·ic** \-ˌkär-dē-ə-ˈgra-fik\ adj — **elec·tro·car·di·og·ra·phy** \-dē-ˈä-grə-fē\ n

elec·tro·chem·is·try \-ˈke-mə-strē\ n : a branch of chemistry that deals with the relation of electricity to chemical changes — **elec·tro·chem·i·cal** \-ˈke-mi-kəl\ adj

elec·tro·cute \i-ˈlek-trə-ˌkyüt\ vb **-cut·ed; -cut·ing 1 :** to kill (a criminal) by electricity **2 :** to kill by electric shock — **elec·tro·cu·tion** \-ˌlek-trə-ˈkyü-shən\ n

elec·trode \i-ˈlek-ˌtrōd\ n : a conductor used to establish electrical contact with a nonmetallic part of a circuit

elec·tro·en·ceph·a·lo·gram \i-ˌlek-trō-in-ˈse-fə-lə-ˌgram\ n : the tracing made by an electroencephalograph

elec·tro·en·ceph·a·lo·graph \-ˌgraf\ n : an apparatus for detecting and recording brain waves — **elec·tro·en·ceph·a·lo·graph·ic** \-ˌse-fə-lə-ˈgra-fik\ adj — **elec·tro·en·ceph·a·log·ra·phy** \-ˈlä-grə-fē\ n

elec·trol·o·gist \i-ˌlek-ˈträ-lə-jist\ n : one that uses electrical means to remove hair, warts, moles, and birthmarks from the body

elec·trol·y·sis \i-ˌlek-ˈträ-lə-səs\ n **1 :** the production of chemical changes by passage of an electric current through an electrolyte **2 :** the destruction of hair roots with an electric current — **elec·tro·lyt·ic** \-trə-ˈli-tik\ adj

elec·tro·lyte \i-ˈlek-trə-ˌlīt\ n : a nonmetallic electric conductor in which current is carried by the movement of ions; *also* : a substance whose solution or molten form is such a conductor

elec·tro·mag·net \i-ˌlek-trō-'mag-nət\ *n* : a core of magnetic material (as iron) surrounded by a coil of wire through which an electric current is passed to magnetize the core

elec·tro·mag·net·ic \-mag-'ne-tik\ *adj* : of, relating to, or produced by electromagnetism — **elec·tro·mag·net·i·cal·ly** *adv*

electromagnetic radiation *n* : energy in the form of electromagnetic waves; *also* : a series of electromagnetic waves

electromagnetic wave *n* : a wave (as a radio wave, an X-ray, or a wave of visible light) that consists of associated electric and magnetic effects and that travels at the speed of light

elec·tro·mag·ne·tism \i-ˌlek-trō-'mag-nə-ˌti-zəm\ *n* **1** : magnetism developed by a current of electricity **2** : a natural force responsible for interactions between charged particles which result from their charge

elec·tro·mo·tive force \i-ˌlek-trə-'mō-tiv-\ *n* : the potential difference derived from an electrical source per unit quantity of electricity passing through the source

elec·tron \i-'lek-ˌträn\ *n* : a negatively charged elementary particle

elec·tron·ic \i-ˌlek-'trä-nik\ *adj* **1** : of or relating to electrons or electronics **2** : involving a computer — **elec·tron·i·cal·ly** \-ni-k(ə-)lē\ *adv*

electronic mail *n* : E-MAIL

elec·tron·ics \i-ˌlek-'trä-niks\ *n* **1** : the physics of electrons and electronic devices **2** : electronic components, devices, or equipment

electron microscope *n* : an instrument in which a beam of electrons is used to produce an enlarged image of a minute object

electron tube *n* : a device in which electrical conduction by electrons takes place within a sealed container and which is used for the controlled flow of electrons

electron volt *n* : a unit of energy equal to 1.60×10^{-19} joule

elec·tro·pho·re·sis \i-ˌlek-trə-fə-'rē-səs\ *n* : the movement of suspended particles through a medium (as paper or gel) by an electromotive force — **elec·tro·pho·ret·ic** \-'re-tik\ *adj*

elec·tro·plate \i-'lek-trə-ˌplāt\ *vb* : to coat (as with metal) by electrolysis

elec·tro·shock therapy \i-'lek-trō-ˌshäk-\ *n* : the treatment of mental disorder by applying electric current to the head and inducing convulsions

elec·tro·stat·ics \i-ˌlek-trə-'sta-tiks\ *n* : physics dealing with the interactions of stationary electric charges

el·ee·mos·y·nary \ˌe-li-'mäs-sə-ˌner-ē\ *adj* : CHARITABLE

el·e·gance \'e-li-gəns\ *n* **1** : refined gracefulness; *also* : tasteful richness (as of design) **2** : something marked by ele-

gance — **el·e·gant** \-gənt\ *adj* — **el·e·gant·ly** *adv*

ele·gi·ac \ˌe-lə-'jī-ək, -ˌak\ *adj* : of or relating to an elegy

el·e·gy \'e-lə-jē\ *n, pl* **-gies** : a song, poem, or speech expressing grief for one who is dead; *also* : a reflective poem usu. melancholy in tone

elem *abbr* elementary

el·e·ment \'e-lə-mənt\ *n* **1** *pl* : weather conditions; *esp* : severe weather ⟨boards exposed to the ∼s⟩ **2** : natural environment ⟨in her ∼⟩ **3** : a constituent part **4** *pl* : the simplest principles (as of an art or science) : RUDIMENTS **5** : a member of a mathematical set **6** : any of the fundamental substances that consist of atoms of only one kind ♦ **Synonyms** COMPONENT, INGREDIENT, CONSTITUENT — **el·e·men·tal** \ˌe-lə-'ment-ᵊl\ *adj*

☞ the ELEMENT table is on page 232

el·e·men·ta·ry \ˌe-lə-'men-trē, -tə-rē\ *adj* **1** : SIMPLE, RUDIMENTARY; *also* : of, relating to, or teaching the basic subjects of education

elementary particle *n* : a subatomic particle of matter and energy that does not appear to be made up of other smaller particles

elementary school *n* : a school usu. including the first six or the first eight grades

el·e·phant \'e-lə-fənt\ *n, pl* **elephants** *also* **elephant** : any of a family of huge thickset nearly hairless mammals that have the snout lengthened into a trunk and two long curving pointed ivory tusks

el·e·phan·ti·a·sis \ˌe-lə-fən-'tī-ə-səs\ *n, pl* **-a·ses** \-ˌsēz\ : enlargement and thickening of tissues in response esp. to infection by minute parasitic worms

el·e·phan·tine \ˌe-lə-'fan-ˌtēn, -ˌtīn, 'e-lə-fən-\ *adj* **1** : of great size or strength **2** : CLUMSY, PONDEROUS ⟨∼ verse⟩

elev *abbr* elevation

el·e·vate \'e-lə-ˌvāt\ *vb* **-vat·ed; -vat·ing** **1** : to lift up : RAISE **2** : EXALT, ENNOBLE ⟨great books that ∼ their readers⟩ **3** : ELATE

el·e·va·tion \ˌe-lə-'vā-shən\ *n* **1** : the height to which something is raised (as above sea level) **2** : a lifting up **3** : something (as a hill) that is elevated

el·e·va·tor \'e-lə-ˌvā-tər\ *n* **1** : a cage or platform for conveying people or things from one level to another **2** : a building for storing and discharging grain **3** : a movable surface on an airplane to produce motion up or down

elev·en \i-'le-vən\ *n* **1** : one more than 10 **2** : the 11th in a set or series **3** : something having 11 units; *esp* : a football team — **eleven** *adj or pron* — **elev·enth** \-vənth\ *adj or n*

elf \'elf\ *n, pl* **elves** \'elvz\ : a mischievous fairy — **elf·ish** \'el-fish\ *adj*

ELF *abbr* extremely low frequency

elf·in \'el-fən\ *adj* : of, relating to, or resembling an elf

elic·it \i-'li-sət\ *vb* : to draw out or forth ♦ **Synonyms** EVOKE, EDUCE, EXTRACT, EXTORT

CHEMICAL ELEMENTS

ELEMENT NAME	SYMBOL & ATOMIC NUMBER	ATOMIC WEIGHT[1]	ELEMENT NAME	SYMBOL & ATOMIC NUMBER	ATOMIC WEIGHT[1]
actinium	(Ac = 89)	227.0277	meitnerium	(Mt = 109)	(268)
aluminum	(Al = 13)	26.98154	mendelevium	(Md = 101)	(258)
americium	(Am = 95)	(243)	mercury	(Hg = 80)	200.59
antimony	(Sb = 51)	121.760	molybdenum	(Mo = 42)	95.94
argon	(Ar = 18)	39.948	neodymium	(Nd = 60)	144.24
arsenic	(As = 33)	74.92160	neon	(Ne = 10)	20.180
astatine	(At = 85)	(210)	neptunium	(Np = 93)	(237)
barium	(Ba = 56)	137.33	nickel	(Ni = 28)	58.6934
berkelium	(Bk = 97)	(247)	niobium	(Nb = 41)	92.90638
beryllium	(Be = 4)	9.012182	nitrogen	(N = 7)	14.0067
bismuth	(Bi = 83)	208.98038	nobelium	(No = 102)	(259)
bohrium	(Bh = 107)	(264)	osmium	(Os = 76)	190.23
boron	(B = 5)	10.81	oxygen	(O = 8)	15.9994
bromine	(Br = 35)	79.904	palladium	(Pd = 46)	106.42
cadmium	(Cd = 48)	112.41	phosphorus	(P = 15)	30.973761
calcium	(Ca = 20)	40.078	platinum	(Pt = 78)	195.078
californium	(Cf = 98)	(251)	plutonium	(Pu = 94)	(244)
carbon	(C = 6)	12.011	polonium	(Po = 84)	(209)
cerium	(Ce = 58)	140.116	potassium	(K = 19)	39.0983
cesium	(Cs = 55)	132.90545	praseodymium	(Pr = 59)	140.90765
chlorine	(Cl = 17)	35.453	promethium	(Pm = 61)	(145)
chromium	(Cr = 24)	51.996	protactinium	(Pa = 91)	(231)
cobalt	(Co = 27)	58.93320	radium	(Ra = 88)	(226)
copernicium	(Cn = 112)	(285)	radon	(Rn = 86)	(222)
copper	(Cu = 29)	63.546	rhenium	(Re = 75)	186.207
curium	(Cm = 96)	(247)	rhodium	(Rh = 45)	102.90550
darmstadtium	(Ds = 110)	(269)	roentgenium	(Rg = 111)	(280)
dubnium	(Db = 105)	(262)	rubidium	(Rb = 37)	85.4678
dysprosium	(Dy = 66)	162.50	ruthenium	(Ru = 44)	101.07
einsteinium	(Es = 99)	(252)	rutherfordium	(Rf = 104)	(261)
erbium	(Er = 68)	167.259	samarium	(Sm = 62)	150.36
europium	(Eu = 63)	151.964	scandium	(Sc = 21)	44.95591
fermium	(Fm = 100)	(257)	seaborgium	(Sg = 106)	(266)
fluorine	(F = 9)	18.998403	selenium	(Se = 34)	78.96
francium	(Fr = 87)	(223)	silicon	(Si = 14)	28.0855
gadolinium	(Gd = 64)	157.25	silver	(Ag = 47)	107.8682
gallium	(Ga = 31)	69.723	sodium	(Na = 11)	22.989770
germanium	(Ge = 32)	72.64	strontium	(Sr = 38)	87.62
gold	(Au = 79)	196.96655	sulfur	(S = 16)	32.07
hafnium	(Hf = 72)	178.49	tantalum	(Ta = 73)	180.9479
hassium	(Hs = 108)	(277)	technetium	(Tc = 43)	(98)
helium	(He = 2)	4.002602	tellurium	(Te = 52)	127.60
holmium	(Ho = 67)	164.93032	terbium	(Tb = 65)	158.92534
hydrogen	(H = 1)	1.0079	thallium	(Tl = 81)	204.3833
indium	(In = 49)	114.818	thorium	(Th = 90)	232.0381
iodine	(I = 53)	126.90447	thulium	(Tm = 69)	168.93421
iridium	(Ir = 77)	192.217	tin	(Sn = 50)	118.71
iron	(Fe = 26)	55.845	titanium	(Ti = 22)	47.867
krypton	(Kr = 36)	83.80	tungsten	(W = 74)	183.84
lanthanum	(La = 57)	138.9055	uranium	(U = 92)	(238)
lawrencium	(Lr = 103)	(262)	vanadium	(V = 23)	50.9415
lead	(Pb = 82)	207.2	xenon	(Xe = 54)	131.29
lithium	(Li = 3)	6.941	ytterbium	(Yb = 70)	173.04
lutetium	(Lu = 71)	174.967	yttrium	(Y = 39)	88.90585
magnesium	(Mg = 12)	24.305	zinc	(Zn = 30)	65.39
manganese	(Mn = 25)	54.93805	zirconium	(Zr = 40)	91.224

[1]Weights are based on the naturally occurring isotope compositions and scaled to $^{12}C = 12$. For elements lacking stable isotopes, the mass number of the most stable nuclide is shown in parentheses.

elide \i-'līd\ *vb* **elid·ed; elid·ing** : to suppress or alter by elision

el·i·gi·ble \'e-lə-jə-bəl\ *adj* : qualified to participate or to be chosen — **el·i·gi·bil·i·ty** \,e-lə-jə-'bi-lə-tē\ *n* — **eligible** *n*

elim·i·nate \i-'li-mə-,nāt\ *vb* **-nat·ed; -nat·ing** [L *eliminatus*, pp. of *eliminare*, fr. *limen* threshold] **1** : REMOVE, ERADICATE **2** : to pass (wastes) from the body **3** : to leave out : IGNORE — **elim·i·na·tion** \-,li-mə-'nā-shən\ *n*

eli·sion \i-'li-zhən\ *n* : the omission of a final or initial sound or of a word; *esp* : the omission of an unstressed vowel or syllable in a verse to achieve a uniform rhythm

elite \ā-'lēt, ē-\ *n* [F *élite*] **1** : the choice part; *also* : a superior group **2** : a typewriter type providing 12 characters to the inch — **elite** *adj*

elit·ism \-'lē-,ti-zəm\ *n* : leadership or rule by an elite; *also* : advocacy of such elitism — **elit·ist** \-tist\ *n or adj*

elix·ir \i-'lik-sər\ *n* [ME, fr. ML, fr. Ar *al-iksīr* the elixir, fr. *al* the + *iksīr* elixir] **1** : a substance held capable of prolonging life indefinitely; *also* : PANACEA **2** : a sweetened alcoholic medicinal solution

Eliz·a·be·than \i-,li-zə-'bē-thən\ *adj* : of, relating to, or characteristic of Elizabeth I of England or her times

elk \'elk\ *n, pl* **elk** *or* **elks** **1** : MOOSE — used for one of the Old World **2** : a large gregarious deer of No. America, Europe, Asia, and northwestern Africa with curved antlers having many branches

¹**ell** \'el\ *n* [ME *eln*, fr. OE; akin to L *ulna* forearm, Gk *ōlenē* elbow] : a former English cloth measure of 45 inches

²**ell** *n* : an extension at right angles to a building

el·lipse \i-'lips, e-\ *n* : a closed curve of oval shape

el·lip·sis \i-'lip-səs, e-\ *n, pl* **el·lip·ses** \-,sēz\ **1** : omission from an expression of a word clearly implied **2** : marks (as . . .) to show omission

el·lip·soid \i-'lip-,sȯid, e-\ *n* : a surface all plane sections of which are circles or ellipses — **el·lip·soi·dal** \-,lip-'sȯi-d⁰l\ *also* **ellipsoid** *adj*

el·lip·ti·cal \i-'lip-ti-kəl, e-\ *or* **el·lip·tic** \-tik\ *adj* **1** : of, relating to, or shaped like an ellipse **2** : of, relating to, or marked by ellipsis — **el·lip·ti·cal·ly** \-ti-k(ə-)lē\ *adv*

elm \'elm\ *n* : any of a genus of large trees that have toothed leaves and nearly circular one-seeded winged fruits and are often grown as shade trees; *also* : the wood of an elm

El Ni·ño \el-'nē-nyō\ *n* : a flow of unusually warm Pacific Ocean water moving toward and along the west coast of So. America

el·o·cu·tion \,e-lə-'kyü-shən\ *n* : the art of effective public speaking — **el·o·cu·tion·ist** \-shə-nist\ *n*

elon·gate \i-'lȯŋ-,gāt\ *vb* **-gat·ed; -gat·ing** : to make or grow longer ◆ *Synonyms* EXTEND, LENGTHEN, PROLONG,

PROTRACT — **elon·ga·tion** \(,)ē-,lȯŋ-'gā-shən\ *n*

elope \i-'lōp\ *vb* **eloped; elop·ing** : to run away esp. to be married — **elope·ment** *n* — **elop·er** *n*

el·o·quent \'e-lə-kwənt\ *adj* **1** : having or showing clear and forceful expression ⟨an ~ speaker⟩ **2** : clearly showing some feeling or meaning — **el·o·quence** \-kwəns\ *n* — **el·o·quent·ly** *adv*

¹**else** \'els\ *adv* **1** : in a different or additional manner or place or at a different or additional time ⟨where ~ can we meet⟩ **2** : OTHERWISE ⟨obey or ~ you'll be sorry⟩

²**else** *adj* : OTHER; *esp* : being in addition ⟨what ~ do you want⟩

else·where \-,hwer\ *adv* : in or to another place ⟨took my business ~⟩

elu·ci·date \i-'lü-sə-,dāt\ *vb* **-dat·ed; -dat·ing** : to make clear usu. by explanation ◆ *Synonyms* CLARIFY, EXPLAIN, ILLUMINATE — **elu·ci·da·tion** \-,lü-sə-'dā-shən\ *n*

elude \ē-'lüd\ *vb* **elud·ed; elud·ing** **1** : EVADE **2** : to escape the notice of

elu·sive \ē-'lü-siv\ *adj* : tending to elude : EVASIVE ⟨the solution remains ~⟩ — **elu·sive·ly** *adv* — **elu·sive·ness** *n*

el·ver \'el-vər\ *n* [alter. of *eelfare* migration of eels] : a young eel

elves *pl of* ELF

Ely·si·um \i-'li-zhē-əm, -zē-\ *n, pl* **-si·ums** *or* **-sia** \-zhē-ə, -zē-\ : PARADISE 2 — **Ely·sian** \-'li-zhən\ *adj*

em \'em\ *n* : a length approximately the width of the letter *M*

EM *abbr* **1** electromagnetic **2** electron microscope **3** enlisted man

ema·ci·ate \i-'mā-shē-,āt\ *vb* **-at·ed; -at·ing** : to become or cause to become very thin — **ema·ci·a·tion** \-,mā-shē-'ā-shən, -sē-\ *n*

e-mail \'ē-,māl\ *n* **1** : a system for transmitting messages between computers on a network **2** : a message or messages sent and received through an e-mail system

em·a·nate \'e-mə-,nāt\ *vb* **-nat·ed; -nat·ing** : to come out from a source ◆ *Synonyms* PROCEED, SPRING, RISE, ARISE, ORIGINATE — **em·a·na·tion** \,e-mə-'nā-shən\ *n*

eman·ci·pate \i-'man-sə-,pāt\ *vb* **-pat·ed; -pat·ing** : to set free ◆ *Synonyms* LIBERATE, RELEASE, DELIVER, DISCHARGE — **eman·ci·pa·tion** \-,man-sə-'pā-shən\ *n* — **eman·ci·pa·tor** \-'man-sə-,pā-tər\ *n*

emas·cu·late \i-'mas-kyü-,lāt\ *vb* **-lat·ed; -lat·ing** : to deprive of virility : CASTRATE; *also* : WEAKEN — **emas·cu·la·tion** \-,mas-kyü-'lā-shən\ *n*

em·balm \im-'bäm, -'bälm\ *vb* : to treat (a corpse) so as to protect from decay — **em·balm·er** *n*

em·bank·ment \im-'baŋk-mənt\ *n* : a raised structure (as of earth) to hold back water or carry a roadway

em·bar·go \im-'bär-gō\ *n, pl* **-goes** [Sp, fr. *embargar* to bar] : a prohibition on commerce — **embargo** *vb*

em·bark \im-'bärk\ *vb* **1** : to put or go on

board a ship or airplane **2** : to make a start — **em·bar·ka·tion** \,em-,bär-'kā-shən\ *n*

em·bar·rass \im-'ber-əs\ *vb* **1** : CONFUSE, DISCONCERT **2** : to involve in financial difficulties **3** : to cause to experience self-conscious distress **4** : HINDER, IMPEDE — **em·bar·rass·ing·ly** *adv* — **em·bar·rass·ment** *n*

em·bas·sy \'em-bə-sē\ *n, pl* **-sies 1** : a group of representatives headed by an ambassador **2** : the function, position, or mission of an ambassador **3** : the official residence and offices of an ambassador

em·bat·tle \im-'ba-t³l\ *vb* : to arrange in order for battle; *also* : FORTIFY

em·bat·tled *adj* **1** : engaged in battle, conflict, or controversy **2** : being a site of battle, conflict, or controversy **3** : characterized by conflict or controversy ⟨an ∼ presidency⟩

em·bed \im-'bed\ *vb* **em·bed·ded; em·bed·ding 1** : to enclose closely in a surrounding mass **2** : to make something an integral part of

em·bel·lish \im-'be-lish\ *vb* **1** : ADORN, DECORATE **2** : to add ornamental details to ◆ *Synonyms* BEAUTIFY, DECK, BEDECK, GARNISH, ORNAMENT, DRESS — **em·bel·lish·er** *n* — **em·bel·lish·ment** *n*

em·ber \'em-bər\ *n* **1** : a glowing or smoldering fragment from a fire **2** *pl* : the smoldering remains of a fire

em·bez·zle \im-'be-zəl\ *vb* **-zled; -zling** : to steal (as money) by falsifying records — **em·bez·zle·ment** *n* — **em·bez·zler** *n*

em·bit·ter \im-'bi-tər\ *vb* **1** : to arouse bitter feelings in **2** : to make bitter

em·bla·zon \im-'blā-z³n\ *vb* **1** : to adorn with heraldic devices **2** : to display conspicuously

em·blem \'em-bləm\ *n* : something (as an object or picture) suggesting another object or an idea : SYMBOL — **em·blem·at·ic** \,em-blə-'ma-tik\ *also* **em·blem·at·i·cal** \-ti-kəl\ *adj*

em·body \im-'bä-dē\ *vb* **em·bod·ied; em·body·ing 1** : INCARNATE **2** : to express in definite form **3** : to incorporate into a system or body **4** : PERSONIFY ◆ *Synonyms* COMBINE, INTEGRATE — **em·bodi·ment** \-di-mənt\ *n*

em·bold·en \im-'bōl-dən\ *vb* : to inspire with courage ⟨his speech ∼ed the soldiers⟩

em·bo·lism \'em-bə-,li-zəm\ *n* : the obstruction of a blood vessel by a foreign or abnormal particle

em·bon·point \äⁿ-bōⁿ-'pwäⁿ\ *n* [F] : plumpness of person : STOUTNESS

em·boss \im-'bäs, -'bòs\ *vb* : to ornament with raised work

em·bou·chure \'äm-bu̇-,shu̇r, ,äm-bu̇-'shu̇r\ *n* [F, ultim. fr. *bouche* mouth] : the position and use of the lips, tongue, and teeth in playing a wind instrument

em·bow·er \im-'bau̇-(ə)r\ *vb* : to shelter or enclose in a bower

¹**em·brace** \im-'brās\ *vb* **em·braced; em·brac·ing 1** : to clasp in the arms; *also* : CHERISH, LOVE **2** : ENCIRCLE **3** : TAKE UP, ADOPT ⟨*embraced* the cause⟩; *also*

: WELCOME ⟨*embraced* the opportunity⟩ **4** : INCLUDE **5** : to participate in an embrace ◆ *Synonyms* COMPREHEND, INVOLVE, ENCOMPASS, EMBODY

²**embrace** *n* : an encircling with the arms

em·bra·sure \im-'brā-zhər\ *n* **1** : an opening in a wall through which a cannon is fired **2** : a recess of a door or window

em·bro·ca·tion \,em-brə-'kā-shən\ *n* : LINIMENT

em·broi·der \im-'bròi-dər\ *vb* **1** : to ornament with or do needlework **2** : to elaborate with exaggerated detail

em·broi·dery \im-'bròi-də-rē\ *n, pl* **-der·ies 1** : the forming of decorative designs with needlework **2** : something embroidered

em·broil \im-'bròi(-ə)l\ *vb* **1** : to throw into confusion or disorder **2** : to involve in conflict or difficulties ⟨∼ed in a dispute⟩ — **em·broil·ment** *n*

em·bryo \'em-brē-,ō\ *n, pl* **embryos** : a living thing in its earliest stages of development — **em·bry·on·ic** \,em-brē-'ä-nik\ *adj*

em·bry·ol·o·gy \,em-brē-'ä-lə-jē\ *n* : a branch of biology dealing with embryos and their development — **em·bry·o·log·i·cal** \-brē-ə-'lä-ji-kəl\ *adj* — **em·bry·ol·o·gist** \-brē-'ä-lə-jist\ *n*

em·cee \'em-'sē\ *n* : MASTER OF CEREMONIES — **emcee** *vb*

emend \ē-'mend\ *vb* : to correct usu. by altering the text of ◆ *Synonyms* RECTIFY, REVISE, AMEND — **emen·da·tion** \,ē-,men-'dā-shən\ *n*

emer *abbr* emeritus

¹**em·er·ald** \'em-rəld, 'e-mə-\ *n* : a green beryl prized as a gem

²**emerald** *adj* : brightly or richly green

emerge \i-'mərj\ *vb* **emerged; emerging** : to rise, come forth, or come out into view — **emer·gence** \-'mər-jəns\ *n* — **emer·gent** \-jənt\ *adj*

emer·gen·cy \i-'mər-jən-sē\ *n, pl* **-cies** : an unforeseen event or condition requiring prompt action ◆ *Synonyms* EXIGENCY, CONTINGENCY, CRISIS, JUNCTURE

emergency room *n* : a hospital room for receiving and treating persons needing immediate medical care

emer·i·ta \i-'mer-ə-tə\ *adj* : EMERITUS — used of a woman

emer·i·tus \i-'mer-ə-təs\ *adj* [L] : retired from active duty ⟨professor ∼⟩

em·ery \'e-mə-rē\ *n, pl* **em·er·ies** : a dark granular mineral consisting primarily of corundum and used as an abrasive

emet·ic \i-'me-tik\ *n* : an agent that induces vomiting — **emetic** *adj*

emf *n* [electromotive *force*] : POTENTIAL DIFFERENCE

em·i·grate \'e-mə-,grāt\ *vb* **-grat·ed; -grat·ing** : to leave a place (as a country) to settle elsewhere — **em·i·grant** \-mi-grənt\ *n* — **em·i·gra·tion** \,e-mə-'grā-shən\ *n*

émi·gré *also* **emi·gré** \'e-mə-,grā, ,e-mi-'grā\ *n* [F] : a person who emigrates esp. because of political conditions

em·i·nence \'e-mə-nəns\ *n* **1** : high rank or position; *also* : a person of high rank or attainment **2** : a lofty place

em·i·nent \'e-mə-nənt\ *adj* **1** : CONSPICUOUS, EVIDENT **2** : DISTINGUISHED, PROMINENT ⟨an ∼ physician⟩ — **em·i·nent·ly** *adv*

eminent domain *n* : a right of a government to take private property for public use

emir *or* **amir** \ə-'mir, ā-\ *n* [Ar *amīr* commander] : a ruler, chief, or commander in Islamic countries — **emir·ate** \'e-mər-ət\ *n*

em·is·sary \'e-mə-ˌser-ē\ *n, pl* **-sar·ies** : AGENT; *esp* : a secret agent

emis·sion \ē-'mi-shən\ *n* : something emitted; *esp* : substances discharged into the air

emit \ē-'mit\ *vb* **emit·ted; emit·ting 1** : to give off or out ⟨∼ light⟩; *also* : EJECT **2** : EXPRESS, UTTER ⟨emitted a groan⟩ — **emit·ter** *n*

emol·lient \i-'mäl-yənt\ *adj* : making soft or supple; *also* : soothing esp. to the skin or mucous membrane ⟨an ∼ hand lotion⟩ — **emol·lient** *n*

emol·u·ment \i-'mäl-yə-mənt\ *n* [ME, fr. L *emolumentum* advantage, fr. *emolere* to produce by grinding] : the product (as salary or fees) of an employment

emote \i-'mōt\ *vb* **emot·ed; emot·ing** : to give expression to emotion in or as if in a play

emo·ti·con \i-'mō-ti-ˌkän\ *n* : a group of keyboard characters (as :)) that represents a facial expression esp. in online communications

emo·tion \i-'mō-shən\ *n* : a usu. intense feeling (as of love, hate, or despair) — **emo·tion·al** \-shə-nəl\ *adj* — **emo·tion·al·ly** *adv*

emo·tive \i-'mō-tiv\ *adj* **1** : of or relating to the emotions **2** : appealing to or expressing emotion

emp *abbr* emperor; empress

empanel *var of* IMPANEL

em·pa·thy \'em-pə-thē\ *n* : the experiencing as one's own of the feelings of another; *also* : the capacity for this — **em·path·ic** \im-'pa-thik\ *adj*

em·pen·nage \ˌäm-pə-'näzh, ˌem-\ *n* [F] : the tail assembly of an airplane

em·per·or \'em-pər-ər\ *n* : the sovereign male ruler of an empire

em·pha·sis \'em-fə-səs\ *n, pl* **-pha·ses** \-ˌsēz\ : particular prominence given (as to a syllable in speaking or to a phase of action)

em·pha·sise *Brit var of* EMPHASIZE

em·pha·size \-ˌsīz\ *vb* **-sized; -siz·ing** : to place emphasis on : STRESS

em·phat·ic \im-'fa-tik, em-\ *adj* : uttered with emphasis : STRESSED ⟨an ∼ refusal⟩ — **em·phat·i·cal·ly** \-'ti-k(ə-)lē\ *adv*

em·phy·se·ma \ˌem-fə-'zē-mə, -'sē-\ *n* : a condition marked esp. by abnormal expansion of the air spaces of the lungs resulting in severe breathlessness

em·pire \'em-ˌpī(-ə)r\ *n* **1** : a large state or a group of states under a single sovereign who is usu. an emperor; *also* : something resembling a political empire **2** : imperial sovereignty or dominion

em·pir·i·cal \im-'pir-i-kəl\ *also* **em·pir·ic** \-ik\ *adj* : based on observation; *also* : subject to verification by observation or experiment ⟨∼ laws⟩ — **em·pir·i·cal·ly** \-i-k(ə-)lē\ *adv*

em·pir·i·cism \im-'pir-ə-ˌsi-zəm, em-\ *n* : the practice of relying on observation and experiment esp. in the natural sciences — **em·pir·i·cist** \-sist\ *n*

em·place·ment \im-'plās-mənt\ *n* **1** : a prepared position for weapons or military equipment **2** : PLACEMENT

¹em·ploy \im-'ploi\ *vb* **1** : to make use of **2** : to use the services of **3** : OCCUPY, DEVOTE — **em·ploy·er** *n*

²em·ploy \im-'ploi; 'im-ˌploi, 'em-\ *n* : EMPLOYMENT

em·ploy·ee *also* **em·ploye** \im-ˌploi-'ē, ˌem-; im-'ploi-ē, em-\ *n* : a person who works for another

em·ploy·ment \im-'ploi-mənt\ *n* **1** : OCCUPATION, ACTIVITY **2** : the act of employing : the condition of being employed

em·po·ri·um \im-'pȯr-ē-əm, em-\ *n, pl* **-ri·ums** *also* **-ria** \-ē-ə\ [L, fr. Gk *emporion*, fr. *emporos* traveler, trader] : a commercial center; *esp* : a store carrying varied articles

em·pow·er \im-'pau̇(-ə)r\ *vb* : to give authority or power to; *also* : ENABLE — **em·pow·er·ment** \-mənt\ *n*

em·press \'em-prəs\ *n* **1** : the wife or widow of an emperor **2** : a sovereign female ruler of an empire

¹emp·ty \'emp-tē\ *adj* **emp·ti·er; -est** [ME, fr. OE *ǣmettig* unoccupied, fr. *ǣmetta* leisure] **1** : containing nothing ⟨∼ shelves⟩ **2** : UNOCCUPIED, UNINHABITED ⟨an ∼ building⟩ **3** : lacking value, force, sense, or purpose ♦ **Synonyms** VACANT, BLANK, VOID, STARK, VACUOUS — **emp·ti·ness** *n*

²empty *vb* **emp·tied; emp·ty·ing 1** : to make or become empty **2** : to discharge contents; *also* : to remove from what holds or encloses

³empty *n, pl* **empties** : an empty bottle or can

emp·ty-hand·ed \ˌemp-tē-'han-dəd\ *adj* **1** : having or bringing nothing **2** : having acquired or gained nothing

em·py·re·an \ˌem-ˌpī-'rē-ən, -pə-\ *n* **1** : the highest heaven; *also* : FIRMAMENT **2** : an ideal place or realm

EMT \ˌē-(ˌ)em-'tē\ *n* [emergency medical technician] : a specially trained medical technician certified to provide basic medical services before and during transport to a hospital

¹emu \'ē-myü, -mü\ *n* : a swift-running flightless Australian bird smaller than the related ostrich

²emu *abbr* electromagnetic unit

em·u·late \'em-yù-ˌlāt\ *vb* **-lat·ed; -lat·ing** : to strive to equal or excel : IMITATE — **em·u·la·tion** \ˌem-yù-'lā-shən\ *n* — **em·u·lous** \'em-yù-ləs\ *adj*

emul·si·fi·er \i-'məl-sə-ˌfī(-ə)r\ *n* : a substance (as a soap) that helps to form and stabilize an emulsion

emul·si·fy \-ˌfī\ *vb* **-fied; -fy·ing** : to disperse (as an oil) in an emulsion — **emul·si·fi·ca·tion** \-ˌməl-sə-fə-ˈkā-shən\ *n*

emul·sion \i-ˈməl-shən\ *n* **1** : a mixture of mutually insoluble liquids in which one is dispersed in droplets throughout the other ⟨an ∼ of oil in water⟩ **2** : a light-sensitive coating on photographic film or paper

en \ˈen\ *n* : a length approximately half the width of the letter *M*

¹-en *also* **-n** *adj suffix* : made of : consisting of ⟨earth*en*⟩

²-en *vb suffix* **1** : become or cause to be ⟨sharp*en*⟩ **2** : cause or come to have ⟨length*en*⟩

en·able \i-ˈnā-bəl\ *vb* **en·abled; en·abling 1** : to make able or feasible ⟨wings that ∼ one to fly⟩ **2** : to give legal power, capacity, or sanction to

en·act \i-ˈnakt\ *vb* **1** : to make into law **2** : to act out — **en·act·ment** *n*

enam·el \i-ˈna-məl\ *n* **1** : a glasslike substance used to coat the surface of metal or pottery **2** : the hard outer layer of a tooth **3** : a usu. glossy paint that forms a hard coat — **enamel** *vb*

enam·el·ware \-ˌwer\ *n* : metal utensils coated with enamel

en·am·or \i-ˈna-mər\ *vb* : to inflame with love

en·am·our *chiefly Brit var of* ENAMOR

en bloc \äⁿ-ˈbläk\ *adv or adj* : as a whole : in a mass

enc *or* **encl** *abbr* enclosure

en·camp \in-ˈkamp\ *vb* : to make camp — **en·camp·ment** *n*

en·cap·su·late \in-ˈkap-sə-ˌlāt\ *vb* **-lated; -lat·ing** : to encase or become encased in a capsule **2** : SUMMARIZE — **en·cap·su·la·tion** \-ˌkap-sə-ˈlā-shən\ *n*

en·case \in-ˈkās\ *vb* : to enclose in or as if in a case — **en·case·ment** \-ˈkā-smənt\ *n*

-ence *n suffix* **1** : action or process ⟨emerg*ence*⟩ : instance of an action or process ⟨refer*ence*⟩ **2** : quality or state ⟨depend*ence*⟩

en·ceinte \äⁿ-ˈsant\ *adj* : PREGNANT 1

en·ceph·a·li·tis \in-ˌse-fə-ˈlī-təs\ *n, pl* **-lit·i·des** \-ˈli-tə-ˌdēz\ : inflammation of the brain — **en·ceph·a·lit·ic** \-ˈli-tik\ *adj*

en·ceph·a·lop·a·thy \in-ˌse-fə-ˈlä-pə-thē\ *n, pl* **-thies** : a disease of the brain

en·chain \in-ˈchān\ *vb* : FETTER, CHAIN

en·chant \in-ˈchant\ *vb* **1** : BEWITCH **2** : ENRAPTURE, FASCINATE ⟨was ∼ed by his poetry⟩ — **en·chant·er** *n* — **en·chant·ing·ly** *adv* — **en·chant·ment** *n* — **en·chant·ress** \-ˈchan-trəs\ *n*

en·chi·la·da \ˌen-chə-ˈlä-də\ *n* : a tortilla rolled around a filling, covered with chili sauce, and usu. baked

en·ci·pher \in-ˈsī-fər, en-\ *vb* : ENCODE

en·cir·cle \in-ˈsər-kəl\ *vb* : to pass completely around : SURROUND — **en·cir·cle·ment** *n*

en·clave \ˈen-ˌklāv, ˈän-ˌklāv\ *n* : a distinct territorial, cultural, or social unit

enclosed within or as if within foreign territory

en·close \in-ˈklōz\ *vb* **1** : to shut up or in; *esp* : to surround with a fence **2** : to include along with something else in a parcel or envelope ⟨∼ a check⟩ — **en·clo·sure** \-ˈklō-zhər\ *n*

en·code \in-ˈkōd, en-\ *vb* : to convert (a message) into code

en·co·mi·um \en-ˈkō-mē-əm\ *n, pl* **-mi·ums** *also* **-mia** \-mē-ə\ : high or glowing praise

en·com·pass \in-ˈkəm-pəs\ *vb* **1** : ENCIRCLE **2** : ENVELOP, INCLUDE

en·core \ˈän-ˌkȯr\ *n* **1** : a demand for repetition or reappearance **2** : a further performance or appearance demanded by an audience **3** : a second achievement that usu. surpasses the first — **encore** *vb*

¹en·coun·ter \in-ˈkaun-tər\ *vb* **1** : to meet as an enemy : FIGHT **2** : to meet usu. unexpectedly ⟨∼ problems⟩

²encounter *n* **1** : a hostile usu. violent meeting **2** : a chance meeting **3** : an experience shared with another ⟨a romantic ∼⟩

en·cour·age \in-ˈkər-ij\ *vb* **-aged; -ag·ing 1** : to inspire with courage and hope **2** : STIMULATE, INCITE ⟨tax cuts to ∼ spending⟩ **3** : FOSTER — **en·cour·age·ment** *n* — **en·cour·ag·ing·ly** *adv*

en·croach \in-ˈkrōch\ *vb* [ME *encrochen* to seize, fr. AF *encrocher*, fr. *croche* hook] : to enter gradually or stealthily upon another's property or rights — **en·croach·er** *n* — **en·croach·ment** *n*

en·crust *also* **in·crust** \in-ˈkrəst\ *vb* : to provide with or form a crust

en·crus·ta·tion \(ˌ)in-ˌkrəs-ˈtā-shən, ˌen-\ *var of* INCRUSTATION

en·cum·ber \in-ˈkəm-bər\ *vb* **1** : to weigh down : BURDEN **2** : to hinder the function or activity of ⟨relations ∼ed by mistrust⟩ — **en·cum·brance** \-brəns\ *n*

ency *or* **encyc** *abbr* encyclopedia

-en·cy *n suffix* : quality or state ⟨despondency⟩

¹en·cyc·li·cal \in-ˈsi-kli-kəl, en-\ *adj* : addressed to all the individuals of a group

²encyclical *n* : an encyclical letter; *esp* : a papal letter to the bishops of the church

en·cy·clo·pae·dia, en·cy·clo·pae·dic *chiefly Brit var of* ENCYCLOPEDIA, ENCYCLOPEDIC

en·cy·clo·pe·dia \in-ˌsī-klə-ˈpē-dē-ə\ *n* [ML *encyclopaedia* course of general education, fr. Gk *enkyklios paideia* general education] : a work treating the various branches of learning — **en·cy·clo·pe·dic** \-ˈpē-dik\ *adj*

en·cyst \in-ˈsist, en-\ *vb* : to form or become enclosed in a cyst — **en·cyst·ment** *n*

¹end \ˈend\ *n* **1** : the part of an area that lies at the boundary; *also* : a point which marks the extent or limit of something or at which something ceases to exist **2** : a ceasing of a course (as of action or activity); *also* : DEATH **3** : the ultimate state; *also* : RESULT, ISSUE **4** : REMNANT **5** : PURPOSE, OBJECTIVE **6** : a player stationed at the extremity of a line (as in football) **7** : a share, operation, or aspect of an undertaking

²**end** *vb* **1** : to bring or come to an end **2** : DESTROY; *also* : DIE **3** : to form or be at the end of ♦ *Synonyms* CLOSE, CONCLUDE, TERMINATE, FINISH, COMPLETE

en·dan·ger \in-'dān-jər\ *vb* : to bring into danger; *also* : to create danger

en·dan·gered *adj* : being or relating to an endangered species

endangered species *n* : a species threatened with extinction

en·dear \in-'dir\ *vb* : to cause to become beloved or admired

en·dear·ment \-mənt\ *n* : a sign of affection : CARESS

en·deav·or \in-'de-vər\ *vb* : TRY, ATTEMPT — endeavor *n*

en·deav·our *chiefly Brit var of* ENDEAVOR

en·dem·ic \en-'de-mik, in-\ *adj* : restricted to a particular place ⟨~ plants⟩ ⟨an ~ disease⟩ — **endemic** *n*

end·ing \'en-diŋ\ *n* : something that forms an end; *esp* : SUFFIX

en·dive \'en-ˌdīv\ *n* **1** : an herb related to chicory and grown as a salad plant **2** : the blanched shoot of chicory

end·less \'end-ləs\ *adj* **1** : having or seeming to have no end : ETERNAL ⟨~ debates⟩ **2** : united at the ends : CONTINUOUS ⟨an ~ belt⟩ ♦ *Synonyms* INTERMINABLE, EVERLASTING, UNCEASING, CEASELESS, UNENDING — **end·less·ly** *adv*

end·most \-ˌmōst\ *adj* : situated at the very end

end·note \-ˌnōt\ *n* : a note placed at the end of a text

en·do·crine \'en-də-krən, -ˌkrīn, -ˌkrēn\ *adj* : producing secretions that are distributed by way of the bloodstream ⟨~ glands⟩ — **endocrine** *n* — **en·do·cri·nol·o·gist** \ˌkri-'nä-lə-jist\ *n* — **en·do·cri·nol·o·gy** \-jē\ *n*

en·dog·e·nous \en-'dä-jə-nəs\ *adj* : caused or produced by factors inside the organism or system ⟨~ depression⟩ — **en·dog·e·nous·ly** *adv*

en·do·me·tri·um \ˌen-dō-'mē-trē-əm\ *n, pl* -**tria** \-trē-ə\ : the mucous membrane lining the uterus — **en·do·me·tri·al** \-trē-əl\ *adj*

en·dor·phin \en-'dȯr-fən\ *n* : any of a group of endogenous morphinelike proteins found esp. in the brain

en·dorse *also* **in·dorse** \in-'dȯrs\ *vb* en·dorsed; en·dors·ing [ME *endosen*, fr. AF *endosser* to put on, don, write on the back of, fr. *dos* back, fr. L *dorsum*] **1** : to sign one's name on the back of (as a check) **2** : APPROVE, SANCTION **3** : to recommend (as a product) esp. for financial compensation — **en·dorse·ment** *also* **in·dorse·ment** *n*

en·do·scope \'en-də-ˌskōp\ *n* : an illuminated usu. fiber-optic instrument for visualizing the interior of a hollow organ or part (as the colon or esophagus) — **en·do·scop·ic** \ˌen-də-'skä-pik\ *adj* — **en·dos·co·py** \en-'däs-kə-pē\ *n*

en·do·ther·mic \ˌen-də-'thər-mik\ *adj* : characterized by or formed with absorption of heat

en·dow \in-'daú\ *vb* **1** : to furnish with funds for support ⟨~ a school⟩ **2** : to furnish with something freely or naturally ⟨~ed with intellect⟩ — **en·dow·ment** *n*

en·due \in-'dü, -'dyü\ *vb* en·dued; en·du·ing : PROVIDE, ENDOW

en·dur·ance \in-'dúr-əns, -'dyúr-\ *n* **1** : DURATION **2** : the ability to withstand hardship or stress : FORTITUDE

en·dure \in-'dúr, -'dyúr\ *vb* en·dured; en·dur·ing **1** : LAST, PERSIST **2** : to suffer firmly or patiently : BEAR **3** : TOLERATE — **en·dur·able** *adj*

end·ways \'end-ˌwāz\ *adv or adj* **1** : LENGTHWISE **2** : with the end forward **3** : on end

end·wise \-ˌwīz\ *adv or adj* : ENDWAYS

ENE *abbr* east-northeast

en·e·ma \'e-nə-mə\ *n, pl* enemas *also* **ene·ma·ta** \ˌe-nə-'mä-tə, 'e-nə-mə-tə\ : injection of liquid into the rectum; *also* : material so injected

en·e·my \'e-nə-mē\ *n, pl* -**mies** [ME *enemi*, fr. AF, fr. L *inimicus*, fr. *in-* not + *amicus* friend] : one that attacks or tries to harm another : FOE; *esp* : a military opponent

en·er·get·ic \ˌe-nər-'je-tik\ *adj* : marked by energy : ACTIVE, VIGOROUS ♦ *Synonyms* STRENUOUS, LUSTY, DYNAMIC, VITAL — **en·er·get·i·cal·ly** \-ti-k(ə-)lē\ *adv*

en·er·gise *Brit var of* ENERGIZE

en·er·gize \'e-nər-ˌjīz\ *vb* -gized; -giz·ing : to give energy to

en·er·gy \'e-nər-jē\ *n, pl* -gies **1** : vigorous action : EFFORT **2** : capacity for action **3** : a fundamental entity of nature usu. regarded as the capacity for performing work **4** : usable power (as heat or electricity); *also* : the resources for producing such power

energy level *n* : one of the stable states of constant energy that may be assumed by a physical system (as the electrons in an atom)

en·er·vate \'e-nər-ˌvāt\ *vb* -vat·ed; -vat·ing : to lessen the strength or vigor of : weaken in mind or body ⟨*enervated* by work⟩ — **en·er·vat·ing·ly** \-ˌvā-tiŋ-lē\ *adv* — **en·er·va·tion** \ˌe-nər-'vā-shən\ *n*

en·fee·ble \in-'fē-bəl\ *vb* -bled; -bling : to make feeble ♦ *Synonyms* WEAKEN, DEBILITATE, SAP, UNDERMINE, CRIPPLE — **en·fee·ble·ment** *n*

en·fi·lade \'en-fə-ˌlād, -ˌläd\ *n* : gunfire directed along the length of an enemy battle line — **enfilade** *vb*

en·fold \in-'fōld\ *vb* **1** : ENVELOP ⟨darkness ~ed the city⟩ **2** : EMBRACE

en·force \in-'fȯrs\ *vb* **1** : COMPEL ⟨~ obedience by threats⟩ **2** : to execute effectively ⟨~ the law⟩ — **en·force·able** *adj* — **en·force·ment** *n*

en·forc·er \in-'fȯr-sər\ *n* : one that enforces; *esp* : a player (as in ice hockey) known for rough play

en·fran·chise \in-'fran-ˌchīz\ *vb* -chised; -chis·ing **1** : to set free (as from slavery)

2 : to admit to citizenship; *also* : to grant the vote to — **en·fran·chise·ment** \-ˌchīz-mənt, -chəz-\ *n*

eng *abbr* engine; engineer; engineering

Eng *abbr* England; English

en·gage \in-ˈgāj\ *vb* **en·gaged; en·gag·ing** **1** : PLEDGE; *esp* : to bind by a pledge to marry **2** : EMPLOY, HIRE **3** : to attract and hold esp. by interesting; *also* : to cause to participate **4** : to commence or take part in a venture ⟨*engaged* in shady deals⟩ **5** : to bring or enter into conflict ⟨~ the enemy⟩ **6** : to connect or interlock with : MESH; *also* : to cause to mesh

en·gage·ment \in-ˈgāj-mənt\ *n* **1** : APPOINTMENT **2** : EMPLOYMENT **3** : a mutual promise to marry : BETROTHAL **4** : a hostile encounter

en·gag·ing *adj* : ATTRACTIVE ⟨an ~ smile⟩ — **en·gag·ing·ly** *adv*

en·gen·der \in-ˈjen-dər\ *vb* **1** : BEGET **2** : BRING ABOUT, CREATE ⟨~ controversy⟩ ◆ **Synonyms** GENERATE, BREED, OCCASION, PRODUCE

en·gine \ˈen-jən\ *n* [ME *engin*, fr. AF, fr. L *ingenium* natural disposition, talent] **1** : a mechanical device **2** : a machine for converting energy into mechanical motion **3** : LOCOMOTIVE **4** : software that performs a fundamental function esp. of a larger program — **en·gine·less** *adj*

¹en·gi·neer \ˌen-jə-ˈnir\ *n* **1** : a member of a military unit specializing in engineering work **2** : a designer or builder of engines **3** : one trained in engineering **4** : one that operates an engine

²engineer *vb* **1** : to lay out or manage as an engineer **2** : to guide the course of ⟨~ a rally⟩ ◆ **Synonyms** PILOT, LEAD, STEER

en·gi·neer·ing *n* : the practical applications of scientific and mathematical principles

En·glish \ˈiŋ-glish\ *n* **1** : the language of England, the U.S., and many areas now or formerly under British rule **2** English *pl* : the people of England **3** : spin imparted to a ball that is driven or rolled — **English** *adj* — **En·glish·man** \-mən\ *n* — **En·glish·wom·an** \-ˌwu̇-mən\ *n*

English horn *n* : a woodwind instrument longer than and having a range lower than the oboe

English setter *n* : any of a breed of hunting dogs with a flat silky coat of white or white with color

English sparrow *n* : HOUSE SPARROW

English system *n* : a system of weights and measures in which the foot is the principal unit of length and the pound is the principal unit of weight

engr *abbr* **1** engineer **2** engraved

en·gram \ˈen-ˌgram\ *n* : a hypothetical change in neural tissue postulated in order to account for persistence of memory

en·grave \in-ˈgrāv\ *vb* **en·graved; en·grav·ing 1** : to produce (as letters or lines) by incising a surface **2** : to cut figures, letters, or designs on for printing; *also* : to print from an engraved plate ⟨~ an invitation⟩ **3** : PHOTOENGRAVE — **en·grav·er** *n*

en·grav·ing \in-ˈgrā-viŋ\ *n* **1** : the art of one who engraves **2** : an engraved plate; *also* : a print made from it

en·gross \in-ˈgrōs\ *vb* : to take up the whole interest or attention of ◆ **Synonyms** MONOPOLIZE, ABSORB, CONSUME

en·gulf \in-ˈgəlf\ *vb* : to flow over and enclose : OVERWHELM ⟨~ed in flames⟩

en·hance \in-ˈhans\ *vb* **en·hanced; en·hanc·ing** : to increase or improve (as in value or desirability) ◆ **Synonyms** HEIGHTEN, INTENSIFY, MAGNIFY — **en·hance·ment** *n*

enig·ma \i-ˈnig-mə\ *n* [L *aenigma*, fr. Gk *ainigma*, fr. *ainissesthai* to speak in riddles, fr. *ainos* fable] : something obscure or hard to understand

enig·mat·ic \ˌen-ig-ˈma-tik\ *adj* : resembling an enigma ◆ **Synonyms** OBSCURE, CRYPTIC, MYSTIFYING — **en·ig·mat·i·cal·ly** \-ti-k(ə-)lē\ *adv*

en·join \in-ˈjȯin\ *vb* **1** : COMMAND, ORDER ⟨~ed us to desist⟩ **2** : FORBID ◆ **Synonyms** DIRECT, BID, CHARGE, COMMAND, INSTRUCT

en·joy \in-ˈjȯi\ *vb* **1** : to have for one's benefit or use ⟨~ good health⟩ **2** : to take pleasure or satisfaction in ⟨~ed the concert⟩ — **en·joy·able** *adj* — **en·joy·ment** *n*

enl *abbr* **1** enlarged **2** enlisted

en·large \in-ˈlärj\ *vb* **en·larged; en·larg·ing 1** : to make or grow larger **2** : ELABORATE ◆ **Synonyms** INCREASE, AUGMENT, MULTIPLY, EXPAND — **en·large·ment** *n*

en·light·en \in-ˈlī-tᵊn\ *vb* **1** : INSTRUCT, INFORM **2** : to give spiritual insight to — **en·light·en·ment** *n*

en·list \in-ˈlist\ *vb* **1** : to secure the aid or support of **2** : to engage for service in the armed forces — **en·list·ee** \-ˌlis-ˈtē\ *n* — **en·list·ment** \-ˈlist-mənt\ *n*

en·list·ed \in-ˈlis-təd\ *adj* : of, relating to, or forming the part of a military force below commissioned or warrant officers

enlisted man *n* : a man or woman in the armed forces ranking below a commissioned or warrant officer

en·liv·en \in-ˈlī-vən\ *vb* : to give life, action, or spirit to : ANIMATE

en masse \äⁿ-ˈmas\ *adv* [F] : in a body : as a whole

en·mesh \in-ˈmesh\ *vb* : to catch or entangle in or as if in meshes

en·mi·ty \ˈen-mə-tē\ *n, pl* **-ties** : ILL WILL; *esp* : mutual hatred ◆ **Synonyms** HOSTILITY, ANTIPATHY, ANIMOSITY, RANCOR, ANTAGONISM

en·no·ble \i-ˈnō-bəl\ *vb* **-bled; -bling** : EXALT, ELEVATE; *esp* : to raise to noble rank — **en·no·ble·ment** *n*

en·nui \ˌän-ˈwē\ *n* [F] : BOREDOM

enor·mi·ty \i-ˈnȯr-mə-tē\ *n, pl* **-ties 1** : an outrageous, vicious, or immoral act **2** : great wickedness **3** : IMMENSITY

enor·mous \i-ˈnȯr-məs\ *adj* [L *enormis*, fr. *e, ex* out of + *norma* rule] **1** : exceedingly wicked **2** : great in size, number, or degree : HUGE ◆ **Synonyms** IMMENSE,

VAST, GIGANTIC, COLOSSAL, MAMMOTH, ELEPHANTINE — **enor·mous·ly** *adv*

¹enough \i-'nəf\ *adj* : SUFFICIENT

²enough *adv* **1** : SUFFICIENTLY **2** : FULLY, QUITE **3** : TOLERABLY

³enough *pron* : a sufficient number, quantity, or amount

en·quire \in-'kwī(-ə)r\, **en·qui·ry** \'in-,kwī(-ə)r-ē, in-'; 'in-kwə-rē, 'iŋ-\ *chiefly Brit var of* INQUIRE, INQUIRY

en·rage \in-'rāj\ *vb* : to fill with rage

en·rap·ture \in-'rap-chər\ *vb* **en·rap·tured; en·rap·tur·ing** : DELIGHT

en·rich \in-'rich\ *vb* **1** : to make rich or richer **2** : ORNAMENT, ADORN — **en·rich·ment** *n*

en·roll *also* **en·rol** \in-'rōl\ *vb* **en·rolled; en·roll·ing 1** : to enter or register on a roll or list **2** : to offer (oneself) for enrolling — **en·roll·ment** *n*

en route \än-'rüt, en-\ *adv or adj* : on or along the way ⟨stalled while *en route* to work⟩

ENS *abbr* ensign

en·sconce \in-'skäns\ *vb* **en·sconced; en·sconc·ing 1** : SHELTER, CONCEAL **2** : to settle snugly or securely ♦ *Synonyms* SECRETE, HIDE, CACHE, STASH

en·sem·ble \än-'säm-bəl\ *n* [F, fr. *ensemble* together, fr. L *insimul* at the same time] : a group (as of singers, dancers, or players) or a set (as of clothes) producing a single effect

en·sheathe \in-'shēth\ *vb* : to cover with or as if with a sheath

en·shrine \in-'shrīn\ *vb* **1** : to enclose in or as if in a shrine **2** : to cherish as sacred — **en·shrine·ment** \-mənt\ *n*

en·shroud \in-'shraúd\ *vb* : SHROUD, OBSCURE

en·sign \'en-sən, *1 also* -,sīn\ *n* **1** : FLAG; *also* : BADGE, EMBLEM **2** : a commissioned officer in the navy ranking next below a lieutenant junior grade

en·slave \in-'slāv\ *vb* : to make a slave of — **en·slave·ment** *n*

en·snare \in-'sner\ *vb* : SNARE, TRAP ♦ *Synonyms* ENTRAP, BAG, CATCH, CAPTURE

en·sue \in-'sü\ *vb* **en·sued; en·su·ing** : to follow in time or as a result ⟨the birds escaped and chaos *ensued*⟩

en·sure \in-'shúr\ *vb* **en·sured; en·sur·ing** : INSURE, GUARANTEE

en·tail \in-'tāl\ *vb* **1** : to limit the inheritance of (property) to the owner's lineal descendants or to a class thereof **2** : to include or involve as a necessary step or result ⟨the sacrifices that parenting *~s*⟩ — **en·tail·ment** *n*

en·tan·gle \in-'taŋ-gəl\ *vb* : TANGLE, CONFUSE — **en·tan·gle·ment** *n*

en·tente \än-'tänt\ *n* [F] : an understanding providing for joint action; *also* : parties linked by such an entente

en·ter \'en-tər\ *vb* **1** : to go or come in or into **2** : to become a member of : JOIN ⟨~ the ministry⟩ **3** : BEGIN **4** : to take part in : CONTRIBUTE **5** : to go into or upon and take possession **6** : to set down (as in a list) : REGISTER ⟨~ the data⟩ **7**

: to place (a complaint) before a court; *also* : to put on record ⟨~ a complaint⟩

en·ter·i·tis \,en-tə-'rī-təs\ *n* : intestinal inflammation; *also* : a disease marked by this

en·ter·prise \'en-tər-,prīz\ *n* **1** : UNDERTAKING, PROJECT **2** : readiness for daring action : INITIATIVE **3** : a business organization

en·ter·pris·ing \-,prī-ziŋ\ *adj* : bold and vigorous in action : ENERGETIC

en·ter·tain \,en-tər-'tān\ *vb* **1** : to treat or receive as a guest **2** : AMUSE, DIVERT ⟨~ed us with jokes⟩ **3** : to hold in mind ⟨~ed thoughts of retirement⟩ ♦ *Synonyms* HARBOR, SHELTER, LODGE, HOUSE, BILLET — **en·ter·tain·er** *n* — **en·ter·tain·ment** *n*

en·thrall *or* **en·thral** \in-'thról\ *vb* **en·thralled; en·thrall·ing 1** : ENSLAVE **2** : to hold spellbound

en·throne \in-'thrōn\ *vb* **1** : to seat on or as if on a throne **2** : EXALT

en·thuse \in-'thüz, -'thyüz\ *vb* **en·thused; en·thus·ing 1** : to make enthusiastic **2** : to show enthusiasm

en·thu·si·asm \in-'thü-zē-,a-zəm, -'thyü-\ *n* [Gk *enthousiasmos*, fr. *enthousiazein* to be inspired, irreg. fr. *entheos* inspired, fr. *theos* god] **1** : strong warmth of feeling : keen interest : FERVOR **2** : a cause of fervor — **en·thu·si·ast** \-,ast, -əst\ *n* — **en·thu·si·as·tic** \in-,thü-zē-'as-tik, -,thyü-\ *adj* — **en·thu·si·as·ti·cal·ly** \-ti-k(ə-)lē\ *adv*

en·tice \in-'tīs\ *vb* **en·ticed; en·tic·ing** : ALLURE, TEMPT — **en·tice·ment** *n*

en·tire \in-'tī(-ə)r\ *adj* : COMPLETE, WHOLE ♦ *Synonyms* SOUND, PERFECT, INTACT, UNDAMAGED — **en·tire·ly** *adv*

en·tire·ty \in-'tī-rə-tē, -'tī(-ə)r-tē\ *n, pl* **-ties 1** : COMPLETENESS **2** : WHOLE, TOTALITY

en·ti·tle \in-'tī-t°l\ *vb* **en·ti·tled; en·ti·tling 1** : NAME, DESIGNATE **2** : to give a right or claim to ⟨*entitled* to a fair trial⟩

en·ti·tle·ment \in-'tī-t°l-mənt\ *n* : a government program providing benefits to members of a specified group

en·ti·ty \'en-tə-tē\ *n, pl* **-ties 1** : EXISTENCE, BEING **2** : something with separate and real existence

en·tomb \in-'tüm\ *vb* : to place in a tomb : BURY — **en·tomb·ment** *n*

en·to·mol·o·gy \,en-tə-'mä-lə-jē\ *n* : a branch of zoology that deals with insects — **en·to·mo·log·i·cal** \-mə-'lä-ji-kəl\ *adj* — **en·to·mol·o·gist** \-jist\ *n*

en·tou·rage \,än-tú-'räzh\ *n* [F] : RETINUE

en·tr'acte \'än-,trakt\ *n* [F] **1** : something (as a dance) performed between two acts of a play **2** : the interval between two acts of a play

en·trails \'en-,trālz\ *n pl* : VISCERA; *esp* : INTESTINES

¹en·trance \'en-trəns\ *n* **1** : permission or right to enter **2** : the act of entering **3** : a means or place of entry

²en·trance \in-'trans\ *vb* **en·tranced; en·tranc·ing** : CHARM, DELIGHT

en·trant \'en-trənt\ *n* : one that enters esp. as a competitor

en·trap \in-'trap\ *vb* : ENSNARE, TRAP — **en·trap·ment** *n*

en·treat \in-'trēt\ *vb* : to ask urgently : BESEECH ♦ *Synonyms* BEG, IMPLORE, PLEAD, SUPPLICATE — **en·treaty** \-'trē-tē\ *n*

en·trée *or* **en·tree** \'än-,trā\ *n* [F *entrée*] 1 : freedom of entry or access 2 : the main course of a meal in the U.S. ♦ *Synonyms* ADMISSION, ADMITTANCE, ENTRANCE

en·trench \in-'trench\ *vb* 1 : to place within or surround with a trench esp. for defense; *also* : to establish solidly 〈~ed customs〉 2 : ENCROACH, TRESPASS — **en·trench·ment** *n*

en·tre·pre·neur \,än-trə-prə-'nər, -'nu̇r, -'nyu̇r\ *n* [F, fr. OF, fr. *entreprendre* to undertake] : one who organizes and assumes the risk of a business or enterprise — **en·tre·pre·neur·ial** \-'nu̇r-ē-əl, -'nyu̇r-, -'nər-\ *adj* — **en·tre·pre·neur·ship** \-,ship\ *n*

en·tro·py \'en-trə-pē\ *n, pl* **-pies** 1 : the degree of disorder in a system 2 : an ultimate state of inert uniformity

en·trust \in-'trəst\ *vb* 1 : to commit something to another as a trust 2 : to commit to another with confidence ♦ *Synonyms* CONFIDE, CONSIGN, RELEGATE, COMMEND

en·try \'en-trē\ *n, pl* **entries** 1 : ENTRANCE 2 2 : ENTRANCE 3; *also* : VESTIBULE 1 3 : an entering in a record; *also* : an item so entered 4 : a headword with its definition or identification; *also* : VOCABULARY ENTRY 5 : one entered in something (as a contest or market)

en·twine \in-'twīn\ *vb* : to twine together or around

enu·mer·ate \i-'nü-mə-,rāt, -'nyü-\ *vb* **-at·ed; -at·ing** 1 : to determine the number of : COUNT 2 : LIST — **enu·mer·a·tion** \-,nü-mə-'rā-shən, -,nyü-\ *n*

enun·ci·ate \ē-'nən-sē-,āt\ *vb* **-at·ed; -at·ing** 1 : to state definitely; *also* : ANNOUNCE, PROCLAIM 2 : PRONOUNCE, ARTICULATE 〈~ every syllable〉 — **enun·ci·a·tion** \-,nən-sē-'ā-shən\ *n*

en·ure·sis \,en-yu̇-'rē-səs\ *n* : involuntary discharge of urine : BED-WETTING

env *abbr* envelope

en·vel·op \in-'ve-ləp\ *vb* : to enclose completely with or as if with a covering — **en·vel·op·ment** *n*

en·ve·lope \'en-və-,lōp, 'än-\ *n* 1 : a usu. paper container for a letter 2 : WRAPPER, COVERING 3 : a conventionally accepted limit 〈fashions that push the ~〉

en·ven·om \in-'ve-nəm\ *vb* 1 : to make poisonous 2 : EMBITTER

en·vi·able \'en-vē-ə-bəl\ *adj* : highly desirable — **en·vi·ably** \-blē\ *adv*

en·vi·ous \'en-vē-əs\ *adj* : feeling or showing envy — **en·vi·ous·ly** *adv* — **en·vi·ous·ness** *n*

en·vi·ron·ment \in-'vī-rən-mənt, -'vī(-ə)rn-\ *n* 1 : SURROUNDINGS 2 : the whole complex of factors (as soil, climate, and living things) that influence the form and the ability to survive of a plant or animal or ecological community — **en·vi·ron·men·tal** \-,vī-rən-'men-t°l, -,vī(-ə)rn-\ *adj* — **en·vi·ron·men·tal·ly** \-t°l-ē\ *adv*

en·vi·ron·men·tal·ist \-,vī-rən-'men-tə-list, -,vī(-ə)rn-\ *n* : a person concerned about environmental quality esp. with respect to control of pollution — **en·vi·ron·men·tal·ism** \-,vī-rən-'men-tə-,li-zəm, -,vī(-ə)rn-\

en·vi·rons \in-'vī-rənz\ *n pl* 1 : SUBURBS 2 : SURROUNDINGS; *also* : VICINITY

en·vis·age \in-'vi-zij\ *vb* **-aged; -ag·ing** : to have a mental picture of

en·vi·sion \in-'vi-zhən, en-\ *vb* : to picture to oneself 〈~s world peace〉

en·voy \'en-,vȯi, 'än-\ *n* 1 : a diplomatic agent 2 : REPRESENTATIVE, MESSENGER

¹en·vy \'en-vē\ *n, pl* **envies** [ME *envie*, fr. AF, fr. L *invidia*, fr. *invidus* envious, fr. *invidēre* to look askance at, envy, fr. *vidēre* to see] : painful or resentful awareness of another's advantages; *also* : an object of envy

²envy *vb* **en·vied; en·vy·ing** : to feel envy toward or on account of

en·zyme \'en-,zīm\ *n* : any of various complex proteins produced by living cells that catalyze specific biochemical reactions at body temperatures — **en·zy·mat·ic** \,en-zə-'ma-tik\ *adj*

Eo·cene \'ē-ə-,sēn\ *adj* : of, relating to, or being the epoch of the Tertiary between the Paleocene and the Oligocene — **Eocene** *n*

EOE *abbr* equal opportunity employer

eo·lian \ē-'ō-lē-ən\ *adj* : borne, deposited, or produced by the wind

EOM *abbr* end of month

eon *var of* AEON

EP *abbr* European plan

EPA *abbr* Environmental Protection Agency

ep·au·let *also* **ep·au·lette** \,e-pə-'let\ *n* [F *épaulette*, dim. of *épaule* shoulder] : a shoulder ornament esp. on a coat or military uniform

épée \'e-,pā, ā-'pā\ *n* [F] : a fencing or dueling sword

Eph *or* **Ephes** *abbr* Ephesians

ephed·rine \i-'fe-drən\ *n* : a stimulant drug used to treat asthma and nasal congestion

ephem·era \i-'fe-mər-ə\ *n pl* : paper items (as posters or tickets) of little original value collected usu. as a hobby

ephem·er·al \i-'fe-mə-rəl\ *adj* [Gk *ephēmeros* lasting a day, daily, fr. *epi-* on + *hēmera* day] : SHORT-LIVED, TRANSITORY ♦ *Synonyms* PASSING, FLEETING, TRANSIENT, EVANESCENT — **ephem·er·al·i·ty** \i-,fe-mə-'ra-lə-tē\ *n*

Ephe·sians \i-'fē-zhənz\ *n* — see BIBLE table

ep·ic \'e-pik\ *n* : a long poem in elevated style narrating the deeds of a hero — **epic** *adj*

epi·cen·ter \'e-pi-,sen-tər\ *n* : the point on the earth's surface directly above the point of origin of an earthquake

ep·i·cure \'e-pi-,kyu̇r\ *n* : a person with

sensitive and discriminating tastes esp. in food and wine

ep·i·cu·re·an \e-pi-kyù-'rē-ən, -'kyùr-ē-\ *n* : EPICURE — **epicurean** *adj*

¹ep·i·dem·ic \e-pə-'de-mik\ *adj* : affecting many persons at one time ⟨~ disease⟩; *also* : excessively prevalent

²epidemic *n* : an epidemic outbreak esp. of disease

ep·i·de·mi·ol·o·gy \ep-ə-dē-mē-'ä-lə-jē\ *n* : the study of the incidence, distribution, and control of disease in a population — **ep·i·de·mi·o·log·i·cal** \-dē-mē-ə-'lä-ji-kəl\ *also* **ep·i·de·mi·o·log·ic** \-jik\ *adj* — **ep·i·de·mi·ol·o·gist** \-'ä-lə-jist\ *n*

epi·der·mis \e-pə-'dər-məs\ *n* : an outer layer esp. of skin — **epi·der·mal** \-məl\ *adj*

epi·du·ral \e-pi-'d(y)ùr-əl\ *adj* : administered into the space outside the membrane that envelops the spinal cord ⟨~ anesthesia⟩ — **epidural** *n*

epi·glot·tis \e-pə-'glä-təs\ *n* : a thin plate of flexible tissue protecting the tracheal opening during swallowing

ep·i·gram \e-pə-,gram\ *n* : a short witty poem or saying — **ep·i·gram·mat·ic** \e-pə-grə-'ma-tik\ *adj*

ep·i·lep·sy \e-pə-,lep-sē\ *n, pl* **-sies** [ultim. fr. Gk *epilēpsia*, fr. *epilambanein* to seize] : a disorder marked by abnormal electrical discharges in the brain and typically manifested by sudden periods of diminished consciousness or by convulsions — **ep·i·lep·tic** \e-pə-'lep-tik\ *adj or n*

ep·i·logue *also* **ep·i·log** \e-pə-,lòg, -,läg\ *n* **1** : a concluding section of a literary work **2** : a speech addressed to the spectators by an actor at the end of a play

epi·neph·rine \e-pə-'ne-frən\ *n* : an adrenal hormone used medicinally esp. as a heart stimulant, a muscle relaxant, and a vasoconstrictor

epiph·a·ny \i-'pi-fə-nē\ *n, pl* **-nies 1** *cap* : January 6 observed as a church festival in commemoration of the coming of the Magi to Jesus at Bethlehem **2** : a sudden striking understanding of something

epis·co·pa·cy \i-'pis-kə-pə-sē\ *n, pl* **-cies 1** : government of a church by bishops **2** : EPISCOPATE

epis·co·pal \i-'pis-kə-pəl\ *adj* **1** : of or relating to a bishop or episcopacy **2** *cap* : of or relating to the Protestant Episcopal Church

Epis·co·pa·lian \i-,pis-kə-'pāl-yən\ *n* : a member of the Protestant Episcopal Church

epis·co·pate \i-'pis-kə-pət, -,pāt\ *n* **1** : the rank, office, or term of a bishop **2** : a body of bishops

ep·i·sode \e-pə-,sōd\ *n* [Gk *epeisodion*, fr. *epeisodios* coming in besides, fr. *eisodios* coming in, fr. *eis* into + *hodos* road, journey] **1** : a unit of action in a dramatic or literary work **2** : an incident in a course of events : OCCURRENCE ⟨a feverish ~⟩ — **ep·i·sod·ic** \e-pə-'sä-dik\ *adj*

epis·tle \i-'pi-səl\ *n* **1** *cap* : one of the letters of the New Testament **2** : LETTER — **epis·to·lary** \i-'pis-tə-,ler-ē\ *adj*

ep·i·taph \e-pə-,taf\ *n* : an inscription in memory of a dead person

ep·i·tha·la·mi·um \e-pə-thə-'lä-mē-əm\ *or* **ep·i·tha·la·mi·on** \-mē-ən\ *n, pl* **-ums** *or* **-mia** \-mē-ə\ : a song or poem in honor of a bride and bridegroom

ep·i·the·li·um \e-pə-'thē-lē-əm\ *n, pl* **-lia** \-lē-ə\ : a cellular membrane covering a bodily surface or lining a cavity — **ep·i·the·li·al** \-lē-əl\ *adj*

ep·i·thet \e-pə-,thet, -thət\ *n* : a characterizing and often abusive word or phrase ⟨a racial ~⟩

epit·o·me \i-'pi-tə-mē\ *n* **1** : ABSTRACT, SUMMARY **2** : EMBODIMENT ⟨the ~ of elegance⟩ — **epit·o·mize** \-,mīz\ *vb*

ep·och \e-pək, -,päk\ *n* : a usu. extended period : ERA, AGE — **ep·och·al** \-pə-kəl, -,pä-\ *adj*

ep·onym \e-pə-,nim\ *n* **1** : one for whom something is or is believed to be named **2** : a name (as of a disease) based on or derived from an eponym — **epon·y·mous** \i-'pä-nə-məs\ *adj*

ep·oxy \e-'päk-sē\ *vb* **ep·ox·ied** *or* **ep·oxyed; ep·oxy·ing** : to glue, fill, or coat with epoxy resin

epoxy resin *n* : a synthetic resin used in coatings and adhesives

ep·si·lon \ep-sə-län, -lən\ *n* : the 5th letter of the Greek alphabet — E or ε

Ep·som salts \ep-səm-\ *n* : a bitter colorless or white magnesium salt with cathartic properties

eq *abbr* **1** equal **2** equation

equa·ble \e-kwə-bəl, 'ē-\ *adj* : UNIFORM, EVEN; *esp* : free from unpleasant extremes — **eq·ua·bil·i·ty** \e-kwə-'bi-lə-tē, ,ē-\ *n* — **eq·ua·bly** \e-kwə-blē, 'ē-\ *adv*

¹equal \ē-kwəl\ *adj* **1** : of the same measure, quantity, value, quality, number, degree, or status as another ⟨~ opportunity⟩ **2** : IMPARTIAL ⟨~ justice⟩ **3** : free from extremes **4** : able to cope with a situation or task — **equal·i·ty** \i-'kwä-lə-tē\ *n* — **equal·ly** *adv*

²equal *vb* **equaled** *or* **equalled; equaling** *or* **equal·ling** : to be or become equal to; *also* : to be identical in value to

³equal *n* : one that is equal

equal·ise, equal·is·er *Brit var of* EQUALIZE, EQUALIZER

equal·ize \ē-kwə-,līz\ *vb* **-ized; -iz·ing** : to make equal, uniform, or constant — **equal·i·za·tion** \ē-kwə-lə-'zā-shən\ *n* — **equal·iz·er** *n*

equals sign *or* **equal sign** *n* : a sign = indicating equivalence

equa·nim·i·ty \ē-kwə-'ni-mə-tē, ,e-\ *n, pl* **-ties** : COMPOSURE

equate \i-'kwāt\ *vb* **equat·ed; equat·ing** : to make, treat, or regard as equal or comparable ⟨~s liars with thieves⟩

equa·tion \i-'kwā-zhən\ *n* **1** : an act of equating : the state of being equated **2** : a usu. formal statement of equivalence esp. of mathematical expressions

equa·tor \i-'kwā-tər, 'ē-,\ *n* : an imaginary circle around the earth that is everywhere equally distant from the two poles — **equa·to·ri·al** \ˌē-kwə-ˈtór-ē-əl, ˌe-\ *adj*

equer·ry \ˈe-kwə-rē, i-ˈkwer-ē\ *n, pl* **-ries** **1** : an officer in charge of the horses of a prince or noble **2** : a personal attendant of a member of the British royal family

¹**eques·tri·an** \i-ˈkwes-trē-ən\ *adj* : of or relating to horseback riding ⟨∼ competition⟩; *also* : representing a person on horseback ⟨an ∼ statue⟩

²**equestrian** *n* : one who rides a horse

eques·tri·enne \i-ˌkwes-trē-ˈen\ *n* : a female rider on horseback

equi·dis·tant \ˌē-kwə-ˈdis-tənt\ *adj* : equally distant

equi·lat·er·al \ˌē-kwə-ˈla-tə-rəl\ *adj* : having all sides or faces equal ⟨∼ triangles⟩

equi·lib·ri·um \ˌē-kwə-ˈli-brē-əm, ˌe-\ *n, pl* **-ri·ums** *or* **-ria** \-brē-ə\ : a state of intellectual or emotional balance; *also* : a state of balance between opposing forces or actions ♦ **Synonyms** POISE, BALANCE, EQUIPOISE

equine \ˈē-ˌkwīn, ˈe-\ *adj* [L *equinus,* fr. *equus* horse] : of or relating to the horse — **equine** *n*

equi·noc·tial \ˌē-kwə-ˈnäk-shəl, ˌe-\ *adj* : relating to an equinox

equi·nox \ˈē-kwə-ˌnäks, ˈe-\ *n* : either of the two times each year when the sun appears directly overhead at the equator and day and night are everywhere on earth of equal length

equip \i-ˈkwip\ *vb* **equipped; equipping** [AF *eskiper* to load on board a ship, outfit, man, of Gmc origin] **1** : to supply with needed resources **2** : to make ready : PREPARE ⟨*equipped* for the challenge⟩

eq·ui·page \ˈe-kwə-pij\ *n* : a horse-drawn carriage usu. with its servants

equip·ment \i-ˈkwip-mənt\ *n* **1** : things used in equipping : SUPPLIES, OUTFIT **2** : the equipping of a person or thing : the state of being equipped

equi·poise \ˈe-kwə-ˌpóiz, ˈē-\ *n* **1** : BALANCE, EQUILIBRIUM **2** : COUNTERBALANCE

eq·ui·ta·ble \ˈe-kwə-tə-bəl\ *adj* : JUST, FAIR — **eq·ui·ta·bly** \-blē\ *adv*

eq·ui·ta·tion \ˌe-kwə-ˈtā-shən\ *n* : the act or art of riding on horseback

eq·ui·ty \ˈe-kwə-tē\ *n, pl* **-ties** **1** : JUSTNESS, IMPARTIALITY **2** : value of a property or of an interest in it in excess of claims against it

equiv *abbr* equivalent

equiv·a·lent \i-ˈkwi-və-lənt\ *adj* : EQUAL; *also* : virtually identical — **equiv·a·lence** \-ləns\ *n* — **equivalent** *n*

equiv·o·cal \i-ˈkwi-və-kəl\ *adj* **1** : AMBIGUOUS ⟨∼ answers⟩ **2** : UNCERTAIN, UNDECIDED **3** : SUSPICIOUS, DUBIOUS ⟨∼ behavior⟩ ♦ **Synonyms** OBSCURE, DARK, VAGUE, ENIGMATIC — **equiv·o·cal·ly** *adv*

equiv·o·cate \i-ˈkwi-və-ˌkāt\ *vb* **-cat·ed; -cat·ing** **1** : to use misleading language **2** : to avoid giving a definite answer — **equiv·o·ca·tion** \-ˌkwi-və-ˈkā-shən\ *n*

¹**-er** \ər\ *adj suffix or adv suffix* — used to form the comparative degree of adjectives and adverbs of one or two syllables ⟨hot*ter*⟩ ⟨dri*er*⟩ ⟨silli*er*⟩ and sometimes of longer ones

²**-er** \ər\ *also* **-ier** \ē-ər, yər\ *or* **-yer** \yər\ *suffix* **1** : a person occupationally connected with ⟨furri*er*⟩ ⟨lawy*er*⟩ **2** : a person or thing belonging to or associated with ⟨old-tim*er*⟩ **3** : a native of : resident of ⟨New Zealand*er*⟩ **4** : one that has ⟨double-deck*er*⟩ **5** : one that produces or yields ⟨pork*er*⟩ **6** : one that does or performs ⟨a specified action⟩ ⟨batt*er*⟩ **7** : one that is a suitable object of ⟨a specified action⟩ ⟨broil*er*⟩ **8** : one that is ⟨foreign*er*⟩

Er *symbol* erbium

ER *abbr* emergency room

era \ˈer-ə, ˈe-rə, ˈir-ə\ *n* [LL *aera,* fr. L, counters, pl. of *aes* copper, money] **1** : a chronological order or system of notation reckoned from a given date as basis **2** : a period identified by some special feature ⟨the ∼ of industrialization⟩ **3** : any of the four major divisions of geologic time ♦ **Synonyms** AGE, EPOCH, PERIOD, TIME

ERA *abbr* **1** earned run average **2** Equal Rights Amendment

erad·i·cate \i-ˈra-də-ˌkāt\ *vb* **-cat·ed; -cat·ing** [L *eradicatus,* pp. of *eradicare,* fr. *e-* out + *radix* root] : UPROOT, ELIMINATE ♦ **Synonyms** EXTERMINATE, ANNIHILATE, ABOLISH, EXTINGUISH — **erad·i·ca·ble** \-di-kə-bəl\ *adj* — **erad·i·ca·tion** \-ˌra-də-ˈkā-shən\ *n*

erase \i-ˈrās\ *vb* **erased; eras·ing** : to rub or scratch out (as written words); *also* : OBLITERATE ♦ **Synonyms** CANCEL, EFFACE, DELETE, EXPUNGE — **eras·er** *n* — **era·sure** \i-ˈrā-shər\ *n*

er·bi·um \ˈər-bē-əm\ *n* : a rare metallic element found with yttrium

¹**ere** \ˈer\ *prep* : BEFORE

²**ere** *conj* : BEFORE

¹**erect** \i-ˈrekt\ *adj* **1** : not leaning or lying down : UPRIGHT **2** : being in a state of physiological erection

²**erect** *vb* **1** : BUILD **2** : to fix or set in an upright position ⟨∼ an antenna⟩ **3** : SET UP; *also* : ESTABLISH, DEVELOP

erec·tile \i-ˈrek-tᵊl, -ˈrek-ˌtī(-ə)l\ *adj* : capable of becoming erect ⟨∼ tissue⟩ ⟨∼ feathers of a bird⟩

erec·tion \i-ˈrek-shən\ *n* **1** : the turgid state of a previously flaccid bodily part when it becomes dilated with blood **2** : CONSTRUCTION ⟨the ∼ of a building⟩

ere·long \er-ˈlón\ *adv* : before long

er·e·mite \ˈer-ə-ˌmīt\ *n* : HERMIT

er·go \ˈer-gō, ˈər-\ *adv* [L] : THEREFORE

er·go·nom·ics \ˌər-gə-ˈnä-miks\ *n sing or pl* : an applied science concerned with designing and arranging things people use in order to improve efficiency and safety — **er·go·nom·ic** \-mik\ *adj*

er·got \ˈər-gət, -ˌgät\ *n* **1** : a disease of rye and other cereals caused by a fungus; *also* : this fungus **2** : a medicinal compound or preparation derived from an ergot fungus

er·mine \ˈər-mən\ *n, pl* **ermines 1** : any of several weasels with winter fur mostly white; *also* : this white fur **2** : a rank or office whose official robe is ornamented with ermine

erode \i-ˈrōd\ vb **erod·ed; erod·ing** : to diminish or destroy by degrees; *esp* : to gradually eat into or wear away ⟨soil *eroded* by wind and water⟩ — **erod·ible** *also* **erod·able** \-ˈrō-də-bəl\ *adj*

erog·e·nous \i-ˈrä-jə-nəs\ *adj* **1** : sexually sensitive ⟨∼ zones⟩ **2** : of, relating to, or arousing sexual feelings

ero·sion \i-ˈrō-zhən\ *n* : the process or state of being eroded — **ero·sion·al** \-ˈrō-zhə-nəl\ *adj* — **ero·sion·al·ly** *adv*

ero·sive \i-ˈrō-siv\ *adj* : tending to erode — **ero·sive·ness** *n*

erot·ic \i-ˈrä-tik\ *adj* : relating to or dealing with sexual love : AMATORY ⟨∼ art⟩ — **erot·i·cal·ly** \-ti-k(ə-)lē\ *adv* — **erot·i·cism** \-tə-ˌsi-zəm\ *n*

err \ˈer, ˈər\ *vb* : to be or do wrong

er·rand \ˈer-ənd\ *n* : a short trip taken to do something; *also* : the object or purpose of such a trip

er·rant \ˈer-ənt\ *adj* **1** : WANDERING ⟨an ∼ knight⟩ **2** : straying outside proper bounds ⟨an ∼ throw⟩ **3** : behaving wrongly ⟨an ∼ child⟩

er·ra·ta \e-ˈrä-tə\ *n* : a list of corrigenda

er·rat·ic \i-ˈra-tik\ *adj* **1** : having no fixed course **2** : INCONSISTENT ⟨∼ dieting⟩; *also* : ECCENTRIC ⟨∼ behavior⟩ — **er·rat·i·cal·ly** \-ti-k(ə-)lē\ *adv*

er·ra·tum \e-ˈrä-təm\ *n, pl* **-ta** \-tə\ : CORRIGENDUM

er·ro·ne·ous \i-ˈrō-nē-əs, e-ˈrō-\ *adj* : INCORRECT — **er·ro·ne·ous·ly** *adv*

er·ror \ˈer-ər\ *n* **1** : a usu. ignorant or unintentional deviating from accuracy or truth ⟨made an ∼ in adding⟩ **2** : a defensive misplay in baseball **3** : the state of one that errs ⟨to be in ∼⟩ **4** : a product of mistake ⟨a typographical ∼⟩ — **er·ror·less** *adj*

er·satz \ˈer-ˌzäts\ *adj* [G *ersatz-*, fr. *Ersatz*, n., substitute] : being usu. an artificial and inferior substitute ⟨∼ diamonds⟩

erst \ˈərst\ *adv, archaic* : ERSTWHILE

¹erst·while \-ˌhwī(-ə)l\ *adv* : in the past : FORMERLY

²erstwhile *adj* : FORMER, PREVIOUS ⟨∼ friends⟩

er·u·di·tion \ˌer-ə-ˈdi-shən, ˌer-yə-\ *n* : SCHOLARSHIP, LEARNING — **er·u·dite** \ˈer-ə-ˌdīt, ˈer-yə-\ *adj*

erupt \i-ˈrəpt\ *vb* **1** : to burst forth or cause to burst forth : EXPLODE **2** : to break through a surface ⟨teeth ∼*ing* through the gum⟩ **3** : to break out with or as if with a skin rash — **erup·tion** \-ˈrəp-shən\ *n* — **erup·tive** \-tiv\ *adj*

-ery *n suffix* **1** : qualities collectively : character ⟨-NESS ⟨snobb*ery*⟩ **2** : art : practice ⟨cook*ery*⟩ **3** : place of doing, keeping, producing, or selling (the thing specified) ⟨fish*ery*⟩ ⟨bak*ery*⟩ **4** : collection : aggregate ⟨fin*ery*⟩ **5** : state or condition ⟨slav*ery*⟩

ery·sip·e·las \ˌer-ə-ˈsi-pə-ləs, ˌir-\ *n* : an acute bacterial disease marked by fever and severe skin inflammation

er·y·the·ma \ˌer-ə-ˈthē-mə\ *n* : abnormal redness of the skin due to capillary congestion (as in inflammation)

eryth·ro·cyte \i-ˈri-thrə-ˌsīt\ *n* : RED BLOOD CELL

Es *symbol* einsteinium

¹-es \əz, iz *after* s, z, sh, ch; z *after* v or a vowel\ *n pl suffix* — used to form the plural of most nouns that end in s ⟨glass*es*⟩, z ⟨fuzz*es*⟩, sh ⟨bush*es*⟩, ch ⟨peach*es*⟩, or a final y that changes to i ⟨lad*ies*⟩ and of some nouns ending in f that changes to v ⟨loav*es*⟩

²-es *vb suffix* — used to form the third person singular present of most verbs that end in s ⟨bless*es*⟩, z ⟨fizz*es*⟩, sh ⟨hush*es*⟩, ch ⟨catch*es*⟩, or a final y that changes to i ⟨defi*es*⟩

es·ca·late \ˈes-kə-ˌlāt\ *vb* **-lat·ed; -lat·ing** : to increase in extent, volume, number, intensity, or scope ⟨the violence escalat*ed*⟩ — **es·ca·la·tion** \ˌes-kə-ˈlā-shən\ *n*

es·ca·la·tor \ˈes-kə-ˌlā-tər\ *n* : a moving set of stairs

escallop *var of* SCALLOP

es·ca·pade \ˈes-kə-ˌpād\ *n* [F, action of escaping] : a mischievous adventure

¹es·cape \is-ˈkāp\ *vb* **es·caped; es·cap·ing** [ME, fr. AF *escaper, eschaper*, fr. VL *excappare*, fr. L *ex-* out + LL *cappa* head covering, cloak] **1** : to get free or away **2** : to avoid a threatening evil **3** : AVOID 2 ⟨∼ injury⟩ **4** : ELUDE ⟨his name ∼*s* me⟩ **5** : to be produced or uttered involuntarily ⟨let a sob ∼ him⟩

²escape *n* **1** : flight from or avoidance of something unpleasant **2** : LEAKAGE **3** : a means of escape

³escape *adj* : providing a means or way of escape

es·cap·ee \is-ˌkā-ˈpē, ˌes-(ˌ)kā-\ *n* : one that has escaped esp. from prison

escape velocity *n* : the minimum velocity needed by a body (as a rocket) to escape from the gravitational field of a celestial body (as the earth)

es·cap·ism \is-ˈkā-ˌpi-zəm\ *n* : diversion of the mind to imaginative activity as an escape from routine — **es·cap·ist** \-pist\ *adj or n*

es·car·got \ˌes-ˌkär-ˈgō\ *n, pl* **-gots** \-ˈgō(z)\ : a snail prepared for use as food

es·ca·role \ˈes-kə-ˌrōl\ *n* : ENDIVE 1

es·carp·ment \is-ˈkärp-mənt\ *n* **1** : a steep slope in front of a fortification **2** : a long cliff

es·chew \is-ˈchü\ *vb* : SHUN, AVOID

¹es·cort \ˈes-ˌkort\ *n* : one (as a person or warship) accompanying another esp. as a protection or courtesy

²es·cort \is-ˈkort, es-\ *vb* : to accompany as an escort

es·crow \ˈes-ˌkrō\ *n* [AF *escrowe* scroll, strip of parchment] : something (as a deed or a sum of money) delivered by one person to another to be delivered to a third party only upon the fulfillment of a condition; *also* : a fund or deposit serving as an escrow

es·cu·do \is-ˈkü-dō\ *n, pl* **-dos** **1** : the former basic monetary unit of Portugal **2** — see MONEY table

es·cutch·eon \is-ˈkə-chən\ *n* : the usu.

shield-shaped surface on which a coat of arms is shown

Esd *abbr* Esdras

Es·dras \'ez-drəs\ *n* — see BIBLE table

ESE *abbr* east-southeast

Es·ki·mo \'es-kə-ˌmō\ *n* **1** : a member of a group of peoples of northern Canada, Greenland, Alaska, and eastern Siberia **2** : any of the languages of the Eskimo peoples

Eskimo dog *n* : a sled dog of American origin

ESL *abbr* English as a second language

esoph·a·gus \i-'sä-fə-gəs\ *n, pl* **-gi** \-ˌgī, -ˌjī\ : a muscular tube that leads from the cavity behind the mouth to the stomach — **esoph·a·geal** \-ˌsä-fə-'jē-əl\ *adj*

es·o·ter·ic \ˌe-sə-'ter-ik\ *adj* **1** : designed for or understood only by the specially initiated **2** : PRIVATE, SECRET

esp *abbr* especially

ESP \ˌē-(ˌ)es-'pē\ *n* : EXTRASENSORY PERCEPTION

es·pa·drille \'es-pə-ˌdril\ *n* [F] : a flat sandal usu. having a fabric upper and a flexible sole

es·pal·ier \is-'pal-yər, -ˌyā\ *n* : a plant (as a fruit tree) trained to grow flat against a support — **espalier** *vb*

es·pe·cial \is-'pe-shəl\ *adj* : SPECIAL, PARTICULAR — **es·pe·cial·ly** *adv*

Es·pe·ran·to \ˌes-pə-'ran-tō, -'rän-\ *n* : an artificial international language based esp. on words common to the chief European languages

es·pi·o·nage \'es-pē-ə-ˌnäzh, -nij\ *n* [F *espionnage*] : the practice of spying

es·pla·nade \'es-plə-ˌnäd\ *n* : a level open stretch or area; *esp* : one for walking or driving along a shore

es·pous·al \i-'spaů-zəl\ *n* **1** : BETROTHAL; *also* : WEDDING **2** : a taking up (as of a cause) as a supporter ⟨∼ of human rights⟩ — **es·pouse** \i-'spaůz\ *vb*

espres·so \e-'spre-sō\ *n, pl* **-sos** : coffee brewed by forcing steam or hot water through finely ground darkly roasted coffee beans

es·prit \i-'sprē\ *n* : sprightly wit

es·prit de corps \i-ˌsprē-də-'kȯr\ *n* [F] : the common spirit existing in the members of a group

es·py \i-'spī\ *vb* **es·pied; es·py·ing** : to catch sight of ♦ *Synonyms* BEHOLD, SEE, VIEW, DESCRY

Esq *or* **Esqr** *abbr* esquire

es·quire \'es-ˌkwī(-ə)r\ *n* [ME, fr. AF *esquier* squire, fr. LL *scutarius*, fr. L *scutum* shield] **1** : a man of the English gentry ranking next below a knight **2** : a candidate for knighthood serving as attendant to a knight **3** — used as a title of courtesy

-ess \əs, ˌes\ *n suffix* : female ⟨author*ess*⟩

¹es·say \e-'sā, 'e-ˌsā\ *vb* : ATTEMPT, TRY

²es·say *n* **1** \'e-ˌsā, e-'sā\ : ATTEMPT **2** \'e-ˌsā\ : a literary composition usu. dealing with a subject from a limited or personal point of view — **es·say·ist** \'e-ˌsā-ist\ *n*

es·sence \'e-s°ns\ *n* **1** : fundamental nature or quality **2** : a substance distilled or extracted from another substance (as a plant or drug) and having the special qualities of the original substance **3** : PERFUME **4** : the most significant element or aspect of something ⟨the ∼ of the issue⟩

¹es·sen·tial \i-'sen-chəl\ *adj* **1** : of, relating to, or constituting an essence ⟨voting is an ∼ right of citizenship⟩ ⟨∼ oils⟩ **2** : of the utmost importance : INDISPENSABLE ⟨water is ∼ for life⟩ **3** : being a substance that must be obtained from the diet because it is not sufficiently produced by the body ⟨∼ amino acids⟩ ♦ *Synonyms* IMPERATIVE, NECESSARY, NECESSITOUS — **es·sen·tial·ly** *adv*

²essential *n* : something essential

est *abbr* **1** established **2** estimate; estimated

EST *abbr* eastern standard time

¹-est \əst, ist\ *adj suffix or adv suffix* — used to form the superlative degree of adjectives and adverbs of one or two syllables ⟨fatt*est*⟩ ⟨lat*est*⟩ ⟨lucki*est*⟩ ⟨often-*est*⟩ and less often of longer ones

²-est \əst, ist\ *or* **-st** \st\ *vb suffix* — used to form the archaic second person singular of English verbs (with *thou*) ⟨did*st*⟩

es·tab·lish \i-'sta-blish\ *vb* **1** : to institute permanently ⟨∼ a law⟩ **2** : FOUND ⟨∼ a settlement⟩; *also* : EFFECT **3** : to make firm or stable **4** : to put on a firm basis : SET UP ⟨∼ a son in business⟩ **5** : to gain acceptance or recognition of ⟨the movie ∼ed her as a star⟩; *also* : PROVE ⟨∼ed his innocence⟩

es·tab·lish·ment \-mənt\ *n* **1** : something established **2** : a place of residence or business with its furnishings and staff **3** : an established ruling or controlling group ⟨the literary ∼⟩ **4** : the act or state of establishing or being established

es·tate \i-'stāt\ *n* **1** : STATE, CONDITION; *also* : social standing : STATUS **2** : a social or political class ⟨the three ∼s of nobility, clergy, and commons⟩ **3** : a person's possessions : FORTUNE **4** : a landed property

¹es·teem \i-'stēm\ *n* : high regard

²esteem *vb* **1** : REGARD ⟨was highly ∼ed⟩ **2** : to set a high value on ♦ *Synonyms* RESPECT, ADMIRE, REVERE

es·ter \'es-tər\ *n* : an often fragrant organic compound formed by the reaction of an acid and an alcohol

Esth *abbr* Esther

Es·ther \'es-tər\ *n* — see BIBLE table

esthete, esthetic, esthetically, esthetics *var of* AESTHETE, AESTHETIC, AESTHETICALLY, AESTHETICS

es·ti·ma·ble \'es-tə-mə-bəl\ *adj* : worthy of esteem ⟨an ∼ adversary⟩

¹es·ti·mate \'es-tə-ˌmāt\ *vb* **-mat·ed; -mat·ing** **1** : to give or form an approximation (as of value, size, or cost) **2** : JUDGE, CONCLUDE ♦ *Synonyms* EVALUATE, VALUE, RATE, APPRAISE, ASSAY, ASSESS — **es·ti·ma·tor** \-ˌmā-tər\ *n*

²es·ti·mate \'es-tə-mət\ *n* **1** : OPINION, JUDGMENT **2** : a rough or approximate calculation **3** : a statement of the cost of work to be done

es·ti·ma·tion \ˌes-tə-ˈmā-shən\ n   1 : JUDGMENT, OPINION 2 : ESTIMATE 3 : ESTEEM, HONOR

es·ti·vate \ˈes-tə-ˌvāt\ vb **-vat·ed; -vat·ing** : to pass the summer in an inactive or resting state ⟨creatures *estivating* in the cool mud⟩ — **es·ti·va·tion** \ˌes-tə-ˈvā-shən\ n

es·trange \i-ˈstrānj\ vb **es·tranged; es·trang·ing** : to alienate the affections or confidence of — **es·trange·ment** n

es·tro·gen \ˈes-trə-jən\ n : a steroid (as a sex hormone) that tends to cause estrus and the development of female secondary sex characteristics — **es·tro·gen·ic** \ˌes-trə-ˈje-nik\ adj

estrous cycle n : the cycle of changes in the endocrine and reproductive systems of a female mammal from the beginning of one period of estrus to the beginning of the next

es·trus \ˈes-trəs\ n : a periodic state of sexual excitability during which the female of most mammals is willing to mate with the male and is capable of becoming pregnant : HEAT — **es·trous** \-trəs\ adj

es·tu·ary \ˈes-chə-ˌwer-ē\ n, pl **-ar·ies** : an arm of the sea at the mouth of a river — **es·tu·a·rine** \-wə-ˌrīn, -ˌrēn, -rin\ adj

ET abbr eastern time

eta \ˈā-tə\ n : the 7th letter of the Greek alphabet — H or η

ETA abbr estimated time of arrival

et al \et-ˈal\ abbr [L et alii (masc.), et aliae (fem.), or et alia (neut.)] and others

etc abbr et cetera

et cet·era \et-ˈse-tə-rə, -ˈse-trə\ [L] and others esp. of the same kind

etch \ˈech\ vb [D etsen, fr. G ätzen to etch, corrode, fr. OHG azzen to feed] 1 : to produce (as a design) on a hard material by corroding its surface (as by acid) 2 : to delineate clearly — **etch·er** n

etch·ing n 1 : the action, process, or art of etching 2 : a design produced on or print made from an etched plate

ETD abbr estimated time of departure

eter·nal \i-ˈtər-nᵊl\ adj : EVERLASTING, PERPETUAL — **eter·nal·ly** adv

eter·ni·ty \i-ˈtər-nə-tē\ n, pl **-ties** 1 : infinite duration 2 : IMMORTALITY

¹**-eth** \əth, ith\ or **-th** \th\ vb suffix — used to form the archaic third person singular present of verbs ⟨doth⟩

²**-eth** — see ²**-TH**

eth·ane \ˈe-ˌthān\ n : a colorless odorless gaseous hydrocarbon found in natural gas and used esp. as a fuel

eth·a·nol \ˈe-thə-ˌnȯl\ n : ALCOHOL 1

ether \ˈē-thər\ n 1 : the upper regions of space; also : the gaseous element formerly held to fill these regions 2 : a light flammable liquid used as an anesthetic and solvent

ethe·re·al \i-ˈthir-ē-əl\ adj 1 : CELESTIAL, HEAVENLY 2 : exceptionally delicate : AIRY, DAINTY ⟨∼ flaky pastry⟩ — **ethe·re·al·ly** adv — **ethe·re·al·ness** n

Ether·net \ˈē-thər-ˌnet\ n : a computer network architecture for local area networks

eth·i·cal \ˈe-thi-kəl\ adj 1 : of or relating

to ethics 2 : conforming to accepted and esp. professional standards of conduct

♦ **Synonyms** VIRTUOUS, MORAL, PRINCIPLED — **eth·i·cal·ly** adv

eth·ics \ˈe-thiks\ n sing or pl 1 : a discipline dealing with good and evil and with moral duty 2 : moral principles or practice

¹**eth·nic** \ˈeth-nik\ adj [ME, heathen, fr. LL ethnicus, fr. Gk ethnikos national, gentile, fr. ethnos nation, people] : of or relating to races or large groups of people classed according to common traits and customs — **eth·ni·cal·ly** adv

²**ethnic** n : a member of a minority ethnic group who retains its customs, language, or social views

eth·nol·o·gy \eth-ˈnä-lə-jē\ n : a science dealing with the races of human beings, their origin, distribution, characteristics, and relations — **eth·no·log·i·cal** \ˌeth-nə-ˈlä-ji-kəl\ adj — **eth·nol·o·gist** \eth-ˈnä-lə-jist\ n

ethol·o·gy \ē-ˈthä-lə-jē\ n : the scientific and objective study of animal behavior — **etho·log·i·cal** \ˌē-thə-ˈlä-ji-kəl, ˌe-\ adj — **ethol·o·gist** \ē-ˈthä-lə-jist\ n

ethos \ˈē-ˌthäs\ n : the distinguishing character, sentiment, moral nature, or guiding beliefs of a person, group, or institution

ethyl alcohol n : ALCOHOL 1

eth·yl·ene \ˈe-thə-ˌlēn\ n : a colorless flammable gas found in coal gas or obtained from petroleum

eti·ol·o·gy \ˌē-tē-ˈä-lə-jē\ n : the causes of a disease or abnormal condition; also : a branch of medicine concerned with the causes and origins of diseases — **eti·o·log·ic** \ˌē-tē-ə-ˈlä-jik\ or **eti·o·log·i·cal** \-ji-kəl\ adj

et·i·quette \ˈe-ti-kət, -ˌket\ n [F étiquette, lit., label, list] : the forms prescribed by custom or authority to be observed in social, official, or professional life

♦ **Synonyms** PROPRIETY, DECORUM, DECENCY, DIGNITY

Etrus·can \i-ˈtrəs-kən\ n 1 : the language of the Etruscans 2 : an inhabitant of ancient Etruria — **Etruscan** adj

et seq abbr [L et sequens] and the following one; [L et sequentes (masc. & fem. pl.) or et sequentia (neut. pl.)] and the following ones

-ette \ˈet, ˌet, ət, it\ n suffix 1 : little one ⟨dinette⟩ 2 : female ⟨usherette⟩

étude \ˈā-ˌtüd, -ˌtyüd\ n [F, lit., study] : a musical composition for practice to develop technical skill

et·y·mol·o·gy \ˌe-tə-ˈmä-lə-jē\ n, pl **-gies** 1 : the history of a linguistic form (as a word) shown by tracing its development and relationships 2 : a branch of linguistics dealing with etymologies — **et·y·mo·log·i·cal** \-mə-ˈlä-ji-kəl\ adj — **et·y·mol·o·gist** \-ˈmä-lə-jist\ n

Eu symbol europium

EU abbr European Union

eu·ca·lyp·tus \ˌyü-kə-ˈlip-təs\ n, pl **-ti** \-ˌtī\ or **-tus·es** : any of a genus of mostly Australian evergreen trees widely grown for shade or their wood, oils, resins, and gums

Eu·cha·rist \'yü-kə-rəst\ n : COMMUNION 2 — **eu·cha·ris·tic** \,yü-kə-'ris-tik\ adj, often cap

¹**eu·chre** \'yü-kər\ n : a card game in which the side naming the trump must take three of five tricks to win

²**euchre** vb **eu·chred; eu·chring** : CHEAT, TRICK

eu·clid·e·an also **eu·clid·i·an** \yü-'kli-dē-ən\ adj, often cap : of or relating to the geometry of Euclid or a geometry based on similar axioms

eu·gen·ics \yü-'je-niks\ n : a science dealing with the improvement (as by selective breeding) of hereditary qualities esp. of human beings — **eu·gen·ic** \-nik\ adj

eu·lo·gy \'yü-lə-jē\ n, pl **-gies** 1 : a speech in praise of some person or thing esp. in honor of a deceased person 2 : high praise — **eu·lo·gis·tic** \,yü-lə-'jis-tik\ adj — **eu·lo·gize** \'yü-lə-,jīz\ vb

eu·nuch \'yü-nək\ n : a castrated man

eu·phe·mism \'yü-fə-,mi-zəm\ n [Gk euphēmismos, fr. euphēmos auspicious, sounding good, fr. eu- good + phēmē speech] : the substitution of a mild or pleasant expression for one offensive or unpleasant; also : the expression substituted — **eu·phe·mis·tic** \,yü-fə-'mis-tik\ adj — **eu·phe·mis·ti·cal·ly** \-tī-k(ə-)lē\ adv

eu·pho·ni·ous \yü-'fō-nē-əs\ adj : pleasing to the ear — **eu·pho·ni·ous·ly** adv

eu·pho·ny \'yü-fə-nē\ n, pl **-nies** : the effect produced by words so combined as to please the ear

eu·pho·ria \yü-'fór-ē-ə\ n : a marked feeling of well-being or elation — **eu·phor·ic** \-'fór-ik\ adj

Eur abbr Europe; European

Eur·asian \yù-'rā-zhən, -shən\ adj 1 : of mixed European and Asian origin 2 : of or relating to Europe and Asia — **Eurasian** n

eu·re·ka \yù-'rē-kə\ interj [Gk heurēka I have found, fr. heuriskein to find; fr. the exclamation attributed to Archimedes on discovering a method for determining the purity of gold] — used to express triumph on a discovery

eu·ro \'yür-ō\ n, pl **euros** : the common basic monetary unit of most countries of the European Union — see MONEY table

Eu·ro–Amer·i·can \,yür-ō-ə-'mer-ə-kən\ n 1 : a person of mixed European and American ancestry 2 : CAUCASIAN

Eu·ro·bond \'yür-ō-,bänd\ n : a bond of a U.S. corporation that is sold outside the U.S. but that is valued and paid for in dollars and yields interest in dollars

Eu·ro·cur·ren·cy \,yür-ō-'kər-ən-sē\ n : moneys (as of the U.S. and Japan) held outside their countries of origin and used in the money markets of Europe

Eu·ro·dol·lar \'yür-ō-,dä-lər\ n : a U.S. dollar held as Eurocurrency

Eu·ro·pe·an \,yür-ə-'pē-ən\ n 1 : a native or inhabitant of Europe 2 : a person of

European descent — **European** adj —
Eu·ro·pe·an·ize \-ə-,nīz\ vb

European–American n : EURO-AMERI-CAN

Eu·ro·pe·an·ism \yür-,ō-'pē-ə-ni-zəm\ n 1 : allegiance to the traditions, interests, or ideals of Europeans 2 : advocacy of political and economic integration of Europe — **eu·ro·pe·an·ist** \-nist\ n

European plan n : a hotel plan whereby the daily rates cover only the cost of the room

eu·ro·pi·um \yù-'rō-pē-əm\ n : a rare metallic chemical element

eu·sta·chian tube \yü-'stā-shən-\ n, often cap E : a tube connecting the inner cavity of the ear with the throat and equalizing air pressure on both sides of the eardrum

eu·tha·na·sia \,yü-thə-'nā-zhə\ n [Gk, easy death, fr. eu- good + thanatos death] : the act or practice of killing or permitting the death of hopelessly sick or injured persons or animals with as little pain as possible for reasons of mercy

EVA abbr extravehicular activity

evac·u·ate \i-'va-kyə-,wāt\ vb **-at·ed; -at·ing** 1 : EMPTY 2 : to discharge wastes from the body 3 : to remove or withdraw from : VACATE — **evac·u·a·tion** \-,va-kyə-'wā-shən\ n

evac·u·ee \i-,va-kyə-'wē\ n : a person removed from a dangerous place

evade \i-'vād\ vb **evad·ed; evad·ing** : to manage to avoid esp. by dexterity or slyness : ELUDE, ESCAPE ⟨evaded capture⟩

eval·u·ate \i-'val-yü-,wāt\ vb **-at·ed; -at·ing** : APPRAISE, VALUE ⟨~ the candidates⟩ — **eval·u·a·tion** \-,val-yü-'wā-shən\ n

ev·a·nes·cent \,e-və-'ne-sᵊnt\ adj : tending to vanish like vapor ⟨~ pleasures⟩
♦ **Synonyms** PASSING, TRANSIENT, TRANSITORY, MOMENTARY — **ev·a·nes·cence** \-sᵊns\ n

evan·gel·i·cal \,ē-,van-'je-li-kəl, ,e-vən-\ adj [LL evangelium gospel, fr. Gk evangelion, fr. euangelos bringing good news, fr. eu- good + angelos messenger] 1 : of or relating to the Christian gospel esp. as presented in the four Gospels 2 : of or relating to certain Protestant churches emphasizing the authority of Scripture and the importance of preaching as contrasted with ritual 3 : ZEALOUS ⟨~ fervor⟩ — **Evangelical** n — **Evan·gel·i·cal·ism** \-kə-,li-zəm\ n — **Evan·gel·i·cal·ly** adv

evan·ge·lism \i-'van-jə-,li-zəm\ n 1 : the winning or revival of personal commitments to Christ 2 : militant or crusading zeal — **evan·ge·lis·tic** \-,van-jə-'lis-tik\ adj — **evan·ge·lis·ti·cal·ly** adv

evan·ge·list \i-'van-jə-list\ n 1 often cap : the writer of any of the four Gospels 2 : a person who evangelizes; esp : a Protestant minister or layman who preaches at special services

evan·ge·lize \i-'van-jə-,līz\ vb **-lized; -liz·ing** 1 : to preach the gospel 2 : to convert to Christianity

evap abbr evaporate

evap·o·rate \i-'va-pə-,rāt\ vb **-rat·ed;**

-rat·ing **1** : to pass off or cause to pass off in vapor **2** : to disappear quickly **3** : to drive out the moisture from (as by heat) — **evap·o·ra·tion** \-ˌva-pə-ˈrā-shən\ n — **evap·o·ra·tor** \-ˌrā-tər\ n

evap·o·rite \i-ˈva-pə-ˌrīt\ n : a sedimentary rock that originates by the evaporation of seawater in an enclosed basin

eva·sion \i-ˈvā-zhən\ n **1** : a means of evading **2** : an act or instance of evading ⟨arrested for tax ∼⟩ — **eva·sive** \i-ˈvā-siv\ adj — **eva·sive·ness** n

eve \ˈēv\ n **1** : EVENING **2** : the period just before some important event

¹**even** \ˈē-vən\ adj **1** : LEVEL, FLAT ⟨∼ ground⟩ **2** : REGULAR, SMOOTH **3** : EQUAL, FAIR ⟨an ∼ exchange⟩ **4** : BALANCED; also : fully revenged **5** : divisible by two **6** : EXACT ⟨an ∼ dollar⟩ — **even·ly** adv — **even·ness** n

²**even** adv **1** : EXACTLY, PRECISELY **2** : FULLY, QUITE **3** : at the very time **4** — used as an intensive to stress identity ⟨∼ I know that⟩ **5** — used as an intensive to emphasize something extreme or highly unlikely ⟨so simple ∼ a child can do it⟩ **6** — used as an intensive to stress the comparative degree ⟨did ∼ better⟩ **7** — used as an intensive to indicate a small or minimum degree ⟨didn't ∼ try⟩

³**even** vb : to make or become even

even·hand·ed \ˌē-vən-ˈhan-dəd\ adj : FAIR, IMPARTIAL ⟨an ∼ assessment⟩ — **even·hand·ed·ly** adv

eve·ning \ˈēv-niŋ\ n **1** : the end of the day and early part of the night **2** chiefly Southern & Midland : AFTERNOON

evening primrose n : a coarse biennial herb with yellow flowers that open in the evening

evening star n : a bright planet (as Venus) seen esp. in the western sky at or after sunset

even·song \ˈē-vən-ˌsȯŋ\ n, often cap **1** : VESPERS **2** : evening prayer esp. when sung

event \i-ˈvent\ n [MF or L; MF, fr. L eventus, fr. evenire to happen, fr. venire to come] **1** : OCCURRENCE **2** : a noteworthy happening **3** : CONTINGENCY ⟨in the ∼ of rain⟩ **4** : a contest in a program of sports — **event·ful** adj

even·tide \ˈē-vən-ˌtīd\ n : EVENING

even·tu·al \i-ˈven-chü-wəl\ adj : coming at some later time : ULTIMATE — **even·tu·al·ly** adv

even·tu·al·i·ty \i-ˌven-chü-ˈwa-lə-tē\ n, pl **-ties** : a possible event or outcome

even·tu·ate \i-ˈven-chü-ˌwāt\ vb **-at·ed; -at·ing** : to result finally

ev·er \ˈe-vər\ adv **1** : ALWAYS ⟨∼ faithful⟩ **2** : at any time **3** : in any way : AT ALL ⟨how can I ∼ thank you⟩

ev·er·glade \ˈe-vər-ˌglād\ n : a low-lying tract of swampy or marshy land

ev·er·green \-ˌgrēn\ adj : having foliage that remains green ⟨most coniferous trees are ∼⟩ — **evergreen** n

¹**ev·er·last·ing** \ˌe-vər-ˈlas-tiŋ\ adj **1** : enduring forever : ETERNAL **2** : having or being flowers or foliage that retain form

or color for a long time when dried — **ev·er·last·ing·ly** adv

²**everlasting** n **1** : ETERNITY ⟨from ∼⟩ **2** : a plant with everlasting flowers; also : its flower

ev·er·more \ˌe-vər-ˈmȯr\ adv : FOREVER

ev·ery \ˈev-rē\ adj [ME everich, every, fr. OE ǣfre ǣlc, fr. ǣfre ever + ǣlc each] **1** : being each one of a group **2** : all possible ⟨given ∼ chance⟩; also : COMPLETE ⟨have ∼ confidence⟩

ev·ery·body \ˈev-ri-ˌbä-dē, -bə-\ pron : every person

ev·ery·day \ˈev-rē-ˌdā\ adj : encountered or used routinely : ORDINARY

ev·ery·one \-(ˌ)wən\ pron : EVERYBODY

ev·ery·thing \ˈev-rē-ˌthiŋ\ pron **1** : all that exists **2** : all that is relevant

ev·ery·where \ˈev-rē-ˌhwer\ adv : in every place or part

evg abbr evening

evict \i-ˈvikt\ vb **1** : to put (a person) out from a property by legal process **2** : EXPEL ♦ **Synonyms** EJECT, OUST, DISMISS — **evic·tion** \-ˈvik-shən\ n

¹**ev·i·dence** \ˈe-və-dəns\ n **1** : an outward sign **2** : PROOF, TESTIMONY; esp : matter submitted in court to determine the truth of alleged facts

²**evidence** vb : PROVE, EVINCE

ev·i·dent \-dənt\ adj : clear to the vision and understanding ♦ **Synonyms** MANIFEST, DISTINCT, OBVIOUS, APPARENT, PLAIN

ev·i·dent·ly \ˈe-və-dənt-lē, ˌe-və-ˈdent-\ adv **1** : in an evident manner **2** : on the basis of available evidence

¹**evil** \ˈē-vəl\ adj **evil·er** or **evil·ler; evil·est** or **evil·lest 1** : WICKED **2** : causing or threatening distress or harm : PERNICIOUS — **evil·ly** adv

²**evil** n **1** : the fact of suffering, misfortune, and wrongdoing **2** : a source of sorrow, distress, or calamity

evil·do·er \ˌē-vəl-ˈdü-ər\ n : one who does evil

evil–mind·ed \-ˈmīn-dəd\ adj : having an evil disposition or evil thoughts — **evil–mind·ed·ly** adv

evince \i-ˈvins\ vb **evinced; evinc·ing** : SHOW, REVEAL ⟨evinced an interest in art⟩

evis·cer·ate \i-ˈvi-sə-ˌrāt\ vb **-at·ed; -at·ing 1** : to remove the entrails of **2** : to deprive of vital content or force — **evis·cer·a·tion** \-ˌvi-sə-ˈrā-shən\ n

evoke \i-ˈvōk\ vb **evoked; evok·ing** : to call forth or up — **evo·ca·tion** \ˌē-vō-ˈkā-shən, ˌe-və-\ n — **evoc·a·tive** \i-ˈvä-kə-tiv\ adj

evo·lu·tion \ˌe-və-ˈlü-shən\ n **1** : one of a set of prescribed movements (as in a dance) **2** : a process of change in a particular direction **3** : a theory that the various kinds of plants and animals are descended from other kinds that lived in earlier times and that the differences are due to inherited changes that occurred over many generations — **evo·lu·tion·ary** \-shə-ˌner-ē\ adj — **evo·lu·tion·ist** \-shə-nist\ n

evolve \i-ˈvälv\ vb **evolved; evolv·ing** [L

evolvere to unroll] : to develop or change
by or as if by evolution

EW *abbr* enlisted woman

e-waste \'ē-,wāst\ *n* : waste consisting of
discarded electronic products

ewe \'yü\ *n* : a female sheep

ew·er \'yü-ər\ *n* : a water pitcher

¹**ex** \'eks\ *prep* [L] : out of : FROM

²**ex** *n* : a former spouse

³**ex** *abbr* **1** example **2** express **3** extra

Ex *abbr* Exodus

ex- \ *also occurs in this prefix where only
i is shown below (as in* "express") *and ks
sometimes occurs where only gz is shown
(as in* "exact") *\ prefix* **1** : out of : outside
2 : former ⟨*ex*-president⟩

ex·ac·er·bate \ig-'za-sər-,bāt\ *vb* **-bat·ed;
-bat·ing** : to make more violent, bitter,
or severe ⟨comments that ∼ the dispute⟩
— **ex·ac·er·ba·tion** \-,za-sər-'bā-shən\ *n*

¹**ex·act** \ig-'zakt\ *vb* **1** : to compel to furnish **2** : to call for as suitable or necessary — **ex·ac·tion** \-'zak-shən\ *n*

²**exact** *adj* : precisely accurate or correct
— **ex·act·ly** *adv* — **ex·act·ness** *n*

ex·act·ing \ig-'zak-tiŋ\ *adj* **1** : greatly demanding ⟨an ∼ taskmaster⟩ **2** : requir-
ing close attention and precision

ex·ac·ti·tude \ig-'zak-tə-,tüd, -,tyüd\ *n*
: the quality or state of being exact

ex·ag·ger·ate \ig-'za-jə-,rāt\ *vb* **-at·ed;
-at·ing** [L *exaggeratus*, pp. of *exaggerare*,
lit., to heap up, fr. *agger* heap] : to enlarge
(as a statement) beyond normal : OVER-
STATE — **ex·ag·ger·at·ed·ly** *adv* — **ex·
ag·ger·a·tion** \-,za-jə-'rā-shən\ *n* — **ex·
ag·ger·a·tor** \-'za-jə-,rā-tər\ *n*

ex·alt \ig-'zólt\ *vb* **1** : to raise up esp. in
rank, power, or dignity **2** : GLORIFY ⟨the
poem ∼s her beauty⟩ — **ex·al·ta·tion**
\,eg-,zól-'tā-shən, ,ek-,sól-\ *n*

ex·am \ig-'zam\ *n* : EXAMINATION

ex·am·ine \ig-'za-mən\ *vb* **ex·am·ined;
ex·am·in·ing** **1** : to inspect closely
: QUESTION; *esp* : to test by questioning
♦ Synonyms INTERROGATE, QUERY,
QUIZ, CATECHIZE — **ex·am·i·na·tion**
\-,za-mə-'nā-shən\ *n*

ex·am·ple \ig-'zam-pəl\ *n* **1** : something
forming a model to be followed or avoided **2** : a representative sample **3** : a problem to be solved in order to show the
application of some rule

ex·as·per·ate \ig-'zas-pə-,rāt\ *vb* **-at·ed;
-at·ing** : VEX, IRRITATE — **ex·as·per·a·
tion** \ig-,zas-pə-'rā-shən\ *n*

exc *abbr* **1** excellent **2** except

ex·ca·vate \'ek-skə-,vāt\ *vb* **-vat·ed; -vat·
ing** **1** : to hollow out; *also* : to form by
hollowing out **2** : to dig out and remove
(as earth) **3** : to reveal to view by digging
away a covering — **ex·ca·va·tion** \,ek-
skə-'vā-shən\ *n* — **ex·ca·va·tor** \'ek-skə-
,vā-tər\ *n*

ex·ceed \ik-'sēd\ *vb* **1** : to go or be beyond the limit of **2** : SURPASS ⟨∼ed our
expectations⟩ — **ex·ceed·ance** \-'sē-
dᵊns\ *n*

ex·ceed·ing·ly \-'sē-diŋ-lē\ *also* **ex·ceed·
ing** *adv* : EXTREMELY, VERY

ex·cel \ik-'sel\ *vb* **ex·celled; ex·cel·ling**
: SURPASS, OUTDO

ex·cel·lence \'ek-sə-ləns\ *n* **1** : the quality of being excellent **2** : an excellent or
valuable quality : VIRTUE **3** : EXCEL-
LENCY 2

ex·cel·len·cy \-lən-sē\ *n, pl* **-cies** **1** : EX-
CELLENCE **2** — used as a title of honor

ex·cel·lent \-lənt\ *adj* : very good of its
kind : FIRST-CLASS — **ex·cel·lent·ly** *adv*

ex·cel·si·or \ik-'sel-sē-ər\ *n* : fine curled
wood shavings used esp. for packing fragile items

¹**ex·cept** \ik-'sept\ *also* **ex·cept·ing** *prep*
: with the exclusion or exception of ⟨dai-
ly ∼ Sundays⟩

²**except** *vb* **1** : to take or leave out ⟨chil-
dren were ∼ed from the study⟩ **2** : OB-
JECT

³**except** *also* **excepting** *conj* **1** : UNLESS
⟨∼ you repent⟩ **2** : ONLY ⟨I'd go, ∼ it's
too far⟩

ex·cep·tion \ik-'sep-shən\ *n* **1** : the act of
excepting **2** : something excepted ⟨an ∼
to the rule⟩ **3** : OBJECTION

ex·cep·tion·able \ik-'sep-shə-nə-bəl\ *adj*
: OBJECTIONABLE

ex·cep·tion·al \ik-'sep-shə-nəl\ *adj* **1**
: UNUSUAL ⟨an ∼ number of rainy days⟩
2 : SUPERIOR ⟨∼ skill⟩ — **ex·cep·tion·
al·ly** *adv*

ex·cerpt \'ek-,sərpt, 'eg-,zərpt\ *n* : a passage selected or copied : EXTRACT — **ex·
cerpt** \ek-'sərpt, eg-'zərpt; 'ek-,sərpt, 'eg-
,zərpt\ *vb*

ex·cess \ik-'ses, 'ek-,ses\ *n* **1** : SUPER-
FLUITY, SURPLUS **2** : the amount by
which one quantity exceeds another **3**
: INTEMPERANCE; *also* : an instance of
intemperance ⟨the dictator's ∼es⟩ —
excess *adj* — **ex·ces·sive** \ik-'se-siv\
adj — **ex·ces·sive·ly** *adv*

exch *abbr* exchange; exchanged

¹**ex·change** \iks-'chānj\ *n* **1** : the giving or
taking of one thing in return for another
: TRADE **2** : a substituting of one thing
for another **3** : interchange of valuables
and esp. of bills of exchange or money of
different countries **4** : a place where
things and services are exchanged; *also* : a
marketplace for securities **5** : a central
office in which telephone lines are connected for communication

²**exchange** *vb* **ex·changed; ex·chang·
ing** : to transfer in return for some equivalent : BARTER, SWAP — **ex·change·
able** \iks-'chān-jə-bəl\ *adj*

ex·che·quer \'eks-,che-kər\ *n* [ME *es-
cheker*, fr. AF, chessboard, counting table, office charged with revenue collection, fr. *eschec* check (in chess), chess]
: TREASURY; *esp* : a national treasury

ex·cise \'ek-,sīz\ *n* : a tax on the manufacture, sale, or consumption of a commodity

ex·ci·sion \ik-'si-zhən\ *n* : removal by or
as if by cutting out esp. by surgical means
— **ex·cise** \ik-'sīz\ *vb*

ex·cit·able \ik-'sī-tə-bəl\ *adj* : easily excited — **ex·cit·abil·i·ty** \-,sī-tə-'bi-lə-tē\ *n*

ex·cite \ik-'sīt\ *vb* **ex·cit·ed; ex·cit·ing** **1**
: to stir up the emotions of : ROUSE **2** : to
increase the activity of : STIMULATE
♦ Synonyms PROVOKE, PIQUE, QUICK-

EN — **ex·ci·ta·tion** \ˌek-ˌsī-'tā-shən, ˌek-sə-\ n — **ex·cit·ed·ly** adv — **ex·cit·ing·ly** adv

ex·cite·ment \ik-'sīt-mənt\ n : AGITATION, STIR

ex·claim \iks-'klām\ vb : to cry out, speak, or utter sharply or vehemently — **ex·cla·ma·tion** \ˌeks-klə-'mā-shən\ n — **ex·clam·a·to·ry** \iks-'kla-mə-ˌtȯr-ē\ adj

exclamation point n : a punctuation mark ! used esp. after an interjection or exclamation

ex·clude \iks-'klüd\ vb **ex·clud·ed; ex·clud·ing** 1 : to prevent from using or participating : BAR 2 : to put out : EXPEL — **ex·clu·sion** \-'klü-zhən\ n — **ex·clu·sion·ary** \-zhə-ˌner-ē\ adj

ex·clu·sive \iks-'klü-siv\ adj 1 : reserved for particular persons 2 : snobbishly aloof; also : STYLISH 3 : SOLE ⟨~ rights⟩; also : UNDIVIDED ⟨my ~ attention⟩ ♦ **Synonyms** CHIC, MODISH, SMART, SWANK, FASHIONABLE — **exclusive** n — **ex·clu·sive·ly** adv — **ex·clu·sive·ness** n — **ex·clu·siv·i·ty** \ˌeks-ˌklü-si-və-tē, iks-, -zi-\ n

exclusive of prep : not taking into account

ex·cog·i·tate \ek-'skä-jə-ˌtāt\ vb : to think out : DEVISE

ex·com·mu·ni·cate \ˌek-skə-'myü-nə-ˌkāt\ vb : to cut off officially from the rites of the church — **ex·com·mu·ni·ca·tion** \-ˌmyü-nə-'kā-shən\ n

ex·co·ri·ate \ek-'skȯr-ē-ˌāt\ vb **-at·ed; -at·ing** : to criticize severely — **ex·co·ri·a·tion** \(ˌ)ek-ˌskȯr-ē-'ā-shən\ n

ex·cre·ment \'ek-skrə-mənt\ n : waste discharged from the body; esp : FECES — **ex·cre·men·tal** \ˌek-skrə-'men-tᵊl\ adj

ex·cres·cence \ik-'skre-sᵊns\ n : OUTGROWTH; esp : an abnormal outgrowth (as a wart)

ex·cre·ta \ik-'skrē-tə\ n pl : waste matter (as feces) separated or eliminated from the body

ex·crete \ik-'skrēt\ vb **ex·cret·ed; ex·cret·ing** : to separate and eliminate wastes from the body esp. in urine or sweat — **ex·cre·tion** \-'skrē-shən\ n — **ex·cre·to·ry** \'ek-skrə-ˌtȯr-ē\ adj

ex·cru·ci·at·ing \ik-'skrü-shē-ˌā-tin\ adj [L excruciare to torture, fr. cruciare to crucify, fr. crux cross] : intensely painful or distressing ♦ **Synonyms** AGONIZING, HARROWING, TORTUROUS — **ex·cru·ci·at·ing·ly** adv

ex·cul·pate \'ek-(ˌ)skəl-ˌpāt\ vb **-pat·ed; -pat·ing** : to clear from alleged fault or guilt ♦ **Synonyms** ABSOLVE, EXONERATE, ACQUIT, VINDICATE, CLEAR

ex·cur·sion \ik-'skər-zhən\ n 1 : EXPEDITION; esp : a pleasure trip 2 : DIGRESSION — **ex·cur·sion·ist** \-zhə-nist\ n

ex·cur·sive \-'skər-siv\ adj : constituting or characterized by digression

¹**ex·cuse** \ik-'skyüz\ vb **ex·cused; ex·cus·ing** [ME, fr. AF excuser, fr. L excusare, fr. causa cause, explanation] 1 : to make apology for 2 : PARDON 3 : to release from an obligation 4 : JUSTIFY — **ex·cus·able** adj

²**excuse** \ik-'skyüs\ n 1 : an act of excusing 2 : something that excuses or is a reason for excusing : JUSTIFICATION

exec n : EXECUTIVE

ex·e·cra·ble \'ek-si-krə-bəl\ adj 1 : DETESTABLE ⟨~ crimes⟩ 2 : very bad ⟨~ spelling⟩

ex·e·crate \'ek-sə-ˌkrāt\ vb **-crat·ed; -crat·ing** [L exsecratus, pp. of exsecrari to put under a curse, fr. ex- out of + sacer sacred] : to denounce as evil or detestable; also : DETEST — **ex·e·cra·tion** \ˌek-sə-'krā-shən\ n

ex·e·cute \'ek-si-ˌkyüt\ vb **-cut·ed; -cut·ing** 1 : to carry out fully : put completely into effect 2 : to do what is called for (as by a law) 3 : to put to death in accordance with a legal sentence 4 : to produce by carrying out a design 5 : to do what is needed to give validity to ⟨~ a deed⟩ — **ex·e·cu·tion** \ˌek-si-'kyü-shən\ n — **ex·e·cu·tion·er** n

¹**ex·ec·u·tive** \ig-'ze-kyə-tiv\ adj 1 : of or relating to the enforcement of laws and the conduct of affairs 2 : designed for or related to carrying out plans or purposes

²**executive** n 1 : the branch of government with executive duties 2 : one having administrative or managerial responsibility

ex·ec·u·tor \ig-'ze-kyə-tər\ n : the person named in a will to execute it

ex·ec·u·trix \ig-'ze-kyə-ˌtriks\ n, pl **ex·ec·u·tri·ces** \-ˌze-kyə-'trī-ˌsēz\ or **ex·ec·u·trix·es** \-'ze-kyə-ˌtrik-səz\ : a woman who is an executor

ex·e·ge·sis \ˌek-sə-'jē-səs\ n, pl **-ge·ses** \-'jē-ˌsēz\ : explanation or critical interpretation of a text

ex·e·gete \'ek-sə-ˌjēt\ n : one who practices exegesis — **ex·e·get·i·cal** \ˌek-sə-'je-ti-kəl\ adj

ex·em·plar \ig-'zem-ˌplär, -plər\ n 1 : one that serves as a model or example; esp : an ideal model ⟨an ~ of courage⟩ 2 : a typical instance or example

ex·em·pla·ry \ig-'zem-plə-rē\ adj : serving as a pattern; also : COMMENDABLE ⟨~ courage⟩

ex·em·pli·fy \ig-'zem-plə-ˌfī\ vb **-fied; -fy·ing** : to illustrate by example : serve as an example of — **ex·em·pli·fi·ca·tion** \-ˌzem-plə-fə-'kā-shən\ n

¹**ex·empt** \ig-'zempt\ adj : free from some liability to which others are subject ⟨~ from taxation⟩

²**exempt** vb : to make exempt : EXCUSE — **ex·emp·tion** \ig-'zemp-shən\ n

¹**ex·er·cise** \'ek-sər-ˌsīz\ n 1 : EMPLOYMENT, USE ⟨~ of authority⟩ 2 : exertion made for the sake of training or physical fitness 3 : a task or problem done to develop skill 4 pl : a public exhibition or ceremony

²**exercise** vb **-cised; -cis·ing** 1 : EXERT ⟨~ control⟩ 2 : to train by or engage in exercise 3 : WORRY, DISTRESS ⟨issues that ~ voters⟩ — **ex·er·cis·er** n

ex·ert \ig-'zərt\ vb : to bring or put into action ⟨~ influence⟩ ⟨~ed himself⟩ — **ex·er·tion** \-'zər-shən\ n

ex·fo·li·ate \eks-'fō-lē-ˌāt\ vb **-at·ed; -at**

ing : to cast off in scales, layers, or splinters — **ex·fo·li·a·tion** \-,fō-lē-'ā-shən\ *n*

ex·hale \eks-'hāl\ *vb* **ex·haled; ex·hal·ing** **1** : to breathe out **2** : to give or pass off in the form of vapor — **ex·ha·la·tion** \,eks-hə-'lā-shən\ *n*

¹**ex·haust** \ig-'zost\ *vb* **1** : to use up wholly **2** : to tire or wear out **3** : to draw off or let out completely; *also* : EMPTY **4** : to develop (a subject) completely

²**exhaust** *n* **1** : the escape of used vapor or gas from an engine; *also* : the gas that escapes **2** : a system of pipes through which exhaust escapes

ex·haus·tion \ig-'zòs-chən\ *n* : extreme weariness : FATIGUE

ex·haus·tive \ig-'zò-stiv\ *adj* : covering all possibilities : THOROUGH ⟨an ∼ investigation⟩ — **ex·haus·tive·ly** *adv*

¹**ex·hib·it** \ig-'zi-bət\ *vb* **1** : to display esp. publicly **2** : to present to a court in legal form ♦ *Synonyms* DISPLAY, SHOW, PARADE, FLAUNT — **ex·hi·bi·tion** \,ek-sə-'bi-shən\ *n* — **ex·hib·i·tor** \ig-'zi-bə-tər\ *n*

²**exhibit** *n* **1** : an act or instance of exhibiting; *also* : something exhibited **2** : something produced and identified in court for use as evidence

ex·hi·bi·tion·ism \,ek-sə-'bi-shə-,ni-zəm\ *n* **1** : a perversion marked by a tendency to indecently expose one's genitals **2** : the act or practice of behaving so as to attract attention to oneself — **ex·hi·bi·tion·ist** \-nist\ *n or adj*

ex·hil·a·rate \ig-'zi-lə-,rāt\ *vb* **-rat·ed; -rat·ing** : ENLIVEN, STIMULATE — **ex·hil·a·ra·tion** \-,zi-lə-'rā-shən\ *n*

ex·hort \ig-'zòrt\ *vb* : to urge, advise, or warn earnestly — **ex·hor·ta·tion** \,ek-,sòr-tā-shən, ,eg-,zòr-, -zər-\ *n*

ex·hume \ig-'züm, iks-'hyüm\ *vb* **ex·humed; ex·hum·ing** [ME fr. ML *exhumare*, fr. L *ex* out of + *humus* earth] : DISINTER — **ex·hu·ma·tion** \,eks-hyü-'mā-shən, ,eg-zü-\ *n*

ex·i·gen·cy \'ek-sə-jən-sē, ig-'zi-jən-\ *n, pl* **-cies 1** *pl* : REQUIREMENTS **2** : urgent need — **ex·i·gent** \'ek-sə-jənt\ *adj*

ex·ig·u·ous \ig-'zi-gyə-wəs\ *adj* : scanty in amount — **ex·i·gu·i·ty** \,eg-zi-'gyü-ə-tē\ *n*

¹**ex·ile** \'eg-,zī(-ə)l, 'ek-,sī(-ə)l\ *n* **1** : BANISHMENT; *also* : voluntary absence from one's country or home **2** : a person driven from his or her native place

²**exile** *vb* **ex·iled; ex·il·ing** : BANISH, EXPEL ♦ *Synonyms* EXPATRIATE, DEPORT, OSTRACIZE

ex·ist \ig-'zist\ *vb* **1** : to have being **2** : to continue to be : LIVE

ex·is·tence \ig-'zis-təns\ *n* **1** : continuance in living **2** : actual or present occurrence ⟨∼ of a state of war⟩ — **ex·is·tent** \-tənt\ *adj*

ex·is·ten·tial \,eg-zis-'ten-chəl, ,ek-sis-\ *adj* **1** : of or relating to existence **2** : EMPIRICAL **3** : having being in time and space **4** : of or relating to existentialism or existentialists

ex·is·ten·tial·ism \,eg-zis-'ten-chə-,li-zəm\ *n* : a philosophy centered on individual existence and personal responsibility for acts of free will in the absence of certain knowledge of what is right or wrong — **ex·is·ten·tial·ist** \-list\ *adj or n*

ex·it \'eg-zət, 'ek-sət\ *n* **1** : a departure from a stage **2** : a going out or away; *also* : DEATH **3** : a way out of an enclosed space **4** : a point of departure from an expressway — **exit** *vb*

exo·bi·ol·o·gy \,ek-sō-bī-'ä-lə-jē\ *n* : biology concerned with life originating or existing outside the earth or its atmosphere — **exo·bi·ol·o·gist** \-jist\ *n*

exo·crine gland \'ek-sə-krən, -,krīn, -,krēn\ *n* : a gland (as a salivary gland) that releases a secretion externally by means of a canal or duct

Exod *abbr* Exodus

ex·o·dus \'ek-sə-dəs\ *n* **1** *cap* — see BIBLE table **2** : a mass departure : EMIGRATION

ex of·fi·cio \,ek-sə-'fi-shē-,ō\ *adv or adj* : by virtue of or because of an office ⟨*ex officio* chairman⟩

ex·og·e·nous \ek-'sä-jə-nəs\ *adj* : caused or produced by factors outside the organism or system — **ex·og·e·nous·ly** *adv*

ex·on·er·ate \ig-'zä-nə-,rāt\ *vb* **-at·ed; -at·ing** [ME, fr. L *exoneratus*, pp. of *exonerare* to unburden, fr. *ex-* out + *onus* load] : to free from blame ♦ *Synonyms* ACQUIT, ABSOLVE, EXCULPATE, VINDICATE — **ex·on·er·a·tion** \-,zä-nə-'rā-shən\ *n*

exo·plan·et \'ek-sō-,pla-nət\ *n* : a planet orbiting a star that is not our sun

ex·or·bi·tant \ig-'zòr-bə-tənt\ *adj* : exceeding what is usual or proper

ex·or·cise \'ek-,sòr-,sīz, -sər-\ *vb* **-cised; -cis·ing 1** : to get rid of by or as if by solemn command **2** : to free of an evil spirit — **ex·or·cism** \-,si-zəm\ *n* — **ex·or·cist** \-,sist\ *n*

exo·sphere \'ek-sō-,sfir\ *n* : the outermost region of the atmosphere

exo·ther·mic \,ek-sō-'thər-mik\ *adj* : characterized by or formed with evolution of heat

ex·ot·ic \ig-'zä-tik\ *adj* **1** : introduced from another country ⟨∼ plants⟩ **2** : strikingly, excitingly, or mysteriously different or unusual ⟨∼ flavors⟩ — **exotic** *n* — **ex·ot·i·cal·ly** \-ti-k(ə-)lē\ *adv* — **ex·ot·i·cism** \-tə-,si-zəm\ *n*

exp *abbr* **1** expense **2** experiment **3** export **4** express

ex·pand \ik-'spand\ *vb* **1** : to open up : UNFOLD **2** : ENLARGE **3** : to develop in detail ♦ *Synonyms* AMPLIFY, SWELL, DISTEND, INFLATE, DILATE — **ex·pand·able** \-'span-də-bəl\ *adj* — **ex·pand·er** *n*

ex·panse \ik-'spans\ *n* : a broad extent (as of land or sea)

ex·pan·sion \ik-'span-chən\ *n* **1** : the act or process of expanding **2** : the quality or state of being expanded **3** : an expanded part or thing

expansion slot *n* : a socket on a motherboard for a circuit board (**expansion card**) offering additional capabilities

ex·pan·sive \ik-'span-siv\ *adj* **1** : tending to expand or to cause expansion **2**

: warmly benevolent, generous, or ready to talk **3** : of large extent or scope — **ex·pan·sive·ly** adv — **ex·pan·sive·ness** n

ex par·te \eks-'pär-tē\ adv or adj [ML] : from a one-sided point of view

ex·pa·ti·ate \ek-'spā-shē-ˌāt\ vb **-at·ed; -at·ing** : to talk or write at length — **ex·pa·ti·a·tion** \-ˌspā-shē-'ā-shən\ n

¹**ex·pa·tri·ate** \ek-'spā-trē-ˌāt\ vb **-at·ed; -at·ing** : EXILE — **ex·pa·tri·a·tion** \ek-ˌspā-trē-'ā-shən\ n

²**ex·pa·tri·ate** \ek-'spā-trē-ˌāt, -trē-ət\ adj : living in a foreign country — **expatriate** n

ex·pect \ik-'spekt\ vb **1** : SUPPOSE, THINK **2** : to look forward to : ANTICIPATE **3** : to consider reasonable, due, or necessary **4** : to consider to be obliged

ex·pec·tan·cy \ik-'spek-tən-sē\ n, pl **-cies 1** : EXPECTATION **2** : the expected amount (as of years of life)

ex·pec·tant \-tənt\ adj : marked by expectation; esp : expecting the birth of a child ⟨~ parents⟩ — **ex·pec·tant·ly** adv

ex·pec·ta·tion \ˌek-ˌspek-'tā-shən\ n **1** : the act or state of expecting **2** : prospect of inheritance — usu. used in pl. **3** : something expected

ex·pec·to·rant \ik-'spek-tə-rənt\ n : an agent that promotes the discharge or expulsion of mucus from the respiratory tract — **expectorant** adj

ex·pec·to·rate \-ˌrāt\ vb **-rat·ed; -rat·ing** : SPIT — **ex·pec·to·ra·tion** \-ˌspek-tə-'rā-shən\ n

ex·pe·di·ence \ik-'spē-dē-əns\ n : EXPEDIENCY

ex·pe·di·en·cy \-ən-sē\ n, pl **-cies 1** : fitness to some end **2** : use of expedient means and methods; also : something expedient

¹**ex·pe·di·ent** \-ənt\ adj [ME, fr. AF or L; AF, fr. L expediens, prp. of expedire to extricate, prepare, be useful, fr. ex- out + ped-, pes foot] **1** : adapted for achieving a particular end **2** : marked by concern with what is advantageous; esp : governed by self-interest

²**expedient** n : something expedient; esp : a temporary means to an end

ex·pe·dite \'ek-spə-ˌdīt\ vb **-dit·ed; -dit·ing** : to carry out promptly; also : to speed up ⟨~ a lawsuit⟩

ex·pe·dit·er \-ˌdī-tər\ n : one that expedites; esp : one employed to ensure efficient movement of goods or supplies in a business

ex·pe·di·tion \ˌek-spə-'di-shən\ n **1** : a journey for a particular purpose; also : the persons making it **2** : efficient promptness

ex·pe·di·tion·ary \-'di-shə-ˌner-ē\ adj : of, relating to, or constituting an expedition; also : sent on military service abroad

ex·pe·di·tious \-'di-shəs\ adj : marked by or acting with prompt efficiency ♦ **Synonyms** SWIFT, FAST, RAPID, SPEEDY

ex·pel \ik-'spel\ vb **ex·pelled; ex·pelling** : to drive or force out : EJECT

ex·pend \ik-'spend\ vb **1** : to pay out

: SPEND **2** : UTILIZE ⟨~ resources⟩; also : USE UP — **ex·pend·able** adj

ex·pen·di·ture \ik-'spen-di-chər, -ˌchúr\ n **1** : the act or process of expending **2** : something expended

ex·pense \ik-'spens\ n **1** : EXPENDITURE **2** : COST **3** : a cause of expenditure **4** : SACRIFICE ⟨had a laugh at my ~⟩

ex·pen·sive \ik-'spen-siv\ adj : COSTLY, DEAR — **ex·pen·sive·ly** adv

¹**ex·pe·ri·ence** \ik-'spir-ē-əns\ n **1** : observation of or participation in events resulting in or tending toward knowledge **2** : knowledge, practice, or skill derived from observation or participation in events; also : the length of such participation **3** : something encountered, undergone, or lived through (as by a person or community)

²**experience** vb **-enced; -enc·ing 1** : FIND OUT, DISCOVER **2** : to have experience of : UNDERGO ⟨~ the loss of a pet⟩

ex·pe·ri·enced adj : made capable through experience ⟨an ~ pilot⟩

¹**ex·per·i·ment** \ik-'sper-ə-mənt\ n : a controlled procedure carried out to discover, test, or demonstrate something; also : the process of testing — **ex·per·i·men·tal** \-ˌsper-ə-'men-tᵊl\ adj — **ex·per·i·men·tal·ly** \-'men-tᵊl-ē\ adv

²**ex·per·i·ment** \-ˌment\ vb : to make experiments — **ex·per·i·men·ta·tion** \ik-ˌsper-ə-mən-'tā-shən\ n — **ex·per·i·ment·er** n

¹**ex·pert** \'ek-ˌspərt\ adj : showing special skill or knowledge — **ex·pert·ly** adv — **ex·pert·ness** n

²**ex·pert** \'ek-ˌspərt\ n : an expert person : SPECIALIST ⟨a computer ~⟩

ex·per·tise \ˌek-(ˌ)spər-'tēz\ n : the skill of an expert ⟨~ in legal matters⟩

expert system n : computer software that attempts to mimic the reasoning of a human specialist

ex·pi·ate \'ek-spē-ˌāt\ vb **-at·ed; -at·ing** : to give satisfaction for : ATONE ⟨~ sin⟩ — **ex·pi·a·tion** \ˌek-spē-'ā-shən\ n

ex·pi·a·to·ry \'ek-spē-ə-ˌtór-ē\ adj : serving to expiate

expiration date n **1** : the date after which something is no longer in effect **2** : the date after which a product is expected to decline in quality or effectiveness

ex·pire \ik-'spī(-ə)r, ek-\ vb **ex·pired; ex·pir·ing 1** : to breathe one's last breath : DIE **2** : to come to an end **3** : to breathe out from or as if from the lungs — **ex·pi·ra·tion** \ˌek-spə-'rā-shən\ n

ex·plain \ik-'splān\ vb [ME explanen, fr. L explanare, lit., to make level, fr. planus level, flat] **1** : to make clear **2** : to give the reason for — **ex·pla·na·tion** \ˌek-splə-'nā-shən\ n — **ex·plan·a·to·ry** \ik-'splan-ə-ˌtór-ē\ adj

ex·ple·tive \'ek-splə-tiv\ n : a usu. profane exclamation

ex·pli·ca·ble \ek-'spli-kə-bəl, 'ek-(ˌ)spli-\ adj : capable of being explained

ex·pli·cate \'ek-splə-ˌkāt\ vb **-cat·ed; -cat·ing** : to give a detailed explanation of — **ex·pli·ca·tion** \ˌek-spli-'kā-shən\ n

ex·plic·it \ik-'spli-sət\ *adj* : clearly and precisely expressed ⟨∼ directions⟩ — **ex·plic·it·ly** *adv* — **ex·plic·it·ness** *n*

ex·plode \ik-'splōd\ *vb* **ex·plod·ed; explod·ing** [L *explodere* to drive off the stage by clapping, fr. *ex-* out + *plaudere* to clap] **1** : DISCREDIT ⟨∼ a belief⟩ **2** : to burst or cause to burst violently and noisily ⟨∼ a bomb⟩ ⟨the boiler *exploded*⟩ **3** : to undergo a rapid chemical or nuclear reaction with production of heat and violent expansion of gas ⟨dynamite ∼s⟩ **4** : to give forth a sudden strong and noisy outburst of emotion **5** : to increase rapidly ⟨the city's population *exploded*⟩

exploded *adj* : showing the parts separated but in correct relationship to each other ⟨an ∼ view of a carburetor⟩

¹ex·ploit \'ek-,splȯit\ *n* : DEED; *esp* : a notable or heroic act

²ex·ploit \ik-'splȯit\ *vb* **1** : to make productive use of : UTILIZE ⟨∼ natural resources⟩ **2** : to use unfairly for one's own advantage ⟨∼ migrant workers⟩ — **ex·ploi·ta·tion** \,ek-,splȯi-'tā-shən\ *n*

ex·plore \ik-'splȯr\ *vb* **ex·plored; explor·ing 1** : to look into or travel over thoroughly **2** : to examine carefully ⟨∼ a wound⟩ — **ex·plo·ra·tion** \,ek-splə-'rā-shən\ *n* — **ex·plor·ato·ry** \ik-'splȯr-ə-,tȯr-ē\ *adj* — **ex·plor·er** *n*

ex·plo·sion \ik-'splō-zhən\ *n* : the act or an instance of exploding

ex·plo·sive \ik-'splō-siv\ *adj* **1** : relating to or able to cause explosion **2** : tending to explode ⟨an ∼ temper⟩ — **explosive** *n* — **ex·plo·sive·ly** *adv*

ex·po \'ek-,spō\ *n, pl* **expos** : EXPOSITION 2

ex·po·nent \ik-'spō-nənt, 'ek-,spō-\ *n* **1** : a symbol written above and to the right of a mathematical expression (as ^{3} in a^3) to signify how many times it is to be used as a factor **2** : INTERPRETER, EXPOUNDER **3** : ADVOCATE, CHAMPION — **ex·po·nen·tial** \,ek-spə-'nen-chəl\ *adj* — **ex·po·nen·tial·ly** *adv*

ex·po·nen·ti·a·tion \,ek-spə-,nen-chē-'ā-shən\ *n* : the mathematical operation of raising a quantity to a power

¹ex·port \ek-'spȯrt, 'ek-,spȯrt\ *vb* : to send (as merchandise) to foreign countries — **ex·por·ta·tion** \,ek-,spȯr-'tā-shən, -spər-\ *n* — **ex·port·er** *n*

²ex·port \'ek-,spȯrt\ *n* **1** : something exported esp. for trade **2** : the act of exporting

ex·pose \ik-'spōz\ *vb* **ex·posed; ex·pos·ing 1** : to deprive of shelter or protection **2** : to submit or subject to an action or influence; *esp* : to subject (as photographic film) to radiant energy (as light) **3** : to bring to light : DISCLOSE ⟨∼ a scam⟩ **4** : to cause to be open to view

ex·po·sé \,ek-spō-'zā\ *n* : an exposure of something discreditable

ex·po·si·tion \,ek-spə-'zi-shən\ *n* **1** : a setting forth of the meaning or purpose (as of a writing); *also* : discourse designed to convey information **2** : a public exhibition

ex·pos·i·tor \ik-'spä-zə-tər\ *n* : one who explains : COMMENTATOR

ex post fac·to \,eks-'pōst-,fak-tō\ *adv or adj* : after the fact

ex·pos·tu·late \ik-'späs-chə-,lāt\ *vb* : to reason earnestly with a person esp. in dissuading : REMONSTRATE — **ex·pos·tu·la·tion** \-,späs-chə-'lā-shən\ *n*

ex·po·sure \ik-'spō-zhər\ *n* **1** : the fact or condition of being exposed **2** : the act or an instance of exposing **3** : the length of time for which a film is exposed **4** : a section of a photographic film for one picture

ex·pound \ik-'spaȯnd\ *vb* **1** : STATE **2** : INTERPRET, EXPLAIN — **ex·pound·er** *n*

¹ex·press \ik-'spres\ *adj* **1** : EXPLICIT; *also* : EXACT, PRECISE **2** : SPECIFIC ⟨this ∼ purpose⟩ **3** : traveling at high speed and esp. with few stops ⟨an ∼ train⟩; *also* : adapted to high-speed use ⟨∼ roads⟩ — **ex·press·ly** *adv*

²express *adv* : by express ⟨ship it ∼⟩

³express *n* **1** : a system for the prompt transportation of goods; *also* : a company operating such a service or the shipments so transported **2** : an express vehicle

⁴express *vb* **1** : to make known : SHOW, STATE ⟨∼ regret⟩; *also* : SYMBOLIZE **2** : to squeeze out : extract by pressing **3** : to send by express **4** : to manifest or produce by a genetic process

ex·pres·sion \ik-'spre-shən\ *n* **1** : UTTERANCE **2** : something that represents or symbolizes : SIGN; *esp* : a mathematical symbol or combination of signs and symbols representing a quantity or operation **3** : the detectable effect of a gene **4** : a significant word or phrase; *also* : manner of expressing (as in writing or music) **5** : facial aspect or vocal intonation indicative of feeling — **ex·pres·sion·less** *adj*

ex·pres·sion·ism \ik-'spre-shə-,ni-zəm\ *n* : a theory or practice in art of seeking to depict the artist's subjective responses to objects and events — **ex·pres·sion·ist** \-nist\ *n or adj* — **ex·pres·sion·is·tic** \-,spre-shə-'nis-tik\ *adj*

ex·pres·sive \ik-'spre-siv\ *adj* **1** : of or relating to expression **2** : serving to express ⟨an ∼ gesture⟩ — **ex·pres·sive·ly** *adv* — **ex·pres·sive·ness** *n*

ex·press·way \ik-'spres-,wā\ *n* : a divided superhighway with limited access

ex·pro·pri·ate \ek-'sprō-prē-,āt\ *vb* **-at·ed; -at·ing** : to deprive of possession or the right to own — **ex·pro·pri·a·tion** \(,)ek-,sprō-prē-'ā-shən\ *n*

expt *abbr* experiment

ex·pul·sion \ik-'spəl-shən\ *n* : an expelling or being expelled : EJECTION

ex·punge \ik-'spənj\ *vb* **ex·punged; ex·pung·ing** [L *expungere* to mark for deletion by dots, fr. *ex-* out + *pungere* to prick] : OBLITERATE, ERASE

ex·pur·gate \'ek-spər-,gāt\ *vb* **-gat·ed; -gat·ing** : to clear (as a book) of objectionable passages — **ex·pur·ga·tion** \,ek-spər-'gā-shən\ *n*

ex·qui·site \ek-'skwi-zət, 'ek-(,)skwi-\ *adj* [ME *exquisit*, fr. L *exquisitus*, pp. of *ex-*

quirere to search out, fr. *ex* out + *quaer-ere* to seek] **1** : marked by flawless form or workmanship **2** : keenly appreciative or sensitive **3** : pleasingly beautiful or delicate ♦ INTENSE ⟨~ pain⟩

ext *abbr* **1** extension **2** exterior **3** external **4** extra **5** extract

ex·tant \ˈek-stənt; ek-ˈstant\ *adj* : EXISTENT; *esp* : not lost or destroyed

ex·tem·po·ra·ne·ous \ek-ˌstem-pə-ˈrā-nē-əs\ *adj* : not planned beforehand : IMPROMPTU — **ex·tem·po·ra·ne·ous·ly** *adv*

ex·tem·po·rary \ik-ˈstem-pə-ˌrer-ē\ *adj* : EXTEMPORANEOUS

ex·tem·po·re \ik-ˈstem-pə-(ˌ)rē\ *adv* : EXTEMPORANEOUSLY

ex·tem·po·rise *Brit var of* EXTEMPORIZE

ex·tem·po·rize \ik-ˈstem-pə-ˌrīz\ *vb* **-rized; -riz·ing** : to do something extemporaneously ⟨~ a speech⟩

ex·tend \ik-ˈstend\ *vb* **1** : to spread or stretch forth or out (as in reaching) **2** : to exert or cause to exert to full capacity **3** : PROFFER ⟨~ credit⟩ **4** : PROLONG ⟨~ a note⟩ **5** : to make greater or broader ⟨~ knowledge⟩ ⟨~ a business⟩ **6** : to stretch out or reach across a distance, space, or time ♦ *Synonyms* LENGTHEN, ELONGATE, PROTRACT — **ex·tend·able** *also* **ex·tend·ible** \-ˈsten-də-bəl\ *adj*

ex·ten·sion \ik-ˈsten-chən\ *n* **1** : an extending or being extended **2** : a program that geographically extends the educational resources of an institution **3** : an additional part; *also* : an extra telephone connected to a line

ex·ten·sive \ik-ˈsten-siv\ *adj* : of considerable extent : FAR-REACHING, BROAD ⟨~ training⟩ — **ex·ten·sive·ly** *adv*

ex·tent \ik-ˈstent\ *n* **1** : the range or space over which something extends ⟨a property of large ~⟩ **2** : the point or degree to which something extends ⟨to the fullest ~ of the law⟩

ex·ten·u·ate \ik-ˈsten-yū-ˌwāt\ *vb* **-at·ed; -at·ing** : to lessen the seriousness of — **ex·ten·u·a·tion** \-ˌsten-yū-ˈwā-shən\ *n*

¹**ex·te·ri·or** \ek-ˈstir-ē-ər\ *adj* **1** : EXTERNAL **2** : suitable for use on an outside surface ⟨~ paint⟩

²**exterior** *n* : an exterior part or surface

ex·ter·mi·nate \ik-ˈstər-mə-ˌnāt\ *vb* **-nat·ed; -nat·ing** : to get rid of completely usu. by killing off ♦ *Synonyms* EXTIRPATE, ERADICATE, ABOLISH, ANNIHILATE — **ex·ter·mi·na·tion** \-ˌstər-mə-ˈnā-shən\ *n* — **ex·ter·mi·na·tor** \-ˈstər-mə-ˌnā-tər\ *n*

¹**ex·ter·nal** \ek-ˈstər-nᵊl\ *adj* **1** : outwardly perceivable; *also* : SUPERFICIAL **2** : of, relating to, or located on the outside or an outer part **3** : arising or acting from without; *also* : FOREIGN ⟨~ affairs⟩ — **ex·ter·nal·ly** *adv*

²**external** *n* : an external feature

ex·tinct \ik-ˈstiŋkt\ *adj* **1** : EXTINGUISHED; *also* : no longer active ⟨an ~ volcano⟩ **2** : no longer existing or in use ⟨dinosaurs are ~⟩ ⟨~ languages⟩ — **ex·tinc·tion** \ik-ˈstiŋk-shən\ *n*

ex·tin·guish \ik-ˈstiŋ-gwish\ *vb* : to cause

to stop burning; *also* : to bring to an end (as by destroying) — **ex·tin·guish·able** *adj* — **ex·tin·guish·er** *n*

ex·tir·pate \ˈek-stər-ˌpāt\ *vb* **-pat·ed; -pat·ing** [L *exstirpatus*, pp. of *exstirpare*, fr. *ex-* out + *stirps* trunk, root] **1** : to destroy completely ⟨~ a heresy⟩ **2** : UPROOT ♦ *Synonyms* EXTERMINATE, ERADICATE, ABOLISH, ANNIHILATE — **ex·tir·pa·tion** \ek-stər-ˈpā-shən\ *n*

ex·tol *also* **ex·toll** \ik-ˈstōl\ *vb* **ex·tolled; ex·tol·ling** : to praise highly : GLORIFY

ex·tort \ik-ˈstȯrt\ *vb* [L *extortus*, pp. of *extorquēre* to wrench out, extort, fr. *ex-* out + *torquēre* to twist] : to obtain by force or improper pressure ⟨~ a bribe⟩ — **ex·tor·tion** \-ˈstȯr-shən\ *n* — **ex·tor·tion·er** *n* — **ex·tor·tion·ist** *n*

ex·tor·tion·ate \ik-ˈstȯr-shə-nət\ *adj* : EXCESSIVE, EXORBITANT ⟨~ prices⟩ — **ex·tor·tion·ate·ly** *adv*

¹**ex·tra** \ˈek-strə\ *adj* **1** : ADDITIONAL ⟨~ work⟩ **2** : SUPERIOR ⟨~ quality⟩

²**extra** *n* **1** : a special edition of a newspaper **2** : an added charge **3** : an additional worker or performer (as in a motion picture)

³**extra** *adv* : beyond what is usual ⟨~ large⟩

¹**ex·tract** \ik-ˈstrakt, *esp for 3* ˈek-ˌstrakt\ *vb* **1** : to draw out; *esp* : to pull out forcibly ⟨~ a tooth⟩ **2** : to withdraw (as a juice or a constituent) by a physical or chemical process **3** : to select for citation : QUOTE — **ex·tract·able** *adj* — **ex·trac·tion** \ik-ˈstrak-shən\ *n* — **ex·trac·tor** \-tər\ *n*

²**ex·tract** \ˈek-ˌstrakt\ *n* **1** : EXCERPT, CITATION **2** : a product (as a juice or a concentrate) obtained by extracting

ex·tra·cur·ric·u·lar \ˌek-strə-kə-ˈri-kyə-lər\ *adj* : lying outside the regular curriculum; *esp* : of or relating to school-connected activities (as sports) usu. carrying no academic credit

ex·tra·dite \ˈek-strə-ˌdīt\ *vb* **-dit·ed; -dit·ing** : to obtain by or deliver up to extradition

ex·tra·di·tion \ˌek-strə-ˈdi-shən\ *n* : the surrender of an alleged criminal to a different jurisdiction for trial

ex·tra·mar·i·tal \ˌek-strə-ˈma-rə-tᵊl\ *adj* : of or relating to sexual intercourse by a married person with someone other than his or her spouse

ex·tra·mu·ral \-ˈmyür-əl\ *adj* : existing or functioning beyond the bounds of an organized unit

ex·tra·ne·ous \ek-ˈstrā-nē-əs\ *adj* **1** : coming from without ⟨~ light⟩ **2** : not forming a vital part; *also* : IRRELEVANT — **ex·tra·ne·ous·ly** *adv*

ex·tra·net \ˈek-strə-ˌnet\ *n* : a network like an intranet but also allowing access by certain outside parties

ex·traor·di·nary \ik-ˈstrȯr-də-ˌner-ē, ˌek-strə-ˈȯr-\ *adj* **1** : notably unusual or exceptional **2** : employed on special service ⟨an ambassador ~⟩ — **ex·traor·di·nar·i·ly** \-ˌstrȯr-də-ˈner-ə-lē, ˌek-strə-ˌȯr-\ *adv*

ex·trap·o·late \ik-ˈstra-pə-ˌlāt\ *vb* **-lat·ed; -lat·ing** : to infer (unknown data) from known data — ex·trap·o·la·tion \-ˌstra-pə-ˈlā-shən\ n

ex·tra·sen·so·ry \ˌek-strə-ˈsen-sə-rē\ adj : not acting or occurring through the known senses

extrasensory perception n : perception (as in telepathy) of events external to the self not gained through the senses and not deducible from previous experience

ex·tra·so·lar \-ˈsō-lər\ adj : originating or existing outside the solar system

ex·tra·ter·res·tri·al \-tə-ˈres-trē-əl\ adj : originating or existing outside the earth or its atmosphere ⟨~ life⟩ — **extraterrestrial** n

ex·tra·ter·ri·to·ri·al \-ˌter-ə-ˈtòr-ē-əl\ adj : existing or taking place outside the territorial limits of a jurisdiction

ex·tra·ter·ri·to·ri·al·i·ty \-ˌtòr-ē-ˈa-lə-tē\ n : exemption from the application or jurisdiction of local law or tribunals ⟨diplomats enjoy ~⟩

ex·trav·a·gant \ik-ˈstra-vi-gənt\ adj 1 : EXCESSIVE ⟨~ claims⟩ 2 : unduly lavish : WASTEFUL 3 : too costly ♦ **Synonyms** IMMODERATE, EXORBITANT, EXTREME, INORDINATE, UNDUE — **ex·trav·a·gance** \-gəns\ n — **ex·trav·a·gant·ly** adv

ex·trav·a·gan·za \ik-ˌstra-və-ˈgan-zə\ n 1 : a literary or musical work marked by extreme freedom of style and structure 2 : a spectacular show

ex·tra·ve·hic·u·lar \ˌek-strə-vē-ˈhi-kyə-lər\ adj : taking place outside a vehicle (as a spacecraft) ⟨~ activity⟩

¹ex·treme \ik-ˈstrēm\ adj 1 : very great or intense ⟨~ cold⟩ 2 : very severe or radical ⟨~ measures⟩ 3 : going to great lengths or beyond normal limits ⟨politically ~⟩ 4 : most remote ⟨the ~ end⟩ 5 : UTMOST; also : MAXIMUM — **ex·treme·ly** adv

²extreme n 1 : something located at one end or the other of a range or series 2 : EXTREMITY 4

extremely low frequency n : a radio frequency in the lowest range of the radio spectrum

ex·trem·ism \ik-ˈstrē-ˌmi-zəm\ n : the quality or state of being extreme; also : advocacy of extreme political measures — **ex·trem·ist** \-mist\ n or adj

ex·trem·i·ty \ik-ˈstre-mə-tē\ n, pl **-ties** 1 : the most remote part or point 2 : a limb of the body; esp : a human hand or foot 3 : the greatest need or danger 4 : the utmost degree ⟨the extremities of suffering⟩ 5 : a drastic or desperate measure

ex·tri·cate \ˈek-strə-ˌkāt\ vb **-cat·ed; -cat·ing** [L extricatus, pp. of extricare, fr. ex- out + tricae trifles, perplexities] : to free from an entanglement or difficulty ♦ **Synonyms** DISENTANGLE, UNTANGLE, DISENCUMBER — **ex·tri·ca·ble** \ik-ˈstri-kə-bəl, ˈek-(ˌ)stri-\ adj — **ex·tri·ca·tion** \ˌek-strə-ˈkā-shən\ n

ex·trin·sic \ek-ˈstrin-zik, -sik\ adj 1 : not forming part of or belonging to a thing 2 : EXTERNAL — **ex·trin·si·cal·ly** \-zi-k(ə-)lē, -si-\ adv

ex·tro·vert also **ex·tra·vert** \ˈek-strə-ˌvərt\ n : a gregarious and unreserved person — **ex·tro·ver·sion** or **ex·tra·ver·sion** \ˌek-strə-ˈvər-zhən\ n — **ex·tro·vert·ed** also **ex·tra·vert·ed** adj

ex·trude \ik-ˈstrüd\ vb **ex·trud·ed; ex·trud·ing** 1 : to force, press, or push out 2 : to shape (as plastic) by forcing through a die — **ex·tru·sion** \-ˈstrü-zhən\ n — **ex·trud·er** n

ex·u·ber·ant \ig-ˈzü-bə-rənt\ adj 1 : unrestrained in enthusiasm or style 2 : PROFUSE ⟨~ vegetation⟩ — **ex·u·ber·ance** \-rəns\ n — **ex·u·ber·ant·ly** adv

ex·ude \ig-ˈzüd\ vb **ex·ud·ed; ex·ud·ing** [L exsudare, fr. ex- out + sudare to sweat] 1 : to discharge slowly through pores or cuts : OOZE 2 : to display conspicuously or abundantly ⟨~s charm⟩ — **ex·u·date** \ˈek-sù-ˌdāt, -syù-\ n — **ex·u·da·tion** \ˌek-sù-ˈdā-shən, -syù-\ n

ex·ult \ig-ˈzəlt\ vb : REJOICE, GLORY ⟨~ed in their victory⟩ — **ex·ul·tant** \-ˈzəl-tᵊnt\ adj — **ex·ul·tant·ly** adv — **ex·ul·ta·tion** \ˌek-(ˌ)səl-ˈtā-shən, ˌeg-(ˌ)zəl-\ n

ex·urb \ˈek-ˌsərb, ˈeg-ˌzərb\ n : a region outside a city and its suburbs inhabited chiefly by well-to-do families — **ex·ur·ban** \ek-ˈsər-bən, eg-ˈzər-\ adj

ex·ur·ban·ite \ek-ˈsər-bə-ˌnīt; eg-ˈzər-\ n : one who lives in an exurb

ex·ur·bia \ek-ˈsər-bē-ə, eg-ˈzər-\ n : the generalized region of exurbs

-ey — see -Y

¹eye \ˈī\ n 1 : an organ of sight typically consisting in vertebrates of a globular structure that is located in a socket of the skull, is lined with a sensitive retina, and is normally paired 2 : VISION, PERCEPTION; also : faculty of discrimination ⟨an ~ for bargains⟩ 3 : POINT OF VIEW, JUDGMENT — often used in pl. ⟨in the ~s of the law⟩ 4 : something suggesting an eye (as the hole of a needle or the bud of a potato) 5 : the calm center of a cyclone — **eyed** \ˈīd\ adj

²eye vb **eyed; eye·ing** or **ey·ing** : to look at : WATCH

¹eye·ball \ˈī-ˌból\ n : the globular capsule of the vertebrate eye

²eyeball vb : to look at intently

eye·brow \-ˌbraủ\ n : the ridge over the eye or the hair growing on it

eye·drop·per \-ˌdrä-pər\ n : DROPPER 2

eye·glass \-ˌglas\ n : a lens worn to aid vision; also, pl : GLASSES

eye·lash \-ˌlash\ n 1 : the fringe of hair edging the eyelid — usu. used in pl. 2 : a single hair of the eyelashes

eye·let \-lət\ n 1 : a small hole intended for ornament or for passage of a cord or lace 2 : a typically metal ring for reinforcing an eyelet : GROMMET

eye·lid \-ˌlid\ n : either of the movable folds of skin and muscle that can be closed over the eyeball

eye·lin·er \-ˌlī-nər\ n : makeup used to emphasize the contour of the eyes

eye–open·er \-ˌō-pə-nər\ n : something startling or surprising — **eye–open·ing** adj

eye·piece \-ˌpēs\ n : the lens or combination of lenses at the eye end of an optical instrument

eye shadow *n* : a colored cosmetic applied to the eyelids to accent the eyes

eye·sight \-ˌsīt\ *n* : SIGHT, VISION

eye·sore \-ˌsȯr\ *n* : something offensive to view

eye·strain \-ˌstrān\ *n* : weariness or a strained state of the eye

eye·tooth \-ˈtüth\ *n* : a canine tooth of the upper jaw

eye·wash \-ˌwȯsh, -ˌwäsh\ *n* **1** : an eye lotion **2** : misleading or deceptive statements, actions, or procedures

eye·wit·ness \-ˈwit-nəs\ *n* : a person who actually sees something happen

ey·rie *chiefly Brit var of* AERIE

ey·rir \ˈā-ˌrir\ *n*, *pl* **au·rar** \ˈau̇-ˌrär\ — see *krona* at MONEY table

Ez *or* **Ezr** *abbr* Ezra

Ezech *abbr* Ezechiel

Eze·chiel \i-ˈzē-kyəl\ *n* — see BIBLE table

Ezek *abbr* Ezekiel

Eze·kiel \i-ˈzē-kyəl\ *n* — see BIBLE table

e–zine \ˈē-ˌzēn\ *n* : an online magazine

Ez·ra \ˈez-rə\ *n* — see BIBLE table

F

f \ˈef\ *n*, *pl* **f's** *or* **fs** \ˈefs\ *often cap* **1** : the 6th letter of the English alphabet **2** : a grade rating a student's work as failing

²f *abbr*, *often cap* **1** Fahrenheit **2** false **3** family **4** farad **5** female **6** feminine **7** forte **8** French **9** frequency **10** Friday

³f *symbol* focal length

F *symbol* fluorine

FAA *abbr* Federal Aviation Administration

fab \ˈfab\ *adj* : FABULOUS

Fa·bi·an \ˈfā-bē-ən\ *adj* : of, relating to, or being a society of socialists organized in England in 1884 to spread socialist principles gradually — **Fabian** *n* — **Fa·bi·an·ism** *n*

fa·ble \ˈfā-bəl\ *n* **1** : a legendary story of supernatural happenings **2** : a narration intended to teach a lesson; *esp* : one in which animals speak and act like people **3** : FALSEHOOD

fa·bled \ˈfā-bəld\ *adj* **1** : FICTITIOUS **2** : told or celebrated in fable ⟨~ deeds⟩

fab·ric \ˈfa-brik\ *n* [MF *fabrique*, fr. L *fabrica* workshop, structure] **1** : STRUCTURE, FRAMEWORK ⟨the ~ of society⟩ **2** : CLOTH; *also* : a material that resembles cloth

fab·ri·cate \ˈfa-bri-ˌkāt\ *vb* **-cat·ed; -cat·ing** **1** : INVENT, CREATE **2** : to make up for the sake of deception ⟨reporters *fabricating* news stories⟩ **3** : CONSTRUCT, MANUFACTURE ⟨~ tools⟩ — **fab·ri·ca·tion** \ˌfa-bri-ˈkā-shən\ *n*

fab·u·lous \ˈfa-byə-ləs\ *adj* **1** : resembling a fable; *also* : INCREDIBLE, MARVELOUS ⟨had a ~ time⟩ **2** : told in or based on fable — **fab·u·lous·ly** *adv*

fac *abbr* **1** facsimile **2** faculty

fa·cade *also* **fa·çade** \fə-ˈsäd\ *n* [F *façade*, fr. It *facciata*, fr. *faccia* face] **1** : the principal face or front of a building **2** : a false, superficial, or artificial appearance ◆ **Synonyms** MASK, DISGUISE, FRONT, GUISE, PRETENSE, VENEER

¹face \ˈfās\ *n* **1** : the front part of the head **2** : PRESENCE ⟨in the ~ of danger⟩ **3** : facial expression : LOOK ⟨put a sad ~ on⟩ **4** : GRIMACE ⟨made a ~⟩ **5** : outward appearance ⟨looks easy on the ~

of it⟩ **6** : CONFIDENCE; *also* : BOLDNESS **7** : DIGNITY, PRESTIGE ⟨afraid to lose ~⟩ **8** : SURFACE; *esp* : a front, principal, bounding, or contacting surface ⟨~ of a cliff⟩ ⟨the ~s of a cube⟩ ⟨the ~ of a golf club⟩ — **faced** \ˈfāst, ˈfā-səd\ *adj*

²face *vb* **faced; fac·ing** **1** : to confront brazenly **2** : to line near the edge esp. with a different material; *also* : to cover the front or surface of ⟨~ a building with marble⟩ **3** : to meet or bring in direct contact or confrontation ⟨*faced* the problem⟩ **4** : to stand or sit with the face toward ⟨~ the sun⟩ **5** : to have the front oriented toward ⟨a house *facing* the park⟩ **6** : to have as or be a prospect ⟨~ a grim future⟩ **7** : to turn the face or body in a specified direction — **face the music** : to meet the unpleasant consequences of one's actions

face·down \ˌfās-ˈdau̇n\ *adv* : with the face downward ⟨cards turned ~⟩

face·less \-ləs\ *n* **1** : lacking character or individuality **2** : lacking a face

face–lift \ˈfās-ˌlift\ *n* **1** : plastic surgery on the face and neck to remove defects (as wrinkles) typical of aging **2** : MODERNIZATION — **face–lift** *vb*

face–off \ˈfās-ˌȯf\ *n* **1** : a method of beginning play by dropping a puck or ball (as in hockey) between two opposing players each of whom attempts to control it **2** : CONFRONTATION — **face off** *vb*

fac·et \ˈfa-sət\ *n* [F *facette*, dim. of *face*] **1** : a small plane surface of a cut gem **2** : ASPECT, PHASE

fa·ce·tious \fə-ˈsē-shəs\ *adj* **1** : joking often inappropriately ⟨~ remarks⟩ **2** : JOCULAR, JOCOSE ◆ **Synonyms** WITTY, HUMOROUS — **fa·ce·tious·ly** *adv* — **fa·ce·tious·ness** *n*

¹fa·cial \ˈfā-shəl\ *adj* **1** : of or relating to the face **2** : used to improve the appearance of the face

²facial *n* : a facial treatment

fac·ile \ˈfa-səl\ *adj* **1** : easily accomplished, handled, or attained **2** : SIMPLISTIC **3** : readily manifested and often insincere ⟨~ prose⟩ **4** : READY, FLUENT ⟨a ~ writer⟩

fa·cil·i·tate \fə-'si-lə-ˌtāt\ *vb* **-tat·ed; -tat·ing** : to make easier — **fa·cil·i·ta·tion** \-ˌsi-lə-'tā-shən\ *n* — **fa·cil·i·ta·tor** \-'si-lə-ˌtā-tər\ *n*

fa·cil·i·ty \fə-'si-lə-tē\ *n, pl* **-ties 1** : the quality of being easily performed **2** : ease in performance : APTITUDE **3** : PLIANCY **4** : something that makes easier an action, operation, or course of conduct; *also* : REST ROOM — often used in pl. **5** : something (as a hospital) built or installed for a particular purpose

fac·ing \'fā-siŋ\ *n* **1** : a lining at the edge esp. of a garment **2** *pl* : the collar, cuffs, and trimmings of a uniform coat **3** : an ornamental or protective layer **4** : material for facing

fac·sim·i·le \fak-'si-mə-lē\ *n* [L *fac simile* make similar] **1** : an exact copy **2** : a system of transmitting and reproducing printed matter or pictures by means of signals sent over telephone lines

fact \'fakt\ *n* **1** : DEED; *esp* : CRIME ⟨accessory after the ~⟩ **2** : the quality of being actual **3** : something that exists or occurs **4** : a piece of information — **in fact** : in truth

fac·tion \'fak-shən\ *n* : a group or combination (as in a government) acting together within and usu. against a larger body : CLIQUE — **fac·tion·al·ism** \-shə-nə-ˌli-zəm\ *n*

fac·tious \'fak-shəs\ *adj* **1** : of, relating to, or caused by faction **2** : inclined to faction or the formation of factions : causing dissension ♦ *Synonyms* INSUBORDINATE, CONTUMACIOUS, INSURGENT, SEDITIOUS, REBELLIOUS

fac·ti·tious \fak-'ti-shəs\ *adj* : ARTIFICIAL, SHAM ⟨a ~ display of grief⟩

fac·toid \'fak-ˌtȯid\ *n* **1** : an invented fact believed to be true because of its appearance in print **2** : a brief usu. trivial fact

¹fac·tor \'fak-tər\ *n* **1** : AGENT **2** : something that actively contributes to a result ⟨a ~ in her decision⟩ **3** : GENE **4** : any of the numbers or symbols in mathematics that when multiplied together form a product; *esp* : any of the integers that divide a given integer without a remainder

²factor *vb* **1** : to work as a factor **2** : to find the mathematical factors of and esp. the prime mathematical factors of

¹fac·to·ri·al \fak-'tȯr-ē-əl\ *adj* : of, relating to, or being a factor

²factorial *n* : the product of all the positive integers from 1 to a given integer *n*

fac·to·ry \'fak-trē, -tə-rē\ *n, pl* **-ries 1** : a trading post where resident brokers trade **2** : a building or group of buildings used for manufacturing

fac·to·tum \fak-'tō-təm\ *n* [NL, lit., do everything, fr. L *fac* do + *totum* everything] : a person (as a servant) having numerous or varied duties

facts of life : the physiological processes and behavior involved in sex and reproduction

fac·tu·al \'fak-chə-wəl\ *adj* : of or relating to facts; *also* : based on fact — **fac·tu·al·ly** *adv*

fac·ul·ty \'fa-kəl-tē\ *n, pl* **-ties 1** : ability

to act or do : POWER; *also* : natural aptitude **2** : one of the powers of the mind or body ⟨the ~ of hearing⟩ **3** : the teachers in a school or college or one of its divisions

fad \'fad\ *n* : a practice or interest followed for a time with exaggerated zeal : CRAZE — **fad·dish** *adj* — **fad·dish·ly** *adv* — **fad·dist** *n*

¹fade \'fād\ *vb* **fad·ed; fad·ing 1** : WITHER **2** : to lose or cause to lose freshness or brilliance of color **3** : VANISH ⟨a *fading* memory⟩ **4** : to grow dim or faint

²fade *n* : a short haircut in which hair on top of the head stands high

FADM *abbr* fleet admiral

fae·cal, fae·ces *chiefly Brit var of* FECAL, FECES

fa·er·ie *also* **fa·ery** \'fā-rē, 'fer-ē\ *n, pl* **fa·er·ies 1** : FAIRYLAND **2** : FAIRY

¹fag \'fag\ *vb* **fagged; fag·ging 1** : DRUDGE **2** : TIRE, EXHAUST ⟨*fagged* by the work⟩

²fag *n* : MENIAL, DRUDGE

³fag *n* : an English public-school boy who acts as servant to another

⁴fag *vb* : to act as a fag

⁵fag *n* : CIGARETTE

fag end *n* **1** : REMNANT **2** : the extreme end **3** : the last part or coarser end of a web of cloth **4** : the untwisted end of a rope

fag·ot *or* **fag·got** \'fa-gət\ *n* : a bundle of sticks or twigs

fag·ot·ing *or* **fag·got·ing** *n* : an embroidery produced by tying threads in hourglass-shaped clusters

Fah *or* **Fahr** *abbr* Fahrenheit

Fahr·en·heit \'fer-ən-ˌhīt\ *adj* : relating to, conforming to, or having a thermometer scale with the boiling point of water at 212 degrees and the freezing point at 32 degrees above zero

fa·ience *or* **fa·ïence** \fā-'äns\ *n* [F] : earthenware decorated with opaque colored glazes

¹fail \'fāl\ *vb* **1** : to become feeble; *esp* : to decline in health **2** : to die away **3** : to stop functioning **4** : to fall short ⟨~*ed* in his duty⟩ **5** : to be or become absent or inadequate **6** : to be unsuccessful esp. in achieving a passing grade **7** : to become bankrupt **8** : DISAPPOINT **9** : NEGLECT ⟨~*ed* to lock the door⟩

²fail *n* : FAILURE ⟨without ~⟩

¹fail·ing \'fā-liŋ\ *n* : WEAKNESS, SHORTCOMING

²failing *prep* : in the absence or lack of

faille \'fī(-ə)l\ *n* : a somewhat shiny closely woven ribbed fabric (as silk)

fail-safe \'fāl-ˌsāf\ *adj* **1** : incorporating a counteractive feature for a possible source of failure **2** : having no chance of failure — **fail-safe** *n*

fail·ure \'fāl-yər\ *n* **1** : a failing to do or perform **2** : a state of inability to perform a normal function adequately ⟨heart ~⟩; *also* : an abrupt cessation of functioning ⟨a power ~⟩ **3** : a fracturing or giving way under stress **4** : a lack of success **5** : BANKRUPTCY **6** : DEFICIEN-

CY ⟨crop ∼⟩ 7 : DETERIORATION, DE-
CAY 8 : one that has failed

¹fain \'fān\ adj 1 archaic : GLAD; also : IN-
CLINED 2 : being obliged or compelled
²fain adv 1 : with pleasure 2 : by preference

¹faint \'fānt\ adj [ME faint, feint, fr. AF, fr.
faindre, feindre to feign, lose heart] 1
: COWARDLY, SPIRITLESS ⟨∼ of heart⟩ 2
: weak, dizzy, and likely to faint 3 : lacking vigor or strength : FEEBLE ⟨∼
praise⟩ 4 : hardly perceptible ⟨∼ hand-
writing⟩ — faint·ly adv — faint·ness n
²faint vb : to lose consciousness
³faint n : the action of fainting; also : the
resulting condition

faint-heart·ed \ˌfānt-'här-təd\ adj : lacking courage : TIMID

¹fair \'fer\ adj 1 : pleasing in appearance
: BEAUTIFUL 2 : superficially pleasing
: SPECIOUS 3 : CLEAN, PURE 4 : CLEAR,
LEGIBLE 5 : not stormy or cloudy 6
: JUST 7 : conforming with the rules : AL-
LOWED; also : being within the foul lines
⟨∼ ball⟩ 8 : open to legitimate pursuit
or attack ⟨∼ game⟩ 9 : PROMISING,
LIKELY ⟨a ∼ chance of winning⟩ 10
: favorable to a ship's course ⟨a ∼ wind⟩
11 : light in complexion : BLOND 12
: ADEQUATE 13 : significant in size ⟨a ∼
amount of traffic⟩ — fair·ness n
²fair adv 1 : in a fair manner ⟨play ∼⟩ 2
chiefly Brit : FAIRLY 4
³fair n 1 : a gathering of buyers and sellers
at a stated time and place for trade 2 : a
competitive exhibition (as of farm products) 3 : a sale of assorted articles usu.
for a charitable purpose ⟨a book ∼⟩ 4
: an exhibition that promotes available
services ⟨a job ∼⟩

fair·ground \-ˌgraund\ n : an area where
outdoor fairs, circuses, or exhibitions are
held

fair·ing \'fer-iŋ\ n : a structure for producing a smooth outline and reducing
drag (as on an airplane)

fair·ly \'fer-lē\ adv 1 : HANDSOMELY 2
: in a manner of speaking ⟨∼ bursting
with pride⟩ 3 : without bias 4 : to a full
degree or extent : PLAINLY, DISTINCTLY
5 : SOMEWHAT, RATHER ⟨a ∼ easy job⟩

fair–spo·ken \'fer-'spō-kən\ adj : pleasant and courteous in speech

fair–trade \-'trād\ adj : of, relating to, or
being an agreement between a producer
and a seller that branded merchandise
will be sold at or above a specified price
— fair–trade vb

fair·way \-ˌwā\ n : the mowed part of a
golf course between tee and green

fairy \'fer-ē\ n, pl fair·ies [ME fairie fairyland, enchantment, fr. AF faerie, fr. fee
fairy, fr. L Fata, goddess of fate, fr. fatum
fate] : an imaginary being of folklore and
romance usu. having diminutive human
form and magic powers — fairy adj

fairy·land \-ˌland\ n 1 : the land of fairies
2 : a beautiful or charming place

fairy tale n 1 : a children's story usu.
about mythical beings (as fairies) 2 : FIB

fait ac·com·pli \ˌfät-ˌä-kōⁿ-'plē\ n, pl
faits accomplis \same or -'plēz\ [F, ac-

complished fact] : a thing accomplished
and presumably irreversible

faith \'fāth\ n, pl faiths \'fāths, 'fāthz\
[ME feith, fr. AF feid, fei, fr. L fides] 1
: allegiance to duty or a person : LOYAL-
TY 2 : belief and trust in God 3 : complete trust 4 : a system of religious beliefs — faith·ful \-fəl\ adj — faith·ful·ly
adv — faith·ful·ness n

faith·less \'fāth-ləs\ adj 1 : DISLOYAL 2
: not to be relied on ♦ Synonyms
FALSE, TRAITOROUS, TREACHEROUS, UN-
FAITHFUL — faith·less·ly adv — faith-
less·ness n

fa·ji·ta \fə-'hē-tə\ n : a marinated strip
usu. of beef or chicken grilled or broiled
and served usu. with a flour tortilla and
savory fillings

¹fake \'fāk\ adj : COUNTERFEIT, SHAM
²fake n 1 : IMITATION, FRAUD; also : IM-
POSTOR 2 : a simulated move in sports
(as a pretended pass)
³fake vb faked; fak·ing 1 : to treat so as
to falsify 2 : COUNTERFEIT 3 : to deceive
(an opponent) in a sports contest by making a fake — fak·er n

fa·kir \fə-'kir\ n [Ar faqīr, lit., poor man]
1 : a Muslim mendicant : DERVISH 2 : a
wandering Hindu ascetic

fal·con \'fal-kən, 'fȯl-\ n 1 : a hawk
trained for use in falconry 2 : any of
various swift long-winged long-tailed
hawks having a notched beak and usu.
inhabiting open areas

fal·con·ry \'fal-kən-rē, 'fȯl-\ n 1 : the art
of training hawks to hunt in cooperation
with a person 2 : the sport of hunting
with hawks — fal·con·er n

¹fall \'fȯl\ vb fell \'fel\; fall·en \'fȯ-lən\;
fall·ing 1 : to descend freely by the force
of gravity 2 : to hang freely 3 : to come
or go as if by falling ⟨darkness fell⟩ 4 : to
become uttered 5 : to lower or become
lowered : DROP ⟨her eyes fell⟩ 6 : to
leave an erect position suddenly and involuntarily 7 : STUMBLE, STRAY 8 : to
drop down wounded or dead esp. in battle 9 : to become captured ⟨the city fell
to the enemy⟩ 10 : to suffer ruin, defeat,
or failure 11 : to commit an immoral act
12 : to move or extend in a downward
direction 13 : SUBSIDE, ABATE 14 : to
decline in quality, activity, quantity, or
value 15 : to assume a look of shame or
dejection ⟨her face fell⟩ 16 : to occur at
a certain time 17 : to come by chance
18 : DEVOLVE ⟨the duties fell to him⟩ 19
: to have the proper place or station ⟨the
accent ∼s on the first syllable⟩ 20 : to
come within the scope of something 21
: to pass from one condition to another
⟨fell ill⟩ 22 : to set about heartily or actively ⟨∼ to work⟩ — fall all over oneself or fall over backward : to display
excessive eagerness — fall flat : to produce no response or result — fall for 1
: to fall in love with 2 : to become a victim of — fall from grace : BACKSLIDE —
fall into line : to comply with a certain
course of action — fall short 1 : to be
deficient 2 : to fail to attain
²fall n 1 : the act of falling 2 : a falling

out, off, or away : DROPPING **3** : AUTUMN **4** : a thing or quantity that falls ⟨a light ∼ of snow⟩ **5** : COLLAPSE, DOWNFALL **6** : the surrender or capture of a besieged place **7** : departure from virtue or goodness **8** : SLOPE **9** : WATERFALL — usu. used in pl. **10** : a decrease in size, quantity, degree, or value ⟨a ∼ in price⟩ **11** : the distance which something falls **12** : an act of forcing a wrestler's shoulders to the mat; *also* : a bout of wrestling

fal·la·cious \fə-ˈlā-shəs\ *adj* **1** : embodying a fallacy ⟨a ∼ argument⟩ **2** : MISLEADING, DECEPTIVE

fal·la·cy \ˈfa-lə-sē\ *n, pl* **-cies** **1** : a false or mistaken idea **2** : an often plausible argument using false or illogical reasoning

fall back *vb* : RETREAT, RECEDE

fall guy *n* : SCAPEGOAT

fal·li·ble \ˈfa-lə-bəl\ *adj* **1** : liable to be erroneous **2** : capable of making a mistake — **fal·li·bly** \-blē\ *adv*

fall·ing–out \ˌfȯ-liŋ-ˈaût\ *n, pl* **fallings–out** *or* **falling–outs** : QUARREL

falling star *n* : METEOR

fal·lo·pi·an tube \fə-ˈlō-pē-ən-\ *n, often cap F* : either of the pair of anatomical tubes that carry the eggs from the ovary to the uterus

fall·out \ˈfȯl-ˌaût\ *n* **1** : the often radioactive particles that result from a nuclear explosion and descend through the air **2** : a secondary and often lingering effect or result

fall out *vb* : QUARREL

¹fal·low \ˈfa-(ˌ)lō\ *n* : fallow land; *also* : the state of being or lying fallow — **fallow** *vb*

²fallow *adj* **1** : left without tilling or sowing after plowing **2** : DORMANT, INACTIVE ⟨a writer's ∼ period⟩

false \ˈfȯls\ *adj* **fals·er; fals·est** **1** : not genuine : ARTIFICIAL ⟨∼ teeth⟩ **2** : intentionally untrue **3** : adjusted or made so as to deceive ⟨∼ scales⟩ **4** : tending to mislead : DECEPTIVE ⟨∼ promises⟩ **5** : not true ⟨∼ concepts⟩ **6** : not faithful or loyal : TREACHEROUS **7** : not essential or permanent ⟨∼ front⟩ **8** : inaccurate in pitch **9** : based on mistaken ideas — **false·ly** *adv* — **false·ness** *n* — **fal·si·ty** \ˈfȯl-sə-tē\ *n*

false·hood \ˈfȯls-ˌhùd\ *n* **1** : LIE **2** : absence of truth or accuracy **3** : the practice of lying

fal·set·to \fȯl-ˈse-tō\ *n, pl* **-tos** [It, fr. dim. of *falso* false] : an artificially high voice; *esp* : an artificial singing voice that overlaps and extends above the range of the full voice esp. of a tenor

fal·si·fy \ˈfȯl-sə-ˌfī\ *vb* **-fied; -fy·ing** **1** : to prove to be false **2** : to alter so as to deceive **3** : LIE; *also* : MISREPRESENT — **fal·si·fi·able** \ˌfȯl-sə-ˈfī-ə-bəl\ *adj* — **fal·si·fi·ca·tion** \ˌfȯl-sə-fə-ˈkā-shən\ *n*

fal·ter \ˈfȯl-tər\ *vb* **1** : to move unsteadily : STUMBLE, TOTTER **2** : to hesitate in speech : STAMMER **3** : to hesitate in purpose or action : WAVER, FLINCH **4** : to lose effectiveness ⟨a ∼*ing* business⟩ — **fal·ter·ing·ly** *adv*

fam *abbr* **1** familiar **2** family

fame \ˈfām\ *n* : public reputation : RENOWN — **famed** \ˈfāmd\ *adj*

fa·mil·ial \fə-ˈmil-yəl\ *adj* **1** : of, relating to, or suggestive of a family **2** : tending to occur in more members of a family than expected by chance alone ⟨a ∼ disorder⟩

¹fa·mil·iar \fə-ˈmil-yər\ *n* **1** : COMPANION **2** : a spirit held to attend and serve or guard a person **3** : one who frequents a place

²familiar *adj* **1** : closely acquainted : INTIMATE **2** : of or relating to a family **3** : INFORMAL ⟨a ∼ style⟩ **4** : FORWARD, PRESUMPTUOUS **5** : frequently seen or experienced ⟨a ∼ face⟩ **6** : of everyday occurrence — **fa·mil·iar·ly** *adv*

fa·mil·iar·ise *Brit var of* FAMILIARIZE

fa·mil·iar·i·ty \fə-ˌmil-ˈyer-ə-tē, -ˌmi-lē-ˈer-\ *n, pl* **-ties** **1** : close friendship : INTIMACY **2** : INFORMALITY **3** : an unduly bold or forward act or expression : IMPROPRIETY **4** : close acquaintance with something ⟨∼ with current software⟩

fa·mil·iar·ize \fə-ˈmil-yə-ˌrīz\ *vb* **-ized; -iz·ing** **1** : to make known or familiar **2** : to make thoroughly acquainted

fam·i·ly \ˈfam-lē, ˈfa-mə-\ *n, pl* **-lies** [ME *familie*, fr. L *familia* household, fr. *famulus* servant] **1** : a group of individuals living under one roof and under one head : HOUSEHOLD **2** : a group of persons of common ancestry : CLAN **3** : a group of things having common characteristics; *esp* : a group of related plants or animals ranking in biological classification above a genus and below an order **4** : a social unit esp. consisting of one or two parents and their children

family planning *n* : planning intended to determine the number and spacing of one's children by using birth control

family tree *n* : GENEALOGY; *also* : a genealogical diagram

fam·ine \ˈfa-mən\ *n* **1** : an extreme scarcity of food **2** : a great shortage

fam·ish \ˈfa-mish\ *vb* **1** : STARVE **2** : to suffer for lack of something necessary

fa·mous \ˈfā-məs\ *adj* **1** : widely known **2** : honored for achievement **3** : EXCELLENT, FIRST-RATE ♦ *Synonyms* RENOWNED, CELEBRATED, NOTED, NOTORIOUS, DISTINGUISHED, EMINENT, ILLUSTRIOUS

fa·mous·ly *adv* : SPLENDIDLY, EXCELLENTLY ⟨got along ∼⟩

¹fan \ˈfan\ *n* : a device (as a hand-waved triangular piece or a mechanism with blades) for producing a current of air

²fan *vb* **fanned; fan·ning** **1** : to drive away the chaff from grain by winnowing **2** : to move (air) with or as if with a fan **3** : to direct a current of air upon ⟨∼ a fire⟩ **4** : to stir up to activity : STIMULATE **5** : to spread like a fan **6** : to strike out in baseball

³fan *n* : an enthusiastic follower or admirer

fa·nat·ic \fə-ˈna-tik\ *or* **fa·nat·i·cal** \-ti-kəl\ *adj* [L *fanaticus* inspired by a deity, frenzied, fr. *fanum* temple] : marked by excessive enthusiasm and often intense uncritical devotion — **fanatic** n — **fa·nat·i·cism** \-tə-ˌsi-zəm\ n

fan·ci·er \'fan-sē-ər\ n 1 : one that has a special liking or interest 2 : a person who breeds or grows some kind of animal or plant for points of excellence

fan·ci·ful \'fan-si-fəl\ adj 1 : marked by, existing in, or given to unrestrained imagination or whim rather than reason 2 : curiously made or shaped ⟨a ~ design⟩ — **fan·ci·ful·ly** adv

¹**fan·cy** \'fan-sē\ vb **fan·cied; fan·cy·ing** 1 : LIKE 2 : IMAGINE 3 : to believe without evidence or certainty 4 : to visualize or interpret as

²**fancy** n, pl **fancies** [ME fantasie, fantsy imagination, image, preference, fr. AF fantasie illusion, fr. L phantasia, fr. Gk. appearance, imagination] 1 : LIKING, INCLINATION; also : LOVE 2 : WHIM, NOTION, IDEA ⟨a passing ~⟩ 3 : IMAGINATION 4 : TASTE, JUDGMENT ♦ **Synonyms** CAPRICE, CROTCHET, VAGARY

³**fancy** adj **fan·ci·er; -est** 1 : WHIMSICAL 2 : not plain : ORNAMENTAL, POSH 3 : of particular excellence 4 : bred esp. for a showy appearance 5 : EXCESSIVE 6 : executed with technical skill and style — **fan·ci·ly** \'fan-sə-lē\ adv

fancy dress n : a costume (as for a masquerade) chosen to suit a fancy

fan·cy–free \ˌfan-sē-'frē\ adj : free from amorous attachment; also : free to imagine

fan·cy·work \'fan-sē-ˌwərk\ n : ornamental needlework (as embroidery)

fan·dan·go \fan-'daŋ-gō\ n, pl **-gos** 1 : a lively Spanish or Spanish-American dance 2 : TOMFOOLERY

fane \'fān\ n 1 : TEMPLE 2 : CHURCH

fan·fare \'fan-ˌfer\ n 1 : a flourish of trumpets 2 : a showy display

fan fiction n : stories involving fictional characters that are written by fans

fang \'faŋ\ n : a long sharp tooth; esp : a grooved or hollow tooth of a venomous snake — **fanged** \'faŋd\ adj

fan·light \'fan-ˌlīt\ n : a semicircular window with radiating bars like a fan that is set over a door or window

fan·ny \'fa-nē\ n, pl **fannies** : BUTTOCKS

fan·tail \'fan-ˌtāl\ n 1 : a fan-shaped tail or end 2 : an overhang at the stern of a ship

fan·ta·sia \fan-'tä-zhə, -zhē-ə, -zē-ə; ˌfan-tə-'zē-ə\ n : a musical composition free and fanciful in form

fan·ta·sise Brit var of FANTASIZE

fan·ta·size \'fan-tə-ˌsīz\ vb **-sized; -sizing** : IMAGINE, DAYDREAM

fan·tas·tic \fan-'tas-tik\ also **fan·tas·ti·cal** \-ti-kəl\ adj 1 : IMAGINARY, UNREAL 2 : conceived by unrestrained fancy 3 : exceedingly or unbelievably great 4 : ECCENTRIC ♦ **Synonyms** CHIMERICAL, FANCIFUL, IMAGINARY — **fan·tas·ti·cal·ly** \-ti-k(ə-)lē\ adv

fan·ta·sy also **phan·ta·sy** \'fan-tə-sē\ n, pl **-sies** 1 : IMAGINATION, FANCY 2 : a product of the imagination : ILLUSION 3 : FANTASIA — **fantasy** vb

FAQ abbr frequently asked question

¹**far** \'fär\ adv **far·ther** \-thər\ or **fur·ther** \'fər-\; **far·thest** or **fur·thest** \-thəst\ 1 : at or to a considerable distance in space or time ⟨~ from home⟩ 2 : by a broad interval : WIDELY, MUCH ⟨~ better⟩ 3 : to or at a definite distance, point, or degree ⟨as ~ as I know⟩ 4 : to an advanced point or extent ⟨go ~ in his field⟩ — **by far** : by a considerable margin — **far and away** : DECIDEDLY — **so far** : until now

²**far** adj **farther** or **further; farthest** or **furthest** 1 : remote in space or time 2 : DIFFERENT 3 : LONG ⟨a ~ journey⟩ 4 : being the more distant of two ⟨on the ~ side of the lake⟩

far·ad \'fer-ˌad, -əd\ n : a unit of capacitance equal to the capacitance of a capacitor having a potential difference of one volt between its plates when it is charged with one coulomb of electricity

far·away \'fär-ə-ˌwā\ adj 1 : DISTANT, REMOTE ⟨~ lands⟩ 2 : DREAMY

farce \'färs\ n 1 : a broadly satirical comedy with an improbable plot 2 : the humor characteristic of farce or pretense 3 : a ridiculous or empty display — **far·ci·cal** \'fär-si-kəl\ adj

far cry n 1 : a long distance 2 : something notably different ⟨a far cry from what we expected⟩

¹**fare** \'fer\ vb **fared; far·ing** 1 : GO, TRAVEL 2 : GET ALONG, SUCCEED ⟨fared well in math⟩ 3 : EAT, DINE

²**fare** n 1 : range of food : DIET; also : material provided for use, consumption, or enjoyment 2 : the price charged to transport a person 3 : a person paying a fare : PASSENGER

¹**fare·well** \fer-'wel\ vb imper : get along well — used interjectionally to or by one departing

²**farewell** n 1 : a wish of well-being at parting : GOOD-BYE 2 : LEAVE-TAKING

³**fare·well** \'fer-ˌwel\ adj : PARTING, FINAL ⟨a ~ concert⟩

far–fetched \'fär-'fecht\ adj : not easily or naturally deduced or introduced : IMPROBABLE ⟨a ~ story⟩

far–flung \-'fləŋ\ adj : widely spread or distributed ⟨a ~ empire⟩

fa·ri·na \fə-'rē-nə\ n [L, meal, flour] : a fine meal (as of wheat) used in puddings or as a breakfast cereal

far·i·na·ceous \ˌfer-ə-'nā-shəs\ adj 1 : having a mealy texture or surface 2 : containing or rich in starch

¹**farm** \'färm\ n [ME ferme rent, lease, fr. AF, fr. fermer to fix, rent, fr. L firmare to make firm, fr. firmus firm] 1 : a tract of land used for raising crops or livestock 2 : a minor-league subsidiary of a major-league team

²**farm** vb : to use (land) as a farm ⟨~ed 200 acres⟩; also : to raise crops or livestock — **farm·er** n

farm·hand \'färm-ˌhand\ n : a farm laborer

farm·house \-ˌhau̇s\ n : a dwelling on a farm

farm·ing \'fär-miŋ\ n : the occupation or business of a person who farms

farmland • fat

farm·land \'färm-ˌland\ *n* : land used or suitable for farming

farm out *vb* : to turn over (as a task) to another

farm·stead \'färm-ˌsted\ *n* : a farm with its buildings

farm·yard \-ˌyärd\ *n* : land around or enclosed by farm buildings

far-off \'fär-'óf\ *adj* : remote in time or space : DISTANT

fa·rouche \fə-'rüsh\ *adj* [F] 1 : WILD 2 : marked by shyness and lack of polish

far-out \'fär-'aút\ *adj* : very unconventional ⟨∼ clothes⟩

far·ra·go \fə-'rä-gō, -'rā-\ *n, pl* **-goes** [L, mixed fodder, mixture] : a confused collection : MIXTURE

far-reach·ing \'fär-'rē-chiŋ\ *adj* : having a wide range or effect

far·ri·er \'fer-ē-ər\ *n* [alter. of ME *ferrour*, fr. AF, blacksmith, fr. *ferrer* to shoe (horses)] : a person who shoes horses

¹far·row \'fer-ō\ *vb* : to give birth to a litter of pigs

²farrow *n* : a litter of pigs

far-see·ing \'fär-ˌsē-iŋ\ *adj* 1 : FARSIGHTED 1 2 : FARSIGHTED 2

far·sight·ed \'fär-ˌsī-təd\ *adj* 1 : seeing or able to see to a great distance 2 : JUDICIOUS, WISE, SHREWD 3 : affected with an eye condition in which vision is better for distant than near objects — **far·sight·ed·ness** *n*

¹far·ther \'fär-thər\ *adv* 1 : at or to a greater distance or more advanced point 2 : to a greater degree or extent

²farther *adj* 1 : more distant 2 : ADDITIONAL

far·ther·most \-ˌmōst\ *adj* : FARTHEST

¹far·thest \'fär-thəst\ *adj* : most distant

²farthest *adv* 1 : to or at the greatest distance : REMOTEST ⟨hit the ball ∼⟩ 2 : to the most advanced point 3 : by the greatest degree or extent : MOST

far·thing \'fär-thiŋ\ *n* 1 : a former British monetary unit equal to ¹/₄ of a penny; *also* : a coin representing this unit 2 : something of small value

fas·cia \1 *is usu* 'fā-sh(ē-)ə, 2 *is usu* 'fa-\ *n, pl* **-ci·ae** \-shē-ˌē\ *or* **-cias** 1 : a flat usu. horizontal part (as a band or board) of or on a building 2 : a sheet of connective tissue covering body structures (as muscles)

fas·ci·cle \'fa-si-kəl\ *n* 1 : a small or slender bundle (as of pine needles or nerve fibers) 2 : one of the divisions of a book published in parts — **fas·ci·cled** \-kəld\ *adj*

fas·ci·nate \'fa-sə-ˌnāt\ *vb* **-nat·ed; -nat·ing** [L *fascinare*, fr. *fascinum* evil spell] 1 : to transfix and hold spellbound by an irresistible power 2 : ALLURE 3 : to be irresistibly attractive — **fas·ci·na·tion** \ˌfa-sə-'nā-shən\ *n*

fas·cism \'fa-ˌshi-zəm\ *n, often cap* : a political philosophy, movement, or regime that exalts nation and often race and stands for a centralized autocratic often militaristic government — **fas·cist** \-shist\ *n or adj, often cap* — **fas·cis·tic** \fa-'shis-tik\ *adj, often cap*

¹fash·ion \'fa-shən\ *n* 1 : the make or form of something 2 : MANNER, WAY 3 : a prevailing custom, usage, or style 4 : the prevailing style (as in dress) ♦ *Synonyms* MODE, VOGUE, RAGE, TREND

²fashion *vb* 1 : MOLD, CONSTRUCT ⟨∼ a vase out of clay⟩ 2 : FIT, ADAPT

fash·ion·able \'fa-shə-nə-bəl\ *adj* 1 : dressing or behaving according to fashion : STYLISH 2 : of or relating to the world of fashion ⟨∼ resorts⟩ ♦ *Synonyms* CHIC, MODISH, SMART, SWANK — **fash·ion·ably** \-blē\ *adv*

¹fast \'fast\ *adj* 1 : firmly fixed 2 : tightly shut 3 : adhering firmly 4 : STUCK 5 : STAUNCH ⟨∼ friends⟩ 6 : characterized by quick motion, operation, or effect ⟨a ∼ trip⟩ ⟨a ∼ track⟩ 7 : indicating ahead of the correct time ⟨the clock is ∼⟩ 8 : not easily disturbed : SOUND ⟨a ∼ sleep⟩ 9 : permanently dyed; *also* : being proof against fading ⟨colors ∼ to sunlight⟩ 10 : DISSIPATED, WILD ⟨a ∼ crowd⟩ 11 : sexually promiscuous ♦ *Synonyms* RAPID, SWIFT, FLEET, QUICK, SPEEDY, HASTY

²fast *adv* 1 : in a firm or fixed manner ⟨stuck ∼ in the mud⟩ 2 : SOUNDLY, DEEPLY ⟨∼ asleep⟩ 3 : SWIFTLY 4 : RECKLESSLY

³fast *vb* 1 : to abstain from food 2 : to eat sparingly or abstain from some foods

⁴fast *n* 1 : the act or practice of fasting 2 : a time of fasting

fast·back \'fast-ˌbak\ *n* : an automobile having a roof with a long slope to the rear

fast·ball \-ˌból\ *n* : a baseball pitch thrown at full speed

fas·ten \'fa-sᵊn\ *vb* 1 : to attach or join by or as if by pinning, tying, or nailing 2 : to make fast : fix securely 3 : to become fixed or joined 4 : to focus attention ⟨∼ed onto the newest trends⟩ — **fas·ten·er** *n*

fas·ten·ing *n* : something that fastens : FASTENER

fast-food \ˌfast-'füd\ *adj* : specializing in food that is prepared and served quickly ⟨a ∼ restaurant⟩

fast-for·ward \-'fór-wərd\ *n* 1 : a function of an electronic device that advances a recording rapidly 2 : a state of rapid advancement — **fast-forward** *vb*

fas·tid·i·ous \fa-'sti-dē-əs\ *adj* 1 : overly difficult to please 2 : showing a meticulous or demanding attitude ⟨∼ workmanship⟩ ♦ *Synonyms* NICE, FINICKY, FUSSY, PARTICULAR, PERSNICKETY, SQUEAMISH — **fas·tid·i·ous·ly** *adv* — **fas·tid·i·ous·ness** *n*

fast·ness \'fast-nəs\ *n* 1 : the quality or state of being fast 2 : a fortified or secure place : STRONGHOLD

fast-talk \'fast-ˌtók\ *vb* : to influence by persuasive and usu. deceptive talk

fast-track \'fast-ˌtrak\ *vb* : to speed up the processing or production of

fast track *n* : a course leading to rapid advancement or success

¹fat \'fat\ *adj* **fat·ter; fat·test** 1 : PLUMP, OBESE 2 : OILY, GREASY 3 : well filled out : BIG 4 : well stocked : ABUNDANT 5 : richly rewarding — **fat·ness** n

²**fat** n 1 : animal tissue rich in greasy or oily matter 2 : any of various energy-rich esters that occur naturally in animal fats and in plants and are soluble in organic solvents (as ether) but not in water 3 : the best or richest portion ⟨lived on the ~ of the land⟩ 4 : OBESITY 5 : excess matter ⟨trim the ~ from the budget⟩

fa·tal \'fāt-ᵊl\ adj 1 : FATEFUL ⟨that ~ day⟩ 2 : causing death or ruin ⟨a ~ mistake⟩ — **fa·tal·ly** adv

fa·tal·ism \-ᵢ-zəm\ n : the belief that events are determined by fate — **fa·tal·ist** \-ist\ n — **fa·tal·is·tic** \ˌfāt-ᵊl-'is-tik\ adj — **fa·tal·is·ti·cal·ly** \-ti-k(ə-)lē\ adv

fa·tal·i·ty \fā-'ta-lə-tē, fə-\ n, pl **-ties** 1 : DEADLINESS 2 : FATE 3 : death resulting from a disaster or accident; also : one who suffers such a death

fat·back \'fat-ˌbak\ n : a fatty strip from the back of the hog usu. cured by salting and drying

fat cat n 1 : a wealthy contributor to a political campaign 2 : a wealthy privileged person

fate \'fāt\ n [ME, fr. MF or L; MF, fr. L fatum, lit., what has been spoken, fr. fari to speak] 1 : the cause or will that is held to determine events : DESTINY 2 : LOT, FORTUNE 3 : DISASTER; esp : DEATH 4 : END, OUTCOME 5 pl, cap : the three goddesses of classical mythology who determine the course of human life

fat·ed \'fā-təd\ adj : decreed, controlled, or marked by fate

fate·ful \'fāt-fəl\ adj 1 : OMINOUS, PROPHETIC 2 : IMPORTANT, DECISIVE 3 : DEADLY, DESTRUCTIVE 4 : determined by fate — **fate·ful·ly** adv

fath abbr fathom

fat·head \'fat-ˌhed\ n : a stupid person — **fat·head·ed** \-'he-dəd\ adj

¹**fa·ther** \'fä-thər\ n 1 : a male parent 2 cap : God esp. as the first person of the Trinity 3 : FOREFATHER 4 : one deserving the respect and love given to a father 5 often cap : an early Christian writer accepted by the church as an authoritative witness to its teaching and practice 6 : ORIGINATOR ⟨the ~ of modern radio⟩; also : SOURCE 7 : PRIEST — used esp. as a title 8 : one of the leading men ⟨city ~s⟩ — **fa·ther·hood** \-ˌhüd\ n — **fa·ther·less** adj — **fa·ther·ly** adj

²**father** vb 1 : BEGET 2 : to be the founder, producer, or author of 3 : to treat or care for as a father

father–in–law \'fä-thə-rən-ˌlò\ n, pl **fathers–in–law** \-thər-zən-\ : the father of one's husband or wife

fa·ther·land \'fä-thər-ˌland\ n 1 : the native land of one's ancestors 2 : one's native land

¹**fath·om** \'fa-thəm\ n [ME fadme, fr. OE fæthm length of the outstretched arms] : a unit of length equal to 6 feet (about 1.8 meters) used esp. for measuring the depth of water

²**fathom** vb 1 : to measure by a sounding line 2 : PROBE 3 : to penetrate and come

to understand ⟨~ the problem⟩ — **fath·om·able** \'fa-thə-mə-bəl\ adj

fath·om·less \'fa-thəm-ləs\ adj : incapable of being fathomed

¹**fa·tigue** \fə-'tēg\ n [F] 1 : manual or menial work performed by military personnel 2 pl : the uniform or work clothing worn on fatigue and in the field 3 : weariness from labor or stress 4 : the tendency of a material to break under repeated stress

²**fatigue** vb **fa·tigued; fa·tigu·ing** : WEARY, TIRE

fat·ten \'fa-tᵊn\ vb : to make or grow fat

Fat Tuesday n : MARDI GRAS

¹**fat·ty** \'fa-tē\ adj **fat·ti·er; -est** 1 : containing fat esp. in unusual amounts 2 : GREASY

²**fatty** n, pl **fat·ties** : a fat person

fatty acid n : any of numerous acids that contain only carbon, hydrogen, and oxygen and that occur naturally in fats and various oils

fa·tu·ity \fə-'tü-ə-tē, -'tyü-\ n, pl **-ities** : FOOLISHNESS, STUPIDITY

fat·u·ous \'fa-chú-wəs\ adj : FOOLISH, INANE, SILLY — **fat·u·ous·ly** adv

fau·bourg \fō-'bùr\ n 1 : a suburb esp. of a French city 2 : a city quarter

fau·ces \'fò-ˌsēz\ n pl [L, throat] : the narrow passage located between the soft palate and the base of the tongue that joins the mouth to the pharynx

fau·cet \'fò-sət, 'fä-\ n : a fixture for drawing off a liquid (as from a pipe)

¹**fault** \'fólt\ n 1 : a weakness in character : FAILING 2 : IMPERFECTION, IMPAIRMENT, DEFECT 3 : an error esp. in service in a net or racket game 4 : MISDEMEANOR; also : MISTAKE 5 : responsibility for something wrong 6 : a fracture in the earth's crust accompanied by a displacement of one side relative to the other — **fault·i·ly** \'fól-tə-lē\ adv — **fault·less** adj — **fault·less·ly** adv — **faulty** adj

²**fault** vb 1 : to commit a fault : ERR 2 : to fracture so as to produce a geologic fault 3 : to find a fault in 4 : BLAME, CRITICIZE

fault·find·er \'fólt-ˌfīn-dər\ n : a person who tends to find fault or complain ♦ **Synonyms** CRITIC, CARPER, CAVILER, COMPLAINER — **fault·find·ing** n or adj

faun \'fòn\ n : a Roman god similar to but gentler than a satyr

fau·na \'fò-nə\ n, pl **faunas** also **fau·nae** \-ˌnē, -ˌnī\ [NL, fr. L Fauna, sister of Faunus (the Roman god of animals)] : animals or animal life esp. of a region, period, or environment — **fau·nal** \-nᵊl\ adj

fau·vism \'fō-ˌvi-zəm\ n, often cap : a movement in painting characterized by vivid colors, free treatment of form, and a vibrant and decorative effect — **fau·vist** \-vist\ n, often cap

faux pas \'fō-ˌpä, fō-'\ n, pl **faux pas** \same or -ˌpäz, -'päz\ [F, lit., false step] : BLUNDER; esp : a social blunder

fa·va bean \'fä-və-\ n : the large flat edible seed of an Old World vetch; also : this plant

¹**fa·vor** \'fā-vər\ n 1 : friendly regard

shown toward another esp. by a superior **2** : APPROVAL **3** : PARTIALITY **4** : POPULARITY **5** : gracious kindness; *also* : an act of such kindness **6** *pl* : effort in one's behalf : ATTENTION **7** : a token of love (as a ribbon) usu. worn conspicuously **8** : a small gift or decorative item given out at a party **9** : a special privilege **10** : sexual privileges — usu. used in pl. **11** *archaic* : LETTER **12** : BEHALF, INTEREST ⟨acted in his own ∼⟩

²**favor** *vb* **1** : to regard or treat with favor **2** : OBLIGE **3** : ENDOW ⟨∼ed by nature⟩ **4** : to treat gently or carefully : SPARE ⟨∼ a lame leg⟩ **5** : PREFER **6** : SUPPORT, SUSTAIN ⟨∼ed the tax reform⟩ **7** : FACILITATE ⟨darkness ∼s attack⟩ **8** : RESEMBLE ⟨he ∼s his father⟩

fa·vor·a·ble \\'fā-və-rə-bəl\\ *adj* **1** : APPROVING ⟨a ∼ response⟩ **2** : HELPFUL, PROMISING, ADVANTAGEOUS ⟨∼ weather⟩ — **fa·vor·a·bly** \\-blē\\ *adv*

fa·vor·ite \\'fā-və-rət, -vrət\\ *n* **1** : a person or a thing that is favored above others **2** : a competitor regarded as most likely to win — **favorite** *adj*

favorite son *n* : a candidate supported by the delegates of his state at a presidential nominating convention

fa·vor·it·ism \\'fā-və-rə-ˌti-zəm\\ *n* : PARTIALITY, BIAS

fa·vour *chiefly Brit var of* FAVOR

¹**fawn** \\'fȯn, 'fän\\ *vb* **1** : to show affection ⟨a dog ∼ing on its master⟩ **2** : to court favor by a cringing or flattering manner ♦ **Synonyms** GROVEL, KOWTOW, TOADY, TRUCKLE

²**fawn** *n* **1** : a young deer **2** : a light grayish brown — **fawny** \\'fȯ-nē, 'fä-\\ *adj*

fax \\'faks\\ *n* **1** : FACSIMILE 2 **2** : a device used to send or receive facsimile communications; *also* : such a communication — **fax** *vb*

fay \\'fā\\ *n* : FAIRY, ELF — **fay** *adj*

faze \\'fāz\\ *vb* **fazed; faz·ing** : to disturb the composure or courage of : DAUNT

FBI *abbr* Federal Bureau of Investigation

FCC *abbr* Federal Communications Commission

FD *abbr* fire department

FDA *abbr* Food and Drug Administration

FDIC *abbr* Federal Deposit Insurance Corporation

Fe *symbol* [L *ferrum*] iron

fe·al·ty \\'fē(-ə)l-tē\\ *n, pl* **-ties** : LOYALTY, ALLEGIANCE ♦ **Synonyms** FIDELITY, DEVOTION, FAITHFULNESS, PIETY

¹**fear** \\'fir\\ *vb* **1** : to have a reverent awe of ⟨∼ God⟩ **2** : to be afraid of ⟨∼s spiders⟩ **3** : to be apprehensive

²**fear** *n* **1** : an unpleasant often strong emotion caused by expectation or awareness of danger; *also* : an instance of or a state marked by this emotion **2** : anxious concern : SOLICITUDE **3** : profound reverence esp. toward God ♦ **Synonyms** DREAD, FRIGHT, ALARM, PANIC, TERROR, TREPIDATION

fear·ful \\-fəl\\ *adj* **1** : causing fear **2** : filled with fear **3** : showing or caused by fear **4** : extremely bad, intense, or large ⟨paid a ∼ price⟩ — **fear·ful·ly** *adv*

fear·less \\-ləs\\ *adj* : free from fear : BRAVE — **fear·less·ly** *adv* — **fear·less·ness** *n*

fear·some \\-səm\\ *adj* **1** : causing fear **2** : TIMID **3** : INTENSE ⟨∼ determination⟩

fea·si·ble \\'fē-zə-bəl\\ *adj* [ME *faisible*, fr. AF *faisable*, fr. *fais-*, stem of *faire* to make, do] **1** : capable of being done or carried out ⟨a ∼ plan⟩ **2** : SUITABLE **3** : REASONABLE, LIKELY ♦ **Synonyms** POSSIBLE, PRACTICABLE, VIABLE, WORKABLE — **fea·si·bil·i·ty** \\ˌfē-zə-'bi-lə-tē\\ *n* — **fea·si·bly** \\'fē-zə-blē\\ *adv*

¹**feast** \\'fēst\\ *n* **1** : an elaborate meal : BANQUET **2** : ABUNDANCE ⟨a ∼ of good books⟩ **3** : FESTIVAL 1

²**feast** *vb* **1** : to take part in a feast; *also* : to give a feast for **2** : to enjoy some unusual pleasure or delight **3** : DELIGHT, GRATIFY

feat \\'fēt\\ *n* : DEED, EXPLOIT, ACHIEVEMENT; *esp* : an act notable for courage, skill, endurance, or ingenuity

¹**feath·er** \\'fe-thər\\ *n* **1** : any of the light horny outgrowths that form the external covering of the body of a bird **2** : the vane of an arrow **3** : PLUMAGE **4** : KIND, NATURE ⟨birds of a ∼⟩ **5** : ATTIRE, DRESS ⟨in full ∼⟩ **6** : CONDITION, MOOD ⟨in fine ∼⟩ — **feath·ered** \\-thərd\\ — **feath·er·less** *adj* — **feath·ery** *adj* — **a feather in one's cap** : a mark of distinction : HONOR

²**feather** *vb* **1** : to furnish with a feather ⟨∼ an arrow⟩ **2** : to cover, clothe, line, or adorn with or as if with feathers — **feather one's nest** : to provide for oneself financially esp. while exploiting a position of trust

feath·er·bed·ding \\'fe-thər-ˌbe-diŋ\\ *n* : the requiring of an employer usu. under a union rule or safety statute to employ more workers than are needed

feath·er·edge \\-ˌej\\ *n* : a very thin sharp edge

feath·er·weight \\-ˌwāt\\ *n* : one that is very light in weight; *esp* : a boxer weighing more than 118 but not over 126 pounds

¹**fea·ture** \\'fē-chər\\ *n* [ME *feture*, fr. AF, fr. L *factura* act of making, fr. *facere* to make] **1** : the shape or appearance of the face or its parts **2** : a part of the face ⟨her eyes are her best ∼⟩ **3** : a prominent part or characteristic **4** : a special attraction (as in a newspaper) **5** : something offered to the public or advertised as particularly attractive ⟨a new car's ∼s⟩ — **fea·ture·less** *adj*

²**feature** *vb* **1** : to picture in the mind : IMAGINE **2** : to give special prominence to ⟨the show ∼s new artists⟩ **3** : to play an important part

Feb *abbr* February

fe·brile \\'fe-ˌbrī(-ə)l\\ *adj* : FEVERISH

Feb·ru·ary \\'fe-b(y)ə-ˌwer-ē, 'fe-brə-\\ *n* [ME *Februarie*, fr. L *Februarius*, fr. *Februa*, pl., feast of purification] : the 2d month of the year

fe·ces \\'fē-ˌsēz\\ *n pl* : bodily waste discharged from the intestine : EXCREMENT — **fe·cal** \\-kəl\\ *adj*

feck·less \'fek-ləs\ adj 1 : WEAK, INEF-FECTIVE 2 : WORTHLESS, IRRESPONSI-BLE ⟨~ drifters⟩

fe·cund \'fe-kənd, 'fē-\ adj : FRUITFUL, PROLIFIC ⟨~ fields⟩ — **fe·cun·di·ty** \fi-'kən-də-tē, fe-\ n

fe·cun·date \'fe-kən-ˌdāt, 'fē-\ vb **-dat·ed; -dat·ing** 1 : to make fecund 2 : IM-PREGNATE — **fe·cun·da·tion** \ˌfe-kən-'dā-shən, ˌfē-\ n

fed abbr federal; federation

fed·er·al \'fe-də-rəl, -drəl\ adj 1 : formed by a compact between political units that surrender individual sovereignty to a central authority but retain certain limited powers 2 : of or constituting a form of government in which power is distributed between a central authority and constituent territorial units 3 : of or relating to the central government of a federation 4 cap : FEDERALIST 5 often cap : of, relating to, or loyal to the federal government or the Union armies of the U.S. in the American Civil War — **fed·er·al·ly** adv

Federal n : a supporter of the U.S. government in the Civil War; esp : a soldier in the federal armies

federal district n : a district (as the District of Columbia) set apart as the seat of the central government of a federation

fed·er·al·ism \'fe-də-rə-li-zəm, -drə-\ n often cap 1 : the distribution of power in an organization (as a government) between a central authority and the constituent units 2 : support or advocacy of federalism 3 cap : the principles of the Federalists

fed·er·al·ist \-list\ n 1 : an advocate of federalism 2 often cap : an advocate of a federal union between the American colonies after the Revolution and of adoption of the U.S. Constitution 3 cap : a member of a major political party in the early years of the U.S. favoring a strong centralized national government — **federalist** adj, often cap

fed·er·al·ize \'fe-də-rə-ˌlīz, -drə-\ vb **-ized; -iz·ing** 1 : to unite in or under a federal system 2 : to bring under the jurisdiction of a federal government

fed·er·ate \'fe-də-ˌrāt\ vb **-at·ed; -at·ing** : to join in a federation

fed·er·a·tion \ˌfe-də-'rā-shən\ n 1 : a political or societal entity formed by uniting smaller entities 2 : a federal government 3 : a union of organizations 4 : the forming of a federal union

fedn abbr federation

fe·do·ra \fi-'dȯr-ə\ n : a low soft felt hat with the crown creased lengthwise

fed up adj : utterly disgusted, tired, or disgusted ⟨fed up with bureaucracy⟩

fee \'fē\ n [ME, fr. AF fé, fief, of Gmc origin; akin to OE feoh cattle, property] 1 : an estate in land held from a feudal lord 2 : an inherited or heritable estate in land 3 : a fixed charge; also : a charge for a service

fee·ble \'fē-bəl\ adj **fee·bler** \-bə-lər\; **fee·blest** \-bə-ləst\ [ME feble, fr. AF, fr. L flebilis lamentable, wretched, fr. flēre to

weep] 1 : DECREPIT, FRAIL 2 : INEFFEC-TIVE, INADEQUATE ⟨a ~ protest⟩ — **fee·ble·ness** n — **fee·bly** \-blē\ adv

fee·ble·mind·ed \ˌfē-bəl-'mīn-dəd\ adj : lacking normal intelligence — **fee·ble·mind·ed·ness** n

¹**feed** \'fēd\ vb **fed** \'fed\; **feed·ing** 1 : to give food to; also : to give as food 2 : EAT 1; also : PREY 3 : to furnish what is necessary to the development or function of ⟨used wood to ~ the fire⟩ 4 : to supply for another to use ⟨~ a pass⟩ ⟨fed the actor his lines⟩ — **feed·er** n

²**feed** n 1 : a usu. large meal 2 : food for livestock 3 : a mechanism for feeding material to a machine

feed·back \'fēd-ˌbak\ n 1 : the return to the input of a part of the output of a machine, system, or process 2 : response esp. to one in authority about an activity or policy 3 : sound (as whistling) resulting from the retransmission of an amplified or broadcast signal

feed·lot \'fēd-ˌlät\ n : land on which cattle are fattened for market

feed·stuff \-ˌstəf\ n : FEED 2

¹**feel** \'fēl\ vb **felt** \'felt\; **feel·ing** 1 : to perceive or examine through physical contact : TOUCH, HANDLE 2 : EXPERI-ENCE; also : to suffer from 3 : to ascertain by cautious trial ⟨~ out public sentiment⟩ 4 : to be aware of 5 : to be conscious of an inward impression, state of mind, or physical condition 6 : BELIEVE, THINK ⟨say what you ~⟩ 7 : to search for something with the fingers : GROPE 8 : SEEM ⟨it ~s like spring⟩ 9 : to have sympathy or pity

²**feel** n 1 : the sense of touch 2 : SENSA-TION, FEELING 3 : the quality of a thing as imparted through touch

feel·er \'fē-lər\ n 1 : one that feels; esp : a tactile organ (as on the head of an insect) 2 : a proposal or remark made to find out the views of other people

¹**feel·ing** \'fē-liŋ\ n 1 : the sense of touch; also : a sensation perceived by this 2 : a state of mind ⟨a ~ of loneliness⟩ 3 pl : general emotional condition : SENSIBIL-ITIES ⟨hurt their ~s⟩ 4 : OPINION, BE-LIEF 5 : capacity to respond emotionally

²**feeling** adj 1 : SENSITIVE; esp : easily moved emotionally 2 : expressing emotion or sensitivity — **feel·ing·ly** adv

feet pl of FOOT

feign \'fān\ vb 1 : to give a false appearance of : SHAM ⟨~ illness⟩ 2 : to assert as if true : PRETEND

feint \'fānt\ n : something feigned; esp : a mock blow or attack intended to distract attention from the real point of attack — **feint** vb

feisty \'fī-stē\ adj **feist·i·er; -est** : having or showing a lively aggressiveness ⟨a ~ heroine⟩

feld·spar \'feld-ˌspär\ n : any of a group of crystalline minerals consisting of silicates of aluminum with another element (as potassium or sodium)

fe·lic·i·tate \fi-'li-sə-ˌtāt\ vb **-tat·ed; -tat·ing** : CONGRATULATE ⟨felicitated the winner⟩ — **fe·lic·i·ta·tion** \-ˌli-sə-ˈtā-shən\ n

fe·lic·i·tous \fi-ˈli-sə-təs\ adj 1 : well chosen : APT 2 : PLEASANT, DELIGHTFUL — **fe·lic·i·tous·ly** adv

fe·lic·i·ty \fi-ˈli-sə-tē\ n, pl **-ties** 1 : the quality or state of being happy; esp : great happiness 2 : something that causes happiness 3 : a pleasing manner or quality esp. in art or language ⟨her ∼ with words⟩ 4 : an apt expression

fe·line \ˈfē-ˌlīn\ adj [L felinus, fr. felis cat] 1 : of or relating to cats or their kin 2 : sleekly graceful 3 : SLY, TREACHEROUS 4 : STEALTHY — **feline** n

¹**fell** \ˈfel\ n : SKIN, HIDE, PELT

²**fell** vb 1 : to cut, beat, or knock down; also : KILL 2 : to sew (a seam) by folding one raw edge under the other

³**fell** past of FALL

⁴**fell** adj : CRUEL, FIERCE; also : DEADLY — **in one fell swoop** also **at one fell swoop** : all at once : with a single effort

fel·lah \ˈfe-lə, fə-ˈlä\ n, pl **fel·la·hin** or **fel·la·heen** \ˌfe-lə-ˈhēn\ : a peasant or agricultural laborer in Arab countries (as Egypt or Syria)

fel·la·tio \fə-ˈlā-shē-ˌō\ also **fel·la·tion** \-shən\ n : oral stimulation of the penis

fel·low \ˈfe-lō\ n [ME felawe, fr. OE fēolaga, fr. ON fēlagi, fr. fēlag partnership (fr. fē cattle, money) + lag act of laying)] 1 : COMRADE, ASSOCIATE 2 : EQUAL, PEER 3 : one of a pair : MATE 4 : a member of an incorporated literary or scientific society 5 : MAN, BOY 6 : BOYFRIEND 7 : a person granted a stipend for advanced study

fellow man n : a kindred human being

fel·low·ship \ˈfe-lō-ˌship\ n 1 : the condition of friendly relationship existing among persons : COMRADESHIP 2 : a community of interest or feeling 3 : a group with similar interests 4 : the position of a fellow (as of a university) 5 : the stipend granted a fellow

fellow traveler n : a sympathetic supporter of another's cause; esp : a person who sympathizes with and often furthers the ideals and program of an organized group (as the Communist party) without joining it

fel·on \ˈfe-lən\ n 1 : one who has committed a felony 2 : WHITLOW

fel·o·ny \ˈfe-lə-nē\ n, pl **-nies** : a serious crime punishable by a heavy sentence — **fe·lo·ni·ous** \fə-ˈlō-nē-əs\ adj

fel·spar chiefly Brit var of FELDSPAR

¹**felt** \ˈfelt\ n 1 : a cloth made of wool and fur often mixed with natural or synthetic fibers 2 : a material resembling felt

²**felt** past and past part of FEEL

fem abbr 1 female 2 feminine

FEMA abbr Federal Emergency Management Agency

fe·male \ˈfē-ˌmāl\ adj [ME, alter. of femel, fr. AF femele, fr. ML femella, fr. L, girl, dim. of femina woman] 1 : of, relating to, or being the sex that bears young; also : PISTILLATE 2 : characteristic of girls or women ⟨∼ voices⟩ ◆ **Synonyms** FEMI-

NINE, WOMANLY, WOMANLIKE, WOMANISH, EFFEMINATE — **female** n

¹**fem·i·nine** \ˈfe-mə-nən\ adj 1 : of the female sex; also : characteristic of or appropriate or peculiar to women 2 : of, relating to, or constituting the gender that includes most words or grammatical forms referring to females — **fem·i·nin·i·ty** \ˌfe-mə-ˈni-nə-tē\ n

²**feminine** n : a noun, pronoun, adjective, or inflectional form or class of the feminine gender; also : the feminine gender

fem·i·nism \ˈfe-mə-ˌni-zəm\ n 1 : the theory of the political, economic, and social equality of the sexes 2 : organized activity on behalf of women's rights and interests — **fem·i·nist** \-nist\ n or adj

femme fa·tale \ˌfem-fə-ˈtal\ n, pl **femmes fa·tales** \same or -ˈtalz\ [F, lit., disastrous woman] : a seductive woman

fe·mur \ˈfē-mər\ n, pl **fe·murs** or **fem·o·ra** \ˈfe-mə-rə\ : the long leg bone extending from the hip to the knee — **fem·o·ral** \ˈfe-mə-rəl\ adj

¹**fen** \ˈfen\ n : low swampy land

²**fen** \ˈfən\ n, pl **fen** — see yuan at MONEY table

¹**fence** \ˈfens\ n [ME fens, short for defens defense] 1 : a barrier (as of wood or wire) to prevent escape or entry or to mark a boundary 2 : a person who receives stolen goods; also : a place where stolen goods are disposed of — **on the fence** : in a position of neutrality or indecision

²**fence** vb **fenced; fenc·ing** 1 : to enclose with a fence 2 : to keep in or out with a fence 3 : to practice fencing 4 : to use tactics of attack and defense esp. in debate — **fenc·er** n

fenc·ing n 1 : the art or practice of attack and defense with the foil, épée, or saber 2 : the fences of a property or region 3 : material used for building fences

fend \ˈfend\ vb 1 : to keep or ward off : REPEL 2 : SHIFT ⟨∼ for yourself⟩

fend·er \ˈfen-dər\ n : a protective device (as a guard over the wheel of an automobile)

fen·es·tra·tion \ˌfe-nə-ˈstrā-shən\ n : the arrangement and design of windows and doors in a building

Fe·ni·an \ˈfē-nē-ən\ n : a member of a secret 19th century Irish and Irish-American organization dedicated to overthrowing British rule in Ireland

fen·ing \ˈfe-niŋ\ n, pl **fening** or **fen·inga** \-niŋ-ə\ — see marka at MONEY table

fen·nel \ˈfe-nᵊl\ n : a garden plant related to the carrot and grown for its aromatic foliage and seeds

FEPC abbr Fair Employment Practices Commission

fe·ral \ˈfir-əl, ˈfer-\ adj 1 : SAVAGE 2 : WILD 3 : having escaped from domestication and become wild

fer-de-lance \ˈfer-də-ˈlans\ n, pl **fer-de-lance** [F, lit., lance iron, spearhead] : a large venomous pit viper of Central and So. America

¹**fer·ment** \fər-ˈment\ vb 1 : to cause or undergo fermentation 2 : to be or cause

to be in a state of agitation or intense activity

²fer·ment \'fər-ˌment\ n 1 : a living organism (as a yeast) causing fermentation by its enzymes; also : ENZYME 2 : AGITATION, TUMULT

fer·men·ta·tion \ˌfər-mən-'tā-shən, -ˌmen-\ n 1 : chemical decomposition of an organic substance (as in the souring of milk or the formation of alcohol from sugar) by enzymatic action in the absence of oxygen often with formation of gas 2 : FERMENT 2

fer·mi·um \'fer-mē-əm, 'fər-\ n : an artificially produced radioactive metallic chemical element

fern \'fərn\ n : any of an order of vascular plants resembling seed plants in having roots, stems, and leaflike fronds but reproducing by spores instead of by flowers and seeds

fern·ery \'fər-nə-rē\ n, pl -er·ies 1 : a place for growing ferns 2 : a collection of growing ferns

fe·ro·cious \fə-'rō-shəs\ adj 1 : FIERCE, SAVAGE 2 : extremely intense — fe·ro·cious·ly adv — fe·ro·cious·ness n

fe·roc·i·ty \fə-'rä-sə-tē\ n : the quality or state of being ferocious

¹fer·ret \'fer-ət\ n : a partially domesticated usu. white European mammal related to the weasels

²ferret vb 1 : to hunt game with ferrets 2 : to drive out of a hiding place 3 : to find and bring to light by searching ⟨~ out the truth⟩

fer·ric \'fer-ik\ adj : of, relating to, or containing iron

ferric oxide n : an oxide of iron found in nature as hematite and as rust and used esp. as a pigment, for polishing, and in magnetic materials

Fer·ris wheel \'fer-əs-\ n : an amusement device consisting of a large upright power-driven wheel with seats that remain horizontal around its rim

fer·ro·mag·net·ic \ˌfer-ō-mag-'ne-tik\ adj : of or relating to substances that are easily magnetized

fer·rous \'fer-əs\ adj : of, relating to, or containing iron

fer·rule \'fer-əl\ n : a metal ring or cap around a slender wooden shaft to prevent splitting

¹fer·ry \'fer-ē\ vb fer·ried; fer·ry·ing [ME ferien, fr. OE ferian to carry, convey] 1 : to carry by boat across a body of water 2 : to cross by a ferry 3 : to convey from one place to another

²ferry n, pl ferries 1 : a place where persons or things are ferried 2 : FERRYBOAT

fer·ry·boat \'fer-ē-ˌbōt\ n : a boat used in ferrying

fer·tile \'fər-t³l\ adj 1 : producing plentifully : PRODUCTIVE ⟨~ soils⟩ ⟨a ~ mind⟩ 2 : capable of developing or reproducing ⟨~ seed⟩ ⟨a ~ bull⟩ ♦ Synonyms FRUITFUL, PROLIFIC, FECUND, PRODUCTIVE — fer·til·i·ty \(ˌ)fər-'ti-lə-tē\ n

fer·til·ize \'fər-tə-ˌlīz\ vb -ized; -iz·ing 1 : to unite with in the process of fertiliza-

tion ⟨a sperm ~s an egg⟩ 2 : to apply fertilizer to — fer·til·i·za·tion \ˌfər-tə-lə-'zā-shən\ n

fer·til·iz·er \'fər-tə-ˌlī-zər\ n : material (as manure or a chemical mixture) for enriching land

fer·ule \'fer-əl\ n : a rod or ruler used to punish children

fer·ven·cy \'fər-vən-sē\ n, pl -cies : FERVOR

fer·vent \'fər-vənt\ adj 1 : very hot : GLOWING 2 : marked by great intensity of feeling ♦ Synonyms IMPASSIONED, ARDENT, FERVID, FIERY, PASSIONATE — fer·vent·ly adv

fer·vid \-vəd\ adj 1 : very hot 2 : ARDENT, ZEALOUS — fer·vid·ly adv

fer·vor \'fər-vər\ n 1 : intense heat 2 : intensity of feeling or expression

fer·vour chiefly Brit var of FERVOR

fes·cue \'fes-kyü\ n : any of a genus of tufted perennial grasses

fes·tal \'fes-t³l\ adj : FESTIVE

fes·ter \'fes-tər\ vb 1 : to form pus 2 : PUTREFY, ROT 3 : RANKLE

fes·ti·val \'fes-tə-vəl\ n 1 : a time of celebration marked by special observances; esp : an occasion marked with religious ceremonies 2 : a periodic season or program of cultural events or entertainment ⟨a dance ~⟩

fes·tive \'fes-tiv\ adj 1 : of, relating to, or suitable for a feast or festival 2 : JOYFUL, GAY — fes·tive·ly adv

fes·tiv·i·ty \fes-'ti-və-tē\ n, pl -ties 1 : FESTIVAL 1 2 : the quality or state of being festive 3 : festive activity

¹fes·toon \fes-'tün\ n [F feston, fr. It festone, fr. festa festival] 1 : a decorative chain or strip hanging between two points 2 : a carved, molded, or painted ornament representing a decorative chain

²festoon vb 1 : to hang or form festoons on 2 : to shape into festoons

fe·ta \'fe-tə\ n : a white crumbly Greek cheese made from sheep's or goat's milk

fe·tal \'fē-t³l\ adj : of, relating to, or being a fetus

fetch \'fech\ vb 1 : to go or come after and bring or take back ⟨teach a dog to ~ a stick⟩ 2 : to bring in (as a price) 3 : to cause to come : bring out ⟨~ed tears from the eyes⟩ 4 : to give by striking ⟨~ him a blow⟩

fetch·ing adj : ATTRACTIVE, PLEASING ⟨a ~ smile⟩ — fetch·ing·ly adv

¹fete or fête \'fāt, 'fet\ n [F fête, fr. OF feste] 1 : FESTIVAL 2 : a large elaborate entertainment or party

²fete or fête vb fet·ed or fêt·ed; fet·ing or fêt·ing 1 : to honor or commemorate with a fete 2 : to pay high honor to

fet·id \'fe-təd\ adj : having an offensive smell : STINKING

fe·tish also fe·tich \'fe-tish\ n [F & Pg; F fétiche, fr. Pg feitiço, fr. feitiço artificial, false, fr. L facticius factitious] 1 : an object (as an idol or image) believed to have magical powers (as in curing disease) 2 : an object of unreasoning devotion or concern 3 : an object whose real or fantasied presence is psychologically necessary for sexual gratification

fe·tish·ism \'ti-,shi-zəm\ *n* **1** : belief in or devotion to fetishes **2** : the pathological transfer of sexual interest and gratification to a fetish — **fe·tish·ist** \-shist\ *n* — **fe·tish·is·tic** \,fe-ti-'shis-tik\ *adj*

fe·tish·ize \-ti-,shīz\ *vb* **-ized -iz·ing** : to make a fetish of

fet·lock \'fet-,läk\ *n* : a projection on the back of a horse's leg above the hoof; *also* : a tuft of hair on this

fet·ter \'fe-tər\ *n* **1** : a chain or shackle for the feet **2** : something that confines : RESTRAINT — **fetter** *vb*

fet·tle \'fe-t³l\ *n* : a state of fitness or order : CONDITION ⟨in fine ∼⟩

fe·tus \'fē-təs\ *n* : an unborn or unhatched vertebrate esp. after its basic structure is laid down; *esp* : a developing human in the uterus from usu. three months after conception to birth

feud \'fyüd\ *n* : a prolonged quarrel; *esp* : a lasting conflict between families or clans marked by violent attacks made for revenge — **feud** *vb*

feu·dal \'fyü-d³l\ *adj* **1** : of, relating to, or having the characteristics of a medieval fee **2** : of, relating to, or characteristic of feudalism

feu·dal·ism \'fyü-də-,li-zəm\ *n* : a system of political organization prevailing in medieval Europe in which a vassal renders service to a lord and receives protection and land in return; *also* : a similar political or social system — **feu·dal·is·tic** \,fyü-d³l-'is-tik\ *adj*

¹feu·da·to·ry \'fyü-də-,tór-ē\ *adj* : owing feudal allegiance

²feudatory *n, pl* **-ries 1** : FIEF **2** : a person who holds lands by feudal law or usage

fe·ver \'fē-vər\ *n* **1** : a rise in body temperature above the normal; *also* : a disease of which this is a chief symptom **2** : a state of heightened emotion or activity **3** : CRAZE ⟨football ∼⟩ — **fe·ver·ish** *adj* — **fe·ver·ish·ly** *adv*

¹few \'fyü\ *pron* : not many : a small number

²few *adj* **1** : consisting of or amounting to a small number **2** : not many but some ⟨caught a ∼ fish⟩ — **few·ness** *n* — **few and far between** : RARE **3**

³few *n* **1** : a small number of units or individuals ⟨a ∼ of them⟩ **2** : a special limited number ⟨among the ∼⟩

few·er \'fyü-ər\ *pron* : a smaller number of persons or things

fey \'fā\ *adj* **1** *chiefly Scot* : fated to die; *also* : marked by a foreboding of death or calamity **2** : able to see into the future : VISIONARY **3** : marked by an otherworldly air or attitude **4** : CRAZY, TOUCHED

fez \'fez\ *n, pl* **fez·zes** *also* **fez·es** : a round red felt hat that has a flat top and a tassel but no brim

ff *abbr* **1** folios **2** [following] and the following ones **3** fortissimo

FHA *abbr* Federal Housing Administration

fi·an·cé \,fē-,än-'sā\ *n* [F, fr. MF, fr. pp. of *fiancer* to promise, betroth, fr. OF *fiancier*, fr. *fiance* promise, trust, fr. *fier* to trust, ultim. fr. L *fidere*] : a man engaged to be married

fi·an·cée \,fē-,än-'sā\ *n* : a woman engaged to be married

fi·as·co \fē-'as-kō\ *n, pl* **-coes** [F] : a complete failure

fi·at \'fē-ət, -,at, -,ät; 'fī-ət, -,at\ *n* [L, let it be done] : an authoritative and often arbitrary order or decree

¹fib \'fib\ *n* : a trivial or childish lie

²fib *vb* **fibbed; fib·bing** : to tell a fib — **fib·ber** *n*

fi·ber \'fī-bər\ *n* **1** : a threadlike substance or structure (as a muscle cell or fine root); *esp* : a natural (as wool or flax) or artificial (as rayon) filament capable of being spun or woven **2** : indigestible material in food that stimulates the intestine to move its contents along **3** : an element that gives texture or substance **4** : basic toughness : STRENGTH ⟨moral ∼⟩ — **fi·brous** \-brəs\ *adj*

fi·ber·board \'fī-bər-,bórd\ *n* : a material made by compressing fibers (as of wood) into stiff sheets

fi·ber·fill \-,fil\ *n* : synthetic fibers used as a filling material (as for cushions)

fi·ber·glass \-,glas\ *n* : glass in fibrous form used in making various products (as insulation)

fiber optics *n* **1** *pl* : thin transparent fibers of glass or plastic that are enclosed by a less refractive material and that transmit light by internal reflection; *also* : a bundle of such fibers used in an instrument **2** : the technique of the use of fiber optics — **fiber-optic** *adj*

fibre *chiefly Brit var of* FIBER

fi·bril \'fī-brəl, 'fi-\ *n* : a small fiber

fi·bril·la·tion \,fi-brə-'lā-shən, ,fī-\ *n* : rapid irregular contractions of the heart muscle fibers resulting in a lack of synchronism between heartbeat and pulse — **fib·ril·late** \'fi-brə-,lāt, 'fī-\ *vb*

fi·brin \'fī-brən\ *n* : a white insoluble fibrous protein formed in the clotting of blood

¹fi·broid \'fī-bróid, 'fi-\ *adj* : resembling, forming, or consisting of fibrous tissue ⟨∼ tumors⟩

fibroid *n* : a benign tumor of the uterus

fi·bro·my·al·gia \,fī-,brō-,mī-'al-jə\ *n* : any of a group of rheumatic disorders affecting soft tissues (as muscles or tendons)

fi·bro·sis \fī-'brō-səs\ *n* : a condition marked by abnormal increase of fiber-containing tissue

fib·u·la \'fi-byə-lə\ *n, pl* **-lae** \-lē, -,lī\ *or* **-las** : the outer and usu. the smaller of the two bones between the knee and ankle — **fib·u·lar** \-lər\ *adj*

FICA *abbr* Federal Insurance Contributions Act

-fication *n comb form* : making : production ⟨simpli*fication*⟩

fiche \'fēsh\ *n, pl* **fiche** : MICROFICHE

fi·chu \'fi-shü\ *n* [F] : a woman's light triangular scarf draped over the shoulders and fastened in front

fick·le \'fi-kəl\ *adj* : not firm or steadfast in disposition or character : INCONSTANT ⟨~ friends⟩ — **fick·le·ness** *n*

fic·tion \'fik-shən\ *n* 1 : something (as a story) invented by the imagination 2 : fictitious literature (as novels) — **fic·tion·al** \-shə-nəl\ *adj* — **fic·tion·al·ly** *adv*

fic·ti·tious \fik-'ti-shəs\ *adj* 1 : of, relating to, or characteristic of fiction : IMAGINARY 2 : FALSE, ASSUMED ⟨a ~ name⟩ 3 : FEIGNED ♦ *Synonyms* CHIMERICAL, FANCIFUL, FANTASTIC, UNREAL

¹fid·dle \'fi-dᵊl\ *n* 1 : VIOLIN

²fiddle *vb* **fid·dled; fid·dling** 1 : to play on a fiddle 2 : to move the hands or fingers restlessly 3 : PUTTER 4 : MEDDLE, TAMPER — **fid·dler** *n*

fid·dle·head \'fi-dᵊl-,hed\ *n* : one of the young unfurling fronds of some ferns that are often eaten as greens

fiddler crab *n* : any of a genus of burrowing crabs with one claw much enlarged in the male

fid·dle·stick \'fi-dᵊl-,stik\ *n* 1 : a violin bow 2 *pl* : NONSENSE — used as an interjection

fi·del·i·ty \fə-'de-lə-tē, fī-\ *n, pl* **-ties** 1 : the quality or state of being faithful 2 : ACCURACY ⟨~ in sound reproduction⟩ ♦ *Synonyms* ALLEGIANCE, LOYALTY, DEVOTION, FEALTY

¹fidg·et \'fi-jət\ *n* 1 : uneasiness or restlessness as shown by nervous movements — usu. used in pl. 2 : one that fidgets — **fidg·ety** *adj*

²fidget *vb* : to move or cause to move or act restlessly or nervously

fi·du·cia·ry \fə-'dü-shē-,er-ē, -'dyü-, -shə-rē\ *adj* 1 : involving a confidence or trust 2 : held or holding in trust for another ⟨~ accounts⟩ — **fiduciary** *n*

fie \'fī\ *interj* — used to express disgust or disapproval

fief \'fēf\ *n* [F, fr. OF] : a feudal estate : FEE

¹field \'fēld\ *n* 1 : open country 2 : a piece of cleared land for cultivation or pasture 3 : a piece of land yielding some special product 4 : the place where a battle is fought; *also* : BATTLE 5 : an area, division, or sphere of activity ⟨the ~ of science⟩ ⟨salesmen in the ~⟩ 6 : an area for military exercises 7 : an area for sports 8 : a background on which something is drawn or projected ⟨a flag with white stars on a ~ of blue⟩ 9 : a region or space in which a given effect (as magnetism) exists — **field** *adj*

²field *vb* 1 : to handle a batted or thrown baseball while on defense 2 : to put into the field 3 : to answer satisfactorily ⟨~ a tough question⟩ — **field·er** *n*

field day *n* 1 : a day devoted to outdoor sports and athletic competition 2 : a time of extraordinary pleasure or opportunity

field event *n* : a track-and-field event (as weight-throwing) other than a race

field glass *n* : a hand-held binocular telescope — usu. used in pl.

field guide *n* : a manual for identifying natural objects, plants, or animals

field hockey *n* : a field game played between two teams of 11 players each whose object is to knock a ball into the opponent's goal with a curved stick

field marshal *n* : an officer (as in the British army) of the highest rank

field–test \-,test\ *vb* : to test (as a new product) in actual situations reflecting intended use — **field test** *n*

fiend \'fēnd\ *n* 1 : DEVIL 1 2 : DEMON 3 : an extremely wicked or cruel person 4 : a person excessively devoted to a pursuit ⟨a golf ~⟩ 5 : ADDICT ⟨a dope ~⟩ — **fiend·ish** *adj* — **fiend·ish·ly** *adv*

fierce \'firs\ *adj* **fierc·er; fierc·est** 1 : violently hostile or aggressive in temperament 2 : PUGNACIOUS 3 : INTENSE ⟨~ pain⟩ 4 : furiously active or determined 5 : wild or menacing in appearance ♦ *Synonyms* FEROCIOUS, BARBAROUS, SAVAGE, CRUEL — **fierce·ly** *adv* — **fierce·ness** *n*

fi·ery \'fī-ə-rē\ *adj* **fi·er·i·er; -est** 1 : consisting of fire 2 : BURNING, BLAZING 3 : FLAMMABLE 4 : hot like a fire : INFLAMED, FEVERISH 5 : RED ⟨a ~ sunset⟩ 6 : full of emotion or spirit 7 : IRRITABLE — **fi·eri·ness** \-ē-nəs\ *n*

fi·es·ta \fē-'es-tə\ *n* [Sp] : FESTIVAL

fife \'fīf\ *n* [G *Pfeife* pipe, fife] : a small flute

FIFO *abbr* first in, first out

fif·teen \fif-'tēn\ *n* : one more than 14 — **fifteen** *adj or pron* — **fif·teenth** \-'tēnth\ *adj or n*

fifth \'fifth\ *n* 1 : one that is number five in a countable series 2 : one of five equal parts of something 3 : a unit of measure for liquor equal to ¹/₅ U.S. gallon (0.757 liter) — **fifth** *adj or adv*

fifth column *n* : a group of secret supporters of a nation's enemy that engage in espionage or sabotage within the country — **fifth columnist** *n*

fifth wheel *n* : one that is unnecessary and often burdensome

fif·ty \'fif-tē\ *n, pl* **fifties** : five times 10 — **fif·ti·eth** \-tē-əth\ *adj or n* — **fifty** *adj or pron*

fif·ty–fif·ty \,fif-tē-'fif-tē\ *adj* 1 : shared equally ⟨a ~ proposition⟩ 2 : half favorable and half unfavorable

¹fig \'fig\ *n* : a soft usu. pear-shaped edible fruit of a tree related to the mulberry; *also* : a tree bearing figs

²fig *abbr* 1 figurative; figuratively 2 figure

¹fight \'fīt\ *vb* **fought** \'fȯt\; **fight·ing** 1 : to contend against another in battle or physical combat 2 : BOX 3 : to put forth a determined effort 4 : STRUGGLE, CONTEND 5 : to attempt to prevent the success or effectiveness of 6 : WAGE ⟨~ a war⟩ 7 : to gain by struggle

²fight *n* 1 : a hostile encounter : BATTLE 2 : a boxing match 3 : a verbal disagreement 4 : a struggle for a goal or an objective 5 : strength or disposition for fighting ⟨full of ~⟩

fight·er \'fī-tər\ *n* 1 : one that fights; *esp* : WARRIOR 2 : BOXER 1 3 : a fast maneuverable warplane for destroying enemy aircraft

fig·ment \'fig-mənt\ *n* : something imagined or made up

fig·u·ra·tion \ˌfi-gyə-'rā-shən, -gə-\ *n* 1 : FORM, OUTLINE 2 : an act or instance of representation in figures and shapes

fig·u·ra·tive \'fi-gyə-rə-tiv, -gə-\ *adj* 1 : EMBLEMATIC 2 : SYMBOLIC, METAPHORICAL ⟨~ language⟩ — **fig·u·ra·tive·ly** *adv*

¹**fig·ure** \'fi-gyər, -gər\ *n* [ME, fr. AF, fr. L *figura*, fr. *fingere* to shape] 1 : NUMERAL 2 *pl* : arithmetical calculations 3 : a written or printed character 4 : PRICE, SUM ⟨sold at a low ~⟩ 5 : a combination of points, lines, or surfaces in geometry ⟨a circle is a closed plane ~⟩ 6 : SHAPE, FORM, OUTLINE 7 : the graphic representation of a form esp. of a person 8 : a diagram or pictorial illustration of textual matter 9 : PATTERN, DESIGN 10 : appearance made or impression produced ⟨they cut quite a ~⟩ 11 : a series of movements (as in a dance) 12 : PERSONAGE ⟨a well-known sports ~⟩

²**figure** *vb* **fig·ured; fig·ur·ing** 1 : to represent by or as if by a figure or outline 2 : to decorate with a pattern 3 : to indicate or represent by numerals 4 : REGARD, CONSIDER 5 : to be or appear important or conspicuous 6 : COMPUTE, CALCULATE ⟨*figured* the cost⟩

fig·ure·head \'fi-gyər-ˌhed, -gər-\ *n* 1 : a figure on the bow of a ship 2 : a head or chief in name only

figure of speech : a form of expression (as a simile or metaphor) that often compares or identifies one thing with another to convey meaning or heighten effect

figure out *vb* 1 : FIND OUT, DISCOVER 2 : SOLVE ⟨*figure out* a math problem⟩

figure skating *n* : skating that includes various jumps, spins, and dance movements

fig·u·rine \ˌfi-gyə-'rēn, -gə-\ *n* : a small carved or molded figure

fil·a·ment \'fi-lə-mənt\ *n* : a fine thread or threadlike object, part, or process — **fil·a·men·tous** \ˌfi-lə-'men-təs\ *adj*

fil·bert \'fil-bərt\ *n* : the sweet thick-shelled nut of either of two European hazels; *also* : a shrub or small tree bearing filberts

filch \'filch\ *vb* : to steal furtively

¹**file** \'fī(-ə)l\ *n* : a usu. steel tool with a ridged or toothed surface used esp. for smoothing a hard substance

²**file** *vb* **filed; fil·ing** : to rub, smooth, or cut away with a file

³**file** *vb* **filed; fil·ing** [ME, fr. ML *filare* to string documents on a string or wire, fr. *filum* file of documents, lit., thread, fr. L] 1 : to arrange in order 2 : to enter or record officially or as prescribed by law ⟨~ a lawsuit⟩ 3 : to send (copy) to a newspaper

⁴**file** *n* 1 : a device (as a folder or cabinet) by means of which papers may be kept in order 2 : a collection of papers or publications usu. arranged or classified 3 : a collection of data (as text) treated by a computer as a unit

⁵**file** *n* : a row of persons, animals, or things arranged one behind the other

⁶**file** *vb* **filed; fil·ing** : to march or proceed in file

fi·let mi·gnon \ˌfi-(ˌ)lā-mēn-'yōⁿ, fi-ˌlā-\ *n, pl* **filets mignons** \-(ˌ)lā-mēn-'yōⁿz, -ˌlā-\ [F, lit., dainty fillet] : a thick slice of beef cut from the narrow end of a beef tenderloin

fil·ial \'fil-ē-əl, 'fil-yəl\ *adj* : of, relating to, or befitting a son or daughter

fil·i·bus·ter \'fi-lə-ˌbəs-tər\ *n* [Sp *filibustero*, lit., freebooter] 1 : a military adventurer; *esp* : an American engaged in fomenting 19th century Latin American uprisings 2 : the use of delaying tactics (as extremely long speeches) esp. in a legislative assembly; *also* : an instance of this practice — **filibuster** *vb* — **fil·i·bus·ter·er** *n*

fil·i·cide \'fi-lə-ˌsīd\ *n* : the murder of one's own daughter or son

fil·i·gree \'fi-lə-ˌgrē\ *n* [F *filigrane*] : ornamental openwork (as of fine wire) — **fil·i·greed** \-ˌgrēd\ *adj*

fil·ing \'fī-liŋ\ *n* 1 : the act or instance of using a file 2 : a small piece scraped off by a file ⟨iron ~s⟩

Fil·i·pi·no \ˌfi-lə-'pē-nō\ *n, pl* **Filipinos** : a native or inhabitant of the Philippines — **Filipino** *adj*

¹**fill** \'fil\ *vb* 1 : to make or become full 2 : to stop up : PLUG ⟨~ a cavity⟩ 3 : FEED, SATIATE 4 : SATISFY, FULFILL ⟨~ all requirements⟩ 5 : to occupy fully 6 : to spread through ⟨laughter ~ed the room⟩ 7 : OCCUPY ⟨~ the office of president⟩ 8 : to put a person in ⟨~ a vacancy⟩ 9 : to supply as directed ⟨~ a prescription⟩

²**fill** *n* 1 : a full supply; *esp* : a quantity that satisfies or satiates 2 : material used esp. for filling a low place

¹**fill·er** \'fi-lər\ *n* 1 : one that fills 2 : a substance added to another substance (as to increase bulk or weight) 3 : a material used for filling cracks and pores in wood before painting

²**fil·ler** \'fi-ˌler\ *n, pl* **fillers** or **filler** — see *forint* at MONEY table

¹**fil·let** \'fi-lət, *in sense 2* fi-'lā, 'fi-(ˌ)lā\ *also* **fi·let** \fi-'lā, 'fi-(ˌ)lā\ *n* [ME *filet*, fr. AF, dim. of *fil* thread] 1 : a narrow band, strip, or ribbon 2 : a piece or slice of boneless meat or fish; *esp* : the tenderloin of beef

²**fil·let** \'fi-lət, *in sense 2 also* fi-'lā, 'fi-(ˌ)lā\ *vb* 1 : to bind or adorn with or as if with a fillet 2 : to cut into fillets

fill in *vb* 1 : to provide necessary or recent information 2 : to serve as a temporary substitute

fill·ing \'fi-liŋ\ *n* 1 : material used to fill something ⟨a ~ for a tooth⟩ 2 : the yarn interlacing the warp in a fabric 3 : a food mixture used to fill pastry or sandwiches

filling station *n* : GAS STATION

fil·lip \'fi-ləp\ *n* 1 : a blow or gesture made by a flick or snap of the finger across the thumb 2 : something that serves to arouse or excite — **fillip** *vb*

fill–up \'fil-‚əp\ n : an act or instance of filling something

fil·ly \'fi-lē\ n, pl **fillies** : a young female horse. usu. less than four years old

¹**film** \'film\ n 1 : a thin skin or membrane 2 : a thin coating or layer 3 : a flexible strip of chemically treated material used in taking pictures 4 : MOTION PICTURE — **filmy** adj

²**film** vb 1 : to cover with a film 2 : to make a motion picture of

film·dom \'film-dəm\ n : the motion-picture industry

film·og·ra·phy \fil-'mä-grə-fē\ n, pl **-phies** : a list of motion pictures featuring the work of a film figure or a particular topic

film·strip \'film-‚strip\ n : a strip of film bearing a sequence of images for projection as still pictures

¹**fils** \'fēs\ n [F] : SON — used after a family name to distinguish a son from his father

²**fils** \'fils\ n, pl **fils** — see dinar, dirham, rial at MONEY table

¹**fil·ter** \'fil-tər\ n 1 : a porous material through which a fluid is passed to separate out matter in suspension; also : a device containing such material 2 : a device for suppressing waves of certain frequencies; esp : one (as for a camera) that absorbs light of certain colors 3 : software for sorting or blocking certain online material

²**filter** vb 1 : to remove by means of a filter 2 : to pass through a filter — **fil·ter·able** also **fil·tra·ble** \-tə-rə-bəl, -trə-\ adj — **fil·tra·tion** \fil-'trā-shən\ n

filth \'filth\ n [ME, fr. OE fylth, fr. fūl foul] 1 : foul matter; esp : loathsome dirt or refuse 2 : moral corruption 3 : OBSCENITY — **filth·i·ness** n — **filthy** \'fil-thē\ adj

filthy adv : VERY, EXTREMELY ⟨∼ dirty⟩ ⟨∼ rich⟩

fil·trate \'fil-‚trāt\ n : fluid that has passed through a filter

¹**fin** \'fin\ n 1 : a thin external process by which an aquatic animal (as a fish) moves through water 2 : a fin-shaped part (as on an airplane) 3 : FLIPPER 2 — **finned** \'find\ adj

²**fin** abbr 1 finance; financial 2 finish

fi·na·gle \fə-'nā-gəl\ vb **-gled; -gling** 1 : to obtain by indirect or dishonest means : WANGLE 2 : to use devious dishonest methods to achieve one's ends — **fi·na·gler** n

¹**fi·nal** \'fī-nᵊl\ adj 1 : not to be altered or undone ⟨all sales are ∼⟩ 2 : ULTIMATE 3 : relating to or occurring at the end or conclusion ⟨the ∼ results⟩ — **fi·nal·i·ty** \fī-'na-lə-tē, fə-\ n — **fi·nal·ly** adv

²**final** n 1 : a deciding match or game — usu. used in pl. 2 : the last examination in a course — often used in pl.

fi·na·le \fə-'na-lē, fi-'nä-\ n : the close or end of something; esp : the last section of a musical composition

fi·nal·ise Brit var of FINALIZE

fi·nal·ist \'fī-nə-list\ n : a contestant in the finals of a competition

fi·nal·ize \'fī-nə-‚līz\ vb **-ized; -iz·ing** : to put in final or finished form

¹**fi·nance** \fə-'nans, 'fī-‚nans\ n [ME, ending, payment, fr. AF, fr. finer to end, pay, fr. fin end, fr. L finis boundary, end] 1 pl : money resources available esp. to a government or business 2 : management of money affairs

²**finance** vb **fi·nanced; fi·nanc·ing** 1 : to raise or provide funds for 2 : to furnish with necessary funds 3 : to sell or supply on credit

finance company n : a company that makes usu. small short-term loans usu. to individuals

fi·nan·cial \fə-'nan-chəl, fī-\ adj : relating to finance or financiers ⟨∼ problems⟩ — **fi·nan·cial·ly** adv

fi·nan·cials \-shəlz\ n pl : financial statistics

fi·nan·cier \‚fi-nən-'sir, ‚fī-‚nan-\ n 1 : a person skilled in managing public moneys 2 : a person who deals with large-scale finance and investment

finch \'finch\ n : any of numerous songbirds with strong conical bills

¹**find** \'find\ vb **found** \'faůnd\; **find·ing** 1 : to meet with either by chance or by searching or study : ENCOUNTER, DISCOVER 2 : to obtain by effort or management ⟨∼ time to read⟩ 3 : to arrive at : REACH ⟨the bullet found its mark⟩ 4 : EXPERIENCE, FEEL ⟨found happiness⟩ 5 : to gain or regain the use of ⟨found his voice again⟩ 6 : to determine and make a statement about ⟨∼ a verdict⟩

²**find** n 1 : an act or instance of finding 2 : something found; esp : a valuable item of discovery

find·er \'fīn-dər\ n : one that finds; esp : VIEWFINDER

fin de siè·cle \‚faⁿ-də-sē-'eklᵊ\ adj [F, end of century] 1 : of, relating to, or characteristic of the close of the 19th century 2 : of or relating to the end of a century

find·ing \'fīn-diŋ\ n 1 : the act of finding 2 : FIND 2 3 : the result of a judicial proceeding or inquiry

find out vb : to learn by study, observation, or search : DISCOVER

¹**fine** \'fin\ n : money exacted as a penalty for an offense

²**fine** vb **fined; fin·ing** : to impose a fine on : punish by a fine

³**fine** adj **fin·er; fin·est** 1 : free from impurity 2 : very thin in gauge or texture 3 : not coarse ⟨∼ sand⟩ 4 : SUBTLE, SENSITIVE ⟨a ∼ distinction⟩ 5 : superior in quality or appearance 6 : ELEGANT, REFINED ⟨∼ manners⟩ — **fine·ly** adv — **fine·ness** n

⁴**fine** adv 1 : very well 2 — used to express agreement

fine art n : art (as painting, sculpture, or music) concerned primarily with the creation of beautiful objects — usu. used in pl.

fin·ery \'fī-nə-rē\ n, pl **-er·ies** : ORNAMENT, DECORATION; esp : showy clothing and jewels

fine·spun \'fīn-'spən\ adj : developed

with extremely or excessively fine delicacy or detail

fi·nesse \fə-'nes\ *n* **1** : refinement or delicacy of workmanship, structure, or texture **2** : CUNNING, SUBTLETY ⟨handled the questions with ∼⟩ — **finesse** *vb*

fine–tune \'fīn-'tün\ *vb* : to adjust so as to bring to the highest level of performance or effectiveness

fin·fish \'fin-ˌfish\ *n* : FISH 2

¹fin·ger \'fiŋ-gər\ *n* **1** : any of the five divisions at the end of the hand; *esp* : one other than the thumb **2** : something that resembles or does the work of a finger **3** : a part of a glove into which a finger is inserted

²finger *vb* **fin·gered; fin·ger·ing** **1** : to touch or feel with the fingers : HANDLE **2** : to perform with the fingers or with a certain fingering **3** : to mark the notes of a piece of music as a guide in playing **4** : to point out ⟨was ∼*ed* as a suspect⟩

fin·ger·board \'fiŋ-gər-ˌbȯrd\ *n* : the part of a stringed instrument against which the fingers press the strings to vary the pitch

finger bowl *n* : a small water bowl for rinsing the fingers at the table

fin·ger·ing \'fiŋ-gə-riŋ\ *n* **1** : handling or touching with the fingers **2** : the act or method of using the fingers in playing an instrument **3** : the marking of the method of fingering

fin·ger·ling \'fiŋ-gər-liŋ\ *n* : a small fish

fin·ger·nail \'fiŋ-gər-ˌnāl\ *n* : the nail of a finger

fin·ger·print \-ˌprint\ *n* : the pattern of marks made by pressing the tip of a finger or thumb on a surface; *esp* : an ink impression of such a pattern taken for the purpose of identification — **fingerprint** *vb*

fin·ger·tip \-ˌtip\ *n* : the tip of a finger

fin·i·al \'fi-nē-əl\ *n* : an ornamental projection or end (as on a spire)

fin·ick·ing \'fi-ni-kiŋ\ *adj* : FINICKY

fin·icky \'fi-ni-kē\ *adj* : excessively particular in taste or standards ⟨a ∼ eater⟩

fi·nis \'fi-nəs\ *n* : END, CONCLUSION

¹fin·ish \'fi-nish\ *vb* **1** : TERMINATE **2** : to use or dispose of entirely **3** : to bring to completion : ACCOMPLISH **4** : to put a final coat or surface on **5** : to come to the end of a course or undertaking ⟨my horse ∼*ed* third⟩ — **fin·ish·er** *n*

²finish *n* **1** : END, CONCLUSION **2** : something that completes or perfects **3** : the final treatment or coating of a surface

fi·nite \'fī-ˌnīt\ *adj* **1** : having definite or definable limits; *also* : having a limited nature or existence **2** : being less than some positive integer in number or measure and greater than its negative **3** : showing distinction of grammatical person and number ⟨a ∼ verb⟩

fink \'fiŋk\ *n* **1** : a contemptible person **2** : STRIKEBREAKER **3** : INFORMER

Finn \'fin\ *n* : a native or inhabitant of Finland

fin·nan had·die \ˌfi-nən-'ha-dē\ *n* : smoked haddock

¹Finn·ish \'fi-nish\ *adj* : of or relating to Finland, the Finns, or Finnish

²Finnish *n* : the language of the Finns

fin·ny \'fi-nē\ *adj* **1** : having or characterized by fins **2** : relating to or being fish

fiord *var of* FJORD

fir \'fər\ *n* : any of a genus of usu. large evergreen trees related to the pines; *also* : the light soft wood of a fir

¹fire \'fī(-ə)r\ *n* **1** : the light or heat and esp. the flame of something burning **2** : ENTHUSIASM, ZEAL **3** : fuel that is burning (as in a stove or fireplace) **4** : destructive burning (as of a house) **5** : the firing of weapons — **fire·less** *adj*

²fire *vb* **fired; fir·ing** **1** : KINDLE, IGNITE ⟨∼ a house⟩ **2** : STIR, ENLIVEN ⟨∼ the imagination⟩ **3** : to dismiss from employment **4** : SHOOT ⟨∼ a gun⟩ ⟨∼ an arrow⟩ **5** : BAKE ⟨*firing* pottery in a kiln⟩ **6** : to apply fire or fuel to something ⟨∼ a furnace⟩

fire ant *n* : either of two small fiercely stinging So. American ants introduced into the southeastern U.S. where they are agricultural pests

fire·arm \'fī(-ə)r-ˌärm\ *n* : a weapon (as a pistol) from which a shot is discharged by gunpowder

fire·ball \-ˌbȯl\ *n* **1** : a ball of fire **2** : a very bright meteor **3** : the highly luminous cloud of vapor and dust created by a nuclear explosion **4** : a highly energetic person

fire·boat \-ˌbōt\ *n* : a boat equipped for fighting fires

fire·bomb \-ˌbäm\ *n* : an incendiary bomb — **firebomb** *vb*

fire·box \-ˌbäks\ *n* **1** : a chamber (as of a furnace) that contains a fire **2** : a box containing a fire alarm

fire·brand \-ˌbrand\ *n* **1** : a piece of burning wood **2** : a person who creates unrest or strife : AGITATOR

fire·break \-ˌbrāk\ *n* : a barrier of cleared or plowed land intended to check a forest or grass fire

fire·bug \-ˌbəg\ *n* : a person who deliberately sets destructive fires

fire·crack·er \-ˌkra-kər\ *n* : a usu. paper tube containing an explosive and a fuse and set off to make a noise

fire department *n* : an organization for preventing or extinguishing fires; *also* : its members

fire engine *n* : a motor vehicle with equipment for extinguishing fires

fire escape *n* : a stairway or ladder for escape from a burning building

fire·fight·er \'fī(-ə)r-ˌfī-tər\ *n* : a person who fights fires; *esp* : a member of a fire department

fire·fly \-ˌflī\ *n* : any of various small night-flying beetles that produce flashes of light for courtship purposes

fire·house \-ˌhau̇s\ *n* : FIRE STATION

fire irons *n pl* : tools for tending a fire esp. in a fireplace

fire·man \'fī(-ə)r-mən\ *n* **1** : STOKER **2** : FIREFIGHTER

fire off *vb* : to write and send

fire·place \-ˌplās\ *n* **1** : a framed opening

made in a chimney to hold an open fire **2**
: an outdoor structure of brick or stone
for an open fire

fire·plug \-ˌpləg\ n : HYDRANT

fire·pow·er \-ˌpaů-(-ə)r\ n : the ability to
deliver gunfire or warheads on a target

¹**fire·proof** \-ˈprüf\ adj : resistant to fire

²**fireproof** vb : to make fireproof

fire–sale \-ˌsāl\ adj : heavily discounted
⟨∼ prices⟩

fire screen n : a protective screen before
a fireplace

¹**fire·side** \ˈfi(-ə)r-ˌsīd\ n **1** : a place near
the fire or hearth **2** : HOME

²**fireside** adj : having an informal or intimate quality

fire station n : a building housing fire engines and usu. firefighters

fire·storm \ˈfi(-ə)r-ˌstȯrm\ n **1** : a large
destructive very hot fire **2** : a sudden or
violent outburst ⟨∼ of criticism⟩

fire tower n : a tower (as in a forest) from
which a watch for fires is kept

fire·trap \ˈfi(-ə)r-ˌtrap\ n : a building or
place apt to catch on fire or difficult to
escape from in case of fire

fire truck n : FIRE ENGINE

fire·wall \-ˌwȯl\ n : computer hardware or
software for preventing unauthorized access to data

fire·wa·ter \ˈfi(-ə)r-ˌwȯ-tər, -ˌwä-\ n : intoxicating liquor

fire·wood \-ˌwůd\ n : wood used for fuel

fire·work \-ˌwərk\ n : a device designed to
produce a striking display by the burning
of explosive or flammable materials

firing line n **1** : a line from which fire is
delivered against a target **2** : the forefront of an activity

¹**firm** \ˈfərm\ adj **1** : securely fixed in place
2 : SOLID, VIGOROUS ⟨a ∼ handshake⟩ **3**
: having a solid or compact texture **4**
: not subject to change or fluctuation
: STEADY ⟨∼ prices⟩ **5** : STEADFAST **6**
: indicating firmness or resolution —
firm·ly adv — **firm·ness** n

²**firm** vb : to make or become firm

³**firm** n [G Firma, fr. It, signature, ultim. fr.
L firmare to make firm, confirm] **1** : the
name under which a company transacts
business **2** : a business partnership of
two or more persons **3** : a business enterprise

fir·ma·ment \ˈfər-mə-mənt\ n : the arch
of the sky : HEAVENS

firm·ware \ˈfirm-ˌwer\ n : computer programs contained permanently in a hardware device

¹**first** \ˈfərst\ adj : preceding all others as in
time, order, or importance

²**first** adv **1** : before any other **2** : for the
first time **3** : in preference to something
else

³**first** n **1** : number one in a countable series **2** : something that is first **3** : the
lowest forward gear in an automotive vehicle **4** : the winning or highest place in
a competition or examination

first aid n : emergency care or treatment
given an injured or ill person

first·born \ˈfərst-ˈbȯrn\ adj : ELDEST —
firstborn n

first class n : the best or highest group in
a classification — **first–class** adj or adv

first·hand \ˈfərst-ˈhand\ adj : coming
from direct personal observation or experience — **firsthand** adv

first lady n, often cap F&L : the wife or
hostess of the chief executive of a political unit (as a country)

first lieutenant n : a commissioned officer (as in the army) ranking next below a
captain

first·ling \ˈfərst-liŋ\ n : one that comes or
is produced first

first·ly \-lē\ adv : in the first place : FIRST

¹**first–rate** \-ˈrāt\ adj : of the first order of
size, importance, or quality

²**first–rate** adv : very well

first sergeant n **1** : a noncommissioned
officer serving as the chief assistant to
the commander of a military unit **2** : a
rank in the army below a sergeant major
and in the marine corps below a master
gunnery sergeant

first strike n : a preemptive nuclear attack

first–string \ˈfərst-ˈstriŋ\ adj : being a
regular as distinguished from a substitute
— **first–string·er** \-ˌstriŋ-ər\ n

firth \ˈfərth\ n [ME, fr. ON fjorthr] : ESTU-
ARY

fis·cal \ˈfis-kəl\ adj [L fiscalis, fr. fiscus
basket, treasury] **1** : of or relating to
taxation, public revenues, or public debt
2 : of or relating to financial matters —
fis·cal·ly adv

¹**fish** \ˈfish\ n, pl **fish** or **fish·es** **1** : a water-
dwelling animal — usu. used in combina-
tion ⟨starfish⟩ ⟨shellfish⟩ **2** : any of numerous cold-blooded water-breathing
vertebrates with fins, gills, and usu. scales
that include the bony fishes and usu. the
cartilaginous and jawless fishes **3** : the
flesh of fish used as food

²**fish** vb **1** : to attempt to catch fish **2** : to
seek something by roundabout means
⟨∼ for praise⟩ **3** : to search for something underwater **4** : to engage in a
search by groping **5** : to draw forth

fish–and–chips n pl : fried fish and
french fried potatoes

fish·bowl \ˈfish-ˌbōl\ n **1** : a bowl for the
keeping of live fish **2** : a place or condition that affords no privacy

fish·er \ˈfi-shər\ n **1** : one that fishes **2** : a
dark brown No. American carnivorous
mammal related to the weasels

fish·er·man \-mən\ n **1** : a person engaged in fishing **2** : a fishing boat

fish·ery \ˈfi-shə-rē\ n, pl **-er·ies** **1** : the
business of catching fish **2** : a place for
catching fish

fish·hook \ˈfish-ˌhůk\ n : a usu. barbed
hook for catching fish

fish ladder n : an arrangement of pools in
steps by which fish can pass over a dam
in going upstream

fish·net \ˈfish-ˌnet\ n **1** : netting for
catching fish **2** : a coarse open-mesh fabric

fish·tail \-ˌtāl\ vb : to have the rear end
slide from side to side out of control
while moving forward

fish·wife \-\,wīf\ *n* **1** : a woman who sells fish **2** : a vulgar abusive woman

fishy \'fi-shē\ *adj* **fish·i·er; -est 1** : of or resembling fish **2** : QUESTIONABLE 〈the story sounds ∼ to me〉

fis·sion \'fi-shən, -zhən\ *n* [L *fissio,* fr. *findere* to split] **1** : a cleaving into parts **2** : a method of reproduction in which a living cell or body divides into two or more parts each of which grows into a whole new individual **3** : the splitting of an atomic nucleus resulting in the release of large amounts of energy — **fis·sion·able** \'fi-shə-nə-bəl, -zhə-\ *adj*

fis·sure \'fi-shər\ *n* : a narrow opening or crack

fist \'fist\ *n* **1** : the hand with fingers folded into the palm **2** : INDEX 6

fist bump *n* : a gesture in which two people bump their fists together — **fist–bump** *vb*

fist·ful \'fist-,fùl\ *n* : HANDFUL

fist·i·cuffs \'fis-ti-,kəfs\ *n pl* : a fight with the fists

fist pump *n* : a celebratory gesture in which the fist is raised and lowered quickly and vigorously — **fist–pump** *vb*

fis·tu·la \'fis-chə-lə\ *n, pl* **-las** *or* **-lae** : an abnormal passage leading from an abscess or hollow organ — **fis·tu·lous** \-ləs\ *adj*

¹fit \'fit\ *adj* **fit·ter; fit·test 1** : adapted to a purpose : APPROPRIATE **2** : PROPER, RIGHT 〈a movie ∼ for children〉 **3** : PREPARED, READY **4** : physically and mentally sound — **fit·ly** *adv* — **fit·ness** *n*

²fit *n* **1** : a sudden violent attack (as in epilepsy) **2** : a sudden outburst

³fit *vb* **fit·ted** *also* **fit; fit·ting 1** : to be suitable for or to **2** : to be correctly adjusted to or shaped for **3** : to insert or adjust until correctly in place **4** : to make a place or room for **5** : to be in agreement or accord with **6** : PREPARE **7** : ADJUST **8** : SUPPLY, EQUIP 〈*fitted* out with gear〉 **9** : BELONG — **fit·ter** *n*

⁴fit *n* : the fact, condition, or manner of fitting or being fitted

fit·ful \'fit-fəl\ *adj* : not regular : INTERMITTENT 〈∼ sleep〉 — **fit·ful·ly** *adv*

¹fit·ting \'fi-tin\ *adj* : APPROPRIATE, SUITABLE 〈a ∼ tribute〉 — **fit·ting·ly** *adv*

²fitting *n* **1** : the action or act of one that fits; *esp* : a trying on of clothes being made or altered **2** : a small often standardized part 〈a plumbing ∼〉

five \'fīv\ *n* **1** : one more than four **2** : the 5th in a set or series **3** : something having five units; *esp* : a basketball team **4** : a 5-dollar bill — **five** *adj or pron*

¹fix \'fiks\ *vb* **1** : to make firm, stable, or fast **2** : to give a permanent or final form to **3** : AFFIX, ATTACH **4** : to hold or direct steadily 〈∼es his eyes on the horizon〉 **5** : ESTABLISH, SET **6** : ASSIGN 〈∼ the blame〉 **7** : to set in order : ADJUST **8** : PREPARE **9** : to make whole or sound again **10** : to get even with **11** : to influence by improper or illegal methods 〈∼ a race〉 — **fix·er** *n*

²fix *n* **1** : PREDICAMENT **2** : a determination of position (as of a ship) **3** : an accurate determination or understanding **4** : an act of improper influence **5** : a supply or dose of something (as an addictive drug) strongly desired or craved **6** : something that fixes or restores

fix·a·tion \fik-'sā-shən\ *n* : an obsessive or unhealthy preoccupation or attachment — **fix·ate** \'fik-,sāt\ *vb*

fix·a·tive \'fik-sə-tiv\ *n* : something that stabilizes or sets

fixed \'fikst\ *adj* **1** : securely placed or fastened : STATIONARY **2** : not volatile **3** : SETTLED, FINAL **4** : INTENT, CONCENTRATED 〈a ∼ stare〉 **5** : supplied with a definite amount of something needed (as money) — **fixed·ly** \'fik-səd-lē\ *adv* — **fixed·ness** \'fik-səd-nəs\ *n*

fix·i·ty \'fik-sə-tē\ *n, pl* **-ties** : the quality or state of being fixed or stable

fix·ture \'fiks-chər\ *n* **1** : something firmly attached as a permanent part of some other thing **2** : a familiar feature in a particular setting; *esp* : a person associated with a place or activity

¹fizz \'fiz\ *vb* : to make a hissing or sputtering sound

²fizz *n* : an effervescent beverage

¹fiz·zle \'fi-zəl\ *vb* **fiz·zled; fiz·zling 1** : FIZZ **2** : to fail after a good start — often used with *out*

²fizzle *n* : FAILURE

fjord \fē-'ȯrd\ *n* [Norw] : a narrow inlet of the sea between cliffs or steep slopes

fl *abbr* **1** [L *floruit*] flourished **2** fluid

FL *or* **Fla** *abbr* Florida

flab \'flab\ *n* : soft flabby body tissue

flab·ber·gast \'fla-bər-,gast\ *vb* : ASTOUND

flab·by \'fla-bē\ *adj* **flab·bi·er; -est** : lacking firmness : FLACCID 〈∼ muscles〉 — **flab·bi·ness** \-bē-nəs\ *n*

flac·cid \'fla-səd\ *adj* : lacking firmness 〈∼ muscles〉

¹flag \'flag\ *n* : any of various irises; *esp* : a wild iris

²flag *n* **1** : a usu. rectangular piece of fabric of distinctive design that is used as a symbol (as of a nation) or as a signaling device **2** : something used like a flag to signal or attract attention **3** : one of the cross strokes of a musical note less than a quarter note in value

³flag *vb* **flagged; flag·ging 1** : to signal with or as if with a flag; *esp* : to signal to stop 〈∼ a taxi〉 **2** : to mark or identify with or as if with a flag **3** : to call a penalty on 〈∼ a football player〉

⁴flag *vb* **flagged; flag·ging 1** : to hang loose or limp **2** : to become unsteady, feeble, or spiritless **3** : to decline in interest or attraction 〈the topic *flagged*〉

⁵flag *n* : a hard flat stone suitable for paving

flag·el·late \'fla-jə-,lāt\ *vb* **-lat·ed; -lat·ing** : to punish by whipping — **flag·el·la·tion** \,fla-jə-'lā-shən\ *n*

fla·gel·lum \flə-'je-ləm\ *n, pl* **-la** \-lə\ *also* **-lums** : a long whiplike process that is the primary organ of motion of many microorganisms — **fla·gel·lar** \-lər\ *adj*

fla·geo·let \,fla-jə-'let, -'lā\ *n* [F] : a small

woodwind instrument belonging to the flute class

fla·gi·tious \flə-'ji-shəs\ adj : grossly wicked : VILLAINOUS

flag·on \'fla-gən\ n : a container for liquids usu. with a handle, spout, and lid

flag·pole \'flag-ˌpōl\ n : a pole on which to raise a flag

fla·grant \'flā-grənt\ adj [L flagrans, prp. of flagrare to burn] : conspicuously bad ⟨∼ abuse of power⟩ — **fla·grant·ly** adv

fla·gran·te de·lic·to \flə-ˌgran-tē-di-'lik-tō\ adv : IN FLAGRANTE DELICTO

flag·ship \'flag-ˌship\ n 1 : the ship that carries the commander of a fleet or subdivision thereof and flies his flag 2 : the most important one of a group

flag·staff \-ˌstaf\ n : FLAGPOLE

flag·stone \-ˌstōn\ n : ⁵FLAG

¹flail \'flāl\ n : a tool for threshing grain by hand

²flail vb : to strike or swing with or as if with a flail

flair \'fler\ n [F, lit., sense of smell, fr. OF, odor, fr. flairier to give off an odor, fr. VL *flagrare, alter. of L fragrare] 1 : ability to appreciate or make good use of something : BENT, TALENT 2 : a unique style

flak \'flak\ n, pl flak [G, fr. Fliegerabwehrkanonen, fr. Flieger flyer + Abwehr defense + Kanonen cannons] 1 : antiaircraft guns or bursting shells fired from them : CRITICISM, OPPOSITION

¹flake \'flāk\ n 1 : a small loose mass or bit 2 : a thin flattened piece or layer : CHIP — **flaky** adj

²flake vb flaked; flak·ing : to form or separate into flakes

³flake n : a markedly eccentric person : ODDBALL — **flak·i·ness** \'flā-kē-nəs\ n — **flaky** adj

flam·beau \'flam-ˌbō\ n, pl flambeaux \-ˌbōz\ or flambeaus [F, fr. MF, fr. flambe flame] : a flaming torch

flam·boy·ant \flam-'bȯi-ənt\ adj : marked by or given to strikingly elaborate or colorful display or behavior — **flam·boy·ance** \-əns\ n — **flam·boy·an·cy** \-ən-sē\ n — **flam·boy·ant·ly** adv

flame \'flām\ n 1 : the glowing gaseous part of a fire 2 : a state of blazing combustion 3 : a flamelike condition 4 : burning zeal or passion 5 : BRILLIANCE 6 : SWEETHEART 7 : an angry, hostile, or abusive electronic message — **flame** vb

fla·men·co \flə-'meŋ-kō\ n, pl -cos [Sp, fr. flamenco of the Gypsies, lit., Flemish, fr. MD Vlaminc Fleming] : a vigorous rhythmic dance style of the Spanish Gypsies

flame·throw·er \'flām-ˌthrō-ər\ n : a device that expels from a nozzle a burning stream of liquid or semiliquid fuel under pressure

fla·min·go \flə-'miŋ-gō\ n, pl -gos also -goes : any of several long-legged long-necked tropical water birds with scarlet wings and a broad bill bent downward

flam·ma·ble \'fla-mə-bəl\ adj : easily ignited and quick-burning — **flam·ma·bil·i·ty** \ˌfla-mə-'bi-lə-tē\ n — **flammable** n

flan \'flan, 'flän\ n 1 : an open pie with a sweet or savory filling 2 : custard baked with a caramel glaze

flange \'flanj\ n : a rim used for strengthening or guiding something or for attachment to another object

¹flank \'flaŋk\ n 1 : the fleshy part of the side between the ribs and the hip; also : the side of a quadruped 2 : SIDE 3 : the right or left of a formation

²flank vb 1 : to be situated on the side of : BORDER 2 : to attack or threaten the flank of

flank·er \'flaŋ-kər\ n : a football player stationed wide of the formation slightly behind the line of scrimmage as a pass receiver

flan·nel \'fla-nᵊl\ n 1 : a soft twilled wool or worsted fabric with a napped surface 2 : a stout cotton fabric napped on one side 3 pl : flannel underwear or pants

¹flap \'flap\ n 1 : a stroke with something broad : SLAP 2 : something broad, limber, or flat and usu. thin that hangs loose 3 : the motion or sound of something broad and limber as it swings to and fro 4 : a state of excitement or confusion

²flap vb flapped; flap·ping 1 : to beat with something broad and flat 2 : FLING 3 : to move (as wings) with a beating motion 4 : to sway loosely usu. with a noise of striking

flap·jack \'flap-ˌjak\ n : PANCAKE

flap·per \'fla-pər\ n 1 : one that flaps 2 : a young woman of the 1920s who showed freedom from conventions (as in conduct)

¹flare \'fler\ n 1 : a blaze of light used esp. to signal or illuminate; also : a device for producing such a blaze 2 : an unsteady glaring light

²flare vb flared; flar·ing 1 : to flame with a sudden unsteady light 2 : to become suddenly excited or angry ⟨after his harangue, I flared up⟩ 3 : to spread outward

flare-up \-ˌəp\ n : a sudden outburst or intensification

¹flash \'flash\ vb 1 : to break forth in or like a sudden flame 2 : to appear or pass suddenly or with great speed 3 : to send out in or as if in flashes ⟨∼ a message⟩ 4 : to make a sudden display (as of brilliance or feeling) 5 : to gleam or glow intermittently 6 : to fill by a sudden rush of water 7 : to expose to view very briefly ⟨∼ a badge⟩ ♦ Synonyms GLANCE, GLINT, SPARKLE, TWINKLE — **flash·er** n

²flash n 1 : a sudden burst of light 2 : a movement of a flag or light in signaling 3 : a sudden and brilliant burst (as of wit) 4 : a brief time 5 : SHOW, DISPLAY; esp : ostentatious display 6 : one that attracts notice; esp : an outstanding athlete 7 : GLIMPSE, LOOK 8 : a first brief news report 9 : FLASHLIGHT 10 : a device for producing a brief and very bright flash of light for taking photographs 11 : a quick-spreading flame or momentary intense outburst of radiant heat

³flash adj : of sudden origin and short duration ⟨a ∼ fire⟩ ⟨a ∼ flood⟩

⁴flash adv : by very brief exposure to an

intense agent (as heat or cold) ⟨∼ fry⟩ ⟨∼ freeze⟩

flash·back \'flash-ˌbak\ *n* **1** : interruption of the chronological sequence (as of a film or literary work) by an event of earlier occurrence **2** : a past event remembered vividly

flash back *vb* **1** : to vividly remember a past incident **2** : to employ a flashback

flash·bulb \-ˌbəlb\ *n* : an electric bulb that can be used only once to produce a brief and very bright flash of light for taking photographs

flash card *n* : a card bearing words, numbers, or pictures briefly displayed usu. as a learning aid

flash·gun \-ˌgən\ *n* : a device for producing a bright flash of light for photography

flash·ing \'fla-shiŋ\ *n* : sheet metal used in waterproofing (as at the angle between a chimney and a roof)

flash·light \'flash-ˌlīt\ *n* : a battery-operated portable electric light

flash memory *n* : a computer memory chip not requiring connection to a power source to retain its data

flashy \'fla-shē\ *adj* **flash·i·er; -est** **1** : momentarily dazzling **2** : superficially attractive or impressive : SHOWY ⟨∼ clothes⟩ — **flash·i·ly** \-shə-lē\ *adv* — **flash·i·ness** \-shē-nəs\ *n*

flask \'flask\ *n* : a flattened bottle-shaped container ⟨a whiskey ∼⟩

¹flat \'flat\ *adj* **flat·ter; flat·test** **1** : spread out along a surface; *also* : being or characterized by a horizontal line **2** : having a smooth, level, or even surface **3** : having a broad smooth surface and little thickness **4** : DOWNRIGHT, POSITIVE ⟨a ∼ refusal⟩ **5** : FIXED, UNCHANGING ⟨charge a ∼ rate⟩ **6** : EXACT, PRECISE ⟨in four minutes ∼⟩ **7** : DULL, UNINTERESTING; *also* : INSIPID **8** : DEFLATED ⟨a ∼ tire⟩ **9** : lower than the true pitch; *also* : lower by a half step **10** : free from gloss ⟨a ∼ paint⟩ **11** : lacking depth of characterization — **flat·ly** *adv* — **flat·ness** *n*

²flat *n* **1** : a level surface of land : PLAIN **2** : a flat part or surface **3** : a character ♭ that indicates that a specified note is to be lowered by a half step; *also* : the resulting note **4** : something flat **5** : an apartment on one floor **6** : a deflated tire

³flat *adv* **1** : FLATLY **2** : COMPLETELY ⟨∼ broke⟩ **3** : below the true musical pitch

⁴flat *vb* **flat·ted; flat·ting** **1** : FLATTEN **2** : to lower in pitch esp. by a half step

flat·bed \'flat-ˌbed\ *n* : a truck or trailer with a body in the form of a platform or shallow box

flat·boat \-ˌbōt\ *n* : a flat-bottomed boat used esp. for carrying bulky freight

flat·car \-ˌkär\ *n* : a railroad freight car without sides or roof

flat·fish \-ˌfish\ *n* : any of an order of flattened marine bony fishes with both eyes on the upper side

flat·foot \-ˌfút, -ˈfút\ *n, pl* **flat·feet** \-ˌfēt, -ˈfēt\ : a condition in which the arch of the foot is flattened so that the entire sole

rests upon the ground — **flat–foot·ed** \-ˈfú-təd\ *adj*

Flat·head \-ˌhed\ *n, pl* **Flatheads** *or* **Flathead** : a member of an American Indian people of Montana

flat·iron \-ˌī(-ə)rn\ *n* : IRON 3

flat·land \-ˌland\ *n* : land lacking significant variation in elevation

flat–out \'flat-ˌaút\ *adj* **1** : being or going at maximum effort or speed **2** : OUTAND-OUT, DOWNRIGHT ⟨it was a ∼ lie⟩

flat out *adv* **1** : BLUNTLY, DIRECTLY **2** : at top speed **3** *usu* **flat–out** : to the greatest degree : COMPLETELY ⟨is just *flat-out* confusing⟩

flat–pan·el \-ˈpa-nᵊl\ *adj* : relating to or being a thin flat video display

flat·ten \'fla-tᵊn\ *vb* : to make or become flat

flat·ter \'fla-tər\ *vb* [ME *flateren*, fr. AF *flater* to lap, flatter] **1** : to praise too much or without sincerity **2** : to represent too favorably ⟨the portrait ∼s him⟩ **3** : to display to advantage **4** : to judge (oneself) favorably or too favorably — **flat·ter·er** *n*

flat·tery \'fla-tə-rē\ *n, pl* **-ter·ies** : flattering speech or attentions : insincere or excessive praise

flat·top \'flat-ˌtäp\ *n* **1** : AIRCRAFT CARRIER **2** : CREW CUT

flat·u·lent \'fla-chə-lənt\ *adj* **1** : full of gas ⟨a ∼ stomach⟩ **2** : INFLATED, POMPOUS — **flat·u·lence** \-ləns\ *n*

fla·tus \'flā-təs\ *n* : gas formed in the intestine or stomach

flat·ware \'flat-ˌwer\ *n* : eating and serving utensils

flat·worm \-ˌwùrm\ *n* : any of a phylum of flattened mostly parasitic segmented worms (as trematodes and tapeworms)

flaunt \'flónt\ *vb* **1** : to display oneself to public notice **2** : to wave or flutter showily **3** : to display ostentatiously or impudently : PARADE — **flaunt** *n*

flau·ta \'flaù-tə\ *n* : a tortilla rolled around a filling and deep-fried

flau·tist \'flò-tist, 'flaù-\ *n* [It *flautista*] : FLUTIST

¹fla·vor \'flā-vər\ *n* **1** : the quality of something that affects the sense of taste or of taste and smell **2** : a substance that adds flavor **3** : characteristic or predominant quality — **fla·vored** \-vərd\ *adj* — **fla·vor·ful** *adj* — **fla·vor·less** *adj* — **fla·vor·some** *adj*

²flavor *vb* : to give or add flavor to

fla·vor·ing *n* : FLAVOR 2

fla·vour *chiefly Brit var of* FLAVOR

flaw \'flò\ *n* : a small often hidden defect — **flaw·less** *adj* — **flaw·less·ly** *adv* — **flaw·less·ness** *n*

flax \'flaks\ *n* : a fiber that is the source of linen; *also* : a blue-flowered plant grown for this fiber and its oily seeds

flax·en \'flak-sən\ *adj* **1** : made of flax **2** : resembling flax esp. in pale soft straw color

flay \'flā\ *vb* **1** : to strip off the skin or surface of **2** : to criticize harshly

fl dr *abbr* fluid dram

flea \'flē\ n : any of an order of small wingless leaping bloodsucking insects

flea·bane \'flē-,bān\ n : any of various plants of the daisy family once believed to drive away fleas

flea–bit·ten \-,bi-t²n\ adj : bitten by or infested with fleas

flea market n : a usu. open-air market for secondhand articles and antiques

¹fleck \'flek\ vb : STREAK, SPOT

²fleck n 1 : SPOT, MARK 2 : FLAKE, PARTICLE

fledge \'flej\ vb fledged; fledg·ing : to develop the feathers necessary for flying or independent activity

fledg·ling \'flej-liŋ\ n 1 : a young bird just fledged 2 : an immature or inexperienced person

flee \'flē\ vb fled \'fled\; flee·ing 1 : to run away often from danger or evil 2 : VANISH 3 : to run away from : SHUN

¹fleece \'flēs\ n 1 : the woolly coat of an animal and esp. a sheep 2 : a soft or woolly covering — **fleecy** adj

²fleece vb fleeced; fleec·ing 1 : to strip of money or property by fraud or extortion 2 : SHEAR

¹fleet \'flēt\ vb : to pass rapidly

²fleet n [ME flete, fr. OE flēot ship, fr. flēotan to float] 1 : a group of warships under one command 2 : a group (as of ships, planes, or trucks) under one management

⁴fleet adj 1 : SWIFT, NIMBLE 2 : not enduring : FLEETING — **fleet·ness** n

fleet admiral n : an admiral of the highest rank in the navy

fleet·ing \'flē-tiŋ\ adj : passing swiftly

Flem·ing \'fle-miŋ\ n : a member of a Germanic people inhabiting chiefly northern Belgium

Flem·ish \'fle-mish\ n 1 : the Dutch language as spoken by the Flemings 2 **Flemish** pl — FLEMINGS — **Flemish** adj

¹flesh \'flesh\ n 1 : the soft parts of an animal's body; esp : muscular tissue 2 : MEAT 3 : the physical nature of humans as distinguished from the soul 4 : human beings; also : living beings 5 : STOCK, KINDRED 6 : fleshy plant tissue (as fruit pulp) — **fleshed** \'flesht\ adj

²flesh vb : to make fuller or more nearly complete — usu. used with out ⟨flesh out a schedule⟩

flesh fly n : a dipteran fly whose maggots feed on flesh

flesh·ly \'flesh-lē\ adj 1 : CORPOREAL, BODILY 2 : not spiritual : WORLDLY 3 : CARNAL, SENSUAL ⟨~ appetites⟩

flesh·pot \'flesh-,pät\ n 1 pl : bodily comfort : LUXURY 2 : a place of lascivious entertainment — usu. used in pl.

fleshy \'fle-shē\ adj flesh·i·er; -est 1 : consisting of or resembling animal flesh 2 : PLUMP, FAT

flew past of ¹FLY

flex \'fleks\ vb : to bend esp. repeatedly — **flex** n

flex·i·ble \'flek-sə-bəl\ adj 1 : capable of being flexed : PLIANT 2 : yielding to influence : TRACTABLE 3 : readily changed or changing : ADAPTABLE ♦ **Synonyms** ELASTIC, SUPPLE, RESILIENT, SPRINGY — **flex·i·bil·i·ty** \,flek-sə-'bi-lə-tē\ n

flex·or \'flek-sər, -,sór\ n : a muscle serving to bend a body part

flex·ure \'flek-shər\ n : TURN, FOLD

flib·ber·ti·gib·bet \,fli-bər-tē-'ji-bət\ n : a silly flighty person

¹flick \'flik\ n 1 : a light sharp jerky stroke or movement 2 : a sound produced by a flick 3 : ²FLICKER

²flick vb 1 : to strike lightly with a quick sharp motion 2 : FLUTTER, FLIT

³flick n : MOVIE

¹flick·er \'fli-kər\ vb 1 : to move irregularly or unsteadily : FLUTTER 2 : to burn fitfully or with a fluctuating light — **flick·er·ing·ly** adv

²flicker n 1 : an act of flickering 2 : a sudden brief movement ⟨a ~ of an eyelid⟩ 3 : a momentary stirring ⟨a ~ of interest⟩ 4 : a slight indication : HINT 5 : a wavering light

³flicker n : a large barred and spotted No. American woodpecker with a brown back that occurs as an eastern form with yellow on the underside of the wings and tail and a western form with red in these areas

flied past and past part of ³FLY

fli·er \'flī(-ə)r\ n 1 : one that flies; esp : PILOT 2 : a reckless or speculative undertaking 3 usu **fly·er** : an advertising circular

¹flight \'flīt\ n 1 : an act or instance of flying 2 : the ability to fly 3 : a passing through air or space 4 : the distance covered in a flight 5 : swift movement 6 : a trip made by or in an airplane or spacecraft 7 : a group of similar individuals (as birds or airplanes) flying as a unit 8 : a passing (as of the imagination) beyond ordinary limits 9 : a series of stairs from one landing to another — **flight·less** adj

²flight n : an act or instance of running away

flight bag n 1 : a lightweight traveling bag with zippered outside pockets 2 : a small canvas satchel

flight line n : a parking and servicing area for airplanes

flighty \'flī-tē\ adj flight·i·er; -est 1 : easily upset : VOLATILE 2 : easily excited : SKITTISH 3 : CAPRICIOUS, SILLY — **flight·i·ness** \-tē-nəs\ n

flim·flam \'flim-,flam\ n : DECEPTION, FRAUD — **flim·flam·mery** \-,fla-mə-re\ n

flim·sy \'flim-zē\ adj flim·si·er; -est 1 : lacking strength or substance 2 : of inferior materials and workmanship 3 : having little worth or plausibility ⟨a ~ excuse⟩ — **flim·si·ly** \-zə-lē\ adv — **flim·si·ness** \-zē-nəs\ n

flinch \'flinch\ vb [MF flenchir to bend] : to shrink from or as if from pain ⟨~ WINCE⟩ — **flinch** n

¹fling \'fliŋ\ vb flung \'fləŋ\; fling·ing 1 : to move hastily, brusquely, or violently ⟨flung out of the room⟩ 2 : to kick or plunge vigorously 3 : to throw with force or recklessness; also : to cast as if by throwing 4 : to put suddenly into a state or condition

fling • florid

²fling n 1 : an act or instance of flinging 2 : a casual try : ATTEMPT 3 : a period of self-indulgence

flint \'flint\ n 1 : a hard dark quartz that produces a spark when struck by steel 2 : an alloy used for producing a spark in lighters — **flinty** adj

flint glass n : heavy glass containing an oxide of lead and used in lenses and prisms

flint·lock \'flint-ˌläk\ n 1 : a lock for a gun using a flint to ignite the charge 2 : a firearm fitted with a flintlock

¹flip \'flip\ vb **flipped; flip·ping** 1 : to turn by tossing ⟨~ a coin⟩ 2 : to turn over; also : to leaf through ⟨a FLICK, JERK ⟨~ a light switch⟩ 4 : to lose self-control — **flip** n

²flip adj : FLIPPANT, IMPERTINENT

flip·pant \'fli-pənt\ adj : lacking proper respect or seriousness — **flip·pan·cy** \'fli-pən-sē\ n

flip·per \'fli-pər\ n 1 : a broad flat limb (as of a seal) adapted for swimming 2 : a paddlelike shoe used in skin diving

flip side n : the reverse and usu. less popular side of a phonograph record

¹flirt \'flərt\ vb 1 : to move erratically : FLIT 2 : to behave amorously without serious intent 3 : to show casual interest ⟨~ed with the idea⟩; also : to come close to ⟨~ with danger⟩ — **flir·ta·tion** \ˌflər-'tā-shən\ n — **flir·ta·tious** \-shəs\ adj

²flirt n 1 : an act or instance of flirting 2 : a person who flirts

flit \'flit\ vb **flit·ted; flit·ting** : to pass or move quickly or abruptly from place to place : DART — **flit** n

flitch \'flich\ n : a side of cured meat; esp : a side of bacon

fliv·ver \'fli-vər\ n : a small cheap usu. old automobile

¹float \'flōt\ n 1 : something (as a raft) that floats 2 : a cork buoying up the baited end of a fishing line 3 : a hollow ball that floats at the end of a lever in a cistern or tank and regulates the liquid level 4 : a vehicle with a platform to carry an exhibit 5 : a soft drink with ice cream floating in it

²float vb 1 : to rest on the surface of or be suspended in a fluid 2 : to move gently on or through a fluid 3 : to cause to float 4 : WANDER 5 : to offer (securities) in order to finance an enterprise 6 : to finance by floating an issue of stocks or bonds 7 : to arrange for ⟨~ a loan⟩ — **float·er** n

floaty \'flō-tē\ adj **float·i·er; -est** 1 : tending to float : BUOYANT 2 : light and billowy ⟨a ~ skirt⟩

¹flock \'fläk\ n 1 : a group of animals (as birds or sheep) assembled or herded together 2 : a group of people under the guidance of a leader; esp : CONGREGATION 3 : a large number ⟨a ~ of tourists⟩

²flock vb : to gather or move in a flock ⟨people ~ed to the beach⟩

floe \'flō\ n : a flat mass of floating ice

flog \'fläg\ vb **flogged; flog·ging** 1 : to

beat with or as if with a rod or whip 2 : SELL ⟨~ encyclopedias⟩ — **flog·ger** n

¹flood \'fləd\ n 1 : a great flow of water over the land 2 : the flowing in of the tide 3 : an overwhelming volume

²flood vb 1 : to cover or become filled with a flood 2 : to fill abundantly or excessively; esp : to supply an excess of fuel to 3 : to pour forth in a flood — **flood·er** n

flood·gate \'fləd-ˌgāt\ n : a gate for controlling a body of water : SLUICE

flood·light \-ˌlīt\ n : a lamp that throws a broad beam of light; also : the beam itself — **floodlight** vb

flood·plain \-ˌplān\ n : a plain along a river or stream subject to periodic flooding

flood tide n 1 : a rising tide 2 : an overwhelming quantity 3 : a high point

flood·wa·ter \'fləd-ˌwȯ-tər, -ˌwä-\ n : the water of a flood

¹floor \'flȯr\ n 1 : the bottom of a room on which one stands 2 : a ground surface 3 : a story of a building 4 : a main level space (as in a legislative chamber) distinguished from a platform or gallery 5 : AUDIENCE 6 : the right to address an assembly 7 : a lower limit ⟨put a ~ under wheat prices⟩ — **floor·ing** n

²floor vb 1 : to furnish with a floor 2 : to knock down 3 : AMAZE, DUMBFOUND ⟨was ~ed by the news⟩ 4 : to press (a vehicle's accelerator) to the floorboard esp. rapidly

floor·board \-ˌbȯrd\ n 1 : a board in a floor 2 : the floor of an automobile

floor leader n : a member of a legislative body who has charge of a party's organization and strategy on the floor

floor show n : a series of acts presented in a nightclub

floor·walk·er \'flȯr-ˌwȯ-kər\ n : a person employed in a retail store to oversee the sales force and aid customers

floo·zy or **floo·zie** \'flü-zē\ n, pl **floozies** : a usu. young woman of loose morals

flop \'fläp\ vb **flopped; flop·ping** 1 : FLAP 2 : to throw oneself down heavily, clumsily, or in a relaxed manner ⟨flopped into a chair⟩ 3 : FAIL ⟨the show flopped⟩ — **flop** n — **flop** adv — **flop·per** n

flop·house \'fläp-ˌhau̇s\ n : a cheap hotel

¹flop·py \'flä-pē\ adj **flop·pi·er; -est** : tending to flop; esp : soft and flexible — **flop·pi·ly** \-pə-lē\ adv

²floppy n, pl **flop·pies** : FLOPPY DISK

floppy disk n : a thin plastic disk with a magnetic coating on which computer data can be stored

flop sweat n : sweat caused by the fear of failing

flo·ra \'flȯr-ə\ n, pl **floras** also **flo·rae** \-ˌē, -ˌī\ [L Flora, Roman goddess of flowers] : plants or plant life esp. of a region or period

flo·ral \'flȯr-əl\ adj : of, relating to, or depicting flowers ⟨a ~ design⟩

flo·res·cence \flȯ-'re-sᵊns, flə-\ n : a state or period of being in bloom or flourishing — **flo·res·cent** \-ᵊnt\ adj

flor·id \'flȯr-əd\ adj 1 : very flowery in

style : ORNATE ⟨~ prose⟩ **2** : tinged with red : RUDDY **3** : marked by emotional or sexual fervor ⟨~ love letters⟩

flo·rin \'flȯr-ən\ n **1** : an old gold coin first struck at Florence, Italy, in 1252 **2** : a gold coin of a European country patterned after the florin of Florence **3** : any of several modern silver coins issued in Commonwealth countries **4** : GULDEN

flo·rist \'flȯr-ist\ n : a person who sells flowers or ornamental plants

¹**floss** \'fläs\ n **1** : soft thread of silk or mercerized cotton for embroidery **2** : DENTAL FLOSS **3** : fluffy fibrous material

²**floss** vb : to use dental floss on (one's teeth)

flossy \'flä-sē\ adj **floss·i·er; -est 1** : of, relating to, or having the characteristics of floss **2** : STYLISH, GLAMOROUS ⟨~ hotels⟩ — **floss·i·ly** \-sə-lē\ adv

flo·ta·tion \flō-'tā-shən\ n : the process or an instance of floating

flo·til·la \flō-'ti-lə\ n [Sp, dim. of flota fleet] : a fleet esp. of small ships

flot·sam \'flät-səm\ n : floating wreckage of a ship or its cargo

¹**flounce** \'flaůns\ vb **flounced; flounc·ing 1** : to move with exaggerated jerky or bouncy motions **2** : to go with sudden determination

²**flounce** n : an act or instance of flouncing — **flouncy** \'flaůn-sē\ adj

³**flounce** n : a strip of fabric attached by one edge; also : a wide ruffle

¹**floun·der** \'flaůn-dər\ n, pl **flounder** or **flounders** : FLATFISH; esp : any of various important marine food fishes

²**flounder** vb **1** : to struggle to move or obtain footing **2** : to proceed clumsily ⟨~ed through the speech⟩

¹**flour** \'flaů(-ə)r\ n [ME, flower, best of anything, flour, fr. AF flur flower] : finely ground and sifted meal of a grain (as wheat); also : a fine soft powder — **floury** adj

²**flour** vb : to coat with or as if with flour

¹**flour·ish** \'flər-ish\ vb **1** : THRIVE, PROSPER **2** : to be in a state of activity or production ⟨~ed about 1850⟩ **3** : to reach a height of development or influence **4** : to make bold and sweeping gestures **5** : BRANDISH ⟨~ed his sword⟩

²**flourish** n **1** : a florid bit of speech or writing; also : an ornamental touch or decorative detail **2** : FANFARE ⟨a ~ of trumpets⟩ **3** : WAVE ⟨with a ~ of his cane⟩ **4** : showiness in doing something

¹**flout** \'flaůt\ vb : to treat with contemptuous disregard ⟨~ the law⟩ — **flout·er** n

²**flout** n : TAUNT

¹**flow** \'flō\ vb **1** : to issue or move in a stream **2** : RISE ⟨the tide ebbs and ~s⟩ **3** : ABOUND **4** : to proceed smoothly and readily **5** : to have a smooth continuity **6** : to hang loose and billowing **7** : COME, ARISE **8** : MENSTRUATE

²**flow** n **1** : an act of flowing **2** : FLOOD **1**, **2** **3** : a smooth uninterrupted movement **4** : STREAM; also : a mass of material that has flowed when molten **5** : the quantity

that flows in a certain time **6** : MENSTRUATION **7** : a continuous transfer of energy — **flow·age** \'flō-ij\ n

flow·chart \'flō-,chärt\ n : a symbolic diagram showing step-by-step progression through a procedure

flow diagram n : FLOWCHART

¹**flow·er** \'flaů(-ə)r\ n [ME flour, fr. AF flur, flour, fr. L flor-, flos] **1** : a plant shoot modified for reproduction and bearing leaves specialized into floral organs; esp : one of a seed plant consisting of a calyx, corolla, stamens, and carpels **2** : a plant cultivated for its blossoms **3** : the best part or example **4** : the finest most vigorous period **5** : a state of blooming or flourishing — **flow·ered** \'flaů(-ə)rd\ adj — **flow·er·less** adj — **flow·er·like** \-,līk\ adj

²**flower** vb **1** : DEVELOP; also : FLOURISH **2** : to produce flowers : BLOOM

flower girl n : a little girl who carries flowers at a wedding

flower head n : a compact cluster of small flowers without stems suggesting a single flower

flowering plant n : any of a major group of vascular plants (as magnolias, grasses, or roses) that produce flowers and fruit and have the seeds enclosed in an ovary

flow·er·pot \'flaů(-ə)r-,pät\ n : a pot in which to grow plants

flow·ery \'flaů(-ə)r-ē\ adj **1** : of, relating to, or resembling flowers **2** : full of fine words or phrases ⟨a ~ speech⟩ — **flow·er·i·ness** \-ē-nəs\ n

flown \'flōn\ past part of ¹FLY

fl oz abbr fluid ounce

flu \'flü\ n **1** : INFLUENZA **2** : any of several virus diseases marked esp. by respiratory or intestinal symptoms — **flu·like** \-,līk\ adj

flub \'fləb\ vb **flubbed; flub·bing** : BOTCH, BLUNDER — **flub** n

fluc·tu·ate \'flək-chə-,wāt\ vb **-at·ed; -at·ing 1** : WAVER **2** : to move up and down or back and forth — **fluc·tu·a·tion** \,flək-chə-'wā-shən\ n

flue \'flü\ n : a passage (as in a chimney) for directing a current (as of smoke or gases)

flu·ent \'flü-ənt\ adj **1** : capable of flowing : FLUID **2** : ready or facile in speech ⟨~ in French⟩; also : having or showing mastery in a subject or skill **3** : effortlessly smooth and rapid ⟨~ speech⟩ — **flu·en·cy** \-ən-sē\ n — **flu·ent·ly** adv

flue pipe n : an organ pipe whose tone is produced by an air current striking the beveled opening of the pipe

¹**fluff** \'fləf\ n **1** : ¹DOWN **1** ⟨~ from a pillow⟩ **2** : something fluffy **3** : something inconsequential **4** : BLUNDER; esp : an actor's lapse of memory

²**fluff** vb **1** : to make or become fluffy ⟨~ up a pillow⟩ **2** : to make a mistake

fluffy \'flə-fē\ adj **fluff·i·er; -est 1** : covered with or resembling fluff **2** : being light and soft or airy ⟨a ~ omelet⟩ **3** : lacking in meaning or substance — **fluff·i·ly** \-fə-lē\ adv

¹**flu·id** \'flü-əd\ adj **1** : capable of flowing

2 : subject to change or movement **3** : showing a smooth easy style ⟨~ movements⟩ **4** : available for a different use; *esp* : LIQUID **5** ⟨~ assets⟩ — **flu·id·i·ty** \flü-'i-də-tē\ n — **flu·id·ly** adv

²fluid n : a substance (as a liquid or gas) tending to flow or take the shape of its container

fluid dram or **flu·i·dram** \,flü-ə-'dram\ n — see WEIGHT table

fluid ounce n — see WEIGHT table

¹fluke \'flük\ n : any of various trematode flatworms

²fluke n **1** : the part of an anchor that fastens in the ground **2** : a lobe of a whale's tail

³fluke n : a stroke of luck — **fluky** also **fluk·ey** \'flü-kē\ adj

flume \'flüm\ n **1** : an inclined channel for carrying water **2** : a ravine or gorge with a stream running through it

flung past and past part of FLING

flunk \'fləŋk\ vb : to fail esp. in an examination or course — **flunk** n

flun·ky also **flun·key** or **flun·kie** \'fləŋ-kē\ n, pl **flunkies** also **flunkeys 1** : a liveried servant; also : one performing menial or miscellaneous duties **2** : YES-MAN

fluo·res·cence \flô-'re-sᵊns\ n : luminescence caused by radiation absorption that ceases almost immediately after the incident radiation has stopped; also : the emitted radiation — **fluo·resce** \-'res\ vb — **fluo·res·cent** \-'re-sᵊnt\ adj

fluorescent lamp n : a tubular electric lamp in which light is produced by the action of ultraviolet light on a fluorescent material that coats the inner surface of the lamp

fluo·ri·date \'flôr-ə-,dāt\ vb **-dat·ed; -dat·ing** : to add a fluoride to (as drinking water) to reduce tooth decay — **fluo·ri·da·tion** \,flôr-ə-'dā-shən\ n

fluo·ride \'flôr-,īd\ n : a compound of fluorine

fluo·ri·nate \'flôr-ə-,nāt\ vb **-nat·ed; -nat·ing** : to treat or cause to combine with fluorine or a compound of fluorine — **fluo·ri·na·tion** \,flôr-ə-'nā-shən\ n

fluo·rine \'flôr-,ēn, -ən\ n : a pale yellowish flammable irritating toxic gaseous chemical element

fluo·rite \'flôr-,īt\ n : a mineral that consists of the fluoride of calcium used as a flux and in making glass

fluo·ro·car·bon \,flôr-ō-'kär-bən\ n : a compound containing fluorine and carbon used chiefly as a lubricant, refrigerant, or nonstick coating; also : CHLOROFLUOROCARBON

fluo·ro·scope \'flôr-ə-,skōp\ n : an instrument for observing the internal structure of an opaque object (as the living body) by means of X-rays — **fluo·ro·scop·ic** \,flôr-ə-'skä-pik\ adj — **fluo·ros·co·py** \-'ä-skə-pē\ n

fluo·ro·sis \flu-'rō-səs, ,flô-\ n : an abnormal condition (as spotting of the teeth) caused by fluorine or its compounds

flu·ox·e·tine \flü-'äk-sə-,tēn\ n : an antidepressant drug that enhances serotonin activity

flur·ry \'flər-ē\ n, pl **flurries 1** : a gust of wind **2** : a brief light snowfall **3** : COMMOTION, BUSTLE **4** : a brief outburst of activity ⟨a ~ of trading⟩ — **flurry** vb

¹flush \'fləsh\ vb : to cause (a bird) to fly away suddenly

²flush n : a hand of cards all of the same suit

³flush n **1** : a sudden flow (as of water) **2** : a surge esp. of emotion ⟨a ~ of triumph⟩ **3** : a tinge of red : BLUSH **4** : a fresh and vigorous state ⟨in the ~ of youth⟩ **5** : a passing sensation of extreme heat

⁴flush vb **1** : to flow and spread suddenly and freely **2** : to glow brightly **3** : BLUSH **4** : to wash out with a rush of fluid **5** : INFLAME, EXCITE ⟨was ~ed with anger⟩ **6** : to cause to blush

⁵flush adj **1** : of a ruddy healthy color **2** : full of life and vigor **3** : filled to overflowing : AFFLUENT **5** : readily available : ABUNDANT **6** : having an unbroken or even surface **7** : directly abutting : immediately adjacent **8** : set even with an edge of a type page or column — **flushness** n

⁶flush adv **1** : in a flush manner **2** : SQUARELY ⟨a blow ~ on the chin⟩

⁷flush vb : to make flush

flus·ter \'fləs-tər\ vb : to put into a state of agitated confusion — **fluster** n

flute \'flüt\ n **1** : a hollow pipelike musical instrument **2** : a grooved pleat **3** : GROOVE — **flute** vb — **flut·ed** adj

flut·ing n : fluted decoration

flut·ist \'flü-tist\ n : a flute player

¹flut·ter \'flə-tər\ vb [ME *floteren* to float, flutter, fr. OE *floterian*, fr. *flotian* to float] **1** : to flap the wings rapidly **2** : to move with quick wavering or flapping motions **3** : to vibrate in irregular spasms **4** : to move about or behave in an agitated aimless manner — **flut·tery** \-tə-rē\ adj

²flutter n **1** : an act of fluttering **2** : a state of nervous confusion **3** : FLURRY

¹flux \'fləks\ n **1** : an act of flowing **2** : a state of continuous change **3** : a substance used to aid in fusing metals

²flux vb : ¹FUSE

¹fly \'flī\ vb **flew** \'flü\; **flown** \'flōn\; **fly·ing 1** : to move in or pass through the air with wings **2** : to move through the air or before the wind **3** : to float or cause to float, wave, or soar in the air **4** : FLEE **5** : to fade and disappear : VANISH **6** : to move or pass swiftly ⟨time *flies*⟩ **7** : to become expended or dissipated rapidly **8** : to operate or travel in an aircraft or spacecraft **9** : to journey over by flying **10** : AVOID, SHUN **11** : to transport by flying

²fly n, pl **flies 1** : the action or process of flying : FLIGHT **2** pl : the space over a theater stage **3** : a garment closing concealed by a fold of cloth **4** : the length of an extended flag from its staff or support **5** : a baseball hit high into the air **6** : the outer canvas of a tent with a double top — **on the fly** : while still in the air

³fly *vb* **flied; fly·ing** : to hit a fly in baseball

⁴fly *n, pl* **flies 1** : a winged insect — usu. used in combination ⟨butter*fly*⟩ **2** : any of a large order of insects mostly with one pair of functional wings and another pair that if present are reduced to balancing organs and often with larvae without a head, eyes, or legs; *esp* : one (as a housefly) that is large and stout-bodied **3** : a fishhook dressed to suggest an insect

fly·able \'flī-ə-bəl\ *adj* : suitable for flying or being flown

fly ball *n* : ²FLY 5

fly·blown \'flī-ˌblōn\ *adj* : not pure : TAINTED, CORRUPT

fly·by \-ˌbī\ *n, pl* **flybys 1** : a usu. low-altitude flight by an aircraft over a public gathering **2** : a flight of a spacecraft past a heavenly body (as Jupiter) close enough to obtain scientific data

fly–by–night \-bī-ˌnīt\ *adj* **1** : seeking a quick profit usu. by shady acts **2** : TRANSITORY, PASSING ⟨~ fashions⟩

fly casting *n* : the casting of artificial flies in fly-fishing or as a competitive sport

fly-catch·er \-ˌka-chər, -ˌke-\ *n* : any of various passerine birds that feed on insects caught in flight

flyer *var of* FLIER

fly–fish·ing \'flī-ˌfi-shiŋ\ *n* : a method of fishing in which an artificial fly is used for bait

flying boat *n* : a seaplane with a hull designed for floating

flying buttress *n* : a projecting arched structure to support a wall or building

flying fish *n* : any of numerous marine bony fishes capable of long gliding flights out of water by spreading their large finlike wings

flying saucer *n* : an unidentified flying object reported to be saucer-shaped or disk-shaped

flying squirrel *n* : either of two small nocturnal No. American squirrels with folds of skin connecting the forelegs and hind legs that enable them to make long gliding leaps

fly·leaf \'flī-ˌlēf\ *n, pl* **fly·leaves** \-ˌlēvz\ : a blank leaf at the beginning or end of a book

fly·pa·per \-ˌpā-pər\ *n* : paper poisoned or coated with a sticky substance for killing or catching flies

fly·speck \-ˌspek\ *n* **1** : a speck of fly dung **2** : something small and insignificant

fly·way \-ˌwā\ *n* : an established air route of migratory birds

fly·wheel \-ˌhwēl\ *n* : a heavy wheel for regulating the speed of machinery

fm *abbr* fathom

Fm *symbol* fermium

FM \'ef-ˌem\ *n* : a broadcasting system using frequency modulation; *also* : a radio receiver of such a system

fn *abbr* footnote

fo *or* **fol** *abbr* folio

FO *abbr* foreign office

¹foal \'fōl\ *n* : a young horse or related animal; *esp* : one under one year

²foal *vb* : to give birth to a foal

¹foam \'fōm\ *n* **1** : a mass of bubbles formed on the surface of a liquid : FROTH, SPUME **2** : material (as rubber) in a lightweight cellular form — **foamy** *adj*

²foam *vb* : to form foam : FROTH

fob \'fäb\ *n* **1** : a short strap, ribbon, or chain attached esp. to a pocket watch **2** : a small ornament worn on a fob

FOB *abbr* free on board

fob off *vb* **1** : to put off with a trick, excuse, or inferior substitute **2** : to pass or offer as genuine **3** : to put aside

FOC *abbr* free of charge

focal length *n* : the distance of a focus from a lens or curved mirror

fo'c's'le *var of* FORECASTLE

¹fo·cus \'fō-kəs\ *n, pl* **fo·ci** \-ˌsī\ *also* **fo·cus·es** [NL, fr. L, hearth] **1** : a point at which rays (as of light, heat, or sound) meet or diverge or appear to diverge; *esp* : the point at which an image is formed by a mirror, lens, or optical system **2** : FOCAL LENGTH **3** : adjustment (as of eyes or eyeglasses) that gives clear vision **4** : central point : CENTER — **fo·cal** \'fō-kəl\ *adj* — **fo·cal·ly** *adv*

²focus *vb* **-cused** *also* **-cussed; -cus·ing** *also* **-cus·sing 1** : to bring or come to a focus ⟨~ rays of light⟩ **2** : CENTER ⟨~ attention on a problem⟩ **3** : to adjust the focus of

fod·der \'fä-dər\ *n* **1** : coarse dry food (as cornstalks) for livestock **2** : available material used to supply a heavy demand

foe \'fō\ *n* [ME *fo*, fr. OE *fāh*, fr. *fāh* hostile] : ENEMY

FOE *abbr* Fraternal Order of Eagles

foehn *or* **föhn** \'fərn, 'fēn, 'fān\ *n* [G *Föhn*] : a warm dry wind blowing down a mountainside

foe·man \'fō-mən\ *n* : FOE

foe·tal, foe·tus *chiefly Brit var of* FETAL, FETUS

¹fog \'fóg, 'fäg\ *n* **1** : fine particles of water suspended in the lower atmosphere **2** : mental confusion ⟨was in a ~ as what to do next⟩ — **fog·gy** *adj*

²fog *vb* **fogged; fog·ging** : to obscure or be obscured with or as if with fog

fog·horn \'fóg-ˌhórn, 'fäg-\ *n* : a horn sounded in a fog to give warning

fo·gy *also* **fo·gey** \'fō-gē\ *n, pl* **fogies** *also* **fogeys** : a person with old-fashioned ideas ⟨an old ~⟩

foi·ble \'fói-bəl\ *n* : a minor failing or weakness in character or behavior

foie gras \'fwä-ˌgrä\ *n* [F, lit., fat liver] : the fattened liver of an animal and esp. of a goose usu. served as a pâté

¹foil \'fói(-ə)l\ *vb* [ME, alter. of *fullen* to full cloth, fr. AF *foller*] **1** : to prevent from attaining an end : DEFEAT **2** : to bring to naught : THWART

²foil *n* [ME, leaf, fr. AF *fuille, foille*, fr. L *folia*, pl. of *folium* leaf] **1** : a very thin sheet of metal ⟨aluminum ~⟩ **2** : one that serves as a contrast to another ⟨acted as a ~ for a comedian⟩

³foil *n* : a light fencing sword with a flexible blade tapering to a blunt point

foist \'fȯist\ vb : to pass off (something false or worthless) as genuine

¹fold \'fōld\ n 1 : an enclosure for sheep 2 : a group of people with a common faith, belief, or interest

²fold vb : to house (sheep) in a fold

³fold vb 1 : to lay one part over or against another part 2 : to clasp together 3 : EMBRACE 4 : to bend (as a layer of rock) into folds 5 : to incorporate into a mixture by overturning repeatedly without stirring or beating 6 : to become doubled or pleated 7 : FAIL, COLLAPSE ⟨the business ~ed⟩

⁴fold n 1 : a doubling or folding over 2 : a part doubled or laid over another part

fold·away \'fōld-ə-ˌwā\ adj : designed to fold out of the way or out of sight

fold·er \'fōl-dər\ n 1 : one that folds 2 : a folded printed circular 3 : a folded cover or large envelope for loose papers 4 : an object in a computer operating system used to organize files or other folders

fol·de·rol \'fäl-də-ˌräl\ n 1 : a useless trifle 2 : NONSENSE

fold·out \'fōld-ˌaut\ n : a folded leaf (as in a magazine) larger in some dimension than the page

fo·li·age \'fō-lē-ij\ n : a mass of leaves (as of a plant or forest)

fo·li·at·ed \'fō-lē-ˌā-təd\ adj : composed of or separable into layers

fo·lic acid \ˌfō-lik-\ n : a vitamin of the vitamin B complex used esp. to treat nutritional anemias

fo·lio \'fō-lē-ˌō\ n, pl **fo·li·os** 1 : a leaf of a book; also : a page number 2 : the size of a piece of paper cut two from a sheet 3 : a book printed on folio pages

¹folk \'fōk\ n, pl **folk** or **folks** 1 : the largest number or most characteristic part of a group of people forming a tribe or nation 2 pl : PEOPLE, PERSONS ⟨country ~⟩ ⟨old ~⟩ 3 folks pl : the persons of one's own family

²folk adj : of, relating to, or originating among the common people ⟨~ music⟩

folk art n : the traditional anonymous art of usu. untrained people

folk·lore \'fōk-ˌlȯr\ n : customs, beliefs, stories, and sayings of a people handed down from generation to generation — **folk·lor·ic** \-ˌlȯr-ik\ adj — **folk·lor·ist** \-ist\ n

folk mass n : a mass in which traditional liturgical music is replaced by folk music

folk·sing·er \'fōk-ˌsiŋ-ər\ n : a singer of folk songs — **folk·sing·ing** n

folksy \'fōk-sē\ adj **folks·i·er; -est** 1 : SOCIABLE, FRIENDLY 2 : informal, casual, or familiar in manner or style ⟨~ humor⟩

folk·way \'fōk-ˌwā\ n : a way of thinking, feeling, or acting common to a given group of people; esp : a traditional social custom

fol·li·cle \'fä-li-kəl\ n 1 : a small anatomical cavity or gland ⟨a hair ~⟩ 2 : a small fluid-filled cavity in the ovary of a mammal enclosing a developing egg — **fol·lic·u·lar** \fə-'li-kyə-lər\ adj

fol·low \'fä-lō\ vb 1 : to go or come after

2 : to proceed along ⟨~ the path⟩ 3 : to engage in as a way of life ⟨~ the sea⟩ ⟨~ a profession⟩ 4 : OBEY ⟨~ instructions⟩ 5 : PURSUE 6 : to come after in order or rank or natural sequence 7 : to keep one's attention fixed on 8 : to result from ♦ **Synonyms** SUCCEED, ENSUE, SUPERVENE — **fol·low·er** n — **follow suit** 1 : to play a card of the same suit as the card led 2 : to follow an example set

¹fol·low·ing \'fä-lə-wiŋ\ adj 1 : next after : SUCCEEDING ⟨the ~ day⟩ 2 : that immediately follows ⟨trains will leave at the ~ times⟩

²following n : a group of followers, adherents, or partisans

³following prep : subsequent to : AFTER ⟨~ the lecture tea was served⟩

follow–up \'fä-lō-ˌəp\ n : a system or instance of pursuing an initial effort by supplementary action

fol·ly \'fä-lē\ n, pl **follies** [ME folie, fr. AF, fr. fol fool] 1 : lack of good sense 2 : a foolish act or idea : FOOLISHNESS 3 : an excessively costly or unprofitable undertaking

fo·ment \fō-'ment\ vb : INCITE

fo·men·ta·tion \ˌfō-mən-'tā-shən, -ˌmen-\ n 1 : a hot moist material (as a damp cloth) applied to the body to ease pain 2 : the act of fomenting : INSTIGATION

fond \'fänd\ adj [ME, fr. fonne fool] 1 : FOOLISH, SILLY ⟨~ pride⟩ 2 : prizing highly : DESIROUS ⟨~ of praise⟩ 3 : strongly attracted or predisposed ⟨~ of music⟩ 4 : foolishly tender : INDULGENT; also : LOVING, AFFECTIONATE 5 : CHERISHED, DEAR ⟨his ~est hopes⟩ — **fond·ly** adv — **fond·ness** n

fon·dant \'fän-dənt\ n : a creamy preparation of sugar used as a basis for candies or icings

fon·dle \'fän-dᵊl\ vb **fon·dled; fon·dling** : to touch or handle lovingly : CARESS

fon·due also **fon·du** \fän-'dü, -'dyü\ n [F] : a preparation of melted cheese often flavored with white wine

¹font \'fänt\ n 1 : a receptacle for baptismal or holy water 2 : FOUNTAIN, SOURCE ⟨a ~ of information⟩

²font n : an assortment of printing type of one style and sometimes one size

food \'füd\ n 1 : material taken into an organism and used for growth, repair, and vital processes and as a source of energy; also : organic material produced by green plants and used by them as food 2 : nourishment in solid form 3 : something that nourishes, sustains, or supplies ⟨~ for thought⟩

food chain n 1 : a hierarchical arrangement of organisms in an ecological community such that each uses the next usu. lower member as a food source 2 : a hierarchy based on power or importance

food court n : an area (as within a shopping mall) set apart for food concessions

food poisoning n : a digestive illness caused by bacteria or by chemicals in food

food·stuff \'füd-ˌstəf\ n : a substance with

food value; *esp* : a specific nutrient (as fat or protein)

¹**fool** \'fül\ *n* [ME, fr. AF *fol*, fr. LL *follis*, fr. L, bellows, bag] **1** : a person who lacks sense or judgment **2** : JESTER **3** : DUPE **4** : IDIOT

²**fool** *vb* **1** : to spend time idly or aimlessly **2** : to meddle or tamper thoughtlessly or ignorantly **3** : JOKE **4** : DECEIVE **5** : FRITTER 〈*~ed* away his time〉

fool·ery \'fü-lə-rē\ *n, pl* **-er·ies 1** : a foolish act, utterance, or belief **2** : foolish behavior

fool·har·dy \'fül-,här-dē\ *adj* : foolishly daring : RASH — **fool·har·di·ness** \-dē-nəs\ *n*

fool·ish \'fü-lish\ *adj* **1** : showing or arising from folly or lack of judgment **2** : ABSURD, RIDICULOUS **3** : ABASHED — **fool·ish·ly** *adv* — **fool·ish·ness** *n*

fool·proof \'fül-,prüf\ *adj* : so simple or reliable as to leave no opportunity for error, misuse, or failure 〈a *~* plan〉

fools·cap \'fül-,skap\ *n* [fr. the watermark of a fool's cap formerly applied to such paper] : a size of paper typically 16x13 inches

fool's gold *n* : PYRITE

¹**foot** \'fút\ *n, pl* **feet** \'fēt\ *also* **foot 1** : the end part of the leg below the ankle of a vertebrate animal **2** — see WEIGHT table **3** : a group of syllables forming the basic unit of verse meter **4** : something resembling an animal's foot in position or use **5** : the lowest part : BOTTOM **6** : the part at the opposite end from the head **7** : the part (as of a stocking) that covers the foot

²**foot** *vb* **1** : DANCE **2** : to go on foot **3** : to add up **4** : to pay or provide for paying

foot·age \'fü-tij\ *n* **1** : length expressed in feet **2** : the length of film used for a scene; *also* : the material contained on such footage

foot–and–mouth disease *n* : an acute contagious viral disease esp. of cattle

foot·ball \'fút-,bȯl\ *n* **1** : any of several games played by two teams on a rectangular field with goalposts at each end in which the object is to get the ball over the goal line or between goalposts by running, passing, or kicking **2** : the ball used in football

foot·board \-,bȯrd\ *n* **1** : a narrow platform on which to stand or brace the feet **2** : a board forming the foot of a bed

foot·bridge \-,brij\ *n* : a bridge for pedestrians

foot·ed \'fù-təd\ *adj* : having a foot or feet of a specified kind or number 〈flat= footed〉 〈four-footed〉

-foot·er \'fù-tər\ *comb form* : one that is a specified number of feet in height, length, or breadth 〈a six-*footer*〉

foot·fall \'fút-,fȯl\ *n* : the sound of a footstep

foot·hill \-,hil\ *n* : a hill at the foot of higher hills or mountains

foot·hold \-,hōld\ *n* **1** : a hold for the feet : FOOTING **2** : a position usable as a base for further advance

foot·ing *n* **1** : the placing of one's feet in a stable position **2** : the act of moving on foot **3** : a place or space for standing : FOOTHOLD **4** : position with respect to one another : STATUS **5** : BASIS

foot·less \'fút-ləs\ *adj* **1** : having no feet 〈*~* tights〉 **2** : INEPT, INEFFECTUAL

foot·lights \-,līts\ *n pl* **1** : a row of lights along the front of a stage floor **2** : the stage as a profession 〈succeeded in the *~*〉

foo·tling \'füt-liŋ\ *adj* **1** : INEPT 〈*~* amateurs〉 **2** : TRIVIAL

foot·lock·er \'fút-,lä-kər\ *n* : a small trunk designed to be placed at the foot of a bed (as in a barracks)

foot·loose \-,lüs\ *adj* : having no ties : FREE, UNTRAMMELED

foot·man \-mən\ *n* : a male servant who attends a carriage or waits on table, admits visitors, and runs errands

foot·note \-,nōt\ *n* **1** : a note of reference, explanation, or comment placed usu. at the bottom of a page **2** : COMMENTARY

foot·pad \-,pad\ *n* : a round somewhat flat foot on the leg of a spacecraft for distributing weight to minimize sinking into a surface

foot·path \-,path, -,päth\ *n* : a narrow path for pedestrians

foot·print \-,print\ *n* **1** : an impression of the foot **2** : the area on a surface covered by something 〈a tire with a wide *~*〉

foot·race \-,rās\ *n* : a race run on foot

foot·rest \-,rest\ *n* : a support for the feet

foot·sore \-,sȯr\ *adj* : having sore or tender feet (as from much walking)

foot·step \-,step\ *n* **1** : the mark of the foot : TRACK **2** : TREAD **3** : distance covered by a step : PACE **4** : a step on which to ascend or descend **5** : a way of life, conduct, or action

foot·stool \-,stül\ *n* : a low stool to support the feet

foot·wear \-,wer\ *n* : apparel (as shoes or boots) for the feet

foot·work \-,wərk\ *n* : the management of the feet (as in boxing)

fop \'fäp\ *n* : DANDY **1** — **fop·pery** \'fä-pə-rē\ *n* — **fop·pish** *adj*

¹**for** \fər, 'fȯr\ *prep* **1** : as a preparation toward 〈dress *~* dinner〉 **2** : toward the purpose or goal of 〈need time *~* study〉 〈money *~* a trip〉 **3** : so as to reach or attain 〈run *~* cover〉 **4** : as being 〈took him *~* a fool〉 **5** : because of 〈cry *~* joy〉 **6** — used to indicate a recipient 〈a letter *~* you〉 **7** : in support of 〈fought *~* his country〉 **8** : directed at : AFFECTING 〈a cure *~* what ails you〉 **9** — used with a noun or pronoun followed by an infinitive to form the equivalent of a noun clause 〈*~* you to go would be silly〉 **10** : in exchange as equal to : so as to return the value of 〈a lot of trouble *~* nothing〉 〈pay $10 *~* a hat〉 **11** : CONCERNING 〈a stickler *~* detail〉 **12** : CONSIDERING 〈tall *~* her age〉 **13** : through the period of 〈served *~* three years〉 **14** : in honor of 〈named *~* her grandmother〉

²**for** *conj* : BECAUSE

³for *abbr* **1** foreign **2** forestry

fora *pl of* FORUM

¹for·age \'fȯr-ij\ *n* [ME, fr. AF, fr. *fuerre, foer* fodder, straw, of Gmc origin] **1** : food for animals esp. when taken by browsing or grazing **2** : a search for food or supplies

²forage *vb* **for·aged; for·ag·ing 1** : to collect forage from **2** : to search for food or supplies **3** : to get by foraging **4** : to make a search : RUMMAGE

for·ay \'fȯr-ˌā, fȯ-'rā\ *vb* : to raid esp. in search of plunder : PILLAGE — **foray** *n*

¹for·bear \fȯr-'ber\ *vb* **-bore** \-'bȯr\; **-borne** \-'bȯrn\; **-bear·ing 1** : to refrain from : ABSTAIN **2** : to be patient — **for·bear·ance** \-'ber-əns\ *n*

²forbear *var of* FOREBEAR

for·bid \fər-'bid\ *vb* **-bade** \-'bad, -'bād\ *also* **-bad** \-'bad\; **-bid·den** \-'bi-d°n\; **-bid·ding 1** : to command against : PROHIBIT **2** : HINDER, PREVENT ♦ *Synonyms* ENJOIN, INTERDICT, INHIBIT, BAN

forbidding *adj* : DISAGREEABLE, REPELLENT ⟨a ~ task⟩

¹force \'fȯrs\ *n* **1** : strength or energy esp. of an exceptional degree : active power **2** : capacity to persuade or convince **3** : military strength; *also, pl* : the whole military strength (as of a nation) **4** : a body (as of persons or ships) available for a particular purpose **5** : VIOLENCE, COMPULSION **6** : an influence (as a push or pull) that causes motion or a change of motion — **force·ful** \-fəl\ *adj* — **force·ful·ly** *adv* — **in force 1** : in great numbers **2** : VALID, OPERATIVE ⟨the ban remains *in force*⟩

²force *vb* **forced; forc·ing 1** : COMPEL, COERCE **2** : to cause through necessity ⟨*forced* to admit defeat⟩ **3** : to press, attain to, or effect against resistance or inertia ⟨~ your way through⟩ **4** : to raise or accelerate to the utmost ⟨~ the pace⟩ **5** : to produce with unnatural or unwilling effort ⟨*forced* a smile⟩ **6** : to hasten (as in growth) by artificial means

for·ceps \'fȯr-səps\ *n, pl* **forceps** [L] : a handheld instrument for grasping, holding, or pulling objects esp. for delicate operations (as by a surgeon)

forc·ible \'fȯr-sə-bəl\ *adj* **1** : obtained or done by force **2** : showing force or energy : POWERFUL — **forc·i·bly** \-blē\ *adv*

¹ford \'fȯrd\ *n* : a place where a stream may be crossed by wading

²ford *vb* : to cross (a body of water) by wading

¹fore \'fȯr\ *adv* : in, toward, or adjacent to the front : FORWARD

²fore *adj* : being or coming before in time, order, or space

³fore *n* : something that occupies a front position

⁴fore *interj* — used by a golfer to warn anyone within range of the probable line of flight of the ball

fore–and–aft \ˌfȯr-ə-'naft\ *adj* : lying, running, or acting along the length of a structure (as a ship)

¹fore·arm \(ˌ)fȯr-'ärm\ *vb* : to arm in advance : PREPARE

²fore·arm \'fȯr-ˌärm\ *n* : the part of the arm between the elbow and the wrist

fore·bear \-ˌber\ *n* : ANCESTOR, FOREFATHER

fore·bode *also* **for·bode** \fȯr-'bōd\ *vb* **1** : to have a premonition esp. of misfortune **2** : FORETELL, PREDICT ♦ *Synonyms* AUGUR, BODE, FORESHADOW, PORTEND, PROMISE — **fore·bod·ing** *n or adj* — **fore·bod·ing·ly** *adv*

fore·cast \'fȯr-ˌkast\ *vb* **-cast** *also* **-cast·ed; -cast·ing 1** : PREDICT, CALCULATE ⟨~ weather conditions⟩ **2** : to indicate as likely to occur — **forecast** *n* — **fore·cast·er** *n*

fore·cas·tle *or* **fo'c's'le** \'fōk-səl\ *n* **1** : the forward part of the upper deck of a ship **2** : the crew's quarters usu. in a ship's bow

fore·close \fȯr-'klōz\ *vb* **1** : to shut out : PRECLUDE **2** : to take legal measures to terminate a mortgage and take possession of the mortgaged property

fore·clo·sure \-'klō-zhər\ *n* : the act of foreclosing; *esp* : the legal procedure of foreclosing a mortgage

fore·doom \fȯr-'düm\ *vb* : to doom beforehand

fore·fa·ther \'fȯr-ˌfä-thər\ *n* **1** : ANCESTOR **2** : a person of an earlier period and common heritage

forefend *var of* FORFEND

fore·fin·ger \-ˌfiŋ-gər\ *n* : INDEX FINGER

fore·foot \-ˌfu̇t\ *n* : either of the front feet of a quadruped; *also* : the front part of the human foot

fore·front \-ˌfrənt\ *n* : the foremost part or place

foregather *var of* FORGATHER

¹fore·go \fȯr-'gō\ *vb* **-went** \-'went\; **-gone** \-'gȯn\; **-go·ing** : PRECEDE

²forego *var of* FORGO

foregoing *adj* : PRECEDING ⟨the ~ statement can be proven⟩

fore·gone \'fȯr-ˌgȯn\ *adj* : determined in advance ⟨a ~ conclusion⟩

fore·ground \-ˌgrau̇nd\ *n* **1** : the part of a scene or representation that appears nearest to and in front of the spectator **2** : a position of prominence

fore·hand \-ˌhand\ *n* : a stroke (as in tennis) made with the palm of the hand turned in the direction in which the hand is moving; *also* : the side on which such a stroke is made — **forehand** *adj*

fore·hand·ed \(ˌ)fȯr-'han-dəd\ *adj* : mindful of the future : PRUDENT

fore·head \'fȯr-əd, 'fȯr-ˌhed\ *n* : the part of the face above the eyes

for·eign \'fȯr-ən\ *adj* [ME *forein*, fr. AF, fr. LL *foranus* on the outside, fr. L *foris* outside] **1** : situated outside a place or country and esp. one's own country **2** : born in, belonging to, or characteristic of some place or country other than the one under consideration ⟨~ language⟩ **3** : not connected, pertinent, or characteristically present **4** : related to or dealing with other nations ⟨~ affairs⟩ **5**

: occurring in an abnormal situation in the living body ⟨a ∼ body in the eye⟩

for·eign·er \ˈfȯr-ə-nər\ *n* : a person belonging to or owing allegiance to a foreign country

foreign minister *n* : a governmental minister for foreign affairs

fore·know \fȯr-ˈnō\ *vb* **-knew** \-ˈnü, -ˈnyü\; **-known** \-ˈnōn\; **-know·ing** : to have previous knowledge of — **fore·knowl·edge** \ˈfȯr-ˌnä-lij, fȯr-ˈnä-\ *n*

fore·la·dy \ˈfȯr-ˌlā-dē\ *n* : FOREWOMAN

fore·leg \-ˌleg\ *n* : a front leg

fore·limb \-ˌlim\ *n* : a front or upper limb (as a wing, arm, fin, or leg)

fore·lock \-ˌläk\ *n* : a lock of hair growing from the front part of the head

fore·man \-mən\ *n* **1** : a spokesperson of a jury **2** : a person in charge of a group of workers

fore·mast \-ˌmast\ *n* : the mast nearest the bow of a ship

fore·most \-ˌmōst\ *adj* : first in time, place, or order : most important : PREEMINENT — **foremost** *adv*

fore·name \-ˌnām\ *n* : a first name

fore·named \-ˌnāmd\ *adj* : previously named : AFORESAID

fore·noon \-ˌnün\ *n* : MORNING

¹fo·ren·sic \fə-ˈren-sik\ *adj* [L *forensis* public, forensic, fr. *forum* forum] **1** : belonging to, used in, or suitable to courts of law or to public speaking or debate **2** : relating to the application of scientific knowledge to legal problems ⟨∼ medicine⟩

²forensic *n* **1** : an argumentative exercise **2** *pl* : the art or study of argumentative discourse **3** *pl* : scientific analysis of physical evidence (as from a crime scene)

fore·or·dain \ˌfȯr-ȯr-ˈdān\ *vb* : to ordain or decree beforehand : PREDESTINE

fore·part \ˈfȯr-ˌpärt\ *n* **1** : the anterior part of something **2** : the earlier part of a period of time

fore·quar·ter \-ˌkwȯr-tər\ *n* : the front half of a lateral half of the body or carcass of a quadruped ⟨a ∼ of beef⟩

fore·run·ner \-ˌrə-nər\ *n* **1** : one that goes before to give notice of the approach of others : HARBINGER **2** : PREDECESSOR, ANCESTOR ♦ *Synonyms* PRECURSOR, HERALD

fore·sail \-ˌsāl, -səl\ *n* **1** : the lowest sail on the foremast of a square-rigged ship or schooner **2** : the principal sail forward of the foremast (as of a sloop)

fore·see \fȯr-ˈsē\ *vb* **-saw** \-ˈsȯ\; **-seen** \-ˈsēn\; **-see·ing** : to see or realize beforehand : EXPECT ♦ *Synonyms* FOREKNOW, DIVINE, APPREHEND, ANTICIPATE — **fore·see·able** *adj*

fore·shad·ow \-ˈsha-dō\ *vb* : to give a hint or suggestion of beforehand

fore·short·en \fȯr-ˈshȯr-t⁸n\ *vb* : to shorten (a detail) in a drawing or painting so that it appears to have depth

fore·sight \ˈfȯr-ˌsīt\ *n* **1** : the act or power of foreseeing **2** : care or provision for the future : PRUDENCE **3** : an act of looking forward; *also* : a view forward —

fore·sight·ed \-ˌsī-təd\ *adj* — **fore·sight·ed·ly** *adv* — **fore·sight·ed·ness** *n*

fore·skin \-ˌskin\ *n* : a fold of skin enclosing the end of the penis

for·est \ˈfȯr-əst\ *n* [ME, fr. AF, fr. LL *forestis (silva)* unenclosed (woodland), fr. L *foris* outside] : a large thick growth of trees and underbrush — **for·est·ed** \ˈfȯr-ə-stəd\ *adj* — **for·est·land** \ˈfȯr-əst-ˌland\ *n*

fore·stall \fȯr-ˈstȯl\ *vb* : to counter, hinder, or prevent by measures taken in advance ⟨his comments ∼ed the criticism⟩

forest ranger *n* : a person in charge of the management and protection of a portion of a forest

for·est·ry \ˈfȯr-ə-strē\ *n* : the science of growing and caring for forests — **for·est·er** \ˈfȯr-ə-stər\ *n*

foreswear *var of* FORSWEAR

¹fore·taste \ˈfȯr-ˌtāst\ *n* : an advance indication, warning, or notion ⟨a ∼ of winter⟩

²fore·taste \fȯr-ˈtāst\ *vb* : to taste beforehand : ANTICIPATE

fore·tell \fȯr-ˈtel\ *vb* **-told** \-ˈtōld\; **-tell·ing** : to tell of beforehand : PREDICT ♦ *Synonyms* FORECAST, PROPHESY, PROGNOSTICATE

fore·thought \ˈfȯr-ˌthȯt\ *n* **1** : PREMEDITATION **2** : consideration for the future

fore·to·ken \fȯr-ˈtō-kən\ *vb* : to indicate in advance

fore·top \ˈfȯr-ˌtäp\ *n* : a platform near the top of a ship's foremast

for·ev·er \fȯr-ˈe-vər\ *adv* **1** : for a limitless time **2** : at all times : ALWAYS

for·ev·er·more \-ˌe-vər-ˈmȯr\ *adv* : FOREVER

fore·warn \fȯr-ˈwȯrn\ *vb* : to warn beforehand — **fore·warn·ing** \-ˈwȯr-niŋ\ *n*

forewent *past of* FOREGO

fore·wing \ˈfȯr-ˌwiŋ\ *n* : either of the anterior wings of a 4-winged insect

fore·wom·an \-ˌwu̇-mən\ *n* : a woman having the responsibilities of a foreman

fore·word \-ˌwərd\ *n* : PREFACE

¹for·feit \ˈfȯr-fət\ *n* [ME *forfait*, fr. AF, fr. pp. of *forfaire, forsfaire* to commit a crime, forfeit, fr. *fors* outside + *faire* to do] **1** : something forfeited : PENALTY, FINE **2** : FORFEITURE **3** : something deposited and then redeemed on payment of a fine **4** *pl* : a game in which forfeits are exacted

²forfeit *vb* : to lose or lose the right to esp. by some error, offense, or crime

for·fei·ture \ˈfȯr-fə-ˌchu̇r\ *n* **1** : the act of forfeiting **2** : something forfeited : PENALTY

for·fend \fȯr-ˈfend\ *vb* **1** : PREVENT **2** : PROTECT, PRESERVE

for·gath·er *or* **fore·gath·er** \fȯr-ˈga-thər\ *vb* **1** : to come together : ASSEMBLE **2** : to meet someone usu. by chance

¹forge \ˈfȯrj\ *n* [ME, fr. AF, fr. L *fabrica*, fr. *faber* smith] : a furnace or shop with its furnace where metal is heated and worked

²forge *vb* **forged; forg·ing 1** : to form (metal) by heating and hammering **2**

: FASHION, SHAPE ⟨∼ an agreement⟩ 3
: to make or imitate falsely esp. with intent to defraud ⟨∼ a signature⟩ — **forg-
er** n — **forg-ery** \'fȯr-jə-rē\ n
³**forge** vb **forged; forg-ing** : to move
ahead steadily but gradually
for-get \fər-'get\ vb **-got** \-'gät\; **-got-ten**
\-'gät-³n\ or **-got; -get-ting** 1 : to be unable to think of or recall 2 : to fail to
become mindful of at the proper time 3
: NEGLECT, DISREGARD ⟨forgot their old
friends⟩ 4 : to give up hope for or expectation of — **for-get-ful** \-'get-fəl\ adj —
for-get-ful-ly adv — **for-get-ful-ness** n
for-get-me-not \fər-'get-mē-,nät\ n : any
of a genus of small herbs with bright blue
or white flowers
forg-ing n : a piece of forged work
for-give \fər-'giv\ vb **-gave** \-'gāv\; **-giv-
en** \-'gi-vən\; **-giv-ing** 1 : to give up resentment of 2 : PARDON, ABSOLVE 3 : to
grant relief from payment of ⟨∼ a debt⟩
— **for-giv-able** adj — **for-give-ness** n
— **for-giv-er** n
forgiving adj 1 : willing or able to forgive
2 : allowing room for error or weakness
⟨a ∼ recipe⟩
for-go \fȯr-'gō\ vb **-went** \-'went\; **-gone**
\-'gȯn\; **-go-ing** : to give up the enjoyment or advantage of : do without
fo-rint \'fȯr-int\ n, pl **forints** also **forint**
— see MONEY table
¹**fork** \'fȯrk\ n 1 : an implement with two
or more prongs for taking up (as in eating), pitching, or digging 2 : a forked
part, tool, or piece of equipment 3 : a
dividing into branches or a place where
something branches; also : a branch of
such a fork
²**fork** vb 1 : to divide into two or more
branches 2 : to give the form of a fork to
⟨∼ing her fingers⟩ 3 : to raise or pitch
with a fork ⟨∼ hay⟩ 4 : PAY, CONTRIB-
UTE — used with over, out, or up
forked \'fȯrkt, 'fȯr-kəd\ adj : having a
fork : shaped like a fork ⟨∼ lightning⟩
fork-lift \'fȯrk-,lift\ n : a machine for lifting heavy objects by means of steel fingers inserted under the load
for-lorn \fər-'lȯrn, fȯr-\ adj 1 : sad and
lonely because of isolation or desertion 2
: WRETCHED 3 : nearly hopeless — **for-
lorn-ly** adv — **for-lorn-ness** n
¹**form** \'fȯrm\ n 1 : SHAPE, STRUCTURE 2
: a body esp. of a person : FIGURE 3 : the
essential nature of a thing 4 : established
manner of doing or saying something 5
: FORMULA 6 : a document with blank
spaces for insertion of information ⟨tax
∼⟩ 7 : CEREMONY 8 : manner of performing according to recognized standards 9 : a long seat : BENCH 10 : a
model of the human figure used for displaying clothes 11 : MOLD ⟨a ∼ for con-
crete⟩ 12 : type or plates in a frame
ready for printing 13 : MODE, KIND, VA-
RIETY ⟨coal is a ∼ of carbon⟩ 14 : orderly method of arrangement; also : a
particular kind or instance of such arrangement ⟨the sonnet ∼ in poetry⟩ 15
: the structural element, plan, or design
of a work of art 16 : a bounded surface

or volume 17 : a grade in a British school
or in some American private schools 18
: RACING FORM 19 : known ability to
perform; also : condition (as of an athlete) suitable for performing 20 : one of
the ways in which a word is changed to
show difference in use ⟨the plural ∼ of a
noun⟩ — **form-less** adj
²**form** vb 1 : to give form or shape to
: FASHION, MAKE 2 : TRAIN, INSTRUCT 3
: CONSTITUTE, COMPOSE 4 : DEVELOP,
ACQUIRE ⟨∼ a habit⟩ 5 : to arrange in
order ⟨∼ a battle line⟩ 6 : to take form
: ARISE ⟨clouds are ∼ing⟩ 7 : to take a
definite form, shape, or arrangement
¹**for-mal** \'fȯr-məl\ adj 1 : according with
conventional forms and rules ⟨a ∼ dinner party⟩ 2 : done in due or lawful form
⟨a ∼ contract⟩ 3 : CEREMONIOUS, PRIM
⟨a ∼ manner⟩ 4 : NOMINAL — **for-mal-
ly** adv
²**formal** n : something (as a social event)
formal in character
form-al-de-hyde \fȯr-'mal-də-,hīd\ n : a
colorless pungent gas used in water solution as a preservative and disinfectant
for-mal-ise Brit var of FORMALIZE
for-mal-ism \'fȯr-mə-,li-zəm\ n : strict adherence to set forms
for-mal-i-ty \fȯr-'ma-lə-tē\ n, pl **-ties** 1
: compliance with formal or conventional
rules 2 : the quality or state of being formal 3 : an established form that is required or conventional
for-mal-ize \'fȯr-mə-,līz\ vb **-ized; -iz-ing**
1 : to give a certain or definite form to 2
: to make formal; also : to give formal
status or approval to
¹**for-mat** \'fȯr-,mat\ n 1 : the general composition or style of a publication 2 : the
general plan or arrangement of something 3 : a method of organizing data
⟨various file ∼s⟩
²**format** vb **for-mat-ted; for-mat-ting** : to
arrange (as material to be printed) in a
particular format — **for-mat-ter** n
for-ma-tion \fȯr-'mā-shən\ n 1 : an act of
giving form to something : DEVELOP-
MENT 2 : something that is formed 3
: STRUCTURE, SHAPE 4 : an arrangement
of persons or things in a prescribed manner or for a certain purpose
for-ma-tive \'fȯr-mə-tiv\ adj 1 : giving or
capable of giving form : CONSTRUCTIVE
2 : of, relating to, or characterized by
important growth or formation ⟨a child's ∼
years⟩
for-mer \'fȯr-mər\ adj 1 : PREVIOUS,
EARLIER 2 : FOREGOING ⟨the ∼ part of
the chapter⟩ 3 : being first mentioned or
in order of two or more things
for-mer-ly \-lē\ adv : in time past : PREVI-
OUSLY
form-fit-ting \'fȯrm-,fi-tiŋ\ adj : conforming to the outline of the body ⟨a ∼
sweater⟩
for-mi-da-ble \'fȯr-mə-də-bəl, fȯr-'mi-\
adj 1 : exciting fear, dread, or awe ⟨a ∼
foe⟩ 2 : imposing serious difficulties ⟨a
∼ barrier⟩ — **for-mi-da-bly** \-blē\ adv
form letter n 1 : a letter on a frequently
recurring topic that can be sent to differ-

ent people at different times **2** : a letter for mass circulation sent out in many printed copies

for·mu·la \ˈfȯr-myə-lə\ *n, pl* **-las** *or* **-lae** \-ˌlē, -ˌlī\ **1** : a set form of words for ceremonial use **2** : RECIPE, PRESCRIPTION **3** : a milk mixture or substitute for a baby **4** : a group of symbols or figures joined to express information concisely **5** : a customary or set form or method

for·mu·late \-ˌlāt\ *vb* **-lat·ed; -lat·ing 1** : to express in a formula **2** : DESIGN, DEVISE ⟨∼ a policy⟩ **3** : to prepare according to a formula — **for·mu·la·tion** \ˌfȯr-myə-ˈlā-shən\ *n*

for·ni·ca·tion \ˌfȯr-nə-ˈkā-shən\ *n* : consensual sexual intercourse between two persons not married to each other — **for·ni·cate** \ˈfȯr-nə-ˌkāt\ *vb* — **for·ni·ca·tor** \-ˌkā-tər\ *n*

for·sake \fər-ˈsāk, fȯr-\ *vb* **for·sook** \-ˈsu̇k\; **for·sak·en** \-ˈsā-kən\; **for·sak·ing** [ME, fr. OE *forsacan*, fr. *sacan* to dispute] : to renounce or turn away from entirely ⟨forsook teaching for a film career⟩

for·sooth \fər-ˈsüth\ *adv* : in truth : INDEED

for·swear \fȯr-ˈswer\ *vb* **-swore** \-ˈswȯr\; **-sworn** \-ˈswȯrn\; **-swear·ing 1** : to swear falsely : commit perjury **2** : to renounce earnestly or under oath **3** : to deny under oath

for·syth·ia \fər-ˈsi-thē-ə\ *n, pl* **-ias** *also* **-ia** : any of a genus of shrubs related to the olive and having yellow bell-shaped flowers appearing before the leaves in early spring

fort \ˈfȯrt\ *n* [ME *forte*, fr. AF *fort*, fr. *fort* strong, fr. L *fortis*] **1** : a fortified place **2** : a permanent army post

¹forte \ˈfȯrt, ˈfȯr-ˌtā\ *n* [F *fort*, fr. *fort*, adj., strong] : one's strong point

²for·te \ˈfȯr-ˌtā\ *adv or adj* [It, fr. *forte* strong] : LOUD — used as a direction in music

forth \ˈfȯrth\ *adv* **1** : FORWARD, ONWARD ⟨from that day ∼⟩ **2** : out into view ⟨plants putting ∼ leaves⟩

forth·com·ing \ˈfȯrth-ˈkə-miŋ\ *adj* **1** : coming or available soon ⟨the ∼ holidays⟩ **2** : marked by openness and candor : OUTGOING

forth·right \ˈfȯrth-ˌrīt\ *adj* : free from ambiguity or evasiveness : going straight to the point ⟨a ∼ answer⟩ — **forth·right·ly** *adv* — **forth·right·ness** *n*

forth·with \ˌfȯrth-ˈwith\ *adv* : IMMEDIATELY

for·ti·fy \ˈfȯr-tə-ˌfī\ *vb* **-fied; -fy·ing 1** : to strengthen by military defenses **2** : to give physical strength or endurance to **3** : ENCOURAGE **4** : to strengthen or enrich with a material ⟨∼ bread with vitamins⟩ — **for·ti·fi·ca·tion** \ˌfȯr-tə-fə-ˈkā-shən\ *n*

for·tis·si·mo \fȯr-ˈti-sə-ˌmō\ *adv or adj* : very loud — used as a direction in music

for·ti·tude \ˈfȯr-tə-ˌtüd, -ˌtyüd\ *n* : strength of mind that enables one to meet danger or bear pain or adversity

with courage ♦ *Synonyms* GRIT, BACKBONE, PLUCK, GUTS

fort·night \ˈfȯrt-ˌnīt\ *n* [ME *fourtenight*, alter. of *fourtene night* fourteen nights] : two weeks — **fort·night·ly** \-lē\ *adj or adv*

for·tress \ˈfȯr-trəs\ *n* : FORT 1

for·tu·itous \fȯr-ˈtü-ə-təs, -ˈtyü-\ *adj* **1** : happening by chance ⟨a ∼ discovery⟩ **2** : FORTUNATE — **for·tu·itous·ly** *adv*

for·tu·ity \-ə-tē\ *n, pl* **-ities 1** : the quality or state of being fortuitous **2** : a chance event or occurrence

for·tu·nate \ˈfȯr-chə-nət\ *adj* **1** : bringing some good thing not foreseen **2** : LUCKY

for·tu·nate·ly \-lē\ *adv* **1** : in a fortunate manner **2** : it is fortunate that

for·tune \ˈfȯr-chən\ *n* **1** : prosperity attained partly through luck; *also* : CHANCE, LUCK **2** : what happens to a person : good or bad luck **3** : FATE, DESTINY **4** : RICHES, WEALTH

fortune hunter *n* : a person who seeks wealth esp. by marriage

for·tune–tell·er \-ˌte-lər\ *n* : a person who professes to foretell future events — **for·tune–tell·ing** *n or adj*

for·ty \ˈfȯr-tē\ *n, pl* **forties** : four times 10 — **for·ti·eth** \ˈfȯr-tē-əth\ *adj or n* — **forty** *adj or pron*

for·ty–five \ˌfȯr-tē-ˈfīv\ *n* **1** : a .45 caliber handgun — usu. written .45 **2** : a phonograph record designed to be played at 45 revolutions per minute — usu. written 45

for·ty–nin·er \-ˈnī-nər\ *n* : a person in the rush to California for gold in 1849

forty winks *n sing or pl* : a short sleep

fo·rum \ˈfȯr-əm\ *n, pl* **forums** *also* **fo·ra** \-ə\ [L] **1** : the marketplace or central meeting place of an ancient Roman city **2** : a medium (as a publication or online service) of open discussion **3** : COURT **4** : a public assembly, lecture, or program involving audience or panel discussion

¹for·ward \ˈfȯr-wərd\ *adj* **1** : being near or at or belonging to the front **2** : EAGER, READY **3** : BRASH, BOLD **4** : notably advanced or developed : PRECOCIOUS **5** : moving, tending, or leading toward a position in front **6** : EXTREME, RADICAL **7** : of, relating to, or getting ready for the future — **for·ward·ness** *n*

²forward *adv* : to or toward what is ahead or in front

³forward *vb* **1** : to help onward : ADVANCE **2** : to send forward : TRANSMIT **3** : to send or ship onward

⁴forward *n* : a player who plays at the front of a team's offensive formation near the opponent's goal

for·ward·er \-wər-dər\ *n* : one that forwards; *esp* : an agent who forwards goods

for·wards \ˈfȯr-wərdz\ *adv* : FORWARD

forwent *past of* FORGO

¹fos·sil \ˈfä-səl\ *adj* [L *fossilis* obtained by digging, fr. *fodere* to dig] **1** : preserved from a past geologic age ⟨∼ plants⟩ **2** : of or relating to fossil fuels

²fossil *n* **1** : a trace or impression or the remains of a plant or animal of a past geologic age preserved in the earth's

fossil fuel • 4WD

286

crust **2** : a person whose ideas are out-of-date — **fos·sil·ize** \'fä-sə-ˌlīz\ vb

fossil fuel n : a fuel (as coal or oil) that is formed in the earth from plant or animal remains

¹fos·ter \'fȯs-tər\ adj [ME, fr. OE fōstor-, fr. fōstor food, feeding] : affording, receiving, or sharing nourishment or parental care though not related by blood or legal ties ⟨~ parent⟩ ⟨~ child⟩

²foster vb **1** : to give parental care to : NURTURE **2** : to promote the growth or development of : ENCOURAGE

foster home n : a household in which an orphaned, neglected, or delinquent child is placed for care

fos·ter·ling \-tər-liŋ\ n : a foster child

Fou·cault pendulum \ˌfü-ˈkō\ n : a device that consists of a heavy weight hung by a long wire and that swings in a constant direction which appears to change showing that the earth rotates

fought past and past part of FIGHT

¹foul \'fau̇(-ə)l\ adj **1** : offensive to the senses : LOATHSOME; also : clogged with dirt **2** : ODIOUS, DETESTABLE ⟨a ~ crime⟩ **3** : OBSCENE, ABUSIVE ⟨~ language⟩ **4** : DISAGREEABLE, STORMY ⟨~ weather⟩ **5** : TREACHEROUS, DISHONORABLE, UNFAIR ⟨by fair means or ~⟩ **6** : marking the bounds of a playing field ⟨~ lines⟩; also : being outside the foul line ⟨~ ball⟩ ⟨~ territory⟩ **7** : containing marked-up corrections **8** : ENTANGLED — **foul·ly** adv — **foul·ness** n

²foul n **1** : an entanglement or collision in fishing or sailing **2** : an infraction of the rules in a game or sport; also : a baseball hit outside the foul line

³foul vb **1** : to make or become foul or filthy **2** : to entangle or become entangled **3** : OBSTRUCT, BLOCK **4** : to collide with **5** : to make or hit a foul

⁴foul adv : in a foul manner

fou·lard \fu̇-ˈlärd\ n : a lightweight silk of plain or twill weave usu. decorated with a printed pattern

foul-mouthed \ˈfau̇(-ə)l-ˈmau̇thd, -ˈmau̇tht\ adj : given to the use of obscene, profane, or abusive language

foul of prep : AFOUL OF

foul play n : VIOLENCE; esp : MURDER

foul–up \ˈfau̇(-ə)l-ˌəp\ n **1** : a state of being fouled up **2** : a mechanical difficulty

foul up vb **1** : to spoil by mistakes or poor judgment **2** : to cause a foul-up : BUNGLE

¹found \'fau̇nd\ past and past part of FIND

²found vb [ME, fr. AF funder, fonder, fr. L fundare, fr. fundus bottom] **1** : to take the first steps in building **2** : to set or ground on something solid : BASE **3** : to establish (as an institution) often with provision for future maintenance — **found·er** n

foun·da·tion \fau̇n-ˈdā-shən\ n **1** : the act of founding **2** : a basis upon which something stands or is supported ⟨suspicions without ~⟩ **3** : funds given for the permanent support of an institution : ENDOWMENT; also : an institution so endowed **4** : supporting structure : BASE **5** : CORSET — **foun·da·tion·al** \-shə-nəl\ adj

foun·der \ˈfau̇n-dər\ vb **1** : to make or become lame ⟨the horse ~ed⟩ **2** : COLLAPSE **3** : SINK ⟨a ~ing ship⟩ **4** : FAIL

found·ling \ˈfau̇nd-liŋ\ n : an infant found after its unknown parents have abandoned it

found·ry \ˈfau̇n-drē\ n, pl **foundries** : a building or works where metal is cast

fount \'fau̇nt\ n : SOURCE, FOUNTAIN

foun·tain \ˈfau̇n-tᵊn\ n **1** : a spring of water **2** : SOURCE **3** : an artificial jet of water **4** : a container for liquid that can be drawn off as needed

foun·tain·head \-ˌhed\ n : SOURCE

fountain pen n : a pen with a reservoir that feeds the writing point with ink

four \'fȯr\ n **1** : one more than three **2** : the 4th in a set or series **3** : something having four units — **four** adj or pron

4x4 also **four–by–four** \ˈfȯr-bī-ˌfȯr\ n : a four-wheel automobile with four-wheel drive

four–flush \-ˌfləsh\ vb : to make a false claim : BLUFF — **four–flush·er** n

four·fold \-ˌfōld, -ˈfōld\ adj **1** : being four times as great or as many **2** : having four units or members — **four·fold** \-ˈfōld\ adv

4–H \ˈfȯr-ˈāch\ adj [fr. the fourfold aim of improving the head, heart, hands, and health] : of or relating to a program set up by the U.S. Department of Agriculture to help young people become productive citizens — **4–H'er** n

Four Hundred or **400** n : the exclusive social set of a community — used with the

four–in–hand \ˈfȯr-ən-ˌhand\ n **1** : a team of four horses driven by one person; also : a vehicle drawn by such a team **2** : a necktie tied in a slipknot with long ends overlapping vertically in front

four–o'clock \ˈfȯr-ə-ˌkläk\ n : a garden plant with fragrant yellow, red, or white flowers without petals that open late in the afternoon

four–post·er \ˌfȯr-ˈpō-stər\ n : a bed with tall corner posts orig. designed to support curtains or a canopy

four·score \ˈfȯr-ˈskȯr\ adj : being four times twenty : EIGHTY

four·some \ˈfȯr-səm\ n **1** : a group of four persons or things **2** : a golf match between two pairs of partners

four·square \-ˈskwer\ adj **1** : SQUARE **2** : marked by boldness and conviction : FORTHRIGHT — **foursquare** adv

four·teen \fȯr-ˈtēn\ n : one more than 13 — **fourteen** adj or pron — **four·teenth** \-ˈtēnth\ adj or n

fourth \'fȯrth\ n **1** : one that is number four in a countable series **2** : one of four equal parts of something — **fourth** adj or adv

fourth estate n, often cap F&E : the public press

fourth wall n : an imaginary wall that keeps performers from recognizing or directly addressing their audience

4WD abbr four-wheel drive

four–wheel \'fȯr-ˌhwēl\ *or* **four–wheeled** \-ˌhwēld\ *adj* : acting on or by means of four wheels of a motor vehicle ⟨∼ disc brakes⟩

four–wheel drive *n* : an automotive drive mechanism that acts on all four wheels of the vehicle; *also* : a vehicle with such a drive

¹**fowl** \'faů(-ə)l\ *n, pl* **fowl** *or* **fowls** 1 : BIRD 2 : a cock or hen of the domestic chicken; *also* : the flesh of these used as food

²**fowl** *vb* : to hunt wildfowl

¹**fox** \'fäks\ *n, pl* **fox·es** *also* **fox** 1 : any of various flesh-eating mammals related to the wolves but smaller and with shorter legs and a more pointed muzzle; *also* : the fur of a fox 2 : a clever crafty person 3 *cap* : a member of an American Indian people formerly living in what is now Wisconsin

²**fox** *vb* : TRICK, OUTWIT

fox·glove \'fäks-ˌgləv\ *n* : a common plant related to the snapdragons that is grown for its showy spikes of dotted white or purple tubular flowers and as a source of digitalis

fox·hole \-ˌhōl\ *n* : a pit dug for protection against enemy fire

fox·hound \-ˌhaůnd\ *n* : any of various large swift powerful hounds used in hunting foxes

fox·ing \'fäk-siŋ\ *n* : brownish spots on old paper

fox terrier *n* : a small lively terrier that occurs in varieties with smooth dense coats or with harsh wiry coats

fox–trot \'fäks-ˌträt\ *n* 1 : a short broken slow trotting gait 2 : a ballroom dance in duple time

foxy \'fäk-sē\ *adj* **fox·i·er; -est** 1 : resembling or suggestive of a fox 2 : WILY 3 : physically attractive

foy·er \'fȯi-(ə)r, 'fȯi-ˌyā\ *n* [F, lit., fireplace, fr. OF *foier*, fr. VL **focarium*, fr. L *focus* hearth] : LOBBY; *also* : an entrance hallway

fpm *abbr* feet per minute

FPO *abbr* fleet post office

fps *abbr* feet per second

fr *abbr* 1 father 2 franc 3 friar 4 from

¹**Fr** *abbr* 1 France; French 2 Friday

²**Fr** *symbol* francium

fra·cas \'frā-kəs, 'fra-\ *n, pl* **fra·cas·es** \-kə-səz\ [F, din, row, fr. It *fracasso*, fr. *fracassare* to shatter] : BRAWL

frack·ing \'fra-kiŋ\ *n* [by shortening & alter. fr. *hydraulic) fracturing*] : the injection of fluid into shale beds so as to free up petroleum — **frack** \'frak\ *vb*

frac·tal \'frak-t°l\ *n* : an irregular curve or shape that repeats itself at any scale on which it is examined — **fractal** *adj*

frac·tion \'frak-shən\ *n* 1 : a numerical representation (as ¹/₂, ³/₄, or 3.323) indicating the quotient of two numbers 2 : FRAGMENT 3 : PORTION ⟨a small ∼ of voters⟩ — **frac·tion·al** \-shə-nəl\ *adj* — **frac·tion·al·ly** *adv*

frac·tious \'frak-shəs\ *adj* 1 : tending to be troublesome : hard to handle or control 2 : QUARRELSOME, IRRITABLE

frac·ture \'frak-chər\ *n* 1 : a breaking of something and esp. a bone 2 : CRACK, CLEFT — **fracture** *vb*

frag·ile \'fra-jəl, -ˌjī(-ə)l\ *adj* : easily broken : DELICATE — **fra·gil·i·ty** \frə-'ji-lə-tē\ *n*

¹**frag·ment** \'frag-mənt\ *n* : a part broken off, detached, or incomplete

²**frag·ment** \-ˌment\ *vb* : to break into fragments — **frag·men·ta·tion** \ˌfrag-mən-'tā-shən, -ˌmən-\ *n*

frag·men·tary \'frag-mən-ˌter-ē\ *adj* : made up of fragments : INCOMPLETE ⟨a ∼ account⟩

fra·grant \'frā-grənt\ *adj* : sweet or agreeable in smell — **fra·grance** \-grəns\ *n* — **fra·grant·ly** *adv*

frail \'frāl\ *adj* [ME, fr. AF *fraile*, fr. L *fragilis* fragile, fr. *frangere* to break] 1 : morally or physically weak 2 : FRAGILE, DELICATE

frail·ty \'frāl-tē\ *n, pl* **frailties** 1 : the quality or state of being frail 2 : a fault due to weakness

¹**frame** \'frām\ *vb* **framed; fram·ing** 1 : PLAN, CONTRIVE 2 : SHAPE, CONSTRUCT 3 : FORMULATE 4 : DRAW UP ⟨∼ a constitution⟩ 5 : to make appear guilty 6 : to fit or adjust for a purpose : ARRANGE 7 : to provide with or enclose in a frame — **fram·er** *n*

²**frame** *n* 1 : something made of parts fitted and joined together 2 : the physical makeup of the body 3 : an arrangement of structural parts that gives form or support 4 : a supporting or enclosing border or open case (as for a window or picture) 5 : one picture of a series (as on a length of film) 6 : FRAME-UP

³**frame** *adj* : having a wood frame ⟨∼ houses⟩

frame of mind *n* : mental attitude or outlook : MOOD

frame–up \'frā-ˌməp\ *n* 1 : an act or series of actions in which someone is framed 2 : an action that is planned, contrived, or formulated

frame·work \'frām-ˌwərk\ *n* : a basic supporting part or structure

franc \'fraŋk\ *n* 1 : any of various former basic monetary units (as of Belgium, France, and Luxembourg) 2 — see MONEY table

fran·chise \'fran-ˌchīz\ *n* [ME, fr. AF, fr. *franchir* to free, fr. *franc* free] 1 : a right or license granted to an individual or group ⟨a ∼ to operate a ferry⟩ 2 : a constitutional or statutory right or privilege; *esp* : the right to vote 3 : the right of membership in a professional sports league; *also* : a team having such membership

fran·chi·see \ˌfran-ˌchī-'zē, -chə-\ *n* : one granted a franchise

fran·chis·er \'fran-ˌchī-zər\ *n* 1 : FRANCHISEE 2 : FRANCHISOR

fran·chi·sor \ˌfran-ˌchī-'zȯr, -chə-\ *n* : one that grants a franchise

fran·ci·um \'fran-sē-əm\ *n* : a radioactive metallic chemical element

Fran·co–Amer·i·can \ˌfraŋ-kō-ə-'mer-ə-kən\ *n* : an American of French or esp.

French-Canadian descent — **Franco-American** *adj*

fran·gi·ble \'fran-jə-bəl\ *adj* : BREAKABLE — **fran·gi·bil·i·ty** \,fran-jə-'bi-lə-tē\ *n*

¹frank \'fraŋk\ *adj* : marked by free, forthright, and sincere expression — **frank·ness** *n*

²frank *vb* : to mark (a piece of mail) with an official sign so that it can be mailed free; *also* : to mail free

³frank *n* **1** : the signature or mark on a piece of mail indicating free or paid postage **2** : the privilege of sending mail free

⁴frank *n* : FRANKFURTER

Fran·ken·stein \'fraŋ-kən-,stīn\ *n* **1** : a monstrous creation that usu. ruins its originator **2** : a monster in the shape of a man

frank·furt·er \'fraŋk-fər-tər, -,fər-\ or **frank·furt** \-fərt\ *n* : a seasoned sausage (as of beef or beef and pork)

frank·in·cense \'fraŋ-kən-,sens\ *n* : a fragrant resin burned as incense

frank·ly \'fraŋ-klē\ *adv* **1** : in a frank manner **2** : in truth : INDEED ⟨~, I don't know⟩

fran·tic \'fran-tik\ *adj* : marked by uncontrolled emotion or disordered anxious activity — **fran·ti·cal·ly** \-ti-k(ə-)lē\ *adv*

frap·pé \fra-'pā\ or **frappe** *same or* **¹frap**\ *n* [F *frappé*, fr. pp. of *frapper* to strike, chill] **1** : an iced or frozen drink **2** : a thick milk shake — **frap·pé** \fra-'pā\ *adj*

fra·ter·nal \frə-'tər-nᵊl\ *adj* **1** : of, relating to, or involving brothers **2** : of, relating to, or being a fraternity or society **3** : derived from two ova ⟨~ twins⟩ **4** : FRIENDLY, BROTHERLY — **fra·ter·nal·ly** *adv*

fra·ter·ni·ty \frə-'tər-nə-tē\ *n, pl* **-ties 1** : a social, honorary, or professional group; *esp* : a men's student organization **2** : BROTHERLINESS, BROTHERHOOD **3** : persons of the same class, profession, or tastes

frat·er·nize \'fra-tər-,nīz\ *vb* **-nized; -nizing 1** : to mingle as friends **2** : to associate on close terms with members of a hostile group — **frat·er·ni·za·tion** \,fratər-nə-'zā-shən\ *n*

frat·ri·cide \'fra-trə-,sīd\ *n* **1** : one that kills a sibling or countryman **2** : the act of a fratricide — **frat·ri·cid·al** \,fra-trə-'si-dᵊl\ *adj*

fraud \'frȯd\ *n* **1** : DECEIT, TRICKERY **2** : TRICK **3** : IMPOSTOR, CHEAT

fraud·ster \'frȯd-stər\ *n, chiefly Brit* : a person who engages in fraud

fraud·u·lent \'frȯ-jə-lənt\ *adj* : characterized by, based on, or done by fraud : DECEITFUL — **fraud·u·lence** \-ləns\ *n* — **fraud·u·lent·ly** *adv*

fraught \'frȯt\ *adj* : full of or accompanied by something specified ⟨~ with danger⟩

¹fray \'frā\ *n* : FIGHT, STRUGGLE; *also* : QUARREL, DISPUTE

²fray *vb* **1** : to wear (as an edge of cloth) by rubbing **2** : to separate the threads at the

edge of **3** : STRAIN, IRRITATE ⟨~ed nerves⟩

fraz·zle \'fra-zəl\ *vb* **fraz·zled; fraz·zling 1** : FRAY **2** : to put in a state of extreme physical or nervous fatigue — **frazzle** *n*

¹freak \'frēk\ *n* **1** : WHIM, CAPRICE **2** : a strange, abnormal, or unusual person or thing **3** *slang* : a person who uses an illicit drug **4** : an ardent enthusiast — **freak·ish** *adj* — **freaky** \'frē-kē\ *adj*

²freak *vb* **1** : to experience the effects (as hallucinations) of taking illicit drugs — often used with *out* **2** : to distress or become distressed — often used with *out* — **freak–out** \'frē-,kaut\ *n*

freck·le \'fre-kəl\ *n* : a small brownish spot on the skin — **freckle** *vb*

¹free \'frē\ *adj* **fre·er; fre·est 1** : having liberty **2** : enjoying political or personal independence; *also* : not subject to or allowing slavery **3** : made or done voluntarily : SPONTANEOUS **4** : relieved from or lacking something unpleasant **5** : not subject to a duty, tax, or charge **6** : not obstructed : CLEAR **7** : not being used or occupied ⟨waved with my ~ hand⟩ **8** : not fastened ⟨the ~ end of the rope⟩ **9** : LAVISH **10** : OPEN, FRANK ⟨a ~ exchange of ideas⟩ **11** : given without charge **12** : not literal or exact ⟨~ translation⟩ **13** : not restricted by conventional forms ⟨~ skating⟩ — **free·ly** *adv*

²free *vb* **freed; free·ing 1** : to set free **2** : RELIEVE, RID **3** : DISENTANGLE, CLEAR ♦ **Synonyms** RELEASE, LIBERATE, DISCHARGE, EMANCIPATE, LOOSE

³free *adv* **1** : FREELY **2** : without charge

free·base \'frē-,bās\ *n* : purified cocaine smoked as crack or heated to produce vapors for inhalation — **freebase** *vb*

free·bie or **free·bee** \'frē-bē\ *n* : something given without charge

free·board \'frē-,bȯrd\ *n* : the vertical distance between the waterline and the upper edge of the side of a boat

free·boo·ter \-,bü-tər\ *n* [D *vrijbuiter*, fr. *vrijbuit* plunder, fr. *vrij* free + *buit* booty] : PLUNDERER, PIRATE

free·born \-'bȯrn\ *adj* **1** : not born in vassalage or slavery **2** : of, relating to, or befitting one that is freeborn

freed·man \'frēd-mən, -,man\ *n* : a person freed from slavery

free·dom \'frē-dəm\ *n* **1** : the quality or state of being free : INDEPENDENCE **2** : EXEMPTION, RELEASE **3** : EASE, FACILITY ⟨spoke the language with ~⟩ **4** : FRANKNESS **5** : unrestricted use **6** : a political right; *also* : FRANCHISE, PRIVILEGE

freedom fighter *n* : a person who takes part in a resistance movement against an oppressive political or social establishment

free enterprise *n* : freedom of private business to operate with little regulation by the government

free–for–all \'frē-fə-,rȯl\ *n* : a competition or fight open to all comers and usu. with no rules : BRAWL — **free–for–all** *adj*

free·hand \-,hand\ *adj* : done without mechanical aids or devices ⟨∼ drawing⟩

free·hold \'frē-,hōld\ *n* : ownership of an estate for life usu. with the right to bequeath it to one's heirs; *also* : an estate thus owned — **free·hold·er** *n*

free·lance \-,lans\ *n* : one who pursues a profession (as writing) without a long-term commitment to any one employer — **free·lance** *adj or vb*

free-living \'frē-'li-viŋ\ *adj* 1 : unrestricted in pursuing personal pleasures 2 : being neither parasitic nor symbiotic ⟨∼ organisms⟩

free·load \'frē-,lōd\ *vb* : to impose upon another's hospitality — **free·load·er** *n*

free love *n* 1 : the practice of living openly with one of the opposite sex without marriage 2 : sexual relations without any commitments by either partner

free·man \'frē-mən, -,man\ *n* 1 : one who has civil or political liberty 2 : one having the full rights of a citizen

Free·ma·son \-,mā-sᵊn\ *n* : a member of a secret fraternal society called Free and Accepted Masons — **Free·ma·son·ry** \-rē\ *n*

free radical *n* : an esp. reactive atom or group of atoms with one or more unpaired electrons; *esp* : one that can cause bodily damage (as by altering the chemical structure of cells)

free–range \'frē-,rānj\ *adj* : allowed to range and forage with relative freedom ⟨∼ chickens⟩; *also* : produced by free-range animals ⟨∼ eggs⟩

free speech *n* : speech that is protected by the First Amendment to the U.S. Constitution

free spirit *n* : NONCONFORMIST

free·stand·ing \'frē-'stan-diŋ\ *adj* : standing alone or on its own foundation free of support

free·stone \'frē-,stōn\ *n* 1 : a stone that may be cut freely without splitting 2 : a fruit stone to which the flesh does not cling; *also* : a fruit (as a peach or cherry) having such a stone

free·think·er \-'thiŋ-kər\ *n* : one who forms opinions on the basis of reason independently of authority; *esp* : one who doubts or denies religious dogma — **free·think·ing** *n or adj*

free trade *n* : trade between nations without restrictions (as high taxes on imports)

free verse *n* : verse whose meter is irregular or whose rhythm is not metrical

free·ware \'frē-,wer\ *n* : software that is free or that has a small usu. optional cost

free·way \'frē-,wā\ *n* : an expressway without tolls

free·wheel \-'hwēl\ *vb* : to move, live, or play freely or irresponsibly

free·will \'frē-,wil\ *adj* : VOLUNTARY

free will *n* : voluntary choice or decision

¹**freeze** \'frēz\ *vb* **froze** \'frōz\; **fro·zen** \'frō-zᵊn\; **freez·ing** 1 : to harden or cause to harden into a solid (as ice) by loss of heat 2 : to withstand freezing 3 : to chill or become chilled with cold 4 : to damage by frost 5 : to adhere solidly by or as if by freezing 6 : to become

fixed, motionless, or incapable of speech 7 : to cause to grip tightly 8 : to become clogged with ice 9 : to fix at a certain stage or level ⟨∼ wages⟩

²**freeze** *n* 1 : an act or instance of freezing 2 : the state of being frozen 3 : a state of weather marked by low temperature

freeze–dry \'frēz-'drī\ *vb* : to dry in a frozen state under vacuum esp. for preservation — **freeze–dried** *adj*

freez·er \'frē-zər\ *n* : a compartment, device, or room for freezing food or keeping it frozen

¹**freight** \'frāt\ *n* 1 : payment for carrying goods 2 : CARGO 3 : BURDEN 4 : the carrying of goods by a common carrier 5 : a train that carries freight

²**freight** *vb* 1 : to load with goods for transportation 2 : BURDEN, CHARGE 3 : to ship or transport by freight

freight·er \'frā-tər\ *n* : a ship or airplane used chiefly to carry freight

French \'french\ *n* 1 : the language of France 2 **French** *pl* : the people of France 3 : strong language ⟨pardon my ∼⟩ — **French** *adj* — **French·man** \-mən\ *n* — **French·wom·an** \-,wu̇-mən\ *n*

French door *n* : a door with small panes of glass extending the full length

French dressing *n* 1 : a thin salad dressing usu. made of vinegar and oil with spices 2 : a creamy salad dressing flavored with tomatoes

french fry *n, often cap 1st F* : a strip of potato fried in deep fat until brown — **french fry** *vb, often cap 1st F*

French horn *n* : a curved brass instrument with a funnel-shaped mouthpiece and a flaring bell

French press *n* : a coffeepot in which ground beans are infused and then pressed by a plunger

French toast *n* : bread dipped in a mixture of eggs and milk and fried at a low heat

French twist *n* : a woman's hairstyle in which the hair is coiled at the rear and secured in place

fren·e·my \'fre-nə-mē\ *n, pl* **-mies** : one who pretends to be a friend but is actually an enemy

fre·net·ic \fri-'ne-tik\ *adj* : FRANTIC — **fre·net·i·cal·ly** \-ti-k(ə-)lē\ *adv*

fren·zy \'fren-zē\ *n, pl* **frenzies** 1 : temporary madness or a violently agitated state 2 : intense often disordered activity — **fren·zied** \-zēd\ *adj*

freq *abbr* frequency; frequent; frequently

fre·quen·cy \'frē-kwən-sē\ *n, pl* **-cies** 1 : the fact or condition of occurring frequently 2 : rate of occurrence 3 : the number of cycles per second of an alternating current 4 : the number of waves (as of sound or electromagnetic energy) that pass a fixed point each second

frequency modulation *n* : variation of the frequency of a carrier wave according to another signal; *also* : FM

¹**fre·quent** \frē-'kwent, 'frē-kwənt\ *vb* : to associate with, be in, or resort to habitually — **fre·quent·er** *n*

²**fre·quent** \'frē-kwənt\ adj 1 : happening often or at intervals ⟨making ~ stops⟩ 2 : HABITUAL ⟨a ~ visitor⟩ — **fre·quent·ly** adv

fre·quent–fli·er \'frē-kwənt-'flī-ər\ adj : of, relating to, or being an airline program offering awards for specified numbers of air miles traveled

fres·co \'fres-kō\ n, pl **frescoes** [It, fr. fresco fresh] : the art of painting on fresh plaster; also : a painting done by this method

fresh \'fresh\ adj 1 : VIGOROUS, REFRESHED 2 : not stale, sour, or decayed ⟨~ bread⟩ 3 : not faded 4 : not worn or rumpled 5 : not altered by processing (as freezing or canning) 6 : not containing salt 7 : free from taint : PURE ⟨~ air⟩ 8 : fairly strong : BRISK ⟨~ breeze⟩ 9 : experienced, made, or received newly or anew 10 : ADDITIONAL, ANOTHER ⟨made a ~ start⟩ 11 : ORIGINAL, VIVID ⟨a ~ portrayal⟩ 12 : INEXPERIENCED 13 : newly come or arrived ⟨~ from school⟩ 14 : IMPUDENT — **fresh·ly** adv — **fresh·ness** n

fresh·en \'fre-shən\ vb : to make, grow, or become fresh

fresh·et \'fre-shət\ n : an overflowing of a stream (as by heavy rains)

fresh·man \'fresh-mən\ n 1 : a 1st-year student 2 : BEGINNER, NEWCOMER

fresh·wa·ter \-, wȯ-tər, -, wä-\ n : water that is not salty — **freshwater** adj

¹**fret** \'fret\ vb **fret·ted; fret·ting** [ME, to devour, fret, fr. OE fretan to devour] 1 : WEAR, CORRODE; also : FRAY 2 : RUB, CHAFE 3 : to make by wearing away 4 : to become irritated : WORRY, VEX ⟨fretted over his taxes⟩ 5 : GRATE; also : AGITATE

²**fret** n : an irritated or worried state ⟨in a ~ about the interview⟩

³**fret** n : ornamental work esp. of straight lines in symmetrical patterns

⁴**fret** n : one of a series of ridges across the fingerboard of a stringed musical instrument — **fret·ted** adj

fret·ful \'fret-fəl\ adj : IRRITABLE — **fret·ful·ly** adv — **fret·ful·ness** n

fret·saw \-,sȯ\ n : a narrow-bladed handsaw used for cutting outlines

fret·work \-,wərk\ n 1 : decoration consisting of frets 2 : ornamental openwork or work in relief

Fri abbr Friday

fri·a·ble \'frī-ə-bəl\ adj : easily crumbled or pulverized ⟨~ soil⟩

fri·ar \'frī(-ə)r\ n [ME frere, fryer, fr. AF frere, friere, lit., brother, fr. L frater] : a member of a religious order that orig. lived by alms

fri·ary \'frī(-ə)r-ē\ n, pl **-ar·ies** : a monastery of friars

¹**fric·as·see** \'fri-kə-,sē, ,fri-kə-'sē\ n : a dish made of meat (as chicken) cut into pieces, stewed in stock, and served in sauce

²**fricassee** vb **-seed; -see·ing** : to cook as a fricassee

fric·tion \'frik-shən\ n 1 : the rubbing of one body against another 2 : the force

that resists motion between bodies in contact 3 : clash in opinions between persons or groups : DISAGREEMENT — **fric·tion·al** adj

friction tape n : a usu. cloth adhesive tape impregnated with insulating material and used esp. to protect and insulate electrical conductors

Fri·day \'frī-dē, -(,)dā\ n : the sixth day of the week

fridge \'frij\ n : REFRIGERATOR

fried·cake \'frīd-,kāk\ n : DOUGHNUT, CRULLER

fried rice n : a dish of boiled or steamed rice that is stir-fried with soy sauce and typically includes egg, meat, and vegetables

friend \'frend\ n 1 : one attached to another by respect or affection 2 : ACQUAINTANCE 3 : one who is not hostile 4 : one who supports or favors something ⟨a ~ of art⟩ 5 cap : a member of the Society of Friends : QUAKER — **friend·less** adj — **friend·li·ness** \-lē-nəs\ n — **friend·ly** adj — **friend·ship** \-,ship\ n

frieze \'frēz\ n : an ornamental often sculptured band extending around something (as a building or room)

frig·ate \'fri-gət\ n 1 : a square-rigged warship 2 : a warship smaller than a destroyer

fright \'frīt\ n 1 : sudden terror : ALARM 2 : something that is ugly or shocking

fright·en \'frī-t⁹n\ vb 1 : to make afraid 2 : to drive away or out by frightening 3 : to become frightened — **fright·en·ing·ly** adv

fright·ful \'frīt-fəl\ adj 1 : TERRIFYING 2 : STARTLING 3 : EXTREME ⟨~ thirst⟩ — **fright·ful·ly** adv — **fright·ful·ness** n

frig·id \'fri-jəd\ adj 1 : intensely cold 2 : lacking warmth or ardor : INDIFFERENT 3 : abnormally averse to or unable to achieve orgasm during sexual intercourse — used esp. of women — **fri·gid·i·ty** \fri-'ji-də-tē\ n

frigid zone n : the area or region between the arctic circle and the north pole or between the antarctic circle and the south pole

frill \'fril\ n 1 : a gathered, pleated, or ruffled edging 2 : something unessential — **frilly** adj

fringe \'frinj\ n [ME frenge, fr. AF, fr. VL *frimbia, alter. of L fimbriae (pl.)] 1 : an ornamental border consisting of short threads or strips hanging from an edge or band 2 : something that resembles a fringe : EDGE ⟨operated on the ~s of the law⟩ 3 : something that is additional or secondary to an activity, process, or subject — **fringe** vb

fringe benefit n 1 : an employment benefit paid for by an employer without affecting basic wage rates 2 : any additional benefit

frip·pery \'fri-pə-rē\ n, pl **-per·ies** [MF friperie] 1 : FINERY 2 : pretentious display

frisk \'frisk\ vb 1 : to leap, skip, or dance in a lively or playful way : GAMBOL 2 : to search (a person) esp. for concealed weapons by running the hand rapidly over the clothing

frisky \'fris-kē\ *adj* **frisk·i·er; -est** : PLAYFUL — **frisk·i·ly** \-kə-lē\ *adv* — **frisk·i·ness** \-kē-nəs\ *n*

¹**frit·ter** \'fri-tər\ *n* : a small lump of fried batter often containing fruit or meat

²**fritter** *vb* **1** : to reduce or waste piecemeal **2** : to break into small fragments

fritz \'frits\ *n* : a state of disorder or disrepair — used in the phrase *on the fritz*

friv·o·lous \'fri-və-ləs\ *adj* **1** : of little importance : TRIVIAL **2** : lacking in seriousness — **fri·vol·i·ty** \fri-'vä-lə-tē\ *n* — **friv·o·lous·ly** *adv*

frizz \'friz\ *vb* : to form into small tight curls — **frizz** *n* — **frizzy** *adj*

friz·zies \'fri-zēz\ *n pl* : hair which has become difficult to manage (as due to humidity)

¹**friz·zle** \'fri-zəl\ *vb* **friz·zled; friz·zling** : FRIZZ, CURL — **frizzle** *n*

²**frizzle** *vb* **friz·zled; friz·zling 1** : to fry until crisp and curled **2** : to cook with a sizzling noise

fro \'frō\ *adv* : BACK, AWAY — used in the phrase *to and fro*

frock \'fräk\ *n* **1** : an outer garment worn by monks and friars **2** : an outer garment worn esp. by men **3** : a woman's or girl's dress

frock coat *n* : a man's knee-length usu. double-breasted coat

frog \'frȯg, 'fräg\ *n* **1** : any of various largely aquatic smooth-skinned tailless leaping amphibians **2** : an ornamental braiding for fastening the front of a garment by a loop through which a button passes **3** : a condition in the throat causing hoarseness **4** : a small holder (as of metal, glass, or plastic) with perforations or spikes that is placed in a bowl or vase to keep cut flowers in position

frog·man \'frȯg-,man, 'fräg-, -mən\ *n* : a swimmer equipped to work underwater for long periods of time

¹**frol·ic** \'frä-lik\ *vb* **frol·icked; frol·ick·ing 1** : to make merry **2** : to play about happily : ROMP

²**frolic** *n* **1** : a playful or mischievous action **2** : FUN, MERRIMENT — **frol·ic·some** \-səm\ *adj*

from \'frəm, 'främ\ *prep* **1** — used to show a starting point ⟨a letter ~ home⟩ **2** — used to show removal or separation ⟨subtract 3 ~ 9⟩ **3** — used to show a material, source, or cause ⟨suffering ~ a cold⟩

frond \'fränd\ *n* : a usu. large divided leaf esp. of a fern or palm tree

¹**front** \'frənt\ *n* **1** : FOREHEAD; *also* : the whole face **2** : external and often feigned appearance **3** : a region of active fighting; *also* : a sphere of activity **4** : a political coalition **5** : the side of a building containing the main entrance **6** : the forward part or surface **7** : FRONTAGE **8** : a boundary between two dissimilar air masses **9** : a position directly before or ahead of something else **10** : a person, group, or thing used to mask the identity of the actual controlling agent

²**front** *vb* **1** : to have the principal side adjacent to something **2** : to serve as a front **3** : CONFRONT

front·age \'frən-tij\ *n* **1** : a piece of land lying adjacent (as to a street or the ocean) **2** : the length of a frontage **3** : the front side of a building

front·al \'frən-t³l\ *adj* **1** : of, relating to, or next to the forehead **2** : of, relating to, or directed at the front ⟨a ~ attack⟩ — **fron·tal·ly** *adv*

fron·tier \,frən-'tir\ *n* **1** : a border between two countries **2** : a region that forms the margin of settled territory **3** : the outer limits of knowledge or achievement ⟨the ~s of science⟩ — **fron·tiers·man** \-'tirz-mən\ *n*

fron·tis·piece \'frən-tə-,spēs\ *n* : an illustration preceding and usu. facing the title page of a book

front man *n* : a person serving as a front or figurehead

front·ward \'frənt-wərd\ *or* **front·wards** \-wərdz\ *adv or adj* : toward the front

¹**frost** \'frȯst\ *n* **1** : freezing temperature **2** : a covering of tiny ice crystals on a cold surface — **frosty** *adj*

²**frost** *vb* **1** : to cover with frost **2** : to put icing on (as a cake) **3** : to produce a slightly roughened surface on (as glass) **4** : to injure or kill by frost

¹**frost·bite** \'frȯst-,bīt\ *vb* **-bit** \-,bit\; **-bit·ten** \-,bi-t³n\; **-bit·ing** : to injure by frost or frostbite

²**frostbite** *n* : the freezing or the local effect of a partial freezing of some part of the body

frost heave *n* : an upthrust of pavement caused by freezing of moist soil

frost·ing \'frȯs-tiŋ\ *n* **1** : ICING **2** : a dull finish on metal or glass

froth \'frȯth\ *n, pl* **froths** \'frȯths, 'frȯthz\ [ME, fr. ON *frotha*] **1** : bubbles formed in or on a liquid **2** : something light or worthless — **frothy** *adj*

frou-frou \'frü-,frü\ *n* [F] **1** : a rustling esp. of a woman's skirts **2** : showy or frilly ornamentation

fro·ward \'frō-wərd\ *adj* : DISOBEDIENT, WILLFUL

frown \'fraun\ *vb* **1** : to wrinkle the forehead (as in displeasure or thought) **2** : to look with disapproval **3** : to express with a frown — **frown** *n*

frow·sy *or* **frow·zy** \'frau-zē\ *adj* **frow·si·er** *or* **frow·zi·er; -est** : having a slovenly or uncared-for appearance

froze *past of* FREEZE

fro·zen \'frō-z³n\ *adj* **1** : treated, affected, or crusted over by freezing **2** : subject to long and severe cold **3** : incapable of being changed, moved, or undone : FIXED ⟨~ wages⟩ **4** : not available for present use ⟨~ capital⟩ **5** : expressing or characterized by cold unfriendliness

FRS *abbr* Federal Reserve System

frt *abbr* freight

fruc·ti·fy \'frək-tə-,fī, 'frùk-\ *vb* **-fied; -fy·ing 1** : to bear fruit **2** : to make fruitful or productive

fruc·tose \'frək-,tōs, 'frùk-\ *n* : a very

sweet soluble sugar that occurs esp. in fruit juices and honey

fru·gal \'frü-gəl\ adj : ECONOMICAL, THRIFTY — **fru·gal·i·ty** \frü-'ga-lə-tē\ n — **fru·gal·ly** adv

¹**fruit** \'früt\ n [ME, fr. AF frut, fruit, fr. L fructus fruit, use, fr. frui to enjoy, have the use of] 1 : a product of plant growth; esp : a usu. edible and sweet reproductive body (as a strawberry or apple) of a seed plant 2 : a product of fertilization in a plant; esp : the ripe ovary of a seed plant with its contents and appendages 3 : CONSEQUENCE, RESULT — **fruit·ed** \'frü-təd\ adj

²**fruit** vb : to bear or cause to bear fruit

fruit·cake \'früt-ˌkāk\ n : a rich cake containing nuts, dried or candied fruits, and spices

fruit fly n : any of various small dipteran flies whose larvae feed on fruit or decaying vegetable matter

fruit·ful \'früt-fəl\ adj 1 : yielding or producing fruit 2 : very productive; also : bringing results ⟨a ~ idea⟩ — **fruit·ful·ly** adv — **fruit·ful·ness** n

fru·ition \frü-'i-shən\ n 1 : ENJOYMENT 2 : the state of bearing fruit 3 : REALIZATION, ACCOMPLISHMENT ⟨guided the project to ~⟩

fruit·less \'früt-ləs\ adj 1 : not bearing fruit 2 : UNSUCCESSFUL ⟨a ~ attempt⟩ — **fruit·less·ly** adv

fruity \'frü-tē\ adj **fruit·i·er; -est** : resembling a fruit esp. in flavor

frumpy \'frəm-pē\ adj **frump·i·er; -est** : DOWDY, DRAB ⟨a ~ dress⟩

frus·trate \'frəs-ˌtrāt\ vb **frus·trat·ed; frus·trat·ing** 1 : to balk or defeat in an endeavor 2 : to induce feelings of insecurity, discouragement, or dissatisfaction in 3 : to bring to nothing — **frus·trat·ing·ly** adv — **frus·tra·tion** \ˌfrəs-'trā-shən\ n

frus·tum \'frəs-təm\ n, pl **frustums** or **frus·ta** \-tə\ : the part of a cone or pyramid formed by cutting off the top by a plane parallel to the base

frwy abbr freeway

¹**fry** \'frī\ vb **fried; fry·ing** [ME frien, fr. AF frire, fr. L frigere to roast] 1 : to cook in a pan or on a griddle over heat esp. with the use of fat 2 : to undergo frying 3 : to damage or destroy by overheating esp. by high voltage

²**fry** n, pl **fries** 1 : a social gathering where fried food is eaten 2 : a dish of something fried; esp, pl : FRENCH FRIES

³**fry** n, pl **fry** [ME, fr. AF frie, fr. freier, frier to rub, spawn, fr. L fricare to rub] 1 : recently hatched fishes; also : very small adult fishes 2 : members of a group or class ⟨small ~⟩

fry·er \'frī(-ə)r\ n 1 : something (as a young chicken) suitable for frying 2 : a deep utensil for frying foods

FSLIC abbr Federal Savings and Loan Insurance Corporation

ft abbr 1 feet; foot 2 fort

FTC abbr Federal Trade Commission

FTP \ˌef-ˌtē-'pē\ n [file transfer protocol] : a system for transferring computer files esp. via the Internet — **FTP** vb

fuch·sia \'fyü-shə\ n 1 : any of a genus of shrubs related to the evening primrose and grown for their showy nodding often red or purple flowers 2 : a vivid reddish purple color

fud·dle \'fə-dᵊl\ vb **fud·dled; fud·dling** : MUDDLE, CONFUSE

fud·dy–dud·dy \'fə-dē-ˌdə-dē\ n, pl **-dies** : one that is old-fashioned, unimaginative, or conservative

¹**fudge** \'fəj\ vb **fudged; fudg·ing** 1 : to exceed the proper bounds of something 2 : CHEAT; also : FALSIFY ⟨fudged their data⟩ 3 : to fail to come to grips with

²**fudge** n 1 : NONSENSE 2 : a soft candy of milk, sugar, butter, and flavoring

¹**fu·el** \'fyü-əl, 'fyül\ n : a material used to produce heat or power by burning; also : a material from which nuclear energy can be liberated

²**fuel** vb **-eled** or **-elled; -el·ing** or **-el·ling** : to provide with or take in fuel

fuel cell n : a device that continuously changes the chemical energy of a fuel directly into electrical energy

fuel injection n : a system for injecting a precise amount of atomized fuel into an internal combustion engine — **fuel–in·ject·ed** \'fyül-in-ˌjek-təd\ adj

¹**fu·gi·tive** \'fyü-jə-tiv\ adj 1 : running away or trying to escape 2 : likely to vanish suddenly : not fixed or lasting

²**fugitive** n 1 : one who flees or tries to escape 2 : something elusive or hard to find

fugue \'fyüg\ n 1 : a musical composition in which different parts successively repeat the theme 2 : a disturbed state of consciousness characterized by acts that are not recalled upon recovery

füh·rer or **fueh·rer** \'fyür-ər, 'fir-\ n [G] : LEADER; esp : TYRANT

¹**-ful** \fəl\ adj suffix, sometimes **-ful·ler**; sometimes **-ful·lest** 1 : full of ⟨prideful⟩ 2 : characterized by ⟨peaceful⟩ 3 : having the qualities of ⟨masterful⟩ 4 : tending, given, or liable to ⟨helpful⟩

²**-ful** \ˌfül\ n suffix : number or quantity that fills or would fill ⟨roomful⟩

ful·crum \'fül-krəm, 'fəl-\ n, pl **ful·crums** or **ful·cra** \-krə\ [LL, fr. L, bedpost] : the support on which a lever turns

ful·fill or **ful·fil** \fül-'fil\ vb **ful·filled; ful·fill·ing** 1 : to put into effect 2 : to bring to an end 3 : SATISFY ⟨~ed expectations⟩ — **ful·fill·ment** or **ful·fil·ment** n

¹**full** \'fül\ adj 1 : FILLED 2 : complete esp. in detail, number, or duration 3 : having all the distinguishing characteristics ⟨a ~ member⟩ 4 : MAXIMUM ⟨~ strength⟩ 5 : rounded in outline ⟨a ~ figure⟩ 6 : possessing an abundance ⟨~ of wrinkles⟩ 7 : having an abundance of material ⟨a ~ skirt⟩ 8 : satisfied esp. with food or drink 9 : having volume or depth of sound 10 : completely occupied with a thought or plan — **full·ness** also **ful·ness** n

²**full** adv 1 : VERY, EXTREMELY 2 : ENTIRELY ⟨fill a glass ~⟩ 3 : STRAIGHT, SQUARELY ⟨hit him ~ in the face⟩

³**full** n 1 : the highest or fullest state or

degree **2** : the utmost extent — **in full** : to the requisite or complete amount

⁴**full** vb : to shrink and thicken (woolen cloth) by moistening, heating, and pressing — **full·er** n

full·back \'fùl-ˌbak\ n : a football back stationed behind the halfbacks

full–blood·ed \'fùl-'blə-dəd\ adj : of unmixed ancestry : PUREBRED

full–blown \-'blōn\ adj **1** : being at the height of bloom **2** : fully mature or developed

full–bod·ied \-'bä-dēd\ adj : marked by richness and fullness

full dress n : the style of dress worn for ceremonial or formal occasions

full–fledged \'fùl-'flejd\ adj **1** : fully developed **2** : having attained complete status ⟨a ~ lawyer⟩

full house n : a poker hand containing three of a kind and a pair

full moon n : the moon with its whole disk illuminated

full–on \-ˌón, -ˌän\ adj : COMPLETE, FULL-FLEDGED

full–scale \'fùl-'skāl\ adj **1** : identical to an original in proportion and size ⟨~ drawing⟩ **2** : involving full use of available resources ⟨a ~ revolt⟩

full–term \-ˌtərm\ adj : retained in the uterus for the normal period of gestation before birth ⟨a ~ baby⟩

full tilt adv : at high speed

full–time \'fùl-'tīm\ adj or adv : involving or working a normal or standard schedule

ful·ly \'fù-lē\ adv **1** : in a full manner or degree : COMPLETELY **2** : at least ⟨~ nine tenths of us⟩

ful·mi·nate \'fùl-mə-ˌnāt, 'fəl-\ vb **-nat·ed; -nat·ing** [ME, fr. ML fulminatus, pp. of fulminare, fr. L, to strike (of lightning), fr. fulmen lightning] : to utter or send out censure or invective : condemn severely ⟨fulminated against the tax increase⟩ — **ful·mi·na·tion** \ˌfùl-mə-'nā-shən, ˌfəl-\ n

ful·some \'fùl-səm\ adj **1** : COPIOUS, ABUNDANT ⟨~ detail⟩ **2** : generous in amount or extent ⟨a ~ victory⟩ **3** : excessively flattering ⟨~ praise⟩

fu·ma·role \'fyü-mə-ˌrōl\ n : a hole in a volcanic region from which hot gases issue

fum·ble \'fəm-bəl\ vb **fum·bled; fum·bling 1** : to grope about clumsily **2** : to fail to hold, catch, or handle properly — **fumble** n

¹**fume** \'fyüm\ n : a usu. irritating smoke, vapor, or gas

²**fume** vb **fumed; fum·ing 1** : to treat with fumes **2** : to give off fumes **3** : to express anger or annoyance

fu·mi·gant \'fyü-mi-gənt\ n : a substance used for fumigation

fu·mi·gate \'fyü-mə-ˌgāt\ vb **-gat·ed; -gat·ing** : to treat with fumes to disinfect or destroy pests — **fu·mi·ga·tion** \ˌfyü-mə-'gā-shən\ n — **fu·mi·ga·tor** \'fyü-mə-ˌgā-tər\ n

¹**fun** \'fən\ n [E dial. fun to hoax] **1** : something that provides amusement or enjoyment **2** : ENJOYMENT

²**fun** adj : full of fun ⟨a ~ person⟩ ⟨had a ~ time⟩

¹**func·tion** \'fəŋk-shən\ n **1** : OCCUPATION **2** : special purpose **3** : the particular purpose for which a person or thing is specially fitted or used or for which a thing exists ⟨the ~ of a hammer⟩; also : the natural or proper action of a bodily part in a living thing ⟨the ~ of the heart⟩ **4** : a formal ceremony or social affair **5** : a mathematical relationship that assigns to each element of a set one and only one element of the same or another set **6** : a variable (as a quality, trait, or measurement) that depends on and varies with another ⟨height is a ~ of age in children⟩ **7** : a computer subroutine that performs a calculation with variables provided by a program — **func·tion·al** \-shə-nəl\ adj — **func·tion·al·ly** adv

²**function** vb : to have or carry on a function ⟨the computer ~s well⟩

func·tion·ary \'fəŋk-shə-ˌner-ē\ n, pl **-ar·ies** : one who performs a certain function; esp : OFFICIAL

function word n : a word (as a preposition, auxiliary verb, or conjunction) expressing the grammatical relationship between other words

¹**fund** \'fənd\ n [L fundus bottom, country estate] **1** : a sum of money or resources intended for a special purpose **2** : STORE, SUPPLY **3** pl : available money **4** : an organization administering a special fund

²**fund** vb **1** : to provide funds for ⟨~ed cancer research⟩ **2** : to convert (a short-term obligation) into a long-term interest-bearing debt — **fund·er** n

fun·da·men·tal \ˌfən-də-'men-tᵊl\ adj **1** : serving as an origin : PRIMARY **2** : BASIC, ESSENTIAL **3** : RADICAL ⟨~ change⟩ **4** : of central importance : PRINCIPAL ⟨~ purpose⟩ — **fundamental** n — **fun·da·men·tal·ly** adv

fun·da·men·tal·ism \-tə-ˌli-zəm\ n **1** often cap : a Protestant religious movement emphasizing the literal infallibility of the Bible **2** : a movement or attitude stressing strict adherence to a set of basic principles — **fun·da·men·tal·ist** \-list\ adj or n

¹**fu·ner·al** \'fyü-nə-rəl\ adj **1** : of, relating to, or constituting a funeral **2** : FUNEREAL **2**

²**funeral** n : the ceremonies held for a dead person usu. before burial

fu·ner·ary \'fyü-nə-ˌrer-ē\ adj : of, used for, or associated with burial ⟨~ rites⟩

fu·ne·re·al \fyü-'nir-ē-əl\ adj **1** : of or relating to a funeral **2** : suggesting a funeral ⟨a ~ mood⟩

fun·gi·cide \'fən-jə-ˌsīd, 'fəŋ-gə-\ n : an agent that kills or checks the growth of fungi — **fun·gi·cid·al** \ˌfən-jə-'sī-dᵊl, ˌfəŋ-gə-\ adj

fun·gus \'fəŋ-gəs\ n, pl **fun·gi** \'fən-ˌjī, 'fəŋ-ˌgī\ also **fun·gus·es** \'fəŋ-gə-səz\ : any of a kingdom of parasitic spore-producing organisms (as molds, mildews, and mushrooms) formerly classified as plants — **fun·gal** \-gəl\ adj — **fun·gous** \-gəs\ adj

fu·nic·u·lar \fyu̇-'ni-kyə-lər, fə-\ n : a cable railway ascending a mountain

¹funk \'fəŋk\ n : a strong offensive smell

²funk n : a depressed state of mind

funky \'fəŋ-kē\ adj **funk·i·er; -est 1** : having an earthy unsophisticated style and feeling; *esp* : having the style and feeling of older black American music **2** : odd or quaint in appearance or style ⟨a ~ little restaurant⟩ — **funk·i·ness** n

¹fun·nel \'fə-nᵊl\ n **1** : a cone-shaped utensil with a tube used for catching and directing a downward flow (as of liquid) **2** : FLUE, SMOKESTACK

²funnel vb **-neled** also **-nelled; -nel·ing** also **-nel·ling 1** : to pass through or as if through a funnel **2** : to move to a central point or into a central channel

fun·nies \'fə-nēz\ n pl : a comic strip or a comic section (as of a newspaper) — used with *the*

fun·ny \'fə-nē\ adj **fun·ni·er; -est 1** : AMUSING **2** : FACETIOUS **3** : PECULIAR **3 4** : UNDERHANDED — **funny** adv

funny bone n : a place at the back of the elbow where a blow easily compresses a nerve and causes a painful tingling sensation

fun·plex \'fən-ˌpleks\ n : a center containing various entertainment facilities

¹fur \'fər\ n **1** : an article of clothing made of or with fur **2** : the hairy coat of a mammal esp. when fine, soft, and thick; *also* : this coat dressed for use — **fur** adj — **furred** \'fərd\ adj

²fur abbr furlong

fur·be·low \'fər-bə-ˌlō\ n **1** : FLOUNCE, RUFFLE **2** : showy trimming

fur·bish \'fər-bish\ vb **1** : to make lustrous : POLISH **2** : to give a new look to : RENOVATE

fu·ri·ous \'fyu̇r-ē-əs\ adj **1** : FIERCE, ANGRY, VIOLENT **2** : BOISTEROUS **3** : INTENSE ⟨~ growth⟩ — **fu·ri·ous·ly** adv

furl \'fərl\ vb **1** : to wrap or roll (as a sail or a flag) close to or around something **2** : to curl in furls — **furl** n

fur·long \'fər-ˌlȯŋ\ n [ME, fr. OE *furlang*, fr. *furh* furrow + *lang* long] : a unit of distance equal to 220 yards (about 201 meters)

fur·lough \'fər-lō\ n [D *verlof*, lit., permission] : a leave of absence from duty granted esp. to a soldier — **furlough** vb

fur·nace \'fər-nəs\ n : an enclosed structure in which heat is produced

fur·nish \'fər-nish\ vb **1** : to provide with what is needed : EQUIP **2** : SUPPLY, GIVE ⟨~ed them with food⟩

fur·nish·ings \-ni-shiŋz\ n pl **1** : articles or accessories of dress **2** : FURNITURE

fur·ni·ture \'fər-ni-chər\ n : equipment that is necessary or desirable; *esp* : movable articles (as chairs or beds) for a room

fu·ror \'fyu̇r-ˌȯr\ n **1** : ANGER, RAGE **2** : a contagious excitement; *esp* : a fashionable craze **3** : UPROAR

fu·rore \-ˌȯr\ n [It] : FUROR 2, 3

fur·ri·er \'fər-ē-ər\ n : one who prepares or deals in furs

fur·ring \'fər-iŋ\ n : wood or metal strips applied to a wall or ceiling to form a level surface or an air space

fur·row \'fər-ō\ n **1** : a trench in the earth made by a plow **2** : a narrow groove or wrinkle — **furrow** vb

fur·ry \'fər-ē\ adj **fur·ri·er; -est 1** : resembling or consisting of fur **2** : covered with fur

¹fur·ther \'fər-thər\ adv **1** : FARTHER 1 **2** : in addition : MOREOVER **3** : to a greater extent or degree

²further vb : to help forward — **fur·ther·ance** \'fər-thə-rəns\ n

³further adj **1** : FARTHER 1 **2** : ADDITIONAL ⟨~ education⟩

fur·ther·more \'fər-thər-ˌmȯr\ adv : in addition to what precedes : BESIDES

fur·ther·most \-ˌmōst\ adj : most distant : FARTHEST

fur·thest \'fər-thəst\ adv or adj : FARTHEST

fur·tive \'fər-tiv\ adj [F or L; F *furtif*, fr. L *furtivus*, fr. *furtum* theft, fr. *fur* thief] : done by stealth : SLY ⟨a ~ glance⟩ — **fur·tive·ly** adv — **fur·tive·ness** n

fu·ry \'fyu̇r-ē\ n, pl **furies 1** : intense and often destructive rage **2** : extreme fierceness or violence **3** : FRENZY

furze \'fərz\ n : GORSE

¹fuse \'fyüz\ vb **fused; fus·ing 1** : MELT **2** : to unite by or as if by melting together — **fus·ible** adj

²fuse n : an electrical safety device having a metal wire or strip that melts and interrupts the circuit when the current becomes too strong

³fuse n : a cord or cable that is set afire to ignite an explosive charge **2** usu **fuze** : a mechanical or electrical device for setting off the explosive charge of a projectile, bomb, or torpedo

⁴fuse also **fuze** \'fyüz\ vb **fused** also **fuzed; fus·ing** also **fuz·ing 1** : to equip with a fuse

fu·se·lage \'fyü-sə-ˌläzh, -zə-\ n : the central body portion of an aircraft

fu·sil·lade \'fyü-sə-ˌläd, -ˌläd\ n : a number of shots fired simultaneously or in rapid succession

fu·sion \'fyü-zhən\ n **1** : the act or process of melting or making plastic by heat **2** : union by or as if by melting **3** : the union of light atomic nuclei to form heavier nuclei with the release of huge quantities of energy

¹fuss \'fəs\ n **1** : needless bustle or excitement : COMMOTION **2** : effusive praise **3** : a state of agitation **4** : OBJECTION, PROTEST **5** : DISPUTE

²fuss vb : to make a fuss ⟨~ed over the baby⟩

fuss·bud·get \'fəs-ˌbə-jət\ n : one who fusses or is fussy about trifles

fussy \'fə-sē\ adj **fuss·i·er; -est 1** : IRRITABLE **2** : overly decorative ⟨a ~ wallpaper pattern⟩ **3** : requiring or giving close attention or concern to details or niceties — **fuss·i·ly** \-sə-lē\ adv — **fuss·i·ness** \-sē-nəs\ n

fus·tian \'fəs-chən\ n **1** : a strong usu. cotton fabric **2** : pretentious writing or speech — **fustian** adj

fus·ty \'fəs-tē\ *adj* **fus·ti·er; -est** [prob. alter. of ME *foisted, foist* musty, fr. *foist* wine cask, fr. AF *fust, fuist* wood, tree trunk, cask] 1 : MUSTY 2 : OLD-FASH-IONED ⟨~ notions⟩

fut *abbr* future

fu·tile \'fyü-t³l, 'fyü-¸tī(-ə)l\ *adj* 1 : USE-LESS, VAIN 2 : FRIVOLOUS, TRIVIAL — **fu·tile·ly** *adv* — **fu·til·i·ty** \fyü-'til-ə-tē\ *n*

fu·ton \'fü-¸tän\ *n* [Jp] : a usu. cotton-filled mattress used on the floor or in a frame as a bed, couch, or chair

¹fu·ture \'fyü-chər\ *adj* 1 : of, relating to, or constituting a verb tense that express-es time yet to come 2 : coming after the present

²future *n* 1 : time that is to come 2 : what is going to happen 3 : an expectation of advancement or progressive develop-ment 4 : the future tense; *also* : a verb form in it

fu·tur·ism \'fyü-chə-¸ri-zəm\ *n* : a modern movement in art, music, and literature that tries esp. to express the energy and activity of mechanical processes — **fu·tur·ist** \'fyü-chə-rist\ *n*

fu·tur·is·tic \¸fyü-chə-'ris-tik\ *adj* : of or relating to the future or to futurism; *also* : very modern

fu·tu·ri·ty \fyü-'túr-ə-tē, -'tyúr-\ *n, pl* **-ties** 1 : FUTURE 2 : the quality or state of be-ing future 3 *pl* : future events or prospects

fuze *var of* FUSE

fuzz \'fəz\ *n* : fine light particles or fibers (as of down or fluff)

fuzzy \'fə-zē\ *adj* **fuzz·i·er; -est** 1 : hav-ing or resembling fuzz 2 : INDISTINCT ⟨~ photos⟩ 3 : being or relating to pleasant usu. sentimental emotions ⟨~ feelings⟩ — **fuzz·i·ness** \-zē-nəs\ *n*

fuzzy logic *n* : a system of logic in which a statement can be true, false, or any of a continuum of values in between

fwd *abbr* forward

FWD *abbr* front-wheel drive

FY *abbr* fiscal year

-fy *vb suffix* : make : form into ⟨dandi*fy*⟩

FYI *abbr* for your information

¹g \'jē\ *n, pl* **g's** *or* **gs** \'jēz\ *often cap* 1 : the 7th letter of the English alphabet 2 : a unit of force equal to the force exerted by gravity on a body at rest and used to indicate the force to which a body is sub-jected when accelerated 3 *slang* : a sum of $1000

²g *abbr, often cap* 1 game 2 gauge 3 good 4 gram 5 gravity

ga *abbr* gauge

¹Ga *abbr* Georgia

²Ga *symbol* gallium

GA *abbr* 1 general assembly 2 general average 3 general of the army 4 Georgia

gab \'gab\ *vb* **gabbed; gab·bing** : to talk in a rapid or thoughtless manner : CHAT-TER — **gab** *n*

gab·ar·dine \'ga-bər-¸dēn\ *n* 1 : GABER-DINE 1 2 : a firm durable twilled fabric having diagonal ribs and made of various fibers; *also* : a garment of gabardine

gab·ble \'ga-bəl\ *vb* **gab·bled; gab·bling** : JABBER, BABBLE

gab·by \'ga-bē\ *adj* **gab·bi·er; -est** : TALKATIVE, GARRULOUS

gab·er·dine \'ga-bər-¸dēn\ *n* 1 : a long loose outer garment worn in medieval times and associated esp. with Jews 2 : GABARDINE 2

gab·fest \'gab-¸fest\ *n* 1 : an informal gathering for general talk 2 : an extend-ed conversation

ga·ble \'gā-bəl\ *n* : the vertical triangular end of a building formed by the sides of the roof sloping from the ridge down to the eaves — **ga·bled** \-bəld\ *adj*

gad \'gad\ *vb* **gad·ded; gad·ding** : to be constantly active without specific pur-pose — usu. used with *about* ⟨*gadded* about Europe for a year⟩ — **gad·der** *n*

gad·about \'ga-də-¸baút\ *n* : a person who flits about in social activity

gad·fly \'gad-¸flī\ *n* 1 : a fly that bites or harasses livestock 2 : a person who an-noys esp. by persistent criticism

gad·get \'ga-jət\ *n* : DEVICE, CONTRIV-ANCE — **gad·get·ry** \'ga-jə-trē\ *n*

gad·o·lin·i·um \¸ga-də-'li-nē-əm\ *n* : a magnetic metallic chemical element

¹Gael \'gāl\ *n* : a Celtic inhabitant of Ire-land or Scotland

²Gael *abbr* Gaelic

Gael·ic \'gā-lik\ *adj* : of or relating to the Gaels or their languages — **Gaelic** *n*

gaff \'gaf\ *n* 1 : a spear used in taking fish or turtles; *also* : a metal hook for holding or lifting heavy fish 2 : the spar support-ing the top of a fore-and-aft sail 3 : rough treatment : ABUSE — **gaff** *vb*

gaffe \'gaf\ *n* 1 : a social blunder

gaf·fer \'ga-fər\ *n* 1 : an old man 2 : a lighting electrician on a motion-picture or television set

¹gag \'gag\ *vb* **gagged; gag·ging** 1 : to re-strict use of the mouth of with a gag 2 : to prevent from speaking freely 3 : to retch or cause to retch 4 : OBSTRUCT, CHOKE 5 : BALK 6 : to make quips — **gag·ger** *n*

²gag *n* 1 : something thrust into the mouth esp. to prevent speech or outcry 2 : an official check or restraint on free speech 3 : a laugh-provoking remark or act 4 : PRANK, TRICK

¹gage \'gāj\ *n* 1 : a token of defiance; *esp* : a glove or cap cast on the ground as a pledge of combat 2 : SECURITY

²**gage** *var of* GAUGE

gag·gle \'ga-gəl\ *n* [ME *gagyll,* fr. *gagelen* to cackle] **1** : a flock of geese **2** : an unorganized group

gai·ety *also* **gay·ety** \'gā-ə-tē\ *n, pl* **-eties 1** : festive activity : MERRYMAKING **2** : MERRIMENT **3** : FINERY ♦ *Synonyms* MIRTH, FESTIVITY, GLEE, HILARITY, JOLLITY

gai·ly *also* **gay·ly** \'gā-lē\ *adv* : in a gay manner ⟨chatting ~⟩

¹**gain** \'gān\ *n* **1** : PROFIT **2** : ACQUISITION, ACCUMULATION **3** : INCREASE

²**gain** *vb* **1** : to get possession of : EARN **2** : WIN ⟨~ a victory⟩ **3** : to increase in ⟨~ momentum⟩ **4** : PERSUADE **5** : to arrive at **6** : ACHIEVE ⟨~ strength⟩ **7** : to run fast ⟨the watch ~s a minute a day⟩ **8** : PROFIT **9** : INCREASE **10** : to improve in health ♦ *Synonyms* ACCOMPLISH, ATTAIN, REALIZE — **gain·er** *n*

gain·ful \'gān-fəl\ *adj* : PROFITABLE ⟨~ employment⟩ — **gain·ful·ly** *adv*

gain·say \ˌgān-'sā\ *vb* **-said** \-'sād, -'sed\; **-say·ing; -says** \-'sāz, -'sez\ [ME *gainsayen,* fr. *gain-* against + *sayen* to say] **1** : DENY, DISPUTE **2** : to speak against ♦ *Synonyms* CONTRADICT, CONTRAVENE, IMPUGN, NEGATE — **gain·say·er** *n*

gait \'gāt\ *n* : manner of moving on foot; *also* : a particular pattern or style of such moving — **gait·ed** *adj*

gai·ter \'gā-tər\ *n* **1** : a leg covering reaching from the instep to ankle, midcalf, or knee **2** : an overshoe with a fabric upper **3** : an ankle-high shoe with elastic gores in the sides

¹**gal** \'gal\ *n* : GIRL

²**gal** *abbr* gallon

Gal *abbr* Galatians

ga·la \'gā-lə, 'ga-, 'gä-\ *n* : a festive celebration : FESTIVITY — **gala** *adj*

ga·lac·tic \gə-'lak-tik\ *adj* : of or relating to a galaxy

Ga·la·tians \gə-'lā-shənz\ *n* — see BIBLE table

gal·axy \'ga-lək-sē\ *n, pl* **-ax·ies** [ME *galaxie, galaxias,* fr. LL *galaxias,* fr. Gk, fr. *galakt-, gala* milk] **1** : MILKY WAY GALAXY — used with *the* **2** : a very large group of stars **3** : an assemblage of brilliant or famous persons or things

gale \'gāl\ *n* **1** : a strong wind **2** : an emotional outburst ⟨~s of laughter⟩

ga·le·na \gə-'lē-nə\ *n* : a lustrous bluish gray mineral that consists of the sulfide of lead and is the chief ore of lead

¹**gall** \'gȯl\ *n* **1** : BILE **2** : something bitter to endure **3** : RANCOR **4** : IMPUDENCE ♦ *Synonyms* EFFRONTERY, BRASS, CHEEK, CHUTZPAH, AUDACITY, PRESUMPTION

²**gall** *n* : a skin sore caused by chafing

³**gall** *vb* **1** : CHAFE; *esp* : to become sore or worn by rubbing **2** : VEX, HARASS

⁴**gall** *n* : an abnormal outgrowth of plant tissue usu. due to parasites

¹**gal·lant** \gə-'lant, -'länt; 'ga-lənt\ *n* **1** : a young man of fashion **2** : a man who

shows a marked fondness for the company of women and who is esp. attentive to them **3** : SUITOR

²**gal·lant** \'ga-lənt *(usual for 2, 3, 4);* gə-'lant, -'länt *(usual for 5)*\ *adj* **1** : showy in dress or bearing : SMART **2** : SPLENDID, STATELY **3** : SPIRITED, BRAVE **4** : CHIVALROUS, NOBLE **5** : polite and attentive to women — **gal·lant·ly** *adv*

gal·lant·ry \'ga-lən-trē\ *n, pl* **-ries 1** *archaic* : gallant appearance **2** : an act of marked courtesy **3** : courteous attention to a woman **4** : conspicuous bravery ♦ *Synonyms* HEROISM, VALOR, PROWESS

gall·blad·der \'gȯl-ˌbla-dər\ *n* : a membranous muscular sac attached to the liver and serving to store bile

gal·le·on \'ga-lē-ən\ *n* : a large square-rigged sailing ship formerly used esp. by the Spanish

gal·le·ria \ˌga-lə-'rē-ə\ *n* [It] : a roofed and usu. glass-enclosed promenade or court

gal·lery \'ga-lə-rē\ *n, pl* **-ler·ies 1** : an outdoor balcony; *also* : PORCH, VERANDA **2** : a long narrow passage, apartment, or hall **3** : a narrow passage (as one made underground by a miner or through wood by an insect) **4** : a room where works of art are exhibited; *also* : an organization dealing in works of art **5** : a balcony in a theater, auditorium, or church; *esp* : the highest one in a theater **6** : the spectators at a sporting event (as a tennis or golf match) **7** : a photographer's studio — **gal·ler·ied** \-rēd\ *adj*

gal·ley \'ga-lē\ *n, pl* **galleys 1** : a long low ship propelled esp. by oars and formerly used esp. in the Mediterranean Sea **2** : the kitchen esp. of a ship or airplane **3** : a proof of typeset matter esp. in a single column

Gal·lic \'ga-lik\ *adj* : of or relating to Gaul or France

gal·li·mau·fry \ˌga-lə-'mȯ-frē\ *n, pl* **-fries** [MF *galimafree* stew] : HODGEPODGE

gal·li·nule \'ga-lə-ˌnül, -ˌnyül\ *n* : any of several aquatic birds related to the rails

gal·li·um \'ga-lē-əm\ *n* : a bluish-white metallic chemical element used esp. in semiconductors

gal·li·vant \'ga-lə-ˌvant\ *vb* : to travel, roam, or move about for pleasure

gal·lon \'ga-lən\ *n* — see WEIGHT table

¹**gal·lop** \'ga-ləp\ *vb* **1** : to go or cause to go at a gallop **2** : to run fast — **gal·lop·er** *n*

²**gallop** *n* **1** : a bounding gait of a quadruped; *esp* : a fast 3-beat gait of a horse **2** : a ride or run at a gallop

gal·lows \'ga-lōz\ *n, pl* **gallows** *or* **gallows·es** : a frame usu. of two upright posts and a crosspiece from which criminals are hanged; *also* : the punishment of hanging

gall·stone \'gȯl-ˌstōn\ *n* : an abnormal concretion occurring in the gallbladder or bile passages

gal·lus·es \'ga-lə-səz\ *n pl* : SUSPENDERS

ga·lore \gə-'lȯr\ adj [Ir go leor enough] : ABUNDANT, PLENTIFUL

ga·losh \gə-'läsh\ n : a high overshoe

galv abbr galvanized

gal·va·nise Brit var of GALVANIZE

gal·va·nize \'gal-və-ˌnīz\ vb **-nized; -niz·ing** 1 : to stimulate as if by an electric shock ⟨~ public opinion⟩ 2 : to coat (iron or steel) with zinc — **gal·va·ni·za·tion** \ˌgal-və-nə-'zā-shən\ n — **gal·va·niz·er** n

gal·va·nom·e·ter \ˌgal-və-'nä-mə-tər\ n : an instrument for detecting or measuring a small electric current

gam·bit \'gam-bət\ n [It gambetto, lit., act of tripping someone, fr. gamba leg] 1 : a chess opening in which a player risks one or more minor pieces to gain an advantage in position 2 : a calculated move : STRATAGEM ♦ **Synonyms** TRICK, ARTIFICE, GIMMICK, MANEUVER, PLAY, RUSE

¹gam·ble \'gam-bəl\ vb **gam·bled; gam·bling** 1 : to play a game for money or property 2 : BET, WAGER 3 : VENTURE, HAZARD — **gam·bler** n

²gamble n : a risky undertaking

gam·bol \'gam-bəl\ vb **-boled** or **-bolled; -bol·ing** or **-bol·ling** : to skip about in play : FRISK — **gambol** n

gam·brel roof \'gam-brəl-\ n : a roof with a lower steeper slope and an upper flatter one on each side

¹game \'gām\ n 1 : AMUSEMENT, DIVERSION 2 : SPORT, FUN ⟨made ~ of the strange boy⟩ 3 : SCHEME, PROJECT 4 : a line of work : PROFESSION 5 : CONTEST 6 : animals hunted for sport or food; also : the flesh of a game animal

²game vb **gamed; gam·ing** 1 : to play for a stake 2 : to take dishonest advantage of ⟨~ the tax system⟩

³game adj : PLUCKY, RESOLUTE — **game·ly** adv — **game·ness** n

⁴game adj : LAME ⟨a ~ leg⟩

game·cock \'gām-ˌkäk\ n : a rooster trained for fighting

game fish n : SPORT FISH

game·keep·er \'gām-ˌkē-pər\ n : a person in charge of the breeding and protection of game animals or birds on a private preserve

game show n : a television program on which contestants compete usu. for prizes in a game

game·some \'gām-səm\ adj : MERRY ♦ **Synonyms** PLAYFUL, FROLICSOME, SPORTIVE, ANTIC

game·ster \'gām-stər\ n : GAMBLER

gam·ete \'ga-ˌmēt\ n : a mature germ cell — **ga·met·ic** \gə-'me-tik\ adj

game theory n : the analysis of a situation involving conflicting interests (as in business) in terms of gains and losses among opposing players

gam·in \'ga-mən\ n [F] 1 : a boy who hangs around on the streets 2 : GAMINE 2

ga·mine \ga-'mēn\ n 1 : a girl who hangs around on the streets 2 : a small playfully mischievous girl

gam·ma \'ga-mə\ n : the 3d letter of the Greek alphabet — Γ or γ

gamma globulin n : a blood protein fraction rich in antibodies; also : a solution of this from human blood donors that is given to provide immunity against some infectious diseases (as measles)

gamma ray n : a photon emitted by a radioactive substance; also : a photon of higher energy than that of an X-ray — usu. used in pl.

gam·mon \'ga-mən\ n, chiefly Brit : a cured ham or side of bacon

gam·ut \'ga-mət\ n : an entire range or series ♦ **Synonyms** SCALE, SPECTRUM

gamy or **gam·ey** \'gā-mē\ adj **gam·i·er; -est** 1 : GAME, PLUCKY 2 : having the flavor of game esp. when near tainting ⟨~ meat⟩ 3 : SCANDALOUS; also : DISREPUTABLE — **gam·i·ness** \-mē-nəs\ n

¹gan·der \'gan-dər\ n : a male goose

²gander n : LOOK, GLANCE

¹gang \'gaŋ\ n 1 : a set of implements or devices arranged to operate together 2 : a group of persons working or associated together; esp : a group of criminals or young delinquents

²gang vb 1 : to attack in a gang — usu. used with up 2 : to form into or move or act as a gang

gang·land \'gaŋ-ˌland\ n : the world of organized crime

gan·gling \'gaŋ-gliŋ\ adj : loosely and awkwardly built : LANKY

gan·gli·on \'gaŋ-glē-ən\ n, pl **-glia** \-ə\ also **-gli·ons** : a mass of nerve tissue containing cell bodies of neurons outside the central nervous system; also : NUCLEUS 3 — **gan·gli·on·ic** \ˌgaŋ-glē-'ä-nik\ adj

gan·gly \'gaŋ-glē\ adj : GANGLING

gang·plank \'gaŋ-ˌplaŋk\ n : a movable bridge from a ship to the shore

gang·plow \-ˌplau̇\ n : a plow that turns two or more furrows at one time

gan·grene \'gaŋ-ˌgrēn, gaŋ-'grēn\ n : the death of soft tissues in a local area of the body due to loss of the blood supply — **gangrene** vb — **gan·gre·nous** \'gaŋ-grə-nəs\ adj

gang·sta \'gaŋ-stə\ n : a member of an urban street gang

gangsta rap n : rap music with usu. hostile lyrics portraying urban gang life

gang·ster \'gaŋ-stər\ n : a member of a gang of criminals : RACKETEER

gang·way \'gaŋ-ˌwā\ n 1 : PASSAGEWAY; also : GANGPLANK 2 : clear passage through a crowd

gan·net \'ga-nət\ n, pl **gannets** also **gannet** : any of several large fish-eating usu. white and black seabirds that breed chiefly on offshore islands

gant·let var of GAUNTLET

gan·try \'gan-trē\ n, pl **gantries** : a frame structure on side supports over or around something

GAO abbr General Accounting Office

gaol \'jāl\, **gaol·er** \'jā-lər\ chiefly Brit var of JAIL, JAILER

gap \'gap\ n 1 : BREACH, CLEFT 2 : a

mountain pass 3 : a blank space; *also* : an incomplete or deficient area 4 : a wide difference in character or attitude 5 : a problem caused by a disparity ⟨credibility ∼⟩

gape \'gāp\ *vb* gaped; gap·ing 1 : to open the mouth wide 2 : to open or part widely 3 : to stare with mouth open 4 : YAWN — gape *n*

¹gar \'gär\ *n* : any of several fishes that have a long body resembling that of a pike and long narrow jaws

²gar *abbr* garage

GAR *abbr* Grand Army of the Republic

¹ga·rage \gə-'räzh, -'räj\ *n* [F, act of docking, garage, fr. *garer* to dock, fr. MF *garrer*, prob. ultim. fr. ON *vara* to beware, take care] : a shelter or repair shop for automobiles

²garage *vb* ga·raged; ga·rag·ing : to keep or put in a garage

garage sale *n* : a sale of used household or personal articles held on the seller's own premises

garb \'gärb\ *n* 1 : style of dress 2 : outward form : APPEARANCE — garb *vb*

gar·bage \'gär-bij\ *n* 1 : food waste 2 : unwanted or useless material

gar·bage·man \-,man\ *n* : a person who collects and removes garbage

gar·ble \'gär-bəl\ *vb* gar·bled; gar·bling : to distort the meaning of ⟨∼ a story⟩

gar·çon \gär-'sōⁿ\ *n, pl* garçons *same or* gär-'sōⁿz\ [F, boy, servant] : WAITER

¹gar·den \'gär-dᵊn\ *n* 1 : a plot for growing fruits, flowers, or vegetables 2 : a public recreation area; *esp* : one for displaying plants or animals

²garden *vb* : to lay out or work in a garden — gar·den·er *n*

gar·de·nia \gär-'dē-nyə\ *n* [NL, genus name, fr. Alexander *Garden* †1791 Scot. naturalist] : any of a genus of tropical trees or shrubs that are related to the madder and have fragrant white or yellow flowers

garden–variety *adj* : COMMONPLACE, ORDINARY ⟨∼ police dramas⟩

gar·fish \'gär-,fish\ *n* : GAR

gar·gan·tuan \gär-'gan-chə-wən\ *adj, often cap* : tremendous in size, volume, or degree ⟨∼ waterfalls⟩ ♦ *Synonyms* HUGE, COLOSSAL, GIGANTIC, MAMMOTH, MONSTROUS, TITANIC

gar·gle \'gär-gəl\ *vb* gar·gled; gar·gling : to rinse the throat with liquid agitated by air forced through it from the lungs — gargle *n*

gar·goyle \'gär-,goi(-ə)l\ *n* 1 : a waterspout in the form of a grotesque human or animal figure projecting from the roof or eaves of a building 2 : a grotesquely carved figure

gar·ish \'ger-ish\ *adj* : FLASHY, GLARING, SHOWY, GAUDY ⟨a ∼ wardrobe⟩

¹gar·land \'gär-lənd\ *n* : WREATH, CHAPLET

²garland *vb* : to form into or deck with a garland

gar·lic \'gär-lik\ *n* [ME *garlek*, fr. OE *gārlēac*, fr. *gār* spear + *lēac* leek] : an herb related to the lilies and grown for its pun-

gent bulbs used in cooking; *also* : its bulb — gar·licky \-li-kē\ *adj*

gar·ment \'gär-mənt\ *n* : an article of clothing

gar·ner \'gär-nər\ *vb* 1 : to gather into storage 2 : to acquire by effort ⟨∼ evidence⟩ 3 : ACCUMULATE, COLLECT

gar·net \'gär-nət\ *n* [ME *gernet*, fr. AF *gernete*, fr. *gernet* dark red, fr. *pume gernete* pomegranate] : a transparent deep red mineral sometimes used as a gem

gar·nish \'gär-nish\ *vb* 1 : DECORATE, EMBELLISH 2 : to add decorative or savory touches to (food) 3 : GARNISHEE — garnish *n*

gar·nish·ee \,gär-nə-'shē\ *vb* -eed; -ee·ing 1 : to serve with a garnishment 2 : to take (as a debtor's wages) by legal authority

gar·nish·ment \'gär-nish-mənt\ *n* 1 : GARNISH 2 : a legal warning concerning the attachment of property to satisfy a debt; *also* : the attachment of such property

gar·ni·ture \-ni-chər, -,chùr\ *n* : EMBELLISHMENT, TRIMMING

gar·ret \'ger-ət\ *n* : the part of a house just under the roof : ATTIC

gar·ri·son \'ger-ə-sən\ *n* [ME *garisoun* protection, fr. AF *garisun* healing, protection, fr. *garir* to heal, protect, of Gmc origin] 1 : a military post; *esp* : a permanent military installation 2 : the troops stationed at a garrison — garrison *vb*

garrison state *n* : a state organized on a primarily military basis

gar·rote *or* ga·rotte \gə-'rät, -'rōt\ *n* [Sp *garrote*] 1 : a method of execution by strangulation; *also* : the apparatus used 2 : an implement (as a wire with handles) for strangulation — garrote *or* garotte *vb*

gar·ru·lous \'ger-ə-ləs\ *adj* : TALKATIVE, WORDY — gar·ru·li·ty \gə-'rü-lə-tē\ *n* — gar·ru·lous·ly *adv* — gar·ru·lous·ness *n*

gar·ter \'gär-tər\ *n* : a band or strap worn to hold up a stocking or sock

garter snake *n* : any of a genus of harmless American snakes with longitudinal stripes on the back

¹gas \'gas\ *n, pl* gas·es *also* gas·ses [NL, alter. of L *chaos* space, chaos] 1 : a fluid (as hydrogen or air) that tends to expand indefinitely 2 : a gas or mixture of gases used as a fuel or anesthetic 3 : a substance that can be used to produce a poisonous, asphyxiating, or irritant atmosphere 4 : GASOLINE — gas·eous \'ga-sē-əs, -shəs\ *adj*

²gas *vb* gassed; gas·sing 1 : to treat with gas; *also* : to poison with gas 2 : to fill with gasoline ⟨∼ up the car⟩

gash \'gash\ *n* : a deep long cut — gash *vb*

gas·ket \'gas-kət\ *n* : material (as rubber) or a part used to seal a joint

gas·light \'gas-,līt\ *n* 1 : light made by burning illuminating gas 2 : a gas flame; *also* : a gas lighting fixture

gas mask *n* : a mask with a chemical air

filter used to protect the face and lungs against poison gas

gas·o·line \'ga-sə-,lēn, ,ga-sə-'lēn\ n : a flammable liquid mixture made from petroleum and used esp. as a motor fuel

gasp \'gasp\ vb 1 : to catch the breath audibly (as with shock) 2 : to breathe laboriously : PANT 3 : to utter in a gasping manner — **gasp** n

gas station n : a retail station for servicing and fueling motor vehicles

gas·tric \'gas-trik\ adj : of or relating to the stomach

gastric juice n : the acid digestive secretion of the stomach

gas·tri·tis \gas-'trī-təs\ n : inflammation of the lining of the stomach

gas·tro·en·ter·i·tis \,gas-trō-,en-tə-'rī-təs\ n : inflammation of the lining membrane of the stomach and intestine

gas·tro·en·ter·ol·o·gy \,gas-trō-,en-tə-'rä-lə-jē\ n : a branch of medicine concerned with the structure, functions, and diseases of the stomach and intestines — **gas·tro·en·ter·ol·o·gist** \-jist\ n

gas·tro·in·tes·ti·nal \,gas-trō-in-'tes-tə-nᵊl\ adj : of, relating to, affecting, or including both the stomach and intestine ⟨∼ tract⟩ ⟨∼ distress⟩

gas·tron·o·my \gas-'trä-nə-mē\ n [F gastronomie, fr. Gk Gastronomia, title of a 4th cent. B.C. poem, fr. gastēr belly + -nomia system of laws] : the art of good eating — **gas·tro·nom·ic** \,gas-trə-'nä-mik\ also **gas·tro·nom·i·cal** \-mi-kəl\ adj — **gas·tro·nom·i·cal·ly** \-k(ə-)lē\ adv

gas·tro·pod \'gas-trə-,päd\ n : any of a large class of mollusks (as snails and slugs) with a muscular foot and a spiral shell or none — **gastropod** adj

gas·works \'gas-,wərks\ n sing or pl : a plant for manufacturing gas

gate \'gāt\ n 1 : an opening for passage in a wall or fence 2 : a city or castle entrance often with defensive structures 3 : the frame or door that closes a gate 4 : a device (as a valve) for controlling the passage of a fluid or signal 5 : the total admission receipts or the number of people at an event

-gate \,gāt\ n comb form [Watergate, scandal that resulted in the resignation of President Richard Nixon in 1974] : usu. political scandal often involving the concealment of wrongdoing

gate·crash·er \'gāt-,kra-shər\ n : a person who enters without paying admission or attends without invitation

gate·keep·er \-,kē-pər\ n : a person who tends or guards a gate

gate·post \-,pōst\ n : the post to which a gate is hung or the one against which it closes

gate·way \-,wā\ n 1 : an opening for a gate 2 : a means of entrance or exit

¹**gath·er** \'ga-thər\ vb 1 : to bring together : COLLECT 2 : PICK, HARVEST 3 : to pick up little by little 4 : to scoop up from a resting place ⟨∼ed up the child⟩ 5 : to gain or win by gradual increase 6 : ATTRACT, ACCUMULATE ⟨∼ dust⟩ 7 : to summon up ⟨∼ courage to dive⟩ 8 : to

gain control of ⟨∼ed his wits⟩ 9 : to draw about or close to something 10 : to pull (fabric) along a line of stitching into puckers 11 : GUESS, DEDUCE, INFER 12 : ASSEMBLE 13 : to swell out and fill with pus 14 : GROW, INCREASE ♦ **Synonyms** CONGREGATE, FORGATHER ♦ **gath·er·er** n

²**gather** n : a puckering in cloth made by gathering

GATT \'gat\ abbr General Agreement on Tariffs and Trade

gauche \'gōsh\ adj [F, lit., left] 1 : lacking social experience or grace; also : not tactful 2 : crudely made or done ♦ **Synonyms** CLUMSY, HEAVY-HANDED, INEPT, MALADROIT

gau·che·rie \,gō-shə-'rē\ n : a tactless or awkward action

gau·cho \'gau̇-chō\ n, pl **gauchos** : a cowboy of the So. American pampas

gaud \'gȯd\ n : ORNAMENT, TRINKET

gaudy \'gȯ-dē\ adj **gaud·i·er; -est** : ostentatiously or tastelessly ornamented 2 : marked by showiness or extravagance : OUTLANDISH 3 : EXCEPTIONAL ⟨a ∼ batting average⟩ ♦ **Synonyms** GARISH, FLASHY, GLARING, TAWDRY — **gaud·i·ly** \-də-lē\ adv — **gaud·i·ness** \-dē-nəs\ n

¹**gauge** also **gage** \'gāj\ n 1 : measurement according to some standard or system 2 : DIMENSIONS, SIZE 3 usu **gage** : an instrument for measuring, testing, or registering

²**gauge** also **gage** vb **gauged** also **gaged; gaug·ing** also **gag·ing** 1 : MEASURE 2 : to determine the capacity or contents of 3 : ESTIMATE, JUDGE

gaunt \'gȯnt\ adj 1 : excessively thin and angular ⟨a ∼ face⟩ 2 : BARREN, DESOLATE ♦ **Synonyms** BONY, LANK, LANKY, LEAN, RAWBONED, SKINNY — **gaunt·ness** n

¹**gaunt·let** also **gant·let** \'gȯnt-lət\ n 1 : a protective glove 2 : an open challenge (as to combat) 3 : a dress glove extending above the wrist

²**gauntlet** also **gantlet** n 1 : a double file of men armed with weapons (as clubs) with which to strike at an individual who is made to run between them 2 : ORDEAL 3 : a line or series of something to be greeted or managed

gauss \'gau̇s\ n : the centimeter-gram-second unit of magnetic flux density that is equal to 1×10^{-4} tesla

gauze \'gȯz\ n : a very thin often transparent fabric used esp. for draperies and surgical dressings

gauzy \'gȯ-zē\ adj **gauz·i·er; -est** 1 : made of or resembling gauze 2 : marked by vagueness or fuzziness ⟨a ∼ memory⟩

gave past of GIVE

gav·el \'ga-vəl\ n : a mallet used by a presiding officer or auctioneer

ga·votte \gə-'vät\ n : a dance of French peasant origin marked by the raising rather than sliding of the feet

gawk \'gȯk\ vb : to gape or stare stupidly — **gawk·er** n

gawky \'gȯ-kē\ *adj* **gawk·i·er; -est** : AWKWARD, CLUMSY — **gawk·i·ly** \-kə-lē\ *adv* — **gawk·i·ness** *n*

gay \'gā\ *adj* **1** : MERRY **2** : BRIGHT, LIVELY **3** : brilliant in color **4** : given to social pleasures; *also* : LICENTIOUS **5** : HOMOSEXUAL; *also* : of, relating to, or used by homosexuals ⟨a ∼ bar⟩

gayety, gayly *var of* GAIETY, GAILY

gaz *abbr* gazette

gaze \'gāz\ *vb* **gazed; gaz·ing** : to fix the eyes in a steady intent look ♦ **Synonyms** GAPE, GAWK, GLARE, GOGGLE, PEER, STARE — **gaze** *n* — **gaz·er** *n*

ga·ze·bo \gə-'zē-bō\ *n, pl* **-bos 1** : BELVEDERE **2** : a freestanding roofed structure usu. open on the sides

ga·zelle \gə-'zel\ *n, pl* **gazelles** *also* **gazelle** : any of numerous small swift graceful antelopes

ga·zette \gə-'zet\ *n* **1** : NEWSPAPER **2** : an official journal

gaz·et·teer \ˌga-zə-'tir\ *n* : a geographical dictionary

ga·zil·lion \gə-'zil-yən\ *n* : ZILLION — **gazillion** *adj* — **ga·zil·lionth** \-yənth\ *adj*

gaz·pa·cho \gəz-'pä-(ˌ)chō, gə-'spä-\ *n, pl* **-chos** [Sp] : a spicy soup usu. made from raw vegetables and served cold

GB *abbr* Great Britain

GCA *abbr* ground-controlled approach

gd *abbr* good

Gd *symbol* gadolinium

GDR *abbr* German Democratic Republic

Ge *symbol* germanium

gear \'gir\ *n* **1** : CLOTHING **2** : movable property : GOODS **3** : EQUIPMENT ⟨fishing ∼⟩ **4** : a mechanism that performs a specific function ⟨steering ∼⟩ **5** : a toothed wheel **6** : working order or adjustment ⟨got her career in ∼⟩ **7** : an adjustment of transmission gears (as of an automobile or bicycle) that determines speed and direction of travel — **gear** *vb*

gear·box \'gir-ˌbäks\ *n* : TRANSMISSION 3

gear·shift \-ˌshift\ *n* : a mechanism by which transmission gears are shifted

gear·wheel \-ˌhwēl\ *n* : GEAR 5

gecko \'ge-kō\ *n, pl* **geck·os** *also* **geck·oes** : any of numerous small chiefly tropical insect-eating lizards

GED *abbr* general equivalency diploma

geek \'gēk\ *n* : a person of an intellectual bent who is often disliked — **geek·i·ness** *n* — **geeky** *adj*

geese *pl of* GOOSE

gee·zer \'gē-zər\ *n* : an odd or eccentric person usu. of old age

Gei·ger counter \'gī-gər-\ *n* : an electronic instrument for detecting the presence of cosmic rays or radioactive substances

gei·sha \'gā-shə, 'gē-\ *n, pl* **geisha** *or* **geishas** [Jp, fr. *gei* art + *-sha* person] : a Japanese girl or woman who is trained to provide entertaining company for men

gel \'jel\ *n* : a solid jellylike colloid (as gelatin dessert) — *vb*

gel·a·tin *also* **gel·a·tine** \'je-lə-tən\ *n* : glutinous material and esp. protein obtained from animal tissues by boiling and used as a food, in dyeing, and in photography; *also* : an edible jelly formed with gelatin — **ge·lat·i·nous** \jə-'la-tə-nəs\ *adj*

geld \'geld\ *vb* : CASTRATE

geld·ing *n* : a castrated male horse

gel·id \'je-ləd\ *adj* : extremely cold

gem \'jem\ *n* **1** : JEWEL **2** : a usu. valuable stone cut and polished for ornament **3** : something valued for beauty or perfection ⟨a ∼ of colonial architecture⟩

Gem·i·ni \'je-mə-(ˌ)nē, -ˌnī; 'ge-mə-ˌnē\ *n* **1** : a zodiacal constellation between Taurus and Cancer usu. pictured as twins sitting together **2** : the 3d sign of the zodiac in astrology; *also* : one born under this sign

gem·ol·o·gy *or* **gem·mol·o·gy** \je-'mä-lə-jē, jə-\ *n* : the science of gems — **gem·olog·i·cal** \ˌje-mə-'lä-ji-kəl\ *adj* — **gem·ol·o·gist** *also* **gem·mol·o·gist** \-jist\ *n*

gem·stone \'jem-ˌstōn\ *n* : a mineral or petrified material that when cut and polished can be used in jewelry

gen *abbr* **1** general **2** genitive

Gen *abbr* Genesis

Gen AF *abbr* general of the air force

gen·darme \'zhän-ˌdärm, 'jän-\ *n* [F, intended as sing. of *gensdarmes*, pl. of *gent d'armes*, lit., armed people] : a member of a body of soldiers esp. in France serving as an armed police force

gen·der \'jen-dər\ *n* [ME *gendre*, fr. AF *genre, gendre*, fr. L *gener-, genus* birth, race, kind, gender] **1** : any of two or more divisions within a grammatical class that determine agreement with and selection of other words or grammatical forms **2** : SEX 1

gene \'jēn\ *n* : a part of DNA or RNA that contains chemical information needed to make a particular protein (as an enzyme) controlling or influencing an inherited bodily trait (as eye color) or activity (as metabolism) or that influences or controls the activity of another gene or genes — **gen·ic** \'jē-nik, 'je-\ *adj*

ge·ne·al·o·gy \ˌjē-nē-'ä-lə-jē, ˌje-, -'a-\ *n, pl* **-gies** : PEDIGREE, LINEAGE; *also* : the study of family pedigrees — **ge·ne·a·log·i·cal** \ˌjē-nē-ə-'lä-ji-kəl, ˌje-\ *adj* — **ge·ne·a·log·i·cal·ly** \-k(ə-)lē\ *adv* — **ge·ne·al·o·gist** \ˌjē-nē-'ä-lə-jist, ˌje-; -'a-\ *n*

gene pool *n* : the total genetic information contained in a population of interbreeding organisms

genera *pl of* GENUS

¹**gen·er·al** \'je-nə-rəl, 'jen-rəl\ *adj* **1** : of or relating to the whole **2** : taken as a whole **3** : relating to or covering all instances **4** : not special or specialized **5** : common to many ⟨a ∼ custom⟩ **6** : not limited in meaning : not specific **7** : holding superior rank ⟨inspector ∼⟩ ♦ **Synonyms** GENERIC, UNIVERSAL

²**general** *n* **1** : something that involves or is applicable to the whole **2** : a commissioned officer ranking next below a general of the army or a general of the air force **3** : a commissioned officer of the highest rank in the marine corps — **in general** : for the most part

general assembly *n* **1** : a legislative assembly; *esp* : a U.S. state legislature **2** *cap G&A* : the supreme deliberative body of the United Nations

gen·er·al·i·sa·tion, gen·er·al·ise, gen·er·al·ised *Brit var of* GENERALIZATION, GENERALIZE, GENERALIZED

gen·er·a·lis·si·mo \ˌje-nə-rə-ˈli-sə-ˌmō\ *n, pl* **-mos** [It, fr. *generale* general] : the chief commander of an army

gen·er·al·i·ty \ˌje-nə-ˈra-lə-tē\ *n, pl* **-ties** **1** : the quality or state of being general **2** : GENERALIZATION **2** **3** : a vague or inadequate statement **4** : the greatest part : BULK

gen·er·al·i·za·tion \ˌje-nə-rə-lə-ˈzā-shən, ˌjen-rə-\ *n* **1** : the act or process of generalizing **2** : a general statement, law, principle, or proposition

gen·er·al·ize \ˈje-nə-rə-ˌlīz, ˈjen-rə-\ *vb* **-ized; -iz·ing** **1** : to make general **2** : to draw general conclusions from **3** : to reach a general conclusion esp. on the basis of particular instances **4** : to extend throughout the body

gen·er·al·ly \ˈjen-rə-lē, ˈje-nə-\ *adv* **1** : in a general manner **2** : as a rule

general of the air force : a commissioned officer of the highest rank in the air force

general of the army : a commissioned officer of the highest rank in the army

general practitioner *n* : a physician or veterinarian whose practice is not limited to a specialty

gen·er·al·ship \ˈje-nə-rəl-ˌship, ˈjen-rəl-\ *n* **1** : office or tenure of office of a general **2** : LEADERSHIP **3** : military skill as a high commander

general store *n* : a retail store that carries a wide variety of goods but is not divided into departments

gen·er·ate \ˈje-nə-ˌrāt\ *vb* **-at·ed; -at·ing** : to bring into existence : PRODUCE ⟨~ electricity⟩ ♦ *Synonyms* CREATE, ORIGINATE, PROCREATE, SPAWN

gen·er·a·tion \ˌje-nə-ˈrā-shən\ *n* **1** : a body of living beings constituting a single step in the line of descent from an ancestor; *also* : the average period between generations **2** : PRODUCTION

Generation X *n* : the generation of Americans born in the 1960s and 1970s

gen·er·a·tive \ˈje-nə-rə-tiv, -ˌrā-tiv\ *adj* : having the power or function of generating, originating, producing, or reproducing ⟨~ organs⟩

gen·er·a·tor \ˈje-nə-ˌrā-tər\ *n* : one that generates; *esp* : a machine by which mechanical energy is changed into electrical energy

ge·ner·ic \jə-ˈner-ik\ *adj* **1** : not specific : GENERAL **2** : not protected by a trademark ⟨a ~ drug⟩ **3** : of or relating to a biological genus **4** : having no particularly distinctive quality ⟨~ towns⟩ — **generic** *n* — **ge·ner·i·cal·ly** \-i-k(ə-)lē\ *adv*

gen·er·ous \ˈje-nə-rəs\ *adj* **1** : free in giving or sharing ⟨~ donors⟩ **2** : HIGH-MINDED, NOBLE **3** : ABUNDANT, AMPLE, COPIOUS ⟨a ~ salary⟩ ♦ *Synonyms* LIBERAL, BOUNTIFUL, MUNIFICENT, OPENHANDED — **gen·er·os·i·ty** \ˌje-nə-ˈrä-sə-tē\ *n* — **gen·er·ous·ly** \ˈje-nə-rəs-lē\ *adv* — **gen·er·ous·ness** *n*

gen·e·sis \ˈje-nə-səs\ *n, pl* **-e·ses** \-ˌsēz\ : the origin or coming into existence of something

Genesis *n* — see BIBLE table

gene–splic·ing \-ˌsplī-sin\ *n* : the process of preparing recombinant DNA

gene therapy *n* : the insertion of normal or altered genes into cells esp. to replace defective genes in the treatment of genetic disorders or to provide a specialized disease-fighting function

ge·net·ic \jə-ˈne-tik\ *adj* : of or relating to the origin, development, or causes of something; *also* : of, relating to, or caused by genes or genetics ⟨~ research⟩ — **ge·net·i·cal·ly** \-ti-k(ə-)lē\ *adv*

genetic code *n* : the chemical code that is the basis of genetic inheritance and consists of units of three linked chemical groups in DNA and RNA which specify particular amino acids used to make proteins or which start or stop the process of making proteins

genetic engineering *n* : the alteration of genetic material esp. by cutting up and joining together DNA from one or more species of organism and inserting the result into an organism — **genetically engineered** *adj*

ge·net·ics \jə-ˈne-tiks\ *n* : a branch of biology dealing with heredity and variation — **ge·net·i·cist** \-tə-sist\ *n*

ge·nial \ˈjē-nyəl, ˈjē-nē-əl\ *adj* **1** : favorable to growth or comfort ⟨~ sunshine⟩ **2** : CHEERFUL, KINDLY ⟨a ~ host⟩ ♦ *Synonyms* AFFABLE, CONGENIAL, CORDIAL, GRACIOUS, SOCIABLE — **ge·nial·i·ty** \ˌjē-nē-ˈa-lə-tē, jēn-ˈya-\ *n* — **ge·nial·ly** *adv*

-gen·ic \ˈje-nik\ *adj comb form* **1** : producing : forming **2** : produced by : formed from **3** : suitable for production or reproduction by (such) a medium

ge·nie \ˈjē-nē\ *n, pl* **ge·nies** *also* **ge·nii** \-nē-ˌī\ [F *génie*, fr. Ar *jinnī*] : a supernatural spirit that often takes human form usu. serving the person who calls on it

gen·i·tal \ˈje-nə-tᵊl\ *adj* **1** : concerned with reproduction ⟨~ organs⟩ **2** : of, relating to, or characterized by the stage of psychosexual development in psychoanalytic theory in which oral and anal impulses are subordinated to adaptive interpersonal mechanisms — **gen·i·tal·ly** *adv*

gen·i·ta·lia \ˌje-nə-ˈtāl-yə\ *n pl* : reproductive organs; *esp* : the external genital organs — **gen·i·ta·lic** \-ˈta-lik, -ˈtā-\ *adj*

gen·i·tals \ˈje-nə-tᵊlz\ *n pl* : GENITALIA

gen·i·tive \ˈje-nə-tiv\ *adj* : of, relating to, or constituting a grammatical case marking typically a relationship of possessor or source — **genitive** *n*

gen·i·to·uri·nary \ˌje-nə-tō-ˈyu̇r-ə-ˌner-ē\ *adj* : of or relating to the genital and urinary organs or functions

ge·nius \ˈjē-nyəs\ *n, pl* **ge·nius·es** *or* **ge·**

nii \-nē-ˌi\ [L, tutelary spirit, natural inclinations, fr. *gignere* to beget] **1** *pl* **genii** : an attendant spirit of a person or place; *also* : a person who influences another for good or evil **2** : a strong leaning or inclination **3** : a peculiar or distinctive character or spirit (as of a nation or a language) **4** *pl usu* **genii** : SPIRIT, GENIE **5** *pl usu* **geniuses** : a single strongly marked capacity or aptitude **6** : extraordinary intellectual power; *also* : a person having such power ♦ **Synonyms** GIFT, FACULTY, FLAIR, KNACK, TALENT

genl *abbr* general

geno·cide \ˈje-nə-ˌsīd\ *n* : the deliberate and systematic destruction of a racial, political, or cultural group

ge·nome \ˈjē-ˌnōm\ *n* **1** : one haploid set of chromosomes **2** : the genetic material of an organism

ge·no·mics \jē-ˈnō-miks\ *n* : a branch of biotechnology concerned esp. with investigating and collecting data about the structure and function of all or part of an organism's genome

-genous \jə-nəs\ *adj comb form* **1** : producing : yielding ⟨*erogenous*⟩ **2** : having (such) an origin ⟨*endogenous*⟩

genre \ˈzhän-rə, ˈzhäⁿ-; ˈzhäⁿrˈ; ˈjän-rə\ *n* **1** : a distinctive type or category esp. of literary composition **2** : a style of painting in which everyday subjects are treated realistically

gens \ˈjenz, ˈgens\ *n, pl* **gen·tes** \ˈjen-ˌtēz, ˈgen-ˌtās\ [L] : a Roman clan embracing the families of the same stock in the male line

gent *n* : GENTLEMAN

gen·teel \jen-ˈtēl\ *adj* **1** : ARISTOCRATIC **2** : ELEGANT, STYLISH **3** : POLITE, REFINED **4** : maintaining the appearance of superior social status **5** : marked by false delicacy, prudery, or affectation — **gen·teel·ly** *adv* — **gen·teel·ness** *n*

gen·tian \ˈjen-chən\ *n* : any of numerous herbs with opposite leaves and showy usu. blue flowers in the fall

gen·tile \ˈjen-ˌtī(-ə)l\ *n* [ME, fr. LL *gentilis* heathen, pagan, fr. L *gent-, gens* clan, nation] **1** *often cap* : a person who is not Jewish; *esp* : a Christian as distinguished from a Jew **2** : HEATHEN, PAGAN — **gentile** *adj, often cap*

gen·til·i·ty \jen-ˈti-lə-tē\ *n, pl* **-ties** **1** : good birth and family **2** : the qualities characteristic of a well-bred person **3** : good manners **4** : superior social status shown in manners or mode of life

¹gen·tle \ˈjen-tˀl\ *adj* **gen·tler** \ˈjent-lər, -tˀl-ər\; **gen·tlest** \ˈjent-ləst, -tˀl-əst\ **1** : belonging to a family of high social station **2** : of, relating to, or characteristic of a gentleman **3** : KIND, AMIABLE ⟨a ~ pastor⟩ **4** : TRACTABLE, DOCILE ⟨a ~ dog⟩ **5** : not harsh, stern, or violent **6** : SOFT, DELICATE **7** : MODERATE — **gen·tle·ness** *n* — **gen·tly** *adv*

²gentle *vb* **gen·tled; gen·tling** **1** : to make or become mild, docile, soft, or moderate **2** : MOLLIFY, PLACATE

gen·tle·folk \ˈjen-tˀl-ˌfōk\ *also* **gen·tle·folks** \-ˌfōks\ *n* : persons of good family and breeding

gen·tle·man \-mən\ *n* **1** : a man of good family **2** : a well-bred man **3** : MAN — used in pl. as a form of address — **gen·tle·man·ly** *adj*

gen·tle·wom·an \-ˌwu̇-mən\ *n* **1** : a woman of good family **2** : a woman attending a lady of rank **3** : a woman with very good manners : LADY

gen·tri·fi·ca·tion \ˌjen-trə-fə-ˈkā-shən\ *n* : the process of renewal accompanying the influx of middle-class people into deteriorating areas that often displaces earlier usu. poorer residents — **gen·tri·fy** \ˈjen-trə-ˌfī\ *vb*

gen·try \ˈjen-trē\ *n, pl* **gentries** **1** : people of good birth, breeding, and education : ARISTOCRACY **2** : the class of English people between the nobility and the yeomanry **3** : persons of a designated class

gen·u·flect \ˈjen-yə-ˌflekt\ *vb* : to bend the knee esp. in worship — **gen·u·flec·tion** \ˌjen-yə-ˈflek-shən\ *n*

gen·u·ine \ˈjen-yə-wən\ *adj* **1** : AUTHENTIC, REAL ⟨a ~ signature⟩ **2** : SINCERE, HONEST ⟨their love is ~⟩ ♦ **Synonyms** BONA FIDE, TRUE, VERITABLE — **gen·u·ine·ly** *adv* — **gen·u·ine·ness** *n*

ge·nus \ˈjē-nəs\ *n, pl* **gen·era** \ˈje-nə-rə\ [L, birth, race, kind] : a category of biological classification that ranks between the family and the species and contains related species

geo·cen·tric \ˌjē-ō-ˈsen-trik\ *adj* **1** : relating to or measured from the earth's center **2** : having or relating to the earth as a center

geo·chem·is·try \-ˈke-mə-strē\ *n* : a branch of geology that deals with the chemical composition of and chemical changes in the earth — **geo·chem·i·cal** \-mi-kəl\ *adj* — **geo·chem·ist** \-ˈmist\ *n*

ge·ode \ˈjē-ˌōd\ *n* : a nodule of stone having a cavity lined with mineral matter

¹geo·de·sic \ˌjē-ə-ˈde-sik\ *adj* : made of light straight structural elements ⟨a ~ dome⟩

²geodesic *n* : the shortest line between two points on a surface

geo·det·ic \ˌjē-ə-ˈde-tik\ *adj* : of, relating to, or being precise measurement of the earth and its features ⟨a ~ survey⟩

geog *abbr* geographic; geographical; geography

ge·og·ra·phy \jē-ˈä-grə-fē\ *n, pl* **-phies** **1** : a science that deals with the natural features of the earth and its climate, products, and inhabitants **2** : the natural features of a region — **ge·og·ra·pher** \-fər\ *n* — **geo·graph·ic** \ˌjē-ə-ˈgra-fik\ *or* **geo·graph·i·cal** \-fi-kəl\ *adj* — **geo·graph·i·cal·ly** \-fi-k(ə-)lē\ *adv*

geol *abbr* geologic; geological; geology

ge·ol·o·gy \jē-ˈä-lə-jē\ *n, pl* **-gies** **1** : a science that deals with the history of the earth and its life esp. as recorded in rocks; *also* : a study of the features of a celestial body (as the moon) **2** : the geologic features of an area — **geo·log·ic** \ˌjē-ə-ˈlä-jik\ *or* **geo·log·i·cal** \-ji-kəl\ *adj*

— **geo·log·i·cal·ly** \-ji-k(ə-)lē\ *adv*
ge·ol·o·gist \jē-ˈä-lə-jist\ *n*
geom *abbr* geometric; geometrical; geometry
geo·mag·net·ic \ˌjē-ō-mag-ˈne-tik\ *adj* : of or relating to the magnetism of the earth — **geo·mag·ne·tism** \-ˈmag-nə-ˌti-zəm\ *n*
geometric mean *n* : the *n*th root of the product of *n* numbers; *esp* : a number that is the second term of three consecutive terms of a geometric progression ⟨the *geometric mean* of 9 and 4 is 6⟩
geometric progression *n* : a progression (as 1, $\frac{1}{2}$, $\frac{1}{4}$) in which the ratio of a term to its predecessor is always the same
ge·om·e·try \jē-ˈä-mə-trē\ *n, pl* **-tries** [ultim. fr. Gk *geōmetria*, fr. *geōmetrein* to measure the earth, fr. *gē* earth + *metron* measure] : a branch of mathematics dealing with the relations, properties, and measurements of solids, surfaces, lines, points, and angles — **ge·om·e·ter** \-tər\ *n* — **geo·met·ric** \ˌjē-ə-ˈme-trik\ *or* **geo·met·ri·cal** \-tri-kəl\ *adj*
geo·phys·ics \ˌjē-ō-ˈfi-ziks\ *n* : the physics of the earth — **geo·phys·i·cal** \-zi-kəl\ *adj* — **geo·phys·i·cist** \-zə-sist\ *n*
geo·pol·i·tics \-ˈpä-lə-ˌtiks\ *n* : a combination of political and geographic factors relating to a state — **geo·po·lit·i·cal** \-pə-ˈli-ti-kəl\ *adj*
geo·ther·mal \ˌjē-ō-ˈthər-məl\ *adj* : of, relating to, or using the heat of the earth's interior ⟨∼ energy⟩
ger *abbr* gerund
Ger *abbr* German; Germany
ge·ra·ni·um \jə-ˈrā-nē-əm\ *n* [L, fr. Gk *geranion*, fr. *geranos* crane] : any of a genus of herbs with usu. deeply cut leaves and typically pink, purple, or white flowers; *also* : any of a related genus of herbs that are native to southern Africa and are widely grown for their clusters of showy usu. red, pink, or white flowers
ger·bil *also* **ger·bile** \ˈjər-bəl\ *n* : any of numerous Old World burrowing desert rodents with long hind legs
ge·ri·at·ric \ˌjer-ē-ˈa-trik\ *adj* **1** : of or relating to geriatrics or the process of aging **2** : of, relating to, or appropriate for elderly people **3** : OLD
ge·ri·at·rics \-triks\ *n* : a branch of medicine dealing with the problems and diseases of old age and aging
germ \ˈjərm\ *n* **1** : a bit of living matter capable of growth and development (as into an organism) **2** : SOURCE, RUDIMENTS **3** : MICROORGANISM; *esp* : one causing disease
Ger·man \ˈjər-mən\ *n* **1** : a native or inhabitant of Germany **2** : the language of Germany, Austria, and parts of Switzerland — **German** *adj* — **Ger·man·ic** \jər-ˈma-nik\ *adj*
ger·mane \jər-ˈmān\ *adj* [ME *germain*, lit., having the same parents, fr. AF, fr. L *germanus*, fr. *germen* sprout, bud] : RELEVANT, APPROPRIATE ♦ **Synonyms** APPLICABLE, MATERIAL, PERTINENT
ger·ma·ni·um \jər-ˈmā-nē-əm\ *n* : a grayish white hard chemical element used

esp. in semiconductor and optical materials and as a catalyst
German measles *n sing or pl* : an acute contagious virus disease milder than typical measles but damaging to the fetus when occurring early in pregnancy
German shepherd *n* : any of a breed of intelligent responsive working dogs of German origin often used in police work and as guide dogs for the blind
germ cell *n* : an egg or sperm or one of their antecedent cells
ger·mi·cide \ˈjər-mə-ˌsīd\ *n* : an agent that destroys germs — **ger·mi·cid·al** \ˌjər-mə-ˈsī-dᵊl\ *adj*
ger·mi·nal \ˈjər-mə-nəl\ *adj* : of or relating to a germ or germ cell; *also* : EMBRYONIC
ger·mi·nate \ˈjər-mə-ˌnāt\ *vb* **-nat·ed; -nat·ing** **1** : to cause to develop : begin to develop : SPROUT **2** : to come into being : EVOLVE — **ger·mi·na·tion** \ˌjər-mə-ˈnā-shən\ *n*
ger·on·tol·o·gy \ˌjer-ən-ˈtä-lə-jē\ *n* : a scientific study of aging and the problems of the aged — **ge·ron·to·log·i·cal** \jə-ˌrän-tə-ˈlä-ji-kəl\ *adj* — **ger·on·tol·o·gist** \ˌjer-ən-ˈtä-lə-jist\ *n*
ger·ry·man·der \ˈjer-ē-ˌman-dər\ *vb* : to divide into election districts so as to give one political party an advantage — **gerrymander** *n*
ger·und \ˈjer-ənd\ *n* : a word having the characteristics of both verb and noun
ge·sta·po \gə-ˈstä-pō\ *n, pl* **-pos** [G, fr. *Geheime Staatspolizei*, lit., secret state police] : a usu. terrorist secret-police organization operating against persons suspected of disloyalty
ges·ta·tion \je-ˈstā-shən\ *n* : PREGNANCY, INCUBATION — **ges·tate** \ˈjes-ˌtāt\ *vb*
ges·tic·u·late \je-ˈsti-kyə-ˌlāt\ *vb* **-lat·ed; -lat·ing** : to make gestures esp. when speaking — **ges·tic·u·la·tion** \-ˌsti-kyə-ˈlā-shən\ *n*
ges·ture \ˈjes-chər\ *n* **1** : a movement usu. of the body or limbs that expresses or emphasizes an idea, sentiment, or attitude **2** : something said or done by way of formality or courtesy, as a symbol or token, or for its effect on the attitudes of others — **ges·tur·al** \-chə-rəl\ *adj* — **gesture** *vb*
ge·sund·heit \gə-ˈzùnt-ˌhīt\ *interj* [G, lit., health] — used to wish good health esp. to one who has just sneezed
¹**get** \ˈget\ *vb* **got** \ˈgät\; **got** *or* **got·ten** \ˈgä-tᵊn\; **get·ting** **1** : to gain possession of (as by receiving, acquiring, earning, buying, or winning) : PROCURE, OBTAIN, FETCH **2** : to succeed in coming or going ⟨*got* away to the lake⟩ **3** : to cause to come or go ⟨*got* the car to the station⟩ **4** : BEGET **5** : to cause to be in a certain condition or position ⟨don't ∼ wet⟩ **6** : BECOME ⟨∼ sick⟩ **7** : PREPARE **8** : SEIZE **9** : to move emotionally; *also* : IRRITATE **10** : BAFFLE, PUZZLE **11** : KILL **12** : HIT **13** : to be subjected to ⟨∼ the measles⟩ **14** : to receive as punishment **15** : to find out by calculation **16** : HEAR; *also* : UNDERSTAND ⟨*got* the joke⟩ **17**

: PERSUADE, INDUCE 18 : HAVE ⟨he's *got* no money⟩ 19 : to have as an obligation or necessity ⟨you have *got* to come⟩ 20 : to establish communication with 21 : to be able ⟨finally *got* to go to med school⟩ 22 : to come to be ⟨*got* talking about old times⟩ 23 : to leave at once — **get ahead** : to achieve success — **get a move on** : HURRY — **get away with** : to avoid punishment for (as a crime) — **get into** : to become strongly involved or interested in ⟨*got into* music⟩ — **get over** : to reconcile oneself to ⟨*got over* the breakup⟩

²**get** \'get\ *n* : OFFSPRING, PROGENY

get along *vb* 1 : GET BY 2 : to be on friendly terms

get-away \'ge-tə-,wā\ *n* 1 : ESCAPE 2 : START 3 : a usu. brief vacation

get by *vb* : to meet one's needs

get–to-geth-er \'get-tə-,ge-thər\ *n* : an informal social gathering

get-up \'get-,əp\ *n* 1 : OUTFIT, COSTUME 2 : general composition or structure

gew·gaw \'gü-,gȯ, 'gyü-\ *n* : a showy trifle : BAUBLE, TRINKET

gey·ser \'gī-zər\ *n* [Icelandic *Geysir*, hot spring in Iceland] : a spring that intermittently shoots up hot water and steam

g–force \'jē-,fȯrs\ *n* : the force of gravity or acceleration on a body

ghast·ly \'gast-lē\ *adj* **ghast·li·er; -est** 1 : HORRIBLE, SHOCKING 2 : resembling a ghost : DEATHLIKE, PALE ♦ **Synonyms** GRUESOME, GRIM, LURID, GRISLY, MACABRE

ghat \'gȯt\ *n* [Hindi & Urdu *ghāṭ*] : a broad flight of steps on an Indian riverbank that provides access to the water

gher·kin \'gər-kən\ *n* 1 : a small prickly fruit of a vine related to the cucumber used to make pickles 2 : an immature cucumber

ghet·to \'ge-tō\ *n, pl* **ghettos** *or* **ghet·toes** : a quarter of a city in which members of a minority group live because of social, legal, or economic pressure

¹**ghost** \'gōst\ *n* 1 : the seat of life : SOUL 2 : a disembodied soul; *esp* : the soul of a dead person believed to be an inhabitant of the unseen world or to appear in bodily form to living people 3 : SPIRIT, DEMON 4 : a faint trace ⟨a ~ of a smile⟩ 5 : a false image in a photographic negative or on a television screen — **ghost·ly** *adv*

²**ghost** *vb* : GHOSTWRITE

ghost·write \-,rīt\ *vb* **-wrote** \-,rōt\; **-writ·ten** \-,ri-t³n\ : to write for and in the name of another — **ghost·writ·er** *n*

ghoul \'gül\ *n* [Ar *ghūl*] : a legendary evil being that robs graves and feeds on corpses — **ghoul·ish** *adj*

GHQ *abbr* general headquarters

gi *abbr* gill

¹**GI** \jē-'ī\ *adj* [galvanized *i*ron; fr. abbr. used in listing such articles as garbage cans, but taken as abbr. for *government issue*] 1 : provided by an official U.S. military supply department ⟨~ shoes⟩ 2 : of, relating to, or characteristic of U.S. military personnel 3 : conforming to military regulations or customs ⟨a ~ haircut⟩

²**GI** *n, pl* **GIs** *or* **GI's** \-'īz\ : a member or former member of the U.S. armed forces; *esp* : an enlisted person

³**GI** *abbr* 1 galvanized iron 2 gastrointestinal 3 general issue 4 government issue

gi·ant \'jī-ənt\ *n* 1 : a legendary humanlike being of great size and strength 2 : a living being or thing of extraordinary size or powers — **giant** *adj*

gi·ant·ess \'jī-ən-təs\ *n* : a female giant

giant panda *n* : PANDA 2

gib·ber \'ji-bər\ *vb* : to speak rapidly, inarticulately, and often foolishly

gib·ber·ish \'ji-bə-rish\ *n* : unintelligible or confused speech or language

¹**gib·bet** \'ji-bət\ *n* : GALLOWS

²**gibbet** *vb* 1 : to hang on a gibbet 2 : to expose to public scorn 3 : to execute by hanging

gib·bon \'gi-bən\ *n* : any of several tailless apes of southeastern Asia

gib·bous \'ji-bəs, 'gi-\ *adj* 1 : rounded like the exterior of a sphere or circle 2 : seen with more than half but not all of the apparent disk illuminated ⟨~ moon⟩ 3 : having a hump : HUMPBACKED

gibe *or* **jibe** \'jīb\ *vb* **gibed** *or* **jibed**; **gib·ing** *or* **jib·ing** : to utter taunting words : SNEER — **gibe** *or* **jibe** *n*

gib·lets \'jib-ləts\ *n pl* : the edible viscera of a fowl

Gib·son girl \'gib-sən-\ *adj* : of or relating to a style in women's clothing characterized by high necks, full sleeves, and slender waistlines

gid·dy \'gi-dē\ *adj* **gid·di·er; -est** 1 : DIZZY 2 : causing dizziness ⟨a ~ height⟩ 3 : not serious : FRIVOLOUS, SILLY — **gid·di·ness** \-dē-nəs\ *n*

gid·dy·ap \,gi-dē-'ap, -'əp\ *or* **gid·dy·up** \-'əp\ *vb imper* — a command (as to a horse) to go ahead or go faster

GIF \'gif, 'jif\ *n* [graphic *i*nterchange *f*ormat] : a computer file format for digital images; *also* : the image itself

gift \'gift\ *n* 1 : a special ability : TALENT 2 : something given : PRESENT 3 : the act or power of giving

gift card *n* : a card entitling the recipient to goods or services of a specified value from the issuer

gift·ed \'gif-təd\ *adj* : TALENTED

¹**gig** \'gig\ *n* 1 : a long light ship's boat 2 : a light 2-wheeled one-horse carriage

²**gig** *n* : a pronged spear for catching fish — **gig** *vb*

³**gig** *n* : a job for a specified time; *esp* : an entertainer's engagement

⁴**gig** *n* : a military demerit — **gig** *vb*

giga·byte \'ji-gə-,bīt, 'gi-\ *n* : 1024 megabytes or 1,073,741,824 bytes; *also* : one billion bytes

gi·gan·tic \jī-'gan-tik\ *adj* : exceeding the usual (as in size or force)

gig·gle \'gi-gəl\ *vb* **gig·gled; gig·gling** : to laugh with repeated short catches of the breath — **giggle** *n* — **gig·gly** \-gə-lē\ *adj*

GIGO *abbr* garbage in, garbage out

gig·o·lo \'ji-gə-,lō\ *n, pl* **-los** 1 : a man

supported by a woman usu. in return for his attentions **2** : a professional dancing partner or male escort

Gi·la monster \'hē-lə-\ *n* : a large orange and black venomous lizard of the southwestern U.S.

¹**gild** \'gild\ *vb* **gild·ed** *or* **gilt** \'gilt\; **gild·ing** **1** : to overlay with or as if with a thin covering of gold **2** : to give an attractive but often deceptive appearance to

²**gild** *var of* GUILD

¹**gill** \'jil\ *n* — see WEIGHT table

²**gill** \'gil\ *n* : an organ (as of a fish) for obtaining oxygen from water

¹**gilt** \'gilt\ *adj* : of the color of gold

²**gilt** *n* : gold or a substance resembling gold laid on the surface of an object

³**gilt** *n* : a young female swine

¹**gim·crack** \'jim-ˌkrak\ *n* : a showy object of little use or value

²**gimcrack** *adj* : CHEAP, SHODDY

gim·let \'gim-lət\ *n* : a small tool with screw point and cross handle for boring holes

gim·me cap \'gi-mē-\ *n* : an adjustable visored cap featuring a corporate logo or slogan

gim·mick \'gi-mik\ *n* **1** : CONTRIVANCE, GADGET **2** : an important feature that is not immediately apparent : CATCH **3** : a new and ingenious scheme **4** : a device used to attract business or attention — **gim·micky** \-mi-kē\ *adj*

gim·mick·ry \'gi-mi-krē\ *n, pl* **-ries** : an array of or the use of gimmicks

gimpy \'gim-pē\ *adj* : LAME 1

¹**gin** \'jin\ *n* [ME *gin*, fr. AF, short for *engin* engine] **1** : TRAP, SNARE **2** : a machine to separate seeds from cotton — **gin** *vb*

²**gin** *n* [by shortening & alter. fr. *geneva*, kind of gin] : a liquor distilled from a grain mash and flavored with juniper berries

gin·ger \'jin-jər\ *n* : the pungent aromatic rootstock of a tropical plant used esp. as a spice and in medicine; *also* : the spice or the plant

ginger ale *n* : a carbonated soft drink flavored with ginger

gin·ger·bread \'jin-jər-ˌbred\ *n* **1** : a cake made with molasses and flavored with ginger **2** : lavish or superfluous ornament esp. in architecture

gin·ger·ly \'jin-jər-lē\ *adj* : very cautious or careful — **gingerly** *adv*

gin·ger·snap \-ˌsnap\ *n* : a thin brittle molasses cookie flavored with ginger

ging·ham \'giŋ-əm\ *n* : a cotton cloth that is often marked with a pattern of colored squares

gin·gi·vi·tis \ˌjin-jə-'vī-təs\ *n* : inflammation of the gums

gink·go *also* **ging·ko** \'giŋ-(ˌ)kō\ *n, pl* **ginkgoes** *or* **ginkgos** *also* **gingkos** *or* **gingkoes** **1** : a tree of eastern China with fan-shaped leaves often grown as a shade tree **2** : GINKGO BILOBA

ginkgo bi·lo·ba \-ˌbī-'lō-bə\ *n* : an extract of the leaves of ginkgo that is held to enhance mental functioning

gin·seng \'jin-ˌseŋ\ *n* : an aromatic root of a Chinese or No. American herb used

esp. in Chinese medicine; *also* : one of these herbs

Gip·sy *chiefly Brit var of* GYPSY

gi·raffe \jə-'raf\ *n, pl* **giraffes** [It *giraffa*, fr. Ar *zirāfa*] : an African ruminant mammal with a very long neck and a short coat with dark blotches

gird \'gərd\ *vb* **gird·ed** *or* **girt** \'gərt\; **gird·ing** **1** : to encircle or fasten (as a sword) with or as if with a belt **2** : to invest esp. with power or authority **3** : PREPARE, BRACE

gird·er \'gər-dər\ *n* : a horizontal main supporting beam

gir·dle \'gər-dᵊl\ *n* **1** : something (as a belt or sash) that encircles or confines **2** : a woman's supporting undergarment that extends from the waist to below the hips — **girdle** *vb*

girl \'gərl\ *n* **1** : a female child **2** : a young woman **3** : SWEETHEART — **girl·hood** \-ˌhud\ *n* — **girl·ish** *adj*

girl Friday *n* : a female assistant (as in an office) entrusted with a wide variety of tasks

girl·friend \'gərl-ˌfrend\ *n* **1** : a female friend **2** : a regular female companion in a romantic or sexual relationship

Girl Scout *n* : a member of any of the scouting programs of the Girl Scouts of the United States of America

girth \'gərth\ *n* **1** : a band around an animal by which something (as a saddle) may be fastened on its back **2** : a measure around something

gist \'jist\ *n* [AF, it lies, fr. *gesir* to lie, ultim. fr. L *jacēre*] : the main point or part ⟨the ~ of his speech⟩

git *dial var of* GET

give \'giv\ *vb* **gave** \'gāv\; **giv·en** \'gi-vən\; **giv·ing** **1** : to make a present of **2** : to bestow by formal action **3** : to accord or yield to another **4** : to yield to force, strain, or pressure **5** : to put into the possession or keeping of another **6** : PROFFER ⟨*gave* her his hand⟩ **7** : DELIVER ⟨*gave* the bride away⟩ **8** : to present in public performance or to view **9** : PROVIDE ⟨~ a party⟩ **10** : ATTRIBUTE **11** : to make, form, or yield as a product or result ⟨cows ~ milk⟩ **12** : PAY **13** : to deliver by some bodily action ⟨*gave* me a push⟩ **14** : to offer as a pledge ⟨I ~ you my word⟩ **15** : DEVOTE **16** : to cause to have or receive ⟨~ me time⟩

²**give** *n* **1** : capacity or tendency to yield to force or strain **2** : the quality or state of being springy

give–and–take \ˌgiv-ən-'tāk\ *n* **1** : COMPROMISE **2** : a usu. good-natured exchange (as of ideas)

give·away \'gi-və-ˌwā\ *n* **1** : an unintentional revelation or betrayal **2** : something given away free; *esp* : PREMIUM

give in *vb* : SUBMIT, SURRENDER

¹**giv·en** \'gi-vən\ *adj* **1** : DISPOSED, INCLINED ⟨~ to swearing⟩ **2** : SPECIFIED, PARTICULAR ⟨at a ~ time⟩

²**given** *n* : something taken for granted : a basic condition or assumption

³**given** *prep* : CONSIDERING

given name *n* : a name that precedes one's surname

give out *vb* **1** : EMIT **2** : BREAK DOWN **3** : to become exhausted : COLLAPSE

give up *vb* **1** : SURRENDER **2** : to abandon (oneself) to a feeling, influence, or activity **3** : QUIT ⟨*give up* his job⟩

giz·mo *also* **gis·mo** \'giz-mō\ *n, pl* **giz·mos** *also* **gismos** : GADGET

giz·zard \'gi-zərd\ *n* : the muscular usu. horny-lined enlargement of the alimentary canal of a bird used for churning and grinding up food

gla·cial \'glā-shəl\ *adj* **1** : extremely cold **2** : of or relating to glaciers **3** : being or relating to a past period of time when a large part of the earth was covered by glaciers **4** *cap* : PLEISTOCENE **5** : very slow ⟨a ~ pace⟩ — **gla·cial·ly** *adv*

gla·ci·ate \'glā-shē-ˌāt\ *vb* **-at·ed; -at·ing** **1** : to subject to glacial action **2** : to produce glacial effects in or on — **gla·ci·a·tion** \ˌglā-shē-ˈā-shən, -sē-\ *n*

gla·cier \'glā-shər\ *n* [F, fr. MF dial. (Savoy), fr. *glace* ice, fr. L *glacies*] : a large body of ice moving slowly down a slope or spreading outward on a land surface

¹glad \'glad\ *adj* **glad·der; glad·dest** **1** : experiencing pleasure, joy, or delight **2** : PLEASED **3** : very willing ⟨was ~ to help⟩ **4** : PLEASANT, JOYFUL **5** : CHEERFUL ⟨a ~ morning⟩ — **glad·ly** *adv* — **glad·ness** *n*

²glad *n* : GLADIOLUS

glad·den \'gla-dᵊn\ *vb* : to make glad

glade \'glād\ *n* : a grassy open space surrounded by woods

glad·i·a·tor \'gla-dē-ˌā-tər\ *n* **1** : a person engaged in a fight to the death for public entertainment in ancient Rome **2** : a person engaging in a public fight or controversy; *also* : PRIZEFIGHTER — **glad·i·a·to·ri·al** \ˌgla-dē-ə-ˈtȯr-ē-əl\ *adj*

glad·i·o·lus \ˌgla-dē-ˈō-ləs\ *n, pl* **-oli** \-ˈō-(ˌ)lē, -ˌlī\ *or* **-olus** *also* **-o·lus·es** [L, fr. dim. of *gladius* sword] : any of a genus of chiefly African plants related to the irises and having erect sword-shaped leaves and stalks of bright-colored flowers

glad·some \'glad-səm\ *adj* : giving or showing joy : CHEERFUL

glad·stone \'glad-ˌstōn\ *n, often cap* : a suitcase with flexible sides on a rigid frame that opens flat into two compartments

glam \'glam\ *n* : extravagantly showy glamour — **glam** *adj*

glam·or·ise *Brit var of* GLAMORIZE

glam·or·ize *also* **glam·our·ize** \'gla-mə-ˌrīz\ *vb* **-ized; -iz·ing** : to make or look upon as glamorous

glam·our *also* **glam·or** \'gla-mər\ *n* [Sc *glamour* magic spell, alter. of E *grammar*; fr. the popular association of erudition with occult practices] : an exciting and often illusory and romantic attractiveness; *esp* : alluring personal attraction — **glam·or·ous** *also* **glam·our·ous** \-mə-rəs\ *adj*

¹glance \'glans\ *vb* **glanced; glanc·ing** **1** : to strike and fly off to one side **2** : GLEAM **3** : to give a quick look

²glance *n* **1** : a quick intermittent flash or gleam **2** : a deflected impact or blow **3** : a quick look

gland \'gland\ *n* : a cell or group of cells that prepares and secretes a substance (as saliva or sweat) for further use in or discharge from the body

glan·du·lar \'glan-jə-lər\ *adj* : of, relating to, or involving glands

glans \'glanz\ *n, pl* **glan·des** \'glan-ˌdēz\ [L, lit., acorn] : a conical vascular body forming the extremity of the penis or clitoris

¹glare \'gler\ *vb* **glared; glar·ing** **1** : to shine with a harsh dazzling light **2** : to stare fiercely or angrily

²glare *n* **1** : a harsh dazzling light **2** : an angry or fierce stare

glar·ing *adj* : very conspicuous ⟨a ~ error⟩ — **glar·ing·ly** *adv*

glass \'glas\ *n* **1** : a hard brittle amorphous usu. transparent or translucent material consisting typically of silica **2** : something made of glass; *esp* : TUMBLER **2 3** *pl* : a pair of lenses used to correct defects of vision : SPECTACLES **4** : the quantity held by a glass container — **glass** *adj* — **glass·ful** \-ˌfu̇l\ *n* — **glassy** *adj*

glass-blow·ing \-ˌblō-iŋ\ *n* : the art of shaping a mass of glass that has been softened by heat by blowing air into it through a tube — **glass-blow·er** *n*

glass·ware \-ˌwer\ *n* : articles made of glass

glau·co·ma \glau̇-ˈkō-mə, glȯ-\ *n* : a disease of the eye marked by increased pressure within the eyeball resulting in damage to the retina and gradual loss of vision

¹glaze \'glāz\ *vb* **glazed; glaz·ing** **1** : to furnish (as a window frame) with glass **2** : to apply glaze to

²glaze *n* : a glassy coating or surface

gla·zier \'glā-zhər\ *n* : a person who sets glass in window frames

¹gleam \'glēm\ *n* **1** : a transient subdued or partly obscured light **2** : GLINT **3** : a faint trace ⟨a ~ of hope⟩

²gleam *vb* **1** : to shine with subdued light or moderate brightness **2** : to appear briefly or faintly ♦ *Synonyms* FLASH, GLIMMER, GLISTEN, GLITTER, SHIMMER, SPARKLE

glean \'glēn\ *vb* **1** : to gather grain left by reapers **2** : to collect little by little or with patient effort ⟨antiques ~ed from flea markets⟩ — **glean·able** *adj* — **glean·er** *n*

glean·ings \'glē-niŋz\ *n pl* : things acquired by gleaning

glee \'glē\ *n* [ME, fr. OE *glēo* entertainment, music] **1** : JOY, HILARITY **2** : a part-song for three usu. male voices — **glee·ful** *adj* — **glee·ful·ly** *adv*

glee club *n* : a chorus organized for singing usu. short choral pieces

glen \'glen\ *n* : a narrow hidden valley

glen·gar·ry \glen-ˈga-rē\ *n, pl* **-ries** *often cap* : a woolen cap of Scottish origin

glib \'glib\ *adj* **glib·ber; glib·best**

: speaking or spoken with careless ease — **glib·ly** adv

glide \ˈglīd\ vb **glid·ed; glid·ing 1** : to move smoothly and effortlessly **2** : to descend gradually without engine power ⟨∼ in an airplane⟩ — **glide** n

glid·er \ˈglī-dər\ n **1** : one that glides **2** : an aircraft resembling an airplane but having no engine **3** : a porch seat suspended from an upright frame

¹**glim·mer** \ˈgli-mər\ vb : to shine faintly or unsteadily

²**glimmer** n **1** : a faint unsteady light **2** : INKLING **3** : a small amount : HINT

¹**glimpse** \ˈglimps\ vb **glimpsed; glimps·ing** : to take a brief look : see momentarily or incompletely

²**glimpse** n **1** : a faint idea : GLIMMER **2** : a short hurried look

glint \ˈglint\ vb **1** : to shine by reflection : SPARKLE, GLITTER, GLEAM **2** : to appear briefly or faintly — **glint** n

glis·san·do \gli-ˈsän-(ˌ)dō\ n, pl **-di** \-(ˌ)dē\ or **-dos** : a rapid sliding up or down the musical scale

¹**glis·ten** \ˈgli-sᵊn\ vb : to shine by reflection with a soft luster or sparkle

²**glisten** n : GLITTER, SPARKLE

glis·ter \ˈglis-tər\ vb : GLITTER

glitch \ˈglich\ n : MALFUNCTION; also : SNAG

¹**glit·ter** \ˈgli-tər\ vb **1** : to shine with brilliant or metallic luster : SPARKLE **2** : to shine with strong emotion : FLASH ⟨eyes ∼ing in anger⟩ **3** : to be brilliantly attractive esp. in a superficial way

²**glitter** n **1** : sparkling brilliancy, showiness, or attractiveness **2** : small glittering objects used for ornamentation — **glit·tery** \ˈgli-tə-rē\ adj

glitz \ˈglits\ n : extravagant showiness — **glitzy** \ˈglit-sē\ adj

²**glitz** vb : to make flashy or extravagant in appearance — often used with up

gloam·ing \ˈglō-miŋ\ n : TWILIGHT, DUSK

gloat \ˈglōt\ vb : to think about something with triumphant and often malicious delight ⟨∼ing over their victory⟩

glob \ˈgläb\ n **1** : a small drop **2** : a large rounded mass

glob·al \ˈglō-bəl\ adj **1** : WORLDWIDE **2** : COMPREHENSIVE, GENERAL — **glob·al·ly** adv

glob·al·i·za·tion \ˌglō-bə-lə-ˈzā-shən\ n : the development of an increasingly integrated global economy

Global Positioning System n : GPS

global warming n : an increase in the earth's atmospheric and oceanic temperatures due to an increase in the greenhouse effect

globe \ˈglōb\ n **1** : BALL, SPHERE **2** : EARTH; also : a spherical representation of the earth

globe-trot·ter \ˈglōb-ˌträ-tər\ n : a person who travels widely — **globe-trot·ting** n or adj

glob·u·lar \ˈglä-byə-lər\ adj : having the shape of a globe or globule

glob·ule \ˈglä-(ˌ)byül\ n : a tiny globe or ball esp. of a liquid

glob·u·lin \ˈglä-byə-lən\ n : any of a class of simple proteins insoluble in pure water but soluble in dilute salt solutions that occur widely in plant and animal tissues

glock·en·spiel \ˈglä-kən-ˌshpēl, -ˌspēl\ n [G, fr. Glocke bell + Spiel play] : a percussion musical instrument consisting of a series of metal bars played with two hammers

gloom \ˈglüm\ n **1** : partial or total darkness **2** : lowness of spirits : DEJECTION **3** : an atmosphere of despondency ⟨a ∼ fell over the household⟩ — **gloom·i·ly** \ˈglü-mə-lē\ adv — **gloom·i·ness** \-mē-nəs\ n — **gloomy** \ˈglü-mē\ adj

Gloomy Gus \-ˈgəs\ n, pl **Gloomy Gus·es** : a person who is habitually gloomy

glop \ˈgläp\ n : a messy mass or mixture

glo·ri·fy \ˈglȯr-ə-ˌfī\ vb **-fied; -fy·ing 1** : to raise to heavenly glory **2** : to light up brilliantly **3** : EXTOL **4** : to give glory to (as in worship) — **glo·ri·fi·ca·tion** \ˌglȯr-ə-fə-ˈkā-shən\ n

glo·ri·ous \ˈglȯr-ē-əs\ adj **1** : possessing or deserving glory : PRAISEWORTHY **2** : conferring glory : RESPLENDENT, MAGNIFICENT ⟨a ∼ sunset⟩ **4** : DELIGHTFUL, WONDERFUL ⟨had a ∼ weekend⟩ — **glo·ri·ous·ly** adv

¹**glo·ry** \ˈglȯr-ē\ n, pl **glories 1** : RENOWN **2** : honor and praise rendered in worship **3** : something that secures praise or renown **4** : a distinguishing quality or asset **5** : RESPLENDENCE, MAGNIFICENCE **6** : heavenly bliss **7** : a height of prosperity or achievement

²**glory** vb **glo·ried; glo·ry·ing** : to rejoice proudly : EXULT

¹**gloss** \ˈgläs, ˈglȯs\ n **1** : LUSTER, SHEEN, BRIGHTNESS **2** : outward show

²**gloss** vb **1** : to give a false appearance of acceptableness to ⟨∼ over inadequacies⟩ **2** : to deal with too lightly or not at all ⟨∼ed over the problem⟩

³**gloss** n [alter. of gloze, fr. ME glose, fr. AF, fr. ML glosa, glossa, fr. Gk glōssa, glōtta tongue, language, unusual word] **1** : an explanatory note (as in the margin of a text) **2** : GLOSSARY **3** : an interlinear translation **4** : a continuous commentary accompanying a text

⁴**gloss** vb : to furnish glosses for

glos·sa·ry \ˈglä-sə-rē, ˈglȯ-\ n, pl **-ries** : a collection of difficult or specialized terms with their meanings — **glos·sar·i·al** \glä-ˈser-ē-əl, glȯ-\ adj

glos·so·la·lia \ˌglä-sə-ˈlā-lē-ə, ˌglȯ-\ n [ultim. fr. Gk glōssa tongue, language + lalia chatter] : TONGUE 6

¹**glossy** \ˈglä-sē, ˈglȯ-\ adj **gloss·i·er; -est** : having a surface luster or brightness — **gloss·i·ly** \-sə-lē\ adv — **gloss·i·ness** \-sē-nəs\ n

²**glossy** n, pl **gloss·ies** : a photograph printed on smooth shiny paper

glot·tis \ˈglä-təs\ n, pl **glot·tis·es** or **glot·ti·des** \-tə-ˌdēz\ : the slitlike opening between the vocal cords in the larynx — **glot·tal** \ˈglä-tᵊl\ adj

glove \ˈgləv\ n **1** : a covering for the hand having separate sections for each finger **2** : a padded leather covering for the hand for use in a sport

¹glow \'glō\ *vb* **1** : to shine with or as if with intense heat **2** : to have a rich warm usu. ruddy color : FLUSH, BLUSH **3** : to feel hot **4** : to show exuberance or elation ⟨~ with pride⟩

²glow *n* **1** : brightness or warmth of color; *esp* : REDNESS **2** : warmth of feeling or emotion **3** : a sensation of warmth **4** : light such as is emitted from a heated substance

glow·er \'glau̇(-ə)r\ *vb* : to stare angrily : SCOWL — **glower** *n*

glow-worm \'glō-,wǝrm\ *n* : any of various insect larvae or adults that give off light

glox·in·ia \gläk-'si-nē-ə\ *n* : any of a genus of tropical herbs related to the African violets; *esp* : one with showy bell-shaped or slipper-shaped flowers

gloze \'glōz\ *vb* **glozed; gloz·ing** : to make appear right or acceptable : GLOSS

glu·cose \'glü-,kōs\ *n* **1** : a form of crystalline sugar; *esp* : DEXTROSE **2** : a sweet light-colored syrup made from cornstarch

glue \'glü\ *n* : a jellylike protein substance made from animal materials and used for sticking things together; *also* : any of various other strong adhesives — **glue** *vb* — **glu·ey** \'glü-ē\ *adj*

glum \'glǝm\ *adj* **glum·mer; glum·mest** **1** : broodingly morose : SULLEN **2** : DREARY, GLOOMY ⟨a ~ countenance⟩ ♦ **Synonyms** CRABBED, DOUR, SATURNINE, SULKY

¹glut \'glǝt\ *vb* **glut·ted; glut·ting** **1** : OVERSUPPLY **2** : to fill esp. with food to satiety : SATIATE

²glut *n* : an excessive supply

glu·ten \'glü-t²n\ *n* : a gluey protein substance that causes dough to be sticky

glu·ti·nous \'glü-tə-nəs\ *adj* : STICKY

glut·ton \'glǝ-t²n\ *n* : one that eats to excess — **glut·ton·ous** \'glǝ-tə-nəs\ *adj* — **glut·tony** \'glǝ-tə-nē\ *n*

glyc·er·in *or* **glyc·er·ine** \'gli-sə-rən\ *n* : GLYCEROL

glyc·er·ol \'gli-sə-,rȯl, -,rōl\ *n* : a sweet syrupy alcohol usu. obtained from fats and used esp. as a solvent

gly·co·gen \'gli-kə-jən\ *n* : a white tasteless substance that is the chief storage carbohydrate of animals

gm *abbr* gram

GM *abbr* **1** general manager **2** guided missile

G–man \'jē-,man\ *n* : a special agent of the Federal Bureau of Investigation

GMT *abbr* Greenwich mean time

gnarled \'närld\ *adj* **1** : KNOTTY ⟨~ hands⟩ **2** : GLOOMY, SULLEN

gnash \'nash\ *vb* : to grind (as teeth) together

gnat \'nat\ *n* : any of various small usu. biting dipteran flies

gnaw \'nȯ\ *vb* **1** : to consume, wear away, or make by persistent biting or nibbling **2** : to affect as if by gnawing — **gnaw·er** *n*

gneiss \'nīs\ *n* : a layered rock similar in composition to granite

gnome \'nōm\ *n* : a dwarf of folklore who lives inside the earth and guards precious ore or treasure — **gnome·like** \-,līk\ *adj* — **gnom·ish** *adj*

GNP *abbr* gross national product

gnu \'nü\ *n, pl* **gnu** *or* **gnus** : WILDEBEEST

¹go \'gō\ *vb* **went** \'went\; **gone** \'gȯn, 'gän\; **go·ing; goes** \'gōz\ **1** : to move on a course : PROCEED ⟨~ slow⟩ **2** : LEAVE, DEPART **3** : to take a certain course or follow a certain procedure ⟨reports ~ through department channels⟩ **4** : EXTEND, RUN ⟨his land ~es to the river⟩; *also* : LEAD ⟨that door ~es to the cellar⟩ **5** : to be habitually in a certain state ⟨~es barefoot⟩ **6** : to become lost, consumed, or spent; *also* : DIE **7** : ELAPSE, PASS ⟨went for a good price⟩ **9** : to become impaired or weakened ⟨his hearing started to ~⟩ **10** : to give way under force or pressure : BREAK **11** : to move along in a specified manner ⟨it went well⟩ **12** : to be in general or on an average ⟨cheap, as yachts ~⟩ **13** : to become esp. as the result of a contest ⟨the decision went against him⟩ **14** : to put or subject oneself ⟨~ to great expense⟩ **15** : RESORT ⟨went to court to recover damages⟩ **16** : to begin or maintain an action or motion **17** : to function properly ⟨the clock doesn't ~⟩ **18** : to be known ⟨~es by an alias⟩ **19** : to be or act in accordance ⟨a good rule to ~ by⟩ **20** : to come to be applied **21** : to pass by award, assignment, or lot **22** : to contribute to a result ⟨qualities that ~ to make a hero⟩ **23** : to be about, intending, or expecting something ⟨is ~ing to leave town⟩ **24** : to arrive at a certain state or condition ⟨~ to sleep⟩ **25** : to come to be ⟨the tire went flat⟩ **26** : to be capable of being sung or played ⟨the tune ~es like this⟩ **27** : to be suitable or becoming : HARMONIZE **28** : to be capable of passing, extending, or being contained or inserted ⟨this coat will ~ in the trunk⟩ **29** : to have a usual or proper place or position : BELONG ⟨these books ~ on the top shelf⟩ **30** : to be capable of being divided ⟨3 ~es into 6 twice⟩ **31** : to have a tendency ⟨that ~es to show that he is honest⟩ **32** : to be acceptable, satisfactory, or adequate ⟨any color will ~ with black⟩ **33** : to empty the bladder or bowels **34** : to proceed along or according to : FOLLOW **35** : TRAVERSE **36** : BET, BID ⟨willing to ~ $50⟩ **37** : to assume the function or obligation of ⟨~ bail for a friend⟩ **38** : to participate to the extent of ⟨~ halves⟩ **39** : WEIGH **40** : ENDURE, TOLERATE **41** : AFFORD ⟨can't ~ the price⟩ **42** : SAY — used chiefly in oral narration of speech **43** : to engage in ⟨don't ~ telling everyone⟩ — **go at 1** : ATTACK, ATTEMPT **2** : UNDERTAKE — **go back on 1** : ABANDON **2** : BETRAY **3** : FAIL — **go by the board** : to be discarded — **go for 1** : to pass for or serve as **2** : to try to secure **3** : FAVOR — **go one better** : OUTDO, SURPASS — **go over 1** : EXAMINE **2** : REPEAT **3** : STUDY, REVIEW — **go places** : to be on the way to success — **go steady** : to date one person exclusively — **go to bat for** : DEFEND, CHAMPION — **go to town 1** : to work or act efficiently **2** : to be very successful

²**go** *n, pl* **goes 1** : the act or manner of going **2** : the height of fashion ⟨boots are all the ~⟩ **3** : a turn of affairs : OCCURRENCE **4** : ENERGY, VIGOR **5** : ATTEMPT, TRY ⟨give it a ~⟩ **6** : a spell of activity ⟨finished the job at one ~⟩ — **no go** : USELESS, HOPELESS — **on the go** : constantly active

³**go** *adj* : functioning properly ⟨declared all systems ~⟩

goad \'gōd\ *n* [ME *gode,* fr. OE *gād* spear, goad] **1** : a pointed rod used to urge on an animal **2** : something that urges
♦ *Synonyms* STIMULUS, IMPETUS, INCENTIVE, SPUR, STIMULANT — **goad** *vb*

go-ahead \'gō-ə-ˌhed\ *n* : authority to proceed ⟨got the ~ for the project⟩

goal \'gōl\ *n* **1** : the mark set as limit to a race; *also* : an area to be reached safely in children's games **2** : AIM, PURPOSE **3** : an area or object toward which play is directed to score; *also* : a successful attempt to score

goal·ie \'gō-lē\ *n* : GOALKEEPER

goal·keep·er \'gōl-ˌkē-pər\ *n* : a player who defends the goal in various games

goal·post \-ˌpōst\ *n* : one of the two vertical posts with a crossbar that constitute the goal in various games

goat \'gōt\ *n, pl* **goats** *or* **goat** : any of various hollow-horned ruminant mammals related to the sheep that have backward-curving horns, a short tail, and usu. straight hair

goa·tee \gō-'tē\ *n* : a small trim pointed or tufted beard on a man's chin

goat·herd \'gōt-ˌhərd\ *n* : a person who tends goats

goat·skin \-ˌskin\ *n* : the skin of a goat or a leather made from it

¹**gob** \'gäb\ *n* **1** : LUMP, MASS

²**gob** *n* : SAILOR

gob·bet \'gä-bət\ *n* : LUMP, MASS

¹**gob·ble** \'gä-bəl\ *vb* **gob·bled; gob·bling 1** : to swallow or eat greedily **2** : to take eagerly : GRAB

²**gobble** *vb* **gob·bled; gob·bling** : to make the natural guttural noise of a male turkey

gob·ble·dy·gook *also* **gob·ble·de·gook** \'gä-bəl-dē-ˌgúk, -ˌgük\ *n* : generally unintelligible jargon

gob·bler \'gä-blər\ *n* : a male turkey

go-be·tween \'gō-bə-ˌtwēn\ *n* : an intermediate agent : BROKER

gob·let \'gä-blət\ *n* : a drinking glass with a foot and stem

gob·lin \'gä-blən\ *n* : an ugly or grotesque sprite that is mischievous and sometimes evil and malicious

go·by \'gō-bē\ *n, pl* **gobies** *also* **goby** : any of numerous spiny-finned fishes usu. having the pelvic fins united to form a ventral sucking disk

god \'gäd, 'gód\ *n* **1** *cap* : the supreme reality; *esp* : the Being worshiped as the creator and ruler of the universe **2** : a

being or object believed to have supernatural attributes and powers and to require worship **3** : a thing of supreme value **4** : an extraordinarily attractive person

god·child \'gäd-ˌchī(-ə)ld, 'gód-\ *n* : a person for whom another person stands as sponsor at baptism

god·daugh·ter \-ˌdó-tər\ *n* : a female godchild

god·dess \'gä-dəs, 'gó-\ *n* **1** : a female god **2** : a woman whose charm or beauty arouses adoration

god·fa·ther \'gäd-ˌfä-thər, 'gód-\ *n* **1** : a man who sponsors a person at baptism **2** : the leader of an organized crime syndicate

god·head \-ˌhed\ *n* **1** : divine nature or essence **2** *cap* : GOD 1; *also* : the nature of God esp. as existing in three persons

god·hood \-ˌhúd\ *n* : DIVINITY

god·less \-ləs\ *adj* : not acknowledging a deity or divine law — **god·less·ness** *n*

god·like \-ˌlīk\ *adj* : resembling or having the qualities of God or a god

god·ly \-lē\ *adj* **god·li·er; -est 1** : DIVINE **2** : PIOUS, DEVOUT — **god·li·ness** *n*

god·moth·er \-ˌmə-thər\ *n* : a woman who sponsors a person at baptism

god·par·ent \-ˌper-ənt\ *n* : a sponsor at baptism

god·send \-ˌsend\ *n* : a desirable or needed thing or event that comes unexpectedly

god·son \-ˌsən\ *n* : a male godchild

God·speed \-'spēd\ *n* : a prosperous journey : SUCCESS ⟨bade him ~⟩

go·fer *or* **go·pher** \'gō-fər\ *n* [alter. of *go for*] : an employee whose duties include running errands

go-get·ter \'gō-ˌge-tər\ *n* : an aggressively enterprising person — **go-get·ting** *adj or n*

gog·gle \'gä-gəl\ *vb* **gog·gled; gog·gling** : to stare with wide or protuberant eyes

gog·gles \'gä-gəlz\ *n pl* : protective glasses set in a flexible frame that fits snugly against the face

go-go \'gō-ˌgō\ *adj* **1** : related to, being, or employed to entertain in a disco ⟨~ dancers⟩ **2** : aggressively enterprising and energetic ⟨~ entrepreneurs⟩

go·ings-on \ˌgō-iŋ-'zón, -'zän\ *n pl* : ACTIONS, EVENTS

goi·ter \'gói-tər\ *n* : an abnormally enlarged thyroid gland visible as a swelling at the base of the neck — **goi·trous** \-trəs, -tə-rəs\ *adj*

goi·tre *chiefly Brit var of* GOITER

go-kart \'gō-ˌkärt\ *n* : a small motorized vehicle used esp. for racing

gold \'gōld\ *n* **1** : a malleable yellow metallic chemical element used esp. for coins and jewelry **2** : gold coins; *also* : MONEY **3** : a yellow color

gold·brick \'gōld-ˌbrik\ *n* : a person who shirks assigned work — **goldbrick** *vb*

gold coast *n, often cap G&C* : an exclusive residential district

gold digger *n* : a person who uses charm to extract money or gifts from others

gold·en \'gōl-dən\ *adj* **1** : made of or relating to gold **2** : having the color of gold; *also* : BLOND **3** : SHINING, LUSTROUS **4** : SUPERB **5** : FLOURISHING, PROSPEROUS **6** : radiantly youthful and vigorous **7** : FAVORABLE, ADVANTAGEOUS ⟨a ∼ opportunity⟩ **8** : MELLOW, RESONANT ⟨a ∼ tenor⟩

gold·en-ag·er \ˈgōl-dən-ˈā-jər\ *n* : an elderly and often retired person usu. engaging in club activities

golden eagle *n* : a large dark brown eagle with gold-colored feathers on the back of the head and neck

golden hamster *n* : a small tawny hamster often kept as a pet

golden handcuffs *n pl* : special benefits offered to an employee as an inducement to continue service

golden handshake *n* : a generous severance agreement given esp. as an inducement to early retirement

golden retriever *n* : any of a breed of retrievers with a flat golden coat

gold·en·rod \ˈgōl-dən-ˌräd\ *n* : any of numerous herbs related to the daisies that have tall slender stalks with many tiny usu. yellow flower heads

golden years *n pl* : the advanced years in a lifetime

gold·finch \-ˌfinch\ *n* **1** : a small largely red, black, and yellow Old World finch often kept in a cage **2** : any of three small related American finches of which the males usu. become bright yellow and black in summer

gold·fish \-ˌfish\ *n* : a small usu. golden-orange carp often kept as an aquarium or pond fish

gold·smith \-ˌsmith\ *n* : a person who makes or deals in articles of gold

golf \ˈgälf, ˈgȯlf\ *n* : a game played with a small ball and various clubs on a course having 9 or 18 holes — **golf** *vb* — **golf·er** *n*

-gon \ˌgän\ *n comb form* : figure having (so many) angles ⟨hexa*gon*⟩

go·nad \ˈgō-ˌnad\ *n* : a sperm- or egg-producing gland : OVARY, TESTIS — **go·nad·al** \gō-ˈna-d²l\ *adj*

go·nad·o·trop·ic \gō-ˌna-də-ˈträ-pik\ *also* **go·nad·o·tro·phic** \-ˈtrō-fik, -ˈträ-\ *adj* : acting on or stimulating the gonads

go·nad·o·tro·pin \-ˈtrō-pən\ *also* **go·nad·o·tro·phin** \-fən\ *n* : a gonadotropic hormone

gon·do·la \ˈgän-də-lə (*usual for 1*), gän-ˈdō-\ *n* [It. dial. (Venice), prob. fr. MGk *kontoura* small vessel] **1** : a long narrow boat used on the canals of Venice **2** : a railroad car used for hauling loose freight (as coal) **3** : an enclosure beneath an airship or balloon **4** : an enclosed car suspended from a cable and used esp. for transporting skiers

gon·do·lier \ˌgän-də-ˈlir\ *n* : a person who propels a gondola

¹gone \ˈgȯn\ *past part of* GO

²gone *adj* **1** : LOST, RUINED **2** : DEAD **3** : SINKING, WEAK **4** : INVOLVED, ABSORBED **5** : INFATUATED **6** : PREGNANT **7** : PAST

gon·er \ˈgȯ-nər\ *n* : one whose case is hopeless

gong \ˈgäŋ, ˈgȯŋ\ *n* : a metallic disk that produces a resounding tone when struck

gono·coc·cus \ˌgä-nə-ˈkä-kəs\ *n, pl* **-coc·ci** \-ˈkäk-ˌsī, -(ˌ)sē, -ˈkä-ˌkī, -(ˌ)kē\ : a pus-producing bacterium causing gonorrhea — **gono·coc·cal** \-ˈkä-kəl\ *adj*

gon·or·rhea \ˌgä-nə-ˈrē-ə\ *n* : a contagious sexually transmitted inflammation of the genital tract caused by the gonococcus — **gon·or·rhe·al** \-ˈrē-əl\ *adj*

goo \ˈgü\ *n* **1** : a viscid or sticky substance **2** : sentimental tripe — **goo·ey** \-ē\ *adj*

goo·ber \ˈgü-bər, ˈgù-\ *n, Southern & Midland* : PEANUT

¹good \ˈgùd\ *adj* **bet·ter** \ˈbe-tər\; **best** \ˈbest\ **1** : of a favorable character or tendency **2** : BOUNTIFUL, FERTILE ⟨∼ land⟩ **3** : COMELY, ATTRACTIVE **4** : SUITABLE, FIT **5** : SOUND, WHOLE ⟨only one ∼ arm⟩ **6** : AGREEABLE, PLEASANT ⟨had a ∼ time⟩ **7** : SALUTARY, WHOLESOME **8** : CONSIDERABLE, AMPLE ⟨a ∼ bit of time⟩ **9** : FULL ⟨waited a ∼ hour⟩ **10** : WELL-FOUNDED **11** : TRUE ⟨holds ∼ for everybody⟩ **12** : legally valid or effectual **13** : ADEQUATE, SATISFACTORY **14** : conforming to a standard ⟨∼ English⟩ **15** : DISCRIMINATING **16** : COMMENDABLE, VIRTUOUS **17** : KIND **18** : UPPER-CLASS **19** : COMPETENT **20** : LOYAL, CLOSE ⟨a ∼ friend⟩ — **good·ish** *adj*

²good *n* **1** : something good **2** : GOODNESS **3** : BENEFIT, WELFARE ⟨for the ∼ of mankind⟩ **4** : something that has economic utility **5** *pl* : personal property **6** *pl* : CLOTH **7** *pl* : WARES, MERCHANDISE ⟨canned ∼s⟩ **8** : good persons ⟨the ∼ die young⟩ **9** *pl* : proof of wrongdoing — **for good** : FOREVER, PERMANENTLY — **to the good** : in a position of net gain or profit ⟨$10 *to the good*⟩

³good *adv* : WELL

good–bye *or* **good–by** \gùd-ˈbī, gə-\ *n* : a concluding remark at parting

good cholesterol *n* : HDL

good–for–noth·ing \ˈgùd-fər-ˌnə-thiŋ\ *adj* : of no use or value — **good–for–nothing** *n*

Good Friday *n* : the Friday before Easter observed as the anniversary of the crucifixion of Christ

good–heart·ed \ˈgùd-ˈhär-təd\ *adj* : having a kindly generous disposition — **good–heart·ed·ly** *adv* — **good–heart·ed·ness** *n*

good–look·ing \ˈgùd-ˈlù-kiŋ\ *adj* : having an attractive appearance

good·ly \ˈgùd-lē\ *adj* **good·li·er**; **-est** **1** : of pleasing appearance **2** : LARGE, CONSIDERABLE ⟨a ∼ sum of money⟩

good·man \ˈgùd-mən\ *n, archaic* : MR.

good–na·tured \ˈgùd-ˈnā-chərd\ *adj* : of a cheerful disposition — **good–na·tured·ly** \-chərd-lē\ *adv*

good·ness \-nəs\ *n* : EXCELLENCE, VIRTUE

good·wife \-ˌwīf\ *n, archaic* : MRS.

good·will \-ˈwil\ *n* **1** : BENEVOLENCE **2**

: the value of the trade a business has built up over time **3** : cheerful consent **4** : willing effort

goody *or* **good·ie** \\'gu̇-dē\ *n, pl* **good·ies** : something that is good esp. to eat

goody–goody \\'gu̇-dē-'gu̇-dē\ *adj* : affectedly good — **goody–goody** *n*

goof \\'gu̇f\ *vb* **1** : to spend time idly or foolishly — usu. used with *off* **2** : BLUNDER — usu. used with *up* — **goof** *n*

goof·ball \\'gu̇f-,bȯl\ *n* **1** *slang* : a barbiturate sleeping pill **2** : a goofy person

go off *vb* **1** : EXPLODE **2** : to follow a course ⟨the party *went off* well⟩

goof–off \\'gu̇f-,ȯf\ *n* : one who evades work or responsibility

goofy \\'gü-fē\ *adj* **goof·i·er; -est** : CRAZY, SILLY — **goof·i·ness** \-fē-nəs\ *n*

goo·gle \\'gü-gəl\ *vb* **goo·gled; goo·gling** [*Google*, trademark for a search engine] : to use the Google search engine to obtain information on the World Wide Web

goon \\'gün\ *n* : a man hired to terrorize or kill opponents

go on *vb* **1** : to continue in a course of action **2** : to take place : HAPPEN

goose \\'güs\ *n, pl* **geese** \\'gēs\ **1** : any of numerous long-necked web-footed birds related to the swans and ducks; *also* : a female goose as distinguished from a gander **2** : a foolish person **3** *pl* **goos·es** : a tailor's smoothing iron

goose·ber·ry \\'güs-,ber-ē, 'güz-, -bə-rē\ *n* : the acid berry of any of several shrubs related to the currant and used esp. in jams and pies

goose bumps *n pl* : roughening of the skin caused usu. by cold, fear, or a sudden feeling of excitement

goose·flesh \-,flesh\ *n* : GOOSE BUMPS

goose pimples *n pl* : GOOSE BUMPS

go out *vb* **1** : to become extinguished **2** : to become a candidate ⟨*went out* for the football team⟩

go over *vb* : SUCCEED

GOP *abbr* Grand Old Party (Republican)

¹go·pher \\'gō-fər\ *n* **1** : a burrowing American land tortoise **2** : any of a family of No. American burrowing rodents with large cheek pouches opening beside the mouth **3** : any of several small ground squirrels of the prairie region of No. America

²gopher *var of* GOFER

go·pik \gȯ-'pēk, -'pik\ *n, pl* **gopik** — see *manat* at MONEY table

¹gore \\'gȯr\ *n* : a tapering or triangular piece (as of cloth) in a skirt)

²gore *vb* **gored; gor·ing** : to pierce or wound with something pointed

³gore *n* **1** : BLOOD **2** : gruesomeness depicted in vivid detail

¹gorge \\'gȯrj\ *n* **1** : THROAT **2** : a narrow ravine **3** : a mass of matter that chokes up a passage

²gorge *vb* **gorged; gorg·ing** : to eat greedily : stuff to capacity : GLUT

gor·geous \\'gȯr-jəs\ *adj* : resplendently beautiful

Gor·gon·zo·la \,gȯr-gən-'zō-lə\ *n* : a pungent blue cheese of Italian origin

go·ril·la \gə-'ri-lə\ *n* [NL, fr. Gk *Gorillai*, tribe of hairy women in an account of a voyage around Africa] : an African anthropoid ape related to but much larger than the chimpanzee

gor·man·dise *chiefly Brit var of* GORMANDIZE

gor·man·dize \\'gȯr-mən-,dīz\ *vb* **-dized; -diz·ing** : to eat ravenously — **gor·man·diz·er** *n*

gorp \\'gȯrp\ *n* : a snack consisting of high-calorie food (as raisins and nuts)

gorse \\'gȯrs\ *n* : a spiny yellow-flowered European evergreen shrub of the legume family

gory \\'gȯr-ē\ *adj* **gor·i·er; -est** **1** : BLOODSTAINED **2** : HORRIBLE, SENSATIONAL ⟨the ~ details⟩

gos·hawk \\'gäs-,hȯk\ *n* : any of several long-tailed hawks with short rounded wings

gos·ling \\'gäz-liŋ, 'gȯz-\ *n* : a young goose

¹gos·pel \\'gäs-pəl\ *n* [ME, fr. OE *gōdspel*, fr. *gōd* good + *spell* message, news] **1** : the teachings of Christ and the apostles **2** *cap* : any of the first four books of the New Testament **3** : something accepted or promoted as infallible truth

²gospel *adj* **1** : of, relating to, or emphasizing the gospel **2** : relating to or being American religious songs associated with evangelism

gos·sa·mer \\'gä-sə-mər\ *n* [ME *gossomer*, fr. *gos* goose + *somer* summer] **1** : a film of cobwebs floating in the air **2** : something light, delicate, or tenuous

¹gos·sip \\'gä-səp\ *n* **1** : a person who habitually reveals personal or sensational facts **2** : rumor or report of an intimate nature **3** : an informal conversation — **gos·sipy** *adj*

²gossip *vb* : to spread gossip

got *past and past part of* GET

Goth \\'gäth\ *n* : a member of a Germanic people that early in the Christian era overran the Roman Empire

¹Goth·ic \\'gä-thik\ *adj* **1** : of or relating to the Goths **2** : of or relating to a style of architecture prevalent in western Europe from the middle 12th to the early 16th century

²Gothic *n* **1** : the Germanic language of the Goths **2** : the Gothic architectural style or decoration

gotten *past part of* GET

Gou·da \\'gü-də\ *n* : a mild Dutch milk cheese shaped in balls

¹gouge \\'gau̇j\ *n* **1** : a rounded troughlike chisel **2** : a hole or groove made with or as if with a gouge

²gouge *vb* **gouged; goug·ing** **1** : to cut holes or grooves in with or as if with a gouge **2** : DEFRAUD, CHEAT

gou·lash \\'gü-,läsh, -,lash\ *n* [Hungarian *gulyás*] : a stew made with meat, assorted vegetables, and paprika

go under *vb* : to be overwhelmed, defeated, or destroyed : FAIL

gourd \\'gȯrd, 'gu̇rd\ *n* **1** : any of a family of tendril-bearing vines including the cucumber, squash, and melon **2** : the fruit of a gourd; *esp* : any of various inedible hard-shelled fruits used esp. for ornament or implements

gourde \'gu̇rd\ *n* — see MONEY table

gour·mand \'gu̇r-ˌmänd\ *n* 1 : one who is excessively fond of eating and drinking 2 : GOURMET

gour·met \'gu̇r-ˌmā, gu̇r-'mā\ *n* [F, fr. MF, alter. of *gromet* boy servant, vintner's assistant] : a connoisseur of food and drink

gout \'gau̇t\ *n* : a metabolic disease marked by painful inflammation and swelling of the joints — **gouty** *adj*

gov *abbr* 1 government 2 governor 3 governmental institution — used in World Wide Web addresses

gov·ern \'gə-vərn\ *vb* [ME, fr. AF *governer*, fr. L *gubernare* to steer, govern, fr. Gk *kybernan*] 1 : to control and direct the making and administration of policy in : RESTRAIN — **gov·ern·able** \-vər-nə-bəl\ *adj* — **gov·er·nance** \-vər-nəns\ *n* 2 : CONTROL, DIRECT, INFLUENCE 3 : DETERMINE, REGULATE 4

gov·ern·ess \'gə-vər-nəs\ *n* : a woman who teaches and trains a child esp. in a private home

gov·ern·ment \'gə-vərn-mənt\ *n* 1 : authoritative direction or control : RULE 2 : the making of policy 3 : the organization or agency through which a political unit exercises authority 4 : the complex of institutions, laws, and customs through which a political unit is governed 5 : the governing body — **gov·ern·men·tal** \ˌgə-vərn-'men-tᵊl\ *adj* — **gov·ern·men·tal·ly** \-'tᵊl-ē\ *adv*

gov·er·nor \'gə-vər-nər\ *n* 1 : one that governs; *esp* : a ruler, chief executive, or head of a political unit (as a state) 2 : an attachment to a machine for automatic control of speed — **gov·er·nor·ship** *n*

govt *abbr* government

gown \'gau̇n\ *n* 1 : a loose flowing outer garment 2 : an official robe worn esp. by a judge, clergyman, or teacher 3 : a woman's dress 〈evening ∼s〉 4 : a loose robe 5 : an academic community within a town or city — **gown** *vb*

gp *abbr* group

GP *abbr* general practitioner

GPO *abbr* 1 general post office 2 Government Printing Office

GPS \ˌjē-ˌpē-'es\ *n* [*Global Positioning System*] : a navigation system that uses satellite signals to fix location; *also* : the signal receiver itself

GQ *abbr* general quarters

gr *abbr* 1 grade 2 grain 3 gram 4 gravity 5 gross

grab \'grab\ *vb* **grabbed; grab·bing** : to take hastily : SNATCH — **grab** *n*

¹grace \'grās\ *n* 1 : unmerited help given to people by God (as in overcoming temptation) 2 : freedom from sin through divine grace 3 : a virtue coming from God 4 — used as a title for a duke, a duchess, or an archbishop 5 : a short prayer at a meal 6 : a temporary respite (as from the payment of a debt) 7 : APPROVAL, ACCEPTANCE 〈in his good ∼s〉

8 : CHARM 9 : ATTRACTIVENESS, BEAUTY 10 : fitness or proportion of line or expression 11 : ease of movement 12 : a musical trill or ornament — **grace·ful** \-fəl\ *adj* — **grace·ful·ly** *adv* — **grace·ful·ness** *n* — **grace·less** *adj*

²grace *vb* **graced; grac·ing** 1 : HONOR 2 : ADORN, EMBELLISH

gra·cious \'grā-shəs\ *adj* 1 : marked by kindness and courtesy 〈a ∼ host〉 2 : GRACEFUL 3 : characterized by charm and good taste 4 : MERCIFUL — **gra·cious·ly** *adv* — **gra·cious·ness** *n*

grack·le \'gra-kəl\ *n* : any of several large American blackbirds with glossy iridescent plumage

grad *abbr* graduate; graduated

gra·da·tion \grā-'dā-shən, grə-\ *n* 1 : a series forming successive stages 2 : a step, degree, or stage in a series 3 : an advance by regular degrees 4 : the act or process of grading

¹grade \'grād\ *n* [L *gradus* step, degree, fr. *gradi* to step, go] 1 : a position in a scale of rank, quality, or order 2 : a stage in a process or ranking 3 : a division of the school course representing one year's work; *also* : the pupils in such a division 4 : a class of persons or things of the same rank or quality 5 : a mark or rating esp. of accomplishment in school 6 : the degree of slope (as of a road); *also* : SLOPE 7 *pl* : the elementary school system

²grade *vb* **grad·ed; grad·ing** 1 : to arrange in grades : SORT 2 : to make level or evenly sloping 〈∼ a highway〉 3 : to give a grade to 〈∼ a pupil in history〉 4 : to assign to a grade

grade inflation *n* : the assigning of grades higher than previously assigned for given levels of achievement

grad·er \'grā-dər\ *n* 1 : a machine for leveling earth 2 : a pupil in a school grade

grade school *n* : ELEMENTARY SCHOOL

gra·di·ent \'grā-dē-ənt\ *n* : SLOPE, GRADE

grad·u·al \'gra-jə-wəl\ *adj* : proceeding or changing by steps or degrees 〈∼ improvements〉 — **grad·u·al·ly** *adv*

grad·u·al·ism \-wə-ˌli-zəm\ *n* : the policy of approaching a desired end gradually

¹grad·u·ate \'gra-jə-wət\ *n* 1 : a holder of an academic degree or diploma 2 : a graduated container for measuring contents

²graduate *adj* 1 : holding an academic degree or diploma 2 : of or relating to studies beyond the first or bachelor's degree 〈∼ school〉

³grad·u·ate \'gra-jə-ˌwāt\ *vb* **-at·ed; -at·ing** 1 : to grant or receive an academic degree or diploma 2 : to divide into grades, classes, or intervals 3 : to admit to a particular standing or grade

grad·u·a·tion \ˌgra-jə-'wā-shən\ *n* 1 : a mark that graduates something 2 : an act or process of graduating 3 : COMMENCEMENT 2

graf·fi·ti \grə-'fē-(ˌ)tē\ *n* : unauthorized writing or drawing on a public surface

graf·fi·to \grə-'fē-tō, grə-\ *n, pl* **-ti** \-(ˌ)tē\

: an inscription or drawing made on a public surface (as a wall)

¹**graft** \'graft\ *n* **1** : a grafted plant; *also* : the point of union in this **2** : material (as skin) used in grafting **3** : the getting of money or advantage dishonestly; *also* : the money or advantage so gained

²**graft** *vb* **1** : to insert a shoot from one plant into another so that they join and grow; *also* : to join one thing to another as in plant grafting ⟨~ skin over a burn⟩ **2** : to get (as money) dishonestly — **graft·er** *n*

gra·ham cracker \'grā-əm-, 'gram-\ *n* : a slightly sweet cracker made chiefly of whole wheat flour

Grail \'grāl\ *n* **1** : the cup or platter used according to medieval legend by Christ at the Last Supper and thereafter the object of knightly quests **2** *not cap* : the object of an extended or difficult quest

grain \'grān\ *n* **1** : a seed or fruit of a cereal grass **2** : seeds or fruits of various food plants and esp. cereal grasses; *also* : a plant (as wheat) producing grain **3** : a small hard particle **4** : a unit of weight based on the weight of a grain of wheat — see WEIGHT table **5** : TEXTURE; *also* : the arrangement of fibers in wood **6** : natural disposition ⟨lying goes against my ~⟩ — **grained** \'grānd\ *adj*

grain alcohol *n* : ALCOHOL 1

grainy \'grā-nē\ *adj* **grain·i·er; -est 1** : resembling or having some characteristic of grain : not smooth or fine **2** *of a photograph* : appearing to be composed of grain-like particles

¹**gram** \'gram\ *n* [F *gramme*, fr. LL *gramma*, a small weight, fr. Gk *gramma* letter, writing, a small weight, fr. *graphein* to write] : a metric unit of mass and weight equal to ¹/₁₀₀₀ kilogram — see METRIC SYSTEM table

²**gram** *abbr* grammar; grammatical

-gram \,gram\ *n comb form* : drawing : writing : record ⟨telegram⟩

gram·mar \'gra-mər\ *n* **1** : the study of the classes of words, their inflections, and their functions and relations in the sentence **2** : a study of what is to be preferred and what avoided in inflection and syntax **3** : speech or writing evaluated according to its conformity to grammatical rules — **gram·mar·i·an** \grə-'mer-ē-ən, -'mar-\ *n* — **gram·mat·i·cal** \-'ma-ti-kəl\ *adj* — **gram·mat·i·cal·ly** \-k(ə-)lē\ *adv*

grammar school *n* **1** : a secondary school emphasizing Latin and Greek in preparation for college; *also* : a British college preparatory school **2** : a school intermediate between the primary grades and high school **3** : ELEMENTARY SCHOOL

gramme \'gram\ *chiefly Brit var of* GRAM

gram-o-phone \'gra-mə-,fōn\ *n* : PHONOGRAPH

gra·na·ry \'grā-nə-rē, 'gra-\ *n, pl* **-ries 1** : a storehouse for grain **2** : a region producing grain in abundance

¹**grand** \'grand\ *adj* **1** : higher in rank or importance : FOREMOST, CHIEF **2** : great

in size **3** : INCLUSIVE, COMPLETE ⟨a ~ total⟩ **4** : MAGNIFICENT, SPLENDID **5** : showing wealth or high social standing **6** : IMPRESSIVE, STATELY **7** : very good : FINE ⟨had a ~ time⟩ — **grand·ly** *adv* — **grand·ness** *n*

²**grand** *n, pl* **grand** *slang* : a thousand dollars

gran·dam \'gran-,dam, -dəm\ *or* **gran·dame** \-,dām, -dəm\ *n* : an old woman

grand·child \'grand-,chī(-ə)ld\ *n* : a child of one's son or daughter

grand·daugh·ter \'gran-,dȯ-tər\ *n* : a daughter of one's son or daughter

grande dame \'grän-'däm\ *n, pl* **grandes dames** \-'däm\ : a usu. elderly woman of great prestige or ability

gran·dee \gran-'dē\ *n* : a high-ranking Spanish or Portuguese nobleman

gran·deur \'gran-jər\ *n* **1** : the quality or state of being grand : MAGNIFICENCE **2** : something that is grand

grand·fa·ther \'grand-,fä-thər\ *n* : the father of one's father or mother; *also* : ANCESTOR

grandfather clock *n* : a tall clock that stands on the floor

gran·dil·o·quence \gran-'di-lə-kwəns\ *n* : pompous eloquence — **gran·dil·o·quent** \-kwənt\ *adj*

gran·di·ose \'gran-dē-,ōs, ,gran-dē-'ōs\ *adj* : IMPRESSIVE, IMPOSING; *also* : affectedly splendid — **gran·di·ose·ly** *adv* — **gran·di·os·i·ty** \,gran-dē-'ä-sə-tē\ *n*

grand jury *n* : a jury that examines accusations of crime against persons and makes formal charges on which the persons are later tried

grand mal \'grän-,mäl; 'grand-,mal\ *n* [F, lit., great illness] : severe epilepsy

grand·moth·er \'grand-,mə-thər\ *n* : the mother of one's father or mother; *also* : a female ancestor

grand·par·ent \-,per-ənt\ *n* : a parent of one's father or mother

grand piano *n* : a piano with horizontal frame and strings

grand prix \'grän-'prē\ *n, pl* **grand prix** *same or* -'prēz\ *often cap G&P* : a long-distance auto race over a road course; *also* : a high-level competition in another sport (as sailing)

grand slam *n* **1** : a total victory or success **2** : a home run hit with three runners on base

grand·son \'grand-,sən\ *n* : a son of one's son or daughter

grand·stand \-,stand\ *n* : a usu. roofed stand for spectators at a racecourse or stadium

grange \'grānj\ *n* **1** : a farm or farmhouse with its various buildings **2** *cap* : one of the lodges of a national association originally made up of farmers; *also* : the association itself — **Grang·er** \'grān-jər\ *n*

gran·ite \'gra-nət\ *n* : a hard granular igneous rock used esp. for building — **gra·nit·ic** \gra-'ni-tik\ *adj*

gran·ite·ware \'gra-nət-,wer\ *n* : ironware with mottled enamel

gra·no·la \grə-'nō-lə\ n : a cereal made of rolled oats and usu. raisins and nuts

¹**grant** \'grant\ vb 1 : to consent to : ALLOW, PERMIT 2 : GIVE, BESTOW ⟨~ed land to settlers⟩ 3 : to admit as true — **grant·er** n — **grant·or** \'gran-tər, -,tȯr\ n

²**grant** n 1 : the act of granting 2 : something granted; esp : a gift for a particular purpose ⟨a ~ for study abroad⟩ 3 : a transfer of property by deed or writing; also : the instrument by which such a transfer is made 4 : the property transferred by grant — **grant·ee** \gran-'tē\ n

gran·u·lar \'gra-nyə-lər\ adj : consisting of or appearing to consist of granules — **gran·u·lar·i·ty** \,gra-nyə-'lar-ə-tē\ n

gran·u·late \'gra-nyə-,lāt\ vb -lat·ed; -lating : to form into grains or crystals — **gran·u·la·tion** \,gra-nyə-'lā-shən\ n

gran·ule \'gra-nyül\ n : a small grain or particle

grape \'grāp\ n [ME, fr. AF, grape stalk, bunch of grapes, grape, of Gmc origin] 1 : a smooth-skinned juicy edible greenish white, deep red, or purple berry that is the chief source of wine 2 : any of numerous woody vines widely grown for their bunches of grapes

grape·fruit \'grāp-,früt\ n 1 pl **grapefruit** or **grapefruits** : a large edible yellowskinned citrus fruit 2 : a tree bearing grapefruit

grape hyacinth n : any of several small bulbous herbs related to the lilies that produce clusters of usu. blue flowers in the spring

grape·shot \'grāp-,shät\ n : a cluster of small iron balls formerly fired at people from short range by a cannon

grape·vine \-,vīn\ n 1 : GRAPE 2 2 : RUMOR; also : an informal means of circulating information or gossip

graph \'graf\ n : a diagram that usu. by means of dots and lines shows change in one variable factor in comparison with one or more other factors — **graph** vb

-graph \,graf\ n comb form 1 : something written ⟨autograph⟩ 2 : instrument for making or transmitting records ⟨seismograph⟩

¹**graph·ic** \'gra-fik\ also **graph·i·cal** \-fi-kəl\ adj 1 : of or relating to the arts (**graphic arts**) of representation, decoration, and printing on flat surfaces 2 : being written, drawn, or engraved 3 : vividly described ⟨~ details⟩ — **graph·i·cal·ly** \-fi-k(ə-)lē\ adv

²**graphic** n 1 : a picture, map, or graph used for illustration 2 : a pictorial image displayed on a computer screen

graphical user interface n : a computer program designed to allow easy user interaction esp. by having graphic menus or icons

graph·ics tablet \-fiks-\ n : a computer input device for entering pictorial information by drawing or tracing

graph·ite \'gra-,fīt\ n [G Graphit, fr. Gk graphein to write] : a soft black form of carbon used esp. for lead pencils and lubricants

grap·nel \'grap-nəl\ n : a small anchor

used esp. to recover a sunken object or to anchor a small boat

¹**grap·ple** \'gra-pəl\ n : the act of grappling

²**grapple** vb **grap·pled; grap·pling** 1 : to seize or hold with or as if with a hooked implement 2 : to come to grips with : WRESTLE

¹**grasp** \'grasp\ vb 1 : to make the motion of seizing 2 : to take or seize firmly 3 : to enclose and hold with the fingers or arms 4 : COMPREHEND

²**grasp** n 1 : HANDLE 2 : EMBRACE 3 : HOLD, CONTROL 4 : the reach of the arms 5 : the power of seizing and holding or attaining 6 : COMPREHENSION

grasp·ing adj : GREEDY, AVARICIOUS

grass \'gras\ n 1 : herbage for grazing animals 2 : any of a large family of plants (as wheat, bamboo, or sugarcane) with jointed stems and narrow leaves 3 : grass-covered land 4 : MARIJUANA — **grass·like** \-,līk\ adj — **grassy** adj

grass·hop·per \-,hä-pər\ n : any of numerous leaping plant-eating insects

grass·land \-,land\ n : land covered naturally or under cultivation with grasses and low-growing herbs

grass roots n pl : society at the local level as distinguished from the centers of political leadership

¹**grate** \'grāt\ vb **grat·ed; grat·ing** 1 : to pulverize by rubbing against something rough 2 : to grind or rub against with a rasping noise 3 : IRRITATE — **grat·er** n — **grat·ing·ly** adv

²**grate** n 1 : GRATING 2 : a frame of iron bars for holding fuel while it burns

grate·ful \'grāt-fəl\ adj 1 : THANKFUL, APPRECIATIVE; also : expressing gratitude 2 : PLEASING — **grate·ful·ly** adv — **grate·ful·ness** n

grat·i·fy \'gra-tə-,fī\ vb -fied; -fy·ing : to afford pleasure to — **grat·i·fi·ca·tion** \,gra-tə-fə-'kā-shən\ n

grat·ing \'grā-tiŋ\ n : a framework with parallel bars or crossbars

gra·tis \'gra-təs, 'grā-\ adv or adj : without charge or recompense : FREE

grat·i·tude \'gra-tə-,tüd, -,tyüd\ n : THANKFULNESS

gra·tu·itous \grə-'tü-ə-təs, -'tyü-\ adj 1 : done or provided without recompense : FREE 2 : UNWARRANTED ⟨a ~ assumption⟩ ⟨~ violence in movies⟩

gra·tu·ity \-ə-tē\ n, pl -ities : ¹⁰TIP

gra·va·men \grə-'vä-mən\ n, pl **-va·mens** or **-vam·i·na** \-'va-mə-nə\ [LL, burden] : the basic or significant part of a grievance or complaint

¹**grave** \'grāv\ vb **graved; grav·en** \'grā-vən\ or **graved; grav·ing** : SCULPTURE, ENGRAVE

²**grave** n : an excavation in the earth as a place of burial; also : TOMB

³**grave** \'grāv; 5 also 'gräv\ adj 1 : IMPORTANT 2 : threatening sharp harm or danger 3 : DIGNIFIED, SOLEMN 4 : drab in color : SOMBER 5 : of, marked by, or being an accent mark having the form ` — **grave·ly** adv — **grave·ness** n

grav·el \'gra-vəl\ n : pebbles and small

pieces of rock larger than grains of sand
— **grav·el·ly** adj

Graves' disease \'grāvz-\ n : hyperthyroidism characterized by goiter and often protrusion of the eyeballs

grave·stone \'grāv-ˌstōn\ n : a burial monument

grave·yard \-ˌyärd\ n : CEMETERY

grav·id \'gra-vəd\ adj [L gravidus, fr. gravis heavy] : PREGNANT

gra·vi·me·ter \gra-'vi-mə-tər, 'gra-və-ˌmē-\ n : a device for measuring variations in a gravitational field

grav·i·tate \'gra-və-ˌtāt\ vb -tat·ed; -tating : to move or tend to move toward something

grav·i·ta·tion \ˌgra-və-'tā-shən\ n 1 : a natural force of attraction that tends to draw bodies together and that occurs because of the mass of the bodies 2 : the action or process of gravitating — **grav·i·ta·tion·al** \-shə-nəl\ adj — **grav·i·ta·tion·al·ly** adv

grav·i·ty \'gra-və-tē\ n, pl **-ties** 1 : IMPORTANCE; esp : SERIOUSNESS 2 : ²MASS 5 3 : the gravitational attraction of the mass of a celestial object (as earth) for bodies close to it; also : GRAVITATION 1

gra·vure \grə-'vyùr\ n [F] : PHOTOGRAVURE

gra·vy \'grā-vē\ n, pl **gravies** 1 : a sauce made from the thickened and seasoned juices of cooked meat 2 : unearned or illicit gain : GRAFT

¹**gray** also **grey** \'grā\ adj 1 : of the color gray; also : dull in color 2 : having gray hair 3 : CHEERLESS, DISMAL ⟨a ~ day⟩ 4 : intermediate in position or character ⟨an ethically ~ area⟩ — **gray·ish** adj — **gray·ness** n

²**gray** also **grey** n 1 : something of a gray color 2 : a neutral color ranging between black and white

³**gray** also **grey** vb : to make or become gray

gray·beard \'grā-ˌbird\ n : an old man

gray·ling \'grā-liŋ\ n, pl **grayling** also **graylings** : any of several slender freshwater food and sport fishes related to the trouts

gray matter n 1 : the grayish part of nervous tissue consisting mostly of the cell bodies of neurons 2 : INTELLIGENCE

gray wolf n : a large wolf of northern No. America and Asia that is usu. gray

¹**graze** \'grāz\ vb **grazed; graz·ing** [ME grasen, fr. OE grasian, fr. græs grass] 1 : to feed on herbage or pasture 2 : to feed (livestock) on grass or pasture — **graz·er** n

²**graze** vb **grazed; graz·ing** 1 : to touch lightly in passing 2 : SCRATCH, ABRADE

¹**grease** \'grēs\ n 1 : rendered animal fat 2 : oily material 3 : a thick lubricant — **greasy** \'grē-sē, -zē\ adj

²**grease** \'grēs, 'grēz\ vb **greased; greasing** : to smear or lubricate with grease

grease·paint \'grēs-ˌpānt\ n : theater makeup

¹**great** \'grāt\ adj 1 : large in size : BIG 2 : ELABORATE, AMPLE ⟨in ~ detail⟩ 3 : large in number : NUMEROUS 4 : being

beyond the average : MIGHTY, INTENSE ⟨a ~ weight⟩ ⟨in ~ pain⟩ 5 : EMINENT, GRAND 6 : long continued ⟨a ~ while⟩ 7 : MAIN, PRINCIPAL ⟨a reception in the ~ hall⟩ 8 : more distant in a family relationship by one generation ⟨a great-grandfather⟩ 9 : markedly superior in character, quality, or skill ⟨~ at bridge⟩ 10 : EXCELLENT, FINE ⟨had a ~ time⟩ — **great·ly** adv — **great·ness** n

great ape n : any of a family of primates including the gorilla, orangutan, and chimpanzees

great blue heron n : a large crested grayish-blue American heron

great circle n : a circle on the surface of a sphere that has the same center as the sphere; esp : one on the surface of the earth an arc of which is the shortest travel distance between two points

great·coat \'grāt-ˌkōt\ n : a heavy overcoat

Great Dane n : any of a breed of very tall powerful smooth-coated dogs

great·er adj, often cap : consisting of a central city together with adjacent areas ⟨~ London⟩

great·heart·ed \'grāt-'här-təd\ adj 1 : COURAGEOUS 2 : MAGNANIMOUS

great power n, often cap G&P : one of the nations that figure most decisively in international affairs

great white shark n : a large and dangerous shark of warm seas that has large saw-edged teeth and is whitish below and bluish or brownish above

grebe \'grēb\ n : any of a family of lobe-toed diving birds related to the loons

Gre·cian \'grē-shən\ adj : GREEK

greed \'grēd\ n : acquisitive or selfish desire beyond reason — **greed·i·ly** \'grē-də-lē\ adv — **greed·i·ness** \-dē-nəs\ n — **greedy** \'grē-dē\ adj

¹**Greek** \'grēk\ n 1 : a native or inhabitant of Greece 2 : the ancient or modern language of Greece

²**Greek** adj 1 : of, relating to, or characteristic of Greece, the Greeks, or Greek 2 : ORTHODOX 3

¹**green** \'grēn\ adj 1 : of the color green 2 : covered with verdure; also : consisting of green plants or of the leafy parts of plants ⟨a ~ salad⟩ 3 : UNRIPE; also : IMMATURE 4 : having a sickly appearance 5 : not fully processed or treated ⟨~ liquor⟩ ⟨~ hides⟩ 6 : INEXPERIENCED; also : NAIVE 7 : concerned with or supporting environmentalism ⟨~ companies⟩ — **green·ish** adj — **green·ness** n

²**green** vb : to make or become green

³**green** n 1 : a color between blue and yellow in the spectrum : the color of growing fresh grass or of the emerald 2 : something of a green color 3 : green vegetation; esp, pl : leafy herbs or leafy parts of a vegetable ⟨collard ~s⟩ ⟨beet ~s⟩ 4 : a grassy plot; esp : a smooth grassy area around the hole into which the ball must be played in golf

green·back \'grēn-ˌbak\ n : a U.S. legal-tender note

green bean n : a kidney bean that is used

as a snap bean when the pods are colored green

green·belt \'grēn-ˌbelt\ *n* : a belt of parks or farmlands around a community

green card *n* : an identity card attesting the permanent resident status of an alien in the U.S.

green·ery \'grē-nə-rē\ *n, pl* **-er·ies** : green foliage or plants

green–eyed \'grē-ˈnīd\ *adj* : JEALOUS

green·gro·cer \'grēn-ˌgrō-sər\ *n, chiefly Brit* : a retailer of fresh vegetables and fruit

green·horn \-ˌhȯrn\ *n* : an inexperienced person; *also* : NEWCOMER

green·house \-ˌhau̇s\ *n* : a glass structure for the growing of tender plants

greenhouse effect *n* : warming of a planet's atmosphere that occurs when the sun's radiation passes through the atmosphere, is absorbed by the planet, and is reradiated as radiation of longer wavelength that can be absorbed by atmospheric gases

green manure *n* : an herbaceous crop (as clover) plowed under when green to enrich the soil

green onion *n* : a young onion pulled before the bulb has enlarged and used esp. in salads : SCALLION

green pepper *n* : a sweet pepper before it turns red at maturity

green·room \'grēn-ˌrüm, -ˌru̇m\ *n* : a room (as in a theater or studio) where performers can relax before, between, or after appearances

green·sward \-ˌswȯrd\ *n* : turf that is green with growing grass

green thumb *n* : an unusual ability to make plants grow

green·wash·ing \'grēn-ˌwȯ-shiŋ, -ˌwä-\ *n* : expressions of environmentalist concerns as a cover for products, policies, or activities deleterious to the environment

Green·wich mean time \'gri-nij-, 'gre-, -nich-\ *n* [*Greenwich*, England] : the time of the meridian of Greenwich used historically as the basis of worldwide standard time

Greenwich time *n* : GREENWICH MEAN TIME

green·wood \'grēn-ˌwu̇d\ *n* : a forest that is green with foliage

greet \'grēt\ *vb* **1** : to address with expressions of kind wishes **2** : to meet or react to in a specified manner **3** : to be perceived by — **greet·er** *n*

greet·ing *n* **1** : a salutation on meeting **2** *pl* : best wishes : REGARDS

greeting card *n* : a card that bears a message usu. sent on a special occasion

gre·gar·i·ous \gri-ˈger-ē-əs\ *adj* [L *gregarius* of a flock or herd, fr. *greg-, grex* flock, herd] **1** : SOCIAL, COMPANIONABLE **2** : tending to flock together — **gre·gar·i·ous·ly** *adv* — **gre·gar·i·ous·ness** *n*

grem·lin \'grem-lən\ *n* : a cause of error or equipment malfunction conceived of as a small gnome

gre·nade \grə-ˈnād\ *n* [MF, lit., pomegranate, fr. LL *granata*, fr. L, fem. of *granatus* seedy, fr. *granum* grain] : a small bomb that is thrown by hand or launched (as by a rifle)

gren·a·dier \ˌgre-nə-ˈdir\ *n* : a member of a European regiment formerly armed with grenades

gren·a·dine \ˌgre-nə-ˈdēn, 'gre-nə-ˌdēn\ *n* : a syrup flavored with pomegranates and used in mixed drinks

grew *past of* GROW

grey *var of* GRAY

grey·hound \'grā-ˌhau̇nd\ *n* : any of a breed of tall slender dogs noted for speed and keen sight

grid \'grid\ *n* **1** : GRATING **2** : a network of conductors for distributing electric power **3** : a network of horizontal and perpendicular lines (as for locating points on a map) **4** : GRIDIRON 2; *also* : FOOTBALL

grid·dle \'gri-dᵊl\ *n* : a flat usu. metal surface for cooking food

griddle cake *n* : PANCAKE

grid·iron \'grid-ˌī(-ə)rn\ *n* **1** : a grate for broiling food **2** : a football field

grid·lock \-ˌläk\ *n* : a traffic jam in which an intersection is so blocked that vehicles cannot move

grief \'grēf\ *n* **1** : emotional distress caused by or as if by bereavement; *also* : a cause of such distress **2** : DISASTER ⟨the expedition came to ∼⟩; *also* : MISHAP

griev·ance \'grē-vəns\ *n* **1** : a cause of distress affording reason for complaint or resistance **2** : COMPLAINT

grieve \'grēv\ *vb* **grieved; griev·ing** [ME *greven*, fr. AF *grever*, fr. L *gravare* to burden, fr. *gravis* heavy, grave] **1** : to cause grief or sorrow to : DISTRESS **2** : to feel grief : SORROW

griev·ous \'grē-vəs\ *adj* **1** : causing suffering, grief, or sorrow : SEVERE ⟨a ∼ wound⟩ **2** : OPPRESSIVE, ONEROUS ⟨∼ costs of war⟩ **3** : SERIOUS, GRAVE ⟨a ∼ fault⟩ — **griev·ous·ly** *adv*

¹grill \'gril\ *vb* **1** : to broil on a grill; *also* : to fry or toast on a griddle **2** : to question intensely ⟨∼ a suspect⟩

²grill *n* **1** : a cooking utensil of parallel bars on which food is grilled **2** : a usu. informal restaurant

grille *or* **grill** \'gril\ *n* : a grating that forms a barrier or screen

grill·work \'gril-ˌwərk\ *n* : work constituting or resembling a grille

grim \'grim\ *adj* **grim·mer; grim·mest 1** : CRUEL, FIERCE **2** : harsh and forbidding in appearance **3** : ghastly or repellent in character **4** : RELENTLESS — **grim·ly** *adv* — **grim·ness** *n*

gri·mace \'gri-məs, gri-ˈmās\ *n* : a facial expression usu. of disgust or disapproval — **grimace** *vb*

grime \'grīm\ *n* : soot, smut, or dirt adhering to or embedded in a surface; *also* : accumulated dirtiness and disorder — **grimy** *adj*

grin \'grin\ *vb* **grinned; grin·ning** : to draw back the lips so as to show the teeth esp. in amusement — **grin** *n*

¹grind \'grīnd\ *vb* **ground** \'grau̇nd\; **grind·ing 1** : to reduce to small particles

2 : to wear down, polish, or sharpen by friction 3 : OPPRESS 4 : to press with a grating noise : GRIT ⟨~ the teeth⟩ 5 : to operate or produce by turning a crank 6 : DRUDGE; *esp* : to study hard 7 : to move with difficulty or friction ⟨gears ~*ing*⟩

²**grind** *n* 1 : dreary monotonous labor, routine, or study 2 : one who works or studies excessively

grind·er \'grīn-dər\ *n* 1 : MOLAR 2 *pl* : TEETH 3 : one that grinds 4 : SUBMARINE 2 5 : an athlete who succeeds through hard work and determination

grind·stone \'grīnd-ˌstōn\ *n* : a flat circular stone of natural sandstone that revolves on an axle and is used for grinding, shaping, or smoothing

¹**grip** \'grip\ *vb* **gripped; grip·ping** 1 : to seize or hold firmly 2 : to hold the interest of strongly ⟨*gripped* by the story⟩

²**grip** *n* 1 : GRASP; *also* : strength in gripping 2 : a firm tenacious hold 3 : UNDERSTANDING 4 : a device for gripping 5 : TRAVELING BAG

gripe \'grīp\ *vb* **griped; grip·ing** 1 : IRRITATE, VEX 2 : to cause or experience spasmodic pains in the bowels 3 : COMPLAIN — **gripe** *n*

grippe \'grip\ *n* : INFLUENZA

gris–gris \'grē-ˌgrē\ *n, pl* **gris–gris** \-ˌgrēz\ [F] : an amulet or incantation used chiefly by people of black African ancestry

gris·ly \'griz-lē\ *adj* **gris·li·er; -est** : HORRIBLE, GRUESOME

grist \'grist\ *n* : grain to be ground or already ground

gris·tle \'gri-səl\ *n* : CARTILAGE — **gris·tly** \'gris-lē\ *adj*

grist·mill \'grist-ˌmil\ *n* : a mill for grinding grain

¹**grit** \'grit\ *n* 1 : a hard sharp granule (as of sand); *also* : material composed of such granules 2 : unyielding courage ⟨the pioneers' ~⟩ — **grit·ty** *adj*

²**grit** *vb* **grit·ted; grit·ting** : GRIND, GRATE

grits \'grits\ *n pl* : coarsely ground hulled grain ⟨hominy ~⟩

griz·zled \'gri-zəld\ *adj* : streaked or mixed with gray; *also* : having gray hair

griz·zly \'griz-lē\ *adj* **griz·zli·er; -est** : GRIZZLED

grizzly bear *n* : a large powerful brownish bear of western No. America

gro *abbr* gross

groan \'grōn\ *vb* 1 : MOAN 2 : to make a harsh sound under sudden or prolonged strain ⟨the chair ~*ed* under his weight⟩ — **groan** *n*

groat \'grōt\ *n* : an old British coin worth four pennies

gro·cer \'grō-sər\ *n* [ME, fr. AF *groser* wholesaler, fr. *gros* coarse, wholesale, fr. L *grossus* coarse] : a dealer esp. in staple foodstuffs — **gro·cery** \'grōs-rē, 'grōsh-, 'grō-sə-\ *n*

grog \'gräg\ *n* [*Old Grog*, nickname of Edward Vernon †1757 Eng. admiral responsible for diluting the sailors' rum] : alcoholic liquor; *esp* : liquor (as rum) mixed with water

grog·gy \'grä-gē\ *adj* **grog·gi·er; -est**

: weak and unsteady on the feet or in action — **grog·gi·ly** \-gə-lē\ *adv* — **grog·gi·ness** \-gē-nəs\ *n*

groin \'groin\ *n* 1 : the juncture of the lower abdomen and inner part of the thigh; *also* : the region of this juncture 2 : the curved line or rib on a ceiling along which two vaults meet

grok \'gräk\ *vb* **grokked grok·king** : to understand profoundly and intuitively

grom·met \'grä-mət, 'grə-\ *n* 1 : a ring of rope 2 : an eyelet of firm material to strengthen or protect an opening

¹**groom** \'grüm, 'grum\ *n* 1 : a person responsible for the care of horses 2 : BRIDEGROOM

²**groom** *vb* 1 : to clean and care for (an animal) 2 : to make neat or attractive 3 : PREPARE

grooms·man \'grümz-mən, 'grumz-\ *n* : a male friend who attends a bridegroom at his wedding

groove \'grüv\ *n* 1 : a long narrow channel 2 : a fixed routine — **groove** *vb*

groovy \'grü-vē\ *adj* **groov·i·er; -est** 1 : EXCELLENT 2 : HIP

grope \'grōp\ *vb* **groped; grop·ing** 1 : to feel about or search for blindly or uncertainly ⟨~ for the right word⟩ 2 : to feel one's way by groping

gros·beak \'grōs-ˌbēk\ *n* : any of several finches of Europe or America with large stout conical bills

gro·schen \'grō-shən\ *n, pl* **groschen** : a former Austrian monetary unit equal to ¹/₁₀₀ schilling

gros·grain \'grō-ˌgrān\ *n* [F *gros grain* coarse texture] : a silk or rayon fabric with crosswise cotton ribs

¹**gross** \'grōs\ *adj* 1 : glaringly noticeable 2 : OUT-AND-OUT, UTTER 3 : BIG, BULKY; *esp* : excessively fat 4 : GENERAL, BROAD 5 : consisting of an overall total exclusive of deductions ⟨~ earnings⟩ 6 : CARNAL, EARTHY ⟨~ pleasures⟩ 7 : UNREFINED; *also* : crudely vulgar 8 : lacking knowledge — **gross·ly** *adv* — **gross·ness** *n*

²**gross** *n* : an overall total exclusive of deductions — **gross** *vb*

³**gross** *n, pl* **gross** : a total of 12 dozen things ⟨a ~ of pencils⟩

gross domestic product *n* : the gross national product excluding the value of net income earned abroad

gross national product *n* : the total value of the goods and services produced in a nation during a year

gro·szy \'grō-shē\ *n, pl* **groszy** — see *zloty* at MONEY table

grot \'grät\ *n* : GROTTO

gro·tesque \grō-'tesk\ *adj* 1 : FANCIFUL, BIZARRE 2 : absurdly incongruous 3 : ECCENTRIC — **gro·tesque·ly** *adv*

grot·to \'grä-tō\ *n, pl* **grottoes** *also* **grottos** 1 : CAVE 2 : an artificial cavelike structure

grouch \'grauch\ *n* 1 : a fit of bad temper 2 : a habitually irritable or complaining person — **grouch** *vb* — **grouchy** *adj*

¹**ground** \'graund\ *n* 1 : the bottom of a body of water 2 *pl* : sediment at the bottom of a liquid 3 : a basis for belief, ac-

tion, or argument **4** : BACKGROUND **5** : the surface of the earth; *also* : SOIL **6** : an area with a particular use ⟨fishing ∼s⟩ **7** *pl* : the area about and belonging to a building **8** : a conductor that makes electrical connection with the earth — **ground·less** *adj*

²**ground** *vb* **1** : to bring to or place on the ground **2** : to run or cause to run aground **3** : to provide a reason or justification for **4** : to furnish with a foundation of knowledge **5** : to connect electrically with a ground **6** : to restrict to the ground; *also* : prohibit from some activity ⟨∼ed for a week⟩

³**ground** *past and past part of* GRIND

ground ball *n* : a batted baseball that rolls or bounces along the ground

ground cover *n* : low plants that grow over and cover the soil; *also* : a plant suitable for use as ground cover

ground·ed \'graún-dəd\ *adj* : mentally and emotionally stable

ground·er \'graún-dər\ *n* : GROUND BALL

ground·hog \'graund-ˌhóg, -ˌhäg\ *n* : WOODCHUCK

ground·ling \'graúnd-lin\ *n* : a spectator in the pit of an Elizabethan theater

ground rule *n* **1** : a sports rule adopted to modify play on a particular field, court, or course **2** : a rule of procedure

ground squirrel *n* : any of various burrowing squirrels of No. America and Eurasia that often live in colonies in open areas

ground swell *n* **1** : a broad deep ocean swell caused by an often distant gale or earthquake **2** *usu* **ground·swell** : a rapid spontaneous growth (as of political opinion)

ground·wa·ter \'graúnd-ˌwó-tər, -ˌwä-\ *n* : water within the earth that supplies wells and springs

ground·work \-ˌwərk\ *n* : FOUNDATION, BASIS

ground zero *n* **1** : the point above, below, or at which a nuclear explosion occurs **2** : the center or origin of rapid, intense, or violent activity

¹**group** \'grüp\ *n* **1** : a number of individuals related by a common factor (as physical association, community of interests, or blood) **2** : a combination of atoms commonly found together in a molecule ⟨a methyl ∼⟩

²**group** *vb* : to associate in groups : CLUSTER, AGGREGATE

grou·per \'grü-pər\ *n, pl* **groupers** *also* **grouper** : any of numerous large solitary bottom fishes of warm seas

group home *n* : a residence for persons requiring care or supervision

group·ie \'grü-pē\ *n* : a fan of a rock group who usu. follows the group around on concert tours; *also* : ENTHUSIAST, FAN

group therapy *n* : therapy in the presence of a therapist in which several patients discuss their personal problems

groupware \'grüp-ˌwer\ *n* : software that enables users to work jointly via a network on projects or files

¹**grouse** \'graús\ *n, pl* **grouse** *or* **grouses**

: any of various chiefly ground-dwelling game birds that have feathered legs and are usu. of reddish brown or other protective color

²**grouse** *vb* **groused; grous·ing** : COMPLAIN, GRUMBLE

grout \'graút\ *n* : material (as mortar) used for filling spaces — **grout** *vb*

grove \'grōv\ *n* : a small wood usu. without underbrush

grov·el \'grä-vəl, 'grə-\ *vb* **-eled** *or* **-elled; -el·ing** *or* **-el·ling** **1** : to creep or lie with the body prostrate in fear or humility **2** : to abase oneself

grow \'grō\ *vb* **grew** \'grü\; **grown** \'grōn\; **grow·ing** **1** : to spring up and develop to maturity **2** : to be able to grow : THRIVE **3** : to take on some relation through or as if through growth ⟨tree limbs grown together⟩ **4** : INCREASE, EXPAND **5** : to develop from a parent source **6** : BECOME **7** : to have an increasing influence **8** : to cause to grow ⟨∼ a business⟩ — **grow·er** *n*

growing pains *n pl* **1** : pains in the legs of growing children having no known relation to growth **2** : the stresses and strains attending a new project or development

growl \'graú(-ə)l\ *vb* **1** : RUMBLE **2** : to utter a deep throaty sound **3** : GRUMBLE — **growl** *n*

grown–up \'grō-ˌnəp\ *adj* : not childish : ADULT — **grown–up** *n*

growth \'grōth\ *n* **1** : stage or condition attained in growing **2** : a process of growing esp. through progressive development or increase **3** : a result or product of growing ⟨a fine ∼ of hair⟩; *also* : an abnormal mass of tissue (as a tumor)

growth hormone *n* : a vertebrate hormone that is secreted by the pituitary gland and regulates growth

growth industry *n* : a business, interest, or activity that is increasingly popular, profitable, or trendy

¹**grub** \'grəb\ *vb* **grubbed; grub·bing** **1** : to clear or root out by digging **2** : to dig in the ground usu. for a hidden object **3** : to search about

²**grub** *n* **1** : a soft thick wormlike insect larva ⟨beetle ∼s⟩ **2** : DRUDGE; *also* : a slovenly person **3** : FOOD

grub·by \'grə-bē\ *adj* **grub·bi·er; -est** : DIRTY, SLOVENLY ⟨∼ clothes⟩ — **grub·bi·ness** \-bē-nəs\ *n*

grub·stake \'grəb-ˌstāk\ *n* : supplies or funds furnished a mining prospector in return for a share in his finds

¹**grudge** \'grəj\ *vb* **grudged; grudg·ing** : to be reluctant to give : BEGRUDGE

²**grudge** *n* : a feeling of deep-seated resentment or ill will

gru·el \'grü-əl\ *n* : a thin porridge

gru·el·ing *or* **gru·el·ling** \'grü-liŋ, 'grü-ə-\ *adj* : requiring extreme effort : EXHAUSTING ⟨a ∼ race⟩

grue·some \'grü-səm\ *adj* [fr. earlier *growsome*, fr. E dial. *grow, grue* to shiver] : inspiring horror or repulsion — **grue·some·ly** *adv* — **grue·some·ness** *n*

gruff \'grəf\ *adj* **1** : rough in speech or

manner **2** : being deep and harsh : HOARSE — **gruff·ly** adv

grum·ble \'grəm-bəl\ vb **grum·bled; grum·bling 1** : to mutter in discontent **2** : GROWL, RUMBLE — **grum·bler** n

grumpy \'grəm-pē\ adj **grump·i·er; -est** : moodily cross : SURLY — **grump·i·ly** \-pə-lē\ adv — **grump·i·ness** \-pē-nəs\ n

grunge \'grənj\ n **1** : one that is grungy **2** : heavy metal rock music expressing alienation and discontent **3** : untidy or tattered clothing typically worn by grunge fans

grun·gy \'grən-jē\ adj **grun·gi·er; -est** : shabby or dirty in character or condition

grun·ion \'grən-yən\ n : a fish of the California coast which comes inshore to spawn at nearly full moon

grunt \'grənt\ n : a deep throaty sound (as that of a hog) — **grunt** vb

GSA abbr **1** General Services Administration **2** Girl Scouts of America

G suit n [gravity] : a suit for a pilot or astronaut designed to counteract the physiological effects of acceleration

GSUSA abbr Girl Scouts of the United States of America

gt abbr great

Gt Brit abbr Great Britain

gtd abbr guaranteed

GU abbr Guam

gua·ca·mo·le \ˌgwä-kə-'mō-lē\ n [MexSp, fr. Nahuatl āhuacamōlli, fr. āhuacatl avocado + mōlli sauce] : mashed and seasoned avocado

gua·nine \'gwä-ˌnēn\ n : a purine base that codes genetic information in the molecular chain of DNA and RNA

gua·no \'gwä-nō\ n [Sp, fr. Quechua wanu fertilizer, dung] : excrement esp. of seabirds or bats; also : a fertilizer composed chiefly of this excrement

gua·ra·ni \ˌgwär-ə-'nē\ n, pl **guaranies** also **guaranis** — see MONEY table

¹**guar·an·tee** \ˌger-ən-'tē\ n **1** : GUARANTOR **2** : GUARANTY **3** : an agreement by which one person undertakes to secure another in the possession or enjoyment of something **4** : an assurance of the quality of or of the length of use to be expected from a product offered for sale **5** : GUARANTY 4

²**guarantee** vb **-teed; -tee·ing 1** : to undertake to answer for the debt, failure to perform, or faulty performance of (another) **2** : to undertake an obligation to establish, perform, or continue **3** : to give security to

guar·an·tor \ˌger-ən-'tòr\ n : one who gives a guarantee

¹**guar·an·ty** \'ger-ən-tē\ n, pl **-ties 1** : an undertaking to answer for another's failure to pay a debt or perform a duty **2** : GUARANTEE **3** : GUARANTOR **4** : PLEDGE, SECURITY

²**guaranty** vb **-tied; -ty·ing** : GUARANTEE

¹**guard** \'gärd\ n **1** : a person or a body of persons on sentinel duty **2** pl : troops assigned to protect a sovereign **3** : a defensive position (as in boxing) **4** : the act or duty of protecting or defending **5** : PRO-

TECTION **6** : a protective or safety device **7** : a football lineman playing between center and tackle; also : a basketball player stationed farthest from the goal — **on guard** : WATCHFUL, ALERT

²**guard** vb **1** : PROTECT, DEFEND **2** : to watch over **3** : to be on guard

guard·house \'gärd-ˌhaús\ n **1** : a building occupied by a guard or used as a headquarters by soldiers on guard duty **2** : a military jail

guard·ian \'gär-dē-ən\ n **1** : CUSTODIAN **2** : one who has the care of the person or property of another — **guard·ian·ship** n

guard·room \'gärd-ˌrüm\ n **1** : a room used by a military guard while on duty **2** : a room where military prisoners are confined

guards·man \'gärdz-mən\ n : a member of a military body called guard or guards

gua·va \'gwä-və\ n : the sweet yellow or pink acid fruit of a shrubby tropical American tree used esp. for making jam and jelly; also : the tree

gu·ber·na·to·ri·al \ˌgü-bər-nə-'tòr-ē-əl\ adj : of or relating to a governor

guer·don \'gər-dⁿn\ n : REWARD, RECOMPENSE

Guern·sey \'gərn-zē\ n, pl **Guernseys** : any of a breed of usu. reddish-brown and white dairy cattle that produce rich yellowish milk

guer·ril·la or **gue·ril·la** \gə-'ri-lə\ n [Sp guerrilla, fr. dim. of guerra war, of Gmc origin] : one who engages in irregular warfare esp. as a member of an independent unit

guess \'ges\ vb **1** : to form an opinion from little or no evidence **2** : BELIEVE, SUPPOSE **3** : to conjecture correctly about : DISCOVER — **guess** n

guest \'gest\ n **1** : a person to whom hospitality (as of a house or a club) is extended **2** : a patron of a commercial establishment (as a hotel) **3** : a person not a regular member of a cast who appears on a program

guest·house \'gest-ˌhaús\ n : a house run as a boarding house or bed-and-breakfast

guf·faw \(ˌ)gə-'fò\ n : a loud burst of laughter — **guf·faw** vb

guid·ance \'gī-dⁿns\ n **1** : the act or process of guiding **2** : ADVICE, DIRECTION

¹**guide** \'gīd\ n **1** : one who leads or directs another's course **2** : one who shows and explains points of interest **3** : something that provides guiding information; also : SIGNPOST **4** : a device to direct the motion of something

²**guide** vb **guid·ed; guid·ing 1** : to act as a guide to **2** : MANAGE, DIRECT **3** : to superintend the training of — **guid·able** \'gī-də-bəl\ adj

guide·book \'gīd-ˌbúk\ n : a book of information for travelers

guided missile n : a missile whose course may be altered during flight

guide dog n : a dog trained to lead the blind

guide·line \'gīd-ˌlīn\ n : an indication or outline of policy or conduct

guide word n : a term at the head of a

page of an alphabetical reference work that indicates the alphabetically first or last word on that page

gui·don \'gī-ˌdän, 'gī-dᵊn\ *n* : a small flag (as of a military unit)

guild \'gild\ *n* : an association of people with common aims and interests; *esp* : a medieval association of merchants or craftsmen — **guild·hall** \-ˌhȯl\ *n*

guil·der \'gil-dər\ *n* : GULDEN

guile \'gī(-ə)l\ *n* : deceitful cunning : DUPLICITY — **guile·ful** *adj* — **guile·less** *adj* — **guile·less·ness** *n*

guil·lo·tine \'gi-lə-ˌtēn, ˌgē-ə-'tēn\ *n* [F, fr. Joseph *Guillotin* †1814 Fr. physician] : a machine for beheading persons — **guillotine** *vb*

guilt \'gilt\ *n* 1 : the fact of having committed an offense esp. against the law 2 : BLAMEWORTHINESS 3 : a feeling of responsibility for wrongdoing — **guilt·less** *adj*

guilt–trip \'gilt-ˌtrip\ *vb* : to cause feelings of guilt in

guilty \'gil-tē\ *adj* **guilt·i·er; -est** 1 : having committed a breach of conduct or a crime 2 : suggesting or involving guilt 3 : aware of or suffering from guilt — **guilt·i·ly** \-tə-lē\ *adv* — **guilt·i·ness** \-tē-nəs\ *n*

guin·ea \'gi-nē\ *n* 1 : a British gold coin no longer issued worth 21 shillings 2 : a unit of value equal to 21 shillings

guinea fowl *n* : a gray and white spotted West African bird related to the pheasants and widely raised for food; *also* : any of several related birds

guinea hen *n* : a female guinea fowl; *also* : GUINEA FOWL

guinea pig *n* 1 : a small stocky short-eared and nearly tailless So. American rodent often kept as a pet or used in lab research 2 : a subject of research or testing

guise \'gīz\ *n* 1 : a form or style of dress : COSTUME 2 : external appearance : SEMBLANCE

gui·tar \gi-'tär\ *n* : a musical instrument with usu. six strings plucked with a pick or with the fingers

gulch \'gəlch\ *n* : RAVINE

gul·den \'gül-dən, 'gúl-\ *n, pl* **guldens** or **gulden** 1 : the basic monetary unit of the Netherlands until 2002 2 : the basic monetary unit of Suriname until 2004

gulf \'gəlf\ *n* [ME *goulf*, fr. MF *golfe*, fr. It *golfo*, fr. LL *colpus*, fr. Gk *kolpos* bosom, gulf] 1 : a part of an ocean or sea partly or mostly surrounded by land 2 : ABYSS, CHASM 3 : a wide separation ⟨the ∼ between generations⟩

¹**gull** \'gəl\ *n* : any of numerous mostly white or gray long-winged web-footed seabirds

²**gull** *vb* : to make a dupe of : DECEIVE

³**gull** *n* : DUPE

gul·let \'gə-lət\ *n* : ESOPHAGUS; *also* : THROAT

gull·ible \'gə-lə-bəl\ *adj* : easily duped or cheated

gul·ly \'gə-lē\ *n, pl* **gullies** : a trench worn

in the earth by and often filled with running water after rains

gulp \'gəlp\ *vb* 1 : to swallow hurriedly or greedily 2 : SUPPRESS ⟨∼ down a sob⟩ 3 : to catch the breath as if in taking a long drink — **gulp** *n*

¹**gum** \'gəm\ *n* : the oral tissue that surrounds the necks of the teeth

²**gum** *n* [ME *gomme*, fr. MF, fr. L *cummi, gummi*, fr. Gk *kommi*, fr. Egyptian *qmy.t*] 1 : a sticky plant exudate; *esp* : one that hardens on drying 2 : a sticky substance 3 : a preparation usu. of a plant gum sweetened and flavored and used for chewing — **gum·my** *adj*

gum arabic *n* : a water-soluble gum obtained from several acacias and used esp. in making inks, adhesives, confections, and pharmaceuticals

gum·bo \'gəm-bō\ *n* [AmerF *gombo*, of Bantu origin] : a rich thick soup usu. thickened with okra

gum·drop \'gəm-ˌdräp\ *n* : a candy made usu. from corn syrup with gelatin and coated with sugar crystals

gump·tion \'gəmp-shən\ *n* 1 *chiefly dial* : shrewd common sense 2 : ENTERPRISE, INITIATIVE ⟨lacked the ∼ to try⟩

gum·shoe \'gəm-ˌshü\ *n* : DETECTIVE — **gumshoe** *vb*

¹**gun** \'gən\ *n* 1 : CANNON 2 : a portable firearm 3 : a discharge of a gun 4 : something suggesting a gun in shape or function 5 : THROTTLE — **gunned** \'gənd\ *adj*

²**gun** *vb* **gunned; gun·ning** 1 : to hunt with a gun 2 : SHOOT 3 : to open up the throttle of so as to increase speed

gun·boat \'gən-ˌbōt\ *n* : a small lightly armed ship for use in shallow waters

gun·fight \-ˌfīt\ *n* : a duel with guns — **gun·fight·er** *n*

gun·fire \-ˌfī(-ə)r\ *n* : the firing of guns

gung ho \'gəŋ-'hō\ *adj* : extremely zealous or enthusiastic

gun·man \-mən\ *n* : a man armed with a gun; *esp* : a professional killer

gun·ner \'gə-nər\ *n* 1 : a soldier or airman who operates or aims a gun 2 : one who hunts with a gun

gun·nery \'gə-nə-rē\ *n* : the use of guns; *esp* : the science of the flight of projectiles and effective use of guns

gunnery sergeant *n* : a noncommissioned officer in the marine corps ranking next below a master sergeant

gun·ny·sack \'gə-nē-ˌsak\ *n* : a sack made of a coarse heavy fabric (as burlap)

gun·point \'gən-ˌpȯint\ *n* : the muzzle of a gun — **at gunpoint** : under a threat of death by being shot

gun·pow·der \-ˌpaú-dər\ *n* : an explosive powder used in guns and blasting

gun·shot \-ˌshät\ *n* 1 : shot fired from a gun 2 : the range of a gun ⟨within ∼⟩

gun–shy \-ˌshī\ *adj* : afraid of a loud noise 2 : markedly distrustful

gun·sling·er \-ˌsliŋ-ər\ *n* : a skilled gunman esp. in the American West

gun·smith \-ˌsmith\ *n* : one who designs, makes, or repairs firearms

gun·wale also **gun·nel** \'gə-nᵊl\ n : the upper edge of a ship's or boat's side

gup·py \'gə-pē\ n, pl **guppies** [R.J.L. *Guppy* †1916 Trinidadian naturalist] : a small brightly colored tropical fish

gur·gle \'gər-gəl\ vb **gur·gled**; **gur·gling** : to make a sound like that of an irregularly flowing or gently splashing liquid — **gurgle** n

Gur·kha \'gùr-kə, 'gər-\ n : a soldier from Nepal in the British or Indian army

gur·ney \'gər-nē\ n, pl **gurneys** : a wheeled cot or stretcher

gu·ru \'gùr-ü\ n, pl **gurus** [ultim. fr. Sanskrit *guru*, fr. *guru*, adj., heavy, venerable] **1** : a personal religious and spiritual teacher in Hinduism **2** : a teacher in matters of fundamental concern **3** : EXPERT ⟨a fitness ∼⟩

gush \'gəsh\ vb **1** : to issue or pour forth copiously or violently : SPOUT **2** : to make an effusive display of affection or enthusiasm

gush·er \'gə-shər\ n : one that gushes; *esp* : an oil well with a large natural flow

gushy \'gə-shē\ adj **gush·i·er**; **-est** : marked by effusive sentimentality

gus·set \'gə-sət\ n : a triangular insert (as in a seam of a sleeve) to give width or strength — **gusset** vb

gus·sy up \'gə-sē-\ vb **gus·sied up**; **gus·sy·ing up** **1** : to dress in best or formal clothes **2** : to make more attractive, glamorous, or fancy

¹gust \'gəst\ n **1** : a sudden brief rush of wind **2** : a sudden outburst : SURGE ⟨a ∼ of emotion⟩ — **gusty** adj

²gust vb : to blow in gusts

gus·ta·to·ry \'gəs-tə-ˌtôr-ē\ adj : relating to or associated with the sense of taste

gus·to \'gəs-tō\ n, pl **gustoes** : enthusiastic enjoyment; *also* : VITALITY **4**

¹gut \'gət\ n **1** pl : BOWELS, ENTRAILS **2** : the alimentary canal or a part of it (as the intestine); *also* : BELLY, ABDOMEN **3** pl : the inner essential parts ⟨a car's ∼s⟩ **4** pl : COURAGE, PLUCK

²gut vb **gut·ted**; **gut·ting** **1** : EVISCERATE **2** : to destroy the inside of ⟨fire *gutted* the building⟩

gut check n : a test of courage, character, or determination

gutsy \'gət-sē\ adj **guts·i·er**; **-est** : marked by courage and determination

gut·ter \'gə-tər\ n : a groove or channel for carrying off esp. rainwater

gut·ter·snipe \-ˌsnīp\ n : a street urchin

gut·tur·al \'gə-tə-rəl\ adj **1** : sounded in the throat **2** : being or marked by an utterance that is strange, unpleasant, or disagreeable — **guttural** n

gut·ty \'gə-tē\ adj **gut·ti·er**; **-est** **1** : GUTSY **2** : having a vigorous challenging quality ⟨a ∼ role in a play⟩

gut–wrench·ing \'gət-ˌren-chiŋ\ adj : causing emotional anguish

¹guy \'gī\ n : a rope, chain, or rod attached to something as a brace or guide

²guy vb : to steady or reinforce with a guy

³guy n : MAN, FELLOW; *also, pl* : PERSONS

⁴guy vb : to make fun of : RIDICULE

guz·zle \'gə-zəl\ vb **guz·zled**; **guz·zling** : to drink greedily

gym \'jim\ n : GYMNASIUM

gym·kha·na \jim-'kä-nə\ n : a meet featuring sports contests; *esp* : a contest of automobile-driving skill

gym·na·si·um \for 1 jim-'nä-zē-əm, -zhəm, for 2 gim-'nä-zē-əm\ n, pl **-si·ums** or **-na·sia** \-'nä-zē-ə, -'nä-zhə; -'nä-zē-ə\ [L, exercise ground, school, fr. Gk *gymnasion*, fr. *gymnazein* to exercise naked, fr. *gymnos* naked] **1** : a room or building for indoor sports **2** : a European secondary school that prepares students for the university

gym·nas·tics \jim-'nas-tiks\ n : a competitive sport developed from physical exercises designed to demonstrate strength, balance, and body control — **gym·nast** \'jim-ˌnast\ n — **gym·nas·tic** adj

gym·no·sperm \'jim-nə-ˌspərm\ n : any of a group of woody vascular seed plants (as conifers) that produce naked seeds not enclosed in an ovary

gyn or **gynecol** abbr gynecology

gy·nae·col·o·gy chiefly Brit var of GYNECOLOGY

gy·ne·col·o·gy \ˌgī-nə-'kä-lə-jē\ n : a branch of medicine that deals with the diseases and routine care of the reproductive system of women — **gy·ne·co·log·ic** \-ni-kə-'lä-jik\ or **gy·ne·co·log·i·cal** \-ji-kəl\ adj — **gy·ne·col·o·gist** \-nə-'kä-lə-jist\ n

gy·no·cen·tric \ˌgī-nə-'sen-trik\ adj : emphasizing feminine interests or a feminine point of view

gyp \'jip\ n **1** : CHEAT, SWINDLER **2** : FRAUD, SWINDLE — **gyp** vb

gyp·sum \'jip-səm\ n : a calcium-containing mineral used in making plaster of paris

Gyp·sy \'jip-sē\ n, pl **Gypsies** [by shortening & alter. fr. *Egyptian*] : a member of a traditionally traveling people coming orig. from India and living chiefly in Europe, Asia, and No. America; *also* : the language of the Gypsies

gypsy moth n : an Old World moth that was introduced into the U.S. where its caterpillar is a destructive defoliator of many trees

gy·rate \'jī-ˌrāt\ vb **gy·rat·ed**; **gy·rat·ing** **1** : to revolve around a point or axis **2** : to oscillate with or as if with a circular or spiral motion — **gy·ra·tion** \jī-'rā-shən\ n

gyr·fal·con \'jər-ˌfal-kən, -ˌfól-\ n : an arctic falcon with several color forms that is the largest of all falcons

¹gy·ro \'jī-rō\ n, pl **gyros** : GYROSCOPE

²gy·ro \'yē-ˌrō, 'zhir-ō\ n, pl **gyros** : a sandwich esp. of lamb and beef, tomato, onion, and yogurt sauce on pita bread

gy·ro·scope \'jī-rō-ˌskōp\ n : a wheel or disk mounted to spin rapidly about an axis that is free to turn in various directions

Gy Sgt abbr gunnery sergeant

gyve \'jīv, 'gīv\ n : FETTER — **gyve** vb

¹h \'āch\ *n, pl* h's *or* hs \'ā-chəz\ *often cap* : the 8th letter of the English alphabet

²h *abbr, often cap* 1 hard; hardness 2 heroin 3 hit 4 husband

H *symbol* hydrogen

¹ha \'hä\ *interj* — used esp. to express surprise or joy

²ha *abbr* hectare

Hab *abbr* Habacuc; Habakkuk

Ha·ba·cuc \'ha-bə-ˌkək, hə-'ba-kək\ *n* : HABAKKUK

Ha·bak·kuk \'ha-bə-ˌkək, hə-'ba-kək\ *n* — see BIBLE table

ha·ba·ne·ra \ˌhä-bə-'ner-ə\ *n* [Sp *(danza) habanera*, lit., dance of Havana] 1 : a Cuban dance in slow time; *also* : the music for this dance

ha·ba·ne·ro *also* ha·ba·ñe·ro \ˌ(h)ä-bə-'n(y)er-ō\ *n* : a very hot chili pepper that is usu. orange when mature

ha·be·as cor·pus \'hā-bē-əs-'kòr-pəs\ *n* [ME, fr. ML, lit., you should have the body (the opening words of the writ)] : a writ issued to bring a party before a court

hab·er·dash·er \'ha-bər-ˌda-shər\ *n* : a dealer in men's clothing and accessories

hab·er·dash·ery \-ˌda-shə-rē\ *n, pl* -er·ies 1 : goods sold by a haberdasher 2 : a haberdasher's shop

ha·bil·i·ment \hə-'bi-lə-mənt\ *n* 1 *pl* : TRAPPINGS, EQUIPMENT 2 : DRESS; *esp* : the dress characteristic of an occupation or occasion — usu. used in pl.

hab·it \'ha-bət\ *n* 1 : DRESS, GARB 2 : BEARING, CONDUCT 3 : PHYSIQUE 4 : mental makeup 5 : a usual manner of behavior : CUSTOM 6 : a behavior pattern acquired by frequent repetition ⟨has a ∼ of swearing⟩ 7 : ADDICTION ⟨a drug ∼⟩ 8 : mode of growth or occurrence ⟨trees with a spreading ∼⟩

hab·it·able \'ha-bə-tə-bəl\ *adj* : capable of being lived in — hab·it·abil·i·ty \ˌha-bə-tə-'bi-lə-tē\ *n*

hab·i·tat \'ha-bə-ˌtat\ *n* [L, it inhabits] : the place or environment where a plant or animal naturally occurs

hab·i·ta·tion \ˌha-bə-'tā-shən\ *n* 1 : OCCUPANCY 2 : a dwelling place : RESIDENCE 3 : SETTLEMENT

hab·it-form·ing \'ha-bət-ˌfòr-miŋ\ *adj* : causing addiction : ADDICTIVE

ha·bit·u·al \hə-'bi-chə-wəl\ *adj* 1 : CUSTOMARY 2 : doing, practicing, or acting by force of habit 3 : inherent in an individual ⟨∼ grace⟩ — ha·bit·u·al·ly *adv* — ha·bit·u·al·ness *n*

ha·bit·u·ate \hə-'bi-chə-ˌwāt\ *vb* -at·ed; -at·ing 1 : ACCUSTOM 2 : to cause or undergo habituation

ha·bit·u·a·tion \hə-ˌbi-chə-'wā-shən\ *n* 1 : the process of making habitual 2 : psychological dependence on a drug after a period of use

ha·bi·tué *also* ha·bi·tue \hə-'bi-chə-ˌwā\ *n* [F] 1 : one who may be regularly found in or at (as a place of entertainment) 2 : DEVOTEE

ha·ci·en·da \ˌhä-sē-'en-də\ *n* 1 : a large estate in a Spanish-speaking country 2 : the main building of a farm or ranch

¹hack \'hak\ *vb* 1 : to cut or sever with repeated irregular blows 2 : to cough in a short dry manner 3 : to manage successfully; *also* : TOLERATE ⟨can't ∼ the pressure⟩ 4 : to gain access to a computer illegally

²hack *n* 1 : an implement for hacking 2 : a short dry cough 3 : a hacking blow

³hack *n* 1 : a horse hired or used for varied work 2 : a horse worn out in service 3 : a light easy often 3-gaited saddle horse 4 : HACKNEY, TAXICAB 5 : a person who works solely for mercenary reasons; *esp* : a writer working solely for commercial success — hack *adj*

⁴hack *vb* : to operate a taxicab

hack·er \'ha-kər\ *n* 1 : one that hacks; *also* : a person unskilled at something 2 : an expert at using a computer 3 : a person who illegally gains access to and sometimes tampers with information in a computer system

hack·ie \'ha-kē\ *n* : a taxicab driver

hack·le \'ha-kəl\ *n* 1 : one of the long feathers on the neck or back of a bird 2 *pl* : hairs (as on a dog's neck) that can be erected 3 *pl* : TEMPER, DANDER

hack·man \'hak-mən\ *n* : HACKIE

¹hack·ney \'hak-nē\ *n, pl* hackneys 1 : a horse for riding or driving 2 : a carriage or automobile kept for hire

²hackney *vb* : to make trite

hack·neyed \'hak-nēd\ *adj* : lacking in freshness or originality ⟨∼ slogans⟩

hack·saw \'hak-ˌsò\ *n* : a fine-tooth saw in a frame for cutting metal

hack·work \-ˌwərk\ *n* : work done on order usu. according to a formula

had *past and past part of* HAVE

had·dock \'ha-dək\ *n, pl* haddock *also* haddocks : an Atlantic food fish usu. smaller than the related cod

Ha·des \'hā-(ˌ)dēz\ *n* 1 : the abode of the dead in Greek mythology 2 *often not cap* : HELL

haem *chiefly Brit var of* HEME

hae·ma·tite *Brit var of* HEMATITE

haf·ni·um \'haf-nē-əm\ *n* : a gray metallic chemical element

haft \'haft\ *n* : the handle of a weapon or tool

hag \'hag\ *n* 1 : an ugly or evil-looking old woman 2 : WITCH 1

Hag *abbr* Haggai

Hag·gai \'ha-gē-ˌī, 'ha-ˌgī\ *n* — see BIBLE table

hag·gard \'ha-gərd\ *adj* : having a worn or emaciated appearance ⟨∼ faces⟩

♦ **Synonyms** CAREWORN, WASTED,

DRAWN — **hag·gard·ly** *adv* — **hag·gard·ness** *n*

hag·gis \ˈha-gəs\ *n* : a traditionally Scottish dish made of the heart, liver, and lungs of a sheep or a calf minced with suet, onions, oatmeal, and seasonings

hag·gle \ˈha-gəl\ *vb* **hag·gled; hag·gling** : to argue in bargaining — **hag·gler** *n*

Ha·gi·og·ra·pha \ˌha-gē-ˈä-grə-fə, ˌhä-jē-\ *n pl* — see WRITINGS

ha·gio·graph·ic \ˌha-gē-ə-ˈgra-fik, ˌhä-, -jē-\ *adj* : of or relating to hagiography; *esp* : excessively flattering

ha·gi·og·ra·phy \ˌha-gē-ˈä-grə-fē, ˌhä-jē-\ *n* 1 : biography of saints or venerated persons 2 : idealizing or idolizing biography — **ha·gi·og·ra·pher** \-fər\ *n*

hai·ku \ˈhī-(ˌ)kü\ *n, pl* **haiku** [Jp] : an unrhymed Japanese verse form of three lines containing usu. five, seven, and five syllables respectively; *also* : a poem in this form

¹**hail** \ˈhāl\ *n* 1 : precipitation in the form of small lumps of ice 2 : something that gives the effect of falling hail

²**hail** *vb* 1 : to precipitate hail 2 : to pour down and strike like hail

³**hail** *interj* [ME, fr. ON *heill*, fr. *heill* healthy] — used to express acclamation

⁴**hail** *vb* 1 : SALUTE, GREET 2 : SUMMON

⁵**hail** *n* 1 : an expression of greeting, approval, or praise 2 : hearing distance

Hail Mary *n* 1 : a salutation and prayer to the Virgin Mary 2 : a long forward pass in football thrown as a final attempt to score

hail·stone \ˈhāl-ˌstōn\ *n* : a pellet of hail

hail·storm \-ˌstórm\ *n* : a storm accompanied by hail

hair \ˈher\ *n* : a threadlike outgrowth esp. from the skin of a mammal; *also* : a covering or growth of hairs of an animal or a body part — **haired** \ˈherd\ *adj* — **hairless** *adj*

hair·breadth \ˈher-ˌbredth\ *or* **hairsbreadth** \ˈherz-\ *n* : a very small distance or margin

hair·brush \-ˌbrəsh\ *n* : a brush for the hair

hair·cloth \-ˌklòth\ *n* : a stiff wiry fabric used esp. for upholstery

hair·cut \-ˌkət\ *n* : the act, process, or style of cutting and shaping the hair

hair·do \-ˌdü\ *n, pl* **hairdos** : HAIRSTYLE

hair·dress·er \-ˌdre-sər\ *n* : a person who dresses or cuts hair — **hair·dress·ing** *n*

hair·line \-ˌlīn\ *n* 1 : a very thin line 2 : the outline of the hair on the head

hair·piece \-ˌpēs\ *n* 1 : supplementary hair (as a switch) used in some women's hairdos 2 : TOUPEE

hair·pin \-ˌpin\ *n* 1 : a U-shaped pin to hold the hair in place 2 : a sharp U-shaped turn in a road — **hairpin** *adj*

hair–rais·ing \ˈher-ˌrā-ziŋ\ *adj* : causing terror or astonishment

hair·split·ter \-ˌspli-tər\ *n* : a person who makes excessively fine distinctions in reasoning — **hair·split·ting** \-ˌspli-tiŋ\ *adj or n*

hair·spray \ˈher-ˌsprā\ *n* : a liquid sprayed onto the hair to hold it in place

hair·style \-ˌstī(-ə)l\ *n* : a way of wearing the hair — **hair·styl·ing** *n*

hair·styl·ist \-ˌstī-list\ *n* : HAIRDRESSER

hair–trigger *adj* : immediately responsive to the slightest stimulus

hairy \ˈher-ē\ *adj* **hair·i·er; -est** 1 : covered with or as if with hair 2 : tending to cause nervous tension ⟨a few ∼ moments⟩ 3 : difficult to deal with — **hair·i·ness** \-ē-nəs\ *n*

hairy woodpecker *n* : a common No. American woodpecker with a white back that is larger than the similarly marked downy woodpecker

hajj \ˈhaj\ *n* : a pilgrimage to Mecca prescribed as a religious duty for Muslims

hajji \ˈha-jē\ *n* : one who has made a pilgrimage to Mecca — often used as a title

hake \ˈhāk\ *n* : any of several marine food fishes related to the cod

ha·la·la \hə-ˈlä-lə\ *n, pl* **halala** *or* **halalas** — see *riyal* at MONEY table

hal·berd \ˈhal-bərd, ˈhòl-\ *also* **hal·bert** \-bərt\ *n* : a weapon esp. of the 15th and 16th centuries consisting of a battle-ax and pike on a long handle

hal·cy·on \ˈhal-sē-ən\ *adj* [Gk *halkyōn, alkyōn*, a mythical bird believed to nest at sea and to calm the waves] 1 : CALM, PEACEFUL ⟨a ∼ lake⟩ 2 : being a time of happiness, success, or prosperity

¹**hale** \ˈhāl\ *adj* : free from defect, disease, or infirmity ♦ **Synonyms** HEALTHY, SOUND, ROBUST, WELL

²**hale** *vb* **haled; hal·ing** 1 : HAUL, PULL 2 : to compel to go

ha·ler \ˈhä-lər\ *n, pl* **ha·le·ru** \ˈhä-lə-ˌrü\ — see *koruna* at MONEY table

¹**half** \ˈhaf, ˈhäf\ *n, pl* **halves** \ˈhavz, ˈhävz\ 1 : either of two equal parts into which something is divisible 2 : one of a pair

²**half** *adj* 1 : being one of two equal parts 2 : amounting to nearly half 3 : PARTIAL, INCOMPLETE — **half** *adv*

half–and–half \ˌhaf-ᵊn-ˈhaf, ˌhäf-ᵊn-ˈhäf\ *n* : something that is half one thing and half another

half·back \ˈhaf-ˌbak, ˈhäf-\ *n* 1 : a football back stationed on or near the flank 2 : a player stationed immediately behind the forward line

half–baked \-ˈbākt\ *adj* 1 : poorly planned 2 : lacking common sense 3 : not thoroughly baked

half–breed \-ˌbrēd\ *n, often disparaging* : one of mixed racial descent — **half–breed** *adj, often disparaging*

half brother *n* : a brother related through one parent only

half–caste \ˈhaf-ˌkast, ˈhäf-\ *n* : HALF-BREED — **half–caste** *adj*

half–cocked \ˈhaf-ˈkäkt, ˈhäf-\ *adj* : lacking adequate preparation

half–dol·lar \-ˈdä-lər\ *n* 1 : a coin representing one half of a dollar 2 : the sum of fifty cents

half·heart·ed \-ˈhär-təd\ *adj* : lacking spirit or interest — **half·heart·ed·ly** *adv* — **half·heart·ed·ness** *n*

half–life \-ˌlīf\ *n* : the time required for

half of something (as atoms or a drug) to undergo a process

half–mast \-'mast\ *n* : a point about halfway down from the top of a mast or staff

half note *n* : a musical note equal in time to one half that of a whole note

half·pen·ny \-ˌtrak-nē\ *n, pl* **half·pence** \'hā-pəns\ *or* **halfpennies** : a former British coin representing one half of a penny

half–pint \'haf-ˌpīnt, 'häf-\ *adj* : of less than average size — **half–pint** *n*

half sister *n* : a sister related through one parent only

half sole *n* : a shoe sole extending from the shank forward — **half–sole** *vb*

half–staff \'haf-'staf, 'häf-\ *n* : HALF-MAST

half step *n* : a musical interval equivalent to one twelfth of an octave

half–time \'haf-ˌtīm, 'häf-\ *n* : an intermission between halves of a game

half–track \-ˌtrak\ *n* : a motor vehicle propelled by an endless chain-track drive system; *esp* : such a vehicle lightly armored for military use

half–truth \-ˌtrüth\ *n* : a statement that is only partially true; *esp* : one that deliberately mixes truth and falsehood

half·way \-'wā\ *adj* **1** : midway between two points **2** : PARTIAL — **halfway** *adv*

half–wit \-ˌwit\ *n* : a foolish or imbecilic person — **half–wit·ted** \-'wi-təd\ *adj* — **half–wit·ted·ness** *n*

hal·i·but \'ha-lə-bət\ *n, pl* **halibut** *also* **halibuts** [ME *halybutte*, fr. *haly, holy* holy + *butte* flatfish; fr. its being eaten on holy days] : any of several large edible marine flatfishes

ha·lite \'ha-ˌlīt, 'hā-\ *n* : ROCK SALT

hal·i·to·sis \ˌha-lə-'tō-səs\ *n* : the condition of having fetid breath

hall \'hȯl\ *n* **1** : the residence of a medieval king or noble; *also* : the house of a landed proprietor **2** : a large public building **3** : a college or university building; *also* : DORMITORY **4** : LOBBY; *also* : CORRIDOR **5** : AUDITORIUM

hal·le·lu·jah \ˌha-lə-'lü-yə\ *interj* [Heb *hallĕlūyāh* praise (ye) the Lord] — used to express praise, joy, or thanks

hall·mark \'hȯl-ˌmärk\ *n* **1** : a mark put on an article to indicate origin, purity, or genuineness **2** : a distinguishing characteristic

hal·low \'ha-lō\ *vb* **1** : CONSECRATE **2** : REVERE, VENERATE ⟨our ∼*ed* leader⟩ — **hal·lowed** \-lōd, -ə-wəd\ *adj*

Hal·low·een *also* **Hal·low·e'en** \ˌha-lə-'wēn, ˌhä-\ *n* : the evening of October 31 observed esp. by children in merrymaking and masquerading

hal·lu·ci·nate \hə-'lü-sə-ˌnāt\ *vb* **-nat·ed; -nat·ing** : to have hallucinations or experience as a hallucination

hal·lu·ci·na·tion \hə-ˌlü-sə-'nā-shən\ *n* : perception of objects with no reality due usu. to use of drugs (as LSD) or to disorder of the nervous system; *also* : something so perceived ♦ *Synonyms* DELUSION, ILLUSION, MIRAGE — **hal·lu·ci·na·to·ry** \-'lü-sə-nə-ˌtȯr-ē\ *adj*

hal·lu·ci·no·gen \hə-'lü-sə-nə-jən\ *n* : a substance that induces hallucinations — **hal·lu·ci·no·gen·ic** \-ˌlü-sə-nə-'je-nik\ *adj or n*

hall·way \'hȯl-ˌwā\ *n* **1** : an entrance hall **2** : CORRIDOR

ha·lo \'hā-lō\ *n, pl* **halos** *or* **haloes** [L *halos,* fr. Gk *halōs* threshing floor, disk, halo] **1** : a circle of light appearing to surround a shining body (as the sun) **2** : the aura of glory surrounding an idealized person or thing

¹hal·o·gen \'ha-lə-jən\ *n* : any of the five elements fluorine, chlorine, bromine, iodine, and astatine

²halogen *adj* : containing, using, or being a halogen ⟨a ∼ lamp⟩

¹halt \'hȯlt\ *adj* : LAME 1

²halt *n* : STOP

³halt *vb* **1** : to stop marching or traveling **2** : DISCONTINUE, END ⟨∼ protests⟩

¹hal·ter \'hȯl-tər\ *n* **1** : a rope or strap for leading or tying an animal; *also* : HEADSTALL **2** : NOOSE **3** : a brief blouse held in place by straps around the neck and across the back

²halter *vb* **hal·tered; hal·ter·ing 1** : to catch with or as if with a halter; *also* : to put a halter on (as a horse) **2** : HANG **3** : IMPEDE, RESTRAIN

halt·ing \'hȯl-tiŋ\ *adj* : UNCERTAIN, FALTERING — **halt·ing·ly** *adv*

halve \'hav, 'häv\ *vb* **halved; halv·ing 1** : to divide into two equal parts **2** : to reduce to one half

halv·ers \'ha-vərz, 'hä-\ *n pl* : half shares : HALVES

halves *pl of* HALF

hal·yard \'hal-yərd\ *n* : a rope or tackle for hoisting and lowering (as sails)

¹ham \'ham\ *n* **1** : a buttock with its associated thigh — usu. used in pl. **2** : a cut of meat and esp. pork from the thigh **3** : a showy performer **4** : an operator of an amateur radio station — **ham** *adj*

²ham *vb* **hammed; ham·ming** : to overplay a part : OVERACT

ham·burg·er \'ham-ˌbər-gər\ *or* **ham·burg** \-ˌbərg\ *n* [G *Hamburger* of Hamburg, Germany] **1** : ground beef **2** : a sandwich consisting of a ground-beef patty in a round roll

ham·let \'ham-lət\ *n* : a small village

¹ham·mer \'ha-mər\ *n* **1** : a hand tool used for pounding; *also* : something resembling a hammer in form or function **2** : the part of a gun whose striking action causes explosion of the charge **3** : a metal sphere hurled by a flexible handle for distance in a track-and-field event (**hammer throw**) **4** : ACCELERATOR 2

²hammer *vb* **1** : to beat, drive, or shape with repeated blows of a hammer : POUND **2** : to produce or bring about as if by repeated blows — usu. used with *out* **3** : to criticize severely

ham·mer·head \'ha-mər-ˌhed\ *n* **1** : the striking part of a hammer **2** : any of a family of medium-sized sharks with eyes at the ends of lateral extensions of the flattened head

ham·mer·lock \-ˌläk\ *n* : a wrestling hold

in which an opponent's arm is held bent behind the back

ham·mer·toe \-ˌtō\ n : a toe deformed by having one or more joints permanently flexed

¹ham·mock \'ha-mək\ n [Sp *hamaca*, of AmerInd origin] : a swinging couch hung by cords at each end

²hammock n : a fertile elevated area of the southern U.S. and esp. Florida with hardwood vegetation and soil rich in humus

¹ham·per \'ham-pər\ vb : IMPEDE; *also* : RESTRAIN ◆ **Synonyms** TRAMMEL, CLOG, FETTER, SHACKLE

²hamper n : a large usu. lidded basket

ham·ster \'ham-stər\ n [G, fr. OHG *hamustro*, of Slavic origin] : any of a subfamily of small Old World rodents with large cheek pouches

¹ham·string \'ham-ˌstriŋ\ n : any of several muscles at the back of the thigh or tendons at the back of the knee

²hamstring vb **-strung** \-ˌstrəŋ\; **-string·ing** **1** : to make ineffective or powerless ⟨*hamstrung* by guilt⟩ **2** : to cripple by cutting the leg tendons

¹hand \'hand\ n **1** : the end of a front limb when modified (as in humans) for grasping **2** : an indicator or pointer on a dial **3** : personal possession — usu. used in pl.; *also* : CONTROL **4** : SIDE **5** **5** : a pledge esp. of betrothal **6** : HANDWRITING **7** : SKILL, ABILITY; *also* : a significant part ⟨had a ∼ in the victory⟩ **8** : ASSISTANCE; *also* : PARTICIPATION ⟨had no ∼ in the affair⟩ **9** : an outburst of applause **10** : a single round in a card game; *also* : the cards held by a player after a deal **11** : WORKER, EMPLOYEE; *also* : a member of a ship's crew — **hand·less** adj — **at hand** : near in time or place — **on hand** : in present possession or readily available — **out of hand** : out of control

²hand vb **1** : to lead, guide, or assist with the hand **2** : to give, pass, or transmit with the hand ⟨∼ed her the letter⟩

hand·bag \'hand-ˌbag\ n : a bag for carrying small personal articles and money

hand·ball \-ˌbȯl\ n : a game played by striking a small rubber ball against a wall with the hand

hand·bill \-ˌbil\ n : a small printed sheet for distribution by hand

hand·book \-ˌbu̇k\ n : a concise reference book : MANUAL

hand·car \-ˌkär\ n : a small 4-wheeled railroad car propelled by hand or by a small motor

hand·clasp \-ˌklasp\ n : HANDSHAKE

hand·craft \-ˌkraft\ vb : to fashion by manual skill

¹hand·cuff \-ˌkəf\ n : a metal fastening that can be locked around a wrist and is usu. connected with another such fastening — usu. used in pl.

²handcuff vb : MANACLE

hand·ed \'han-dəd\ adj : having or using such or so many hands ⟨a left-*handed* person⟩ — **hand·ed·ness** n

hand·ful \'hand-ˌfu̇l\ n, pl **hand·fuls** \-ˌfu̇lz\ *also* **hands·ful** \'handz-ˌfu̇l\ **1** : as much or as many as the hand will grasp **2** : a small number **3** : as much as one can manage

hand·gun \-ˌgən\ n : a firearm held and fired with one hand

hand-held \-ˌheld\ adj : designed for use while being held in the hand — **hand-held** n

¹hand·i·cap \'han-di-ˌkap\ n [obs. E *handicap*, a game in which forfeit money was held in a cap, fr. *hand in cap*] **1** : a contest in which an artificial advantage is given or disadvantage imposed on a contestant to equalize chances of winning; *also* : the advantage given or disadvantage imposed **2** : a disadvantage that makes achievement difficult

²handicap vb **-capped**; **-cap·ping** **1** : to give a handicap to **2** : to put at a disadvantage

hand·i·capped adj, *sometimes offensive* : having a physical or mental disability

hand·i·cap·per \-ˌka-pər\ n : a person who predicts the winners in a contest

hand·i·craft \'han-di-ˌkraft\ n **1** : manual skill **2** : an occupation requiring manual skill **3** : the articles fashioned by those engaged in handicraft — **hand·i·craft·er** \-ˌkraf-tər\ n — **hand·i·crafts·man** \-ˌkrafts-mən\ n

hand in glove *or* **hand and glove** adv : in an extremely close relationship

hand·i·work \'han-di-ˌwərk\ n : work done personally or by the hands

hand·ker·chief \'haŋ-kər-chəf, -ˌchēf\ n, pl **-chiefs** \-chəfs, -ˌchēfs\ *also* **-chieves** \-ˌchēvz\ : a small piece of cloth used for various personal purposes (as the wiping of the face)

¹han·dle \'han-dᵊl\ n **1** : a part (as of a tool) designed to be grasped by the hand **2** : NAME; *also* : NICKNAME — **han·dled** \-dᵊld\ adj — **off the handle** : into a state of sudden and violent anger — usu. used with *fly*

²handle vb **han·dled**; **han·dling** **1** : to touch, hold, or manage with the hands **2** : to have responsibility for **3** : to deal or trade in **4** : to behave in a certain way when managed or directed ⟨a car that ∼s well⟩ — **han·dler** n

han·dle·bar \'han-dᵊl-ˌbär\ n : a usu. bent bar with a grip at each end (as for steering a bicycle) — usu. used in pl.

hand·made \'hand-ˈmād\ adj : made by hand or by a hand process

hand·maid·en \-ˌmā-dᵊn\ *also* **hand·maid** \-ˌmād\ n : a female attendant

hand–me–down \-ˌme-ˌdau̇n\ adj : used by one person after having been used by another — **hand–me–down** n

hand·out \'hand-ˌau̇t\ n **1** : a portion (as of food) given to a beggar **2** : a piece of printed information for free distribution; *also* : a prepared statement released to the press

hand over vb : to yield control of

hand·pick \'hand-ˈpik\ vb : to select personally ⟨a ∼ed candidate⟩

hand·rail \-ˌrāl\ n : a narrow rail for grasping as a support

hand·saw \-ˌsȯ\ *n* : a saw designed to be used with one hand

hands down *adv* **1** : with little effort **2** : without question

hand·sel \ˈhan-səl\ *n* **1** : a gift made as a token of good luck **2** : a first installment : earnest money

hand·set \ˈhand-ˌset\ *n* : a combined telephone transmitter and receiver mounted on a handheld device

hand·shake \-ˌshāk\ *n* : a clasping usu. of right hands by two people

hands-off \ˈhandz-ˈȯf\ *adj* : characterized by noninterference

hand·some \ˈhan-səm\ *adj* **hand·som·er; -est** [ME *handsom* easy to manipulate] **1** : SIZABLE, AMPLE ⟨a ~ profit⟩ **2** : GENEROUS, LIBERAL **3** : pleasing and usu. impressive in appearance ♦ **Synonyms** BEAUTIFUL, LOVELY, PRETTY, COMELY, FAIR — **hand·some·ly** *adv* — **hand·some·ness** *n*

hands-on \ˈhandz-ˈȯn, -ˈän\ *adj* **1** : being or providing direct practical experience in the operation of something **2** : characterized by active personal involvement ⟨~ management⟩

hand·spring \ˈhand-ˌspriŋ\ *n* : an acrobatic feat in which the body turns in a full circle from a standing position and lands first on the hands and then on the feet

hand·stand \-ˌstand\ *n* : an act of supporting the body on the hands with the trunk and legs balanced in the air

hand-to-hand *adj* : involving physical contact or very close range ⟨~ fighting⟩ — **hand to hand** *adv*

hand-to-mouth *adj* : having or providing nothing to spare ⟨lived a ~ existence⟩ — **hand to mouth** *adv*

hand·wo·ven \ˈhand-ˌwō-vən\ *adj* : produced on a hand-operated loom

hand·writ·ing \-ˌrī-tiŋ\ *n* : writing done by hand; *also* : the form of writing peculiar to a person — **hand·writ·ten** \-ˌri-tᵊn\ *adj*

handy \ˈhan-dē\ *adj* **hand·i·er; -est 1** : conveniently near **2** : easily used ⟨a ~ tool⟩ **3** : DEXTEROUS — **hand·i·ly** \-də-lē\ *adv* — **hand·i·ness** \-dē-nəs\ *n*

handy·man \-ˌman\ *n* **1** : one who does odd jobs **2** : one competent in a variety of small skills or repair work

¹hang \ˈhaŋ\ *vb* **hung** \ˈhəŋ\ *also* **hanged; hang·ing 1** : to fasten or remain fastened to an elevated point without support from below; *also* : to fasten or be fastened so as to allow free motion on the point of suspension ⟨~ a door⟩ **2** : to suspend by the neck until dead; *also* : to die by hanging **3** : DROOP ⟨hung his head in shame⟩ **4** : to fasten to a wall ⟨~ wallpaper⟩ **5** : to prevent (a jury) from coming to a decision **6** : to display (pictures) in a gallery **7** : to remain stationary in the air **8** : to be imminent **9** : DEPEND **10** : to take hold for support **11** : to be burdensome **12** : to undergo delay **13** : to incline downward; *also* : to fit or fall from the figure in easy lines **14** : to be raptly attentive **15** : to pass time idly by

relaxing or socializing ⟨~ing at the mall⟩ — often used with *around* or *out* —

hang out to dry : to subject to ruin by abandonment

²hang *n* **1** : the manner in which a thing hangs **2** : an understanding of something ⟨got the ~ of skiing⟩

han·gar \ˈhaŋ-ər\ *n* [F] : a covered and usu. enclosed area for housing and repairing aircraft

hang·dog \ˈhaŋ-ˌdȯg\ *adj* **1** : SAD, DEJECTED ⟨a ~ look on his face⟩ **2** : SHEEPISH

hang·er \ˈhaŋ-ər\ *n* **1** : one that hangs **2** : a device that fits inside or around a garment for hanging from a hook or rod

hang·er-on \ˈhaŋ-ər-ˈȯn, -ˈän\ *n, pl* **hangers-on** : one who hangs around a person or place esp. for personal gain

hang in *vb* : to persist tenaciously

hang·ing *n* **1** : an execution by strangling or snapping the neck by a suspended noose **2** : something hung

hang·man \ˈhaŋ-mən\ *n* **1** : a public executioner **2** : a game in which players must identify an unknown word by guessing the letters that comprise it within a designated number of chances

hang·nail \-ˌnāl\ *n* : a bit of skin hanging loose at the edge of a fingernail

hang on *vb* **1** : to keep hold onto something **2** : HANG IN **3** : to await something desired

hang·out \ˈhaŋ-ˌaút\ *n* : a favorite place for spending time

hang·over \-ˌō-vər\ *n* **1** : something that remains from what is past **2** : disagreeable physical effects following heavy drinking or the use of drugs

hang-up \ˈhaŋ-ˌəp\ *n* : a source of mental or emotional difficulty

hang up *vb* **1** : to place on a hook or hanger **2** : to end a telephone conversation by breaking the connection **3** : to keep delayed or suspended

hank \ˈhaŋk\ *n* : COIL, LOOP ⟨a ~ of rope⟩

han·ker \ˈhaŋ-kər\ *vb* : to desire strongly or persistently — **han·ker·ing** *n*

han·kie *or* **han·ky** \ˈhaŋ-kē\ *n, pl* **hankies** : HANDKERCHIEF

han·ky-pan·ky \ˌhaŋ-kē-ˈpaŋ-kē\ *n* **1** : questionable or underhanded activity **2** : sexual dalliance

hansel *var of* HANDSEL

han·som \ˈhan-səm\ *n* : a 2-wheeled covered carriage with the driver's seat elevated at the rear

han·ta·virus \ˈhän-tə-ˌvī-rəs, ˈhən-, ˈhan-\ *n* : any of a genus of viruses including some transmitted by rodents that cause pneumonia or hemorrhagic fevers

Ha·nuk·kah *also* **Cha·nu·kah** \ˈḵä-nə-kə, ˈhä-\ *n* [Heb *ḥănukkāh* dedication] : an 8-day Jewish holiday commemorating the rededication of the Temple of Jerusalem after its defilement by Antiochus of Syria

hap \ˈhap\ *n* **1** : HAPPENING **2** : CHANCE, FORTUNE

¹hap·haz·ard \hap-ˈha-zərd\ *n* : CHANCE

²haphazard *adj* : marked by lack of plan

or order — **hap·haz·ard·ly** *adv* — **hap·haz·ard·ness** *n*

hap·less \'hap-ləs\ *adj* : UNFORTUNATE — **hap·less·ly** *adv* — **hap·less·ness** *n*

hap·loid \'hap-ˌlȯid\ *adj* : having the number of chromosomes characteristic of gametic cells — **haploid** *n*

hap·ly \'hap-lē\ *adv* : by chance

hap·pen \'ha-pən\ *vb* **1** : to occur by chance **2** : to take place **3** : CHANCE 2

¹hap·pen·ing *n* **1** : OCCURRENCE **2** : an event that is especially interesting, entertaining, or important

²happening *adj* **1** : very fashionable **2** : offering much stimulating activity ⟨a ∼ nightclub⟩

hap·pi·ly \'ha-pə-lē\ *adv* **1** : LUCKILY **2** : in a happy manner or state ⟨lived ∼ ever after⟩ **3** : APTLY, SUCCESSFULLY

hap·pi·ness \'ha-pē-nəs\ *n* **1** : a state of well-being and contentment; *also* : a pleasurable satisfaction **2** : APTNESS

hap·py \'ha-pē\ *adj* **hap·pi·er; -est 1** : FORTUNATE **2** : APT, FELICITOUS **3** : enjoying well-being and contentment ⟨a ∼ childhood⟩ **4** : PLEASANT ⟨a ∼ ending⟩; *also* : PLEASED, GRATIFIED ⟨∼ to meet you⟩ **5** : quick or enthusiastic to use or do something ⟨trigger-*happy*⟩ ⟨a cliché-*happy* writer⟩ **♦ Synonyms** GLAD, CHEERFUL, LIGHTHEARTED, JOYFUL, JOYOUS

hap·py-go-lucky \ˌha-pē-gō-'lə-kē\ *adj* : CAREFREE

happy hour *n* : a period of time when the price of drinks at a bar is reduced

hara-kiri \ˌha-ri-'kir-ē, -'ka-rē\ *n* [Jp *harakiri,* fr. *hara* belly + *kiri* cutting] : ritual suicide by disembowelment

ha·rangue \hə-'raŋ\ *n* **1** : a ranting speech or writing **2** : LECTURE — **harangue** *vb* — **ha·rangu·er** *n*

ha·rass \hə-'ras, 'ha-rəs\ *vb* [F *harasser,* fr. MF, fr. *harer* to set a dog on, fr. OF *hare,* interj. used to incite dogs, fr. of Gmc origin] **1** : EXHAUST, FATIGUE **2** : to worry and impede by repeated raids **3** : to annoy continually **4** : to create an unpleasant or hostile situation for esp. by one's verbal or physical conduct **♦ Synonyms** HARRY, PLAGUE, PESTER, TEASE, BEDEVIL — **ha·rass·ment** *n*

har·bin·ger \'här-bən-jər\ *n* : one that announces or foreshadows what is coming : PRECURSOR; *also* : PORTENT

¹har·bor \'här-bər\ *n* **1** : a place of security and comfort **2** : a part of a body of water protected and deep enough to furnish anchorage : PORT

²harbor *vb* **1** : to give or take refuge : SHELTER ⟨∼ a fugitive⟩ ⟨∼ed in the barn⟩ **2** : to be the home or habitat of; *also* : LIVE **3** : to hold a thought or feeling ⟨∼ a grudge⟩

har·bor·age \'här-bən-rij\ *n* : HARBOR

har·bour *chiefly Brit var of* HARBOR

hard \'härd\ *adj* **1** : not easily penetrated : not easily yielding to pressure **2** : high in alcoholic content **3** : containing salts that prevent lathering with soap ⟨∼ water⟩ **4** : stable in value ⟨∼ currency⟩ **5** : physically fit **6** : FIRM, DEFINITE ⟨∼

agreement⟩; *also* : based on clear fact ⟨∼ evidence⟩ **7** : CLOSE, SEARCHING ⟨a ∼ look⟩ **8** : REALISTIC ⟨good ∼ sense⟩ **9** : OBDURATE, UNFEELING ⟨a ∼ heart⟩ **10** : difficult to bear ⟨∼ times⟩; *also* : HARSH, SEVERE **11** : RESENTFUL ⟨∼ feelings⟩ **12** : STRICT, UNRELENTING ⟨a ∼ bargain⟩ **13** : INCLEMENT ⟨a ∼ winter⟩ **14** : intense in force or manner ⟨a ∼ gust of wind⟩ **15** : ARDUOUS, STRENUOUS ⟨∼ work⟩ **16** : sounding as in *arcing* and *geese* respectively — used of *c* and *g* **17** : TROUBLESOME ⟨a ∼ problem⟩ **18** : having difficulty in doing something ⟨∼ of hearing⟩ **19** : addictive and gravely detrimental to health ⟨∼ drugs⟩ **20** : of or relating to the natural sciences and esp. the physical sciences — **hard** *adv* — **hard·ness** *n*

hard-and-fast *adj* : rigidly binding : STRICT ⟨a ∼ rule⟩

hard·back \'härd-ˌbak\ *n* : a hardcover book

hard·ball \-ˌbȯl\ *n* **1** : BASEBALL **2** : forceful uncompromising methods

hard-bit·ten \-'bi-tᵊn\ *adj* : SEASONED, TOUGH ⟨∼ campaigners⟩

hard·board \-ˌbȯrd\ *n* : a very dense fiberboard

hard-boiled \-'bȯi(-ə)ld\ *adj* **1** *of an egg* : boiled until both white and yolk have solidified **2** : lacking sentiment : TOUGH; *also* : HARDHEADED 2

hard·bound \-ˌbau̇nd\ *adj* : HARDCOVER

hard copy *n* : a copy of textual or graphic information (as from computer storage) produced on paper

hard-core \'härd-'kȯr\ *adj* **1** : extremely resistant to solution or improvement **2** : being the most determined or dedicated members of a specified group **3** : containing explicit depictions of sex acts — **hard core** *n*

hard·cov·er \-'kə-vər\ *adj* : having rigid boards on the sides covered in cloth or paper ⟨∼ books⟩

hard disk *n* : a sealed rigid metal disk used as a computer storage device; *also* : HARD DRIVE

hard drive *n* : a data-storage device consisting of a drive and one or more hard disks

hard·en \'här-dᵊn\ *vb* **1** : to make or become hard or harder **2** : to confirm or become confirmed in disposition or action — **hard·en·er** *n*

hard·hack \'härd-ˌhak\ *n* : an American spirea with dense clusters of pink or white flowers and leaves having a hairy rusty yellow underside

hard hat *n* **1** : a protective hat worn esp. by construction workers **2** : a construction worker

hard·head·ed \'härd-'he-dəd\ *adj* **1** : STUBBORN, WILLFUL **2** : SOBER, REALISTIC ⟨some ∼ advice⟩ — **hard·head·ed·ly** *adv* — **hard·head·ed·ness** *n*

hard·heart·ed \-'här-təd\ *adj* : PITILESS, CRUEL — **hard·heart·ed·ly** *adv* — **hard·heart·ed·ness** *n*

har·di·hood \'här-dē-ˌhu̇d\ *n* **1** : resolute

courage and fortitude **2** : VIGOR, ROBUSTNESS

hard–line \'härd-'līn\ *adj* : advocating or involving a rigidly uncompromising course of action ⟨a ∼ conservative⟩ — **hard–lin·er** \-'lī-nər\ *n*

hard–luck \-,lək\ *adj* : marked by or relating to bad luck ⟨∼ losing teams⟩

hard·ly \'härd-lē\ *adv* **1** : with force **2** : SEVERELY **3** : with difficulty **4** : only just : BARELY ⟨can ∼ tell the difference⟩ **5** : certainly not ⟨is ∼ a friend of mine⟩

hard–nosed \'härd-'nōzd\ *adj* : TOUGH, UNCOMPROMISING; *also* : HARDHEADED 2

hard palate *n* : the bony anterior part of the palate forming the roof of the mouth

hard·pan \'härd-,pan\ *n* : a compact layer in soil that is impenetrable by roots

hard–pressed \-'prest\ *adj* : HARD PUT; *esp* : being under financial strain

hard put *adj* **1** : barely able **2** : faced with difficulty or perplexity

hard rock *n* : rock music marked by a heavy beat, high amplification, and usu. frenzied performances

hard–shell \'härd-,shel\ *or* **hard–shelled** \-,sheld\ *adj* **1** : having a hard shell **2** : HIDEBOUND, UNCOMPROMISING ⟨a ∼ conservative⟩

hard·ship \-,ship\ *n* **1** : SUFFERING, PRIVATION **2** : something that causes suffering or privation

hard·tack \-,tak\ *n* : a saltless hard biscuit, bread, or cracker

hard·top \-,täp\ *n* : an automobile having a permanent rigid top

hard·ware \-,wer\ *n* **1** : ware (as cutlery or tools) made of metal **2** : the physical components (as electronic devices) of a vehicle (as a spacecraft) or an apparatus (as a computer)

hard–wired \-,wī(-ə)rd\ *adj* **1** : connected or incorporated by or as if by permanent electrical connections **2** : genetically or innately determined or predisposed ⟨∼ reactions⟩ ⟨is ∼ to avoid change⟩

hard·wood \-,wud\ *n* : the wood of a broad-leaved usu. deciduous tree as distinguished from that of a conifer; *also* : such a tree — **hardwood** *adj*

hard·work·ing \-'wər-kiŋ\ *adj* : INDUSTRIOUS, DILIGENT

har·dy \'här-dē\ *adj* **har·di·er; -est 1** : BOLD, BRAVE ⟨∼ pioneers⟩ **2** : AUDACIOUS, BRAZEN **3** : ROBUST; *also* : able to withstand adverse conditions (as of weather) ⟨∼ shrubs⟩ — **har·di·ly** \-də-lē\ *adv* — **har·di·ness** \-dē-nəs\ *n*

hare \'her\ *n, pl* **hare** *or* **hares** : any of various swift timid long-eared mammals like the related rabbits but born with open eyes and fur

hare·bell \'her-,bel\ *n* : a slender herb with bright blue bell-shaped flowers

hare·brained \-'brānd\ *adj* : FOOLISH, ABSURD ⟨∼ notions⟩

hare·lip \-'lip\ *n, sometimes offensive* : CLEFT LIP

ha·rem \'her-əm\ *n* [Ar *ḥarīm*, lit., something forbidden & *ḥaram*, lit., sanctuary] **1** : a house or part of a house allotted to

women in a Muslim household **2** : the women and servants occupying a harem **3** : a group of females associated with one male

hark \'härk\ *vb* : LISTEN

harken *var of* HEARKEN

har·le·quin \'här-li-kən, -kwən\ *n* **1** *cap* : a character (as in comedy) with a shaved head, masked face, variegated tights, and wooden sword **2** : CLOWN 2

har·lot \'här-lət\ *n* : PROSTITUTE

¹**harm** \'härm\ *n* **1** : physical or mental damage : INJURY **2** : MISCHIEF, HURT — **harm·ful** \-fəl\ *adj* — **harm·ful·ly** *adv* — **harm·ful·ness** *n* — **harm·less** *adj* — **harm·less·ly** *adv* — **harm·less·ness** *n*

²**harm** *vb* : to cause harm to : INJURE

¹**har·mon·ic** \här-'mä-nik\ *adj* **1** : of or relating to musical harmony or harmonics **2** : pleasing to the ear — **har·mon·i·cal·ly** \-ni-k(ə-)lē\ *adv*

²**harmonic** *n* : a musical overtone

har·mon·i·ca \här-'mä-ni-kə\ *n* : a small wind instrument in which the sound is produced by metal reeds

har·mo·ni·ous \här-'mō-nē-əs\ *adj* **1** : musically concordant **2** : CONGRUOUS **3** : marked by accord in sentiment or action ⟨a ∼ relationship⟩ — **har·mo·ni·ous·ly** *adv* — **har·mo·ni·ous·ness** *n*

har·mo·nise *Brit var of* HARMONIZE

har·mo·ni·um \här-'mō-nē-əm\ *n* : a keyboard wind instrument in which the wind acts on a set of metal reeds

har·mo·nize \'här-mə-,nīz\ *vb* **-nized; -niz·ing 1** : to play or sing in harmony **2** : to be in harmony **3** : to bring into consonance or accord — **har·mo·ni·za·tion** \,här-mə-nə-'zā-shən\ *n*

har·mo·ny \'här-mə-nē\ *n, pl* **-nies** [ME *armony*, fr. AF *armonie*, fr. L *harmonia*, fr. Gk, joint, harmony, fr. *harmos* joint] **1** : musical agreement of sounds; *esp* : the combination of tones into chords and progressions of chords **2** : a pleasing arrangement of parts; *also* : ACCORD **3** : internal calm

¹**har·ness** \'här-nəs\ *n* **1** : the gear other than a yoke of a draft animal **2** : something that resembles a harness

²**harness** *vb* **1** : to put a harness on; *also* : YOKE **2** : UTILIZE ⟨∼ one's potential⟩

¹**harp** \'härp\ *n* : a musical instrument consisting of a triangular frame set with strings plucked by the fingers — **harp·ist** \'här-pist\ *n*

²**harp** *vb* **1** : to play on a harp **2** : to dwell on a subject tiresomely — **harp·er** *n*

har·poon \här-'pün\ *n* : a barbed spear used esp. in hunting whales — **harpoon** *vb* — **har·poon·er** *n*

harp·si·chord \'härp-si-,kórd\ *n* : a keyboard instrument producing tones by the plucking of its strings with quills or with leather or plastic points

har·py \'här-pē\ *n, pl* **harpies** [L *Harpyia*, a malign creature of myth having a woman's head and a bird's body, fr. Gk] **1** : a predatory person : LEECH **2** : a shrewish woman

har·ri·dan \'her-ə-dən\ *n* : SHREW 2

¹**har·ri·er** \'her-ē-ər\ *n* **1** : any of a breed

of medium-sized foxhounds **2** : a runner on a cross-country team

²**harrier** *n* : a slender long-legged hawk

¹**har·row** \'her-ō\ *n* : a cultivating tool that has spikes, spring teeth, or disks and is used esp. to pulverize and smooth the soil

²**harrow** *vb* **1** : to cultivate with a harrow **2** : TORMENT, VEX

har·rumph \hə-'rəmf\ *vb* : to comment disapprovingly as though clearing the throat

har·ry \'her-ē\ *vb* **har·ried; har·ry·ing 1** : RAID, PILLAGE **2** : to torment by or as if by constant attack ♦ *Synonyms* WORRY, ANNOY, PLAGUE, PESTER

harsh \'härsh\ *adj* **1** : disagreeably rough **2** : causing discomfort or pain **3** : unduly exacting : SEVERE — **harsh·ly** *adv* — **harsh·ness** *n*

harsh·en \'här-shən\ *vb* : to make or become harsh ⟨~ed his voice⟩

hart \'härt\ *n, chiefly Brit* : STAG

har·um–scar·um \,har-əm-'skar-əm\ *adj* : RECKLESS, IRRESPONSIBLE

¹**har·vest** \'här-vəst\ *n* **1** : the season for gathering in crops; *also* : the act of gathering in a crop **2** : a mature crop **3** : the product or reward of effort

²**harvest** *vb* **1** : to gather in a crop : REAP **2** : to gather, hunt, or kill (as deer) for human use or population control **3** : to remove cells, tissues, or organs from a living or recently deceased body esp. for transplanting — **har·vest·er** *n*

has *pres 3d sing of* HAVE

has–been \'haz-,bin\ *n* : one that has passed the peak of ability, power, effectiveness, or popularity

¹**hash** \'hash\ *vb* [F *hacher*, fr. OF *hachier*, fr. *hache* battle-ax, of Gmc origin] **1** : to chop into small pieces **2** : to talk about — often used with *over* or *out*

²**hash** *n* **1** : chopped meat mixed with potatoes and browned **2** : HODGEPODGE, JUMBLE

³**hash** *n* : HASHISH

hash browns *n pl* : boiled potatoes that have been diced, mixed with chopped onions and shortening, and fried

hash·ish \'ha-,shēsh, ha-'shēsh\ *n* [Ar *ḥashīsh*] : the intoxicating concentrated resin from the flowering tops of the female hemp plant

hash·tag \'hash-,tag\ *n* : a word or phrase preceded by the symbol # that classifies the accompanying text

hasp \'hasp\ *n* : a fastener (as for a door) consisting of a hinged metal strap that fits over a staple and is secured by a pin or padlock

has·si·um \'ha-sē-əm\ *n* : an artificially produced radioactive metallic chemical element

has·sle \'ha-səl\ *n* **1** : WRANGLE; *also* : FIGHT **2** : an annoying or troublesome concern — **hassle** *vb*

has·sock \'ha-sək\ *n* : a cushion that serves as a seat or leg rest; *also* : a cushion to kneel on in prayer

haste \'hāst\ *n* **1** : rapidity of motion or action : SPEED **2** : rash or headlong action **3** : excessive eagerness — **hast·i·ly**

\'hā-stə-lē\ *adv* — **hast·i·ness** \-stē-nəs\ *n* — **hasty** \'hā-stē\ *adj*

has·ten \'hā-sᵊn\ *vb* **1** : to urge on **2** : to move or act quickly : HURRY ♦ *Synonyms* SPEED, ACCELERATE, QUICKEN

hat \'hat\ *n* : a covering for the head usu. having a shaped crown and brim — **under one's hat** : SECRET ⟨kept the plans *under his hat*⟩

hat-box \'hat-,bäks\ *n* : a round piece of luggage esp. for carrying hats

¹**hatch** \'hach\ *n* **1** : a small door or opening **2** : a door or cover for access down into a compartment of a ship

²**hatch** *vb* **1** : to produce by incubation; *also* : INCUBATE **2** : to emerge from an egg or pupa; *also* : to give forth young **3** : ORIGINATE ⟨~ a scheme⟩ — **hatch·ery** \'ha-chə-rē\ *n*

hatch·back \'hach-,bak\ *n* : an automobile with a rear hatch that opens upward

hatch·et \'ha-chət\ *n* **1** : a short-handled ax with a hammerlike part opposite the blade **2** : TOMAHAWK

hatchet man *n* : a person hired for murder, coercion, or unscrupulous attack

hatch·ing \'ha-chiŋ\ *n* : the engraving or drawing of closely spaced fine lines chiefly to give an effect of shading; *also* : the pattern so created

hatch·way \'hach-,wā\ *n* : a hatch giving access usu. by a ladder or stairs

¹**hate** \'hāt\ *n* **1** : intense hostility and aversion **2** : an object of hatred — **hate·ful** \-fəl\ *adj* — **hate·ful·ly** *adv* — **hate·ful·ness** *n*

²**hate** *vb* **hat·ed; hat·ing 1** : to express or feel extreme enmity **2** : to find distasteful ♦ *Synonyms* DETEST, ABHOR, ABOMINATE, LOATHE — **hat·er** *n*

ha·tred \'hā-trəd\ *n* : HATE; *also* : prejudiced hostility or animosity

hat·ter \'ha-tər\ *n* : one that makes, sells, or cleans and repairs hats

hau·berk \'hȯ-bərk\ *n* : a coat of mail

haugh·ty \'hȯ-tē\ *adj* **haugh·ti·er; -est** [obs. *haught*, fr. ME *haute*, fr. AF *halt, haut*, lit., high, fr. L *altus*] : disdainfully proud ♦ *Synonyms* INSOLENT, LORDLY, OVERBEARING, ARROGANT — **haugh·ti·ly** \-tə-lē\ *adv* — **haugh·ti·ness** \-tē-nəs\ *n*

¹**haul** \'hȯl\ *vb* **1** : to exert traction on : DRAW, PULL **2** : to furnish transportation : CART — **haul·er** *n*

²**haul** *n* **1** : PULL, TUG **2** : the result of an effort to obtain, collect, or win **3** : the length or course of a transportation route; *also* : LOAD

haul·age \'hȯ-lij\ *n* **1** : the act or process of hauling **2** : a charge for hauling

haunch \'hȯnch\ *n* **1** : ²HIP 1 **2** : HINDQUARTER 2 — usu. used in pl. **3** : HINDQUARTER 1

¹**haunt** \'hȯnt\ *vb* **1** : to visit often : FREQUENT **2** : to have a disquieting effect on ⟨was ~ed by his past⟩; *also* : to reappear continually in **3** : to visit or inhabit as a ghost — **haunt·er** *n* — **haunt·ing·ly** *adv*

²**haunt** \'hȯnt, *2 is usu* 'hant\ *n* **1** : a place habitually frequented **2** *chiefly dial* : GHOST

haute cou·ture \ˌōt-kù-'tùr\ *n* [F] : the establishments or designers that create exclusive and often trend-setting fashions for women; *also* : the fashions created

haute cui·sine \-kwi-'zēn\ *n* : artful or elaborate cuisine

hau·teur \hō-'tər, ō-, hō-\ *n* : ARROGANCE, HAUGHTINESS

¹**have** \'hav, həv, v; *in sense 2 before "to" usu* 'haf\ *vb* **had** \'had, həd\; **hav·ing; has** \'haz, həz, *in sense 2 before "to" usu* 'has\ **1** : to hold in possession; *also* : to hold in one's use, service, or regard ⟨*has* a good job⟩ **2** : to be compelled or forced ⟨~ to go now⟩ **3** : to stand in relationship to ⟨*has* many enemies⟩ **4** : OBTAIN; *also* : RECEIVE, ACCEPT **5** : to be marked by ⟨*has* red hair⟩ **6** : SHOW; *also* : USE, EXERCISE ⟨~ mercy⟩ **7** : EXPERIENCE; *also* : TAKE ⟨~ a look⟩ **8** : to entertain in the mind ⟨~ an idea⟩ **9** : to cause to **10** : ALLOW **11** : to be competent in **12** : to hold in a disadvantageous position; *also* : TRICK **13** : BEGET **14** : to partake of **15** — used as an auxiliary with the past participle to form the present perfect, past perfect, or future perfect — **have at** : ATTACK — **have coming** : DESERVE — **have done with** : to be finished with — **have had it** : to have endured all one will permit or can stand — **have to do with** : to have in the way of relation with or effect on

²**have** \'hav\ *n* : one that has material wealth

ha·ven \'hā-vən\ *n* **1** : HARBOR, PORT **2** : a place of safety **3** : a place offering favorable conditions ⟨an artist's ~⟩

have–not \'hav-ˌnät, -'nät\ *n* : one that is poor in material wealth

hav·er·sack \'ha-vər-ˌsak\ *n* [F *havresac*, fr. G *Habersack* bag for oats] : a bag similar to a knapsack but worn over one shoulder

hav·oc \'ha-vək\ *n* **1** : wide and general destruction **2** : great confusion and disorder

haw \'hò\ *n* : a hawthorn berry; *also* : HAWTHORN

Ha·wai·ian \hə-'wä-yən\ *n* **1** : a native or resident of Hawaii; *esp* : one of Polynesian ancestry **2** : the Polynesian language of Hawaii

¹**hawk** \'hòk\ *n* **1** : any of numerous mostly small or medium-sized day-flying birds of prey (as a falcon or kite) **2** : a supporter of a war or a warlike policy — **hawk·ish** *adj*

²**hawk** *vb* : to make a harsh coughing sound in or as if in clearing the throat; *also* : to raise by hawking

³**hawk** *vb* : to offer goods for sale by calling out in the street — **hawk·er** *n*

hawk·weed \'hòk-ˌwēd\ *n* : any of several plants related to the daisies usu. having yellow flowers

haw·ser \'hò-zər\ *n* : a large rope for towing, mooring, or securing a ship

haw·thorn \'hò-ˌthȯrn\ *n* : any of a genus of spiny spring-flowering shrubs or small trees related to the apple

¹**hay** \'hā\ *n* **1** : herbage (as grass) mowed and cured for fodder **2** : REWARD **3** *slang* : BED ⟨hit the ~⟩ **4** : a small amount of money

²**hay** *vb* : to cut, cure, and store for hay

hay·cock \'hā-ˌkäk\ *n* : a small conical pile of hay

hay fever *n* : an acute allergic reaction esp. to plant pollen that resembles a cold

hay·loft \'hā-ˌlòft\ *n* : a loft for hay

hay·mow \-ˌmaù\ *n* : a mow of or for hay

hay·rick \-ˌrik\ *n* : a large sometimes thatched outdoor stack of hay

hay·seed \-ˌsēd\ *n, pl* **hayseed** *or* **hayseeds 1** : clinging bits of straw or chaff from hay **2** : BUMPKIN, YOKEL

hay·stack \-ˌstak\ *n* : a stack of hay

hay·wire \-ˌwī(-ə)r\ *adj* : being out of order or control : CRAZY ⟨things went ~⟩

¹**haz·ard** \'ha-zərd\ *n* [ME, a dice game, fr. AF *hasard*, fr. Sp *azar*, Ar *al-zahr* the die] **1** : a source of danger **2** : CHANCE; *also* : ACCIDENT **3** : an obstacle on a golf course — **haz·ard·ous** *adj*

²**hazard** *vb* : VENTURE, RISK ⟨~ a guess⟩

¹**haze** \'hāz\ *n* **1** : fine dust, smoke, or light vapor causing lack of transparency in the air **2** : vagueness of mind or perception

²**haze** *vb* **hazed; haz·ing** : to harass by abusive and humiliating tricks usu. by way of initiation

ha·zel \'hā-zəl\ *n* **1** : any of a genus of shrubs or small trees related to the birches and bearing edible brown nuts (**ha·zel·nuts** \-ˌnəts\) **2** : a light brown color

hazy \'hā-zē\ *adj* **haz·i·er; -est 1** : obscured or darkened by haze **2** : VAGUE, INDEFINITE ⟨a ~ memory⟩; *also* : UNCERTAIN — **haz·i·ly** \-zə-lē\ *adv* — **haz·i·ness** \-zē-nəs\ *n*

Hb *abbr* hemoglobin

HBM *abbr* Her Britannic Majesty; His Britannic Majesty

H–bomb \'āch-ˌbäm\ *n* : HYDROGEN BOMB

HC *abbr* **1** Holy Communion **2** House of Commons

hd *abbr* head

HD *abbr* **1** heavy-duty **2** high definition

hdbk *abbr* handbook

hdkf *abbr* handkerchief

HDL \ˌāch-(ˌ)dē-'el\ *n* [*high-density lipoprotein*] : a cholesterol-poor protein-rich lipoprotein of blood plasma correlated with reduced risk of atherosclerosis

hdwe *abbr* hardware

he \'hē\ *pron* **1** : that male one **2** : a person : the person ⟨~ who hesitates is lost⟩

He *symbol* helium

HE *abbr* **1** Her Excellency **2** His Eminence **3** His Excellency

¹**head** \'hed\ *n* **1** : the front or upper part of the body containing the brain, the chief sense organs, and the mouth **2** : MIND; *also* : natural aptitude ⟨has a ~ for math⟩ **3** : POISE ⟨a level ~⟩ **4** : the obverse of a coin **5** : INDIVIDUAL; *also, pl* **head** : one of a number (as of cattle) **6** : the end that is upper or higher or opposite the foot; *also* : either end of something (as a drum) whose two ends need not be distinguished **7** : a compact mass

of plant parts (as leaves or flowers) **8** : the source of a stream **9** : DIRECTOR, LEADER; *also* : a leading element (as of a procession) **10** : a projecting part; *also* : the striking part of a weapon **11** : the place of leadership or honor **12** : a separate part or topic **13** : the foam on a fermenting or effervescing liquid **14** : a critical point ⟨events came to a ∼⟩ — **head·ed** \'he-dəd\ *adj* — **head·less** *adj* — **over one's head** : beyond one's comprehension or competence

²**head** *adj* : PRINCIPAL, CHIEF ⟨∼ chef⟩

³**head** *vb* **1** : to provide with or form a head; *also* : to form the head of **2** : LEAD, CONDUCT ⟨∼ed the search⟩ **3** : to get in front of esp. so as to stop; *also* : SURPASS **4** : to put or stand at the head **5** : to point or proceed in a certain direction ⟨∼ed west⟩

head·ache \'he-,dāk\ *n* **1** : pain in the head **2** : a baffling situation or problem — **head·achy** *also* **head·achey** \-,ā-kē\ *adj*

head·band \'hed-,band\ *n* : a band worn on or around the head

head·bang·er \-,baŋ-ər\ *n* : one who performs or enjoys hard rock

head·board \-,bòrd\ *n* : a board forming the head (as of a bed)

head cold *n* : a common cold centered in the nasal passages and adjacent mucous tissues

head·dress \'hed-,dres\ *n* : an often elaborate covering for the head

head·first \-'fərst\ *adv* : HEADLONG 1 ⟨dove ∼ into the water⟩ — **headfirst** *adj*

head·gear \-,gir\ *n* : a covering or protective device for the head

head·hunt·er \-,hən-tər\ *n* **1** : one that engages in head-hunting **2** : a recruiter of esp. executive personnel

head–hunt·ing \-,hən-tiŋ\ *n* : the practice of seeking out and decapitating enemies and preserving their heads as trophies

head·ing \'he-diŋ\ *n* **1** : the compass direction in which the longitudinal axis of a ship or airplane points **2** : something that appears at the top or beginning of something else (as a document)

head·land \'hed-lənd, -,land\ *n* : PROMONTORY

head·light \-,līt\ *n* : a light mounted on the front of a vehicle to illuminate the road ahead

¹**head·line** \-,līn\ *n* : a head of a newspaper story or article usu. printed in large type

²**headline** *vb* **1** : to provide with a headline **2** : to publicize highly **3** : to be a leading performer in

head·lock \-,läk\ *n* : a wrestling hold in which one encircles the opponent's head with one arm

¹**head·long** \-,lòŋ\ *adv* **1** : with the head foremost **2** : RECKLESSLY **3** : without delay

²**head·long** \-,lòŋ\ *adj* **1** : PRECIPITATE, RASH ⟨∼ flight⟩ **2** : plunging with the head foremost

head·man \'hed-'man, -,man\ *n* : one who is a leader : CHIEF

head·mas·ter \-,mas-tər\ *n* : a man who is head of a private school

head·mis·tress \-,mis-trəs\ *n* : a woman who is head of a private school

head of steam : strong driving force : MOMENTUM

head–on \'hed-'òn, -'än\ *adj* : having the front facing in the direction of initial contact or line of sight ⟨∼ collision⟩ — **head–on** *adv*

head·phone \-,fōn\ *n* : an earphone held on by a band over the head

head·piece \-,pēs\ *n* : a covering for the head

head·pin \-,pin\ *n* : a bowling pin that stands foremost in the arrangement of pins

head·quar·ters \-,kwòr-tərz\ *n sing or pl* **1** : a place from which a commander exercises command **2** : the administrative center of an enterprise

head·rest \-,rest\ *n* **1** : a support for the head **2** : a pad at the top of the back of an automobile seat

head·room \-,rüm, -,rùm\ *n* : vertical space in which to stand, sit, or move

head–scratcher \-,skra-chər\ *n* : PUZZLE, MYSTERY

head·set \-,set\ *n* : a pair of headphones

head·ship \-,ship\ *n* : the position, office, or dignity of a head

heads·man \'hedz-mən\ *n* : EXECUTIONER

head·stall \'hed-,stòl\ *n* : a part of a bridle or halter that encircles the head

head·stone \-,stōn\ *n* : a memorial stone at the head of a grave

head·strong \'hed-,stròŋ\ *adj* **1** : not easily restrained **2** : directed by ungovernable will ♦ **Synonyms** UNRULY, INTRACTABLE, WILLFUL, PERTINACIOUS, REFRACTORY, STUBBORN

heads–up \'hedz-'əp\ *n* : WARNING

head·wait·er \-'wā-tər\ *n* : the head of the dining-room staff of a restaurant or hotel

head·wa·ter \-,wò-tər, -,wä-\ *n* : the source of a stream — usu. used in pl.

head·way \-,wā\ *n* : forward motion; *also* : PROGRESS

head·wind \-,wind\ *n* : a wind blowing in a direction opposite to a course esp. of a ship or aircraft

head·word \'hed-,wərd\ *n* **1** : a word or term placed at the beginning **2** : a word qualified by a modifier

head·work \-,wərk\ *n* : mental work or effort : THINKING

heady \'he-dē\ *adj* **head·i·er; -est** **1** : WILLFUL, RASH; *also* : IMPETUOUS **2** : INTOXICATING ⟨a ∼ wine⟩ **3** : SHREWD

heal \'hēl\ *vb* **1** : to make or become healthy, sound, or whole **2** : CURE, REMEDY — **heal·er** *n*

health \'helth\ *n* **1** : sound physical or mental condition; *also* : overall condition of the body ⟨in poor ∼⟩ **2** : WELL-BEING **3** : a toast to someone's health or prosperity

health care *n* : efforts made to maintain

or restore health — usu. hyphenated when used attributively

health club n : a commercial establishment providing health and fitness facilities and equipment for members

health·ful \'helth-fəl\ adj 1 : beneficial to health 2 : HEALTHY — **health·ful·ly** adv — **health·ful·ness** n

health maintenance organization n : HMO

healthy \'hel-thē\ adj **health·i·er; -est** 1 : enjoying or typical of good health : WELL 2 : evincing or conducive to health 3 : PROSPEROUS ⟨a ~ economy⟩; also : CONSIDERABLE 2 ⟨a ~ savings⟩ — **health·i·ly** \-thə-lē\ adv — **health·i·ness** \-thē-nəs\ n

¹**heap** \'hēp\ n : PILE ⟨rubbish ~⟩; also : LOT 5 ⟨a ~ of fun⟩

²**heap** vb 1 : to throw or lay in a heap 2 : to give in large quantities; also : to load heavily

hear \'hir\ vb **heard** \'hərd\; **hear·ing** 1 : to perceive by the ear 2 : to gain knowledge of by hearing : LEARN 3 : HEED; also : ATTEND 4 : to give a legal hearing to or take testimony from — **hear·er** n

hear·ing n 1 : the process, function, or power of perceiving sound; esp : the special sense by which noises and tones are received as stimuli 2 : EARSHOT 3 : opportunity to be heard 4 : a listening to arguments (as in a court); also : a session (as of a legislative committee) in which testimony is taken from witnesses

hear·ken \'här-kən\ vb : to give attention : LISTEN ♦ **Synonyms** HEAR, HARK, HEED

hear·say \'hir-ˌsā\ n : RUMOR

hearse \'hərs\ n : a vehicle for carrying the dead to the grave

heart \'härt\ n 1 : a hollow muscular organ that by rhythmic contraction keeps up the circulation of the blood in the body; also : something resembling a heart in shape 2 : any of a suit of playing cards marked with a red figure of a heart; also, pl : a card game in which the object is to avoid taking tricks containing hearts 3 : the whole personality; also : the emotional or moral as distinguished from the intellectual nature 4 : COURAGE 5 : one's innermost being ⟨knew it in his ~⟩ 6 : CENTER; also : the essential part 7 : the younger central part of a compact leafy cluster (as of lettuce) — **heart·ed** \'här-təd\ adj — **by heart** : by rote or from memory

heart·ache \-ˌāk\ n : anguish of mind

heart attack n : an acute episode of heart disease due to insufficient blood supply to the heart muscle

heart·beat \'härt-ˌbēt\ n : one complete pulsation of the heart

heart·break \-ˌbrāk\ n : crushing grief

heart·break·ing \-ˌbrā-kiŋ\ adj : causing extreme sorrow or distress — **heart·break·er** \-ˌbrā-kər\ n — **heart·break·ing·ly** adv

heart·bro·ken \-ˌbrō-kən\ adj : overcome by sorrow

heart·burn \-ˌbərn\ n : a burning distress

behind the sternum due esp. to the backward flow of acid from the stomach to the esophagus

heart disease n : an abnormal organic condition of the heart or of the heart and circulation

heart·en \'här-t²n\ vb : ENCOURAGE, CHEER ⟨were ~ed by the victory⟩

heart·felt \'härt-ˌfelt\ adj : deeply felt : SINCERE ⟨~ thanks⟩

hearth \'härth\ n 1 : an area (as of brick) in front of a fireplace; also : the floor of a fireplace 2 : HOME

hearth·stone \'härth-ˌstōn\ n 1 : stone forming a hearth 2 : HOME

heart·less \'härt-ləs\ adj : CRUEL

heart·rend·ing \-ˌren-diŋ\ adj : HEART-BREAKING

heart·sick \-ˌsik\ adj : very despondent — **heart·sick·ness** n

heart–stop·ping \-ˌstä-piŋ\ adj : extremely thrilling or exciting

heart·strings \-ˌstriŋz\ n pl : the deepest emotions or affections

heart·throb \-ˌthräb\ n 1 : the throb of a heart 2 : sentimental emotion 3 : SWEET-HEART 4 : an entertainer noted for his sex appeal

heart–to–heart adj : SINCERE, FRANK

heart·warm·ing \'härt-ˌwȯr-miŋ\ adj : inspiring sympathetic feeling

heart·wood \-ˌwu̇d\ n : the older harder nonliving and usu. darker wood of the central part of a tree trunk

¹**hearty** \'här-tē\ adj **heart·i·er; -est** 1 : giving full support; also : JOVIAL 2 : vigorously healthy 3 : ABUNDANT; also : NOURISHING ⟨~ soups⟩ ♦ **Synonyms** SINCERE, WHOLEHEARTED, UNFEIGNED, HEARTFELT — **heart·i·ly** \-tə-lē\ adv — **heart·i·ness** \-tē-nəs\ n

²**hearty** n, pl **heart·ies** : an enthusiastic jovial fellow; also : SAILOR

¹**heat** \'hēt\ vb 1 : to make or become warm or hot 2 : EXCITE ⟨a ~ed discussion⟩ — **heat·ed·ly** adv — **heat·er** n

²**heat** n 1 : a condition of being hot : WARMTH 2 : a form of energy that when added to a body causes the body to rise in temperature, to fuse, to evaporate, or to expand 3 : high temperature 4 : intensity of feeling; also : sexual excitement esp. in a female mammal 5 : a preliminary race for narrowing the competition 6 : pungency of flavor 7 slang : POLICE 8 : PRESSURE, COERCION; also : ABUSE, CRITICISM ⟨took ~ for my mistakes⟩

heat exchanger n : a device (as an automobile radiator) for transferring heat from one fluid to another without allowing them to mix

heat exhaustion n : a condition marked by weakness, nausea, dizziness, and profuse sweating resulting from physical exertion in a hot environment

heath \'hēth\ n 1 : a tract of wasteland 2 : any of a family of often evergreen shrubby plants (as a blueberry or heather) of wet acid soils — **heathy** adj

hea·then \'hē-thən\ n, pl **heathens** or **heathen** 1 : an unconverted member of a people or nation that does not acknowledge the God of the Bible **2** : an uncivilized or irreligious person — **heathen** *adj* — **hea·then·dom** *n* — **hea·then·ish** *adj* — **hea·then·ism** *n*

heath·er \'he-thər\ *n* : a northern and alpine evergreen heath with usu. lavender flowers — **heath·ery** *adj*

heat lightning *n* : flashes of light without thunder ascribed to distant lightning reflected by high clouds

heat·stroke \'hēt-,strōk\ *n* : a disorder marked esp. by high body temperature without sweating and that follows prolonged exposure to excessive heat

¹heave \'hēv\ *vb* **heaved** *or* **hove** \'hōv\; **heav·ing 1** : to rise or lift upward **2** : THROW **3** : to rise and fall rhythmically; *also* : PANT **4** : RETCH **5** : PULL, PUSH — **heav·er** *n*

²heave *n* **1** : an effort to lift or raise **2** : THROW, CAST **3** : an upward motion **4** *pl* : a chronic lung disease of horses marked by difficult breathing and persistent cough

heav·en \'he-vən\ *n* **1** : FIRMAMENT — usu. used in pl. **2** *often cap* : the abode of the Deity and of the blessed dead; *also* : a spiritual state of everlasting communion with God **3** *cap* : GOD **1 4** : a place of supreme happiness — **heav·en·ly** *adj* — **heav·en·ward** *adv or adj*

¹heavy \'he-vē\ *adj* **heavi·er; -est 1** : having great weight **2** : hard to bear **3** : SERIOUS **4** : DEEP, PROFOUND ⟨a ∼ silence⟩ **5** : burdened with something oppressive; *also* : PREGNANT **6** : SLUGGISH **7** : DRAB; *also* : DOLEFUL **8** : DROWSY **9** : greater than the average of its kind or class **10** : very rich and hard to digest; *also* : not properly raised or leavened **11** : producing goods (as steel) used in the production of other goods — **heavi·ly** \-və-lē\ *adv* — **heavi·ness** \-vē-nəs\ *n*

²heavy *n, pl* **heav·ies** : a theatrical role representing a dignified or imposing person; *also* : a villain esp. in a story

heavy–duty \,he-vē-'dü-tē, -'dyü-\ *adj* : able to withstand unusual strain

heavy–hand·ed \-'han-dəd\ *adj* **1** : CLUMSY **2** : OPPRESSIVE, HARSH

heavy–heart·ed \-'här-təd\ *adj* : SADDENED, DESPONDENT

heavy lifting *n* : a burdensome or laborious duty

heavy metal *n* : energetic and highly amplified electronic rock music

heavy·set \,he-vē-'set\ *adj* : stocky and compact in build

heavy water *n* : water enriched in deuterium

heavy·weight \'he-vē-,wāt\ *n* : one above average in weight; *esp* : a boxer in an unlimited weight division

Heb *abbr* Hebrews

He·bra·ism \'hē-brā-,i-zəm\ *n* : the thought, spirit, or practice characteristic of the Hebrews — **He·bra·ic** \hi-'brā-ik\ *adj*

He·bra·ist \'hē-,brā-ist\ *n* : a specialist in Hebrew and Hebraic studies

He·brew \'hē-brü\ *n* **1** : the language of the Hebrews **2** : a member of or descendant from a group of Semitic peoples; *esp* : ISRAELITE — **Hebrew** *adj*

He·brews \'hē-(,)brüz\ *n* — see BIBLE table

hec·a·tomb \'he-kə-,tōm\ *n* : an ancient Greek and Roman sacrifice of 100 oxen or cattle

heck·le \'he-kəl\ *vb* **heck·led; heck·ling** : to harass with questions or gibes : BADGER — **heck·ler** *n*

hect·are \'hek-,ter\ *n* — see METRIC SYSTEM table

hec·tic \'hek-tik\ *adj* **1** : being hot and flushed **2** : filled with excitement, activity, or confusion — **hec·ti·cal·ly** \-ti-k(ə-)lē\ *adv*

hec·to·gram \'hek-tə-,gram\ *n* — see METRIC SYSTEM table

hec·to·li·ter \'hek-tə-,lē-tər\ *n* — see METRIC SYSTEM table

hec·to·me·ter \'hek-tə-,mē-tər, hek-'tä-mə-tər\ *n* — see METRIC SYSTEM table

hec·tor \'hek-tər\ *vb* [*hector* bully, fr. *Hector*, champion of Troy in Greek legend] **1** : SWAGGER **2** : to intimidate by bluster or personal pressure

¹hedge \'hej\ *n* **1** : a fence or boundary formed of shrubs or small trees **2** : BARRIER **3** : a means of protection (as against financial loss)

²hedge *vb* **hedged; hedg·ing 1** : ENCIRCLE **2** : HINDER **3** : to protect oneself financially by a counterbalancing action **4** : to evade the risk of commitment — **hedg·er** *n*

hedge·hog \'hej-,hóg, -,häg\ *n* : a small Old World insect-eating mammal covered with spines; *also* : PORCUPINE

hedge·hop \-,häp\ *vb* : to fly an airplane very close to the ground

hedge·row \-,rō\ *n* : a row of shrubs or trees bounding or separating fields

he·do·nism \'hē-də-,ni-zəm\ *n* [Gk *hēdonē* pleasure] : the doctrine that pleasure is the chief good in life; *also* : a way of life based on this — **he·do·nist** \-nist\ *n* — **he·do·nis·tic** \,hēdə-'ni-stik\ *adj*

¹heed \'hēd\ *vb* : to pay attention

²heed *n* : ATTENTION, NOTICE — **heed·ful** \-fəl\ *adj* — **heed·ful·ly** *adv* — **heed·ful·ness** *n* — **heed·less** *adj* — **heed·less·ly** *adv* — **heed·less·ness** *n*

¹heel \'hēl\ *n* **1** : the hind part of the foot **2** : one of the crusty ends of a loaf of bread **3** : a solid attachment forming the back of the sole of a shoe **4** : a rear, low, or bottom part **5** : a contemptible person

²heel *vb* : to tilt to one side : LIST

¹heft \'heft\ *n* : WEIGHT, HEAVINESS

²heft *vb* : to test the weight of by lifting

hefty \'hef-tē\ *adj* **heft·i·er; -est 1** : marked by bigness, bulk, and usu. strength **2** : impressively large ⟨got a ∼ raise⟩

he·ge·mo·ny \hi-'je-mə-nē\ *n* : preponderant influence or authority over others : DOMINATION

he·gi·ra \hi-'jī-rə\ *n* [the *Hegira*, flight of Muhammad from Mecca in A.D. 622, fr. ML, fr. Ar *hijra*, lit., departure] : a journey esp. when undertaken to escape a dangerous or undesirable environment

heif·er \'he-fər\ *n* : a young cow; *esp* : one that has not had a calf

height \'hīt\ *n* **1** : the highest part or point **2** : the distance from the bottom to the top of something standing upright **3** : ALTITUDE

height·en \'hī-tᵊn\ *vb* **1** : to increase in amount or degree **2** : to make or become high or higher ◆ **Synonyms** ENHANCE, INTENSIFY, AGGRAVATE, MAGNIFY

Heim·lich maneuver \'hīm-lik-\ *n* [Henry J. *Heimlich* b1920 Am. surgeon] : the manual application of sudden upward pressure on the upper abdomen of a choking victim to force a foreign object from the trachea

hei·nous \'hā-nəs\ *adj* [ME, fr. AF *hainus, heinous,* fr. *haine* hate, fr. *hair* to hate] : hatefully or shockingly evil — **hei·nous·ly** *adv* — **hei·nous·ness** *n*

heir \'er\ *n* : one who inherits or is entitled to inherit property, rank, title, or office — **heir·ship** *n*

heir apparent *n, pl* **heirs apparent** : an heir whose right to succeed (as to a title) cannot be taken away if he or she survives the present holder

heir·ess \'er-əs\ *n* : a female heir esp. to great wealth

heir·loom \'er-ˌlüm\ *n* **1** : a piece of personal property that descends by inheritance **2** : something handed on from one generation to another

heir presumptive *n, pl* **heirs presumptive** : an heir whose present right to inherit could be lost through the birth of a nearer relative

heist \'hīst\ *vb* : to commit armed robbery on; *also* : STEAL — **heist** *n*

held *past and past part of* HOLD

he·li·cal \'he-li-kəl, 'hē-\ *adj* : SPIRAL

he·li·cop·ter \'he-lə-ˌkäp-tər, 'hē-\ *n* [F *hélicoptère,* fr. Gk *helik-, helix* spiral + *pteron* wing] : an aircraft that is supported in the air by one or more rotors revolving on substantially vertical axes

he·lio·cen·tric \ˌhē-lē-ō-'sen-trik\ *adj* : having or relating to the sun as center

he·li·o·sphere \'hē-lē-ə-ˌsfir, -ō-\ *n* : the region in space influenced by the sun or solar wind

he·lio·trope \'hē-lē-ə-ˌtrōp\ *n* [L *heliotropium,* fr. Gk *hēliotropion,* fr. *hēlios* sun + *tropos* turn; fr. its flowers' turning toward the sun] : any of a genus of herbs or shrubs related to the forget-me-nots that have small white or purple flowers

he·li·port \'he-lə-ˌpȯrt\ *n* : a landing and takeoff place for a helicopter

he·li·um \'hē-lē-əm\ *n* [NL, fr. Gk *hēlios* sun] : a very light inert gaseous chemical element occurring in various natural gases

he·lix \'hē-liks\ *n, pl* **he·li·ces** \'he-lə-ˌsēz, 'hē-\ *also* **he·lix·es** \'hē-lik-səz\ : something spiral in form

hell \'hel\ *n* **1** : a nether world in which the dead continue to exist **2** : the realm of the devil in which the damned suffer everlasting punishment **3** : a place or

state of torment or destruction — **hell·ish** *adj*

hel·la·cious \ˌhe-'lā-shəs\ *adj* **1** : exceptionally powerful or violent ⟨∼ winds⟩ **2** : remarkably good **3** : extremely difficult ⟨a ∼ schedule⟩ **4** : extraordinarily large

hell–bent \'hel-ˌbent\ *adj* : stubbornly determined ⟨∼ on revenge⟩

hell–cat \-ˌkat\ *n* **1** : WITCH 2 **2** : a violently temperamental person; *esp* : an ill-tempered woman

hel·le·bore \'he-lə-ˌbȯr\ *n* **1** : any of a genus of poisonous herbs related to the buttercups; *also* : the dried root of a hellebore **2** : a poisonous plant related to the lilies; *also* : its dried roots used in medicine and insecticides

Hel·lene \'he-ˌlēn\ *n* : GREEK

Hel·le·nism \'he-lə-ˌni-zəm\ *n* : a body of humanistic and classical ideals associated with ancient Greece — **Hel·len·ic** \he-'le-nik\ *adj* — **Hel·le·nist** \'he-lə-nist\ *n*

Hel·le·nis·tic \ˌhe-lə-'nis-tik\ *adj* : of or relating to Greek history, culture, or art after Alexander the Great

hell–for–leather \'hel-fər-'le-thər\ *adv* : at full speed : STEERSMAN

hell·gram·mite \'hel-grə-ˌmīt\ *n* : an aquatic insect larva that is used as bait in fishing

hell·hole \'hel-ˌhōl\ *n* : a place of extreme misery or squalor

hel·lion \'hel-yən\ *n* : a troublesome or mischievous person

hel·lo \hə-'lō, he-\ *n, pl* **hellos** : an expression of greeting — used interjectionally

helm \'helm\ *n* **1** : a lever or wheel for steering a ship **2** : a position of control

hel·met \'hel-mət\ *n* : a protective covering for the head

helms·man \'helmz-mən\ *n* : the person at the helm : STEERSMAN

helms·per·son \-ˌpər-sᵊn\ *n* : HELMSMAN

hel·ot \'he-lət\ *n* : SLAVE, SERF

¹**help** \'help\ *vb* **1** : AID, ASSIST **2** : IMPROVE, RELIEVE **3** : to be of use; *also* : PROMOTE **4** : to change for the better **5** : to refrain from; *also* : PREVENT **6** : to serve with food or drink ⟨∼ yourself⟩ — **help·er** *n*

²**help** *n* **1** : AID, ASSISTANCE; *also* : a source of aid **2** : REMEDY, RELIEF **3** : one who assists another **4** : EMPLOYEE — **help·ful** \-fəl\ *adj* — **help·ful·ly** *adv* — **help·ful·ness** *n* — **help·less** *adj* — **help·less·ly** *adv* — **help·less·ness** *n*

helper T cell *n* : a T cell that participates in the immune response by recognizing foreign antigens and has a protein on its surface to which HIV attaches

help·ing *n* : a portion of food

help·mate \'help-ˌmāt\ *n* **1** : HELPER **2** : WIFE

help·meet \-ˌmēt\ *n* : HELPMATE

hel·ter–skel·ter \ˌhel-tər-'skel-tər\ *adv* **1** : in undue haste or disorder **2** : HAPHAZARDLY

helve \'helv\ *n* : a handle of a tool or weapon

Hel·ve·tian \hel-'vē-shən\ *adj* : SWISS — **Helvetian** *n*

¹**hem** \'hem\ *n* **1** : a border of an article (as of cloth) doubled back and stitched down **2** : RIM, MARGIN

²**hem** *vb* **hemmed; hem·ming 1** : to make a hem in sewing; *also* : BORDER, EDGE **2** : to surround restrictively

he–man \'hē-,man\ *n* : a strong virile man

he·ma·tite \'hē-mə-,tīt\ *n* : a mineral that consists of an oxide of iron and that constitutes an important iron ore

he·ma·tol·o·gy \,hē-mə-'tä-lə-jē\ *n* : a branch of biology that deals with the blood and blood-forming organs — **he·ma·to·log·ic** \-tə-'lä-jik\ *also* **he·ma·to·log·i·cal** \-ji-kəl\ *adj* — **he·ma·tol·o·gist** \-'tä-lə-jist\ *n*

he·ma·to·ma \-'tō-mə\ *n, pl* **-mas** *also* **-ma·ta** \-mə-tə\ : a usu. clotted mass of blood forming as a result of a broken blood vessel

heme \'hēm\ *n* : the deep red iron-containing part of hemoglobin

hemi·sphere \'he-mə-,sfir\ *n* **1** : one of the halves of the earth as divided by the equator into northern and southern parts or by a meridian into eastern and western parts **2** : either of two half spheres formed by a plane through the sphere's center — **hemi·spher·ic** \,he-mə-'sfir-ik, -'sfer-\ *or* **hemi·spher·i·cal** \-'sfir-i-kəl, -'sfer-\ *adj*

hem·line \'hem-,līn\ *n* : the line formed by the lower edge of a garment

hem·lock \'hem-,läk\ *n* **1** : any of several poisonous herbs related to the carrot **2** : an evergreen tree related to the pines; *also* : its soft light wood

he·mo·glo·bin \'hē-mə-,glō-bən\ *n* : an iron-containing compound found in red blood cells that carries oxygen from the lungs to the body tissues

he·mo·phil·ia \,hē-mə-'fi-lē-ə\ *n* : a hereditary blood defect usu. of males that slows blood clotting with resulting difficulty in stopping bleeding — **he·mo·phil·i·ac** \-lē-,ak\ *adj or n*

hem·or·rhage \'hem-rij, 'he-mə-\ *n* : a large discharge of blood from the blood vessels — **hemorrhage** *vb* — **hem·or·rhag·ic** \,he-mə-'ra-jik\ *adj*

hemorrhagic fever *n* : any of a group of virus diseases characterized chiefly by sudden onset, fever, aching, and bleeding in the internal organs

hem·or·rhoid \'hem-,rȯid, 'he-mə-\ *n* : a swollen mass of dilated veins at or just within the anus — usu. used in pl.

hemp \'hemp\ *n* : a tall widely grown Asian herb that is the source of a tough fiber used in rope and of marijuana and hashish from its flowers and leaves; *also* : the fiber — **hemp·en** \'hem-pən\ *adj*

hem·stitch \'hem-,stich\ *vb* : to embroider (fabric) by drawing out parallel threads and stitching the exposed threads in groups to form designs

hen \'hen\ *n* : a female chicken esp. over a year old; *also* : a female bird

hence \'hens\ *adv* **1** : AWAY **2** : from this time ⟨four years ~⟩ **3** : CONSEQUENTLY **4** : from this source or origin

hence·forth \hens-,fȯrth\ *adv* : from this point on

hence·for·ward \-'fȯr-wərd\ *adv* : HENCEFORTH

hench·man \'hench-mən\ *n* [ME *hengestman* groom, fr. *hengest* stallion] : a trusted follower or supporter

hen·na \'he-nə\ *n* **1** : an Old World tropical shrub with fragrant white flowers; *also* : a reddish brown dye obtained from its leaves and used esp. on hair **2** : the color of henna dye

hen·peck \'hen-,pek\ *vb* : to nag and boss one's husband

hep \'hep\ *adj* : HIP

hep·a·rin \'he-pə-rən\ *n* : a compound found esp. in liver that slows the clotting of blood and is used medically

he·pat·ic \hi-'pa-tik\ *adj* : of, relating to, or associated with the liver

he·pat·i·ca \hi-'pa-ti-kə\ *n* : any of a genus of herbs related to the buttercups that have lobed leaves and delicate white, pink, or bluish flowers

hep·a·ti·tis \,he-pə-'tī-təs\ *n, pl* **-tit·i·des** \-'ti-tə-,dēz\ : inflammation of the liver; *also* : a virus disease of which this is a feature

hep·tam·e·ter \hep-'ta-mə-tər\ *n* : a line of verse containing seven metrical feet

hep·tath·lon \hep-'tath-lən, -,län\ *n* : a 7-event athletic contest for women

¹**her** \'hər\ *adj* : of or relating to her or herself

²**her** *pron, objective case of* SHE

¹**her·ald** \'her-əld\ *n* **1** : an official crier or messenger **2** : HARBINGER **3** : ANNOUNCER **4** : ADVOCATE

²**herald** *vb* **1** : to give notice of **2** : HAIL, GREET; *also* : PUBLICIZE

he·ral·dic \he-'ral-dik, hə-\ *adj* : of or relating to heralds or heraldry

her·ald·ry \'her-əl-drē\ *n, pl* **-ries 1** : the practice of devising and granting armorial insignia and of tracing genealogies **2** : INSIGNIA **3** : PAGEANTRY

herb \'ərb, 'hərb\ *n* **1** : a seed plant that lacks woody tissue and dies to the ground at the end of a growing season **2** : a plant or plant part valued for medicinal or savory qualities — **her·ba·ceous** \,ər-'bā-shəs, ,hər-\ *adj*

herb·age \'ər-bij, 'hər-\ *n* : green plants esp. when used or fit for grazing

her·bal \'ər-bəl, 'hər-\ *adj* : of, relating to, utilizing, or made of herbs

herb·al·ist \'ər-bə-list, 'hər-\ *n* **1** : a person who practices healing by the use of herbs **2** : a person who collects or grows herbs

her·bar·i·um \,ər-'ber-ē-əm, ,hər-\ *n, pl* **-ia** \-ē-ə\ **1** : a collection of dried plant specimens **2** : a place that houses an herbarium

her·bi·cide \'ər-bə-,sīd, 'hər-\ *n* : an agent used to destroy or inhibit plant growth — **her·bi·cid·al** \,ər-bə-'sī-d'l, ,hər-\ *adj*

her·biv·o·rous \,ər-'bi-və-rəs, ,hər-\ *adj* : feeding on plants — **her·bi·vore** \'ər-bə-,vȯr, 'hər-\ *n*

her·cu·le·an \,hər-kyə-'lē-ən, ,hər-'kyü-lē-\ *adj, often cap* [*Hercules*, hero of

Greek myth renowned for his strength] : of extraordinary power, size, or difficulty ⟨a ~ task⟩

¹herd \'hərd\ n 1 : a group of animals of one kind kept or living together 2 : a group of people with a common bond ⟨a ~ of tourists⟩ 3 : MOB

²herd vb 1 : to assemble or move in a herd — herd·er n

herds·man \'hərdz-mən\ n : one who manages, breeds, or tends livestock

¹here \'hir\ adv 1 : in or at this place; also : NOW 2 : at or in this point, particular, or case 3 : in the present life or state 4 : to this place ⟨come ~⟩

²here n : this place ⟨get away from ~⟩

here·abouts \'hir-ə-,baůts\ or here·about \-,baůt\ adv : in this vicinity

¹here·af·ter \hir-'af-tər\ adv 1 : after this in sequence or in time 2 : in some future time or state

²hereafter n, often cap 1 : FUTURE 2 : an existence beyond earthly life

here·by \-'bī\ adv : by means of this

he·red·i·tary \hə-'re-də-,ter-ē\ adj 1 : genetically passed or passable from parent to offspring 2 : passing by inheritance; also : having title or possession through inheritance 3 : of a kind established by tradition

he·red·i·ty \-də-tē\ n : the characteristics and potentialities genetically derived from one's ancestors; also : the passing of these from ancestor to descendant

Her·e·ford \'hər-fərd\ n : any of a breed of red-coated beef cattle with white faces and markings

here·in \hir-'in\ adv : in this

here·of \-'əv, -'äv\ adv : of this

here·on \-'ȯn, -'än\ adv : on this

her·e·sy \'her-ə-sē\ n, pl -sies [ME heresie, fr. AF, fr. LL haeresis, fr. LGk hairesis, fr. Gk, action of taking, choice, sect, fr. hairein to take] 1 : adherence to a religious opinion contrary to church dogma 2 : an opinion or doctrine contrary to church dogma 3 : dissent from a dominant theory, opinion, or practice — her·e·tic \-,tik\ n — he·ret·i·cal \hə-'re-ti-kəl\ adj

here·to \hir-'tü\ adv : to this document

here·to·fore \'hir-tə-,fȯr\ adv : up to this time

here·un·der \hir-'ən-dər\ adv : under this or according to this writing

here·un·to \hir-'ən-tü\ adv : to this

here·upon \'hir-ə-,pȯn, -,pän\ adv : on this or immediately after this

here·with \hir-'with, -'with\ adv 1 : with this 2 : HEREBY

her·i·ta·ble \'her-ə-tə-bəl\ adj : capable of being inherited

her·i·tage \'her-ə-tij\ n 1 : property that descends to an heir 2 : LEGACY 3 : BIRTHRIGHT

her·maph·ro·dite \(,)hər-'ma-frə-,dīt\ n : an animal or plant having both male and female reproductive organs — hermaphrodite adj — her·maph·ro·dit·ic \(,)hər-,ma-frə-'di-tik\ adj

her·met·ic \hər-'me-tik\ also her·met·i-cal \-ti-kəl\ adj : AIRTIGHT — her·met·i·cal·ly \-ti-k(ə-)lē\ adv

her·mit \'hər-mət\ n [ME heremite, eremite, fr. AF, fr. LL eremita, fr. LGk erēmitēs, fr. Gk, adj., living in the desert, fr. erēmia desert, fr. erēmos desolate] : one who lives in solitude esp. for religious reasons

her·mit·age \-mə-tij\ n 1 : the dwelling of a hermit 2 : a secluded dwelling

hermit crab n : any of numerous crabs that occupy empty mollusk shells

her·nia \'hər-nē-ə\ n, pl -ni·as or -ni·ae \-nē-,ē, -nē-,ī\ : a protrusion of a bodily part (as a loop of intestine) into a pouch of the weakened wall of a cavity in which it is normally enclosed — her·ni·ate \-nē-,āt\ vb — her·ni·a·tion \,hər-nē-'ā-shən\ n

he·ro \'hē-rō\ n, pl heroes 1 : a mythological or legendary figure of great strength or ability 2 : a man admired for his achievements and qualities 3 : the chief male character in a literary or dramatic work 4 pl usu heros : SUBMARINE 2 — he·ro·ic \hi-'rō-ik\ adj — he·ro·i·cal·ly \-i-k(ə-)lē\ adv

heroic couplet n : a rhyming couplet in iambic pentameter

he·ro·ics \hi-'rō-iks\ n pl : heroic or showy behavior

her·o·in \'her-ə-wən\ n : an illicit addictive narcotic drug made from morphine

her·o·ine \'her-ə-wən\ n 1 : a woman admired for her achievements and qualities 2 : the chief female character in a literary or dramatic work

her·o·ism \'her-ə-,wi-zəm\ n 1 : heroic conduct 2 : the qualities of a hero ♦ Synonyms VALOR, PROWESS, GALLANTRY

her·on \'her-ən\ n, pl herons also heron : any of various long-legged long-billed wading birds with soft plumage

her·pes \'hər-pēz\ n : any of several virus diseases characterized by the formation of blisters on the skin or mucous membranes

herpes sim·plex \-'sim-,pleks\ n : either of two virus diseases marked in one by watery blisters above the waist (as on the mouth and lips) and in the other on the sex organs

herpes zos·ter \-'zäs-tər\ n : SHINGLES

her·pe·tol·o·gy \,hər-pə-'tä-lə-jē\ n : a branch of zoology dealing with reptiles and amphibians — her·pe·tol·o·gist \,hər-pə-'tä-lə-jist\ n

her·ring \'her-iŋ\ n, pl herring or herrings : a valuable narrow-bodied food fish of the No. Atlantic; also : a related fish of the No. Pacific harvested esp. for its roe

her·ring·bone \'her-iŋ-,bōn\ n : a pattern made up of rows of parallel lines with adjacent rows slanting in reverse directions; also : a twilled fabric with this pattern

hers \'hərz\ pron : one or the ones belonging to her

her·self \hər-'self\ pron : SHE, HER — used reflexively, for emphasis, or in absolute constructions

hertz \'hərts, 'herts\ *n, pl* **hertz** : a unit of frequency equal to one cycle per second
hes·i·tant \'he-zə-tənt\ *adj* : tending to hesitate — **hes·i·tance** \-təns\ *n* — **hes·i·tan·cy** \-tən-sē\ *n* — **hes·i·tant·ly** *adv*
hes·i·tate \'he-zə-ˌtāt\ *vb* **-tat·ed; -tat·ing** **1** : to hold back (as in doubt) **2** : PAUSE
♦ **Synonyms** WAVER, VACILLATE, FALTER, SHILLY-SHALLY — **hes·i·ta·tion** \ˌhe-zə-'tā-shən\ *n*
het·ero·dox \'he-tə-rə-ˌdäks\ *adj* **1** : differing from an acknowledged standard **2** : holding unorthodox opinions — **het·er·o·doxy** \-ˌdäk-sē\ *n*
het·er·o·ge·neous \ˌhe-tə-rə-'jē-nē-əs, -nyəs\ *adj* : consisting of dissimilar ingredients or constituents : MIXED — **het·er·o·ge·ne·ity** \-jə-'nē-ə-tē\ *n* — **het·er·o·ge·neous·ly** *adv*
het·er·o·glos·sia \ˌhe-tə-rō-'glä-sē-ə, -'glò-\ *n* : a diversity of voices, styles of discourse, or points of view in a literary work
het·er·o·sex·ism \ˌhe-tə-rō-'sek-si-zəm\ *n* : discrimination or prejudice by heterosexuals against homosexuals
het·er·o·sex·u·al \ˌhe-tə-rō-ˌsek-shə-wəl\ *adj* **1** : of, relating to, or marked by sexual interest in the opposite sex; *also* : of, relating to, or involving sexual intercourse between members of opposite sex **2** : of or relating to different sexes — **heterosexual** *n* — **het·er·o·sex·u·al·i·ty** \-ˌsek-shə-'wa-lə-tē\ *n*
hew \'hyü\ *vb* **hewed; hewed** *or* **hewn** \'hyün\; **hew·ing** **1** : to cut or fell with blows (as of an ax) **2** : to give shape to with or as if with an ax **3** : to conform strictly ⟨*—ed* to the rules⟩ — **hew·er** *n*
HEW *abbr* Department of Health, Education, and Welfare
¹hex \'heks\ *vb* **1** : to practice witchcraft **2** : JINX
²hex *n* : SPELL, JINX
³hex *adj* : HEXAGONAL
⁴hex *abbr* hexagon
hexa·gon \'hek-sə-ˌgän\ *n* [ultim. fr. Gk *hex* six + *gōnia* angle] : a polygon having six angles and six sides — **hex·ag·o·nal** \hek-'sa-gən-ᵊl\ *adj*
hex·am·e·ter \hek-'sa-mə-tər\ *n* : a line of verse containing six metrical feet
hey \'hā\ *interj* — used esp. to call attention or to express doubt, surprise, or joy
hey·day \'hā-ˌdā\ *n* : a period of greatest strength, vigor, or prosperity
hf *abbr* half
Hf *symbol* hafnium
HF *abbr* high frequency
hg *abbr* hectogram
Hg *symbol* [NL *hydrargyrum,* lit., water silver] mercury
hgt *abbr* height
hgwy *abbr* highway
HH *abbr* **1** Her Highness **2** His Highness **3** His Holiness
HHS *abbr* Department of Health and Human Services
HI *abbr* **1** Hawaii **2** humidity index
hi·a·tus \hī-'ā-təs\ *n* [L, fr. *hiare* to yawn] **1** : a break in an object : GAP **2** : a period

when something is suspended or interrupted
hi·ba·chi \hi-'bä-chē\ *n* [Jp] : a charcoal brazier
hi·ber·nate \'hī-bər-ˌnāt\ *vb* **-nat·ed; -nat·ing** : to pass the winter in a torpid or resting state — **hi·ber·na·tion** \ˌhī-bər-'nā-shən\ *n* — **hi·ber·na·tor** \'hī-bər-ˌnā-tər\ *n*
hi·bis·cus \hī-'bis-kəs, hə-\ *n* : any of a genus of herbs, shrubs, and trees related to the mallows and noted for large showy flowers
hic·cup *also* **hic·cough** \'hi-(ˌ)kəp\ *n* **1** : a spasmodic breathing movement checked by sudden closing of the glottis accompanied by a peculiar sound; *also, pl* : an attack of hiccuping **2** : a slight irregularity, error, or malfunction **3** : a brief minor interruption or change — **hiccup** *vb*
hick \'hik\ *n* [*Hick,* nickname for *Richard*] : an unsophisticated provincial person — **hick** *adj*
hick·o·ry \'hi-kə-rē\ *n, pl* **-ries** : any of a genus of No. American hardwood trees related to the walnuts; *also* : the wood of a hickory — **hickory** *adj*
hi·dal·go \hi-'dal-gō\ *n, pl* **-gos** *often cap* [Sp, fr. earlier *fijo dalgo,* lit., son of something] : a member of the lower nobility of Spain
hidden tax *n* **1** : a tax ultimately paid by someone other than the person on whom it is formally levied **2** : an economic injustice that reduces one's income or buying power
¹hide \'hīd\ *vb* **hid** \'hid\; **hid·den** \'hid-ᵊn\ *or* **hid; hid·ing** **1** : to put or remain out of sight **2** : to conceal for shelter or protection; *also* : to seek protection **3** : to keep secret **4** : to turn away in shame or anger — **hid·er** *n*
²hide *n* : the skin of an animal
hide-and-seek \ˌhīd-ᵊn-'sēk\ *n* : a children's game in which everyone hides from one player who tries to find them
hide·away \'hī-də-ˌwā\ *n* : HIDEOUT
hide·bound \'hīd-ˌbaùnd\ *adj* : being inflexible or conservative
hid·eous \'hi-dē-əs\ *adj* [ME *hidous,* fr. AF *hidus, hisdos,* fr. *hisde,* *hide* terror] **1** : offensive to one of the senses : UGLY **2** : morally offensive : SHOCKING ♦ **Synonyms** GHASTLY, GRISLY, GRUESOME, HORRIBLE, LURID, MACABRE — **hid·eous·ly** *adv* — **hid·eous·ness** *n*
hide·out \'hīd-ˌaùt\ *n* : a place of refuge or concealment
hie \'hī\ *vb* **hied; hy·ing** *or* **hie·ing** : HASTEN
hi·er·ar·chy \'hī-ə-ˌrär-kē\ *n, pl* **-chies** **1** : a ruling body of clergy organized into ranks **2** : persons or things arranged in a graded series — **hi·er·ar·chi·cal** \ˌhī-ə-'rär-ki-kəl\ *adj* — **hi·er·ar·chi·cal·ly** \-k(ə-)lē\ *adv*
hi·er·o·glyph·ic \ˌhī-ə-rə-'gli-fik\ *n* [MF *hieroglyphique,* adj., ultim. fr. Gk *hieroglyphikos,* fr. *hieros* sacred + *glyphein* to carve] **1** : a character in a system of pic-

ture writing (as of the ancient Egyptians) 2 : a symbol or sign difficult to decipher

hi-fi \'hī-'fī\ n 1 : HIGH FIDELITY 2 : equipment for reproduction of sound with high fidelity

hig·gle·dy–pig·gle·dy \ˌhi-gəl-dē-'pi-gəl-dē\ adv : in confusion

¹**high** \'hī\ adj 1 : ELEVATED; also : TALL 2 : advanced toward fullness or culmination; also : slightly tainted 3 : advanced esp. in complexity ⟨∼er mathematics⟩ 4 : long past 5 : SHRILL, SHARP 6 : far from the equator ⟨∼ latitudes⟩ 7 : exalted in character 8 : of greater degree, size, or amount than average ⟨∼ in cholesterol⟩ 9 : of relatively great importance 10 : FORCIBLE, STRONG ⟨∼ winds⟩ 11 : showing elation or excitement 12 : INTOXICATED; also : excited or stupefied by or as if by a drug — **high·ly** adv

²**high** adv 1 : at or to a high place or degree 2 : LUXURIOUSLY ⟨living ∼⟩

³**high** n 1 : an elevated place 2 : a region of high barometric pressure 3 : a high point or level 4 : the gear of a vehicle giving the highest speed 5 : an excited or stupefied state produced by or as if by a drug

high·ball \'hī-ˌbȯl\ n : a usu. tall drink of liquor mixed with water or a carbonated beverage

high beam n : a vehicle headlight with a long-range focus

high·born \'hī-'bȯrn\ adj : of noble birth

high·boy \-ˌbȯi\ n : a high chest of drawers mounted on a base with legs

high·bred \-'bred\ adj : coming from superior stock

high·brow \-ˌbrau̇\ n : a person of superior learning or culture — **highbrow** adj — **high·brow·ism** \-ˌbrau̇-ˌi-zəm\ n

high–definition adj : being or relating to a television system with twice as many scan lines per frame as a conventional system

high–density li·po·pro·tein \-ˌlī-pō-'prō-tēn, -ˌli-\ n : HDL

high·er–up \ˌhī-ər-'əp\ n : a superior officer or official

high–fa·lu·tin \ˌhī-fə-'lü-t°n\ adj : PRETENTIOUS, POMPOUS

high fashion n 1 : HIGH STYLE 2 : HAUTE COUTURE

high fidelity n : the reproduction of sound or image with a high degree of faithfulness to the original

high five n : a slapping of upraised right hands by two people (as in celebration) — **high–five** vb

high–flown \'hī-'flōn\ adj 1 : EXALTED 2 : BOMBASTIC

high frequency n : a radio frequency between 3 and 30 megahertz

high gear n 1 : HIGH 4 2 : a state of intense or maximum activity

high–hand·ed \'hī-'han-dəd\ adj : OVERBEARING — **high–hand·ed·ly** adv — **high–hand·ed·ness** n

high–hat \-'hat\ adj : SUPERCILIOUS, SNOBBISH — **high–hat** vb

high·land \'hī-lənd\ n : elevated or mountainous land

high·land·er \-lən-dər\ n 1 : an inhabitant of a highland 2 cap : an inhabitant of the Scottish Highlands

high–level \'hī-'le-vəl\ adj 1 : being of high importance or rank 2 : being or relating to highly concentrated and environmentally hazardous nuclear waste

¹**high·light** \-ˌlīt\ n : an event or detail of major importance

²**highlight** vb 1 : EMPHASIZE 2 : to constitute a highlight of 3 : to mark (text) with a highlighter 4 : to cause to be displayed in a way that stands out on a computer screen

high·light·er \-ˌlīt-ər\ n : a pen with transparent ink used for marking text passages

high–mind·ed \-'mīn-dəd\ adj : marked by elevated principles and feelings — **high–mind·ed·ness** n

high·ness \-nəs\ n 1 : the quality or state of being high 2 — used as a title (as for kings)

high–pres·sure \-'pre-shər\ adj : using or involving aggressive and insistent sales techniques

high–rise \-'rīz\ adj 1 : having several stories and being equipped with elevators ⟨∼ apartments⟩ 2 : of or relating to high-rise buildings

high road n : HIGHWAY

high school n : a school usu. including grades 9 to 12 or 10 to 12

high sea n : the open sea outside territorial waters — usu. used in pl.

high–sound·ing \'hī-'sauṅ-din̄\ adj : POMPOUS, IMPOSING ⟨∼ rhetoric⟩

high–spir·it·ed \-'spir-ə-təd\ adj : characterized by a bold or energetic spirit

high–strung \-'strən̄\ adj : having an extremely nervous or sensitive temperament

high style n : the newest in fashion or design

high·tail \'hī-ˌtāl\ vb : to retreat at full speed

high tech \-'tek\ n : HIGH TECHNOLOGY

high technology n : technology involving the use of advanced devices

high–ten·sion \'hī-'ten-chən\ adj : having or using a high voltage

high–test \-'test\ adj : having a high octane number

high–tick·et \-'ti-kət\ adj : EXPENSIVE

high–toned \-'tōnd\ adj 1 : high in social, moral, or intellectual quality 2 : PRETENTIOUS, POMPOUS

high·way \'hī-ˌwā\ n : a main direct road

high·way·man \'hī-ˌwā-mən\ n : a thief who robs travelers on a road

hi·jab \hē-'jäb, -'jab\ n [Ar ḥijāb cover, screen, veil] : the covering for the hair and neck that is worn by Muslim women

hi·jack also **high·jack** \'hī-jak\ vb : to steal esp. by stopping a vehicle on the highway; also : to commandeer a flying airplane — **hijack** n — **hi·jack·er** n

¹**hike** \'hīk\ vb **hiked**; **hik·ing** 1 : to move or raise with a sudden motion 2 : to take a long walk — **hik·er** n

²**hike** n **1** : a long walk **2** : RISE, INCREASE ⟨price ∼⟩

hi·lar·i·ous \hi-ˈler-ē-əs, hī-\ adj : marked by or providing boisterous merriment — **hi·lar·i·ous·ly** adv — **hi·lar·i·ty** \-ə-tē\ n

hill \ˈhil\ n **1** : a usu. rounded elevation of land **2** : a little heap or mound (as of earth) — **hilly** adj

hill·bil·ly \ˈhil-ˌbi-lē\ n, pl **-lies** : a person from a backwoods area

hill·ock \ˈhi-lək\ n : a small hill

hill·side \ˈhil-ˌsīd\ n : the part of a hill between the summit and the foot

hill·top \-ˌtäp\ n : the top of a hill

hilt \ˈhilt\ n : a handle esp. of a sword or dagger

him \ˈhim\ pron, objective case of HE

him·self \him-ˈself\ pron : HE, HIM — used reflexively, for emphasis, or in absolute constructions

¹**hind** \ˈhīnd\ n, pl **hinds** also **hind** : a female of a common Eurasian deer

²**hind** adj : REAR ⟨the dog's ∼ legs⟩

hin·der \ˈhin-dər\ vb **1** : to impede the progress of **2** : to hold back ♦ Synonyms OBSTRUCT, BLOCK, BAR, IMPEDE

²**hind·er** \ˈhīn-dər\ adj : HIND

Hin·di \ˈhin-dē\ n : a literary and official language of northern India

hind·most \ˈhīnd-ˌmōst\ adj : farthest to the rear

hind·quar·ter \-ˌkwȯr-tər\ n **1** : one side of the back half of the carcass of a quadruped **2** pl : the part of the body of a quadruped behind the junction of hind limbs and trunk

hin·drance \ˈhin-drəns\ n **1** : the state of being hindered **2** : IMPEDIMENT 1 **3** : the action of hindering

hind·sight \ˈhīnd-ˌsīt\ n : understanding of an event after it has happened

Hin·du–Ara·bic adj : relating to, being, or composed of Arabic numerals

Hin·du·ism \ˈhin-dü-ˌi-zəm\ n : a body of religious beliefs and practices native to India — **Hin·du** n or adj

hind wing n : either of the posterior wings of a 4-winged insect

¹**hinge** \ˈhinj\ n : a jointed device on which a swinging part (as a door, gate, or lid) turns

²**hinge** vb **hinged; hing·ing 1** : to attach by or furnish with hinges **2** : to be contingent on a single construction

hint \ˈhint\ n **1** : an indirect or summary suggestion **2** : CLUE **3** : a very slight amount ♦ Synonyms DASH, SOUPÇON, SUSPICION, TINCTURE, TOUCH — **hint** vb

hin·ter·land \ˈhin-tər-ˌland\ n **1** : a region behind a coast **2** : a region remote from cities

¹**hip** \ˈhip\ n : the fruit of a rose

²**hip** n **1** : the part of the body on either side below the waist consisting of the side of the pelvis and the upper thigh **2** : HIP JOINT

³**hip** adj **hip·per; hip·pest** : keenly aware of or interested in the newest developments or styles — **hip·ness** n

⁴**hip** vb **hipped; hip·ping** : TELL, INFORM

hip·bone \ˈhip-ˌbōn, -ˌbōn\ n : the large flaring bone that makes a lateral half of the pelvis in mammals

hip–hop \ˈhip-ˌhäp\ n **1** : a subculture esp. of inner-city youths who are devotees of rap music **2** : the stylized rhythmic music that accompanies rap — **hip–hop** adj

hip–hug·gers \ˈhip-ˌhə-gərz\ n pl : low-slung close-fitting pants that rest on the hips

hip joint n : the articulation between the femur and the hipbone

hipped \ˈhipt\ adj : having hips esp. of a specified kind ⟨broad-hipped⟩

hip·pie or **hip·py** \ˈhi-pē\ n, pl **hippies** : a usu. young person who rejects established mores and advocates nonviolence; also : a long-haired unconventionally dressed young person

hip·po \ˈhi-pō\ n, pl **hippos** : HIPPOPOTAMUS

hip·po·drome \ˈhi-pə-ˌdrōm\ n : an arena for equestrian performances

hip·po·pot·a·mus \ˌhi-pə-ˈpä-tə-məs\ n, pl **-mus·es** or **-mi** \-ˌmī\ [L, fr. Gk hippopotamos, alter. of hippos potamios, lit., river horse] : a large thick-skinned aquatic mammal of sub-Saharan Africa that is related to the swine

¹**hire** \ˈhī(-ə)r\ n **1** : payment for labor or personal services : WAGES **2** : EMPLOYMENT **3** : one who is hired

²**hire** vb **hired; hir·ing 1** : to employ for pay **2** : to engage the temporary use of for pay **3** : to take employment

hire·ling \ˈhī(-ə)r-liŋ\ n : a hired person; esp : one with mercenary motives

hir·sute \ˈhər-ˌsüt, ˈhir-\ adj : HAIRY

¹**his** \ˈhiz\ adj : of or relating to him or himself

²**his** pron : one or the ones belonging to him

His·pan·ic \hi-ˈspa-nik\ adj : of, relating to, or being a person of Latin-American descent living in the U.S. — **Hispanic** n

hiss \ˈhis\ vb : to make a sharp sibilant sound; also : to express disapproval of by hissing — **hiss** n

hissy fit \ˈhi-sē-\ n : TANTRUM

hist abbr historian; historical; history

his·ta·mine \ˈhis-tə-ˌmēn, -mən\ n : a compound widespread in animal tissues that plays a major role in allergic reactions (as hay fever)

his·to·gram \ˈhis-tə-ˌgram\ n : a representation of statistical data by rectangles whose widths represent class intervals and whose heights usu. represent corresponding frequencies

his·tol·o·gy \hi-ˈstä-lə-jē\ n, pl **-gies 1** : a branch of anatomy dealing with tissue structure **2** : tissue structure or organization — **his·to·log·i·cal** \ˌhis-tə-ˈlä-ji-kəl\ or **his·to·log·ic** \-ˈlä-jik\ adj — **his·tol·o·gist** \-ˈtä-lə-jist\ n

his·to·ri·an \hi-ˈstȯr-ē-ən\ n : a student or writer of history

his·to·ric·i·ty \ˌhis-tə-ˈri-sə-tē\ n : historical actuality

his·to·ri·og·ra·pher \hi-ˌstȯr-ē-ˈä-grə-fər\ n : HISTORIAN

his·to·ry \ˈhis-tə-rē\ n, pl **-ries** [ultim. fr.

L *historia,* fr. Gk, inquiry, history, fr. *histōr, istōr* knowing, learned] **1** : a chronological record of significant events often with an explanation of their causes **2** : a branch of knowledge that records and explains past events **3** : events that form the subject matter of history **4** : an established record ⟨a convict's ~ of violence⟩ — **his·tor·ic** \hi-'stòr-ik\ *adj* — **his·tor·i·cal** \-i-kəl\ *adj* — **his·tor·i·cal·ly** \-k(ə-)lē\ *adv*

his·tri·on·ic \ˌhis-trē-'ä-nik\ *adj* [LL *histrionicus,* fr. L *histrio* actor] **1** : deliberately affected **2** : of or relating to actors, acting, or the theater — **his·tri·on·i·cal·ly** \-ni-k(ə-)lē\ *adv*

his·tri·on·ics \-niks\ *n pl* **1** : theatrical performances **2** : deliberate display of emotion for effect

¹**hit** \'hit\ *vb* **hit; hit·ting** **1** : to reach with a blow : STRIKE; *also* : to arrive with a force like a blow ⟨the storm ~⟩ **2** : to make or bring into contact : COLLIDE **3** : to affect detrimentally ⟨was ~ by the flu⟩ **4** : to make a request of **5** : to come upon **6** : to accord with : SUIT **7** : REACH, ATTAIN **8** : to indulge in often to excess — **hit·ter** *n*

²**hit** *n* **1** : an act or instance of hitting or being hit **2** : a great success **3** : BASE HIT **4** : a dose of a drug **5** : a murder committed by a gangster **6** : an instance of connecting to a particular website **7** : a successful match in a search (as of the Internet)

¹**hitch** \'hich\ *vb* **1** : to move by jerks **2** : to catch or fasten esp. by a hook or knot **3** : HITCHHIKE

²**hitch** *n* **1** : JERK, PULL **2** : a sudden halt **3** : a connection between something towed and its mover **4** : KNOT

hitch·hike \'hich-ˌhīk\ *vb* : to travel by securing free rides from passing vehicles — **hitch·hik·er** *n*

¹**hith·er** \'hi-thər\ *adv* : to this place

²**hither** *adj* : being on the near or adjacent side

hith·er·to \-ˌtü\ *adv* : up to this time

HIV \ˌāch-(ˌ)ī-'vē\ *n* [*human immunodeficiency virus*] : any of several retroviruses that infect and destroy helper T cells causing the great reduction in their numbers that is diagnostic of AIDS

hive \'hīv\ *n* **1** : a container for housing honeybees **2** : a colony of bees **3** : a place swarming with busy occupants — **hive** *vb*

hives \'hīvz\ *n sing or pl* : an allergic disorder marked by raised itching patches on the skin or mucous membranes

hl *abbr* hectoliter

HL *abbr* House of Lords

hm *abbr* hectometer

HM *abbr* **1** Her Majesty; Her Majesty's **2** His Majesty; His Majesty's

HMO \ˌāch-(ˌ)em-'ō\ *n* [*health maintenance organization*] : a comprehensive health-care organization financed by periodic fixed payments by voluntarily enrolled individuals and families

HMS *abbr* **1** Her Majesty's ship **2** His Majesty's ship

Ho *symbol* holmium

hoa·gie *also* **hoa·gy** \'hō-gē\ *n, pl* **hoa·gies** : SUBMARINE 2

hoard \'hòrd\ *n* : a hidden accumulation — **hoard** *vb* — **hoard·er** *n*

hoar·frost \'hòr-ˌfròst\ *n* : FROST 2

hoarse \'hòrs\ *adj* **hoars·er; hoars·est** **1** : rough and harsh in sound **2** : having a grating voice — **hoarse·ly** *adv* — **hoarse·ness** *n*

hoary \'hòr-ē\ *adj* **hoar·i·er; -est** **1** : gray or white with or as if with age **2** : ANCIENT — **hoar·i·ness** \'hòr-ē-nəs\ *n*

hoax \'hōks\ *n* : an act intended to trick or dupe; *also* : something accepted or established by fraud — **hoax** *vb* — **hoax·er** *n*

hob \'häb\ *n* : MISCHIEF, TROUBLE ⟨raising ~⟩

¹**hob·ble** \'hä-bəl\ *vb* **hob·bled, hob·bling** **1** : to limp along; *also* : to make lame **2** : FETTER

²**hobble** *n* **1** : a hobbling movement **2** : something used to hobble an animal

hob·by \'hä-bē\ *n, pl* **hobbies** : a pursuit or interest engaged in for relaxation — **hob·by·ist** \-ist\ *n*

hob·by·horse \'hä-bē-ˌhòrs\ *n* **1** : a stick with a horse's head on which children pretend to ride **2** : a toy horse mounted on rockers **3** : a topic to which one constantly reverts

hob·gob·lin \'häb-ˌgäb-lən\ *n* **1** : a mischievous goblin **2** : BOGEY 1

hob·nail \-ˌnāl\ *n* : a short large-headed nail for studding shoe soles — **hob·nailed** \-ˌnāld\ *adj*

hob·nob \-ˌnäb\ *vb* **hob·nobbed; hob·nob·bing** : to associate familiarly

ho·bo \'hō-bō\ *n, pl* **hoboes** *also* **hobos** : TRAMP 2

¹**hock** \'häk\ *n* : a joint or region in the hind limb of a quadruped just above the foot and corresponding to the human ankle

²**hock** *n* [D *hok* pen, prison] : ²PAWN 2 ⟨got his watch out of ~⟩; *also* : DEBT 2 ⟨trying to get out of ~⟩ — **hock** *vb*

hock·ey \'hä-kē\ *n* **1** : FIELD HOCKEY **2** : ICE HOCKEY

ho·cus–po·cus \ˌhō-kəs-'pō-kəs\ *n* **1** : SLEIGHT OF HAND **2** : nonsense or sham used to conceal deception

hod \'häd\ *n* : a long-handled carrier for mortar or bricks

hodge·podge \'häj-ˌpäj\ *n* : a heterogeneous mixture : JUMBLE

Hodgkin's disease \'häj-kinz-\ *n* : a neoplastic disease of lymphoid tissue characterized esp. by enlargement of lymph nodes, spleen, and liver

hoe \'hō\ *n* : a long-handled implement with a thin flat blade used esp. for cultivating, weeding, or loosening the earth around plants — **hoe** *vb*

hoe·cake \'hō-ˌkāk\ *n* : a small cornmeal cake

hoe·down \-ˌdaùn\ *n* **1** : SQUARE DANCE **2** : a gathering featuring hoedowns

¹**hog** \'hòg, 'häg\ *n, pl* **hogs** *also* **hog** **1** : a domestic swine esp. when grown **2** : a

selfish, gluttonous, or filthy person —
hog·gish *adj*

²**hog** *vb* **hogged; hog·ging** : to take or
hold selfishly ⟨*hogged* the limelight⟩

ho·gan \'hō-ˌgän\ *n* : a Navaho Indian
dwelling usu. made of logs and mud

hog·back \'hȯg-ˌbak, 'häg-\ *n* : a ridge
with a sharp summit and steep sides

hog·nose snake \'hȯg-ˌnōz-, 'häg-\ or
hog·nosed snake \-ˌnōzd-\ *n* : any of a
genus of rather small harmless stout-
bodied No. American snakes that seldom
bite but hiss wildly and often play dead
when disturbed

hogs·head \'hȯgz-ˌhed, 'hägz-\ *n* 1 : a
large cask or barrel 2 : a liquid measure
equal to 63 U.S. gallons

hog-tie \'hȯg-ˌtī, 'häg-\ *vb* 1 : to tie together the feet of ⟨∼ a calf⟩ 2 : to make
helpless

hog·wash \-ˌwȯsh, -ˌwäsh\ *n* 1 : SWILL,
SLOP 2 : NONSENSE, BALONEY

hog wild *adj* : lacking in restraint

hoi pol·loi \ˌhȯi-pə-'lȯi\ *n pl* [Gk, the
many] : the general populace

hoi·sin sauce \'hȯi-ˌsin-\ *n* : a thick reddish sauce of soybeans, spices, and garlic
used in Asian cookery

¹**hoist** \'hȯist\ *vb* : RAISE, LIFT

²**hoist** *n* 1 : LIFT 2 : an apparatus for
hoisting

hoke \'hōk\ *vb* **hoked; hok·ing** : FAKE
— usu. used with *up*

hok·ey \'hō-kē\ *adj* **hok·i·er; -est** 1
: CORNY ⟨∼ songs⟩ 2 : PHONY ⟨a ∼
excuse⟩

ho·kum \'hō-kəm\ *n* : NONSENSE

¹**hold** \'hōld\ *vb* **held** \'held\; **hold·ing** 1
: POSSESS; *also* : KEEP 2 : RESTRAIN 3
: to have a grasp on 4 : to support, remain, or keep in a particular situation or
position 5 : SUSTAIN; *also* : RESERVE 6
: BEAR, COMPORT 7 : to maintain in being or action : PERSIST 8 : CONTAIN, AC-
COMMODATE 9 : HARBOR, ENTERTAIN;
also : CONSIDER, REGARD 10 : to carry
on by concerted action; *also* : CONVOKE
11 : to occupy esp. by appointment or
election 12 : to be valid 13 : HALT,
PAUSE — **hold·er** *n* — **hold forth** : to
speak at length — **hold to** : to adhere to
: MAINTAIN — **hold with** : to agree with
or approve of

²**hold** *n* 1 : STRONGHOLD 2 : CONFINE-
MENT; *also* : PRISON 3 : the act or manner of holding : GRIP 4 : a restraining,
dominating, or controlling influence 5
: something that may be grasped as a support 6 : an order or indication that something is to be reserved or delayed — **on
hold** : in a temporary state of waiting (as
during a phone call); *also* : in a state of
postponement ⟨plans *on hold*⟩

³**hold** *n* 1 : the interior of a ship below
decks; *esp* : a ship's cargo deck 2 : an
airplane's cargo compartment

hold·ing *n* 1 : land or other property
owned ⟨2 : a ruling of a court esp. on an
issue of law

holding pattern *n* : a course flown by an
aircraft waiting to land

hold out *vb* 1 : to continue to fight or

work 2 : to refuse to come to an agreement — **hold-out** \'hōl-ˌdaůt\ *n*

hold·over \'hōl-ˌdō-vər\ *n* : one that is
held over

hold·up \'hōl-ˌdəp\ *n* 1 : DELAY 2 : robbery at the point of a gun

hole \'hōl\ *n* 1 : an opening into or
through something 2 : a hollow place (as
a pit or cave) 3 : DEN, BURROW 4 : a
wretched or dingy place 5 : a unit of play
from tee to cup in golf 6 : an awkward
position — **hole** *vb*

hol·i·day \'hä-lə-ˌdā\ *n* [ME, fr. OE *hāligdæg*,
fr. *hālig* holy + *dæg* day] 1 : a day
set aside for special religious observance
2 : a day of freedom from work; *esp* : one
in commemoration of an event 3 : VACA-
TION — **holiday** *vb*

ho·li·ness \'hō-lē-nəs\ *n* : the quality or
state of being holy — used as a title for
various high religious officials

ho·lis·tic \hō-'lis-tik\ *adj* : relating to or
concerned with integrated wholes or
complete systems rather than with the
analysis or treatment of separate parts
⟨∼ medicine⟩ ⟨∼ ecology⟩

hol·lan·daise \ˌhä-lən-'dāz\ *n* : a rich
sauce made basically of butter, egg yolks,
and lemon juice or vinegar

hol·ler \'hä-lər\ *vb* : to cry out : SHOUT —
holler *n*

¹**hol·low** \'hä-lō\ *n* 1 : CAVITY, HOLE 2 : a
surface depression

²**hollow** *adj* **hol·low·er** \'hä-lə-wər\; **hol·low·est**
\-lə-wəst\ 1 : CONCAVE, SUNKEN
2 : having a cavity within 3 : lacking in
real value, sincerity, or substance; *also*
: FALSE 4 : MUFFLED ⟨a ∼ sound⟩ —
hol·low·ness *n*

³**hollow** *vb* : to make or become hollow

hol·low·ware *or* **hol·lo·ware** \'hä-lə-ˌwar\ *n*
: vessels (as bowls or cups) with a
significant depth and volume

hol·ly \'hä-lē\ *n, pl* **hollies** : either of two
trees or shrubs with branches of usu. evergreen glossy spiny-margined leaves and
red berries

hol·ly·hock \'hä-lē-ˌhäk, -ˌhȯk\ *n* [ME *holihoc*,
fr. *holi* holy + *hoc* mallow] : a biennial or perennial herb related to the mallows that is widely grown for its tall
stalks of showy flowers

hol·mi·um \'hōl-mē-əm\ *n* : a metallic
chemical element

ho·lo·caust \'hä-lə-ˌkȯst, 'hō-\ *n* 1 : a
thorough destruction esp. by fire 2 *often
cap* : the killing of European Jews by the
Nazis during World War II; *also* : GENO-
CIDE

Ho·lo·cene \'hō-lə-ˌsēn\ *adj* : of, relating
to, or being the present geologic epoch
— **Holocene** *n*

ho·lo·gram \'hō-lə-ˌgram, 'hä-\ *n* : a
three-dimensional image produced by an
interference pattern of light (as laser
light)

ho·lo·graph \'hō-lə-ˌgraf, 'hä-\ *n* : a document wholly in the handwriting of its author

ho·log·ra·phy \hō-'lä-grə-fē\ *n* : the process of making a hologram — **ho·lo·graph·ic**
\ˌhō-lə-'gra-fik, ˌhä-\ *adj*

Hol·stein \'hōl-ˌstēn, -ˌstīn\ n : any of a breed of large black-and-white dairy cattle that produce large quantities of comparatively low-fat milk

Hol·stein–Frie·sian \-'frē-zhən\ n : HOLSTEIN

hol·ster \'hōl-stər\ n [D] : a usu. leather case for a firearm

ho·ly \'hō-lē\ adj **ho·li·er; -est** 1 : worthy of absolute devotion 2 : SACRED 3 : having a divine quality ◆ **Synonyms** HALLOWED, BLESSED, SANCTIFIED, CONSECRATED — **ho·li·ly** \-lə-lē\ adv

Holy Spirit n : the third person of the Christian Trinity

ho·ly·stone \'hō-lē-ˌstōn\ n : a soft sandstone used to scrub a ship's wooden decks — **holystone** vb

hom·age \'ä-mij, 'hä-\ n [ME, fr. AF homage, omage, fr. home man, vassal, fr. L homo human being] : expression of high regard; also : TRIBUTE 3

hom·bre \'äm-ˌbrā, 'əm-, -brē\ n : GUY, FELLOW

hom·burg \'häm-ˌbərg\ n [Homburg, Germany] : a man's felt hat with a stiff curled brim and a high crown creased lengthwise

¹**home** \'hōm\ n 1 : one's residence; also : HOUSE 2 : the social unit formed by a family living together 3 : a congenial environment; also : HABITAT 4 : a place of origin 5 : the objective in various games

²**home** vb homed; hom·ing 1 : to go or return home 2 : to proceed to or toward a source of radiated energy used as a guide

home·body \'hōm-ˌbä-dē\ n : one whose life centers on home

home·boy \-ˌbȯi\ n 1 : a boy or man from one's neighborhood, hometown, or region 2 : a fellow member of a youth gang 3 : an inner-city youth

home·bred \-'bred\ adj : produced at home : INDIGENOUS

home·com·ing \-ˌkə-miŋ\ n 1 : a return home 2 : an annual celebration for alumni at a college or university

home computer n : a small inexpensive microcomputer

home economics n : the theory and practice of homemaking

home·girl \'hōm-ˌgərl\ n 1 : a girl or woman from one's neighborhood, hometown, or region 2 : a girl or woman who is a member of one's peer group 3 : an inner-city girl or woman

home·grown \'hōm-'grōn\ adj 1 : grown domestically ⟨∼ peaches⟩ 2 : LOCAL, INDIGENOUS ⟨a ∼ artist⟩

home·land \-ˌland\ n 1 : native land 2 : an area set aside to be a state for a people of a particular national, cultural, or racial origin

home·less \-ləs\ adj : having no home or permanent residence — **home·less·ness** n

home·ly \'hōm-lē\ adj **home·li·er; -est** 1 : FAMILIAR 2 : unaffectedly natural 3 : lacking beauty or proportion — **home·li·ness** \-lē-nəs\ n

home·made \'hōm-ˌmād\ adj : made in

the home, on the premises, or by one's own efforts

home·mak·er \-ˌmā-kər\ n : one who manages a household esp. as a wife and mother — **home·mak·ing** \-kiŋ\ n

ho·me·op·a·thy \ˌhō-mē-'ä-pə-thē\ n : a system of medical practice that treats disease esp. with minute doses of a remedy that would in larger amounts produce symptoms in healthy persons similar to those of the disease — **ho·meo·path** \'hō-mē-ə-ˌpath\ n — **ho·meo·path·ic** \ˌhō-mē-ə-'pa-thik\ adj

ho·meo·sta·sis \ˌhō-mē-ō-'stā-səs\ n : the maintenance of a relatively stable state of equilibrium between interrelated physiological, psychological, or social factors characteristic of an individual or group — **ho·meo·stat·ic** \-'sta-tik\ adj

home page n : the page usu. encountered first at a website that usu. contains hyperlinks to the other pages of the site

home plate n : a slab at the apex of a baseball diamond that a base runner must touch in order to score

hom·er \'hō-mər\ n : HOME RUN — **homer** vb

home·room \'hōm-ˌrüm, -ˌrùm\ n : a classroom where pupils report at the beginning of each school day

home run n : a hit in baseball that enables the batter to go around all the bases and score a run

home·school \'hōm-ˌskül\ vb : to teach school subjects to one's children at home — **home·school·er** \-ˌskü-lər\ n

home·sick \'hōm-ˌsik\ adj : longing for home and family while absent from them — **home·sick·ness** n

home·spun \-ˌspən\ adj 1 : spun or made at home; also : made of a loosely woven usu. woolen or linen fabric 2 : SIMPLE, HOMELY

¹**home·stead** \-ˌsted\ n : the home and land occupied by a family

²**homestead** vb : to acquire or settle on public land — **home·stead·er** n

home·stretch \-'strech\ n 1 : the part of a racecourse between the last curve and the winning post 2 : a final stage (as of a project)

home theater n : an entertainment system (as a television with surround sound and a DVD player) for the home

home video n : prerecorded videocassettes or videodiscs for home viewing

¹**home·ward** \-wərd\ or **home·wards** \-wərdz\ adv : toward home

²**homeward** adj : being or going toward home

home·work \-ˌwərk\ n 1 : an assignment given a student to be completed outside the classroom 2 : preparatory reading or research

¹**hom·ey** \'hō-mē\ adj **hom·i·er; -est** : characteristic of home

²**homey** or **hom·ie** \'hō-mē\ n, pl **homeys** or **homies** : HOMEBOY

ho·mi·cide \'hä-mə-ˌsīd, 'hō-\ n [L homicida murderer & homicidium manslaughter; both fr. homo human being + caedere to cut, kill] 1 : a person who kills another **2** : a killing of one human being by another — **hom·i·cid·al** \ˌhä-mə-'sī-dᵊl\ *adj*

hom·i·ly \'hä-mə-lē\ *n, pl* **-lies** : SERMON — **hom·i·let·ic** \ˌhä-mə-'le-tik\ *adj*

homing pigeon *n* : a racing pigeon trained to return home

hom·i·nid \'hä-mə-nəd, -ˌnid\ *n* : any of a family of primate mammals that comprise all living humans and extinct ancestral and related forms — **hominid** *adj*

hom·i·ny \'hä-mə-nē\ *n* : hulled corn with the germ removed

ho·mo·cys·te·ine \ˌhō-mō-'sis-tə-ˌēn\ *n* : an amino acid associated with an increased risk of heart disease when occurring at high levels in the blood

ho·mo·erot·ic \ˌhō-mō-i-'rä-tik\ *adj* : marked by or portraying homosexual desire — **ho·mo·erot·i·cism** \-'rä-tə-ˌsi-zəm\ *n*

ho·mo·ge·neous \ˌhō-mə-'jē-nē-əs, -nyəs\ *adj* : of the same or a similar kind; *also* : of uniform structure — **ho·mo·ge·ne·i·ty** \-jə-'nē-ə-tē\ *n* — **ho·mo·ge·neous·ly** *adv*

ho·mo·ge·ni·sa·tion, ho·mog·e·nise *Brit var of* HOMOGENIZATION, HOMOGENIZE

ho·mog·e·nize \hō-'mä-jə-ˌnīz, hə-\ *vb* **-nized; -niz·ing 1** : to make homogeneous **2** : to reduce the particles in (as milk) to uniform size and distribute them evenly throughout the liquid — **ho·mog·e·ni·za·tion** \-ˌmä-jə-nə-'zā-shən\ *n* — **ho·mog·e·niz·er** *n*

ho·mo·graph \'hä-mə-ˌgraf, 'hō-\ *n* : one of two or more words spelled alike but different in origin, meaning, or pronunciation (as the *bow* of a ship, a *bow* and arrow)

ho·mol·o·gy \hō-'mä-lə-jē, hə-\ *n, pl* **-gies 1** : structural likeness between corresponding parts of different plants or animals due to evolution from a common ancestor **2** : structural likeness between different parts of the same individual — **ho·mol·o·gous** \-'mä-lə-gəs\ *adj*

hom·onym \'hä-mə-ˌnim, 'hō-\ *n* **1** : HOMOPHONE, HOMOGRAPH **2** : one of two or more words spelled and pronounced alike but different in meaning (as *pool* of water and *pool* the game)

ho·mo·pho·bia \ˌhō-mə-'fō-bē-ə\ *n* : irrational fear of, aversion to, or discrimination against homosexuality or homosexuals — **ho·mo·phobe** \'hō-mə-ˌfōb\ *n* — **ho·mo·pho·bic** \-'fō-bik\ *adj*

ho·mo·phone \'hä-mə-ˌfōn, 'hō-\ *n* : one of two or more words (as *to*, *too*, *two*) pronounced alike but different in meaning or derivation or spelling

Ho·mo sa·pi·ens \ˌhō-mō-'sä-pē-ənz, -ˌsa-\ *n* : HUMANKIND

ho·mo·sex·u·al \ˌhō-mō-'sek-shə-wəl\ *adj* : of, relating to, or marked by sexual interest in the same sex as oneself; *also* : of, relating to, or involving sexual intercourse between members of the same sex — **homosexual** *n* — **ho·mo·sex·u·al·i·ty** \-ˌsek-shə-'wa-lə-tē\ *n*

hon *abbr* honor; honorable; honorary

hone \'hōn\ *n* : WHETSTONE — **hone** *vb* — **hon·er** *n*

hone in *vb* : to move toward or direct attention to an objective

¹**hon·est** \'ä-nəst\ *adj* [ME, fr. AF, fr. L *honestus* honorable, fr. *honos, honor* honor] **1** : free from deception : TRUTHFUL; *also* : GENUINE, REAL **2** : REPUTABLE **3** : CREDITABLE ⟨an ~ day's work⟩ **4** : marked by integrity **5** : FRANK ♦ *Synonyms* UPRIGHT, JUST, CONSCIENTIOUS, HONORABLE — **hon·est·ly** *adv* — **hon·es·ty** \-nə-stē\ *n*

²**honest** *adv* : HONESTLY; *also* : with all sincerity ⟨I didn't do it, ~⟩

hon·ey \'hə-nē\ *n, pl* **honeys** : a sweet sticky substance made by honeybees from the nectar of flowers — **hon·eyed** \-nēd\ *adj*

hon·ey·bee \-hə-nē-ˌbē\ *n* : a honey-producing bee often kept in hives

¹**hon·ey·comb** \-ˌkōm\ *n* : a mass of 6-sided wax cells built by honeybees; *also* : something of similar structure or appearance

²**honeycomb** *vb* : to make or become full of cavities like a honeycomb

hon·ey·dew \-ˌdü, -ˌdyü\ *n* : a sweetish deposit secreted on plants by aphids, scale insects, or fungi

honeydew melon *n* : a smooth-skinned muskmelon with sweet green flesh

honey locust *n* : a tall usu. spiny No. American leguminous tree with hard durable wood and long twisted pods

hon·ey·moon \'hə-nē-ˌmün\ *n* **1** : a period of harmony esp. just after marriage **2** : a holiday taken by a newly married couple — **honeymoon** *vb* — **hon·ey·moon·er** *n*

hon·ey·suck·le \'hə-nē-ˌsə-kəl\ *n* : any of a genus of shrubs with fragrant tube-shaped flowers rich in nectar

honk \'häŋk, 'hȯŋk\ *n* : the cry of a goose; *also* : a similar sound (as of a horn) — **honk** *vb* — **honk·er** *n*

honk·y-tonk \'häŋ-kē-ˌtäŋk, 'hȯŋ-kē-ˌtȯŋk\ *n* : a tawdry nightclub or dance hall — **honky-tonk** *adj*

¹**hon·or** \'ä-nər\ *n* **1** : good name : REPUTATION; *also* : outward respect **2** : PRIVILEGE **3** : a person of superior standing — used esp. as a title **4** : one who brings respect or fame ⟨an ~ to the class⟩ **5** : an evidence or symbol of distinction **6** : CHASTITY, PURITY **7** : INTEGRITY ♦ *Synonyms* HOMAGE, REVERENCE, DEFERENCE, OBEISANCE

²**honor** *vb* **1** : to regard or treat with honor **2** : to confer honor on **3** : to fulfill the terms of; *also* : to accept as payment — **hon·or·ee** \ˌä-nə-'rē\ *n* — **hon·or·er** *n*

hon·or·able \'ä-nə-rə-bəl\ *adj* **1** : deserving of honor **2** : of great renown **3** : accompanied with marks of honor **4** : doing credit to the possessor **5** : characterized by integrity — **hon·or·able·ness** *n* — **hon·or·ably** \-blē\ *adv*

hon·o·rar·i·um \ˌä-nə-'rer-ē-əm\ *n, pl* **-ia** \-ē-ə\ *also* **-iums** : a reward usu. for services on which custom or propriety forbids a price to be set

hon·or·ary \'ä-nə-ˌrer-ē\ adj 1 : having or conferring distinction 2 : conferred in recognition of achievement without the usual prerequisites ⟨∼ degree⟩ 3 : UNPAID, VOLUNTARY ⟨an ∼ chairman⟩ — **hon·or·ari·ly** \ˌä-nə-'rer-ə-lē\ adv

hon·or·if·ic \ˌä-nə-'ri-fik\ adj : conferring or conveying honor ⟨∼ titles⟩

hon·our, hon·our·able chiefly Brit var of HONOR, HONORABLE

¹**hood** \'hu̇d\ n 1 : a covering for the head and neck and sometimes the face 2 : an ornamental fold (as at the back of an ecclesiastical vestment) 3 : a cover for parts of mechanisms; esp : the covering over an automobile engine — **hood·ed** \'hu̇-dəd\ adj

²**hood** \'hu̇d, 'hu̇d\ n : HOODLUM

³**hood** \'hu̇d\ n : an inner-city neighborhood; also : INNER CITY

-hood \ˌhu̇d\ n suffix 1 : state : condition : quality : character ⟨boyhood⟩ ⟨hardihood⟩ 2 : instance of a (specified) state or quality ⟨falsehood⟩ 3 : individuals sharing a (specified) state or character ⟨brotherhood⟩

hood·ie \'hu̇-dē\ n : a hooded sweatshirt

hood·lum \'hu̇d-ləm, 'hu̇d-\ n 1 : THUG 2 : a young ruffian

hoo·doo \'hü-dü\ n, pl **hoodoos** 1 : a body of magical practices traditional esp. among blacks in the southern U.S. 2 : something that brings bad luck — **hoo·doo** n

hood·wink \'hu̇d-ˌwiŋk\ vb : to deceive by false appearance

hoo·ey \'hü-ē\ n : NONSENSE

hoof \'hu̇f, 'hüf\ n, pl **hooves** \'hu̇vz, 'hüvz\ also **hoofs** : a horny covering that protects the ends of the toes of ungulate mammals (as horses or cattle); also : a hoofed foot — **hoofed** \'hu̇ft, 'hüft\ adj

¹**hook** \'hu̇k\ n 1 : a curved or bent device for catching, holding, or pulling 2 : something curved or bent like a hook 3 : a flight of a ball (as in golf) that curves in a direction opposite to the dominant hand of the player propelling it 4 : a short punch delivered with a circular motion and with the elbow bent and rigid

²**hook** vb 1 : CURVE, CROOK 2 : to seize or make fast with a hook 3 : STEAL 4 : to work as a prostitute

hoo·kah \'hu̇-kə, 'hü-\ n [Ar ḥuqqa bottle of a water pipe] : WATER PIPE

hook·er \'hu̇-kər\ n 1 : one that hooks 2 : PROSTITUTE

hook·up \'hu̇k-ˌkəp\ n : an assemblage (as of apparatus or circuits) used for a specific purpose (as in radio)

hook up vb : to become involved in a working, social, or sexual relationship

hook·worm \'hu̇k-ˌwərm\ n : any of several parasitic intestinal nematode worms having hooks or plates around the mouth; also : infestation with or disease caused by hookworms

hoo·li·gan \'hü-li-gən\ n : RUFFIAN, HOODLUM — **hoo·li·gan·ism** \-gə-ˌni-zəm\ n

hoop \'hu̇p, 'hüp\ n 1 : a circular strip used esp. for holding together the staves

of a barrel 2 : a circular figure or object : RING 3 : a circle of flexible material for expanding a woman's skirt 4 : BASKETBALL — usu. used in pl.

hoop·la \'hu̇p-ˌlä, 'hu̇p-\ n [F houp-là, interj.] : TO-DO; also : BALLYHOO

hoop·ster \'hu̇p-stər\ n : a basketball player

hoo·ray \hu̇-'rā\ interj — used to express joy, approval, or encouragement

hoose·gow \'hu̇s-ˌgau̇\ n [Sp juzgado panel of judges, courtroom] : JAIL

¹**hoot** \'hu̇t\ vb 1 : to shout or laugh usu. in contempt 2 : to make the natural throat noise of an owl — **hoot·er** n

²**hoot** n 1 : a sound of hooting 2 : the least bit ⟨don't give a ∼⟩ 3 : something or someone amusing ⟨the play is a real ∼⟩

hoo·te·nan·ny \'hü-tə-ˌna-nē\ n, pl **-nies** : a gathering at which folksingers entertain often with the audience joining in

¹**hop** \'häp\ vb **hopped; hop·ping** 1 : to move by quick springy leaps 2 : to make a quick trip 3 : to ride on esp. surreptitiously and without authorization

²**hop** n 1 : a short brisk leap esp. on one leg 2 : DANCE 3 : a short trip by air

³**hop** n : a vine related to the hemp plant whose ripe dried pistillate catkins are used esp. in flavoring malt liquors; also, pl : its pistillate catkins

¹**hope** \'hōp\ vb **hoped; hop·ing** : to desire with expectation of fulfillment

²**hope** n 1 : TRUST, RELIANCE 2 : desire accompanied by expectation of fulfillment; also : something hoped for 3 : one that gives promise for the future — **hope·ful** \-fəl\ adj — **hope·ful·ness** n — **hope·less** adj — **hope·less·ly** adv — **hope·less·ness** n

HOPE abbr Health Opportunity for People Everywhere

hope·ful·ly \'hōp-fə-lē\ adv 1 : in a hopeful manner 2 : it is hoped

Ho·pi \'hō-pē\ n, pl **Hopi** or **Hopis** : a member of an American Indian people of Arizona; also : the language of the Hopi people

hopped–up \'häpt-'əp\ adj 1 : being under the influence of a narcotic; also : full of enthusiasm or excitement 2 : having more than usual power ⟨a ∼ engine⟩

hop·per \'hä-pər\ n 1 : a usu. immature hopping insect (as a grasshopper) 2 : a usu. funnel-shaped container for delivering material (as grain) 3 : a freight car with hinged doors in a sloping bottom 4 : a box into which a bill is to be considered by a legislative body is dropped 5 : a tank holding a liquid and having a device for releasing its contents through a pipe

hop·scotch \'häp-ˌskäch\ n : a child's game in which a player tosses an object (as a stone) into areas of a figure drawn on the ground and hops through the figure to pick up the object

hor abbr horizontal

horde \'hȯrd\ n : THRONG, SWARM

ho·ri·zon \hə-'rī-zᵊn\ n [ME, fr. LL, fr. Gk horizont-, horizōn, fr. prp. of horizein to bound, fr. horos limit, boundary] 1

: the apparent junction of earth and sky **2** : range of outlook or experience

hor·i·zon·tal \ˌhȯr-ə-'zän-tᵊl\ *adj* : parallel to the horizon : LEVEL — **horizontal** *n* — **hor·i·zon·tal·ly** *adv*

hor·mon·al \hȯr-'mō-nᵊl\ *adj* : of, relating to, or effected by hormones — **hor·mon·al·ly** \-nᵊl-ē\ *adv*

hor·mone \'hȯr-ˌmōn\ *n* [Gk *hormōn*, prp. of *horman* to stir up, fr. *hormē* impulse, assault] : a product of living cells that circulates in body fluids and has a specific effect on the activity of cells remote from its point of origin

horn \'hȯrn\ *n* **1** : one of the hard projections of bone or keratin on the head of many hoofed mammals **2** : something resembling or suggesting a horn **3** : a brass wind instrument **4** : a usu. electrical device that makes a noise ⟨an automobile ∼⟩ — **horned** \'hȯrnd\ *adj* — **horn·less** *adj*

horn·book \'hȯrn-ˌbůk\ *n* **1** : a child's primer consisting of a sheet of parchment or paper protected by a sheet of transparent horn **2** : a rudimentary treatise

horned toad *n* : any of several small harmless insect-eating lizards with spines on the head resembling horns and spiny scales on the body

hor·net \'hȯr-nət\ *n* : any of the larger social wasps

horn in *vb* : to participate without invitation : INTRUDE

horn·pipe \'hȯrn-ˌpīp\ *n* : a lively folk dance of the British Isles

horny \'hȯr-nē\ *adj* **horn·i·er; -est 1** : of or made of horn; *also* : HARD, CALLOUS **2** : having horns **3** : desiring sexual gratification; *also* : excited sexually

ho·rol·o·gy \hə-'rä-lə-jē\ *n* : the science of measuring time or constructing time-indicating instruments — **hor·o·log·i·cal** \ˌhȯr-ə-'lä-ji-kəl\ *adj* — **ho·rol·o·gist** \hə-'rä-lə-jist\ *n*

horo·scope \'hȯr-ə-ˌskōp\ *n* [ME *horoscopum*, fr. L *horoscopus*, fr. Gk *hōroskopos*, fr. *hōra* hour + *skopos* watcher] **1** : a diagram of the relative positions of planets and signs of the zodiac at a particular time for use by astrologers to foretell events of a person's life **2** : an astrological forecast

hor·ren·dous \hȯ-'ren-dəs\ *adj* : DREADFUL, HORRIBLE

hor·ri·ble \'hȯr-ə-bəl\ *adj* **1** : marked by or conducive to horror **2** : highly disagreeable ⟨a ∼ mistake⟩ — **hor·ri·ble·ness** *n* — **hor·ri·bly** \-blē\ *adv*

hor·rid \'hȯr-əd\ *adj* **1** : HIDEOUS **2** : REPULSIVE — **hor·rid·ly** *adv*

hor·rif·ic \hȯ-'ri-fik\ *adj* : having the power to horrify ⟨a ∼ crime⟩ — **hor·rif·i·cal·ly** \-fi-k(ə-)lē\ *adv*

hor·ri·fy \'hȯr-ə-ˌfī\ *vb* **-fied; -fy·ing** : to cause to feel horror ♦ *Synonyms* APPALL, DAUNT, DISMAY

hor·ror \'hȯr-ər\ *n* **1** : painful and intense fear, dread, or dismay **2** : intense repugnance **3** : something that horrifies

horror story *n* : an account of an unsettling or unfortunate occurrence

hors de com·bat \ˌȯr-də-kōⁿ-'bä\ *adv or adj* : in a disabled condition

hors d'oeuvre \ȯr-'dərv\ *n, pl* **hors d'oeuvres** *same or* -'dərvz\ *also* **hors d'oeuvre** [F *hors-d'oeuvre*, lit., outside of the work] : any of various savory foods usu. served as appetizers

horse \'hȯrs\ *n, pl* **hors·es** *also* **horse 1** : a large solid-hoofed herbivorous mammal domesticated as a draft and saddle animal **2** : a supporting framework usu. with legs — **horse·less** *adj*

¹horse·back \'hȯrs-ˌbak\ *n* : the back of a horse

²horseback *adv* : on horseback

horse chestnut *n* : a large tree with palmate leaves, erect conical clusters of showy flowers, and large glossy brown seeds enclosed in a prickly bur; *also* : its seed

horse·flesh \'hȯrs-ˌflesh\ *n* : horses for riding, driving, or racing

horse·fly \-ˌflī\ *n* : any of a family of large dipteran flies with bloodsucking females

horse·hair \-ˌher\ *n* **1** : the hair of a horse esp. from the mane or tail **2** : cloth made from horsehair

horse·hide \-ˌhīd\ *n* **1** : the dressed or raw hide of a horse **2** : the ball used in baseball

horse latitudes *n pl* : either of two calm regions near 30°N and 30°S latitude

horse·laugh \'hȯrs-ˌlaf, -ˌläf\ *n* : a loud boisterous laugh

horse·man \-mən\ *n* **1** : one who rides horseback; *also* : one skilled in managing horses **2** : a breeder or raiser of horses — **horse·man·ship** *n*

horse·play \-ˌplā\ *n* : rough boisterous play

horse·play·er \-ər\ *n* : a bettor on horse races

horse·pow·er \'hȯrs-ˌpaů(-ə)r\ *n* : a unit of power equal in the U.S. to 746 watts

horse·rad·ish \-ˌra-dish\ *n* : a tall white-flowered herb related to the mustards whose pungent root is used as a condiment; *also* : the pungent condiment

horse·shoe \'hȯrs-ˌshü\ *n* **1** : a usu. U-shaped protective metal plate fitted to the rim of a horse's hoof **2** *pl* : a game in which horseshoes are pitched at a fixed object — **horse·shoe** *vb* — **horse·sho·er** *n*

horseshoe crab *n* : any of several marine arthropods with a broad crescent-shaped combined head and thorax

horse·tail \'hȯrs-ˌtāl\ *n* : any of a genus of primitive spore-producing plants with hollow jointed stems and leaves reduced to sheaths about the joints

horse·whip \-ˌhwip\ *vb* : to flog with a whip made to be used on a horse

horse·wom·an \-ˌwů-mən\ *n* **1** : a woman skilled in riding horseback or in caring for or managing horses **2** : a woman who breeds or raises horses

hors·ey *also* **horsy** \'hȯr-sē\ *adj* **hors·i·er; -est 1** : of, relating to, or suggesting a horse **2** : having to do with horses or horse racing

hort *abbr* horticultural; horticulture

hor·ta·tive \'hȯr-tə-tiv\ *adj* : giving exhortation ⟨a ∼ appeal⟩

hor·ta·to·ry \'hȯr-tə-ˌtōr-ē\ *adj* : HORTATIVE

hor·ti·cul·ture \'hȯr-tə-ˌkəl-chər\ *n* : the science and art of growing fruits, vegetables, flowers, and ornamental plants — **hor·ti·cul·tur·al** \ˌhȯr-tə-'kəl-chə-rəl\ *adj* — **hor·ti·cul·tur·ist** \-rist\ *n*

Hos *abbr* Hosea

ho·san·na \hō-'za-nə, -'zä-\ *interj* [Gk *hōsanna*, fr. Heb *hōshīʿāh-nnā* pray, save (us)!] — used as a cry of acclamation and adoration — **hosanna** *n*

¹**hose** \'hōz\ *n, pl* **hose** *or* **hos·es** 1 *pl* **hose** : STOCKING, SOCK; *also* : a close-fitting garment covering the legs and waist 2 : a flexible tube for conveying fluids (as from a faucet)

²**hose** *vb* **hosed; hos·ing** : to spray, water, or wash with a hose

Ho·sea \hō-'zā-ə, -'zē-\ *n* — see BIBLE table

ho·siery \'hō-zhə-rē, -zə-\ *n* : STOCKINGS, SOCKS

hosp *abbr* hospital

hos·pice \'häs-pəs\ *n* 1 : a lodging for travelers or for young persons or the underprivileged 2 : a facility or program for caring for dying persons

hos·pi·ta·ble \hä-'spi-tə-bəl, 'häs-(ˌ)pi-\ *adj* 1 : given to generous and cordial reception of guests 2 : readily receptive — **hos·pi·ta·bly** \-blē\ *adv*

hos·pi·tal \'häs-ˌpi-t°l\ *n* [ME, fr. AF, fr. ML *hospitale* hospice, guest house, fr. neut. of L *hospitalis* of a guest, fr. *hospit-, hospes* guest, host] : an institution where the sick or injured receive medical or surgical care

hos·pi·ta·lise *Brit var of* HOSPITALIZE

hos·pi·tal·i·ty \ˌhäs-pə-'ta-lə-tē\ *n, pl* **-ties** : hospitable treatment, reception, or disposition

hos·pi·tal·ize \'häs-ˌpi-tə-ˌlīz\ *vb* **-ized; -iz·ing** : to place in a hospital as a patient — **hos·pi·tal·i·za·tion** \ˌhäs-ˌpi-t°l-ə-'zā-shən\ *n*

¹**host** \'hōst\ *n* [ME, fr. AF *ost*, fr. LL *hostis*, fr. L, stranger, enemy] 1 : ARMY 2 : MULTITUDE ⟨a ∼ of options⟩

²**host** *n* [ME *hoste* host, guest, fr. AF, fr. L *hospit-, hospes*] 1 : one who receives or entertains guests 2 : an animal or plant on or in which a parasite lives 3 : one into which something (as an organ) is transplanted 4 : SERVER 2 — **host** *vb*

³**host** *n, often cap* [ultim. fr. L *hostia* sacrifice] : the eucharistic bread

hos·tage \'häs-tij\ *n* 1 : a person kept as a pledge pending the fulfillment of an agreement 2 : a person taken by force to secure the taker's demands

hos·tel \'häs-t°l\ *n* [ME, fr. AF, fr. ML *hospitale* hospice] 1 : INN 2 : a supervised lodging for youth — **hos·tel·er** *or* **hos·tel·ler** *n*

hos·tel·ry \-rē\ *n, pl* **-ries** : INN, HOTEL

host·ess \'hō-stəs\ *n* : a woman who acts as host

hos·tile \'häs-t°l, -ˌtī(-ə)l\ *adj* : marked by

usu. overt antagonism : UNFRIENDLY — **hostile** *n* — **hos·tile·ly** *adv*

hos·til·i·ty \hä-'sti-lə-tē\ *n, pl* **-ties** 1 : an unfriendly state or action 2 *pl* : overt acts of war

hos·tler \'häs-lər, 'äs-\ *n* : one who takes care of horses or mules

hot \'hät\ *adj* **hot·ter; hot·test** 1 : marked by a high temperature or an uncomfortable degree of body heat 2 : giving a sensation of heat or of burning 3 : ARDENT, FIERY 4 : sexually excited 5 : EAGER 6 : newly made or received 7 : PUNGENT 8 : unusually lucky or favorable ⟨∼ dice⟩ 9 : recently and illegally obtained ⟨∼ jewels⟩ — **hot** *adv* — **hot·ly** *adv* — **hot·ness** *n*

hot·bed \-ˌbed\ *n* 1 : a glass-covered bed of soil heated (as by fermenting manure) and used esp. for raising seedlings 2 : an environment that favors rapid growth or development

hot–blood·ed \-'blə-dəd\ *adj* : easily roused or excited ⟨∼ rebels⟩

hot·box \-ˌbäks\ *n* : a bearing (as of a railroad car) overheated by friction

hot button *n* : an emotional issue or concern that triggers immediate intense reaction

hot·cake \-ˌkāk\ *n* : PANCAKE

hot dog *n* : a cooked frankfurter usu. served in a long split roll

ho·tel \hō-'tel\ *n* [F *hôtel*, fr. OF *hostel*, fr. ML *hospitale* hospice] : a building where lodging and usu. meals, entertainment, and various personal services are provided for the public

hot flash *n* : a sudden brief flushing and sensation of heat usu. associated with menopausal endocrine imbalance

hot·head·ed \'hät-'he-dəd\ *adj* : FIERY, IMPETUOUS ⟨a ∼ troublemaker⟩ — **hot·head** \-ˌhed\ *n* — **hot·head·ed·ly** *adv* — **hot·head·ed·ness** *n*

hot·house \-ˌhaus\ *n* : a heated greenhouse esp. for raising tropical plants

hotline *n* : a telephone line for emergency use (as between governments or to a counseling service)

hot pants *n pl* : very short shorts

hot pepper *n* : a small usu. thin-walled pepper with a pungent taste; *also* : a plant bearing hot peppers

hot plate *n* : a simple portable appliance for heating or for cooking

hot potato *n* : an embarrassing or controversial issue

hot rod *n* : an automobile modified for high speed and fast acceleration — **hot·rod·der** \-'rä-dər\ *n*

hots \'häts\ *n pl* : strong sexual desire — usu. used with *the*

hot seat *n* : a position of anxiety or embarrassment

hot·shot \'hät-ˌshät\ *n* : a showily skillful person ⟨a ∼ lawyer⟩

hot tub *n* : a large tub of hot water for one or more bathers

hot water *n* : TROUBLE, DIFFICULTY

hot–wire \'hät-ˌwī(-ə)r\ *vb* : to start (an automobile) by short-circuiting the ignition system

¹**hound** \ˈhau̇nd\ *n* **1** : any of various hunting dogs that track prey by scent or sight **2** : FAN, ADDICT ⟨autograph ∼s⟩

²**hound** *vb* : to pursue relentlessly

hour \ˈau̇(-ə)r\ *n* **1** : the 24th part of a day : 60 minutes **2** : the time of day **3** : a particular or customary time **4** : a class session — **hour·ly** *adv or adj*

hour·glass \ˈau̇(-ə)r-ˌglas\ *n* : a glass vessel for measuring time in which sand runs from an upper compartment to a lower compartment in an hour

hou·ri \ˈhu̇r-ē\ *n* [F, fr. Pers *hūri*, fr. Ar *hūrīya*] : one of the beautiful maidens of the Muslim paradise

¹**house** \ˈhau̇s\ *n, pl* **hous·es** \ˈhau̇-zəz\ **1** : a building for human habitation **2** : an animal shelter (as a den or nest) **3** : a building in which something is stored **4** : HOUSEHOLD; *also* : FAMILY **5** : a residence for a religious community or for students; *also* : those in residence **6** : a legislative body **7** : a place of business or entertainment **8** : a business organization **9** : the audience in a theater or concert hall — **house·ful** *n*

²**house** \ˈhau̇z\ *vb* **housed; hous·ing 1** : to provide with or take shelter : LODGE **2** : STORE ⟨paintings *housed* in a gallery⟩

house·boat \ˈhau̇s-ˌbōt\ *n* : a pleasure boat fitted for use as a dwelling or for leisurely cruising

house·boy \-ˌbȯi\ *n* : a boy or man hired to act as a household servant

house·break \-ˌbrāk\ *vb* **-broke; -broken; -break·ing** : to train (a pet) in excretory habits acceptable in indoor living

house·break·ing \-ˌbrā-kiŋ\ *n* : the act of breaking into a dwelling with the intent of committing a felony

house·clean \-ˌklēn\ *vb* : to clean a house and its furniture — **house·clean·ing** *n*

house·coat \-ˌkōt\ *n* : a woman's often long-skirted informal garment for wear around the house

house·fly \-ˌflī\ *n* : a dipteran fly that is common about human habitations

¹**house·hold** \-ˌhōld\ *n* : those who dwell as a family under the same roof — **house·hold·er** *n*

²**household** *adj* **1** : DOMESTIC **2** : FAMILIAR, COMMON ⟨a ∼ name⟩

house·keep·er \-ˌkē-pər\ *n* : a woman employed to take care of a house

house·keep·ing \-ˌkē-piŋ\ *n* : the care and management of a house or institutional property

house·lights \-ˌlīts\ *n pl* : the lights that illuminate the auditorium of a theater

house·maid \-ˌmād\ *n* : a girl or woman who is a servant employed to do housework

house·moth·er \-ˌmə-thər\ *n* : a woman acting as hostess, chaperone, and often housekeeper in a group residence

house·plant \-ˌplant\ *n* : a plant grown or kept indoors

house sparrow *n* : a Eurasian sparrow widely introduced in urban and agricultural areas

house·top \ˈhau̇s-ˌtäp\ *n* : ROOF

house·wares \-ˌwerz\ *n pl* : small articles of household equipment

house·warm·ing \-ˌwȯr-miŋ\ *n* : a party to celebrate the taking possession of a house or premises

house·wife \-ˌwīf\ *n* : a married woman in charge of a household — **house·wife·ly** *adj* — **house·wif·ery** \-ˌwī-fə-rē\ *n*

house·work \-ˌwərk\ *n* : the work of housekeeping

¹**hous·ing** \ˈhau̇-ziŋ\ *n* **1** : SHELTER; *also* : dwellings provided for people **2** : something that covers or protects

²**housing** *n* : CAPARISON 1

HOV *abbr* high-occupancy vehicle

hove *past and past part of* HEAVE

hov·el \ˈhə-vəl, ˈhä-\ *n* : a small, wretched, and often dirty house : HUT

hov·er \ˈhə-vər, ˈhä-\ *vb* **hov·ered; hov·er·ing 1** : FLUTTER; *also* : to move to and fro **2** : to be in an uncertain state

hov·er·craft \-ˌkraft\ *n* : a vehicle that rides on a cushion of air over a surface

¹**how** \ˈhau̇\ *adv* **1** : in what way or manner ⟨∼ was it done⟩ **2** : with what meaning ⟨∼ do we interpret such behavior⟩ **3** : for what reason ⟨∼ could you have done such a thing⟩ **4** : to what extent or degree ⟨∼ deep is it⟩ **5** : in what state or condition ⟨∼ are you⟩ — **how about** : what do you say to or think of ⟨*how about* coming with me⟩ — **how come** : why is it that

²**how** *conj* **1** : the way or manner in which ⟨remember ∼ they fought⟩ **2** : HOWEVER ⟨do it ∼ you like⟩

¹**how·be·it** \hau̇-ˈbē-ət\ *conj* : ALTHOUGH

²**howbeit** *adv* : NEVERTHELESS

how·dah \ˈhau̇-də\ *n* [Hindi & Urdu *haudā*, fr. Ar *haudaj*] : a seat or covered pavilion on the back of an elephant or camel

¹**how·ev·er** \hau̇-ˈe-vər\ *conj* : in whatever manner that

²**however** *adv* **1** : in whatever manner; *also* : to whatever degree **2** : in spite of that

how·it·zer \ˈhau̇-ət-sər\ *n* : a short cannon that shoots shells at a high angle

howl \ˈhau̇(-ə)l\ *vb* **1** : to emit a loud long doleful sound characteristic of dogs **2** : to cry loudly — **howl** *n*

howl·er \ˈhau̇-lər\ *n* **1** : one that howls **2** : a humorous and ridiculous blunder

howl·ing *adj* **1** : DESOLATE, WILD **2** : very great ⟨a ∼ success⟩

how·so·ev·er \ˌhau̇-sə-ˈwe-vər\ *adv* : HOWEVER 1

hoy·den \ˈhȯi-dᵊn\ *n* : a girl or woman of saucy, boisterous, or carefree behavior — **hoy·den·ish** *adj*

hp *abbr* horsepower

HP *abbr* high pressure

HPF *abbr* highest possible frequency

HQ *abbr* headquarters

hr *abbr* **1** here **2** hour

HR *abbr* House of Representatives

HRH *abbr* **1** Her Royal Highness **2** His Royal Highness

hryv·nia \ˈ(h)riv-nē-ə\ *n, pl* **hryvnia** *or* **hryvnias** — see MONEY table

hrzn *abbr* horizon

Hs *symbol* hassium

HS *abbr* high school

HST *abbr* Hawaiian standard time

ht *abbr* height

HT *abbr* **1** Hawaii time **2** high-tension

HTML \ˌāch-ˌtē-ˌem-ˈel\ *n* [*hypertext markup language*] : a computer language used to create World Wide Web documents

http *abbr* hypertext transfer protocol

hua·ra·che \wə-ˈrä-chē\ *n* [MexSp] : a sandal with an upper made of interwoven leather strips

hub \ˈhəb\ *n* **1** : the central part of a circular object (as a wheel) **2** : a center of activity; *esp* : an airport or city through which an airline routes most of its traffic

hub·bub \ˈhə-ˌbəb\ *n* : UPROAR ⟨the ~ in the stadium⟩; *also* : TURMOIL ⟨the ~ following the war⟩

hub·cap \ˈhəb-ˌkap\ *n* : a removable metal cap over the end of an axle

hu·bris \ˈhyü-brəs\ *n* : exaggerated pride or self-confidence

huck·le·ber·ry \ˈhə-kəl-ˌber-ē\ *n* **1** : any of a genus of American shrubs of the heath family; *also* : its edible dark blue berry **2** : BLUEBERRY

huck·ster \ˈhək-stər\ *n* : PEDDLER, HAWKER — **huck·ster·ism** \-stə-ˌri-zəm\ *n*

HUD *abbr* Department of Housing and Urban Development

¹**hud·dle** \ˈhə-dᵊl\ *vb* **hud·dled; hud·dling** **1** : to crowd together **2** : CONFER

²**huddle** *n* **1** : a closely packed group **2** : MEETING, CONFERENCE

hue \ˈhyü\ *n* **1** : COLOR; *also* : gradation of color **2** : the attribute of colors that permits them to be classed as red, yellow, green, blue, or an intermediate color — **hued** \ˈhyüd\ *adj*

hue and cry *n* : a clamor of pursuit or protest

huff \ˈhəf\ *n* : a fit of anger or pique — **huff** *vb* — **huff·i·ly** \ˈhə-fə-lē\ *adv* — **huffy** \ˈhə-fē\ *adj*

hug \ˈhəg\ *vb* **hugged; hug·ging** **1** : EMBRACE **2** : to stay close to — **hug** *n*

huge \ˈhyüj\ *adj* **hug·er; hug·est** : very large or extensive — **huge·ly** *adv* — **huge·ness** *n*

hug·ger–mug·ger \ˈhə-gər-ˌmə-gər\ *n* **1** : SECRECY **2** : CONFUSION, MUDDLE

Hu·gue·not \ˈhyü-gə-ˌnät\ *n* : a French Protestant of the 16th and 17th centuries

hu·la \ˈhü-lə\ *n* : a sinuous Polynesian dance usu. accompanied by chants

hulk \ˈhəlk\ *n* **1** : a heavy clumsy ship **2** : an old ship unfit for service **3** : a bulky or unwieldy person or thing

hulk·ing \ˈhəl-kiŋ\ *adj* : BURLY, MASSIVE

¹**hull** \ˈhəl\ *n* **1** : the outer covering of a fruit or seed **2** : the frame or body esp. of a ship or boat

²**hull** *vb* : to remove the hulls of — **hull·er** *n*

hul·la·ba·loo \ˈhə-lə-bə-ˌlü\ *n, pl* **-loos** : a confused noise : UPROAR

hul·lo \ˌhə-ˈlō\ *chiefly Brit var of* HELLO

hum \ˈhəm\ *vb* **hummed; hum·ming** **1** : to utter a sound like that of the speech sound \m\ prolonged **2** : DRONE **3** : to be busily active **4** : to run smoothly **5** : to sing with closed lips — **hum** *n* — **hum·mer** *n*

¹**hu·man** \ˈhyü-mən, ˈyü-\ *adj* **1** : of, relating to, being, or characteristic of humans **2** : having human form or attributes — **hu·man·ly** *adv* — **hu·man·ness** *n*

²**human** *n* : any of a species of bipedal primate mammals comprising all living persons and their recent ancestors; *also* : HOMINID — **hu·man·like** \-ˌlīk\ *adj*

hu·mane \hyü-ˈmān, yü-\ *adj* **1** : marked by compassion, sympathy, or consideration for others **2** : HUMANISTIC — **hu·mane·ly** *adv* — **hu·mane·ness** *n*

human immunodeficiency virus *n* : HIV

hu·man·ism \ˈhyü-mə-ˌni-zəm, ˈyü-\ *n* **1** : devotion to the humanities; *also* : the revival of classical letters characteristic of the Renaissance **2** : a doctrine or way of life centered on human interests or values — **hu·man·ist** \-nist\ *n or adj* — **hu·man·is·tic** \ˌhyü-mə-ˈnis-tik, ˌyü-\ *adj*

hu·man·i·tar·i·an \hyü-ˌma-nə-ˈter-ē-ən, yü-\ *n* : one who practices philanthropy — **humanitarian** *adj* — **hu·man·i·tar·i·an·ism** *n*

hu·man·i·ty \hyü-ˈma-nə-tē, yü-\ *n, pl* **-ties** **1** : the quality or state of being human or humane **2** *pl* : the branches of learning dealing with human concerns (as philosophy) as opposed to natural processes (as physics) **3** : the human race

hu·man·ize \ˈhyü-mə-ˌnīz, ˈyü-\ *vb* **-ized; -iz·ing** : to make human or humane — **hu·man·i·za·tion** \ˌhyü-mə-nə-ˈzā-shən, ˌyü-\ *n* — **hu·man·iz·er** *n*

hu·man·kind \ˈhyü-mən-ˌkīnd, ˈyü-\ *n* : the human race

hu·man·oid \ˈhyü-mə-ˌnȯid, ˈyü-\ *adj* : having human form or characteristics — **humanoid** *n*

human pap·il·lo·ma·virus \-ˌpa-pə-ˈlō-mə-ˌvī-rəs\ *n* : any of numerous DNA-containing viruses that cause various human warts

¹**hum·ble** \ˈhəm-bəl\ *adj* **hum·bler** \-bə-lər\; **hum·blest** \-bə-ləst\ [ME, fr. AF, fr. L *humilis* low, humble, fr. *humus* earth] **1** : not proud or haughty **2** : not pretentious : UNASSUMING **3** : INSIGNIFICANT ◆ *Synonyms* MEEK, MODEST, LOWLY — **hum·ble·ness** *n* — **hum·bly** *adv*

²**humble** *vb* **hum·bled; hum·bling** **1** : to make humble **2** : to destroy the power or prestige of — **hum·bler** *n*

¹**hum·bug** \ˈhəm-ˌbəg\ *n* **1** : HOAX, FRAUD **2** : NONSENSE

²**humbug** *vb* **hum·bugged; hum·bug·ging** : DECEIVE

hum·ding·er \ˈhəm-ˈdiŋ-ər\ *n* : a person or thing of striking excellence

hum·drum \ˈhəm-ˌdrəm\ *adj* : MONOTONOUS, DULL — **humdrum** *n*

hu·mer·us \ˈhyü-mə-rəs\ *n, pl* **hu·meri** \ˈhyü-mə-ˌrī, -ˌrē\ : the long bone extending from shoulder to elbow

hu·mid \ˈhyü-məd, ˈyü-\ *adj* : containing or characterized by perceptible moisture : DAMP — **hu·mid·ly** *adv*

hu·mid·i·fy \hyü-ˈmi-də-ˌfī\ *vb* **-fied; -fy-**

ing : to make humid — **hu·mid·i·fi·ca·tion** \-₁mi-də-fə-'kā-shən\ n — **hu·mid·i·fi·er** \-'mi-də-₁fī-ər\ n

hu·mid·i·ty \hyü-'mi-də-tē, yü-\ n, pl **-ties** : the amount of atmospheric moisture

hu·mi·dor \'hyü-mə-₁dòr, 'yü-\ n : a case (as for storing cigars) in which the air is kept properly humidified

hu·mil·i·ate \hyü-'mi-lē-₁āt, yü-\ vb **-at·ed; -at·ing** : to injure the self-respect of : MORTIFY — **hu·mil·i·at·ing·ly** adv — **hu·mil·i·a·tion** \-₁mi-lē-'ā-shən\ n

hu·mil·i·ty \hyü-'mi-lə-tē, yü-\ n : the quality or state of being humble

hum·ming·bird \'hə-miŋ-₁bərd\ n : any of a family of tiny brightly colored American birds related to the swifts

hum·mock \'hə-mək\ n : a rounded mound : KNOLL — **hum·mocky** \-mə-kē\ adj

hum·mus \'hə-məs, 'hu̇-\ n [Ar ḥummuṣ chickpeas] : a paste of pureed chickpeas usu. mixed with sesame oil or paste

hu·mon·gous \hyü-'məŋ-gəs, -'mäŋ-\ adj [perh. alter. of huge + monstrous] : extremely large ⟨a ~ stadium⟩

¹hu·mor \'hyü-mər, 'yü-\ n **1** : TEMPERAMENT **2** : MOOD **3** : WHIM **4** : a quality that appeals to a sense of the ludicrous or incongruous; also : a keen perception of the ludicrous or incongruous **5** : comical or amusing entertainment — **hu·mor·ist** \'hyü-mə-rist, 'yü-\ n — **hu·mor·less** \'hyü-mər-ləs, 'yü-\ adj — **hu·mor·less·ly** adv — **hu·mor·less·ness** n — **hu·mor·ous** \'hyü-mə-rəs, 'yü-\ adj — **hu·mor·ous·ly** adv — **hu·mor·ous·ness** n

²humor vb : to comply with the wishes or mood of ⟨~ the boss⟩

hu·mour chiefly Brit var of HUMOR

hump \'həmp\ n **1** : a rounded protuberance (as on the back of a camel) **2** : a difficult phase or obstacle ⟨over the ~⟩ — **humped** adj

hump·back \'həmp-₁bak; 1 also -'bak\ n **1** : HUNCHBACK **2** : HUMPBACK WHALE — **hump·backed** adj

humpback whale n : a large baleen whale having very long flippers

hu·mus \'hyü-məs, 'yü-\ n : the dark organic part of soil formed from decaying matter

Hun \'hən\ n : a member of an Asian people that invaded Europe about A.D. 450

¹hunch \'hənch\ vb **1** : to thrust oneself forward **2** : to assume or cause to assume a bent or crooked posture

²hunch n **1** : PUSH **2** : a strong intuitive feeling about what will happen

hunch·back \'hənch-₁bak\ n : a person with a crooked back; also : a back with a hump — **hunch·backed** adj

hun·dred \'hən-drəd\ n, pl **hundreds** or **hundred** : 10 times 10 — **hundred** adj — **hun·dredth** \-drədth\ adj or n

hun·dred·weight or **hundredweights** n, pl **hundred-weight** or **hundredweights** — see WEIGHT table

¹hung past and past part of HANG

²hung adj : unable to reach a decision or verdict ⟨a ~ jury⟩

Hung abbr Hungarian; Hungary

Hun·gar·i·an \₁həŋ-'ger-ē-ən\ n **1** : a native or inhabitant of Hungary **2** : the language of the Hungarians — **Hungarian** adj

hun·ger \'həŋ-gər\ n **1** : a craving or urgent need for food **2** : a strong desire — **hunger** vb — **hun·gri·ly** adv — **hun·gry** adj

hung·over \'həŋ-'ō-vər\ adj : having a hangover

hung up adj **1** : DELAYED **2** : ENTHUSIASTIC; also : PREOCCUPIED — usu. used with on ⟨hung up on winning⟩

hunk \'həŋk\ n **1** : a large piece **2** : an attractive well-built man — **hunky** adj

hun·ker \'həŋ-kər\ vb **1** : CROUCH, SQUAT — usu. used with down **2** : to settle in for a sustained period — used with down

hun·ky-do·ry \₁həŋ-kē-'dòr-ē\ adj : quite satisfactory : FINE

¹hunt \'hənt\ vb **1** : to pursue for food or in sport; also : to take part in a hunt **2** : to try to find : SEEK **3** : to drive or chase esp. by harrying **4** : to traverse in search of prey — **hunt·er** n

²hunt n : an act, practice, or instance of hunting

Hun·ting·ton's disease \'hən-tiŋ-tənz-\ n : a chorea that usu. begins in middle age and leads to dementia

hunt·ress \'hən-trəs\ n : a woman who hunts game

hunts·man \'hənts-mən\ n **1** : HUNTER **2** : a person who manages a hunt and looks after the hounds

hur·dle \'hər-dᵊl\ n **1** : a barrier to leap over in a race **2** : OBSTACLE — **hurdle** vb — **hur·dler** n

hur·dy-gur·dy \₁hər-dē-'gər-dē, 'hər-dē-₁gər-dē\ n, pl **-gur·dies** : a musical instrument in which the sound is produced by turning a crank

hurl \'hərl\ vb **1** : to move or cause to move vigorously **2** : to throw down with violence **3** : FLING; also : PITCH — **hurl** n — **hurl·er** n

hur·ly-bur·ly \₁hər-lē-'bər-lē\ n : UPROAR, TUMULT

Hu·ron \'hyu̇r-ən, 'hyu̇r-₁än\ n, pl **Hurons** or **Huron** : a member of a confederacy of American Indian peoples formerly living between Georgian Bay and Lake Ontario

hur·rah \hu̇-'rȯ, -'rä\ also **hur·ray** \hu̇-'rā\ interj — used to express joy, approval, or encouragement

hur·ri·cane \'hər-ə-₁kān\ n [Sp huracán, of AmerInd origin] : a tropical cyclone with winds of 74 miles (118 kilometers) per hour or greater that is usu. accompanied by rain, thunder, and lightning

¹hur·ry \'hər-ē\ vb **hur·ried; hur·ry·ing** **1** : to carry or cause to go with haste **2** : to impel to a greater speed **3** : to move or act with haste — **hurried** adj — **hur·ried·ly** adv

²hurry n : extreme haste or eagerness

¹hurt \'hərt\ vb **hurt; hurt·ing** **1** : to feel or cause to feel physical or emotional pain **2** : to do harm to : DAMAGE **3** : OF-

FEND 4 : HAMPER 5 : to be in need — usu. used with *for* — **hurt** *adj*

²hurt *n* 1 : a bodily injury or wound 2 : SUFFERING 3 : HARM, WRONG — **hurtful** *adj* — **hurt·ful·ness** *n*

hur·tle \'hər-t⁰l\ *vb* **hur·tled; hur·tling** 1 : to move rapidly or forcefully 2 : HURL, FLING

¹hus·band \'həz-bənd\ *n* [ME *husbonde,* fr. OE *hūsbonda* master of a house, fr. ON *hūsbōndi,* fr. *hūs* house + *bōndi* householder] : a male partner in a marriage

²husband *vb* : to manage prudently

hus·band·man \'həz-bənd-mən\ *n* : FARMER

hus·band·ry \'həz-bən-drē\ *n* 1 : the control or judicious use of resources 2 : AGRICULTURE 3 : the production and care of domestic animals

¹hush \'həsh\ *vb* 1 : to make or become quiet or calm 2 : SUPPRESS

²hush *n* : SILENCE, QUIET

hush–hush \'həsh-,həsh\ *adj* : SECRET, CONFIDENTIAL

¹husk \'həsk\ *n* 1 : a usu. thin dry outer covering of a seed or fruit 2 : an outer layer : SHELL

²husk *vb* : to strip the husk from — **husk·er** *n*

¹hus·ky \'həs-kē\ *adj* **hus·ki·er; -est** : HOARSE — **hus·ki·ly** \-kə-lē\ *adv* — **hus·ki·ness** \-kē-nəs\ *n*

²husky *n, pl* **huskies** 1 : a heavy-coated working dog of the New World Arctic 2 : SIBERIAN HUSKY

³husky *adj* 1 : BURLY, ROBUST 2 : LARGE

hus·sar \(,)hə-'zär\ *n* [Hung *huszár*] : a member of any of various European cavalry units

hus·sy \'hə-zē, -sē\ *n, pl* **hussies** [alter. of *housewife*] 1 : a lewd or brazen woman 2 : a pert or mischievous girl

hus·tings \'həs-tiŋz\ *n pl* : a place where political campaign speeches are made; *also* : the proceedings in an election campaign

hus·tle \'hə-səl\ *vb* **hus·tled; hus·tling** 1 : JOSTLE, SHOVE 2 : HASTEN, HURRY 3 : to work energetically — **hustle** *n* — **hus·tler** \'həs-lər\ *n*

hut \'hət\ *n* : a small and often temporary dwelling : SHACK

hutch \'həch\ *n* 1 : a chest or compartment for storage 2 : a cupboard usu. surmounted with open shelves 3 : a pen or coop for an animal 4 : HUT

huz·zah *or* **huz·za** \(,)hə-'zä\ *n* : a shout of acclaim — often used interjectionally to express joy or approbation

HV *abbr* 1 high velocity 2 high voltage

HVAC *abbr* heating, ventilating and air-conditioning

hvy *abbr* heavy

HW *abbr* hot water

hwy *abbr* highway

hy·a·cinth \'hī-ə-(,)sinth\ *n* : a bulbous Mediterranean herb related to the lilies that is widely grown for its spikes of fragrant bell-shaped flowers

hy·brid \'hī-brəd\ *n* 1 : an offspring of genetically differing parents (as members of different breeds or species) 2 : one of mixed origin or composition — **hybrid** *adj* — **hy·brid·i·za·tion** \,hī-brə-də-'zā-shən\ *n* — **hy·brid·ize** \'hī-brə-,dīz\ *vb* — **hy·brid·iz·er** *n*

hy·dra \'hī-drə\ *n* : any of numerous small tubular freshwater coelenterates that are polyps having at one end a mouth surrounded by tentacles

hy·dran·gea \hī-'drān-jə\ *n* : any of a genus of shrubs related to the currants and grown for their showy clusters of white, pink, or bluish flowers

hy·drant \'hī-drənt\ *n* : a pipe with a valve and spout at which water may be drawn from a main pipe

hy·drate \'hī-,drāt\ *n* : a compound formed by union of water with some other substance — **hydrate** *vb*

hy·drau·lic \hī-'drò-lik\ *adj* [ultim. fr. Gk *hydraulis* pipe organ using water pressure, fr. *hydōr* water + *aulos* reed instrument] 1 : operated, moved, or effected by means of water 2 : of or relating to hydraulics 3 : operated by the resistance offered or the pressure transmitted when a quantity of liquid is forced through a small orifice or through a tube 4 : hardening or setting under water

hy·drau·lics \-liks\ *n* : a science that deals with practical applications of liquid (as water) in motion

hydro \'hī-drō\ *n* : HYDROPOWER

hy·dro·car·bon \'hī-drō-,kär-bən\ *n* : an organic compound containing only carbon and hydrogen

hy·dro·ceph·a·lus \,hī-drō-'se-fə-ləs\ *n* : abnormal increase in the amount of fluid in the cranial cavity accompanied by enlargement of the skull and atrophy of the brain

hy·dro·chlo·ric acid \,hī-drə-'klòr-ik-\ *n* : a sharp-smelling corrosive acid used in the laboratory and in industry and present in dilute form in gastric juice

hy·dro·dy·nam·ics \,hī-drō-dī-'na-miks\ *n* : a science that deals with the motion of fluids and the forces acting on moving bodies immersed in fluids — **hy·dro·dy·nam·ic** *adj*

hy·dro·elec·tric \,hī-drō-i-'lek-trik\ *adj* : of or relating to production of electricity by waterpower — **hy·dro·elec·tric·i·ty** \-,lek-'tri-sə-tē\ *n*

hy·dro·foil \'hī-drə-,fòi(-ə)l\ *n* : a boat that has fins attached to the bottom by struts for lifting the hull clear of the water to allow faster speeds

hy·dro·gen \'hī-drə-jən\ *n* [F *hydrogène,* fr. Gk *hydōr* water + *-genēs* born; fr. the fact that water is generated by its combustion] : a gaseous colorless odorless highly flammable chemical element that is the lightest of the elements — **hy·drog·e·nous** \hī-'drä-jə-nəs\ *adj*

hy·dro·ge·nate \hī-'drä-jə-,nāt, 'hī-drə-\ *vb* **-nat·ed; -nat·ing** : to combine or treat with hydrogen; *esp* : to add hydrogen to the molecule of — **hy·dro·ge·na·tion** \hī-,drä-jə-'nā-shən, ,hī-drə-\ *n*

hydrogen bomb *n* : a bomb whose violent explosive power is due to the sudden release of atomic energy resulting from the fusion of light nuclei (as of hydrogen atoms)

hydrogen peroxide *n* : an unstable compound of hydrogen and oxygen used esp. as an oxidizing and bleaching agent, an antiseptic, and a propellant

hy·dro·graph·ic \ˌhī-drə-ˈgra-fik\ *adj* : of or relating to the description and study of bodies of water — **hy·drog·ra·pher** *n* — **hy·drog·ra·phy** \hī-ˈdrä-grə-fē\ *n*

hy·drol·o·gy \hī-ˈdrä-lə-jē\ *n* : a science dealing with the properties, distribution, and circulation of water — **hy·dro·log·ic** \ˌhī-drə-ˈlä-jik\ *or* **hy·dro·log·i·cal** \-ji-kəl\ *adj* — **hy·drol·o·gist** \hī-ˈdrä-lə-jist\ *n*

hy·dro·ly·sis \hī-ˈdrä-lə-səs\ *n* : a chemical decomposition involving the addition of the elements of water

hy·drom·e·ter \hī-ˈdrä-mə-tər\ *n* : a floating instrument for determining specific gravities of liquids and hence the strength (as of alcoholic liquors)

hy·dro·pho·bia \ˌhī-drə-ˈfō-bē-ə\ *n* [LL, fr. Gk, fr. *hydōr* water + *phobos* fear] : RABIES

hy·dro·phone \ˈhī-drə-ˌfōn\ *n* : an underwater listening device

¹**hy·dro·plane** \ˈhī-drə-ˌplān\ *n* 1 : a powerboat designed for racing that skims the surface of the water 2 : SEAPLANE

²**hydroplane** *vb* : to skid on a wet road due to loss of contact between the tires and road

hy·dro·pon·ics \ˌhī-drə-ˈpä-niks\ *n* : the growing of plants in nutrient solutions — **hy·dro·pon·ic** *adj*

hy·dro·pow·er \ˈhī-drə-ˌpaù-(ə)r\ *n* : hydroelectric power

hy·dro·sphere \ˈhī-drə-ˌsfir\ *n* : the water (as vapor or lakes) of the earth

hy·dro·stat·ic \ˌhī-drə-ˈsta-tik\ *adj* : of or relating to fluids at rest or to the pressures they exert or transmit

hy·dro·ther·a·py \ˌhī-drə-ˈther-ə-pē\ *n* : the use of water esp. externally in the treatment of disease or disability

hy·dro·ther·mal \ˌhī-drə-ˈthər-məl\ *adj* : of or relating to hot water

hy·drous \ˈhī-drəs\ *adj* : containing water

hy·drox·ide \hī-ˈdräk-ˌsīd\ *n* 1 : a negatively charged ion consisting of one atom of oxygen and one atom of hydrogen 2 : a compound of hydroxide with an element or group

hy·e·na \hī-ˈē-nə\ *n* [ME *hyene*, fr. L *hyaena*, fr. Gk *hyaina*, fr. *hys* hog] : any of several large doglike carnivorous mammals of Asia and Africa

hy·giene \ˈhī-ˌjēn\ *n* 1 : a science concerned with establishing and maintaining good health 2 : conditions or practices conducive to health — **hy·gien·ic** \hī-ˈje-nik, -ˈjē-\ *adj* — **hy·gien·i·cal·ly** \-ni-k(ə-)lē\ *adv* — **hy·gien·ist** \hī-ˈjē-nist, ˈhī-ˌjē-, hī-ˈje-\ *n*

hy·grom·e·ter \hī-ˈgrä-mə-tər\ *n* : any of several instruments for measuring the humidity of the atmosphere

hy·gro·scop·ic \ˌhī-grə-ˈskä-pik\ *adj* : readily taking up and retaining moisture

hying *pres part of* HIE

hy·men \ˈhī-mən\ *n* : a fold of mucous membrane partly closing the opening of the vagina

hy·me·ne·al \ˌhī-mə-ˈnē-əl\ *adj* : NUPTIAL

hymn \ˈhim\ *n* : a song of praise esp. to God — **hymn** *vb*

hym·nal \ˈhim-nəl\ *n* : a book of hymns

hyp *abbr* hypothesis; hypothetical

¹**hype** \ˈhīp\ *vb* **hyped; hyp·ing** 1 : STIMULATE — usu. used with *up* 2 : INCREASE — **hyped–up** *adj*

²**hype** *vb* **hyped; hyping** 1 : DECEIVE 2 : PUBLICIZE

³**hype** *n* 1 : DECEPTION, PUT-ON 2 : PUBLICITY

hy·per \ˈhī-pər\ *adj* 1 : HIGH-STRUNG, EXCITABLE 2 : extremely active

hy·per·acid·i·ty \ˌhī-pər-ə-ˈsi-də-tē\ *n* : the condition of containing excessive acid esp. in the stomach — **hy·per·ac·id** \-ˈa-səd\ *adj*

hy·per·ac·tive \-ˈak-tiv\ *adj* : excessively or pathologically active — **hy·per·ac·tiv·i·ty** \-ˌak-ˈti-və-tē\ *n*

hy·per·bar·ic \ˌhī-pər-ˈber-ik\ *adj* : of, relating to, or utilizing greater than normal pressure (as of oxygen)

hy·per·bo·la \hī-ˈpər-bə-lə\ *n, pl* **-las** *or* **-lae** \-(ˌ)lē\ : a curve formed by the intersection of a double right circular cone with a plane that cuts both halves of the cone — **hy·per·bol·ic** \ˌhī-pər-ˈbä-lik\ *adj*

hy·per·bo·le \hī-ˈpər-bə-(ˌ)lē\ *n* : extravagant exaggeration used as a figure of speech

hy·per·crit·i·cal \ˌhī-pər-ˈkri-ti-kəl\ *adj* : excessively critical — **hy·per·crit·i·cal·ly** \-k(ə-)lē\ *adv*

hy·per·drive \ˈhī-pər-ˌdrīv\ *n* : a state of extremely heightened activity

hy·per·ex·tend \ˌhī-pər-ik-ˈstend\ *vb* : to extend beyond the normal range of motion — **hy·per·ex·ten·sion** \-ˈsten-shən\ *n*

hy·per·gly·ce·mia \ˌhī-pər-glī-ˈsē-mē-ə\ *n* : excess of sugar in the blood — **hy·per·gly·ce·mic** \-mik\ *adj*

hy·per·ki·net·ic \-kə-ˈne-tik\ *adj* : characterized by fast-paced or frenetic activity

hy·per·link \ˈhī-pər-ˌliŋk\ *n* : a connecting element (as highlighted text) between one place in a hypertext or hypermedia document and another

hy·per·me·dia \ˈhī-pər-ˌmē-dē-ə\ *n* : a database format offering direct access to text, sound, or images related to that on display

hy·per·opia \ˌhī-pə-ˈrō-pē-ə\ *n* : a condition in which visual images come to focus behind the retina resulting esp. in defective vision for near objects — **hy·per·opic** \-ˈrō-pik, -ˈrä-\ *adj*

hy·per·sen·si·tive \-ˈsen-sə-tiv\ *adj* 1 : excessively or abnormally sensitive 2 : abnormally susceptible physiologically to a specific agent (as a drug) — **hy·per·sen·si·tive·ness** *n* — **hy·per·sen·si·tiv·i·ty** \-ˌsen-sə-ˈti-və-tē\ *n*

hy·per·ten·sion \'hī-pər-ˌten-chən\ *n* : high blood pressure — **hy·per·ten·sive** \ˌhī-pər-'ten-siv\ *adj or n*

hy·per·text \'hī-pər-ˌtekst\ *n* : a database format in which information related to that on display can be accessed directly from the display

hy·per·thy·roid·ism \ˌhī-pər-'thī-ˌròi-ˌdi-zəm\ *n* : excessive activity of the thyroid gland; *also* : the resulting bodily condition — **hy·per·thy·roid** \-'thī-ˌròid\ *adj*

hy·per·tro·phy \hī-'pər-trə-fē\ *n, pl* **-phies** : excessive development of a body part — **hy·per·tro·phic** \ˌhī-pər-'trō-fik\ *adj* — **hypertrophy** *vb*

hy·per·ven·ti·late \ˌhī-pər-'ven-tə-ˌlāt\ *vb* : to breathe rapidly and deeply esp. to the point of losing an abnormal amount of carbon dioxide from the blood — **hy·per·ven·ti·la·tion** \-ˌven-tə-'lā-shən\ *n*

hy·phen \'hī-fən\ *n* : a punctuation mark - used esp. to divide or to compound words or word parts — **hyphen** *vb*

hy·phen·ate \'hī-fə-ˌnāt\ *vb* **-at·ed; -at·ing** : to connect or divide with a hyphen — **hy·phen·ation** \ˌhī-fə-'nā-shən\ *n*

hyp·no·sis \hip-'nō-səs\ *n, pl* **-no·ses** \-ˌsēz\ : an induced state that resembles sleep and in which the subject is responsive to suggestions of the inducer (**hyp·no·tist** \'hip-nə-tist\) — **hyp·no·tism** \'hip-nə-ˌti-zəm\ *n* — **hyp·no·tiz·able** \'hip-nə-ˌtī-zə-bəl\ *adj* — **hyp·no·tize** \-ˌtīz\ *vb*

¹**hyp·not·ic** \hip-'nä-tik\ *adj* **1** : inducing sleep : SOPORIFIC **2** : of or relating to hypnosis or hypnotism **3** : readily holding the attention — **hyp·not·i·cal·ly** \-ti-k(ə-)lē\ *adv*

²**hypnotic** *n* : a sleep-inducing drug

hy·po \'hī-pō\ *n, pl* **hypos** : SODIUM THIOSULFATE; *also* : a solution of sodium thiosulfate

hy·po·al·ler·gen·ic \ˌhī-pō-ˌa-lər-'je-nik\ *adj* : having little likelihood of causing an allergic response

hy·po·cen·ter \'hī-pə-ˌsen-tər\ *n* : the point of origin of an earthquake

hy·po·chon·dria \ˌhī-pə-'kän-drē-ə\ *n* [NL, fr. LL, pl., upper abdomen (formerly regarded as the seat of hypochondria), fr. Gk, lit., the parts under the cartilage (of the breastbone), fr. *hypo-* under + *chondros* cartilage] : depression of mind often centered on imaginary physical ailments — **hy·po·chon·dri·ac** \-drē-ˌak\ *adj or n*

hy·poc·ri·sy \hi-'pä-krə-sē\ *n, pl* **-sies** : a

feigning to be what one is not or to believe what one does not; *esp* : the false assumption of an appearance of virtue or religion — **hyp·o·crite** \'hi-pə-ˌkrit\ *n* — **hyp·o·crit·i·cal** \ˌhi-pə-'kri-ti-kəl\ *adj* — **hyp·o·crit·i·cal·ly** \-k(ə-)lē\ *adv*

¹**hy·po·der·mic** \ˌhī-pə-'dər-mik\ *adj* : administered by or used in making an injection beneath the skin

²**hypodermic** *n* : HYPODERMIC SYRINGE; *also* : an injection made with this

hypodermic needle *n* : NEEDLE 3; *also* : HYPODERMIC SYRINGE

hypodermic syringe *n* : a small syringe with a hollow needle for injecting material into or through the skin

hy·po·gly·ce·mia \ˌhī-pō-glī-'sē-mē-ə\ *n* : abnormal decrease of sugar in the blood — **hy·po·gly·ce·mic** \-mik\ *adj*

hy·pot·e·nuse \hī-'pä-tə-ˌnüs, -ˌnyüs, -ˌnüz, -ˌnyüz\ *n* : the side of a right triangle that is opposite the right angle; *also* : its length

hy·po·thal·a·mus \ˌhī-pō-'tha-lə-məs\ *n* : a part of the brain that lies beneath the thalamus and is a control center for the autonomic nervous system

hy·poth·e·sis \hī-'pä-thə-səs\ *n, pl* **-e·ses** \-ˌsēz\ : an assumption made esp. in order to test its logical or empirical consequences — **hy·po·thet·i·cal** \ˌhī-pə-'the-ti-kəl\ *adj* — **hy·po·thet·i·cal·ly** \-k(ə-)lē\ *adv*

hy·poth·e·size \-ˌsīz\ *vb* **-sized; -siz·ing** : to adopt as a hypothesis

hy·po·thy·roid·ism \ˌhī-pō-'thī-ˌròi-ˌdi-zəm\ *n* : deficient activity of the thyroid gland; *also* : a resultant lowered metabolic rate and general loss of vigor — **hy·po·thy·roid** *adj*

hys·sop \'hi-səp\ *n* : a European mint sometimes used as a potherb

hys·ter·ec·to·my \ˌhis-tə-'rek-tə-mē\ *n, pl* **-mies** : surgical removal of the uterus

hys·te·ria \hi-'ster-ē-ə, -'stir-\ *n* [NL, fr. E *hysteric*, adj., fr. L *hystericus*, fr. Gk *hysterikos*, fr. *hystera* womb; fr. the Greek notion that hysteria was peculiar to women and caused by disturbances in the uterus] **1** : a nervous disorder marked esp. by defective emotional control **2** : unmanageable fear or outburst of emotion — **hys·ter·ic** \-'ster-ik\ *n* — **hys·ter·i·cal** \-'ster-i-kəl\ *also* **hysteric** *adj* — **hys·ter·i·cal·ly** \-k(ə-)lē\ *adv*

hys·ter·ics \-'ster-iks\ *n pl* : a fit of uncontrollable laughter or crying

Hz *abbr* hertz

¹i \ˈī\ n, pl i's or is \ˈīz\ often cap : the 9th letter of the English alphabet

²i abbr, often cap island; isle

³i symbol Imaginary unit

¹I \ˈī, ə\ pron : the one speaking or writing

²I abbr interstate

³I symbol iodine

Ia or IA abbr Iowa

-ial adj suffix : ¹-AL ⟨manorial⟩

iamb \ˈī-ˌam\ or iam-bus \ī-ˈam-bəs\ n, pl iambs \ˈī-ˌamz\ or iam-bus-es : a metrical foot of one unaccented syllable followed by one accented syllable — iam-bic \ī-ˈam-bik\ adj or n

-ian — see -AN

-iatric also -iatrical adj comb form : of or relating to (such) medical treatment or healing ⟨pediatric⟩

-iatrics n pl comb form : medical treatment ⟨pediatrics⟩

ib or ibid abbr ibidem

ibex \ˈī-ˌbeks\ n, pl ibex or ibex-es [L] : any of several Old World wild goats with large curved horns

ibi-dem \ˈi-bə-ˌdem, i-ˈbī-dəm\ adv [L] : in the same place

-ibility — see -ABILITY

ibis \ˈī-bəs\ n, pl ibis or ibis-es [L, fr. Gk, fr. Egypt hbw] : any of various wading birds related to the herons but having a downwardly curved bill

-ible — see -ABLE

ibu-pro-fen \ˌī-byù-ˈprō-fən\ n : a nonsteroidal anti-inflammatory drug used to relieve pain and fever

IC \ˌī-ˈsē\ n : INTEGRATED CIRCUIT

¹-ic adj suffix 1 : of, relating to, or having the form of : being ⟨panoramic⟩ 2 : related to, derived from, or containing ⟨alcoholic⟩ 3 : in the manner of : like that of : characteristic of 4 : associated or dealing with : utilizing ⟨electronic⟩ 5 : characterized by : exhibiting ⟨nostalgic⟩ : affected with ⟨allergic⟩ 6 : caused by 7 : tending to produce ⟨analgesic⟩

²-ic n suffix : one having the character or nature of : one belonging to or associated with : one exhibiting or affected by : one that produces

-ical adj suffix : -IC ⟨symmetrical⟩ ⟨geological⟩ — -ically adv suffix

ICBM \ˌī-(ˌ)sē-(ˌ)bē-ˈem\ n, pl ICBM's or ICBMs \-ˈemz\ : an intercontinental ballistic missile

ICC abbr Interstate Commerce Commission

¹ice \ˈīs\ n 1 : frozen water 2 : a substance resembling ice 3 : a state of coldness (as from formality or reserve) 4 : a flavored frozen dessert; esp : one containing no milk or cream

²ice vb iced; ic-ing 1 : FREEZE 2 : CHILL 3 : to cover with or as if with icing

ice age n : a time of widespread glaciation

ice bag n : a waterproof bag to hold ice for local application of cold to the body

ice-berg \ˈīs-ˌbərg\ n : a large floating mass of ice broken off from a glacier

iceberg lettuce n : any of various crisp light green lettuces that form a compact head like a cabbage

ice-boat \ˈīs-ˌbōt\ n : a boatlike frame on runners propelled on ice by sails

ice-bound \-ˌbaund\ adj : surrounded, obstructed, or covered by ice

ice-box \-ˌbäks\ n : REFRIGERATOR

ice-break-er \-ˌbrā-kər\ n : a ship equipped (as with a reinforced bow) to make a channel through thick ice

ice cap n : a glacier forming on relatively level land and flowing outward from its center

ice cream n : a frozen food containing sweetened or flavored cream or butterfat

ice hockey n : a game in which two teams of ice-skating players try to shoot a puck into the opponent's goal

ice-house \ˈīs-ˌhaus\ n : a building in which ice is made or stored

¹Ice-lan-dic \īs-ˈlan-dik\ adj : of, relating to, or characteristic of Iceland, the Icelanders, or their language

²Icelandic n : the language of Iceland

ice-man \ˈīs-ˌman\ n : one who sells or delivers ice

ice milk n : a sweetened frozen food made of skim milk

ice pick n : a hand tool ending in a spike for chipping ice

ice-skate \ˈīs-ˌskāt\ vb : to skate on ice — ice-skater n

ice storm n : a storm in which falling rain freezes on contact

ice water n : chilled or iced water esp. for drinking

ich-thy-ol-o-gy \ˌik-thē-ˈä-lə-jē\ n : a branch of zoology dealing with fishes — ich-thy-ol-o-gist \-jist\ n

ici-cle \ˈī-ˌsi-kəl\ n [ME isikel, fr. is ice + ikel icicle, fr. OE gicel] : a hanging mass of ice formed by the freezing of dripping water

ic-ing \ˈī-siŋ\ n : a sweet usu. creamy mixture used to coat baked goods

ICJ abbr International Court of Justice

icky \ˈi-kē\ adj ick-i-er; -est : OFFENSIVE, DISTASTEFUL — ick-i-ness n

icon also ikon \ˈī-ˌkän\ n 1 : IMAGE; esp : a religious image painted on a wood panel 2 : a small picture on a computer display that suggests the purpose of an available function — icon-ic \ī-ˈkä-nik\ adj

icon-o-clasm \ī-ˈkä-nə-ˌkla-zəm\ n : the doctrine, practice, or attitude of an iconoclast

icon-o-clast \-ˌklast\ n [ML iconoclastes, fr. MGk eikonoklastēs, lit., image destroyer, fr. Gk eikōn image + klan to break] **1** : one who destroys religious images or opposes their veneration **2** : one who attacks cherished beliefs or institutions

-ics \iks\ *n sing or pl suffix* **1** : study : knowledge : skill : practice ⟨linguis*tics*⟩ ⟨electro*nics*⟩ **2** : characteristic actions or activities ⟨acroba*tics*⟩ **3** : characteristic qualities, operations, or phenomena ⟨mecha*nics*⟩

ic·tus \'ik-təs\ *n* : the recurring stress or beat in a rhythmic or metrical series of sounds

ICU *abbr* intensive care unit

icy \'ī-sē\ *adj* **ic·i·er; -est** **1** : covered with, abounding in, or consisting of ice **2** : intensely cold **3** : being cold and unfriendly — **ic·i·ly** \'ī-sə-lē\ *adv* — **ic·i·ness** \-sē-nəs\ *n*

¹id \'id\ *n* [L, it] : the part of the psyche in psychoanalytic theory that is completely unconscious and concerned with instinctual needs and drives

²id *abbr* idem

¹ID \'ī-'dē\ *n* : a document with identifying information about an individual whose name appears on it

²ID *vb* **ID'd** *or* **IDed; ID'ing** *or* **IDing** : IDENTIFY

³ID *abbr* **1** Idaho **2** identification

idea \ī-'dē-ə\ *n* **1** : a plan for action : DESIGN **2** : something imagined or pictured in the mind **3** : a central meaning or purpose ♦ *Synonyms* CONCEPT, CONCEPTION, NOTION, IMPRESSION

¹ide·al \ī-'dēl\ *adj* **1** : existing only in the mind : IMAGINARY; *also* : lacking practicality **2** : of or relating to an ideal or to perfection : PERFECT

²ideal *n* **1** : a standard of excellence **2** : one regarded as a model worthy of imitation **3** : GOAL ♦ *Synonyms* ARCHETYPE, EXAMPLE, EXEMPLAR, PARADIGM, PATTERN

ide·al·ise *Brit var of* IDEALIZE

ide·al·ism \ī-'dē-ə-ˌli-zəm\ *n* : the practice of forming ideals or living under their influence; *also* : an idealized representation — **ide·al·ist** \-list\ *n* — **ide·al·is·tic** \ī-ˌdē-ə-'lis-tik\ *adj* — **ide·al·is·ti·cal·ly** \-ti-k(ə-)lē\ *adv*

ide·al·ize \ī-'dē-ə-ˌlīz\ *vb* **-ized; -iz·ing** : to think of or represent as ideal — **ide·al·i·za·tion** \-ˌdē-ə-lə-'zā-shən\ *n*

ide·al·ly \ī-'dē-lē, -'dē-ə-lē\ *adv* **1** : in idea or imagination : MENTALLY **2** : in agreement with an ideal : PERFECTLY

ide·a·tion \ˌī-dē-'ā-shən\ *n* : the forming or entertaining of ideas — **ide·ate** \'ī-dē-ˌāt\ *vb* — **ide·a·tion·al** \ˌī-dē-'ā-shə-nəl\ *adj*

idem \'ī-ˌdem, 'ē-, 'i-\ *pron* [L, same] : the same as something previously mentioned

iden·ti·cal \ī-'den-ti-kəl\ *adj* **1** : being the same **2** : essentially alike ♦ *Synonyms* EQUIVALENT, EQUAL, TANTAMOUNT

iden·ti·fi·ca·tion \ī-ˌden-tə-fə-'kā-shən\ *n* **1** : an act of identifying : the state of being identified **2** : evidence of identity **3** : an unconscious psychological process by which an individual models thoughts,

feelings, and actions after another person or an object

iden·ti·fy \ī-'den-tə-ˌfī\ *vb* **-fied; -fy·ing** **1** : to regard as identical **2** : ASSOCIATE **3** : to establish the identity of **4** : to practice psychological identification — **iden·ti·fi·able** \-ˌden-tə-'fī-ə-bəl\ *adj* — **iden·ti·fi·ably** \-blē\ *adv* — **iden·ti·fi·er** \-ˌfī(-ə)r\ *n*

iden·ti·ty \ī-'den-tə-tē\ *n, pl* **-ties** **1** : sameness of essential character **2** : INDIVIDUALITY **3** : the fact of being the same person or thing as claimed

identity crisis *n* : psychological conflict esp. in adolescence involving confusion about one's social role and one's personality

identity theft *n* : the illegal use of someone else's personal information to obtain money or credit

ideo·gram \'ī-dē-ə-ˌgram, 'i-\ *n* **1** : a picture or symbol used in a system of writing to represent a thing or an idea **2** : a character or symbol used in a system of writing to represent an entire word

ideo·logue *also* **idea·logue** \'ī-dē-ə-ˌlȯg\ *n* : a partisan advocate or adherent of a particular ideology

ide·ol·o·gy \ˌī-dē-'ä-lə-jē, ˌi-\ *n, also* **ide·al·o·gy** \-'ä-lə-jē, -'a-\ *n, pl* **-gies** **1** : the body of ideas characteristic of a particular individual, group, or culture **2** : the assertions, theories, and aims that constitute a political, social, and economic program — **ide·o·log·i·cal** \ˌī-dē-ə-'lä-ji-kəl, ˌi-\ *adj* — **ide·o·log·i·cal·ly** \-'lä-ji-k(ə-)lē\ *adv* — **ide·ol·o·gist** \-dē-'ä-lə-jist\ *n*

ides \'īdz\ *n sing or pl* : the 15th day of March, May, July, or October or the 13th day of any other month in the ancient Roman calendar

id·i·o·cy \'i-dē-ə-sē\ *n, pl* **-cies** **1** *usu offensive* : extreme mental retardation **2** : something notably stupid or foolish

id·i·om \'i-dē-əm\ *n* **1** : the language peculiar to a person or group **2** : the characteristic form or structure of a language **3** : an expression that cannot be understood from the meanings of its separate words (as *give way*) — **id·i·o·mat·ic** \ˌi-dē-ə-'ma-tik\ *adj* — **id·i·o·mat·i·cal·ly** \-ti-k(ə)lē\ *adv*

id·i·o·path·ic \ˌi-dē-ə-'pa-thik\ *adj* : arising spontaneously or from an obscure or unknown cause ⟨an ∼ disease⟩

id·i·o·syn·cra·sy \ˌi-dē-ə-'siŋ-krə-sē\ *n, pl* **-sies** : personal peculiarity — **id·i·o·syn·crat·ic** \ˌi-dē-ō-sin-'kra-tik\ *adj* — **id·i·o·syn·crat·i·cal·ly** \-'kra-ti-k(ə-)lē\ *adv*

id·i·ot \'i-dē-ət\ *n* [ME, fr. AF *ydiote*, fr. L *idiota* ignorant person, fr. Gk *idiōtēs* one in a private station, layman, ignorant person, fr. *idios* one's own, private] **1** *usu offensive* : a person affected with idiocy **2** : a foolish or stupid person — **id·i·ot·ic** \ˌi-dē-'ä-tik\ *adj* — **id·i·ot·i·cal·ly** \-ti-k(ə)lē\ *adv*

id·i·ot-proof \'i-dē-ət-ˌprüf\ *adj* : extremely easy to operate or maintain

¹idle \'ī-dᵊl\ *adj* **idler** \'ī-də-lər\; **idlest** \'ī-də-ləst\ **1** : GROUNDLESS, WORTHLESS, USELESS ⟨∼ talk⟩ **2** : not occupied or employed : INACTIVE **3** : LAZY — **idle·ness** *n* — **idly** \'īd-lē\ *adv*

²**idle** *vb* **idled; idling 1** : to spend time doing nothing **2** : to make idle **3** : to run without being connected so that power is not used for useful work — **idler** *n*

idol \'ī-d^əl\ *n* **1** : an image worshipped as a god; *also* : a false god **2** : an object of passionate devotion ⟨a sports ∼⟩

idol·a·ter *or* **idol·a·tor** \ī-'dä-lə-tər\ *n* : a worshiper of idols

idol·a·try \-trē\ *n, pl* **-tries 1** : the worship of a physical object as a god **2** : excessive devotion — **idol·a·trous** \-trəs\ *adj*

idol·ize \'ī-də-,līz\ *vb* **-ized; -iz·ing** : to make an idol of ⟨*idolized* his father⟩ — **idol·i·za·tion** \,ī-də-lə-'zā-shən\ *n*

idyll \'ī-d^əl\ *n* **1** : a simple work of writing or poetry that describes country life or suggests a peaceful setting **2** : a fit subject for an idyll — **idyl·lic** \ī-'di-lik\ *adj*

i.e. \'ī-'ē\ *abbr* [L *id est*] that is

IE *abbr* industrial engineer

IED *abbr* improvised explosive device

-ier — see -ER

if \'if\ *conj* **1** : in the event that ⟨∼ he stays, I leave⟩ **2** : WHETHER ⟨ask ∼ he left⟩ **3** — used as a function word to introduce an exclamation expressing a wish ⟨∼ it would only rain⟩ **4** : even though ⟨an interesting ∼ untenable argument⟩ **5** : and perhaps not even ⟨few ∼ any changes are expected⟩

IF *abbr* intermediate frequency

if·fy \'i-fē\ *adj* : full of contingencies or unknown conditions

-i·fy \ə-,fī\ *vb suffix* : -FY

IG *abbr* inspector general

ig·loo \'i-glü\ *n, pl* **igloos** [Inuit (an Eskimo language) *iglu* house] : an Eskimo house or hut often made of snow blocks and in the shape of a dome

ig·ne·ous \'ig-nē-əs\ *adj* **1** : FIERY **2** : formed by solidification of molten rock

ig·nite \ig-'nīt\ *vb* **ig·nit·ed; ig·nit·ing** : to set afire or catch fire — **ig·nit·able** \-'nī-tə-bəl\ *adj*

ig·ni·tion \ig-'ni-shən\ *n* **1** : a setting on fire **2** : the process or means (as an electric spark) of igniting the fuel mixture in an engine **3** : a device that activates an ignition system

ig·no·ble \ig-'nō-bəl\ *adj* **1** : of common birth **2** : not honorable : BASE, MEAN ✦ **Synonyms** DESPICABLE, SCURVY, SORDID, VILE, WRETCHED — **ig·no·bly** *adv*

ig·no·min·i·ous \,ig-nə-'mi-nē-əs\ *adj* **1** : DISHONORABLE **2** : DESPICABLE **3** : HUMILIATING, DEGRADING ✦ **Synonyms** DISREPUTABLE, DISCREDITABLE, DISGRACEFUL, INGLORIOUS — **ig·no·min·i·ous·ly** *adv* — **ig·no·mi·ny** \'ig-nə-,mi-nē, ig-'nä-mə-nē\ *n*

ig·no·ra·mus \,ig-nə-'rā-məs\ *n, pl* **-mus·es** *also* **-mi** \-mī\ [*Ignoramus*, ignorant lawyer in *Ignoramus* (1615), play by George Ruggle] : an utterly ignorant person

ig·no·rance \'ig-nə-rəns\ *n* : the state of being ignorant

ig·no·rant \'ig-nə-rənt\ *adj* **1** : lacking knowledge **2** : resulting from or showing lack of knowledge or intelligence **3** : UNAWARE, UNINFORMED ✦ **Synonyms** BENIGHTED, ILLITERATE, UNEDUCATED, UNLETTERED, UNTUTORED — **ig·no·rant·ly** *adv*

ig·nore \ig-'nȯr\ *vb* **ig·nored; ig·nor·ing** : to refuse to take notice of ✦ **Synonyms** OVERLOOK, SLIGHT, NEGLECT

igua·na \i-'gwä-nə\ *n* : any of various large tropical American lizards

ihp *abbr* indicated horsepower

IHS \,ī-,āch-'es\ [LL, part transliteration of Gk IHΣ, abbr. for IHΣΟΥΣ *Iēsous* Jesus] — used as a Christian symbol and monogram for *Jesus*

ikon *var of* ICON

IL *abbr* Illinois

il·e·itis \,i-lē-'ī-təs\ *n* : inflammation of the ileum

il·e·um \'i-lē-əm\ *n, pl* **il·ea** \-lē-ə\ : the part of the small intestine between the jejunum and the large intestine

il·i·ac \'i-lē-,ak\ *adj* : of, relating to, or located near the ilium

il·i·um \'i-lē-əm\ *n, pl* **il·ia** \-lē-ə\ : the uppermost and largest of the three bones making up either side of the pelvis

ilk \'ilk\ *n* : SORT, KIND

¹**ill** \'il\ *adj* **worse** \'wərs\; **worst** \'wərst\ **1** : attended or caused by an evil intent ⟨∼ deeds⟩ **2** : not normal or sound ⟨∼ health⟩; *also* : not in good health : SICK **3** : BAD, UNLUCKY ⟨an ∼ omen⟩ **4** : not right or proper ⟨∼ manners⟩ **5** : UNFRIENDLY, HOSTILE ⟨∼ feeling⟩

²**ill** *adv* **worse; worst 1** : with displeasure **2** : in a harsh manner **3** : HARDLY, SCARCELY ⟨can ∼ afford it⟩ **4** : BADLY, UNLUCKILY **5** : in a faulty way

³**ill** *n* **1** : EVIL **2** : MISFORTUNE, DISTRESS **3** : AILMENT, SICKNESS; *also* : TROUBLE

⁴**ill** *abbr* illustrated; illustration; illustrator

Ill *abbr* Illinois

ill-ad·vised \,il-əd-'vīzd\ *adj* : not well counseled ⟨∼ efforts⟩ — **ill-ad·vis·ed·ly** \-'vī-zəd-lē\ *adv*

ill-bred \-'bred\ *adj* : badly brought up : IMPOLITE ⟨an ∼ child⟩

il·le·gal \il-'lē-gəl\ *adj* **1** : not lawful; *also* : not sanctioned by official rules ✦ **Synonyms** UNLAWFUL, CRIMINAL, ILLEGITIMATE, ILLICIT, WRONGFUL — **il·le·gal·i·ty** \i-li-'ga-lə-tē\ *n* — **il·le·gal·ly** *adv*

il·leg·i·ble \il-'le-jə-bəl\ *adj* : not legible — **il·leg·i·bil·i·ty** \il-,le-jə-'bi-lə-tē\ *n* — **il·leg·i·bly** \il-'le-jə-blē\ *adv*

il·le·git·i·mate \,i-li-'ji-tə-mət\ *adj* **1** : born of unmarried parents **2** : ILLOGICAL **3** : ILLEGAL — **il·le·git·i·ma·cy** \-'ji-tə-mə-sē\ *n* — **il·le·git·i·mate·ly** *adv*

ill-fat·ed \'il-'fā-təd\ *adj* : UNFORTUNATE ⟨an ∼ expedition⟩

ill-fa·vored \-'fā-vərd\ *adj* : UGLY, UNATTRACTIVE

ill-got·ten \'gä-t^ən\ *adj* : acquired by improper means ⟨∼ gains⟩

ill-hu·mored \-'hyü-mərd, -'yü-\ *adj* : SURLY, IRRITABLE

il·lib·er·al \il-'li-bə-rəl\ *adj* : not liberal : NARROW, BIGOTED

il·lic·it \il-'li-sət\ *adj* : not permitted : UNLAWFUL — **il·lic·it·ly** *adv*

il·lim·it·able \il-'li-mə-tə-bəl\ *adj* : BOUNDLESS, MEASURELESS — **il·lim·it·ably** \-blē\ *adv*

Il·li·nois \‚i-lə-'nöi *also* -'nöiz\ *n, pl* **Illinois** : a member of an American Indian people of Illinois, Iowa, and Wisconsin

il·lit·er·ate \il-'li-tə-rət\ *adj* **1** : having little or no education; *esp* : unable to read or write **2** : showing a lack of familiarity with the fundamentals of a particular field of knowledge — **il·lit·er·a·cy** \-'li-tə-rə-sē\ *n* — **illiterate** *n*

ill–man·nered \'il-'ma-nərd\ *adj* : marked by bad manners : RUDE

ill–na·tured \'nā-chərd\ *adj* : CROSS, SURLY — **ill–na·tured·ly** *adv*

ill·ness \'il-nəs\ *n* : SICKNESS

il·log·i·cal \il-'lä-ji-kəl\ *adj* : lacking sound reasoning; *also* : SENSELESS — **il·log·i·cal·ly** \-k(ə-)lē\ *adv*

ill–starred \'il-'stärd\ *adj* : UNLUCKY 1 ⟨an ~ venture⟩

ill–tem·pered \-'tem-pərd\ *adj* : CROSS

ill–treat \-'trēt\ *vb* : to treat cruelly or improperly : MALTREAT — **ill–treat·ment** *n*

il·lu·mi·nate \i-'lü-mə-‚nāt\ *vb* **-nat·ed; -nat·ing 1** : to supply or brighten with light : light up **2** : to make clear : ELUCIDATE; *also* : to bring to the fore **3** : to decorate (as a manuscript) with designs or pictures in gold or colors — **il·lu·mi·nat·ing·ly** *adv* — **il·lu·mi·na·tion** \-‚lü-mə-'nā-shən\ *n* — **il·lu·mi·na·tor** \'lü-mə-‚nā-tər\ *n*

il·lu·mine \i-'lü-mən\ *vb* **-mined; -min·ing** : ILLUMINATE

ill–us·age \'il-'yü-sij\ *n* : harsh, unkind, or abusive treatment

ill–use \-'yüz\ *vb* : MALTREAT, ABUSE

il·lu·sion \i-'lü-zhən\ *n* [ME, fr. AF, fr. LL *illusio*, fr. L, action of mocking, fr. *illudere* to mock at, fr. *ludere* to play, mock] **1** : a mistaken idea : MISCONCEPTION **2** : a misleading visual image; *also* : HALLUCINATION

il·lu·sion·ist \i-'lü-zhə-nist\ *n* : one that produces illusions; *esp* : a sleight-of-hand performer

il·lu·sive \i-'lü-siv\ *adj* : DECEPTIVE

il·lu·so·ry \i-'lü-sə-rē, -zə-\ *adj* : DECEPTIVE ⟨~ hopes⟩

illust *or* **illus** *abbr* illustrated; illustration

il·lus·trate \'i-ləs-‚trāt\ *vb* **-trat·ed; -trat·ing** [L *illustrare*, fr. *lustrare* to purify, make bright] **1** : to explain by use of examples : CLARIFY; *also* : DEMONSTRATE **2** : to provide with pictures or figures that explain or decorate **3** : to serve to explain or decorate — **il·lus·tra·tor** \'i-ləs-‚strā-tər\ *n*

il·lus·tra·tion \‚i-lə-'strā-shən\ *n* **1** : the act of illustrating : the condition of being illustrated **2** : an example or instance that helps make something clear **3** : a picture or diagram that explains or decorates

il·lus·tra·tive \i-'ləs-trə-tiv, 'i-lə-‚strā-\ *adj* : serving, tending, or designed to illustrate — **il·lus·tra·tive·ly** *adv*

il·lus·tri·ous \i-'ləs-trē-əs\ *adj* : notably outstanding because of rank or achievement ♦ *Synonyms* DISTINGUISHED, EMINENT, FAMOUS, GREAT, NOTABLE, PROMINENT — **il·lus·tri·ous·ness** *n*

ill will *n* : unfriendly feeling

ILS *abbr* instrument landing system

¹im·age \'i-mij\ *n* **1** : a likeness or imitation of a person or thing; *esp* : STATUE **2** : a picture of an object formed by a device (as a mirror or lens) **3** : a visual representation of something ⟨a computer ~⟩ **4** a person strikingly like another person ⟨he is the ~ of his father⟩ **5** : a mental picture or conception : IMPRESSION, IDEA, CONCEPT **6** : a vivid representation or description

²image *vb* **im·aged; im·ag·ing 1** : to call up a mental picture of **2** : to describe or portray in words **3** : to create a representation of **4** : REFLECT, MIRROR **5** : to make appear : PROJECT

im·ag·ery \'i-mij-rē\ *n, pl* **-er·ies 1** : IMAGES; *also* : the art of making images **2** : figurative language **3** : mental images; *esp* : the products of imagination

imag·in·able \i-'ma-jə-nə-bəl\ *adj* : capable of being imagined : CONCEIVABLE — **imag·in·ably** *adv*

imag·in·ary \i-'ma-jə-‚ner-ē\ *adj* **1** : existing only in the imagination **2** : containing or relating to a quantity (**imaginary unit**) that is the positive square root of minus 1 (√-1)

imaginary number *n* : a complex number (as $2 + 3i$) with a nonzero term (**imaginary part**) containing the imaginary unit as a factor

imag·i·na·tion \i-‚ma-jə-'nā-shən\ *n* **1** : the act or power of forming a mental image of something not present to the senses or not previously known or experienced **2** : creative ability **3** : RESOURCEFULNESS **4** : a mental image : a creation of the mind — **imag·i·na·tive** \i-'ma-jə-nə-tiv, -‚nā-\ *adj* — **imag·i·na·tive·ly** *adv*

imag·ine \i-'ma-jən\ *vb* **imag·ined; imag·in·ing 1** : to form a mental picture of something not present **2** : THINK, GUESS ⟨I ~ it will rain⟩

imag·in·ings \-'maj-niŋz, -'ma-jə-\ *n pl* : products of the imagination

im·ag·ism \'i-mi-‚ji-zəm\ *n, often cap* : a movement in poetry advocating free verse and the expression of ideas and emotions through clear precise images — **im·ag·ist** \-jist\ *n*

ima·go \i-'mā-gō, -'mä-\ *n, pl* **imagoes** *or* **ima·gi·nes** \-'mā-gə-‚nēz, -'mä-\ [NL, fr. L, image] : an insect in its final adult stage — **ima·gi·nal** \i-'mā-gə-n²l, -'mä-\ *adj*

im·bal·ance \'im-'ba-ləns\ *n* : lack of balance : the state of being out of equilibrium or out of proportion

im·be·cile \'im-bə-səl, -‚sil\ *n* **1** *usu offensive* : a person affected with moderate mental retardation **2** : FOOL, IDIOT — **imbecile** *or* **im·be·cil·ic** \‚im-bə-'si-lik\ *adj* — **im·be·cil·i·ty** \‚im-bə-'si-lə-tē\ *n*

imbed *var of* EMBED

im·bibe \im-'bīb\ *vb* **im·bibed; im·bib-**

ing 1 : to receive and retain in the mind **2** : to drink alcoholic beverages **3** : to take in or up : ABSORB — **im·bib·er** n

im·bri·ca·tion \ˌim-brə-ˈkā-shən\ n **1** : an overlapping of edges (as of tiles) **2** : a pattern showing imbrication — **im·bri·cate** \ˈim-bri-kət\ adj

im·bro·glio \im-ˈbrōl-yō\ n, pl **-glios** [It, fr. *imbrogliare* to entangle] **1** : a confused mass **2** : a complicated situation; *also* : a serious or embarrassing misunderstanding

im·brue \-ˈbrü\ vb **im·brued; im·bru·ing** : STAIN ⟨hands *imbrued* with blood⟩

im·bue \-ˈbyü\ vb **im·bued; im·bu·ing 1** : to permeate or influence as if by dyeing **2** : to tinge or dye deeply

IMF abbr International Monetary Fund

imit abbr imitative

im·i·ta·ble \ˈi-mə-tə-bəl\ adj : capable or worthy of being imitated or copied

im·i·tate \ˈi-mə-ˌtāt\ vb **-tat·ed; -tat·ing 1** : to follow as a model : COPY **2** : RESEMBLE **3** : REPRODUCE **4** : MIMIC, COUNTERFEIT — **im·i·ta·tor** \-ˌtā-tər\ n

im·i·ta·tion \ˌi-mə-ˈtā-shən\ n **1** : an act of imitating **2** : COPY, COUNTERFEIT **3** : a literary work that reproduces the style of another author — **imitation** adj

im·i·ta·tive \ˈi-mə-ˌtā-tiv\ adj **1** : marked by imitation **2** : inclined to imitate **3** : COUNTERFEIT

im·mac·u·late \i-ˈma-kyə-lət\ adj **1** : being without stain or blemish : PURE **2** : spotlessly clean ⟨∼ linen⟩ — **im·mac·u·late·ly** adv

im·ma·nent \ˈi-mə-nənt\ adj **1** INHERENT **2** : being within the limits of experience or knowledge — **im·ma·nence** \-nəns\ n — **im·ma·nen·cy** \-nən-sē\ n

im·ma·te·ri·al \ˌi-mə-ˈtir-ē-əl\ adj **1** : not consisting of matter : SPIRITUAL **2** : UNIMPORTANT, TRIFLING   ♦ *Synonyms* BODILESS, DISEMBODIED, INCORPOREAL, INSUBSTANTIAL, NONPHYSICAL — **im·ma·te·ri·al·i·ty** \-(ˌ)i-ˌtir-ē-ˈa-lə-tē\ n

im·ma·ture \ˌi-mə-ˈtur, -ˈtyur\ adj : lacking complete development : not yet mature ⟨∼ behavior⟩ — **im·ma·tu·ri·ty** \-ˈtur-ə-tē, -ˈtyur-\ n

im·mea·sur·able \(ˌ)i-ˈme-zhə-rə-bəl\ adj : not capable of being measured : indefinitely extensive : ILLIMITABLE — **im·mea·sur·ably** \-blē\ adv

im·me·di·a·cy \i-ˈmē-dē-ə-sē\ n, pl **-cies 1** : the quality or state of being immediate **2** : something that is of immediate importance

im·me·di·ate \i-ˈmē-dē-ət\ adj **1** : acting directly and alone : DIRECT ⟨the ∼ cause of death⟩ **2** : being next in line or relation ⟨members of the ∼ family⟩ **3** : not distant : CLOSE **4** : made or done at once ⟨an ∼ response⟩ **5** : near to or related to the present time ⟨the ∼ future⟩ — **im·me·di·ate·ly** adv

im·me·mo·ri·al \ˌi-mə-ˈmȯr-ē-əl\ adj : extending beyond the reach of memory, record, or tradition ⟨from time ∼⟩

im·mense \i-ˈmens\ adj [ME, fr. MF, fr. L *immensus* immeasurable, fr. *mensus*, pp. of *metiri* to measure] **1** : very great in

size or degree : VAST, HUGE **2** : EXCELLENT — **im·mense·ly** adv — **im·men·si·ty** \-ˈmen-sə-tē\ n

im·merse \i-ˈmərs\ vb **im·mersed; im·mers·ing 1** : to plunge or dip esp. into a fluid **2** : ENGROSS, ABSORB **3** : to baptize by immersing — **im·mer·sion** \-ˈmər-zhən\ n

im·mi·grant \ˈi-mi-grənt\ n **1** : a person who immigrates **2** : a plant or animal that becomes established where it did not previously occur

im·mi·grate \ˈi-mə-ˌgrāt\ vb **-grat·ed; -grat·ing** : to come into a foreign country and take up residence — **im·mi·gra·tion** \ˌi-mə-ˈgrā-shən\ n

im·mi·nent \ˈi-mə-nənt\ adj : ready to take place; esp : hanging threateningly over one's head ⟨in ∼ danger⟩ — **im·mi·nence** \-nəns\ n — **im·mi·nent·ly** adv

im·mis·ci·ble \(ˌ)i-ˈmi-sə-bəl\ adj : incapable of mixing — **im·mis·ci·bil·i·ty** \-ˌmi-sə-ˈbi-lə-tē\ n

im·mis·er·a·tion \(ˌ)i-ˌmi-zə-ˈrā-shən\ n : IMPOVERISHMENT

im·mo·bile \(ˌ)i-ˈmō-bəl\ adj : incapable of being moved : FIXED — **im·mo·bil·i·ty** \ˌi-mō-ˈbi-lə-tē\ n

im·mo·bi·lize \i-ˈmō-bə-ˌlīz\ vb : to make immobile — **im·mo·bi·li·za·tion** \ˌi-ˌmō-bə-lə-ˈzā-shən\ n

im·mod·er·ate \(ˌ)i-ˈmä-də-rət\ adj : lacking in moderation : EXCESSIVE ⟨∼ drinking⟩ — **im·mod·er·a·cy** \-rə-sē\ n — **im·mod·er·ate·ly** adv

im·mod·est \(ˌ)i-ˈmä-dəst\ adj : not modest : BRAZEN, INDECENT ⟨an ∼ dress⟩ ⟨∼ conduct⟩ — **im·mod·est·ly** adv — **im·mod·es·ty** \-də-stē\ n

im·mo·late \ˈi-mə-ˌlāt\ vb **-lat·ed; -lat·ing** [L *immolare*, to sprinkle with meal before sacrificing, sacrifice, fr. *mola* sacrificial barley cake, lit., millstone] : to offer in sacrifice; esp : to kill as a sacrificial victim — **im·mo·la·tion** \ˌi-mə-ˈlā-shən\ n

im·mor·al \(ˌ)i-ˈmȯr-əl\ adj : not moral — **im·mor·al·ly** adv

im·mor·al·i·ty \ˌi-mȯ-ˈra-lə-tē, ˌi-mə-\ n **1** : WICKEDNESS; esp : UNCHASTITY **2** : an immoral act or practice

¹**im·mor·tal** \(ˌ)i-ˈmȯr-t⁸l\ adj **1** : not mortal : exempt from death ⟨∼ gods⟩ **2** : destined to be remembered forever ⟨those ∼ words⟩ — **im·mor·tal·ly** adv

²**immortal** n **1** : one exempt from death **2** pl, often cap : the gods in Greek and Roman mythology **3** : a person whose fame is lasting ⟨an ∼ of baseball⟩

im·mor·tal·ise Brit var of IMMORTALIZE

im·mor·tal·i·ty \ˌi-mȯr-ˈta-lə-tē\ n : the quality or state of being immortal; esp : unending existence

im·mor·tal·ize \i-ˈmȯr-tə-ˌlīz\ vb **-ized; -iz·ing** : to make immortal

im·mov·able \(ˌ)i-ˈmü-və-bəl\ adj **1** : firmly fixed, settled, or fastened : FAST, STATIONARY ⟨∼ mountains⟩ **2** : STEADFAST, UNYIELDING **3** : IMPASSIVE — **im·mov·abil·i·ty** \-ˌmü-və-ˈbi-lə-tē\ n — **im·mov·ably** \-blē\ adv

im·mune \i-ˈmyün\ adj **1** : EXEMPT **2** : having a special capacity for resistance (as to a disease) **3** : containing or producing antibodies — **im·mu·ni·ty** \\-'myü-nə-tē\ *n*

immune response *n* : a response of the body to an antigen resulting in the formation of antibodies and cells designed to react with the antigen and render it harmless

immune system *n* : the bodily system that protects the body from foreign substances, cells, and tissues by producing the immune response and that includes esp. the thymus, spleen, lymph nodes, and lymphocytes

im·mu·nize \'i-myə-ˌnīz\ *vb* **-nized; -nizing** : to make immune — **im·mu·ni·za·tion** \ˌi-myə-nə-'zā-shən\ *n*

im·mu·no·de·fi·cien·cy \ˌi-myə-nō-di-'fishən-sē\ *n* : inability to produce the normal number of antibodies or immunologically sensitized cells esp. in response to specific antigens — **im·mu·no·de·fi·cient** \-'fi-shənt\ *adj*

im·mu·no·glob·u·lin \ˌi-myə-nō-'glä-byələn\ *n* : ANTIBODY

im·mu·nol·o·gy \ˌi-myə-'nä-lə-jē\ *n* : a science that deals with the immune system, immunity, and the immune response — **im·mu·no·log·ic** \-nə-'lä-jik\ *or* **im·mu·no·log·i·cal** \-ji-kəl\ *adj* — **im·mu·no·log·i·cal·ly** \-ji-k(ə-)lē\ *adv* — **im·mu·nol·o·gist** \-'nä-lə-jist\ *n*

im·mu·no·sup·pres·sion \ˌi-myə-nō-sə-'pre-shən\ *n* : suppression (as by drugs) of natural immune responses — **im·mu·no·sup·press** \-'pres\ *vb* — **im·mu·no·sup·pres·sant** \-'pre-sⁿnt\ *n or adj* — **im·mu·no·sup·pres·sive** \-'pre-siv\ *adj*

im·mu·no·ther·a·py \-'ther-ə-pē\ *n* : the treatment or prevention of disease by attempting to induce immunity

im·mure \i-'myùr\ *vb* **im·mured; im·mur·ing** **1** : to enclose within or as if within walls **2** : to build into a wall; *esp* : to entomb in a wall

im·mu·ta·ble \(ˌ)i-'myü-tə-bəl\ *adj* : UNCHANGEABLE, UNCHANGING — **im·mu·ta·bil·i·ty** \-ˌmyü-tə-'bi-lə-tē\ *n* — **im·mu·ta·bly** \-'myü-tə-blē\ *adv*

¹**imp** \'imp\ *n* **1** : a small demon : FIEND **2** : a mischievous child

²**imp** *abbr* **1** imperative **2** imperfect **3** imperial **4** import; imported

¹**im·pact** \im-'pakt\ *vb* **1** : to press together **2** : to have an impact on

²**im·pact** \'im-ˌpakt\ *n* **1** : a forceful contact, collision, or onset; *also* : the impetus communicated in or as if in a collision **2** : EFFECT

im·pact·ed \im-'pak-təd\ *adj* **1** : packed or wedged in **2** : wedged between the jawbone and another tooth

im·pair \im-'per\ *vb* : to diminish in quantity, value, excellence, or strength : DAMAGE, LESSEN — **im·pair·ment** *n*

im·paired \-'pard\ *adj* : being in a less than perfect or whole condition; *esp* : disabled or functionally defective — often used in combination ⟨hearing-*impaired*⟩

im·pa·la \im-'pa-lə\ *n, pl* **impalas** *or* **impala** : a large brownish African antelope that in the male has slender curved horns with ridges

im·pale \im-'pāl\ *vb* **im·paled; im·paling** : to pierce with or as if with something pointed — **im·pale·ment** *n*

im·pal·pa·ble \(ˌ)im-'pal-pə-bəl\ *adj* **1** : unable to be felt by touch : INTANGIBLE **2** : not easily seen or understood — **im·pal·pa·bly** \-blē\ *adv*

im·pan·el *or* **em·pan·el** \im-'pan-ᵊl\ *vb* : to enter in or on a panel : ENROLL ⟨~ a jury⟩

im·part \im-'pärt\ *vb* **1** : to give from one's store or abundance ⟨the sun ~s warmth⟩ **2** : to make known

im·par·tial \(ˌ)im-'pär-shəl\ *adj* : not partial : UNBIASED, JUST — **im·par·tial·i·ty** \-ˌpär-shē-'a-lə-tē\ *n* — **im·par·tial·ly** *adv*

im·pass·able \(ˌ)im-'pa-sə-bəl\ *adj* : incapable of being passed, traversed, or crossed ⟨~ roads⟩ — **im·pass·ably** \-blē\ *adv*

im·passe \'im-ˌpas\ *n* **1** : a predicament from which there is no obvious escape **2** : an impassable road or way

im·pas·si·ble \(ˌ)im-'pa-sə-bəl\ *adj* : incapable of feeling : IMPASSIVE

im·pas·sioned \im-'pa-shənd\ *adj* : filled with passion or zeal : showing great warmth or intensity of feeling ♦ **Synonyms** PASSIONATE, ARDENT, FERVENT, FERVID

im·pas·sive \(ˌ)im-'pa-siv\ *adj* : showing no signs of feeling, emotion, or interest : EXPRESSIONLESS, INDIFFERENT ♦ **Synonyms** STOIC, PHLEGMATIC, APATHETIC, STOLID — **im·pas·sive·ly** *adv* — **im·pas·siv·i·ty** \ˌim-ˌpa-'si-və-tē\ *n*

im·pas·to \im-'pas-tō, -'päs-\ *n* : the thick application of a pigment to a canvas or panel in painting; *also* : the body of pigment so applied

im·pa·tiens \im-'pā-shənz, -shəns\ *n* : any of a genus of herbs with usu. spurred flowers and seed capsules that readily split open

im·pa·tient \(ˌ)im-'pā-shənt\ *adj* **1** : not patient : restless or short of temper esp. under irritation, delay, or opposition **2** : INTOLERANT ⟨~ of poverty⟩ **3** : prompted or marked by impatience ⟨an ~ reply⟩ **4** : ANXIOUS — **im·pa·tience** \-shəns\ *n* — **im·pa·tient·ly** *adv*

im·peach \im-'pēch\ *vb* [ME *empechen* to accuse, fr. AF *empecher, enpechier* to ensnare, impede, prosecute, fr. LL *impedicare* to fetter, fr. L *pedica* fetter, fr. *ped-, pes* foot] **1** : to charge (a public official) before an authorized tribunal with misconduct in office **2** : to challenge the credibility or validity of **3** : to remove from public office for misconduct — **im·peach·ment** *n*

im·pec·ca·ble \(ˌ)im-'pe-kə-bəl\ *adj* **1** : not capable of sinning or wrongdoing **2** : FAULTLESS, IRREPROACHABLE ⟨a man of ~ character⟩ — **im·pec·ca·bil·i·ty** \ˌpe-kə-'bi-lə-tē\ *n* — **im·pec·ca·bly** \-'pe-kə-blē\ *adv*

im·pe·cu·nious \ˌim-pi-'kyü-nyəs, -nē-əs\ *adj* : having little or no money — **im·pe·cu·nious·ness** *n*

im·ped·ance \im-'pē-d°ns\ n : the opposition in an electrical circuit to the flow of an alternating current

im·pede \im-'pēd\ vb **im·ped·ed; im·ped·ing** [L *impedire,* fr. *ped-, pes* foot] : to interfere with the progress of

im·ped·i·ment \im-'pe-də-mənt\ n 1 : something that impedes, hinders, or obstructs 2 : a speech defect

im·ped·i·men·ta \im-ˌpe-də-'men-tə\ n pl : things that impede

im·pel \im-'pel\ vb **im·pelled; im·pel·ling** : to urge or drive forward or on : FORCE; *also* : PROPEL

im·pel·ler *also* **im·pel·lor** \im-'pe-lər\ n : a rotor esp. in a pump

im·pend \im-'pend\ vb 1 : to hover or hang over threateningly : MENACE 2 : to be about to occur

im·pen·e·tra·ble \(ˌ)im-'pe-nə-trə-bəl\ adj 1 : incapable of being penetrated or pierced ⟨an ~ jungle⟩ 2 : incapable of being comprehended : INSCRUTABLE ⟨an ~ mystery⟩ — **im·pen·e·tra·bil·i·ty** \-ˌpe-nə-trə-'bi-lə-tē\ n — **im·pen·e·tra·bly** \-'pe-nə-trə-blē\ adv

im·pen·i·tent \(ˌ)im-'pe-nə-tənt\ adj : not penitent : not repenting of sin — **im·pen·i·tence** \-təns\ n

im·per·a·tive \im-'per-ə-tiv\ adj 1 : expressing a command, request, or encouragement ⟨~ sentence⟩ 2 : having power to restrain, control, or direct 3 : NECESSARY ⟨an ~ duty⟩ — **imperative** n — **im·per·a·tive·ly** adv

im·per·cep·ti·ble \ˌim-pər-'sep-tə-bəl\ adj : not perceptible; *esp* : too slight to be perceived ⟨~ changes⟩ — **im·per·cep·ti·bly** \-blē\ adv

im·per·cep·tive \ˌim-pər-'sep-tiv\ adj : not perceptive ⟨an ~ reader⟩

imperf abbr imperfect

¹**im·per·fect** \(ˌ)im-'pər-fikt\ adj 1 : not perfect : DEFECTIVE, INCOMPLETE 2 : of, relating to, or being a verb tense used to designate a continuing state or an incomplete action esp. in the past — **im·per·fect·ly** adv

²**imperfect** n : the imperfect tense; *also* : a verb form in it

im·per·fec·tion \ˌim-pər-'fek-shən\ n : the quality or state of being imperfect; *also* : FAULT, BLEMISH

im·pe·ri·al \im-'pir-ē-əl\ adj 1 : of, relating to, or befitting an empire or an emperor; *also* : of or relating to the United Kingdom or to the Commonwealth or British Empire 2 : ROYAL, SOVEREIGN; *also* : REGAL, IMPERIOUS 3 : of unusual size or excellence

im·pe·ri·al·ism \im-'pir-ē-ə-ˌli-zəm\ n : the policy of seeking to extend the power, dominion, or territories of a nation — **im·pe·ri·al·ist** \-list\ n or adj — **im·pe·ri·al·is·tic** \-ˌpir-ē-ə-'lis-tik\ adj — **im·pe·ri·al·is·ti·cal·ly** \-ti-k(ə-)lē\ adv

im·per·il \im-'per-əl\ vb **-iled** or **-illed; -il·ing** or **-il·ling** : ENDANGER

im·pe·ri·ous \im-'pir-ē-əs\ adj 1 : COMMANDING, LORDLY 2 : ARROGANT, DOMINEERING 3 : IMPERATIVE, URGENT ⟨~ problems⟩ — **im·pe·ri·ous·ly** adv

im·per·ish·able \(ˌ)im-'per-i-shə-bəl\ adj : not perishable or subject to decay

im·per·ma·nent \(ˌ)im-'pər-mə-nənt\ adj : not permanent : TRANSIENT - - **im·per·ma·nent·ly** adv

im·per·me·able \(ˌ)im-'pər-mē-ə-bəl\ adj : not permitting passage (as of a fluid) through its substance

im·per·mis·si·ble \ˌim-pər-'mi-sə-bəl\ adj : not permissible ⟨~ by law⟩

im·per·son·al \(ˌ)im-'pər-sə-nəl\ adj 1 : not referring to any particular person or thing 2 : not involving human emotions — **im·per·son·al·i·ty** \-ˌpər-sə-'na-lə-tē\ n — **im·per·son·al·ly** adv

im·per·son·ate \im-'pər-sə-ˌnāt\ vb **-at·ed; -at·ing** : to assume or act the character of — **im·per·son·a·tion** \-ˌpər-sə-'nā-shən\ n — **im·per·son·a·tor** \-'pər-sə-ˌnā-tər\ n

im·per·ti·nent \(ˌ)im-'pər-tə-nənt\ adj 1 : IRRELEVANT 2 : not restrained within due or proper bounds : RUDE, INSOLENT, SAUCY ⟨an ~ reply⟩ — **im·per·ti·nence** \-nəns\ n — **im·per·ti·nent·ly** adv

im·per·turb·able \ˌim-pər-'tər-bə-bəl\ adj : marked by extreme calm, impassivity, and steadiness : SERENE

im·per·vi·ous \(ˌ)im-'pər-vē-əs\ adj 1 : incapable of being penetrated (as by moisture) 2 : not capable of being affected or disturbed ⟨~ to criticism⟩

im·pe·ti·go \ˌim-pə-'tē-gō, -'tī-\ n : a contagious skin disease characterized by vesicles, pustules, and yellowish crusts

im·pet·u·ous \im-'pe-chə-wəs\ adj 1 : marked by impulsive vehemence ⟨~ temper⟩ 2 : marked by force and violence ⟨with ~ speed⟩ — **im·pet·u·os·i·ty** \(ˌ)im-ˌpe-chə-'wä-sə-tē\ n — **im·pet·u·ous·ly** adv

im·pe·tus \'im-pə-təs\ n [L, assault, impetus, fr. *impetere* to attack, fr. *petere* to go to, seek] 1 : a driving force : IMPULSE; *also* : INCENTIVE 2 : MOMENTUM

im·pi·e·ty \(ˌ)im-'pī-ə-tē\ n, pl **-ties** 1 : the quality or state of being impious 2 : an impious act

im·pinge \im-'pinj\ vb **im·pinged; im·ping·ing** 1 : to strike or dash esp. with a sharp collision 2 : ENCROACH, INFRINGE — **im·pinge·ment** n

im·pi·ous \'im-pē-əs, (ˌ)im-'pī-\ adj : not pious : IRREVERENT, PROFANE

imp·ish \'im-pish\ adj : of, relating to, or befitting an imp; *esp* : MISCHIEVOUS — **imp·ish·ly** adv — **imp·ish·ness** n

im·pla·ca·ble \(ˌ)im-'pla-kə-bəl, -'plā-\ adj : not capable of being appeased, pacified, mitigated, or changed ⟨an ~ enemy⟩ — **im·pla·ca·bil·i·ty** \-ˌpla-kə-'bi-lə-tē, -ˌplā-\ n — **im·pla·ca·bly** \-'pla-kə-blē\ adv

im·plant \im-'plant\ vb 1 : to set firmly or deeply 2 : to fix in the mind or spirit 3 : to insert in living tissue (as for growth or absorption) — **im·plant** \'im-ˌplant\ n — **im·plan·ta·tion** \ˌim-ˌplan-'tā-shən\ n

im·plau·si·ble \(ˌ)im-'plȯ-zə-bəl\ adj : not plausible — **im·plau·si·bil·i·ty** \-ˌplȯ-'bi-lə-tē\ n — **im·plau·si·bly** \-'plȯ-zə-blē\ adv

¹im·ple·ment \'im-plə-mənt\ n [ME, fr. AF, fr. ML *implementum* item making a full complement, appurtenance, tool, fr. LL, act of filling up, fr. L *implēre* to fill up] : TOOL, UTENSIL, INSTRUMENT

²im·ple·ment \-ˌment\ vb 1 : CARRY OUT; *esp* : to put into practice ⟨~ a plan⟩ 2 : to provide implements for — im·ple·men·ta·tion \ˌim-plə-mən-'tā-shən\ n

im·pli·cate \'im-plə-ˌkāt\ vb -cat·ed; -cat·ing 1 : IMPLY 2 : INVOLVE — im·pli·ca·tion \-'kā-shən\ n

im·plic·it \im-'pli-sət\ adj 1 : understood though not directly stated or expressed : IMPLIED; *also* : POTENTIAL 2 : COMPLETE, UNQUESTIONING, ABSOLUTE ⟨~ faith⟩ — im·plic·it·ly adv

im·plode \im-'plōd\ vb im·plod·ed; im·plod·ing 1 : to burst or collapse inward 2 : SELF-DESTRUCT — im·plo·sion \-'plō-zhən\ n — im·plo·sive \-siv\ adj

im·plore \im-'plȯr\ vb im·plored; im·plor·ing : BESEECH, ENTREAT ⟨implored him not to go⟩ ♦ **Synonyms** SUPPLICATE, BEG, IMPORTUNE, PLEAD

im·ply \im-'plī\ vb im·plied; im·ply·ing 1 : to involve or indicate by inference, association, or necessary consequence rather than by direct statement ⟨war *implies* fighting⟩ 2 : to express indirectly : hint at : SUGGEST

im·po·lite \ˌim-pə-'līt\ adj : not polite : RUDE, DISCOURTEOUS

im·pol·i·tic \(ˌ)im-'pä-lə-ˌtik\ adj : not politic : UNWISE

im·pon·der·a·ble \(ˌ)im-'pän-də-rə-bəl\ adj : incapable of being weighed or evaluated with exactness — imponderable n

¹im·port \im-'pȯrt\ vb 1 : MEAN, SIGNIFY 2 : to bring (as merchandise) into a place or country from a foreign or external source — im·port·er n

²im·port \'im-ˌpȯrt\ n 1 : IMPORTANCE, SIGNIFICANCE 2 : MEANING, SIGNIFICATION 3 : something (as merchandise) brought in from another country

im·por·tance \im-'pȯr-t°ns\ n : the quality or state of being important : MOMENT, SIGNIFICANCE ♦ **Synonyms** CONSEQUENCE, IMPORT, WEIGHT

im·por·tant \im-'pȯr-t°nt\ adj 1 : marked by importance : SIGNIFICANT 2 : giving an impression of importance — im·por·tant·ly adv

im·por·ta·tion \ˌim-ˌpȯr-'tā-shən, -pər-\ n 1 : the act or practice of importing 2 : something imported

im·por·tu·nate \im-'pȯr-chə-nət\ adj 1 : troublesomely urgent or persistent 2 : BURDENSOME, TROUBLESOME

im·por·tune \ˌim-pər-'tün, -'tyün; -'pȯr-chən\ vb -tuned; -tun·ing : to urge or beg with troublesome persistence — im·por·tu·ni·ty \-pər-'tü-nə-tē, -'tyü-\ n

im·pose \im-'pōz\ vb im·posed; im·pos·ing 1 : to establish or apply by authority ⟨~ a tax⟩; *also* : to establish by force ⟨imposed a government⟩ 2 : OBTRUDE ⟨imposed herself on others⟩ 3 : to take unwarranted advantage of something ⟨~ on her good nature⟩ — im·po·si·tion \ˌim-pə-'zi-shən\ n

im·pos·ing adj : impressive because of size, bearing, dignity, or grandeur — im·pos·ing·ly adv

im·pos·si·ble \(ˌ)im-'pä-sə-bəl\ adj 1 : incapable of being or of occurring 2 : enormously difficult 3 : extremely undesirable : UNACCEPTABLE — im·pos·si·bil·i·ty \-ˌpä-sə-'bi-lə-tē\ n — im·pos·si·bly \-'pä-sə-blē\ adv

¹im·post \'im-ˌpōst\ n : TAX, DUTY

²im·post n : a block, capital, or molding from which an arch springs

im·pos·tor or im·post·er \im-'päs-tər\ n : one that assumes an identity or title not one's own in order to deceive

im·pos·ture \im-'päs-chər\ n : DECEPTION; *esp* : fraudulent impersonation

im·po·tent \'im-pə-tənt\ adj 1 : lacking in power or strength : HELPLESS 2 : unable to copulate; *also* : STERILE — im·po·tence \-təns\ n — im·po·ten·cy \-tən-sē\ n — im·po·tent·ly adv

im·pound \im-'paund\ vb 1 : CONFINE, ENCLOSE ⟨~ stray dogs⟩ 2 : to seize and hold in legal custody 3 : to collect in a reservoir ⟨~ water⟩ — im·pound·ment n

im·pov·er·ish \im-'pä-və-rish\ vb : to make poor; *also* : to deprive of strength, richness, or fertility — im·pov·er·ish·ment n

im·prac·ti·ca·ble \(ˌ)im-'prak-ti-kə-bəl\ adj : not practicable : incapable of being put into practice or use ⟨an ~ plan⟩

im·prac·ti·cal \(ˌ)im-'prak-ti-kəl\ adj : not practical : IMPRACTICABLE

im·pre·cate \'im-pri-ˌkāt\ vb -cat·ed; -cat·ing : CURSE — im·pre·ca·tion \ˌim-pri-'kā-shən\ n

im·pre·cise \ˌim-pri-'sīs\ adj : not precise — im·pre·cise·ly adv — im·pre·cise·ness n — im·pre·ci·sion \-'si-zhən\ n

im·preg·na·ble \im-'preg-nə-bəl\ adj : incapable of being taken by assault : UNCONQUERABLE, UNASSAILABLE — im·preg·na·bil·i·ty \(ˌ)im-ˌpreg-nə-'bi-lə-tē\ n

im·preg·nate \im-'preg-ˌnāt\ vb -nat·ed; -nat·ing 1 : to fertilize or make pregnant 2 : to cause to be filled, permeated, or saturated — im·preg·na·tion \ˌim-ˌpreg-'nā-shən\ n

im·pre·sa·rio \ˌim-prə-'sär-ē-ˌō\ n, pl -ri·os [It, fr. *impresa* undertaking, fr. *imprendere* to undertake] 1 : the manager or conductor of an opera or concert company 2 : one who puts on an entertainment 3 : MANAGER, PRODUCER

¹im·press \im-'pres\ vb 1 : to apply with or produce (as a mark) by pressure : IMPRINT 2 : to press, stamp, or print in or upon 3 : to produce a vivid impression of 4 : to affect esp. forcibly or deeply — im·press·ible adj

²im·press \'im-ˌpres\ n 1 : a characteristic or distinctive mark 2 : IMPRESSION, EFFECT 3 : an impression or image of something formed by or as if by pressure; *also* : a product of pressure or influence

³im·press \im-'pres\ vb 1 : to force into naval service 2 : to get the aid or services

of by forcible argument or persuasion — **im·press·ment** n

im·pres·sion \im-'pre-shən\ n **1** : a characteristic trait or feature resulting from influence : IMPRESS **2** : a stamp, form, or figure made by impressing : IMPRINT **3** : an esp. marked influence or effect on feeling, sense, or mind **4** : a single print or copy (as from type or from an engraved plate or book) **5** : all the copies of a publication (as a book) printed for one issue : PRINTING **6** : a usu. vague notion or remembrance **7** : an imitation in caricature of a noted personality as a form of entertainment

im·pres·sion·able \im-'pre-shə-nə-bəl\ *adj* : capable of being easily impressed : easily molded or influenced

im·pres·sion·ism \im-'pre-shə-,ni-zəm\ n, *often cap* : a theory or practice in modern art of depicting the natural appearances of objects by dabs or strokes of primary unmixed colors in order to simulate actual reflected light — **im·pres·sion·is·tic** \-,pre-shə-'nis-tik\ *adj*

im·pres·sion·ist \im-'pre-shə-nist\ n **1** *often cap* : a painter who practices impressionism **2** : an entertainer who does impressions

im·pres·sive \im-'pre-siv\ *adj* : making or tending to make a marked impression ⟨an ~ speech⟩ — **im·pres·sive·ly** *adv* — **im·pres·sive·ness** n

im·pri·ma·tur \,im-prə-'mä-,tùr\ n [NL, let it be printed] **1** : a license to print or publish; *also* : official approval of a publication by a censor **2** : SANCTION, APPROVAL

¹im·print \im-'print, 'im-,print\ *vb* **1** : to stamp or mark by or as if by pressure : IMPRESS **2** : to fix firmly (as on the memory)

²im·print \'im-,print\ n **1** : something imprinted or printed **2** : a publisher's name printed at the foot of a title page **3** : an indelible distinguishing effect or influence ⟨put her ~ on the company⟩

im·pris·on \im-'pri-z°n\ *vb* : to put in or as if in prison : CONFINE — **im·pris·on·ment** n

im·prob·a·ble \(,)im-'prä-bə-bəl\ *adj* : unlikely to be true or to occur — **im·prob·a·bil·i·ty** \-,prä-bə-'bi-lə-tē\ n — **im·prob·a·bly** \-'prä-bə-blē\ *adv*

im·promp·tu \im-'prämp-tü, -tyü\ *adj* [F, fr. *impromptu* extemporaneously, fr. L *in promptu* in readiness] **1** : made or done on or as if on the spur of the moment **2** : EXTEMPORANEOUS, UNREHEARSED ⟨an ~ speech⟩ — **impromptu** *adv or n*

im·prop·er \(,)im-'prä-pər\ *adj* **1** : not proper, fit, or suitable **2** : INCORRECT, INACCURATE **3** : not in accord with propriety, modesty, or good manners — **im·prop·er·ly** *adv*

improper fraction n : a fraction whose numerator is equal to or larger than the denominator

im·pro·pri·e·ty \,im-prə-'prī-ə-tē\ n, *pl* **-ties 1** : an improper act or remark; *esp* : an unacceptable use of a word or of language **2** : the quality or state of being improper

im·prov \'im-,präv\ *adj* : of, relating to, or being an improvised comedy routine — **improv** n

im·prove \im-'prüv\ *vb* **im·proved; im·prov·ing 1** : to enhance or increase in value or quality **2** : to grow or become better ⟨your work is *improving*⟩ **3** : to make good use of ⟨~ the time by reading⟩ — **im·prov·able** \-'prü-və-bəl\ *adj*

im·prove·ment \im-'prüv-mənt\ n **1** : the act or process of improving **2** : increased value or excellence of something **3** : something that adds to the value or appearance of a thing

im·prov·i·dent \(,)im-'prä-və-dənt\ *adj* : not providing for the future — **im·prov·i·dence** \-dəns\ n

im·pro·vise \'im-prə-,vīz\ *vb* **-vised; -vis·ing** [F *improviser*, fr. It *improvvisare*, fr. *improvviso* sudden, fr. L *improvisus*, lit., unforeseen] **1** : to compose, recite, play, or sing on the spur of the moment : EXTEMPORIZE ⟨~ on the piano⟩ **2** : to make, invent, or arrange offhand ⟨~ a sail out of shirts⟩ — **im·pro·vi·sa·tion** \im-,prä-və-'zā-shən, ,im-prə-və-\ n — **im·pro·vis·er** *or* **im·pro·vi·sor** \,im-prə-'vī-zər, 'im-prə-,vī-\ n

im·pru·dent \(,)im-'prü-d°nt\ *adj* : not prudent : lacking discretion, wisdom, or good judgement — **im·pru·dence** \-d°ns\ n — **im·pru·dent·ly** *adv*

im·pu·dent \'im-pyü-dənt\ *adj* : marked by contemptuous boldness or disregard of others — **im·pu·dence** \-dəns\ n — **im·pu·dent·ly** *adv*

im·pugn \im-'pyün\ *vb* [ME, to assail, fr. AF *empugner*, fr. L *inpugnare*, fr. *pugnare* to fight] : to attack by words or arguments : oppose or attack as false or as lacking integrity ⟨~ed his rival's character⟩

im·puis·sance \im-'pwi-s°ns, -'pyü-ə-səns\ n [ME, fr. MF] : the quality or state of being powerless : WEAKNESS

im·pulse \'im-,pəls\ n **1** : a force that starts a body into motion; *also* : the motion produced by such a force **2** : an arousing of the mind and spirit to some usu. unpremeditated action **3** : NERVE IMPULSE

im·pul·sion \im-'pəl-shən\ n **1** : the act of impelling : the state of being impelled **2** : a force that impels **3** : IMPULSE 2; *also* : COMPULSION 3

im·pul·sive \im-'pəl-siv\ *adj* **1** : having the power of or actually driving or impelling **2** : arising from or prone to act on impulse — **im·pul·sive·ly** *adv* — **im·pul·sive·ness** n

im·pu·ni·ty \im-'pyü-nə-tē\ n [MF or L; MF *impunité*, fr. L *impunitas*, fr. *impune* without punishment, fr. *poena* penalty, punishment] : exemption from punishment, harm, or loss

im·pure \(,)im-'pyùr\ *adj* **1** : not pure : UNCHASTE, OBSCENE **2** : DIRTY, FOUL ⟨~ water⟩ **3** : ADULTERATED, MIXED — **im·pu·ri·ty** \-'pyùr-ə-tē\ n

im·pute \im-ˈpyüt\ *vb* **im·put·ed; im·put·ing** **1** : to lay the responsibility or blame for often falsely or unjustly **2** : to credit to a person or a cause : ATTRIBUTE — **im·put·able** \-ˈpyü-tə-bəl\ *adj* — **im·pu·ta·tion** \im-pyü-ˈtā-shən\ *n*

¹in \ˈin\ *prep* **1** — used to indicate physical surroundings ⟨swim ~ the lake⟩ **2** : INTO **1** ⟨ran ~ the house⟩ **3** : DURING ⟨~ the summer⟩ **4** : WITH ⟨written ~ pencil⟩ **5** — used to indicate one's situation or state of being ⟨~ luck⟩ ⟨~ love⟩ **6** — used to indicate manner or purpose ⟨~ a hurry⟩ ⟨said ~ reply⟩ **7** : INTO **2** ⟨broke ~ pieces⟩

²in *adv* **1** : to or toward the inside ⟨come ~⟩; *also* : to or toward some destination or place ⟨flew ~ from the South⟩ **2** : at close quarters : NEAR ⟨the enemy closed ~⟩ **3** : into the midst of something ⟨mix ~ the flour⟩ **4** : to or at its proper place ⟨fit a piece ~⟩ **5** : WITHIN ⟨locked ~⟩ **6** : in vogue or season **7** : in one's presence, possession, or control ⟨the results are ~⟩

³in *adj* **1** : located inside or within **2** : that is in position, operation, or power ⟨the ~ party⟩ **3** : directed inward : INCOMING ⟨the ~ train⟩ **4** : keenly aware of and responsive to what is new and fashionable ⟨the ~ crowd⟩; *also* : extremely fashionable ⟨the ~ thing to do⟩

⁴in *n* **1** : one who is in office or power or on the inside **2** : INFLUENCE, PULL ⟨he has an ~ with the owner⟩

⁵in *abbr* **1** inch **2** inlet

IN *abbr* Indiana

In *symbol* indium

in- \(ˌ)in\ *prefix* : not : absence of : NON-, UN-

in·abil·i·ty \ˌi-nə-ˈbi-lə-tē\ *n* : the quality or state of being unable

in ab·sen·tia \ˌin-ab-ˈsen-chə, -chē-ə\ *adv* : in one's absence

in·ac·ti·vate \(ˌ)i-ˈnak-tə-ˌvāt\ *vb* : to make inactive — **in·ac·ti·va·tion** \(ˌ)i-ˌnak-tə-ˈvā-shən\ *n*

in·ad·e·quate \(ˌ)i-ˈna-di-kwət\ *adj* : not adequate : INSUFFICIENT — **in·ad·e·qua·cy** \-kwə-sē\ *n* — **in·ad·e·quate·ly** *adv* — **in·ad·e·quate·ness** *n*

in·ad·ver·tent \ˌi-nəd-ˈvər-tᵊnt\ *adj* **1** : HEEDLESS, INATTENTIVE **2** : UNINTENTIONAL ⟨an ~ omission⟩ — **in·ad·ver·tence** \-tᵊns\ *n* — **in·ad·ver·ten·cy** \-tᵊn-sē\ *n* — **in·ad·ver·tent·ly** *adv*

in·alien·able \(ˌ)i-ˈnāl-yə-nə-bəl, -ˈnā-lē-ə-\ *adj* : incapable of being alienated, surrendered, or transferred ⟨~ rights⟩ — **in·alien·abil·i·ty** \(ˌ)i-ˌnāl-yə-nə-ˈbi-lə-tē, -ˌnā-lē-ə-\ *n* — **in·alien·ably** *adv*

in·amo·ra·ta \i-ˌna-mə-ˈrä-tə\ *n* : a woman with whom one is in love

inane \i-ˈnān\ *adj* **inan·er; -est** : EMPTY, INSUBSTANTIAL; *also* : SHALLOW, SILLY — **inane·ly** *adv* — **inan·i·ty** \i-ˈna-nə-tē\ *n*

in·an·i·mate \(ˌ)i-ˈna-nə-mət\ *adj* : not animate or animated : lacking the qualities of living things — **in·an·i·mate·ly** *adv* — **in·an·i·mate·ness** *n*

in·ap·pre·cia·ble \ˌi-nə-ˈprē-shə-bəl\ *adj* : too small to be perceived — **in·ap·pre·cia·bly** \-blē\ *adv*

in·apt \(ˌ)i-ˈnapt\ *adj* **1** : not suitable ⟨an ~ analogy⟩ **2** : INEPT — **in·apt·ly** *adv* — **in·apt·ness** *n*

in·ar·tic·u·late \ˌi-när-ˈti-kyə-lət\ *adj* **1** : not understandable as spoken words **2** : MUTE **3** : incapable of being expressed by speech ⟨~ fear⟩; *also* : UNSPOKEN **4** : not having the power of distinct utterance or effective expression — **in·ar·tic·u·late·ly** *adv*

in·as·much as \ˌi-nəz-ˈməch-\ *conj* : seeing that : SINCE

in·at·ten·tion \ˌi-nə-ˈten-chən\ *n* : failure to pay attention : DISREGARD — **in·at·ten·tive** \-ˈten-tiv\ *adj*

¹in·au·gu·ral \i-ˈnȯ-gyə-rəl, -gə-\ *adj* **1** : of or relating to an inauguration **2** : marking a beginning

²inaugural *n* **1** : an inaugural address **2** : INAUGURATION

in·au·gu·rate \i-ˈnȯ-gyə-ˌrāt, -gə-\ *vb* **-rat·ed; -rat·ing** **1** : to introduce into an office with suitable ceremonies : INSTALL **2** : to dedicate ceremoniously **3** : BEGIN, INITIATE — **in·au·gu·ra·tion** \-ˌnȯ-gyə-ˈrā-shən, -gə-\ *n*

in·board \ˈin-ˌbȯrd\ *adv* **1** : inside the hull of a ship **2** : close or closest to the center line of a vehicle or craft — **inboard** *adj*

in·born \ˈin-ˈbȯrn\ *adj* **1** : present from or as if from birth **2** : HEREDITARY, INHERITED ♦ *Synonyms* INNATE, CONGENITAL, NATIVE

in·bound \ˈin-ˌbaund\ *adj* : inward bound ⟨~ traffic⟩

in·box \ˈin-ˌbäks\ *n* : a receptacle for incoming interoffice letters; *also* : a computer folder for incoming e-mail

in·bred \ˈin-ˈbred\ *adj* **1** : ingrained in one's nature as deeply as if by heredity **2** : subjected to or produced by inbreeding

in·breed·ing \ˈin-ˌbrē-diŋ\ *n* **1** : the interbreeding of closely related individuals esp. to preserve and fix desirable characters of and to eliminate unfavorable characters from a stock **2** : confinement to a narrow range or a local or limited field of choice — **in·breed** \-ˈbrēd\ *vb*

inc *abbr* **1** incomplete **2** incorporated **3** increase

In·ca \ˈiŋ-kə\ *n* [Sp, fr. Quechua *inka* ruler of the Inca empire] **1** : a noble or a member of the ruling family of an Indian empire of Peru, Bolivia, and Ecuador until the Spanish conquest **2** : a member of any people under Inca influence

in·cal·cu·la·ble \\(ˌ)in-ˈkal-kyə-lə-bəl\ *adj* **1** : not capable of being calculated; *esp* : very great **2** : not predictable ⟨~ consequences⟩ — **in·cal·cu·la·bly** \-blē\ *adv*

in·can·des·cent \ˌin-kən-ˈde-sᵊnt\ *adj* **1** : glowing with heat **2** : SHINING, BRILLIANT — **in·can·des·cence** \-sᵊns\ *n*

incandescent lamp *n* : LIGHT BULB 1

in·can·ta·tion \ˌin-ˌkan-ˈtā-shən\ *n* : a use of spells or verbal charms spoken or sung as a part of a ritual of magic; *also* : a formula of words used in or as if in such a ritual

in·ca·pa·ble \(ˌ)in-ˈkā-pə-bəl\ *adj* : lacking ability or qualification for a particular purpose; *also* : UNQUALIFIED — **in·ca·pa·bil·i·ty** \-ˌkā-pə-ˈbi-lə-tē\ *n*

in·ca·pac·i·tate \ˌin-kə-ˈpa-sə-ˌtāt\ *vb* **-tat·ed; -tat·ing** : to make incapable or unfit

in·ca·pac·i·ty \ˌin-kə-ˈpa-sə-tē\ *n, pl* **-ties** : the quality or state of being incapable

in·car·cer·ate \in-ˈkär-sə-ˌrāt\ *vb* **-at·ed; -at·ing** : IMPRISON, CONFINE — **in·car·cer·a·tion** \(ˌ)in-ˌkär-sə-ˈrā-shən\ *n*

in·car·na·dine \in-ˈkär-nə-ˌdīn, -ˌdēn\ *vb* **-dined; -din·ing** : REDDEN

in·car·nate \in-ˈkär-nət, -ˌnāt\ *adj* **1** : having bodily and esp. human form and substance **2** : PERSONIFIED — **in·car·nate** \-ˌnāt\ *vb*

in·car·na·tion \ˌin-ˌkär-ˈnā-shən\ *n* **1** : the embodiment of a deity or spirit in an earthly form **2** *cap* : the union of divine and human natures in Jesus Christ **3** : a person showing a trait or typical character to a marked degree **4** : the act of incarnating : the state of being incarnate

in·cen·di·ary \in-ˈsen-dē-ˌer-ē\ *adj* **1** : of or relating to a deliberate burning of property **2** : tending to excite or inflame **3** : designed to start fires ⟨an ~ bomb⟩ — **incendiary** *n*

¹**in·cense** \ˈin-ˌsens\ *n* **1** : material used to produce a fragrant odor when burned **2** : the perfume or smoke from some spices and gums when burned

²**in·cense** \in-ˈsens\ *vb* **in·censed; in·cens·ing** : to make extremely angry

in·cen·tive \in-ˈsen-tiv\ *n* [ME, fr. LL *incentivum*, fr. *incentivus* stimulating, fr. L, setting the tune, fr. *incinere* to play (a tune), fr. *canere* to sing] : something that incites or is likely to incite to determination or action

in·cep·tion \in-ˈsep-shən\ *n* : BEGINNING, COMMENCEMENT

in·cer·ti·tude \(ˌ)in-ˈsər-tə-ˌtüd, -ˌtyüd\ *n* **1** : UNCERTAINTY, DOUBT, INDECISION **2** : INSECURITY, INSTABILITY

in·ces·sant \(ˌ)in-ˈse-sᵊnt\ *adj* : continuing or flowing without interruption ⟨~ rains⟩ — **in·ces·sant·ly** *adv*

in·cest \ˈin-ˌsest\ *n* [ME, fr. L *incestus* sexual impurity, fr. *incestus* impure, fr. *castus* pure] : sexual intercourse between persons so closely related that marriage is illegal — **in·ces·tu·ous** \in-ˈses-chü-wəs\ *adj*

¹**inch** \ˈinch\ *n* [ME, fr. OE *ynce*, fr. L *un-*

cia twelfth part, inch, ounce] — see WEIGHT table

²**inch** *vb* : to move by small degrees

in·cho·ate \in-ˈkō-ət, ˈin-kə-ˌwāt\ *adj* : being only partly in existence or operation : INCOMPLETE ⟨~ yearnings⟩

inch·worm \ˈinch-ˌwərm\ *n* : LOOPER

in·ci·dence \ˈin-sə-dəns\ *n* : rate of occurrence or effect

¹**in·ci·dent** \-dənt\ *n* **1** : OCCURRENCE, HAPPENING **2** : an action likely to lead to grave consequences esp. in diplomatic matters

²**incident** *adj* **1** : occurring or likely to occur esp. in connection with some other happening **2** : falling or striking on something ⟨~ light rays⟩

¹**in·ci·den·tal** \ˌin-sə-ˈden-tᵊl\ *adj* **1** : subordinate, nonessential, or attendant in position or significance ⟨~ expenses⟩ **2** : CASUAL, CHANCE

²**incidental** *n* **1** *pl* : minor items (as of expense) that are not individually accounted for **2** : something incidental

in·ci·den·tal·ly \ˌin-sə-ˈden-tə-lē, -ˈdent-lē\ *adv* **1** : in an incidental manner **2** : by the way

in·cin·er·ate \in-ˈsi-nə-ˌrāt\ *vb* **-at·ed; -at·ing** : to burn to ashes — **in·cin·er·a·tion** \-ˌsi-nə-ˈrā-shən\ *n*

in·cin·er·a·tor \in-ˈsi-nə-ˌrā-tər\ *n* : a furnace for burning waste

in·cip·i·ent \in-ˈsi-pē-ənt\ *adj* : beginning to be or become apparent

in·cise \in-ˈsīz\ *vb* **in·cised; in·cis·ing** **1** : to cut into **2** : CARVE, ENGRAVE

in·ci·sion \in-ˈsi-zhən\ *n* : CUT, GASH; *esp* : a surgical cut

in·ci·sive \in-ˈsī-siv\ *adj* : impressively direct and decisive — **in·ci·sive·ly** *adv*

in·ci·sor \in-ˈsī-zər\ *n* : a front tooth typically adapted for cutting

in·cite \in-ˈsīt\ *vb* **in·cit·ed; in·cit·ing** : to arouse to action : stir up — **in·cite·ment** *n* — **in·cit·er** *n*

in·ci·vil·i·ty \ˌin-sə-ˈvi-lə-tē\ *n* **1** : RUDENESS, DISCOURTESY **2** : a rude or discourteous act

incl *abbr* include; included; including; inclusive

in·clem·ent \(ˌ)in-ˈkle-mənt\ *adj* : SEVERE, STORMY ⟨~ weather⟩ — **in·clem·en·cy** \-mən-sē\ *n*

in·cli·na·tion \ˌin-klə-ˈnā-shən\ *n* **1** : PROPENSITY, BENT; *esp* : LIKING **2** : BOW, NOD ⟨an ~ of the head⟩ **3** : a tilting of something **4** : SLANT, SLOPE

¹**in·cline** \in-ˈklīn\ *vb* **in·clined; in·clin·ing** **1** : BOW, BEND **2** : to be drawn toward an opinion or course of action **3** : to deviate from the vertical or horizontal : SLOPE **4** : INFLUENCE, PERSUADE — **in·clin·er** *n*

²**in·cline** \ˈin-ˌklīn\ *n* : SLOPE

inclose, inclosure *var of* ENCLOSE, ENCLOSURE

in·clude \in-ˈklüd\ *vb* **in·clud·ed; in·clud·ing** : to take in or comprise as a part of a whole ⟨the price ~s tax⟩ — **in·clu·sion** \in-ˈklü-zhən\ *n*

in·clu·sive \in-ˈklü-siv\ *adj* **1** : including stated limits or extremes ⟨from Monday to Friday ⁓⟩ **2** : broad in scope; *esp* : covering all items, costs, or services — **in·clu·sive·ly** *adj* — **in·clu·sive·ness** *n*

incog *abbr* incognito

¹**in·cog·ni·to** \ˌin-ˌkäg-ˈnē-to, in-ˈkäg-nə-ˌto\ *adv or adj* [It, fr. L *incognitus* unknown, fr. *cognoscere* to know] : with one's identity concealed

²**incognito** *n, pl* **-tos 1** : one appearing or living incognito **2** : the state or disguise of an incognito

in·co·her·ent \ˌin-kō-ˈhir-ənt, -ˈher-\ *adj* **1** : not sticking closely or compactly together : LOOSE **2** : lacking normal clarity or intelligibility in speech or thought ⟨an ⁓ patient⟩ — **in·co·her·ence** \-əns\ *n* — **in·co·her·ent·ly** *adv*

in·come \ˈin-ˌkəm\ *n* : a gain usu. measured in money that derives from labor, business, or property

income tax *n* : a tax on the net income of an individual or business concern

in·com·ing \ˈin-ˌkə-miŋ\ *adj* : coming in ⟨the ⁓ tide⟩ ⟨⁓ freshmen⟩

in·com·men·su·rate \ˌin-kə-ˈmen-sə-rət, -ˈmen-chə-\ *adj* : not commensurate; *esp* : INADEQUATE

in·com·mode \ˌin-kə-ˈmōd\ *vb* **-mod·ed; -mod·ing** : INCONVENIENCE, DISTURB

in·com·mu·ni·ca·ble \ˌin-kə-ˈmyü-ni-kə-bəl\ *adj* : not communicable : not capable of being communicated or imparted; *also* : UNCOMMUNICATIVE

in·com·mu·ni·ca·do \ˌin-kə-ˌmyü-nə-ˈkä-dō\ *adv or adj* : without means of communication; *also* : in solitary confinement ⟨a prisoner held ⁓⟩

in·com·pa·ra·ble \(ˌ)in-ˈkäm-pə-rə-bəl, -prə-\ *adj* **1** : eminent beyond comparison : MATCHLESS **2** : not suitable for comparison — **in·com·pa·ra·bly** \-blē\ *adv*

in·com·pat·i·ble \ˌin-kəm-ˈpa-tə-bəl\ *adj* : incapable of or unsuitable for association or use together ⟨⁓ colors⟩ ⟨temperamentally ⁓⟩ — **in·com·pat·i·bil·i·ty** \ˌin-kəm-ˌpa-tə-ˈbi-lə-tē\ *n*

in·com·pe·tent \(ˌ)in-ˈkäm-pə-tənt\ *adj* **1** : not legally qualified **2** : not competent : lacking sufficient knowledge, skill, or ability — **in·com·pe·tence** \-təns\ *n* — **in·com·pe·ten·cy** \-tən-sē\ *n* — **incompetent** *n*

in·com·plete \ˌin-kəm-ˈplēt\ *adj* : lacking a part or parts : UNFINISHED, IMPERFECT — **in·com·plete·ly** *adv* — **in·com·plete·ness** *n*

in·com·pre·hen·si·ble \ˌin-ˌkäm-prē-ˈhen-sə-bəl\ *adj* : impossible to comprehend : UNINTELLIGIBLE ⟨⁓ muttering⟩

in·con·ceiv·able \ˌin-kən-ˈsē-və-bəl\ *adj* **1** : impossible to comprehend **2** : UNBELIEVABLE

in·con·gru·ous \(ˌ)in-ˈkäŋ-grü-wəs\ *adj* : not consistent with or suitable to the surroundings or associations — **in·con·gru·i·ty** \ˌin-kən-ˈgrü-ə-tē, -ˌkän-\ *n* — **in·con·gru·ous·ly** *adv*

in·con·se·quen·tial \ˌin-ˌkän-sə-ˈkwen-chəl\ *adj* **1** : ILLOGICAL; *also* : IRRELEVANT **2** : of no significance : UNIMPORTANT — **in·con·se·quence** \(ˌ)in-ˈkän-sə-ˌkwens\ *n* — **in·con·se·quen·tial·ly** *adv*

in·con·sid·er·able \ˌin-kən-ˈsi-də-rə-bəl\ *adj* : SLIGHT, TRIVIAL ⟨the cost was not ⁓⟩

in·con·sid·er·ate \ˌin-kən-ˈsi-də-rət\ *adj* : HEEDLESS, THOUGHTLESS; *esp* : not respecting the rights or feelings of others — **in·con·sid·er·ate·ly** *adv* — **in·con·sid·er·ate·ness** *n*

in·con·sol·able \ˌin-kən-ˈsō-lə-bəl\ *adj* : incapable of being consoled — **in·con·sol·ably** *adv*

in·con·spic·u·ous \ˌin-kən-ˈspi-kyə-wəs\ *adj* : not readily noticeable — **in·con·spic·u·ous·ly** *adv*

in·con·stant \(ˌ)in-ˈkän-stənt\ *adj* : not constant : CHANGEABLE ♦ *Synonyms* FICKLE, CAPRICIOUS, MERCURIAL, UNSTABLE, VOLATILE — **in·con·stan·cy** \-stən-sē\ *n* — **in·con·stant·ly** *adv*

in·con·test·able \ˌin-kən-ˈtes-tə-bəl\ *adj* : not contestable : INDISPUTABLE — **in·con·test·ably** \-ˈtes-tə-blē\ *adv*

in·con·ti·nent \(ˌ)in-ˈkänt-ᵊn-ənt\ *adj* **1** : lacking self-restraint **2** : unable to retain urine or feces voluntarily — **in·con·ti·nence** \-əns\ *n*

in·con·tro·vert·ible \ˌin-ˌkän-trə-ˈvər-tə-bəl\ *adj* : not open to question : INDISPUTABLE ⟨⁓ evidence⟩ — **in·con·tro·vert·ibly** \-blē\ *adv*

¹**in·con·ve·nience** \ˌin-kən-ˈvē-nyəns\ *n* **1** : something that is inconvenient **2** : the quality or state of being inconvenient

²**inconvenience** *vb* **-nienced; -nienc·ing** : to subject to inconvenience

in·con·ve·nient \ˌin-kən-ˈvē-nyənt\ *adj* : not convenient : causing trouble or annoyance : INOPPORTUNE — **in·con·ve·nient·ly** *adv*

in·cor·po·rate \in-ˈkȯr-pə-ˌrāt\ *vb* **-rat·ed; -rat·ing 1** : to unite closely or so as to form one body : BLEND **2** : to form, form into, or become a corporation **3** : to give material form to : EMBODY — **in·cor·po·ra·tion** \-ˌkȯr-pə-ˈrā-shən\ *n*

in·cor·po·re·al \ˌin-kȯr-ˈpȯr-ē-əl\ *adj* : having no material body or form

in·cor·rect \ˌin-kə-ˈrekt\ *adj* **1** : INACCURATE, FAULTY ⟨an ⁓ transcription⟩ **2** : not true : WRONG **3** : UNBECOMING, IMPROPER — **in·cor·rect·ly** *adv* — **in·cor·rect·ness** *n*

in·cor·ri·gi·ble \(ˌ)in-ˈkȯr-ə-jə-bəl\ *adj* : incapable of being corrected, amended, or reformed — **in·cor·ri·gi·bil·i·ty** \(ˌ)in-ˌkȯr-ə-jə-ˈbi-lə-tē\ *n* — **in·cor·ri·gi·bly** \-ˈkȯr-ə-jə-blē\ *adv*

in·cor·rupt·ible \ˌin-kə-ˈrəp-tə-bəl\ *adj* **1** : not subject to decay or dissolution **2** : incapable of being bribed or morally corrupted — **in·cor·rupt·ibil·i·ty** \-ˌrəp-tə-ˈbi-lə-tē\ *n* — **in·cor·rupt·ibly** \-ˈrəp-tə-blē\ *adv*

incr *abbr* increase; increased

¹**in·crease** \in-ˈkrēs, ˈin-ˌkrēs\ *vb* **in-**

| incombustible | inconclusive | inconsistency | incoordination |
| incomprehension | incongruent | inconsistent | |

creased; **in·creas·ing** [ME *encresen*, fr. AF *encreistre*, fr. L. *increscere*, fr. *crescere* to grow] **1** : to become greater : GROW **2** : to multiply by the production of young ⟨rabbits ~ rapidly⟩ **3** : to make greater — **increased** *adj* — **in·creas·ing·ly** \-'krē-siŋ-lē\ *adv*

²**in·crease** \'in-ˌkrēs, in-'krēs\ *n* **1** : addition or enlargement in size, extent, or quantity : GROWTH **2** : something that is added to an original stock or amount (as by growth)

in·cred·i·ble \(ˌ)in-'kre-də-bəl\ *adj* : too extraordinary and improbable to be believed; *also* : hard to believe — **in·cred·i·bil·i·ty** \(ˌ)in-ˌkre-də-'bi-lə-tē\ *n* — **in·cred·i·bly** \-'kre-də-blē\ *adv*

in·cred·u·lous \-'kre-jə-ləs\ *adj* **1** : SKEPTICAL **2** : expressing disbelief — **in·cre·du·li·ty** \ˌin-kri-'dü-lə-tē, -'dyü-\ *n* — **in·cred·u·lous·ly** *adv*

in·cre·ment \'iŋ-krə-mənt, 'in-\ *n* **1** : the action or process of increasing esp. in quantity or value : ENLARGEMENT **2** : something gained or added; *esp* : one of a series of regular consecutive additions — **in·cre·men·tal** \ˌiŋ-krə-'men-t³l, ˌin-\ *adj* — **in·cre·men·tal·ly** *adv*

in·crim·i·nate \in-'kri-mə-ˌnāt\ *vb* **-nat·ed; -nat·ing** : to charge with or prove involvement in a crime or fault : ACCUSE — **in·crim·i·na·tion** \-ˌkri-mə-'nā-shən\ *n* — **in·crim·i·na·to·ry** \-'kri-mə-nə-ˌtȯr-ē\ *adj*

incrust *var of* ENCRUST

in·crus·ta·tion *also* **en·crus·ta·tion** \ˌin-ˌkrəs-'tā-shən\ *n* **1** : CRUST; *also* : an accumulation (as of habits, opinions, or customs) resembling a crust **2** : the act of encrusting : the state of being encrusted

in·cu·bate \'iŋ-kyü-ˌbāt, 'in-\ *vb* **-bat·ed; -bat·ing** : to sit on (eggs) to hatch by the warmth of the body; *also* : to keep (as an embryo) under conditions favorable for development — **in·cu·ba·tion** \ˌiŋ-kyü-'bā-shən, ˌin-\ *n*

in·cu·ba·tor \'iŋ-kyü-ˌbāt-ər, 'in-\ *n* : one that incubates; *esp* : an apparatus providing suitable conditions (as of warmth and moisture) for incubating something (as a premature baby)

in·cu·bus \'iŋ-kyə-bəs, 'in-\ *n, pl* **-bi** \-ˌbī, -ˌbē\ *also* **-bus·es** [ME, fr. LL, fr. L *incubare* to lie on] **1** : a spirit supposed to work evil on persons in their sleep **2** : NIGHTMARE **1** **3** : one that oppresses like a nightmare

in·cul·cate \in-'kəl-ˌkāt, 'in-(ˌ)kəl-\ *vb* **-cat·ed; -cat·ing** [L *inculcare*, lit., to tread on, fr. *calcare* to trample, fr. *calx* heel] : to teach and impress by frequent repetitions or admonitions — **in·cul·ca·tion** \ˌin-(ˌ)kəl-'kā-shən\ *n*

in·cul·pa·ble \(ˌ)in-'kəl-pə-bəl\ *adj* : free from guilt : INNOCENT

in·cul·pate \in-'kəl-ˌpāt, 'in-(ˌ)kəl-\ *vb* **-pat·ed; -pat·ing** : INCRIMINATE

in·cum·ben·cy \in-'kəm-bən-sē\ *n, pl* **-cies** **1** : something that is incumbent **2** : the quality or state of being incumbent

3 : the office or period of office of an incumbent

¹**in·cum·bent** \in-'kəm-bənt\ *n* : the holder of an office or position

²**incumbent** *adj* **1** : imposed as a duty **2** : occupying a specified office **3** : lying or resting on something else

in·cu·nab·u·lum \ˌin-kyə-'na-byə-ləm, iŋ-\ *n, pl* **-la** \-lə\ [NL, fr. L *incunabula*, pl., bands holding the baby in a cradle, fr. *cunae* cradle] : a book printed before 1501

in·cur \in-'kər\ *vb* **in·curred; in·cur·ring** : to become liable or subject to : bring down upon oneself

in·cur·able \(ˌ)in-'kyùr-ə-bəl\ *adj* **1** : not curable **2** : not likely to be changed — **incurable** *n* — **in·cur·ably** \(ˌ)in-'kyùr-ə-blē\ *adv*

in·cur·sion \in-'kər-zhən\ *n* **1** : a sudden hostile invasion : RAID **2** : an entering or into (as an activity)

in·cus \'iŋ-kəs\ *n, pl* **in·cu·des** \iŋ-'kyü-(ˌ)dēz\ [NL, fr. L, anvil] : the middle bone of a chain of three small bones in the middle ear of a mammal

ind *abbr* **1** independent **2** index **3** industrial; industry

Ind *abbr* **1** Indian **2** Indiana

in·debt·ed \in-'de-təd\ *adj* **1** : owing gratitude or recognition to another **2** : owing money — **in·debt·ed·ness** *n*

in·de·cent \(ˌ)in-'dē-s³nt\ *adj* : not decent; *esp* : grossly improper or offensive — **in·de·cen·cy** \-s³n-sē\ *n* — **in·de·cent·ly** *adv*

in·de·ci·sion \ˌin-di-'si-zhən\ *n* : a wavering between two or more possible courses of action : IRRESOLUTION

in·de·ci·sive \ˌin-di-'sī-siv\ *adj* **1** : INCONCLUSIVE ⟨an ~ battle⟩ **2** : marked by or prone to indecision **3** : INDEFINITE — **in·de·ci·sive·ly** *adv* — **in·de·ci·sive·ness** *n*

in·de·co·rous \(ˌ)in-'de-kə-rəs; ˌin-di-'kȯr-əs\ *adj* : conflicting with accepted standards of good conduct or good taste

♦ *Synonyms* IMPROPER, UNSEEMLY, INDECENT, UNBECOMING, INDELICATE — **in·de·co·rous·ly** *adv* — **in·de·co·rous·ness** *n*

in·deed \in-'dēd\ *adv* **1** : without any question : TRULY — often used interjectionally to express irony, disbelief, or surprise **2** : in reality **3** : all things considered

in·de·fat·i·ga·ble \ˌin-di-'fa-ti-gə-bəl\ *adj* : UNTIRING ⟨an ~ worker⟩ — **in·de·fat·i·ga·bly** \-blē\ *adv*

in·de·fea·si·ble \-'fē-zə-bəl\ *adj* : not capable of being annulled or voided — **in·de·fea·si·bly** \-blē\ *adv*

in·de·fen·si·ble \-'fen-sə-bəl\ *adj* **1** : incapable of being maintained as right or valid **2** : INEXCUSABLE ⟨~ comments⟩ **3** : incapable of being protected against physical attack

in·de·fin·able \-'fī-nə-bəl\ *adj* : incapable of being precisely described or analyzed — **in·de·fin·ably** \-blē\ *adv*

in·def·i·nite \(_)in-'def-ə-nət\ *adj* **1** : not defining or identifying ⟨*an* is an ~ article⟩ **2** : not precise : VAGUE **3** : having no fixed limits — **in·def·i·nite·ly** *adv* — **in·def·i·nite·ness** *n*

in·del·i·ble \in-'de-lə-bəl\ *adj* [ME, fr. ML *indelibilis,* alter. of L *indelebilis,* fr. *delēre* to delete, destroy] **1** : not capable of being removed or erased **2** : making marks that cannot be erased **3** : LASTING, UNFORGETTABLE ⟨an ~ performance⟩ — **in·del·i·bly** \in-'de-lə-blē\ *adv*

in·del·i·cate \(_)in-'de-li-kət\ *adj* : not delicate; *esp* : IMPROPER, COARSE, TACTLESS ♦ **Synonyms** INDECENT, UNSEEMLY, INDECOROUS, UNBECOMING — **in·del·i·ca·cy** \in-'de-lə-kə-sē\ *n*

in·dem·ni·fy \in-'dem-nə-‚fī\ *vb* **-fied; -fy·ing** [L *indemnis* unharmed, fr. *in-* not + *damnum* damage] **1** : to secure against hurt, loss, or damage **2** : to make compensation to for hurt, loss, or damage — **in·dem·ni·fi·ca·tion** \-‚dem-nə-fə-'kā-shən\ *n*

in·dem·ni·ty \in-'dem-nə-tē\ *n, pl* **-ties 1** : security against hurt, loss, or damage; *also* : exemption from incurred penalties or liabilities **2** : something that indemnifies

¹in·dent \in-'dent\ *vb* [ME, fr. AF *endenter,* fr. *dent* tooth, fr. L *dent-, dens*] **1** : to notch the edge of **2** : INDENTURE **3** : to set (as a line of a paragraph) in from the margin

²indent *vb* **1** : to force inward so as to form a depression **2** : to form a dent in

in·den·ta·tion \‚in-‚den-'tā-shən\ *n* **1** : NOTCH; *also* : a recess in a surface **2** : the action of indenting : the condition of being indented **3** : DENT **4** : INDENTION 2

in·den·tion \in-'den-chən\ *n* **1** : INDENTATION 2 **2** : the blank space produced by indenting

¹in·den·ture \in-'den-chər\ *n* **1** : a written certificate or agreement; *esp* : a contract binding one person (as an apprentice) to work for another for a given period of time — often used in pl. **2** : INDENTATION 1 : DENT

²indenture *vb* **in·den·tured; in·den·tur·ing** : to bind (as an apprentice) by indentures

in·de·pen·dence \‚in-də-'pen-dəns\ *n* : the quality or state of being independent : FREEDOM

Independence Day *n* : July 4 observed as a legal holiday in the U.S. in commemoration of the adoption of the Declaration of Independence in 1776

in·de·pen·dent \‚in-də-'pen-dənt\ *adj* **1** : SELF-GOVERNING; *also* : not affiliated with a larger controlling unit **2** : not requiring or relying on something else or somebody else ⟨an ~ conclusion⟩ ⟨~ of her parents⟩ **3** : not easily influenced : showing self-reliance and personal freedom ⟨an ~ mind⟩ **4** : not committed to a political party ⟨an ~ voter⟩ **5** : MAIN

⟨an ~ clause⟩ — **independent** *n* — **in·de·pen·dent·ly** *adv*

independent variable *n* : a variable whose value is not determined by that of any other variable in a function

in·de·scrib·able \‚in-di-'skrī-bə-bəl\ *adj* **1** : that cannot be described **2** : being too intense or great for description — **in·de·scrib·ably** \-blē\ *adv*

in·de·ter·mi·nate \‚in-di-'tər-mə-nət\ *adj* **1** : VAGUE; *also* : not known in advance **2** : not limited in advance; *also* : not leading to a definite end or result — **in·de·ter·mi·na·cy** \-nə-sē\ *n* — **in·de·ter·mi·nate·ly** *adv*

¹in·dex \'in-‚deks\ *n, pl* **in·dex·es** *or* **in·di·ces** \-də-‚sēz\ **1** : POINTER **2** : SIGN, INDICATION ⟨an ~ of character⟩ **3** : a guide for facilitating references; *esp* : an alphabetical list of items treated in a printed work with the page number where each item may be found **4** : a list of restricted or prohibited material **5** *pl usu* **indices** : a number or symbol or expression (as an exponent) associated with another to indicate a mathematical operation or use or position in an arrangement or expansion **6** : a character ☞ used to direct attention (as to a note) **7** : INDEX NUMBER

²index *vb* **1** : to provide with or put into an index **2** : to serve as an index of **3** : to regulate by indexation

in·dex·a·tion \‚in-‚dek-'sā-shən\ *n* : a system of economic control in which a body of variables (as wages and interest) rise or fall at the same rate as an index of the cost of living

index finger *n* : the finger next to the thumb

in·dex·ing *n* : INDEXATION

index number *n* : a number used to indicate change in magnitude (as of cost) as compared with the magnitude at some specified time

index of refraction : REFRACTIVE INDEX

in·dia ink \'in-dē-ə-\ *n, often cap 1st I* **1** : a solid black pigment used in drawing **2** : a fluid made from india ink

In·di·an \'in-dē-ən\ *n* **1** : a native or inhabitant of India or of the East Indies; *also* : a person of Indian descent **2** : AMERICAN INDIAN — **Indian** *adj*

Indian corn *n* **1** : CORN 2 **2** : corn having hard kernels of various colors (as reddish-brown or purple) used esp. for ornament

Indian meal *n* : CORNMEAL

Indian paintbrush *n* : any of a genus of herbaceous plants related to the snapdragons that have brightly colored bracts

Indian pipe *n* : a waxy white leafless saprophytic herb of Asia and the U.S.

Indian summer *n* : a period of mild weather in late autumn or early winter

In·dia paper \'in-dē-ə-\ *n* **1** : a thin absorbent paper used esp. for taking impressions (as of steel engravings) **2** : a thin tough opaque printing paper

in·di·cate \'in-də-‚kāt\ *vb* **-cat·ed; -cat·ing 1** : to point out or to **2** : to show

---

indemonstrable   indestructible   indeterminable

indirectly **3** : to state briefly — **in·di·ca·tion** \ˌin-də-ˈkā-shən\ *n* — **in·di·ca·tor** \ˈin-də-ˌkā-tər\ *n*

¹**in·dic·a·tive** \in-ˈdi-kə-tiv\ *adj* **1** : of, relating to, or being a verb form that represents an act or state as a fact ⟨~ mood⟩ **2** : serving to indicate ⟨actions ~ of fear⟩

²**indicative** *n* **1** : the indicative mood of a language **2** : a form in the indicative mood

in·di·cia \in-ˈdi-shə, -shē-ə\ *n pl* **1** : distinctive marks **2** : postal markings often imprinted on mail or mailing labels

in·dict \in-ˈdīt\ *vb* [alter. of earlier *indite*, fr. ME, fr. AF *enditer* to write, point out, indict, ultim. fr. L *indicere* to make known formally, fr. *dicere* to say] **1** : to charge with a fault or offense **2** : to charge with a crime by the finding of a jury — **in·dict·able** *adj* — **in·dict·ment** *n*

in·die \ˈin-dē\ *n* **1** : one that is independent; *esp* : an unaffiliated record or motion-picture production company **2** : something produced by an indie — **indie** *adj*

in·dif·fer·ent \in-ˈdi-frənt, -fə-rənt\ *adj* **1** : UNBIASED, UNPREJUDICED **2** : of no importance one way or the other **3** : marked by no special liking for or dislike of something **4** : being neither excessive nor inadequate **5** : PASSABLE, MEDIOCRE **6** : being neither right nor wrong — **in·dif·fer·ence** \-frəns, -fə-rəns\ *n* — **in·dif·fer·ent·ly** *adv*

in·dig·e·nous \in-ˈdi-jə-nəs\ *adj* : produced, growing, or living naturally in a particular region

in·di·gent \ˈin-di-jənt\ *adj* : IMPOVERISHED, NEEDY — **in·di·gence** \-jəns\ *n*

in·di·gest·ible \ˌin-dī-ˈjes-tə-bəl, -də-\ *adj* : not readily digested

in·di·ges·tion \-ˈjes-chən\ *n* : inadequate or difficult digestion : DYSPEPSIA

in·dig·nant \in-ˈdig-nənt\ *adj* : filled with or marked by indignation — **in·dig·nant·ly** *adv*

in·dig·na·tion \ˌin-dig-ˈnā-shən\ *n* : anger aroused by something unjust, unworthy, or mean

in·dig·ni·ty \in-ˈdig-nə-tē\ *n, pl* **-ties** : an offense against personal dignity or self-respect; *also* : humiliating treatment

in·di·go \ˈin-di-ˌgō\ *n, pl* **-gos** *or* **-goes** [It dial., fr. L *indicum*, fr. Gk *indikon*, fr. *indikos* Indic, fr. *Indos* India] **1** : a blue dye obtained from plants or synthesized **2** : a deep reddish blue color

in·di·rect \ˌin-də-ˈrekt, -dī-\ *adj* **1** : not straight ⟨an ~ route⟩ **2** : not straightforward and open ⟨~ methods⟩ **3** : not having a plainly seen connection ⟨an ~ cause⟩ **4** : not directly to the point ⟨an ~ answer⟩ — **in·di·rec·tion** \-ˈrek-shən\ *n* — **in·di·rect·ly** *adv* — **in·di·rect·ness** *n*

in·dis·creet \ˌin-di-ˈskrēt\ *adj* : not discreet : IMPRUDENT — **in·dis·creet·ly** *adv*

in·dis·cre·tion \ˌin-di-ˈskre-shən\ *n* **1** : IMPRUDENCE ⟨dietary ~⟩ **2** : something marked by lack of discretion; *esp* : an act deviating from accepted morality

in·dis·crim·i·nate \ˌin-di-ˈskri-mə-nət\ *adj* **1** : not careful in making choices **2** : HAPHAZARD, RANDOM ⟨an ~ application of a law⟩ **3** : UNRESTRAINED **4** : MOTLEY — **in·dis·crim·i·nate·ly** *adv*

in·dis·pens·able \ˌin-di-ˈspen-sə-bəl\ *adj* : absolutely essential : REQUISITE — **in·dis·pens·abil·i·ty** \-ˌspen-sə-ˈbi-lə-tē\ *n* — **indispensable** *n* — **in·dis·pens·ably** \-ˈspen-sə-blē\ *adv*

in·dis·posed \-ˈspōzd\ *adj* **1** : slightly ill **2** : AVERSE — **in·dis·po·si·tion** \ˌ(ˌ)in-ˌdis-pə-ˈzi-shən\ *n*

in·dis·put·able \ˌin-di-ˈspyü-tə-bəl, (ˌ)in-ˈdis-pyə-\ *adj* : not disputable : UNQUESTIONABLE ⟨~ proof⟩ — **in·dis·put·ably** \-blē\ *adv*

in·dis·sol·u·ble \ˌin-di-ˈsäl-yə-bəl\ *adj* : not capable of being dissolved, undone, or broken : PERMANENT ⟨an ~ contract⟩

in·dis·tinct \ˌin-di-ˈstiŋkt\ *adj* **1** : not sharply outlined or separable : BLURRED, FAINT, DIM **2** : not readily distinguishable : UNCERTAIN — **in·dis·tinct·ly** *adv* — **in·dis·tinct·ness** *n*

in·dite \in-ˈdīt\ *vb* **in·dit·ed; in·dit·ing** : COMPOSE ⟨~ a poem⟩; *also* : to put in writing ⟨~ a letter⟩

in·di·um \ˈin-dē-əm\ *n* : a malleable silvery metallic chemical element

indiv *abbr* individual

¹**in·di·vid·u·al** \ˌin-də-ˈvi-jə-wəl\ *adj* **1** : of, relating to, or associated with an individual ⟨~ traits⟩ **2** : being an individual : existing as an indivisible whole **3** : intended for one person **4** : SEPARATE ⟨~ copies⟩ **5** : having marked individuality ⟨an ~ style⟩ — **in·di·vid·u·al·ly** *adv*

²**individual** *n* **1** : a single member of a category : a particular person, animal, or thing **2** : PERSON ⟨a disagreeable ~⟩

in·di·vid·u·al·ise *Brit var of* INDIVIDUALIZE

in·di·vid·u·al·ism \ˌin-də-ˈvi-jə-wə-ˌli-zəm\ *n* **1** : a doctrine that the interests of the individual are primary **2** : a doctrine holding that the individual has political or economic rights with which the state must not interfere **3** : INDIVIDUALITY

in·di·vid·u·al·ist \-list\ *n* **1** : one that pursues a markedly independent course in thought or action **2** : one that advocates or practices individualism — **individualist** *or* **in·di·vid·u·al·is·tic** \-ˌvi-jə-wə-ˈlis-tik\ *adj*

in·di·vid·u·al·i·ty \-ˌvi-jə-ˈwa-lə-tē\ *n, pl* **-ties** **1** : the sum of qualities that characterize and distinguish an individual from all others; *also* : PERSONALITY **2** : separate or distinct existence **3** : INDIVIDUAL, PERSON

in·di·vid·u·al·ize \-ˈvi-jə-wə-ˌlīz\ *vb* **-ized;**

-iz·ing : to make individual in character **2** : to treat or notice individually : PARTICULARIZE **3** : to adapt to the needs of an individual

individual retirement account *n* : IRA

in·di·vid·u·ate \ˌin-də-ˈvi-jə-ˌwāt\ *vb* **-at·ed; -at·ing** : to give individuality to : form into an individual — **in·di·vid·u·a·tion** \-ˌvi-jə-ˈwā-shən\ *n*

in·di·vis·i·ble \ˌin-də-ˈvi-zə-bəl\ *adj* : impossible to divide or separate — **in·di·vis·i·bil·i·ty** \-ˌvi-zə-ˈbi-lə-tē\ *n* — **in·di·vis·i·bly** *adv*

In·do-Ar·y·an \ˌin-dō-ˈer-ē-ən\ *n* : a branch of the Indo-European language family that includes Hindi and other languages of south Asia

in·doc·tri·nate \in-ˈdäk-trə-ˌnāt\ *vb* **-nat·ed; -nat·ing** : to instruct esp. in fundamentals or rudiments : TEACH **2** : to teach the beliefs and doctrines of a particular group — **in·doc·tri·na·tion** \(ˌ)in-ˌdäk-trə-ˈnā-shən\ *n* — **in·doc·tri·na·tor** *n*

In·do-Eu·ro·pe·an \ˌin-dō-ˌyùr-ə-ˈpē-ən\ *adj* : of, relating to, or constituting a family of languages comprising those spoken in most of Europe and in the parts of the world colonized by Europeans since 1500 and also in Persia, the subcontinent of India, and some other parts of Asia

in·do·lent \ˈin-də-lənt\ *adj* [LL *indolens* insensitive to pain, fr. L *dolēre* to feel pain] **1** : slow to develop or heal ⟨~ ulcers⟩ **2** : LAZY — **in·do·lence** \-ləns\ *n* — **in·do·lent·ly** *adv*

in·dom·i·ta·ble \in-ˈdä-mə-tə-bəl\ *adj* : UNCONQUERABLE ⟨~ courage⟩ — **in·dom·i·ta·bly** \-blē\ *adv*

in·door \ˈin-ˌdòr\ *adj* **1** : of or relating to the inside of a building **2** : living, located, or carried on within a building

in·doors \in-ˈdòrz\ *adv* : in or into a building

indorse, indorsement *var of* ENDORSE, ENDORSEMENT

in·du·bi·ta·ble \(ˌ)in-ˈdü-bə-tə-bəl, -ˈdyü-\ *adj* : UNQUESTIONABLE ⟨~ truths⟩ — **in·du·bi·ta·bly** \-blē\ *adv*

in·duce \in-ˈdüs, -ˈdyüs\ *vb* **in·duced; in·duc·ing** **1** : PERSUADE, INFLUENCE **2** : BRING ABOUT **3** : to produce (as an electric current) by induction **4** : to determine by induction; *esp* : to infer from particulars — **in·duc·er** *n*

in·duce·ment \-mənt\ *n* **1** : something that induces : MOTIVE **2** : the act or process of inducing

in·duct \in-ˈdəkt\ *vb* **1** : to place in office **2** : to admit as a member **3** : to enroll for military training or service — **in·duct·ee** \-ˌdək-ˈtē\ *n*

in·duc·tance \in-ˈdək-təns\ *n* : a property of an electric circuit by which a varying current produces an electromotive force in that circuit or in a nearby circuit; *also* : the measure of this property

in·duc·tion \in-ˈdək-shən\ *n* **1** : the act or process of inducting; *also* : INITIATION **2** : the formality by which a civilian is inducted into military service **3** : inference of a generalized conclusion from particular instances; *also* : a conclusion so reached **4** : the act of causing or bringing on or about **5** : the process by which an electric current, an electric charge, or magnetism is produced in a body by the proximity of an electric or magnetic field

in·duc·tive \in-ˈdək-tiv\ *adj* : of, relating to, or employing induction

in·duc·tor \in-ˈdək-tər\ *n* : an electrical component that acts upon another or is itself acted upon by induction

in·dulge \in-ˈdəlj\ *vb* **in·dulged; in·dulg·ing** **1** : to give free rein to : GRATIFY **2** : HUMOR **3** : to gratify one's taste or desire for ⟨~ in alcohol⟩

in·dul·gence \in-ˈdəl-jəns\ *n* **1** : remission of temporal punishment due in Roman Catholic doctrine for sins whose eternal punishment has been remitted by reception of the sacrifice of penance **2** : the act of indulging : the state of being indulgent **3** : an indulgent act **4** : the thing indulged in **5** : SELF-INDULGENCE — **in·dul·gent** \-jənt\ *adj* — **in·dul·gent·ly** *adv*

in·du·rat·ed \ˈin-dyù-ˌrā-təd, -dú-\ *adj* : physically or emotionally hardened — **in·du·ra·tion** \ˌin-dyù-ˈrā-shən, -dú-\ *n*

in·dus·tri·al \in-ˈdəs-trē-əl\ *adj* **1** : of or relating to industry **2** : HEAVY-DUTY ⟨an ~ zipper⟩ **3** : characterized by highly developed industries — **in·dus·tri·al·ly** *adv*

in·dus·tri·al·ise *Brit var of* INDUSTRIALIZE

in·dus·tri·al·ist \-ə-list\ *n* : a person owning or engaged in the management of an industry

in·dus·tri·al·ize \in-ˈdəs-trē-ə-ˌlīz\ *vb* **-ized; -iz·ing** : to make or become industrial — **in·dus·tri·al·i·za·tion** \-ˌdəs-trē-ə-lə-ˈzā-shən\ *n*

in·dus·tri·ous \in-ˈdəs-trē-əs\ *adj* : DILIGENT, BUSY — **in·dus·tri·ous·ly** *adv* — **in·dus·tri·ous·ness** *n*

in·dus·try \ˈin-(ˌ)dəs-trē\ *n, pl* **-tries** **1** : DILIGENCE **2** : a department or branch of a craft, art, business, or manufacture; *esp* : one that employs a large personnel and capital **3** : a distinct group of productive enterprises **4** : manufacturing activity as a whole

in·dwell \(ˌ)in-ˈdwel\ *vb* : to exist within as an activating spirit or force

In·dy car \ˈin-dē-\ *n* : a single-seat, open-cockpit racing car with the engine in the rear

¹**in·ebri·ate** \i-ˈnē-brē-ˌāt\ *vb* **-at·ed; -at·ing** : to make drunk : INTOXICATE — **in·ebri·a·tion** \-ˌnē-brē-ˈā-shən\ *n*

²**in·ebri·ate** \-ət\ *n* : one that is drunk; *esp* : DRUNKARD

in·ef·fa·ble \(ˌ)in-ˈe-fə-bəl\ *adj* **1** : incapable of being expressed in words : INDESCRIBABLE ⟨~ joy⟩ **2** : UNSPEAKABLE ⟨~ disgust⟩ **3** : not to be uttered : TABOO — **in·ef·fa·bly** \-blē\ *adv*

in·ef·fec·tive \ˌi-nə-ˈfek-tiv\ *adj* **1** : INEF-

---

inedible   ineducable   ineffaceable

FECTUAL 2 : not able to perform efficiently or as expected : INCAPABLE — in·ef·fec·tive·ly adv — in·ef·fec·tive·ness n

in·ef·fec·tu·al \-'fek-chə-wəl\ adj 1 : not producing the proper or usual effect 2 : INEFFECTIVE 2 — in·ef·fec·tu·al·ly adv

in·ef·fi·cient \ˌi-nə-'fi-shənt\ adj 1 : not producing the desired effect 2 : wasteful of time or energy 3 : INCAPABLE, INCOMPETENT — in·ef·fi·cien·cy \-'fi-shən-sē\ n — in·ef·fi·cient·ly adv

in·el·e·gant \(ˌ)i-'ne-li-gənt\ adj : lacking in refinement, grace, or good taste — in·el·e·gance \-gəns\ n — in·el·e·gant·ly adv

in·el·i·gi·ble \(ˌ)i-'ne-lə-jə-bəl\ adj : not qualified for an office or position — in·el·i·gi·bil·i·ty \(ˌ)i-ˌne-lə-jə-'bi-lə-tē\ n

in·eluc·ta·ble \ˌi-ni-'lək-tə-bəl\ adj : not to be avoided, changed, or resisted ⟨an ∼ conclusion⟩ — in·eluc·ta·bly \-blē\ adv

in·ept \i-'nept\ adj 1 : lacking in fitness or aptitude : UNFIT 2 : FOOLISH 3 : being out of place : INAPPROPRIATE 4 : generally incompetent : BUNGLING — in·ept·ly adv — in·ept·ness n

in·ep·ti·tude \(ˌ)i-'nep-ti-ˌtüd, -ˌtyüd\ n : the quality or state of being inept; esp : INCOMPETENCE

in·equal·i·ty \ˌi-ni-'kwä-lə-tē\ n 1 : the quality of being unequal or uneven; esp : UNEVENNESS, DISPARITY 2 : an instance of being unequal

in·ert \i-'nərt\ adj [L inert-, iners unskilled, idle, fr. art-, ars skill] 1 : powerless to move 2 : SLUGGISH 3 : lacking in active properties ⟨chemically ∼⟩ — in·ert·ly adv — in·ert·ness n

in·er·tia \i-'nər-shə, -shē-ə\ n 1 : a property of matter whereby it remains at rest or continues in uniform motion unless acted upon by some outside force 2 : INERTNESS, SLUGGISHNESS — in·er·tial \-shəl\ adj

in·es·cap·able \ˌi-nə-'skā-pə-bəl\ adj : incapable of being escaped : INEVITABLE — in·es·cap·ably \-blē\ adv

in·es·ti·ma·ble \(ˌ)i-'nes-tə-mə-bəl\ adj 1 : incapable of being estimated or computed ⟨∼ errors⟩ 2 : too valuable or excellent to be fully appreciated — in·es·ti·ma·bly \-blē\ adv

in·ev·i·ta·ble \i-'ne-və-tə-bəl\ adj : incapable of being avoided or evaded : bound to happen ⟨the ∼ result⟩ — in·ev·i·ta·bil·i·ty \(ˌ)i-ˌne-və-tə-'bi-lə-tē\ n

in·ev·i·ta·bly \-blē\ adv 1 : in an inevitable way 2 : as is to be expected

in·ex·act \ˌi-nig-'zakt\ adj 1 : not precisely correct or true : INACCURATE 2 : not rigorous and careful — in·ex·act·ly adv — in·ex·act·ness n

in·ex·cus·able \ˌi-nik-'skyü-zə-bəl\ adj : impossible to excuse or justify ⟨∼ rudeness⟩ — in·ex·cus·ably \-blē\ adv

in·ex·haust·ible \ˌi-nig-'zȯ-stə-bəl\ adj 1

: incapable of being used up ⟨an ∼ supply⟩ 2 : UNTIRING ⟨an ∼ hiker⟩ — in·ex·haust·ibly \-blē\ adv

in·ex·o·ra·ble \(ˌ)i-'nek-sə-rə-bəl\ adj : not to be persuaded, moved, or stopped : RELENTLESS — in·ex·o·ra·bly adv

in·ex·pe·ri·ence \ˌi-nik-'spir-ē-əns\ n : lack of experience or of knowledge gained by experience — in·ex·pe·ri·enced \-ənst\ adj

in·ex·pert \(ˌ)i-'nek-ˌspərt\ adj : not expert : UNSKILLED — in·ex·pert·ly adv

in·ex·pi·a·ble \(ˌ)i-'nek-spē-ə-bəl\ adj : not capable of being atoned for

in·ex·pli·ca·ble \ˌi-nik-'spli-kə-bəl, (ˌ)i-'nek-(ˌ)spli-\ adj : incapable of being explained or accounted for ⟨an ∼ mistake⟩ — in·ex·pli·ca·bly \-blē\ adv

in·ex·press·ible \-'spre-sə-bəl\ adj : not capable of being expressed ⟨∼ joy⟩ — in·ex·press·ibly \-blē\ adv

in ex·tre·mis \ˌin-ik-'strā-məs, -'strē-\ adv : in extreme circumstances; esp : at the point of death

in·ex·tri·ca·ble \ˌi-nik-'stri-kə-bəl, (ˌ)i-'nek-(ˌ)stri-\ adj 1 : forming a maze or tangle from which it is impossible to get free 2 : incapable of being disentangled or untied — in·ex·tri·ca·bly \-blē\ adv

inf abbr 1 infantry 2 infinitive

in·fal·li·ble \(ˌ)in-'fa-lə-bəl\ adj 1 : incapable of error : UNERRING ⟨an ∼ marksman⟩ 2 : SURE, CERTAIN ⟨an ∼ remedy⟩ — in·fal·li·bil·i·ty \(ˌ)in-ˌfa-lə-'bi-lə-tē\ n — in·fal·li·bly \(ˌ)in-'fa-lə-blē\ adv

in·fa·mous \'in-fə-məs\ adj 1 : having a reputation of the worst kind 2 : DISGRACEFUL — in·fa·mous·ly adv

in·fa·my \-mē\ n, pl -mies 1 : evil reputation brought about by something grossly criminal, shocking, or brutal 2 : an extreme and publicly known criminal or evil act 3 : the state of being infamous

in·fan·cy \'in-fən-sē\ n, pl -cies 1 : early childhood 2 : a beginning or early period of existence

in·fant \'in-fənt\ n [ME enfaunt, fr. AF enfant, fr. L infant-, infans, adj., incapable of speech, young, fr. fant-, fans, prp. of fari to speak] : BABY; also : a person who is a legal minor

in·fan·ti·cide \in-'fan-tə-ˌsīd\ n : the killing of an infant

in·fan·tile \'in-fən-ˌtī(-ə)l, -t³l, -ˌtēl\ adj : of or relating to infants; also : CHILDISH

infantile paralysis n : POLIOMYELITIS

in·fan·try \'in-fən-trē\ n, pl -tries [MF & It; MF infanterie, fr. It infanteria, fr. infante boy, foot soldier] : soldiers trained, armed, and equipped to fight on foot — in·fan·try·man \-mən\ n

in·farct \'in-ˌfärkt\ n [L infarctus, pp. of infarcire to stuff] : an area of dead tissue (as of the heart wall) caused by blocking of local blood circulation — in·farc·tion \in-'färk-shən\ n

in·fat·u·ate \in-'fa-chə-ˌwāt\ vb -at·ed; -at·ing : to inspire with a foolish or ex-

---

inefficacious	inelasticity
inefficacy	inequitable
inelastic	inequity

ineradicable	inexpensive
inerrant	inexpressive
inexpedient	inextinguishable

travagant love or admiration — **in·fat·u·a·tion** \-ˌfa-chə-ˈwā-shən\ *n*

in·fect \in-ˈfekt\ *vb* **1** : to contaminate with disease-producing matter **2** : to communicate a pathogen or disease to **3** : to cause to share one's feelings ⟨~*ed* us with his enthusiasm⟩

in·fec·tion \in-ˈfek-shən\ *n* **1** : a disease or condition caused by a germ or parasite; *also* : such a germ or parasite **2** : an act or process of infecting — **in·fec·tious** \-shəs\ *adj* — **in·fec·tive** \-ˈfek-tiv\ *adj*

infectious mononucleosis *n* : an acute infectious disease characterized by fever, swelling of lymph glands, and increased numbers of lymph cells in the blood

in·fe·lic·i·tous \ˌin-fi-ˈli-sə-təs\ *adj* : not appropriate in application or expression ⟨~ comments⟩ — **in·fe·lic·i·ty** \-sə-tē\ *n*

in·fer \in-ˈfər\ *vb* **-ferred; -fer·ring 1** : to derive as a conclusion from facts or premises **2** : GUESS, SURMISE **3** : to lead to as a conclusion or consequence **4** : HINT, SUGGEST ♦ *Synonyms* DEDUCE, CONCLUDE, JUDGE, GATHER — **in·fer·ence** \ˈin-fə-rəns, -frəns\ *n* — **in·fer·en·tial** \ˌin-fə-ˈren-chəl\ *adj*

in·fe·ri·or \in-ˈfir-ē-ər\ *adj* **1** : situated lower down **2** : of low or lower degree or rank **3** : of lesser quality **4** : of little or less importance, value, or merit ⟨an ~ opponent⟩ — **inferior** *n* — **in·fe·ri·or·i·ty** \-ˌfir-ē-ˈór-ə-tē\ *n*

in·fer·nal \in-ˈfər-nᵊl\ *adj* **1** : of or relating to hell **2** : HELLISH, FIENDISH ⟨~ schemes⟩ **3** : DAMNABLE ⟨an ~ pest⟩ — **in·fer·nal·ly** *adv*

in·fer·no \in-ˈfər-nō\ *n, pl* **-nos** [It, hell, fr. LL *infernus,* fr. L, lower] : a place or a state that resembles or suggests hell; *also* : intense heat

in·fer·tile \(ˌ)in-ˈfər-tᵊl\ *adj* : not fertile or productive : BARREN — **in·fer·til·i·ty** \ˌin-fər-ˈti-lə-tē\ *n*

in·fest \in-ˈfest\ *vb* : to trouble by spreading or swarming in or over; *also* : to live in or on as a parasite — **in·fes·ta·tion** \ˌin-ˌfes-ˈtā-shən\ *n*

in·fi·del \ˈin-fə-dᵊl, -fə-ˌdel\ *n* **1** : one who is not a Christian or opposes Christianity **2** : an unbeliever esp. with respect to a particular religion

in·fi·del·i·ty \ˌin-fə-ˈde-lə-tē, -fī-\ *n, pl* **-ties 1** : lack of belief in a religion **2** : unfaithfulness or an instance of it esp. in marriage

in·field \ˈin-ˌfēld\ *n* : the part of a baseball field inside the baselines — **in·field·er** *n*

in·fight·ing \ˈin-ˌfī-tiŋ\ *n* **1** : fighting at close quarters **2** : dissension or rivalry among members of a group

in·fil·trate \in-ˈfil-ˌtrāt, ˈin-(ˌ)fil-\ *vb* **-trat·ed; -trat·ing 1** : to enter or filter into or through something **2** : to pass into or through by or as if by filtering or permeating — **in·fil·tra·tion** \ˌin-(ˌ)fil-ˈtrā-shən\ *n* — **in·fil·tra·tor** *n*

in·fi·nite \ˈin-fə-nət\ *adj* **1** : LIMITLESS, BOUNDLESS, ENDLESS ⟨~ space⟩ ⟨~ pa-

tience⟩ **2** : VAST, IMMENSE; *also* : INEXHAUSTIBLE ⟨~ wealth⟩ **3** : greater than any preassigned finite value however large ⟨~ number of positive integers⟩; *also* : extending to infinity ⟨~ plane surface⟩ — **infinite** *n* — **in·fi·nite·ly** *adv*

in·fin·i·tes·i·mal \(ˌ)in-ˌfi-nə-ˈte-sə-məl\ *adj* : immeasurably or incalculably small — **in·fin·i·tes·i·mal·ly** *adv*

in·fin·i·tive \in-ˈfi-nə-tiv\ *n* : a verb form having the characteristics of both verb and noun and in English usu. being used with *to*

in·fin·i·tude \in-ˈfi-nə-ˌtüd, -ˌtyüd\ *n* **1** : the quality or state of being infinite **2** : something that is infinite esp. in extent

in·fin·i·ty \in-ˈfi-nə-tē\ *n, pl* **-ties 1** : the quality of being infinite **2** : unlimited extent of time, space, or quantity **3** : an indefinitely great number or amount

in·firm \in-ˈfərm\ *adj* **1** : deficient in vitality; *esp* : feeble from age **2** : weak of mind, will, or character : IRRESOLUTE **3** : not solid or stable : INSECURE

in·fir·ma·ry \in-ˈfər-mə-rē\ *n, pl* **-ries** : a place for the care of the infirm or sick

in·fir·mi·ty \in-ˈfər-mə-tē\ *n, pl* **-ties 1** : FEEBLENESS **2** : DISEASE, AILMENT **3** : a personal failing : FOIBLE

in fla·gran·te de·lic·to \ˌin-flə-ˈgrän-tē-di-ˈlik-tō, -ˈgran-\ *adv* **1** : in the very act of committing a misdeed **2** : in the midst of sexual activity

in·flame \in-ˈflām\ *vb* **in·flamed; in·flam·ing 1** : KINDLE **2** : to excite to excessive or uncontrollable action or feeling; *also* : INTENSIFY **3** : to affect or become affected with inflammation

in·flam·ma·ble \in-ˈfla-mə-bəl\ *adj* **1** : FLAMMABLE **2** : easily inflamed, excited, or angered : IRASCIBLE

in·flam·ma·tion \ˌin-flə-ˈmā-shən\ *n* : a bodily response to injury in which an affected area becomes red, hot, and painful and congested with blood

in·flam·ma·to·ry \in-ˈfla-mə-ˌtór-ē\ *adj* **1** : tending to excite the senses or to arouse anger, disorder, or tumult : SEDITIOUS **2** : causing or accompanied by inflammation ⟨an ~ disease⟩

in·flate \in-ˈflāt\ *vb* **in·flat·ed; in·flat·ing 1** : to swell with air or gas ⟨~ a balloon⟩ **2** : to puff up : ELATE ⟨~ one's ego⟩ **3** : to expand or increase abnormally ⟨~ prices⟩ — **in·flat·able** *adj*

in·fla·tion \in-ˈflā-shən\ *n* **1** : an act of inflating **2** : the state of being inflated : empty pretentiousness : POMPOSITY **3** : a continuing rise in the general price level usu. attributed to an increase in the volume of money and credit

in·fla·tion·ary \-shə-ˌner-ē\ *adj* : of, characterized by, or productive of inflation

in·flect \in-ˈflekt\ *vb* **1** : to turn from a direct line or course : CURVE **2** : to vary a word by inflection **3** : to change or vary the pitch of the voice

in·flec·tion \in-ˈflek-shən\ *n* **1** : the act or result of curving or bending **2** : a change

infeasible

in pitch or loudness of the voice **3** : the change of form that words undergo to mark case, gender, number, tense, person, mood, or voice — **in·flec·tion·al** \-shə-nəl\ *adj*

in·flex·i·ble \(ˌ)in-ˈflek-sə-bəl\ *adj* **1** : UN-YIELDING **2** : RIGID **3** : incapable of change ⟨an ∼ deadline⟩ — **in·flex·i·bil·i·ty** \-ˌflek-sə-ˈbi-lə-tē\ *n* — **in·flex·i·bly** \-ˈflek-sə-blē\ *adv*

in·flex·ion \in-ˈflek-shən\ *chiefly Brit var of* INFLECTION

in·flict \in-ˈflikt\ *vb* : AFFLICT; *also* : to give by or as if by striking ⟨∼ pain⟩ — **in·flic·tion** \-ˈflik-shən\ *n*

in·flo·res·cence \ˌin-flə-ˈre-sᵊn(t)s\ *n* : the manner of development and arrangement of flowers on a stem; *also* : a flowering stem with its appendages : a flower cluster

in·flow \ˈin-ˌflō\ *n* : a flowing in

¹in·flu·ence \ˈin-ˌflü-əns\ *n* **1** : the act or power of producing an effect without apparent force or direct authority **2** : the power or capacity of causing an effect in indirect or intangible ways **3** : one that exerts influence — **in·flu·en·tial** \ˌin-flü-ˈen-chəl\ *adj* — **under the influence** : affected by alcohol

²influence *vb* **-enced; -enc·ing 1** : to affect or alter by influence : SWAY **2** : to have an effect on the condition or development of : MODIFY

in·flu·en·za \ˌin-flü-ˈen-zə\ *n* [It, lit., influence, fr. ML *influentia*; fr. the belief that epidemics were due to the influence of the stars] **1** : an acute and highly contagious virus disease marked by fever, prostration, aches and pains, and respiratory inflammation; *also* : any of various feverish usu. virus diseases typically with respiratory symptoms

in·flux \ˈin-ˌfləks\ *n* : a coming in

in·fo \ˈin-(ˌ)fō\ *n* : INFORMATION

in·fold \in-ˈfōld\ *vb* **1** : ENFOLD **2** : to fold inward or toward one another

in·fo·mer·cial \ˈin-fō-ˌmər-shəl\ *n* : a television program that is an extended advertisement often including a discussion or demonstration

in·form \in-ˈfȯrm\ *vb* **1** : to communicate knowledge to : TELL **2** : to give information or knowledge **3** : to act as an informer ♦ *Synonyms* ACQUAINT, APPRISE, ADVISE, NOTIFY

in·for·mal \(ˌ)in-ˈfȯr-məl\ *adj* **1** : conducted or carried out without formality or ceremony ⟨an ∼ party⟩ **2** : characteristic of or appropriate to ordinary, casual, or familiar use ⟨∼ clothes⟩ — **in·for·mal·i·ty** \ˌin-fȯr-ˈma-lə-tē, -fər-\ *n* — **in·for·mal·ly** \(ˌ)in-ˈfȯr-mə-lē\ *adv*

in·for·mant \in-ˈfȯr-mənt\ *n* : a person who gives information : INFORMER

in·for·ma·tion \ˌin-fər-ˈmā-shən\ *n* **1** : the communication or reception of knowledge or intelligence **2** : knowledge obtained from investigation, study, or instruction : FACTS, DATA **3** : the attribute communicated by one of two or more alternative sequences of something (as nucleotides in DNA or binary digits in a

computer program) — **in·for·ma·tion·al** \-shə-nəl\ *adj*

information superhighway *n* : INTERNET

information technology *n* : technology involving computer systems and networks for the processing and distribution of data

in·for·ma·tive \in-ˈfȯr-mə-tiv\ *adj* : imparting knowledge : INSTRUCTIVE

in·formed \in-ˈfȯrmd\ *adj* **1** : having or based on information ⟨an ∼ decision⟩ **2** : EDUCATED, KNOWLEDGEABLE

informed consent *n* : consent to a medical procedure by someone who understands what is involved

in·form·er \-ˈfȯr-mər\ *n* : one that informs; *esp* : a person who informs against others for illegalities esp. for financial gain

in·fo·tain·ment \ˌin-fō-ˈtān-mənt\ *n* : a television program that presents information (as news) in a manner intended to be entertaining

in·frac·tion \in-ˈfrak-shən\ *n* [ME, fr. ML *infractio*, fr. L, subduing, fr. *infringere* to break, crush] : the act of infringing : VIOLATION

in·fra dig \ˌin-frə-ˈdig\ *adj* [short for L *infra dignitatem*] : being beneath one's dignity

in·fra·red \ˌin-frə-ˈred\ *adj* : being, relating to, or using radiation having wavelengths longer than those of red light — **infrared** *n*

in·fra·struc·ture \ˈin-frə-ˌstrək-chər\ *n* **1** : the underlying foundation or basic framework (as of a system or organization) **2** : the system of public works of a country, state, or region; *also* : the resources (as buildings or equipment) required for an activity

in·fre·quent \(ˌ)in-ˈfrē-kwənt\ *adj* **1** : seldom happening : RARE **2** : placed or occurring at wide intervals in space or time ♦ *Synonyms* UNCOMMON, SCARCE, SPORADIC — **in·fre·quent·ly** *adv*

in·fringe \in-ˈfrinj\ *vb* **in·fringed; in·fring·ing 1** : VIOLATE, TRANSGRESS ⟨∼ a patent⟩ **2** : ENCROACH, TRESPASS ⟨∼ on our rights⟩ — **in·fringe·ment** *n*

in·fu·ri·ate \in-ˈfyu̇r-ē-ˌāt\ *vb* **-at·ed; -at·ing** : to make furious : ENRAGE — **in·fu·ri·at·ing·ly** *adv*

in·fuse \in-ˈfyüz\ *vb* **in·fused; in·fus·ing 1** : to instill a principle or quality in ⟨*infused* the team with confidence⟩ **2** : INSPIRE, ANIMATE **3** : to steep (as tea) without boiling — **in·fu·sion** \-ˈfyü-zhən\ *n*

¹-ing \iŋ\ *n suffix* **1** : action or process ⟨sleep*ing*⟩ : instance of an action or process ⟨a meet*ing*⟩ **2** : product or result of an action or process ⟨an engrav*ing*⟩ ⟨earn*ings*⟩ **3** : something used in an action or process ⟨a bed cover*ing*⟩ **4** : something connected with, consisting of, or used in making (a specified thing) ⟨scaffold*ing*⟩ **5** : something related to (a specified concept) ⟨off*ing*⟩

²-ing *n suffix* : one of a (specified) kind

³-ing *vb suffix or adj suffix* — used to form the present participle ⟨sail*ing*⟩ and sometimes to form an adjective resembling a present participle but not derived from a verb ⟨swashbuckl*ing*⟩

in·ga·ther \'in-,ga‑*h*ər\ *vb* : to gather in : ASSEMBLE

in·ge·nious \in-'jēn-yəs\ *adj* **1** : marked by special aptitude at discovering, inventing, or contriving **2** : marked by originality, resourcefulness, and cleverness in conception or execution — **in·ge·nious·ly** *adv* — **in·ge·nious·ness** *n*

in·ge·nue *or* **in·gé·nue** \'an-jə-,nü, 'än-; 'aⁿ-zhə-, 'äⁿ-\ *n* : a naive girl or young woman; *esp* : an actress portraying such a person

in·ge·nu·i·ty \,in-jə-'nü-ə-tē, -'nyü-\ *n*, *pl* **-ties** : skill or cleverness in planning or inventing : INVENTIVENESS

in·gen·u·ous \in-'jen-yə-wəs\ *adj* [L *ingenuus* native, freeborn, fr. *gignere* to beget] **1** : innocently straightforward ⟨her ∼ curiosity⟩ **2** : lacking craft or subtlety ⟨∼ comments⟩ — **in·gen·u·ous·ly** *adv* — **in·gen·u·ous·ness** *n*

in·gest \in-'jest\ *vb* : to take in for or as if for digestion — **in·ges·tion** \-'jes-chən\ *n*

in·gle·nook \'iŋ-gəl-,nu̇k\ *n* : a nook by a large open fireplace; *also* : a bench occupying this nook

in·glo·ri·ous \(,)in-'glōr-ē-əs\ *adj* **1** : SHAMEFUL **2** : not glorious : lacking fame or honor — **in·glo·ri·ous·ly** *adv*

in·got \'iŋ-gət\ *n* : a mass of metal cast in a form convenient for storage or transportation

¹in·grain \(,)in-'grān\ *vb* : to work indelibly into the natural texture or mental or moral constitution — **in·grained** *adj*

²in·grain \'in-,grān\ *adj* **1** : made of fiber that is dyed before being spun into yarn **2** : made of yarn that is dyed before being woven or knitted **3** : INNATE — **in·grain** *n*

in·grate \'in-,grāt\ *n* : an ungrateful person

in·gra·ti·ate \in-'grā-shē-,āt\ *vb* **-at·ed; -at·ing** : to gain favor by deliberate effort

in·gra·ti·at·ing *adj* **1** : capable of winning favor : PLEASING ⟨an ∼ smile⟩ **2** : FLATTERING ⟨an ∼ manner⟩

in·grat·i·tude \(,)in-'gra-tə-,tüd, -,tyüd\ *n* : lack of gratitude

in·gre·di·ent \in-'grē-dē-ənt\ *n* : one of the substances that make up a mixture or compound : CONSTITUENT

in·gress \'in-,gres\ *n* : ENTRANCE, ACCESS — **in·gres·sion** \in-'gre-shən\ *n*

in·grow·ing \'in-,grō-iŋ\ *adj* : growing or tending inward

in·grown \-,grōn\ *adj* : grown in; *esp* : having the free tip or edge embedded in the flesh ⟨an ∼ toenail⟩

in·gui·nal \'iŋ-gwə-n³l\ *adj* : of, relating to, or situated in or near the region of the groin ⟨an ∼ hernia⟩

in·hab·it \in-'ha-bət\ *vb* : to live or dwell in ⟨spiders that ∼ caves⟩ — **in·hab·it·able** *adj* — **in·hab·i·ta·tion** \in-,ha-bə-'tā-shən\ *n*

in·hab·i·tant \in-'ha-bə-tənt\ *n* : a permanent resident in a place

in·hal·ant \in-'hā-lənt\ *n* : something (as a medicine) that is inhaled

in·ha·la·tor \'in-hə-,lā-tər\ *n* : a device that provides a mixture of carbon dioxide and oxygen for breathing

in·hale \in-'hāl\ *vb* **in·haled; in·hal·ing** : to breathe in — **in·ha·la·tion** \,in-hə-'lā-shən\ *n*

in·hal·er \in-'hā-lər\ *n* : a device by means of which medicinal material is inhaled

in·here \in-'hir\ *vb* **in·hered; in·her·ing** : to be inherent

in·her·ent \in-'hir-ənt, -'her-\ *adj* : established as an essential part of something : INTRINSIC ⟨risks ∼ in the venture⟩ — **in·her·ent·ly** *adv*

in·her·it \in-'her-ət\ *vb* **1** : to receive esp. from one's ancestors **2** : to receive by genetic transmission — **in·her·it·able** \-ə-tə-bəl\ *adj* — **in·her·i·tance** \-ə-təns\ *n* — **in·her·i·tor** \-ə-tər\ *n*

in·hib·it \in-'hi-bət\ *vb* **1** : PROHIBIT, FORBID **2** : to hold in check : RESTRAIN ⟨∼ed by fear⟩ — **in·hib·i·tor** \-bə-tər\ *n* — **in·hib·i·to·ry** \-bə-,tȯr-ē\ *adj*

in·hi·bi·tion \,in-hə-'bi-shən\ *n* **1** : PROHIBITION, RESTRAINT **2** : a usu. inner check on free activity, expression, or functioning

in–house \'in-,hȧu̇s, -'hȧu̇s\ *adj* : existing, originating, or carried on within a group or organization

in·hu·man \(,)in-'hyü-mən, -'yü-\ *adj* **1** : lacking pity, kindness, or mercy : SAVAGE ⟨an ∼ tyrant⟩ **2** : COLD, IMPERSONAL **3** : not worthy of or conforming to the needs of human beings ⟨∼ living conditions⟩ **4** : of or suggesting a nonhuman class of beings — **in·hu·man·ly** *adv* — **in·hu·man·ness** *n*

in·hu·mane \,in-hyü-'mān, -yü-\ *adj* : not humane : INHUMAN **1**

in·hu·man·i·ty \-'ma-nə-tē\ *n*, *pl* **-ties** **1** : the quality or state of being cruel or barbarous **2** : a cruel or barbarous act

in·im·i·cal \i-'ni-mi-kəl\ *adj* **1** : being adverse often by reason of hostility ⟨forces ∼ to change⟩ **2** : HOSTILE, UNFRIENDLY ⟨∼ factions⟩ — **in·im·i·cal·ly** *adv*

in·im·i·ta·ble \(,)i-'ni-mə-tə-bəl\ *adj* : not capable of being imitated

in·iq·ui·ty \i-'ni-kwə-tē\ *n*, *pl* **-ties** [ME *iniquite*, fr. AF *iniquité*, fr. L *iniquitas*, fr. *iniquus* uneven, fr. *aequus* equal] **1** : WICKEDNESS **2** : a wicked act — **in·iq·ui·tous** \-təs\ *adj*

¹ini·tial \i-'ni-shəl\ *adj* **1** : of or relating to the beginning : INCIPIENT ⟨my ∼ reaction⟩ **2** : being at the beginning — **ini·tial·ly** *adv*

²initial *n* : the first letter of a word or name

³initial *vb* **-tialed** *or* **-tialled; -tial·ing** *or* **-tial·ling** : to affix an initial to

¹ini·ti·ate \i-'ni-shē-,āt\ *vb* **-at·ed; -at·ing** **1** : START, BEGIN **2** : to induct into membership by or as if by special ceremonies **3** : to instruct in the rudiments or princi-

---

inharmonious   **inhospitable**   **injudicious**

ples of something — **ini·ti·a·tion** \-ˌni-shē-ˈā-shən\ n

²**ini·ti·ate** \i-ˈni-shē-ət\ n **1** : a person who is undergoing or has passed an initiation **2** : a person who is instructed or adept in some special field

ini·tia·tive \i-ˈni-shə-tiv\ n **1** : an introductory step **2** : self-reliant enterprise ⟨showed great ∼⟩ **3** : a process by which laws may be introduced or enacted directly by vote of the people

ini·tia·to·ry \i-ˈni-shē-ə-ˌtȯr-ē\ adj **1** : INTRODUCTORY **2** : tending or serving to initiate ⟨∼ rites⟩

in·ject \in-ˈjekt\ vb **1** : to force into something ⟨∼ serum with a needle⟩ **2** : to introduce as an element into some situation or subject ⟨∼ a note of suspicion⟩ — **in·jec·tion** \-ˈjek-shən\ n

in·junc·tion \in-ˈjəŋk-shən\ n **1** : ORDER, ADMONITION **2** : a court writ whereby one is required to do or to refrain from doing a specified act

in·jure \ˈin-jər\ vb **in·jured**; **in·jur·ing 1** : WRONG **2** : to damage or hurt esp. physically ◆ **Synonyms** HARM, IMPAIR, MAR, SPOIL

in·ju·ry \ˈin-jə-rē\ n, pl **-ries 1** : an act that damages or hurts : WRONG **2** : hurt, damage, or loss sustained — **in·ju·ri·ous** \in-ˈju̇r-ē-əs\ adj

in·jus·tice \(ˌ)in-ˈjəs-təs\ n **1** : violation of a person's rights : UNFAIRNESS **2** : an unjust act or deed : WRONG

¹**ink** \ˈiŋk\ n [ME enke, fr. AF encre, enke, fr. LL encaustum, fr. L encaustus burned in, fr. Gk enkaustos, fr. enkaiein to burn in] : a usu. liquid and colored material for writing and printing — **inky** adj

²**ink** vb : to put ink on; esp : SIGN

ink·blot test \ˈiŋk-ˌblät-\ n : any of several psychological tests based on the interpretation of irregular figures

ink·horn \-ˌhȯrn\ n : a small bottle (as of horn) for holding ink

in-kind \ˈin-ˈkīnd\ adj : consisting of something (as goods) other than money

ink-jet n : a computer printer that sprays electrically charged droplets of ink onto paper — **ink-jet** adj

in·kling \ˈiŋ-kliŋ\ n **1** : HINT, INTIMATION **2** : a vague idea

ink·stand \ˈiŋk-ˌstand\ n : INKWELL; also : a pen and ink stand

ink·well \-ˌwel\ n : a container for ink

in·laid \ˈin-ˈlād\ adj : decorated with material set into a surface

¹**in·land** \ˈin-ˌland, -lənd\ adj **1** chiefly Brit : not foreign : DOMESTIC ⟨∼ revenue⟩ **2** : of or relating to the interior of a country ⟨the ∼ states⟩

²**inland** n : the interior of a country

³**inland** adv : into or toward the interior

in-law \ˈin-ˌlȯ\ n : a relative by marriage

¹**in·lay** \(ˌ)in-ˈlā, ˈin-ˌlā\ vb **in·laid** \-ˈlād\; **in·lay·ing** : to set (a material) into a surface or ground material esp. for decoration

²**in·lay** \ˈin-ˌlā\ n **1** : inlaid work **2** : a shaped filling cemented into a tooth

in·let \ˈin-ˌlet, -lət\ n **1** : a small or narrow

bay **2** : an opening for intake esp. of a fluid

in-line skate n : a roller skate whose four wheels are set in a straight line — **in-line skater** n — **in-line skating** n

in·mate \ˈin-ˌmāt\ n : any of a group occupying a single place of residence; esp : a person confined (as in a hospital or prison)

in me·di·as res \in-ˌmā-dē-əs-ˈräs\ adv [L, lit., into the midst of things] : in or into the middle of a narrative or plot

in me·mo·ri·am \ˌin-mə-ˈmȯr-ē-əm\ prep [L] : in memory of

in·most \ˈin-ˌmōst\ adj : deepest within : INNERMOST

inn \ˈin\ n : HOTEL, TAVERN

in·nards \ˈi-nərdz\ n pl [alter. of inwards] **1** : the internal organs of a human being or animal; esp : VISCERA **2** : the internal parts of a structure or mechanism

in·nate \i-ˈnāt\ adj **1** : existing in, belonging to, or determined by factors present in an individual from birth : NATIVE **2** : INHERENT, INTRINSIC ⟨the ∼ defects of a plan⟩ — **in·nate·ly** adv

in·ner \ˈi-nər\ adj **1** : situated farther in ⟨the ∼ bark⟩ **2** : near a center esp. of influence ⟨the ∼ circle⟩ **3** : of or relating to the mind or spirit ⟨an ∼ voice⟩ **4** : being a usu. repressed part of one's psychological makeup ⟨the ∼ child⟩

inner city : the usu. older, poorer, and more densely populated section of a city — **inner–city** adj

in·ner-di·rect·ed \ˌi-nər-də-ˈrek-təd, -(ˌ)dī-\ adj : directed in thought and action by one's own scale of values as opposed to external norms

inner ear : the part of the ear that is most important for hearing, is located in a cavity in the temporal bone, and contains sense organs of hearing and of awareness of position in space

in·ner·most \ˈi-nər-ˌmōst\ adj : farthest inward : INMOST

in·ner·sole \ˈi-nər-ˈsōl\ n : INSOLE

in·ner·spring \ˈi-nər-ˈspriŋ\ adj : having coil springs inside a padded casing ⟨an ∼ mattress⟩

inner tube n : an airtight rubber tube inside a tire to hold air under pressure

in·ning \ˈi-niŋ\ n **1** sing or pl : a division of a cricket match **2** : a baseball team's turn at bat; also : a division of a baseball game consisting of a turn at bat for each team

inn·keep·er \ˈin-ˌkē-pər\ n **1** : a proprietor of an inn **2** : a hotel manager

in·no·cence \ˈi-nə-səns\ n **1** : BLAMELESSNESS; also : freedom from legal guilt **2** : GUILELESSNESS, SIMPLICITY; also : IGNORANCE

in·no·cent \-sənt\ adj [ME, fr. AF, fr. L innocens, fr. nocens wicked, fr. nocēre to harm] **1** : free from guilt or sin : BLAMELESS **2** : harmless in effect or intention; also : CANDID ⟨an ∼ remark⟩ **3** : free from legal guilt or fault : LAWFUL **4** : INGENUOUS ⟨an ∼ question⟩ **5** : UNAWARE — **innocent** n — **in·no·cent·ly** adv

in·noc·u·ous \i-'nä-kyə-wəs\ *adj* **1** : HARMLESS **2** : not offensive; *also* : INSIPID ⟨~ jokes⟩

in·nom·i·nate \i-'nä-mə-nət\ *adj* : having no name; *also* : ANONYMOUS

in·no·vate \'i-nə-‚vāt\ *vb* **-vat·ed; -vat·ing** : to introduce as or as if new : make changes — **in·no·va·tive** \-‚vā-tiv\ *adj* — **in·no·va·tor** \-‚vā-tər\ *n*

in·no·va·tion \‚i-nə-'vā-shən\ *n* **1** : the introduction of something new **2** : a new idea, method, or device

in·nu·en·do \‚in-yə-'wen-dō\ *n, pl* **-dos** or **-does** [L, by nodding, fr. *innuere* to nod to, make a sign to, fr. *nuere* to nod] : HINT, INSINUATION; *esp* : a veiled reflection on character or reputation

in·nu·mer·a·ble \i-'nü-mə-rə-bəl, -'nyü-\ *adj* : too many to be numbered

in·oc·u·late \i-'nä-kyə-‚lāt\ *vb* **-lat·ed; -lat·ing** [ME, to insert a bud in a plant, fr. L *inoculare*, fr. *oculus* eye, bud] : to introduce something into; *esp* : to introduce a serum or antibody into (an organism) to treat or prevent a disease — **in·oc·u·la·tion** \-‚nä-kyə-'lā-shən\ *n*

in·op·er·a·ble \(‚)in-'ä-pə-rə-bəl\ *adj* **1** : not suitable for surgery ⟨an ~ tumor⟩ **2** : not operable ⟨~ vehicles⟩

in·op·er·a·tive \-'ä-pə-rə-tiv, -'ä-pə-‚rā-\ *adj* : not functioning

in·op·por·tune \(‚)in-‚ä-pər-'tün, -'tyün\ *adj* : INCONVENIENT, INAPPROPRIATE — **in·op·por·tune·ly** *adv*

in·or·di·nate \in-'ȯr-d°n-ət\ *adj* : exceeding reasonable limits : IMMODERATE ⟨drank an ~ amount of water⟩ — **in·or·di·nate·ly** *adv*

in·or·gan·ic \‚in-ȯr-'ga-nik\ *adj* : being or composed of matter of other than plant or animal origin : MINERAL

in·pa·tient \'in-‚pā-shənt\ *n* : a hospital patient who receives lodging and food as well as treatment

in·put \'in-‚pu̇t\ *n* **1** : something put in **2** : power or energy put into a machine or system **3** : information fed into a computer or data processing system **4** : ADVICE, OPINION — **input** *vb*

in·quest \'in-‚kwest\ *n* **1** : an official inquiry or examination esp. before a jury **2** : INQUIRY, INVESTIGATION

in·qui·e·tude \(‚)in-'kwī-ə-‚tüd, -‚tyüd\ *n* : UNEASINESS, RESTLESSNESS

in·quire \in-'kwī(-ə)r\ *vb* **in·quired; in·quir·ing 1** : to ask about : ASK **2** : INVESTIGATE, EXAMINE — **in·quir·er** *n* — **in·quir·ing·ly** *adv*

in·qui·ry \'in-‚kwī(-ə)r-ē, in-'kwī(-ə)r-ē; 'in-kwə-rē, 'iŋ-\ *n, pl* **-ries 1** : a request for information; *also* : RESEARCH **2** : a systematic investigation of a matter of public interest

in·qui·si·tion \‚in-kwə-'zi-shən, ‚iŋ-\ *n* **1** : a judicial or official inquiry usu. before a jury **2** *cap* : a former Roman Catholic tribunal for the discovery and punishment of heresy **3** : a severe questioning — **in·quis·i·tor** \in-'kwi-zə-tər\ *n* — **in·quis·i·to·ri·al** \-‚kwi-zə-'tȯr-ē-əl\ *adj*

in·quis·i·tive \in-'kwi-zə-tiv\ *adj* **1** : given to examination or investigation ⟨an ~ mind⟩ **2** : unduly curious — **in·quis·i·tive·ly** *adv* — **in·quis·i·tive·ness** *n*

in re \in-'rā, -'rē\ *prep* : in the matter of

INRI *abbr* [L *Iesus Nazarenus Rex Iudaeorum*] Jesus of Nazareth, King of the Jews

in·road \'in-‚rōd\ *n* **1** : INVASION, RAID **2** : an advance made usu. at the expense of another ⟨made ~s toward getting the job⟩

in·rush \'in-‚rəsh\ *n* : a crowding or flooding in

ins *abbr* **1** inches **2** insurance

INS *abbr* Immigration and Naturalization Service

in·sa·lu·bri·ous \‚in-sə-'lü-brē-əs\ *adj* : UNWHOLESOME, NOXIOUS ⟨~ air⟩

ins and outs *n pl* **1** : characteristic peculiarities **2** : RAMIFICATIONS

in·sane \(‚)in-'sān\ *adj* **1** : exhibiting serious and debilitating mental disorder; *also* : used by or for the insane **2** : ABSURD **3** : greatly exceeding the ordinary, usual, or expected — **in·sane·ly** *adv* — **in·san·i·ty** \in-'sa-nə-tē\ *n*

in·sa·tia·ble \(‚)in-'sā-shə-bəl\ *adj* : incapable of being satisfied ⟨an ~ thirst⟩ — **in·sa·tia·bil·i·ty** \(‚)in-‚sā-shə-'bi-lə-tē\ *n* — **in·sa·tia·bly** *adv*

in·sa·tiate \(‚)in-'sā-shē-ət, -shät\ *adj* : INSATIABLE — **in·sa·tiate·ly** *adv*

in·scribe \in-'skrīb\ *vb* **1** : to write, engrave, or print as a lasting record **2** : ENROLL **3** : to write, engrave, or print characters upon **4** : to dedicate to someone **5** : to draw within a figure so as to touch in as many places as possible — **in·scrip·tion** \-'skrip-shən\ *n*

in·scru·ta·ble \in-'skrü-tə-bəl\ *adj* : not readily comprehensible : MYSTERIOUS ⟨an ~ smile⟩ — **in·scru·ta·bly** \-blē\ *adv*

in·seam \'in-‚sēm\ *n* : the seam on the inside of the leg of a pair of pants; *also* : the length of this seam

in·sect \'in-‚sekt\ *n* [L *insectum*, fr. *insectus*, pp. of *insecare* to cut into, fr. *secare* to cut] : any of a class of small usu. winged arthropod animals (as flies, bees, beetles, and moths) with usu. three pairs of legs as adults

in·sec·ti·cide \in-'sek-tə-‚sīd\ *n* : an agent for destroying insects — **in·sec·ti·cid·al** \(‚)in-‚sek-tə-'sī-d°l\ *adj*

in·sec·tiv·o·rous \‚in-‚sek-'ti-və-rəs\ *adj* : feeding on insects

in·se·cure \‚in-si-'kyu̇r\ *adj* **1** : UNCERTAIN **2** : not protected : UNSAFE ⟨an ~ investment⟩ **3** : LOOSE, SHAKY ⟨an ~ hinge⟩ **4** : not highly stable ⟨an ~ marriage⟩; *also* : lacking assurance : ANXIOUS, FEARFUL — **in·se·cure·ly** *adv* — **in·se·cu·ri·ty** \-'kyu̇r-ə-tē\ *n*

in·sem·i·nate \in-'se-mə-‚nāt\ *vb* **-nat·ed; -nat·ing** : to introduce semen into the genital tract of (a female) — **in·sem·i·na·tion** \-‚se-mə-'nā-shən\ *n*

in·sen·sate \(‚)in-'sen-‚sāt, -sət\ *adj* **1** : lacking sense or understanding; *also*

: FOOLISH **2** : INANIMATE **3** : BRUTAL, INHUMAN ⟨~ rage⟩

in·sen·si·ble \(ˌ)in-ˈsen-sə-bəl\ *adj* **1** : IMPERCEPTIBLE; *also* : SLIGHT, GRADUAL **2** : INANIMATE **3** : UNCONSCIOUS **4** : lacking sensory perception or ability to react ⟨~ to pain⟩ **5** : APATHETIC, INDIFFERENT; *also* : UNAWARE ⟨~ of their danger⟩ **6** : MEANINGLESS **7** : lacking delicacy or refinement — **in·sen·si·bil·i·ty** \-ˌsen-sə-ˈbi-lə-tē\ *n* — **in·sen·si·bly** \-ˈsen-sə-blē\ *adv*

in·sen·tient \(ˌ)in-ˈsen-chē-ənt\ *adj* : lacking perception, consciousness, or animation — **in·sen·tience** \-chē-əns\ *n*

in·sep·a·ra·ble \(ˌ)in-ˈse-prə-bəl, -pə-rə-\ *adj* **1** : incapable of being separated or disjoined **2** : very close or intimate ⟨~ friends⟩ — **in·sep·a·ra·bil·i·ty** \-ˌse-prə-ˈbi-lə-tē, -pə-rə-\ *n* — **inseparable** *n* — **in·sep·a·ra·bly** \-ˈse-prə-blē, -pə-rə-\ *adv*

¹**in·sert** \in-ˈsərt\ *vb* **1** : to put or thrust in ⟨~ a key in a lock⟩ ⟨~ a comma⟩ **2** : INTERPOLATE **3** : to set in (as a piece of fabric) and make fast

²**in·sert** \ˈin-ˌsərt\ *n* : something that is inserted or is for insertion; *esp* : written or printed material inserted (as between the leaves of a book)

in·ser·tion \in-ˈsər-shən\ *n* **1** : something that is inserted **2** : the act or process of inserting

in·set \ˈin-ˌset\ *vb* inset *or* in·set·ted; in·set·ting : to set in : INSERT — **inset** *n*

¹**in·shore** \ˈin-ˈshȯr\ *adj* **1** : situated, living, or carried on near shore **2** : moving toward shore ⟨an ~ current⟩

²**inshore** *adv* : to or toward shore

¹**in·side** \in-ˈsīd, ˈin-ˌsīd\ *n* **1** : an inner side or surface : INTERIOR **2** : inward nature, thoughts, or feeling **3** *pl* : VISCERA, ENTRAILS **4** : a position of power, trust, or familiarity — **inside** *adj*

²**inside** *adv* **1** : on the inner side **2** : in or into the interior

³**inside** *prep* **1** : in or into the inside of ⟨~ the house⟩ **2** : WITHIN ⟨~ an hour⟩

inside of *prep* : INSIDE

inside out *adv* **1** : in such a manner that the inner surface becomes the outer ⟨turned the shirt *inside out*⟩ **2** : in a state of disarray or reorganization ⟨turned his life *inside out*⟩

in·sid·er \in-ˈsī-dər\ *n* : a person who is in a position of power or has access to confidential information

in·sid·i·ous \in-ˈsi-dē-əs\ *adj* [L *insidiosus*, fr. *insidiae* ambush, fr. *insidēre* to sit in, sit on, fr. *sedēre* to sit] **1** : SLY, TREACHEROUS **2** : SEDUCTIVE **3** : having a gradual and cumulative effect : SUBTLE — **in·sid·i·ous·ly** *adv* — **in·sid·i·ous·ness** *n*

in·sight \ˈin-ˌsīt\ *n* : the power, act, or result of seeing into a situation : UNDERSTANDING ⟨a leader of great ~⟩ — **in·sight·ful** \ˈin-ˌsīt-fəl, in-ˈsīt-\ *adj*

in·sig·nia \in-ˈsig-nē-ə\ *also* **in·sig·ne** \-(ˌ)nē\ *n, pl* **-nia** *or* **-ni·as** : a distinguishing mark esp. of authority or honor : BADGE

in·sin·cere \ˌin-sin-ˈsir\ *adj* : not sincere : HYPOCRITICAL — **in·sin·cere·ly** *adv* — **in·sin·cer·i·ty** \-ˈser-ə-tē\ *n*

in·sin·u·ate \in-ˈsin-yə-ˌwāt\ *vb* **-at·ed; -at·ing** [L *insinuare*, fr. *sinuare* to bend, curve, fr. *sinus* curve] **1** : to introduce gradually or in a subtle, indirect, or artful way **2** : to imply in a subtle or devious way — **in·sin·u·a·tion** \(ˌ)in-ˌsin-yə-ˈwā-shən\ *n*

in·sin·u·at·ing *adj* **1** : winning favor and confidence by imperceptible degrees **2** : tending gradually to cause doubt, distrust, or change of outlook

in·sip·id \in-ˈsi-pəd\ *adj* **1** : lacking taste or savor **2** : DULL, FLAT ⟨an ~ movie⟩ — **in·si·pid·i·ty** \ˌin-sə-ˈpi-də-tē\ *n*

in·sist \in-ˈsist\ *vb* [MF *or* L; MF *insister*, fr. L *insistere* to stand upon, persist, fr. *sistere* to take a stand] : to take a resolute stand ⟨~ed on paying⟩

in·sis·tence \in-ˈsis-təns\ *n* : the act of insisting; *also* : an insistent attitude or quality : URGENCY

in·sis·tent \in-ˈsis-tənt\ *adj* : disposed to insist — **in·sis·tent·ly** *adv*

in si·tu \in-ˈsī-tü, -ˈsē-\ *adv or adj* [L, in position] : in the natural or original position ⟨an *in situ* cancer⟩

in·so·far as \ˌin-sə-ˈfär-\ *conj* : to the extent or degree that

insol *abbr* insoluble

in·so·la·tion \ˌin-(ˌ)sō-ˈlā-shən\ *n* : solar radiation that has been received

in·sole \ˈin-ˌsōl\ *n* **1** : an inside sole of a shoe **2** : a loose thin strip placed inside a shoe for warmth or comfort

in·so·lent \ˈin-sə-lənt\ *adj* : contemptuous, rude, disrespectful, or bold in behavior or language — **in·so·lence** \-ləns\ *n*

in·sol·u·ble \(ˌ)in-ˈsäl-yə-bəl\ *adj* **1** : having or admitting of no solution or explanation **2** : difficult or impossible to dissolve — **in·sol·u·bil·i·ty** \ˌsäl-yə-ˈbi-lə-tē\ *n*

in·sol·vent \(ˌ)in-ˈsäl-vənt\ *adj* **1** : unable or insufficient to pay all debts ⟨an ~ estate⟩ **2** : IMPOVERISHED, DEFICIENT — **in·sol·ven·cy** \-vən-sē\ *n*

in·som·nia \in-ˈsäm-nē-ə\ *n* : prolonged and usu. abnormal sleeplessness — **in·som·ni·ac** \-nē-ˌak\ *n*

in·so·much as \ˌin-sə-ˈməch-\ *conj* : INASMUCH AS

insomuch that *conj* : to such a degree that : SO

in·sou·ci·ance \in-ˈsü-sē-əns, aⁿ-süs-ˈyäⁿs\ *n* [F] : lighthearted unconcern ⟨youthful ~⟩ — **in·sou·ci·ant** \in-ˈsü-sē-ənt, aⁿ-süs-ˈyäⁿ\ *adj*

insp *abbr* inspector

in·spect \in-ˈspekt\ *vb* : to view closely and critically : EXAMINE ⟨~ the gem for flaws⟩ — **in·spec·tion** \-ˈspek-shən\ *n* — **in·spec·tor** \-tər\ *n*

inspector general *n* : the head of a system of inspection (as of an army)

in·spi·ra·tion \ˌin-spə-ˈrā-shən\ *n* **1** : the act or power of moving the intellect or emotions **2** : INHALATION **3** : the quality or state of being inspired; *also* : something that is inspired **4** : an inspiring agent or influence — **in·spi·ra·tion·al** \-shə-nəl\ *adj*

in·spire \in-ˈspīr\ *vb* **in·spired; in·spir·ing** **1** : to influence, move, or guide by divine or supernatural inspiration **2** : to exert an animating, enlivening, or exalting influence upon ⟨a painter *inspired* by cubism⟩; *also* : AFFECT **3** : to communicate to an agent supernaturally; *also* : bring out or about **4** : INHALE **5** : INCITE **6** : to spread by indirect means — **in·spir·er** *n*

in·spir·it \in-ˈspir-ət\ *vb* : ENCOURAGE, HEARTEN ⟨—*ed* the team⟩

inst *abbr* **1** instant **2** institute; institution; institutional

in·sta·bil·i·ty \ˌin-stə-ˈbi-lə-tē\ *n* : lack of steadiness; *esp* : lack of emotional or mental stability

in·stal *chiefly Brit var of* INSTALL

in·stall \in-ˈstȯl\ *vb* **1** : to place formally in office : induct into an office, rank, or order **2** : to establish in an indicated place, condition, or status **3** : to set up for use or service — **in·stal·la·tion** \ˌin-stə-ˈlā-shən\ *n*

¹in·stall·ment *also* **in·stal·ment** \in-ˈstȯl-mənt\ *n* : INSTALLATION

²installment *also* **instalment** *n* **1** : one of the parts into which a debt or sum is divided for payment **2** : one of several parts presented at intervals

¹in·stance \ˈin-stəns\ *n* **1** : INSTIGATION, REQUEST **2** : EXAMPLE ⟨for —⟩ **3** : an event or step that is part of a process or series ✦ *Synonyms* CASE, ILLUSTRATION, SAMPLE, SPECIMEN

²instance *vb* **in·stanced; in·stanc·ing** : to mention as a case or example

¹in·stant \ˈin-stənt\ *n* **1** : MOMENT ⟨the — we met⟩ **2** : the present or current month

²instant *adj* **1** : URGENT **2** : PRESENT, CURRENT **3** : IMMEDIATE ⟨— relief⟩ **4** : premixed or precooked for easy final preparation ⟨— cake mix⟩; *also* : immediately soluble in water ⟨— coffee⟩

in·stan·ta·neous \ˌin-stən-ˈtā-nē-əs\ *adj* : done or occurring in an instant or without delay ⟨an — chemical reaction⟩ — **in·stan·ta·neous·ly** *adv*

in·stan·ter \in-ˈstan-tər\ *adv* : at once

in·stan·ti·ate \in-ˈstan-chē-ˌāt\ *vb* **-at·ed; -at·ing** : to represent (an abstraction) by a concrete example — **in·stan·ti·a·tion** \-ˌstan-chē-ˈā-shən\ *n*

in·stant·ly \ˈin-stənt-lē\ *adv* : at once : IMMEDIATELY

in·state \in-ˈstāt\ *vb* : to establish in a rank or office : INSTALL

in·stead \in-ˈsted\ *adv* **1** : as a substitute or equivalent **2** : as an alternative

instead of *prep* : as a substitute for or alternative ⟨use glue *instead of* paste⟩

in·step \ˈin-ˌstep\ *n* : the arched part of the human foot in front of the ankle joint; *esp* : its upper surface

in·sti·gate \ˈin-stə-ˌgāt\ *vb* **-gat·ed; -gat·ing** : to goad or urge forward : PROVOKE, INCITE ⟨— a revolt⟩ — **in·sti·ga·tion**

\ˌin-stə-ˈgā-shən\ *n* — **in·sti·ga·tor** \ˈin-stə-ˌgā-tər\ *n*

in·stil *chiefly Brit var of* INSTILL

in·still \in-ˈstil\ *vb* **1** : to cause to enter drop by drop **2** : to impart gradually

¹in·stinct \ˈin-ˌstiŋkt\ *n* **1** : a natural aptitude **2** : a largely inheritable and unalterable tendency of an organism to make a complex and specific response to environmental stimuli without involving reason; *also* : behavior originating below the conscious level — **in·stinc·tive** \in-ˈstiŋk-tiv\ *adj* — **in·stinc·tive·ly** *adv*

²instinct \in-ˈstiŋkt, ˈin-ˌstiŋkt\ *adj* : IMBUED, INFUSED

in·stinc·tu·al \in-ˈstiŋk-chə-wəl\ *adj* : of, relating to, or based on instinct

¹in·sti·tute \ˈin-stə-ˌtüt, -ˌtyüt\ *vb* **-tut·ed; -tut·ing** **1** : to establish in a position or office **2** : ORGANIZE **3** : INAUGURATE, INITIATE ⟨— a new policy⟩

²institute *n* **1** : an elementary principle recognized as authoritative; *also, pl* : a collection of such principles and precepts **2** : an organization for the promotion of a cause : ASSOCIATION **3** : an educational institution **4** : a brief course of instruction on a particular field

in·sti·tu·tion \ˌin-stə-ˈtü-shən, -ˈtyü-\ *n* **1** : an act of originating, setting up, or founding **2** : an established practice, law, or custom **3** : a society or corporation esp. of a public character ⟨a charitable —⟩; *also* : ASYLUM **3** — **in·sti·tu·tion·al** \-ˈtü-shə-nəl, -ˈtyü-\ *adj* — **in·sti·tu·tion·al·ize** \-nə-ˌlīz\ *vb* — **in·sti·tu·tion·al·ly** *adv*

instr *abbr* **1** instructor **2** instrument; instrumental

in·struct \in-ˈstrəkt\ *vb* [ME, fr. L *instructus*, pp. of *instruere*, fr. *struere* to build] **1** : TEACH **2** : INFORM **3** : to give an order or a command to

in·struc·tion \in-ˈstrək-shən\ *n* **1** : LESSON, PRECEPT **2** : COMMAND, ORDER **3** *pl* : DIRECTIONS **4** : the action, practice, or profession of a teacher — **in·struc·tion·al** \-shə-nəl\ *adj*

in·struc·tive \in-ˈstrək-tiv\ *adj* : carrying a lesson : ENLIGHTENING ⟨an — book⟩

in·struc·tor \in-ˈstrək-tər\ *n* : one that instructs; *esp* : a college teacher below professorial rank — **in·struc·tor·ship** *n*

in·stru·ment \ˈin-strə-mənt\ *n* **1** : a device used to produce music **2** : a means by which something is done **3** : a device for doing work and esp. precision work ⟨a drafting —⟩ **4** : a legal document (as a deed) **5** : a device used in navigating an airplane — **in·stru·ment** \-ˌment\ *vb*

in·stru·men·tal \ˌin-strə-ˈmen-tᵊl\ *adj* **1** : acting as a crucial agent or means ⟨was — in arranging the deal⟩ **2** : of, relating to, or done with an instrument **3** : relating to, composed for, or performed on a musical instrument

in·stru·men·tal·ist \-ˈmen-tə-list\ *n* : a player on a musical instrument

in·stru·men·tal·i·ty \ˌin-strə-mən-ˈta-lə-tē, -ˌmen-\ *n, pl* **-ties** **1** : the quality or state of being instrumental **2** : MEANS, AGENCY

in·stru·men·ta·tion \ˌin-strə-mən-ˈtā-shən, -ˌmen-\ *n* **1** : ORCHESTRATION **2** : instruments for a particular purpose

instrument panel *n* : DASHBOARD

in·sub·or·di·nate \ˌin-sə-ˈbȯr-də-nət\ *adj* : disobedient to authority — **in·sub·or·di·na·tion** \-ˌbȯr-də-ˈnā-shən\ *n*

in·sub·stan·tial \ˌin-səb-ˈstan-chəl\ *adj* **1** : lacking substance or reality **2** : lacking firmness or solidity

in·suf·fer·able \(ˌ)in-ˈsə-fə-rə-bəl\ *adj* : not to be endured : INTOLERABLE ⟨an ~ bore⟩ — **in·suf·fer·ably** \-blē\ *adv*

in·suf·fi·cient \ˌin-sə-ˈfish-ənt\ *adj* : not sufficient ⟨~ funds⟩; *also* : lacking capacity — **in·suf·fi·cien·cy** \-shən-sē\ *n* — **in·suf·fi·cient·ly** *adv*

in·su·lar \ˈin-sə-lər, -syə-\ *adj* **1** : of, relating to, or forming an island **2** : dwelling or situated on an island **3** : NARROW-MINDED ⟨an ~ perspective⟩ — **in·su·lar·i·ty** \ˌin-sə-ˈlar-ə-tē, -syə-\ *n*

in·su·late \ˈin-sə-ˌlāt\ *vb* **-lat·ed; -lat·ing** [L *insula* island] : ISOLATE; *esp* : to separate a conductor of electricity, heat, or sound from other conducting bodies by means of a nonconductor — **in·su·la·tion** \ˌin-sə-ˈlā-shən\ *n* — **in·su·la·tor** \ˈin-sə-ˌlā-tər\ *n*

in·su·lin \ˈin-sə-lən\ *n* : a pancreatic hormone essential esp. for the metabolism of carbohydrates and the regulation of glucose levels in the blood

¹in·sult \in-ˈsəlt\ *vb* [MF *or* L; MF *insulter*, fr. L *insultare*, lit., to spring upon, fr. *saltare* to leap] : to treat with insolence or contempt : AFFRONT ⟨were ~ed by his rudeness⟩ — **in·sult·ing·ly** *adv*

²in·sult \ˈin-ˌsəlt\ *n* : a gross indignity

in·su·per·a·ble \(ˌ)in-ˈsü-pə-rə-bəl\ *adj* : incapable of being surmounted, overcome, passed over, or solved — **in·su·per·a·bly** \-blē\ *adv*

in·sup·port·able \ˌin-sə-ˈpȯr-tə-bəl\ *adj* **1** : UNENDURABLE **2** : UNJUSTIFIABLE

in·sur·able \in-ˈshu̇r-ə-bəl\ *adj* : capable of being or proper to be insured

in·sur·ance \in-ˈshu̇r-əns\ *n* **1** : the business of insuring persons or property **2** : coverage by contract whereby one party agrees to guarantee another against a specified loss **3** : the sum for which something is insured **4** : a means of guaranteeing protection or safety

in·sure \in-ˈshu̇r\ *vb* **in·sured; in·sur·ing** **1** : to provide or obtain insurance on or for : UNDERWRITE **2** : to make certain : ENSURE

in·sured \in-ˈshu̇rd\ *n* : a person whose life or property is insured

in·sur·er \in-ˈshu̇r-ər\ *n* : one that insures; *esp* : an insurance company

in·sur·gent \in-ˈsər-jənt\ *n* **1** : a person who revolts against civil authority or an established government : REBEL **2** : a member of a political party who rebels against it — **in·sur·gence** \-jəns\ *n* — **in·sur·gen·cy** \-jən-sē\ *n* — **in·sur·gent** *adj*

in·sur·mount·able \ˌin-sər-ˈmau̇n-tə-bəl\ *adj* : INSUPERABLE ⟨~ problems⟩ — **in·sur·mount·ably** \-blē\ *adv*

in·sur·rec·tion \ˌin-sə-ˈrek-shən\ *n* : an act or instance of revolting against civil authority or an established government — **in·sur·rec·tion·ist** \-shə-nist\ *n*

int *abbr* **1** interest **2** interior **3** intermediate **4** internal **5** international **6** intransitive

in·tact \in-ˈtakt\ *adj* : untouched esp. by anything that harms or diminishes

in·ta·glio \in-ˈtal-yō\ *n, pl* **-glios** [It] : an engraving cut deeply into the surface of a hard material (as stone)

in·take \ˈin-ˌtāk\ *n* **1** : an opening through which fluid enters **2** : the act of taking in **3** : something taken in

¹in·tan·gi·ble \(ˌ)in-ˈtan-jə-bəl\ *adj* : incapable of being touched : IMPALPABLE ⟨~ benefits⟩ — **in·tan·gi·bly** \-blē\ *adv*

²intangible *n* **1** : an incorporeal asset **2** : an abstract quality or attribute

in·te·ger \ˈin-ti-jər\ *n* [L, adj., whole, entire] : a number (as 1, 2, 3, 12, 432) that is not a fraction and does not include a fraction, is the negative of such a number, or is 0

¹in·te·gral \ˈin-ti-grəl\ *adj* **1** : essential to completeness ⟨~ to the company⟩ **2** : formed as a unit with another part **3** : composed of parts that make up a whole **4** : ENTIRE

²integral *n* : the result of a mathematical integration

in·te·grate \ˈin-tə-ˌgrāt\ *vb* **-grat·ed; -grat·ing** **1** : to find a function that has a given derivative **2** : to form, coordinate, or blend into a functioning whole : UNITE **3** : to incorporate into a larger unit **4** : to end the segregation of and bring into equal membership in society or an organization; *also* : DESEGREGATE — **in·te·gra·tion** \ˌin-tə-ˈgrā-shən\ *n*

integrated circuit *n* : a group of tiny electronic components and their connections that is produced in or on a small slice of material (as silicon)

in·teg·ri·ty \in-ˈte-grə-tē\ *n* **1** : adherence to a code of values : INCORRUPTIBILITY **2** : SOUNDNESS **3** : COMPLETENESS

in·teg·u·ment \in-ˈte-gyə-mənt\ *n* : a covering layer (as a skin or cuticle) of an organism or one of its parts

in·tel·lect \ˈin-tə-ˌlekt\ *n* **1** : the power of knowing : the capacity for knowledge **2** : the capacity for rational or intelligent thought esp. when highly developed **3** : a person with great intellectual powers

in·tel·lec·tu·al \ˌin-tə-ˈlek-chə-wəl\ *adj* **1** : of, relating to, or performed by the intellect : RATIONAL **2** : given to study, reflection, and speculation ⟨~ games⟩ **3** : engaged in activity requiring the creative use of the intellect — **intellectual** *n* — **in·tel·lec·tu·al·ly** *adv*

in·tel·lec·tu·al·ism \-chə-wə-ˌli-zəm\ *n* : devotion to the exercise of intellect or to intellectual pursuits

in·tel·li·gence \in-ˈte-lə-jəns\ *n* **1** : ability to learn and understand or to deal with new or trying situations **2** : mental acuteness **3** : INFORMATION, NEWS **4** : an agency engaged in obtaining information esp. concerning an enemy or possible enemy; *also* : the information so gained

intelligence quotient *n* : IQ

in·tel·li·gent \in-'te-lə-jənt\ *adj* [L *intelligens,* fr. *intelligere* to understand, fr. *inter* between + *legere* to select] : having or showing intelligence or intellect ⟨an ∼ decision⟩ — **in·tel·li·gent·ly** *adv*

in·tel·li·gen·tsia \in-ˌte-lə-'jent-sē-ə, -'gent-\ *n* [Russ *intelligentsiya,* fr. L *intelligentia* intelligence] : intellectuals forming a vanguard or elite

in·tel·li·gi·ble \in-'te-lə-jə-bəl\ *adj* : capable of being understood or comprehended ⟨a very ∼ plan⟩ — **in·tel·li·gi·bil·i·ty** \-ˌte-lə-jə-'bi-lə-tē\ *n* — **in·tel·li·gi·bly** \-'te-lə-jə-blē\ *adv*

in·tem·per·ance \(ˌ)in-'tem-pə-rəns\ *n* : lack of moderation; *esp* : habitual or excessive drinking of intoxicants — **in·tem·per·ate** \-pə-rət\ *adj* — **in·tem·per·ate·ness** *n*

in·tend \in-'tend\ *vb* [ME *entenden, intenden,* fr. AF *entendre,* fr. L *intendere* to stretch out, direct, aim at, fr. *tendere* to stretch] **1** : to have in mind as a purpose or aim ⟨∼s to retire⟩ **2** : to design for a specified use or future ⟨programs ∼ed to help students⟩

in·ten·dant \in-'ten-dənt\ *n* : an official (as a governor) esp. under the French, Spanish, or Portuguese monarchies

¹in·tend·ed *adj* **1** : expected to be such in the future; *esp* : BETROTHED **2** : INTENTIONAL ⟨an ∼ pun⟩

²intended *n* : an engaged person

in·tense \in-'tens\ *adj* **1** : existing in an extreme degree ⟨∼ pain⟩ **2** : marked by great zeal, energy, or eagerness ⟨∼ effort⟩ **3** : showing strong feeling; *also* : deeply felt — **in·tense·ly** *adv*

in·ten·si·fy \in-'ten-sə-ˌfī\ *vb* **-fied; -fy·ing 1** : to make or become intense or more intensive **2** : to make more acute : SHARPEN ♦ *Synonyms* AGGRAVATE, HEIGHTEN, ENHANCE, MAGNIFY — **in·ten·si·fi·ca·tion** \-ˌten-sə-fə-'kā-shən\ *n*

in·ten·si·ty \in-'ten-sə-tē\ *n, pl* **-ties 1** : the quality or state of being intense; *esp* : degree of strength, energy, or force

¹in·ten·sive \in-'ten-siv\ *adj* **1** : highly concentrated **2** : serving to give emphasis — **in·ten·sive·ly** *adv*

²intensive *n* : an intensive word, particle, or prefix (the word "very" is an ∼)

intensive care *n* : continuous monitoring and treatment of seriously ill patients; *also* : an area of a hospital providing this treatment

¹in·tent \in-'tent\ *n* **1** : the state of mind with which an act is done : VOLITION **2** : PURPOSE, AIM ⟨the artist's ∼⟩ **3** : MEANING, SIGNIFICANCE

²intent *adj* **1** : directed with keen attention ⟨an ∼ gaze⟩ **2** : ENGROSSED; *also* : DETERMINED ⟨∼ on winning⟩ — **in·tent·ly** *adv* — **in·tent·ness** *n*

in·ten·tion \in-'ten-chən\ *n* **1** : a determination to act in a certain way **2** : PUR-

POSE, AIM, END ♦ *Synonyms* INTENT, DESIGN, OBJECT, OBJECTIVE, GOAL

in·ten·tion·al \in-'ten-chə-nəl\ *adj* : done by intention or design : INTENDED — **in·ten·tion·al·ly** *adv*

in·ter \in-'tər\ *vb* **in·terred; in·ter·ring** : BURY

in·ter·ac·tion \ˌin-tər-'ak-shən\ *n* : mutual or reciprocal action or influence — **in·ter·act** \-'akt\ *vb*

in·ter·ac·tive \-'ak-tiv\ *adj* **1** : mutually or reciprocally active **2** : involving the actions or input of a user ⟨∼ exhibits⟩ **3** : allowing two-way electronic communications (as between a person and a computer) — **in·ter·ac·tive·ly** *adv* — **in·ter·ac·tiv·i·ty** \-ˌak-'ti-və-tē\ *n*

in·ter alia \ˌin-tər-'ā-lē-ə, -'ä-\ *adv* : among other things

in·ter·atom·ic \ˌin-tər-ə-'tä-mik\ *adj* : existing or acting between atoms

in·ter·breed \-'brēd\ *vb* **-bred** \-'bred\; **-breed·ing** : to breed together

in·ter·ca·la·ry \in-'tər-kə-ˌler-ē\ *adj* **1** : INTERCALATED ⟨February 29 is an ∼ day⟩ **2** : INTERPOLATED

in·ter·ca·late \-ˌlāt\ *vb* **-lat·ed; -lat·ing 1** : to insert (as a day) in a calendar **2** : to insert between or among existing elements or layers — **in·ter·ca·la·tion** \-ˌtər-kə-'lā-shən\ *n*

in·ter·cede \ˌin-tər-'sēd\ *vb* **-ced·ed; -ced·ing** : to act between parties with a view to reconciling differences

¹in·ter·cept \ˌin-tər-'sept\ *vb* **1** : to stop or interrupt the progress or course of **2** : to include (as part of a curve or solid) between two points, curves, or surfaces **3** : to gain possession of (an opponent's pass) — **in·ter·cep·tion** \-'sep-shən\ *n*

²in·ter·cept \'in-tər-ˌsept\ *n* : INTERCEPTION; *esp* : the interception of a target by an interceptor or missile

in·ter·cep·tor \ˌin-tər-'sep-tər\ *n* : a fighter plane designed for defense against attacking bombers

in·ter·ces·sion \ˌin-tər-'se-shən\ *n* **1** : MEDIATION **2** : prayer or petition in favor of another — **in·ter·ces·sor** \-'se-sər\ *n* — **in·ter·ces·so·ry** \-'se-sə-rē\ *adj*

¹in·ter·change \ˌin-tər-'chānj\ *vb* **1** : to put each in the place of the other **2** : EXCHANGE **3** : to change places mutually — **in·ter·change·able** \-'chān-jə-bəl\ *adj* — **in·ter·change·ably** \-blē\ *adv*

²in·ter·change \'in-tər-ˌchānj\ *n* **1** : EXCHANGE **2** : a highway junction that by separated levels permits passage between highways without crossing traffic streams

in·ter·col·le·giate \ˌin-tər-kə-'lē-jət\ *adj* : existing or carried on between colleges ⟨∼ sports⟩

in·ter·com \'in-tər-ˌkäm\ *n* : a two-way system for localized communication

in·ter·con·nect \ˌin-tər-kə-'nekt\ *vb* : to connect with one another — **in·ter·con·nec·tion** \-'nek-shən\ *n*

in·ter·con·ti·nen·tal \-ˌkän-tə-'nen-t°l\ *adj* **1** : extending among or carried on between continents ⟨∼ trade⟩ **2** : capable of traveling between continents ⟨∼ ballistic missiles⟩

in·ter·course \'in-tər-ˌkȯrs\ *n* 1 : connection or dealings between persons or nations 2 : physical sexual contact between individuals that involves the genitalia of at least one person ⟨anal ∼⟩; *esp* : SEXUAL INTERCOURSE

in·ter·de·nom·i·na·tion·al \ˌin-tər-di-ˌnä-mə-ˈnā-shə-nəl\ *adj* : involving different denominations

in·ter·de·part·men·tal \ˌin-tər-di-ˌpärt-ˈmen-tᵊl, -ˌdē-\ *adj* : carried on between or involving different departments (as of a college)

in·ter·de·pen·dent \ˌin-tər-di-ˈpen-dənt\ *adj* : dependent upon one another — **in·ter·de·pen·dence** \-dəns\ *n*

in·ter·dict \ˌin-tər-ˈdikt\ *vb* 1 : to prohibit by decree 2 : to destroy, cut off, or damage (as an enemy line of supply) : INTERCEPT ⟨∼ed drug shipments⟩ — **in·ter·dic·tion** \-ˈdik-shən\ *n*

in·ter·dis·ci·plin·ary \-ˈdi-sə-plə-ˌner-ē\ *adj* : involving two or more academic, scientific, or artistic disciplines

¹**in·ter·est** \'in-trəst; 'in-tə-rəst, -ˌrest\ *n* 1 : right, title, or legal share in something 2 : a charge for borrowed money that is generally a percentage of the amount borrowed; *also* : the return received by capital on its investment 3 : WELFARE, BENEFIT; *also* : SELF-INTEREST 4 : CURIOSITY, CONCERN 5 : readiness to be concerned with or moved by an object or class of objects 6 : a quality in a thing that arouses interest

²**interest** *vb* 1 : to persuade to participate or engage 2 : to engage the attention of

in·ter·est·ing *adj* : holding the attention — **in·ter·est·ing·ly** *adv*

¹**in·ter·face** \'in-tər-ˌfās\ *n* 1 : a surface forming a common boundary of two bodies, spaces, or phases ⟨an oil-water ∼⟩ 2 : the place at which two independent systems meet and act on or communicate with each other ⟨the man-machine ∼⟩ 3 : the means by which interaction or communication is achieved at an interface — **in·ter·fa·cial** \ˌin-tər-ˈfā-shəl\ *adj*

²**interface** *vb* **-faced; -fac·ing** 1 : to connect by means of an interface 2 : to serve as an interface

in·ter·faith \ˌin-tər-ˈfāth\ *adj* : involving persons of different religious faiths

in·ter·fere \ˌin-tər-ˈfir\ *vb* **-fered; -fer·ing** [ME *enterferen*, fr. AF *(s')entreferir* to strike one another, fr. *entre* between, among + *ferir* to strike, fr. L *ferire*] 1 : to come in collision or be in opposition : CLASH 2 : to enter into the affairs of others 3 : to affect one another

in·ter·fer·ence \-ˈfir-əns\ *n* 1 : the act or process of interfering 2 : something that interferes : OBSTRUCTION 3 : the mutual effect on meeting of two waves resulting in areas of increased and decreased amplitude 4 : the blocking of an opponent in football to make way for the ballcarrier 5 : the illegal hindering of an opponent in sports

in·ter·fer·om·e·ter \ˌin-tər-fə-ˈrä-mə-tər\ *n* : an apparatus that uses the interference of waves (as of light) for making precise measurements — **in·ter·fer·om·e·try** \-fə-ˈrä-mə-trē\ *n*

in·ter·fer·on \ˌin-tər-ˈfir-ˌän\ *n* : any of a group of antiviral proteins of low molecular weight produced usu. by animal cells in response to a virus, a parasite in the cell, or a chemical

in·ter·ga·lac·tic \ˌin-tər-gə-ˈlak-tik\ *adj* : relating to or situated in the spaces between galaxies

in·ter·gen·er·a·tion·al \-ˌje-nə-ˈrā-shə-nəl\ *adj* : existing or occurring between generations ⟨∼ conflicts⟩

in·ter·gla·cial \-ˈglā-shəl\ *n* : a warm period between successive glaciations

in·ter·gov·ern·men·tal \-ˌgə-vərn-ˈmen-tᵊl\ *adj* : existing or occurring between two governments or levels of government

in·ter·im \'in-tə-rəm\ *n* [L, adv., meanwhile, fr. *inter* between] : a time intervening : INTERVAL — **interim** *adj*

¹**in·te·ri·or** \in-ˈtir-ē-ər\ *adj* 1 : lying, occurring, or functioning within the limiting boundaries : INSIDE, INNER 2 : remote from the surface, border, or shore : INLAND

²**interior** *n* 1 : the inland part (as of a country) 2 : INSIDE 3 : the internal affairs of a state or nation 4 : a scene or view of the interior of a building

interior decoration *n* : INTERIOR DESIGN — **interior decorator** *n*

interior design *n* : the art or practice of planning and supervising the design and execution of architectural interiors and their furnishings — **interior designer** *n*

interj *abbr* interjection

in·ter·ject \ˌin-tər-ˈjekt\ *vb* : to throw in between or among other things

in·ter·jec·tion \ˌin-tər-ˈjek-shən\ *n* : an exclamatory word (as *ouch*) — **in·ter·jec·tion·al·ly** \-shə-nə-lē\ *adv*

in·ter·lace \ˌin-tər-ˈlās\ *vb* 1 : to unite by or as if by lacing together : INTERWEAVE 2 : INTERSPERSE

in·ter·lard \ˌin-tər-ˈlärd\ *vb* : to vary by inserting or interjecting something ⟨a speech ∼ed with anecdotes⟩

in·ter·leave \ˌin-tər-ˈlēv\ *vb* **-leaved; -leav·ing** : to arrange in alternate layers

in·ter·leu·kin \ˌin-tər-ˈlü-kən\ *n* : any of several proteins of low molecular weight that are produced by cells of the body and regulate the immune system and immune responses

¹**in·ter·line** \ˌin-tər-ˈlīn\ *vb* : to insert between lines already written or printed

²**interline** *vb* : to provide (as a coat) with an interlining

in·ter·lin·ear \ˌin-tər-ˈli-nē-ər\ *adj* : inserted between lines already written or printed ⟨an ∼ translation of a text⟩

in·ter·lin·gual \ˌin-tər-ˈliŋ-gwəl\ *adj* : of, relating to, or existing between two or more languages

in·ter·lin·ing \'in-tər-ˌlī-niŋ\ *n* : a lining (as of a coat) between the ordinary lining and the outside fabric

in·ter·link \ˌin-tər-ˈliŋk\ *vb* : to link together

in·ter·lock \ˌin-tər-ˈläk\ *vb* 1 : to engage or interlace together : lock together

: UNITE **2** : to connect so that action of one part affects action of another part — **in·ter·lock** \'in-tər-ˌläk\ n

in·ter·loc·u·tor \ˌin-tər-'lä-kyə-tər\ n : one who takes part in dialogue or conversation

in·ter·loc·u·to·ry \-ˌtȯr-ē\ adj : made during the progress of a legal action and not final or definite ⟨an ~ decree⟩

in·ter·lope \ˌin-tər-'lōp\ vb **-loped; -lop·ing 1** : to encroach on the rights (as in trade) of others **2** : INTRUDE, INTERFERE — **in·ter·lop·er** n

in·ter·lude \'in-tər-ˌlüd\ n **1** : a usu. short simple play or dramatic entertainment **2** : an intervening period, space, or event **3** : a piece of music inserted between the parts of a longer composition or a religious service

in·ter·mar·riage \ˌin-tər-'mer-ij\ n **1** : marriage within one's own group as required by custom **2** : marriage between members of different groups

in·ter·mar·ry \-'mer-ē\ vb **1** : to marry each other **2** : to marry within a group **3** : to become connected by intermarriage

¹in·ter·me·di·ary \ˌin-tər-'mē-dē-ˌer-ē\ adj **1** : INTERMEDIATE **2** : acting as a mediator

²intermediary n, pl **-ar·ies** : MEDIATOR, GO-BETWEEN

¹in·ter·me·di·ate \ˌin-tər-'mē-dē-ət\ adj : being or occurring at the middle place or degree or between extremes

²intermediate n **1** : one that is intermediate **2** : INTERMEDIARY

intermediate school n **1** : JUNIOR HIGH SCHOOL **2** : a school usu. comprising grades 4–6

in·ter·ment \in-'tər-mənt\ n : BURIAL

in·ter·mez·zo \ˌin-tər-'met-sō, -'med-zō\ n, pl **-zi** \-sē, -zē\ or **-zos** [It, ultim. fr. L intermedius intermediate] : a short movement connecting major sections of an extended musical work (as a symphony); also : a short independent instrumental composition

in·ter·mi·na·ble \(ˌ)in-'tər-mə-nə-bəl\ adj : ENDLESS; esp : wearisomely protracted — **in·ter·mi·na·bly** \-blē\ adv

in·ter·min·gle \ˌin-tər-'miŋ-gəl\ vb : to mingle or mix together

in·ter·mis·sion \ˌin-tər-'mi-shən\ n **1** : INTERRUPTION, BREAK **2** : a temporary halt esp. in a public performance

in·ter·mit \-'mit\ vb **-mit·ted; -mit·ting** : DISCONTINUE; also : to be intermittent

in·ter·mit·tent \-'mi-t²nt\ adj : coming and going at intervals ⟨~ rain⟩ ♦ **Synonyms** RECURRENT, PERIODIC, ALTERNATE — **in·ter·mit·tent·ly** adv

in·ter·mix \ˌin-tər-'miks\ vb : to mix together : INTERMINGLE — **in·ter·mix·ture** \-'miks-chər\ n

in·ter·mo·lec·u·lar \-mə-'le-kyə-lər\ adj : existing or acting between molecules

in·ter·mon·tane \ˌin-tər-'män-ˌtān\ adj : situated between mountains

¹in·tern \'in-ˌtərn, in-'tərn\ vb : to confine or impound esp. during a war — **in·tern·ee** \(ˌ)in-ˌtər-'nē\ n — **in·tern·ment** \-'tərn-mənt\ n

²in·tern also **in·terne** \'in-ˌtərn\ n : an advanced student or recent graduate (as in medicine) gaining supervised practical experience — **in·tern·ship** n

³in·tern \'in-ˌtərn\ vb : to work as an intern

in·ter·nal \in-'tər-n²l\ adj **1** : INWARD, INTERIOR **2** : relating to or located in the inside of the body ⟨~ pain⟩ **3** : of, relating to, or occurring within the confines of an organized structure ⟨~ affairs⟩ **4** : of, relating to, or existing within the mind **5** : INTRINSIC, INHERENT ⟨~ evidence⟩ — **in·ter·nal·ly** adv

internal combustion engine n : an engine in which the fuel is ignited within the engine cylinder

in·ter·nal·ise Brit var of INTERNALIZE

in·ter·nal·ize \in-'tər-nə-ˌlīz\ vb **-ized; -iz·ing** : to incorporate (as values) within the self through learning or socialization ⟨internalized their parents' values⟩ — **in·ter·nal·i·za·tion** \-ˌtər-nə-lə-'zā-shən\ n

internal medicine n : a branch of medicine that deals with the diagnosis and treatment of diseases not requiring surgery

¹in·ter·na·tion·al \ˌin-tər-'na-shə-nəl\ adj **1** : common to or affecting two or more nations ⟨~ trade⟩ **2** : of, relating to, or constituting a group having members in two or more nations — **in·ter·na·tion·al·ly** adv

²international n : one that is international; esp : an organization of international scope

in·ter·na·tion·al·ise Brit var of INTERNATIONALIZE

in·ter·na·tion·al·ism \-'na-shə-nə-ˌli-zəm\ n : a policy of cooperation among nations; also : an attitude favoring such a policy — **in·ter·na·tion·al·ist** \-ˌlist\ n or adj

in·ter·na·tion·al·ize \-'na-shə-nə-ˌlīz\ vb : to make international; esp : to place under international control

International System of Units n : a system of units based on the metric system and used by international convention esp. for scientific work

in·ter·ne·cine \ˌin-tər-'ne-ˌsēn, -'nē-ˌsīn\ adj [L internecinus, fr. internecare to destroy, kill, fr. necare to kill, fr. nec-, nex violent death] **1** : DEADLY; esp : mutually destructive **2** : of, relating to, or involving conflict within a group ⟨~ feuds⟩

In·ter·net \'in-tər-ˌnet\ n : an electronic communications network that connects computer networks worldwide

in·ter·nist \'in-ˌtər-nist\ n : a physician who specializes in internal medicine

in·ter·nun·cio \ˌin-tər-'nən-sē-ˌō, -'nùn-\ n [It internunzio] : a papal legate of lower rank than a nuncio

in·ter·of·fice \-'ȯ-fəs\ adj : functioning or communicating between the offices of an organization

in·ter·per·son·al \-'pər-sə-nəl\ adj : being, relating to, or involving relations between persons ⟨~ communication⟩ — **in·ter·per·son·al·ly** adv

in·ter·plan·e·tary \ˌin-tər-'pla-nə-ˌter-ē\

adj : existing, carried on, or operating between planets ⟨∼ space⟩

in·ter·play \'in-tər-ˌplā\ *n* : INTERACTION

in·ter·po·late \in-'tər-pə-ˌlāt\ *vb* **-lat·ed; -lat·ing 1** : to change (as a text) by inserting new or foreign matter **2** : to insert (as words) into a text or into a conversation **3** : to estimate values of (data or a function) between two known values — **in·ter·po·la·tion** \-ˌtər-pə-'lā-shən\ *n*

in·ter·pose \ˌin-tər-'pōz\ *vb* **-posed; -pos·ing 1** : to place between **2** : to thrust in : INTRUDE, INTERRUPT **3** : to inject between parts of a conversation or argument **4** : to come or be between

♦ *Synonyms* INTERFERE, INTERCEDE, INTERMEDIATE, INTERVENE — **in·ter·po·si·tion** \-pə-'zi-shən\ *n*

in·ter·pret \in-'tər-prət\ *vb* **1** : to explain the meaning of; *also* : to act as an interpreter : TRANSLATE **2** : to understand according to individual belief, judgment, or interest **3** : to represent artistically — **in·ter·pret·er** *n* — **in·ter·pre·tive** \-'tər-prə-tiv\ *adj*

in·ter·pre·ta·tion \in-ˌtər-prə-'tā-shən\ *n* **1** : EXPLANATION ⟨∼ of the law⟩ **2** : an instance of artistic interpretation in performance or adaptation — **in·ter·pre·ta·tive** \-'tər-prə-ˌtā-tiv\ *adj*

in·ter·ra·cial \-'rā-shəl\ *adj* : of, involving, or designed for members of different races

in·ter·reg·num \ˌin-tə-'reg-nəm\ *n, pl* **-nums** *or* **-na** \-nə\ **1** : the time during which a throne is vacant between two successive reigns or regimes **2** : a pause in a continuous series

in·ter·re·late \ˌin-tər-ri-'lāt\ *vb* : to bring into or have a mutual relationship — **in·ter·re·lat·ed·ness** \-'lā-təd-nəs\ *n* — **in·ter·re·la·tion** \-'lā-shən\ *n* — **in·ter·re·la·tion·ship** *n*

interrog *abbr* interrogative

in·ter·ro·gate \in-'ter-ə-ˌgāt\ *vb* **-gat·ed; -gat·ing** : to question esp. formally and systematically ⟨∼ a suspect⟩ — **in·ter·ro·ga·tion** \-ˌter-ə-'gā-shən\ *n* — **in·ter·ro·ga·tor** \-'ter-ə-ˌgā-tər\ *n*

in·ter·rog·a·tive \ˌin-tə-'rä-gə-tiv\ *adj* : asking a question ⟨∼ sentence⟩ — **interrogative** *n* — **in·ter·rog·a·tive·ly** *adv*

in·ter·rog·a·to·ry \ˌin-tə-'rä-gə-ˌtȯr-ē\ *adj* : INTERROGATIVE

in·ter·rupt \ˌin-tə-'rəpt\ *vb* **1** : to stop or hinder by breaking in **2** : to break the uniformity or continuity of **3** : to break in by speaking while another is speaking — **in·ter·rupt·er** *n* — **in·ter·rup·tion** \-'rəp-shən\ *n* — **in·ter·rup·tive** \-'rəp-tiv\ *adv*

in·ter·scho·las·tic \ˌin-tər-skə-'las-tik\ *adj* : existing or carried on between schools ⟨∼ sports⟩

in·ter·sect \ˌin-tər-'sekt\ *vb* **1** : to divide by passing through or across **2** : to meet and cross (as at a point); *also* : OVERLAP — **in·ter·sec·tion** \-'sek-shən\ *n*

in·ter·sperse \ˌin-tər-'spərs\ *vb* **-spersed; -spers·ing 1** : to place something at intervals in or among **2** : to insert at intervals among other things — **in·ter·sper·sion** \-'spər-zhən\ *n*

¹in·ter·state \ˌin-tər-'stāt\ *adj* : relating to, including, or connecting two or more states esp. of the U.S. ⟨∼ commerce⟩

²in·ter·state \'in-tər-ˌstāt\ *n* : an interstate highway

in·ter·stel·lar \ˌin-tər-'ste-lər\ *adj* : located or taking place among the stars

in·ter·stice \in-'tər-stəs\ *n, pl* **-stic·es** \-stə-ˌsēz, -stə-səz\ : a space that intervenes between things : CHINK — **in·ter·sti·tial** \ˌin-tər-'sti-shəl\ *adj*

in·ter·tid·al \ˌin-tər-'tī-dᵊl\ *adj* : of, relating to, or being the area that is above low-tide mark but exposed to tidal flooding ⟨life in the ∼ mud⟩

in·ter·twine \-'twīn\ *vb* : to twine or cause to twine about one another : INTERLACE — **in·ter·twine·ment** *n*

in·ter·twist \-'twist\ *vb* : INTERTWINE

in·ter·ur·ban \-'ər-bən\ *adj* : connecting cities or towns

in·ter·val \'in-tər-vəl\ *n* [ME *intervalle*, fr. AF & L; AF *entreval*, fr. L *intervallum* space between ramparts, interval, fr. *inter*- between + *vallum* rampart] **1** : a space of time between events or states : PAUSE **2** : a space between objects, units, or states **3** : the difference in pitch between two tones

in·ter·vene \ˌin-tər-'vēn\ *vb* **-vened; -ven·ing 1** : to occur, fall, or come between points of time or between events **2** : to enter or appear as an unrelated feature or circumstance ⟨rain *intervened* and we postponed the trip⟩ **3** : to come in or between in order to stop, settle, or modify ⟨∼ in a quarrel⟩ **4** : to occur or lie between two things — **in·ter·ven·tion** \-'ven-chən\ *n*

in·ter·ven·tion·ism \-'ven-chə-ˌni-zəm\ *n* : interference by one country in the political affairs of another — **in·ter·ven·tion·ist** \-'ven-chə-nist\ *n or adj*

in·ter·view \'in-tər-ˌvyü\ *n* **1** : a formal consultation usu. to evaluate qualifications **2** : a meeting at which a writer or reporter obtains information from a person; *also* : the recorded or written account of such a meeting — **interview** *vb* — **in·ter·view·ee** \ˌin-tər-(ˌ)vyü-'ē\ *n* — **in·ter·view·er** *n*

in·ter·vo·cal·ic \ˌin-tər-vō-'ka-lik\ *adj* : immediately preceded and immediately followed by a vowel ⟨an ∼ consonant⟩

in·ter·weave \ˌin-tər-'wēv\ *vb* **-wove** \-'wōv\ *also* **-weaved; -wo·ven** \-'wō-vən\ *also* **-weaved; -weav·ing** : to weave or blend together : INTERTWINE, INTERMINGLE — **interwoven** *adj*

in·tes·tate \in-'tes-ˌtāt, -tət\ *adj* **1** : having made no valid will ⟨died ∼⟩ **2** : not disposed of by will ⟨∼ estate⟩

in·tes·tine \in-'tes-tən\ *n* : the tubular part of the alimentary canal that extends from stomach to anus and consists of a long narrow upper part (**small intestine**) followed by a broader shorter lower part (**large intestine**) — **in·tes·ti·nal** \-tə-nᵊl\ *adj*

in·ti·fa·da \ˌin-tə-'fä-də\ *n* : an armed uprising of Palestinians against Israeli occupation of the West Bank and Gaza Strip

¹in·ti·mate \'in-tə-ˌmāt\ *vb* **-mat·ed; -mat·ing** [LL *intimare* to put in, announce, fr. L *intimus* innermost] **1** : ANNOUNCE, NOTIFY **2** : to communicate indirectly : HINT — **in·ti·ma·tion** \ˌin-tə-mā-shən\ *n*

²in·ti·mate \'in-tə-mət\ *adj* **1** : INTRINSIC; *also* : INNERMOST **2** : marked by very close association, contact, or familiarity **3** : marked by a warm friendship ⟨~ friends⟩ **4** : suggesting informal warmth or privacy **5** : of a very personal or private nature ⟨~ feelings⟩ — **in·ti·ma·cy** \'in-tə-mə-sē\ *n* — **in·ti·mate·ly** *adv*

³in·ti·mate \'in-tə-mət\ *n* : an intimate friend, associate, or confidant

in·tim·i·date \in-'ti-mə-ˌdāt\ *vb* **-dat·ed; -dat·ing** : to make timid or fearful : FRIGHTEN; *esp* : to compel or deter by or as if by threats ♦ *Synonyms* COW, BULLDOZE, BULLY, BROWBEAT — **in·tim·i·dat·ing·ly** *adv* — **in·tim·i·da·tion** \-ˌti-mə-'dā-shən\ *n*

intl *or* **intnl** *abbr* international

in·to \'in-tü\ *prep* **1** : to the inside of ⟨ran ~ the house⟩ **2** : to the state, condition, or form of ⟨got ~ trouble⟩ **3** : AGAINST ⟨ran ~ a wall⟩

in·tol·er·a·ble \(ˌ)in-'tä-lə-rə-bəl\ *adj* **1** : UNBEARABLE ⟨~ pain⟩ **2** : EXCESSIVE — **in·tol·er·a·bly** \-blē\ *adv*

in·tol·er·ant \(ˌ)in-'tä-lə-rənt\ *adj* **1** : unable or unwilling to endure ⟨is lactose ~⟩ **2** : unwilling to grant equality, freedom, or other social rights : BIGOTED — **in·tol·er·ance** \-rəns\ *n*

in·to·na·tion \ˌin-tō-'nā-shən\ *n* **1** : something that is intoned **2** : the act of intoning and esp. of chanting **3** : the manner of singing, playing, or uttering tones; *esp* : the rise and fall in pitch of the voice in speech

in·tone \in-'tōn\ *vb* **in·toned; in·ton·ing** : to utter in musical or prolonged tones : CHANT ⟨~ a prayer⟩

in to·to \in-'tō-tō\ *adv* [L, on the whole] : TOTALLY, ENTIRELY

in·tox·i·cant \in-'täk-si-kənt\ *n* : something that intoxicates; *esp* : an alcoholic drink — **intoxicant** *adj*

in·tox·i·cate \-sə-ˌkāt\ *vb* **-cat·ed; -cat·ing** **1** : to affect by a drug (as alcohol or cocaine) esp. to the point of physical or mental impairment **2** : to excite to enthusiasm or frenzy ⟨*intoxicated* by his power⟩ — **in·tox·i·ca·tion** \-ˌtäk-sə-'kā-shən\ *n*

in·trac·ta·ble \(ˌ)in-'trak-tə-bəl\ *adj* : not easily controlled

in·tra·mu·ral \-'myùr-əl\ *adj* : being or occurring within the walls or limits (as of a city or college) ⟨~ sports⟩

in·tra·mus·cu·lar \-'məs-kyə-lər\ *adj* : situated within, occurring in, or administered by entering a muscle — **in·tra·mus·cu·lar·ly** *adv*

in·tra·net \'in-trə-ˌnet\ *n* a network similar to the World Wide Web but having access limited to certain authorized users

intrans *abbr* intransitive

in·tran·si·gent \-jənt\ *adj* : UNCOMPRO-

MISING ⟨an ~ attitude⟩ — **in·tran·si·gence** \-jəns\ *n* — **intransigent** *n*

in·tran·si·tive \(ˌ)in-'tran-sə-tiv, -zə-\ *adj* : not transitive; *esp* : not having or containing an object ⟨an ~ verb⟩ — **in·tran·si·tive·ly** *adv* — **in·tran·si·tive·ness** *n*

in·tra·state \ˌin-trə-'stāt\ *adj* : existing or occurring within a state ⟨~ rivals⟩

in·tra·uter·ine device \-'yü-tə-rən-, -ˌrīn-\ *n* : a device inserted into and left in the uterus to prevent pregnancy

in·tra·ve·nous \ˌin-trə-'vē-nəs\ *adj* : being within or entering by way of the veins ⟨~ feeding⟩; *also* : used in or using intravenous procedures ⟨~ needles⟩ — **in·tra·ve·nous·ly** *adv*

intrench *var of* ENTRENCH

in·trep·id \in-'tre-pəd\ *adj* : characterized by resolute fearlessness, fortitude, and endurance ⟨an ~ explorer⟩ — **in·tre·pid·i·ty** \ˌin-trə-'pi-də-tē\ *n*

in·tri·cate \'in-tri-kət\ *adj* [ME, fr. L *intricatus*, pp. of *intricare* to entangle, fr. *tri-cae* trifles, complications] **1** : having many complexly interrelated parts : COMPLICATED **2** : difficult to follow, understand, or solve — **in·tri·ca·cy** \-tri-kə-sē\ *n* — **in·tri·cate·ly** *adv*

¹in·trigue \'in-ˌtrēg, in-'trēg\ *n* **1** : a secret scheme : PLOT **2** : a clandestine love affair

²in·trigue \in-'trēg\ *vb* **in·trigued; in·trigu·ing** **1** to accomplish by intrigue **2** : to carry on an intrigue; *esp* : PLOT, SCHEME **3** : to arouse the interest, desire, or curiosity of — **in·trigu·ing·ly** *adv*

in·trin·sic \in-'trin-zik, -sik\ *adj* : belonging to the essential nature or constitution of a thing — **in·trin·si·cal·ly** \-zi-k(ə-)lē, -si-\ *adv*

introd *abbr* introduction

in·tro·duce \ˌin-trə-'düs, -'dyüs\ *vb* **-duced; -duc·ing** **1** : to lead or bring in esp. for the first time **2** : to bring into practice or use **3** : to cause to be acquainted **4** : to present for discussion **5** : PLACE, INSERT ♦ *Synonyms* INSINUATE, INTERPOLATE, INTERPOSE, INTERJECT — **in·tro·duc·tion** \-'dək-shən\ *n* — **in·tro·duc·to·ry** \-'dək-tə-rē\ *adj*

in·troit \'in-ˌtroit, -ˌtrō-ət\ *n* **1** *often cap* : the first part of the traditional proper of the Mass **2** : a piece of music sung or played at the beginning of a worship service

in·tro·spec·tion \-'spek-shən\ *n* : a reflective looking inward : an examination of one's own thoughts or feelings — **in·tro·spect** \ˌin-trə-'spekt\ *vb* — **in·tro·spec·tive** \-'spek-tiv\ *adj* — **in·tro·spec·tive·ly** *adv*

in·tro·vert \'in-trə-ˌvərt\ *n* : a reserved or shy person — **in·tro·ver·sion** \ˌin-trə-'vər-zhən\ *n* — **introvert** *adj* — **in·tro·vert·ed** \'in-trə-ˌvər-təd\ *adj*

in·trude \in-'trüd\ *vb* **in·trud·ed; in·trud·ing** **1** : to thrust, enter, or force in or upon **2** : ENCROACH, TRESPASS — **in·trud·er** *n* — **in·tru·sion** \-'trü-zhən\ *n* — **in·tru·sive** \-'trü-siv\ *adj* — **in·tru·sive·ness** *n*

intrust *var of* ENTRUST

in·tu·it \in-'tü-ət, -'tyü-\ *vb* : to know, sense, or understand by intuition

in·tu·ition \,in-tü-'wi-shən, -tyü-\ *n* 1 : quick and ready insight 2 : the power or faculty of knowing things without conscious reasoning — **in·tu·itive** \in-'tü-ə-tiv, -'tyü-\ *adj* — **in·tu·itive·ly** *adv*

In·u·it \'i-nü-wət, 'in-yü-\ *n* [Inuit *inuit*, pl. of *inuk* person] 1 *pl* **Inuit** or **Inuits** : a member of the indigenous people of No. America and Greenland 2 : the language of the Inuit people

in·un·date \'i-nən-,dāt\ *vb* **-dat·ed; -dat·ing** : to cover with or as if with a flood : OVERFLOW — **in·un·da·tion** \,i-nən-'dā-shən\ *n*

in·ure \i-'nür, -'nyür\ *vb* **in·ured; in·ur·ing** [ME *enuren*, fr. *in ure* customary, fr. *putten in ure* to use, put into practice, part. trans. of AF *mettre en ovre, en uevre*] 1 : to accustom to accept something undesirable ⟨*inured* to violence⟩ 2 : to become of advantage

in utero \in-'yü-tə-,rō\ *adv or adj* [L] : in the uterus : before birth

inv *abbr* 1 inventor 2 invoice

in vac·uo \in-'va-kyü-,wō\ *adv* [L] : in a vacuum

in·vade \in-'vād\ *vb* **in·vad·ed; in·vad·ing** 1 : to enter for conquest or plunder 2 : to encroach upon 3 : to spread through and usu. harm ⟨germs ∼ the tissues⟩ — **in·vad·er** *n*

¹**in·val·id** \(,)in-'va-ləd\ *adj* : being without foundation or force in fact, reason, or law — **in·va·lid·i·ty** \,in-və-'li-də-tē\ *n* — **in·val·id·ly** *adv*

²**in·va·lid** \'in-və-ləd\ *adj* : being in ill health : SICKLY

³**invalid** \'in-və-ləd\ *n* : a person in usu. chronic ill health — **in·va·lid·ism** \-lə-,di-zəm\ *n*

⁴**in·va·lid** \'in-və-ləd, -,lid\ *vb* 1 : to remove from active duty by reason of sickness or disability 2 : to make sickly or disabled

in·val·i·date \(,)in-'va-lə-,dāt\ *vb* : to make invalid ⟨*invalidate* a contract⟩; *esp* : to weaken or make valueless — **in·val·i·da·tion** \in-,va-lə-'dā-shən\ *n*

in·valu·able \-'val-yə-bəl, -yə-wə-bəl\ *adj* : valuable beyond estimation

in·vari·able \-'ver-ē-ə-bəl\ *adj* : not changing or capable of change : CONSTANT — **in·vari·ably** \-blē\ *adv*

in·va·sion \in-'vā-zhən\ *n* : an act or instance of invading; *esp* : entry of an army into a country for conquest

in·va·sive \in-'vā-siv, -ziv\ *adj* 1 : tending to spread ⟨∼ cancer cells⟩ 2 : involving entry into the living body (as by surgery) ⟨∼ therapy⟩

in·vec·tive \in-'vek-tiv\ *n* 1 : an abusive expression or speech 2 : abusive language — **invective** *adj*

in·veigh \in-'vā\ *vb* : to protest or complain bitterly or vehemently : RAIL

in·vei·gle \in-'vā-gəl, -'vē-\ *vb* **in·vei·gled; in·vei·gling** [AF *enveegler, aveogler* to blind, hoodwink, fr. *avogle, enveugle* blind, fr. ML *ab oculis*, lit., lacking eyes] 1 : to win over by flattery : ENTICE 2 : to acquire by ingenuity or flattery ⟨*inveigled* his way into her confidence⟩

in·vent \in-'vent\ *vb* 1 : to think up 2 : to create or produce for the first time — **in·ven·tor** \-'ven-tər\ *n*

in·ven·tion \in-'ven-chən\ *n* 1 : INVENTIVENESS 2 : a creation of the imagination; *esp* : a false conception 3 : a device, contrivance, or process originated after study and experiment 4 : the act or process of inventing

in·ven·tive \in-'ven-tiv\ *adj* 1 : CREATIVE, INGENIOUS ⟨an ∼ composer⟩ 2 : characterized by invention ⟨an ∼ turn of mind⟩ — **in·ven·tive·ness** *n*

in·ven·to·ry \'in-vən-,tȯr-ē\ *n, pl* **-ries** 1 : an itemized list of current goods or assets 2 : SURVEY, SUMMARY 3 : STOCK, SUPPLY 4 : the act or process of taking an inventory — **inventory** *vb*

¹**in·verse** \(,)in-'vərs, 'in-,vərs\ *adj* : opposite in order, nature, or effect : REVERSED — **in·verse·ly** *adv*

²**inverse** *n* : something inverse or resulting in or from inversion : OPPOSITE

in·ver·sion \in-'vər-zhən\ *n* 1 : a reversal of position, order, or relationship; *esp* : an increase of temperature with altitude through a layer of air 2 : the act or process of inverting

in·vert \in-'vərt\ *vb* 1 : to reverse in position, order, or relationship 2 : to turn upside down or inside out 3 : to turn inward

in·ver·te·brate \(,)in-'vər-tə-brət, -,brāt\ *adj* : lacking a backbone; *also* : of or relating to invertebrate animals — **invertebrate** *n*

¹**in·vest** \in-'vest\ *vb* 1 : to install formally in an office or honor 2 : to furnish with power or authority : VEST 3 : to cover completely : ENVELOP 4 : CLOTHE, ADORN 5 : BESIEGE 6 : to endow with a quality or characteristic

²**invest** *vb* 1 : to commit (money) in order to earn a financial return ⟨∼ed in real estate⟩ 2 : to expend for future benefits or advantages 3 : to make an investment — **in·ves·tor** \-'ves-tər\ *n*

in·ves·ti·gate \in-'ves-tə-,gāt\ *vb* **-gat·ed; -gat·ing** [L *investigare* to track, investigate, fr. *vestigium* footprint, track] : to study by close examination and systematic inquiry — **in·ves·ti·ga·tion** \-,ves-tə-'gā-shən\ *n* — **in·ves·ti·ga·tive** \'ves-tə-,gā-tiv\ *adj* — **in·ves·ti·ga·tor** \-,gā-tər\ *n*

in·ves·ti·ture \in-'ves-tə-,chùr, -chər\ *n* 1 : the act of ratifying or establishing in office 2 : something that covers or adorns

¹**in·vest·ment** \in-'vest-mənt\ *n* 1 : an outer layer : ENVELOPE 2 : INVESTITURE 1 3 : BLOCKADE, SIEGE

²**investment** *n* : the outlay of money for income or profit; *also* : the sum invested or the property purchased

in·vet·er·ate \in-'ve-tə-rət\ *adj* 1 : firmly established by age or long persistence 2 : confirmed in a habit ⟨an ∼ liar⟩

in·vi·a·ble \(,)in-'vī-ə-bəl\ *adj* : incapable of surviving

in·vid·i·ous \in-'vi-dē-əs\ *adj* 1 : tending

to cause discontent, animosity, or envy ⟨an ~ comparison⟩ **2** : ENVIOUS **3** : OBNOXIOUS ⟨~ remarks⟩ — **in·vid·i·ous·ly** adv

in·vig·o·rate \in-'vi-gə-,rāt\ vb **-rat·ed; -rat·ing** : to give life and energy to : ANIMATE ⟨~ the economy⟩ — **in·vig·o·ra·tion** \-,vi-gə-'rā-shən\ n

in·vin·ci·ble \(,)in-'vin-sə-bəl\ adj : incapable of being conquered, overcome, or subdued — **in·vin·ci·bil·i·ty** \-,vin-sə-'bi-lə-tē\ n — **in·vin·ci·bly** \-'vin-sə-blē\ adv

in·vi·o·la·ble \-'vī-ə-lə-bəl\ adj **1** : safe from violation or profanation **2** : UNASSAILABLE ⟨~ borders⟩ — **in·vi·o·la·bil·i·ty** \-,vī-ə-lə-'bi-lə-tē\ n

in·vi·o·late \-'vī-ə-lət\ adj : not violated or profaned : PURE ⟨an ~ oath⟩

in·vis·i·ble \-'vi-zə-bəl\ adj **1** : incapable of being seen ⟨~ to the naked eye⟩ **2** : HIDDEN **3** : IMPERCEPTIBLE, INCONSPICUOUS ⟨~ barriers⟩ — **in·vis·i·bil·i·ty** \-,vi-zə-'bi-lə-tē\ n — **in·vis·i·bly** \-'vi-zə-blē\ adv

invisible hand n : a hypothetical economic force that works for the benefit of all

in·vi·ta·tion·al \,in-və-'tā-shə-nəl\ adj : limited to invited participants ⟨an ~ tournament⟩ — **invitational** n

in·vite \in-'vīt\ vb **in·vit·ed; in·vit·ing** **1** : ENTICE, TEMPT **2** : to increase the likelihood of ⟨~ trouble⟩ **3** : to request the presence or participation of : ASK **4** : to request formally **5** : ENCOURAGE ⟨~ suggestions⟩ — **in·vi·ta·tion** \,in-və-'tā-shən\ n

in·vit·ing adj : ATTRACTIVE, TEMPTING

in vi·tro \in-'vē-trō, -'vi-, -'vi-\ adv or adj [NL, lit., in glass] : outside the living body and in an artificial environment ⟨in vitro fertilization⟩

in·vo·ca·tion \,in-və-'kā-shən\ n **1** : SUPPLICATION; esp : a prayer at the beginning of a service **2** : a formula for conjuring : INCANTATION

¹**in·voice** \'in-,vois\ n [modif. of MF envois, pl. of envoi message] : an itemized list of goods shipped usu. specifying the price and the terms of sale : BILL

²**invoice** vb **in·voiced; in·voic·ing** : to send an invoice to or for : BILL

in·voke \in-'vōk\ vb **in·voked; in·vok·ing** **1** : to petition for help or support **2** : to appeal to or cite as authority ⟨~ a law⟩ **3** : to call forth by incantation : CONJURE ⟨~ spirits⟩ **4** : to make an earnest request for : SOLICIT ⟨invoked mercy⟩ **5** : to put into effect or operation **6** : to bring about : CAUSE

in·vol·un·tary \(,)in-'vä-lən-,ter-ē\ adj **1** : done contrary to or without choice **2** : COMPULSORY ⟨~ servitude⟩ **3** : not controlled by the will : REFLEX ⟨~ contractions⟩ — **in·vol·un·tari·ly** \-,vä-lən-'ter-ə-lē\ adv

in·vo·lute \'in-və-,lüt\ adj : INVOLVED, INTRICATE ⟨an ~ maneuver⟩

in·vo·lu·tion \,in-və-'lü-shən\ n **1** : the act or an instance of enfolding or entangling **2** : COMPLEXITY, INTRICACY

in·volve \in-'välv\ vb **in·volved; in·volv·ing** **1** : to draw in as a participant **2** : ENVELOP **3** : to occupy (as oneself) absorbingly; esp : to commit oneself emotionally **4** : to relate closely : CONNECT **5** : to have as part of itself : INCLUDE **6** : ENTAIL, IMPLY ⟨the job ~s traveling⟩ **7** : ²AFFECT — **in·volve·ment** n

in·volved \-'välvd\ adj : INTRICATE, COMPLEX ⟨an ~ plot⟩

in·vul·ner·a·ble \(,)in-'vəl-nə-rə-bəl\ adj **1** : incapable of being wounded, injured, or damaged **2** : immune to or proof against attack — **in·vul·ner·a·bil·i·ty** \-,vəl-nə-rə-'bi-lə-tē\ n — **in·vul·ner·a·bly** \-'vəl-nə-rə-blē\ adv

¹**in·ward** \'in-wərd\ adj **1** : situated on the inside **2** : MENTAL; also : SPIRITUAL **3** : directed toward the interior

²**inward** or **in·wards** \-wərdz\ adv **1** : toward the inside, center, or interior **2** : toward the inner being ⟨turned his thoughts ~⟩

in·ward·ly \'in-wərd-lē\ adv **1** : MENTALLY, SPIRITUALLY **2** : INTERNALLY ⟨bled ~⟩ **3** : to oneself ⟨cursed ~⟩

IOC abbr International Olympic Committee

io·dide \'ī-ə-,dīd\ n : a compound of iodine with another element or group

io·dine \'ī-ə-,dīn, -dᵊn\ n **1** : a nonmetallic chemical element used esp. in medicine and photography **2** : a solution of iodine used as a local antiseptic

io·dise Brit var of IODIZE

io·dize \'ī-ə-,dīz\ vb **io·dized; io·diz·ing** : to treat with iodine or an iodide

ion \'ī-ən, 'ī-,än\ n [Gk, neut. of iōn, prp. of ienai to go; so called because in electrolysis it goes to one of the two poles] : an electrically charged particle, atom, or group of atoms — **ion·ic** \ī-'ä-nik\ adj

-ion n suffix : act, process, state, or condition ⟨validation⟩

ion·ise Brit var of IONIZE

ion·ize \'ī-ə-,nīz\ vb **ion·ized; ion·iz·ing** **1** : to convert wholly or partly into ions **2** : to become ionized — **ion·iz·able** \ī-ə-'nī-zə-bəl\ adj — **ion·i·za·tion** \,ī-ə-nə-'zā-shən\ n — **ion·iz·er** \'ī-ə-,nī-zər\ n

ion·o·sphere \ī-'ä-nə-,sfir\ n : the part of the earth's atmosphere extending from about 30 miles (50 kilometers) to the exosphere that contains ionized atmospheric gases — **ion·o·spher·ic** \ī-,ä-nə-'sfir-ik, -'sfer-\ adj

IOOF abbr Independent Order of Odd Fellows

io·ta \ī-'ō-tə\ n [L, fr. Gk iōta] **1** : the 9th letter of the Greek alphabet — I or ι **2** : a very small quantity : JOT

IOU \ī-(,)ō-'yü\ n : an acknowledgement of a debt

IP abbr innings pitched

IP address \'ī-'pē-\ n [Internet protocol] : the numeric address of a computer on the Internet

ip·e·cac \'i-pi-,kak\ n [Pg ipecacuanha] : an emetic and expectorant drug used esp. as a syrup in treating accidental poisoning; also : either of two tropical American plants or their rhizomes and roots used to make ipecac

IPO \ˌī-ˌpē-'ō\ *n, pl* **IPOs** : an initial public offering of a company's stock

ip·so fac·to \ˌip-sō-'fak-tō\ *adv* [NL, lit., by the fact itself] : by the very nature of the case

iq *abbr* [L *idem quod*] the same as

IQ \'ī-'kyü\ *n* : a number used to express a person's relative intelligence as determined by a standardized test

¹**Ir** *abbr* Irish

²**Ir** *symbol* iridium

IR *abbr* infrared

¹**IRA** \ˌī-(ˌ)är-'ā; 'ī-rə\ *n* [*i*ndividual *r*etirement *a*ccount] : a retirement savings account in which income taxes are deferred until withdrawals are made

²**IRA** *abbr* Irish Republican Army

irai·mbi·lan·ja \ē-ˌrīm-bē-'län(d)-zə\ *n, pl* **iraimbilanja** — see *ariary* at MONEY table

iras·ci·ble \i-'ra-sə-bəl\ *adj* : marked by hot temper and easily provoked anger
♦ **Synonyms** CHOLERIC, TESTY, TOUCHY, CRANKY, CROSS — **iras·ci·bil·i·ty** \-ˌra-sə-'bi-lə-tē\ *n*

irate \ī-'rāt\ *adj* **1** : roused to ire ⟨an ∼ customer⟩ **2** : arising from anger — **irate·ly** *adv*

ire \'ī(-ə)r\ *n* : ANGER, WRATH — **ire·ful** *adj*

Ire *abbr* Ireland

ire·nic \ī-'re-nik\ *adj* : favoring, conducive to, or operating toward peace or conciliation ⟨∼ measures⟩

ir·i·des·cence \ˌir-ə-'de-sᵊns\ *n* : a rainbowlike play of colors — **ir·i·des·cent** \-sᵊnt\ *adj*

irid·i·um \ir-'i-dē-əm\ *n* : a hard brittle heavy metallic chemical element

iris \'ī-rəs\ *n, pl* **iris·es** *also* **iri·des** \'ī-rə-ˌdēz, 'ir-ə-\ [ME, fr. L *iris* rainbow, iris plant, fr. Gk, rainbow, iris plant, iris of the eye] **1** : the colored part around the pupil of the eye **2** : any of a large genus of plants with linear basal leaves and large showy flowers

Irish \'ī-rish\ *n* **1 Irish** *pl* : the people of Ireland **2** : the Celtic language of Ireland — **Irish** *adj* — **Irish·man** \-mən\ *n* — **Irish·wom·an** \-ˌwu̇-mən\ *n*

Irish bull *n* : an incongruous statement (as "it was hereditary in his family to have no children")

Irish coffee *n* : hot sugared coffee with Irish whiskey and whipped cream

Irish moss *n* : the dried and bleached plants of a red alga that is a source of carrageenan; *also* : this red alga

Irish setter *n* : any of a breed of hunting dogs with a mahogany-red coat

irk \'ərk\ *vb* : to make weary, irritated, or bored : ANNOY

irk·some \'ərk-səm\ *adj* : tending to irk : ANNOYING — **irk·some·ly** *adv*

¹**iron** \'ī(-ə)rn\ *n* [ME, fr. OE *īsern, īren*] **1** : a heavy malleable magnetic metallic chemical element that rusts easily and is vital to biological processes **2** : something made of metal and esp. iron; *also* : something (as handcuffs) used to bind or restrain ⟨put them in ∼s⟩ **3** : a household device with a flat base that is heated and used for pressing cloth **4** : STRENGTH, HARDNESS

²**iron** *vb* **1** : to press or smooth with or as if with a heated iron **2** : to remove (as wrinkles) by ironing — **iron·er** *n*

¹**iron·clad** \-'klad\ *adj* **1** : sheathed in iron armor **2** : so firm or secure as to be unbreakable

²**iron·clad** \-ˌklad\ *n* : an armored naval vessel esp. of the 19th century

iron curtain *n* : a political, military, and ideological barrier that isolates an area; *esp, often cap* : one formerly isolating an area under Soviet control

iron·ic \ī-'rä-nik\ *also* **iron·i·cal** \-ni-kəl\ *adj* **1** : of, relating to, or marked by irony **2** : given to irony

iron·i·cal·ly \-ni-k(ə-)lē\ *adv* **1** : in an ironic manner **2** : it is ironic

iron·ing *n* : clothes ironed or to be ironed

iron lung *n* : a device for artificial respiration that encloses the chest in a chamber in which changes of pressure force air into and out of the lungs

iron out *vb* : to remove or lessen difficulties in or extremes of

iron oxide *n* : FERRIC OXIDE

iron·stone \'ī(-ə)rn-ˌstōn\ *n* **1** : a hard iron-rich sedimentary rock **2** : a hard heavy durable pottery developed in England in the 19th century

iron·ware \-ˌwer\ *n* : articles made of iron

iron·weed \-ˌwēd\ *n* : any of a genus of mostly weedy plants related to the asters that have terminal heads of red, purple, or white flowers

iron·wood \-ˌwu̇d\ *n* : any of numerous trees or shrubs with exceptionally hard wood; *also* : the wood

iron·work \-ˌwərk\ *n* **1** : work in iron **2** *pl* : a mill or building where iron or steel is smelted or heavy iron or steel products are made — **iron·work·er** *n*

iro·ny \'ī-rə-nē\ *n, pl* **-nies** [L *ironia*, fr. Gk *eirōnia*, fr. *eirōn* dissembler] **1** : the use of words to express the opposite of what one really means **2** : incongruity between the actual result of a sequence of events and the expected result

Ir·o·quois \'ir-ə-ˌkwȯi\ *n, pl* **Iroquois** *same or* -ˌkwȯiz\ **1** *pl* : an American Indian confederacy orig. of New York that consisted of the Cayuga, Mohawk, Oneida, Onondaga, and Seneca and later included the Tuscarora **2** : a member of any of the Iroquois peoples

ir·ra·di·ate \i-'rā-dē-ˌāt\ *vb* **-at·ed; -at·ing** **1** : ILLUMINATE **2** : ENLIGHTEN **3** : to treat by exposure to radiation **4** : RADIATE — **ir·ra·di·a·tion** \-ˌrā-dē-'ā-shən\ *n*

¹**ir·ra·tio·nal** \(ˌ)i-'ra-shə-nəl\ *adj* **1** : incapable of reasoning ⟨∼ beasts⟩; *also* : defective in mental power ⟨∼ with fever⟩ **2** : not based on reason ⟨∼ fears⟩ **3** : being or numerically equal to an irrational number — **ir·ra·tio·nal·i·ty** \(ˌ)i-ˌra-shə-'na-lə-tē\ *n* — **ir·ra·tio·nal·ly** *adv*

²**irrational** *n* : IRRATIONAL NUMBER

irrational number *n* : a real number that cannot be expressed as the quotient of two integers

ir·rec·on·cil·able \(ˌ)i-ˌre-kən-'sī-lə-bəl,

-'re-kən-ˌsī-\ *adj* : impossible to reconcile, adjust, or harmonize — **ir·rec·on·cil·abil·i·ty** \(ˌ)i-ˌre-kən-ˌsī-lə-'bi-lə-tē\ *n*

ir·re·cov·er·able \ˌir-i-'kə-və-rə-bəl\ *adj* : not capable of being recovered or rectified : IRREPARABLE ⟨an ∼ loss⟩ — **ir·re·cov·er·ably** \-blē\ *adv*

ir·re·deem·able \ˌir-i-'dē-mə-bəl\ *adj* 1 : not redeemable; *esp* : not terminable by payment of the principal ⟨an ∼ bond⟩ 2 : not convertible into gold or silver at the will of the holder 3 : being beyond remedy : HOPELESS ⟨∼ villains⟩

ir·re·den·tism \-'den-ˌti-zəm\ *n* : a principle or policy directed toward the incorporation of a territory historically or ethnically part of another into that other — **ir·re·den·tist** \-tist\ *n or adj*

ir·re·duc·ible \ˌir-i-'dü-sə-bəl, -'dyü-\ *adj* : not reducible ⟨an ∼ fraction⟩ — **ir·re·duc·ibly** \-blē\ *adv*

ir·re·fut·able \ˌir-i-'fyü-tə-bəl, (ˌ)i-'refyət-\ *adj* : impossible to refute

irreg *abbr* irregular

ir·reg·u·lar \(ˌ)i-'re-gyə-lər\ *adj* 1 : not regular : not natural or uniform 2 : not conforming to the normal or usual manner of inflection ⟨∼ verbs⟩ 3 : not belonging to a regular or organized army ⟨∼ troops⟩ — **irregular** *n* — **ir·reg·u·lar·ly** *adv*

ir·reg·u·lar·i·ty \i-ˌre-gyə-'la-rə-tē\ *n, pl* -ties 1 : something that is irregular 2 : the quality or state of being irregular 3 : occasional constipation

ir·rel·e·vant \(ˌ)i-'re-lə-vənt\ *adj* : not relevant — **ir·rel·e·vance** \-vəns\ *n*

ir·re·li·gious \ˌir-i-'li-jəs\ *adj* : lacking religious emotions, doctrines, or practices

ir·re·me·di·a·ble \ˌir-i-'mē-dē-ə-bəl\ *adj* : impossible to remedy or correct

ir·re·mov·able \ˌir-i-'mü-və-bəl\ *adj* : not removable

ir·rep·a·ra·ble \(ˌ)i-'re-pə-rə-bəl\ *adj* : impossible to make good, undo, repair, or remedy ⟨∼ damage⟩

ir·re·place·able \ˌir-i-'plā-sə-bəl\ *adj* : not replaceable ⟨∼ antiques⟩

ir·re·press·ible \-'pre-sə-bəl\ *adj* : impossible to repress or control ⟨∼ curiosity⟩

ir·re·proach·able \-'prō-chə-bəl\ *adj* : not reproachable : BLAMELESS

ir·re·sist·ible \ˌir-i-'zis-tə-bəl\ *adj* : impossible to successfully resist ⟨an ∼ craving⟩ — **ir·re·sist·ibly** \-blē\ *adv*

ir·res·o·lute \(ˌ)i-'re-zə-ˌlüt\ *adj* : uncertain how to act or proceed : VACILLATING — **ir·res·o·lute·ly** \-ˌlüt-lē; (ˌ)i-ˌrezə-'lüt-\ *adv* — **ir·res·o·lu·tion** \(ˌ)i-ˌrezə-'lü-shən\ *n*

ir·re·spec·tive of \ˌir-i-'spek-tiv-\ *prep* : without regard to

ir·re·spon·si·ble \-'spän-sə-bəl\ *adj* : not responsible ⟨∼ wastrels⟩ — **ir·re·spon·si·bil·i·ty** \-ˌspän-sə-'bi-lə-tē\ *n* — **ir·re·spon·si·bly** \-'spän-sə-blē\ *adv*

ir·re·triev·able \ˌir-i-'trē-və-bəl\ *adj* : not retrievable : IRRECOVERABLE

ir·rev·er·ence \(ˌ)i-'re-və-rəns\ *n* 1 : lack of reverence 2 : an irreverent act or utterance — **ir·rev·er·ent** \-rənt\ *adj* — **ir·rev·er·ent·ly** *adv*

ir·re·vers·ible \ˌir-i-'vər-sə-bəl\ *adj* : incapable of being reversed ⟨an ∼ loss⟩

ir·rev·o·ca·ble \(ˌ)i-'re-və-kə-bəl\ *adj* : incapable of being revoked or recalled ⟨∼ change⟩ — **ir·rev·o·ca·bly** \-blē\ *adv*

ir·ri·gate \'ir-ə-ˌgāt\ *vb* -gat·ed; -gat·ing : to supply (as land) with water by artificial means; *also* : to flush with liquid — **ir·ri·ga·tion** \ˌir-ə-'gā-shən\ *n*

ir·ri·ta·bil·i·ty \ˌir-ə-tə-'bi-lə-tē\ *n* 1 : the property of living things and of protoplasm that enables reaction to stimuli 2 : the quality or state of being irritable; *esp* : readiness to become annoyed or angry

ir·ri·ta·ble \'ir-ə-tə-bəl\ *adj* : capable of being irritated; *esp* : readily or easily irritated — **ir·ri·ta·bly** \-blē\ *adv*

ir·ri·tate \'ir-ə-ˌtāt\ *vb* -tat·ed; -tat·ing 1 : to excite to anger : EXASPERATE 2 : to make sore or inflamed — **ir·ri·tant** \'ir-ə-tənt\ *adj or n* — **ir·ri·tat·ing·ly** *adv* — **ir·ri·ta·tion** \ˌir-ə-'tā-shən\ *n*

ir·rupt \(ˌ)i-'rəpt\ *vb* 1 : to rush in forcibly or violently 2 : to increase suddenly in numbers ⟨rabbits ∼ in cycles⟩ — **ir·rup·tion** \-'rəp-shən\ *n*

IRS *abbr* Internal Revenue Service

Isa *abbr* Isaiah

Is *or* **Is** *abbr* Isaiah

Isa·iah \ī-'zā-ə\ *n* — see BIBLE table

Isa·ias \ī-'zā-əs\ *n* : ISAIAH

ISBN *abbr* International Standard Book Number

is·che·mia \is-'kē-mē-ə\ *n* : deficient supply of blood to a body part (as the brain) — **is·che·mic** \-mik\ *adj*

-ish *adj suffix* 1 : of, relating to, or being ⟨Finn*ish*⟩ 2 : characteristic of ⟨boy*ish*⟩ ⟨mul*ish*⟩ 3 : inclined or liable to ⟨book*ish*⟩ 4 : having a touch or trace of : somewhat ⟨purpl*ish*⟩ 5 : having the approximate age of ⟨forty*ish*⟩

isin·glass \'ī-zᵊn-ˌglas, 'ī-ziŋ-\ *n* 1 : a gelatin obtained from various fish 2 : mica esp. in thin sheets

isl *abbr* island

Is·lam \is-'läm, iz-, -'lam, 'is-ˌ, 'iz-ˌ\ *n* [Ar *islām* submission (to the will of God)] : the religious faith of Muslims including belief in Allah as the sole deity and in Muhammad as his prophet; *also* : the civilization built on this faith — **Is·lam·ic** \is-'lä-mik, iz-, -'la-\ *adj*

is·land \'ī-lənd\ *n* [ME *iland*, fr. OE *īgland*, fr. *īg* island + *land* land] 1 : a body of land smaller than a continent surrounded by water 2 : something resembling an island in its isolation

is·land·er \'ī-lən-dər\ *n* : a native or inhabitant of an island

isle \'ī(-ə)l\ *n* : ISLAND; *esp* : a small island

is·let \'ī-lət\ *n* : a small island

ism \'i-zəm\ *n* : a distinctive doctrine, cause, or theory

-ism *n suffix* 1 : act : practice : process ⟨critic*ism*⟩ 2 : manner of action or behavior characteristic of a (specified) person or thing ⟨fanatic*ism*⟩ 3 : state : condition : property ⟨dual*ism*⟩ 4 : abnormal state or condition ⟨alcohol*ism*⟩ 5 : doctrine : theory : cult ⟨Buddh*ism*⟩ 6 : adherence to a set of principles ⟨stoic*ism*⟩

7 : prejudice or discrimination on the basis of a (specified) attribute ⟨*racism*⟩ ⟨*sexism*⟩ **8** : characteristic or peculiar feature or trait ⟨colloquial*ism*⟩

iso·bar \ˈī-sə-ˌbär\ *n* : a line on a map connecting places of equal barometric pressure — **iso·bar·ic** \ˌī-sə-ˈbär-ik, -ˈber-\ *adj*

iso·late \ˈī-sə-ˌlāt\ *vb* **-lat·ed; -lat·ing** [fr. *isolated* set apart, fr. F *isolé*, fr. It *isolato*, fr. *isola* island, fr. L *insula*] : to place or keep by itself : separate from others — **iso·la·tion** \ˌī-sə-ˈlā-shən\ *n*

isolated *adj* **1** : occurring alone or once : UNIQUE **2** : SPORADIC ⟨∼ outbreaks⟩

iso·la·tion·ism \ˌī-sə-ˈlā-shə-ˌni-zəm\ *n* : a policy of national isolation by abstention from international political and economic relations — **iso·la·tion·ist** \-shə-nist\ *n or adj*

iso·mer \ˈī-sə-mər\ *n* : any of two or more chemical compounds that contain the same numbers of atoms of the same elements but differ in structural arrangement and properties — **iso·mer·ic** \ˌī-sə-ˈmer-ik\ *adj* — **isom·er·ism** \ī-ˈsä-mə-ˌri-zəm\ *n*

iso·met·rics \ˌī-sə-ˈme-triks\ *n sing or pl* : exercise involving a series of brief and intense contractions of muscles against each other or against an immovable resistance — **iso·met·ric** *adj*

iso·prene \ˈī-sə-ˌprēn\ *n* : a hydrocarbon used esp. in making synthetic rubber

isos·ce·les \ī-ˈsä-sə-ˌlēz\ *adj* : having two equal sides ⟨an ∼ triangle⟩

iso·therm \ˈī-sə-ˌthərm\ *n* : a line on a map connecting points having the same temperature

iso·ther·mal \ˌī-sə-ˈthər-məl\ *adj* : of, relating to, or marked by equality of temperature

iso·tope \ˈī-sə-ˌtōp\ *n* [Gk *isos* equal + *topos* place] : any of the forms of a chemical element that differ chiefly in the number of neutrons in an atom — **iso·to·pic** \ˌī-sə-ˈtä-pik, -ˈtō-\ *adj* — **iso·top·i·cal·ly** \-ˈtä-pi-k(ə-)lē, -ˈtō-\ *adv*

Isr *abbr* Israel; Israeli

Is·ra·el·ite \ˈiz-rē-ə-ˌlīt\ *n* : a member of the Hebrew people descended from Jacob

is·su·ance \ˈi-shü-wəns\ *n* : the act of issuing or giving out esp. officially

¹is·sue \ˈi-shü\ *n* [ME, exit, proceeds, fr. AF, fr. *issir* to come out, go out, fr. L *exire*, fr. *ire* to go] **1** : the action of going, coming, or flowing out : EGRESS, EMERGENCE **2** : EXIT, OUTLET, VENT **3** : OFFSPRING, PROGENY **4** : OUTCOME, RESULT **5** : a point of debate or controversy; *also* : the point at which an unsettled matter is ready for a decision **6** : a discharge (as of blood) from the body **7** : something coming forth from a specified source **8** : the act of officially giving out or printing : PUBLICATION; *also* : the quantity of things given out at one time

²issue *vb* **is·sued; is·su·ing 1** : to go, come, or flow out **2** : to come forth or cause to come forth : EMERGE, DISCHARGE, EMIT **3** : ACCRUE **4** : to de-

scend from a specified parent or ancestor **5** : to result in **6** : to put forth or distribute officially **7** : PUBLISH **8** : EMANATE, RESULT — **is·su·er** *n*

¹-ist *n suffix* **1** : one that performs a (specified) action ⟨cyc*list*⟩ : one that makes or produces ⟨novel*ist*⟩ **2** : one that plays a (specified) musical instrument ⟨harp*ist*⟩ **3** : one that operates a (specified) mechanical instrument or contrivance ⟨machin*ist*⟩ **4** : one that specializes in a (specified) art or science or skill ⟨geolog*ist*⟩ **5** : one that adheres to or advocates a (specified) doctrine or system or code of behavior ⟨social*ist*⟩ or that of a (specified) individual ⟨Darwin*ist*⟩

²-ist *adj suffix* : -ISTIC

isth·mi·an \ˈis-mē-ən\ *adj* : of, relating to, or situated in or near an isthmus

isth·mus \ˈis-məs\ *n* : a narrow strip of land connecting two larger portions of land

¹it \ˈit, ət\ *pron* **1** : that one — used of a lifeless thing, a plant, a person or animal, or an abstract entity ⟨∼'s a big building⟩ ⟨∼'s a shade tree⟩ ⟨who is ∼⟩ ⟨beauty is everywhere and ∼ is a source of joy⟩ **2** — used as a subject of an impersonal verb that expresses a condition or action without reference to an agent ⟨∼ is raining⟩ **3** — used as an anticipatory subject or object ⟨∼'s good to see you⟩

²it \ˈit\ *n* : the player in a game who performs the principal action of the game (as trying to find others in hide-and-seek)

It *abbr* Italian; Italy

ital *abbr* italic; italicized

Ital *abbr* Italian

Ital·ian \i-ˈtal-yən\ *n* **1** : a native or inhabitant of Italy **2** : the language of Italy — **Italian** *adj*

ital·ic \i-ˈta-lik, ī-\ *adj* : relating to type in which the letters slope up toward the right (as in "italic") — **italic** *n*

ital·i·cise *Brit var of* ITALICIZE

ital·i·cize \i-ˈta-lə-ˌsīz, ī-\ *vb* **-cized; -ciz·ing** : to print in italics — **ital·i·ci·za·tion** \-ˌta-lə-sə-ˈzā-shən\ *n*

itch \ˈich\ *n* **1** : an uneasy irritating skin sensation that evokes a desire to scratch the affected area **2** : a skin disorder accompanied by an itch **3** : a persistent desire — **itch** *vb* — **itchy** *adj*

-ite *n suffix* **1** : native : resident ⟨suburban*ite*⟩ **2** : adherent : follower ⟨Lenin*ite*⟩ **3** : product ⟨metabol*ite*⟩ **4** : mineral : rock ⟨quartz*ite*⟩

item \ˈī-təm\ *n* [L, likewise, also] **1** : a separate particular in a list, account, or series : ARTICLE **2** : a separate piece of news (as in a newspaper)

item·ise *Brit var of* ITEMIZE

item·ize \ˈī-tə-ˌmīz\ *vb* **-ized; -iz·ing** : to set down in detail : LIST — **item·i·za·tion** \ˌī-tə-mə-ˈzā-shən\ *n*

it·er·ate \ˈi-tə-ˌrāt\ *vb* **-at·ed; -at·ing** : REITERATE, REPEAT ⟨*iterated* his innocence⟩

it·er·a·tion \ˌi-tə-ˈrā-shən\ *n* **1** : REPETITION; *esp* : a computational process in which a series of operations is repeated until a condition is met **2** : one repetition

of the series of operations in iteration **3**
: VERSION

itin·er·ant \ī-'ti-nə-rənt, ə-\ *adj* : traveling from place to place; *esp* : covering a circuit ⟨an ~ preacher⟩

itin·er·ary \ī-'ti-nə-ˌrer-ē, ə-\ *n, pl* **-ar·ies** **1** : the route of a journey or the proposed outline of one **2** : a travel diary **3** : GUIDEBOOK

its \'its\ *adj* : of or relating to it or itself

it·self \it-'self\ *pron* : that identical one — used reflexively, for emphasis, or in absolute constructions

-ity *n suffix* : quality : state : degree ⟨alkalinity⟩

IUD \ˌī-(ˌ)yü-'dē\ *n* : INTRAUTERINE DEVICE

IV \ˌī-'vē\ *n, pl* **IVs** [*intravenous*] : an apparatus used to administer a fluid (as of nutrients) intravenously; *also* : a fluid administered by IV

-ive *adj suffix* : that performs or tends toward an (indicated) action ⟨corrective⟩

ivo·ry \'ī-vrē, -və-rē\ *n, pl* **-ries** [ME *ivo-*

rie, fr. AF *ivoire, iuurie,* fr. L *eboreus* of ivory, fr. *ebur* ivory] **1** : the hard creamy-white material composing the tusks of an elephant or walrus **2** : a pale yellow color **3** : something made of ivory or of a similar substance

ivory tower *n* **1** : an impractical lack of concern with urgent problems **2** : a place of learning

ivy \'ī-vē\ *n, pl* **ivies** : a trailing woody evergreen vine with small black berries that is related to ginseng

IWW *abbr* Industrial Workers of the World

-ize *vb suffix* **1** : cause to be or conform to or resemble ⟨Americanize⟩ : cause to be formed into ⟨unionize⟩ **2** : subject to a (specified) action ⟨satirize⟩ **3** : saturate, treat, or combine with ⟨macadamize⟩ **4** : treat like ⟨idolize⟩ **5** : become : become like ⟨crystallize⟩ **6** : be productive in or of : engage in a (specified) activity ⟨philosophize⟩ **7** : adopt or spread the manner of activity or the teaching of ⟨Christianize⟩

J

¹j \'jā\ *n, pl* **j's** *or* **js** \'jāz\ *often cap* : the 10th letter of the English alphabet

²j *abbr, often cap* **1** jack **2** journal **3** judge **4** justice

¹jab \'jab\ *vb* **jabbed; jab·bing** : to thrust quickly or abruptly : POKE

²jab *n* : a usu. short straight punch

jab·ber \'ja-bər\ *vb* : to talk rapidly, indistinctly, or unintelligibly : CHATTER — **jabber** *n* — **jab·ber·er** *n*

jab·ber·wocky \'ja-bər-ˌwä-kē\ *n* : meaningless speech or writing

ja·bot \zha-'bō, 'ja-ˌbō\ *n* : a ruffle worn down the front of a dress or shirt

jac·a·ran·da \ˌja-kə-'ran-də\ *n* : any of a genus of pinnate-leaved tropical American trees with clusters of showy blue flowers

¹jack \'jak\ *n* **1** : a mechanical device; *esp* : one used to raise a heavy body a short distance **2** : a male donkey **3** : a small target ball in lawn bowling **4** : a small national flag flown by a ship **5** : a small 6-pointed metal object used in a game (**jacks**) **6** : a playing card bearing the figure of a soldier or servant **7** : a socket into which a plug is inserted for connecting electric circuits

²jack *vb* **1** : to raise by means of a jack **2** : INCREASE ⟨~ up prices⟩

jack·al \'ja-kəl\ *n* [Turk *çakal,* fr. Pers *shaqāl*] : any of several mammals of Asia and Africa related to the wolves

jack·a·napes \'ja-kə-ˌnāps\ *n* **1** : MONKEY, APE **2** : an impudent or conceited person

jack·ass \'jak-ˌas\ *n* **1** : DONKEY; *esp* : a male donkey **2** : a stupid person : FOOL

jack·boot \-ˌbüt\ *n* **1** : a heavy military boot of glossy black leather extending

above the knee **2** : a laceless military boot reaching to the calf

jack·daw \'jak-ˌdo\ *n* : a black and gray Old World crowlike bird

jack·et \'ja-kət\ *n* [ME *jaket,* fr. AF *jackés,* pl., dim. of MF *jaque* short jacket, fr. *jacques* peasant, fr. the name *Jacques* James] **1** : a garment for the upper body usu. having a front opening, collar, and sleeves **2** : an outer covering or casing ⟨a book ~⟩

Jack Frost *n* : frost or frosty weather personified

jack·ham·mer \'jak-ˌha-mər\ *n* : a pneumatic percussion tool for drilling rock or breaking pavement

jack-in-the-box *n, pl* **jack-in-the-boxes** *or* **jacks-in-the-box** : a toy consisting of a small box out of which a figure springs when the lid is raised

jack-in-the-pulpit *n, pl* **jack-in-the-pulpits** *also* **jacks-in-the-pulpit** : a No. American spring-flowering woodland herb having an upright club-shaped spadix arched over by a green and purple spathe

¹jack·knife \'jak-ˌnīf\ *n* **1** : a large pocketknife **2** : a dive in which the diver bends from the waist and touches the ankles before straightening out

²jackknife *vb* : to fold like a jackknife ⟨the trailer truck *jackknifed*⟩

jack·leg \'jak-ˌleg\ *adj* **1** : lacking skill or training **2** : MAKESHIFT

jack-of-all-trades *n, pl* **jacks-of-all-trades** : one who is able to do passable work at various tasks

jack-o'-lan·tern \'ja-kə-ˌlan-tərn\ *n* : a lantern made of a pumpkin cut to look like a human face

jack·pot \'jak-ˌpät\ *n* **1** : a large sum of money formed by the accumulation of stakes from previous play (as in poker) **2** : an impressive and often unexpected success or reward

jack·rab·bit \-ˌra-bət\ *n* : any of several large hares of western No. America with very long ears and hind legs

Jack Russell terrier \'jak-'rə-səl-\ *n* : any of a breed of small terriers having a white coat with dark markings

jack·straw \-ˌstrȯ\ *n* **1** *pl* : a game in which straws or thin sticks are let fall in a heap and each player in turn tries to remove them one at a time without disturbing the rest **2** : one of the pieces used in jackstraws

jack·tar \-'tär\ *n, often cap* : SAILOR

Ja·cob's ladder \'jā-kəbz-\ *n* : any of several perennial herbs related to phlox that have pinnate leaves and blue or white bell-shaped flowers

jac·quard \'ja-ˌkärd\ *n, often cap* : a fabric of intricate variegated weave or pattern

¹jade \'jād\ *n* **1** : a broken-down, vicious, or worthless horse **2** : a disreputable woman

²jade *vb* **jad·ed; jad·ing 1** : to wear out by overwork or abuse **2** : to become weary
   ♦ *Synonyms* EXHAUST, FATIGUE, TIRE

³jade *n* [F, fr. obs. Sp *(piedra de la) ijada*, lit., loin stone; fr. the belief that jade cures renal colic] : a usu. green gemstone that takes a high polish

jad·ed *adj* : made dull, apathetic, or cynical by experience or by surfeit

¹jag \'jag\ *n* : a sharp projecting part

²jag *n* : SPREE ⟨a crying ~⟩

jag·ged \'ja-gəd\ *adj* : sharply notched

jag·uar \'ja-ˌgwär\ *n* : a black-spotted tropical American cat that is larger and stockier than the Old World leopard

jai alai \'hī-ˌlī\ *n* [Sp, fr. Basque, fr. *jai* festival + *alai* merry] : a court game played by usu. two or four players with a ball and a curved wicker basket strapped to the wrist

jail \'jāl\ *n* [ME *jaiole*, fr. AF *gaiole, jaiole*, fr. LL *caveola*, dim. of L *cavea* cage] : PRISON; *esp* : one for persons held in lawful custody — **jail** *vb*

jail·bird \-ˌbȯrd\ *n* : a habitual criminal

jail·break \-ˌbrāk\ *n* : a forcible escape from jail

jail·er *also* **jail·or** \'jā-lər\ *n* : a keeper of a jail

jal·ap \'ja-ləp, 'jä-\ *n* : a powdered purgative drug from the root of a Mexican plant related to the morning glory; *also* : this root or plant

ja·la·pe·ño \ˌhä-lə-'pān-(ˌ)yō\ *n* : a small plump dark green chili pepper

ja·lopy \jə-'lä-pē\ *n, pl* **ja·lop·ies** : a dilapidated vehicle (as an automobile)

jal·ou·sie \'ja-lə-sē\ *n* [F, lit., jealousy] : a blind, window, or door with adjustable horizontal slats or louvers

¹jam \'jam\ *vb* **jammed; jam·ming 1** : to press into a close or tight position **2** : to cause to become wedged so as to be unworkable; *also* : to make or become un-

workable through the jamming of a movable part **3** : to push forcibly ⟨~ on the brakes⟩ **4** : CRUSH, BRUISE ⟨*jammed* a finger in the door⟩ **5** : to make unintelligible by sending out interfering signals or messages **6** : to take part in a jam session — **jam·mer** *n*

²jam *n* **1** : a crowded mass that impedes or blocks ⟨traffic ~⟩ **2** : a difficult state of affairs

³jam *n* : a food made by boiling fruit and sugar to a thick consistency

Jam *abbr* Jamaica

jamb \'jam\ *n* [ME *jambe*, fr. AF *jambe, gambe*, lit., leg] : an upright piece forming the side of an opening (as of a door)

jam·ba·laya \ˌjəm-bə-'lī-ə\ *n* [LaF] : rice cooked with ham, sausage, chicken, shrimp, or oysters and seasoned with herbs

jam·bo·ree \ˌjam-bə-'rē\ *n* : a large festive gathering

James \'jāmz\ *n* — see BIBLE table

jam–pack \'jam-'pak\ *vb* : to pack tightly or to excess

jam session *n* : an impromptu performance esp. by jazz musicians

Jan *abbr* January

jan·gle \'jaŋ-gəl\ *vb* **jan·gled; jan·gling** : to make a harsh or discordant sound — **jangle** *n*

jan·i·tor \'ja-nə-tər\ *n* [L, doorkeeper, fr. *janus* arch, gate] : a person who has the care of a building — **jan·i·to·ri·al** \ˌja-nə-'tȯr-ē-əl\ *adj*

Jan·u·ary \'ja-nyə-ˌwer-ē\ *n* [ME *Januarie*, fr. L *Januarius*, first month of the ancient Roman year, fr. *Janus*, two-faced god of gates and beginnings] : the 1st month of the year

¹ja·pan \jə-'pan\ *n* : a varnish giving a hard brilliant finish

²japan *vb* **ja·panned; ja·pan·ning** : to cover with a coat of japan

Jap·a·nese \ˌja-pə-'nēz, -'nēs\ *n, pl* **Japanese 1** : a native or inhabitant of Japan **2** : the language of Japan — **Japanese** *adj*

Japanese beetle *n* : a small metallic green and brown scarab beetle introduced from Japan that is a pest on the roots of grasses as a grub and on foliage and fruits as an adult

¹jape \'jāp\ *vb* **japed; jap·ing 1** : JOKE **2** : MOCK

²jape *n* : JEST, GIBE

¹jar \'jär\ *vb* **jarred; jar·ring 1** : to make a harsh or discordant sound **2** : to have a harsh or disagreeable effect **3** : VIBRATE, SHAKE ⟨tremors *jarred* the house⟩

²jar *n* **1** : a state of conflict **2** : a harsh discordant sound **3** : JOLT **4** : a painful effect : SHOCK

³jar *n* : a widemouthed container usu. of glass or earthenware

jar·di·niere \ˌjär-də-'nir\ *n* : an ornamental stand for plants or flowers

jar·gon \'jär-gən\ *n* **1** : confused unintelligible language **2** : the special vocabulary of a particular group or activity **3** : obscure and often pretentious language

Jas *abbr* James

jas·mine \\'jaz-mən\\ *also* **jes·sa·mine** \\'jes-mən, 'je-sə-\\ *n* [MF *jasmin,* fr. Ar *yāsamīn,* fr. Pers] : any of various climbing shrubs with fragrant flowers

jas·per \\'jas-pər\\ *n* : a usu. red, yellow, or brown opaque quartz

jaun·dice \\'jȯn-dəs\\ *n* : yellowish discoloration of skin, tissues, and body fluids by bile pigments; *also* : an abnormal condition marked by jaundice

jaun·diced \\-dəst\\ *adj* **1** : affected with or as if with jaundice **2** : exhibiting envy, distaste, or hostility ⟨a ~ critic⟩

jaunt \\'jȯnt\\ *n* : a short trip usu. for pleasure

jaun·ty \\'jȯn-tē\\ *adj* **jaun·ti·er; -est** : sprightly in manner or appearance : LIVELY ⟨~ tunes⟩ — **jaun·ti·ly** \\-tə-lē\\ *adv* — **jaun·ti·ness** \\-tē-nəs\\ *n*

jav·e·lin \\'ja-və-lən\\ *n* **1** : a light spear **2** : a slender shaft thrown for distance in a track-and-field contest

¹jaw \\'jȯ\\ *n* **1** : either of the bony or cartilaginous structures that support the soft tissues enclosing the mouth and that usu. bear teeth **2** : the parts forming the walls of the mouth and serving to open and close it — usu. used in pl. **3** : one of a pair of movable parts for holding or crushing something — **jawed** \\'jȯd\\ *adj*

²jaw *vb* : to talk abusively, indignantly, or at length ⟨~*ing* with her sister⟩

¹jaw·bone \\-,bōn\\ *n* : JAW 1

²jawbone *vb* : to talk forcefully and persuasively

jaw·break·er \\-,brā-kər\\ *n* **1** : a word difficult to pronounce **2** : a round hard candy

jaw–drop·ping \\'jȯ-,dra-piŋ\\ *adj* : causing great surprise or astonishment

jaw·less fish \\'jȯ-ləs-\\ *n* : any of a group of primitive vertebrates (as lampreys) without jaws

jay \\'jā\\ *n* : any of various noisy brightly colored often largely blue birds smaller than the related crows

jay·bird \\'jā-,bərd\\ *n* : JAY

jay·vee \\jā-'vē\\ *n* **1** : JUNIOR VARSITY **2** : a member of a junior varsity team

jay·walk \\'jā-,wȯk\\ *vb* : to cross a street carelessly without regard for traffic regulations — **jay·walk·er** *n*

¹jazz \\'jaz\\ *n* **1** : American music characterized by improvisation, syncopated rhythms, and contrapuntal ensemble playing **2** : empty talk **3** : similar but unspecified things : STUFF

²jazz *vb* : ENLIVEN ⟨~ things up⟩

jazzy \\'ja-zē\\ *adj* **jazz·i·er; -est 1** : having the characteristics of jazz **2** : marked by unrestraint, animation, or flashiness

JCS *abbr* joint chiefs of staff

jct *abbr* junction

JD *abbr* **1** [L *juris doctor*] doctor of jurisprudence; doctor of law **2** [L *jurum doctor*] doctor of laws **3** justice department **4** juvenile delinquent

jeal·ous \\'je-ləs\\ *adj* **1** : demanding complete devotion **2** : suspicious of a rival or of one believed to enjoy an advantage ⟨~ of his rich friends⟩ **3** : VIGILANT — **jeal·ous·ly** *adv* — **jeal·ou·sy** \\-lə-sē\\ *n*

jeans \\'jēnz\\ *n pl* [pl. of *jean* twilled cloth, short for *jean fustian,* fr. ME *Gene* Genoa, Italy] : pants made of durable twilled cotton cloth

jeep \\'jēp\\ *n* : a small four-wheel drive general-purpose motor vehicle used in World War II

¹jeer \\'jir\\ *vb* : to speak or cry out in derision : MOCK ⟨~ed the umpire⟩

²jeer *n* : TAUNT ⟨~ed by the bully⟩

Je·ho·vah \\ji-'hō-və\\ *n* : GOD 1

je·hu \\'jē-hü, -hyü\\ *n* : a driver of a coach or cab

je·june \\ji-'jün\\ *adj* [L *jejunus* empty of food, hungry, meager] : lacking interest or significance : DULL

je·ju·num \\ji-'jü-nəm\\ *n* [L] : the section of the small intestine between the duodenum and the ileum — **je·ju·nal** \\-'jü-n⁰l\\ *adj*

jell \\'jel\\ *vb* **1** : to come to the consistency of jelly **2** : to take shape ⟨my idea began to ~⟩

jel·ly \\'je-lē\\ *n, pl* **jellies 1** : a food with a soft elastic consistency due usu. to the presence of gelatin or pectin; *esp* : a fruit product made by boiling sugar and the juice of a fruit **2** : a substance resembling jelly — **jelly** *vb* — **jel·ly·like** *adj*

jelly bean *n* : a bean-shaped candy

jel·ly·fish \\'je-lē-,fish\\ *n* : a marine coelenterate with a nearly transparent jellylike body and stinging tentacles

jen·net \\'je-nət\\ *n* **1** : a small Spanish horse **2** : a female donkey

jen·ny \\'je-nē\\ *n, pl* **jennies 1** : a female bird or donkey

jeop·ar·dy \\'je-pər-dē\\ *n* [ME *jeopardie,* fr. AF *juparti, jeuparti* alternative, lit., divided game] : exposure to death, loss, or injury ♦ **Synonyms** PERIL, HAZARD, RISK, DANGER — **jeop·ar·dize** \\-,dīz\\ *vb*

Jer *abbr* Jeremiah; Jeremias

jer·e·mi·ad \\,jer-ə-'mī-əd, -,ad\\ *n* : a prolonged lamentation or complaint; *also* : a cautionary or angry harangue

Jer·e·mi·ah \\,jer-ə-'mī-ə\\ *n* — see BIBLE table

Jer·e·mi·as \\,jer-ə-'mī-əs\\ *n* : JEREMIAH

¹jerk \\'jərk\\ *n* **1** : a short quick pull or twist : TWITCH **2** : an annoyingly stupid or foolish person — **jerk·i·ly** \\'jər-kə-lē\\ *adv* — **jerky** \\'jər-kē\\ *adj*

²jerk *vb* **1** : to give a sharp quick push, pull, or twist **2** : to move in short abrupt motions

jer·kin \\'jər-kən\\ *n* : a close-fitting usu. sleeveless jacket

jerk·wa·ter \\'jərk-,wȯ-tər, -,wä-\\ *adj* [fr. *jerkwater* rural train] : of minor importance : INSIGNIFICANT ⟨~ towns⟩

jer·ry–built \\'jer-ē-,bilt\\ *adj* : built cheaply and flimsily

jer·ry–rigged \\-,rigd\\ *adj* : organized or constructed in a crude or improvised manner

jer·sey \\'jər-zē\\ *n, pl* **jerseys** [*Jersey,* one of the Channel islands] **1** : a plain weft-knitted fabric **2** : a close-fitting knitted shirt **3** *often cap* : any of a breed of small usu. fawn-colored dairy cattle

Jersey barrier *n* : a concrete slab that is

used with others to block or reduce traffic or to divide a highway

Je·ru·sa·lem artichoke \jə-'rü-sə-ləm-\ *n* : a No. American sunflower widely grown for its edible tubers that are used as a vegetable; *also* : its tubers

jess \'jes\ *n* : a leg strap by which a captive bird of prey may be controlled

jessamine *var of* JASMINE

¹**jest** \'jest\ *n* **1** : an act intended to provoke laughter **2** : a witty remark **3** : a frivolous mood ⟨said in ∼⟩ — **jest** *vb*

jest·er \'jes-tər\ *n* : a retainer formerly kept to provide casual entertainment

¹**jet** \'jet\ *n* : a velvet-black coal that takes a good polish and is often used for jewelry

²**jet** *vb* **jet·ted; jet·ting** : to spout or emit in a stream

³**jet** *n* **1** : a forceful rush (as of liquid or gas) through a narrow opening; *also* : a nozzle for a jet of fluid **2** : a jet-propelled airplane

⁴**jet** *vb* **jet·ted; jet·ting** : to travel by jet

jet lag *n* : a condition that is marked esp. by fatigue and irritability and occurs following a long flight through several time zones — **jet-lagged** *adj*

jet·lin·er \'jet-,lī-nər\ *n* : a jet-propelled airliner

jet·port \-,pȯrt\ *n* : an airport designed to handle jets

jet-pro·pelled \,jet-prə-'peld\ *adj* : driven by an engine (**jet engine**) that produces propulsion (**jet propulsion**) by the rearward discharge of a jet of fluid (as heated air and exhaust gases)

jet·sam \'jet-səm\ *n* : jettisoned goods; *esp* : such goods washed ashore

jet set *n* : an international group of wealthy people who frequent fashionable resorts

jet stream *n* : a long narrow high-altitude current of high-speed winds blowing generally from the west

jet·ti·son \'je-tə-sən\ *vb* **1** : to throw (goods) overboard to lighten a ship or aircraft in distress **2** : DISCARD ⟨∼ed their old computers⟩ — **jettison** *n*

jet·ty \'je-tē\ *n, pl* **jetties 1** : a pier built to influence the current or to protect a harbor **2** : a landing wharf

jeu d'es·prit \zhœ-des-'prē\ *n, pl* **jeux d'esprit** *same*\ [F, lit., play of the mind] : a witty comment or composition

Jew \'jü\ *n* **1** : ISRAELITE **2** : one whose religion is Judaism — **Jew·ish** *adj*

¹**jew·el** \'jü-əl\ *n* [ME *juel*, fr. AF, dim. of *ju, jeu* game, play, fr. L *jocus* game, joke] **1** : an ornament of precious metal **2** : GEMSTONE, GEM

²**jewel** *vb* **-eled** *or* **-elled; -el·ing** *or* **-el·ling** : to adorn or equip with jewels

jewel box *n* : a thin plastic case for a CD or DVD

jew·el·er *or* **jew·el·ler** \'jü-ə-lər\ *n* : a person who makes or deals in jewelry and related articles

jew·el·lery *chiefly Brit var of* JEWELRY

jew·el·ry \'jü-əl-rē\ *n* : JEWELS; *esp* : objects of precious metal set with gems and worn for personal adornment

Jew·ry \'jůr-ē, 'jù-ər-ē, 'jü-rē\ *n* : the Jewish people

jg *abbr* junior grade

¹**jib** \'jib\ *n* : a triangular sail set on a line running from the bow to the mast

²**jib** *vb* **jibbed; jib·bing** : to refuse to proceed further

¹**jibe** *var of* GIBE

²**jibe** \'jīb\ *vb* **jibed; jib·ing** : to be in accord : AGREE ⟨his conclusion does not ∼ with theirs⟩

ji·ca·ma \'hē-kə-mə\ *n* : an edible starchy tuber of a tropical American vine of the legume family

jif·fy \'ji-fē\ *n, pl* **jiffies** : MOMENT, INSTANT ⟨I'll be ready in a ∼⟩

¹**jig** \'jig\ *n* **1** : a lively dance in triple rhythm **2** : TRICK, GAME ⟨the ∼ is up⟩ **3** : a device used to hold work during manufacture or assembly

²**jig** *vb* **jigged; jig·ging** : to dance a jig

jig·ger \'ji-gər\ *n* : a measure usu. holding 1 to 2 ounces (30 to 60 milliliters) used in mixing drinks

jig·gle \'ji-gəl\ *vb* **jig·gled; jig·gling** : to move with quick little jerks — **jiggle** *n*

jig·saw \'jig-,sȯ\ *n* : SCROLL SAW 2

jigsaw puzzle *n* : a puzzle consisting of small irregularly cut pieces to be fitted together to form a picture

ji·had \ji-'häd, -'had\ *n* **1** : a Muslim holy war **2** : CRUSADE 2

ji·had·ist \ji-'hä-dist, -'ha-\ *n* : a Muslim who advocates or participates in a jihad

¹**jilt** \'jilt\ *vb* : to drop (as a lover) capriciously or unfeelingly

²**jilt** *n* : one who jilts a lover

jim crow \'jim-'krō\ *n, often cap J&C* : discrimination against blacks esp. by legal enforcement or traditional sanctions — **jim crow** *adj, often cap J&C* — **jim crow·ism** \-'krō-,i-zəm\ *n, often cap J&C*

jim-dan·dy \'jim-'dan-dē\ *n* : something excellent of its kind — **jim-dandy** *adj*

jim·mies \'ji-mēz\ *n pl* : tiny rod-shaped bits of usu. chocolate-flavored candy often sprinkled on ice cream

¹**jim·my** \'ji-mē\ *n, pl* **jimmies** : a small crowbar

²**jimmy** *vb* **jim·mied; jim·my·ing** : to force open with a jimmy

jim·son·weed \'jim-sən-,wēd\ *n, often cap* : a coarse poisonous weed related to the tomato that has large trumpet-shaped white or violet flowers

¹**jin·gle** \'jiŋ-gəl\ *vb* **jin·gled; jin·gling** : to make a light clinking or tinkling sound

²**jingle** *n* **1** : a light clinking or tinkling sound **2** : a short verse or song with catchy repetition

jin·go·ism \'jiŋ-gō-,i-zəm\ *n* : extreme chauvinism or nationalism marked esp. by a belligerent foreign policy — **jin·go·ist** \-ist\ *n* — **jin·go·is·tic** \,jiŋ-gō-'is-tik\ *adj*

jin·rik·sha \jin-'rik-,shȯ\ *n* : RICKSHAW

¹**jinx** \'jiŋks\ *n* : one that brings bad luck

²**jinx** *vb* : to foredoom to failure or misfortune

jit·ney \'jit-nē\ *n, pl* **jitneys** : a small bus

that serves a regular route on a flexible schedule

jit·ter·bug \'ji-tər-ˌbəg\ n : a dance in which couples two-step, balance, and twirl vigorously in standardized patterns — **jitterbug** vb

jit·ters \'ji-tərz\ n pl : extreme nervousness — **jit·tery** \-tə-rē\ adj

¹jive \'jīv\ n 1 : swing music or dancing performed to it 2 : glib, deceptive, or foolish talk 3 : the jargon of jazz enthusiasts

²jive vb **jived; jiv·ing** 1 : KID, TEASE 2 : to dance to or play jive

Jn or **Jno** abbr John

Jo abbr Joel

¹job \'jäb\ n 1 : a piece of work 2 : something that has to be done : TASK 3 : a regular remunerative position — **job·less** adj

²job vb **jobbed; job·bing** 1 : to do occasional pieces of work for hire 2 : to hire or let by the job

Job \'jōb\ n — see BIBLE table

job action n : a protest action by workers to force compliance with demands

job·ber \'jä-bər\ n 1 : a person who buys goods and then sells them to other dealers : MIDDLEMAN 2 : a person who does work by the job

job·hold·er \'jäb-ˌhōl-dər\ n : one having a regular job

jock \'jäk\ n [jockstrap] : ATHLETE; esp : a school or college athlete

¹jock·ey \'jä-kē\ n, pl **jockeys** : one who rides a horse esp. as a professional in a race

²jockey vb **jock·eyed; jock·ey·ing** : to maneuver or manipulate by adroit or devious means ⟨rivals ∼ed for power⟩

jock·strap \'jäk-ˌstrap\ n [E slang jock penis] : ATHLETIC SUPPORTER

jo·cose \jō-'kōs\ adj 1 : MERRY ⟨∼ partygoers⟩ 2 : HUMOROUS ♦ Synonyms JOCULAR, FACETIOUS, WITTY

joc·u·lar \'jä-kyə-lər\ adj : marked by jesting : PLAYFUL — **joc·u·lar·i·ty** \ˌjäk-yə-'lar-ə-tē\ n — **joc·u·lar·ly** adv

jo·cund \'jä-kənd\ adj : marked by mirth or cheerfulness ⟨a ∼ celebration⟩

jodh·pur \'jäd-pər\ n 1 pl : riding breeches loose above the knee and tight-fitting below 2 : an ankle-high boot fastened with a strap

Joe Blow \'jō-\ n : an average or ordinary man

Jo·el \'jō-əl\ n — see BIBLE table

Joe Six–Pack \'jō-\ n : a blue-collar worker

¹jog \'jäg\ vb **jogged; jog·ging** 1 : to give a slight shake or push to 2 : to go at a slow monotonous pace 3 : to run or ride at a slow trot — **jog·ger** n

²jog n 1 : a slight shake 2 : a jogging movement or pace

³jog n 1 : a projecting or retreating part of a line or surface 2 : a brief abrupt change in direction

jog·gle \'jä-gəl\ vb **jog·gled; jog·gling** : to shake slightly — **joggle** n

john \'jän\ n 1 : TOILET 2 : a prostitute's client

John \'jän\ n — see BIBLE table

john·ny \'jä-nē\ n, pl **johnnies** : a short-sleeved gown opening in the back that is worn by hospital patients

John·ny–jump–up \ˌjä-nē-'jəmp-ˌəp\ n : any of various small-flowered cultivated pansies

joie de vi·vre \ˌzhwä-də-'vēvrᵃ\ n [F] : keen enjoyment of life

join \'jȯin\ vb 1 : to come or bring together so as to form a unit 2 : to come or bring into close association 3 : to become a member of 4 : ADJOIN 5 : to take part in a collective activity

join·er \'jȯi-nər\ n 1 : a worker who constructs articles by joining pieces of wood 2 : a gregarious person who joins many organizations

¹joint \'jȯint\ n 1 : the point of contact between bones of an animal skeleton with the parts that surround and support it 2 : a cut of meat suitable for roasting 3 : a place where two things or parts are connected 4 : ESTABLISHMENT; esp : a shabby or disreputable establishment 5 : a marijuana cigarette — **joint·ed** adj

²joint adj 1 : UNITED 2 : common to two or more — **joint·ly** adv

³joint vb 1 : to unite by or provide with a joint 2 : to separate the joints of

joist \'jȯist\ n : any of the small beams ranged parallel from wall to wall in a building to support a floor or ceiling

¹joke \'jōk\ n : something said or done to provoke laughter; esp : a brief narrative with a humorous climax

²joke vb **joked; jok·ing** : to make jokes — **jok·ing·ly** adv

jok·er \'jō-kər\ n 1 : a person who jokes 2 : an extra card used in some card games 3 : a misleading part of an agreement that works to one party's disadvantage

jol·li·fi·ca·tion \ˌjä-li-fə-'kā-shən\ n : a festive celebration

jol·li·ty \'jä-lə-tē\ n, pl **-ties** : GAIETY, MERRIMENT

jol·ly \'jä-lē\ adj **jol·li·er; -est** : full of high spirits : MERRY

¹jolt \'jōlt\ vb 1 : to give a quick hard knock or blow to 2 : to move with a sudden jerky motion — **jolt·er** n

²jolt n 1 : an abrupt jerky blow or movement 2 : a sudden shock

Jon abbr Jonah; Jonas

Jo·nah \'jō-nə\ n — see BIBLE table

Jo·nas \'jō-nəs\ n : JONAH

¹jones \'jōnz\ n 1 slang : addiction to heroin 2 slang : HEROIN 3 slang : a craving for something

²jones vb, slang : to have a craving for something

jon·gleur \zhōⁿ-'glər\ n : an itinerant medieval minstrel

jon·quil \'jän-kwəl\ n [F jonquille, fr. Sp junquillo, dim. of junco reed, fr. L juncus] : a narcissus with fragrant clustered white or yellow flowers

josh \'jäsh\ vb : TEASE, JOKE

Josh abbr Joshua

Josh·ua \'jä-shə-wə\ n — see BIBLE table

Joshua tree n : a tall branched yucca of the southwestern U.S.

jos·tle \'jä-səl\ vb **jos·tled; jos·tling 1** : to come in contact or into collision **2** : to make one's way by pushing and shoving ⟨*jostled* his way onto the bus⟩

Jos·ue \'jä-shü-ē\ n : JOSHUA

¹jot \'jät\ n : the least bit : IOTA

²jot vb **jot·ted; jot·ting** : to write briefly and hurriedly

jot·ting \'jä-tiŋ\ n : a brief note

joule \'jül\ n : a unit of work or energy equal to the work done by a force of one newton acting through a distance of one meter

jounce \'jauns\ vb **jounced; jounc·ing** : JOLT — **jounce** n

jour abbr **1** journal **2** journeyman

jour·nal \'jər-nᵊl\ n [ME, service book containing the day hours, fr. AF *jurnal*, fr. *jurnal* daily, fr. L *diurnalis*, fr. *dies* day] **1** : a brief account of daily events **2** : a record of proceedings (as of a legislative body) **3** : a periodical (as a newspaper) dealing esp. with current events **4** : the part of a rotating axle or spindle that turns in a bearing

jour·nal·ese \ˌjər-nə-'lēz, -'lēs\ n : a style of writing held to be characteristic of newspapers

jour·nal·ism \'jər-nə-ˌli-zəm\ n **1** : the business of writing for, editing, or publishing periodicals (as newspapers) **2** : writing designed for or characteristic of newspapers — **jour·nal·ist** \-list\ n — **jour·nal·is·tic** \ˌjər-nə-'lis-tik\ adj

¹jour·ney \'jər-nē\ n, pl **journeys** [ME, fr. OF *journee* day's journey, fr. *jour* day] : a traveling from one place to another

²journey vb **jour·neyed; jour·ney·ing** : to go on a journey : TRAVEL

jour·ney·man \-mən\ n **1** : a worker who has learned a trade and works for another person **2** : an experienced reliable worker

¹joust \'jaust\ vb : to engage in a joust

²joust n : a combat on horseback between two knights with lances esp. as part of a tournament

jo·vial \'jō-vē-əl\ adj : marked by good humor ⟨in a ~ mood⟩ — **jo·vi·al·i·ty** \ˌjō-vē-'a-lə-tē\ n — **jo·vi·al·ly** adv

¹jowl \'jaú-(ə)l\ n : loose flesh about the lower jaw or throat

²jowl n **1** : the lower jaw **2** : CHEEK

¹joy \'jói\ n [ME, fr. AF *joie*, fr. L *gaudia*] **1** : a feeling of happiness that comes from success, good fortune, or a sense of well-being **2** : a source of happiness ✦ **Synonyms** BLISS, DELIGHT, ENJOYMENT, PLEASURE — **joy·less** adj

²joy vb : REJOICE

joy·ful \-fəl\ adj : experiencing, causing, or showing joy ⟨~ news⟩ — **joy·ful·ly** adv

joy·ous \'jói-əs\ adj : JOYFUL — **joy·ous·ly** adv — **joy·ous·ness** n

joy·ride \'jói-ˌrīd\ n : a ride for pleasure often marked by reckless driving — **joy·ride** vb — **joy·rid·er** n — **joy·rid·ing** n

joy·stick \-ˌstik\ n : a control device (as for a computer) consisting of a lever capable of motion in two or more directions

JP abbr **1** jet propulsion **2** justice of the peace

JPEG \'jā-ˌpeg\ n [*Joint Photographic Experts Group*] : a computer file format for usu. high-quality digital images

Jr abbr junior

jt or **jnt** abbr joint

ju·bi·lant \'jü-bə-lənt\ adj [L *jubilans*, prp. of *jubilare* to rejoice] : EXULTANT ⟨~ winners⟩ — **ju·bi·lant·ly** adv

ju·bi·la·tion \ˌjü-bə-'lā-shən\ n : EXULTATION

ju·bi·lee \'jü-bə-ˌlē, ˌjü-bə-'lē\ n [ME, fr. AF & LL; AF *jubilé*, fr. LL *jubilaeus*, fr. LGk *iōbēlaios*, fr. Heb *yōbhēl* ram's horn, trumpet, jubilee] **1** : a 50th anniversary **2** : a season or occasion of celebration

ju·co \'jü-ˌkō\ n, pl **jucos** : JUNIOR COLLEGE; *also* : an athlete at a junior college

Jud abbr Judith

Ju·da·ic \jü-'dā-ik\ *also* **Ju·da·i·cal** \-'dā-ə-kəl\ adj : of, relating to, or characteristic of Jews or Judaism

Ju·da·ism \'jü-də-ˌi-zəm, -dā-, -dē-\ n : a religion developed among the ancient Hebrews and marked by belief in one God and by the moral and ceremonial laws of the Old Testament and the rabbinic tradition

Jude \'jüd\ n — see BIBLE table

Judg abbr Judges

¹judge \'jəj\ vb **judged; judg·ing 1** : to form an authoritative opinion **2** : to decide as a judge : TRY **3** : to form an estimate or evaluation about something : THINK ✦ **Synonyms** CONCLUDE, DEDUCE, GATHER, INFER

²judge n **1** : a public official authorized to decide questions brought before a court **2** : UMPIRE **3** : one who gives an authoritative opinion : CRITIC — **judge·ship** n

Judges n — see BIBLE table

judg·ment or **judge·ment** \'jəj-mənt\ n **1** : a decision or opinion given after judging; *esp* : a formal decision given by a court **2** cap : the final judging of mankind by God **3** : the process of forming an opinion by discerning and comparing **4** : the capacity for judging : DISCERNMENT

judg·men·tal \ˌjəj-'men-təl\ adj **1** : of, relating to, or involving judgment **2** : characterized by a tendency to judge harshly — **judg·men·tal·ly** adv

judgment call n : a subjective decision, ruling, or opinion

Judgment Day n : the day of the final judging of all human beings by God

ju·di·ca·ture \'jü-di-kə-ˌchùr\ n **1** : the administration of justice **2** : JUDICIARY 1

ju·di·cial \jü-'di-shəl\ adj **1** : of or relating to the administration of justice or the judiciary **2** : ordered or enforced by a court **3** : CRITICAL — **ju·di·cial·ly** adv

ju·di·cia·ry \jü-'di-shē-ˌer-ē, -shə-rē\ n **1** : a system of courts of law; *also* : the judges of these courts **2** : a branch of government in which judicial power is vested — **judiciary** adj

ju·di·cious \jü-'di-shəs\ adj : having, exercising, or characterized by sound judgment ⟨a ~ decision⟩ ✦ **Synonyms**

PRUDENT, SAGE, SANE, SENSIBLE, WISE — **ju·di·cious·ly** adv

Ju·dith \ˈjü-dəth\ n — see BIBLE table

ju·do \ˈjü-dō\ n [Jp, fr. jū weakness, gentleness + dō art] : a sport derived from jujitsu that emphasizes the use of quick movement and leverage to throw an opponent — **ju·do·ist** \-ist\ n

ju·do·ka \ˈjü-dō-ˌkä\ n, pl judoka or judokas : one who participates in judo

¹**jug** \ˈjəg\ n 1 : a large deep container with a narrow mouth and a handle 2 : JAIL, PRISON

²**jug** vb jugged; jug·ging : JAIL, IMPRISON

jug–eared \ˈjəg-ˌird\ adj : having protuberant ears

jug·ger·naut \ˈjə-gər-ˌnȯt\ n [Hindi Jagannāth, title of Vishnu (a Hindu god), lit., lord of the world] : a massive inexorable force or object that crushes everything in its path

jug·gle \ˈjə-gəl\ vb jug·gled; jug·gling 1 : to keep several objects in motion in the air at the same time 2 : to manipulate esp. in order to achieve a desired and often fraudulent end — **jug·gler** \ˈjə-glər\ n

jug·u·lar \ˈjə-gyə-lər\ adj : of, relating to, or situated in or on the throat or neck ⟨the ~ veins⟩

juice \ˈjüs\ n 1 : the extractable fluid contents of cells or tissues 2 pl : the natural fluids of an animal body 3 : something that supplies power; esp : ELECTRICITY 2

juic·er \ˈjü-sər\ n : an appliance for extracting juice (as from fruit)

juice up vb : to give life, energy, or spirit to ⟨juice up the music⟩

juicy \ˈjü-sē\ adj juic·i·er; -est 1 : SUCCULENT 2 : rich in interest; also : RACY ⟨~ gossip⟩ — **juic·i·ly** \-sə-lē\ adv — **juic·i·ness** \-sē-nəs\ n

ju·jit·su also **ju·jut·su** or **jiu·jit·su** \jü-ˈjit-sü\ n : an art of fighting employing holds, throws, and paralyzing blows

ju·ju \ˈjü-jü\ n : a style of African music characterized by a rapid beat, use of percussion instruments, and vocal harmonies

ju·jube \ˈjü-ˌjüb, ˈjü-jü-ˌbē\ n : a fruit-flavored gumdrop or lozenge

juke·box \ˈjük-ˌbäks\ n : a coin-operated machine that automatically plays selected recordings

Jul abbr July

ju·lep \ˈjü-ləp\ n [ME, sweetened water, fr. MF, fr. Ar julāb, fr. Pers gulāb, fr. gul rose + āb water] : a drink made of bourbon, sugar, and mint served over crushed ice

Ju·ly \ju̇-ˈlī\ n [ME Julie, fr. OE Julius, fr. L, fr. Gaius Julius Caesar] : the 7th month of the year

¹**jum·ble** \ˈjəm-bəl\ vb jum·bled; jum·bling : to mix in a confused mass

²**jumble** n : a disorderly mass or pile

jum·bo \ˈjəm-bō\ n, pl jumbos [Jumbo, a huge elephant exhibited by P.T. Barnum] : a very large specimen of its kind ⟨a ~ TV screen⟩ — **jumbo** adj

¹**jump** \ˈjəmp\ vb 1 : to spring into the air : leap over 2 : to give a start 3 : to rise or

increase suddenly or sharply 4 : to make a sudden attack 5 : to leave hurriedly and often furtively ⟨~ town⟩ 6 : to act or move before (as a signal) — **jump bail** : to abscond after being released from custody on bail — **jump ship** 1 : to leave the company of a ship without authority 2 : to desert a cause — **jump the gun** : to begin something before the proper time

²**jump** n 1 : a spring into the air; esp : one made for height or distance in a track meet 2 : a sharp sudden increase 3 : an initial advantage ⟨got the ~ on his rival⟩

¹**jump·er** \ˈjəm-pər\ n : one that jumps

²**jumper** n 1 : a loose blouse 2 : a sleeveless one-piece dress worn usu. with a blouse 3 pl : a child's sleeveless coverall

jumping bean n : a seed of any of several Mexican shrubs that tumbles about because of the movements of a small moth larva inside it

jumping–off place n 1 : a remote or isolated place 2 : a place from which an enterprise is launched

jump·mas·ter \ˈjəmp-ˌmas-tər\ n : a person who supervises parachutists

jump–start \ˈjəmp-ˌstärt\ vb : to start (an engine or vehicle) by connection to an external power source

jump·suit \ˈjəmp-ˌsüt\ n 1 : a coverall worn by parachutists in jumping 2 : a one-piece garment consisting of a blouse or shirt with attached pants or shorts

jumpy \ˈjəm-pē\ adj jump·i·er; -est : NERVOUS, JITTERY

jun abbr junior

Jun abbr June

junc abbr junction

jun·co \ˈjəŋ-kō\ n, pl juncos or juncoes : any of a genus of small common pink-billed No. American finches that are largely gray with conspicuous white tail feathers

junc·tion \ˈjəŋk-shən\ n 1 : an act of joining 2 : a place or point of meeting

junc·ture \ˈjəŋk-chər\ n 1 : JOINT, CONNECTION 2 : UNION 3 : a critical time or state of affairs

June \ˈjün\ n [ME, fr. L Junius] : the 6th month of the year

jun·gle \ˈjəŋ-gəl\ n [Hindi & Urdu jangal forest] 1 : a thick tangled mass of tropical vegetation; also : a tract overgrown with vegetation 2 : a place of ruthless struggle for survival

¹**ju·nior** \ˈjü-nyər\ adj 1 : YOUNGER 2 : lower in rank ⟨a ~ partner⟩ 3 : of or relating to juniors

²**junior** n 1 : a person who is younger or of lower rank than another 2 : a student in the next-to-last year before graduating

junior college n : a school that offers studies corresponding to those of the 1st two years of college

junior high school n : a school usu. including grades 7–9

junior varsity n : a team whose members lack the experience or qualifications required for the varsity

ju·ni·per \ˈjü-nə-pər\ n : any of numerous coniferous shrubs or trees with leaves like needles or scales and female cones like berries

¹junk \'jəŋk\ *n* **1** : old iron, glass, paper, or waste; *also* : discarded articles **2** : a shoddy product **3** : something of little meaning, worth, or significance **4** *slang* : NARCOTICS; *esp* : HEROIN — **junky** *adj*

²junk *vb* : DISCARD, SCRAP

³junk *n* : a ship of eastern Asia with a high stern and 4-cornered sails

junk·er \'jəŋ-kər\ *n* : something (as an old automobile) ready for scrapping

Jun·ker \'yún-kər\ *n* [G] : a member of the Prussian landed aristocracy

jun·ket \'jəŋ-kət\ *n* **1** : a pudding of sweetened flavored milk set by rennet **2** : a trip made by an official at public expense

junk food *n* : food that is high in calories but low in nutritional content

junk·ie *also* **junky** \'jəŋ-kē\ *n, pl* **junkies** **1** : a narcotics peddler or addict **2** : one that derives inordinate pleasure from or is dependent on something ⟨a sugar ∼⟩

jun·ta \'hùn-tə, 'jən-, 'hən-\ *n* [Sp, fr. *junto* joined, fr. L *junctus*, pp. of *jungere* to join] : a group of persons controlling a government esp. after a revolutionary seizure of power

Ju·pi·ter \'jü-pə-tər\ *n* : the largest of the planets and the one 5th in order of distance from the sun

Ju·ras·sic \jù-'ra-sik\ *adj* : of, relating to, or being the period of the Mesozoic era between the Triassic and the Cretaceous that is marked esp. by the presence of dinosaurs — **Jurassic** *n*

ju·rid·i·cal \jù-'ri-di-kəl\ *also* **ju·rid·ic** \-dik\ *adj* **1** : of or relating to the administration of justice **2** : LEGAL — **ju·rid·i·cal·ly** \-k(ə-)lē\ *adv*

ju·ris·dic·tion \ˌjùr-əs-'dik-shən\ *n* **1** : the power, right, or authority to interpret and apply the law **2** : the authority of a sovereign power **3** : the limits or territory within which authority may be exercised — **ju·ris·dic·tion·al** \-shə-nəl\ *adj*

ju·ris·pru·dence \-'prü-dᵊns\ *n* **1** : the science or philosophy of law **2** : a system of laws

ju·rist \'jùr-ist\ *n* : one having a thorough knowledge of law; *esp* : JUDGE

ju·ris·tic \jù-'ris-tik\ *adj* **1** : of or relating to a jurist or jurisprudence **2** : of, relating to, or recognized in law

ju·ror \'jùr-ər, -ˌȯr\ *n* : a member of a jury

¹ju·ry \'jùr-ē\ *n, pl* **juries 1** : a body of persons sworn to inquire into a matter submitted to them and to give their verdict **2** : a committee for judging and awarding prizes

²jury *adj* : improvised for temporary use esp. in an emergency ⟨a ∼ mast⟩

jury nullification *n* : the acquitting of a defendant by a jury in disregard of the judge's instructions and contrary to the jury's findings of fact

jury–rig \'jùr-ē-ˌrig\ *vb* : to construct or arrange in a makeshift fashion

¹just \'jəst\ *adj* **1** : having a basis in or conforming to fact or reason : REASONABLE ⟨∼ comment⟩ **2** : CORRECT, PROPER ⟨∼ proportions⟩ **3** : morally or legally right ⟨a ∼ title⟩ **4** : DESERVED, MERITED ⟨∼ punishment⟩ ♦ **Synonyms** UPRIGHT, HONORABLE, CONSCIENTIOUS, HONEST — **just·ly** *adv* — **just·ness** *n*

²just \'jəst, 'jist\ *adv* **1** : EXACTLY ⟨∼ right⟩ **2** : very recently ⟨has ∼ left⟩ **3** : BARELY ⟨∼ too late⟩ **4** : DIRECTLY ⟨∼ west of here⟩ **5** : ONLY ⟨∼ last year⟩ **6** : QUITE ⟨∼ wonderful⟩ **7** : POSSIBLY ⟨it ∼ might work⟩

jus·tice \'jəs-təs\ *n* **1** : the administration of what is just (as by assigning merited rewards or punishments) **2** : JUDGE **3** : the administration of law **4** : FAIRNESS; *also* : RIGHTEOUSNESS

justice of the peace : a local magistrate empowered chiefly to try minor cases, to administer oaths, and to perform marriages

jus·ti·fy \'jəs-tə-ˌfī\ *vb* **-fied; -fy·ing 1** : to prove to be just, right, or reasonable **2** : to pronounce free from guilt or blame **3** : to adjust spaces in a line of printed text so the margins are even — **jus·ti·fi·able** *adj* — **jus·ti·fi·ca·tion** \ˌjəs-tə-fə-'kā-shən\ *n*

jut \'jət\ *vb* **jut·ted; jut·ting** : PROJECT, PROTRUDE

jute \'jüt\ *n* : a strong glossy fiber from either of two tropical plants used esp. for making sacks and twine

juv *abbr* juvenile

¹ju·ve·nile \'jü-və-ˌnī(-ə)l, -nəl\ *adj* **1** : showing incomplete development **2** : of, relating to, or characteristic of children or young people

²juvenile *n* **1** : a young person; *esp* : one below the legally established age of adulthood **2** : a young animal (as a fish or a bird) or plant **3** : an actor or actress who plays youthful parts

juvenile delinquency *n* : violation of the law or antisocial behavior by a juvenile — **juvenile delinquent** *n*

jux·ta·pose \'jək-stə-ˌpōz\ *vb* **-posed; -pos·ing** : to place side by side — **jux·ta·po·si·tion** \ˌjək-stə-pə-'zi-shən\ *n*

JV *abbr* junior varsity

¹**k** \'kā\ *n, pl* **k's** *or* **ks** \'kāz\ **1** *often cap*
: the 11th letter of the English alphabet **2**
cap : STRIKEOUT

²**k** *abbr* **1** karat **2** kitchen **3** knit **4** kosher
— often enclosed in a circle

¹**K** *abbr* **1** Kelvin **2** kindergarten

²**K** *symbol* [NL *kalium*] potassium

kab·ba·lah *also* **kab·ba·la** *or* **ka·ba·la** *or*
ca·ba·la \kə-'bä-lə, 'ka-bə-lə\ *n, often cap*
1 : a medieval Jewish mysticism marked
by belief in creation through emanation
and a cipher method of interpreting
Scripture **2** : esoteric or mysterious doctrine

kabob *var of* KEBAB

Ka·bu·ki \kə-'bü-kē\ *n* : traditional Japanese popular drama with highly stylized
singing and dancing

kad·dish \'kä-dish\ *n, often cap* : a Jewish
prayer recited in the daily synagogue ritual and by mourners at public services
after the death of a close relative

kaf·fee·klatsch \'kȯ-fē-,klach, 'kä-\ *n, often cap* [G] : an informal social gathering
for coffee and conversation

kai·ser \'kī-zər\ *n* : EMPEROR; *esp* : the
ruler of Germany from 1871 to 1918

Ka·lash·ni·kov \kə-'lash-nə-,kȯf\ *n* [M. T.
Kalashnikov b1919 Soviet weapons de-
signer] : a Soviet-designed assault rifle

kale \'kāl\ *n* : a hardy cabbage with
curled leaves that do not form a head

ka·lei·do·scope \kə-'lī-də-,skōp\ *n* : a
tube containing loose bits of colored material (as glass) and two mirrors at one
end that shows many different patterns
as it is turned — **ka·lei·do·scop·ic** \-,lī-
də-'skä-pik\ *adj* — **ka·lei·do·scop·i·cal-
ly** \-pi-k(ə-)lē\ *adv*

ka·ma·ai·na \,kä-mə-'ī-nə\ *n* [Hawaiian
kama'aina, fr. *kama* child + *'aina* land]
: one who has lived in Hawaii for a long
time

kame \'kām\ *n* [Sc, lit., comb] : a short
ridge or mound of material deposited by
water from a melting glacier

ka·mi·ka·ze \,kä-mi-'kä-zē\ *n* [Jp, lit., divine wind] : a member of a corps of Japanese pilots assigned to make a suicidal
crash on a target; *also* : an airplane flown
in such an attack

Kan *or* **Kans** *abbr* Kansas

kan·ga·roo \,kaŋ-gə-'rü\ *n, pl* **-roos** : any
of various large leaping marsupial mammals of Australia and adjacent islands
with powerful hind legs and a long thick
tail used as a support

kangaroo court *n* : a court or an illegal
self-appointed tribunal characterized by
irresponsible, perverted, or irregular procedures

ka·o·lin \'kā-ə-lən\ *n* : a fine usu. white
clay used in ceramics and refractories
and for the treatment of diarrhea

ka·pey·ka \kä-'pā-kä\ *n, pl* **ka·pe·ek** \kä-
'pā-ək\ — see *rubel* at MONEY table

ka·pok \'kä-,päk\ *n* : silky fiber from the
seeds of a tropical tree used esp. as a filling (as for life preservers)

Kap·o·si's sar·co·ma \'ka-pə-sēz-sär-
'kō-mə\ *n* : a neoplastic disease associated esp. with AIDS that affects esp. the
skin and mucous membranes and is characterized usu. by the formation of pink
to reddish-brown or bluish plaques

kap·pa \'ka-pə\ *n* : the 10th letter of the
Greek alphabet — K or κ

ka·put *also* **ka·putt** \kä-'pu̇t, kə-, -'pu̇t\
adj [G, fr. F *capot*] not having made a
trick at piquet] **1** : utterly defeated or
destroyed **2** : unable to function : USE-
LESS

kar·a·kul \'ker-ə-kəl\ *n* : the usu. curly
glossy black coat of a very young lamb of
a hardy Asian breed of sheep

kar·a·o·ke \,ker-ē-'ō-kē\ *n* [Jp] : a device
that plays instrumental accompaniments
for songs to which the user sings along

kar·at \'ker-ət\ *n* : a unit for expressing
proportion of gold in an alloy equal to
¹⁄₂₄ part of pure gold

ka·ra·te \kə-'rä-tē\ *n* [Jp, lit., empty hand]
: an art of self-defense in which an attacker is disabled by crippling kicks and
punches

kar·ma \'kär-mə\ *n, often cap* [Skt] : the
force generated by a person's actions
held in Hinduism and Buddhism to per-
petuate reincarnation and to determine
the nature of the person's next existence
— **kar·mic** \-mik\ *adj*

karst \'kärst\ *n* [G] : an irregular limestone region with sinks, underground
streams, and caverns

ka·ty·did \'kä-tē-,did\ *n* : any of several
large green tree-dwelling American grasshoppers with long antennae

kay·ak \'kī-,ak\ *n* : an Eskimo canoe
made of a skin-covered frame with a
small opening and propelled by a double-
bladed paddle; *also* : a similar portable
boat — **kay·ak·er** *n*

kayo \(,)kā-'ō, 'kā-ō\ *n* : KNOCKOUT —
kayo *vb*

ka·zoo \kə-'zü\ *n, pl* **kazoos** : a toy musical instrument consisting of a tube with a
membrane sealing one end and a side
hole to sing or hum into

KB *abbr* kilobyte

kc *abbr* kilocycle

KC *abbr* **1** Kansas City **2** King's Counsel
3 Knights of Columbus

kc/s *abbr* kilocycles per second

KD *abbr* knocked down

ke·bab *or* **ke·bob** *also* **ka·bob** \kə-'bäb\
n : cubes of meat cooked with vegetables
usu. on a skewer

kedge \'kej\ *n* : a small anchor

¹**keel** \'kēl\ *n* **1** : the chief structural mem-

ber of a ship running lengthwise along the center of its bottom **2** : something (as a bird's breastbone) like a ship's keel in form or use — **keeled** \'kēld\ *adj*

²**keel** *vb* : FAINT, SWOON — usu. used with *over* ⟨~ed over from the heat⟩

keel·boat \'kēl-ˌbōt\ *n* : a shallow covered keeled riverboat for freight that is usu. rowed, poled, or towed

keel·haul \-ˌhȯl\ *vb* : to haul under the keel of a ship as punishment

¹**keen** \'kēn\ *adj* **1** : SHARP ⟨a ~ knife⟩ **2** : SEVERE ⟨a ~ wind⟩ **3** : ENTHUSIASTIC ⟨~ about swimming⟩ **4** : mentally alert ⟨a ~ mind⟩ **5** : STRONG, ACUTE ⟨~ eyesight⟩ **6** : WONDERFUL, EXCELLENT — **keen·ly** *adv* — **keen·ness** *n*

²**keen** *n* : a lamentation for the dead uttered in a loud wailing voice or in a wordless cry — **keen** *vb*

¹**keep** \'kēp\ *vb* **kept** \'kept\; **keep·ing 1** : FULFILL, OBSERVE ⟨~ a promise⟩ ⟨~ a holiday⟩ **2** : GUARD ⟨~ us from harm⟩; *also* : to take care of ⟨~ a neighbor's children⟩ **3** : MAINTAIN ⟨~ silence⟩ **4** : to have in one's service or at one's disposal ⟨~ a horse⟩ **5** : to preserve a record in ⟨~ a diary⟩ **6** : to have in stock for sale **7** : to retain in one's possession ⟨~ what you find⟩ **8** : to carry on (as a business) : CONDUCT **9** : HOLD, DETAIN ⟨~ him in jail⟩ **10** : to refrain from revealing ⟨~ a secret⟩ **11** : to continue in good condition ⟨meat will ~ in a freezer⟩ **12** : ABSTAIN, REFRAIN — **keep·er** *n*

²**keep** *n* **1** : FORTRESS **2** : the means or provisions by which one is kept — **for keeps 1** : with the provision that one keep what one has won ⟨play marbles *for keeps*⟩ **2** : PERMANENTLY ⟨came home *for keeps*⟩

keep·away \'kēp-ə-ˌwā\ *n* : a game in which players try to keep an object from one or more other players

keeping *n* : CONFORMITY ⟨in ~ with good taste⟩

keeping room *n* : a common room used for multiple purposes

keep·sake \'kēp-ˌsāk\ *n* : MEMENTO

keep up *vb* **1** : to persevere in **2** : MAINTAIN, SUSTAIN **3** : to keep informed **4** : to continue without interruption

keg \'keg\ *n* : a small cask or barrel

keg·ger \'ke-gər\ *n* : a party featuring one or more kegs of beer

keg·ler \'ke-glər\ *n* : ¹BOWLER

kelp \'kelp\ *n* : any of various coarse brown seaweeds; *also* : a mass of these or their ashes often used as fertilizer

kel·vin \'kel-vən\ *n* : a unit of temperature equal to ¹⁄₂₇₃.₁₆ of the Kelvin scale temperature of the triple point of water and equal to the Celsius degree

Kelvin *adj* : relating to, conforming to, or being a temperature scale according to which absolute zero is 0 K, the equivalent of −273.15°C

ken \'ken\ *n* **1** : range of vision : SIGHT **2** : range of understanding

ken·nel \'ke-nᵊl\ *n* : a shelter for a dog or cat; *also* : an establishment for the breed-

ing or boarding of dogs or cats — **kennel** *vb*

ke·no \'kē-nō\ *n* : a game resembling bingo

ke·no·sis \kə-'nō-səs\ *n* : the relinquishment of divine attributes by Jesus Christ in becoming human — **ke·not·ic** \-'nä-tik\ *adj*

ken·te cloth \'ken-ˌtā-\ *n* : colorfully patterned cloth traditionally woven by hand in Ghana

Ken·tucky bluegrass \kən-'tə-kē-\ *n* : a valuable pasture and meadow grass of both Europe and America

Ke·ogh plan \'kē-(ˌ)ō-\ *n* [Eugene James *Keogh* †1989 Am. politician] : an individual retirement account for the self-employed

ke·pi \'kā-pē, 'ke-\ *n* [F] : a military cap with a round flat top and a visor

ker·a·tin \'ker-ə-tən\ *n* : any of various sulfur-containing proteins that make up hair and horny tissues

kerb \'kərb\ *n, Brit* : CURB 3

ker·chief \'kər-chəf, -ˌchēf\ *n, pl* **ker·chiefs** \-chəfs, -ˌchēfs\ *also* **kerchieves** \-ˌchēvz\ [ME *courchef*, fr. AF *coverchef*, *cuerchief*, fr. *coverir* to cover + *chef* head] **1** : a square of cloth worn esp. as a head covering **2** : HANDKERCHIEF

kerf \'kərf\ *n* : a slit or notch made by a saw or cutting torch

ker·nel \'kər-nᵊl\ *n* **1** : the inner softer part of a seed, fruit stone, or nut **2** : a whole seed of a cereal ⟨a ~ of corn⟩ **3** : a central or essential part : CORE

ker·o·sene *also* **ker·o·sine** \'ker-ə-ˌsēn, ˌker-ə-'sēn\ *n* : a flammable oil produced from petroleum and used for a fuel and as a solvent

kes·trel \'kes-trəl\ *n* : any of various small falcons that usu. hover in the air while searching for prey

ketch \'kech\ *n* : a large fore-and-aft rigged boat with two masts

ketch·up *also* **catch·up** \'ke-chəp, 'ka-\ *or* **cat·sup** \'ke-chəp, 'ka-; 'kat-səp\ *n* : a seasoned tomato puree

ket·tle \'ke-tᵊl\ *n* : a metallic vessel for boiling liquids

ket·tle·drum \-ˌdrəm\ *n* : a brass, copper, or fiberglass drum with calfskin or plastic stretched across the top

¹**key** \'kē\ *n* **1** : a usu. metal instrument by which the bolt of a lock is turned; *also* : a device having the form or function of a key **2** : a means of gaining or preventing entrance, possession, or control **3** : EXPLANATION, SOLUTION **4** : one of the levers pressed by a finger in operating or playing an instrument **5** : a leading individual or principle **6** : a system of seven tones based on their relationship to a tonic; *also* : the tone or pitch of a voice **7** : a small switch for opening or closing an electric circuit ⟨a telegraph ~⟩

²**key** *vb* **1** : SECURE, FASTEN **2** : to regulate the musical pitch of **3** : to bring into harmony or conformity **4** : to make nervous — usu. used with *up*

³**key** *adj* : BASIC, CENTRAL ⟨~ issues⟩

⁴**key** *n* : a low island or reef (as off the southern coast of Florida)

⁵**key** *n, slang* : a kilogram esp. of marijuana or heroin

key·board \-ˌbȯrd\ *n* **1** : a row of keys (as on a piano) **2** : an assemblage of keys for operating a machine

key club *n* : a private club serving liquor and providing entertainment

key·hole \ˈkē-ˌhōl\ *n* : a hole for receiving a key

¹**key·note** \-ˌnōt\ *n* **1** : the first and harmonically fundamental tone of a scale **2** : the central fact, idea, or mood

²**keynote** *vb* **1** : to set the keynote of **2** : to deliver the major address (as at a convention) — **key·not·er** *n*

key·punch \ˈkē-ˌpənch\ *n* : a machine with a keyboard used to cut holes or notches in punch cards — **keypunch** *vb* — **key·punch·er** *n*

key·stone \-ˌstōn\ *n* : the wedge-shaped piece at the crown of an arch that locks the other pieces in place

key·stroke \-ˌstrōk\ *n* : an act or instance of depressing a key on a keyboard

key word *n* : a word that is a key; *esp, usu* **key·word** : a significant word from a title or document used esp. as an indication of the content

kg *abbr* kilogram

KGB *abbr* [Russ *Komitet gosudarstvennoĭ bezopasnosti*] (Soviet) State Security Committee

kha·ki \ˈka-kē, ˈkä-\ *n* [Hindi & Urdu *khākī* dust-colored, fr. *khāk* dust, fr. Pers] **1** : a light yellowish brown color **2** : a khaki-colored cloth; *also* : a military uniform of this cloth

khan \ˈkän, ˈkan\ *n* : a Mongol leader; *esp* : a successor of Genghis Khan

khe·dive \kə-ˈdēv\ *n* : a ruler of Egypt from 1867 to 1914 governing as a viceroy of the sultan of Turkey

khoum \ˈküm\ *n* — see ouguiya at MONEY table

kHz *abbr* kilohertz

KIA *abbr* killed in action

kib·ble \ˈki-bəl\ *vb* **kib·bled; kib·bling** : to grind coarsely — **kibble** *n*

kib·butz \ki-ˈbu̇ts, -ˈbüts\ *n, pl* **kib·but·zim** \-ˌbu̇t-ˈsēm, -ˌbüt-\ [ModHeb *qibbūṣ*] : a communal farm or settlement in Israel

ki·bitz·er \ˈki-bət-sər, kə-ˈbit-\ *n* : one who looks on and usu. offers unwanted advice — **kib·itz** \ˈki-bəts\ *vb*

ki·bosh \ˈki-ˌbäsh\ *n* : something that serves as a check or stop ⟨put the ∼ on his plan⟩

¹**kick** \ˈkik\ *vb* **1** : to strike out or hit with the foot; *also* : to score by kicking a ball **2** : to object strongly **3** : to recoil when fired — **kick·er** *n*

²**kick** *n* **1** : a blow or thrust with the foot; *esp* : a propelling of a ball with the foot **2** : the recoil of a gun **3** : a feeling or expression of objection **4** : stimulating effect esp. of pleasure

kick·back \ˈkik-ˌbak\ *n* **1** : a sharp violent reaction **2** : a secret return of a part of a sum received

kick back *vb* : to assume a relaxed position or attitude

kick·box·ing \ˈkik-ˌbäk-siŋ\ *n* : boxing in which boxers are permitted to kick with bare feet — **kick·box·er** \-sər\ *n*

kick in *vb* **1** : CONTRIBUTE **2** *slang* : DIE **3** : to begin operating or having an effect ⟨the caffeine started to *kick in*⟩

kick·off \ˈkik-ˌȯf\ *n* **1** : a kick that puts the ball in play (as in football) **2** : COMMENCEMENT ⟨campaign ∼⟩

kick off *vb* **1** : to start or resume play with a placekick **2** : to begin proceedings ⟨*kick off* a campaign⟩ **3** *slang* : DIE

kick over *vb* : to begin or cause to begin to fire — used of an internal combustion engine

kick·shaw \ˈkik-ˌshȯ\ *n* [modif. of F *quelque chose* something] **1** : DELICACY **2** : TRINKET

kick·stand \ˈkik-ˌstand\ *n* : a swiveling metal bar attached to a 2-wheeled vehicle for holding it up when not in use

kick–start \ˈkik-ˌstärt\ *vb* : JUMP-START

kicky \ˈki-kē\ *adj* : providing a kick or thrill : EXCITING; *also* : excitingly fashionable

¹**kid** \ˈkid\ *n* **1** : a young goat **2** : the flesh, fur, or skin of a young goat; *also* : something made of kid **3** : CHILD, YOUNGSTER — **kid·dish** *adj*

²**kid** *vb* **kid·ded; kid·ding 1** : FOOL **2** : TEASE — **kid·der** *n* — **kid·ding·ly** *adv*

kid·do \ˈki-dō\ *n, pl* **kiddos 1** — used as a familiar form of address ⟨you're okay, ∼⟩ **2** : CHILD, KID

kid·nap \ˈkid-ˌnap\ *vb* **kid·napped** *also* **kid·naped** \-ˌnapt\; **kid·nap·ping** *also* **kid·nap·ing** \-ˌna-piŋ\ : to hold or carry a person away by unlawful force or by fraud against one's will — **kid·nap·per** *also* **kid·nap·er** \-ˌna-pər\ *n*

kid·ney \ˈkid-nē\ *n, pl* **kidneys** : either of a pair of organs lying near the backbone that excrete waste products of the body in the form of urine

kidney bean *n* **1** : an edible seed of the common cultivated bean; *esp* : one that is large and dark red **2** : a plant bearing kidney beans

kid·skin \ˈkid-ˌskin\ *n* : the skin of a young goat used for leather

kiel·ba·sa \kēl-ˈbä-sə, kil-\ *n, pl* **-basas** *also* **-ba·sy** \-ˈbä-sē\ [Pol *kiełbasa*] : a smoked sausage of Polish origin

¹**kill** \ˈkil\ *vb* **1** : to deprive of life **2** : to put an end to ⟨∼ competition⟩; *also* : DEFEAT ⟨∼ a proposed amendment⟩ **3** : USE UP ⟨∼ time⟩ **4** : to mark for omission ◆ **Synonyms** SLAY, MURDER, ASSASSINATE, EXECUTE — **kill·er** *n*

²**kill** *n* **1** : an act of killing **2** : an animal or animals killed (as in a hunt); *also* : an aircraft, ship, or vehicle destroyed by military action

kill·deer \ˈkil-ˌdir\ *n, pl* **killdeers** *or* **killdeer** [imit.] : an American plover with a plaintive penetrating cry

killer app \-ˈap\ *n* : a component (as a computer application) that in itself makes something worth having or using

killer bee *n* : AFRICANIZED BEE

killer whale *n* : a small gregarious black and white flesh-eating whale with a white oval patch behind each eye

kill·ing *n* : a sudden notable gain or profit

killing field *n* : a scene of mass killing

kill·joy \'kil-ˌjȯi\ *n* : one who spoils the pleasures of others

kiln \'kil, 'kiln\ *n* [ME *kilne*, fr. OE *cyln*, fr. L *culina* kitchen] : a heated enclosure (as an oven) for processing a substance by burning, firing, or drying — **kiln** *vb*

ki·lo \'kē-lō\ *n, pl* **kilos** : KILOGRAM

ki·lo·byte \'ki-lə-ˌbīt, 'kē-\ *n* : 1024 bytes

kilo·cy·cle \'ki-lə-ˌsī-kəl\ *n* : KILOHERTZ

ki·lo·gram \'kē-lə-ˌgram, 'ki-\ *n* **1** : the basic metric unit of mass that is nearly equal to the mass of 1000 cubic centimeters of water at its maximum density — see METRIC SYSTEM table **2** : the weight of a kilogram mass under earth's gravity

ki·lo·hertz \'ki-lə-ˌhərts, 'kē-, -ˌherts\ *n* : 1000 hertz

kilo·li·ter \'ki-lə-ˌlē-tər\ *n* — see METRIC SYSTEM table

ki·lo·me·ter \ki-'lä-mə-tər, 'ki-lə-ˌmē-\ *n* : a metric unit of length equal to 1000 meters — see METRIC SYSTEM table

ki·lo·ton \'ki-lə-ˌtən, 'kē-lō-\ *n* **1** : 1000 tons **2** : an explosive force equivalent to that of 1000 tons of TNT

ki·lo·volt \-ˌvōlt\ *n* : 1000 volts

kilo·watt \'ki-lə-ˌwät\ *n* : 1000 watts

kilowatt–hour *n* : a unit of energy equal to that expended by one kilowatt in one hour

kilt \'kilt\ *n* : a knee-length pleated skirt usu. of tartan worn by men in Scotland

kil·ter \'kil-tər\ *n* : proper condition ⟨out of ∼⟩

ki·mo·no \kə-'mō-nə\ *n, pl* **-nos** **1** : a loose robe with wide sleeves traditionally worn with a wide sash as an outer garment by the Japanese **2** : a loose dressing gown or jacket

kin \'kin\ *n* **1** : an individual's relatives **2** : KINSMAN

ki·na \'kē-nə\ *n, pl* **kina** — see MONEY table

ki·na·ra \kē-'nä-rə\ *n* : a candelabra with seven candlesticks used during Kwanzaa

¹**kind** \'kīnd\ *n* **1** : essential quality or character **2** : a group united by common traits or interests : CATEGORY; *also* : VARIETY **3** : goods or commodities as distinguished from money

²**kind** *adj* **1** : of a sympathetic, forbearing, or pleasant nature **2** : arising from sympathy or forbearance ⟨∼ deeds⟩ ♦ **Synonyms** BENEVOLENT, BENIGN, BENIGNANT, KINDLY — **kind·ness** *n*

kin·der·gar·ten \'kin-dər-ˌgär-tᵊn\ *n* [G, lit., children's garden] : a school or class for children usu. from four to six years old

kin·der·gart·ner \-ˌgärt-nər\ *n* **1** : a kindergarten teacher **2** : a kindergarten pupil

kind·heart·ed \ˌkīnd-'här-təd\ *adj* : marked by a sympathetic nature

kin·dle \'kin-dᵊl\ *vb* **kin·dled; kin·dling** **1** : to set on fire : start burning **2** : to stir up : AROUSE **3** : ILLUMINATE, GLOW

kin·dling \'kind-liŋ, 'kin-lən\ *n* : easily combustible material for starting a fire

¹**kind·ly** \'kīnd-lē\ *adj* **kind·li·er; -est** **1** : of an agreeable or beneficial nature **2** : of a sympathetic or generous nature — **kind·li·ness** *n*

²**kindly** *adv* **1** : READILY ⟨does not take ∼ to criticism⟩ **2** : SYMPATHETICALLY **3** : COURTEOUSLY, OBLIGINGLY

kind of *adv* : to a moderate degree ⟨it's *kind of* late to begin⟩

¹**kin·dred** \'kin-drəd\ *n* **1** : a group of related individuals **2** : one's relatives

²**kindred** *adj* : of a like nature or character

kine \'kīn\ *archaic pl of* COW

kin·e·ma \'ki-nə-mə\ *Brit var of* CINEMA

ki·ne·mat·ics \ˌki-nə-'ma-tiks\ *n* : a science that deals with motion apart from considerations of mass and force — **ki·ne·mat·ic** \-tik\ *or* **ki·ne·mat·i·cal** \-ti-kəl\ *adj*

kin·es·the·sia \ˌki-nəs-'thē-zhə, -zhē-ə\ *or* **kin·es·the·sis** \-'thē-səs\ *n, pl* **-sias** *or* **-ses** \-ˌsēz\ : a sense that perceives bodily position, and weight and is mediated by nervous receptors in tendons, muscles, and joints; *also* : sensory experience derived from this sense — **kin·es·thet·ic** \-'the-tik\ *adj*

ki·net·ic \kə-'ne-tik\ *adj* : of or relating to the motion of material bodies and the forces and energy **(kinetic energy)** associated with them

ki·net·ics \-tiks\ *n sing or pl* : a science that deals with the effects of forces upon the motions of material bodies or with changes in a physical or chemical system

kin·folk \'kin-ˌfōk\ *or* **kinfolks** *n pl* : RELATIVES

king \'kiŋ\ *n* **1** : a male sovereign **2** : a chief among competitors ⟨home-run ∼⟩ **3** : the principal piece in the game of chess **4** : a playing card bearing the figure of a king **5** : a checker that has been crowned — **king·less** *adj* — **king·ly** *adj* — **king·ship** *n*

king crab *n* **1** : HORSESHOE CRAB **2** : a large crab of the No. Pacific caught commercially for food

king·dom \'kiŋ-dəm\ *n* **1** : a country whose head is a king or queen **2** : a realm or region in which something or someone is dominant ⟨a cattle ∼⟩ **3** : one of the three primary divisions of lifeless material, plants, and animals into which natural objects are grouped; *also* : a biological category that ranks above the phylum

king·fish·er \-ˌfi-shər\ *n* : any of numerous usu. bright-colored crested birds that feed chiefly on fish

king·pin \'kiŋ-ˌpin\ *n* **1** : HEADPIN **2** : the leader in a group or undertaking

Kings *n* — see BIBLE table

king–size \'kiŋ-ˌsīz\ *or* **king–sized** \-ˌsīzd\ *adj* **1** : longer than the regular or standard size **2** : unusually large **3** : having dimensions of about 76 by 80 inches (1.9 by 2.0 meters) ⟨a ∼ bed⟩; *also* : of a size that fits a king-size bed

kink \'kiŋk\ *n* **1** : a short tight twist or curl **2** : a mental peculiarity : QUIRK **3** : CRAMP ⟨a ∼ in the back⟩ **4** : an imperfection likely to cause difficulties in operation — **kinky** *adj*

kin·ship \'kin-ˌship\ *n* : RELATIONSHIP

kins·man \'kinz-mən\ *n* : RELATIVE; *esp* : a male relative

kins·wom·an \-ˌwu̇-mən\ *n* : a female relative

ki·osk \'kē-ˌäsk\ *n* **1** : a small structure with one or more open sides **2** : a stand-alone device providing information and services on a computer screen ⟨interactive ∼s at the museum⟩

Ki·o·wa \'kī-ə-ˌwo̅, -ˌwä, -ˌwä\ *n, pl* **Kiowa** *or* **Kiowas** : a member of an American Indian people of Colorado, Kansas, New Mexico, Oklahoma, and Texas

kip \'kip, 'gip\ *n, pl* **kip** *or* **kips** — see MONEY table

kip·per \'ki-pər\ *n* : a fish (as a herring) preserved by salting and drying or smoking — **kipper** *vb*

kirk \'kərk, 'kirk\ *n, chiefly Scot* : CHURCH

kir·tle \'kər-tᵊl\ *n* : a long gown or dress worn by women

kis·met \'kiz-ˌmet, -mət\ *n, often cap* [Turk, fr. Ar *qisma* portion, lot] : FATE

¹kiss \'kis\ *vb* **1** : to touch or caress with the lips as a mark of affection or greeting **2** : to touch gently or lightly

²kiss *n* **1** : a caress with the lips **2** : a gentle touch or contact **3** : a bite-size candy

kiss·er \'ki-sər\ *n* **1** : one that kisses *slang* : MOUTH **2** *slang* : FACE

kit \'kit\ *n* **1** : a set of articles for personal use; *also* : a set of tools or implements or of parts to be assembled **2** : a container (as a case) for a kit

kitch·en \'ki-chən\ *n* **1** : a room with cooking facilities **2** : the personnel that prepares, cooks, and serves food

kitch·en·ette \ˌki-chə-'net\ *n* : a small kitchen or an alcove containing cooking facilities

kitchen police *n* **1** : KP **2** : the work of KPs

kitch·en·ware \'ki-chən-ˌwer\ *n* : utensils and appliances for kitchen use

kite \'kīt\ *n* **1** : any of various long-winged hawks often with deeply forked tails **2** : a light frame covered with paper or cloth and designed to be flown in the air at the end of a long string

kith \'kith\ *n* [ME, fr. OE *cȳthth,* fr. *cūth* known] : familiar friends, neighbors, or relatives ⟨∼ and kin⟩

kitsch \'kich\ *n* [G] : something often of poor quality that appeals to popular or lowbrow taste — **kitschy** \'ki-chē\ *adj*

kit·ten \'ki-tᵊn\ *n* : a young cat — **kit·ten·ish** *adj*

¹kit·ty \'ki-tē\ *n, pl* **kitties** : CAT; *esp* : KITTEN

²kitty *n, pl* **kitties** : a fund in a poker game made up of contributions from each pot; *also* : POOL

kit·ty-cor·ner *also* **cat·ty-cor·ner** *or* **cat·er·cor·ner** \'ki-tē-ˌkȯr-nər, 'ka-, 'ka-tə-\ *or* **kit·ty-cor·nered** *or* **cat·ty-cor·nered** *or* **cat·er-cornered** \-nərd\ *adv or adj* : in a diagonal or oblique position

ki·wi \'kē-(ˌ)wē\ *n* **1** : any of a small genus of flightless New Zealand birds **2** : KIWIFRUIT

ki·wi·fruit \-ˌfrüt\ *n* : a brownish hairy egg-shaped fruit of a subtropical vine that has sweet bright green flesh and small edible black seeds

KJV *abbr* King James Version

KKK *abbr* Ku Klux Klan

kl *abbr* kiloliter

klatch *also* **klatsch** \'klach\ *n* [G *Klatsch* gossip] : a gathering marked by informal conversation

klep·toc·ra·cy \klep-'tä-krə-sē\ *n, pl* **-cies** : government by those who seek chiefly status and personal gain at the expense of the governed

klep·to·ma·nia \ˌklep-tə-'mā-nē-ə\ *n* : a persistent neurotic impulse to steal esp. without economic motive — **klep·to·ma·ni·ac** \-nē-ˌak\ *n*

klieg light *or* **kleig light** \'klēg-\ *n* : a very bright lamp used in making motion pictures

klutz \'kləts\ *n* [Yiddish *klots,* lit., wooden beam] : a clumsy person — **klutzy** *adj*

km *abbr* kilometer

kn *abbr* knot

knack \'nak\ *n* **1** : a clever way of doing something **2** : natural aptitude

knap·sack \'nap-ˌsak\ *n* : a bag (as of canvas) strapped on the back and used esp. for carrying supplies

knave \'nāv\ *n* **1** : ROGUE **2** : JACK 6 — **knav·ery** \'nā-və-rē\ *n* — **knav·ish** \'nā-vish\ *adj*

knead \'nēd\ *vb* : to work and press into a mass with the hands; *also* : MASSAGE — **knead·er** *n*

knee \'nē\ *n* : the joint in the middle part of the leg — **kneed** \'nēd\ *adj*

knee·cap \'nē-ˌkap\ *n* : a thick flat triangular movable bone forming the front of the knee

knee·hole \-ˌhōl\ *n* : a space (as under a desk) for the knees

knee-jerk \'nē-ˌjərk\ *adj* : readily predictable ⟨a ∼ reaction⟩

kneel \'nēl\ *vb* **knelt** \'nelt\ *or* **kneeled**; **kneel·ing** : to bend the knee : fall or rest on the knees

¹knell \'nel\ *vb* **1** : to ring esp. for a death or disaster **2** : to summon, announce, or proclaim by a knell

²knell *n* **1** : a stroke of a bell esp. when tolled (as for a funeral) **2** : an indication of the end or failure of something

knew *past of* KNOW

knick·ers \'ni-kərz\ *n pl* : loose-fitting short pants gathered at the knee

knick-knack \'nik-ˌnak\ *n* : a small trivial article intended for ornament

¹knife \'nīf\ *n, pl* **knives** \'nīvz\ **1** : a cutting instrument consisting of a sharp blade fastened to a handle **2** : a sharp cutting tool in a machine

²knife *vb* **knifed**; **knif·ing** : to stab, slash, or wound with a knife

¹knight \'nīt\ *n* **1** : a mounted warrior of feudal times serving a king **2** : a man honored by a sovereign for merit and in Great Britain ranking below a baronet **3** : a man devoted to the service of a lady **4**

: a member of an order or society **5** : a chess piece having an L-shaped move — **knight·ly** adj

²knight vb : to make a knight of

knight·hood \'nīt-‚hůd\ n **1** : the rank, dignity, or profession of a knight **2** : CHIVALRY **3** : knights as a class or body

knish \kə-'nish\ n [Yiddish] : a small round or square of dough stuffed with a filling (as of meat or fruit) and baked or fried

¹knit \'nit\ vb knit or knit·ted; knit·ting **1** : to link firmly or closely **2** : WRINKLE ⟨~ her brows⟩ **3** : to form a fabric by interlacing yarn or thread in connected loops with needles **4** : to grow together ⟨the fractured bone knitted slowly⟩ — **knit·ter** n

²knit n **1** : a basic knitting stitch **2** : a knitted garment or fabric

knit·wear \-‚wer\ n : knitted clothing

knob \'näb\ n **1** : a rounded protuberance; also : a small rounded ornament or handle **2** : a rounded usu. isolated hill — **knobbed** \'näbd\ adj — **knob·by** \'nä-bē\ adj

¹knock \'näk\ vb **1** : to strike with a sharp blow **2** : BUMP, COLLIDE **3** : to make a pounding noise; esp : to have engine knock **4** : to find fault with

²knock n **1** : a sharp blow **2** : a pounding noise; esp : one caused by abnormal ignition in an automobile engine

knock·down \'näk-‚daůn\ n **1** : the action of knocking down **2** : something (as a blow) that knocks down **3** : something that can be easily assembled or disassembled

knock down vb **1** : to strike to the ground with or as if with a sharp blow **2** : to take apart : DISASSEMBLE **3** : to receive as income or salary : EARN **4** : to make a reduction in

knock·er \'nä-kər\ n : one that knocks; esp : a device hinged to a door for use in knocking

knock–knee \'näk-‚nē\ n : a condition in which the legs curve inward at the knees — **knock–kneed** \-‚nēd\ adj

knock–off \'näk-‚ȯf\ n : a copy or imitation of someone or something popular

knock off vb **1** : to stop doing something **2** : to do quickly, carelessly, or routinely **3** : to deduct from a price **4** : KILL **5** : ROB **6** : COPY, IMITATE

knock·out \'näk-‚aůt\ n **1** : a blow that fells and immobilizes an opponent (as in boxing) **2** : something sensationally striking or attractive

knock out vb **1** : to defeat by a knockout **2** : to make unconscious or inoperative **3** : to tire out : EXHAUST

knock·wurst also **knack·wurst** \'näk-‚wǝrst, -‚vůrst\ n : a short thick heavily seasoned sausage

knoll \'nōl\ n : a small round hill

¹knot \'nät\ n **1** : an interlacing (as of string) forming a lump or knob and often used for fastening or tying together **2** : PROBLEM **3** : a bond of union; esp : the marriage bond **4** : a protuberant lump or swelling in tissue **5** : a rounded cross-

grained area in lumber that is a section through the junction of a tree branch with the trunk; also : the woody tissue forming this junction in a tree **6** : GROUP, CLUSTER **7** : an ornamental bow of ribbon **8** : one nautical mile per hour; also : one nautical mile — **knot·ty** adj

²knot vb knot·ted; knot·ting **1** : to tie in or with a knot **2** : ENTANGLE

knot·hole \-‚hōl\ n : a hole in a board or tree trunk where a knot has come out

knout \'naůt, 'nůt\ n : a whip used for flogging

know \'nō\ vb knew \'nü, 'nyü\; known \'nōn\; know·ing **1** : to perceive directly : have understanding or direct cognition of; also : to recognize the nature of **2** : to be acquainted or familiar with **3** : to be aware of the truth of **4** : to have a practical understanding of — **know·able** adj — **know·er** n — **in the know** : possessing confidential information

know–how \'nō-‚haů\ n : knowledge of how to do something smoothly and efficiently

knowing adj **1** : having or reflecting knowledge, intelligence, or information **2** : shrewdly and keenly alert : DELIBERATE ⟨~ interference⟩ ♦ **Synonyms** CLEVER, BRIGHT, SMART — **know·ing·ly** adv

knowl·edge \'nä-lij\ n **1** : understanding gained by actual experience ⟨a ~ of carpentry⟩ **2** : range of information ⟨to the best of my ~⟩ **3** : clear perception of truth **4** : something learned and kept in the mind

knowl·edge·able \'nä-li-jə-bəl\ adj : having or showing knowledge or intelligence

knuck·le \'nə-kəl\ n : the rounded knob at a joint and esp. at a finger joint

knuckle down vb : to apply oneself earnestly ⟨knuckled down to the task⟩

knuckle under vb : SUBMIT, SURRENDER

knurl \'nərl\ n **1** : KNOB **2** : one of a series of small ridges on a metal surface to aid in gripping — **knurled** \'nərld\ adj — **knurly** adj

¹KO \(‚)kä-'ō, 'kä-ō\ n : KNOCKOUT

²KO vb KO'd; KO'·ing : to knock out in boxing

ko·ala \kō-'ä-lə\ n : a gray furry Australian marsupial that has large hairy ears and feeds on eucalyptus leaves

ko·bo \'kō-(‚)bō\ n, pl kobo — see naira at MONEY table

K of C abbr Knights of Columbus

kohl·ra·bi \kōl-'rä-bē\ n, pl -bies [G, fr. It cavolo rapa, lit., cabbage turnip] : a cabbage that forms no head but has a swollen fleshy edible stem

koi \'kȯi\ n, pl koi [Jp] : a carp bred for large size and a variety of colors and often stocked in ornamental ponds

ko·lin·sky \kə-'lin-skē\ n, pl -skies : the fur of various Asian minks

Ko·mo·do dragon \kə-'mō-dō-\ n [Komodo Island, Indonesia] : a carnivorous lizard of Indonesia that is the largest of all known lizards

kook \'kük\ n : SCREWBALL 2

kooky also **kook·ie** \'kü-kē\ adj kook·i-

er; -est : having the characteristics of a kook : CRAZY, ECCENTRIC ⟨a ∼ radical⟩ — **kook·i·ness** *n*

Koo·te·nai *or* **Ku·te·nai** \'kü-tə-ˌnā\ *n, pl* **-nai** *or* **-nais** : a member of an American Indian people of the Rocky Mountains in both the U.S. and Canada; *also* : their language

ko·peck *or* **ko·pek** \'kō-ˌpek\ *n* [Russ *kopeīka*] — see *ruble* at MONEY table

ko·piy·ka \ˌkō-'pē-kə\ *n* — see *hryvnia* at MONEY table

ko·ra \'kor-ə\ *n* : a 21-stringed African musical instrument

Ko·ran *or* **Qur·an** *also* **Qur'an** \kə-'ran, -'rän\ *n* [Ar *qur'ān*] : a sacred book of Islam that contains revelations made to Muhammad by Allah

ko·ru·na \'kor-ə-ˌnä\ *n, pl* **ko·ru·ny** \-ə-nē\ *or* **korunas** *or* **ko·run** \-ən\ 1 — see MONEY table 2 : the basic monetary unit of Slovakia from 1992 to 2009

ko·sher \'kō-shər\ *adj* [Yiddish, fr. Heb *kāshēr* fit, proper] 1 : ritually fit for use according to Jewish law 2 : selling or serving kosher food

kow·tow \kaủ-'taủ, 'kaủ-ˌtaủ\ *vb* [Chin *kôutóu*, fr. *kòu* to knock + *tóu* head] 1 : to show obsequious deference 2 : to kneel and touch the forehead to the ground as a sign of homage or deep respect

KP \ˌkā-'pē\ *n* 1 : an enlisted person detailed to help the cooks in a military mess 2 : the work of KPs

kph *abbr* kilometers per hour

Kr *symbol* krypton

kraal \'kräl, 'krol\ *n* 1 : a native village in southern Africa 2 : an enclosure for domestic animals in southern Africa

kraut \'kraủt\ *n* : SAUERKRAUT

Krem·lin \'krem-lən\ *n* : the Russian government

Krem·lin·ol·o·gist \ˌkrem-lə-'nä-lə-jist\ *n* : a specialist in the policies and practices of the government of the Soviet Union

¹**kro·na** \'krō-nə\ *n, pl* **kro·nor** \-ˌnor\ [Sw] — see MONEY table

²**kro·na** \'krō-nə\ *n, pl* **kro·nur** \-nər\ [Icel] — see MONEY table

kro·ne \'krō-nə\ *n, pl* **kro·ner** \-nər\ — see MONEY table

kroon \'krōn\ *n, pl* **kroo·ni** \'krō-nē\ *or* **kroons** : the basic monetary unit of Estonia from 1928 to 1940 and from 1991 to 2011

Kru·ger·rand \'krü-gər-ˌrand, -ˌränd\ *n* : a 1-ounce gold coin of the Republic of South Africa

kryp·ton \'krip-ˌtän\ *n* : a gaseous chemical element used esp. in electric lamps

KS *abbr* Kansas

kt *abbr* 1 karat 2 knight

ku·do \'kü-dō, 'kyü-\ *n, pl* **kudos** [fr. *kudos* (taken as pl.)] 1 : AWARD, HONOR 2 : COMPLIMENT, PRAISE

ku·dos \'kü-ˌdäs, 'kyü-\ *n* : fame and renown resulting from achievement

kud·zu \'kud-zü, 'kəd-\ *n* [Jp *kuzu*] : a fast-growing weedy leguminous vine used for forage and erosion control

ku·lak \kü-'lak, kyü-, -'läk\ *n* [Russ, lit., fist] 1 : a wealthy peasant farmer in 19th century Russia 2 : a farmer characterized by Communists as too wealthy

kum·quat \'kəm-ˌkwät\ *n* : any of several small citrus fruits with sweet spongy rind and acid pulp

ku·na \'kü-ˌnä\ *n, pl* **kuna** *or* **ku·ne** \-nä\ — see MONEY table

kung fu \kəŋ-'fü, ˌkùŋ-\ *n* : a Chinese art of self-defense resembling karate

kung pao \'kəŋ-'paủ, 'küŋ-, 'kùŋ-\ *adj* : being stir-fried or deep-fried and served in a spicy hot sauce usu. with peanuts

kur·ta \'kər-tə\ *n* : a long loose-fitting collarless shirt

ku·rus \kə-'rüsh\ *n, pl* **kurus** — see *lira* at MONEY table

kV *abbr* kilovolt

kvell \'kvel\ *vb* : to be extraordinarily proud

kvetch \'kvech, 'kfech\ *vb* : to complain habitually — **kvetch** *n*

kW *abbr* kilowatt

kwa·cha \'kwä-chə\ *n, pl* **kwacha** — see MONEY table

kwan·za \'kwän-zə\ *n, pl* **kwanzas** *or* **kwanza** — see MONEY table

Kwan·zaa *also* **Kwan·za** \'kwän-zə\ [Swahili *kwanza* first] : an African-American cultural festival held from December 26 to January 1

kwash·i·or·kor \ˌkwä-shē-'or-kor, -or-'kor\ *n* : a disease of young children caused by deficient intake of protein

kWh *abbr* kilowatt-hour

Ky *or* **KY** *abbr* Kentucky

kyat \'chät\ *n, pl* **kyats** *or* **kyat** — see MONEY table

ky·bosh *chiefly Brit var of* KIBOSH

¹**l** \'el\ *n, pl* **l's** *or* **ls** \'elz\ *often cap* : the 12th letter of the English alphabet

²**l** *abbr, often cap* 1 lake 2 large 3 left 4 [L *libra*] pound 5 line 6 liter

¹**La** *abbr* Louisiana

²**La** *symbol* lanthanum

LA *abbr* 1 law agent 2 Los Angeles 3 Louisiana

laa·ri \'lä-rē\ *n, pl* **laari** — see *rufiyaa* at MONEY table

lab \'lab\ *n* : LABORATORY

Lab *n* : LABRADOR RETRIEVER

¹**la·bel** \'lā-bəl\ *n* 1 : a slip attached to something for identification or description 2 : a descriptive or identifying word or phrase 3 : BRAND 3

label *vb* **-beled** *or* **-belled; -bel·ing** *or*
-bel·ling **1 :** to affix a label to **2 :** to
describe or name with a label
la·bi·al \'lā-bē-əl\ *adj* **:** of, relating to, or
situated near the lips or labia
la·bia ma·jo·ra \'lā-bē-ə-mə-'jòr-ə\ *n pl*
: the outer fatty folds of the vulva
labia mi·no·ra \-mə-'nòr-ə\ *n pl* **:** the inner highly vascular folds of the vulva
la·bile \'lā-,bī(-ə)l, -bəl\ *adj* **1 :** UNSTABLE
⟨~ a mineral⟩ **2 :** ADAPTABLE
la·bi·um \'lā-bē-əm\ *n, pl* **la·bia** \-ə\ [NL,
fr. L, lip] **:** any of the folds at the margin
of the vulva
¹la·bor \'lā-bər\ *n* **1 :** physical or mental
effort; *also* **:** human activity that provides
the goods or services in an economy **2**
: the physical efforts of giving birth; *also*
: the period of such labor **3 :** TASK **4**
: those who do manual labor or work for
wages; *also* **:** labor unions or their officials
²labor *vb* **1 :** WORK **2 :** to move with great
effort **3 :** to be in the labor of giving
birth **4 :** to suffer from some disadvantage or distress ⟨~ under a delusion⟩ **5**
: to treat or work out laboriously — **la-
bor·er** *n*
lab·o·ra·to·ry \'la-brə-,tòr-ē, -bə-rə-\ *n, pl*
-ries : a place equipped for making scientific experiments or tests
Labor Day *n* **:** the 1st Monday in September observed as a legal holiday in recognition of the working people
la·bored \'lā-bərd\ *adj* **:** not freely or easily done ⟨~ breathing⟩
la·bo·ri·ous \lə-'bòr-ē-əs\ *adj* **1 :** INDUS-
TRIOUS **2 :** requiring great effort — **la-
bo·ri·ous·ly** *adv*
la·bor-sav·ing \'lā-bər-,sā-viŋ\ *adj* **:** designed to replace or decrease labor
labor union *n* **:** an organization of workers formed to advance its members' interest in respect to wages and working conditions
la·bour *chiefly Brit var of* LABOR
lab·ra·dor·ite \'la-brə-,dòr-,īt\ *n* **:** an iridescent feldspar used in jewelry
Lab·ra·dor retriever \'la-brə-,dòr-\ *n*
: any of a breed of strongly built retrievers having a short dense black, yellow, or
chocolate coat
la·bur·num \lə-'bər-nəm\ *n* **:** any of a genus of leguminous shrubs or trees with
hanging clusters of yellow flowers
lab·y·rinth \'la-bə-,rinth\ *n* **:** a place constructed of or filled with confusing intricate passageways **:** MAZE
lab·y·rin·thine \,la-bə-'rin-thən, -,thīn,
-,thēn\ *adj* **:** INTRICATE, INVOLVED ⟨a ~
plot⟩ ⟨~ hallways⟩
lac \'lak\ *n* **:** a resinous substance secreted
by a scale insect and used chiefly in the
form of shellac
¹lace \'lās\ *vb* **laced; lac·ing 1 :** TIE **2 :** to
adorn with lace **3 :** INTERTWINE **4**
: BEAT, LASH **5 :** to add something that
taints (as a drug) or enhances flavor (as a
spice) **6 :** to criticize sharply — used
with *into* ⟨*laced* into his opponent⟩
²lace *n* [ME, fr. AF *lace, laz*, fr. L *laqueus*
snare] **1 :** a cord or string used for draw-

ing together two edges **2 :** an ornamental
braid **3 :** a fine openwork usu. figured
fabric made of thread — **lacy** \'lā-sē\ *adj*
lac·er·ate \'la-sə-,rāt\ *vb* **-at·ed; -at·ing**
: to tear roughly — **lac·er·a·tion** \,la-sə-
'rā-shən\ *n*
lace·wing \'lās-,wiŋ\ *n* **:** any of various
insects with delicate wing veins, long antennae, and often brilliant eyes
lach·ry·mal *or* **lac·ri·mal** \'la-krə-məl\
adj **1** *usu* **lacrimal :** of, relating to, or being glands that produce tears **2 :** of, relating to, or marked by tears
lach·ry·mose \'la-krə-,mōs\ *adj* **1**
: TEARFUL **2 :** MOURNFUL ⟨~ songs⟩
lack \'lak\ *vb* **1 :** to be wanting or missing
2 : to be deficient in ⟨~s experience⟩
lack *n* **:** the fact or state of being wanting
or deficient **:** NEED
lack·a·dai·si·cal \,la-kə-'dā-zi-kəl\ *adj*
: lacking life, spirit, or zest — **lack·a·dai-
si·cal·ly** \-k(ə-)lē\ *adv*
lack·ey \'la-kē\ *n, pl* **lackeys 1 :** FOOT-
MAN, SERVANT **2 :** TOADY
lack·lus·ter \'lak-,ləs-tər\ *adj* **:** DULL
la·con·ic \lə-'kä-nik\ *adj* [L *laconicus*
Spartan, fr. Gk *lakōnikos;* fr. the Spartan
reputation for terseness of speech] **:** sparing of words **:** TERSE ♦ **Synonyms** CON-
CISE, CURT, SHORT, SUCCINCT, BRUSQUE
— **la·con·i·cal·ly** \-ni-k(ə-)lē\ *adv*
lac·quer \'la-kər\ *n* **:** a clear or colored
usu. glossy and quick-drying surface
coating — **lacquer** *vb*
lac·ri·ma·tion \,la-krə-'mā-shən\ *n* **:** secretion of tears
la·crosse \lə-'kròs\ *n* [CanF *la crosse*, lit.,
the crooked stick] **:** a goal game in which
players use a long-handled triangular-
headed stick having a mesh pouch for
catching, carrying, and throwing the ball
lac·tate \'lak-,tāt\ *vb* **lac·tat·ed; lac·tat-
ing :** to secrete milk — **lac·ta·tion** \lak-
'tā-shən\ *n*
lac·tic \'lak-tik\ *adj* **1 :** of or relating to
milk **2 :** obtained from sour milk or
whey
lactic acid *n* **:** a syrupy acid present in
blood and muscle tissue and used esp. in
food and medicine
lac·tose \'lak-,tōs\ *n* **:** a sugar present in
milk
la·cu·na \lə-'kü-nə, -'kyü-\ *n, pl* **la·cu-
nae** \-nē\ *also* **la·cu·nas** [L, pool, pit,
gap, fr. *lacus* lake] **:** a blank space or
missing part **:** GAP, DEFICIENCY
lad \'lad\ *n* **:** YOUTH; *also* **:** FELLOW
lad·der \'la-dər\ *n* **1 :** a structure for
climbing that consists of two parallel
sidepieces joined at intervals by crosspieces **2 :** something resembling a ladder
in having ascending steps or stages ⟨a
tournament ~⟩
lad·die \'la-dē\ *n* **:** a young lad
lad·en \'lā-d°n\ *adj* **:** LOADED, BURDENED
lad·ing \'lā-diŋ\ *n* **:** CARGO, FREIGHT
la·dle \'lā-d°l\ *n* **:** a deep-bowled long-
handled spoon used in taking up and
conveying liquids — **ladle** *vb*
la·dy \'lā-dē\ *n, pl* **ladies** [ME, fr. OE
hlǣfdīge, fr. *hlāf* bread + *-dīge* (akin to
dǣge kneader of bread)] **1 :** a woman of

property, rank, or authority; *also* : a woman of superior social position or of refinement **2** : WOMAN **3** : WIFE

lady beetle *n* : LADYBUG

la·dy·bird \'lā-dē-ˌbərd\ *n* : LADYBUG

la·dy·bug \-ˌbəg\ *n* : any of various small nearly hemispherical and usu. brightly colored beetles that feed mostly on other insects

la·dy·fin·ger \-ˌfiŋ-gər\ *n* : a small finger=shaped sponge cake

lady–in–waiting *n, pl* **ladies–in–waiting** : a lady appointed to attend or wait on a queen or princess

la·dy·like \'lā-dē-ˌlīk\ *adj* : WELL-BRED

la·dy·ship \-ˌship\ *n* : the condition of being a lady : rank of lady

lady's slipper *also* **lady slipper** *n* : any of several No. American orchids with slipper-shaped flowers

¹lag \'lag\ *n* **1** : a slowing up or falling behind; *also* : the amount by which one lags **2** : INTERVAL

²lag *vb* **lagged; lag·ging** **1** : to fail to keep up : stay behind **2** : to slacken gradually ♦ *Synonyms* DAWDLE, DALLY, TARRY, LOITER

la·ger \'lä-gər\ *n* : a usu. dry beer slowly brewed and matured under refrigeration

lag·gard \'la-gərd\ *adj* : tending to lag ⟨~ workers⟩ — **laggard** *n* — **lag·gard·ly** *adv or adj* — **lag·gard·ness** *n*

la·gniappe \'lan-ˌyap\ *n* : something given en free esp. with a purchase

la·goon \lə-'gün\ *n* : a shallow sound, channel, or pond near or connected to a larger body of water

laid *past and past part of* LAY

laid–back \'lād-'bak\ *adj* : having a relaxed style or character ⟨~ music⟩

lain *past part of* LIE

lair \'ler\ *n* **1** : the resting or living place of a wild animal : DEN **2** : a usu. hidden refuge

laird \'lerd\ *n, chiefly Scot* : a landed proprietor

lais·ser–faire *chiefly Brit var of* LAISSEZ-FAIRE

lais·sez–faire \ˌle-ˌsā-'fer, ˌlā-, -ˌzā-\ *n* [F *laissez faire* let do] : a doctrine opposing governmental control of economic affairs beyond that necessary to maintain peace and property rights

la·ity \'lā-ə-tē\ *n* **1** : the people of a religious faith as distinct from its clergy **2** : the mass of people as distinct from those of a particular field

lake \'lāk\ *n* : an inland body of standing water of considerable size; *also* : a pool of liquid (as lava or pitch)

La·ko·ta \lə-'kō-tə\ *n, pl* **Lakota** *also* **La·kotas** : a member of a western division of the Dakota peoples; *also* : their language

¹lam \'lam\ *vb* **lammed; lam·ming** : to flee hastily — **lam** *n*

²lam *abbr* laminated

Lam *abbr* Lamentations

la·ma \'lä-mə\ *n* : a Buddhist monk of Tibet or Mongolia

la·ma·sery \'lä-mə-ˌser-ē\ *n, pl* **-ser·ies** : a monastery for lamas

¹lamb \'lam\ *n* **1** : a young sheep; *also* : its

flesh used as food **2** : an innocent or gentle person

²lamb *vb* : to bring forth a lamb

lam·baste *or* **lam·bast** \lam-'bāst, -'bast\ *vb* **1** : BEAT **2** : EXCORIATE ♦ *Synonyms* CASTIGATE, FLAY, LASH

lamb·da \'lam-də\ *n* : the 11th letter of the Greek alphabet — Λ *or* λ

lam·bent \'lam-bənt\ *adj* [L *lambens*, prp. of *lambere* to lick] **1** : FLICKERING ⟨a ~ flame⟩ **2** : softly radiant ⟨~ eyes⟩ **3** : marked by lightness or brilliance ⟨~ humor⟩ ♦ *Synonyms* EFFULGENT, INCANDESCENT, LUCENT, LUMINOUS — **lam·ben·cy** \-bən-sē\ *n* — **lam·bent·ly** *adv*

lamb·skin \'lam-ˌskin\ *n* : a lamb's skin or a small fine-grade sheepskin or the leather made from either

¹lame \'lām\ *adj* **lam·er; lam·est** **1** : having a body part and esp. a limb so disabled as to impair freedom of movement; *also* : marked by stiffness and soreness **2** : lacking substance : WEAK ⟨~ excuses⟩ **3** : INFERIOR, PITIFUL ⟨a ~ school⟩ — **lame·ly** *adv* — **lame·ness** *n*

²lame *vb* **lamed; lam·ing** : to make lame : DISABLE ⟨was *lamed* by a broken leg⟩

la·mé \lä-'mā, la-\ *n* [F] : a brocaded clothing fabric with tinsel filling threads (as of gold or silver)

lame·brain \'lām-ˌbrān\ *n* : DOLT

lame duck *n* : an elected official continuing to hold office between an election and the inauguration of a successor — **lame–duck** *adj*

¹la·ment \lə-'ment\ *vb* **1** : to mourn aloud : WAIL **2** : to express sorrow or regret for : BEWAIL — **lam·en·ta·ble** \'la-mən-tə-bəl, lə-'men-tə-\ *adj* — **lam·en·ta·bly** \-blē\ *adv* — **lam·en·ta·tion** \ˌla-mən-'tā-shən\ *n*

²lament *n* **1** : a crying out in grief : WAIL **2** : DIRGE, ELEGY **3** : COMPLAINT

Lamentations *n* — see BIBLE table

la·mia \'lā-mē-ə\ *n* : a female demon

lam·i·na \'la-mə-nə\ *n, pl* **-nae** \-ˌnē\ *or* **-nas** : a thin plate or scale

¹lam·i·nate \'la-mə-ˌnāt\ *vb* **-nat·ed; -nat·ing** : to make by uniting layers of one or more materials — **lam·i·na·tion** \ˌla-mə-'nā-shən\ *n*

²lam·i·nate \-nət\ *n* : a product manufactured by laminating

lamp \'lamp\ *n* **1** : a vessel with a wick for burning a flammable liquid (as oil) to produce light **2** : a device for producing light or heat

lamp·black \-ˌblak\ *n* : black soot used esp. as a pigment

lamp·light·er \-ˌlī-tər\ *n* : one that lights a lamp

lam·poon \lam-'pün\ *n* : SATIRE; *esp* : a harsh satire directed against an individual — **lampoon** *vb*

lam·prey \'lam-prē\ *n, pl* **lampreys** : any of a family of eel-shaped jawless fishes that have well-developed eyes and a large disk-shaped sucking mouth armed with horny teeth

LAN \'lan, ˌel-ˌā-'en\ *n* : LOCAL AREA NETWORK

la·nai \lə-ˈnī\ *n* [Hawaiian *lānai*] : PORCH, VERANDA

¹lance \ˈlans\ *n* 1 : a spear carried by mounted soldiers 2 : any of various sharp-pointed implements; *esp* : LANCET

²lance *vb* lanced; lanc·ing : to pierce or open with a lance ⟨~ a boil⟩

lance corporal *n* : an enlisted person in the marine corps ranking above a private first class and below a corporal

lanc·er \ˈlan-sər\ *n* : a cavalryman of a unit formerly armed with lances

lan·cet \ˈlan-sət\ *n* : a sharp-pointed and usu. 2-edged surgical instrument

¹land \ˈland\ *n* 1 : the solid part of the surface of the earth; *also* : a part of the earth's surface ⟨fenced ~⟩ ⟨marshy ~⟩ 2 : NATION 3 : REALM, DOMAIN ⟨the ~ of the living⟩ — **land·less** *adj*

²land *vb* 1 : DISEMBARK; *also* : to touch at a place on shore 2 : to alight or cause to alight on a surface ⟨~ a punch⟩ 3 : to bring to or arrive at a destination 4 : to catch and bring in ⟨~ a fish⟩; *also* : GAIN, SECURE ⟨~ a job⟩

lan·dau \ˈlan-ˌdau̇\ *n* : a 4-wheeled carriage with a top divided into two sections that can be lowered, thrown back, or removed

land·ed *adj* : having an estate in land ⟨~ gentry⟩

land·er \ˈlan-dər\ *n* : a space vehicle designed to land on a celestial body

land·fall \ˈland-ˌfȯl\ *n* : a sighting or making of land (as after a voyage); *also* : the land first sighted

land·fill \-ˌfil\ *n* : a low-lying area on which refuse is buried between layers of earth — **landfill** *vb*

land·form \-ˌfȯrm\ *n* : a natural feature of a land surface

land·hold·er \-ˌhōl-dər\ *n* : a holder or owner of land — **land·hold·ing** \-diŋ\ *adj or n*

land·ing \ˈlan-diŋ\ *n* 1 : the action of one that lands 2 : a place for discharging or taking on passengers and cargo 3 : a level part of a staircase

landing gear *n* : the part that supports the weight of an aircraft when it is on the ground

land·la·dy \ˈland-ˌlā-dē\ *n* : a woman who is a landlord

land·locked \-ˌläkt\ *adj* 1 : enclosed or nearly enclosed by land ⟨a ~ country⟩ 2 : confined to fresh water by some barrier ⟨~ salmon⟩

land·lord \-ˌlȯrd\ *n* 1 : the owner of property leased or rented to another 2 : a person who rents lodgings : INNKEEPER

land·lub·ber \-ˌlə-bər\ *n* : one who knows little of the sea or seamanship

land·mark \-ˌmärk\ *n* 1 : an object that marks a course or boundary or serves as a guide 2 : an event that marks a turning point 3 : a structure of unusual historical and usu. aesthetic interest

land·mass \-ˌmas\ *n* : a large area of land

land mine *n* 1 : a mine placed on or just below the surface of the ground and designed to be exploded by the weight of

someone or something passing over it 2 : a trap for the unwary

land·own·er \-ˌō-nər\ *n* : an owner of land

¹land·scape \-ˌskāp\ *n* 1 : a picture of natural inland scenery 2 : a portion of land that can be seen in one glance

²landscape *vb* land·scaped; land·scap·ing : to modify (a natural landscape) by grading, clearing, or decorative planting

land·slide \-ˌslīd\ *n* 1 : the slipping down of a mass of rocks or earth on a steep slope; *also* : the mass of material that slides 2 : an overwhelming victory esp. in a political contest

lands·man \ˈlandz-mən\ *n* : a person who lives on land; *esp* : LANDLUBBER

land·ward \ˈland-wərd\ *adv or adj* : to or toward the land

lane \ˈlān\ *n* 1 : a narrow passageway (as between fences) 2 : a relatively narrow way or track ⟨traffic ~⟩

lan·guage \ˈlaŋ-gwij\ *n* [ME, fr. AF *langage*, fr. *langue* tongue, language, fr. L *lingua*] 1 : the words, their pronunciation, and the methods of combining them used and understood by a community 2 : form or style of verbal expression ⟨legal ~⟩ 3 : a system of signs and symbols and rules for using them that is used to carry information

lan·guid \ˈlaŋ-gwəd\ *adj* 1 : WEAK 2 : sluggish in character or disposition : LISTLESS ⟨a ~ summer day⟩ 3 : SLOW — **lan·guid·ly** *adv* — **lan·guid·ness** *n*

lan·guish \ˈlaŋ-gwish\ *vb* 1 : to become languid 2 : to become dispirited : PINE 3 : to appeal for sympathy by assuming an expression of grief

lan·guor \ˈlaŋ-gər\ *n* 1 : a languid feeling 2 : listless indolence or inertia ♦ *Synonyms* LETHARGY, LASSITUDE, TORPIDITY, TORPOR — **lan·guor·ous** *adj* — **languor·ous·ly** *adv*

La Ni·ña \lä-ˈnē-nyə\ *n* : an upwelling of unusually cold ocean water along the west coast of So. America that often follows an El Niño

lank \ˈlaŋk\ *adj* 1 : not well filled out 2 : hanging straight and limp ⟨~ hair⟩

lanky \ˈlaŋ-kē\ *adj* lank·i·er; -est : ungracefully tall and thin

lan·o·lin \ˈlan-ᵊl-ən\ *n* : the fatty coating of sheep's wool esp. when refined for use in ointments and cosmetics

lan·ta·na \lan-ˈtä-nə\ *n* : any of a genus of tropical shrubs related to the vervains with showy heads of small bright flowers

lan·tern \ˈlan-tərn\ *n* [ME *lanterne*, fr. AF, fr. L *lanterna*, fr. Gk *lamptēr*, fr. *lampein* to shine] 1 : a usu. portable light with a protective covering 2 : the chamber in a lighthouse containing the light 3 : a projector for slides

lan·tha·num \ˈlan-thə-nəm\ *n* : a soft malleable metallic chemical element

lan·yard \ˈlan-yərd\ *n* : a piece of rope for fastening something in ships; *also* : any of various cords

¹lap \ˈlap\ *n* 1 : a loose panel of a garment 2 : the clothing that lies on the knees, thighs, and lower part of the trunk when one sits; *also* : the front part of the lower trunk and thighs of a seated person **3** : an environment of nurture ⟨the ∼ of luxury⟩ **4** : CHARGE, CONTROL ⟨in the ∼ of the gods⟩

²lap *vb* **lapped; lap·ping 1** : FOLD **2** : WRAP **3** : to lay over or near so as to partly cover

³lap *n* **1** : the amount by which an object overlaps another; *also* : the part of an object that overlaps another **2** : an act or instance of going over a course (as a track or swimming pool)

⁴lap *vb* **lapped; lap·ping 1** : to scoop up food or drink with the tip of the tongue; *also* : DEVOUR — usu. used with *up* **2** : to splash gently ⟨*lapping* waves⟩

⁵lap *n* **1** : an act or instance of lapping **2** : a gentle splashing sound

lap·a·ros·co·py \ˌla-pə-ˈräs-kə-pē\ *n, pl* **-pies** : visual examination of the abdomen by means of an endoscope; *also* : surgery using laparoscopy — **lap·a·ro·scope** \ˈla-pə-rə-ˌskōp\ *n* — **lap·a·ro·scop·ic** \ˌla-pə-rə-ˈskä-pik\ *adj*

lap·dog \ˈlap-ˌdȯg\ *n* : a small dog that may be held in the lap

la·pel \lə-ˈpel\ *n* : the fold of the front of a coat that is usu. a continuation of the collar

¹lap·i·dary \ˈla-pə-ˌder-ē\ *n, pl* **-dar·ies** : a person who cuts, polishes, or engraves precious stones

²lapidary *adj* **1** : of, relating to, or suitable for engraved inscriptions **2** : of, relating to, or suggestive of precious stones or the art of cutting them

lap·in \ˈla-pən\ *n* : rabbit fur usu. sheared and dyed

la·pis la·zu·li \ˌla-pəs-ˈla-zə-lē, -zhə-\ *n* : a usu. blue semiprecious stone often having sparkling bits of pyrite

lap·pet \ˈla-pət\ *n* : a fold or flap on a garment

¹lapse \ˈlaps\ *n* [L *lapsus,* fr. *labi* to slip] **1** : a slight error ⟨a mental ∼⟩ **2** : a fall from a higher to a lower state **3** : the termination of a right or privilege through failure to meet requirements **4** : INTERRUPTION **5** : APOSTASY **6** : a passage of time; *also* : INTERVAL ♦ **Synonyms** BLOOPER, BLUNDER, BONER, GOOF, MISTAKE, SLIP

²lapse *vb* **lapsed; laps·ing 1** : to commit apostasy **2** : SINK, SLIP ⟨*lapsed* into a coma⟩ **3** : CEASE

lap·top \ˈlap-ˌtäp\ *adj* : of a size that can be used conveniently on one's lap ⟨a ∼ computer⟩ — **laptop** *n*

lap·wing \ˈlap-ˌwiŋ\ *n* : an Old World crested plover

lar·board \ˈlär-bərd\ *n* : ⁵PORT

lar·ce·ny \ˈlär-sə-nē\ *n, pl* **-nies** [ME, fr. AF *larecin* theft, fr. L *latrocinium* robbery, fr. *latro* mercenary soldier] : THEFT — **lar·ce·nous** \-nəs\ *adj*

larch \ˈlärch\ *n* : any of a genus of trees related to the pines that shed their needles in the fall

¹lard \ˈlärd\ *vb* **1** : to insert strips of usu.

pork fat into (meat) before cooking; *also* : GREASE **2** *obs* : ENRICH

²lard *n* : a soft white fat obtained by rendering fatty tissue of the hog

lar·der \ˈlär-dər\ *n* : a place where foods (as meat) are kept

large \ˈlärj\ *adj* **larg·er; larg·est 1** : having more than usual power, capacity, or scope **2** : exceeding most other things of like kind in quantity or size ♦ **Synonyms** BIG, GREAT, OVERSIZE — **large** *adv* — **large·ness** *n* — **at large 1** : UNCONFINED **2** : as a whole

large·ly \ˈlärj-lē\ *adv* : to a large extent

lar·gesse *or* **lar·gess** \lär-ˈzhes, -ˈjes\ *n* **1** : liberal giving **2** : a generous gift

¹lar·go \ˈlär-gō\ *adv or adj* [It, slow, broad, fr. L *largus* abundant] : at a very slow tempo — used as a direction in music

²largo *n, pl* **largos** : a largo movement

lari \ˈlä-rē\ *n, pl* **lari** — see MONEY table

lar·i·at \ˈlar-ē-ət\ *n* [AmerSp *la reata* the lasso, fr. Sp *la* the + AmerSp *reata* lasso, fr. Sp *reatar* to tie again] : a long rope used to catch or tether livestock : LASSO

¹lark \ˈlärk\ *n* : any of a family of small songbirds; *esp* : SKYLARK

²lark *n* : a source or quest for fun or adventure

³lark *vb* : to engage in harmless fun or mischief — often used with *about*

lark·spur \ˈlärk-ˌspər\ *n* : DELPHINIUM; *esp* : any of the widely cultivated annual delphiniums

lar·va \ˈlär-və\ *n, pl* **lar·vae** \-(ˌ)vē\ *also* **larvas** [NL, fr. L, specter, mask] : the wingless often wormlike form in which insects hatch from the egg; *also* : any young animal (as a tadpole) that is fundamentally unlike its parent — **lar·val** \-vəl\ *adj*

lar·yn·gi·tis \ˌlar-ən-ˈjī-təs\ *n* : inflammation of the larynx

lar·ynx \ˈlar-iŋks\ *n, pl* **la·ryn·ges** \lə-ˈrin-ˌjēz\ *or* **lar·ynx·es** : the upper part of the trachea containing the vocal cords — **la·ryn·ge·al** \lə-ˈrin-jəl\ *adj*

la·sa·gna \lə-ˈzän-yə\ *n* [It] : boiled broad flat noodles baked with a sauce usu. of tomatoes, cheese, and meat

las·car \ˈlas-kər\ *n* : an Indian sailor

las·civ·i·ous \lə-ˈsi-vē-əs\ *adj* : LUSTFUL, LEWD ♦ **Synonyms** LICENTIOUS, LECHEROUS, LIBIDINOUS, SALACIOUS — **las·civ·i·ous·ness** *n*

la·ser \ˈlā-zər\ *n* [*l*ight *a*mplification by *s*timulated *e*mission of *r*adiation] **1** : a device that produces an intense monochromatic beam of light **2** : something thrown or directed straight with high speed or intensity ⟨threw a ∼ into the end zone⟩

laser disc *n* : OPTICAL DISK; *esp* : one containing a video recording

¹lash \ˈlash\ *vb* **1** : to move violently or suddenly **2** : WHIP **3** : to attack verbally

²lash *n* **1** : a stroke esp. with a whip; *also* : WHIP **2** : a stinging rebuke **3** : EYELASH

³lash *vb* : to bind with or as if with a line

lass \ˈlas\ *n* : GIRL

lass·ie \ˈla-sē\ *n* : LASS

las·si·tude \'la-sə-,tüd, -,tyüd\ n 1 : WEARINESS, FATIGUE 2 : LANGUOR

las·so \'la-sō, la-'sü\ n, pl **lassos** or **lassoes** [Sp *lazo*] : a rope or long leather thong with a noose used for catching livestock — **lasso** vb

¹last \'last\ vb 1 : to continue in existence or operation 2 : to remain fresh or unimpaired : ENDURE 3 : to manage to continue 4 : to be enough for the needs of

²last n : a foot-shaped form on which a shoe is shaped or repaired

³last vb : to shape with a last

⁴last adv 1 : at the end 2 : most recently 3 : in conclusion

⁵last adj 1 : following all the rest : FINAL 2 : next before the present ⟨~ week⟩ 3 : most up-to-date 4 : farthest from a specified quality, attitude, or likelihood ⟨the ~ thing we want⟩ 5 : CONCLUSIVE; also : SUPREME — **last·ly** adv

⁶last n : something that is last ⟨the ~ of them⟩ — **at last** : FINALLY

last-ditch \'last-,dich\ adj : made as a final effort esp. to avert disaster

last laugh n : an ultimate satisfaction or triumph despite previous doubt or criticism

Last Supper n : the supper eaten by Jesus and his disciples on the night of his betrayal

lat abbr latitude

Lat abbr Latin

¹latch \'lach\ vb : to catch or get hold

²latch n : a catch that holds a door or gate closed

³latch vb : to make fast with a latch

latch·et \'la-chət\ n : a strap, thong, or lace for fastening a shoe or sandal

latch·key \'lach-,kē\ n : a key for opening a door latch esp. from the outside

latch·string \-,strin\ n : a string on a latch that may be left hanging outside the door for raising the latch

¹late \'lāt\ adj **lat·er**; **lat·est** 1 : coming or remaining after the due, usual, or proper time 2 : far advanced toward the close or end 3 : recently deceased 4 : made, appearing, or happening just previous to the present : RECENT ⟨~ news⟩ — **late·ly** adv — **late·ness** n

²late adv **lat·er**; **lat·est** 1 : after the usual or proper time; also : at or to an advanced point in time 2 : RECENTLY

late·com·er \'lāt-,kə-mər\ n : one who arrives late

la·teen \la-'tēn\ adj : relating to or being a triangular sail extended by a long spar slung to a low mast

la·tent \'lāt-ᵊnt\ adj : present but not visible or active ♦ *Synonyms* DORMANT, QUIESCENT, POTENTIAL — **la·ten·cy** \-ᵊn-sē\ n

¹lat·er·al \'la-tə-rəl\ adj : situated on, directed toward, or coming from the side ⟨a ~ view⟩ — **lat·er·al·ly** adv

²lateral n 1 : a branch from the main part 2 : a football pass thrown parallel to the line of scrimmage or away from the opponent's goal

la·tex \'lā-,teks\ n, pl **la·ti·ces** \'lā-tə-,sēz, 'la-\ or **la·tex·es** 1 : a milky juice produced by various plant cells (as of milkweeds, poppies, and the rubber tree) 2 : a water emulsion of a synthetic rubber or plastic used esp. in paint

lath \'lath, 'lȧth\ n, pl **laths** or **lath** : a thin narrow strip of wood used esp. as a base for plaster; also : a building material in sheets used for the same purpose — **lath** vb

lathe \'lāth\ n : a machine in which a piece of material is held and turned while being shaped by a tool

¹lath·er \'la-thər\ n 1 : a foam or froth formed when a detergent is agitated in water; also : foam from profuse sweating (as by a horse) 2 : DITHER

²lather vb : to spread lather over ⟨~ed his face before shaving⟩; also : to form a lather

Lat·in \'lat-ᵊn\ n 1 : the language of ancient Rome 2 : a member of any of the peoples whose languages derive from Latin — **Latin** adj

La·ti·na \lə-'tē-nə\ n : a woman or girl who is a native or inhabitant of Latin America; also : a woman or girl of Latin-American origin living in the U.S.

Latin American n : a native or inhabitant of any of the countries of No., Central, or So. America whose official language is Spanish or Portuguese — **Latin-American** adj

La·ti·no \lə-'tē-nō\ n, pl **-nos** : a native or inhabitant of Latin America; also : a person of Latin-American origin living in the U.S. — **Latino** adj

lat·i·tude \'la-tə-,tüd, -,tyüd\ n 1 : angular distance north or south from the earth's equator measured in degrees 2 : a region marked by its latitude 3 : freedom of action or choice

lat·i·tu·di·nar·i·an \,la-tə-,tü-də-'ner-ē-ən, -,tyü-\ n : a person who is liberal in religious belief and conduct

la·trine \lə-'trēn\ n : TOILET

lats \'lȧts\ n, pl **la·ti** \'lä-tē\ or **la·tu** \'lä-tü\ : the basic monetary unit of Latvia from 1922 to 1940 and from 1991 through 2013

lat·ter \'la-tər\ adj 1 : more recent; also : FINAL 2 : of, relating to, or being the second of two things referred to

lat·ter-day adj 1 : of present or recent times 2 : of a later or subsequent time

Latter-day Saint n : a member of a religious body founded by Joseph Smith in 1830 and accepting the Book of Mormon as divine revelation : MORMON

lat·ter·ly \'la-tər-lē\ adv 1 : LATER 2 : of late : RECENTLY ⟨the business has grown ~⟩

lat·tice \'la-təs\ n 1 : a framework of crossed wood or metal strips; also : a window, door, or gate having a lattice 2 : a regular geometrical arrangement

lat·tice·work \-,wərk\ n : LATTICE; also : work made of lattices

Lat·vi·an \'lat-vē-ən\ n 1 : a native or inhabitant of Latvia 2 : the language of the Latvians — **Latvian** adj

¹laud \'lȯd\ n : PRAISE, ACCLAIM

²laud vb : PRAISE, EXTOL ♦ *Synonyms*

CELEBRATE, EULOGIZE, GLORIFY, MAGNIFY — **laud·able** adj — **laud·ably** adv

lau·da·num \'lȯd-ᵊn-əm\ n : a tincture of opium

lau·da·to·ry \'lȯ-də-ˌtōr-ē\ adj : of, relating to, or expressive of praise

¹**laugh** \'laf, 'låf\ vb [ME, fr. OE *hliehhan*] : to show mirth, joy, or scorn with a chuckle or explosive vocal sound; *also* : to become amused or derisive — **laugh·able** adj — **laugh·ing·ly** adv

²**laugh** n 1 : the act of laughing 2 : JOKE; *also* : JEER 3 pl : SPORT 1

laughing gas n : NITROUS OXIDE

laugh·ing·stock \'la-fiŋ-ˌstäk, 'lå-\ n : an object of ridicule

laugh·ter \'laf-tər, 'låf-\ n : the action or sound of laughing

¹**launch** \'lȯnch\ vb 1 : THROW, HURL; *also* : to send off ⟨~ a rocket⟩ 2 : to set afloat 3 : to set in operation : START ⟨~ a business⟩ — **launch·er** n

²**launch** n : an act or instance of launching

³**launch** n : a small open or half-decked motorboat

launch·pad \'lȯnch-ˌpad\ n : a platform from which a rocket is launched

laun·der \'lȯn-dər\ vb 1 : to wash or wash and iron clothing and household linens 2 : to transfer (as money of an illegal origin) through an outside party to conceal the true source — **laun·der·er** n

laun·dress \'lȯn-drəs\ n : a woman who is a laundry worker

laun·dry \'lȯn-drē\ n, pl **laundries** [fr. obs. *launder* launderer, fr. AF *lavandere*, fr. ML *lavandarius*, fr. L *lavandus* needing to be washed, fr. *lavare* to wash] 1 : a place where laundering is done 2 : clothes or linens that have been or are to be laundered — **laun·dry·man** \-mən\ n

lau·re·ate \'lȯr-ē-ət\ n : the recipient of honor for achievement in an art or science — **lau·re·ate·ship** n

lau·rel \'lȯr-əl\ n 1 : an evergreen tree or shrub of southern Europe that is related to the sassafras and cinnamon and has glossy aromatic leaves 2 : MOUNTAIN LAUREL 3 : a crown of laurel awarded as an honor — usu. used in pl.

lav abbr lavatory

la·va \'lä-və, 'la-\ n [It] : melted rock coming from a volcano; *also* : such rock that has cooled and hardened

la·vage \lə-'väzh\ n [F] : WASHING; *esp* : the washing out (as of an organ) esp. for medicinal reasons

lav·a·to·ry \'la-və-ˌtōr-ē\ n, pl **-ries** 1 : a fixed washbowl with running water and drainpipe 2 : BATHROOM

lave \'läv\ vb **laved; lav·ing** : WASH

lav·en·der \'la-vən-dər\ n 1 : a Mediterranean mint or its dried leaves and flowers used to perfume clothing and bed linen 2 : a pale purple color

¹**lav·ish** \'la-vish\ adj [ME *laves, lavage*, prob. fr. MF *lavasse, lavache* downpour, fr. *laver* to wash] 1 : expending or bestowing profusely 2 : expended or produced in abundance ⟨~ gifts⟩ 3

: marked by excess ⟨~ decor⟩ — **lav·ish·ly** adv — **lav·ish·ness** n

²**lavish** vb : to expend or give freely

law \'lȯ\ n 1 : a rule of conduct or action established by custom or laid down and enforced by a governing authority; *also* : the whole body of such rules 2 : the control brought about by enforcing rules 3 cap : the revelation of the divine will set forth in the Old Testament; *also* : the first part of the Jewish scriptures — see BIBLE table 4 : a rule or principle of construction or procedure 5 : the science that deals with laws and their interpretation and application 6 : the profession of a lawyer 7 : a rule or principle stating something that always works in the same way under the same conditions

law·break·er \'lȯ-ˌbrā-kər\ n : a person who violates the law

law·ful \'lȯ-fəl\ adj 1 : permitted by law 2 : RIGHTFUL — **law·ful·ly** adv

law·giv·er \-ˌgi-vər\ n : LEGISLATOR

law·less \'lȯ-ləs\ adj 1 : having no laws 2 : UNRULY, DISORDERLY ⟨a ~ mob⟩ — **law·less·ly** adv — **law·less·ness** n

law·mak·er \-ˌmā-kər\ n : LEGISLATOR

law·man \'lȯ-mən\ n : a law enforcement official (as a sheriff or marshal)

¹**lawn** \'lȯn\ n : ground (as around a house) covered with mowed grass

²**lawn** n : a fine sheer linen or cotton fabric

lawn bowling n : a bowling game played on a green with wooden balls which are rolled at a jack

law·ren·ci·um \lȯ-'ren-sē-əm\ n : a short-lived radioactive element

law·suit \'lȯ-ˌsüt\ n : a suit in law

law·yer \'lȯ-yər\ n : one who conducts lawsuits for clients or advises as to legal rights and obligations in other matters — **law·yer·ly** adj

lax \'laks\ adj 1 : not strict ⟨~ discipline⟩ 2 : not tense or rigid ♦ *Synonyms* REMISS, NEGLIGENT, NEGLECTFUL, DELINQUENT, DERELICT — **lax·i·ty** \'lak-sə-tē\ n — **lax·ly** adv — **lax·ness** n

¹**lax·a·tive** \'lak-sə-tiv\ adj : relieving constipation

²**laxative** n : a usu. mild laxative drug

¹**lay** \'lā\ vb **laid** \'lād\; **lay·ing** 1 : to beat or strike down 2 : to put on or set down : PLACE 3 : to produce and deposit eggs 4 : SETTLE; *also* : ALLAY 5 : SPREAD 6 : PREPARE, CONTRIVE 7 : WAGER 8 : to impose esp. as a duty or burden 9 : to set in order or position 10 : to bring to a specified condition ⟨*laid* waste the land⟩ 11 : to put forward : SUBMIT

²**lay** n : the way in which something lies or is laid in relation to something else

³**lay** past of ¹LIE

⁴**lay** n 1 : a simple narrative poem 2 : SONG

⁵**lay** adj 1 : of or relating to the laity 2 : not of a particular profession; *also* : lacking extensive knowledge of a particular subject

lay·away \'lā-ə-ˌwā\ n : a purchasing agreement by which a retailer agrees to hold merchandise secured by a deposit until the price is paid in full

lay·er \'lā-ər\ *n* **1** : one that lays **2** : one thickness, course, or fold laid or lying over or under another

lay·ette \lā-'et\ *n* [F, fr. MF, dim. of *laye* box] : an outfit of clothing and equipment for a newborn infant

lay·man \'lā-mən\ *n* : a person who is a member of the laity

lay·off \'lā-ˌȯf\ *n* **1** : a period of inactivity **2** : the act of laying off an employee

lay off *vb* **1** : to cease to employ (a worker) often temporarily **2** : to leave undisturbed **3** : to stop doing something

lay·out \'lā-ˌau̇t\ *n* : the final arrangement, plan, or design of something

lay·over \-ˌō-vər\ *n* : STOPOVER

lay·per·son \-ˌpər-sən\ *n* : a member of the laity

lay·wom·an \'lā-ˌwu̇-mən\ *n* : a woman who is a member of the laity

la·zar \'la-zər, 'lā-\ *n* : LEPER

laze \'lāz\ *vb* **lazed; laz·ing** : to pass time in idleness or relaxation

la·zy \'lā-zē\ *adj* **la·zi·er; -est 1** : disliking activity or exertion **2** : encouraging idleness ⟨a ~ day⟩ **3** : SLUGGISH **4** : DROOPY, LAX **5** : not rigorous or strict ⟨~ work habits⟩ — **la·zi·ly** \-zə-lē\ *adv* — **la·zi·ness** \-zē-nəs\ *n*

la·zy·bones \-ˌbōnz\ *n sing or pl* : a lazy person

lazy Su·san \ˌlā-zē-'süz-ᵊn\ *n* : a revolving tray used for serving food

lb *abbr* [L *libra*] pound

lc *abbr* lowercase

LC *abbr* Library of Congress

¹LCD \ˌel-(ˌ)sē-'dē\ *n* [*liquid crystal display*] : a display (as of the time in a digital watch) that consists of segments of a liquid crystal whose reflectivity varies with the voltage applied to them

²LCD *abbr* least common denominator; lowest common denominator

LCDR *abbr* lieutenant commander

LCM *abbr* least common multiple; lowest common multiple

LCpl *abbr* lance corporal

LCS *abbr* League Championship Series

ld *abbr* **1** load **2** lord

LD *abbr* learning disabled; learning disability

LDC *abbr* less developed country

ldg *abbr* **1** landing **2** loading

LDL \ˌel-(ˌ)dē-'el\ *n* [*low-density lipoprotein*] : a cholesterol-rich protein-poor lipoprotein of blood plasma correlated with increased probability of developing atherosclerosis

L-do·pa \'el-'dō-pə\ *n* : an isomer of dopa used esp. in the treatment of Parkinson's disease

LDS *abbr* Latter-day Saints

lea \'lē, 'lā\ *n* : PASTURE, MEADOW

leach \'lēch\ *vb* : to pass a liquid (as water) through to carry off the soluble components; *also* : to dissolve out by such means ⟨~ alkali from ashes⟩

¹lead \'lēd\ *vb* **led** \'led\; **lead·ing 1** : to guide on a way **2** : LIVE ⟨~ a quiet life⟩ **3** : to direct the operations, activity, or performance of ⟨~ an orchestra⟩ **4** : to go at the head of : be first ⟨~ a parade⟩ **5** : to begin play with; *also* : BEGIN, OPEN **6** : to tend toward a definite result ⟨study ~ing to a degree⟩ — **lead·er** *n* — **lead·er·less** *adj* — **lead·er·ship** *n*

²lead \'lēd\ *n* **1** : a position at the front; *also* : a margin by which one leads **2** : the privilege of leading in cards; *also* : the card or suit led **3** : EXAMPLE *n* : one that leads **5** : a principal role (as in a play); *also* : one who plays such a role **6** : INDICATION, CLUE **7** : an insulated electrical conductor

³lead \'led\ *n* **1** : a heavy malleable bluish white chemical element **2** : an article made of lead; *esp* : a weight for sounding at sea **3** : a thin strip of metal used to separate lines of type in printing **4** : a thin stick of marking substance in or for a pencil

⁴lead \'led\ *vb* **1** : to cover, line, or weight with lead **2** : to fix (glass) in position with lead **3** : to treat or mix with lead or a lead compound

lead·en \'led-ᵊn\ *adj* **1** : made of lead; *also* : of the color of lead **2** : SLUGGISH, DULL ⟨a ~ lecture⟩

lead off *vb* : OPEN, BEGIN; *esp* : to bat first in an inning — **lead-off** \'led-ˌȯf\ *n or adj*

¹leaf \'lēf\ *n, pl* **leaves** \'lēvz\ **1** : a usu. flat and green outgrowth of a plant stem that is a unit of foliage and functions esp. in photosynthesis; *also* : FOLIAGE **2** : something (as a page or a flat moving part) that is suggestive of a leaf — **leaf·less** *adj* — **leafy** *adj*

²leaf *vb* **1** : to produce leaves **2** : to turn the pages of a book

leaf·age \'lē-fij\ *n* : FOLIAGE

leafed \'lēft\ *adj* : LEAVED

leaf·hop·per \'lēf-ˌhä-pər\ *n* : any of a family of small leaping insects related to the cicadas that suck the juices of plants

leaf·let \'lē-flət\ *n* **1** : a division of a compound leaf **2** : PAMPHLET, FOLDER

leaf mold *n* : a compost or layer composed chiefly of decayed leaves

leaf·stalk \'lēf-ˌstȯk\ *n* : PETIOLE

¹league \'lēg\ *n* : a unit of distance equal to about three miles (five kilometers)

²league *n* **1** : an association or alliance (as of nations or sports teams) for a common purpose **2** : CLASS, CATEGORY — **league** *vb* — **leagu·er** \'lē-gər\ *n*

¹leak \'lēk\ *vb* **1** : to enter or escape through a leak **2** : to let a substance in or out through an opening **3** : to become or make known ⟨~ed the news⟩

²leak *n* **1** : a crack or hole that accidentally admits a fluid or light or lets it escape; *also* : something that secretly or accidentally permits the admission or escape of something else **2** : LEAKAGE — **leaky** *adj*

leak·age \'lē-kij\ *n* **1** : the act of leaking **2** : the thing or amount that leaks

¹lean \'lēn\ *vb* **1** : to bend from a vertical position : INCLINE **2** : to cast one's weight to one side for support **3** : to rely on for support **4** : to incline in opinion, taste, or desire — **lean** *n*

²lean *adj* **1** : lacking or deficient in flesh and esp. in fat ⟨~ meat⟩ **2** : lacking richness or productiveness ⟨∼ profits⟩ **3** : low in fuel content — **lean·ness** *n*

leant \'lent\ *chiefly Brit past of* LEAN

lean–to \'lēn-ˌtü\ *n, pl* **lean–tos** \-ˌtüz\ : a wing or extension of a building having a roof of only one slope; *also* : a rough shed or shelter with a similar roof

¹**leap** \'lēp\ *vb* **leapt** \'lept, 'lēpt\ *or* **leaped; leap·ing** : to spring free from a surface or over an obstacle : JUMP

²**leap** *n* : JUMP

leap·frog \'lēp-ˌfróg, -ˌfräg\ *n* : a game in which a player bends down and is vaulted over by another — **leapfrog** *vb*

leap year *n* : a year containing 366 days with February 29 as the extra day

learn \'lərn\ *vb* **learned** \'lərnd, 'lərnt\; **learn·ing 1** : to gain knowledge, understanding, or skill by study or experience; *also* : MEMORIZE ⟨∼ the poem⟩ **2** : to find out : ASCERTAIN ⟨∼ the truth⟩ — **learn·er** *n*

learn·ed \'lər-nəd\ *adj* : SCHOLARLY, ERUDITE — **learn·ed·ly** *adv* — **learn·ed·ness** *n*

learn·ing \'lər-niŋ\ *n* : KNOWLEDGE, ERUDITION

learning disability *n* : any of various conditions (as dyslexia) that interfere with a person's ability to learn and so result in impaired functioning (as in language) — **learning disabled** *adj*

learnt \'lərnt\ *chiefly Brit past and past part of* LEARN

¹**lease** \'lēs\ *n* : a contract transferring real estate for a term of years or at will usu. for a specified rent

²**lease** *vb* **leased; leas·ing** [AF *lesser, lescher* to leave, hand over, lease, fr. L *laxare* to loosen, fr. *laxus* slack] **1** : to grant by lease **2** : to hold under a lease
♦ **Synonyms** LET, CHARTER, HIRE, RENT

lease·hold \'lēs-ˌhōld\ *n* **1** : a tenure by lease **2** : land held by lease — **lease·hold·er** *n*

leash \'lēsh\ *n* [ME *lees, leshe,* fr. AF **lesche, lesse* prob. fr. *lesser* to leave, let go] **1** : a line for leading or restraining an animal **2** : a state of restraint ⟨kept spending on a tight ∼⟩ — **leash** *vb*

¹**least** \'lēst\ *adj* **1** : lowest in importance or position **2** : smallest in size or degree **3** : SLIGHTEST ⟨the ∼ sign of trouble⟩

²**least** *n* : one that is least

³**least** *adv* : in the smallest or lowest degree

least common denominator *n* : the least common multiple of two or more denominators

least common multiple *n* : the smallest common multiple of two or more numbers

least·wise \'lēst-ˌwīz\ *adv* : at least

leath·er \'le-thər\ *n* : animal skin dressed for use — **leath·ern** \-thərn\ *adj* — **leath·ery** *adj*

leath·er·back \-ˌbak\ *n* : the largest existing sea turtle with a flexible leathery carapace

leath·er·neck \-ˌnek\ *n* : MARINE

¹**leave** \'lēv\ *vb* **left** \'left\; **leav·ing 1** : to allow or cause to remain behind **2** : to have as a remainder **3** : BEQUEATH **4** : to

let stay without interference **5** : to go away : depart from **6** : GIVE UP, ABANDON ⟨*left* his wife for another woman⟩

²**leave** *n* **1** : PERMISSION; *also* : authorized absence from duty **2** : DEPARTURE

³**leave** *vb* **leaved; leav·ing** : LEAF

leaved \'lēvd\ *adj* : having leaves

¹**leav·en** \'le-vən\ *n* **1** : a substance (as yeast) used to produce fermentation (as in dough) **2** : something that modifies or lightens

²**leaven** *vb* : to raise (dough) with a leaven; *also* : to permeate with a modifying or vivifying element ⟨lectures ∼ed with humor⟩

leav·en·ing *n* : LEAVEN

leaves *pl of* LEAF

leave–tak·ing \'lēv-ˌtā-kiŋ\ *n* : DEPARTURE, FAREWELL

leav·ings \'lē-viŋz\ *n pl* : REMNANT, RESIDUE ⟨the ∼ of a meal⟩

lech·ery \'le-chə-rē\ *n* : inordinate indulgence in sexual activity — **lech·er** \'le-chər\ *n* — **lech·er·ous** \'le-chə-rəs\ *adj* — **lech·er·ous·ly** *adv* — **lech·er·ous·ness** *n*

lec·i·thin \'le-sə-thən\ *n* : any of several waxy phosphorus-containing substances that are common in animals and plants, form colloidal solutions in water, and have emulsifying and wetting properties

lect *abbr* lecture; lecturer

lec·tern \'lek-tərn\ *n* : a stand to support a book for a standing reader

lec·tor \-tər\ *n* : one whose chief duty is to read the lessons in a church service

lec·ture \'lek-chər\ *n* **1** : a discourse given before an audience esp. for instruction **2** : REPRIMAND — **lecture** *vb* — **lec·tur·er** *n* — **lec·ture·ship** *n*

led *past and past part of* LEAD

LED \ˌel-(ˌ)ē-'dē\ *n* [*light-emitting diode*] : a semiconductor diode that emits light when a voltage is applied to it and is used esp. for electronic displays

le·der·ho·sen \'lā-dər-ˌhōz-ᵊn\ *n pl* : leather shorts often with suspenders worn esp. in Bavaria

ledge \'lej\ *n* [ME *legge* bar of a gate] **1** : a shelflike projection from a top or an edge **2** : REEF

led·ger \'le-jər\ *n* : a book containing accounts to which debits and credits are transferred in final form

lee \'lē\ *n* **1** : a protecting shelter **2** : the side (as of a ship) that is sheltered from the wind — **lee** *adj*

leech \'lēch\ *n* **1** : any of various bloodsucking segmented usu. freshwater worms that are related to the earthworms and have a sucker at each end **2** : a hanger-on who seeks gain

leek \'lēk\ *n* : an onionlike herb grown for its mildly pungent leaves and stalk

leer \'lir\ *n* : a suggestive, knowing, or malicious look — **leer** *vb*

leery \'lir-ē\ *adj* : SUSPICIOUS, WARY

lees \'lēz\ *n pl* : DREGS ⟨∼ in the bottle⟩

¹**lee·ward** \'lē-wərd, 'lü-ərd\ *n* : the lee side

²**leeward** *adj* : situated away from the wind

lee·way \'lē-ˌwā\ *n* **1** : lateral movement

of a ship when under way **2** : an allowable margin of freedom or variation

¹left \'left\ *adj* [ME, fr. OE, weak; fr. the left hand's being the weaker in most individuals] **1** : of, relating to, or being the side of the body in which the heart is mostly located; *also* : located nearer to this side than to the right **2** *often cap* : of, adhering to, or constituted by the political left — **left** *adv*

²left *n* **1** : the left hand; *also* : the side or part that is on or toward the left side **2** *often cap* : those professing political views marked by desire to reform the established order and usu. to give greater freedom to the common people — **leftward** \-wərd\ *adv or adj*

³left *past and past part of* LEAVE

³left–hand *adj* **1** : situated on the left **2** : LEFT-HANDED

left–hand·ed \'left-'han-dəd\ *adj* **1** : using the left hand habitually or more easily than the right **2** : designed for or done with the left hand **3** : INSINCERE, BACKHANDED ⟨a ~ compliment⟩ **4** : COUNTERCLOCKWISE — **left–handed** *adv* — **left–hand·ed·ness** *n* — **left–hand·er** \-dər\ *n*

left·ism \'lef-,ti-zəm\ *n* **1** : the principles and views of the left **2** : advocacy of the doctrines of the left — **left·ist** \-tist\ *n or adj*

left·over \'left-,ō-vər\ *n* : something that remains unused or unconsumed

lefty \'lef-tē\ *n, pl* **left·ies** **1** : a left-handed person **2** : an advocate of leftism

¹leg \'leg\ *n* **1** : a limb of an animal used esp. for supporting the body and in walking; *also* : the part of the vertebrate leg between knee and foot **2** : something resembling or analogous to an animal leg ⟨table ~⟩ **3** : the part of an article of clothing that covers the leg **4** : a portion of a trip **5** *pl* : long-term appeal or interest ⟨a musical that has ~s⟩ — **leg·ged** \'le-gəd\ *adj* — **leg·less** *adj*

²leg *vb* **legged; leg·ging** : to use the legs in walking or esp. in running

³leg *abbr* **1** legal **2** legislative; legislature

leg·a·cy \'le-gə-sē\ *n, pl* **-cies** : INHERITANCE; *also* : something that has come from a predecessor or the past

le·gal \'lē-gəl\ *adj* **1** : of or relating to law or lawyers **2** : LAWFUL; *also* : STATUTORY **3** : enforced in courts of law — **le·gal·i·ty** \li-'ga-lə-tē\ *n* — **le·gal·ize** \'lē-gə-,līz\ *vb* — **le·gal·ly** *adv*

le·gal·ese \,lē-gə-'lēz\ *n* : the specialized language of the legal profession

le·gal·ism \'lē-gə-,li-zəm\ *n* **1** : strict, literal, or excessive conformity to the law or to a religious or moral code **2** : a legal term — **le·gal·is·tic** \,lē-gə-'lis-tik\ *adj*

leg·ate \'le-gət\ *n* : an official representative

leg·a·tee \,le-gə-'tē\ *n* : a person to whom a legacy is bequeathed

le·ga·tion \li-'gā-shən\ *n* **1** : a diplomatic mission headed by a minister **2** : the official residence and office of a minister in a foreign country

le·ga·to \li-'gä-tō\ *adv or adj* [It, lit., tied]

: in a smooth and connected manner (as of music)

leg·end \'le-jənd\ *n* [ME *legende*, fr. AF & ML; AF *legende*, fr. ML *legenda*, fr. L *legere* to read] **1** : a story coming down from the past; *esp* : one popularly accepted as historical though not verifiable **2** : an inscription on an object; *also* : CAPTION **3** : an explanatory list of the symbols on a map or chart

leg·end·ary \'le-jən-,der-ē\ *adj* **1** : of, relating to, or characteristic of a legend **2** : FAMOUS ⟨~ actors⟩ — **leg·en·dari·ly** \-,der-ə-lē\ *adv*

leg·er·de·main \,le-jər-də-'mān\ *n* [ME, fr. MF *leger de main* light of hand] : SLEIGHT OF HAND

leg·ging *or* **leg·gin** \'le-gən, -gin\ *n* : a covering for the leg; *also* : TIGHTS

leg·gy \'le-gē\ *adj* **leg·gi·er; -est** **1** : having unusually long legs **2** : having long and attractive legs **3** : SPINDLY — used of a plant

leg·horn \'leg-,hörn, 'le-gərn\ *n* **1** : a fine plaited straw; *also* : a hat made of this straw **2** : any of a Mediterranean breed of small hardy chickens

leg·i·ble \'le-jə-bəl\ *adj* : capable of being read : CLEAR — **leg·i·bil·i·ty** \,le-jə-'bi-lə-tē\ *n* — **leg·i·bly** \'le-jə-blē\ *adv*

¹le·gion \'lē-jən\ *n* **1** : a unit of the Roman army comprising 3000 to 6000 soldiers **2** : MULTITUDE ⟨~s of fans⟩ **3** : an association of ex-servicemen — **le·gion·ary** \-jə-,ner-ē\ *n* — **le·gion·naire** \,lē-jə-'nar\ *n*

²legion *adj* : MANY, NUMEROUS

Legionnaires' disease *also* **Legionnaire's disease** \-'nerz-\ *n* : a lobar pneumonia caused by a bacterium

legis *abbr* legislation; legislative; legislature

leg·is·late \'le-jəs-,lāt\ *vb* **-lat·ed; -lat·ing** : to make or enact laws; *also* : to bring about by legislation — **leg·is·la·tor** \-,lā-tər\ *n*

leg·is·la·tion \,le-jəs-'lā-shən\ *n* **1** : the action of legislating **2** : laws made by a legislative body

leg·is·la·tive \'le-jəs-,lā-tiv\ *adj* **1** : having the power of legislating **2** : of or relating to a legislature or legislation

leg·is·la·ture \'le-jəs-,lā-chər\ *n* : an organized body of persons having the authority to make laws

le·git \li-'jit\ *adj, slang* : LEGITIMATE

¹le·git·i·mate \li-'ji-tə-mət\ *adj* **1** : lawfully begotten **2** : GENUINE **3** : LAWFUL **4** : conforming to recognized principles or accepted rules or standards — **le·git·i·ma·cy** \-mə-sē\ *n* — **le·git·i·mate·ly** *adv*

²le·git·i·mate \-,māt\ *vb* : to make legitimate

le·git·i·mise *Brit var of* LEGITIMIZE

le·git·i·mize \li-'ji-tə-,mīz\ *vb* **-mized; -miz·ing** : LEGITIMATE

leg·man \'leg-,man\ *n* **1** : a reporter assigned usu. to gather information **2** : an assistant who gathers information and runs errands

le·gume \'le-,gyüm, li-'gyüm\ *n* [F] **1** : any of a large family of plants having fruits that are dry pods and split when ripe and including important food and forage plants (as beans and clover); *also* : the part (as seeds or pods) of a legume used as food **2** : the pod of a legume — **le·gu·mi·nous** \li-'gyü-mə-nəs\ *adj*

¹lei \'lā, 'lā-,ē\ *n* : a wreath or necklace usu. of flowers

²lei \'lā\ *pl of* LEU

lei·sure \'lē-zhər, 'le-, 'lā-\ *n* : time free from work or duties **2** : EASE; *also* : CONVENIENCE ⟨read it at your ~⟩ ♦ *Synonyms* RELAXATION, REST, REPOSE — **lei·sure·ly** *adj or adv*

leit·mo·tif *also* **leit·mo·tiv** \'līt-mō-,tēf\ *n* [G *Leitmotiv*, fr. *leiten* to lead + *Motiv* motive] : a dominant recurring theme

lek \'lek\ *n, pl* **leks** *or* **le·ke** *or* **lekë** \'le-kə\ — see MONEY table

lem·ming \'le-miŋ\ *n* [Norw] : any of various short-tailed rodents found mostly in northern regions and noted for recurrent mass migrations

lem·on \'le-mən\ *n* **1** : an acid yellow usu. nearly oblong citrus fruit; *also* : a citrus tree that bears lemons **2** : something (as an automobile) unsatisfactory or defective — **lem·ony** *adj*

lem·on·ade \,le-mə-'nād\ *n* : a beverage of lemon juice, sugar, and water

lemon curd *n* : a custard made with lemon juice, butter, sugar, and eggs

lem·on·grass \'le-mən-,gras\ *n* : a tropical Asian grass grown for its lemon-scented foliage used as a seasoning

lem·pi·ra \lem-'pir-ə\ *n* — see MONEY table

le·mur \'lē-mər\ *n* : any of various arboreal primates largely of Madagascar that have large eyes, very soft woolly fur, and a long furry tail

Len·a·pe \'le-nə-pē, lə-'nä-pē\ *n, pl* **Lenape** *or* **Lenapes** : DELAWARE

lend \'lend\ *vb* **lent** \'lent\; **lend·ing** **1** : to give for temporary use on condition that the same or its equivalent be returned **2** : AFFORD, FURNISH **3** : ACCOMMODATE — **lend·er** *n*

lend–lease \-'lēs\ *n* : the transfer of goods and services to an ally to aid in a common cause with payment made by a return of the items or their use in the cause or by a similar transfer of other goods and services

length \'leŋth\ *n* **1** : the longer or longest dimension of an object; *also* : a measured distance **2** : duration or extent in time or space **3** : the length of something taken as a unit of measure **4** : a single piece of a series of pieces that may be joined together ⟨a ~ of pipe⟩ — **at length 1** : in full **2** : FINALLY

length·en \'leŋ-thən\ *vb* : to make or become longer ♦ *Synonyms* EXTEND, ELONGATE, PROLONG, PROTRACT

length·wise \'leŋth-,wīz\ *adv* : in the direction of the length — **lengthwise** *adj*

lengthy \'leŋ-thē\ *adj* **length·i·er; -est** **1** : protracted excessively **2** : EXTENDED, LONG ⟨a ~ journey⟩

le·nient \'lē-nē-ənt, -nyənt\ *adj* : of mild and tolerant disposition or effect ♦ *Syn-*

onyms INDULGENT, FORBEARING, MERCIFUL, TOLERANT — **le·ni·en·cy** \'lē-nē-ən-sē, -nyən-sē\ *n* — **le·ni·ent·ly** *adv*

len·i·tive \'le-nə-tiv\ *adj* : alleviating pain or harshness

len·i·ty \'le-nə-tē\ *n* : LENIENCY

lens \'lenz\ *n* [L *lent-, lens* lentil; so called fr. the shape of a convex lens] **1** : a curved piece of glass or plastic used singly or combined in an optical instrument for forming an image; *also* : a device for focusing radiation other than light **2** : a transparent body in the eye that focuses light rays on receptors at the back of the eye

Lent \'lent\ *n* : a 40-day period of penitence and fasting observed from Ash Wednesday to Easter by many churches — **Lent·en** \'len-tᵊn\ *adj*

len·til \'len-tᵊl\ *n* : a Eurasian annual legume grown for its flat edible seeds and for fodder; *also* : its seed

Leo \'lē-ō\ *n* [L, lit., lion] **1** : a zodiacal constellation between Cancer and Virgo usu. pictured as a lion **2** : the 5th sign of the zodiac in astrology; *also* : one born under this sign

le·one \lē-'ōn\ *n, pl* **leones** *or* **leone** — see MONEY table

le·o·nine \'lē-ə-,nīn\ *adj* : of, relating to, or resembling a lion

leop·ard \'le-pərd\ *n* : a large usu. tawny and black-spotted cat of southern Asia and Africa

le·o·tard \'lē-ə-,tärd\ *n* : a close-fitting garment worn esp. by dancers and for exercise

lep·er \'le-pər\ *n* **1** : a person affected with leprosy **2** : OUTCAST

lep·re·chaun \'le-prə-,kän\ *n* : a mischievous elf of Irish folklore

lep·ro·sy \'le-prə-sē\ *n* : a chronic bacterial disease marked esp. if not treated by slow-growing swellings with deformity and loss of sensation of affected parts — **lep·rous** \-prəs\ *adj*

lep·tin \'lep-tən\ *n* : a hormone that is produced by fat-containing cells and plays a role in body weight regulation

lep·ton \lep-'tän\ *n, pl* **lep·ta** \-'tä\ : a former monetary unit equal to $1/100$ drachma

les·bi·an \'lez-bē-ən\ *n* [fr. the reputed homosexual group associated with the poet Sappho of Lesbos] : a woman who is a homosexual — **lesbian** *adj* — **les·bi·an·ism** \-ə-,ni-zəm\ *n*

lèse ma·jes·té *or* **lese maj·es·ty** \'läz-'ma-jə-stē, 'lez-, 'lēz-\ *n* [MF *lese majesté*, fr. L *laesa majestas*, lit., injured majesty] : an offense violating the dignity of a sovereign

le·sion \'lē-zhən\ *n* : an abnormal structural change in the body due to injury or disease; *esp* : one clearly marked off from healthy tissue around it

¹less \'les\ *adj, comparative of* ¹LITTLE **1** : FEWER ⟨~ than six⟩ **2** : of lower rank, degree, or importance **3** : SMALLER; *also* : more limited in quantity ⟨~ than a year⟩

²less *adv, comparative of* ²LITTLE : to a lesser extent or degree

³**less** *n, pl* **less** **1** : a smaller portion **2** : something of less importance

⁴**less** *prep* : diminished by : MINUS ⟨list price ~ the discount⟩

-less \ləs\ *adj suffix* **1** : destitute of : not having ⟨child*less*⟩ **2** : unable to be acted on or to act (in a specified way) ⟨daunt*less*⟩

les·see \le-'sē\ *n* : a tenant under a lease

less·en \'le-sᵊn\ *vb* : to make or become less **♦ Synonyms** DECREASE, DIMINISH, DWINDLE, ABATE

less·er \'le-sər\ *adj, comparative of* ¹LITTLE : of less size, quality, or significance

les·son \'le-sᵊn\ *n* **1** : a passage from sacred writings read in a service of worship **2** : a reading or exercise to be studied by a pupil; *also* : something learned **3** : a period of instruction **4** : an instructive example

les·sor \'le-ˌsȯr, le-'sȯr\ *n* : one who conveys property by a lease

lest \'lest\ *conj* : for fear that

¹**let** \'let\ *n* [ME *lette,* fr. *letten* to delay, hinder, fr. OE *lettan*] **1** : HINDRANCE, OBSTACLE **2** : a shot or point in racket games that does not count

²**let** *vb* **let; let·ting** [ME *leten,* fr. OE *lǣtan*] **1** : to cause to : MAKE ⟨~ it be known⟩ **2** : RENT, LEASE; *also* : to assign esp. after bids **3** : ALLOW, PERMIT ⟨~ me go⟩

-let *n suffix* **1** : small one ⟨book*let*⟩ **2** : article worn on ⟨wrist*let*⟩

let·down \'let-ˌdaȯn\ *n* **1** : DISAPPOINTMENT **2** : a slackening of effort

le·thal \'lē-thəl\ *adj* : DEADLY, FATAL ⟨~ weapons⟩ — **le·thal·ly** *adv*

leth·ar·gy \'le-thər-jē\ *n* **1** : abnormal drowsiness **2** : the quality or state of being lazy or indifferent **♦ Synonyms** LANGUOR, LASSITUDE, TORPOR — **le·thar·gic** \li-'thär-jik\ *adj*

let on *vb* **1** : REVEAL ⟨knows a lot more than he *lets on*⟩ **2** : PRETEND

¹**let·ter** \'le-tər\ *n* **1** : a symbol that stands for a speech sound and constitutes a unit of an alphabet **2** : a written or printed communication **3** *pl* : LITERATURE; *also* : LEARNING **4** : the literal meaning ⟨the ~ of the law⟩ **5** : a single piece of type

²**letter** *vb* : to mark with letters : INSCRIBE — **let·ter·er** *n*

letter bomb *n* : an explosive device concealed in an envelope and mailed to the intended victim

let·ter·boxed \'le-tər-ˌbäkst\ *adj* : being a video recording formatted to display a frame size proportional to a standard theater screen

letter carrier *n* : a person who delivers mail

let·ter·head \'le-tər-ˌhed\ *n* : stationery with a printed or engraved heading; *also* : the heading itself

let·ter–per·fect \ˌle-tər-'pər-fikt\ *adj* : correct to the smallest detail

let·ter·press \'le-tər-ˌpres\ *n* : printing done directly by impressing the paper on an inked raised surface

letters of marque \-'märk\ : a license granted to a private person by a government to fit out an armed ship to capture enemy shipping

letters patent *n pl* : a written grant from a government to a person in a form readily open for inspection by all

let·tuce \'le-təs\ *n* [ME *letuse,* fr. AF, prob. fr. pl. of *letue* lettuce plant, fr. L *lactuca,* fr. *lac* milk; fr. its milky juice] : a garden composite plant with crisp leaves used esp. in salads

let-up \'let-ˌəp\ *n* : a lessening of effort

leu \'leȯ\ *n, pl* **lei** \'lā\ — see MONEY table

leu·kae·mia *chiefly Brit var of* LEUKEMIA

leu·ke·mia \lü-'kē-mē-ə\ *n* : a malignant disease characterized by an abnormal increase in the number of white blood cells in the blood-forming tissues — **leu·ke·mic** \-mik\ *adj or n*

leu·ko·cyte \'lü-kə-ˌsīt\ *n* : WHITE BLOOD CELL

lev \'lef\ *n, pl* **le·va** \'le-və\ — see MONEY table

Lev *or* **Levit** *abbr* Leviticus

¹**le·vee** \'le-vē; lə-'vē, -'vā\ *n* [F *lever* act of arising] : a reception held by or for a person of distinction

²**lev·ee** \'le-vē\ *n* : an embankment to prevent or confine flooding; *also* : a river landing place

¹**lev·el** \'le-vəl\ *n* **1** : a device for establishing a horizontal line or plane **2** : horizontal condition **3** : a horizontal position, line, or surface often taken as an index of altitude; *also* : a flat area of ground **4** : height, position, rank, or size in a scale

²**level** *vb* **-eled** *or* **-elled; -el·ing** *or* **-el·ling** **1** : to make flat or even; *also* : to come to a level **2** : AIM, DIRECT **3** : EQUALIZE **4** : RAZE — **lev·el·er** *n*

³**level** *adj* **1** : having a flat even surface **2** : HORIZONTAL **3** : of the same height or rank; *also* : UNIFORM **4** : steady and cool in judgment ⟨keep a ~ head when in danger⟩ — **lev·el·ly** *adv* — **lev·el·ness** *n*

lev·el·head·ed \ˌle-vəl-'he-dəd\ *adj* : having or showing sound judgment : SENSIBLE ⟨a ~ decision⟩

le·ver \'le-vər, 'lē-\ *n* **1** : a bar used for prying or dislodging something; *also* : a means for achieving one's purpose **2** : a rigid piece turning about an axis and used for transmitting and changing force and motion

le·ver·age \'le-vrij, 'lē-, -və-rij\ *n* : the action or mechanical effect of a lever

le·vi·a·than \li-'vī-ə-thən\ *n* **1** : a large sea animal **2** : something large or formidable ⟨the ocean liner is a ~⟩

lev·i·tate \'le-və-ˌtāt\ *vb* **-tat·ed; -tat·ing** : to rise or cause to rise in the air in seeming defiance of gravitation — **lev·i·ta·tion** \ˌle-və-'tā-shən\ *n*

Le·vit·i·cus \li-'vi-tə-kəs\ *n* — see BIBLE table

lev·i·ty \'le-və-tē\ *n* : lack of seriousness **♦ Synonyms** LIGHTNESS, FLIPPANCY, FRIVOLITY

levo·do·pa \ˌle-və-'dō-pə\ *n* : L-DOPA

¹**levy** \'le-vē\ *n, pl* **lev·ies** **1** : the imposition or collection of an assessment; *also* : an amount levied **2** : the enlistment or

conscription of men for military service; *also* : troops raised by levy

²**levy** *vb* **lev·ied; levy·ing 1** : to impose or collect by legal authority ⟨~ taxes⟩ **2** : to enlist for military service **3** : WAGE ⟨~ war⟩ **4** : to seize property

lewd \'lüd\ *adj* [ME *lewed* vulgar, fr. OE *lǣwede* lay, ignorant] : sexually unchaste; *also* : OBSCENE, VULGAR — **lewd·ly** *adv* — **lewd·ness** *n*

lex·i·cog·ra·phy \ˌlek-sə-'kä-grə-fē\ *n* **1** : the editing or making of a dictionary **2** : the principles and practices of dictionary making — **lex·i·cog·ra·pher** \-fər\ *n* — **lex·i·co·graph·i·cal** \-kō-'gra-fi-kəl\ *or* **lex·i·co·graph·ic** \-fik\ *adj*

lex·i·con \'lek-sə-ˌkän\ *n, pl* **lex·i·ca** \-si-kə\ *or* **lexicons 1** : DICTIONARY **2** : the vocabulary of a language, speaker, or subject

lg *abbr* **1** large **2** long

LH *abbr* **1** left hand **2** lower half

li *abbr* link

Li *symbol* lithium

LI *abbr* Long Island

li·a·bil·i·ty \ˌlī-ə-'bil-ə-tē\ *n, pl* **-ties 1** : the quality or state of being liable **2** *pl* : DEBTS **3** : DISADVANTAGE

li·a·ble \'lī-ə-bəl\ *adj* **1** : legally obligated : RESPONSIBLE **2** : LIKELY, APT ⟨~ to fall⟩ **3** : SUSCEPTIBLE ⟨~ to disease⟩

li·ai·son \'lē-ə-ˌzän, lē-'ā-\ *n* [F] **1** : a close bond : INTERRELATIONSHIP **2** : an illicit sexual relationship **3** : communication for mutual understanding (as between parts of an armed force); *also* : one that carries on a liaison

li·ar \'lī-(ə)r\ *n* : a person who lies

¹**lib** \'lib\ *n* : LIBERATION

²**lib** *abbr* **1** liberal **2** librarian; library

li·ba·tion \lī-'bā-shən\ *n* **1** : an act of pouring a liquid as a sacrifice (as to a god); *also* : the liquid poured **2** : DRINK

¹**li·bel** \'lī-bəl\ *n* [ME, written declaration, fr. AF, fr. L *libellus*, dim. of *liber* book] **1** : a spoken or written statement or a representation that gives an unjustly unfavorable impression of a person or thing **2** : the action or crime of publishing a libel — **li·bel·ous** *or* **li·bel·lous** \-bə-ləs\ *adj*

²**libel** *vb* **-beled** *or* **-belled; -bel·ing** *or* **-bel·ling** : to make or publish a libel — **li·bel·er** *n* — **li·bel·ist** *n*

¹**lib·er·al** \'li-brəl, -bə-rəl\ *adj* [ME, fr. AF, fr. L *liberalis* suitable for a freeman, generous, fr. *liber* free] **1** : of, relating to, or based on the liberal arts **2** : GENEROUS, BOUNTIFUL ⟨a ~ serving⟩ **3** : not literal **4** : not narrow in opinion or judgment : TOLERANT; *also* : not orthodox **5** : not conservative — **lib·er·al·i·ty** \ˌli-bə-'ra-lə-tē\ *n* — **lib·er·al·ize** \'li-brə-ˌlīz, -bə-rə-\ *vb* — **lib·er·al·ly** *adv*

²**liberal** *n* : a person who holds liberal views

liberal arts *n pl* : the studies (as language, philosophy, history, literature, or abstract science) in a college or university intended to provide chiefly general knowledge and to develop the general intellectual capacities

lib·er·al·ism \'li-brə-ˌli-zəm, -bə-rə-\ *n* : liberal principles and theories

lib·er·ate \'li-bə-ˌrāt\ *vb* **-at·ed; -at·ing 1** : to free from bondage or restraint; *also* : to raise to equal rights and status **2** : to free (as a gas) from combination — **lib·er·a·tion** \ˌli-bə-'rā-shən\ *n* — **lib·er·a·tor** \'li-bə-ˌrā-tər\ *n*

liberated *adj* : freed from or opposed to traditional social and sexual attitudes or roles ⟨a ~ marriage⟩

lib·er·tar·i·an \ˌli-bər-'ter-ē-ən\ *n* **1** : an advocate of the doctrine of free will **2** : one who upholds the principles of unrestricted liberty

lib·er·tine \'li-bər-ˌtēn\ *n* : a person who leads a dissolute life

lib·er·ty \'li-bər-tē\ *n, pl* **-ties 1** : FREEDOM **2** : an action going beyond normal limits; *esp* : FAMILIARITY **3** : a short leave from naval duty

li·bid·i·nous \lə-'bi-də-nəs\ *adj* **1** : LASCIVIOUS **2** : LIBIDINAL

li·bi·do \lə-'bē-dō\ *n, pl* **-dos** [NL, fr. L, desire, lust] **1** : psychic energy derived from basic biological urges **2** : sexual drive — **li·bid·i·nal** \lə-'bi-də-nəl\ *adj*

Li·bra \'lē-brə\ *n* [L, lit., scales] **1** : a zodiacal constellation between Virgo and Scorpio usu. pictured as a balance scale **2** : the 7th sign of the zodiac in astrology; *also* : one born under this sign

li·brar·i·an \lī-'brer-ē-ən\ *n* : a specialist in the management of a library

li·brary \'lī-ˌbrer-ē\ *n, pl* **-brar·ies 1** : a place in which books and related materials are kept for use but not for sale **2** : a collection of books

li·bret·to \lə-'bre-tō\ *n, pl* **-tos** *or* **-ti** \-tē\ [It, dim. of *libro* book, fr. L *liber*] : the text esp. of an opera — **li·bret·tist** \-tist\ *n*

lice *pl of* LOUSE

li·cense *or* **li·cence** \'lī-sᵊns\ *n* **1** : permission to act **2** : a permission granted by authority to engage in an activity **3** : a document, plate, or tag providing proof of a license **4** : freedom used irresponsibly — **license** *vb*

licensed practical nurse *n* : a specially trained person who is licensed (as by a state) to provide routine care for the sick

li·cens·ee \ˌlī-sᵊn-'sē\ *n* : a licensed person

licente *pl of* SENTE

li·cen·ti·ate \lī-'sen-chē-ət\ *n* : one licensed to practice a profession

li·cen·tious \lī-'sen-chəs\ *adj* : LEWD, LASCIVIOUS — **li·cen·tious·ly** *adv* — **li·cen·tious·ness** *n*

lichee *var of* LITCHI

li·chen \'lī-kən\ *n* : any of various complex plantlike organisms made up of an alga and a fungus growing as a unit on a solid surface — **li·chen·ous** *adj*

lic·it \'li-sət\ *adj* : LAWFUL

¹**lick** \'lik\ *vb* **1** : to draw the tongue over; *also* : to flicker over like a tongue **2** : THRASH; *also* : DEFEAT

²**lick** *n* **1** : a stroke of the tongue **2** : a small amount **3** : a hasty careless effort

4 : BLOW 5 : a natural deposit of salt that animals lick

lick·e·ty–split \,li-kə-tē-'split\ *adv* : at great speed

lick·spit·tle \'lik-,spi-t³l\ *n* : a fawning subordinate : TOADY

lic·o·rice \'li-kə-rish, -rəs\ *n* [ME, fr. AF *licoris*, fr. LL *liquiritia*, alter. of L *glycyrrhiza*, fr. Gk *glykyrrhiza*, fr. *glykys* sweet + *rhiza* root] 1 : the dried root of a European leguminous plant; *also* : an extract from it used esp. as a flavoring and in medicine 2 : a candy flavored with licorice 3 : a plant yielding licorice

lid \'lid\ *n* 1 : a movable cover 2 : EYELID 3 : something that confines or suppresses — **lid·ded** \'li-dəd\ *adj*

li·do \'lē-dō\ *n, pl* **lidos** : a fashionable beach resort

¹lie \'lī\ *vb* **lay** \'lā\; **lain** \'lān\; **ly·ing** \'lī-iŋ\ 1 : to be in, stay at rest in, or assume a horizontal position; *also* : to be in a helpless or defenseless state 2 : EXTEND ⟨our route *lay* to the west⟩ 3 : to occupy a certain relative position 4 : to have an effect esp. through mere presence

²lie *n* : the position in which something lies

³lie *vb* **lied; ly·ing** \'lī-iŋ\ : to tell a lie

⁴lie *n* : an untrue statement made with intent to deceive

lied \'lēt\ *n, pl* **lie·der** \'lē-dər\ [G] : a German song esp. of the 19th century

lie detector *n* : a polygraph for detecting physiological evidence of the tension that accompanies lying

lief \'lēv, 'lēf\ *adv* : GLADLY, WILLINGLY

¹liege \'lēj\ *adj* : LOYAL, FAITHFUL

²liege *n* 1 : VASSAL 2 : a feudal superior

lien \'lēn, 'lē-ən\ *n* : a legal claim on the property of another for the satisfaction of a debt or duty

lieu \'lü\ *n, archaic* : PLACE, STEAD — **in lieu of** : in the place of

lieut *abbr* lieutenant

lieu·ten·ant \lü-'te-nənt\ *n* [ME, fr. AF *lieu tenant*, fr. *liu, lieu* place + *tenant* holding, fr. *tenir* to hold, fr. L *tenēre*] 1 : a representative of another in the performance of duty 2 : FIRST LIEUTENANT; *also* : SECOND LIEUTENANT 3 : a commissioned officer in the navy ranking next below a lieutenant commander — **lieu·ten·an·cy** \-nən-sē\ *n*

lieutenant colonel *n* : a commissioned officer (as in the army) ranking next below a colonel

lieutenant commander *n* : a commissioned officer in the navy ranking next below a commander

lieutenant general *n* : a commissioned officer (as in the army) ranking next below a general

lieutenant governor *n* : a deputy or subordinate governor

lieutenant junior grade *n, pl* **lieutenants junior grade** : a commissioned officer in the navy ranking next below a lieutenant

life \'līf\ *n, pl* **lives** \'līvz\ 1 : the quality that distinguishes a vital and functional being from a dead body or inanimate matter; *also* : a state of an organism char-

acterized esp. by capacity for metabolism, growth, reaction to stimuli, and reproduction 2 : the physical and mental experiences of an individual 3 : BIOGRAPHY 4 : a specific phase or period ⟨adult ∼⟩ 5 : the period from birth to death; *also* : a sentence of imprisonment for the remainder of a person's life 6 : a way of living 7 : PERSON ⟨many *lives* were lost in the fire⟩ 8 : ANIMATION, SPIRIT ⟨dancing without ∼⟩ 9 : living beings ⟨forest ∼⟩ 10 : animate activity ⟨signs of ∼⟩ 11 : one providing interest and vigor ⟨∼ of the party⟩ — **life·less** *adj* — **life·like** *adj*

life·blood \'līf-,bləd\ *n* : a basic source of strength and vitality

life·boat \-,bōt\ *n* : a sturdy boat designed for use in saving lives at sea

life·guard \-,gärd\ *n* : a usu. expert swimmer employed to safeguard bathers

life·line \-,līn\ *n* 1 : a line to which persons may cling for safety 2 : something considered vital for survival

life·long \-,lȯŋ\ *adj* : continuing through life

life preserver *n* : a buoyant device designed to save a person from drowning

lif·er \'lī-fər\ *n* 1 : a person sentenced to life imprisonment 2 : a person who makes a career in the armed forces

life raft *n* : a raft for use by people forced into the water

life·sav·ing \'līf-,sā-viŋ\ *n* : the skill or practice of saving or protecting lives esp. of drowning persons — **life·sav·er** \-,sā-vər\ *n*

life science *n* : a branch of science (as biology, medicine, and sometimes anthropology or sociology) that deals with living organisms and life processes — usu. used in pl. — **life scientist** *n*

life·style \'līf-,stī(-ə)l\ *n* : a way of living

²lifestyle *adj* : associated with, reflecting, or promoting an enhanced or more desirable lifestyle

life·time \-,tīm\ *n* : the duration of an individual's existence

life·work \-'wərk\ *n* : the entire or principal work of one's lifetime; *also* : a work extending over a lifetime

life·world \-,wər(-ə)ld\ *n* : the total of an individual's physical surroundings and everyday experiences

LIFO *abbr* last in, first out

¹lift \'lift\ *vb* 1 : RAISE, ELEVATE; *also* : RISE, ASCEND 2 : to put an end to : STOP ⟨∼ a ban⟩ 3 : to pay off ⟨∼ a mortgage⟩ — **lift·er** *n*

²lift *n* 1 : LOAD 2 : the action or an instance of lifting 3 : HELP; *also* : a ride along one's way 4 : RISE, ADVANCE 5 *chiefly Brit* : ELEVATOR 6 : an elevation of the spirits 7 : the upward force that is developed by a moving airfoil and that opposes the pull of gravity

lift–off \-,ȯf\ *n* : a vertical takeoff (as by a rocket)

lift truck *n* : a small truck for lifting and transporting loads

lig·a·ment \'li-gə-mənt\ *n* : a band of

tough fibrous tissue that holds bones together or supports an organ in place

li·gate \'lī-ˌgāt\ vb **li·gat·ed; li·gat·ing** : to tie with a ligature — **li·ga·tion** \lī-'gā-shən\ n

lig·a·ture \'lig-ə-ˌchùr, -chər\ n **1** : something that binds or ties; also : a thread used in surgery esp. for tying blood vessels **2** : a printed or written character consisting of two or more letters or characters (as æ) united

¹light \'līt\ n **1** : something that makes vision possible : electromagnetic radiation visible to the human eye; also : the sensation aroused by stimulation of the visual sense organs **2** : DAYLIGHT **3** : a source of light (as a candle) **4** : ENLIGHTENMENT; also : TRUTH **5** : public knowledge ⟨facts brought to ~⟩ **6** : a particular aspect presented to view ⟨saw the matter in a different ~⟩ **7** : WINDOW **8** pl : STANDARDS ⟨according to his ~s⟩ **9** : CELEBRITY **10** : LIGHTHOUSE, BEACON; also : TRAFFIC LIGHT **11** : a flame for lighting something

²light adj **1** : having light : BRIGHT **2** : PALE 2 ⟨~ blue⟩ — **light·ness** n

³light vb **lit** \'lit\ or **light·ed; light·ing 1** : to make or become light **2** : to cause to burn : BURN **3** : to conduct with a light **4** : ILLUMINATE

⁴light adj **1** : not heavy **2** : not serious ⟨~ reading⟩ **3** : SCANTY ⟨~ rain⟩ **4** : easily disturbed ⟨a ~ sleeper⟩ **5** : GENTLE ⟨a ~ blow⟩ **6** : easily endurable ⟨a ~ cold⟩; also : requiring little effort ⟨~ exercise⟩ **7** : SWIFT, NIMBLE **8** : FRIVOLOUS **9** : DIZZY **10** : made with lower calorie content or less of some ingredient than usual ⟨~ salad dressing⟩ **11** : producing goods for direct consumption by the consumer ⟨~ industry⟩ — **light·ly** adv — **light·ness** n

⁵light adv **1** : LIGHTLY **2** : with little baggage ⟨travel ~⟩

⁶light vb **lit** \'lit\ or **light·ed; light·ing 1** : SETTLE, ALIGHT **2** : to fall unexpectedly **3** : HAPPEN ⟨~ed on a solution⟩

light bulb n **1** : a lamp in which an electrically heated filament emits light **2** : FLUORESCENT LAMP

light–emitting diode n : LED

¹light·en \'līt-ᵊn\ vb **1** : ILLUMINATE, BRIGHTEN **2** : to give out flashes of lightning

²lighten vb **1** : to relieve of a burden **2** : GLADDEN **3** : to become lighter

lighten up vb : to take things less seriously ⟨lighten up and relax⟩

ligh·ter \'li-tər\ n : a barge used esp. in loading or unloading ships

²light·er \'lī-tər\ n : one that lights; esp : a device for lighting (as a fire or cigarette)

light-face \'līt-ˌfās\ n : a type having light thin lines — **light-faced** \-ˌfāst\ adj

light–head·ed \'līt-ˌhe-dəd\ adj **1** : feeling confused or dizzy **2** : lacking maturity or seriousness

light-heart·ed \-ˌhär-təd\ adj : free from worry — **light-heart·ed·ly** adv — **light-heart·ed·ness** n

light·house \-ˌhaùs\ n : a structure with a powerful light for guiding sailors

light meter n : a usu. handheld device for indicating correct photographic exposure

¹light·ning \'līt-niŋ\ n : the flashing of light produced by a discharge of atmospheric electricity; also : the discharge itself

²lightning adj : extremely fast

lightning bug n : FIREFLY

lightning rod n : a grounded metallic rod set up on a structure to protect it from lightning

light out vb : to leave in a hurry

light·proof \'līt-ˌprüf\ adj : impenetrable by light

lights \'līts\ n pl : the lungs esp. of a slaughtered animal

light·ship \'līt-ˌship\ n : a ship with a powerful light moored at a place dangerous to navigation

light show n : a kaleidoscopic display (as of colored lights)

light·some \'līt-səm\ adj **1** : free from care **2** : NIMBLE

¹light·weight \'līt-ˌwāt\ n : one of less than average weight; esp : a boxer weighing not over 135 pounds

²lightweight adj **1** : INCONSEQUENTIAL **2** : of less than average weight

light–year \'līt-ˌyir\ n **1** : an astronomical unit of distance equal to the distance that light travels in one year in a vacuum or about 5.88 trillion miles (9.46 trillion kilometers) **2** : an extremely large measure of comparison ⟨saw it ~s ago⟩

lig·nin \'lig-nən\ n : a substance related to cellulose that occurs in the woody cell walls of plants and in the cementing material between them

lig·nite \'lig-ˌnīt\ n : brownish black soft coal

¹like \'līk\ vb **liked; lik·ing 1** : ENJOY ⟨~s baseball⟩ **2** : WANT ⟨would ~ a drink⟩ **3** : CHOOSE ⟨does as she ~s⟩ — **lik·able** or **like·able** \'lī-kə-bəl\ adj

²like n : PREFERENCE

³like adj : SIMILAR ♦ **Synonyms** ALIKE, ANALOGOUS, COMPARABLE, PARALLEL, UNIFORM

⁴like prep **1** : similar or similarly to ⟨seems ~ a dream⟩ **2** : typical of **3** : comparable to **4** : as though there would be ⟨looks ~ rain⟩ **5** : such as ⟨a subject ~ physics⟩

⁵like n **1** : COUNTERPART **2** : one that is similar to another ⟨we may never see his ~ again⟩ — **and the like** : ET CETERA

⁶like conj **1** : AS IF ⟨acted ~ they were scared⟩ **2** : in the same way that ⟨do it ~ mom said⟩

-like adj comb form : resembling or characteristic of ⟨ladylike⟩ ⟨lifelike⟩

like·li·hood \'lī-klē-ˌhùd\ n : PROBABILITY

¹like·ly \'lī-klē\ adj **like·li·er; -est 1** : very probable **2** : BELIEVABLE **3** : PROMISING ⟨a ~ place to fish⟩

²likely adv : in all probability

lik·en \'lī-kən\ vb : COMPARE

like·ness \'līk-nəs\ n **1** : COPY, PORTRAIT **2** : SEMBLANCE **3** : RESEMBLANCE

like·wise \-ˌwīz\ *adv* **1** : in like manner **2** : in addition : ALSO

lik·ing \ˈlī-kiŋ\ *n* : favorable regard ⟨took a ∼ to the newcomer⟩; *also* : TASTE

li·lac \ˈlī-lək, -ˌlak, -ˌläk\ *n* [obs. F (now *lilas*), fr. Ar *līlak*, fr. Pers *nīlak* bluish, fr. *nīl* blue, fr. Skt *nīla* dark blue] **1** : a shrub related to the olive that produces large clusters of fragrant grayish pink, purple, or white flowers **2** : a moderate purple color

lil·an·ge·ni \ˌli-lən-ˈge-nē\ *n, pl* **em·a·lan·ge·ni** \ˌe-mə-lən-ˈge-nē\ — see MONEY table

lil·li·pu·tian \ˌli-lə-ˈpyü-shən\ *adj, often cap* **1** : SMALL, MINIATURE **2** : PETTY

lilt \ˈlilt\ *n* **1** : a cheerful lively song or tune **2** : a rhythmical swing or flow

lily \ˈli-lē\ *n, pl* **lil·ies** : any of a genus of tall bulbous herbs with leafy stems and usu. funnel-shaped flowers; *also* : any of various related plants

lily of the valley : a low perennial herb related to the lilies that produces a raceme of fragrant nodding bell-shaped white flowers

li·ma bean \ˈlī-mə-\ *n* : a bushy or tall-growing bean widely cultivated for its flat edible usu. pale green or whitish seeds; *also* : the seed

limb \ˈlim\ *n* **1** : one of the projecting paired appendages (as legs, arms, or wings) used by an animal esp. in moving or grasping **2** : a large branch of a tree : BOUGH — **limb·less** *adj*

¹lim·ber \ˈlim-bər\ *adj* **1** : FLEXIBLE, SUPPLE **2** : LITHE, NIMBLE

²limber *vb* : to make or become limber

lim·bic \ˈlim-bik\ *adj* : of, relating to, or being a group of structures of the brain (**limbic system**) concerned esp. with emotion and motivation

¹lim·bo \ˈlim-bō\ *n, pl* **limbos** [ME, fr. ML, abl. of *limbus* limbo, fr. L, border] **1** *often cap* : an abode of souls barred from heaven through no fault of their own **2** : a place or state of confinement, oblivion, or uncertainty ⟨a ∼ of forgotten things⟩

²limbo *n, pl* **limbos** : an acrobatic dance or contest that involves passing under a horizontal pole

Lim·burg·er \ˈlim-ˌbər-gər\ *n* : a pungent semisoft surface-ripened cheese

¹lime \ˈlīm\ *n* : a caustic powdery white solid that consists of calcium and oxygen, is obtained from limestone or shells, and is used in making cement and in fertilizer — **lime** *vb* — **limy** \ˈlī-mē\ *adj*

²lime *n* : a small yellowish green citrus fruit with juicy acid pulp

lime·ade \ˌlīm-ˈād, ˈlī-ˌmād\ *n* : a beverage of lime juice, sugar, and water

lime·light \ˈlīm-ˌlīt\ *n* **1** : a device in which flame is directed against a cylinder of lime formerly used in the theater to cast a strong white light on the stage **2** : the center of public attention

lim·er·ick \ˈli-mə-rik\ *n* : a light or humorous poem of 5 lines

lime·stone \ˈlīm-ˌstōn\ *n* : a rock that is formed by accumulation of organic remains (as shells), is used in building, and yields lime when burned

¹lim·it \ˈli-mət\ *n* **1** : something that restrains or confines; *also* : the utmost extent **2** : BOUNDARY; *also, pl* : BOUNDS **3** : a prescribed maximum or minimum **4** : a number whose value becomes arbitrarily close to that of a function as its independent variable approaches a given value — **lim·it·less** *adj* — **lim·it·less·ness** *n*

²limit *vb* **1** : to set limits to **2** : to reduce in quantity or extent — **lim·i·ta·tion** \ˌli-mə-ˈtā-shən\ *n*

lim·it·ed *adj* **1** : confined within limits **2** : offering faster service esp. by making fewer stops ⟨a ∼ train⟩

limn \ˈlim\ *vb* **limned; limn·ing** \ˈli-miŋ, ˈlim-niŋ\ **1** : DRAW; *also* : PAINT **2** : DELINEATE **3** : DESCRIBE

limo \ˈli-(ˌ)mō\ *n, pl* **limos** : LIMOUSINE

li·mo·nite \ˈlī-mə-ˌnīt\ *n* : a ferric oxide that is a major ore of iron — **li·mo·nit·ic** \ˌlī-mə-ˈni-tik\ *adj*

lim·ou·sine \ˈli-mə-ˌzēn, ˌli-mə-ˈzēn\ *n* [F] **1** : a large luxurious often chauffeur-driven sedan **2** : a large vehicle for transporting passengers to and from an airport

¹limp \ˈlimp\ *vb* : to walk lamely; *also* : to proceed with difficulty

²limp *n* : a limping movement or gait

³limp *adj* **1** : having no defined shape; *also* : not stiff or rigid **2** : lacking in strength or firmness ⟨went ∼ from fatigue⟩ — **limp·ly** *adv* — **limp·ness** *n*

lim·pet \ˈlim-pət\ *n* : any of numerous gastropod sea mollusks with a conical shell that clings to rocks or timbers

lim·pid \ˈlim-pəd\ *adj* : CLEAR, TRANSPARENT ⟨∼ water⟩

lin *abbr* **1** lineal **2** linear

lin·age \ˈlī-nij\ *n* : the number of lines of written or printed matter

linch·pin \ˈlinch-ˌpin\ *n* : a locking pin inserted crosswise (as through the end of an axle)

lin·den \ˈlin-dən\ *n* : any of a genus of trees with large heart-shaped leaves and clustered yellowish flowers; *also* : the light white wood of a linden

¹line \ˈlīn\ *n* **1** : CORD, ROPE, WIRE; *also* : a length of material used in measuring and leveling **2** : pipes for conveying a fluid ⟨a gas ∼⟩ **3** : a horizontal row of written or printed characters; *also* : VERSE **4** : NOTE **5** : the words making up a part in a drama — usu. used in pl. **6** : something distinct, long, and narrow; *also* : ROUTE **7** : a state of agreement **8** : a course of conduct, action, or thought; *also* : OCCUPATION **9** : LIMIT **10** : an arrangement of persons or objects of one kind in an orderly series ⟨waiting in ∼⟩ **11** : a transportation system **12 a** : the football players who are stationed on the line of scrimmage **b** : a group of three players who play together as a unit in hockey **13** : a long narrow mark; *also* : EQUATOR **14** : a geometric element that is the path of a moving point **15** : CONTOUR **16** : a general plan ⟨thinking along these ∼*s*⟩ **17** : an indication based on insight or investigation

²line *vb* **lined; lin·ing 1** : to mark with a line **2** : to place or form a line along **3** : ALIGN ⟨∼ up the sheets of paper⟩

³line *vb* **lined; lin·ing** : to cover the inner surface of ⟨∼ the box with paper⟩

lin·eage \'li-nē-ij\ *n* : lineal descent from a common progenitor; *also* : FAMILY

lin·eal \'li-nē-əl\ *adj* **1** : LINEAR **2** : consisting of or being in a direct line of ancestry; *also* : HEREDITARY

lin·ea·ment \'li-nē-ə-mənt\ *n* : an outline, feature, or contour of a body and esp. of a face — usu. used in pl.

lin·ear \'li-nē-ər\ *adj* **1** : of, relating to, resembling, or having a graph that is a line and esp. a straight line : STRAIGHT **2** : composed of simply drawn lines with little attempt at pictorial representation ⟨∼ script⟩ **3** : being long and uniformly narrow

line·back·er \'līn-,ba-kər\ *n* : a defensive football player who lines up just behind the line of scrimmage

line drive *n* : a batted baseball hit in a flatter path than a fly ball

line–item veto *n* : the power of a government executive to veto specific items in an appropriations bill

line·man \'līn-mən\ *n* **1** : a person who sets up or repairs communication or power lines **2** : a player in the line in football

lin·en \'li-nən\ *n* **1** : cloth made of flax; *also* : thread or yarn spun from flax **2** : clothing or household articles made of linen cloth or similar fabric

line of scrimmage : an imaginary line in football parallel to the goal lines and tangent to the nose of the ball laid on the ground before a play

¹lin·er \'lī-nər\ *n* : a ship or airplane of a regular transportation line

²liner *n* : one that lines or is used as a lining — **lin·er·less** *adj*

line score *n* : a score of a baseball game giving the runs, hits, and errors made by each team

lines·man \'līnz-mən\ *n* **1** : LINEMAN 1 **2** : an official who assists a referee

line·up \'lī-,nəp\ *n* **1** : a list of players taking part in a game (as of baseball) **2** : a line of persons arranged esp. for identification by police

ling \'liŋ\ *n* : any of various fishes related to the cod

-ling *n suffix* **1** : one associated with ⟨nestling⟩ **2** : young, small, or minor one ⟨duckling⟩

lin·ger \'liŋ-gər\ *vb* : TARRY; *also* : PROCRASTINATE — **lin·ger·er** *n*

lin·ge·rie \,län-jə-'rā, ,läⁿ-zhə-, -'rē\ *n* [F, fr. MF, fr. *linge* linen, fr. L *lineus* made of linen, fr. *linum* flax, linen] : women's intimate apparel

lin·go \'liŋ-gō\ *n, pl* **lingoes** : a usu. strange or incomprehensible language

lin·gua fran·ca \,liŋ-gwə-'fraŋ-kə\ *n, pl* **lingua francas** *or* **lin·guae fran·cae** \-gwē-'fraŋ-,kē\ [It] **1** *often cap* : a common language consisting of Italian mixed

with French, Spanish, Greek, and Arabic that was formerly spoken in Mediterranean ports **2** : a common or commercial tongue among speakers of different languages

lin·gual \'liŋ-gwəl\ *adj* : of, relating to, or produced by the tongue

lin·gui·ca \liŋ-'gwē-sə\ *n* : a spicy Portuguese sausage

lin·guist \'liŋ-gwist\ *n* **1** : a person skilled in languages **2** : a person who specializes in linguistics

lin·guis·tics \liŋ-'gwis-tiks\ *n* : the study of human speech including the units, nature, structure, and modification of language — **lin·guis·tic** \-tik\ *adj*

lin·i·ment \'li-nə-mənt\ *n* : a liquid preparation rubbed on the skin esp. to relieve pain

lin·ing \'lī-niŋ\ *n* : material used to line esp. an inner surface

link \'liŋk\ *n* **1** : a connecting structure; *esp* : a single ring of a chain **2** : BOND, TIE **3** : HYPERLINK — **link** *vb* — **link·er** *n*

link·age \'liŋ-kij\ *n* **1** : the manner or style of being united **2** : the quality or state of being linked **3** : a system of links

linking verb *n* : a word or expression (as a form of *be, become, feel,* or *seem*) that links a subject with its predicate

links \'liŋks\ *n pl* : a golf course

link·up \'liŋ-,kəp\ *n* **1** : MEETING **2** : something that serves as a linking device or factor

lin·net \'li-nət\ *n* : an Old World finch

li·no·leum \lə-'nō-lē-əm\ *n* [L *linum* flax + *oleum* oil] : a floor covering with a canvas back and a surface of hardened linseed oil and a filler

lin·seed \'lin-,sēd\ *n* : the seeds of flax yielding a yellowish oil (**linseed oil**) used esp. in paints and linoleum

lin·sey–wool·sey \,lin-zē-'wul-zē\ *n* : a coarse sturdy fabric of wool and linen or cotton

lint \'lint\ *n* **1** : linen made into a soft fleecy substance **2** : fine ravels and short fibers of yarn or fabric **3** : the fibers that surround cotton seeds and form the cotton staple

lin·tel \'lin-tᵊl\ *n* : a horizontal piece across the top of an opening (as of a door) that carries the weight of the structure above it

linz·er torte \'lin-sər-, -zər-\ *n, often cap L* : a baked buttery torte made with chopped almonds, sugar, and spices and filled with jam or preserves

li·on \'lī-ən\ *n, pl* **lions** : a large heavily built cat of Africa and southern Asia with a shaggy mane in the male

li·on·ess \'lī-ə-nəs\ *n* : a female lion

li·on·heart·ed \,lī-ən-'här-təd\ *adj* : COURAGEOUS, BRAVE

li·on·ise *Brit var of* LIONIZE

li·on·ize \'lī-ə-,nīz\ *vb* **-ized; -iz·ing** : to treat as an object of great interest or importance — **li·on·i·za·tion** \,lī-ə-nə-'zā-shən\ *n*

lion's den *n* : a place or state of extreme disadvantage, antagonism, or hostility

lip \'lip\ *n* **1** : either of the two fleshy folds that surround the mouth; *also* : the margin of the human lip **2** : a part or projection suggesting a lip **3** : the edge of a hollow vessel or cavity — **lipped** \'lipt\ *adj*

li·pa \'lē-ˌpä, -pə\ *n, pl* **lipa** — see *kuna* at MONEY table

lip·id \'li-pəd\ *n* : any of various substances (as fats and waxes) that with proteins and carbohydrates make up the principal structural parts of living cells

lip·lock \'lip-ˌläk\ *n* : a long amorous kiss

li·po·pro·tein \ˌlī-pō-'prō-ˌtēn, ˌli-\ *n* : a protein that is a complex of protein and lipid

li·po·suc·tion \'li-pə-ˌsək-shən, 'lī-\ *n* : surgical removal of local fat deposits (as in the thighs) esp. for cosmetic purposes

lip-read·ing \'lip-ˌrē-diŋ\ *n* : the interpreting of a speaker's words by watching lip and facial movements without hearing the voice

lip service *n* : an avowal of allegiance that is not matched by action

lip·stick \'lip-ˌstik\ *n* : a waxy solid colored cosmetic in stick form for the lips — **lip·sticked** \-ˌstikt\ *adj*

liq *abbr* **1** liquid **2** liquor

liq·ue·fy *also* **liq·ui·fy** \'li-kwə-ˌfī\ *vb* **-fied; -fy·ing** : to make or become liquid — **liq·ue·fi·er** \-ˌfī(-ə)r\ *n*

li·queur \li-'kər\ *n* [F] : a distilled alcoholic liquor flavored with aromatic substances and usu. sweetened

¹liq·uid \'li-kwəd\ *adj* **1** : flowing freely like water **2** : neither solid nor gaseous **3** : shining and clear ⟨large ∼ eyes⟩ **4** : smooth and musical in tone; *also* : smooth and unconstrained in movement **5** : consisting of or capable of ready conversion into cash ⟨∼ assets⟩ — **li·quid·i·ty** \li-'kwi-də-tē\ *n*

²liquid *n* : a liquid substance

liq·ui·date \'li-kwə-ˌdāt\ *vb* **-dat·ed; -dat·ing** **1** : to settle the accounts and distribute the assets of (as a business) **2** : to pay off ⟨∼ a debt⟩ **3** : to get rid of; *esp* : KILL — **liq·ui·da·tion** \ˌli-kwə-'dā-shən\ *n*

liquid crystal *n* : an organic liquid that resembles a crystal in having ordered molecular arrays

liquid crystal display *n* : LCD

liquid measure *n* : a unit or series of units for measuring liquid capacity — see METRIC SYSTEM table, WEIGHT table

li·quor \'li-kər\ *n* [ME *licour*, fr. AF, fr. L *liquor*, fr. *liquēre* to be fluid] : a liquid substance; *esp* : a distilled alcoholic beverage

li·quo·rice *chiefly Brit var of* LICORICE

li·ra \'lir-ə, 'lē-rə\ *n* **1** *pl* **li·re** \'lē-rā\ : the former basic monetary unit of Italy **2** : the basic monetary unit of Turkey — see MONEY table **3** *pl* **li·ri** \'lē-rē\ : the basic monetary unit of Malta until 2008

lisente *pl of* SENTE

lisle \'līl\ *n* : a smooth tightly twisted thread usu. made of long-staple cotton

lisp \'lisp\ *vb* : to pronounce \s\ and \z\ imperfectly esp. by turning them into \th\ and \t͟h\; *also* : to speak childishly — **lisp** *n* — **lisp·er** *n*

lis·some *also* **lis·som** \'li-səm\ *adj* **1** : easily flexed **2** : LITHE **2** ⟨a ∼ dancer⟩ **3** : NIMBLE — **lis·some·ly** *adv*

¹list \'list\ *vb, archaic* : PLEASE; *also* : WISH

²list *vb, archaic* : LISTEN

³list *n* : a leaning to one side : TILT

⁴list *vb* : TILT

⁵list *n* **1** : a simple series of words or numerals; *also* : an official roster **2** : CATALOG, CHECKLIST

⁶list *vb* : to make a list of; *also* : to include on a list — **list·ee** \li-'stē\ *n*

lis·ten \'li-sᵊn\ *vb* **1** : to pay attention in order to hear **2** : HEED — **lis·ten·er** *n*

lis·ten·er·ship \'li-sᵊn-ər-ˌship\ *n* : the audience for a radio program or recording

list·ing \'lis-tiŋ\ *n* **1** : an act or instance of making or including in a list **2** : something that is listed

list·less \'list-ləs\ *adj* : SPIRITLESS, LANGUID ⟨a ∼ performance⟩ — **list·less·ly** *adv* — **list·less·ness** *n*

list price *n* : the price of an item as published in a catalog, price list, or advertisement before being discounted

lists \'lists\ *n pl* : an arena for combat (as jousting)

¹lit \'lit\ *past and past part of* LIGHT

²lit *abbr* **1** liter **2** literal; literally **3** literary **4** literature

lit·a·ny \'li-tə-nē\ *n, pl* **-nies** [ME *letanie*, fr. AF & LL, fr. AF; fr. LL *litania*, fr. LGk *litaneia*, fr. Gk, entreaty, fr. *litanos* suppliant] **1** : a prayer consisting of a series of supplications and responses said alternately by a leader and a group **2** : a lengthy recitation ⟨a ∼ of complaints⟩

li·tas \'lē-ˌtäs\ *n, pl* **li·tai** \-ˌtī\ *or* **li·tu** \-ˌtü\ : the basic monetary unit of Lithuania from 1923 to 1940 and from 1991 through 2014

litchi *var of* LYCHEE

lite \'līt\ *adj* **1** : ⁴LIGHT 10 ⟨∼ beer⟩ **2** : lacking in substance or seriousness ⟨∼ news⟩

li·ter \'lē-tər\ *n* — see METRIC SYSTEM table

lit·er·al \'li-tə-rəl\ *adj* **1** : adhering to fact or to the ordinary or usual meaning (as of a word) **2** : UNADORNED; *also* : PROSAIC **3** : VERBATIM

lit·er·al·ism \-rə-ˌli-zəm\ *n* **1** : adherence to the explicit substance (as of an idea) **2** : fidelity to observable fact — **lit·er·al·ist** \-list\ *n* — **lit·er·al·is·tic** \ˌli-tə-rə-'lis-tik\ *adj*

lit·er·al·ly \'li-tə-rə-lē, 'li-trə-\ *adv* **1** : ACTUALLY ⟨was ∼ insane⟩ **2** : VIRTUALLY ⟨∼ poured out new ideas⟩

lit·er·ary \'li-tə-ˌrer-ē\ *adj* **1** : of or relating to literature **2** : WELL-READ

lit·er·ate \'li-trət, -tə-rət\ *adj* **1** : EDUCATED; *also* : able to read and write **2** : LITERARY; *also* : POLISHED, LUCID — **lit·er·a·cy** \'li-trə-sē, -tə-rə-\ *n* — **literate** *n*

li·te·ra·ti \ˌli-tə-'rä-tē\ *n pl* **1** : the educated class **2** : persons interested in literature or the arts

lit·er·a·ture \'li-trə-ˌchùr, -tə-rə-, -chər\ *n*

1 : the production of written works having excellence of form or expression and dealing with ideas of permanent interest **2** : the written works produced in a particular language, country, or age

lithe \ˈlīth̯, ˈlīth\ adj **1** : SUPPLE **2** : characterized by effortless grace; also : athletically slim ⟨a ~ body⟩

lithe·some \ˈlīth̯-səm, ˈlīth-\ adj : LISSOME

lith·i·um \ˈli-thē-əm\ n : a light silver-white metallic chemical element

li·thog·ra·phy \li-ˈthä-grə-fē\ n : the process of printing from a plane surface (as a smooth stone or metal plate) on which the image to be printed is ink-receptive and the blank area ink-repellent — **lith·o·graph** \ˈli-thə-ˌgraf\ vb — **lithograph** n — **li·thog·ra·pher** \li-ˈthä-grə-fər, ˈli-thə-ˌgra-fər\ n — **lith·o·graph·ic** \ˌli-thə-ˈgra-fik\ adj — **lith·o·graph·i·cal·ly** \-fi-k(ə-)lē\ adv

li·thol·o·gy \li-ˈthä-lə-jē\ n, pl **-gies** : the study of rocks — **lith·o·log·ic** \ˌli-thə-ˈlä-jik\ or **lith·o·log·i·cal** \-ji-kəl\ adj

lith·o·sphere \ˈli-thə-ˌsfir\ n : the outer part of the solid earth

Lith·u·a·nian \ˌli-thə-ˈwā-nē-ən, -thyù-\ n **1** : a native or inhabitant of Lithuania **2** : the language of the Lithuanians — **Lithuanian** adj

lit·i·gant \ˈli-ti-gənt\ n : a party to a lawsuit — **litigant** adj

lit·i·gate \-ˌgāt\ vb **-gat·ed; -gat·ing** : to carry on a legal contest by judicial process; also : to contest at law — **lit·i·ga·tion** \ˌli-tə-ˈgā-shən\ n

li·ti·gious \lə-ˈti-jəs\ adj **1** : CONTENTIOUS **2** : prone to engage in lawsuits **3** : of or relating to litigation — **li·ti·gious·ly** adv — **li·ti·gious·ness** n

lit·mus \ˈlit-məs\ n : a coloring matter from lichens that turns red in acid solutions and blue in alkaline

litmus test n : a test in which a single factor (as an attitude) is decisive

Litt D or **Lit D** abbr [ML litterarum doctor] : doctor of letters; doctor of literature

¹**lit·ter** \ˈli-tər\ n [ME, fr. AF litere, fr. lit bed, fr. L lectus] **1** : a covered and curtained couch with shafts that is used to carry a single passenger; also : a device (as a stretcher) for carrying a sick or injured person **2** : material used as bedding for animals; also : material used to absorb the urine and feces of animals **3** : the offspring of an animal at one birth **4** : RUBBISH

²**litter** vb **1** : to give birth to young **2** : to strew or mark with scattered objects

lit·ter·bug \ˈli-tər-ˌbəg\ n : one who litters a public area

¹**lit·tle** \ˈli-tᵊl\ adj **lit·tler** \ˈli-tᵊl-ər\ or **less** \ˈles\ or **less·er** \ˈle-sər\; **lit·tlest** \ˈli-tᵊl-əst\ or **least** \ˈlēst\ **1** : not big; also : YOUNG **2** : not important **3** : PETTY **3** **4** : not much — **lit·tle·ness** n

²**little** adv **less** \ˈles\; **least** \ˈlēst\ **1** : SLIGHTLY; also : not at all **2** : INFREQUENTLY

³**little** n **1** : a small amount or quantity **2** : a short time or distance

Little Dipper n : the seven bright stars of Ursa Minor arranged in a form resembling a dipper

little finger n : PINKIE

little theater n : a small theater for low-cost dramatic productions designed for a limited audience

lit·to·ral \ˈli-tə-rəl, ˌli-tə-ˈral\ adj : of, relating to, or growing on or near a shore esp. of the sea — **littoral** n

lit·ur·gy \ˈli-tər-jē\ n, pl **-gies** : a rite or body of rites prescribed for public worship — **li·tur·gi·cal** \lə-ˈtər-ji-kəl\ adj — **li·tur·gi·cal·ly** \-k(ə-)lē\ adv — **lit·ur·gist** \ˈli-tər-jist\ n

liv·able also **live·able** \ˈli-və-bəl\ adj **1** : suitable for living in or with ⟨a ~ house⟩ ⟨~wages⟩ **2** : ENDURABLE — **liv·a·bil·i·ty** \ˌli-və-ˈbi-lə-tē\ n

¹**live** \ˈliv\ vb **lived; liv·ing 1** : to be or continue alive ⟨lived 80 years⟩ **2** : SUBSIST **3** : RESIDE ⟨~s next door⟩ **4** : to conduct one's life **5** : to remain in human memory or record ⟨his legacy ~s⟩

²**live** \ˈlīv\ adj **1** : having life ⟨~ worms⟩ **2** : ACTUAL ⟨a real ~ celebrity⟩ **3** : BURNING, GLOWING ⟨a ~ cigar⟩ **4** : connected to electric power ⟨a ~ wire⟩ **5** : UNEXPLODED ⟨a ~ bomb⟩ **6** : of continuing interest ⟨a ~ issue⟩ **7** : of or involving the actual presence of real people ⟨~ audience⟩; also : broadcast directly at the time of production **8** : being in play ⟨a ~ ball⟩

lived–in \ˈlivd-ˌin\ adj : of or suggesting long-term human habitation or use

live down vb : to live so as to wipe out the memory or effects of

live in vb : to live in one's place of employment — used of a servant — **live–in** \ˈliv-ˌin\ adj

live·li·hood \ˈlīv-lē-ˌhùd\ n : means of support or subsistence

live·long \ˈliv-ˌlòŋ\ adj [ME lef long, fr. lef dear + long long] : WHOLE, ENTIRE ⟨the ~ day⟩

live·ly \ˈlīv-lē\ adj **live·li·er; -est 1** : ANIMATED ⟨~ debate⟩ **2** : KEEN, VIVID ⟨~ interest⟩ **3** : showing activity or vigor ⟨a ~ manner⟩ **4** : quick to rebound ⟨a ~ ball⟩ **5** : full of life ♦ Synonyms VIVACIOUS, SPRIGHTLY, GAY, SPIRITED — **live·li·ness** n — **live·ly** adv

liv·en \ˈlī-vən\ vb : ENLIVEN

live oak n : any of several American evergreen oaks; esp : one of the southeastern U.S. that is often planted as a shade tree

¹**liv·er** \ˈli-vər\ n **1** : a large glandular organ of vertebrates that secretes bile and is a center of metabolic activity **2** : the liver of an animal (as a calf or chicken) eaten as food

²**liver** n : one that lives esp. in a specified way ⟨a fast ~⟩

liv·er·ish \ˈli-və-rish\ adj **1** : resembling liver esp. in color **2** : BILIOUS **3** : PEEVISH — **liv·er·ish·ness** n

liver spots n pl : AGE SPOTS

liv·er·wort \ˈli-vər-ˌwərt\ n : any of a class of flowerless plants resembling the related mosses

liv·er·wurst \-ˌwərst, -ˌwùrst\ n [part

trans. of G *Leberwurst,* fr. *Leber* liver + *Wurst* sausage] : a sausage consisting chiefly of liver

liv·ery \'li-və-rē\ *n, pl* **-er·ies** 1 : a servant's uniform; *also* : distinctive dress 2 : the feeding, care, and stabling of horses for pay; *also* : an establishment (as a stable or business) keeping horses or vehicles for hire — **liv·er·ied** \-rēd\ *adj*

liv·ery·man \'li-və-rē-mən\ *n*

lives *pl of* LIFE

live·stock \'līv-ˌstäk\ *n* : farm animals kept for use and profit

live wire *n* : an alert, active, or aggressive person — **live–wire** *adj*

liv·id \'li-vəd\ *adj* [F *livide,* fr. L *lividus,* fr. *livēre* to be blue] 1 : discolored by bruising 2 : ASHEN, PALLID 3 : REDDISH 4 : ENRAGED — **li·vid·i·ty** \li-'vi-də-tē\ *n*

¹**liv·ing** \'li-viŋ\ *adj* 1 : having life 2 : NATURAL 3 : full of life and vigor; *also* : VIVID ⟨in ~ color⟩

²**living** *n* 1 : the condition of being alive 2 : LIVELIHOOD 3 : manner of life

living room *n* : a room in a residence used for the common social activities of the occupants

living wage *n* : a wage sufficient to provide an acceptable standard of living

living will *n* : a document requesting that the signer not be kept alive by artificial means unless there is a reasonable expectation of recovery

livre \'lēvrᵊ\ *n* : the pound of Lebanon

liz·ard \'li-zərd\ *n* : any of a group of 4-legged reptiles with long tapering tails

Lk *abbr* Luke

ll *abbr* lines

lla·ma \'lä-mə\ *n* [Sp, fr. Quechua] : any of a genus of wild or domesticated So. American mammals related to the camels but smaller and without a hump

lla·no \'lä-nō\ *n, pl* **llanos** : an open grassy plain esp. of Latin America

LLD *abbr* [NL *legum doctor*] doctor of laws

LNG *abbr* liquefied natural gas

¹**load** \'lōd\ *n* 1 : PACK; *also* : CARGO 2 : a mass of weight supported by something 3 : something that burdens the mind or spirits 4 : a large quantity — usu. used in pl. 5 : a standard, expected, or authorized burden

²**load** *vb* 1 : to put a load in or on; *also* : to receive a load 2 : to encumber with an obligation or something heavy or disheartening 3 : to increase the weight of by adding something 4 : to supply abundantly 5 : to put a charge in (as a firearm) 6 : to copy or transfer into a computer's memory esp. from an external source

load·ed *adj* 1 *slang* : HIGH 12 2 : having a large amount of money 3 : equipped with an abundance of options ⟨a ~ car⟩

load·stone *var of* LODESTONE

¹**loaf** \'lōf\ *n, pl* **loaves** \'lōvz\ : a shaped or molded mass esp. of bread

²**loaf** *vb* : to spend time in idleness : LOUNGE

loaf·er \'lō-fər\ *n* 1 : one that loafs : IDLER 2 : a low step-in shoe

loam \'lōm, 'lüm\ *n* : SOIL; *esp* : a loose soil of mixed clay, sand, and silt — **loamy** *adj*

¹**loan** \'lōn\ *n* 1 : money lent at interest; *also* : something lent for the borrower's temporary use 2 : the grant of temporary use

²**loan** *vb* : LEND

loan shark *n* : a person who lends money at excessive rates of interest — **loan-shark·ing** \'lōn-ˌshär-kiŋ\ *n*

loan·word \'lōn-ˌwərd\ *n* : a word taken from another language and at least partly naturalized

loath *also* **loth** \'lōth, 'lōth\ *or* **loathe** \'lōth, 'lōth\ *adj* : RELUCTANT

loathe \'lōth\ *vb* **loathed; loath·ing** : to dislike greatly ◆ *Synonyms* ABOMINATE, ABHOR, DETEST, HATE

loath·ing \'lō-thiŋ\ *n* : extreme disgust

loath·some \'lōth-səm, 'lōth-\ *adj* : exciting loathing : REPULSIVE

lob \'läb\ *vb* **lobbed; lob·bing** 1 : to throw, hit, or propel something in a high arc 2 : to direct (as a question) so as to elicit a response — **lob** *n*

¹**lob·by** \'lä-bē\ *n, pl* **lobbies** 1 : a corridor used esp. as a passageway or waiting room 2 : a group of persons engaged in lobbying

²**lobby** *vb* **lob·bied; lob·by·ing** : to try to influence public officials and esp. legislators — **lob·by·ist** *n*

lobe \'lōb\ *n* : a curved or rounded part esp. of a bodily organ — **lo·bar** \'lō-bər\ *adj* — **lobed** \'lōbd\ *adj*

lo·be·lia \lō-'bēl-yə\ *n* : any of a genus of plants often grown for their clusters of showy flowers

lo·bot·o·my \lō-'bä-tə-mē\ *n, pl* **-mies** : surgical severance of certain nerve fibers in the brain used esp. formerly to relieve some mental disorders

lob·ster \'läb-stər\ *n* [ME, fr. OE *loppestre,* fr. *loppe* spider] : any of a family of edible marine crustaceans with two large pincerlike claws and four other pairs of legs; *also* : SPINY LOBSTER

¹**lo·cal** \'lō-kəl\ *adj* 1 : of, relating to, or occupying a particular place 2 : serving a particular limited district; *also* : making all stops ⟨a ~ train⟩ 3 : affecting a small part of the body ⟨a ~ infection⟩ — **lo·cal·ly** *adv*

²**local** *n* : one that is local

local area network *n* : a network of personal computers in a small area (as an office)

lo·cale \lō-'kal\ *n* : a place that is the setting for a particular event

lo·cal·ise *Brit var of* LOCALIZE

lo·cal·i·ty \lō-'ka-lə-tē\ *n, pl* **-ties** : a particular spot, situation, or location

lo·cal·ize \'lō-kə-ˌlīz\ *vb* **-ized; -iz·ing** : to fix in or confine to a definite place or locality — **lo·cal·i·za·tion** \ˌlō-kə-lə-'zā-shən\ *n*

lo·cate \'lō-ˌkāt, lō-'kāt\ *vb* **lo·cat·ed; lo·cat·ing** 1 : STATION, SETTLE 2 : to determine the site of 3 : to find or fix the place of in a sequence

lo·ca·tion \lō-'kā-shən\ *n* 1 : SITUATION,

PLACE **2** : the process of locating **3** : a place outside a studio where a motion picture is filmed

lo·ca·vore \'lō-kə-ˌvȯr\ *n* [*local* + *-vore* (as in *carnivore*)] : one who eats foods grown locally whenever possible

loc cit *abbr* [L *loco citato*] in the place cited

loch \'läk, 'läḵ\ *n, Scot* : LAKE; *also* : a bay or arm of the sea esp. when nearly land-locked

¹lock \'läk\ *n* : a tuft, strand, or ringlet of hair; *also* : a cohering bunch (as of wool or flax)

²lock *n* **1** : a fastening in which a bolt is operated **2** : the mechanism of a firearm by which the charge is exploded **3** : an enclosure (as in a canal) used in raising or lowering boats from level to level **4** : AIR LOCK **5** : a wrestling hold

³lock *vb* **1** : to fasten the lock of; *also* : to make fast with a lock **2** : to confine or exclude by means of a lock **3** : INTER-LOCK **4** : to make or become motionless by the interlocking of parts

lock·er \'lä-kər\ *n* **1** : a drawer, cup-board, or compartment for individual storage use **2** : an insulated compart-ment for storing frozen food

lock·et \'lä-kət\ *n* : a small usu. metal case for a memento worn suspended from a chain or necklace

lock·jaw \'läk-ˌjȯ\ *n* : a symptom of teta-nus marked by spasms of the jaw muscles and inability to open the jaws; *also* : TET-ANUS

lock·nut \-ˌnət\ *n* **1** : a nut screwed tight on another to prevent it from slacking back **2** : a nut designed to lock itself when screwed tight

lock·out \-ˌaut\ *n* : the suspension of work by an employer during a labor dis-pute in order to make employees accept the terms being offered

lock·smith \-ˌsmith\ *n* : one who makes or repairs locks

lock·step \-ˌstep\ *n* : a mode of marching in step by a body of men moving in a very close single file

lock·up \-ˌəp\ *n* : JAIL

lo·co \'lō-kō\ *adj* [Sp] *slang* : CRAZY, FRENZIED

lo·co·mo·tion \ˌlō-kə-'mō-shən\ *n* **1** : the act or power of moving from place to place **2** : TRAVEL

¹lo·co·mo·tive \ˌlō-kə-'mō-tiv\ *adj* : of or relating to locomotion or a locomotive

²locomotive *n* : a self-propelled vehicle used to move railroad cars

lo·co·mo·tor \ˌlō-kə-'mō-tər\ *adj* : of or relating to locomotion or organs used in locomotion

lo·co·weed \'lō-kō-ˌwēd\ *n* : any of sev-eral leguminous plants of western No. America that are poisonous to livestock

lo·cus \'lō-kəs\ *n, pl* **lo·ci** \'lō-ˌsī\ [L] **1** : PLACE, LOCALITY **2** : the set of all points whose location is determined by stated conditions

lo·cust \'lō-kəst\ *n* **1** : a usu. destructive migratory grasshopper **2** : CICADA **3** : any of various leguminous trees; *also* : the wood of a locust

lo·cu·tion \lō-'kyü-shən\ *n* : a particular form of expression; *also* : PHRASEOLOGY

lode \'lōd\ *n* : an ore deposit

lode·stone \-ˌstōn\ *n* : an iron-containing rock with magnetic properties

¹lodge \'läj\ *vb* **lodged; lodg·ing** **1** : to provide quarters for; *also* : to settle in a place **2** : CONTAIN **3** : to come to a rest and remain ⟨*lodged* in his throat⟩ **4** : to deposit for safekeeping **5** : to vest (as au-thority) in an agent **6** : FILE ⟨~ a com-plaint⟩

²lodge *n* **1** : a house set apart for resi-dence in a special season or by an em-ployee on an estate; *also* : INN **2** : a den or lair esp. of gregarious animals **3** : the meeting place of a branch of a fraternal organization; *also* : the members of such a branch

lodg·er \'lä-jər\ *n* : a person who occupies a rented room in another's house

lodg·ing \'lä-jiṇ\ *n* **1** : DWELLING **2** : a room or suite of rooms in another's house rented as a dwelling place — usu. used in pl.

lodg·ment *or* **lodge·ment** \'läj-mənt\ *n* **1** : a lodging place **2** : the act or manner of lodging **3** : DEPOSIT

loess \'les, 'ləs\ *n* : a usu. yellowish brown loamy deposit believed to be chiefly deposited by the wind

lo–fi \'lō-ˌfī\ *n* : audio production of rough or unpolished sound quality — **lo-fi** *adj*

¹loft \'lȯft\ *n* [ME, fr. OE, air, sky, fr. ON *lopt*] **1** : ATTIC **2** : GALLERY ⟨organ ~⟩ **3** : an upper floor in a warehouse or barn) esp. when not partitioned **4** : the thickness of a fabric or insulated material (as of a sleeping bag)

²loft *vb* : to strike or throw a ball so that it rises high in the air

lofty \'lȯf-tē\ *adj* **loft·i·er; -est** **1** : NO-BLE; *also* : SUPERIOR ⟨~ ideals⟩ **2** : ex-tremely proud **3** : HIGH, TALL — **loft·i·ly** \'lȯf-tə-lē\ *adv* — **loft·i·ness** \-tē-nəs\ *n*

¹log \'lȯg, 'läg\ *n* **1** : a bulky piece of a cut or fallen tree **2** : an apparatus for mea-suring a ship's speed **3** : the daily record of a ship's progress; *also* : a regularly kept record of performance or events ⟨a pi-lot's ~⟩ ⟨a runner's ~⟩

²log *vb* **logged; log·ging** **1** : to cut (trees) for lumber; *also* : to clear (land) of trees in lumbering **2** : to enter in a log **3** : to sail a ship or fly an airplane for (an indi-cated distance or period of time) **4** : to have (an indicated record) to one's credit : ACHIEVE — **log·ger** \'lȯ-gər, 'lä-\ *n*

³log *n* : LOGARITHM

lo·gan·ber·ry \'lō-gən-ˌber-ē\ *n* : a red-fruited upright-growing dewberry; *also* : its berry

log·a·rithm \'lȯ-gə-ˌri-thəm, 'lä-\ *n* : the exponent that indicates the power to which a base is raised to produce a given number ⟨the ~ of 100 to base 10 is 2 since $10^2 = 100$⟩ — **log·a·rith·mic** \ˌlȯ-gə-'rith-mik, ˌlä-\ *adj*

loge \'lōzh\ *n* : a small compartment;

also : a box in a theater **2** : a small partitioned area; *also* : the forward section of a theater mezzanine **3** : a raised level of seats in a stadium

log·ger·head \'lȯ-gər-ˌhed, 'lä-\ *n* : a large sea turtle of subtropical and temperate waters — **at loggerheads** : in a state of quarrelsome disagreement

log·gia \'lȯ-jē-ə, 'lȯ-jä\ *n, pl* **loggias** \'lȯ-jē-əz, 'lȯ-jäz\ : a roofed open gallery

log·ic \'lä-jik\ *n* **1** : a science that deals with the rules and tests of sound thinking and proof by reasoning **2** : sound reasoning **3** : the arrangement of circuit elements for arithmetic computation in a computer — **log·i·cal** \-ji-kəl\ *adj* — **log·i·cal·ly** \-ji-k(ə-)lē\ *adv* — **lo·gi·cian** \lō-'ji-shən\ *n*

lo·gis·tics \lō-'jis-tiks\ *n sing or pl* : the procurement, maintenance, and transportation of matériel, facilities, and personnel — **lo·gis·tic** \-tik\ *or* **lo·gis·ti·cal** \-ti-kəl\ *adj*

log·jam \'lȯg-ˌjam, 'läg-\ *n* **1** : a deadlocked jumble of logs in a watercourse **2** : DEADLOCK — **logjam** *vt*

logo \'lō-gō\ *n, pl* **log·os** \-gōz\ : an identifying symbol (as for advertising)

log off *vb* : to end the connection of a computer to a network or system

log on *vb* : to start the connection of a computer to a network or system

logo·type \'lō-gə-ˌtīp, 'lä-\ *n* : LOGO

log·roll·ing \-ˌrō-liŋ\ *n* : the trading of votes by legislators to secure favorable action on projects of individual interest

lo·gy \'lō-gē\ *also* **log·gy** \'lȯ-gē, 'lä-\ *adj* **lo·gi·er; -est** : deficient in vitality : SLUGGISH

loin \'lȯin\ *n* [ME *loyne*, fr. AF *loigne*, fr. VL **lumbea*, fr. L *lumbus*] **1** : the part of the body on each side of the spinal column and between the hip and the lower ribs; *also* : a cut of meat from this part of an animal **2** *pl* : the pubic region; *also* : the organs of reproduction

loin·cloth \-ˌklȯth\ *n* : a cloth worn about the loins often as the sole article of clothing in warm climates

loi·ter \'lȯi-tər\ *vb* **1** : LINGER **2** : to hang around idly ◆ *Synonyms* DAWDLE, DALLY, PROCRASTINATE, LAG, TARRY — **loi·ter·er** *n*

loll \'läl\ *vb* **1** : DROOP, DANGLE **2** : LOUNGE ⟨~ing by the pool⟩

lol·la·pa·loo·za \ˌlä-lə-pə-'lü-zə\ *n* : something extraordinarily impressive or outstanding

lol·li·pop *or* **lol·ly·pop** \'lä-li-ˌpäp\ *n* : a lump of hard candy on a stick

lol·ly·gag \'lä-lē-ˌgag\ *vb* **-gagged; -gagging** : DAWDLE

Lond *abbr* London

lone \'lōn\ *adj* **1** : SOLITARY ⟨a ~ sentinel⟩ **2** : SOLE, ONLY ⟨the ~ theater in town⟩ **3** : ISOLATED ⟨a ~ tree⟩

lone·ly \'lōn-lē\ *adj* **lone·li·er; -est** **1** : being without company **2** : UNFREQUENTED ⟨a ~ spot⟩ **3** : LONESOME — **lone·li·ness** *n*

lon·er \'lō-nər\ *n* : one that avoids others

lone·some \'lōn-səm\ *adj* **1** : sad from

lack of companionship **2** : REMOTE; *also* : SOLITARY ⟨a ~ road⟩ — **lone·some·ly** *adv* — **lone·some·ness** *n*

¹long \'lȯŋ\ *adj* **lon·ger** \'lȯŋ-gər\; **longest** \'lȯŋ-gəst\ **1** : extending for a considerable distance ⟨a ~ corridor⟩; *also* : TALL, ELONGATED ⟨~ legs⟩ **2** : having a specified length **3** : extending over a considerable time; *also* : TEDIOUS ⟨~ lectures⟩ **4** : containing many items in a series ⟨a ~ list⟩ **5** : being a syllable or speech sound of relatively great duration **6** : extending far into the future **7** : well furnished with something — used with *on* ⟨~ on talent⟩

²long *adv* : for or during a long time

³long *n* : a long period of time

⁴long *vb* **longed; long·ing** \'lȯŋ-iŋ\ : to feel a strong desire or wish ◆ *Synonyms* YEARN, HANKER, PINE, HUNGER, THIRST

⁵long *abbr* longitude

long·boat \'lȯŋ-ˌbōt\ *n* : a large boat usu. carried by a merchant sailing ship

long·bow \-ˌbō\ *n* : a wooden bow drawn by hand and used esp. by medieval English archers

lon·gev·i·ty \län-'je-və-tē\ *n* [LL *longaevitas*, fr. L *longaevus* long-lived, fr. *longus* long + *aevum* age] : a long duration of individual life; *also* : length of life

long·hair \'lȯŋ-ˌher\ *n* **1** : a lover of classical music **2** : HIPPIE **3** : a domestic cat having long outer fur — **long–haired** \-ˌherd\ *or* **long·hair** *adj*

long·hand \-ˌhand\ *n* : HANDWRITING

long·horn \-ˌhȯrn\ *n* : any of the cattle with long horns formerly common in the southwestern U.S.

long hundredweight *n, Brit* — see WEIGHT table

long·ing \'lȯŋ-iŋ\ *n* : a strong desire esp. for something unattainable — **long·ing·ly** *adv*

lon·gi·tude \'län-jə-ˌtüd, -ˌtyüd\ *n* : angular distance expressed usu. in degrees east or west from the prime meridian through Greenwich, England

lon·gi·tu·di·nal \ˌlän-jə-'tü-dᵊn-əl, -'tyüd-\ *adj* **1** : extending lengthwise **2** : of or relating to length — **lon·gi·tu·di·nal·ly** *adv*

long–range \'lȯŋ-'rānj\ *adj* **1** : relating to or fit for long distances **2** : involving a long period of time

long·shore·man \'lȯŋ-ˌshȯr-mən\ *n* : a laborer at a wharf who loads and unloads cargo

long–suf·fer·ing \-'sə-friŋ, -fə-riŋ\ *n* : patiently enduring lasting offense or hardship

long–term \'lȯŋ-'tərm\ *adj* **1** : extending over or involving a long period of time **2** : constituting a financial obligation based on a term usu. of more than 10 years ⟨~ bonds⟩

long·time \'lȯŋ-'tīm\ *adj* : of long duration ⟨~ friends⟩

long ton *n* — see WEIGHT table

lon·gueur \lōⁿ-'gœr\ *n, pl* **longueurs** *same or* -'gœrz\ [F, lit., length] : a dull tedious portion (as of a book)

long–wind·ed \ˌlȯŋ-ˈwin-dəd\ *adj* : tediously long in speaking or writing

loo·fah \ˈlü-fə\ *n* : a sponge consisting of the fibrous skeleton of a gourd

¹**look** \ˈlu̇k\ *vb* 1 : to exercise the power of vision : SEE ⟨~ what I won⟩ 2 : EXPECT 3 : to have an appearance that befits ⟨~s the part⟩ 4 : SEEM ⟨~s thin⟩ 5 : to direct one's attention : HEED ⟨~ at the sign⟩ 6 : POINT, FACE ⟨~s east⟩ 7 : to show a tendency — **look after** : to take care of — **look at** 1 : CONSIDER ⟨*looking at* all possibilities⟩ 2 : CONFRONT, FACE ⟨*looking at* stiff fines⟩ — **look for** 1 : EXPECT — **look forward** : to anticipate with pleasure ⟨*look forward* to summer⟩

²**look** *n* 1 : the action of looking : GLANCE 2 : EXPRESSION; *also* : physical appearance 3 : ASPECT

look down *vb* : to regard with contempt — used with *on* or *upon*

looking glass *n* : MIRROR

look·out \ˈlu̇k-ˌau̇t\ *n* 1 : a person assigned to watch (as on a ship) 2 : a careful watch 3 : VIEW 4 : a matter of concern

look up *vb* 1 : IMPROVE ⟨business is *looking up*⟩ 2 : to search for in or as if in a reference work 3 : to seek out esp. for a brief visit

¹**loom** \ˈlüm\ *n* : a frame or machine for weaving together threads or yarns into cloth

²**loom** *vb* 1 : to come into sight in an unnaturally large, indistinct, or distorted form 2 : to appear in an impressively exaggerated form

loon \ˈlün\ *n* : any of several web-footed black-and-white fish-eating diving birds

loo·ny *or* **loo·ney** \ˈlü-nē\ *adj* **loo·ni·er; -est** : CRAZY, FOOLISH

loony bin *n* : a psychiatric hospital

loop \ˈlüp\ *n* 1 : a fold or doubling of a line through which another line or hook can be passed; *also* : a loop-shaped figure or course ⟨a ~ in a river⟩ 2 : a circular airplane maneuver executed in the vertical plane 3 : a continuously repeated segment of film, music, or sound — **loop** *vb*

loop·er \ˈlü-pər\ *n* : any of numerous rather small hairless moth caterpillars that move with a looping motion

loop·hole \ˈlüp-ˌhōl\ *n* 1 : a small opening in a wall through which firearms may be discharged 2 : a means of escape; *esp* : an ambiguity or omission that allows one to evade the intent of a law or contract

loopy \ˈlü-pē\ *adj* **loop·i·er; -est** 1 : having loops 2 : CRAZY, BIZARRE — **loop·i·ly** \-pə-lē\ *adv* — **loop·i·ness** \-pē-nəs\ *n*

¹**loose** \ˈlüs\ *adj* **loos·er; loos·est** 1 : not rigidly fastened 2 : free from restraint or obligation 3 : not dense or compact in structure 4 : not chaste : LEWD 5 : SLACK 6 : not precise or exact — **loose·ly** *adv* — **loose·ness** *n*

²**loose** *vb* **loosed; loos·ing** 1 : RELEASE 2 : UNTIE 3 : DETACH 4 : DISCHARGE 5 : RELAX, SLACKEN

³**loose** *adv* : LOOSELY

loos·en \ˈlü-sᵊn\ *vb* 1 : FREE 2 : to make

or become loose 3 : to relax the severity of ⟨~ rules⟩

loot \ˈlüt\ *n* [Hindi & Urdu *lūṭ;* akin to Skt *luṇṭati* he plunders] : goods taken in war or by robbery : PLUNDER — **loot** *vb* — **loot·er** *n*

¹**lop** \ˈläp\ *vb* **lopped; lop·ping** 1 : to cut branches or twigs from : TRIM; *also* : to cut off

²**lop** *vb* **lopped; lop·ping** 1 : to hang downward; *also* : to flop or sway loosely

lope \ˈlōp\ *n* : an easy bounding gait — **lope** *vb*

lop·sid·ed \ˈläp-ˈsī-dəd\ *adj* 1 : leaning to one side 2 : UNSYMMETRICAL — **lop·sid·ed·ly** *adv* — **lop·sid·ed·ness** *n*

lo·qua·cious \lō-ˈkwā-shəs\ *adj* : excessively talkative — **lo·quac·i·ty** \-ˈkwa-sə-tē\ *n*

¹**lord** \ˈlȯrd\ *n* [ME *loverd, lord,* fr. OE *hlāford,* fr. *hlāf* loaf + *weard* keeper] 1 : one having power and authority over others; *esp* : a person from whom a feudal fee or estate is held 2 *cap* : GOD 1 3 : a man of rank or high position; *esp* : a British nobleman 4 *pl, cap* : the upper house of the British parliament 5 : a person of great power in some field

²**lord** *vb* : to act like a lord; *esp* : to put on airs — usu. used with *it*

lord chancellor *n, pl* **lords chancellor** : a British officer of state who presides over the House of Lords, serves as head of the British judiciary, and is usu. a leading member of the cabinet

lord·ly \-lē\ *adj* **lord·li·er; -est** 1 : DIGNIFIED; *also* : NOBLE 2 : HAUGHTY

lord·ship \-ˌship\ *n* 1 : the rank or dignity of a lord — used as a title 2 : the authority or territory of a lord

Lord's Supper *n* : COMMUNION

lore \ˈlȯr\ *n* : KNOWLEDGE; *esp* : traditional knowledge or belief

lor·gnette \lȯrn-ˈyet\ *n* [F, fr. *lorgner* to take a sidelong look at, fr. MF, fr. *lorgne* squinting] : a pair of eyeglasses or opera glasses with a handle

lorn \ˈlȯrn\ *adj* : FORSAKEN, DESOLATE

lor·ry \ˈlȯr-ē\ *n, pl* **lorries** *chiefly Brit* : MOTORTRUCK

lose \ˈlüz\ *vb* **lost** \ˈlȯst\; **los·ing** \ˈlü-ziŋ\ 1 : DESTROY 2 : to miss from a customary place : MISLAY 3 : to suffer deprivation of 4 : to fail to use : WASTE ⟨no time to ~⟩ 5 : to fail to win or obtain ⟨~ the game⟩ 6 : to fail to keep or maintain ⟨~ his balance⟩ 7 : to wander from ⟨~ her way⟩ 8 : to get rid of ⟨should ~ the beard⟩ — **los·er** *n* — **lose it** 1 : to go crazy 2 : to fail to keep one's composure

loss \ˈlȯs\ *n* 1 : RUIN 2 : the harm resulting from losing 3 : something that is lost 4 *pl* : killed, wounded, or captured soldiers 5 : failure to win 6 : an amount by which the cost exceeds the selling price 7 : decrease in amount or degree

loss leader *n* : an article sold at a loss in order to draw customers

lost \ˈlȯst\ *adj* 1 : not used, won, or claimed 2 : no longer possessed or known 3 : ruined or destroyed physically or morally : DENIED; *also* : HARDENED

5 : unable to find the way; *also* : HELP-LESS **6** : ABSORBED, RAPT **7** : not appreciated or understood ⟨his jokes were ~ on me⟩ **8** : made obscure : OVERLOOKED ⟨~ in translation⟩ **9** : FUTILE ⟨a ~ cause⟩

lot \'lät\ *n* **1** : an object used in deciding something by chance; *also* : the use of lots to decide something **2** : SHARE, POR-TION; *also* : FORTUNE, FATE **3** : a plot of land **4** : a group of individuals : SET **5** : a considerable quantity ⟨a ~ of trouble⟩

loth *var of* LOATH

lo•ti \'lō-tē\ *n, pl* **ma•lo•ti** \mə-'lō-tē\ — see MONEY table

lo•tion \'lō-shən\ *n* : a liquid preparation for cosmetic and external medicinal use

lot•tery \'lä-tə-rē\ *n, pl* **-ter•ies** **1** : a drawing of lots in which prizes are given to the winning names or numbers **2** : a matter determined by chance

lo•tus \'lō-təs\ *n* **1** : a fruit held in Greek legend to cause dreamy contentment and forgetfulness **2** : any of various water lilies represented esp. in ancient Egyptian and Hindu art **3** : any of several leguminous forage plants

loud \'laud\ *adj* **1** : marked by intensity or volume of sound **2** : CLAMOROUS, NOISY **3** : obtrusive or offensive in color or pattern ⟨a ~ tie⟩ — **loud** *adv* — **loud•ly** *adv* — **loud•ness** *n*

loud•mouthed \-,maŭtht, -,maŭthd\ *adj* : given to loud offensive talk

loud•speak•er \-,spē-kər\ *n* : a device that changes electrical signals into sound

¹**lounge** \'laŭnj\ *vb* **lounged; loung•ing** : to act or move lazily or listlessly

²**lounge** *n* **1** : a room with comfortable furniture; *also* : a room (as in a theater) with lounging, smoking, and toilet facilities **2** : a long couch

lour, loury *var of* LOWER, LOWERY

louse \'laŭs\ *n, pl* **lice** \'līs\ **1** : any of various small wingless usu. flattened insects parasitic on warm-blooded animals **2** : a plant pest (as an aphid) **3** *pl* **lous•es** \'laŭ-səz\ : a contemptible person

lousy \'laŭ-zē\ *adj* **lous•i•er; -est 1** : infested with lice **2** : POOR, INFERIOR **3** : somewhat ill **4** : amply supplied ⟨~ with money⟩ — **lous•i•ly** \-zə-lē\ *adv* — **lous•i•ness** \-zē-nəs\ *n*

lout \'laŭt\ *n* : a stupid awkward fellow — **lout•ish** *adj* — **lout•ish•ly** *adv*

lou•ver *or* **lou•vre** \'lü-vər\ *n* **1** : an opening having parallel slanted slats to allow flow of air but to exclude rain or sun or to provide privacy; *also* : a slat in such an opening **2** : a device with movable slats for controlling the flow of air or light

¹**love** \'ləv\ *n* **1** : strong affection **2** : warm attachment ⟨~ of the sea⟩ **3** : attraction based on sexual desire **4** : a beloved person **5** : unselfish loyal and benevolent concern for others **6** : a score of zero in tennis — **love•less** *adj*

²**love** *vb* **loved; lov•ing 1** : CHERISH **2** : to feel a passion, devotion, or tenderness for **3** : CARESS **4** : to take pleasure in ⟨~s to play bridge⟩ — **lov•able** *also* **love•able** \'lə-və-bəl\ *adj* — **lov•er** *n*

love•bird \'ləv-,bərd\ *n* : any of various small usu. gray or green parrots that seem to show caring behavior for their mates

love•lorn \-,lȯrn\ *adj* : deprived of love or of a lover

love•ly \'ləv-lē\ *adj* **love•li•er; -est** : BEAUTIFUL — **love•li•ly** \'ləv-lə-lē\ *adv* — **love•li•ness** *n* — **lovely** *adv*

love•mak•ing \-,mā-kiŋ\ *n* **1** : COURT-SHIP **2** : sexual activity; *esp* : COPULA-TION

love•sick \-,sik\ *adj* **1** : YEARNING ⟨a ~ suitor⟩ **2** : expressing a lover's longing — **love•sick•ness** *n*

lov•ing \'lə-viŋ\ *adj* **1** : AFFECTIONATE **2** : PAINSTAKING — **lov•ing•ly** *adv*

¹**low** \'lō\ *vb* : MOO

²**low** *n* : MOO

³**low** *adj* **low•er** \'lō-ər\; **low•est** \'lō-əst\ **1** : not high or tall ⟨~ wall⟩; *also* : DÉCOLLETÉ **2** : situated or passing below the normal level or surface ⟨~ ground⟩; *also* : marking a nadir **3** : not loud ⟨~ voice⟩ **4** : being near the equator **5** : humble in status **6** : WEAK; *also* : DEPRESSED **7** : STRICKEN, PROSTRATE **8** : less than usual in number, amount, or value; *also* : of lesser degree than average **9** : falling short of a standard **10** : UNFAVORABLE — **low** *adv* — **low•ness** *n*

⁴**low** *n* **1** : something that is low **2** : a region of low barometric pressure **3** : the arrangement of gears in an automobile transmission that gives the slowest speed and greatest power

low-ball \'lō-,bȯl\ *vb* : to give a deceptively low price, cost estimate, or offer to

low beam *n* : a vehicle headlight beam with short-range focus

low blow *n* : an unprincipled attack

low-brow \'lō-,braŭ\ *adj* : having little taste or intellectual interest ⟨~ humor⟩ — **lowbrow** *n*

low–density lipoprotein *n* : LDL

low•down \-,daŭn\ *n* : pertinent and esp. guarded information

low–down \-,daŭn\ *adj* **1** : MEAN, CONTEMPTIBLE **2** : deeply emotional

low–end \-,end\ *adj* : of, relating to, or being the lowest-priced merchandise in a manufacturer's line

¹**low•er** *also* **lour** \'laŭ(-ə)r\ *vb* **1** : FROWN **2** : to become dark, gloomy, and threatening — **lower** *adj* — **lour** *n*

²**low•er** \'lō-ər\ *adj* **1** : relatively low (as in rank) **2** : SOUTHERN ⟨the ~ states⟩ **3** : less advanced in the scale of evolutionary development ⟨~ animals⟩ **4** : situated beneath the earth's surface **5** : constituting the popular and more representative branch of a bicameral legislative body

³**low•er** \'lō-ər\ *vb* **1** : DROP; *also* : DIMINISH **2** : to let descend by its own weight; *also* : to reduce the height of **3** : to reduce in value, number, or amount **4** : DEGRADE; *also* : HUMBLE

low•er•case \,lō-ər-'kās\ *adj* : being a letter that belongs to or conforms to the series a, b, c, etc., rather than A, B, C, etc. — **lowercase** *n*

lower class *n* : a social class occupying a position below the middle class and having the lowest status in a society — **lower-class** \-'klas\ *adj*

low-er-most \'lō-ər-,mōst\ *adj* : LOWEST

low-ery *also* **loury** \'laü-(ə-)rē\ *adj* : GLOOMY, LOWERING ⟨a ∼ sky⟩

lowest common denominator *n* 1 : LEAST COMMON DENOMINATOR 2 : something designed to appeal to a low-brow audience; *also* : such an audience

lowest common multiple *n* : LEAST COMMON MULTIPLE

low-key \'lō-'kē\ *also* **low-keyed** \-'kēd\ *adj* : of low intensity : RESTRAINED

low-land \'lō-lənd, -,land\ *n* : low and usu. level country

low-lev-el \'lō-'le-vəl\ *adj* 1 : being of low importance or rank 2 : being or relating to nuclear waste of low concentration

low-life \'lō-,līf\ *n, pl* **low-lifes** \-,līfs\ *also* **low-lives** \-,līvz\ : a person of low social status or moral character

low-ly \'lō-lē\ *adj* **low-li-er; -est** 1 : HUMBLE, MEEK 2 : ranking low in some hierarchy — **low-li-ness** *n*

low-rise \'lō-'rīz\ *adj* 1 : having few stories and not equipped with elevators ⟨a ∼ building⟩ 2 : of, relating to, or characterized by low-rise buildings

low-slung \'lō-,sləŋ\ *adj* : relatively low to the ground or floor ⟨a ∼ building⟩ ⟨∼ pants⟩

low-tech \'lō-'tek\ *adj* : technologically simple or unsophisticated

¹**lox** \'läks\ *n* : liquid oxygen

²**lox** *n, pl* **lox** *or* **lox-es** : salmon cured in brine and sometimes smoked

loy-al \'lȯi(-ə)l\ *adj* [MF, fr. OF *leial, leel,* fr. L *legalis* legal] 1 : faithful in allegiance to one's government 2 : faithful esp. to a cause or ideal : CONSTANT — **loy-al-ly** \'lȯi-(ə)l-lē\ *adv* — **loy-al-ty** \'lȯi-(ə)l-tē\ *n*

loy-al-ist \'lȯi-ə-list\ *n* : one who is or remains loyal to a political party, government, or sovereign

loz-enge \'lä-zənj\ *n* 1 : a diamond-shaped figure 2 : a small flat often medicated candy

LP *abbr* low pressure

LPG *abbr* liquefied petroleum gas

LPGA *abbr* Ladies Professional Golf Association

LPN \'el-'pē-'en\ *n* : LICENSED PRACTICAL NURSE

Lr *symbol* Lawrencium

LSD \,el-(,)es-'dē\ *n* [G *Lysergsäure-Diäthylamid* lysergic acid diethylamide] : an illicit and highly potent hallucinogenic drug derived from ergot or produced synthetically

lt *abbr* light

Lt *abbr* lieutenant

LT *abbr* long ton

LTC *or* **Lt Col** *abbr* lieutenant colonel

Lt Comdr *abbr* lieutenant commander

ltd *abbr* limited

LTG *or* **Lt Gen** *abbr* lieutenant general

LTJG *abbr* lieutenant, junior grade

ltr *abbr* letter

Lu *symbol* lutetium

lu-au \'lü-,aü\ *n* : a Hawaiian feast

lub *abbr* lubricant; lubricating

lub-ber \'lə-bər\ *n* 1 : LOUT 2 : an unskilled seaman — **lub-ber-ly** *adj*

lube \'lüb\ *n* : LUBRICANT; *also* : application of a lubricant

lu-bri-cant \'lü-bri-kənt\ *n* : a material capable of reducing friction when applied between moving parts

lu-bri-cate \'lü-brə-,kāt\ *vb* **-cat-ed; -cat-ing** : to apply a lubricant to — **lu-bri-ca-tion** \,lü-brə-'kā-shən\ *n* — **lu-bri-ca-tor** \'lü-brə-,kā-tər\ *n*

lu-bri-cious \lü-'bri-shəs\ *or* **lu-bri-cous** \'lü-bri-kəs\ *adj* 1 : SMOOTH, SLIPPERY 2 : LECHEROUS; *also* : SALACIOUS — **lu-bric-i-ty** \lü-'bri-sə-tē\ *n*

lu-cent \'lü-s³nt\ *adj* 1 : LUMINOUS 2 : CLEAR, LUCID — **lu-cent-ly** *adv*

lu-cerne \lü-'sərn\ *n, chiefly Brit* : ALFALFA

lu-cid \'lü-səd\ *adj* 1 : SHINING 2 : mentally sound 3 : easily understood ⟨a ∼ explanation⟩ — **lu-cid-i-ty** \lü-'si-də-tē\ *n* — **lu-cid-ly** *adv* — **lu-cid-ness** *n*

Lu-ci-fer \'lü-sə-fər\ *n* [ME, the morning star, a fallen rebel archangel, the Devil, fr. OE, fr. L, the morning star, fr. *lucifer* light-bearing] : DEVIL, SATAN

¹**luck** \'lək\ *n* 1 : CHANCE, FORTUNE 2 : good fortune — **luck-less** *adj*

²**luck** *vb* 1 : to prosper or succeed esp. through chance or good fortune — usu. used with *out* 2 : to come upon something desirable by chance — usu. used with *out, on, onto,* or *into*

luck-i-ly \'lə-kə-lē\ *adv* 1 : in a lucky manner 2 : FORTUNATELY 2

lucky \'lə-kē\ *adj* **luck-i-er; -est** 1 : favored by luck : FORTUNATE 2 : FORTUITOUS 3 : seeming to bring good luck ⟨a ∼ penny⟩ — **luck-i-ness** *n*

lu-cra-tive \'lü-krə-tiv\ *adj* : PROFITABLE ⟨∼ business deals⟩ — **lu-cra-tive-ly** *adv* — **lu-cra-tive-ness** *n*

lu-cre \'lü-kər\ *n* [ME, fr. AF, fr. L *lucrum*] : PROFIT; *also* : MONEY

lu-cu-bra-tion \,lü-kyə-'brā-shən, -kə-\ *n* : laborious study : MEDITATION

Lud-dite \'lə-,dīt\ *n* [perh. fr. Ned *Ludd,* 18th cent. Eng. workman who destroyed a knitting frame] : one who is opposed to technological change

lu-di-crous \'lü-də-krəs\ *adj* : LAUGHABLE, RIDICULOUS ⟨a ∼ idea⟩ — **lu-di-crous-ly** *adv* — **lu-di-crous-ness** *n*

luff \'ləf\ *vb* : to turn the head of a ship toward the wind

¹**lug** \'ləg\ *vb* **lugged; lug-ging** 1 : DRAG, PULL 2 : to carry laboriously

²**lug** *n* 1 : a projecting piece (as for fastening, support, or traction) 2 : a nut securing a wheel on an automobile

lug-gage \'lə-gij\ *n* : containers (as suitcases) for carrying personal belongings : BAGGAGE

lu-gu-bri-ous \lü-'gü-brē-əs\ *adj* : mournful often to an exaggerated degree ⟨∼ music⟩ — **lu-gu-bri-ous-ly** *adv* — **lu-gu-bri-ous-ness** *n*

Luke \'lük\ *n* — see BIBLE table

luke·warm \'lük-'wȯrm\ adj **1** : moderately warm : TEPID **2** : not enthusiastic ⟨∼ praise⟩ — **luke·warm·ly** adv

¹**lull** \'ləl\ vb **1** : SOOTHE, CALM **2** : to cause to relax vigilance

²**lull** n **1** : a temporary calm (as during a storm) **2** : a temporary drop in activity ⟨a ∼ in sales⟩

lul·la·by \'lə-lə-ˌbī\ n, pl **-bies** : a song to lull children to sleep

lu·ma \ˌlü-'mä\ n — see dram at MONEY table

lum·ba·go \ˌləm-'bā-gō\ n : acute or chronic pain in the lower back

lum·bar \'ləm-bər, -ˌbär\ adj : of, relating to, or constituting the loins or the vertebrae between the thoracic vertebrae and sacrum ⟨∼ region⟩

¹**lum·ber** \'ləm-bər\ vb : to move heavily or clumsily ⟨an elephant ∼ed along the road⟩

²**lumber** n **1** : surplus or disused articles that are stored away **2** : timber or logs esp. when dressed for use

³**lumber** vb : to cut logs; also : to saw logs into lumber — **lum·ber·man** \-mən\ n

lum·ber·jack \-ˌjak\ n : LOGGER

lum·ber·yard \-ˌyärd\ n : a place where lumber is kept for sale

lu·mi·nary \'lü-mə-ˌner-ē\ n, pl **-nar·ies 1** : a very famous person **2** : a source of light; esp : a celestial body

lu·mi·nes·cence \ˌlü-mə-'ne-sᵊns\ n : the low-temperature emission of light (as by a chemical or physiological process); also : such light — **lu·mi·nes·cent** \-sᵊnt\ adj

lu·mi·nous \'lü-mə-nəs\ adj **1** : emitting light; also : LIGHTED **2** : CLEAR, INTELLIGIBLE **3** : ILLUSTRIOUS — **lu·mi·nance** \-nəns\ n — **lu·mi·nos·i·ty** \ˌlü-mə-'nä-sə-tē\ n — **lu·mi·nous·ly** adv

lum·mox \'lə-məks\ n : a clumsy person

¹**lump** \'ləmp\ n **1** : a piece or mass of indefinite size and shape **2** : AGGREGATE, TOTALITY **3** : a usu. abnormal swelling — **lump·ish** adj — **lumpy** adj

²**lump** vb **1** : to heap together in a lump **2** : to form into lumps

³**lump** adj : not divided into parts ⟨a ∼ sum⟩

lump·ec·to·my \ˌləm-'pek-tə-mē\ n, pl **-mies** : excision of a breast tumor

lu·na·cy \'lü-nə-sē\ n, pl **-cies 1** : INSANITY **2** : extreme folly

lu·nar \'lü-nər\ adj : of or relating to the moon ⟨a ∼ eclipse⟩

lu·nate \'lü-ˌnāt\ adj : shaped like a crescent

lu·na·tic \'lü-nə-ˌtik\ adj [ME lunatik, fr. AF & LL; AF lunatik, fr. LL lunaticus, fr. L luna moon; fr. the belief that lunacy fluctuated with the phases of the moon] **1** : INSANE; also : used for insane persons **2** : extremely foolish — **lunatic** n

¹**lunch** \'lənch\ n **1** : a light meal usu. eaten in the middle of the day **2** : the food prepared for a lunch

²**lunch** vb : to eat lunch

lun·cheon \'lən-chən\ n : a usu. formal lunch

lun·cheon·ette \ˌlən-chə-'net\ n : a small restaurant serving light lunches

lunch·room \'lənch-ˌrüm, -ˌrùm\ n **1** : LUNCHEONETTE **2** : a room (as in a school) where lunches are sold and eaten or lunches brought from home may be eaten

lu·nette \lü-'net\ n : something shaped like a crescent

lung \'ləŋ\ n **1** : one of the usu. paired baglike breathing organs in the chest of an air-breathing vertebrate **2** : a mechanical device to promote breathing and make it easier — **lunged** \'ləŋd\ adj

lunge \'lənj\ n **1** : a sudden thrust or pass (as with a sword) **2** : a sudden forward stride or leap — **lunge** vb

lu·pine \'lü-pən\ n : any of a genus of leguminous plants with long upright clusters of pealike flowers

lu·pus \'lü-pəs\ n [ML, fr. L, wolf] : any of several diseases characterized by skin lesions; esp : SYSTEMIC LUPUS ERYTHEMATOSUS

lurch \'lərch\ n : a sudden swaying or tipping movement — **lurch** vb

¹**lure** \'lur\ n **1** : ENTICEMENT; also : APPEAL ⟨the ∼ of easy money⟩ **2** : an artificial bait for catching fish

²**lure** vb **lured; lur·ing** : to draw on with a promise of pleasure or gain

lu·rid \'lur-əd\ adj **1** : GRUESOME; also : SENSATIONAL **2** : wan and ghostly pale in appearance **3** : shining with the red glow of fire seen through smoke or cloud

♦ **Synonyms** GHASTLY, GRISLY, GRIM, HORRIBLE, MACABRE — **lu·rid·ly** adv

lurk \'lərk\ vb **1** : to move furtively : SNEAK **2** : to lie concealed

lus·cious \'lə-shəs\ adj **1** : having a pleasingly sweet taste or smell **2** : sensually appealing ⟨a ∼ voice⟩ — **lus·cious·ly** adv — **lus·cious·ness** n

¹**lush** \'ləsh\ adj : having or covered with abundant growth ⟨∼ pastures⟩

²**lush** n : a habitual heavy drinker

lust \'ləst\ n **1** : usu. intense or unbridled sexual desire : LASCIVIOUSNESS **2** : an intense longing ⟨a ∼ to succeed⟩ — **lust** vb — **lust·ful** adj

lus·ter or **lus·tre** \'ləs-tər\ n **1** : a shine or sheen esp. from reflected light **2** : BRIGHTNESS, GLITTER **3** : GLORY, SPLENDOR — **lus·ter·less** adj — **lus·trous** \-trəs\ adj

lus·tral \'ləs-trəl\ adj : serving or intended to purify ⟨∼ water⟩

lusty \'ləs-tē\ adj **lust·i·er; -est** : full of vitality : ROBUST — **lust·i·ly** \'ləs-tə-lē\ adv — **lust·i·ness** \-tē-nəs\ n

lute \'lüt\ n : a stringed musical instrument with a large pear-shaped body and a fretted fingerboard — **lu·te·nist** or **lu·ta·nist** \'lü-tᵊn-ist\ n

lu·te·tium also **lu·te·cium** \lü-'tē-shē-əm, -shəm\ n : a metallic chemical element

Lu·ther·an \'lü-thə-rən\ n : a member of a Protestant denomination adhering to the doctrines of Martin Luther — **Lu·ther·an·ism** \-rə-ˌni-zəm\ n

lux·u·ri·ant \ˌləg-'zhùr-ē-ənt, ˌlək-'shùr-\ adj **1** : yielding or growing abundantly : LUSH, PRODUCTIVE ⟨∼ vegetation⟩ **2** : abundantly rich and varied; also : FLOR-

ID ⟨a ~ fabric⟩ ♦ *Synonyms* EXUBER-ANT, LAVISH, OPULENT, PRODIGAL, PRO-FUSE, RIOTOUS — **lux·u·ri·ance** \-ē-əns\ *n* — **lux·u·ri·ant·ly** *adv*

lux·u·ri·ate \-ē-ˌāt\ *vb* **-at·ed; -at·ing 1** : to grow profusely **2** : REVEL

lux·u·ry \ˈlək-shə-rē, ˈləg-zhə-\ *n, pl* **-ries 1** : great ease and comfort **2** : something adding to pleasure or comfort but not absolutely necessary — **lux·u·ri·ous** \ˌləg-ˈzhúr-ē-əs, ˌlək-ˈshúr-\ *adj* — **lux·u·ri·ous·ly** *adv*

lv *abbr* leave

lwei \lə-ˈwā\ *n, pl* **lwei** — see *kwanza* at MONEY table

LWV *abbr* League of Women Voters

¹**-ly** \lē\ *adj suffix* **1** : like in appearance, manner, or nature ⟨queen*ly*⟩ **2** : charac-terized by regular recurrence in (speci-fied) units of time : every ⟨hour*ly*⟩ ⟨week*ly*⟩

²**-ly** *adv suffix* **1** : in a (specified) manner ⟨slow*ly*⟩ **2** : from a (specified) point of view ⟨grammatical*ly*⟩

ly·ce·um \lī-ˈsē-əm, ˈlī-sē-\ *n* **1** : a hall for public lectures **2** : an association provid-ing public lectures, concerts, and enter-tainments

ly·chee *or* **li·tchi** \ˈlē-chē, ˈli-\ *n* [Ch(Beijing) *lìzhī*] **1** : an oval fruit with a hard scaly outer covering, a small hard seed, and edi-ble flesh **2** : an Asian tree bearing lychees

lye \ˈlī\ *n* : a corrosive alkaline substance used esp. in making soap

ly·ing \ˈlī-iŋ\ *adj* : UNTRUTHFUL, FALSE

ly·ing-in \ˌlī-iŋ-ˈin\ *n, pl* **lyings-in** *or* **ly·ing-ins** : the state during and conse-quent to childbirth : CONFINEMENT

Lyme disease \ˈlīm-\ *n* [*Lyme*, Connecti-cut, where it was first reported] : an acute inflammatory disease that is caused by a spirochete transmitted by ticks, is charac-terized usu. by chills and fever, and if left untreated may result in joint pain, arthri-tis, and cardiac and neurological disorders

lymph \ˈlimf\ *n* : a usu. clear fluid con-sisting chiefly of blood plasma and white blood cells, circulating in thin-walled tubes (**lymphatic vessels**), and bathing the body tissues — **lym·phat·ic** \lim-ˈfa-tik\ *adj*

lymph·ade·nop·a·thy \ˌlim-ˌfa-də-ˈnä-pə-thē\ *n, pl* **-thies** : abnormal enlargement of the lymph nodes

lymph node *n* : any of the rounded mass-es of lymphoid tissue surrounded by a capsule of connective tissue

lym·pho·cyte \ˈlim-fə-ˌsīt\ *n* : any of the white blood cells arising from lymphoid tissue that are typically found in lymph and blood and that include the cellular mediators (as a B cell or a T cell) of im-munity — **lym·pho·cyt·ic** \ˌlim-fə-ˈsi-tik\ *adj*

lym·phoid \ˈlim-ˌfóid\ *adj* **1** : of, relating to, or being tissue (as of the lymph nodes) containing lymphocytes **2** : of, relating to, or resembling lymph

lym·pho·ma \lim-ˈfō-mə\ *n, pl* **-mas** *also* **-ma·ta** \-mə-tə\ : a usu. malignant tumor of lymphoid tissue

lynch \ˈlinch\ *vb* : to put to death by mob action without legal sanction or due pro-cess of law — **lynch·er** *n*

lynx \ˈliŋks\ *n, pl* **lynx** *or* **lynx·es** : any of several wildcats with a short tail, long legs, and usu. tufted ears

lyre \ˈlī(-ə)r\ *n* : a stringed musical instru-ment of the harp class having a U-shaped frame and used by the ancient Greeks

¹**lyr·ic** \ˈlir-ik\ *n* **1** : a lyric poem **2** *pl* : the words of a popular song — **lyr·i·cal** \-i-kəl\ *adj*

²**lyric** *adj* **1** : suitable for singing : MELOD-IC **2** : expressing direct and usu. intense personal emotion ⟨~ poetry⟩

ly·ser·gic acid di·eth·yl·am·ide \lə-ˈsər-jik . . . ˌdī-ˌe-thə-ˈla-ˌmīd, lī-, -ˈla-məd\ *n* : LSD

LZ *abbr* landing zone

¹**m** \ˈem\ *n, pl* **m's** *or* **ms** \ˈemz\ *often cap* : the 13th letter of the English alphabet

²**m** *abbr, often cap* **1** Mach **2** male **3** mar-ried **4** masculine **5** medium **6** [L *meri-dies*] noon **7** meter **8** mile **9** [L *mille*] thousand **10** minute **11** month **12** moon

ma \ˈmä, ˈmó\ *n* : MOTHER

MA *abbr* **1** [ML *magister artium*] master of arts **2** Massachusetts **3** mental age

ma'am \ˈmam, *after "yes" often* əm\ *n* : MADAM

Mac *abbr* Machabees

Mac *or* **Macc** *abbr* Maccabees

ma·ca·bre \mə-ˈkäb; ˈkä-brə, -bər\ *adj* [F] **1** : having death as a subject **2** : GRUE-SOME **3** : HORRIBLE

mac·ad·am \mə-ˈka-dəm\ *n* [John L. Mc-Adam †1836 Brit. engineer] : a roadway

or pavement of small closely packed bro-ken stone — **mac·ad·am·ize** \-də-ˌmīz\ *vb*

mac·a·da·mia nut \ˌma-kə-ˈdā-mē-ə-\ *n* : a hard-shelled richly flavored nut of any of several Australian trees

ma·caque \mə-ˈkak, -ˈkäk\ *n* : any of a genus of short-tailed chiefly Asian mon-keys; *esp* : RHESUS MONKEY

mac·a·ro·ni \ˌma-kə-ˈrō-nē\ *n* **1** : pasta made chiefly of wheat flour and shaped in the form of slender tubes **2** *pl* **-nis** *or* **-nies** : FOP, DANDY

mac·a·roon \ˌma-kə-ˈrün\ *n* : a small cookie made chiefly of egg whites, sugar, and ground almonds or coconut

ma·caw \mə-ˈkó\ *n* : any of numerous parrots of Central and So. America

Mac·ca·bees \'ma-kə-ˌbēz\ n — see BI-BLE table

¹**mace** \'mās\ n : a spice made from the fibrous coating of the nutmeg

²**mace** n **1** : a heavy often spiked club used as a weapon esp. in the Middle Ages **2** : an ornamental staff carried as a symbol of authority

mac·er·ate \'ma-sə-ˌrāt\ vb **-at·ed; -at·ing 1** : to cause to waste away **2** : to soften by steeping or soaking so as to separate the parts — **mac·er·a·tion** \ˌma-sə-'rā-shən\ n

Mac·Guf·fin or **Mc·Guf·fin** \mə-'gə-fən\ n : an object, event, or character whose main purpose is to advance the plot of a motion picture

mach abbr machine; machinery; machinist

Mach \'mäk\ n : a speed expressed by a Mach number

Mach·a·bees \'ma-kə-ˌbēz\ n : MACCA-BEES

ma·chete \mə-'she-tē\ n : a large heavy knife used for cutting sugarcane and underbrush and as a weapon

Ma·chi·a·vel·lian \ˌma-kē-ə-'ve-lē-ən\ adj [Niccolò Machiavelli, †1527 Ital. political philosopher] : characterized by cunning, duplicity, and bad faith — **Ma·chi·a·vel·lian·ism** n

mach·i·na·tion \ˌma-kə-'nā-shən, ˌma-shə-\ n : an act of planning esp. to do harm; esp : PLOT — **mach·i·nate** \'ma-kə-ˌnāt, 'ma-shə-\ vb

¹**ma·chine** \mə-'shēn\ n **1** : CONVEYANCE, VEHICLE; esp : AUTOMOBILE **2** : a combination of mechanical parts that transmit forces, motion, and energy one to another **3** : an instrument (as a lever) for transmitting or modifying force or motion **4** : an electrical, electronic, or mechanical device for performing a task ⟨a sewing ~⟩ **5** : a highly organized political group under the leadership of a boss or small clique

²**machine** vb **ma·chined; ma·chin·ing** : to shape or finish by machine-operated tools — **ma·chin·able** \-'shē-nə-bəl\ adj

machine gun n : an automatic gun capable of rapid continuous firing — **ma·chine–gun** vb — **machine gunner** n

machine language n : the set of symbolic instruction codes used to represent operations and data in a machine (as a computer)

machine–readable adj : directly usable by a computer

ma·chin·ery \mə-'shē-nə-rē\ n, pl **-er·ies 1** : MACHINES; also : the working parts of a machine **2** : the means by which something is done

ma·chin·ist \mə-'shē-nist\ n : a person who makes or works on machines

ma·chis·mo \mä-'chēz-(ˌ)mō, -'chiz-\ n : a strong or exaggerated pride in one's masculinity

Mach number \'mäk-\ n : a number representing the ratio of the speed of a body (as an aircraft) to the speed of sound in the surrounding atmosphere

ma·cho \'mä-chō\ adj [Sp, lit., male, fr. L masculus] : characterized by machismo

mack·er·el \'ma-kə-rəl\ n, pl **mackerel** or **mackerels** : a No. Atlantic food fish greenish above and silvery below

mack·i·naw \'ma-kə-ˌnò\ n : a short heavy plaid coat

mack·in·tosh also **mac·in·tosh** \'ma-kən-ˌtäsh\ n **1** chiefly Brit : RAINCOAT **2** : a lightweight waterproof fabric

mac·ra·mé also **mac·ra·me** \'ma-krə-ˌmā\ n [ultim. fr. Ar miqrama coverlet] : a coarse lace or fringe made by knotting threads or cords in a geometrical pattern

¹**mac·ro** \'ma-(ˌ)krō\ adj : very large; also : involving large quantities or being on a large scale ⟨~ economic policies⟩

²**macro** n, pl **macros** : a single computer instruction that stands for a sequence of operations

mac·ro·bi·ot·ic \ˌma-krō-bī-'ä-tik, -bē-\ adj : relating to or being a very restricted diet (as one containing chiefly whole cereals or grains)

mac·ro·cosm \'ma-krə-ˌkä-zəm\ n : the great world : UNIVERSE

ma·cron \'mā-ˌkrän, 'ma-\ n : a mark placed over a vowel (as in \māk\) to show that the vowel is long

mac·ro·scop·ic \ˌma-krə-'skä-pik\ adj : visible to the naked eye — **mac·ro·scop·i·cal·ly** \-pi-k(ə-)lē\ adv

mac·u·la \'ma-kyə-lə\ n, pl **-lae** \-ˌlē, -ˌlī\ also **-las** : an anatomical spot distinguishable from surrounding tissues — **mac·u·lar** \-lər\ adj

mad \'mad\ adj **mad·der; mad·dest 1** : disordered in mind : INSANE **2** : being rash and foolish **3** : FURIOUS, ENRAGED **4** : carried away by enthusiasm ⟨~ about football⟩ **5** : RABID **6** : marked by wild gaiety and merriment **7** : FRANTIC ⟨a ~ rush⟩ — **mad·ly** adv — **mad·ness** n

mad·am \'ma-dəm\ n **1** pl **mes·dames** \mā-'däm\ — used as a form of polite address to a woman **2** pl **madams** : the female head of a house of prostitution

ma·dame \mə-'dam, before a surname also 'ma-dəm\ n, pl **mes·dames** \mā-'däm\ : MISTRESS — used as a title equivalent to Mrs. for a married woman not of English-speaking nationality

mad·cap \'mad-ˌkap\ adj : WILD, RECKLESS ⟨a ~ scheme⟩ — **madcap** n

mad cow disease n : a fatal encephalopathy of cattle that affects the nervous system causing the brain tissue to resemble a porous sponge

mad·den \'ma-dᵊn\ vb : to make mad — **mad·den·ing·ly** adv

mad·der \'ma-dər\ n : a Eurasian herb with yellow flowers and fleshy red roots; also : its root or a dye prepared from it

made past and past part of MAKE

Ma·dei·ra \mə-'dir-ə\ n : an amber-colored dessert wine

ma·de·moi·selle \ˌma-də-mə-'zel, -mwə-, mam-'zel\ n, pl **ma·de·moi·selles** \-'zelz\ or **mes·de·moi·selles** \ˌmā-də-me-'zel, -mwə-\ : an unmarried girl or woman — used as a title for an unmarried woman not of English-speaking nationality

made–to–measure *adj* : CUSTOM-MADE

made–up \'mād-'əp\ *adj* **1** : fancifully conceived or falsely devised **2** : marked by the use of makeup

mad·house \'mad-ˌhau̇s\ *n* **1** : a place for the detention and care of the insane **2** : a place of great uproar

mad·man \'mad-ˌman, -mən\ *n* : LUNATIC

Ma·don·na \mə-'dä-nə\ *n* : a representation (as a picture or statue) of the Virgin Mary

ma·dras \'ma-drəs; ˌmə-'dras, -'dräs\ *n* [*Madras*, India] : a fine usu. cotton fabric with various designs (as plaid)

ma·dras·sa or **ma·dra·sa** \mə-'dra-sə, -'drä-\ *n* : a Muslim school, college, or university that is often part of a mosque

mad·ri·gal \'ma-dri-gəl\ *n* [It *madrigale*] **1** : a short lyrical poem in a strict poetic form **2** : an elaborate part-song esp. of the 16th and 17th centuries

mad·wom·an \'mad-ˌwu̇-mən\ *n* : a woman who is insane

mael·strom \'māl-strəm\ *n* **1** : a violent whirlpool **2** : TUMULT

mae·stro \'mī-strō\ *n, pl* **maestros** or **mae·stri** \-ˌstrē\ [It] : a master in an art; *esp* : an eminent composer, conductor, or teacher of music

Ma·fia \'mä-fē-ə\ *n* [It] : a secret criminal society of Sicily or Italy; *also* : a similar organization elsewhere

ma·fi·o·so \ˌmä-fē-'ō-(ˌ)sō\ *n, pl* **-si** \-(ˌ)sē\ : a member of the Mafia

¹mag \'mag\ *n* : MAGAZINE

²mag *abbr* **1** magnetism **2** magneto **3** magnitude

mag·a·zine \'ma-gə-ˌzēn\ *n* [MF, fr. Old Occitan, fr. Ar *makhāzin*, pl. of *makhzan* storehouse] **1** : a storehouse esp. for military supplies **2** : a place for keeping gunpowder in a fort or ship **3** : a publication usu. containing stories, articles, or poems and issued periodically **4** : a container in a gun for holding cartridges; *also* : a chamber (as on a camera) for film

ma·gen·ta \mə-'jen-tə\ *n* : a deep purplish red color

mag·got \'ma-gət\ *n* : the legless wormlike larva of a dipteran fly — **mag·goty** *adj*

ma·gi \'mā-ˌjī\ *n pl, often cap* : the three wise men from the East who paid homage to the infant Jesus

mag·ic \'ma-jik\ *n* **1** : the use of means (as charms or spells) believed to have supernatural power over natural forces **2** : an extraordinary power or influence seemingly from a supernatural force **3** : SLEIGHT OF HAND — **magic** *adj* — **mag·i·cal** \-ji-kəl\ *adj* — **mag·i·cal·ly** \-ji-k(ə-)lē\ *adv*

ma·gi·cian \mə-'ji-shən\ *n* : a person skilled in magic

mag·is·te·ri·al \ˌma-jə-'stir-ē-əl\ *adj* **1** : AUTHORITATIVE ⟨a ∼ attitude⟩ **2** : of or relating to a magistrate or a magistrate's office or duties

ma·gis·tral \'ma-jə-strəl\ *adj* : AUTHORITATIVE

mag·is·trate \'ma-jə-ˌstrāt\ *n* : an official entrusted with administration of the laws — **mag·is·tra·cy** \-strə-sē\ *n*

mag·lev \'mag-lev\ *n* **1** : the use of magnetic fields to float an object above a solid surface **2** : a train using maglev technology

mag·ma \'mag-mə\ *n* : molten rock material within the earth — **mag·mat·ic** \mag-'ma-tik\ *adj*

mag·nan·i·mous \mag-'na-nə-məs\ *adj* **1** : showing or suggesting a lofty and courageous spirit **2** : NOBLE, GENEROUS — **mag·na·nim·i·ty** \ˌmag-nə-'ni-mə-tē\ *n* — **mag·nan·i·mous·ly** *adv* — **mag·nan·i·mous·ness** *n*

mag·nate \'mag-ˌnāt\ *n* : a person of rank, influence, or distinction

mag·ne·sia \mag-'nē-shə, -zhə\ *n* [NL, fr. *magnes carneus*, a white earth, lit., flesh magnet] : a light white oxide of magnesium used as a laxative

mag·ne·sium \mag-'nē-zē-əm, -zhəm\ *n* : a silver-white light malleable metallic chemical element

mag·net \'mag-nət\ *n* **1** : LODESTONE **2** : a body that is able to attract iron **3** : something that attracts

mag·net·ic \mag-'ne-tik\ *adj* **1** : having an unusual ability to attract ⟨a ∼ leader⟩ **2** : of or relating to a magnet or magnetism **3** : magnetized or capable of being magnetized — **mag·net·i·cal·ly** \-ti-k(ə-)lē\ *adv*

magnetic disk *n* : DISK 3

magnetic levitation *n* : MAGLEV 1

magnetic north *n* : the northerly direction in the earth's magnetic field indicated by the north-seeking pole of a compass needle

magnetic resonance imaging *n* : a noninvasive diagnostic technique that produces computerized images of internal body tissues based on electromagnetically induced activity of atoms within the body

magnetic tape *n* : a ribbon coated with a magnetic material on which information (as sound) may be stored

mag·ne·tise *Brit var of* MAGNETIZE

mag·ne·tism \'mag-nə-ˌti-zəm\ *n* **1** : the power (as of a magnet) to attract iron **2** : the science that deals with magnetic phenomena **3** : an ability to attract or charm

mag·ne·tite \'mag-nə-ˌtīt\ *n* : a black mineral that is an important iron ore

mag·ne·tize \'mag-nə-ˌtīz\ *vb* **-tized; -tiz·ing 1** : to induce magnetic properties in **2** : to attract like a magnet : CHARM — **mag·ne·tiz·able** *adj* — **mag·ne·ti·za·tion** \ˌmag-nə-tə-'zā-shən\ *n* — **mag·ne·tiz·er** *n*

mag·ne·to \mag-'nē-tō\ *n, pl* **-tos** : a generator used to produce sparks in an internal combustion engine

mag·ne·tom·e·ter \ˌmag-nə-'tä-mə-tər\ *n* : an instrument for measuring the strength of a magnetic field

mag·ne·to·sphere \mag-'nē-tə-ˌsfir,

-'ne-\ *n* : a region around a celestial object (as the earth) in which charged particles are trapped by its magnetic field

mag·ne·to·spher·ic \-ˌnē-tə-'sfir-ik, -'sfer-\ *adj*

mag·ni·fi·ca·tion \ˌmag-nə-fə-'kā-shən\ *n* 1 : the act of magnifying 2 : the amount by which an optical lens or instrument magnifies

mag·nif·i·cent \mag-'ni-fə-sənt\ *adj* : characterized by grandeur or beauty : SPLENDID 2 : EXALTED, NOBLE ♦ *Synonyms* IMPOSING, STATELY, GRAND, MAJESTIC — **mag·nif·i·cence** \-səns\ *n* — **mag·nif·i·cent·ly** *adv*

mag·nif·i·co \mag-'ni-fi-ˌkō\ *n, pl* **-coes** *or* **-cos** 1 : a nobleman of Venice 2 : a person of high position

mag·ni·fy \'mag-nə-ˌfī\ *vb* **-fied; -fy·ing** 1 : EXTOL, LAUD; *also* : to cause to be held in greater esteem 2 : INTENSIFY; *also* : EXAGGERATE 3 : to enlarge in fact or in appearance ⟨a microscope *magnifies* an object⟩ — **mag·ni·fi·er** \'mag-nə-ˌfī(-ə)r\ *n*

mag·nil·o·quent \mag-'ni-lə-kwənt\ *adj* : characterized by an exalted and often bombastic style or manner — **mag·nil·o·quence** \-kwəns\ *n*

mag·ni·tude \'mag-nə-ˌtüd, -tyüd\ *n* 1 : greatness of size or extent 2 : SIZE 3 : QUANTITY 4 : a number representing the brightness of a celestial object 5 : a number representing the intensity of an earthquake

mag·no·lia \mag-'nōl-yə\ *n* : any of a genus of usu. spring-flowering shrubs and trees with large often fragrant flowers

mag·num opus \'mag-nəm-'ō-pəs\ *n* [L] : the greatest achievement of an artist or writer

mag·pie \'mag-ˌpī\ *n* : any of various long-tailed often black-and-white birds related to the jays

Mag·yar \'mag-ˌyär, 'mäg-; 'mä-ˌjär\ *n* : a member of the dominant people of Hungary — **Magyar** *adj*

ma·ha·ra·ja *or* **ma·ha·ra·jah** \ˌmä-hə-'rä-jə\ *n* : a Hindu prince ranking above a raja

ma·ha·ra·ni *or* **ma·ha·ra·nee** \-'rä-nē\ *n* 1 : the wife of a maharaja 2 : a Hindu princess ranking above a rani

ma·ha·ri·shi \ˌmä-hə-'rē-shē\ *n* : a Hindu teacher of mystical knowledge

ma·hat·ma \mə-'hät-mə, -'hat-\ *n* [Skt *mahātman*, fr. *mahātman* great-souled, fr. *mahat* great + *ātman* soul] : a person revered for high-mindedness, wisdom, and selflessness

Ma·hi·can \mə-'hē-kən\ *or* **Mo·hi·can** \mō-, mə-\ *n, pl* **-can** *or* **-cans** : a member of an American Indian people of the upper Hudson River valley

ma·hog·a·ny \mə-'hä-gə-nē\ *n, pl* **-nies** : the reddish wood of any of various chiefly tropical trees that is used in furniture; *also* : a tree yielding this wood

ma·hout \mə-'haůt\ *n* [Hindi & Urdu *mahāwat, mahāut*] : a keeper and driver of an elephant

maid \'mād\ *n* 1 : an unmarried girl or young woman 2 : MAIDSERVANT; *also* : a woman or girl employed to do domestic work

¹maid·en \'mā-dᵊn\ *n* : MAID 1 — **maiden·ly** *adj*

²maiden *adj* 1 : UNMARRIED; *also* : VIRGIN 2 : of, relating to, or befitting a maiden 3 : FIRST ⟨a ship's ~ voyage⟩

maid·en·hair fern \-ˌher-\ *n* : any of a genus of ferns with delicate feathery fronds

maid·en·head \'mā-dᵊn-ˌhed\ *n* 1 : VIRGINITY 2 : HYMEN

maid·en·hood \-ˌhůd\ *n* : the condition or time of being a maiden

maid–in–waiting *n, pl* **maids–in–waiting** : a young woman appointed to attend a queen or princess

maid of honor : a bride's principal unmarried wedding attendant

maid·ser·vant \'mād-ˌsər-vənt\ *n* : a girl or woman who is a servant

¹mail \'māl\ *n* [ME *male* bag, fr. AF, of Gmc origin] 1 : material sent or carried in the postal system 2 : a nation's postal system — often used in pl. 3 : E-MAIL

²mail *vb* : to send by mail

³mail *n* [ME *maille* metal link, mail, fr. AF, fr. L *macula* spot, mesh] : armor made of metal links or plates

mail·box \'māl-ˌbäks\ *n* 1 : a public box for the collection of mail 2 : a private box for the delivery of mail

mail·man \-ˌman\ *n* : a man who delivers mail

¹main \'mām\ *vb* : to mutilate, disfigure, or wound seriously

¹main \'mān\ *n* 1 : FORCE ⟨with might and ~⟩ 2 : MAINLAND; *also* : HIGH SEA 3 : the chief part 4 : a principal pipe, duct, or circuit of a utility system

²main *adj* 1 : CHIEF, PRINCIPAL ⟨the ~ idea⟩ 2 : fully exerted ⟨~ force⟩ 3 : expressing the chief predication in a complex sentence ⟨the ~ clause⟩ — **main·ly** *adv*

main·frame \'mān-ˌfrām\ *n* : a large fast computer

main·land \-ˌland, -lənd\ *n* : a continuous body of land constituting the chief part of a country or continent

main·line \-ˌlīn\ *vb, slang* : to inject a narcotic drug into a vein

main line *n* : a principal highway or railroad line

main·mast \'mān-ˌmast, -məst\ *n* : the principal mast on a sailing ship

main·sail \-ˌsāl, -səl\ *n* : the largest sail on the mainmast

main·spring \-ˌspriŋ\ *n* 1 : the chief spring in a mechanism (as of a watch) 2 : the chief motive, agent, or cause

main·stay \-ˌstā\ *n* 1 : a stay running from the head of the mainmast to the foot of the foremast 2 : a chief support

main·stream \-ˌstrēm\ *n* : a prevailing current or direction of activity or influence — **mainstream** *adj*

main·tain \mān-'tān\ *vb* [ME *mainteinen*, fr. AF *maintenir, maynteiner*, fr. ML *manutenēre*, fr. L *manu tenēre* to hold in the hand] 1 : to keep in an existing state (as of repair) 2 : to sustain against opposition or danger **3** : to continue in ⟨CARRY ON **4** : to provide for : SUPPORT **5** : ASSERT ⟨~ed his innocence⟩ — **main·tain·abil·i·ty** \-,tā-nə-'bil-ə-tē\ n — **main·tain·able** \-'tā-nə-bəl\ adj — **main·te·nance** \'mān-tə-nəns\ n

main·top \'mān-,täp\ n : a platform at the head of the mainmast of a square-rigged ship

mai·son·ette \,mā-zə-'net\ n **1** : a small house **2** : an apartment often on two floors

mai tai \'mī-,tī\ n : a cocktail made with liquors and fruit juices

maî·tre d' or **mai·tre d'** \,mā-trə-'dē, ,me-\ n, pl **maî·tre d's** or **maitre d's** \-'dēz\ : MAÎTRE D'HÔTEL

maî·tre d'hô·tel \,mā-trə-dō-'tel, ,me-\ n, pl **maîtres d'hôtel** ⟨same⟩ [F, lit., master of house] **1** : MAJORDOMO **2** : HEADWAITER

maize \'māz\ n : CORN 2

Maj abbr major

maj·es·ty \'ma-jə-stē\ n, pl **-ties 1** : sovereign power, authority, or dignity; also : the person of a sovereign — used as a title **2** : GRANDEUR, SPLENDOR — **ma·jes·tic** \mə-'jes-tik\ adj — **ma·jes·ti·cal·ly** \-ti-k(ə-)lē\ adv

Maj Gen abbr Major General

ma·jol·i·ca \mə-'jä-li-kə\ also **ma·iol·i·ca** \-'yä-\ n : any of several faiences; esp : an Italian tin-glazed pottery

¹ma·jor \'mā-jər\ adj **1** : greater in number, extent, or importance ⟨a ~ poet⟩ **2** : notable or conspicuous in effect or scope ⟨a ~ improvement⟩ **3** : SERIOUS ⟨a ~ illness⟩ **4** : having half steps between the 3d and 4th and the 7th and 8th degrees ⟨~ scale⟩; also : based on a major scale ⟨~ key⟩ ⟨~ chord⟩

²major n **1** : a commissioned officer (as in the army) ranking next below a lieutenant colonel **2** : an academic subject chosen as a field of specialization; also : a student specializing in such a field ⟨a history ~⟩

³major vb : to pursue an academic major

ma·jor-do·mo \,mā-jər-'dō-mō\ n, pl **-mos** [Sp mayordomo or obs. It maiordomo, fr. ML major domus, lit., chief of the house] **1** : a head steward **2** : BUTLER

ma·jor·ette \,mā-jə-'ret\ n : DRUM MAJORETTE

major general n : a commissioned officer (as in the army) ranking next below a lieutenant general

ma·jor·i·ty \mə-'jòr-ə-tē\ n, pl **-ties 1** : the age at which full civil rights are accorded; also : the status of one who has attained this age **2** : a number greater than half of a total; also : the excess of this greater number over the remainder **3** : the rank of a major

ma·jus·cule \'ma-jəs-,kyül, mə-'jəs-\ n : a large letter (as a capital)

Ma·kah \'mä-kä\ n, pl **Makah** or **Makahs** : a member of an American Indian people of the northwest coast of No. America

¹make \'māk\ vb **made** \'mād\; **mak·ing 1** : to cause to exist, occur, or appear; also : DESTINE ⟨was made to be an actor⟩

2 : FASHION ⟨~ a dress⟩; also : COMPOSE **3** : to formulate in the mind ⟨~ plans⟩ **4** : CONSTITUTE ⟨house made of stone⟩ **5** : to compute to be **6** : to set in order : PREPARE ⟨~ a bed⟩ **7** : to cause to be or become; also : APPOINT **8** : ENACT; also : EXECUTE ⟨~ a will⟩ **9** : CONCLUDE ⟨didn't know what to ~ of it⟩ **10** : CARRY OUT, PERFORM ⟨~ a gesture⟩ **11** : COMPEL **12** : to assure the success of ⟨will ~ us or break us⟩ **13** : to amount to in significance ⟨~s no difference⟩ **14** : to be capable of developing or being fashioned into **15** : REACH, ATTAIN; also : GAIN **16** : to start out : GO **17** : to have weight or effect ⟨courtesy ~s for safer driving⟩ ◆ **Synonyms** FORM, SHAPE, FABRICATE, MANUFACTURE — **mak·er** n — **make believe** : PRETEND — **make do** : to manage with the means at hand — **make fun of** : RIDICULE, MOCK — **make good 1** : INDEMNIFY ⟨make good the loss⟩; also : to carry out successfully ⟨make good his promise⟩ **2** : SUCCEED — **make way 1** : to give room for passing, entering, or occupying **2** : to make progress

²make n **1** : the manner or style of construction; also : BRAND 3 **2** : MAKEUP 3 : the action of manufacturing — **on the make** : in search of wealth, social status, or sexual adventure

¹make-be·lieve \'māk-bə-,lēv\ n : a pretending that what is not real is real

²make-believe adj : IMAGINED, PRETENDED

make-do \-,dü\ adj : MAKESHIFT

make out vb **1** : to draw up in writing ⟨make out a list⟩ **2** : to find or grasp the meaning of ⟨can you make that out⟩ **3** : to represent as being **4** : to pretend to be true **5** : DISCERN ⟨make out a ship in the fog⟩ **6** : GET ALONG, FARE ⟨make out well in life⟩ **7** : to engage in amorous kissing and caressing

make over vb : REMAKE, REMODEL — **make-over** \'mā-,kō-vər\ n

make·shift \'māk-,shift\ n : a temporary expedient — **makeshift** adj

make·up \'mā-,kəp\ n **1** : the way in which something is put together; also : physical, mental, and moral constitution **2** : cosmetics esp. for the face; also : materials (as wigs and cosmetics) used in making up

make up vb **1** : FORM, COMPOSE **2** : to compensate for a deficiency **3** : SETTLE ⟨made up my mind⟩ **4** : INVENT, IMPROVISE **5** : to become reconciled **6** : to put on makeup (as for a play)

make-work \'māk-,wərk\ n : BUSYWORK

mak·ings \'mā-kiŋz\ n pl : the material from which something is made

Mal abbr Malachi

Mal·a·chi \'ma-lə-,kī\ n — see BIBLE table

Mal·a·chi·as \,ma-lə-'kī-əs\ n : MALACHI

mal·a·chite \'ma-lə-,kīt\ n : a green mineral that is a carbonate of copper used for making ornamental objects

mal·adapt·ed \,ma-lə-'dap-təd\ adj : poorly suited to a particular use, purpose, or situation

mal·ad·just·ed \ˌma-lə-'jəs-təd\ *adj* : poorly or inadequately adjusted (as to one's environment) — **mal·ad·just·ment** \-'jəst-mənt\ *n*

mal·adroit \ˌma-lə-'droit\ *adj* : not adroit : INEPT ⟨the ~ handling of the crisis⟩

mal·a·dy \'ma-lə-dē\ *n, pl* **-dies** : a disease or disorder of body or mind

mal·aise \mə-'lāz, ma-\ *n* [F] : a hazy feeling of not being well

mal·a·mute \'ma-lə-ˌmyüt\ *n* : a dog often used to draw sleds esp. in northern No. America

mal·a·prop·ism \'ma-lə-ˌprä-ˌpi-zəm\ *n* : a usu. humorous misuse of a word

mal·ap·ro·pos \ˌma-ˌla-prə-'pō, ma-'la-prə-ˌpō\ *adv* : in an inappropriate or inopportune way — **malapropos** *adj*

ma·lar·ia \mə-'ler-ē-ə\ *n* [It, fr. *mala aria* bad air] : a disease marked by recurring chills and fever and caused by a protozoan parasite of the blood that is transmitted by anopheles mosquitoes — **ma·lar·i·al** \-əl\ *adj*

ma·lar·key \mə-'lär-kē\ *n* : insincere or foolish talk

mal·a·thi·on \ˌma-lə-'thī-ən, -ˌän\ *n* : an insecticide with a relatively low toxicity for mammals

Ma·lay \mə-'lā, 'mā-ˌlā\ *n* **1** : a member of a people of the Malay Peninsula and Archipelago **2** : the language of the Malays — **Malay** *adj* — **Ma·lay·an** \mə-'lā-ən, 'mā-ˌlā-\ *n or adj*

mal·con·tent \ˌmal-kən-'tent\ *adj* : marked by a dissatisfaction with the existing state of affairs : DISCONTENTED — **malcontent** *n*

mal de mer \ˌmal-də-'mer\ *n* [F] : SEASICKNESS

¹**male** \'māl\ *n* : a male individual

²**male** *adj* : of, relating to, or being the sex that produces germ cells which fertilize the eggs of a female; *also* : STAMINATE **2** : MASCULINE — **male·ness** *n*

male·dic·tion \ˌma-lə-'dik-shən\ *n* : CURSE, EXECRATION

male·fac·tor \'ma-lə-ˌfak-tər\ *n* : EVILDOER; *esp* : one who commits an offense against the law — **male·fac·tion** \ˌma-lə-'fak-shən\ *n*

ma·lef·ic \mə-'le-fik\ *adj* **1** : BALEFUL ⟨~ influences⟩ **2** : MALICIOUS

ma·lef·i·cent \-fə-sənt\ *adj* : working or productive of harm or evil

ma·lev·o·lent \mə-'le-və-lənt\ *adj* : having, showing, or arising from ill will, spite, or hatred ♦ *Synonyms* MALIGNANT, MALIGN, MALICIOUS, SPITEFUL — **ma·lev·o·lence** \-ləns\ *n*

mal·fea·sance \mal-'fē-zᵊns\ *n* : wrongful conduct esp. by a public official

mal·for·ma·tion \ˌmal-for-'mā-shən\ *n* : irregular or faulty formation or structure; *also* : an instance of this — **malformed** \mal-'förmd\ *adj*

mal·func·tion \mal-'fəŋk-shən\ *vb* : to fail to operate normally — **malfunction** *n*

mal·ice \'ma-ləs\ *n* : desire to cause injury or distress to another — **ma·li·cious** \mə-'li-shəs\ *adj* — **ma·li·cious·ly** *adv*

¹**ma·lign** \mə-'līn\ *adj* **1** : evil in nature, influence, or effect; *also* : MALIGNANT 2 **2** : moved by ill will

²**malign** *vb* : to speak evil of : DEFAME

ma·lig·nant \mə-'lig-nənt\ *adj* **1** : INJURIOUS, MALIGN **2** : tending to produce death or deterioration ⟨a ~ tumor⟩ — **ma·lig·nan·cy** \-nən-sē\ *n* — **ma·lig·nant·ly** *adv* — **ma·lig·ni·ty** \-nə-tē\ *n*

ma·lin·ger \mə-'liŋ-gər\ *vb* [F *malingre* sickly] : to pretend illness so as to avoid duty — **ma·lin·ger·er** *n*

mal·i·son \'ma-lə-sən, -zən\ *n* : CURSE

mall \'mol, 'mal\ *n* **1** : a shaded walk : PROMENADE **2** : an urban shopping area featuring a variety of shops surrounding a concourse **3** : a usu. large enclosed suburban shopping area containing various shops

mal·lard \'ma-lərd\ *n, pl* **mallard** or **mallards** : a common wild duck that is the source of domestic ducks

mal·lea·ble \'ma-lē-ə-bəl\ *adj* **1** : capable of being extended or shaped by beating with a hammer or by the pressure of rollers **2** : ADAPTABLE, PLIABLE ⟨~ young minds⟩ ♦ *Synonyms* PLASTIC, PLIANT, DUCTILE, SUPPLE — **mal·le·a·bil·i·ty** \ˌma-lē-ə-'bi-lə-tē\ *n*

mal·let \'ma-lət\ *n* **1** : a tool with a large head for driving another tool or for striking a surface without marring it **2** : a long-handled hammerlike implement for striking a ball (as in croquet)

mal·le·us \'ma-lē-əs\ *n, pl* **mal·lei** \-lē-ˌī, -lē-ˌē\ [NL, fr. L, hammer] : the outermost of the three small bones of the mammalian middle ear

mal·low \'ma-lō\ *n* : any of a genus of herbs with lobed leaves, usu. showy flowers, and a disk-shaped fruit

malm·sey \'mälm-zē\ *n, often cap* : the sweetest variety of Madeira

mal·nour·ished \mal-'nər-isht\ *adj* : UNDERNOURISHED

mal·nu·tri·tion \ˌmal-nü-'tri-shən, -nyü-\ *n* : faulty and esp. inadequate nutrition

mal·oc·clu·sion \ˌma-lə-'klü-zhən\ *n* : faulty coming together of teeth in biting

mal·odor·ous \ma-'lō-də-rəs\ *adj* : ill-smelling — **mal·odor·ous·ly** *adv* — **mal·odor·ous·ness** *n*

maloti *pl of* LOTI

mal·prac·tice \mal-'prak-təs\ *n* : a dereliction of professional duty or a failure of professional skill that results in injury, loss, or damage

malt \'molt\ *n* **1** : grain and esp. barley steeped in water until it has sprouted and used in brewing and distilling **2** : liquor made with malt — **malty** *adj*

malted milk \'mol-təd-\ *n* : a powder prepared from dried milk and an extract from malt; *also* : a beverage of this powder in milk or other liquid

Mal·thu·sian \mal-'thü-zhən, -'thyü-\ *adj* : of or relating to a theory that population unless checked (as by war) tends to increase faster than its means of subsistence — **Malthusian** *n* — **Mal·thu·sian·ism** \-zhə-ˌni-zəm\ *n*

malt·ose \'mȯl-ˌtōs\ *n* : a sugar formed esp. from starch by the action of enzymes

mal·treat \mal-'trēt\ *vb* : to treat cruelly or roughly : ABUSE — **mal·treat·ment** *n*

mal·ware \'mal-ˌwer\ *n* : software designed to interfere with a computer's normal functioning

ma·ma *or* **mam·ma** \'mä-mə\ *n* : MOTHER

mam·bo \'mäm-bō\ *n, pl* **mambos** : a dance of Cuban origin related to the rumba — **mambo** *vb*

mam·mal \'ma-məl\ *n* [NL *Mammalia,* fr. LL, neut. pl. of *mammalis* of the breast, fr. L *mamma* breast] : any of a class of warm-blooded vertebrates that includes humans and all other animals which nourish their young with milk and have the skin more or less covered with hair — **mam·ma·li·an** \mə-'mā-lē-ən, ma-\ *adj or n*

mam·ma·ry \'ma-mə-rē\ *adj* : of, relating to, or being the glands (**mammary glands**) that in female mammals secrete milk

mam·mo·gram \'ma-mə-ˌgram\ *n* : an X-ray photograph of the breasts

mam·mog·ra·phy \ma-'mä-grə-fē\ *n* : X-ray examination of the breasts (as for early detection of cancer)

mam·mon \'ma-mən\ *n, often cap* : material wealth having a debasing influence

¹**mam·moth** \'ma-məth\ *n* : any of a genus of large hairy extinct elephants

²**mammoth** *adj* : of very great size : GIGANTIC ♦ **Synonyms** COLOSSAL, ENORMOUS, IMMENSE, VAST, ELEPHANTINE

¹**man** \'man\ *n, pl* **men** \'men\ **1** : a human being; *esp* : an adult male **2** : the human race : MANKIND **3** : one possessing in high degree the qualities considered distinctive of manhood **4** : an adult male servant or employee **5** : the individual who can fulfill one's requirements ⟨he's your ~⟩ **6 a** : one of the pieces with which various games (as chess) are played **b** : one of the players on a team **7** *often cap* : white society or people

²**man** *vb* **manned; man·ning 1** : to supply with men ⟨~ a fleet⟩ **2** : FORTIFY, BRACE

³**man** *abbr* manual

Man *abbr* Manitoba

man–about–town *n, pl* **men–about–town** : a worldly and socially active man

man·a·cle \'ma-ni-kəl\ *n* **1** : a shackle for the hand or wrist **2** : something used as a restraint

man·age \'ma-nij\ *vb* **man·aged; man·ag·ing 1** : HANDLE, CONTROL ⟨~s her skis well⟩; *also* : to direct or carry on business or affairs **2** : to make and keep compliant **3** : to treat with care : HUSBAND **4** : to achieve one's purpose : CONTRIVE — **man·age·abil·i·ty** \ˌma-ni-jə-'bi-lə-tē\ *n* — **man·age·able** \'ma-ni-jə-bəl\ *adj* — **man·age·able·ness** *n* — **man·age·ably** \-blē\ *adv*

managed care *n* : a health-care system that controls costs by limiting doctor's fees and by restricting the patient's choice of doctors

man·age·ment \'ma-nij-mənt\ *n* **1** : the act or art of managing : CONTROL **2** : judicious use of means to accomplish an end **3** : the group of those who manage or direct an enterprise

man·ag·er \'ma-ni-jər\ *n* : one that manages — **man·a·ge·ri·al** \ˌma-nə-'jir-ē-əl\ *adj*

ma·ña·na \mən-'yä-nə\ *n* [Sp, lit., tomorrow] : an indefinite time in the future

ma·nat \ma-'nat\ *n, pl* **manat** *or* **manats** — see MONEY table

man–at–arms *n, pl* **men–at–arms** : SOLDIER; *esp* : one who is heavily armed and mounted

man·a·tee \'ma-nə-ˌtē\ *n* : any of a genus of chiefly tropical plant-eating aquatic mammals having a broad rounded tail

man·ci·ple \'man-sə-pəl\ *n* : a steward or purveyor esp. for a college or monastery

man·da·mus \man-'dā-məs\ *n* [L, we enjoin] : a writ issued by a superior court commanding that an official act or duty be performed

man·da·rin \'man-də-rən\ *n* **1** : a public official of high rank under the Chinese Empire **2** *cap* : the chief dialect group of China **3** : a yellow to reddish orange loose-skinned citrus fruit; *also* : a tree that bears mandarins

man·date \'man-ˌdāt\ *n* **1** : an authoritative command **2** : an authorization to act given to a representative **3** : a commission granted by the League of Nations to a member nation for governing conquered territory; *also* : a territory so governed

man·da·to·ry \'man-də-ˌtȯr-ē\ *adj* **1** : containing or constituting a command : OBLIGATORY **2** : of or relating to a League of Nations mandate

man·di·ble \'man-də-bəl\ *n* **1** : JAW; *esp* : a lower jaw **2** : either segment of a bird's bill — **man·dib·u·lar** \man-'di-byə-lər\ *adj*

man·do·lin \ˌman-də-'lin, 'man-də-lən\ *n* : a stringed musical instrument with a pear-shaped body and a fretted neck

man·drake \'man-ˌdrāk\ *n* **1** : an Old World herb related to the nightshades or its large forked root formerly credited with magical properties **2** : MAYAPPLE

man·drel *also* **man·dril** \'man-drəl\ *n* **1** : an axle or spindle inserted into a hole in a piece of work to support it during machining **2** : a metal bar used as a core around which material may be cast, shaped, or molded

man·drill \'man-drəl\ *n* : a large baboon of western central Africa

mane \'mān\ *n* : long heavy hair growing about the neck of some mammals (as horses) — **maned** \'mānd\ *adj*

man–eat·er \'man-ˌē-tər\ *n* : one (as a shark or cannibal) that has or is thought to have an appetite for human flesh — **man–eat·ing** *adj*

ma·nège \ma-'nezh, mə-\ *n* : the art of horsemanship or of training horses

ma·nes \'mä-ˌnās, 'mā-ˌnēz\ *n pl, often cap* : the spirits of the dead and gods of the lower world in ancient Roman belief

ma·neu·ver \mə-'nü-vər, -'nyü-\ *n* [F *manœuvre*, fr. OF *maneuvre* work done by hand, fr. ML *manuopera*, fr. *manu operare* to work by hand] **1** : a military or naval movement; *also* : an armed forces training exercise — often used in pl. **2** : a procedure involving expert physical movement **3** : an evasive movement or shift of tactics; *also* : an action taken to gain a tactical end — **maneuver** *vb* — **ma·neu·ver·abil·i·ty** \-,nü-və-rə-'bi-lə-tē, -,nyü-\ *n* — **ma·neu·ver·able** \-'nü-və-rə-bəl, -'nyü-\ *adj*

man Friday *n* : an efficient and devoted aide or employee

man·ful \'man-fəl\ *adj* : having or showing courage and resolution ⟨a ~ struggle⟩ — **man·ful·ly** *adv*

man·ga \'maŋ-gə\ *n* [Jp, comic, cartoon, fr. *man-* involuntary, aimless + *-ga* picture] : a Japanese comic book or graphic novel

man·ga·nese \'maŋ-gə-,nēz, -,nēs\ *n* : a metallic chemical element resembling iron but not magnetic

mange \'mānj\ *n* : any of several contagious itchy skin diseases esp. of domestic animals — **mangy** \'mān-jē\ *adj*

man·ger \'mān-jər\ *n* : a trough or open box for livestock feed or fodder

¹man·gle \'maŋ-gəl\ *vb* **man·gled; man·gling** **1** : to cut, bruise, or hack with repeated blows **2** : to spoil or injure esp. through ineptitude — **man·gler** *n*

²mangle *n* : a machine with heated rollers for ironing laundry

man·go \'maŋ-gō\ *n, pl* **mangoes** *also* **mangos** [Pg *manga*, prob. fr. Malayalam (Dravidian language of India) *māṅṅa*] : an edible juicy yellowish-red fruit borne by a tropical evergreen tree related to the sumacs; *also* : this tree

man·grove \'man-,grōv\ *n* : any of a genus of tropical maritime trees that send out many prop roots and form dense thickets important in coastal land building

man·han·dle \'man-,han-d°l\ *vb* : to handle roughly

man·hat·tan \man-'ha-t°n\ *n, often cap* : a cocktail made of whiskey and vermouth

man·hole \'man-,hōl\ *n* : a hole through which a person may go esp. to gain access to an underground or enclosed structure

man·hood \-,hůd\ *n* **1** : the condition of being an adult male **2** : qualities associated with men : MANLINESS **3** : MEN ⟨the nation's ~⟩

man–hour \-'aů-(-ə)r\ *n* : a unit of one hour's work by one person

man·hunt \-,hənt\ *n* : an organized hunt for a person and esp. for one charged with a crime

ma·nia \'mā-nē-ə, -nyə\ *n* **1** : excitement manifested by mental and physical hyperactivity, disorganized behavior, and elevated mood **2** : excessive enthusiasm

ma·ni·ac \'mā-nē-,ak\ *n* : LUNATIC, MADMAN

ma·ni·a·cal \mə-'nī-ə-kəl\ *also* **ma·ni·ac** \'mā-nē-ak\ *adj* **1** : affected with or sug-

gestive of madness **2** : FRANTIC ⟨a ~ mob⟩

man·ic \'ma-nik\ *adj* : affected with, relating to, characterized by, or resulting from mania — **manic** *n* — **man·i·cal·ly** \-ni-k(ə-)lē\ *adv*

manic depression *n* : BIPOLAR DISORDER

man·ic–de·pres·sive \,ma-nik-di-'pre-siv\ *adj* : characterized by or affected with either mania or depression or alternating episodes of mania and depression — **manic–depressive** *n*

¹man·i·cure \'ma-nə-,kyůr\ *n* **1** : MANICURIST **2** : a treatment for the care of the hands and nails

²manicure *vb* **-cured; -cur·ing** **1** : to do manicure work on **2** : to trim closely and evenly

man·i·cur·ist \-,kyůr-ist\ *n* : a person who gives manicure treatments

¹man·i·fest \'ma-nə-,fest\ *adj* [ME, fr. AF or L; AF *manifeste*, fr. L *manifestus*, caught in the act, flagrant, obvious, perh. fr. *manus* hand + *-festus* (akin to L in*festus* hostile)] **1** : readily perceived by the senses and esp. by the sight **2** : easily understood : OBVIOUS — **man·i·fest·ly** *adv*

²manifest *vb* : to make evident or certain by showing or displaying ♦ **Synonyms** EVINCE, DEMONSTRATE, EXHIBIT

³manifest *n* : a list of passengers or an invoice of cargo for a ship or plane

man·i·fes·ta·tion \,ma-nə-fə-'stā-shən\ *n* : DISPLAY, DEMONSTRATION

man·i·fes·to \,ma-nə-'fes-tō\ *n, pl* **-tos** *or* **-toes** : a public declaration of intentions, motives, or views

¹man·i·fold \'ma-nə-,fōld\ *adj* **1** : marked by diversity or variety **2** : consisting of or operating many of one kind combined

²manifold *n* : a pipe fitting with several lateral outlets for connecting it with other pipes

³manifold *vb* **1** : MULTIPLY **2** : to make a number of copies of (as a letter)

man·i·kin *also* **man·ni·kin** \'ma-ni-kən\ *n* **1** : MANNEQUIN **2** : a little man : DWARF

Ma·nila hemp \mə-'ni-lə-\ *n* : a tough fiber from a Philippine plant related to the banana that is used for cordage

manila paper *n, often cap M* : a tough brownish paper made orig. from Manila hemp

man·i·oc \'ma-nē-,äk\ *n* : CASSAVA

ma·nip·u·late \mə-'ni-pyə-,lāt\ *vb* **-lat·ed; -lat·ing** **1** : to treat or operate manually or mechanically esp. with skill **2** : to manage or use skillfully **3** : to influence esp. with intent to deceive — **ma·nip·u·la·tion** \-,ni-pyə-'lā-shən\ *n* — **ma·nip·u·la·tive** \-'ni-pyə-,lā-tiv\ *adj* — **ma·nip·u·la·tor** \-,lā-tər\ *n*

ma·nip·u·la·tives \mə-'ni-pyə-,lā-tivz\ *n pl* : objects that a student is instructed to use in a way that teaches or reinforces a lesson

man·kind *n* **1** \'man-'kīnd\ : the human race **2** \-,kīnd\ : men as distinguished from women

¹man·ly \'man-lē\ *adv* : in a manly manner

²manly *adj* **man·li·er; -est** : having qualities appropriate to or generally associated with a man : BOLD, RESOLUTE ⟨a ~ competitor⟩ — **man·li·ness** n

man–made \'man-'mād\ adj : made by humans rather than nature ⟨~ systems⟩; esp : SYNTHETIC ⟨~ fibers⟩

man·na \'ma-nə\ n 1 : food miraculously supplied to the Israelites in the wilderness 2 : something of value that comes unexpectedly : WINDFALL

manned \'mand\ adj : carrying or performed by a person ⟨~ spaceflight⟩

man·ne·quin \'ma-ni-kən\ n 1 : a form representing the human figure used esp. for displaying clothes 2 : a person employed to model clothing

man·ner \'ma-nər\ n 1 : KIND, SORT ⟨what ~ of man is he⟩ 2 : a way of acting or proceeding ⟨worked in a brisk ~⟩; also : normal behavior ⟨spoke bluntly as was his ~⟩ 3 : a method of artistic execution 4 pl : social conduct; also : BEARING 5 pl : BEHAVIOR ⟨taught the child good ~s⟩

man·nered \'ma-nərd\ adj 1 : having manners of a specified kind ⟨well-mannered⟩ 2 : having an artificial character ⟨a highly ~ style⟩

man·ner·ism \'ma-nə-,ri-zəm\ n 1 : ARTIFICIALITY, PRECIOSITY 2 : a peculiarity of action, bearing, or treatment ♦ *Synonyms* POSE, AIR, AFFECTATION

man·ner·ly \'ma-nər-lē\ adj : showing good manners : POLITE — **man·ner·li·ness** n — **mannerly** adv

man·nish \'ma-nish\ adj 1 : resembling or suggesting a man rather than a woman 2 : generally associated with or characteristic of a man ⟨a ~ voice⟩ — **man·nish·ly** adv — **man·nish·ness** n

ma·no a ma·no \,mä-nō-ä-'mä-nō\ adv or adj : in direct competition or conflict

ma·noeu·vre \mə-'nü-vər, -'nyü-\ chiefly Brit var of MANEUVER

man–of–war \,man-əv-'wȯr\ n, pl **men–of–war** \,men-\ : WARSHIP

ma·nom·e·ter \ma-'nä-mə-tər\ n : an instrument for measuring the pressure of gases and vapors — **mano·met·ric** \,ma-nə-'me-trik\ adj

man·or \'ma-nər\ n 1 : the house or hall of an estate; also : a landed estate 2 : an English estate of a feudal lord — **ma·no·ri·al** \mə-'nȯr-ē-əl\ adj — **ma·no·ri·al·ism** \-ə-,li-zəm\ n

man power n 1 : power available from or supplied by the physical effort of human beings 2 usu **man·pow·er** : the total supply of persons available and fitted for service

man·qué \mäⁿ-'kā\ adj [F, fr. pp. of manquer to lack, fail] : short of or frustrated in the fulfillment of one's aspirations or talents ⟨a poet ~⟩

man·sard \'man-,särd, -sərd\ n : a roof having two slopes on all sides with the lower slope steeper than the upper one

manse \'mans\ n : the residence esp. of a Presbyterian minister

man·ser·vant \'man-,sər-vənt\ n, pl **men·ser·vants** \'men-,sər-vənts\ : a male servant

man·sion \'man-chən\ n : a large imposing residence; also : a separate apartment in a large structure

man–size \'man-,sīz\ or **man–sized** \-,sīzd\ adj : suitable for or requiring a man ⟨a ~ job⟩

man·slaugh·ter \-,slȯ-tər\ n : the unlawful killing of a human being without express or implied malice

man·ta \'man-tə\ n : a square piece of cloth or blanket used in southwestern U.S. and Latin America as a cloak or shawl

man·teau \man-'tō\ n : a loose cloak, coat, or robe

man·tel \'man-tᵊl\ n : a beam, stone, or arch serving as a lintel to support the masonry above a fireplace; also : a shelf above a fireplace

man·tel·piece \'man-tᵊl-,pēs\ n : the shelf of a mantel

man·til·la \man-'tē-yə, -'ti-lə\ n : a light scarf worn over the head and shoulders esp. by Spanish and Latin-American women

man·tis \'man-təs\ n, pl **man·tis·es** also **man·tes** \-,tēz\ [NL, fr. Gk, lit., diviner, prophet] : any of a group of large usu. green insect-eating insects that hold their prey in forelimbs folded as if in prayer

man·tis·sa \man-'ti-sə\ n : the part of a logarithm to the right of the decimal point

¹man·tle \'man-tᵊl\ n 1 : a loose sleeveless garment worn over other clothes 2 : something that covers, enfolds, or envelops 3 : a lacy sheath that gives light by incandescence when placed over a flame 4 : the portion of the earth lying between the crust and the core 5 : MANTEL

²mantle vb **man·tled; man·tling** 1 : to cover with a mantle 2 : BLUSH

man·tra \'man-trə\ n : a mystical formula of invocation or incantation (as in Hinduism)

¹man·u·al \'man-yə-wəl\ adj 1 : of, relating to, or involving the hands; also : worked or made by hand ⟨a ~ pump⟩ 2 : requiring or using physical skill and energy ⟨~ labor⟩ — **man·u·al·ly** adv

²manual n 1 : a small book; esp : HANDBOOK 2 : the prescribed movements in the handling of a military item and esp. a weapon during a drill or ceremony ⟨the ~ of arms⟩ 3 : a keyboard esp. of an organ

man·u·fac·to·ry \,man-yə-'fak-tə-rē\ n : FACTORY

¹man·u·fac·ture \,man-yə-'fak-chər\ n [MF, fr. ML manufactura, L manu factus made by hand] 1 : something made from raw materials 2 : the process of making wares by hand or by machinery; also : a productive industry using machinery

²manufacture vb **-tured; -tur·ing** 1 : to make from raw materials by hand or by machinery; also : to engage in manufacture 2 : INVENT, FABRICATE; also : CREATE — **man·u·fac·tur·er** n

man·u·mit \,man-yə-'mit\ vb **-mit·ted; -mit·ting** : to free from slavery — **man·u·mis·sion** \-'mi-shən\ n

¹ma·nure \mə-ˈnu̇r, -ˈnyu̇r\ vb ma·nured; ma·nur·ing : to fertilize land with manure

²manure n : FERTILIZER; esp : refuse from stables and barnyards — ma·nu·ri·al \-ˈnu̇r-ē-əl, -ˈnyu̇r-\ adj

man·u·script \ˈman-yə-ˌskript\ n [L manu scriptus written by hand] 1 : a written or typewritten composition or document; also : a document submitted for publication 2 : writing as opposed to print

Manx \ˈmaŋks\ n pl : the people of the Isle of Man — Manx adj

¹many \ˈme-nē\ adj more \ˈmȯr\; most \ˈmōst\ : consisting of or amounting to a large but indefinite number ⟨∼ years ago⟩

²many pron : a large number ⟨∼ are called⟩

³many n : a large but indefinite number ⟨a good ∼ of them⟩

many·fold \ˌme-nē-ˈfōld\ adv : by many times

many–sid·ed \-ˈsī-dəd\ adj 1 : having many sides or aspects 2 : VERSATILE

Mao·ism \ˈmau̇-ˌi-zəm\ n : the theory and practice of Communism developed in China chiefly by Mao Zedong — Mao·ist \ˈmau̇-ist\ n or adj

Mao·ri \ˈmau̇(-ə)r-ē\ n, pl Maori or Mao·ris : a member of a Polynesian people native to New Zealand

¹map \ˈmap\ n [ML mappa, fr. L, napkin, towel] 1 : a representation usu. on a flat surface of the whole or part of an area 2 : a representation of the celestial sphere or part of it

²map vb mapped; map·ping 1 : to make a map of 2 : to plan in detail ⟨∼ out a program⟩ — map·pa·ble \ˈma-pə-bəl\ adj — map·per n

MAP abbr modified American plan

ma·ple \ˈmā-pəl\ n : any of a genus of trees or shrubs with 2-winged dry fruit and opposite leaves; also : the hard light-colored wood of a maple used esp. for floors and furniture

maple sugar n : sugar made by boiling maple syrup

maple syrup n : syrup made by concentrating the sap of maple trees and esp. the sugar maple

mar \ˈmär\ vb marred; mar·ring : to detract from the wholeness or perfection of : SPOIL ♦ Synonyms INJURE, HURT, HARM, DAMAGE, IMPAIR, BLEMISH

Mar abbr March

ma·ra·ca \mə-ˈrä-kə, -ˈra-\ n [Pg maracá] : a rattle usu. made from a gourd and used as a percussion instrument

mar·a·schi·no \ˌmer-ə-ˈskē-nō-, -ˈshē-\ n, often cap : a cherry preserved in a sweet liqueur made from the juice of a bitter wild cherry

mar·a·thon \ˈmer-ə-ˌthän\ n [Marathon, Greece, site of a victory of Greeks over Persians in 490 B.C. the news of which was carried to Athens by a long-distance runner] 1 : a long-distance race esp. on foot 2 : an endurance contest

mar·a·thon·er \ˈmer-ə-ˌthä-nər\ n : a person who takes part in a marathon — mar·a·thon·ing n

ma·raud \mə-ˈrȯd\ vb : to roam about and raid in search of plunder : PILLAGE — ma·raud·er n

mar·ble \ˈmär-bəl\ n 1 : a limestone that can be polished and used in fine building work 2 : something resembling marble (as in coldness) 3 : a small ball (as of glass) used in various games; also, pl : a children's game played with these small balls — marble adj

mar·bling \-bə-liŋ, -bliŋ\ n : an intermixture of fat through the lean of a cut of meat

mar·cel \mär-ˈsel\ n : a deep soft wave made in the hair by the use of a heated curling iron — marcel vb

¹march \ˈmärch\ n : a border region : FRONTIER

²march vb 1 : to move along in or as if in military formation 2 : to walk in a direct purposeful manner; also : PROGRESS, ADVANCE 3 : TRAVERSE ⟨∼ed 10 miles⟩ — march·er n

³march n 1 : the action of marching; also : the distance covered (as by a military unit) in a march 2 : a regular measured stride or rhythmic step used in marching 3 : forward movement 4 : a piece of music with marked rhythm suitable for marching to

March n [ME, fr. AF, fr. L martius, fr. martius of Mars, fr. Mart-, Mars, Roman god of war] : the 3d month of the year

mar·chio·ness \ˈmär-shə-nəs\ n 1 : the wife or widow of a marquess 2 : a woman holding the rank of a marquess in her own right

Mar·di Gras \ˈmär-dē-ˌgrä\ n [F, lit., fat Tuesday] : the Tuesday before Ash Wednesday often observed with parades and merrymaking

¹mare \ˈmer\ n : an adult female of the horse or a related mammal

²ma·re \ˈmär-(ˌ)ä\ n, pl ma·ria \ˈmär-ē-ə\ : any of several large dark areas on the surface of the moon or Mars

mar·ga·rine \ˈmär-jə-rən\ n : a food product made usu. from vegetable oils churned with skimmed milk and used as a substitute for butter

mar·ga·ri·ta \ˌmär-gə-ˈrē-tə\ n : a cocktail consisting of tequila, lime or lemon juice, and an orange-flavored liqueur

mar·gin \ˈmär-jən\ n 1 : the part of a page outside the main body of printed or written matter 2 : EDGE ⟨continental ∼⟩ 3 : a spare amount, measure, or degree allowed for use if needed ⟨a safety ∼⟩ 4 : measure or degree of difference ⟨a one-vote ∼⟩

mar·gin·al \-jə-nəl\ adj 1 : written or printed in the margin 2 : of, relating to, or situated at a margin or border 3 : close to the lower limit of quality or acceptability 4 : excluded from or existing outside the mainstream of society or a group — mar·gin·al·ly adv

mar·gi·na·lia \ˌmär-jə-ˈnā-lē-ə\ n pl : marginal notes or embellishments

mar·gin·al·ize \ˈmär-jə-nᵊl-ˌīz\ vb -ized;

-iz·ing : to relegate to an unimportant position within a society or group

mar·grave \'mär-ˌgräv\ *n* : the military governor esp. of a medieval German border province

ma·ri·a·chi \ˌmär-ē-'ä-chē, ˌmer-\ *n* : a Mexican street band; *also* : a member of or the music of such a band

mari·gold \'mer-ə-ˌgōld\ *n* : any of a genus of tropical American herbs related to the daisies that are grown for their showy usu. yellow, orange, or maroon flower heads

mar·i·jua·na *also* **mar·i·hua·na** \ˌmer-ə-'wä-nə, -'hwä-\ *n* [MexSp *marihuana*] : the dried leaves and flowering tops of the female hemp plant smoked usu. illegally for their intoxicating effect; *also* : HEMP

ma·rim·ba \mə-'rim-bə\ *n* : a xylophone of southern Africa and Central America; *also* : a modern version of it

ma·ri·na \mə-'rē-nə\ *n* : a dock or basin providing secure moorings for pleasure boats

mar·i·nade \ˌmer-ə-'nād\ *n* : a savory usu. acidic sauce in which meat, fish, or a vegetable is soaked to enrich its flavor or to tenderize it

mar·i·na·ra \ˌmer-ə-'ner-ə\ *adj* [It *(alla) marinara*, lit., in sailor style] : made with tomatoes, onions, garlic, and spices; *also* : served with marinara sauce

mar·i·nate \'mer-ə-ˌnāt\ *vb* **-nat·ed; -nat·ing** : to steep (as meat or fish) in a marinade

¹**ma·rine** \mə-'rēn\ *adj* **1** : of or relating to the sea or its navigation or commerce **2** : of or relating to marines

²**marine** *n* **1** : the mercantile and naval shipping of a country **2** : any of a class of soldiers serving on shipboard or with a naval force

mar·i·ner \'mer-ə-nər\ *n* : SAILOR

mar·i·o·nette \ˌmer-ē-ə-'net\ *n* : a puppet moved by strings or by hand

mar·i·tal \'mer-ə-t⁰l\ *adj* : of or relating to marriage : CONJUGAL ♦ *Synonyms* MATRIMONIAL, CONNUBIAL, NUPTIAL

mar·i·time \'mer-ə-ˌtīm\ *adj* **1** : of, relating to, or bordering on the sea **2** : of or relating to navigation or commerce of the sea

mar·jo·ram \'mär-jə-rəm\ *n* : any of various fragrant mints often used as seasoning

¹**mark** \'märk\ *n* **1** : something (as a line or fixed object) designed to record position; *also* : the starting line or position in a track event **2** : TARGET; *also* : GOAL, OBJECT **3** : an object of abuse or ridicule **4** : the question under discussion **5** : NORM ⟨not up to the ∼⟩ **6** : a visible sign : INDICATION; *also* : CHARACTERISTIC **7** : a written or printed symbol **8** : GRADE **5** ⟨a ∼ of B+⟩ **9** : IMPORTANCE, DISTINCTION **10** : a lasting impression ⟨making his ∼ in the world⟩; *also* : a damaging impression left on a surface

²**mark** *vb* **1** : to set apart by a line or boundary **2** : to designate by a mark or make a mark on **3** : CHARACTERIZE ⟨the

vehemence that ∼s his speeches⟩; *also* : SIGNALIZE ⟨this year ∼s our 50th anniversary⟩ **4** : to take notice of : OBSERVE ⟨∼ my words⟩ — **mark·er** *n*

³**mark** *n* : DEUTSCHE MARK

Mark \'märk\ *n* — see BIBLE table

mar·ka \'mär-kə\ *n, pl* **mar·a·ka** \'mär-kə\ *or* **marka** *or* **mar·kas** — see MONEY table

mark·down \'märk-ˌdaun\ *n* **1** : a lowering of price **2** : the amount by which an original price is reduced

mark down *vb* : to put a lower price on

marked \'märkt\ *adj* **1** : NOTICEABLE — **mark·ed·ly** \'mär-kəd-lē\ *adv*

¹**mar·ket** \'mär-kət\ *n* **1** : a meeting together of people for trade by purchase and sale; *also* : a public place where such a meeting is held **2** : the rate or price offered for a commodity or security **3** : the course of commercial activity by which the exchange of commodities is effected **4** : a geographical area of demand for commodities; *also* : extent of demand **5** : a retail establishment usu. of a specific kind

²**market** *vb* : to go to a market to buy or sell; *also* : SELL — **mar·ket·able** *adj*

mar·ket·place \'mär-kət-ˌplās\ *n* **1** : an open square in a town where markets are held **2** : the world of trade or economic activity

mark·ka \'mär-ˌkä\ *n, pl* **mark·kaa** \'mär-ˌkä\ *or* **markkas** \-ˌkäz\ : the basic monetary unit of Finland from 1917 to 2001

marks·man \'märks-mən\ *n* : a person skillful at hitting a target — **marks·man·ship** *n*

mark·up \'mär-ˌkəp\ *n* **1** : a raising of price **2** : an amount added to the cost price of an article to determine the selling price

mark up *vb* : to put a higher price on

markup language *n* : a system for marking the components and layout of a computer document

marl \'märl\ *n* : an earthy deposit rich in lime used esp. as fertilizer — **marly** \'mär-lē\ *adj*

mar·lin \'mär-lən\ *n* : any of several large oceanic sport fishes related to sailfishes

mar·line·spike *also* **mar·lin·spike** \'mär-lən-ˌspīk\ *n* : a pointed iron tool used to separate strands of rope or wire (as in splicing)

mar·ma·lade \'mär-mə-ˌlād\ *n* : a clear jelly holding in suspension pieces of fruit and fruit rind

mar·mo·re·al \mär-'mȯr-ē-əl\ *adj* : of, relating to, or suggestive of marble

mar·mo·set \'mär-mə-ˌset\ *n* : any of numerous small bushy-tailed monkeys of Central and So. America

mar·mot \'mär-mət\ *n* : any of a genus of stout short-legged burrowing No. American rodents

¹**ma·roon** \mə-'rün\ *vb* **1** : to put ashore (as on a desolate island) and leave to one's fate **2** : to leave in isolation and without hope of escape

²**maroon** *n* : a dark red color

¹**mar·quee** \mär-'kē\ *n* [modif. of F *mar-*

quise, lit., marchioness] **1** : a large tent set up (as for an outdoor party) **2** : a usu. metal and glass canopy over an entrance (as of a theater) **3** : a sign over the entrance of a theater or arena advertising a performance

²marquee *adj* : having or being a great attraction : PREEMINENT ⟨~ athletes⟩

mar·quess \ˈmär-kwəs\ *or* **mar·quis** \ˈmär-kwəs, mär-ˈkē\ *n* **1** : a nobleman of hereditary rank in Europe and Japan **2** : a member of the British peerage ranking below a duke and above an earl

mar·que·try \ˈmär-kə-trē\ *n* : inlaid work of wood, shell, or ivory (as on a table or cabinet)

mar·quise \mär-ˈkēz\ *n, pl* **mar·quises** *same or* -ˈkē-zəz\ : MARCHIONESS

mar·riage \ˈmer-ij\ *n* **1** : the state of being united to another person as a usu. contractual relationship according to law or custom **2** : a wedding ceremony and attendant festivities **3** : a close union ⟨a ~ of light and shadow⟩ — **mar·riage·able** *adj*

married name *n* : a woman's surname acquired through marriage

mar·row \ˈmer-ō\ *n* : a soft vascular tissue that fills the cavities of most bones

mar·row·bone \ˈmer-ə-ˌbōn, ˈmer-ō-\ *n* : a bone (as a shinbone) rich in marrow

mar·ry \ˈmer-ē\ *vb* **mar·ried; mar·ry·ing 1** : to join in marriage **2** : to take as a spouse : WED **3** : to enter into a close union **4** : COMBINE, UNITE — **mar·ried** *adj or n*

Mars \ˈmärz\ *n* : the planet 4th from the sun and conspicuous for its red color

marsh \ˈmärsh\ *n* : a tract of soft wet land — **marshy** *adj*

¹mar·shal \ˈmär-shəl\ *n* [ME, fr. AF *mareschal,* of Gmc origin; akin to OHG *marahscalc* marshal, fr. *marah* horse + *scalc* servant] **1** : a high official in a medieval household; *also* : a person in charge of the ceremonial aspects of a gathering **2** : a general officer of the highest military rank **3** : an administrative officer (as of a U.S. judicial district) having duties similar to a sheriff's **4** : the administrative head of a city police or fire department

²marshal *vb* **mar·shaled** *or* **mar·shalled; mar·shal·ing** *or* **mar·shal·ling 1** : to arrange in order, rank, or position ⟨~ troops⟩ **2** : to bring together ⟨~ arguments⟩ **3** : to lead with ceremony : USHER

marsh gas *n* : METHANE

marsh·mal·low \ˈmärsh-ˌme-lō, -ˌma-\ *n* : a light spongy confection made from corn syrup, sugar, albumen, and gelatin

marsh marigold *n* : a swamp herb related to the buttercups that has bright yellow flowers

mar·su·pi·al \mär-ˈsü-pē-əl\ *n* : any of an order of primitive mammals (as opossums, kangaroos, or wombats) that bear very immature young which are nourished in a pouch on the abdomen of the female — **marsupial** *adj*

mart \ˈmärt\ *n* : MARKET

mar·ten \ˈmär-tᵊn\ *n, pl* **marten** *or* **martens** : a slender mammal that is larger than the related weasels and has soft gray or brown fur; *also* : this fur

mar·tial \ˈmär-shəl\ *adj* [L *martialis* of Mars, fr. *Mart-, Mars* Mars, Roman god of war] **1** : of, relating to, or suited for war or a warrior ⟨~ music⟩ **2** : of or relating to an army or military life **3** : WARLIKE

martial art *n* : any of several arts of combat (as karate and judo) practiced as sport

martial law *n* **1** : the law applied in occupied territory by the occupying military forces **2** : the established law of a country administered by military forces in an emergency when civilian law enforcement agencies are unable to maintain public order and safety

mar·tian \ˈmär-shən\ *adj, often cap* : of or relating to the planet Mars or its hypothetical inhabitants — **martian** *n, often cap*

mar·tin \ˈmär-tᵊn\ *n* : any of several swallows and esp. one of No. America with purplish blue plumage

mar·ti·net \ˌmär-tə-ˈnet\ *n* : a strict disciplinarian

mar·tin·gale \ˈmär-tᵊn-ˌgāl\ *n* : a strap connecting a horse's girth to the bit or reins so as to hold down its head

mar·ti·ni \mär-ˈtē-nē\ *n* : a cocktail made of gin or vodka and dry vermouth

¹mar·tyr \ˈmär-tər\ *n* [ME, fr. OE, fr. LL, fr. Gk *martyr-, martys* witness] **1** : a person who dies rather than renounce a religion; *also* : a person who makes a great sacrifice for the sake of principle **2** : a great or constant sufferer

²martyr *vb* **1** : to put to death for adhering to a belief **2** : TORTURE

mar·tyr·dom \ˈmär-tər-dəm\ *n* **1** : the suffering and death of a martyr **2** : TORTURE

¹mar·vel \ˈmär-vəl\ *n* **1** : one that causes wonder or astonishment **2** : intense surprise or interest

²marvel *vb* **mar·veled** *or* **mar·velled; mar·vel·ing** *or* **mar·vel·ling** : to feel surprise, wonder, or amazed curiosity ⟨~ed at the circus act⟩

mar·vel·ous *or* **mar·vel·lous** \ˈmär-və-ləs\ *adj* **1** : causing wonder **2** : of the highest kind or quality — **mar·vel·ous·ly** *adv* — **mar·vel·ous·ness** *n*

Marx·ism \ˈmärk-ˌsi-zəm\ *n* : the political, economic, and social principles and policies advocated by Karl Marx — **Marx·ist** \-sist\ *n or adj*

mar·zi·pan \ˈmärt-sə-ˌpän, -ˌpan; ˈmär-zə-ˌpan\ *n* [G, fr. It *marzapane*] : a confection of almond paste, sugar, and egg whites

masc *abbr* masculine

mas·cara \ma-ˈsker-ə\ *n* : a cosmetic esp. for darkening the eyelashes

mas·car·po·ne \ˌmas-kär-ˈpō-nā\ *n* : an Italian cream cheese

mas·cot \ˈmas-ˌkät, -kət\ *n* [F *mascotte,* fr. Occitan *mascoto,* fr. *masco* witch, fr. ML *masca*] : a person, animal, or object adopted usu. by a group to bring good luck

¹**mas·cu·line** \'mas-kyə-lən\ *adj* **1** : MALE; *also* : MANLY **2** : of, relating to, or constituting the gender that includes most words or grammatical forms referring to males — **mas·cu·lin·i·ty** \ˌmas-kyə-'li-nə-tē\ *n*

²**masculine** *n* : a noun, pronoun, adjective, or inflectional form or class of the masculine gender; *also* : the masculine gender

¹**mash** \'mash\ *n* **1** : a mixture of ground feeds for livestock **2** : crushed malt or grain steeped in hot water to make wort **3** : a soft pulpy mass

²**mash** *vb* **1** : to reduce to a soft pulpy state **2** : CRUSH, SMASH ⟨∼ a finger⟩ — **mash·er** *n*

MASH *abbr* mobile army surgical hospital

mash–up \'mash-ˌəp\ *n* : something created by combining elements from two or more sources

¹**mask** \'mask\ *n* **1** : a cover for the face usu. for disguise or protection **2** : MASQUE **3** : a figure of a head worn on the stage in antiquity **4** : a copy of a face made by means of a mold ⟨death ∼⟩ **5** : something that conceals or disguises : the face of an animal

²**mask** *vb* **1** : to conceal from view : DISGUISE **2** : to cover for protection

mask·er \'mas-kər\ *n* : a participant in a masquerade

mas·och·ism \'ma-sə-ˌki-zəm, 'ma-zə-\ *n* **1** : a sexual perversion characterized by pleasure in being subjected to pain or humiliation **2** : pleasure in being abused or dominated — **mas·och·ist** \-kist\ *n* — **mas·och·is·tic** \ˌma-sə-'kis-tik, ˌma-zə-\ *adj*

ma·son \'mā-sᵊn\ *n* **1** : a skilled worker who builds with stone, brick, or concrete **2** *cap* : FREEMASON

Ma·son·ic \mə-'sä-nik\ *adj* : of or relating to Freemasons or Freemasonry

ma·son·ry \'mā-sᵊn-rē\ *n, pl* **-ries** **1** : something constructed of materials used by masons **2** : the art, trade, or work of a mason **3** *cap* : FREEMASONRY

masque \'mask\ *n* **1** : MASQUERADE **2** : a short allegorical dramatic performance (as of the 17th century)

¹**mas·quer·ade** \ˌmas-kə-'rād\ *n* **1** : a social gathering of persons wearing masks; *also* : a costume for wear at such a gathering **2** : DISGUISE

²**masquerade** *vb* **-ad·ed; -ad·ing** **1** : to disguise oneself : POSE **2** : to take part in a masquerade — **mas·quer·ad·er** *n*

¹**mass** \'mas\ *n* **1** *cap* : a sequence of prayers and ceremonies forming the eucharistic service of the Roman Catholic Church **2** *often cap* : a celebration of the Eucharist **3** : a musical setting for parts of the Mass

²**mass** *n* **1** : a quantity or aggregate of matter usu. of considerable size **2** : EXPANSE, BULK; *also* : MASSIVENESS **3** : the principal part **4** : AGGREGATE, WHOLE **5** : the quantity of matter that a body possesses as measured by its inertia **6** : a

large quantity, amount, or number **7** : the great body of people — usu. used in pl. — **massy** *adj*

³**mass** *vb* : to form or collect into a mass

Mass *abbr* Massachusetts

mas·sa·cre \'ma-si-kər\ *n* **1** : the killing of many persons under cruel or atrocious circumstances **2** : a wholesale slaughter — **massacre** *vb*

¹**mas·sage** \mə-'säzh, -'säj\ *n* : manipulation of tissues (as by rubbing and kneading) for therapeutic purposes

²**massage** *vb* **mas·saged; mas·sag·ing** **1** : to subject to massage **2** : to treat flatteringly; *also* : MANIPULATE, DOCTOR ⟨∼ data⟩

mas·seur \ma-'sər\ *n* : a man who practices massage

mas·seuse \-'sərz, -'süz\ *n* : a woman who practices massage

mas·sif \ma-'sēf\ *n* : a principal mountain mass

mas·sive \'ma-siv\ *adj* **1** : forming or consisting of a large mass **2** : large in structure, scope, or degree — **mas·sive·ly** *adv* — **mas·sive·ness** *n*

mass·less \'mas-ləs\ *adj* : having no mass ⟨∼ particles⟩

mass medium *n, pl* **mass media** : a medium of communication (as the newspapers or television) that is designed to reach the mass of the people

mass–pro·duce \ˌmas-prə-'düs, -'dyüs\ *vb* : to produce in quantity usu. by machinery — **mass production** *n*

¹**mast** \'mast\ *n* **1** : a long pole or spar rising from the keel or deck of a ship and supporting the yards, booms, and rigging **2** : a slender vertical structure — **mast·ed** \'mas-təd\ *adj*

²**mast** *n* : nuts (as acorns) accumulated on the forest floor and often serving as food for animals (as hogs)

mas·tec·to·my \ma-'stek-tə-mē\ *n, pl* **-mies** : surgical removal of the breast

¹**mas·ter** \'mas-tər\ *n* **1** : a male teacher; *also* : a person holding an academic degree higher than a bachelor's but lower than a doctor's **2** : one highly skilled (as in an art or profession) **3** : one having authority or control **4** : VICTOR, SUPERIOR **5** : the commander of a merchant ship **6** : a youth or boy too young to be called *mister* — used as a title **7** : an original from which copies are made

²**master** *vb* **1** : to become master of : OVERCOME **2** : to become skilled or proficient in **3** : to produce a master recording of (as a musical performance)

master chief petty officer *n* : a petty officer of the highest rank in the navy

mas·ter·ful \'mas-tər-fəl\ *adj* **1** : inclined and usu. competent to act as master **2** : having or reflecting the skill of a master ⟨∼ verse⟩ — **mas·ter·ful·ly** *adv* — **mas·ter·ful·ness** *n*

master gunnery sergeant *n* : a noncommissioned officer in the marine corps ranking above a master sergeant

master key *n* : a key designed to open several different locks

mas·ter·ly \'mas-tər-lē\ *adj* **1** : indicating

thorough knowledge or superior skill ⟨∼ performance⟩ **2** : having the skill of a master ⟨a ∼ writer⟩ — **mas·ter·ly** adv

mas·ter·mind \'-ˌmīnd\ n : a person who directs or provides creative intelligence for a project — **mastermind** vb

master of ceremonies : a person who acts as host at a formal event or a program of entertainment

mas·ter·piece \'mas-tər-ˌpēs\ n : a work done with extraordinary skill

master plan n : an overall plan

mas·ter's \'mas-tərz\ n : a master's degree

master sergeant n **1** : a noncommissioned officer in the army ranking next below a sergeant major **2** : a noncommissioned officer in the air force ranking next below a senior master sergeant **3** : a noncommissioned officer in the marine corps ranking next below a master gunnery sergeant

mas·ter·stroke \'mas-tər-ˌstrōk\ n : a masterly performance or move

mas·ter·work \-ˌwərk\ n : MASTERPIECE

mas·tery \'mas-tə-rē\ n **1** : DOMINION; also : SUPERIORITY **2** : possession or display of great skill or knowledge

mast·head \'mast-ˌhed\ n **1** : the top of a mast **2** : the printed matter in a newspaper or periodical giving the title and details of ownership and rates of subscription or advertising

mas·tic \'mas-tik\ n : a pasty material used as a coating or cement

mas·ti·cate \'mas-tə-ˌkāt\ vb **-cat·ed; -cat·ing** : CHEW — **mas·ti·ca·tion** \ˌmas-tə-'kā-shən\ n

mas·tiff \'mas-təf\ n : any of a breed of large smooth-coated dogs used esp. as guard dogs

mast·odon \'mas-tə-ˌdän\ n [NL, fr. Gk mastos breast + odōn, odous tooth] : any of numerous huge extinct mammals related to the mammoths

mas·toid \'mas-ˌtȯid\ n : a bony prominence behind the ear — **mastoid** adj

mas·tur·ba·tion \ˌmas-tər-'bā-shən\ n : stimulation of the genital organs apart from sexual intercourse, usu. to orgasm, and esp. by use of one's own hand — **mas·tur·bate** \'mas-tər-ˌbāt\ vb — **mas·tur·ba·to·ry** \'mas-tər-bə-ˌtȯr-ē\ adj

¹mat \'mat\ n **1** : a piece of coarse woven or plaited fabric **2** : something made up of many intertwined strands **3** : a large thick pad used as a surface for wrestling and gymnastics

²mat vb **mat·ted; mat·ting 1** : to provide with a mat **2** : to form into a tangled mass ⟨dirt matted her hair⟩

³mat vb **mat·ted; mat·ting 1** also **matte** or **matt** : to make (as a color) matte **2** : to provide (a picture) with a mat

⁴mat var of ²MATTE

⁵mat or **matt** or **matte** n : a border going around a picture between picture and frame or serving as the frame

mat·a·dor \'ma-tə-ˌdȯr\ n [Sp, fr. matar to kill] : a bullfighter whose role is to kill the bull in a bullfight

¹match \'mach\ n **1** : a person or thing equal or similar to another; also : one able to cope with another : RIVAL **2** : a suitable pairing of persons or objects **3** : a contest or game between two or more individuals **4** : a marriage union; also : a prospective marriage partner — **match·less** adj

²match vb **1** : to meet as an antagonist; also : PIT ⟨∼ wits⟩ **2** : to provide with a worthy competitor; also : to set in comparison with **3** : MARRY **4** : to combine suitably or congenially ⟨∼ed the drapes with the rug⟩; also : ADAPT, SUIT **5** : to act in harmony ⟨his shoes and belt ∼⟩ **6** : to provide with a counterpart

³match n : a short slender piece of flammable material (as wood) tipped with a combustible mixture that ignites through friction

match·book \'mach-ˌbůk\ n : a small folder containing rows of paper matches

match·lock \-ˌläk\ n : a musket with a slow-burning cord lowered over a hole in the breech to ignite the charge

match·mak·er \-ˌmā-kər\ n : one who arranges a match and esp. a marriage

match·wood \-ˌwůd\ n : small pieces of wood

¹mate \'māt\ vb **mat·ed; mat·ing** : CHECKMATE — **mate** n

²mate n **1** : ASSOCIATE, COMPANION; also : HELPER **2** : a deck officer on a merchant ship ranking below the captain **3** : one of a pair; esp : either member of a married couple or a breeding pair of animals

³mate vb **mat·ed; mat·ing 1** : to join or fit together **2** : to come or bring together as mates **3** : COPULATE

¹ma·te·ri·al \mə-'tir-ē-əl\ adj **1** : PHYSICAL ⟨∼ world⟩; also : BODILY ⟨∼ needs⟩ **2** : of or relating to matter rather than form ⟨∼ cause⟩; also : EMPIRICAL ⟨∼ knowledge⟩ **3** : highly important : SIGNIFICANT ⟨∼ progress⟩ — **ma·te·ri·al·ly** adv

²material n **1** : the elements or substance of which something is composed or made **2** : apparatus necessary for doing or making something

ma·te·ri·al·ise Brit var of MATERIALIZE

ma·te·ri·al·ism \mə-'tir-ē-ə-ˌli-zəm\ n **1** : a theory that everything can be explained as being or coming from matter **2** : a preoccupation with material rather than intellectual or spiritual things — **ma·te·ri·al·ist** \-list\ n or adj — **ma·te·ri·al·is·tic** \-ˌtir-ē-ə-'lis-tik\ adj — **ma·te·ri·al·is·ti·cal·ly** \-ti-k(ə-)lē\ adv

ma·te·ri·al·ize \mə-'tir-ē-ə-ˌlīz\ vb **-ized; -iz·ing 1** : to give material form to; also : to assume bodily form **2** : to make an often unexpected appearance — **ma·te·ri·al·i·za·tion** \mə-ˌtir-ē-ə-lə-'zā-shən\ n

ma·té·ri·el or **ma·te·ri·el** \mə-ˌtir-ē-'el\ n [F matériel] : equipment, apparatus, and supplies used by an organization

ma·ter·nal \mə-'tər-n³l\ adj **1** : MOTHERLY **2** : related through or inherited or derived from a female parent ⟨his ∼ grandparents⟩ — **ma·ter·nal·ly** adv

¹ma·ter·ni·ty \mə-'tər-nə-tē\ n, pl **-ties 1**

: the quality or state of being a mother; *also* : MOTHERLINESS **2** : a hospital facility for the care of women before and during childbirth and for newborn babies

²**maternity** *adj* **1** : designed for wear during pregnancy ⟨a ~ dress⟩ **2** : effective for the period close to and including childbirth ⟨~ leave⟩

¹**math** \'math\ *n* : MATHEMATICS

²**math** *abbr* mathematical; mathematician

math·e·mat·ics \ˌma-thə-'ma-tiks\ *n* : the science of numbers and their properties, operations, and relations and with shapes in space and their structure and measurement — **math·e·mat·i·cal** \-'ma-ti-kəl\ *adj* — **math·e·mat·i·cal·ly** \-ti-k(ə-)lē\ *adv* — **math·e·ma·ti·cian** \ˌma-thə-mə-'ti-shən\ *n*

mat·i·nee *or* **mat·i·née** \ˌma-tə-'nā\ *n* [F *matinée*, lit., morning, fr. OF, fr. *matin* morning, fr. L *matutinum*, fr. neut. of *matutinus* of the morning, fr. *Matuta*, goddess of morning] : a musical or dramatic performance in the daytime and esp. the afternoon

mat·ins \'ma-tᵊnz\ *n pl, often cap* **1** : special prayers said between midnight and 4 a.m. **2** : a morning service of liturgical prayer in Anglican churches

ma·tri·arch \'mā-trē-ˌärk\ *n* : a woman who rules or dominates a family, group, or state — **ma·tri·ar·chal** \ˌmā-trē-'är-kəl\ *adj* — **ma·tri·ar·chy** \'mā-trē-ˌär-kē\ *n*

ma·tri·cide \'ma-trə-ˌsīd, 'mā-\ *n* : the murder of a mother by her child — **ma·tri·cid·al** \ˌma-trə-'sī-dᵊl, ˌmā-\ *adj*

ma·tric·u·late \mə-'tri-kyə-ˌlāt\ *vb* **-lat·ed; -lat·ing** : to enroll as a member of a body and esp. of a college or university — **ma·tric·u·la·tion** \-ˌtri-kyə-'lā-shən\ *n*

mat·ri·mo·ny \'ma-trə-ˌmō-nē\ *n* [ME, fr. AF *matrimoignie*, fr. L *matrimonium*, fr. *mater* mother, matron] : MARRIAGE — **mat·ri·mo·nial** \ˌma-trə-'mō-nē-əl\ *adj* — **mat·ri·mo·nial·ly** *adv*

ma·trix \'mā-triks\ *n, pl* **ma·tri·ces** \'mā-trə-ˌsēz, 'ma-\ *or* **ma·trix·es** \'mā-trik-səz\ **1** : something within or from which something else originates, develops, or takes form **2** : a mold from which a relief surface (as a piece of type) is made

ma·tron \'mā-trən\ *n* **1** : a married woman usu. of dignified maturity or social distinction **2** : a woman supervisor (as in a school or police station) — **ma·tron·ly** *adj*

Matt *abbr* Matthew

¹**matte** *or* **matt** *var of* ³MAT

²**matte** *also* **matt** \'mat\ *adj* : not shiny : DULL

¹**mat·ter** \'ma-tər\ *n* **1** : a subject of interest or concern **2** *pl* : events or circumstances of a particular situation **3** : the subject of a discourse or writing **4** : TROUBLE, DIFFICULTY ⟨what's the ~⟩ **5** : the substance of which a physical object is composed **6** : PUS **7** : an indefinite amount or quantity ⟨a ~ of a few days⟩ **8** : something written or printed **9** : MAIL — **as a matter of fact** : ACTUALLY — **no matter** : without regard to ⟨will follow

no matter where you go⟩ — **no matter what** : regardless of the consequences ⟨must win, *no matter what*⟩

²**matter** *vb* : to be of importance

mat·ter-of-fact \ˌma-tə-rəv-'fakt\ *adj* : adhering to fact; *also* : being plain, straightforward, or unemotional — **mat·ter-of-fact·ly** *adv* — **mat·ter-of-fact·ness** *n*

Mat·thew \'ma-thyü\ *n* — see BIBLE table

mat·tins *often cap, chiefly Brit var of* MATINS

mat·tock \'ma-tək\ *n* : a digging and grubbing tool with features of an adze and an ax or pick

mat·tress \'ma-trəs\ *n* **1** : a fabric case filled with resilient material used as or for a bed **2** : an inflatable airtight sack for use as a mattress

mat·u·rate \'ma-chə-ˌrāt\ *vb* **-rat·ed; -rat·ing** : MATURE

mat·u·ra·tion \ˌma-chə-'rā-shən\ *n* **1** : the process of becoming mature **2** : the emergence of personal and behavioral characteristics through growth processes — **mat·u·ra·tion·al** \-shə-nəl\ *adj*

¹**ma·ture** \mə-'túr, -'tyúr\ *adj* **ma·tur·er; -est** **1** : based on slow careful consideration **2** : having attained a final or desired state **3** : of or relating to a condition of full development **4** : suitable only for adults ⟨~ content⟩ **5** : due for payment — **ma·ture·ly** *adv*

²**mature** *vb* **ma·tured; ma·tur·ing** : to reach or bring to maturity or completion

ma·tu·ri·ty \mə-'túr-ə-tē, -'tyúr-\ *n* **1** : the quality or state of being mature; *esp* : full development **2** : the date when a note becomes due for payment

mat·u·ti·nal \ˌma-chü-'tī-nᵊl; mə-'tü-tə-nᵊl, -'tyü-\ *adj* : of, relating to, or occurring in the morning : EARLY

mat·zo *or* **mat·zoh** \'mät-sə\ *n, pl* **mat·zoth** \-ˌsōt, -ˌsōth, -sōs\ *or* **mat·zos** *or* **mat·zohs** [Yiddish *matse*, fr. Heb *maṣé ṣāh*] : unleavened bread eaten esp. at the Passover

maud·lin \'mȯd-lən\ *adj* [alter. of Mary *Magdalene;* fr. her depiction as a weeping, penitent sinner] **1** : drunk enough to be silly **2** : weakly and effusively sentimental ⟨a ~ love story⟩

¹**maul** \'mȯl\ *n* : a heavy hammer often with a wooden head used esp. for driving wedges

²**maul** *vb* **1** : BEAT, BRUISE; *also* : MANGLE **2** : to handle roughly

maun·der \'mȯn-dər\ *vb* **1** : to wander slowly and idly **2** : to speak indistinctly or disconnectedly

mau·so·le·um \ˌmȯ-sə-'lē-əm, ˌmȯ-zə-\ *n, pl* **-leums** *or* **-lea** \-'lē-ə\ [L, fr. Gk *mausōleion*, fr. *Mausōlos* Mausolus † *ab* 353 B.C. ruler of Caria whose tomb was one of the seven wonders of the ancient world] : a large tomb; *esp* : a usu. stone building for entombment of the dead above ground

mauve \'mōv, 'mȯv\ *n* : a moderate purple, violet, or lilac color

ma·ven *also* **ma·vin** \'mā-vən\ *n* [Yiddish *meyvn*, fr. LHeb *mēbhīn*] : EXPERT

mav·er·ick \'ma-vrik, -və-rik\ *n* [Samuel A. *Maverick* † 1870 Am. pioneer who did not brand his calves] **1** : an unbranded range animal **2** : NONCONFORMIST

maw \'mȯ\ *n* **1** : STOMACH; *also* : the crop of a bird **2** : the throat, gullet, or jaws esp. of a voracious animal

mawk·ish \'mȯ-kish\ *adj* : sickly sentimental ⟨~ poetry⟩ — **mawk·ish·ly** *adv* — **mawk·ish·ness** *n*

max *abbr* maximum

maxi \'mak-sē\ *n, pl* **max·is** : a long skirt, dress, or coat

maxi- *comb form* **1** : extra long ⟨*maxi*-kilt⟩ **2** : extra large ⟨*maxi*-problems⟩

max·il·la \mak-'si-lə\ *n, pl* **max·il·lae** \-'si-(,)lē\ *or* **maxillas** : JAW 1; *esp* : an upper jaw — **max·il·lary** \'mak-sə-,ler-ē\ *adj*

max·im \'mak-səm\ *n* : a proverbial saying

max·i·mal \'mak-sə-məl\ *adj* : MAXIMUM — **max·i·mal·ly** *adv*

max·i·mise *Brit var of* MAXIMIZE

max·i·mize \'mak-sə-,mīz\ *vb* **-mized; -miz·ing** **1** : to increase to a maximum **2** : to make the most of — **max·i·mi·za·tion** \,mak-sə-mə-'zā-shən\ *n*

max·i·mum \'mak-sə-məm\ *n, pl* **-ma** \-mə\ *or* **-mums** **1** : the greatest quantity, value, or degree **2** : an upper limit allowed by authority **3** : the largest of a set of numbers — **maximum** *adj*

max out *vb* **1** : to push to or reach a limit or an extreme **2** : to use up all available credit on (a credit card)

may \'mā\ *verbal auxiliary, past* **might** \'mīt\ *pres sing & pl* **may** **1** : have permission or liberty to ⟨you ~ go now⟩ **2** : be in some degree likely to ⟨you ~ be right⟩ **3** — used as an auxiliary to express a wish, purpose, contingency, or concession ⟨~ the best man win⟩

May \'mā\ *n* [ME, fr. OF *mai*, fr. L *Maius*, fr. *Maia*, Roman goddess] : the 5th month of the year

Ma·ya \'mī-ə\ *n, pl* **Maya** *or* **Mayas** : a member of a group of American Indian peoples of Yucatán, Guatemala, and adjacent areas — **Ma·yan** \'mī-ən\ *n or adj*

may·ap·ple \'mā-,a-pəl\ *n* : a No. American woodland herb related to the barberry that has a poisonous root, one or two large leaves, and an edible egg-shaped yellow fruit

may·be \'mā-bē, 'me-\ *adv* : PERHAPS

May Day \'mā-,dā\ *n* : May 1 celebrated as a springtime festival and in some countries as Labor Day

may·flow·er \'mā-,flau̇(-ə)r\ *n* : any of several spring blooming herbs (as the trailing arbutus or an anemone)

may·fly \'mā-flī\ *n* : any of an order of insects with an aquatic nymph and a short-lived fragile adult having membranous wings

may·hem \'mā-,hem, 'mā-əm\ *n* **1** : willful and permanent crippling, mutilation, or disfigurement of a person **2** : needless or wilful damage

may·on·naise \'mā-ə-,nāz\ *n* [F] : a dressing made of egg yolks, vegetable oil, and vinegar or lemon juice

may·or \'mā-ər\ *n* : an official elected to act as chief executive or nominal head of a city or borough — **may·or·al** \-əl\ *adj* — **may·or·al·ty** \-əl-tē\ *n*

may·pole \'mā-,pōl\ *n, often cap* : a tall flower-wreathed pole forming a center for May Day sports and dances

maze \'māz\ *n* : a confusing intricate network of passages — **mazy** *adj*

ma·zur·ka \mə-'zər-kə\ *n* : a Polish dance in moderate triple measure

MB *abbr* Manitoba

MBA *abbr* master of business administration

mc *abbr* megacycle

¹MC *n* : MASTER OF CEREMONIES

²MC *abbr* member of Congress

Mc- \mək; mə *before forms beginning with* k *or* g\ *prefix* : used to indicate a convenient, low-quality version of a specified thing ⟨*Mc*Book⟩

Mc·Coy \mə-'kȯi\ *n* : something that is neither imitation nor substitute ⟨the real ~⟩

McGuffin *var of* MACGUFFIN

MCPO *abbr* master chief petty officer

¹Md *abbr* Maryland

²Md *symbol* mendelevium

MD *abbr* **1** [NL *medicinae doctor*] doctor of medicine **2** Maryland **3** muscular dystrophy

MDMA \,em-,dē-,em-'ā\ *n* : ECSTASY 2

mdnt *abbr* midnight

mdse *abbr* merchandise

MDT *abbr* mountain daylight (saving) time

me \'mē\ *pron, objective case of* I

Me *abbr* Maine

ME *abbr* **1** Maine **2** mechanical engineer **3** medical examiner

¹mead \'mēd\ *n* : an alcoholic beverage brewed from water and honey, malt, and yeast

²mead *n, archaic* : MEADOW

mead·ow \'me-dō\ *n* : land in or mainly in grass; *esp* : a tract of moist low-lying usu. level grassland — **mead·ow·land** \-,land\ *n* — **mead·owy** \'me-də-wē\ *adj*

mead·ow·lark \'me-dō-,lärk\ *n* : any of several American songbirds related to the orioles that are streaked brown above and in northernmost forms have a yellow breast marked with a black crescent

mead·ow·sweet \-,swēt\ *n* : a No. American native or naturalized spirea

mea·ger *or* **mea·gre** \'mē-gər\ *adj* **1** : THIN **2** : lacking richness, fertility, or strength; *also* : POOR ⟨a ~ income⟩
♦ **Synonyms** SCANTY, SCANT, SPARE, SPARSE — **mea·ger·ly** *adv* — **mea·ger·ness** *n*

¹meal \'mēl\ *n* **1** : an act or the time of eating a portion of food **2** : the portion of food eaten at a meal

²meal *n* **1** : usu. coarsely ground seeds of a cereal **2** : a product resembling seed meal — **mealy** *adj*

meal·time \'mēl-,tīm\ *n* : the usual time at which a meal is served

mealy·bug \'mē-lē-,bəg\ *n* : any of a family of scale insects with a white cottony or waxy covering that are destructive pests esp. of fruit trees

mealy-mouthed \ˈmē-lē-ˌmau̇thd, -ˌmau̇tht\ *adj* : not plain and straightforward : DEVIOUS 〈a ~ politician〉

¹**mean** \ˈmēn\ *vb* **meant** \ˈment\; **meaning 1** : to have in the mind as a purpose **2** : to serve to convey, show, or indicate : SIGNIFY 〈red ~s stop〉 **3** : to have importance to the degree of 〈~s the world to me〉 **4** : to direct to a particular individual 〈a gift *meant* for me〉

²**mean** *adj* **1** : HUMBLE **2** : lacking acumen : DULL **3** : SHABBY, CONTEMPTIBLE 〈no ~ feat〉 **4** : IGNOBLE, BASE 〈a ~ trick〉 **5** : STINGY **6** : pettily selfish or malicious **7** : VEXATIOUS 〈a ~ dog〉 **8** : EXCELLENT 〈throws a ~ slider〉 — **mean-ly** *adv* — **mean-ness** *n*

³**mean** *adj* **1** : occupying a middle position (as in space, order, or time) **2** : being a mean : AVERAGE 〈a ~ value〉

⁴**mean** *n* **1** : a middle point between extremes **2** *pl* : something helpful in achieving a desired end **3** *pl* : material resources affording a secure life **4** : ARITHMETIC MEAN

¹**me-an-der** \mē-ˈan-dər\ *n* [L *maeander*, fr. Gk *maiandros*, fr. *Maiandros* (now *Menderes*), river in Asia Minor] **1** : a winding course **2** : a winding of a stream — **me-an-drous** \-drəs\ *adj*

²**meander** *vb* **1** : to follow a winding course **2** : to wander aimlessly or casually

mean-ing *n* **1** : the thing one intends to convey esp. by language; *also* : the thing that is thus conveyed **2** : AIM **3** : SIGNIFICANCE; *esp* : implication of a hidden significance **4** : CONNOTATION; *also* : DENOTATION — **mean-ing-ful** \-fəl\ *adj* — **mean-ing-ful-ly** *adv* — **mean-ing-less** *adj*

¹**mean-time** \ˈmēn-ˌtīm\ *n* : the intervening time

²**meantime** *adv* : MEANWHILE

¹**mean-while** \-ˌhwī(-ə)l\ *n* : MEANTIME

²**meanwhile** *adv* **1** : during the intervening time **2** : at the same time

meas *abbr* measure

mea-sles \ˈmē-zəlz\ *n sing or pl* : an acute virus disease marked by fever and an eruption of distinct circular red spots

mea-sly \ˈmēz-lē, -zə-lē\ *adj* **mea-sli-er; -est** : contemptibly small or insignificant

¹**mea-sure** \ˈme-zhər, ˈmā-\ *n* **1** : an adequate or moderate portion; *also* : a suitable limit **2** : the dimensions, capacity, or amount of something ascertained by measuring; *also* : an instrument for measuring **3** : a unit of measurement; *also* : a system of such units **4** : the act or process of measuring **5** : rhythmic structure or movement **6** : the part of a musical staff between two bars **7** : CRITERION **8** : a means to an end **9** : a legislative bill — **mea-sure-less** *adj*

²**measure** *vb* **mea-sured; mea-sur-ing 1** : to mark or fix in multiples of a specific unit 〈~ off five centimeters〉 **2** : to find out the size, extent, or amount of **3** : to

bring into comparison or competition **4** : to serve as a means of measuring **5** : to have a specified measurement — **mea-sur-able** \ˈme-zhə-rə-bəl, ˈmā-\ *adj* — **mea-sur-ably** \-blē\ *adv* — **mea-sur-er** *n*

mea-sure-ment \ˈme-zhər-mənt, ˈmā-\ *n* **1** : the act or process of measuring **2** : a figure, extent, or amount obtained by measuring

measure up *vb* **1** : to have necessary or fitting qualifications **2** : to equal esp. in ability

meat \ˈmēt\ *n* **1** : FOOD; *esp* : solid food as distinguished from drink **2** : animal and esp. mammal flesh considered as food **3** : the edible part inside a covering (as a shell or rind) — **meaty** *adj*

meat-ball \-ˌbȯl\ *n* : a small ball of chopped or ground meat

meat loaf *n* : a dish of ground meat seasoned and baked in the form of a loaf

mec-ca \ˈme-kə\ *n, often cap* [*Mecca*, Saudi Arabia, a destination of pilgrims in the Islamic world] : a center of a specified activity or interest 〈a shopping ~〉

mech *abbr* mechanical; mechanics

¹**me-chan-ic** \mi-ˈka-nik\ *adj* : of or relating to manual work or skill

²**mechanic** *n* **1** : a manual worker **2** : MACHINIST; *esp* : one who repairs cars

me-chan-i-cal \mi-ˈka-ni-kəl\ *adj* **1** : of or relating to machinery, to manual operations, or to mechanics **2** : done as if by a machine : AUTOMATIC 〈a ~ response〉 ♦ **Synonyms** INSTINCTIVE, IMPULSIVE, SPONTANEOUS — **me-chan-i-cal-ly** \-k(ə-)lē\ *adv*

mechanical drawing *n* : drawing done with the aid of instruments

me-chan-ics \mi-ˈka-niks\ *n sing or pl* **1** : a branch of physics that deals with energy and forces and their effect on bodies **2** : the practical application of mechanics (as to the operation of machines) **3** : mechanical or functional details 〈the ~ of the brain〉

mech-a-nism \ˈme-kə-ˌni-zəm\ *n* **1** : a piece of machinery; *also* : a process or technique for achieving a result **2** : mechanical operation or action **3** : the fundamental processes involved in or responsible for a natural phenomenon 〈the visual ~〉

mech-a-nis-tic \ˌme-kə-ˈnis-tik\ *adj* **1** : mechanically determined 〈~ universe〉 **2** : MECHANICAL — **mech-a-nis-ti-cal-ly** \-ti-k(ə-)lē\ *adv*

mech-a-nize \ˈme-kə-ˌnīz\ *vb* **-nized; -niz-ing 1** : to make mechanical **2** : to equip with machinery esp. in order to replace human or animal labor **3** : to equip with armed and armored motor vehicles — **mech-a-ni-za-tion** \ˌme-kə-nə-ˈzā-shən\ *n* — **mech-a-niz-er** *n*

¹**med** \ˈmed\ *adj* : MEDICAL 〈~ school〉

²**med** *n* : MEDICINE 1 — usu. used in pl.

³**med** *abbr* **1** medical; medicine **2** medieval **3** medium

MEd *abbr* master of education

med-al \ˈme-dᵊl\ *n* [MF *medaille*, fr. OIt *medaglia* coin worth half a denarius, medal, fr. VL *medalis half, alter. of LL medialis middle, fr. L medius] **1** : a small usu. metal object bearing a religious emblem or picture **2** : a piece of metal issued to commemorate a person or event or to award excellence or achievement

med·al·ist or **med·al·list** \'me-dᵊl-ist\ n **1** : a designer or maker of medals **2** : a recipient of a medal as an award

me·dal·lion \mə-'dal-yən\ n **1** : a large medal **2** : a tablet or panel bearing a portrait or an ornament

med·dle \'me-dᵊl\ vb **med·dled; med·dling** : to interfere without right or propriety — **med·dler** \'me-dᵊl-ər\ n

med·dle·some \'me-dᵊl-səm\ adj : inclined to meddle ⟨a ~ neighbor⟩

med·e·vac also **med·i·vac** \'me-də-,vak\ n **1** : emergency evacuation of the sick or wounded **2** : a helicopter used for medevac

me·dia \'mē-dē-ə\ n, pl **me·di·as 1** : MEDIUM 4 **2** sing or pl in constr : MASS MEDIA

me·di·al \'mē-dē-əl\ adj : occurring in or extending toward the middle

¹me·di·an \'mē-dē-ən\ n **1** : a value in an ordered set of values below and above which there are an equal number of values **2** : MEDIAN STRIP

²median adj **1** : being in the middle or in an intermediate position **2** : relating to or constituting a statistical median

median strip n : a strip dividing a highway into lanes according to the direction of travel

me·di·ate \'mē-dē-,āt\ vb **-at·ed; -at·ing 1** : to act as an intermediary; esp : to work with opposing sides in order to resolve (as a dispute) or bring about (as a settlement) **2** : to bring about, influence, or transmit (as a physical process or effect) by acting as an intermediate or controlling agent or mechanism ♦ Synonyms INTERCEDE, INTERVENE, INTERPOSE, INTERPOSE — **me·di·a·tion** \,mē-dē-'ā-shən\ n — **me·di·a·tor** \'mē-dē-,ā-tər\ n

med·ic \'me-dik\ n : one engaged in medical work; esp : CORPSMAN

med·i·ca·ble \'me-di-kə-bəl\ adj : CURABLE

Med·ic·aid \'me-di-,kād\ n : a program of financial assistance for medical care designed for those unable to afford regular medical service and financed jointly by the state and federal governments

med·i·cal \'me-di-kəl\ adj : of or relating to the science or practice of medicine or the treatment of disease — **med·i·cal·ly** \-k(ə-)lē\ adv

medical examiner n : a public officer who performs autopsies on bodies to find the cause of death

me·di·ca·ment \mi-'di-kə-mənt, 'me-di-kə-\ n : a substance used in therapy

Medi·care \'me-di-,ker\ n : a government program of financial assistance for medical care esp. for the aged

med·i·cate \'me-də-,kāt\ vb **-cat·ed; -cat·ing** : to treat with medicine

med·i·ca·tion \,me-də-'kā-shən\ n **1** : the act or process of medicating **2** : MEDICINE 1

me·dic·i·nal \mə-'di-sᵊn-əl\ adj : tending or used to cure disease or relieve pain — **me·dic·i·nal·ly** adv

med·i·cine \'me-də-sən\ n **1** : a substance or preparation used in treating disease **2** : a science and art dealing with the prevention, alleviation, and cure of disease

medicine ball n : a heavy stuffed leather ball used for conditioning exercises

medicine man n : a priestly healer or sorcerer esp. among the American Indians : SHAMAN

med·i·co \'me-di-,kō\ n, pl **-cos** : a medical practitioner or student

me·di·e·val also **me·di·ae·val** \,mē-dē-'ē-vəl, ,me-, mē-'dē-vəl\ adj **1** : of, relating to, or characteristic of the Middle Ages **2** : having a quality (as cruelty) associated with the Middle Ages **3** : extremely outmoded or antiquated — **me·di·e·val·ism** \-və-,li-zəm\ n — **me·di·e·val·ist** \-list\ n

me·di·o·cre \,mē-dē-'ō-kər\ adj [MF, fr. L mediocris, fr. medius middle + ocris stony mountain] : of moderate or low quality : ORDINARY ⟨did a ~ job⟩ — **me·di·oc·ri·ty** \-'ä-krə-tē\ n

med·i·tate \'me-də-,tāt\ vb **-tat·ed; -tat·ing 1** : to muse over : CONTEMPLATE, PONDER **2** : to engage in deep mental exercise directed toward a heightened level of spiritual awareness **3** : INTEND, PLAN — **med·i·ta·tion** \,me-də-'tā-shən\ n — **med·i·ta·tive** \'me-də-,tā-tiv\ adj — **med·i·ta·tive·ly** adv

Med·i·ter·ra·nean \,me-də-tə-'rā-nē-ən, -'rā-nyən\ adj : of or relating to the Mediterranean Sea or to the lands or people around it

¹me·di·um \'mē-dē-əm\ n, pl **mediums** or **me·dia** \-dē-ə\ [L] **1** : something in a middle position; also : a middle position or degree **2** : a means of effecting or conveying something **3** : a surrounding or enveloping substance **4** : a channel or system of communication, information, or entertainment **5** : a mode of artistic expression **6** : an individual held to be a channel of communication between the earthly world and a world of spirits **7** : a condition or environment in which something may function or flourish

²medium adj : intermediate in amount, quality, position, or degree

me·di·um·is·tic \,mē·dē-ə-'mis-tik\ adj : of, relating to, or being a spiritualistic medium

medivac var of MEDEVAC

med·ley \'med-lē\ n, pl **medleys 1** : HODGEPODGE **2** : a musical composition made up esp. of a series of songs

me·dul·la \mə-'də-lə\ n, pl **-las** or **-lae** \-(,)lē, -,lī\ : an inner or deep anatomical part; also : the posterior part (**medulla ob·lon·ga·ta** \-,ä-,blòn-'gä-tə\) of the vertebrate brain that is continuous with the spinal cord

meed \'mēd\ n : a fitting return

meek \'mēk\ adj **1** : enduring injury with patience and without resentment **2** : de-

ficient in spirit and courage **3** : MODER-
ATE — **meek·ly** *adv* — **meek·ness** *n*

meer·schaum \'mir-shəm, -ˌshȯm\ *n* [G,
fr. *Meer* sea + *Schaum* foam] : a tobacco
pipe made of a light white clayey mineral

¹**meet** \'mēt\ *vb* **met** \'met\; **meet·ing**
1 : to come upon : FIND **2** : JOIN, INTER-
SECT **3** : to appear to the perception of **4**
: OPPOSE, FIGHT **5** : to join in conversation or discussion; *also* : ASSEMBLE **6** : to
conform to ⟨∼s requirements⟩ **7** : to
pay fully **8** : to cope with **9** : to provide
for **10** : to be introduced to

²**meet** *n* : an assembling esp. for a hunt or
for competitive sports

³**meet** *adj* : SUITABLE, PROPER

meet·ing \'mē-tiŋ\ *n* **1** : an act of coming
together : ASSEMBLY **2** : JUNCTION, IN-
TERSECTION

meet·ing·house \-ˌhau̇s\ *n* : a building
for public assembly and esp. for Protestant worship

meg \'meg\ *n* : MEGABYTE

mega- *or* **meg-** *comb form* **1** : great
: large ⟨*megahit*⟩ **2** : million ⟨*megahertz*⟩

mega·byte \'me-gə-ˌbīt\ *n* : 1024 kilo-
bytes or 1,048,576 bytes; *also* : one million bytes

mega·cy·cle \-ˌsī-kəl\ *n* : MEGAHERTZ

mega·death \-ˌdeth\ *n* : one million
deaths — used as a unit in reference to
nuclear warfare

mega·hertz \'me-gə-ˌhərts, -ˌherts\ *n* : a
unit of frequency equal to one million
hertz

mega·lith \'me-gə-ˌlith\ *n* : a large stone
used in prehistoric monuments — **mega·
lith·ic** \ˌme-gə-ˈli-thik\ *adj*

meg·a·lo·ma·nia \ˌme-gə-lō-ˈmā-nē-ə,
-nyə\ *n* : a mental disorder marked by
feelings of personal omnipotence and
grandeur — **meg·a·lo·ma·ni·ac** \-ˈmā-
nē-ˌak\ *adj or n* — **meg·a·lo·ma·ni·a·cal**
\-mə-ˈnī-ə-kəl\ *adj*

meg·a·lop·o·lis \ˌme-gə-ˈlä-pə-ləs\ *n* : a
very large urban unit

mega·phone \'me-gə-ˌfōn\ *n* : a cone-
shaped device used to intensify or direct
the voice — **megaphone** *vb*

mega·pix·el \'me-gə-ˌpik-səl\ *n* : one million pixels

mega·plex \-ˌpleks\ *n* : a cineplex having
usu. at least 16 movie theaters

mega·ton \-ˌtən\ *n* : an explosive force
equivalent to that of one million tons of
TNT

mega·vi·ta·min \-ˌvī-tə-mən\ *adj* : relating to or consisting of very large doses of
vitamins — **mega·vi·ta·mins** *n pl*

meh \'me\ *interj* — used to express indifference or mild disappointment

mei·o·sis \mī-ˈō-səs\ *n* : a process of cell
division in gamete-producing cells in
which the number of chromosomes is reduced to one half — **mei·ot·ic** \mī-ˈä-tik\
adj

meit·ner·i·um \mīt-ˈnir-ē-əm, -ˈner-\ *n*
: an artificially produced radioactive
chemical element

mel·an·cho·lia \ˌme-lən-ˈkō-lē-ə\ *n* : a

mental condition marked by extreme depression often with delusions

mel·an·chol·ic \ˌme-lən-ˈkä-lik\ *adj* **1**
: DEPRESSED **2** : of or relating to melan-
cholia

mel·an·choly \'me-lən-ˌkä-lē\ *n, pl* **-chol-
ies** [ME *malencolie*, fr. AF, fr. LL *melan-
cholia*, fr. Gk, fr. *melan-, melas* black +
cholē bile; so called fr. the former belief
that it was caused by an excess of black
bile] : depression of spirits : DEJECTION
— **melancholy** *adj*

Mel·a·ne·sian \ˌme-lə-ˈnē-zhən\ *n* : a
member of the dominant native group of
the Pacific island grouping of Melanesia
— **Melanesian** *adj*

mé·lange \mā-ˈlä⁴zh, -ˈlänj\ *n* : a mixture
esp. of incongruous elements

mel·a·nin \'me-lə-nən\ *n* : any of various
dark brown pigments of animal or plant
structures (as skin or hair)

mel·a·nism \'me-lə-ˌni-zəm\ *n* : an increased amount of black or nearly black
pigmentation

mel·a·no·ma \ˌme-lə-ˈnō-mə\ *n, pl* **-mas**
also **-ma·ta** \-mə-tə\ : a usu. malignant
tumor containing dark pigment

¹**meld** \'meld\ *vb* : to show or announce
for a score in a card game

²**meld** *n* : a card or combination of cards
that is or can be melded

me·lee \'mā-ˌlā, mā-ˈlā\ *n* [F *mêlée*] : a
confused struggle ♦ **Synonyms** FRA-
CAS, ROW, BRAWL, DONNYBROOK

me·lio·rate \'mēl-yə-ˌrāt, 'mē-lē-ə-\ *vb*
-rat·ed; -rat·ing : AMELIORATE — **me·
lio·ra·tion** \ˌmēl-yə-ˈrā-shən, ˌmē-lē-ə-\
n — **me·lio·ra·tive** \'mēl-yə-ˌrā-tiv, 'mē-lē-
ə-\ *adj*

mel·lif·lu·ous \me-ˈli-flə-wəs, mə-\ *adj*
[ME *mellyfluous*, fr. LL *mellifluus*, fr. L
mel honey + *fluere* to flow] : sweetly flowing ⟨a ∼ voice⟩ — **mel·lif·lu·ous·ly** *adv*
— **mel·lif·lu·ous·ness** *n*

¹**mel·low** \'me-lō\ *adj* **1** : soft aged and
sweet because of ripeness; *also* : well aged and
pleasingly mild ⟨∼ wine⟩ **2** : made gentle by age or experience **3** : being rich
and full but not garish or strident ⟨∼
colors⟩ **4** : of soft loamy consistency ⟨∼
soil⟩ — **mel·low·ness** *n*

²**mellow** *vb* : to make or become mellow
— often used with *out*

me·lo·di·ous \mə-ˈlō-dē-əs\ *adj* : pleasing
to the ear ⟨∼ chimes⟩ — **me·lo·di·ous·
ly** *adv* — **me·lo·di·ous·ness** *n*

melo·dra·ma \'me-lə-ˌdrä-mə, -ˌdra-\ *n* **1**
: an extravagantly theatrical play in
which action and plot predominate over
characterization **2** : something having a
sensational or theatrical quality — **melo·
dra·mat·ic** \ˌme-lə-drə-ˈma-tik\ *adj* —
melo·dra·mat·i·cal·ly \-ti-k(ə-)lē\ *adv* —
melo·dra·ma·tist \ˌme-lə-ˈdra-mə-tist,
-ˈdrä-\ *n*

mel·o·dy \'me-lə-dē\ *n, pl* **-dies** **1** : sweet
or agreeable sound **2** : a particular succession of notes : TUNE, AIR — **me·lod·ic**
\mə-ˈlä-dik\ *adj* — **me·lod·i·cal·ly** \-di-
k(ə-)lē\ *adv*

mel·on \'me-lən\ *n* : any of various typically sweet fruits (as a muskmelon or

447

watermelon) of the gourd family usu. eaten raw

¹melt \'melt\ *vb* **1** : to change from a solid to a liquid state usu. by heat **2** : DISSOLVE, DISINTEGRATE; *also* : to cause to disperse or disappear ⟨her anger ~*ed* away⟩ **3** : to make or become tender or gentle

²melt *n* : a melted substance

melt·down \'melt-ˌdau̇n\ *n* **1** : the melting of the core of a nuclear reactor **2** : a collapse of something (as one's self-control)

melting pot *n* : a place where different races, cultures, or individuals assimilate into a cohesive whole

melt·wa·ter \-ˌwȯ-tər, -ˌwä-\ *n* : water derived from the melting of ice and snow

mem *abbr* **1** member **2** memoir **3** memorial

mem·ber \'mem-bər\ *n* **1** : a part (as an arm, leg, leaf, or branch) of an animal or plant **2** : one of the individuals composing a group **3** : a part of a whole ⟨~*s* of a set⟩

mem·ber·ship \-ˌship\ *n* **1** : the state or status of being a member **2** : the body of members

mem·brane \'mem-ˌbrān\ *n* : a thin pliable layer esp. of animal or plant origin — **mem·bra·nous** \-brə-nəs\ *adj*

me·men·to \mə-'men-tō\ *n, pl* **-tos** *or* **-toes** [ME, fr. L, remember, imper. of *meminisse* to remember]: something that serves to warn or remind; *also* : SOUVENIR

memo \'me-mō\ *n, pl* **mem·os** : MEMORANDUM

mem·oir \'mem-ˌwär\ *n* **1** : MEMORANDUM **2** : AUTOBIOGRAPHY — usu. used in pl. **3** : an account of something noteworthy; *also, pl* : the record of the proceedings of a learned society

mem·o·ra·bil·ia \ˌme-mə-rə-'bi-lē-ə, -'bil-yə\ *n pl* [L] **1** : things worthy of remembrance **2** : things associated with a particular interest and that are usu. collected : MEMENTOS

mem·o·ra·ble \'me-mə-rə-bəl\ *adj* : worth remembering : NOTABLE ⟨a ~ quotation⟩ — **mem·o·ra·bil·i·ty** \ˌme-mə-rə-ˈbi-lə-tē\ *n* — **mem·o·ra·ble·ness** *n* — **mem·o·ra·bly** \-blē\ *adv*

mem·o·ran·dum \ˌme-mə-'ran-dəm\ *n, pl* **-dums** *or* **-da** \-də\ **1** : an informal record; *also* : a written reminder **2** : an informal written note

¹me·mo·ri·al \mə-'mȯr-ē-əl\ *adj* : serving to preserve remembrance

²memorial *n* **1** : something designed to keep remembrance alive; *esp* : MONUMENT **2** : a statement of facts often accompanied with a petition — **me·mo·ri·al·ize** *vb*

Memorial Day *n* : the last Monday in May or formerly May 30 observed as a legal holiday in honor of those who died in war

mem·o·rise *Brit var of* MEMORIZE

mem·o·rize \'me-mə-ˌrīz\ *vb* **-rized; -rizing** : to learn by heart — **mem·o·ri·za-**

tion \ˌme-mə-rə-'zā-shən\ *n* — **mem·o·riz·er** *n*

mem·o·ry \'me-mə-rē\ *n, pl* **-ries** **1** : the power or process of remembering **2** : the store of things remembered **3** : COMMEMORATION **4** : something remembered **5** : the time within which past events are remembered **6** : a device (as in a computer) in which information can be stored; *esp* : RAM **7** : capacity for storing information ⟨512 megabytes of ~⟩
♦ **Synonyms** REMEMBRANCE, RECOLLECTION, REMINISCENCE

men *pl of* MAN

¹men·ace \'me-nəs\ *n* **1** : THREAT **2** : DANGER ⟨those dogs are a ~⟩; *also* : NUISANCE

²menace *vb* **men·aced; men·ac·ing** **1** : THREATEN **2** : ENDANGER — **men·ac·ing·ly** *adv*

mé·nage \mā-'näzh\ *n* [F] : HOUSEHOLD

ménage à trois \-ä-'trwä\ *n* : an arrangement in which three persons share sexual relations esp. while living together

me·nag·er·ie \mə-'na-jə-rē\ *n* : a collection of wild animals esp. for exhibition

¹mend \'mend\ *vb* **1** : to improve in manners or morals **2** : to put into good shape : REPAIR **3** : to improve in or restore to health : HEAL — **mend·er** *n*

²mend *n* **1** : an act of mending **2** : a mended place

men·da·cious \men-'dā-shəs\ *adj* : given to deception or falsehood : UNTRUTHFUL
♦ **Synonyms** DISHONEST, DECEITFUL — **men·da·cious·ly** *adv* — **men·dac·i·ty** \-'da-sə-tē\ *n*

men·de·le·vi·um \ˌmen-də-'lē-vē-əm, -'lā-\ *n* : a radioactive metallic chemical element artificially produced

men·di·cant \'men-di-kənt\ *n* **1** : BEGGAR **2** *often cap* : FRIAR — **men·di·can·cy** \-kən-sē\ *n* — **mendicant** *adj*

men·folk \'men-ˌfōk\ *or* **men·folks** \-ˌfōks\ *n pl* **1** : men in general **2** : the men of a family or community

men·ha·den \men-'hā-dᵊn, mən-\ *n, pl* **-den** *also* **-dens** : a marine fish related to the herring that is abundant along the Atlantic coast of the U.S.

¹me·nial \'mē-nē-əl, -nyəl\ *n* : a domestic servant

²menial *adj* **1** : of or relating to servants **2** : HUMBLE, SERVILE ⟨answered in ~ tones⟩ — **me·ni·al·ly** *adv*

men·in·gi·tis \ˌme-nən-'jī-təs, *n, pl* **-git·i·des** \-'ji-tə-ˌdēz\ *also* **men·in·gi·ti·des** : inflammation of the membranes enclosing the brain and spinal cord; *also* : a usu. bacterial disease marked by this

me·ninx \'mē-niŋks, 'me-\ *n, pl* **me·nin·ges** \mə-'nin-(ˌ)jēz\ : any of the three membranes that envelop the brain and spinal cord — **men·in·ge·al** \ˌme-nən-'jē-əl\ *adj*

me·nis·cus \mə-'nis-kəs\ *n, pl* **me·nis·ci** \-'nis-ˌkī, -ˌkē\ *also* **me·nis·cus·es** **1** : CRESCENT **2** : the curved upper surface of a column of liquid

men·o·pause \'me-nə-ˌpȯz\ *n* : the period of life when menstruation stops natu-

rally — **men·o·paus·al** \ˌme-nə-ˈpȯ-zəl\ *adj*

me·no·rah \mə-ˈnȯr-ə\ *n* [Heb *měnōrāh* candlestick] : a candelabrum that is used in Jewish worship

men·ses \ˈmen-ˌsēz\ *n sing or pl* : the menstrual flow

menstrual cycle *n* : the complete cycle of physiological changes from the beginning of one menstrual period to the beginning of the next

men·stru·a·tion \ˌmen-strə-ˈwā-shən, men-ˈstrā-\ *n* : a discharging of bloody matter at approximately monthly intervals from the uterus of breeding-age nonpregnant primate females; *also* : PERIOD 6 — **men·stru·al** \ˈmen-strə-wəl\ *adj* — **men·stru·ate** \ˈmen-strə-ˌwāt, -ˌstrāt\ *vb*

men·su·ra·ble \ˈmen-sə-rə-bəl, ˈ-chə-\ *adj* : MEASURABLE

men·su·ra·tion \ˌmen-sə-ˈrā-shən, ˌmen-chə-\ *n* : MEASUREMENT

-ment *n suffix* **1** : concrete result, object, or agent of a (specified) action ⟨embank*ment*⟩ ⟨entangle*ment*⟩ **2** : concrete means or instrument of a (specified) action ⟨entertain*ment*⟩ **3** : action : process ⟨encircle*ment*⟩ ⟨develop*ment*⟩ **4** : place of a (specified) action ⟨encamp*ment*⟩ **5** : state : condition ⟨amaze*ment*⟩

men·tal \ˈmen-tᵊl\ *adj* **1** : of or relating to the mind **2** : of, relating to, or affected with a disorder of the mind ⟨∼ illness⟩ — **men·tal·ly** *adv*

mental age *n* : a measure of a child's mental development in terms of the number of years it takes an average child to reach the same level

mental deficiency *n* : MENTAL RETARDATION

men·tal·i·ty \men-ˈta-lə-tē\ *n, pl* **-ties** **1** : mental power or capacity **2** : mode or way of thought

mental retardation *n* : subaverage intellectual ability present from infancy that is characterized by an IQ of 70 or less and problems in development, learning, and social adjustment — **mentally retarded** *adj*

men·tee \men-ˈtē\ *n* : PROTÉGÉ

men·thol \ˈmen-ˌthȯl, -ˌthōl\ *n* : an alcohol occurring esp. in mint oils that has the odor and cooling properties of peppermint — **men·tho·lat·ed** \-thə-ˌlā-təd\ *adj*

¹men·tion \ˈmen-chən\ *n* **1** : a brief or casual reference **2** : a formal citation for outstanding achievement

²mention *vb* **1** : to refer to : CITE **2** : to cite for superior achievement — **not to mention** : not even yet counting or considering

men·tor \ˈmen-ˌtȯr, -tər\ *n* : a trusted counselor or guide; *also* : TUTOR, COACH — **mentor** *vb*

menu \ˈmen-yü, ˈmān-\ *n, pl* **menus** [F, fr. *menu* small, detailed, fr. OF, fr. L *minutus* minute (adj.)] **1** : a list of the dishes available (as in a restaurant) for a meal; *also* : the dishes served **2** : a list of offerings or options

me·ow \mē-ˈȧu̇\ *vb* : to make the characteristic cry of a cat — **meow** *n*

mer *abbr* meridian

mer·can·tile \ˈmər-kən-ˌtēl, -ˌtī(-ə)l\ *adj* : of or relating to merchants or trading

¹mer·ce·nary \ˈmər-sə-ˌner-ē\ *n, pl* **-nar·ies** : a person who serves merely for wages; *esp* : a soldier hired into foreign service

²mercenary *adj* **1** : serving merely for pay or gain **2** : hired for service in a foreign army

mer·cer \ˈmər-sər\ *n, Brit* : a dealer in usu. expensive fabrics

mer·cer·ise *Brit var of* MERCERIZE

mer·cer·ize \ˈmər-sə-ˌrīz\ *vb* **-ized; -iz·ing** : to treat cotton yarn or cloth with alkali so that it looks silky or takes a better dye

¹mer·chan·dise \ˈmər-chən-ˌdīz, -ˌdīs\ *n* : the commodities or goods that are bought and sold in business

²mer·chan·dise \-ˌdīz\ *vb* **-dised; -dis·ing** : to buy and sell in business : TRADE — **mer·chan·dis·er** *n*

mer·chant \ˈmər-chənt\ *n* **1** : a buyer and seller of commodities for profit **2** : STOREKEEPER

mer·chant·able \ˈmər-chən-tə-bəl\ *adj* : acceptable to buyers : MARKETABLE

mer·chant·man \ˈmər-chənt-mən\ *n* : a ship used in commerce

merchant marine *n* : the commercial ships of a nation

merchant ship *n* : MERCHANTMAN

mer·ci·ful·ly \ˈmər-si-fə-lē\ *adv* **1** : in a merciful manner **2** : FORTUNATELY 2 ⟨∼ we didn't have to attend⟩

mer·cu·ri·al \ˌmər-ˈkyu̇r-ē-əl\ *adj* **1** : unpredictably changeable ⟨a ∼ personality⟩ **2** : MERCURIC — **mer·cu·ri·al·ly** *adv* — **mer·cu·ri·al·ness** *n*

mer·cu·ric \ˌmər-ˈkyu̇r-ik\ *adj* : of, relating to, or containing mercury

mercuric chloride *n* : a poisonous compound of mercury and chlorine used as an antiseptic and fungicide

mer·cu·ry \ˈmər-kyə-rē\ *n, pl* **-ries** **1** : a heavy silver-white liquid metallic chemical element used esp. in scientific instruments **2** *cap* : the planet nearest the sun

mer·cy \ˈmər-sē\ *n, pl* **mercies** [ME, fr. AF *merci*, fr. ML *merced-, merces*, fr. L, price paid, wages, fr. *merc-, merx* merchandise] **1** : compassion shown to an offender; *also* : imprisonment rather than death for first-degree murder **2** : a blessing resulting from divine favor or compassion; *also* : a fortunate circumstance **3** : compassion shown to victims of misfortune — **mer·ci·ful** \-si-fəl\ *adj* — **mer·ci·less** \-si-ləs\ *adj* — **mer·ci·less·ly** *adv* — **mercy** *adj*

mercy killing *n* : EUTHANASIA

¹mere \ˈmir\ *n* : LAKE, POOL

²mere *adj, superlative* **mer·est** **1** : not diluted : PURE **2** : being nothing more than ⟨a ∼ child⟩ — **mere·ly** *adv*

mer·e·tri·cious \ˌmer-ə-ˈtri-shəs\ *adj* [L *meretricius*, fr. *meretrix* prostitute, fr. *merēre* to earn] : tawdrily attractive ⟨∼

trinkets); *also* : SPECIOUS — **mer·e·tri·cious·ly** *adv* — **mer·e·tri·cious·ness** *n*

mer·gan·ser \(ˌ)mər-ˈgan-sər\ *n* : any of various fish-eating wild ducks with a usu. crested head and a slender bill hooked at the end and serrated along the margins

merge \ˈmərj\ *vb* **merged**; **merg·ing** **1** : to blend gradually **2** : to combine, unite, or coalesce into one ✦ **Synonyms** MINGLE, AMALGAMATE, FUSE, INTERFUSE, INTERMINGLE

merg·er \ˈmər-jər\ *n* **1** : the act or process of merging **2** : absorption by a corporation of one or more others

me·rid·i·an \mə-ˈri-dē-ən\ *n* [ME, fr. AF *meridien*, fr. *meridien* of noon, fr. L *meridianus*, fr. *meridies* noon, south, irreg. fr. *medius* mid + *dies* day] **1** : the highest point : CULMINATION **2** : any of the imaginary circles on the earth's surface passing through the north and south poles **3** : any of the pathways along which the body's vital energy flows according to the theory behind acupuncture — **meridian** *adj*

me·ringue \mə-ˈraŋ\ *n* [F] : a baked dessert topping of stiffly beaten egg whites and powdered sugar

me·ri·no \mə-ˈrē-nō\ *n, pl* **-nos** [Sp] **1** : any of a breed of sheep noted for fine soft wool **2** : a fine soft fabric or yarn of wool or wool and cotton

¹**mer·it** \ˈmer-ət\ *n* **1** : laudable or blameworthy traits or actions **2** : a praiseworthy quality; *also* : character or conduct deserving reward or honor **3** *pl* : the intrinsic nature of a legal case; *also* : legal significance

²**merit** *vb* : EARN, DESERVE

mer·i·toc·ra·cy \ˌmer-ə-ˈtä-krə-sē\ *n, pl* **-cies** : a system in which the talented are chosen and moved ahead based on their achievement; *also* : leadership by the talented

mer·i·to·ri·ous \ˌmer-ə-ˈtȯr-ē-əs\ *adj* : deserving honor or esteem — **mer·i·to·rious·ly** *adv* — **mer·i·to·ri·ous·ness** *n*

mer·lin \ˈmər-lən\ *n* : a small compact falcon of the northern hemisphere

mer·lot \mer-ˈlō, mər-\ *n* : a dry red wine made from a widely grown grape; *also* : the grape itself

mer·maid \ˈmər-ˌmād\ *n* : a legendary sea creature with a woman's upper body and a fish's tail

mer·man \-ˌman, -mən\ *n* : a legendary sea creature with a man's upper body and a fish's tail

mer·ri·ment \ˈmer-i-mənt\ *n* **1** : HILARITY **2** : FESTIVITY

mer·ry \ˈmer-ē\ *adj* **mer·ri·er**; **-est** **1** : full of gaiety or high spirits **2** : marked by festivity **3** : BRISK 〈a ~ pace〉 ✦ **Synonyms** BLITHE, JOCUND, JOVIAL, JOLLY, MIRTHFUL

merry–go–round \ˈmer-ē-gō-ˌrau̇nd\ *n* **1** : a circular revolving platform with benches and figures of animals on which people sit for a ride **2** : a busy round of activities

mer·ry·mak·ing \ˈmer-ē-ˌmā-kiŋ\ *n* **1**

: jovial or festive activity **2** : a festive occasion — **mer·ry·mak·er** \-ˌmā-kər\ *n*

me·sa \ˈmā-sə\ *n* [Sp, lit., table, fr. L *mensa*] : a flat-topped hill with steep sides

mes·cal \me-ˈskal, mə-\ *n* **1** : PEYOTE **2** **2** : a usu. colorless liquor distilled from the leaves of an agave; *also* : this agave

mes·ca·line \ˈmes-kə-lən, -ˌlēn\ *n* : a hallucinatory alkaloid from the peyote cactus

mes·clun \ˈmes-klən\ *n* : a mixture of young tender greens; *also* : a salad made with mesclun

mes·dames *pl of* MADAM *or of* MADAME *or of* MRS.

mes·de·moi·selles *pl of* MADEMOISELLE

¹**mesh** \ˈmesh\ *n* **1** : one of the openings between the threads or cords of a net; *also* : one of the similar spaces in a network **2** : the fabric of a net **3** : NETWORK **4** : working contact (as of the teeth of gears) 〈in ~〉 — **meshed** \ˈmesht\ *adj*

²**mesh** *vb* **1** : to catch in or as if in a mesh **2** : to be in or come into mesh : ENGAGE **3** : to fit together properly

mesh·work \ˈmesh-ˌwərk\ *n* : NETWORK

me·si·al \ˈmē-zē-əl, -sē-\ *adj* : of, relating to, or being the surface of a tooth that is closest to the middle of the front of the jaw

mes·mer·ise *Brit var of* MESMERIZE

mes·mer·ize \ˈmez-mə-ˌrīz\ *vb* **-ized**; **-izing** : HYPNOTIZE — **mes·mer·ic** \mez-ˈmer-ik\ *adj* — **mes·mer·ism** \ˈmez-mə-ˌri-zəm\ *n*

Me·so·lith·ic \ˌme-zə-ˈli-thik\ *adj* : of, relating to, or being a transitional period of the Stone Age between the Paleolithic and the Neolithic periods

me·so·sphere \ˈme-zə-ˌsfir\ *n* : a layer of the atmosphere between the stratosphere and the thermosphere

Me·so·zo·ic \ˌme-zə-ˈzō-ik, ˌmē-\ *adj* : of, relating to, or being the era of geologic history between the Paleozoic and the Cenozoic and extending from about 245 million years ago to about 65 million years ago — **Mesozoic** *n*

mes·quite \mə-ˈskēt, me-\ *n* : any of several spiny leguminous trees and shrubs chiefly of the southwestern U.S. with sugar-rich pods important as fodder; *also* : mesquite wood used esp. in grilling food

¹**mess** \ˈmes\ *n* [ME *mes*, fr. AF, fr. LL *missus* course at a meal, fr. *missus*, pp. of *mittere* to put, fr. L, to send] **1** : a quantity of food; *also* : enough food of a specified kind for a dish or meal 〈a ~ of beans〉 **2** : a group of persons who regularly eat together; *also* : a meal eaten by such a group **3** : a place where meals are regularly served to a group **4** : a confused, dirty, or offensive state — **messy** *adj*

²**mess** *vb* **1** : to supply with meals; *also* : to take meals with a mess **2** : to make dirty or untidy; *also* : BUNGLE **3** : INTERFERE, MEDDLE 〈don't ~ with me〉 **4** : PUTTER, TRIFLE

mes·sage \ˈme-sij\ *n* : a communication sent by one person to another

message board *n* : BULLETIN BOARD 2

messeigneurs *pl of* MONSEIGNEUR

mes·sen·ger \'me-sᵊn-jər\ *n* : one who carries a message or does an errand

messenger RNA *n* : an RNA that carries the code for a particular protein from DNA in the nucleus to a ribosome in the cytoplasm and acts as a template for the formation of that protein

Mes·si·ah \mə-'sī-ə\ *n* **1** : the expected king and deliverer of the Jews **2** : Jesus **3** *not cap* : a professed or accepted leader of a cause — **mes·si·an·ic** \ˌme-sē-'a-nik\ *adj*

messieurs *pl of* MONSIEUR

mess·mate \'mes-ˌmāt\ *n* : a member of a group who eat regularly together

Messrs. \'me-sərz\ *pl of* MR.

mes·ti·zo \me-'stē-zō\ *n, pl* **-zos** [Sp] : a person of mixed blood

¹met *past and past part of* MEET

²met *abbr* metropolitan

me·tab·o·lism \mə-'ta-bə-ˌli-zəm\ *n* : the processes by which the substance of plants and animals incidental to life is built up and broken down; *also* : the processes by which a substance is handled in the living body (the ~ of sugar) — **met·a·bol·ic** \ˌme-tə-'bä-lik\ *adj* — **me·tab·o·lize** \mə-'ta-bə-ˌlīz\ *vb*

me·tab·o·lite \-ˌlīt\ *n* **1** : a product of metabolism **2** : a substance essential to the metabolism of a particular organism or to a metabolic process

meta·car·pal \ˌme-tə-'kär-pəl\ *n* : any of usu. five more or less elongated bones of the part of the hand or forefoot between the wrist and the bones of the digits — **metacarpal** *adj*

meta·car·pus \-'kär-pəs\ *n* : the part of the hand or forefoot that contains the metacarpals

met·al \'me-tᵊl\ *n* **1** : any of various opaque, fusible, ductile, and typically lustrous substances that are good conductors of electricity and heat **2** : METTLE; *also* : the material out of which a person or thing is made — **me·tal·lic** \mə-'ta-lik\ *adj*

met·al·lur·gy \'me-tᵊl-ˌər-jē\ *n* : the science and technology of metals — **met·al·lur·gi·cal** \ˌme-tᵊl-'ər-ji-kəl\ *adj* — **met·al·lur·gist** \'me-tᵊl-ˌər-jist\ *n*

met·al·ware \'me-tᵊl-ˌwer\ *n* : metal utensils for household use

met·al·work \-ˌwərk\ *n* : work and esp. artistic work made of metal — **met·al·work·er** \-ˌwər-kər\ *n* — **met·al·work·ing** *n*

meta·mor·phism \ˌme-tə-'mȯr-ˌfi-zəm\ *n* : a change in the structure of rock; *esp* : a change to a more compact and more highly crystalline form produced by pressure, heat, and water — **meta·mor·phic** \-'mȯr-fik\ *adj*

meta·mor·pho·sis \ˌme-tə-'mȯr-fə-səs\ *n, pl* **-pho·ses** \-ˌsēz\ **1** : a change of physical form, structure, or substance esp. by supernatural means; *also* : a striking alteration (as in appearance or character) **2** : a fundamental change in form and often habits of an animal accompa-

nying the transformation of a larva into an adult — **meta·mor·phose** \-ˌfōz, -ˌfōs\ *vb*

met·a·phor \'me-tə-ˌfȯr\ *n* : a figure of speech in which a word for one idea or thing is used in place of another to suggest a likeness between them (as in "the ship plows the sea") — **met·a·phor·ic** \ˌme-tə-'fȯr-ik\ *or* **met·a·phor·i·cal** \-tə-'fȯr-i-kəl\ *adj* — **met·a·phor·i·cal·ly** \-i-k(ə-)lē\ *adv*

meta·phys·ics \ˌme-tə-'fi-ziks\ *n* [ML *Metaphysica*, title of Aristotle's treatise on the subject, fr. Gk *(ta) meta (ta) physika*, lit., the (works) after the physical (works); fr. its position in his collected works] : the philosophical study of the ultimate causes and underlying nature of things — **meta·phys·i·cal** \-'fi-zi-kəl\ *adj* — **meta·phy·si·cian** \-fə-'zi-shən\ *n*

me·tas·ta·sis \mə-'tas-tə-səs\ *n, pl* **-ta·ses** \-ˌsēz\ : the spread of a health-impairing agency (as cancer cells) from the initial or primary site of disease to another part of the body; *also* : a secondary growth of a malignant tumor — **me·tas·ta·size** \-tə-ˌsīz\ *vb* — **met·a·stat·ic** \ˌme-tə-'sta-tik\ *adj*

meta·tar·sal \ˌme-tə-'tär-səl\ *n* : any of the bones of the foot between the tarsus and the bones of the digits that in humans include five elongated bones — **metatarsal** *adj*

meta·tar·sus \-'tär-səs\ *n* : the part of the human foot or the hind foot in quadrupeds that contains the metatarsals

¹mete \'mēt\ *vb* **met·ed; met·ing 1** *archaic* : MEASURE **2** : ALLOT — usu. used with *out* (~ out punishment)

²mete *n* : BOUNDARY (~s and bounds)

me·te·or \'mē-tē-ər, -ˌȯr\ *n* **1** : a small particle of matter in the solar system directly observable only by its glow from frictional heating on falling into the earth's atmosphere **2** : the streak of light produced by a meteor

me·te·or·ic \ˌmē-tē-'ȯr-ik\ *adj* **1** : of, relating to, or resembling a meteor **2** : transiently brilliant (a ~ career) — **me·te·or·i·cal·ly** \-i-k(ə-)lē\ *adv*

me·te·or·ite \'mē-tē-ə-ˌrīt\ *n* : a meteor that reaches the surface of the earth

me·te·or·oid \'mē-tē-ə-ˌrȯid\ *n* : a small particle of matter in the solar system

me·te·o·rol·o·gy \ˌmē-tē-ə-'rä-lə-jē\ *n* : a science that deals with the atmosphere and its phenomena and esp. with weather forecasting — **me·te·o·ro·log·ic** \ˌmē-tē-ˌȯr-ə-'lä-jik\ *or* **me·te·o·ro·log·i·cal** \-'lä-ji-kəl\ *adj* — **me·te·o·rol·o·gist** \ˌmē-tē-ə-'rä-lə-jist\ *n*

¹me·ter \'mē-tər\ *n* : rhythm in verse or music

²meter *n* : the basic metric unit of length — see METRIC SYSTEM table

³meter *n* : a measuring and sometimes recording instrument

⁴meter *vb* **1** : to measure by means of a meter **2** : to print postal indicia on by means of a postage meter (~ed mail)

meter–kilogram–second *adj* : of, relating to, or being a system of units based on the meter, the kilogram, and the second

meter maid *n* : a woman assigned to write tickets for parking violations

meth·a·done \'me-thə-ˌdōn\ *also* **meth·a·don** \-ˌdän\ *n* : a synthetic addictive narcotic drug used esp. as a substitute narcotic in the treatment of heroin addiction

meth·am·phet·amine \ˌme-tham-'fe-tə-ˌmēn, -thə-, -mən\ *n* : a drug used medically in the form of its hydrochloride in the treatment of obesity and often illicitly as a stimulant

meth·ane \'me-ˌthān\ *n* : a colorless odorless flammable gas produced by decomposition of organic matter or from coal and used esp. as a fuel

meth·a·nol \'me-thə-ˌnól, -ˌnōl\ *n* : a volatile flammable poisonous liquid alcohol used esp. as a solvent and as an antifreeze

meth·aqua·lone \me-'tha-kwə-ˌlōn\ *n* : a sedative and hypnotic habit-forming drug that is not a barbiturate

meth·od \'me-thəd\ *n* [ME, prescribed treatment, fr. L *methodus*, fr. Gk *methodos*, fr. *meta* with + *hodos* way] **1** : a procedure or process for achieving an end **2** : orderly arrangement : PLAN ♦ *Synonyms* MODE, MANNER, WAY, FASHION, SYSTEM — **me·thod·i·cal** \mə-'thä-di-kəl\ *adj* — **me·thod·i·cal·ly** \-k(ə-)lē\ *adv* — **me·thod·i·cal·ness** *n*

meth·od·ise *Brit var of* METHODIZE

Meth·od·ist \'me-thə-dist\ *n* : a member of a Protestant denomination adhering to the doctrines of John Wesley — **Meth·od·ism** \-ˌdi-zəm\ *n*

meth·od·ize \'me-thə-ˌdīz\ *vb* **-ized; -izing** : SYSTEMATIZE

meth·od·ol·o·gy \ˌme-thə-'dä-lə-jē\ *n, pl* **-gies** **1** : a body of methods and rules followed in a science or discipline **2** : the study of the principles or procedures of inquiry in a particular field

meth·yl \'me-thəl\ *n* : a chemical radical consisting of carbon and hydrogen

methyl alcohol *n* : METHANOL

meth·yl·mer·cury \ˌme-thəl-'mər-kyə-rē\ *n* : any of various toxic compounds of mercury that often occur as pollutants which accumulate in animals esp. at the top of a food chain

met·i·cal \'me-ti-kəl\ *n, pl* **met·i·cais** \-kī\ *also* **meticals** — see MONEY table

me·tic·u·lous \mə-'ti-kyə-ləs\ *adj* [L *meticulosus* fearful, fr. *metus* fear] : extremely careful in attending to details — **me·tic·u·lous·ly** *adv* — **me·tic·u·lous·ness** *n*

mé·tier \'me-ˌtyā, me-'tyā\ *n* : an area of activity in which one is expert or successful

me·tre \'mē-tər\ *chiefly Brit var of* METER

met·ric \'me-trik\ *adj* **1** : of or relating to measurement; *esp* : of or relating to the metric system **2** : METRICAL

met·ri·cal \'me-tri-kəl\ *adj* **1** : of, relating to, or composed in meter **2** : METRIC 1 — **met·ri·cal·ly** \-k(ə-)lē\ *adv*

met·ri·ca·tion \ˌme-tri-'kā-shən\ *n* : the

act or process of converting into or expressing in the metric system

met·ri·cize \'me-trə-ˌsīz\ *vb* **-cized; -cizing** : to change into or express in the metric system

metric system *n* : a decimal system of weights and measures based on the meter and on the kilogram

☞ the METRIC SYSTEM table is on page 452

metric ton *n* — see METRIC SYSTEM table

¹me·tro \'me-trō\ *n, pl* **metros** : SUBWAY

²metro *adj* : of, relating to, or characteristic of a metropolis and sometimes including its suburbs

me·tro·nome \'me-trə-ˌnōm\ *n* : an instrument for marking exact time by a regularly repeated tick

me·trop·o·lis \mə-'trä-pə-ləs\ *n* [ME, fr. LL, fr. Gk *mētropolis*, fr. *mētēr* mother + *polis* city] : the chief or capital city of a country, state, or region — **met·ro·pol·i·tan** \ˌme-trə-'pä-lə-tən\ *adj*

met·tle \'me-t³l\ *n* **1** : SPIRIT, COURAGE **2** : quality of temperament

met·tle·some \'me-t³l-səm\ *adj* : full of mettle : COURAGEOUS ⟨a ~ opponent⟩

MeV *abbr* million electron volts

¹mew \'myü\ *vb* : MEOW — **mew** *n*

²mew *vb* : CONFINE

mews \'myüz\ *n sing or pl, chiefly Brit* : stables usu. with living quarters built around a court; *also* : a narrow street with dwellings converted from stables

Mex *abbr* Mexican; Mexico

mez·za·nine \'me-zə-ˌnēn, ˌme-zə-'\ *n* **1** : a low-ceilinged story between two main stories of a building **2** : the lowest balcony in a theater; *also* : the first few rows of such a balcony

mez·zo for·te \ˌmet-(ˌ)sō-'fór-ˌtā, ˌmed-(ˌ)zō-, -tē\ *adj or adv* [It] : moderately loud — used as a direction in music

mez·zo pia·no \-pē-'ä-(ˌ)nō\ *adj or adv* [It] : moderately soft — used as a direction in music

mez·zo-so·pra·no \-sə-'pra-nō, -'prä-\ *n* : a woman's voice having a range between that of the soprano and contralto; *also* : a singer having such a voice

MFA *abbr* master of fine arts

mfr *abbr* manufacture; manufacturer

mg *abbr* milligram

Mg *symbol* magnesium

MG *abbr* **1** machine gun **2** major general **3** military government

mgr *abbr* **1** manager **2** monseigneur **3** monsignor

mgt *or* **mgmt** *abbr* management

MGy Sgt *abbr* master gunnery sergeant

MHz *abbr* megahertz

mi *abbr* **1** mile; mileage **2** mill

MI *abbr* **1** Michigan **2** military intelligence

MIA \ˌem-(ˌ)ī-'ā\ *n* [*missing in action*] : a member of the armed forces whose whereabouts following a combat mission are unknown

Mi·ami \mī-'a-mē, -mə\ *n, pl* **Mi·ami** *or* **Mi·am·is** : a member of an American Indian people orig. of Wisconsin and Indiana

mi·as·ma \mī-'az-mə, mē-\ *n, pl* **-mas** *also* **-ma·ta** \-mə-tə\ **1** : a vapor from a

METRIC SYSTEM

LENGTH

UNIT	SYMBOL	METRIC EQUIVALENT	U.S. EQUIVALENT
kilometer	km	1,000 meters	0.62 mile
hectometer	hm	100 meters	328.08 feet
dekameter	dam	10 meters	32.81 feet
meter	m		39.37 inches
decimeter	dm	0.1 meter	3.94 inches
centimeter	cm	0.01 meter	0.39 inch
millimeter	mm	0.001 meter	0.039 inch
micrometer	μm	0.000001 meter	0.000039 inch

AREA

UNIT	SYMBOL	METRIC EQUIVALENT	U.S. EQUIVALENT
square kilometer	sq km or km^2	1,000,000 square meters	0.39 square miles
hectare	ha	10,000 square meters	2.47 acres
are	a	100 square meters	119.60 square yards
square centimeter	sq cm or cm^2	0.0001 square meter	0.16 square inch

VOLUME

UNIT	SYMBOL	METRIC EQUIVALENT	U.S. EQUIVALENT
cubic meter	m^3		1.31 cubic yards
cubic decimeter	dm^3	0.001 cubic meter	61.02 cubic inches
cubic centimeter	cu cm or cm^3 $also$ cc	0.000001 cubic meter	0.061 cubic inch

MASS AND WEIGHT

UNIT	SYMBOL	METRIC EQUIVALENT	U.S. EQUIVALENT
metric ton	t	1,000,000 grams	1.10 short tons
kilogram	kg	1,000 grams	2.20 pounds
hectogram	hg	100 grams	3.53 ounces
dekagram	dag	10 grams	0.35 ounce
gram	g		0.035 ounce
decigram	dg	0.1 gram	1.54 grains
centigram	cg	0.01 gram	0.15 grain
milligram	mg	0.001 gram	0.015 grain
microgram	μg or mcg	0.000001 gram	0.000015 grain

CAPACITY

UNIT	METRIC EQUIVALENT	U.S. EQUIVALENT UNITS		
		CUBIC	DRY	LIQUID
kiloliter (kl)	1,000 liters	1.31 cubic yards	28.38 bushels	264.17 gallons
hectoliter (hl)	100 liters	3.53 cubic feet	2.84 bushels	26.42 gallons
dekaliter (dal)	10 liters	0.35 cubic foot	1.14 pecks	2.64 gallons
liter (l)		61.02 cubic inches	0.91 quart	1.06 quarts
deciliter (dl)	0.1 liter	6.10 cubic inches	0.18 pint	0.21 pint
centiliter (cl)	0.01 liter	0.61 cubic inch		0.34 fluid ounce
milliliter (ml)	0.001 liter	0.061 cubic inch		0.27 fluid dram
microliter (μl)	0.000001 liter	0.000061 cubic inch		0.00027 fluid dram

For metric system equivalents of U.S. system units, see WEIGHTS AND MEASURES table.

swamp formerly believed to cause disease
2 : a harmful influence or atmosphere ⟨a
~ of smog⟩ — **mi·as·mal** \-məl\ *adj* —
mi·as·mic \-mik\ *adj*

mic \'mik\ *n* : MICROPHONE

Mic *abbr* Micah

mi·ca \'mī-kə\ *n* [NL, fr. L, grain, crumb]
: any of various mineral silicates readily
separable into thin transparent sheets

Mi·cah \'mī-kə\ *n* — see BIBLE table

mice *pl of* MOUSE

Mich *abbr* Michigan

Mi·che·as \'mī-kē-əs, mī-'kē-əs\ *n* : MI-CAH

Mic·mac \'mik-ˌmak\ *n, pl* Micmac *or*
Micmacs : a member of an American
Indian people of eastern Canada

micr- *or* **micro-** *comb form* **1** : small
: minute ⟨*micro*capsule⟩ **2** : one millionth part of a specified unit ⟨*micro*sec-
ond⟩

¹mi·cro \'mī-krō\ *adj* **1** : very small; *esp*
: MICROSCOPIC **2** : involving minute
quantities or variations

²micro *n, pl* micros : MICROCOMPUTER

mi·crobe \'mī-ˌkrōb\ *n* : MICROORGAN-
ISM; *esp* : one causing disease — **mi·cro-
bi·al** \mī-'krō-bē-əl\ *adj*

mi·cro·bi·ol·o·gy \ˌmī-krō-bī-'ä-lə-jē\ *n*
: a branch of biology dealing esp. with
microscopic forms of life — **mi·cro·bio-
log·i·cal** \-ˌbī-ə-'lä-ji-kəl\ *adj* — **mi·cro-
bi·ol·o·gist** \-bī-'ä-lə-jist\ *n*

mi·cro·brew·ery \'mī-krō-ˌbrü-ə-rē\ *n* : a
small brewery making specialty beer in
limited quantities

mi·cro·burst \-ˌbərst\ *n* : a violent short-
lived localized downdraft that creates
extreme wind shears at low altitudes

mi·cro·cap·sule \'mī-krō-ˌkap-səl, -ˌsül\ *n*
: a tiny capsule containing material (as a
medicine) released when the capsule is
broken, melted, or dissolved

mi·cro·chip \-ˌchip\ *n* : INTEGRATED CIR-
CUIT

mi·cro·cir·cuit \-ˌsər-kət\ *n* : a compact
electronic circuit

mi·cro·com·put·er \-kəm-ˌpyü-tər\ *n* : a
small computer that uses a microprocessor; *esp* : PERSONAL COMPUTER

mi·cro·cosm \'mī-krə-ˌkä-zəm\ *n* : an individual or community thought of as a
miniature world or universe

mi·cro·elec·tron·ics \ˌmī-krō-i-ˌlek-'trä-
niks\ *n* : a branch of electronics that
deals with the miniaturization of electronic circuits and components — **mi·
cro·elec·tron·ic** \-nik\ *adj*

mi·cro·en·cap·su·late \ˌmī-krō-in-'kap-
sə-ˌlāt\ *vb* : to enclose (as a drug) in a
microcapsule — **mi·cro·en·cap·su·la-
tion** \-in-ˌkap-sə-'lā-shən\ *n*

mi·cro·fi·ber \'mī-krō-ˌfī-bər\ *n* : a fine
usu. soft polyester fiber; *also* : fabric
made from such fibers

mi·cro·fiche \'mī-krō-ˌfēsh, -ˌfish\ *n, pl*
-fiche *or* **-fiches** *same or* -ˌfē-shəz, -ˌfi-\
: a sheet of microfilm containing rows of
images of pages of printed matter

mi·cro·film \-ˌfilm\ *n* : a film bearing a
photographic record (as of print) on a
reduced scale — **microfilm** *vb*

mi·cro·graph \'mī-krə-ˌgraf\ *n* : a graphic
reproduction of the image of an object
formed by a microscope

mi·cro·man·age \ˌmī-krō-'ma-nij\ *vb* : to
manage esp. with excessive control or attention to details — **mi·cro·man·age-
ment** \-mənt\ *n* — **mi·cro·man·ag·er**
\-ni-jər\ *n*

mi·cro·me·te·or·ite \ˌmī-krō-'mē-tē-ə-
ˌrīt\ *n* : a very small particle in interplan-
etary space

mi·crom·e·ter \mī-'krä-mə-tər\ *n* : an instrument used with a telescope or microscope for measuring minute distances

mi·cro·min·ia·tur·iza·tion \ˌmī-kro-ˌmi-
nē-ə-ˌchür-ə-'zā-shən,   -ˌmi-ni-ˌchür-,
-ˌchər-\ *n* : the process of producing
things in a very small size and esp. in a
size smaller than one considered miniature — **mi·cro·min·ia·tur·ized** \-'mi-nē-
ə-chə-ˌrīzd, -'mi-ni-chə-\ *adj*

mi·cron \'mī-ˌkrän\ *n* : one millionth of a
meter

mi·cro·or·gan·ism \ˌmī-krō-'òr-gə-ˌni-
zəm\ *n* : an organism (as a bacterium) too
tiny to be seen by the unaided eye

mi·cro·phone \'mī-krə-ˌfōn\ *n* : an instrument for converting sound waves
into variations of an electric current for
transmitting or recording sound

mi·cro·pho·to·graph \ˌmī-krə-'fō-tə-
ˌgraf\ *n* : PHOTOMICROGRAPH

mi·cro·pro·ces·sor \ˌmī-krō-'prä-ˌse-sər\
n : a computer processor contained on a
microchip

mi·cro·scope \'mī-krə-ˌskōp\ *n* : an instrument for making magnified images of
minute objects usu. using light — **mi-
cros·co·py** \mī-'kräs-kə-pē\ *n*

mi·cro·scop·ic \ˌmī-krə-'skä-pik\ *also*
mi·cro·scop·i·cal \-pi-kəl\ *adj* **1** : of,
relating to, or involving the use of the
microscope **2** : too tiny to be seen without the use of a microscope : very small
— **mi·cro·scop·i·cal·ly** \-pi-k(ə-)lē\ *adv*

mi·cro·sec·ond \'mī-krō-ˌse-kənd\ *n*
: one millionth of a second

mi·cro·sur·gery \ˌmī-krō-'sər-jə-rē\ *n*
: minute dissection or manipulation (as
by a laser beam) of living structures or
tissue — **mi·cro·sur·gi·cal** \-'sər-ji-kəl\
adj

mi·cro·tech·nol·o·gy \-tek-'nä-lə-jē\ *n*
: technology on a small or microscopic
scale

¹mi·cro·wave \'mī-krə-ˌwāv\ *n* **1** : a radio
wave between one millimeter and one
meter in wavelength **2** : MICROWAVE
OVEN

²microwave *vb* : to heat or cook in a microwave oven — **mi·cro·wav·able** *or* **mi-
cro·wave·able** \ˌmī-krə-'wā-və-bəl\ *adj*

microwave oven *n* : an oven in which
food is cooked by the absorption of microwave energy by water molecules in
the food

¹mid \'mid\ *adj* : MIDDLE

²mid *abbr* middle

mid·air \'mid-'er\ *n* : a point or region in
the air well above the ground

mid·day \'mid-ˌdā, -'dā\ *n* : NOON

mid·den \'mi-dᵊn\ *n* : a refuse heap

¹**mid·dle** \'mi-d°l\ *adj* **1** : equally distant from the extremes : MEDIAL, CENTRAL **2** : being at neither extreme : INTERMEDIATE **3** *cap* : constituting an intermediate period

²**middle** *n* **1** : a middle part, point, or position **2** : WAIST

middle age *n* : the period of life from about 45 to about 64 — **mid·dle–aged** \,mi-d°l-'äjd\ *adj*

Middle Ages *n pl* : the period of European history from about A.D. 500 to about 1500

mid·dle·brow \'mi-d°l-,braů\ *n* : a person who is moderately but not highly cultivated — **middlebrow** *adj*

middle class *n* : a social class holding a position between the upper class and the lower class — **middle–class** *adj*

middle ear *n* : a small membrane-lined cavity of the ear through which sound waves are transmitted by a chain of tiny bones

middle finger *n* : the midmost of the five digits of the hand

mid·dle·man \'mi-d°l-,man\ *n* : INTERMEDIARY; *esp* : one intermediate between the producer of goods and the retailer or consumer

middle–of–the–road *adj* : standing for or following a course of action midway between extremes; *esp* : being neither liberal nor conservative in politics — **mid·dle–of–the–road·er** \-'rō-dər\ *n* — **mid·dle–of–the–road·ism** \-'rō-,di-zəm\ *n*

middle school *n* : a school usu. including grades 5 to 8 or 6 to 8

mid·dle·weight \'mi-d°l-,wāt\ *n* : one of average weight; *esp* : a boxer weighing not over 160 pounds

mid·dling \'mid-liŋ, -lən\ *adj* **1** : of middle, medium, or moderate size, degree, or quality **2** : MEDIOCRE

mid·dy \'mi-dē\ *n, pl* **middies** : MIDSHIPMAN

midge \'mij\ *n* : a very small fly : GNAT

midg·et \'mi-jət\ *n* **1** : something (as an animal) very small for its kind **2** *sometimes offensive* : a very small person

midi \'mi-dē\ *n* : a calf-length dress, coat, or skirt

MIDI \'mi-dē\ *n* [*musical instrument digital interface*] : a proctocol for the transmission of digitally encoded music

mid·land \'mid-lənd, -,land\ *n* : the interior or central region of a country

mid·life \'mid-'līf\ *n* : MIDDLE AGE

midlife crisis *n* : a period of emotional turmoil in middle age characterized esp. by a strong desire for change

mid·most \-,mōst\ *adj* : being in or near the exact middle — **midmost** *adv*

mid·night \-,nīt\ *n* : 12 o'clock at night

mid–ocean ridge \'mid-'ō-shən-\ *n* : an elevation on an ocean floor at the boundary of diverging tectonic plates

mid·point \'mid-,pȯint, -'pȯint\ *n* : a point at or near the center or middle

mid·riff \'mi-,drif\ *n* [ME *midrif*, fr. OE *midhrif*, fr. *midde* mid + *hrif* belly] **1** : DIAPHRAGM 1 **2** : the mid-region of the human torso

mid·sec·tion \-,sek-shən\ *n* : a section midway between the extremes; *esp* : MIDRIFF 2

mid·ship·man \'mid-,ship-mən, (,)mid-'ship-\ *n* : a student in a naval academy

mid·ships \-,ships\ *adv* : AMIDSHIPS

midst \'midst\ *n* **1** : the interior or central part or point **2** : a position of proximity to the members of a group ⟨in our ∼⟩ **3** : the condition of being surrounded or beset — **midst** *prep*

mid·stream \'mid-'strēm, -,strēm\ *n* : the middle of a stream

mid·sum·mer \-'sə-mər, -,sə-\ *n* **1** : the middle of summer **2** : the summer solstice

mid·town \'mid-,taůn, -'taůn\ *n* : a central section of a city; *esp* : one situated between sections called *downtown* and *uptown* — **midtown** *adj*

¹**mid·way** \'mid-,wā, -'wā\ *adv* : in the middle of the way or distance

²**mid·way** \-,wā\ *n* : an avenue (as at a carnival) for concessions and amusements

mid·week \-,wēk\ *n* : the middle of the week — **mid·week·ly** \-,wē-klē, -'wē-\ *adj or adv*

mid·wife \'mid-,wīf\ *n* : a person who helps women in childbirth — **mid·wife·ry** \-,wī-f(ə-)rē\ *n*

mid·win·ter \'mid-'win-tər, -,win-\ *n* **1** : the winter solstice **2** : the middle of winter

mid·year \-,yir\ *n* **1** : the middle of a year **2** : a midyear examination — **midyear** *adj*

mien \'mēn\ *n* **1** : air or bearing esp. as expressive of mood or personality : DEMEANOR **2** : APPEARANCE, ASPECT ⟨dresses of formal ∼⟩

miff \'mif\ *vb* : to put into an ill humor

¹**might** \'mīt\ *verbal auxiliary, past of* MAY — used as an auxiliary to express permission or possibility in the past, a present condition contrary to fact, less probability or possibility than *may*, or as a polite alternative to *may, ought*, or *should*

²**might** *n* : the power, authority, or resources of an individual or a group

mighty \'mī-tē\ *adj* **might·i·er; -est** **1** : very strong : POWERFUL **2** : GREAT, NOTABLE — **might·i·ly** \'mī-tə-lē\ *adv* — **might·i·ness** \-tē-nəs\ *n* — **mighty** *adv*

mi·gnon·ette \,min-yə-'net\ *n* : an annual garden herb with spikes of tiny fragrant flowers

mi·graine \'mī-,grān\ *n* [ME *mygreyn*, fr. MF *migraine*, fr. LL *hemicrania* pain in one side of the head, fr. Gk *hēmikrania*, fr. *hēmi-* half + *kranion* cranium] : a condition marked by recurrent severe headache and often nausea; *also* : an attack of migraine

mi·grant \'mī-grənt\ *n* : one that migrates; *esp* : a person who moves in order to find work (as picking crops) — **migrant** *adj*

mi·grate \'mī-,grāt\ *vb* **mi·grat·ed; mi·grat·ing** **1** : to move from one country or place to another **2** : to pass usu. periodically from one region or climate to another for feeding or breeding — **mi-**

gra·tion \mī-'grā-shən\ n — **mi·gra·to·ry** \'mī-grə-ˌtór-ē\ adj

mi·ka·do \mə-'kä-dō\ n, pl **-dos** : an emperor of Japan

mike \'mīk\ n : MICROPHONE

¹mil \'mil\ n : a unit of length equal to ¹⁄₁₀₀₀ inch

²mil abbr military

milch \'milk, 'milch\ adj : giving milk ⟨∼ cow⟩

mild \'mī(-ə)ld\ adj 1 : gentle in nature or behavior 2 : moderate in action or effect 3 : TEMPERATE ⟨∼ weather⟩ ♦ **Synonyms** EASY, COMPLAISANT, AMIABLE, LENIENT — **mild·ly** adv — **mild·ness** n

mil·dew \'mil-ˌdü, -ˌdyü\ n : a superficial usu. whitish growth produced on organic matter and on plants by a fungus; also : a fungus producing this growth — **mildew** vb

mile \'mī(-ə)l\ n [ME, fr. OE mīl, fr. L milia miles, fr. milia passuum, lit., thousands of paces] 1 — see WEIGHT table 2 : NAUTICAL MILE

mile·age \'mī-lij\ n 1 : an allowance for traveling expenses at a certain rate per mile 2 : distance in miles traveled (as in a day) 3 : the amount of service yielded (as by a tire) expressed in terms of miles of travel 4 : the average number of miles a motor vehicle will travel on a gallon of gasoline

mile·post \'mī(-ə)l-ˌpōst\ n : a post indicating the distance in miles from a given point

mile·stone \-ˌstōn\ n 1 : a stone serving as a milepost 2 : a significant point in development

mi·lieu \mēl-'yər, -'yü, -'yœ\ n, pl **milieus** or **mi·lieux** \same or -'yərz, -'yüz, -'yœz\ [F] : ENVIRONMENT, SETTING

mil·i·tant \'mi-lə-tənt\ adj 1 : engaged in warfare 2 : aggressively active esp. in a cause — **mil·i·tance** \-təns\ n — **mil·i·tan·cy** \-tən-sē\ n — **militant** n — **mil·i·tant·ly** adv

mil·i·ta·rise Brit var of MILITARIZE

mil·i·ta·rism \'mi-lə-tə-ˌri-zəm\ n 1 : predominance of the military class or its ideals 2 : a policy of aggressive military preparedness — **mil·i·ta·rist** \-rist\ n — **mil·i·ta·ris·tic** \ˌmi-lə-tə-'ris-tik\ adj

mil·i·ta·rize \'mi-lə-tə-ˌrīz\ vb **-rized; -rizing** 1 : to equip with military forces and defenses ⟨∼ a region⟩ 2 : to give a military character to

¹mil·i·tary \'mi-lə-ˌter-ē\ adj 1 : of or relating to soldiers, arms, war, or the army 2 : performed by armed forces; also : supported by armed force ♦ **Synonyms** MARTIAL, WARLIKE — **mil·i·tar·i·ly** \ˌmi-lə-'ter-ə-lē\ adv

²military n, pl military also **mil·i·tar·ies** 1 : the military, naval, and air forces of a nation 2 : military persons

military police n : a branch of an army that exercises guard and police functions

mil·i·tate \'mi-lə-ˌtāt\ vb **-tat·ed; -tat·ing** : to have weight or effect ⟨disagreements ∼ against an alliance⟩

mi·li·tia \mə-'li-shə\ n : a part of the organized armed forces of a country liable to call only in emergency — **mi·li·tia·man** \-mən\ n

¹milk \'milk\ n 1 : a nutritive usu. whitish fluid secreted by female mammals for feeding their young 2 : a milklike liquid (as a plant juice) — **milk·i·ness** \'mil-kē-nəs\ n — **milky** adj

²milk vb 1 : to draw off the milk of ⟨∼ a cow⟩ 2 : to draw something from as if by milking

milk·maid \'milk-ˌmād\ n : DAIRYMAID

milk·man \-ˌman, -mən\ n : a person who sells or delivers milk

milk of magnesia : a milk-white mixture of hydroxide of magnesium and water used as an antacid and laxative

milk shake n : a thoroughly blended drink made of milk, a flavoring syrup, and often ice cream

milk·sop \'milk-ˌsäp\ n : an unmanly man

milk·weed \-ˌwēd\ n : any of a genus of herbs with milky juice and clustered flowers

Milky Way n 1 : a broad irregular band of light that stretches across the sky and is caused by the light of a very great number of faint stars 2 : MILKY WAY GALAXY

Milky Way galaxy n : the galaxy of which the sun is a member and which includes the stars that create the light of the Milky Way

¹mill \'mil\ n 1 : a building with machinery for grinding grain into flour 2 : a machine used in processing (as by grinding, stamping, cutting, or finishing) raw material 3 : FACTORY

²mill vb 1 : to process in a mill 2 : to move in a circle or in an eddying mass

³mill n : one tenth of a cent

mill·age \'mi-lij\ n : a rate (as of taxation) expressed in mills

¹mil·len·ni·al \mə-'le-nē-əl\ adj : of or relating to a millennium

²millennial n : a person born in the 1980s or 1990s — usually pl.

mil·len·ni·um \mə-'le-nē-əm\ n, pl **-nia** \-nē-ə\ or **-niums** 1 : a period of 1000 years; also : a 1000th anniversary or its celebration 2 : the 1000 years mentioned in Revelation 20 when holiness is to prevail and Christ is to reign on earth 3 : a period of great happiness or human perfection

mill·er \'mi-lər\ n 1 : one that operates a mill and esp. a flour mill 2 : any of various moths having powdery wings

mil·let \'mi-lət\ n : any of several small-seeded cereal and forage grasses cultivated for grain or hay; also : the grain of a millet

milli- comb form : one thousandth part of

mil·li·am·pere \ˌmi-lē-'am-ˌpir\ n : one thousandth of an ampere

mil·liard \'mil-ˌyärd, 'mi-lē-ˌärd\ n, Brit : a thousand millions

mil·li·bar \'mi-lə-ˌbär\ n : a unit of atmospheric pressure

mil·li·gram \-ˌgram\ n — see METRIC SYSTEM table

mil·li·li·ter \-ˌlē-tər\ n — see METRIC SYSTEM table

mil·lime \mə-'lēm\ n — see *dinar* at MONEY table

mil·li·me·ter \'mi-lə-ˌmē-tər\ n — see METRIC SYSTEM table

mil·li·ner \'mi-lə-nər\ n [irreg. fr. *Milan*, Italy; fr. the importation of women's finery from Italy in the 16th century] : a person who designs, makes, trims, or sells women's hats

mil·li·nery \'mi-lə-ˌner-ē\ n 1 : women's apparel for the head 2 : the business or work of a milliner

mill·ing \'mi-liŋ\ n : a corrugated edge on a coin

mil·lion \'mil-yən\ n, pl **millions** or **million** : a thousand thousands — **million** adj — **mil·lionth** \-yənth\ adj or n

mil·lion·aire \ˌmil-yə-'ner, 'mil-yə-ˌner\ n : one whose wealth is estimated at a million or more (as of dollars or pounds)

mil·li·pede \'mi-lə-ˌpēd\ n : any of a class of arthropods related to the centipedes and having a long segmented body with a hard covering, two pairs of legs on most segments, and no poison fangs

mil·li·sec·ond \-ˌse-kənd\ n : one thousandth of a second

mil·li·volt \-ˌvōlt\ n : one thousandth of a volt

mill·pond \'mil-ˌpänd\ n : a pond made by damming a stream to produce a fall of water for operating a mill

mill·race \-ˌrās\ n : a canal in which water flows to and from a mill wheel

mill·stone \-ˌstōn\ n : either of two round flat stones used for grinding grain

mill·stream \-ˌstrēm\ n : a stream whose flow is used to run a mill; *also* : the stream in a millrace

mill wheel n : a waterwheel that drives a mill

mill·wright \'mil-ˌrīt\ n : a person who builds mills or sets up or maintains their machinery

milt \'milt\ n : the sperm-containing fluid of a male fish

mime \'mīm\ n 1 : MIMIC 2 : PANTOMIME — **mime** vb

mim·eo·graph \'mi-mē-ə-ˌgraf\ n : a machine for making many copies by means of a stencil through which ink is pressed — **mimeograph** vb

mi·me·sis \mə-'mē-səs, mī-\ n : IMITATION, MIMICRY

mi·met·ic \-'me-tik\ adj 1 : IMITATIVE 2 : relating to, characterized by, or exhibiting mimicry

¹mim·ic \'mi-mik\ n : one that mimics

²mimic vb **mim·icked** \-mikt\; **mim·ick·ing** 1 : to imitate closely 2 : to ridicule by imitation 3 : to resemble by biological mimicry

mim·ic·ry \'mi-mi-krē\ n, pl **-ries** 1 : an instance of mimicking 2 : a superficial resemblance of one organism to another or to natural objects among which it lives that gives it an advantage (as protection from predation)

mi·mo·sa \mə-'mō-sə, mī-, -zə\ n : any of a genus of trees, shrubs, and herbs of the legume family that occur in warm regions and have ball-shaped heads of small white or pink flowers

min abbr 1 minim 2 minimum 3 mining 4 minister 5 minor 6 minute

min·a·ret \ˌmi-nə-'ret\ n [F, fr. Turk *minare*, fr. Ar *manāra* lighthouse] : a tall slender tower of a mosque from which a muezzin calls the faithful to prayer

mi·na·to·ry \'mi-nə-ˌtōr-ē, 'mī-\ adj : THREATENING, MENACING

mince \'mins\ vb **minced**; **minc·ing** [ME, fr. AF *mincer*, fr. VL **minutiare*, fr. L *minutia* smallness, fr. *minutus* small, fr. pp. of *minuere* to lessen] 1 : to cut into very small pieces 2 : to restrain (words) within the bounds of decorum 3 : to walk in a prim affected manner

mince·meat \'mins-ˌmēt\ n : a finely chopped mixture esp. of raisins, apples, spices, and often meat used as a filling for a pie

¹mind \'mīnd\ n 1 : MEMORY 2 : the part of an individual that feels, perceives, thinks, wills, and esp. reasons 3 : INTENTION, DESIRE 4 : normal mental condition 5 : OPINION, VIEW ⟨changed her ∼⟩ 6 : MOOD 7 : mental qualities of a person or group 8 : intellectual ability 9 : ATTENTION ⟨pay him no ∼⟩

²mind vb 1 chiefly dial : REMEMBER 2 : to attend to closely 3 : HEED, OBEY 4 : to be concerned about; *also* : DISLIKE 5 : to be careful or cautious ⟨∼ the broken stair⟩ 6 : to take charge of 7 : to regard with attention

mind–bend·ing \'mīnd-ˌben-diŋ\ adj : MIND-BLOWING — **mind–bend·ing·ly** adv

mind–blow·ing \-ˌblō-iŋ\ adj : PSYCHEDELIC 1; *also* : MIND-BOGGLING — **mind–blow·er** \-ˌblō-ər\ n — **mind–blow·ing·ly** adv

mind–bog·gling \-ˌbä-gə-liŋ\ adj : mentally or emotionally exciting or overwhelming ⟨∼ special effects⟩

mind·ed \'mīn-dəd\ adj 1 : INCLINED, DISPOSED 2 : having a mind of a specified kind or concerned with a specific thing — usu. used in combination ⟨narrow-*minded*⟩ ⟨health-*minded*⟩

mind·ful \'mīnd-fəl\ adj : bearing in mind : AWARE ⟨∼ of their needs⟩ — **mind·ful·ly** adv — **mind·ful·ness** n

mind·less \-ləs\ adj 1 : marked by a lack of mind or consciousness; *esp* : marked by no use of the intellect 2 : not mindful : HEEDLESS — **mind·less·ly** adv — **mind·less·ness** n

¹mine \'mīn\ pron : that which belongs to me

²mine n 1 : an excavation in the earth from which minerals are taken; *also* : an ore deposit 2 : an underground passage beneath an enemy position 3 : an explosive device for destroying enemy personnel, vehicles, or ships 4 : a rich source of supply

³mine vb **mined**; **min·ing** 1 : to dig a mine 2 : UNDERMINE 3 : to get ore from the earth 4 : to place military mines in — **min·er** n

mine·field \'mīn-ˌfēld\ n 1 : an area set

with mines **2** : something resembling a minefield esp. in having many dangers ⟨a political ∼⟩

mine·lay·er \-,lā-ər\ *n* : a naval vessel for laying underwater mines

min·er·al \'mi-nə-rəl\ *n* **1** : a crystalline substance (as diamond or quartz) of inorganic origin **2** : a naturally occurring substance (as coal, salt, or water) obtained usu. from the ground — **mineral** *adj*

min·er·al·ise *Brit var of* MINERALIZE

min·er·al·ize \'mi-nə-rə-,līz\ *vb* **-ized; -izing 1** : to impregnate or supply with minerals **2** : to change into mineral form — **min·er·al·i·za·tion** \-rə-lə-'zā-shən\ *n*

min·er·al·o·gy \,mi-nə-'rä-lə-jē, -'ra-\ *n* : a science dealing with minerals — **mineral·og·i·cal** \,mi-nə-rə-'lä-ji-kəl\ *adj* — **min·er·al·o·gist** \,mi-nə-'rä-lə-jist, -'ra-\ *n*

mineral oil *n* : an oil of mineral origin; *esp* : a refined petroleum oil used as a laxative

mineral water *n* : water infused with mineral salts or gases

min·e·stro·ne \,mi-nə-'strō-nē, -'strōn\ *n* [It, fr. *minestra*, fr. *minestrare* to serve, dish up, fr. L *ministrare*, fr. *minister* servant] : a rich thick vegetable soup

mine·sweep·er \'mīn-,swē-pər\ *n* : a warship for removing or neutralizing underwater mines

min·gle \'miŋ-gəl\ *vb* **min·gled; mingling 1** : to bring or combine together : MIX ⟨*mingling* odors⟩ **2** : ASSOCIATE; *also* : to move about socially ⟨*mingled* with the guests⟩

ming tree \'miŋ-\ *n* : a dwarfed usu. evergreen tree grown as bonsai; *also* : an artificial plant resembling this

mini \'mi-nē\ *n, pl* **min·is** : something small of its kind — **mini** *adj*

mini- *comb form* : smaller or briefer than usual, normal, or standard

min·ia·ture \'mi-nē-ə-,chùr, 'mi-ni-,chùr, -chər\ *n* [It *miniatura* art of illuminating a manuscript, fr. ML, fr. L *miniare* to color with red lead, fr. *minium* red lead] **1** : a copy on a much reduced scale; *also* : something small of its kind **2** : a small painting (as on ivory or metal) — **miniature** *adj* — **min·ia·tur·ist** \-,chùr-ist, -chər-\ *n*

min·ia·tur·ize \'mi-nē-ə-,chə-,rīz, 'mi-ni-\ *vb* **-ized; -iz·ing** : to design or construct in small size — **min·ia·tur·i·za·tion** \,mi-nē-ə-,chùr-ə-'zā-shən, ,mi-ni-, -chər-\ *n*

mini·bar \'mi-nē-,bär\ *n* : a small refrigerator in a hotel room that is stocked with beverages and snacks

mini·bike \'mi-nē-,bīk\ *n* : a small one-passenger motorcycle

mini·bus \-,bəs\ *n* : a small bus or van

mini·com·put·er \-kəm-,pyü-tər\ *n* : a computer between a mainframe and a microcomputer in size and speed

mini·disc \'mi-nē-,disk\ *n* : a miniature optical disk

min·im \'mi-nəm\ *n* — see WEIGHT table

min·i·mal \'mi-nə-məl\ *adj* **1** : relating to or being a minimum : LEAST **2** : of or relating to minimalism or minimal art — **min·i·mal·ly** *adv*

minimal art *n* : abstract art consisting primarily of simple geometric forms executed in an impersonal style — **minimal artist** *n*

min·i·mal·ism \'mi-nə-mə-,li-zəm\ *n* : MINIMAL ART; *also* : a style (as in music or literature) marked by extreme spareness or simplicity — **min·i·mal·ist** \-list\ *n*

mini·mart \'mi-nē-,märt\ *n* : CONVENIENCE STORE

min·i·mise *Brit var of* MINIMIZE

min·i·mize \'mi-nə-,mīz\ *vb* **-mized; -miz·ing 1** : to reduce or keep to a minimum **2** : to underestimate intentionally ⟨∼ the defects⟩ ♦ **Synonyms** DEPRECIATE, DECRY, DISPARAGE

min·i·mum \'mi-nə-məm\ *n, pl* **-ma** \-mə\ *or* **-mums 1** : the least quantity assignable, admissible, or possible **2** : the least of a set of numbers **3** : the lowest degree or amount of variation (as of temperature) reached or recorded — **minimum** *adj*

min·ion \'min-yən\ *n* [MF *mignon* darling] **1** : a servile dependent, follower, or underling **2** : one highly favored **3** : a subordinate official

min·is·cule \'mi-nəs-,kyül\ *var of* MINUSCULE

mini·se·ries \'mi-nē-,sir-ēz\ *n* : a television story presented in sequential episodes

mini·skirt \-,skərt\ *n* : a skirt with the hemline several inches above the knee

¹min·is·ter \'mi-nə-stər\ *n* **1** : AGENT **2** : a member of the clergy esp. of a Protestant communion **3** : a high officer of state who heads a division of governmental activities **4** : a diplomatic representative to a foreign state — **min·is·te·ri·al** \,mi-nə-'stir-ē-əl\ *adj*

²minister *vb* **1** : to perform the functions of a minister of religion **2** : to give aid or service — **min·is·tra·tion** \,mi-nə-'strā-shən\ *n*

¹min·is·trant \'mi-nə-strənt\ *adj, archaic* : performing service as a minister

²ministrant *n* : one that ministers

min·is·try \'mi-nə-strē\ *n, pl* **-tries 1** : MINISTRATION **2** : the office, duties, or functions of a minister; *also* : the period of service or office **3** : CLERGY **4** : AGENCY **5** *often cap* : the body of ministers governing a nation or state; *also* : a government department headed by a minister

mini·tow·er \'mi-nē-,taù(-ə)r\ *n* : a computer tower of intermediate size

mini·van \'mi-nē-,van\ *n* : a small van

mink \'miŋk\ *n, pl* **mink** *or* **minks** : either of two slender flesh-eating mammals resembling the related weasels; *also* : the soft lustrous typically dark brown fur of a mink

min·ke whale \'miŋ-kə-\ *n* : a small grayish baleen whale with a whitish underside

Minn *abbr* Minnesota

min·ne·sing·er \'mi-ni-,siŋ-ər, -,ziŋ-\ *n* [G, fr. Middle High German, fr. *minne* love + *singer* singer] : any of a class of German lyric poets and musicians of the 12th to the 14th centuries

min·now \'mi-nō\ *n, pl* **minnows** *also* **minnow** : any of numerous small freshwater fishes

¹**mi·nor** \'mī-nər\ *adj* **1** : inferior in importance, size, or degree **2** : not having reached majority **3** : having the third, sixth, and sometimes the seventh degrees lowered by a half step ⟨~ scale⟩; *also* : based on a minor scale ⟨~ key⟩ **4** : not serious ⟨~ illness⟩

²**minor** *n* **1** : a person who has not attained majority **2** : a subject of academic study chosen as a secondary field of specialization

³**minor** *vb* : to pursue an academic minor ⟨~ed in philosophy⟩

mi·nor·i·ty \mə-'nȯr-ə-tē, mī-\ *n, pl* **-ties** **1** : the period or state of being a minor **2** : the smaller in number of two groups; *esp* : a group having less than the number of votes necessary for control **3** : a part of a population differing from others (as in race); *also* : a member of a minority

mi·nox·i·dil \mə-'näk-sə-,dil\ *n* : a drug used orally to treat hypertension and topically in solution to promote hair regrowth in some forms of baldness

min·ster \'min-stər\ *n* : a large or important church

min·strel \'min-strəl\ *n* **1** : a medieval singer of verses; *also* : MUSICIAN, POET **2** : any of a group of performers usu. with blackened faces in a program of black American songs, jokes, and impersonations ⟨a ~ show⟩

min·strel·sy \-sē\ *n* : the singing and playing of a minstrel; *also* : a body of minstrels

¹**mint** \'mint\ *n* **1** : any of a large family of aromatic square-stemmed herbs and shrubs; *esp* : one (as spearmint) that is fragrant and is the source of a flavoring oil **2** : a mint-flavored piece of candy — **minty** *adj*

²**mint** *n* **1** : a place where coins are made **2** : a vast sum ⟨worth a ~⟩

³**mint** *vb* **1** : to make (as coins) out of metal **2** : CREATE; *also* : to give a certain status to ⟨newly ~ed lawyers⟩ — **mint·age** \-ij\ *n* — **mint·er** *n*

⁴**mint** *adj* : unmarred as if fresh from a mint ⟨in ~ condition⟩

min·u·end \'min-yə-,wend\ *n* : a number from which another is to be subtracted

min·u·et \,min-yə-'wet\ *n* : a slow graceful dance

¹**mi·nus** \'mī-nəs\ *prep* **1** : diminished by : LESS ⟨seven ~ three equals four⟩ **2** : LACKING, WITHOUT ⟨~ his hat⟩

²**minus** *n* : a negative quantity or quality

³**minus** *adj* **1** : algebraically negative ⟨~ quantity⟩ **2** : having a negative quality

¹**mi·nus·cule** \'mi-nəs-,kyül\ *n* : a lowercase letter

²**minuscule** *also* **min·is·cule** *adj* : very small

minus sign *n* : a sign — used in mathematics to indicate subtraction or a negative quantity

¹**min·ute** \'mi-nət\ *n* **1** : the 60th part of an hour or of a degree : 60 seconds **2** : a short space of time **3** *pl* : the official record of the proceedings of a meeting

²**mi·nute** \mī-'nüt, mə-, -'nyüt\ *adj* **mi·nut·er; -est** **1** : very small **2** : of little importance : TRIFLING **3** : marked by close attention to details ♦ **Synonyms** DIMINUTIVE, TINY, MINIATURE, WEE — **mi·nute·ly** *adv* — **mi·nute·ness** *n*

min·ute·man \'mi-nət-,man\ *n* : a member of a group of armed men pledged to take the field at a minute's notice during and immediately before the American Revolution

mi·nu·tia \mə-'nü-shə, -'nyü-, -shē-ə\ *n, pl* **-ti·ae** \-shē-,ē\ [L] : a minute or minor detail — usu. used in pl.

minx \'miŋks\ *n* : a pert girl

Mio·cene \'mī-ə-,sēn\ *adj* : of, relating to, or being the epoch of the Tertiary between the Oligocene and the Pliocene — **Miocene** *n*

mir·a·cle \'mir-i-kəl\ *n* **1** : an extraordinary event manifesting divine intervention in human affairs **2** : an unusual event, thing, or accomplishment : WONDER, MARVEL — **mi·rac·u·lous** \mə-'rak-yə-ləs\ *adj* — **mi·rac·u·lous·ly** *adv*

miracle drug *n* : a usu. newly discovered drug that elicits a dramatic response in a patient's condition

mi·rage \mə-'räzh\ *n* **1** : an illusion that often appears as a pool of water or a mirror in which distant objects are seen inverted, is sometimes seen at sea, in the desert, or over a hot pavement, and results from atmospheric conditions **2** : something illusory and unattainable

¹**mire** \'mī(-ə)r\ *n* : heavy and often deep mud or slush — **miry** *adj*

²**mire** *vb* **mired; mir·ing** : to stick or sink in or as if in mire

mire·poix \mir-'pwä\ *n, pl* **mirepoix** : a mixture of diced vegetables and sometimes meats used in soups, stews, and sauces

¹**mir·ror** \'mir-ər\ *n* **1** : a polished or smooth surface (as of glass) that forms images by reflection **2** : a true representation

²**mirror** *vb* **1** : to reflect in or as if in a mirror **2** : RESEMBLE ⟨her mood ~s the gloomy weather⟩

mirth \'mərth\ *n* : gladness or gaiety accompanied with laughter ♦ **Synonyms** GLEE, JOLLITY, HILARITY, MERRIMENT — **mirth·ful** \-fəl\ *adj* — **mirth·ful·ly** *adv* — **mirth·ful·ness** *n* — **mirth·less** *adj*

MIRV \'mərv\ *n* [multiple independently targeted reentry vehicle] : an ICBM with multiple warheads that have different targets — **MIRV** *vb*

mis·ad·ven·ture \,mi-səd-'ven-chər\ *n* : MISFORTUNE, MISHAP

mis·aligned \,mi-sə-'līnd\ *adj* : not properly aligned — **mis·align·ment** \-'līn-mənt\ *n*

mis·al·li·ance \,mi-sə-'lī-əns\ *n* : an improper or unsuitable marriage

mis·al·lo·ca·tion \,mi-,sa-lə-'kā-shən\ *n* : faulty or improper allocation

mis·an·dry \'mi-ˌsan-drē\ n : a hatred of men — **mis·an·drist** \-drist\ n or adj

mis·an·thrope \'mi-sⁿn-ˌthrōp\ n : one who hates humankind — **mis·an·throp·ic** \ˌmi-sⁿn-'thrä-pik\ adj — **mis·an·throp·i·cal·ly** \-pi-k(ə-)lē\ adv — **mis·an·thro·py** \mi-'san-thrə-pē\ n

mis·ap·ply \ˌmi-sə-'plī\ vb : to apply wrongly — **mis·ap·pli·ca·tion** \ˌmi-ˌsa-plə-'kā-shən\ n

mis·ap·pre·hend \ˌmi-ˌsa-pri-'hend\ vb : MISUNDERSTAND — **mis·ap·pre·hen·sion** \-'hen-chən\ n

mis·ap·pro·pri·ate \ˌmi-sə-'prō-prē-ˌāt\ vb : to appropriate wrongly (as by embezzlement) — **mis·ap·pro·pri·a·tion** \-ˌprō-prē-'ā-shən\ n

mis·be·got·ten \-bi-'gä-tⁿn\ adj : ILLEGITIMATE; also : ill-conceived

mis·be·have \ˌmis-bi-'hāv\ vb : to behave improperly — **mis·be·hav·er** n — **mis·be·hav·ior** \-'hā-vyər\ n

mis·be·liev·er \-bə-'lē-vər\ n : one who holds a false or unorthodox belief

mis·brand \mis-'brand\ vb : to brand falsely or in a misleading manner

misc abbr miscellaneous

mis·cal·cu·late \mis-'kal-kyə-ˌlāt\ vb : to calculate wrongly — **mis·cal·cu·la·tion** \ˌmis-ˌkal-kyə-'lā-shən\ n

mis·call \mis-'kȯl\ vb : MISNAME

mis·car·riage \-'ker-ij\ n 1 : failure in the administration of justice 2 : spontaneous expulsion of a fetus before it is capable of independent life

mis·car·ry \-'ker-ē\ vb 1 : to have a miscarriage of a fetus 2 : to go wrong; also : to be unsuccessful

mis·ce·ge·na·tion \ˌmi-se-jə-'nā-shən, ˌmi-si-jə-'nā-\ n [L miscēre to mix + genus race] : marriage, cohabitation, or sexual intercourse between persons of different races

mis·cel·la·neous \ˌmi-sə-'lā-nē-əs\ adj 1 : consisting of diverse things or members 2 : having various traits; also : dealing with or interested in diverse subjects — **mis·cel·la·neous·ly** adv — **mis·cel·la·neous·ness** n

mis·cel·la·ny \'mi-sə-ˌlā-nē\ n, pl -nies : a collection of writings on various subjects 2 : HODGEPODGE

mis·chance \mis-'chans\ n : bad luck; also : MISHAP

mis·chief \'mis-chəf\ n [ME meschief, fr. AF, misfortune, hardship, fr. OF meschever to come out badly, fr. mes- badly + chief head, end] 1 : injury caused by a particular agent 2 : a source of harm or irritation 3 : action that annoys; also : MISCHIEVOUSNESS

mis·chie·vous \'mis-chə-vəs\ adj 1 : HARMFUL, INJURIOUS 2 : causing annoyance or minor injury 3 : irresponsibly playful (~ children) — **mis·chie·vous·ly** adv — **mis·chie·vous·ness** n

mis·ci·ble \'mi-sə-bəl\ adj : capable of being mixed

mis·com·mu·ni·ca·tion \ˌmis-kə-ˌmyü-nə-'kā-shən\ n : failure to communicate clearly

mis·con·ceive \ˌmis-kən-'sēv\ vb : to interpret incorrectly — **mis·con·cep·tion** \-'sep-shən\ n

mis·con·duct \mis-'kän-(ˌ)dəkt\ n 1 : MISMANAGEMENT 2 : intentional wrongdoing 3 : improper behavior; also : a penalty in a sport for improper behavior

mis·con·strue \ˌmis-kən-'strü\ vb : MISINTERPRET — **mis·con·struc·tion** \-'strək-shən\ n

mis·count \mis-'kaunt\ vb : to count incorrectly : MISCALCULATE

mis·cre·ant \'mis-krē-ənt\ n : one who behaves criminally or viciously — **miscreant** adj

mis·cue \mis-'kyü\ n : MISTAKE, ERROR — **miscue** vb

mis·deed \mis-'dēd\ n : a wrong deed

mis·de·mean·or \ˌmis-di-'mē-nər\ n 1 : a crime less serious than a felony 2 : MISDEED

mis·di·rect \ˌmis-də-'rekt, -dī-\ vb : to give a wrong direction to — **mis·di·rec·tion** \-'rek-shən\ n

mis·do·ing \mis-'dü-iŋ\ n : WRONGDOING — **mis·do** \-'dü\ vb — **mis·do·er** \-'dü-ər\ n

mise–en–scène \ˌmē-ˌzäⁿ-'sen, -'sän\ n, pl mise–en–scènes \same or -'senz, -'sänz\ [F] 1 : the arrangement of the scenery, property, and actors on a stage 2 : SETTING; also : ENVIRONMENT

mi·ser \'mī-zər\ n [L miser miserable] : a person who hoards and is stingy with money — **mi·ser·li·ness** \-lē-nəs\ n — **mi·ser·ly** adj

mis·er·a·ble \'mi-zə-rə-bəl, 'miz-rə-\ adj 1 : wretchedly deficient; also : causing extreme discomfort 2 : being in a state of distress 3 : SHAMEFUL — **mis·er·a·ble·ness** n — **mis·er·a·bly** \-blē\ adv

mis·ery \'mi-zə-rē\ n, pl -er·ies 1 : suffering and want caused by poverty or affliction 2 : a cause of suffering or discomfort 3 : emotional distress

mis·fea·sance \mis-'fē-zⁿns\ n : the performance of a lawful action in an illegal or improper manner

mis·file \-'fī(-ə)l\ vb : to file in the wrong place

mis·fire \-'fī(-ə)r\ vb 1 : to fail to fire 2 : to miss an intended effect — **misfire** n

mis·fit \'mis-ˌfit, sense 1 also mis-'fit\ n 1 : something that fits badly 2 : a person who is poorly adjusted to a situation or environment

mis·for·tune \mis-'fȯr-chən\ n 1 : bad luck 2 : an unfortunate condition or event

mis·giv·ing \-'gi-viŋ\ n : a feeling of doubt or suspicion esp. concerning a future event

mis·gov·ern \-'gə-vərn\ vb : to govern badly — **mis·gov·ern·ment** n

mis·guid·ance \-'gī-dⁿns\ n : faulty guidance — **mis·guide** \-'gīd\ vb

mis·guid·ed \-'gī-dəd\ adj : led or prompted by wrong or inappropriate motives or ideals — **mis·guid·ed·ly** adv

mis·han·dle \-'han-dⁿl\ vb 1 : MALTREAT 2 : to manage wrongly

mis·hap \'mis-ˌhap\ *n* : an unfortunate accident

mish·mash \'mish-ˌmash, -ˌmäsh\ *n* : HODGEPODGE, JUMBLE

mis·in·form \ˌmi-sᵊn-'fȯrm\ *vb* : to give false or misleading information to — **mis·in·for·ma·tion** \ˌmi-ˌsin-fər-'mā-shən\ *n*

mis·in·ter·pret \ˌmi-sᵊn-'tər-prət\ *vb* : to understand or explain wrongly — **mis·in·ter·pre·ta·tion** \-ˌtər-prə-'tā-shən\ *n*

mis·judge \mis-'jəj\ *vb* 1 : to estimate wrongly 2 : to have an unjust opinion of — **mis·judg·ment** \mis-'jəj-mənt\ *n*

mis·la·bel \-'lā-bəl\ *vb* : to label incorrectly or falsely \was ~*ed* a liar\

mis·lay \mis-'lā\ *vb* **-laid** \-'lād\; **-lay·ing** : MISPLACE, LOSE *mislaid* his keys\

mis·lead \mis-'lēd\ *vb* **-led** \-'led\; **-lead·ing** : to lead in a wrong direction or into a mistaken action or belief — **mis·lead·ing·ly** *adv*

mis·like \-'līk\ *vb* : DISLIKE — **mis·like** *n*

mis·man·age \-'ma-nij\ *vb* : to manage badly — **mis·man·age·ment** *n*

mis·match \-'mach\ *vb* : to match unsuitably or badly — **mis·match** \mis-'mach, 'mis-ˌmach\ *n*

mis·name \-'nām\ *vb* : to name incorrectly : MISCALL

mis·no·mer \mis-'nō-mər\ *n* : a wrong or inappropriate name or designation

mi·so \'mē-sō\ *n* : a high-protein fermented food paste consisting chiefly of soybeans, salt, and usu. grain

mi·sog·y·ny \mə-'sä-jə-nē\ *n* [Gk *misogynia*, fr. *misein* to hate + *gynē* woman] : a hatred of women — **mi·sog·y·nist** \-nist\ *n or adj* — **mi·sog·y·nis·tic** \mə-ˌsä-jə-'nis-tik\ *adj*

mis·ori·ent \mi-'sȯr-ē-ˌent\ *vb* : to orient improperly or incorrectly — **mis·ori·en·ta·tion** \mi-ˌsȯr-ē-ən-'tā-shən\ *n*

mis·place \mis-'plās\ *vb* 1 : to put in a wrong or unremembered place 2 : to set on a wrong object \~ trust\

mis·play \-'plā\ *n* : a wrong or unskillful play — **mis·play** \mis-'plā, 'mis-ˌplā\ *vb*

mis·print \'mis-ˌprint\ *n* : a mistake in printed matter — **mis·print** \mis-'print\ *vb*

mis·pro·nounce \ˌmis-prə-'naùns\ *vb* : to pronounce incorrectly — **mis·pro·nun·ci·a·tion** \-prə-ˌnən-sē-'ā-shən\ *n*

mis·quote \mis-'kwōt\ *vb* : to quote incorrectly — **mis·quo·ta·tion** \ˌmis-kwō-'tā-shən\ *n*

mis·read \-'rēd\ *vb* **-read** \-'red\; **-read·ing** \-'rē-diŋ\ : to read or interpret incorrectly \~ her expression\

mis·rep·re·sent \ˌmis-ˌre-pri-'zent\ *vb* : to represent falsely or unfairly \~ the facts\ — **mis·rep·re·sen·ta·tion** \-ˌzen-'tā-shən\ *n*

¹mis·rule \mis-'rül\ *vb* : MISGOVERN

²misrule *n* 1 : MISGOVERNMENT 2 : DISORDER

¹miss \'mis\ *vb* 1 : to fail to hit, reach, or contact 2 : to feel the absence of 3 : to fail to obtain 4 : AVOID \just ~*ed* hitting the other car\ 5 : OMIT 6 : to fail to understand \~ the point\ 7 : to fail to perform or attend; *also* : MISFIRE

²miss *n* 1 : a failure to hit or to attain a result 2 : MISFIRE

³miss *n* 1 *cap* — used as a title prefixed to the name of an unmarried woman or girl 2 : a young unmarried woman or girl

Miss *abbr* Mississippi

mis·sal \'mi-səl\ *n* : a book containing all that is said or sung at mass during the entire year

mis·send \mis-'send\ *vb* : to send incorrectly (as to a wrong destination)

mis·shap·en \-'shā-pən\ *adj* : badly shaped : having an ugly shape

mis·sile \'mi-səl\ *n* [L, fr. neut. of *missilis* capable of being thrown, fr. *mittere* to let go, send] : an object (as a stone, bullet, or rocket) thrown or projected usu. so as to strike a target

miss·ing \'mi-siŋ\ *adj* : ABSENT; *also* : LOST \~ in action\

mis·sion \'mi-shən\ *n* 1 : a group of missionaries; *also* : a place where missionaries work 2 : a group of envoys to a foreign country; *also* : a team of specialists or cultural leaders sent to a foreign country 3 : TASK, OBJECTIVE

¹mis·sion·ary \'mi-shə-ˌner-ē\ *adj* : of, relating to, or engaged in missions

²missionary *n, pl* **-ar·ies** : a person commissioned by a church to spread its faith or carry on humanitarian work

mis·sion·er \'mi-shə-nər\ *n* : MISSIONARY

Mis·sis·sip·pi·an \ˌmi-sə-'si-pē-ən\ *adj* 1 : of or relating to Mississippi, its people, or the Mississippi River 2 : of, relating to, or being the period of the Paleozoic era between the Devonian and the Pennsylvanian — **Mississippian** *n*

mis·sive \'mi-siv\ *n* : LETTER

mis·speak \mis-'spēk\ *vb* : to say imperfectly or incorrectly

mis·spell \-'spel\ *vb* : to spell incorrectly — **mis·spell·ing** *n*

mis·spend \-'spend\ *vb* **-spent** \-'spent\; **-spend·ing** : WASTE, SQUANDER \my *misspent* youth\

mis·state \mis-'stāt\ *vb* : to state incorrectly — **mis·state·ment** *n*

mis·step \-'step\ *n* 1 : a wrong step 2 : MISTAKE, BLUNDER

mist \'mist\ *n* 1 : water in the form of particles suspended or falling in the air 2 : something that obscures understanding — **mist** *vb*

mis·tak·able \mə-'stā-kə-bəl\ *adj* : capable of being misunderstood or mistaken

¹mis·take \mi-'stāk\ *vb* **-took** \-'stùk\; **-tak·en** \-'stā-kən\; **-tak·ing** 1 : to blunder in the choice of 2 : MISINTERPRET 3 : to make a wrong judgment of the character or ability of 4 : to confuse with another — **mis·tak·en·ly** *adv* — **mis·tak·er** *n*

²mistake *n* 1 : a wrong judgment : MISUNDERSTANDING 2 : a wrong action or statement : ERROR

¹mis·ter \'mis-tər\ *n* 1 *cap* — used sometimes instead of *Mr.* 2 : SIR — used without a name in addressing a man

²**mist·er** \'mis-tər\ *n* : a device for spraying mist

mis·tle·toe \'mi-səl-ˌtō\ *n* : a European parasitic green shrub that grows on trees and has yellowish flowers and waxy white berries

mis·tral \'mis-trəl, mi-'sträl\ *n* [F, fr. Occitan, fr. *mistral* masterful, fr. LL *magistralis* of a teacher, fr. L *magister* master] : a strong cold dry northerly wind of southern France

mis·treat \mis-'trēt\ *vb* : to treat badly : ABUSE — **mis·treat·ment** *n*

mis·tress \'mis-trəs\ *n* 1 : a woman who has power, authority, or ownership ⟨∼ of the house⟩ 2 : something personified as female that rules or dominates ⟨when Rome was ∼ of the world⟩ 3 : a woman other than his wife with whom a married man has sexual relations; *also, archaic* : SWEETHEART 4 — used archaically as a title prefixed to the name of a married or unmarried woman

mis·tri·al \'mis-ˌtrī-(-ə)l\ *n* : a trial that has no legal effect

¹**mis·trust** \mis-'trəst\ *n* : a lack of confidence : DISTRUST — **mis·trust·ful** \-fəl\ *adj* — **mis·trust·ful·ly** *adv* — **mis·trust·ful·ness** *n*

²**mistrust** *vb* : to have no trust or confidence in : SUSPECT

misty \'mis-tē\ *adj* **mist·i·er; -est** 1 : obscured by or as if by mist : INDISTINCT ⟨a ∼ memory⟩ 2 : TEARFUL — **mist·i·ly** \-tə-lē\ *adv* — **mist·i·ness** \-tē-nəs\ *n*

mis·un·der·stand \ˌmi-ˌsən-dər-'stand\ *vb* **-stood** \-'stůd\; **-stand·ing** 1 : to fail to understand 2 : to interpret incorrectly

mis·un·der·stand·ing \-'stan-diŋ\ *n* 1 : MISINTERPRETATION 2 : DISAGREEMENT, QUARREL

mis·us·age \mis-'yü-sij\ *n* 1 : bad treatment : ABUSE 2 : wrong or improper use

mis·use \mis-'yüz\ *vb* 1 : to use incorrectly 2 : ABUSE, MISTREAT — **mis·use** \-'yüs\ *n*

¹**mite** \'mīt\ *n* 1 : any of numerous tiny arthropod animals related to the spiders that often live and feed on animals or plants

²**mite** *n* 1 : a small coin or sum of money 2 : a small amount : BIT

¹**mi·ter** *or* **mi·tre** \'mī-tər\ *n* [ME *mitre*, fr. AF, fr. L *mitra* headband, turban, fr. Gk] 1 : a headdress worn by bishops and abbots 2 : MITER JOINT

²**miter** *or* **mitre** *vb* **mi·tered** *or* **mi·tred; mi·ter·ing** *or* **mi·tring** \'mī-tə-riŋ\ 1 : to match or fit together in a miter joint 2 : to bevel the ends of for making a miter joint

miter joint *n* : a usu. perpendicular joint made by fitting together two parts with the ends cut at an angle

mit·i·gate \'mi-tə-ˌgāt\ *vb* **-gat·ed; -gat·ing** 1 : to make less harsh or hostile 2 : to make less severe or painful — **mit·i·ga·tion** \ˌmi-tə-'gā-shən\ *n* — **mit·i·ga·tive** \'mi-tə-ˌgā-tiv\ *adj*

mi·to·chon·dri·on \ˌmī-tə-'kän-drē-ən\ *n, pl* **-dria** \-drē-ə\ : any of various round or long cellular organelles that produce energy for the cell — **mi·to·chon·dri·al** \-drē-əl\ *adj*

mi·to·sis \mī-'tō-səs\ *n, pl* **-to·ses** \-ˌsēz\ : a process that takes place in the nucleus of a dividing cell and results in the formation of two new nuclei each of which has the same number of chromosomes as the parent nucleus; *also* : cell division in which mitosis occurs — **mi·tot·ic** \-'tä-tik\ *adj*

mitt \'mit\ *n* 1 : a baseball catcher's or first baseman's glove 2 *slang* : HAND

mit·ten \'mi-tᵊn\ *n* : a covering for the hand having a separate section for the thumb only — **mit·tened** \-tᵊnd\ *adj*

¹**mix** \'miks\ *vb* 1 : to combine into one mass 2 : ASSOCIATE 3 : to form by mingling components 4 : to produce (a recording) by electronically combining sounds from different sources 5 : HYBRIDIZE 6 : CONFUSE ⟨∼es up the facts⟩ 7 : to become involved ♦ **Synonyms** BLEND, MERGE, COALESCE, AMALGAMATE, FUSE — **mix·able** *adj* — **mix it up** : to engage in a fight, contest, or dispute

²**mix** *n* : a product of mixing; *esp* : a commercially prepared mixture of food ingredients

mixed \'mikst\ *adj* 1 : combining features of more than one kind 2 : made up of or involving individuals or items of more than one kind 3 : including or accompanied by different or opposing elements ⟨a ∼ blessing⟩ 4 : resulting from the crossing or breeding of individuals of different races or breeds ⟨a stallion of ∼ blood⟩

mixed number *n* : a number (as $5^2/_3$) composed of an integer and a fraction

mixed-up \'mikst-'əp\ *adj* : CONFUSED

mix·er \'mik-sər\ *n* 1 : one that mixes; *esp* : a machine or device for mixing 2 : an event (as a dance) that encourages meeting and socializing 3 : a nonalcoholic beverage used in a cocktail

mixt *abbr* mixture

mix·ture \'miks-chər\ *n* 1 : the act or process of mixing; *also* : the state of being mixed 2 : a product of mixing

mix-up \'miks-ˌəp\ *n* 1 : an instance of confusion 2 : CONFLICT, FIGHT

miz·zen *also* **miz·en** \'mi-zᵊn\ *n* 1 : a fore-and-aft sail set on the mizzenmast 2 : MIZZENMAST — **mizzen** *also* **mizen** *adj*

miz·zen·mast \-ˌmast, -məst\ *n* : the mast aft or next aft of the mainmast

mk *abbr* 1 mark 2 markka

Mk *abbr* Mark

mks *abbr* meter-kilogram-second

mkt *abbr* market

mktg *abbr* marketing

ml *abbr* milliliter

Mlle *abbr* [F] mademoiselle

Mlles *abbr* [F] mesdemoiselles

mm *abbr* millimeter

MM *abbr* [F] messieurs

Mme *abbr* [F] madame

Mmes *abbr* [F] mesdames

Mn *symbol* manganese

MN *abbr* Minnesota

mne·mon·ic \ni-'mä-nik\ *adj* : assisting

or designed to assist memory; *also* : of or relating to memory

mo *abbr* month

¹**Mo** *abbr* **1** Missouri **2** Monday

²**Mo** *symbol* molybdenum

MO *abbr* **1** mail order **2** medical officer **3** Missouri **4** modus operandi **5** money order

moan \'mōn\ *n* : a low prolonged sound indicative of pain or grief — **moan** *vb*

moat \'mōt\ *n* : a deep wide usu. water-filled trench around a castle

¹**mob** \'mäb\ *n* [L *mobile vulgus* vacillating crowd] **1** : MASSES, RABBLE **2** : a disorderly crowd **3** : a criminal gang

²**mob** *vb* **mobbed; mob·bing 1** : to crowd about and attack or annoy ⟨*mobbed* by fans⟩ **2** : to crowd into or around ⟨shoppers *mobbed* the stores⟩

¹**mo·bile** \'mō-bəl, -ˌbī(-ə)l, -ˌbēl\ *adj* **1** : capable of moving or being moved **2** : changeable in appearance, mood, or purpose; *also* : ADAPTABLE **3** : having the opportunity for or undergoing a shift in social status **4** : using vehicles for transportation ⟨~ warfare⟩ **5** : CELLULAR 2 — **mo·bil·i·ty** \mō-'bi-lə-tē\ *n*

²**mo·bile** \'mō-ˌbēl\ *n* : a construction or sculpture (as of wire and sheet metal) with parts that can be set in motion by air currents; *also* : a similar structure suspended so that it is moved by a current of air

mobile home *n* : a trailer used as a permanent dwelling

mo·bi·lise *chiefly Brit var of* MOBILIZE

mo·bi·lize \'mō-bə-ˌlīz\ *vb* **-lized; -liz·ing 1** : to put into movement or circulation **2** : to assemble and make ready for action ⟨~ army reserves⟩ — **mo·bi·li·za·tion** \ˌmō-bə-lə-'zā-shən\ *n* — **mo·bi·liz·er** \'mō-bə-ˌlī-zər\ *n*

mob·ster \'mäb-stər\ *n* : a member of a criminal gang

moc·ca·sin \'mä-kə-sən\ *n* **1** : a soft leather heelless shoe **2** : WATER MOCCASIN

mo·cha \'mō-kə\ *n* [*Mocha*, port in Yemen] **1** : choice coffee grown in Arabia **2** : a mixture of coffee and chocolate or cocoa **3** : a dark chocolate-brown color

¹**mock** \'mäk, 'mȯk\ *vb* **1** : to treat with contempt or ridicule **2** : DELUDE **3** : DEFY **4** : to mimic in sport or derision — **mock·er** *n* — **mock·ery** \'mä-kə-rē, 'mȯ-\ *n* — **mock·ing·ly** *adv*

²**mock** *adj* : SIMULATED ⟨a ~ trial⟩

mock-he·ro·ic \ˌmäk-hi-'rō-ik, ˌmȯk-\ *adj* : ridiculing or burlesquing heroic style, character, or action ⟨a ~ poem⟩

mock·ing·bird \'mä-kiŋ-ˌbərd, 'mȯ-\ *n* : a grayish No. American songbird related to the catbirds and thrashers that mimics the calls of other birds

mock-up \'mä-ˌkəp, 'mȯ-\ *n* **1** : a full-sized structural model built for study, testing, or display ⟨a ~ of a car⟩ **2** : a working sample (as of a magazine) for review

¹**mod** \'mäd\ *adj* **1** : of, relating to, or being the style of the 1960s British youth culture **2** : HIP, TRENDY

²**mod** *abbr* **1** moderate **2** modern **3** modification; modified

mode \'mōd\ *n* **1** : a particular form or variety of something; *also* : STYLE **2** : a manner of doing something **3** : the most frequent value of a set of data — **mod·al** \'mō-dᵊl\ *adj*

¹**mod·el** \'mä-dᵊl\ *n* **1** : structural design **2** : a miniature representation; *also* : a pattern of something to be made **3** : an example for imitation or emulation **4** : one who poses (as for an artist or to display clothes) **5** : TYPE, DESIGN ⟨a new car ~⟩

²**model** *vb* **mod·eled** *or* **mod·elled; mod·el·ing** *or* **mod·el·ling 1** : SHAPE, FASHION, CONSTRUCT ⟨~ed in clay⟩ **2** : to work as a fashion model

³**model** *adj* **1** : serving as or worthy of being a pattern ⟨a ~ student⟩ **2** : being a miniature representation of something ⟨a ~ airplane⟩

mo·dem \'mō-dəm, -ˌdem\ *n* : a device that converts signals from one device (as a computer) to a form compatible with another (as a telephone)

¹**mod·er·ate** \'mä-də-rət\ *adj* **1** : avoiding extremes; *also* : TEMPERATE **2** : AVERAGE; *also* : MEDIOCRE **3** : limited in scope or effect **4** : not expensive — **moderate** *n* — **mod·er·ate·ly** *adv* — **mod·er·ate·ness** *n*

²**mod·er·ate** \'mä-də-ˌrāt\ *vb* **-at·ed; -at·ing 1** : to lessen the intensity of : TEMPER **2** : to act as a moderator — **mod·er·a·tion** \ˌmä-də-'rā-shən\ *n*

mod·er·a·tor \'mä-də-ˌrā-tər\ *n* **1** : MEDIATOR **2** : one who presides over an assembly, meeting, or discussion

mod·ern \'mä-dərn\ *adj* [LL *modernus*, fr. L *modo* just now, fr. *modus* measure] : of, relating to, or characteristic of the present or the immediate past : CONTEMPORARY ⟨~ art⟩ — **modern** *n* — **mo·der·ni·ty** \mə-'dər-nə-tē\ *n* — **mod·ern·ly** *adv* — **mod·ern·ness** *n*

mod·ern·ise, mod·ern·i·sa·tion *Brit var of* MODERNIZE, MODERNIZATION

mod·ern·ism \'mä-dər-ˌni-zəm\ *n* : a practice, movement, or belief peculiar to modern times

mod·ern·ize \'mä-dər-ˌnīz\ *vb* **-ized; -iz·ing** : to make or become modern — **mod·ern·i·za·tion** \ˌmä-dər-nə-'zā-shən\ *n* — **mod·ern·iz·er** *n*

mod·est \'mä-dəst\ *adj* **1** : having a moderate estimate of oneself; *also* : DIFFIDENT **2** : observing the proprieties of dress and behavior **3** : limited in size, amount, or scope ⟨a ~ income⟩ — **mod·est·ly** *adv* — **mod·es·ty** \-də-stē\ *n*

mod·i·cum \'mä-di-kəm\ *n* : a small amount ⟨a ~ of privacy⟩

modif *abbr* modification

mod·i·fy \'mä-də-ˌfī\ *vb* **-fied; -fy·ing 1** : MODERATE **2** : to limit the meaning of esp. in a grammatical construction **3** : CHANGE, ALTER — **mod·i·fi·ca·tion** \ˌmä-də-fə-'kā-shən\ *n* — **mod·i·fi·er** \'mä-də-ˌfī-ər\ *n*

mod·ish \'mō-dish\ *adj* : FASHIONABLE,

STYLISH ⟨∼ decor⟩ — **mod·ish·ly** *adv* — **mod·ish·ness** *n*

mo·diste \mō-ˈdēst\ *n* : a maker of fashionable dresses and hats

mod·u·lar \ˈmä-jə-lər\ *adj* : constructed with standardized units ⟨∼ homes⟩

mod·u·lar·ized \ˈmä-jə-lə-ˌrīzd\ *adj* : containing or consisting of modules

mod·u·late \ˈmä-jə-ˌlāt\ *vb* -**lat·ed;** -**lat·ing 1** : to tune to a key or pitch **2** : to keep in proper measure or proportion : TEMPER **3** : to vary the amplitude or frequency of a carrier wave for the transmission of information (as in radio or television) — **mod·u·la·tion** \ˌmä-jə-ˈlā-shən\ *n* — **mod·u·la·tor** \ˈmä-jə-ˌlā-tər\ *n* — **mod·u·la·to·ry** \-lə-ˌtȯr-ē\ *adj*

mod·ule \ˈmä-jül\ *n* **1** : any in a series of standardized units for use together **2** : an assembly of wired electronic parts for use with other such assemblies **3** : an independent unit that constitutes a part of the total structure of a space vehicle ⟨a propulsion ∼⟩

mo·dus ope·ran·di \ˌmō-dəs-ˌä-pə-ˈran-dē, -ˌdī\ *n, pl* **mo·di operandi** \ˌmō-ˌdē-, ˌmō-ˌdī-\ [NL] : a method of procedure

¹**mo·gul** \ˈmō-gəl, mō-ˈgəl\ *n* [fr. *Mogul*, member of a Muslim dynasty ruling northern India] : an important person : MAGNATE ⟨a media ∼⟩

²**mogul** \ˈmō-gəl\ *n* : a bump in a ski run

mo·hair \ˈmō-ˌher\ *n* [modif. of obs. It *mocaiarro*, fr. Ar *mukhayyar*, lit., choice] : a fabric or yarn made wholly or in part from the long silky hair of the Angora goat; *also* : this goat hair

Mo·ham·med·an *also* **Mu·ham·mad·an** \mō-ˈha-mə-dən, -ˈhä-, mü-\ *n* : MUSLIM — **Mo·ham·med·an·ism** *also* **Mu·ham·mad·an·ism** \-də-ˌni-zəm\ *n*

Mo·hawk \ˈmō-ˌhȯk\ *n, pl* **Mohawk** or **Mohawks 1** : a member of an American Indian people of the Mohawk River valley, New York; *also* : the language of the Mohawk people **2** : a hairstyle with a narrow strip of upright hair down the center and the sides shaved

Mo·he·gan \mō-ˈhē-gən, mə-\ or **Mo·hi·can** \-ˈhē-kən\ *n, pl* **Mohegan** or **Mohegans** or **Mohican** or **Mohicans** : a member of an American Indian people of southeastern Connecticut

mo·hel \ˈmō-(h)el, ˈmȯi-(ə)l\ *n, pl* **hels** *also* **mo·ha·lim** \ˌmō-hä-ˈlēm\ *also* **mo·hel·im** \-(h)e-ˈlēm\ : a person who performs Jewish circumcisions

Mohican *var of* MAHICAN

moi·e·ty \ˈmȯi-ə-tē\ *n, pl* -**ties** : one of two equal or approximately equal parts

moil \ˈmȯi(-ə)l\ *vb* : to work hard : DRUDGE — **moil** *n* — **moil·er** *n*

moi·ré \mȯ-ˈrā, mwä-\ or **moire** \same or ˈmȯir, ˈmwär\ *n* : a fabric (as silk) having a watered appearance

moist \ˈmȯist\ *adj* : slightly or moderately wet — **moist·ly** *adv* — **moist·ness** *n*

moist·en \ˈmȯi-sᵊn\ *vb* : to make or become moist — **moist·en·er** *n*

mois·ture \ˈmȯis-chər\ *n* : the small amount of liquid that causes dampness

mois·tur·ise *Brit var of* MOISTURIZE

mois·tur·ize \ˈmȯis-chə-ˌrīz\ *vb* -**ized;** -**iz·ing** : to add moisture to ⟨∼ the skin⟩ — **mois·tur·iz·er** *n*

mo·ji·to \mō-ˈhē-tō\ *n, pl* -**tos** [AmerSp, dim. of *moje, mojo* citrus marinade, fr. Sp *mojar* to moisten] : a cocktail made of rum, sugar, mint, lime juice and soda water

mol *abbr* molecular; molecule

mo·lar \ˈmō-lər\ *n* [ME *molares*, pl., fr. L *molaris*, fr. *molaris* of a mill, fr. *mola* millstone] : any of the broad teeth adapted to grinding food and located in the back of the jaw — **molar** *adj*

mo·las·ses \mə-ˈla-səz\ *n* : the thick brown syrup that is separated from raw sugar in sugar manufacture

¹**mold** \ˈmōld\ *n* : crumbly soil rich in organic matter

²**mold** *n* **1** : distinctive nature or character **2** : the frame on or around which something is constructed **3** : a cavity in which something is shaped; *also* : an object so shaped **4** : MOLDING

³**mold** *vb* **1** : to shape in or as if in a mold **2** : to ornament with molding — **mold·er** *n*

⁴**mold** *n* : a surface growth of fungus esp. on damp or decaying matter; *also* : a fungus that produces mold — **mold·i·ness** \ˈmōl-dē-nəs\ *n* — **moldy** *adj*

⁵**mold** *vb* : to become moldy

mold·board \ˈmōld-ˌbȯrd\ *n* : a curved iron plate attached above the plowshare to lift and turn the soil

mold·er \ˈmōl-dər\ *vb* : to crumble into small pieces

mold·ing \ˈmōl-diŋ\ *n* **1** : an act or process of shaping in a mold; *also* : an object so shaped **2** : a decorative surface, plane, or curved strip

¹**mole** \ˈmōl\ *n* : a small often pigmented spot or protuberance on the skin

²**mole** *n* **1** : any of numerous small burrowing insect-eating mammals related to the shrews and hedgehogs **2** : a spy embedded within an organization

³**mole** *n* : a massive breakwater or jetty

molecular biology *n* : a branch of biology dealing with the ultimate physical and chemical organization of living matter and esp. with the molecular basis of inheritance and protein synthesis — **molecular biologist** *n*

molecular weight *n* : the mass of a molecule that is equal to the sum of the masses of all atoms contained in the molecule's formula

mol·e·cule \ˈmä-li-ˌkyül\ *n* : the smallest particle of matter that is the same chemically as the whole mass — **mo·lec·u·lar** \mə-ˈle-kyə-lər\ *adj*

mole·hill \ˈmōl-ˌhil\ *n* : a little ridge of earth thrown up by a mole

mole·skin \-ˌskin\ *n* **1** : the skin of the mole used as fur **2** : a heavy durable cotton fabric

mo·lest \mə-ˈlest\ *vb* **1** : ANNOY, DISTURB **2** : to make annoying sexual advances to; *esp* : to force physical and usu. sexual contact on — **mo·les·ta·tion** \ˌmō-ˌles-ˈtā-shən\ *n* — **mo·lest·er** *n*

moll • monism

moll \\'mäl\\ *n* : a gangster's girlfriend

mol·li·fy \\'mä-lə-ˌfī\\ *vb* **-fied; -fy·ing 1** : to soothe in temper : APPEASE **2** : SOFTEN **3** : to reduce in intensity : ASSUAGE ⟨~ ill feelings⟩ — **mol·li·fi·ca·tion** \\ˌmä-lə-fə-'kā-shən\\ *n*

mol·lusk *or* **mol·lusc** \\'mä-ləsk\\ *n* : any of a large phylum of usu. shelled and aquatic invertebrate animals (as snails, clams, and squids) — **mol·lus·can** *also* **mol·lus·kan** \\mə-'ləs-kən\\ *adj*

¹**mol·ly·cod·dle** \\'mä-lē-ˌkä-d⁰l\\ *n* : a pampered man or boy

²**mollycoddle** *vb* **mol·ly·cod·dled; mol·ly·cod·dling** : PAMPER

Mo·lo·tov cocktail \\'mä-lə-ˌtȯf-, 'mȯ-\\ *n* [Vyacheslav M. *Molotov* †1986 Soviet foreign minister] : a crude bomb made of a bottle filled usu. with gasoline and fitted with a wick (as a saturated rag) that is ignited just prior to hurling

¹**molt** \\'mōlt\\ *vb* : to shed hair, feathers, outer skin, or horns periodically with the cast-off parts being replaced by new growth — **molt·er** *n*

²**molt** *n* : the act or process of molting

mol·ten \\'mōl-t⁰n\\ *adj* **1** : fused or liquefied by heat **2** : GLOWING

mo·ly \\'mō-lē\\ *n* : a mythical herb with black root, white flowers, and magic powers

mo·lyb·de·num \\mə-'lib-də-nəm\\ *n* : a metallic chemical element used in strengthening and hardening steel

mom \\'mäm, 'məm\\ *n* : MOTHER

mom–and–pop *adj* : being a small owner-operated business

mo·ment \\'mō-mənt\\ *n* **1** : a minute portion of time : INSTANT **2** : a time of excellence ⟨he has his ~s⟩ **3** : IMPORTANCE ⟨an event of great ~⟩ ♦ *Synonyms* CONSEQUENCE, SIGNIFICANCE, WEIGHT, IMPORT

mo·men·tar·i·ly \\ˌmō-mən-'ter-ə-lē\\ *adv* **1** : for a moment **2** *archaic* : INSTANTLY **3** : at any moment : SOON

mo·men·tary \\'mō-mən-ˌter-ē\\ *adj* **1** : continuing only a moment ⟨a ~ pause⟩; *also* : EPHEMERAL **2** : recurring at every moment — **mo·men·tar·i·ness** \\-ˌter-ē-nəs\\ *n*

mo·men·tous \\mō-'men-təs\\ *adj* : very important ⟨a ~ decision⟩ — **mo·men·tous·ly** *adv* — **mo·men·tous·ness** *n*

mo·men·tum \\mō-'men-təm\\ *n, pl* **mo·men·ta** \\-'men-tə\\ *or* **momentums** : a property that a moving body has due to its mass and motion; *also* : IMPETUS

mom·my \\'mä-mē, 'mə-\\ *n, pl* **mom·mies** : MOTHER

Mon *abbr* Monday

mon·arch \\'mä-nərk, -ˌnärk\\ *n* **1** : a person who reigns over a kingdom or an empire **2** : one holding preeminent position or power **3** : MONARCH BUTTERFLY — **mo·nar·chi·cal** \\mə-'när-ki-kəl\\ *also* **mo·nar·chic** \\-'när-kik\\ *adj*

monarch butterfly *n* : a large orange and black migratory American butterfly whose larva feeds on milkweed

mon·ar·chist \\'mä-nər-kist\\ *n* : a believer in monarchical government — **mon·ar·chism** \\-ˌki-zəm\\ *n*

mon·ar·chy \\'mä-nər-kē\\ *n, pl* **-chies** : a nation or state governed by a monarch

mon·as·tery \\'mä-nə-ˌster-ē\\ *n, pl* **-ter·ies** : a house for persons under religious vows (as monks)

mo·nas·tic \\mə-'nas-tik\\ *adj* : of or relating to monasteries or to monks or nuns — **monastic** *n* — **mo·nas·ti·cal·ly** \\-ti-k(ə-)lē\\ *adv* — **mo·nas·ti·cism** \\-tə-ˌsi-zəm\\ *n*

mon·au·ral \\mä-'nȯr-əl\\ *adj* : MONOPHONIC — **mon·au·ral·ly** *adv*

Mon·day \\'mən-dē, -ˌdā\\ *n* : the second day of the week

mon·e·tary \\'mä-nə-ˌter-ē, 'mə-\\ *adj* : of or relating to money or to the mechanisms by which it is supplied and circulated in the economy

mon·ey \\'mə-nē\\ *n, pl* **moneys** *or* **monies** \\'mə-nēz\\ **1** : something (as metal currency) accepted as a medium of exchange **2** : wealth reckoned in monetary terms **3** : the 1st, 2d, and 3d places in a horse or dog race

☞ the MONEY TABLE is on pages 465–466

mon·eyed \\'mə-nēd\\ *adj* **1** : having money : WEALTHY **2** : consisting in or derived from money

mon·ey·lend·er \\'mə-nē-ˌlen-dər\\ *n* : one (as a bank or pawnbroker) whose business is lending money

money market *n* : the trade in short-term negotiable financial instruments

money of account : a denominator of value or basis of exchange used in keeping accounts

money order *n* : an order purchased at a post office, bank, or telegraph office directing another office to pay a sum of money to a party named on it

mon·ger \\'məŋ-gər, 'mäŋ-\\ *n* **1** : DEALER **2** : one who tries to stir up or spread something — usu. used in combination ⟨warmonger⟩

mon·go \\'mäŋ-(ˌ)gō\\ *n, pl* **mongo** — see *tugrik* at MONEY table

Mon·gol \\'mäŋ-gəl, 'mäŋ-ˌgōl\\ *n* : a member of any of several traditionally pastoral peoples of Mongolia — **Mongol** *adj*

Mon·go·lian \\män-'gōl-yən, mäŋ-, -'gō-lē-ən\\ *n* **1** : a native or inhabitant of Mongolia **2** : a member of the Mongoloid racial stock — **Mongolian** *adj*

Mon·gol·oid \\'mäŋ-gə-ˌlȯid\\ *adj* : of or relating to a major racial stock native to Asia that includes peoples of northern and eastern Asia, Malaysians, Eskimos, and often American Indians — **Mongoloid** *n*

mon·goose \\'mäŋ-ˌgüs, 'mäŋ-\\ *n, pl* **mon·goos·es** *also* **mon·geese** \\-ˌgēs\\ : any of a group of small agile Old World mammals that are related to the civet cats and feed chiefly on small animals and fruits

mon·grel \\'mäŋ-grəl, 'məŋ-\\ *n* : an offspring of parents of different breeds; *esp* : one of uncertain ancestry

mon·i·ker \\'mä-ni-kər\\ *n* : NAME, NICKNAME

mo·nism \\'mō-ˌni-zəm, 'mä-\\ *n* : a view

465

MONEY — WORLD CURRENCIES

NAME	SUBDIVISION	COUNTRY	NAME	SUBDIVISION	COUNTRY
afghani	100 puls	Afghanistan	dram	100 luma	Armenia
ariary	5 iraimbilanja	Madagascar	escudo	100 centavos	Cape Verde
baht *or* tical	100 satang	Thailand	euro[5]	100 cents	Austria, Belgium, Cyprus, Estonia, Finland, France, Germany, Greece, Ireland, Italy, Latvia, Lithuania, Luxembourg, Malta, Netherlands, Portugal, Slovakia, Slovenia, Spain
balboa[1]	100 centesimos	Panama			
birr	100 cents	Ethiopia			
bolivar	100 centimos	Venezuela			
boliviano	100 centavos	Bolivia			
cedi	100 pesewas	Ghana	forint	100 fillérs[2]	Hungary
colón	100 centimos	Costa Rica	franc[6]	100 centimes	Cameroon, Central African Republic, Chad, Republic of the Congo, Equatorial Guinea[7], Gabon
córdoba	100 centavos	Nicaragua			
dalasi	100 bututs	Gambia			
denar	100 deni[2]	Macedonia			
dinar	100 centimes	Algeria			
dinar	1000 fils	Bahrain	franc[8]	100 centimes	Benin, Burkina Faso, Guinea-Bissau, Ivory Coast, Mali, Niger, Senegal, Togo
dinar	1000 fils	Iraq			
dinar	1000 fils	Jordan			
dinar	1000 fils	Kuwait			
dinar	1000 dirhams	Libya	franc	100 centimes	Burundi
dinar	1000 millimes	Tunisia	franc	100 centimes	Comoros
dirham	100 centimes	Morocco	franc	100 centimes	Democratic Republic of the Congo
dirham	100 fils	United Arab Emirates			
			franc	100 centimes	Djibouti
dobra	100 centimos	São Tomé and Príncipe	franc	100 centimes	Guinea
			franc	100 centimes[2]	Rwanda
dollar[3]	100 cents	Antigua and Barbuda, Dominica, Grenada, St. Kitts-Nevis, St. Lucia, St. Vincent and the Grenadines	franc	100 centimes *or* rappen	Switzerland
			gourde	100 centimes	Haiti
dollar	100 cents	Australia	guarani	100 centimos	Paraguay
dollar	100 cents	Bahamas	hryvnia	100 kopiykas	Ukraine
dollar	100 cents	Barbados	kina	100 toea	Papua New Guinea
dollar	100 cents	Belize			
dollar	100 sen *or* cents	Brunei	kip	100 at	Laos
			koruna	100 haleru	Czech Republic
dollar	100 cents	Canada	krona	100 aurar (*sing* eyrir)	Iceland
dollar	100 cents	Fiji			
dollar	100 cents	Guyana	krona	100 ore	Sweden
dollar	100 cents	Hong Kong	krone	100 ore	Denmark
dollar	100 cents	Jamaica	krone	100 ore	Norway
dollar	100 cents	Liberia	kuna	100 lipa	Croatia
dollar	100 cents	Namibia	kwacha	100 tambala	Malawi
dollar	100 cents	New Zealand	kwacha	100 ngwee	Zambia
dollar	100 cents	Singapore	kwanza	100 lwei	Angola
dollar	100 cents	Solomon Islands	kyat	100 pyas	Myanmar
			lari	100 tetri	Republic of Georgia
dollar	100 cents	Suriname			
dollar	100 cents	Taiwan	lek	100 qindarka (*sing* qintar)	Albania
or yuan					
			lempira	100 centavos	Honduras
dollar	100 cents	Trinidad and Tobago	leone	100 cents	Sierra Leone
			leu	100 bani (*sing* ban)	Moldova
dollar	100 cents	United States			
dollar[4]	100 cents	Zimbabwe	leu	100 bani (*sing* ban)	Romania
dollar — see RINGGIT, below					
dong	100 xu	Vietnam	lev	100 stotinki	Bulgaria

See footnotes at end of table, p. 466.

MONEY — WORLD CURRENCIES

NAME	SUBDIVISION	COUNTRY	NAME	SUBDIVISION	COUNTRY
lilangeni (*pl* emalangeni)	100 cents	Swaziland	rial *also* riyal	100 fils	Yemen
lira *or* pound	100 kurus	Turkey	rial — see RIYAL, below		
			riel	100 sen	Cambodia
livre — see POUND, below			ringgit *or* dollar	100 sen	Malaysia
loti	100 licente (*sing* sente)	Lesotho	riyal	100 dirhams	Qatar
manat	100 gopik	Azerbaijan	riyal *also* rial	100 halala	Saudi Arabia
manat	100 tenesi (*sing* tenne)	Turkmenistan	riyal — see RIAL, above		
marka	100 fening	Bosnia and Herzegovina	rubel *or* ruble	100 kapeek (*sing* kapeyka)	Belarus
metical	100 centavos	Mozambique	ruble	100 kopecks	Russia
naira	100 kobo	Nigeria	rufiyaa	100 laari	Maldives
nakfa	100 cents	Eritrea	rupee	100 paisa	India
ngultrum	100 chetrums	Bhutan	rupee	100 cents	Mauritius
ouguiya	5 khoums	Mauritania	rupee	100 paisa	Nepal
pa'anga	100 seniti	Tonga	rupee	100 paisa	Pakistan
pataca	100 avos	Macao	rupee	100 cents	Seychelles
peso	100 centavos	Argentina	rupee	100 cents	Sri Lanka
peso	100 centavos	Chile	rupiah	100 sen	Indonesia
peso	100 centavos	Colombia	shekel	100 agorot	Israel
peso	100 centavos	Cuba	shilling	100 cents	Kenya
peso	100 centavos	Dominican Republic	shilling	100 cents	Somalia
			shilling	100 cents	Tanzania
peso	100 centavos	Mexico	shilling	100 cents	Uganda
peso *or* piso	100 sentimos *or* centavos	Philippines	sol	100 centimos	Peru
			som	100 tyiyn	Kyrgyzstan
peso	100 centesimos	Uruguay	som *or* sum	100 tiyin	Uzbekistan
pound	100 piastres	Egypt			
pound *or* livre	100 piastres	Lebanon	somoni	100 dirams	Tajikistan
			taka	100 paisa *or* poisha	Bangladesh
pound	100 piastres	South Sudan			
pound	100 piastres	Sudan	tala	100 sene	Samoa
pound	100 piastres	Syria	tenge	100 tiyins	Kazakhstan
pound	100 pence (*sing* penny)	United Kingdom	tical — see BAHT, above		
			tugrik	100 mongo	Mongolia
pound — see LIRA, above			vatu		Vanuatu
pula	100 thebe	Botswana	won	100 chon	North Korea
quetzal	100 centavos	Guatemala	won	100 chon	South Korea
rand	100 cents	South Africa	yen	100 sen[2]	Japan
real	100 centavos	Brazil	yuan	100 fen	China
rial	100 dinars	Iran	yuan — see DOLLAR, above		
rial	1000 baiza	Oman	zloty	100 groszy	Poland

[1]A monetary unit in name only; replaced by the U.S. dollar.
[2]Now a subdivision in name only.
[3]Issued by the Eastern Caribbean Central Bank.
[4]A monetary unit in name only; replaced by multiple foreign currencies.
[5]Replaced the individual monetary units of participating European Union countries.
[6]Issued by the Bank of Central African States.
[7]The franc of Equatorial Guinea is also called the *franco*.
[8]Issued by the West African Economic and Monetary Union.

that reality is basically one unitary organic whole — **mo·nist** \'mō-nist, 'mä-\ *n*

mo·ni·tion \mō-'ni-shən, mə-\ *n* : WARNING, CAUTION

¹mon·i·tor \'mä-nə-tər\ *n* **1** : a student appointed to assist a teacher **2** : one that monitors; *esp* : a video display screen (as for a computer)

²monitor *vb* : to watch, check, or observe for a special purpose

mon·i·to·ry \'mä-nə-ˌtȯr-ē\ *adj* : giving admonition : WARNING

¹monk \'məŋk\ *n* [ME, fr. OE *munuc*, fr. LL *monachus*, fr. LGk *monachos*, fr. Gk, adj., single, fr. *monos* alone] : a man belonging to a religious order and living in a monastery — **monk·ish** *adj*

²monk *n* : MONKEY

¹mon·key \'məŋ-kē\ *n, pl* **monkeys** : a nonhuman primate mammal; *esp* : one of the smaller, longer-tailed, and usu. more arboreal primates as contrasted with the apes

²monkey *vb* **mon·keyed; mon·key·ing 1** : FOOL, TRIFLE — often used with *around* **2** : TAMPER — usu. used with *with* ⟨don't ~ around with the controls⟩

monkey bars *n pl* : a framework of bars on which children can play

mon·key·shine \'məŋ-kē-ˌshīn\ *n* : PRANK — usu. used in pl.

monkey wrench *n* : a wrench with one fixed and one adjustable jaw at right angles to a handle

monk·fish \'məŋk-ˌfish\ *n* : either of two marine bony fishes that have a large flattened head and are used for food

monks·hood \'məŋks-ˌhu̇d\ *n* : any of a genus of poisonous plants related to the buttercups; *esp* : a tall Eurasian herb with white or purplish flowers

¹mono \'mä-nō\ *adj* : MONOPHONIC

²mono *n* : INFECTIOUS MONONUCLEOSIS

mono·chro·mat·ic \ˌmä-nə-krō-'ma-tik\ *adj* **1** : having or consisting of one color **2** : consisting of radiation (as light) of a single wavelength

mono·chrome \'mä-nə-ˌkrōm\ *adj* : involving or producing visual images in a single color or in varying tones of a single color ⟨~ television⟩

mon·o·cle \'mä-ni-kəl\ *n* : an eyeglass for one eye

mono·clo·nal \ˌmä-nə-'klō-nəl\ *adj* : produced by, being, or composed of cells derived from a single cell ⟨~ antibodies⟩

mono·cot·y·le·don \ˌmä-nə-ˌkät-tə-'lē-dᵊn\ *n* : any of a class or subclass of chiefly herbaceous seed plants having an embryo with a single cotyledon and usu. parallel-veined leaves

mon·o·dy \'mä-nə-dē\ *n, pl* **-dies** [LGk *monōidia*, fr. Gk *monos* single + *aeidein* to sing] : ELEGY, DIRGE — **mo·nod·ic** \mə-'nä-dik\ *or* **mo·nod·i·cal** \-di-kəl\ *adj* — **mon·o·dist** \'mä-nə-dist\ *n*

mo·nog·a·my \mə-'nä-gə-mē\ *n* **1** : marriage with but one person at a time **2** : the practice of having a single mate during a period of time — **mo·nog·a·mist** \-mist\ *n* — **mo·nog·a·mous** \-məs\ *adj*

mono·gram \'mä-nə-ˌgram\ *n* : a sign of identity composed of the combined initials of a name — **monogram** *vb*

mono·graph \'mä-nə-ˌgraf\ *n* : a learned treatise on a small area of learning

mono·lin·gual \ˌmä-nə-'liŋ-gwəl\ *adj* : knowing or using only one language

mono·lith \'mä-nə-ˌlith\ *n* **1** : a single great stone often in the form of a monument or column **2** : something large and powerful that acts as a single unified force ⟨a bureaucratic ~⟩ — **mono·lith·ic** \ˌmä-nə-'li-thik\ *adj*

mono·logue *also* **mono·log** \'mä-nə-ˌlȯg\ *n* **1** : a dramatic soliloquy; *also* : a long speech monopolizing conversation **2** : the routine of a stand-up comic — **mono·logu·ist** \-ˌlȯg-ist\ *or* **mo·nol·o·gist** \'mä-nə-lə-jist; 'mä-nə-ˌlȯ-gist\ *n*

mono·ma·nia \ˌmä-nə-'mä-nē-ə, -nyə\ *n* **1** : mental disorder limited in expression to one area of thought **2** : excessive concentration on a single object or idea — **mono·ma·ni·ac** \-nē-ˌak\ *n or adj*

mono·mer \'mä-nə-mər\ *n* : a simple chemical compound that can be polymerized

mono·nu·cle·o·sis \ˌmä-nō-ˌnü-klē-'ō-səs, -ˌnyü-\ *n* : INFECTIOUS MONONUCLEOSIS

mono·phon·ic \ˌmä-nə-'fä-nik\ *adj* : of or relating to sound recording or reproduction involving a single transmission path

mono·plane \'mä-nə-ˌplān\ *n* : an airplane with only one set of wings

mo·nop·o·ly \mə-'nä-pə-lē\ *n, pl* **-lies** [L *monopolium*, fr. Gk *monopōlion*, fr. *monos* alone, single + *pōlein* to sell] **1** : exclusive ownership (as through command of supply) **2** : a commodity controlled by one party **3** : one that has a monopoly — **mo·nop·o·list** \-list\ *n* — **mo·nop·o·lis·tic** \mə-ˌnä-pə-'lis-tik\ *adj* — **mo·nop·o·li·za·tion** \-lə-'zā-shən\ *n* — **mo·nop·o·lize** \mə-'nä-pə-ˌlīz\ *vb*

mono·rail \'mä-nə-ˌrāl\ *n* : a single rail serving as a track for a vehicle; *also* : a vehicle traveling on such a track

mono·so·di·um glu·ta·mate \ˌmä-nə-ˌsō-dē-əm-'glü-tə-ˌmāt\ *n* : a crystalline salt used to enhance the flavor of food

mono·syl·la·ble \'mä-nə-ˌsi-lə-bəl\ *n* : a word of one syllable — **mono·syl·lab·ic** \ˌmä-nə-sə-'la-bik\ *adj* — **mono·syl·lab·i·cal·ly** \-bi-k(ə-)lē\ *adv*

mono·the·ism \'mä-nə-(ˌ)thē-ˌi-zəm\ *n* : a doctrine or belief that there is only one deity — **mono·the·ist** \-ˌthē-ist\ *n* — **mono·the·is·tic** \-thē-'is-tik\ *adj*

mono·tone \'mä-nə-ˌtōn\ *n* : a succession of syllables, words, or sentences in unvaried key or pitch

mo·not·o·nous \mə-'nä-tə-nəs\ *adj* **1** : uttered or sounded in one unvarying tone **2** : tediously uniform — **mo·not·o·nous·ly** *adv* — **mo·not·o·nous·ness** *n* — **mo·not·o·ny** \mə-'nä-tə-nē\ *n* : tedious sameness or uniformity

mono·un·sat·u·rat·ed \ˌmä-nō-ˌən-'sa-chə-ˌrā-təd\ *adj* : containing one double or triple bond per molecule — used esp. of an oil, fat, or fatty acid

mon·ox·ide \mə-'näk-ˌsīd\ *n* : an oxide

containing one atom of oxygen in a molecule

mon·sei·gneur \ˌmōⁿ-ˌsān-ˈyər\ *n, pl* **mes·sei·gneurs** \ˌmā-ˌsān-ˈyər, -ˈyərz\ : a French dignitary — used as a title

mon·sieur \məs-ˈyər\ *n, pl* **mes·sieurs** \same or -ˈyərz\ : a Frenchman of high rank or station — used as a title equivalent to *Mister*

mon·si·gnor \män-ˈsē-nyər\ *n, pl* **monsignors** *or* **mon·si·gno·ri** \ˌmän-ˌsēn-ˈyȯr ē\ [It *monsignore*] : a Roman Catholic prelate — used as a title

mon·soon \män-ˈsün\ *n* [obs. Dutch *monssoen,* fr. Pg *monção,* fr. Ar *mawsim* time, season] 1 : a periodic wind esp. in the Indian Ocean and southern Asia 2 : the season of the southwest monsoon esp. in India 3 : rainfall associated with the monsoon

¹**mon·ster** \ˈmän-stər\ *n* 1 : an abnormally developed plant or animal 2 : an animal of strange or terrifying shape; *also* : one unusually large of its kind 3 : an extremely ugly, wicked, or cruel person — **mon·stros·i·ty** \män-ˈsträ-sə-tē\ *n* — **mon·strous** \ˈmän-strəs\ *adj* — **mon·strous·ly** *adv*

²**monster** *adj* : very large : ENORMOUS

mon·strance \ˈmän-strəns\ *n* : a vessel in which the consecrated Host is exposed for the adoration of the faithful

Mont *abbr* Montana

mon·tage \män-ˈtäzh\ *n* [F] 1 : a composite photograph made by combining several separate pictures 2 : an artistic composition made up of several different kinds of elements 3 : a varied mixture : JUMBLE

month \ˈmənth\ *n, pl* **months** \ˈməns, ˈmənths\ : one of the 12 parts into which the year is divided — **month·ly** *adv or adj or n*

month·long \ˈmənth-ˈlȯn\ *adj* : lasting a month

mon·u·ment \ˈmän-yə-mənt\ *n* 1 : a lasting reminder; *esp* : a structure erected in remembrance of a person or event 2 : NATIONAL MONUMENT

mon·u·men·tal \ˌmän-yə-ˈmen-tᵊl\ *adj* 1 : of or relating to a monument 2 : MASSIVE; *also* : OUTSTANDING ⟨a ~ achievement⟩ 3 : very great ⟨a ~ task⟩ — **mon·u·men·tal·ly** *adv*

moo \ˈmü\ *vb* : to make the natural throat noise of a cow — **moo** *n*

¹**mood** \ˈmüd\ *n* 1 : a conscious state of mind or predominant emotion : FEELING 2 : a prevailing attitude : DISPOSITION 3 : a distinctive atmosphere

²**mood** *n* : distinction of form of a verb to express whether its action or state is conceived as fact or in some other manner (as wish)

moody \ˈmü-dē\ *adj* **mood·i·er; -est** 1 : GLOOMY 2 : subject to moods : TEMPERAMENTAL — **mood·i·ly** \-də-lē\ *adv* — **mood·i·ness** \-dē-nəs\ *n*

¹**moon** \ˈmün\ *n* 1 : the earth's natural satellite 2 : SATELLITE 2

²**moon** *vb* : to engage in idle reverie

moon·beam \ˈmün-ˌbēm\ *n* : a ray of light from the moon

¹**moon·light** \-ˌlīt\ *n* : the light of the moon — **moon·lit** \-ˌlit\ *adj*

²**moonlight** *vb* **moon·light·ed; moon·light·ing** : to hold a second job in addition to a regular one — **moon·light·er** *n*

moon·roof \-ˌrüf, -ˌru̇f\ *n* : a glass sunroof

moon·scape \-ˌskāp\ *n* : the surface of the moon as seen or as pictured

moon·shine \-ˌshīn\ *n* 1 : MOONLIGHT 2 : empty talk 3 : intoxicating liquor usu. illegally distilled

moon·stone \-ˌstōn\ *n* : a transparent or translucent feldspar of pearly luster used as a gem

moon·struck \-ˌstrək\ *adj* 1 : mentally unbalanced 2 : romantically sentimental 3 : lost in fantasy

¹**moor** \ˈmu̇r\ *n* 1 *chiefly Brit* : an expanse of open rolling infertile land 2 : a boggy area; *esp* : one that is peaty and dominated by grasses and sedges

²**moor** *vb* : to make fast with or as if with cables, lines, or anchors

Moor \ˈmu̇r\ *n* : one of the Arab and Berber conquerors of Spain — **Moor·ish** *adj*

moor·ing \ˈmu̇r-iŋ\ *n* 1 : a place where or an object to which a craft can be made fast 2 : an established practice or stabilizing influence — usu. used in pl.

moor·land \-lənd, -ˌland\ *n* : land consisting of moors

moose \ˈmüs\ *n, pl* **moose** : a large heavy-antlered ruminant mammal related to the deer that has humped shoulders and long legs and inhabits northern forested areas

¹**moot** \ˈmüt\ *vb* : to bring up for discussion; *also* : DEBATE

²**moot** *adj* 1 : open to question; *also* : DISPUTED ⟨a ~ assertion⟩ 2 : having no practical significance ⟨the discussion became ~⟩

¹**mop** \ˈmäp\ *n* : an implement made of absorbent material fastened to a handle and used esp. for cleaning floors

²**mop** *vb* **mopped; mop·ping** : to use a mop on : clean with a mop

mope \ˈmōp\ *vb* **moped; mop·ing** 1 : to become dull, dejected, or listless 2 : DAWDLE

mo·ped \ˈmō-ˌped\ *n* : a light low-powered motorbike that can be pedaled

mop·pet \ˈmä-pət\ *n* [obs. E *mop* fool, child] : CHILD

mo·raine \mə-ˈrān\ *n* : an accumulation of earth and stones left by a glacier

¹**mor·al** \ˈmȯr-əl\ *adj* 1 : of or relating to principles of right and wrong 2 : conforming to a standard of right behavior; *also* : capable of right and wrong action 3 : probable but not proved ⟨a ~ certainty⟩ 4 : perceptual or psychological rather than tangible or practical in nature or effect ⟨a ~ victory⟩ ♦ *Synonyms* VIRTUOUS, RIGHTEOUS, NOBLE, ETHICAL, PRINCIPLED — **mor·al·ly** *adv*

²**moral** *n* 1 : the practical meaning (as of a story) 2 *pl* : moral practices or teachings ⟨protecting the public ~s⟩

mo·rale \mə-'ral\ *n* **1** : MORALITY **2** : the mental and emotional attitudes of an individual to the tasks at hand; *also* : ESPRIT DE CORPS

mor·al·ise *Brit var of* MORALIZE

mor·al·ist \'mȯr-ə-list\ *n* **1** : one who leads a moral life **2** : a thinker or writer concerned with morals **3** : one concerned with regulating the morals of others — **mor·al·is·tic** \ˌmȯr-ə-'lis-tik\ *adj* — **mor·al·is·ti·cal·ly** \-ti-k(ə-)lē\ *adv*

mo·ral·i·ty \mə-'ra-lə-tē\ *n, pl* **-ties** : moral conduct : VIRTUE

mor·al·ize \'mȯr-ə-ˌlīz\ *vb* **-ized; -iz·ing** : to make moral reflections — **mor·al·i·za·tion** \ˌmȯr-ə-lə-'zā-shən\ *n* — **mor·al·iz·er** \'mȯr-ə-ˌlī-zər\ *n*

mo·rass \mə-'ras\ *n* [D *moeras,* fr. OF *maresc,* of Gmc origin; akin to OE *mersc* marsh] : SWAMP; *also* : something that entangles, impedes, or confuses

mor·a·to·ri·um \ˌmȯr-ə-'tȯr-ē-əm\ *n, pl* **-ri·ums** *or* **-ria** \-ē-ə\ [ultim. fr. L *mora* delay] : a suspension of activity

mo·ray eel \mə-'rā-, 'mȯr-ˌā-\ *n* : any of numerous often brightly colored biting eels of warm seas

mor·bid \'mȯr-bəd\ *adj* **1** : of, relating to, or typical of disease; *also* : DISEASED, SICKLY **2** : characterized by gloomy or unwholesome ideas or feelings **3** : GRISLY, GRUESOME 〈~ details〉 — **mor·bid·i·ty** \mȯr-'bi-də-tē\ *n* — **mor·bid·ly** *adv* — **mor·bid·ness** *n*

mor·dant \'mȯr-dᵊnt\ *adj* **1** : biting or caustic in manner or style **2** : BURNING, PUNGENT — **mor·dant·ly** *adv*

¹more \'mȯr\ *adj* **1** : GREATER 〈something ~ than I expected〉 **2** : ADDITIONAL 〈wanted ~ coffee〉

²more *adv* **1** : in addition **2** : to a greater or higher degree 〈~ evenly matched〉

³more *n* **1** : a greater quantity, number, or amount 〈the ~ the merrier〉 **2** : an additional amount 〈costs a little ~〉

⁴more *pron* : additional persons or things or a greater amount

mo·rel \mə-'rel\ *n* : any of several pitted edible fungi

more·over \mȯr-'ō-vər\ *adv* : in addition : FURTHER

mo·res \'mȯr-ˌāz\ *n pl* [L, pl. of *mor-, mos* custom] **1** : the fixed morally binding customs of a group **2** : HABITS, MANNERS 〈cultural ~〉

Mor·gan \'mȯr-gən\ *n* : any of an American breed of lightly built horses

morgue \'mȯrg\ *n* : a place where the bodies of dead persons are kept until released for burial or autopsy

mor·i·bund \'mȯr-ə-(ˌ)bənd\ *adj* : being in a dying condition

Mor·mon \'mȯr-mən\ *n* : a member of the Church of Jesus Christ of Latter-day Saints — **Mor·mon·ism** \-mə-ˌni-zəm\ *n*

morn \'mȯrn\ *n* : MORNING

morn·ing \'mȯr-niŋ\ *n* **1** : the early part of the day; *esp* : the time from the sunrise to noon **2** : BEGINNING

morn·ing-after pill \ˌmȯr-niŋ-'af-tər-\ *n* : a contraceptive drug taken up to usu. three days after sexual intercourse

morning glory *n* : any of various twining plants related to the sweet potato that have often showy bell-shaped or funnel-shaped flowers

morning sickness *n* : nausea and vomiting that typically occur in the morning esp. during early pregnancy

morning star *n* : a bright planet (as Venus) seen in the eastern sky before or at sunrise

mo·roc·co \mə-'rä-kō\ *n* : a fine leather made of goatskins tanned with sumac

mo·ron \'mȯr-ˌän\ *n* **1** *usu. offensive* : a mildly mentally retarded person **2** : a very stupid person — **mo·ron·ic** \mə-'rä-nik\ *adj* — **mo·ron·i·cal·ly** \-ni-k(ə-)lē\ *adv*

mo·rose \mə-'rōs\ *adj* [L *morosus* hard to please, exacting, fr. *mor-, mos* custom, disposition] : having a sullen disposition; *also* : GLOOMY — **mo·rose·ly** *adv* — **mo·rose·ness** *n*

morph \'mȯrf\ *vb* : to change the form or character of : TRANSFORM

mor·pheme \'mȯr-ˌfēm\ *n* : a meaningful linguistic unit that contains no smaller meaningful parts — **mor·phe·mic** \mȯr-'fē-mik\ *adj*

mor·phia \'mȯr-fē-ə\ *n* : MORPHINE

mor·phine \'mȯr-ˌfēn\ *n* [F, fr. Gk *Morpheus,* Greek god of dreams] : an addictive drug obtained from opium and used to ease pain or induce sleep

mor·phol·o·gy \mȯr-'fä-lə-jē\ *n* **1** : a branch of biology dealing with the form and structure of organisms **2** : a study and description of word formation in a language — **mor·pho·log·i·cal** \ˌmȯr-fə-'lä-ji-kəl\ *adj* — **mor·phol·o·gist** \mȯr-'fä-lə-jist\ *n*

mor·ris \'mȯr-əs\ *n* : a vigorous English dance traditionally performed by men wearing costumes and bells

mor·row \'mär-ō\ *n* : the next day

Morse code \'mȯrs-\ *n* : either of two codes consisting of dots and dashes or long and short sounds used for transmitting messages

mor·sel \'mȯr-səl\ *n* [ME, fr. AF, dim. of *mors* bite, fr. L *morsus,* fr. *mordēre* to bite] **1** : a small piece or quantity 〈chocolate ~s〉 **2** : a tasty dish

mor·tal \'mȯr-tᵊl\ *adj* **1** : causing death : FATAL; *also* : leading to eternal punishment 〈~ sin〉 **2** : subject to death 〈~ man〉 **3** : implacably hostile 〈~ foe〉 **4** : very great : EXTREME 〈~ fear〉 **5** : HUMAN 〈~ limitations〉 — **mortal** *n* — **mor·tal·i·ty** \mȯr-'ta-lə-tē\ *n* — **mor·tal·ly** \'mȯr-tᵊl-ē\ *adv*

¹mor·tar \'mȯr-tər\ *n* **1** : a strong bowl in which substances are pounded or crushed with a pestle **2** : a short-barreled cannon used to fire shells at high angles

²mortar *n* : a building material (as a mixture of lime and cement with sand and water) that is spread between bricks or stones to bind them together as it hardens — **mortar** *vb*

mor·tar·board \'mȯr-tər-ˌbȯrd\ *n* **1** : a square board for holding mortar **2** : an academic cap with a flat square top

mort·gage \'mȯr-gij\ n [ME morgage, fr. AF mortgage, fr. mort dead + gage pledge] : a transfer of rights to a piece of property usu. as security for the payment of a loan or debt that becomes void when the debt is paid — **mortgage** vb — **mort·gag·ee** \ˌmȯr-gi-'jē\ n — **mort·gag·or** \ˌmȯr-gi-'jȯr\ n

mor·ti·cian \mȯr-'ti-shən\ n [L mort-, mors death + E -ician (as in physician)] : UNDERTAKER

mor·ti·fy \'mȯr-tə-ˌfī\ vb -fied; -fy·ing 1 : to subdue (as the body) esp. by abstinence or self-inflicted pain 2 : HUMILIATE ⟨her behavior mortified her parents⟩ 3 : to become necrotic or gangrenous — **mor·ti·fi·ca·tion** \ˌmȯr-tə-fə-'kā-shən\ n

mor·tise also **mor·tice** \'mȯr-təs\ n : a hole cut in a piece of wood into which another piece fits to form a joint

mor·tu·ary \'mȯr-chə-ˌwer-ē\ n, pl -ar·ies : a place in which dead bodies are kept until burial

mos abbr months

mo·sa·ic \mō-'zā-ik\ n : a surface decoration made by inlaying small pieces (as of colored glass or stone) to form figures or patterns; also : a design made in mosaic — **mosaic** adj

mo·sey \'mō-zē\ vb **mo·seyed; mo·sey·ing** : SAUNTER ⟨moseyed through the park⟩

mosh \'mäsh\ vb : to engage in rough uninhibited dancing near the stage at a rock concert

mosh pit n : an area in front of a stage where rough dancing takes place at a rock concert

Mos·lem \'mäz-ləm\ var of MUSLIM

mosque \'mäsk\ n : a building used for public worship by Muslims

mos·qui·to \mə-'skē-tō\ n, pl -toes also -tos : any of a family of dipteran flies the female of which sucks the blood of animals

mosquito net n : a net or screen for keeping out mosquitoes

moss \'mȯs\ n : any of a class of green plants that lack flowers but have small leafy stems and often grow in clumps — **mossy** adj

moss·back \'mȯs-ˌbak\ n : an extremely conservative person : FOGY

¹**most** \'mōst\ adj 1 : GREATEST ⟨the ∼ ability⟩ 2 : the majority of ⟨∼ people⟩

²**most** adv 1 : to the greatest or highest degree ⟨∼ beautiful⟩ 2 : to a very great degree ⟨a ∼ careful driver⟩

³**most** n : the greatest amount ⟨the ∼ I can do⟩

⁴**most** pron : the greatest number or part ⟨∼ became discouraged⟩

-most adj suffix : most ⟨innermost⟩ : most toward ⟨endmost⟩

most·ly \'mōst-lē\ adv : MAINLY

mot \'mō\ n, pl **mots** \same or 'mōz\ [F, word, saying, fr. LL muttum grunt] : a witty saying

mote \'mōt\ n : a small particle

mo·tel \mō-'tel\ n [blend of motor and hotel] : a hotel in which the rooms are accessible from the parking area

mo·tet \mō-'tet\ n : a choral work on a sacred text for several voices usu. without instrumental accompaniment

moth \'mȯth\ n, pl **moths** \'mȯthz, 'mȯths\ : any of various insects belonging to the same order as the butterflies but usu. night-flying and with a stouter body and smaller wings

moth·ball \'mȯth-ˌbȯl\ n 1 : a ball (as of naphthalene) used to keep moths out of clothing 2 pl : protective storage ⟨many ships were put in ∼s⟩

¹**moth·er** \'mə-thər\ n 1 : a female parent 2 : the superior of a religious community of women 3 : SOURCE, ORIGIN ⟨necessity is the ∼ of invention⟩ — **moth·er·hood** \-ˌhud\ n — **moth·er·less** adj — **moth·er·li·ness** \-lē-nəs\ n — **moth·er·ly** adj

²**mother** vb 1 : to give birth to; also : PRODUCE 2 : to care for or protect like a mother

moth·er·board \'mə-thər-ˌbȯrd\ n : the main circuit board esp. of a microcomputer

moth·er–in–law \'mə-thər-ən-ˌlȯ\ n, pl **mothers–in–law** \'mə-thərz-\ : the mother of one's spouse

moth·er·land \'mə-thər-ˌland\ n 1 : the land of origin of something 2 : the native land of one's ancestors

moth·er–of–pearl \ˌmə-thər-əv-'pərl\ n : the hard pearly matter forming the inner layer of a mollusk shell

mother ship n : a ship serving smaller craft

mo·tif \mō-'tēf\ n [F, motive, motif] : a dominant idea or central theme (as in a work of art)

mo·tile \'mōt-ᵊl, 'mō-ˌtī(-ə)l\ adj : capable of spontaneous movement ⟨∼ cells⟩ — **mo·til·i·ty** \mō-'ti-lə-tē\ n

¹**mo·tion** \'mō-shən\ n 1 : an act, process, or instance of moving 2 : a proposal for action (as by a deliberative body) 3 pl : ACTIVITIES, MOVEMENTS — **mo·tion·less** adj — **mo·tion·less·ly** adv — **mo·tion·less·ness** n

²**motion** vb : to direct or signal by a movement

motion picture n : a series of pictures projected on a screen so rapidly that they produce a continuous picture in which persons and objects seem to move

motion sickness n : sickness induced by motion and characterized by nausea

mo·ti·vate \'mō-tə-ˌvāt\ vb -vat·ed; -vat·ing : to provide with a motive : IMPEL — **mo·ti·va·tion** \ˌmō-tə-'vā-shən\ n — **mo·ti·va·tion·al** \-shə-nəl\ adj — **mo·ti·va·tor** \'mō-tə-ˌvā-tər\ n

¹**mo·tive** \'mō-tiv, 2 also mō-'tēv\ n 1 : something (as a need or desire) that causes a person to act 2 : a recurrent theme in a musical composition 3 : MOTIF — **mo·tive·less** adj

²**mo·tive** \'mō-tiv\ adj 1 : moving to action 2 : of or relating to motion

mot·ley \'mät-lē\ adj 1 : variegated in color 2 : made up of diverse often incongruous elements ♦ **Synonyms** HETEROGENEOUS, MISCELLANEOUS, ASSORTED, MIXED, VARIED

¹**mo·tor** \'mō-tər\ *n* [L, fr. *movēre* to move] **1** : one that imparts motion **2** : a machine that produces motion or power for doing work **3** : AUTOMOBILE

²**motor** *vb* : to travel or transport by automobile : DRIVE — **mo·tor·ist** *n*

mo·tor·bike \'mō-tər-ˌbīk\ *n* : a small lightweight motorcycle

mo·tor·boat \-ˌbōt\ *n* : a boat propelled by a motor

mo·tor·cade \-ˌkād\ *n* : a procession of motor vehicles

mo·tor·car \-ˌkär\ *n* : AUTOMOBILE

mo·tor·cy·cle \'mō-tər-ˌsī-kəl\ *n* : a 2-wheeled automotive vehicle — **mo·tor·cy·clist** \-k(ə-)list\ *n*

motor home *n* : a large motor vehicle equipped as living quarters

motor inn *n* : MOTEL

mo·tor·ise *Brit var of* MOTORIZE

mo·tor·ize \'mō-tə-ˌrīz\ *vb* **-ized; -iz·ing** **1** : to equip with a motor **2** : to equip with automobiles

mo·tor·man \'mō-tər-mən\ *n* : an operator of a motor-driven vehicle (as a streetcar or subway train)

motor scooter *n* : a low 2- or 3-wheeled automotive vehicle resembling a child's scooter but having a seat

mo·tor·truck \'mō-tər-ˌtrək\ *n* : an automotive truck

motor vehicle *n* : an automotive vehicle (as an automobile) not operated on rails

mot·tle \'mä-t²l\ *vb* **mot·tled; mot·tling** : to mark with spots of different color : BLOTCH

mot·to \'mä-tō\ *n, pl* **mottoes** *also* **mottos** [It, fr. LL *muttum* grunt, fr. L *muttire* to mutter] **1** : a sentence, phrase, or word inscribed on something to indicate its character or use **2** : a short expression of a guiding rule of conduct

moue \'mü\ *n* : a little grimace

mould *chiefly Brit var of* MOLD

moult *chiefly Brit var of* MOLT

mound \'maund\ *n* **1** : an artificial bank or hill of earth or stones **2** : KNOLL **3** : HEAP, PILE ⟨a ~ of work⟩

¹**mount** \'maunt\ *n* : a high hill

²**mount** *vb* **1** : to increase in amount or extent; *also* : RISE, ASCEND **2** : to get up on something; *esp* : to seat oneself on (as a horse) for riding **3** : to put in position ⟨~ artillery⟩ **4** : to set on something that elevates **5** : to attach to a support **6** : to prepare esp. for examination or display — **mount·able** *adj* — **mount·er** *n*

³**mount** *n* **1** : FRAME, SUPPORT **2** : a means of conveyance; *esp* : SADDLE HORSE

moun·tain \'maun-t²n\ *n* : a landmass higher than a hill — **moun·tain·ous** \-tə-nəs\ *adj* — **moun·tainy** \-t²n-ē\ *adj*

mountain ash *n* : any of various trees related to the roses that have pinnate leaves and red or orange-red fruits

mountain bike *n* : a bicycle with wide knobby tires, straight handlebars, and 18 or 21 gears that is designed to operate esp. over unpaved terrain

moun·tain·eer \ˌmaun-tə-'nir\ *n* **1** : a native or inhabitant of a mountainous region **2** : one who climbs mountains for sport

mountain goat *n* : a ruminant mammal of mountainous northwestern No. America that resembles a goat

mountain laurel *n* : a No. American evergreen shrub or small tree of the heath family with glossy leaves and clusters of rose-colored or white flowers

mountain lion *n* : COUGAR

moun·tain·side \'maun-t²n-ˌsīd\ *n* : the side of a mountain

moun·tain·top \-ˌtäp\ *n* : the summit of a mountain

moun·te·bank \'maun-ti-ˌbaŋk\ *n* [It *montimbanco*, fr. *montare* to mount + *in* in, on + *banco, banca* bench] : QUACK, CHARLATAN

Mount·ie \'maun-tē\ *n* : a member of the Royal Canadian Mounted Police

mount·ing \'maun-tiŋ\ *n* : something that serves as a frame or support

mourn \'mōrn\ *vb* : to feel or express grief or sorrow — **mourn·er** *n*

mourn·ful \-fəl\ *adj* : expressing, feeling, or causing sorrow ⟨a ~ song⟩ — **mourn·ful·ly** *adv* — **mourn·ful·ness** *n*

mourn·ing \'mōr-niŋ\ *n* **1** : an outward sign (as black clothes) of grief for a person's death **2** : a period of time during which signs of grief are shown

mouse \'maus\ *n, pl* **mice** \'mīs\ **1** : any of numerous small rodents with pointed snout, long body, and slender tail **2** : a small manual device that controls cursor movement on a computer display

mouse pad *n* : a thin flat pad on which a computer mouse is used

mous·er \'mau-sər\ *n* : a cat proficient at catching mice

mouse·trap \'maus-ˌtrap\ *n* **1** : a trap for catching mice **2** : a stratagem that lures one to defeat or destruction — **mousetrap** *vb*

mousse \'müs\ *n* [F, lit., froth, moss] **1** : a molded chilled dessert made with sweetened and flavored whipped cream or egg whites and gelatin **2** : a foamy preparation used in styling hair — **mousse** *vb*

moustache *var of* MUSTACHE

mousy *or* **mous·ey** \'mau-sē, -zē\ *adj* **mous·i·er; -est** **1** : QUIET, STEALTHY **2** : TIMID **3** : grayish brown — **mous·i·ness** \'mau-sē-nəs, -zē-\ *n*

¹**mouth** \'mauth\ *n, pl* **mouths** \'mauthz, 'mauths\ **1** : the opening through which an animal takes in food; *also* : the cavity that encloses the tongue, lips, and teeth in the typical vertebrate **2** : something resembling a mouth (as in affording entrance) — **mouthed** \'mauthd, 'mautht\ *adj* — **mouth·ful** *n*

²**mouth** \'mauth\ *vb* **1** : SPEAK; *also* : DECLAIM **2** : to repeat without comprehension or sincerity ⟨~ed platitudes⟩ **3** : to form soundlessly with the lips

mouth harp *n* : HARMONICA

mouth·part \'mauth-ˌpärt\ *n* : a structure or appendage near the mouth (as of an insect) esp. when adapted for eating

mouth·piece \-ˌpēs\ *n* **1** : a part (as of a

musical instrument) that goes in the mouth or to which the mouth is applied **2** : SPOKESMAN

mouth-to-mouth *adj* : of, relating to, or being a method of artificial respiration in which air from a rescuer's mouth is forced into a victim's lungs

mouth-wash \-ˌwȯsh, -ˌwäsh\ *n* : a usu. antiseptic liquid preparation for cleaning the mouth and teeth

mou-ton \'mü-ˌtän\ *n* : processed sheepskin that has been sheared or dyed to resemble beaver or seal

¹move \'müv\ *vb* **moved; mov-ing** **1** : to change or cause to change position or posture **2** : to go or cause to go from one point to another; *also* : DEPART **3** : to take or cause to take action **4** : to show marked activity **5** : to stir the emotions **6** : to make a formal request, application, or appeal **7** : to change one's residence **8** : EVACUATE **2** — **mov-able** *or* **move-able** \'mü-və-bəl\ *adj*

²move *n* **1** : an act of moving **2** : a calculated step taken to gain an objective **3** : a change of location **4** : an agile action esp. in sports

move-ment \'müv-mənt\ *n* **1** : the act or process of moving : MOVE **2** : a series of organized activities working toward an objective **3** : the moving parts of a mechanism (as of a watch) **4** : RHYTHM **5** : a section of an extended musical composition **6** : an act of voiding the bowels; *also* : STOOL **4**

mov-er \'mü-vər\ *n* : one that moves; *esp* : one that moves the belongings of others from one location to another

mov-ie \'mü-vē\ *n* **1** : MOTION PICTURE **2** *pl* : a showing of a motion picture **3** *pl* : the motion-picture industry

¹mow \'maů\ *n* : the part of a barn where hay or straw is stored

²mow \'mō\ *vb* **mowed** *or* **mown** \'mōn\; **mow-ing** **1** : to cut (as grass) with a scythe or machine **2** : to cut the standing herbage of ⟨~ the lawn⟩ — **mow-er** *n*

mox-ie \'mäk-sē\ *n* **1** : ENERGY, PEP **2** : COURAGE, DETERMINATION

moz-za-rel-la \ˌmät-sə-'re-lə\ *n* [It] : a moist white unsalted unripened mild cheese of a smooth rubbery texture

¹MP \'em-'pē\ *n* **1** : a member of the military police **2** : an elected member of a parliament

²MP *abbr* **1** melting point **2** metropolitan police

mpg *abbr* miles per gallon

mph *abbr* miles per hour

Mr. \'mis-tər\ *n, pl* **Messrs.** \'me-sərz\ — used as a conventional title of courtesy before a man's surname or his title of office

MRI *n* : MAGNETIC RESONANCE IMAGING; *also* : the procedure in which magnetic resonance imaging is used

Mr. Right *n* : a man who would make the perfect husband

Mrs. \'mi-səz, -səs, *esp Southern* 'mi-zəz, -zəs\ *n, pl* **Mes-dames** \mā-'däm, -'dam\

— used as a conventional title of courtesy before a married woman's surname

Ms. \'miz\ *n, pl* **Mss.** *or* **Mses.** \'mi-zez\ — used instead of *Miss* or *Mrs.*

MS *abbr* **1** manuscript **2** master of science **3** military science **4** Mississippi **5** motor ship **6** multiple sclerosis

msec *abbr* millisecond

msg *abbr* message

MSG *abbr* **1** master sergeant **2** monosodium glutamate

msgr *abbr* **1** monseigneur **2** monsignor

MSgt *abbr* master sergeant

MSS *abbr* manuscripts

MST *abbr* mountain standard time

mt *abbr* mount; mountain

¹Mt *abbr* Matthew

²Mt *symbol* meitnerium

MT *abbr* **1** metric ton **2** Montana **3** mountain time

mtg *abbr* **1** meeting **2** mortgage

mtge *abbr* mortgage

mu \'myü, 'mü\ *n* : the 12th letter of the Greek alphabet — M or μ

¹much \'məch\ *adj* **more** \'mȯr\; **most** \'mōst\ : great in quantity, amount, extent, or degree ⟨~ money⟩

²much *adv* **more; most** **1** : to a great degree or extent ⟨~ happier⟩ **2** : ALMOST, NEARLY ⟨looks ~ as he did before⟩

³much *n* **1** : a great quantity, amount, extent, or degree **2** : something considerable or impressive

mu-ci-lage \'myü-sə-lij\ *n* : a watery sticky solution (as of a gum) used esp. as an adhesive — **mu-ci-lag-i-nous** \ˌmyü-sə-'la-jə-nəs\ *adj*

muck \'mək\ *n* **1** : soft moist barnyard manure **2** : FILTH, DIRT **3** : a dark richly organic soil; *also* : MUD, MIRE — **mucky** *adj*

muck-rake \-ˌrāk\ *vb* : to expose publicly real or apparent misconduct of a prominent individual or business — **muck-rak-er** *n*

mu-cus \'myü-kəs\ *n* : a slimy slippery protective secretion of membranes (**mucous membranes**) lining some body cavities — **mu-cous** \-kəs\ *adj*

mud \'məd\ *n* : soft wet earth : MIRE

mud-dle \'mə-dᵊl\ *vb* **mud-dled; mud-dling** **1** : to make muddy **2** : to confuse esp. with liquor **3** : to mix up or make a mess of ⟨*muddled* the household accounts⟩ **4** : to think or act in a confused way

mud-dle-head-ed \ˌmə-dᵊl-'he-dəd\ *adj* **1** : mentally confused **2** : INEPT

¹mud-dy \'mə-dē\ *adj* **mud-di-er; -est** **1** : full of or covered with mud **2** : suggestive of mud **3** : CLOUDY, OBSCURE — **mud-di-ness** *n*

²muddy *vb* **mud-died; mud-dy-ing** **1** : to soil or stain with or as if with mud **2** : to make cloudy or obscure **3** : CONFUSE

mud-flat \'məd-ˌflat\ *n* : a level tract alternately covered and left bare by the tide

mud-guard \'məd-ˌgärd\ *n* : a guard over or a flap behind a wheel of a vehicle to catch or deflect mud

mud-room \-ˌrüm, -ˌrům\ *n* : a room in a

house for removing dirty or wet footwear and clothing

mud·sling·er \-ˌsliŋ-ər\ n : one who uses invective esp. against a political opponent — **mud·sling·ing** \-ˌsliŋ-iŋ\ n

Muen·ster \ˈmən-stər, ˈmün-, ˈmun-\ n : a semisoft bland cheese

mu·ez·zin \mü-ˈe-zᵊn, myü-\ n : a Muslim crier who calls the hour of daily prayer

¹**muff** \ˈməf\ n : a warm tubular covering for the hands

²**muff** n : a bungling performance; esp : a failure to hold a ball in attempting a catch — **muff** vb

muf·fin \ˈmə-fən\ n : a small soft cake baked in a cup-shaped container

muf·fle \ˈmə-fəl\ vb **muf·fled; muf·fling 1** : to wrap up so as to conceal or protect **2** : to wrap or pad with something to dull the sound of **3** : to keep down : SUP-PRESS ⟨*muffled* his feelings⟩

muf·fler \ˈmə-flər\ n **1** : a scarf worn around the neck **2** : a device (as on a car's exhaust) to deaden noise

muf·ti \ˈməf-tē\ n : civilian clothes

¹**mug** \ˈməg\ n : a usu. metal or earthenware cylindrical drinking cup

²**mug** vb **mugged; mug·ging 1** : to pose or make faces esp. to attract attention or for a camera **2** : PHOTOGRAPH

³**mug** vb **mugged; mug·ging 2** : to assault usu. with intent to rob — **mug·ger** n

mug·gy \ˈmə-gē\ adj **mug·gi·er; -est** : being warm and humid — **mug·gi·ness** \-gē-nəs\ n

mug·wump \ˈməg-ˌwəmp\ n [obs. slang *mugwump* kingpin, fr. Massachusett (Algonquian language of New England) *mugquomp* war leader] : an independent in politics

Muhammadan, Muhammadanism var of **MOHAMMEDAN, MOHAMMEDANISM**

mu·ja·hid·een or **mu·ja·hed·in** \mü-ˌja-hi-ˈdēn, -ˌjä-\ n pl [Ar *mujāhidīn*, pl. of *mujāhid*, lit., person who wages jihad] : Islamic guerrilla fighters esp. in the Middle East

muk·luk \ˈmək-ˌlək\ n **1** : an Eskimo boot of sealskin or reindeer skin **2** : a boot with a soft leather sole worn over several pairs of socks

mu·lat·to \mù-ˈla-tō, myü-, -ˈlä-\ n, pl **-toes** or **-tos** [Sp *mulato*, fr. *mulo* mule, fr. L *mulus*] : a first-generation offspring of a black person and a white person; also : a person of mixed white and black ancestry

mul·ber·ry \ˈməl-ˌber-ē\ n : any of a genus of trees with edible berrylike fruit and leaves used as food for silkworms; also : the fruit

mulch \ˈməlch\ n : a protective covering (as of straw or leaves) spread on the ground esp. to reduce evaporation or control weeds — **mulch** vb

¹**mulct** \ˈməlkt\ n : FINE, PENALTY

²**mulct** vb **1** : FINE **2** : CHEAT, DEFRAUD

¹**mule** \ˈmyül\ n **1** : a hybrid offspring of a male donkey and a female horse **2** : a very stubborn person — **mul·ish** \ˈmyü-lish\ adj — **mul·ish·ly** adv — **mul·ish·ness** n

²**mule** n : a slipper whose upper does not extend around the heel of the foot

mule deer n : a long-eared deer of western No. America

mu·le·teer \ˌmyü-lə-ˈtir\ n : one who drives mules

¹**mull** \ˈməl\ vb : PONDER, MEDITATE

²**mull** vb : to heat, sweeten, and flavor (as wine) with spices

mul·lein \ˈmə-lən\ n : a tall herb related to the snapdragons that has coarse woolly leaves and flowers in spikes

mul·let \ˈmə-lət\ n, pl **mullet** or **mullets** : any of a family of largely gray chiefly marine bony fishes including valuable food fishes

mul·li·gan stew \ˈmə-li-gən-\ n : a stew made from whatever ingredients are available

mul·li·ga·taw·ny \ˌmə-li-gə-ˈtȯ-nē\ n : a soup usu. of chicken stock seasoned with curry

mul·lion \ˈməl-yən\ n : a vertical strip separating windowpanes

multi- comb form **1** : many : multiple ⟨*multi*unit⟩ **2** : many times over ⟨*multi*millionaire⟩

mul·ti·col·ored \ˌməl-ti-ˈkə-lərd\ adj : having many colors

mul·ti·cul·tur·al \ˌməl-tē-ˈkəl-chə-rəl, -ˌtī-\ adj : of, relating to, reflecting, or adapted to diverse cultures ⟨a ~ society⟩ — **mul·ti·cul·tur·al·ism** \-rə-ˌli-zəm\ n — **mul·ti·cul·tur·al·ist** \-rə-list\ n or adj

mul·ti·di·men·sion·al \-ti-də-ˈmen-chə-nəl, -ˌtī-, -dī-\ adj : of, relating to, or having many facets or dimensions ⟨a ~ problem⟩ ⟨~ space⟩

mul·ti·eth·nic \-ˈeth-nik\ adj : including, involving, or made up of people of various ethnic groups

mul·ti·fac·et·ed \-ˈfa-sə-təd\ adj : having many facets or aspects ⟨a ~ concept⟩

mul·ti·fam·i·ly \-ˈfam-lē, -ˈfam-ə-\ adj : designed for use by several families

mul·ti·far·i·ous \ˌməl-tə-ˈfer-ē-əs\ adj : having great variety : DIVERSE ⟨~ activities⟩ — **mul·ti·far·i·ous·ness** n

mul·ti·form \ˈməl-ti-ˌfȯrm\ adj : having many forms or appearances — **mul·ti·for·mi·ty** \ˌməl-ti-ˈfȯr-mə-tē\ n

mul·ti·lat·er·al \ˌməl-ti-ˈla-tə-rəl, -ˌtī-, -ˈla-trəl\ adj : having many sides or participants ⟨~ treaty⟩ — **mul·ti·lat·er·al·ism** \-ˈla-tə-rə-ˌli-zəm\ n — **mul·ti·lat·er·al·ly** adv

mul·ti·lay·ered \-ˈlā-ərd, -ˈlerd\ or **mul·ti·lay·er** \-ˈlā-ər, -ˈler\ adj : having or involving several distinct layers or levels

mul·ti·lev·el \-ˈle-vəl\ adj : having several levels

mul·ti·lin·gual \-ˈliŋ-gwəl\ adj : knowing or using several languages — **mul·ti·lin·gual·ism** \-gwə-ˌli-zəm\ n

¹**mul·ti·me·dia** \-ˈmē-dē-ə\ adj : using, involving, or encompassing several media ⟨a ~ advertising campaign⟩

²**multimedia** n sing or pl : the technique of using several media (as in art); also : something (as software) that uses or facilitates it

mul·ti·mil·lion·aire \ˌməl-ti-ˌmil-yə-ˈnar,

-ˌtī-, -ˈmil-yə-ˌnar\ *n* : a person worth several million dollars

mul·ti·na·tion·al \-ˈna-shə-nəl\ *adj* **1** : of or relating to several nationalities **2** : relating to or involving several nations **3** : having divisions in several countries ⟨a ~ corporation⟩ — **multinational** *n*

mul·ti·pack \ˈməl-tē-ˌpak\ *n* : a package of several individually packed items sold as a unit

¹**mul·ti·ple** \ˈməl-tə-pəl\ *adj* **1** : more than one; *also* : MANY ⟨~ achievements⟩ **2** : VARIOUS

²**multiple** *n* : the product of a quantity by an integer ⟨35 is a ~ of 7⟩

multiple–choice *adj* : having several answers given from which the correct one is to be chosen ⟨a ~ question⟩

multiple personality disorder *n* : a neurosis in which the personality becomes separated into two or more parts each of which controls behavior part of the time

multiple sclerosis *n* : a disease marked by patches of hardened tissue in the brain or spinal cord and associated esp. with partial or complete paralysis and muscular tremor

mul·ti·plex \ˈməl-tə-ˌpleks\ *n* : CINEPLEX

mul·ti·pli·cand \ˌməl-tə-pli-ˈkand\ *n* : the number that is to be multiplied by another

mul·ti·pli·ca·tion \ˌməl-tə-plə-ˈkā-shən\ *n* **1** : INCREASE **2** : a short method of finding the result of adding a figure the number of times indicated by another figure

multiplication sign *n* **1** : TIMES SIGN **2** : a centered dot indicating multiplication

mul·ti·plic·i·ty \ˌməl-tə-ˈpli-sə-tē\ *n, pl* -**ties** : a great number or variety

mul·ti·pli·er \ˈməl-tə-ˌplī-(ə)r\ *n* : one that multiplies; *esp* : a number by which another number is multiplied

mul·ti·ply \ˈməl-tə-ˌplī\ *vb* -**plied; -ply·ing** **1** : to increase in number (as by breeding) **2** : to find the product of by multiplication; *also* : to perform multiplication

mul·ti·pur·pose \ˌməl-ti-ˈpər-pəs, -ˌtī-\ *adj* : having or serving several purposes

mul·ti·ra·cial \-ˈrā-shəl\ *adj* : composed of, involving, or representing various races

mul·ti·sense \-ˌsens\ *adj* : having several meanings ⟨~ words⟩

mul·ti·sto·ry \-ˌstȯr-ē\ *adj* : having several stories ⟨~ buildings⟩

mul·ti·task·ing \ˈməl-tē-ˌtas-kiŋ, -ˌtī-\ *n* **1** : the concurrent performance of several jobs by a computer **2** : the performance of multiple tasks at one time — **mul·ti·task** \ˌtask\ *vb* — **mul·ti·task·er** \-ˌtaskər\ *n*

mul·ti·tude \ˈməl-tə-ˌtüd, -ˌtyüd\ *n* : a great number — **mul·ti·tu·di·nous** \ˌməl-tə-ˈtüd-d°n-əs, -ˈtyüd-\ *adj*

mul·ti·unit \ˌməl-ti-ˈyü-nət, -ˌtī-\ *adj* : having several units

mul·ti·vi·ta·min \-ˈvī-tə-mən\ *adj* : containing several vitamins and esp. all known to be essential to health — **multivitamin** *n*

¹**mum** \ˈməm\ *adj* : SILENT

²**mum** *chiefly Brit var of* MOM

³**mum** *n* : CHRYSANTHEMUM

mum·ble \ˈməm-bəl\ *vb* **mum·bled; mum·bling** : to speak in a low indistinct manner — **mumble** *n* — **mum·bler** *n* — **mum·bly** *adj*

mum·ble·ty–peg \ˈməm-bəl-tē-ˌpeg\ *also* **mum·ble–the–peg** \ˈməm-bəl-thə-\ *n* : a game in which the players try to flip a knife from various positions so that the blade will stick into the ground

mum·bo jum·bo \ˌməm-bō-ˈjəm-bō\ *n* **1** : a complicated ritual with elaborate trappings **2** : GIBBERISH, NONSENSE

mum·mer \ˈmə-mər\ *n* **1** : an actor esp. in a pantomime **2** : a person who goes merrymaking in disguise during festivals — **mum·mery** *n*

mum·my \ˈmə-mē\ *n, pl* **mummies** [ME *mummie* powdered parts of a mummified body used as a drug, fr. AF *mumie*, fr. ML *mumia*, fr. Ar *mūmiya* bitumen, mummy, fr. Per *mūm* wax] : a body embalmed for burial in the manner of the ancient Egyptians — **mum·mi·fi·ca·tion** \ˌmə-mi-fə-ˈkā-shən\ *n* — **mum·mi·fy** \ˈmə-mi-ˌfī\ *vb*

mumps \ˈməmps\ *n sing or pl* [fr. pl. of obs. *mump* grimace] : a virus disease marked by fever and swelling esp. of the salivary glands

mun *or* **munic** *abbr* municipal

munch \ˈmənch\ *vb* : to eat with a chewing action; *also* : to snack on

munch·ies \ˈmən-chēz\ *n pl* **1** : hunger pangs **2** : light snack foods

mun·dane \ˌmən-ˈdān, ˈmən-ˌdān\ *adj* **1** : of or relating to the world **2** : concerned with the practical details of everyday life — **mun·dane·ly** *adv*

mung bean \ˈməŋ-\ *n* : an erect bushy bean widely grown in warm regions for its edible seeds and as the chief source of bean sprouts; *also* : its seed

mu·nic·i·pal \myù-ˈni-sə-pəl\ *adj* **1** : of, relating to, or characteristic of a municipality **2** : restricted to one locality — **mu·nic·i·pal·ly** *adv*

mu·nic·i·pal·i·ty \myù-ˌni-sə-ˈpa-lə-tē\ *n, pl* -**ties** : an urban political unit with corporate status and usu. powers of self-government

mu·nif·i·cent \myù-ˈni-fə-sənt\ *adj* : liberal in giving : GENEROUS — **mu·nif·i·cence** \-səns\ *n*

mu·ni·tion \myù-ˈni-shən\ *n* : ARMAMENT, AMMUNITION

¹**mu·ral** \ˈmyùr-əl\ *adj* **1** : of or relating to a wall **2** : applied to and made part of a wall or ceiling surface

²**mural** *n* : a mural painting — **mu·ral·ist** *n*

¹**mur·der** \ˈmər-dər\ *n* **1** : the crime of unlawfully killing a person esp. with malice aforethought **2** : something unusually difficult or dangerous

²**murder** *vb* **1** : to commit a murder; *also* : to kill brutally **2** : to put an end to **3** : to spoil by performing poorly ⟨~ a song⟩ — **mur·der·er** *n*

mur·der·ess \ˈmər-də-rəs\ *n* : a woman who murders

mur·der·ous \'mər-də-rəs\ adj 1 : having or appearing to have the purpose of murder ⟨∼ impulses⟩ 2 : marked by or causing murder or bloodshed ⟨∼ gunfire⟩ — **mur·der·ous·ly** adv

murk \'mərk\ n : DARKNESS, GLOOM — **murk·i·ly** \'mər-kə-lē\ adv — **murk·i·ness** \-kē-nəs\ n — **murky** adj

mur·mur \'mər-mər\ n 1 : a muttered complaint 2 : a low indistinct often continuous sound — **murmur** vb — **mur·mur·er** n — **mur·mur·ous** adj

mus abbr 1 museum 2 music; musical; musician

mus·ca·tel \ˌməs-kə-'tel\ n : a sweet fortified wine

¹**mus·cle** \'mə-səl\ n [ME, fr. L musculus, fr. dim. of mus mouse] 1 : a body tissue consisting of long cells that contract when stimulated and produce motion; also : an organ consisting of this tissue and functioning in moving a body part 2 : STRENGTH, BRAWN ⟨needs ∼ for lifting weights⟩ — **mus·cled** \'mə-səld\ adj — **mus·cu·lar** \'məs-kyə-lər\ adj — **mus·cu·lar·i·ty** \ˌməs-kyə-'lar-ə-tē\ n

²**muscle** vb **mus·cled; mus·cling** : to force one's way

mus·cle–bound \'mə-səl-ˌbau̇nd\ adj : having some of the muscles abnormally enlarged and lacking in elasticity (as from excessive exercise)

mus·cle·man \-ˌman\ n : a man with a muscular physique

muscular dystrophy n : any of a group of diseases characterized by progressive wasting of muscles

mus·cu·la·ture \'məs-kyə-lə-ˌchu̇r\ n : the muscles of the body or its parts

muscu·lo·skel·e·tal \ˌməs-kyə-lō-'ske-lə-t²l\ adj : of, relating to, or involving both musculature and skeleton

¹**muse** \'myüz\ vb **mused; mus·ing** [ME, fr. AF muser to gape, idle, muse, fr. OF *mus mouth of an animal, fr. ML musus] : to become absorbed in thought ⟨mused about what might have been⟩ — **mus·ing·ly** adv

²**muse** n [fr. Muse any of the nine sister goddesses of learning and the arts in Greek myth, fr. ME, fr. MF, fr. L Musa, fr. Gk Mousa] : a source of inspiration

mu·se·um \myu̇-'zē-əm\ n : an institution devoted to the procurement, care, and display of objects of lasting interest or value

¹**mush** \'məsh\ n 1 : cornmeal boiled in water 2 : sentimental drivel

²**mush** vb : to travel esp. over snow with a sled drawn by dogs

¹**mush·room** \'məsh-ˌrüm, -ˌru̇m\ n : the fleshy usu. caplike spore-bearing organ of various fungi esp. when edible; also : such a fungus

²**mushroom** vb 1 : to spread out : EXPAND 2 : to collect wild mushrooms 3 : to grow rapidly ⟨the population ∼ed⟩

mushy \'mə-shē\ adj **mush·i·er; -est** 1 : soft like mush 2 : excessively sentimental ⟨a ∼ movie⟩

mu·sic \'myü-zik\ n 1 : the science or art of combining tones into a composition having structure and continuity; also : vocal or instrumental sounds having rhythm, melody, or harmony 2 : an agreeable sound

¹**mu·si·cal** \'myü-zi-kəl\ adj 1 : of or relating to music or musicians 2 : having the pleasing tonal qualities of music 3 : fond of or gifted in music ⟨a ∼ family⟩ — **mu·si·cal·ly** \-k(ə-)lē\ adv

²**musical** n : a film or theatrical production consisting of musical numbers and dialogue based on a unifying plot

mu·si·cale \ˌmyü-zi-'kal\ n : a usu. private social gathering featuring music

mu·si·cian \myu̇-'zi-shən\ n : a composer, conductor, or performer of music — **mu·si·cian·ly** adj — **mu·si·cian·ship** n

mu·si·col·o·gy \ˌmyü-zi-'kä-lə-jē\ n : the study of music as a field of knowledge or research — **mu·si·co·log·i·cal** \-kə-'lä-ji-kəl\ adj — **mu·si·col·o·gist** \-'kä-lə-jist\ n

musk \'məsk\ n : a substance obtained esp. from a small Asian deer (**musk deer**) and used as a perfume fixative — **musk·i·ness** \'məs-kē-nəs\ n — **musky** adj

musk·keg \'məs-ˌkeg\ n : BOG; esp : a mossy bog in northern No. America

mus·kel·lunge \'məs-kə-ˌlənj\ n, pl **muskellunge** : a large No. American pike that is a valuable sport fish

mus·ket \'məs-kət\ n [MF mousquet, fr. It moschetto small artillery piece, kind of small hawk, fr. dim. of mosca fly, fr. L musca] : a heavy large-caliber muzzle-loading shoulder firearm — **mus·ke·teer** \ˌməs-kə-'tir\ n

mus·ket·ry \'məs-kə-trē\ n 1 : MUSKETS 2 : MUSKETEERS 3 : musket fire

musk·mel·on \'məsk-ˌme-lən\ n : a small round to oval melon that has usu. a sweet edible green or orange flesh and a musky odor

musk ox n : a heavyset shaggy-coated wild ox of Greenland and the arctic tundra of northern No. America

musk·rat \'məs-ˌkrat\ n, pl **muskrat** or **muskrats** : a large No. American aquatic rodent with webbed feet and dark brown fur; also : its fur

Mus·lim \'məz-ləm\ n : an adherent of Islam — **Muslim** adj

mus·lin \'məz-lən\ n : a plain-woven sheer to coarse cotton fabric

¹**muss** \'məs\ n : a state of disorder — **muss·i·ly** \'mə-sə-lē\ adv — **muss·i·ness** \-sē-nəs\ n — **mussy** adj

²**muss** vb : to make untidy : DISARRANGE

mus·sel \'mə-səl\ n 1 : a dark edible saltwater bivalve mollusk 2 : any of various freshwater bivalve mollusks of the central U.S. having shells with a pearly lining

¹**must** \'məst\ vb — used as an auxiliary esp. to express a command, requirement, obligation, or necessity

²**must** n 1 : an imperative duty 2 : an indispensable item

mus·tache also **mous·tache** \'məs-ˌtash, (ˌ)məs-'tash\ n : the hair growing on the human upper lip — **mus·tached** also **mous·tached** \-ˌtasht, -'tasht\ adj

mus·tang \'məs-ˌtaŋ\ n [MexSp mestengo, fr. Sp, stray, fr. mesteño strayed, fr. mesta annual roundup of cattle that disposed of strays, fr. ML (animalia) mixta mixed animals] : a small hardy naturalized horse of the western plains of America; also : BRONC

mus·tard \'məs-tərd\ n 1 : a pungent yellow powder of the seeds of an herb related to the cabbage and used as a condiment or in medicine 2 : a plant that yields mustard; also : a closely related plant — **mustardy** adj

mustard gas n : a poison gas used in warfare that has violent irritating and blistering effects

¹**mus·ter** \'məs-tər\ n 1 : an act of assembling (as for military inspection); also : critical examination 2 : an assembled group

²**muster** vb [ME mustren to show, muster, fr. AF mustrer, monstrer, fr. L monstrare to show, fr. monstrum evil omen, monster] 1 : CONVENE, ASSEMBLE ⟨∼ an army⟩; also : to call the roll of 2 : ACCUMULATE 3 : to call forth : ROUSE ⟨∼ed support⟩ 4 : to amount to : COMPRISE

muster out vb : to discharge from military service

musty \'məs-tē\ adj **mus·ti·er; -est** : MOLDY, STALE; also : tasting or smelling of damp or decay — **must·i·ly** \-tə-lē\ adv — **must·i·ness** \-tē-nəs\ n

mu·ta·ble \'myü-tə-bəl\ adj 1 : prone to change : FICKLE 2 : capable of or liable to mutation : VARIABLE — **mu·ta·bil·i·ty** \ˌmyü-tə-'bi-lə-tē\ n

mu·tant \'myüt-ᵊnt\ adj : of, relating to, or produced by mutation — **mutant** n

mu·tate \'myü-ˌtāt\ vb **mu·tat·ed; mu·tat·ing** : to undergo or cause to undergo mutation — **mu·ta·tive** \'myü-ˌtā-tiv, -tə-tiv\ adj

mu·ta·tion \myü-'tā-shən\ n 1 : CHANGE 2 : an inherited physical or biochemical change in genetic material; also : the process of producing a mutation 3 : an individual, strain, or trait resulting from mutation — **mu·ta·tion·al** adj

¹**mute** \'myüt\ adj **mut·er; mut·est** 1 : unable to speak 2 : SILENT — **mute·ly** adv — **mute·ness** n

²**mute** n 1 : a person who cannot or does not speak 2 : a device on a musical instrument that reduces, softens, or muffles the tone

³**mute** vb **mut·ed; mut·ing** : to muffle, reduce, or eliminate the sound of

mu·ti·late \'myü-tə-ˌlāt\ vb **-lat·ed; -lat·ing** 1 : to cut up or alter radically so as to make imperfect 2 : MAIM, CRIPPLE — **mu·ti·la·tion** \ˌmyü-tə-'lā-shən\ n — **mu·ti·la·tor** \'myü-tə-ˌlā-tər\ n

mu·ti·ny \'myü-tə-nē\ n, pl **-nies** : willful refusal to obey constituted authority; esp : revolt against a superior officer — **mu·ti·neer** \ˌmyü-tə-'nir\ n — **mu·ti·nous** \'myü-tə-nəs\ adj — **mu·ti·nous·ly** adv

mutt \'mət\ n : MONGREL, CUR

mut·ter \'mə-tər\ vb 1 : to speak indistinctly or with a low voice and lips partly closed 2 : GRUMBLE — **mutter** n

mut·ton \'mə-tᵊn\ n [ME motoun mutton, sheep, fr. AF mutun ram, sheep, mutton] : the flesh of a mature sheep used for food — **mut·tony** adj

mut·ton-chops \'mə-tᵊn-ˌchäps\ n pl : whiskers on the side of the face that are narrow at the temple and broad and round by the lower jaws

mu·tu·al \'myü-chə-wəl\ adj 1 : given and received in equal amount ⟨∼ trust⟩ 2 : having the same feelings one for the other ⟨∼ enemies⟩ 3 : COMMON, JOINT ⟨a ∼ friend⟩ — **mu·tu·al·ly** adv

mutual fund n : an investment company that invests money of its shareholders in a usu. diversified group of securities of other corporations

muu·muu \'mü-ˌmü\ n : a loose dress of Hawaiian origin

¹**muz·zle** \'mə-zəl\ n 1 : the nose and jaws of an animal; also : a covering for the muzzle to prevent biting or eating 2 : the mouth of a gun

²**muzzle** vb **muz·zled; muz·zling** 1 : to put a muzzle on 2 : to restrain from expression : GAG ⟨tried to ∼ the press⟩

mV abbr millivolt

MV abbr motor vessel

MVP abbr most valuable player

MW abbr megawatt

my \'mī\ adj 1 : of or relating to me or myself 2 — used interjectionally esp. to express surprise

my·col·o·gy \mī-'kä-lə-jē\ n : a branch of biology dealing with fungi — **my·co·log·i·cal** \ˌmī-kə-'lä-ji-kəl\ adj — **my·col·o·gist** \mī-'kä-lə-jist\ n

my·elo·ma \ˌmī-ə-'lō-mə\ n, pl **-mas** or **-ma·ta** \-mə-tə\ : a primary tumor of the bone marrow

my·nah or **my·na** \'mī-nə\ n : any of several Asian starlings; esp : a dark brown slightly crested bird sometimes taught to mimic speech

my·o·pia \mī-'ō-pē-ə\ n : a condition in which visual images come to a focus in front of the retina resulting esp. in defective vision of distant objects — **my·o·pic** \-'ō-pik, -'ä-\ adj — **my·o·pi·cal·ly** \-pi-k(ə-)lē\ adv

¹**myr·i·ad** \'mir-ē-əd\ n [Gk myriad-, myrias, fr. myrioi countless, ten thousand] : an indefinitely large number

²**myriad** adj : consisting of a very great but indefinite number

myr·mi·don \'mər-mə-ˌdän\ n : a loyal follower; esp : one who executes orders without protest or pity

myrrh \'mər\ n : a fragrant aromatic plant gum used in perfumes and formerly for incense

myr·tle \'mər-tᵊl\ n : an evergreen shrub of southern Europe with shiny leaves, fragrant flowers, and black berries; also : PERIWINKLE

my·self \mī-'self, mə-\ pron : I, ME — used reflexively, for emphasis, or in absolute constructions ⟨I hurt ∼⟩ ⟨I ∼ did it⟩ ⟨∼ busy, I sent him instead⟩

mys·tery \'mis-tə-rē\ n, pl **-ter·ies** 1 : a

religious truth known by revelation alone **2** : something not understood or beyond understanding **3** : enigmatic quality or character **4** : a work of fiction dealing with the solution of a mysterious crime — **mys·te·ri·ous** \mis-'tir-ē-əs\ *adj* — **mys·te·ri·ous·ly** *adv* — **mys·te·ri·ous·ness** *n*

¹**mys·tic** \'mis-tik\ *adj* **1** : of or relating to mystics or mysticism **2** : MYSTERIOUS; *also* : MYSTIFYING

²**mystic** *n* : a person who follows, advocates, or experiences mysticism

mys·ti·cal \'mis-ti-kəl\ *adj* **1** : SPIRITUAL, SYMBOLIC **2** : of or relating to an intimate knowledge of or direct communion with God (as through contemplation or visions)

mys·ti·cism \'mis-tə-ˌsi-zəm\ *n* : the belief that direct knowledge of God or ultimate reality is attainable through immediate intuition or insight

mys·ti·fy \'mis-tə-ˌfī\ *vb* **-fied; -fy·ing 1** : to perplex the mind of **2** : to make mysterious — **mys·ti·fi·ca·tion** \ˌmis-tə-fə-'kā-shən\ *n*

mys·tique \mi-'stēk\ *n* [F] **1** : an air or attitude of mystery and reverence developing around something or someone **2** : the special esoteric skill essential in a calling or activity

myth \'mith\ *n* **1** : a usu. legendary narrative that presents part of the beliefs of a people or explains a practice or natural phenomenon **2** : an imaginary or unverifiable person or thing — **myth·i·cal** \'mi-thi-kəl\ *or* **myth·ic** \-thik\ *adj*

my·thol·o·gy \mi-'thä-lə-jē\ *n, pl* **-gies** : a body of myths and esp. of those dealing with the gods and heroes of a people — **myth·o·log·i·cal** \ˌmi-thə-'lä-ji-kəl\ *adj* — **my·thol·o·gist** \mi-'thä-lə-jist\ *n* — **my·thol·o·gize** \-ˌjīz\ *vb*

¹**n** \'en\ *n, pl* **n's** *or* **ns** \'enz\ *often cap* **1** : the 14th letter of the English alphabet **2** : an unspecified quantity

²**n** *abbr, often cap* **1** net **2** neuter **3** noon **4** normal **5** north; northern **6** note **7** noun **8** number

N *symbol* nitrogen

-n — see -EN

Na *symbol* [NL *natrium*] sodium

NA *abbr* **1** no account **2** North America **3** not applicable **4** not available

NAACP \ˌen-ˌdə-bəl-ˌā-sē-'pē, ˌen-ˌā-ˌā-ˌsē-\ *abbr* National Association for the Advancement of Colored People

nab \'nab\ *vb* **nabbed; nab·bing** : SEIZE; *esp* : ARREST

NAB *abbr* New American Bible

na·bob \'nā-ˌbäb\ *n* [Hindi *navāb* & Urdu *nawāb*, provincial governor (in the Mogul empire), fr. Ar *nuwwāb*, pl. of *nā'ib* governor] : a person of great wealth or prominence

na·celle \nə-'sel\ *n* : an enclosure (as for an engine) on an aircraft

na·cho \'nä-chō\ *n, pl* **nachos** [AmerSp] : a tortilla chip topped with melted cheese and often additional savory toppings

na·cre \'nā-kər\ *n* : MOTHER-OF-PEARL — **na·cre·ous** \'nā-krē-əs\ *adj*

na·dir \'nā-ˌdir, -dir\ *n* [ME, fr. MF, fr. Ar *nadhīr* opposite] **1** : the point of the celestial sphere that is directly opposite the zenith and directly beneath the observer **2** : the lowest point

¹**nag** \'nag\ *n* : HORSE; *esp* : an old or decrepit horse

²**nag** *vb* **nagged; nag·ging 1** : to find fault incessantly : COMPLAIN **2** : to irritate by constant scolding or urging **3** : to be a continuing source of annoyance ⟨a *nagging* backache⟩

³**nag** *n* : one who nags habitually

Nah *abbr* Nahum

Na·huatl \'nä-ˌwä-t°l\ *n* : a group of American Indian languages of central and southern Mexico

Na·hum \'nā-həm, -əm\ *n* — see BIBLE table

NAIA *abbr* National Association of Intercollegiate Athletes

na·iad \'nā-əd, 'nī-, -ˌad\ *n, pl* **naiads** *or* **na·ia·des** \-ə-ˌdēz\ **1** : one of the nymphs in ancient mythology living in lakes, rivers, springs, and fountains **2** : an aquatic young of some insects (as a dragonfly)

¹**na·if** *or* **na·if** \nä-'ēf\ *adj* : NAIVE

²**naif** *or* **naif** *n* : a naive person

¹**nail** \'nāl\ *n* **1** : a horny sheath protecting the end of each finger and toe in humans and related primates **2** : a slender pointed fastener with a head designed to be pounded in

²**nail** *vb* : to fasten with or as if with a nail — **nail·er** *n*

nail down *vb* : to settle or establish clearly and unmistakably ⟨*nailed down* the victory⟩

nain·sook \'nän-ˌsůk\ *n* : a soft lightweight muslin

nai·ra \'nī-ra\ *n* — see MONEY table

na·ive *or* **na·ïve** \nä-'ēv\ *adj* **na·iv·er; -est** [F *naïve*, fem. of *naïf*, fr. OF, inborn, natural, fr. L *nativus* native] **1** : marked by unaffected simplicity : ARTLESS, INGENUOUS **2** : CREDULOUS ♦ *Synonyms* NATURAL, INNOCENT, SIMPLE, UNAFFECTED, UNSOPHISTICATED, UNSTUDIED — **na·ive·ly** *adv* — **na·ive·ness** *n*

na·ïve·té *also* **na·ive·te** *or* **na·ive·té** \ˌnä-ˌē-və-'tā, nä-'ē-və-ˌtä\ *n* **1** : a naive remark or action **2** : the quality or state of being naive

na·ive·ty *also* **na·ïve·ty** \nä-'ē-və-tē\ *n, pl* **-ties** : NAÏVETÉ na·ked \'nā-kəd\ adj 1 : having no clothes on : NUDE 2 : UNSHEATHED ⟨a ~ sword⟩ 3 : lacking a usual or natural covering (as of foliage or feathers) 4 : PLAIN, UNADORNED ⟨the ~ truth⟩ 5 : not aided by artificial means ⟨seen by the ~ eye⟩ — na·ked·ly adv — na·ked·ness n

¹nak·fa \'näk-,fä\ n, pl nakfa — see MONEY table

nam·by-pam·by \,nam-bē-'pam-bē\ adj 1 : INSIPID 2 : WEAK, INDECISIVE
♦ Synonyms BLAND, FLAT, INANE, JEJUNE, VAPID, WISHY-WASHY

¹name \'nām\ n 1 : a word or words by which a person or thing is known 2 : a disparaging epithet ⟨call him ~s⟩ 3 : REPUTATION; esp : distinguished reputation ⟨made a ~ for herself⟩ 4 : FAMILY, CLAN ⟨was a disgrace to their ~⟩ 5 : appearance as opposed to reality ⟨a friend in ~ only⟩

²name vb named; nam·ing 1 : to give a name to : CALL 2 : to mention or identify by name 3 : NOMINATE, APPOINT 4 : to decide on : CHOOSE ⟨named the wedding date⟩ 5 : to mention explicitly : SPECIFY ⟨~ a price⟩ — name·able adj

³name adj 1 : of, relating to, or bearing a name ⟨~ tag⟩ 2 : having an established reputation ⟨~ brands⟩

name day n : the church feast day of the saint after whom one is named

name·less \'nām-ləs\ adj 1 : having no name 2 : not marked with a name ⟨a ~ grave⟩ 3 : not known by name ⟨a ~ hero⟩ 4 : too distressing to be described ⟨~ fears⟩ — name·less·ly adv

name·ly \-lē\ adv : that is to say : AS ⟨the cat family, ~, lions, tigers, and similar animals⟩

name·plate \-,plāt\ n : a plate or plaque bearing a name (as of a resident)

name·sake \-,sāk\ n : one that has the same name as another; esp : one named after another

nan·keen \nan-'kēn\ n : a durable brownish yellow cotton fabric orig. woven by hand in China

nan·ny goat \'na-nē-\ n : a female domestic goat

nano·me·ter \'na-nə-,mē-tər\ n : one billionth of a meter

nano·scale \-,skāl\ adj : having dimensions measured in nanometers

nano·sec·ond \-,se-kənd\ n : one billionth of a second

nano·tech·nol·o·gy \,na-nō-tek-'nä-lə-jē\ n : the manipulation of materials on an atomic or molecular scale

nano·tube \'na-nō-,tüb\ n : a microscope tube (as of carbon) whose diameter is measured in nanometers

¹nap \'nap\ vb napped; nap·ping 1 : to sleep briefly esp. during the day : DOZE 2 : to be off guard ⟨was caught napping⟩

²nap n : a short sleep esp. during the day

³nap n : a soft downy fibrous surface (as on yarn and cloth) — nap·less adj — napped \'napt\ adj

na·palm \'nā-,pälm, -,päm\ n [naphthalene + palmitate, salt of a fatty acid] 1 : a

thickener used in jelling gasoline (as for incendiary bombs) 2 : fuel jelled with napalm

nape \'nāp, 'nap\ n : the back of the neck

na·pery \'nā-pə-rē\ n : household linen esp. for the table

naph·tha \'naf-thə, 'nap-\ n : any of various liquid hydrocarbon mixtures used chiefly as solvents

naph·tha·lene \-,lēn\ n : a crystalline substance used esp. in organic synthesis and as a moth repellent

nap·kin \'nap-kən\ n 1 : a piece of material (as cloth) used at table to wipe the lips or fingers and protect the clothes 2 : a small cloth or towel

na·po·leon \nə-'pōl-yən, -'pō-lē-ən\ n : an oblong pastry with a filling of cream, custard, or jelly

Na·po·le·on·ic \nə-,pō-lē-'ä-nik\ adj : of, relating to, or characteristic of Napoleon I or his family

narc also nark \'närk\ n, slang : a person (as a government agent) who investigates narcotics violations

nar·cis·sism \'när-sə-,si-zəm\ n [G Narzissismus, fr. Narziss Narcissus, beautiful youth of Greek mythology who fell in love with his own image] 1 : undue dwelling on one's own self or attainments 2 : love of or sexual desire for one's own body — nar·cis·sist \-sist\ n or adj — nar·cis·sis·tic \,när-sə-'sis-tik\ adj

nar·cis·sus \när-'si-səs\ n, pl nar·cis·si \-,sī, -,sē\ or nar·cis·sus·es or narcissus : DAFFODIL; esp : one with short-tubed flowers usu. borne separately

nar·co·lep·sy \'när-kə-,lep-sē\ n, pl -sies : a condition characterized by brief attacks of deep sleep — nar·co·lep·tic \,när-kə-'lep-tik\ adj or n

nar·co·sis \när-'kō-səs\ n, pl -co·ses \-,sēz\ : a state of stupor, unconsciousness, or arrested activity produced by the influence of chemicals (as narcotics)

nar·co·ter·ror·ism \'när-kō-'ter-ər-,i-zəm\ n : terrorism financed by profits from illegal drug trafficking

nar·cot·ic \när-'kä-tik\ n [ME narkotik, fr. MF narcotique, fr. narcotique, adj., fr. ML narcoticus, fr. Gk narkōtikos, fr. narkoun to benumb, fr. narkē numbness] 1 : a drug (as opium) that dulls the senses, relieves pain, and induces sleep 2 : an illegal drug (as marijuana or LSD) — narcotic adj

nar·co·tize \'när-kə-,tīz\ vb -tized; -tizing 1 : to treat with or subject to a narcotic; also : to put into a state of narcosis 2 : to soothe to unconsciousness or unawareness

nard \'närd\ n : a fragrant ointment of the ancients

na·res \'ner-(,)ēz\ n pl [L] : the pair of openings of the nose

Nar·ra·gan·sett \,na-rə-'gan-sət\ n, pl -sett or -setts 1 : a member of an American Indian people of Rhode Island 2 : the Algonquian language of the Narragansett people

nar·rate \'ner-,āt\ vb nar·rat·ed; nar·rating : to recite the details of (as a story)

: RELATE, TELL — **nar·ra·tion** \na-'rā-shən\ *n* — **nar·ra·tor** \'ner-ˌā-tər\ *n*

nar·ra·tive \'ner-ə-tiv\ *n* 1 : something that is narrated : STORY 2 : the art or practice of narrating

¹**nar·row** \'ner-ō\ *adj* 1 : of slender or less than standard width 2 : limited in size or scope : RESTRICTED 3 : not liberal in views : PREJUDICED 4 : interpreted or interpreting strictly 5 : CLOSE ⟨won by a ~ margin⟩; *also* : barely successful ⟨a ~ escape⟩ — **nar·row·ly** *adv* — **nar·row·ness** *n*

²**narrow** *vb* : to lessen in width or extent

³**narrow** *n* : a narrow passage : STRAIT — usu. used in pl.

nar·row-mind·ed \ˌner-ō-'mīn-dəd\ *adj* : not liberal or broad-minded ♦ *Synonyms* ILLIBERAL, BIGOTED, HIDEBOUND, INTOLERANT

nar·whal \'när-ˌhwäl, 'när-wəl\ *n* : an arctic sea mammal about 20 feet (6 meters) long that is related to the dolphins and in the male has a long twisted ivory tusk

NAS *abbr* naval air station

NASA \'na-sə\ *abbr* National Aeronautics and Space Administration

¹**na·sal** \'nā-zəl\ *n* 1 : a nasal part 2 : a nasal consonant or vowel

²**nasal** *adj* 1 : of or relating to the nose 2 : uttered through the nose — **na·sal·ly** *adv*

na·sal·ize \'nā-zə-ˌlīz\ *vb* **-ized; -iz·ing** : to make nasal or pronounce as a nasal sound — **na·sal·i·za·tion** \ˌnā-zə-lə-'zā-shən\ *n*

na·scent \'na-sᵊnt, 'nā-\ *adj* : coming into existence : beginning to grow or develop — **na·scence** \-sᵊns\ *n*

nas·tur·tium \nə-'stər-shəm, na-\ *n* : either of two widely cultivated waterystemmed herbs with showy spurred flowers and pungent edible seeds

nas·ty \'nas-tē\ *adj* **nas·ti·er; -est** 1 : FILTHY 2 : INDECENT, OBSCENE 3 : HARMFUL, DANGEROUS ⟨took a ~ fall⟩ 4 : DISAGREEABLE ⟨~ weather⟩ 5 : MEAN, ILL-NATURED ⟨a ~ temper⟩ 6 : DIFFICULT, VEXATIOUS ⟨a ~ problem⟩ 7 : UNFAIR, DIRTY ⟨a ~ trick⟩ — **nas·ti·ly** \'nas-tə-lē\ *adv* — **nas·ti·ness** \-tē-nəs\ *n*

nat *abbr* 1 national 2 native 3 natural

na·tal \'nā-tᵊl\ *adj* 1 : NATIVE 2 : of, relating to, or present at birth

na·ta·to·ri·um \ˌnā-tə-'tòr-ē-əm, ˌna-\ *n* : a swimming pool esp. indoors

na·tion \'nā-shən\ *n* [ME *nacioun*, fr. AF *naciun* fr. L *nation-, natio* birth, race, nation, fr. *nasci* to be born] 1 : NATIONALITY 5; *also* : a politically organized nationality 2 : a community of people composed of one or more nationalities with its own territory and government 3 : the territory of a nation 4 : a federation of tribes (as of American Indians) — **na·tion·hood** *n*

¹**na·tion·al** \'na-shə-nəl\ *adj* 1 : of or relating to a nation 2 : comprising or characteristic of a nationality 3 : FEDERAL 3 — **na·tion·al·ly** *adv*

²**national** *n* 1 : one who owes allegiance to a nation 2 : a competition that is national in scope — usu. used in pl.

national guard *n* 1 : a military force serving as a national constabulary and defense force 2 *cap N & G* : a militia force recruited by each state of the U.S., equipped by the federal government, and jointly maintained subject to the call of either — **national guardsman** *n, often cap*

na·tion·al·ise *chiefly Brit var of* NATIONALIZE

na·tion·al·ism \'na-shə-nə-ˌli-zəm\ *n* : devotion to national interests, unity, and independence

na·tion·al·ist \-list\ *n* 1 : an advocate of or believer in nationalism 2 : a member of a political party or group advocating national independence or strong national government — **nationalist** *adj* — **na·tion·al·is·tic** \ˌna-shə-nə-'lis-tik\ *adj*

na·tion·al·i·ty \ˌna-shə-'na-lə-tē\ *n, pl* **-ties** 1 : national character 2 : a legal relationship involving allegiance of an individual and protection on the part of the state 3 : membership in a particular nation 4 : political independence or existence as a separate nation 5 : a people having a common origin, tradition, and language and capable of forming a state 6 : an ethnic group within a larger unit (as a nation)

na·tion·al·ize \'na-shə-nə-ˌlīz\ *vb* **-ized; -iz·ing** 1 : to make national : make a nation of 2 : to remove from private ownership and place under government control — **na·tion·al·i·za·tion** \ˌna-shə-nə-lə-'zā-shən\ *n*

national monument *n* : a place of historic, scenic, or scientific interest set aside for preservation usu. by presidential proclamation

national park *n* : an area of special scenic, historical, or scientific importance set aside and maintained by a national government esp. for recreation or study

national seashore *n* : a recreational area adjacent to a seacoast and maintained by the federal government

na·tion·wide \ˌnā-shən-'wīd\ *adj* : extending throughout a nation

¹**na·tive** \'nā-tiv\ *adj* 1 : INBORN, NATURAL ⟨~ talents⟩ 2 : born in a particular place or country 3 : belonging to a person because of the place or circumstances of birth ⟨her ~ language⟩ 4 : grown, produced, or originating in a particular place : INDIGENOUS 5 *cap* : NATIVE AMERICAN ♦ *Synonyms* ABORIGINAL, AUTOCHTHONOUS, ENDEMIC

²**native** *n* : one that is native; *esp* : a person who belongs to a particular country by birth

Native American *n* : a member of any of the aboriginal peoples of No. America and esp. the U.S.

na·tiv·ism \'nā-ti-ˌvi-zəm\ *n* 1 : a policy of favoring native inhabitants over immigrants 2 : the revival or perpetuation of a native culture esp. in opposition to acculturation

na·tiv·i·ty \nə-'ti-və-tē, nā-\ *n, pl* **-ties** 1

: the process or circumstances of being born : BIRTH **2** *cap* : the birth of Christ
natl *abbr* national
NATO \'nā-(,)tō\ *abbr* North Atlantic Treaty Organization
nat·ty \'na-tē\ *adj* **nat·ti·er; -est** : trimly neat and tidy : SMART — **nat·ti·ly** \-tə-lē\ *adv* — **nat·ti·ness** \-tē-nəs\ *n*
¹**nat·u·ral** \'na-chə-rəl\ *adj* **1** : determined by nature : INBORN, INNATE ⟨~ ability⟩ **2** : BORN ⟨a ~ fool⟩ **3** : ILLEGITIMATE ⟨a ~ child⟩ **4** : HUMAN **5** : of or relating to nature **6** : not artificial **7** : being simple and sincere : not affected **8** : LIFELIKE **9** : being neither sharp nor flat ♦ **Synonyms** INGENUOUS, NAIVE, UNSOPHISTICATED, ARTLESS, GUILELESS — **nat·u·ral·ness** *n*
²**natural** *n* **1** : IDIOT **2** : a character ♭ placed on a line or space of the musical staff to nullify the effect of a preceding sharp or flat **3** : one obviously suitable for a purpose ♦ AFRO
natural childbirth *n* : a system of managing childbirth in which the mother prepares to remain conscious and assist in delivery with little or no use of drugs
natural gas *n* : a combustible gaseous mixture of hydrocarbons coming from the earth's crust and used chiefly as a fuel and raw material
natural history *n* **1** : a treatise on some aspect of nature **2** : the study of natural objects esp. from an amateur or popular point of view
nat·u·ral·ise *Brit var of* NATURALIZE
nat·u·ral·ism \'na-chə-rə-,li-zəm\ *n* **1** : action or thought based only on natural desires and instincts **2** : a doctrine that denies a supernatural explanation of the origin or development of the universe and holds that scientific laws account for all of nature **3** : realism in art and literature — **nat·u·ral·is·tic** \,na-chə-rə-'lis-tik\ *adj*
nat·u·ral·ist \-list\ *n* **1** : one that advocates or practices naturalism **2** : a student of animals or plants esp. in the field
nat·u·ral·ize \-,līz\ *vb* **-ized; -iz·ing 1** : to confer the rights of a citizen on **2** : to become or cause to become established as if native ⟨~ new forage crops⟩ — **nat·u·ral·i·za·tion** \,na-chə-rə-lə-'zā-shən\ *n*
nat·u·ral·ly \'na-chə-rə-lē, 'nach-rə-\ *adv* **1** : by nature : by natural character or ability **2** : as might be expected **3** : without artificial aid; *also* : without affectation **4** : REALISTICALLY
natural science *n* : a science (as physics, chemistry, or biology) that deals with matter, energy, and their interrelations and transformations or with objectively measurable phenomena — **natural scientist** *n*
natural selection *n* : the natural process that results in the survival of individuals or groups best adjusted to their environment
na·ture \'nā-chər\ *n* [ME, fr. MF, fr. L *natura*, fr. *natus*, pp. of *nasci* to be born] **1** : the inherent quality or basic constitution of a person or thing; *also* : DISPOSI-

TION, TEMPERAMENT **2** : KIND, SORT ⟨letters of a personal ~⟩ **3** : the physical universe **4** : one's natural instincts or way of life ⟨quirks of human ~⟩; *also* : primitive state ⟨a return to ~⟩ **5** : natural scenery or environment ⟨beauties of ~⟩
¹**naught** *also* **nought** \'nȯt, 'nät\ *pron* : NOTHING ⟨efforts came to ~⟩
²**naught** *also* **nought** *n* **1** : NOTHINGNESS, NONEXISTENCE **2** : the arithmetical symbol 0 : ZERO
naugh·ty \'nȯ-tē, 'nä-\ *adj* **naugh·ti·er; -est 1** : guilty of disobedience or misbehavior **2** : lacking in taste or propriety ⟨~ jokes⟩ — **naugh·ti·ly** \-tə-lē\ *adv* — **naugh·ti·ness** \-tē-nəs\ *n*
nau·sea \'nȯ-zē-ə, -sē-; 'nȯ-zhə, -shə\ *n* [L, seasickness, nausea, fr. Gk *nautia, nausia*, fr. *nautēs* sailor] **1** : sickness of the stomach with a desire to vomit **2** : extreme disgust
nau·se·ate \'nȯ-zē-,āt, -sē-, -zhē-, -shē-\ *vb* **-at·ed; -at·ing** : to affect or become affected with nausea — **nau·se·at·ing·ly** *adv*
nau·seous \'nȯ-shəs, -zē-əs\ *adj* **1** : causing nausea or disgust **2** : affected with nausea or disgust
naut *abbr* nautical
nau·ti·cal \'nȯ-ti-kəl\ *adj* : of or relating to sailors, navigation, or ships ⟨~ terms⟩ — **nau·ti·cal·ly** \-k(ə-)lē\ *adv*
nautical mile *n* : a unit of distance equal to about 6080 feet (1852 meters)
nau·ti·lus \'nȯ-tə-ləs\ *n, pl* **-lus·es** *or* **-li** \,lī, -,lē\ : any of a genus of sea mollusks related to the octopuses but having a spiral chambered shell
nav *abbr* **1** naval **2** navigable; navigation
Na·va·jo *also* **Na·va·ho** \'na-və-,hō, 'nä-\ *n, pl* **-jo** *or* **-jos** *also* **-ho** *or* **-hos** : a member of an American Indian people of northern New Mexico and Arizona; *also* : their language
na·val \'nā-vəl\ *adj* : of, relating to, or possessing a navy ⟨a ~ power⟩
naval stores *n pl* : products (as pitch, turpentine, or rosin) obtained from resinous conifers (as pines)
nave \'nāv\ *n* [ML *navis*, fr. L, ship] : the central part of a church running lengthwise
na·vel \'nā-vəl\ *n* : a depression in the middle of the abdomen that marks the point of attachment of fetus and mother
navel–gaz·ing \'nā-vəl-'gā-zin\ *n* : useless or excessive self-contemplation
navel orange *n* : a seedless orange having a pit at the blossom end where the fruit encloses a small secondary fruit
nav·i·ga·ble \'na-vi-gə-bəl\ *adj* **1** : capable of being navigated ⟨a ~ river⟩ **2** : capable of being steered — **nav·i·ga·bil·i·ty** \,na-vi-gə-'bi-lə-tē\ *n*
nav·i·gate \'na-və-,gāt\ *vb* **-gat·ed; -gat·ing 1** : to sail on or through ⟨~ the Atlantic Ocean⟩ **2** : to steer or direct the course of a ship or aircraft **3** : MOVE; *esp* : WALK ⟨could hardly ~⟩ — **nav·i·ga·tion** \,na-və-'gā-shən\ *n* — **nav·i·ga·tor** \'na-və-,gā-tər\ *n*

na·vy \'nā-vē\ *n, pl* **navies** **1** : FLEET; *also* : the warships belonging to a nation **2** *often cap* : a nation's organization for naval warfare

navy yard *n* : a yard where naval vessels are built or repaired

¹nay \'nā\ *adv* : NO

²nay *n* : a negative vote; *also* : a person casting such a vote

³nay *conj* : not merely this but also : not only so but ⟨he was happy, ∼, ecstatic⟩

nay·say·er \'nā-,sā-ər\ *n* : one who denies, refuses, or opposes something

Na·zi \'nät-sē, 'nat-\ *n* [G, fr. *Nationalsozialist*, lit., national socialist] : a member of a German fascist party controlling Germany from 1933 to 1945 under Adolf Hitler — **Nazi** *adj* — **Na·zism** \'nät-,si-zəm, 'nat-\ *also* **Na·zi·ism** \-sē-,i-zəm\ *n*

Nb *symbol* niobium

NB *abbr* **1** New Brunswick **2** nota bene

NBA *abbr* **1** National Basketball Association **2** National Boxing Association

NBC *abbr* National Broadcasting Company

NBS *abbr* National Bureau of Standards

NC *abbr* **1** no charge **2** North Carolina

NCAA *abbr* National Collegiate Athletic Association

NCO \,en-,sē-'ō\ *n* : NONCOMMISSIONED OFFICER

nd *abbr* no date

Nd *symbol* neodymium

ND *abbr* North Dakota

N Dak *abbr* North Dakota

Ne *symbol* neon

NE *abbr* **1** Nebraska **2** New England **3** northeast

Ne·an·der·thal \nē-'an-dər-,thôl, nā-'ändər-,täl\ *n* **1** : an extinct Old World hominid that lived from 30,000 to 200,000 years ago **2** : a person who resembles or suggests a caveman — **Neanderthal** *or* **Neandertal** *adj*

neap tide \'nēp-\ *n* : a tide of minimum range occurring at the first and third quarters of the moon

¹near \'nir\ *adv* **1** : at, within, or to a short distance or time **2** : ALMOST ⟨was ∼ dead⟩

²near *prep* : close to

³near *adj* **1** : closely related or associated; *also* : INTIMATE **2** : not far away; *also* : being the closer or left-hand member of a pair ⟨the ∼ side of the lake⟩ **3** : barely avoided ⟨a ∼ accident⟩ **4** : DIRECT, SHORT ⟨by the ∼est route⟩ **5** : STINGY **6** : not real but very like ⟨∼ silk⟩ — **near·ly** *adv* — **near·ness** *n*

⁴near *vb* : APPROACH

near beer *n* : any of various malt liquors low in alcohol

near·by \'nir-'bī, 'nir-,bī\ *adv or adj* : close at hand

near·sight·ed \'nir-'sī-təd\ *adj* : able to see near things more clearly than distant ones : MYOPIC — **near·sight·ed·ly** *adv* — **near·sight·ed·ness** *n*

neat \'nēt\ *adj* [MF *net*, fr. L *nitidus* bright, neat, fr. *nitēre* to shine] **1** : being orderly and clean **2** : not mixed or diluted ⟨∼ brandy⟩ **3** : marked by tasteful simplicity **4** : PRECISE, SYSTEMATIC **5** : SKILLFUL, ADROIT **6** : FINE, ADMIRABLE ♦ **Synonyms** SHIPSHAPE, TIDY, TRIG, TRIM — **neat** *adv* — **neat·ly** *adv* — **neat·ness** *n*

neath \'nēth\ *prep, dial* : BENEATH

neat·nik \'nēt-nik\ *n* : a person who is compulsively neat

neb \'neb\ *n* **1** : the beak of a bird or tortoise; *also* : NOSE, SNOUT **2** : NIB

Neb *or* **Nebr** *abbr* Nebraska

NEB *abbr* New English Bible

neb·u·la \'ne-byə-lə\ *n, pl* **-lae** \-,lē, -,lī\ *also* **-las** [NL, fr. L, mist, cloud] **1** : any of numerous clouds of gas or dust in interstellar space **2** : GALAXY — **neb·u·lar** \-lər\ *adj*

neb·u·liz·er \'ne-byə-,lī-zər\ *n* : ATOMIZER

neb·u·lous \'ne-byə-ləs\ *adj* **1** : of or relating to a nebula **2** : HAZY, INDISTINCT

¹nec·es·sary \'ne-sə-,ser-ē\ *adj* **1** : INEVITABLE, INESCAPABLE; *also* : CERTAIN **2** : PREDETERMINED **3** : COMPULSORY **4** : positively needed : INDISPENSABLE ⟨∼ supplies⟩ ♦ **Synonyms** IMPERATIVE, NECESSITOUS, ESSENTIAL — **nec·es·sar·i·ly** \,ne-sə-'ser-ə-lē\ *adv*

²necessary *n, pl* **-sar·ies** : an indispensable item

ne·ces·si·tate \ni-'se-sə-,tāt\ *vb* **-tat·ed; -tat·ing** : to make necessary

ne·ces·si·tous \ni-'se-sə-təs\ *adj* **1** : NEEDY, IMPOVERISHED **2** : URGENT **3** : NECESSARY ⟨∼ bargaining⟩

ne·ces·si·ty \ni-'se-sə-tē\ *n, pl* **-ties** **1** : conditions that cannot be changed **2** : WANT, POVERTY **3** : something that is necessary ⟨water is a ∼⟩ **4** : very great need

¹neck \'nek\ *n* **1** : the part of the body connecting the head and the trunk **2** : the part of a garment covering or near to the neck **3** : a relatively narrow part suggestive of a neck ⟨∼ of a bottle⟩ ⟨∼ of land⟩ **4** : a narrow margin esp. of victory ⟨won by a ∼⟩ — **necked** \'nekt\ *adj*

²neck *vb* : to kiss and caress amorously

neck and neck *adv or adj* : very close (as in a race)

neck·er·chief \'ne-kər-chəf, -,chēf\ *n, pl* **-chiefs** \-chəfs, -,chēfs\ *also* **-chieves** \-,chēvz\ : a square of cloth worn folded about the neck like a scarf

neck·lace \'ne-kləs\ *n* : an ornament worn around the neck

neck·line \'nek-,līn\ *n* : the outline of the neck opening of a garment

neck·tie \-,tī\ *n* : a strip of cloth worn around the neck and tied in front

ne·crol·o·gy \nə-'krä-lə-jē\ *n, pl* **-gies** **1** : OBITUARY **2** : a list of the recently dead

nec·ro·man·cy \'ne-krə-,man-sē\ *n* **1** : the art or practice of conjuring up the spirits of the dead for purposes of magically revealing the future **2** : MAGIC, SORCERY — **nec·ro·man·cer** \-sər\ *n*

ne·crop·o·lis \nə-'krä-pə-ləs, ne-\ *n, pl* **-lis·es** *or* **-les** \-,lēz\ *or* **-leis** \-,läs\ *or* **-li** \-,lī, -,lē\ [LL, fr. Gk *nekropolis*, fr. *nekros* dead body + *polis* city] : CEMETERY; *esp* : a large elaborate cemetery of an ancient city

nec·rop·sy \'ne-ˌkräp-sē\ *n, pl* **-sies** : AUTOPSY; *esp* : an autopsy performed on an animal

ne·cro·sis \nə-'krō-səs, ne-\ *n, pl* **ne·cro·ses** \-ˌsēz\ : usu. local death of body tissue — **ne·crot·ic** \-'krä-tik\ *adj*

nec·tar \'nek-tər\ *n* 1 : the drink of the Greek and Roman gods; *also* : any delicious drink 2 : a sweet plant secretion that is the raw material of honey

nec·tar·ine \ˌnek-tə-'rēn\ *n* : a smooth-skinned peach

née *or* **nee** \'nā\ *adj* [F, lit., born] — used to identify a woman by her maiden family name

¹**need** \'nēd\ *n* 1 : OBLIGATION ⟨no ~ to hurry⟩ 2 : a lack of something requisite, desirable, or useful 3 : a condition requiring supply or relief ⟨when the ~ arises⟩ 4 : POVERTY ♦ **Synonyms** NECESSITY, EXIGENCY

²**need** *vb* 1 : to be in want 2 : to have cause or occasion for : REQUIRE ⟨he ~s advice⟩ 3 : to be under obligation or necessity ⟨we ~ to know the truth⟩

need·ful \'nēd-fəl\ *adj* : NECESSARY, REQUISITE ⟨bought only what was ~⟩

¹**nee·dle** \'nē-dᵊl\ *n* 1 : a slender pointed usu. steel implement used in sewing 2 : a slender rod (as for knitting, controlling a small opening, or transmitting vibrations to or from a recording) ⟨a phonograph ~⟩ 3 : a slender hollow instrument by which material is introduced into or withdrawn from the body 4 : a slender indicator on a dial 5 : a needle-shaped leaf (as of a pine)

²**needle** *vb* **nee·dled; nee·dling** : PROD, GOAD; *esp* : to incite to action by repeated gibes ⟨*needled* him into a fight⟩

nee·dle-nose pliers \'nē-dᵊl-ˌnōz-\ *n pl* : pliers with long slender jaws for grasping small or thin objects

nee·dle·point \'nē-dᵊl-ˌpóint\ *n* 1 : lace worked with a needle over a paper pattern 2 : embroidery done on canvas across counted threads — **needlepoint** *adj*

need·less \'nēd-ləs\ *adj* : UNNECESSARY ⟨~ waste⟩ — **need·less·ly** *adv* — **need·less·ness** *n*

nee·dle·wom·an \'nē-dᵊl-ˌwu̇-mən\ *n* : a woman who does needlework; *esp* : SEAMSTRESS

nee·dle·work \-ˌwərk\ *n* : work done with a needle; *esp* : work (as embroidery) other than plain sewing

needs \'nēdz\ *adv* : of necessity : NECESSARILY ⟨must ~ be recognized⟩

needy \'nē-dē\ *adj* **need·i·er; -est** : being in want : POVERTY-STRICKEN

ne'er \'ner\ *adv* : NEVER

ne'er-do-well \'ner-dü-ˌwel\ *n* : an idle worthless person — **ne'er-do-well** *adj*

ne·far·i·ous \ni-'fer-ē-əs\ *adj* [L *nefarius*, fr. *nefas* crime, fr. *ne-* not + *fas* right, divine law] : very wicked : EVIL ♦ **Synonyms** BAD, IMMORAL, INIQUITOUS, SINFUL, VICIOUS — **ne·far·i·ous·ly** *adv*

neg *abbr* negative

ne·gate \ni-'gāt\ *vb* **ne·gat·ed; ne·gat·ing** 1 : to deny the existence or truth of 2 : to cause to be ineffective or invalid : NULLIFY ⟨~ a contract⟩

ne·ga·tion \ni-'gā-shən\ *n* 1 : the action or operation of negating or making negative 2 : a negative doctrine or statement

¹**neg·a·tive** \'ne-gə-tiv\ *adj* 1 : marked by denial, prohibition, or refusal ⟨a ~ reply⟩ 2 : not positive or constructive; *esp* : not affirming the presence of what is sought or suspected to be present ⟨test results were ~⟩ 3 : less than zero ⟨a ~ number⟩ 4 : being, relating to, or charged with electricity of which the electron is the elementary unit 5 : having the light and dark parts opposite to what they were in the original photographic subject — **neg·a·tive·ly** *adv* — **neg·a·tive·ness** *n* — **neg·a·tiv·i·ty** \ˌne-gə-'ti-və-tē\ *n*

²**negative** *n* 1 : a negative word or statement 2 : a negative vote or reply; *also* : REFUSAL 3 : something that is the opposite or negation of something else 4 : a negative number 5 : the side that votes or argues for the opposition (as in a debate) 6 : a negative photographic image on transparent material

³**negative** *vb* **-tived; -tiv·ing** 1 : to refuse to accept or approve 2 : to vote against 3 : DISPROVE

negative income tax *n* : a system of federal subsidy payments to families with incomes below a stipulated level

neg·a·tiv·ism \'ne-gə-ti-ˌvi-zəm\ *n* : an attitude of skepticism and denial of nearly everything affirmed or suggested by others

¹**ne·glect** \ni-'glekt\ *vb* [L *neglectus*, pp. of *neglegere, neclegere,* fr. *nec-* not + *legere* to gather] 1 : DISREGARD 2 : to leave undone or unattended to esp. through carelessness ♦ **Synonyms** OMIT, IGNORE, OVERLOOK, SLIGHT, FORGET, MISS

²**neglect** *n* 1 : an act or instance of neglecting something 2 : the condition of being neglected — **ne·glect·ful** *adj*

neg·li·gee *also* **neg·li·gé** \ˌne-glə-'zhā\ *n* : a woman's long flowing dressing gown

neg·li·gent \'ne-gli-jənt\ *adj* : marked by neglect ♦ **Synonyms** NEGLECTFUL, REMISS, DELINQUENT, DERELICT — **neg·li·gence** \-jəns\ *n* — **neg·li·gent·ly** *adv*

neg·li·gi·ble \'ne-gli-jə-bəl\ *adj* : so small as to be neglected or disregarded

ne·go·tiant \ni-'gō-shē-ənt\ *n* : NEGOTIATOR

ne·go·ti·ate \ni-'gō-shē-ˌāt\ *vb* **-at·ed; -at·ing** [L *negotiari* to carry on business, fr. *negotium* business, fr. *neg-* not + *otium* leisure] 1 : to confer with another so as to arrive at the settlement of some matter; *also* : to arrange for or bring about by such conferences ⟨~ a treaty⟩ 2 : to transfer to another by delivery or endorsement in return for equivalent value ⟨~ a check⟩ 3 : to get through, around, or over successfully ⟨~ a turn⟩ — **ne·go·tia·ble** \-shə-bəl, -shē-ə-\ *adj* — **ne-**

go·ti·a·tion \ni-ˌgō-sē-ˈā-shən, -shē-\ *n* —
ne·go·ti·a·tor \-ˈgō-shē-ˌā-tər\ *n*
ne·gri·tude \ˈne-grə-ˌtüd, -ˌtyüd, ˈnē-\
n : a consciousness of and pride in one's
African heritage
Ne·gro \ˈnē-grō\ *n, pl* **Negroes** [Sp or Pg,
fr. *negro* black] *sometimes offensive* : a
member of the human race native to Africa and classified according to physical
features (as dark skin pigmentation) —
Negro *adj, sometimes offensive* — **Ne-
groid** \ˈnē-ˌgròid\ *n or adj, often not cap,
sometimes offensive*
Neh *abbr* Nehemiah
Ne·he·mi·ah \ˌnē-ə-ˈmī-ə\ *n* — see BIBLE
table
neigh \ˈnā\ *n* : a loud prolonged cry of a
horse — **neigh** *vb*
¹**neigh·bor** \ˈnā-bər\ *n* **1** : one living or
located near another **2** : FELLOW MAN
²**neighbor** *vb* : to be next to or near to
: border on
neigh·bor·hood \ˈnā-bər-ˌhùd\ *n* **1**
: NEARNESS **2** : a place or region near
: VICINITY; *also* : a number or amount
near ⟨costs in the ∼ of $10⟩ **3** : the peo-
ple living near one another **4** : a section
lived in by neighbors and usu. having distinguishing characteristics
neigh·bor·ly \-lē\ *adj* : befitting congenial neighbors; *esp* : FRIENDLY ⟨a ∼ wel-
come⟩ — **neigh·bor·li·ness** *n*
neigh·bour *chiefly Brit var of* NEIGHBOR
¹**nei·ther** \ˈnē-thər, ˈnī-\ *conj* **1** : not either
⟨∼ good nor bad⟩ **2** : NOR ⟨∼ did I⟩
²**neither** *pron* : neither one : not the one
and not the other ⟨∼ of the two⟩
³**neither** *adj* : not either ⟨∼ hand⟩
nel·son \ˈnel-sən\ *n* : a wrestling hold in
which one applies leverage against an opponent's arm, neck, and head
nem·a·tode \ˈne-mə-ˌtōd\ *n* : any of a
phylum of elongated cylindrical worms
parasitic in animals or plants or free-living in soil or water
nem·e·sis \ˈne-mə-səs\ *n, pl* **-e·ses** \-ˌsēz\
[L *Nemesis*, goddess of divine retribution,
fr. Gk] **1** : one that inflicts retribution or
vengeance **2** : a formidable and usu. victorious rival **3** : an act or effect of retribution; *also* : CURSE
neo·clas·sic \ˌnē-ō-ˈkla-sik\ *or* **neo·clas-
si·cal** \-si-kəl\ *adj* : of or relating to a revival or adaptation of the classical style
esp. in literature, art, or music
neo·co·lo·nial·ism \ˌnē-ō-kə-ˈlō-nē-ə-ˌli-
zəm\ *n* : the economic and political policies by which a nation indirectly maintains or extends its influence over other
areas or peoples — **neo·co·lo·nial** *adj* —
neo·co·lo·nial·ist \-list\ *n or adj*
neo·con \ˈnē-ō-ˌkän\ *n* : NEOCONSERVA-
TIVE
neo·con·ser·va·tive \-kən-ˈsər-və-tiv\ *n*
: a former liberal espousing political con-
servatism — **neo·con·ser·va·tism** \-və-
ˌti-zəm\ *n* — **neoconservative** *adj*
neo·dym·i·um \ˌnē-ō-ˈdi-mē-əm\ *n* : a
silver-white to yellow metallic chemical
element
neo·im·pres·sion·ism \ˌnē-ō-im-ˈpre-
shə-ˌni-zəm\ *n, often cap N&I* : a late 19th

century French art movement that attempted to make impressionism more
precise and to use a pointillist painting
technique
Neo·lith·ic \ˌnē-ə-ˈli-thik\ *adj* : of or relating to the latest period of the Stone Age
characterized by polished stone implements
ne·ol·o·gism \nē-ˈä-lə-ˌji-zəm\ *n* : a new
word or expression
ne·on \ˈnē-ˌän\ *n* [Gk, neut. of *neos* new]
1 : a gaseous colorless chemical element
used in electric lamps **2** : a lamp in which
a discharge through neon gives a reddish
glow — **neon** *adj*
neo·na·tal \ˌnē-ō-ˈnā-tᵊl\ *adj* : of, relating
to, or affecting the newborn ⟨a ∼ infec-
tion⟩ — **neo·na·tal·ly** *adv*
neo·nate \ˈnē-ə-ˌnāt\ *n* : a newborn child
neo·pa·gan \ˌnē-ō-ˈpā-gən\ *n* : a person
who practices a contemporary form of
paganism
neo·phyte \ˈnē-ə-ˌfīt\ *n* **1** : a new convert
: PROSELYTE **2** : NOVICE **3** : BEGINNER
♦ **Synonyms** APPRENTICE, FRESHMAN,
NEWCOMER, ROOKIE, TENDERFOOT,
TYRO
neo·plasm \ˈnē-ə-ˌpla-zəm\ *n* : a new
growth of tissue serving no useful purpose in the body : TUMOR — **neo·plas-
tic** \ˌnē-ə-ˈplas-tik\ *adj*
neo·prene \ˈnē-ə-ˌprēn\ *n* : a synthetic
rubber used esp. for special-purpose
clothing (as wet suits)
neo·trop·i·cal \ˌnē-ō-ˈträ-pi-kəl\ *adj, often cap* : of or relating to a zoogeographic
region of America that extends south
from the central plateau of Mexico
ne·pen·the \nə-ˈpen-thē\ *n* **1** : a potion
used by the ancients to dull pain and sorrow **2** : something capable of making
one forget grief or suffering
neph·ew \ˈne-fyü, *chiefly Brit* -vyü\ *n* [ME
nevew, fr. AF *neveu*, fr. LL *nepot-*, *nepos*,
fr. L, grandson, descendant] : a son of
one's brother, sister, brother-in-law, or
sister-in-law
ne·phrit·ic \ni-ˈfri-tik\ *adj* **1** : RENAL **2**
: of, relating to, or affected with nephritis
ne·phri·tis \ni-ˈfrī-təs\ *n, pl* **ne·phrit·i-
des** \-ˈfri-tə-ˌdēz\ : kidney inflammation
ne plus ul·tra \ˌnē-ˌpləs-ˈəl-trə\ *n* [NL,
(go) no more beyond] : the highest point
capable of being attained
nep·o·tism \ˈne-pə-ˌti-zəm\ *n* [F *népo-
tisme*, fr. It *nepotismo*, fr. *nepote* nephew,
fr. LL *nepot-*, *nepos*] : favoritism shown to
a relative (as in the granting of jobs)
Nep·tune \ˈnep-ˌtün, -ˌtyün\ *n* : the planet
8th in order from the sun — **Nep·tu·ni-
an** \nep-ˈtü-nē-ən, -ˈtyü-\ *adj*
nep·tu·ni·um \nep-ˈtü-nē-əm, -ˈtyü-\ *n* : a
short-lived radioactive element
nerd \ˈnərd\ *n* : an unstylish or socially
inept person; *esp* : one slavishly devoted
to intellectual pursuits — **nerdy** *adj*
Ne·re·id \ˈnir-ē-əd\ *n* : a sea nymph in
Greek mythology
¹**nerve** \ˈnərv\ *n* **1** : SINEW, TENDON
⟨strain every ∼⟩ **2** : any of the strands
of nervous tissue that carry nerve impulses between the brain and spinal cord and

every part of the body **3** : power of endurance or control : FORTITUDE; *also* : BOLDNESS, DARING **4** *pl* : NERVOUSNESS **5** : a vein of a leaf or insect wing — **nerved** \'nərvd\ *adj* — **nerve·less** *adj*

²**nerve** *vb* **nerved; nerv·ing** : to give strength or courage to

nerve cell *n* : NEURON; *also* : CELL BODY

nerve gas *n* : a chemical weapon damaging esp. to the nervous and respiratory systems

nerve impulse *n* : a physical and chemical change that moves along a process of a neuron after stimulation and carries a record of sensation or an instruction to act

nerve–rack·ing *or* **nerve–wrack·ing** \'nərv-,ra-kiŋ\ *adj* : extremely trying on the nerves ⟨~ noise⟩

ner·vous \'nər-vəs\ *adj* **1** : FORCIBLE, SPIRITED **2** : of, relating to, or made up of neurons or nerves **3** : easily excited or annoyed : JUMPY ⟨a ~ horse⟩ **4** : TIMID, APPREHENSIVE ⟨a ~ smile⟩ **5** : UNEASY, UNSTEADY — **ner·vous·ly** *adv* — **ner·vous·ness** *n*

nervous breakdown *n* : an attack of mental or emotional disorder of sufficient severity to be incapacitating esp. when requiring hospitalization

nervous system *n* : a bodily system that in vertebrates is made up of the brain and spinal cord, nerves, ganglia, and parts of the sense organs and that receives and interprets stimuli and transmits nerve impulses

nervy \'nər-vē\ *adj* **nerv·i·er; -est** **1** : showing calm courage ⟨a ~ performer⟩ **2** : marked by impudence or presumption ⟨a ~ salesperson⟩ **3** : EXCITABLE, NERVOUS ♦ *Synonyms* BOLD, CHEEKY, FORWARD, FRESH, IMPUDENT, SAUCY

-ness \nəs\ *n suffix* : state : condition : quality : degree ⟨good*ness*⟩

¹**nest** \'nest\ *n* **1** : the shelter prepared by a bird for its eggs and young **2** : a place where eggs (as of insects or fish) are laid and hatched **3** : a place of rest, retreat, or lodging **4** : DEN, HANGOUT ⟨a ~ of thieves⟩ **5** : the occupants of a nest **6** : a series of objects (as bowls or tables) fitting inside or under one another

²**nest** *vb* **1** : to build or occupy a nest **2** : to fit compactly together or within one another

nest egg *n* : a fund of money accumulated as a reserve

nes·tle \'ne-səl\ *vb* **nes·tled; nes·tling** **1** : to settle snugly or comfortably **2** : to press closely and affectionately : CUDDLE **3** : to settle, shelter, or house as if in a nest

nest·ling \'nest-liŋ\ *n* : a bird too young to leave its nest

¹**net** \'net\ *n* **1** : a meshed fabric twisted, knotted, or woven together at regular intervals **2** : a device made all or partly of net and used esp. to catch birds, fish, or insects **3** : something made of net used esp. for protecting, confining, carrying, or dividing ⟨a tennis ~⟩ **4** : SNARE, TRAP **5** *often cap* : INTERNET

²**net** *vb* **net·ted; net·ting** **1** : to cover or enclose with or as if with a net **2** : to catch in or as if in a net

³**net** *adj* : free from all charges or deductions ⟨~ profit⟩ ⟨~ weight⟩

⁴**net** *vb* **net·ted; net·ting** : to gain or produce as profit : CLEAR, YIELD ⟨his business *netted* $50,000 a year⟩

⁵**net** *n* : a net amount, profit, weight, or price

Neth *abbr* Netherlands

neth·er \'ne-thər\ *adj* : situated down or below ⟨the ~ regions of the earth⟩

neth·er·most \-,mōst\ *adj* : LOWEST

neth·er·world \-,wərld\ *n* **1** : the world of the dead **2** : UNDERWORLD

net·i·quette \'ne-ti-kət, -,ket\ *n* : etiquette governing communication on the Internet

net·roots \'net-,rüts, -,rüts\ *n pl* : the grass-roots political activists who communicate via the Internet

nett *Brit var of* NET

net·ting *n* **1** : NETWORK **2** : the act or process of making a net or network

¹**net·tle** \'ne-t⁰l\ *n* : any of a genus of coarse herbs with stinging hairs

²**nettle** *vb* **net·tled; net·tling** : PROVOKE, VEX, IRRITATE

net·tle·some \'ne-t⁰l-səm\ *adj* : causing vexation : IRRITATING

net·work \'net-,wərk\ *n* **1** : NET **2** : a system of elements (as lines or channels) that cross in the manner of the threads in a net **3** : a group or system of related or connected parts; *esp* : a chain of radio or television stations **4** : a system of computers that are connected (as by telephone wires)

net·work·ing \'net-,wər-kiŋ\ *n* **1** : the exchange of information or services among individuals, groups, or institutions **2** : the cultivation of productive business relationships

neu·ral \'nùr-əl, 'nyùr-\ *adj* : of, relating to, or involving a nerve or the nervous system ⟨~ pathways⟩

neu·ral·gia \nù-'ral-jə, nyù-\ *n* : acute pain that follows the course of a nerve — **neu·ral·gic** \-jik\ *adj*

neur·as·the·nia \,nùr-əs-'thē-nē-ə, ,nyùr-\ *n* [NL, fr. Gk *neuron* nerve + *asthenia* weakness, fr. *asthenēs* weak, fr. *a-* not + *sthenos* strength] : a psychological disorder marked esp. by fatiguing easily, lack of motivation, feelings of inadequacy, and psychosomatic symptoms — **neur·as·then·ic** \-the-nik, -'thē-\ *adj or n*

neu·ri·tis \nù-'rī-təs, nyù-\ *n, pl* **-rit·i·des** \-'ri-tə-,dēz\ *or* **-ri·tis·es** : inflammation of a nerve — **neu·rit·ic** \-'ri-tik\ *adj or n*

neu·ro·bi·ol·o·gy \,nùr-ō-bī-'ä-lə-jē\ *n* : a branch of biology that deals with the nervous system — **neu·ro·bi·o·log·i·cal** \-,bī-ə-'lä-ji-kəl\ *adj* — **neu·ro·bi·ol·o·gist** \-bī-'ä-lə-jist\ *n*

neu·rol·o·gy \nù-'rä-lə-jē, nyù-\ *n* : the scientific study of the nervous system — **neu·ro·log·i·cal** \,nùr-ə-'lä-ji-kəl, ,nyùr-\ *or* **neu·ro·log·ic** \-jik\ *adj* — **neu·ro·log·i·cal·ly** \-ji-k(ə-)lē\ *adv* — **neu·rol·o·gist** \nù-'rä-lə-jist, nyù-\ *n*

neu·ro·mus·cu·lar \,nùr-ō-'məs-kyə-lər, ,nyùr-\ *adj* : of, relating to, or affecting nerves and muscles ⟨a ~ disease⟩

neu·ron \'nü-,rän, 'nyü-\ *n* : a cell with specialized processes that is the fundamental functional unit of nervous tissue — **neu·ro·nal** \'nùr-ə-n³l, 'nyùr-\ *adj*

neu·rone \-,rōn\ *chiefly Brit var of* NEURON

neu·ro·sci·ence \,nùr-ō-'sī-əns, ,nyùr-\ *n* : a branch of the life sciences that deals with the anatomy, physiology, biochemistry, or molecular biology of nerves and nervous tissue and esp. with their relation to behavior and learning — **neu·ro·sci·en·tist** \-ən-tist\ *n*

neu·ro·sis \nù-'rō-səs, nyù-\ *n, pl* **-ro·ses** \-,sēz\ : a mental and emotional disorder that is less serious than a psychosis, is not characterized by disturbance of the use of language, and is accompanied by various bodily and mental disturbances (as visceral symptoms, anxieties, or phobias)

neu·ro·sur·gery \,nùr-ō-'sər-jə-rē, ,nyùr-\ *n* : surgery of nervous structures (as nerves, the brain, or the spinal cord) — **neu·ro·sur·geon** \-'sər-jən\ *n*

¹neu·rot·ic \nù-'rä-tik, nyù-\ *adj* : relating to, being, or affected with a neurosis — **neu·rot·i·cal·ly** \-ti-k(ə-)lē\ *adv*

²neurotic *n* : an emotionally unstable or neurotic person

neu·ro·trans·mit·ter \,nùr-ō-trans-'mi-tər, ,nyùr-, -tranz-\ *n* : a substance (as acetylcholine) that transmits nerve impulses across a synapse

neut *abbr* neuter

¹neu·ter \'nü-tər, 'nyü-\ *adj* [ME *neutre*, fr. MF & L; MF *neutre*, fr. L *neuter*, lit., neither, fr. *ne-* not + *uter* which of two] 1 : of, relating to, or constituting the gender that includes most words or grammatical forms referring to things classed as neither masculine nor feminine 2 : lacking or having imperfectly developed sex organs

²neuter *n* 1 : a noun, pronoun, adjective, or inflectional form or class of the neuter gender; *also* : the neuter gender 2 : WORKER 2; *also* : a spayed or castrated animal

³neuter *vb* 1 : CASTRATE, SPAY 2 : to remove the force or effectiveness of

¹neu·tral \'nü-trəl, 'nyü-\ *n* 1 : one that is neutral 2 : a neutral color 3 : a position of disengagement (as of gears)

²neutral *adj* 1 : not favoring either side in a quarrel, contest, or war 2 : of or relating to a neutral state or power 3 : MIDDLING, INDIFFERENT 4 : having no hue : GRAY; *also* : not decided in color 5 : neither acid nor basic ⟨a ~ solution⟩ 6 : not electrically charged

neu·tral·ise *Brit var of* NEUTRALIZE

neu·tral·ism \'nü-trə-,li-zəm, 'nyü-\ *n* : a policy or the advocacy of neutrality esp. in international affairs

neu·tral·i·ty \nü-'tra-lə-tē, nyü-\ *n* : the quality or state of being neutral; *esp* : refusal to take part in a war between other powers

neu·tral·ize \'nü-trə-,līz, 'nyü-\ *vb* **-ized;**

-iz·ing : to make neutral; *esp* : COUNTERACT — **neu·tral·i·za·tion** \,nü-trə-lə-'zā-shən, ,nyü-\ *n*

neu·tri·no \nü-'trē-nō, nyü-\ *n, pl* **-nos** : an uncharged elementary particle held to be massless or very light

neu·tron \'nü-,trän, 'nyü-\ *n* : an uncharged atomic particle that is nearly equal in mass to the proton

neutron bomb *n* : a nuclear bomb designed to produce lethal neutrons but less blast and fire damage than other nuclear bombs

neutron star *n* : a dense celestial object that results from the collapse of a large star

Nev *abbr* Nevada

nev·er \'ne-vər\ *adv* 1 : not ever 2 : not in any degree, way, or condition

nev·er·more \,ne-vər-'mór\ *adv* : never again

nev·er–nev·er land \,ne-vər-'ne-vər-\ *n* : an ideal or imaginary place

nev·er·the·less \,ne-vər-thə-'les\ *adv* : in spite of that : HOWEVER

ne·vus \'nē-vəs\ *n, pl* **ne·vi** \-,vī\ : a usu. pigmented area on the skin : MOLE

¹new \'nü, 'nyü\ *adj* 1 : not old : RECENT, MODERN 2 : recently discovered, recognized, or learned about ⟨~ drugs⟩ 3 : UNFAMILIAR ⟨visit ~ places⟩ 4 : different from the former 5 : not accustomed ⟨~ to the work⟩ 6 : beginning as a repetition of a previous act or thing ⟨a ~ year⟩ 7 : REFRESHED, REGENERATED ⟨rest made a ~ man of him⟩ 8 : being in a position or place for the first time ⟨a ~ member⟩ 9 *cap* : having been in use after medieval times : MODERN ⟨*New* Latin⟩
♦ *Synonyms* NOVEL, NEWFANGLED, FRESH — **new·ish** *adj* — **new·ness** *n*

²new *adv* : NEWLY ⟨*new*-mown hay⟩

¹new age *adj, often cap N&A* 1 : of, relating to, or being New Age 2 : CONTEMPORARY, MODERN

²new age *n* 1 *cap* : a group of late 20th century social attitudes adapted from a variety of ancient and modern beliefs relating to spirituality, right living, and health 2 : a soft soothing form of instrumental music

new·bie \'nü-bē, 'nyü-\ *n* : a newcomer esp. to cyberspace

new blood *n* : persons accepted into a group or organization and expected to provide fresh ideas and vitality

¹new·born \-,bórn\ *adj* 1 : recently born 2 : born anew ⟨~ hope⟩

²newborn *n, pl* **newborn** *or* **newborns** : a newborn individual

new·com·er \-,kə-mər\ *n* 1 : one recently arrived 2 : BEGINNER

New Deal *n* : the legislative and administrative program of President F. D. Roosevelt to promote economic recovery and social reform during the 1930s — **New Dealer** *n*

new·el \'nü-əl, 'nyü-\ *n* : a post about which the steps of a circular staircase wind; *also* : a post at the foot of a stairway or one at a landing

new·fan·gled \'nü-'faŋ-gəld, 'nyü-\ *adj* 1

: attracted to novelty **2** : of the newest style : NOVEL ⟨∼ gadgets⟩

new–fash·ioned \-'fa-shənd\ adj **1** : made in a new fashion or form ⟨∼ automobiles⟩ **2** : UP-TO-DATE

new·found \'faund\ adj : newly found

New Left n : a radical political movement originating in the 1960s

new·ly \'nü-lē, 'nyü-\ adv **1** : LATELY, RECENTLY ⟨a ∼ married couple⟩ **2** : ANEW, AFRESH ⟨∼ painted⟩

new·ly·wed \-,wed\ n : a person recently married

new moon n : the phase of the moon with its dark side toward the earth; also : the thin crescent moon seen for a few days after the new moon phase

news \'nüz, 'nyüz\ n **1** : a report of recent events : TIDINGS **2** : material reported in a newspaper or news periodical or on a newscast

news·boy \'nüz-,bȯi, 'nyüz-\ n : one who delivers or sells newspapers

news·cast \-,kast\ n : a radio or television broadcast of news — **news·cast·er** \-,kas-tər\ n

news·group \-,grüp\ n : an Internet bulletin board devoted to a certain topic

news·let·ter \'nüz-,le-tər, 'nyüz-\ n : a small newspaper containing news or information of interest chiefly to a special group

news·mag·a·zine \-,ma-gə-,zēn\ n : a usu. weekly magazine devoted chiefly to summarizing and analyzing news

news·man \-mən, -,man\ n : a person who gathers, reports, or comments on the news : REPORTER

news·pa·per \-,pā-pər\ n : a paper that is published at regular intervals and contains news, articles of opinion, features, and advertising

news·pa·per·man \-,pā-pər-,man\ n : a person who owns or is employed by a newspaper

news·print \-,print\ n : paper made chiefly from wood pulp and used mostly for newspapers

news·reel \-,rēl\ n : a short motion picture portraying current events

news·stand \-,stand\ n : a place where newspapers and periodicals are sold

news·week·ly \-,wēk-lē\ n : a weekly newspaper or newsmagazine

news·wire \-,wī(-ə)r\ n : WIRE SERVICE

news·wom·an \-,wu̇-mən\ n : a woman who is a reporter

news·wor·thy \-,wər-thē\ adj : sufficiently interesting to the general public to warrant reporting

newsy \'nü-zē, 'nyü-\ adj **news·i·er; -est** : filled with news; esp : TALKATIVE

newt \'nüt, 'nyüt\ n [ME, alter. (from misdivision of an ewte) of ewt, evete, fr. OE efete] : any of various small chiefly aquatic salamanders

New Testament n : the second of the two chief divisions of the Christian Bible — see BIBLE table

new·ton \'nü-t³n, 'nyü-\ n : the unit of force in the metric system equal to the force required to impart an acceleration

of one meter per second per second to a mass of one kilogram

new wave n, often cap N&W : the latest and esp. the most outrageous style — **new–wave** adj

New Year n **1** : NEW YEAR'S DAY; also : the first days of the year **2** : ROSH HASHANAH

New Year's Day n : January 1 observed as a legal holiday

¹**next** \'nekst\ adj : immediately preceding or following : NEAREST

²**next** prep : nearest or adjacent to

³**next** adv **1** : in the time, place, or order nearest or immediately succeeding **2** : on the first occasion to come

⁴**next** n : one that is next

nex·us \'nek-səs\ n, pl **nex·us·es** \-sə-səz\ or **nex·us** \-səs, -,süs\ : CONNECTION, LINK

Nez Percé \'nez-'pərs\ n : a member of an American Indian people of Idaho, Washington, and Oregon; also : the language of the Nez Percé

NF abbr Newfoundland

NFC abbr National Football Conference

NFL abbr National Football League

Nfld abbr Newfoundland

NG abbr **1** National Guard **2** no good

ngul·trum \en-'gul-trəm\ n — see MONEY table

ngwee \en-'gwē\ n, pl **ngwee** — see kwacha at MONEY table

NH abbr New Hampshire

NHL abbr National Hockey League

Ni symbol nickel

ni·a·cin \'nī-ə-sən\ n : an organic acid of the vitamin B complex found widely in plants and animals and used esp. against pellagra

¹**nib** \'nib\ n : POINT; esp : a pen point

²**nib·ble** \'ni-bəl\ vb **nib·bled; nib·bling** : to bite gently or bit by bit

²**nibble** n : a small or cautious bite

ni·cad \'nī-,kad\ n : a rechargeable dry cell that has a nickel cathode and a cadmium anode

nice \'nīs\ adj **nic·er; nic·est** [ME, foolish, wanton, fr. AF, silly, simple, fr. L nescius ignorant, fr. nescire to not know] **1** : FASTIDIOUS, DISCRIMINATING **2** : marked by delicate discrimination or treatment ⟨a ∼ distinction between those two words⟩ **3** : PLEASING, AGREEABLE ⟨had a ∼ time⟩; also : well-executed ⟨a ∼ shot⟩ **4** : WELL-BRED ⟨∼ people⟩ **5** : VIRTUOUS, RESPECTABLE ♦ **Synonyms** CHOOSY, FINICKY, PARTICULAR, PERSNICKETY, PICKY — **nice·ly** adv — **nice·ness** n

nice–nel·ly \'nīs-'ne-lē\ adj, often cap 2d N **1** : marked by euphemism **2** : PRUDISH ⟨his ∼ sweetheart⟩ — **nice nelly** n, often cap 2d N — **nice–nel·ly·ism** \-,i-zəm\ n, often cap 2d N

nice·ty \'nī-sə-tē\ n, pl **-ties** **1** : a dainty, delicate, or elegant thing ⟨enjoy the niceties of life⟩ **2** : a fine point or distinction ⟨niceties of workmanship⟩ **3** : EXACTNESS, PRECISION, ACCURACY

niche \'nich\ n [F] **1** : a recess in a wall esp. for a statue **2** : a place, employment, or activity for which a person or thing is best fitted **3** : the living space or role of an organism in an ecological community esp. with regard to food consumption

¹nick \'nik\ *n* **1** : a small notch, groove, or chip **2** : the final critical moment ⟨in the ~ of time⟩

²nick *vb* : NOTCH, CHIP

nick·el \'ni-kəl\ *n* **1** : a hard silver-white metallic chemical element capable of a high polish and used in alloys **2** : the U.S. 5-cent piece made of copper and nickel; *also* : the Canadian 5-cent piece

nick·el·ode·on \,ni-kə-'lō-dē-ən\ *n* **1** : an early movie theater to which admission cost five cents **2** : JUKEBOX

nick·er \'ni-kər\ *vb* : NEIGH, WHINNY — **nicker** *n*

nick·name \'nik-,nām\ *n* [ME *nekename* additional name, alter. (from misdivision of *an ekename*) of *ekename*, fr. *eke* also + *name*] **1** : a usu. descriptive name given instead of or in addition to the one belonging to a person, place, or thing **2** : a familiar form of a proper name — **nickname** *vb*

nic·o·tine \'ni-kə-,tēn\ *n* : a poisonous and addictive substance in tobacco that is used as an insecticide

nic·o·tin·ic acid \,ni-kə-'tē-nik-, -'ti-\ *n* : NIACIN

niece \'nēs\ *n* : a daughter of one's brother, sister, brother-in-law, or sister-in-law

nif·ty \'nif-tē\ *adj* **nif·ti·er; -est** : very good : very attractive

nig·gard \'ni-gərd\ *n* : a stingy person : MISER — **nig·gard·li·ness** \-lē-nəs\ *n* — **nig·gard·ly** *adj or adv*

nig·gling \'ni-gə-liŋ\ *adj* **1** : PETTY ⟨~ details⟩ **2** : bothersome in a petty way

♦ **Synonyms** INCONSEQUENTIAL, MEASLY, PICAYUNE, PIDDLING, TRIFLING, TRIVIAL

¹nigh \'nī\ *adv* **1** : near in place, time, or relationship **2** : NEARLY, ALMOST

²nigh *adj* : CLOSE, NEAR

³nigh *prep* : NEAR

night \'nīt\ *n* **1** : the period between dusk and dawn **2** : the darkness of night **3** : a period of misery or unhappiness **4** : NIGHTFALL — **night** *adj*

night blindness *n* : reduced visual capacity in faint light (as at night)

night·cap \'nīt-,kap\ *n* **1** : a cloth cap worn with nightclothes **2** : a usu. alcoholic drink taken at bedtime

night·clothes \-,klōthz, -,klōz\ *n pl* : garments worn in bed

night·club \-,kləb\ *n* : a place of entertainment open at night usu. serving food and liquor and providing music for dancing

night crawl·er \-,kró-lər\ *n* : EARTHWORM; *esp* : a large earthworm found on the soil surface at night

night·dress \'nīt-,dres\ *n* : NIGHTGOWN

night·fall \-,fól\ *n* : the coming of night

night·gown \-,gaún\ *n* : a loose garment for wear in bed

night·hawk \-,hók\ *n* : any of a genus of American birds related to and resembling the whip-poor-will

night·in·gale \'nī-t°n-,gāl, 'nī-tiŋ-\ *n* [ME, fr. OE *nihtegale*, fr. *niht* night + *galan* to sing] : any of several Old World thrushes noted for the sweet usu. nocturnal song of the male

night·life \'nīt-,līf\ *n* : the activity of pleasure-seekers at night

night·ly \'nīt-lē\ *adj* **1** : happening, done, or produced by night or every night **2** : of or relating to the night or every night — **nightly** *adv*

night·mare \'nīt-,mer\ *n* **1** : a frightening dream **2** : a frightening or horrible experience — **nightmare** *adj* — **night·mar·ish** *adj*

night rider *n* : a member of a secret band who ride masked at night doing violence to punish or terrorize

night·shade \'nīt-,shād\ *n* : any of a large genus of herbs, shrubs, and trees that includes poisonous forms (as the belladonna), ornamentals (as the petunias), and important food plants (as the potato and eggplant)

night·shirt \-,shərt\ *n* : a nightgown resembling a shirt

night soil *n* : human feces used esp. for fertilizing the soil

night·stick \'nīt-,stik\ *n* : a police officer's club

night·time \-,tīm\ *n* : the time from dusk to dawn

night·walk·er \-,wó-kər\ *n* : a person who roves about at night esp. with criminal or immoral intent

ni·hil·ism \'nī-ə-,li-zəm, 'nē-hə-\ *n* **1** : a viewpoint that traditional values and beliefs are unfounded and that existence is senseless and useless **2** : ANARCHISM — **ni·hil·ist** \-list\ *n or adj* — **ni·hil·is·tic** \,nī-ə-'lis-tik, ,nē-hə-\ *adj*

nil \'nil\ *n* : ZERO, NOTHING

nim·ble \'nim-bəl\ *adj* **nim·bler; nim·blest** [ME *nimel*, fr. OE *numol* holding much, fr. *niman* to take] **1** : quick and light in motion : AGILE ⟨a ~ dancer⟩ **2** : quick in understanding and learning : CLEVER ⟨a ~ mind⟩ ♦ **Synonyms** ACTIVE, BRISK, SPRIGHTLY, SPRY, ZIPPY — **nim·ble·ness** *n* — **nim·bly** \-blē\ *adv*

nim·bus \'nim-bəs\ *n, pl* **nim·bi** \-,bī, -bē\ *or* **nim·bus·es** **1** : a figure (as a disk) in an art work suggesting radiant light about the head of a divinity, saint, or sovereign **2** : a rain cloud; *also* : THUNDERHEAD

NIMBY \'nim-bē\ *n* [*not in my backyard*] : opposition to the placement of something undesirable (as a prison) in one's neighborhood

nim·rod \'nim-,räd\ *n* **1** : HUNTER **2** : IDIOT, JERK

nin·com·poop \'nin-kəm-,püp\ *n* : FOOL, SIMPLETON

nine \'nīn\ *n* **1** : one more than eight **2** : the 9th in a set or series **3** : something having nine units; *esp* : a baseball team — **nine** *adj or pron* — **ninth** \'nīnth\ *adj or adv or n* — **to the nines** **1** : to perfection **2** : in an elaborate manner ⟨dressed *to the nines*⟩

nine days' wonder *n* : something that creates a short-lived sensation

nine·pins \'nīn-ˌpinz\ *n* : a bowling game using nine pins arranged usu. in a diamond-shaped configuration

nine·teen \'nīn-'tēn\ *n* : one more than 18 — **nineteen** *adj or pron* — **nine·teenth** \-'tēnth\ *adj or n*

nine·ty \'nīn-tē\ *n, pl* **nineties** : nine times 10 — **nine·ti·eth** \-tē-əth\ *adj or n* — **ninety** *adj or pron*

nin·ja \'nɪn-jə, -ˌ(ˌ)jä\ *n, pl* **ninja** *or* **ninjas** [Jp] : a person trained in ancient Japanese martial arts and employed esp. for espionage and assassinations

nin·ny \'ni-nē\ *n, pl* **ninnies** : FOOL

ni·o·bi·um \nī-'ō-bē-əm\ *n* : a gray metallic chemical element used in alloys

¹nip \'nip\ *vb* **nipped; nip·ping** **1** : to catch hold of and squeeze tightly between two surfaces, edges, or points **2** : ³CLIP **3** : to destroy the growth, progress, or fulfillment of ⟨*nipped* in the bud⟩ **4** : to injure or make numb with cold : CHILL **5** : SNATCH, STEAL

²nip *n* **1** : a sharp stinging cold **2** : a biting or pungent flavor **3** : PINCH, BITE **4** : a small portion : BIT

³nip *n* : a small quantity of liquor : SIP

⁴nip *vb* **nipped; nip·ping** : to take liquor in nips : TIPPLE

nip and tuck *adj or adv* : so close that the lead shifts rapidly from one contestant to another

nip·per \'ni-pər\ *n* **1** : one that nips **2** *pl* : PINCERS **3** : CHILD; *esp* : a small boy

nip·ple \'ni-pəl\ *n* : the protuberance of a mammary gland through which milk is drawn off : TEAT; *also* : something resembling a nipple

nip·py \'ni-pē\ *adj* **nip·pi·er; -est** **1** : PUNGENT, SHARP **2** : CHILLY

nir·va·na \nər-'vä-nə\ *n, often cap* [Skt *nirvāṇa*, lit., act of extinguishing, fr. *nis-* out + *vāti* it blows] **1** : the final freeing of a soul from all that enslaves it; *esp* : the supreme happiness that according to Buddhism comes when all passion, hatred, and delusion die out and the soul is released from the necessity of further purification **2** : OBLIVION; *also* : PARADISE

ni·sei \nē-'sā, 'nē-ˌsā\ *n, pl* **nisei** *often cap* : a son or daughter of immigrant Japanese parents who is born and educated in America

ni·si \'nī-ˌsī\ *adj* [L, unless, fr. *ne-* not + *si* if] : taking effect at a specified time unless previously modified or voided ⟨a divorce decree ~⟩

nit \'nit\ *n* **1** : the egg of a parasitic insect (as a louse); *also* : the young insect **2** : a minor shortcoming

nite *var of* NIGHT

ni·ter \'nī-tər\ *n* : POTASSIUM NITRATE

nit–pick·ing \'nit-ˌpi-kiŋ\ *n* : minute and usu. unjustified criticism — **nit·pick·er** *n*

¹ni·trate \'nī-ˌtrāt, -trət\ *n* **1** : a salt or ester of nitric acid **2** : sodium nitrate or potassium nitrate used as a fertilizer

²ni·trate \-ˌtrāt\ *vb* **ni·trat·ed; ni·trat·ing** : to treat or combine with nitric acid or a nitrate — **ni·tra·tion** \nī-'trā-shən\ *n*

ni·tre *chiefly Brit var of* NITER

ni·tric acid \'nī-trik-\ *n* : a corrosive liquid acid used esp. in making dyes, explosives, and fertilizers

ni·tri·fi·ca·tion \ˌnī-trə-fə-'kā-shən\ *n* : the oxidation (as by bacteria) of ammonium salts to nitrites and then to nitrates — **ni·tri·fy·ing** \'nī-trə-fī-iŋ\ *adj*

ni·trite \'nī-ˌtrīt\ *n* : a salt of nitrous acid

ni·tro \'nī-trō\ *n, pl* **nitros** : any of various nitrated products; *esp* : NITROGLYCERIN

ni·tro·gen \'nī-trə-jən\ *n* : a tasteless odorless gaseous chemical element constituting 78 percent of the atmosphere by volume — **ni·trog·e·nous** \nī-'trä-jə-nəs\ *adj*

nitrogen narcosis *n* : a state of euphoria and confusion caused by nitrogen forced into a diver's bloodstream from atmospheric air under pressure

ni·tro·glyc·er·in *or* **ni·tro·glyc·er·ine** \ˌnī-trə-'gli-sə-rən\ *n* : an oily explosive liquid used to make dynamite and in medicine to dilate blood vessels

ni·trous acid \'nī-trəs-\ *n* : an unstable nitrogen-containing acid known only in solution or in the form of its salts

nitrous oxide *n* : a colorless gas used esp. as an anesthetic in dentistry

nit·ty–grit·ty \'ni-tē-ˌgri-tē, ˌni-tē-'gri-tē\ *n* : what is essential and basic : specific practical details

nit·wit \'nit-ˌwit\ *n* : a scatterbrained or stupid person

¹nix \'niks\ *n* : NOTHING

²nix *vb* : VETO, REJECT

³nix *adv* : NO

NJ *abbr* New Jersey

NL *abbr* National League

NLRB *abbr* National Labor Relations Board

NM *abbr* **1** nautical mile **2** New Mexico

N Mex *abbr* New Mexico

NMI *abbr* no middle initial

NNE *abbr* north-northeast

NNW *abbr* north-northwest

¹no \'nō\ *adv* **1** — used to express the negative of an alternative ⟨shall we continue or ~⟩ **2** : in no respect or degree ⟨he is ~ better than the others⟩ **3** : not so ⟨~, I'm not ready⟩ **4** — used with an adjective to imply a meaning opposite to the positive statement ⟨in ~ uncertain terms⟩ **5** — used to introduce a more emphatic or explicit statement ⟨has the right, ~, the duty to continue⟩ **6** — used as an interjection to express surprise or doubt ⟨~—you don't say⟩ **7** — used in combination with a verb to form a compound adjective ⟨*no*-bake pie⟩ **8** : in negation ⟨shook his head ~⟩

²no *adj* **1** : not any; *also* : hardly any **2** : not a ⟨she's ~ expert⟩

³no \'nō\ *n, pl* **noes** *or* **nos** \'nōz\ **1** : REFUSAL, DENIAL ⟨got a ~ in reply⟩ **2** : a negative vote or decision; *also, pl* : persons voting in the negative

⁴no *abbr* **1** north; northern **2** [L *numero*, abl. of *numerus*] number

¹No *var of* NOH

²**No** *symbol* nobelium

No·bel·ist \nō-'be-list\ *n* : a winner of a Nobel prize

no·bel·i·um \nō-'be-lē-əm\ *n* : a radioactive metallic chemical element produced artificially

No·bel prize \nō-'bel-, 'nō-,bel-\ *n* : any of various annual prizes (as in peace, literature, or medicine) established by the will of Alfred Nobel for the encouragement of persons who work for the interests of humanity

no·bil·i·ty \nō-'bi-lə-tē\ *n* 1 : the quality or state of being noble 2 : nobles considered as forming a class

¹**no·ble** \'nō-bəl\ *adj* **no·bler; no·blest** [ME, fr. AF, fr. L *nobilis* well known, noble, fr. *noscere* to come to know] 1 : ILLUSTRIOUS; *also* : FAMOUS, NOTABLE 2 : of high birth, rank, or station : ARISTOCRATIC 3 : EXCELLENT 4 : STATELY, IMPOSING ⟨a ∼ edifice⟩ 5 : of a superior nature ♦ *Synonyms* AUGUST, BARONIAL, GRAND, GRANDIOSE, MAGNIFICENT, MAJESTIC — **no·ble·ness** *n* — **no·bly** \-blē\ *adv*

²**noble** *n* : a person of noble rank or birth

no·ble·man \'nō-bəl-mən\ *n* : a member of the nobility : PEER

no·blesse oblige \nō-,bles-ə-'blēzh\ *n* [F, lit., nobility obligates] : the obligation of honorable, generous, and responsible behavior associated with high rank or birth

no·ble·wom·an \'nō-bəl-,wú-mən\ *n* : a woman of noble rank : PEERESS

¹**no·body** \'nō-,bä-dē, -bə-\ *pron* : no person

²**nobody** *n, pl* **no·bod·ies** : a person of no influence or importance

no-brain·er \'nō-'brā-nər\ *n* : something that requires a minimum of thought

noc·tur·nal \näk-'tər-n°l\ *adj* 1 : of, relating to, or occurring in the night 2 : active at night ⟨a ∼ bird⟩

noc·turne \'näk-,tərn\ *n* : a work of art dealing with night; *esp* : a dreamy pensive composition for the piano

noc·u·ous \'nä-kyə-wəs\ *adj* : HARMFUL — **noc·u·ous·ly** *adv*

nod \'näd\ *vb* **nod·ded; nod·ding** 1 : to bend the head downward or forward (as in bowing, going to sleep, or giving assent) 2 : to move up and down ⟨tulips *nodding* in the breeze⟩ 3 : to show by a nod of the head ⟨∼ agreement⟩ 4 : to make a slip or error in a moment of abstraction ⟨did many good things, but sometimes he *nodded*⟩ — **nod** *n*

nod·dle \'nä-d°l\ *n* : HEAD

nod·dy \'nä-dē\ *n, pl* **noddies** 1 : FOOL 2 : a stout-bodied tropical tern

node \'nōd\ *n* : a thickened, swollen, or differentiated area (as of tissue); *esp* : the part of a stem from which a leaf arises — **nod·al** \-°l\ *adj*

nod·ule \'nä-jül\ *n* : a small lump or swelling — **nod·u·lar** \'nä-jə-lər\ *adj*

no·el \nō-'el\ *n* [F *noël* Christmas, carol, fr. OF *Nael* (*Deu*), *Noel* Christmas, fr. L *natalis* birthday] 1 : a Christmas carol 2 *cap* : the Christmas season

noes *pl of* NO

no–fault \'nō-'fȯlt\ *adj* 1 : of, relating to, or being a motor vehicle insurance plan under which someone involved in an accident is compensated usu. up to a stipulated limit for actual losses by that person's own insurance company regardless of who is responsible 2 : of, relating to, or being a divorce law under which neither party is held responsible for the breakup of the marriage

nog·gin \'nä-gən\ *n* 1 : a small mug or cup; *also* : a small quantity of drink 2 : a person's head

no–good \'nō-'gùd\ *adj* : having no worth, virtue, use, or chance of success — **no-good** \'nō-,gùd\ *n*

Noh *also* **No** \'nō\ *n, pl* **Noh** *also* **No** : classic Japanese dance-drama having a heroic theme, a chorus, and highly stylized action, costuming, and scenery

no–hit·ter \(,)nō-'hi-tər\ *n* : a baseball game or part of a game in which a pitcher allows no base hits

no·how \'nō-,haú\ *adv* : in no manner

¹**noise** \'nȯiz\ *n* [ME, fr. AF, disturbance, noise, fr. L *nausea* nausea] 1 : loud, confused, or senseless shouting or outcry 2 : SOUND; *esp* : one that lacks agreeable musical quality or is noticeably unpleasant 3 : unwanted electronic signal or disturbance — **noise·less** *adj* — **noise·ly** *adv*

²**noise** *vb* **noised; nois·ing** : to spread by rumor or report ⟨the story was *noised* abroad⟩

noise·mak·er \'nȯiz-,mā-kər\ *n* : one that makes noise; *esp* : a device used to make noise at parties

noise pollution *n* : annoying or harmful noise in an environment

noi·some \'nȯi-səm\ *adj* 1 : HARMFUL, UNWHOLESOME 2 : offensive to the senses (as smell) : DISGUSTING ⟨∼ habits⟩ ♦ *Synonyms* INSALUBRIOUS, NOXIOUS, SICKLY, UNHEALTHFUL, UNHEALTHY

noisy \'nȯi-zē\ *adj* **nois·i·er; -est** 1 : making loud noises 2 : full of noises : LOUD — **nois·i·ly** \-zə-lē\ *adv* — **nois·i·ness** \-zē-nəs\ *n*

nol·le pro·se·qui \,nä-lē-'prä-sə-,kwī\ *n* [L, to be unwilling to pursue] : an entry on the record of a legal action that the prosecutor or plaintiff will proceed no further in an action or suit or in some aspect of it

no·lo con·ten·de·re \,nō-lō-kən-'ten-də-rē\ *n* [L, I do not wish to contend] : a plea in a criminal prosecution that subjects the defendant to conviction but does not admit guilt or preclude denying the charges in another proceeding

nol–pros \'näl-'präs\ *vb* **nol-prossed; nol–pros·ing** : to discontinue by entering a nolle prosequi

nom *abbr* nominative

no·mad \'nō-,mad\ *n* 1 : a member of a people who have no fixed residence but move from place to place 2 : an individual who roams about aimlessly — **no·mad** *adj* — **no·mad·ic** \nō-'ma-dik\ *adj*

no–man's–land \'nō-,manz-,land\ *n* 1 : an area of unowned, unclaimed, or uninhabited land **2** : an unoccupied area between opposing troops

nom de guerre \,näm-di-'ger\ *n, pl* **noms de guerre** *same or* ,nämz-\ [F, lit., war name] : PSEUDONYM

nom de plume \-'plüm\ *n, pl* **noms de plume** *same or* ,nämz-\ [F, pen name; prob. coined in E] : PEN NAME

no·men·cla·ture \'nō-mən-,klā-chər\ *n* **1** : NAME, DESIGNATION **2** : a system of terms used in a science or art

nom·i·nal \'nä-mə-n³l\ *adj* **1** : being something in name or form only ⟨∼ head of a party⟩ **2** : TRIFLING ⟨a ∼ price⟩ — **nom·i·nal·ly** *adv*

nom·i·nate \'nä-mə-,nāt\ *vb* **-nat·ed; -nat·ing** : to choose as a candidate for election, appointment, or honor ♦ *Synonyms* APPOINT, DESIGNATE, NAME, TAP — **nom·i·na·tion** \,nä-mə-'nā-shən\ *n*

nom·i·na·tive \'nä-mə-nə-tiv\ *adj* : of, relating to, or constituting a grammatical case marking typically the subject of a verb — **nominative** *n*

nom·i·nee \,nä-mə-'nē\ *n* : a person nominated for an office, duty, or position

non- \('\)nän *or* ,nän *before stressed syllables;* ,nän *elsewhere*\ *prefix* **1** : not : reverse of **2** : absence of **2** : having no importance

non·age \'nä-nij, 'nō-\ *n* **1** : legal minority **2** : a period of youth **3** : IMMATURITY

no·na·ge·nar·i·an \,nō-nə-jə-'ner-ē-ən, ,nä-\ *n* : a person whose age is in the nineties

non·aligned \,nän-ə-'līnd\ *adj* : not allied with other nations

no–name \'nō-,näm\ *adj* : not having a readily recognizable name ⟨∼ brands⟩

non·book \'nän-,bůk\ *n* : a book of little literary merit that is often a compilation (as of pictures or speeches)

¹nonce \'näns\ *n* : the one, particular, or present occasion or purpose ⟨for the ∼⟩

²nonce *adj* : occurring, used, or made only once or for a special occasion ⟨a ∼ word⟩

non·cha·lant \,nän-shə-'länt\ *adj* [F, fr. OF, fr. prp. of *nonchaloir* to disregard, fr. *non-* not + *chaloir* to concern, fr. L *calēre* to be warm] : giving an effect of unconcern or indifference ♦ *Synonyms* COLLECTED, COMPOSED, COOL, IMPERTURBABLE, UNFLAPPABLE, UNRUFFLED —

non·cha·lance \-'läns\ *n* — **non·cha·lant·ly** *adv*

non-com \'nän-,käm\ *n* : NONCOMMISSIONED OFFICER

non·com·ba·tant \,nän-kəm-'ba-t³nt, nän-'käm-bə-tənt\ *n* : a member (as a chaplain) of the armed forces whose duties do not include fighting; *also* : CIVILIAN — **noncombatant** *adj*

non·com·mis·sioned officer \,nän-kə-'mi-shənd-\ *n* : a subordinate officer in the armed forces appointed from enlisted personnel

non·com·mit·tal \,nän-kə-'mi-t³l\ *adj* : indicating neither consent nor dissent ⟨a ∼ reply⟩

non com·pos men·tis \,nän-,käm-pəs-'men-təs\ *adj* : not of sound mind

non·con·duc·tor \,nän-kən-'dək-tər\ *n* : a substance that is a very poor conductor of heat, electricity, or sound

non·con·form·ist \-kən-'fȯr-mist\ *n* **1** *often cap* : a person who does not conform to an established church and esp. the Church of England **2** : a person who does not conform to a generally accepted pattern of thought or action ♦ *Synonyms* DISSENTER, DISSIDENT, HERETIC, SCHISMATIC, SECTARY, SEPARATIST — **non·con·for·mi·ty** \-'fȯr-mə-tē\ *n*

non·co·op·er·a·tion \,nän-kō-,ä-pə-'rā-shən\ *n* : failure or refusal to cooperate; *esp* : refusal through civil disobedience of a people to cooperate with the government of a country

non·cred·it \(,)nän-'kre-dət\ *adj* : not offering credit toward a degree

non·cus·to·di·al \,nän-kə-'stō-dē-əl\ *adj* : of or being a parent who does not have legal custody of a child

non·dairy \'nän-'der-ē\ *adj* : containing no milk or milk products ⟨∼ margarine⟩

non·de·script \,nän-di-'skript\ *adj* **1** : not belonging to any particular class or kind **2** : lacking distinctive qualities ⟨a ∼ building⟩

non·drink·er \-'driŋ-kər\ *n* : a person who abstains from alcohol

¹none \'nən\ *pron* **1** : not any ⟨∼ of them went⟩ **2** : not one ⟨∼ of the family⟩ **3** : not any such thing or person ⟨half a loaf is better than ∼⟩

²none *adj, archaic* : not any : NO

nonabrasive	nonbeliever	noncompliance	nondemocratic
nonabsorbent	nonbelligerent	noncomplying	nondenomination-
nonacademic	nonbiodegradable	nonconducting	al
nonacceptance	nonbreakable	nonconfidence	nondepartmental
nonaccredited	noncaloric	nonconflicting	nondestructive
nonacid	noncancerous	nonconformance	nondevelopment
nonactivated	noncandidate	nonconforming	nondiscrimination
nonadaptive	noncellular	nonconsensual	nondiscriminatory
nonaddictive	noncitizen	nonconstructive	nondistinctive
nonadhesive	nonclerical	noncontagious	nondurable
nonadjacent	noncoital	noncontinuous	noneconomic
nonadjustable	noncombat	noncorroding	noneducational
nonaggression	noncombative	noncorrosive	nonelastic
nonalcoholic	noncombustible	noncriminal	nonelection
nonappearance	noncommercial	noncritical	nonelective
nonaromatic	noncommunist	noncrystalline	nonelectric
nonathletic	noncompeting	nondeductible	nonelectrical
nonattendance	noncompetitive	nondelivery	nonemotional

³**none** *adv* : by no means : not at all ⟨he got there ∼ too soon⟩

non·en·ti·ty \ˌnän-ˈen-tə-tē\ *n* **1** : something that does not exist or exists only in the imagination **2** : one of no consequence or significance ♦ *Synonyms*
NOBODY, NOTHING, WHIPPERSNAPPER

nones \ˈnōnz\ *n sing or pl* : the 7th day of March, May, July, or October or the 5th day of any other month in the ancient Roman calendar

non·es·sen·tial \ˌnän-i-ˈsen-shəl\ *adj* **1** : not essential **2** : being a substance synthesized by the body in sufficient quantity to satisfy dietary needs

none·such \ˈnən-ˌsəch\ *n* : one without an equal — **nonesuch** *adj*

none·the·less \ˌnən-thə-ˈles\ *adv* : NEVERTHELESS

non·event \ˈnän-i-ˌvent\ *n* **1** : an event that fails to take place or to satisfy expectations **2** : a highly promoted event of little intrinsic interest

non·fat \ˈˈfat\ *adj* : lacking fat solids : having fat solids removed ⟨∼ milk⟩

non·gono·coc·cal \ˌnän-ˌgä-nə-ˈkä-kəl\ *adj* : not caused by a gonococcus

non·he·ro \ˈnän-ˈhē-rō\ *n* : ANTIHERO

non–Hodg·kin's lymphoma \ˈnän-ˈhäj-kənz-\ *n* : any of numerous malignant lymphomas not classified as Hodgkin's disease

non·in·ter·ven·tion \ˌnän-ˌin-tər-ˈven-chən\ *n* : refusal or failure to intervene (as in the affairs of other countries)

non·is·sue \ˈnän-ˈi-shü\ *n* : an issue of little importance or concern

non·met·al \ˈnän-ˈme-tᵊl\ *n* : a chemical element (as carbon) that lacks the characteristics of a metal — **non·me·tal·lic** \ˌnän-mə-ˈta-lik\ *adj*

non·neg·a·tive \-ˈne-gə-tiv\ *adj* : not negative : being either positive or zero

non·nu·cle·ar \ˈnän-ˈnü-klē-ər\ *adj* **1** : not nuclear **2** : not having, using, or involving nuclear weapons

non·ob·jec·tive \ˌnän-əb-ˈjek-tiv\ *adj* **1** : not objective **2** : representing no natural or actual object, figure, or scene ⟨∼ art⟩

¹**non·pa·reil** \-pə-ˈrel\ *adj* : having no equal : PEERLESS ⟨a ∼ performer⟩

²**nonpareil** *n* **1** : an individual of unequaled excellence : PARAGON **2** : a small flat disk of chocolate covered with white sugar pellets

non·par·ti·san \ˈnän-ˈpär-tə-zən\ *adj* : not partisan; *esp* : not influenced by political party spirit or interests

non·per·son \-ˈpər-sᵊn\ *n* **1** : UNPERSON **2** : a person having no social or legal status

non·plus \ˈnän-ˈpləs\ *vb* **-plussed** *also* **-plused** \-ˈpləst\; **-plus·sing** *also* **-plus-ing** : PUZZLE, PERPLEX

non·pre·scrip·tion \ˌnän-pri-ˈskrip-shən\ *adj* : available for sale legally without a doctor's prescription

non·prof·it \ˈnän-ˈprä-fət\ *adj* : not conducted or maintained for the purpose of making a profit ⟨a ∼ organization⟩

non·pro·lif·er·a·tion \ˌnän-prə-ˌli-fə-ˈrā-shən\ *adj* : providing for the stoppage of proliferation (as of nuclear arms) ⟨a ∼ treaty⟩

non·read·er \ˈnän-ˈrē-dər\ *n* : one who does not read or has difficulty reading

non·rep·re·sen·ta·tion·al \ˌnän-ˌre-pri-ˌzen-ˈtā-shə-nəl\ *adj* : NONOBJECTIVE 2

non·res·i·dent \ˈnän-ˈre-zə-dənt\ *adj* : not living in a particular place — **non·res·i·dence** \-dəns\ *n* — **nonresident** *n*

non·re·sis·tance \ˌnän-ri-ˈzis-təns\ *n* : the principles or practice of passive submission to authority even when unjust or oppressive

non·re·stric·tive \-ri-ˈstrik-tiv\ *adj* **1** : not serving or tending to restrict **2** : not limiting the reference of the word or phrase modified ⟨a ∼ clause⟩

non·sched·uled \ˈnän-ˈske-jüld\ *adj* : li-

nonenforcement	nonhereditary	nonmaterial	nonpolitical
nonethical	nonhomogeneous	nonmember	nonporous
non-euclidean	nonhomologous	nonmembership	nonpregnant
nonexclusive	nonhuman	nonmigratory	nonproductive
nonexempt	nonidentical	nonmilitary	nonprofessional
nonexistence	nonimportation	nonmoral	nonprotein
nonexistent	nonindustrial	nonmotile	nonradioactive
nonexplosive	noninfectious	nonmoving	nonrandom
nonfarm	noninflammable	nonnegotiable	nonrated
nonfatal	nonintellectual	nonobservance	nonreactive
nonfattening	nonintercourse	nonoccurrence	nonreciprocal
nonfederated	noninterference	nonofficial	nonrecognition
nonferrous	nonintoxicant	nonoily	nonrecurrent
nonfiction	nonintoxicating	nonorthodox	nonrecurring
nonfictional	noninvasive	nonparallel	nonrefillable
nonfilamentous	nonionizing	nonparasitic	nonreligious
nonfilterable	nonirritating	nonparticipant	nonrenewable
nonflammable	nonlegal	nonparticipating	nonresidential
nonflowering	nonlethal	nonpathogenic	nonrestricted
nonfood	nonlife	nonpaying	nonreturnable
nonfreezing	nonlinear	nonpayment	nonreusable
nonfulfillment	nonliterary	nonperformance	nonreversible
nonfunctional	nonliving	nonperishable	nonrigid
nonglare	nonlogical	nonphysical	nonruminant
nongraded	nonmagnetic	nonpoisonous	nonsalable
nonhazardous	nonmalignant	nonpolar	

censed to carry passengers or freight by air without a regular schedule

non·sense \\'nän-,sens, -səns\\ *n* 1 : foolish or meaningless words or actions 2 : things of no importance or value —
non·sen·si·cal \\nän-'sen-si-kəl\\ *adj* —
non·sen·si·cal·ly \\-k(ə-)lē\\ *adv*

non se·qui·tur \\nän-'se-kwə-tər\\ *n* [L, it does not follow] : an inference that does not follow from the premises

non·skid \\'nän-'skid\\ *adj* : designed to prevent skidding ⟨a ~ surface⟩

non·slip \\-'slip\\ *adj* : designed to prevent slipping ⟨a ~ handle⟩

non·stan·dard \\,nän-'stan-dərd\\ *adj* 1 : not standard 2 : not conforming to the usage characteristic of educated native speakers of a language

non·start·er \\'nän-'stär-tər\\ *n* 1 : one that does not start 2 : one that is not productive or effective

non·stick \\-'stik\\ *adj* : allowing easy removal of cooked food particles

¹non·stop \\-'stäp\\ *adj* : done or made without a stop ⟨~ action⟩ — **nonstop** *adv*

²nonstop *n* : a nonstop airplane flight

non·sup·port \\,nän-sə-'pȯrt\\ *n* : failure to support; *esp* : failure on the part of one under obligation to provide maintenance

non·threat·en·ing \\-'thret-nin, -'thre-tᵊn-in\\ *adj* : not likely to cause danger or anxiety ⟨a ~ illness⟩ ⟨a ~ environment⟩

non–U \\'nän-'yü\\ *adj* : not characteristic of the upper classes ⟨~ speech⟩

non·union \\-'yü-nyən\\ *adj* 1 : not belonging to a trade union ⟨~ carpenters⟩ 2 : not recognizing or favoring trade unions or their members ⟨~ employers⟩

non·us·er \\-'yü-zər\\ *n* : one who does not make use of something (as drugs)

non·vi·o·lence \\'nän-'vī-ə-ləns\\ *n* 1 : abstention from violence as a matter of principle 2 : avoidance of violence 3 : nonviolent political demonstrations —
non·vi·o·lent \\-lənt\\ *adj*

non·white \\,nän-'hwīt, -'wīt\\ *n* : a person whose features and esp. skin color are different from those of peoples of northwestern Europe — **nonwhite** *adj*

non·wo·ven \\'nän-'wō-vən\\ *adj* : made of fibers held together by interlocking or bonding (as by chemical or thermal means) — **nonwoven** *n*

noo·dle \\'nü-dᵊl\\ *n* [G *Nudel*] : a food paste made usu. with egg and shaped typically in ribbon form

nook \\'nuk\\ *n* 1 : an interior angle or corner formed usu. by two walls ⟨a chimney ~⟩ 2 : a sheltered or hidden place ⟨searched every ~ and cranny⟩ 3 : a usu. recessed section of a larger room ⟨a breakfast ~⟩

noon \\'nün\\ *n* : the middle of the day : 12 o'clock in the daytime — **noon** *adj*

noon·day \\'nün-,dā\\ *n* : NOON, MIDDAY

no one *pron* : NOBODY

noon·tide \\'nün-,tīd\\ *n* : NOON

noon·time \\-,tīm\\ *n* : NOON

noose \\'nüs\\ *n* : a loop with a slipknot that binds closer the more it is drawn

nope \\'nōp\\ *adv* : NO

nor \\'nȯr\\ *conj* : and not ⟨not for you ~ for me⟩ — used esp. to introduce and negate the second member and each later member of a series of items preceded by *neither* ⟨neither here ~ there⟩

Nor·dic \\'nȯr-dik\\ *adj* 1 : of or relating to the Germanic peoples of northern Europe and esp. of Scandinavia 2 : of or relating to competitive ski events involving cross-country racing, ski jumping, or biathlon — **Nordic** *n*

nor·epi·neph·rine \\'nȯr-,e-pə-'ne-frən\\ *n* : a nitrogen-containing neurotransmitter in parts of the sympathetic and central nervous systems

norm \\'nȯrm\\ *n* [L *norma*, lit., carpenter's square] 1 : an authoritative standard or model; *esp* : a set standard of development or achievement usu. derived from the average or median achievement of a large group 2 : a typical or widespread practice, procedure, or custom ♦ *Synonyms* AVERAGE, MEAN, MEDIAN, PAR

¹nor·mal \\'nȯr-məl\\ *adj* 1 : REGULAR, STANDARD, NATURAL 2 : of average intelligence; *also* : sound in mind and body — **nor·mal·cy** \\-sē\\ *n* — **nor·mal·i·ty** \\nȯr-'ma-lə-tē\\ *n* — **nor·mal·ly** *adv*

²normal *n* 1 : one that is normal 2 : the usual condition, level, or quantity

nor·mal·ise *Brit var of* NORMALIZE

nor·mal·ize \\'nȯr-mə-,līz\\ *vb* **-ized; -iz·ing** : to make or restore to normal ⟨*normalizing* relations⟩ — **nor·mal·i·za·tion** \\,nȯr-mə-lə-'zā-shən\\ *n*

Nor·man \\'nȯr-mən\\ *n* 1 : a native or inhabitant of Normandy 2 : one of the 10th century Scandinavian conquerors of Normandy 3 : one of the Norman-French conquerors of England in 1066 — **Norman** *adj*

nor·ma·tive \\'nȯr-mə-tiv\\ *adj* : of, relating to, or determining norms — **nor·ma·tive·ly** *adv* — **nor·ma·tive·ness** *n*

Norse \\'nȯrs\\ *n*, *pl* **Norse** 1 : NORWE-

---

nonscientific	nonsmoking	nontemporal	nonveteran
nonscientist	nonsocial	nontenured	nonviable
nonseasonal	nonspeaking	nontheistic	nonvisual
nonsectarian	nonspecialist	nonthreatening	nonvocal
nonsegregated	nonspecific	nontoxic	nonvolatile
nonselective	nonsteroidal	nontraditional	nonvoter
non-self-governing	nonstudent	nontransferable	nonvoting
nonsexist	nonsuccess	nontypical	nonworker
nonsexual	nonsurgical	nonuniform	nonworking
nonshrinkable	nontaxable	nonvascular	nonzero
nonsinkable	nonteaching	nonvenomous	
nonsmoker	nontechnical	nonverbal	

GIAN; *also* : any of the western Scandinavian dialects or languages **2** *pl* : SCANDINAVIANS; *also* : NORWEGIANS

Norse·man \-mən\ *n* : any of the ancient Scandinavians

¹**north** \'nȯrth\ *adv* : to, toward, or in the north

²**north** *adj* **1** : situated toward or at the north **2** : coming from the north

³**north** *n* **1** : the direction to the left of one facing east **2** : the compass point directly opposite to south **3** *cap* : regions or countries north of a specified or implied point — **north·er·ly** \'nȯr-thər-lē\ *adv or adj* — **north·ern** \-thərn\ *adj* — **North·ern·er** \-thər-nər\ *n* — **north·ern·most** \-thərn-ˌmōst\ *adj* — **north·ward** \'nȯrth-wərd\ *adv or adj* — **north·wards** \-wərdz\ *adv*

north·east \nȯrth-'ēst\ *n* **1** : the general direction between north and east **2** : the compass point midway between north and east **3** *cap* : regions or countries northeast of a specified or implied point — **northeast** *adj or adv* — **north·east·er·ly** \-'thē-stər-lē\ *adv or adj* — **north·east·ern** \-stərn\ *adj*

north·east·er \-'ēs-tər\ *n* **1** : a strong northeast wind **2** : a storm with northeast winds

north·er \'nȯr-thər\ *n* **1** : a strong north wind **2** : a storm with north winds

northern lights *n pl* : AURORA BOREALIS

north pole *n, often cap N&P* **1** : the northernmost point of the earth

North Star *n* : the star toward which the northern end of the earth's axis points

north·west \nȯrth-'west\ *n* **1** : the general direction between north and west **2** : the compass point midway between north and west **3** *cap* : regions or countries northwest of a specified or implied point — **northwest** *adj or adv* — **north·west·er·ly** \-'we-stər-lē\ *adv or adj* — **north·west·ern** \-'we-stərn\ *adj*

Norw *abbr* Norway; Norwegian

Nor·we·gian \nȯr-'wē-jən\ *n* **1** : a native or inhabitant of Norway **2** : the language of Norway — **Norwegian** *adj*

nos *abbr* numbers

¹**nose** \'nōz\ *n* **1** : the part of the face or head containing the nostrils and covering the front of the nasal cavity **2** : the sense of smell **3** : something (as a point, edge, or projecting front part) that resembles a nose ⟨the ~ of a plane⟩ — **nosed** \'nōzd\ *adj* — **on the nose** : on target : ACCURATE — **under one's nose** : extremely near : in one's presence

²**nose** *vb* **nosed; nos·ing 1** : to detect by or as if by smell : SCENT **2** : to push or move with the nose **3** : to touch or rub with the nose : NUZZLE **4** : PRY **5** : to move ahead slowly ⟨the ship *nosed* into her berth⟩

nose·bleed \'nōz-ˌblēd\ *n* : a bleeding from the nose

nose cone *n* : a protective cone constituting the forward end of an aerospace vehicle

nose·dive \'nōz-ˌdīv\ *n* **1** : a downward nose-first plunge (as of an airplane) **2** : a sudden extreme drop (as in prices)

nose·gay \'nōz-ˌgā\ *n* : a small bunch of flowers : POSY

nose out *vb* **1** : to discover often by prying **2** : to defeat by a narrow margin

nose·piece \-ˌpēs\ *n* **1** : a fitting at the lower end of a microscope tube to which the objectives are attached **2** : the bridge of a pair of eyeglasses

no–show \'nō-'shō\ *n* : a person who does not show up for an event as expected

nos·tal·gia \nä-'stal-jə\ *n* [NL, fr. Gk *nostos* return home + *algos* pain, grief] **1** : HOMESICKNESS **2** : a wistful yearning for something past or irrecoverable — **nos·tal·gic** \-jik\ *adj* — **nos·tal·gist** \-jist\ *n*

nos·tril \'näs-trəl\ *n* [ME *nosethirl*, fr. OE *nosthyrl*, fr. *nosu* nose + *thyrel* hole] **1** : either of the nares usu. with the adjoining nasal wall and passage **2** : either fleshy lateral wall of the nose

nos·trum \'näs-trəm\ *n* [L, neut. of *noster* our, ours, fr. *nos* we] : a questionable medicine or remedy

nosy *or* **nos·ey** \'nō-zē\ *adj* **nos·i·er; -est** : INQUISITIVE, PRYING ⟨~ neighbors⟩

not \'nät\ *adv* **1** — used to make negative a group of words or a word ⟨the boys are ~ here⟩ **2** — used to stand for the negative of a preceding group of words ⟨sometimes hard to see and sometimes ~⟩

no·ta be·ne \ˌnō-tə-'be-nē, -'be-\ [L, mark well] — used to call attention to something important

no·ta·bil·i·ty \ˌnō-tə-'bi-lə-tē\ *n, pl* **-ties 1** : the quality or state of being notable **2** : NOTABLE

¹**no·ta·ble** \'nō-tə-bəl\ *adj* **1** : NOTEWORTHY, REMARKABLE ⟨a ~ achievement⟩ **2** : DISTINGUISHED, PROMINENT ⟨two ~ politicians made speeches⟩

²**notable** *n* : a person of note ♦ **Synonyms** BIGWIG, EMINENCE, NABOB, PERSONAGE, SOMEBODY, VIP

no·ta·bly \'nō-tə-blē\ *adv* **1** : in a notable manner **2** : ESPECIALLY, PARTICULARLY

no·tar·i·al \nō-'ter-ē-əl\ *adj* : of, relating to, or done by a notary public

no·ta·rize \'nō-tə-ˌrīz\ *vb* **-rized; -riz·ing** : to acknowledge or make legally authentic as a notary public

no·ta·ry public \'nō-tə-rē-\ *n, pl* **notaries public** *or* **notary publics** : a public official who attests or certifies writings (as deeds) to make them legally authentic

no·ta·tion \nō-'tā-shən\ *n* **1** : ANNOTATION, NOTE : the act, process, or method of representing data by marks, signs, figures, or characters; *also* : a system of symbols (as letters, numerals, or musical notes) used in such notation

¹**notch** \'näch\ *n* **1** : a V-shaped hollow in an edge or surface **2** : a narrow pass between two mountains

²**notch** *vb* **1** : to cut or make notches in **2** : to score or record by or as if by cutting

a series of notches ⟨~ed 20 points for the team⟩

notch·back \'näch-ˌbak\ *n* : an automobile with a trunk whose lid forms a distinct deck

¹**note** \'nōt\ *vb* **not·ed; not·ing** 1 : to notice or observe with care ⟨noted her reaction⟩; *also* : to record or preserve in writing 2 : to make special mention of : REMARK

²**note** *n* 1 : a musical sound 2 : a cry, call, or sound esp. of a bird 3 : a special tone in a person's words or voice ⟨a ~ of fear⟩ 4 : a character in music used to indicate duration of a tone by its shape and pitch by its position on the staff 5 : a characteristic feature : MOOD, QUALITY ⟨a ~ of optimism⟩ 6 : MEMORANDUM 7 : a brief and informal record; *also* : a written or printed comment or explanation 8 : a written promise to pay a debt 9 : a piece of paper money 10 : a short informal letter 11 : a formal diplomatic or official communication 12 : DISTINCTION, REPUTATION ⟨an artist of ~⟩ 13 : OBSERVATION, NOTICE, HEED ⟨take ~ of the time⟩

note·book \'nōt-ˌbùk\ *n* 1 : a book for notes or memoranda 2 : a portable microcomputer smaller than a laptop computer

not·ed \'nō-təd\ *adj* : well known by reputation : EMINENT ⟨a ~ violinist⟩

note·wor·thy \'nōt-ˌwər-thē\ *adj* : worthy of note : REMARKABLE

¹**noth·ing** \'nə-thiŋ\ *pron* 1 : no thing ⟨leaves ~ to the imagination⟩ 2 : no part 3 : one of no interest, value, or importance ⟨she's ~ to me⟩ 4 : a light playful remark ⟨sweet ~s⟩

²**nothing** *adv* : not at all : in no degree

³**nothing** *n* 1 : something that does not exist 2 : ZERO 3 : a person or thing of little or no value or importance

⁴**nothing** *adj* : of no account : WORTHLESS

noth·ing·ness \'nə-thiŋ-nəs\ *n* 1 : the quality or state of being nothing 2 : NONEXISTENCE; *also* : utter insignificance 3 : something insignificant or valueless

¹**no·tice** \'nō-təs\ *n* 1 : WARNING, ANNOUNCEMENT 2 : notification of the termination of an agreement or contract at a specified time 3 : ATTENTION, HEED ⟨bring the matter to my ~⟩ 4 : a written or printed announcement 5 : a short critical account or examination (as of a play) : REVIEW

²**notice** *vb* **no·ticed; no·tic·ing** 1 : to make mention of : remark on : NOTE 2 : to take notice of : OBSERVE, MARK

no·tice·able \'nō-tə-sə-bəl\ *adj* : worthy of notice 2 : likely to be noticed ⟨a ~ scar⟩ — **no·tice·ably** \-blē\ *adv*

no·ti·fy \'nō-tə-ˌfī\ *vb* **-fied; -fy·ing** 1 : to give notice of : report the occurrence of 2 : to give notice to — **no·ti·fi·ca·tion** \ˌnō-tə-fə-'kā-shən\ *n*

no·tion \'nō-shən\ *n* 1 : IDEA, CONCEPTION ⟨have a ~ of what he means⟩ 2 : a belief held : OPINION, VIEW 3 : WHIM, FANCY ⟨a sudden ~ to go⟩ 4 *pl* : small

useful articles (as pins, needles, or thread)

no·tion·al \'nō-shə-nəl\ *adj* 1 : existing in the mind only : IMAGINARY, UNREAL 2 : given to foolish or fanciful moods or ideas : WHIMSICAL

no·to·ri·ous \nō-'tòr-ē-əs\ *adj* : generally known and talked of; *esp* : widely and unfavorably known — **no·to·ri·ety** \ˌnō-ta-'rī-ə-tē\ *n* — **no·to·ri·ous·ly** \nō-'tòr-ē-əs-lē\ *adv*

¹**not·with·stand·ing** \ˌnät-with-'stan-diŋ, -with-\ *prep* : in spite of

²**notwithstanding** *adv* : NEVERTHELESS

³**notwithstanding** *conj* : ALTHOUGH

nou·gat \'nü-gət\ *n* [F, fr. Occitan, fr. Old Occitan, nogat, fr. noga nut, ultim. fr. L nuc-, nux] : a confection of nuts or fruit pieces in a sugar paste

nought *var of* NAUGHT

noun \'naún\ *n* : a word that is the name of a subject of discourse (as a person or place)

nour·ish \'nər-ish\ *vb* : to promote the growth or development of

nour·ish·ing *adj* : giving nourishment

nour·ish·ment \'nər-ish-mənt\ *n* 1 : FOOD, NUTRIENT 2 : the action or process of nourishing

nou·veau riche \ˌnü-ˌvō-'rēsh\ *n, pl* **nou·veaux riches** \same\ [F] : a person newly rich : PARVENU

Nov *abbr* November

no·va \'nō-və\ *n, pl* **novas** or **no·vae** \-(ˌ)vē, -ˌvī\ [NL, fem. of L novus new] : a star that suddenly increases greatly in brightness and then within a few months or years grows dim again

¹**nov·el** \'nä-vəl\ *adj* 1 : having no precedent : NEW 2 : STRANGE, UNUSUAL

²**novel** *n* : a long invented prose narrative dealing with human experience through a connected sequence of events — **nov·el·ist** \-və-list\ *n*

nov·el·ette \ˌnä-və-'let\ *n* : a brief novel or long short story

nov·el·ize \'nä-və-ˌlīz\ *vb* **-ized; -iz·ing** : to convert into the form of a novel — **nov·el·i·za·tion** \ˌnä-və-lə-'zā-shən\ *n*

no·vel·la \nō-'ve-lə\ *n, pl* **novellas** or **no·vel·le** \-'ve-lē\ : NOVELETTE

nov·el·ty \'nä-vəl-tē\ *n, pl* **-ties** 1 : something new or unusual 2 : NEWNESS 3 : a small manufactured article intended mainly for personal or household adornment — usu. used in pl.

No·vem·ber \nō-'vem-bər\ *n* [ME November, fr. AF, fr. L November ninth month of the early Roman calendar, fr. novem nine] : the 11th month of the year

no·ve·na \nō-'vē-nə\ *n* : a Roman Catholic nine-day period of prayer

nov·ice \'nä-vəs\ *n* 1 : a new member of a religious order who is preparing to take the vows of religion 2 : one who is inexperienced or untrained

no·vi·tiate \nō-'vi-shət\ *n* 1 : the period or state of being a novice 2 : a house where novices are trained 3 : NOVICE

¹**now** \'naú\ *adv* 1 : at the present time or moment 2 : in the time immediately before the present 3 : IMMEDIATELY,

FORTHWITH **4** — used with the sense of present time weakened or lost (as to express command, introduce an important point, or indicate a transition) ⟨~ hear this⟩ **5** : SOMETIMES ⟨~ one and ~ another⟩ **6** : under the present circumstances **7** : at the time referred to **8** : by this time

²now *conj* : in view of the fact ⟨~ that you're here, we'll start⟩

³now *n* : the present time or moment : PRESENT

⁴now *adj* **1** : of or relating to the present time ⟨the ~ president⟩ **2** : excitingly new ⟨~ clothes⟩; *also* : constantly aware of what is new ⟨~ people⟩

NOW *abbr* **1** National Organization for Women **2** negotiable order of withdrawal

now·a·days \ˈnau̇-ə-ˌdāz\ *adv* : at the present time

no·way \ˈnō-ˌwā\ *or* **no·ways** \-ˌwāz\ *adv* : NOWISE

no·where \-ˌhwer\ *adv* **1** : not anywhere **2** : not at all — usu. used with *near* ⟨~ near enough⟩ — **nowhere** *n*

no·wise \ˈnō-ˌwīz\ *adv* : in no way

nox·ious \ˈnäk-shəs\ *adj* : harmful esp. to health or morals

noz·zle \ˈnä-zəl\ *n* : a short tube constricted in the middle or at one end and used (as on a hose) to speed up or direct a flow of fluid

np *abbr* **1** no pagination **2** no place (of publication)

Np *symbol* neptunium

NP *abbr* notary public

NR *abbr* not rated

NRA *abbr* National Rifle Association

NS *abbr* **1** not specified **2** Nova Scotia

NSA *abbr* National Security Agency

NSC *abbr* National Security Council

NSF *abbr* **1** National Science Foundation **2** not sufficient funds

NSW *abbr* New South Wales

NT *abbr* **1** New Testament **2** Northern Territory **3** Northwest Territories

nth \ˈenth\ *adj* **1** : numbered with an unspecified or indefinitely large ordinal number ⟨for the ~ time⟩ **2** : EXTREME, UTMOST ⟨to the ~ degree⟩

NTP *abbr* normal temperature and pressure

nt wt *or* **n wt** *abbr* net weight

nu \ˈnü, ˈnyü\ *n* : the 13th letter of the Greek alphabet — N or ν

NU *abbr* name unknown

nu·ance \ˈnü-ˌäns, ˈnyü-, nü-ˈäns, nyü-\ *n* [F] : a shade of difference : a delicate variation (as in tone or meaning)

nub \ˈnəb\ *n* **1** : KNOB, LUMP **2** : GIST, POINT ⟨the ~ of the story⟩

nub·bin \ˈnə-bən\ *n* **1** : something (as an ear of corn) that is small for its kind, stunted, undeveloped, or imperfect **2** : a small projecting bit

nu·bile \ˈnü-ˌbī(-ə)l, ˈnyü-, -bəl\ *adj* **1** : of marriageable condition or age **2** : sexually attractive ⟨~ young women⟩

nu·cle·ar \ˈnü-klē-ər, ˈnyü-\ *adj* **1** : of, relating to, or constituting a nucleus **2** : of, relating to, or using the atomic nu-

cleus or energy derived from it **3** : of, relating to, or being a weapon whose destructive power results from an uncontrolled nuclear reaction

nu·cle·ate \ˈnü-klē-ˌāt, ˈnyü-\ *vb* **-at·ed; -at·ing** : to form, act as, or have a nucleus — **nu·cle·ation** \ˌnü-klē-ˈā-shən, ˌnyü-\ *n*

nu·cle·ic acid \nü-ˈklē-ik-, nyü-, -ˈklā-\ *n* : any of various complex organic acids (as DNA or RNA) found esp. in cell nuclei

nu·cle·o·tide \ˈnü-klē-ə-ˌtīd, ˈnyü-\ *n* : any of several compounds that are the basic structural units of nucleic acids

nu·cle·us \ˈnü-klē-əs, ˈnyü-\ *n, pl* **nu·clei** \-klē-ˌī\ *also* **nu·cle·us·es** [NL, fr. L, kernel, dim. of *nuc-*, *nux* nut] **1** : a central mass or part about which matter gathers or is collected : CORE **2** : a cell part that is characteristic of all living things except viruses, bacteria, and certain algae, that is necessary for heredity and for making proteins, that contains the chromosomes with their genes, and that is enclosed in a membrane **3** : a mass of gray matter or group of cell bodies of neurons in the central nervous system **4** : the central part of an atom that comprises nearly all of the atomic mass **5** : a basic or essential part

¹nude \ˈnüd, ˈnyüd\ *adj* **nud·er; nud·est 1** : BARE, NAKED, UNCLOTHED **2** : featuring or catering to naked people ⟨a ~ beach⟩ — **nu·di·ty** \ˈnü-də-tē, ˈnyü-\ *n*

²nude *n* **1** : a nude human figure esp. as depicted in art **2** : the condition of being nude ⟨in the ~⟩

nudge \ˈnəj\ *vb* **nudged; nudg·ing** : to touch or push gently (as with the elbow) usu. in order to seek attention — **nudge** *n*

nud·ism \ˈnü-ˌdi-zəm, ˈnyü-\ *n* : the practice of going nude esp. in mixed groups at specially secluded places — **nud·ist** \-dist\ *n*

nu·ga·to·ry \ˈnü-gə-ˌtȯr-ē\ *adj* **1** : INCONSEQUENTIAL, WORTHLESS ⟨his efforts were rendered ~⟩ **2** : having no force : INEFFECTUAL

nug·get \ˈnə-gət\ *n* **1** : a lump of precious metal (as gold) **2** : TIDBIT

nui·sance \ˈnü-s⁰ns, ˈnyü-\ *n* : an annoying or troublesome person or thing

nuisance tax *n* : an excise tax collected in small amounts directly from the consumer

¹nuke \ˈnük, ˈnyük\ *n* **1** : a nuclear weapon **2** : a nuclear power plant

²nuke *vb* **nuked; nuk·ing 1** : to attack with nuclear weapons **2** : MICROWAVE

null \ˈnəl\ *adj* **1** : having no legal or binding force : INVALID, VOID **2** : amounting to nothing **3** : INSIGNIFICANT — **nul·li·ty** \ˈnə-lə-tē\ *n*

null and void *adj* : having no force, binding power, or validity

nul·li·fy \ˈnə-lə-ˌfī\ *vb* **-fied; -fy·ing** : to make null or valueless; *also* : ANNUL — **nul·li·fi·ca·tion** \ˌnə-lə-fə-ˈkā-shən\ *n*

num *abbr* numeral

Num *or* **Numb** *abbr* Numbers

numb \'nəm\ *adj* : lacking sensation or emotion : BENUMBED — **numb** *vb* — **numb·ly** *adv* — **numb·ness** *n*

¹**num·ber** \'nəm-bər\ *n* 1 : the total of individuals or units taken together 2 : an indefinite total ⟨a small ∼ of tickets remain unsold⟩ 3 : an ascertainable total ⟨the sands of the desert are without ∼⟩ 4 : a distinction of word form to denote reference to one or more than one 5 : a unit belonging to a mathematical system and subject to its laws; *also, pl* : ARITHMETIC 6 : a symbol used to represent a mathematical number; *also* : such a number used to identify or designate ⟨a phone ∼⟩ 7 : one in a series of musical or theatrical performances 8 : an act of transforming or impairing ⟨tripped and did a ∼ on her knee⟩

²**number** *vb* 1 : COUNT, ENUMERATE 2 : to include with or be one of a group 3 : to restrict to a small or definite number 4 : to assign a number to 5 : to comprise in number : TOTAL

num·ber·less \-ləs\ *adj* : INNUMERABLE, COUNTLESS ⟨∼ stars in the sky⟩

Numbers *n* — see BIBLE table

numb·ing \'nəm-miŋ\ *adj* : tending to make numb ⟨a ∼ lecture⟩ ⟨a ∼ realization⟩

numbskull *var of* NUMSKULL

nu·mer·a·cy \'nü-mə-rə-sē, 'nyü-\ *n* : the capacity for quantitative thought or expression

nu·mer·al \'nü-mə-rəl, 'nyü-\ *n* : a conventional symbol representing a number — **numeral** *adj*

nu·mer·ate \'nü-mə-ˌrāt, 'nyü-\ *vb* **-at·ed; -at·ing** : ENUMERATE

nu·mer·a·tor \-ˌrā-tər\ *n* : the part of a fraction above the line

nu·mer·ic \nü-'mer-ik, nyü-\ *adj* : NUMERICAL; *esp* : denoting a number or a system of numbers

nu·mer·i·cal \-'mer-i-kəl\ *adj* 1 : of or relating to numbers ⟨in ∼ order⟩ 2 : expressed in or involving numbers — **nu·mer·i·cal·ly** \-k(ə-)lē\ *adv*

nu·mer·ol·o·gy \ˌnü-mə-'rä-lə-jē, ˌnyü-\ *n* : the study of the occult significance of numbers — **nu·mer·ol·o·gist** \-jist\ *n*

nu·mer·ous \'nü-mə-rəs, 'nyü-\ *adj* : consisting of, including, or relating to a great number : MANY

nu·mis·mat·ics \ˌnü-məz-'ma-tiks, ˌnyü-\ *n* : the study or collection of monetary objects — **nu·mis·mat·ic** \-'ma-tik\ *adj* — **nu·mis·ma·tist** \nü-'miz-mə-tist, nyü-\ *n*

num·skull *also* **numb·skull** \'nəm-ˌskəl\ *n* : a stupid person : DUNCE

nun \'nən\ *n* : a woman belonging to a religious order; *esp* : one under solemn vows of poverty, chastity, and obedience

nun·cio \'nən-sē-ˌō, 'nün-\ *n*, *pl* **-ci·os** [It, fr. L *nuntius* messenger] : a permanent high-ranking papal representative to a civil government

nun·nery \'nə-nə-rē\ *n*, *pl* **-ner·ies** : a convent of nuns

¹**nup·tial** \'nəp-shəl\ *adj* : of or relating to marriage or a wedding ⟨∼ vows⟩

²**nuptial** *n* : MARRIAGE, WEDDING — usu. used in pl.

¹**nurse** \'nərs\ *n* [ME *norice, nurse,* fr. AF *nurice,* fr. LL *nutricia,* fr. L, fem. of *nutricius* nourishing] 1 : a girl or woman employed to take care of children 2 : a person trained to care for sick people

²**nurse** *vb* **nursed; nurs·ing** 1 : SUCKLE 2 : to take charge of and watch over 3 : TEND ⟨∼ an invalid⟩ 4 : to treat with special care ⟨∼ a headache⟩ 5 : to hold in one's mind or consideration ⟨∼ a grudge⟩ 6 : to act or serve as a nurse

nurse-maid \'nərs-ˌmād\ *n* : NURSE 1

nurse-prac·ti·tion·er \-prak-'ti-shə-nər\ *n* : a registered nurse who is qualified to assume some of the duties formerly assumed only by a physician

nurs·ery \'nər-sə-rē\ *n*, *pl* **-er·ies** 1 : a room for children 2 : a place where children are temporarily cared for in their parents' absence 3 : a place where young plants are grown usu. for transplanting

nurs·ery·man \-mən\ *n* : a man who keeps or works in a plant nursery

nursery school *n* : a school for children under kindergarten age

nursing home *n* : a private establishment providing care for persons (as the aged or the chronically ill) who are unable to care for themselves

nurs·ling \'nərs-liŋ\ *n* 1 : one that is solicitously cared for 2 : a nursing child

¹**nur·ture** \'nər-chər\ *n* 1 : TRAINING, UPBRINGING; *also* : the influences that modify the expression of an individual's heredity 2 : FOOD, NOURISHMENT

²**nurture** *vb* **nur·tured; nur·tur·ing** 1 : to care for : FEED, NOURISH 2 : EDUCATE, TRAIN ⟨∼ students⟩ 3 : FOSTER ⟨∼ creativity⟩

nut \'nət\ *n* 1 : a dry fruit or seed with a hard shell and a firm inner kernel; *also* : its kernel 2 : a metal block with a hole through it that is fastened to a bolt or screw by means of a screw thread within the hole 3 : the ridge on the upper end of the fingerboard in a stringed musical instrument over which the strings pass 4 : a foolish, eccentric, or crazy person 5 : ENTHUSIAST

nut·crack·er \'nət-ˌkra-kər\ *n* : an instrument for cracking nuts

nut·hatch \-ˌhach\ *n* : any of various small tree-climbing chiefly insect-eating birds

nut·meg \-ˌmeg, -ˌmāg\ *n* [ME *notemuge,* ultim. fr. Old Occitan *noz muscada,* lit., musky nut] : a spice made by grinding the nutlike aromatic seed of a tropical tree; *also* : the seed or tree

nu·tria \'nü-trē-ə, 'nyü-\ *n* [Sp] 1 : the durable usu. light brown fur of a nutria 2 : a large So. American aquatic rodent with webbed hind feet

¹**nu·tri·ent** \'nü-trē-ənt, 'nyü-\ *adj* : NOURISHING ⟨∼ deficiencies⟩

²**nutrient** *n* : a nutritive substance or ingredient ⟨fruits and vegetables are important ∼s⟩

nu·tri·ment \-trə-mənt\ *n* : NUTRIENT

nu·tri·tion \nü-'tri-shən, nyü-\ *n* : the act or process of nourishing; *esp* : the processes by which an individual takes in and utilizes food material — **nu·tri·tion·al** \-shə-nəl\ *adj* — **nu·tri·tion·al·ly** *adv* — **nu·tri·tion·ist** \-shə-nist\ *n* — **nu·tri·tive** \'nü-trə-tiv, 'nyü-\ *adj*

nu·tri·tious \-shəs\ *adj* : NOURISHING — **nu·tri·tious·ly** *adv*

nuts \'nəts\ *adj* 1 : ENTHUSIASTIC, KEEN 2 : CRAZY, DEMENTED

nut·shell \'nət-,shel\ *n* : the shell of a nut — **in a nutshell** : in a few words ⟨that's the story *in a nutshell*⟩

nut·ty \'nə-tē\ *adj* **nut·ti·er; -est** 1 : containing or suggesting nuts ⟨a ~ flavor⟩ 2 : mentally unbalanced

nuz·zle \'nə-zəl\ *vb* **nuz·zled; nuz·zling** 1 : to root around, push, or touch with or as if with the nose 2 : NESTLE, SNUGGLE

NV *abbr* Nevada

NW *abbr* northwest

NWT *abbr* Northwest Territories

NY *abbr* New York

NYC *abbr* New York City

ny·lon \'nī-,län\ *n* 1 : any of numerous strong tough elastic synthetic materials used esp. in textiles and plastics 2 *pl* : stockings made of nylon

nymph \'nimf\ *n* 1 : any of the lesser goddesses in ancient mythology represented as maidens living in the mountains, forests, meadows, and waters 2 : GIRL 3 : an immature insect resembling the adult but smaller, less differentiated, and usu. lacking developed wings

nym·pho·ma·nia \,nim-fə-'mā-nē-ə, -nyə\ *n* : excessive sexual desire by a female — **nym·pho·ma·ni·ac** \-nē-,ak\ *n or adj*

NZ *abbr* New Zealand

¹o \'ō\ *n, pl* **o's** *or* **os** \'ōz\ *often cap* 1 : the 15th letter of the English alphabet 2 : ZERO

²o *abbr, often cap* 1 ocean 2 Ohio 3 ohm

¹O *var of* OH

²O *symbol* oxygen

o/a *abbr* on or about

oaf \'ōf\ *n* : a stupid or awkward person — **oaf·ish** *adj*

oak \'ōk\ *n, pl* **oaks** *or* **oak** : any of a genus of trees or shrubs related to the beech and chestnut and bearing a rounded thin-shelled nut surrounded at the base by a hardened cup; *also* : the usu. tough hard durable wood of an oak — **oak·en** \'ō-kən\ *adj*

oa·kum \'ō-kəm\ *n* [ME *okum*, fr. OE *ācumba* flax fiber, from *ā-* out + *-cumba* (akin to OE *camb* comb)] : loosely twisted hemp or jute fiber impregnated with tar and used esp. in caulking ships

oar \'ȯr\ *n* : a long pole with a broad blade at one end used for propelling or steering a boat

oar·lock \'ȯr-,läk\ *n* : a U-shaped device for holding an oar in place

oars·man \'ȯrz-mən\ *n* : one who rows esp. in a racing crew

OAS *abbr* Organization of American States

oa·sis \ō-'ā-səs\ *n, pl* **oa·ses** \-,sēz\ : a fertile or green area in an arid region

oat \'ōt\ *n* : a cereal grass widely grown for its edible seed; *also* : this seed — **oat·en** \'ō-t³n\ *adj*

oat·cake \'ōt-,kāk\ *n* : a thin flat oatmeal cake

oath \'ōth\ *n, pl* **oaths** \'ōthz, 'ōths\ 1 : a solemn appeal to God to witness to the truth of a statement or the sacredness of a promise 2 : an irreverent or careless use of a sacred name

oat·meal \'ōt-,mēl\ *n* 1 : ground or rolled oats 2 : porridge made from ground or rolled oats

Ob *or* **Obad** *abbr* Obadiah

Oba·di·ah \,ō-bə-'dī-ə\ *n* — see BIBLE table

ob·bli·ga·to \,ä-blə-'gä-tō\ *n, pl* **-tos** *also* **-ti** \-'gä-tē\ [It] : an accompanying part usu. played by a solo instrument

ob·du·rate \'äb-də-rət, -dyə-\ *adj* : stubbornly resistant : UNYIELDING ⟨an ~ denial⟩ ♦ **Synonyms** INFLEXIBLE, ADAMANT, RIGID, UNCOMPROMISING — **ob·du·ra·cy** \-rə-sē\ *n*

obe·di·ent \ō-'bē-dē-ənt\ *adj* : submissive to the restraint or command of authority ♦ **Synonyms** DOCILE, TRACTABLE, AMENABLE, BIDDABLE — **obe·di·ence** \-əns\ *n* — **obe·di·ent·ly** *adv*

obei·sance \ō-'bē-səns, -'bā-\ *n* 1 : a bow made to show respect or submission 2 : DEFERENCE, HOMAGE ⟨makes ~ to her mentors⟩

obe·lisk \'ä-bə-,lisk\ *n* [MF *obelisque*, fr. L *obeliscus*, fr. Gk *obeliskos*, fr. dim. of *obelos* spit, pointed pillar] : a 4-sided pillar that tapers toward the top and ends in a pyramid

obese \ō-'bēs\ *adj* [L *obesus*, fr. *obagainst* + *esus*, pp. of *edere* to eat] : having excessive body fat ♦ **Synonyms** CORPULENT, FLESHY, GROSS, OVERWEIGHT, PORTLY, STOUT — **obe·si·ty** \-'bē-sə-tē\ *n*

obey \ō-'bā\ *vb* **obeyed; obey·ing** 1 : to follow the commands or guidance of : behave obediently 2 : to comply with ⟨~ orders⟩ ♦ **Synonyms** CONFORM, KEEP, MIND, OBSERVE

ob·fus·cate \'äb-fə-,skāt\ *vb* **-cat·ed; -cat·ing** 1 : to make dark or obscure 2 : to make difficult to understand — **ob·fus·ca·tion** \,äb-fəs-'kā-shən\ *n*

OB–GYN *abbr* obstetrician gynecologist; obstetrics gynecology

obi \'ō-bē\ *n* [Jp] : a broad sash worn esp. with a Japanese kimono

obit \ō-'bit, 'ō-bət\ *n* : OBITUARY

obi·ter dic·tum \ˌō-bə-tər-ˈdik-təm\ *n, pl* **obiter dic·ta** \-tə\ [LL, lit., something said in passing] : an incidental remark or observation

obit·u·ary \ə-ˈbi-chə-ˌwer-ē\ *n, pl* **-ar·ies** : a notice of a person's death usu. with a short biographical account

obj *abbr* object; objective

¹**ob·ject** \ˈäb-jikt\ *n* **1** : something that may be seen or felt; *also* : something that may be perceived or examined mentally **2** : something that arouses an emotional response (as of affection or pity) **3** : AIM, PURPOSE ⟨the ~ is to raise money⟩ **4** : a word or word group denoting that on or toward which the action of a verb is directed; *also* : a noun or noun equivalent in a prepositional phrase

²**ob·ject** \əb-ˈjekt\ *vb* **1** : to offer in opposition **2** : to oppose something; *also* : DISAPPROVE ♦ **Synonyms** PROTEST, REMONSTRATE, EXPOSTULATE — **ob·jec·tor** \-ˈjek-tər\ *n*

object code *n* : a computer program after translation from source code

ob·jec·ti·fy \əb-ˈjek-tə-ˌfī\ *vb* **-fied; -fy·ing** : to make objective

ob·jec·tion \əb-ˈjek-shən\ *n* **1** : the act of objecting **2** : a reason for or a feeling of disapproval

ob·jec·tion·able \əb-ˈjek-shə-nə-bəl\ *adj* : UNDESIRABLE, OFFENSIVE — **ob·jec·tion·ably** \-blē\ *adv*

¹**ob·jec·tive** \əb-ˈjek-tiv\ *adj* **1** : of or relating to an object or end **2** : existing outside and independent of the mind **3** : of, relating to, or constituting a grammatical case marking typically the object of a verb or preposition **4** : treating or dealing with facts without distortion by personal feelings or prejudices — **ob·jec·tive·ly** *adv* — **ob·jec·tive·ness** *n* — **ob·jec·tiv·i·ty** \ˌäb-ˌjek-ˈti-və-tē\ *n*

²**objective** *n* **1** : the lens (as in a microscope) nearest the object and forming an image of it **2** : an aim, goal, or end of action

ob·jet d'art \ˌòb-ˌzhä-ˈdär\ *n, pl* **ob·jets d'art** *same*\ [F] : an article of artistic worth **2** : CURIO ♦ **Synonyms** KNICKKNACK, BAUBLE, BIBELOT, GEWGAW, NOVELTY, TRINKET

ob·jet trou·vé \ˈòb-ˌzhä-trü-ˈvä\ *n, pl* **objets trouvés** *same*\ [F, lit., found object] : a found natural or discarded object (as a piece of driftwood or an old bathtub) held to have aesthetic value

ob·jur·ga·tion \ˌäb-jər-ˈgä-shən\ *n* : a harsh rebuke — **ob·jur·gate** \ˈäb-jər-ˌgät\ *vb*

obl *abbr* 1 oblique 2 oblong

ob·late \ä-ˈblät\ *adj* : flattened or depressed at the poles ⟨an ~ spheroid⟩

ob·la·tion \ə-ˈblä-shən\ *n* : a religious offering

ob·li·gate \ˈä-blə-ˌgāt\ *vb* **-gat·ed; -gat·ing** : to bind legally or morally

ob·li·ga·tion \ˌä-blə-ˈgä-shən\ *n* **1** : an act of obligating oneself to a course of action **2** : something (as a promise or a contract) that binds one to a course of action **3** : INDEBTEDNESS; *also* : LIABILITY **4**

: DUTY — **ob·lig·a·to·ry** \ə-ˈbli-gə-ˌtòr-ē\ *adj*

oblige \ə-ˈblīj\ *vb* **obliged; oblig·ing** [ME, fr. AF *obliger*, fr. L *obligare*, lit., to bind to, fr. *ob-* toward + *ligare* to bind] **1** : FORCE, COMPEL ⟨the soldiers were *obliged* to retreat⟩ **2** : to bind by a favor; *also* : to do a favor for or do something as a favor

oblig·ing *adj* : willing to do favors — **oblig·ing·ly** *adv*

oblique \ō-ˈblēk\ *adj* **1** : neither perpendicular nor parallel : SLANTING **2** : not straightforward : INDIRECT — **oblique·ly** *adv* — **oblique·ness** *n* — **obliq·ui·ty** \-ˈbli-kwə-tē\ *n*

oblique case *n* : a grammatical case other than the nominative or vocative

oblit·er·ate \ə-ˈbli-tə-ˌrāt\ *vb* **-at·ed; -at·ing** [L *oblitterare*, fr. *ob* in the way of + *littera* letter] **1** : to remove from recognition or memory **2** : to make undecipherable by wiping out or covering over **3** : CANCEL — **oblit·er·a·tion** \-ˌbli-tə-ˈrā-shən\ *n*

obliv·i·on \ə-ˈbli-vē-ən\ *n* **1** : the condition of being oblivious **2** : the condition or state of being forgotten

obliv·i·ous \ə-ˈbli-vē-əs\ *adj* **1** : lacking memory or mindful attention **2** : UNAWARE ⟨~ of the risks⟩ — **obliv·i·ous·ly** *adv* — **obliv·i·ous·ness** *n*

ob·long \ˈä-ˌblòŋ\ *adj* : deviating from a square, circular, or spherical form by elongation in one dimension — **oblong** *n*

ob·lo·quy \ˈä-blə-kwē\ *n, pl* **-quies** **1** : strongly condemnatory utterance or language **2** : bad repute : DISGRACE ♦ **Synonyms** DISHONOR, SHAME, INFAMY, DISREPUTE, IGNOMINY

ob·nox·ious \äb-ˈnäk-shəs\ *adj* : REPUGNANT, OFFENSIVE ⟨~ behavior⟩ — **ob·nox·ious·ly** *adv* — **ob·nox·ious·ness** *n*

oboe \ˈō-bō\ *n* [It, fr. F *hautbois*, fr. *haut* high + *bois* wood] : a woodwind instrument with a slender conical tube and a double reed mouthpiece — **obo·ist** \ˈō-ˌbō-ist\ *n*

ob·scene \äb-ˈsēn\ *adj* **1** : REPULSIVE **2** : deeply offensive to morality or decency; *esp* : designed to incite to lust or depravity ♦ **Synonyms** GROSS, VULGAR, COARSE, CRUDE, INDECENT — **ob·scene·ly** *adv* — **ob·scen·i·ty** \-ˈse-nə-tē\ *n*

ob·scu·ran·tism \äb-ˈskyùr-ən-ˌti-zəm, ˌäb-skyù-ˈran-\ *n* **1** : opposition to the spread of knowledge **2** : deliberate vagueness or abstruseness — **ob·scu·ran·tist** \-tist\ *n or adj*

¹**ob·scure** \äb-ˈskyùr\ *adj* **1** : DIM, GLOOMY **2** : not readily understood : VAGUE **3** : REMOTE; *also* : HUMBLE ♦ **Synonyms** DARK, DUSKY, MURKY, TENEBROUS — **ob·scure·ly** *adv* — **ob·scu·ri·ty** \-ˈskyùr-ə-tē\ *n*

²**obscure** *vb* **ob·scured; ob·scur·ing** **1** : to make dark, dim, or indistinct **2** : to conceal or hide by or as if by covering

ob·se·qui·ous \əb-ˈsē-kwē-əs\ *adj* : humbly or excessively attentive (as to a person in authority) : FAWNING, SYCOPHAN-

TIC ♦ *Synonyms* MENIAL, SERVILE, SLAVISH, SUBSERVIENT — **ob·se·qui·ous·ly** *adv* — **ob·se·qui·ous·ness** *n*

ob·se·quy \'äb-sə-kwē\ *n, pl* **-quies** : a funeral or burial rite — usu. used in pl.

ob·serv·able \əb-'zər-və-bəl\ *adj* 1 : NOTEWORTHY 2 : capable of being observed — **ob·serv·abil·i·ty** \-'bi-lə-tē\ *n*

ob·ser·vance \əb-'zər-vəns\ *n* 1 : a customary practice or ceremony 2 : an act or instance of following a custom, rule, or law 3 : OBSERVATION

ob·ser·vant \-vənt\ *adj* 1 : WATCHFUL ⟨~ spectators⟩ 2 : KEEN, PERCEPTIVE 3 : MINDFUL ⟨~ of the amenities⟩

¹**ob·ser·va·tion** \ˌäb-sər-'vā-shən, -zər-\ *n* 1 : an act or instance of observing 2 : the gathering of information (as for scientific studies) by noting facts or occurrences 3 : a conclusion drawn from observing; *also* : REMARK, STATEMENT 4 : the fact of being observed — **ob·ser·va·tion·al** \-shə-nəl\ *adj*

²**observation** *adj* : designed for use in viewing or in making observations

ob·ser·va·to·ry \əb-'zər-və-ˌtȯr-ē\ *n, pl* **-ries** : a place or institution equipped for observation of natural phenomena (as in astronomy)

ob·serve \əb-'zərv\ *vb* **ob·served; ob·serv·ing** 1 : to conform one's action or practice to 2 : CELEBRATE 3 : to make a scientific observation of 4 : to see or sense esp. through careful attention 5 : to come to realize esp. through consideration of noted facts 6 : REMARK — **ob·serv·er** *n*

ob·sess \əb-'ses\ *vb* : to preoccupy intensely or abnormally

ob·ses·sion \äb-'se-shən\ *n* : a persistent disturbing preoccupation with an idea or feeling; *also* : an emotion or idea causing such a preoccupation — **ob·ses·sive** \-'se-siv\ *adj or n* — **ob·ses·sive·ly** *adv*

obsessive–compulsive *adj* : relating to, characterized by, or affected with recurring obsessions and compulsions esp. as symptoms of a neurotic state

ob·sid·i·an \əb-'si-dē-ən\ *n* : a dark natural glass formed by the cooling of molten lava

ob·so·les·cent \ˌäb-sə-'le-s³nt\ *adj* : going out of use : becoming obsolete ⟨~ computers⟩ — **ob·so·les·cence** \-s³ns\ *n*

ob·so·lete \ˌäb-sə-'lēt, 'äb-sə-ˌlēt\ *adj* : no longer in use; *also* : OLD-FASHIONED ⟨an ~ technology⟩ ♦ *Synonyms* EXTINCT, OUTWORN, PASSÉ, SUPERSEDED

ob·sta·cle \'äb-sti-kəl\ *n* : something that stands in the way or opposes

ob·stet·rics \əb-'ste-triks\ *n sing or pl* : a branch of medicine that deals with birth and with its antecedents and sequels — **ob·stet·ric** \-trik\ *or* **ob·stet·ri·cal** \-tri-kəl\ *adj* — **ob·ste·tri·cian** \ˌäb-stə-'tri-shən\ *n*

ob·sti·nate \'äb-stə-nət\ *adj* : fixed and unyielding (as in an opinion or course) despite reason or persuasion : STUBBORN ⟨~ opposition⟩ — **ob·sti·na·cy** \-nə-sē\ *n* — **ob·sti·nate·ly** *adv*

ob·strep·er·ous \əb-'stre-pə-rəs\ *adj* 1 : uncontrollably noisy 2 : stubbornly resistant to control : UNRULY — **ob·strep·er·ous·ness** *n*

ob·struct \əb-'strəkt\ *vb* 1 : to block by an obstacle 2 : to impede the passage, action, or operation of 3 : to cut off from sight — **ob·struc·tive** \-'strək-tiv\ *adj* — **ob·struc·tor** \-tər\ *n*

ob·struc·tion \əb-'strək-shən\ *n* 1 : an act of obstructing : the state of being obstructed 2 : something that obstructs : HINDRANCE

ob·struc·tion·ist \-shə-nist\ *n* : a person who hinders progress or business esp. in a legislative body — **ob·struc·tion·ism** \-shə-ˌni-zəm\ *n*

ob·tain \əb-'tān\ *vb* 1 : to gain or attain usu. by planning or effort 2 : to be generally recognized or established ♦ *Synonyms* PROCURE, SECURE, WIN, EARN, ACQUIRE — **ob·tain·able** *adj*

ob·trude \əb-'trüd\ *vb* **ob·trud·ed; ob·trud·ing** 1 : to thrust out 2 : to thrust forward without warrant or request 3 : INTRUDE — **ob·tru·sion** \-'trü-zhən\ *n* — **ob·tru·sive** \-'trü-siv\ *adj* — **ob·tru·sive·ly** *adv* — **ob·tru·sive·ness** *n*

ob·tuse \äb-'tüs, -'tyüs\ *adj* **ob·tus·er; -est** 1 : exceeding 90 degrees but less than 180 degrees ⟨~ angle⟩ 2 : not pointed or acute : BLUNT 3 : not sharp or quick of wit ⟨is too ~ to take a hint⟩ — **ob·tuse·ly** *adv* — **ob·tuse·ness** *n*

obv *abbr* obverse

¹**ob·verse** \äb-'vərs, 'äb-ˌvərs\ *adj* 1 : facing the observer or opponent 2 : being a counterpart or complement — **ob·verse·ly** *adv*

²**ob·verse** \'äb-ˌvərs, äb-'vərs\ *n* 1 : the side (as of a coin) bearing the principal design and lettering 2 : a front or principal surface 3 : a counterpart having the opposite orientation or force

ob·vi·ate \'äb-vē-ˌāt\ *vb* **-at·ed; -at·ing** : to anticipate and prevent (as a situation) or make unnecessary (as an action) ♦ *Synonyms* PREVENT, AVERT, FORESTALL, FORFEND, PRECLUDE — **ob·vi·a·tion** \ˌäb-vē-'ā-shən\ *n*

ob·vi·ous \'äb-vē-əs\ *adj* [L *obvius,* fr. *obviam* in the way, fr. *ob* in the way of + *viam,* acc. of *via* way] : easily found, seen, or understood : PLAIN ♦ *Synonyms* EVIDENT, MANIFEST, PATENT, CLEAR — **ob·vi·ous·ly** *adv* — **ob·vi·ous·ness** *n*

OC *abbr* officer candidate

oc·a·ri·na \ˌä-kə-'rē-nə\ *n* [It] : a wind instrument typically having an oval body with finger holes and a projecting mouthpiece

occas *abbr* occasionally

¹**oc·ca·sion** \ə-'kā-zhən\ *n* 1 : a favorable opportunity 2 : a direct or indirect cause 3 : the time of an event 4 : EXIGENCY 5 *pl* : AFFAIRS, BUSINESS 6 : a special event : CELEBRATION

²**occasion** *vb* : BRING ABOUT, CAUSE

oc·ca·sion·al \ə-'kā-zhə-nəl\ *adj* 1 : happening or met with now and then ⟨~ visits⟩ 2 : used or designed for a special occasion ⟨~ verse⟩ ♦ *Synonyms* IN-

FREQUENT, RARE, SPORADIC — **oc·ca·sion·al·ly** adv

oc·ci·den·tal \ˌäk-sə-ˈden-tᵊl\ adj, often cap [fr. *Occident* West, fr. ME, fr. AF, fr. L *occident-, occidens*, fr. prp. of *occidere* to fall, set (of the sun)] : WESTERN — **Occidental** n

Oc·ci·tan \ˈäk-sə-ˌtan\ n [F, fr. ML *occitanus*, fr. Old Occitan *oc* yes (contrasted with OF *oïl* yes)] : a Romance language spoken in southern France

oc·clude \ə-ˈklüd\ vb **oc·clud·ed; oc·clud·ing** **1** : OBSTRUCT ⟨an *occluded* artery⟩ **2** : to come together with opposing surfaces in contact — used of teeth — **oc·clu·sion** \-ˈklü-zhən\ n — **oc·clu·sive** \-ˈklü-siv\ adj

¹**oc·cult** \ə-ˈkəlt\ adj **1** : not revealed : SECRET **2** : ABSTRUSE, MYSTERIOUS **3** : of or relating to supernatural agencies, their effects, or knowledge of them ⟨the ∼ arts⟩ — **oc·cult·ism** \-ˈkəl-ˌti-zəm\ n — **oc·cult·ist** \-tist\ n

²**occult** n : occult matters — used with *the*

oc·cu·pan·cy \ˈä-kyə-pən-sē\ n, pl **-cies** **1** : the act of occupying : the state of being occupied **2** : an occupied building or part of a building

oc·cu·pant \-pənt\ n : one who occupies something; esp : RESIDENT

oc·cu·pa·tion \ˌä-kyə-ˈpā-shən\ n **1** : an activity in which one engages; esp : VOCATION **2** : the taking possession of property; also : the taking possession of an area by a foreign military force — **oc·cu·pa·tion·al** \-shə-nəl\ adj — **oc·cu·pa·tion·al·ly** adv

occupational therapy n : therapy by means of activity; esp : creative activity prescribed for its effect in promoting recovery or rehabilitation — **occupational therapist** n

oc·cu·py \ˈä-kyə-ˌpī\ vb **-pied; -py·ing** **1** : to engage the attention or energies of **2** : to fill up (an extent in space or time) **3** : to take or hold possession of **4** : to reside in as owner or tenant — **oc·cu·pi·er** n

oc·cur \ə-ˈkər\ vb **oc·curred; oc·cur·ring** [L *occurrere*, fr. *ob-* in the way + *currere* to run] **1** : to be found or met with : APPEAR **2** : HAPPEN ⟨the event will ∼ at noon⟩ **3** : to come to mind

oc·cur·rence \ə-ˈkər-əns\ n **1** : something that takes place **2** : the action or process of occurring

ocean \ˈō-shən\ n **1** : the whole body of salt water that covers nearly three fourths of the surface of the earth **2** : any of the large bodies of water into which the great ocean is divided — **ocean·ic** \ˌō-shē-ˈa-nik\ adj

ocean·ar·i·um \ˌō-shə-ˈnar-ē-əm\ n, pl **-iums** or **-ia** \-ē-ə\ : a large marine aquarium

ocean·front \ˈō-shən-ˌfrənt\ n : a shore area on the ocean

ocean·go·ing \-ˌgō-iŋ\ adj : of, relating to, or suitable for travel on the ocean

ocean·og·ra·phy \ˌō-shə-ˈnä-grə-fē\ n : a science dealing with the ocean and its

phenomena — **ocean·og·ra·pher** \-fər\ n — **ocean·o·graph·ic** \-nə-ˈgra-fik\ adj

oce·lot \ˈä-sə-ˌlät, ˈō-\ n : a medium-sized American wildcat ranging southward from Texas to northern Argentina and having a tawny yellow or gray coat with black markings

ocher or **ochre** \ˈō-kər\ n : an earthy usu. red or yellow iron ore used as a pigment; also : the color esp. of yellow ocher

o'·clock \ə-ˈkläk\ adv : according to the clock

OCR abbr optical character reader; optical character recognition

OCS abbr officer candidate school

oct abbr octavo

Oct abbr October

oc·ta·gon \ˈäk-tə-ˌgän\ n : a polygon of eight angles and eight sides — **oc·tag·o·nal** \äk-ˈta-gə-nᵊl\ adj

oc·tane \ˈäk-ˌtān\ n : OCTANE NUMBER

octane number n : a number used to measure the antiknock properties of gasoline that increases as the likelihood of knocking decreases

oc·tave \ˈäk-tiv\ n **1** : a musical interval embracing eight degrees; also : a tone or note at this interval or the whole series of notes, tones, or keys within this interval **2** : a group of eight

oc·ta·vo \äk-ˈtā-vō, -ˈtä-\ n, pl **-vos** **1** : the size of a piece of paper cut eight from a sheet **2** : a book printed on octavo pages

oc·tet \äk-ˈtet\ n **1** : a musical composition for eight voices or eight instruments; also : the performers of such a composition **2** : a group or set of eight

Oc·to·ber \äk-ˈtō-bər\ n [ME *Octobre*, fr. OE *October*, fr. L, eighth month of the early Roman calendar, fr. *octo* eight] : the 10th month of the year

oc·to·ge·nar·i·an \ˌäk-tə-jə-ˈner-ē-ən\ n : a person whose age is in the eighties

oc·to·pus \ˈäk-tə-pəs\ n, pl **-pus·es** or **-pi** \-ˌpī\ : any of various sea mollusks with eight long muscular arms furnished with suckers

oc·to·syl·lab·ic \ˌäk-tə-sə-ˈla-bik\ adj : composed of verses having eight syllables — **octosyllabic** n

¹**oc·u·lar** \ˈä-kyə-lər\ adj **1** : VISUAL **2** : of or relating to the eye or the eyesight

²**ocular** n : EYEPIECE

oc·u·list \ˈä-kyə-list\ n **1** : OPHTHALMOLOGIST **2** : OPTOMETRIST

¹**OD** \ˌō-ˈdē\ n : an overdose of a drug and esp. a narcotic

²**OD** vb **OD'd** or **ODed; OD'ing; OD's** : to become ill or die from an OD

³**OD** abbr **1** doctor of optometry **2** [L *oculus dexter*] right eye **3** officer of the day **4** olive drab **5** overdraft **6** overdrawn

odd \ˈäd\ adj [ME *odde*, fr. ON *oddi* point of land, triangle, odd number] **1** : being only one of a pair or set ⟨an ∼ shoe⟩ **2** : somewhat more than the number mentioned ⟨forty ∼ years ago⟩ **3** : being an integer (as 1, 3, or 5) not divisible by two without leaving a remainder **4** : additional to what is usual ⟨∼ jobs⟩ **5**

: STRANGE ⟨an ∼ way of behaving⟩ —
odd·ness *n*
odd·ball \'äd-,bȯl\ *n* : one that is eccentric — **oddball** *adj*
odd·i·ty \'ä-də-tē\ *n, pl* **-ties 1** : one that
is odd **2** : the quality or state of being
odd
odd·ly \'äd-lē\ *adv* **1** : in an odd manner
⟨an ∼ shaped roof⟩ **2** : as is odd
odd·ment \'äd-mənt\ *n* : something left
over : REMNANT
odds \'ädz\ *n pl* **1** : a difference by which
one thing is favored over another **2** : DIS-
AGREEMENT — usu. used with *at* **3** : the
ratio between the amount to be paid for
a winning bet and the amount of the bet
⟨the horse went off at ∼ of 6–1⟩
odds and ends *n pl* : miscellaneous
things or matters
odds-on \'ädz-'ȯn, -'än\ *adj* : having a
better than even chance to win
ode \'ōd\ *n* : a lyric poem that expresses a
noble feeling with dignity
odi·ous \'ō-dē-əs\ *adj* : arousing or deserving hatred or repugnance — **odi-
ous·ly** *adv* — **odi·ous·ness** *n*
odi·um \'ō-dē-əm\ *n* **1** : merited loathing
: HATRED **2** : DISGRACE ⟨the ∼ of de-
feat⟩
odom·e·ter \ō-'dä-mə-tər\ *n* [F *odomètre,*
fr. Gk *hodometron,* fr. *hodos* way, road +
metron measure] : an instrument for measuring distance traveled (as by a vehicle)
odor \'ō-dər\ *n* **1** : the quality of something that stimulates the sense of smell;
also : a sensation resulting from such
stimulation **2** : REPUTE, ESTIMATION —
odored \'ō-dərd\ *adj* — **odor·less** *adj*
— **odor·ous** *adj*
odor·if·er·ous \,ō-də-'ri-fə-rəs\ *adj* : having or yielding an odor
odour *chiefly Brit var of* ODOR
od·ys·sey \'ä-də-sē\ *n, pl* **-seys** [the *Od-
yssey,* epic poem attributed to Homer re-
counting the long wanderings of Odys-
seus] : a long wandering marked usu. by
many changes of fortune
oe·cu·men·i·cal \esp Brit ,ē-\ *chiefly Brit
var of* ECUMENICAL
OED *abbr* Oxford English Dictionary
oe·de·ma *chiefly Brit var of* EDEMA
oe·di·pal \'e-də-pəl, 'ē-\ *adj, often cap*
: of, relating to, or resulting from the Oedipus complex
Oe·di·pus complex \-pəs-\ *n* : the positive sexual feelings of a child toward the
parent of the opposite sex and hostile or
jealous feelings toward the parent of the
same sex that may be a source of adult
personality disorder when unresolved
OEO *abbr* Office of Economic Opportunity
o'er \'ȯr\ *adv or prep* : OVER
OES *abbr* Order of the Eastern Star
oe·soph·a·gus *chiefly Brit var of* ESOPH-
AGUS
oeu·vre \'ər-vrə, 'œvr³\ *n, pl* **oeuvres**
\same\ : a substantial body of work constituting the lifework of a writer, an artist, or a composer
of \'əv, 'äv\ *prep* **1** : FROM ⟨a man ∼ the
West⟩ **2** : having as a significant back-

ground or character element ⟨a man ∼
noble birth⟩ ⟨a woman ∼ ability⟩ **3**
: owing to ⟨died ∼ flu⟩ **4** : BY ⟨the plays
∼ Shakespeare⟩ **5** : having as component parts or material, contents, or members ⟨a house ∼ brick⟩ ⟨a glass ∼ wa-
ter⟩ ⟨a pack ∼ fools⟩ **6** : belonging to or
included by ⟨the front ∼ the house⟩ ⟨a
time ∼ life⟩ ⟨one ∼ you⟩ ⟨the best ∼
its kind⟩ ⟨the son ∼ a doctor⟩ **7** : ABOUT
⟨tales ∼ the West⟩ **8** : connected with
: OVER ⟨the queen ∼ England⟩ **9** : that
is : signified as ⟨the city ∼ Rome⟩ **10** —
used to indicate apposition of the words
it joins ⟨that fool ∼ a husband⟩ **11** : as
concerns : FOR ⟨love ∼ nature⟩ **12** —
used to indicate the application of an adjective ⟨fond ∼ candy⟩ **13** : BEFORE
⟨quarter ∼ ten⟩
OF *abbr* outfield
¹off \'ȯf\ *adv* **1** : from a place or position
⟨drove ∼ in a new car⟩; *also* : ASIDE
⟨turned ∼ into a side road⟩ **2** : at a distance in time or space ⟨stood ∼ a few
yards⟩ ⟨several years ∼⟩ **3** : so as to be
unattached or removed ⟨the lid blew ∼⟩
4 : to a state of discontinuance, exhaustion, or completion ⟨shut the radio ∼⟩ **5**
: away from regular work ⟨took time ∼
for lunch⟩
²off *prep* **1** : away from ⟨just ∼ the high-
way⟩ ⟨take it ∼ the table⟩ **2** : to seaward
of ⟨two miles ∼ the coast⟩ **3** : FROM
⟨borrowed a dollar ∼ me⟩ **4** : at the expense of ⟨lives ∼ his parents⟩ **5** : not
now engaged in ⟨∼ duty⟩ **6** : abstaining
from ⟨∼ liquor⟩ **7** : below the usual
level of ⟨∼ his game⟩
³off *adj* **1** : more removed or distant **2**
: started on the way **3** : not operating **4**
: not correct **5** : REMOTE, SLIGHT ⟨an ∼
chance⟩ **6** : INFERIOR ⟨∼ grade of oil⟩
7 : provided for ⟨well ∼⟩
⁴off *abbr* office; officer; official
of·fal \'ȯ-fəl\ *n* [ME, fr. *off* + *fall*] **1**
: the waste or by-product of a process;
esp : the viscera and trimmings of a
butchered animal removed in dressing
off and on *adv* : INTERMITTENTLY
— **rained** *off and on*⟩
¹off·beat \'ȯf-,bēt\ *n* : the unaccented part
of a musical measure
²offbeat *adj* : ECCENTRIC, UNCONVEN-
TIONAL ⟨an ∼ style⟩
off-col·or \'ȯf-'kə-lər\ *or* **off-col·ored**
\-lərd\ *adj* **1** : not having the right or
standard color **2** : of doubtful propriety
: verging on indecency ⟨∼ stories⟩
of·fend \ə-'fend\ *vb* **1** : SIN, TRANSGRESS
2 : to cause discomfort or pain : HURT **3**
: to cause dislike or vexation : ANNOY
♦ *Synonyms* AFFRONT, INSULT, OUT-
RAGE — **of·fend·er** *n*
of·fense *or* **of·fence** \ə-'fens, *esp for 2 &*
3 'ä-,fens\ *n* **1** : something that outrages
the senses **2** : ATTACK, ASSAULT **3** : the
offensive team or members of a team
playing offensive positions **4** : DISPLEA-
SURE **5** : SIN, MISDEED **6** : an infraction
of law : CRIME
¹of·fen·sive \ə-'fen-siv, *esp for 1 & 2* 'ä-
,fen-\ *adj* **1** : AGGRESSIVE **2** : of or relat-

ing to an attempt to score in a game; *also* : of or relating to a team in possession of the ball or puck 3 : OBNOXIOUS ⟨an ∼ odor⟩ 4 : INSULTING ⟨∼ remarks⟩ — **of·fen·sive·ly** *adv* — **of·fen·sive·ness** *n*

²offensive *n* : ATTACK

¹of·fer \'ȯ-fər\ *vb* **of·fered; of·fer·ing** 1 : SACRIFICE 2 : to present for acceptance : TENDER; *also* : to propose as payment 3 : PROPOSE, SUGGEST; *also* : to declare one's readiness 4 : to try or begin to exert ⟨∼ resistance⟩ 5 : to place on sale — **of·fer·ing** *n*

²offer *n* 1 : PROPOSAL 2 : BID 3 : TRY

of·fer·to·ry \'ȯ-fər-ˌtȯr-ē\ *n, pl* **-ries** : the presentation of offerings at a church service; *also* : the musical accompaniment during it

off-gas·sing \'ȯf-ˌga-siŋ\ *n* : the emission of esp. noxious gases (as from a building material)

off·hand \'ȯf-'hand\ *adv or adj* : without previous thought or preparation

off-hour \-ˌaù(-ə)r-\ *n* : a period of time other than a rush hour; *also* : a period of time other than business hours

of·fice \'ȯ-fəs\ *n* 1 : a special duty or position; *esp* : a position of authority in government ⟨run for ∼⟩ 2 : a prescribed form or service of worship; *also* : RITE 3 : an assigned or assumed duty or role 4 : a place where a business is transacted or a service is supplied

of·fice·hold·er \'ȯ-fəs-ˌhōl-dər\ *n* : one holding a public office

of·fi·cer \'ȯ-fə-sər\ *n* 1 : one charged with the enforcement of law 2 : one who holds an office of trust or authority 3 : a person who holds a position of authority or command in the armed forces; *esp* : COMMISSIONED OFFICER

¹of·fi·cial \ə-'fi-shəl\ *n* : OFFICER 2

²official *adj* 1 : of or relating to an office or to officers 2 : AUTHORIZED, AUTHORITATIVE ⟨∼ statement⟩ 3 : befitting or characteristic of a person in office — **of·fi·cial·ly** *adv*

of·fi·cial·dom \ə-'fi-shəl-dəm\ *n* : officials as a class

of·fi·cial·ism \ə-'fi-shə-ˌli-zəm\ *n* : lack of flexibility and initiative combined with excessive adherence to regulations

of·fi·ci·ant \ə-'fi-shē-ənt\ *n* : one (as a priest) who officiates at a religious rite

of·fi·ci·ate \ə-'fi-shē-ˌāt\ *vb* **-at·ed; -at·ing** 1 : to perform a ceremony, function, or duty 2 : to act in an official capacity

of·fi·cious \ə-'fi-shəs\ *adj* : volunteering one's services where they are neither asked for nor needed ⟨an ∼ busybody⟩ — **of·fi·cious·ly** *adv* — **of·fi·cious·ness** *n*

off·ing \'ȯ-fiŋ\ *n* : the near or foreseeable future

off-line \'ȯf-'līn\ *adj or adv* : not connected to or controlled directly by a computer

off of *prep* : OFF

off·print \'ȯf-ˌprint\ *n* : a separately printed excerpt (as from a magazine)

off-road \-'rōd\ *adj* : of, relating to, or being a vehicle designed for use away

from public roads — **off–road·er** \-'rō-dər\ *n*

off-sea·son \-ˌsē-z³n\ *n* : a time of suspended or reduced activity

¹off·set \-ˌset\ *n* 1 : a sharp bend (as in a pipe) by which one part is turned aside out of line 2 : a printing process in which an inked impression is first made on a rubber-blanketed cylinder and then transferred to the paper

²off·set *vb* **off·set; off·set·ting** 1 : to place over against : BALANCE 2 : to compensate for 3 : to form an offset in ⟨∼ a wall⟩

off·shoot \'ȯf-ˌshüt\ *n* 1 : a collateral or derived branch, descendant, or member 2 : a branch of a main stem (as of a plant)

¹off·shore \'ȯf-ˌshȯr\ *adv* 1 : at a distance from the shore 2 : outside the country : ABROAD

²off·shore \'ȯf-ˌshȯr\ *adj* 1 : moving away from the shore 2 : situated off the shore but within waters under a country's control

off·side \-'sīd\ *adv or adj* : illegally in advance of the ball or puck

off·spring \-ˌspriŋ\ *n, pl* **offspring** *also* **offsprings** : PROGENY, YOUNG

off·stage \'ȯf-ˌstāj, -ˌstāj\ *adv or adj* 1 : off or away from the stage 2 : out of the public view ⟨deals made ∼⟩

off-the-record *adj* : given or made in confidence and not for publication

off-the-shelf *adj* : available as a stock item : not specially designed or made

off-the-wall *adj* : highly unusual : BIZARRE ⟨an ∼ sense of humor⟩

off·track \'ȯf-'trak\ *adv or adj* : away from a racetrack

off-white \'ȯf-'hwīt\ *n* : a yellowish or grayish white color

off year *n* 1 : a year in which no major election is held 2 : a year of diminished activity or production

oft \'ȯft\ *adv* : OFTEN

of·ten \'ȯ-fən\ *adv* : many times : FREQUENTLY

of·ten·times \-ˌtīmz\ *or* **oft·times** \'ȯf-ˌtīmz, 'ȯft-\ *adv* : OFTEN

ogle \'ō-gəl\ *vb* **ogled; ogling** : to look at in a flirtatious way — **ogle** *n* — **ogler** *n*

ogre \'ō-gər\ *n* 1 : a monster of fairy tales and folklore that eats people 2 : a dreaded person or object

ogress \'ō-grəs\ *n* : a female ogre

oh *also* **O** \'ō\ *interj* 1 — used to express an emotion or in response to physical stimuli 2 — used in direct address

OH *abbr* Ohio

ohm \'ōm\ *n* : a unit of electrical resistance equal to the resistance of a circuit in which a potential difference of one volt produces a current of one ampere — **ohm·ic** \'ō-mik\ *adj*

ohm·me·ter \'ōm-ˌmē-tər\ *n* : an instrument for indicating resistance in ohms directly

¹oil \'ȯi(-ə)l\ *n* [ME *oile*, fr. AF, fr. L *oleum* olive oil, fr. Gk *elaion*, fr. *elaia* olive] 1 : any of numerous fatty or greasy liquid substances obtained from plants, animals, or minerals and used for fuel, food,

medicines, and manufacturing **2** : PE-
TROLEUM **3** : artists' colors made with
oil; *also* : a painting in such colors — **oil-
i-ness** \\'oi-lē-nəs\ *n* — **oily** \\'oi-lē\ *adj*

²oil *vb* : to put oil in or on — **oil-er** *n*

oil-cloth \\'oi-(ə)l-ˌklȯth\ *n* : cloth treated
with oil or paint and used for table and
shelf coverings

oil pan *n* : the lower section of a crank-
case used as an oil reservoir

oil shale *n* : a rock (as shale) from which
oil can be recovered

oil-skin \\'oi-(ə)l-ˌskin\ *n* **1** : an oiled waterproof cloth **2** : an oilskin raincoat **3**
pl : an oilskin coat and pants

oink \\'oiŋk\ *n* : the natural noise of a hog
— **oink** *vb*

oint-ment \\'oint-mənt\ *n* : a salve for use
on the skin

OJ *abbr* orange juice

Ojib-wa *or* **Ojib-way** *or* **Ojibwe** \ō-'jib-
ˌwä\ *n, pl* **Ojibwa** *or* **Ojibwas** *or* **Ojib-
way** *or* **Ojibways** *or* **Ojibwe** *or* **Ojibwes**
1 : a member of an American Indian
people of the region around Lake Superior and westward **2** : the Algonquian
language of the Ojibwa people

OJT *abbr* on-the-job training

¹OK *or* **okay** \ō-'kā\ *adv or adj* : all right

²OK *or* **okay** *vb* **OK'd** *or* **okayed; OK'-ing**
or **okay-ing** : APPROVE, AUTHORIZE —
OK *or* **okay** *n*

³OK *abbr* Oklahoma

Okla *abbr* Oklahoma

okra \\'ō-krə\ *n* : a tall annual plant related to the mallows that has edible green
pods; *also* : these pods

¹old \\'ōld\ *adj* **1** : ANCIENT; *also* : of long
standing **2** *cap* : belonging to an early
period ⟨*Old* Irish⟩ **3** : having existed for
a specified period of time **4** : of or relating to a past era **5** : advanced in years **6**
: showing the effects of age or use **7** : no
longer in use — **old-ish** \\'ōl-dish\ *adj*

²old *n* : old or earlier time ⟨days of ∼⟩

old-en \\'ōl-dən\ *adj* : of or relating to a
bygone era

¹old–fash-ioned \\'ōld-'fa-shənd\ *adj* **1**
: OUT-OF-DATE, ANTIQUATED **2** : CON-
SERVATIVE

²old–fashioned *n* : a cocktail usu. made
with whiskey, bitters, sugar, a twist of
lemon peel, and water or soda water

old–growth \\'ōld-'grōth\ *adj* : of, relating
to, or being a forest with large old trees,
numerous snags and woody debris, and a
multilayered canopy

old guard *n, often cap O&G* : the conservative members of an organization

old hat *adj* **1** : OLD-FASHIONED ⟨equip-
ment that is now *old hat*⟩ **2** : STALE,
TRITE

old-ie \\'ōl-dē\ *n* : something old; *esp* : a
popular song from the past

old–line \\'ōld-'līn\ *adj* **1** : ORIGINAL, ES-
TABLISHED ⟨an ∼ business⟩ **2** : adher-
ing to old policies or practices

old maid *n* **1** : SPINSTER **2** : a prim fussy
person — **old–maid-ish** \\'ōld-'mā-dish\
adj

old man *n* **1** : HUSBAND **2** : FATHER

old–school *adj* : adhering to traditional
policies or practices ⟨an ∼ politician⟩

old-ster \\'ōld-stər\ *n* : an old or elderly
person

Old Testament *n* : the first of the two
chief divisions of the Christian Bible —
see BIBLE table

old–time \\'ōld-'tīm\ *adj* **1** : of, relating
to, or characteristic of an earlier period
2 : of long standing

old–tim-er \-'tī-mər\ *n* : VETERAN; *also*
: OLDSTER

old–world \-'wərld\ *adj* : having old-fashioned charm ⟨an ∼ hotel⟩

ole-ag-i-nous \ˌō-lē-'a-jə-nəs\ *adj* : OILY

ole-an-der \\'ō-lē-ˌan-dər\ *n* : a poisonous
evergreen shrub often grown for its fragrant white to red flowers

oleo \\'ō-lē-ˌō\ *n, pl* **ole-os** : MARGARINE

oleo-mar-ga-rine \ˌō-lē-ō-'mär-jə-rən\ *n*
: MARGARINE

ol-fac-to-ry \äl-'fak-tə-rē, ōl-\ *adj* : of or
relating to the sense of smell

oli-gar-chy \\'ä-lə-ˌgär-kē, 'ō-\ *n, pl* **-chies**
1 : a government in which power is in the
hands of a few **2** : a state having an oli-
garchy; *also* : the group holding power in
such a state — **oli-garch** \-ˌgärk\ *n* —
oli-gar-chic \ˌä-lə-'gär-kik, ˌō-\ *or* **oli-
gar-chi-cal** \-ki-kəl\ *adj*

Oli-go-cene \\'ä-li-gō-ˌsēn, ə-'li-gə-ˌsēn\
adj : of, relating to, or being the epoch of
the Tertiary between the Eocene and the
Miocene — **Oligocene** *n*

olio \\'ō-lē-ˌō\ *n, pl* **oli-os** : HODGEPODGE,
MEDLEY

ol-ive \\'ä-liv\ *n* **1** : an Old World evergreen tree grown in warm regions for its
fruit that is a food and the source of an
edible oil (**olive oil**); *also* : the fruit **2** : a
dull yellowish green color

olive drab *n* **1** : a grayish olive color **2**
: an olive drab wool or cotton fabric; *also*
: a uniform of this fabric

ol-i-vine \\'ä-lə-ˌvēn\ *n* : a usu. greenish
mineral that is a complex silicate of magnesium and iron

Olym-pic Games \ō-'lim-pik-\ *n pl* : a
modified revival of an ancient Greek festival consisting of international athletic
contests that are held at separate winter
and summer gatherings at four-year intervals

om \\'ōm\ *n* : a mantra consisting of the
sound "om" used in contemplating ultimate reality

Oma-ha \\'ō-mə-ˌhä, -ˌhȯ\ *n, pl* **Omaha** *or*
Omahas : a member of an American Indian people of northeastern Nebraska

om-buds-man \\'äm-ˌbu̇dz-mən, äm-
'bu̇dz-\ *n, pl* **-men** \-mən\ **1** : a government official appointed to investigate
complaints made by individuals against
abuses or capricious acts of public officials **2** : one that investigates reported
complaints (as from students or consumers)

ome-ga \ō-'mā-gə\ *n* : the 24th and last
letter of the Greek alphabet — Ω or ω

om-elet *or* **om-elette** \\'äm-lət, 'ä-mə-\ *n*
[F *omelette*, alter. of MF *amelette*,
alemele, alter. of *alemelle* thin plate, ul-

tim. fr. L *lamella*, dim. of *lamina*] : eggs beaten with milk or water, cooked without stirring until set, and folded over

omen \'ō-mən\ *n* : an event or phenomenon believed to be a sign or warning of a future occurrence

omi·cron \'ä-mə-ˌkrän, 'ō-\ *n* : the 15th letter of the Greek alphabet — O or o

om·i·nous \'ä-mə-nəs\ *adj* : foretelling evil : THREATENING — **om·i·nous·ly** *adv* — **om·i·nous·ness** *n*

omis·si·ble \ō-'mi-sə-bəl\ *adj* : that may be omitted ⟨~ details⟩

omis·sion \ō-'mi-shən\ *n* **1** : something neglected or left undone **2** : the act of omitting : the state of being omitted

omit \ō-'mit\ *vb* **omit·ted; omit·ting 1** : to leave out or leave unmentioned **2** : to leave undone: FAIL

¹**om·ni·bus** \'äm-ni-(ˌ)bəs\ *n* : BUS

²**omnibus** *adj* : of, relating to, or providing for many things at once ⟨an ~ bill⟩

om·nip·o·tent \äm-'ni-pə-tənt\ *adj* **1** *often cap* : ALMIGHTY 1 **2** : having unlimited authority or influence ⟨an ~ ruler⟩ — **om·nip·o·tence** \-təns\ *n* — **om·nip·o·tent·ly** *adv*

om·ni·pres·ent \ˌäm-ni-'pre-z³nt\ *adj* : present in all places at all times ⟨an ~ problem⟩ — **om·ni·pres·ence** \-z³ns\ *n*

om·ni·scient \äm-'ni-shənt\ *adj* : having infinite awareness, understanding, and insight — **om·ni·science** \-shəns\ *n* — **om·ni·scient·ly** *adv*

om·ni·um–gath·er·um \ˌäm-nē-əm-'ga-thə-rəm\ *n, pl* **omnium–gatherums** : a miscellaneous collection

om·niv·o·rous \äm-'ni-və-rəs\ *adj* : feeding on both animal and vegetable substances **2** : AVID ⟨an ~ reader⟩ — **om·niv·o·rous·ly** *adv* — **om·niv·o·rous·ness** *n*

¹**on** \'ȯn, 'än\ *prep* **1** : in or to a position over and in contact with ⟨jumped ~ his horse⟩ **2** : touching the surface of ⟨shadows ~ the wall⟩ **3** : AT, TO ⟨~ the right were the mountains⟩ **4** : IN, ABOARD ⟨went ~ the train⟩ **5** : during or at the time of ⟨came ~ Monday⟩ ⟨every hour ~ the hour⟩ **6** : through the agency of ⟨was cut ~ a tin can⟩ **7** : in a state or process of ⟨~ fire⟩ ⟨~ the wane⟩ **8** : connected with as a member or participant ⟨~ a committee⟩ ⟨~ tour⟩ **9** — used to indicate a basis, source, or standard of computation ⟨has it ~ good authority⟩ ⟨10 cents ~ the dollar⟩ **10** : with regard to ⟨a monopoly ~ wheat⟩ **11** : at or toward as an object ⟨crept up ~ her⟩ **12** : ABOUT, CONCERNING ⟨a book ~ minerals⟩

²**on** *adv* **1** : in or into a position of contact with or attachment to a surface **2** : FORWARD **3** : into operation

³**on** *adj* : being in operation or in progress

ON *abbr* Ontario

¹**once** \'wəns\ *adv* [ME *ones*, fr. genitive of *on* one] **1** : one time only **2** : at any one time ⟨didn't ~ thank me⟩ **3** : FORMERLY ⟨was ~ young⟩ **4** : by one degree of relationship ⟨first cousin ~ removed⟩

²**once** *n* : one single time — **at once 1** : at the same time **2** : IMMEDIATELY

³**once** *adj* : FORMER ⟨a ~ successful actor⟩

⁴**once** *conj* : AS SOON AS ⟨~ we're finished, we can leave⟩

once–over \'wəns-ˌō-vər\ *n* : a swift examination or survey

on·co·gene \'äŋ-kō-ˌjēn\ *n* : a gene having the potential to cause a normal cell to become cancerous

on·col·o·gy \än-'kä-lə-jē\ *n* : the study of tumors — **on·co·log·i·cal** \ˌäŋ-kə-'lä-ji-kəl\ *also* **on·co·log·ic** \-jik\ *adj* — **on·col·o·gist** \än-'kä-lə-jist\ *n*

on·com·ing \'ȯn-ˌkə-miŋ, 'än-\ *adj* : APPROACHING ⟨~ traffic⟩

¹**one** \'wən\ *adj* **1** : being a single unit or thing ⟨~ person went⟩ **2** : being one in particular ⟨early ~ morning⟩ **3** : being the same in kind or quality ⟨members of ~ race⟩; *also* : UNITED **4** : being not specified or fixed ⟨~ day soon⟩

²**one** *n* **1** : the number denoting unity **2** : the 1st in a set or series **3** : a single person or thing — **one·ness** \'wən-nəs\ *n*

³**one** *pron* **1** : a certain indefinitely indicated person or thing ⟨saw ~ of his friends⟩ **2** : a person in general ⟨~ never knows⟩ **3** — used in place of a first-person pronoun

Onei·da \ō-'nī-də\ *n, pl* **Oneida** *or* **Oneidas** : a member of an American Indian people orig. of New York

one–man band *n* **1** : a musician who plays several instruments during a solo performance **2** : a person who alone undertakes or is responsible for several tasks

oner·ous \'ä-nə-rəs, 'ō-\ *adj* : imposing or constituting a burden : TROUBLESOME ⟨an ~ task⟩ ♦ *Synonyms* OPPRESSIVE, EXACTING, BURDENSOME, WEIGHTY

one·self \(ˌ)wən-'self\ *also* **one's self** *pron* : one's own self — usu. used reflexively or for emphasis

one–sid·ed \'wən-'sī-dəd\ *adj* **1** : having or occurring on one side only; *also* : having one side prominent or more developed **2** : PARTIAL ⟨a ~ interpretation⟩

one–time \-ˌtīm\ *adj* : FORMER ⟨a ~ actor⟩

one–to–one \ˌwən-tə-'wən\ *adj* : pairing each element of a set uniquely with an element of another set

one up *adj* : being in a position of advantage ⟨was *one up* on the others⟩

one–way *adj* : moving, allowing movement, or functioning in only one direction ⟨~ streets⟩

on·go·ing \'ȯn-ˌgō-iŋ, 'än-\ *adj* : continuously moving forward

on·ion \'ən-yən\ *n* : the pungent edible bulb of a widely cultivated plant related to the lilies; *also* : this plant

on·ion·skin \-ˌskin\ *n* : a thin strong translucent paper of very light weight

on–line \'ȯn-'līn, 'än-\ *adj or adv* : connected to, served by, or available through a computer network (as the Internet);

also : done while online ⟨∼ shopping⟩ — **online** *adv*

on·look·er \'ȯn-ˌlu̇-kər, 'än-\ *n* : SPECTATOR

¹on·ly \'ōn-lē\ *adj* **1** : unquestionably the best **2** : SOLE ⟨the ∼ one left⟩

²only *adv* **1** : MERELY, JUST ⟨∼ $2⟩ **2** : SOLELY ⟨known ∼ to me⟩ **3** : at the very least ⟨was ∼ too true⟩ **4** : as a final result ⟨will ∼ make you sick⟩

³only *conj* : except that

on·o·mato·poe·ia \ˌä-nə-ˌmä-tə-'pē-ə\ *n* [LL, fr. Gk *onomatopoiia*, fr. *onoma* name + *poiein* to make] **1** : formation of words in imitation of natural sounds (as *buzz* or *hiss*) **2** : the use of words whose sound suggests the sense — **on·o·mato·poe·ic** \-'pē-ik\ *or* **on·o·mato·po·et·ic** \-pō-'e-tik\ *adj* — **on·o·mato·poe·i·cal·ly** \-'pē-ə-k(ə-)lē\ *or* **on·o·mato·po·et·i·cal·ly** \-pō-'e-ti-k(ə-)lē\ *adv*

On·on·da·ga \ˌä-nən-'dȯ-gə, -'dä-, -'dä-\ *n*, *pl* **-ga** *or* **-gas** : a member of an American Indian people of New York and Canada

on·rush \'ȯn-ˌrəsh, 'än-\ *n* : a rushing onward — **on·rush·ing** *adj*

on-screen \'ȯn-'skrēn, 'än-\ *adv or adj* : on a computer or television screen

on·set \-ˌset\ *n* **1** : ATTACK **2** : BEGINNING ⟨the ∼ of winter⟩

on·shore \-ˌshȯr\ *adj* **1** : moving toward the shore **2** : situated on or near the shore — **on·shore** \-'shȯr\ *adv*

on·slaught \'ȯn-ˌslȯt, 'än-\ *n* : a fierce attack; *also* : something resembling such an attack ⟨an ∼ of questions⟩

Ont *abbr* Ontario

on·to \'ȯn-tü, 'än-\ *prep* : to a position or point on

onus \'ō-nəs\ *n* **1** : BURDEN **2** : OBLIGATION **3** : BLAME

¹on·ward \'ȯn-wərd, 'än-\ *also* **on·wards** \-wərdz\ *adv* : FORWARD ⟨kept moving ∼⟩

²onward *adj* : directed or moving onward : FORWARD

on·yx \'ä-niks\ *n* [ME *oniche, onyx*, fr. AF & L; AF, fr. L *onyx*, fr. Gk, lit., claw, nail] : a translucent chalcedony in parallel layers of different colors

oo·dles \'ü-dᵊlz\ *n pl* : a great quantity

oo·lite \'ō-ə-ˌlīt\ *n* : a rock consisting of small round grains cemented together — **oo·lit·ic** \ˌō-ə-'li-tik\ *adj*

¹ooze \'üz\ *n* [ME *wose*, fr. OE *wāse* mire] **1** : a soft deposit (as of mud) on the bottom of a body of water **2** : soft wet ground : MUD — **oozy** \'ü-zē\ *adj*

²ooze *vb* **oozed; ooz·ing 1** : to flow or leak out slowly or imperceptibly **2** : EXUDE ⟨∼ confidence⟩

³ooze *n* : something that oozes

op *abbr* **1** operation; operative; operator **2** opportunity **3** opus

OP *abbr* **1** observation post **2** out of print

opac·i·ty \ō-'pa-sə-tē\ *n*, *pl* **-ties 1** : obscurity of meaning **2** : mental dullness **3** : the quality or state of being opaque **4** : an opaque spot in a normally transparent structure

opal \'ō-pəl\ *n* : a mineral with iridescent colors that is used as a gem

opal·es·cent \ˌō-pə-'le-sᵊnt\ *adj* : IRIDESCENT — **opal·es·cence** \-sᵊns\ *n*

opaque \ō-'pāk\ *adj* **1** : blocking the passage of radiant energy and esp. light **2** : not easily understood; *also* : OBTUSE — **opaque·ly** *adv* — **opaque·ness** *n*

op art \'äp-\ *n* : OPTICAL ART — **op artist** *n*

op cit *abbr* [L *opere citato*] in the work cited

ope \'ōp\ *vb* **oped; op·ing** *archaic* : OPEN

OPEC *abbr* Organization of Petroleum Exporting Countries

op–ed \'äp-'ed\ *n*, *often cap O&E* : a page of special features usu. opposite the editorial page of a newspaper

¹open \'ō-pən\ *adj* **open·er; open·est 1** : not shut or shut up ⟨an ∼ door⟩ **2** : not secret or hidden; *also* : FRANK **3** : not enclosed or covered ⟨an ∼ fire⟩; *also* : not protected **4** : free to be entered or used ⟨an ∼ tournament⟩ **5** : easy to get through or see ⟨∼ country⟩ **6** : spread out : EXTENDED **7** : not decided ⟨an ∼ question⟩ **8** : readily accessible and cooperative; *also* : GENEROUS **9** : having openings, interruptions, or spaces ⟨an ∼ mesh⟩; *also* : having components separated by a space in writing and printing ⟨the name *Spanish moss* is an ∼ compound⟩ **10** : ready to operate ⟨stores are ∼⟩ **11** : free from restraints or controls ⟨∼ season⟩ — **open·ly** *adv* — **open·ness** *n*

²open \'ō-pən\ *vb* **opened; open·ing 1** : to change or move from a shut position; *also* : to make open by clearing away obstacles **2** : to make accessible **3** : to make openings in **4** : to make or become functional ⟨∼ a store⟩ **5** : REVEAL; *also* : ENLIGHTEN **6** : BEGIN ⟨∼ talks⟩ — **open·er** *n*

³open *n* **1** : OUTDOORS **2** : a contest or tournament open to all

open–air *adj* : OUTDOOR ⟨∼ theaters⟩

open arms *n pl* : an eager or warm welcome

open–faced \-'fāst\ *also* **open–face** \-'fās\ *adj* : served without a covering layer of bread ⟨an ∼ sandwich⟩

open·hand·ed \ˌō-pən-'han-dəd\ *adj* : GENEROUS — **open·hand·ed·ly** *adv*

open–heart *adj* : of, relating to, or performed on a heart temporarily relieved of circulatory function and laid open for repair of defects or damage

open–hearth *adj* : of, relating to, or being a process of making steel in a furnace that reflects the heat from the roof onto the material

opening *n* **1** : an act or instance of making or becoming open **2** : BEGINNING **3** : something that is open **4** : OCCASION; *also* : an opportunity for employment

open mike *n* : an event in which amateurs may perform

open–mind·ed \ˌō-pən-'mīn-dəd\ *adj* : free from rigidly fixed preconceptions — **open–mind·ed·ness** *n*

open sentence *n* : a statement (as in

mathematics) containing at least one blank or unknown so that when the blank is filled or a quantity substituted for the unknown the statement becomes a complete statement that is either true or false

open shop *n* : an establishment having members and nonmembers of a labor union on the payroll

open·work \'ō-pən-,wərk\ *n* : work so made as to show openings through its substance ⟨a railing of wrought-iron ∼⟩ — **open–worked** \-,wərkt\ *adj*

¹**opera** *pl of* OPUS

²**op·era** \'ä-prə, -pə-rə\ *n* : a drama set to music — **op·er·at·ic** \,ä-pə-'ra-tik\ *adj*

op·er·a·ble \'ä-pə-rə-bəl\ *adj* 1 : fit, possible, or desirable to use 2 : likely to result in a favorable outcome after surgical treatment

opera glasses *n pl* : small binoculars for use in a theater

op·er·ate \'ä-pə-,rāt\ *vb* **-at·ed; -at·ing** 1 : to perform work : FUNCTION 2 : to produce an effect 3 : to put or keep in operation 4 : to perform or subject to an operation — **op·er·a·tor** \-,rā-tər\ *n*

operating system *n* : software that controls the operation of a computer

op·er·a·tion \,ä-pə-'rā-shən\ *n* 1 : a doing or performing of a practical work 2 : an exertion of power or influence; *also* : method or manner of functioning 3 : a surgical procedure 4 : a process of deriving one mathematical expression from others according to a rule 5 : a military action or mission 6 : a usu. small business — **op·er·a·tion·al** \-shə-nəl\ *adj*

¹**op·er·a·tive** \'ä-pə-rə-tiv, -,rā-\ *adj* 1 : producing an appropriate effect; *also* : most significant or essential 2 : OPERATING ⟨an ∼ force⟩ 3 : having to do with physical operations; *also* : WORKING ⟨an ∼ craftsman⟩ 4 : based on or consisting of an operation ⟨∼ dentistry⟩

²**operative** *n* 1 : OPERATOR; *esp* : a secret agent 2 : a person who works toward achieving the objectives of a larger interest

op·er·et·ta \,ä-pə-'re-tə\ *n* [It, dim. of *opera* opera] : a light musical-dramatic work with a romantic plot, spoken dialogue, and dancing scenes

oph·thal·mic \äf-'thal-mik, äp-\ *adj* [Gk *ophthalmikos*, fr. *ophthalmos* eye] : of, relating to, or located near the eye

oph·thal·mol·o·gy \,äf-,thal-'mä-lə-jē, ,äp-\ *n* : a branch of medicine dealing with the structure, functions, and diseases of the eye — **oph·thal·mol·o·gist** \-jist\ *n*

oph·thal·mo·scope \äf-'thal-mə-,skōp, äp-\ *n* : an instrument for use in viewing the interior of the eye and esp. the retina

opi·ate \'ō-pē-ət, -pē-,āt\ *n* : a preparation or derivative of opium; *also* : a narcotic or a substance with similar activity — **opiate** *adj*

opine \ō-'pīn\ *vb* **opined; opin·ing** : to express an opinion : STATE

opin·ion \ə-'pin-yən\ *n* 1 : JUDGMENT 2 : a belief stronger than impression and

less strong than positive knowledge 3 : a formal statement by an expert after careful study

opin·ion·at·ed \ə-'pin-yə-,nā-təd\ *adj* : obstinately adhering to personal opinions

opi·um \'ō-pē-əm\ *n* [ME, fr. L, fr. Gk *opion*, fr. dim. of *opos* sap] : an addictive narcotic drug that is the dried latex of a Eurasian poppy

opos·sum \ə-'pä-səm\ *n, pl* **opossums** *also* **opossum** : an omnivorous tree=dwelling No. American marsupial that is active chiefly at night and has a pointed snout and a prehensile tail

opp *abbr* opposite

op·po·nent \ə-'pō-nənt\ *n* : one that opposes : ADVERSARY

op·por·tune \,ä-pər-'tün, -'tyün\ *adj* [ME, fr. MF *opportun*, fr. L *opportunus*, fr. *ob-* toward + *portus* port, harbor] : SUITABLE ⟨an ∼ moment⟩ — **op·por·tune·ly** *adv*

op·por·tun·ism \,ä-pər-'tü-,ni-zəm, -'tyü-\ *n* : a taking advantage of opportunities or circumstances esp. with little regard for principles or ultimate consequences — **op·por·tun·ist** \-nist\ *n* — **op·por·tu·nis·tic** \-tü-'nis-tik, -tyü-\ *adj*

op·por·tu·ni·ty \,ä-pər-'tü-nə-tē, -'tyü-\ *n, pl* **-ties** 1 : a favorable combination of circumstances, time, and place 2 : a chance for advancement

op·pose \ə-'pōz\ *vb* **op·posed; op·pos·ing** 1 : to place opposite or against something (as to provide resistance or contrast) 2 : to strive against : RESIST — **op·po·si·tion** \,ä-pə-'zi-shən\ *n*

¹**op·po·site** \'ä-pə-zət\ *adj* 1 : set over against something that is at the other end or side 2 : OPPOSED, HOSTILE; *also* : CONTRARY 3 : contrarily turned or moving 4 : being the other of a matching or contrasting pair ⟨the ∼ sex⟩ — **op·po·site·ly** *adv* — **op·po·site·ness** *n*

²**opposite** *n* : one that is opposed or contrary

³**opposite** *adv* : on or to an opposite side

⁴**opposite** *prep* : across from and usu. facing ⟨the house ∼ ours⟩

op·press \ə-'pres\ *vb* 1 : to crush by abuse of power or authority ⟨∼ed minorities⟩ 2 : to weigh down : BURDEN

♦ **Synonyms** AGGRIEVE, WRONG, PERSECUTE — **op·pres·sive** \-'pre-siv\ *adj* — **op·pres·sive·ly** *adv* — **op·pres·sor** \-'pre-sər\ *n*

op·pres·sion \ə-'pre-shən\ *n* 1 : unjust or cruel exercise of power or authority 2 : DEPRESSION

op·pro·bri·ous \ə-'prō-brē-əs\ *adj* : expressing or deserving opprobrium — **op·pro·bri·ous·ly** *adv*

op·pro·bri·um \-brē-əm\ *n* 1 : something that brings disgrace 2 : public disgrace or ill fame

¹**opt** \'äpt\ *vb* : to make a choice; *esp* : to decide in favor of something

²**opt** *abbr* 1 optical; optician; optics 2 optional

op·tic \'äp-tik\ *adj* : of or relating to vision or the eye

op·ti·cal \'äp-ti-kəl\ *adj* 1 : relating to

optics **2** : OPTIC **3** : of, relating to, or using light

optical art *n* : nonobjective art characterized by the use of geometric patterns often for an illusory effect

optical disk *n* : a disk on which information has been recorded digitally and which is read using a laser

optical fiber *n* : a single fiber-optic strand

op·ti·cian \äp-'ti-shən\ *n* **1** : a maker of or dealer in optical items and instruments **2** : a person who makes or orders eyeglasses and contact lenses to prescription and sells them

op·tics \'äp-tiks\ *n* : a science that deals with the nature and properties of light

op·ti·mal \'äp-tə-məl\ *adj* : most desirable or satisfactory — **op·ti·mal·ly** *adv*

op·ti·mism \'äp-tə-ˌmi-zəm\ *n* [F *optimisme*, fr. L *optimum*, n., best, fr. neut. of *optimus* best] **1** : a doctrine that this world is the best possible world **2** : an inclination to anticipate the best possible outcome of actions or events — **op·ti·mist** \-mist\ *n* — **op·ti·mis·tic** \ˌäp-tə-'mis-tik\ *adj* — **op·ti·mis·ti·cal·ly** \-ti-k(ə-)lē\ *adv*

op·ti·mize \'äp-tə-ˌmīz\ *vb* **-mized; -miz·ing** : to make as perfect, effective, or functional as possible — **op·ti·mi·za·tion** \ˌäp-tə-mə-'zā-shən\ *n*

op·ti·mum \'äp-tə-məm\ *n, pl* **-ma** \-mə\ *also* **-mums** [L] : the amount or degree of something most favorable to an end; *also* : greatest degree attained under implied or specified conditions

op·tion \'äp-shən\ *n* **1** : the power or right to choose **2** : a right to buy or sell something at a specified price during a specified period **3** : something offered for choice — **op·tion·al** \-shə-nəl\ *adj*

op·tom·e·try \äp-'tä-mə-trē\ *n* : the health-care profession concerned esp. with examining the eyes for defects of vision and with prescribing corrective lenses or eye exercises — **op·to·met·ric** \ˌäp-tə-'me-trik\ *adj* — **op·tom·e·trist** \äp-'tä-mə-trist\ *n*

opt out *vb* : to choose not to participate

op·u·lence \'ä-pyə-ləns\ *n* **1** : WEALTH **2** : ABUNDANCE

op·u·lent \'ä-pyə-lənt\ *adj* **1** : WEALTHY **2** : richly abundant — **op·u·lent·ly** *adv*

opus \'ō-pəs\ *n, pl* **opera** \'ō-pə-rə, 'ä-\ *also* **opus·es** \'ō-pə-səz\ : WORK; *esp* : a musical composition

or \'ȯr\ *conj* — used as a function word to indicate an alternative ⟨sink ~ swim⟩

OR *abbr* **1** operating room **2** Oregon

-or *n suffix* : one that does a (specified) thing ⟨calculat*or*⟩

or·a·cle \'ȯr-ə-kəl\ *n* **1** : one held to give divinely inspired answers or revelations **2** : an authoritative or wise utterance; *also* : a person of great authority or wisdom — **orac·u·lar** \ȯ-'ra-kyə-lər\ *adj*

¹oral \'ȯr-əl\ *adj* **1** : SPOKEN ⟨an ~ report⟩ **2** : of, given through, or involving the mouth ⟨an ~ vaccine⟩ **3** : of, relating to, or characterized by the first stage of psychosexual development in psychoanalytic theory in which libidinal gratification is derived from intake (as of food), by sucking, and later by biting **4** : relating to or characterized by personality traits of passive dependency and aggressiveness — **oral·ly** *adv*

²oral *n* : an oral examination — usu. used in pl.

oral sex *n* : oral stimulation of the genitals : CUNNILINGUS, FELLATIO

orang \ə-'raŋ\ *n* : ORANGUTAN

or·ange \'är-inj, 'ȯr-\ *n* **1** : a juicy citrus fruit with reddish yellow rind; *also* : an evergreen tree with fragrant white flowers that bears this fruit **2** : a color between red and yellow — **or·ang·ey** *or* **orangy** \'är-in-jē, 'ȯr-\ *adj*

or·ange·ade \ˌär-in-'jād, ˌȯr-\ *n* : a beverage of orange juice, sugar, and water

orange hawkweed *n* : a weedy herb related to the daisies with bright orange-red flower heads

or·ange·ry \'är-inj-rē, 'ȯr-\ *n, pl* **-ries** : a protected place (as a greenhouse) for raising oranges in cool climates

orang·utan \ə-'raŋ-ə-ˌtaŋ, -ˌtan\ *n* [Bazaar Malay *orang*-utan (Malay-based pidgin), fr. Malay *orang* man + *hutan* forest] : a large reddish brown tree-living anthropoid ape of Borneo and Sumatra

orate \ȯ-'rāt\ *vb* **orat·ed; orat·ing** : to speak in a declamatory manner

ora·tion \ə-'rā-shən\ *n* : an elaborate discourse delivered in a formal and dignified manner

or·a·tor \'ȯr-ə-tər\ *n* : one noted for skill and power as a public speaker

or·a·tor·i·cal \ˌȯr-ə-'tȯr-i-kəl\ *adj* : of, relating to, or characteristic of an orator or oratory — **or·a·tor·i·cal·ly** \-'tȯr-i-k(ə-)lē\ *adv*

or·a·to·rio \ˌȯr-ə-'tȯr-ē-ˌō\ *n, pl* **-rios** : a lengthy choral work usu. on a scriptural subject

¹or·a·to·ry \'ȯr-ə-ˌtȯr-ē\ *n, pl* **-ries** : a private or institutional chapel

²oratory *n* : the art of speaking eloquently and effectively in public **♦ Synonyms** RHETORIC, ELOCUTION

orb \'ȯrb\ *n* : a spherical body; *also* : EYE

or·bit \'ȯr-bət\ *n* [L *orbita*, lit., path, rut] **1** : a path described by one body in its revolution about another **2** : range or sphere of activity — **or·bit·al** \-bə-tᵊl\ *adj*

²orbit *vb* **1** : CIRCLE **2** : to send up and make revolve in an orbit ⟨~ a satellite⟩ — **or·bit·er** *n*

or·ca \'ȯr-kə\ *n* : KILLER WHALE

orch *abbr* orchestra

or·chard \'ȯr-chərd\ *n* [ME, fr. OE *ortgeard*, fr. *ort*- (fr. L *hortus* garden) + *geard* yard] : a place where fruit trees, sugar maples, or nut trees are grown; *also* : the trees of such a place — **or·chard·ist** \-chər-dist\ *n*

or·ches·tra \'ȯr-kə-strə\ *n* **1** : the front section of seats on the main floor of a theater **2** : a group of instrumentalists organized to perform ensemble music — **or·ches·tral** \ȯr-'kes-trəl\ *adj* — **or·ches·tral·ly** *adv*

or·ches·trate \'ȯr-kə-ˌstrāt\ *vb* **-trat·ed; -trat·ing** **1** : to compose or arrange for an orchestra **2** : to arrange so as to achieve a desired effect ⟨~ a campaign⟩ — **or·ches·tra·tion** \ˌȯr-kə-ˈstrā-shən\ n

or·chid \ˈȯr-kəd\ n : any of a large family of plants having often showy flowers with three petals of which the middle one is enlarged into a lip; *also* : a flower of an orchid

ord *abbr* **1** order **2** ordnance

or·dain \ȯr-ˈdān\ *vb* **1** : to admit to the ministry or priesthood by the ritual of a church **2** : DECREE, ENACT; *also* : DESTINE — **or·dain·ment** n

or·deal \ȯr-ˈdēl, ˈȯr-ˌdēl\ n : a severe trial or experience

¹**or·der** \ˈȯr-dər\ *vb* **1** : ARRANGE, REGULATE **2** : COMMAND **3** : to place an order

²**order** n **1** : a group of people formally united; *also* : a badge or medal of such a group **2** : any of the several grades of the Christian ministry; *also, pl* : ORDINATION **3** : a rank, class, or special group of persons or things **4** : a category of biological classification ranking above the family and below the class **5** : ARRANGEMENT, SEQUENCE; *also* : the prevailing state of things **6** : a customary mode of procedure; *also* : the rule of law or proper authority **7** : a specific rule, regulation, or authoritative direction **8** : a style of building; *also* : an architectural column forming the unit of a style **9** : condition esp. with regard to repair **10** : a direction to pay money or to buy or sell goods; *also* : goods bought or sold — **in order** : APPROPRIATE, DESIRABLE ⟨apologies are *in order*⟩ — **in order to** : for the purpose of

¹**or·der·ly** \ˈȯr-dər-lē\ *adj* **1** : arranged according to some order; *also* : NEAT, TIDY **2** : well behaved ⟨an ~ crowd⟩ ♦ **Synonyms** METHODICAL, SYSTEMATIC, REGULAR — **or·der·li·ness** n

²**orderly** n, *pl* **-lies** **1** : a soldier who attends a superior officer **2** : a hospital attendant who does general work

or·di·nal \ˈȯr-də-nəl\ *adj* : indicating order or rank (as sixth) in a series

ordinal number n : a number (as first, second, or third) that designates the place of an item in an ordered sequence — compare CARDINAL NUMBER

or·di·nance \ˈȯr-də-nəns\ n : an authoritative decree or law; *esp* : a municipal regulation

or·di·nary \ˈȯr-də-ˌner-ē\ *adj* **1** : to be expected : USUAL **2** : of common quality, rank, or ability ⟨~ kids⟩; *also* : POOR, INFERIOR ⟨~ wine⟩ ♦ **Synonyms** CUSTOMARY, ROUTINE, NORMAL, EVERYDAY — **or·di·nar·i·ly** \ˌȯr-də-ˈner-ə-lē\ *adv* — **or·di·nar·i·ness** \ˈȯr-də-ˌner-ē-nəs\ n

or·di·nate \ˈȯr-də-nət, -ˌnāt\ n : the vertical coordinate of a point in a plane coordinate system obtained by measuring parallel to the y-axis

or·di·na·tion \ˌȯr-də-ˈnā-shən\ n : the act or ceremony by which a person is ordained

ord·nance \ˈȯrd-nəns\ n **1** : military supplies **2** : CANNON, ARTILLERY

Or·do·vi·cian \ˌȯr-də-ˈvi-shən\ *adj* : of, relating to, or being the period of the Paleozoic era between the Cambrian and the Silurian — **Ordovician** n

or·dure \ˈȯr-jər\ n : EXCREMENT

¹**ore** \ˈȯr\ n : a naturally occurring mineral mined to obtain a substance that it contains

²**ore** \ˈȯr-ə\ n, *pl* **ore** — see *krona, krone* at MONEY table

Ore *or* **Oreg** *abbr* Oregon

oreg·a·no \ə-ˈre-gə-ˌnō\ n : a bushy perennial mint used as a seasoning and a source of oil

org *abbr* organization; organized

or·gan \ˈȯr-gən\ n **1** : a musical instrument having sets of pipes sounded by compressed air and controlled by keyboards; *also* : an electronic keyboard instrument that approximates the sounds of the pipe organ **2** : a differentiated animal or plant structure (as a heart or a leaf) made up of cells and tissues and performing some bodily function **3** : a group that performs a specialized function ⟨the various ~s of government⟩ **4** : PERIODICAL ⟨the official ~ of the party⟩

or·gan·dy *also* **or·gan·die** \ˈȯr-gən-dē\ n, *pl* **-dies** [F *organdi*] : a fine transparent muslin with a stiff finish

or·gan·elle \ˌȯr-gə-ˈnel\ n : a specialized cell part that resembles an organ in having a special function

or·gan·ic \ȯr-ˈga-nik\ *adj* **1** : of, relating to, or arising in a bodily organ **2** : of, relating to, or derived from living things **3** : of, relating to, or containing carbon compounds **4** : of or relating to a branch of chemistry dealing with carbon compounds **5** : involving, producing, or dealing in foods produced without the use of laboratory-made fertilizers, growth substances, antibiotics, or pesticides ⟨~ farming⟩ **6** : ORGANIZED ⟨an ~ whole⟩ — **or·gan·i·cal·ly** \-ni-k(ə-)lē\ *adv*

or·ga·ni·sa·tion, or·ga·nise *Brit var of* ORGANIZATION, ORGANIZE

or·gan·ism \ˈȯr-gə-ˌni-zəm\ n : an individual living thing (as a person, animal, or plant) — **or·gan·is·mic** \ˌȯr-gə-ˈniz-mik\ *adj*

or·gan·ist \ˈȯr-gə-nist\ n : a person who plays an organ

or·ga·ni·za·tion \ˌȯr-gə-nə-ˈzā-shən\ n **1** : the act or process of organizing or of being organized; *also* : the condition or manner of being organized **2** : ASSOCIATION, SOCIETY **3** : an administrative structure (as a business or a political party) — **or·ga·ni·za·tion·al** \-shə-nəl\ *adj*

or·ga·nize \ˈȯr-gə-ˌnīz\ *vb* **-nized; -niz·ing** **1** : to develop an organic structure **2** : to form into a complete and functioning whole **3** : to set up an administrative structure for **4** : to arrange by systematic planning and united effort **5** : to join in a union; *also* : UNIONIZE ♦ **Synonyms** INSTITUTE, FOUND, ESTABLISH, CONSTITUTE — **or·ga·niz·er** n

or·gano·chlo·rine \ȯr-ˌga-nə-ˈklȯr-ˌēn\ *adj* : of, relating to, or being a chlorinated hydrocarbon pesticide (as DDT) — **organochlorine** *n*

or·gano·phos·phate \-'fäs-₁fāt\ *n* : an organophosphorus pesticide — **organophosphate** *adj*

or·gano·phos·pho·rus \-'fäs-fə-rəs\ *also* **or·gano·phos·pho·rous** \-'fäs-'fôr-əs\ *adj* : of, relating to, or being a phosphorus-containing organic pesticide (as malathion)

or·gan·za \ôr-'gan-zə\ *n* : a sheer strong fabric resembling organdy and usu. made of silk, rayon, or nylon

or·gasm \'ôr-₁ga-zəm\ *n* : the climax of sexual excitement — **or·gas·mic** \ôr-'gaz-mik\ *adj*

or·gi·as·tic \₁ôr-jē-'as-tik\ *adj* : of, relating to, or marked by orgies

or·gu·lous \'ôr-gyə-ləs, -gə-\ *adj* : PROUD

or·gy \'ôr-jē\ *n, pl* **orgies** : a gathering marked by unrestrained indulgence (as in sexual activity, alcohol, or drugs)

ori·el \'ôr-ē-əl\ *n* : a window built out from a wall—and usu. supported by a bracket

ori·ent \'ôr-ē-ent\ *vb* 1 : to set in a definite position esp. in relation to the points of the compass 2 : to acquaint with an existing situation or environment 3 : to direct toward the interests of a particular group

Orient *n* : EAST 3; *esp* : the countries of eastern Asia

ori·en·tal \₁ôr-ē-'en-t⁰l\ *adj, often cap* [fr. *Orient* East, fr. ME, fr. AF, fr. L *orient-, oriens*, fr. prp. of *oriri* to rise] : of or situated in Asia

ori·en·tate \'ôr-ē-ən-₁tāt\ *vb* **-tat·ed; -tat·ing** 1 : ORIENT 2 : to face east

ori·en·ta·tion \₁ôr-ē-ən-tā-shən\ *n* 1 : the act or state of being oriented 2 : a person's identity based on sexual tendencies

or·i·fice \'ôr-ə-fəs\ *n* : OPENING, MOUTH

ori·flamme \'ôr-ə-₁flam\ *n* : a brightly colored banner used as a standard or ensign in battle

orig *abbr* original; originally

ori·ga·mi \₁ôr-ə-'gä-mē\ *n* : the Japanese art or process of paper folding

ori·gin \'ôr-ə-jən\ *n* 1 : ANCESTRY 2 : rise, beginning, or derivation from a source; *also* : CAUSE 3 : the intersection of coordinate axes

¹**orig·i·nal** \ə-'ri-jə-nəl\ *n* : something from which a copy, reproduction, or translation is made : PROTOTYPE

²**original** *adj* 1 : FIRST, INITIAL 2 : not copied from something else : FRESH 3 : INVENTIVE — **orig·i·nal·i·ty** \-₁ri-jə-la-tē\ *n* — **orig·i·nal·ly** \-'ri-jə-nə-lē\ *adv*

orig·i·nate \ə-'ri-jə-₁nāt\ *vb* **-nat·ed; -nat·ing** 1 : to give rise to : INITIATE 2 : to come into existence : BEGIN — **orig·i·na·tor** \-₁nā-tər\ *n*

ori·ole \'ôr-ē-₁ōl\ *n* : any of various New World birds of which the males are usu. black and yellow or black and orange

or·i·son \'ôr-ə-sən\ *n* : PRAYER

or·mo·lu \'ôr-mə-₁lü\ *n* : a golden or gilded brass used for decorative purposes

¹**or·na·ment** \'ôr-nə-mənt\ *n* : something

that lends grace or beauty — **or·na·men·tal** \₁ôr-nə-'men-t⁰l\ *adj*

²**or·na·ment** \-₁ment\ *vb* : to provide with ornament : ADORN — **or·na·men·ta·tion** \₁ôr-nə-mən-'tā-shən\ *n*

or·nate \ôr-'nāt\ *adj* : elaborately decorated ⟨an ∼ mantel⟩ — **or·nate·ly** *adv* — **or·nate·ness** *n*

or·nery \'ôr-nə-rē, 'ä-nə-\ *adj* : having an irritable disposition

or·ni·thol·o·gy \₁ôr-nə-'thä-lə-jē\ *n, pl* **-gies** : a branch of zoology dealing with birds — **or·ni·tho·log·i·cal** \-thə-'lä-ji-kəl\ *adj* — **or·ni·thol·o·gist** \-'thä-lə-jist\ *n*

oro·tund \'ôr-ə-₁tənd\ *adj* 1 : SONOROUS ⟨an ∼ voice⟩ 2 : POMPOUS ⟨an ∼ speech⟩ — **oro·tun·di·ty** \₁ôr-ə-'tən-di-tē\ *n*

or·phan \'ôr-fən\ *n* : a child deprived by death of one or usu. both parents — **or·phan** *vb*

or·phan·age \'ôr-fə-nij\ *n* : an institution for the care of orphans

or·tho·don·tia \₁ôr-thə-'dän-chə, -chē-ə\ *n* : ORTHODONTICS

or·tho·don·tics \₁ôr-thə-'dän-tiks\ *n* : a branch of dentistry concerned with the correction of faults in the arrangement and placing of the teeth — **or·tho·don·tic** \-tik\ *adj* — **or·tho·don·tist** \-'dän-tist\ *n*

or·tho·dox \'ôr-thə-₁däks\ *adj* [ME *orthodoxe*, fr. MF or LL; MF *orthodoxe*, fr. LL *orthodoxus*, fr. LGk *orthodoxos*, fr. Gk *orthos* right + *doxa* opinion] 1 : conforming to established doctrine esp. in religion 2 : CONVENTIONAL 3 *cap* : of or relating to a Christian church originating in the church of the Eastern Roman Empire — **or·tho·doxy** \-₁däk-sē\ *n*

or·thog·ra·phy \ôr-'thä-grə-fē\ *n* : SPELLING — **or·tho·graph·ic** \₁ôr-thə-'gra-fik\ *adj*

or·tho·pe·dics *also* **or·tho·pae·dics** \₁ôr-thə-'pē-diks\ *n sing or pl* : a branch of medicine concerned with the correction or prevention of skeletal injuries or disorders — **or·tho·pe·dic** *also* **or·tho·pae·dic** \-dik\ *adj* — **or·tho·pe·dist** \-dist\ *n*

-ory *adj suffix* 1 : of, relating to, or characterized by ⟨anticipat*ory*⟩ 2 : serving for, producing, or maintaining ⟨illus*ory*⟩

Os *symbol* osmium

OS *abbr* 1 [L *oculus sinister*] left eye 2 ordinary seaman 3 out of stock

Osage \ō-'sāj\ *n, pl* **Osag·es** *or* **Osage** : a member of an American Indian people orig. of Missouri

os·cil·late \'ä-sə-₁lāt\ *vb* **-lat·ed; -lat·ing** 1 : to swing backward and forward like a pendulum 2 : to move or travel back and forth between two points 3 : VARY, FLUCTUATE — **os·cil·la·tion** \₁ä-sə-'lā-shən\ *n* — **os·cil·la·tor** \'ä-sə-₁lā-tər\ *n* — **os·cil·la·to·ry** \'ä-sə-lə-₁tôr-ē\ *adj*

os·cil·lo·scope \ä-'si-lə-₁skōp\ *n* : an instrument in which variations in current or voltage appear as a visible wave form on a fluorescent screen

os·cu·late \'äs-kyə-₁lāt\ *vb* **-lat·ed; -lat·ing** : KISS — **os·cu·la·tion** \₁äs-kyə-'lā-shən\ *n* — **os·cu·la·to·ry** \'äs-kyə-lə-ˌtōr-ē\ *adj*

Osee \'ō-ˌzē, ō-'zā-ə\ *n* : HOSEA

OSHA \'ō-shə\ *abbr* Occupational Safety and Health Administration

osier \'ō-zhər\ *n* : any of various willows with pliable twigs used esp. in making baskets and furniture; *also* : a twig from an osier

os·mi·um \'äz-mē-əm\ *n* : a very heavy hard brittle metallic chemical element used esp. as a catalyst and in alloys

os·mo·sis \äz-'mō-səs, äs-\ *n* : movement of a solvent through a semipermeable membrane into a solution of higher concentration that tends to equalize the concentrations of the solutions on either side of the membrane — **os·mot·ic** \-'mä-tik\ *adj*

os·prey \'äs-prē, -ˌprā\ *n, pl* **ospreys** : a large dark brown and white fish-eating hawk

os·si·fy \'ä-sə-ˌfī\ *vb* **-fied; -fy·ing** : to make or become hardened or set in one's ways ⟨an ossified regime⟩ — **os·si·fi·ca·tion** \ˌä-sə-fə-'kā-shən\ *n*

os·su·ary \'ä-shə-ˌwer-ē, -syə-\ *n, pl* **-ar·ies** : a depository for the bones of the dead

os·ten·si·ble \ä-'sten-sə-bəl\ *adj* : shown outwardly : PROFESSED, APPARENT — **os·ten·si·bly** \-blē\ *adv*

os·ten·ta·tion \ˌäs-tən-'tā-shən\ *n* : pretentious or excessive display — **os·ten·ta·tious** \-shəs\ *adj* — **os·ten·ta·tious·ly** *adv*

os·te·o·ar·thri·tis \ˌäs-tē-ō-är-'thrī-təs\ *n* : arthritis marked by degeneration of the cartilage and bone of joints

os·teo·path \'äs-tē-ə-ˌpath\ *n* : a practitioner of osteopathy

os·te·op·a·thy \ˌäs-tē-'ä-pə-thē\ *n* : a system of treating diseases emphasizing manipulation (as of joints) but not excluding other agencies (as the use of medicine and surgery) — **os·teo·path·ic** \ˌäs-tē-ə-'pa-thik\ *adj*

os·teo·po·ro·sis \ˌäs-tē-ō-pə-'rō-səs\ *n, pl* **-ro·ses** \-ˌsēz\ : a condition affecting esp. older women and characterized by fragile and porous bones

os·tra·cise *Brit var of* OSTRACIZE

os·tra·cize \'äs-trə-ˌsīz\ *vb* **-cized; -ciz·ing** [Gk *ostrakizein* to banish by voting with potsherds, fr. *ostrakon* shell, potsherd] : to exclude from a group by common consent — **os·tra·cism** \-ˌsi-zəm\ *n*

os·trich \'äs-trich, 'ös-\ *n* : a very large swift-footed flightless bird of Africa

Os·we·go tea \ä-'swē-gō-\ *n* : a No. American mint with showy scarlet flowers

OT *abbr* 1 occupational therapy 2 Old Testament 3 overtime

¹**oth·er** \'ə-thər\ *adj* 1 : being the one left; *also* : being the ones distinct from those first mentioned ⟨every ∼ day⟩ 3 : DIFFERENT 4 : ADDITIONAL 5 : recently past ⟨the ∼ night⟩

²**other** *pron* 1 : remaining one or ones 2 : a different or additional one ⟨something or ∼⟩

oth·er·wise \'ə-thər-ˌwīz\ *adv* 1 : in a different way 2 : in different circumstances 3 : in other respects 4 : if not 5 : NOT — **otherwise** *adj*

oth·er·world \-ˌwərld\ *n* : a world beyond death or beyond present reality

oth·er·world·ly \ˌə-thər-'wərld-lē\ *adj* : not worldly : concerned with spiritual, intellectual, or imaginative matters

oti·ose \'ō-shē-ˌōs, 'ō-tē-\ *adj* 1 : FUTILE 2 : IDLE 3 : USELESS ⟨∼ details⟩

oto·lar·yn·gol·o·gy \ˌō-tō-ˌla-rən-'gä-lə-jē\ *n* : a medical specialty concerned esp. with the ear, nose, and throat — **oto·lar·yn·gol·o·gist** \-jist\ *n*

oto·rhi·no·lar·yn·gol·o·gy \ˌō-tō-ˌrī-nō-ˌla-rən-'gä-lə-jē\ *n* : OTOLARYNGOLOGY — **oto·rhi·no·lar·yn·gol·o·gist** \-jist\ *n*

OTS *abbr* officers' training school

Ot·ta·wa \'ä-tə-wə, -ˌwä, -ˌwȯ\ *n, pl* **Otta·was** *or* **Ottawa** : a member of an American Indian people of Michigan and southern Ontario

ot·ter \'ä-tər\ *n, pl* **otters** *also* **otter** : any of various web-footed fish-eating mammals with dark brown fur that are related to the weasels; *also* : the fur

ot·to·man \'ä-tə-mən\ *n* : an upholstered seat or couch usu. without a back; *also* : an overstuffed footstool

ou·bli·ette \ˌü-blē-'et\ *n* [F, fr. MF, fr. *oublier* to forget, ultim. fr. L *oblivisci*] : a dungeon with an opening at the top

ought \'ȯt\ *verbal auxiliary* — used to express moral obligation, advisability, natural expectation, or logical consequence ⟨you ∼ to apologize⟩

ou·gui·ya \ü-'gwē-ə, -'gē-\ *n, pl* **ouguiya** — see MONEY table

ounce \'aúns\ *n* [ME, fr. AF *unce*, fr. L *uncia* twelfth part, ounce, fr. *unus* one] 1 : a unit of avoirdupois, troy, and apothecaries' weight — see WEIGHT table 2 : FLUID OUNCE

our \är, 'aú(-ə)r\ *adj* : of or relating to us or ourselves

ours \'aúr(-ə)z, 'ärz\ *pron* : that which belongs to us

our·selves \är-'selvz, aú(-ə)r-\ *pron* : our own selves — used reflexively, for emphasis, or in absolute constructions ⟨we pleased ∼⟩ ⟨we'll do it ∼⟩ ⟨we were tourists ∼⟩

-ous *adj suffix* : full of : abounding in : having : possessing the qualities of ⟨clamorous⟩ ⟨poisonous⟩

oust \'aúst\ *vb* : to eject from or deprive of property or position : EXPEL ♦ *Synonyms* EVICT, DISMISS, BANISH, DEPORT

oust·er \'aús-tər\ *n* : EXPULSION

¹**out** \'aút\ *adv* 1 : in a direction away from the inside or center 2 : beyond control 3 : to extinction, exhaustion, or completion 4 : in or into the open 5 : so as to retire a batter or base runner; *also* : so as to be retired

²**out** *vb* : to become known ⟨the truth will ∼⟩

³**out** *prep* 1 : out through ⟨looked ∼ the window⟩ 2 : outward on or along ⟨drive ∼ the river road⟩

⁴**out** *adj* 1 : situated outside or at a dis-

tance **2** : not in : ABSENT; *also* : not being in power **3** : removed from play as a batter or base runner **4** : not being in vogue or fashion : not up-to-date **5** : attempting a particular activity 〈won his first time ∼〉

⁵**out** *n* **1** : one who is out of office **2** : the retiring of a batter or base runner

out-age \'aù-tij\ *n* : a period or instance of interruption esp. of electricity

out-and-out *adj* : COMPLETE, THOROUGHGOING 〈an ∼ fraud〉

out-bid \‚aùt-'bid\ *vb* : to make a higher bid than

¹**out-board** \'aùt-‚bòrd\ *adj* **1** : situated outboard **2** : having or using an outboard motor

²**outboard** *adv* **1** : outside a ship's hull **2** : away from the long axis of a ship **3** : in a position closer to the wing tip of an airplane

outboard motor *n* : a small internal combustion engine with propeller attached for mounting at the stern of a small boat

out-bound \'aùt-‚baùnd\ *adj* : outward bound 〈∼ traffic〉

out-break \-‚bràk\ *n* **1** : a sudden increase in activity, incidence, or numbers **2** : INSURRECTION, REVOLT

out-build-ing \-‚bil-diŋ\ *n* : a building separate from but accessory to a main house

out-burst \-‚bərst\ *n* : ERUPTION; *esp* : a violent expression of feeling

out-cast \-‚kast\ *n* : one that is cast out by society

out-class \aùt-'klas\ *vb* : SURPASS

out-come \'aùt-‚kəm\ *n* : a final consequence : RESULT

out-crop \-‚kräp\ *n* : a coming out of bedrock to the surface of the ground; *also* : the part of a rock formation that thus appears — **outcrop** *vb*

out-cry \-‚krī\ *n* : a loud cry : CLAMOR

out-dat-ed \'dā-təd\ *adj* : OUTMODED

out-dis-tance \-'dis-təns\ *vb* : to go far ahead of (as in a race) : OUTSTRIP

out-do \-'dü\ *vb* **-did** \-'did\; **-done** \-'dən\; **-do-ing; -does** \-'dəz\ : to go beyond in action or performance

out-door \'aùt-‚dòr, -'dòr\ *also* **out-doors** \-‚dòrz, -'dòrz\ *adj* **1** : of or relating to the outdoors **2** : performed outdoors **3** : not enclosed (as by a roof)

¹**out-doors** \'aùt-‚dòrz, -'dòrz\ *adv* : in or into the open air

²**outdoors** *n* **1** : the open air **2** : the world away from human habitation — **outdoorsy** \‚aùt-'dòr-zē\ *adj*

out-draw \aùt-'dròʌ *vb* **-drew** \-'drü\; **-drawn** \-'dròn\; **-draw-ing 1** : to attract a larger audience than **2** : to draw a handgun more quickly than

¹**out-er** \'aù-tər\ *adj* **1** : EXTERNAL **2** : situated farther out; *also* : being away from a center

outer ear *n* : the outer visible portion of the ear that collects and directs sound waves toward the eardrum

out-er-most \-‚mōst\ *adj* : farthest out

outer space *n* : SPACE 5

out-er-wear \'aù-tər-‚wer\ *n* **1** : clothing

for outdoor wear **2** : outer clothing as opposed to underwear

out-face \aùt-'fās\ *vb* **1** : to cause to waver or submit **2** : DEFY

out-field \'aùt-‚fēld\ *n* : the part of a baseball field beyond the infield and within the foul lines; *also* : players in the outfield — **out-field-er** \-‚fēl-dər\ *n*

out-fight \aùt-'fīt\ *vb* : to surpass in fighting : DEFEAT

¹**out-fit** \'aùt-‚fit\ *n* **1** : the equipment or apparel for a special purpose or occasion **2** : GROUP 〈an insurance ∼〉

²**outfit** *vb* **out-fit-ted; out-fit-ting** : EQUIP — **out-fit-ter** *n*

out-flank \aùt-'flaŋk\ *vb* : to get around the flank of (an opposing force)

out-flow \'aùt-‚flō\ *n* **1** : a flowing out **2** : something that flows out

out-fox \aùt-'fäks\ *vb* : OUTWIT

out-go \'aùt-‚gō\ *n, pl* **outgoes** : EXPENDITURES, OUTLAY

out-go-ing \-‚gō-iŋ\ *adj* **1** : going out 〈∼ tide〉 **2** : retiring from a place or position **3** : FRIENDLY

out-grow \aùt-'grō\ *vb* **-grew** \-'grü\; **-grown** \-'grōn\; **-grow-ing 1** : to grow faster than **2** : to grow too large for

out-growth \'aùt-‚grōth\ *n* : a product of growing out : OFFSHOOT; *also* : CONSEQUENCE, RESULT

out-guess \aùt-'ges\ *vb* : OUTWIT

out-gun \-'gən\ *vb* : to surpass in firepower

out-house \'aùt-‚haùs\ *n* : OUTBUILDING; *esp* : an outdoor toilet

out-ing \'aù-tiŋ\ *n* : a brief stay or trip in the open 〈a family ∼〉

out-land-ish \aùt-'lan-dish\ *adj* **1** : of foreign appearance or manner; *also* : BIZARRE **2** : remote from civilization — **out-land-ish-ly** *adv*

out-last \-'last\ *vb* : to last longer than

¹**out-law** \'aùt-‚lò\ *n* **1** : a person excluded from the protection of the law **2** : a lawless person

²**outlaw** *vb* **1** : to deprive of the protection of the law **2** : to make illegal — **out-law-ry** \'aùt-‚lòr-ē\ *n*

out-lay \'aùt-‚lā\ *n* **1** : the act of spending **2** : EXPENDITURE

out-let \'aùt-‚let, -lət\ *n* **1** : EXIT, VENT **2** : a means of release (as for an emotion) **3** : a medium for usu. public expression : a media organization **4** : a market for a commodity **5** : a receptacle for the plug of an electrical device

¹**out-line** \'aùt-‚līn\ *n* **1** : a line marking the outer limits of an object or figure **2** : a drawing in which only contours are marked **3** : SUMMARY, SYNOPSIS 〈an ∼ of the novel〉 **4** : PLAN

²**outline** *vb* **1** : to draw the outline of **2** : to indicate the chief features or parts of

out-live \aùt-'liv\ *vb* : to live longer than

♦ *Synonyms* OUTLAST, SURVIVE

out-look \'aùt-‚lùk\ *n* **1** : a place offering a view; *also* : VIEW **2** : STANDPOINT **3** : the prospect for the future

out-ly-ing \-‚lī-iŋ\ *adj* : distant from a center or main body

out-ma-neu-ver \‚aùt-mə-'nü-vər, -'nyü-\

vb : to defeat by more skillful maneuvering

out·mod·ed \aut-'mō-dəd\ *adj* 1 : no longer in style 2 : no longer acceptable or current ⟨∼ technology⟩

out·num·ber \-'nəm-bər\ *vb* : to exceed in number

out of *prep* 1 : out from within or behind ⟨walk *out of* the room⟩ ⟨look *out of* the window⟩ 2 : from a state of ⟨wake up *out of* a deep sleep⟩ 3 : beyond the limits of ⟨*out of* sight⟩ 4 : BECAUSE OF ⟨asked *out of* curiosity⟩ 5 : FROM, WITH ⟨built it *out of* scrap⟩ 6 : in or into a state of loss or not having ⟨cheated him *out of* $5000⟩ ⟨we're *out of* matches⟩ 7 : from among ⟨one *out of* four⟩ — **out of it** : SQUARE, OLD-FASHIONED

out-of-bounds *adv or adj* : outside the prescribed boundaries or limits

out-of-date *adj* : no longer in fashion or in use : OUTMODED

out-of-door *or* **out-of-doors** *adj* : OUTDOOR

out-of-the-way *adj* 1 : UNUSUAL 2 : being off the beaten track

out·pa·tient \'aut-,pā-shənt\ *n* : a patient who visits a hospital or clinic for diagnosis or treatment without staying overnight

out·per·form \,aut-pər-'fȯrm\ *vb* : to perform better than

out·play \aut-'plā\ *vb* : to play more skillfully than

out·point \-'pȯint\ *vb* : to win more points than

out·post \'aut-,pōst\ *n* 1 : a security detachment dispatched by a main body of troops to protect it from enemy surprise; *also* : a military base established (as by treaty) in a foreign country 2 : an outlying or frontier settlement

out·pour·ing \-,pȯr-iŋ\ *n* : something that pours out or is poured out

out·pull \aut-'pul\ *vb* : OUTDRAW 1

¹**out·put** \'aut-,put\ *n* 1 : the amount produced (as by a machine or factory) : PRODUCTION 2 : the information produced by a computer

²**output** *vb* **out·put·ted** *or* **output; out·put·ting** : to produce as output

¹**out·rage** \'aut-,rāj\ *n* [ME, fr. AF *utrage, outrage* insult, excess, fr. *utre, outre* beyond, fr. L *ultra*] 1 : a violent or shameful act 2 : INJURY, INSULT 3 : the anger or resentment aroused by injury or insult

²**outrage** *vb* **out·raged; out·rag·ing** 1 : RAPE 2 : to subject to violent injury or gross insult 3 : to arouse to extreme resentment

out·ra·geous \aut-'rā-jəs\ *adj* : extremely offensive, insulting, or shameful : SHOCKING — **out·ra·geous·ly** *adv*

out·rank \-'raŋk\ *vb* : to rank higher than

ou·tré \ü-'trā\ *adj* [F] : violating convention or propriety : BIZARRE ⟨∼ creations⟩

¹**out·reach** \aut-'rēch\ *vb* 1 : to surpass in reach 2 : to get the better of by trickery

²**out·reach** \'aut-,rēch\ *n* 1 : the act of reaching out 2 : the extent of reach 3

: the extending of services beyond usual limits

out·rid·er \-,rī-dər\ *n* : a mounted attendant

out·rig·ger \-,ri-gər\ *n* 1 : a frame attached to the side of a boat to prevent capsizing 2 : a craft equipped with an outrigger

¹**out·right** \aut-'rīt\ *adv* 1 : COMPLETELY 2 : INSTANTANEOUSLY

²**out·right** \'aut-,rīt\ *adj* 1 : being exactly what is stated ⟨an ∼ lie⟩ 2 : given or made without reservation or encumbrance ⟨an ∼ sale⟩

out·run \aut-'rən\ *vb* **-ran** \-'ran\; **-run; -run·ning** : to run faster than; *also* : EXCEED

out·sell \-'sel\ *vb* **-sold** \-'sōld\; **-sell·ing** : to exceed in sales

out·set \'aut-,set\ *n* : BEGINNING, START

out·shine \aut-'shīn\ *vb* **-shone** \-'shōn\ *or* **-shined; -shin·ing** 1 : to shine brighter than 2 : SURPASS

¹**out·side** \aut-'sīd, 'aut-,sīd\ *n* 1 : a place or region beyond an enclosure or boundary 2 : EXTERIOR 3 : the utmost limit or extent

²**outside** *adj* 1 : OUTER 2 : coming from without ⟨∼ influences⟩ 3 : being apart from one's regular duties ⟨∼ activities⟩ 4 : REMOTE ⟨an ∼ chance⟩

³**outside** *adv* : on or to the outside

⁴**outside** *prep* 1 : on or to the outside of 2 : beyond the limits of 3 : EXCEPT

outside of *prep* 1 : OUTSIDE 2 : BESIDES

out·sid·er \aut-'sī-dər\ *n* : a person who does not belong to a group

out·size \'aut-,sīz\ *also* **out·sized** \-,sīzd\ *adj* : unusually large : extravagant in size or degree

out·skirts \-,skərts\ *n pl* : the outlying parts (as of a city) : BORDERS

out·smart \aut-'smärt\ *vb* : OUTWIT

out·source \'aut-,sȯrs\ *vb* **-sourced; -sourc·ing** : to obtain (goods or services) from an outside supplier

out·spend \-'spend\ *vb* 1 : to exceed the limits of in spending ⟨∼s his income⟩ 2 : to spend more than

out·spo·ken \aut-'spō-kən\ *adj* : direct and open in speech or expression — **out·spo·ken·ly** *adv* — **out·spo·ken·ness** *n*

out·spread \-'spred\ *vb* **-spread; -spread·ing** : to spread out

out·stand·ing \-'stan-diŋ\ *adj* 1 : PROJECTING 2 : UNPAID; *also* : UNRESOLVED ⟨∼ warrants⟩ 3 : publicly issued and sold 4 : CONSPICUOUS; *also* : DISTINGUISHED — **out·stand·ing·ly** *adv*

out·stay \-'stā\ *vb* 1 : OVERSTAY 2 : to surpass in endurance

out·stretch \aut-'strech\ *vb* : to stretch out : EXTEND

out·strip \-'strip\ *vb* 1 : to go faster than 2 : EXCEL, SURPASS

out·take \'aut-,tāk\ *n* : something taken out; *esp* : a take that is not used in an edited version of a film or videotape

out·vote \-'vōt\ *vb* : to defeat by a majority of votes

¹**out·ward** \'aut-wərd\ *adj* 1 : moving or

directed toward the outside **2** : showing outwardly

²**outward** or **out·wards** \-wərdz\ adv : toward the outside

out·ward·ly \-wərd-lē\ adv : on the outside : EXTERNALLY

out·wear \aut-'wer\ vb **-wore** \-'wōr\; **-worn** \-'wōrn\; **-wear·ing** : to wear longer than : OUTLAST

out·weigh \-'wā\ vb : to exceed in weight, value, or importance

out·wit \-'wit\ vb : to get the better of by superior cleverness

¹**out·work** \-'wərk\ vb : to outdo in working

²**out·work** \'aut-,wərk\ n : a minor defensive position outside a fortified area

out·worn \aut-'wōrn\ adj : OUTMODED

ou·zo \'ü-(,)zō\ n : a colorless anise-flavored unsweetened Greek liqueur

ova pl of OVUM

oval \'ō-vəl\ adj [ML ovalis, fr. LL, of an egg, fr. L ovum egg] : egg-shaped; also : broadly elliptical — **oval** n

ova·ry \'ō-və-rē\ n, pl **-ries** **1** : one of the usu. paired female reproductive organs producing eggs and in vertebrates sex hormones **2** : the part of a flower in which seeds are produced — **ovar·i·an** \ō-'ver-ē-ən\ adj

ovate \'ō-,vāt\ adj : egg-shaped

ova·tion \ō-'vā-shən\ n [L ovation-, ovatio, fr. ovare to exult] : an enthusiastic popular tribute

ov·en \'ə-vən\ n : a chamber (as in a stove) for baking, heating, or drying

oven·bird \-,bərd\ n : a large olive-green American warbler that builds its dome-shaped nest on the ground

¹**over** \'ō-vər\ adv **1** : across a barrier or intervening space **2** : across the brim ⟨boil ~⟩ **3** : so as to bring the underside up **4** : out of a vertical position **5** : beyond some quantity, limit, or norm **6** : ABOVE **7** : at an end **8** : THROUGH ⟨read it ~⟩; also : THOROUGHLY ⟨still thinking it ~⟩ **9** : AGAIN ⟨do it ~⟩

²**over** prep **1** : above in position, authority, or scope ⟨towered ~ her⟩ ⟨obeyed those ~ him⟩ **2** : more than ⟨cost ~ $100⟩ **3** : ON, UPON ⟨a cape ~ her shoulders⟩ **4** : along the length of ⟨~ the road⟩ **5** : through the medium of : ON ⟨spoke ~ TV⟩ **6** : all through ⟨showed me ~ the house⟩ **7** : on or to the other side or beyond ⟨jump ~ a ditch⟩ **8** : DURING ⟨~ the past 25 years⟩ **9** : on account of ⟨trouble ~ money⟩

³**over** adj **1** : UPPER, HIGHER **2** : REMAINING **3** : ENDED ⟨those days are ~⟩

over- prefix **1** : so as to exceed or surpass **2** : excessive; excessively

over·act \,ō-vər-'akt\ vb : to exaggerate in acting

¹**over·age** \,ō-vər-'āj\ adj **1** : too old to be useful **2** : older than is normal for one's position, function, or grade

²**over·age** \'ō-və-rij\ n : SURPLUS

over·all \,ō-vər-'ol\ adj : including everything ⟨~ expenses⟩

over·alls \'ō-vər-,olz\ n pl : pants of strong material usu. with a piece extending up to cover the chest

over·arm \-,ärm\ adj : done with the arm raised above the shoulder

over·awe \,ō-vər-'o\ vb : to restrain or subdue by awe

over·bal·ance \-'ba-ləns\ vb **1** : OUTWEIGH **2** : to cause to lose balance

over·bear·ing \-'ber-iŋ\ adj : ARROGANT, DOMINEERING

over·bite \'ō-vər-,bit\ n : the projection of the upper front teeth over the lower

over·blown \-'blōn\ adj **1** : PORTLY **2** : INFLATED, PRETENTIOUS

over·board \'ō-vər-,bōrd\ adv **1** : over the side of a ship into the water **2** : to extremes of enthusiasm

¹**over·cast** \'ō-vər-,kast\ adj : clouded over : GLOOMY

²**overcast** n : COVERING; esp : a covering of clouds

over·charge \,ō-vər-'chärj\ vb **1** : to charge too much **2** : to fill or load too full — **over·charge** \'ō-vər-,chärj\ n

over·coat \'ō-vər-,kōt\ n : a warm coat worn over indoor clothing

over·come \,ō-vər-'kəm\ vb **-came** \-'kām\; **-come**; **-com·ing** **1** : CONQUER **2** : to make helpless or exhausted

over·do \,ō-vər-'dü\ vb **-did** \-'did\; **-done** \-'dən\; **-do·ing**; **-does** \-'dəz\ **1** : to do too much; also : to tire oneself **2** : EXAGGERATE **3** : to cook too long

over·dose \'ō-vər-,dōs\ n : too great a dose (as of medicine); also : a lethal or toxic amount (as of a drug) — **over·dose** \,ō-vər-'dōs\ vb

over·draft \'ō-vər-,draft\ n : an overdrawing of a bank account; also : the sum overdrawn

over·draw \,ō-vər-'dro\ vb **-drew** \-'drü\; **-drawn** \-'dron\; **-draw·ing** **1** : to draw checks on a bank account for more than the balance **2** : EXAGGERATE

over·drive \'ō-vər-,drīv\ n : an automotive transmission gear that transmits to the driveshaft a speed greater than the engine speed

over·dub \,ō-vər-'dəb\ vb : to transfer (recorded sound) onto an earlier recording for a combined effect — **over·dub** \'ō-vər-,dəb\ n

over·due \-'dü, -'dyü\ adj **1** : unpaid when due ⟨an ~ bill⟩; also : not appearing or presented on time ⟨an ~ train⟩ **2** : more than ready

---

overabundance	overbid	overcareful	overcritical
overabundant	overbold	overcautious	overcrowd
overachiever	overbuild	overcompensation	overdecorated
overactive	overburden	overconfidence	overdependence
overaggressive	overbuy	overconfident	overdetermined
overambitious	overcapacity	overconscientious	overdevelop
overanxious	overcapitalize	overcook	overdress

overexpose • oversee

over·ex·pose \ˌō-vər-ik-ˈspōz\ vb : to expose (as film) for more time than is needed — **over·ex·po·sure** \-ˈspō-zhər\ n

¹**over·flow** \-ˈflō\ vb 1 : INUNDATE; also : to pour forth in a flood 2 : to flow over the brim or top of

²**over·flow** \ˈō-vər-ˌflō\ n 1 : FLOOD; also : SURPLUS 2 : an outlet for surplus liquid

over·fly \ˌō-vər-ˈflī\ vb -flew \-ˈflü\; -flown \-ˈflōn\; -fly·ing : to fly over in an aircraft or spacecraft — **over·flight** \ˈō-vər-ˌflīt\ n

over·grow \ˌō-vər-ˈgrō\ vb -grew \-ˈgrü\; -grown \-ˈgrōn\; -grow·ing 1 : to grow over so as to cover 2 : OUTGROW 3 : to grow excessively — **over·growth** \ˈō-vər-ˌgrōth\ n

over·hand \ˈō-vər-ˌhand\ adj : made with the hand brought down from above — **overhand** adv — **over·hand·ed** \-ˌhan-dəd\ adv or adj

¹**over·hang** \ˈō-vər-ˌhaŋ, ˌō-vər-ˈhaŋ\ vb -hung \-ˌhəŋ, -ˈhəŋ\; -hang·ing 1 : to project over : jut out 2 : to hang over threateningly

²**over·hang** \ˈō-vər-ˌhaŋ\ n : a part (as of a roof) that overhangs

over·haul \ˌō-vər-ˈhol\ vb 1 : to examine thoroughly and make necessary repairs and adjustments 2 : OVERTAKE

¹**over·head** \ˌō-vər-ˈhed\ adv : ALOFT

²**over·head** \ˈō-vər-ˌhed\ adj : operating or lying above ⟨∼ storage bins⟩

³**over·head** \ˈō-vər-ˌhed\ n : business expenses not chargeable to a particular part of the work

over·hear \ˌō-vər-ˈhir\ vb -heard \-ˈhərd\; -hear·ing : to hear without the speaker's knowledge or intention

over·joyed \ˌō-vər-ˈjoid\ adj : filled with great joy

over·kill \ˈō-vər-ˌkil\ n 1 : destructive capacity greatly exceeding that required for a target 2 : a large excess

over·land \ˈō-vər-ˌland, -lənd\ adv or adj : by, on, or across land

over·lap \ˌō-vər-ˈlap\ vb 1 : to lap over 2 : to have something in common — **over·lap** \ˈō-vər-ˌlap\ n

over·lay \ˌō-vər-ˈlā\ vb -laid \-ˈlād\; -lay·ing : to lay or spread over or across — **over·lay** \ˈō-vər-ˌlā\ n

over·leap \ˌō-vər-ˈlēp\ vb -leaped or -leapt \-ˈlēpt, -ˈlept\; -leap·ing 1 : to leap over or across 2 : to defeat (oneself) by going too far

over·lie \ˌō-vər-ˈlī\ vb -lay \-ˈlā\; -lain \-ˈlān\; -ly·ing : to lie over or upon

¹**over·look** \ˌō-vər-ˈlúk\ vb 1 : INSPECT 2 : to look down on from above 3 : to fail

to see 4 : IGNORE ⟨∼ed his faults⟩; also : EXCUSE 5 : SUPERINTEND

²**over·look** \ˈō-vər-ˌlúk\ n : a place from which to look upon a scene below

over·lord \-ˌlórd\ n : a lord who has supremacy over other lords

over·ly \ˈō-vər-lē\ adv : EXCESSIVELY

over·match \ˌō-vər-ˈmach\ vb : to be more than a match for : DEFEAT

over·much \-ˈməch\ adj or adv : too much

¹**over·night** \-ˈnīt\ adv 1 : on or during the night 2 : SUDDENLY ⟨became famous ∼⟩

²**overnight** adj : of, lasting, or staying the night ⟨∼ guests⟩

over·pass \ˈō-vər-ˌpas\ n 1 : a crossing (as of two highways) at different levels by means of a bridge 2 : the upper level of an overpass

over·play \ˌō-vər-ˈplā\ vb 1 : EXAGGERATE; also : OVEREMPHASIZE 2 : to rely too much on the strength of

over·pop·u·la·tion \ˌō-vər-ˌpä-pyə-ˈlā-shən\ n : the condition of having a population so dense as to cause a decline in population or in living conditions — **over·pop·u·lat·ed** \-ˈpä-pyə-ˌlā-təd\ adj

over·pow·er \-ˈpaú-(ə)r\ vb : to overcome by superior force

over·price \ˌō-vər-ˈprīs\ vb : to price too high

over·print \-ˈprint\ vb : to print over with something additional — **over·print** \ˈō-vər-ˌprint\ n

over·qual·i·fied \-ˈkwä-lə-ˌfīd\ adj : having more education, experience, or experience than a job calls for

over·reach \ˌō-vər-ˈrēch\ vb : to defeat (oneself) by too great an effort

over·ride \-ˈrīd\ vb -rode \-ˈrōd\; -rid·den \-ˈri-dᵊn\; -rid·ing 1 : to ride over or across 2 : to prevail over; also : to set aside ⟨∼ a veto⟩

over·rule \-ˈrül\ vb 1 : to prevail over 2 : to rule against 3 : to set aside

¹**over·run** \-ˈrən\ vb -ran \-ˈran\; -run·ning 1 : to defeat and occupy the positions of 2 : OVERSPREAD; also : INFEST 3 : to go beyond 4 : to flow over

²**over·run** \ˈō-vər-ˌrən\ n 1 : an act or instance of overrunning; esp : an exceeding of estimated costs 2 : the amount by which something overruns

over·sea \ˌō-vər-ˈsē, ˈō-vər-ˌsē\ adj or adv : OVERSEAS

over·seas \ˌō-vər-ˈsēz, -ˌsēz\ adv or adj : beyond or across the sea : ABROAD

over·see \ˌō-vər-ˈsē\ vb -saw \-ˈsó\; -seen \-ˈsēn\; -see·ing 1 : OVERLOOK 2

overeager	overfatigued	overindulgent	overproduce
overeat	overfeed	overinflate	overproduction
overeducated	overfill	overlarge	overprotect
overemphasis	overgeneralization	overlearn	overprotective
overemphasize	overgeneralize	overload	overrate
overenthusiastic	overgenerous	overlong	overreact
overestimate	overgraze	overmodest	overreaction
overexcite	overhasty	overnice	overrefinement
overexcited	overheat	overoptimism	overregulate
overexert	overhype	overoptimistic	overreliance
overexertion	overindulge	overpay	overrepresented
overextend	overindulgence	overpraise	overripe

: INSPECT; *also* : SUPERVISE ⟨~ the project⟩ — **over·seer** \'ō-vər-ˌsir\ *n*

over·sell \ˌō-vər-'sel\ *vb* **-sold; -sel·ling** : to sell too much to or too much of

over·sexed \ˌō-vər-'sekst\ *adj* : exhibiting excessive sexual drive or interest

over·shad·ow \-'sha-dō\ *vb* 1 : to cast a shadow over 2 : to exceed in importance

over·shoe \'ō-vər-ˌshü\ *n* : a protective outer shoe; *esp* : GALOSH

over·shoot \ˌō-vər-'shüt\ *vb* **-shot** \-'shät\; **-shoot·ing** 1 : to pass swiftly beyond 2 : to shoot over or beyond

over·sight \'ō-vər-ˌsīt\ *n* 1 : SUPERVISION 2 : an inadvertent omission or error

over·size \ˌō-vər-'sīz\ *or* **over·sized** \-'sīzd\ *adj* : of more than ordinary size

over·sleep \ˌō-vər-'slēp\ *vb* **-slept** \-'slept\; **-sleep·ing** : to sleep beyond the time for waking

over·spread \-'spred\ *vb* **-spread; -spread·ing** : to spread over or above

over·state \-'stāt\ *vb* : EXAGGERATE — **over·state·ment** *n*

over·stay \-'stā\ *vb* : to stay beyond the time or limits of ⟨~ed her welcome⟩

over·step \-'step\ *vb* : EXCEED

over·sub·scribe \-səb-'skrīb\ *vb* : to subscribe for more of than is available, asked for, or offered for sale

overt \ō-'vərt, 'ō-ˌvərt\ *adj* [ME, fr. AF, fr. pp. of *ovrir* to open] : not secret ⟨~ hostility⟩ — **overt·ly** *adv*

over·take \ˌō-vər-'tāk\ *vb* **-took** \-'tůk\; **-tak·en** \-'tā-kən\; **-tak·ing** : to catch up with; *also* : to catch up with and pass by ⟨~ the lead runner⟩

over–the–counter *adj* : sold lawfully without a prescription ⟨~ drugs⟩

over–the–hill *adj* 1 : past one's prime 2 : advanced in age

over–the–top *adj* : extremely flamboyant or outrageous ⟨an ~ performance⟩

over·throw \ˌō-vər-'thrō\ *vb* **-threw** \-'thrü\; **-thrown** \-'thrōn\; **-throw·ing** 1 : UPSET 2 : to bring down : DEFEAT ⟨~ a government⟩ 3 : to throw over or past — **over·throw** \'ō-vər-ˌthrō\ *n*

over·time \'ō-vər-ˌtīm\ *n* : time beyond a set limit; *esp* : working time in excess of a standard day or week — **overtime** *adv*

over·tone \-ˌtōn\ *n* 1 : one of the higher tones in a complex musical tone 2 : IMPLICATION, SUGGESTION ⟨political ~s⟩

over·trick \'ō-vər-ˌtrik\ *n* : a card trick won in excess of the number bid

over·ture \'ō-vər-ˌchůr, -chər\ *n* [ME, lit., opening, fr. AF, fr. VL *opertura*, alter. of L *apertura*] 1 : an opening offer 2 : an orchestral introduction to a musical dramatic work

over·turn \ˌō-vər-'tərn\ *vb* 1 : to turn over : UPSET ⟨~ a vase⟩ 2 : INVALIDATE ⟨~ a court ruling⟩

over·view \'ō-vər-ˌvyü\ *n* : a general survey : SUMMARY

over·ween·ing \ˌō-vər-'wē-niŋ\ *adj* 1 : ARROGANT ⟨~ pride⟩ 2 : IMMODERATE

over·weight \'ō-vər-ˌwāt\ *n* 1 : weight above what is required or allowed 2 : bodily weight greater than normal — **overweight** *adj*

over·whelm \ˌō-vər-'hwelm\ *vb* 1 : OVERTHROW 2 : SUBMERGE 3 : to overcome completely

over·whelm·ing *adj* : EXTREME, GREAT ⟨~ joy⟩ — **over·whelm·ing·ly** *adv*

over·win·ter \-'win-tər\ *vb* : to survive or pass the winter

over·work \-'wərk\ *vb* 1 : to work or cause to work too hard or long 2 : to use too much — **overwork** *n*

over·wrought \ˌō-vər-'rót\ *adj* 1 : extremely excited 2 : elaborated to excess

ovi·duct \'ō-və-ˌdəkt\ *n* : a tube that serves for the passage of eggs from an ovary

ovip·a·rous \ō-'vi-pə-rəs\ *adj* : reproducing by eggs that hatch outside the parent's body

ovoid \'ō-ˌvóid\ *or* **ovoi·dal** \ō-'vói-d°l\ *adj* : egg-shaped : OVAL

ovu·la·tion \ˌäv-yə-'lā-shən, ˌōv-\ *n* : the discharge of a mature egg from the ovary — **ovu·late** \'äv-yə-ˌlāt, 'ōv-\ *vb*

ovule \'äv-yül, 'ōv-\ *n* : any of the bodies in a plant ovary that after fertilization become seeds

ovum \'ō-vəm\ *n, pl* **ova** \-və\ : EGG 2

ow \'au\ *interj* — used esp. to express sudden pain

owe \'ō\ *vb* **owed; ow·ing** 1 : to be under obligation to pay or render 2 : to be indebted to or for; *also* : to be in debt

owing to *prep* : BECAUSE OF

owl \'au̇(-ə)l\ *n* : any of an order of chiefly nocturnal birds of prey with a large head and eyes and strong talons — **owl·ish** *adj* — **owl·ish·ly** *adv*

owl·et \'au̇-lət\ *n* : a young or small owl

¹**own** \'ōn\ *adj* : belonging to oneself — used as an intensive after a possessive adjective ⟨her ~ car⟩

²**own** *vb* 1 : to have or hold as property 2 : to have power or mastery over 3 : ACKNOWLEDGE ⟨would not ~ up to his mistake⟩; *also* : CONFESS — **own·er** *n* — **own·er·ship** *n*

³**own** *pron* : one or ones belonging to oneself — **on one's own** : for or by oneself : left to one's own resources

ox \'äks\ *n, pl* **ox·en** \'äk-sən\ *also* **ox** : any of the large domestic bovine mammals kept for milk, draft, and meat; *esp* : an adult castrated male ox

ox·blood \'äks-ˌbləd\ *n* : a moderate reddish brown

ox·bow \-ˌbō\ *n* 1 : a U-shaped collar worn by a draft ox 2 : a U-shaped bend in a river — **oxbow** *adj*

ox·ford \'äks-fərd\ *n* : a low shoe laced or tied over the instep

ox·i·dant \'äk-sə-dənt\ *n* : OXIDIZING AGENT — **oxidant** *adj*

ox·i·da·tion \ˌäk-sə-'dā-shən\ *n* : the act or process of oxidizing; *also* : the condition of being oxidized — **ox·i·da·tive** \'äk-sə-ˌdā-tiv\ *adj*

ox·ide \'äk-ˌsīd\ *n* : a compound of oxygen with another element or group

ox·i·dize \'äk-sə-ˌdīz\ *vb* **-dized; -diz·ing** : to combine with oxygen ⟨iron rusts because it is oxidized by exposure to the air⟩ — **ox·i·diz·er** *n*

oxidizing agent *n* : a substance (as oxygen or nitric acid) that oxidizes by taking up electrons

ox·y·gen \'äk-si-jən\ *n* [F *oxygène*, fr. Gk *oxys* acidic, lit., sharp + *-genēs* giving rise to; so called because it was once thought to be an essential element of all acids] : a colorless odorless gaseous chemical element that is found in the air, is essential to life, and is involved in combustion

ox·y·gen·ate \'äk-si-jə-ˌnāt\ *vb* **-at·ed; -at·ing** : to impregnate, combine, or supply with oxygen — **ox·y·gen·a·tion** \ˌäk-si-jə-'nā-shən\ *n*

oxygen mask *n* : a device worn over the nose and mouth through which oxygen is supplied

oxygen tent *n* : a canopy which can be placed over a bedridden person and within which a flow of oxygen can be maintained

ox·y·mo·ron \ˌäk-sē-'mȯr-ˌän\ *n* : a combination of contradictory words (as *cruel kindness*) — **ox·y·mo·ron·ic** \-mə-'rä-nik\ *adj*

oys·ter \'ȯis-tər\ *n* : any of various marine mollusks with an irregular 2-valved shell that include commercially important edible shellfish and pearl producers — **oys·ter·ing** *n* — **oys·ter·man** \-mən\ *n*

oz *abbr* [obs. It *onza* (now *oncia*)] ounce; ounces

ozone \'ō-ˌzōn\ *n* **1** : a bluish gaseous reactive form of oxygen that is formed naturally in the atmosphere and is used for disinfecting, deodorizing, and bleaching **2** : pure and refreshing air

ozone layer *n* : an atmospheric layer at heights of about 25 miles (40 kilometers) with high ozone content which blocks most solar ultraviolet radiation

¹p \'pē\ *n, pl* **p's** *or* **ps** \'pēz\ *often cap* : the 16th letter of the English alphabet

²p *abbr, often cap* **1** page **2** participle **3** past **4** pawn **5** pence; penny **6** per **7** petite **8** pint **9** pressure **10** purl

P *symbol* phosphorus

pa \'pä, 'pȯ\ *n* : FATHER

¹Pa *abbr* **1** pascal **2** Pennsylvania

²Pa *symbol* protactinium

¹PA \ˌ(ˌ)pē-'ā\ *n* : PHYSICIAN'S ASSISTANT

²PA *abbr* **1** Pennsylvania **2** per annum **3** power of attorney **4** press agent **5** private account **6** professional association **7** public address **8** purchasing agent

pa·an·ga \pä-'äŋ-gə\ *n* — see MONEY table

pab·u·lum \'pa-byə-ləm\ *n* [L, food, fodder] : usu. soft digestible food

Pac *abbr* Pacific

PAC *abbr* political action committee

¹pace \'pās\ *n* **1** : rate of movement or progress (as in walking or working) **2** : a step in walking; *also* : a measure of length based on such a step **3** : GAIT; *esp* : a horse's gait in which the legs on the same side move together

²pace *vb* **paced; pac·ing** **1** : to go or cover at a pace or with slow steps **2** : to measure off by paces ⟨∼ off a 15-yard penalty⟩ **3** : to set or regulate the pace of

³pa·ce \'pā-sē, 'pä-ˌkā, -ˌchä\ *prep* : contrary to the opinion of

pace·mak·er \'pās-ˌmā-kər\ *n* **1** : one that sets the pace for another **2** : a body part (as of the heart) that serves to establish and maintain a rhythmic activity **3** : an electrical device for stimulating or steadying the heartbeat

pac·er \'pā-sər\ *n* **1** : a horse that paces **2** : PACEMAKER

pachy·derm \'pa-ki-ˌdərm\ *n* [F *pachyderme*, fr. Gk *pachydermos* thick-skinned, fr. *pachys* thick + *derma* skin] : any of various thick-skinned hoofed mammals (as an elephant)

pach·ys·an·dra \ˌpa-ki-'san-drə\ *n* : any of a genus of low perennial evergreen plants used as a ground cover

pa·cif·ic \pə-'si-fik\ *adj* **1** : tending to lessen conflict **2** : CALM, PEACEFUL

pac·i·fi·er \'pa-sə-ˌfī(-ə)r\ *n* : one that pacifies; *esp* : a device for a baby to chew or suck on

pac·i·fism \'pa-sə-ˌfi-zəm\ *n* : opposition to war or violence as a means of settling disputes — **pac·i·fist** \-fist\ *n or adj* — **pac·i·fis·tic** \ˌpa-sə-'fis-tik\ *adj*

pac·i·fy \'pa-sə-ˌfī\ *vb* **-fied; -fy·ing** **1** : to allay anger or agitation in : SOOTHE **2** : SETTLE; *also* : SUBDUE — **pac·i·fi·ca·tion** \ˌpa-sə-fə-'kā-shən\ *n*

¹pack \'pak\ *n* **1** : a compact bundle; *also* : a flexible container for carrying a bundle esp. on the back **2** : a large amount : HEAP **3** : a set of playing cards **4** : a group or band of people or animals **5** : wet absorbent material for application to the body

²pack *vb* **1** : to stow goods in for transportation **2** : to fill in or surround so as to prevent passage of air, steam, or water **3** : to put into a protective container **4** : to load with a pack ⟨∼ a mule⟩ **5** : to crowd in **6** : to make into a pack **7** : to cause to go without ceremony ⟨∼ them off to school⟩ **8** : WEAR, CARRY ⟨∼ a gun⟩

³**pack** *vb* : to make up fraudulently so as to secure a desired result ⟨∼ a jury⟩

¹**pack·age** \'pa-kij\ *n* **1** : BUNDLE, PARCEL **2** : a group of related things offered as a whole

²**package** *vb* **pack·aged; pack·ag·ing** : to make into or enclose in a package

package deal : an offer containing several items all or none of which must be accepted

package store *n* : a store that sells alcoholic beverages in sealed containers for consumption off the premises

pack·er \'pa-kər\ *n* : one that packs; *esp* : a wholesale food dealer

pack·et \'pa-kət\ *n* **1** : a small bundle or package **2** : a passenger boat carrying mail and cargo on a regular schedule

pack·horse \'pak-ˌhȯrs\ *n* : a horse used to carry goods or supplies

pack·ing \'pa-kiŋ\ *n* : material used to pack something

pack·ing·house \-ˌhaủs\ *n* : an establishment for processing and packing food and esp. meat and its by-products

pack rat *n* **1** : a bushy-tailed rodent of western No. America that hoards food and miscellaneous objects; *also* : any of several rodents of similar habit **2** : a person who collects or saves many esp. unneeded items

pack·sad·dle \'pak-ˌsa-dᵊl\ *n* : a saddle for supporting loads on the back of an animal

pack·thread \-ˌthred\ *n* : strong thread for tying

pact \'pakt\ *n* : AGREEMENT, TREATY

¹**pad** \'pad\ *n* **1** : a cushioning part or thing : CUSHION **2** : the cushioned underside of the foot or toes of some mammals **3** : the floating leaf of a water plant **4** : a writing tablet **5** : LAUNCHPAD **6** : living quarters; *also* : BED

²**pad** *vb* **pad·ded; pad·ding** **1** : to furnish with a pad or padding **2** : to expand with needless or fraudulent matter

pad·ding *n* : the material with which something is padded

¹**pad·dle** \'pa-dᵊl\ *vb* **pad·dled; pad·dling** : to move the hands and feet about in shallow water

²**paddle** *n* **1** : an implement with a flat blade used in propelling and steering a small craft (as a canoe) **2** : an implement used for stirring, mixing, or beating **3** : a broad board on the outer rim of a waterwheel or a paddle wheel

³**paddle** *vb* **pad·dled; pad·dling** **1** : to move on or through water by or as if by using a paddle **2** : to beat or stir with a paddle

paddle wheel *n* : a wheel with paddles around its outer edge used to move a boat

paddle wheeler *n* : a steam-driven vessel propelled by a paddle wheel

pad·dock \'pa-dək\ *n* **1** : a usu. enclosed area for pasturing or exercising animals; *esp* : one where racehorses are saddled and paraded before a race **2** : an area at

a racecourse where racing cars are parked

pad·dy \'pa-dē\ *n, pl* **paddies** : wet land where rice is grown

paddy wagon *n* : an enclosed motor-truck for carrying prisoners

pad·lock \'pad-ˌläk\ *n* : a removable lock with a curved piece that snaps into a catch — **padlock** *vb*

pa·dre \'pä-drā\ *n* [Sp or It or Pg, lit., father, fr. L *pater*] **1** : PRIEST **2** : a military chaplain

pad thai \'päd-'tī\ *n, often cap T* : a Thai dish of rice noodles stir-fried with additional ingredients

pae·an \'pē-ən\ *n* : an exultant song of praise or thanksgiving

pae·di·at·ric, pae·di·a·tri·cian, pae·di·at·rics *chiefly Brit var of* PEDIATRIC, PEDIATRICIAN, PEDIATRICS

pa·el·la \pä-'e-lə, -'äl-yə, -'ā-yə\ *n* : a saffron-flavored dish of rice, meat, seafood, and vegetables

pa·gan \'pā-gən\ *n* [ME, fr. LL *paganus*, fr. L, civilian, country dweller, fr. *pagus* country district] : HEATHEN — **pagan** *adj* — **pa·gan·ism** \-gə-ˌni-zəm\ *n*

¹**page** \'pāj\ *n* : ATTENDANT; *esp* : one employed to deliver messages

²**page** *vb* **paged; pag·ing** **1** : to summon by repeatedly calling out the name of **2** : to send a message to via a pager

³**page** *n* **1** : a single leaf (as of a book); *also* : a single side of such a leaf **2** : the information at a single World Wide Web address

⁴**page** *vb* **paged; pag·ing** : to mark or number the pages of

pag·eant \'pa-jənt\ *n* [ME *pagyn, padgeant*, lit., scene of a play, fr. AF *pagine, pagent*, fr. ML *pagina*, perh. fr. L, page] : an elaborate spectacle, show, or procession esp. with tableaux or floats — **pag·eant·ry** \-jən-trē\ *n*

page·boy \'pāj-ˌbȯi\ *n* [¹*page*] : an often shoulder-length hairdo with the ends of the hair turned smoothly under

pag·er \'pā-jər\ *n* : one that pages; *esp* : a small radio receiver that alerts its user to incoming messages

pag·i·nate \'pa-jə-ˌnāt\ *vb* **-nat·ed; -nat·ing** : ⁴PAGE

pag·i·na·tion \ˌpa-jə-'nā-shən\ *n* **1** : the paging of written or printed matter **2** : the number and arrangement of pages (as of a book)

pa·go·da \pə-'gō-də\ *n* : a tower with roofs curving upward at the division of each of several stories

paid *past and past part of* PAY

pail \'pāl\ *n* : a usu. cylindrical vessel with a handle — **pail·ful** \-ˌfủl\ *n*

¹**pain** \'pān\ *n* **1** : PUNISHMENT, PENALTY **2** : suffering or distress of body or mind; *also* : a basic bodily sensation marked by discomfort (as throbbing or aching) **3** *pl* : great care **4** : one that irks or annoys — **pain·ful** \-fəl\ *adj* — **pain·ful·ly** *adv* — **pain·less** *adj* — **pain·less·ly** *adv*

²**pain** *vb* : to cause or experience pain

pain·kill·er \'pān-ˌki-lər\ *n* : something

(as a drug) that relieves pain — **pain·kill·ing** *adj*

pains·tak·ing \-ˌstā·kiŋ\ *adj* : taking pains : showing care — **pains·taking** *n* — **pains·tak·ing·ly** *adv*

¹paint \ˈpānt\ *vb* **1** : to apply color, pigment, or paint to **2** : to produce or portray in lines or colors on a surface; *also* : to practice the art of painting **3** : to decorate with colors **4** : to use cosmetics **5** : to describe vividly **6** : SWAB — **paint·er** *n*

²paint *n* **1** : something produced by painting **2** : MAKEUP **3** : a mixture of a pigment and a liquid that forms a thin adherent coating when spread on a surface; *also* : the dry pigment used in making this mixture **4** : an applied coating of paint

paint-ball \ˈpānt-ˌbȯl\ *n* : a game in which two teams try to capture each other's flag using guns that shoot paint-filled pellets

paint·brush \ˈpānt-ˌbrəsh\ *n* : a brush for applying paint

painted lady *n* : a migratory butterfly with wings mottled in brown, orange, black, and white

painting *n* **1** : a work (as a picture) produced by painting **2** : the art or occupation of painting

¹pair \ˈper\ *n, pl* **pairs** *also* **pair** [ME *paire*, fr. AF, fr. L *paria* equal things, fr. neut. pl. of *par* equal] **1** : two things of a kind designed for use together **2** : something made up of two corresponding pieces ⟨a ~ of pants⟩ **3** : a set of two people or animals

²pair *vb* **1** : to arrange in pairs **2** : to form a pair : MATCH **3** : to become associated with another

pai·sa \ˈpī-ˌsä\ *n, pl* **paisa** *or* **pai·se** \-ˈsä\ — see *rupee, taka* at MONEY table

pais·ley \ˈpāz-lē\ *adj, often cap* : decorated with colorful curved abstract figures ⟨a ~ shawl⟩

Pai·ute \ˈpī-ˌüt, -ˌyüt\ *n* : a member of an American Indian people orig. of Utah, Arizona, Nevada, and California

pa·ja·mas \pə-ˈjä-məz, -ˈja-\ *n pl* : a loose suit for sleeping or lounging

pal \ˈpal\ *n* : a close friend

pal·ace \ˈpa-ləs\ *n* [ME *palais*, fr. AF, fr. L *palatium*, fr. *Palatium*, the Palatine Hill in Rome where the emperors' residences were built] **1** : the official residence of a chief of state **2** : MANSION

pal·a·din \ˈpa-lə-dən\ *n* **1** : a trusted military leader (as for a medieval prince) **2** : a leading champion of a cause

pa·laes·tra \pə-ˈles-trə\ *n, pl* **-trae** \-(ˌ)trē\ : a school in ancient Greece or Rome for sports (as wrestling)

pa·lan·quin \ˌpa-lən-ˈkēn\ *n* : an enclosed couch for one person borne on the shoulders of men by means of poles

pal·at·able \ˈpa-lə-tə-bəl\ *adj* : agreeable to the taste ♦ **Synonyms** APPETIZING, SAVORY, TASTY, TOOTHSOME

pal·a·tal \ˈpa-lə-tᵊl\ *adj* **1** : of or relating to the palate **2** : pronounced with some part of the tongue near or touching the hard palate ⟨the \y\ in *yeast* and the \sh\ in *she* are ~ sounds⟩

pal·a·tal·ize \ˈpa-lə-tə-ˌlīz\ *vb* **-ized; -iz·ing** : to pronounce as or change into a palatal sound — **pal·a·tal·i·za·tion** \ˌpa-lə-tə-lə-ˈzā-shən\ *n*

pal·ate \ˈpa-lət\ *n* **1** : the roof of the mouth separating the mouth from the nasal cavity **2** : TASTE

pa·la·tial \pə-ˈlā-shəl\ *adj* **1** : of, relating to, or being a palace **2** : MAGNIFICENT

pa·lat·i·nate \pə-ˈla-tə-nət\ *n* : the territory of a palatine

¹pal·a·tine \ˈpa-lə-ˌtīn\ *adj* **1** : possessing royal privileges; *also* : of or relating to a palatine or a palatinate **2** : of or relating to a palace : PALATIAL

²palatine *n* **1** : a feudal lord having sovereign power within his domains **2** : a high officer of an imperial palace

pa·la·ver \pə-ˈla-vər, -ˈlä-\ *n* [Pg *palavra* word, speech, fr. LL *parabola* parable, speech] **1** : a long parley **2** : idle talk — **palaver** *vb*

¹pale \ˈpāl\ *n* **1** : a stake or picket of a fence **2** : an enclosed place; *also* : a district or territory within certain bounds or under a particular jurisdiction **3** : LIMITS, BOUNDS ⟨conduct beyond the ~⟩

²pale *vb* **paled; pal·ing** : to enclose with or as if with pales : FENCE

³pale *adj* **pal·er; pal·est** **1** : deficient in color or intensity : WAN ⟨a ~ face⟩ **2** : lacking in brightness : DIM ⟨a ~ star⟩ **3** : not dark or intense in hue ⟨a ~ blue⟩ — **pale·ness** *n*

⁴pale *vb* **paled; pal·ing** : to make or become pale

pale ale *n* : a medium-colored very dry ale

pale·face \ˈpāl-ˌfās\ *n* : a white person

Pa·leo·cene \ˈpā-lē-ə-ˌsēn\ *adj* : of, relating to, or being the earliest epoch of the Tertiary — **Paleocene** *n*

pa·leo·con·ser·va·tive \ˌpā-lē-ō-kən-ˈsər-və-tiv\ *n* : a conservative espousing traditional principles and policies

pa·le·og·ra·phy \ˌpā-lē-ˈä-grə-fē\ *n* [NL *palaeographia*, fr. Gk *palaios* ancient + *graphein* to write] : the study of ancient writings and inscriptions — **pa·le·og·ra·pher** *n*

Pa·leo·lith·ic \ˌpā-lē-ə-ˈli-thik\ *adj* : of or relating to the earliest period of the Stone Age characterized by rough or chipped stone implements

pa·le·on·tol·o·gy \ˌpā-lē-ˌän-ˈtä-lə-jē\ *n* : a science dealing with the life of past geologic periods as known from fossil remains — **pa·le·on·to·log·i·cal** \-ˌän-tə-ˈlä-ji-kəl\ *adj* — **pa·le·on·tol·o·gist** \-ˌän-ˈtä-lə-jist, -ən-\ *n*

Pa·leo·zo·ic \ˌpā-lē-ə-ˈzō-ik\ *adj* : of, relating to, or being the era of geologic history extending from about 570 million years ago to about 245 million years ago — **Paleozoic** *n*

pal·ette \ˈpa-lət\ *n* : a thin often oval board that a painter holds and mixes colors on; *also* : the colors on a palette

pal·frey \ˈpȯl-frē\ *n, pl* **palfreys** *archaic* : a saddle horse that is not a warhorse; *esp* : one suitable for a woman

pa·limp·sest \ˈpa-ləmp-ˌsest\ *n* [L *pa-*

limpsestus, fr. Gk *palimpsēstos* scraped again] : writing material (as a parchment) used after the erasure of earlier writing

pal·in·drome \'pa-lən-ˌdrōm\ *n* : a word, verse, or sentence (as "Able was I ere I saw Elba") or a number (as 1881) that reads the same backward or forward

pal·ing \'pā-liŋ\ *n* **1** : a fence of pales **2** : material for pales **3** : PALE, PICKET

pal·i·sade \ˌpa-lə-'sād\ *n* **1** : a high fence of stakes esp. for defense **2** : a line of steep cliffs

¹pall \'pól\ *vb* **1** : to lose in interest or attraction **2** : SATIATE, CLOY

²pall *n* **1** : a heavy cloth draped over a coffin **2** : something that produces a gloomy atmosphere

pal·la·di·um \pə-'lā-dē-əm\ *n* : a silver-white metallic chemical element used esp. as a catalyst and in alloys

pall-bear·er \'pól-ˌber-ər\ *n* : a person who attends the coffin at a funeral

¹pal·let \'pa-lət\ *n* : a small, hard, or makeshift bed

²pallet *n* : a portable platform for transporting and storing materials

pal·li·ate \'pa-lē-ˌāt\ *vb* **-at·ed; -at·ing 1** : to ease (as a disease) without curing **2** : to cover by excuses and apologies ⟨~ faults⟩ — **pal·li·a·tion** \ˌpa-lē-'ā-shən\ *n* — **pal·li·a·tive** \'pa-lē-ˌā-tiv\ *adj or n*

pal·lid \'pa-ləd\ *adj* : PALE, WAN

pal·lor \'pa-lər\ *n* : PALENESS

¹palm \'päm, 'pälm\ *n* [ME, fr. OE, fr. L *palma* palm of the hand, palm tree; fr. the resemblance of the tree's leaves to the outstretched hand] **1** : any of a family of mostly tropical trees, shrubs, or vines usu. with a tall unbranched stem topped by a crown of large leaves **2** : a symbol of victory; *also* : VICTORY

²palm *n* : the underpart of the hand between the fingers and the wrist

³palm *vb* **1** : to conceal in or with the hand ⟨~ a card⟩ **2** : to impose by fraud

pal·mate \'pal-ˌmāt, 'päl-\ *also* **pal·mat·ed** \-ˌmā-təd\ *adj* : resembling a hand with the fingers spread

pal·met·to \pal-'me-tō\ *n, pl* **-tos** *or* **-toes** : any of several usu. small palms with fan-shaped leaves

palm·is·try \'pä-mə-strē, 'päl-\ *n* : the practice of reading a person's character or future from the markings on the palms — **palm·ist** \'pä-mist, 'päl-\ *n*

Palm Sunday *n* : the Sunday preceding Easter and commemorating Christ's triumphal entry into Jerusalem

palm·top \'päm-ˌtäp, 'pälm-\ *n* : a portable computer small enough to hold in the hand

palmy \'pä-mē, 'päl-\ *adj* **palm·i·er; -est 1** : abounding in or bearing palms **2** : FLOURISHING, PROSPEROUS

pal·o·mi·no \ˌpa-lə-'mē-nō\ *n, pl* **-nos** [AmerSp, fr. Sp, like a dove, fr. L *palumbinus,* fr. *palumbes,* a species of dove] : a horse with a pale cream to golden coat and cream or white mane and tail

pal·pa·ble \'pal-pə-bəl\ *adj* **1** : capable of being touched or felt : TANGIBLE **2** : OBVIOUS, PLAIN ⟨the resentment was ~⟩

♦ **Synonyms** PERCEPTIBLE, SENSIBLE, APPRECIABLE, TANGIBLE, DETECTABLE — **pal·pa·bly** \-blē\ *adv*

pal·pate \'pal-ˌpāt\ *vb* **pal·pat·ed; pal·pat·ing** : to examine by touch esp. medically — **pal·pa·tion** \pal-'pā-shən\ *n*

pal·pi·tate \'pal-pə-ˌtāt\ *vb* **-tat·ed; -tat·ing** : to beat rapidly and strongly : THROB — **pal·pi·ta·tion** \ˌpal-pə-'tā-shən\ *n*

pal·sy \'pól-zē\ *n, pl* **palsies 1** : PARALYSIS **2** : a condition marked by tremor — **pal·sied** \-zēd\ *adj*

pal·ter \'pól-tər\ *vb* **pal·tered; pal·ter·ing 1** : to act insincerely : EQUIVOCATE **2** : HAGGLE

pal·try \'pól-trē\ *adj* **pal·tri·er; -est 1** : TRASHY ⟨a ~ pamphlet⟩ **2** : MEAN, DESPICABLE ⟨a ~ trick⟩ **3** : TRIVIAL ⟨~ excuses⟩ **4** : MEAGER, MEASLY ⟨a ~ sum⟩

pam *abbr* pamphlet

pam·pas \'pam-pəz, 'päm-, -pəs\ *n pl* : wide grassy So. American plains

pam·per \'pam-pər\ *vb* : to treat with excessive attention : INDULGE ♦ **Synonyms** CODDLE, HUMOR, BABY, SPOIL

pam·phlet \'pam-flət\ *n* [ME *pamflet* unbound booklet, fr. *Pamphilus seu De Amore* Pamphilus or On Love, popular Latin love poem of the 12th cent.] : an unbound printed publication

pam·phle·teer \ˌpam-flə-'tir\ *n* : a writer of pamphlets attacking something or urging a cause

¹pan \'pan\ *n* **1** : a usu. broad, shallow, and open container for domestic use; *also* : something resembling such a container **2** : a basin or depression in land **3** : HARDPAN

²pan *vb* **panned; pan·ning 1** : to wash earth or gravel in a pan in searching for gold **2** : to criticize severely

Pan *abbr* Panama

pan·a·cea \ˌpa-nə-'sē-ə\ *n* : a remedy for all ills or difficulties : CURE-ALL

pa·nache \pə-'nash, -'näsh\ *n* [MF *pennache,* ultim. fr. LL *pinnaculum* small wing] **1** : an ornamental tuft (as of feathers) esp. on a helmet **2** : dash or flamboyance in style and action

pan·a·ma \'pa-nə-ˌmä, -ˌmò\ *n, often cap* : a handmade hat braided from strips of the leaves from a tropical American tree

pan·a·tela \ˌpa-nə-'te-lə\ *n* : a long slender cigar with straight sides

pan·cake \'pan-ˌkāk\ *n* : a flat cake made of thin batter and fried on both sides

pan·chro·mat·ic \ˌpan-krō-'ma-tik\ *adj* : sensitive to all colors of visible light ⟨~ film⟩

pan·cre·as \'paŋ-krē-əs, 'pan-\ *n* : a large compound gland of vertebrates that produces insulin and discharges enzymes into the intestine — **pan·cre·at·ic** \ˌpaŋ-krē-'a-tik, ˌpan-\ *adj*

pan·da \'pan-də\ *n* **1** : a long-tailed reddish brown Himalayan mammal related to and resembling the raccoon **2** : a large black-and-white mammal of China usu. classified with the bears

pan·dem·ic \pan-'de-mik\ *n* : a widespread outbreak of disease — **pan·demic** *adj*

pan·de·mo·ni·um \ˌpan-də-ˈmō-nē-əm\ *n* : a wild uproar : TUMULT

¹**pan·der** \ˈpan-dər\ *vb* : to act as a pander ⟨~s to the public's taste for violence⟩

²**pander** *n* 1 : a go-between in love intrigues; *also* : PIMP 2 : a person who caters to or exploits others' desires or weaknesses

P & I *abbr* principal and interest

P & L *abbr* profit and loss

Pan·do·ra's box \pan-ˈdȯr-əz-\ *n* : a prolific source of troubles

pan·dow·dy \pan-ˈdau̇-dē\ *n, pl* **-dies** : a deep-dish apple dessert spiced, sweetened, and covered with a crust

pane \ˈpān\ *n* : a sheet of glass (as in a door or window)

pan·e·gyr·ic \ˌpa-nə-ˈjir-ik\ *n* : a eulogistic oration or writing ⟨a ~ on war heroes⟩ — **pan·e·gyr·ist** \-ˈjir-ist\ *n*

¹**pan·el** \ˈpa-nᵊl\ *n* [ME, piece of cloth, jury list on a piece of parchment, fr. AF, fr. VL *pannellus*, dim. of L *pannus* cloth, rag] 1 : a list of persons appointed for special duty ⟨a jury ~⟩; *also* : a group of people taking part in a discussion or quiz program 2 : a section of something (as a wall or door) often made below the level of the frame; *also* : a flat piece of construction material 3 : a flat piece of wood on which a picture is painted 4 : a mount for controls or dials

²**panel** *vb* **-eled** *or* **-elled**; **-el·ing** *or* **-el·ling** : to decorate with panels

paneling *n* : decorative panels

pan·el·ist \ˈpa-nᵊl-ist\ *n* : a member of a discussion or quiz panel

panel truck *n* : a small motortruck with a fully enclosed body

pang \ˈpaŋ\ *n* : a sudden sharp spasm (as of pain) or attack (as of remorse)

¹**pan·han·dle** \ˈpan-ˌhan-dᵊl\ *n* : a narrow projection of a larger territory (as a state) ⟨the Texas ~⟩

²**panhandle** *vb* **-dled**; **-dling** : to ask for money on the street — **pan·han·dler** *n*

¹**pan·ic** \ˈpa-nik\ *n* : a sudden overpowering fright; *also* : extreme anxiety ⟨a ~ disorder⟩ ⟨~ attacks⟩ ♦ *Synonyms* TERROR, CONSTERNATION, DISMAY, ALARM, DREAD, FEAR — **pan·icky** \-ni-kē\ *adj*

²**panic** *vb* **pan·icked** \-nikt\; **pan·ick·ing** : to affect or be affected with panic

pan·i·cle \ˈpa-ni-kəl\ *n* : a branched flower cluster (as of a lilac) in which each branch from the main stem has one or more flowers

pan·jan·drum \pan-ˈjan-drəm\ *n, pl* **-drums** *also* **-dra** \-drə\ : a powerful personage or pretentious official

pan·nier *also* **pan·ier** \ˈpan-yər\ *n* : a large basket esp. for bearing on the back

pan·o·ply \ˈpa-nə-plē\ *n, pl* **-plies** 1 : a full suit of armor 2 : a protective covering 3 : an impressive array

pan·ora·ma \ˌpa-nə-ˈra-mə, -ˈrä-\ *n* 1 : a picture unrolled before one's eyes 2 : a complete view in every direction — **pan·oram·ic** \-ˈra-mik\ *adj*

pan out *vb* : TURN OUT; *esp* : SUCCEED

pan·sy \ˈpan-zē\ *n, pl* **pansies** [ME *pancy, pensee,* fr. MF *pensée,* fr. *pensée* thought, fr. *penser* to think, fr. L *pensare* to ponder] : a low-growing garden herb related to the violet; *also* : its showy flower

¹**pant** \ˈpant\ *vb* [ME, fr. AF *panteiser,* fr. VL **phantasiare* to have hallucinations, fr. Gk *phantasioun,* fr. *phantasia* appearance, imagination] 1 : to breathe in a labored manner 2 : YEARN 3 : THROB

²**pant** *n* : a panting breath or sound

³**pant** *n* 1 : an outer garment covering each leg separately and usu. extending from the waist to the ankle — usu. used in pl. 2 *pl* : PANTIE

pan·ta·loons \ˌpan-tə-ˈlünz\ *n pl* 1 : close-fitting pants of the 19th century usu. having straps passing under the instep 2 : loose-fitting usu. shorter than ankle-length trousers

pan·the·ism \ˈpan-thē-ˌi-zəm\ *n* : a doctrine that equates God with the forces and laws of the universe — **pan·the·ist** \-ist\ *n* — **pan·the·is·tic** \ˌpan-thē-ˈis-tik\ *adj*

pan·the·on \ˈpan-thē-ˌän, -ən\ *n* 1 : a temple dedicated to all the gods; *also* : the gods of a people 2 : a group of illustrious people ⟨a ~ of great writers⟩

pan·ther \ˈpan-thər\ *n, pl* **panthers** *also* **panther** 1 : LEOPARD; *esp* : a black one 2 : COUGAR 3 : JAGUAR

pant·ie *or* **panty** \ˈpan-tē\ *n, pl* **pant·ies** : a woman's or child's short underpants — usu. used in pl.

pan·to·mime \ˈpan-tə-ˌmīm\ *n* 1 : a play in which the actors use no words 2 : expression of something by bodily or facial movements only — **pantomime** *vb* — **pan·to·mim·ic** \ˌpan-tə-ˈmi-mik\ *adj*

pan·try \ˈpan-trē\ *n, pl* **pantries** : a storage room for food or dishes

pant·suit \ˈpant-ˌsüt\ *n* : a woman's outfit consisting usu. of a long jacket and pants of the same material

panty hose *n pl* : a one-piece undergarment for women consisting of hosiery combined with a pantie

panty·waist \ˈpan-tē-ˌwāst\ *n* : SISSY

pap \ˈpap\ *n* : soft food for infants or invalids

pa·pa \ˈpä-pə\ *n* : FATHER

pa·pa·cy \ˈpā-pə-sē\ *n, pl* **-cies** 1 : the office of pope 2 : a succession of popes 3 : the term of a pope's reign 4 *cap* : the system of government of the Roman Catholic Church

pa·pa·in \pə-ˈpā-ən, -ˈpī-ən\ *n* : an enzyme in papaya juice used esp. as a meat tenderizer and in medicine

pa·pal \ˈpā-pəl\ *adj* : of or relating to the pope or to the Roman Catholic Church

papaw *var of* PAWPAW

pa·pa·ya \pə-ˈpī-ə\ *n* : a tropical American tree with large yellow black-seeded edible fruit; *also* : its fruit

pa·per \ˈpā-pər\ *n* [ME *papir,* fr. AF, fr. L *papyrus* papyrus, paper, fr. Gk *papyros* papyrus] 1 : a pliable substance made usu. of vegetable matter and used to write or print on, to wrap things in, or to cover walls; *also* : a single sheet of this substance 2 : a printed or written document 3 : NEWSPAPER 4 : WALLPAPER — **paper** *adj or vb* — **pa·pery** \'pā-pə-rē\ *adj*

pa·per·back \-ˌbak\ *n* : a paper-covered book

pa·per·board \-ˌbȯrd\ *n* : CARDBOARD

pa·per·hang·er \'pā-pər-ˌhaŋ-ər\ *n* : one that applies wallpaper — **pa·per·hang·ing** *n*

pa·per·weight \-ˌwāt\ *n* : an object used to hold down loose papers by its weight

pa·pier–mâ·ché \ˌpā-pər-mə-ˈshā, ˌpa-ˌpyā-mə-, -ma-\ *n* [F, lit., chewed paper] : a molding material of wastepaper and additives (as glue) — **papier–mâché** *adj*

pa·pil·la \pə-ˈpi-lə\ *n, pl* **-lae** \-(ˌ)lē, -ˌlī\ [L, nipple] : a small projecting bodily part (as one of the nubs on the surface of the tongue) that resembles a tiny nipple in form — **pap·il·lary** \'pa-pə-ˌler-ē, pə-ˈpi-lə-rē\ *adj*

pa·poose \pa-ˈpüs, pə-\ *n* [Narragansett *papoòs*] : a young child of No. American Indian parents

pa·pri·ka \pə-ˈprē-kə, pa-\ *n* [Hung] : a mild red spice made from the fruit of various cultivated sweet peppers

Pap smear \'pap-\ *n* : a method for the early detection of cancer esp. of the uterine cervix

Pap test *n* : PAP SMEAR

pap·ule \'pa-pyül\ *n* : a small solid usu. conical elevation of the skin — **pap·u·lar** \-pyə-lər\ *adj*

pa·py·rus \pə-ˈpī-rəs\ *n, pl* **-ri** \-(ˌ)rē, -ˌrī\ *or* **-rus·es** : a tall grassy sedge of the Nile valley 2 : paper made from papyrus pith

¹**par** \'pär\ *n* 1 : a stated value (as of a security) 2 : a common level : EQUALITY 3 : an accepted standard or normal condition 4 : the score standard set for each hole of a golf course — **par** *adj*

²**par** *abbr* 1 paragraph 2 parallel 3 parish

par·a·ble \'pa-rə-bəl\ *n* : a simple story told to illustrate a moral truth

pa·rab·o·la \pə-ˈra-bə-lə\ *n* : a plane curve formed by a point moving so that its distance from a fixed point is equal to its distance from a fixed line — **par·a·bol·ic** \ˌpar-ə-ˈbä-lik\ *adj*

para·chute \'pa-rə-ˌshüt\ *n* [F, fr. *para-* (as in *parasol*) + *chute* fall] : a device for slowing the descent of a person or object through the air that consists of a usu. hemispherical canopy beneath which the person or object is suspended — **para·chute** *vb* — **para·chut·ist** \-ˌshü-tist\ *n*

parachute pants *n pl* : baggy casual pants of lightweight fabric

¹**pa·rade** \pə-ˈrād\ *n* 1 : a pompous display : EXHIBITION 2 : MARCH, PROCESSION; *esp* : a ceremonial formation and march 3 : a place for strolling

²**parade** *vb* **pa·rad·ed; pa·rad·ing** 1 : to march in a parade 2 : PROMENADE 3 : SHOW OFF ⟨*paraded* her knowledge⟩ 4 : MASQUERADE

par·a·digm \'pa-rə-ˌdīm, -ˌdim\ *n* 1

: MODEL, PATTERN 2 : a systematic inflection of a verb or noun showing a complete conjugation or declension — **par·a·dig·mat·ic** \ˌpa-rə-dig-ˈma-tik\ *adj*

par·a·dise \'pa-rə-ˌdīs, -ˌdīz\ *n* [ME *paradis*, fr. AF, fr. LL *paradisus*, fr. Gk *paradeisos*, lit., enclosed park, of Iranian origin] 1 : HEAVEN 2 : a place or state of bliss

par·a·di·sia·cal \ˌpa-rə-də-ˈsī-ə-kəl\ *or* **par·a·dis·i·ac** \-ˈdi-zē-ˌak, -sē-\ *adj* : of, relating to, or resembling paradise

par·a·dox \'pa-rə-ˌdäks\ *n* : a statement that seems contrary to common sense and yet is perhaps true — **par·a·dox·i·cal** \ˌpa-rə-ˈdäk-si-kəl\ *adj* — **par·a·dox·i·cal·ly** \-k(ə-)lē\ *adv*

par·af·fin \'pa-rə-fən\ *n* : a waxy substance used esp. for making candles and sealing foods

par·a·glid·ing \'pa-rə-ˌglī-diŋ\ *n* : the sport of soaring from a slope or cliff using a modified parachute

par·a·gon \'pa-rə-ˌgän, -gən\ *n* : a model of perfection : PATTERN ⟨a ~ of virtue⟩

¹**para·graph** \'pa-rə-ˌgraf\ *n* : a subdivision of a written composition that deals with one point or gives the words of one speaker; *also* : a character (as ¶) marking the beginning of a paragraph

²**paragraph** *vb* : to divide into paragraphs

par·a·keet \'pa-rə-ˌkēt\ *n* : any of numerous usu. small slender parrots with a long graduated tail

para·le·gal \ˌpa-rə-ˈlē-gəl\ *adj* : of, relating to, or being a paraprofessional who assists a lawyer — **paralegal** *n*

Par·a·li·pom·e·non \ˌpa-rə-lə-ˈpä-mə-ˌnän\ *n* : CHRONICLES

par·al·lax \'pa-rə-ˌlaks\ *n* : the difference in apparent direction of an object as seen from two different points

¹**par·al·lel** \'pa-rə-ˌlel\ *adj* [L *parallelus*, fr. Gk *parallēlos*, fr. *para* beside + *allēlōn* of one another, fr. *allos . . . allos* one . . . another, fr. *allos* other] 1 : lying or moving in the same direction but always the same distance apart 2 : similar in essential parts — **par·al·lel·ism** \-ˌle-ˌli-zəm\ *n*

²**parallel** *n* 1 : a parallel line, curve, or surface 2 : one of the imaginary circles on the earth's surface that parallel the equator and mark the latitude 3 : something essentially similar to another 4 : SIMILARITY, LIKENESS

³**parallel** *vb* 1 : COMPARE 2 : to correspond to 3 : to extend in a parallel direction with

par·al·lel·o·gram \ˌpa-rə-ˈle-lə-ˌgram\ *n* : a 4-sided geometric figure with opposite sides equal and parallel

par·a·lyse *Brit var of* PARALYZE

pa·ral·y·sis \pə-ˈra-lə-səs\ *n, pl* **-y·ses** \-ˌsēz\ : complete or partial loss of function esp. when involving the motion or sensation in a part of the body — **par·a·lyt·ic** \ˌpa-rə-ˈli-tik\ *adj or n*

par·a·lyze \'pa-rə-ˌlīz\ *vb* **-lyzed; -lyz·ing** 1 : to affect with paralysis 2 : to make powerless or inactive ⟨*paralyzed* by fear⟩ — **par·a·lyz·ing·ly** *adv*

par·a·me·cium \ˌpa-rə-ˈmē-shəm, -shē-əm, -sē-əm\ *n, pl* **-cia** \-shə, -shē-ə, -sē-ə\ *also* **-ci·ums** : any of a genus of slipper-shaped protozoans that move by cilia

para·med·ic \ˌpa-rə-ˈme-dik\ *also* **para·med·i·cal** \-di-kəl\ *n* **1** : a person who assists a physician in a paramedical capacity **2** : a specially trained medical technician licensed to provide a wide range of emergency services before or during transportation to a hospital

para·med·i·cal \ˌpa-rə-ˈme-di-kəl\ *also* **para·med·ic** \-ˈme dik\ *adj* : concerned with supplementing the work of trained medical professionals

pa·ram·e·ter \pə-ˈra-mə-tər\ *n* **1** : a quantity whose value characterizes a statistical population or a member of a system (as a family of curves) **2** : a physical property whose value determines the characteristics or behavior of a system **3** : a characteristic element : FACTOR — **para·met·ric** \ˌpa-rə-ˈme-trik\ *adj*

para·mil·i·tary \ˌpa-rə-ˈmi-lə-ˌter-ē\ *adj* : formed on a military pattern esp. as an auxiliary military force

par·a·mount \ˈpa-rə-ˌmaunt\ *adj* : superior to all others : SUPREME ♦ *Synonyms* PREPONDERANT, PREDOMINANT, DOMINANT, CHIEF, SOVEREIGN

par·amour \ˈpa-rə-ˌmur\ *n* : an illicit lover

para·noia \ˌpa-rə-ˈnoi-ə\ *n* : a psychosis marked by delusions and irrational suspicion usu. without hallucinations — **par·a·noid** \ˈpa-rə-ˌnoid\ *adj or n*

para·nor·mal \ˌpa-rə-ˈnor-məl\ *adj* : not scientifically explainable : SUPERNATURAL ⟨∼ phenomena⟩

par·a·pet \ˈpa-rə-pət, -ˌpet\ *n* **1** : a protecting rampart **2** : a low wall or railing (as at the edge of a bridge)

par·a·pher·na·lia \ˌpa-rə-fə-ˈnāl-yə, -fər-\ *n sing or pl* **1** : personal belongings **2** : EQUIPMENT, APPARATUS

para·phrase \ˈpa-rə-ˌfrāz\ *n* : a restatement of a text giving the meaning in different words — **paraphrase** *vb*

para·ple·gia \ˌpa-rə-ˈplē-jə, -jē-ə\ *n* : paralysis of the lower trunk and legs — **para·ple·gic** \-jik\ *adj or n*

para·pro·fes·sion·al \-prə-ˈfe-shə-nəl\ *n* : a trained worker who assists a professional — **paraprofessional** *adj*

para·psy·chol·o·gy \ˌpa-rə-sī-ˈkä-lə-jē\ *n* : a field of study concerned with investigating paranormal psychological phenomena (as extrasensory perception) — **para·psy·chol·o·gist** \-jist\ *n*

par·a·site \ˈpa-rə-ˌsīt\ *n* [MF, fr. L *parasitus*, fr. Gk *parasitos*, fr. *para-* beside + *sitos* grain, food] **1** : a plant or animal living in, with, or on another organism usu. to its harm **2** : one depending on another and not making adequate return — **par·a·sit·ic** \ˌpa-rə-ˈsi-tik\ *adj* — **par·a·sit·ism** \ˈpa-rə-sə-ˌti-zəm, -ˌsī-ˌti-\ *n* — **par·a·sit·ize** \-ˌtīz\ *vb*

par·a·si·tol·o·gy \ˌpa-rə-sə-ˈtä-lə-jē\ *n* : a branch of biology dealing with parasites and parasitism esp. among animals — **par·a·si·tol·o·gist** \-jist\ *n*

para·sol \ˈpa-rə-ˌsol\ *n* [F, It. *parasole*,

fr. *parare* to shield + *sole* sun, fr. L *sol*] : a lightweight umbrella used as a shield against the sun

para·sym·pa·thet·ic nervous system \ˌpa-rə-ˌsim-pə-ˈthe-tik-\ *n* : the part of the autonomic nervous system that tends to induce secretion, to increase the tone and contractility of smooth muscle, and to slow heart rate

para·thi·on \ˌpa-rə-ˈthī-ən, -ˌän\ *n* : an extremely toxic insecticide

para·thy·roid \-ˈthī-ˌroid\ *n* : PARATHYROID GLAND — **parathyroid** *adj*

parathyroid gland *n* : any of usu. four small endocrine glands adjacent to or embedded in the thyroid gland that produce a hormone (**parathyroid hormone**) concerned with calcium and phosphorus metabolism

para·tran·sit \ˌpa-rə-ˈtran-sət, -zət\ *n* : transportation service that provides individualized rules without fixed routes or timetables

para·troop·er \ˈpa-rə-ˌtrü-pər\ *n* : a member of the paratroops

para·troops \-ˌtrüps\ *n pl* : troops trained to parachute from an airplane

para·ty·phoid \ˌpa-rə-ˈtī-ˌfoid\ *n* : a bacterial food poisoning resembling typhoid fever

par·boil \ˈpär-ˌboi(-ə)l\ *vb* : to boil briefly

¹**par·cel** \ˈpär-səl\ *n* **1** : a tract or plot of land **2** : COLLECTION, LOT ⟨the story was a ∼ of lies⟩ **3** : a wrapped bundle : PACKAGE

²**parcel** *vb* **-celed** *or* **-celled; -cel·ing** *or* **-cel·ling** : to divide into portions

parcel post *n* **1** : a mail service handling parcels **2** : packages handled by parcel post

parch \ˈpärch\ *vb* **1** : to toast under dry heat **2** : to shrivel with heat

parch·ment \ˈpärch-mənt\ *n* : the skin of an animal prepared for writing on; *also* : a writing on such material

pard \ˈpärd\ *n* : LEOPARD

¹**par·don** \ˈpär-dᵊn\ *n* : excuse of an offense without penalty; *esp* : an official release from legal punishment

²**pardon** *vb* : to free from penalty : EXCUSE, FORGIVE ⟨∼ a criminal⟩ ⟨∼ a debt⟩ — **par·don·able** \ˈpär-dᵊn-ə-bəl\ *adj*

par·don·er \ˈpär-dᵊn-ər\ *n* **1** : a medieval preacher delegated to raise money for religious works by soliciting offerings and granting indulgences **2** : one that pardons

pare \ˈper\ *vb* **pared; par·ing** **1** : to trim off an outside part (as the skin or rind) of **2** : to reduce as if by paring ⟨∼ expenses⟩ — **par·er** *n*

par·e·gor·ic \ˌper-ə-ˈgor-ik\ *n* : an alcoholic preparation of opium and camphor used esp. to relieve pain

par·ent \ˈper-ənt\ *n* **1** : one that begets or brings forth offspring : FATHER, MOTHER **2** : one who brings up and cares for another **3** : SOURCE, ORIGIN — **par·ent·age** \-ən-tij\ *n* — **pa·ren·tal** \pə-ˈren-tᵊl\ *adj* — **par·ent·hood** *n*

pa·ren·the·sis \pə-ˈren-thə-səs\ *n, pl*

-the·ses \-ˌsēz\ **1** : a word, phrase, or sentence inserted in a passage to explain or modify the thought **2** : one of a pair of punctuation marks ( ) used esp. to enclose parenthetic matter — **par·en·thet·ic** \ˌper-ən-ˈthe-tik\ *or* **par·en·thet·i·cal** \-ti-kəl\ *adj* — **par·en·thet·i·cal·ly** \-k(ə-)lē\ *adv*

pa·ren·the·size \pə-ˈren-thə-ˌsīz\ *vb* **-sized; -siz·ing** : to make a parenthesis of

par·ent·ing \ˈper-ən-tiŋ\ *n* : the raising of a child by its parents

pa·re·sis \pə-ˈrē-səs, ˈpa-rə-\ *n, pl* **pa·re·ses** \-ˌsēz\ : a usu. incomplete paralysis; *also* : insanity caused by syphilitic alteration of the brain that leads to dementia and paralysis

par ex·cel·lence \ˌpär-ˌek-sə-ˈlä⁾s\ *adj* [F, lit., by excellence] : being the best of a kind : PREEMINENT

par·fait \pär-ˈfā\ *n* [F, lit., something perfect] : a cold dessert made of layers of fruit, syrup, ice cream, and whipped cream

pa·ri·ah \pə-ˈrī-ə\ *n* : OUTCAST

pa·ri·etal \pə-ˈrī-ə-tᵊl\ *adj* **1** : of, relating to, or forming the walls of an anatomical structure **2** : of or relating to college living or its regulation

pari-mu·tu·el \ˌper-i-ˈmyü-chə-wəl\ *n* : a betting system in which winners share the total stakes minus a percentage for the management

paring *n* : a pared-off piece

pa·ri pas·su \ˈpa-ri-ˈpa-sü\ *adv or adj* [L, with equal step] : at an equal rate or pace

par·ish \ˈper-ish\ *n* **1** : a church district in the care of one pastor; *also* : the residents of such an area **2** : a local church community **3** : a civil division of the state of Louisiana : COUNTY

pa·rish·io·ner \pə-ˈri-shə-nər\ *n* : a member or resident of a parish

par·i·ty \ˈper-ə-tē\ *n, pl* **-ties** : EQUALITY, EQUIVALENCE

¹**park** \ˈpärk\ *n* **1** : a tract of ground kept as a game preserve or recreation area **2** : a place where vehicles (as automobiles) are parked **3** : an enclosed stadium used esp. for ball games

²**park** *vb* **1** : to leave a vehicle temporarily (as in a parking lot or garage) **2** : to set and leave temporarily

par·ka \ˈpär-kə\ *n* : a very warm jacket with a hood

Par·kin·son's disease \ˈpär-kən-sənz-\ *n* : a chronic progressive neurological disease chiefly of later life marked esp. by tremor and weakness of resting muscles and by a shuffling gait

Parkinson's Law : an observation in office organization: work expands so as to fill the time available for its completion

par·kour \pär-ˈkùr, ˈpär-ˌkùr\ *n* [F, alter. of *parcours* course, route, fr. ML *percursus*, fr. L *percurrere* to run through] : the sport of traversing environmental obstacles by running, climbing, or leaping rapidly

park·way \ˈpärk-ˌwā\ *n* : a broad landscaped thoroughfare

par·lance \ˈpär-ləns\ *n* **1** : SPEECH **2** : manner of speaking 〈military ~〉

¹**par·lay** \ˈpär-ˌlā, -lē\ *vb* : to increase or change into something of much greater value 〈~ed a $1000 loan into a multimillion-dollar company〉

²**parlay** *n* : a series of bets in which the original stake plus its winnings are risked on successive wagers

par·ley \ˈpär-lē\ *n, pl* **parleys** : a conference usu. over matters in dispute : DISCUSSION — **parley** *vb*

par·lia·ment \ˈpär-lə-mənt\ *n* [ME, fr. AF *parlement*, fr. *parler* to speak, fr. ML *parabolare*, fr. LL *parabola* speech, parable] **1** : a formal governmental conference **2** *cap* : an assembly that constitutes the supreme legislative body of a country (as the United Kingdom) — **par·lia·men·ta·ry** \ˌpär-lə-ˈmen-tə-rē\ *adj*

par·lia·men·tar·i·an \ˌpär-lə-ˌmen-ˈter-ē-ən\ *n* **1** *often cap* : an adherent of the parliament during the English Civil War **2** : an expert in parliamentary procedure

par·lor \ˈpär-lər\ *n* **1** : a room for conversation or the reception of guests **2** : a place of business 〈beauty ~〉

par·lour \ˈpär-lər\ *chiefly Brit var of* PARLOR

par·lous \ˈpär-ləs\ *adj* : full of danger or risk : PRECARIOUS — **par·lous·ly** *adv*

Par·me·san \ˈpär-mə-ˌzän, -ˌzhän, -ˌzan\ *n* : a hard dry cheese with a sharp flavor

par·mi·gia·na \ˌpär-mi-ˈjä-nə, ˌpär-mi-ˈzhän\ *or* **par·mi·gia·no** \-ˈjä-(ˌ)nō\ *adj* : made or covered with Parmesan cheese 〈veal ~〉

pa·ro·chi·al \pə-ˈrō-kē-əl\ *adj* **1** : of or relating to a church parish **2** : limited in scope : NARROW, PROVINCIAL — **pa·ro·chi·al·ism** \-ə-ˌli-zəm\ *n*

parochial school *n* : a school maintained by a religious body

par·o·dy \ˈper-ə-dē\ *n, pl* **-dies** [L *parodia*, fr. Gk *parōidia*, fr. *para-* beside + *aidein* to sing] : a humorous or satirical imitation — **parody** *vb*

pa·role \pə-ˈrōl\ *n* : a conditional release of a prisoner whose sentence has not expired — **parole** *vb* — **pa·rol·ee** \-ˌrō-ˈlē, -ˈrō-ˌlē\ *n*

par·ox·ysm \ˈpa-rək-ˌsi-zəm, pə-ˈräk-\ *n* : a sudden sharp attack (as of pain or coughing) : CONVULSION — **par·ox·ys·mal** \ˌpa-rək-ˈsiz-məl, pə-ˌräk-\ *adj*

par·quet \ˈpär-ˌkā, pär-ˈkā\ *n* [F] **1** : a flooring of parquetry **2** : the lower floor of a theater; *esp* : the forward part of the orchestra

par·que·try \ˈpär-kə-trē\ *n, pl* **-tries** : fine woodwork inlaid in patterns

par·ri·cide \ˈpa-rə-ˌsīd\ *n* **1** : one that murders a parent or a close relative **2** : the act of a parricide

par·rot \ˈper-ət\ *n* : any of numerous bright-colored tropical birds that have a stout hooked bill

parrot fever *n* : PSITTACOSIS

par·ry \ˈper-ē\ *vb* **par·ried; par·ry·ing 1** : to ward off a weapon or blow **2** : to

evade esp. by an adroit answer — **parry**
n

parse \'pärs *also* 'pärz\ *vb* **parsed; pars·ing** : to give a grammatical description of
a word or a group of words

par·sec \'pär-,sek\ *n* : a unit of measure
for interstellar space equal to 3.26 light=
years

par·si·mo·ny \'pär-sə-,mō-nē\ *n* : ex·treme or excessive frugality — **par·si·mo·ni·ous** \,pär-sə-'mō-nē-əs\ *adj* —
par·si·mo·ni·ous·ly *adv*

pars·ley \'pär-slē\ *n* : a garden plant re·lated to the carrot that has finely divided
leaves used as a seasoning or garnish; *also*
: the leaves

pars·nip \'pär-snəp\ *n* : a garden plant
related to the carrot that has a long edi·ble usu. whitish root which is cooked as a
vegetable; *also* : the root

par·son \'pär-s⁸n\ *n* [ME *persone*, fr. AF,
fr. ML *persona*, lit., person, fr. L] : MINIS·TER 2, PASTOR

par·son·age \'pär-sə-nij\ *n* : a house pro·vided by a church for its pastor

¹**part** \'pärt\ *n* **1** : a division or portion of
a whole **2** : the melody or score for a
particular voice or instrument **3** : a spare
piece for a machine **4** : DUTY, FUNCTION
5 : one of the sides in a dispute **6** : ROLE;
also : an actor's lines in a play **7** *pl* : TAL·ENTS, ABILITY ⟨a man of many ∼*s*⟩ **8**
: the line where one's hair divides (as in
combing)

²**part** *vb* **1** : to take leave of someone **2**
: to divide or break into parts : SEPARATE
3 : to go away : DEPART; *also* : DIE **4** : to
give up possession ⟨∼ed with her jewels⟩
5 : APPORTION, SHARE

³**part** *abbr* **1** participial; participle **2** par·ticular

par·take \pär-'tāk\ *vb* **-took** \-'tůk\; **-tak·en** \-'tā-kən\; **-tak·ing 1** : to have a share
or part **2** : to take a portion (as of food)
— **par·tak·er** *n*

par·terre \pär-'ter\ *n* [F, fr. MF, fr. *par
terre* on the ground] **1** : an ornamental
garden with paths between the flower
beds **2** : the part of a theater floor behind
the orchestra

par·the·no·gen·e·sis \,pär-thə-nō-'je-nə-səs\ *n* [NL, fr. Gk *parthenos* virgin + L
genesis genesis] : development of a new
individual from an unfertilized usu. fe·male sex cell — **par·the·no·ge·net·ic**
\-jə-'ne-tik\ *adj*

par·tial \'pär-shəl\ *adj* **1** : not total or
general : affecting a part only **2** : favor·ing one party over the other : BIASED **3**
: markedly fond — used with *to* — **par·tial·i·ty** \,pär-shē-'a-lə-tē\ *n* — **par·tial·ly**
adv

par·tic·i·pate \pär-'ti-sə-,pāt\ *vb* **-pat·ed;
-pat·ing 1** : to take part in something
⟨∼ in a game⟩ **2** : SHARE — **par·tic·i·pant** \-pənt\ *adj or n* — **par·tic·i·pa·tion**
\-,ti-sə-'pā-shən\ *n* — **par·tic·i·pa·tor**
\-'ti-sə-,pā-tər\ *n* — **par·tic·i·pa·to·ry**
\-'ti-sə-pə-,tōr-ē\ *adj*

par·ti·ci·ple \'pär-tə-,si-pəl\ *n* : a word
having the characteristics of both verb

and adjective — **par·ti·cip·i·al** \,pär-tə-'si-pē-əl\ *adj*

par·ti·cle \'pär-ti-kəl\ *n* **1** : a very small
bit of matter **2** : a unit of speech (as an
article, preposition, or conjunction) ex·pressing some general aspect of meaning
or some connective or limiting relation

par·ti·cle·board \-,bôrd\ *n* : a board
made of very small pieces of wood bond·ed together

par·ti–col·or \,pär-tē-'kə-lər\ *or* **par·ti–col·ored** \-lərd\ *adj* : showing different
colors or tints; *esp* : having one main
color broken by patches of one or more
other colors

¹**par·tic·u·lar** \pər-'ti-kyə-lər\ *adj* **1** : of or
relating to a specific person or thing ⟨the
laws of a ∼ state⟩ **2** : DISTINCTIVE, SPE·CIAL ⟨the ∼ point of his talk⟩ **3** : SEPA·RATE, INDIVIDUAL ⟨each ∼ hair⟩ **4** : at·tentive to details : PRECISE **5** : hard to
please : EXACTING ⟨is ∼ about her
clothes⟩ — **par·tic·u·lar·i·ty** \-,ti-kyə-'lar-ə-tē\ *n* — **par·tic·u·lar·ly** *adv*

²**particular** *n* : an individual fact or detail

par·tic·u·lar·ise *Brit var of* PARTICULAR·IZE

par·tic·u·lar·ize \pər-'ti-kyə-lə-,rīz\ *vb*
-ized; -iz·ing 1 : to state in detail : SPEC·IFY **2** : to go into details

par·tic·u·late \pər-'ti-kyə-lət, pär-, -,lāt\
adj : relating to or existing as minute
separate particles — **particulate** *n*

¹**part·ing** *n* : a place or point of separation
or divergence

²**parting** *adj* : given, taken, or done at
parting ⟨a ∼ kiss⟩

par·ti·san *also* **par·ti·zan** \'pär-tə-zən,
-sən\ *n* **1** : one that takes the part of an·other : ADHERENT **2** : GUERRILLA —
partisan *adj* — **par·ti·san·ship** *n*

par·tite \'pär-,tīt\ *adj* : divided into a usu.
specified number of parts

par·ti·tion \pär-'ti-shən\ *n* **1** : DIVISION **2**
: something that divides or separates; *esp*
: an interior dividing wall — **partition** *vb*

par·ti·tive \'pär-tə-tiv\ *adj* : of, relating
to, or denoting a part

part·ly \'pärt-lē\ *adv* : in part : in some
measure or degree

part·ner \'pärt-nər\ *n* **1** : ASSOCIATE,
COLLEAGUE **2** : either of two persons
who dance together **3** : one who plays on
the same team with another **4** : SPOUSE
5 : one of two or more persons contractu·ally associated as joint principals in a
business — **part·ner·ship** *n*

part of speech : a class of words (as
nouns or verbs) distinguished according
to the kind of idea denoted and the func·tion performed in a sentence

par·tridge \'pär-trij\ *n, pl* **partridge** *or*
par·tridg·es : any of various stout-bod·ied Old World game birds

part–song \'pärt-,sôn\ *n* : a song with
two or more voice parts

part–time \-'tīm\ *adj or adv* : involving or
working less than a full or regular sched·ule — **part–tim·er** \-,tī-mər\ *n*

par·tu·ri·tion \,pär-tə-'ri-shən, ,pär-chə-,
,pär-tyü-\ *n* : CHILDBIRTH

part·way \'pärt-ˌwā\ *adv* : to some extent : PARTLY

par·ty \'pär-tē\ *n, pl* **parties** **1** : a person or group taking one side of a question; *esp* : a group of persons organized for the purpose of directing the policies of a government **2** : a person or group concerned in an action or affair : PARTICIPANT **3** : a group of persons detailed for a common task **4** : a social gathering

party animal *n* : a person known for frequent attendance at parties

par·ty·go·er \'pär-tē-ˌgō-ər\ *n* : a person who attends a party or who attends parties frequently

par·ve·nu \'pär-və-ˌnü, -ˌnyü\ *n* [F, fr. pp. of *parvenir* to arrive, fr. L *pervenire*, fr. *per* through + *venire* to come] : one who has recently or suddenly risen to wealth or power but has not yet secured the social position associated with it

pas \'pä\ *n, pl* **pas** *same or* 'päz\ : a dance step or combination of steps

pas·cal \pas-'kal\ *n* : a unit of pressure in the metric system equal to one newton per square meter

pas·chal \'pas-kəl\ *adj* : of, relating to, appropriate for, or used during Passover or Easter ceremonies

pa·sha \'pä-shə, 'pa-; pə-'shä\ *n* : a man (as formerly a governor in Turkey) of high rank

pash·mi·na \ˌpəsh-'mē-nə\ *n* : a fine wool from the undercoat of domestic Himalayan goats; *also* : a shawl made from this wool

¹pass \'pas\ *vb* **1** : MOVE, PROCEED **2** : to go away; *also* : DIE **3** : to move past, beyond, or over **4** : to allow to elapse : SPEND **5** : to go or make way through **6** : to go or allow to go unchallenged **7** : to undergo transfer **8** : to render a legal judgment **9** : OCCUR **10** : to secure the approval of (as a legislature) **11** : to go or cause to go through an inspection, test, or course of study successfully **12** : to be regarded **13** : CIRCULATE ⟨~ a note⟩ **14** : VOID **15** : to transfer the ball or puck to another player **16** : to decline to bid or bet on one's hand in a card game **17** : to give a base on balls to **18** : to let something go by without accepting ⟨~ed on his offer⟩ — **pass·er** *n*

²pass *n* : a gap in a mountain range

³pass *n* **1** : the act or an instance of passing **2** : REALIZATION, ACCOMPLISHMENT **3** : a state of affairs **4** : a written authorization to leave, enter, or move about freely **5** : a transfer of a ball or puck from one player to another **6** : BASE ON BALLS **7** : EFFORT, TRY **8** : a sexually inviting gesture or approach

⁴pass *abbr* **1** passenger **2** passive

pass·able \'pa-sə-bəl\ *adj* **1** : capable of being passed or traveled on **2** : just good enough : TOLERABLE ⟨did a ~ job⟩ — **pass·ably** \-blē\ *adv*

pas·sage \'pa-sij\ *n* **1** : a means (as a road or corridor) of passing **2** : the action or process of passing **3** : a voyage esp. by sea or air **4** : a right or permission

to pass **5** : ENACTMENT **6** : a usu. brief portion or section (as of a book)

pas·sage·way \-ˌwā\ *n* : a way that allows passage

pass·book \'pas-ˌbůk\ *n* : BANKBOOK

pas·sé \pa-'sā\ *adj* **1** : past one's prime **2** : not up-to-date : OUTMODED

pas·sel \'pa-səl\ *n* : a large number ⟨a ~ of children⟩

pas·sen·ger \'pa-sᵊn-jər\ *n* : a traveler in a public or private conveyance

pass·er·by \'pa-sər-ˌbī\ *n, pl* **pass·ers·by** : one who passes by

pas·ser·ine \'pa-sə-ˌrīn\ *adj* : of or relating to the large order of birds comprising singing birds that perch

pas·sim \'pa-səm\ *adv* [L, fr. *passus* scattered, fr. pp. of *pandere* to spread] : here and there : THROUGHOUT

pass·ing *n* : the act of one that passes or causes to pass; *esp* : DEATH

pas·sion \'pa-shən\ *n* **1** *often cap* : the sufferings of Christ between the night of the Last Supper and his death **2** : strong feeling; *also, pl* : the emotions as distinguished from reason **3** : RAGE, ANGER **4** : LOVE; *also* : an object of affection or enthusiasm **5** : sexual desire — **pas·sion·ate** \'pa-shə-nət\ *adj* — **pas·sion·ate·ly** *adv* — **pas·sion·less** *adj*

pas·sion·flow·er \'pa-shən-ˌflaů-(ə)r\ *n* [fr. the fancied resemblance of parts of the flower to the instruments of Christ's crucifixion] : any of a genus of chiefly tropical woody climbing vines or erect herbs with showy flowers and pulpy often edible berries (**passion fruit**)

pas·sive \'pa-siv\ *adj* **1** : not active : acted upon **2** : asserting that the grammatical subject is subjected to or affected by the action represented by the verb ⟨~ voice⟩ **3** : making use of the sun's heat usu. without the aid of mechanical devices **4** : SUBMISSIVE, PATIENT — **passive** *n* — **pas·sive·ly** *adv* — **pas·siv·i·ty** \pa-'si-və-tē\ *n*

pas·sive–ma·trix \-'mā-triks\ *adj* : of, relating to, or being on LCD in which pixels are controlled in groups

pass·key \'pas-ˌkē\ *n* : a key for opening two or more locks

pass out *vb* : to lose consciousness

Pass·over \'pas-ˌō-vər\ *n* [fr. the exemption of the Israelites from the slaughter of the firstborn in Egypt (Exod 12:23–27)] : a Jewish holiday celebrated in March or April in commemoration of the Hebrews' liberation from slavery in Egypt

pass·port \'pas-ˌpȯrt\ *n* : an official document issued by a country upon request to a citizen requesting protection during travel abroad

pass up *vb* : DECLINE, REJECT

pass·word \'pas-ˌwərd\ *n* **1** : a word or phrase that must be spoken by a person before being allowed to pass a guard **2** : a sequence of characters required for access to a computer system

¹past \'past\ *adj* **1** : AGO ⟨10 years ~⟩ **2** : just gone or elapsed ⟨the ~ month⟩ **3** : having existed or taken place in a period before the present : BYGONE **4** : of, relating to, or constituting a verb tense that expresses time gone by

²**past** *prep or adv* : BEYOND

³**past** *n* **1** : time gone by **2** : something that happened or was done in a former time **3** : the past tense; *also* : a verb form in it **4** : a secret past life

pas·ta \ˈpäs-tə\ *n* [It] **1** : a paste in processed form (as macaroni) or in the form of fresh dough (as ravioli) **2** : a dish of cooked pasta

¹**paste** \ˈpāst\ *n* [ME, fr. AF, fr. LL *pasta* dough, paste] **1** : DOUGH **2** : a smooth food product made by evaporation or grinding ⟨tomato ~⟩ **3** : a shaped dough (as spaghetti or ravioli) **4** : a preparation (as of flour and water) for sticking things together **5** : a brilliant glass used for artificial gems

²**paste** *vb* **past·ed; past·ing** : to cause to adhere by paste : STICK

paste·board \ˈpāst-ˌbȯrd\ *n* : CARDBOARD

¹**pas·tel** \pas-ˈtel\ *n* **1** : a paste made of powdered pigment; *also* : a crayon of such paste **2** : a drawing in pastel **3** : a pale or light color

²**pastel** *adj* **1** : of or relating to a pastel **2** : pale in color

pas·tern \ˈpas-tərn\ *n* : the part of a horse's foot extending from the fetlock to the top of the hoof

pas·teur·i·za·tion \ˌpas-chə-rə-ˈzā-shən, ˌpas-tə-\ *n* : partial sterilization of a substance (as milk) by heat or radiation — **pas·teur·ize** \ˈpas-chə-ˌrīz, ˈpas-tə-\ *vb* — **pas·teur·iz·er** *n*

pas·tiche \pas-ˈtēsh\ *n* : a composition (as in literature or music) made up of selections from different works

pas·tille \pas-ˈtēl\ *n* : LOZENGE 2

pas·time \ˈpas-ˌtīm\ *n* : DIVERSION; *esp* : something that serves to make time pass agreeably

pas·tor \ˈpas-tər\ *n* [ME *pastour*, fr. AF, fr. L *pastor*, herdsman, fr. *pascere* to feed, pasture, nurture] : a minister or priest serving a local church or parish — **pas·tor·ate** \-tə-rət\ *n*

¹**pas·to·ral** \ˈpas-tə-rəl\ *adj* **1** : of or relating to shepherds or to rural life **2** : of or relating to spiritual guidance esp. of a congregation **3** : of or relating to the pastor of a church

²**pastoral** *n* : a literary work dealing with shepherds or rural life

pas·to·rale \ˌpas-tə-ˈräl, -ˈral\ *n* [It] : a musical composition having a pastoral theme

past participle *n* : a participle that typically expresses completed action, that is one of the principal parts of the verb, and that is used in the formation of perfect tenses in the active voice and of all tenses in the passive voice

pas·tra·mi \pə-ˈsträ-mē\ *n* [Yiddish *pastrame*] : a highly seasoned smoked beef prepared esp. from shoulder cuts

pas·try \ˈpā-strē\ *n, pl* **pastries** : sweet baked goods made of dough or with a crust made of enriched dough

pas·tur·age \ˈpas-chə-rij\ *n* : PASTURE

¹**pas·ture** \ˈpas-chər\ *n* **1** : plants (as grass) for the feeding esp. of grazing livestock **2** : land or a plot of land used for grazing

²**pasture** *vb* **pas·tured; pas·tur·ing 1** : GRAZE **2** : to use as pasture

pasty \ˈpā-stē\ *adj* **past·i·er; -est** : resembling paste; *esp* : pallid and unhealthy in appearance

¹**pat** \ˈpat\ *n* **1** : a light tap esp. with the hand or a flat instrument; *also* : the sound made by it **2** : something (as butter) shaped into a small usu. square individual portion

²**pat** *adv* : in a pat manner : PERFECTLY

³**pat** *vb* **pat·ted; pat·ting 1** : to strike lightly with a flat instrument **2** : to flatten, smooth, or put into place or shape with a pat **3** : to tap gently or lovingly with the hand

⁴**pat** *adj* **1** : exactly suited to the occasion : APT **2** : memorized exactly **3** : UNYIELDING ⟨stood ~ on the issue⟩

PAT *abbr* point after touchdown

pa·ta·ca \pə-ˈtä-kə\ *n* — see MONEY table

¹**patch** \ˈpach\ *n* **1** : a piece used to cover a torn or worn place; *also* : one worn on a garment as an ornament or insignia **2** : a small area distinct from that about it **3** : a shield worn over the socket of an injured or missing eye

²**patch** *vb* **1** : to mend or cover with a patch **2** : to make of fragments **3** : to repair usu. in hasty fashion

patch·ou·li \ˈpa-chə-lē, pə-ˈchü-lē\ *n* : a heavy perfume made from the fragrant essential oil of an Asian mint; *also* : the plant itself

patch test *n* : a test for allergic sensitivity made by applying to the unbroken skin small pads soaked with the allergen to be tested

patch·work \ˈpach-ˌwərk\ *n* : something made of pieces of different materials, shapes, or colors

patchy \ˈpa-chē\ *adj* **patch·i·er; -est** : marked by or consisting of patches; *also* : irregular in appearance or quality — **patch·i·ness** \-chē-nəs\ *n*

pate \ˈpāt\ *n* : HEAD; *esp* : the crown of the head

pâ·té *also* **pate** \pä-ˈtā\ *n* [F] **1** : a meat or fish pie or patty **2** : a spread of finely chopped or pureed seasoned meat

pa·tel·la \pə-ˈte-lə\ *n, pl* **-lae** \-ˈte-(ˌ)lē, -ˌlī\ *or* **-las** [L] : KNEECAP — **pa·tel·lar** \-ˈte-lər\ *adj*

pat·en \ˈpa-tᵊn\ *n* **1** : PLATE; *esp* : one of precious metal for the eucharistic bread **2** : a thin disk

¹**pat·ent** \/ & *4 are* ˈpa-tᵊnt, *Brit also* ˈpā-, *2* & *3 are* ˈpa-tᵊnt, ˈpā-\ *adj* **1** : open to public inspection — used chiefly in the phrase *letters patent* **2** : free from obstruction **3** : EVIDENT, OBVIOUS **4** : protected by a patent ◆ **Synonyms** MANIFEST, DISTINCT, APPARENT, PALPABLE, PLAIN, CLEAR — **pat·ent·ly** *adv*

²**pat·ent** \ˈpa-tᵊnt, *Brit also* ˈpā-\ *n* **1** : an official document conferring a right or privilege **2** : a document securing to an

inventor for a term of years exclusive right to his or her invention **3** : something patented

³pat·ent *vb* : to secure by patent

pat·en·tee \ˌpa-tᵊn-ˈtē, *Brit also* ˌpā-\ *n* : one to whom a grant is made or a privilege secured by patent

patent medicine \ˈpa-tᵊnt-\ *n* : a packaged nonprescription drug protected by a trademark; *also* : any proprietary drug

pa·ter·fa·mil·i·as \ˌpä-tər-fə-ˈmi-lē-əs\ *n*, *pl* **pa·tres·fa·mil·i·as** \ˌpā-ˌtrēz-\ [L] : the father of a family : the male head of a household

pa·ter·nal \pə-ˈtər-nᵊl\ *adj* **1** : FATHERLY **2** : related through or inherited or derived from a father — **pa·ter·nal·ly** *adv*

pa·ter·nal·ism \-nə-ˌli-zəm\ *n* : a system under which an authority treats those under its control paternally (as by regulating their conduct and supplying their needs)

¹pa·ter·ni·ty \pə-ˈtər-nə-tē\ *n* **1** : FATHERHOOD **2** : descent from a father

²paternity *adj* **1** : granted to a father ⟨∼ leave⟩ **2** : of or relating to the determination of paternity ⟨a ∼ suit⟩

¹path \ˈpath, ˈpäth\ *n*, *pl* **paths** \ˈpathz, ˈpaths, ˈpäthz, ˈpäths\ **1** : a trodden way **2** : ROUTE, COURSE — **path·less** *adj*

²path *or* **pathol** *abbr* pathology

path·break·ing \ˈpath-ˌbrā-kiŋ\ *adj* : TRAILBLAZING

pa·thet·ic \pə-ˈthe-tik\ *adj* **1** : evoking tenderness, pity, or sorrow **2** : pitifully inadequate ⟨a ∼ performance⟩ ♦ **Synonyms** PITIFUL, PITEOUS, PITIABLE, POOR — **pa·thet·i·cal·ly** \-ti-k(ə-)lē\ *adv*

path·find·er \ˈpath-ˌfīn-dər, ˈpäth-\ *n* : one that discovers a way; *esp* : one that explores untraveled regions to mark out a new route

patho·gen \ˈpa-thə-jən\ *n* : a specific agent (as a bacterium) causing disease — **patho·gen·ic** \ˌpa-thə-ˈje-nik\ *adj* — **patho·ge·nic·i·ty** \-jə-ˈni-sə-tē\ *n*

pa·thog·ra·phy \pə-ˈthä-grə-fē\ *n* : biography focusing on a person's flaws and misfortunes

pa·thol·o·gy \pə-ˈthä-lə-jē\ *n*, *pl* **-gies 1** : the study of the essential nature of disease **2** : the abnormality of structure and function characteristic of a disease **3** : deviation giving rise to social ills — **path·o·log·i·cal** \ˌpa-thə-ˈlä-ji-kəl\ *adj* — **pa·thol·o·gist** \pə-ˈthä-lə-jist\ *n*

pa·thos \ˈpā-ˌthäs, -ˌthōs\ *n* : an element in experience or artistic representation evoking pity or compassion

path·way \ˈpath-ˌwā, ˈpäth-\ *n* : PATH

pa·tience \ˈpā-shəns\ *n* **1** : the capacity, habit, or fact of being patient **2** *chiefly Brit* : SOLITAIRE 2

¹pa·tient \ˈpā-shənt\ *adj* **1** : bearing pain or trials without complaint **2** : showing self-control : CALM **3** : STEADFAST, PERSEVERING — **pa·tient·ly** *adv*

²patient *n* : one under medical care

pa·ti·na \ˈpa-tə-nə, pə-ˈtē-\ *n*, *pl* **pa·ti·nas** \-nəz\ *or* **pa·ti·nae** \ˈpa-tə-ˌnē, -ˌnī\ **1** : a green film formed on copper and bronze

by exposure to moist air **2** : a superficial covering or exterior

pa·tio \ˈpa-tē-ˌō, ˈpä-\ *n*, *pl* **pa·ti·os 1** : COURTYARD **2** : an often paved area near a dwelling used esp. for outdoor dining

pa·tois \ˈpa-ˌtwä\ *n*, *pl* **pa·tois** \-ˌtwäz\ [F] **1** : a dialect other than the standard dialect; *esp* : uneducated or provincial speech **2** : JARGON 2

pa·tri·arch \ˈpā-trē-ˌärk\ *n* **1** : a man revered as father or founder (as of a tribe) **2** : a venerable old man **3** : an ecclesiastical dignitary (as the bishop of an Eastern Orthodox see) — **pa·tri·ar·chal** \ˌpā-trē-ˈär-kəl\ *adj* — **pa·tri·arch·ate** \ˈpā-trē-ˌär-kət, -ˌkät\ *n* — **pa·tri·ar·chy** \-ˌär-kē\ *n*

pa·tri·cian \pə-ˈtri-shən\ *n* : a person of high birth : ARISTOCRAT — **patrician** *adj*

pat·ri·cide \ˈpa-trə-ˌsīd\ *n* **1** : one who murders his or her own father **2** : the murder of one's own father

pat·ri·mo·ny \ˈpa-trə-ˌmō-nē\ *n* : something (as an estate) inherited or derived esp. from one's father : HERITAGE — **pat·ri·mo·ni·al** \ˌpa-trə-ˈmō-nē-əl\ *adj*

pa·tri·ot \ˈpā-trē-ət, -ˌät\ *n* [MF *patriote* compatriot, fr. LL *patriota*, fr. Gk *patriōtēs*, fr. *patria* lineage, fr. *patr-, patēr* father] : one who loves his or her country — **pa·tri·ot·ic** \ˌpā-trē-ˈä-tik\ *adj* — **pa·tri·ot·i·cal·ly** \-ti-k(ə-)lē\ *adv* — **pa·tri·o·tism** \ˈpā-trē-ə-ˌti-zəm\ *n*

pa·tris·tic \pə-ˈtris-tik\ *adj* : of or relating to the church fathers or their writings

¹pa·trol \pə-ˈtrōl\ *n* : the action of going the rounds (as of an area) for observation or the maintenance of security; *also* : a person or group performing such an action

²patrol *vb* **pa·trolled; pa·trol·ling** : to carry out a patrol

pa·trol·man \pə-ˈtrōl-mən\ *n* : a police officer assigned to a beat

patrol wagon *n* : PADDY WAGON

pa·tron \ˈpā-trən\ *n* [ME, fr. AF, fr. ML & L; ML *patronus* patron saint, patron of a benefice, pattern, fr. L, defender, fr. *patr-, pater* father] **1** : a person chosen or named as special protector **2** : a wealthy or influential supporter ⟨∼ of poets⟩; *also* : BENEFACTOR **3** : a regular client or customer ⟨diner ∼s⟩

pa·tron·age \ˈpa-trə-nij, ˈpā-\ *n* **1** : the support or influence of a patron **2** : the trade of customers **3** : control of appointment to government jobs

pa·tron·ess \ˈpā-trə-nəs\ *n* : a woman who is a patron

pa·tron·ise *Brit var of* PATRONIZE

pa·tron·ize \ˈpā-trə-ˌnīz, ˈpa-\ *vb* **-ized; -iz·ing 1** : to be a customer of **2** : to treat condescendingly, haughtily, or coolly ⟨rich people who ∼ the poor⟩

pat·ro·nym·ic \ˌpa-trə-ˈni-mik\ *n* : a name derived from the name of one's father or a paternal ancestor usu. by the addition of an affix

pa·troon \pə-ˈtrün\ *n* : the proprietor of a manorial estate esp. in New York under Dutch rule

pat·sy \'pat-sē\ *n, pl* **pat·sies** : a person who is easily duped or victimized

¹**pat·ter** \'pa-tər\ *vb* : to talk glibly or mechanically ✦ *Synonyms* CHATTER, PRATE, CHAT, PRATTLE, BABBLE

²**patter** *n* 1 : a specialized lingo 2 : extremely rapid talk ⟨a comedian's ∼⟩

³**patter** *vb* : to strike, pat, or tap rapidly

⁴**patter** *n* : a quick succession of taps or pats ⟨the ∼ of rain⟩

pat·tern \'pa-tərn\ *n* [ME *patron*, fr. AF, fr. ML *patronus*, fr. L, defender, fr. *patr-*, *pater* father] 1 : an ideal model 2 : something used as a model for making things ⟨a dressmaker's ∼⟩ 3 : SAMPLE 4 : an artistic design 5 : CONFIGURATION 6 : a sample of a person's behaviors or characteristics ⟨a ∼ of violence⟩

²**pattern** *vb* : to form according to a pattern

pat·ty *also* **pat·tie** \'pa-tē\ *n, pl* **patties** 1 : a little pie 2 : a small flat cake esp. of chopped food ⟨hamburger *patties*⟩

pau·ci·ty \'pȯ-sə-tē\ *n* : smallness of number or quantity

paunch \'pȯnch\ *n* : a usu. large belly : POTBELLY — **paunchy** *adj*

pau·per \'pȯ-pər\ *n* : a person without means of support except from charity — **pau·per·ism** \-pə-ˌri-zəm\ *n* — **pau·per·ize** \-pə-ˌrīz\ *vb*

¹**pause** \'pȯz\ *n* 1 : a temporary stop; *also* : a period of inaction 2 : a brief suspension of the voice 3 : a sign ⌢ or ⌣ above or below a musical note or rest to show it is to be prolonged 4 : a reason for pausing 5 : a function of an electronic device that pauses a recording

²**pause** *vb* **paused; paus·ing** : to stop, rest, or linger for a time

pave \'pāv\ *vb* **paved; pav·ing** : to cover (as a road) with hard material in order to smooth or firm the surface

pave·ment \'pāv-mənt\ *n* 1 : a paved surface 2 : the material with which something is paved

pa·vil·ion \pə-'vil-yən\ *n* [ME *pavilloun*, *pavillioun*, fr. AF, fr. L *papilion-*, *papilio* butterfly] 1 : a large tent 2 : a usu. open structure (as in a park) used for entertainment or shelter

pav·ing \'pā-viŋ\ *n* : PAVEMENT

¹**paw** \'pȯ\ *n* : the foot of a quadruped (as a dog or lion) having claws

²**paw** *vb* 1 : to touch or strike with a paw; *also* : to scrape with a hoof 2 : to feel or handle clumsily or rudely 3 : to flail about or grab for with the hands

pawl \'pȯl\ *n* : a pivoted tongue or sliding bolt designed to fall into notches on another machine part to permit motion in one direction only

¹**pawn** \'pȯn\ *n* [ME *pown*, fr. AF *peoun*, *paun*, fr. ML *pedon-*, *pedo* foot soldier, fr. LL, one with broad feet, fr. L *ped-*, *pes* foot] 1 : a chess piece of the least value 2 : one used for the purposes of another

²**pawn** *n* 1 : something deposited as security for a loan; *also* : HOSTAGE 2 : the state of being pledged

³**pawn** *vb* : to deposit as a pledge

pawn·bro·ker \'pȯn-ˌbrō-kər\ *n* : one who lends money on goods pledged

Paw·nee \pȯ-'nē\ *n, pl* **Pawnee** *or* **Pawnees** : a member of an American Indian people orig. of Kansas and Nebraska

pawn·shop \'pȯn-ˌshäp\ *n* : a pawnbroker's place of business

paw·paw *also* **pa·paw** \pə-'pȯ\ : PAPAYA 2 \'pä-pȯ, 'pȯ-\ : a No. American tree with green-skinned edible fruit; *also* : its fruit

¹**pay** \'pā\ *vb* **paid** \'pād\ *also in sense 7* **payed; pay·ing** [ME, fr. AF *paier*, fr. L *pacare* to pacify, fr. *pac-*, *pax* peace] 1 : to make due return to for goods or services 2 : to discharge indebtedness for : SETTLE ⟨∼ a bill⟩ 3 : to give in forfeit ⟨∼ the penalty⟩ 4 : REQUITE 5 : to give, offer, or make freely or as fitting ⟨∼ attention⟩ 6 : to be profitable to : RETURN 7 : to make slack and allow to run out ⟨∼ out a rope⟩ — **pay·able** *adj* — **pay·ee** \pā-'ē\ *n* — **pay·er** *n*

²**pay** *n* 1 : something paid; *esp* : WAGES 2 : the status of being paid by an employer : EMPLOY

³**pay** *adj* 1 : containing something valuable (as gold) ⟨∼ dirt⟩ 2 : equipped to receive a fee for use ⟨∼ telephone⟩ 3 : requiring payment

pay·back \'pā-ˌbak\ *n* 1 : a return on an investment equal to the original capital outlay 2 : something given in return, compensation, or retaliation

pay·check \'pā-ˌchek\ *n* 1 : a check in payment of wages or salary 2 : WAGES, SALARY

pay·load \-ˌlōd\ *n* : the load carried by a vehicle in addition to what is necessary for its operation; *also* : the weight of such a load

pay·mas·ter \-ˌmas-tər\ *n* : one who distributes the payroll

pay·ment \'pā-mənt\ *n* 1 : the act of paying 2 : something paid

pay·off \-ˌȯf\ *n* 1 : PROFIT, REWARD; *also* : RETRIBUTION 2 : the climax of an incident or enterprise ⟨the ∼ of a story⟩

pay-per-view *n* : a cable television service by which customers can order access to a single airing of a TV feature

pay·roll \-ˌrōl\ *n* : a list of persons entitled to receive pay; *also* : the money to pay those on such a list

payt *abbr* payment

pay up *vb* : to pay what is due; *also* : to pay in full

Pb *symbol* [L *plumbum*] lead

PBS *abbr* Public Broadcasting Service

PBX \ˌpē-(ˌ)bē-'eks\ *n* [*private branch exchange*] : a private telephone switchboard

¹**PC** \ˌpē-'sē\ *n, pl* **PCs** *or* **PC's** [*personal computer*] : MICROCOMPUTER

²**PC** *abbr* 1 Peace Corps 2 percent; percentage 3 politically correct 4 postcard 5 [L *post cibum*] after meals 6 professional corporation

PCB \ˌpē-ˌsē-'bē\ *n* : POLYCHLORINATED BIPHENYL

PCP \ˌpē-ˌsē-'pē\ *n* : PHENCYCLIDINE

pct *abbr* percent; percentage

pd *abbr* paid

Pd *symbol* palladium

PD *abbr* **1** per diem **2** police department **3** potential difference

PDA \ˌpē-ˌdē-ˈā\ *n* [*personal digital assistant*] : a small microprocessor device for storing and organizing personal information

PDQ \ˌpē-ˌdē-ˈkyü\ *adv, often not cap* [abbr. of *pretty damned quick*] : IMMEDIATELY

PDT *abbr* Pacific daylight (saving) time

PE *abbr* **1** physical education **2** printer's error **3** professional engineer

pea \ˈpē\ *n, pl* **peas** *also* **pease** \ˈpēz\ **1** : the round edible protein-rich seed borne in the pod of a widely grown leguminous vine; *also* : this vine **2** : any of various plants resembling or related to the pea

peace \ˈpēs\ *n* **1** : a state of calm and quiet; *esp* : public security under law **2** : freedom from disturbing thoughts or emotions **3** : a state of concord (as between persons or governments); *also* : an agreement to end hostilities — **peace‧able** \ˈpē-sə-bəl\ *adj* — **peace‧ably** \-blē\ *adv* — **peace‧ful** *adj* — **peace‧ful‧ly** *adv*

peace‧keep‧ing \ˈpēs-ˌkē-piŋ\ *n* : the preserving of peace; *esp* : international enforcement and supervision of a truce — **peace‧keep‧er** *n*

peace‧mak‧er \-ˌmā-kər\ *n* : one who settles an argument or stops a fight

peace‧time \-ˌtīm\ *n* : a time when a nation is not at war

peach \ˈpēch\ *n* [ME *peche,* fr. AF *pesche, peche,* fr. LL *persica,* fr. L (*malum*) *Persicum,* lit., Persian fruit] : a sweet juicy fuzzy-skinned fruit of a small usu. pink-flowered tree related to the cherry and plums; *also* : this tree — **peachy** *adj*

pea‧cock \ˈpē-ˌkäk\ *n* [ME *pecok,* fr. pe- (fr. OE *pēa* peafowl, fr. L *pavo* peacock) + *cok* cock] : the male peafowl that can spread its long tail feathers to make a colorful display

pea‧fowl \-ˌfau̇(-ə)l\ *n* : either of two large domesticated Asian pheasants

pea‧hen \-ˌhen\ *n* : the female peafowl

¹peak \ˈpēk\ *n* **1** : a pointed or projecting part **2** : the top of a hill or mountain; *also* : MOUNTAIN **3** : the front projecting part of a cap **4** : the narrow part of a ship's bow or stern **5** : the highest level or greatest degree — **peak** *adj*

²peak *vb* : to bring to or reach a maximum

peak‧ed \ˈpē-kəd\ *adj* : THIN, SICKLY

¹peal \ˈpēl\ *n* **1** : the loud ringing of bells **2** : a set of tuned bells **3** : a loud sound or succession of sounds

²peal *vb* : to give out peals : RESOUND

pea‧nut \ˈpē-(ˌ)nət\ *n* **1** : an annual herb related to the pea but having pods that ripen underground; *also* : this pod or one of the edible seeds it bears **2** *pl* : a very small amount **3** : a pellet of polystyrene foam

pear \ˈper\ *n* : the fleshy fruit of a tree related to the apple; *also* : this tree

pearl \ˈpərl\ *n* **1** : a small hard often lustrous body formed within the shell of some mollusks used as a gem **2** : one that is choice or precious ⟨~s of wisdom⟩ **3** : a slightly bluish medium gray color — **pearly** \ˈpər-lē\ *adj*

peas‧ant \ˈpe-zᵊnt\ *n* **1** : any of a class of small landowners or laborers tilling the soil **2** : a usu. uneducated person of low social status — **peas‧ant‧ry** \-zᵊn-trē\ *n*

pea‧shoot‧er \ˈpē-ˌshü-tər\ *n* : a toy blowgun for shooting peas

peat \ˈpēt\ *n* : a dark substance formed by partial decay of plants (as mosses) in water — **peaty** *adj*

peat moss *n* : SPHAGNUM

¹peb‧ble \ˈpe-bəl\ *n* : a small usu. round stone — **peb‧bly** \-b(ə-)lē\ *adj*

²pebble *vb* **peb‧bled; peb‧bling** : to produce a rough surface texture in ⟨~ leather⟩

pec \ˈpek\ *n* : PECTORAL MUSCLE

pe‧can \pi-ˈkän, -ˈkan; ˈpē-ˌkan\ *n* : the smooth thin-shelled edible nut of a large American hickory; *also* : this tree

pec‧ca‧dil‧lo \ˌpe-kə-ˈdi-lō\ *n, pl* **-loes** *or* **-los** : a slight offense

pec‧ca‧ry \ˈpe-kə-rē\ *n, pl* **-ries** : any of several American chiefly tropical mammals resembling but smaller than the related pigs

pec‧ca‧vi \pe-ˈkä-ˌvē\ *n* [L, I have sinned, fr. *peccare* to sin] : an acknowledgment of sin

¹peck \ˈpek\ *n* — see WEIGHT table

²peck *vb* **1** : to strike or pierce with or as if with the bill **2** : to make (as a hole) by pecking **3** : to pick up with or as if with the bill

³peck *n* **1** : an impression made by pecking **2** : a quick sharp stroke

pecking order *also* **peck order** *n* : a basic pattern of social organization within a flock of poultry in which each bird pecks another lower in the scale without being pecked in return and submits to pecking by one of higher rank; *also* : a social hierarchy

pec‧tin \ˈpek-tən\ *n* : any of various water-soluble plant substances that cause fruit jellies to set — **pec‧tic** \-tik\ *adj*

pec‧to‧ral \ˈpek-tə-rəl\ *adj* : of or relating to the breast or chest

pectoral muscle *n* : either of two muscles on each side of the body which connect the front walls of the chest with the bones of the upper arm and shoulder

pe‧cu‧liar \pi-ˈkyül-yər\ *adj* [ME *peculier,* fr. L *peculiaris* of private property, special, fr. *peculium* private property, fr. *pecus* cattle] **1** : belonging exclusively to one person or group **2** : CHARACTERISTIC, DISTINCTIVE **3** : QUEER, ODD ⟨her ~ behavior⟩ ♦ **Synonyms** IDIOSYNCRATIC, ECCENTRIC, SINGULAR, STRANGE, WEIRD — **pe‧cu‧liar‧i‧ty** \-ˌkyül-ˈya-rə-tē, -ˌkyü-lē-ˈa-\ *n* — **pe‧cu‧liar‧ly** *adv*

pe‧cu‧ni‧ary \pi-ˈkyü-nē-ˌer-ē\ *adj* : of or relating to money : MONETARY

ped‧a‧gogue *also* **ped‧a‧gog** \ˈpe-də-ˌgäg\ *n* : TEACHER, SCHOOLMASTER

ped‧a‧go‧gy \ˈpe-də-ˌgō-jē, -ˌgä-\ *n* : the

¹**ped·al** \'pe-dᵊl\ *n* : a lever worked by the foot

²**pedal** *adj* : of or relating to the foot

³**pedal** *vb* **ped·aled** *also* **ped·alled; ped·al·ing** *also* **ped·al·ling** 1 : to use or work a pedal (as of a piano or bicycle) 2 : to ride a bicycle

ped·ant \'pe-dᵊnt\ *n* 1 : a person who makes a show of knowledge 2 : a formal uninspired teacher 〈his piano teacher was a ∼〉 — **pe·dan·tic** \pi-'dan-tik\ *adj* — **ped·ant·ry** \'pe-dᵊn-trē\ *n*

ped·dle \'pe-dᵊl\ *vb* **ped·dled; ped·dling** : to sell or offer for sale from place to place — **ped·dler** *also* **ped·lar** \'ped-lər\ *n*

ped·er·ast \'pe-də-ˌrast\ *n* [Gk *paiderastēs*, lit., lover of boys] : one who practices anal intercourse esp. with a boy — **ped·er·as·ty** \'pe-də-ˌras-tē\ *n*

ped·es·tal \'pe-dəs-tᵊl\ *n* 1 : the support or foot of something (as a column, statue, or vase) that is upright 2 : a position of high regard

¹**pe·des·tri·an** \pə-'des-trē-ən\ *adj* 1 : OR-DINARY 2 : going on foot

²**pedestrian** *n* : WALKER

pe·di·at·rics \ˌpē-dē-ˈa-triks\ *n* : a branch of medicine dealing with the development, care, and diseases of children — **pe·di·at·ric** \-trik\ *adj* — **pe·di·a·tri·cian** \ˌpē-dē-ə-ˈtri-shən\ *n*

pedi·cab \'pe-di-ˌkab\ *n* : a pedal-driven tricycle with seats for a driver and two passengers

pedi·cure \'pe-di-ˌkyúr\ *n* : care of the feet, toes, and nails; *also* : a single treatment of these parts — **ped·i·cur·ist** \-ˌkyúr-ist\ *n*

pedi·gree \'pe-də-ˌgrē\ *n* [ME *pedegru*, fr. AF *pé de grue*, lit., crane's foot; fr. the shape made by the lines of a genealogical chart] 1 : a record of a line of ancestors 2 : an ancestral line — **ped·i·greed** \-ˌgrēd\ *adj*

ped·i·ment \'pe-də-mənt\ *n* : a low triangular gablelike decoration (as over a door or window) on a building

pe·dom·e·ter \pi-'dä-mə-tər\ *n* : an instrument that measures the distance one walks

pe·do·phile \'pe-də-ˌfī(-ə)l, 'pē-\ *n* : one affected with pedophilia

pe·do·phil·ia \ˌpe-də-ˈfi-lē-ə, ˌpē-\ *n* : sexual perversion in which children are the preferred sexual object

pe·dun·cle \'pē-ˌdəŋ-kəl\ *n* : a narrow supporting stalk

peek \'pēk\ *vb* 1 : to look furtively 2 : to peer from a place of concealment 3 : GLANCE — **peek** *n*

¹**peel** \'pēl\ *vb* [ME *pelen*, fr. AF *peler*, fr. L *pilare* to remove the hair from, fr. *pilus* hair] 1 : to strip the skin, bark, or rind from 2 : to strip off (as a coat); *also* : to come off 3 : to lose the skin, bark, or rind

²**peel** *n* : a skin or rind esp. of a fruit

peel·ing \'pē-liŋ\ *n* : a peeled-off piece or strip (as of skin or rind)

peen \'pēn\ *n* : the usu. hemispherical or wedge-shaped end of the head of a hammer opposite the face

¹**peep** \'pēp\ *vb* : to utter a feeble shrill sound or the slightest sound

²**peep** *n* : a feeble shrill sound

³**peep** *vb* 1 : to look slyly esp. through an aperture : PEEK 2 : to begin to emerge 3 : to look at : WATCH — **peep·er** *n*

⁴**peep** *n* 1 : a first faint appearance 2 : a brief or furtive look

peep·hole \'pēp-ˌhōl\ *n* : a hole to peep through

¹**peer** \'pir\ *n* 1 : one of equal standing with another : EQUAL 2 : NOBLE — **peer·age** \-ij\ *n*

²**peer** *vb* 1 : to look intently or curiously 2 : to come slightly into view

peer·ess \'pir-əs\ *n* : a woman who is a peer

peer·less \'pir-ləs\ *adj* : having no equal : MATCHLESS 〈a ∼ cellist〉 ♦ *Syn-onyms* SUPREME, UNEQUALED, UNPARALLELED, INCOMPARABLE

¹**peeve** \'pēv\ *vb* **peeved; peev·ing** : to make resentful : ANNOY

²**peeve** *n* 1 : a feeling or mood of resentment 2 : a particular grievance

pee·vish \'pē-vish\ *adj* : querulous in temperament : FRETFUL ♦ *Synonyms* IRRITABLE, PETULANT, HUFFY — **pee·vish·ly** *adv* — **pee·vish·ness** *n*

pee·wee \'pē-ˌwē\ *n* 1 : one that is diminutive or tiny 2 : a level of sports usu. for young children — **peewee** *adj*

¹**peg** \'peg\ *n* 1 : a small pointed piece (as of wood) used to pin down or fasten things or to fit into holes 2 : a projecting piece used as a support or boundary marker 3 : SUPPORT, PRETEXT 4 : STEP, DEGREE 5 : THROW

²**peg** *vb* **pegged; peg·ging** 1 : to put a peg into : fasten, pin down, or attach with or as if with pegs 2 : to work hard and steadily : PLUG 3 : HUSTLE 4 : to mark by pegs 5 : to hold (as prices) at a set level or rate 6 : IDENTIFY 〈was *pegged* as an intellectual〉 7 : THROW

PEI *abbr* Prince Edward Island

pei·gnoir \pān-ˈwär, pen-\ *n* [F, lit., garment worn while combing the hair, fr. MF, fr. *peigner* to comb the hair, fr. L *pectinare*, fr. *pectin-, pecten* comb] : NEGLIGEE

¹**pe·jo·ra·tive** \pi-ˈjór-ə-tiv\ *n* : a pejorative word or phrase

²**pejorative** *adj* : having negative connotations : DISPARAGING — **pe·jo·ra·tive·ly** *adv*

peke \'pēk\ *n, often cap* : PEKINGESE

Pe·king·ese *or* **Pe·kin·ese** \ˌpē-kə-ˈnēz, -ˈnēs; -kin-ˈēz, -ˈēs\ *n, pl* **Pekingese** *or* **Pekinese** : any of a breed of Chinese origin of small short-legged long-haired dogs

pe·koe \'pē-(ˌ)kō\ *n* : a black tea made from young tea leaves

pel·age \'pe-lij\ *n* : the hairy covering of a mammal

pe·lag·ic \pə-ˈla-jik\ *adj* : OCEANIC

pelf \'pelf\ *n* : MONEY, RICHES

pel·i·can \'pe-li-kən\ *n* : any of a genus of large web-footed birds having a pouched lower bill used to scoop in fish

pel·la·gra \pə-'la-grə, -'lä-\ *n* : a disease caused by a diet with too little niacin and protein and marked by a skin rash, disease of the digestive system, and mental disturbances

pel·let \'pe-lət\ *n* **1** : a little ball (as of medicine) **2** : BULLET — **pel·let·al** \-lə-təl\ *adj* — **pel·let·ize** \-ˌtīz\ *vb*

pell–mell \ˌpel-'mel\ *adv* **1** : in mingled confusion ⟨papers strewn ~ on the desk⟩ **2** : HEADLONG ⟨ran ~ for the door⟩

pel·lu·cid \pə-'lü-səd\ *adj* : extremely clear : LIMPID, TRANSPARENT ⟨a ~ stream⟩ ♦ *Synonyms* TRANSLUCENT, LUCID, LUCENT

pe·lo·ton \ˌpe-lə-'tän\ *n* : the main body of riders in a bicycle race

¹pelt \'pelt\ *n* : a skin esp. of a fur-bearing animal

²pelt *vb* : to strike with a succession of blows or missiles

pel·vis \'pel-vəs\ *n, pl* **pel·vis·es** \-və-səz\ *or* **pel·ves** \-ˌvēz\ : a basin-shaped part of the vertebrate skeleton consisting of the large bone of each hip and the nearby bones of the spine — **pel·vic** \-vik\ *adj*

pem·mi·can *also* **pem·i·can** \'pe-mi-kən\ *n* : dried meat pounded fine and mixed with melted fat

¹pen \'pen\ *vb* **penned; pen·ning** : to shut in or as if in a pen

²pen *n* **1** : a small enclosure for animals **2** : a small place of confinement or storage

³pen *n* **1** : an implement for writing or drawing with ink or a similar fluid **2** : a writing instrument regarded as a means of expression **3** : STYLUS 3

⁴pen *vb* **penned; pen·ning** : WRITE

⁵pen *n* : PENITENTIARY

⁶pen *abbr* peninsula

PEN *abbr* International Association of Poets, Playwrights, Editors, Essayists and Novelists

pe·nal \'pē-n°l\ *adj* : of or relating to punishment

pe·nal·ise *Brit var of* PENALIZE

pe·nal·ize \'pē-nə-ˌliz, 'pe-\ *vb* **-ized; -iz·ing** : to put a penalty on

pen·al·ty \'pe-n°l-tē\ *n, pl* **-ties** **1** : punishment for crime or offense **2** : something forfeited when a person fails to do something agreed to **3** : disadvantage, loss, or hardship (as to a competitor) due to some action

pen·ance \'pe-nəns\ *n* **1** : an act performed to show sorrow or repentance for sin **2** : a sacrament (as in the Roman Catholic Church) consisting of confession, absolution, and a penance directed by the confessor

pence \'pens\ *pl of* PENNY

pen·chant \'pen-chənt\ *n* [F, fr. prp. of *pencher* to incline, fr. VL *pendicare*, fr. L *pendere* to weigh] : a strong inclination : LIKING ⟨a ~ for taking risks⟩ ♦ *Synonyms* LEANING, PROPENSITY, PREDILECTION, PREDISPOSITION

¹pen·cil \'pen-səl\ *n* : a writing or drawing tool consisting of or containing a slender cylinder of a solid marking substance

²pencil *vb* **-ciled** *or* **-cilled; -cil·ing** *or* **-cil·ling 1** : to draw or write with a pencil **2** : to plan or designate tentatively ⟨~ed in the appointment⟩

pen·dant *also* **pen·dent** \'pen-dənt\ *n* : a hanging ornament (as on a necklace)

pen·dent *or* **pen·dant** \'pen-dənt\ *adj* : SUSPENDED, OVERHANGING

¹pend·ing \'pen-diŋ\ *prep* **1** : DURING **2** : while awaiting ⟨~ approval⟩

²pending *adj* **1** : not yet decided ⟨a ~ application⟩ **2** : IMMINENT

pen·du·lous \'pen-jə-ləs, -də-\ *adj* : hanging loosely : DROOPING ⟨~ earrings⟩

pen·du·lum \-ləm\ *n* : a body that swings freely from a fixed point

pe·ne·plain *also* **pe·ne·plane** \'pē-ni-ˌplān\ *n* : a large almost flat land surface shaped by erosion

pen·e·trate \'pe-nə-ˌtrāt\ *vb* **-trat·ed; -trat·ing 1** : to enter into : PIERCE **2** : PERMEATE **3** : to see into : UNDERSTAND **4** : to affect deeply — **pen·e·tra·ble** \-trə-bəl\ *adj* — **pen·e·tra·tion** \ˌpe-nə-'trā-shən\ *n* — **pen·e·tra·tive** \'pe-nə-ˌtrā-tiv\ *adj*

penetrating *adj* **1** : having the power of entering, piercing, or pervading ⟨a ~ shriek⟩ ⟨a ~ odor⟩ **2** : ACUTE, DISCERNING ⟨a ~ look⟩

pen·guin \'peŋ-gwən, 'pen-\ *n* : any of various erect short-legged flightless seabirds of the southern hemisphere

pen·i·cil·lin \ˌpe-nə-'si-lən\ *n* : any of several antibiotics produced by molds or synthetically and used against various bacteria

pen·in·su·la \pə-'nin-sə-lə\ *n* [L *paeninsula*, fr. *paene* almost + *insula* island] : a long narrow portion of land extending out into the water — **pen·in·su·lar** \-lər\ *adj*

pe·nis \'pē-nəs\ *n, pl* **pe·nis·es** *also* **pe·nes** \-ˌnēz\ : a male organ of copulation that in the human male also functions as the channel by which urine leaves the body

¹pen·i·tent \'pe-nə-tənt\ *adj* : feeling sorrow for sins or offenses : REPENTANT — **pen·i·tence** \-təns\ *n* — **pen·i·ten·tial** \ˌpe-nə-'ten-chəl\ *adj*

²penitent *n* : a penitent person

¹pen·i·ten·tia·ry \ˌpe-nə-'ten-chə-rē\ *n, pl* **-ries** : a state or federal prison

²penitentiary *adj* : of, relating to, or incurring confinement in a penitentiary

pen·knife \'pen-ˌnīf\ *n* : a small pocket-knife

pen·light *also* **pen·lite** \-ˌlīt\ *n* : a small flashlight resembling a fountain pen in size or shape

pen·man \'pen-mən\ *n* **1** : COPYIST : one skilled in penmanship **3** : AUTHOR

pen·man·ship \-ˌship\ *n* : the art or practice of writing with the pen

Penn *or* **Penna** *abbr* Pennsylvania

pen name *n* : an author's pseudonym

pen·nant \'pe-nənt\ *n* **1** : a tapering flag

used esp. for signaling **2** : a flag symbolic of championship

pen·ne \'pe-nā\ *n* : short diagonally cut tubular pasta

pen·ni \'pe-nē\ *n, pl* **pen·nia** \-nē-ə\ *or* **pen·nis** \-nēz\ : a former monetary unit equal to ¹/₁₀₀ markka

pen·non \'pe-nən\ *n* **1** : a long narrow ribbonlike flag borne on a lance **2** : WING

Penn·syl·va·nian \,pen-səl-'vā-ııyən\ *adj* **1** : of or relating to Pennsylvania or its people **2** : of, relating to, or being the period of the Paleozoic era between the Mississippian and the Permian — **Pennsylvanian** *n*

pen·ny \'pe-nē\ *n, pl* **pennies** \-nēz\ *or* **pence** \'pens\ **1** *pl usu* **pence** : a British monetary unit formerly equal to ¹/₁₂ shilling but now equal to ¹/₁₀₀ pound; *also* : a coin of this value — see *pound* at MONEY table **2** *pl* **pennies** : a cent of the U.S. or Canada **3** : a former monetary unit equal to ¹/₁₀₀ Irish pound — **pen·ni·less** \'pe-ni-ləs\ *adj*

pen·ny–pinch·ing \'pe-nē-,pin-chiŋ\ *n* : PARSIMONY — **pen·ny–pinch·er** *n* — **penny–pinching** *adj*

pen·ny·weight \-,wāt\ *n* — see WEIGHT table

pen·ny–wise \-,wīz\ *adj* : wise or prudent only in small matters

pe·nol·o·gy \pi-'nä-lə-jē\ *n* : a branch of criminology dealing with prisons and the treatment of offenders

¹**pen·sion** \'pen-chən\ *n* : a fixed sum paid regularly esp. to a person retired from service

²**pension** *vb* : to pay a pension to — **pension·er** *n*

pen·sive \'pen-siv\ *adj* : musingly, dreamily, or sadly thoughtful ♦ **Synonyms** REFLECTIVE, SPECULATIVE, CONTEMPLATIVE, MEDITATIVE — **pen·sive·ly** *adv*

pen·stock \'pen-,stäk\ *n* **1** : a sluice or gate for regulating a flow **2** : a pipe for carrying water

pent \'pent\ *adj* : shut up : CONFINED

pen·ta·gon \'pen-tə-,gän\ *n* : a polygon of five angles and five sides — **pen·tag·o·nal** \pen-'ta-gə-nºl\ *adj*

pen·tam·e·ter \pen-'ta-mə-tər\ *n* : a line of verse containing five metrical feet

pen·tath·lon \pen-'tath-lən\ *n* : a composite athletic contest consisting of five events

Pen·te·cost \'pen-ti-,kóst\ *n* : the 7th Sunday after Easter observed as a church festival commemorating the descent of the Holy Spirit on the apostles — **Pen·te·cos·tal** \,pen-ti-'käs-tºl\ *adj*

Pentecostal *n* : a member of a Christian religious body that stresses expressive worship, evangelism, and spiritual gifts — **Pen·te·cos·tal·ism** \,pen-ti-'käs-tə-,li-zəm\

pent·house \'pent-,haůs\ *n* [alter. of ME *pentis*, fr. AF *apentiz*, fr. *apent*, pp. of *apendre* to attach, hang against] **1** : a shed or sloping roof attached to a wall or building **2** : an apartment built on the top floor or roof of a building

pen·ul·ti·mate \pi-'nəl-tə-mət\ *adj* : next to the last ⟨~ syllable⟩

pen·um·bra \pə-'nəm-brə\ *n, pl* **-brae** \-(,)brē\ *or* **-bras** **1** : the partial shadow surrounding a complete shadow (as in an eclipse) **2** : something that covers or obscures ⟨a ~ of secrecy⟩

pe·nu·ri·ous \pə-'nůr-ē-əs, -'nyůr-\ *adj* : **1** : marked by penury **2** : MISERLY ♦ **Synonyms** STINGY, CLOSE, TIGHTFISTED, PARSIMONIOUS

pen·u·ry \'pe-nyə-rē\ *n* **1** : extreme poverty **2** : extreme frugality

pe·on \'pē-,än, -ən\ *n, pl* **peons** *or* **pe·o·nes** \pā-'ō-nēz\ **1** : a member of the landless laboring class in Spanish America **2** : one bound to service for payment of a debt — **pe·on·age** \-ə-nij\ *n*

pe·o·ny \'pē-ə-nē\ *n, pl* **-nies** : any of a genus of chiefly Eurasian plants with large often double red, pink, or white flowers; *also* : the flower

¹**peo·ple** \'pē-pəl\ *n, pl* **people** [ME *peple*, fr. AF *peple, peuple,* fr. L *populus*] **1** *pl* : human beings making up a group or linked by a common characteristic or interest **2** *pl* : human beings — often used in compounds instead of *persons* ⟨*salespeople*⟩ or attributively ⟨~ skills⟩ **3** *pl* : the mass of persons in a community : POPULACE; *also* : ELECTORATE ⟨the ~'s choice⟩ **4** *pl* **peoples** : a body of persons (as a tribe, nation, or race) united by a common culture, sense of kinship, or political organization

²**people** *vb* **peo·pled; peo·pling** : to supply or fill with or as if with people

¹**pep** \'pep\ *n* : brisk energy or initiative — **pep·py** *adj*

²**pep** *vb* **pepped; pep·ping** : to put pep into : STIMULATE ⟨~ the team up⟩

¹**pep·per** \'pe-pər\ *n* **1** : either of two pungent condiments from the berry (**pepper·corn** \-,kórn\) of an Indian climbing plant : BLACK PEPPER, WHITE PEPPER; *also* : this plant **2** : a plant related to the tomato and widely grown for its hot or mild sweet fruit; *also* : this fruit

²**pepper** *vb* **pep·pered; pep·per·ing** **1** : to shower with missiles or rapid blows **2** : to sprinkle or season with or as if with pepper **3** : to deliver something in rapid succession ⟨~*ed* him with questions⟩

pep·per·mint \-,mint, -mənt\ *n* : a pungent aromatic mint; *also* : candy flavored with its oil

pep·per·o·ni \,pe-pə-'rō-nē\ *n* : a highly seasoned beef and pork sausage

pepper spray *n* : a temporarily disabling aerosol that causes irritation and blinding of the eyes and inflammation of the nose, throat, and skin

pep·pery \'pe-pə-rē\ *adj* **1** : having the qualities of pepper : PUNGENT, HOT **2** : having a hot temper : FIERY

pep·sin \'pep-sən\ *n* : an enzyme of the stomach that promotes digestion by breaking down proteins; *also* : a preparation of this used medicinally

pep·tic \'pep-tik\ *adj* [L *pepticus*, fr. Gk

peptikos, fr. *peptos* cooked, *peptein* to cook, digest] **1** : relating to or promoting digestion **2** : caused by digestive juices ⟨a ∼ ulcer⟩

pep·tide \'pep-ˌtīd\ *n* : any of various organic compounds composed of two or more amino acids bonded together

Pe·quot \'pē-ˌkwät\ *n* : a member of an American Indian people of eastern Connecticut

¹per \'pər\ *prep* **1** : by means of **2** : to or for each **3** : ACCORDING TO

²per *adv* : for each : APIECE

³per *abbr* **1** period **2** person

¹per·ad·ven·ture \'pər-əd-a,ven-chər\ *adv, archaic* : PERHAPS

²peradventure *n* **1** : DOUBT **2** : CHANCE 4

per·am·bu·late \pə-'ram-byə-ˌlāt\ *vb* **-lated; -lat·ing** : to travel over esp. on foot — **per·am·bu·la·tion** \-ˌram-byə-'lā-shən\ *n*

per·am·bu·la·tor \pə-'ram-byə-ˌlā-tər\ *n, chiefly Brit* : a baby carriage

per an·num \(ˌ)pər-'a-nəm\ *adv* [ML] : in or for each year : ANNUALLY

per·cale \(ˌ)pər-'kāl, 'pər-ˌ; (ˌ)pər-'kal\ *n* : a fine woven cotton cloth

per cap·i·ta \(ˌ)pər-'ka-pə-tə\ *adv or adj* [ML, by heads] : by or for each person

per·ceive \pər-'sēv\ *vb* **per·ceived; per·ceiv·ing** **1** : to attain awareness : REALIZE **2** : to become aware of through the senses — **per·ceiv·able** *adj*

¹per·cent \pər-'sent\ *adv* [*per* + L *centum* hundred] : in each hundred

²percent *n, pl* **percent** *or* **percents** **1** : one part in a hundred : HUNDREDTH **2** : PERCENTAGE

per·cent·age \pər-'sen-tij\ *n* **1** : a part of a whole expressed in hundredths **2** : the result obtained by multiplying a number by a percent **3** : ADVANTAGE, PROFIT **4** : PROBABILITY; *also* : favorable odds

percentage point : one hundredth of a whole ⟨rates rose one *percentage point* from 6.5 to 7.5 percent⟩

per·cen·tile \pər-'sen-ˌtī(-ə)l\ *n* : a value on a scale of one hundred indicating the standing of a score or grade in terms of the percentage of scores or grades falling with or below it

per·cept \'pər-ˌsept\ *n* : an impression of an object obtained by use of the senses

per·cep·ti·ble \pər-'sep-tə-bəl\ *adj* : capable of being perceived ⟨a barely ∼ light⟩ — **per·cep·ti·bly** \-blē\ *adv*

per·cep·tion \pər-'sep-shən\ *n* **1** : an act or result of perceiving **2** : awareness of one's environment through physical sensation **3** : ability to understand : INSIGHT, COMPREHENSION ♦ *Synonyms* PENETRATION, DISCERNMENT, DISCRIMINATION

per·cep·tive \pər-'sep-tiv\ *adj* : capable of or exhibiting keen perception : OBSERVANT — **per·cep·tive·ly** *adv*

per·cep·tu·al \pər-'sep-chə-wəl\ *adj* : of, relating to, or involving sensory stimulus as opposed to abstract concept ⟨∼ stimulation⟩ — **per·cep·tu·al·ly** *adv*

¹perch \'pərch\ *n* **1** : a roost for a bird **2** : a high station or vantage point

²perch *vb* : ROOST

³perch *n, pl* **perch** *or* **perch·es** : either of two small freshwater bony fishes used for food; *also* : any of various fishes resembling or related to these

per·chance \pər-'chans\ *adv* : PERHAPS

per·cip·i·ent \pər-'si-pē-ənt\ *adj* : capable of or characterized by perception — **per·cip·i·ence** \-əns\ *n*

per·co·late \'pər-kə-ˌlāt\ *vb* **-lat·ed; -lat·ing** **1** : to trickle or filter through a permeable substance **2** : to filter hot water through to extract the essence ⟨∼ coffee⟩ — **per·co·la·tor** \-ˌlā-tər\ *n*

per con·tra \(ˌ)pər-'kän-trə\ *adv* [It, by the opposite side (of the ledger)] **1** : on the contrary **2** : by way of contrast

per·cus·sion \pər-'kə-shən\ *n* **1** : a sharp blow : IMPACT; *esp* : a blow upon a cap (**percussion cap**) designed to explode the charge in a firearm **2** : the beating or striking of a musical instrument; *also* : instruments sounded by striking, shaking, or scraping

per di·em \pər-'dē-əm, -'dī-\ *adv* [ML] : by the day — **per diem** *adj or n*

per·di·tion \pər-'di-shən\ *n* **1** : eternal damnation **2** : HELL

per·du·ra·ble \(ˌ)pər-'dùr-ə-bəl, -'dyùr-\ *adj* : very durable — **per·du·ra·bil·i·ty** \-ˌdùr-ə-'bi-lə-tē, -ˌdyùr-\ *n*

père \'per\ *n* [F, fr. OF *paire, perre,* fr. L *pater*] FATHER — used after a name to distinguish a father from a son

per·e·gri·na·tion \ˌper-ə-grə-'nā-shən\ *n* : a traveling about esp. on foot

per·e·grine falcon \'per-ə-grən, -ˌgrēn\ *n* : a swift nearly cosmopolitan falcon that often nests in cities and is often used in falconry

pe·remp·to·ry \pə-'remp-tə-rē\ *adj* **1** : barring a right of action or delay **2** : expressive of urgency or command : IMPERATIVE **3** : marked by arrogant self-assurance ♦ *Synonyms* IMPERIOUS, MASTERFUL, DOMINEERING, MAGISTERIAL — **pe·remp·to·ri·ly** \-tə-rə-lē\ *adv*

¹per·en·ni·al \pə-'re-nē-əl\ *adj* **1** : present at all seasons of the year ⟨∼ streams⟩ **2** : continuing to live from year to year ⟨∼ plants⟩ **3** : recurring regularly : PERMANENT ⟨∼ problems⟩ ♦ *Synonyms* LASTING, PERPETUAL, ENDURING, EVERLASTING — **pe·ren·ni·al·ly** *adv*

²perennial *n* : a perennial plant

perf *abbr* **1** perfect **2** perforated

¹per·fect \'pər-fikt\ *adj* **1** : being without fault or defect **2** : EXACT, PRECISE **3** : COMPLETE **4** : relating to or being a verb tense that expresses an action or state completed at the time of speaking or at a time spoken of — **per·fect·ly** *adv* — **per·fect·ness** *n*

²per·fect \pər-'fekt\ *vb* : to make perfect

³per·fect \pər-'fikt\ *n* : the perfect tense; *also* : a verb form in it

per·fect·ible \pər-'fek-tə-bəl, 'pər-fik-\ *adj* : capable of improvement or perfection — **per·fect·ibil·i·ty** \pər-ˌfek-tə-'bi-lə-tē, ˌpər-fik-\ *n*

per·fec·tion \pər-'fek-shən\ n **1** : the quality or state of being perfect **2** : the highest degree of excellence **3** : the act or process of perfecting

per·fec·tion·ist \-shə-nist\ n : a person who will not accept or be content with anything less than perfection

per·fec·to \pər-'fek-tō\ n, pl **-tos** : a cigar that is thick in the middle and tapers almost to a point at each end

per·fi·dy \'pər-fə-dē\ n, pl **-dies** [L perfidia, fr. perfidus faithless, fr. per- detrimental to + fides faith] : violation of faith or loyalty : TREACHERY — **per·fid·i·ous** \pər-'fi-dē-əs\ adj — **per·fid·i·ous·ly** adv

per·fo·rate \'pər-fə-ˌrāt\ vb **-rat·ed; -rat·ing** : to bore through : PIERCE; esp : to make a line of holes in to facilitate separation — **per·fo·ra·tion** \ˌpər-fə-'rā-shən\ n

per·force \pər-'fōrs\ adv : of necessity ⟨we attended ∼⟩

per·form \pər-'fōrm\ vb **1** : FULFILL **2** : CARRY OUT, DO **3** : FUNCTION **4** : to do in a set manner **5** : to give a performance — **per·form·er** n

per·for·mance \pər-'fōr-məns\ n **1** : the act or process of performing **2** : DEED, FEAT **3** : a public presentation

¹per·fume \pər-'fyüm, 'pər-ˌfyüm\ n **1** : a usu. pleasant odor : FRAGRANCE **2** : a preparation used for scenting

²per·fume \pər-'fyüm, 'pər-ˌfyüm\ vb **per·fumed; per·fum·ing** : SCENT

per·fum·ery \pər-'fyü-mə-rē\ n, pl **-er·ies 1** : the art or process of making perfume **2** : PERFUMES **3** : an establishment where perfumes are made

per·func·to·ry \pər-'fəŋk-tə-rē\ adj : done merely as a duty — **per·func·to·ri·ly** adv

per·go·la \'pər-gə-lə\ n [It] : a structure consisting of posts supporting an open roof in the form of a trellis

perh abbr perhaps

per·haps \pər-'haps\ adv : possibly but not certainly

per·i·gee \'per-ə-ˌjē\ n [MF, fr. NL perigeum, fr. Gk perigeion, fr. peri around, near + gē earth] : the point at which an orbiting object is nearest the body (as the earth) being orbited

peri·he·lion \ˌper-ə-'hēl-yən\ n, pl **-he·lia** \-'hēl-yə\ : the point in the path of a celestial body (as a planet) that is nearest to the sun

per·il \'per-əl\ n : DANGER; also : a source of danger : RISK — **per·il·ous** adj — **per·il·ous·ly** adv

pe·rim·e·ter \pə-'ri-mə-tər\ n **1** : the boundary of a closed plane figure; also : its length **2** : a line bounding or protecting an area

peri·na·tal \ˌper-ə-'nā-t³l\ adj : occurring in, concerned with, or being in the period around the time of birth ⟨∼ care⟩

¹pe·ri·od \'pir-ē-əd\ n [ultim. fr. Gk periodos circuit, period of time, rhetorical period, fr. peri around + hodos way] **1** : SENTENCE; also : the full pause closing the utterance of a sentence **2** : END, STOP **3** : a punctuation mark . used esp. to mark the end of a declarative sentence or an abbreviation **4** : an extent of time; esp : one regarded as a stage or division in a process or development **5** : a portion of time in which a recurring phenomenon completes one cycle and is ready to begin again **6** : a single cyclic occurrence of menstruation

²period adj : of or relating to a particular historical period ⟨∼ furniture⟩

pe·ri·od·ic \ˌpir-ē-'ä-dik\ adj **1** : occurring at regular intervals of time **2** : happening repeatedly **3** : of or relating to a sentence that has no trailing elements following full grammatical statement of the essential idea

¹pe·ri·od·i·cal \ˌpir-ē-'ä-di-kəl\ adj **1** : PERIODIC **2** : published at regular intervals **3** : of or relating to a periodical — **pe·ri·od·i·cal·ly** \-k(ə-)lē\ adv

²periodical n : a periodical publication

periodic table n : an arrangement of chemical elements based on their atomic structure and on their properties

peri·odon·tal \ˌper-ē-ō-'dän-t³l\ adj **1** : surrounding a tooth **2** : of or affecting periodontal tissues or regions

per·i·pa·tet·ic \ˌper-ə-pə-'te-tik\ adj : performed or performing while moving about : ITINERANT ⟨∼ salesmen⟩

pe·riph·er·al \pə-'ri-fər-əl\ n : a device connected to a computer to provide communication or auxiliary functions

peripheral nervous system n : the part of the nervous system that is outside the central nervous system and comprises the spinal nerves, the cranial nerves except the one supplying the retina, and the autonomic nervous system

pe·riph·ery \pə-'ri-fə-rē\ n, pl **-er·ies 1** : the boundary of a rounded figure **2** : outward bounds : border area — **pe·riph·er·al** \-fə-rəl\ adj

pe·riph·ra·sis \pə-'ri-frə-səs\ n, pl **-ra·ses** \-ˌsēz\ : CIRCUMLOCUTION

peri·scope \'per-ə-ˌskōp\ n : a tubular optical instrument enabling an observer to see an otherwise blocked field of view

per·ish \'per-ish\ vb : to become destroyed or ruined : cease to exist

per·ish·able \'per-i-shə-bəl\ adj : easily spoiled ⟨∼ foods⟩ — **perishable** n

peri·stal·sis \ˌper-ə-'stȯl-səs, -'stal-\ n, pl **-stal·ses** \-ˌsēz\ : waves of contraction passing along the walls of a hollow muscular organ (as the intestine) and forcing its contents onward — **peri·stal·tic** \-'stȯl-tik, -'stal-\ adj

peri·style \'per-ə-ˌstīl\ n : a row of columns surrounding a building or court

peri·to·ne·um \ˌper-ə-tə-'nē-əm\ n, pl **-ne·ums** or **-nea** : the smooth transparent serous membrane that lines the cavity of the abdomen — **peri·to·ne·al** \-'nē-əl\ adj

peri·to·ni·tis \ˌper-ə-tə-'nī-təs\ n : inflammation of the peritoneum

peri·wig \'per-i-ˌwig\ n : WIG

per·i·win·kle \'per-i-ˌwiŋ-kəl\ n : a usu. blue-flowered creeping plant cultivated as a ground cover

PERIODIC TABLE

This is the common long form of the table, with atomic numbers given along with the symbols. Roman numerals and letters heading the vertical columns indicate the groups. (There are differences of opinion regarding the letter designations, but those given here are probably the most generally used. International standards favor numbering the groups 1-18 from left to right using Arabic numerals, but the designations shown below remain quite common.) Horizontal rows represent the periods, with two series removed from the two very long periods and represented below the main table.

IA[1]	IIA[2]	IIIB	IVB	VB	VIB	VIIB	VIII	VIII	VIII	IB	IIB	IIIA	IVA	VA	VIA	VIIA[3]	VIIIA[4]
1 H																	2 He
3 Li	4 Be											5 B	6 C	7 N	8 O	9 F	10 Ne
11 Na	12 Mg											13 Al	14 Si	15 P	16 S	17 Cl	18 Ar
19 K	20 Ca	21 Sc	22 Ti	23 V	24 Cr	25 Mn	26 Fe	27 Co	28 Ni	29 Cu	30 Zn	31 Ga	32 Ge	33 As	34 Se	35 Br	36 Kr
37 Rb	38 Sr	39 Y	40 Zr	41 Nb	42 Mo	43 Tc	44 Ru	45 Rh	46 Pd	47 Ag	48 Cd	49 In	50 Sn	51 Sb	52 Te	53 I	54 Xe
55 Cs	56 Ba	57 *La	72 Hf	73 Ta	74 W	75 Re	76 Os	77 Ir	78 Pt	79 Au	80 Hg	81 Tl	82 Pb	83 Bi	84 Po	85 At	86 Rn
87 Fr	88 Ra	89 #Ac	104 Rf	105 Db	106 Sg	107 Bh	108 Hs	109 Mt	110 Ds	111 Rg	112 Cn						

*LANTHANIDE SERIES	58 Ce	59 Pr	60 Nd	61 Pm	62 Sm	63 Eu	64 Gd	65 Tb	66 Dy	67 Ho	68 Er	69 Tm	70 Yb	71 Lu
#ACTINIDE SERIES	90 Th	91 Pa	92 U	93 Np	94 Pu	95 Am	96 Cm	97 Bk	98 Cf	99 Es	100 Fm	101 Md	102 No	103 Lr

[1] Group IA (excluding hydrogen) comprises the alkali metals.
[2] Group IIA comprises the alkaline earth metals.
[3] Group VIIA (excluding hydrogen) comprises the halogens.
[4] Group VIIIA (also called group Zero) comprises the noble gases.

²**periwinkle** *n* : any of various small edible seashore snails

per·ju·ry \'pər-jə-rē\ *n* : the voluntary violation of an oath to tell the truth : lying under oath — **per·jure** \'pər-jər\ *vb* — **per·jur·er** *n*

¹**perk** \'pərk\ *vb* 1 : to thrust (as the head) up impudently or jauntily 2 : to regain vigor or spirit 3 : to make trim or brisk : FRESHEN — **perky** *adj*

²**perk** *vb* : PERCOLATE

³**perk** *n* : PERQUISITE — usu. used in pl.

per·lite \'pər-ˌlīt\ *n* : volcanic glass that when expanded by heat forms a lightweight material used esp. in concrete and plaster and for potting plants

¹**perm** \'pərm\ *n* : PERMANENT

²**perm** *vb* : to give (hair) a permanent

³**perm** *abbr* permanent

per·ma·frost \'pər-mə-ˌfrȯst\ *n* : a permanently frozen layer below the surface in frigid regions of a planet

¹**per·ma·nent** \'pər-mə-nənt\ *adj* : LASTING, STABLE — **per·ma·nence** \-nəns\ *n* — **per·ma·nen·cy** \-nən-sē\ *n* — **per·ma·nent·ly** *adv*

²**permanent** *n* : a long-lasting hair wave or straightening

permanent press *n* : the process of treating fabrics with chemicals (as resin) and heat for setting the shape and for aiding wrinkle resistance

per·me·able \'pər-mē-ə-bəl\ *adj* : having small openings that permit liquids or gases to seep through — **per·me·a·bil·i·ty** \ˌpər-mē-ə-'bi-lə-tē\ *n*

per·me·ate \'pər-mē-ˌāt\ *vb* **-at·ed; -at·ing** 1 : PERVADE 2 : to seep through the pores of : PENETRATE — **per·me·ation** \ˌpər-mē-'ā-shən\ *n*

Perm·ian \'pər-mē-ən\ *adj* : of, relating to, or being the latest period of the Paleozoic era — **Permian** *n*

per·mis·si·ble \pər-'mi-sə-bəl\ *adj* : that may be permitted : ALLOWABLE

per·mis·sion \pər-'mi-shən\ *n* : formal consent : AUTHORIZATION

per·mis·sive \pər-'mi-siv\ *adj* : granting permission; *esp* : INDULGENT — **per·mis·sive·ly** *adv* — **per·mis·sive·ness** *n*

¹**per·mit** \pər-'mit\ *vb* **per·mit·ted; per·mit·ting** 1 : to consent to : ALLOW 2 : to make possible

²**per·mit** \'pər-ˌmit, pər-'mit\ *n* : a written permission : LICENSE ⟨a fishing ∼⟩

per·mu·ta·tion \ˌpər-myü-'tā-shən\ *n* 1 : a major or fundamental change 2 : the act or process of changing the order of an ordered set of objects ♦ *Synonyms* INNOVATION, MUTATION, VICISSITUDE

per·ni·cious \pər-'ni-shəs\ *adj* [ME, fr. AF, fr. L *perniciosus*, fr. *pernicies* destruction, fr. *per-* through + *nec-, nex* violent death] : very destructive or injurious ⟨a ∼ influence⟩ — **per·ni·cious·ly** *adv*

per·ora·tion \'per-ə-ˌrā-shən, 'pər-\ *n* : the concluding part of a speech

¹**per·ox·ide** \pə-'räk-ˌsīd\ *n* : an oxide containing a large proportion of oxygen; *esp* : HYDROGEN PEROXIDE

²**peroxide** *vb* **-id·ed; -id·ing** : to bleach with hydrogen peroxide

perp *abbr* 1 perpendicular 2 perpetrator

per·pen·dic·u·lar \ˌpər-pən-'di-kyə-lər\ *adj* 1 : standing at right angles to the plane of the horizon 2 : forming a right angle with each other or with a given line or plane — **perpendicular** *n* — **per·pen·dic·u·lar·i·ty** \-ˌdi-kyə-'la-rə-tē\ *n* — **per·pen·dic·u·lar·ly** *adv*

per·pe·trate \'pər-pə-ˌtrāt\ *vb* **-trat·ed; -trat·ing** : to carry out (as a crime) : COMMIT — **per·pe·tra·tion** \ˌpər-pə-'trā-shən\ *n* — **per·pe·tra·tor** \'pər-pə-ˌtrā-tər\ *n*

per·pet·u·al \pər-'pe-chə-wəl\ *adj* 1 : continuing forever : EVERLASTING 2 : occurring continually : CONSTANT ⟨∼ annoyance⟩ ♦ *Synonyms* CEASELESS, UNCEASING, CONTINUAL, CONTINUOUS, INCESSANT, UNREMITTING — **per·pet·u·al·ly** *adv*

per·pet·u·ate \pər-'pe-chə-ˌwāt\ *vb* **-at·ed; -at·ing** : to make perpetual : cause to last indefinitely ⟨∼ a belief⟩ — **per·pet·u·a·tion** \-ˌpe-chə-'wā-shən\ *n*

per·pe·tu·i·ty \ˌpər-pə-'tü-ə-tē, -'tyü-\ *n, pl* **-ties** 1 : ETERNITY 1 2 : the quality or state of being perpetual

per·plex \pər-'pleks\ *vb* : to disturb mentally; *esp* : CONFUSE — **per·plex·i·ty** \-'plek-sə-tē\ *n*

per·plexed \-'plekst\ *adj* 1 : filled with uncertainty : PUZZLED ⟨a ∼ look⟩ 2 : full of difficulty : COMPLICATED — **per·plex·ed·ly** \-'plek-səd-lē\ *adv*

per·qui·site \'pər-kwə-zət\ *n* : a privilege or profit beyond regular pay

pers *abbr* person; personal

¹**per se** \(ˌ)pər-'sā\ *adv* [L] : by, of, or in itself : as such

²**per se** *adj* : being such inherently, clearly, or as a matter of law

per·se·cute \'pər-si-ˌkyüt\ *vb* **-cut·ed; -cut·ing** : to pursue in such a way as to injure or afflict : HARASS; *esp* : to cause to suffer because of belief — **per·se·cu·tion** \ˌpər-si-'kyü-shən\ *n* — **per·se·cu·tor** \'pər-si-ˌkyü-tər\ *n*

per·se·vere \ˌpər-sə-'vir\ *vb* **-vered; -ver·ing** : to persist (as in an undertaking) in spite of difficulties — **per·se·ver·ance** \-'vir-əns\ *n*

Per·sian \'pər-zhən\ *n* 1 : a native or inhabitant of ancient Persia 2 : a member of one of the peoples of modern Iran 3 : the language of the Persians

Persian cat *n* : any of a breed of stocky round-headed domestic cats that have a long silky coat

Persian lamb *n* : a pelt with very silky tightly curled fur that is obtained from newborn lambs which are older than those yielding broadtail

per·si·flage \'pər-si-ˌfläzh, 'per-\ *n* [F, fr. *persifler* to banter, fr. *per-* thoroughly + *siffler* to whistle, hiss, boo, ultim. fr. L *sibilare*] : lightly jesting or mocking talk

per·sim·mon \pər-'si-mən\ *n* : either of two trees related to the ebony; *also* : the edible usu. orange or red plumlike fruit of a persimmon

per·sist \pər-'sist, -'zist\ *vb* 1 : to go on resolutely or stubbornly in spite of difficulties **2** : to continue to exist — **per-sis-tence** \-'sis-təns, -'zis-\ *n* — **per-sis-ten-cy** \-tən-sē\ *n* — **per-sis-tent** \-tənt\ *adj* — **per-sis-tent-ly** *adv*

per-snick-e-ty \pər-'sni-kə-tē\ *adj* : fussy about small details

per-son \'pər-sən\ *n* [ME, fr. AF *persone*, fr. L *persona* actor's mask, character in a play, person, prob. fr. Etruscan *phersu* mask, fr. Gk *prosōpa*, pl. of *prosōpon* face, mask] **1** : a human being : INDI-VIDUAL — used in combination esp. by those who prefer to avoid *man* in com-pounds applicable to both sexes ⟨chair-*person*⟩ **2** : one of the three modes of being in the Godhead as understood by Trinitarians **3** : the body of a human be-ing **4** : the individual personality of a hu-man being : SELF **5** : reference of a seg-ment of discourse to the speaker, to one spoken to, or to one spoken of esp. as indicated by certain pronouns

per-so-na \pər-'sō-nä\ *n, pl* **-nae** \-nē\ *or* **-nas** : the personality that a person proj-ects in public

per-son-able \'pər-sə-nə-bəl\ *adj* : pleas-ant in person : ATTRACTIVE

per-son-age \'pər-sə-nij\ *n* : a person of rank, note, or distinction

¹per-son-al \'pər-sə-nəl\ *adj* **1** : of, relat-ing to, or affecting a person : PRIVATE ⟨~ correspondence⟩ **2** : done in person ⟨a ~ inquiry⟩ **3** : relating to the person or body ⟨~ injuries⟩ **4** : relating to an individual esp. in an offensive way ⟨re-sented such ~ remarks⟩ **5** : of or relat-ing to temporary or movable property as distinguished from real estate **6** : denot-ing grammatical person **7** : intended for use by one person ⟨a ~ stereo⟩

²personal *n* : a short newspaper para-graph relating to a person or group or to personal matters **2** : a short personal or private communication in the classified ads section of a newspaper

personal computer *n* : a computer with a microprocessor designed for an indi-vidual user to run esp. commercial soft-ware

personal digital assistant *n* : PDA

per-son-al-ise *Brit var of* PERSONALIZE

per-son-al-i-ty \,pər-sə-'na-lə-tē\ *n, pl* **-ties** **1** : an offensively personal remark ⟨indulges in *personalities*⟩ **2** : the collec-tion of emotional and behavioral traits that characterize a person **3** : distinction of personal and social traits **4** : a well= known person ⟨a TV ~⟩ ♦ *Synonyms* INDIVIDUALITY, TEMPERAMENT, DISPO-SITION, MAKEUP

per-son-al-ize \'pər-sə-nə-,līz\ *vb* **-ized; -iz-ing** : to make personal or individual; *esp* : to mark as belonging to a particular person ⟨*personalized* stationery⟩

per-son-al-ly \'pər-sə-nə-lē\ *adv* **1** : in person **2** : as a person **3** : as far as oneself is con-cerned ⟨~, I don't want to go⟩

per-son-al-ty \'pər-sə-nəl-tē\ *n, pl* **-ties** : personal property

per-so-na non gra-ta \pər-'sō-nə-,nän-'grä-tə, -'grä-\ *adj* [L] : being personally unacceptable or unwelcome

per-son-ate \'pər-sə-,nāt\ *vb* **-at-ed; -at-ing** : IMPERSONATE, REPRESENT

per-son-i-fy \pər-'sä-nə-,fī\ *vb* **-fied; -fy-ing** **1** : to think of or represent as a per-son **2** : to be the embodiment of : INCAR-NATE ⟨~ the law⟩ — **per-son-i-fi-ca-tion** \-,sä-nə-fə-'kā-shən\ *n*

per-son-nel \,pər-sə-'nel\ *n* : a body of persons employed

per-spec-tive \pər-'spek-tiv\ *n* **1** : the science of painting and drawing so that objects represented have apparent depth and distance **2** : the aspect in which a subject or its parts are mentally viewed; *esp* : a view of things (as objects or events) in their true relationship or rela-tive importance

per-spi-ca-cious \,pər-spə-'kā-shəs\ *adj* : having or showing keen understanding or discernment ⟨a ~ observation⟩ — **per-spi-cac-i-ty** \-'ka-sə-tē\ *n*

per-spic-u-ous \pər-'spi-kyə-wəs\ *adj* : plain to the understanding ⟨a ~ argu-ment⟩ — **per-spi-cu-i-ty** \,pər-spə-'kyü-ə-tē\ *n*

per-spire \pər-'spī-(ə)r\ *vb* **per-spired; per-spir-ing** : SWEAT — **per-spi-ra-tion** \,pər-spə-'rā-shən\ *n*

per-suade \pər-'swād\ *vb* **per-suad-ed; per-suad-ing** : to win over to a belief or course of action by argument or entreaty — **per-sua-sive** \-'swā-siv, -ziv\ *adj* — **per-sua-sive-ly** *adv* — **per-sua-sive-ness** *n*

per-sua-sion \pər-'swā-zhən\ *n* **1** : the act or process of persuading **2** : a system of religious beliefs; *also* : a group holding such beliefs

pert \'pərt\ *adj* [ME, evident, attractive, saucy, short for *apert* evident, fr. AF, fr. L *apertus* open, fr. pp. of *aperire* to open] **1** : saucily free and forward : IMPUDENT **2** : stylishly trim : JAUNTY **3** : LIVELY

per-tain \pər-'tān\ *vb* **1** : to belong to as a part, quality, or function ⟨duties ~*ing* to the office⟩ **2** : to have reference : RE-LATE ⟨books ~*ing* to birds⟩

per-ti-na-cious \,pər-tə-'nā-shəs\ *adj* **1** : holding resolutely to an opinion or pur-pose **2** : obstinately persistent ⟨a ~ bill collector⟩ ♦ *Synonyms* DOGGED, MUL-ISH, HEADSTRONG, PERVERSE — **per-ti-nac-i-ty** \-'na-sə-tē\ *n*

per-ti-nent \'pər-tə-nənt\ *adj* : relating to the matter under consideration ♦ *Syn-onyms* RELEVANT, GERMANE, APPLICA-BLE, APROPOS — **per-ti-nence** \-əns\ *n*

per-turb \pər-'tərb\ *vb* : to disturb greatly esp. in mind : UPSET — **per-tur-ba-tion** \,pər-tər-'bā-shən\ *n*

per-tus-sis \pər-'tə-səs\ *n* : WHOOPING COUGH

pe-ruke \pə-'rük\ *n* : WIG

pe-ruse \pə-'rüz\ *vb* **pe-rused; pe-rus-ing** : READ; *esp* : to read over attentively or leisurely — **pe-rus-al** \-'rü-zəl\ *n*

per-vade \pər-'vād\ *vb* **per-vad-ed; per-vad-ing** : to spread through every part of : PERMEATE ⟨excitement *pervaded* the room⟩ — **per-va-sive** \-'vā-siv, -ziv\ *adj*

per-verse \pər-'vərs\ *adj* **1** : turned away from what is right or good : CORRUPT **2**

: obstinate in opposing what is reasonable or accepted **3** : marked by perversion — **per·verse·ly** *adv* — **per·verse·ness** *n* — **per·ver·si·ty** \-'vǝr-sǝ-tē\ *n*

per·ver·sion \pǝr-'vǝr-zhǝn\ *n* **1** : the action of perverting : the condition of being perverted **2** : a perverted form of something; *esp* : aberrant sexual behavior

¹**per·vert** \pǝr-'vǝrt\ *vb* **1** : to lead astray : CORRUPT 〈~ the young〉 **2** : to divert to a wrong purpose : MISAPPLY 〈~ evidence〉 ◆ **Synonyms** DEPRAVE, DEBASE, DEBAUCH, DEMORALIZE — **per·vert·er** *n*

²**per·vert** \'pǝr-ˌvǝrt\ *n* : one that is perverted; *esp* : one given to sexual perversion

pe·se·ta \pǝ-'sā-tǝ\ *n* : the former basic monetary unit of Spain

pe·se·wa \pǝ-'sā-wǝ\ *n* — see *cedi* at MONEY table

pes·ky \'pes-kē\ *adj* **pes·ki·er; -est** : causing annoyance : TROUBLESOME

pe·so \'pā-sō\ *n, pl* **pesos** — see MONEY table

pes·si·mism \'pe-sǝ-ˌmi-zǝm\ *n* [F *pessimisme*, fr. L *pessimus* worst] : an inclination to take the least favorable view (as of events) or to expect the worst — **pes·si·mist** \-mist\ *n* — **pes·si·mis·tic** \ˌpe-sǝ-'mis-tik\ *adj*

pest \'pest\ *n* **1** : a destructive epidemic disease : PLAGUE **2** : a plant or animal detrimental to humans **3** : one that pesters : NUISANCE — **pesty** *adj*

pes·ter \'pes-tǝr\ *vb* : to harass with petty irritations : ANNOY

pes·ti·cide \'pes-tǝ-ˌsīd\ *n* : an agent used to destroy pests

pes·tif·er·ous \pes-'ti-fǝ-rǝs\ *adj* **1** : PESTILENT 〈~ vermin〉 **2** : ANNOYING

pes·ti·lence \'pes-tǝ-lǝns\ *n* : a destructive infectious swiftly spreading disease; *esp* : BUBONIC PLAGUE

pes·ti·lent \-lǝnt\ *adj* **1** : dangerous to life : DEADLY **2** : PERNICIOUS, HARMFUL **3** : TROUBLESOME **4** : INFECTIOUS, CONTAGIOUS 〈a ~ disease〉

pes·ti·len·tial \ˌpes-tǝ-'len-chǝl\ *adj* **1** : causing or tending to cause pestilence : DEADLY **2** : morally harmful

pes·tle \'pes-ǝl, 'pes-t²l\ *n* : an implement for grinding substances in a mortar — **pestle** *vb*

¹**pet** \'pet\ *n* **1** : FAVORITE, DARLING **2** : a domesticated animal kept for pleasure rather than utility

²**pet** *adj* **1** : kept or treated as a pet 〈~ dog〉 **2** : expressing fondness 〈~ name〉 **3** : particularly liked or favored

³**pet** *vb* **pet·ted; pet·ting** **1** : to stroke gently or lovingly **2** : to make a pet of : PAMPER **3** : to engage in amorous kissing and caressing

⁴**pet** *n* : a fit of peevishness, sulkiness, or anger — **pet·tish** *adj*

Pet *abbr* Peter

pet·al \'pe-t²l\ *n* : one of the modified leaves of a flower's corolla

pe·tard \pǝ-'tärd, -'tär\ *n* : a case containing an explosive to break down a door or gate or breach a wall

pe·ter \'pē-tǝr\ *vb* : to diminish gradually and come to an end 〈his energy ~ed out〉

Pe·ter \'pē-tǝr\ *n* — see BIBLE table

pet·i·ole \'pe-tē-ˌōl\ *n* : a slender stem that supports a leaf

pe·tite \pǝ-'tēt\ *adj* [F] : small and trim of figure 〈a ~ woman〉 — **petite** *n*

pe·tit four \ˌpe-tē-'fór\ *n, pl* **petits fours** *or* **petit fours** \-'fórz\ [F, lit., small oven] : a small cake cut from pound or sponge cake and frosted

¹**pe·ti·tion** \pǝ-'ti-shǝn\ *n* : an earnest request : ENTREATY; *esp* : a formal written request made to an authority

²**petition** *vb* : to make a request to or for — **pe·ti·tion·er** *n*

pe·trel \'pe-trǝl\ *n* : any of numerous seabirds that fly far from land

pe·tri dish \'pē-trē-\ *n* **1** : a small shallow dish used esp. for growing bacteria **2** : something fostering development or innovation

pet·ri·fy \'pe-trǝ-ˌfī\ *vb* **-fied; -fy·ing** **1** : to convert (organic matter) into stone or stony material **2** : to make rigid or inactive (as from fear or awe) — **pet·ri·fac·tion** \ˌpe-trǝ-'fak-shǝn\ *n*

pet·ro·chem·i·cal \ˌpe-trō-'ke-mi-kǝl\ *n* : a chemical isolated or derived from petroleum or natural gas — **pet·ro·chem·is·try** \-'ke-mǝ-strē\ *n*

pet·rol \'pe-trǝl\ *n, chiefly Brit* : GASOLINE

pet·ro·la·tum \ˌpe-trǝ-'lā-tǝm\ *n* : PETROLEUM JELLY

pe·tro·leum \pǝ-'trō-lē-ǝm\ *n* [ML, fr. Gk *petra* rock + L *oleum* oil] : an oily flammable liquid obtained from wells drilled in the ground and refined into gasoline, fuel oils, and other products

petroleum jelly *n* : a tasteless, odorless, and oily or greasy substance from petroleum that is used esp. in ointments and dressings

¹**pet·ti·coat** \'pe-tē-ˌkōt\ *n* **1** : a skirt worn under a dress **2** : an outer skirt

²**petticoat** *adj* : of, relating to, or exercised by women : FEMALE

pet·ti·fog·ger \'pe-tē-ˌfó-gǝr, -ˌfä-\ *n* **1** : a lawyer whose methods are petty, underhanded, or disreputable **2** : one given to quibbling over trifles — **pet·ti·fog·ging** \-gin\ *adj or n*

pet·ty \'pe-tē\ *adj* **pet·ti·er; -est** [ME *pety* small, minor, alter. of *petit*, fr. AF, small] **1** : having secondary rank : MINOR 〈~ prince〉 **2** : of little importance : TRIFLING 〈~ faults〉 **3** : marked by narrowness or meanness — **pet·ti·ly** \'pe-tǝ-lē\ *adv* — **pet·ti·ness** \-tē-nǝs\ *n*

petty officer *n* : a subordinate officer in the navy or coast guard appointed from among the enlisted personnel

petty officer first class *n* : a petty officer ranking below a chief petty officer

petty officer second class *n* : a petty officer ranking below a petty officer first class

petty officer third class *n* : a petty officer ranking below a petty officer second class

pet·u·lant \'pe-chə-lənt\ *adj* : marked by capricious ill humor ◆ *Synonyms* IRRITABLE, PEEVISH, FRETFUL, FRACTIOUS, QUERULOUS — **pet·u·lance** \-ləns\ *n* — **pet·u·lant·ly** *adv*

pe·tu·nia \pi-'tün-yə, -'tyün-\ *n* : any of a genus of tropical So. American herbs related to the potato and having bright funnel-shaped flowers

pew \'pyü\ *n* [ME *pewe*, fr. MF *puie* balustrade, fr. L *podia*, pl. of *podium* parapet, podium, fr. Gk *podion* base, dim. of *pod-*, *pous* foot] : any of the benches with backs fixed in rows in a church

pe·wee \'pē-(ˌ)wē\ *n* : any of various small American flycatchers

pew·ter \'pyü-tər\ *n* **1** : an alloy of tin used esp. for household utensils **2** : a bluish gray color — **pewter** *adj* — **pew·ter·er** *n*

pey·o·te \pā-'ō-tē\ *also* **pey·otl** \-'ō-t²l\ *n* **1** : a hallucinogenic drug derived from the peyote cactus and containing mescaline **2** : a small cactus of the southwestern U.S. and Mexico

pf *abbr* **1** pfennig **2** preferred

PFC *or* **Pfc** *abbr* private first class

pfd *abbr* preferred

pfen·nig \'fe-nig\ *n*, *pl* **pfennig** *also* **pfennigs** *or* **pfen·ni·ge** \'fe-ni-gə\ : a former monetary unit equal to $\frac{1}{100}$ deutsche mark

PFLAG *abbr* parents, families, and friends of lesbians and gays

pg *abbr* page

PG *abbr* postgraduate

PGA *abbr* Professional Golfers' Association

pH \(ˌ)pē-'āch\ *n* : a value used to express acidity and alkalinity; *also* : the condition represented by such a value

PH *abbr* **1** pinch hit **2** public health

pha·eton \'fā-ə-t²n\ *n* [F *phaéton*, fr. Gk *Phaethōn*, son of the sun god who persuaded his father to let him drive the chariot of the sun but who lost control of the horses with disastrous consequences] **1** : a light 4-wheeled horse-drawn vehicle **2** : an open automobile with two cross seats

phage \'fāj\ *n* : BACTERIOPHAGE

pha·lanx \'fā-ˌlaŋks\ *n*, *pl* **pha·lanx·es** *or* **pha·lan·ges** \fə-'lan-ˌjēz\ **1** : a group or body (as of troops) in compact formation **2** *pl* **phalanges** : one of the digital bones of the hand or foot of a vertebrate

phal·a·rope \'fa-lə-ˌrōp\ *n*, *pl* **-ropes** *also* **-rope** : any of a genus of small shorebirds related to sandpipers

phal·lic \'fa-lik\ *adj* **1** : of, relating to, or resembling a phallus **2** : relating to or being the stage of psychosexual development in psychoanalytic theory during which children become interested in their own sexual organs

phal·lus \'fa-ləs\ *n*, *pl* **phal·li** \'fa-ˌlī\ *or* **phal·lus·es** : PENIS; *also* : a symbolic representation of the penis

Phan·er·o·zo·ic \ˌfa-nə-rə-'zō-ik\ *adj* : of, relating to, or being an eon of geologic history comprising the Paleozoic, Mesozoic, and Cenozoic

phan·tasm \'fan-ˌta-zəm\ *n* : a product of the imagination : ILLUSION — **phan·tas·mal** \ˌfan-'taz-məl\ *adj*

phan·tas·ma·go·ria \fan-ˌtaz-mə-'gȯr-ē-ə\ *n* : a constantly shifting complex succession of things seen or imagined; *also* : a scene that constantly changes or fluctuates

phantasy *var of* FANTASY

phan·tom \'fan-təm\ *n* **1** : something (as a specter) that is apparent to sense but has no substantial existence **2** : a mere show : SHADOW — **phantom** *adj*

pha·raoh \'fer-ō, 'fā-rō\ *n*, *often cap* : a ruler of ancient Egypt

phar·i·sa·ical \ˌfa-rə-'sā-ə-kəl\ *adj* : hypocritically self-righteous

phar·i·see \'fa-rə-ˌsē\ *n* **1** *cap* : a member of an ancient Jewish sect noted for strict observance of rites and ceremonies of the traditional law **2** : a self-righteous or hypocritical person — **phar·i·sa·ic** \ˌfa-rə-'sā-ik\ *adj*

pharm *abbr* pharmaceutical; pharmacist; pharmacy

phar·ma·ceu·ti·cal \ˌfär-mə-'sü-ti-kəl\ *adj* : of, relating to, or engaged in pharmacy or the manufacture and sale of medicinal drugs — **pharmaceutical** *n*

phar·ma·col·o·gy \ˌfär-mə-'kä-lə-jē\ *n* **1** : the science of drugs esp. as related to medicinal uses **2** : the reactions and properties of one or more drugs — **phar·ma·co·log·i·cal** \-kə-'lä-ji-kəl\ *also* **phar·ma·co·log·ic** \-kə-'lä-jik\ *adj* — **phar·ma·col·o·gist** \-'kä-lə-jist\ *n*

phar·ma·co·poe·ia *also* **phar·ma·co·pe·ia** \-kə-'pē-ə\ *n* **1** : a book describing drugs and medicinal preparations **2** : a stock of drugs

phar·ma·cy \'fär-mə-sē\ *n*, *pl* **-cies** **1** : the art, practice, or profession of preparing and dispensing medical drugs **2** : DRUGSTORE — **phar·ma·cist** \-sist\ *n*

phar·ynx \'fa-riŋks\ *n*, *pl* **pha·ryn·ges** \fə-'rin-ˌjēz\ *also* **phar·ynx·es** : the muscular tubular passage extending from the back of the nasal cavity and mouth to the esophagus — **pha·ryn·ge·al** \fə-'rin-jəl, ˌfa-rən-'jē-əl\ *adj*

phase \'fāz\ *n* **1** : a particular appearance in a recurring series of changes ⟨∼s of the moon⟩ **2** : a stage or interval in a process or cycle ⟨first ∼ of an experiment⟩ **3** : an aspect or part under consideration — **pha·sic** \'fā-zik\ *adj*

phase down *vb* : to reduce the size or amount of by phases

phase in *vb* : to introduce in stages

phase-out \'fāz-ˌaut\ *n* : a gradual stopping of operations or production

phase out *vb* : to stop production or use of in stages ⟨*phase out* old equipment⟩

PhD *abbr* [L *philosophiae doctor*] doctor of philosophy

pheas·ant \'fe-z²nt\ *n*, *pl* **pheasant** *or* **pheasants** : any of numerous long-tailed brilliantly colored game birds related to the domestic chicken

phen·cy·cli·dine \ˌfen-'sī-klə-ˌdēn\ *n* : a drug used esp. as a veterinary anesthetic and sometimes illicitly as a hallucinogenic drug

phe·no·bar·bi·tal \,fē-nō-'bär-bə-,tȯl\ *n* : a crystalline drug used as a hypnotic and sedative

phe·nol \'fē-,nȯl\ *n* : a corrosive poisonous acidic compound present in coal and wood tars and used in solution as a disinfectant

phe·nom·e·non \fi-'nä-mə-,nän, -nən\ *n*, *pl* **-na** \-nə\ *or* **-nons** [LL *phaenomenon*, fr. Gk *phainomenon*, fr. neut. of *phainomenos*, prp. of *phainesthai* to appear] **1** *pl* **-na** : an observable fact or event **2** : an outward sign of the working of a law of nature **3** *pl* **-nons** : an extraordinary person or thing : PRODIGY — **phe·nom·e·nal** \-'nä-mə-nᵊl\ *adj* — **phe·nom·e·nal·ly** *adv*

pher·o·mone \'fer-ə-,mōn\ *n* : a chemical substance that is usu. produced by an animal and serves to stimulate a behavioral response in other individuals of the same species — **pher·o·mon·al** \,fer-ə-'mō-nᵊl\ *adj*

phi \'fī\ *n* : the 21st letter of the Greek alphabet — Φ or φ

phi·al \'fī-(ə)l\ *n* : VIAL

Phil *abbr* Philippians

phi·lan·der \fə-'lan-dər\ *vb* : to have casual or illicit sexual relations with many women — **phi·lan·der·er** *n*

phi·lan·thro·py \fə-'lan-thrə-pē\ *n*, *pl* **-pies 1** : goodwill toward all people; *esp* : effort to promote human welfare **2** : a charitable act or gift; *also* : an organization that distributes or is supported by donated funds — **phil·an·throp·ic** \,fi-lən-'thrä-pik\ *adj* — **phil·an·throp·i·cal·ly** \-pi-k(ə-)lē\ *adv* — **phi·lan·thro·pist** \fə-'lan-thrə-pist\ *n*

phi·lat·e·ly \fə-'la-tə-lē\ *n* : the collection and study of postage and imprinted stamps — **phil·a·tel·ic** \,fi-lə-'te-lik\ *adj* — **phi·lat·e·list** \fə-'la-tə-list\ *n*

Phi·le·mon \fə-'lē-mən, fī-\ *n* — see BIBLE table

Phi·lip·pi·ans \fə-'li-pē-ənz\ *n* — see BIBLE table

phi·lip·pic \fə-'li-pik\ *n* : TIRADE

phi·lis·tine \'fi-lə-,stēn; fə-'lis-tən\ *n*, *often cap* [*Philistine*, inhabitant of ancient Philistia (Palestine)] : a person who is smugly insensitive or indifferent to intellectual or artistic values — **philistine** *adj*, *often cap*

Phil·lips \'fi-ləps\ *adj* : of, relating to, or being a screw having a head with a cross slot or its corresponding screwdriver

philo·den·dron \,fi-lə-'den-drən\ *n*, *pl* **-drons** *also* **-dra** \-drə\ [NL, fr. Gk, neut. of *philodendros* loving trees, fr. *philos* dear, friendly + *dendron* tree] : any of various plants of the arum family grown for their showy foliage

phi·lol·o·gy \fə-'lä-lə-jē\ *n* **1** : the study of literature and relevant fields **2** : LINGUISTICS; *esp* : historical and comparative linguistics — **phil·o·log·i·cal** \,fi-lə-'lä-ji-kəl\ *adj* — **phi·lol·o·gist** \fə-'lä-lə-jist\ *n*

philos *abbr* philosopher; philosophy

phi·los·o·pher \fə-'lä-sə-fər\ *n* **1** : a reflective thinker : SCHOLAR **2** : a student of or specialist in philosophy **3** : a person whose philosophical perspective makes it possible to meet trouble calmly

phi·los·o·phise *Brit var of* PHILOSOPHIZE

phi·los·o·phize \fə-'lä-sə-,fīz\ *vb* **-phized; -phiz·ing 1** : to reason like a philosopher : THEORIZE **2** : to expound a philosophy esp. superficially

phi·los·o·phy \fə-'lä-sə-fē\ *n*, *pl* **-phies 1** : sciences and liberal arts exclusive of medicine, law, and theology ⟨doctor of ∼⟩ **2** : a critical study of fundamental beliefs and the grounds for them **3** : a system of philosophical concepts ⟨Aristotelian ∼⟩ **4** : a basic theory concerning a particular subject or sphere of activity **5** : the sum of the ideas and convictions of an individual or group ⟨her ∼ of life⟩ **6** : calmness of temper and judgment — **phil·o·soph·i·cal** \,fi-lə-'sä-fi-kəl\ *also* **phil·o·soph·ic** \,fi-lə-'sä-fik\ *adj* — **phil·o·soph·i·cal·ly** \-k(ə-)lē\ *adv*

phil·ter \'fil-tər\ *n* **1** : a magic potion **2** : a potion, drug, or charm held to arouse sexual passion

phil·tre *chiefly Brit var of* PHILTER

phle·bi·tis \fli-'bī-təs\ *n* : inflammation of a vein

phle·bot·o·my \fli-'bä-tə-mē\ *n*, *pl* **-mies** : the opening of a vein esp. for removing or releasing blood

phlegm \'flem\ *n* [ME *fleume*, fr. AF, fr. LL *phlegma*, fr. Gk, flame, inflammation, phlegm, fr. *phlegein* to burn] : thick mucus secreted in abnormal quantity esp. in the nose and throat

phleg·mat·ic \fleg-'ma-tik\ *adj* : having or showing a slow and stolid temperament ⟨was ∼ during the crisis⟩ ♦ **Synonyms** IMPASSIVE, APATHETIC, STOIC

phlo·em \'flō-,em\ *n* : a vascular plant tissue external to the xylem that carries dissolved food material and functions in support and storage

phlox \'fläks\ *n*, *pl* **phlox** *or* **phlox·es** : any of a genus of American herbs that have tall stalks with showy spreading terminal clusters of flowers

pho·bia \'fō-bē-ə\ *n* : an irrational persistent fear or dread — **pho·bic** \'fō-bik\ *adj*

phoe·be \'fē-(,)bē\ *n* : a flycatcher of the eastern U.S. that has a slight crest and is grayish brown above and yellowish white below

phoe·nix \'fē-niks\ *n* : a legendary bird held to live for centuries and then to burn itself to death and rise fresh and young from its ashes

¹phone \'fōn\ *n* **1** : TELEPHONE **2** : EARPHONE

²phone *vb* **phoned; phon·ing** : TELEPHONE

phone card *n* : a prepaid card used in paying for telephone calls

pho·neme \'fō-,nēm\ *n* : one of the elementary units of speech that distinguish one utterance from another — **pho·ne·mic** \fō-'nē-mik\ *adj*

pho·net·ics \fə-'ne-tiks\ *n* : the study and systematic classification of the sounds made in spoken utterance — **pho·net·ic** \-tik\ *adj* — **pho·ne·ti·cian** \ˌfō-nə-'ti-shən\ *n*

pho·nic \'fä-nik\ *adj* **1** : of, relating to, or producing sound **2** : of or relating to the sounds of speech or to phonics — **pho·ni·cal·ly** \-ni-k(ə-)lē\ *adv*

pho·nics \'fä-niks\ *n* : a method of teaching people to read and pronounce words by learning the phonetic value of letters, letter groups, and esp. syllables

pho·no·graph \'fō-nə-ˌgraf\ *n* : an instrument for reproducing sounds by means of the vibration of a needle following a spiral groove on a revolving disc

pho·nol·o·gy \fə-'nä-lə-jē\ *n* : a study and description of the sound changes in a language — **pho·no·log·i·cal** \ˌfō-nə-'lä-ji-kəl\ *adj* — **pho·nol·o·gist** \fə-'nä-lə-jist\ *n*

pho·ny *also* **pho·ney** \'fō-nē\ *adj* **pho·ni·er; -est** : not genuine or real : FAKE ⟨a ~ name⟩ — **phony** *n*

phos·phate \'fäs-ˌfāt\ *n* : a salt of a phosphoric acid — **phos·phat·ic** \fäs-'fa-tik\ *adj*

phos·phor \'fäs-fər\ *n* : a phosphorescent substance

phos·pho·res·cence \ˌfäs-fə-'re-sᵊns\ *n* **1** : luminescence caused by the absorption of radiations (as light or electrons) and continuing after these radiations stop **2** : an enduring luminescence without sensible heat — **phos·pho·res·cent** \-sᵊnt\ *adj* — **phos·pho·res·cent·ly** *adv*

phosphoric acid \fäs-ˈfȯr-ik-, -ˈfär-\ *n* : any of several oxygen-containing acids of phosphorus

phos·pho·rus *also* **phos·pho·rous** \'fäs-fə-rəs\ *n* [NL, fr. Gk *phōsphoros* light=bearing, fr. *phōs* light + *pherein* to carry, bring] : a nonmetallic chemical element that has characteristics similar to nitrogen and occurs widely esp. as phosphates — **phos·pho·ric** \fäs-ˈfȯr-ik, -ˈfär-\ *adj* — **phos·pho·rous** \'fäs-fə-rəs; fäs-ˈfȯr-əs\ *adj*

phot- *or* **photo-** *comb form* **1** : light ⟨*pho*tography⟩ **2** : photograph : photographic ⟨*photo*engraving⟩ **3** : photoelectric ⟨*photo*cell⟩

pho·to \'fō-tō\ *n, pl* **photos** : PHOTOGRAPH — **photo** *vb or adj*

pho·to·cell \'fō-tō-ˌsel\ *n* : PHOTOELECTRIC CELL

pho·to·chem·i·cal \ˌfō-tō-'ke-mi-kəl\ *adj* : of, relating to, or resulting from the chemical action of radiant energy

pho·to·com·pose \-kəm-'pōz\ *vb* : to compose reading matter for reproduction by means of characters photographed on film — **pho·to·com·po·si·tion** \-ˌkäm-pə-'zi-shən\ *n*

pho·to·copy \'fō-tə-ˌkä-pē\ *n* : a photographic reproduction of graphic matter — **photocopy** *vb*

pho·to·elec·tric \ˌfō-tō-i-'lek-trik\ *adj* : relating to an electrical effect due to the interaction of light with matter — **pho·to·elec·tri·cal·ly** \-tri-k(ə-)lē\ *adv*

photoelectric cell *n* : a device whose electrical properties are modified by the action of light

pho·to·en·grave \ˌfō-tō-in-'grāv\ *vb* : to make a photoengraving of

pho·to·en·grav·ing *n* : a process by which an etched printing plate is made from a photograph or drawing; *also* : a print made from such a plate

photo finish *n* : a race finish so close that a photograph of the finish is used to determine the winner

pho·tog \fə-'täg\ *n* : PHOTOGRAPHER

pho·to·gen·ic \ˌfō-tə-'je-nik\ *adj* : eminently suitable esp. aesthetically for being photographed

pho·to·graph \'fō-tə-ˌgraf\ *n* : a picture taken by photography — **photograph** *vb* — **pho·tog·ra·pher** \fə-'tä-grə-fər\ *n*

pho·tog·ra·phy \fə-'tä-grə-fē\ *n* : the art or process of producing images on a sensitive surface (as film or a CCD chip) by the action of light — **pho·to·graph·ic** \ˌfō-tə-'gra-fik\ *adj* — **pho·to·graph·i·cal·ly** \-fi-k(ə-)lē\ *adv*

pho·to·gra·vure \ˌfō-tə-grə-'vyu̇r\ *n* : a process for making prints from an intaglio plate prepared by photographic methods

pho·to·li·thog·ra·phy \ˌfō-tō-li-'thä-grə-fē\ *n* : the process of photographically transferring a pattern to a surface for etching (as in making an integrated circuit)

pho·tom·e·ter \fō-'tä-mə-tər\ *n* : an instrument for measuring the intensity of light — **pho·to·met·ric** \ˌfō-tə-'me-trik\ *adj* — **pho·tom·e·try** \fō-'tä-mə-trē\ *n*

pho·to·mi·cro·graph \ˌfō-tō-'mī-krə-ˌgraf\ *n* : a photograph of a microscope image — **pho·to·mi·crog·ra·phy** \-mī-'krä-grə-fē\ *n*

pho·ton \'fō-ˌtän\ *n* : a quantum of electromagnetic radiation

photo op *n* : a situation or event that lends itself to the taking of pictures which favor the individuals photographed

pho·to·play \'fō-tō-ˌplā\ *n* : MOTION PICTURE

pho·to·sen·si·tive \ˌfō-tə-'sen-sə-tiv\ *adj* : sensitive or sensitized to the action of radiant energy

pho·to·shop \'fō-(ˌ)tō-ˌshäp\ *vb, often cap* : to alter a digital image with image-editing software

pho·to·sphere \'fō-tə-ˌsfir\ *n* : the luminous surface of a star — **pho·to·spher·ic** \ˌfō-tə-'sfir-ik, -'sfer-\ *adj*

pho·to·syn·the·sis \ˌfō-tō-'sin-thə-səs\ *n* : the process by which chlorophyll-containing plants make carbohydrates from water and from carbon dioxide in the air in the presence of light — **pho·to·syn·the·size** \-ˌsīz\ *vb* — **pho·to·syn·thet·ic** \-sin-'the-tik\ *adj*

phr *abbr* phrase

¹phrase \'frāz\ *n* **1** : a brief expression **2** : a group of two or more grammatically related words that form a sense unit expressing a thought

²**phrase** *vb* **phrased; phras·ing** : to express in words

phrase·ol·o·gy \ˌfrā-zē-'ä-lə-jē\ *n, pl* **-gies** : a manner of phrasing : STYLE

phras·ing *n* : style of expression

phre·net·ic *archaic var of* FRENETIC

phren·ic \'fre-nik\ *adj* : of or relating to the diaphragm ⟨~ nerves⟩

phre·nol·o·gy \fri-'nä-lə-jē\ *n* : the study of the conformation of the skull based on the belief that it indicates mental faculties and character traits

phy·lac·tery \fə-'lak-tə-rē\ *n, pl* **-ter·ies** **1** : one of two small square leather boxes containing slips inscribed with scripture passages and traditionally worn on the left arm and forehead by Jewish men during morning weekday prayers **2** : AMULET

phy·lum \'fī-ləm\ *n, pl* **phy·la** \-lə\ [NL, fr. Gk *phylon* tribe, race] : a major category in biological classification esp. of animals that ranks above the class and below the kingdom; *also* : a group (as of people) apparently of common origin

phys *abbr* **1** physical **2** physics

¹**phys·ic** \'fi-zik\ *n* **1** : the profession of medicine **2** : MEDICINE; *esp* : PURGATIVE

²**physic** *vb* **phys·icked; phys·ick·ing** : PURGE

¹**phys·i·cal** \'fi-zi-kəl\ *adj* **1** : of or relating to nature or the laws of nature **2** : material as opposed to mental or spiritual **3** : of, relating to, or produced by the forces and operations of physics **4** : of or relating to the body — **phys·i·cal·ly** \-k(ə-)lē\ *adv*

²**physical** *n* : PHYSICAL EXAMINATION

physical education *n* : instruction in the development and care of the body ranging from simple calisthenics to training in hygiene, gymnastics, and the performance and management of athletic games

physical examination *n* : an examination of the bodily functions and condition of an individual

phys·i·cal·ize \'fi-zə-kə-ˌlīz\ *vb* **-ized; -iz·ing** : to give physical form or expression to

physical science *n* : any of the sciences (as physics and astronomy) that deal primarily with nonliving materials — **physical scientist** *n*

physical therapy *n* : the treatment of disease by physical and mechanical means (as massage, exercise, water, or heat) — **physical therapist** *n*

phy·si·cian \fə-'zi-shən\ *n* : a doctor of medicine

physician's assistant *n* : a person certified to provide basic medical care usu. under a licensed physician's supervision

phys·i·cist \'fi-zə-sist\ *n* : a scientist who specializes in physics

phys·ics \'fi-ziks\ *n* [L *physica*, pl., natural sciences, fr. Gk *physika*, fr. *physis* growth, nature, fr. *phyein* to bring forth] **1** : the science of matter and energy and their interactions **2** : the physical properties and composition of something

phys·i·og·no·my \ˌfi-zē-'äg-nə-mē\ *n, pl* **-mies** : facial appearance esp. as a reflection of inner character

phys·i·og·ra·phy \ˌfi-zē-'ä-grə-fē\ *n* : geography dealing with physical features of the earth — **phys·io·graph·ic** \ˌfi-zē-ō-'gra-fik\ *adj*

phys·i·ol·o·gy \ˌfi-zē-'ä-lə-jē\ *n* **1** : a branch of biology dealing with the functions and functioning of living matter and organisms **2** : functional processes in an organism or any of its parts — **phys·i·o·log·i·cal** \-zē-ə-'lä-ji-kəl\ *or* **phys·i·o·log·ic** \-jik\ *adj* — **phys·i·o·log·i·cal·ly** \-ji-k(ə-)lē\ *adv* — **phys·i·ol·o·gist** \-zē-'ä-lə-jist\ *n*

phys·io·ther·a·py \ˌfi-zē-ō-'ther-ə-pē\ *n* : PHYSICAL THERAPY — **phys·io·ther·a·pist** \-pist\ *n*

phy·sique \fə-'zēk\ *n* : the build of a person's body : bodily constitution

phy·to·chem·i·cal \ˌfi-tō-'ke-mi-kəl\ *n* : a chemical compound occurring naturally in plants

phy·to·plank·ton \'fī-tō-ˌplaŋk-tən\ *n* : plant life of the plankton

pi \'pī\ *n, pl* **pis** \'pīz\ **1** : the 16th letter of the Greek alphabet — Π or π **2** : the symbol π denoting the ratio of the circumference of a circle to its diameter; *also* : the ratio itself equal to approximately 3.1416

PI *abbr* private investigator

pi·a·nis·si·mo \ˌpē-ə-'ni-sə-ˌmō\ *adv or adj* : very softly — used as a direction in music

pi·a·nist \pē-'a-nist, 'pē-ə-\ *n* : a person who plays the piano

¹**pi·a·no** \pē-'ä-nō\ *adv or adj* : SOFTLY — used as a direction in music

²**pi·a·no** \pē-'a-nō\ *n, pl* **pianos** [It, short for *pianoforte*, fr. *gravicembalo col piano e forte*, lit., harpsichord with soft and loud; fr. the fact that its tones could be varied in loudness] : a musical instrument having steel strings sounded by felt-covered hammers operated from a keyboard

pi·ano·forte \pē-ˌa-nō-'fȯr-ˌtā, -tē; pē-'a-nə-ˌfȯrt\ *n* : PIANO

pi·as·tre *also* **pi·as·ter** \pē-'as-tər\ *n* — see *pound* at MONEY table

pi·az·za \pē-'a-zə, *esp for 1* -'at-sə\ *n, pl* **piazzas** *or* **pi·az·ze** \-'ät-(ˌ)sā, -'ät-\ [It, fr. L *platea* broad street] **1** : an open square esp. in an Italian town **2** : a long hall with an arched roof **3** *dial* : VERANDA, PORCH

pi·broch \'pē-ˌbräk\ *n* : a set of variations for the bagpipe

pic \'pik\ *n, pl* **pics** *or* **pix** \'piks\ **1** : PHOTOGRAPH **2** : MOTION PICTURE

pi·ca \'pī-kə\ *n* : a typewriter type with 10 characters to the inch

pi·ca·resque \ˌpi-kə-'resk, ˌpē-\ *adj* : of or relating to rogues ⟨~ fiction⟩

pi·ca·yune \ˌpi-kē-'yün\ *adj* : of little value : TRIVIAL; *also* : PETTY

pic·ca·lil·li \ˌpi-kə-'li-lē\ *n* : a relish of chopped vegetables and spices

pic·co·lo \'pi-kə-ˌlō\ *n, pl* **-los** [It, short for *piccolo flauto* small flute] : a small shrill flute pitched an octave higher than the ordinary flute

pice \'pīs\ *n, pl* **pice** : PAISA

¹pick \'pik\ *vb* **1** : to pierce or break up with a pointed instrument **2** : to remove bit by bit; *also* : to remove covering matter from **3** : to gather by plucking ⟨~ apples⟩ **4** : CULL, SELECT **5** : ROB ⟨~ a pocket⟩ **6** : PROVOKE ⟨~ a quarrel⟩ **7** : to dig into or pull lightly at **8** : to pluck with fingers or a pick ⟨~ a guitar⟩ **9** : to loosen or pull apart with a sharp point ⟨~ wool⟩ **10** : to unlock with a wire **11** : to eat sparingly ⟨~ at a salad⟩ — **pick·er** *n* — **pick on** : to single out for criticism, teasing, or bullying

²pick *n* **1** : the act or privilege of choosing **2** : the best or choicest one **3** : the part of a crop gathered at one time

³pick *n* **1** : a heavy wooden-handled tool pointed at one or both ends **2** : a pointed implement used for picking **3** : a small thin piece (as of plastic) used to pluck the strings of a stringed instrument

pick·a·back \'pi-gē-ˌbak, 'pi-kə-\ *var of* PIGGYBACK

pick·ax \'pik-ˌaks\ *n* : ³PICK 1

pick·er·el \'pi-kə-rəl\ *n, pl* **pickerel** or **pickerels** : either of two bony fishes related to the pikes; *also* : WALLEYE 2

pick·er·el·weed \-ˌwēd\ *n* : a No. American shallow-water herb that bears spikes of purplish blue flowers

¹pick·et \'pi-kət\ *n* **1** : a pointed stake (as for a fence) **2** : a detached body of soldiers on outpost duty; *also* : SENTINEL **3** : a person posted by a labor union where workers are on strike; *also* : a person posted for a protest

²picket *vb* **1** : to guard with pickets **2** : TETHER ⟨~ a horse⟩ **3** : to post pickets at ⟨~ a factory⟩ **4** : to serve as a picket

pick·ings \'pi-kiŋz, -kənz\ *n pl* **1** : gleanable or eatable fragments : SCRAPS **2** : yield for effort expended : RETURN

pick·le \'pi-kəl\ *n* **1** : a brine or vinegar solution for preserving foods; *also* : a food (as a cucumber) preserved in a pickle **2** : a difficult situation : PLIGHT — **pickle** *vb*

pick·lock \'pik-ˌläk\ *n* **1** : BURGLAR, THIEF **2** : a tool for picking locks

pick·pock·et \'pik-ˌpä-kət\ *n* : one who steals from pockets

¹pick·up \'pik-ˌəp\ *n* **1** : a hitchhiker who is given a ride **2** : a temporary chance acquaintance **3** : a picking up **4** : revival of business activity **5** : ACCELERATION **6** : the conversion of mechanical movements into electrical impulses in the reproduction of sound; *also* : a device for making such conversion **7** : a light truck having an enclosed cab and an open body with low sides and a tailgate **8** : a pickup game **9** : a player acquired from another team

²pickup *adj* : using or comprising local or available personnel ⟨a ~ game⟩

pick up *vb* **1** : to take hold of and lift **2** : IMPROVE **3** : to put in order

picky \'pi-kē\ *adj* **pick·i·er; -est** : FUSSY, FINICKY ⟨a ~ eater⟩

¹pic·nic \'pik-ˌnik\ *n* : an outing with food usu. provided by members of the group and eaten in the open

picnic *vb* **pic·nicked; pic·nick·ing** : to go on a picnic : eat in picnic fashion

pi·cot \'pē-ˌkō\ *n* : one of a series of small loops forming an edging on ribbon or lace

pic·to·ri·al \pik-'tȯr-ē-əl\ *adj* : of, relating to, or consisting of pictures

¹pic·ture \'pik-chər\ *n* **1** : a representation made by painting, drawing, or photography **2** : a vivid description in words **3** : IMAGE, COPY ⟨was the ~ of his father⟩ **4** : a transitory visual image (as on a TV screen) **5** : MOTION PICTURE **6** : SITUATION ⟨a bleak economic ~⟩

²picture *vb* **pic·tured; pic·tur·ing** **1** : to paint or draw a picture of **2** : to describe vividly in words **3** : to form a mental image of

pic·tur·esque \ˌpik-chə-'resk\ *adj* **1** : resembling a picture ⟨a ~ landscape⟩ **2** : CHARMING, QUAINT ⟨a ~ character⟩ **3** : GRAPHIC, VIVID ⟨a ~ account⟩ — **pic·tur·esque·ness** *n*

picture tube *n* : a cathode-ray tube on which the picture appears in a television

pid·dle \'pi-dᵊl\ *vb* **pid·dled; pid·dling** : to act or work idly : DAWDLE

pid·dling \'pi-dᵊl-on, -iŋ\ *adj* : TRIVIAL, PALTRY ⟨spent a ~ sum⟩

pid·dly \'pid-lē\ *adj* : TRIVIAL, PIDDLING

pid·gin \'pi-jən\ *n* [fr. *pidgin English*, fr. Chinese Pidgin English *pidgin* business] : a simplified speech used for communication between people with different languages

pie \'pī\ *n* : a dish consisting of a pastry crust and a filling (as of fruit or meat)

¹pie·bald \'pī-ˌbȯld\ *adj* : of different colors; *esp* : blotched with white and black ⟨a ~ horse⟩

²piebald *n* : a piebald animal

¹piece \'pēs\ *n* **1** : a part of a whole : FRAGMENT, PORTION **2** : one of a group, set, or mass ⟨~s of flatware⟩; *also* : a single item or instance ⟨a ~ of nonsense⟩ ⟨a ~ of news⟩ **3** : a movable object used in a board game **4** : a length, weight, or size in which something is made or sold **5** : a product (as an essay) of creative work **6** : FIREARM **7** : COIN

²piece *vb* **pieced; piec·ing** **1** : to repair or complete by adding pieces : PATCH **2** : to join into a whole

pièce de ré·sis·tance \pē-ˌes-də-rā-ˌzē-'stäns\ *n, pl* **pièces de ré·sis·tance** \same\ [F] **1** : the chief dish of a meal **2** : an outstanding item

piece·meal \'pēs-ˌmēl\ *adv or adj* : one piece at a time : GRADUALLY

piece·work \-ˌwərk\ *n* : work done and paid for by the piece — **piece·work·er** *n*

pie chart *n* : a circular chart that shows quantities or frequencies by parts of a circle shaped like pieces of pie

pied \'pīd\ *adj* : of two or more colors in blotches : VARIEGATED

pied-à-terre \pē-ˌä-də-'ter\ *n, pl* **pieds-à-terre** \same\ [F, lit., foot to the ground] : a temporary or second lodging

pier \'pir\ *n* **1** : a support for a bridge

span **2** : a structure built out into the water for use as a landing place or a promenade or to protect or form a harbor **3** : an upright supporting part (as a pillar) of a building or structure

pierce \'pirs\ *vb* **pierced; pierc·ing 1** : to enter or thrust into sharply or painfully : STAB **2** : to make a hole in or through : PERFORATE 〈*pierced* ears〉 **3** : to force or make a way into or through : PENETRATE **4** : to see through : DISCERN — **pierc·er** *n*

piercing *n* : a piece of jewelry attached to pierced flesh

pies *pl of* PI *or of* PIE

pi·ety \'pī-ə-tē\ *n, pl* **pi·et·ies 1** : fidelity to natural obligations (as to parents) **2** : dutifulness in religion : DEVOUTNESS **3** : a pious act

pif·fle \'pi-fəl\ *n* : trifling talk or action

pig \'pig\ *n* **1** : SWINE; *esp* : a young domesticated swine **2** : PORK **3** : a dirty, gluttonous, or repulsive person **4** : a crude casting of metal (as iron)

pi·geon \'pi-jən\ *n* : any of numerous stout-bodied short-legged birds with smooth thick plumage

¹**pi·geon·hole** \'pi-jən-ˌhōl\ *n* : a small open compartment (as in a desk) for keeping letters or documents

²**pigeonhole** *vb* **1** : to place in or as if in a pigeonhole : FILE **2** : to lay aside **3** : to assign to a usu. restrictive category

pi·geon–toed \-ˌtōd\ *adj* : having the toes and forefoot turned inward

pig·gish \'pi-gish\ *adj* **1** : GREEDY **2** : STUBBORN

pig·gy·back \'pi-gē-ˌbak\ *also* **pick·a·back** \'pi-gē-, 'pi-kə-\ *adv or adj* **1** : up on the back and shoulders **2** : on a railroad flatcar

pig·head·ed \'pig-'he-dəd\ *adj* : OBSTINATE, STUBBORN

pig latin *n, often cap L* : a jargon that is made by systematic alteration of English

pig·let \'pi-glət\ *n* : a small usu. young swine

pig·ment \'pig-mənt\ *n* **1** : coloring matter **2** : a powder mixed with a liquid to give color (as in paints) — **pig·ment·ed** \-mən-təd\ *adj*

pig·men·ta·tion \ˌpig-mən-'tā-shən\ *n* : coloration with or deposition of pigment; *esp* : an excessive deposition of bodily pigment

pigmy *var of* PYGMY

pig·nut \'pig-ˌnət\ *n* : the bitter nut of any of several hickory trees; *also* : any of these trees

pig·pen \-ˌpen\ *n* **1** : a pen for pigs **2** : a dirty place

pig·skin \-ˌskin\ *n* **1** : the skin of a swine or leather made of it **2** : FOOTBALL 2

pig·sty \-ˌstī\ *n* : PIGPEN

pig·tail \-ˌtāl\ *n* : a tight braid of hair

pi·ka \'pē-kə, 'pī-\ *n* : any of various small short-eared mammals related to the rabbits and occurring in rocky uplands of Asia and western No. America

¹**pike** \'pīk\ *n* : a sharp point or spike

²**pike** *n, pl* **pike** *or* **pikes** : a large slender long-snouted freshwater bony fish valued for food; *also* : any of various related fishes

³**pike** *n* : a long wooden shaft with a pointed steel head formerly used as a foot soldier's weapon

⁴**pike** *n* : TURNPIKE

pik·er \'pī-kər\ *n* **1** : one who does things in a small way or on a small scale **2** : TIGHTWAD, CHEAPSKATE

pike·staff \'pīk-ˌstaf\ *n* : the staff of a foot soldier's pike

pi·laf *also* **pi·laff** \pi-'läf, 'pē-ˌläf\ *or* **pi·lau** \pi-'lō, -'lȯ, 'pē-lō, -lȯ\ *n* : a dish made of seasoned rice often with meat

pi·las·ter \pi-'las-tər, 'pī-ˌlas-tər\ *n* : an architectural support that looks like a rectangular column and projects slightly from a wall

pil·chard \'pil-chərd\ *n* : a small European marine fish related to the herrings and often packed as a sardine

¹**pile** \'pī(-ə)l\ *n* : a long slender column (as of wood or steel) driven into the ground to support a vertical load

²**pile** *n* **1** : a quantity of things heaped together **2** : PYRE **3** : a great number or quantity : LOT 〈a ~s of money〉

³**pile** *vb* **piled; pil·ing 1** : to lay in a pile : STACK **2** : to heap up : ACCUMULATE **3** : to press forward in a mass : CROWD

⁴**pile** *n* : a velvety surface of fine short hairs or threads (as on cloth) — **piled** \'pī(-ə)ld\ *adj* — **pile·less** *adj*

piles \'pī(-ə)lz\ *n pl* : HEMORRHOIDS

pil·fer \'pil-fər\ *vb* : to steal in small quantities 〈~ pens from work〉

pil·grim \'pil-grəm\ *n* [ME, fr. AF *pelerin, pilegrin,* fr. LL *pelegrinus,* alter. of L *peregrinus* foreigner, fr. *peregrinus* foreign, fr. *peregri* abroad, fr. *per* through + *ager* land] **1** : one who journeys in foreign lands : WAYFARER **2** : one who travels to a shrine or holy place as an act of devotion **3** *cap* : one of the English settlers founding Plymouth colony in 1620

pil·grim·age \-grə-mij\ *n* : a journey of a pilgrim esp. to a shrine or holy place

pil·ing \'pī-liŋ\ *n* : a structure of piles

pill \'pil\ *n* **1** : a small rounded mass usu. of medicine that is swallowed whole **2** : a disagreeable or tiresome person **3** *often cap* : an oral contraceptive — usu. used with *the*

pil·lage \'pi-lij\ *vb* **pil·laged; pil·lag·ing** : to take booty : LOOT, PLUNDER — **pillage** *n* — **pil·lag·er** *n*

pil·lar \'pi-lər\ *n* **1** : a strong upright support (as for a roof) **2** : a column or shaft standing alone esp. as a monument **3** : an integral or upstanding member or part **4** : a fundamental tenet 〈the five ~s of Islam〉 — **pil·lared** \-lərd\ *adj*

pill·box \'pil-ˌbäks\ *n* **1** : a shallow round box for pills **2** : a low concrete emplacement esp. for machine guns

pil·lion \'pil-yən\ *n* **1** : a pad or cushion placed behind a saddle for an extra rider **2** *chiefly Brit* : a motorcycle or bicycle saddle for a passenger

¹**pil·lo·ry** \'pi-lə-rē\ *n, pl* **-ries** : a wooden frame for public punishment having

holes in which the head and hands can be locked

²pillory *vb* **-ried; -ry·ing** **1** : to set in a pillory **2** : to expose to public scorn

¹pil·low \'pi-lō\ *n* : a case filled with springy material (as feathers) and used to support the head of a resting person

²pillow *vb* : to rest or place on or as if on a pillow; *also* : to serve as a pillow for

pil·low·case \-,kās\ *n* : a removable covering for a pillow

¹pi·lot \'pī-lət\ *n* **1** : HELMSMAN, STEERSMAN **2** : a person qualified and licensed to take ships into and out of a port **3** : GUIDE, LEADER **4** : one that flies an aircraft or spacecraft **5** : a television show filmed or taped as a sample of a proposed series — **pi·lot·less** *adj*

²pilot *vb* : CONDUCT, GUIDE; *esp* : to act as pilot of ⟨∼ a ship⟩

³pilot *adj* : serving as a guiding or activating device or as a testing or trial unit ⟨a ∼ light⟩ ⟨a ∼ factory⟩

pi·lot·house \'pī-lət-,haůs\ *n* : a shelter on the upper deck of a ship for the steering gear and the helmsman

pilot whale *n* : either of two mostly black medium-sized whales

pil·sner *also* **pil·sen·er** \'pilz-nər, 'pil-zə-\ *n* [G, lit., of Pilsen (Plzeň), city in the Czech Republic] **1** : a light beer with a strong flavor of hops **2** : a tall slender footed glass for beer

pi·men·to \pə-'men-tō\ *n, pl* **pimentos** *or* **pimento** [Sp *pimienta* allspice, pepper, fr. LL *pigmenta,* pl. of *pigmentum* plant juice, fr. L, pigment] **1** : ALLSPICE **2** : PIMIENTO

pi·mien·to \pə-'men-tō\ *n, pl* **-tos** : any of various mild red sweet pepper fruits used esp. to stuff olives and to make paprika

pimp \'pimp\ *n* : a man who solicits clients for a prostitute — **pimp** *vb*

pim·per·nel \'pim-pər-,nel, -nəl\ *n* : any of a genus of herbs related to the primroses

pim·ple \'pim-pəl\ *n* : a small inflamed swelling on the skin often containing pus — **pim·ply** \-p(ə-)lē\ *adj*

¹pin \'pin\ *n* **1** : a piece of wood or metal used esp. for fastening things together or as a support by which one thing may be suspended from another; *esp* : a small pointed piece of wire with a head used for fastening clothes or attaching papers **2** : an ornament or emblem fastened to clothing with a pin **3** : one of the pieces constituting the target (as in bowling); *also* : the staff of the flag marking a hole on a golf course **4** : LEG

²pin *vb* **pinned; pin·ning** **1** : to fasten, join, or secure with a pin **2** : to hold fast or immobile **3** : ATTACH, HANG ⟨*pinned* their hopes on one man⟩ **4** : to assign the blame for ⟨∼ a crime on someone⟩ **5** : to define clearly : ESTABLISH ⟨∼ down an idea⟩

PIN *abbr* personal identification number

pi·ña co·la·da \,pēn-yə-kō-'lä-də, ,pē-nə-\ *n* [Sp, lit., strained pineapple] : a tall drink made of rum, cream of coconut, and pineapple juice mixed with ice

pin·afore \'pi-nə-,fōr\ *n* : a sleeveless dress or apron fastened at the back

pin·ball machine \'pin-,bȯl-\ *n* : an amusement device in which a ball is maneuvered along a slanted surface among a series of targets for points

pince–nez \pa°s-'nā\ *n, pl* **pince–nez** *same or* -'nāz\ [F, fr. *pincer* to pinch + *nez* nose] : eyeglasses clipped to the nose by a spring

pin·cer \'pin-sər\ *n* **1** *pl* : a gripping instrument with two handles and two grasping jaws **2** : a claw (as of a lobster) resembling pincers

¹pinch \'pinch\ *vb* [ME, fr. AF *pincher, pincer,* fr. VL *pinctiare, punctiare,* fr. L *punctum* puncture] **1** : to squeeze between the finger and thumb or between the jaws of an instrument **2** : to compress painfully **3** : CONTRACT, SHRIVEL **4** : to be miserly; *also* : to subject to strict economy **5** : to confine or limit narrowly **6** : STEAL **7** : ARREST

²pinch *n* **1** : a critical point : EMERGENCY **2** : painful effect **3** : an act of pinching **4** : a very small quantity **5** : ARREST

³pinch *adj* : SUBSTITUTE ⟨a ∼ runner⟩

pinch–hit \,pinch-'hit\ *vb* **1** : to bat in the place of another player esp. when a hit is particularly needed **2** : to act or serve in place of another — **pinch hit** *n* — **pinch hitter** *n*

pin curl *n* : a curl made usu. by dampening a strand of hair, coiling it, and securing it by a hairpin or clip

pin·cush·ion \'pin-,kủ-shən\ *n* : a cushion for pins not in use

¹pine \'pīn\ *n* : any of a genus of evergreen cone-bearing trees; *also* : the light durable resinous wood of a pine

²pine *vb* **pined; pin·ing** **1** : to lose vigor or health through distress **2** : to long for something intensely ⟨*pined* for home⟩

pi·ne·al \'pī-nē-əl, pī-'nē-əl\ *n* : PINEAL GLAND — **pineal** *adj*

pineal gland *n* : a small usu. conical appendage of the brain of all vertebrates with a cranium that functions primarily as an endocrine organ

pine·ap·ple \'pīn-,a-pəl\ *n* : a tropical plant bearing a large edible juicy fruit; *also* : its fruit

pin·feath·er \'pin-,fe-thər\ *n* : a new feather just coming through the skin

ping \'piŋ\ *n* **1** : a sharp sound like that of a bullet striking **2** : engine knock

pin·hole \'pin-,hōl\ *n* : a small hole made by, for, or as if by a pin

¹pin·ion \'pin-yən\ *n* : the end section of a bird's wing; *also* : WING

²pinion *vb* : to restrain by binding the arms; *also* : SHACKLE

³pinion *n* : a gear with a small number of teeth designed to mesh with a larger wheel or rack

¹pink \'piŋk\ *n* **1** : any of a genus of plants with narrow leaves often grown for their showy flowers **2** : the highest degree : HEIGHT ⟨the ∼ of condition⟩

²pink *n* : a light tint of red

³pink *adj* **1** : of the color pink **2** : holding socialistic views — **pink·ish** *adj*

⁴**pink** vb **1** : to perforate in an ornamental pattern **2** : PIERCE, STAB **3** : to cut a saw-toothed edge on

pink·eye \'piŋk-ˌī\ n : an acute contagious eye inflammation

pin·kie or **pin·ky** \'piŋ-kē\ n, pl **pinkies** : the smallest finger of the hand

pin·nace \'pi-nəs\ n **1** : a light sailing ship **2** : a ship's boat

pin·na·cle \'pi-ni-kəl\ n [ME pinnacle, fr. AF, fr. LL pinnaculum small wing, gable, fr. L pinna wing, battlement] **1** : a turret ending in a small spire **2** : a lofty peak **3** : ACME

pin·nate \'pi-ˌnāt\ adj : resembling a feather esp. in having similar parts arranged on each side of an axis ⟨a ~ leaf⟩ — **pin·nate·ly** adv

pi·noch·le \'pē-ˌnə-kəl\ n : a card game played with a 48-card deck

pi·ñon or **pin·yon** \'pin-ˌyōn, -ˌyän\ n, pl **pi·ñons** or **pin·yons** or **pi·ño·nes** \pin-ˈyō-nēz\ [AmerSp piñón] : any of various small pines of western No. America with edible seeds; also : the edible seed of a piñon

pin·point \'pin-ˌpȯint\ vb : to locate, hit, or aim with great precision

pin·prick \-ˌprik\ n **1** : a small puncture made by or as if by a pin **2** : a petty irritation or annoyance

pins and needles n pl : a pricking tingling sensation in a limb growing numb or recovering from numbness — **on pins and needles** : in a nervous or jumpy state of anticipation

pin·stripe \'pin-ˌstrīp\ n : a narrow stripe on a fabric; also : a suit with such stripes — **pin-striped** \-ˌstrīpt\ adj

pint \'pint\ n — see WEIGHT table

pin·to \'pin-ˌtō\ n, pl **pintos** also **pintoes** : a spotted horse or pony

pinto bean n : a spotted seed produced by a kind of kidney bean and used for food

pin-up \'pin-ˌəp\ adj : suitable or designed for hanging on a wall; also : suited (as by beauty) to be the subject of a pin-up photograph

pin·wheel \-ˌhwēl, -ˌwēl\ n **1** : a fireworks device in the form of a revolving wheel of colored fire **2** : a toy consisting of lightweight vanes that revolve at the end of a stick

pin·worm \-ˌwərm\ n : a nematode worm parasitic in the human intestine

pin·yin \'pin-'yin\ n, often cap : a system for writing Chinese ideograms by using Roman letters to represent the sounds

¹**pi·o·neer** \ˌpī-ə-'nir\ n **1** : one that originates or helps open up a new line of thought or activity **2** : an early settler in a territory

²**pioneer** vb **1** : to act as a pioneer **2** : to open or prepare for others to follow ⟨~ed a new cancer treatment⟩; also : SETTLE

pi·ous \'pī-əs\ adj **1** : marked by reverence for deity : DEVOUT **2** : excessively or affectedly religious **3** : SACRED, DEVOTIONAL **4** : showing loyal reverence for a person or thing : DUTIFUL **5**

: marked by sham or hypocrisy ⟨~ hypocrites⟩ — **pi·ous·ly** adv

¹**pip** \'pip\ n : one of the dots used on dice and dominoes to indicate numerical value

²**pip** n : a small fruit seed (as of an apple)

¹**pipe** \'pīp\ n **1** : a tubular musical instrument played by forcing air through it **2** : BAGPIPE **3** : a tube designed to conduct something (as water, steam, or oil) **4** : a device for smoking having a tube with a bowl at one end and a mouthpiece at the other **5** : a means of transmission (as of computer data)

²**pipe** vb **piped**; **pip·ing 1** : to play on a pipe **2** : to speak in a high or shrill voice **3** : to convey by or as if by pipes — **pip·er** n

pipe down vb : to stop talking or making noise

pipe dream n : an illusory or fantastic hope

pipe·line \'pīp-ˌlīn\ n **1** : a line of pipe with pumps, valves, and control devices for conveying fluids **2** : a channel for information **3** : PIPE 5

pi·pette or **pi·pet** \pī-'pet\ n : a device for measuring and transferring small volumes of liquid

pipe up vb : to speak loudly and distinctly; also : to express an opinion freely

pip·ing \'pī-piŋ\ n **1** : the music of pipes **2** : a narrow fold of material used to decorate edges or seams

piping hot adj : very hot

pip·pin \'pi-pən\ n : a crisp tart usu. yellowish apple

pip-squeak \'pip-ˌskwēk\ n : one that is small or insignificant

pi·quant \'pē-kənt\ adj **1** : pleasantly savory : PUNGENT ⟨a ~ sauce⟩ **2** : engagingly provocative; also : having a lively charm — **pi·quan·cy** \-kən-sē\ n

¹**pique** \'pēk\ n [F] : a passing feeling of wounded vanity : RESENTMENT

²**pique** vb **piqued**; **piqu·ing 1** : IRRITATE 1 2 : to arouse by a provocation or challenge : GOAD

pi·qué or **pi·que** \pi-'kā\ n : a durable ribbed clothing fabric

pi·quet \pi-'kā\ n : a 2-handed card game played with 32 cards

pi·ra·cy \'pī-rə-sē\ n, pl **-cies 1** : robbery on the high seas; also : an act resembling such robbery **2** : the unauthorized use of another's production or invention

pi·ra·nha \pə-'rä-nə, -'rän-yə\ n [Pg, fr. Tupi (So. American Indian language) piráia, fr. pirá fish + áia tooth] : any of various usu. small So. American fishes with sharp teeth that include some known to attack humans and large animals

pi·rate \'pī-rət\ n [ME, fr. MF or L; MF, fr. L pirata, fr. Gk peiratēs, fr. peiran to attempt, test] : one who commits piracy — **pirate** vb — **pi·rat·i·cal** \pə-'ra-ti-kəl, pī-\ adj

pir·ou·ette \ˌpir-ə-'wet\ n [F] : a rapid whirling about of the body; esp : a full turn on the toe or ball of one foot in ballet — **pirouette** vb

pis *pl of* PI

pis·ca·to·ri·al \ˌpis-kə-ˈtȯr-ē-əl\ *adj* : of or relating to fishing

Pi·sces \ˈpī-ˌsēz\ *n* [ME, fr. L, lit., fishes]
1 : a zodiacal constellation between Aquarius and Aries usu. pictured as a fish
2 : the 12th sign of the zodiac in astrology; *also* : one born under this sign

pis·mire \ˈpis-ˌmī(-ə)r\ *n* : ANT

pi·so \ˈpē-(ˌ)sō\ *n* : the peso of the Philippines

pis·ta·chio \pə-ˈsta-shē-ˌō, -ˈstä-\ *n, pl* **-chios** : the greenish edible seed of a small Asian tree related to the sumacs; *also* : the tree

pis·til \ˈpis-tᵊl\ *n* : the female reproductive organ in a flower — **pis·til·late** \ˈpis-tə-ˌlāt\ *adj*

pis·tol \ˈpis-tᵊl\ *n* : a handgun whose chamber is integral with the barrel

pis·tol–whip \-ˌhwip\ *vb* : to beat with a pistol

pis·ton \ˈpis-tən\ *n* : a sliding piece that receives and transmits motion and that usu. consists of a short cylinder inside a larger cylinder

¹**pit** \ˈpit\ *n* 1 : a hole, shaft, or cavity in the ground : an often sunken area designed for a particular use; *also* : an enclosed place (as for cockfights) 3 : HELL; *also, pl* : WORST ⟨it's the ∼s⟩ 4 : a natural hollow or indentation in a surface 5 : a small indented mark or scar (as from disease or corrosion) 6 : an area beside a racecourse where cars are fueled and repaired during a race

²**pit** *vb* **pit·ted; pit·ting** 1 : to form pits in or become marred with pits 2 : to match for fighting

³**pit** *n* : the stony seed of some fruits (as the cherry, peach, and date)

⁴**pit** *vb* **pit·ted; pit·ting** : to remove the pit from

pi·ta \ˈpē-tə\ *n* [ModGk] : a thin flat bread

pit–a–pat \ˌpi-ti-ˈpat\ *n* : PITTER-PATTER — **pit–a–pat** *adv or adj*

pit bull *n* : a powerful compact short‑haired dog developed for fighting

¹**pitch** \ˈpich\ *n* 1 : a dark sticky substance left over esp. from distilling tar or petroleum 2 : resin from various conifers — **pitchy** *adj*

²**pitch** *vb* 1 : to erect and fix firmly in place ⟨∼ a tent⟩ 2 : THROW, FLING 3 : to deliver a baseball to a batter 4 : to toss (as coins) toward a mark 5 : to set at a particular level ⟨∼ the voice low⟩ 6 : to fall headlong 7 : to have the front end (as of a ship) alternately plunge and rise 8 : to incline downward : SLOPE

³**pitch** *n* 1 : the action or a manner of pitching 2 : degree of slope ⟨∼ of a roof⟩ 3 : the relative level of some quality or state ⟨a high ∼ of excitement⟩ 4 : highness or lowness of sound; *also* : a standard frequency for tuning instruments 5 : a presentation delivered to sell or promote something 6 : the delivery of a baseball to a batter; *also* : the baseball delivered

pitch·blende \ˈpich-ˌblend\ *n* : a dark mineral that is the chief source of uranium

¹**pitch·er** \ˈpi-chər\ *n* : a container for liquids that usu. has a lip and a handle

²**pitcher** *n* : one that pitches esp. in a baseball game

pitcher plant *n* : any of various plants with leaves modified to resemble pitchers in which insects are trapped and digested

pitch·fork \ˈpich-ˌfȯrk\ *n* : a long-handled fork used esp. in pitching hay

pitch in *vb* 1 : to begin to work 2 : to contribute to a common effort

pitch·man \ˈpich-mən\ *n* : SALESMAN; *esp* : one who sells merchandise on the streets or from a concession

pitch–per·fect \ˈpich-ˈpər-fikt\ *adj* : having just the right tone or style ⟨a ∼ translation⟩

pit·e·ous \ˈpi-tē-əs\ *adj* : arousing pity : PITIFUL — **pit·e·ous·ly** *adv*

pit·fall \ˈpit-ˌfȯl\ *n* 1 : TRAP, SNARE; *esp* : a covered pit used for capturing animals 2 : a hidden danger or difficulty

pith \ˈpith\ *n* 1 : loose spongy tissue esp. in the center of the stem of vascular plants 2 : the essential part : CORE

pithy \ˈpi-thē\ *adj* **pith·i·er; -est** 1 : consisting of or filled with pith 2 : having substance and point : CONCISE

piti·able \ˈpi-tē-ə-bəl\ *adj* : PITIFUL

piti·ful \ˈpi-ti-fəl\ *adj* 1 : arousing or deserving pity ⟨a ∼ sight⟩ 2 : lamentably inadequate : MEAGER — **piti·ful·ly** *adv*

piti·less \ˈpi-ti-ləs\ *adj* : devoid of pity : HARSH, CRUEL — **piti·less·ly** *adv*

pi·ton \ˈpē-ˌtän\ *n* [F] : a spike, wedge, or peg that can be driven into a rock or ice surface as a support

pit·tance \ˈpi-tᵊns\ *n* : a small portion, amount, or allowance

pit·ted \ˈpi-təd\ *adj* : marked with pits

pit·ter–pat·ter \ˈpi-tər-ˌpa-tər, ˈpi-tē-\ *n* : a rapid succession of light taps or sounds ⟨the ∼ of rain⟩ — **pitter–patter** \ˌpi-tər-ˈpa-tər, ˌpi-tē-\ *adv or adj* — **pitter–patter** *same as adv*\ *vb*

pi·tu·i·tary \pə-ˈtü-ə-ˌter-ē, -ˈtyü-\ *n, pl* **-itar·ies** : PITUITARY GLAND — **pituitary** *adj*

pituitary gland *n* : a small oval endocrine gland located at the base of the brain that produces various hormones that affect most basic bodily functions (as growth and reproduction)

pit viper *n* : any of various mostly New World venomous snakes with a sensory pit on each side of the head and hollow perforated fangs

pity \ˈpi-tē\ *n, pl* **pit·ies** [ME *pite*, fr. AF *pité*, fr. L *pietas* piety, pity, fr. *pius* pious]
1 : sympathetic sorrow : COMPASSION 2 : something to be regretted

pity *vb* **pit·ied; pity·ing** : to feel pity for

¹**piv·ot** \ˈpi-vət\ *n* : a fixed pin on which something turns — **pivot** *adj*

²**pivot** *vb* : to turn on or as if on a pivot

piv·ot·al \ˈpi-və-tᵊl\ *adj* 1 : of or relating to a pivot 2 : vitally important : CRITICAL ⟨a ∼ decision⟩

pix *pl of* PIC

pix·el \ˈpik-səl, -ˌsel\ *n* 1 : any of the

small elements that together make up an image (as on a television screen) **2** : any of the detecting elements of a charge-coupled device used as an optical sensor

pix·ie *also* **pixy** \'pik-sē\ *n, pl* **pix·ies** : FAIRY; *esp* : a mischievous sprite

piz·za \'pēt-sə\ *n* [It] : an open pie made of rolled bread dough spread with a spiced mixture (as of tomatoes, cheese, and ground meat) and baked

piz·zazz *or* **pi·zazz** \pə-'zaz\ *n* **1** : GLAMOUR **2** : VITALITY

piz·ze·ria \ˌpēt-sə-'rē-ə\ *n* : an establishment where pizzas are made and sold

piz·zi·ca·to \ˌpit-si-'kä-tō\ *adv or adj* [It] : by means of plucking instead of bowing — used as a direction in music

pj's \'pē-ˌjāz\ *n pl* : PAJAMAS

pk *abbr* **1** park **2** peak **3** peck **4** pike

pkg *abbr* package

pkt *abbr* **1** packet **2** pocket

pkwy *abbr* parkway

pl *abbr* **1** place **2** plate **3** plural

¹plac·ard \'pla-kərd, -ˌkärd\ *n* : a notice posted in a public place : POSTER

²plac·ard \-ˌkärd, -kord\ *vb* **1** : to cover with or as if with placards **2** : to announce by or as if by posting

pla·cate \'plā-ˌkāt, 'pla-\ *vb* **pla·cat·ed; pla·cat·ing** : to soothe esp. by concessions : APPEASE — **pla·ca·ble** \'pla-kə-bəl, 'plā-\ *adj*

¹place \'plās\ *n* [ME, fr. AF, open space, fr. L *platea* broad street, fr. Gk *plateia* (*hodos*), fr. fem. of *platys* broad, flat] **1** : SPACE, ROOM **2** : an indefinite region : AREA **3** : a building or locality used for a special purpose **4** : a center of population **5** : a particular part of a surface : SPOT **6** : relative position in a scale or sequence; *also* : position at the end of a competition ⟨last ∼⟩ **7** : ACCOMMODATION; *esp* : SEAT **8** : the position of a figure within a numeral ⟨12 is a two ∼ number⟩ **9** : JOB; *esp* : public office **10** : a public square **11** : 2d place at the finish (as of a horse race) — **in place of** : INSTEAD OF — **out of place** : not in the proper location : INAPPROPRIATE

²place *vb* **placed; plac·ing 1** : to put in a particular place : SET **2** : to distribute in an orderly manner : ARRANGE **3** : IDENTIFY **4** : to give an order for ⟨∼ a bet⟩ **5** : to earn a given spot in a competition; *esp* : to come in 2d

pla·ce·bo \plə-'sē-bō\ *n, pl* **-bos** [L, I shall please!] : an inert medication used for its psychological effect or for purposes of comparison in an experiment

place·hold·er \'plās-ˌhōl-dər\ *n* : a symbol in a mathematical or logical expression that may be replaced by the name of any element of a set

place·kick \-ˌkik\ *n* : the kicking of a ball placed or held on the ground — **placekick** *vb* — **place·kick·er** *n*

place·ment \'plās-mənt\ *n* : an act or instance of placing

place–name \-ˌnām\ *n* : the name of a geographical locality

pla·cen·ta \plə-'sen-tə\ *n, pl* **-tas** *or* **-tae** \-ˌtē\ [NL, fr. L, flat cake] : the organ in most mammals by which the fetus is joined to the maternal uterus and is nourished — **pla·cen·tal** \-'sen-t³l\ *adj or n*

plac·er \'pla-sər\ *n* : a deposit of sand or gravel containing particles of valuable mineral (as gold)

plac·id \'pla-səd\ *adj* : UNDISTURBED, PEACEFUL ♦ *Synonyms* TRANQUIL, SERENE, CALM — **pla·cid·i·ty** \pla-'si-də-tē\ *n* — **plac·id·ly** *adv*

plack·et \'pla-kət\ *n* : a slit in a garment

pla·gia·rise *Brit var of* PLAGIARIZE

pla·gia·rize \'plā-jə-ˌrīz\ *vb* **-rized; -riz·ing** : to present the ideas or words of another as one's own — **pla·gia·rism** \-ˌri-zəm\ *n* — **pla·gia·rist** \-rist\ *n*

¹plague \'plāg\ *n* **1** : a disastrous evil or influx; *also* : NUISANCE **2** : PESTILENCE; *esp* : a destructive contagious bacterial disease (as bubonic plague)

²plague *vb* **plagued; plagu·ing 1** : to afflict with or as if with disease or disaster **2** : TEASE, TORMENT ⟨*plagued* by guilt⟩

plaid \'plad\ *n* [ScGael *plaide*] **1** : a rectangular length of tartan worn esp. over the left shoulder as part of the Scottish national costume **2** : a twilled woolen fabric with a tartan pattern **3** : a pattern of unevenly spaced repeated stripes crossing at right angles — **plaid** *adj*

¹plain \'plān\ *n* : an extensive area of level or rolling treeless country

²plain *adj* **1** : lacking ornament ⟨a ∼ dress⟩ **2** : free of extraneous matter **3** : OPEN, UNOBSTRUCTED ⟨∼ view⟩ **4** : EVIDENT, OBVIOUS **5** : easily understood : CLEAR **6** : CANDID, BLUNT **7** : SIMPLE, UNCOMPLICATED ⟨∼ cooking⟩ **8** : lacking beauty or ugliness — **plain·ly** *adv* — **plain·ness** *n*

plain·clothes·man \'plān-'klōthz-mən, -'klōz-, -ˌman\ *n* : a police officer who wears civilian clothes instead of a uniform while on duty : DETECTIVE

plain·spo·ken \-'spō-kən\ *adj* : FRANK

plaint \'plānt\ *n* **1** : LAMENTATION, WAIL **2** : PROTEST, COMPLAINT

plain·tiff \'plān-təf\ *n* : the complaining party in a lawsuit

plain·tive \'plān-tiv\ *adj* : expressive of suffering or woe : MELANCHOLY ⟨a ∼ sigh⟩ — **plain·tive·ly** *adv*

plait \'plāt, 'plat\ *n* **1** : PLEAT **2** : a braid esp. of hair or straw — **plait** *vb*

¹plan \'plan\ *n* **1** : a drawing or diagram showing the parts or details of something **2** : a method for accomplishing an objective; *also* : GOAL, AIM

²plan *vb* **planned; plan·ning 1** : to form a plan of ⟨∼ a new city⟩ **2** : INTEND ⟨*planned* to go⟩ — **plan·ner** *n*

¹plane \'plān\ *vb* **planed; plan·ing** : to smooth or level off with or as if with a plane — **plan·er** *n*

²plane *n* : PLANE TREE

³plane *n* : a tool for smoothing or shaping a wood surface

⁴plane *n* **1** : a level or flat surface **2** : a level of existence, consciousness, or development **3** : AIRPLANE

⁵plane *adj* **1** : FLAT, LEVEL **2** : dealing

with flat surfaces or figures ⟨∼ geometry⟩

plane·load \'plān-ˌlōd\ n : a load that fills an airplane

plan·et \'pla-nət\ n [ME planete, fr. AF, fr. LL planeta, fr. Gk planēt-, planēs, lit., wanderer, fr. planasthai to wander] : any of the large bodies in the solar system that revolve around the sun — **plan·e·tary** \-nə-ˌter-ē\ adj

plan·e·tar·i·um \ˌpla-nə-'ter-ē-əm\ n, pl **-i·ums** or **-ia** \-ē-ə\ : a building or room housing a device to project images of celestial bodies

plan·e·tes·i·mal \ˌpla-nə-'tes-ə-məl\ n : any of numerous small solid celestial bodies which may have existed during the formation of the solar system

plan·e·toid \'pla-nə-ˌtȯid\ n : a body resembling a planet; esp : ASTEROID

plane tree n : any of a genus of trees (as a sycamore) with large lobed leaves and globe-shaped fruit

plan·gent \'plan-jənt\ adj 1 : having a loud reverberating sound ⟨a ∼ roar⟩ 2 : having an expressive esp. plaintive quality ⟨∼ lyrics⟩ — **plan·gen·cy** \-jən-sē\ n

¹**plank** \'plaŋk\ n 1 : a heavy thick board 2 : an article in the platform of a political party

²**plank** vb 1 : to cover with planks 2 : to set or lay down forcibly 3 : to cook and serve on a board

plank·ing \'plaŋ-kiŋ\ n : a quantity or covering of planks

plank·ton \'plaŋk-tən\ n [G, fr. Gk. neut. of planktos drifting] : the passively floating or weakly swimming animal and plant life of a body of water — **plank·ton·ic** \plaŋk-'tä-nik\ adj

¹**plant** \'plant\ vb 1 : to set in the ground to grow 2 : ESTABLISH, SETTLE 3 : to stock or provide with something 4 : to place firmly or forcibly 5 : to hide or arrange with intent to deceive

²**plant** n 1 : any of a kingdom of living things that usu. have no locomotor ability or obvious sense organs and have cellulose cell walls and usu. capacity for indefinite growth 2 : the land, buildings, and machinery used in carrying on a trade or business

¹**plan·tain** \'plan-t²n\ n [ME, fr. AF, fr. L plantagin-, plantago, fr. planta sole of the foot; fr. its broad leaves] : any of a genus of weedy herbs with spikes of tiny greenish flowers

²**plantain** n [Sp plántano, plátano plane tree, banana tree, fr. ML plantanus plane tree, alter. of L platanus] : a banana plant with starchy greenish fruit that is eaten cooked; also : its fruit

plan·tar \'plan-tər, -ˌtär\ adj : of or relating to the sole of the foot

plan·ta·tion \plan-'tā-shən\ n 1 : a large group of plants and esp. trees under cultivation 2 : an agricultural estate usu. worked by resident laborers

plant·er \'plan-tər\ n 1 : one that plants or sows; esp : an owner or operator of a plantation 2 : a container for plants

plant louse n : APHID

plaque \'plak\ n [F] 1 : an ornamental brooch 2 : a flat thin piece (as of metal) used for decoration; also : a commemorative tablet 3 : a bacteria-containing film on a tooth

plash \'plash\ n : SPLASH — **plash** vb

plas·ma \'plaz-mə\ n 1 : the fluid part of blood, lymph, or milk 2 : a gas composed of ionized particles 3 : a display (as a television screen) in which cells of plasma emit light upon receiving an electric current — **plas·mat·ic** \plaz-'ma-tik\ adj

¹**plas·ter** \'plas-tər\ n 1 : a dressing consisting of a backing spread with an often medicated substance that clings to the skin ⟨adhesive ∼⟩ 2 : a paste that hardens as it dries and is used for coating walls and ceilings

²**plaster** vb : to cover with or as if with plaster — **plas·ter·er** n

plas·ter·board \'plas-tər-ˌbȯrd\ n : DRYWALL

plaster of par·is \-ˌ'pa-rəs\ often cap 2d P : a white powder made from gypsum and used as a quick-setting paste with water for casts and molds

¹**plas·tic** \'plas-tik\ adj [L plasticus of molding, fr. Gk plastikos, fr. plassein to mold, form] 1 : capable of being molded ⟨∼ clay⟩ 2 : characterized by or using modeling ⟨∼ arts⟩ 3 : made or consisting of a plastic ◆ **Synonyms** PLIABLE, PLIANT, DUCTILE, MALLEABLE, ADAPTABLE — **plas·tic·i·ty** \plas-'ti-sə-tē\ n

²**plastic** n : a plastic substance; esp : a synthetic or processed material that can be formed into rigid objects or into films or filaments

plastic surgery n : surgery to repair, restore, or improve lost, injured, defective, or misshapen body parts — **plastic surgeon** n

¹**plat** \'plat\ n 1 : a small plot of ground 2 : a plan of a piece of land with actual or proposed features (as lots)

²**plat** vb **plat·ted; plat·ting** : to make a plat of

¹**plate** \'plāt\ n 1 : a flat thin piece of material 2 : domestic hollowware made of or plated with gold, silver, or base metals 3 : DISH 4 : HOME PLATE 5 : the molded metal or plastic cast of a page of type to be printed from 6 : a sheet of glass or plastic coated with a chemical sensitive to light and used in photography 7 : the part of a denture that fits to the mouth; also : DENTURE 8 : something printed from an engraving 9 : a huge mobile segment of the earth's crust

²**plate** vb **plat·ed; plat·ing** 1 : to overlay with metal (as gold or silver) 2 : to make a printing plate of

pla·teau \pla-'tō\ n, pl **plateaus** or **plateaux** \-'tōz\ [F] : a large level area of high land

plate glass n : rolled, ground, and polished sheet glass

plate·let \'plāt-lət\ n : a minute flattened body; esp. : a minute colorless disklike body of mammalian blood that assists in blood clotting

plat·en \'pla-t²n\ n 1 : a flat plate; esp

: one that exerts or receives pressure (as in a printing press) **2** : the roller of a typewriter or printer

plate tectonics *n* **1** : a theory in geology that the lithosphere is divided into plates at the boundaries of which much of earth's seismic activity occurs **2** : the process and dynamics of tectonic plate movement — **plate–tectonic** *adj*

plat·form \'plat-,fȯrm\ *n* **1** : a raised flooring or stage for speakers, performers, or workers **2** : a declaration of the principles on which a group of persons (as a political party) stands **3** : OPERATING SYSTEM

plat·ing \'plā-tiŋ\ *n* : a coating of metal plates or plate ⟨the ~ of a ship⟩

plat·i·num \'pla-tə-nəm\ *n* : a heavy grayish white metallic chemical element

plat·i·tude \'pla-tə-,tüd, -,tyüd\ *n* : a flat or trite remark — **plat·i·tu·di·nous** \-'tü-də-nəs, -'tyü-\ *adj*

pla·ton·ic love \plə-'tä-nik-, plā-\ *n, often cap P* : a close relationship between two persons without sexual desire

pla·toon \plə-'tün\ *n* [F *peloton* small detachment, lit., ball, fr. *pelote* little ball] **1** : a subdivision of a company-size military unit usu. consisting of two or more squads or sections **2** : a group of football players trained either for offense or for defense and sent into the game as a body

platoon sergeant *n* : a noncommissioned officer in the army ranking below a first sergeant

plat·ter \'pla-tər\ *n* **1** : a large serving plate **2** : a phonograph record

platy \'pla-tē\ *n, pl* **platy** *or* **platys** *or* **plat·ies** : either of two small stocky usu. brilliantly colored bony fishes often kept in tropical aquariums

platy·pus \'pla-ti-pəs\ *n, pl* **platy·pus·es** *also* **platy·pi** \-,pī\ [NL, fr. Gk *platypous* flat-footed, fr. *platys* broad, flat + *pous* foot] : a small aquatic egg-laying marsupial mammal of Australia with webbed feet and a fleshy bill like a duck's

plau·dit \'plȯ-dət\ *n* : an act of applause

plau·si·ble \'plȯ-zə-bəl\ *adj* [L *plausibilis* worthy of applause, fr. *plausus*, pp. of *plaudere* to applaud] : seemingly worthy of belief — **plau·si·bil·i·ty** \,plȯ-zə-'bi-lə-tē\ *n* — **plau·si·bly** \'plȯ-zə-blē\ *adv*

¹play \'plā\ *n* **1** : brisk handling of something (as a weapon) **2** : the course of a game; *also* : a particular act or maneuver in a game **3** : recreational activity; *esp* : the spontaneous activity of children **4** : JEST ⟨said in ~⟩ **5** : the act or an instance of punning **6** : GAMBLING **7** : OPERATION ⟨bring extra force into ~⟩ **8** : a brisk or light movement **9** : free motion (as of part of a machine) **10** : scope for action **11** : PUBLICITY ⟨an effort to arouse liking ⟨made a ~ for her⟩ **12** : a stage representation of a drama; *also* : a dramatic composition **14** : a function of an electronic device that causes a recording to play — **play·ful** \-fəl\ *adj* — **play·ful·ly** *adv* — **play·ful·ness** *n* — **in play** : in condition or position to be played

²play *vb* **1** : to engage in recreation : FROLIC **2** : to handle or behave lightly or absentmindedly **3** : to make a pun ⟨~ on words⟩ **4** : to take advantage ⟨~ on fears⟩ **5** : to move or operate in a brisk or irregular manner ⟨a flashlight ~ed over the wall⟩ **6** : to perform music ⟨~ on a violin⟩; *also* : to perform (music) on an instrument ⟨~ a waltz⟩ **7** : to perform music upon ⟨~ the piano⟩; *also* : to sound in performance ⟨the organ is ~ing⟩ **8** : to cause to emit sounds ⟨~ a radio⟩; *also* : to cause to reproduce recorded material ⟨~ a DVD⟩ **9** : to act in a dramatic medium; *also* : to act in the character of ⟨~ the hero⟩ **10** : GAMBLE **11** : to produce a specified impression in performance ⟨~s like a comedy⟩ **12** : to behave in a specified way ⟨~ safe⟩; *also* : COOPERATE ⟨~ along with him⟩ **13** : to deal with; *also* : EMPHASIZE ⟨~ up her good qualities⟩ **14** : to perform for amusement ⟨~ a trick⟩ **15** : WREAK **16** : to use as an esp. political strategy **17** : to contend with in a game; *also* : to fill (a certain position) on a team **18** : to make wagers on ⟨~ the races⟩ **19** : WIELD, PLY **20** : to keep in action — **play·er** *n*

play·act·ing \'plā-,ak-tiŋ\ *n* **1** : performance in theatrical productions **2** : insincere or artificial behavior

play·back \-,bak\ *n* : an act of reproducing recorded sound or pictures — **play back** *vb*

play·bill \-,bil\ *n* : a poster advertising the performance of a play

play·book \-,bu̇k\ *n* **1** : a notebook containing diagrammed football plays **2** : a stock of usual tactics or methods

play·boy \-,bȯi\ *n* : a man whose chief interest is the pursuit of pleasure

play·date \-,dāt\ *n* : a usu. prearranged play session for small children

play·go·er \-,gō-ər\ *n* : a person who frequently attends plays

play·ground \-,graund\ *n* : an area used for games and play esp. by children

play·house \-,haus\ *n* **1** : THEATER **2** : a small house for children to play in

playing card *n* : any of a set of 24 to 78 cards marked to show its rank and suit and used to play a game of cards

play·let \'plā-lət\ *n* : a short play

play·mate \-,māt\ *n* : a companion in play

play·off \-,ȯf\ *n* : a contest or series of contests to break a tie or determine a championship

play out *vb* : DEVELOP, UNFOLD ⟨see how things *play out*⟩

play·pen \-,pen\ *n* : a portable enclosure in which a young child may play

play·suit \-,süt\ *n* : a sports and play outfit for women and children

play·thing \-,thiŋ\ *n* : TOY

play·wright \-,rīt\ *n* : a writer of plays

pla·za \'pla-zə, 'plä-\ *n* [Sp, fr. L *platea* broad street] **1** : a public square in a city or town **2** : a shopping center

PLC *abbr, Brit* public limited company

plea \'plē\ *n* **1** : a defendant's answer in law to a charge or indictment **2** : something alleged as an excuse **3** : ENTREATY, APPEAL

plead \'plēd\ *vb* **plead·ed** *or* **pled** \'pled\; **plead·ing 1** : to argue before a court or authority ⟨~ a case⟩ **2** : to answer to a charge or indictment ⟨~ guilty⟩ **3** : to argue for or against something ⟨~ for acquittal⟩ **4** : to appeal earnestly ⟨~s for help⟩ **5** : to offer a plea (as in defense) ⟨~ed illness⟩ — **plead·er** *n*

pleas·ant \'ple-z³nt\ *adj* **1** : giving pleasure : AGREEABLE ⟨a ~ experience⟩ **2** : marked by pleasing behavior or appearance ⟨a ~ person⟩ — **pleas·ant·ly** *adv* — **pleas·ant·ness** *n*

pleas·ant·ry \-z³n-trē\ *n, pl* **-ries** : a pleasant and casual act or speech

¹**please** \'plēz\ *vb* **pleased; pleas·ing 1** : to give pleasure or satisfaction to **2** : LIKE ⟨do as you ~⟩ **3** : to be the will or pleasure of ⟨may it ~ his Majesty⟩

²**please** *adv* — used as a function word to express politeness or emphasis in a request ⟨~ come in⟩

pleas·ing *adj* : giving pleasure ⟨a ~ fragrance⟩ — **pleas·ing·ly** *adv*

plea·sur·able \'ple-zhə-rə-bəl\ *adj* : PLEASANT, GRATIFYING ⟨a ~ cruise⟩ — **plea·sur·ably** \-blē\ *adv*

plea·sure \'ple-zhər\ *n* **1** : DESIRE, INCLINATION ⟨await your ~⟩ **2** : a state of gratification : ENJOYMENT **3** : a source of delight or joy ⟨a ~ to see you dance⟩

¹**pleat** \'plēt\ *vb* **1** : FOLD; *esp* : to arrange in pleats **2** : BRAID

²**pleat** *n* : a fold (as in cloth) made by doubling material over on itself

plebe \'plēb\ *n* : a freshman at a military or naval academy

¹**ple·be·ian** \pli-'bē-ən\ *n* **1** : a member of the Roman plebs **2** : one of the common people

²**plebeian** *adj* **1** : of or relating to plebeians **2** : COMMON, VULGAR ⟨~ tastes⟩

pleb·i·scite \'ple-bə-ˌsīt, -sət\ *n* : a vote of the people (as of a country) on a proposal submitted to them

plebs \'plebz\ *n, pl* **ple·bes** \'plē-bēz\ **1** : the general populace **2** : the common people of ancient Rome

plec·trum \'plek-trəm\ *n, pl* **plec·tra** \-trə\ *or* **plec·trums** [L] : ³PICK 3

¹**pledge** \'plej\ *n* [ME *plegge* security, fr. AF *plege*, fr. LL *plebium*, fr. *plebere* to pledge, prob. of Gmc origin] **1** : something given as security for the performance of an act **2** : the state of being held as a security or guaranty **3** : TOAST **3 4** : PROMISE, VOW

²**pledge** *vb* **pledged; pledg·ing 1** : to deposit as a pledge **2** : TOAST **3** : to bind by a pledge : PLIGHT **4** : PROMISE

Pleis·to·cene \'plī-stə-ˌsēn\ *adj* : of, relating to, or being the earlier epoch of the Quaternary — **Pleistocene** *n*

ple·na·ry \'plē-nə-rē, 'ple-\ *adj* **1** : FULL ⟨~ power⟩ **2** : including all entitled to attend ⟨~ session⟩

pleni·po·ten·tia·ry \ˌple-nə-pə-'ten-chə-rē, -'ten-chē-ˌer-ē\ *n, pl* **-ries** : a diplomatic agent having full authority — **plenipotentiary** *adj*

plen·i·tude \'ple-nə-ˌtüd, -ˌtyüd\ *n* **1** : COMPLETENESS **2** : ABUNDANCE

plen·te·ous \'plen-tē-əs\ *adj* **1** : FRUITFUL **2** : existing in plenty

plen·ti·ful \'plen-ti-fəl\ *adj* **1** : containing or yielding plenty ⟨a ~ harvest⟩ **2** : ABUNDANT — **plen·ti·ful·ly** *adv*

plen·ty \'plen-tē\ *n* : a more than adequate number or amount

ple·num \'ple-nəm, 'plē-\ *n, pl* **-nums** *or* **-na** \-nə\ : a general assembly of all members esp. of a legislative body

pleth·o·ra \'ple-thə-rə\ *n* : an excessive quantity or fullness; *also* : PROFUSION

pleu·ri·sy \'plur-ə-sē\ *n* : inflammation of the membrane that lines the chest and covers the lungs

plex·i·glass \'plek-si-ˌglas\ *n* [alter. of *Plexiglas*, a trademark] : a transparent acrylic plastic often used in place of glass

plex·us \'plek-səs\ *n, pl* **plex·us·es** \-sə-səz\ : an interlacing network esp. of blood vessels or nerves

pli·able \'plī-ə-bəl\ *adj* **1** : FLEXIBLE **2** : yielding easily to others ⟨a ~ child⟩

♦ **Synonyms** PLASTIC, PLIANT, DUCTILE, MALLEABLE, ADAPTABLE — **pli·abil·i·ty** \ˌplī-ə-'bi-lə-tē\ *n*

pli·ant \'plī-ənt\ *adj* **1** : FLEXIBLE **2** : easily influenced : PLIABLE ⟨a ~ senator⟩ — **pli·an·cy** \-ən-sē\ *n*

pli·ers \'plī-ərz\ *n pl* : small pincers for bending or cutting wire or handling small objects

¹**plight** \'plīt\ *vb* : to put or give in pledge : ENGAGE

²**plight** *n* : an unfortunate, difficult, or precarious situation

plinth \'plinth\ *n* : the lowest part of the base of an architectural column

Plio·cene \'plī-ə-ˌsēn\ *adj* : of, relating to, or being the latest epoch of the Tertiary — **Pliocene** *n*

PLO *abbr* Palestine Liberation Organization

plod \'pläd\ *vb* **plod·ded; plod·ding 1** : to walk heavily or slowly : TRUDGE **2** : to work laboriously and monotonously : DRUDGE — **plod·der** *n* — **plod·ding·ly** *adv*

plonk *var of* PLUNK

plop \'pläp\ *vb* **plopped; plop·ping 1** : to fall or move with a sound like that of something dropping into water **2** : to set, drop, or throw heavily or hastily ⟨*plopped* down on the couch⟩ ⟨~ down $20⟩ — **plop** *n*

¹**plot** \'plät\ *n* **1** : a small area of ground **2** : a ground plan (as of an area) **3** : the main story (as of a book or movie) **4** : a secret scheme : INTRIGUE

²**plot** *vb* **plot·ted; plot·ting 1** : to make a plot or plan of **2** : to mark on or as if on a chart **3** : to plan or contrive esp. secretly — **plot·ter** *n*

plo·ver \'plə-vər, 'plō-\ *n, pl* **plover** *or* **plovers** [ME, fr. AF, fr. VL *pluviarius*, fr. L *pluvia* rain] : any of a family of shorebirds that differ from the sandpipers in having shorter stouter bills

¹**plow** *or* **plough** \'plau̇\ *n* **1** : an implement used to cut, lift, turn over, and

partly break up soil **2** : a device (as a snowplow) operating like a plow

²**plow** *or* **plough** *vb* **1** : to open, break up, or work with a plow **2** : to move through like a plow ⟨a ship *~ing* the waves⟩ **3** : to proceed laboriously ⟨*~ed* through his work⟩ — **plow·able** *adj* — **plow·er** *n*

plow·boy \'plau̇-ˌbȯi\ *n* : a boy who leads the horse drawing a plow

plow·man \-mən, -ˌman\ *n* **1** : a man who guides a plow **2** : a farm laborer

plow·share \-ˌsher\ *n* : a part of a plow that cuts the earth

ploy \'plȯi\ *n* : a tactic intended to embarrass or frustrate an opponent

¹**pluck** \'plək\ *vb* **1** : to pull off or out : PICK; *also* : to pull something from **2** : to play (an instrument) by pulling the strings **3** : TUG, TWITCH

²**pluck** *n* **1** : an act or instance of plucking **2** : SPIRIT, COURAGE

plucky \'plə-kē\ *adj* **pluck·i·er; -est** : COURAGEOUS, SPIRITED ⟨*~* recruits⟩

¹**plug** \'pləg\ *n* **1** : STOPPER; *also* : an obstructing mass **2** : a cake of tobacco **3** : a poor or worn-out horse **4** : SPARK PLUG **5** : a lure with several hooks used in fishing **6** : a device on the end of a cord for making an electrical connection **7** : a piece of favorable publicity

²**plug** *vb* **plugged; plug·ging 1** : to stop, make tight, or secure by inserting a plug **2** : HIT, SHOOT **3** : to publicize insistently **4** : PLOD, DRUDGE

plug and play *n* : a computer feature enabling the operating system to automatically detect and configure peripherals — **plug-and-play** *adj*

plugged-in \'pləgd-'in\ *adj* : technologically or socially informed and connected

plug-in \'pləg-ˌin\ *n* : a small piece of software that supplements a larger program

plum \'pləm\ *n* [ME, fr. OE *plūme*, modif. of L *prunum* plum, fr. Gk *proumnon*] **1** : a smooth-skinned juicy fruit borne by trees related to the peach and cherry; *also* : a tree bearing plums **2** : a raisin when used in desserts (as puddings) **3** : something excellent; *esp* : something desirable given in return for a favor

plum·age \'plü-mij\ *n* : the feathers of a bird — **plum·aged** \-mijd\ *adj*

¹**plumb** \'pləm\ *n* : a weight on the end of a line (**plumb line**) used esp. by builders to show vertical direction

²**plumb** *adv* **1** : VERTICALLY **2** : COMPLETELY ⟨*~* tired out⟩ **3** : EXACTLY; *also* : IMMEDIATELY

³**plumb** *vb* : to sound, adjust, or test with a plumb ⟨*~* the depth of a well⟩

⁴**plumb** *adj* **1** : VERTICAL **2** : COMPLETE

plumb·er \'plə-mər\ *n* : a worker who fits or repairs pipes and fixtures

plumb·ing \'plə-miŋ\ *n* : a system of pipes in a building for supplying and carrying off water

¹**plume** \'plüm\ *n* : FEATHER; *esp* : a large, conspicuous, or showy feather — **plumed** \'plümd\ *adj* — **plumy** \'plü-mē\ *adj*

²**plume** *vb* **plumed; plum·ing 1** : to pro-

vide or deck with feathers **2** : to indulge (oneself) in pride

¹**plum·met** \'plə-mət\ *n* : PLUMB; *also* : PLUMB LINE

²**plummet** *vb* : to drop or plunge straight down

¹**plump** \'pləmp\ *vb* **1** : to drop or fall suddenly or heavily **2** : to favor something strongly ⟨*~ing* for change⟩

²**plump** *n* : a sudden heavy fall or blow; *also* : the sound made by it

³**plump** *adv* **1** : straight down; *also* : straight ahead **2** : UNQUALIFIEDLY ⟨came out *~* for free trade⟩

⁴**plump** *adj* : having a full rounded usu. pleasing form ♦ **Synonyms** FLESHY, STOUT, ROLY-POLY, ROTUND — **plump·ness** *n*

¹**plun·der** \'plən-dər\ *vb* : to take the goods of by force or wrongfully : PILLAGE — **plun·der·er** *n*

²**plunder** *n* : something taken by force or theft : LOOT

¹**plunge** \'plənj\ *vb* **plunged; plung·ing 1** : IMMERSE, SUBMERGE **2** : to enter or cause to enter a state or course of action suddenly or violently ⟨*~* into war⟩ **3** : to cast oneself into or as if into water **4** : to gamble heavily and recklessly **5** : to descend suddenly

²**plunge** *n* : a sudden dive, leap, or rush

plung·er \'plən-jər\ *n* **1** : one that plunges **2** : a sliding piece driven by or against fluid pressure : PISTON **3** : a rubber cup on a handle pushed against an opening to free a waste outlet of an obstruction

plunk \'pləŋk\ *or* **plonk** \'pläŋk, 'plȯŋk\ *vb* **1** : to make or cause to make a hollow metallic sound **2** : to drop heavily or suddenly — **plunk** *n*

plu·per·fect \(ˌ)plü-'pər-fikt\ *adj* [ME *pluperfyth*, modif. of LL *plusquamperfectus*, lit., more than perfect] : of, relating to, or constituting a verb tense that denotes an action or state as completed at or before a past time spoken of — **pluperfect** *n*

plu·ral \'plu̇r-əl\ *adj* [ME, fr. AF & L; AF *plurel*, fr. L *pluralis*, fr. *plur-, plus* more] : of, relating to, or constituting a word form used to denote more than one — **plural** *n*

plu·ral·i·ty \plu̇-'ra-lə-tē\ *n, pl* **-ties 1** : the state of being plural **2** : an excess of votes over those cast for an opposing candidate **3** : the greatest number of votes cast when not a majority

plu·ral·ize \'plu̇r-ə-ˌlīz\ *vb* **-ized; -iz·ing** : to make plural or express in the plural form — **plu·ral·i·za·tion** \ˌplu̇r-ə-lə-'zā-shən\ *n*

¹**plus** \'pləs\ *adj* [L, more] **1** : mathematically positive **2** : having or being in addition to what is anticipated **3** : falling high in a specified range ⟨a grade of B *~*⟩

²**plus** *n, pl* **plus·es** \'plə-səz\ *also* **plus·ses 1** : a sign + (**plus sign**) used in mathematics to indicate addition or a positive quantity **2** : an added quantity; *also* : a positive quality **3** : SURPLUS

³**plus** *prep* **1** : increased by : with the addition of ⟨3 *~* 4⟩ **2** : BESIDES

⁴**plus** *conj* : AND ⟨soup ∼ salad and bread⟩

¹**plush** \'pləsh\ *n* : a fabric with a pile longer and less dense than velvet pile — **plushy** *adj*

²**plush** *adj* : notably luxurious ⟨a ∼ suite⟩ — **plush·ly** *adv* — **plush·ness** *n*

plus/minus sign *n* : the sign ± used to indicate a quantity taking on both a positive value and its negative or to indicate a plus or minus quantity

plus or minus *adj* : indicating a quantity whose positive and negative values bracket a range of values ⟨*plus or minus* 3 inches⟩

plus–size \'pləs-ˌsīz\ *also* **plus–sized** \-ˌsīzd\ *adj* : extra large ⟨∼ clothing⟩ ⟨∼ shoppers⟩

Plu·to \'plü-tō\ *n* : a dwarf planet whose orbit crosses the orbit of Neptune — see PLANET table

plu·toc·ra·cy \plü-'tä-krə-sē\ *n, pl* **-cies** 1 : government by the wealthy 2 : a controlling class of the wealthy — **plu·to·crat** \'plü-tə-ˌkrat\ *n* — **plu·to·crat·ic** \ˌplü-tə-'kra-tik\ *adj*

plu·to·ni·um \plü-'tō-nē-əm\ *n* : a radioactive chemical element formed by the decay of neptunium

plu·vi·al \'plü-vē-əl\ *adj* 1 : of or relating to rain 2 : characterized by abundant rain

¹**ply** \'plī\ *vb* **plied; ply·ing** 1 : to use, practice, or work diligently ⟨∼ a trade⟩ 2 : to keep supplying something to ⟨plied them with liquor⟩ 3 : to go or travel regularly esp. by sea

²**ply** *n, pl* **plies** : one of the folds, thicknesses, or strands of which something (as plywood or yarn) is made

³**ply** *vb* **plied; ply·ing** : to twist together ⟨∼ yarns⟩

ply·wood \'plī-ˌwùd\ *n* : material made of thin sheets of wood glued and pressed together

pm *abbr* premium

Pm *symbol* promethium

PM *abbr* 1 paymaster 2 police magistrate 3 postmaster 4 post meridiem — often not cap. and often punctuated 5 postmortem 6 prime minister 7 provost marshal

pmk *abbr* postmark

PMS \ˌpē-ˌem-'es\ *n* : PREMENSTRUAL SYNDROME

pmt *abbr* payment

pneu·mat·ic \nù-'ma-tik, nyù-\ *adj* 1 : of, relating to, or using air or wind 2 : moved by air pressure 3 : filled with compressed air ⟨∼ tires⟩ — **pneu·mat·i·cal·ly** \-ti-k(ə-)lē\ *adv*

pneu·mo·coc·cus \ˌnü-mə-'kä-kəs, ˌnyü-\ *n, pl* **-coc·ci** \-'käk-ˌsī, -ˌsē; -'kä-ˌkī, -ˌkē\ : a bacterium that causes pneumonia — **pneu·mo·coc·cal** \-'kä-kəl\ *adj*

pneu·mo·co·ni·o·sis \ˌnü-mō-ˌkō-nē-'ō-səs, ˌnyü-\ *n* : a disease of the lungs caused by habitual inhalation of irritant mineral or metallic particles

pneu·mo·nia \nù-'mō-nyə, nyù-\ *n* : an inflammatory disease of the lungs

Po *symbol* polonium

PO *abbr* 1 petty officer 2 post office

¹**poach** \'pōch\ *vb* [ME *pochen*, fr. MF *pocher*, fr. OF *poché* poached, lit., bagged, fr. *poche* bag, pouch, of Gmc origin] : to cook (as an egg or fish) in simmering liquid

²**poach** *vb* : to hunt or fish unlawfully — **poach·er** *n*

POB *abbr* post office box

po·bla·no \pō-'blä-nō\ *n, pl* **-nos** : a heart-shaped usu. mild chili pepper esp. when fresh and dark green

po'·boy \'pō-ˌbói\ *also* **poor boy** *n* : SUBMARINE 2

pock \'päk\ *n* : a small swelling on the skin (as in smallpox); *also* : a spot suggesting this

¹**pock·et** \'pä-kət\ *n* 1 : a small bag open at the top or side inserted in a garment 2 : supply of money : MEANS 3 : RECEPTACLE, CONTAINER 4 : a small isolated area or group ⟨∼s of fog⟩ 5 : a small body of ore — **pock·et·ful** *n*

²**pocket** *vb* 1 : to put in or as if in a pocket 2 : STEAL ⟨∼ed the profits⟩

³**pocket** *adj* 1 : small enough to fit in a pocket; *also* : SMALL, MINIATURE ⟨a ∼ park⟩ 2 : carried in or paid from one's own pocket

¹**pock·et·book** \-ˌbùk\ *n* 1 : PURSE; *also* : HANDBAG 2 : financial resources

²**pocketbook** *adj* : relating to money

pocket gopher *n* : GOPHER 2

pock·et·knife \'pä-kət-ˌnīf\ *n* : a knife with a folding blade to be carried in the pocket

pocket veto *n* : an indirect veto of a legislative bill by an executive through retention of the bill unsigned until after adjournment of the legislature

pock·mark \'päk-ˌmärk\ *n* : a pit or scar caused by smallpox or acne — **pock·marked** \-ˌmärkt\ *adj*

po·co \'pō-kō, 'pò-\ *adv* [It, little, fr. L *paucus*] : SOMEWHAT — used to qualify a direction in music ⟨∼ allegro⟩

po·co a po·co \ˌpō-kō-ä-'pō-kō, ˌpò-kō-ä-'pò-\ *adv* : little by little : GRADUALLY — used as a direction in music

pod \'päd\ *n* 1 : a dry fruit (as of a pea) that splits open when ripe 2 : an external streamlined compartment (as for a jet engine) on an airplane 3 : a compartment (as for personnel, a power unit, or an instrument) on a ship or craft

POD *abbr* pay on delivery

pod·cast \'päd-ˌkast\ *n* [*iPod*, trademark for a portable media player + broad*cast*] : a program made available in digital format for download over the Internet — **podcast** *vb* — **pod·cast·er** *n*

po·di·a·try \pə-'dī-ə-trē, pō-\ *n* : the medical care and treatment of the human foot — **po·di·at·ric** \ˌpō-dē-'a-trik\ *adj* — **po·di·a·trist** \pə-'dī-ə-trist, pō-\ *n*

po·di·um \'pō-dē-əm\ *n, pl* **podiums** *or* **po·dia** \-dē-ə\ 1 : a dais esp. for an orchestral conductor 2 : LECTERN

POE *abbr* port of entry

po·em \'pō-əm\ *n* : a composition in verse

po·esy \'pō-ə-zē\ *n* : POETRY

po·et \'pō-ət\ n [ME, fr. AF poete, fr. L poeta, fr. Gk poiētēs maker, poet, fr. poiein to make] : a writer of poetry; also : a creative artist of great sensitivity

po·et·as·ter \'pō-ə-ˌtas-tər\ n : an inferior poet

po·et·ess \'pō-ə-təs\ n : a girl or woman who is a poet

poetic justice n : an outcome in which vice is punished and virtue rewarded usu. in a manner peculiarly or ironically appropriate

po·et·ry \'pō-ə-trē\ n 1 : metrical writing 2 : POEMS — **po·et·ic** \pō-'e-tik\ or **po·et·i·cal** \-ti-kəl\ adj

po·grom \'pō-grəm, pō-'gräm\ n [Yiddish, fr. Russ, lit., devastation] : an organized massacre of helpless people and esp. of Jews

poi \'pói\ n, pl **poi** or **pois** : a food prepared from the cooked corms of taro that are mashed with water to the consistency of a paste or thick liquid

poi·gnant \'pói-nyənt\ adj 1 : painfully affecting the feelings ⟨~ grief⟩ 2 : deeply moving ⟨~ scene⟩ — **poi·gnan·cy** \-nyən-sē\ n

poin·ci·ana \ˌpóin-sē-'a-nə\ n : any of several ornamental tropical leguminous trees or shrubs with bright orange or red flowers

poin·set·tia \póin-'se-tē-ə\ n : a showy tropical American spurge with usu. scarlet bracts that suggest petals and surround small yellow flowers

¹**point** \'póint\ n 1 : an individual detail; also : the most important essential 2 : PURPOSE ⟨no ~ in continuing⟩ 3 : a geometric element that has position but no size 4 : a particular place : LOCALITY 5 : a particular stage or degree 6 : a sharp end : TIP 7 : a projecting piece of land 8 : a punctuation mark; esp : PERIOD 9 : DECIMAL POINT 10 : one of the divisions of the compass 11 : a unit of counting (as in a game score) — **point·less** adj — **pointy** \'póin-tē\ adj — **beside the point** : IRRELEVANT — **to the point** : RELEVANT, PERTINENT ⟨her remark was to the point⟩

²**point** vb 1 : to furnish with a point : SHARPEN 2 : PUNCTUATE 3 : to separate (a decimal fraction) from an integer by a decimal point — usu. used with off 4 : to indicate the position of esp. by extending a finger 5 : to direct attention to ⟨~ out an error⟩ 6 : AIM, DIRECT 7 : to lie extended, aimed, or turned in a particular direction : FACE, LOOK

point–and–click adj : relating to or being a computer interface that allows the activation of a file by selection with a pointing device (as a mouse)

point–and–shoot adj : having or using preset or automatically adjusted controls ⟨a ~ camera⟩

point–blank \'póint-'blaŋk\ adj 1 : so close to the target that a missile fired will travel in a straight line to the mark 2 : DIRECT, BLUNT ⟨a ~ refusal⟩ — **point–blank** adv

point·ed \'póin-təd\ adj 1 : having a

point 2 : being to the point : DIRECT 3 : aimed at a particular person or group; also : CONSPICUOUS, MARKED ⟨~ indifference⟩ — **point·ed·ly** adv

point·er \'póin-tər\ n 1 : one that points out : INDICATOR 2 : a large short-haired hunting dog 3 : HINT, TIP ⟨gave me some ~s on how to play⟩

poin·til·lism \'pwan-tē-ˌyi-zəm, 'póin-tə-ˌli-zəm\ n [F pointillisme, fr pointiller to stipple, fr. point spot, point] : the theory or practice in painting of applying small strokes or dots of color to a surface so that from a distance they blend together — **poin·til·list** \ˌpwan-tē-'yēst, 'póin-tə-list\ n or adj

point man n : a principal spokesman or advocate

point of no return : a critical point at which turning back or reversal is not possible

point of view : a position from which something is considered or evaluated

point spread : the number of points by which a favorite is expected to defeat an underdog

¹**poise** \'póiz\ vb **poised; pois·ing** : BALANCE

²**poise** n 1 : BALANCE 2 : self-possessed calmness ⟨kept her ~ even under attack⟩; also : a particular way of carrying oneself

poi·sha \'pói-shə\ n, pl **poisha** : the paisa of Bangladesh

¹**poi·son** \'pói-zᵊn\ n [ME, fr. AF poisun drink, potion, poison, fr. L potion-, potio drink] : a substance that through its chemical action can injure or kill — **poi·son·ous** \-zᵊn-əs\ adj

²**poison** vb 1 : to injure or kill with poison 2 : to treat or taint with poison 3 : to affect destructively : CORRUPT ⟨~ed her mind⟩ — **poi·son·er** n

poison hemlock n : a large branching poisonous herb with finely divided leaves and white flowers that is related to the carrot

poison ivy n 1 : a usu. climbing plant related to the sumacs that has leaves composed of three shiny leaflets and produces an irritating oil causing a usu. intensely itching skin rash; also : any of several related plants 2 : a skin rash caused by poison ivy

poison oak n : any of several shrubby plants closely related to poison ivy and having similar properties

poison sumac n : a No. American swamp shrub with pinnate leaves, greenish flowers, greenish white berries, and irritating properties

¹**poke** \'pōk\ n, chiefly Southern & Midland : BAG, SACK

²**poke** vb **poked; pok·ing** 1 : PROD; also : to stir up by prodding 2 : to make a prodding or jabbing movement esp. repeatedly 3 : HIT, PUNCH 4 : to thrust forward obtrusively 5 : RUMMAGE ⟨poking around the attic⟩ 6 : MEDDLE, PRY 7 : DAWDLE ⟨poking along toward home⟩ — **poke fun at** : RIDICULE, MOCK

³**poke** n : a quick thrust; also : PUNCH

¹pok·er \'pō-kər\ *n* : a metal rod for stirring a fire

²po·ker \'pō-kər\ *n* : any of several card games in which the player with the highest hand at the end of the betting wins

poke·weed \'pōk-ˌwēd\ *n* : a coarse American perennial herb with clusters of white flowers and dark purple juicy berries

poky *or* **pok·ey** \'pō-kē\ *adj* **pok·i·er; -est 1** : small and cramped **2** : SHABBY, DULL **3** : annoyingly slow

pol \'päl\ *n* : POLITICIAN

po·lar \'pō-lər\ *adj* **1** : of or relating to a geographical pole **2** : of or relating to a pole (as of a magnet)

polar bear *n* : a large creamy-white bear that inhabits arctic regions

Po·lar·is \pə-'ler-əs\ *n* : NORTH STAR

po·lar·ise *Brit var of* POLARIZE

po·lar·i·ty \pō-'ler-ə-tē\ *n, pl* **-ties** : the condition of having poles and esp. magnetic or electrical poles

po·lar·i·za·tion \ˌpō-lə-rə-'zā-shən\ *n* **1** : the action of polarizing : the state of being polarized **2** : concentration about opposing extremes

po·lar·ize \'pō-lə-ˌrīz\ *vb* **-ized; -iz·ing 1** : to cause (light waves) to vibrate in a definite way **2** : to give physical polarity to **3** : to break up into opposing groups

pol·der \'pōl-dər, 'päl-\ *n* [D] : a tract of low land reclaimed from the sea

¹pole \'pōl\ *n* : a long slender piece of wood or metal ⟨telephone ∼⟩

²pole *vb* **poled; pol·ing** : to impel or push with a pole ⟨∼ a boat⟩

³pole *n* **1** : either end of an axis esp. of the earth **2** : either of the terminals of an electric device (as a battery or generator) **3** : one of two or more regions in a magnetized body at which the magnetism is concentrated — **pole·ward** \'pōl-wərd\ *adj or adv*

¹pole·ax \'pōl-ˌaks\ *n* : a battle-ax with a short handle

²poleax *vb* : to attack or fell with or as if with a poleax

pole·cat \'pōl-ˌkat\ *n, pl* **polecats** *or* **polecat 1** : a European carnivorous mammal of which the ferret is considered a domesticated variety **2** : SKUNK

po·lem·ic \pə-'le-mik\ *n* : the art or practice of disputation — usu. used in pl. — **po·lem·i·cal** \-mi-kəl\ *also* **po·lem·ic** \-mik\ *adj* — **po·lem·i·cist** \-sist\ *n*

pole·star \'pōl-ˌstär\ *n* **1** : NORTH STAR **2** : a directing principle : GUIDE

pole vault *n* : a field contest in which each contestant uses a pole to vault for height over a crossbar — **pole–vault** *vb* — **pole–vault·er** *n*

¹po·lice \pə-'lēs\ *vb* **po·liced; po·lic·ing 1** : to control, regulate, or keep in order esp. by use of police ⟨∼ a highway⟩ **2** : to make clean and put in order ⟨policed up the concert site⟩

²police *n, pl* **police** [F, government, fr. OF, fr. LL *politia*, fr. Gk *politeia*, fr. *politēs* citizen, fr. *polis* city, state] **1** : the department of government that keeps public order and safety and enforces the laws; *also* : the members of this department **2** : a private organization resembling a police force; *also* : its members **3** : military personnel detailed to clean and put in order

po·lice·man \-mən\ *n* : POLICE OFFICER

police officer *n* : a member of a police force

police state *n* : a state characterized by repressive, arbitrary, totalitarian rule by means of secret police

po·lice·wom·an \pə-'lēs-ˌwù-mən\ *n* : a woman who is a police officer

¹pol·i·cy \'pä-lə-sē\ *n, pl* **-cies** : a definite course or method of action selected to guide and determine present and future decisions

²policy *n, pl* **-cies** : a writing whereby a contract of insurance is made

pol·i·cy·hold·er \'pä-lə-sē-ˌhōl-dər\ *n* : one granted an insurance policy

po·lio \'pō-lē-ˌō\ *n* : POLIOMYELITIS — **polio** *adj*

po·lio·my·eli·tis \-ˌmī-ə-'lī-təs\ *n* : an acute virus disease marked by inflammation of the gray matter of the spinal cord leading usu. to paralysis

¹pol·ish \'pä-lish\ *vb* **1** : to make smooth and glossy usu. by rubbing **2** : to refine or improve in manners, condition, or style

²polish *n* **1** : a smooth glossy surface : LUSTER **2** : REFINEMENT, CULTURE **3** : the action or process of polishing **4** : a preparation used to produce a gloss

Pol·ish \'pō-lish\ *n* : the Slavic language of the Poles — **Polish** *adj*

polit *abbr* political; politician

po·lit·bu·ro \'pä-lət-ˌbyùr-ō, 'pō-, pə-'lit-\ *n* [Russ *politbyuro*] : the principal policy-making committee of a Communist party

po·lite \pə-'līt\ *adj* **po·lit·er; -est 1** : REFINED, CULTIVATED ⟨∼ society⟩ **2** : marked by correct social conduct : COURTEOUS; *also* : CONSIDERATE, TACTFUL — **po·lite·ly** *adv* — **po·lite·ness** *n*

po·li·tesse \ˌpä-li-'tes\ *n* [F] : formal politeness

pol·i·tic \'pä-lə-ˌtik\ *adj* **1** : wise in promoting a policy ⟨a ∼ statesman⟩ **2** : shrewdly tactful ⟨a ∼ move⟩

po·lit·i·cal \pə-'li-ti-kəl\ *adj* **1** : of or relating to government or politics **2** : involving or charged or concerned with acts against a government or a political system ⟨∼ prisoners⟩ — **po·lit·i·cal·ly** \-k(ə-)lē\ *adv*

politically correct *adj* : conforming to a belief that language and practices which could offend sensibilities (as in matters of sex or race) should be eliminated — **political correctness** *n*

pol·i·ti·cian \ˌpä-lə-'ti-shən\ *n* : a person actively engaged in government or politics

pol·i·tick \'pä-lə-ˌtik\ *vb* : to engage in political discussion or activity

po·lit·i·co \pə-'li-ti-ˌkō\ *n, pl* **-cos** *also* **-coes** : POLITICIAN

pol·i·tics \'pä-lə-ˌtiks\ *n sing or pl* **1** : the art or science of government, of guiding or influencing governmental policy, or of winning and holding control over a government **2** : political affairs or business; *esp* : competition between groups or individuals for power and leadership **3** : political opinions

pol·i·ty \'pä-lə-tē\ *n, pl* **-ties** : a politically organized unit; *also* : the form or constitution of such a unit

pol·ka \'pōl-kə, 'pō-kə\ *n* [Czech, fr. *Polka* Polish woman, fem. of *Polák* Pole] : a lively couple dance of Bohemian origin; *also* : music for this dance — **polka** *vb*

pol·ka dot \'pō-kə-,dät\ *n* : a dot in a pattern of regularly distributed dots — **polka–dot** *or* **polka–dot·ted** \-,dä-təd\ *adj*

¹**poll** \'pōl\ *n* **1** : HEAD **2** : the casting and recording of votes; *also* : the total vote cast **3** : the place where votes are cast — usu. used in pl. **4** : a questioning of persons to obtain information or opinions to be analyzed

²**poll** *vb* **1** : to cut off or shorten a growth or part of : CLIP, SHEAR **2** : to receive and record the votes of **3** : to receive (as votes) in an election **4** : to question in a poll

pol·lack *or* **pol·lock** \'pä-lək\ *n, pl* **pollack** *or* **pollock** : an important No. Atlantic food fish that is related to the cods; *also* : a related food fish of the No. Pacific

pol·len \'pä-lən\ *n* [NL, fr. L, fine flour] : a mass of male spores of a seed plant usu. appearing as a yellow dust

pol·li·na·tion \,pä-lə-'nā-shən\ *n* : the carrying of pollen to the female part of a plant to fertilize the seed — **pol·li·nate** \'pä-lə-,nāt\ *vb* — **pol·li·na·tor** \-,nā-tər\ *n*

poll·ster \'pōl-stər\ *n* : one that conducts a poll or compiles data obtained by a poll

poll tax *n* : a tax of a fixed amount per person levied on adults and often linked to the right to vote

pol·lute \pə-'lüt\ *vb* **pol·lut·ed; pol·lut·ing** : to make impure; *esp* : to contaminate (an environment) esp. with manmade waste — **pol·lut·ant** \-'lü-t³nt\ *n* — **pol·lut·er** *n* — **pol·lu·tion** \-'lü-shən\ *n*

pol·ly·wog *or* **pol·li·wog** \'pä-lē-,wäg\ *n* : TADPOLE

po·lo \'pō-lō\ *n* [Balti (Tibetan language of northern Kashmir), ball] : a game played by two teams on horseback using long-handled mallets to drive a wooden ball

po·lo·ni·um \pə-'lō-nē-əm\ *n* : a radioactive metallic chemical element

pol·ter·geist \'pōl-tər-,gīst\ *n* [G, fr. *poltern* to knock + *Geist* spirit] : a noisy usu. mischievous ghost held to be responsible for unexplained noises

pol·troon \päl-'trün\ *n* : COWARD

poly- *comb form* [Gk, fr. *polys* many] **1** : many : several ⟨*poly*syllabic⟩ **2** : polymeric ⟨*poly*ester⟩

poly·chlo·ri·nat·ed bi·phe·nyl \,pä-li-'klōr-ə-,nā-təd-,bī-'fen-³l, -'fēn-\ *n* : any of several industrial compounds that are toxic environmental pollutants

poly·clin·ic \,pä-li-'kli-nik\ *n* : a clinic or hospital treating diseases of many sorts

poly·es·ter \'pä-lē-,es-tər\ *n* : a polymer composed of ester groups used esp. in making fibers or plastics; *also* : a product (as fabric) composed of polyester

poly·eth·yl·ene \,pä-lē-'e-thə-,lēn\ *n* : a lightweight plastic resistant to chemicals and moisture and used chiefly in packaging

po·lyg·a·my \pə-'li-gə-mē\ *n* : the practice of having more than one wife or husband at one time — **po·lyg·a·mist** \-mist\ *n* — **po·lyg·a·mous** \-məs\ *adj*

poly·glot \'pä-li-,glät\ *adj* **1** : speaking or writing several languages **2** : containing or made up of several languages — **polyglot** *n*

poly·gon \'pä-li-,gän\ *n* : a closed plane figure bounded by straight lines — **po·lyg·o·nal** \pə-'li-gə-n³l\ *adj*

poly·graph \'pä-li-,graf\ *n* : an instrument (as a lie detector) for recording variations of several bodily functions (as blood pressure) simultaneously — **po·lyg·ra·pher** \pə-'li-grə-fər, 'pä-li-,gra-fər\ *n*

poly·he·dron \,pä-li-'hē-drən\ *n* : a solid formed by plane faces that are polygons — **poly·he·dral** \-drəl\ *adj*

poly·math \'pä-li-,math\ *n* : a person of encyclopedic learning

poly·mer \'pä-lə-mər\ *n* : a chemical compound formed by union of small molecules and usu. consisting of repeating structural units — **poly·mer·ic** \,pä-lə-'mer-ik\ *adj*

po·lym·er·i·za·tion \pə-,li-mə-rə-'zā-shən\ *n* : a chemical reaction in which two or more small molecules combine to form polymers — **po·lym·er·ize** \pə-'li-mə-,rīz\ *vb*

Poly·ne·sian \,pä-lə-'nē-zhən\ *n* **1** : a member of any of the indigenous peoples of Polynesia **2** : a group of Austronesian languages spoken in Polynesia — **Polynesian** *adj*

poly·no·mi·al \,pä-lə-'nō-mē-əl\ *n* : an algebraic expression having one or more terms each of which consists of a constant multiplied by one or more variables raised to a nonnegative integral power — **polynomial** *adj*

pol·yp \'pä-ləp\ *n* **1** : an invertebrate animal (as a coral) that is a coelenterate having a hollow cylindrical body closed at one end **2** : a growth projecting from a mucous membrane (as of the colon or vocal cords)

po·lyph·o·ny \pə-'li-fə-nē\ *n* : music consisting of two or more melodically independent but harmonizing voice parts — **poly·phon·ic** \,pä-li-'fä-nik\ *adj*

poly·pro·pyl·ene \,pä-lē-'prō-pə-,lēn\ *n* : any of various polymer plastics or fibers

poly·sty·rene \,pä-li-'stī-,rēn\ *n* : a rigid transparent nonconducting thermoplastic used esp. in molded products and foams

poly·syl·lab·ic \-sə-'la-bik\ *adj* **1** : having more than three syllables **2** : characterized by polysyllabic words

poly·syl·la·ble \'pä-li-ˌsi-lə-bəl\ *n* : a polysyllabic word

poly·tech·nic \ˌpä-li-'tek-nik\ *adj* : of, relating to, or instructing in many technical arts or applied sciences

poly·the·ism \'pä-li-thē-ˌi-zəm\ *n* : belief in or worship of many gods — **poly·the·ist** \-ˌthē-ist\ *adj or n* — **poly·the·is·tic** \ˌpä-li-thē-'is-tik\ *adj*

poly·un·sat·u·rat·ed \ˌpä-lē-ˌən-'sa-chə-ˌrā-təd\ *adj* : having many double or triple bonds in a molecule — used esp. of an oil or fatty acid

poly·ure·thane \ˌpä-lē-'yùr-ə-ˌthän\ *n* : any of various polymers used esp. in foams and in resins (as for coatings)

poly·vi·nyl \ˌpä-li-'vī-nᵊl\ *adj* : of, relating to, or being a polymerized vinyl compound, resin, or plastic — often used in combination

pome·gran·ate \'pä-mə-ˌgra-nət\ *n* [ME *poumgrenet*, fr. AF *pome garnette*, lit., seedy fruit] : a many-seeded reddish fruit that has an edible crimson pulp and is borne by a tropical Asian tree; *also* : the tree

¹**pom·mel** \'pə-məl, 'pä-\ *n* **1** : the knob on the hilt of a sword **2** : the knoblike bulge at the front and top of a saddlebow

²**pom·mel** \'pə-məl\ *vb* **-meled** *or* **-melled; -mel·ing** *or* **-mel·ling** : PUMMEL

pomp \'pämp\ *n* **1** : brilliant display : SPLENDOR **2** : OSTENTATION

pom·pa·dour \'päm-pə-ˌdór\ *n* : a style of dressing the hair high over the forehead

pom·pa·no \'päm-pə-ˌnō, 'päm-\ *n, pl* **-no** *or* **-nos** : a narrow silvery fish of coastal waters of the western Atlantic

pom–pom \'päm-ˌpäm\ *n* **1** : an ornamental ball or tuft used on a cap or costume **2** : a fluffy ball flourished by cheerleaders

pom·pon \'päm-ˌpän\ *n* **1** : POM-POM **2** : a chrysanthemum or dahlia with small rounded flower heads

pomp·ous \'päm-pəs\ *adj* **1** : suggestive of pomp; *esp* : OSTENTATIOUS **2** : pretentiously dignified ⟨~ politicians⟩ **3** : excessively elevated or ornate ◆ **Synonyms** ARROGANT, MAGISTERIAL, SELF-IMPORTANT — **pom·pos·i·ty** \päm-'pä-sə-tē\ *n* — **pomp·ous·ly** *adv*

pon·cho \'pän-chō\ *n, pl* **ponchos** [AmerSp, fr. Mapuche (American Indian language of Chile)] **1** : a blanket with a slit in the middle for the head so that it can be worn as a garment **2** : a waterproof garment resembling a poncho

pond \'pänd\ *n* : a small body of water

pon·der \'pän-dər\ *vb* **pon·dered; pon·der·ing 1** : to weigh in the mind **2** : to consider carefully

pon·der·o·sa pine \'pän-də-ˌrō-sə-, -zə-\ *n* : a tall pine of western No. America with long needles; *also* : its strong reddish wood

pon·der·ous \'pän-də-rəs\ *adj* **1** : of very great weight **2** : UNWIELDY, CLUMSY ⟨a ~ weapon⟩ **3** : oppressively dull ⟨a ~ speech⟩ ◆ **Synonyms** CUMBROUS, CUMBERSOME, WEIGHTY

pone \'pōn\ *n, Southern & Midland* : an oval-shaped cornmeal cake; *also* : corn bread in the form of pones

pon·iard \'pän-yərd\ *n* : DAGGER

pon·tiff \'pän-təf\ *n* : POPE — **pon·tif·i·cal** \pän-'ti-fi-kəl\ *adj*

¹**pon·tif·i·cate** \pän-'ti-fi-kət, -fə-ˌkāt\ *n* : the state, office, or term of office of a pontiff

²**pon·tif·i·cate** \pän-'ti-fə-ˌkāt\ *vb* **-cat·ed; -cat·ing** : to deliver dogmatic opinions

pon·toon \pän-'tün\ *n* **1** : a flat-bottomed boat **2** : a boat or float used in building a floating temporary bridge **3** : a float of a seaplane

po·ny \'pō-nē\ *n, pl* **ponies** : a small horse

po·ny·tail \-ˌtāl\ *n* : a style of arranging hair to resemble the tail of a pony

pooch \'püch\ *n* : DOG

poo·dle \'pü-dᵊl\ *n* [G *Pudel*, short for *Pudelhund*, fr. *pudeln* to splash + *Hund* dog] : any of a breed of active intelligent dogs with a dense curly solid-colored coat

pooh–pooh \'pü-'pü\ *also* **pooh** \'pü\ *vb* **1** : to express contempt or impatience **2** : DERIDE, SCORN ⟨~ed my idea⟩

¹**pool** \'pül\ *n* **1** : a small deep body of usu. fresh water **2** : a small body of standing liquid **3** : SWIMMING POOL

²**pool** *vb* : to form a pool

³**pool** *n* **1** : all the money bet on the result of a particular event **2** : any of several games of billiards played on a table having six pockets **3** : the amount contributed by the participants in a joint venture **4** : a combination between competing firms for mutual profit **5** : a readily available supply

⁴**pool** *vb* : to combine (as resources) in a common fund or effort

¹**poop** \'püp\ *n* : an enclosed superstructure at the stern of a ship

²**poop** *n, slang* : INFORMATION

poop deck *n* : a partial deck above a ship's main afterdeck

poor \'pùr\ *adj* **1** : lacking material possessions ⟨~ people⟩ **2** : less than adequate : MEAGER ⟨a ~ crop⟩ **3** : arousing pity ⟨~ you ~ thing⟩ **4** : inferior in quality or value **5** : UNPRODUCTIVE, BARREN ⟨~ soil⟩ **6** : fairly unsatisfactory ⟨~ prospects⟩; *also* : UNFAVORABLE ⟨~ opinion⟩ — **poor·ly** *adv*

poor boy *var of* PO'BOY

poor·house \'pùr-ˌhaùs\ *n* : a publicly supported home for needy or dependent persons

poor–mouth \-ˌmaùth, -ˌmaùth\ *vb* : to plead poverty as a defense or excuse

¹**pop** \'päp\ *vb* **popped; pop·ping 1** : to go, come, enter, or issue forth suddenly or quickly ⟨~ into bed⟩ **2** : to put or thrust suddenly ⟨~ questions⟩ **3** : to burst or cause to burst with a sharp sound; *also* : to make a sharp sound **4** : to protrude from the sockets **5** : SHOOT **6** : to hit a pop-up

²**pop** *n* **1** : a sharp explosive sound **2** : SHOT **3** : SODA POP

³**pop** *n* : FATHER

⁴**pop** *adj* **1** : POPULAR ⟨~ music⟩ **2** : of

or relating to pop music ⟨~ singer⟩ 3 : of or relating to the popular culture disseminated through the mass media ⟨~ psychology⟩ 4 : of, relating to, or imitating ⟨~ painter⟩

⁵**pop** n : pop music or culture; also : POP ART

⁶**pop** abbr population

pop art n, often cap P&A : art in which commonplace objects (as comic strips or soup cans) are used as subject matter — **pop artist** n

¹**pop·corn** \'päp-ˌkȯrn\ n : a corn whose kernels burst open into a white starchy mass when heated; also : the burst kernels

²**popcorn** adj : having widespread appeal but little artistic merit ⟨~ movies⟩

pope \'pōp\ n, often cap : the head of the Roman Catholic Church

pop-eyed \'päp-ˌīd\ adj : having eyes that bulge (as from disease)

pop fly n : POP-UP

pop·gun \'päp-ˌgən\ n : a toy gun for shooting pellets with compressed air

pop·in·jay \'pä-pən-ˌjā\ n [ME papejay parrot, fr. MF papegai, papejai, fr. Ar babghā] : a strutting supercilious person

pop·lar \'pä-plər\ n 1 : any of a genus of slender quick-growing trees (as a cottonwood) related to the willows 2 : the wood of a poplar

pop·lin \'pä-plən\ n : a strong plain-woven fabric with crosswise ribs

pop·over \'päp-ˌō-vər\ n : a hollow muffin made from a thin batter rich in egg

pop·per \'pä-pər\ n : a utensil for popping corn

pop·py \'pä-pē\ n, pl **poppies** : any of a genus of herbs with showy flowers including one that yields opium

pop·py·cock \-ˌkäk\ n : empty talk or writing : NONSENSE

pop·u·lace \'pä-pyə-ləs\ n 1 : the common people 2 : POPULATION

pop·u·lar \'pä-pyə-lər\ adj 1 : of or relating to the general public ⟨~ government⟩ 2 : suited to the tastes of the general public ⟨~ style⟩ 3 : INEXPENSIVE ⟨~ rates⟩ 4 : frequently encountered or widely accepted ⟨~ notion⟩ 5 : commonly liked or approved ⟨a ~ teacher⟩ — **pop·u·lar·i·ty** \ˌpä-pyə-'la-rə-tē\ n — **pop·u·lar·ize** \'pä-pyə-lə-ˌrīz\ vb — **pop·u·lar·ly** adv

pop·u·late \'pä-pyə-ˌlāt\ vb **-lat·ed; -lat·ing** 1 : to have a place in : INHABIT 2 : PEOPLE

pop·u·la·tion \ˌpä-pyə-'lā-shən\ n 1 : the people or number of people in an area 2 : the organisms inhabiting a particular locality 3 : a group of individuals or items from which samples are taken for statistical measurement

population explosion n : a pyramiding of numbers of a biological population; esp : the recent great increase in human numbers resulting from increased survival and exponential population growth

pop·u·list \'pä-pyə-list\ n : a believer in or advocate of the rights, wisdom, or virtues of the common people — **pop·u·lism** \-ˌli-zəm\ n

pop·u·lous \'pä-pyə-ləs\ adj 1 : densely populated; also : having a large population 2 : CROWDED — **pop·u·lous·ness** n

¹**pop-up** \'päp-ˌəp\ n : a short high fly in baseball

²**pop-up** adj : of, relating to, or having a component or device that pops up

por·ce·lain \'pȯr-sə-lən\ n : a fine-grained translucent ceramic ware

porch \'pȯrch\ n : a covered entrance usu. with a separate roof

por·cine \'pȯr-ˌsīn\ adj : of, relating to, or suggesting swine

por·ci·ni \pȯr-'chē-nē\ n, pl **porcini** [It] : a large edible brownish mushroom

por·ci·no \pȯr-'chē-nō\ n, pl **-ni** : PORCINI

por·cu·pine \'pȯr-kyə-ˌpīn\ n [ME porke despyne, fr. MF porc espin, fr. It porcospino, fr. L porcus pig + spina spine, prickle] : any of various mammals having stiff sharp spines mingled with their hair

¹**pore** \'pȯr\ vb **pored; por·ing** 1 : to read studiously or attentively ⟨~ over a book⟩ 2 : PONDER, REFLECT

²**pore** n : a tiny hole or space (as in the skin or soil) — **pored** \'pȯrd\ adj

pork \'pȯrk\ n : the flesh of swine dressed for use as food

pork barrel n : government projects or appropriations yielding rich patronage benefits

pork·er \'pȯr-kər\ n : HOG; esp : a young pig suitable for use as fresh pork

por·nog·ra·phy \pȯr-'nä-grə-fē\ n : the depiction of erotic behavior intended to cause sexual excitement — **por·no·graph·ic** \ˌpȯr-nə-'gra-fik\ adj

po·rous \'pȯr-əs\ adj 1 : full of pores 2 : permeable to fluids : ABSORPTIVE — **po·ros·i·ty** \pȯ-'rä-sə-tē\ n

por·phy·ry \'pȯr-fə-rē\ n, pl **-ries** : a rock consisting of feldspar crystals embedded in a compact fine-grained base material — **por·phy·rit·ic** \ˌpȯr-fə-'ri-tik\ adj

por·poise \'pȯr-pəs\ n [ME porpoys, fr. AF porpeis, fr. ML porcopiscis, fr. L porcus pig + piscis fish] : any of a family of small gregarious blunt-snouted whales with spadelike teeth; also : DOLPHIN 1

por·ridge \'pȯr-ij\ n : a soft food made by boiling meal of grains or legumes in milk or water

por·rin·ger \'pȯr-ən-jər\ n : a low one-handled metal bowl or cup

¹**port** \'pȯrt\ n 1 : HARBOR 2 : a city with a harbor 3 : AIRPORT

²**port** n 1 : an inlet or outlet (as in an engine) for a fluid : PORTHOLE 3 : JACK 7

³**port** vb : to turn or put a helm to the left

⁴**port** n : the left side of a ship or airplane looking forward — **port** adj

⁵**port** n : a sweet fortified wine

portabella or **portabello** var of PORTOBELLO

por·ta·bil·i·ty \ˌpȯr-tə-'bil-ə-tē\ n, pl **-ties** 1 : the quality or state of being portable 2 : the ability to transfer benefits from one pension fund to another when a worker changes jobs

por·ta·ble \'pòr-tə-bəl\ *adj* : capable of being carried — **portable** *n*

¹**por·tage** \'pòr-tij, pòr-'täzh\ *n* [ME, fr. AF, fr. *porter* to carry] : the carrying of boats and goods overland between navigable bodies of water; *also* : a route for such carrying

²**portage** *vb* **por·taged; por·tag·ing** : to carry gear over a portage

por·tal \'pòrt-²l\ *n* : DOOR, ENTRANCE; *esp* : a grand or imposing one

portal–to–portal *adj* : of or relating to the time spent by a worker in traveling from the entrance to an employer's property to the worker's actual job site (as in a mine)

port·cul·lis \pòrt-'kə-ləs\ *n* : a grating at the gateway of a castle or fortress that can be let down to stop entrance

porte co·chere \,pòrt-kō-'sher\ *n* [F *porte cochère*, lit., coach door] : a roofed structure extending from the entrance of a building over an adjacent driveway and sheltering those getting in or out of vehicles

por·tend \pòr-'tend\ *vb* 1 : to give a sign or warning of beforehand 2 : INDICATE, SIGNIFY ♦ *Synonyms* AUGUR, PROGNOSTICATE, FORETELL, PREDICT, FORECAST, PROPHESY

por·tent \'pòr-,tent\ *n* 1 : something that foreshadows a coming event : OMEN : MARVEL, PRODIGY

por·ten·tous \pòr-'ten-təs\ *adj* 1 : of, relating to, or constituting a portent 2 : PRODIGIOUS 3 : self-consciously solemn : POMPOUS

¹**por·ter** \'pòr-tər\ *n, chiefly Brit* : DOORKEEPER

²**porter** *n* 1 : a person who carries burdens; *esp* : one employed (as at a terminal) to carry baggage 2 : an attendant in a railroad car 3 : a dark heavy ale

por·ter·house \'pòr-tər-,haùs\ *n* : a choice beefsteak with a large tenderloin

port·fo·lio \pòrt-'fō-lē-,ō\ *n, pl* **-li·os** 1 : a portable case for papers or drawings 2 : the office and functions of a minister of state 3 : the securities held by an investor

port·hole \'pòrt-,hōl\ *n* : an opening (as a window) in the side of a ship or aircraft

por·ti·co \'pòr-ti-,kō\ *n, pl* **-coes** *or* **-cos** [It] : a row of columns supporting a roof around or at the entrance of a building

¹**por·tion** \'pòr-shən\ *n* 1 : one's part or share ⟨a ~ of food⟩ 2 : DOWRY 3 : an individual's lot 4 : a part of a whole ⟨a ~ of the sky⟩

²**portion** *vb* 1 : to divide into portions 2 : to allot to as a portion

port·land cement \'pòrt-lənd-\ *n* : a cement made by calcining and grinding a mixture of clay and limestone

port·ly \'pòrt-lē\ *adj* **port·li·er; -est** : somewhat stout

port·man·teau \pòrt-'man-,tō\ *n, pl* **-teaus** *or* **-teaux** \-,tōz\ [MF *portemanteau*, fr. *porter* to carry + *manteau* mantle, fr. L *mantellum*] : a large traveling bag

por·to·bel·lo \,pòr-tə-'be-lō\ *also* **por·ta·bel·la** \-lə\ *or* **por·ta·bel·lo** \-lō\ *n, pl* **-los** *also* **-las** : a large dark mature mushroom noted for its meaty texture

port of call : an intermediate port where ships customarily stop for supplies, repairs, or transshipment of cargo

port of entry 1 : a place where foreign goods may be cleared through a customhouse 2 : a place where an alien may enter a country

por·trait \'pòr-trət, -,trāt\ *n* : a picture (as a painting or photograph) of a person usu. showing the face — **por·trait·ist** \-tra-tist\ *n*

por·trai·ture \'pòr-trə-,chùr\ *n* : the practice or art of making portraits

por·tray \pòr-'trā\ *vb* 1 : to make a picture of : DEPICT 2 : to describe in words 3 : to play the role of — **por·tray·al** *n*

Por·tu·guese \'pòr-chə-,gēz, -,gēs; ,pòr-chə-'gēz, -'gēs\ *n, pl* **Portuguese** 1 : a native or inhabitant of Portugal 2 : the language of Portugal and Brazil — **Portuguese** *adj*

Portuguese man–of–war *n* : any of several large colonial marine invertebrate animals related to the jellyfishes and having a large sac by which the colony floats at the surface

por·tu·la·ca \,pòr-chə-'la-kə\ *n* : any of a genus of succulent herbs cultivated for their showy flowers

pos *abbr* 1 position 2 positive

¹**pose** \'pōz\ *vb* **posed; pos·ing** 1 : to assume or cause to assume a posture usu. for artistic purposes 2 : to set forth : PROPOSE ⟨~ a question⟩ 3 : to affect an attitude or character

²**pose** *n* 1 : a sustained posture; *esp* : one assumed by a model 2 : an attitude assumed for effect : PRETENSE

¹**pos·er** \'pō-zər\ *n* : a puzzling question

²**poser** *n* : a person who poses

po·seur \pō-'zər\ *n* [F, lit., poser] : an affected or insincere person

posh \'päsh\ *adj* : FASHIONABLE ⟨a ~ restaurant⟩

pos·it \'pä-zət\ *vb* : to assume the existence of : POSTULATE

po·si·tion \pə-'zi-shən\ *n* 1 : an arranging in order 2 : the stand taken on a question 3 : the point or area occupied by something : SITUATION 4 : a certain arrangement of bodily parts ⟨exercise in a sitting ~⟩ 5 : RANK, STATUS 6 : EMPLOYMENT, JOB — **position** *vb* — **po·si·tion·al** \-'shə-nəl\ *adj*

¹**pos·i·tive** \'pä-zə-tiv\ *adj* 1 : expressed definitely ⟨her answer was a ~ no⟩ 2 : CONFIDENT, CERTAIN ⟨~ it was my book⟩ 3 : of, relating to, or constituting the degree of grammatical comparison that denotes no increase in quality, quantity, or relation 4 : not fictitious : REAL 5 : active and effective in function ⟨~ leadership⟩ 6 : having the light and shade as existing in the original subject ⟨a ~ photograph⟩ 7 : numerically greater than zero ⟨a ~ number⟩ 8 : being, relating to, or charged with electricity of which the proton is the elementary unit

9 : AFFIRMATIVE ⟨a ~ response⟩ 10 : FAVORABLE; *also* : marked by optimism ⟨a ~ attitude⟩ — **pos·i·tive·ly** *adv* — **pos·i·tive·ness** *n*

²**positive** *n* 1 : the positive degree or a positive form in a language 2 : a positive photograph

pos·i·tron \'pä-zə-ˌträn\ *n* : a positively charged particle having the same mass and magnitude of charge as the electron

po·so·le *or* **po·zo·le** \pō-'sō-lā\ *n* : a thick Mexican soup made with pork, hominy, garlic, and chili

poss *abbr* possessive

pos·se \'pä-sē\ *n* [ML *posse comitatus*, lit., power or authority of the county] 1 : a body of persons organized to assist a sheriff in an emergency 2 : a body of attendants or followers

pos·sess \pə-'zes\ *vb* 1 : to have as property : OWN 2 : to have as an attribute, knowledge, or skill 3 : to enter into and control firmly ⟨~ed by a devil⟩ — **pos·ses·sor** \-'ze-sər\ *n*

pos·ses·sion \-'ze-shən\ *n* 1 : control or occupancy of property 2 : OWNERSHIP 3 : something owned : PROPERTY 4 : domination by something (as an evil spirit, a passion, or an idea) 5 : SELF-CONTROL

pos·ses·sive \pə-'ze-siv\ *adj* 1 : of, relating to, or constituting a grammatical case denoting ownership 2 : showing the desire to possess ⟨a ~ nature⟩ — **possessive** *n* — **pos·ses·sive·ness** *n*

pos·si·ble \'pä-sə-bəl\ *adj* 1 : being within the limits of ability, capacity, or realization 2 : being something that may or may not occur ⟨~ dangers⟩ 3 : able or fitted to become ⟨a ~ site for a bridge⟩ — **pos·si·bil·i·ty** \ˌpä-sə-'bi-lə-tē\ *n* — **pos·si·bly** \'pä-sə-blē\ *adv*

pos·sum \'pä-səm\ *n* : OPOSSUM

¹**post** \'pōst\ *n* 1 : an upright piece of timber or metal serving esp. as a support : PILLAR 2 : a pole or stake set up as a mark or indicator

²**post** *vb* 1 : to affix to a usual place (as a wall) for public notices 2 : to publish or announce by or as if by a public notice ⟨~ grades⟩ 3 : to forbid (property) to trespassers by putting up a notice 4 : SCORE ⟨~ed a 70 in the final round⟩ 5 : to publish in an online forum

³**post** *n* 1 *obs* : COURIER 2 *chiefly Brit* : ¹MAIL; *also* : POST OFFICE 3 : something that is published online

⁴**post** *vb* 1 : to ride or travel with haste : HURRY 2 : ¹MAIL ⟨~ a letter⟩ 3 : to enter in a ledger 4 : INFORM ⟨kept him ~ed on new developments⟩

⁵**post** *n* 1 : the place at which a soldier is stationed; *esp* : a sentry's beat or station 2 : a station or task to which a person is assigned 3 : the place at which a body of troops is stationed : CAMP 4 : OFFICE, POSITION 5 : a trading settlement or station

⁶**post** *vb* 1 : to station in a given place 2 : to put up (as bond)

post·age \'pōs-tij\ *n* : the fee for postal service; *also* : stamps representing this fee

post·al \'pōs-t³l\ *adj* : of or relating to the mails or the post office

postal card *n* : POSTCARD

postal service *n* : a government agency or department handling the transmission of mail

¹**post·card** \'pōst-ˌkärd\ *n* : a card on which a message may be written for mailing without an envelope

²**postcard** *adj* : PICTURESQUE

post chaise *n* : a 4-wheeled closed carriage for two to four persons

post·con·sum·er \ˌpōst-kən-'sü-mər\ *adj* 1 : discarded by a consumer 2 : having been used and recycled for reuse in another product

post·date \ˌpōst-'dāt\ *vb* : to date with a date later than that of execution ⟨~ a check⟩

post·doc·tor·al \-'däk-tə-rəl\ *also* **post·doc·tor·ate** \-tə-rət\ *adj* : of, relating to, or engaged in advanced academic or professional work beyond a doctor's degree

post·er \'pō-stər\ *n* : a bill or placard for posting often in a public place

¹**pos·te·ri·or** \pō-'stir-ē-ər, pä-\ *adj* 1 : later in time 2 : situated behind

²**pos·te·ri·or** \pä-'stir-ē-ər, pō-\ *n* : the hinder bodily parts; *esp* : BUTTOCKS

pos·ter·i·ty \pä-'ster-ə-tē\ *n* 1 : the descendants from one ancestor 2 : all future generations

pos·tern \'pōs-tərn, 'päs-\ *n* 1 : a back door or gate 2 : a private or side entrance

post exchange *n* : a store at a military post that sells to military personnel and authorized civilians

post·grad \'pōst-ˌgrad\ *adj* : POSTGRADUATE

post·grad·u·ate \(ˌ)pōst-'gra-jə-wət\ *adj* : of or relating to studies beyond the bachelor's degree — **postgraduate** *n*

post·haste \'pōst-'hāst\ *adv* : with all possible speed

post·hole \-ˌhōl\ *n* : a hole for a post and esp. a fence post

post·hu·mous \'päs-chə-məs\ *adj* [L *posthumus*, alter. of *postumus* last-born, posthumous, fr. superl. of *posterus* coming after] 1 : born after the death of the father 2 : published after the death of the author — **post·hu·mous·ly** *adv*

post·hyp·not·ic \ˌpōst-hip-'nä-tik\ *adj* : of, relating to, or characteristic of the period following a hypnotic trance

pos·til·ion *or* **pos·til·lion** \pō-'stil-yən\ *n* : a rider on the left-hand horse of a pair drawing a coach

Post·im·pres·sion·ism \ˌpōst-im-'presh-ə-ˌni-zəm\ *n* : a late 19th century French theory or practice of art that stresses variously volume, picture structure, or expressionism

post·lude \'pōst-ˌlüd\ *n* : an organ solo played at the end of a church service

post·man \-mən, -ˌman\ *n* : MAILMAN

post·mark \-ˌmärk\ *n* : an official postal marking on a piece of mail; *esp* : the mark canceling the postage stamp — **postmark** *vb*

post·mas·ter \-ˌmas-tər\ *n* : a person who has charge of a post office

postmaster general *n, pl* **postmasters general** : an official in charge of a national postal service

post·men·o·paus·al \ˌpōst-ˌme-nə-ˈpȯ-zəl\ *adj* 1 : having undergone menopause 2 : occurring or administered after menopause

post me·ri·di·em \ˌpōst-mə-ˈri-dē-əm\ *adj* [L] : being after noon

post·mis·tress \ˈpōst-ˌmis-trəs\ *n* : a woman in charge of a post office

post·mod·ern \ˌpōst-ˈmä-dərn\ *adj* : of, relating to, or being any of various movements in reaction to modernism

¹**post·mor·tem** \ˌpōst-ˈmȯr-təm\ *adj* [L *post mortem* after death] 1 : done, occurring, or collected after death ⟨a ∼ examination⟩ 2 : following the event

²**postmortem** *n* 1 : AUTOPSY 2 : an analysis or discussion of an event after it is over ⟨a ∼ of the election⟩

post·na·sal drip \ˈpōst-ˌnā-zəl-\ *n* : flow of mucous secretion from the posterior part of the nasal cavity onto the wall of the pharynx

post·na·tal \(ˌ)pōst-ˈnā-tᵊl\ *adj* : occurring or being after birth; *esp* : of or relating to a newborn infant

post office *n* 1 : POSTAL SERVICE 2 : a local branch of a post office department

post·op·er·a·tive \(ˌ)pōst-ˈä-prə-tiv, -pə-ˌrā-\ *adj* : following or having undergone a surgical operation ⟨∼ care⟩

post·paid \ˈpōst-ˈpād\ *adj* : having the postage paid by the sender and not chargeable to the receiver

post·par·tum \(ˌ)pōst-ˈpär-təm\ *adj* [NL *post partum* after birth] : following parturition — **postpartum** *adv*

post·pone \pōst-ˈpōn\ *vb* **post·poned; post·pon·ing** : to put off to a later time — **post·pone·ment** *n*

post road *n* : a road over which mail is carried

post·script \ˈpōst-ˌskript\ *n* : a note added esp. to a completed letter

post time *n* : the designated time for the start of a horse race

post–traumatic *adj* : occurring after or as a result of trauma ⟨∼ stress⟩

pos·tu·lant \ˈpäs-chə-lənt\ *n* : a probationary candidate for membership in a religious order

¹**pos·tu·late** \ˈpäs-chə-ˌlāt\ *vb* **-lat·ed; -lat·ing** : to assume as true

²**pos·tu·late** \ˈpäs-chə-lət, -ˌlāt\ *n* : a proposition taken for granted as true esp. as a basis for a chain of reasoning

¹**pos·ture** \ˈpäs-chər\ *n* 1 : the position or bearing of the body or one of its parts 2 : STATE, CONDITION 3 : ATTITUDE ⟨a ∼ of arrogance⟩

²**posture** *vb* **pos·tured; pos·tur·ing** : to strike a pose esp. for effect

post·war \ˈpōst-ˈwȯr\ *adj* : occurring or existing after a war

po·sy \ˈpō-zē\ *n, pl* **posies** 1 : a brief sentiment : MOTTO 2 : a bunch of flowers; *also* : FLOWER

¹**pot** \ˈpät\ *n* 1 : a rounded container used

chiefly for domestic purposes 2 : the total of the bets at stake at one time 3 : RUIN ⟨go to ∼⟩ — **pot·ful** *n*

²**pot** *vb* **pot·ted; pot·ting** 1 : to preserve or place in a pot 2 : SHOOT

³**pot** *n* : MARIJUANA

po·ta·ble \ˈpō-tə-bəl\ *adj* : suitable for drinking — **po·ta·bil·i·ty** \ˌpō-tə-ˈbi-lə-tē\ *n*

po·tage \pō-ˈtäzh\ *n* : a thick soup

pot·ash \ˈpät-ˌash\ *n* [sing. of *pot ashes*] : potassium or any of its various compounds esp. as used in agriculture

po·tas·si·um \pə-ˈta-sē-əm\ *n* : a silver-white soft metallic chemical element that occurs abundantly in nature

potassium bromide *n* : a crystalline salt used as a sedative and in photography

potassium carbonate *n* : a white salt used in making glass and soap

potassium nitrate *n* : a soluble salt used in making gunpowder, as a fertilizer, and in medicine

po·ta·tion \pō-ˈtā-shən\ *n* : a usu. alcoholic drink; *also* : the act of drinking

po·ta·to \pə-ˈtā-tō\ *n, pl* **-toes** : the edible starchy tuber of a plant related to the tomato; *also* : this plant

potato beetle *n* : COLORADO POTATO BEETLE

potato bug *n* : COLORADO POTATO BEETLE

potbellied pig *n* : any of an Asian breed of small pigs having a straight tail, potbelly, and black, white, or black and white coat

pot·bel·ly \ˈpät-ˌbe-lē\ *n* : a protruding abdomen — **pot·bel·lied** \-lēd\ *adj*

pot·boil·er \-ˌbȯi-lər\ *n* : a usu. inferior work of art or literature produced chiefly for profit

po·tent \ˈpō-tᵊnt\ *adj* 1 : having authority or influence : POWERFUL 2 : chemically or medicinally effective 3 : able to copulate — used esp. of the male ♦ *Synonyms* FORCEFUL, FORCIBLE, MIGHTY, PUISSANT — **po·ten·cy** \-tᵊn-sē\ *n*

po·ten·tate \ˈpō-tᵊn-ˌtāt\ *n* : one who wields controlling power : RULER

¹**po·ten·tial** \pə-ˈten-chəl\ *adj* : existing in possibility : capable of becoming actual ⟨a ∼ champion⟩ ♦ *Synonyms* DORMANT, LATENT, QUIESCENT — **po·ten·ti·al·i·ty** \pə-ˌten-chē-ˈa-lə-tē\ *n* — **po·ten·tial·ly** \-ˈten-chə-lē\ *adv*

²**potential** *n* 1 : something that can develop or become actual ⟨a ∼ for violence⟩ 2 : the work required to move a unit positive charge from infinity to a point in question; *also* : POTENTIAL DIFFERENCE

potential difference *n* : the difference in potential between two points that represents the work involved in the transfer of a unit quantity of electricity from one point to the other

potential energy *n* : the energy an object has because of its position or nature or the arrangement of its parts

po·ten·ti·ate \pə-ˈten-chē-ˌāt\ *vb* **-at·ed; -at·ing** : to make potent; *esp* : to augment the activity of (as a drug) synergistically — **po·ten·ti·a·tion** \-,ten-chē-'ā-shən\ *n*

pot·head \'pät-,hed\ *n* : a person who frequently smokes marijuana

poth·er \'pä-thər\ *n* : a noisy disturbance; *also* : FUSS

pot·herb \'pät-,ərb, -,hərb\ *n* : an herb whose leaves or stems are boiled for greens or used to season food

pot·hole \'pät-,hōl\ *n* : a large pit or hole (as in a road surface)

pot·hook \-,hu̇k\ *n* : an S-shaped hook for hanging pots and kettles over an open fire

po·tion \'pō-shən\ *n* : a mixture of liquids (as liquor or medicine)

pot·luck \'pät-'lək\ *n* : the regular meal available to a guest for whom no special preparations have been made

pot·pie \-'pī\ *n* : pastry-covered meat and vegetables cooked in a deep dish

pot·pour·ri \,pō-pu̇-'rē\ *n* [F *pot pourri*, lit., rotten pot] 1 : a mixture of flowers, herbs, and spices used for scent 2 : a miscellaneous collection

pot·sherd \'pät-,shərd\ *n* : a pottery fragment

pot·shot \-,shät\ *n* 1 : a shot taken from ambush or at a random or easy target 2 : a critical remark made in a random or sporadic manner

pot sticker *n* : a crescent-shaped dumpling that is steamed and fried

pot·tage \'pä-tij\ *n* : a thick soup of vegetables and often meat

¹**pot·ter** \'pä-tər\ *n* : one that makes pottery

²**potter** *vb* : PUTTER

pot·tery \'pä-tə-rē\ *n, pl* **-ter·ies** 1 : a place where earthen pots and dishes are made 2 : the art of the potter 3 : dishes, pots, and vases made from clay

pot·ty–mouthed \'pä-tē-,mau̇thd, -,mau̇tht\ *adj* : given to the use of vulgar language

¹**pouch** \'pau̇ch\ *n* [ME *pouche*, fr. AF, of Gmc origin; akin to OE *pocca* bag] 1 : a small bag (as for tobacco) carried on the person 2 : a bag for storing or transporting goods ⟨mail ∼⟩ ⟨diplomatic ∼⟩ : an anatomical sac; *esp* : one for carrying the young on the abdomen of a female marsupial (as a kangaroo)

²**pouch** *vb* : to put or form into or as if into a pouch

poult \'pōlt\ *n* : a young fowl; *esp* : a young turkey

poul·ter·er \'pōl-tər-ər\ *n* : one that deals in poultry

poul·tice \'pōl-təs\ *n* : a soft usu. heated and medicated mass spread on cloth and applied to a sore or injury — **poultice** *vb*

poul·try \'pōl-trē\ *n* : domesticated birds kept for eggs or meat — **poul·try·man** \-mən\ *n*

pounce \'pau̇ns\ *vb* **pounced; pouncing** : to spring or swoop upon and seize something

¹**pound** \'pau̇nd\ *n, pl* **pounds** *also* **pound** 1 : a unit of avoirdupois, troy, and apothecaries' weight — see WEIGHT table 2 — see MONEY table 3 : the former basic monetary unit of Ireland 4 : LIRA 3

²**pound** *n* : a public enclosure where stray animals are kept

³**pound** *vb* 1 : to crush to a powder or pulp by beating 2 : to strike or beat heavily or repeatedly 3 : DRILL 1 4 : to move or move along heavily

pound·age \'pau̇n-dij\ *n* : POUNDS; *also* : weight in pounds

pound cake *n* : a rich cake made with a large proportion of eggs and shortening

pound–fool·ish \'pau̇nd-'fü-lish\ *adj* : imprudent in dealing with large sums or large matters

pour \'pȯr\ *vb* 1 : to flow or cause to flow in a stream or flood 2 : to rain hard 3 : to supply freely and copiously

pour·boire \pu̇r-'bwär\ *n* [F, fr. *pour boire* for drinking] : TIP, GRATUITY

pout \'pau̇t\ *vb* : to show displeasure by thrusting out the lips; *also* : to look sullen — **pout** *n*

pov·er·ty \'pä-vər-tē\ *n* [ME *poverte*, fr. AF *poverté*, fr. L *paupertat-, paupertas*, fr. *pauper* poor] 1 : lack of money or material possessions : WANT 2 : poor quality (as of soil)

poverty line *n* : a level of personal or family income below which one is classified as poor according to government standards

pov·er·ty–strick·en \'pä-vər-tē-,stri-kən\ *adj* : very poor : DESTITUTE

POW \,pē-(,)ō-'də-bəl-(,)yü\ *n* : PRISONER OF WAR

¹**pow·der** \'pau̇-dər\ *vb* 1 : to sprinkle or cover with or as if with powder 2 : to reduce to powder

²**powder** *n* [ME *poudre*, fr. AF *pudre, podre*, fr. L *pulver-, pulvis* dust] 1 : dry material made up of fine particles; *also* : a usu. medicinal or cosmetic preparation in this form 2 : a solid explosive (as gunpowder) — **pow·dery** *adj*

powder room *n* : a rest room for women

¹**pow·er** \'pau̇(-ə)r\ *n* 1 : the ability to act or produce an effect 2 : a position of ascendancy over others : AUTHORITY 3 : one that has control or authority; *esp* : a sovereign state 4 : physical might; *also* : mental or moral vigor 5 : the number of times as indicated by an exponent that a number occurs as a factor in a product ⟨5 to the third ∼ is 125⟩; *also* : the product itself ⟨8 is a ∼ of 2⟩ 6 : force or energy used to do work; *also* : the time rate at which work is done or energy transferred 7 : MAGNIFICATION 2 — **pow·er·ful** \-fəl\ *adj* — **pow·er·ful·ly** *adv* — **pow·er·less** *adj*

²**power** *vb* : to supply with power and esp. motive power

³**power** *adj* 1 : operated mechanically or electrically rather than manually 2 : of, relating to, or utilizing strength

pow·er·boat \-,bōt\ *n* : MOTORBOAT

pow·er·house \'pau̇(-ə)r-,hau̇s\ *n* 1 : POWER PLANT 1 2 : one having great drive, energy, or ability

power plant *n* 1 : a building in which electric power is generated 2 : an engine and related parts supplying the motive power of a self-propelled vehicle

pow·wow \'pau̇-ˌwau̇\ *n* **1** : a No. American Indian ceremony (as for victory in war) **2** : a meeting for discussion : CONFERENCE

pox \'päks\ *n, pl* **pox** *or* **pox·es** : any of various diseases (as smallpox or syphilis) marked by a rash on the skin

pozole *var of* POSOLE

pp *abbr* **1** pages **2** pianissimo

PP *abbr* **1** parcel post **2** past participle **3** postpaid **4** prepaid

ppd *abbr* **1** postpaid **2** prepaid

PPO \ˌpē-ˌpē-'ō\ *n, pl* **PPOs** [*preferred provider organization*] : a health-care organization that gives economic incentives to enrolled individuals who use certain health-care providers

PPS *abbr* [L *post postscriptum*] an additional postscript

ppt *abbr* precipitate

PQ *abbr* Province of Quebec

pr *abbr* **1** pair **2** price

Pr *symbol* praseodymium

¹PR *or* **p.r.** \'pē-'är\ *n* **1** : PUBLIC RELATIONS

²PR *abbr* **1** payroll **2** public relations **3** Puerto Rico

prac·ti·ca·ble \'prak-ti-kə-bəl\ *adj* : capable of being put into practice, done, or accomplished ⟨a ~ method⟩ — **prac·ti·ca·bil·i·ty** \ˌprak-ti-kə-'bi-lə-tē\ *n*

prac·ti·cal \'prak-ti-kəl\ *adj* **1** : of, relating to, or shown in practice ⟨~ questions⟩ **2** : VIRTUAL ⟨~ control⟩ **3** : capable of being put to use ⟨a ~ knowledge of French⟩ **4** : inclined to action as opposed to speculation ⟨a ~ person⟩ **5** : qualified by practice ⟨a good ~ mechanic⟩ — **prac·ti·cal·i·ty** \ˌprak-ti-'ka-lə-tē\ *n* — **prac·ti·cal·ly** \-k(ə-)lē\ *adv*

practical joke *n* : a prank intended to trick or embarrass someone or cause physical discomfort

practical nurse *n* : a professional nurse without all of the qualifications of a registered nurse; *esp* : LICENSED PRACTICAL NURSE

¹prac·tice *also* **prac·tise** \'prak-təs\ *vb* **prac·ticed** *also* **prac·tised; prac·tic·ing** *also* **prac·tis·ing** **1** : CARRY OUT, APPLY ⟨~ what you preach⟩ **2** : to perform or work at repeatedly so as to become proficient ⟨~ tennis strokes⟩ **3** : to do or perform customarily ⟨~ politeness⟩ **4** : to be professionally engaged in ⟨~ law⟩

²practice *also* **practise** *n* **1** : actual performance or application **2** : customary action : HABIT **3** : systematic exercise for proficiency **4** : the exercise of a profession; *also* : a professional business

prac·ti·tion·er \prak-'ti-shə-nər\ *n* : one who practices a profession

prae·tor \'prē-tər\ *n* : an ancient Roman magistrate ranking below a consul — **prae·to·ri·an** \prē-'tȯr-ē-ən\ *adj*

prag·mat·ic \prag-'ma-tik\ *also* **prag·mat·i·cal** \-ti-kəl\ *adj* **1** : of or relating to practical affairs **2** : concerned with the practical consequences of actions or beliefs ⟨a ~ leader⟩ : PRAGMATIC — **prag·mat·i·cal·ly** \-ti-k(ə-)lē\ *adv*

prag·ma·tism \'prag-mə-ˌti-zəm\ *n* : a practical approach to problems and affairs

prai·rie \'prer-ē\ *n* [F, fr. OF *prairie*, fr. VL *prataria*, fr. L *pratum* meadow] : a broad tract of level or rolling grassland

prairie dog *n* : an American burrowing black-tailed rodent related to the squirrels and living in colonies

prairie schooner *n* : a covered wagon used by pioneers in cross-country travel

praise \'prāz\ *vb* **praised; prais·ing 1** : to express approval of : COMMEND **2** : to glorify (a divinity or a saint) esp. in song — **praise** *n*

praise·wor·thy \-ˌwər-thē\ *adj* : LAUDABLE ⟨a ~ effort⟩

pra·line \'prä-ˌlēn, 'prā-\ *n* [F] : a confection of nuts and sugar

pram \'pram\ *n, chiefly Brit* : PERAMBULATOR

prance \'prans\ *vb* **pranced; pranc·ing 1** : to spring from the hind legs ⟨a *prancing* horse⟩ **2** : SWAGGER; *also* : CAPER — **prance** *n* — **pranc·er** *n*

prank \'praŋk\ *n* : a playful or mildly mischievous act : TRICK

prank·ster \'praŋk-stər\ *n* : a person who plays pranks

pra·seo·dym·i·um \ˌprā-zē-ō-'di-mē-əm\ *n* : a yellowish white metallic chemical element

prate \'prāt\ *vb* **prat·ed; prat·ing** : to talk long and idly : chatter foolishly

prat·fall \'prat-ˌfȯl\ *n* **1** : a fall on the buttocks **2** : a humiliating blunder

¹prat·tle \'pra-t⁵l\ *vb* **prat·tled; prat·tling** : PRATE, BABBLE

²prattle *n* : trifling or childish talk

prawn \'prȯn\ *n* : any of various edible shrimplike crustaceans; *also* : SHRIMP 1

pray \'prā\ *vb* **1** : ENTREAT, IMPLORE **2** : to ask earnestly for something **3** : to address God or a god esp. with supplication

prayer \'prer\ *n* **1** : a supplication or expression addressed to God or a god; *also* : a set order of words used in praying **2** : an earnest request or wish **3** : the act or practice of praying to God or a god **4** : a religious service consisting chiefly of prayers — often used in pl. **5** : something prayed for **6** : a slight chance

prayer book *n* : a book containing prayers and often directions for worship

prayer·ful \'prer-fəl\ *adj* **1** : DEVOUT **2** : EARNEST — **prayer·ful·ly** *adv*

praying mantis *n* : MANTIS

PRC *abbr* People's Republic of China

preach \'prēch\ *vb* **1** : to deliver a sermon **2** : to set forth in a sermon **3** : to advocate earnestly ⟨~*ed* tolerance⟩ — **preach·er** *n* — **preach·ment** *n*

pre·ad·o·les·cence \ˌprē-ˌa-də-'le-s⁵ns\ *n* : the period of human development just preceding adolescence — **pre·ad·o·les·cent** \-s⁵nt\ *adj or n*

pre·am·ble \'prē-ˌam-bəl\ *n* [ME, fr. MF *preamble*, fr. ML *preambulum*, fr. LL, neut. of *praeambulus* walking in front of, fr. L *prae* in front of + *ambulare* to walk]

: an introductory part ⟨the ∼ to a constitution⟩

pre·ar·range \ˌprē-ə-ˈrānj\ vb : to arrange beforehand — **pre·ar·range·ment** n

pre·as·sign \ˌprē-ə-ˈsīn\ vb : to assign beforehand

Pre·cam·bri·an \ˈprē-ˈkam-brē-ən, -ˈkām-\ adj : of, relating to, or being the era that is earliest in geologic history and is characterized esp. by the appearance of single-celled organisms — **Precambrian** n

pre·can·cel \(ˌ)prē-ˈkan-səl\ vb : to cancel (a postage stamp) in advance of use — **precancel** n — **pre·can·cel·la·tion** \ˌprē-ˌkan-sə-ˈlā-shən\ n

pre·can·cer·ous \(ˌ)prē-ˈkan-sə-rəs\ adj : likely to become cancerous

pre·car·i·ous \pri-ˈker-ē-əs\ adj : dependent on uncertain conditions : dangerously insecure : UNSTABLE ⟨a ∼ foothold⟩ ⟨∼ prosperity⟩ ♦ Synonyms DELICATE, SENSITIVE, TICKLISH, TOUCHY, TRICKY — **pre·car·i·ous·ly** adv — **pre·car·i·ous·ness** n

pre·cau·tion \pri-ˈkȯ-shən\ n : a measure taken beforehand to prevent harm or secure good — **pre·cau·tion·ary** \-shə-ˌner-ē\ adj

pre·cede \pri-ˈsēd\ vb **pre·ced·ed; pre·ced·ing** : to be, go, or come ahead or in front of (as in rank or time)

pre·ce·dence \ˈpre-sə-dəns, pri-ˈsēd-ᵊns\ n **1** : the act or fact of preceding **2** : consideration based on order of importance : PRIORITY

¹**prec·e·dent** \pri-ˈsē-dᵊnt, ˈpre-sə-dənt\ adj : prior in time, order, or significance

²**prec·e·dent** \ˈpre-sə-dənt\ n : something said or done that may serve to authorize or justify further words or acts of the same or a similar kind

pre·ced·ing \pri-ˈsē-diŋ\ adj : that precedes ♦ Synonyms ANTECEDENT, FOREGOING, PRIOR, FORMER, ANTERIOR

pre·cen·tor \pri-ˈsen-tər\ n : a leader of the singing of a choir or congregation

pre·cept \ˈprē-ˌsept\ n : a command or principle intended as a general rule of action or conduct

pre·cep·tor \pri-ˈsep-tər, ˈprē-ˌsep-\ n : TUTOR

pre·ces·sion \prē-ˈse-shən\ n : a slow gyration of the rotation axis of a spinning body (as the earth) — **pre·cess** \prē-ˈses\ vb — **pre·ces·sion·al** \-ˈsə-shə-nəl\ adj

pre·cinct \ˈprē-ˌsiŋkt\ n **1** : an administrative subdivision (as of a city) : DISTRICT ⟨police ∼⟩ ⟨electoral ∼⟩ **2** : an enclosure bounded by the limits of a building or place — often used in pl. **3** pl : ENVIRONS

pre·ci·os·i·ty \ˌpre-shē-ˈä-sə-tē\ n, pl **-ties** : fastidious refinement

pre·cious \ˈpre-shəs\ adj **1** : of great value ⟨∼ jewels⟩ **2** : greatly cherished : DEAR ⟨∼ memories⟩ **3** : AFFECTED ⟨∼ language⟩

prec·i·pice \ˈpre-sə-pəs\ n : a steep cliff

pre·cip·i·tan·cy \pri-ˈsi-pə-tən-sē\ n : undue hastiness or suddenness

¹**pre·cip·i·tate** \pri-ˈsi-pə-ˌtāt\ vb **-tat·ed; -tat·ing** [L praecipitare, fr. praecipit-, praeceps headlong, fr. prae in front of + caput head] **1** : to throw violently **2** : to throw down **3** : to cause to happen quickly or abruptly ⟨∼ a quarrel⟩ **4** : to cause to separate from solution or suspension **5** : to fall as rain, snow, or hail ♦ Synonyms SPEED, ACCELERATE, QUICKEN, HASTEN, HURRY

²**pre·cip·i·tate** \pri-ˈsi-pə-tət, -ˌtāt\ n : the solid matter that separates from a solution or suspension

³**pre·cip·i·tate** \pri-ˈsi-pə-tət\ adj **1** : showing extreme or unwise haste : RASH **2** : falling with steep descent; also : PRECIPITOUS — **pre·cip·i·tate·ly** adv — **pre·cip·i·tate·ness** n

pre·cip·i·ta·tion \pri-ˌsi-pə-ˈtā-shən\ n **1** : rash haste **2** : the process of precipitating or forming a precipitate **3** : water that falls to earth esp. as rain or snow; also : the quantity of this water

pre·cip·i·tous \pri-ˈsi-pə-təs\ adj **1** : PRECIPITATE **2** : having the character of a precipice : very steep ⟨a ∼ slope⟩; also : containing precipices ⟨∼ trails⟩ — **pre·cip·i·tous·ly** adv

pré·cis \prā-ˈsē\ n, pl **pré·cis** \-ˈsēz\ [F] : a concise summary of essentials

pre·cise \pri-ˈsīs\ adj **1** : exactly defined or stated : DEFINITE **2** : highly accurate : EXACT **3** : conforming strictly to a standard : SCRUPULOUS ⟨a ∼ teacher⟩ — **pre·cise·ly** adv — **pre·cise·ness** n

pre·ci·sion \pri-ˈsi-zhən\ n : the quality or state of being precise

pre·clude \pri-ˈklüd\ vb **pre·clud·ed; pre·clud·ing** : to make impossible : BAR, PREVENT

pre·co·cious \pri-ˈkō-shəs\ adj [L praecoc-, praecox, lit., ripening early, fr. prae-ahead + coquere to cook] : early in development and esp. in mental development — **pre·co·cious·ly** adv — **pre·coc·i·ty** \pri-ˈkä-sə-tē\ n

pre·con·ceive \ˌprē-kən-ˈsēv\ vb : to form an opinion of beforehand — **pre·con·cep·tion** \-ˈsep-shən\ n

pre·con·di·tion \-ˈdi-shən\ vb : to put in proper or desired condition or frame of mind in advance

pre·cook \ˌprē-ˈku̇k\ vb : to cook partially or entirely before final cooking or reheating

pre·cur·sor \pri-ˈkər-sər\ n : one that precedes and indicates the approach of another : FORERUNNER

pred abbr predicate

pre·da·ceous or **pre·da·cious** \pri-ˈdā-shəs\ adj : living by preying on others : PREDATORY

pre·date \ˈprē-ˈdāt\ vb : ANTEDATE

pre·da·tion \pri-ˈdā-shən\ n **1** : the act of preying or plundering **2** : a mode of life in which food is primarily obtained by killing and consuming animals

pred·a·tor \ˈpre-də-tər\ n : an animal that lives by predation

pred·a·to·ry \ˈpre-də-ˌtȯr-ē\ adj **1** : of or relating to plunder ⟨∼ warfare⟩ **2** : disposed to exploit others **3** : preying upon other animals

pre·dawn \(ˌ)prē-ˈdȯn\ adj : of or relating to the time just before dawn

pre·de·cease \ˌprē-di-ˈsēs\ vb **-ceased; -ceas·ing** : to die before another person

pre·de·ces·sor \ˈpre-də-ˌse-sər, ˈprē-\ n : a previous holder of a position to which another has succeeded

pre·des·ig·nate \(ˌ)prē-ˈde-zig-ˌnāt\ vb : to designate beforehand

pre·des·ti·na·tion \ˌprē-ˌdes-tə-ˈnā-shən\ n : the act of foreordaining to an earthly lot or eternal destiny by divine decree; also : the state of being so foreordained — **pre·des·ti·nate** \prē-ˈdes-tə-ˌnāt\ vb

pre·des·tine \prē-ˈdes-tən\ vb : to settle beforehand : FOREORDAIN

pre·de·ter·mine \ˌprē-di-ˈtər-mən\ vb : to determine beforehand

pred·i·ca·ble \ˈpre-di-kə-bəl\ adj : capable of being predicated or affirmed

pre·dic·a·ment \pri-ˈdi-kə-mənt\ n : a difficult or trying situation ✦ *Synonyms* DILEMMA, PICKLE, QUAGMIRE, JAM

¹**pred·i·cate** \ˈpre-di-kət\ n : the part of a sentence or clause that expresses what is said of the subject

²**pred·i·cate** \ˈpre-də-ˌkāt\ vb **-cat·ed; -cat·ing 1** : AFFIRM **2** : to assert to be a quality or attribute **3** : FOUND, BASE — usu. used with *on* — **pred·i·ca·tion** \ˌpre-də-ˈkā-shən\ n

pre·dict \pri-ˈdikt\ vb : to declare in advance — **pre·dict·abil·i·ty** \-ˌdik-tə-ˈbi-lə-tē\ n — **pre·dict·able** \-ˈdik-tə-bəl\ adj — **pre·dict·ably** \-blē\ adv — **pre·dic·tion** \-ˈdik-shən\ n

pre·di·gest \ˌprē-dī-ˈjest\ vb : to simplify for easy use; also : to subject to artificial or natural partial digestion

pre·di·lec·tion \ˌpre-də-ˈlek-shən, ˌprē-\ n : an established preference for something

pre·dis·pose \ˌprē-dis-ˈpōz\ vb : to incline in advance : make susceptible ⟨was *predisposed* to infection⟩ — **pre·dis·po·si·tion** \ˌprē-ˌdis-pə-ˈzi-shən\ n

pre·dom·i·nant \pri-ˈdä-mə-nənt\ adj : greater in importance, strength, influence, or authority — **pre·dom·i·nance** \-nəns\ n

pre·dom·i·nant·ly \-nənt-lē\ adv : for the most part : MAINLY

pre·dom·i·nate \pri-ˈdä-mə-ˌnāt\ vb : to be superior esp. in power or numbers : PREVAIL

pre·dom·i·nate·ly \pri-ˈdä-mə-nət-lē\ adv : PREDOMINANTLY

pree·mie \ˈprē-mē\ n : a premature baby

pre·em·i·nent \prē-ˈe-mə-nənt\ adj : having highest rank : OUTSTANDING — **pre·em·i·nence** \-nəns\ n — **pre·em·i·nent·ly** adv

pre·empt \prē-ˈempt\ vb **1** : to settle upon (public land) with the right to purchase before others; also : to take by such right **2** : to seize upon before someone else can **3** : to take the place of ✦ *Synonyms* USURP, CONFISCATE, APPROPRIATE, EXPROPRIATE — **pre·emp·tion** \-ˈemp-shən\ n

pre·emp·tive \prē-ˈemp-tiv\ adj : marked by the seizing of the initiative : initiated by oneself ⟨~ attack⟩

preen \ˈprēn\ vb [ME *prenen*, alter. of *proynen, prunen*, fr. AF *puroindre, proindre*, fr. *pur-* thoroughly + *oindre* to anoint, rub, fr. L *unguere*] **1** : to groom with the bill — used of a bird **2** : to dress or smooth up : PRIMP **3** : to pride (oneself) for achievement

pre·ex·ist \ˌprē-ig-ˈzist\ vb : to exist before — **pre·ex·is·tence** \-ˈzis-təns\ n — **pre·ex·is·tent** \-tənt\ adj

pref abbr **1** preface **2** preference **3** preferred **4** prefix

¹**pre·fab** \(ˌ)prē-ˈfab, ˈprē-ˌfab\ adj : produced by prefabrication ⟨a ~ house⟩

²**pre·fab** n : a prefabricated structure

pre·fab·ri·cate \(ˌ)prē-ˈfa-brə-ˌkāt\ vb : to manufacture the parts of (a structure) beforehand for later assembly — **pre·fab·ri·ca·tion** \ˌprē-ˌfa-bri-ˈkā-shən\ n

¹**pref·ace** \ˈpre-fəs\ n : the introductory remarks of a speaker or writer — **pref·a·to·ry** \ˈpre-fə-ˌtȯr-ē\ adj

²**preface** vb **pref·aced; pref·ac·ing** : to introduce with a preface

pre·fect \ˈprē-ˌfekt\ n **1** : a high official; esp : a chief officer or magistrate **2** : a student monitor

pre·fec·ture \ˈprē-ˌfek-chər\ n : the office, term, or residence of a prefect

pre·fer \pri-ˈfər\ vb **pre·ferred; pre·fer·ring 1** : PROMOTE **2** : to like better **3** : to bring (as a charge) against a person — **pref·er·a·ble** \ˈpre-fə-rə-bəl\ adj — **pref·er·a·bly** \-blē\ adv

pref·er·ence \ˈpre-frəns, -fə-rəns\ n **1** : a special liking for one thing over another **2** : CHOICE, SELECTION — **pref·er·en·tial** \ˌpre-fə-ˈren-chəl\ adj

pre·fer·ment \pri-ˈfər-mənt\ n : PROMOTION, ADVANCEMENT

preferred provider organization n : PPO

pre·fig·ure \prē-ˈfi-gyər\ vb **1** : FORESHADOW **2** : to imagine beforehand

¹**pre·fix** \ˈprē-ˌfiks, prē-ˈfiks\ vb : to place before ⟨~ a title to a name⟩

²**pre·fix** \ˈprē-ˌfiks\ n : an affix occurring at the beginning of a word

pre·flight \ˈprē-ˈflīt\ adj : preparing for or preliminary to flight

pre·form \(ˌ)prē-ˈfȯrm, ˈprē-ˌfȯrm\ vb : to form or shape beforehand

preg·na·ble \ˈpreg-nə-bəl\ adj : vulnerable to capture ⟨a ~ fort⟩

preg·nant \ˈpreg-nənt\ adj **1** : containing unborn offspring within the body **2** : rich in significance : MEANINGFUL — **preg·nan·cy** \-nən-sē\ n

pre·heat \prē-ˈhēt\ vb : to heat beforehand; esp : to heat (an oven) to a designated temperature before using

pre·hen·sile \prē-ˈhen-səl, -ˌsī(-ə)l\ adj : adapted for grasping esp. by wrapping around ⟨a monkey with a ~ tail⟩

pre·his·tor·ic \ˌprē-his-ˈtȯr-ik\ also **pre·his·tor·i·cal** \-i-kəl\ adj : of, relating to, or existing in the period before written history began

pre·judge \(ˌ)prē-ˈjəj\ vb : to judge before full hearing or examination

¹**prej·u·dice** \ˈpre-jə-dəs\ n **1** : DAMAGE;

esp : detriment to one's rights or claims **2** : an opinion made without adequate basis ⟨racial ∼⟩ — **prej·u·di·cial** \ˌpre-jə-ˈdi-shəl\ *adj*

²**prejudice** *vb* **-diced; -dic·ing 1** : to damage by a judgment or action esp. at law **2** : to cause to have prejudice

pre·kin·der·gar·ten \(ˈ)prē-ˈkin-dər-ˌgärt³n\ *n* **1** : NURSERY SCHOOL **2** : a class or program preceding kindergarten

prel·ate \ˈpre-lət\ *n* : an ecclesiastic (as a bishop) of high rank — **prel·a·cy** \-lə-sē\ *n*

pre·launch \ˈprē-ˈlȯnch\ *adj* : preparing for or preliminary to launch

pre·lim \ˈprē-ˌlim, pri-ˈlim\ *n or adj* : PRELIMINARY

¹**pre·lim·i·nary** \pri-ˈli-mə-ˌner-ē\ *n, pl* **-nar·ies** : something that precedes or introduces the main business or event

²**preliminary** *adj* : preceding the main discourse or business

pre·lude \ˈprel-ˌyüd; ˈpre-ˌlüd, ˈprā-\ *n* **1** : an introductory performance or event **2** : a musical section or movement introducing the main theme; *also* : an organ solo played at the beginning of a church service

pre·mar·i·tal \(ˌ)prē-ˈmer-ə-t³l\ *adj* : existing or occurring before marriage

pre·ma·ture \ˌprē-mə-ˈtu̇r, -ˈtyu̇r, -ˈchu̇r\ *adj* : happening, coming, born, or done before the usual or proper time ⟨a ∼ birth⟩ — **pre·ma·ture·ly** *adv*

¹**pre·med** \ˈprē-ˈmed\ *n* : a premedical student or course of study

²**premed** *adj* : PREMEDICAL

pre·med·i·cal \(ˌ)prē-ˈme-di-kəl\ *adj* : preceding and preparing for the professional study of medicine

pre·med·i·tate \pri-ˈme-də-ˌtāt\ *vb* : to consider and plan beforehand — **pre·med·i·ta·tion** \-ˌme-də-ˈtā-shən\ *n*

pre·men·o·paus·al \(ˌ)prē-ˌme-nə-ˈpȯ-zəl\ *adj* : of, relating to, or being in the period preceding menopause

pre·men·stru·al \(ˌ)prē-ˈmen-strə-wəl\ *adj* : of, relating to, or occurring in the period just before menstruation

premenstrual syndrome *n* : a varying group of symptoms manifested by some women prior to menstruation

premie *var of* PREEMIE

¹**pre·mier** \pri-ˈmir, -ˈmyir, ˈprē-mē-ər\ *adj* [ME *primer, primier,* fr. AF, first, chief, fr. L *primarius* of the first rank] : first in rank or importance : CHIEF; *also* : first in time : EARLIEST

²**premier** *n* : PRIME MINISTER — **pre·mier·ship** *n*

¹**pre·miere** \pri-ˈmyer, -ˈmir\ *n* : a first performance

²**premiere** *also* **pre·mier** *same as* ¹PREMIERE\ *vb* **pre·miered; pre·mier·ing** : to give or receive a first public performance

¹**prem·ise** \ˈpre-məs\ *n* **1** : a statement of fact or a supposition made or implied as a basis of argument **2** *pl* : a piece of land with the structures on it; *also* : the place of business of an enterprise

²**premise** *vb* **prem·ised; prem·is·ing** : to base on certain assumptions

pre·mi·um \ˈprē-mē-əm\ *n* [L *praemium* booty, profit, reward, fr. *prae* before + *emere* to take, buy] **1** : REWARD, PRIZE **2** : a sum over and above the stated value **3** : something paid over and above a fixed wage or price **4** : something given with a purchase **5** : the sum paid for a contract of insurance **6** : an unusually high value

pre·mix \ˌprē-ˈmiks\ *vb* : to mix before use

pre·mo·lar \(ˌ)prē-ˈmō-lər\ *adj* : situated in front of or preceding the molar teeth; *esp* : being or relating to those teeth of a mammal in front of the true molars and behind the canines — **premolar** *n*

pre·mo·ni·tion \ˌprē-mə-ˈni-shən, ˌpre-\ *n* **1** : previous warning **2** : PRESENTIMENT ⟨had a ∼ of disaster⟩ — **pre·mon·i·to·ry** \pri-ˈmä-nə-ˌtȯr-ē\ *adj*

pre·na·tal \ˈprē-ˈnā-t³l\ *adj* : occurring, existing, or taking place before birth

pre·nup·tial \prē-ˈnəp-shəl\ *adj* : made or occurring before marriage

prenuptial agreement *n* : an agreement between a man and a woman before marrying in which they give up future rights to each other's property in the event of divorce or death

pre·oc·cu·pa·tion \prē-ˌä-kyə-ˈpā-shən\ *n* : complete absorption of the mind or interests; *also* : something that causes such absorption

pre·oc·cu·pied \prē-ˈä-kyə-ˌpīd\ *adj* **1** : lost in thought; *also* : absorbed in some preoccupation **2** : already occupied

♦ *Synonyms* ABSTRACTED, ABSENT, ABSENTMINDED

pre·oc·cu·py \-ˌpī\ *vb* **1** : to occupy the attention of beforehand **2** : to take possession of before another

pre·op·er·a·tive \(ˌ)prē-ˈä-prə-tiv, -pə-ˌrā-\ *adj* : occurring before a surgical operation

pre·or·dain \ˌprē-ȯr-ˈdān\ *vb* : FOREORDAIN

pre–owned \(ˌ)prē-ˈōnd\ *adj* : SECONDHAND ⟨∼ vehicles⟩

prep *abbr* **1** preparatory **2** preposition

pre·pack·age \(ˌ)prē-ˈpa-kij\ *vb* : to package (as food) before offering for sale to the customer

preparatory school *n* **1** : a usu. private school preparing students primarily for college **2** *Brit* : a private elementary school preparing students primarily for British public schools

pre·pare \pri-ˈper\ *vb* **pre·pared; pre·par·ing 1** : to make or get ready ⟨∼ dinner⟩ ⟨∼ a student for college⟩ **2** : to get ready beforehand **3** : to put together : COMPOUND ⟨∼ a prescription⟩ — **prep·a·ra·tion** \ˌpre-pə-ˈrā-shən\ *n* — **pre·pa·ra·to·ry** \pri-ˈper-ə-ˌtȯr-ē\ *adj*

pre·pared·ness \pri-ˈper-əd-nəs\ *n* : a state of adequate preparation

pre·pay \(ˌ)prē-ˈpā\ *vb* **-paid** \-ˈpād\; **-pay·ing** : to pay or pay the charge on in advance

pre·pon·der·ant \pri-ˈpän-də-rənt\ *adj* : having greater weight, force, influence, or frequency — **pre·pon·der·ance** \-rəns\ *n* — **pre·pon·der·ant·ly** *adv*

pre·pon·der·ate \pri-'pän-də-ˌrāt\ vb **-at·ed; -at·ing** [L *praeponderare*, fr. *prae-* ahead + *ponder-, pondus* weight] : to exceed in weight, force, influence, or frequency : PREDOMINATE

prep·o·si·tion \ˌpre-pə-'zi-shən\ n : a word that combines with a noun or pronoun to form a phrase — **prep·o·si·tion·al** \-'zi-shə-nəl\ adj

pre·pos·sess \ˌprē-pə-'zes\ vb **1** : to cause to be preoccupied **2** : to influence beforehand esp. favorably

pre·pos·sess·ing adj : tending to create a favorable impression ⟨a ~ manner⟩

pre·pos·ses·sion \-'ze-shən\ n **1** : PREJUDICE **2** : an exclusive concern with one idea or object

pre·pos·ter·ous \pri-'päs-tə-rəs\ adj : contrary to nature or reason : ABSURD

prep·py or **prep·pie** \'pre-pē\ n, pl **prep·pies 1** : a student at or a graduate of a preparatory school **2** : a person deemed to dress or behave like a preppy

pre·puce \'prē-ˌpyüs\ n : FORESKIN

pre·quel \'prē-kwəl\ n : a literary or dramatic work whose story precedes that of an earlier work

pre·re·cord·ed \(ˌ)prē-ri-'kȯr-dəd\ adj : recorded for later broadcast or play

pre·req·ui·site \prē-'re-kwə-zət\ n : something required beforehand or for the end in view — **prerequisite** adj

pre·rog·a·tive \pri-'rä-gə-tiv\ n : an exclusive or special right, power, or privilege ⟨presidential ~s⟩

pres abbr **1** present **2** president

¹pres·age \'pre-sij\ n [ME, fr. L *praesagium*, fr. *praesagus* having a foreboding, fr. *prae* before + *sagus* prophetic] **1** : something that foreshadows a future event : OMEN **2** : FOREBODING

²pre·sage \'pre-sij, pri-'sāj\ vb **pre·saged; pre·sag·ing 1** : to give an omen or warning of : FORESHADOW **2** : FORETELL, PREDICT

pres·by·o·pia \ˌprez-bē-'ō-pē-ə\ n : a visual condition in which loss of elasticity of the lens of the eye causes defective accommodation and inability to focus sharply for near vision — **pres·by·o·pic** \-'ō-pik, -'ä-\ adj or n

pres·by·ter \'prez-bə-tər\ n [LL, elder, priest, fr. Gk *presbyteros*, compar. of *presbys* elder, old man] **1** : PRIEST, MINISTER **2** : an elder in a Presbyterian church

¹Pres·by·te·ri·an \ˌprez-bə-'tir-ē-ən\ n : a member of a Presbyterian church

²Presbyterian adj **1** often not cap : characterized by a graded system of representative ecclesiastical bodies (as presbyteries) exercising legislative and judicial powers **2** : of or relating to a group of Protestant Christian bodies that are presbyterian in government — **Pres·by·te·ri·an·ism** \-ˌni-zəm\ n

pres·by·tery \'prez-bə-ˌter-ē\ n, pl **-ter·ies 1** : the part of a church reserved for the officiating clergy **2** : a ruling body in Presbyterian churches consisting of the ministers and representative elders of a district

¹pre·school \'prē-ˌskül\ adj : of or relating to the period in a child's life from infancy to the age of five or six — **pre·school·er** \-ˌskü-lər\ n

²preschool n : NURSERY SCHOOL

pre·science \'pre-shəns, 'prē-\ n : foreknowledge of events; also : FORESIGHT — **pre·scient** \-shənt, -shē-ənt\ adj

pre·scribe \pri-'skrīb\ vb **pre·scribed; pre·scrib·ing 1** : to lay down as a guide or rule of action **2** : to direct the use of (as a medicine) as a remedy

pre·scrip·tion \pri-'skrip-shən\ n **1** : the action of prescribing rules or directions **2** : a written direction for the preparation and use of a medicine; also : a medicine prescribed

pre·scrip·tive \pri-'skrip-tiv\ adj **1** : serving to prescribe ⟨~ rules⟩ **2** : acquired by, based on, or determined by prescription or by custom

pres·ence \'pre-zᵊns\ n **1** : the fact or condition of being present **2** : the space immediately around a person **3** : one that is present **4** : the bearing of a person; esp : stately bearing

¹pres·ent \'pre-zᵊnt\ n : something presented : GIFT

²pre·sent \pri-'zent\ vb **1** : to bring into the presence or acquaintance of : INTRODUCE **2** : to bring before the public ⟨~ a play⟩ **3** : to make a gift to **4** : to give formally **5** : to lay (as a charge) before a court for inquiry **6** : to aim or direct (as a weapon) so as to face in a particular direction — **pre·sent·able** adj — **pre·sen·ta·tion** \ˌprē-ˌzen-'tā-shən, ˌpre-zᵊn-\ n — **pre·sent·ment** \pri-'zent-mənt\ n

³pres·ent \'pre-zᵊnt\ adj **1** : now existing or in progress ⟨~ conditions⟩ **2** : being in view or at hand ⟨~ at the meeting⟩ **3** : under consideration ⟨the ~ problem⟩ **4** : of, relating to, or constituting a verb tense that expresses present time or the time of speaking

⁴pres·ent \'pre-zᵊnt\ n **1** pl : the present legal document **2** : the present tense; also : a verb form in it **3** : the present time

pres·ent–day \'pre-zᵊnt-'dā\ adj : now existing or occurring : CURRENT

pre·sen·ti·ment \pri-'zen-tə-mənt\ n : a feeling that something is about to happen : PREMONITION ⟨a ~ of danger⟩

pres·ent·ly \'pre-zᵊnt-lē\ adv **1** : SOON ⟨~ they arrived⟩ **2** : NOW ⟨~ busy⟩

present participle n : a participle that typically expresses present action and that in English is formed with the suffix *-ing* and is used in the formation of the progressive tenses

¹pre·serve \pri-'zərv\ vb **pre·served; pre·serv·ing 1** : to keep safe : GUARD, PROTECT **2** : to keep from decaying; esp : to process food (as by canning or pickling) to prevent spoilage **3** : MAINTAIN ⟨~ silence⟩ — **pres·er·va·tion** \ˌpre-zər-'vā-shən\ n — **pre·ser·va·tive** \pri-'zər-və-tiv\ adj or n — **pre·serv·er** n

²preserve n **1** : preserved fruit — often used in pl. **2** : an area for the protection of natural resources (as animals)

pre·set \'prē-ˌset\ vb **-set; -set·ting** : to set beforehand — **preset** n

pre·shrink \prē-'shriŋk\ vb **-shrank** \-'shraŋk\; **-shrunk** \-'shrəŋk\ : to shrink (as a fabric) before making into a garment

pre·side \pri-'zīd\ vb **pre·sid·ed; pre·sid·ing** [L praesidēre to guard, preside over, fr. prae in front of + sedēre to sit] 1 : to exercise guidance or control 2 : to occupy the place of authority; esp : to act as chairman

pres·i·dent \'pre-zə-dənt\ n 1 : one chosen to preside ⟨~ of the assembly⟩ 2 : the chief officer of an organization (as a corporation or society) 3 : an elected official serving as both chief of state and chief political executive; also : a chief of state often with only minimal political powers — **pres·i·den·cy** \-dən-sē\ n — **pres·i·den·tial** \ˌpre-zə-'den-chəl\ adj

pre·si·dio \pri-'sē-dē-ˌō, -'si-\ n, pl **-di·os** [Sp] : a military post or fortified settlement in an area currently or orig. under Spanish control

pre·sid·i·um \pri-'si-dē-əm\ n, pl **-ia** \-dē-ə\ or **-iums** [Russ prezidium, fr. L praesidium garrison] : a permanent executive committee that acts for a larger body in a Communist country

¹**pre·soak** \(ˌ)prē-'sōk\ vb : to soak beforehand

²**pre·soak** \'prē-ˌsōk\ n 1 : an instance of presoaking 2 : a preparation used in presoaking clothes

pre·sort \(ˌ)prē-'sȯrt\ vb : to sort (mail) by zip code usu. before delivery to a post office

¹**press** \'pres\ n 1 : a crowded condition : THRONG 2 : a machine for exerting pressure 3 : CLOSET, CUPBOARD 4 : PRESSURE 5 : the properly creased condition of a freshly pressed garment 6 : PRINTING PRESS; also : the act or the process of printing 7 : a printing or publishing establishment 8 : the media (as newspapers and magazines) of public news and comment; also : persons (as reporters) employed in these media 9 : comment in newspapers and periodicals

²**press** vb 1 : to bear down upon : push steadily against 2 : ASSAIL, COMPEL 3 : to squeeze out the juice or contents of ⟨~ grapes⟩ 4 : to squeeze to a desired density, shape, or smoothness; esp : IRON 5 : to try hard to persuade : URGE 6 : to follow through : PROSECUTE 7 : CROWD ⟨reporters ~ed around the players⟩ 8 : to force one's way 9 : to require haste or speed in action — **press·er** n

press agent n : an agent employed to establish and maintain good public relations through publicity

press·ing adj : URGENT ⟨a ~ need⟩

press·man \'pres-mən, -ˌman\ n : the operator of a press and esp. a printing press

press·room \-ˌrüm, -ˌrum\ n 1 : a room in a printing plant containing the printing presses 2 : a room for the use of reporters

¹**pres·sure** \'pre-shər\ n 1 : the burden of physical or mental distress 2 : the action

of pressing; esp : the application of force to something by something else in direct contact with it 3 : the force exerted over a surface divided by its area 4 : the stress or urgency of matters demanding attention

²**pressure** vb **pres·sured; pres·sur·ing** : to apply pressure to

pressure group n : a group that seeks to influence governmental policy but not to elect candidates to office

pressure suit n : an inflatable suit for high-altitude flight or spaceflight to protect the body from low pressure

pres·sur·ise Brit var of PRESSURIZE

pres·sur·ize \'pre-shə-ˌrīz\ vb **-ized; -iz·ing** 1 : to maintain higher pressure within than without; esp : to maintain normal atmospheric pressure within (as an airplane cabin) during high-altitude flight or spaceflight 2 : to apply pressure to 3 : to design to withstand pressure — **pres·sur·i·za·tion** \ˌpre-shə-rə-'zā-shən\ n

pres·ti·dig·i·ta·tion \ˌpres-tə-ˌdi-jə-'tā-shən\ n : SLEIGHT OF HAND

pres·tige \pres-'tēzh, -'tēj\ n [F, fr. MF, conjuror's trick, illusion, fr. LL praestigium, fr. L praestigiae, pl., conjuror's tricks, fr. praestringere to graze, blunt, constrict, fr. prae- in front of + stringere to bind tight] : standing or estimation in the eyes of people : REPUTATION ♦ **Synonyms** INFLUENCE, AUTHORITY, WEIGHT, CACHET — **pres·ti·gious** \-'ti-jəs, -'tē-\ adj

¹**pres·to** \'pres-tō\ interj [It, quick, quickly] — used to indicate the sudden appearance or occurrence of something

²**presto** adv or adj 1 : suddenly as if by magic : IMMEDIATELY 2 : at a rapid tempo — used as a direction in music

pre·stress \(ˌ)prē-'stres\ vb : to introduce internal stresses into (as a structural beam) to counteract later load stresses

pre·sum·ably \pri-'zü-mə-blē\ adv : by reasonable assumption

pre·sume \pri-'züm\ vb **pre·sumed; pre·sum·ing** 1 : to take upon oneself without leave or warrant : DARE 2 : to take for granted : ASSUME 3 : to act or behave with undue boldness — **pre·sum·able** \-'zü-mə-bəl\ adj

pre·sump·tion \pri-'zəmp-shən\ n 1 : presumptuous attitude or conduct : AUDACITY 2 : an attitude or belief dictated by probability; also : the grounds lending probability to a belief — **pre·sump·tive** \-tiv\ adj

pre·sump·tu·ous \pri-'zəmp-chə-wəs\ adj : overstepping due bounds : taking liberties — **pre·sump·tu·ous·ly** adv

pre·sup·pose \ˌprē-sə-'pōz\ vb 1 : to suppose beforehand 2 : to require beforehand as a necessary condition — **pre·sup·po·si·tion** \(ˌ)prē-ˌsə-pə-'zi-shən\ n

pre·teen \'prē-ˌtēn\ n : a boy or girl not yet 13 years old — **preteen** adj

pre·tend \pri-'tend\ vb 1 : PROFESS ⟨doesn't ~ to be scientific⟩ 2 : FEIGN ⟨~ to be angry⟩ 3 : to lay claim ⟨~ to a throne⟩ — **pre·tend·er** n

pre·tense *or* **pre·tence** \'prē-ˌtens, pri-'tens\ *n* **1** : CLAIM; *esp* : one not supported by fact **2** : mere display : SHOW **3** : an attempt to attain a certain condition ⟨made a ~ at discipline⟩ **4** : false show : PRETEXT ⟨a ~ of objectivity⟩ — **pre·ten·sion** \pri-'ten-chən\ *n*

pre·ten·tious \pri-'ten-chəs\ *adj* **1** : making or possessing usu. unjustified claims (as to excellence) ⟨a ~ literary style⟩ **2** : making demands on one's ability or means : AMBITIOUS ⟨too ~ an undertaking⟩ — **pre·ten·tious·ly** *adv* — **pre·ten·tious·ness** *n*

pret·er·it *or* **pret·er·ite** \'pre-tə-rət\ *n* : a verb form expressing action in the past

pre·term \(ˌ)prē-'tərm, 'prē-ˌ\ *adj* : of, relating to, being, or brought forth by premature birth ⟨a ~ infant⟩

pre·ter·nat·u·ral \ˌprē-tər-'na-chə-rəl\ *adj* **1** : exceeding what is natural ⟨his ~ stamina⟩ **2** : inexplicable by ordinary means — **pre·ter·nat·u·ral·ly** *adv*

pre·text \'prē-ˌtekst\ *n* : a purpose stated or assumed to cloak the real intention or state of affairs

pret·ti·fy \'pri-ti-ˌfī\ *vb* **-fied; -fy·ing** : to make pretty — **pret·ti·fi·ca·tion** \ˌpri-ti-fə-'kā-shən\ *n*

¹pret·ty \'pri-tē\ *adj* **pret·ti·er; -est** [ME *praty, prety,* fr. OE *prættig* tricky, fr. *prætt* trick] **1** : pleasing by delicacy or grace : having conventionally accepted elements of beauty ⟨~ flowers⟩ **2** : MISERABLE, TERRIBLE ⟨a ~ state of affairs⟩ **3** : moderately large ⟨a ~ profit⟩ **4** : PLEASANT — usu. used in negative constructions ⟨the truth was not so ~⟩ ◆ **Synonyms** COMELY, FAIR, BEAUTIFUL, ATTRACTIVE, LOVELY — **pret·ti·ly** \-tə-lē\ *adv* — **pret·ti·ness** \-tē-nəs\ *n*

²pretty *adv* : in some degree : MODERATELY; *also* : QUITE, MAINLY

³pretty *vb* **pret·tied; pret·ty·ing** : to make pretty — usu. used with *up*

pretty boy *n* : a man who is notably good-looking

pret·zel \'pret-səl\ *n* [G *Brezel,* ultim. fr. L *brachiatus* having branches like arms, fr. *brachium* arm] : a brittle or chewy glazed usu. salted slender bread often shaped like a loose knot

prev *abbr* previous; previously

pre·vail \pri-'vāl\ *vb* **1** : to win mastery : TRIUMPH **2** : to be or become effective : SUCCEED **3** : to urge successfully ⟨~ed upon her to sing⟩ **4** : to be frequent : PREDOMINATE — **pre·vail·ing·ly** *adv*

prev·a·lent \'pre-və-lənt\ *adj* : generally or widely existent : WIDESPREAD — **prev·a·lence** \-ləns\ *n*

pre·var·i·cate \pri-'ver-ə-ˌkāt\ *vb* **-cat·ed; -cat·ing** [L *praevaricari* to act in collusion, lit., to straddle, fr. *prae* in front of + *varicare* to straddle, fr. *varus* bow-legged] : to deviate from the truth : EQUIVOCATE — **pre·var·i·ca·tion** \-ˌver-ə-'kā-shən\ *n* — **pre·var·i·ca·tor** \-'ver-ə-ˌkā-tər\ *n*

pre·vent \pri-'vent\ *vb* **1** : to keep from happening or existing ⟨steps to ~ war⟩ **2** : to hold back : HINDER, STOP ⟨~ us

from going⟩ — **pre·vent·able** *also* **pre·vent·ible** \-'ven-tə-bəl\ *adj* — **pre·ven·ta·tive** \-'ven-tə-tiv\ *adj or n* — **pre·ven·tion** \-'ven-chən\ *n* — **pre·ven·tive** \-'ven-tiv\ *adj or n*

pre·ver·bal \ˌprē-'vər-bəl\ *adj* : having not yet acquired the faculty of speech

¹pre·view \'prē-ˌvyü\ *vb* : to see or discuss beforehand; *esp* : to view or show in advance of public presentation

²preview *n* **1** : FORETASTE **2** : an advance showing or viewing **3** *also* **pre·vue** \-ˌvyü\ : a showing of snatches from a motion picture advertised for future appearance

pre·vi·ous \'prē-vē-əs\ *adj* : going before : EARLIER, FORMER ◆ **Synonyms** FOREGOING, PRIOR, PRECEDING, ANTECEDENT — **pre·vi·ous·ly** *adv*

pre·vi·sion \prē-'vi-zhən\ *n* **1** : FORESIGHT, PRESCIENCE **2** : FORECAST, PREDICTION ⟨a ~ of success⟩

pre·war \'prē-'wȯr\ *adj* : occurring or existing before a war

¹prey \'prā\ *n, pl* **prey** *also* **preys 1** : an animal taken for food by a predator; *also* : VICTIM **2** : the act or habit of preying

²prey *vb* **1** : to raid for booty **2** : to seize and devour prey **3** : to have a harmful or wearing effect

prf *abbr* proof

¹price \'prīs\ *n* **1** *archaic* : VALUE **2** : the amount of money paid or asked for the sale of a specified thing; *also* : the cost at which something is obtained

²price *vb* **priced; pric·ing 1** : to set a price on **2** : to ask the price of **3** : to drive by raising prices ⟨priced themselves out of the market⟩

price–fix·ing \'prīs-ˌfik-siŋ\ *n* : the setting of prices artificially (as by producers or government)

price·less \-ləs\ *adj* : having a value beyond any price : INVALUABLE ◆ **Synonyms** PRECIOUS, COSTLY, EXPENSIVE

price support *n* : artificial maintenance of prices of a commodity at a level usu. fixed through government action

price war *n* : a period of commercial competition in which prices are repeatedly cut by the competitors

pric·ey *also* **pricy** \'prī-sē\ *adj* **pric·i·er; -est** : EXPENSIVE ⟨a ~ restaurant⟩

¹prick \'prik\ *n* **1** : a mark or small wound made by a pointed instrument **2** : something sharp or pointed **3** : an instance of pricking; *also* : a sensation of being pricked

²prick *vb* **1** : to pierce slightly with a sharp point; *also* : to have or cause a pricking sensation **2** : to affect with anguish or remorse ⟨~s his conscience⟩ **3** : to outline with punctures ⟨~ out a pattern⟩ **4** : to stand or cause to stand erect ⟨the dog's ears ~ed up at the sound⟩ ◆ **Synonyms** PUNCH, PUNCTURE, PERFORATE, BORE, DRILL

prick·er \'pri-kər\ *n* : BRIAR; *also* : THORN

¹prick·le \'pri-kəl\ *n* **1** : a small sharp process (as on a plant) **2** : a slight stinging pain — **prick·ly** \'pri-klē\ *adj*

²**prickle** vb **prick·led; prick·ling** 1 : to prick lightly 2 : TINGLE

prickly heat n : a red cutaneous eruption with intense itching and tingling caused by inflammation around the ducts of the sweat glands

prickly pear n : any of numerous cacti with usu. yellow flowers and prickly flat or rounded joints; also : the sweet pulpy pear-shaped edible fruit of various prickly pears

¹**pride** \ˈprīd\ n 1 : CONCEIT 2 : justifiable self-respect 3 : elation over an act or possession ⟨took ~ in her work⟩ 4 : haughty behavior : DISDAIN 5 : ostentatious display — **pride·ful** adj

²**pride** vb **prid·ed; prid·ing** : to indulge (as oneself) in pride

priest \ˈprēst\ n [ME preist, fr. OE prēost, ultim. fr. LL presbyter elder, priest, fr. Gk presbyteros, fr. compar. of presbys old man, elder] : a person having authority to perform the sacred rites of a religion; esp : a member of the Anglican, Eastern, or Roman Catholic clergy ranking below a bishop and above a deacon — **priest·hood** n — **priest·li·ness** n — **priest·ly** adj

priest·ess \ˈprēs-təs\ n : a woman authorized to perform the sacred rites of a religion

prig \ˈprig\ n : one who irritates by rigid or pointed observance of proprieties — **prig·gish** \ˈpri-gish\ adj — **prig·gish·ly** adv

¹**prim** \ˈprim\ adj **prim·mer; prim·mest** : stiffly formal and precise — **prim·ly** adv — **prim·ness** n

²**prim** abbr 1 primary 2 primitive

pri·ma·cy \ˈprī-mə-sē\ n 1 : the state of being first (as in rank) 2 : the office, rank, or character of an ecclesiastical primate

pri·ma don·na \ˌpri-mə-ˈdä-nə\ n, pl **prima donnas** [It, lit., first lady] 1 : a principal female singer (as in an opera company) 2 : a vain undisciplined usu. uncooperative person

pri·ma fa·cie \ˈprī-mə-ˈfā-shə, -sē, -shē\ adj or adv [L, at first view] 1 : based on immediate impression : APPARENT 2 : SELF-EVIDENT

pri·mal \ˈprī-məl\ adj 1 : ORIGINAL, PRIMITIVE 2 : first in importance

pri·mar·i·ly \prī-ˈmer-ə-lē\ adv 1 : FUNDAMENTALLY 2 : ORIGINALLY

¹**pri·ma·ry** \ˈprī-ˌmer-ē, -mə-rē\ adj 1 : first in order of time or development; also : PREPARATORY 2 : of first rank or importance; also : FUNDAMENTAL 3 : not derived from or dependent on something else ⟨~ sources⟩

²**primary** n, pl **-ries** : a preliminary election in which voters nominate or express a preference among candidates usu. of their own party

primary care n : health care provided by a medical professional with whom a patient has initial contact

primary color n : any of a set of colors from which all other colors may be derived

primary school n 1 : a school usu. including grades 1-3 and sometimes kindergarten 2 : ELEMENTARY SCHOOL

pri·mate \ˈprī-ˌmāt or esp for 1 -mət\ n 1 often cap : the highest-ranking bishop of a province or nation 2 : any of an order of mammals including humans, apes, and monkeys

¹**prime** \ˈprīm\ n 1 : the earliest stage of something; esp : SPRINGTIME 2 : the most active, thriving, or successful stage or period (as of one's life) 3 : the best individual; also : the best part of something 4 : any integer other than 0, +1, or –1 that is not divisible without remainder by any integer except +1, –1, and plus or minus itself; esp : any such integer that is positive

²**prime** adj 1 : standing first (as in time, rank, significance, or quality) ⟨~ requisite⟩ 2 : of, relating to, or being a number that is prime

³**prime** vb **primed; prim·ing** 1 : FILL, LOAD 2 : to lay a preparatory coating upon (as in painting) 3 : to put in working condition 4 : to instruct beforehand : COACH ⟨primed the witness⟩

prime meridian n : the meridian of 0° longitude which runs through Greenwich, England, and from which other longitudes are reckoned east and west

prime minister n 1 : the chief minister of a ruler or state 2 : the chief executive of a parliamentary government

¹**prim·er** \ˈpri-mər\ n [ME, layperson's prayer book, fr. AF, fr. ML primarium, fr. LL, neut. of primarius primary] 1 : a small book for teaching children to read 2 : a small introductory book on a subject ⟨a ~ of modern art⟩ 3 : a short informative piece of writing

²**prim·er** \ˈprī-mər\ n 1 : one that primes 2 : a device for igniting an explosive 3 : material for priming a surface

prime rate n : an interest rate announced by a bank to be the lowest available to its most credit-worthy customers

prime time n 1 : the time period when the television or radio audience is largest; also : television shows aired in prime time 2 : the choicest or busiest time

pri·me·val \prī-ˈmē-vəl\ adj : of or relating to the earliest ages : PRIMITIVE

¹**prim·i·tive** \ˈpri-mə-tiv\ adj 1 : ORIGINAL, PRIMARY 2 : of, relating to, or characteristic of an early stage of development or evolution 3 : ELEMENTAL, NATURAL 4 : of, relating to, or produced by a tribal people or culture 5 : SELF-TAUGHT; also : produced by a self-taught artist — **prim·i·tive·ly** adv — **prim·i·tive·ness** n — **prim·i·tiv·i·ty** \ˌpri-mə-ˈti-və-tē\ n

²**primitive** n 1 : something primitive 2 : a primitive artist 3 : a member of a primitive people

prim·i·tiv·ism \ˈpri-mə-ti-ˌvi-zəm\ n 1 : primitive practices or procedures; also : a primitive quality or state 2 : belief in the superiority of a simple way of life close to nature 3 : the style of art of primitive peoples or primitive artists

pri·mo·gen·i·tor \\,prī-mō-'je-nə-tər\ *n*
: ANCESTOR, FOREFATHER

pri·mo·gen·i·ture \\-'je-nə-,chùr\ *n* **1**
: the state of being the firstborn of a family **2** : an exclusive right of inheritance belonging to the eldest son

pri·mor·di·al \prī-'mòr-dē-əl\ *adj* : first created or developed : existing in its original state : PRIMEVAL

primp \'primp\ *vb* : to dress in a careful or finicky manner

prim·rose \'prim-,rōz\ *n* : any of a genus of perennial herbs with large leaves arranged at the base of the stem and clusters of showy flowers

prin *abbr* **1** principal **2** principle

prince \'prins\ *n* [ME, fr. AF, fr. L *princeps* leader, initiator, fr. *primus* first + *capere* to take] **1** : MONARCH, KING **2** : a male member of a royal family; *esp* : a son of the monarch **3** : a person of high standing (as in a class) ⟨a ~ of poets⟩ — **prince·dom** \-dəm\ *n* — **prince·ly** *adj*

prince·ling \-liŋ\ *n* : a petty prince

prin·cess \'prin-səs, -,ses\ *n* **1** : a female member of a royal family **2** : the consort of a prince

¹**prin·ci·pal** \'prin-sə-pəl\ *adj* : most important — **prin·ci·pal·ly** *adv*

²**principal** *n* **1** : a leading person (as in a play) **2** : the chief officer of an educational institution **3** : the person from whom an agent's authority derives **4** : a capital sum earning interest or used as a fund

prin·ci·pal·i·ty \\,prin-sə-'pa-lə-tē\ *n, pl* **-ties** : the position, territory, or jurisdiction of a prince

principal parts *n pl* : the inflected forms of a verb

prin·ci·ple \'prin-sə-pəl\ *n* **1** : a general or fundamental law, doctrine, or assumption **2** : a rule or code of conduct; *also* : devotion to such a code **3** : the laws or facts of nature underlying the working of an artificial device **4** : a primary source : ORIGIN; *also* : an underlying faculty or endowment **5** : the active part (as of a drug)

prin·ci·pled \-pəld\ *adj* : exhibiting, based on, or characterized by principle ⟨high-principled⟩

prink \'priŋk\ *vb* : PRIMP

¹**print** \'print\ *n* [ME *prente*, fr. AF, fr. *preint, prient*, pp. of *priendre* to press, fr. L, *premere*] **1** : a mark made by pressure **2** : something stamped with an impression **3** : printed state or form **4** : printed matter **5** : a copy made by printing **6** : cloth with a pattern applied by printing

²**print** *vb* **1** : to stamp (as a mark) in or on something **2** : to produce impressions of (as from type) **3** : to write in letters like those of printer's type **4** : to make (a positive picture) from a photographic negative

print·able \'prin-tə-bəl\ *adj* **1** : capable of being printed or of being printed from **2** : worthy or fit to be published

print·er \'prin-tər\ *n* : one that prints; *esp* : a device that produces printout

print·ing *n* **1** : reproduction in printed

form **2** : the art, practice, or business of a printer **3** : IMPRESSION 5

printing press *n* : a machine that produces printed copies

print·out \'print-,aut\ *n* : a printed output produced by a computer — **print out** *vb*

¹**pri·or** \'prī(-ə)r\ *n* : the superior ranking next to the abbot or abbess of a religious house

²**prior** *adj* **1** : earlier in time or order **2** : taking precedence logically or in importance — **pri·or·i·ty** \prī-'òr-ə-tē\ *n*

pri·or·ess \'prī-ə-rəs\ *n* : a nun corresponding in rank to a prior

pri·or·i·tize \prī-'òr-ə-,tīz, 'prī-ə-rə-,tīz\ *vb* **-tized; -tiz·ing** : to list or rate in order of priority

prior to *prep* : in advance of : BEFORE

pri·o·ry \'prī-ə-rē\ *n, pl* **-ries** : a religious house under a prior or prioress

prise *chiefly Brit var of* ⁵PRIZE

prism \'pri-zəm\ *n* [LL *prisma*, fr. Gk, lit., something sawed, fr. *priein* to saw] **1** : a solid whose sides are parallelograms and whose ends are parallel and alike in shape and size **2** : a usu. 3-sided transparent object that refracts light so that it breaks up into rainbow colors — **pris·mat·ic** \priz-'ma-tik\ *adj*

pris·on \'pri-z³n\ *n* : a place or state of confinement esp. for criminals

pris·on·er \'pri-z³n-ər\ *n* : a person deprived of liberty; *esp* : one on trial or in prison

prisoner of war : a person captured in war

pris·sy \'pri-sē\ *adj* **pris·si·er; -est** : being overly prim and precise : PRIGGISH — **pris·si·ness** \-sē-nəs\ *n*

pris·tine \'pris-,tēn, pris-'tēn\ *adj* **1** : PRIMITIVE **2** : having the purity of its original state : UNSPOILED

prith·ee \'pri-thē\ *interj, archaic* — used to express a wish or request

pri·va·cy \'prī-və-sē\ *n, pl* **-cies** **1** : the quality or state of being apart from others **2** : SECRECY

¹**pri·vate** \'prī-vət\ *adj* **1** : belonging to or intended for a particular individual or group ⟨~ property⟩ **2** : restricted to the individual : PERSONAL ⟨~ opinion⟩ **3** : carried on by the individual independently ⟨~ study⟩ **4** : not holding public office ⟨a ~ citizen⟩ **5** : withdrawn from company or observation ⟨a ~ place⟩ **6** : not known publicly ⟨~ dealings⟩ — **pri·vate·ly** *adv*

²**private** *n* : an enlisted person of the lowest rank in the marine corps or of one of the two lowest ranks in the army — **in private** : not openly or in public

pri·va·teer \\,prī-və-'tir\ *n* : an armed private ship licensed to attack enemy shipping; *also* : a sailor on such a ship

private first class *n* : an enlisted person ranking next below a corporal in the army and next below a lance corporal in the marine corps

pri·va·tion \prī-'vā-shən\ *n* **1** : DEPRIVATION 1 **2** : the state of being deprived; *esp* : lack of what is needed for existence

priv·et \'pri-vət\ *n* : a nearly evergreen

shrub related to the olive and widely used for hedges

¹priv·i·lege \'priv-lij, 'pri-və-\ *n* [ME, fr. AF, fr. L *privilegium* law for or against a private person, fr. *privus* private + *leg-*, *lex* law] : a right or immunity granted as an advantage or favor esp. to some and not others

²privilege *vb* **-leged; -leg·ing** 1 : to grant a privilege to 2 : to accord a higher value to : FAVOR

privileged *adj* 1 : having or enjoying one or more privileges ⟨~ classes⟩ 2 : not subject to disclosure in a court of law ⟨a ~ communication⟩

¹privy \'pri-vē\ *adj* 1 : PERSONAL, PRIVATE 2 : SECRET 3 : admitted as one sharing in a secret ⟨~ to the conspiracy⟩ — **priv·i·ly** \'pri-və-lē\ *adv*

²privy *n, pl* **priv·ies** : TOILET; *esp* : OUTHOUSE

¹prize \'prīz\ *n* 1 : something offered or striven for in competition or in contests of chance 2 : something exceptionally desirable

²prize *adj* 1 : awarded or worthy of a prize ⟨a ~ essay⟩; *also* : awarded as a prize ⟨a ~ medal⟩ 2 : OUTSTANDING

³prize *vb* **prized; priz·ing** : to value highly : ESTEEM ⟨a *prized* possession⟩

⁴prize *n* : property (as a ship) lawfully captured in time of war

⁵prize *vb* **prized; priz·ing** : PRY

prize·fight \'prīz-,fīt\ *n* : a professional boxing match — **prize·fight·er** *n* — **prize·fight·ing** *n*

prize·win·ner \-,wi-nər\ *n* : a winner of a prize — **prize·win·ning** *adj*

¹pro \'prō\ *n, pl* **pros** : a favorable argument, person, or position

²pro *adv* : in favor of : FOR

³pro *n or adj* : PROFESSIONAL

PRO *abbr* public relations officer

pro·ac·tive \prō-'ak-tiv\ *adj* : acting in anticipation of future problems or needs — **pro·ac·tive·ly** *adv*

pro-am \'prō-'am\ *adj* : involving professionals competing alongside or against amateurs ⟨a ~ tournament⟩ — **pro-am** *n*

prob *abbr* 1 probable; probably 2 problem

prob·a·bil·i·ty \,prä-bə-'bi-lə-tē\ *n, pl* **-ties** 1 : the quality or state of being probable 2 : something probable 3 : a measure of how often a particular event will occur if something (as tossing a coin) is done repeatedly which results in any of a number of possible events

prob·a·ble \'prä-bə-bəl\ *adj* 1 : apparently or presumably true ⟨a ~ hypothesis⟩ 2 : likely to be or become true or real ⟨a ~ result⟩ — **prob·a·bly** \-bə-blē\ *adv*

¹pro·bate \'prō-,bāt\ *n* : the judicial determination of the validity of a will

²pro·bate *vb* **pro·bat·ed; pro·bat·ing** : to establish (a will) by probate as genuine and valid

pro·ba·tion \prō-'bā-shən\ *n* 1 : subjection of an individual to a period of testing and trial to ascertain fitness (as for a job)

2 : the action of giving a convicted offender freedom during good behavior under the supervision of a probation officer — **pro·ba·tion·ary** \-shə-,ner-ē\ *adj*

pro·ba·tion·er \-shə-nər\ *n* 1 : a person (as a newly admitted student nurse) whose fitness is being tested during a trial period 2 : a convicted offender on probation

pro·ba·tive \'prō-bə-tiv\ *adj* 1 : serving to test or try 2 : serving to prove

¹probe \'prōb\ *n* 1 : a slender instrument for examining a cavity (as a wound) 2 : an information-gathering device sent into outer space 3 : a penetrating investigation ◆ **Synonyms** INQUIRY, INQUEST, RESEARCH, INQUISITION

²probe *vb* **probed; prob·ing** 1 : to examine with a probe 2 : to investigate thoroughly

pro·bi·ty \'prō-bə-tē\ *n* : UPRIGHTNESS, HONESTY

prob·lem \'prä-bləm\ *n* 1 : a question raised for consideration or solution 2 : an intricate unsettled question 3 : a source of perplexity or vexation — **problem** *adj*

prob·lem·at·ic \,prä-blə-'ma-tik\ *also* **prob·lem·at·i·cal** \-ti-kəl\ *adj* 1 : difficult to solve or decide : PUZZLING 2 : DUBIOUS, QUESTIONABLE

pro·bos·cis \prə-'bä-səs, -'bäs-kəs\ *n, pl* **-bos·cis·es** *also* **-bos·ci·des** \-'bä-sə-,dēz\ [L, fr. Gk *proboskis*, fr. *pro-* before + *boskein* to feed] : a long flexible snout (as the trunk of an elephant)

proc *abbr* proceedings

pro·caine \'prō-,kān\ *n* : a drug used esp. as a local anesthetic

pro·ce·dure \prə-'sē-jər\ *n* 1 : a particular way of doing something ⟨democratic ~⟩ 2 : a series of steps followed in a regular order ⟨a surgical ~⟩ — **pro·ce·dur·al** \-'sē-jə-rəl\ *adj*

pro·ceed \prō-'sēd\ *vb* 1 : to come forth : ISSUE 2 : to go on in an orderly way; *also* : CONTINUE 3 : to begin and carry on an action 4 : to take legal action 5 : to go forward : ADVANCE

pro·ceed·ing *n* 1 : PROCEDURE 2 *pl* : DOINGS 3 *pl* : legal action 4 : TRANSACTION 5 *pl* : an official record of things said or done

pro·ceeds \'prō-,sēdz\ *n pl* : the total amount or the profit arising from a business deal : RETURN

¹pro·cess \'prä-,ses, 'prō-\ *n, pl* **pro·cess·es** \-,se-səz, -sə-səz, -sə-,sēz\ 1 : PROGRESS, ADVANCE 2 : something going on : PROCEEDING 3 : a natural phenomenon marked by gradual changes that lead toward a particular result ⟨the ~ of growth⟩ 4 : a series of actions or operations directed toward a particular result ⟨a manufacturing ~⟩ 5 : legal action 6 : a mandate issued by a court; *esp* : SUMMONS 7 : a projecting part of an organism or organic structure

²process *vb* : to subject to a special process

pro·ces·sion \prə-'se-shən\ *n* : a group of

individuals moving along in an orderly often ceremonial way

pro·ces·sion·al \-'se-shə-nəl\ *n* **1** : music for a procession **2** : a ceremonial procession

pro·ces·sor \'prä-₁se-sər, 'prō-\ *n* : one that processes **2** : CPU

pro–choice \(₁)prō-'chȯis\ *adj* : favoring the legalization of abortion

pro·claim \prō-'klām\ *vb* : to make known publicly : DECLARE

proc·la·ma·tion \₁prä-klə-'mā-shən\ *n* : an official public announcement

pro·cliv·i·ty \prō-'kli-və-tē\ *n, pl* **-ties** : an inherent inclination esp. toward something objectionable

pro·con·sul \-'kän-səl\ *n* **1** : a governor or military commander of an ancient Roman province **2** : an administrator in a modern colony or occupied area — **pro·con·su·lar** \-sə-lər\ *adj*

pro·cras·ti·nate \prə-'kras-tə-₁nāt, prō-\ *vb* **-nat·ed; -nat·ing** [L *procrastinare,* fr. *pro-* forward + *crastinus* of tomorrow, fr. *cras* tomorrow] : to put off usu. habitually doing something that should be done
♦ **Synonyms** DAWDLE, DELAY — **pro·cras·ti·na·tion** \-₁kras-tə-'nā-shən\ *n* — **pro·cras·ti·na·tor** \-'kras-tə-₁nā-tər\ *n*

pro·cre·ate \'prō-krē-₁āt\ *vb* **-at·ed; -at·ing** : to beget or bring forth offspring
♦ **Synonyms** REPRODUCE, BREED, GENERATE, PROPAGATE — **pro·cre·ation** \₁prō-krē-'ā-shən\ *n* — **pro·cre·ative** \'prō-krē-₁ā-tiv\ *adj* — **pro·cre·ator** \-₁ā-tər\ *n*

pro·crus·te·an \prə-'krəs-tē-ən\ *adj, often cap* [fr. *Procrustes,* villain of Greek mythology who made victims fit his bed by stretching them or cutting off their legs] : marked by arbitrary often ruthless disregard of individual differences or special circumstances

proc·tor \'präk-tər\ *n* : one appointed to supervise students (as at an examination) — **proctor** *vb* — **proc·to·ri·al** \präk-'tȯr-ē-əl\ *adj*

proc·u·ra·tor \'prä-kyə-₁rā-tər\ *n* : a Roman provincial administrator

pro·cure \prə-'kyu̇r\ *vb* **pro·cured; pro·cur·ing 1** : to get possession of : OBTAIN **2** : to make women available for promiscuous sexual intercourse **3** : ACHIEVE
♦ **Synonyms** SECURE, ACQUIRE, GAIN, WIN, EARN — **pro·cur·able** \-'kyu̇r-ə-bəl\ *adj* — **pro·cure·ment** *n* — **pro·cur·er** *n*

¹prod \'präd\ *vb* **prod·ded; prod·ding 1** : to thrust a pointed instrument into : GOAD **2** : INCITE, STIR — **prod** *n*

²prod *abbr* product; production

prod·i·gal \'prä-di-gəl\ *adj* **1** : recklessly extravagant; *also* : LUXURIANT **2** : WASTEFUL, LAVISH ♦ **Synonyms** PROFUSE, LUSH, OPULENT — **prodigal** *n* — **prod·i·gal·i·ty** \₁prä-də-'ga-lə-tē\ *n*

pro·di·gious \prə-'di-jəs\ *adj* **1** : exciting wonder **2** : extraordinary in size or degree : ENORMOUS ♦ **Synonyms** MONSTROUS, TREMENDOUS, STUPENDOUS, MONUMENTAL — **pro·di·gious·ly** *adv*

prod·i·gy \'prä-də-jē\ *n, pl* **-gies 1**

: something extraordinary : WONDER **2** : a highly talented child

¹pro·duce \prə-'düs, -'dyüs\ *vb* **pro·duced; pro·duc·ing 1** : to present to view : EXHIBIT **2** : to give birth or rise to : YIELD **3** : EXTEND, PROLONG **4** : to give being or form to : BRING ABOUT, MAKE; *esp* : MANUFACTURE **5** : to sponsor or oversee the making of **6** : to cause to accrue ⟨~ a profit⟩ — **pro·duc·er** *n*

²pro·duce \'prä-(₁)düs, 'prō- *also* -(₁)dyüs\ *n* : PRODUCT **2**; *also* : agricultural products and esp. fresh fruits and vegetables

prod·uct \'prä-(₁)dəkt\ *n* **1** : the number resulting from multiplication **2** : something produced

pro·duc·tion \prə-'dək-shən\ *n* **1** : something produced : PRODUCT **2** : the act or process of producing — **pro·duc·tive** \-'dək-tiv\ *adj* — **pro·duc·tive·ness** *n* — **pro·duc·tiv·i·ty** \(₁)prō-₁dək-'ti-və-tē, ₁prä-(₁)dək-\ *n*

product placement *n* : the inclusion of a product in a television program or film as a means of advertising

pro·em \'prō-₁em\ *n* **1** : preliminary comment : PREFACE **2** : PRELUDE

¹prof \'präf\ *n* : PROFESSOR

²prof *abbr* professional

¹pro·fane \prō-'fān\ *vb* **pro·faned; pro·fan·ing 1** : to treat (something sacred) with irreverence or contempt **2** : to debase by an unworthy use — **prof·a·na·tion** \₁prä-fə-'nā-shən\ *n*

²profane *adj* [ME *prophane,* fr. MF, fr. L *profanus,* fr. *pro-* before + *fanum* temple] **1** : not concerned with religion : SECULAR **2** : not holy because unconsecrated, impure, or defiled **3** : serving to debase what is holy : IRREVERENT **4** : OBSCENE, VULGAR — **pro·fane·ly** *adv* — **pro·fane·ness** *n*

pro·fan·i·ty \prō-'fa-nə-tē\ *n, pl* **-ties 1** : the quality or state of being profane **2** : the use of profane language **3** : profane language

pro·fess \prə-'fes\ *vb* **1** : to declare or admit openly : AFFIRM **2** : to declare in words only : PRETEND **3** : to confess one's faith in **4** : to practice or claim to be versed in (a calling or occupation) — **pro·fess·ed·ly** \-'fe-səd-lē\ *adv*

pro·fes·sion \prə-'fe-shən\ *n* **1** : an open declaration or avowal of a belief or opinion **2** : a calling requiring specialized knowledge and often long academic preparation **3** : the whole body of persons engaged in a calling

¹pro·fes·sion·al \prə-'fe-shə-nəl\ *adj* **1** : of, relating to, or characteristic of a profession **2** : engaged in one of the professions **3** : participating for gain in an activity often engaged in by amateurs — **pro·fes·sion·al·ly** *adv*

²professional *n* : one that engages in an activity professionally

pro·fes·sion·al·ism \-nə-₁li-zəm\ *n* **1** : the conduct, aims, or qualities that characterize or mark a profession or a professional person **2** : the following of a profession (as athletics) for gain or livelihood

pro·fes·sion·al·ize \-nə-,līz\ *vb* **-ized; -iz·ing** : to give a professional nature to

pro·fes·sor \prə-'fe-sər\ *n* : a teacher at a university or college; *esp* : a faculty member of the highest academic rank — **pro·fes·so·ri·al** \,prō-fə-'sȯr-ē-əl, ,prä-\ *adj* — **pro·fes·sor·ship** *n*

prof·fer \'prä-fər\ *vb* **prof·fered; prof·fer·ing** : to present for acceptance : OFFER — **proffer** *n*

pro·fi·cient \prə-'fi-shənt\ *adj* : well advanced in an art, occupation, or branch of knowledge ♦ *Synonyms* ADEPT, SKILLFUL, EXPERT, MASTERFUL, MASTERLY — **pro·fi·cien·cy** \-shən-sē\ *n* — **proficient** *n* — **pro·fi·cient·ly** *adv*

¹**pro·file** \'prō-,fī(-ə)l\ *n* [It *profilo*, fr. *profilare* to draw in outline, fr. *pro-* forward (fr. L) + *filare* to spin, fr. LL, fr. L *filum* thread] **1** : a representation of something in outline; *esp* : a human head seen in side view **2** : a concise biographical sketch **3** : degree or level of public exposure ⟨keep a low ~⟩

²**profile** *vb* **pro·filed; pro·fil·ing** : to write or draw a profile of

profiling *n* : the act of suspecting or targeting a person solely on the basis of observed characteristics or behavior ⟨racial ~⟩

¹**prof·it** \'prä-fət\ *n* **1** : a valuable return : GAIN **2** : the excess of the selling price of goods over their cost — **prof·it·less** *adj*

²**profit** *vb* **1** : to be of use : BENEFIT **2** : to derive benefit : GAIN ⟨~ed from his mistakes⟩ — **prof·it·able** \'prä-fə-tə-bəl\ *adj* — **prof·it·ably** \-blē\ *adv*

prof·i·teer \,prä-fə-'tir\ *n* : one who makes what is considered an unreasonable profit — **profiteer** *vb*

prof·li·gate \'prä-fli-gət, -flə-,gāt\ *adj* **1** : completely given up to dissipation and licentiousness **2** : wildly extravagant — **prof·li·ga·cy** \-gə-sē\ *n* — **profligate** *n* — **prof·li·gate·ly** *adv*

pro for·ma \(,)prō-'fȯr-mə\ *adj* : done or existing as a matter of form

pro·found \prə-'faund, prō-\ *adj* **1** : marked by intellectual depth or insight ⟨a ~ thought⟩ **2** : coming from or reaching to a depth ⟨a ~ sigh⟩ **3** : deeply felt : INTENSE ⟨~ sympathy⟩ — **pro·found·ly** *adv* — **pro·fun·di·ty** \-'fən-də-tē\ *n*

pro·fuse \prə-'fyüs, prō-\ *adj* : pouring forth liberally : ABUNDANT ⟨~ bleeding⟩ ♦ *Synonyms* LAVISH, PRODIGAL, LUXURIANT, EXUBERANT — **pro·fuse·ly** *adv* — **pro·fu·sion** \-'fyü-zhən\ *n*

prog *abbr* program

pro·gen·i·tor \prō-'je-nə-tər\ *n* **1** : a direct ancestor : FOREFATHER **2** : ORIGINATOR, PRECURSOR

prog·e·ny \'prä-jə-nē\ *n, pl* **-nies** : OFFSPRING, CHILDREN, DESCENDANTS

pro·ges·ter·one \prō-'jes-tə-,rōn\ *n* : a female hormone that causes the uterus to undergo changes so as to provide a suitable environment for a fertilized egg

prog·na·thous \'präg-nə-thəs\ *adj* : having the lower jaw projecting beyond the upper part of the face

prog·no·sis \präg-'nō-səs\ *n, pl* **-no·ses** \-,sēz\ **1** : the prospect of recovery from disease **2** : FORECAST

¹**prog·nos·tic** \präg-'näs-tik\ *n* **1** : PORTENT **2** : PROPHECY

²**prognostic** *adj* : of, relating to, or serving as ground for prognostication or a prognosis

prog·nos·ti·cate \präg-'näs-tə-,kāt\ *vb* **-cat·ed; -cat·ing** : to foretell from signs or symptoms — **prog·nos·ti·ca·tion** \-,näs-tə-'kā-shən\ *n* — **prog·nos·ti·ca·tor** \-'näs-tə-,kā-tər\ *n*

¹**pro·gram** \'prō-,gram, -grəm\ *n* [F *programme* agenda, public notice, fr. Gk *programma*, fr. *prographein* to write in advance, fr. *pro-* before + *graphein* to write] **1** : a brief outline of the order to be pursued or the subjects included (as in a public entertainment); *also* : PERFORMANCE **2** : a plan of procedure esp. toward a goal **3** : coded instructions for a computer — **pro·gram·mat·ic** \,prō-grə-'ma-tik\ *adj*

²**program** *also* **programme** *vb* **-grammed** *or* **-gramed; -gram·ming** *or* **-gram·ing** **1** : to arrange or furnish a program of or for **2** : to enter in a program **3** : to provide (as a computer) with a program — **pro·gram·ma·bil·i·ty** \(,)prō-,gra-mə-'bi-lə-tē\ *n* — **pro·gram·ma·ble** \'prō-,gra-mə-bəl\ *adj* — **pro·gram·mer** *also* **pro·gram·er** \'prō-,gra-mər, -grə-\ *n*

programme *chiefly Brit var of* PROGRAM

programmed instruction *n* : instruction through information given in small steps with each requiring a correct response by the learner before going on to the next step

pro·gram·ming *also* **pro·gram·ing** *n* **1** : the planning, scheduling, or performing of a program **2** : the process of instructing or learning by means of an instruction program **3** : the process of preparing an instruction program

¹**prog·ress** \'prä-grəs, -,gres\ *n* **1** : a forward movement : ADVANCE **2** : a gradual betterment ⟨the ~ of science⟩

²**pro·gress** \prə-'gres\ *vb* **1** : to move forward : PROCEED **2** : to develop to a more advanced stage : IMPROVE

pro·gres·sion \prə-'gre-shən\ *n* **1** : an act of progressing : ADVANCE **2** : a continuous and connected series

¹**pro·gres·sive** \prə-'gre-siv\ *adj* **1** : of, relating to, or characterized by progress ⟨a ~ city⟩ **2** : moving forward or onward : ADVANCING **3** : increasing in extent or severity ⟨a ~ disease⟩ **4** *often cap* : of or relating to political Progressives **5** : of, relating to, or constituting a verb form that expresses action in progress at the time of speaking or a time spoken of — **pro·gres·sive·ly** *adv*

²**progressive** *n* **1** : one that is progressive **2** : a person believing in moderate political change and social improvement by government action; *esp, cap* : a member of a Progressive Party in the U.S.

pro·hib·it \prō-'hi-bət\ *vb* **1** : to forbid by

authority 2 : to prevent from doing something

pro·hi·bi·tion \ˌprō-ə-'bi-shən\ *n* 1 : the act of prohibiting 2 : the forbidding by law of the sale or manufacture of alcoholic beverages — **pro·hi·bi·tion·ist** \-'bi-shə-nist\ *n* — **pro·hib·i·tive** \prō-'hi-bə-tiv\ *adj* — **pro·hib·i·tive·ly** *adv* — **pro·hib·i·to·ry** \-'hi-bə-ˌtȯr-ē\ *adj*

¹**proj·ect** \'prä-ˌjekt, -jikt\ *n* 1 : a specific plan or design : SCHEME 2 : a planned undertaking ⟨a research ∼⟩

²**pro·ject** \prə-'jekt\ *vb* 1 : to devise in the mind : DESIGN 2 : to throw forward 3 : PROTRUDE 4 : to cause (light or shadow) to fall into space or (an image) to fall on a surface ⟨∼ a beam of light⟩ 5 : to attribute (a thought, feeling, or personal characteristic) to a person, group, or object 6 : to display outwardly — **pro·jec·tion** \-'jek-shən\ *n*

pro·jec·tile \prə-'jek-t³l, -'jek-tī-(ə)l\ *n* 1 : a body hurled or projected by external force; *esp* : a missile for a firearm 2 : a self-propelling weapon

pro·jec·tion·ist \prə-'jek-shə-nist\ *n* : one that operates a motion-picture projector or television equipment

pro·jec·tor \-'jek-tər\ *n* : one that projects; *esp* : a device for projecting pictures on a screen

pro·lapse \prō-'laps, 'prō-ˌ\ *n* : the falling down or slipping of a body part from its usual position

pro·le·gom·e·non \ˌprō-li-'gä-mə-ˌnän, -nən\ *n, pl* **-e·na** \-nə\ : prefatory remarks

pro·le·tar·i·an \ˌprō-lə-'ter-ē-ən\ *n* [L *proletarius* belonging to the lowest class of citizens, fr. *proles* progeny, fr. *pro-* forth + *-oles* (akin to *alere* to nourish)] : a member of the proletariat — **proletarian** *adj*

pro·le·tar·i·at \-ē-ət\ *n* : the laboring class; *esp* : industrial workers who sell their labor to live

pro–life \ˌprō-'līf\ *n* : ANTIABORTION

pro·lif·er·ate \prə-'li-fə-ˌrāt\ *vb* **-at·ed; -at·ing** : to grow or increase by rapid production of new units (as cells, offspring, or nuclear weapons) — **pro·lif·er·a·tion** \-ˌli-fə-'rā-shən\ *n*

pro·lif·ic \prə-'li-fik\ *adj* 1 : producing young or fruit abundantly 2 : marked by abundant inventiveness or productivity ⟨a ∼ writer⟩ — **pro·lif·i·cal·ly** \-fi-k(ə-)lē\ *adv*

pro·logue *also* **pro·log** \'prō-ˌlȯg, -ˌläg\ *n* : PREFACE ⟨∼ of a play⟩

pro·long \prə-'lȯŋ\ *vb* 1 : to lengthen in time : CONTINUE ⟨∼ a meeting⟩ 2 : to lengthen in extent or range ⟨∼ an airport runway⟩ ♦ *Synonyms* PROTRACT, EXTEND, ELONGATE, STRETCH — **pro·lon·ga·tion** \ˌprō-ˌlȯŋ-'gā-shən\ *n*

prom \'präm\ *n* : a formal dance given by a high school or college class

¹**prom·e·nade** \ˌprä-mə-'nād, -'näd\ *vb*

-nad·ed; -nad·ing 1 : to take a promenade 2 : to walk about in or on

²**promenade** *n* [F, fr. *promener* to take for a walk, fr. MF, alter. of OF *pourmener*, fr. *pour-* completely (fr. L *pro-*) + *mener* to lead, fr. LL *minare* to drive, fr. L *minari* to threaten] 1 : a place for strolling 2 : a leisurely walk for pleasure or display 3 : an opening grand march at a formal ball

pro·me·thi·um \prə-'mē-thē-əm\ *n* : a metallic chemical element obtained from uranium or neodymium

prom·i·nence \'prä-mə-nəns\ *n* 1 : something prominent 2 : the quality, state, or fact of being prominent or conspicuous 3 : a mass of cloudlike gas that arises from the sun's chromosphere

prom·i·nent \-nənt\ *adj* 1 : jutting out : PROJECTING 2 : readily noticeable : CONSPICUOUS 3 : DISTINGUISHED, EMINENT ⟨a ∼ lawyer⟩ ♦ *Synonyms* REMARKABLE, OUTSTANDING, STRIKING, SALIENT — **prom·i·nent·ly** *adv*

pro·mis·cu·ous \prə-'mis-kyə-wəs\ *adj* 1 : consisting of various sorts and kinds : MIXED 2 : not restricted to one class or person 3 : having a number of sexual partners ♦ *Synonyms* MISCELLANEOUS, ASSORTED, HETEROGENEOUS, MOTLEY, VARIED — **pro·mis·cu·i·ty** \ˌprä-mis-'kyü-ə-tē, ˌprō-ˌmis-\ *n* — **pro·mis·cu·ous·ly** *adv* — **pro·mis·cu·ous·ness** *n*

¹**prom·ise** \'prä-məs\ *n* 1 : a pledge to do or not to do something specified 2 : ground for expectation of success or improvement 3 : something promised

²**promise** *vb* **prom·ised; prom·is·ing** 1 : to engage to do, bring about, or provide ⟨∼ help⟩ 2 : to suggest beforehand ⟨dark clouds ∼ rain⟩ 3 : to give ground for expectation ⟨it ∼s to be a good game⟩

promising *adj* : likely to succeed or yield good results ⟨a ∼ new medicine⟩ — **prom·is·ing·ly** *adv*

prom·is·so·ry \'prä-mə-ˌsȯr-ē\ *adj* : containing a promise

prom·on·to·ry \'prä-mən-ˌtȯr-ē\ *n, pl* **-ries** : a point of land jutting into the sea : HEADLAND

pro·mote \prə-'mōt\ *vb* **pro·mot·ed; pro·mot·ing** 1 : to advance in station, rank, or honor 2 : to contribute to the growth or prosperity of : FURTHER 3 : LAUNCH — **pro·mo·tion** \-'mō-shən\ *n* — **pro·mo·tion·al** \-shə-nəl\ *adj*

pro·mot·er \-'mō-tər\ *n* : one that promotes; *esp* : one that assumes the financial responsibilities of a sports event ⟨a boxing ∼⟩

¹**prompt** \'prämpt\ *vb* 1 : INCITE 2 : to assist (one acting or reciting) by suggesting the next words 3 : INSPIRE, URGE — **prompt·er** *n*

²**prompt** *adj* 1 : being ready and quick to act; *also* : PUNCTUAL 2 : performed readily or immediately ⟨∼ service⟩ — **prompt·ly** *adv* — **prompt·ness** *n*

prompt·book \-ˌbuk\ *n* : a copy of a play

with directions for performance used by a theater prompter

promp·ti·tude \'prämp-tə-ˌtüd, -ˌtyüd\ *n* : the quality or habit of being prompt : PROMPTNESS

pro·mul·gate \'prä-məl-ˌgāt; prō-'məl-\ *vb* **-gat·ed; -gat·ing** : to make known or put into force by open declaration — **prom·ul·ga·tion** \ˌprä-məl-'gā-shən, ˌprō-(ˌ)məl-\ *n*

pron *abbr* **1** pronoun **2** pronounced **3** pronunciation

prone \'prōn\ *adj* **1** : having a tendency or inclination : DISPOSED **2** : lying face downward; *also* : lying flat or prostrate ♦ **Synonyms** SUBJECT, EXPOSED, OPEN, LIABLE, SUSCEPTIBLE — **prone·ness** *n*

prong \'prȯŋ\ *n* : one of the sharp points of a fork : TINE; *also* : a slender projecting part (as of an antler) — **pronged** \'prȯŋd\ *adj*

prong·horn \'prȯŋ-ˌhȯrn\ *n, pl* **prong·horn** *or* **pronghorns** : a swift horned ruminant mammal chiefly of grasslands of western No. America that resembles an antelope

pro·noun \'prō-ˌnaún\ *n* : a word used as a substitute for a noun

pro·nounce \prə-'naúns\ *vb* **pro·nounced; pro·nounc·ing 1** : to utter officially or as an opinion ⟨∼ sentence⟩ **2** : to employ the organs of speech in order to produce ⟨∼ a word⟩; *esp* : to say or speak correctly ⟨she can't ∼ his name⟩ — **pro·nounce·able** *adj* — **pro·nun·ci·a·tion** \-ˌnən-sē-'ā-shən\ *n*

pro·nounced *adj* : strongly marked : DECIDED ⟨a ∼ dislike⟩

pro·nounce·ment \prə-'naúns-mənt\ *n* : a formal declaration of opinion; *also* : ANNOUNCEMENT

pron·to \'prän-ˌtō\ *adv* [Sp, fr. L *promptus* prompt] : QUICKLY

pro·nu·clear \'prō-'nü-klē-ər, -'nyü-\ *adj* : supporting the use of nuclear-powered electric generating stations

pro·nun·ci·a·men·to \prō-ˌnən-sē-ə-'men-tō\ *n, pl* **-tos** *or* **-toes** : PROCLAMATION, MANIFESTO

¹proof \'prüf\ *n* [ME *prof, prove,* alter. of *preve,* fr. AF *preove,* fr. LL *proba,* fr. L *probare* to test, prove, fr. *probus* good, honest] **1** : the evidence that compels acceptance by the mind of a truth or fact **2** : a process or operation that establishes validity or truth : TEST **3** : a trial impression (as from type) **4** : a trial print from a photographic negative **5** : alcoholic content (as of a beverage) indicated by a number that is twice the percent by volume of alcohol present ⟨whiskey of 90 ∼ is 45% alcohol⟩

²proof *adj* **1** : successful in resisting or repelling ⟨∼ against tampering⟩ ⟨water-*proof*⟩ **2** : of standard strength or quality or alcoholic content

proof·read \-ˌrēd\ *vb* : to read and mark corrections in — **proof·read·er** *n*

¹prop \'präp\ *n* : something that props

²prop *vb* **propped; prop·ping 1** : to support by placing something under or against **2** : SUSTAIN, STRENGTHEN

³prop *n* : PROPERTY 4

⁴prop *n* : PROPELLER

⁵prop *abbr* **1** property **2** proposition **3** proprietor

pro·pa·gan·da \ˌprä-pə-'gan-də, ˌprō-pə-\ *n* [NL, fr. *Congregatio de propaganda fide* Congregation for propagating the faith, organization established by Pope Gregory XVI] : the spreading of ideas or information to further or damage a cause; *also* : ideas or allegations spread for such a purpose — **pro·pa·gan·dist** \-dist\ *n*

pro·pa·gan·dize \-ˌdīz\ *vb* **-dized; -diz·ing** : to subject to or carry on propaganda

prop·a·gate \'prä-pə-ˌgāt\ *vb* **-gat·ed; -gat·ing 1** : to reproduce or cause to reproduce biologically : MULTIPLY **2** : to cause to spread ⟨*propagating* the faith⟩ — **prop·a·ga·tion** \ˌprä-pə-'gā-shən\ *n*

pro·pane \'prō-ˌpān\ *n* : a heavy flammable gas found in petroleum and natural gas and used esp. as a fuel

pro·pel \prə-'pel\ *vb* **pro·pelled; pro·pel·ling** : to drive forward or onward ♦ **Synonyms** PUSH, SHOVE, THRUST

pro·pel·lant *also* **pro·pel·lent** \-'pe-lənt\ *n* : something (as a fuel) that propels — **propellant** *also* **propellent** *adj*

pro·pel·ler \prə-'pe-lər\ *n* : a device consisting of a hub fitted with blades that is used to propel a vehicle (as a motorboat or an airplane)

pro·pen·si·ty \prə-'pen-sə-tē\ *n, pl* **-ties** : an often intense natural inclination or preference

¹prop·er \'prä-pər\ *adj* **1** : referring to one individual only ⟨∼ noun⟩ **2** : belonging characteristically to a species or individual : PECULIAR **3** : very satisfactory : EXCELLENT **4** : strictly limited to a specified thing ⟨the city ∼⟩ **5** : CORRECT ⟨the ∼ way to proceed⟩ **6** : strictly decorous : GENTEEL **7** : marked by suitability or rightness ⟨∼ punishment⟩ ♦ **Synonyms** MEET, APPROPRIATE, FITTING, SEEMLY — **prop·er·ly** *adv*

²proper *n* : the parts of the Mass that vary according to the liturgical calendar

prop·er·tied \'prä-pər-tēd\ *adj* : owning property and esp. much property

prop·er·ty \'prä-pər-tē\ *n, pl* **-ties 1** : a quality peculiar to an individual or thing **2** : something owned; *esp* : a piece of real estate **3** : OWNERSHIP **4** : an article or object used in a play or motion picture other than painted scenery and actor's costumes

proph·e·cy *also* **proph·e·sy** \'prä-fə-sē\ *n, pl* **-cies** *also* **-sies 1** : an inspired utterance of a prophet **2** : PREDICTION

proph·e·sy \-ˌsī\ *vb* **-sied; -sy·ing 1** : to speak or utter by divine inspiration **2** : PREDICT — **proph·e·si·er** *n*

proph·et \'prä-fət\ *n* [ME *prophete,* fr. AF, fr. L *propheta,* fr. Gk *prophētēs,* fr. *pro* for + *phanai* to speak] **1** : one who utters divinely inspired revelations **2** : one who foretells future events

proph·et·ess \'prä-fə-təs\ *n* : a woman who is a prophet

pro·phet·ic \prə-'fe-tik\ *or* **pro·phet·i·cal**

\-ti-kəl\ *adj* : of, relating to, or characteristic of a prophet or prophecy — **pro·phet·i·cal·ly** \-ti-k(ə-)lē\ *adv*

Proph·ets \'prä-fəts\ *n pl* — see BIBLE table

¹**pro·phy·lac·tic** \ˌprō-fə-'lak-tik, ˌprä-\ *adj* **1** : preventing or guarding from the spread or occurrence of disease or infection **2** : PREVENTIVE

²**prophylactic** *n* : something prophylactic; *esp* : a device (as a condom) for preventing venereal infection or conception

pro·phy·lax·is \-'lak-səs\ *n, pl* **-lax·es** \-'lak-ˌsēz\ : measures designed to preserve health and prevent the spread of disease

pro·pin·qui·ty \prə-'piṇ-kwə-tē\ *n* **1** : KINSHIP **2** : nearness in place or time : PROXIMITY

pro·pi·ti·ate \prō-'pi-shē-ˌāt\ *vb* **-at·ed; -at·ing** : to gain or regain the favor of : APPEASE 〈~ the angry gods〉 — **pro·pi·ti·a·tion** \-ˌpi-shē-'ā-shən\ *n* — **pro·pi·tia·to·ry** \-'pi-shē-ə-ˌtȯr-ē\ *adj*

pro·pi·tious \prə-'pi-shəs\ *adj* **1** : favorably disposed 〈~ deities〉 **2** : being of good omen 〈~ circumstances〉

prop·man \'präp-ˌman\ *n* : one who is in charge of stage properties

pro·po·nent \prə-'pō-nənt\ *n* : one who argues in favor of something

¹**pro·por·tion** \prə-'pȯr-shən\ *n* **1** : BALANCE, SYMMETRY **2** : SHARE, QUOTA **3** : the relation of one part to another or to the whole with respect to magnitude, quantity, or degree : RATIO **4** : SIZE, DEGREE — **in proportion** : PROPORTIONAL

²**proportion** *vb* **-tioned; -tion·ing 1** : to adjust (a part or thing) in size relative to other parts or things **2** : to make the parts of harmonious

pro·por·tion·al \prə-'pȯr-shə-nəl\ *adj* : corresponding in size, degree, or intensity; *also* : having the same or a constant ratio — **pro·por·tion·al·ly** *adv*

pro·por·tion·ate \prə-'pȯr-shə-nət\ *adj* : PROPORTIONAL — **pro·por·tion·ate·ly** *adv*

pro·pose \prə-'pōz\ *vb* **pro·posed; pro·pos·ing 1** : PLAN, INTEND 〈~s to buy a house〉 **2** : to make an offer of marriage **3** : to offer for consideration : SUGGEST 〈~ a policy〉 — **pro·pos·al** \-'pō-zəl\ *n* — **pro·pos·er** *n*

¹**prop·o·si·tion** \ˌprä-pə-'zi-shən\ *n* **1** : something proposed for consideration : PROPOSAL **2** : a request for sexual intercourse **3** : a statement of something to be discussed, proved, or explained **4** : SITUATION, AFFAIR 〈a tough ~〉 — **prop·o·si·tion·al** \-'zi-shə-nəl\ *adj*

²**proposition** *vb* **-tioned; -tion·ing** : to make a proposal to; *esp* : to suggest sexual intercourse to

pro·pound \prə-'paund\ *vb* : to set forth for consideration 〈~ a doctrine〉

pro·pri·etary \prə-'prī-ə-ˌter-ē\ *adj* **1** : of, relating to, or characteristic of a proprietor or proprietorship 〈~ rights〉 **2** : made and sold by one with the sole right to do so 〈~ medicines〉 〈~ software〉

pro·pri·e·tor \prə-'prī-ə-tər\ *n* : OWNER — **pro·pri·e·tor·ship** *n*

pro·pri·e·tress \-'prī-ə-trəs\ *n* : a woman who is a proprietor

pro·pri·e·ty \prə-'prī-ə-tē\ *n, pl* **-ties 1** : the standard of what is socially acceptable in conduct or speech **2** *pl* : the customs of polite society

props \'präps\ *n sing or pl* **1** *slang* : DUE **1** 〈gave him his ~〉 **2** *slang* : RESPECT **2** 〈earned the ~ of his peers〉 **3** *slang* : ACKNOWLEDGMENT 〈deserves ~ for the effort〉

pro·pul·sion \prə-'pəl-shən\ *n* **1** : the action or process of propelling **2** : something that propels — **pro·pul·sive** \-siv\ *adj*

pro ra·ta \(ˌ)prō-'rä-tə, -'rä-\ *adv* : in proportion to the share of each : PROPORTIONATELY

pro·rate \(ˌ)prō-'rāt\ *vb* **pro·rat·ed; pro·rat·ing** : to divide, distribute, or assess proportionately

pro·rogue \prə-'rōg\ *vb* **pro·rogued; pro·rogu·ing** : to suspend or end a session of (a legislative body) — **pro·ro·ga·tion** \ˌprō-rō-'gā-shən\ *n*

pros *pl of* PRO

pro·sa·ic \prō-'zā-ik\ *adj* : lacking imagination or excitement : DULL

pro·sce·ni·um \prō-'sē-nē-əm\ *n* **1** : the part of a stage in front of the curtain **2** : the wall containing the arch that frames the stage

pro·scribe \prō-'skrīb\ *vb* **pro·scribed; pro·scrib·ing 1** : OUTLAW **2** : to condemn or forbid as harmful — **pro·scrip·tion** \-'skrip-shən\ *n*

prose \'prōz\ *n* [ME, fr. AF, fr. L *prosa*, fr. fem. of *prorsus, prosus*, straightforward, being in prose, alter. of *proversus*, pp. of *provertere* to turn forward] : the ordinary language people use in speaking or writing

pros·e·cute \'prä-si-ˌkyüt\ *vb* **-cut·ed; -cut·ing 1** : to follow to the end 〈~ an investigation〉 **2** : to seek legal punishment of 〈~ a forger〉 — **pros·e·cu·tion** \ˌprä-si-'kyü-shən\ *n* — **pros·e·cu·tor** \'prä-si-ˌkyü-tər\ *n* — **pros·e·cu·to·ri·al** \ˌprä-si-kyü-'tȯr-ē-əl\ *adj*

¹**pros·e·lyte** \'prä-sə-ˌlīt\ *n* : a new convert to a religion, belief, or party — **pros·e·ly·tism** \-ˌlī-ˌti-zəm\ *n*

²**proselyte** *vb* **-lyt·ed; -lyt·ing** : PROSELYTIZE

pros·e·ly·tise *Brit var of* PROSELYTIZE

pros·e·ly·tize \'prä-sə-lə-ˌtīz\ *vb* **-tized; -tiz·ing 1** : to induce someone to convert to one's faith **2** : to recruit someone to join one's party, institution, or cause

pros·o·dy \'prä-sə-dē, -zə-\ *n, pl* **-dies** : the study of versification and esp. of metrical structure — **pro·sod·ic** \prə-'sä-dik\ *adj*

¹**pros·pect** \'prä-ˌspekt\ *n* **1** : an extensive view; *also* : OUTLOOK **2** : the act of looking forward **3** : a mental vision of something to come **4** : something that is awaited or expected : POSSIBILITY **5** : a potential buyer or customer; *also* : a likely candidate (as for a job) — **pro·spec-**

tive \prǝ-'spek-tiv, 'prä-ˌspek-\ adj — **pro·spec·tive·ly** adv

²**pros·pect** \'prä-ˌspekt\ vb : to explore esp. for mineral deposits — **pros·pec·tor** \-ˌspek-tǝr, prä-'spek-\ n

pro·spec·tus \prǝ-'spek-tǝs\ n : a preliminary statement that describes an enterprise and is distributed to prospective buyers or participants

pros·per \'präs-pǝr\ vb **pros·pered; pros·per·ing** : SUCCEED; esp : to achieve economic success

pros·per·i·ty \präs-'per-ǝ-tē\ n : thriving condition : SUCCESS; esp : economic well-being

pros·per·ous \'präs-pǝ-rǝs\ adj 1 : FAVORABLE ⟨~ winds⟩ 2 : marked by success or economic well-being ⟨a ~ business⟩

pros·ta·glan·din \ˌpräs-tǝ-'glan-dǝn\ n : any of various oxygenated unsaturated fatty acids of animals that perform a variety of hormonelike actions

pros·tate \'präs-ˌtāt\ n [NL prostata, fr. Gk prostatēs, fr. proïstanai to put in front] : PROSTATE GLAND — **pros·tat·ic** \prä-'sta-tik\ adj

prostate gland n : a glandular body about the base of the male urethra that produces a secretion which is a major part of the fluid ejaculated during an orgasm

pros·ta·ti·tis \ˌpräs-tǝ-'tī-tǝs\ n : inflammation of the prostate gland

pros·the·sis \präs-'thē-sǝs, 'präs-thǝ-\ n, pl **-the·ses** \-ˌsēz\ : an artificial replacement for a missing body part — **pros·thet·ic** \präs-'the-tik\ adj

pros·thet·ics \-'the-tiks\ n pl : the surgical or dental specialty concerned with the design, construction, and fitting of prostheses

¹**pros·ti·tute** \'präs-tǝ-ˌtüt, -ˌtyüt\ vb **-tut·ed; -tut·ing** 1 : to offer indiscriminately for sexual activity esp. for money 2 : to devote to corrupt or unworthy purposes — **pros·ti·tu·tion** \ˌpräs-tǝ-'tü-shǝn, -'tyü-\ n

²**prostitute** n : one who engages in sexual activities for money

¹**pros·trate** \'prä-ˌstrāt\ adj 1 : stretched out with face on the ground in adoration or submission 2 : lying flat 3 : completely overcome ⟨~ with a cold⟩

²**prostrate** vb **pros·trat·ed; pros·trat·ing** 1 : to throw or put into a prostrate position 2 : to reduce to a weak or powerless condition — **pros·tra·tion** \prä-'strā-shǝn\ n

prosy \'prō-zē\ adj **pros·i·er; -est** 1 : PROSAIC, ORDINARY 2 : TEDIOUS

Prot abbr Protestant

prot·ac·tin·i·um \ˌprō-ˌtak-'ti-nē-ǝm\ n : a metallic radioactive chemical element of relatively short life

prot·ag·o·nist \prō-'ta-gǝ-nist\ n 1 : the principal character in a drama or story 2 : a leader or supporter of a cause

pro·te·an \'prō-tē-ǝn\ adj : able to assume different shapes or roles

pro·tect \prǝ-'tekt\ vb : to shield from injury : GUARD

pro·tec·tion \prǝ-'tek-shǝn\ n 1 : the act of protecting : the state of being protected 2 : one that protects ⟨wear a helmet as a ~⟩ 3 : the supervision or support of one that is smaller and weaker 4 : the freeing of producers from foreign competition in their home market by high duties on competitive goods — **pro·tec·tive** \-'tek-tiv\ adj

pro·tec·tion·ist \-shǝ-nist\ n : an advocate of government economic protection for domestic producers through restrictions on foreign competitors — **pro·tec·tion·ism** \-shǝ-ˌni-zǝm\ n

pro·tec·tor \prǝ-'tek-tǝr\ n 1 : one that protects : GUARDIAN 2 : a device used to prevent injury : GUARD 3 : REGENT 1

pro·tec·tor·ate \-tǝ-rǝt\ n 1 : government by a protector 2 : the relationship of superior authority assumed by one state over a dependent one; also : the dependent political unit in such a relationship

pro·té·gé \'prō-tǝ-ˌzhā\ n [F] : one who is protected, trained, or guided by an influential person

pro·tein \'prō-ˌtēn\ n [F protéine, fr. LGk prōteios primary, fr. Gk prōtos first] : any of various complex nitrogen-containing substances that consist of chains of amino acids, are present in all living cells, and are an essential part of the human diet

pro tem \prō-'tem\ adv : PRO TEMPORE

pro tem·po·re \prō-'tem-pǝ-rē\ adv [L] : for the time being

Pro·te·ro·zo·ic \ˌprä-tǝ-rǝ-'zō-ik, ˌprō-\ adj : of, relating to, or being the eon of geologic history between the Archean and the Phanerozoic — **Proterozoic** n

¹**pro·test** \'prō-ˌtest\ n 1 : the act of protesting; esp : an organized public demonstration of disapproval 2 : a complaint or objection against an idea, an act, or a course of action

²**pro·test** \prō-'test\ vb 1 : to assert positively : make solemn declaration of ⟨~s his innocence⟩ 2 : to object strongly : make a protest against ⟨~ a ruling⟩ — **pro·tes·ta·tion** \ˌprä-tǝs-'tā-shǝn\ n — **pro·test·er** or **pro·tes·tor** \-tǝr\ n

Prot·es·tant \'prä-tǝs-tǝnt, 3 also prǝ-'tes-\ n 1 : a member or adherent of one of the Christian churches deriving from the Reformation 2 : a Christian not of a Catholic or Orthodox church 3 not cap : one who makes a protest — **Prot·es·tant·ism** \'prä-tǝs-tǝn-ˌti-zǝm\ n

pro·tha·la·mi·on \ˌprō-thǝ-'lā-mē-ǝn\ or **pro·tha·la·mi·um** \-mē-ǝm\ n, pl **-mia** \-mē-ǝ\ : a song in celebration of a marriage

pro·to·col \'prō-tǝ-ˌkȯl\ n [MF prothocole, fr. ML protocollum, fr. LGk prōtokollon first sheet of a papyrus roll bearing data of manufacture, fr. Gk prōtos first + kollan to glue together, fr. kolla glue] 1 : an original draft or record 2 : a preliminary memorandum of diplomatic negotiation 3 : a code of diplomatic or military etiquette 4 : a set of conventions for formatting data in an electronic communications system

pro·ton \\'prō-ˌtän\\ *n* [Gk *prōton*, neut. of *prōtos* first] : a positively charged atomic particle present in all atomic nuclei — **pro·ton·ic** \\-'tä-nik\\ *adj*

pro·to·plasm \\'prō-tə-ˌpla-zəm\\ *n* : the complex colloidal largely protein substance of living plant and animal cells — **pro·to·plas·mic** \\ˌprō-tə-'plaz-mik\\ *adj*

pro·to·type \\'prō-tə-ˌtīp\\ *n* : an original model : ARCHETYPE

pro·to·zo·an \\ˌprō-tə-'zō-ən\\ *n* : any of a phylum or subkingdom of unicellular lower invertebrate animals that include some pathogenic parasites of humans and domestic animals — **protozoan** *adj*

pro·tract \\prō-'trakt\\ *vb* : to prolong in time or space ♦ **Synonyms** EXTEND, LENGTHEN, ELONGATE, STRETCH

pro·trac·tor \\-'trak-tər\\ *n* : an instrument for drawing and measuring angles

pro·trude \\prō-'trüd\\ *vb* **pro·trud·ed**; **pro·trud·ing** : to stick out or cause to stick out : jut out — **pro·tru·sion** \\-'trü-zhən\\ *n*

pro·tu·ber·ance \\prō-'tü-bə-rəns, -'tyü-\\ *n* : something that protrudes

pro·tu·ber·ant \\-rənt\\ *adj* : extending beyond the surrounding surface in a bulge

proud \\'praud\\ *adj* **1** : having or showing excessive self-esteem : HAUGHTY **2** : highly pleased : EXULTANT **3** : having proper self-respect ⟨too ~ to beg⟩ **4** : GLORIOUS ⟨a ~ occasion⟩ **5** : SPIRITED ⟨a ~ steed⟩ ♦ **Synonyms** ARROGANT, INSOLENT, OVERBEARING, DISDAINFUL — **proud·ly** *adv*

prov *abbr* **1** province; provincial **2** provisional

Prov *abbr* Proverbs

prove \\'prüv\\ *vb* **proved**; **proved** *or* **prov·en** \\'prü-vən\\; **prov·ing** **1** : to test by experiment or by a standard **2** : to establish the truth of by argument or evidence **3** : to show to be correct, valid, or genuine **4** : to turn out esp. after trial or test ⟨the car *proved* to be a good choice⟩ — **prov·able** \\'prü-və-bəl\\ *adj*

prov·e·nance \\'prä-və-nəns\\ *n* : ORIGIN, SOURCE

Pro·ven·çal \\ˌprō-ˌvän-'säl, ˌprä-vən-\\ *n* **1** : a native or inhabitant of Provence **2** : OCCITAN — **Provençal** *adj*

prov·en·der \\'prä-vən-dər\\ *n* **1** : dry food for domestic animals : FEED **2** : FOOD, VICTUALS

pro·ve·nience \\prə-'vē-nyəns\\ *n* : ORIGIN, SOURCE

prov·erb \\'prä-ˌvərb\\ *n* : a pithy popular saying : ADAGE

pro·ver·bi·al \\prə-'vər-bē-əl\\ *adj* **1** : of, relating to, or resembling a proverb **2** : commonly spoken of

Proverbs *n* — see BIBLE table

pro·vide \\prə-'vīd\\ *vb* **pro·vid·ed**; **pro·vid·ing** [ME, fr. L *providēre*, lit., to see ahead, fr. *pro-* forward + *vidēre* to see] **1** : to take measures beforehand ⟨~ against inflation⟩ **2** : to make a proviso or stipulation **3** : to supply what is need-

ed ⟨~ for a family⟩ **4** : EQUIP **5** : to supply for use : YIELD — **pro·vid·er** *n*

pro·vid·ed *conj* : on condition that : IF

prov·i·dence \\'prä-və-dəns\\ *n* **1** *often cap* : divine guidance or care **2** *cap* : GOD **1** **3** : the quality or state of being provident

prov·i·dent \\-dənt\\ *adj* **1** : making provision for the future : PRUDENT **2** : FRUGAL — **prov·i·dent·ly** *adv*

prov·i·den·tial \\ˌprä-və-'den-chəl\\ *adj* **1** : of, relating to, or determined by Providence **2** : OPPORTUNE, LUCKY

providing *conj* : PROVIDED

prov·ince \\'prä-vəns\\ *n* **1** : an administrative district or division of a country **2** *pl* : all of a country except the metropolises **3** : proper business or scope : SPHERE ⟨the ~ of the jury⟩

pro·vin·cial \\prə-'vin-chəl\\ *adj* **1** : of or relating to a province **2** : limited in outlook : NARROW ⟨~ ideas⟩ — **pro·vin·cial·ism** \\-chə-ˌli-zəm\\ *n*

proving ground *n* : a place for scientific experimentation or testing

¹**pro·vi·sion** \\prə-'vi-zhən\\ *n* **1** : the act or process of providing; *also* : a measure taken beforehand **2** : a stock of needed supplies; *esp* : a stock of food — usu. used in pl. **3** : PROVISO

²**provision** *vb* : to supply with provisions

pro·vi·sion·al \\-'vi-zhə-nəl\\ *adj* : provided for a temporary need : CONDITIONAL — **pro·vi·sion·al·ly** *adv*

pro·vi·so \\prə-'vī-zō\\ *n, pl* **-sos** *also* **-soes** [ME, fr. ML *proviso quod* provided that] : an article or clause that introduces a condition : STIPULATION

pro·vo·ca·teur \\prō-ˌvä-kə-'tər\\ *n* : one who provokes

prov·o·ca·tion \\ˌprä-və-'kā-shən\\ *n* **1** : the act of provoking **2** : something that provokes

pro·voc·a·tive \\prə-'vä-kə-tiv\\ *adj* : serving to provoke or excite

pro·voke \\prə-'vōk\\ *vb* **pro·voked**; **pro·vok·ing** **1** : to incite to anger : INCENSE **2** : to call forth : EVOKE ⟨a remark that *provoked* laughter⟩ **3** : to stir up on purpose ⟨~ an argument⟩ ♦ **Synonyms** IRRITATE, EXASPERATE, AGGRAVATE, INFLAME, RILE, PIQUE — **pro·vok·er** *n*

pro·vo·lo·ne \\ˌprō-və-'lō-nē\\ *n* : a usu. firm pliant often smoked Italian cheese

pro·vost \\'prō-ˌvōst, 'prä-vəst\\ *n* : a high official : DIGNITARY; *esp* : a high-ranking university administrative officer

pro·vost mar·shal \\ˌprō-ˌvō-'mär-shəl\\ *n* : an officer who supervises the military police of a command

prow \\'prau\\ *n* : the bow of a ship

prow·ess \\'prau-əs\\ *n* **1** : military valor and skill **2** : extraordinary ability

prowl \\'prau(-ə)l\\ *vb* : to roam about stealthily — **prowl** *n* — **prowl·er** *n*

prox·i·mal \\'präk-sə-məl\\ *adj* **1** : next to or nearest the point of attachment or origin; *esp* : located toward the center of the body **2** : of, relating to, or being the mesial and distal surfaces of a tooth — **prox·i·mal·ly** *adv*

prox·i·mate \\'präk-sə-mət\\ *adj* **1** : DIRECT ⟨the ~ cause⟩ **2** : very near

prox·im·i·ty \präk-ˈsi-mə-tē\ *n* : NEAR-NESS ⟨lives in ∼ to a bus stop⟩

prox·i·mo \ˈpräk-sə-ˌmō\ *adj* [L *proximo mense* in the next month] : of or occurring in the next month after the present

proxy \ˈpräk-sē\ *n, pl* **prox·ies** [ME *proxi, procucie,* alter. of *procuracie,* fr. AF, fr. ML *procuratia,* alter. of L *procuratio* appointment of another as an agent, fr. *procurare* to take care of] : the authority or power to act for another; *also* : a document giving such authorization — **proxy** *adj*

prude \ˈprüd\ *n* : a person who shows or affects extreme modesty — **prud·ery** \ˈprü-də-rē\ *n* — **prud·ish** *adj* — **prud·ish·ly** *adv*

pru·dent \ˈprü-dᵊnt\ *adj* **1** : shrewd in the management of practical affairs **2** : CAUTIOUS, DISCREET **3** : PROVIDENT, FRUGAL ♦ **Synonyms** JUDICIOUS, FORESIGHTED, SENSIBLE, SANE — **pru·dence** \-dᵊns\ *n* — **pru·den·tial** \prü-ˈden-chəl\ *adj* — **pru·dent·ly** *adv*

¹prune \ˈprün\ *n* : a dried plum

²prune *vb* **pruned; prun·ing** : to cut off unwanted parts (as of a tree)

pru·ri·ent \ˈprür-ē-ənt\ *adj* : LASCIVIOUS; *also* : exciting to lasciviousness — **pru·ri·ence** \-ē-əns\ *n*

¹pry \ˈprī\ *vb* **pried; pry·ing** : to look closely or inquisitively; *esp* : SNOOP

²pry *vb* **pried; pry·ing** **1** : to raise, move, or pull apart with a pry or lever **2** : to detach or open with difficulty

³pry *n* : a tool for prying

Ps *or* **Psa** *abbr* Psalms

PS *abbr* **1** [L *postscriptum*] postscript **2** public school

PSA *abbr* public service announcement

psalm \ˈsäm, ˈsälm\ *n, often cap* [ME, fr. OE *psealm,* fr. LL *psalmus,* fr. Gk *psalmos,* lit., twanging of a harp, fr. *psallein* to pluck, play a stringed instrument] : a sacred song or poem; *esp* : one of the hymns collected in the Book of Psalms — **psalm·ist** *n*

psalm·o·dy \ˈsä-mə-dē, ˈsäl-\ *n* : the singing of psalms in worship

Psalms *n* — see BIBLE table

Psal·ter \ˈsȯl-tər\ *n* : the Book of Psalms; *also* : a collection of the Psalms arranged for devotional use

pseud *abbr* pseudonym; pseudonymous

pseu·do \ˈsü-dō\ *adj* : SPURIOUS, SHAM

pseu·do·nym \ˈsü-də-ˌnim\ *n* : a fictitious name — **pseu·don·y·mous** \sü-ˈdä-nə-məs\ *adj*

pseu·do·sci·ence \ˌsü-dō-ˈsī-əns\ *n* : a system of theories, assumptions, and methods erroneously regarded as scientific — **pseu·do·sci·en·tif·ic** \-ˌsī-ən-ˈti-fik\ *adj*

PSG *abbr* platoon sergeant

¹psi \ˈsī, ˈpsī\ *n* : the 23d letter of the Greek alphabet — Ψ or ψ

²psi *abbr* pounds per square inch

psit·ta·co·sis \ˌsi-tə-ˈkō-səs\ *n* : an infectious disease of birds marked by diarrhea and wasting and transmissible to humans

pso·ri·a·sis \sə-ˈrī-ə-səs\ *n* : a chronic skin disease characterized by red patches covered with white scales

PST *abbr* Pacific standard time

¹psych *or* **psyche** \ˈsīk\ *vb* **psych·ing** **1** : OUTWIT, OUTGUESS; *also* : to analyze beforehand **2** : INTIMIDATE; *also* : to prepare oneself psychologically ⟨get *psyched* up for the game⟩

²psych *abbr* psychology

psy·che \ˈsī-kē\ *n* : SOUL, PERSONALITY; *also* : MIND

psy·che·del·ic \ˌsī-kə-ˈde-lik\ *adj* **1** : of, relating to, or causing abnormal psychic effects ⟨∼ drugs⟩ **2** : relating to the taking of psychedelic drugs ⟨∼ experience⟩ **3** : imitating, suggestive of, or reproducing the effects of psychedelic drugs ⟨∼ art⟩ ⟨∼ colors⟩ — **psychedelic** *n* — **psy·che·del·i·cal·ly** \-li-k(ə-)lē\ *adv*

psy·chi·a·try \sə-ˈkī-ə-trē, sī-\ *n* [prob. fr. F *psychiatrie,* fr. *psychiatre* psychiatrist, fr. Gk *psychē* breath, soul + *iatros* physician] : a branch of medicine dealing with mental, emotional, and behavioral disorders — **psy·chi·at·ric** \ˌsī-kē-ˈa-trik\ *adj* — **psy·chi·a·trist** \sə-ˈkī-ə-trist, sī-\ *n*

¹psy·chic \ˈsī-kik\ *also* **psy·chi·cal** \-ki-kəl\ *adj* **1** : of or relating to the psyche **2** : lying outside the sphere of physical science **3** : sensitive to nonphysical or supernatural forces — **psy·chi·cal·ly** \-k(ə-)lē\ *adv*

²psychic *n* : a person apparently sensitive to nonphysical forces; *also* : MEDIUM 6

psy·cho \ˈsī-kō\ *n, pl* **psychos** : a mentally disturbed person — **psycho** *adj*

psy·cho·ac·tive \ˌsī-kō-ˈak-tiv\ *adj* : affecting the mind or behavior

psy·cho·anal·y·sis \ˌsī-kō-ə-ˈna-lə-səs\ *n* : a method of dealing with psychic disorders by having the patient talk freely about personal experiences and esp. about early childhood and dreams — **psy·cho·an·a·lyst** \-ˈa-nə-list\ *n* — **psy·cho·an·a·lyt·ic** \-ˌa-nə-ˈli-tik\ *adj* — **psy·cho·an·a·lyze** \-ˈa-nə-ˌlīz\ *vb*

psy·cho·bab·ble \ˈsī-kō-ˌba-bəl\ *n* : psychological jargon esp. when used in a trite or simplistic manner

psy·cho·dra·ma \ˌsī-kō-ˈdrä-mə, -ˈdra-\ *n* **1** : an extemporized dramatization designed to afford catharsis for one or more of the participants from whose life the plot is taken **2** : a dramatic event or story with psychological overtones

psy·cho·gen·ic \-ˈje-nik\ *adj* : originating in the mind or in mental or emotional conflict

psy·cho·graph·ics \ˌsī-kō-ˈgra-fiks\ *n sing or pl* : market research or statistics classifying population groups according to psychological variables

psychol *abbr* psychologist; psychology

psy·chol·o·gy \sī-ˈkä-lə-jē\ *n, pl* **-gies 1** : the science of mind and behavior **2** : the mental and behavioral characteristics of an individual or group — **psy·cho·log·i·cal** \ˌsī-kə-ˈlä-ji-kəl\ *adj* — **psy·cho·log·i·cal·ly** \-ji-k(ə-)lē\ *adv* — **psy·chol·o·gist** \sī-ˈkä-lə-jist\ *n*

psy·cho·path \ˈsī-kō-ˌpath\ *n* : a mentally ill or unstable person; *esp* : a person who engages in antisocial behavior and exhibits a pervasive disregard for the rights, feelings, and safety of others — **psy·cho·path·ic** \ˌsī-kə-ˈpa-thik\ adj

psy·cho·sex·u·al \ˌsī-kō-ˈsek-shə-wəl\ adj **1** : of or relating to the mental, emotional, and behavioral aspects of sexual development **2** : of or relating to the physiological psychology of sex

psy·cho·sis \sī-ˈkō-səs\ n, pl **-cho·ses** \-ˌsēz\ : a serious mental illness (as schizophrenia) marked by loss of or greatly lessened ability to test whether what one is thinking and feeling about the real world is really true

psy·cho·so·cial \ˌsī-kō-ˈsō-shəl\ adj **1** : involving both psychological and social aspects **2** : relating social conditions to mental health

psy·cho·so·mat·ic \ˌsī-kō-sə-ˈma-tik\ adj : of, relating to, involving, or concerned with bodily symptoms caused by mental or emotional disturbance

psy·cho·ther·a·py \ˌsī-kō-ˈther-ə-pē\ n : treatment of mental or emotional disorder or of related bodily ills by psychological means — **psy·cho·ther·a·pist** \-pist\ n

psy·chot·ic \sī-ˈkä-tik\ adj : of or relating to psychosis ⟨~ behavior⟩ ⟨a ~ patient⟩ — **psychotic** n

psy·cho·tro·pic \ˌsī-kə-ˈtrō-pik\ adj : acting on the mind ⟨~ drugs⟩

pt abbr **1** part **2** payment **3** pint **4** point **5** port

Pt symbol platinum

PT abbr **1** Pacific time **2** part-time **3** physical therapy **4** physical training

PTA abbr Parent-Teacher Association

ptar·mi·gan \ˈtär-mi-gən\ n, pl **-gan** or **-gans** : any of various grouses of northern regions with completely feathered feet

PT boat \ˌ(ˌ)pē-ˈtē-\ n [patrol torpedo] : a small fast patrol craft usu. armed with torpedos

pte abbr, Brit private

ptg abbr printing

PTO abbr **1** Parent-Teacher Organization **2** please turn over

pto·maine \ˈtō-ˌmān\ n : any of various chemical substances formed by bacteria in decaying matter (as meat) and including a few poisonous ones

Pu symbol plutonium

¹pub \ˈpəb\ n **1** chiefly Brit : PUBLIC HOUSE **2** : TAVERN

²pub abbr **1** public **2** publication **3** published; publisher; publishing

pu·ber·ty \ˈpyü-bər-tē\ n : the condition of being or period of becoming first capable of reproducing sexually — **pu·ber·tal** \-bər-tᵊl\ adj

pu·bes \ˈpyü-bēz\ n, pl **pubes** [NL, fr. L. manhood, body hair, pubic region] **1** : the hair that appears upon the lower middle region of the abdomen at puberty **2** : the pubic region

pu·bes·cence \pyü-ˈbe-sᵊns\ n **1** : the quality or state of being pubescent **2** : a pubescent covering or surface

pu·bes·cent \-sᵊnt\ adj **1** : arriving at or having reached puberty **2** : covered with fine soft short hairs

pu·bic \ˈpyü-bik\ adj : of, relating to, or situated near the pubes or the pubis

pu·bis \ˈpyü-bəs\ n, pl **pu·bes** \-bēz\ : the ventral and anterior of the three principal bones composing either half of the pelvis

publ abbr **1** publication **2** published; publisher

¹pub·lic \ˈpə-blik\ adj **1** : exposed to general view ⟨the story became ~⟩ **2** : of, relating to, or affecting the people as a whole ⟨~ opinion⟩ **3** : CIVIC, GOVERNMENTAL ⟨~ expenditures⟩ **4** : of, relating to, or serving the community ⟨~ officials⟩ **5** : not private : SOCIAL ⟨~ morality⟩ **6** : open to all ⟨~ library⟩ **7** : well known : PROMINENT ⟨~ figures⟩ **8** : supported by public funds and private contributions rather than by income from commercials — **pub·lic·ly** adv

²public n **1** : the people as a whole : POPULACE **2** : a group of people having common interests ⟨the movie-going ~⟩

pub·li·can \ˈpə-bli-kən\ n **1** : a Jewish tax collector for the ancient Romans **2** chiefly Brit : the licensee of a pub

pub·li·ca·tion \ˌpə-blə-ˈkā-shən\ n **1** : the act or process of publishing **2** : a published work

public house n **1** : INN **2** chiefly Brit : a licensed saloon or bar

pub·li·cise Brit var of PUBLICIZE

pub·li·cist \ˈpə-blə-sist\ n : one that publicizes; esp : PRESS AGENT

pub·lic·i·ty \(ˌ)pə-ˈbli-sə-tē\ n **1** : information with news value issued to gain public attention or support **2** : public attention or acclaim

pub·li·cize \ˈpə-blə-ˌsīz\ vb **-cized; -ciz·ing** : to bring to public attention : ADVERTISE ⟨publicizing his book⟩

pub·lic–key \ˈpə-blik-ˈkē\ n : the publicly shared element of a code usable only to encode messages

public relations n sing or pl : the business of fostering public goodwill toward a person, firm, or institution; also : the degree of goodwill and understanding achieved

public school n **1** : an endowed secondary boarding school in Great Britain offering a classical curriculum and preparation for the universities or public service **2** : a free tax-supported school controlled by a local governmental authority

public–spirited adj : motivated by devotion to the general or national welfare

public works n pl : works (as schools or highways) constructed with public funds for public use

pub·lish \ˈpə-blish\ vb **1** : to make generally known : announce publicly **2** : to produce or release literature, information, musical scores or sometimes recordings, or art for sale to the public — **pub·lish·er** n

¹puck \ˈpək\ n : a mischievous sprite — **puck·ish** adj — **puck·ish·ly** adv

²puck n : a disk used in ice hockey

¹puck·er \ˈpə-kər\ vb : to contract into folds or wrinkles

²puck·er *n* : FOLD, WRINKLE

pud·ding \\'pu̇-diŋ\\ *n* : a soft, spongy, or thick creamy dessert

pud·dle \\'pə-dᵊl\\ *n* : a very small pool of usu. dirty or muddy water

pu·den·dum \\pyu̇-'den-dəm\\ *n, pl* **-da** \\-də\\ [NL, fr. L *pudēre* to be ashamed] : the human external genital organs esp. of a woman

pudgy \\'pə-jē\\ *adj* **pudg·i·er; -est** : being short and plump : CHUBBY

pueb·lo \\'pwe-blō, pü-'e-\\ *n, pl* **-los** [Sp, village, lit., people, fr. L *populus*] **1** : an American Indian village of Arizona or New Mexico that consists of flat-roofed stone or adobe houses joined in groups sometimes several stories high **2** *cap* : a member of a group of American Indian peoples of the southwestern U.S.

pu·er·ile \\'pyu̇-ə-rəl\\ *adj* : CHILDISH, SILLY ⟨~ remarks⟩ — **pu·er·il·i·ty** \\,pyu̇-ə-'ri-lə-tē\\ *n*

pu·er·per·al \\pyu̇-'ər-pə-rəl\\ *adj* : of, relating to, or occurring during childbirth or the period immediately following ⟨~ infection⟩ ⟨~ depression⟩

puerperal fever *n* : an abnormal condition that results from infection of the placental site following childbirth or abortion

¹puff \\'pəf\\ *vb* **1** : to blow in short gusts **2** : PANT **3** : to emit small whiffs or clouds **4** : BLUSTER, BRAG **5** : INFLATE, SWELL **6** : to make proud or conceited **7** : to praise extravagantly

²puff *n* **1** : a short discharge (as of air or smoke); *also* : a slight explosive sound accompanying it **2** : a light fluffy pastry **3** : a slight swelling **4** : a fluffy mass; *also* : a small pad for applying cosmetic powder **5** : a laudatory notice or review — **puffy** *adj*

³puff *adj* : of, relating to, or designed for promotion or flattery ⟨~ articles on the new TV series⟩

puff·ball \\'pəf-,bȯl\\ *n* : any of various globe-shaped and often edible fungi

puf·fin \\'pə-fən\\ *n* : any of several seabirds having a short neck and a deep grooved parti-colored bill

¹pug \\'pəg\\ *n* **1** : any of a breed of small stocky short-haired dogs with a wrinkled face **2** : a close coil of hair

²pug *n* : ¹BOXER

pu·gi·lism \\'pyü-jə-,li-zəm\\ *n* : BOXING — **pu·gi·list** \\-list\\ *n* — **pu·gi·lis·tic** \\,pyü-jə-'lis-tik\\ *adj*

pug·na·cious \\,pəg-'nā-shəs\\ *adj* : having a quarrelsome or combative nature
♦ **Synonyms** BELLIGERENT, BELLICOSE, CONTENTIOUS, TRUCULENT — **pug·nac·i·ty** \\-'na-sə-tē\\ *n*

puis·sance \\'pwi-səns, 'pyü-ə-\\ *n* : POWER, STRENGTH ⟨the ~ of the king⟩ — **puis·sant** \\-sənt\\ *adj*

puke \\'pyük\\ *vb* **puked; puk·ing** : VOMIT — **puke** *n*

puk·ka \\'pə-kə\\ *adj* [Hindi *pakkā* cooked, ripe, solid, fr. Skt *pakva*] : GENUINE, AUTHENTIC; *also* : FIRST-CLASS, COMPLETE

pul \\'pül\\ *n, pl* **puls** \\'pülz\\ *or* **pul** — see *afghani* at MONEY table

pu·la \\'pü-lə, 'pyü-\\ *n, pl* **pula** — see MONEY table

pul·chri·tude \\'pəl-krə-,tüd, -,tyüd\\ *n* : BEAUTY — **pul·chri·tu·di·nous** \\,pəl-krə-'tüd-ᵊn-əs, -'tyü-\\ *adj*

pule \\'pyül\\ *vb* **puled; pul·ing** : WHINE, WHIMPER

¹pull \\'pu̇l\\ *vb* **1** : to exert force so as to draw (something) toward the force; *also* : MOVE ⟨~ out of a driveway⟩ **2** : PLUCK; *also* : EXTRACT ⟨~ a tooth⟩ **3** : STRETCH, STRAIN ⟨~ a tendon⟩ **4** : to draw apart : TEAR **5** : to make (as a proof) by printing **6** : REMOVE ⟨~ed the pitcher in the third inning⟩ **7** : DRAW ⟨~ a gun⟩ **8** : to carry out esp. with daring ⟨~ a robbery⟩ **9** : PERPETRATE, COMMIT **10** : ATTRACT **11** : to express strong sympathy — **pull·er** *n*

²pull *n* **1** : the act or an instance of pulling **2** : the effort expended in moving **3** : ADVANTAGE ⟨had the ~ of a respected family name⟩; *esp* : special influence **4** : a device for pulling something or for operating by pulling **5** : a force that attracts or compels **6** : an injury from abnormal straining or stretching ⟨a muscle ~⟩

pull·back \\'pu̇l-,bak\\ *n* : an orderly withdrawal of troops

pull–down *adj* : appearing below a selected item (as a menu title) on a computer display ⟨a ~ menu⟩

pul·let \\'pu̇-lət\\ *n* : a young hen esp. of the domestic chicken when less than a year old

pul·ley \\'pu̇-lē\\ *n, pl* **pulleys** : a wheel used to transmit power by means of a belt, rope, or chain; *esp* : one with a grooved rim that forms part of a tackle for hoisting or for changing the direction of a force

Pull·man \\'pu̇l-mən\\ *n* : a railroad passenger car with comfortable furnishings esp. for night travel

pull off *vb* : to accomplish successfully

pull–out \\'pu̇l-,au̇t\\ *n* : PULLBACK

pull·over \\'pu̇l-,ō-vər\\ *adj* : put on by being pulled over the head ⟨~ sweater⟩ — **pull·over** *n*

pull–up \\'pu̇l-,əp\\ *n* : CHIN-UP

pull up *vb* : to bring or come to an often abrupt halt : STOP

pul·mo·nary \\'pu̇l-mə-,ner-ē, 'pəl-\\ *adj* : of, relating to, or carried on by the lungs ⟨the ~ circulation⟩

pulp \\'pəlp\\ *n* **1** : the soft juicy or fleshy part of a fruit or vegetable **2** : a soft moist mass **3** : the soft sensitive tissue that fills the central cavity of a tooth **4** : a material (as from wood) used in making paper **5** : a magazine using cheap paper and often dealing with sensational material — **pulpy** *adj*

pul·pit \\'pu̇l-,pit\\ *n* : a raised platform or high reading desk used in preaching or conducting a worship service

pulp·wood \\'pəlp-,wu̇d\\ *n* : wood used in making pulp for paper

pul·sar \\'pəl-,sär\\ *n* : a celestial source of pulsating electromagnetic radiation (as radio waves)

pul·sate \\'pəl-,sāt\\ *vb* **pul·sat·ed; pul-**

sat·ing : to expand and contract rhythmically : BEAT ⟨an artery ∼s⟩ — **pul·sa·tion** \ˌpəl-ˈsā-shən\ n

pulse \ˈpəls\ n 1 : the regular throbbing in the arteries caused by the contractions of the heart 2 : rhythmical beating, vibrating, or sounding 3 : a brief change in electrical current or voltage — **pulse** vb

pul·ver·ise Brit var of PULVERIZE

pul·ver·ize \ˈpəl-və-ˌrīz\ vb -ized; -iz·ing 1 : to reduce (as by crushing or grinding) or be reduced to very small particles 2 : DEMOLISH

pu·ma \ˈpü-mə, ˈpyü-\ n, pl pumas also puma [Sp, fr. Quechua] : COUGAR

pum·ice \ˈpə-məs\ n : a light porous volcanic glass used esp. for smoothing and polishing

pum·mel \ˈpə-məl\ vb -meled also -melled; -mel·ing also -mel·ling : POUND, BEAT ⟨∼ed the intruder⟩

¹**pump** \ˈpəmp\ n : a device for raising, transferring, or compressing fluids esp. by suction or pressure

²**pump** vb 1 : to raise (as water) with a pump 2 : to draw fluid from with a pump; also : to fill by means of a pump ⟨∼ up a tire⟩ 3 : to force or propel in the manner of a pump — **pump·er** n

³**pump** n : a low shoe that grips the foot chiefly at the toe and heel

pumped \ˈpəmpt\ adj : filled with energetic excitement and enthusiasm

pum·per·nick·el \ˈpəm-pər-ˌni-kəl\ n : a dark rye bread

pump·kin \ˈpəmp-kən, ˈpəŋ-kən\ n : the large usu. orange fruit of a vine of the gourd family that is widely used as food; also : this vine

pun \ˈpən\ n : the humorous use of a word in a way that suggests two or more interpretations — **pun** vb

¹**punch** \ˈpənch\ n : a tool for piercing, stamping, cutting, or forming

²**punch** vb 1 : PROD, POKE; also : DRIVE, HERD ⟨∼ing cattle⟩ 2 : to strike with the fist 3 : to emboss, perforate, or make with a punch 4 : to operate, produce, or enter (as data) by or as if by punching — **punch·er** n

³**punch** n 1 : a quick blow with or as if with the fist 2 : effective energy or forcefulness

⁴**punch** n [perh. fr. Hindi pāc five, fr. Skt pañca; fr. the number of ingredients] : a drink usu. composed of wine or alcoholic liquor and nonalcoholic beverages; also : a drink composed of nonalcoholic beverages

punch card n : a card with holes punched in particular positions to represent data

punch-drunk \ˈpənch-ˌdrəŋk\ adj 1 : suffering from brain injury resulting from repeated head blows received in boxing 2 : DAZED, CONFUSED

pun·cheon \ˈpən-chən\ n : a large cask

punch line n : the sentence or phrase in a joke that makes the point

punch list n : a list of tasks to be completed at the end of a project

punchy \ˈpən-chē\ adj **punch·i·er; -est** 1 : having punch : FORCEFUL 2 : DAZED,

CONFUSED ⟨a ∼ boxer⟩ 3 : VIVID, VIBRANT ⟨∼ graphics⟩

punc·til·io \ˌpəŋk-ˈti-lē-ˌō\ n, pl -i·os 1 : a nice detail of conduct in a ceremony or in observance of a code 2 : careful observance of forms (as in social conduct)

punc·til·i·ous \ˌpəŋk-ˈti-lē-əs\ adj : marked by precise accordance with codes or conventions ♦ **Synonyms** METICULOUS, SCRUPULOUS, CAREFUL, PUNCTUAL

punc·tu·al \ˈpəŋk-chə-wəl\ adj : being on time : PROMPT — **punc·tu·al·i·ty** \ˌpəŋk-chə-ˈwa-lə-tē\ n — **punc·tu·al·ly** adv

punc·tu·ate \ˈpəŋk-chə-ˌwāt\ vb -at·ed; -at·ing 1 : to mark or divide (written matter) with punctuation marks 2 : to break into at intervals 3 : EMPHASIZE

punc·tu·a·tion \ˌpəŋk-chə-ˈwā-shən\ n : the act, practice, or system of inserting standardized marks in written matter to clarify the meaning and separate structural units

¹**punc·ture** \ˈpəŋk-chər\ n 1 : an act of puncturing 2 : a small hole or wound made by puncturing

²**puncture** vb **punc·tured; punc·tur·ing** 1 : to make a hole in : PIERCE 2 : to make useless as if by a puncture

pun·dit \ˈpən-dət\ n [Hindi paṇḍit, fr. Skt paṇḍita, fr. paṇḍita learned] 1 : a learned person : TEACHER 2 : AUTHORITY, CRITIC

pun·dit·oc·ra·cy \ˌpən-dət-ˈä-krə-sē\ n, pl -cies : a group of powerful and influential political commentators

pun·gent \ˈpən-jənt\ adj 1 : having a sharp incisive quality : CAUSTIC ⟨a ∼ editorial⟩ 2 : causing a sharp, intense, or irritating sensation (as of taste or smell); esp : ACRID ⟨a ∼ odor⟩ — **pun·gen·cy** \-jən-sē\ n — **pun·gent·ly** adv

pun·ish \ˈpə-nish\ vb 1 : to impose a penalty on for a fault or crime ⟨∼ an offender⟩ 2 : to inflict a penalty for ⟨∼ treason with death⟩ 3 : to inflict injury on : HURT ♦ **Synonyms** CHASTISE, CASTIGATE, CHASTEN, DISCIPLINE, CORRECT — **pun·ish·able** adj

pun·ish·ment n 1 : retributive suffering, pain, or loss : PENALTY 2 : rough treatment

pu·ni·tive \ˈpyü-nə-tiv\ adj : inflicting, involving, or aiming at punishment

¹**punk** \ˈpəŋk\ n 1 : a young inexperienced person 2 : a petty hoodlum

²**punk** adj : very poor : INFERIOR

³**punk** n : dry crumbly wood useful for tinder; also : a substance made from fungi for use as tinder

pun·ster \ˈpən-stər\ n : one who is given to punning

¹**punt** \ˈpənt\ n : a long narrow flat-bottomed boat with square ends

²**punt** vb : to propel (as a punt) with a pole

³**punt** vb : to kick a football or soccer ball dropped from the hands before it touches the ground

⁴**punt** n : the act or an instance of punting a ball

pu·ny \ˈpyü-nē\ adj **pu·ni·er; -est** [AF

puisné younger, weakly, lit., born afterward, fr. *puis* afterward (fr. L *post*) + *né* born, fr. L *natus*] : slight in power, size, or importance : WEAK ⟨a ~ body⟩ ⟨~ sales⟩

pup \\'pəp\ *n* : a young dog; *also* : one of the young of some other animals

pu·pa \\'pyü-pə\ *n, pl* **pupae** \-(ˌ)pē\ *or* **pupas** [NL, fr. L *pupa* doll] : a form of some insects (as a bee, moth, or beetle) between the larva and the adult that usu. has a protective covering (as a cocoon) — **pu·pal** \-pəl\ *adj*

¹**pu·pil** \\'pyü-pəl\ *n* 1 : a child or young person in school or in the charge of a tutor 2 : DISCIPLE

²**pupil** *n* : the dark central opening of the iris of the eye

pup·pet \\'pə-pət\ *n* [ME *popet* youth, doll, fr. MF *poupette*, ultim. fr. L *pupa* doll] 1 : a small figure of a person or animal moved by hand or by strings or wires 2 : DOLL 3 : one whose acts are controlled by an outside force or influence

pup·pe·teer \ˌpə-pə-'tir\ *n* : one who manipulates puppets

pup·py \\'pə-pē\ *n, pl* **puppies** : a young domestic dog

pu·pu \\'pü-ˌpü\ *n* : an Asian dish consisting of a variety of foods

pur·blind \\'pər-ˌblīnd\ *adj* 1 : partly blind 2 : lacking in insight : OBTUSE

¹**pur·chase** \\'pər-chəs\ *vb* **pur·chased; pur·chas·ing** : to obtain by paying money or its equivalent : BUY — **pur·chas·able** \-chə-sə-bəl\ *adj* — **pur·chas·er** *n*

²**purchase** *n* 1 : an act or instance of purchasing 2 : something purchased 3 : a secure hold or grasp; *also* : advantageous leverage

pur·dah \\'pər-də\ *n* : seclusion of women from public observation among Muslims and some Hindus esp. in India; *also* : a state of seclusion

pure \\'pyür\ *adj* **pur·er; pur·est** 1 : unmixed with any other matter : free from taint ⟨~ gold⟩ ⟨~ water⟩ 2 : SHEER, ABSOLUTE ⟨~ nonsense⟩ 3 : ABSTRACT, THEORETICAL ⟨~ mathematics⟩ 4 : free from what vitiates, weakens, or pollutes ⟨speaks a ~ French⟩ 5 : free from moral fault : INNOCENT 6 : CHASTE, CONTINENT — **pure·ly** *adv*

pure-blood·ed \-ˌblə-dəd\ *or* **pure-blood** \-ˌbləd\ *adj* : FULL-BLOODED — **pure-blood** *n*

pure·bred \-'bred\ *adj* : bred from members of a recognized breed, strain, or kind without crossbreeding over many generations — **pure·bred** \-ˌbred\ *n*

¹**pu·ree** \pyü-'rā, -'rē\ *n* [F *purée*, fr. MF, fr. fem. of *puré*, pp. of *purer* to purify, strain, fr. L *purare* to purify] : a paste or thick liquid suspension usu. made from finely ground cooked food; *also* : a thick soup made of pureed vegetables

²**puree** *vb* **pu·reed; pu·ree·ing** : to make a puree of

pur·ga·tion \ˌpər-'gā-shən\ *n* : the act or result of purging

¹**pur·ga·tive** \\'pər-gə-tiv\ *adj* : purging or tending to purge

²**purgative** *n* : a strong laxative : CATHARTIC

pur·ga·to·ry \\'pər-gə-ˌtȯr-ē\ *n, pl* **-ries** 1 : an intermediate state after death for expiatory purification 2 : a place or state of temporary punishment — **pur·ga·tor·i·al** \ˌpər-gə-'tȯr-ē-əl\ *adj*

¹**purge** \\'pərj\ *vb* **purged; purg·ing** 1 : to cleanse or purify esp. from sin 2 : to have or cause strong and usu. repeated emptying of the bowels 3 : to get rid of ⟨the leaders had been *purged*⟩

²**purge** *n* 1 : something that purges; *esp* : PURGATIVE 2 : an act or result of purging; *esp* : a ridding of persons regarded as treacherous or disloyal

pu·ri·fy \\'pyür-ə-ˌfī\ *vb* **-fied; -fy·ing** : to make or become pure ⟨~ water⟩ ⟨~ the mind⟩ — **pu·ri·fi·ca·tion** \ˌpyür-ə-fə-'kā-shən\ *n* — **pu·ri·fi·ca·to·ry** \pyü-'ri-fi-kə-ˌtȯr-ē\ *adj* — **pu·ri·fi·er** *n*

Pu·rim \\'pur-(ˌ)im\ *n* : a Jewish holiday celebrated in February or March in commemoration of the deliverance of the Jews from the massacre plotted by Haman

pu·rine \\'pyur-ˌēn\ *n* : any of a group of bases including several (as adenine or guanine) that are constituents of DNA or RNA

pur·ism \\'pyür-ˌi-zəm\ *n* : rigid adherence to or insistence on purity or nicety esp. in use of words — **pur·ist** \-ist\ *n* — **pu·ris·tic** \pyü-'ris-tik\ *adj*

pu·ri·tan \\'pyür-ə-tən\ *n* 1 *cap* : a member of a 16th and 17th century Protestant group in England and New England opposing the ceremonies and government of the Church of England 2 : one who practices or preaches a stricter or professedly purer moral code than that which prevails — **pu·ri·tan·i·cal** \ˌpyür-ə-'ta-ni-kəl\ *adj* — **pu·ri·tan·i·cal·ly** *adv*

pu·ri·ty \\'pyür-ə-tē\ *n* : the quality or state of being pure

¹**purl** \\'pərl\ *n* : a stitch in knitting

²**purl** *vb* : to knit in purl stitch

³**purl** *n* : a gentle murmur or movement (as of purling water)

⁴**purl** *vb* 1 : EDDY, SWIRL 2 : to make a soft murmuring sound

pur·lieu \\'pər-lü, 'pər-yü\ *n* 1 : an outlying district : SUBURB 2 *pl* : ENVIRONS

pur·loin \(ˌ)pər-'lȯin, 'pər-ˌlȯin\ *vb* : STEAL, FILCH

¹**pur·ple** \\'pər-pəl\ *adj* **pur·pler; pur·plest** 1 : of the color purple 2 : highly rhetorical ⟨a ~ passage⟩ 3 : PROFANE ⟨~ language⟩ — **pur·plish** *adj*

²**purple** *n* 1 : a bluish red color 2 : a purple robe emblematic esp. of regal rank or authority

¹**pur·port** \\'pər-ˌpȯrt\ *n* [ME, fr. AF, content, tenor, fr. *purporter* to carry, mean, purport, fr. *pur-* thoroughly + *porter* to carry] : meaning conveyed or implied; *also* : GIST ⟨the ~ of her letter⟩

²**pur·port** \(ˌ)pər-'pȯrt\ *vb* : to convey or profess outwardly as the meaning or in-

tention : CLAIM ⟨~s to be objective⟩ — **pur·port·ed·ly** \-\ˈpȯr-təd-lē\ *adv*

¹pur·pose \ˈpər-pəs\ *n* **1** : an object or result aimed at : INTENTION **2** : RESOLUTION, DETERMINATION — **pur·pose·ful** \-fəl\ *adj* — **pur·pose·ful·ly** *adv* — **pur·pose·less** *adj* — **pur·pose·ly** *adv*

²purpose *vb* **pur·posed; pur·pos·ing** : to propose as an aim to oneself

purr \ˈpər\ *n* : a low murmur typical of a contented cat — **purr** *vb*

¹purse \ˈpərs\ *n* **1** : a receptacle (as a pouch) to carry money and often other small objects in **2** : RESOURCES **3** : a sum of money offered as a prize or present

²purse *vb* **pursed; purs·ing** : PUCKER

purs·er \ˈpər-sər\ *n* : an official on a ship who keeps accounts and attends to the comfort of passengers

purs·lane \ˈpər-slən, -ˌslān\ *n* : a fleshy-leaved weedy trailing plant with tiny yellow flowers that is sometimes used in salads

pur·su·ance \pər-ˈsü-əns\ *n* : the act of carrying out or into effect

pur·su·ant to \-ˈsü-ənt-\ *prep* : in carrying out : ACCORDING TO

pur·sue \pər-ˈsü\ *vb* **pur·sued; pur·su·ing 1** : to follow in order to overtake or overcome : CHASE **2** : to seek to accomplish ⟨~ a goal⟩ **3** : to proceed along ⟨~ a course⟩ **4** : to engage in ⟨~ a career⟩ — **pur·su·er** *n*

pur·suit \pər-ˈsüt\ *n* **1** : the act of pursuing **2** : OCCUPATION, BUSINESS

pu·ru·lent \ˈpyur-ə-lənt, -yə-\ *adj* : containing or accompanied by pus ⟨a ~ discharge⟩ — **pu·ru·lence** \-ləns\ *n*

pur·vey \(ˌ)pər-ˈvā\ *vb* **pur·veyed; pur·vey·ing** : to supply (as provisions) usu. as a business — **pur·vey·ance** \-əns\ *n* — **pur·vey·or** \-ər\ *n*

pur·view \ˈpər-ˌvyü\ *n* **1** : the range or limit esp. of authority, responsibility, or intention **2** : range of vision, understanding, or cognizance

pus \ˈpəs\ *n* : thick yellowish white fluid matter (as in a boil) formed at a place of inflammation and infection (as an abscess) and containing germs, white blood cells, and tissue debris

¹push \ˈpush\ *vb* [ME *possen, pusshen*, prob. fr. OF *pousser* to exert pressure, fr. L *pulsare*, fr. *pellere* to drive, strike] **1** : to press against with force in order to drive or impel **2** : to thrust forward, downward, or outward **3** : to urge on : press forward **4** : to cause to increase ⟨~ prices to record levels⟩ **5** : to urge or press the advancement, adoption, or practice of; *esp* : to make aggressive efforts to sell **6** : to engage in the illicit sale of narcotics

²push *n* **1** : a vigorous effort : DRIVE ⟨a ~ for higher wages⟩ **2** : an act of pushing **3** : vigorous enterprise : ENERGY

push–button *adj* **1** : operated or done by means of push buttons **2** : using or depending on complex and more or less automatic mechanisms ⟨~ warfare⟩

push button *n* : a small button or knob

that when pushed operates something esp. by closing an electric circuit

push·cart \ˈpush-ˌkärt\ *n* : a cart or barrow pushed by hand

push·er \ˈpu̇-shər\ *n* : one that pushes; *esp* : one that pushes illegal drugs

push·over \-ˌō-vər\ *n* **1** : something easily accomplished **2** : an opponent easy to defeat **3** : SUCKER ⟨she's nobody's ~⟩

push-up \-ˌəp\ *n* : a conditioning exercise performed in a prone position by raising and lowering the body with the straightening and bending of the arms while keeping the back straight and supporting the body on the hands and toes

pushy \ˈpu̇-shē\ *adj* **push·i·er; -est** : aggressive often to an objectionable degree

pu·sil·lan·i·mous \ˌpyü-sə-ˈla-nə-məs\ *adj* [LL *pusillanimis*, fr. L *pusillus* very small (dim. of *pusus* boy) + *animus* spirit] : contemptibly timid : COWARDLY — **pu·sil·la·nim·i·ty** \ˌpyü-sə-lə-ˈni-mə-tē\ *n*

¹puss \ˈpu̇s\ *n* : CAT

²puss *n, slang* : FACE

¹pussy \ˈpu̇-sē\ *n, pl* **puss·ies** : CAT

²pus·sy \ˈpə-sē\ *adj* **pus·si·er; -est** : full of or resembling pus

pussy·cat \ˈpu̇-sē-\ *n* : CAT

pussy·foot \-ˌfu̇t\ *vb* **1** : to tread or move warily or stealthily **2** : to refrain from committing oneself

pussy willow \ˈpu̇-sē-\ *n* : a willow having large silky catkins

pus·tule \ˈpəs-chül\ *n* : a pus-filled pimple

put \ˈpu̇t\ *vb* **put; put·ting 1** : to bring into a specified position : PLACE ⟨~ the book on the table⟩ **2** : SEND, THRUST **3** : to throw with an upward pushing motion ⟨~ the shot⟩ **4** : to bring into a specified state ⟨~ the plan into effect⟩ **5** : SUBJECT ⟨~ traitors to death⟩ **6** : IMPOSE **7** : to set before one for decision ⟨~ the question⟩ **8** : EXPRESS, STATE ⟨~ my feelings into words⟩ **9** : TRANSLATE, ADAPT **10** : APPLY, ASSIGN ⟨~ them to work⟩ **11** : ESTIMATE ⟨~ the number at 20⟩ **12** : ATTACH, ATTRIBUTE ⟨~ a high value on it⟩ **13** : to take a specified course ⟨the ship ~ out to sea⟩

pu·ta·tive \ˈpyü-tə-tiv\ *adj* **1** : commonly accepted ⟨~ expert⟩ **2** : assumed to exist or to have existed

put–down \ˈpu̇t-ˌdau̇n\ *n* : a belittling remark

put in *vb* **1** : to come in with : INTERPOSE ⟨*put in* a good word for me⟩ **2** : to spend time at some occupation or job ⟨*put in* eight hours at the office⟩

put off *vb* : POSTPONE, DELAY ⟨*put off* my visit⟩

¹put–on \ˈpu̇t-ˌȯn, -ˌän\ *adj* : PRETENDED, ASSUMED ⟨a ~ accent⟩

²put-on *n* **1** : a deliberate act of misleading someone **2** : PARODY, SPOOF

put·out \ˈpu̇t-ˌau̇t\ *n* : the retiring of a base runner or batter in baseball

put out *vb* **1** : EXTINGUISH **2** : ANNOY; *also* : INCONVENIENCE **3** : to cause to be out (as in baseball)

pu·tre·fy \ˈpyü-trə-ˌfī\ *vb* **-fied; -fy·ing** : to make or become putrid : ROT ⟨*putre-*

fied meat\} — **pu·tre·fac·tion** \ˌpyü-trə-ˈfak-shən\ *n* — **pu·tre·fac·tive** \-tiv\ *adj*
pu·tres·cent \pyü-ˈtre-sᵊnt\ *adj* : becoming putrid : ROTTING ⟨∼ carcasses⟩ — **pu·tres·cence** \-sᵊns\ *n*
pu·trid \ˈpyü-trəd\ *adj* 1 : ROTTEN, DECAYED ⟨∼ meat⟩ 2 : VILE, CORRUPT — **pu·trid·i·ty** \pyü-ˈtri-də-tē\ *n*
putsch \ˈpu̇ch\ *n* [G] : a secretly plotted and suddenly executed attempt to overthrow a government
putt \ˈpət\ *n* : a golf stroke made on the green to cause the ball to roll into the hole — **putt** *vb*
put·ta·nes·ca \ˌpü-tä-ˈnes-kä\ *adj* : served with or being a pungent tomato sauce
put·tee \ˌpə-ˈtē, ˈpə-tē\ *n* [Hindi *paṭṭī* strip of cloth] 1 : a cloth strip wrapped around the lower leg 2 : a leather legging
¹**put·ter** \ˈpu̇-tər\ *n* : one that puts
²**putt·er** \ˈpə-tər\ *n* 1 : a golf club used in putting 2 : one that putts
³**put·ter** \ˈpə-tər\ *vb* 1 : to move or act aimlessly or idly 2 : TINKER
put·ty \ˈpə-tē\ *n, pl* **putties** [F *potée* potter's glaze, lit., potful, fr. OF, fr. *pot* pot] 1 : a doughlike cement used esp. to fasten glass in sashes 2 : one who is easily manipulated — **putty** *vb*
put up *vb* 1 : SHEATHE 2 : to prepare so as to preserve for later use 3 : to offer for public sale ⟨*put* the house *up* for auction⟩ 4 : ACCOMMODATE, LODGE ⟨*put* us *up* for the night⟩ 5 : BUILD 6 : to engage in ⟨*put up* a struggle⟩ 7 : CONTRIBUTE, PAY — **put up with** : TOLERATE 2
¹**puz·zle** \ˈpə-zəl\ *vb* **puz·zled; puz·zling** 1 : to bewilder mentally : PERPLEX 2 : to solve with difficulty or ingenuity ⟨∼ out a riddle⟩ 3 : to be in a quandary ⟨∼ over what to do⟩ 4 : to attempt a solution of a puzzle ⟨∼ over a person's words⟩ ♦ *Synonyms* MYSTIFY, BEWILDER, NONPLUS, CONFOUND — **puz·zle·ment** *n* — **puz·zler** *n*
²**puzzle** *n* 1 : something that puzzles 2 : a question, problem, or contrivance designed for testing ingenuity
PVC *abbr* polyvinyl chloride
pvt *abbr* private
PW *abbr* prisoner of war
pwt *abbr* pennyweight
PX *abbr* post exchange
pya \pē-ˈä\ *n* — see *kyat* at MONEY table
pyg·my *also* **pig·my** \ˈpig-mē\ *n, pl* **pygmies** *also* **pigmies** [ME *pigmei*, fr. L *pygmaeus* of a pygmy, dwarfish, fr. Gk *pygmaios*, fr. *pygmē* fist, measure of length] 1 *cap* : any of a small people of equatorial Africa 2 : an unusually small person; *also* : an insignificant or unimpressive person — **pygmy** *adj*
py·ja·mas \pə-ˈjä-məz\ *chiefly Brit var of* PAJAMAS

py·lon \ˈpī-ˌlän, -lən\ *n* 1 : a usu. massive gateway; *esp* : an Egyptian one flanked by flat-topped pyramids 2 : a tower that supports wires over a long span 3 : a post or tower marking the course in an airplane race
py·or·rhea \ˌpī-ə-ˈrē-ə\ *n* : an inflammation with pus of the sockets of the teeth
¹**pyr·a·mid** \ˈpir-ə-ˌmid\ *n* 1 : a massive structure with a square base and four triangular faces meeting at a point 2 : a geometrical solid having a polygon for its base and three or more triangles for its sides that meet at a point to form the top — **py·ra·mi·dal** \pə-ˈra-mə-dᵊl, ˌpir-ə-ˈmid-\ *adj*
²**pyramid** *vb* 1 : to build up in the form of a pyramid : heap up 2 : to increase rapidly on a broadening base
pyramid scheme *n* : a usu. illegal operation in which participants pay to join and profit from payments made by subsequent participants
pyre \ˈpī(-ə)r\ *n* : a combustible heap for burning a dead body as a funeral rite
py·re·thrum \pī-ˈrē-thrəm\ *n* : an insecticide made from the dried heads of any of several Old World chrysanthemums
py·rim·i·dine \pī-ˈri-mə-ˌdēn\ *n* : any of a group of bases including several (as cytosine, thymine, or uracil) that are constituents of DNA or RNA
py·rite \ˈpī-ˌrīt\ *n* : a mineral containing sulfur and iron that is brass-yellow in color
py·rol·y·sis \pī-ˈrä-lə-səs\ *n* : chemical change caused by the action of heat
py·ro·ma·nia \ˌpī-rō-ˈmā-nē-ə\ *n* : an irresistible impulse to start fires — **py·ro·ma·ni·ac** \-nē-ˌak\ *n*
py·ro·tech·nics \ˌpī-rə-ˈtek-niks\ *n pl* 1 : a display of fireworks 2 : a spectacular display (as of extreme virtuosity) ⟨musical ∼⟩ — **py·ro·tech·nic** \-nik\ *also* **py·ro·tech·ni·cal** \-ni-kəl\ *adj*
Pyr·rhic \ˈpir-ik\ *adj* : achieved at excessive cost ⟨a ∼ victory⟩; *also* : costly to the point of outweighing expected benefits
Py·thag·o·re·an theorem \pī-ˌtha-gə-ˈrē-ən-\ *n* : a theorem in geometry: the square of the length of the hypotenuse of a right triangle equals the sum of the squares of the lengths of the other two sides
py·thon \ˈpī-ˌthän, -thən\ *n* [L, monstrous serpent killed by the god Apollo, fr. Gk *Pythōn*] : a large snake (as a boa) that squeezes and suffocates its prey; *esp* : any of the large Old World snakes that include the largest snakes living at the present time
pyx \ˈpiks\ *n* : a small case used to carry the Eucharist to the sick

¹q \'kyü\ *n, pl* **q's** *or* **qs** \'kyüz\ *often cap*
: the 17th letter of the English alphabet
²q *abbr, often cap* **1** quart **2** quarto **3**
queen **4** query **5** question
QB *abbr* quarterback
QED *abbr* [L *quod erat demonstrandum*]
which was to be demonstrated
qin·tar \kin-'tär\ *n, pl* **qin·dar·ka** \kin-
'där-kə\ — see *lek* at MONEY table
qi·vi·ut \'kē-vē-ˌüt\ *n* [Inuit] : the wool of
the undercoat of the musk ox
Qld *abbr* Queensland
QM *abbr* quartermaster
QMC *abbr* quartermaster corps
QMG *abbr* quartermaster general
qq v *abbr* [L *quae vide*] which (*pl*) see
qr *abbr* quarter
Q rating *n* [quotient] : a scale measuring
popularity based on dividing an assessment of familiarity or recognition by an
assessment of favorable opinion; *also*
: position on such a scale
qt *abbr* **1** quantity **2** quart
q.t. \ˌkyü-'tē\ *n, often cap Q&T* : QUIET —
usu. used in the phrase *on the q.t.*
qto *abbr* quarto
qty *abbr* quantity
qu *or* **ques** *abbr* question
¹quack \'kwak\ *vb* : to make the characteristic cry of a duck
²quack *n* : a sound made by quacking
³quack *n* **1** : CHARLATAN **2** : a pretender
to medical skill **♦ Synonyms** FAKER,
IMPOSTOR, MOUNTEBANK — **quack** *adj*
— **quack·ery** \'kwa-kə-rē\ *n* — **quack-
ish** *adj*
¹quad \'kwäd\ *n* : QUADRANGLE
²quad *n* **1** : QUADRUPLET **2** : a ski lift that
accommodates four people
³quad *abbr* quadrant
quad·ran·gle \'kwä-ˌdraŋ-gəl\ *n* **1**
: QUADRILATERAL **2** : a 4-sided courtyard or enclosure — **quad·ran·gu·lar**
\kwä-'draŋ-gyə-lər\ *adj*
quad·rant \'kwä-drənt\ *n* **1** : one quarter
of a circle : an arc of 90° **2** : any of the
four quarters into which something is divided by two lines intersecting each other
at right angles
qua·drat·ic \kwä-'dra-tik\ *adj* : having or
being a term in which the variable (as *x*)
is squared but containing no term in
which the variable is raised to a higher
power than a square ⟨a ~ equation⟩ —
quadratic *n*
qua·dren·ni·al \kwä-'dre-nē-əl\ *adj* **1**
: consisting of or lasting for four years **2**
: occurring every four years
qua·dren·ni·um \-nē-əm\ *n, pl* **-ni·ums**
or **-nia** \-nē-ə\ : a period of four years
quad·ri·ceps \'kwä-drə-ˌseps\ *n* : a muscle of the front of the thigh that is divided
into four parts
¹quad·ri·lat·er·al \ˌkwä-drə-'la-tə-rəl\ *n* : a
polygon of four sides

²quadrilateral *adj* : having four sides
qua·drille \kwä-'dril, kə-\ *n* : a square
dance made up of five or six figures in
various rhythms
quad·ri·par·tite \ˌkwä-drə-'pär-ˌtīt\ *adj* **1**
: consisting of four parts **2** : shared by
four parties or persons
quad·ri·ple·gia \ˌkwä-drə-'plē-jə, -jē-ə\ *n*
: paralysis of both arms and both legs —
quad·ri·ple·gic \-jik\ *adj or n*
qua·driv·i·um \kwä-'dri-vē-əm\ *n* : the
four liberal arts of arithmetic, music, geometry, and astronomy in a medieval
university
quad·ru·ped \'kwä-drə-ˌped\ *n* : an animal having four feet — **qua·dru·pe·dal**
\kwä-'drü-pə-dᵊl, ˌkwä-drə-'pe-\ *adj*
¹qua·dru·ple \kwä-'drü-pəl, -'drə-; 'kwä-
drə-\ *vb* **qua·dru·pled; qua·dru·pling**
: to make or become four times as great
or as many
²quadruple *adj* : FOURFOLD
qua·dru·plet \kwä-'drə-plət, -'drü-; 'kwä-
drə-\ *n* **1** : a combination of four of a
kind **2** : one of four offspring born at
one birth
¹qua·dru·pli·cate \kwä-'drü-pli-kət\ *adj* **1**
: repeated four times **2** : FOURTH
²qua·dru·pli·cate \-plə-ˌkāt\ *vb* **-cat·ed;**
-cat·ing **1** : QUADRUPLE **2** : to prepare
in quadruplicate — **qua·dru·pli·ca·tion**
\-ˌdrü-plə-'kā-shən\ *n*
³qua·dru·pli·cate \-'drü-pli-kət\ *n* **1**
: four copies all alike ⟨typed in ~⟩ **2**
: one of four like things
quaff \'kwäf, 'kwaf\ *vb* : to drink deeply
or repeatedly — **quaff** *n*
quag·mire \'kwag-ˌmī(-ə)r, 'kwäg-\ *n* **1**
: soft miry land that yields under the foot
2 : PREDICAMENT
qua·hog \'kō-ˌhóg, 'kwò-, 'kwō-, -ˌhäg\ *n*
[modif. of Narragansett *poquaûhock*] : a
round thick-shelled edible clam of the
U.S.
quai \'kā\ *n* : QUAY
¹quail \'kwāl\ *n, pl* **quail** *or* **quails** [ME
quaile, fr. AF, fr. ML *quaccula*, of imit.
origin] : any of numerous small short=
winged plump game birds (as a bobwhite)
related to the domestic chicken
²quail *vb* [ME, to grow feeble, fr. MD *quel-
en*] : to lose heart : COWER ⟨~ed at the
daunting task⟩ **♦ Synonyms** RECOIL,
SHRINK, FLINCH, WINCE, BLANCH
quaint \'kwānt\ *adj* : unusual or different in character or appearance; *esp*
: pleasingly old-fashioned or unfamiliar
♦ Synonyms ODD, QUEER, CURIOUS,
STRANGE — **quaint·ly** *adv* — **quaint-
ness** *n*
¹quake \'kwāk\ *vb* **quaked; quak·ing** **1**
: to shake usu. from shock or instability
2 : to tremble usu. from cold or fear
²quake *n* : a shaking or trembling; *esp*
: EARTHQUAKE

Quak·er \'kwā-kər\ n : FRIEND 5

qual abbr quality

qual·i·fi·ca·tion \ˌkwä-lə-fə-'kā-shən\ n 1 : LIMITATION, MODIFICATION ⟨her statement stands without ∼⟩ 2 : a special skill that fits a person for some work or position 3 : REQUIREMENT ⟨a ∼ for membership⟩

qual·i·fied \'kwä-lə-ˌfīd\ adj 1 : fitted for a given purpose or job 2 : limited in some way ⟨∼ approval⟩

qual·i·fi·er \'kwä-lə-ˌfī(-ə)r\ n 1 : one that satisfies requirements 2 : a word or word group that limits the meaning of another word or word group

qual·i·fy \'kwä-lə-ˌfī\ vb -fied; -fy·ing 1 : to reduce from a general to a particular form : MODIFY 2 : to make less harsh 3 : to limit the meaning of (as a noun) 4 : to fit by skill or training for some purpose 5 : to give or have a legal right to do something 6 : to demonstrate the necessary ability ⟨∼ for the finals⟩ ♦ Synonyms MODERATE, TEMPER

qual·i·ta·tive \'kwä-lə-ˌtā-tiv\ adj : of, relating to, or involving quality — **qual·i·ta·tive·ly** adv

¹**qual·i·ty** \'kwä-lə-tē\ n, pl -ties 1 : peculiar and essential character : NATURE 2 : degree of excellence 3 : high social status 4 : a distinguishing attribute

²**quality** adj : being of high quality

qualm \'kwäm, 'kwälm\ n 1 : a sudden attack (as of nausea) 2 : a sudden feeling of doubt, fear, or uneasiness esp. in not following one's conscience or better judgment

qualm·ish \'kwä-mish, 'kwäl-\ adj 1 : feeling qualms : NAUSEATED 2 : overly scrupulous : SQUEAMISH 3 : of, relating to, or producing qualms

quan·da·ry \'kwän-drē\ n, pl -ries : a state of perplexity or doubt

quan·ti·fy \'kwän-tə-ˌfī\ vb -fied; -fy·ing : to determine, express, or measure the quantity of — **quan·ti·fi·able** \ˌkwän-tə-'fī-ə-bəl\ adj

quan·ti·ta·tive \'kwän-tə-ˌtā-tiv\ adj : of, relating to, or involving quantity — **quan·ti·ta·tive·ly** adv

quan·ti·ty \'kwän-tə-tē\ n, pl -ties 1 : AMOUNT, NUMBER 2 : a considerable amount ⟨buys food in ∼⟩

quan·tize \'kwän-ˌtīz\ vb **quan·tized; quan·tiz·ing** : to subdivide (as energy) into small units

¹**quan·tum** \'kwän-təm\ n, pl **quan·ta** \-tə\ [L, neut. of quantus how much] 1 : QUANTITY, AMOUNT 2 : an elemental unit of energy

²**quantum** adj 1 : LARGE, SIGNIFICANT 2 : relating to or employing the principles of quantum mechanics

quantum mechanics n sing or pl : a theory of matter based on the concept of possession of wave properties by elementary particles — **quantum mechanical** adj — **quantum mechanically** adv

quantum theory n 1 : a theory in physics based on the idea that radiant energy (as light) is composed of small separate packets of energy 2 : QUANTUM MECHANICS

quar abbr quarterly

quar·an·tine \'kwȯr-ən-ˌtēn\ n [modif. of It quarantena, lit., period of forty days, fr. quaranta forty, fr. L quadraginta] 1 : a period during which a ship suspected of carrying contagious disease is forbidden contact with the shore 2 : a restraint on the movements of persons or goods to prevent the spread of pests or disease 3 : a place or period of quarantine 4 : a state of enforced isolation — **quarantine** vb

quark \'kwȯrk, 'kwärk\ n : a hypothetical elementary particle that carries a fractional charge and is held to be a constituent of heavier particles (as protons and neutrons)

¹**quar·rel** \'kwȯr-əl\ n 1 : a ground of dispute 2 : a verbal clash : CONFLICT — **quar·rel·some** \-səm\ adj

²**quarrel** vb -reled or -relled; -rel·ing or -rel·ling 1 : to find fault 2 : to dispute angrily : WRANGLE

¹**quar·ry** \'kwȯr-ē\ n, pl quarries [ME querre entrails of game given to the hounds, fr. AF cureie, quereie, fr. quir, cuir skin, hide (on which the entrails were placed), fr. L corium] 1 : game hunted with hawks 2 : PREY

²**quarry** n, pl quarries [ME quarey, alter. of quarrere, fr. AF, fr. VL *quadraria, fr. LL quadrus hewn (lit., squared) stone, fr. L quadrum square] : an open excavation usu. for obtaining building stone or limestone — **quarry** vb

quart \'kwȯrt\ n — see WEIGHT table

¹**quar·ter** \'kwȯr-tər\ n 1 : one of four equal parts 2 : a fourth of a dollar; also : a coin of this value 3 : a district of a city 4 pl : LODGINGS ⟨moved into new ∼s⟩ 5 : MERCY, CLEMENCY ⟨gave no ∼⟩ 6 : a fourth part of the moon's period

²**quarter** vb 1 : to divide into four equal parts 2 : to provide with shelter

¹**quar·ter·back** \-ˌbak\ n : a football player who calls the signals and directs the offensive play for the team

²**quarterback** vb 1 : to direct the offensive play of a football team 2 : LEAD, BOSS

quar·ter·deck \-ˌdek\ n : the stern area of a ship's upper deck

quarter horse n : any of a breed of compact muscular saddle horses characterized by great endurance and by high speed for short distances

¹**quar·ter·ly** \'kwȯr-tər-lē\ adv : at 3-month intervals

²**quarterly** adj : occurring, issued, or payable at 3-month intervals

³**quarterly** n, pl -lies : a periodical published four times a year

quar·ter·mas·ter \-ˌmas-tər\ n 1 : a petty officer who attends to a ship's helm, binnacle, and signals 2 : an army officer who provides clothing and subsistence for troops

quar·ter·staff \-ˌstaf\ n, pl -staves \-ˌstavz, -ˌstāvz\ : a long stout staff formerly used as a weapon

quar·tet also **quar·tette** \kwȯr-'tet\ n 1

: a musical composition for four instruments or voices **2** : a group of four and esp. of four musicians

quar·to \'kwȯr-tō\ *n, pl* **quartos** **1** : the size of a piece of paper cut four from a sheet **2** : a book printed on quarto pages

quartz \'kwȯrts\ *n* : a common often transparent crystalline mineral that is a form of silica

quartz·ite \'kwȯrt-ˌsīt\ *n* : a compact granular rock composed of quartz and derived from sandstone

qua·sar \'kwā-ˌzär, -ˌsär\ *n* : any of a class of extremely distant starlike celestial objects

¹**quash** \'kwäsh, 'kwȯsh\ *vb* : to suppress or extinguish summarily and completely : QUELL

²**quash** *vb* : to nullify by judicial action

qua·si \'kwā-ˌzī, -ˌsī; 'kwä-zē, -sē-sē\ *adj* : being in some sense or degree ⟨a ∼ corporation⟩

quasi- *comb form* [L, as if, as it were, approximately, fr. *quam* as + *si* if] : in some sense or degree ⟨*quasi*-historical⟩

qua·si–gov·ern·men·tal \-gə-vərn-'men-tᵊl\ *adj* : supported by the government but managed privately

Qua·ter·na·ry \'kwä-tər-ˌner-ē, kwə-'tər-nə-rē\ *adj* : of, relating to, or being the geologic period from the end of the Tertiary to the present — **Quaternary** *n*

qua·train \'kwä-ˌtrān\ *n* : a unit of four lines of verse

qua·tre·foil \'ka-tər-ˌfȯi(-ə)l, 'ka-trə-\ *n* : a stylized figure often of a flower with four petals

qua·ver \'kwā-vər\ *vb* **1** : TREMBLE, SHAKE ⟨∼ed with nervousness⟩ **2** : TRILL **3** : to speak in tremulous tones ◆ *Synonyms* SHUDDER, QUAKE, TWITTER, QUIVER, SHIVER — **quaver** *n*

quay \'kē, 'kwā, 'kā\ *n* : WHARF

Que *abbr* Quebec

quean \'kwēn\ *n* : PROSTITUTE

quea·sy \'kwē-zē\ *adj* **quea·si·er; -est** : NAUSEATED — **quea·si·ly** \-zə-lē\ *adv* — **quea·si·ness** \-zē-nəs\ *n*

Que·chua \'ke-chə-wə, 'kech-wə\ *n* : a family of languages spoken in Peru and adjacent countries of the So. American Andes

queen \'kwēn\ *n* [ME *quene*, fr. OE *cwēn* woman, wife, queen] **1** : the wife or widow of a king **2** : a female monarch **3** : a woman notable for rank, power, or attractiveness **4** : the most powerful piece in the game of chess **5** : a playing card bearing the figure of a queen **6** : a fertile female of a social insect (as a bee or termite) — **queen·ly** *adj*

Queen Anne's lace \-'anz-\ *n* : a widely naturalized Eurasian herb from which the cultivated carrot originated

queen consort *n, pl* **queens consort** : the wife of a reigning king

queen mother *n* : a dowager queen who is mother of the reigning sovereign

queen–size *adj* : having dimensions of approximately 60 inches by 80 inches ⟨a ∼ bed⟩; *also* : of a size that fits a queen-size bed

¹**queer** \'kwir\ *adj* **1** : COUNTERFEIT ⟨∼ money⟩ **2** : differing from the usual or normal : PECULIAR, STRANGE **3** *often disparaging* : HOMOSEXUAL; *also, sometimes offensive* : of, relating to, or used by homosexuals ◆ *Synonyms* WEIRD, BIZARRE, ECCENTRIC, CURIOUS — **queer** *n* — **queer·ly** *adv* — **queer·ness** *n*

²**queer** *vb* : to spoil the effect of : DISRUPT ⟨∼ed our plans⟩

queer theory *n* : an approach to literary and cultural study that rejects traditional categories of gender and sexuality

quell \'kwel\ *vb* **1** : to put an end to by force ⟨∼ a riot⟩ **2** : CALM, PACIFY ⟨∼ fears⟩

quench \'kwench\ *vb* **1** : PUT OUT, EXTINGUISH **2** : SUBDUE **3** : SLAKE, SATISFY ⟨∼ed his thirst⟩ — **quench·able** *adj* — **quench·er** *n* — **quench·less** *adj*

quer·u·lous \'kwer-ə-ləs, -yə-\ *adj* **1** : constantly complaining **2** : FRETFUL, WHINING ⟨a ∼ voice⟩ ◆ *Synonyms* PETULANT, PETTISH, IRRITABLE, PEEVISH, HUFFY — **quer·u·lous·ly** *adv* — **quer·u·lous·ness** *n*

que·ry \'kwir-ē, 'kwer-\ *n, pl* **queries** : QUESTION — **query** *vb*

que·sa·dil·la \ˌkā-sə-'dē-ə\ *n* : a tortilla filled with a savory mixture, folded, and usu. fried

quest \'kwest\ *n* : SEARCH ⟨in ∼ of game⟩ — **quest** *vb*

¹**ques·tion** \'kwes-chən\ *n* **1** : an interrogative expression **2** : a subject for debate; *also* : a proposition to be voted on **3** : INQUIRY **4** : DISPUTE ⟨true beyond ∼⟩

²**question** *vb* **1** : to ask questions **2** : DOUBT, DISPUTE ⟨∼ed the verdict⟩ **3** : to subject to analysis : EXAMINE ◆ *Synonyms* INTERROGATE, QUIZ, QUERY — **ques·tion·er** *n*

ques·tion·able \'kwes-chə-nə-bəl\ *adj* **1** : not certain or exact : DOUBTFUL **2** : not believed to be true, sound, or moral ◆ *Synonyms* DUBIOUS, PROBLEMATICAL, MOOT, DEBATABLE — **ques·tion·ably** \-blē\ *adv*

question mark *n* : a punctuation mark ? used esp. at the end of a sentence to indicate a direct question

ques·tion·naire \ˌkwes-chə-'ner\ *n* : a set of questions for obtaining information

quet·zal \ket-'säl, -'sal\ *n, pl* **quetzals** *or* **quet·za·les** \-'sä-ˌläs, -'sa-\ **1** : a Central American bird with brilliant plumage **2** *pl* **quetzales** — see MONEY table

¹**queue** \'kyü\ *n* [F, lit., tail, fr. OF *cue, coe*, fr. L *cauda, coda*] **1** : a braid of hair usu. worn hanging at the back of the head **2** : a waiting line (as of persons)

²**queue** *vb* **queued; queu·ing** *or* **queue·ing** : to line up in a queue

quib·ble \'kwi-bəl\ *n* **1** : an evasion of or shifting from the point at issue **2** : a minor objection or criticism — **quibble** *vb* — **quib·bler** *n*

¹**quick** \'kwik\ *adj* **1** : LIVING **2** : RAPID, SPEEDY ⟨∼ steps⟩ **3** : prompt to understand, think, or perceive : ALERT **4** : easily aroused ⟨a ∼ temper⟩ **5** : turning or

bending sharply ⟨a ~ turn in the road⟩ ♦ **Synonyms** FLEET, FAST, HASTY, EXPEDITIOUS — **quick** adv — **quick·ly** adv — **quick·ness** n

²**quick** n **1** : a sensitive area of living flesh **2** : a vital part : HEART

quick bread n : a bread made with a leavening agent that permits immediate baking of the dough or batter

quick·en \'kwi-kən\ vb **1** : to come to life : REVIVE **2** : AROUSE, STIMULATE ⟨curiosity ~ed my interest⟩ **3** : to increase in speed : HASTEN **4** : to show vitality (as by growing or moving) ♦ **Synonyms** ANIMATE, ENLIVEN, LIVEN, VIVIFY

quick-freeze \'kwik-'frēz\ vb **-froze** \-'frōz\; **-fro·zen** \-'frō-zⁿn\; **-freez·ing** : to freeze (food) for preservation so rapidly that the natural juices and flavor are not lost

quick·ie \'kwi-kē\ n : something hurriedly done or made

quick·lime \'kwik-,līm\ n : ¹LIME

quick·sand \-,sand\ n : a deep mass of loose sand mixed with water

quick·sil·ver \-,sil-vər\ n : MERCURY 1

quick·step \-,step\ n : a spirited march tune or dance

quick-wit·ted \'kwik-'wi-təd\ adj : mentally alert ♦ **Synonyms** CLEVER, BRIGHT, SMART, INTELLIGENT

quid \'kwid\ n : a lump of something chewable ⟨a ~ of tobacco⟩

quid pro quo \,kwid-,prō-'kwō\ n [NL, something for something] : something given or received for something else

qui·es·cent \kwī-'e-sⁿnt\ adj : being at rest : QUIET ⟨a ~ state⟩ ♦ **Synonyms** LATENT, DORMANT, POTENTIAL — **qui·es·cence** \-sⁿns\ n

¹**qui·et** \'kwī-ət\ n : REPOSE

²**quiet** adj **1** : marked by little motion or activity : CALM **2** : GENTLE, MILD ⟨a ~ disposition⟩ **3** : enjoyed in peace and relaxation ⟨a ~ cup of tea⟩ **4** : free from noise or uproar **5** : not showy : MODEST ⟨~ clothes⟩ **6** : SECLUDED ⟨a ~ nook⟩ — **quiet** adv — **qui·et·ly** adv — **qui·et·ness** n

³**quiet** vb **1** : CALM, PACIFY **2** : to become quiet — usu. used with down

qui·etude \'kwī-ə-,tüd, -,tyüd\ n : QUIETNESS, REPOSE

qui·etus \kwī-'ē-təs\ n [ME quietus est, fr. ML, he is quit, formula of discharge from obligation] **1** : final settlement (as of a debt) **2** : DEATH

quill \'kwil\ n **1** : a large stiff feather; also : the hollow tubular part of a feather **2** : one of the hollow sharp spines of a hedgehog or porcupine **3** : a pen made from a feather

¹**quilt** \'kwilt\ n : a padded bed coverlet

²**quilt** vb **1** : to fill, pad, or line like a quilt **2** : to stitch or sew in layers with padding in between **3** : to make quilts

quince \'kwins\ n : a hard yellow applelike fruit; also : a tree related to the roses that bears this fruit

qui·nine \'kwī-,nīn\ n : a bitter white drug obtained from cinchona bark and used esp. in treating malaria

qui·noa \'kēn-,wä, kē-'nō-ə\ n [Sp, fr. Quechua kinua] : the starchy seeds of an annual herb related to spinach which are used as food and ground into flour; also : this herb

quint \'kwint\ n : QUINTUPLET

quin·tal \'kwin-tⁿl, 'kan-\ n : HUNDREDWEIGHT

quin·tes·sence \kwin-'te-sⁿns\ n **1** : the purest essence of something **2** : the most typical example ⟨the ~ of self-control⟩ — **quin·tes·sen·tial** \,kwin-tə-'sen-chəl\ adj — **quin·tes·sen·tial·ly** adv

quin·tet \kwin-'tet\ n **1** : a musical composition for five instruments or voices **2** : a group of five and esp. five musicians

¹**quin·tu·ple** \kwin-'tü-pəl, -'tyü-, -'tə-\ adj **1** : having five units or members **2** : being five times as great or as many — **quintuple** n

²**quintuple** vb **quin·tu·pled**; **quin·tu·pling** : to make or become five times as great or as many

quin·tu·plet \kwin-'tə-plət, -'tü-, -'tyü-\ n **1** : a group of five of a kind **2** : one of five offspring born at one birth

¹**quin·tu·pli·cate** \kwin-'tü-pli-kət, -'tyü-\ adj **1** : repeated five times **2** : FIFTH ⟨file the ~ copy⟩

²**quintuplicate** n **1** : one of five like things **2** : five copies all alike ⟨typed in ~⟩

³**quin·tu·pli·cate** \-plə-,kāt\ vb **-cat·ed**; **-cat·ing 1** : QUINTUPLE **2** : to provide in quintuplicate

¹**quip** \'kwip\ n : a clever remark : GIBE

²**quip** vb **quipped**; **quip·ping 1** : to make quips : GIBE **2** : to jest or gibe at

quire \'kwī(-ə)r\ n : a set of 24 or sometimes 25 sheets of paper of the same size and quality

quirk \'kwərk\ n : a peculiarity of action or behavior — **quirky** adj

quirt \'kwərt\ n : a riding whip with a short handle and a rawhide lash

quis·ling \'kwiz-liŋ\ n [Vidkun Quisling †1945 Norw. politician who collaborated with the Nazis] : one who helps the invaders of one's own country

quit \'kwit\ vb **quit** also **quit·ted**; **quit·ting 1** : CONDUCT, BEHAVE ⟨~ themselves well⟩ **2** : to depart from : LEAVE; also : to bring to an end **3** : to give up for good ⟨~ smoking⟩ ⟨~ my job⟩ ♦ **Synonyms** ACQUIT, COMPORT, DEPORT, DEMEAN — **quit·ter** n

quite \'kwīt\ adv **1** : COMPLETELY, WHOLLY ⟨not ~ finished⟩ **2** : to an extreme : POSITIVELY **3** : to a considerable extent : RATHER ⟨~ rich⟩

quits \'kwits\ adj : even or equal with another

quit·tance \'kwi-tⁿns\ n : REQUITAL

¹**quiv·er** \'kwi-vər\ n : a case for carrying arrows

²**quiver** vb **quiv·ered**; **quiv·er·ing** : to shake with a slight trembling motion ⟨~ed with rage⟩ ♦ **Synonyms** SHIVER, SHUDDER, QUAVER, QUAKE, TREMBLE — **quiv·er·ing·ly** adv

³**quiver** n : the act or action of quivering : TREMOR

qui vive \kē-'vēv\ n [F *qui-vive,* fr. *qui vive?* long live who?, challenge of a French sentry] : ALERT ⟨on the *qui vive* for prowlers⟩

quix·ot·ic \kwĭk-'sä-tik\ adj [fr. *Don Quixote,* hero of the novel *Don Quixote de la Mancha* by Cervantes] : foolishly impractical esp. in the pursuit of ideals — **quix·ot·i·cal·ly** \-ti-kə-lē\ adv

¹quiz \'kwiz\ n, pl **quiz·zes** 1 : an eccentric person 2 : PRACTICAL JOKE 3 : a short oral or written test

²quiz vb **quizzed; quiz·zing** 1 : MOCK 2 : to look at inquisitively 3 : to question closely ◆ **Synonyms** ASK, INTERROGATE, QUERY

quiz·zi·cal \'kwi-zi-kəl\ adj 1 : comically quaint 2 : mildly teasing or mocking 3 : expressive of puzzlement, curiosity, or disbelief ⟨gave me a ∼ look⟩

quoit \'kwāt, 'kwȯit, 'kȯit\ n 1 : a flattened ring of iron or circle of rope used in a throwing game 2 pl : a game in which quoits are thrown at an upright pin in an attempt to ring the pin

quon·dam \'kwän-dəm, -,dam\ adj [L, at one time, formerly, fr. *quom, cum* when] : FORMER ⟨a ∼ friend⟩

quo·rum \'kwȯr-əm\ n : the number of members required to be present for business to be legally transacted

quot abbr quotation

quo·ta \'kwō-tə\ n : a proportional part esp. when assigned : SHARE

quot·able \'kwō-tə-bəl\ adj : fit for or worth quoting ⟨a ∼ comment⟩ — **quot·abil·i·ty** \-'bi-lə-tē\ n

quo·ta·tion \kwō-'tā-shən\ n 1 : the act or process of quoting 2 : the price currently bid or offered for something 3 : something that is quoted

quotation mark n : one of a pair of punctuation marks " " or ' ' used esp. to indicate the beginning and end of a quotation in which exact phraseology is directly cited

quote \'kwōt\ vb **quot·ed; quot·ing** [ML *quotare* to mark the number of, number references, fr. L *quotus* of what number or quantity, fr. *quot* how many, (as) many as] 1 : to speak or write a passage from another usu. with acknowledgment; *also* : to repeat a passage in substantiation or illustration 2 : to state the market price of a commodity, stock, or bond 3 : to inform a hearer or reader that matter following is quoted — **quote** n

quoth \'kwōth\ vb past [ME, past of *quethen* to say, fr. OE *cwethan*] archaic : SAID — usu. used in the 1st and 3d persons with the subject following

quo·tid·i·an \kwō-'ti-dē-ən\ adj 1 : DAILY 2 : COMMONPLACE, ORDINARY ⟨∼ concerns⟩

quo·tient \'kwō-shənt\ n : the number obtained by dividing one number by another

Quran also **Qur'an** var of KORAN

qv abbr [L *quod vide*] which see

qy abbr query

¹r \'är\ n, pl **r's** or **rs** \'ärz\ often cap : the 18th letter of the English alphabet

²r abbr, often cap 1 rabbi 2 radius 3 rare 4 Republican 5 rerun 6 resistance 7 right 8 river 9 roentgen 10 rook 11 run

Ra symbol radium

RA abbr 1 regular army 2 Royal Academy 3 research assistant

¹rab·bet \'ra-bət\ n : a groove in the edge or face of a surface (as a board) esp. to receive another piece

²rabbet vb : to cut a rabbet in; *also* : to join by means of a rabbet

rab·bi \'ra-,bī\ n [ME, fr. OE, fr. LL, fr. Gk *rhabbi,* fr. Heb *rabbī* my master, fr. *rabh* master + *-ī* my] 1 : MASTER, TEACHER — used by Jews as a term of address 2 : a Jew trained and ordained for professional religious leadership — **rab·bin·ic** \rə-'bi-nik\ or **rab·bin·i·cal** \-ni-kəl\ adj

rab·bin·ate \'ra-bə-nət, -,nāt\ n 1 : the office of a rabbi 2 : the whole body of rabbis

rab·bit \'ra-bət\ n, pl **rabbit** or **rabbits** : any of various long-eared short-tailed burrowing mammals distinguished from the related hares by being blind, furless, and helpless at birth; *also* : the pelt of a rabbit

rabbit ears n pl : an indoor V-shaped television antenna

rab·ble \'ra-bəl\ n 1 : MOB 2 2 : the lowest class of people

rab·ble–rous·er \'ra-bəl-,raú-zər\ n : one that stirs up (as to hatred or violence) the masses of the people

rab·id \'ra-bəd\ adj 1 : VIOLENT, FURIOUS 2 : being fanatical or extreme ⟨∼ supporters⟩ 3 : affected with rabies — **ra·bid·ly** adv

ra·bies \'rā-bēz\ n, pl **rabies** [NL, fr. L, madness] : an acute deadly virus disease of the nervous system transmitted by the bite of an affected animal

rac·coon \ra-'kün\ n, pl **raccoon** or **rac·coons** : a gray No. American chiefly tree-dwelling mammal with a black mask, a bushy ringed tail, and nocturnal habits; *also* : its pelt

¹race \'rās\ n 1 : a strong current of running water; *also* : its channel 2 : an onward course (as of time or life) 3 : a contest of speed 4 : a contest for a desired end (as election to office)

²race vb **raced; rac·ing** 1 : to run in a race 2 : to run swiftly : RUSH 3 : to engage in a race with 4 : to drive or ride at high speed — **rac·er** n

³**race** *n* **1** : a family, tribe, people, or nation of the same stock **2** : a group of individuals within a biological species able to breed together **3** : a category of humankind that shares certain distinctive physical traits — **ra·cial** \'rā-shəl\ *adj* — **ra·cial·ly** *adv*

race·course \'rās-ˌkȯrs\ *n* : a course for racing

race·horse \-ˌhȯrs\ *n* : a horse bred or kept for racing

ra·ceme \rā-'sēm\ *n* [L *racemus* bunch of grapes] : a flower cluster with flowers borne along a stem and blooming from the base toward the tip — **rac·e·mose** \'ra-sə-ˌmōs\ *adj*

race·track \'rās-ˌtrak\ *n* : a usu. oval course on which races are run

race·way \-ˌwā\ *n* **1** : a channel for a current of water **2** : RACECOURSE

ra·cial·ism \'rā-shə-ˌli-zəm\ *n* : a theory that race determines human traits and capacities; *also* : RACISM — **ra·cial·ist** \-list\ *n* — **ra·cial·is·tic** \ˌrā-shə-'lis-tik\ *adj*

ra·cial·ize \'rā-shə-ˌlīz\ *vb* **-ized; -iz·ing** : to give a racial character to

racing form *n* : a paper giving data about racehorses for use by bettors

rac·ism \'rā-ˌsi-zəm\ *n* : a belief that some races are by nature superior to others; *also* : discrimination based on such belief — **rac·ist** \-sist\ *n*

¹**rack** \'rak\ *n* **1** : an instrument of torture on which a body is stretched **2** : a framework on or in which something may be placed (as for display or storage) **3** : a bar with teeth on one side to mesh with a pinion or worm gear

²**rack** *vb* **1** : to torture on or as if on a rack **2** : to stretch or strain by force **3** : TORMENT **4** : to place on or in a rack

¹**rack·et** *or* **rac·quet** \'ra-kət\ *n* [MF *raquette*, ultim. fr. ML *rasceta* wrist, carpus, fr. Ar *rusgh* wrist] : a light bat made of netting stretched in an oval open frame having a handle and used for striking a ball or shuttlecock

²**racket** *n* **1** : confused noise : DIN **2** : a fraudulent or dishonest scheme or activity ⟨a criminal ∼⟩

³**racket** *vb* : to make a racket

rack·e·teer \ˌra-kə-'tir\ *n* : a person who obtains money by an illegal enterprise usu. involving intimidation — **rack·e·teer·ing** *n*

rack up *vb* : ACHIEVE, GAIN ⟨racked up their 10th victory⟩

ra·con·teur \ˌra-ˌkän-'tər\ *n* : one good at telling anecdotes

rac·quet·ball \'ra-kət-ˌbȯl\ *n* : a game similar to handball that is played on a 4-walled court with a short-handled racket

racy \'rā-sē\ *adj* **rac·i·er; -est 1** : full of zest **2** : PUNGENT, SPICY **3** : RISQUÉ, SUGGESTIVE ⟨∼ jokes⟩ — **rac·i·ly** \'rā-sə-lē\ *adv* — **rac·i·ness** \-sē-nəs\ *n*

rad *abbr* **1** radical **2** radio **3** radius

ra·dar \'rā-ˌdär\ *n* [*radio detecting and ranging*] : a device that emits radio waves for detecting and locating an object by the reflection of the radio waves and that may use this reflection to determine the object's direction and speed

radar gun *n* : a handheld device that uses radar to measure the speed of a moving object

ra·dar·scope \'rā-ˌdär-ˌskōp\ *n* : a visual display for a radar receiver

¹**ra·di·al** \'rā-dē-əl\ *adj* : arranged or having parts arranged like rays around a common center ⟨the ∼ form of a starfish⟩ — **ra·di·al·ly** *adv*

²**radial** *n* : a pneumatic tire with cords laid perpendicular to the center line

radial engine *n* : an internal combustion engine with cylinders arranged radially like the spokes of a wheel

ra·di·an \'rā-dē-ən\ *n* : a unit of measure for angles that is equal to approximately 57.3 degrees

ra·di·ant \'rā-dē-ənt\ *adj* **1** : SHINING, GLOWING **2** : beaming with happiness ⟨a ∼ smile⟩ **3** : transmitted by radiation
  ♦ **Synonyms** BRILLIANT, BRIGHT, LUMINOUS, LUSTROUS — **ra·di·ance** \-əns\ *n* — **ra·di·ant·ly** *adv*

radiant energy *n* : energy traveling as electromagnetic waves

ra·di·ate \'rā-dē-ˌāt\ *vb* **-at·ed; -at·ing 1** : to send out rays : SHINE, GLOW **2** : to issue in or as if in rays ⟨light ∼s⟩ **3** : to spread around as from a center

ra·di·a·tion \ˌrā-dē-'ā-shən\ *n* **1** : the action or process of radiating **2** : the process of emitting radiant energy in the form of waves or particles; *also* : something (as an X-ray beam) that is radiated

radiation sickness *n* : sickness that results from exposure to radiation and is commonly marked by fatigue, nausea, vomiting, loss of teeth and hair, and in more severe cases by damage to blood-forming tissue

radiation therapy *n* : RADIOTHERAPY

ra·di·a·tor \'rā-dē-ˌā-tər\ *n* : any of various devices (as a set of pipes or tubes) for transferring heat from a fluid within to an area or object outside

¹**rad·i·cal** \'ra-di-kəl\ *adj* [ME, fr. LL *radicalis*, fr. L *radic-, radix* root] **1** : FUNDAMENTAL, EXTREME, THOROUGHGOING **2** : of or relating to radicals in politics — **rad·i·cal·ism** \-kə-ˌli-zəm\ *n* — **rad·i·cal·ly** *adv*

²**radical** *n* **1** : a person who favors rapid and sweeping changes in laws and methods of government **2** : FREE RADICAL; *also* : a group of atoms considered as a unit in certain reactions or as a subunit of a larger molecule **3** : a mathematical expression indicating a root by means of a radical sign; *also* : RADICAL SIGN

rad·i·cal·ise *Brit var of* RADICALIZE

rad·i·cal·ize \-kə-ˌlīz\ *vb* **-ized; -iz·ing** : to make radical esp. in politics — **rad·i·cal·i·za·tion** \ˌra-di-kə-lə-'zā-shən\ *n*

radical sign *n* : the sign √ placed before a mathematical expression to indicate that its root is to be taken

ra·dic·chio \ra-'di-kē-ō\ *n, pl* **-chios** : a chicory with reddish variegated leaves

radii *pl of* RADIUS

¹**ra·dio** \'rā-dē-ˌō\ *n, pl* **ra·di·os** 1 : the wireless transmission or reception of signals using electromagnetic waves 2 : a radio receiving set 3 : the radio broadcasting industry — **radio** *adj*

²**radio** *vb* : to communicate or send a message to by radio

ra·dio·ac·tiv·i·ty \ˌrā-dē-ō-ˌak-'ti-və-tē\ *n* : the property that some elements or isotopes have of spontaneously emitting energetic particles by the disintegration of their atomic nuclei — **ra·dio·ac·tive** \-'ak-tiv\ *adj*

radio astronomy *n* : astronomy dealing with radio waves received from outside the earth's atmosphere

ra·dio·car·bon \ˌrā-dē-ō-'kär-bən\ *n* : CARBON 14

radio frequency *n* : an electromagnetic wave frequency intermediate between audio frequencies and infrared frequencies used esp. for communication and radar signals

ra·dio·gram \'rā-dē-ō-ˌgram\ *n* : a message transmitted by radio

ra·dio·graph \-ˌgraf\ *n* : a photograph made by some form of radiation other than light; *esp* : an X-ray photograph — **radiograph** *vb* — **ra·dio·graph·ic** \ˌrā-dē-ō-'gra-fik\ *adj* — **ra·dio·graph·i·cal·ly** \-fi-k(ə-)lē\ *adv* — **ra·di·og·ra·phy** \ˌrā-dē-'ä-grə-fē\ *n*

ra·dio·iso·tope \ˌrā-dē-ō-'ī-sə-ˌtōp\ *n* : a radioactive isotope

ra·di·ol·o·gy \ˌrā-dē-'ä-lə-jē\ *n* : the use of radiant energy (as X-rays and radium radiations) in medicine — **ra·di·ol·o·gist** \-jist\ *n*

ra·dio·man \'rā-dē-ō-ˌman\ *n* : a radio operator or technician

ra·di·om·e·ter \ˌrā-dē-'ä-mə-tər\ *n* : an instrument for measuring the intensity of radiant energy — **ra·dio·met·ric** \ˌrā-dē-ō-'me-trik\ *adj* — **ra·di·om·e·try** \-mə-trē\ *n*

ra·dio·phone \'rā-dē-ə-ˌfōn\ *n* : RADIOTELEPHONE

ra·dio·sonde \'rā-dē-ō-ˌsänd\ *n* : a small radio transmitter carried aloft (as by balloon) and used to transmit meteorological data

ra·dio·tele·phone \ˌrā-dē-ō-'te-lə-ˌfōn\ *n* : a telephone that uses radio waves wholly or partly instead of connecting wires — **ra·dio·te·le·pho·ny** \-tə-'le-fə-nē, -'te-lə-ˌfō-nē\ *n*

radio telescope *n* : a radio receiver-antenna combination used for observation in radio astronomy

ra·dio·ther·a·py \ˌrā-dē-ō-'ther-ə-pē\ *n* : the treatment of disease by means of radiation (as X-rays) — **ra·dio·ther·a·pist** \-pist\ *n*

rad·ish \'ra-dish\ *n* [ME, alter. of OE *rǣdic*, fr. L *radic-*, *radix* root, radish] : a pungent fleshy root usu. eaten raw; *also* : a plant related to the mustards that produces this root

ra·di·um \'rā-dē-əm\ *n* [NL, fr. L *radius* ray] : a very radioactive metallic chemical element that is used in the treatment of cancer

ra·di·us \'rā-dē-əs\ *n, pl* **ra·dii** \-ē-ˌī\ *also* **ra·di·us·es** 1 : a straight line extending from the center of a circle or a sphere to the circumference or surface; *also* : the length of a radius 2 : the bone on the thumb side of the human forearm 3 : a circular area defined by the length of its radius ◆ *Synonyms* RANGE, REACH, SCOPE, COMPASS

RADM *abbr* rear admiral

ra·don \'rā-ˌdän\ *n* : a heavy radioactive gaseous chemical element

RAF *abbr* Royal Air Force

raf·fia \'ra-fē-ə\ *n* : fiber used esp. for making baskets and hats that is obtained from the stalks of the leaves of a tropical African palm (**raffia palm**)

raff·ish \'ra-fish\ *adj* : jaunty or sporty esp. in a flashy or vulgar manner — **raff·ish·ly** *adv* — **raff·ish·ness** *n*

¹**raf·fle** \'ra-fəl\ *vb* **raf·fled; raf·fling** : to dispose of by a raffle

²**raffle** *n* : a lottery in which the prize is won by one of a number of persons buying chances

¹**raft** \'raft\ *n* 1 : a number of logs or timbers fastened together to form a float 2 : a flat structure for support or transportation on water

²**raft** *vb* 1 : to travel or transport by raft 2 : to make into a raft

³**raft** *n* : a large amount or number

raf·ter \'raf-tər\ *n* : any of the parallel beams that support a roof

¹**rag** \'rag\ *n* 1 : a waste piece of cloth 2 : a sleazy newspaper

²**rag** *n* : a composition in ragtime

ra·ga \'rä-gə\ *n* 1 : a traditional melodic pattern or mode in Indian music 2 : an improvisation based on a raga

rag·a·muf·fin \'ra-gə-ˌmə-fən\ *n* [ME *Ragamuffyn*, name for a ragged, oafish person] : a ragged dirty person; *esp* : a poorly clothed often dirty child

¹**rage** \'rāj\ *n* 1 : violent and uncontrolled anger 2 : VOGUE, FASHION

²**rage** *vb* **raged; rag·ing** 1 : to be furiously angry : RAVE 2 : to continue out of control ⟨the fire *raged*⟩

rag·ged \'ra-gəd\ *adj* 1 : TORN, TATTERED ⟨a ~ dress⟩; *also* : wearing tattered clothes 2 : done in an uneven way ⟨a ~ performance⟩ — **rag·ged·ly** *adv* — **rag·ged·ness** *n*

rag·lan \'ra-glən\ *n* : an overcoat with sleeves (**raglan sleeves**) sewn in with seams slanting from neck to underarm

ra·gout \ra-'gü\ *n* [F *ragoût*, fr. *ragoûter* to revive the taste, fr. MF *ragouster*, fr. *re-* + *a-* to (fr. L *ad-*) + *goust* taste, fr. L *gustus*] : a highly seasoned meat stew with vegetables

rag·pick·er \'rag-ˌpi-kər\ *n* : one who collects rags and refuse for a living

rag·time \-ˌtīm\ *n* : music in which there is more or less continuous syncopation in the melody

rag·top \'rag-ˌtäp\ *n* : CONVERTIBLE

rag·weed \-ˌwēd\ *n* : any of several chiefly No. American weedy composite herbs with allergenic pollen

¹raid \'rād\ *n* : a sudden usu. surprise attack or invasion : FORAY

²raid *vb* : to make a raid on — **raid·er** *n*

¹rail \'rāl\ *n* [ME *raile*, fr. AF *raille, reille* bar, rule, fr. L *regula* straightedge, rule, fr. *regere* to keep straight, direct] **1** : a bar extending from one support to another as a guard or barrier **2** : a bar of steel forming a track for wheeled vehicles **3** : RAILROAD

²rail *vb* : to provide with a railing

³rail *n, pl* **rail** *or* **rails** : any of numerous small wading birds often hunted as game birds

⁴rail *vb* [ME, fr. MF *railler* to mock, prob. fr. OF *reillier* to growl, mutter, fr. VL **ragulare* to bray, fr. LL *ragere* to neigh] : to complain angrily : SCOLD, REVILE — **rail·er** *n*

rail·ing \'rā-liŋ\ *n* : a barrier of rails

rail·lery \'rā-lə-rē\ *n, pl* **-ler·ies** : good-natured ridicule : BANTER

¹rail·road \'rāl-ˌrōd\ *n* : a permanent road with rails fixed to ties providing a track for cars; *also* : such a road and its assets constituting a property

²railroad *vb* **1** : to put through (as a law) too hastily **2** : to convict hastily or with insufficient or improper evidence **3** : to send by rail **4** : to work on a railroad — **rail·road·er** *n* — **rail·road·ing** *n*

rail·way \-ˌwā\ *n* : RAILROAD

rai·ment \'rā-mənt\ *n* : CLOTHING

¹rain \'rān\ *n* **1** : water falling in drops from the clouds **2** : a shower of objects ⟨a ~ of bullets⟩ — **rainy** *adj*

²rain *vb* **1** : to send down rain **2** : to fall as or like rain **3** : to pour down

¹rain·bow \-ˌbō\ *n* : an arc or circle of colors formed by the refraction and reflection of the sun's rays in rain, spray, or mist

²rainbow *adj* **1** : having many colors **2** : of, relating to, or made up of people of different races or cultural backgrounds

rainbow trout *n* : a large stout-bodied fish of western No. America closely related to the salmons of the Pacific and usu. having red or pink stripes with black dots along its sides

rain check *n* **1** : a ticket stub good for a later performance when the scheduled one is rained out **2** : an assurance of a deferred extension of an offer

rain·coat \'rān-ˌkōt\ *n* : a waterproof or water-repellent coat

rain date *n* : an alternative date for an event postponed due to rain

rain·drop \-ˌdräp\ *n* : a drop of rain

rain·fall \-ˌfol\ *n* **1** : amount of precipitation measured by depth **2** : a fall of rain

rain forest *n* : a tropical woodland having an annual rainfall of at least 100 inches (254 centimeters) and marked by lofty broad-leaved evergreen trees forming a continuous canopy

rain·mak·ing \'rān-ˌmā-kiŋ\ *n* : the action or process of producing or attempting to produce rain by artificial means — **rain·mak·er** *n*

rain out *vb* : to interrupt or prevent by rain

rain·storm \'rān-ˌstorm\ *n* : a storm of or with rain

rain·wa·ter \-ˌwo-tər, -ˌwä-\ *n* : water fallen as rain

¹raise \'rāz\ *vb* **raised; rais·ing** **1** : to cause or help to rise : LIFT ⟨~ a window⟩ **2** : AWAKEN, AROUSE ⟨enough to ~ the dead⟩ **3** : BUILD, ERECT ⟨~ a monument⟩ **4** : PROMOTE ⟨was *raised* to captain⟩ **5** : END ⟨~ a siege⟩ **6** : COLLECT ⟨~ money⟩ **7** : BREED, GROW ⟨~ cattle⟩ ⟨~ corn⟩; *also* : BRING UP ⟨~ a family⟩ **8** : PROVOKE ⟨~ a laugh⟩ **9** : to bring to notice ⟨~ an objection⟩ **10** : INCREASE ⟨~ prices⟩; *also* : to bet more than **11** : to make light and spongy ⟨~ dough⟩ **12** : to multiply a quantity by itself a specified number of times ⟨~ 2 to the third power⟩ **13** : to cause to form ⟨~ a blister⟩ ♦ *Synonyms* LIFT, HOIST, BOOST, ELEVATE — **rais·er** *n* —
raise the bar : to set a higher standard

²raise *n* : an increase in amount (as of a bid or bet); *also* : an increase in pay

rai·sin \'rā-zⁿn\ *n* [ME, fr. AF, grape, raisin, fr. L *racemus* cluster of grapes or berries] : a grape dried for food

rai·son d'être \ˌrā-ˌzōⁿ-ˈdetrⁿ\ *n, pl* **rai·sons d'être** \-ˌzōⁿz-\ : reason or justification for existence

ra·ja *or* **ra·jah** \'rä-jə\ *n* [Hindi *rājā*, fr. Skt *rājan* king] : an Indian prince

¹rake \'rāk\ *n* : a long-handled garden tool having a crossbar with prongs

²rake *vb* **raked; rak·ing** **1** : to gather, loosen, or smooth with or as if with a rake **2** : to sweep the length of (as a trench or ship) with gunfire

³rake *n* : inclination from either perpendicular or horizontal : SLANT

⁴rake *n* : a dissolute man : LIBERTINE

rake–off \'rāk-ˌof\ *n* : a percentage or cut taken

rak·ish \'rā-kish\ *adj* : DISSOLUTE — **rak·ish·ly** *adv* — **rak·ish·ness** *n*

²rakish *adj* **1** : having a trim appearance indicative of speed ⟨a ~ sloop⟩ **2** : JAUNTY, SPORTY ⟨~ clothes⟩ — **rak·ish·ly** *adv* — **rak·ish·ness** *n*

¹ral·ly \'ra-lē\ *vb* **ral·lied; ral·ly·ing** **1** : to bring together for a common purpose; *also* : to bring back to order ⟨a leader ~ing his forces⟩ **2** : to arouse to activity or from depression or weakness **3** : to make a comeback ♦ *Synonyms* STIR, ROUSE, AWAKEN, WAKEN, KINDLE

²rally *n, pl* **rallies** **1** : an act of rallying **2** : a mass meeting to arouse enthusiasm **3** : a competitive automobile event run over public roads

³rally *vb* **ral·lied; ral·ly·ing** : BANTER

rallying cry *n* : WAR CRY 2

¹ram \'ram\ *n* **1** : a male sheep **2** : BATTERING RAM

²ram *vb* **rammed; ram·ming** **1** : to force or drive in or through **2** : CRAM, CROWD **3** : to strike against violently

RAM \'ram\ *n* : a computer memory that provides the main internal storage for programs and data

¹ram·ble \'ram-bəl\ *vb* **ram·bled; ram-**

bling : to go about aimlessly : ROAM, WANDER

²ram·ble *n* : a leisurely excursion; *esp* : an aimless walk

ram·bler \'ram-blər\ *n* **1** : a person who rambles **2** : any of various climbing roses with large clusters of small often double flowers

ram·bunc·tious \ram-'bəŋk-shəs\ *adj* : UNRULY

ra·mie \'rā-mē, 'ra-\ *n* : a strong lustrous bast fiber from an Asian nettle

ram·i·fi·ca·tion \,ra-mə-fə-'kā-shən\ *n* **1** : the act or process of branching **2** : CONSEQUENCE, OUTGROWTH ⟨the ∼s of the decision⟩

ram·i·fy \'ra-mə-,fī\ *vb* **-fied; -fy·ing** : to branch out

ramp \'ramp\ *n* : a sloping passage or roadway connecting different levels

¹ram·page \'ram-,pāj, (,)ram-'pāj\ *vb* **rampaged; ram·pag·ing** : to rush about wildly ⟨*rampaging* soccer fans⟩

²ram·page \'ram-,pāj\ *n* : a course of violent or riotous action or behavior — **ram·pa·geous** \ram-'pā-jəs\ *adj*

ram·pant \'ram-pənt\ *adj* : unchecked in growth or spread : RIFE ⟨fear was ∼ in the town⟩ — **ram·pan·cy** \-pən-sē\ *n* — **ram·pant·ly** *adv*

ram·part \'ram-,pärt\ *n* **1** : a protective barrier **2** : a broad embankment raised as a fortification

¹ram·rod \'ram-,räd\ *n* **1** : a rod used to ram a charge into a muzzle-loading gun **2** : a cleaning rod for small arms **3** : BOSS, OVERSEER

²ramrod *adj* : marked by rigidity or severity ⟨his ∼ posture⟩

³ramrod *vb* : to direct, supervise, and control ⟨*ramrodded* the project forward⟩

ram·shack·le \'ram-,sha-kəl\ *adj* : RICKETY, TUMBLEDOWN

ran *past of* RUN

¹ranch \'ranch\ *n* [MexSp *rancho* small ranch, fr. Sp, camp, hut & Sp dial., small farm, fr. Old Spanish *ranchear* (se) to take up quarters, fr. MF (se) *ranger* to take up a position, fr. *ranger* to set in a row] **1** : an establishment for the raising and grazing of livestock (as cattle, sheep, or horses) **2** : a large farm devoted to a specialty **3** : RANCH HOUSE 2

²ranch *vb* : to live or work on a ranch — **ranch·er** *n*

ranch house *n* **1** : the main house on a ranch **2** : a one-story house typically with a low-pitched roof

ran·cho \'ran-chō, 'rän-\ *n, pl* **ranchos** : RANCH 1

ran·cid \'ran-səd\ *adj* **1** : having a rank smell or taste **2** : OFFENSIVE **3** — **ran·cid·i·ty** \ran-'si-də-tē\ *n*

ran·cor \'raŋ-kər\ *n* : bitter deep-seated ill will ♦ *Synonyms* ANTAGONISM, ANIMOSITY, ANTIPATHY, ENMITY, HOSTILITY — **ran·cor·ous** *adj*

ran·cour *Brit var of* RANCOR

rand \'rand, 'ränd, 'ränt\ *n, pl* **rand** — see MONEY table

R & B *abbr* rhythm and blues

R & D *abbr* research and development

ran·dom \'ran-dəm\ *adj* : CHANCE, HAPHAZARD — **ran·dom·ly** *adv* — **ran·dom·ness** *n*

random–access *adj* : allowing access to stored data in any order the user desires

random–access memory *n* : RAM

ran·dom·ize \'ran-də-,mīz\ *vb* **-ized; -izing** : to select, assign, or arrange in a random way — **ran·dom·i·za·tion** \,ran-də-mə-'zā-shən\ *n*

R & R *abbr* rest and recreation; rest and recuperation

rang *past of* RING

¹range \'rānj\ *n* **1** : a series of things in a row **2** : a cooking stove having an oven and a flat top with burners **3** : open land where animals (as livestock) may roam and graze **4** : the region throughout which an organism occurs **5** : the act of ranging about **6** : the distance a weapon will shoot or is to be shot **7** : a place where shooting is practiced **8** : the space or extent included, covered, or used : SCOPE **9** : a variation within limits ♦ *Synonyms* REACH, COMPASS, RADIUS, CIRCLE

²range *vb* **ranged; rang·ing** [ME, fr. AF *renger*, fr. *renc, reng* line, place, row, of Gmc origin] **1** : to set in a row or in proper order **2** : to set in place among others of the same kind **3** : to roam over or through : EXPLORE **4** : to roam at large or freely **5** : to correspond in direction or line **6** : to vary within limits **7** : to find the range of an object by instrument (as radar)

rang·er \'rān-jər\ *n* **1** : FOREST RANGER **2** : a member of a body of troops who range over a region **3** : an expert in close-range fighting and raiding tactics

rangy \'rān-jē\ *adj* **rang·i·er; -est** : being long-limbed and slender ⟨a ∼ teenager⟩ — **rang·i·ness** \'rān-jē-nəs\ *n*

ra·ni *or* **ra·nee** \rä-'nē, 'rä-,nē\ *n* : a raja's wife

¹rank \'raŋk\ *adj* **1** : strong and vigorous and usu. coarse in growth **2** : unpleasantly strong-smelling — **rank·ly** *adv* — **rank·ness** *n*

²rank *n* **1** : ROW ⟨∼s of houses⟩ **2** : a line of soldiers ranged side by side **3** *pl* : the body of enlisted personnel ⟨rose from the ∼s⟩ **4** : position in a group **5** : superior position **6** : a grade of official standing (as in an army) **7** : an orderly arrangement **8** : CLASS, DIVISION — usu. used in pl.

³rank *vb* **1** : to arrange in lines or in regular formation **2** : RATE **3** : to rate above (as in official standing) **4** : to take or have a relative position

rank and file *n* : the general membership of a body as contrasted with its leaders

rank·ing \'raŋ-kiŋ\ *adj* **1** : having a high position : of the highest rank **2** : being next to the chairman in seniority

ran·kle \'raŋ-kəl\ *vb* **ran·kled; ran·kling** [ME *ranclen* to fester, fr. AF *rancler*, fr. OF *draoncler, raoncler*, fr. *draoncle, raoncle* festering sore, fr. ML *dracunculus*, fr. L, dim. of *draco* serpent] : to cause anger, irritation, or bitterness

ran·sack \'ran-,sak\ *vb* : to search thoroughly; *esp* : to search through and rob

¹ran·som \'ran-səm\ *n* [ME *ransoun*, fr. OF *rançun*, fr. L *redemption-*, *redemptio* act of buying back, fr. *redimere* to buy back, redeem] **1** : something paid or demanded for the freedom of a captive **2** : the act of ransoming

²ransom *vb* : to free from captivity or punishment by paying a price — **ran·som·er** *n*

rant \'rant\ *vb* **1** : to talk loudly and wildly **2** : to scold violently ⟨~ed against his opponent⟩ — **rant·er** *n* — **rant·ing·ly** *adv*

¹rap \'rap\ *n* **1** : a sharp blow **2** : a sharp rebuke **3** : a negative often undeserved reputation ⟨a bum ~⟩ **4** : responsibility for or consequences of an action ⟨take the ~⟩

²rap *vb* **rapped; rap·ping 1** : to strike sharply : KNOCK **2** : to utter sharply **3** : to criticize sharply

³rap *vb* **rapped; rap·ping 1** : to talk freely and frankly **2** : to perform rap music — **rap·per** *n*

⁴rap *n* **1** : TALK, CONVERSATION **2** : a rhythmic chanting of rhymed couplets to a musical accompaniment; *also* : a piece so performed

ra·pa·cious \rə-'pā-shəs\ *adj* **1** : excessively greedy or covetous **2** : living on prey **3** : RAVENOUS ⟨a ~ appetite⟩ — **ra·pa·cious·ly** *adv* — **ra·pa·cious·ness** *n* — **ra·pac·i·ty** \-'pa-sə-tē\ *n*

¹rape \'rāp\ *n* : an Old World herb related to the mustards that is grown as a forage crop and for its seeds (**rapeseed** \-,sēd\)

²rape *vb* **raped; rap·ing** : to commit rape on — **rap·er** *n* — **rap·ist** \'rā-pist\ *n*

³rape *n* **1** : a carrying away by force **2** : unlawful sexual activity and usu. sexual intercourse carried out forcibly or under threat of injury

¹rap·id \'ra-pəd\ *adj* [L *rapidus* strong-flowing, rapid, fr. *rapere* to seize, carry away] : very fast : SWIFT ♦ *Synonyms* FLEET, QUICK, SPEEDY — **ra·pid·i·ty** \rə-'pi-də-tē\ *n* — **rap·id·ly** *adv*

²rapid *n* : a place in a stream where the current flows very fast usu. over obstructions — usu. used in pl.

rapid eye movement *n* : rapid conjugate movement of the eyes associated with REM sleep

rapid transit *n* : fast passenger transportation (as by subway) in cities

¹ra·pi·er \'rā-pē-ər\ *n* : a straight 2-edged sword with a narrow pointed blade

²rapier *adj* : extremely sharp or keen ⟨~ wit⟩

rap·ine \'ra-pən, -,pīn\ *n* : PILLAGE, PLUNDER

rap·pel \ra-'pel, ra-\ *vb* **-pelled; -pel·ling** : to descend (as from a cliff) by sliding down a rope

rap·pen \'rä-pən\ *n, pl* **rappen** : the centime of Switzerland

rap·port \ra-'pȯr\ *n* : RELATION; *esp* : relation characterized by harmony

rap·proche·ment \,ra-prȯsh-'mäⁿ, ra-

'prȯsh-,mäⁿ\ *n* : the establishment of or a state of having cordial relations

rap·scal·lion \rap-'skal-yən\ *n* : RASCAL, SCAMP

rapt \'rapt\ *adj* **1** : carried away with emotion **2** : ABSORBED, ENGROSSED ⟨listened with ~ attention⟩ — **rapt·ly** \'rapt-lē\ *adv* — **rapt·ness** *n*

rap·tor \'rap-tər, -,tȯr\ *n* **1** : BIRD OF PREY **2** : a usu. small-to-medium-sized predatory dinosaur

rap·ture \'rap-chər\ *n* : spiritual or emotional ecstasy — **rap·tur·ous** \-chə-rəs\ *adj* — **rap·tur·ous·ly** *adv*

rapture of the deep : NITROGEN NARCOSIS

ra·ra avis \,rer-ə-'ā-vəs, ,rär-ə-'ä-wəs\ *n, pl* **ra·ra avis·es** \-'ā-və-səz\ *or* **ra·rae aves** \,rär-,ī-'ä-,wās\ [L, rare bird] : a rare person or thing : RARITY

¹rare \'rer\ *adj* **rar·er; rar·est 1** : not thick or dense : THIN ⟨~ air⟩ **2** : unusually fine : EXCELLENT, SPLENDID **3** : seldom met with — **rare·ly** *adv* — **rare·ness** *n* — **rar·i·ty** \'rar-ə-tē\ *n*

²rare *adj* **rar·er; rar·est** : cooked so that the inside is still red ⟨~ beef⟩

rare·bit \'rer-bət\ *n* : WELSH RABBIT

rar·efac·tion \,rer-ə-'fak-shən\ *n* **1** : the action or process of rarefying **2** : the state of being rarefied

rar·e·fy *also* **rar·i·fy** \'rer-ə-,fī\ *vb* **-fied; -fy·ing** : to make or become rare, thin, or less dense

rar·ing \'rer-ən, -iŋ\ *adj* : full of enthusiasm or eagerness ⟨~ to go⟩

ras·cal \'ras-kəl\ *n* [ME *rascaile* foot soldiers, commoners, worthless person, fr. AF *rascaille*, fr. OF dial. **rasquer* to scrape, clean off, ultim. fr. L *radere* to scrape, shave] **1** : a mean or dishonest person **2** : a mischievous person — **ras·cal·i·ty** \ra-'ska-lə-tē\ *n* — **ras·cal·ly** \'ras-kə-lē\ *adj*

rash \'rash\ *adj* : having or showing little regard for consequences : too hasty in decision, action, or speech : RECKLESS ♦ *Synonyms* DARING, FOOLHARDY, ADVENTUROUS, VENTURESOME — **rash·ly** *adv* — **rash·ness** *n*

²rash *n* : an eruption on the body

rash·er \'ra-shər\ *n* : a thin slice of bacon or ham broiled or fried; *also* : a portion consisting of several such slices

¹rasp \'rasp\ *vb* **1** : to rub with or as if with a rough file **2** : to grate harshly on (as one's nerves) **3** : to speak in a grating tone ⟨"Don't touch me," she ~ed⟩

²rasp *n* : a coarse file with cutting points instead of ridges

rasp·ber·ry \'raz-,ber-ē, -bə-rē\ *n* **1** : any of various edible usu. black or red berries produced by some brambles; *also* : such a bramble **2** : a sound of contempt made by protruding the tongue through the lips and expelling air forcibly

¹rat \'rat\ *n* **1** : any of numerous rodents larger than the related mice **2** : a contemptible person; *esp* : one that betrays friends or associates

²rat *vb* **rat·ted; rat·ting 1** : to betray or

inform on one's associates **2** : to hunt or catch rats

rat cheese *n* : CHEDDAR

ratch·et \'ra-chət\ *n* : a device that consists of a bar or wheel having slanted teeth into which a pawl drops so as to allow motion in only one direction

¹**rate** \'rāt\ *vb* **rat·ed; rat·ing** : to scold violently

²**rate** *n* **1** : quantity, amount, or degree measured by some standard **2** : an amount (as of payment) measured by its relation to some other amount (as of time) **3** : a charge, payment, or price fixed according to a ratio, scale, or standard ⟨tax ∼⟩ **4** : RANK, CLASS

³**rate** *vb* **rat·ed; rat·ing 1** : ESTIMATE **2** : CONSIDER, REGARD ⟨*rated* as a good pianist⟩ **3** : to settle the relative rank or class of **4** : to be classed : RANK **5** : to have a right to : DESERVE ⟨the new museum ∼s a visit⟩ **6** : to be of consequence — **rat·er** *n*

rath·er \'ra-thər, 'rä-, 'rə-\ *adv* [ME, fr. OE *hrathor*, compar. of *hrathe* quickly] **1** : more properly **2** : PREFERABLY ⟨I'd ∼ not go⟩ **3** : more correctly speaking **4** : to the contrary : INSTEAD **5** : SOMEWHAT ⟨∼ warm⟩

rather than *prep* : INSTEAD OF

raths·kel·ler \'rät-,ske-lər, 'rat-\ *n* [obs. G (now *Ratskeller*), city-hall basement restaurant, fr. *Rat* council + *Keller* cellar] : a usu. basement tavern or restaurant

rat·i·fy \'ra-tə-,fī\ *vb* **-fied; -fy·ing** : to approve and accept formally — **rat·i·fi·ca·tion** \,ra-tə-fə-'kā-shən\ *n*

rat·ing \'rā-tiŋ\ *n* **1** : a classification according to grade : RANK **2** *Brit* : an enlisted person in the navy **3** : an estimate of the credit standing and business responsibility of a person or firm

ra·tio \'rā-shō, -shē-ō\ *n, pl* **ra·tios 1** : the indicated quotient of two numbers or mathematical expressions **2** : the relationship in number, quantity, or degree between two or more things

ra·ti·o·ci·na·tion \,ra-tē-,ō-sə-'nā-shən, -,ä-\ *n* : exact thinking : REASONING — **ra·ti·o·ci·nate** \-'ō-sə-,nāt, -'ä-\ *vb* — **ra·ti·o·ci·na·tive** \-'ō-sə-,nā-tiv, -'ä-\ *adj* — **ra·ti·o·ci·na·tor** \-'ō-sə-,nā-tər, -'ä-sə-\ *n*

¹**ra·tion** \'ra-shən, 'rā-\ *n* **1** : a food allowance for one day **2** : FOOD, PROVISIONS, DIET — usu. used in pl. **3** : SHARE, ALLOTMENT

²**ration** *vb* **1** : to supply with or allot as rations **2** : to use or allot sparingly
♦ *Synonyms* APPORTION, PORTION, PRORATE, PARCEL

¹**ra·tio·nal** \'ra-shə-nəl\ *adj* **1** : having reason or understanding **2** : of or relating to reason **3** : relating to, consisting of, or being one or more rational numbers — **ra·tio·nal·ly** *adv*

²**rational** *n* : RATIONAL NUMBER

ra·tio·nale \,ra-shə-'nal\ *n* **1** : an explanation of principles controlling belief or practice **2** : an underlying reason

ra·tio·nal·ise *Brit var of* RATIONALIZE

ra·tio·nal·ism \'ra-shə-nə-,li-zəm\ *n* : the practice of guiding one's actions and

opinions solely by what seems reasonable — **ra·tio·nal·ist** \-list\ *n* — **rationalist** *or* **ra·tio·nal·is·tic** \,ra-shə-nə-'lis-tik\ *adj* — **ra·tio·nal·is·ti·cal·ly** \-ti-k(ə-)lē\ *adv*

ra·tio·nal·i·ty \,ra-shə-'na-lə-tē\ *n, pl* **-ties** : the quality or state of being rational

ra·tio·nal·ize \'ra-shə-nə-,līz\ *vb* **-ized; -iz·ing 1** : to make (something irrational) appear rational or reasonable **2** : to provide a natural explanation of (as a myth) **3** : to justify (as one's behavior or weaknesses) esp. to oneself **4** : to find plausible but untrue reasons for conduct — **ra·tio·nal·i·za·tion** \,ra-shə-nə-lə-'zā-shən\ *n*

rational number *n* : a number that can be expressed as an integer or the quotient of an integer divided by a nonzero integer

rat race *n* : strenuous, tiresome, and usu. competitive activity or rush

rat·tan \ra-'tan, rə-\ *n* : a cane or switch made from one of the long stems of an Asian climbing palm; *also* : this palm

rat·ter \'ra-tər\ *n* : a rat-catching dog or cat

¹**rat·tle** \'ra-t³l\ *vb* **rat·tled; rat·tling 1** : to make or cause to make a series of clattering sounds **2** : to move with a clattering sound **3** : to say or do in a brisk lively fashion ⟨∼ off the answers⟩ **4** : CONFUSE, UPSET ⟨∼ a witness⟩

²**rattle** *n* **1** : a toy that produces a rattle when shaken **2** : a series of clattering and knocking sounds **3** : a rattling organ at the end of a rattlesnake's tail

rat·tler \'rat-lər\ *n* : RATTLESNAKE

rat·tle·snake \'ra-t³l-,snāk\ *n* : any of various American pit vipers with a rattle at the end of the tail

rat·tle·trap \'ra-t³l-,trap\ *n* : something (as an old car) rickety and full of rattles

rat·tling \'rat-liŋ\ *adj* **1** : LIVELY, BRISK ⟨moved at a ∼ pace⟩ **2** : FIRST-RATE, SPLENDID

rat·trap \'rat-,trap\ *n* **1** : a trap for rats **2** : a dilapidated building

rat·ty \'ra-tē\ *adj* **rat·ti·er; -est 1** : infested with rats **2** : of, relating to, or suggestive of rats **3** : SHABBY ⟨a ∼ old coat⟩

rau·cous \'rò-kəs\ *adj* **1** : HARSH, HOARSE, STRIDENT ⟨∼ voices⟩ **2** : boisterously disorderly — **rau·cous·ly** *adv* — **rau·cous·ness** *n*

raun·chy \'ròn-chē, 'rän-\ *adj* **raun·chi·er; -est 1** : SLOVENLY, DIRTY **2** : OBSCENE, SMUTTY ⟨∼ jokes⟩ — **raun·chi·ness** \-chē-nəs\ *n*

¹**rav·age** \'ra-vij\ *n* [F] : an act or result of ravaging : DEVASTATION

²**ravage** *vb* **rav·aged; rav·ag·ing** : to lay waste : DEVASTATE — **rav·ag·er** *n*

¹**rave** \'rāv\ *vb* **raved; rav·ing 1** : to talk wildly in or as if in delirium : STORM, RAGE **2** : to talk with extreme enthusiasm ⟨*raved* about the show⟩ — **rav·er** *n*

²**rave** *n* **1** : an act or instance of raving **2** : an extravagantly favorable criticism

¹**rav·el** \'ra-vəl\ *vb* **-eled** *or* **-elled; -el·ing** *or* **-el·ling 1** : UNRAVEL, UNTWIST **2** : TANGLE, CONFUSE

²**ravel** *n* **1** : something tangled **2** : something raveled out; *esp* : a loose thread

¹**ra·ven** \ˈrā-vən\ *n* : a large black bird related to the crow

²**raven** *adj* : black and glossy like a raven's feathers

³**rav·en** \ˈra-vən\ *vb* **1** : to devour greedily **2** : DESPOIL, PLUNDER **3** : PREY

rav·en·ous \ˈra-və-nəs\ *adj* **1** : RAPACIOUS, VORACIOUS ⟨~ wolves⟩ **2** : eager for food : very hungry — **rav·en·ous·ly** *adv* — **rav·en·ous·ness** *n*

ra·vine \rə-ˈvēn\ *n* : a small narrow steepsided valley larger than a gully

rav·i·o·li \ˌra-vē-ˈō-lē\ *n, pl* **ravioli** *also* **raviolis** [It, fr. It dial., pl. of *raviolo*, lit., little turnip, dim. of *rava* turnip, fr. L *rapa*] : small cases of dough with a savory filling (as of meat or cheese)

rav·ish \ˈra-vish\ *vb* **1** : to seize and take away by violence **2** : to overcome with emotion and esp. with joy or delight ⟨~ed by her beauty⟩ **3** : RAPE — **rav·ish·er** *n* — **rav·ish·ment** *n*

¹**raw** \ˈrȯ\ *adj* **raw·er** \ˈrȯ-ər\; **raw·est** \ˈrȯ-əst\ **1** : not cooked **2** : changed little from the original form : not processed ⟨~ materials⟩ **3** : having the surface abraded or irritated ⟨a ~ sore⟩ **4** : not trained or experienced ⟨~ recruits⟩ **5** : VULGAR, COARSE ⟨~ language⟩ **6** : disagreeably cold and damp ⟨a ~ day⟩ **7** : UNFAIR ⟨~ deal⟩ — **raw·ness** *n*

²**raw** *n* : a raw place or state — **in the raw** : NAKED

raw·boned \ˈrȯ-ˌbōnd\ *adj* : LEAN, GAUNT; *also* : having a heavy frame that seems to have little flesh

raw·hide \ˈrȯ-ˌhīd\ *n* : the untanned skin of cattle; *also* : a whip made of this

¹**ray** \ˈrā\ *n* : any of an order of large flat cartilaginous fishes that have the eyes on the upper surface and the hind end of the body slender and taillike

²**ray** *n* [ME, fr. AF *rai*, fr. L *radius* rod, ray] **1** : any of the lines of light that appear to radiate from a bright object **2** : a thin beam of radiant energy (as light) **3** : light from a beam **4** : a thin line like a beam of light **5** : an animal or plant structure resembling a ray **6** : a tiny bit : PARTICLE ⟨a ~ of hope⟩

ray·on \ˈrā-ˌän\ *n* : a fiber made from cellulose; *also* : a yarn, thread, or fabric made from such fibers

raze \ˈrāz\ *vb* **razed**; **raz·ing** **1** : to scrape, cut, or shave off **2** : to destroy to the ground : DEMOLISH

ra·zor \ˈrā-zər\ *n* : a sharp cutting instrument used to shave off hair

ra·zor–backed \ˈrā-zər-ˌbakt\ *or* **ra·zor-back** \-ˌbak\ *adj* : having a sharp narrow back ⟨a ~ horse⟩

razor clam *n* : any of a family of marine bivalve mollusks having a long narrow curved thin shell

razor wire *n* : coiled wire fitted with sharp edges and used as an obstacle or barrier

¹**razz** \ˈraz\ *n* : RASPBERRY 2

²**razz** *vb* : RIDICULE, TEASE ⟨fans ~ed visiting players⟩

Rb *symbol* rubidium

RBC *abbr* red blood cells

RBI \ˌär-(ˌ)bē-ˈī, ˈri-bē\ *n, pl* **RBIs** *or* **RBI** [*run batted in*] : a run in baseball that is driven in by a batter

RC *abbr* **1** Red Cross **2** Roman Catholic

RCAF *abbr* Royal Canadian Air Force

RCMP *abbr* Royal Canadian Mounted Police

RCN *abbr* Royal Canadian Navy

rct *abbr* recruit

rd *abbr* **1** road **2** rod **3** round

RD *abbr* rural delivery

RDA *abbr* recommended daily allowance; recommended dietary allowance

re \ˈrā, ˈrē\ *prep* : with regard to

Re *symbol* rhenium

re- \rē, ˌrē, ˈrē\ *prefix* **1** : again : for a second time **2** : anew : in a new or different form **3** : back : backward

¹**reach** \ˈrēch\ *vb* **1** : to stretch out **2** : to touch or attempt to touch or seize **3** : to extend to **4** : to communicate with **5** : to arrive at ♦ **Synonyms** GAIN, REALIZE, ACHIEVE, ATTAIN — **reach·able** *adj* — **reach·er** *n*

²**reach** *n* **1** : an unbroken stretch of a river **2** : the act of reaching **3** : a reachable distance; *also* : ability to reach **4** : a range of knowledge or comprehension

re·act \rē-ˈakt\ *vb* **1** : to exert a return or counteracting influence **2** : to have or show a reaction **3** : to act in opposition to a force or influence **4** : to move or tend in a reverse direction **5** : to undergo chemical change

re·ac·tant \rē-ˈak-tənt\ *n* : a chemically reacting substance

re·ac·tion \rē-ˈak-shən\ *n* **1** : the act or process of reacting **2** : a counter tendency; *esp* : a tendency toward a former esp. outmoded political or social order or policy **3** : bodily, mental, or emotional response to a stimulus **4** : chemical change **5** : a process involving change in atomic nuclei

re·ac·tion·ary \rē-ˈak-shə-ˌner-ē\ *adj* : relating to, marked by, or favoring esp. political reaction — **reactionary** *n*

re·ac·tive \rē-ˈak-tiv\ *adj* : reacting or tending to react ⟨a ~ chemical⟩

re·ac·tor \rē-ˈak-tər\ *n* **1** : one that reacts **2** : a device for the controlled release of nuclear energy

¹**read** \ˈrēd\ *vb* **read** \ˈred\; **read·ing** [ME *reden* to advise, interpret, read, fr. OE *rǣdan*] **1** : to understand language by interpreting written symbols for speech sounds **2** : to utter aloud written or printed words **3** : to learn by observing ⟨~ nature's signs⟩ **4** : to study by a course of reading ⟨~s law⟩ **5** : to discover the meaning of ⟨~ the clues⟩ **6** : to recognize or interpret as if by reading **7** : to attribute (a meaning) to something ⟨~ guilt in his manner⟩ **8** : INDICATE ⟨thermometer ~s 10°⟩ **9** : to consist in phrasing or meaning ⟨the two versions

reabsorb   reacquire   reactivate   reactivation

~ differently⟩ — **read·abil·i·ty** \ˌrē-də-'bi-lə-tē\ n — **read·able** \'rē-də-bəl\ adj — **read·ably** \-blē\ adv — **read·er** n

²**read** \'red\ adj : informed by reading ⟨widely ~⟩

read·er·ship \'rē-dər-ˌship\ n : the mass or a particular group of readers

read·ing n **1** : something read or for reading **2** : a particular version **3** : data indicated by an instrument ⟨thermometer ~⟩ **4** : a particular interpretation (as of a law) **5** : a particular performance (as of a musical work) **6** : an indication of a certain state of affairs

read–only memory n : ROM

read·out \'rēd-ˌau̇t\ n **1** : the process of removing information from an automatic device (as a computer) and displaying it in an understandable form; also : the information removed from such a device **2** : an electronic device that presents information in visual form

read out vb **1** : to read aloud **2** : to expel from an organization

¹**ready** \'re-dē\ adj **read·i·er; -est 1** : prepared for use or action **2** : likely to do something indicated; also : willingly disposed : INCLINED **3** : spontaneously prompt ⟨her ~ wit⟩ **4** : immediately available ⟨~ cash⟩ — **read·i·ly** \'re-də-lē\ adv — **read·i·ness** \-dē-nəs\ n — **at the ready** : ready for immediate use

²**ready** vb **read·ied; ready·ing** : to make ready : PREPARE

ready–made \ˌre-dē-'mād\ adj : already made up for general sale : not specially made — **ready–made** n

ready room n : a room in which pilots are briefed and await orders

re·agent \rē-'ā-jənt\ n : a substance that takes part in or brings about a particular chemical reaction

¹**re·al** \'rēl\ adj [ME, real, relating to things (in law), fr. AF, fr. ML & LL; ML realis relating to things (in law), fr. LL, real, fr. L res thing, fact] **1** : of or relating to fixed or immovable things (as land) ⟨~ property⟩ **2** : not artificial : GENUINE; also : not imaginary — **re·al·ness** n — **for real 1** : in earnest **2** : GENUINE ⟨the threat was for real⟩

²**real** adv : VERY ⟨had a ~ good time⟩

³**re·al** \rā-'äl\ n — see MONEY table

real estate n : property in buildings and land

re·al·ism \'rē-ə-ˌli-zəm\ n **1** : the disposition to face facts and to deal with them practically **2** : true and faithful portrayal of nature and of people in art or literature — **re·al·ist** \-list\ adj or n — **re·al·is·tic** \ˌrē-ə-'lis-tik\ adj — **re·al·is·ti·cal·ly** \-ti-k(ə-)lē\ adv

re·al·i·ty \rē-'a-lə-tē\ n, pl **-ties 1** : the quality or state of being real **2** : something real **3** : the totality of real things and events

re·al·ize \'rē-ə-ˌlīz\ vb **-ized; -iz·ing 1** : to make actual : ACCOMPLISH **2** : to convert into money ⟨~ assets⟩ **3** : OBTAIN, GAIN ⟨~ a profit⟩ **4** : to be aware of : UNDERSTAND — **re·al·iz·able** adj — **re·al·i·za·tion** \ˌrē-ə-lə-'zā-shən\ n

re·al·ly \'rē-lē, 'ri-\ adv : in truth : in fact : ACTUALLY

realm \'relm\ n **1** : KINGDOM **2** : SPHERE, DOMAIN ⟨within the ~ of possibility⟩

real number n : a number that has no imaginary part ⟨the set of all real numbers comprises the rationals and the irrationals⟩

re·al·po·li·tik \rā-'äl-ˌpō-li-ˌtēk\ n, often cap [G] : politics based on practical and material factors rather than on theoretical or ethical objectives

real time n : the actual time during which something takes place — **real–time** adj

re·al·ty \'rēl-tē\ n : REAL ESTATE

¹**ream** \'rēm\ n [ME reme, fr. AF, ultim. fr. Ar rizma, lit., bundle] : a quantity of paper that is variously 480, 500, or 516 sheets

²**ream** vb : to enlarge, shape, or clear with a reamer

ream·er \'rē-mər\ n : a tool with cutting edges that is used to enlarge or shape a hole

reap \'rēp\ vb **1** : to cut or clear with a scythe, sickle, or machine **2** : to gather by or as if by cutting : HARVEST ⟨~ a reward⟩ — **reap·er** n

¹**rear** \'rir\ vb **1** : to erect by building **2** : to set or raise upright **3** : to breed and raise for use or market ⟨~ livestock⟩ **4** : BRING UP, FOSTER **5** : to lift or rise up; esp : to rise on the hind legs

²**rear** n **1** : the unit (as of an army) or area farthest from the enemy **2** : BACK; also : the position at the back of something

³**rear** adj : being at the back

rear admiral n : a commissioned officer in the navy or coast guard ranking next below a vice admiral

¹**rear·ward** \'rir-wərd\ adj **1** : being at or toward the rear **2** : directed toward the rear ⟨a ~ glance⟩

²**rear·ward** also **rear·wards** \-wərdz\ adv : at or toward the rear ⟨looking ~⟩

reas abbr reasonable

¹**rea·son** \'rē-zʰn\ n [ME resoun, fr. AF raisun, fr. L ration-, ratio reason, computation] **1** : a statement offered in explanation or justification **2** : GROUND, CAUSE **3** : the power to think : INTELLECT **4** : a sane or sound mind **5** : due exercise of the faculty of logical thought

²**reason** vb **1** : to talk with another to

readdress	reallocate	reappearance	rearm
readjust	reallocation	reapplication	rearmament
readjustment	reanalysis	reapply	rearouse
readmission	reanalyze	reappoint	rearrange
readmit	reanimate	reappointment	rearrangement
reaffirm	reanimation	reapportion	rearrest
reaffirmation	reannex	reapportionment	reascend
realign	reannexation	reappraisal	
realignment	reappear	reappraise	

cause a change of mind **2** : to use the faculty of reason : THINK **3** : to discover or formulate by the use of reason — **rea·son·er** n — **rea·son·ing** n

rea·son·able \'rē-z°n-ə-bəl\ adj **1** : being within the bounds of reason : not extreme **2** : INEXPENSIVE **3** : able to reason : RATIONAL — **rea·son·able·ness** n — **rea·son·ably** \-blē\ adv

re·as·sure \ˌrē-ə-'shùr\ vb **1** : to assure again **2** : to restore confidence to : free from fear — **re·as·sur·ance** \-'shùr-əns\ n — **re·as·sur·ing·ly** adv

¹**re·bate** \'rē-ˌbāt\ vb re·bat·ed; re·bat·ing : to make or give a rebate

²**rebate** n : a return of part of a payment ♦ **Synonyms** DEDUCTION, ABATEMENT, DISCOUNT

¹**reb·el** \'re-bəl\ adj [ME, fr. AF, fr. L re·bellis, fr. re- + bellum war] : of or relating to rebels

²**rebel** n : one that rebels against authority

³**re·bel** \ri-'bel\ vb re·belled; re·bel·ling **1** : to resist the authority of one's government **2** : to act in or show disobedience **3** : to feel or exhibit anger or revulsion

re·bel·lion \ri-'bel-yən\ n : resistance to authority; esp : defiance against a government through uprising or revolt

re·bel·lious \-yəs\ adj **1** : given to or engaged in rebellion **2** : inclined to resist authority — **re·bel·lious·ly** adv — **re·bel·lious·ness** n

re·birth \ˌrē-'bərth\ n **1** : a new or second birth **2** : RENAISSANCE, REVIVAL

re·born \-'bórn\ adj : born again : REGENERATED, REVIVED

¹**re·bound** \ˌrē-'baùnd, 'rē-ˌbaùnd\ vb **1** : to spring back on or as if on striking another body **2** : to recover from a setback or frustration ⟨~ed quickly from the loss⟩

²**re·bound** \'rē-ˌbaùnd\ n **1** : the action of rebounding **2** : a rebounding ball **3** : a reaction to setback or frustration

re·buff \ri-'bəf\ vb : to reject or criticize sharply : SNUB — **rebuff** n

re·build \ˌrē-'bild\ vb -built \-'bilt\; -build·ing **1** : REPAIR, RECONSTRUCT; also : REMODEL **2** : to build again

¹**re·buke** \ri-'byük\ vb re·buked; re·buk·ing : to reprimand sharply : REPROVE

²**rebuke** n : a sharp reprimand

re·bus \'rē-bəs\ n [L, by things, abl. pl. of res thing] : a representation of syllables or words by means of pictures; also : a riddle composed of such pictures

re·but \ri-'bət\ vb re·but·ted; re·but·ting : to refute esp. formally (as in debate) by evidence and arguments ♦ **Synonyms** DISPROVE, CONTROVERT, CONFUTE — **re·but·ter** n

re·but·tal \ri-'bə-t°l\ n : the act of rebutting

rec abbr **1** receipt **2** record; recording **3** recreation

re·cal·ci·trant \ri-'kal-sə-trənt\ adj [LL recalcitrant-, recalcitrans, prp. of recalcitrare to be stubbornly disobedient, fr. L, to kick back, fr. re- back, again + calcitrare to kick, fr. calc-, calx heel] **1** : stubbornly resisting authority ⟨a ~ prisoner⟩ **2** : resistant to handling or treatment ♦ **Synonyms** REFRACTORY, HEADSTRONG, WILLFUL, UNRULY, UNGOVERNABLE — **re·cal·ci·trance** \-trəns\ n

¹**re·call** \ri-'kól\ vb **1** : REVOKE, CANCEL **2** : to call back **3** : REMEMBER, RECOLLECT ⟨~ed their last meeting⟩

²**re·call** \ri-'kól, 'rē-ˌkól\ n **1** : a summons to return **2** : the procedure of removing an official by popular vote **3** : remembrance of things learned or experienced **4** : the act of revoking **5** : a call by a manufacturer for the return of a product that may be defective or contaminated

re·cant \ri-'kant\ vb : to take back (something one has said) publicly : make an open confession of error — **re·can·ta·tion** \ˌrē-ˌkan-'tā-shən\ n

¹**re·cap** \'rē-ˌkap, rē-'kap\ vb re·capped; re·cap·ping : RECAPITULATE — **re·cap** \'rē-ˌkap\ n

²**recap** vb re·capped; re·cap·ping : RETREAD — **re·cap** \'rē-ˌkap\ n

re·ca·pit·u·late \ˌrē-kə-'pi-chə-ˌlāt\ vb -lat·ed; -lat·ing : to restate briefly : SUMMARIZE ⟨~ recent news stories⟩ — **re·ca·pit·u·la·tion** \-ˌpi-chə-'lā-shən\ n

re·cap·ture \(ˌ)rē-'kap-chər\ vb **1** : to capture again **2** : to experience again ⟨~ happy times⟩

re·cast \(ˌ)rē-'kast\ vb **1** : to cast again **2** : REVISE, REMODEL ⟨~ a sentence⟩

recd abbr received

re·cede \ri-'sēd\ vb re·ced·ed; re·ced·ing **1** : to move back or away ⟨a receding hairline⟩ **2** : to slant backward **3** : DIMINISH, CONTRACT ⟨a receding deficit⟩

¹**re·ceipt** \ri-'sēt\ n **1** : RECIPE **2** : the act of receiving **3** : something received — usu. used in pl. **4** : a written acknowledgment of something received

²**receipt** vb **1** : to give a receipt for **2** : to mark as paid

re·ceiv·able \ri-'sē-və-bəl\ adj **1** : capable of being received; esp : acceptable as legal ⟨~ certificates⟩ **2** : subject to call for payment ⟨notes ~⟩

re·ceive \ri-'sēv\ vb re·ceived; re·ceiv·ing **1** : to take in or accept (as something sent or paid) : come into possession of : GET **2** : CONTAIN, HOLD **3** : to permit to enter : GREET, WELCOME **4** : to be at home to visitors **5** : to accept as true or authoritative **6** : to be the subject of : UNDERGO, EXPERIENCE ⟨~ a shock⟩ **7**

reassemble	reassume	reawaken	reburial
reassembly	reattach	rebaptism	rebury
reassert	reattachment	rebaptize	recalculate
reassess	reattain	rebid	recalculation
reassessment	reattempt	rebind	
reassign	reauthorization	reboil	
reassignment	reauthorize	rebroadcast	

: to change incoming radio waves into sounds or pictures ⟨∼ a broadcast⟩

re·ceiv·er \ri-ˈsē-vər\ *n* **1** : one that receives **2** : a person legally appointed to receive and have charge of property or money involved in a lawsuit **3** : a device for converting electromagnetic waves or signals into audio or visual form ⟨telephone ∼⟩

re·ceiv·er·ship \-,ship\ *n* **1** : the office or function of a receiver **2** : the condition of being in the hands of a receiver

re·cen·cy \ˈrē-sᵊn-sē\ *n* : RECENTNESS

re·cent \ˈrē-sᵊnt\ *adj* **1** : of the present time or time just past ⟨∼ history⟩ **2** : having lately come into existence : NEW, FRESH ⟨∼ buds⟩ **3** *cap* : HOLOCENE — **re·cent·ly** *adv* — **re·cent·ness** *n*

re·cep·ta·cle \ri-ˈsep-ti-kəl\ *n* **1** : something used to receive and hold something else : CONTAINER **2** : the enlarged end of a flower stalk upon which the parts of the flower grow **3** : an electrical fitting containing the live parts of a circuit

re·cep·tion \ri-ˈsep-shən\ *n* **1** : the act of receiving **2** : a social gathering at which guests are formally welcomed

re·cep·tion·ist \ri-ˈsep-shə-nist\ *n* : a person employed to greet callers

re·cep·tive \ri-ˈsep-tiv\ *adj* : able or inclined to receive; *esp* : open and responsive to ideas, impressions, or suggestions ⟨a ∼ audience⟩ — **re·cep·tive·ly** *adv* — **re·cep·tive·ness** *n* — **re·cep·tiv·i·ty** \,rē-,sep-ˈti-və-tē\ *n*

re·cep·tor \ri-ˈsep-tər\ *n* **1** : one that receives stimuli : SENSE ORGAN **2** : a chemical group or molecule in the outer cell membrane or in the cell interior that has an affinity for a specific chemical group, molecule, or virus

¹re·cess \ˈrē-,ses, ri-ˈses\ *n* **1** : a secret or secluded place **2** : an indentation in a line or surface (as an alcove in a room) **3** : a suspension of business or procedure for rest or relaxation

²recess *vb* **1** : to put into a recess **2** : to make a recess in **3** : to interrupt for a recess **4** : to take a recess

re·ces·sion \ri-ˈse-shən\ *n* **1** : the act of receding : WITHDRAWAL **2** : a departing procession (as at the end of a church service) **3** : a period of reduced economic activity

re·ces·sion·al \ri-ˈse-shə-nəl\ *n* **1** : a hymn or musical piece at the conclusion of a service or program **2** : RECESSION 2

¹re·ces·sive \ri-ˈse-siv\ *adj* **1** : tending to recede **2** : producing or being a bodily characteristic that is masked or not expressed when a contrasting dominant gene or trait is present ⟨∼ genes⟩ ⟨∼ traits⟩

²recessive *n* : a recessive characteristic or gene; *also* : an individual that has one or more recessive characteristics

re·cher·ché \rə-,sher-ˈshā, -ˈsher-,shā\ *adj* [F] **1** : CHOICE, RARE **2** : excessively refined ⟨∼ poetry⟩

re·cid·i·vism \ri-ˈsi-də-,vi-zəm\ *n* : a ten-

dency to relapse into a previous condition; *esp* : relapse into criminal behavior — **re·cid·i·vist** \-vist\ *n*

rec·i·pe \ˈre-sə-(,)pē\ *n* [L, take, imperative of *recipere* to take, receive, fr. *re-* back + *capere* to take] **1** : a set of instructions for making something from various ingredients **2** : a method of procedure : FORMULA

re·cip·i·ent \ri-ˈsi-pē-ənt\ *n* : one that receives

¹re·cip·ro·cal \ri-ˈsi-prə-kəl\ *adj* **1** : inversely related **2** : MUTUAL, SHARED **3** : serving to reciprocate **4** : mutually corresponding — **re·cip·ro·cal·ly** *adv*

²reciprocal *n* **1** : something in a reciprocal relationship to another **2** : one of a pair of numbers (as ⅔ and 3/2) whose product is one

re·cip·ro·cate \-,kāt\ *vb* **-cat·ed; -cat·ing** **1** : to move backward and forward alternately **2** : to give and take mutually **3** : to make a return for something done or given — **re·cip·ro·ca·tion** \-,si-prə-ˈkā-shən\ *n*

rec·i·proc·i·ty \,re-sə-ˈprä-sə-tē\ *n, pl* **-ties** **1** : the quality or state of being reciprocal **2** : mutual exchange of privileges (as trade advantages between countries)

re·cit·al \ri-ˈsī-tᵊl\ *n* **1** : an account or instance of reciting : ACCOUNT **2** : a public reading or recitation ⟨a poetry ∼⟩ **3** : a concert given by a musician, dancer, or dance troupe **4** : a public exhibition of skill given by music or dance pupils — **re·cit·al·ist** \-tᵊl-ist\ *n*

rec·i·ta·tion \,re-sə-ˈtā-shən\ *n* **1** : RECITING, RECITAL **2** : delivery before an audience usu. of something memorized ⟨∼ of a poem⟩ **3** : a classroom exercise in which pupils answer questions on a lesson they have studied

re·cite \ri-ˈsīt\ *vb* **re·cit·ed; re·cit·ing** **1** : to repeat verbatim (as something memorized) **2** : to recount in some detail : RELATE **3** : to reply to a teacher's questions on a lesson — **re·cit·er** *n*

reck·less \ˈre-kləs\ *adj* : lacking caution ⟨a ∼ driver⟩ ♦ *Synonyms* HASTY, BRASH, HOTHEADED, THOUGHTLESS — **reck·less·ly** *adv* — **reck·less·ness** *n*

reck·on \ˈre-kən\ *vb* **1** : COUNT, CALCULATE, COMPUTE **2** : CONSIDER, REGARD ⟨was ∼ed as the leader⟩ **3** *chiefly dial* : THINK, SUPPOSE, GUESS

reck·on·ing *n* **1** : an act or instance of reckoning **2** : a settling of accounts ⟨day of ∼⟩

re·claim \ri-ˈklām\ *vb* **1** : to recall from wrong conduct : REFORM **2** : to change from an undesirable to a desired condition ⟨∼ marshy land⟩ **3** : to obtain from a waste product or by-product ⟨∼ed plastic⟩ **4** : to demand or obtain the return of — **re·claim·able** *adj* — **rec·la·ma·tion** \,re-klə-ˈmā-shən\ *n*

re·cline \ri-ˈklīn\ *vb* **re·clined; re·clin-**

rechannel	rechargeable	recheck	reclassification
recharge	recharter	rechristen	reclassify

recliner • record

ing 1 : to lean or incline backward **2 :** to lie down : REST

re·clin·er \ri-ˈklī-nər\ *n* : a chair with an adjustable back and footrest

re·cluse \ˈre-ˌklüs, ri-ˈklüs\ *n* : a person who leads a secluded or solitary life : HERMIT — **re·clu·sive** \ri-ˈklü-siv\ *adj*

rec·og·nise *chiefly Brit var of* RECOGNIZE

rec·og·ni·tion \ˌre-kəg-ˈni-shən\ *n* **1 :** the act of recognizing : the state of being recognized : ACKNOWLEDGMENT ⟨in ~ of their achievements⟩ **2 :** special notice or attention

re·cog·ni·zance \ri-ˈkäg-nə-zəns\ *n* : a promise recorded before a court or magistrate to do something (as to appear in court or to keep the peace) usu. under penalty of a money forfeiture

rec·og·nize \ˈre-kəg-ˌnīz\ *vb* **-nized; -niz·ing 1 :** to acknowledge (as a speaker in a meeting) as one entitled to be heard at the time **2 :** to acknowledge the existence or the independence of (a country or government) **3 :** to take notice of **4 :** to acknowledge with appreciation **5 :** to acknowledge acquaintance with **6 :** to identify as previously known **7 :** to perceive clearly : REALIZE — **rec·og·niz·able** \ˈre-kəg-ˌnī-zə-bəl\ *adj* — **rec·og·niz·ably** \-blē\ *adv*

¹re·coil \ri-ˈkȯi(-ə)l\ *vb* [ME *reculen, recoilen,* fr. AF *reculer, recuiler,* fr. *re-* back + *cul* backside, fr. L *culus*] **1 :** to draw back : RETREAT **2 :** to spring back to or as if to a starting point ◆ **Synonyms** SHRINK, FLINCH, WINCE, QUAIL, BLENCH

²re·coil \ˈrē-ˌkȯil, ri-ˈkȯil\ *n* : the action of recoiling (as by a gun or spring)

re·coil·less \-ˌkȯi(-ə)l-ləs, -ˈkȯi(-ə)l-\ *adj* : venting expanding propellant gas before recoil is produced ⟨~ gun⟩

rec·ol·lect \ˌre-kə-ˈlekt\ *vb* : to recall to mind : REMEMBER ◆ **Synonyms** RECALL, REMIND, REMINISCE, BETHINK

rec·ol·lec·tion \ˌre-kə-ˈlek-shən\ *n* **1 :** the act or power of recollecting **2 :** something recollected

re·com·bi·nant \(ˌ)rē-ˈkäm-bə-nənt\ *adj* **1 :** relating to genetic recombination **2 :** containing or produced by recombinant DNA ⟨~ vaccines⟩

recombinant DNA *n* : genetically engineered DNA prepared in vitro by joining together DNA usu. from more than one species of organism

re·com·bi·na·tion \ˌrē-ˌkäm-bə-ˈnā-shən\ *n* : the formation of new combinations of genes

rec·om·mend \ˌre-kə-ˈmend\ *vb* **1 :** to present as deserving of acceptance or trial **2 :** to give in charge : COMMIT **3 :** to make acceptable **4 :** ADVISE, COUNSEL

— **rec·om·mend·able** \-ˈmen-də-bəl\ *adj*

rec·om·men·da·tion \ˌre-kə-mən-ˈdā-shən\ *n* **1 :** the act of recommending **2 :** something recommended **3 :** something that recommends

¹re·com·pense \ˈre-kəm-ˌpens\ *vb* **-pensed; -pens·ing 1 :** to give compensation to : pay for ⟨was *recompensed* for their losses⟩ **2 :** to return in kind : REQUITE ◆ **Synonyms** REIMBURSE, INDEMNIFY, REPAY, COMPENSATE

²recompense *n* : COMPENSATION

rec·on·cile \ˈre-kən-ˌsī(-ə)l\ *vb* **-ciled; -cil·ing 1 :** to cause to be friendly or harmonious again **2 :** ADJUST, SETTLE ⟨~ differences⟩ **3 :** to bring to submission or acceptance ◆ **Synonyms** CONFORM, ACCOMMODATE, HARMONIZE, COORDINATE — **rec·on·cil·able** *adj* — **rec·on·cile·ment** *n* — **rec·on·cil·er** *n*

rec·on·cil·i·a·tion \ˌre-kən-ˌsi-lē-ˈā-shən\ *n* **1 :** the action of reconciling **2 :** the Roman Catholic sacrament of penance

re·con·dite \ˈre-kən-ˌdīt\ *adj* **1 :** hard to understand : ABSTRUSE ⟨~ terminology⟩ **2 :** little known : OBSCURE

re·con·di·tion \ˌrē-kən-ˈdi-shən\ *vb* **1 :** to restore to good condition (as by replacing parts) **2 :** to condition anew

re·con·nais·sance \ri-ˈkä-nə-zəns, -səns\ *n* [F, lit., recognition] : a preliminary survey of an area; *esp* : an exploratory military survey of enemy territory

re·con·noi·ter *or* **re·con·noi·tre** \ˌrē-kə-ˈnȯi-tər, ˌre-\ *vb* **-noi·tered** *or* **-noi·tred; -noi·ter·ing** *or* **-noi·tring :** to make a reconnaissance of : engage in reconnaissance ⟨~ed to locate enemy positions⟩

re·con·sid·er \ˌrē-kən-ˈsi-dər\ *vb* : to consider again with a view to changing or reversing ⟨~ed his decision⟩ — **re·con·sid·er·a·tion** \-ˌsi-də-ˈrā-shən\ *n*

re·con·sti·tute \ˌrē-ˈkän-stə-ˌtüt, -ˌtyüt\ *vb* : to restore to a former condition by adding water ⟨~ powdered milk⟩

re·con·struct \ˌrē-kən-ˈstrəkt\ *vb* : to construct again : REBUILD

re·con·struc·tion \ˌrē-kən-ˈstrək-shən\ *n* **1 :** the act of reconstructing : the state of being reconstructed **2** *often cap* : the reorganization and reestablishment of the seceded states in the Union after the American Civil War **3 :** something reconstructed

¹re·cord \ri-ˈkȯrd\ *vb* [ME, lit., to recall, fr. AF *recorder,* fr. L *recordari,* fr. *re-* back, again + *cord-, cors* heart] **1 :** to set down in writing ⟨~ed her observations⟩ **2 :** to register permanently **3 :** INDICATE, READ **4 :** to give evidence of **5 :** to cause (as sound or visual images) to be registered

recoin	recompile	recondense	recontact
recolonization	recompose	reconfirm	recontaminate
recolonize	recomputation	reconfirmation	recontamination
recolor	recompute	reconnect	reconvene
recombine	reconceive	reconquer	reconvert
recommence	reconcentrate	reconquest	recook
recommission	reconception	reconsecrate	recopy
recommit	recondensation	reconsecration	

(as on a disc or a magnetic tape) in a form that permits reproduction

²**rec·ord** \'re-kərd\ *n* **1** : the act of being recorded **2** : a written account of proceedings **3** : known facts about a person; *also* : a collection of items of information (as in a database) treated as a unit **4** : an attested top performance **5** : something on which sound or visual images have been recorded

³**re·cord** \ri-'kȯrd\ *n* : a function of an electronic device that causes it to record

re·cord·er \ri-'kȯr-dər\ *n* **1** : a judge in some city courts **2** : one who records transactions officially **3** : a recording device **4** : a wind instrument with a whistle mouthpiece and eight fingerholes

re·cord·ing *n* : RECORD 5

re·cord·ist \ri-'kȯr-dist\ *n* : one who records sound esp. on film

¹**re·count** \ri-'kaunt\ *vb* : to relate in detail : TELL   ♦ *Synonyms* RECITE, REHEARSE, NARRATE, DESCRIBE, STATE, REPORT

²**re·count** \'rē-ˌkaunt, (ˌ)rē-'kaunt\ *vb* : to count again

³**re·count** \'rē-ˌkaunt, (ˌ)rē-'kaunt\ *n* : a second or fresh count

re·coup \ri-'küp\ *vb* : to get an equivalent or compensation for : make up for something lost ⟨∼ed their costs⟩

re·course \'rē-ˌkȯrs, ri-'kȯrs\ *n* **1** : a turning to someone or something for assistance or protection **2** : a source of aid : RESORT

re·cov·er \ri-'kə-vər\ *vb* **1** : to get back again : REGAIN, RETRIEVE **2** : to regain normal health, poise, or status **3** : to make up for : RECOUP ⟨∼ed all his losses⟩ **4** : RECLAIM ⟨∼ land from the sea⟩ **5** : to obtain a legal judgment in one's favor — **re·cov·er·able** *adj*

re–cov·er \ˌrē-'kə-vər\ *vb* : to cover again

recovering *adj* : being in the process of overcoming a shortcoming or problem ⟨a ∼ alcoholic⟩

re·cov·ery \ri-'kə-və-rē\ *n* **1** : an act or instance of recovering; *esp* : an economic upturn **2** : the process of combating a disorder or problem

¹**rec·re·ant** \'re-krē-ənt\ *adj* [ME, fr. AF, fr. prp. of (*se*) *recreire* to give up, yield, fr. ML (*se*) *recredere* to resign oneself (to a judgment), fr. L *re-* back + *credere* to believe] **1** : COWARDLY **2** : UNFAITHFUL ⟨were ∼ to their duties⟩

²**recreant** *n* **1** : COWARD **2** : DESERTER

rec·re·ate \'re-krē-ˌāt\ *vb* **-at·ed; -at·ing** **1** : to give new life or freshness to **2** : to take recreation ⟨*recreated* at the beach⟩ — **rec·re·ative** \-ˌā-tiv\ *adj*

re–cre·ate \ˌrē-krē-'āt\ *vb* : to create again ⟨*re-created* the battle scene⟩ — **re–cre·ation** \-'ā-shən\ *n* — **re–cre·ative** \-'ā-tiv\ *adj*

rec·re·ation \ˌre-krē-'ā-shən\ *n* : a refreshing of strength or spirits after work; *also* : a means of refreshment   ♦ *Synonyms* DIVERSION, ENTERTAINMENT,

AMUSEMENT — **rec·re·ation·al** \-shə-nəl\ *adj*

recreational vehicle *n* : a vehicle designed for recreational use (as camping)

re·crim·i·na·tion \ri-ˌkri-mə-'nā-shən\ *n* : a retaliatory accusation — **re·crim·i·nate** \-'kri-mə-ˌnāt\ *vb* — **re·crim·i·na·tory** \-'kri-mə-nə-ˌtȯr-ē\ *adj*

re·cru·des·cence \ˌrē-krü-'de-s³ns\ *n* : a renewal or breaking out again esp. of something unhealthful or dangerous

¹**re·cruit** \ri-'krüt\ *vb* **1** : to form or strengthen with new members ⟨∼ an army⟩ **2** : to enlist as a member of an armed service **3** : to secure the services of **4** : to seek to enroll **5** : to restore or increase in health or vigor ⟨resting to ∼ his strength⟩ — **re·cruit·er** *n* — **re·cruit·ment** *n*

²**recruit** *n* [F *recrute, recrue* fresh growth, new levy of soldiers, fr. MF, fr. *recroistre* to grow up again, fr. L *recrescere*] : a newcomer to an activity or field; *esp* : a newly enlisted member of the armed forces

rec·tal \'rek-t³l\ *adj* : of or relating to the rectum — **rec·tal·ly** *adv*

rect·an·gle \'rek-ˌtaŋ-gəl\ *n* : a 4-sided figure with four right angles; *esp* : one with adjacent sides of unequal length — **rect·an·gu·lar** \rek-'taŋ-gyə-lər\ *adj*

rec·ti·fi·er \'rek-tə-ˌfī(-ə)r\ *n* : one that rectifies; *esp* : a device for converting alternating current into direct current

rec·ti·fy \'rek-tə-ˌfī\ *vb* **-fied; -fy·ing** : to make or set right : CORRECT   ♦ *Synonyms* EMEND, AMEND, MEND, RIGHT — **rec·ti·fi·ca·tion** \ˌrek-tə-fə-'kā-shən\ *n*

rec·ti·lin·ear \ˌrek-tə-'li-nē-ər\ *adj* **1** : moving in a straight line ⟨∼ motion⟩ **2** : characterized by straight lines

rec·ti·tude \'rek-tə-ˌtüd, -ˌtyüd\ *n* **1** : moral integrity **2** : correctness of procedure   ♦ *Synonyms* VIRTUE, GOODNESS, MORALITY, PROBITY

rec·to \'rek-tō\ *n, pl* **rectos** : a right-hand page

rec·tor \'rek-tər\ *n* **1** : a priest or minister in charge of a parish **2** : the head of a university or school — **rec·to·ri·al** \rek-'tȯr-ē-əl\ *adj*

rec·to·ry \'rek-tə-rē\ *n, pl* **-ries** : the residence of a rector or a parish priest

rec·tum \'rek-təm\ *n, pl* **rectums** *or* **rec·ta** \-tə\ [ME, fr. ML, fr. *rectum intestinum*, lit., straight intestine] : the last part of the intestine joining the colon and anus

re·cum·bent \ri-'kəm-bənt\ *adj* : lying down : RECLINING

re·cu·per·ate \ri-'kü-pə-ˌrāt, -'kyü-\ *vb* **-at·ed; -at·ing** : to get back (as health or strength) : RECOVER — **re·cu·per·a·tion** \-ˌkü-pə-'rā-shən, -ˌkyü-\ *n* — **re·cu·per·a·tive** \-'kü-pə-ˌrā-tiv, -'kyü-\ *adj*

re·cur \ri-'kər\ *vb* **re·curred; re·cur·ring** **1** : to go or come back in thought or in discussion **2** : to occur or appear again esp. after an interval : occur time after time ⟨*recurring* headaches⟩ — **re·cur·rence** \-'kər-əns\ *n* — **re·cur·rent** \-ənt\ *adj* re·cy·cle \rē-'sī-kəl\ vb 1 : to pass again through a cycle of changes or treatment 2 : to process (as liquid body waste, glass, or cans) in order to regain materials for human use — re·cy·cla·bil·i·ty \-ˌsī-klə-'bil-ə-tē\ n — re·cy·cla·ble \-k(ə)lə-bəl\ adj — recycle n

¹red \'red\ adj red·der; red·dest 1 : of the color red 2 : endorsing radical social or political change esp. by force 3 often cap : of or relating to the former U.S.S.R. or its allies 4 : tending to support Republican candidates ⟨~ states⟩ — red·ly adv — red·ness n

²red n 1 : the color of blood or of the ruby 2 : a revolutionary in politics 3 cap : COMMUNIST 4 : the condition of showing a loss ⟨in the ~⟩

re·dact \ri-'dakt\ vb 1 : to put in writing : FRAME ⟨~ed the proclamation⟩ 2 : EDIT — re·dac·tor \-'dak-tər\ n

re·dac·tion \-'dak-shən\ n 1 : an act or instance of redacting 2 : EDITION

red alga n : any of a group of reddish usu. marine algae

red blood cell n : any of the hemoglobin-containing cells that carry oxygen from the lungs to the tissues and are responsible for the red color of vertebrate blood

red·breast \'red-ˌbrest\ n : ROBIN

red–carpet n : marked by ceremonial courtesy ⟨was given the ~ treatment⟩

red cedar n : an American juniper with scalelike leaves and fragrant close-grained red wood; also : its wood

red clover n : a European clover that has globe-shaped heads of reddish flowers and is widely cultivated for hay and forage

red·coat \'red-ˌkōt\ n : a British soldier esp. during the Revolutionary War

red·den \'red-dᵊn\ vb : to make or become red or reddish : FLUSH, BLUSH

red·dish \'re-dish\ adj : tinged with red — red·dish·ness n

red dwarf n : a star with lower temperature and less mass than the sun

re·deem \ri-'dēm\ vb [ME redemen, fr. AF redeimer, modif. of L redimere, fr. re-, red- back, again + emere to take, buy] 1 : to recover (property) by discharging an obligation 2 : to ransom, free, or rescue by paying a price 3 : to free from the consequences of sin 4 : to remove the obligation of by payment ⟨the government ~s savings bonds⟩; also : to convert into something of value 5 : to make good (a promise) by performing : FULFILL 6 : to atone for — re·deem·able adj — re·deem·er n

re·demp·tion \ri-'demp-shən\ n : the act of redeeming : the state of being redeemed — re·demp·tive \-tiv\ adj — re·demp·to·ry \-tə-rē\ adj

re·de·ploy \ˌrē-di-'ploi\ vb 1 : to transfer from one area or activity to another 2 : to relocate men or equipment — re·de·ploy·ment n

red–eye \'red-ˌī\ n 1 : cheap whiskey 2 : a late night or overnight flight

red·fish \'red-ˌfish\ n : any of various reddish marine fishes of the Atlantic including some used for food

red fox n : a fox with orange-red to reddish brown fur

red giant n : a very large star with a relatively low surface temperature

red–hand·ed \'red-'han-dəd\ adv or adj : in the act of committing a misdeed

red·head \-ˌhed\ n : a person having red hair — red·head·ed \-ˌhe-dəd\ adj

red herring n : a diversion intended to distract attention from the real issue

red–hot \'red-'hät\ adj 1 : extremely hot; esp : glowing with heat 2 : EXCITED, FURIOUS 3 : very new ⟨~ news⟩

re·di·al \'rē-ˌdī-(-ə)l\ n : a telephone function that automatically repeats the dialing of the last number called — redial vb

re·dis·trib·ute \ˌrē-də-'stri-byüt\ vb 1 : to alter the distribution of 2 : to spread to other areas — re·dis·tri·bu·tion \(ˌ)rē-ˌdis-trə-'byü-shən\ n

re·dis·trict \ˌrē-'dis-(ˌ)trikt\ vb : to organize into new territorial and esp. political divisions

red–let·ter \'red-ˌle-tər\ adj : of special significance : MEMORABLE ⟨a ~ day⟩

red–light adj : having many houses of prostitution ⟨a ~district⟩

re·do \(ˌ)rē-'dü\ vb : to do over or again; esp : REDECORATE

red oak n : any of various No. American oaks with leaves usu. having spiny-tipped lobes and acorns that take two years to mature; also : the wood of a red oak

red·o·lent \'re-də-lənt\ adj 1 : FRAGRANT, AROMATIC 2 : having a specified fragrance ⟨a room ~ of cooked cabbage⟩ 3 : REMINISCENT, SUGGESTIVE ⟨a tavern ~ of colonial times⟩ — red·o·lence \-ləns\ n — red·o·lent·ly adv

re·dou·ble \(ˌ)rē-'də-bəl\ vb 1 : to make twice as great in size or amount; also : INTENSIFY

re·doubt \ri-'daut\ n [F redoute, fr. It ridotto, fr. ML reductus secret place, fr. L, withdrawn, fr. reducere to lead back, fr. re- back + ducere to lead] : a small usu. temporary fortification

re·doubt·able \ri-'dau-tə-bəl\ adj [ME redoutable, fr. AF, fr. reduter to dread, fr. re- back, again + duter to doubt] : arousing dread or fear : FORMIDABLE

re·dound \ri-'daund\ vb 1 : to have an effect ⟨the change may ~ to her benefit⟩ 2 : to become added or transferred : ACCRUE

red pepper n 1 : CAYENNE PEPPER 2 : a mature red hot pepper or sweet pepper

¹**re·dress** \ri-'dres\ *vb* **1** : to set right : REMEDY ⟨∼ injustice⟩ **2** : COMPENSATE **3** : to remove the cause of (a grievance) **4** : AVENGE

²**redress** *n* **1** : relief from distress **2** : means or possibility of seeking a remedy **3** : compensation for loss or injury **4** : an act or instance of redressing

red·shift \'red-'shift\ *n* : displacement of the spectrum of a heavenly body toward longer wavelengths; *also* : a measure of this displacement

red snapper *n* : any of various reddish fishes including several food fishes

red spider *n* : SPIDER MITE

red squirrel *n* : a common No. American squirrel with the upper parts chiefly red

red–tailed hawk \'red-,tāld-\ *n* : a rodent-eating No. American hawk with a rather short tyically reddish tail

red tape *n* [fr. the red tape formerly used to bind legal documents in England] : official routine or procedure marked by excessive complexity which results in delay or inaction

red tide *n* : seawater discolored by the presence of large numbers of dinoflagellates which produce a toxin that renders infected shellfish poisonous

re·duce \ri-'dūs, -'dyüs\ *vb* **re·duced; re·duc·ing** **1** : LESSEN **2** : to bring to a specified state or condition ⟨reduced them to tears⟩ **3** : to put in a lower rank or grade **4** : CONQUER ⟨∼ a fort⟩ **5** : to bring into a certain order or classification **6** : to correct (as a fracture) by restoration of displaced parts **7** : to lessen one's weight ♦ *Synonyms* DECREASE, DIMINISH, ABATE, DWINDLE, RECEDE — **re·duc·er** *n* — **re·duc·ible** \-'dü-sə-bəl, -'dyü-\ *adj*

re·duc·tion \ri-'dək-shən\ *n* **1** : the act of reducing : the state of being reduced **2** : something made by reducing **3** : the amount taken off in reducing something

re·dun·dan·cy \ri-'dən-dən-sē\ *n, pl* **-cies** **1** : the quality or state of being redundant : SUPERFLUITY **2** : something redundant or in excess **3** : the use of surplus words

re·dun·dant \-dənt\ *adj* **1** : exceeding what is needed or normal : SUPERFLUOUS; *esp* : using more words than necessary **2** : marked by repetition — **re·dun·dant·ly** *adv*

red–winged blackbird \'red-,wiŋd-\ *n* : a No. American blackbird of which the adult male is black with a patch of bright scarlet on the wings

red·wood \'red-,wůd\ *n* : a tall coniferous timber tree esp. of coastal California; *also* : its durable wood

reed \'rēd\ *n* **1** : any of various tall slender grasses of wet areas; *also* : a stem or growth of reed **2** : a musical instrument made from the hollow stem of a reed **3** : an elastic tongue of cane, wood, or metal by which tones are produced in organ pipes and certain other wind instruments — **reedy** *adj*

re·ed·u·cate \(,)rē-'e-jə-,kāt\ *vb* : to train again; *esp* : to rehabilitate through education — **re·ed·u·ca·tion** *n*

¹**reef** \'rēf\ *n* **1** : a part of a sail taken in or let out in regulating the sail's size **2** : reduction in sail area by reefing

²**reef** *vb* : to reduce the area of a sail by rolling or folding part of it

³**reef** *n* : a ridge of rocks, sand or coral at or near the surface of the water

reef·er \'rē-fər\ *n* : a marijuana cigarette

¹**reek** \'rēk\ *n* : a strong or disagreeable fume or odor

²**reek** *vb* **1** : to give off or become permeated with a strong or offensive odor **2** : to give a strong impression of some constituent quality ⟨an excuse that ∼ed of falsehood⟩ — **reek·er** *n* — **reeky** \'rē-kē\ *adj*

¹**reel** \'rēl\ *n* : a revolvable device on which something flexible (as film or tape) is wound; *also* : a quantity of something wound on such a device

²**reel** *vb* **1** : to wind on or as if on a reel **2** : to pull or draw (as a fish) by reeling a line — **reel·able** *adj* — **reel·er** *n*

³**reel** *vb* **1** : WHIRL; *also* : to be giddy **2** : to waver or fall back (as from a blow) **3** : to walk or move unsteadily

⁴**reel** *n* : a reeling motion

⁵**reel** *n* : a lively Scottish dance or its music

reel off *vb* **1** : to tell or recite rapidly and easily ⟨reeled off the right answers⟩ **2** : to achieve usu. consecutively ⟨reeled off six straight wins⟩

re·en·try \rē-'en-trē\ *n* **1** : a second or new entry **2** : the action of reentering the earth's atmosphere from space

reeve \'rēv\ *vb* **rove** \'rōv\ *or* **reeved; reev·ing** : to pass (as a rope) through a hole in a block or cleat

¹**ref** \'ref\ *n* : REFEREE 2

²**ref** *abbr* **1** reference **2** referred **3** reformed **4** refunding

re·fec·tion \ri-'fek-shən\ *n* **1** : refreshment esp. after hunger or fatigue **2** : food and drink together : REPAST

re·fec·to·ry \ri-'fek-tə-rē\ *n, pl* **-ries** : a dining hall (as in a monastery or college)

re·fer \ri-'fər\ *vb* **re·ferred; re·fer·ring** [ME *referren*, fr. AF *referer, referir*, fr. L *referre* to bring back, report, refer, fr. *re-* back + *ferre* to carry] **1** : to assign to a certain source, cause, or relationship **2** : to direct or send to some person or place (as for information or help) **3** : to submit to someone else for consideration or action **4** : to have recourse (as for information or aid) **5** : to have connection

reecho	reemphasize	reenlist	reevaluate
reedit	reemploy	reenlistment	reevaluation
reelect	reemployment	reenter	reexamination
reelection	reenact	reequip	reexamine
reemerge	reenactment	reestablish	reexport
reemergence	reenergize	reestablishment	refashion
reemphasis			

: RELATE **6** : to direct attention : speak of
: MENTION, ALLUDE ♦ **Synonyms** RE-
CUR, REPAIR, RESORT, APPLY, GO, TURN
— **re·fer·able** \'re-fə-rə-bəl, ri-'fər-ə-\
adj

ref·er·ee \ˌre-fə-'rē\ *n* **1** : a person to
whom an issue esp. in law is referred for
investigation or settlement **2** : an umpire
in certain games

referee *vb* **-eed; -ee·ing** : to act as referee

ref·er·ence \'re-frəns, -fə-rəns\ *n* **1** : the
act of referring **2** : RELATION, RESPECT
3 : ALLUSION, MENTION **4** : something
that refers a reader to another passage or
book **5** : consultation esp. for obtaining
information ⟨books for ∼⟩ **6** : a person
of whom inquiries as to character or ability can be made **7** : a written recommendation of a person for employment

ref·er·en·dum \ˌre-fə-'ren-dəm\ *n, pl* **-da**
\-də\ *or* **-dums** : the submitting of legislative measures to the voters for approval
or rejection; *also* : a vote on a measure so
submitted

ref·er·ent \'re-frənt, -fə-rənt\ *n* : one that
refers or is referred to; *esp* : the thing a
word stands for — **referent** *adj*

re·fer·ral \ri-'fər-əl\ *n* **1** : the act or an
instance of referring **2** : one that is referred

re·fill \ˌrē-'fil\ *vb* : to fill again : REPLEN-
ISH — **re·fill·able** *adj*

re·fill \'rē-ˌfil\ *n* : a new or fresh supply of
something

re·fi·nance \ˌrē-fə-'nans, (ˌ)rē-'fī-nans\ *vb*
: to renew or reorganize the financing of

re·fine \ri-'fīn\ *vb* **re·fined; re·fin·ing 1**
: to free from impurities or waste matter
2 : IMPROVE, PERFECT **3** : to free or become free of what is coarse or uncouth **4**
: to make improvements by introducing
subtle changes — **re·fin·er** *n*

re·fined \ri-'fīnd\ *adj* **1** : freed from impurities **2** : CULTURED, CULTIVATED **3**
: PRECISE, EXACT

re·fine·ment \ri-'fīn-mənt\ *n* **1** : the action of refining **2** : the quality or state of
being refined **3** : a refined feature or
method; *also* : something intended to improve or perfect

re·fin·ery \ri-'fī-nə-rē\ *n, pl* **-er·ies** : a
building and equipment for refining met-
als, oil, or sugar

re·flect \ri-'flekt\ *vb* [ME, fr. L *reflectere*
to bend back, fr. *re-* back + *flectere* to
bend] **1** : to bend or cast back (as light,
heat, or sound) **2** : to give back a likeness
or image of as a mirror does **3** : to bring
as a result ⟨∼ed credit on him⟩ **4** : to
make apparent : SHOW ⟨figures that ∼
economic growth⟩ **5** : to cast reproach
or blame ⟨their bad conduct ∼ed on
their training⟩ **6** : PONDER, MEDITATE
— **re·flec·tion** \-'flek-shən\ *n* — **re·flec-
tive** \-tiv\ *adj* — **re·flec·tiv·i·ty** \(ˌ)rē-
ˌflek-'ti-və-tē\ *n*

re·flec·tor \ri-'flek-tər\ *n* : one that re-

flects; *esp* : a polished surface for reflecting radiation (as light)

¹re·flex \'rē-ˌfleks\ *n* **1** : an automatic and
usu. inborn response to a stimulus not
involving higher mental centers **2** *pl* : the
power of acting or responding with
enough speed ⟨an athlete with great
∼es⟩

²reflex *adj* **1** : bent or directed back **2**
: of, relating to, or produced by a reflex
⟨a ∼ action⟩ — **re·flex·ly** *adv*

¹re·flex·ive \ri-'flek-siv\ *adj* : of or relating
to an action directed back upon the doer
or the grammatical subject ⟨a ∼ verb⟩
⟨the ∼ pronoun *himself*⟩ — **re·flex·ive-
ly** *adv* — **re·flex·ive·ness** *n*

²reflexive *n* : a reflexive verb or pronoun

re·flex·ol·o·gy \ˌrē-ˌflek-'sä-lə-jē\ *n* : massage in which pressure is applied to specific points on the hands or feet

re·flux \'rē-ˌfləks\ *n* : a flowing back

re·fo·cus \(ˌ)rē-'fō-kəs\ *vb* **1** : to focus
again **2** : to change the emphasis or direction of ⟨∼ed her life⟩

re·for·es·ta·tion \ˌrē-ˌfȯr-ə-'stā-shən\ *n*
: the action of renewing forest cover by
planting seeds or young trees — **re·for-
est** \rē-'fȯr-əst\ *vb*

¹re·form \ri-'fȯrm\ *vb* **1** : to make better
or improve by removal of faults **2** : to
correct or improve one's own character
or habits ♦ **Synonyms** CORRECT, REC-
TIFY, EMEND, REMEDY, REDRESS, RE-
VISE — **re·form·able** *adj* — **re·for·ma-
tive** \-'fȯr-mə-tiv\ *adj*

²reform *n* : improvement or correction of
what is corrupt or defective

re–form \ˌrē-'fȯrm\ *vb* : to form again

ref·or·ma·tion \ˌre-fər-'mā-shən\ *n* **1**
: the act of reforming **2** *cap* : a 16th century religious
movement marked by the establishment
of the Protestant churches

¹re·for·ma·to·ry \ri-'fȯr-mə-ˌtȯr-ē\ *adj*
: aiming at or tending toward reformation : REFORMATIVE

²reformatory *n, pl* **-ries** : a penal institution for reforming esp. young or first offenders

re·form·er \ri-'fȯr-mər\ *n* **1** : one that
works for or urges reform **2** *cap* : a leader of the Protestant Reformation

refr *abbr* refraction

re·fract \ri-'frakt\ *vb* [L *refractus*, pp. of
refringere to break open, break up, fr. *re-*
back + *frangere* to break] : to subject to
refraction

re·frac·tion \ri-'frak-shən\ *n* : the bending of a ray (as of light) when it passes
obliquely from one medium into another
in which its speed is different — **re·frac-
tive** \-tiv\ *adj*

refractive index *n* : the ratio of the speed
of radiation in one medium to that in another medium

re·frac·to·ry \ri-'frak-tə-rē\ *adj* **1** : OBSTI-
NATE, STUBBORN, UNMANAGEABLE **2**
: capable of enduring high temperature

refight	refit	refold	reformulation
refigure	refix	reforge	refortify
refinish	refloat	reformulate	refound

⟨~ bricks⟩ ♦ *Synonyms* RECALCI-
TRANT, INTRACTABLE, UNGOVERNABLE,
UNRULY, HEADSTRONG, WILLFUL — **re-
frac·to·ri·ness** \ri-'f(r)ak-tə-rē-nəs\ *n* —
refractory *n*

¹**re·frain** \ri-'frān\ *vb* : to hold oneself back
: FORBEAR ⟨~ from interfering⟩ — **re-
frain·ment** *n*

²**refrain** *n* : a phrase or verse recurring
regularly in a poem or song

re·fresh \ri-'fresh\ *vb* 1 : to make or become fresh or fresher 2 : to revive by or
as if by renewal of supplies ⟨~ one's
memory⟩ 3 : to freshen up 4 : to supply
or take refreshment 5 : to update or renew esp. by sending a new signal ⟨~ the
Web page⟩ ♦ *Synonyms* RESTORE, RE-
JUVENATE, RENOVATE, REFURBISH —
re·fresh·er *n* — **re·fresh·ing·ly** *adv*

re·fresh·ment \-mənt\ *n* 1 : the act of
refreshing : the state of being refreshed 2
: something that refreshes 3 *pl* : a light
meal; *also* : assorted light foods

re·fried beans \'rē-ˌfrīd-\ *n pl* : beans
cooked with seasonings, fried, then
mashed and fried again

refrig *abbr* refrigerating; refrigeration

re·frig·er·ate \ri-'fri-jə-ˌrāt\ *vb* **-at·ed;
-at·ing** : to make cool; *esp* : to chill or
freeze (food) for preservation — **re·frig-
er·ant** \-jə-rənt\ *adj or n* — **re·frig·er·a-
tion** \-ˌfri-jə-'rā-shən\ *n* — **re·frig·er·a-
tor** \-'fri-jə-ˌrā-tər\ *n*

ref·uge \'re-(ˌ)fyü\ *n* 1 : shelter or protection from danger or distress 2 : a place
that provides protection

ref·u·gee \ˌre-fyü-'jē\ *n* : one who flees
for safety esp. to a foreign country

re·ful·gence \ri-'ful-jəns, -'fəl-\ *n* : a radiant or resplendent quality or state — **re-
ful·gent** \-jənt\ *adj*

¹**re·fund** \ri-'fənd, 'rē-ˌfənd\ *vb* : to give or
put back (money) : REPAY — **re·fund-
able** *adj*

²**re·fund** \'rē-ˌfənd\ *n* 1 : the act of refunding 2 : a sum refunded

re·fur·bish \ri-'fər-bish\ *vb* : to brighten
or freshen up : RENOVATE

¹**re·fuse** \ri-'fyüz\ *vb* **re·fused; re·fus·ing**
1 : to decline to accept : REJECT 2 : to
decline to do, give, or grant : DENY — **re-
fus·al** \-'fyü-zəl\ *n*

²**re·fuse** \'re-ˌfyüs, -ˌfyüz\ *n* : rejected or
worthless matter : RUBBISH, TRASH

re·fute \ri-'fyüt\ *vb* **re·fut·ed; re·fut·ing**
[L *refutare* to check, suppress, refute] : to
prove to be false by argument or evidence — **ref·u·ta·tion** \ˌre-fyü-'tā-shən\
n — **re·fut·er** *n*

¹**reg** \'reg\ *n* : REGULATION

²**reg** *abbr* 1 region 2 register; registered;
registration 3 regular

re·gal \'rē-gəl\ *adj* 1 : of, relating to, or
befitting a king : ROYAL 2 : STATELY,
SPLENDID — **re·gal·ly** *adv*

re·gale \ri-'gāl\ *vb* **re·galed; re·gal·ing**
1 : to entertain richly or agreeably 2 : to
give pleasure or amusement to ⟨regaled

us with stories⟩ ♦ *Synonyms* GRATIFY,
DELIGHT, PLEASE, REJOICE, GLADDEN

re·ga·lia \ri-'gāl-yə\ *n pl* 1 : the emblems,
symbols, or paraphernalia of royalty (as
the crown and scepter) 2 : the insignia of
an office or order 3 : special costume
: FINERY

¹**re·gard** \ri-'gärd\ *n* 1 : CONSIDERATION,
HEED; *also* : CARE, CONCERN 2 : GAZE,
GLANCE, LOOK 3 : RESPECT, ESTEEM
⟨held in high ~⟩ 4 *pl* : friendly greetings
implying respect and esteem 5 : an aspect to be considered : PARTICULAR —
re·gard·ful *adj* — **re·gard·less** *adj*

²**regard** *vb* 1 : to think of : CONSIDER 2
: to pay attention to 3 : to show respect
for : HEED ⟨~s *his elders*⟩ 4 : to hold in
high esteem : care for 5 : to look at : gaze
upon ⟨~ed the landscape⟩ 6 *archaic* : to
relate to

re·gard·ing *prep* : CONCERNING

regardless of \ri-'gärd-ləs-\ *prep* : in spite
of

re·gat·ta \ri-'gä-tə, -'ga-\ *n* : a boat race or
a series of boat races

re·gen·cy \'rē-jən-sē\ *n, pl* **-cies** 1 : the
office or government of a regent or body
of regents 2 : a body of regents 3 : the
period during which a regent governs

re·gen·er·a·cy \ri-'je-nə-rə-sē\ *n* : the
state of being regenerated

¹**re·gen·er·ate** \ri-'je-nə-rət\ *adj* 1
: formed or created again 2 : spiritually
reborn or converted

²**re·gen·er·ate** \ri-'je-nə-ˌrāt\ *vb* 1 : to subject to spiritual renewal 2 : to reform
completely 3 : to replace (a body part)
by a new growth of tissue 4 : to give new
life to : REVIVE — **re·gen·er·a·tion** \-ˌje-
nə-'rā-shən\ *n* — **re·gen·er·a·tive** \-'je-
nə-ˌrā-tiv\ *adj* — **re·gen·er·a·tor** \-ˌrā-
tər\ *n*

re·gent \'rē-jənt\ *n* 1 : a person who rules
during the childhood, absence, or incapacity of the sovereign 2 : a member of a
governing board (as of a state university)
— **regent** *adj*

reg·gae \'re-ˌgā\ *n* : popular music of Jamaican origin that combines native styles
with elements of rock and soul music

reg·i·cide \'re-jə-ˌsīd\ *n* 1 : one who murders a king 2 : murder of a king

re·gift \(ˌ)rē-'gift\ *vb* : to give a previously
received gift to someone else

re·gime *also* **ré·gime** \rā-'zhēm, ri-\ *n* 1
: REGIMEN 2 : a form or system of government 3 : a government in power; *also*
: a period of rule

reg·i·men \'re-jə-mən\ *n* [ME, fr. ML, position of authority, direction, set of rules,
fr. L, steering, control, fr. *regere* to direct]
1 : a systematic course of treatment or
training ⟨a strict dietary ~⟩ 2 : GOV-
ERNMENT

¹**reg·i·ment** \'re-jə-mənt\ *n* : a military
unit consisting usu. of a number of bat-
talions — **reg·i·men·tal** \ˌre-jə-'ment-təl\
adj

---

refreeze   refurnish   regain   regather
refuel

²reg·i·ment \'re-jə-,ment\ *vb* : to organize rigidly esp. for regulation or central control; *also* : to subject to order or uniformity — **reg·i·men·ta·tion** \,re-jə-mən-'tā-shən\ *n*

reg·i·men·tals \,re-jə-'men-təlz\ *n pl* **1** : a regimental uniform **2** : military dress

re·gion \'rē-jən\ *n* [ME, fr. AF *regiun*, fr. L *region-, regio*, line, direction, area, fr. *regere* to rule] : an often indefinitely defined part or area

re·gion·al \'rē-jə-nəl\ *adj* **1** : affecting a particular region : LOCALIZED **2** : of, relating to, characteristic of, or serving a region — **re·gion·al·ly** *adv*

¹reg·is·ter \'re-jə-stər\ *n* **1** : a record of items or details; *also* : a book or system for keeping such a record **2** : the range of a voice or instrument **3** : a device to regulate ventilation or heating **4** : an automatic device recording a number or quantity **5** : CASH REGISTER

²register *vb* **-tered; -ter·ing 1** : to enter in a register (as in a list of guests) **2** : to record automatically **3** : to secure special care for (mail matter) by paying additional postage **4** : to convey an impression of : EXPRESS **5** : to make or adjust so as to correspond exactly

registered nurse *n* : a graduate trained nurse who has been licensed to practice by a state authority after passing qualifying examinations

reg·is·trant \'re-jə-strənt\ *n* : one that registers or is registered

reg·is·trar \-,strär\ *n* : an official recorder or keeper of records (as at an educational institution)

reg·is·tra·tion \,re-jə-'strā-shən\ *n* **1** : the act of registering **2** : an entry in a register **3** : the number of persons registered : ENROLLMENT **4** : a document certifying an act of registering

reg·is·try \'re-jə-strē\ *n, pl* **-tries 1** : ENROLLMENT, REGISTRATION **2** : a place of registration **3** : an official record book or an entry in one

reg·nant \'reg-nənt\ *adj* **1** : REIGNING **2** : DOMINANT **3** : of common or widespread occurrence

¹re·gress \'rē-gres\ *n* **1** : an act or the privilege of going or coming back **2** : RETROGRESSION

²re·gress \ri-'gres\ *vb* : to go or cause to go back or to a lower level — **re·gres·sive** *adj* — **re·gres·sor** \-'gre-sər\ *n*

re·gres·sion \ri-'gre-shən\ *n* : the act or an instance of regressing; *esp* : reversion to an earlier mental or behavioral level

¹re·gret \ri-'gret\ *vb* **re·gret·ted; re·gret·ting 1** : to mourn the loss or death of **2** : to be very sorry for **3** : to experience regret — **re·gret·ta·ble** \-'gre-tə-bəl\ *adj* — **re·gret·ter** *n*

²regret *n* **1** : sorrow caused by something beyond one's power to remedy **2** : an expression of sorrow **3** *pl* : a note politely declining an invitation — **re·gret·ful** \-fəl\ *adj* — **re·gret·ful·ly** *adv*

re·gret·ta·bly \-'gre-tə-blē\ *adv* **1** : to a regrettable extent **2** : it is to be regretted

re·group \(,)rē-'grüp\ *vb* : to form into a new grouping

regt *abbr* regiment

¹reg·u·lar \'re-gyə-lər\ *adj* [ME *reguler*, fr. AF, fr. LL *regularis* regular, fr. L, of a bar, fr. *regula* rule, straightedge, fr. *regere* to keep straight, direct] **1** : belonging to a religious order **2** : made, built, or arranged according to a rule, standard, or type; *also* : even or symmetrical in form or structure **3** : ORDERLY, METHODICAL ⟨∼ habits⟩; *also* : not varying : STEADY ⟨a ∼ pace⟩ **4** : made, selected, or conducted according to rule or custom **5** : properly qualified ⟨not a ∼ lawyer⟩ **6** : conforming to the normal or usual manner or inflection **7** : of, relating to, or constituting the permanent standing military force of a state — **reg·u·lar·i·ty** \,re-gyə-'la-rə-tē\ *n* — **reg·u·lar·ize** \'re-gyə-lə-,rīz\ *vb* — **reg·u·lar·ly** *adv*

²regular *n* **1** : one that is regular (as in attendance) **2** : a member of the regular clergy **3** : a soldier in a regular army **4** : a player on an athletic team who is usu. in the starting lineup

reg·u·late \'re-gyə-,lāt\ *vb* **-lat·ed; -lat·ing 1** : to govern or direct according to rule : CONTROL **2** : to bring under the control of law or authority **3** : to put in good order **4** : to fix or adjust the time, amount, degree, or rate of — **reg·u·la·tive** \-,lā-tiv\ *adj* — **reg·u·la·tor** \-,lā-tər\ *n* — **reg·u·la·to·ry** \-lə-,tȯr-ē\ *adj*

reg·u·la·tion \,re-gyə-'lā-shən\ *n* **1** : the act of regulating : the state of being regulated **2** : a rule dealing with details of procedure **3** : an order issued by an executive authority of a government and having the force of law

re·gur·gi·tate \rē-'gər-jə-,tāt\ *vb* **-tat·ed; -tat·ing** [ML *regurgitare*, fr. L re- re- + LL *gurgitare* to engulf, fr. L *gurgit-, gurges* whirlpool] : to throw or be thrown back, up, or out ⟨∼ food⟩ — **re·gur·gi·ta·tion** \-,gər-jə-'tā-shən\ *n*

re·hab \'rē-,hab\ *n* **1** : REHABILITATION **2** : a rehabilitated building — **rehab** *vb*

re·ha·bil·i·tate \,rē-hə-'bi-lə-,tāt, ,rē-ə-\ *vb* **-tat·ed; -tat·ing 1** : to restore to a former capacity, rank, or right : REINSTATE **2** : to restore to good condition or health — **re·ha·bil·i·ta·tion** \-,bi-lə-'tā-shən\ *n* — **re·ha·bil·i·ta·tive** \-,tā-tiv\ *adj*

re·hash \rē-'hash\ *vb* : to present again in another form without real change or improvement — **rehash** *n*

re·hear·ing \,rē-'hir-iŋ\ *n* : a second or new hearing by the same tribunal

re·hears·al \ri-'hər-səl\ *n* **1** : something told again : RECITAL **2** : a private performance or practice session preparatory to a public appearance

re·hearse \ri-'hərs\ *vb* **re·hearsed; re·hears·ing 1** : to say again : REPEAT **2** : to recount in order : ENUMERATE; *also* : RELATE 1 **3** : to give a rehearsal of **4**

: to train by rehearsal **5** : to engage in a rehearsal — **re·hears·er** *n*

¹reign \'rān\ *n* **1** : the authority or rule of a sovereign **2** : the time during which a sovereign rules

²reign *vb* **1** : to rule as a sovereign **2** : to be predominant or prevalent

re·im·burse \‚rē-əm-'bərs\ *vb* **-bursed; -burs·ing** [*re-* re- + obs. E *imburse* to put in the pocket, pay, fr. ML *imbursare* to put into a purse, fr. L *in-* in + ML *bursa* purse, fr. LL, hide of an ox, fr. Gk *byrsa*] : to pay back : make restitution : REPAY ⟨was *reimbursed* for her travel expenses⟩ ♦ **Synonyms** INDEMNIFY, RECOMPENSE, REQUITE, COMPENSATE — **re·im·burs·able** *adj* — **re·im·burse·ment** *n*

¹rein \'rān\ *n* **1** : a strap fastened to a bit by which a rider or driver controls an animal **2** : a restraining influence : CHECK **3** : controlling or guiding power **4** : complete freedom — usu. used in the phrase *give rein to*

²rein *vb* : to check or direct by reins

re·in·car·na·tion \‚rē-(‚)in-(‚)kär-'nā-shən\ *n* : rebirth of the soul in a new body — **re·in·car·nate** \‚rē-in-'kär-‚nāt\ *vb*

rein·deer \'rān-‚dir\ *n* [ME *reindere*, fr. ON *hreinn* reindeer + ME *deer* animal, deer] : CARIBOU — used esp. for one of the Old World

reindeer moss *n* : a gray, erect, tufted, and much-branched edible lichen of northern regions that is an important food of reindeer

re·in·fec·tion \‚rē-in-'fek-shən\ *n* : infection following another infection of the same type

re·in·force \‚rē-ən-'fōrs\ *vb* **1** : to strengthen with additional forces ⟨∼ our troops⟩ **2** : to strengthen with new force, aid, material, or support — **re·in·force·ment** *n* — **re·in·forc·er** *n*

re·in·scribe \‚rē-ən-'skrīb\ *vb* : to reestablish or rename in a new and esp. stronger form or context

re·in·state \‚rē-in-'stāt\ *vb* **-stat·ed; -stat·ing** : to restore to a former position, condition, or capacity — **re·in·state·ment** *n*

re·in·vent \‚rē-in-'vent\ *vb* **1** : to make as if for the first time something already invented ⟨∼ the wheel⟩ **2** : to remake completely

re·it·er·ate \rē-'i-tə-‚rāt\ *vb* **-at·ed; -at·ing** : to state or do over again or repeatedly — **re·it·er·a·tion** \-‚i-tə-'rā-shən\ *n*

¹re·ject \ri-'jekt\ *vb* **1** : to refuse to accept, consider, use, or submit to **2** : to refuse to hear, receive, or admit : REPEL **3** : to rebuff or withhold love from **4** : to throw out esp. as useless or unsatisfactory **5** : to subject (a transplanted tissue) to an attack by immune system components of the recipient organism — **re·jec·tion** \-'jek-shən\ *n*

²re·ject \'rē-‚jekt\ *n* : a rejected person or thing

re·joice \ri-'jȯis\ *vb* **re·joiced; re·joic·ing 1** : to give joy to : GLADDEN **2** : to feel joy or great delight — **re·joic·er** *n*

re·join \(‚)rē-'jȯin *for 1,* ri- *for 2*\ *vb* **1** : to join again **2** : to say in answer (as to a plaintiff's plea in court) : REPLY

re·join·der \ri-'jȯin-dər\ *n* : REPLY; *esp* : an answer to a reply

re·ju·ve·nate \ri-'jü-və-‚nāt\ *vb* **-nat·ed; -nat·ing** : to make young or youthful again : give new vigor to ♦ **Synonyms** RENEW, REFRESH, RENOVATE, RESTORE — **re·ju·ve·na·tion** \-‚jü-və-'nā-shən\ *n*

rel *abbr* **1** relating; relative **2** religion; religious

¹re·lapse \ri-'laps, 'rē-‚laps\ *n* [ME, fr. ML *relapsus*, fr. L *relabi* to slide back] : the act or process of backsliding or worsening **2** : a recurrence of illness after a period of improvement

²re·lapse \ri-'laps\ *vb* **re·lapsed; re·laps·ing** : to slip or fall back into a former worse state (as of illness)

re·late \ri-'lāt\ *vb* **re·lat·ed; re·lat·ing 1** : to give an account of : TELL, NARRATE **2** : to show or establish logical or causal connection between **3** : to have relationship or connection **4** : to have or establish relationship (the way a child ∼s to a teacher) **5** : to respond favorably ⟨can't ∼ to that kind of music⟩ — **re·lat·able** *adj* — **re·lat·er** *or* **re·la·tor** \-'lā-tər\ *n*

re·lat·ed *adj* **1** : connected by some understood relationship **2** : connected through membership in the same family — **re·lat·ed·ness** *n*

re·la·tion \ri-'lā-shən\ *n* **1** : NARRATION, ACCOUNT **2** : CONNECTION, RELATIONSHIP **3** : connection by blood or marriage : KINSHIP; *also* : RELATIVE **4** : REFERENCE, RESPECT ⟨in ∼ to⟩ **5** : the state of being mutually interested or involved (as in social or commercial matters) **6** *pl* : DEALINGS, AFFAIRS ⟨foreign ∼s⟩ **7** *pl* : SEXUAL INTERCOURSE — **re·la·tion·al** \-shnəl\ *adj*

re·la·tion·ship \-‚ship\ *n* : the state of being related or interrelated

¹rel·a·tive \'re-lə-tiv\ *n* **1** : a word referring grammatically to an antecedent **2** : a thing having a relation to or a dependence upon another thing **3** : a person connected with another by blood or marriage

²relative *adj* **1** : introducing a subordinate clause qualifying an expressed or implied antecedent ⟨∼ pronoun⟩; *also* : introduced by such a connective ⟨∼ clause⟩ **2** : PERTINENT, RELEVANT ⟨matters ∼ to world peace⟩ **3** : not absolute or independent : COMPARATIVE **4** : expressed as the ratio of the specified quantity to the total magnitude or to the mean of all quantities involved ♦ **Synonyms** DE-

reheat
rehouse
reimpose
reimposition
reincorporate
reinsert

reinsertion
reintegrate
reinterpret
reinterpretation
reintroduce
reintroduction

reinvention
reinvest
reinvestment
reinvigorate
reinvigoration

reissue
rejudge
rekindle
reknit

PENDENT, CONTINGENT, CONDITIONAL — **rel·a·tive·ly** adv — **rel·a·tive·ness** n

relative humidity n : the ratio of the amount of water vapor actually present in the air to the greatest amount possible at the same temperature

rel·a·tiv·is·tic \ˌre-lə-ti-'vis-tik\ adj 1 : of, relating to, or characterized by relativity 2 : moving at a velocity that is a significant fraction of the speed of light so that effects predicted by the theory of relativity become evident ⟨a ∼ electron⟩ — **rel·a·tiv·is·ti·cal·ly** \-ti-k(ə-)lē\ adv

rel·a·tiv·i·ty \ˌre-lə-'ti-və-tē\ n, pl **-ties** 1 : the quality or state of being relative 2 : a theory in physics that considers mass and energy to be equivalent and that predicts changes in mass, dimension, and time which are related to speed but are noticeable esp. at speeds approaching that of light; also : an extension of the theory to include gravitation and related acceleration phenomena

re·lax \ri-'laks\ vb 1 : to make or become less firm, tense, or rigid 2 : to make less severe or strict 3 : to seek rest or recreation — **re·lax·er** n

¹**re·lax·ant** \ri-'lak-sənt\ adj : of, relating to, or producing relaxation

²**relaxant** n : a relaxing agent; esp : a drug that induces muscular relaxation

re·lax·ation \ˌrē-ˌlak-'sā-shən\ n 1 : the act of relaxing or state of being relaxed : a lessening of tension 2 : DIVERSION, RECREATION

¹**re·lay** \'rē-ˌlā\ n [ME, set of fresh hounds, fr. relayen to release fresh hounds, take a fresh horse, fr. MF relaier, fr. re- again + laier to let go, leave] 1 : a fresh supply (as of horses or men) arranged beforehand to relieve others 2 : a race between teams in which each team member covers a specified part of a course 3 : an electromagnetic device in which the opening or closing of one circuit activates another device (as a switch in another circuit) 4 : the act of passing along by stages

²**re·lay** \'rē-ˌlā, ri-'lā\ vb **re·layed**; **re·lay·ing** 1 : to place in or provide with relays 2 : to pass along by relays 3 : to control or operate by a relay

³**re·lay** \(ˌ)rē-'lā\ vb **-laid** \-'lād\; **-lay·ing** : to lay again

¹**re·lease** \ri-'lēs\ vb **re·leased**; **re·leas·ing** 1 : to set free from confinement or restraint; also : DISMISS ⟨released from her job⟩ 2 : to relieve from something that oppresses, confines, or burdens 3 : RELINQUISH ⟨∼ a claim⟩ 4 : to permit publication, performance, exhibition, or sale of; also : to make available to the public ♦ **Synonyms** EMANCIPATE, DISCHARGE, FREE, LIBERATE

²**release** n 1 : relief or deliverance from sorrow, suffering, or trouble 2 : discharge from an obligation or responsibility 3 : an act of setting free : the state of being freed 4 : a document effecting a legal release 5 : a releasing for performance or publication; also : the matter

released (as to the press) 6 : a device for holding or releasing a mechanism as required

rel·e·gate \'re-lə-ˌgāt\ vb **-gat·ed**; **-gat·ing** 1 : to send into exile : BANISH 2 : to remove or dismiss to some less prominent position 3 : to assign to a particular class or sphere 4 : to submit to someone or something for appropriate action : DELEGATE ♦ **Synonyms** COMMIT, ENTRUST, CONSIGN, COMMEND — **rel·e·ga·tion** \ˌre-lə-'gā-shən\ n

re·lent \ri-'lent\ vb 1 : to become less stern, severe, or harsh 2 : SLACKEN

re·lent·less \-ləs\ adj : showing or promising no abatement of severity, intensity, or pace ⟨∼ pressure⟩ — **re·lent·less·ly** adv — **re·lent·less·ness** n

rel·e·vance \'re-lə-vəns\ n : relation to the matter at hand; also : practical and esp. social applicability

rel·e·van·cy \-vən-sē\ n : RELEVANCE

rel·e·vant \'re-lə-vənt\ adj : bearing on the matter at hand : PERTINENT ♦ **Synonyms** GERMANE, MATERIAL, APPLICABLE, APROPOS — **rel·e·vant·ly** adv

re·li·able \ri-'lī-ə-bəl\ adj : fit to be trusted or relied on : BANISH 2 : DEPENDABLE, TRUSTWORTHY — **re·li·abil·i·ty** \-ˌlī-ə-'bi-lə-tē\ n — **re·li·able·ness** n — **re·li·ably** \-'lī-ə-blē\ adv

re·li·ance \ri-'lī-əns\ n 1 : the act of relying 2 : the state of being reliant 3 : one relied on

re·li·ant \ri-'lī-ənt\ adj : having reliance on someone or something : DEPENDENT

rel·ic \'re-lik\ n 1 : an object venerated because of its association with a saint or martyr 2 : SOUVENIR, MEMENTO 3 pl : REMAINS, RUINS 4 : a remaining trace : VESTIGE

rel·ict \'re-likt\ n : WIDOW

re·lief \ri-'lēf\ n 1 : removal or lightening of something oppressive, painful, or distressing 2 : WELFARE 2 3 : military assistance to an endangered post or force 4 : release from a post or from performance of a duty; also : one that takes the place of another on duty 5 : legal remedy or redress 6 : projection of figures or ornaments from the background (as in sculpture) 7 : the state of being distinguished by contrast 8 : the elevations of a land surface

relief pitcher n : a baseball pitcher who takes over for another during a game

re·lieve \ri-'lēv\ vb **re·lieved**; **re·liev·ing** 1 : to free partly or wholly from a burden or from distress 2 : to bring about the removal or alleviation of : MITIGATE 3 : to release from a post or duty; also : to take the place of 4 : to break the monotony of 5 : to discharge the bladder or bowels of (oneself) ♦ **Synonyms** ALLEVIATE, LIGHTEN, ASSUAGE, ALLAY — **re·liev·er** n

relig abbr religion

re·li·gion \ri-'li-jən\ n 1 : the service and worship of God or the supernatural 2 : devotion to a religious faith 3 : a per-

---

relaunch   relearn   relight

sonal set or institutionalized system of religious beliefs, attitudes, and practices **4** : a cause, principle, or belief held to with faith and ardor — **re·li·gion·ist** *n*

¹re·li·gious \ri-'li-jəs\ *adj* **1** : relating or devoted to an acknowledged ultimate reality or deity **2** : of or relating to religious beliefs or observances **3** : scrupulously and conscientiously faithful **4** : FERVENT, ZEALOUS ⟨∼ about football⟩ — **re·li·gious·ly** *adv*

²religious *n, pl* **religious** : a member of a religious order under monastic vows

re·lin·quish \ri-'liŋ-kwish, -'lin-\ *vb* **1** : to withdraw or retreat from : ABANDON, QUIT **2** : GIVE UP ⟨∼ a title⟩ **3** : to let go of : RELEASE ♦ *Synonyms* YIELD, LEAVE, RESIGN, SURRENDER, CEDE, WAIVE — **re·lin·quish·ment** *n*

rel·i·quary \'re-lə-ˌkwer-ē\ *n, pl* **-quar·ies** : a container for religious relics

¹rel·ish \'re-lish\ *n* [ME *reles* taste, fr. OF, something left behind, release, fr. *relessier* to relax, release, fr. L *relaxare*] **1** : characteristic flavor : SAVOR **2** : keen enjoyment or delight in something : GUSTO **3** : APPETITE, INCLINATION ⟨has no ∼ for sports⟩ **4** : a highly seasoned sauce (as of pickles) eaten with other food to add flavor

²relish *vb* **1** : to add relish to **2** : to take pleasure in : ENJOY **3** : to eat with pleasure — **rel·ish·able** *adj*

re·live \(ˌ)rē-'liv\ *vb* : to live again or over again; *esp* : to experience again in the imagination

re·lo·cate \(ˌ)rē-'lō-ˌkāt, ˌrē-lō-'kāt\ *vb* **1** : to locate again **2** : to move to a new location — **re·lo·ca·tion** \ˌrē-lō-'kā-shən\ *n*

re·luc·tant \ri-'lək-tənt\ *adj* : feeling or showing aversion, hesitation, or unwillingness ⟨∼ to get involved⟩ ♦ *Synonyms* DISINCLINED, INDISPOSED, HESITANT, LOATH, AVERSE — **re·luc·tance** \-təns\ *n* — **re·luc·tant·ly** *adv*

re·ly \ri-'lī\ *vb* **-lied; re·ly·ing** [ME *relien* to rally, fr. AF *relier* to retie, gather, rally, fr. L *religare* to tie out of the way, fr. *re-* back + *ligare* to tie] : to place faith or confidence : DEPEND

REM \'rem\ *n* : RAPID EYE MOVEMENT

re·main \ri-'mān\ *vb* **1** : to be left after others have been removed, subtracted, or destroyed **2** : to be something yet to be shown, done, or treated ⟨it ∼s to be seen⟩ **3** : to stay after others have gone **4** : to continue unchanged

re·main·der \ri-'mān-dər\ *n* **1** : that which is left over : a remaining group, part, or trace **2** : the number left after a subtraction **3** : the number that is left over from the dividend after division and that is less than the divisor **4** : a book sold at a reduced price by the publisher after sales have slowed ♦ *Synonyms* LEAVINGS, REST, BALANCE, REMNANT, RESIDUE

re·mains \-'mānz\ *n pl* **1** : a remaining part or trace ⟨the ∼ of a meal⟩ **2** : a dead body

¹re·make \(ˌ)rē-'māk\ *vb* **-made** \-'mād\; **-mak·ing** : to make anew or in a different form

²re·make \'rē-ˌmāk\ *n* : one that is remade; *esp* : a new version of a motion picture

re·mand \ri-'mand\ *vb* : to order back; *esp* : to return to custody pending trial or for further detention

¹re·mark \ri-'märk\ *n* **1** : the act of remarking : OBSERVATION, NOTICE **2** : a passing observation or comment

²remark *vb* **1** : to take notice of : OBSERVE **2** : to express as an observation or comment : SAY

re·mark·able \ri-'mär-kə-bəl\ *adj* : worthy of being or likely to be noticed : UNUSUAL, EXTRAORDINARY, NOTEWORTHY — **re·mark·able·ness** *n*

re·mark·ably \ri-'mär-kə-blē\ *adv* **1** : in a remarkable manner **2** : as is remarkable ⟨∼, no one was hurt⟩

re·me·di·a·ble \ri-'mē-dē-ə-bəl\ *adj* : capable of being remedied

re·me·di·al \ri-'mē-dē-əl\ *adj* : intended to remedy or improve ⟨a class in ∼ math⟩

¹rem·e·dy \'re-mə-dē\ *n, pl* **-dies** [ME *remedie*, fr. AF, fr. L *remedium*, fr. *re-* back, again + *mederi* to heal] **1** : a medicine or treatment that cures or relieves a disease or condition **2** : something that corrects or counteracts an evil or compensates for a loss

²remedy *vb* **-died; -dy·ing** : to provide or serve as a remedy for

re·mem·ber \ri-'mem-bər\ *vb* **-bered; -ber·ing** **1** : to bring to mind or think of again : RECOLLECT **2** : to keep from forgetting : keep in mind **3** : to convey greetings from ⟨∼ greetings from⟩ **4** : COMMEMORATE

re·mem·brance \-brəns\ *n* **1** : an act of remembering : RECOLLECTION **2** : the ability to remember : MEMORY **3** : the period over which one's memory extends **4** : a memory of a person, thing, or event **5** : something that serves to bring to mind : REMINDER **6** : a greeting or gift recalling or expressing friendship or affection

re·mind \ri-'mīnd\ *vb* : to put in mind of something : cause to remember — **re·mind·er** *n*

rem·i·nisce \ˌre-mə-'nis\ *vb* **-nisced; -nisc·ing** : to indulge in reminiscence

rem·i·nis·cence \-'ni-s²ns\ *n* **1** : a recalling or telling of a past experience **2** : an account of a memorable experience

rem·i·nis·cent \-s²nt\ *adj* **1** : of or relating to reminiscence **2** : marked by or given to reminiscence **3** : serving to remind : SUGGESTIVE — **rem·i·nis·cent·ly** *adv*

re·miss \ri-'mis\ *adj* **1** : negligent or careless in the performance of work or duty **2** : showing neglect or inattention

---

reline	remap	remarry	remelt
reload	remarriage	rematch	remigration
remanufacture			

♦ *Synonyms* LAX, NEGLECTFUL, DELIN-QUENT, DERELICT — **re·miss·ness** *n*

re·mis·sion \ri-'mi-shən\ *n* 1 : the act or process of remitting 2 : a state or period during which something is remitted

re·mit \ri-'mit\ *vb* **re·mit·ted; re·mit·ting** 1 : FORGIVE, PARDON ⟨~ sins⟩ 2 : to give or gain relief from (as pain) 3 : to refer for consideration, report, or decision 4 : to refrain from exacting or enforcing (as a penalty) 5 : to send (money) in payment of a bill

re·mit·tal \ri-'mi-t³l\ *n* : REMISSION

re·mit·tance \ri-'mi-t³ns\ *n* 1 : a sum of money remitted 2 : transmittal of money (as to a distant place)

rem·nant \'rem-nənt\ *n* 1 : a usu. small part or trace remaining 2 : an unsold or unused end of a fabric that is sold by the yard

re·mod·el \,rē-'mä-d³l\ *vb* : to alter the structure of : MAKE OVER

re·mon·strance \ri-'män-strəns\ *n* : an act or instance of remonstrating

re·mon·strant \-strənt\ *adj* : vigorously objecting or opposing — **remonstrant** *n* — **re·mon·strant·ly** *adv*

re·mon·strate \ri-'män-,strāt\ *vb* **-strated; -strat·ing** : to plead in opposition to something : speak in protest or reproof ♦ *Synonyms* EXPOSTULATE, OBJECT, PROTEST — **re·mon·stra·tion** \ri-,män-'strā-shon, ,re-mən-\ *n* — **re·mon·stra·tor** \ri-'män-,strā-tər\ *n*

rem·o·ra \'re-mə-rə\ *n* : any of a family of marine bony fishes with sucking organs on the head by which they cling esp. to other fishes

re·morse \ri-'mórs\ *n* [ME, fr. AF *remors*, fr. ML *remorsus*, fr. LL, act of biting again, fr. L *remordēre* to bite again, fr. *re-* again + *mordēre* to bite] : a gnawing distress arising from a sense of guilt for past wrongs ♦ *Synonyms* PENITENCE, REPENTANCE, CONTRITION — **re·morse·ful** *adj*

re·morse·less \-ləs\ *adj* 1 : MERCILESS 2 : PERSISTENT, RELENTLESS

¹**re·mote** \ri-'mōt\ *adj* **re·mot·er; -est** 1 : far off in place or time : not near 2 : not closely related : DISTANT 3 : located out of the way : SECLUDED 4 : acting, acted on, or controlled indirectly or from a distance 5 : small in degree : SLIGHT ⟨a ~ chance⟩ 6 : distant in manner ⟨became ~ in old age⟩ — **re·mote·ly** *adv* — **re·mote·ness** *n*

²**remote** *n* 1 : a radio or television program or a portion of a program originating outside the studio 2 : REMOTE CONTROL 2

remote control *n* 1 : control (as by radio signal) of operation from a point at some distance removed 2 : a device or mechanism for controlling something from a distance

¹**re·mount** \(,)rē-'maúnt\ *vb* 1 : to mount again 2 : to furnish remounts to

²**re·mount** \'rē-,maúnt\ *n* : a fresh horse to replace one no longer available

¹**re·move** \ri-'müv\ *vb* **re·moved; re·mov·ing** 1 : to move from one place to another : TRANSFER 2 : to move by lifting or taking off or away 3 : DISMISS, DISCHARGE 4 : to get rid of : ELIMINATE ⟨~ a fire hazard⟩ 5 : to change one's residence or location 6 : to go away : DEPART 7 : to be capable of being removed — **re·mov·able** *adj* — **re·mov·al** \-'mü-vəl\ *n* — **re·mov·er** *n*

²**remove** *n* 1 : a transfer from one location to another : MOVE 2 : a degree or stage of separation

REM sleep *n* : a state of sleep that recurs cyclically several times during normal sleep and is associated with rapid eye movements and dreaming

re·mu·ner·ate \ri-'myü-nə-,rāt\ *vb* **-at·ed; -at·ing** : to pay an equivalent for or to : RECOMPENSE ⟨their services were *remunerated*⟩ — **re·mu·ner·a·tor** \-,rā-tər\ *n*

re·mu·ner·a·tion \ri-,myü-nə-'rā-shon\ *n* : COMPENSATION, PAYMENT

re·mu·ner·a·tive \ri-'myü-nə-rə-tiv, -,rā-\ *adj* : serving to remunerate : GAINFUL

re·nais·sance \,re-nə-'säns, -'zäns\ *n* 1 *cap* : the cultural revival and beginnings of modern science in Europe in the 14th–17th centuries; *also* : the period of the Renaissance 2 *often cap* : a movement or period of vigorous artistic and intellectual activity 3 : REBIRTH, REVIVAL

re·nal \'rē-n³l\ *adj* : of, relating to, or located in or near the kidneys

re·na·scence \ri-'na-s³ns, -'nä-\ *n, often cap* : RENAISSANCE

rend \'rend\ *vb* **rent** \'rent\; **rend·ing** 1 : to remove by violence : WREST 2 : to tear forcibly apart : SPLIT

ren·der \'ren-dər\ *vb* 1 : to extract (as lard) by heating 2 : to give to another; *also* : YIELD 3 : to give in return 4 : to do (a service) for another ⟨~ aid⟩ 5 : to cause to be or become : MAKE 6 : to reproduce or represent by artistic or verbal means 7 : TRANSLATE ⟨~ into English⟩

¹**ren·dez·vous** \'rän-di-,vü, -dā-\ *n, pl* **ren·dez·vous** \-,vüz\ [MF, fr. *rendez vous* present yourselves] 1 : a place appointed for a meeting; *also* : a meeting at an appointed place 2 : a place of popular resort 3 : the process of bringing two spacecraft together

²**rendezvous** *vb* **-voused** \-,vüd\; **-vous·ing** \-,vü-in\; **-vouses** \-,vüz\ : to come or bring together at a rendezvous

ren·di·tion \ren-'di-shon\ *n* : an act or a result of rendering ⟨first ~ of the work into English⟩

ren·e·gade \'re-ni-,gād\ *n* [Sp *renegado*, fr. ML *renegatus*, fr. pp. of *renegare* to deny, fr. L *re-* re- + *negare* to deny] : a deserter from one faith, cause, principle, or party for another

re·nege \ri-'neg\ *vb* **re·neged; re·neg·ing** 1 : to go back on a promise or commitment 2 : to fail to follow suit when able in a card game in violation of the rules — **re·neg·er** *n*

---

remold   rename   renegotiate   renegotiation

re·new \ri-'nü, -'nyü\ vb **1** : to make or become new, fresh, or strong again **2** : to restore to existence : RECREATE, REVIVE **3** : to make or do again : REPEAT ⟨∼ a complaint⟩ **4** : to begin again : RESUME ⟨∼ed his efforts⟩ **5** : REPLACE ⟨∼ the lining of a coat⟩ **6** : to grant or obtain an extension of or on ⟨∼ a lease⟩ ⟨∼ a subscription⟩ — **re·new·er** n

re·new·able \ri-'nü-ə-bal, -'nyü-\ adj **1** : capable of being renewed **2** : capable of being replaced by natural ecological cycles or sound management procedures ⟨∼ resources⟩

re·new·al \ri-'nü-əl, -'nyü-\ n **1** : the act of renewing : the state of being renewed **2** : something renewed

ren·net \'re-nət\ n **1** : the contents of the stomach of an unweaned animal (as a calf) or the lining membrane of the stomach used for curdling milk **2** : rennin or a substitute known as rennin to curdle milk

ren·nin \'re-nən\ n : a stomach enzyme that coagulates casein and is used commercially to curdle milk in the making of cheese

re·nounce \ri-'naúns\ vb **re·nounced**; **re·nounc·ing** **1** : to give up, refuse, or resign usu. by formal declaration **2** : to refuse further to follow, obey, or recognize : REPUDIATE — **re·nounce·ment** n

ren·o·vate \'re-nə-ˌvāt\ vb **-vat·ed**; **-vat·ing** **1** : to make like new again : put in good condition : REPAIR ⟨renovated the kitchen⟩ **2** : to restore to vigor or activity — **ren·o·va·tion** \ˌre-nə-'vā-shən\ n — **ren·o·va·tor** \'re-nə-ˌvā-tər\ n

re·nown \ri-'naún\ n : a state of being widely acclaimed and honored : FAME, CELEBRITY ⟨writers of ∼⟩ ♦ **Synonyms** HONOR, GLORY, REPUTATION, REPUTE — **re·nowned** \-'naúnd\ adj

¹rent \'rent\ n **1** : money or the amount of money paid or due at intervals for the use of another's property **2** : property rented or for rent

²rent vb **1** : to give possession and use of in return for rent **2** : to take and hold under an agreement to pay rent **3** : to be for rent ⟨∼s for $100 a month⟩ — **rent·er** n

³rent n **1** : a tear made by or as if by rending **2** : a split in a party or organized group : SCHISM

¹rent·al \'ren-təl\ n **1** : an amount paid or collected as rent **2** : something that is rented **3** : an act of renting

²rental adj : of or relating to rent

re·nun·ci·a·tion \ri-ˌnən-sē-'ā-shən\ n : the act of renouncing : REPUDIATION

¹rep \'rep\ n : REPRESENTATIVE ⟨sales ∼s⟩

²rep abbr **1** repair **2** repeat **3** report; reporter **4** republic

Rep abbr Republican

re·pack·age \(ˌ)rē-'pa-kij\ vb : to package again or anew; esp : to put into a more attractive form

¹re·pair \ri-'per\ vb [ME, fr. AF repairer to go back, return, fr. LL repatriare to go home again, fr. L re- back + patria native country] : to make one's way : GO ⟨∼ed to the drawing room⟩

²repair vb [ME, fr. AF reparer, fr. L reparare, fr. re- back + parare to prepare] **1** : to restore to good condition : FIX **2** : to restore to a healthy state **3** : REMEDY ⟨∼ a wrong⟩ — **re·pair·er** n — **re·pair·man** \-ˌman\ n

³repair n **1** : a result of repairing **2** : an act of repairing **3** : condition with respect to need of repairing ⟨in bad ∼⟩

rep·a·ra·tion \ˌre-pə-'rā-shən\ n **1** : the act of making amends for a wrong **2** : amends made for a wrong; esp : money paid by a defeated nation in compensation for damages caused during hostilities — usu. used in pl. ♦ **Synonyms** REDRESS, RESTITUTION, INDEMNITY

re·par·a·tive \ri-'pa-rə-tiv\ adj **1** : of, relating to, or effecting repairs **2** : serving to make amends

rep·ar·tee \ˌre-pər-'tē\ n **1** : a witty reply **2** : a succession of clever replies; also : skill in making such replies

re·past \ri-'past, 'rē-ˌpast\ n : a supply of food and drink served as a meal

re·pa·tri·ate \rē-'pā-trē-ˌāt\ vb **-at·ed**; **-at·ing** : to send or bring back to the country of origin or citizenship ⟨∼ prisoners of war⟩ — **re·pa·tri·ate** \-trē-ət, -trē-ˌāt\ n — **re·pa·tri·a·tion** \-ˌpā-trē-'ā-shən\ n

re·pay \rē-'pā\ vb **-paid** \-'pād\; **-pay·ing** **1** : to pay back : REFUND **2** : to give or do in return or requital **3** : to make a return payment to : RECOMPENSE, REQUITE ♦ **Synonyms** REMUNERATE, COMPENSATE, REIMBURSE, INDEMNIFY — **re·pay·able** adj — **re·pay·ment** n

re·peal \ri-'pēl\ vb [ME repelen, fr. AF repeler, lit., to call back, fr. re- back + apeler to appeal, call] : to annul by authoritative and esp. legislative action ⟨∼ a law⟩ — **repeal** n — **re·peal·er** n

¹re·peat \ri-'pēt\ vb **1** : to say again **2** : to do again **3** : to say over from memory — **re·peat·able** adj — **re·peat·er** n

²re·peat \ri-'pēt, 'rē-ˌpēt\ n **1** : the act of repeating **2** : something repeated or to be repeated (as a radio or television program)

³re·peat \ri-'pēt\ adj : of, relating to, or being one that repeats an offense, achievement, or action

re·peat·ed \ri-'pē-təd\ adj : done or recurring again and again : FREQUENT ⟨∼ requests⟩ — **re·peat·ed·ly** adv

re·pel \ri-'pel\ vb **re·pelled**; **re·pel·ling** **1** : to drive away : REPULSE **2** : to fight against : RESIST **3** : to turn away : REJECT **4** : to cause aversion in : DISGUST

¹re·pel·lent also **re·pel·lant** \ri-'pe-lənt\ adj **1** : tending to drive away ⟨a mosquito-repellent spray⟩ **2** : causing disgust

²repellent also **repellant** n : something

renominate   reoccur   reorganize   repack
renomination   reopen   reorient   repaint
renumber   reorder   reorientation   repass
reoccupy   reorganization

that repels; *esp* : a substance that repels insects

re·pent \ri-'pent\ *vb* **1** : to turn from sin and resolve to reform one's life **2** : to feel sorry for (something done) : REGRET ⟨~ed his decision⟩ — **re·pen·tance** \ri-'pen-t⁰ns\ *n* — **re·pen·tant** \-t⁰nt\ *adj*

re·per·cus·sion \ˌrē-pər-'kə-shən, ˌre-\ *n* **1** : REVERBERATION **2** : a reciprocal action or effect **3** : a widespread, indirect, or unforeseen effect of something done or said

rep·er·toire \'re-pər-ˌtwär\ *n* [F] **1** : a list of plays, operas, pieces, or parts which a company or performer is prepared to present **2** : a list of the skills or devices possessed by a person or needed in a person's occupation

rep·er·to·ry \'re-pər-ˌtȯr-ē\ *n, pl* **-ries 1** : REPOSITORY **2** : REPERTOIRE **3** : a company that presents its repertoire in the course of one season at one theater

rep·e·ti·tion \ˌre-pə-'ti-shən\ *n* **1** : the act or an instance of repeating **2** : the fact of being repeated

rep·e·ti·tious \-'ti-shəs\ *adj* : marked by repetition; *esp* : tediously repeating ⟨~ work⟩ — **rep·e·ti·tious·ly** *adv* — **rep·e·ti·tious·ness** *n*

re·pet·i·tive \ri-'pe-tə-tiv\ *adj* : REPETITIOUS — **re·pet·i·tive·ly** *adv* — **re·pet·i·tive·ness** *n*

re·pine \ri-'pīn\ *vb* **re·pined; re·pin·ing 1** : to feel or express discontent or dejection **2** : to long for something

repl *abbr* replace; replacement

re·place \ri-'plās\ *vb* **1** : to restore to a former place or position **2** : to take the place of : SUPPLANT **3** : to put something new in the place of — **re·place·able** *adj* — **re·plac·er** *n*

re·place·ment \ri-'plās-mənt\ *n* **1** : the act of replacing **2** : the state of being replaced **2** : one that replaces another esp. in a job or function

¹re·play \ˌ(ˌ)rē-'plā\ *vb* : to play again or over

²re·play \'rē-ˌplā\ *n* **1** : an act or instance of replaying **2** : the playing of a tape (as a videotape)

re·plen·ish \ri-'ple-nish\ *vb* : to fill or build up again : stock or supply anew — **re·plen·ish·ment** *n*

re·plete \ri-'plēt\ *adj* **1** : fully provided ⟨a kit ~ with instructions⟩ **2** : FULL; *esp* : full of food — **re·plete·ness** *n* — **re·ple·tion** \ri-'plē-shən\ *n*

rep·li·ca \'re-pli-kə\ *n* [It, repetition, fr. *replicare* to repeat, fr. LL, fr. L, to fold back, fr. *re-* back + *plicare* to fold] **1** : an exact reproduction (as of a painting) executed by the original artist **2** : a copy exact in all details : DUPLICATE

¹rep·li·cate \'re-plə-ˌkāt\ *vb* **-cat·ed; -cat·ing** : DUPLICATE, REPEAT

²rep·li·cate \-pli-kət\ *n* : one of several identical experiments or procedures

rep·li·ca·tion \ˌre-plə-'kā-shən\ *n* **1** : ANSWER, REPLY **2** : precise copying or re-

production; *also* : an act or process of this ⟨~ of DNA⟩

¹re·ply \ri-'plī\ *vb* **re·plied; re·ply·ing** : to say or do in answer : RESPOND

²reply *n, pl* **replies** : ANSWER, RESPONSE

repo \'rē-ˌpō\ *adj* : of, relating to, or being in the business of repossessing property (as a car)

¹re·port \ri-'pȯrt\ *n* [ME, fr. AF, fr. *reporter* to bring back, report, fr. L *reportare*, fr. *re-* back + *portare* to carry] **1** : common talk : RUMOR **2** : FAME, REPUTATION ⟨a person of good ~⟩ **3** : a usu. detailed account or statement **4** : an explosive noise

²report *vb* **1** : to give an account of : RELATE, TELL **2** : to serve as carrier of (a message) **3** : to prepare or present (as an account of an event) for a newspaper or a broadcast **4** : to make a charge of misconduct against **5** : to present oneself (as for work) **6** : to make known to the authorities ⟨~ a fire⟩ **7** : to return or present (as a matter referred to a committee) with conclusions and recommendations **8** : to work as a subordinate ⟨~s to the vice president⟩ — **re·port·able** *adj*

re·port·age \ri-'pȯr-tij, ˌre-pȯr-'täzh, ˌre-ˌpȯr-'\ *n* [F] **1** : the act or process of reporting news **2** : writing intended to give an account of observed or documented events

report card *n* : a periodic report on a student's grades

re·port·ed·ly \ri-'pȯr-təd-lē\ *adv* : according to report ⟨is ~ about to be fired⟩

re·port·er \ri-'pȯr-tər\ *n* : one that reports; *esp* : a person who gathers and reports news for a news medium — **re·por·to·ri·al** \ˌre-pər-'tȯr-ē-əl\ *adj*

¹re·pose \ri-'pōz\ *vb* **re·posed; re·pos·ing 1** : to lay at rest **2** : to lie at rest **3** : to lie dead **4** : to take a rest **5** : to rest for support : LIE

²repose *n* **1** : a state of resting (as after exertion); *esp* : SLEEP **2** : eternal or heavenly rest **3** : CALM, PEACE ⟨the ~ of the bayous⟩ **4** : cessation or absence of activity, movement, or animation **5** : composure of manner : POISE — **re·pose·ful** *adj*

³repose *vb* **re·posed; re·pos·ing 1** : to place (as trust) in someone or something **2** : to place for control, management, or use

re·pos·i·to·ry \ri-'pä-zə-ˌtȯr-ē\ *n, pl* **-ries 1** : a place where something is deposited or stored **2** : a person to whom something is entrusted

re·pos·sess \ˌrē-pə-'zes\ *vb* **1** : to regain possession of **2** : to take possession of in default of the payment of installments due — **re·pos·ses·sion** \-'ze-shən\ *n*

rep·re·hend \ˌre-pri-'hend\ *vb* : to express disapproval of : CENSURE ♦ **Synonyms** CRITICIZE, CONDEMN, DENOUNCE, BLAME, PAN — **rep·re·hen·sion** \-'hen-chən\ *n*

rep·re·hen·si·ble \-'hen-sə-bəl\ *adj* : de-

---

repeople   rephrase   replant   repopulate
rephotograph

serving blame or censure : CULPABLE — **rep·re·hen·si·bly** \-blē\ *adv*

rep·re·sent \ˌre-pri-ˈzent\ *vb* **1** : to present a picture or a likeness of : PORTRAY, DEPICT **2** : to serve as a sign or symbol of **3** : to act the role of **4** : to stand in the place of : act or speak for; *also* : to manage the legal and business affairs of **5** : to be a member or example of : TYPIFY **6** : to serve as an elected representative of **7** : to describe as having a specified quality or character **8** : to state with the purpose of affecting judgment or action

rep·re·sen·ta·tion \ˌre-pri-ˌzen-ˈtā-shən\ *n* **1** : the act of representing **2** : one (as a picture or image) that represents something else **3** : the state of being represented in a legislative body; *also* : the body of persons representing a constituency **4** : a usu. formal statement made to effect a change

¹rep·re·sen·ta·tive \ˌre-pri-ˈzen-tə-tiv\ *adj* **1** : serving to represent **2** : standing or acting for another **3** : founded on the principle of representation : carried on by elected representatives ⟨∼ government⟩ — **rep·re·sen·ta·tive·ly** *adv* — **rep·re·sen·ta·tive·ness** *n*

²representative *n* **1** : one that represents another; *esp* : one representing a district in a legislative body as a member of a lower house **2** : a typical example of a group, class, or quality

re·press \ri-ˈpres\ *vb* **1** : CURB, SUBDUE **2** : RESTRAIN, SUPPRESS **3** : to exclude from consciousness ⟨∼ a painful memory⟩ — **re·pres·sion** \-ˈpre-shən\ *n* — **re·pres·sive** \-ˈpre-siv\ *adj*

¹re·prieve \ri-ˈprēv\ *vb* **re·prieved**; **re·priev·ing** **1** : to delay the punishment or execution of **2** : to give temporary relief to

²reprieve *n* **1** : the act of reprieving : the state of being reprieved **2** : a formal temporary suspension of a sentence esp. of death **3** : a temporary respite

¹rep·ri·mand \ˈre-prə-ˌmand\ *n* : a severe or formal reproof

²reprimand *vb* : to reprove severely or formally ⟨∼ed the sergeant⟩

¹re·print \ˌ(ˌ)rē-ˈprint\ *vb* : to print again

²re·print \ˈrē-ˌprint\ *n* : a reproduction of printed matter

re·pri·sal \ri-ˈprī-zəl\ *n* : an act in retaliation for something done by another

re·prise \ri-ˈprēz\ *n* : a recurrence, renewal, or resumption of an action; *also* : a musical repetition

¹re·proach \ri-ˈprōch\ *n* **1** : an expression of disapproval **2** : DISGRACE, DISCREDIT **3** : the act of reproaching : REBUKE **4** : a cause or occasion of blame or disgrace — **re·proach·ful** \-fəl\ *adj* — **re·proach·ful·ly** *adv* — **re·proach·ful·ness** *n*

²reproach *vb* **1** : CENSURE, REBUKE **2** : to cast discredit on ♦ *Synonyms* CHIDE, ADMONISH, REPROVE, REPRIMAND — **re·proach·able** *adj*

rep·ro·bate \ˈre-prə-ˌbāt\ *n* **1** : a person

foreordained to damnation **2** : a thoroughly bad person : SCOUNDREL — **reprobate** *adj*

rep·ro·ba·tion \ˌre-prə-ˈbā-shən\ *n* : strong disapproval : CONDEMNATION

re·pro·duce \ˌrē-prə-ˈdüs, -ˈdyüs\ *vb* **1** : to produce again or anew **2** : to produce offspring — **re·pro·duc·ible** \-ˈdü-sə-bəl, -ˈdyü-\ *adj* — **re·pro·duc·tion** \-ˈdək-shən\ *n* — **re·pro·duc·tive** \-ˈdək-tiv\ *adj*

re·proof \ri-ˈprüf\ *n* : blame or censure for a fault

re·prove \ri-ˈprüv\ *vb* **re·proved**; **re·prov·ing** **1** : to administer a rebuke to **2** : to express disapproval of ♦ *Synonyms* REPRIMAND, ADMONISH, REPROACH, CHIDE — **re·prov·er** *n*

rept *abbr* report

rep·tile \ˈrep-tī(-ə)l, -tᵊl\ *n* [ME *reptil*, fr. MF or LL; MF *reptile*, fr. LL *reptile*, fr. L *repere* to crawl] : any of a large class of air-breathing scaly vertebrates including snakes, lizards, alligators, turtles, and extinct related forms (as dinosaurs) — **rep·til·i·an** \rep-ˈti-lē-ən\ *adj or n*

re·pub·lic \ri-ˈpə-blik\ *n* [F *république*, fr. MF *republique*, fr. L *respublica*, fr. *res* thing, wealth + *publica*, fem. of *publicus* public] **1** : a government having a chief of state who is not a monarch and is usu. a president; *also* : a nation or other political unit having such a government **2** : a government in which supreme power is held by the citizens entitled to vote and is exercised by elected officers and representatives governing according to law; *also* : a nation or other political unit having such a form of government **3** : a constituent political and territorial unit of the former nations of Czechoslovakia, the U.S.S.R., or Yugoslavia

¹re·pub·li·can \-bli-kən\ *n* **1** : one that favors or supports a republican form of government **2** *cap* : a member of a republican party and esp. of the Republican party of the U.S.

²republican *adj* **1** : of, relating to, or resembling a republic **2** : favoring or supporting a republic **3** *cap* : of, relating to, or constituting one of the two major political parties in the U.S. evolving in the mid-19th century — **re·pub·li·can·ism** *n*, *often cap*

re·pu·di·ate \ri-ˈpyü-dē-ˌāt\ *vb* **-at·ed**; **-at·ing** [L *repudiare* to cast off, divorce, fr. *repudium* rejection of a prospective spouse, divorce] **1** : to cast off : DISOWN **2** : to refuse to have anything to do with : refuse to acknowledge, accept, or pay ⟨∼ a charge⟩ ⟨∼ a debt⟩ ♦ *Synonyms* SPURN, REJECT, DECLINE — **re·pu·di·a·tion** \-ˌpyü-dē-ˈā-shən\ *n* — **re·pu·di·a·tor** \-ˈpyü-dē-ˌā-tər\ *n*

re·pug·nance \ri-ˈpəg-nəns\ *n* **1** : the quality or fact of being contradictory or inconsistent **2** : strong dislike, distaste, or antagonism

re·pug·nant \-nənt\ *adj* **1** : marked by

repugnance **2** : contrary to a person's tastes or principles : exciting distaste or aversion ♦ *Synonyms* REPELLENT, AB-HORRENT, DISTASTEFUL, OBNOXIOUS, REVOLTING, LOATHSOME — **re·pug·nant·ly** *adv*

¹**re·pulse** \ri-ˈpəls\ *vb* **re·pulsed; re·puls·ing 1** : to drive or beat back : REPEL **2** : to repel by discourtesy or denial : RE-BUFF **3** : to cause a feeling of repulsion in : DISGUST ⟨*repulsed* by the violence⟩

²**repulse** *n* **1** : REBUFF, REJECTION **2** : the action of repelling an attacker : the fact of being repelled

re·pul·sion \ri-ˈpəl-shən\ *n* **1** : the action of repulsing : the state of being repulsed **2** : the force with which bodies, particles, or like forces repel one another **3** : a feeling of aversion

re·pul·sive \-siv\ *adj* **1** : serving or tending to repel or reject **2** : arousing aversion or disgust ♦ *Synonyms* REPUG-NANT, REVOLTING, LOATHSOME, NOI-SOME — **re·pul·sive·ly** *adv* — **re·pul·sive·ness** *n*

re·pur·pose \(ˌ)rē-ˈpər-pəs\ *vb* : to give a new purpose or use to

rep·u·ta·ble \ˈre-pyə-tə-bəl\ *adj* : having a good reputation : ESTIMABLE ⟨a ~ law-yer⟩ — **rep·u·ta·bly** \-blē\ *adv*

rep·u·ta·tion \ˌre-pyù-ˈtā-shən\ *n* **1** : overall quality or character as seen or judged by people in general **2** : place in public esteem or regard

¹**re·pute** \ri-ˈpyüt\ *vb* **re·put·ed; re·put·ing** : BELIEVE, CONSIDER ⟨*reputed* to be a millionaire⟩

²**repute** *n* **1** : REPUTATION ⟨knew her by ~⟩ **2** : the state of being favorably known or spoken of

re·put·ed \ri-ˈpyü-təd\ *adj* **1** : REPUTA-BLE **2** : according to reputation : SUP-POSED — **re·put·ed·ly** *adv*

req *abbr* **1** request **2** require; required **3** requisition

¹**re·quest** \ri-ˈkwest\ *n* **1** : an act or instance of asking for something **2** : a thing asked for **3** : the condition of being asked for ⟨available on ~⟩

²**request** *vb* **1** : to make a request to or of **2** : to ask for — **re·quest·er** *or* **re·quest·or** *n*

re·qui·em \ˈre-kwē-əm, ˈrā-\ *n* [ME, fr. L (first word of the requiem mass), acc. of *requies* rest, fr. *quies* quiet, rest] **1** : a mass for a dead person; *also* : a musical setting for this **2** : a musical service or hymn in honor of the dead

re·quire \ri-ˈkwī(-ə)r\ *vb* **re·quired; re·quir·ing 1** : to demand as necessary or essential **2** : COMMAND, ORDER ⟨the law ~s that everyone pay the tax⟩

re·quire·ment \-mənt\ *n* **1** : something (as a condition or quality) required ⟨en-trance ~s⟩ **2** : NECESSITY ⟨production was sufficient to satisfy military ~s⟩

req·ui·site \ˈre-kwə-zət\ *adj* : REQUIRED, NECESSARY — **requisite** *n*

req·ui·si·tion \ˌre-kwə-ˈzi-shən\ *n* **1** : formal application or demand (as for supplies) **2** : the state of being in demand or use — **requisition** *vb*

re·quite \ri-ˈkwīt\ *vb* **re·quit·ed; re·quit·ing 1** : to make return for : REPAY **2** : to make retaliation for : AVENGE **3** : to make return to — **re·quit·al** \-ˈkwī-tᵊl\ *n*

rere·dos \ˈrer-ə-ˌdäs\ *n* : a usu. ornamental wood or stone screen or partition wall behind an altar

re·run \ˈrē-ˌrən, (ˌ)rē-ˈrən\ *n* : the act or an instance of running again or anew; *esp* : a showing of a motion picture or television program after its first run — **re·run** \(ˌ)rē-ˈrən\ *vb*

res *abbr* **1** research **2** reservation; reserve **3** reservoir **4** residence; resident **5** resolution

re·sale \ˈrē-ˌsāl, (ˌ)rē-ˈsāl\ *n* : the act of selling again usu. to a new party — **re·sal·able** \(ˌ)rē-ˈsā-lə-bəl\ *adj*

re·scind \ri-ˈsind\ *vb* : REPEAL, CANCEL, ANNUL — **re·scis·sion** \-ˈsi-zhən\ *n*

re·script \ˈrē-ˌskript\ *n* : an official or authoritative order or decree

res·cue \ˈres-kyü\ *vb* **res·cued; res·cu·ing** [ME *rescouen, rescuen,* fr. AF *rescure,* fr. *re-* back, again + *escure* to shake off, fr. L *excutere*] : to free from danger, harm, or confinement — **rescue** *n* — **res·cu·er** *n*

re·search \ri-ˈsərch, ˈrē-ˌsərch\ *n* **1** : careful or diligent search **2** : studious inquiry or examination aimed at the discovery and interpretation of new knowledge **3** : the collecting of information about a particular subject — **research** *vb* — **re·search·er** *n*

re·sec·tion \ri-ˈsek-shən\ *n* : the surgical removal of part of an organ or structure

re·sem·blance \ri-ˈzem-bləns\ *n* : the quality or state of resembling

re·sem·ble \ri-ˈzem-bəl\ *vb* **-bled; -bling** : to be like or similar to

re·sent \ri-ˈzent\ *vb* : to feel or exhibit annoyance or indignation at ⟨~ed his interference⟩ — **re·sent·ful** \-fəl\ *adj* — **re·sent·ful·ly** *adv* — **re·sent·ment** *n*

re·ser·pine \ri-ˈsər-ˌpēn, -pən\ *n* : a drug used in treating high blood pressure and nervous tension

res·er·va·tion \ˌre-zər-ˈvā-shən\ *n* **1** : act of reserving **2** : something (as a room in a hotel) arranged for in advance **3** : something reserved; *esp* : a tract of public land set aside for special use **4** : a limiting condition

¹**re·serve** \ri-ˈzərv\ *vb* **re·served; re·serv·ing 1** : to store for future or special use **2** : to hold back for oneself **3** : to set aside or arrange to have set aside or held for special use

²**reserve** *n* **1** : something reserved : STOCK, STORE **2** : a military force with-

repurchase	rerecord	rescore	reseed
reradiate	reroute	rescreen	resell
reread	reschedule	reseal	
rereading			

held from action for later use — usu. used in pl. **3** : the military forces of a country not part of the regular services; *also* : RESERVIST **4** : a tract set apart : RESERVATION **5** : an act of reserving **6** : restraint or caution in one's words or bearing **7** : money or its equivalent kept in hand or set apart to meet liabilities

re·served \ri-ˈzərvd\ *adj* **1** : restrained in words and actions **2** : set aside for future or special use — **re·serv·ed·ly** \-ˈzər-vəd-lē\ *adv* — **re·serv·ed·ness** \-vəd-nəs\ *n*

re·serv·ist \ri-ˈzər-vist\ *n* : a member of a military reserve

res·er·voir \ˈre-zə-ˌvwär, -zər-, -ˌvwȯr\ *n* [F] : a place where something is kept in store; *esp* : an artificial lake where water is collected and kept for use

re·shuf·fle \rē-ˈshə-fəl\ *vb* **1** : to shuffle again **2** : to reorganize usu. by redistribution of existing elements ⟨*reshuffled* our schedule⟩ — **reshuffle** *n*

re·side \ri-ˈzīd\ *vb* **re·sid·ed; re·sid·ing** **1** : to make one's home : DWELL **2** : to be present as a quality or vested as a right

res·i·dence \ˈre-zə-dəns\ *n* **1** : the act or fact of residing in a place as a dweller or in discharge of a duty or an obligation **2** : the place where one actually lives **3** : a building used as a home : DWELLING **4** : the period of living in a place

res·i·den·cy \ˈre-zə-dən-sē\ *n, pl* **-cies** **1** : the residence of or the territory under a diplomatic resident **2** : a period of advanced training in a medical specialty

¹res·i·dent \-dənt\ *adj* **1** : RESIDING **2** : being in residence **3** : not migratory

²resident *n* **1** : one who resides in a place **2** : a diplomatic representative with governing powers (as in a protectorate) **3** : a physician serving a residency

res·i·den·tial \ˌre-zə-ˈden-chəl\ *adj* **1** : used as a residence or by residents **2** : occupied by or restricted to residences — **res·i·den·tial·ly** *adv*

¹re·sid·u·al \ri-ˈzi-jə-wəl\ *n* **1** : a residual product or substance **2** : a payment (as to an actor or writer) for each rerun after an initial showing (as of a taped TV show)

²residual *adj* : being a residue or remainder

re·sid·u·ary \ri-ˈzi-jə-ˌwer-ē\ *adj* : of, relating to, or constituting a residue esp. of an estate

res·i·due \ˈre-zə-ˌdü, -ˌdyü\ *n* : a part remaining after another part has been taken away : REMAINDER

re·sid·u·um \ri-ˈzi-jə-wəm\ *n, pl* **re·sid·ua** \-jə-wə\ [L] **1** : something remaining or residual after certain deductions are made **2** : a residual product

re·sign \ri-ˈzīn\ *vb* [ME, fr. AF *resigner*, fr. L *resignare*, lit., to unseal, cancel, fr. *signare* to sign, seal] **1** : to give up deliberately (as one's position) esp. by a formal act **2** : to give (oneself) over (as to grief or despair) without resistance — **re·sign·ed·ly** \-ˈzī-nəd-lē\ *adv*

re–sign \(ˌ)rē-ˈsīn\ *vb* : to sign again

res·ig·na·tion \ˌre-zig-ˈnā-shən\ *n* **1** : an act or instance of resigning; *also* : a formal notification of such an act **2** : the quality or state of being resigned

re·sil·ience \ri-ˈzil-yəns\ *n* **1** : the ability of a body to regain its original size and shape after being compressed, bent, or stretched **2** : an ability to recover from or adjust easily to change or misfortune

re·sil·ien·cy \-yən-sē\ *n* : RESILIENCE

re·sil·ient \-yənt\ *adj* : marked by resilience ⟨~ players⟩

res·in \ˈre-zᵊn\ *n* : any of various substances obtained from the gum or sap of some trees and used esp. in varnishes, plastics, and medicine; *also* : a comparable synthetic product — **res·in·ous** *adj*

¹re·sist \ri-ˈzist\ *vb* **1** : to fight against : OPPOSE ⟨~ aggression⟩ **2** : to withstand the force or effect of ⟨~ed temptation⟩ ⟨~ disease⟩ ♦ *Synonyms* COMBAT, REPEL — **re·sist·ible** \-ˈzis-tə-bəl\ *adj* — **re·sist·less** *adj*

²resist *n* : something (as a coating) that resists or prevents a particular action

re·sis·tance \ri-ˈzis-təns\ *n* **1** : the act or an instance of resisting : OPPOSITION **2** : the power or capacity to resist; *esp* : the inherent ability of an organism to resist harmful influences (as disease or infection) **3** : the opposition offered by a body to the passage through it of a steady electric current

re·sis·tant \-tənt\ *adj* : giving, capable of, or exhibiting resistance

re·sis·tor \ri-ˈzis-tər\ *n* : a device used to provide resistance to the flow of an electric current in a circuit

res·o·lute \ˈre-zə-ˌlüt\ *adj* : firmly determined in purpose : RESOLVED ⟨a ~ leader⟩ ♦ *Synonyms* STEADFAST, STAUNCH, FAITHFUL, TRUE, LOYAL — **res·o·lute·ly** *adv* — **res·o·lute·ness** *n*

res·o·lu·tion \ˌre-zə-ˈlü-shən\ *n* **1** : the act or process of resolving **2** : the action of solving; *also* : SOLUTION **3** : the quality of being resolute : FIRMNESS, DETERMINATION **4** : a formal statement expressing the opinion, will, or intent of a body of persons **5** : a measure of the sharpness of an image or of the fineness with which a device can produce or record such an image

¹re·solve \ri-ˈzälv\ *vb* **re·solved; re·solv·ing** **1** : to break up into constituent parts : ANALYZE **2** : to distinguish between or make visible adjacent parts of **3** : to find an answer to : SOLVE ⟨~ a dispute⟩ **4** : DETERMINE, DECIDE **5** : to make or pass a formal resolution — **re·solv·able** *adj*

²resolve *n* **1** : fixity of purpose **2** : something resolved

res·o·nance \ˈre-zə-nəns\ *n* **1** : the quality or state of being resonant **2** : a reinforcement of sound in a vibrating body caused by waves from another body vibrating at nearly the same rate

reset
resettle
resettlement
resew
reshow
resocialization

res·o·nant \-nənt\ adj 1 : continuing to sound : RESOUNDING 2 : relating to or exhibiting resonance 3 : intensified and enriched by or as if by resonance — **res·o·nant·ly** adv

res·o·nate \-,nāt\ vb **-nat·ed; -nat·ing** 1 : to produce or exhibit resonance 2 : REVERBERATE, RESOUND 3 : to relate harmoniously ⟨~ with voters⟩

res·o·na·tor \-,nā-tər\ n : something that resounds or exhibits resonance

re·sorp·tion \rē-'sorp-shən, -'zorp-\ n : the action or process of breaking down and assimilating something (as a tooth or an embryo)

¹re·sort \ri-'zort\ n [ME, return, source of aid, fr. AF, fr. *resortir* to rebound, resort, fr. *sortir* to go out, leave] 1 : one looked to for help : REFUGE 2 : RECOURSE 3 : frequent or general visiting ⟨place of ~⟩ 4 : a frequently visited place : HAUNT 5 : a place providing recreation esp. to vacationers

²resort vb 1 : to go often or habitually 2 : to have recourse ⟨~ed to violence⟩

re·sound \ri-'zaund\ vb 1 : to become filled with sound : REVERBERATE, RING 2 : to sound loudly

re·sound·ing adj 1 : RESONATING, RESONANT 2 : impressively sonorous ⟨~ name⟩ 3 : EMPHATIC, UNEQUIVOCAL ⟨a ~ success⟩ — **re·sound·ing·ly** adv

re·source \'rē-,sors, ri-'sors\ n [F *ressource*, fr. OF *ressourdre* relief, resource, fr. *resourdre* to relieve, lit., to rise again, fr. L *resurgere*, fr. *re-* again + *surgere* to rise] 1 : a source of supply or support — usu. used in pl. 2 : a natural feature or phenomenon that enhances the quality of human life 3 pl : available funds 4 : a possibility of relief or recovery 5 : a means of spending leisure time 6 : ability to meet and handle situations — **re·source·ful** \ri-'sors-fəl\ adj — **re·source·ful·ness** n

¹re·spect \ri-'spekt\ n 1 : relation to something usu. specified : REGARD ⟨in ~ to⟩ 2 : high or special regard : ESTEEM 3 pl : an expression of respect or deference 4 : DETAIL, PARTICULAR — **re·spect·ful** \-fəl\ adj — **re·spect·ful·ly** adv — **re·spect·ful·ness** n

²respect vb 1 : to consider deserving of high regard : ESTEEM 2 : to refrain from interfering with ⟨~ another's privacy⟩ 3 : to have reference to : CONCERN — **re·spect·er** n

re·spect·able \ri-'spek-tə-bəl\ adj 1 : worthy of respect : ESTIMABLE 2 : decent or correct in conduct : PROPER 3 : fair in size, quantity, or quality ⟨a ~ score⟩ : MODERATE, TOLERABLE 4 : fit to be seen : PRESENTABLE — **re·spect·a·bil·i·ty** \-,spek-tə-'bi-lə-tē\ n — **re·spect·ably** \-'spek-tə-blē\ adv

re·spect·ing prep : with regard to

re·spec·tive \-tiv\ adj : PARTICULAR, SEPARATE ⟨returned to their ~ homes⟩

re·spec·tive·ly \-lē\ adv 1 : as relating to each 2 : each in the order given

res·pi·ra·tion \,res-pə-'rā-shən\ n 1 : an act or the process of breathing 2 : the physical and chemical processes (as breathing and oxidation) by which a living thing obtains oxygen and eliminates waste gases (as carbon dioxide) — **re·spi·ra·to·ry** \'res-pə-rə-,tor-ē, ri-'spī-rə-\ adj — **re·spire** \ri-'spī(-ə)r\ vb

res·pi·ra·tor \'res-pə-,rā-tər\ n 1 : a device covering the mouth and nose esp. to prevent inhaling harmful vapors 2 : a device for artificial respiration

re·spite \'res-pət\ n [ME *respit*, fr. AF, fr. ML *respectus*, fr. L, act of looking back] 1 : a temporary delay 2 : an interval of rest or relief

re·splen·dent \ri-'splen-dənt\ adj : shining brilliantly : gloriously bright : SPLENDID ⟨~ uniforms⟩ — **re·splen·dence** \-dəns\ n — **re·splen·dent·ly** adv

re·spond \ri-'spänd\ vb 1 : ANSWER, REPLY 2 : REACT ⟨~ed to a call for help⟩ 3 : to show favorable reaction ⟨~ to medication⟩ — **re·spond·er** n

re·spon·dent \ri-'spän-dənt\ n : one who responds; esp : one who answers in various legal proceedings — **respondent** adj

re·sponse \ri-'späns\ n 1 : an act of responding 2 : something constituting a reply or a reaction

re·spon·si·bil·i·ty \ri-,spän-sə-'bi-lə-tē\ n, pl **-ties** 1 : the quality or state of being responsible 2 : something for which one is responsible

re·spon·si·ble \ri-'spän-sə-bəl\ adj 1 : liable to be called upon to answer for one's acts or decisions : ANSWERABLE 2 : able to fulfill one's obligations : RELIABLE, TRUSTWORTHY 3 : able to choose for oneself between right and wrong 4 : involving accountability or important duties ⟨~ position⟩ — **re·spon·si·ble·ness** n — **re·spon·si·bly** \-blē\ adv

re·spon·sive \-siv\ adj 1 : RESPONDING 2 : quick to respond : SENSITIVE 3 : using responses ⟨~ readings⟩ — **re·spon·sive·ly** adv — **re·spon·sive·ness** n

¹rest \'rest\ n 1 : REPOSE, SLEEP 2 : freedom from work or activity 3 : a state of motionlessness or inactivity 4 : a place of shelter or lodging 5 : a silence in music equivalent in duration to a note of the same value; also : a character indicating this 6 : something used as a support — **rest·ful** \-fəl\ adj — **rest·ful·ly** adv

²rest vb 1 : to get rest by lying down; esp : SLEEP 2 : to cease from action or motion 3 : to give rest to : set at rest 4 : to sit or lie fixed or supported 5 : to place on or against a support 6 : to remain based or founded 7 : to cause to be firmly fixed : GROUND 8 : to remain for action : DEPEND

³rest n : something left over

res·tau·rant \'res-trənt, -tə-,ränt\ n [F, fr. prp. of *restaurer* to restore, fr. L *restaurare*] : a public eating place

res·tau·ra·teur \,res-tə-rə-'tər\ *also* **res·tau·ran·teur** \-,rän-\ n : the operator or proprietor of a restaurant

---

resow　　　respell　　　restaff　　　restart　　　restate　　　restatement

rest home n : an establishment that gives care for the aged or convalescent

res·ti·tu·tion \ˌres-tə-ˈtü-shən, -ˈtyü-\ n : the act of restoring : the state of being restored; *esp* : restoration of something to its rightful owner ♦ **Synonyms** AMENDS, REDRESS, REPARATION, INDEMNITY, COMPENSATION

res·tive \ˈres-tiv\ *adj* [ME *restyf*, fr. AF *restif*, fr. *rester* to stop, resist, remain, fr. L *restare*, fr. *re-* back + *stare* to stand] 1 : BALKY 2 : UNEASY, FIDGETY ♦ **Synonyms** RESTLESS, IMPATIENT, NERVOUS — **res·tive·ly** *adv* — **res·tive·ness** n

rest·less \ˈrest-ləs\ *adj* 1 : lacking or denying rest ⟨a ~ night⟩ 2 : never resting or settled : always moving ⟨the ~ sea⟩ 3 : marked by or showing unrest esp. of mind ⟨~ pacing back and forth⟩ ♦ **Synonyms** RESTIVE, IMPATIENT, NERVOUS, FIDGETY — **rest·less·ly** *adv* — **rest·less·ness** n

re·stor·able \ri-ˈstȯr-ə-bəl\ *adj* : fit for restoring or reclaiming

res·to·ra·tion \ˌres-tə-ˈrā-shən\ n 1 : an act of restoring : the state of being restored 2 : something (as a building) that has been restored

re·stor·ative \ri-ˈstȯr-ə-tiv\ n : something that restores esp. to consciousness or health — **restorative** *adj*

re·store \ri-ˈstȯr\ *vb* **re·stored; re·stor·ing** 1 : to give back : RETURN 2 : to put back into use or service 3 : to put or bring back into a former or original state 4 : to put again in possession of something — **re·stor·er** n

re·strain \ri-ˈstrān\ *vb* 1 : to prevent from doing something 2 : to limit, restrict, or keep under control : CURB 3 : to place under restraint or arrest — **re·strain·able** *adj* — **re·strain·er** n

re·strained \ri-ˈstrānd\ *adj* : marked by restraint : DISCIPLINED — **re·strain·ed·ly** \-ˈstrā-nəd-lē\ *adv*

restraining order n : a legal order directing one person to stay away from another

re·straint \ri-ˈstrānt\ n 1 : an act of restraining : the state of being restrained 2 : a restraining force, agency, or device 3 : deprivation or limitation of liberty : CONFINEMENT 4 : control over one's feelings : RESERVE

re·strict \ri-ˈstrikt\ *vb* 1 : to confine within bounds : LIMIT 2 : to place under restriction as to use — **re·stric·tive** *adj* — **re·stric·tive·ly** *adv*

re·stric·tion \ri-ˈstrik-shən\ n 1 : something (as a law or rule) that restricts 2 : an act of restricting : the state of being restricted

rest room n : a room or suite of rooms that includes sinks and toilets

¹**re·sult** \ri-ˈzəlt\ *vb* [ME, fr. ML *resultare*, fr. L, to rebound, fr. *re-* re- + *saltare* to leap] : to come about as an effect or consequence ⟨an injury ~*ing* from a fall⟩ — **re·sul·tant** \-ˈzəl-tᵊnt\ *adj or* n

²**result** n 1 : something that results : EFFECT, CONSEQUENCE 2 : beneficial or discernible effect 3 : something obtained by calculation or investigation

re·sume \ri-ˈzüm\ *vb* **re·sumed; re·sum·ing** 1 : to take or assume again 2 : to return to or begin again after interruption 3 : to take back to oneself — **re·sump·tion** \-ˈzəmp-shən\ n

ré·su·mé *or* **re·su·me** *or* **re·su·mé** \ˈre-zə-ˌmā, ˌre-zə-ˈmā\ n [F *résumé*] 1 : SUMMARY; *esp* : a short account of one's career and qualifications usu. prepared by a job applicant 2 : a set of accomplishments ⟨a musical ~⟩

re·sur·gence \ri-ˈsər-jəns\ n : a rising again into life, activity, or prominence — **re·sur·gent** \-jənt\ *adj*

res·ur·rect \ˌre-zə-ˈrekt\ *vb* 1 : to raise from the dead 2 : to bring to attention or use again

res·ur·rec·tion \ˌre-zə-ˈrek-shən\ n 1 *cap* : the rising of Christ from the dead 2 *often cap* : the rising to life of all human dead before the final judgment 3 : REVIVAL ⟨the ~ of her career⟩

re·sus·ci·tate \ri-ˈsə-sə-ˌtāt\ *vb* **-tat·ed; -tat·ing** : to revive from apparent death or unconsciousness; *also* : REVITALIZE — **re·sus·ci·ta·tion** \ri-ˌsə-sə-ˈtā-shən, ˌrē-\ n — **re·sus·ci·ta·tor** \ri-ˈsə-sə-ˌtā-tər\ n

ret *abbr* retired

¹**re·tail** \ˈrē-ˌtāl, *esp for 2 also* ri-ˈtāl\ *vb* 1 : to sell in small quantities directly to the ultimate consumer 2 : to tell in detail or to one person after another — **re·tail·er** n

²**re·tail** \ˈrē-ˌtāl\ n : the sale of goods in small amounts to ultimate consumers — **retail** *adj or adv*

re·tain \ri-ˈtān\ *vb* 1 : to hold in possession or use 2 : to engage (as a lawyer) by paying a fee in advance 3 : to keep in a fixed place or position ♦ **Synonyms** DETAIN, WITHHOLD, RESERVE

¹**re·tain·er** \ri-ˈtā-nər\ n 1 : one that retains 2 : a servant in a wealthy household; *also* : EMPLOYEE 3 : a device that holds something (as teeth) in place

²**retainer** n : a fee paid to secure services (as of a lawyer)

¹**re·take** \(ˌ)rē-ˈtāk\ *vb* **-took** \-ˈtůk\; **-tak·en** \-ˈtā-kən\; **-tak·ing** 1 : to take or seize again 2 : to photograph again

²**re·take** \ˈrē-ˌtāk\ n : a second photographing of a motion-picture scene

re·tal·i·ate \ri-ˈta-lē-ˌāt\ *vb* **-at·ed; -at·ing** : to return like for like; *esp* : to get revenge — **re·tal·i·a·tion** \-ˌta-lē-ˈā-shən\ n — **re·tal·ia·to·ry** \-ˈtal-yə-ˌtȯr-ē\ *adj*

re·tard \ri-ˈtärd\ *vb* : to hold back : delay the progress of ♦ **Synonyms** SLOW, SLACKEN, DETAIN — **re·tar·da·tion** \ˌrē-ˌtär-ˈdā-shən, ri-\ n — **re·tard·er** n

re·tar·dant \ri-'tär-dᵊnt\ *adj* : serving or tending to retard — **retardant** *n*

re·tard·ed *adj, sometimes offensive* : slow or limited in intellectual, emotional, or academic progress

retch \'rech\ *vb* : to try to vomit; *also* : VOMIT

re·ten·tion \ri-'ten-chən\ *n* **1** : the act of retaining : the state of being retained **2** : the power of retaining esp. in the mind : RETENTIVENESS

re·ten·tive \-'ten-tiv\ *adj* : having the power of retaining; *esp* : retaining knowledge easily — **re·ten·tive·ness** *n*

re·think \(ₒ)rē-'thiŋk\ *vb* **-thought** \-'thȯt\; **-think·ing** : to think about again : RECONSIDER

ret·i·cent \'re-tə-sənt\ *adj* **1** : tending not to talk or give out information **2** : RELUCTANT ♦ *Synonyms* RESERVED, TACITURN, CLOSEMOUTHED — **ret·i·cence** \-səns\ *n* — **ret·i·cent·ly** *adv*

ret·i·na \'re-tə-nə\ *n, pl* **retinas** *or* **ret·i·nae** \-,nē\ : the sensory membrane lining the eye that receives the image formed by the lens — **ret·i·nal** \'re-tə-nᵊl\ *adj*

ret·i·nue \'re-tə-,nü, -,nyü\ *n* : the body of attendants or followers of a distinguished person

re·tire \ri-'tī(-ə)r\ *vb* **re·tired; re·tir·ing 1** : RETREAT **2** : to withdraw esp. for privacy **3** : to withdraw from one's occupation or position : conclude one's career **4** : to withdraw from use or service **5** : to go to bed **6** : to cause to be out in baseball — **re·tire·ment** *n*

re·tired \ri-'tī(-ə)rd\ *adj* **1** : SECLUDED, QUIET **2** : withdrawn from active duty or from one's career

re·tir·ee \ri-,tī-'rē\ *n* : a person who has retired from a career

re·tir·ing *adj* : SHY, RESERVED

re·tool \(ₒ)rē-'tül\ *vb* **1** : to reequip with tools **2** : to modify with usu. minor improvements ⟨~ed the team for next year⟩

¹**re·tort** \ri-'tȯrt\ *vb* [L *retortus,* pp. of *re·torquēre,* lit., to twist back, hurl back, fr. *re-* back + *torquēre* to twist] **1** : to say in reply : answer back usu. sharply **2** : to answer (an argument) by a counter argument **3** : RETALIATE

²**retort** *n* : a quick, witty, or cutting reply

³**re·tort** \ri-'tȯrt, 'rē-,tȯrt\ *n* [MF *retorte,* fr. ML *retorta,* fr. L, fem. of *retortus,* pp. of *retorquēre* to twist back; fr. its shape] : a vessel in which substances are distilled or broken up by heat

re·touch \(ₒ)rē-'təch\ *vb* : TOUCH UP; *esp* : to change (as a photographic negative) in order to produce a more desirable appearance

re·trace \(ₒ)rē-'trās\ *vb* : to go over again or in a reverse direction ⟨*retraced* his steps⟩

re·tract \ri-'trakt\ *vb* **1** : to draw back or in **2** : to withdraw (as a charge or promise) : DISAVOW — **re·tract·able** *adj* — **re·trac·tion** \-'trak-shən\ *n*

re·trac·tile \ri-'trak-tᵊl, -'trak-,tī(-ə)l\ *adj* : capable of being drawn back or in ⟨~ claws⟩

¹**re·tread** \(ₒ)rē-'tred\ *vb* **re·tread·ed; re·tread·ing** : to put a new tread on (a worn tire)

²**re·tread** \'rē-,tred\ *n* **1** : a retreaded tire **2** : one pressed into service again; *also* : REMAKE

¹**re·treat** \ri-'trēt\ *n* **1** : an act of withdrawing esp. from something dangerous, difficult, or disagreeable **2** : a military signal for withdrawal; *also* : a military flag-lowering ceremony **3** : a place of privacy or safety : REFUGE **4** : a group withdrawal for prayer, meditation, or study

²**retreat** *vb* **1** : to make a retreat : WITHDRAW **2** : to slope backward

re·trench \ri-'trench\ *vb* [obs. F *retrencher* (now *retrancher*), fr. MF *retrenchier,* fr. *re-* + *trenchier* to cut] **1** : to cut down or pare away : REDUCE, CURTAIL **2** : to cut down expenses : ECONOMIZE ⟨the company had to ~⟩ — **re·trench·ment** *n*

ret·ri·bu·tion \,re-trə-'byü-shən\ *n* : something administered or exacted in recompense; *esp* : PUNISHMENT ♦ *Synonyms* REPRISAL, VENGEANCE, REVENGE, RETALIATION — **re·trib·u·tive** \ri-'tri-byə-tiv\ *adj* — **re·trib·u·to·ry** \-byə-,tȯr-ē\ *adj*

re·trieve \ri-'trēv\ *vb* **re·trieved; re·triev·ing 1** : to search about for and bring in (killed or wounded game) **2** : RECOVER, RESTORE — **re·triev·able** *adj* — **re·triev·al** \-'trē-vəl\ *n*

re·triev·er \ri-'trē-vər\ *n* : one that retrieves; *esp* : a dog of any of several breeds used esp. for retrieving game

ret·ro \'re-trō\ *adj* : relating to or being the styles and fashions of the past ⟨~ clothing⟩

ret·ro·ac·tive \,re-trō-'ak-tiv\ *adj* : made effective as of a date prior to enactment ⟨a ~ pay raise⟩ — **ret·ro·ac·tive·ly** *adv*

ret·ro·fit \'re-trō-,fit, ,re-trō-'fit\ *vb* **1** : to furnish (as an aircraft) with newly available equipment **2** : to adapt to a new purpose or need : MODIFY — **ret·ro·fit** \'re-trō-,fit\ *n*

¹**ret·ro·grade** \'re-trə-,grād\ *adj* **1** : moving or tending backward **2** : tending toward or resulting in a worse condition

²**retrograde** *vb* **1** : RETREAT **2** : DETERIORATE, DEGENERATE

ret·ro·gres·sion \,re-trə-'gre-shən\ *n* : return to a former and less complex level of development or organization — **ret·ro·gress** \,re-trə-'gres\ *vb* — **ret·ro·gres·sive** \,re-trə-'gre-siv\ *adj*

ret·ro·rock·et \'re-trō-,rä-kət\ *n* : an auxiliary rocket engine (as on a spacecraft) used to slow forward motion

¹**ret·ro·spect** \'re-trə-,spekt\ *n* : a review of past events — **ret·ro·spec·tion** \,re-trə-'spek-shən\ *n*

ret·ro·spec·tive \,re-trə-'spek-tiv\ *n* **1** : a comprehensive examination of an artist's work over many years **2** : REVIEW **4** ⟨a

retaste   retest   retransmission   retrial
retell   retrain   retransmit

war ~〉 — **retrospective** adj — **ret·ro·spec·tive·ly** adv

ret·ro·vi·rus \'re-trō-,vī-rəs\ n : any of a group of RNA-containing viruses (as HIV) that make DNA using RNA instead of the reverse — **re·tro·vi·ral** \-rəl\ adj

¹**re·turn** \ri-'tərn\ vb 1 : to go or come back 2 : to pass, give, or send back to an earlier possessor 3 : to put back to or in a former place or state 4 : REPLY, ANSWER 5 : to report esp. officially 6 : to elect to office 7 : to bring in (as profit) : YIELD 8 : to give or perform in return 〈~ a favor〉 — **re·turn·er** n

²**return** n 1 : an act of coming or going back to or from a former place or state 2 : RECURRENCE 3 : a report of the results of balloting 4 : a formal statement of taxable income 5 : the profit from labor, investment, or business : YIELD 6 : the act of returning something 7 : something that returns or is returned; also : a means for conveying something (as water) back to its starting point 8 : something given in repayment or reciprocation; also : ANSWER, RETORT 9 : an answering play — **return** adj

¹**re·turn·able** \ri-'tər-nə-bəl\ adj : capable of being returned (as for reuse); also : permitted to be returned

²**returnable** n : a returnable beverage container

re·turn·ee \ri-,tər-'nē\ n : one who returns

re·union \rē-'yün-yən\ n 1 : an act of reuniting : the state of being reunited 2 : a meeting of persons after separation

¹**rev** \'rev\ n : a revolution of a motor

²**rev** vb **revved**; **rev·ving** 1 : to increase the revolutions per minute of (a motor) 2 : STIMULATE, EXCITE

³**rev** abbr 1 revenue 2 reverse 3 review; reviewed 4 revised; revision 5 revolution

Rev abbr 1 Revelation 2 Reverend

re·vamp \(,)rē-'vamp\ vb : RECONSTRUCT, REVISE; also : RENOVATE

re·vanche \rə-'vänsh\ n [F] : REVENGE; esp : a usu. political policy designed to recover lost territory or status

re·veal \ri-'vēl\ vb 1 : to make known 2 : to show plainly : open up to view

re·veil·le \'re-və-lē\ n [modif. of F réveillez, imper. pl. of réveiller to awaken, fr. MF eveiller to awaken, fr. VL *exvigilare, fr. L vigilare to keep watch, stay awake] : a military signal sounded at about sunrise

¹**rev·el** \'re-vəl\ vb **-eled** or **-elled**; **-el·ing** or **-el·ling** 1 : to take part in a revel 2 : to take great pleasure or satisfaction 〈~ed in the quiet〉 — **rev·el·er** or **rev·el·ler** n — **rev·el·ry** \-vəl-rē\ n

²**revel** n : a usu. wild party or celebration

rev·e·la·tion \,re-və-'lā-shən\ n 1 : an act of revealing 2 : something revealed; esp : an enlightening or astonishing disclosure

Revelation n — see BIBLE table

¹**re·venge** \ri-'venj\ vb **re·venged**; **re·veng·ing** : to inflict harm or injury in return for (a wrong) : AVENGE — **re·veng·er** n

²**revenge** n 1 : a desire for revenge 2 : an act or instance of retaliation to get even 3 : an opportunity for getting satisfaction
♦ **Synonyms** VENGEANCE, RETRIBUTION, REPRISAL — **re·venge·ful** adj

rev·e·nue \'re-və-,nü, -,nyü\ n [ME, return, revenue, fr. AF, fr. revenir to return, fr. L revenire, fr. re- back + venire to come] 1 : investment income 2 : money collected by a government (as through taxes)

rev·e·nu·er \'re-və-,nü-ər, -,nyü-\ n : a revenue officer or boat

re·verb \ri-'vərb, 'rē-,vərb\ n : an electronically produced echo effect in recorded music; also : a device for producing reverb

re·ver·ber·ate \ri-'vər-bə-,rāt\ vb **-at·ed**; **-at·ing** 1 : REFLECT 〈~ light or heat〉 2 : to resound in or as if in a series of echoes — **re·ver·ber·a·tion** \-,vər-bə-'rā-shən\ n

re·vere \ri-'vir\ vb **re·vered**; **re·ver·ing** : to show honor and devotion to : VENERATE 〈a teacher revered by students〉
♦ **Synonyms** REVERENCE, WORSHIP, ADORE

¹**rev·er·ence** \'re-vrəns, -və-rəns\ n 1 : honor or respect felt or shown 2 : a gesture (as a bow or curtsy) of respect

²**reverence** vb **-enced**; **-enc·ing** : to regard or treat with reverence

¹**rev·er·end** \'re-vrənd, -və-rənd\ adj 1 : worthy of reverence : REVERED 2 : being a member of the clergy — used as a title

²**reverend** n : a member of the clergy

rev·er·ent \'re-vrənt, -və-rənt\ adj : expressing reverence — **rev·er·ent·ly** adv

rev·er·en·tial \,re-və-'ren-chəl\ adj : REVERENT

rev·er·ie also **rev·ery** \'re-və-rē\ n, pl **-er·ies** [F rêverie, fr. MF, delirium, fr. resver, rever to wander, be delirious] 1 : DAYDREAM 2 : the state of being lost in thought

re·ver·sal \ri-'vər-səl\ n : an act or process of reversing

¹**re·verse** \ri-'vərs\ adj 1 : opposite to a previous or normal condition 〈in ~ order〉 2 : acting or working in a manner opposite the usual 3 : bringing about reverse movement 〈~ gear〉 — **re·verse·ly** adv

²**reverse** vb **re·versed**; **re·vers·ing** 1 : to turn upside down or completely about in position or direction 2 : to set aside or change (as a legal decision) 3 : to change to the contrary 〈~ a policy〉 4 : to go or cause to go in the opposite direction 5 : to put (as a car) in reverse — **re·vers·ible** \-'vər-sə-bəl\ adj

³**reverse** n 1 : something contrary to

reunification	reusable	revaluation
reunify	reuse	revalue
reunite	revaluate	

something else : OPPOSITE **2** : an act or instance of reversing; *esp* : a change for the worse **3** : the back side of something (as a coin or card) **4** : a gear that reverses something

reverse engineer *vb* : to disassemble or analyze in detail in order to discover concepts involved in manufacture — **reverse engineering** *n*

re·ver·sion \ri-ˈvər-zhən\ *n* **1** : the right of succession or future possession (as to a title or property) **2** : return toward some former or ancestral condition; *also* : a product of this — **re·ver·sion·ary** \-zhə-ˌner-ē\ *adj*

re·vert \ri-ˈvərt\ *vb* **1** : to come or go back ⟨*~ed* to savagery⟩ **2** : to return to a proprietor or his or her heirs **3** : to return to an ancestral type

¹**re·view** \ri-ˈvyü\ *n* **1** : an act of revising **2** : a formal military inspection **3** : a general survey **4** : INSPECTION, EXAMINATION; *esp* : REEXAMINATION **5** : a critical evaluation (as of a book) **6** : a magazine devoted to reviews and essays **7** : a renewed study of previously studied material **8** : REVUE

²**re·view** \ri-ˈvyü, *1 also* ˈrē-\ *vb* **1** : to examine or study again; *esp* : to reexamine judicially **2** : to hold a review of ⟨*~* troops⟩ **3** : to write a critical examination of ⟨*~* a novel⟩ **4** : to look back over ⟨*~ed* her accomplishments⟩ **5** : to study material again

re·view·er \ri-ˈvyü-ər\ *n* : one that reviews; *esp* : a writer of critical reviews

re·vile \ri-ˈvī(-ə)l\ *vb* **re·viled; re·vil·ing** : to abuse verbally : rail at ♦ *Synonyms* VITUPERATE, BERATE, RATE, UPBRAID, SCOLD — **re·vile·ment** *n* — **re·vil·er** *n*

re·vise \ri-ˈvīz\ *vb* **re·vised; re·vis·ing** **1** : to look over something written in order to correct or improve ⟨*~* an essay⟩ **2** : to make a new version of ⟨*~* an almanac⟩ — **re·vis·able** *adj* — **re·vise** *n* — **re·vis·er** *or* **re·vi·sor** \-ˈvī-zər\ *n* — **re·vi·sion** \-ˈvi-zhən\ *n*

re·vi·tal·ise *Brit var of* REVITALIZE

re·vi·tal·ize \ˌrē-ˈvīt-tə-ˌlīz\ *vb* **-ized; -iz·ing** : to give new life or vigor to ⟨*~* the shopping district⟩ — **re·vi·tal·i·za·tion** \(ˌ)rē-ˌvīt-tə-lə-ˈzā-shən\ *n*

re·viv·al \ri-ˈvī-vəl\ *n* **1** : an act of reviving : the state of being revived **2** : a new publication or presentation (as of a book or play) **3** : an evangelistic meeting or series of meetings

re·vive \ri-ˈvīv\ *vb* **re·vived; re·viv·ing** **1** : to bring back to life, consciousness, or activity : make or become fresh or strong again **2** : to bring back into use ⟨*revived* its native language⟩ — **re·viv·er** *n*

re·viv·i·fy \rē-ˈvi-və-ˌfī\ *vb* : REVIVE — **re·viv·i·fi·ca·tion** \-ˌvi-və-fə-ˈkā-shən\ *n*

re·vo·ca·ble \ˈre-və-kə-bəl *also* ri-ˈvō-kə-bəl\ *adj* : capable of being revoked

re·vo·ca·tion \ˌre-və-ˈkā-shən\ *n* : an act or instance of revoking

re·voke \ri-ˈvōk\ *vb* **re·voked; re·vok-**

ing **1** : to annul by recalling or taking back : REPEAL, RESCIND ⟨*~* a license⟩ **2** : RENEGE **2** — **re·vok·er** *n*

¹**re·volt** \ri-ˈvōlt\ *vb* [MF *revolter*, fr. It *rivoltare* to overthrow, fr. VL **revolvitare*, fr. L *revolvere* to revolve, roll back] **1** : to throw off allegiance to a ruler or government : REBEL **2** : to experience disgust or shock **3** : to turn or cause to turn away with disgust or abhorrence ⟨violence *~ed* her⟩ — **re·volt·er** *n*

²**revolt** *n* : REBELLION, INSURRECTION

re·volt·ing *adj* : extremely offensive ⟨a *~* odor⟩ — **re·volt·ing·ly** *adv*

rev·o·lu·tion \ˌre-və-ˈlü-shən\ *n* **1** : the action by a heavenly body of going round in an orbit **2** : ROTATION **3** : a sudden, radical, or complete change; *esp* : the overthrow or renunciation of one ruler or government and substitution of another by the governed

¹**rev·o·lu·tion·ary** \-shə-ˌner-ē\ *adj* **1** : of or relating to revolution **2** : tending to or promoting revolution **3** : constituting or bringing about a major change

²**revolutionary** *n, pl* **-ar·ies** : one who takes part in a revolution or who advocates revolutionary doctrines

rev·o·lu·tion·ise *Brit var of* REVOLUTIONIZE

rev·o·lu·tion·ist \ˌre-və-ˈlü-shə-nist\ *n* : REVOLUTIONARY — **revolutionist** *adj*

rev·o·lu·tion·ize \-ˌnīz\ *vb* **-ized; -iz·ing** : to change fundamentally or completely ⟨*~* an industry⟩ — **rev·o·lu·tion·iz·er** *n*

re·volve \ri-ˈvälv\ *vb* **re·volved; re·volv·ing** **1** : to turn over in the mind : reflect upon : PONDER **2** : to move in an orbit; *also* : ROTATE **3** : to have a specified focus ⟨the debate *revolved* around taxes⟩ — **re·volv·able** *adj*

re·volv·er \ri-ˈväl-vər\ *n* : a pistol with a revolving cylinder of several chambers

re·vue \ri-ˈvyü\ *n* : a theatrical production consisting typically of brief often satirical sketches and songs

re·vul·sion \ri-ˈvəl-shən\ *n* **1** : a strong sudden reaction or change of feeling **2** : a feeling of complete distaste or repugnance

revved *past and past part of* REV

revving *pres part of* REV

¹**re·ward** \ri-ˈwórd\ *vb* **1** : to give a reward to or for **2** : RECOMPENSE

²**reward** *n* **1** : something given in return for good or evil done or received or for some service or attainment **2** : a stimulus that is administered to an organism after a response and that increases the probability of occurrence of the response ♦ *Synonyms* PREMIUM, PRIZE, AWARD

¹**re·wind** \(ˌ)rē-ˈwīnd\ *vb* **-wound; -wind·ing** **1** : to wind again **2** : to reverse the winding of (as film)

²**re·wind** \ˈrē-ˌwīnd\ *n* **1** : something that rewinds **2** : an act of rewinding **3** : a function of an electronic device that reverses a recording to a previous portion

---

revisit	rewash	rewed
rewarm	reweave	reweigh	rewire

re·work \(ˌ)rē-ˈwərk\ *vb* **1** : REVISE **2** : to reprocess for further use

¹**re·write** \(ˌ)rē-ˈrīt\ *vb* **-wrote; -writ·ten; -writ·ing** : to make a revision of : REVISE

²**re·write** \ˈrē-ˌrīt\ *n* : an instance or a piece of rewriting

RF *abbr* radio frequency

RFD *abbr* rural free delivery

Rg *abbr* roentgenium

Rh *symbol* rhodium

RH *abbr* right hand

rhap·so·dy \ˈrap-sə-dē\ *n, pl* **-dies** [L *rhapsodia* portion of an epic poem adapted for recitation, fr. Gk *rhapsōidia* recitation of selections from epic poetry, ultim. fr. *rhaptein* to sew, stitch together + *aidein* to sing] **1** : an expression of extravagant praise or ecstasy **2** : a musical composition of irregular form — **rhap·sod·ic** \rap-ˈsä-dik\ *adj* — **rhap·sod·i·cal·ly** \-di-k(ə-)lē\ *adv* — **rhap·so·dize** \ˈrap-sə-ˌdīz\ *vb*

rhea \ˈrē-ə\ *n* : either of two large flightless 3-toed So. American birds that resemble but are smaller than the African ostrich

rhe·ni·um \ˈrē-nē-əm\ *n* : a rare heavy metallic chemical element

rheo·stat \ˈrē-ə-ˌstat\ *n* : a resistor for regulating an electric current by means of variable resistances — **rheo·stat·ic** \ˌrē-ə-ˈsta-tik\ *adj*

rhe·sus monkey \ˈrē-səs-\ *n* : a pale brown Asian monkey often used in medical research

rhet·o·ric \ˈre-tə-rik\ *n* [ME *rethorik*, fr. AF *rethorique*, fr. L *rhetorica*, fr. Gk *rhētorikē*, lit., art of oratory, fr. *rhētōr* public speaker, fr. *eirein* to speak] : the art of speaking or writing effectively — **rhet·o·ri·cian** \ˌre-tə-ˈri-shən\ *n*

rhe·tor·i·cal \ri-ˈtȯr-i-kəl\ *adj* **1** : of or relating to rhetoric **2** : asked merely for effect with no answer expected ⟨a ∼ question⟩

rheum \ˈrüm\ *n* : a watery discharge from the mucous membranes esp. of the eyes or nose — **rheumy** *adj*

rheu·mat·ic fever \rü-ˈma-tik-\ *n* : an acute disease chiefly of children and young adults that is characterized by fever, by inflammation and pain in and around the joints, and by inflammation of the membranes surrounding the heart and the heart valves

rheu·ma·tism \ˈrü-mə-ˌti-zəm, ˈrü-\ *n* **1** : any of various conditions marked by stiffness, pain, or swelling in muscles or joints **2** : RHEUMATOID ARTHRITIS — **rheu·mat·ic** \rü-ˈma-tik\ *adj*

rheu·ma·toid arthritis \-ˌtȯid-\ *n* : a usu. chronic progressive autoimmune disease characterized by inflammation and swelling of joint structures

rheu·ma·tol·o·gy \ˌrü-mə-ˈtä-lə-jē, ˌrü-\ *n* : a medical science dealing with rheumatic diseases — **rheu·ma·tol·o·gist** \-jist\ *n*

Rh factor \ˌär-ˈāch-\ *n* [*rhesus* monkey (in which it was first detected)] : any of one or more inherited substances in red blood cells that may cause dangerous reactions in some infants or in transfusions

rhine·stone \ˈrīn-ˌstōn\ *n* : a colorless imitation stone of high luster made of glass, paste, or gem quartz

rhi·no \ˈrī-no\ *n, pl* **rhinos** *also* **rhino** : RHINOCEROS

rhi·noc·er·os \rī-ˈnä-sə-rəs\ *n, pl* **-noc·er·os·es** *also* **-noc·er·os** *or* **-noc·eri** \-ˈnä-sə-ˌrī\ [ME *rinoceros*, fr. AF, fr. L *rhinoceros*, fr. Gk *rhinokerōs*, fr. *rhin-, rhis* nose + *keras* horn] : any of a family of large thick-skinned mammals of Africa and Asia with one or two upright horns of keratin on the snout and three toes on each foot

rhi·zome \ˈrī-ˌzōm\ *n* : a fleshy, rootlike, and usu. horizontal underground plant stem that forms shoots above and roots below — **rhi·zom·a·tous** \rī-ˈzä-mə-təs\ *adj*

Rh–neg·a·tive \ˌär-ˌāch-ˈne-gə-tiv\ *adj* : lacking Rh factors in the red blood cells

rho \ˈrō\ *n* : the 17th letter of the Greek alphabet — P or ρ

rho·di·um \ˈrō-dē-əm\ *n* : a rare hard ductile metallic chemical element

rho·do·den·dron \ˌrō-də-ˈden-drən\ *n* : any of a genus of shrubs or trees of the heath family with clusters of large bright flowers

rhom·boid \ˈräm-ˌbȯid\ *n* : a parallelogram with unequal adjacent sides and angles that are not right angles — **rhomboid** *or* **rhom·boi·dal** \räm-ˈbȯi-dᵊl\ *adj*

rhom·bus \ˈräm-bəs\ *n, pl* **rhom·bus·es** *or* **rhom·bi** \-ˌbī\ : a parallelogram having all four sides equal

Rh–pos·i·tive \ˌär-ˌāch-ˈpä-zə-tiv\ *adj* : containing one or more Rh factors in the red blood cells

rhu·barb \ˈrü-ˌbärb\ *n* [ME *rubarbe*, fr. AF *reubarbe*, fr. ML *reubarbarum*, alter. of *rha barbarum*, lit., barbarian rhubarb] : a garden plant related to the buckwheat having leaves with thick juicy edible pink and red stems

¹**rhyme** *also* **rime** \ˈrīm\ *n* **1** : a composition in verse that rhymes; *also* : POETRY **2** : correspondence in terminal sounds (as of two lines of verse)

²**rhyme** *also* **rime** *vb* **rhymed** *also* **rimed; rhym·ing** *also* **rim·ing 1** : to make rhymes; *also* : to write poetry **2** : to have rhymes : be in rhyme

rhythm \ˈri-thəm\ *n* **1** : regular rise and fall in the flow of sound in speech **2** : a movement or activity in which some action or element recurs regularly — **rhyth·mic** \ˈrith-mik\ *or* **rhyth·mi·cal** \-mi-kəl\ *adj* — **rhyth·mi·cal·ly** \-k(ə-)lē\ *adv*

rhythm and blues *n* : popular music based on blues and black folk music

rhythm method *n* : birth control by refraining from sexual intercourse during the time when ovulation is most likely to occur

RI *abbr* Rhode Island

ri·al \rē-ˈȯl, -ˈäl\ *n* — see MONEY table

¹**rib** \ˈrib\ *n* **1** : any of the series of curved bones of the chest of most vertebrates

that are joined to the backbone in pairs and help to support the body wall and protect the organs inside **2** : something resembling a rib in shape or function **3** : an elongated ridge (as in fabric)

²**rib** vb **ribbed; rib·bing** **1** : to furnish or strengthen with ribs **2** : to knit so as to form ridges

³**rib** vb **ribbed; rib·bing** : to poke fun at : TEASE — **rib·ber** n

rib·ald \'ri-bəld\ adj : coarse or indecent esp. in language ⟨~ jokes⟩ — **rib·ald·ry** \-bəl-drē\ n

rib·and \'ri-bənd\ n : RIBBON

rib·bon \'ri-bən\ n **1** : a narrow fabric typically of silk or velvet used for trimming and for badges **2** : a strip of inked cloth (as in a typewriter) **3** : TATTER, SHRED ⟨torn to ~s⟩

ri·bo·fla·vin \ˌrī-bə-'flā-vən, 'rī-bə-ˌflā-vən\ n : a growth-promoting vitamin of the vitamin B complex occurring esp. in milk and liver

ri·bo·nu·cle·ic acid \ˌrī-bō-nü-ˌklē-ik-, -nyü-, -ˌklā-\ n : RNA

ri·bose \'rī-ˌbōs\ n : a sugar with five carbon atoms and five oxygen atoms in each molecule that is part of RNA

ri·bo·some \'rī-bə-ˌsōm\ n : any of the RNA-rich cytoplasmic granules in a cell that are sites of protein synthesis — **ri·bo·som·al** \ˌrī-bə-'sō-məl\ adj

rice \'rīs\ n : the starchy seeds of an annual grass that are cooked and used for food; also : this widely cultivated grass of warm wet areas

rich \'rich\ adj **1** : possessing or controlling great wealth : WEALTHY **2** : COSTLY, VALUABLE **3** : deep and pleasing in color or tone **4** : ABUNDANT **5** : containing much sugar, fat, or seasoning; also : high in combustible content **6** : FRUITFUL, FERTILE — **rich·ly** adv — **rich·ness** n

rich·es \'ri-chəz\ n pl [ME, sing. or pl., fr. richesse wealth, fr. AF richesce, fr. riche rich] : things that make one rich : WEALTH

Rich·ter scale \'rik-tər-\ n : a scale for expressing the magnitude of a seismic disturbance (as an earthquake) in terms of the energy dissipated in it

rick \'rik\ n : a large stack (as of hay) in the open air

rick·ets \'ri-kəts\ n : a childhood deficiency disease marked esp. by soft deformed bones and caused by lack of vitamin D

rick·ett·sia \ri-'ket-sē-ə\ n, pl **-si·as** or **-si·ae** \-sē-ˌē\ : any of a group of usu. rod-shaped bacteria that cause various diseases (as typhus)

rick·ety \'ri-kə-tē\ adj **1** : affected with rickets **2** : SHAKY; also : in unsound physical condition ⟨~ stairs⟩

rick·shaw also **rick·sha** \'rik-ˌshò\ n : a small covered 2-wheeled carriage pulled by one person and used orig. in Japan

¹**ric·o·chet** \'ri-kə-ˌshā, Brit also -ˌshet\ n [F] : a bouncing off at an angle (as of a bullet off a wall); also : an object that ricochets

²**ricochet** vb **-cheted** \-ˌshād\ also **-chet-**

ted \-ˌshe-təd\; **-chet·ing** \-ˌshā-iŋ\ or **-chet·ting** \-ˌshe-tiŋ\ : to bounce or skip with or as if with a glancing rebound

ri·cot·ta \ri-'kä-tə, -'kò-\ n : a white unripened whey cheese of Italy that resembles cottage cheese

rid \'rid\ vb **rid** also **rid·ded; rid·ding** : to make free : CLEAR, RELIEVE ⟨~ the house of mice⟩ — **rid·dance** \'ri-dᵊns\ n

rid·den \'ri-dᵊn\ adj : harassed, oppressed, or obsessed by ⟨debt-ridden⟩ **2** : excessively full of or supplied with ⟨slum-ridden⟩

¹**rid·dle** \'ri-dᵊl\ n : a puzzling question to be solved or answered by guessing

²**riddle** vb **rid·dled; rid·dling** **1** : EXPLAIN, SOLVE **2** : to speak in riddles

³**riddle** n : a coarse sieve

⁴**riddle** vb **rid·dled; rid·dling** **1** : to sift with a riddle **2** : to pierce with many holes **3** : PERMEATE

¹**ride** \'rīd\ vb **rode** \'rōd\; **rid·den** \'ri-dᵊn\; **rid·ing** **1** : to go on an animal's back or in a conveyance (as a boat, car, or airplane); also : to sit on and control so as to be carried along ⟨~ a bicycle⟩ **2** : to float or move on water ⟨~ at anchor⟩; also : to move like a floating object **3** : to bear along : CARRY ⟨rode her on their shoulders⟩ **4** : to travel over a surface ⟨the car ~s well⟩ **5** : to proceed over on horseback **6** : to torment by nagging or teasing

²**ride** n **1** : an act of riding; esp : a trip on horseback or by vehicle **2** : a way (as a road or path) suitable for riding **3** : a mechanical device (as a merry-go-round) for riding on **4** : a means of transportation

rid·er \'rī-dər\ n **1** : one that rides **2** : an addition to a document often attached on a separate piece of paper **3** : a clause dealing with an unrelated matter attached to a legislative bill during passage — **rid·er·less** adj

¹**ridge** \'rij\ n [ME rigge, fr. OE hrycg] **1** : an elevated body part or structure **2** : a range of hills **3** : a raised line or strip **4** : the line made where two sloping surfaces (as of a roof) meet — **ridgy** adj

²**ridge** vb **ridged; ridg·ing** **1** : to form into a ridge **2** : to extend in ridges

¹**rid·i·cule** \'ri-də-ˌkyül\ n : the act of ridiculing : DERISION, MOCKERY

²**ridicule** vb **-culed; -cul·ing** : to laugh at or make fun of mockingly or contemptuously ⟨was ridiculed by his peers⟩

♦ **Synonyms** DERIDE, TAUNT, TWIT, MOCK

ri·dic·u·lous \rə-'di-kyə-ləs\ adj : arousing or deserving ridicule : ABSURD, PREPOSTEROUS ♦ **Synonyms** LAUGHABLE, LUDICROUS, FARCICAL, RISIBLE — **ri·dic·u·lous·ly** adv — **ri·dic·u·lous·ness** n

rid·ley \'rid-lē\ n : either of two relatively small sea turtles

ri·el \rē-'el\ n — see MONEY table

Ries·ling \'rēz-liŋ, 'rēs-\ n : a sweet to very dry white wine made from a single variety of grape orig. grown in Germany

RIF abbr reduction in force

rife \'rīf\ *adj* : WIDESPREAD, PREVALENT, ABOUNDING — **rife** *adv* — **rife·ly** *adv*

¹riff \'rif\ *n* **1** : a repeated phrase in jazz typically supporting a solo improvisation; *also* : a piece based on such a phrase **2** : a usu. witty or improvised remark or outpouring **3** : a distinct variation : TAKE — **riff** *vb*

riff·raff \'rif-ˌraf\ *n* [ME *riffe raffe*, fr. *rif and raf* every single one, fr. AF *rif et raf* altogether] **1** : RABBLE ⟨did not associate with the ∼⟩ **2** : REFUSE, RUBBISH

¹ri·fle \'rī-fəl\ *vb* **ri·fled**; **ri·fling** : to ransack esp. with the intent to steal — **ri·fler** *n*

²rifle *vb* **ri·fled**; **ri·fling** : to cut spiral grooves into the bore of ⟨*rifled* pipe⟩ — **rifling** *n*

³rifle *n* **1** : a shoulder weapon with a rifled bore **2** *pl* : soldiers armed with rifles — **ri·fle·man** \-fəl-mən\ *n*

rift \'rift\ *n* **1** : CLEFT, FISSURE **2** : FAULT 6 **3** : ESTRANGEMENT, SEPARATION ⟨a ∼ between spouses⟩ — **rift** *vb*

¹rig \'rig\ *vb* **rigged**; **rig·ging 1** : to fit out (as a ship) with rigging **2** : CLOTHE, DRESS **3** : EQUIP **4** : to set up esp. as a makeshift ⟨∼ up a shelter⟩

²rig *n* **1** : the distinctive shape, number, and arrangement of sails and masts of a ship **2** : a carriage with its horse **3** : CLOTHING, DRESS **4** : EQUIPMENT

³rig *vb* **rigged**; **rig·ging 1** : to manipulate or control esp. by deceptive or dishonest means **2** : to fix in advance for a desired result — **rig·ger** *n*

rig·ging \'ri-gin, -gən\ *n* **1** : the ropes and chains that hold and move masts, sails, and spars of a ship **2** : a network (as in theater scenery) used for support and manipulation

¹right \'rīt\ *adj* **1** : RIGHTEOUS, UPRIGHT **2** : JUST, PROPER **3** : conforming to truth or fact : CORRECT **4** : APPROPRIATE, SUITABLE **5** : STRAIGHT ⟨a ∼ line⟩ **6** : GENUINE, REAL **7** : of, relating to, or being the side of the body which is away from the side on which the heart is mostly located **8** : located nearer to the right hand; *esp* : being on the right when facing in the same direction as the observer **9** : made to be placed or worn outward ⟨∼ side of a rug⟩ **10** : NORMAL, SOUND ⟨not in her ∼ mind⟩ ♦ *Synonyms* CORRECT, ACCURATE, EXACT, PRECISE, NICE — **right·ness** *n*

²right *n* **1** : qualities that constitute what is correct, just, proper, or honorable **2** : something (as a power or privilege) to which one has a just or lawful claim **3** : just action or decision : the cause of justice **4** : the side or part that is on or toward the right side **5** *cap* : political conservatives **6** *often cap* : a conservative position — **right·ward** \-wərd\ *adj or adv*

³right *adv* **1** : according to what is right ⟨live ∼⟩ **2** : EXACTLY, PRECISELY ⟨∼ here and now⟩ **3** : DIRECTLY ⟨went ∼ home⟩ **4** : according to fact or truth ⟨guess ∼⟩ **5** : all the way : COMPLETELY ⟨∼ to the end⟩ **6** : IMMEDIATELY ⟨∼ after lunch⟩ **7** : QUITE, VERY ⟨∼ nice

weather⟩ **8** : on or to the right ⟨looked ∼ and left⟩

⁴right *vb* **1** : to relieve from wrong **2** : to adjust or restore to a proper state or position **3** : to bring or restore to an upright position **4** : to become upright — **right·er** *n*

right angle *n* : an angle whose measure is 90° : an angle whose sides are perpendicular to each other — **right–an·gled** \'rīt-'aŋ-gəld\ *or* **right–an·gle** \-gəl\ *adj*

right circular cone *n* : CONE 2

righ·teous \'rī-chəs\ *adj* : acting or being in accordance with what is just, honorable, and free from guilt or wrong : UPRIGHT ♦ *Synonyms* VIRTUOUS, NOBLE, MORAL, ETHICAL — **righ·teous·ly** *adv* — **righ·teous·ness** *n*

right·ful \'rīt-fəl\ *adj* **1** : JUST; *also* : FITTING **2** : having or held by a legally just claim — **right·ful·ly** *adv* — **right·ful·ness** *n*

right–hand \'rīt-ˌhand\ *adj* **1** : situated on the right **2** : RIGHT-HANDED **3** : chiefly relied on ⟨his ∼ man⟩

right–hand·ed \-'han-dəd\ *adj* **1** : using the right hand habitually or better than the left **2** : designed for or done with the right hand **3** : CLOCKWISE ⟨a ∼ twist⟩ — **right–handed** *adv* — **right–hand·ed·ly** *adv* — **right–hand·ed·ness** *n*

right·ly \'rīt-lē\ *adv* **1** : FAIRLY, JUSTLY **2** : PROPERLY **3** : CORRECTLY, EXACTLY

right–of–way *n*, *pl* **rights–of–way 1** : a legal right of passage over another person's ground **2** : the area over which a right-of-way exists **3** : the land on which a public road is built **4** : the land occupied by a railroad **5** : the land used by a public utility **6** : the right of traffic to take precedence over other traffic

right on *interj* — used to express agreement or give encouragement

right–to–life *adj* : ANTIABORTION — **right–to–lifer** *n*

right triangle *n* : a triangle having one right angle

right whale *n* : any of a family of large baleen whales having a very large head on a stocky body

rig·id \'ri-jəd\ *adj* **1** : lacking flexibility **2** : strictly observed ♦ *Synonyms* SEVERE, STERN, RIGOROUS, STRINGENT — **ri·gid·i·ty** \rə-'ji-də-tē\ *n* — **rig·id·ly** *adv*

rig·ma·role \'ri-gə-mə-ˌrōl\ *n* [alter. of obs. *ragman roll* long list, catalog] **1** : confused or senseless talk **2** : a complex and ritualistic procedure

rig·or \'ri-gər\ *n* **1** : the quality of being inflexible or unyielding : STRICTNESS **2** : HARSHNESS, SEVERITY **3** : a tremor caused by a chill **4** : strict precision : EXACTNESS ⟨scientific ∼⟩ — **rig·or·ous** *adj* — **rig·or·ous·ly** *adv*

rig·or mor·tis \ˌri-gər-'mȯr-təs\ *n* [NL, stiffness of death] : temporary rigidity of muscles occurring after death

rig·our *chiefly Brit var of* RIGOR

rile \'rī(-ə)l\ *vb* **riled**; **ril·ing 1** : to make angry **2** : ROIL 1

rill \'ril\ *n* : a very small brook

¹rim \'rim\ *n* **1** : the outer part of a wheel

2 : an outer edge esp. of something curved : BORDER, MARGIN

²**rim** vb **rimmed; rim·ming 1** : to serve as a rim for : BORDER **2** : to run around the rim of

¹**rime** \'rīm\ n : FROST 2 — **rimy** \'rī-mē\ adj

²**rime** var of RHYME

rind \'rīnd\ n : a usu. hard or tough outer layer ⟨lemon ∼⟩

¹**ring** \'riŋ\ n **1** : a circular band worn as an ornament or token or used for holding or fastening ⟨wedding ∼⟩ ⟨key ∼⟩ **2** : something circular in shape ⟨smoke ∼⟩ **3** : a place for contest or display ⟨boxing ∼⟩; also : PRIZEFIGHTING **4** : ANNUAL RING **5** : a group of people who work together for selfish or dishonest purposes ⟨a ∼ of smugglers⟩ — **ringed** adj — **ring·like** \'riŋ-ˌlīk\ adj

²**ring** vb **ringed; ring·ing** \'riŋ-iŋ\ **1** : EN-CIRCLE **2** : to throw a ring over (a mark) in a game (as quoits) **3** : to move in a ring or spirally

³**ring** vb **rang** \'raŋ\; **rung** \'rəŋ\; **ring·ing** \'riŋ-iŋ\ **1** : to sound resonantly when struck; also : to feel as if filled with such sound **2** : to cause to make a clear metallic sound by striking **3** : to announce or call by or as if by striking a bell ⟨∼ an alarm⟩ **4** : to repeat loudly and persistently **5** : to summon esp. by a bell ⟨∼ for the butler⟩ — **ring a bell** : to arouse a response ⟨that name rings a bell⟩

⁴**ring** n **1** : a set of bells **2** : the clear resonant sound of vibrating metal **3** : resonant tone : SONORITY **4** : a sound or character expressive of a particular quality **5** : an act or instance of ringing; esp : a telephone call

¹**ring·er** \'riŋ-ər\ n **1** : one that sounds by ringing **2** : one that enters a competition under false representations **3** : one that closely resembles another

²**ringer** n : one that encircles or puts a ring around

ring finger n : the third finger of the left hand counting the index finger as the first

ring·git \'riŋ-git\ n — see MONEY table

ring·lead·er \'riŋ-ˌlē-dər\ n : a leader esp. of a group of troublemakers

ring·let \-lət\ n : a long curl

ring·mas·ter \-ˌmas-tər\ n : one in charge of performances in a circus ring

ring up vb **1** : to total and record esp. by means of a cash register **2** : ACHIEVE ⟨rang up many triumphs⟩

ring·worm \'riŋ-ˌwərm\ n : any of several contagious skin diseases caused by fungi and marked by ring-shaped discolored patches

rink \'riŋk\ n : a level extent of ice marked off for skating or various games; also : a similar surface (as of wood) marked off or enclosed for a sport or game ⟨roller-skating ∼⟩

¹**rinse** \'rins\ vb **rinsed; rins·ing** [ME rincen, AF rincer, alter. of OF recincier, fr. VL *recentiare, fr. L recent-, recens fresh, recent] **1** : to wash lightly or in water only **2** : to cleanse (as of soap) with

clear water **3** : to treat (hair) with a rinse — **rins·er** n

²**rinse** n **1** : an act of rinsing **2** : a liquid used for rinsing **3** : a solution that temporarily tints hair

ri·ot \'rī-ət\ n **1** archaic : disorderly behavior **2** : disturbance of the public peace; esp : a violent public disorder **3** : random or disorderly profusion ⟨a ∼ of color⟩ **4** : one that is wildly amusing ⟨the comedy is a ∼⟩ — **riot** vb — **ri·ot·er** n — **ri·ot·ous** adj

¹**rip** \'rip\ vb **ripped; rip·ping 1** : to cut or tear open **2** : to saw or split (wood) with the grain **3** : CRITICIZE, DISPARAGE ⟨ripped into the team⟩ — **rip·per** n

²**rip** n : a rent made by ripping

RIP abbr [L requiescat in pace] may he rest in peace, may she rest in peace; [L requiescant in pace] may they rest in peace

ri·par·i·an \rə-'per-ē-ən\ adj : of or relating to the bank of a stream, river, or lake ⟨∼ trees⟩

rip cord n : a cord that is pulled to release a parachute out of its container

ripe \'rīp\ adj **rip·er; rip·est 1** : fully grown and developed : MATURE ⟨∼ fruit⟩ **2** : fully prepared : READY ⟨slaves ∼ for a revolt⟩ — **ripe·ly** adv — **ripe·ness** n

rip·en \'rī-pən\ vb **rip·ened; rip·en·ing 1** : to grow or make ripe **2** : to bring to completeness or perfection; also : to age or cure (cheese) to develop characteristic flavor, odor, body, texture, and color

rip–off \'rip-ˌof\ n **1** : an act of stealing : THEFT **2** : a cheap imitation — **rip off** vb

ri·poste \ri-'pōst\ n [F, modif. of It risposta, lit., answer] **1** : a fencer's return thrust after a parry **2** : a retaliatory maneuver or response; esp : a quick retort — **riposte** vb

ripped \'ript\ adj : having high muscle definition ⟨a ∼ body⟩

rip·ple \'ri-pəl\ vb **rip·pled; rip·pling 1** : to become lightly ruffled on the surface **2** : to make a sound like that of rippling water — **ripple** n

rip·saw \'rip-ˌsó\ n : a coarse-toothed saw used to cut wood in the direction of the grain

rip·stop \-ˌstäp\ adj : being a fabric woven in such a way that small tears do not spread ⟨∼ nylon⟩ — **ripstop** n

¹**rise** \'rīz\ vb **rose** \'rōz\; **ris·en** \'riz-ᵊn\; **ris·ing 1** : to get up from sitting, kneeling, or lying **2** : to get up from sleep or from one's bed **3** : to return from death **4** : to take up arms **5** : to end a session : ADJOURN **6** : to appear above the horizon **7** : to move upward : ASCEND **8** : to extend above other objects **9** : to attain a higher level or rank **10** : to increase in quantity, intensity, or pitch **11** : to come into being : HAPPEN, BEGIN, ORIGINATE

²**rise** n **1** : a spot higher than surrounding ground **2** : an upward slope **3** : an act of rising : a state of being risen **4** : BEGINNING, ORIGIN **5** : the elevation of one point above another **6** : an increase in

amount, number, or volume **7** : an angry reaction ⟨tried to get a ∼ out of me⟩

ris·er \'rī-zər\ *n* **1** : one that rises **2** : the upright part between stair treads

ris·i·bil·i·ty \₁ri-zə-'bi-lə-tē\ *n, pl* **-ties** : the ability or inclination to laugh — often used in pl.

ris·i·ble \'ri-zə-bəl\ *adj* **1** : able or inclined to laugh **2** : arousing laughter; *esp* : amusingly ridiculous

¹**risk** \'risk\ *n* **1** : exposure to possible loss or injury : DANGER, PERIL ⟨health ∼*s*⟩ **2** : the chance that an investment will lose value — **risk·i·ness** \'ris-kē-nəs\ *n* — **risky** *adj*

²**risk** *vb* **1** : to expose to danger ⟨∼*ed* his life⟩ **2** : to incur the danger of

ri·sot·to \ri-'sȯ-tō, -'zȯ-\ *n, pl* **-tos** : rice cooked usu. in meat or seafood stock and seasoned

ris·qué \ris-'kā\ *adj* [F] : verging on impropriety or indecency ⟨∼ jokes⟩

ri·tard \ri-'tärd\ *adv or adj* : with a gradual slackening in tempo — used as a direction in music

rite \'rīt\ *n* **1** : a set form for conducting a ceremony **2** : the liturgy of a church **3** : a ceremonial act or action

rit·u·al \'ri-chə-wəl\ *n* **1** : the established form esp. for a religious ceremony **2** : a system of rites **3** : a ceremonial act or action **4** : an act or series of acts regularly repeated in a precise manner — **ritual** *adj* — **rit·u·al·ism** \-wə-₁li-zəm\ *n* — **rit·u·al·is·tic** \₁ri-chə-wə-'lis-tik\ *adj* — **rit·u·al·is·ti·cal·ly** \-ti-k(ə-)lē\ *adv* — **rit·u·al·ly** *adv*

ritzy \'rit-sē\ *adj* **ritz·i·er; -est** : showily elegant : POSH

riv *abbr* river

¹**ri·val** \'rī-vəl\ *n* [MF or L; MF, fr. L *rivalis* one using the same stream as another, rival in love, fr. *rivalis* of a stream, fr. *rivus* stream] **1** : one of two or more trying to get what only one can have **2** : one striving for competitive advantage **3** : one that equals another esp. in desired qualities : MATCH, PEER

²**rival** *adj* : COMPETING

³**rival** *vb* **-valed** *or* **-valled; -val·ing** *or* **-val·ling** **1** : to be in competition with **2** : to try to equal or excel **3** : to have qualities that approach or equal another's

ri·val·ry \'rī-vəl-rē\ *n, pl* **-ries** : COMPETITION

rive \'rīv\ *vb* **rived** \'rīvd\; **riv·en** \'ri-vən\ *also* **rived; riv·ing 1** : SPLIT, REND **2** : SHATTER ⟨nations *riven* by war⟩

riv·er \'ri-vər\ *n* **1** : a natural stream larger than a brook **2** : a large stream or flow

riv·er·bank \-₁baŋk\ *n* : the bank of a river

riv·er·bed \-₁bed\ *n* : the channel occupied by a river

riv·er·boat \-₁bōt\ *n* : a boat for use on a river

riv·er·front \-₁frənt\ *n* : the land or area along a river

riv·er·side \-₁sīd\ *n* : the side or bank of a river

¹**riv·et** \'ri-vət\ *n* : a metal bolt with a head at one end used to join parts by being put

through holes in them and then being flattened on the plain end to make another head

²**rivet** *vb* : to fasten with or as if with a rivet — **riv·et·er** *n*

riv·u·let \'ri-vyə-lət, -və-\ *n* : a small stream

ri·yal *also* **ri·al** \rē-'äl, -'al\ *n* — see MONEY table

rm *abbr* room

Rn *symbol* radon

¹**RN** \₁är-'en\ *n* : REGISTERED NURSE

²**RN** *abbr* Royal Navy

RNA \₁är-(₁)en-'ā\ *n* : any of various nucleic acids (as messenger RNA) that are found esp. in the cytoplasm of cells, have ribose as the 5-carbon sugar, and are associated with the control of cellular chemical activities

rnd *abbr* round

¹**roach** \'rōch\ *n, pl* **roach** *also* **roach·es** : any of various bony fishes related to the carp; *also* : any of several sunfishes

²**roach** *n* **1** : COCKROACH **2** : the butt of a marijuana cigarette

road \'rōd\ *n* [ME *rode*, fr. OE *rād* ride, journey] **1** : ROADSTEAD — often used in pl. **2** : an open way for vehicles, persons, and animals : HIGHWAY **3** : a way to a conclusion or end ⟨the ∼ to success⟩ **4** : a series of scheduled visits (as games or performances) in several locations or the travel necessary to make these visits ⟨the team is on the ∼⟩

road·bed \'rōd-₁bed\ *n* **1** : the foundation of a road or railroad **2** : the part of the surface of a road on which vehicles travel

road·block \-₁bläk\ *n* **1** : a barricade on the road ⟨a police ∼⟩ **2** : an obstruction to progress

road·ie \'rō-dē\ *n* : a person who works for traveling entertainers

road·kill \'rōd-₁kil\ *n* **1** : the remains of an animal that has been killed on a road by a motor vehicle **2** : one that falls victim to intense competition ⟨political ∼⟩

road·run·ner \-₁rə-nər\ *n* : a largely terrestrial bird of the southwestern U.S. and Mexico that is a speedy runner

road·side \'rōd-₁sīd\ *n* : the strip of land along a road — **roadside** *adj*

road·stead \-₁sted\ *n* : an anchorage for ships usu. less sheltered than a harbor

road·ster \'rōd-stər\ *n* **1** : a driving horse **2** : an open automobile that seats two or ten with a storage compartment or rumble seat in the rear

road·way \-₁wā\ *n* : ROAD; *esp* : ROADBED

road·work \-₁wərk\ *n* **1** : work done in constructing or repairing roads **2** : conditioning for an athletic contest (as a boxing match) consisting mainly of long runs

roam \'rōm\ *vb* **1** : WANDER, ROVE **2** : to range or wander over or about **3** : to use a cell phone outside one's local calling area

¹**roan** \'rōn\ *adj* : of dark color (as black, red, or brown) sprinkled with white ⟨a ∼ horse⟩

²**roan** *n* : an animal (as a horse) with a roan coat; *also* : its color

¹roar \\'rȯr\\ vb **1** : to utter a full loud prolonged sound **2** : to make a loud confused sound (as of wind or waves) — **roar·er** n

²roar n : a sound of roaring

¹roast \\'rōst\\ vb **1** : to cook by exposure to dry heat or an open flame **2** : to criticize severely or kiddingly

²roast n **1** : a piece of meat suitable for roasting **2** : an outing at which food is roasted ⟨corn ~⟩ **3** : severe criticism or kidding

³roast adj : ROASTED

roast·er \\'rō-stər\\ n **1** : one that roasts **2** : a device for roasting **3** : something (as a young chicken) fit for roasting

rob \\'räb\\ vb **robbed; rob·bing 1** : to steal from **2** : to deprive of something due or expected **3** : to commit robbery — **rob·ber** n

robber fly n : any of a family of predaceous flies resembling bumblebees

rob·bery \\'rä-bə-rē\\ n, pl **-ber·ies** : the act or practice of robbing; esp : theft of something from a person by use of violence or threat

¹robe \\'rōb\\ n **1** : a long flowing outer garment; esp : one used for ceremonial occasions **2** : a wrap or covering for the lower body (as for sitting outdoors)

²robe vb **robed; rob·ing 1** : to clothe with or as if with a robe **2** : DRESS

rob·in \\'rä-bən\\ n **1** : a small chiefly European thrush with a somewhat orange face and breast **2** : a large No. American thrush with a grayish back, a streaked throat, and a chiefly dull reddish breast

ro·bo·call \\'rō-bō-ˌkȯl\\ n : a telephone call from an automated source that delivers a message to a large number of people

ro·bot \\'rō-ˌbät, -bət\\ n [Czech, fr. robota compulsory labor] **1** : a machine that looks and acts like a human being **2** : an efficient but insensitive person **3** : a device that automatically performs esp. repetitive tasks **4** : something guided by automatic controls — **ro·bot·ic** \\rō-'bä-tik\\ adj

ro·bot·ics \\rō-'bä-tiks\\ n : technology dealing with the design, construction, and operation of robots

ro·bust \\rō-'bəst, 'rō-(ˌ)bəst\\ adj [L robustus oaken, strong, fr. robur oak, strength] **1** : strong and vigorously healthy **2** : capable of performing without failure under a wide range of conditions ⟨~ software⟩ — **ro·bust·ly** adv — **ro·bust·ness** n

ROC abbr Republic of China (Taiwan)

¹rock \\'räk\\ vb **1** : to move back and forth in or as if in a cradle **2** : to sway or cause to sway back and forth **3** : to arouse to excitement (as with rock music) ⟨~ed the crowd⟩ **4** slang : to be extremely enjoyable or effective ⟨this car ~s⟩

²rock n **1** : a rocking movement **2** : popular music usu. played on electric instruments and characterized by a strong beat and much repetition

³rock n **1** : a mass of stony material; also : broken pieces of stone **2** : solid mineral deposits **3** : something like a rock in firmness **4** : GEM; esp : DIAMOND — **rock** adj — **rock·like** adj — **rocky** adj — **on the rocks 1** : in a state of ruin ⟨a marriage on the rocks⟩ **2** : on ice cubes ⟨bourbon on the rocks⟩

rock and roll n : ²ROCK 2

rock·bound \\'räk-ˌbau̇nd\\ adj : fringed or covered with rocks

rock·er \\'rä-kər\\ n **1** : one of the curved pieces on which something (as a chair or cradle) rocks **2** : a chair that rocks on rockers **3** : a device that works with a rocking motion **4** : a rock performer, song, or enthusiast

¹rock·et \\'rä-kət\\ n [It rocchetta, lit., small distaff] **1** : a firework that is propelled through the air by the discharge of gases produced by a burning substance **2** : a jet engine that operates on the same principle as a firework rocket but carries the oxygen needed for burning its fuel **3** : a rocket-propelled bomb or missile

²rocket vb **1** : to convey by means of a rocket **2** : to rise abruptly and rapidly

rock·et·ry \\'rä-kə-trē\\ n : the study or use of rockets

rocket ship n : a rocket-propelled spacecraft

rock·fall \\'räk-ˌfȯl\\ n : a mass of falling or fallen rocks

rock·fish \\-ˌfish\\ n : any of various bony fishes that live among rocks or on rocky bottoms

rock salt n : common salt in rocklike masses or large crystals

Rocky Mountain sheep n : BIGHORN

ro·co·co \\rə-'kō-kō\\ adj [F, irreg. fr. rocaille style of ornament, lit., stone debris] : of or relating to an artistic style esp. of the 18th century marked by fanciful curved forms and elaborate ornamentation — **rococo** n

rod \\'räd\\ n **1** : a straight slender stick **2** : a stick or bundle of twigs used in punishing a person; also : PUNISHMENT **3** : a staff borne to show rank **4** — see WEIGHT table **5** : any of the rod-shaped receptor cells of the retina that are sensitive to faint light **6** slang : HANDGUN

rode past of RIDE

ro·dent \\'rō-dᵊnt\\ n [ultim. fr. L rodent-, rodens, prp. of rodere to gnaw] : any of an order of relatively small mammals (as mice, squirrels, and beavers) with sharp front teeth used for gnawing

ro·deo \\'rō-dē-ˌō, rə-'dā-ō\\ n, pl **ro·de·os** [Sp, fr. rodear to surround, fr. rueda wheel, fr. L rota] **1** : ROUNDUP 1 **2** : a public performance featuring cowboy skills (as riding and roping)

¹roe \\'rō\\ n, pl **roe** or **roes** : DOE

²roe n : the eggs of a fish esp. while bound together in a mass

roe·buck \\'rō-ˌbək\\ n, pl **roebuck** or **roe·bucks** : a male roe deer

roe deer n : either of two small nimble European or Asian deers

roent·gen \\'rent-gən, 'rənt-, -jən\\ n : the international unit of measurement for X-rays and gamma rays

roent·gen·i·um \\rent-'ge-nē-əm, rənt-,

-'je-\ *n* : a short-lived radioactive chemical element

rog·er \'rä-jər\ *interj* — used esp. in radio and signaling to indicate that a message has been received and understood

¹**rogue** \'rōg\ *n* **1** : a dishonest person : SCOUNDREL **2** : of or being a nation whose : SCAMP — **rogu·ery** \'rō-gə-rē\ *n* — **rogu·ish** \-gish\ *adj* — **rogu·ish·ly** *adv* — **rogu·ish·ness** *n*

²**rogue** *adj* **1** : CORRUPT, DISHONEST ⟨∼ cops⟩ **2** : of or being a nation whose leaders defy international law or norms

roil \'rȯi(-ə)l, *for 2 also* 'rī(-ə)l\ *vb* **1** : to make cloudy or muddy by stirring up **2** : RILE **1** — **roily** \'rȯi-lē\ *adj*

rois·ter \'rȯi-stər\ *vb* **rois·tered; rois·ter·ing** : to engage in noisy revelry : CAROUSE — **rois·ter·er** *n* — **rois·ter·ous** \-stə-rəs\ *adj*

ROK *abbr* Republic of Korea (South Korea)

role *also* **rôle** \'rōl\ *n* **1** : an assigned or assumed character; *also* : a part played (as by an actor) **2** : FUNCTION

role model *n* : a person whose behavior in a particular role is imitated by others

¹**roll** \'rōl\ *n* [ME *rolle* scroll, fr. AF, fr. ML *rolla*, alter. of *rotula*, fr. L, dim. of *rota* wheel] **1** : a document containing an official record **2** : an official list of names **3** : bread baked in a small rounded mass **4** : something that rolls : ROLLER

²**roll** *vb* **1** : to move by turning over and over ⟨∼ dice⟩ ⟨∼*ed* her eyes⟩ **2** : to press with a roller ⟨∼ dough⟩ **3** : to move on wheels **4** : to sound with a full reverberating tone **5** : to make a continuous beating sound (as on a drum) **6** : to utter with a trill **7** : to move onward as if by completing a revolution ⟨years ∼*ed* by⟩ **8** : to flow or seem to flow in a continuous stream or with a rising and falling motion ⟨the river ∼*ed* on⟩ **9** : to swing or sway from side to side **10** : to shape or become shaped in rounded form ⟨∼ up the paper⟩ **11** : to move by or as if by turning a crank ⟨∼ down the window⟩

³**roll** *n* **1** : a sound produced by rapid strokes on a drum **2** : a heavy reverberating sound **3** : a rolling movement or action **4** : a swaying movement (as of a ship) **5** : a somersault made in contact with the ground

roll·back \'rōl-,bak\ *n* : the act or an instance of rolling back

roll back *vb* **1** : to reduce (as a commodity price) on a national scale **2** : to cause to withdraw : push back

roll bar *n* : an overhead metal bar on an automobile designed to protect riders in case the automobile overturns

roll call *n* : the act or an instance of calling off a list of names (as of soldiers); *also* : a time for a full roll call

roll·er \'rō-lər\ *n* **1** : a revolving cylinder used for moving, pressing, shaping, applying, or smoothing something **2** : a rod on which something is rolled up **3** : a long heavy ocean wave

roll·er coast·er \'rō-lər-,kō-stər\ *n* : an amusement ride consisting of an elevated railway having sharp curves and steep slopes

roller skate *n* : a skate with wheels instead of a runner — **roller–skate** *vb* — **roller skater** *n*

rol·lick \'rä-lik\ *vb* : ROMP, FROLIC

rol·lick·ing *adj* : full of fun and good spirits ⟨a ∼ good time⟩

roly–poly \,rō-lē-'pō-lē\ *adj* : ROTUND

Rom *abbr* **1** Roman **2** Romance **3** Romania; Romanian **4** Romans

ROM \'räm\ *n* : a computer memory that contains special-purpose information (as a program) which cannot be altered

ro·maine \rō-'mān\ *n* [F, lit., Roman] : a garden lettuce with a tall loose head of long crisp leaves

¹**Ro·man** \'rō-mən\ *n* **1** : a native or resident of Rome **2** *not cap* : roman letters or type

²**Roman** *adj* **1** : of or relating to Rome or the Romans and esp. the ancient Romans **2** *not cap* : relating to type in which the letters are upright **3** : of or relating to the Roman Catholic Church

Roman candle *n* : a cylindrical firework that discharges balls of fire

Roman Catholic *adj* : of, relating to, or being a Christian church led by the pope and having a liturgy centered in the Mass — **Roman Catholicism** *n*

¹**ro·mance** \rō-'mans, 'rō-,mans\ *n* [ME *romauns*, fr. AF *romanz* French, something written in French, tale in verse, fr. ML *Romanice* in a vernacular language, ultim. fr. L *Romanus* Roman] **1** : a medieval tale of knightly adventure **2** : a prose narrative dealing with heroic or mysterious events set in a remote time or place **3** : a love story **4** : a romantic attachment or episode between lovers — **ro·manc·er** *n*

²**romance** *vb* **ro·manced; ro·manc·ing 1** : to exaggerate or invent detail or incident **2** : to have romantic fancies **3** : to carry on a romantic episode with

Ro·mance \rō-'mans, 'rō-,mans\ *adj* : of or relating to any of several languages developed from Latin

Ro·ma·nian \rů-'mā-nē-ən, rō-, -nyən\ *also* **Ru·ma·nian** \rů-\ *n* **1** : a native or inhabitant of Romania **2** : the language of the Romanians

Roman numeral *n* : a numeral in a system of notation that is based on the ancient Roman system

Ro·ma·no \rō-'mä-nō\ *n* : a hard Italian cheese that is sharper than Parmesan

Ro·mans \'rō-mənz\ *n* — see BIBLE table

¹**ro·man·tic** \rō-'man-tik\ *adj* **1** : IMAGINARY **2** : VISIONARY **3** : having an imaginative or emotional appeal **4** : of, relating to, or having the characteristics of romanticism — **ro·man·ti·cal·ly** \-ti-k(ə-)lē\ *adv*

²**romantic** *n* : a romantic person; *esp* : a romantic writer, composer, or artist

ro·man·ti·cism \rō-'man-tə-,si-zəm\ *n*, *often cap* : a literary movement (as in early 19th century England) marked esp. by emphasis on the imagination and the emotions and by the use of autobiographical material — **ro·man·ti·cist** \-sist\ *n, often cap*

ro·man·ti·cize \-'man-tə-ˌsīz\ *vb* **-cized; -ciz·ing** 1 : to make romantic 2 : to have romantic ideas

romp \'rämp\ *vb* 1 : to play actively and noisily 2 : to win a contest easily — **romp** *n*

romp·er \'räm-pər\ *n* 1 : one that romps 2 : a jumpsuit usu. for infants — usu. used in pl.

rood \'rüd\ *n* : CROSS, CRUCIFIX

¹**roof** \'rüf, 'rüf\ *n, pl* **roofs** \'rüfs, 'rüfs, 'rüvz, 'rüvz\ 1 : the upper covering part of a building 2 : something suggesting a roof of a building — **roofed** \'rüft, 'rüft\ *adj* — **roof·ing** *n* — **roof·less** *adj* — **through the roof** : to an extremely high level ⟨prices went *through the roof*⟩

²**roof** *vb* : to cover with a roof

roof·top \-ˌtäp\ *n* : a roof esp. of a house

¹**rook** \'rük\ *n* : a crow that nests and roosts in usu. treetop colonies

²**rook** *vb* : CHEAT, SWINDLE

³**rook** *n* : a chess piece that can move parallel to the sides of the board across any number of unoccupied squares

rook·ery \'rü-kə-rē\ *n, pl* **-er·ies** : a breeding ground or haunt of gregarious birds or mammals; *also* : a colony of such birds or mammals

rook·ie \'rü-kē\ *n* : BEGINNER, RECRUIT; *esp* : a first-year player in a professional sport

¹**room** \'rüm, 'rùm\ *n* 1 : an extent of space occupied by or sufficient or available for something 2 : a partitioned part of a building : CHAMBER; *also* : the people in a room 3 : OPPORTUNITY, CHANCE ⟨∼ to develop his talents⟩ — **room·ful** *n* — **roomy** *adj*

²**room** *vb* : to occupy or share lodgings : LODGE — **room·er** *n*

room·ette \rü-'met, rù-\ *n* : a small private room on a railroad sleeping car

room·mate \'rüm-ˌmāt, 'rùm-\ *n* : one of two or more persons sharing the same room or dwelling

¹**roost** \'rüst\ *n* : a support on which or a place where birds perch

²**roost** *vb* : to settle on or as if on a roost

roost·er \'rüs-tər, 'rùs-\ *n* : an adult male domestic chicken : COCK

¹**root** \'rüt, 'rùt\ *n* 1 : the leafless usu. underground part of a seed plant that functions in absorption, aeration, and storage or as a means of anchorage; *also* : an underground plant part esp. when fleshy and edible 2 : something (as the basal part of a tooth or hair) resembling a root 3 : SOURCE, ORIGIN; *esp* : ANCESTRY — usu. used in pl. 4 : the essential core : HEART ⟨get to the ∼ of the matter⟩ 5 : a number that when taken as a factor an indicated number of times gives a specified number 6 : the lower part — **root·less** *adj* — **root·like** *adj*

²**root** *vb* 1 : to form roots 2 : to fix or become fixed by or as if by roots : ESTABLISH 3 : UPROOT

³**root** *vb* 1 : to turn up or dig with the snout ⟨pigs ∼ing⟩ 2 : to poke or dig around (as in search of something)

⁴**root** \'rüt\ *vb* 1 : to applaud or encourage noisily : CHEER 2 : to wish success or lend support to — **root·er** *n*

root beer *n* : a sweetened carbonated beverage flavored with extracts of roots and herbs

root canal *n* : a dental operation to save a tooth by removing the pulp in the root of the tooth and filling the cavity with a protective substance

root·let \'rüt-lət, 'rùt-\ *n* : a small root

root·stock \-ˌstäk\ *n* : an underground part of a plant that resembles a rhizome

¹**rope** \'rōp\ *n* 1 : a large strong cord made of strands of fiber 2 : a hangman's noose 3 : a thick string (as of pearls) made by twisting or braiding

²**rope** *vb* **roped; rop·ing** 1 : to bind, tie, or fasten together with a rope 2 : to separate or divide by means of a rope 3 : LASSO

Ror·schach test \'ror-ˌshäk-\ *n* : a psychological test in which a subject interprets ink-blot designs in terms that reveal intellectual and emotional factors

ro·sa·ry \'rō-zə-rē\ *n, pl* **-ries** 1 *often cap* : a Roman Catholic devotion consisting of meditation on sacred mysteries during recitation of Hail Marys 2 : a string of beads used in praying

¹**rose** *past of* RISE

²**rose** \'rōz\ *n* 1 : any of a genus of usu. prickly often climbing shrubs with divided leaves and bright often fragrant flowers; *also* : one of these flowers 2 : something resembling a rose in form 3 : a moderate purplish red color — **rose** *adj*

ro·sé \rō-'zā\ *n* [F] : a light pink wine

ro·se·ate \'rō-zē-ət, -zē-ˌāt\ *adj* 1 : resembling a rose esp. in color 2 : OPTIMISTIC ⟨a ∼ view of the future⟩

rose·bud \'rōz-ˌbəd\ *n* : the flower of a rose when it is at most partly open

rose·bush \-ˌbùsh\ *n* : a shrubby rose

rose·mary \'rōz-ˌmer-ē\ *n, pl* **-mar·ies** [ME *rosmarine*, fr. AF *rosmarin*, fr. L *ros marinus*, fr. *ros* dew + *marinus* of the sea, fr. *mare* sea] : a fragrant shrubby Mediterranean mint; *also* : its leaves used as a seasoning

ro·sette \rō-'zet\ *n* [F] 1 : a usu. small badge or ornament of ribbon gathered in the shape of a rose 2 : a circular ornament filled with representations of leaves

rose wa·ter \'rōz-ˌwȯ-tər, -ˌwä-\ *n* : a watery solution of the fragrant constituents of the rose used as a perfume

rose·wood \-ˌwùd\ *n* : any of various tropical trees with dark red wood streaked with black; *also* : this wood

Rosh Ha·sha·nah \ˌräsh-hə-'shä-nə, ˌrōsh-, -'shȯ-\ *n* [Heb *rōsh hashshānāh*, lit., beginning of the year] : the Jewish New Year observed as a religious holiday in September or October

ros·in \'rä-zᵊn\ *n* : a brittle resin obtained esp. from pine trees and used esp. in varnishes and on violin bows

ros·ter \'räs-tər\ *n* 1 : a list of personnel;

also : the persons listed on a roster **2** : an itemized list

ros·trum \'räs-trəm\ *n, pl* **rostrums** or **ros·tra** \-trə\ [L *Rostra*, pl., a platform for speakers in the Roman Forum decorated with the beaks of captured ships, fr. pl. of *rostrum* beak, ship's beak, fr. *rodere* to gnaw] : a stage or platform for public speaking

rosy \'rō-zē\ *adj* **ros·i·er; -est 1** : of the color rose **2** : HOPEFUL, PROMISING ⟨a ∼ outlook⟩ — **ros·i·ly** \'rō-zə-lē\ *adv* — **ros·i·ness** \-zē-nəs\ *n*

¹**rot** \'rät\ *vb* **rot·ted; rot·ting** : to undergo decomposition : DECAY

²**rot** *n* **1** : DECAY **2** : any of various diseases of plants or animals in which tissue breaks down **3** : NONSENSE

¹**ro·ta·ry** \'rō-tə-rē\ *adj* **1** : turning on an axis like a wheel **2** : having a rotating part ⟨a ∼ telephone⟩

²**rotary** *n, pl* **-ries 1** : a rotary machine **2** : a one-way circular road junction

ro·tate \'rō-ˌtāt\ *vb* **ro·tat·ed; ro·tat·ing 1** : to turn or cause to turn about an axis or a center : REVOLVE **2** : to alternate in a series ♦ **Synonyms** TURN, CIRCLE, SPIN, WHIRL, TWIRL — **ro·ta·tion** \rō-'tā-shən\ *n* — **ro·ta·tor** \'rō-ˌtā-tər\ *n* — **ro·ta·to·ry** \'rō-tə-ˌtōr-ē\ *adj*

ROTC *abbr* Reserve Officers' Training Corps

rote \'rōt\ *n* **1** : repetition from memory often without attention to meaning ⟨learn by ∼⟩ **2** : mechanical or unthinking routine or repetition — **rote** *adj*

ro·tis·se·rie \rō-'ti-sə-rē\ *n* [F] **1** : a restaurant specializing in broiled and barbecued meats **2** : an appliance fitted with a spit on which food is rotated before or over a source of heat

ro·to·gra·vure \ˌrō-tə-grə-'vyùr\ *n* : PHOTOGRAVURE

ro·tor \'rō-tər\ *n* **1** : a part that rotates; *esp* : the rotating part of an electrical machine **2** : a system of rotating horizontal blades for supporting a helicopter

ro·to·till·er \'rō-tō-ˌti-lər\ *n* : an engine-powered machine with rotating blades used to lift and turn over soil

rot·ten \'rä-t²n\ *adj* **1** : having rotted **2** : CORRUPT **3** : extremely unpleasant or inferior — **rot·ten·ness** *n*

rot·ten·stone \'rä-t²n-ˌstōn\ *n* : a decomposed siliceous limestone used for polishing

rott·wei·ler \'rät-ˌwī-lər\ *n, often cap* : any of a breed of tall powerful black-and-tan short-haired dogs

ro·tund \rō-'tənd\ *adj* : rounded out ♦ **Synonyms** PLUMP, CHUBBY, PORTLY, STOUT — **ro·tun·di·ty** \-'tən-də-tē\ *n*

ro·tun·da \rō-'tən-də\ *n* **1** : a round building; *esp* : one covered by a dome **2** : a large round room

rouble *var of* RUBLE

roué \rü-'ā\ *n* [F, lit., broken on the wheel, fr. pp. of *rouer* to break on the wheel, fr. ML *rotare*, fr. L, to rotate; fr. the feeling that such a person deserves this punishment] : a man devoted to a life of sensual pleasure : RAKE

rouge \'rüzh, 'rüj\ *n* [F, lit., red] : a cosmetic used to give a red color to cheeks and lips — **rouge** *vb*

¹**rough** \'rəf\ *adj* **rough·er; rough·est 1** : uneven in surface : not smooth **2** : SHAGGY **3** : not calm : TURBULENT, TEMPESTUOUS **4** : marked by harshness or violence **5** : DIFFICULT, TRYING **6** : coarse or rugged in character or appearance **7** : marked by lack of refinement **8** : CRUDE, UNFINISHED **9** : done or made hastily or tentatively ⟨a ∼ estimate⟩ — **rough·ly** *adv* — **rough·ness** *n*

²**rough** *n* **1** : uneven ground covered with high grass esp. along a golf fairway **2** : a crude, unfinished, or preliminary state; *also* : something in such a state **3** : ROWDY, TOUGH

³**rough** *vb* **1** : ROUGHEN **2** : MANHANDLE **3** : to make or shape roughly esp. in a preliminary way — **rough·er** *n*

rough·age \'rə-fij\ *n* : FIBER 2; *also* : food containing much indigestible material acting as fiber

rough–and–ready \ˌrə-fən-'re-dē\ *adj* : rude or unpolished in nature, method, or manner but effective in action or use ⟨a ∼ solution⟩

rough–and–tum·ble \-'təm-bəl\ *n* : rough unrestrained fighting or struggling — **rough–and–tumble** *adj*

rough·en \'rə-fən\ *vb* **rough·ened; rough·en·ing** : to make or become rough

rough–hewn \'rəf-'hyün\ *adj* **1** : being rough and unfinished ⟨∼ beams⟩ **2** : lacking smooth manners or social grace — **rough–hew** \-'hyü\ *vb*

rough·house \'rəf-ˌhaùs\ *vb* **rough·housed; rough·hous·ing** : to participate in rough noisy behavior — **rough·house** *n*

rough·neck \'rəf-ˌnek\ *n* **1** : ROWDY, TOUGH **2** : a worker on a crew drilling oil wells

rough·shod \'rəf-ˌshäd\ *adv* : in a roughly forceful manner ⟨rode ∼ over the opposition⟩

rou·lette \rü-'let\ *n* [F, lit., small wheel] **1** : a gambling game in which a whirling wheel is used **2** : a wheel or disk with teeth around the outside

¹**round** \'raùnd\ *adj* **1** : having every part of the surface or circumference the same distance from the center **2** : CYLINDRICAL **3** : COMPLETE, FULL **4** : approximately correct; *esp* : exact only to a specific decimal or place ⟨∼ numbers⟩ **5** : liberal or ample in size or amount **6** : BLUNT, OUTSPOKEN **7** : moving in or forming a circle **8** : having curves rather than angles — **round·ish** *adj* — **round·ness** *n*

²**round** *prep or adv* : AROUND

³**round** *n* **1** : something round (as a circle, globe, or ring) **2** : a curved or rounded part (as a rung of a ladder) **3** : an indirect path or course; *also* : a regularly covered route (as of a security guard) **4** : a series or cycle of recurring actions or events **5** : one shot fired by a soldier or a gun; *also* : ammunition for one shot **6** : a period of

time or a unit of play in a game or contest **7** : a cut of meat (as beef) esp. between the rump and the lower leg — **in the round 1** : FREESTANDING **2** : with a center stage surrounded by an audience ⟨theater *in the round*⟩

4round *vb* **1** : to make or become round **2** : to go or pass around or part way around **3** : COMPLETE, FINISH **4** : to become plump or shapely **5** : to express as a round number — often used with *off* **6** : to follow a winding course : BEND

1round·about \'raùn-də-,baùt\ *adj* : INDI-RECT, CIRCUITOUS ⟨a ~ explanation⟩

2roundabout *n* **1** *Brit* : MERRY-GO-ROUND **2** *Brit* : ROTARY 2

roun·de·lay \'raùn-də-,lā\ *n* **1** : a simple song with a refrain **2** : a poem with a recurring refrain

round·house \'raùnd-,haùs\ *n* **1** : a circular building for housing and repairing locomotives **2** : a blow with the hand made with a wide swing — **roundhouse** *adj*

round·ly \'raùnd-lē\ *adv* **1** : in a complete manner; *also* : WIDELY **2** : in a blunt way **3** : with vigor

round–rob·in \'raùnd-,rä-bən\ *n* : a tournament in which each contestant meets every other contestant in turn

round–shoul·dered \-,shōl-dərd\ *adj* : having the shoulders stooping or rounded

round–trip *n* : a trip to a place and back

round–up \'raùnd-,əp\ *n* **1** : the gathering together of cattle on the range by riding around them and driving them in; *also* : the ranch hands and horses engaged in a roundup **2** : a gathering in of scattered persons or things **3** : SUMMARY ⟨news ~⟩ — **round up** *vb*

round·worm \-,wərm\ *n* : NEMATODE

rouse \'raùz\ *vb* **roused; rous·ing 1** : to excite to activity : stir up **2** : to wake from sleep — **rous·er** *n*

roust·about \'raùs-tə-,baùt\ *n* **1** : one who does heavy unskilled labor (as on a dock or in an oil field) **2** : a laborer at a circus **3** : a person with no established home or occupation

1rout \'raùt\ *n* **1** : MOB 1, 2 : DISTUR-BANCE **2** : a fashionable gathering

2rout *vb* **1** : RUMMAGE **2** : to gouge out **3** : to expel by force ⟨~ed out of their homes⟩

3rout *n* **1** : a state of wild confusion or disorderly retreat **2** : a disastrous defeat

4rout *vb* **1** : to put to flight **2** : to defeat decisively

1route \'rüt, 'raùt\ *n* [ME, fr. AF *rute*, fr. VL *rupta* (*via*), lit., broken way] **1** : a traveled way **2** : CHANNEL **3** : a line of travel

2route *vb* **rout·ed; rout·ing** : to send by a selected route : DIRECT

route·man \-mən, -,man\ *n* : a person who sells and makes deliveries on an assigned route

rout·er \'raù-tər\ *n* : a machine with a revolving spindle and cutter for shaping a surface (as of wood)

rou·tine \rü-'tēn\ *n* [F, fr. MF, fr. *route*

traveled way] **1** : a regular course of procedure **2** : an often repeated speech or formula **3** : a part fully worked out ⟨a comedy ~⟩ **4** : a set of computer instructions that will perform a certain task — **routine** *adj* — **rou·tine·ly** *adv* — **rou·tin·ize** \-'tē-,nīz\ *vb*

1rove \'rōv\ *vb* **roved; rov·ing** : to wander over or through — **rov·er** *n*

2rove *past and past part of* REEVE

1row \'rō\ *vb* **1** : to propel a boat with oars **2** : to transport in a rowboat **3** : to pull an oar in a crew — **row·er** \'rō-ər\ *n*

2row *n* : an act or instance of rowing

3row *n* **1** : a number of objects in an orderly sequence **2** : WAY, STREET

4row \'raù\ *n* : a noisy quarrel

5row \'raù\ *vb* : to engage in a row

row·boat \'rō-,bōt\ *n* : a small boat designed to be rowed

row·dy \'raù-dē\ *adj* **row·di·er; -est** : coarse or boisterous in behavior : ROUGH ⟨a ~ crowd⟩ — **row·di·ness** \'raù-dē-nəs\ *n* — **rowdy** *n* — **row·dy·ish** *adj* — **row·dy·ism** *n*

row·el \'raù-(ə)l\ *n* : a small pointed wheel on a rider's spur — **rowel** *vb*

1roy·al \'rȯi(-ə)l\ *adj* [ME *roial*, fr. AF *real*, *roial*, fr. L *regalis*, fr. *reg-*, *rex* king] **1** : of or relating to a sovereign : REGAL **2** : fit for a king or queen ⟨a ~ welcome⟩ — **roy·al·ly** *adv*

2royal *n* : a person of royal blood

royal flush *n* : a straight flush having an ace as the highest card

roy·al·ist \'rȯi-ə-list\ *n* : an adherent of a king or of monarchical government

roy·al·ty \'rȯi-əl-tē\ *n, pl* **-ties 1** : the state of being royal **2** : royal persons **3** : a share of a product or profit (as of a mine or oil well) claimed by the owner for allowing another person to use the property **4** : a payment made to an author or composer for each copy of a work sold or to an inventor for each article sold under a patent

RP *abbr* **1** relief pitcher **2** Republic of the Philippines

rpm *abbr* revolutions per minute

rps *abbr* revolutions per second

rpt *abbr* **1** repeat **2** report

RR *abbr* **1** railroad **2** rural route

RS *abbr* **1** recording secretary **2** revised statutes **3** Royal Society

RSV *abbr* Revised Standard Version

RSVP *abbr* [F *répondez s'il vous plaît*] please reply

rt *abbr* **1** right **2** route

RT *abbr* round-trip

rte *abbr* route

Ru *symbol* ruthenium

1rub \'rəb\ *vb* **rubbed; rub·bing 1** : to use pressure and friction on a body or object **2** : to fret or chafe with friction **3** : to scour, polish, erase, or smear by pressure and friction

2rub *n* **1** : DIFFICULTY, OBSTRUCTION **2** : something grating to the feelings

1rub·ber \'rə-bər\ *n* **1** : one that rubs **2** : ERASER **3** : a flexible waterproof elastic substance made from the milky juice of various tropical plants or made synthetically; *also* : something made of this material **4** : CONDOM — **rubber** *adj* — **rubber·ize** \'rə-bə-ˌrīz\ *vb* — **rub·bery** *adj*

²**rubber** *n* **1** : a contest that consists of an odd number of games and is won by the side that takes a majority **2** : an extra game played to decide a tie

¹**rub·ber·neck** \-ˌnek\ *n* **1** : an idly or overly inquisitive person **2** : a person on a guided tour

²**rubberneck** *vb* : to look about, stare, or listen with excessive curiosity ⟨∼*ing* drivers⟩ — **rub·ber·neck·er** *n*

rub·bish \'rə-bish\ *n* **1** : useless waste or rejected matter : TRASH **2** : something worthless or nonsensical

rub·ble \'rə-bəl\ *n* : broken fragments esp. of a destroyed building

ru·bel *or* **ruble** \'rü-bəl\ — see MONEY table

ru·bel·la \rü-'be-lə\ *n* : GERMAN MEASLES

ru·bi·cund \'rü-bi-(ˌ)kənd\ *adj* : RED, RUDDY ⟨a ∼ face⟩

ru·bid·i·um \rü-'bi-dē-əm\ *n* : a soft silvery metallic chemical element

ru·ble *also* **rou·ble** \'rü-bəl\ *n* — see MONEY table

ru·bric \'rü-brik\ *n* [ME *rubrike* from ocher, heading in red letters of part of a book, fr. AF, fr. L *rubrica*, fr. *ruber* red] **1** : HEADING, TITLE; *also* : CLASS, CATEGORY **2** : a rule esp. for the conduct of a religious service

ru·by \'rü-bē\ *n, pl* **rubies** : a clear red precious stone — **ruby** *adj*

ru·by–throat·ed hummingbird \'rü-bē-ˌthrō-təd-\ *n* : a bright green and whitish hummingbird of eastern No. America with a red throat in the male

ruck·us \'rə-kəs\ *n* : ROW, DISTURBANCE

rud·der \'rə-dər\ *n* : a movable flat piece attached at the rear of a ship or aircraft for steering

rud·dy \'rə-dē\ *adj* **rud·di·er; -est** : REDDISH; *esp* : of a healthy reddish complexion — **rud·di·ness** \'rə-dē-nəs\ *n*

rude \'rüd\ *adj* **rud·er; rud·est** **1** : roughly made : CRUDE **2** : UNDEVELOPED, PRIMITIVE **3** : IMPOLITE **4** : UNSKILLED — **rude·ly** *adv* — **rude·ness** *n*

ru·di·ment \'rü-də-mənt\ *n* **1** : an elementary principle or basic skill — usu. used in pl. ⟨the ∼s of mathematics⟩ **2** : something not fully developed — usu. used in pl. ⟨the ∼s of a plan⟩ — **ru·di·men·ta·ry** \ˌrü-də-'men-tə-rē\ *adj*

¹**rue** \'rü\ *n* : REGRET, SORROW — **rue·ful** \-fəl\ *adj* — **rue·ful·ly** *adv* — **rue·ful·ness** *n*

²**rue** *vb* **rued; ru·ing** : to feel regret, remorse, or penitence for ⟨∼s his decision now⟩

³**rue** *n* : a European strong-scented woody herb with bitter-tasting leaves

ruff \'rəf\ *n* **1** : a large round pleated collar worn about 1600 **2** : a fringe of long hair or feathers around the neck of an animal — **ruffed** \'rəft\ *adj*

ruf·fi·an \'rə-fē-ən\ *n* : a brutal person — **ruf·fi·an·ly** *adj*

¹**ruf·fle** \'rə-fəl\ *vb* **ruf·fled; ruf·fling** **1** : to roughen the surface of **2** : IRRITATE,

VEX **3** : to erect (as hair or feathers) in or like a ruff **4** : to flip through (as pages) **5** : to draw into or provide with plaits or folds

²**ruffle** *n* **1** : a strip of fabric gathered or pleated on one edge **2** : RUFF **3** : RIPPLE — **ruf·fly** \'rə-fə-lē, -flē\ *adj*

ru·fi·yaa \'rü-fē-ˌyä\ *n, pl* **rufiyaa** — see MONEY table

RU–486 \ˌär-ˌyü-ˌfȯr-ˌā-tē-'siks\ *n* : a drug taken orally to induce abortion esp. early in pregnancy

rug \'rəg\ *n* **1** : a covering for the legs, lap, and feet **2** : a piece of heavy fabric usu. with a nap or pile used as a floor covering

rug·by \'rəg-bē\ *n, often cap* [*Rugby* School, Rugby, England, where it was first played] : a football game in which play is continuous and interference and forward passing are not permitted

rug·ged \'rə-gəd\ *adj* **1** : having a rough uneven surface **2** : TURBULENT, STORMY **3** : HARSH, STERN **4** : ROBUST, STURDY — **rug·ged·ize** \'rə-gə-ˌdīz\ *vb* — **rug·ged·ly** *adv* — **rug·ged·ness** *n*

¹**ru·in** \'rü-ən\ *n* **1** : complete collapse or destruction **2** : the remains of something destroyed — usu. used in pl. **3** : a cause of destruction **4** : the action of destroying

²**ruin** *vb* **1** : DESTROY **2** : to damage beyond repair **3** : BANKRUPT

ru·in·ation \ˌrü-ə-'nā-shən\ *n* : RUIN, DESTRUCTION

ru·in·ous \'rü-ə-nəs\ *adj* **1** : RUINED, DILAPIDATED **2** : causing ruin ⟨∼ conflicts⟩ — **ru·in·ous·ly** *adv*

¹**rule** \'rül\ *n* [ME *reule*, fr. AF, fr. L *regula* straightedge, rule, fr. *regere* to keep straight, direct] **1** : a guide or principle for governing action : REGULATION **2** : the usual way of doing something **3** : the exercise of authority or control : GOVERNMENT **4** : RULER 2

²**rule** *vb* **ruled; rul·ing** **1** : CONTROL; *also* : GOVERN **2** : to be supreme or outstanding in **3** : to give or state as a considered decision **4** : to mark on paper with or as if with a ruler **5** *slang* : to be extremely cool or popular

rul·er \'rü-lər\ *n* **1** : SOVEREIGN **2** : a straight strip of material (as wood or metal) marked off in units and used for measuring or as a straightedge

rum \'rəm\ *n* **1** : an alcoholic liquor made from sugarcane products (as molasses) **2** : alcoholic liquor

Ru·ma·nian *var of* ROMANIAN

rum·ba \'rəm-bə, 'rùm-\ *n* : a dance of Cuban origin marked by strong rhythmic movements

¹**rum·ble** \'rəm-bəl\ *vb* **rum·bled; rum·bling** : to make a low heavy rolling sound; *also* : to move along with such a sound — **rum·bler** *n*

²**rumble** *n* **1** : a low heavy rolling sound **2** : a street fight esp. among gangs

rumble seat *n* : a folding seat in the back of an automobile that is not covered by the top

rum·bling \'rəm-bliŋ\ *n* **1** : RUMBLE **2**

: widespread talk or complaints — usu. used in pl.

ru·men \'rü-mən\ *n, pl* **ru·mi·na** \-mə-nə\ *or* **rumens** : the large first compartment of the stomach of a ruminant (as a cow)

¹**ru·mi·nant** \'rü-mə-nənt\ *n* : a ruminant mammal

²**ruminant** *adj* **1** : chewing the cud; *also* : of or relating to a group of hoofed mammals (as cattle, deer, and camels) that chew the cud and have a complex 3- or 4-chambered stomach **2** : MEDITATIVE

ru·mi·nate \'rü-mə-ˌnāt\ *vb* **-nat·ed; -nat·ing** [L *ruminari* to chew the cud, muse upon, fr. *rumin-, rumen* first stomach chamber of a ruminant] **1** : MEDITATE, MUSE **2** : to chew the cud — **ru·mi·na·tion** \ˌrü-mə-ˈnā-shən\ *n*

¹**rum·mage** \'rə-mij\ *vb* **rum·maged; rum·mag·ing** : to search thoroughly ⟨*rummaged* the room for his key⟩ — **rum·mag·er** *n*

²**rummage** *n* **1** : a miscellaneous collection **2** : an act of rummaging

rum·my \'rə-mē\ *n* : any of several card games for two or more players

ru·mor \'rü-mər\ *n* **1** : common talk **2** : a statement or report current but not authenticated — **rumor** *vb*

ru·mour *chiefly Brit var of* RUMOR

rump \'rəmp\ *n* **1** : the rear part of an animal; *also* : a cut of meat (as beef) behind the upper sirloin **2** : a small or inferior remnant (as of a group)

rum·ple \'rəm-pəl\ *vb* **rum·pled; rum·pling** : TOUSLE, MUSS, WRINKLE — **rum·ple** *n* — **rum·ply** \'rəm-pə-lē\ *adj*

rum·pus \'rəm-pəs\ *n* : DISTURBANCE, RUCKUS

rumpus room *n* : a room usu. in the basement of a home that is used for games, parties, and recreation

¹**run** \'rən\ *vb* **ran** \'ran\; **run; run·ning 1** : to go faster than a walk **2** : to take to flight : FLEE **3** : to go without restraint ⟨let chickens ∼ loose⟩ **4** : to go rapidly or hurriedly : HASTEN, RUSH **5** : to make a quick or casual trip or visit **6** : to contend in a race; *esp* : to enter an election ⟨∼ for mayor⟩ **7** : to put forward as a candidate for office **8** : to move on or as if on wheels : pass or slide freely **9** : to go back and forth : PLY **10** : to move in large numbers esp. to a spawning ground ⟨shad are *running*⟩ **11** : FUNCTION, OPERATE ⟨∼s on gasoline⟩ ⟨software that ∼s on her computer⟩ **12** : to continue in force ⟨two years to ∼⟩ **13** : to flow rapidly or under pressure : MELT, FUSE, DISSOLVE; *also* : DISCHARGE **7** ⟨my nose is *running*⟩ **14** : to tend to produce or to recur ⟨family ∼s to blonds⟩ ⟨stubbornness ∼s in the family⟩ **15** : to take a certain direction **16** : to be worded or written **17** : to be current ⟨rumors *running* wild⟩ **18** : to cause to produce a flow ⟨*ran* the faucet⟩ **19** : TRACE ⟨∼ down a rumor⟩ **20** : to perform or bring about by running **21** : to cause to pass ⟨∼ a wire from the antenna⟩ **22** : to cause to collide **23** : SMUGGLE **24**

: MANAGE, CONDUCT, OPERATE ⟨∼ a business⟩ **25** : INCUR ⟨∼ a risk⟩ **26** : to permit to accumulate before settling ⟨∼ up a bill⟩ **27** : PRINT, PUBLISH ⟨∼ a news story⟩

²**run** *n* **1** : an act or the action of running **2** : a migration of fish; *also* : the migrating fish **3** : a score in baseball **4** : BROOK, CREEK **5** : a continuous series esp. of similar things **6** : persistent heavy demands from depositors, creditors, or customers **7** : the quantity of work turned out in a continuous operation; *also* : a period of operation (as of a machine or plant) **8** : the usual or normal kind ⟨the ordinary ∼ of students⟩ **9** : the distance covered in continuous travel or sailing **10** : a regular course or trip **11** : freedom of movement in a place or area ⟨has the ∼ of the house⟩ **12** : an enclosure for animals **13** : an inclined course (as for skiing) **14** : a lengthwise ravel (as in a stocking) — **run·less** *adj*

run·about \'rə-nə-ˌbaùt\ *n* : a light wagon, automobile, or motorboat

run·a·gate \'rə-nə-ˌgāt\ *n* **1** : VAGABOND **2** : FUGITIVE

run·around \'rə-nə-ˌraùnd\ *n* : evasive or delaying action esp. in response to a request

¹**run·away** \'rə-nə-ˌwā\ *n* **1** : one that runs away : FUGITIVE **2** : the act of running away out of control; *also* : something (as a horse) that is running out of control

²**runaway** *adj* **1** : FUGITIVE **2** : won by a long lead; *also* : extremely successful **3** : subject to uncontrolled changes ⟨∼ inflation⟩ **4** : operating out of control ⟨a ∼ locomotive⟩

run·down \'rən-ˌdaùn\ *n* : an item-by-item report or review : SUMMARY

run–down \'rən-'daùn\ *adj* **1** : EXHAUSTED, WORN-OUT ⟨that ∼ feeling⟩ **2** : being in poor repair ⟨a ∼ farm⟩

run down *vb* **1** : to collide with and knock down or cause **2** : to chase until exhausted or captured **3** : to find by search **4** : DISPARAGE **5** : to cease to operate for lack of motive power **6** : to decline in physical condition

rune \'rün\ *n* **1** : any of the characters of any of several alphabets formerly used by the Germanic peoples **2** : MYSTERY, MAGIC **3** : a poem esp. in Finnish or Old Norse — **ru·nic** \'rü-nik\ *adj*

¹**rung** *past part of* RING

²**rung** \'rəŋ\ *n* **1** : a rounded crosspiece between the legs of a chair **2** : one of the crosspieces of a ladder

run–in \'rən-ˌin\ *n* **1** : ALTERCATION, QUARREL **2** : something run in

run in *vb* **1** : to insert as additional matter **2** : to arrest esp. for a minor offense **3** : to pay a casual visit

run·nel \'rə-nºl\ *n* : BROOK, STREAMLET

run·ner \'rə-nər\ *n* **1** : one that runs **2** : BASE RUNNER **3** : BALLCARRIER **4** : a thin piece or part on which something (as a sled or an ice skate) slides **5** : the support of a drawer or a sliding door **6** : a horizontal branch from the base of a plant that produces new plants **7** : a plant producing runners **8** : a long narrow carpet **9** : a narrow decorative cloth cover for a table or dresser top

run·ner-up \ˈrə-nər-ˌəp\ *n, pl* **runners-up** *also* **runner-ups** : the competitor in a contest who finishes second

¹**run·ning** *adj* **1** : FLOWING **2** : FLUID, RUNNY **3** : CONTINUOUS, INCESSANT **4** : measured in a straight line ⟨cost per ∼ foot⟩ **5** : of or relating to an act of running **6** : made or trained for running ⟨∼ horse⟩ ⟨∼ shoes⟩

²**running** *adv* : in succession

running light *n* : any of the lights carried by a vehicle (as a ship) at night

run·ny \ˈrə-nē\ *adj* : having a tendency to run ⟨a ∼ dough⟩ ⟨a ∼ nose⟩

run·off \ˈrən-ˌȯf\ *n* : a final contest (as an election) to decide a previous indecisive contest

run–of–the–mill *adj* : not outstanding : AVERAGE ⟨a ∼ performance⟩

run on *vb* **1** : to talk at length **2** : to continue (matter in type) without a break or a new paragraph **3** : to place or add (as an entry in a dictionary) at the end of a paragraphed item — **run–on** \ˈrən-ˌȯn, -ˌän\ *n*

run out *vb* : to use up or exhaust a supply ⟨*ran out* of gas⟩

runt \ˈrənt\ *n* : an unusually small person or animal : DWARF — **runty** *adj*

run·way \ˈrən-ˌwā\ *n* **1** : a beaten path made by animals; *also* : a passage for animals **2** : a paved strip of ground for the landing and takeoff of aircraft **3** : a narrow platform from a stage into an auditorium **4** : a support (as a track) on which something runs

ru·pee \rü-ˈpē, ˈrü-ˌpē\ *n* — see MONEY table

ru·pi·ah \rü-ˈpē-ə\ *n, pl* **rupiah** or **rupiahs** — see MONEY table

¹**rup·ture** \ˈrəp-chər\ *n* : a breaking or tearing apart; *also* : HERNIA

²**rupture** *vb* **rup·tured; rup·tur·ing** : to cause or undergo rupture

ru·ral \ˈru̇r-əl\ *adj* : of or relating to the country, country people, or agriculture

ruse \ˈrüs, ˈrüz\ *n* : a wily subterfuge : TRICK, ARTIFICE

¹**rush** \ˈrəsh\ *n* : any of various often tufted and hollow-stemmed grasslike marsh plants — **rushy** *adj*

²**rush** *vb* [ME *russhen*, fr. AF *reuser, ruser, russher* to drive back, repulse, fr. L *recusare* to oppose] **1** : to move forward or act with too great haste or eagerness or without preparation **2** : to perform in a short time or at high speed **3** : ATTACK, CHARGE **4** : to advance a football by running — **rush·er** *n*

³**rush** *n* **1** : a violent forward motion **2** : unusual demand or activity **3** : a crowding of people to one place **4** : a running

play in football **5** : a sudden feeling of pleasure

⁴**rush** *adj* : requiring or marked by special speed or urgency ⟨∼ orders⟩

rush hour *n* : a time when the amount of traffic or business is at a peak

rusk \ˈrəsk\ *n* : a sweet or plain bread baked, sliced, and baked again until dry and crisp

rus·set \ˈrə-sət\ *n* **1** : a coarse reddish brown cloth **2** : a reddish brown **3** : a baking potato — **russet** *adj*

Rus·sian \ˈrə-shən\ *n* **1** : a native or inhabitant of Russia **2** : a Slavic language of the Russian people — **Russian** *adj*

rust \ˈrəst\ *n* **1** : a reddish coating formed on iron when it is exposed to esp. moist air **2** : any of numerous plant diseases characterized by usu. reddish spots; *also* : a fungus causing rust **3** : a strong reddish brown — **rust** *vb* — **rusty** *adj*

¹**rus·tic** \ˈrəs-tik\ *adj* : of, relating to, or suitable for the country or country people ⟨a ∼ inn⟩ — **rus·ti·cal·ly** \-ti-k(ə-)lē\ *adv* — **rus·tic·i·ty** \ˌrəs-ˈti-sə-tē\ *n*

²**rustic** *n* : a rustic person

rus·ti·cate \ˈrəs-ti-ˌkāt\ *vb* **-cat·ed; -cat·ing** : to go into or reside in the country — **rus·ti·ca·tion** \ˌrəs-ti-ˈkā-shən\ *n*

¹**rus·tle** \ˈrə-səl\ *vb* **rus·tled; rus·tling 1** : to make or cause a rustle **2** : to cause to rustle ⟨∼ a newspaper⟩ **3** : to act or move with energy or speed; *also* : to procure in this way **4** : to forage food **5** : to steal cattle from the range — **rus·tler** *n*

²**rustle** *n* : a quick series of small sounds ⟨∼ of leaves⟩

¹**rut** \ˈrət\ *n* : state or period of sexual excitement esp. in male deer — **rut** *vb*

²**rut** *n* **1** : a track worn by wheels or by habitual passage of something **2** : a usual or fixed routine

ru·ta·ba·ga \ˌrü-tə-ˈbā-gə, ˌrü-\ *n* : a turnip with a large yellowish root

Ruth \ˈrüth\ *n* — see BIBLE table

ru·the·ni·um \rü-ˈthē-nē-əm\ *n* : a rare hard metallic chemical element

ruth·er·ford·i·um \ˌrə-thər-ˈfȯr-dē-əm\ *n* : an artificially produced radioactive chemical element

ruth·less \ˈrüth-ləs\ *adj* [fr. *ruth* compassion, pity, fr. ME *ruthe*, fr. *ruen* to rue, fr. OE *hrēowan*] : having no pity : MERCILESS, CRUEL ⟨a ∼ tyrant⟩ — **ruth·less·ly** *adv* — **ruth·less·ness** *n*

¹**RV** \ˌär-ˈvē\ *n* : RECREATIONAL VEHICLE

²**RV** *abbr* Revised Version

R–value \ˈär-ˌval-yü\ *n* : a measure of resistance to the flow of heat through a substance (as insulation)

RW *abbr* **1** right worshipful **2** right worthy

rwy *or* **ry** *abbr* railway

-ry *n suffix* : -ERY ⟨bigot*ry*⟩

rye \ˈrī\ *n* **1** : a hardy annual grass grown for grain or as a cover crop; *also* : its seed **2** : a whiskey distilled from a rye mash

¹s \'es\ *n, pl* **s's** *or* **ss** \'e-səz\ *often cap* : the 19th letter of the English alphabet

²s *abbr, often cap* **1** saint **2** second **3** senate **4** series **5** shilling **6** singular **7** small **8** son **9** south; southern

¹-s \s *after sounds* f, k, k̠, p, t, th; əz *after sounds* ch, j, s, sh, z, zh; z *after other sounds*\ *n pl suffix* — used to form the plural of most nouns that do not end in *s, z, sh,* or *ch* or *y* following a consonant ⟨heads⟩ ⟨books⟩ ⟨boys⟩ ⟨beliefs⟩, to form the plural of proper nouns that end in *y* following a consonant ⟨Marys⟩, and with or without a preceding apostrophe to form the plural of abbreviations, numbers, letters, and symbols used as nouns ⟨MCs⟩ ⟨4s⟩ ⟨#s⟩ ⟨B's⟩

²-s *adv suffix* — used to form adverbs denoting usual or repeated action or state ⟨works nights⟩

³-s *vb suffix* — used to form the third person singular present of most verbs that do not end in *s, z, sh,* or *ch* or *y* following a consonant ⟨falls⟩ ⟨takes⟩ ⟨plays⟩

S *symbol* sulfur

SA *abbr* **1** Salvation Army **2** seaman apprentice **3** sex appeal **4** [L *sine anno* without year] without date **5** South Africa **6** South America **7** subject to approval

Saami *var of* SAMI

Sab·bath \'sa-bəth\ *n* [ME *sabat,* fr. AF & OE, fr. L *sabbatum,* fr. Gk *sabbaton,* fr. Heb *shabbāth,* lit., rest] : the 7th day of the week observed as a day of worship by Jews and some Christians **2** : Sunday observed among Christians as a day of worship

sab·bat·i·cal \sə-'ba-ti-kəl\ *n* : a leave of ten with pay granted (as to a college professor) usu. every 7th year for rest, travel, or research

sa·ber *or* **sa·bre** \'sā-bər\ *n* [F *sabre*] : a cavalry sword with a curved blade and thick back

saber saw *n* : a portable electric saw with a pointed reciprocating blade; *esp* : JIGSAW

sa·ble \'sā-bəl\ *n, pl* **sables** **1** : the color black **2** *pl* : mourning garments **3** : a dark brown mammal chiefly of northern Asia related to the weasels; *also* : its fur or pelt

¹sab·o·tage \'sa-bə-ˌtäzh\ *n* [F] **1** : deliberate destruction of an employer's property or hindering of production by workers **2** : destructive or hampering action by enemy agents or sympathizers in time of war

²sabotage *vb* **-taged; -tag·ing** : to practice sabotage on : WRECK

sab·o·teur \ˌsa-bə-'tər\ *n* : a person who practices sabotage

sac \'sak\ *n* : a pouch in an animal or plant often containing a fluid

SAC *abbr* Strategic Air Command

sac·cha·rin \'sa-kə-rən\ *n* : a white crystalline compound used as an artificial calorie-free sweetener

sac·cha·rine \'sa-kə-rən\ *adj* : nauseatingly sweet ⟨∼ poetry⟩

sac·er·do·tal \ˌsa-sər-'dō-tᵊl, -kər-\ *adj* : PRIESTLY

sac·er·do·tal·ism \-tə-ˌli-zəm\ *n* : a religious belief emphasizing the powers of priests as essential mediators between God and man

sa·chem \'sā-chəm\ *n* [Narragansett *sâchim*] : a No. American Indian chief

sa·chet \sa-'shā\ *n* [MF, fr. OF, dim. of *sac* bag] : a small bag filled with perfumed powder for scenting clothes

¹sack \'sak\ *n* **1** : a usu. rectangular-shaped bag (as of paper or burlap) **2** : a loose jacket or short coat

²sack *vb* : DISMISS, FIRE

³sack *n* [modif. of MF *sec* dry, fr. L *siccus*] : a white wine popular in England in the 16th and 17th centuries

⁴sack *vb* : to plunder a captured town

sack·cloth \-ˌklȯth\ *n* : a rough garment worn as a sign of penitence

sac·ra·ment \'sa-krə-mənt\ *n* **1** : a formal religious act or rite; *esp* : one (as baptism or the Eucharist) held to have been instituted by Christ **2** : the elements of the Eucharist — **sac·ra·men·tal** \ˌsa-krə-'men-tᵊl\ *adj*

sa·cred \'sā-krəd\ *adj* **1** : set apart for the service or worship of deity **2** : devoted exclusively to one service or use **3** : worthy of veneration or reverence **4** : of or relating to religion : RELIGIOUS

♦ **Synonyms** BLESSED, DIVINE, HALLOWED, HOLY, SANCTIFIED — **sa·cred·ly** *adv* — **sa·cred·ness** *n*

sacred cow *n* : one that is often unreasonably immune from criticism

¹sac·ri·fice \'sa-krə-ˌfīs\ *n* **1** : the offering of something precious to deity **2** : something offered in sacrifice **3** : LOSS, DEPRIVATION **4** : a bunt allowing a base runner to advance while the batter is put out; *also* : a fly ball allowing a runner to score after the catch — **sac·ri·fi·cial** \ˌsa-krə-'fi-shəl\ *adj* — **sac·ri·fi·cial·ly** *adv*

²sac·ri·fice *vb* **-ficed; -fic·ing** **1** : to offer up or kill as a sacrifice **2** : to accept the loss or destruction of for an end, cause, or ideal ⟨*sacrificed* her career for her family⟩ **3** : to make a sacrifice in baseball

sac·ri·lege \'sa-krə-lij\ *n* [ME, fr. AF, fr. L *sacrilegium,* fr. *sacrilegus* one who robs sacred property fr. *sacr-, sacer* sacred + *legere* to gather, steal] **1** : violation of something consecrated to God **2** : gross irreverence toward a hallowed person, place, or thing — **sac·ri·le·gious** \ˌsa-krə-'li-jəs, -'lē-\ *adj* — **sac·ri·le·gious·ly** *adv*

sac·ris·tan \'sa-krə-stən\ *n* **1** : a church officer in charge of the sacristy **2** : SEXTON

sac·ris·ty \'sa-krə-stē\ *n, pl* **-ties** : VESTRY

sac·ro·il·i·ac \₁sa-krō-'i-lē-₁ak\ *n* : the joint between the upper part of the hip-bone and the sacrum

sac·ro·sanct \'sa-krō-₁saŋkt\ *adj* : SACRED, INVIOLABLE

sa·crum \'sa-krəm, 'sä-\ *n, pl* **sa·cra** \'sa-krə, 'sä-\ : the part of the vertebral column that is directly connected with or forms a part of the pelvis and in humans consists of five fused vertebrae

sad \'sad\ *adj* **sad·der; sad·dest** **1** : GRIEVING, MOURNFUL, DOWNCAST **2** : causing sorrow **3** : DULL, SOMBER — **sad·ly** *adv* — **sad·ness** *n*

sad·den \'sa-dᵊn\ *vb* : to make sad

¹**sad·dle** \'sa-dᵊl\ *n* : a usu. padded leather-covered seat (as for a rider on horseback)

²**saddle** *vb* **sad·dled; sad·dling** **1** : to put a saddle on **2** : OPPRESS, BURDEN

sad·dle·bow \'sa-dᵊl-₁bō\ *n* : the arch in the front of a saddle

saddle horse *n* : a horse suited for or trained for riding

Sad·du·cee \'sa-jə-₁sē, 'sa-dyə-\ *n* : a member of an ancient Jewish sect consisting of a ruling class of priests and rejecting certain doctrines — **Sad·du·ce·an** \₁sa-jə-'sē-ən, ₁sa-dyə-\ *adj*

sad·iron \'sa-₁dī-ərn\ *n* : a flatiron with a removable handle

sa·dism \'sā-₁di-zəm, 'sa-\ *n* : a sexual perversion in which gratification is obtained by inflicting physical or mental pain on others — **sa·dist** \'sā-dist, 'sa-\ *n* — **sa·dis·tic** \sə-'dis-tik\ *adj* — **sa·dis·ti·cal·ly** \-ti-k(ə-)lē\ *adv*

sa·do·mas·och·ism \₁sā-(₁)dō-'ma-sə-₁ki-zəm, ₁sa-, -'ma-zə-\ *n* : the derivation of pleasure from the infliction of physical or mental pain either on others or on oneself — **sa·do·mas·och·is·tic** \-₁ma-sə-'kis-tik, -₁ma-zə-\ *adj*

SAE *abbr* **1** self-addressed envelope **2** Society of Automotive Engineers **3** stamped addressed envelope

sa·fa·ri \sə-'fär-ē\ *n* [Swahili, trip, fr. Ar *safarī* of a trip] **1** : a hunting expedition esp. in eastern Africa **2** : JOURNEY, TRIP

¹**safe** \'sāf\ *adj* **saf·er; saf·est** **1** : free from harm or risk **2** : affording safety; *also* : secure from danger or loss **3** : RELIABLE — **safe·ly** *adv*

²**safe** *n* : a container for keeping articles (as valuables) safe

safe–con·duct \-'kän-(₁)dəkt\ *n* : a pass permitting a person to go through enemy lines

¹**safe·guard** \-₁gärd\ *n* : a measure or device for preventing accident

²**safeguard** *vb* : to provide a safeguard for : PROTECT ⟨~ your valuables⟩

safe·keep·ing \'sāf-'kē-piŋ\ *n* : a keeping or being kept in safety

safer sex *n* : SAFE SEX

safe sex *n* : sexual activity and esp. sexu-al intercourse in which various measures (as the use of latex condoms) are taken to avoid disease (as AIDS) transmitted by sexual contact

safe·ty \'sāf-tē\ *n, pl* **safeties** **1** : freedom from danger : SECURITY **2** : a protective device **3** : a football play in which the ball is downed by the offensive team behind its own goal line **4** : a defensive football back in the deepest position — **safety** *adj*

safety glass *n* : shatter-resistant material formed of two sheets of glass with a sheet of clear plastic between them

safety match *n* : a match that ignites only when struck on a special surface

saf·flow·er \'sa-₁flau̇(-ə)r\ *n* : a widely grown Old World herb related to the daisies that has large orange or red flower heads yielding a dyestuff and seeds rich in edible oil

saf·fron \'sa-frən\ *n* : a deep orange powder from the flower of a crocus used to color and flavor foods

sag \'sag\ *vb* **sagged; sag·ging** **1** : to droop or settle from or as if from pressure ⟨a *sagging* mattress⟩ **2** : to lose firmness or vigor — **sag** *n*

sa·ga \'sä-gə\ *n* [ON] : a narrative of heroic deeds; *esp* : one recorded in Iceland in the 12th and 13th centuries

sa·ga·cious \sə-'gā-shəs\ *adj* : of keen mind : SHREWD ⟨a ~ counselor⟩ — **sa·gac·i·ty** \-'ga-sə-tē\ *n*

sag·a·more \'sa-gə-₁mȯr\ *n* : a subordinate No. American Indian chief

¹**sage** \'sāj\ *adj* [ME, fr. AF, fr. VL *sapius*, fr. L *sapere* to taste, have good taste, be wise] : WISE, PRUDENT — **sage·ly** *adv*

²**sage** *n* : one who is distinguished for wisdom

³**sage** *n* [ME, fr. AF *sage, salge,* fr. L *salvia,* fr. *salvus* healthy; fr. its use as a medicinal herb] **1** : a perennial mint with aromatic leaves used in flavoring; *also* : its leaves **2** : SAGEBRUSH **3** : a light grayish green

sage·brush \'sāj-₁brəsh\ *n* : any of several low shrubby No. American composite plants; *esp* : one of the western U.S. with a sagelike odor

Sag·it·tar·i·us \₁sa-jə-'ter-ē-əs\ *n* [L, lit., archer] **1** : a zodiacal constellation between Scorpio and Capricorn usu. pictured as a centaur **2** : the 9th sign of the zodiac in astrology; *also* : one born under this sign

sa·go \'sā-gō\ *n, pl* **sagos** : a dry granulated starch esp. from the pith of various tropical palms (**sago palm**)

sa·gua·ro \sə-'wär-ə, -'gwär-, -ō\ *n, pl* **-ros** [MexSp] : a tall columnar usu. sparsely-branched cactus of dry areas of the southwestern U.S. and Mexico that may attain a height of up to 50 feet (16 meters)

said *past and past part of* SAY

¹**sail** \'sāl\ *n* **1** : a piece of fabric by means of which the wind is used to propel a ship **2** : a sailing ship **3** : something resembling a sail **4** : a trip on a sailboat

²**sail** *vb* **1** : to travel on a sailing ship **2** : to

sail·board \'sāl-ˌbȯrd\ n : a modified surfboard having a mast and sailed by a standing person

sail·boat \-ˌbōt\ n : a boat propelled primarily by sail

sail·cloth \-ˌklȯth\ n : a heavy canvas used for sails, tents, or upholstery

sail·fish \-ˌfish\ n : any of a genus of large marine bony fishes with a large dorsal fin that are related to marlins

sail·ing n : the sport of handling or riding in a sailboat

sail·or \'sā-lər\ n : one that sails; esp : a member of a ship's crew

sail·plane \'sāl-ˌplān\ n : a glider designed to rise in an upward air current

saint \'sānt, before a name (ˌ)sānt or sənt\ n 1 : one officially recognized as preeminent for holiness 2 : one of the spirits of the departed in heaven 3 : a holy or godly person — **saint·ed** \-'sān-təd\ adj — **saint·hood** \-ˌhu̇d\ n

Saint Ber·nard \-bər-'närd\ n : any of a Swiss alpine breed of tall powerful working dogs used esp. formerly in aiding lost travelers

Saint–John's–wort \'sānt-'jänz-ˌwərt, -ˌwȯrt\ n 1 : any of a genus of herbs and shrubs with showy yellow flowers 2 : the dried aerial parts of a Saint-John's-wort used esp. in herbal remedies

saint·ly \'sānt-lē\ adj : relating to, resembling, or befitting a saint ⟨~ zeal⟩ — **saint·li·ness** \-lē-nəs\ n

Saint Val·en·tine's Day \-'va-lən-ˌtīnz-\ n : VALENTINE'S DAY

¹**sake** \'sāk\ n 1 : END, PURPOSE 2 : personal or social welfare, safety, or well-being

²**sa·ke** or **sa·ki** \'sä-kē\ n : a Japanese alcoholic beverage of fermented rice

sa·laam \sə-'läm\ n [Ar salām, lit., peace] 1 : a salutation or ceremonial greeting in the East 2 : an obeisance performed by bowing very low and placing the right palm on the forehead — **salaam** vb

sa·la·cious \sə-'lā-shəs\ adj 1 : arousing sexual desire or imagination 2 : LUSTFUL — **sa·la·cious·ly** adv — **sa·la·cious·ness** n

sal·ad \'sa-ləd\ n : a cold dish (as of lettuce, vegetables, fish, eggs, or fruit) served with dressing

sal·a·man·der \'sa-lə-ˌman-dər\ n : any of numerous amphibians that look like lizards but have scaleless usu. smooth moist skin

sa·la·mi \sə-'lä-mē\ n [It] : a highly seasoned sausage of pork and beef

sal·a·ry \'sa-lə-rē\ n, pl **-ries** [ME salarie, fr. AF, fr. L salarium pension, salary, fr. neut. of salarius of salt, fr. sal salt] : payment made at regular intervals for services

sale \'sāl\ n 1 : transfer of ownership of property from one person to another in return for money 2 : ready market : DEMAND 3 : AUCTION 4 : a selling of goods at bargain prices — **sal·able** or **sale·able** \'sā-lə-bəl\ adj

sales·girl \'sālz-ˌgərl\ n : SALESWOMAN

sales·man \-mən\ n : a person who sells in a store or to outside customers — **sales·man·ship** n

sales·per·son \-ˌpər-sən\ n : a salesman or saleswoman

sales·wom·an \-ˌwu̇-mən\ n : a woman who sells merchandise

sal·i·cyl·ic acid \ˌsa-lə-'si-lik-\ n : a crystalline organic acid used in making aspirin and other medicinal preparations (as skin lotions)

¹**sa·lient** \'sāl-yənt, 'sā-lē-ənt\ adj : jutting forward beyond a line; also : PROMINENT ⟨a ~ feature⟩ ♦ **Synonyms** CONSPICUOUS, STRIKING, NOTICEABLE

²**salient** n : a projecting part in a line of defense

¹**sa·line** \'sā-ˌlēn, -ˌlīn\ adj : consisting of or containing salt : SALTY — **sa·lin·i·ty** \sā-'li-nə-tē, sə-\ n

²**saline** n 1 : a metallic salt esp. with a purgative action 2 : a saline solution

sa·li·va \sə-'lī-və\ n : a liquid secreted into the mouth that helps digestion — **sal·i·vary** \'sa-lə-ˌver-ē\ adj

sal·i·vate \'sa-lə-ˌvāt\ vb **-vat·ed; -vat·ing** : to produce saliva esp. in excess — **sal·i·va·tion** \ˌsa-lə-'vā-shən\ n

sal·low \'sa-lō\ adj : of a yellowish sickly color ⟨a ~ face⟩

sal·ly \'sa-lē\ n, pl **sallies** 1 : a rushing attack on besiegers by troops of a besieged place 2 : a witty remark or retort 3 : a brief excursion — **sally** vb

salm·on \'sa-mən\ n, pl **salmon** also **salmons** 1 : any of several bony fishes with pinkish flesh that are used for food and are related to the trouts 2 : a strong yellowish pink color

sal·mo·nel·la \ˌsal-mə-'ne-lə\ n, pl **-nel·lae** \-'ne-(ˌ)lē, -ˌlī\ or **-nellas** or **-nella** : any of a genus of rod-shaped bacteria that cause various illnesses (as food poisoning)

sa·lon \sə-'län, 'sa-ˌlän, sa-'lōⁿ\ n [F] : an elegant drawing room; also : a fashionable shop ⟨beauty ~⟩

sa·loon \sə-'lün\ n 1 : a large public cabin on a ship 2 : a place where liquors are sold and drunk : BARROOM 3 Brit : SEDAN 2

sal·sa \'sȯl-sə, 'säl-\ n : a spicy sauce of tomatoes, onions, and hot peppers

¹**salt** \'sȯlt\ n 1 : a white crystalline substance that consists of sodium and chlorine and is used in seasoning foods 2 : a saltlike cathartic substance (as Epsom salts) 3 : a compound formed usu. by action of an acid on metal 4 : SAILOR — **salt·i·ness** \'sȯl-tē-nəs\ n — **salty** \'sȯl-tē\ adj

²**salt** vb : to preserve, season, or feed with salt

³**salt** adj : preserved or treated with salt ⟨~ pork⟩; also : SALTY

SALT abbr Strategic Arms Limitation Talks

salt away vb : to lay away safely : SAVE

salt·box \'sȯlt-ˌbäks\ n : a frame dwelling

with two stories in front and one behind and a long sloping roof

salt·cel·lar \-ˌse-lər\ n : a small container for holding salt at the table

sal·tine \sȯl-ˈtēn\ n : a thin crisp cracker sprinkled with salt

salt lick n : LICK 5

salt·pe·ter \ˈsȯlt-ˈpē-tər\ n [ME salt petre, alter. of salpetre, fr. ML sal petrae, lit., salt of the rock] 1 : POTASSIUM NITRATE 2 : SODIUM NITRATE

salt·wa·ter \-ˌwȯ-tər, -ˌwä-\ adj : of, relating to, or living in salt water

sa·lu·bri·ous \sə-ˈlü-brē-əs\ adj : favorable to health ⟨a ∼ climate⟩

sal·u·tary \ˈsal-yə-ˌter-ē\ adj : healthgiving; also : BENEFICIAL ⟨∼ effects⟩

sal·u·ta·tion \ˌsal-yə-ˈtā-shən\ n : an expression of greeting, goodwill, or courtesy usu. by word or gesture

sa·lu·ta·to·ri·an \sə-ˌlü-tə-ˈtȯr-ē-ən\ n : the student having the 2d highest rank in a graduating class who delivers the salutatory address

sa·lu·ta·to·ry \sə-ˈlü-tə-ˌtȯr-ē\ adj : relating to or being the welcoming oration delivered at an academic commencement

¹**sa·lute** \sə-ˈlüt\ vb **sa·lut·ed; sa·lut·ing** 1 : GREET 2 : to honor by special ceremonies 3 : to show respect to (a superior officer) by a formal position of hand, rifle, or sword

²**salute** n 1 : GREETING 2 : the formal position assumed in saluting a superior

¹**sal·vage** \ˈsal-vij\ n 1 : money paid for saving a ship, its cargo, or passengers when the ship is wrecked or in danger 2 : the saving of a ship 3 : the saving of possessions in danger of being lost 4 : things saved from loss or destruction (as by a wreck or fire)

²**salvage** vb **sal·vaged; sal·vag·ing** : to rescue from destruction

sal·va·tion \sal-ˈvā-shən\ n 1 : the saving of a person from sin or its consequences esp. in the life after death 2 : the saving from danger, difficulty, or evil 3 : something that saves ⟨tourism has been the island's ∼⟩

¹**salve** \ˈsav, ˈsäv\ n 1 : a medicinal substance applied to the skin 2 : a soothing influence

²**salve** vb **salved; salv·ing** : EASE, SOOTHE

sal·ver \ˈsal-vər\ n [F salve, fr. Sp salva sampling of food to detect poison, tray, fr. salvar to save, sample food to detect poison, fr. LL salvare to save, fr. L salvus safe] : a small serving tray

sal·vo \ˈsal-vō\ n, pl **salvos** or **salvoes** : a simultaneous discharge of guns

Sam or **Saml** abbr Samuel

SAM \ˈsam, ˌes-ˌā-ˈem\ n [surface-to-air missile] : a guided missile for use against aircraft by ground units

Sa·mar·i·tan \sə-ˈmer-ə-tən\ n 1 : a native or inhabitant of Samaria 2 : a person who is generous in helping those in distress

sa·mar·i·um \sə-ˈmer-ē-əm\ n : a silvery-white lustrous rare metallic chemical element

¹**same** \ˈsām\ adj 1 : being the one referred to : not different 2 : SIMILAR — **same·ness** n

²**same** pron : the same one or ones

³**same** adv : in the same manner

Sa·mi also **Saa·mi** \ˈsä-mē\ n, pl **Sami** or **Samis** also **Saami** or **Saamis** : a member of a people of northern Scandinavia, Finland, and the Kola Peninsula of Russia

Sa·mo·an \sə-ˈmō-ən\ n : a native or inhabitant of Samoa — **Samoan** adj

sa·mo·sa \sə-ˈmō-sə\ n : a small triangular pastry filled with spiced meat or vegetables and fried

sam·o·var \ˈsa-mə-ˌvär\ n [Russ, fr. samo-self + varit' to boil] : an urn with a spigot at the base used esp. in Russia to boil water for tea

sam·pan \ˈsam-ˌpan\ n : a flat-bottomed skiff of eastern Asia usu. propelled by two short oars

¹**sam·ple** \ˈsam-pəl\ n : a representative piece, item, or set of individuals that shows the quality or nature of the whole from which it was taken : EXAMPLE, SPECIMEN

²**sample** vb **sam·pled; sam·pling** : to judge the quality of by a sample

sam·pler \ˈsam-plər\ n 1 : a piece of needlework; esp : one testing skill in embroidering 2 : a collection of various examples of something ⟨a chocolate ∼⟩

Sam·u·el \ˈsam-yə-wəl\ n — see BIBLE table

sam·u·rai \ˈsa-mə-ˌrī, ˈsam-yə-\ n, pl **samurai** : a military retainer of a Japanese feudal lord who adhered to strict principles of honor and duty

san·a·to·ri·um \ˌsa-nə-ˈtȯr-ē-əm\ n, pl **-ri·ums** or **-ria** \-ē-ə\ 1 : a health resort 2 : an establishment for the care esp. of convalescents or the chronically ill

sanc·ti·fy \ˈsaŋk-tə-ˌfī\ vb **-fied; -fy·ing** 1 : to make holy : CONSECRATE 2 : to free from sin — **sanc·ti·fi·ca·tion** \ˌsaŋk-tə-fə-ˈkā-shən\ n

sanc·ti·mo·nious \ˌsaŋk-tə-ˈmō-nē-əs\ adj : hypocritically pious ⟨∼ politicians⟩ — **sanc·ti·mo·nious·ly** adv

¹**sanc·tion** \ˈsaŋk-shən\ n 1 : authoritative approval 2 : a measure (as a threat or fine) designed to enforce a law or standard ⟨economic ∼s⟩

²**sanction** vb : to give approval to : RATIFY

♦ **Synonyms** ENDORSE, ACCREDIT, CERTIFY, APPROVE

sanc·ti·ty \ˈsaŋk-tə-tē\ n, pl **-ties** 1 : GODLINESS 2 : SACREDNESS

sanc·tu·ary \ˈsaŋk-chə-ˌwer-ē\ n, pl **-aries** 1 : a consecrated place (as the part of a church in which the altar is placed) 2 : a place of refuge ⟨bird ∼⟩

sanc·tum \ˈsaŋk-təm\ n, pl **sanctums** also **sanc·ta** \-tə\ : a private office or study : DEN ⟨an editor's ∼⟩

¹**sand** \ˈsand\ n : loose particles of hard broken rock — **sandy** adj

²**sand** vb 1 : to cover or fill with sand 2 : to scour, smooth, or polish with an abrasive (as sandpaper) — **sand·er** n

san·dal \ˈsan-dᵊl\ n : a shoe consisting of

a sole strapped to the foot; *also* : a low or open slipper or rubber overshoe

san·dal·wood \-ˌwu̇d\ *n* : the fragrant yellowish heartwood of a parasitic tree of southern Asia that is much used in ornamental carving and cabinetwork; *also* : the tree

sand·bag \'sand-ˌbag\ *n* : a bag filled with sand and used in fortifications, as ballast, or as a weapon

sand·bank \-ˌbaŋk\ *n* : a deposit of sand (as in a bar or shoal)

sand·bar \-ˌbär\ *n* : a ridge of sand formed in water by tides or currents

sand·blast \-ˌblast\ *vb* : to treat with a stream of sand blown (as for cleaning stone) by compressed air — **sand·blast·er** *n*

sand dollar *n* : any of numerous flat circular sea urchins living chiefly on sandy bottoms in shallow water

S & H *abbr* shipping and handling

sand·hog \'sand-ˌhȯg, -ˌhäg\ *n* : a laborer who builds underwater tunnels

sand·lot \-ˌlät\ *n* : a vacant lot esp. when used for the unorganized sports of children — **sand·lot** *adj* — **sand·lot·ter** *n*

sand·man \-ˌman\ *n* : the genie of folklore who makes children sleepy

sand·pa·per \-ˌpā-pər\ *n* : paper with abrasive (as sand) glued on one side used in smoothing and polishing surfaces — **sandpaper** *vb*

sand·pip·er \-ˌpī-pər\ *n* : any of various shorebirds with a soft-tipped bill longer than that of the related plovers

sand·stone \-ˌstōn\ *n* : rock made of sand united by a natural cement

sand·storm \-ˌstȯrm\ *n* : a windstorm that drives clouds of sand

sand trap *n* : a hazard on a golf course consisting of a hollow containing sand

¹sand·wich \'sand-(ˌ)wich\ *n* [after John Montagu, 4th Earl of *Sandwich* †1792 Eng. diplomat] 1 : two or more slices of bread with a layer (as of meat or cheese) spread between them 2 : something resembling a sandwich

²sandwich *vb* : to squeeze or crowd in

sane \'sān\ *adj* **san·er; san·est** : mentally sound and healthy; *also* : SENSIBLE, RATIONAL — **sane·ly** *adv*

sang *past of* SING

sang·froid \sä⁻'frwä\ *n* [F *sang-froid*, lit., cold blood] : self-possession or an imperturbable state esp. under strain

san·gui·nary \'saŋ-gwə-ˌner-ē\ *adj* : BLOODY ⟨∼ battle⟩

san·guine \'saŋ-gwən\ *adj* 1 : RUDDY 2 : CHEERFUL, HOPEFUL ⟨a ∼ disposition⟩

sanit *abbr* sanitary; sanitation

san·i·tar·i·an \ˌsa-nə-'ter-ē-ən\ *n* : a specialist in sanitation and public health

san·i·tar·i·um \ˌsa-nə-'ter-ē-əm\ *n, pl* -**i·ums** *or* -**ia** \-ē-ə\ : SANATORIUM

san·i·tary \'sa-nə-ˌter-ē\ *adj* 1 : of or relating to health : HYGIENIC 2 : free from filth or infective matter

sanitary napkin *n* : a disposable absorbent pad used to absorb uterine flow (as during menstruation)

san·i·ta·tion \ˌsa-nə-'tā-shən\ *n* : the act

or process of making sanitary; *also* : protection of health by maintenance of sanitary conditions

san·i·tize \'sa-nə-ˌtīz\ *vb* -**tized; -tiz·ing** 1 : to make sanitary 2 : to make more acceptable by removing unpleasant features

san·i·ty \'sa-nə-tē\ *n* : soundness of mind

sank *past of* SINK

sans \'sanz\ *prep* : WITHOUT

San·skrit \'san-ˌskrit\ *n* : an ancient language that is the classical language of India and of Hinduism — **Sanskrit** *adj*

San·ta Ana \ˌsan-tə-'a-nə\ *n* [*Santa Ana Mountains* in southern Calif.] : a hot dry wind from the north, northeast, or east in southern California

san·tims \'sän-ˌtims\ *n, pl* **san·ti·mi** \-ti-ˌmē\ : a monetary unit equal to ¹⁄₁₀₀ lats formerly used in Latvia

¹sap \'sap\ *n* 1 : a vital fluid; *esp* : a watery fluid that circulates through a vascular plant 2 : a foolish gullible person — **sap·less** *adj*

²sap *vb* **sapped; sap·ping** 1 : UNDERMINE 2 : to weaken gradually

sap·id \'sa-pəd\ *adj* : FLAVORFUL

sa·pi·ent \'sa-pē-ənt, 'sa-\ *adj* : WISE, DISCERNING — **sa·pi·ence** \-əns\ *n*

sap·ling \'sa-pliŋ\ *n* : a young tree

sap·phire \'sa-ˌfī(-ə)r\ *n* : a hard transparent usu. rich blue gem

sap·py \'sa-pē\ *adj* **sap·pi·er; -est** 1 : full of sap 2 : overly sentimental ⟨a ∼ movie⟩ 3 : SILLY, FOOLISH

sap·ro·phyte \'sa-prə-ˌfīt\ *n* : a living thing and esp. a plant living on dead or decaying organic matter — **sap·ro·phyt·ic** \ˌsa-prə-'fi-tik\ *adj*

sap·suck·er \'sap-ˌsə-kər\ *n* : any of a genus of No. American woodpeckers

sap·wood \-ˌwu̇d\ *n* : the younger active and usu. lighter and softer outer layer of wood (as of a tree trunk)

sar·casm \'sär-ˌka-zəm\ *n* 1 : a cutting or contemptuous remark 2 : ironic criticism or reproach — **sar·cas·tic** \sär-'kas-tik\ *adj* — **sar·cas·ti·cal·ly** \-ti-k(ə-)lē\ *adv*

sar·co·ma \sär-'kō-mə\ *n, pl* -**mas** *also* -**ma·ta** \-mə-tə\ : a malignant tumor esp. of connective tissue, bone, cartilage, or striated muscle

sar·coph·a·gus \sär-'kä-fə-gəs\ *n, pl* -**gi** \-ˌgī, -ˌjī\ *also* -**gus·es** [L *sarcophagus* (*lapis*) limestone used for coffins, fr. Gk (*lithos*) *sarkophagos*, lit., flesh-eating stone, fr. *sark-, sarx* flesh + *phagein* to eat] : a large stone coffin

sar·dine \sär-'dēn\ *n, pl* **sardines** *also* **sardine** : a young or small fish preserved for use as food

sar·don·ic \sär-'dä-nik\ *adj* : disdainfully or skeptically humorous : derisively mocking ♦ **Synonyms** IRONIC, SATIRIC, SARCASTIC — **sar·don·i·cal·ly** \-ni-k(ə-)lē\ *adv*

sa·ri *also* **sa·ree** \'sär-ē\ *n* [Hindi *sāṛī*] : a garment worn by women in southern Asia that consists of a long cloth draped around the body and head or shoulder

sa·rin \'sär-ən, zä-'rēn\ *n* : an extremely

toxic chemical weapon used as a lethal nerve gas

sa·rong \sə-'rȯŋ, -'räŋ\ *n* : a loose garment wrapped around the body and worn by men and women of the Malay Archipelago and the Pacific islands

sar·sa·pa·ril·la \ˌsas-pə-'ri-lə, ˌsärs-\ *n* **1** : the dried roots of a tropical American smilax used esp. for flavoring; *also* : the plant **2** : a sweetened carbonated beverage flavored with sassafras and an oil from a birch

sar·to·ri·al \sär-'tȯr-ē-əl\ *adj* : of or relating to a tailor or tailored clothes — **sar·to·ri·al·ly** *adv*

SASE *abbr* self-addressed stamped envelope

¹sash \'sash\ *n* : a broad band worn around the waist or over the shoulder

²sash *n, pl* **sash** *also* **sash·es** : a frame for panes of glass in a door or window; *also* : the movable part of a window

sa·shay \sa-'shā\ *vb* **1** : WALK, GLIDE, GO **2** : to strut or move about in an ostentatious manner **3** : to proceed in a diagonal or sideways manner

Sask *abbr* Saskatchewan

Sas·quatch \'sas-ˌkwach, -ˌkwäch\ *n* [Halkomelem (American Indian language of British Columbia) *sésqəc*] : a large hairy humanlike creature reported to exist in the northwestern U.S. and western Canada

sas·sa·fras \'sa-sə-ˌfras\ *n* [Sp *sasafrás*] : an aromatic No. American tree related to the laurel; *also* : its carcinogenic dried root bark

sassy \'sa-sē\ *adj* **sass·i·er; -est** : SAUCY

¹sat *past and past part of* SIT

²sat *abbr* **1** satellite **2** saturated

Sat *abbr* Saturday

Sa·tan \'sā-t³n\ *n* : DEVIL

sa·tang \sə-'täŋ\ *n, pl* **satang** *or* **satangs** — see *baht* at MONEY table

sa·tan·ic \sə-'ta-nik, sā-\ *adj* **1** : of or characteristic of Satan **2** : extremely malicious or wicked — **sa·tan·i·cal·ly** \-ni-k(ə-)lē\ *adv*

satch·el \'sa-chəl\ *n* : SUITCASE

sate \'sāt\ *vb* **sat·ed; sat·ing** : to satisfy to the full; *also* : SURFEIT, GLUT

sa·teen \sa-'tēn, sə-\ *n* : a cotton cloth finished to resemble satin

sat·el·lite \'sa-tə-ˌlīt\ *n* [MF, fr. L *satelles* attendant] **1** : an obsequious follower of a distinguished person : TOADY **2** : a celestial body that orbits a larger body **3** : a manufactured object that orbits a celestial body

satellite dish *n* : a microwave dish for receiving usu. television transmissions from an orbiting satellite

sa·ti·ate \'sā-shē-ˌāt\ *vb* **-at·ed; -at·ing** : to satisfy fully or to excess

sa·ti·ety \sə-'tī-ə-tē\ *n* : fullness to the point of excess

sat·in \'sa-t³n\ *n* : a fabric (as of silk) with a glossy surface — **sat·iny** *adj*

sat·in·wood \'sa-t³n-ˌwu̇d\ *n* : a hard yellowish brown wood of satiny luster; *also* : a tree yielding this wood

sat·ire \'sa-ˌtī(-ə)r\ *n* : biting wit, irony, or sarcasm used to expose vice or folly; *also* : a literary work having these qualities — **sa·tir·ic** \sə-'tir-ik\ *or* **sa·tir·i·cal** \-i-kəl\ *adj* — **sa·tir·i·cal·ly** *adv* — **sat·i·rist** \'sa-tə-rist\ *n* — **sat·i·rize** \-ˌrīz\ *vb*

sat·is·fac·tion \ˌsa-təs-'fak-shən\ *n* **1** : payment through penance of punishment incurred by sin **2** : CONTENTMENT, GRATIFICATION **3** : reparation for an insult **4** : settlement of a claim

sat·is·fac·to·ry \-'fak-tə-rē\ *adj* : giving satisfaction : ADEQUATE — **sat·is·fac·to·ri·ly** \-'fak-tə-rə-lē\ *adv*

sat·is·fy \'sa-təs-ˌfī\ *vb* **-fied; -fy·ing** **1** : to answer or discharge (a claim) in full **2** : to make happy : GRATIFY **3** : to pay what is due to **4** : CONVINCE **5** : to meet the requirements of — **sat·is·fy·ing·ly** *adv*

sa·trap \'sā-ˌtrap, 'sa-\ *n* [ME, fr. L *satrapes*, fr. Gk *satrapēs*, fr. OPers *khshathrapāvan*, lit., protector of the dominion] : a petty prince : a subordinate ruler

sat·u·rate \'sa-chə-ˌrāt\ *vb* **-rat·ed; -rat·ing** **1** : to soak thoroughly **2** : to treat or charge with something to the point where no more can be absorbed, dissolved, or retained — **sat·u·ra·ble** \'sa-chə-rə-bəl\ *adj* — **sat·u·ra·tion** \ˌsa-chə-'rā-shən\ *n*

saturated *adj* **1** : full of moisture **2** : having no double or triple bonds between carbon atoms ⟨~ fats⟩

Sat·ur·day \'sa-tər-dē, -ˌdā\ *n* : the 7th day of the week

Saturday night special *n* : a cheap easily concealed handgun

Sat·urn \'sa-tərn\ *n* : the planet 6th in order from the sun

sat·ur·nine \'sa-tər-ˌnīn\ *adj* : SULLEN, SARDONIC

sa·tyr \'sā-tər\ *n* **1** *often cap* : a woodland deity in Greek mythology having certain characteristics of a horse or goat **2** : a lecherous man

¹sauce \'sȯs, *3 usu* 'sas\ *n* **1** : a fluid dressing or topping for food **2** : stewed fruit **3** : IMPUDENCE

²sauce \'sȯs, *2 usu* 'sas\ *vb* **sauced; sauc·ing** **1** : to put sauce on; *also* : to add zest to **2** : to be impudent to

sauce·pan \'sȯs-ˌpan\ *n* : a small deep cooking pan with a handle

sau·cer \'sȯ-sər\ *n* : a rounded shallow dish for use under a cup

saucy \'sa-sē, 'sȯ-\ *adj* **sauc·i·er; -est** : IMPUDENT, PERT — **sauc·i·ly** \-sə-lē\ *adv* — **sauc·i·ness** \-sē-nəs\ *n*

Sau·di \'sau̇-dē, 'sȯ-, sä-'ü-dē\ *n* : SAUDI ARABIAN — **Saudi** *adj*

Saudi Arabian *n* : a native or inhabitant of Saudi Arabia — **Saudi Arabian** *adj*

sau·er·kraut \'saù(-ə)r-ˌkraù t\ *n* [G, fr. *sauer* sour + *Kraut* greens] : finely cut cabbage fermented in brine

Sauk \'sȯk\ *or* **Sac** \'sȯk, 'sȯk\ *n, pl* **Sauk** *or* **Sauks** *or* **Sac** *or* **Sacs** : a member of an American Indian people formerly living in what is now Wisconsin

sau·na \'sȯ-nə, 'saù-nə\ *n* **1** : a Finnish steam bath in which the steam is provided by water thrown on hot stones **2** : a dry heat bath; *also* : a room or cabinet used for such a bath

saun·ter \'sȯn-tər, 'sän-\ *vb* : STROLL

sau·ro·pod \'sȯr-ə-ˌpäd\ *n* : any of a suborder of plant-eating dinosaurs (as a brontosaurus) with a long neck and tail and a small head — **sauropod** *adj*

sau·sage \'sȯ-sij\ *n* [ME *sausige*, fr. AF *sauseche*, fr. LL *salsicia*, fr. L *salsus* salted] : minced and highly seasoned meat (as pork) usu. enclosed in a tubular casing

S Aust *abbr* South Australia

sau·té \sȯ-'tā, sō-\ *vb* **sau·téed** *or* **sau·téd; sau·té·ing** [F] : to fry lightly in a little fat — **sauté** *n*

sau·terne \sō-'tərn, sȯ-\ *n, often cap* : a usu. semisweet American white wine

¹**sav·age** \'sa-vij\ *adj* [ME, fr. AF *salvage, savage*, fr. LL *salvaticus*, alter. of L *silvaticus* of the woods, wild, fr. *silva* forest] **1** : WILD, UNTAMED **2** : UNCIVILIZED, BARBAROUS **3** : CRUEL, FIERCE — **sav·age·ly** *adv* — **sav·age·ness** *n* — **sav·age·ry** \-rē\ *n*

²**savage** *n* **1** : a member of a primitive human society **2** : a rude, unmannerly, or brutal person

sa·van·na *or* **sa·van·nah** \sə-'va-nə\ *n* [Sp *zavana*] : grassland containing scattered trees

sa·vant \sa-'vänt, sə-, 'sa-vənt\ *n* : a learned person : SCHOLAR

¹**save** \'sāv\ *vb* **saved; sav·ing 1** : to redeem from sin **2** : to rescue from danger **3** : to preserve or guard from destruction or loss; *also* : to store (data) in a computer or on a storage device **4** : to put aside as a store or reserve — **sav·er** *n*

²**save** *n* : a play that prevents an opponent from scoring or winning

³**save** *prep* : EXCEPT

⁴**save** *conj* : BUT

savings and loan association *n* : a cooperative association that holds savings of members in the form of dividend-bearing shares and that invests chiefly in mortgage loans

savings bank *n* : a bank that holds funds of individual depositors in interest-bearing accounts and makes long-term investments (as mortgage loans)

savings bond *n* : a registered U.S. bond issued in denominations of $50 to $10,000

sav·ior *or* **sav·iour** \'sāv-yər\ *n* **1** : one who saves **2** *cap* : Jesus Christ

sa·voir faire \ˌsav-ˌwär-'fer\ *n* [F *savoir-faire*, lit., knowing how to do] : sureness in social behavior

¹**sa·vor** *also* **sa·vour** \'sā-vər\ *n* **1** : the taste and odor of something **2** : a special flavor or quality — **sa·vory** *adj*

²**savor** *also* **savour** *vb* **1** : to have a specified taste, smell, or quality **2** : to taste with pleasure ⟨~*ed* every morsel⟩

sa·vo·ry \'sā-və-rē\ *n, pl* **-ries** : either of two aromatic mints used in cooking

¹**sav·vy** \'sa-vē\ *vb* **sav·vied; sav·vy·ing** : UNDERSTAND, COMPREHEND

²**savvy** *n* : practical know-how ⟨political ~⟩ — **savvy** *adj*

¹**saw** *past of* SEE

²**saw** \'sȯ\ *n* : a cutting tool with a blade having a line of teeth along its edge

³**saw** *vb* **sawed** \'sȯd\; **sawed** *or* **sawn** \'sȯn\; **saw·ing** : to cut or shape with or as if with a saw

⁴**saw** *n* : a common saying : MAXIM

saw·dust \'sȯ-(ˌ)dəst\ *n* : fine particles made by a saw in cutting

saw·fly \-ˌflī\ *n* : any of numerous insects belonging to the same order as bees and wasps and including many whose larvae are plant-feeding pests

saw·horse \-ˌhȯrs\ *n* : a rack on which wood is rested while being sawed by hand

saw·mill \-ˌmil\ *n* : a mill for sawing logs

saw palmetto *n* **1** : any of several shrubby palms with spiny-toothed petioles **2** : the fruit of a saw palmetto used esp. in herbal remedies

saw·yer \'sȯ-yər\ *n* : a person who saws timber

sax \'saks\ *n* : SAXOPHONE

sax·i·frage \'sak-sə-frij, -ˌfrāj\ *n* [ME, fr. AF, fr. LL *saxifraga*, fr. L, fem. of *saxifragus*, breaking rocks] : any of a genus of plants with showy flowers and usu. with leaves growing in tufts close to the ground

sax·o·phone \'sak-sə-ˌfōn\ *n* : a musical instrument having a conical metal tube with a reed mouthpiece and finger keys — **sax·o·phon·ist** \-ˌfō-nist\ *n*

¹**say** \'sā\ *vb* **said** \'sed\; **say·ing; says** \'sez\ **1** : to express in words ⟨~ what you mean⟩ **2** : to state as opinion or belief **3** : PRONOUNCE; *also* : RECITE, REPEAT ⟨~ your prayers⟩ **4** : INDICATE ⟨the clock ~s noon⟩

²**say** *n, pl* **says** \'sāz\ **1** : an expression of opinion **2** : power of decision

say·ing *n* : a commonly repeated statement

say-so \'sā-(ˌ)sō\ *n* : an esp. authoritative assertion or decision; *also* : the right to decide ⟨he has the ~ on this matter⟩

sb *abbr* substantive

Sb *symbol* [L *stibium*] antimony

SB *abbr* [NL *scientiae baccalaureus*] bachelor of science

SBA *abbr* Small Business Administration

sc *abbr* **1** scene **2** science

Sc *symbol* scandium

SC *abbr* **1** South Carolina **2** supreme court

¹**scab** \'skab\ *n* **1** : scabies of domestic animals **2** : a crust of hardened blood forming over a wound **3** : a worker who replaces a striker or works under conditions not authorized by a union **4** : any of various bacterial or fungus plant diseases marked by crusted spots on stems or leaves — **scab·by** *adj*

²**scab** *vb* **scabbed; scab·bing 1** : to become covered with a scab **2** : to work as a scab

scab·bard \'ska-bərd\ *n* : a sheath for the blade of a weapon (as a sword)

sca·bies \'skā-bēz\ *n* [L] : contagious itch or mange caused by mites living as parasites under the skin

sca·brous \'ska-brəs, 'skā-\ *adj* **1** : DIFFICULT, KNOTTY **2** : rough to the touch

: SCALY, SCURFY ⟨a ~ leaf⟩ 3 : dealing with suggestive, indecent, or scandalous themes ⟨~ lyrics⟩; *also* : SQUALID

scad \\'skad\\ *n* : a large number or quantity — usu. used in pl.

scaf·fold \\'ska-fəld, -ˌfōld\\ *n* 1 : a raised platform for workers to sit or stand on 2 : a platform on which a criminal is executed (as by hanging)

scaf·fold·ing *n* : a system of scaffolds; *also* : materials for scaffolds

scal·a·wag *or* **scal·ly·wag** \\'ska-li-ˌwag\\ *n* : RASCAL

¹**scald** \\'skȯld\\ *vb* 1 : to burn with or as if with hot liquid or steam 2 : to heat to just below the boiling point

²**scald** *n* : a burn caused by scalding

¹**scale** \\'skāl\\ *n* 1 : either pan of a balance 2 : BALANCE — usu. used in pl. 3 : a weighing instrument

²**scale** *vb* **scaled; scal·ing** : WEIGH

³**scale** *n* 1 : one of the small thin plates that cover the body esp. of a fish or reptile 2 : a thin plate or flake 3 : a thin coating, layer, or incrustation 4 : SCALE INSECT — **scaled** \\'skāld\\ *adj* — **scale·less** \\'skāl-ləs\\ *adj* — **scaly** *adj*

⁴**scale** *vb* **scaled; scal·ing** : to strip of scales

⁵**scale** *n* [ME, fr. LL *scala* ladder, staircase, fr. L *scalae*, pl., stairs, rungs, ladder] 1 : something divided into regular spaces as a help in drawing or measuring 2 : a graduated series 3 : the size of a sample (as a model) in proportion to the size of the actual thing 4 : a standard of estimation or judgment 5 : a series of musical tones going up or down in pitch according to a specified scheme

⁶**scale** *vb* **scaled; scal·ing** 1 : to climb by or as if by a ladder 2 : to arrange in a graded series

scale insect *n* : any of numerous small insects with wingless scale-covered females that are related to aphids and feed on and are often pests of plants

scale·pan \\'skāl-ˌpan\\ *n* : ¹SCALE 1

scal·lion \\'skal-yən\\ *n* [ultim. fr. L *ascalonia (caepa)* onion of Ascalon (seaport in Palestine)] : an onion without an enlarged bulb; *also* : GREEN ONION

¹**scal·lop** \\'skä-ləp, 'ska-\\ *n* 1 : any of numerous marine bivalve mollusks with radially ridged shells; *also* : a large edible muscle of this mollusk 2 : one of a continuous series of rounded projections forming an edge

²**scallop** *vb* 1 : to bake in a casserole ⟨~ed potatoes⟩ 2 : to shape, cut, or finish in scallops ⟨~ed edges⟩

¹**scalp** \\'skalp\\ *n* : the part of the skin and flesh of the head usu. covered with hair

²**scalp** *vb* 1 : to remove the scalp from 2 : to resell at greatly increased prices ⟨~ tickets⟩ — **scalp·er** *n*

scal·pel \\'skal-pəl\\ *n* : a small straight knife with a thin blade used esp. in surgery

scam \\'skam\\ *n* : a fraudulent or deceptive act or operation

scamp \\'skamp\\ *n* : RASCAL

scam·per \\'skam-pər\\ *vb* : to run nimbly and playfully — **scamper** *n*

scam·pi \\'skam-pē\\ *n, pl* **scampi** [It] : a usu. large shrimp; *also* : large shrimp prepared with a garlic-flavored sauce

¹**scan** \\'skan\\ *vb* **scanned; scan·ning** 1 : to read (verses) so as to show metrical structure 2 : to examine closely 3 : to input or examine systematically in order to obtain data esp. for display or storage 4 : to make a scan of (as the human body) — **scan·ner** *n*

²**scan** *n* 1 : the act or process of scanning 2 : a picture of the distribution of radioactive material in something; *also* : an image of a bodily part produced (as by computer) by combining radiographic data obtained from several angles or sections

Scand *abbr* Scandinavia

scan·dal \\'skan-dᵊl\\ *n* [ME, fr. LL *scandalum* stumbling block, offense, fr. Gk *skandalon*] 1 : DISGRACE, DISHONOR 2 : malicious gossip : SLANDER — **scan·dal·ize** *vb* — **scan·dal·ous** *adj* — **scan·dal·ous·ly** *adv*

scan·dal·mon·ger \\-ˌmən-gər, -ˌmän-\\ *n* : a person who circulates scandal

Scan·di·na·vian \\ˌskan-də-'nā-vē-ən\\ *n* : a native or inhabitant of Scandinavia — **Scandinavian** *adj*

scan·di·um \\'skan-dē-əm\\ *n* : a silvery-white metallic chemical element

scan·ner \\'ska-nər\\ *n* 1 : a radio receiver that sequentially scans a range of frequencies for a signal 2 : a device that scans an image or document esp. for use or storage on a computer

¹**scant** \\'skant\\ *adj* 1 : barely sufficient ⟨food is in ~ supply⟩ 2 : having scarcely enough ♦ *Synonyms* SCANTY, SKIMPY, MEAGER, SPARSE, EXIGUOUS

²**scant** *vb* 1 : SKIMP 2 : STINT

scant·ling \\'skant-liŋ\\ *n* : a small piece of lumber (as an upright in a house)

scanty \\'skan-tē\\ *adj* **scant·i·er; -est** : barely sufficient : SCANT ⟨wore ~ outfits⟩ — **scant·i·ly** \\'skan-tə-lē\\ *adv* — **scant·i·ness** \\-tē-nəs\\ *n*

scape·goat \\'skāp-ˌgōt\\ *n* : one that bears the blame for others

scape·grace \\-ˌgrās\\ *n* [*scape* (escape)] : an incorrigible rascal

scap·u·la \\'ska-pyə-lə\\ *n, pl* **-lae** \\-ˌlē\\ *or* **-las** [L] : SHOULDER BLADE

scap·u·lar \\-lər\\ *n* : a pair of small cloth squares worn on the breast and back under the clothing esp. for religious purposes

scar \\'skär\\ *n* : a mark left after injured tissue has healed — **scar** *vb*

scar·ab \\'ska-rəb\\ *n* [MF *scarabee*, fr. L *scarabaeus*] : any of a family of large stout beetles; *also* : an ornament (as a gem) representing such a beetle

scarce \\'skers\\ *adj* **scarc·er; scarc·est** 1 : deficient in quantity or number : not plentiful 2 : intentionally absent ⟨made himself ~ at inspection time⟩ — **scar·ci·ty** \\'sker-sə-tē\\ *n*

scarce·ly \\-lē\\ *adv* 1 : BARELY ⟨can ~

see them⟩ **2** : almost not **3** : very probably not

¹**scare** \'sker\ *vb* **scared; scar·ing** : FRIGHTEN, STARTLE

²**scare** *n* : FRIGHT — **scary** *adj*

scare·crow \'sker-ˌkrō\ *n* : a crude figure set up to scare birds away from crops

¹**scarf** \'skärf\ *n, pl* **scarves** \'skärvz\ *or* **scarfs** **1** : a broad band (as of cloth) worn about the shoulders, around the neck, over the head, or about the waist **2** : a long narrow cloth cover for a table or dresser top

²**scarf** *vb* [alter. of earlier *scoff* eat greedily] : to eat greedily ⟨*~ed* down his lunch⟩

scar·i·fy \'skar-ə-ˌfī\ *vb* **-fied; -fy·ing** **1** : to make scratches or small cuts in ⟨*~* skin for vaccination⟩ ⟨*~* seeds to help them germinate⟩ **2** : to lacerate the feelings of **3** : to break up and loosen the surface of (as a road) — **scar·i·fi·ca·tion** \ˌskar-ə-fə-'kā-shən\ *n*

scar·let \'skär-lət\ *n* : a bright red color — **scarlet** *adj*

scarlet fever *n* : an acute contagious disease marked by fever, sore throat, and red rash and caused by certain streptococci

scarp \'skärp\ *n* : a line of cliffs produced by faulting or erosion

scath·ing \'skā-thiŋ\ *adj* : bitterly severe ⟨a *~* condemnation⟩

scat·o·log·i·cal \ˌska-tə-'lä-ji-kəl\ *adj* : concerned with obscene matters

scat·ter \'ska-tər\ *vb* **1** : to distribute or strew about irregularly **2** : DISPERSE

scat·ter·brain \'ska-tər-ˌbrān\ *n* : a silly careless person — **scat·ter·brained** \-ˌbrānd\ *adj*

scav·enge \'ska-vənj\ *vb* **scav·enged; scav·eng·ing** : to work or function as a scavenger

scav·en·ger \'ska-vən-jər\ *n* [alter. of earlier *scavager,* fr. AF *scawageour* collector of scavage (duty imposed on nonresident street merchants), fr. *skawage* scavage, fr. MF dial. (Flanders) *escauver* to inspect, fr. MD *scouwen*] : a person or animal that collects, eats, or disposes of refuse or waste

sce·nar·io \sə-'ner-ē-ˌō\ *n, pl* **-i·os** : the plot or outline of a dramatic work; *also* : an account of a possible action

scene \'sēn\ *n* [MF, stage, fr. L *scena, scaena* stage, scene, prob. fr. Etruscan, fr. Gk *skēnē* temporary shelter, tent, building forming the background for a dramatic performance, stage] **1** : a division of one act of a play **2** : a single situation or sequence in a play or motion picture **3** : a stage setting **4** : VIEW, PROSPECT **5** : the place of an occurrence or action **6** : a display of strong feeling and esp. anger **7** : a sphere of activity ⟨the fashion *~*⟩ — **sce·nic** \'sē-nik\ *adj*

scen·ery \'sē-nə-rē\ *n, pl* **-er·ies** **1** : the painted scenes or hangings and accessories used on a theater stage **2** : a picturesque view or landscape

¹**scent** \'sent\ *n* **1** : ODOR, SMELL **2** : sense of smell **3** : course of pursuit

: TRACK **4** : PERFUME **2** — **scent·ed** \'sen-təd\ *adj* — **scent·less** *adj*

²**scent** *vb* **1** : SMELL **2** : to imbue or fill with odor

scep·ter \'sep-tər\ *n* : a staff borne by a sovereign as an emblem of authority

sceptic *var of* SKEPTIC

scep·tre *Brit var of* SCEPTER

sch *abbr* school

¹**sched·ule** \'ske-jül, *esp Brit* 'she-dyül\ *n* **1** : a list of items or details **2** : TIMETABLE

²**schedule** *vb* **sched·uled; sched·ul·ing** **1** : to appoint, assign, or designate for a fixed time **2** : to make a schedule of; *also* : to enter on a schedule

sche·ma \'skē-mə\ *n, pl* **sche·ma·ta** \-mə-tə\ *also* **schemas** : a diagrammatic presentation or plan : OUTLINE

sche·mat·ic \ski-'ma-tik\ *adj* : of or relating to a scheme or diagram : DIAGRAMMATIC — **schematic** *n* — **sche·mat·i·cal·ly** \-ti-k(ə-)lē\ *adv*

¹**scheme** \'skēm\ *n* **1** : a plan for doing something; *esp* : a crafty plot **2** : a systematic design ⟨a color *~*⟩

²**scheme** *vb* **schemed; schem·ing** : to form a plot : INTRIGUE — **schem·er** *n*

schil·ling \'shi-liŋ\ *n* : a former basic monetary unit of Austria

schism \'si-zəm, 'ski-\ *n* **1** : DIVISION, SPLIT; *also* : DISCORD, DISSENSION **2** : a formal division in or separation from a religious body

schis·mat·ic \siz-'ma-tik, ski-\ *n* : one who creates or takes part in schism — **schismatic** *adj*

schist \'shist\ *n* : a metamorphic crystalline rock

schizo·phre·nia \ˌskit-sə-'frē-nē-ə\ *n* [NL, fr. Gk *schizein* to split + *phrēn* diaphragm, mind] : a psychotic mental illness that is characterized by a distorted view of the real world, by a greatly reduced ability to carry out one's daily tasks, and by abnormal ways of thinking, feeling, perceiving, and behaving — **schiz·oid** \'skit-ˌsȯid\ *adj or n* — **schizo·phren·ic** \ˌskit-sə-'fre-nik\ *adj or n*

schle·miel *also* **shle·miel** \shlə-'mēl\ *n* : an unlucky bungler : CHUMP

schlep *or* **schlepp** \'shlep\ *vb* [Yiddish *shlepn*] **1** : DRAG, HAUL **2** : to move slowly or awkwardly

schlock \'shläk\ *or* **schlocky** \'shlä-kē\ *adj* : of low quality or value — **schlock** *n*

schlub *also* **shlub** \'shləb\ *n* [Yiddish *zhlob, zhlub* yokel, boor] *slang* : a stupid, ineffectual, or unattractive person

schmaltz *also* **schmalz** \'shmȯlts, 'shmälts\ *n* [Yiddish *shmalts,* lit., rendered fat] : sentimental or florid music or art — **schmaltzy** *adj*

schmooze *or* **shmooze** \'shmüz\ *vb* : to chat informally esp. to gain favor — **schmooze** *n*

schnapps \'shnaps\ *n, pl* **schnapps** : a liquor (as gin) of high alcoholic content

schnau·zer \'shnaú-zər, 'shnaút-sər\ *n* [G, fr. *Schnauze* snout] : a dog of any of three breeds that are characterized by a wiry coat, long head, pointed ears, heavy eyebrows, and long hair on the muzzle

schol·ar \'skä-lər\ *n* **1** : STUDENT, PUPIL **2** : a learned person : SAVANT — **schol·ar·ly** *adj*

schol·ar·ship \-ˌship\ *n* **1** : the qualities or learning of a scholar **2** : money awarded to a student to help pay for further education

scho·las·tic \skə-'las-tik\ *adj* : of or relating to schools, scholars, or scholarship

¹school \'skül\ *n* **1** : an institution for teaching and learning; *also* : the pupils in attendance **2** : a body of persons of like opinions or beliefs ⟨the radical ∼⟩

²school *vb* : TEACH, TRAIN, DRILL

³school *n* : a large number of one kind of water animal swimming and feeding together

school·boy \-ˌbȯi\ *n* : a boy attending school

school·fel·low \-ˌfe-lō\ *n* : SCHOOLMATE

school·girl \-ˌgərl\ *n* : a girl attending school

school·house \-ˌhau̇s\ *n* : a building used as a school

school·marm \-ˌmärm\ *or* **school·ma'am** \-ˌmam, -ˌmäm\ *n* **1** : a woman who is a schoolteacher **2** : a person who exhibits characteristics popularly attributed to schoolteachers

school·mas·ter \-ˌmas-tər\ *n* : a man who is a schoolteacher

school·mate \-ˌmāt\ *n* : a school companion

school·mis·tress \-ˌmis-trəs\ *n* : a woman who is a schoolteacher

school·room \-ˌrüm, -ˌru̇m\ *n* : CLASSROOM

school·teach·er \-ˌtē-chər\ *n* : one who teaches in a school

schoo·ner \'skü-nər\ *n* : a fore-and-aft rigged sailing ship

schtick *var of* SHTICK

schuss \'shu̇s, 'shüs\ *vb* [G *Schuss*, n., lit., shot] : to ski down a slope at high speed — **schuss** *n*

sci *abbr* science; scientific

sci·at·i·ca \sī-'a-ti-kə\ *n* : pain in the region of the hips or along the course of the nerve at the back of the thigh

sci·ence \'sī-əns\ *n* [ME, fr. AF, fr. L *scientia*, fr. *scient-*, *sciens* having knowledge, fr. prp. of *scire* to know] **1** : an area of knowledge that is an object of study; *esp* : NATURAL SCIENCE **2** : knowledge covering general truths or the operation of general laws especially as obtained and tested through the scientific method — **sci·en·tif·ic** \ˌsī-ən-'ti-fik\ *adj* — **sci·en·tif·i·cal·ly** \-fi-k(ə-)lē\ *adv* — **sci·en·tist** \'sī-ən-tist\ *n*

science fiction *n* : fiction dealing principally with the impact of actual or imagined science on society or individuals

scientific method *n* : the rules and methods for the pursuit of knowledge involving the finding and stating of a problem, the collection of facts through observation and experiment, and the making and testing of ideas that need to be proven right or wrong

scim·i·tar \'si-mə-tər\ *n* : a curved sword used chiefly by Arabs and Turks

scin·til·la \sin-'ti-lə\ *n* : SPARK, TRACE ⟨isn't a ∼ of evidence⟩

scin·til·late \'sin-tə-ˌlāt\ *vb* **-lat·ed; -lat·ing** : SPARKLE, GLEAM — **scin·til·la·tion** \ˌsin-tə-'lā-shən\ *n*

sci·on \'sī-ən\ *n* **1** : a shoot of a plant joined to a stock in grafting **2** : DESCENDANT ⟨a ∼ of a powerful family⟩

scis·sors \'si-zərz\ *n pl* : a cutting instrument like shears but usu. smaller

scissors kick *n* : a swimming kick in which the legs move like scissors

scle·ro·der·ma \ˌskler-ə-'dər-mə\ *n* : a chronic disease characterized by the usu. progressive hardening and thickening of the skin

scle·ro·sis \sklə-'rō-səs\ *n* : abnormal hardening of tissue (as of an artery); *also* : a disease characterized by this — **scle·rot·ic** \-'rä-tik\ *adj*

scoff \'skäf\ *vb* : MOCK, JEER ⟨∼ed at his proposal⟩ — **scoff·er** *n*

scoff·law \-ˌlȯ\ *n* : a contemptuous law violator

¹scold \'skōld\ *n* : a person who scolds

²scold *vb* : to censure severely or angrily

sconce \'skäns\ *n* : a candlestick or an electric light fixture fastened to a wall

scone \'skōn, 'skän\ *n* : a biscuit (as of oatmeal) baked on a griddle

¹scoop \'sküp\ *n* **1** : a large shovel; *also* : a utensil with a shovellike or rounded end **2** : the amount contained by a scoop **3** : an act of scooping **4** : information of immediate interest

²scoop *vb* **1** : to take out or up or empty with or as if with a scoop **2** : to make hollow **3** : to report a news item in advance of ⟨∼ed the other newspapers⟩

scoot \'sküt\ *vb* : to move swiftly

scoot·er \'skü-tər\ *n* **1** : a child's vehicle consisting of a narrow board mounted between two wheels tandem with an upright steering handle attached to the front wheel **2** : MOTOR SCOOTER

¹scope \'skōp\ *n* [It *scopo* purpose, goal, fr. Gk *skopos*] **1** : space or opportunity for action or thought **2** : extent covered : RANGE ⟨is beyond the ∼ of this essay⟩

²scope *n* : an instrument (as a microscope or telescope) for viewing

scorch \'skȯrch\ *vb* : to burn the surface of; *also* : to dry or shrivel with heat ⟨∼ed lawns⟩

¹score \'skȯr\ *n, pl* **scores** **1** *or pl* **score** : TWENTY **2** : CUT, SCRATCH, SLASH **3** : a record of points made (as in a game) **4** : DEBT **5** : REASON, GROUND **6** : the music of a composition or arrangement with different parts indicated **7** : success in obtaining something (as drugs) esp. illegally

²score *vb* **scored; scor·ing 1** : RECORD **2** : to keep score in a game **3** : to mark with lines, grooves, scratches, or notches **4** : to gain or tally in or as if in a game ⟨*scored* a point⟩ **5** : to assign a grade or score to ⟨∼ the tests⟩ **6** : to compose a score for **7** : SUCCEED **8** : ACQUIRE

⟨*scored* tickets to the game⟩ — **score-less** *adj* — **scor·er** *n*

¹scorn \'skȯrn\ *n* : an emotion involving both anger and disgust : CONTEMPT — **scorn·ful** \-fəl\ *adj* — **scorn·ful·ly** *adv*

²scorn *vb* : to hold in contempt : DISDAIN ⟨were ∼ed as fanatics⟩ — **scorn·er** *n*

Scor·pio \'skȯr-pē-,ō\ *n* [L, lit., scorpion] **1** : a zodiacal constellation between Libra and Sagittarius usu. pictured as a scorpion **2** : the 8th sign of the zodiac in astrology; *also* : one born under this sign

scor·pi·on \'skȯr-pē-ən\ *n* : any of an order of arthropods related to the spiders that have a poisonous stinger at the tip of a long jointed tail

¹Scot \'skät\ *n* : a native or inhabitant of Scotland

²Scot *abbr* Scotland; Scottish

Scotch \'skäch\ *n* **1** : SCOTS **2 Scotch** *pl* : the people of Scotland **3** : a whiskey distilled in Scotland esp. from malted barley — **Scotch** *adj* — **Scotch·man** \-mən\ *n* — **Scotch·wom·an** \-,wu̇-mən\ *n*

Scotch bonnet *n* : a small roundish very hot chili pepper esp. of the Caribbean

Scotch pine *n* : a pine that is naturalized in the U.S. from northern Europe and Asia and is a valuable timber tree

Scotch terrier *n* : SCOTTISH TERRIER

scot-free \'skät-'frē\ *adj* : free from obligation, harm, or penalty

Scots \'skäts\ *n* : the English language of Scotland

Scots·man \'skäts-mən\ *n* : SCOT

Scots·wom·an \-,wu̇-mən\ *n* : a woman who is a Scot

Scot·tie \'skä-tē\ *n* : SCOTTISH TERRIER

Scot·tish \'skä-tish\ *adj* : of, relating to, or characteristic of Scotland, Scots, or the Scots

Scottish terrier *n* : any of an old Scottish breed of terrier with short legs, a long head with small erect ears, a broad deep chest, and a thick rough coat

scoun·drel \'skau̇n-drəl\ *n* : a disreputable person : VILLAIN

¹scour \'skau̇(-ə)r\ *vb* **1** : to rub (as with a gritty substance) in order to clean **2** : to cleanse by or as if by rubbing

²scour *vb* **1** : to move rapidly through : RUSH **2** : to examine thoroughly

¹scourge \'skərj\ *n* **1** : LASH, WHIP **2** : PUNISHMENT; *also* : a cause of affliction (as a plague)

²scourge *vb* **scourged; scourg·ing 1** : LASH, FLOG **2** : to punish severely

¹scout \'skau̇t\ *vb* [ME, fr. AF *escuter* to listen, fr. L *auscultare*] **1** : to look around : RECONNOITER **2** : to inspect or observe to get information

²scout *n* **1** : a person sent out to get information; *also* : a soldier, airplane, or ship sent out to reconnoiter **2** : BOY SCOUT **3** : GIRL SCOUT — **scout·mas·ter** \-,mas-tər\ *n*

³scout *vb* : SCORN, SCOFF

scow \'skau̇\ *n* : a large flat-bottomed boat with square ends

scowl \'skau̇(-ə)l\ *vb* : to make a frowning expression of displeasure — **scowl** *n*

SCPO *abbr* senior chief petty officer

scrab·ble \'skra-bəl\ *vb* **scrab·bled; scrab·bling 1** : SCRAPE, SCRATCH **2** : CLAMBER, SCRAMBLE ⟨*scrabbled* on the slippery rocks⟩ **3** : to work hard and long **4** : SCRIBBLE — **scrabble** *n* — **scrab·bler** *n*

scrag·gly \'skra-glē\ *adj* : IRREGULAR; *also* : RAGGED, UNKEMPT ⟨a ∼ beard⟩

scram \'skram\ *vb* **scrammed; scram·ming** : to go away at once

scram·ble \'skram-bəl\ *vb* **scram·bled; scram·bling 1** : to clamber clumsily around **2** : to struggle for or as if for possession of something **3** : to spread irregularly **4** : to mix together **5** : to cook (eggs) by stirring during frying — **scramble** *n*

¹scrap \'skrap\ *n* **1** : FRAGMENT, PIECE **2** : discarded material : REFUSE

²scrap *vb* **scrapped; scrap·ping 1** : to make into scrap ⟨∼ a battleship⟩ **2** : to get rid of as useless ⟨*scrapped* the plans⟩

³scrap *n* : FIGHT

⁴scrap *vb* **scrapped; scrap·ping** : FIGHT, QUARREL — **scrap·per** *n*

scrap·book \'skrap-,bu̇k\ *n* : a blank book in which mementos are kept

¹scrape \'skrāp\ *vb* **scraped; scrap·ing 1** : to remove by drawing a knife over; *also* : to clean or smooth by rubbing off the covering **2** : to damage or injure the surface of by contact with something rough **3** : to draw across a surface with a grating sound **4** : to get together (money) by strict economy **5** : to get along with difficulty ⟨barely *scraping* by on her income⟩ — **scrap·er** *n*

²scrape *n* **1** : the act or the effect of scraping **2** : a bow accompanied by a drawing back of the foot **3** : an unpleasant predicament

scra·pie \'skrā-pē\ *n* : a usu. fatal degenerative disease of the brain esp. of sheep that is related to mad cow disease

¹scrap·py \'skra-pē\ *adj* **scrap·pi·er; -est** : DISCONNECTED, FRAGMENTARY

²scrappy *adj* **scrap·pi·er; -est 1** : QUARRELSOME **2** : having an aggressive and determined spirit ⟨a ∼ competitor⟩

¹scratch \'skrach\ *vb* **1** : to scrape, dig, or rub with or as if with claws or nails ⟨a dog ∼ing at the door⟩ ⟨∼ed my arm⟩ **2** : SCRAPE **3** ⟨∼ed his nails across the blackboard⟩ **3** : SCRAPE **4 4** : to cancel or erase by or as if by drawing a line through **5** : to withdraw from a contest — **scratchy** *adj* — **scratch one's head** : to become confused or perplexed

²scratch *n* **1** : a mark or injury made by or as if by scratching; *also* : a sound so made **2** : the starting line in a race — **from scratch** : with no steps completed or ingredients prepared ahead of time ⟨built from ∼⟩

³scratch *adj* **1** : made or done by chance ⟨a ∼ hit⟩ **2** : made as or used for a trial attempt ⟨∼ paper⟩

scratch card *n* : a card with a small area covered by an opaque coating which may be scraped away to reveal hidden information

scrawl \'skrȯl\ *vb* : to write hastily and carelessly — **scrawl** *n*

scraw·ny \'skrȯ-nē\ *adj* **scraw·ni·er; -est** : very thin : SKINNY

¹**scream** \'skrēm\ *vb* : to cry out loudly and shrilly

²**scream** *n* : a loud shrill cry

scream·ing \'skrē-min\ *adj* : so striking as to attract notice as if by screaming ⟨∼ headlines⟩

screech \'skrēch\ *vb* : SHRIEK — **screech** *n* — **screechy** \'skrē-chē\ *adj*

screech·ing \'skrē-chin\ *adj* : ABRUPT ⟨came to a ∼ halt⟩

¹**screen** \'skrēn\ *n* **1** : a device or partition used to hide, restrain, protect, or decorate ⟨a window ∼⟩; *also* : something that shelters, protects, or conceals **2** : a sieve or perforated material for separating finer from coarser parts (as of sand) **3** : a surface on which an image is made to appear (as in television); *also* : the information displayed on a computer screen at one time **4** : the motion-picture industry

²**screen** *vb* **1** : to shield with or as if with a screen **2** : to separate with a screen; *also* : to select or categorize methodically ⟨∼ contestants⟩ **3** : to present (as a motion picture) on the screen

screen·ing \'skrē-nin\ *n* **1** : metal or plastic mesh (as for window screens) **2** : a showing of a motion picture

screen saver *n* : a computer program that displays something (as images) on the screen of a computer that is on but not in use

¹**screw** \'skrü\ *n* [ME, fr. MF *escroe* female screw, nut, fr. ML *scrofa*, fr. L, sow] **1** : a machine consisting of a solid cylinder with a spiral groove around it and a corresponding hollow cylinder into which it fits **2** : a naillike metal piece with a spiral groove and a head with a slot that is inserted into material by rotating and is used to fasten pieces of solid material together **3** : PROPELLER

²**screw** *vb* **1** : to fasten or close by means of a screw **2** : to operate or adjust by means of a screw **3** : to move or cause to move spirally; *also* : to close or set in position by such an action

screw·ball \'skrü-ˌbȯl\ *n* **1** : a baseball pitch breaking in a direction opposite to a curve **2** : a whimsical, eccentric, or crazy person

screw·driv·er \-ˌdrī-vər\ *n* **1** : a tool for turning screws **2** : a drink made of vodka and orange juice

screw·worm \'skrü-ˌwərm\ *n* : an American blowfly of warm regions whose larva matures in wounds or sores of mammals and may cause disease or death; *esp* : its larva

screwy \'skrü-ē\ *adj* **screw·i·er; -est** **1** : crazily absurd, eccentric, or unusual ⟨a ∼ idea⟩ **2** : CRAZY, INSANE

scrib·ble \'skri-bəl\ *vb* **scrib·bled; scrib·bling** : to write hastily or carelessly — **scribble** *n* — **scrib·bler** *n*

scribe \'skrīb\ *n* **1** : a scholar of Jewish law in New Testament times **2** : a person

whose business is the copying of writing **3** : JOURNALIST

scrim \'skrim\ *n* : a light loosely woven cotton or linen cloth

scrim·mage \'skri-mij\ *n* : the play between two football teams beginning with the snap of the ball; *also* : practice play between two teams — **scrimmage** *vb*

scrimp \'skrimp\ *vb* : to economize greatly ⟨∼ and save⟩

scrim·shaw \'skrim-ˌshȯ\ *n* : carved or engraved articles made orig. by American whalers usu. from baleen or whale ivory — **scrimshaw** *vb*

scrip \'skrip\ *n* **1** : a certificate showing its holder is entitled to something (as stock or land) **2** : paper money issued for temporary use in an emergency

¹**script** \'skript\ *n* **1** : written matter (as lines for a play or broadcast) **2** : HANDWRITING

²**script** *abbr* scripture

scrip·ture \'skrip-chər\ *n* **1** *cap* : the books of the Bible — often used in pl. **2** : the sacred writings of a religion — **scrip·tur·al** \'skrip-chə-rəl\ *adj* — **scrip·tur·al·ly** *adv*

scriv·en·er \'skri-və-nər\ *n* : SCRIBE, COPYIST, WRITER

scrod \'skräd\ *n* [prob. fr. Brit. dial. (Cornwall) *scrawed*, pp. of *scraw, scrawl* to split, salt, and dry (young fish)] : a young fish (as a cod or haddock); *esp* : one split and boned for cooking

scrof·u·la \'skrȯ-fyə-lə\ *n* : tuberculosis of lymph nodes esp. in the neck

¹**scroll** \'skrōl\ *n* : a roll of paper or parchment for writing a document; *also* : a spiral or coiled ornamental form suggesting a loosely or partly rolled scroll

²**scroll** *vb* : to move or cause to move text or graphics up, down, or across a display screen

scroll saw *n* **1** : FRETSAW **2** : a machine saw with a narrow vertically reciprocating blade for cutting curved lines or openwork

scro·tum \'skrō-təm\ *n, pl* **scro·ta** \-tə\ *or* **scrotums** [L] : a pouch that in most male mammals contains the testes

scrounge \'skraünj\ *vb* **scrounged; scroung·ing** : to collect by or as if by foraging

¹**scrub** \'skrəb\ *n* **1** : a thick growth of stunted trees or shrubs; *also* : an area of land covered with scrub **2** : an inferior domestic animal **3** : a person of insignificant size or standing **4** : a player not on the first team — **scrub** *adj* — **scrub·by** *adj*

²**scrub** *vb* **scrubbed; scrub·bing 1** : to clean or wash by rubbing ⟨∼ clothes⟩ ⟨∼ out a spot⟩ **2** : CANCEL

³**scrub** *n* **1** : an act or instance of scrubbing ⟨gave the clothes a good ∼⟩ **2** *pl* : loose-fitting clothing worn by hospital staff ⟨surgical ∼s⟩

scrub·ber \'skrə-bər\ *n* : one that scrubs; *esp* : an apparatus for removing impurities esp. from gases

scruff \'skrəf\ *n* : the loose skin of the back of the neck : NAPE

scruffy \'skrə-fē\ adj **scruff·i·er; -est** : UNKEMPT, SLOVENLY ⟨a ~ tramp⟩

scrump·tious \'skrəmp-shəs\ adj : DELIGHTFUL, EXCELLENT; esp : DELICIOUS ⟨a ~ cake⟩ — **scrump·tious·ly** adv

scrunch·ie or **scrunchy** \'skrən-chē, 'skrún-\ n : a fabric-covered elastic for the hair

¹**scru·ple** \'skrü-pəl\ n [ME scrupil, scriple, fr. AF scruble, fr. L scrupulus, dim. of scrupus source of uneasiness, lit., sharp stone] **1** : a point of conscience or honor **2** : hesitation due to ethical considerations

²**scruple** vb **scru·pled; scru·pling** : to be reluctant on grounds of conscience : HESITATE

scru·pu·lous \'skrü-pyə-ləs\ adj **1** : having moral integrity **2** : PAINSTAKING ⟨was ~ about her work⟩ — **scru·pu·lous·ly** adv — **scru·pu·lous·ness** n

scru·ti·nise Brit var of SCRUTINIZE

scru·ti·nize \'skrü-tə-ˌnīz\ vb **-nized; -niz·ing** : to examine closely

scru·ti·ny \'skrü-tə-nē\ n, pl **-nies** [L scrutinium, fr. scrutari to search, examine, prob. fr. scruta trash] : a careful looking over ♦ Synonyms INSPECTION, EXAMINATION, ANALYSIS

scu·ba \'skü-bə\ n [self-contained underwater breathing apparatus] : an apparatus for breathing while swimming underwater

scuba diver n : one who swims underwater with the aid of scuba gear

¹**scud** \'skəd\ vb **scud·ded; scud·ding** : to move speedily

²**scud** n : light clouds driven by the wind

¹**scuff** \'skəf\ vb **1** : to scrape the feet while walking : SHUFFLE **2** : to scratch or become scratched or worn away

²**scuff** n **1** : a mark or injury caused by scuffing **2** : a flat-soled slipper without heel strap

scuf·fle \'skə-fəl\ vb **scuf·fled; scuf·fling 1** : to struggle confusedly at close quarters ⟨scuffled with the police⟩ **2** : to shuffle one's feet — **scuffle** n

¹**scull** \'skəl\ n **1** : an oar for use in sculling; also : one of a pair of short oars for a single oarsman **2** : a racing shell propelled by one or two persons using sculls

²**scull** vb : to propel (a boat) by an oar over the stern

scul·lery \'skə-lə-rē\ n, pl **-ler·ies** [ME squilerie, sculerie department of household in charge of dishes, fr. AF esquilerie, fr. escuele bowl, fr. L scutella drinking bowl] : a small room near the kitchen used for cleaning dishes, cooking utensils, and vegetables

scul·lion \'skəl-yən\ n : a kitchen helper

sculpt \'skəlpt\ vb : CARVE, SCULPTURE

sculp·tor \'skəlp-tər\ n : a person who produces works of sculpture

¹**sculp·ture** \'skəlp-chər\ n : the act, process, or art of carving or molding material (as stone, wood, or plastic); also : work produced this way — **sculp·tur·al** \'skəlp-chə-rəl\ adj

²**sculpture** vb **sculp·tured; sculp·tur·ing**

: to form or alter as or as if a work of sculpture ⟨sculptured hedges⟩

scum \'skəm\ n **1** : a slimy or filmy covering on the surface of a liquid **2** : waste matter **3** : RABBLE

scup·per \'skə-pər\ n [ME skopper-, perh. fr. AF *escopir, fr. escopir to spit out] : an opening in the side of a ship through which water on deck is drained overboard

scurf \'skərf\ n : thin dry scales of skin (as dandruff); also : a scaly deposit or covering — **scurfy** \'skər-fē\ adj

scur·ri·lous \'skər-ə-ləs\ adj : coarsely jesting : OBSCENE, VULGAR

scur·ry \'skər-ē\ vb **scur·ried; scur·ry·ing** : SCAMPER ⟨scurried for cover⟩

¹**scur·vy** \'skər-vē\ n : a disease caused by a lack of vitamin C and characterized by spongy gums, loosened teeth, and bleeding under the skin

²**scurvy** adj : MEAN, CONTEMPTIBLE — **scur·vi·ly** \-və-lē\ adv

scutch·eon \'skə-chən\ n : ESCUTCHEON

¹**scut·tle** \'skə-t°l\ n : a pail for carrying coal

²**scuttle** n : a small opening with a lid esp. in the deck, side, or bottom of a ship

³**scuttle** vb **scut·tled; scut·tling** : to cut a hole in the deck, side, or bottom of (a ship) in order to sink

⁴**scuttle** vb **scut·tled; scut·tling** : SCURRY, SCAMPER

scut·tle·butt \'skə-t°l-ˌbət\ n : GOSSIP

scythe \'sīth\ n : an implement for mowing (as grass or grain) by hand — **scythe** vb

SD abbr **1** South Dakota **2** special delivery

S Dak abbr South Dakota

SDI abbr Strategic Defense Initiative

Se symbol selenium

SE abbr southeast

sea \'sē\ n **1** : a large body of salt water **2** : OCEAN **3** : rough water; also : a large wave **4** : something likened to the sea esp. in vastness ⟨a ~ of wheat⟩ — **sea** adj — **at sea** : LOST, BEWILDERED

sea anemone n : any of numerous coelenterate polyps whose form, bright and varied colors, and cluster of tentacles superficially resemble a flower

sea·bird \'sē-ˌbərd\ n : a bird (as a gull) frequenting the open ocean

sea·board \-ˌbȯrd\ n : SEACOAST; also : the land bordering a coast

sea·borg·i·um \sē-'bȯr-gē-əm\ n : a short-lived radioactive chemical element produced artificially

sea·coast \-ˌkōst\ n : the shore of the sea

sea·far·er \-ˌfer-ər\ n : SEAMAN 1

sea·far·ing \-ˌfer-iŋ\ n : the use of the sea for travel or transportation — **seafaring** adj

sea·food \-ˌfüd\ n : edible marine fish and shellfish

sea·go·ing \-ˌgō-iŋ\ adj : OCEANGOING

sea·gull \'sē-ˌgəl\ n : GULL

sea horse n : any of a genus of small marine fishes with the head and forepart of the body sharply flexed like the head and neck of a horse

¹**seal** \'sēl\ *n, pl* **seals** *also* **seal** [ME *sele*, fr. OE *seolh*] **1** : any of numerous large carnivorous sea mammals occurring chiefly in cold regions and having limbs adapted for swimming **2** : the pelt of a seal

²**seal** *vb* : to hunt seals

³**seal** *n* [ME *sele, seel*, fr. AF *seal, sel*, fr. L *sigillum*, fr. dim. of *signum* sign, seal] **1** : GUARANTEE, PLEDGE **2** : a device having a raised design that can be stamped on clay or wax; *also* : the impression made by stamping with such a device **3** : something that seals or closes up ⟨safety ~⟩

⁴**seal** *vb* **1** : to affix a seal to; *also* : AUTHENTICATE **2** : to fasten with or as if with a seal to prevent tampering **3** : to close or make secure against access, leakage, or passage **4** : to determine irrevocably ⟨~*ed* his fate⟩

sea-lane \'sē-ˌlān\ *n* : an established sea route

seal-ant \'sē-lənt\ *n* : a sealing agent

seal-er \'sē-lər\ *n* : a coat applied to prevent subsequent coats of paint or varnish from sinking in

sea level *n* : the level of the surface of the sea esp. at its mean midway between mean high and low water

sea-lift \'sē-ˌlift\ *n* : transport of military personnel and equipment by ship

sea lion *n* : any of several large Pacific seals with small external ears

seal-skin \'sēl-ˌskin\ *n* **1** : ¹SEAL 2 **2** : a garment of sealskin

¹**seam** \'sēm\ *n* **1** : the line of junction of two edges and esp. of edges of fabric sewn together **2** : a layer of mineral matter **3** : WRINKLE

²**seam** *vb* **1** : to join by or as if by sewing **2** : WRINKLE, FURROW

sea-man \'sē-mən\ *n* **1** : one who assists in the handling of ships : MARINER **2** : an enlisted person in the navy ranking next below a petty officer third class

seaman apprentice *n* : an enlisted person in the navy ranking next below a seaman

seaman recruit *n* : an enlisted person of the lowest rank in the navy

sea-man-ship \'sē-mən-ˌship\ *n* : the art or skill of handling a ship

seam-less \'sēm-ləs\ *adj* : having no flaws or interruptions ⟨a ~ transition⟩ — **seam-less-ly** *adv*

sea-mount \'sē-ˌmaunt\ *n* : an underwater mountain

seam-stress \'sēm-strəs\ *n* : a woman who does sewing

seamy \'sē-mē\ *adj* **seam-i-er; -est** **1** : UNPLEASANT **2** : DEGRADED, SORDID ⟨the ~ part of town⟩

sé-ance \'sā-ˌäns\ *n* [F] : a meeting to receive communications from spirits

sea-plane \'sē-ˌplān\ *n* : an airplane that can take off from and land on water

sea-port \-ˌpȯrt\ *n* : a port for oceangoing ships

sear \'sir\ *vb* **1** : WITHER **2** : to cook, burn, or scorch esp. on the surface; *also* : BRAND — **sear** *n*

¹**search** \'sərch\ *vb* [ME *cerchen*, fr. AF *cercher* to travel about, investigate, search, fr. LL *circare* to go about, fr. L *circum* round about] **1** : to look through in trying to find something **2** : SEEK **3** : PROBE — **search-er** *n*

²**search** *n* : the act of searching

search engine *n* : computer software or a website used to search data (as text or other websites) for specified information

search-light \-ˌlīt\ *n* : an apparatus for projecting a powerful beam of light; *also* : the light projected

sear-ing \'sir-iŋ\ *adj* : very sharp, harsh or intense ⟨~ pain⟩ ⟨a ~ review⟩

sea scallop *n* : a large scallop of the Atlantic coast of No. America that is harvested for food

sea-scape \'sē-ˌskāp\ *n* **1** : a view of the sea **2** : a picture representing a scene at or of the sea

sea-shell \'sē-ˌshel\ *n* : the shell of a marine animal and esp. a mollusk

sea-shore \-ˌshȯr\ *n* : the shore of a sea

sea-sick \-ˌsik\ *adj* : nauseated by or as if by the motion of a ship — **sea-sick-ness** *n*

sea-side \'sē-ˌsīd\ *n* : SEASHORE

¹**sea-son** \'sē-zən\ *n* [ME *sesoun*, fr. AF *seison* natural season, appropriate time, fr. L *sation-, satio* action of sowing, fr. *serere* to sow] **1** : one of the divisions of the year (as spring or summer) **2** : a period of the year associated with a particular activity, event, or holiday ⟨the Easter ~⟩ ⟨hunting ~⟩ — **sea-son-al** \-zə-nəl\ *adj* — **sea-son-al-ly** *adv*

²**season** *vb* **1** : to make pleasant to the taste by use of salt, pepper, or spices **2** : to make (as by aging or drying) suitable for use **3** : to accustom or habituate to something (as hardship) ♦ **Synonyms** HARDEN, INURE, ACCLIMATE, TOUGHEN — **sea-son-er** *n*

sea-son-able \'sē-zə-nə-bəl\ *adj* : occurring at a good or proper time ⟨~ weather⟩ ♦ **Synonyms** TIMELY, PROPITIOUS, OPPORTUNE — **sea-son-ably** \-blē\ *adv*

seasonal affective disorder *n* : depression that recurs as the days grow shorter during the fall and winter

sea-son-ing \'sē-zə-niŋ\ *n* : something that seasons : CONDIMENT

¹**seat** \'sēt\ *n* **1** : a chair, bench, or stool for sitting on **2** : a place which serves as a capital or center

²**seat** *vb* **1** : to place in or on a seat **2** : to provide seats for

seat belt *n* : straps designed to hold a person in a seat

SEATO \'sē-ˌtō\ *abbr* Southeast Asia Treaty Organization

seat-of-the-pants *adj* : employing or based on personal experience, judgment, and effort rather than technological aids ⟨~ navigation⟩

sea turtle *n* : any of two families of marine turtles that have the feet modified into paddles

sea urchin *n* : any of numerous spiny marine echinoderms having thin brittle globular shells

sea·wall \'sē-ˌwȯl\ *n* : an embankment to protect the shore from erosion

¹**sea·ward** \'sē-wərd\ *n* : the direction or side away from land and toward the open sea

²**seaward** *also* **sea·wards** \-wərdz\ *adv* : toward the sea

³**seaward** *adj* **1** : directed or situated toward the sea **2** : coming from the sea

sea·wa·ter \'sē-ˌwȯ-tər, -ˌwä-\ *n* : water in or from the sea

sea·way \-ˌwā\ *n* : an inland waterway that admits ocean shipping

sea·weed \-ˌwēd\ *n* : a marine alga (as a kelp); *also* : a mass of marine algae

sea·wor·thy \-ˌwər-thē\ *adj* : fit for a sea voyage ⟨a ~ ship⟩

se·ba·ceous \si-'bā-shəs\ *adj* : of, relating to, or secreting fatty material

sec *abbr* **1** second; secondary **2** secretary **3** section **4** [L *secundum*] according to

SEC *abbr* Securities and Exchange Commission

se·cede \si-'sēd\ *vb* **se·ced·ed; se·ced·ing** : to withdraw from an organized body and esp. from a political body

se·ces·sion \si-'se-shən\ *n* : the act of seceding — **se·ces·sion·ist** *n*

se·clude \si-'klüd\ *vb* **se·clud·ed; se·clud·ing** : to keep or shut away from others ⟨*secluded* herself in her room⟩

se·clu·sion \si-'klü-zhən\ *n* : the act of secluding : the state of being secluded — **se·clu·sive** \-siv\ *adj*

¹**sec·ond** \'se-kənd\ *adj* [ME, fr. AF *secund*, fr. L *secundus* second, following, favorable, fr. *sequi* to follow] **1** : being number two in a countable series **2** : next after the first **3** : ALTERNATE ⟨every ~ year⟩ — **second** *or* **sec·ond·ly** *adv*

²**second** *n* **1** : one that is second **2** : one who assists another (as in a duel) **3** : an inferior or flawed article **4** : the second forward gear in a motor vehicle

³**second** *n* [ME *secounde*, fr. ML *secunda*, fr. L, fem. of *secundus* second; fr. its being the second division of a unit into 60 parts, as a minute is the first] **1** : the 60th part of a minute of time or angular measure **2** : an instant of time

⁴**second** *vb* **1** : to encourage or give support to **2** : to act as a second to **3** : to support (a motion) by adding one's voice to that of a proposer

¹**sec·ond·ary** \'se-kən-ˌder-ē\ *adj* **1** : second in rank, value, or occurrence : LESSER **2** : belonging to a second or later stage of development **3** : coming after the primary or elementary ⟨~ schools⟩
♦ *Synonyms* SUBORDINATE, COLLATERAL, DEPENDENT

²**secondary** *n, pl* **-ar·ies** : the defensive backfield of a football team

secondary sex characteristic *n* : a physical characteristic that appears in members of one sex at puberty or in seasonal breeders at breeding season and is not directly concerned with reproduction

second fiddle *n* : one that plays a supporting or subservient role

sec·ond–guess \ˌse-kənd-'ges\ *vb* **1** : to think out other strategies or explanations for after the event **2** : to seek to anticipate or predict ⟨~ the stock market⟩

sec·ond·hand \-'hand\ *adj* **1** : not original **2** : not new : USED ⟨~ clothes⟩ **3** : dealing in used goods

secondhand smoke *n* : tobacco smoke that is exhaled by smokers or is given off by burning tobacco and is inhaled by persons nearby

second lieutenant *n* : a commissioned officer (as in the army) ranking next below a first lieutenant

sec·ond–rate \ˌse-kənd-'rāt\ *adj* : INFERIOR ⟨~ hotels⟩

sec·ond–string \'se-kənd-'striŋ\ *adj* : being a substitute or replacement

se·cre·cy \'sē-krə-sē\ *n, pl* **-cies** **1** : the habit or practice of being secretive **2** : the condition of being hidden or concealed

¹**se·cret** \'sē-krət\ *adj* **1** : HIDDEN, CONCEALED ⟨a ~ staircase⟩ **2** : COVERT, STEALTHY; *also* : engaged in detecting or spying ⟨a ~ agent⟩ **3** : kept from general knowledge — **se·cret·ly** *adv*

²**secret** *n* **1** : MYSTERY **2** : something kept from the knowledge of others

sec·re·tar·i·at \ˌse-krə-'ter-ē-ət\ *n* **1** : the office of a secretary **2** : the secretarial staff in an office **3** : the administrative department of a governmental organization ⟨the UN ~⟩

sec·re·tary \'se-krə-ˌter-ē\ *n, pl* **-tar·ies** **1** : a person employed to handle records, correspondence, and routine work for another person **2** : an officer of a corporation or business who is in charge of correspondence and records **3** : an official at the head of a department of government **4** : a writing desk — **sec·re·tar·i·al** \ˌse-krə-'ter-ē-əl\ *adj* — **sec·re·tary·ship** \'se-krə-ˌter-ē-ˌship\ *n*

¹**se·crete** \si-'krēt\ *vb* **se·cret·ed; se·cret·ing** : to form and give off (a secretion)

²**se·crete** \si-'krēt, 'sē-krət\ *vb* **se·cret·ed; se·cret·ing** : HIDE, CONCEAL

se·cre·tion \si-'krē-shən\ *n* **1** : the process of secreting something **2** : a product of glandular activity; *esp* : one (as a hormone) useful in the organism **3** : the act of hiding something — **se·cre·to·ry** \'sē-krə-ˌtȯr-ē\ *adj*

se·cre·tive \'sē-krə-tiv, si-'krē-\ *adj* : tending to keep secrets or to act secretly ⟨~ about his work⟩ — **se·cre·tive·ly** *adv* — **se·cre·tive·ness** *n*

¹**sect** \'sekt\ *n* **1** : a dissenting religious body **2** : a religious denomination **3** : a group adhering to a distinctive doctrine or to a leader

²**sect** *abbr* section; sectional

¹**sec·tar·i·an** \sek-'ter-ē-ən\ *adj* **1** : of or relating to a sect or sectarian **2** : limited in character or scope — **sec·tar·i·an·ism** *n*

²**sectarian** *n* **1** : an adherent of a sect **2** : a narrow or bigoted person

sec·ta·ry \'sek-tə-rē\ *n, pl* **-ries** : a member of a sect

¹**sec·tion** \'sek-shən\ *n* **1** : a part cut off or

separated **2** : a distinct part **3** : the appearance that a thing has or would have if cut straight through

²**section** vb **1** : to separate or become separated into sections ⟨∼ an orange⟩ **2** : to represent in sections

sec·tion·al \'sek-shə-nəl\ adj **1** : of, relating to, or characteristic of a section **2** : local or regional rather than general in character **3** : divided into sections — **sec·tion·al·ism** n

sec·tor \'sek-tər\ n **1** : a part of a circle between two radii **2** : an area assigned to a military leader to defend **3** : a subdivision of society

sec·u·lar \'se-kyə-lər\ adj **1** : not sacred or ecclesiastical **2** : not bound by monastic vows ⟨a ∼ priest⟩

sec·u·lar·ise Brit var of SECULARIZE

sec·u·lar·ism \'se-kyə-lə-ˌri-zəm\ n : indifference to or exclusion of religion — **sec·u·lar·ist** \-rist\ n — **secularist** also **sec·u·lar·is·tic** \ˌse-kyə-lə-'ris-tik\ adj

sec·u·lar·ize \'se-kyə-lə-ˌrīz\ vb **-ized; -iz·ing 1** : to make secular **2** : to transfer from ecclesiastical to civil or lay use, possession, or control — **sec·u·lar·i·za·tion** \ˌse-kyə-lə-rə-'zā-shən\ n — **sec·u·lar·iz·er** \-kyə-lə-ˌrī-zər\ n

¹**se·cure** \si-'kyur\ adj **se·cur·er; -est** [L securus safe, secure, fr. se without + cura care] **1** : easy in mind : free from fear **2** : free from danger or risk of loss : SAFE **3** : CERTAIN, SURE — **se·cure·ly** adv

²**secure** vb **se·cured; se·cur·ing 1** : to make safe : GUARD **2** : to assure payment of by giving a pledge or collateral **3** : to fasten safely ⟨∼ a door⟩ **4** : GET, ACQUIRE ⟨∼ permission⟩

se·cu·ri·ty \si-'kyur-ə-tē\ n, pl **-ties 1** : SAFETY **2** : freedom from worry **3** : something given as pledge of payment ⟨a ∼ deposit⟩ **4** pl : bond or stock certificates **5** : PROTECTION

secy abbr secretary

se·dan \si-'dan\ n **1** : a covered chair borne on poles by two men **2** : an automobile seating four or more people and usu. having a permanent top

¹**se·date** \si-'dāt\ adj : quiet and dignified in behavior ♦ Synonyms STAID, SOBER, SERIOUS, SOLEMN — **se·date·ly** adv

²**sedate** vb **se·dat·ed; se·dat·ing** : to dose with sedatives — **se·da·tion** \si-'dā-shən\ n

¹**sed·a·tive** \'se-də-tiv\ adj : serving or tending to relieve tension

²**sedative** n : a sedative drug

sed·en·tary \'se-dⁿn-ˌter-ē\ adj : characterized by or requiring much sitting

sedge \'sej\ n : any of a family of plants esp. of marshy areas that differ from the related grasses esp. in having solid stems — **sedgy** \'se-jē\ adj

sed·i·ment \'se-də-mənt\ n **1** : the material that settles to the bottom of a liquid **2** : material (as stones and sand) deposited by water, wind, or a glacier — **sed·i·men·ta·ry** \ˌse-də-'men-tə-rē\ adj — **sed·i·men·ta·tion** \-mən-'tā-shən, -ˌmen-\ n

se·di·tion \si-'di-shən\ n : the causing of discontent, insurrection, or resistance against a government — **se·di·tious** \-shəs\ adj

se·duce \si-'düs, -'dyüs\ vb **se·duced; se·duc·ing 1** : to persuade to disobedience or disloyalty **2** : to lead astray **3** : to entice to sexual intercourse ♦ Synonyms TEMPT, ENTICE, INVEIGLE, LURE — **se·duc·er** n — **se·duc·tion** \-'dək-shən\ n — **se·duc·tive** \-tiv\ adj

sed·u·lous \'se-jə-ləs\ adj [L sedulus, fr. sedulo sincerely, diligently, fr. se without + dolus guile] : DILIGENT, PAINSTAKING

¹**see** \'sē\ vb **saw** \'so\; **seen** \'sēn\; **see·ing 1** : to perceive by the eye; also : to have the power of sight **2** : EXPERIENCE **3** : UNDERSTAND **4** : to make sure ⟨∼ that order is kept⟩ **5** : to meet with **6** : to keep company with esp. in dating **7** : ACCOMPANY, ESCORT ⟨∼ the guests to the door⟩ ♦ Synonyms BEHOLD, DESCRY, ESPY, VIEW, OBSERVE, NOTE, DISCERN — **see red** : to become very angry — **see the light** : to realize an obscured truth

²**see** n : the authority or jurisdiction of a bishop

¹**seed** \'sēd\ n, pl **seed** or **seeds 1** : the grains of plants used for sowing **2** : a ripened ovule of a flowering plant that may develop into a new plant; also : a plant structure (as a spore or small dry fruit) capable of producing a new plant **3** : DESCENDANTS **4** : SOURCE, ORIGIN **5** : a competitor seeded in a tournament — **seed·less** adj — **go to seed** or **run to seed 1** : to develop seed **2** : DECAY, DETERIORATE

²**seed** vb **1** : SOW, PLANT ⟨∼ land with grass⟩ **2** : to bear or shed seeds **3** : to remove seeds from **4** : to rank or schedule (contestants) in a tournament — **seed·er** n

seed·bed \-ˌbed\ n : soil or a bed of soil prepared for planting seed

seed·ling \'sēd-liŋ\ n **1** : a young plant grown from seed **2** : a young tree before it becomes a sapling

seed·time \'sēd-ˌtīm\ n : the season for sowing

seedy \'sē-dē\ adj **seed·i·er; -est 1** : containing or full of seeds **2** : SHABBY

seek \'sēk\ vb **sought** \'sot\; **seek·ing 1** : to search for **2** : to try to reach or obtain **3** : ATTEMPT — **seek·er** n

seem \'sēm\ vb **1** : to appear to the observation or understanding **2** : to give the impression of being : APPEAR

seem·ing adj : outwardly apparent ⟨∼ indifference⟩ — **seem·ing·ly** adv

seem·ly \'sēm-lē\ adj **seem·li·er; -est 1** : conventionally proper **2** : FIT

seep \'sēp\ vb : to flow or pass slowly through fine pores or cracks — **seep·age** \'sē-pij\ n

seer \'sir\ n : a person who foresees or predicts events : PROPHET

seer·suck·er \'sir-ˌsə-kər\ n [Hindi śīrśakar, fr. Pers shīr-o-shakar, lit., milk and sugar] : a light fabric of linen, cotton, or rayon usu. striped and slightly puckered

see·saw \'sē-ˌsò\ n 1 : a contest in which each side assumes then relinquishing the lead 2 : a children's sport of riding up and down on the ends of a plank supported in the middle; *also* : the plank so used — **seesaw** vb

seethe \'sēth\ vb **seethed; seeth·ing** [archaic *seethe* boil] : to become violently agitated ⟨~ with jealousy⟩

seg·ment \'seg-mənt\ n 1 : a part cut off from a geometrical figure (as a circle) by one or more points, lines, or planes 2 : a division of a thing : SECTION — **seg·men·tal** \seg-'men-t³l\ adj — **seg·men·ta·tion** \ˌseg-mən-'tā-shən\ n — **seg·ment·ed** \'seg-ˌmen-təd\ adj

seg·re·gate \'se-gri-ˌgāt\ vb **-gat·ed; -gat·ing** [L *segregare,* fr. *se-* apart + *greg-, grex* herd, flock] : to cut off from others; *esp* : to separate esp. by races or ethnic groups — **seg·re·ga·tion** \ˌse-gri-'gā-shən\ n

seg·re·ga·tion·ist \ˌse-gri-'gā-shə-nist\ n : one who believes in or practices the segregation of races

¹**se·gue** \'se-(ˌ)gwā, 'sā-\ vb **se·gued; se·gue·ing** 1 : to proceed without pause from one musical number to another 2 : to make a transition without interruption from one activity, topic, scene, or part to another

²**segue** n : the act or an instance of segueing

sei·gneur \sān-'yər\ n, *often cap* [MF, fr. ML *senior,* fr. L, adj., elder] : a feudal lord

¹**seine** \'sān\ n : a large weighted fishing net

²**seine** vb **seined; sein·ing** : to fish or catch with a seine — **sein·er** n

seis·mic \'sīz-mik, 'sīs-\ adj : of, relating to, resembling, or caused by an earthquake — **seis·mi·cal·ly** \-mi-k(ə-)lē\ adv — **seis·mic·i·ty** \sīz-'mi-sə-tē, sīs-\ n

seis·mo·gram \'sīz-mə-ˌgram, 'sīs-\ n : the record of an earth tremor made by a seismograph

seis·mo·graph \-ˌgraf\ n : an apparatus to measure and record seismic vibrations — **seis·mo·graph·ic** \ˌsīz-mə-'gra-fik, ˌsīs-\ adj — **seis·mog·ra·phy** \sīz-'mä-grə-fē, sīs-\ n

seis·mol·o·gy \sīz-'mä-lə-jē, sīs-\ n : a science that deals with earthquakes — **seis·mo·log·i·cal** \ˌsīz-mə-'lä-ji-kəl, ˌsīs-\ adj — **seis·mol·o·gist** \sīz-'mä-lə-jist, sīs-\ n

seis·mom·e·ter \sīz-'mä-mə-tər, sīs-\ n : a seismograph measuring the actual movement of the ground

seize \'sēz\ vb **seized; seiz·ing** 1 : to lay hold of or take possession of by force 2 : ARREST 3 : UNDERSTAND 4 : to attack or overwhelm physically : AFFLICT ⟨*seized* by panic⟩ ♦ **Synonyms** TAKE, GRASP, CLUTCH, SNATCH, GRAB

sei·zure \'sē-zhər\ n 1 : the act of seizing : the state of being seized 2 : a sudden attack (as of disease)

sel *abbr* select; selected; selection

sel·dom \'sel-dəm\ adv : not often : RARELY

¹**se·lect** \sə-'lekt\ adj 1 : CHOSEN, PICKED; *also* : CHOICE 2 : judicious or restrictive in choice : DISCRIMINATING

²**select** vb : to choose from a number or group : pick out

se·lec·tion \sə-'lek-shən\ n 1 : the act or process of selecting 2 : something selected : CHOICE 3 : a natural or artificial process that tends to favor the survival and reproduction of individuals with certain traits but not those with others

se·lec·tive \sə-'lek-tiv\ adj : of or relating to selection : selecting or tending to select ⟨~ shoppers⟩

selective service n : a system for calling men up for military service : DRAFT

se·lect·man \si-'lekt-ˌman, -mən\ n : one of a board of officials elected in towns of most New England states to administer town affairs

se·le·ni·um \sə-'lē-nē-əm\ n : a photosensitive chemical element

self \'self\ n, *pl* **selves** \'selvz\ 1 : the essential person distinct from all other persons in identity 2 : a particular side of a person's character 3 : personal interest : SELFISHNESS ⟨put service before ~⟩

self- *comb form* 1 : oneself : itself 2 : of oneself or itself 3 : by oneself or itself; *also* : automatic 4 : to, for, or toward oneself

self-cen·tered \'self-'sen-tərd\ adj : concerned only with one's own self — **self-cen·tered·ness** n

self-com·posed \ˌself-kəm-'pōzd\ adj : having control over one's emotions

self-con·scious \'self-'kän-chəs\ adj : uncomfortably conscious of oneself as an object of observation by others — **self-con·scious·ly** adv — **self-con·scious·ness** n

self-con·tained \ˌself-kən-'tānd\ adj 1 : complete in itself 2 : showing self-control; *also* : reserved in manner

self–abasement	self–aggrandizing	self–cleaning	self–contempt
self–absorbed	self–analysis	self–closing	self–contradiction
self–absorption	self–anointed	self–complacent	self–contradictory
self–acceptance	self–appointed	self–conceit	self–control
self–accusation	self–appraisal	self–concern	self–correcting
self–acting	self–asserting	self–condemned	self–created
self–addressed	self–assertion	self–confessed	self–criticism
self–adjusting	self–assertive	self–confidence	self–cultivation
self–administer	self–assurance	self–confident	self–deceit
self–advancement	self–assured	self–congratulation	self–deception
self–aggrandize-	self–awareness	self–congratulatory	self–defeating
ment	self–betrayal	self–constituted	

self–de·fense \'self-di-'fens\ *n* **1** : a plea of justification for the use of force or for homicide **2** : the act of defending oneself, one's property, or a close relative

self–ef·fac·ing \-ə-'fā-siŋ\ *adj* : RETIRING, SHY ⟨is quiet and ∼⟩

self–ev·i·dent \,self-'e-və-dənt\ *adj* : evident without proof or reasoning

self–fer·til·i·za·tion \,self-,fər-tə-lə-'zā-shən\ *n* : fertilization of a plant or animal by its own pollen or sperm

self–ful·fill·ing \,self-fül-'fi-liŋ\ *adj* : becoming real or true by virtue of having been predicted or expected ⟨a ∼ prophecy⟩

self–help \'self-'help\ *n* : the process of bettering oneself or coping with one's problems without the aid of others — **self–help** *adj*

self·ish \'sel-fish\ *adj* : concerned with one's own welfare excessively or without regard for others — **self·ish·ly** *adv* — **self·ish·ness** *n*

self·less \'self-ləs\ *adj* : UNSELFISH ⟨∼ dedication⟩ — **self·less·ness** *n*

self–made \'self-'mād\ *adj* : having achieved success or prominence by one's own efforts ⟨a ∼ man⟩

self–pol·li·na·tion \,self-,pä-lə-ə-'nā-shən\ *n* : pollination of a flower by its own pollen or sometimes by pollen from another flower on the same plant

self–reg·u·lat·ing \'self-'re-gyə-,lā-tiŋ\ *adj* : AUTOMATIC

self–righ·teous \-'rī-chəs\ *adj* : strongly convinced of one's own righteousness — **self–righ·teous·ly** *adv*

self·same \'self-,sām\ *adj* : precisely the same : IDENTICAL

self–seal·ing \'self-'sē-liŋ\ *adj* : capable of sealing itself (as after puncture)

self–seek·ing \'self-'sē-kiŋ\ *adj* : seeking only to further one's own interests — **self–seeking** *n*

self–start·er \-'stär-tər\ *n* : a person who has initiative

self–will \'self-'wil\ *n* : OBSTINACY

sell \'sel\ *vb* **sold** \'sōld\; **sell·ing 1** : to transfer (property) in return for money or something else of value **2** : to deal in as a business **3** : to be sold ⟨cars are ∼*ing* well⟩ — **sell·er** *n*

sell out *vb* **1** : to dispose of entirely by sale; *esp* : to sell one's business **2** : BETRAY — **sell·out** \'sel-,aut\ *n*

selt·zer \'selt-sər\ *n* [modif. of G *Selterser (Wasser)* water of Selters, fr. Nieder *Selters,* Germany] : artificially carbonated water

sel·vage *or* **sel·vedge** \'sel-vij\ *n* : the edge of a woven fabric so formed as to prevent raveling

selves *pl of* SELF

sem *abbr* **1** semicolon **2** seminar **3** seminary

se·man·tic \si-'man-tik\ *also* **se·man·ti·cal** \-ti-kəl\ *adj* : of or relating to meaning in language ⟨∼ change⟩

se·man·tics \si-'man-tiks\ *n sing or pl* : the study of meanings in language

sema·phore \'se-mə-,fōr\ *n* **1** : a visual signaling apparatus with movable arms **2** : signaling by hand-held flags

sem·blance \'sem-bləns\ *n* **1** : outward appearance **2** : IMAGE, LIKENESS

se·men \'sē-mən\ *n* [NL, fr. L, seed] : a sticky whitish fluid of the male reproductive tract that contains the sperm

se·mes·ter \sə-'mes-tər\ *n* [G, fr. L *semestris* half-yearly, fr. *sex* six + *mensis* month] **1** : half a year **2** : one of the two terms into which many colleges divide the school year

semi \'se-,mī\ *n, pl* **sem·is** : SEMITRAILER

semi- \'se-mi, -,mī\ *prefix* **1** : precisely half of **2** : half in quantity or value; *also* : half of or occurring halfway through a specified period **3** : partly : incompletely **4** : partial : incomplete **5** : having some of the characteristics of

semi·au·to·mat·ic \,se-mē-,ȯ-tə-'ma-tik\ *adj, of a firearm* : able to fire repeatedly

self–definition	self–explaining	self–limiting	self–renewing
self–delusion	self–explanatory	self–love	self–reproach
self–denial	self–expression	self–lubricating	self–respect
self–denying	self–forgetful	self–luminous	self–respecting
self–deprecating	self–giving	self–operating	self–restraint
self–deprecation	self–governing	self–perception	self–revelation
self–depreciation	self–government	self–perpetuating	self–rule
self–described	self–hate	self–pity	self–sacrifice
self–despair	self–hypnosis	self–portrait	self–sacrificing
self–destruct	self–identity	self–possessed	self–satisfaction
self–destruction	self–image	self–possession	self–satisfied
self–destructive	self–importance	self–preservation	self–service
self–determination	self–important	selves–proclaimed	self–serving
self–directed	self–imposed	self–professed	self–starting
self–discipline	self–improvement	self–promotion	self–styled
self–distrust	self–incrimination	self–propelled	self–sufficiency
self–doubt	self–induced	self–propelling	self–sufficient
self–educated	self–indulgence	self–protection	self–supporting
self–employed	self–indulgent	self–realization	self–sustaining
self–employment	self–inflicted	self–referential	self–taught
self–enhancement	self–instruction	self–regard	self–torment
self–esteem	self–interest	self–reliance	self–winding
self–examination	self–knowledge	self–reliant	self–worth

semiannual	semiarid

but requiring release and another press of the trigger for each successive shot

semi·co·lon \'se-mi-ˌkō-lən\ *n* : a punctuation mark ; used esp. to separate major sentence elements

semi·con·duc·tor \ˌse-mi-kən-'dək-tər\ *n* : a substance whose electrical conductivity is between that of a conductor and an insulator — **semi·con·duct·ing** *adj*

¹**semi·fi·nal** \ˌse-mi-'fīn-ⁿl\ *adj* : being next to the last in an elimination tournament

²**semi·fi·nal** \'se-mi-ˌfī-nⁿl\ *n* : a semifinal round or match — **semi·fi·nal·ist** \-ist\ *n*

semi·lu·nar \-'lü-nər\ *adj* : LUNATE

sem·i·nal \'se-mə-nⁿl\ *adj* **1** : of, relating to, or consisting of seed or semen **2** : containing or contributing the seeds of later development : CREATIVE, ORIGINAL — **sem·i·nal·ly** *adv*

sem·i·nar \'se-mə-ˌnär\ *n* **1** : a course of study pursued by a group of advanced students doing original research under a professor **2** : CONFERENCE

sem·i·nary \'se-mə-ˌner-ē\ *n, pl* **-nar·ies** [ME, seedbed, nursery, fr. L *seminarium,* fr. *semen* seed] : an educational institution; *esp* : one that gives theological training — **sem·i·nar·i·an** \ˌse-mə-'ner-ē-ən\ *n*

Sem·i·nole \'se-mə-ˌnōl\ *n, pl* **Seminoles** or **Seminole** : a member of an American Indian people of Florida

semi·per·me·able \ˌse-mi-'pər-mē-ə-bəl\ *adj* : partially but not freely or wholly permeable; *esp* : permeable to some usu. small molecules but not to other usu. larger particles ⟨a ∼ membrane⟩ — **semi·per·me·abil·i·ty** \-ˌpər-mē-ə-'bi-lə-tē\ *n*

Sem·ite \'se-ˌmīt\ *n* : a member of any of a group of peoples (as the Hebrews or Arabs) of southwestern Asia — **Se·mit·ic** \sə-'mi-tik\ *adj*

semi·trail·er \'se-mi-ˌtrā-lər, -ˌmī-\ *n* : a freight trailer that when attached is supported at its forward end by the truck tractor; *also* : a semitrailer with attached tractor

sem·o·li·na \ˌse-mə-'lē-nə\ *n* : the purified hard grains produced from the milling of wheat and used esp. for pasta

sempstress *var of* SEAMSTRESS

¹**sen** \'sen\ *n, pl* **sen** — see *yen* at MONEY table

²**sen** *n, pl* **sen** — see *dollar, ringgit, rupiah* at MONEY table

³**sen** *n, pl* **sen** — see *riel* at MONEY table

⁴**sen** *abbr* **1** senate; senator **2** senior

sen·ate \'se-nət\ *n* : the second of two chambers of a legislature

sen·a·tor \'se-nə-tər\ *n* : a member of a senate — **sen·a·to·ri·al** \ˌse-nə-'tòr-ē-əl\ *adj*

send \'send\ *vb* **sent** \'sent\; **send·ing 1** : to cause to go **2** : EMIT **3** : to propel or drive esp. with force **4** : to put or bring into a certain condition ⟨*sent* them into a rage⟩ **5** : to convey or transmit by an agent — **send·er** *n*

send–off \'send-ˌòf\ *n* : a demonstration of goodwill and encouragement at the start of a new venture (as a trip)

send–up \'send-ˌəp\ *n* : PARODY

se·ne \'sā-(ˌ)nä\ *n, pl* **sene** — see *tala* at MONEY table

Sen·e·ca \'se-ni-kə\ *n, pl* **Seneca** or **Senecas** : a member of an American Indian people of western New York

Sen·e·ga·lese \ˌse-ni-gə-'lēz, -'lēs\ *n, pl* **Senegalese** : a native or inhabitant of Senegal — **Senegalese** *adj*

se·nes·cence \si-'ne-sⁿns\ *n* : the state of being old; *also* : the process of becoming old — **se·nes·cent** \-ⁿnt\ *adj*

se·nile \'sē-ˌnī(-ə)l, 'se-\ *adj* : OLD, AGED; *esp* : exhibiting a loss of cognitive abilities associated with old age — **se·nil·i·ty** \si-'ni-lə-tē\ *n*

¹**se·nior** \'sē-nyər\ *n* **1** : a person older or of higher rank than another **2** : a member of the graduating class of a high school or college

²**senior** *adj* [ME, fr. L, older, elder, compar. of *senex* old] **1** : ELDER **2** : more advanced in dignity or rank **3** : belonging to the final year of a school or college course

senior airman *n* : an enlisted person in the air force ranking next below a staff sergeant

senior chief petty officer *n* : a petty officer in the navy or coast guard ranking next below a master chief petty officer

senior citizen *n* : an elderly person; *esp* : one who has retired

senior high school *n* : a school usu. including grades 10 to 12

se·nior·i·ty \sēn-'yòr-ə-tē\ *n* **1** : the quality or state of being senior **2** : a privileged status owing to length of continuous service

senior master sergeant *n* : a noncommissioned officer in the air force ranking next below a chief master sergeant

sen·i·ti \'se-nə-tē\ *n, pl* **seniti** — see *pa'anga* at MONEY table

sen·na \'se-nə\ *n* **1** : CASSIA 2; *esp* : one used medicinally **2** : the dried leaflets or pods of a cassia used as a purgative

sen·sa·tion \sen-'sā-shən\ *n* **1** : awareness (as of noise or heat) or a mental process (as seeing or hearing) due to stimulation of a sense organ; *also* : an indefinite bodily feeling **2** : a condition of excitement; *also* : the thing that causes this condition

semicentennial	semiformal	semipermanent	semiskilled
semicircle	semigloss	semipolitical	semisoft
semicircular	semi–independent	semiprecious	semisolid
semicivilized	semiliquid	semiprivate	semisweet
semiclassical	semiliterate	semiprofessional	semitransparent
semiconscious	semimonthly	semireligious	semiweekly
semidarkness	semiofficial	semiretired	semiyearly
semidivine			

sen·sa·tion·al \-shə-nəl\ *adj* **1** : of or relating to sensation or the senses **2** : arousing an intense and usu. superficial interest or emotional reaction — **sen·sa·tion·al·ly** *adv*

sen·sa·tion·al·ise *Brit var of* SENSATIONALIZE

sen·sa·tion·al·ism \-nə-ˌli-zəm\ *n* : the use or effect of sensational subject matter or treatment — **sen·sa·tion·al·ist** \-nə-list\ *adj or n* — **sen·sa·tion·al·is·tic** \-ˌsā-shə-nə-'lis-tik\ *adj*

sen·sa·tion·al·ize \-shə-nə-ˌlīz\ *vb* **-ized; -iz·ing** : to present in a sensational manner

¹sense \'sens\ *n* **1** : semantic content : MEANING **2** : the faculty of perceiving by means of sense organs; *also* : a bodily function or mechanism (as sight, hearing, or smell) involving the action and effect of a stimulus on a sense organ **3** : SENSATION, AWARENESS **4** : INTELLIGENCE, JUDGMENT **5** : OPINION ⟨the ~ of the meeting⟩ — **sense·less** *adj* — **sense·less·ly** *adv* — **sense·less·ness** *n*

²sense *vb* **sensed; sens·ing 1** : to be or become aware of ⟨~ danger⟩; *also* : to perceive by the senses **2** : to detect (as radiation) automatically

sense organ *n* : a bodily structure (as an eye or ear) that receives stimuli (as heat or light) which excite neurons to send information to the brain

sen·si·bil·i·ty \ˌsen-sə-'bi-lə-tē\ *n, pl* **-ties** : delicacy of feeling : SENSITIVITY

sen·si·ble \'sen-sə-bəl\ *adj* **1** : capable of being perceived by the senses or the mind; *also* : capable of receiving sense impressions **2** : AWARE, CONSCIOUS **3** : REASONABLE, RATIONAL ⟨a ~ decision⟩ — **sen·si·bly** \-blē\ *adv*

sen·si·tive \'sen-sə-tiv\ *adj* **1** : subject to excitation by or responsive to stimuli **2** : having power of feeling **3** : of such a nature as to be easily affected **4** : TOUCHY ⟨a ~ issue⟩ — **sen·si·tive·ly** *adv* — **sen·si·tive·ness** *n* — **sen·si·tiv·i·ty** \ˌsen-sə-'ti-və-tē\ *n*

sensitive plant *n* : any of several mimosas with leaves that fold or droop when touched

sen·si·tize \'sen-sə-ˌtīz\ *vb* **-tized; -tiz·ing** : to make or become sensitive or hypersensitive — **sen·si·ti·za·tion** \ˌsen-sə-tə-'zā-shən\ *n*

sen·sor \'sen-ˌsȯr, -sər\ *n* : a device that responds to a physical stimulus

sen·so·ry \'sen-sə-rē\ *adj* **1** : of or relating to sensation or the senses ⟨~ perception⟩ **2** : AFFERENT

sen·su·al \'sen-shə-wəl\ *adj* **1** : relating to gratification of the senses **2** : devoted to the pleasures of the senses — **sen·su·al·ist** *n* — **sen·su·al·i·ty** \ˌsen-shə-'wa-lə-tē\ *n* — **sen·su·al·ly** *adv*

sen·su·ous \'sen-shə-wəs\ *adj* **1** : relating to the senses or to things that can be perceived by the senses **2** : VOLUPTUOUS ⟨~ lips⟩ — **sen·su·ous·ly** *adv* — **sen·su·ous·ness** *n*

¹sent *past and past part of* SEND

²sent \'sent\ *n, pl* **sen·ti** \'sen-tē\ : a monetary unit equal to ¹⁄₁₀₀ kroon formerly used in Estonia

sen·te \'sen-tē\ *n, pl* **li·cen·te** *or* **li·sen·te** \li-'sen-tē\ — see *loti* at MONEY table

¹sen·tence \'sen-t⁰ns, -ˌt⁰nz\ *n* [ME, fr. AF, fr. L *sententia*, lit., feeling, opinion, fr. *sentire* to feel] **1** : the punishment set by a court **2** : a grammatically self-contained speech unit that expresses an assertion, a question, a command, a wish, or an exclamation

²sentence *vb* **sen·tenced; sen·tenc·ing** : to impose a sentence on

sen·ten·tious \sen-'ten-chəs\ *adj* : using wise sayings or proverbs; *also* : using pompous language — **sen·ten·tious·ly** *adv* — **sen·ten·tious·ness** *n*

sen·tient \'sen-chənt, -chē-ənt\ *adj* : capable of feeling : having perception

sen·ti·ment \'sen-tə-mənt\ *n* **1** : FEELING; *also* : thought and judgment influenced by feeling : emotional attitude **2** : OPINION, NOTION

sen·ti·men·tal \ˌsen-tə-'men-t⁰l\ *adj* **1** : influenced by tender feelings **2** : affecting the emotions ♦ **Synonyms** BATHETIC, MAUDLIN, MAWKISH, MUSHY — **sen·ti·men·tal·ism** *n* — **sen·ti·men·tal·ist** *n* — **sen·ti·men·tal·i·ty** \-ˌmen-'ta-lə-tē, -mən-\ *n* — **sen·ti·men·tal·ly** *adv*

sen·ti·men·tal·ise *Brit var of* SENTIMENTALIZE

sen·ti·men·tal·ize \-'men-tə-ˌlīz\ *vb* **-ized; -iz·ing 1** : to indulge in sentiment **2** : to look upon or imbue with sentiment ⟨~s the past⟩ — **sen·ti·men·tal·i·za·tion** \-ˌmen-tə-lə-'zā-shən\ *n*

sen·ti·mo \sen-'tē-(ˌ)mō\ *n, pl* **-mos** — see *peso* at MONEY table

sen·ti·nel \'sen-t⁰n-əl\ *n* [MF *sentinelle*, fr. It *sentinella*, fr. *sentina* vigilance, fr. *sentire* to perceive, fr. L] : SENTRY

sen·try \'sen-trē\ *n, pl* **sentries** : a guard at a point of passage

sep *abbr* separate, separated

Sep *abbr* September

SEP *abbr* simplified employee pension

se·pal \'sē-pəl, 'se-\ *n* : one of the modified leaves comprising a flower calyx

sep·a·ra·ble \'se-pə-rə-bəl\ *adj* : capable of being separated — **sep·a·ra·bil·i·ty** \ˌse-pə-rə-'bi-lə-tē\

¹sep·a·rate \'se-pə-ˌrāt\ *vb* **-rat·ed; -rat·ing 1** : to set or keep apart : DISCONNECT, SEVER **2** : to keep apart by something intervening **3** : to cease to be together : PART ⟨the couple decided to ~⟩

²sep·a·rate \'se-prət, -pə-rət\ *adj* **1** : not connected or joined **2** : divided from each other **3** : SINGLE, PARTICULAR ⟨the ~ pieces of the puzzle⟩ — **sep·a·rate·ly** *adv*

³sep·a·rate \'se-prət, -pə-rət\ *n* : an article of dress designed to be worn interchangeably with others to form various combinations

sep·a·ra·tion \ˌse-pə-'rā-shən\ *n* **1** : the act or process of separating : the state of being separated **2** : a point, line, means, or area of division **3** : a formal separating of a married couple by agreement but without divorce

sep·a·rat·ist \'se-prə-tist, 'se-pə-ˌrā-\ *n*

: an advocate of separation (as from a political body) — **sep·a·rat·ism** \'se-prə-,ti-zəm\ n

sep·a·ra·tive \'se-pə-,rā-tiv, 'se-prə-tiv\ adj : tending toward, causing, or expressing separation ⟨∼ influences⟩

sep·a·ra·tor \'se-pə-,rā-tər\ n : one that separates; esp : a device for separating cream from milk

se·pia \'sē-pē-ə\ n : a brownish gray to dark brown color

sep·sis \'sep-səs\ n, pl **sep·ses** \'sep-,sēz\ : a toxic condition due to spread of bacteria or their toxic products in the body

Sept abbr September

Sep·tem·ber \sep-'tem-bər\ n [ME Septembre, fr. AF & OE, both fr. L September (seventh month), fr. septem seven] : the 9th month of the year having 30 days

sep·tic \'sep-tik\ adj 1 : PUTREFACTIVE 2 : relating to or involving sepsis 3 : of, relating to, or used for sewage treatment and disposal

sep·ti·ce·mia \,sep-tə-'sē-mē-ə\ n : BLOOD POISONING

septic tank n : a tank in which sewage is disintegrated by bacteria

sep·tu·a·ge·nar·i·an \sep-,tü-ə-jə-'ner-ē-ən, -,tyü-\ n : a person whose age is in the seventies — **septuagenarian** adj

Sep·tu·a·gint \sep-'tü-ə-jənt, -'tyü-\ n : a Greek version of the Old Testament prepared in the 3d and 2d centuries B.C. by Jewish scholars

sep·tum \'sep-təm\ n, pl **sep·ta** \-tə\ : a dividing wall or membrane esp. between bodily spaces or masses of soft tissue

se·pul·chral \sə-'pəl-krəl\ adj : relating to burial or the grave 2 : GLOOMY

¹sep·ul·chre or **sep·ul·cher** \'se-pəl-kər\ n : a burial vault : TOMB

²sepulchre or **sepulcher** vb -chred or -chered; -chring or -chering : BURY, ENTOMB

sep·ul·ture \'se-pəl-,chûr\ n 1 : BURIAL 2 : SEPULCHRE

se·quel \'sē-kwəl\ n 1 : logical consequence 2 : a literary or cinematic work continuing a story begun in a preceding one

¹se·quence \'sē-kwəns\ n 1 : SERIES 2 : chronological order of events 3 : RESULT, SEQUEL ♦ Synonyms SUCCESSION, CHAIN, PROGRESSION, TRAIN — **se·quen·tial** \si-'kwen-chəl\ adj — **se·quen·tial·ly** adv

²sequence vb -quenced; -quenc·ing 1 : to arrange in a sequence 2 : to determine the sequence of chemical constituents in ⟨∼ DNA⟩

se·quent \'sē-kwənt\ adj 1 : SUCCEEDING, CONSECUTIVE 2 : RESULTANT

se·ques·ter \si-'kwes-tər\ vb : to set apart : SEGREGATE ⟨∼ a jury⟩

se·ques·trate \'sē-kwəs-,trāt, si-'kwes-\ vb -trat·ed; -trat·ing : SEQUESTER — **se·ques·tra·tion** \,sē-kwəs-'trā-shən, ,se-\ n

se·quin \'sē-kwən\ n 1 : an old gold coin of Turkey and Italy 2 : a small metal or plastic plate used for ornamentation esp.

on clothing — **se·quined** or **se·quinned** \-kwənd\ adj

se·quoia \si-'kwȯi-ə\ n : either of two huge California coniferous trees

ser abbr 1 serial 2 series 3 service

sera pl of SERUM

se·ra·glio \sə-'ral-yō\ n, pl **-glios** [It serraglio] : HAREM

se·ra·pe \sə-'rä-pē\ n : a colorful woolen shawl worn over the shoulders esp. by Mexican men

ser·aph \'ser-əf\ n, pl **ser·a·phim** \-ə-,fim, -,fēm\ or **seraphs** : one of the 6-winged angels standing in the presence of God

ser·a·phim \'ser-ə-,fim, -,fēm\ n pl 1 : the highest order of angels 2 sing, pl **seraphim** : SERAPH — **se·raph·ic** \sə-'ra-fik\ adj

Ser·bi·an \'sər-bē-ən\ n 1 : SERB 2 : a south Slavic language spoken by the Serbian people — **Serbian** adj

Ser·bo–Cro·a·tian \,sər-(,)bō-krō-'ā-shən\ n : the Serbian and Croatian languages together with the Slavic speech of Bosnia, Herzegovina, and Montenegro taken as a single language with regional variants

sere \'sir\ adj : DRY, WITHERED

¹ser·e·nade \,ser-ə-'nād\ n [F, fr. It serenata, fr. sereno clear, calm (of weather) fr. L serenus] : music sung or played as a compliment esp. outdoors at night for a woman being courted

²serenade vb -nad·ed; -nad·ing : to entertain with or perform a serenade

ser·en·dip·i·ty \,ser-ən-'di-pə-tē\ n [fr. its possession by the heroes of the Persian fairy tale The Three Princes of Serendip] : the gift of finding valuable or agreeable things not sought for — **ser·en·dip·i·tous** \-təs\ adj — **ser·en·dip·i·tous·ly** adv

se·rene \sə-'rēn\ adj 1 : CLEAR ⟨∼ skies⟩ 2 : QUIET, CALM ♦ Synonyms TRANQUIL, PEACEFUL, PLACID — **se·rene·ly** adv — **se·ren·i·ty** \sə-'re-nə-tē\ n

serf \'sərf\ n : a member of a servile class bound to the land and subject to the will of the landowner — **serf·dom** \-dəm\ n

serge \'sərj\ n : a twilled woolen cloth

ser·geant \'sär-jənt\ n [ME, servant, attendant, sergeant, fr. AF sergant, serjant, fr. L servient-, serviens, prp. of servire to serve] 1 : a noncommissioned officer (as in the army) ranking next below a staff sergeant 2 : an officer in a police force

sergeant at arms : an officer of an organization who preserves order and executes commands

sergeant first class n : a noncommissioned officer in the army ranking next below a master sergeant

sergeant major n, pl **sergeants major** or **sergeant majors** 1 : a noncommissioned officer in the army or marine corps serving as chief administrative assistant in a headquarters 2 : a noncommissioned officer in the marine corps ranking above a first sergeant

¹se·ri·al \'sir-ē-əl\ adj 1 : appearing in parts that follow regularly ⟨a ∼ story⟩ 2

: performing a series of similar acts over a period of time ⟨a ~ killer⟩; *also* : occurring in such acts — **se·ri·al·ly** *adv*
²**serial** *n* : a serial story or other writing — **se·ri·al·ist** \-ə-list\ *n*
se·ries \ˈsir-ēz\ *n, pl* **series** : a number of things or events arranged in order and connected by being alike in some way ♦ *Synonyms* SUCCESSION, PROGRESSION, SEQUENCE, CHAIN, TRAIN, STRING
seri·graph \ˈser-ə-ˌgraf\ *n* : an original silk-screen print — **se·rig·ra·pher** \sə-ˈri-grə-fər\ *n* — **se·rig·ra·phy** \-fē\ *n*
se·ri·ous \ˈsir-ē-əs\ *adj* 1 : thoughtful or subdued in appearance or manner : SOBER 2 : requiring much thought or work 3 : EARNEST, DEVOTED 4 : DANGEROUS, HARMFUL ⟨a ~ illness⟩ 5 : excessive or impressive in quantity or degree ⟨making ~ money⟩ ♦ *Synonyms* GRAVE, SEDATE, STAID — **se·ri·ous·ly** *adv* — **se·ri·ous·ness** *n*
ser·mon \ˈsər-mən\ *n* [ME, fr. AF *sermun*, fr. ML *sermon, sermo*, fr. L, speech, conversation, fr. *serere* to link together] 1 : a religious discourse esp. as part of a worship service 2 : a lecture on conduct or duty
ser·mon·ize \ˈsər-mə-ˌnīz\ *vb* **-ized; -iz·ing** 1 : to compose or deliver a sermon 2 : to preach to or on at length
se·rol·o·gy \sə-ˈrä-lə-jē\ *n* : a science dealing with serums and esp. their reactions and properties — **se·ro·log·i·cal** \ˌsir-ə-ˈlä-ji-kəl\ *or* **se·ro·log·ic** \-jik\ *adj* — **se·ro·log·i·cal·ly** \-ji-k(ə-)lē\ *adv*
se·ro·to·nin \ˌsir-ə-ˈtō-nən, ˌser-\ *n* : a neurotransmitter that is a powerful vasoconstrictor
se·rous \ˈsir-əs\ *adj* : of, relating to, resembling, or producing serum; *esp* : of thin watery constitution
ser·pent \ˈsər-pənt\ *n* : SNAKE
¹**ser·pen·tine** \ˈsər-pən-ˌtēn, -ˌtīn\ *adj* 1 : SLY, CRAFTY 2 : WINDING, TURNING
²**ser·pen·tine** \-ˌtēn\ *n* : a dull-green mineral having a mottled appearance
ser·rate \ˈser-ˌāt\ *adj* : having a saw-toothed edge ⟨a ~ leaf⟩
ser·ried \ˈser-ēd\ *adj* : crowded together
se·rum \ˈsir-əm\ *n, pl* **serums** *or* **se·ra** \-ə\ [L, whey, wheylike fluid] : the clear yellowish antibody-containing fluid that can be separated from blood when it clots; *also* : a preparation of animal serum containing specific antibodies and used to prevent or cure disease
serv *abbr* service
ser·vant \ˈsər-vənt\ *n* : one that serves others; *esp* : a person employed for domestic or personal work
¹**serve** \ˈsərv\ *vb* **served; serv·ing** 1 : to work as a servant 2 : to render obedience and worship to (God) 3 : to comply with the commands or demands of 4 : to work through or perform a term of service (as in the army) 5 : PUT IN ⟨*served* five years in jail⟩ 6 : to be of use : ANSWER ⟨pine boughs *served* for a bed⟩ 7 : BENEFIT 8 : to prove adequate or satisfactory for ⟨a pie that ~*s* eight people⟩ 9 : to make ready and pass out ⟨~ drinks⟩ 10 : to

furnish or supply with something ⟨one power company *serving* the whole state⟩ 11 : to wait on ⟨~ a customer⟩ 12 : to treat or act toward in a specified way ⟨*served* as her maid⟩ 13 : to put the ball in play (as in tennis)
²**serve** *n* : the act of serving a ball (as in tennis)
serv·er \ˈsər-vər\ *n* 1 : one that serves 2 : a computer in a network that is used to provide services (as access to files) to other computers in the network
¹**ser·vice** \ˈsər-vəs\ *n* 1 : the occupation of a servant 2 : HELP, BENEFIT 3 : a meeting for worship; *also* : a form followed in worship or in a ceremony ⟨burial ~⟩ 4 : the act, fact, or means of serving 5 : performance of official or professional duties 6 : SERVE 7 : a set of dishes or silverware 8 : a branch of public employment; *also* : the persons in it ⟨civil ~⟩ 9 : military or naval duty
²**service** *vb* **ser·viced; ser·vic·ing** : to do maintenance or repair work on or for
ser·vice·able \ˈsər-və-sə-bəl\ *adj* : prepared for service : USEFUL, USABLE
ser·vice·man \ˈsər-vəs-ˌman, -mən\ *n* 1 : a man who is a member of the armed forces 2 : a man employed to repair or maintain equipment
service mark *n* : a mark or device used to identify a service (as transportation or insurance) offered to customers
service station *n* : GAS STATION
ser·vice·wom·an \ˈsər-vəs-ˌwù-mən\ *n* : a woman who is a member of the armed forces
ser·vile \ˈsər-vəl, -ˌvī(-ə)l\ *adj* 1 : befitting a slave or servant 2 : behaving like a slave : SUBMISSIVE — **ser·vile·ly** *adv* — **ser·vil·i·ty** \ˌsər-ˈvi-lə-tē\ *n*
serv·ing \ˈsər-vin\ *n* : HELPING
ser·vi·tor \ˈsər-və-tər\ *n* : a male servant
ser·vi·tude \ˈsər-və-ˌtüd, -ˌtyüd\ *n* : SLAVERY, BONDAGE
ser·vo \ˈsər-vō\ *n, pl* **servos** 1 : SERVOMOTOR 2 : SERVOMECHANISM
ser·vo·mech·a·nism \ˈsər-vō-ˌme-kə-ˌni-zəm\ *n* : a device for automatically correcting the performance of a mechanism
ser·vo·mo·tor \-ˌmō-tər\ *n* : a mechanism that supplements a primary control
ses·a·me \ˈse-sə-mē\ *n* : a widely cultivated annual herb of warm regions; *also* : its seeds that yield an edible oil (**sesame oil**) and are used in flavoring
ses·qui·cen·ten·ni·al \ˌses-kwi-sen-ˈte-nē-əl\ *n* [L *sesqui*- one and a half, half again] : a 150th anniversary or its celebration — **sesquicentennial** *adj*
ses·qui·pe·da·lian \ˌses-kwə-pə-ˈdāl-yən\ *adj* 1 : having many syllables : LONG 2 : using long words
ses·sile \ˈse-ˌsī(-ə)l, -səl\ *adj* : permanently attached and not free to move about
ses·sion \ˈse-shən\ *n* 1 : a meeting or series of meetings of a body (as a court or legislature) for the transaction of business 2 : a meeting or period devoted to a particular activity
¹**set** \ˈset\ *vb* **set; set·ting** 1 : to cause to sit 2 : PLACE 3 : ARRANGE, ADJUST 4

: to cause to be or do   **5** : SETTLE, DE-
CREE   **6** : to fix in a frame   **7** : to fix at a
certain amount   **8** : WAGER, STAKE   **9** : to
make or become fast or rigid   **10** : to
adapt (as words) to something (as music)
11 : to become fixed or firm or solid   **12**
: to be suitable : FIT   **13** : BROOD   **14** : to
have a certain direction   **15** : to pass below the horizon   **16** : to defeat in bridge
— **set about** : to begin to do — **set
forth** : to begin a trip — **set off 1** : to
start out on a course or a trip   **2** : to cause
to explode — **set out** : to begin a trip or
undertaking — **set sail** : to begin a voyage — **set upon** : to attack usu. with violence

²set *n*   **1** : a setting or a being set   **2** : DI-
RECTION, COURSE; *also* : TENDENCY   **3**
: FORM, BUILD   **4** : the fit of something
(as a coat)   **5** : an artificial setting for the
scene of a play or motion picture   **6** : a
group of tennis games in which one side
wins at least six   **7** : a group of persons or
things of the same kind or having a common characteristic usu. classed together
8 : a collection of things and esp. of
mathematical elements (as numbers or
points)   **9** : an electronic apparatus ⟨a
television ∼⟩

³set *adj*   **1** : DELIBERATE, INTENT   **2** : fixed
by authority or custom ⟨a ∼ price⟩   **3**
: RIGID ⟨a ∼ frown⟩   **4** : PERSISTENT

set·back \'set-ˌbak\ *n* : a temporary defeat : REVERSE

set back *vb*   **1** : HINDER, DELAY; *also*
: REVERSE   **2** : COST

set piece   **1** : a composition (as in literature or music) executed in fixed or ideal
form often with brilliant effect   **2** : a
scene, depiction, speech, or event obviously designed to have an imposing effect

set·screw \'set-ˌskrü\ *n* : a screw screwed
through one part tightly upon or into another part to prevent relative movement

set·tee \se-'tē\ *n* : a bench or sofa with a
back and arms

set·ter \'se-tər\ *n* : a large long-coated
hunting dog

set·ting \'se-tiŋ\ *n* **1** : the frame in which
a gem is set   **2** : the time, place, and circumstances in which something occurs
or develops; *also* : SCENERY   **3** : music
written for a text (as of a poem)   **4** : the
eggs that a fowl sits on for hatching at
one time

set·tle \'se-t³l\ *vb* **set·tled; set·tling** [ME
settlen to seat, bring to rest, come to rest,
fr. OE *setlan*, fr. *setl* seat]   **1** : to place so
as to stay   **2** : COLONIZE   **3** : to make compact   **4** : QUIET, CALM   **5** : to establish or
secure permanently   **6** : to direct one's efforts   **7** : to fix by agreement   **8** : to give
legally   **9** : ADJUST, ARRANGE   **10** : DECIDE,
DETERMINE   **11** : to make a final disposition
of ⟨∼ an account⟩   **12** : to come to rest   **13**
: to reach an agreement on   **14** : to
sink gradually to a lower level   **15** : to
become clear by depositing sediment —
set·tler *n*

set·tle·ment \'se-t³l-mənt\ *n*   **1** : the act
or process of settling   **2** : BESTOWAL ⟨a

marriage ∼⟩   **3** : payment or adjustment
of an account   **4** : COLONY   **5** : a small
village   **6** : an institution providing various community services esp. to large city
populations   **7** : adjustment of doubts and
differences

set–to \'set-ˌtü\ *n, pl* **set–tos** : FIGHT

set·up \'set-ˌəp\ *n*   **1** : the manner or act
of arranging   **2** : glass, ice, and nonalcoholic beverage for mixing served to patrons who supply their own liquor   **3**
: something (as a plot) that has been constructed or contrived; *also* : FRAME-UP

set up *vb*   **1** : to place in position; *also*
: ASSEMBLE   **2** : CAUSE   **3** : FOUND, ES-
TABLISH ⟨*set up* a school⟩   **4** : FRAME 5

sev·en \'se-vən\ *n*   **1** : one more than six
2 : the 7th in a set or series   **3** : something
having seven units — **seven** *adj or pron*
— **sev·enth** \-vənth\ *adj or adv or n*

sev·en·teen \ˌse-vən-'tēn\ *n* : one more
than 16 — **seventeen** *adj or pron* —
sev·en·teenth \-'tēnth\ *adj or n*

seventeen–year locust *n* : a cicada of
the U.S. that has in the North a life of 17
years and in the South of 13 years of
which most is spent underground as a
nymph and only a few weeks as a winged
adult

sev·en·ty \'se-vən-tē\ *n, pl* **-ties** : seven
times 10 — **sev·en·ti·eth** \-tē-əth\ *adj or
n* — **seventy** *adj or pron*

sev·er \'se-vər\ *vb* **sev·ered; sev·er·ing**
: DIVIDE; *esp* : to separate by or as if by
cutting ⟨∼*ed* ties with his brother⟩ —
sev·er·ance \'sev-rəns, 'se-və-\ *n*

sev·er·al \'sev-rəl, 'se-və-\ *adj* [ME, fr.
AF, fr. ML *separalis*, fr. L *separ* separate,
fr. *separare* to separate]   **1** : INDIVIDUAL,
DISTINCT ⟨federal union of the ∼ states⟩
2 : consisting of an indefinite number but
yet not very many ⟨ate ∼ cookies⟩ —
sev·er·al·ly *adv*

severance pay *n* : extra pay given an employee on termination of employment

se·vere \sə-'vir\ *adj* **se·ver·er; -est   1**
: marked by strictness or sternness : AUS-
TERE   **2** : strict in discipline   **3** : causing
distress and esp. physical discomfort or
pain ⟨∼ weather⟩ ⟨a ∼ wound⟩   **4**
: hard to endure ⟨∼ trials⟩   **5** : SERIOUS
⟨∼ depression⟩   ♦ **Synonyms** STERN,
ASCETIC, ASTRINGENT — **se·vere·ly** *adv*
— **se·ver·i·ty** \-'ver-ə-tē\ *n*

sew \'sō\ *vb* **sewed; sewn** \'sōn\ *or*
sewed; sew·ing   1 : to unite or fasten by
stitches   **2** : to engage in sewing

sew·age \'sü-ij\ *n* : waste materials carried off by sewers

¹sew·er \'sō-ər\ *n* : one that sews

²sew·er \'sü-ər\ *n* : an artificial pipe or
channel to carry off waste matter

sew·er·age \'sü-ə-rij\ *n*   **1** : a system of
sewers   **2** : SEWAGE

sew·ing *n*   **1** : the activity of one who
sews   **2** : material that has been or is to be
sewed

sex \'seks\ *n*   **1** : either of the two major
forms that occur in many living things
and are designated male or female according to their role in reproduction; *also*
: the qualities by which these sexes are

differentiated and which directly or indirectly function in reproduction involving two parents **2** : sexual activity or behavior; *also* : SEXUAL INTERCOURSE — **sexed** \'sekst\ *adj*

sex·a·ge·nar·i·an \ˌsek-sə-jə-'ner-ē-ən\ *n* : a person whose age is in the sixties — **sexagenarian** *adj*

sex appeal *n* : personal appeal or physical attractiveness esp. for members of the opposite sex

sex cell *n* : an egg cell or sperm cell

sex chromosome *n* : one of usu. a pair of chromosomes that are usu. similar in one sex but different in the other sex and are concerned with the inheritance of sex

sex hormone *n* : a steroid hormone (as estrogen or testosterone) that is produced esp. by the gonads or adrenal cortex and chiefly affects the growth or function of the reproductive organs

sex·ism \'sek-ˌsi-zəm\ *n* : prejudice or discrimination based on sex; *esp* : discrimination against women — **sex·ist** \'sek-sist\ *adj or n*

sex·ol·o·gy \sek-'sä-lə-jē\ *n* : the study of sex or of the interactions of the sexes — **sex·ol·o·gist** \-jist\ *n*

sex·pot \'seks-ˌpät\ *n* : a conspicuously sexy woman

sex symbol *n* : a usu. renowned person (as an entertainer) noted and admired for conspicuous attractiveness

sex·tant \'sek-stənt\ *n* [NL *sextant-, sextans* sixth part of a circle, fr. L, sixth part, fr. *sextus* sixth] : a navigational instrument for determining latitude

sex·tet \sek-'tet\ *n* **1** : a musical composition for six voices or instruments; *also* : the performers of such a composition **2** : a group or set of six

sex·ton \'sek-stən\ *n* : one who takes care of church property

sex·u·al \'sek-shə-wəl\ *adj* : of, relating to, or involving sex or the sexes ⟨a ~ spore⟩ ⟨~ relations⟩ — **sex·u·al·i·ty** \ˌsek-shə-'wa-lə-tē\ *n* — **sex·u·al·ly** \'sek-shə-wə-lē\ *adv*

sexual intercourse *n* **1** : intercourse between a male and a female in which the penis is inserted into the vagina **2** : intercourse between individuals involving genital contact other than insertion of the penis into the vagina

sexually transmitted disease *n* : a disease (as syphilis, gonorrhea, AIDS, or the genital form of herpes simplex) that is caused by a microorganism or virus usu. or often transmitted by direct sexual contact

sexual relations *n pl* : SEXUAL INTERCOURSE

sexy \'sek-sē\ *adj* **sex·i·er; -est** : sexually suggestive or stimulating : EROTIC — **sex·i·ly** \-sə-lē\ *adv* — **sex·i·ness** \-sē-nəs\ *n*

SF *abbr* **1** sacrifice fly **2** science fiction **3** square feet

SFC *abbr* sergeant first class

¹**SG** *abbr* **1** sergeant **2** solicitor general **3** surgeon general

²**SG** *symbol* seaborgium

sgd *abbr* signed

Sgt *abbr* sergeant

Sgt Maj *abbr* sergeant major

sh *abbr* share

shab·by \'sha-bē\ *adj* **shab·bi·er; -est** **1** : dressed in worn clothes **2** : threadbare and faded from wear **3** : DESPICABLE, MEAN; *also* : UNFAIR ⟨~ treatment⟩ — **shab·bi·ly** \'sha-bə-lē\ *adv* — **shab·bi·ness** \-bē-nəs\ *n*

shack \'shak\ *n* : HUT, SHANTY

¹**shack·le** \'sha-kəl\ *n* **1** : something (as a manacle or fetter) that confines the legs or arms **2** : a check on free action made as if by fetters **3** : a device for making something fast or secure

²**shackle** *vb* **shack·led; shack·ling** : to bind or fasten with shackles

shad \'shad\ *n, pl* **shad** : any of several sea fishes related to the herrings that swim up rivers to spawn and include some important food fishes

¹**shade** \'shād\ *n* **1** : partial obscurity **2** : space sheltered from the light esp. of the sun **3** : PHANTOM **4** : something that shelters from or intercepts light or heat; *also, pl* : SUNGLASSES **5** : a dark color or a variety of a color **6** : a small difference

²**shade** *vb* **shad·ed; shad·ing** **1** : to shelter from light and heat **2** : DARKEN, OBSCURE **3** : to mark with degrees of light or color **4** : to show slight differences esp. in color or meaning

shad·ing *n* : the color and lines representing darkness or shadow in a drawing or painting

¹**shad·ow** \'sha-dō\ *n* **1** : partial darkness in a space from which light rays are cut off **2** : SHELTER **3** : shade cast upon a surface by something intercepting rays from a light ⟨the ~ of a tree⟩ **4** : PHANTOM **5** : a shaded portion of a picture **6** : a small portion or degree : TRACE ⟨a ~ of doubt⟩ **7** : a source of gloom or unhappiness — **shad·owy** *adj*

²**shadow** *vb* **1** : to cast a shadow on **2** : to represent faintly or vaguely **3** : to follow and watch closely : TRAIL

shad·ow·box \'sha-dō-ˌbäks\ *vb* : to box with an imaginary opponent esp. for training

shady \'shā-dē\ *adj* **shad·i·er; -est** **1** : affording shade **2** : of questionable honesty or reputation ⟨a ~ politician⟩

¹**shaft** \'shaft\ *n, pl* **shafts** **1** : the long handle of a spear or lance **2** : SPEAR, LANCE **3** *or pl* **shaves** \'shavz\ : POLE; *esp* : one of two poles between which a horse is hitched to pull a vehicle **4** : something (as a column) long and slender **5** : a bar to support a rotating piece or to transmit power by rotation **6** : an inclined opening in the ground (as for finding or mining ore) **7** : a vertical opening (as for an elevator) through the floors of a building **8** : harsh or unfair treatment — usu. used with *the*

²**shaft** *vb* **1** : to fit with a shaft **2** : to treat unfairly or harshly

shag \'shag\ *n* : a shaggy tangled mass or covering (as of wool) : long coarse or matted fiber, nap, or pile

shag·gy \'sha-gē\ *adj* **shag·gi·er; -est 1** : rough with or as if with long hair or wool **2** : tangled or rough in surface

shah \'shä, 'shò\ *n, often cap* : a sovereign of Iran

Shak *abbr* Shakespeare

¹**shake** \'shāk\ *vb* **shook** \'shùk\; **shak·en** \'shā-kən\; **shak·ing 1** : to move or cause to move jerkily or irregularly **2** : BRANDISH, WAVE ⟨*shaking* his fist⟩ **3** : to disturb emotionally ⟨*shaken* by her death⟩ **4** : WEAKEN ⟨*shook* his faith⟩ **5** : to bring or come into a certain position, condition, or arrangement by or as if by moving jerkily **6** : to clasp (hands) in greeting or as a sign of goodwill or agreement ♦ *Synonyms* TREMBLE, QUAKE, QUAVER, SHIVER, QUIVER — **shak·able** *or* **shake·able** \'shā-kə-bəl\ *adj*

²**shake** *n* **1** : the act or a result of shaking **2** : DEAL, TREATMENT ⟨a fair ∼⟩

shake·down \'shāk-ˌdaùn\ *n* **1** : an improvised beg ⟨a ∼⟩ **2** : EXTORTION ⟨was a victim of a ∼⟩ **3** : a process or period of adjustment **4** : a test (as of a new ship or airplane) under operating conditions

shake down *vb* **1** : to take up temporary quarters **2** : to occupy a makeshift bed **3** : to become accustomed esp. to new surroundings or duties **4** : to settle down **5** : to give a shakedown test to **6** : to obtain money from in a deceitful or illegal manner **7** : to bring about a reduction of

shak·er \'shā-kər\ *n* **1** : one that shakes ⟨pepper ∼⟩ **2** *cap* : a member of a religious sect founded in England in 1747

Shake·spear·ean *or* **Shake·spear·ian** \shāk-ˈspir-ē-ən\ *adj* : of, relating to, or having the characteristics of Shakespeare or his writings

shake–up \'shāk-ˌəp\ *n* : an extensive often drastic reorganization

shaky \'shā-kē\ *adj* **shak·i·er; -est** : UNSOUND, WEAK ⟨a ∼ ladder⟩ — **shak·i·ly** \'shā-kə-lē\ *adv* — **shak·i·ness** \-kē-nəs\ *n*

shale \'shāl\ *n* : a finely layered rock formed from clay, mud, or silt

shall \shəl, 'shal\ *vb, past* **should** \shəd, 'shùd\ *pres sing & pl* **shall** — used as an auxiliary to express a command, what seems inevitable or likely in the future, simple futurity, or determination

shal·lop \'sha-ləp\ *n* : a light open boat

shal·lot \shə-ˈlät, 'sha-lət\ *n* [modif. of F *échalote*] **1** : a small clustered bulb that is used in seasoning and is produced by a perennial herb belonging to a subspecies of the onion; *also* : this herb **2** : GREEN ONION

¹**shal·low** \'sha-lō\ *adj* **1** : not deep **2** : not intellectually profound

²**shallow** *n* : a shallow place in a body of water — usu. used in pl.

¹**sham** \'sham\ *n* **1** : an ornamental covering for a pillow **2** : COUNTERFEIT, IMITATION **3** : a person who shams

²**sham** *vb* **shammed; sham·ming** : FEIGN, PRETEND — **sham·mer** *n*

³**sham** *adj* : not genuine : FALSE, FEIGNED

sha·man \'shä-mən, 'shā-\ *n* [ultim. fr. Evenki (a language of Siberia) *šamán*] : a priest or priestess who uses magic to cure the sick, to divine the hidden, and to control events

sham·ble \'sham-bəl\ *vb* **sham·bled; sham·bling** : to shuffle along — **shamble** *n*

sham·bles \'sham-bəlz\ *n* **1** : a scene of great slaughter **2** : a scene or state of great destruction or disorder; *also* : MESS

¹**shame** \'shām\ *n* **1** : a painful sense of having done something wrong, improper, or immodest **2** : DISGRACE, DISHONOR **3** : a cause of feeling shame **4** : something to be regretted ⟨it's a ∼ you'll miss the party⟩ — **shame·ful** \-fəl\ *adj* — **shame·ful·ly** *adv* — **shame·less** *adj* — **shame·less·ly** *adv*

²**shame** *vb* **shamed; sham·ing 1** : DISGRACE **2** : to make ashamed

shame·faced \'shām-ˌfāst\ *adj* : ASHAMED, ABASHED — **shame·faced·ly** \-ˌfā-səd-lē, -ˌfāst-lē\ *adv*

¹**sham·poo** \sham-ˈpü\ *vb* [Hindi *cãpo*, imper. of *cãpnā* to press, shampoo] : to wash (as the hair) with soap and water or with a special preparation; *also* : to clean (as a rug) similarly

²**shampoo** *n, pl* **shampoos 1** : the act or an instance of shampooing **2** : a preparation for use in shampooing

sham·rock \'sham-ˌräk\ *n* [Ir *seamróg*, dim. of *seamar* clover] : a plant of folk legend with leaves composed of three leaflets that is associated with St. Patrick and Ireland

shang·hai \shaŋ-ˈhī\ *vb* **shang·haied; shang·hai·ing** [*Shanghai*, China] : to force aboard a ship for service as a sailor; *also* : to trick or force into an undesirable position

Shan·gri–la \ˌshaŋ-gri-ˈlä\ *n* [*Shangri-La*, imaginary land depicted in the novel *Lost Horizon* (1933) by James Hilton] : a remote idyllic hideaway

shank \'shaŋk\ *n* **1** : the part of the leg between the knee and the human ankle or a corresponding part of a quadruped **2** : a cut of meat from the leg **3** : the narrow part of the sole of a shoe beneath the instep **4** : the part of a tool or instrument (as a key or anchor) connecting the functioning part with a part by which it is held or moved

shan·tung \ˌshan-ˈtəŋ\ *n* : a fabric in plain weave having a slightly irregular surface

shan·ty \'shan-tē\ *n, pl* **shanties** [prob. fr. CanF *chantier* lumber camp, hut, fr. F, builder's yard, ways, support for barrels, fr. OF, support, fr. L *cantherius* rafter, trellis] : a small roughly built shelter or dwelling

¹**shape** \'shāp\ *vb* **shaped; shap·ing 1** : to form esp. in a particular shape **2** : DESIGN **3** : ADAPT, ADJUST **4** : REGULATE ♦ *Synonyms* MAKE, FASHION, FABRICATE, MANUFACTURE, FRAME, MOLD

²**shape** *n* **1** : APPEARANCE ⟨the ∼ of an apple⟩ **2** : surface configuration : FORM **3** : bodily contour apart from the head

and face : FIGURE 4 : PHANTOM 5 : CONDITION ⟨was in fine ∼⟩ — **shaped** adj

shape·less \'shā-pləs\ adj 1 : having no definite shape 2 : not shapely — **shape·less·ly** adv — **shape·less·ness** n

shape·ly \'shā-plē\ adj **shape·li·er; -est** : having a pleasing shape ⟨a ∼ model⟩ — **shape·li·ness** n

shape–shift·er \'shāp-ˌshif-tər\ n : one that seems able to change form or identity at will

shard \'shärd\ also **sherd** \'shərd\ n : a broken piece : FRAGMENT

¹**share** \'sher\ n : PLOWSHARE

²**share** n 1 : a portion belonging to one person or group 2 : any of the equal interests into which the capital stock of a corporation is divided

³**share** vb **shared; shar·ing** 1 : APPORTION 2 : to use or enjoy with others 3 : PARTICIPATE — **shar·er** n

share·crop·per \-ˌkrä-pər\ n : a farmer who works another's land in return for a share of the crop — **share·crop** vb

share·hold·er \-ˌhōl-dər\ n : STOCKHOLDER

share·ware \'sher-ˌwer\ n : software available for usu. limited trial use at little or no cost but that can be upgraded for a fee

¹**shark** \'shärk\ n : any of various active, usu. predatory, and mostly large marine cartilaginous fishes

²**shark** n : a greedy crafty person

shark·skin \-ˌskin\ n 1 : the hide of a shark or leather made from it 2 : a fabric woven from strands of many fine threads and having a sleek appearance and silky feel

¹**sharp** \'shärp\ adj 1 : having a thin cutting edge or fine point : not dull or blunt 2 : COLD, NIPPING ⟨a ∼ wind⟩ 3 : keen in intellect, perception, or attention 4 : BRISK, ENERGETIC 5 : IRRITABLE ⟨a ∼ temper⟩ 6 : causing intense distress ⟨a ∼ pain⟩ 7 : HARSH, CUTTING ⟨a ∼ rebuke⟩ 8 : affecting the senses as if cutting or piercing ⟨a ∼ sound⟩ ⟨a ∼ smell⟩ 9 : not smooth or rounded ⟨∼ features⟩ 10 : involving an abrupt or extreme change ⟨a ∼ turn⟩ 11 : CLEAR, DISTINCT ⟨mountains in ∼ relief⟩; also : easy to perceive ⟨a ∼ contrast⟩ 12 : higher than the true pitch; also : raised by a half step 13 : STYLISH ⟨a ∼ dresser⟩ ♦ Synonyms KEEN, ACUTE, QUICK-WITTED, PENETRATIVE — **sharp·ly** adv — **sharp·ness** n

²**sharp** adv 1 : in a sharp manner 2 : EXACTLY, PRECISELY ⟨left at 8 ∼⟩

³**sharp** n 1 : a sharp edge or point 2 : a character # which indicates that a specified note is to be raised by a half step; also : the resulting note 3 : SHARPER

⁴**sharp** vb : to raise in pitch by a half step

shar–pei \ˌshä-'pā, ˌshär-\ n, pl **shar-peis** often cap S&P [Chin (Guangdong dial.) sà sand + pêi fur] : any of a Chinese breed of dogs that have loose wrinkled skin esp. when young

sharp·en \'shär-pən\ vb : to make or become sharp — **sharp·en·er** n

sharp·er \'shär-pər\ n : SWINDLER; esp : a cheating gambler

sharp·ie or **sharpy** \'shär-pē\ n, pl **sharp·ies** 1 : SHARPER 2 : a person who is exceptionally keen or alert

sharp·shoot·er \'shärp-ˌshü-tər\ n : a proficient marksman — **sharp·shoot·ing** n

shat·ter \'sha-tər\ vb : to dash or burst into fragments — **shat·ter·proof** \'sha-tər-ˌprüf\ adj

¹**shave** \'shāv\ vb **shaved; shaved** or **shav·en** \'shā-vən\; **shav·ing** 1 : to slice in thin pieces 2 : to make bare or smooth by cutting the hair from 3 : to cut or pare off by the sliding movement of a razor 4 : to skim along or near the surface of

²**shave** n 1 : any of various tools for cutting thin slices 2 : an act or process of shaving

shav·er \'shā-vər\ n 1 : an electric razor 2 : BOY, YOUNGSTER

shaves pl of SHAFT

shaving n 1 : the act of one that shaves 2 : something shaved off

shawl \'shól\ n : a square or oblong piece of fabric used esp. by women as a loose covering for the head or shoulders

Shaw·nee \shó-'nē, shä-\ n, pl **Shawnee** or **Shawnees** : a member of an American Indian people orig. of the central Ohio valley; also : their language

shd abbr should

she \'shē\ pron : that female one ⟨who is ∼⟩; also : that one regarded as feminine ⟨∼'s a fine ship⟩

sheaf \'shēf\ n, pl **sheaves** \'shēvz\ 1 : a bundle of stalks and ears of grain 2 : a group of things bound together

¹**shear** \'shir\ vb **sheared; sheared** or **shorn** \'shórn\; **shear·ing** 1 : to cut the hair or wool from : CLIP, TRIM 2 : to deprive by or as if by cutting ⟨a tyrant shorn of power⟩ 3 : to cut or break sharply

²**shear** n 1 : any of various cutting tools that consist of two blades fastened together so that the edges slide one by the other — usu. used in pl. 2 chiefly Brit : the act, an instance, or the result of shearing 3 : an action or stress caused by applied forces that causes two parts of a body to slide on each other

shear·wa·ter \'shir-ˌwò-tər, -ˌwä-\ n : any of several seabirds related to the petrels that often skim along waves in flight

sheath \'shēth\ n, pl **sheaths** \'shēthz, 'shēths\ 1 : a case for a blade (as of a knife); also : an anatomical covering suggesting such a case 2 : a close-fitting dress usu. worn without a belt

sheathe \'shēth\ also **sheath** \'shēth\ vb **sheathed; sheath·ing** 1 : to put into a sheath 2 : to cover with something that guards or protects

sheath·ing \'shē-thiŋ, -thiŋ\ n : material used to sheathe something; esp : the first covering of boards or of waterproof material on the outside wall of a frame house or on a timber roof

sheave \'shiv, 'shēv\ *n* : a grooved wheel or pulley (as on a pulley block)

she-bang \shi-'baŋ\ *n* : everything involved in what is under consideration ⟨sold the whole ∼⟩

¹**shed** \'shed\ *vb* **shed; shed·ding 1** : to cause to flow from a cut or wound ⟨∼ blood⟩ **2** : to pour down in drops ⟨∼ tears⟩ **3** : to give out (as light) : DIFFUSE **4** : to throw off (as a natural covering) : DISCARD ⟨∼ skin⟩

²**shed** *n* : a slight structure built for shelter or storage

sheen \'shēn\ *n* : a subdued luster

sheep \'shēp\ *n, pl* **sheep 1** : any of various cud-chewing mammals that are stockier than the related goats and lack a beard in the male; *esp* : one raised for meat or for its wool or skin **2** : a timid or defenseless person **3** : SHEEPSKIN

sheep·dog \'shēp-,dȯg\ *n* : a dog used to tend, drive, or guard sheep

sheep·fold \'shēp-,fōld\ *n* : a pen or shelter for sheep

sheep·herd·er \-,hər-dər\ *n* : a worker in charge of sheep esp. on open range — **sheep·herd·ing** *n*

sheep·ish \'shē-pish\ *adj* : BASHFUL, TIMID; *esp* : embarrassed by consciousness of a fault — **sheep·ish·ly** *adv*

sheep·skin \'shēp-,skin\ *n* **1** : the hide of a sheep or leather prepared from it; *also* : PARCHMENT **2** : DIPLOMA

¹**sheer** \'shir\ *vb* : to turn from a course

²**sheer** *adj* **1** : very thin or transparent **2** : UNQUALIFIED ⟨∼ folly⟩ **3** : very steep ⟨∼ of ice⟩
♦ **Synonyms** PURE, SIMPLE, ABSOLUTE, UNADULTERATED, UNMITIGATED — **sheer** *adv*

¹**sheet** \'shēt\ *n* **1** : a broad piece of cloth (as for a bed); *also* : SAIL **1 2** : a single piece of paper **3** : a broad flat surface ⟨a ∼ of ice⟩ **4** : something broad and long and relatively thin

²**sheet** *n* : a rope used to trim a sail

sheet·ing \'shē-tiŋ\ *n* : material in the form of sheets or suitable for forming into sheets

sheikh *or* **sheik** \'shēk, 'shāk\ *n* : an Arab chief — **sheikh·dom** *or* **sheik·dom** \-dəm\ *n*

shek·el \'she-kəl\ *n* — see MONEY table

shelf \'shelf\ *n, pl* **shelves** \'shelvz\ **1** : a thin flat usu. long and narrow structure fastened horizontally (as on a wall) above the floor to hold things **2** : something (as a sandbar) that suggests a shelf

shelf life *n* : the period of storage time during which a material will remain useful

¹**shell** \'shel\ *n* **1** : a hard or tough often thin outer covering of an animal (as a beetle, turtle, or mollusk) or of an egg or a seed or fruit (as a nut); *also* : something that resembles a shell ⟨a pastry ∼⟩ **2** : a light narrow racing boat propelled by oarsmen **3** : a case holding an explosive and designed to be fired from a cannon; *also* : a case holding the charge of powder and shot or bullet for small arms **4** : a plain usu. sleeveless blouse or sweater —

shelled \'sheld\ *adj* — **shelly** \'she-lē\ *adj*

²**shell** *vb* **1** : to remove from a shell or husk **2** : BOMBARD — **shell·er** *n*

¹**shel·lac** \shə-'lak\ *n* **1** : a purified lac **2** : lac dissolved in alcohol and used as a wood filler or finish

²**shellac** *vb* **shel·lacked; shel·lack·ing 1** : to coat or treat with shellac **2** : to defeat decisively ⟨*shellacked* their opponents⟩

shellacking *n* : a sound drubbing

shell bean *n* : a bean grown esp. for its edible seeds; *also* : its edible seed

shell·fish \-,fish\ *n* : an invertebrate water animal (as an oyster or lobster) with a shell

shell out *vb* : PAY

shell shock *n* : COMBAT FATIGUE — **shell–shocked** \'shel-,shäkt\ *adj*

¹**shel·ter** \'shel-tər\ *n* : something that gives protection : REFUGE

²**shelter** *vb* **shel·tered; shel·ter·ing** : to give protection or refuge to

shelve \'shelv\ *vb* **shelved; shelv·ing 1** : to slope gradually **2** : to store on shelves **3** : to dismiss from service or use **4** : to put aside : DEFER ⟨∼ a proposal⟩

shelv·ing \'shel-viŋ\ *n* : material for shelves; *also* : SHELVES

she·nan·i·gan \shə-'na-ni-gən\ *n* **1** : an underhand trick **2** : questionable conduct — usu. used in pl. **3** : high-spirited or mischievous activity — usu. used in pl.

¹**shep·herd** \'she-pərd\ *n* **1** : one who tends sheep **2** : GERMAN SHEPHERD

²**shepherd** *vb* : to tend as or in the manner of a shepherd

shep·herd·ess \'she-pər-dəs\ *n* : a woman who tends sheep

shepherd's pie *n* : a meat pie with a mashed potato crust

sheqel *n, pl* **sheqalim** *var of* SHEKEL

sher·bet \'shər-bət\ *n* [Turk *şerbet*, fr. Pers *sharbat*, fr. Ar *sharba* drink] **1** : a drink of sweetened diluted fruit juice **2** *also* **sher·bert** \-,bərt\ : a frozen dessert of fruit juices, sugar, milk or water, and egg whites or gelatin

sherd *var of* SHARD

sher·iff \'sher-əf\ *n* [ME *shirreve*, fr. OE *scīrgerēfa*, lit., shire reeve (local official)] : a county officer charged with the execution of the law and the preservation of order

sher·ry \'sher-ē\ *n, pl* **sherries** [alter. of earlier *sherris* (taken as pl.), fr. *Xeres* (now *Jerez*), Spain] : a fortified wine with a nutty flavor

Shet·land pony \'shet-lənd-\ *n* : any of a breed of small stocky hardy ponies

shew \'shō\ *Brit var of* SHOW

shi·at·su *also* **shi·at·zu** \shē-'ät-sü\ *n* : a form of acupressure originating in Japan

shib·bo·leth \'shi-bə-ləth\ *n* [Heb *shibbōleth* stream; fr. the use of this word as a test to distinguish the men of Gilead from members of the tribe of Ephraim (Judges 12:5, 6)] **1** : CATCHPHRASE **2** : language that is a criterion for distinguishing members of a group

¹**shield** \'shēld\ *n* **1** : a broad piece of de-

fensive armor carried on the arm **2** : something that protects or hides **3** : a police officer's badge

²**shield** *vb* : to protect or hide with a shield
♦ **Synonyms** PROTECT, GUARD, SAFEGUARD

shier *comparative of* SHY
shiest *superlative of* SHY

¹**shift** \'shift\ *vb* **1** : EXCHANGE, REPLACE **2** : to change place, position, or direction : MOVE; *also* : to change gears **3** : GET BY, MANAGE

²**shift** *n* **1** : SCHEME, TRICK **2** : a woman's slip or loose-fitting dress **3** : a change in direction, emphasis, or attitude **4** : a group working together alternating with other groups **5** : TRANSFER **6** : GEARSHIFT

shift·less \'shift-ləs\ *adj* : LAZY, INEFFICIENT — **shift·less·ness** *n*

shifty \'shif-tē\ *adj* **shift·i·er; -est 1** : TRICKY; *also* : ELUSIVE **2** : indicative of a tricky nature ⟨~ eyes⟩

shih tzu \'shēd-'zü, 'shēt-'sü\ *n, pl* **shih tzus** *also* **shih tzu** *often cap S&T* [Chin (Beijing) *shīzi (gǒu)*, fr. *shīzi* lion + *gǒu* dog] : any of a breed of small shortlegged dogs of Chinese origin that have a short muzzle and a long dense coat

shii·ta·ke \shē-'tä-kē\ *n* [Jp] : a dark Asian mushroom widely cultivated for its edible cap

shill \'shil\ *n* : one who acts as a decoy (as for a pitchman) — **shill** *vb*

shil·le·lagh *also* **shil·la·lah** \shə-'lā-lē\ *n* [*Shillelagh*, town in Ireland] : CUDGEL, CLUB

shil·ling \'shi-liŋ\ *n* — see MONEY table

shil·ly–shal·ly \'shi-lē-,sha-lē\ *vb* **shilly-shal·lied; shil·ly–shal·ly·ing 1** : to show hesitation or lack of decisiveness **2** : to waste time

shim \'shim\ *n* : a thin often tapered piece of wood, metal, or stone used (as in leveling) to fill in space

shim·mer \'shi-mər\ *vb* : to shine waveringly or tremulously : GLIMMER ⟨~ing light⟩ ♦ **Synonyms** FLASH, GLEAM, GLINT, SPARKLE, GLITTER — **shimmer** *n* — **shim·mery** *adj*

shim·my \'shi-mē\ *n, pl* **shimmies** : an abnormal vibration esp. in the front wheels of a motor vehicle — **shimmy** *vb*

¹**shin** \'shin\ *n* : the front part of the leg below the knee

²**shin** *vb* **shinned; shin·ning** : to climb (as a pole) by gripping alternately with arms or hands and legs

shin·bone \'shin-,bōn\ *n* : TIBIA

¹**shine** \'shīn\ *vb* **shone** \'shōn\ *or* **shined; shin·ing 1** : to give or cause to give light **2** : GLEAM, GLITTER **3** : to be eminent, conspicuous, or distinguished ⟨gave her a chance to ~⟩ **4** : POLISH ⟨~ your shoes⟩

²**shine** *n* **1** : BRIGHTNESS, RADIANCE **2** : LUSTER, BRILLIANCE **3** : fair weather : SUNSHINE ⟨rain or ~⟩ **4** : LIKING, FANCY ⟨took a ~ to them⟩ **5** : a polish given to shoes

shin·er \'shī-nər\ *n* **1** : a silvery fish; *esp* : any of numerous small freshwater

American fishes related to the carp **2** : BLACK EYE

¹**shin·gle** \'shiŋ-gəl\ *n* **1** : a small thin piece of building material used in overlapping rows for covering a roof or outside wall **2** : a small sign

²**shingle** *vb* **shin·gled; shin·gling** : to cover with shingles

³**shingle** *n* : a beach strewn with gravel; *also* : coarse gravel (as on a beach)

shin·gles \'shiŋ-gəlz\ *n* : an acute inflammation of the spinal and cranial nerves caused by reactivation of the chicken pox virus and associated with eruptions and pain along the course of the affected nerves

shin·ny \'shi-nē\ *vb* **shin·nied; shin·ny·ing** : SHIN

shin splints *n sing or pl* : a condition marked by pain and sometimes tenderness and swelling in the shin caused by repeated small injuries to muscles and associated tissue esp. from running

Shin·to \'shin-,tō\ *n* : the indigenous religion of Japan consisting esp. in reverence of the spirits of natural forces and imperial ancestors — **Shin·to·ism** *n* — **Shin·to·ist** *n or adj*

shiny \'shī-nē\ *adj* **shin·i·er; -est** : BRIGHT, RADIANT; *also* : POLISHED

¹**ship** \'ship\ *n* **1** : a large oceangoing boat **2** : a ship's officers and crew **3** : AIRSHIP, AIRCRAFT, SPACECRAFT

²**ship** *vb* **shipped; ship·ping 1** : to put or receive on board a ship for transportation **2** : to have transported by a carrier **3** : to take or draw into a boat ⟨~ oars⟩ ⟨~ water⟩ **4** : to engage to serve on a ship — **ship·per** *n*

-ship \ship\ *n suffix* **1** : state : condition : quality ⟨friend*ship*⟩ **2** : office : dignity : profession ⟨lord*ship*⟩ ⟨clerk*ship*⟩ **3** : art : skill ⟨horseman*ship*⟩ **4** : something showing, exhibiting, or embodying a quality or state ⟨town*ship*⟩ **5** : one entitled to a (specified) rank, title, or appellation ⟨his Lord*ship*⟩ **6** : the body of persons engaged in a specified activity ⟨reader*ship*⟩

ship·board \'ship-,bȯrd\ *n* : SHIP

ship·build·er \-,bil-dər\ *n* : one who designs or builds ships

ship·fit·ter \-,fi-tər\ *n* **1** : one who constructs ships **2** : a naval enlisted person who works as a plumber

ship·mate \-,māt\ *n* : a fellow sailor

ship·ment \-mənt\ *n* : the process of shipping; *also* : the goods shipped

shipping *n* **1** : SHIPS; *esp* : ships in one port or belonging to one country **2** : transportation of goods

ship·shape \'ship-,shāp\ *adj* : TRIM, TIDY ⟨kept the garage ~⟩

ship·worm \-,wərm\ *n* : any of various wormlike marine clams that have a shell used for burrowing in wood and damage wooden ships and wharves

¹**ship·wreck** \-,rek\ *n* **1** : a wrecked ship **2** : destruction or loss of a ship **3** : total loss or failure : RUIN

²**shipwreck** *vb* : to cause or meet disaster at sea through destruction or foundering

ship·wright \'ship-ˌrīt\ n : a carpenter skilled in ship construction and repair

ship·yard \-ˌyärd\ n : a place where ships are built or repaired

shire \'shī(-ə)r, *in place-name compounds* ˌshir, shər\ n : a county in Great Britain

shirk \'shərk\ vb : to avoid performing (duty or work) — **shirk·er** n

shirr \'shər\ vb 1 : to make shirring in 2 : to bake (eggs removed from the shell) until set

shirr·ing \'shər-iŋ\ n : a decorative gathering in cloth made by drawing up parallel lines of stitches

shirt \'shərt\ n 1 : a loose cloth garment usu. having a collar, sleeves, a front opening, and a tail long enough to be tucked inside pants or a skirt 2 : UNDERSHIRT — **shirt·less** adj

shirt·ing \'shər-tiŋ\ n : cloth suitable for making shirts

shish ke·bab \'shish-kə-ˌbäb\ n [Turk *şiş kebabı*, fr. *şiş* spit + *kebap* roast meat] : kebab cooked on skewers

shiv \'shiv\ n, slang : KNIFE

¹**shiv·er** \'shi-vər\ vb : TREMBLE, QUIVER
♦ *Synonyms* SHUDDER, QUAVER, SHAKE, QUAKE

²**shiver** n : an instance of shivering — **shiv·ery** adj

shlemiel var of SCHLEMIEL

shlub var of SCHLUB

shmooze var of SCHMOOZE

Sho·ah \'shō-ə, -ˌä\ n : HOLOCAUST 2

¹**shoal** \'shōl\ n 1 : SHALLOW 2 : a sandbank or bar creating a shallow

²**shoal** n : a large group (as of fish)

shoat \'shōt\ n : a weaned young pig

¹**shock** \'shäk\ n : a pile of sheaves of grain or cornstalks set up in a field

²**shock** n [MF *choc*, fr. *choquer* to strike against] 1 : a sharp impact or violent shake or jar 2 : a sudden violent mental or emotional disturbance 3 : a state of bodily collapse that is often marked by a drop in blood pressure and volume and that is caused esp. by crushing wounds, blood loss, or burns 4 : the effect of a charge of electricity passing through the body 5 : SHOCK ABSORBER — **shock·proof** \-ˌprüf\ adj

³**shock** vb 1 : to strike with surprise, horror, or disgust 2 : to subject to the action of an electrical discharge

⁴**shock** n : a thick bushy mass (as of hair)

shock absorber n : any of several devices for absorbing the energy of sudden shocks in machinery

shock·er \'shä-kər\ n : one that shocks; *esp* : a sensational work of fiction or drama

shock·ing \'shä-kiŋ\ adj : extremely startling and offensive — **shock·ing·ly** adv

shock therapy n : the treatment of mental disorder by induction of coma or convulsions by drugs or electricity

shock wave n : a wave formed by the sudden violent compression of the medium through which it travels

¹**shod·dy** \'shä-dē\ n 1 : wool reclaimed from old rags; *also* : a fabric made from it 2 : inferior or imitation material

²**shoddy** adj **shod·di·er; -est** 1 : made of shoddy 2 : poorly done or made ⟨∼ workmanship⟩ — **shod·di·ly** \'shä-də-lē\ adv — **shod·di·ness** \-dē-nəs\ n

¹**shoe** \'shü\ n 1 : a covering for the human foot 2 : HORSESHOE 3 : the part of a brake that presses on the wheel

²**shoe** vb **shod** \'shäd\ *also* **shoed** \'shüd\; **shoe·ing** : to put a shoe or shoes on

shoe·horn \-ˌhórn\ n : a curved implement (as of horn or plastic) used in putting on a shoe

shoe·lace \'shü-ˌlās\ n : a lace or string for fastening a shoe

shoe·mak·er \-ˌmā-kər\ n : one who makes or repairs shoes

shoe·string \-ˌstriŋ\ n 1 : SHOELACE 2 : a small sum of money

sho·gun \'shō-gən\ n [Jp *shōgun* general] : any of a line of military governors ruling Japan in the revolution of 1867–68 — **sho·gun·ate** \'shō-gə-nət, -ˌnät\ n

shone *past and past part of* SHINE

shook *past of* SHAKE

shook–up \(ˌ)shúk-'əp\ adj : nervously upset : AGITATED

¹**shoot** \'shüt\ vb **shot** \'shät\; **shoot·ing** 1 : to drive (as an arrow or bullet) forward quickly or forcibly 2 : to hit, kill, or wound with a missile 3 : to cause a missile to be driven forth or forth from ⟨∼ a gun⟩ 4 : to send forth (as a ray of light) 5 : to thrust forward or out 6 : to pass rapidly along ⟨∼ the rapids⟩ 7 : PHOTOGRAPH, FILM 8 : to move swiftly : DART 9 : to grow by or as if by sending out shoots; *also* : MATURE, DEVELOP — **shoot·er** n

²**shoot** n 1 : a plant stem with its leaves and branches esp. when not yet mature 2 : an act of shooting 3 : a shooting match

shooting iron n : FIREARM

shooting star n : METEOR 2

shoot up vb : to inject a narcotic into a vein

¹**shop** \'shäp\ n [ME *shoppe*, fr. OE *sceoppa* booth] 1 : a place where things are made or worked on : FACTORY, MILL 2 : a retail store ⟨dress ∼⟩

²**shop** vb **shopped; shop·ping** : to visit stores for purchasing or examining goods — **shop·per** n

shop·keep·er \'shäp-ˌkē-pər\ n : a retail merchant

shop·lift \-ˌlift\ vb : to steal goods on display from a store — **shop·lift·er** n

shop·talk \-ˌtók\ n : talk about one's business or special interests

shop·worn \-ˌwórn\ adj : soiled or frayed from much handling in a store

¹**shore** \'shór\ n : land along the edge of a body of water — **shore·less** adj

²**shore** vb **shored; shor·ing** : to give support to : BRACE

³**shore** n : ¹PROP

shore·bird \-ˌbərd\ n : any of a suborder of birds (as the plovers and sandpipers) found mostly along the seashore

shore patrol n : a branch of a navy that exercises guard and police functions

shor·ing \'shór-iŋ\ n : a group of things that shore something up

shorn *past part of* SHEAR
¹short \'shȯrt\ *adj* **1** : not long or tall **2** : not great in distance **3** : brief in time **4** : not coming up to standard or to an expected amount **5** : CURT, ABRUPT ⟨was ~ with the busybody⟩ **6** : insufficiently supplied ⟨~ of cash⟩ **7** : made with shortening : FLAKY **8** : consisting of or relating to a sale of securities or commodities that the seller does not possess or has not contracted for at the time of the sale ⟨~ sale⟩ — **short·ness** *n*
²short *adv* **1** : ABRUPTLY, CURTLY **2** : at some point before a goal aimed at
³short *n* **1** : something shorter than normal or standard **2** *pl* : drawers or pants of less than knee length **3** : SHORT CIRCUIT
⁴short *vb* : SHORT-CIRCUIT
short·age \'shȯr-tij\ *n* : LACK, DEFICIT
short·cake \'shȯrt-ˌkāk\ *n* : a dessert consisting of short biscuit spread with sweetened fruit
short·change \-'chānj\ *vb* : to cheat esp. by giving less than the correct amount of change
short circuit *n* : a connection made between points in an electric circuit where current is not intended to flow — **short-circuit** *vb*
short·com·ing \'shȯrt-ˌkə-miŋ\ *n* : FAULT 1, FLAW
short·cut \-ˌkət\ *n* **1** : a route more direct than that usu. taken **2** : a quicker way of doing something
short·en \'shȯr-t²n\ *vb* : to make or become short ♦ *Synonyms* CURTAIL, ABBREVIATE, ABRIDGE, RETRENCH
short·en·ing \'shȯr-t²n-iŋ\ *n* : a substance (as lard or butter) that makes pastry tender and flaky
short·hand \'shȯrt-ˌhand\ *n* : a method of writing rapidly by using symbols and abbreviations for letters, words, or phrases : STENOGRAPHY
short·hand·ed \ˌshȯrt-'han-dəd\ *adj* : short of the needed number of people
short·horn \'shȯrt-ˌhȯrn\ *n, often cap* : any of a breed of red, roan, or white cattle of English origin
short hundredweight *n* — see WEIGHT table
short–lived \'shȯrt-ˌlivd, -'līvd\ *adj* : of short life or duration
short·ly \'shȯrt-lē\ *adv* **1** : in a few words **2** : in a short time : SOON
short–or·der \'shȯrt-ˌȯr-dər\ *adj* : preparing or serving food that can be quickly cooked ⟨a ~ cook⟩
short shrift *n* **1** : a brief respite from death **2** : little consideration
short·sight·ed \'shȯrt-ˌsī-təd\ *adj* **1** : lacking foresight **2** : NEARSIGHTED — **short·sight·ed·ness** *n*
short·stop \-ˌstäp\ *n* : a baseball player defending the area between second and third base
short story *n* : a short work of fiction usu. dealing with a few characters and a single event
short–tem·pered \ˌshȯrt-'tem-pərd\ *adj* : having a quick temper

short–term \'shȯrt-ˌtərm\ *adj* **1** : occurring over or involving a relatively short period of time **2** : of or relating to a financial transaction based on a term usu. of less than a year
short ton *n* — see WEIGHT table
short·wave \'shȯrt-ˌwāv\ *n* : a radio wave with a wavelength between 10 and 100 meters
Sho·sho·ne *or* **Sho·sho·ni** \shə-'shō-nē\ *n, pl* **Shoshones** *or* **Shoshoni** : a member of an American Indian people orig. ranging through California, Idaho, Nevada, Utah, and Wyoming
¹shot \'shät\ *n* **1** : an act of shooting **2** : a stroke or throw in some games **3** : something that is shot : MISSILE, PROJECTILE; *esp* : small pellets forming a charge for a shotgun **4** : a metal sphere that is thrown for distance in the shot put **5** : RANGE, REACH **6** : MARKSMAN **7** : a single photographic exposure **8** : a single sequence of a motion picture or a television program made by one camera **9** : an injection (as of medicine) into the body **10** : a small serving of undiluted liquor or other beverage
²shot *past and past part of* SHOOT
shot·gun \'shät-ˌgən\ *n* : a gun with a smooth bore used to fire shot at short range
shot put *n* : a field event in which a shot is heaved for distance
should \'shu̇d, shəd\ *past of* SHALL — used as an auxiliary to express condition, obligation or propriety, probability, or futurity from a point of view in the past
¹shoul·der \'shōl-dər\ *n* **1** : the part of the body of a person or animal where the arm or foreleg joins the body **2** : either edge of a roadway **3** : a rounded or sloping part (as of a bottle) where the neck joins the body
²shoulder *vb* **1** : to push or thrust with the shoulder **2** : to bear on the shoulder **3** : to take the responsibility of
shoulder belt *n* : an automobile safety belt worn across the torso and over the shoulder
shoulder blade *n* : a flat triangular bone at the back of each shoulder
shout \'shȧu̇t\ *vb* : to utter a sudden loud cry — **shout** *n*
shove \'shəv\ *vb* **shoved; shov·ing** : to push along, aside, or away — **shove** *n*
¹shov·el \'shə-vəl\ *n* **1** : a broad long-handled scoop used to lift and throw material **2** : the amount a shovel will hold — **shov·el·ful** \-ˌfu̇l\ *n*
²shovel *vb* **-eled** *or* **-elled; -el·ing** *or* **-el·ling** **1** : to take up and throw with a shovel **2** : to dig or clean out with a shovel
¹show \'shō\ *vb* **showed** \'shōd\; **shown** \'shōn\ *or* **showed; show·ing** **1** : to cause or permit to be seen : EXHIBIT ⟨~ anger⟩ **2** : CONFER, BESTOW ⟨~ mercy⟩ **3** : REVEAL, DISCLOSE ⟨~ed courage in battle⟩ **4** : INSTRUCT ⟨~ me how⟩ **5** : PROVE ⟨~s he was guilty⟩ **6** : APPEAR **7** : to be noticeable **8** : to be third in a horse race

²**show** *n* **1** : a demonstrative display **2** : outward appearance ⟨a ∼ of resistance⟩ **3** : SPECTACLE **4** : a theatrical presentation **5** : a radio or television program **6** : third place in a horse race

¹**show·case** \'shō-ˌkās\ *n* : a cabinet for displaying items (as in a store)

²**showcase** *vb* **show·cased; show·cas·ing** : EXHIBIT

show·down \'shō-ˌdaun\ *n* : a decisive confrontation or contest; *esp* : the showing of poker hands to determine the winner of a pot

¹**show·er** \'shau̇(-ə)r\ *n* **1** : a brief fall of rain **2** : a party given by friends who bring gifts **3** : a bath in which water is showered on the person; *also* : a facility (as a stall) for such a bath — **show·ery** *adj*

²**shower** *vb* **1** : to rain or fall in a shower **2** : to bathe in a shower

show·man \'shō-mən\ *n* : a notably spectacular, dramatic, or effective performer — **show·man·ship** *n*

show-off \'shō-ˌȯf\ *n* : one that seeks to attract attention by conspicuous behavior

show off *vb* **1** : to display proudly **2** : to act as a show-off

show·piece \'shō-ˌpēs\ *n* : an outstanding example used for exhibition

show·place \-ˌplās\ *n* : an estate or building that is a showpiece

show up *vb* : ARRIVE

showy \'shō-ē\ *adj* **show·i·er; -est** : superficially impressive or striking ⟨a ∼ orchid⟩ — **show·i·ly** \'shō-ə-lē\ *adv* — **show·i·ness** \-ē-nəs\ *n*

shpt *abbr* shipment

shrap·nel \'shrap-nəl\ *n, pl* **shrapnel** [Henry *Shrapnel* †1842 Eng. artillery officer] : bomb, mine, or shell fragments

¹**shred** \'shred\ *n* : a narrow strip cut or torn off : a small fragment

²**shred** *vb* **shred·ded; shred·ding** : to cut or tear into shreds

shrew \'shrü\ *n* **1** : any of a family of very small mammals with short velvety fur that are related to the moles **2** : a scolding woman

shrewd \'shrüd\ *adj* : CLEVER, ASTUTE — **shrewd·ly** *adv* — **shrewd·ness** *n*

shrew·ish \'shrü-ish\ *adj* : having an irritable disposition : ILL-TEMPERED — **shrew·ish·ly** *adv* — **shrew·ish·ness** *n*

shriek \'shrēk\ *n* : a shrill cry : SCREAM, YELL — **shriek** *vb*

shrift \'shrift\ *n, archaic* : the act of shriving : CONFESSION

shrike \'shrīk\ *n* : any of numerous usu. largely grayish or brownish birds that often impale their usu. insect prey upon thorns before devouring it

¹**shrill** \'shril\ *vb* : to make a high-pitched piercing sound

²**shrill** *adj* : high-pitched : PIERCING ⟨∼ whistle⟩ — **shril·ly** *adv*

shrimp \'shrimp\ *n, pl* **shrimps** *or* **shrimp** **1** : any of various small marine crustaceans related to the lobsters **2** : a small or puny person

shrine \'shrīn\ *n* [ME, receptacle for the relics of a saint, fr. OE *scrīn*, fr. L *scrinium* case, chest] **1** : the tomb of a saint; *also* : a place where devotion is paid to a saint or deity **2** : a place or object hallowed by its associations

¹**shrink** \'shriŋk\ *vb* **shrank** \'shraŋk\ *or* **shrunk** \'shrəŋk\; **shrunk** *or* **shrunk·en** \'shrəŋ-kən\; **shrink·ing** **1** : to draw back or away **2** : to become smaller or more compact **3** : to lessen in value

♦ **Synonyms** CONTRACT, CONSTRICT, COMPRESS, CONDENSE — **shrink·able** *adj*

²**shrink** *n* : a clinical psychiatrist or psychologist

shrink·age \'shriŋ-kij\ *n* **1** : the act of shrinking **2** : the amount lost by shrinkage

shrive \'shrīv\ *vb* **shrived** *or* **shrove** \'shrōv\; **shriv·en** \'shri-vən\ *or* **shrived** [ME, fr. OE *scrīfan* to prescribe, allot, shrive, fr. L *scribere* to write] : to administer the sacrament of reconciliation to

shriv·el \'shri-vəl\ *vb* **-eled** *or* **-elled; -el·ing** *or* **-el·ling** : to shrink and draw into wrinkles : DWINDLE

¹**shroud** \'shrau̇d\ *n* **1** : something that covers or screens **2** : a cloth placed over a dead body **3** : any of the ropes leading from the masthead of a ship to the side to support the mast

²**shroud** *vb* : to veil or screen from view

shrub \'shrəb\ *n* : a low usu. several-stemmed woody plant — **shrub·by** *adj*

shrub·bery \'shrə-bə-rē\ *n, pl* **-ber·ies** : a planting or growth of shrubs

shrug \'shrəg\ *vb* **shrugged; shrug·ging** : to hunch (the shoulders) up to express aloofness, indifference, or uncertainty — **shrug** *n*

shrug off *vb* **1** : to brush aside : MINIMIZE ⟨she *shrugged* off their concerns⟩ **2** : to shake off **3** : to remove (a garment) by wriggling out

shtick *also* **schtick** *or* **shtik** \'shtik\ *n* [Yiddish *shtik* pranks, lit., piece] **1** : a usu. comic or repetitious performance or routine **2** : one's special trait, interest, or activity

¹**shuck** \'shək\ *n* : SHELL, HUSK

²**shuck** *vb* : to strip of shucks

shud·der \'shə-dər\ *vb* : TREMBLE, QUAKE — **shudder** *n*

shuf·fle \'shə-fəl\ *vb* **shuf·fled; shuf·fling** **1** : to mix in a disorderly mass **2** : to rearrange the order of (cards in a pack) by mixing two parts of the pack together **3** : to shift from place to place **4** : to move with a sliding or dragging gait **5** : to dance in a slow lagging manner — **shuffle** *n*

shuf·fle·board \'shə-fəl-ˌbȯrd\ *n* : a game in which players use long-handled cues to shove disks into scoring areas marked on a smooth surface

shun \'shən\ *vb* **shunned; shun·ning** : to avoid deliberately or habitually

♦ **Synonyms** EVADE, ELUDE, ESCAPE, DUCK

¹**shunt** \'shənt\ *vb* [ME, to turn away] : to turn off to one side; *esp* : to switch (a train) from one track to another

²shunt *n* **1** : a method or device for turning or thrusting aside **2** : a conductor joining two points in an electrical circuit forming an alternate path through which a portion of the current may pass

shut \'shət\ *vb* **shut; shut·ting 1** : CLOSE **2** : to forbid entrance into **3** : to lock up **4** : to fold together ⟨~ a penknife⟩ **5** : to cease or suspend activity ⟨~ down an assembly line⟩

shut·down \-ˌdau̇n\ *n* : a temporary cessation of activity (as in a factory)

shut–in \'shət-ˌin\ *n* : a person confined to home, a room, or bed because of illness or incapacity

shut·out \'shət-ˌau̇t\ *n* : a game or contest in which one side fails to score

shut out *vb* **1** : EXCLUDE **2** : to prevent (an opponent) from scoring in a game or contest

shut·ter \'shə-tər\ *n* **1** : a movable cover for a door or window : BLIND **2** : the part of a camera that opens and closes to allow light to enter

shut·ter·bug \'shə-tər-ˌbəg\ *n* : a photography enthusiast

¹shut·tle \'shə-tᵊl\ *n* **1** : an instrument used in weaving for passing the horizontal threads between the vertical threads **2** : a vehicle traveling back and forth over a short route ⟨a ~ bus⟩ **3** : SPACE SHUTTLE

²shuttle *vb* **shut·tled; shut·tling** : to move back and forth frequently

shut·tle·cock \'shə-tᵊl-ˌkäk\ *n* : a light conical object (as of cork or plastic) used in badminton

shut up *vb* : to cease or cause to cease talking

¹shy \'shī\ *adj* **shi·er** *or* **shy·er** \'shī-ər\; **shi·est** *or* **shy·est** \'shī-əst\ **1** : easily frightened : TIMID **2** : WARY **3** : BASHFUL **4** : DEFICIENT, LACKING ⟨a nickel ~ of a quarter⟩ — **shy·ly** *adv* — **shy·ness** *n*

²shy *vb* **shied; shy·ing 1** : to show a dislike : RECOIL **2** : to start suddenly aside through fright ⟨the horse *shied*⟩

shy·ster \'shī-stər\ *n* : an unscrupulous lawyer or politician

Si *symbol* silicon

SI *abbr* [F *Système International d'Unités*] International System of Units

Si·a·mese \ˌsī-ə-ˈmēz, -ˈmēs\ *n, pl* **Siamese** : THAI — **Siamese** *adj*

Siamese cat *n* : any of a breed of slender blue-eyed short-haired domestic cats of Asian origin

Siamese twin *n* [fr. Chang †1874 and Eng †1874 twins born in Siam with bodies united] : one of a pair of twins with bodies joined together at birth

Siberian husky *n* : any of a breed of thick-coated compact dogs orig. developed in Siberia to pull sleds

¹sib·i·lant \'si-bə-lənt\ *adj* : having, containing, or producing the sound of or a sound resembling that of the *s* or the *sh* in *sash* — **sib·i·lant·ly** *adv*

²sibilant *n* : a sibilant speech sound (as English \s\, \z\, \sh\, \zh\, \ch (=tsh)\, *or* \j (=dzh)\)

sib·ling \'si-bliŋ\ *n* : a brother or sister considered irrespective of sex; *also* : one of two or more offspring having one common parent

sib·yl \'si-bəl\ *n, often cap* : PROPHETESS — **sib·yl·line** \-bə-ˌlīn, -ˌlēn\ *adj*

sic \'sik, 'sēk\ *adv* : intentionally so written — used after a printed word or passage to indicate that it exactly reproduces an original ⟨said he seed ☐ it all⟩

sick \'sik\ *adj* **1** : not in good health : ILL; *also* : of, relating to, or intended for use in sickness ⟨~ pay⟩ **2** : NAUSEATED **3** : DISGUSTED **4** : PINING **5** : mentally or emotionally unsound **6** : MACABRE, SADISTIC ⟨~ jokes⟩ — **sick·ly** *adj*

sick·bed \'sik-ˌbed\ *n* : a bed on which one lies sick

sick·en \'si-kən\ *vb* : to make or become sick — **sick·en·ing·ly** *adv*

sick·le \'si-kəl\ *n* : a cutting tool consisting of a curved metal blade with a short handle

sickle–cell anemia *n* : an inherited anemia in which red blood cells tend to become crescent-shaped and clog small blood vessels and which occurs esp. in individuals of African, Mediterranean, or southwest Asian ancestry

sick·ness \'sik-nəs\ *n* **1** : ill health; *also* : a specific disease **2** : NAUSEA

side \'sīd\ *n* **1** : the right or left part of the trunk of a body **2** : a place away from a central point or line **3** : a border of an object; *esp* : one of the longer borders as contrasted with an end **4** : an outer surface of an object **5** : a position regarded as opposite to another **6** : a body of contestants — **side** *adj* — **on the side** : in addition to the main portion

side·arm \-ˌärm\ *adj* : made with a sideways sweep of the arm ⟨a ~ pitch⟩ — **sidearm** *adv*

side arm *n* : a weapon worn at the side or in the belt

side·bar \'sīd-ˌbär\ *n* : a short news story accompanying a major story and presenting related information

side·board \-ˌbȯrd\ *n* : a piece of dining-room furniture for holding articles of table service

side·burns \-ˌbərnz\ *n pl* : whiskers on the side of the face in front of the ears

side by side *adv* **1** : beside one another **2** : in the same place, time, or circumstance — **side–by–side** *adj*

side·car \-ˌkär\ *n* : a one-wheeled passenger car attached to the side of a motorcycle

side effect *n* : a secondary and usu. adverse effect (as of a drug)

side·kick \'sīd-ˌkik\ *n* : PAL, PARTNER

side·line \'sīd-ˌlīn\ *n* **1** : an activity pursued in addition to one's regular occupation **2** : the space immediately outside the lines of an athletic field or court **3** : a sphere of little or no participation — usu. used in pl.

¹side·long \'sīd-ˌlȯŋ\ *adv* : in the direction of or along the side : OBLIQUELY

²sidelong *adj* : directed to one side ⟨~ look⟩

side·man \'sīd-,man\ n : a member of a jazz or swing orchestra

side-piece \-,pēs\ n : a piece forming or contained in the side of something

si·de·re·al \sī-'dir-ē-əl, sə-\ adj [L sidereus, fr. sider-, sidus star, constellation] 1 : of or relating to the stars 2 : measured by the apparent motion of the stars

side·sad·dle \'sīd-,sa-d'l\ n : a saddle for women on which the rider sits with both legs on the same side of the horse — **sidesaddle** adv

side·show \'sīd-,shō\ n 1 : a minor show offered in addition to a main exhibition (as of a circus) 2 : an incidental diversion

side·step \-,step\ vb 1 : to step aside 2 : AVOID, EVADE ⟨sidestepped the question⟩

side·stroke \-,strōk\ n : a swimming stroke which is executed on the side and in which the arms are swept backward and downward and the legs do a scissors kick

side·swipe \-,swīp\ vb : to strike with a glancing blow along the side — **side-swipe** n

¹side·track \-,trak\ n : SIDING 1

²sidetrack vb 1 : to switch from a main railroad line to a siding 2 : to turn aside from a purpose

side·walk \'sīd-,wȯk\ n : a paved walk at the side of a road or street

side·wall \-,wȯl\ n 1 : a wall forming the side of something 2 : the side of an automobile tire

side·ways \-,wāz\ adv or adj 1 : from the side 2 : with one side to the front 3 : to, toward, or at one side

side·wind·er \-,wīn-dər\ n : a small pale-colored desert rattlesnake of the southwestern U.S.

sid·ing \'sī-diŋ\ n 1 : a short railroad track connected with the main track 2 : material (as boards) covering the outside of frame buildings

si·dle \'sī-d'l\ vb **si·dled**; **si·dling** : to move sideways or with one side foremost

SIDS abbr sudden infant death syndrome

siege \'sēj\ n 1 : the placing of an army around or before a fortified place to force its surrender 2 : a persistent attack (as of illness)

sie·mens \'sē-mənz, 'zē-\ n : a unit of conductance equivalent to one ampere per volt

si·er·ra \sē-'er-ə\ n [Sp, lit., saw, fr. L serra] : a range of mountains esp. with jagged peaks

si·es·ta \sē-'es-tə\ n [Sp, fr. L sexta (hora) noon, lit., sixth hour] : a midday rest or nap

sieve \'siv\ n : a utensil with meshes or holes to separate finer particles from coarser or solids from liquids

sift \'sift\ vb 1 : to pass through a sieve 2 : to separate with or as if with a sieve 3 : to examine carefully 4 : to scatter by or as if by passing through a sieve — **sift·er** n

sig abbr signature

SIG abbr special interest group

sigh \'sī\ vb : to let out a deep audible breath (as in weariness or sorrow) 2 : GRIEVE, YEARN — **sigh** n

¹sight \'sīt\ n 1 : something seen or worth seeing 2 : the process or power of seeing; esp : the sense of which the eye is the receptor and by which qualities of appearance (as position, shape, and color) are perceived 3 : INSPECTION 4 : a device (as a small bead on a gun barrel) that aids the eye in aiming 5 : VIEW, GLIMPSE 6 : the range of vision — **sight·less** adj

²sight vb 1 : to get sight of 2 : to aim by means of a sight

sight·ed \'sī-təd\ adj : having sight

sight·ly \-lē\ adj : pleasing to the sight

sight·see·ing \'sīt-,sē-iŋ\ adj : engaged in or used for seeing sights of interest — **sight·seer** \-,sē-ər\ n

sig·ma \'sig-mə\ n : the 18th letter of the Greek alphabet — Σ or σ or ς

¹sign \'sīn\ n 1 : a gesture expressing a command, wish, or thought 2 : SYMBOL 3 : a notice publicly displayed for advertising purposes or for giving direction or warning 4 : OMEN, PORTENT 5 : TRACE, VESTIGE ⟨left without a ∼⟩

²sign vb 1 : to mark with a sign 2 : to represent by a sign 3 : to make a sign or signal 4 : to write one's name on in token of assent or obligation 5 : to assign legally 6 : to use sign language — **sign·er** n

¹sig·nal \'sig-nəl\ n 1 : a sign agreed on as the start of some joint action 2 : a sign giving warning or notice of something 3 : the message, sound, or image transmitted in electronic communication (as radio)

²signal vb **-naled** or **-nalled**; **-nal·ing** or **-nal·ling** 1 : to notify by a signal 2 : to communicate by signals

³signal adj : DISTINGUISHED ⟨a ∼ honor⟩ — **sig·nal·ly** adv

sig·nal·ize \'sig-nə-,līz\ vb **-ized**; **-iz·ing** : to point out or make conspicuous — **sig·nal·i·za·tion** \,sig-nə-lə-'zā-shən\ n

sig·nal·man \'sig-nəl-mən, -,man\ n : a person who signals or works with signals

sig·na·to·ry \'sig-nə-,tōr-ē\ n, pl **-ries** : a person or government that signs jointly with others — **signatory** adj

sig·na·ture \'sig-nə-,chùr\ n 1 : the name of a person written by himself or herself 2 : the sign placed after the clef to indicate the key or the meter of a piece of music

sign·board \'sīn-,bȯrd\ n : a board bearing a sign or notice

sig·net \'sig-nət\ n : a small intaglio seal (as in a ring)

sig·nif·i·cance \sig-'ni-fi-kəns\ n 1 : something signified : MEANING 2 : SUGGESTIVENESS 3 : CONSEQUENCE, IMPORTANCE ⟨the ∼ of the treaty⟩

sig·nif·i·cant \-kənt\ adj 1 : having meaning; esp : having a hidden or special meaning 2 : having or likely to have considerable influence or effect : IMPORTANT — **sig·nif·i·cant·ly** adv

sig·ni·fy \'sig-nə-,fī\ vb **-fied**; **-fy·ing** 1 : to show by a sign 2 : MEAN, IMPORT 3

: to have significance — **sig·ni·fi·ca·tion** \ˌsig-nə-fə-ˈkā-shən\ n

sign in vb : to make a record of arrival (as by signing a register)

sign language n : a formal system of hand gestures used for communication (as by the deaf)

sign off vb : to announce the end (as of a program or broadcast)

sign of the cross : a gesture of the hand forming a cross (as to invoke divine blessing)

sign on vb 1 : ENLIST 2 : to announce the start of broadcasting for the day

sign out vb : to make a record of departure (as by signing a register)

sign·post \ˈsīn-ˌpōst\ n : a post bearing a sign

sign up vb : to sign one's name in order to obtain, do, or join something

Sikh \ˈsēk\ n : an adherent of a religion of India marked by rejection of caste — **Sikh·ism** n

si·lage \ˈsī-lij\ n : fodder fermented (as in a silo) to produce a rich moist animal feed

¹**si·lence** \ˈsī-ləns\ n 1 : the state of being silent 2 : STILLNESS 3 : SECRECY

²**silence** vb **si·lenced; si·lenc·ing** 1 : to reduce to silence : STILL 2 : to cause to cease hostile firing or criticism

si·lenc·er \ˈsī-lən-sər\ n : a device for muffling the noise of a gunshot

si·lent \ˈsī-lənt\ adj 1 : not speaking : MUTE; also : TACITURN 2 : STILL, QUIET 3 : performed or borne without utterance ⟨a ~ prayer⟩ ♦ **Synonyms** RETICENT, RESERVED, CLOSEMOUTHED, CLOSE — **si·lent·ly** adv

¹**sil·hou·ette** \ˌsil-ə-ˈwet\ n [F] 1 : a representation of the outlines of an object filled in with black or some other uniform color 2 : OUTLINE ⟨~ of a ship⟩

²**silhouette** vb **-ett·ed; -ett·ing** : to represent by a silhouette; also : to show against a light background

sil·i·ca \ˈsi-li-kə\ n : a mineral that consists of silicon and oxygen

sil·i·cate \ˈsi-lə-ˌkāt, ˈsi-li-kət\ n : a chemical salt that consists of a metal combined with silicon and oxygen

si·li·ceous also **si·li·cious** \sə-ˈli-shəs\ adj : of, relating to, or containing silica or a silicate

sil·i·con \ˈsi-li-kən, ˈsi-lə-ˌkän\ n : a nonmetallic chemical element that occurs in combination as the most abundant element next to oxygen in the earth's crust and is used esp. in alloys and semiconductors

sil·i·cone \ˈsi-lə-ˌkōn\ n : an organic silicon compound used esp. for lubricants and varnishes

sil·i·co·sis \ˌsi-lə-ˈkō-səs\ n : a lung disease caused by prolonged inhaling of silica dusts

silk \ˈsilk\ n 1 : a fine strong lustrous protein fiber produced by insect larvae usu. for their cocoons; esp : one from moth larvae (**silk·worms** \-ˌwərmz\) used for cloth 2 : thread or cloth made from silk — **silk·en** \ˈsil-kən\ adj — **silky** adj

silk screen n : a stencil process in which coloring matter is forced through the meshes of a prepared silk or organdy screen; also : a print made by this process — **silk–screen** vb

sill \ˈsil\ n : a heavy crosspiece (as of wood or stone) that forms the bottom member of a window frame or a doorway; also : a horizontal supporting piece at the base of a structure

sil·ly \ˈsi-lē\ adj **sil·li·er; -est** [ME sely, silly happy, innocent, pitiable, feeble, fr. OE sǣlig, fr. sǣl happiness] : FOOLISH, ABSURD, STUPID — **sil·li·ness** n

si·lo \ˈsī-lō\ n, pl **silos** [Sp] 1 : a trench, pit, or esp. a tall cylinder for making and storing silage 2 : an underground structure for housing a guided missile

¹**silt** \ˈsilt\ n 1 : fine earth; esp : particles of such soil floating in rivers, ponds, or lakes 2 : a deposit (as by a river) of silt — **silty** adj

²**silt** vb : to obstruct or cover with silt — **silt·ation** \sil-ˈtā-shən\ n

Si·lu·ri·an \sī-ˈlu̇r-ē-ən\ adj : of, relating to, or being the period of the Paleozoic era between the Ordovician and the Devonian marked by the appearance of the first land plants — **Silurian** n

¹**sil·ver** \ˈsil-vər\ n 1 : a white ductile metallic chemical element that takes a high polish and is a better conductor of heat and electricity than any other substance 2 : coin made of silver 3 : FLATWARE 4 : a grayish white color — **sil·very** adj

²**silver** adj 1 : relating to, made of, or coated with silver 2 : SILVERY

³**silver** vb **sil·vered; sil·ver·ing** : to coat with or as if with silver — **sil·ver·er** n

silver bromide n : a light-sensitive compound used esp. in photography

sil·ver·fish \ˈsil-vər-ˌfish\ n : any of various small wingless insects found in houses and sometimes injurious esp. to sized paper and starched clothes

silver iodide n : a light-sensitive compound used in photography, rainmaking, and medicine

silver maple n : a No. American maple with deeply cut leaves that are green above and silvery white below

silver nitrate n : a soluble compound used in photography and as an antiseptic

sil·ver·ware \ˈsil-vər-ˌwer\ n : FLATWARE

sim abbr simulation; simulator

sim·i·an \ˈsi-mē-ən\ n : MONKEY, APE — **simian** adj

simian immunodeficiency virus n : SIV

sim·i·lar \ˈsi-mə-lər\ adj : marked by correspondence or resemblance ♦ **Synonyms** ALIKE, AKIN, COMPARABLE, PARALLEL — **sim·i·lar·i·ty** \ˌsi-mə-ˈler-ə-tē\ n — **sim·i·lar·ly** adv

sim·i·le \ˈsi-mə-(ˌ)lē\ n [ME, fr. L, likeness, comparison, fr. neut. of similis like, similar] : a figure of speech in which two dissimilar things are compared by the use of like or as (as in "cheeks like roses")

si·mil·i·tude \sə-ˈmi-lə-ˌtüd, -ˌtyüd\ n : LIKENESS, RESEMBLANCE

sim·mer \ˈsi-mər\ vb **sim·mered; sim·mer·ing** 1 : to stew at or just below the boiling point **2** : to be on the point of bursting out with violence or emotional disturbance — **simmer** n

simmer down vb : to become calm or peaceful

si·mo·nize \'sī-mə-ˌnīz\ vb **-nized; -niz·ing** : to polish with or as if with wax

si·mo·ny \'sī-mə-nē, 'si-\ n [ME *symonie*, fr. AF *simonie*, fr. LL *simonia*, fr. *Simon Magus* sorcerer of Samaria in Acts 8:9–24] : the buying or selling of a church office

sim·pa·ti·co \sim-'pä-ti-ˌkō, -'pa-\ adj : CONGENIAL, LIKABLE

sim·per \'sim-pər\ vb : to smile in a silly manner — **simper** n

sim·ple \'sim-pəl\ adj **sim·pler** \-pə-lər\; **sim·plest** \-pə-ləst\ [ME, fr. AF, plain, uncomplicated, artless, fr. L *simplus*, *simplex*, lit., single; L *simplus* fr. *sim-* one + *-plus* multiplied by; L *simplex* fr. *sim-* + *-plex* -fold] **1** : free from dishonesty or vanity : INNOCENT **2** : free from ostentation **3** : of humble origin or modest position **4** : STUPID **5** : not complex : PLAIN ⟨a ~ melody⟩ ⟨~ directions⟩ **6** : lacking education, experience, or intelligence **7** : developing from a single ovary ⟨a ~ fruit⟩ ♦ **Synonyms** EASY, FACILE, LIGHT, EFFORTLESS — **sim·ple·ness** n — **sim·ply** adv

simple interest n : interest paid or computed on the original principal only of a loan or on the amount of an account

sim·ple·ton \'sim-pəl-tən\ n : FOOL

sim·plic·i·ty \sim-'pli-sə-tē\ n, pl **-ties 1** : lack of complication : CLEARNESS ⟨the ~ of his reasoning⟩ **2** : CANDOR, ARTLESSNESS **3** : plainness in manners or way of life **4** : SILLINESS, FOLLY

sim·pli·fy \'sim-plə-ˌfī\ vb **-fied; -fy·ing** : to make less complex — **sim·pli·fi·ca·tion** \ˌsim-plə-fə-'kā-shən\ n

sim·plis·tic \sim-'plis-tik\ adj : excessively simple : tending to overlook complexities ⟨a ~ solution⟩

sim·u·late \'sim-yə-ˌlāt\ vb **-lat·ed; -lat·ing** : to give or create the effect or appearance of : IMITATE; also : to make a simulation of — **sim·u·la·tor** \'sim-yə-ˌlā-tər\ n

sim·u·la·tion \ˌsim-yə-'lā-shən\ n **1** : the act or process of simulating **2** : an object that is not genuine **3** : the imitation by one system or process of the way in which another system or process works

si·mul·ta·ne·ous \ˌsī-məl-'tā-nē-əs, ˌsi-\ adj : occurring or operating at the same time — **si·mul·ta·ne·ous·ly** adv — **si·mul·ta·ne·ous·ness** n

¹sin \'sin\ n **1** : an offense esp. against God **2** : FAULT **3** : a weakened state of human nature in which the self is estranged from God — **sin·less** adj

²sin vb **sinned; sin·ning** : to commit a sin — **sin·ner** n

³sin abbr sine

¹since \'sins\ adv **1** : from a past time until now **2** : backward in time : AGO **3** : after a time in the past

²since conj **1** : from the time when **2** : seeing that : BECAUSE

³since prep **1** : in the period after ⟨changes made ~ the war⟩ **2** : continuously from ⟨has been here ~ 1980⟩

sin·cere \sin-'sir\ adj **sin·cer·er; sin·cer·est 1** : free from hypocrisy : HONEST **2** : GENUINE, REAL — **sin·cere·ly** adv — **sin·cer·i·ty** \-'ser-ə-tē\ n

sine \'sīn\ n [ML *sinus*, fr. L, curve] : the trigonometric function that is the ratio between the side opposite an acute angle in a right triangle and the hypotenuse

si·ne·cure \'sī-ni-ˌkyùr, 'si-\ n : a paying job that requires little or no work

si·ne die \ˌsī-ni-'dī-ˌē, ˌsi-nä-'dē-ˌä\ adv [L, without day] : INDEFINITELY ⟨the meeting adjourned *sine die*⟩

si·ne qua non \ˌsi-ni-ˌkwä-'nän, -'nōn\ n, pl **sine qua nons** also **sine qui·bus non** \-ˌkwi-(ˌ)bùs-\ [LL, without which not] : something indispensable or essential

sin·ew \'sin-yü\ n **1** : TENDON **2** : physical strength — **sin·ewy** adj

sin·ful \'sin-fəl\ adj : marked by or full of sin : WICKED — **sin·ful·ly** adv — **sin·ful·ness** n

¹sing \'siŋ\ vb **sang** \'saŋ\ or **sung** \'səŋ\; **sung; sing·ing 1** : to produce musical tones with the voice; also : to utter with musical tones **2** : to make a prolonged shrill sound ⟨locusts ~ing⟩ **3** : to produce harmonious sustained sounds ⟨birds ~ing⟩ **4** : CHANT, INTONE **5** : to write poetry; also : to celebrate in song or verse **6** : to give information or evidence — **sing·er** n

²sing abbr singular

singe \'sinj\ vb **singed; singe·ing** : to scorch lightly the outside of; esp : to remove the hair or down from usu. by passing over a flame

¹sin·gle \'siŋ-gəl\ adj **1** : UNMARRIED **2** : being alone : being the only one **3** : having only one feature or part **4** : made for one person ♦ **Synonyms** SOLE, UNIQUE, LONE, SOLITARY, SEPARATE, PARTICULAR — **sin·gle·ness** n — **sin·gly** adv

²single n **1** : a separate person or thing; also : an unmarried person **2** : a hit in baseball that enables the batter to reach first base **3** pl : a tennis match with one player on each side

³single vb **sin·gled; sin·gling 1** : to select (one) from a group **2** : to hit a single

single bond n : a chemical bond in which one pair of electrons is shared by two atoms in a molecule

single–lens reflex n : a camera having a single lens that forms an image which is reflected to the viewfinder or recorded on film

sin·gle–mind·ed \ˌsiŋ-gəl-'mīn-dəd\ adj : having one driving purpose or resolve ⟨~ determination⟩ — **sin·gle–mind·ed·ly** adv — **sin·gle–mind·ed·ness** n

sing·song \'siŋ-ˌsóŋ\ n **1** : verse with marked and regular rhythm and rhyme **2** : a voice delivery marked by monotonous rhythm — **sing·songy** \-ˌsóŋ-ē\ adj

sin·gu·lar \'siŋ-gyə-lər\ adj **1** : of, relating to, or constituting a word form denoting one person, thing, or instance **2** : OUTSTANDING, EXCEPTIONAL **3** : of unusual quality **4** : ODD, PECULIAR — **sin·gu·lar** *n* — **sin·gu·lar·i·ty** \ˌsiŋ-gyə-ˈler-ə-tē\ *n* — **sin·gu·lar·ly** *adv*

sin·is·ter \ˈsi-nəs-tər\ *adj* [ME *sinistre*, fr. AF *senestre* on the left, fr. L *sinister* on the left side, inauspicious] **1** : singularly evil or productive of evil **2** : accompanied by or leading to disaster ♦ *Synonyms* BALEFUL, MALIGN, MALEFIC, MALEFICENT — **sin·is·ter·ly** *adv*

¹sink \ˈsiŋk\ *vb* **sank** \ˈsaŋk\ *or* **sunk** \ˈsəŋk\; **sunk**; **sink·ing 1** : SUBMERGE **2** : to descend lower and lower **3** : to grow less in volume or height **4** : to slope downward **5** : to penetrate downward **6** : to fail in health or strength **7** : LAPSE, DEGENERATE **8** : to cause (a ship) to descend to the bottom **9** : to make (a hole or shaft) by digging, boring, or cutting **10** : INVEST — **sink·able** *adj*

²sink *n* **1** : DRAIN, SEWER **2** : a basin connected with a drain **3** : an extensive depression in the land surface

sink·er \ˈsiŋ-kər\ *n* : a weight for sinking a fishing line or net

sink·hole \ˈsiŋk-ˌhōl\ *n* : a hollow place in which drainage collects

si·nol·o·gy \sī-ˈnä-lə-jē\ *n, often cap* : the study of the Chinese and esp. their language, history, and culture — **si·no·log·i·cal** \ˌsī-nə-ˈlä-ji-kəl\ *adj, often cap* — **si·nol·o·gist** \sī-ˈnä-lə-jist\ *n, often cap*

sin tax *n* : a tax on substances or activities considered sinful or harmful

sin·u·ous \ˈsin-yə-wəs\ *adj* : bending in and out : WINDING — **sin·u·os·i·ty** \ˌsin-yə-ˈwä-sə-tē\ *n* — **sin·u·ous·ly** *adv*

si·nus \ˈsī-nəs\ *n* [ME, fr. ML, fr. L, curve, hollow] **1** : any of several cavities of the skull usu. connecting with the nostrils **2** : a space forming a channel (as for the passage of blood)

si·nus·itis \ˌsī-nə-ˈsī-təs\ *n* : inflammation of a sinus of the skull

Sioux \ˈsü\ *n, pl* **Sioux** *same or* ˈsüz\ [AmerF, short for *Nadouessioux*, fr. Ojibwa *na·towe·ssiw-*, prob. fr. Algonquian *a·towe*- speak another language] : DAKOTA

sip \ˈsip\ *vb* **sipped**; **sip·ping** : to drink in small quantities — **sip** *n*

¹si·phon *also* **sy·phon** \ˈsī-fən\ *n* **1** : a bent tube through which a liquid can be transferred by means of air pressure up and over the edge of one container and into another container placed at a lower level **2** *usu* **sy·phon** : a bottle that ejects soda water through a tube when a valve is opened

²siphon *also* **syphon** *vb* **si·phoned** *also* **sy·phoned**; **si·phon·ing** *also* **sy·phon·ing** : to draw off by means of a siphon

sip·py cup \ˈsi-pē-\ *n* : a cup having a lid with a perforated spout for a young child

sir \ˈsər\ *n* [ME *sir*, *sire*, fr. AF, lord, feudal superior, fr. VL **seior*, alter. of L *senior*, compar. of *senex* old, old man] **1** : a man of rank or position — used as a title before the given name of a knight or baronet **2** — used as a usu. respectful form of address

Si·rach \ˈsī-rak, sə-ˈräk\ *n* — see BIBLE table

¹sire \ˈsī(-ə)r\ *n* **1** : FATHER; *also, archaic* : FOREFATHER **2** *archaic* : LORD — used as a form of address and a title **3** : the male parent of an animal (as a horse or dog)

²sire *vb* **sired**; **sir·ing** : BEGET

si·ren \ˈsī-rən\ *n* **1** : a seductive or alluring woman **2** : an electrically operated device for producing a loud shrill warning signal — **siren** *adj*

sir·loin \ˈsər-ˌlȯin\ *n* [alter. of earlier *surloin*, modif. of MF *surlonge*, fr. *sur* over (fr. L *super*) + *longe* loin] : a cut of beef taken from the part in front of the round

sirup *var of* SYRUP

si·sal \ˈsī-səl, -zəl\ *n* : a strong cordage fiber from an agave; *also* : this agave

sis·sy \ˈsi-sē\ *n, pl* **sissies** : an effeminate boy or man; *also* : a timid or cowardly person

sis·ter \ˈsis-tər\ *n* **1** : a female having one or both parents in common with another individual **2** : a member of a religious order of women : NUN **3** *chiefly Brit* : NURSE **4 a** : a girl or woman regarded as a comrade **b** : a girl or woman who shares with another a common national or racial origin — **sis·ter·ly** *adj*

sis·ter·hood \-ˌhud\ *n* **1** : the state of being a sister **2** : a community or society of sisters **3** : the solidarity of women based on shared conditions

sis·ter–in–law \ˈsis-tə-rən-ˌlȯ\ *n, pl* **sisters–in–law** : the sister of one's spouse; *also* : the wife of one's brother

sit \ˈsit\ *vb* **sat** \ˈsat\; **sit·ting 1** : to rest upon the buttocks or haunches **2** : ROOST, PERCH **3** : to occupy a seat **4** : to hold a session **5** : to cover eggs for hatching : BROOD **6** : to pose for a portrait **7** : to remain quiet or inactive **8** : FIT **9** : to cause (oneself) to be seated **10** : to place in position **11** : to keep one's seat on ⟨~ a horse⟩ **12** : BABYSIT — **sit·ter** *n*

si·tar \si-ˈtär\ *n* [Hindi & Urdu *sitār*] : an Indian lute with a long neck and a varying number of strings

sit·com \ˈsit-ˌkäm\ *n* : SITUATION COMEDY

site \ˈsīt\ *n* **1** : LOCATION **2** : WEBSITE

sit–in \ˈsit-ˌin\ *n* : an act of sitting in the seats or on the floor of an establishment as a means of organized protest

sit·u·at·ed \ˈsi-chə-ˌwā-təd\ *adj* : LOCATED, PLACED

sit·u·a·tion \ˌsi-chə-ˈwā-shən\ *n* **1** : LOCATION, SITE **2** : JOB **3** : CONDITION, CIRCUMSTANCES — **sit·u·a·tion·al** \-shə-nəl\ *adj*

situation comedy *n* : a radio or television comedy series that involves a continuing cast of characters in a succession of episodes

sit–up \ˈsit-ˌəp\ *n* : an exercise performed from a supine position by raising the torso to a sitting position and returning to the original position without lifting the feet

SIV \ˌes-ˌī-ˈvē\ *n* [simian immunodeficiency

virus] : a retrovirus related to HIV that causes a disease in monkeys similar to AIDS

six \'siks\ *n* **1** : one more than five **2** : the 6th in a set or series **3** : something having six units — **six** *adj or pron* — **sixth** \'siksth\ *adj or adv or n*

six-gun \'siks-ˌgən\ *n* : a 6-chambered revolver

six-pack \-ˌpak\ *n* : six bottles or cans (as of beer) packaged and purchased together; *also* : the contents of a six-pack

six-pence \-pəns, *US also* -ˌpens\ *n* : the sum of six pence; *also* : an English silver coin of this value

six–shoot-er \'siks-ˌshü-tər\ *n* : SIX-GUN

six-teen \siks-'tēn\ *n* : one more than 15 — **sixteen** *adj or pron* — **six-teenth** \-'tēnth\ *adj or n*

six-ty \'siks-tē\ *n, pl* **sixties** : six times 10 — **six-ti-eth** \'siks-tē-əth\ *adj or n* — **sixty** *adj or pron*

siz-able *or* **size-able** \'sī-zə-bəl\ *adj* : quite large — **siz-ably** \-blē\ *adv*

¹size \'sīz\ *n* [ME *sise* assize, judgment, quantity, fr. AF, short for *assise* assize] : physical extent or bulk : DIMENSIONS; *also* : considerable proportions — **sized** \'sīzd\ *adj*

²size *vb* **sized; siz-ing** **1** : to grade or classify according to size **2** : to form a judgment of ⟨∼ up the situation⟩

³size *n* : a gluey material used for filling the pores in paper, plaster, or textiles — **siz-ing** *n*

⁴size *vb* **sized; siz-ing** : to cover, stiffen, or glaze with size

siz-zle \'si-zəl\ *vb* **siz-zled; siz-zling** : to fry or shrivel up with a hissing sound — **sizzle** *n*

SJ *abbr* Society of Jesus

SK *abbr* Saskatchewan

ska \'skä\ *n* : popular music of Jamaican origin combining traditional Caribbean rhythms and jazz

¹skate \'skāt\ *n, pl* **skates** *also* **skate** : any of a family of rays with thick broad winglike fins

²skate *n* **1** : a metal frame and runner attached to a shoe and used for gliding over ice **2** : ROLLER SKATE; *esp* : IN-LINE SKATE — **skate** *vb* — **skat-er** *n*

skate-board \'skāt-ˌbȯrd\ *n* : a short board mounted on small wheels — **skateboard** *vb* — **skate-board-er** *n*

skeet \'skēt\ *n* : trapshooting in which clay targets are thrown in such a way that their angle of flight simulates that of a flushed game bird

skein \'skān\ *n* : a loosely twisted quantity of yarn or thread wound on a reel

skel-e-ton \'ske-lə-t²n\ *n* **1** : a usu. bony supporting framework of an animal body **2** : a bare minimum **3** : FRAMEWORK — **skel-e-tal** \-lə-t²l\ *adj*

skep-tic \'skep-tik\ *n* **1** : one who believes in skepticism **2** : a person disposed to skepticism esp. regarding religion — **skep-ti-cal** \-ti-kəl\ *adj* — **skep-ti-cal-ly** \-k(ə-)lē\ *adv*

skep-ti-cism \'skep-tə-ˌsi-zəm\ *n* **1** : a doubting state of mind **2** : a doctrine that

certainty of knowledge cannot be attained **3** : doubt concerning religion

sketch \'skech\ *n* [D *schets*, fr. It *schizzo*, lit., splash] **1** : a rough drawing or outline **2** : a short or light literary composition (as a story or essay); *also* : a short comedy piece — **sketch** *vb* — **sketchy** *adj*

¹skew \'skyü\ *vb* : TWIST, SWERVE

²skew *n* : SLANT

skew-er \'skyü-ər\ *n* : a long pin for holding small pieces of meat and vegetables for broiling — **skewer** *vb*

¹ski \'skē\ *n, pl* **skis** [Norw., fr. ON *skīth* stick of wood, ski] : one of a pair of long strips (as of wood, metal or plastic) curving upward in front that are used for gliding over snow or water

²ski *vb* **skied** \'skēd\; **ski-ing** : to glide on skis — **ski-able** \'skē-ə-bəl\ *adj* — **ski-er** *n*

¹skid \'skid\ *n* **1** : a plank for supporting something above the ground **2** : a device placed under a wheel to prevent turning **3** : a timber or rail over or on which something is slid or rolled **4** : the act of skidding **5** : a runner on the landing gear of an aircraft **6** : ²PALLET

²skid *vb* **skid-ded; skid-ding** **1** : to slide without rotating ⟨a *skidding* wheel⟩ **2** : to slide sideways on the road ⟨the car *skidded* on ice⟩ **3** : SLIDE, SLIP

skid row *n* : a district of cheap saloons frequented by vagrants and alcoholics

skiff \'skif\ *n* : a small boat

ski jump *n* : a jump made by a person wearing skis; *also* : a course or track prepared for such jumping — **ski jump** *vb* — **ski jumper** *n*

skil-ful *chiefly Brit var of* SKILLFUL

ski lift *n* : a mechanical device (as a chairlift) for carrying skiers up a long slope

skill \'skil\ *n* **1** : ability to use one's knowledge effectively in doing something **2** : developed or acquired ability ♦ *Synonyms* ART, CRAFT, CUNNING, DEXTERITY, EXPERTISE, KNOW-HOW — **skilled** \'skild\ *adj*

skil-let \'ski-lət\ *n* : a frying pan

skill-ful \'skil-fəl\ *adj* **1** : having or displaying skill : EXPERT **2** : accomplished with skill — **skill-ful-ly** *adv* — **skill-ful-ness** *n*

¹skim \'skim\ *vb* **skimmed; skim-ming** **1** : to take off from the top of a liquid; *also* : to remove (scum or cream) from ⟨∼ milk⟩ **2** : to read rapidly and superficially **3** : to pass swiftly over — **skim-mer** *n*

²skim *adj* : having the cream removed

skimp \'skimp\ *vb* : to give insufficient attention, effort, or funds; *also* : to save by skimping

skimpy \'skim-pē\ *adj* **skimp-i-er; -est** : deficient in supply or execution — **skimp-i-ly** \-pə-lē\ *adv*

¹skin \'skin\ *n* **1** : the outer limiting layer of an animal body; *also* : the usu. thin tough tissue of which this is made **2** : an outer or surface layer (as a rind or peel) — **skin-less** *adj* — **skinned** *adj*

²**skin** *vb* **skinned; skin·ning** : to free from skin : remove the skin of ⟨∼ a rabbit⟩

³**skin** *adj* : devoted to showing nudes ⟨∼ magazines⟩

skin div·ing *n* : the sport of swimming under water with a face mask and flippers and esp. without a portable breathing device — **skin–dive** *vb* — **skin diver** *n*

skin·flint \'skin-ˌflint\ *n* : a very stingy person

skin graft *n* : a piece of skin surgically removed from one area to replace skin in another area — **skin grafting** *n*

skin·head \'skin-ˌhed\ *n* : a person whose hair is cut very short

¹**skin·ny** \'ski-nē\ *adj* **skin·ni·er; -est** 1 : resembling skin 2 : very thin

²**skinny** *n* : inside information

skin·ny–dip \'ski-nē-ˌdip\ *vb* : to swim in the nude — **skin·ny–dip·per** \-ˌdi-pər\ *n*

skin·tight \'skin-'tīt\ *adj* : closely fitted to the figure ⟨∼ pants⟩

¹**skip** \'skip\ *vb* **skipped; skip·ping** 1 : to move with leaps and bounds 2 : to leap lightly over 3 : to pass from point to point (as in reading) disregarding what is in between 4 : to pass over without notice or mention

²**skip** *n* : a light bouncing step; *also* : a gait of alternate hops and steps

skip·jack \'skip-ˌjak\ *n* : a small sailboat with vertical sides and a bottom similar to a flat V

skip·per \'ski-pər\ *n* [ME, fr. MD *schipper,* fr. *schip* ship] : the master of a ship; *also* : the manager of a baseball team — **skipper** *vb*

skir·mish \'skər-mish\ *n* : a minor engagement in war; *also* : a minor dispute or contest — **skirmish** *vb*

¹**skirt** \'skərt\ *n* : a free-hanging garment or part of a garment extending from the waist down

²**skirt** *vb* 1 : to pass around the outer edge of 2 : BORDER 3 : EVADE ⟨∼ the issue⟩

skit \'skit\ *n* : a brief dramatic sketch

ski tow *n* : SKI LIFT

skit·ter \'ski-tər\ *vb* : to glide or skip lightly or quickly : skim along a surface

skit·tish \'ski-tish\ *adj* 1 : CAPRICIOUS 2 : easily frightened ⟨a ∼ horse⟩; *also* : WARY ⟨∼ investors⟩

ski·wear \'skē-ˌwer\ *n* : clothing suitable for wear while skiing

skosh \'skōsh\ *n* [Jp *sukoshi*] : a small amount : BIT ⟨has a ∼ more room⟩

skul·dug·gery *or* **skull·dug·gery** \ˌskəl-'də-gə-rē\ *n, pl* **-ger·ies** : underhanded or unscrupulous behavior

skulk \'skəlk\ *vb* : to move furtively : SNEAK, LURK — **skulk·er** *n*

skull \'skəl\ *n* : the skeleton of the head of a vertebrate that protects the brain and supports the jaws

skull and crossbones *n, pl* **skulls and crossbones** : a depiction of a human skull over crossbones usu. indicating a danger

skull·cap \'skəl-ˌkap\ *n* : a close-fitting brimless cap

¹**skunk** \'skəŋk\ *n, pl* **skunks** *also* **skunk** 1 : any of various black-and-white New World mammals related to the weasels that can forcibly eject an ill-smelling fluid when startled 2 : a contemptible person

²**skunk** *vb* : to defeat decisively; *esp* : to prevent entirely from scoring in a game

skunk cabbage *n* : either of two No. American perennial herbs related to the arums that occur in shaded wet to swampy areas and have a fetid odor suggestive of a skunk

sky \'skī\ *n, pl* **skies** [ME, sky, cloud, fr. ON *skȳ* cloud] 1 : the upper air 2 : HEAVEN — **sky·ey** \'skī-ē\ *adj*

sky·cap \-ˌkap\ *n* : a person employed to carry luggage at an airport

sky·div·ing \-ˌdī-viŋ\ *n* : the sport of jumping from an airplane and executing various body maneuvers before opening a parachute — **skydiver** *n*

sky·jack \-ˌjak\ *vb* : to commandeer an airplane in flight by threat of violence — **sky·jack·er** *n* — **sky·jack·ing** *n*

¹**sky·lark** \-ˌlärk\ *n* : a European lark noted for singing during flight

²**skylark** *vb* : FROLIC, SPORT

sky·light \'skī-ˌlīt\ *n* : a window in a roof or ceiling — **sky·light·ed** \-ˌlī-təd\ *adj*

sky·line \-ˌlīn\ *n* 1 : HORIZON 2 : an outline (as of buildings) against the sky

¹**sky·rock·et** \-ˌrä-kət\ *n* : ROCKET 1

²**skyrocket** *vb* : ROCKET 2

sky·scrap·er \-ˌskrā-pər\ *n* : a very tall building

sky·surf·ing \-ˌsər-fiŋ\ *n* : skydiving with a short modified surfboard attached to the feet — **sky·surf·er** \-fər\ *n*

sky·walk \-ˌwȯk\ *n* : an aerial walkway connecting two buildings

sky·ward \-wərd\ *adv* : toward the sky

sky·writ·ing \-ˌrī-tiŋ\ *n* : writing in the sky formed by smoke emitted from an airplane — **sky·writ·er** *n*

sl *abbr* 1 slightly 2 slip 3 slow

slab \'slab\ *n* : a thick flat piece or slice

¹**slack** \'slak\ *adj* 1 : CARELESS, NEGLIGENT 2 : SLUGGISH, LISTLESS 3 : not taut : LOOSE 4 : not busy or active ⟨a ∼ season⟩ ♦ **Synonyms** LAX, REMISS, NEGLECTFUL, DELINQUENT, DERELICT — **slack·ly** *adv* — **slack·ness** *n*

²**slack** *vb* 1 : to make or become slack : LOOSEN, RELAX 2 : SLAKE 2

³**slack** *n* 1 : cessation of movement or flow : LETUP 2 : a part that hangs loose without strain ⟨∼ of a rope⟩ 3 : pants esp. for casual wear — usu. used in pl.

slack·en \'sla-kən\ *vb* : to make or become slack

slack·er \'sla-kər\ *n* 1 : one that shirks work or evades military duty 2 : a young person perceived to be disaffected, apathetic, cynical, or lacking ambition

slag \'slag\ *n* : the waste left after the melting of ores and the separation of metal from them

slain *past part of* SLAY

slake \'slāk, *for 2 also* 'slak\ *vb* **slaked; slak·ing** 1 : to relieve or satisfy with or as if with refreshing drink ⟨∼ thirst⟩ 2 : to cause (lime) to crumble by mixture with water

sla·lom \'slä-ləm\ *n* [Norw *slalam*, lit., sloping track] : skiing in a zigzag course between obstacles

¹**slam** \'slam\ *n* : the winning of every trick or of all tricks but one in bridge

²**slam** *n* 1 : a heavy jarring impact : BANG 2 : harsh criticism 3 : a poetry competition

³**slam** *vb* **slammed; slam·ming** 1 : to shut violently and noisily 2 : to throw or strike with a loud impact 3 : to criticize harshly ⟨was *slammed* in the press⟩

slam·mer \'sla-mər\ *n* : JAIL, PRISON

¹**slan·der** \'slan-dər\ *vb* : to utter slander against : DEFAME — **slan·der·er** *n*

²**slander** *n* [ME *sclaundre, slaundre*, fr. AF *esclaundre*, alter. of *escandle*, fr. LL *scandalum* stumbling block, offense] : a false report maliciously uttered and tending to injure the reputation of a person — **slan·der·ous** *adj*

slang \'slaŋ\ *n* : an informal nonstandard vocabulary composed typically of invented words, arbitrarily changed words, and extravagant figures of speech — **slangy** *adj*

¹**slant** \'slant\ *n* 1 : a sloping direction, line, or plane 2 : a particular or personal viewpoint ⟨has a liberal ∼⟩ — **slant** *adj* — **slant·wise** \-ˌwīz\ *adv or adj*

²**slant** *vb* 1 : SLOPE 2 : to interpret or present in accordance with a special viewpoint or bias ⟨∼ed the story for their benefit⟩ ♦ *Synonyms* INCLINE, LEAN, LIST, TILT, HEEL — **slant·ing·ly** *adv*

slap \'slap\ *vb* **slapped; slap·ping** 1 : to strike sharply with the open hand 2 : REBUFF, INSULT — **slap** *n*

slap·stick \-ˌstik\ *n* : comedy stressing horseplay

¹**slash** \'slash\ *vb* 1 : to cut with sweeping strokes 2 : to cut slits in (a garment) 3 : to reduce sharply ⟨∼ed prices⟩ — **slash·er** \'sla-shər\ *n*

²**slash** *n* 1 : GASH 2 : an ornamental slit in a garment 3 : a mark / used to denote "or" (as in *and/or*), "and or" (as in *straggler/deserter*), or "per" (as in *feet/second*)

slat \'slat\ *n* : a thin narrow flat strip

¹**slate** \'slāt\ *n* 1 : a dense fine-grained rock that splits into thin layers 2 : a roofing tile or a writing tablet made from this rock 3 : a written or unwritten record ⟨start with a clean ∼⟩ 4 : a list of candidates for election

²**slate** *vb* **slat·ed; slat·ing** 1 : to cover with slate 2 : to designate for action or appointment ⟨is *slated* to open soon⟩

slath·er \'sla-ðər\ *vb* : to spread with or on thickly or lavishly

slat·tern \'sla-tərn\ *n* : a slovenly woman — **slat·tern·ly** *adj*

¹**slaugh·ter** \'slȯ-tər\ *n* 1 : the butchering of livestock for market 2 : great destruction of lives esp. in battle

²**slaughter** *vb* 1 : to kill (animals) for food : BUTCHER 2 : to kill in large numbers or in a bloody way : MASSACRE

slaugh·ter·house \-ˌhau̇s\ *n* : an establishment where animals are butchered

Slav \'släv, 'slav\ *n* : a person speaking a Slavic language

¹**slave** \'slāv\ *n* [ME *sclave*, fr. AF or ML; AF *esclave*, fr. ML *sclavus*, fr. *Sclavus* Slav; fr. the enslavement of Slavs in central Europe in the Middle Ages] 1 : a person held in servitude as property 2 : a device (as the printer of a computer) that is directly responsive to another — **slave** *adj*

²**slave** *vb* **slaved; slav·ing** : to work like a slave : DRUDGE ⟨*slaved* away at his work⟩

sla·ver \'sla-vər, 'slä-\ *n* : SLOBBER — **slaver** *vb*

slav·er \'slā-vər\ *n* : a ship or a person engaged in transporting slaves

slav·ery \'slāv-rē, 'slā-və-\ *n* 1 : wearisome drudgery 2 : the condition of being a slave 3 : the practice of owning slaves ♦ *Synonyms* SERVITUDE, BONDAGE, ENSLAVEMENT

¹**Slav·ic** \'sla-vik, 'slä-\ *n* : a branch of the Indo-European language family including various languages (as Russian or Polish) of eastern Europe

²**Slavic** *adj* : of or relating to the Slavs or their languages

slav·ish \'slā-vish\ *adj* 1 : SERVILE 2 : obeying or imitating with no freedom of judgment or choice — **slav·ish·ly** *adv*

slaw \'slȯ\ *n* : COLESLAW

slay \'slā\ *vb* **slew** \'slü\; **slain** \'slān\; **slay·ing** : KILL — **slay·er** *n*

SLBM *abbr* submarine-launched ballistic missile

sleaze \'slēz\ *n* : a sleazy quality, appearance, or behavior

slea·zy \'slē-zē\ *adj* **slea·zi·er; -est** 1 : FLIMSY, SHODDY 2 : marked by low character or quality ⟨a ∼ lawyer⟩

sled \'sled\ *n* : a vehicle usu. on runners adapted esp. for sliding on snow

sled *vb* **sled·ded; sled·ding** : to ride or carry on a sled

¹**sledge** \'slej\ *n* : SLEDGEHAMMER

²**sledge** *n* : a strong heavy sled

sledge·ham·mer \'slej-ˌha-mər\ *n* : a large heavy hammer wielded with both hands — **sledgehammer** *adj or vb*

¹**sleek** \'slēk\ *vb* 1 : to make smooth or glossy 2 : to gloss over

²**sleek** *adj* 1 : having a smooth well-groomed look 2 : trim and graceful in design ⟨a ∼ car⟩

¹**sleep** \'slēp\ *n* 1 : the natural periodic suspension of consciousness during which bodily powers are restored 2 : a state (as death or coma) suggesting sleep — **sleep·less** *adj* — **sleep·less·ness** *n*

²**sleep** *vb* **slept** \'slept\; **sleep·ing** 1 : to rest or be in a state of sleep; *also* : to spend in sleep 2 : to have sexual intercourse — usu. used with *with* 3 : to provide sleeping space for

sleep·er \'slē-pər\ *n* 1 : one that sleeps 2 : a horizontal beam to support something on or near ground level 3 : SLEEPING CAR 4 : someone or something unpromising or unnoticed that suddenly attains prominence or value

sleeping bag n : a warmly lined bag for sleeping esp. outdoors

sleeping car n : a railroad car with berths for sleeping

sleeping pill n : a drug in tablet or capsule form taken to induce sleep

sleeping sickness n : a serious disease of tropical Africa that is marked by fever, lethargy, confusion, and sleep disturbances and is caused by protozoans transmitted by the tsetse fly

sleep·over \'slēp-ˌō-vər\ n : an overnight stay (as at another's home)

sleep·walk·er \'slēp-ˌwȯ-kər\ n : one that walks while or as if while asleep — **sleep·walk** \-ˌwȯk\ vb

sleepy \'slē-pē\ adj **sleep·i·er; -est** 1 : ready for sleep 2 : quietly inactive — **sleep·i·ly** \'slē-pə-lē\ adv — **sleep·i·ness** \-pē-nəs\ n

sleet \'slēt\ n : frozen or partly frozen rain — **sleet** vb — **sleety** adj

sleeve \'slēv\ n 1 : a part of a garment covering an arm 2 : a tubular part designed to fit over another part — **sleeved** adj — **sleeve·less** adj

¹**sleigh** \'slā\ n : an open usu. horse-drawn vehicle on runners for use on snow or ice

²**sleigh** vb : to drive or travel in a sleigh

sleight \'slīt\ n 1 : TRICK 2 : DEXTERITY

sleight of hand : a trick requiring skillful manual manipulation

slen·der \'slen-dər\ adj 1 : SLIM, THIN 2 : WEAK, SLIGHT 3 : MEAGER, INADEQUATE ⟨~ opportunities⟩

slen·der·ize \-də-ˌrīz\ vb **-ized; -iz·ing** : to make slender

sleuth \'slüth\ n [short for *sleuthhound* bloodhound, fr. ME (Sc) *sleuth hund*, fr. ME *sleuth, sloith, sloth* track of an animal or person, fr. ON *slōth*] : DETECTIVE

¹**slew** \'slü\ past of SLAY

²**slew** vb : TURN, VEER, SKID

¹**slice** \'slīs\ vb **sliced; slic·ing** 1 : to cut a slice from; *also* : to cut into slices 2 : to hit (a ball) so that a slice results

²**slice** n 1 : a thin flat piece cut from something 2 : a flight of a ball (as in golf) that curves in the direction of the dominant hand of the player hitting it

¹**slick** \'slik\ vb : to make smooth or sleek

²**slick** adj 1 : very smooth : SLIPPERY 2 : CLEVER, SMART ⟨a ~ salesperson⟩

³**slick** n 1 : a smooth patch of water covered with a film of oil 2 : a popular magazine printed on coated paper

slick·er \'sli-kər\ n 1 : a long loose raincoat 2 : a sly tricky person 3 : a city dweller esp. of natty appearance or sophisticated mannerisms

¹**slide** \'slīd\ vb **slid** \'slid\; **slid·ing** \'slī-diŋ\ 1 : to move smoothly along a surface 2 : to fall by a loss of support 3 : to pass unobtrusively 4 : to move or pass smoothly; *also* : to pass unnoticed ⟨let it ~ by⟩ 5 : to fall or dive toward a base in baseball

²**slide** n 1 : an act or instance of sliding 2 : something (as a cover or fastener) that operates by sliding 3 : a fall of a mass of earth or snow down a hillside 4 : a surface on which something slides 5 : a glass plate on which a specimen is mounted for examination under a microscope 6 : a small transparent photograph that can be projected on a screen

slid·er \'slī-dər\ n 1 : one that slides 2 : a baseball pitch that looks like a fastball but curves slightly 3 : a small hamburger

slide rule n : a manual device for calculation consisting of a ruler and a movable middle piece graduated with logarithmic scales

slier comparative of SLY

sliest superlative of SLY

¹**slight** \'slīt\ adj 1 : SLENDER; *also* : FRAIL 2 : UNIMPORTANT ⟨a ~ movie⟩ 3 : small of its kind or in amount ⟨a ~ odor⟩ — **slight·ly** adv

²**slight** vb 1 : to treat as unimportant 2 : to ignore discourteously ⟨~ed the mayor⟩ 3 : to perform or attend to carelessly

³**slight** n : a humiliating discourtesy

slim \'slim\ adj **slim·mer; slim·mest** [D, bad, inferior, fr. MD, *slimp* crooked, bad] 1 : SLENDER, SLIGHT, THIN 2 : SMALL, SLIGHT ⟨a ~ chance⟩

²**slim** vb **slimmed; slim·ming** : to make or become slender

slime \'slīm\ n 1 : sticky mud 2 : a slippery substance (as on the skin of a slug or catfish) — **slimy** adj

¹**sling** \'sliŋ\ vb **slung** \'sləŋ\; **sling·ing** 1 : to throw forcibly : FLING 2 : to hurl with or as if with a sling

²**sling** n 1 : a short strap with strings attached for hurling stones or shot 2 : something (as a rope or chain) used to hoist, lower, support, or carry; *esp* : a bandage hanging from the neck to support an arm or hand

sling·shot \'sliŋ-ˌshät\ n : a forked stick with elastic bands for shooting small stones or shot

slink \'sliŋk\ vb **slunk** \'sləŋk\ *also* **slinked** \'sliŋkt\; **slink·ing** 1 : to move stealthily or furtively 2 : to move sinuously — **slinky** adj

¹**slip** \'slip\ vb **slipped; slip·ping** 1 : to escape quietly or secretly 2 : to slide along or cause to slide along smoothly 3 : to make a mistake 4 : to pass unnoticed or undone 5 : to fall off from a standard or level

²**slip** n 1 : a ramp for repairing ships 2 : a ship's berth between two piers 3 : secret or hurried departure, escape, or evasion 4 : BLUNDER 5 : a sudden mishap 6 : a woman's one-piece garment worn under a dress 7 : PILLOWCASE

³**slip** n 1 : a shoot or twig from a plant for planting or grafting 2 : a long narrow strip; *esp* : one of paper used for a record ⟨deposit ~⟩

⁴**slip** vb **slipped; slip·ping** : to take slips from (a plant)

slip·knot \'slip-ˌnät\ n : a knot that slips along the rope around which it is made

slipped disk n : a protrusion of one of the disks of cartilage between vertebrae with pressure on spinal nerves resulting esp. in low back pain

slip·per \'sli-pər\ n : a light low shoe that may be easily slipped on and off

slip·pery \'sli-pə-rē\ adj **slip·per·i·er; -est 1 :** icy, wet, smooth, or greasy enough to cause one to fall or lose one's hold **2 :** not to be trusted : TRICKY (a ~ salesman⟩ — **slip·per·i·ness** n

slip·shod \'slip-ˌshäd\ adj : SLOVENLY, CARELESS ⟨~ work⟩

slip·stream \'slip-ˌstrēm\ n : a stream (as of air) driven aft by a propeller

slip-up \'slip-ˌəp\ n **1 :** MISTAKE **2 :** ACCIDENT

¹**slit** \'slit\ vb **slit; slit·ting 1 :** SLASH **2 :** to cut off or away

²**slit** n : a long narrow cut or opening

slith·er \'sli-thər\ vb : to slip or glide along like a snake — **slith·ery** adj

sliv·er \'sli-vər\ n : SPLINTER

slob \'släb\ n : a slovenly or boorish person

slob·ber \'slä-bər\ vb **slob·bered; slob·ber·ing :** to dribble saliva — **slobber** n

sloe \'slō\ n : the fruit of the blackthorn

slog \'släg\ vb **slogged; slog·ging 1 :** to hit hard : BEAT **2 :** to work hard and steadily

slo·gan \'slō-gən\ n [alter. of earlier slogorn, fr. ScGael sluagh-ghairm, fr. sluagh army, host + gairm cry] : a word or phrase expressing the spirit or aim of a party, group, or cause

slo-mo \'slō-ˌmō\ n : SLOW MOTION — **slo-mo** adj

sloop \'slüp\ n [D sloep] : a single-masted sailboat with a jib and a fore-and-aft mainsail

¹**slop** \'släp\ n **1 :** thin tasteless drink or liquid food — usu. used in pl. **2 :** food waste for animal feed : SWILL **3 :** excreted body waste — usu. used in pl.

²**slop** vb **slopped; slop·ping 1 :** SPILL **2 :** to feed with slop ⟨~ hogs⟩

¹**slope** \'slōp\ vb **sloped; slop·ing :** SLANT, INCLINE

²**slope** n **1 :** upward or downward slant or degree of slant **2 :** ground that forms an incline **3 :** the part of a landmass draining into a particular ocean

slop·py \'slä-pē\ adj **slop·pi·er; -est 1 :** MUDDY, SLUSHY **2 :** SLOVENLY, MESSY

sloppy joe \-ˈjō\ n : ground beef cooked in a thick spicy sauce and usu. served on a bun

slosh \'släsh\ vb **1 :** to flounder through or splash about in or with water, mud, or slush **2 :** to move with a splashing motion

slot \'slät\ n **1 :** a long narrow opening or groove **2 :** a position in a sequence

slot car n : an electric toy racing car that runs on a grooved track

sloth \'slȯth\ n, pl **sloths** \'slȯths, 'slȯthz\ **1 :** LAZINESS, INDOLENCE **2 :** any of several slow-moving plant-eating arboreal mammals of So. and Central America — **sloth·ful** adj

slot machine n **1 :** a machine whose operation is begun by dropping a coin into a slot **2 :** a coin-operated gambling machine that pays off according to the matching of symbols on wheels spun by a handle

slouch \'slaùch\ n **1 :** a lazy or incompe-tent person **2 :** a loose or drooping gait or posture

²**slouch** vb : to walk, stand, or sit with a slouch : SLUMP

¹**slough** \'slü, 2 usu 'slaù\ n **1 :** a wet and marshy or muddy place (as a swamp) **2 :** a discouraged state of mind

²**slough** \'sləf\ also **sluff** n : something that has been or may be shed or cast off

³**slough** \'sləf\ also **sluff** vb : to cast off

Slo·vak \'slō-ˌväk, -ˌvak\ n **1 :** a member of a Slavic people of Slovakia **2 :** the language of the Slovaks — **Slovak** adj — **Slo·va·ki·an** \slō-ˈvä-kē-ən, -ˈva-\ adj or n

slov·en \'slə-vən\ n [ME sloveyn slut, rascal, perh. fr. MD slof negligent] : an untidy person

Slo·vene \'slō-ˌvēn\ n **1 :** a member of a Slavic people living largely in Slovenia **2 :** the language of the Slovenes — **Slovene** adj — **Slo·ve·nian** \slō-ˈvē-nē-ən\ adj or n

slov·en·ly \'slə-vən-lē\ adj **1 :** untidy in dress or person **2 :** lazily or carelessly done : SLIPSHOD ⟨~ thinking⟩

¹**slow** \'slō\ adj **1 :** SLUGGISH; also : dull in mind : STUPID **2 :** moving, flowing, or proceeding at less than the usual speed **3 :** taking more than the usual time **4 :** registering behind the correct time **5 :** not lively : BORING ♦ **Synonyms** DILATORY, LAGGARD, DELIBERATE, LEISURELY — **slow** adv — **slow·ly** adv — **slow·ness** n

²**slow** vb **1 :** to make slow : hold back **2 :** to go slower

slow motion n : motion-picture action photographed so as to appear much slower than normal — **slow-motion** adj

SLR abbr single-lens reflex

sludge \'sləj\ n : a slushy mass : OOZE; esp : solid matter produced by sewage treatment processes

slue var of ²SLEW

¹**slug** \'sləg\ n **1 :** a small mass of metal; esp : BULLET **2 :** a metal disk for use (as in a slot machine) in place of a coin **3 :** any of numerous wormlike mollusks related to the snails **4 :** a quantity of liquor drunk

²**slug** vb **slugged; slug·ging :** to strike forcibly and heavily — **slug·ger** n

slug·gard \'slə-gərd\ n : a lazy person

slug·gish \'slə-gish\ adj **1 :** SLOTHFUL, LAZY **2 :** slow in movement, flow, or growth ⟨a ~ economy⟩ **3 :** STAGNANT, DULL — **slug·gish·ly** adv — **slug·gish·ness** n

¹**sluice** \'slüs\ n [ME sluse, scluse, fr. AF escluse, fr. LL exclusa, fr. L, fem. of exclusus, pp. of excludere to shut out, exclude] **1 :** an artificial passage for water with a gate for controlling the flow; also : the gate so used **2 :** a channel that carries off surplus water **3 :** an inclined trough or flume for washing ore or floating logs

²**sluice** vb **sluiced; sluic·ing 1 :** to draw off through a sluice **2 :** to wash with running water : FLUSH

¹**slum** \'sləm\ n : a thickly populated area

marked by poverty and dirty or deteriorated houses — **slum·my** \'slə-mē\ *adj*

²**slum** *vb* **slummed; slum·ming** : to visit slums esp. out of curiosity; *also* : to go somewhere or do something that might be considered beneath one's station

¹**slum·ber** \'sləm-bər\ *vb* **slum·bered; slum·ber·ing** 1 : DOZE; *also* : SLEEP 2 : to be in a sluggish or torpid state

²**slumber** *n* : SLEEP

slum·ber·ous \'sləm-bə-rəs\ *or* **slum·brous** \-brəs\ *adj* 1 : SLUMBERING, SLEEPY 2 : PEACEFUL, INACTIVE

slum·lord \'sləm-‚lȯrd\ *n* : a landlord who receives unusually large profits from substandard properties

slump \'sləmp\ *vb* 1 : to sink down suddenly : COLLAPSE 2 : SLOUCH 3 : to decline sharply — **slump** *n*

slung *past and past part of* SLING

slunk *past and past part of* SLINK

¹**slur** \'slər\ *n* : a slighting remark : ASPERSION — **slur** *vb*

²**slur** *vb* **slurred; slur·ring** 1 : to slide or slip over without due mention or emphasis 2 : to perform two or more successive notes of different pitch in a smooth or connected way

³**slur** *n* : a curved line connecting notes to be slurred; *also* : a group of slurred notes

slurp \'slərp\ *vb* : to eat or drink noisily — **slurp** *n*

slur·ry \'slər-ē\ *n, pl* **slur·ries** : a watery mixture of insoluble matter

slush \'sləsh\ *n* 1 : partly melted or watery snow 2 : soft mud — **slushy** *adj*

slush fund *n* : an unregulated fund often for illicit purposes

slut \'slət\ *n* 1 : a slovenly woman 2 : a promiscuous woman

sly \'slī\ *adj* **sly·er** *also* **sli·er** \'slī-ər\; **sly·est** *also* **sli·est** \'slī-əst\ 1 : CRAFTY, CUNNING 2 : SECRETIVE, FURTIVE 3 : ROGUISH ♦ *Synonyms* TRICKY, WILY, ARTFUL, FOXY, GUILEFUL — **sly·ly** *also* **sli·ly** *adv* — **sly·ness** *n*

sm *abbr* small

Sm *symbol* samarium

SM *abbr* 1 master of science 2 sergeant major 3 service mark 4 stage manager

SMA *abbr* sergeant major of the army

¹**smack** \'smak\ *n* : characteristic flavor; *also* : a slight trace

²**smack** *vb* 1 : to have a taste 2 : to have a trace or suggestion 〈~s of treason〉

³**smack** *vb* 1 : to move (the lips) so as to make a sharp noise 2 : to kiss or slap with a loud noise

⁴**smack** *n* 1 : a sharp noise made by the lips 2 : a loud kiss or slap

⁵**smack** *adv* : squarely and sharply

⁶**smack** *n* : a sailing ship used in fishing

⁷**smack** *n, slang* : HEROIN

smack·down \'smak-‚daůn\ *n* 1 : the act of knocking down an opponent 2 : a wrestling match 3 : a decisive defeat 4 : a competition between rivals

SMaj *abbr* sergeant major

¹**small** \'smȯl\ *adj* 1 : little in size or amount 2 : operating on a limited scale 3 : little or close to zero (as in number or value) 4 : made up of little things 5

: TRIFLING, UNIMPORTANT 6 : MEAN, PETTY ♦ *Synonyms* DIMINUTIVE, PETITE, WEE, TINY, MINUTE — **small·ish** *adj* — **small·ness** *n*

²**small** *n* : a small part or product 〈the ~ of the back〉

small·pox \'smȯl-‚päks\ *n* : a contagious virus disease of humans formerly common but now eradicated

small talk *n* : light or casual conversation

small-time \'smȯl-‚tīm\ *adj* : insignificant in performance and standing : MINOR — **small-tim·er** *n*

smarmy \'smär-mē\ *adj* **smarm·i·er; -est** : marked by a smug, ingratiating, or false earnestness 〈~ politeness〉

¹**smart** \'smärt\ *adj* 1 : making one smart 〈a ~ blow〉 2 : mentally quick : BRIGHT 3 : WITTY, CLEVER 4 : STYLISH 5 : being a guided missile 6 : containing a microprocessor for limited computing capability 〈~ terminal〉 ♦ *Synonyms* KNOWING, QUICK-WITTED, INTELLIGENT, BRAINY, SHARP — **smart·ly** *adv* — **smart·ness** *n*

²**smart** *vb* 1 : to cause or feel a stinging pain 2 : to feel or endure distress — **smart** *n*

smart al·eck \'smärt-‚a-lik\ *n* : a person given to obnoxious cleverness

smart card *n* : a small plastic card that has a built-in microprocessor to store and handle data

smart·en \'smär-tᵊn\ *vb* : to make smart or smarter — usu. used with *up*

smart phone *n* : a cell phone that includes additional software functions (as e-mail or an Internet browser)

¹**smash** \'smash\ *n* 1 : a smashing blow 2 : a hard, overhand stroke in tennis 3 : the act or sound of smashing 4 : collision of vehicles : CRASH 5 : COLLAPSE, RUIN; *esp* : BANKRUPTCY 6 : a striking success : HIT — **smash** *adj*

²**smash** *vb* 1 : to break or be broken into pieces 2 : to move forward with force and shattering effect 3 : to destroy utterly : WRECK

smat·ter·ing \'sma-tə-riŋ\ *n* 1 : superficial knowledge 2 : a small scattered number or amount

¹**smear** \'smir\ *n* 1 : a spot left by an oily or sticky substance 2 : material smeared on a surface (as of a microscope slide)

²**smear** *vb* 1 : to overspread esp. with something oily or sticky 2 : SMUDGE, SOIL 3 : to injure by slander or insults

¹**smell** \'smel\ *vb* **smelled** \'smeld\ *or* **smelt** \'smelt\; **smell·ing** 1 : to perceive the odor of by sense organs of the nose; *also* : to detect or seek with or as if with these organs 2 : to have or give off an odor

²**smell** *n* 1 : ODOR, SCENT 2 : the process or power of perceiving odor; *also* : the sense by which one perceives odor 3 : an act of smelling — **smelly** *adj*

smelling salts *n pl* : an aromatic preparation used as a stimulant and restorative (as to relieve faintness)

¹**smelt** \'smelt\ *n, pl* **smelts** *or* **smelt** : any of a family of small food fishes of coastal

²smelt *vb* : to melt or fuse (ore) in order to separate the metal; *also* : REFINE

smelt·er \'smel-tər\ *n* 1 : one that smelts 2 : an establishment for smelting

smid·gen *also* **smid·geon** *or* **smid·gin** \'smi-jən\ *n* : a small amount : BIT

smi·lax \'smī-,laks\ *n* 1 : any of various mostly climbing and prickly plants related to the lilies 2 : an ornamental plant related to the asparagus

¹smile \'smī(-ə)l\ *vb* **smiled**; **smil·ing** 1 : to look with a smile 2 : to be favorable 3 : to express by a smile

²smile *n* : a change of facial expression to express amusement, pleasure, or affection — **smile·less** \'smī(-ə)l-ləs\ *adj*

smil·ey \'smī-lē\ *adj* : exhibiting a smile : frequently smiling

smiley face *n* : a line drawing that symbolizes a smiling face

smirch \'smərch\ *vb* : to make dirty or stained 2 : to bring disgrace on — **smirch** *n*

smirk \'smərk\ *vb* : to smile in an affected or smug manner : SIMPER — **smirk** *n*

smite \'smīt\ *vb* **smote** \'smōt\; **smit·ten** \'smi-t³n\ *or* **smote**; **smit·ing** \'smī-tiŋ\ 1 : to strike heavily; *also* : to kill by striking 2 : to affect as if by a heavy blow

smith \'smith\ *n* : a worker in metals; *esp* : BLACKSMITH

smith·er·eens \,smi-thə-'rēnz\ *n pl* [perh. fr. Ir *smidiríní*] : FRAGMENTS, BITS

smithy \'smi-thē\ *n, pl* **smith·ies** 1 : a smith's workshop 2 : BLACKSMITH

¹smock \'smäk\ *n* : a loose garment worn over other clothes as a protection

²smock *vb* : to gather (cloth) in regularly spaced tucks — **smock·ing** *n*

smog \'smäg, 'smóg\ *n* [blend of *smoke* and *fog*] : a thick haze caused by the action of sunlight on air polluted by smoke and automobile exhaust fumes — **smog·gy** *adj*

¹smoke \'smōk\ *n* 1 : the gas from burning material (as coal, wood, or tobacco) in which are suspended particles of soot 2 : a mass or column of smoke 3 : something (as a cigarette) to smoke; *also* : the act of smoking — **smoke·less** *adj* — **smoky** *adj*

²smoke *vb* **smoked**; **smok·ing** 1 : to emit smoke 2 : to inhale and exhale the fumes of burning tobacco; *also* : to use in smoking ⟨∼ a pipe⟩ 3 : to stupefy or drive away by smoke 4 : to discolor with smoke 5 : to cure (as meat) with smoke — **smok·er** *n*

smoke detector *n* : an alarm that sounds automatically when it detects smoke

smoke jumper *n* : a forest firefighter who parachutes to locations otherwise difficult to reach

smoke screen *n* 1 : a screen of smoke to hinder enemy observation 2 : something designed to obscure, confuse, or mislead

smoke·stack \'smōk-,stak\ *n* : a pipe or funnel through which smoke and gases are discharged

smol·der *or* **smoul·der** \'smōl-dər\ *vb*

smol·dered *or* **smoul·dered**; **smol·der·ing** *or* **smoul·der·ing** 1 : to burn and smoke without flame 2 : to burn inwardly — **smolder** *n*

smooch \'smüch\ *vb* : KISS, PET — **smooch** *n*

¹smooth \'smüth\ *adj* 1 : not rough or uneven 2 : not jarring or jolting 3 : BLAND, MILD 4 : fluent in speech and agreeable in manner — **smooth·ly** *adv* — **smooth·ness** *n*

²smooth *vb* 1 : to make smooth 2 : to free from trouble or difficulty

smooth muscle *n* : muscle with no cross striations that is typical of visceral organs (as the stomach and bladder) and is not under voluntary control

smoothy *or* **smooth·ie** \'smü-thē\ *n, pl* **smooth·ies** 1 : an artfully suave person 2 *smoothie* : a creamy beverage of fruit blended with juice, milk, or yogurt

s'more \'smór\ *n* : a dessert of marshmallow and pieces of chocolate sandwiched between graham crackers

smor·gas·bord \'smór-gəs-,bórd\ *n* [Sw *smörgåsbord*, fr. *smörgås* open sandwich + *bord* table] : a luncheon or supper buffet consisting of many foods

smote *past and past part of* SMITE

¹smoth·er \'smə-thər\ *n* 1 : thick stifling smoke 2 : a dense cloud (as of fog or dust) 3 : a confused multitude of things

²smother *vb* **smoth·ered**; **smoth·er·ing** 1 : to be overcome by or die from lack of air 2 : to kill by depriving of air 3 : SUPPRESS 4 : to cover thickly

SMSgt *abbr* senior master sergeant

¹smudge \'sməj\ *vb* **smudged**; **smudg·ing** : to soil or blur by rubbing or smearing ⟨his face was *smudged* with grease⟩

²smudge *n* : a dirty or blurred spot — **smudgy** *adj*

smug \'sməg\ *adj* **smug·ger**; **smug·gest** : conscious of one's virtue and importance : SELF-SATISFIED ⟨was ∼ about her victory⟩ — **smug·ly** *adv* — **smug·ness** *n*

smug·gle \'smə-gəl\ *vb* **smug·gled**; **smug·gling** 1 : to import or export secretly, illegally, or without paying the duties required by law 2 : to convey secretly — **smug·gler** \'smə-glər\ *n*

smut \'smət\ *n* 1 : something (as soot) that smudges; *also* : SMUDGE, SPOT 2 : any of various destructive diseases of plants caused by fungi; *also* : a fungus causing smut 3 : indecent language or matter — **smut·ty** *adj*

smutch \'sməch\ *n* : SMUDGE

Sn *symbol* [LL *stannum*] tin

SN *abbr* seaman

snack \'snak\ *n* : a light meal : BITE — **snack** *vb*

snaf·fle \'sna-fəl\ *n* : a simple jointed bit for a horse's bridle

¹snag \'snag\ *n* 1 : a stump or piece of a tree esp. when under water 2 : an unexpected difficulty ♦ *Synonyms* OBSTACLE, OBSTRUCTION, IMPEDIMENT, BAR

²snag *vb* **snagged**; **snag·ging** 1 : to become caught on or as if on a snag 2 : to seize quickly : SNATCH

snail \'snāl\ *n* : any of numerous small gastropod mollusks with a spiral shell into which they can withdraw

snail mail *n* : mail delivered by a postal system **2** : MAIL 2

snake \'snāk\ *n* **1** : any of numerous long-bodied limbless reptiles **2** : a treacherous person **3** : something that resembles a snake — **snake·like** \-ˌlīk\ *adj* — **snaky** *adj*

snake·bite \-ˌbīt\ *n* : the bite of a snake and esp. a venomous snake

¹**snap** \'snap\ *vb* **snapped**; **snap·ping 1** : to grasp or slash at something with the teeth **2** : to get or buy quickly **3** : to utter sharp or angry words **4** : to break suddenly with a sharp sound **5** : to give a sharp cracking noise **6** : to throw with a quick motion **7** : FLASH ⟨her eyes *snapped*⟩ **8** : to put a football into play — **snap·per** *n* — **snap·pish** *adj*

²**snap** *n* **1** : the act or sound of snapping **2** : something very easy to do : CINCH **3** : a short period of cold weather **4** : a catch or fastening that closes with a click **5** : a thin brittle cookie **6** : ENERGY, VIM; *also* : smartness of movement **7** : the putting of the ball into play in football

snap bean *n* : a bean grown primarily for its long pods that are cooked as a vegetable when young and tender

snap·drag·on \'snap-ˌdra-gən\ *n* : any of a genus of herbs with long spikes of showy flowers

snapping turtle *n* : either of two large American turtles with powerful jaws and a strong musky odor

snap·py \'sna-pē\ *adj* **1** : quickly made or done **2** : marked by vigor **3** : STYLISH ⟨a ~ dresser⟩

snap·shot \'snap-ˌshät\ *n* : a photograph taken usu. with an inexpensive hand-held camera

snare \'sner\ *n* : a trap often consisting of a noose for catching birds or mammals — **snare** *vb*

¹**snarl** \'snärl\ *vb* : to cause to become knotted and intertwined

²**snarl** *n* : TANGLE — **snarly** \'snär-lē\ *adj*

³**snarl** *vb* : to growl angrily or threateningly

⁴**snarl** *n* : an angry ill-tempered growl

¹**snatch** \'snach\ *vb* **1** : to try to grasp something suddenly **2** : to seize or take away suddenly ♦ *Synonyms* CLUTCH, SEIZE, GRAB, NAB

²**snatch** *n* **1** : a short period **2** : an act of snatching **3** : something brief or fragmentary ⟨~*es* of song⟩

¹**sneak** \'snēk\ *vb* **sneaked** \'snēkt\ *or* **snuck** \'snək\; **sneak·ing** : to move, act, or take in a furtive manner ⟨~*ed* past the guard⟩ — **sneak·ing·ly** *adv*

²**sneak** *n* **1** : one who acts in a furtive or shifty manner **2** : a stealthy or furtive move or escape — **sneak·i·ly** \'snē-kə-lē\ *adv* — **sneaky** *adj*

sneak·er \'snē-kər\ *n* : a sports shoe with a pliable rubber sole

sneer \'snir\ *vb* : to show scorn or contempt by curling the lip or by a jeering tone — **sneer** *n*

sneeze \'snēz\ *vb* **sneezed**; **sneez·ing** [ME *snesen*, alter. of *fnesen*, fr. OE *fnēosan*] : to force the breath out suddenly and violently as a reflex act — **sneeze** *n*

SNF *abbr* skilled nursing facility

snick·er \'sni-kər\ *n* : a partly suppressed laugh — **snicker** *vb*

snide \'snīd\ *adj* **1** : MEAN, LOW ⟨a ~ trick⟩ **2** : slyly disparaging ⟨a ~ remark⟩ — **snide·ly** *adv* — **snide·ness** *n*

sniff \'snif\ *vb* **1** : to draw air audibly up the nose esp. for smelling **2** : to show disdain or scorn **3** : to detect by or as if by smelling — **sniff** *n*

snif·fle \'sni-fəl\ *n* **1** *pl* : a head cold marked by nasal discharge **2** : SNUFFLE — **sniffle** *vb*

¹**snip** \'snip\ *n* **1** : a fragment snipped off **2** : a simple stroke of the scissors or shears

²**snip** *vb* **snipped**; **snip·ping** : to cut off by bits : CLIP; *also* : to remove by cutting off ⟨~ a flower⟩

¹**snipe** \'snīp\ *n, pl* **snipes** *or* **snipe** : any of several long-billed game birds esp. of marshy areas that belong to the same family as the sandpipers

²**snipe** *vb* **sniped**; **snip·ing** : to shoot at an exposed enemy from a concealed position — **snip·er** *n*

snip·py \'sni-pē\ *adj* **snip·pi·er; -est** : CURT, SNAPPISH ⟨~ comments⟩ — **snip·pi·ly** \'sni-pə-lē\ *adv*

snips \'snips\ *n pl* : hand shears used esp. for cutting sheet metal ⟨tin ~⟩

snitch \'snich\ *vb* **1** : INFORM, TATTLE **2** : PILFER, SNATCH — **snitch** *n*

sniv·el \'sni-vəl\ *vb* **-eled** *or* **-elled; -el·ing** *or* **-el·ling 1** : to have a running nose; *also* : SNUFFLE **2** : to whine in a snuffling manner — **snivel** *n*

snob \'snäb\ *n* : one who seeks association with persons of higher social position and looks down on those considered inferior — **snob·bish** *adj* — **snob·bish·ly** *adv* — **snob·bish·ness** *n* — **snob·by** \'snä-bē\ *adj*

snob·bery \'snä-bə-rē\ *n, pl* **-ber·ies** : snobbish conduct

¹**snoop** \'snüp\ *vb* [D *snoepen* to buy or eat on the sly] : to pry in a furtive or meddlesome way

²**snoop** *n* : a prying meddlesome person

snoopy \'snü-pē\ *adj* **snoop·i·er; -est** : given to snooping

snooty \'snü-tē\ *adj* **snoot·i·er; -est** : DISDAINFUL, SNOBBISH ⟨~ rich people⟩ — **snoot·i·ly** \'snü-tə-lē\ *adv*

snooze \'snüz\ *vb* **snoozed**; **snooz·ing** : to take a nap : DOZE — **snooze** *n*

snore \'snȯr\ *vb* **snored**; **snor·ing** : to breathe with a rough hoarse noise while sleeping — **snore** *n*

snor·kel \'snȯr-kəl\ *n* [G *Schnorchel*] : a tube projecting above the water used by swimmers for breathing with the face under water — **snorkel** *vb*

snort \'snȯrt\ *vb* **1** : to force air violently and noisily through the nose ⟨his horse ~*ed*⟩ **2** : to inhale (a drug) through the nostrils — **snort** *n*

snot \'snät\ *n* : nasal mucus

snot·ty \'snä-tē\ *adj* **snot·ti·er; -est** **1** : soiled with snot **2** : meanly contemptible ⟨a ~ reply⟩

snout \'snaut\ *n* **1** : a long projecting muzzle (as of a pig) **2** : a usu. large or grotesque nose

¹**snow** \'snō\ *n* **1** : crystals of ice formed from water vapor in the air **2** : a descent or shower of snow crystals

²**snow** *vb* **1** : to fall or cause to fall in or as snow **2** : to cover or shut in with or as if with snow

¹**snow·ball** \'snō-,bȯl\ *n* : a round mass of snow pressed into shape in the hand for throwing

²**snowball** *vb* **1** : to throw snowballs at **2** : to increase or expand at a rapidly accelerating rate

snow·bank \-,baŋk\ *n* : a mound or slope of snow

snow·belt \-,belt\ *n, often cap* : a region that receives an appreciable amount of annual snowfall

snow·blow·er \-,blō-ər\ *n* : a machine in which a rotating spiral blade picks up and propels snow aside

snow·board \-,bȯrd\ *n* : a board like a wide ski ridden in a surfing position downhill over snow

snow·drift \-,drift\ *n* : a bank of drifted snow

snow·drop \-,dräp\ *n* : a plant with narrow leaves and a nodding white flower that blooms early in the spring

snow·fall \-,fȯl\ *n* : a fall of snow

snow fence *n* : a fence across the path of prevailing winds to protect something (as a road) from drifting snow

snow·field \'snō-,fēld\ *n* : a mass of perennial snow at the head of a glacier

snow·mo·bile \'snō-mō-,bēl\ *n* : any of various automotive vehicles for travel on snow — **snow·mo·bil·er** \-,bē-lər\ *n* — **snow·mo·bil·ing** \-liŋ\ *n*

snow pea *n* : a cultivated pea with flat edible pods

snow·plow \'snō-,plaů\ *n* **1** : a device for clearing away snow **2** : a skiing maneuver in which the heels of both skis are slid outward for slowing down or stopping

¹**snow·shoe** \-,shü\ *n* : a lightweight platform for the foot designed to enable a person to walk on soft snow without sinking

²**snowshoe** *vb* **snow·shoed; snow·shoe·ing** : to travel on snowshoes

snow·storm \-,stȯrm\ *n* : a storm of falling snow

snow thrower *n* : SNOWBLOWER

snowy \'snō-ē\ *adj* **snow·i·er; -est** **1** : marked by snow **2** : white as snow

snowy egret *n* : a white American egret with a slender black bill

snub \'snəb\ *vb* **snubbed; snub·bing** : to treat with disdain : SLIGHT — **snub** *n*

snub–nosed \'snəb-,nōzd\ *adj* : having a nose slightly turned up at the end

snuck *past and past part of* SNEAK

¹**snuff** \'snəf\ *vb* **1** : to pinch off the charred end of (a candle) **2** : to put out (a candle) — **snuff·er** *n*

²**snuff** *vb* **1** : to draw forcibly into or through the nose **2** : SMELL

³**snuff** *n* : SNIFF

⁴**snuff** *n* : pulverized tobacco

snuf·fle \'snə-fəl\ *vb* **snuf·fled; snuf·fling** **1** : to snuff or sniff audibly and repeatedly **2** : to breathe with a sniffing sound — **snuf·fle** *n*

snug \'snəg\ *adj* **snug·ger; snug·gest** **1** : fitting closely and comfortably **2** : CONCEALED ⟨a ~ position⟩ — **snug·ly** *adv* — **snug·ness** *n*

snug·gle \'snə-gəl\ *vb* **snug·gled; snug·gling** : to curl up or draw close comfortably : NESTLE

¹**so** \'sō\ *adv* **1** : in the manner indicated **2** : in the same way ⟨he's hungry and ~ am I⟩ **3** : THUS **4** : FINALLY **5** : to an indicated or great extent ⟨I'm ~ bored⟩ **6** : THEREFORE

²**so** *conj* : for that reason ⟨he wanted it, ~ he took it⟩

³**so** *pron* **1** : the same ⟨became chairman and remained ~⟩ **2** : approximately that ⟨a dozen or ~⟩

⁴**so** *abbr* south; southern

SO *abbr* strikeout

¹**soak** \'sōk\ *vb* **1** : to remain in a liquid **2** : WET, SATURATE **3** : to draw in by or as if by absorption ⟨~ up the sunshine⟩
  ♦ **Synonyms** DRENCH, STEEP, IMPREGNATE

²**soak** *n* **1** : the act of soaking **2** : the liquid in which something is soaked **3** : DRUNKARD

soap \'sōp\ *n* : a cleansing substance made usu. by action of alkali on fat — **soap** *vb* — **soapy** *adj*

soap·box \'sōp-,bäks\ *n* : an improvised platform used for delivering informal speeches

soap opera *n* [fr. its sponsorship by soap manufacturers] : a radio or television daytime serial drama

soap·stone \'sōp-,stōn\ *n* : a soft talc-containing stone with a soapy feel

soar \'sȯr\ *vb* **1** : to fly upward or at a height on or as if on wings

sob \'säb\ *vb* **sobbed; sob·bing** : to weep with convulsive heavings of the chest or contractions of the throat — **sob** *n*

so·ba \'sō-bə\ *n* [Jp] : a Japanese noodle made from buckwheat flour

so·ber \'sō-bər\ *adj* **so·ber·er** \-bər-ər\; **so·ber·est** \-bə-rəst\ **1** : temperate in the use of liquor **2** : not drunk **3** : serious or grave in mood or disposition **4** : having a quiet tone or color ♦ **Synonyms** SOLEMN, EARNEST, STAID, SEDATE — **so·ber·ly** *adv* — **so·ber·ness** *n*

so·bri·ety \sō-'brī-ə-tē\ *n* : the quality or state of being sober

so·bri·quet \'sō-bri-,kā, -,ket\ *n* [F] : NICKNAME

soc *abbr* **1** social; society **2** sociology

so·ca \'sō-kə, -kä\ *n* : soul music blended with calypso

so–called \'sō-'kȯld\ *adj* : commonly but often inaccurately so termed

soc·cer \'sä-kər\ *n* [by shortening & alter. fr. *association football*] : a game played on a field by two teams with a round inflated ball that is kicked or hit with any body part other than the hands or arms

¹so·cia·ble \'sō-shə-bəl\ *adj* **1** : liking companionship : FRIENDLY **2** : characterized by pleasant social relations ◆ *Synonyms* GRACIOUS, CORDIAL, AFFABLE, GENIAL — **so·cia·bil·i·ty** \ˌsō-shə-'bi-lə-tē\ *n* — **so·cia·bly** \'sō-shə-blē\ *adv*

²sociable *n* : SOCIAL

¹so·cial \'sō-shəl\ *adj* **1** : marked by pleasant companionship with one's friends **2** : naturally living and breeding in organized communities ⟨∼ insects⟩ **3** : of or relating to human society ⟨∼ institutions⟩ **4** : of, relating to, or based on rank in a particular society ⟨∼ circles⟩; *also* : of or relating to fashionable society — **so·cial·ly** *adv*

²social *n* : a social gathering

so·cial·ise *Brit var of* SOCIALIZE

so·cial·ism \'sō-shə-ˌli-zəm\ *n* : any of various social systems based on shared or government ownership and administration of the means of production and distribution of goods — **so·cial·ist** \'sō-shə-list\ *n or adj* — **so·cial·is·tic** \ˌsō-shə-'lis-tik\ *adj*

so·cial·ite \'sō-shə-ˌlīt\ *n* : a person prominent in fashionable society

so·cial·ize \'sō-shə-ˌlīz\ *vb* **-ized; -iz·ing** **1** : to regulate according to the theory and practice of socialism **2** : to adapt to social needs or uses **3** : to participate actively in a social gathering — **so·cial·i·za·tion** \ˌsō-shə-lə-'zā-shən\ *n*

social media *n pl* : forms of electronic communication (as websites) for sharing information or videos with other users

social science *n* : a science (as economics or political science) dealing with a particular aspect of human society — **social scientist** *n*

social work *n* : services, activities, or methods providing social services esp. to the economically or socially disadvantaged — **social worker** *n*

so·ci·ety \sə-'sī-ə-tē\ *n, pl* **-ties** [MF *societé,* fr. L *societat-, societas,* fr. *socius* companion] **1** : COMPANIONSHIP **2** : a voluntary association of persons for common ends **3** : a part of a community bound together by common interests and standards; *esp* : the group or set of fashionable people

so·cio·eco·nom·ic \ˌsō-sē-ō-ˌe-kə-'nä-mik, ˌsō-shē-, -ˌē-kə-\ *adj* : of, relating to, or involving both social and economic factors

sociol *abbr* sociologist; sociology

so·ci·ol·o·gy \ˌsō-sē-'ä-lə-jē, ˌsō-shē-\ *n* : the science of society, social institutions, and social relationships — **so·cio·log·i·cal** \ˌsō-sē-ə-'lä-ji-kəl, ˌsō-shē-\ *adj* — **so·ci·ol·o·gist** \-'ä-lə-jist\ *n*

so·cio·path \'sō-sē-ə-ˌpath, 'sō-sh(ē-)ə-\ *n* : a person exhibiting antisocial behavior : PSYCHOPATH — **so·cio·path·ic** \ˌsō-sē-ə-'pa-thik, ˌsō-sh(ē-)ə-\ *adj*

¹sock \'säk\ *n, pl* **socks** *or* **sox** \'säks\ : a stocking with a short leg

²sock *vb* : to hit, strike, or apply forcefully

³sock *n* : a vigorous blow : PUNCH

sock·et \'sä-kət\ *n* : an opening or hollow that forms a holder for something

socket wrench *n* : a wrench usu. in the form of a bar and removable socket made to fit a bolt or nut

sock·eye salmon \'säk-ˌī-\ *n* : a commercially important Pacific salmon

¹sod \'säd\ *n* : TURF 1

²sod *vb* **sod·ded; sod·ding** : to cover with sod

so·da \'sō-də\ *n* **1** : SODIUM CARBONATE **2** : SODIUM BICARBONATE **3** : SODIUM **4** : SODA WATER **5** : SODA POP **6** : a sweet drink of soda water, flavoring, and often ice cream

soda pop *n* : a carbonated, sweetened, and flavored soft drink

soda water *n* : a beverage of water charged with carbon dioxide

sod·den \'sä-dᵊn\ *adj* **1** : lacking spirit : DULLED **2** : SOAKED, DRENCHED **3** : heavy or doughy from being improperly cooked ⟨∼ biscuits⟩

so·di·um \'sō-dē-əm\ *n* : a soft waxy silver white metallic chemical element occurring in nature in combined form (as in salt)

sodium bicarbonate *n* : a white weakly alkaline salt used esp. in baking powders, fire extinguishers, and medicine

sodium carbonate *n* : a carbonate of sodium used esp. in washing and bleaching textiles

sodium chloride *n* : SALT 1

sodium fluoride *n* : a salt used chiefly in tiny amounts (as in fluoridation) to prevent tooth decay

sodium hydroxide *n* : a white brittle caustic substance used in making soap and rayon and in bleaching

sodium nitrate *n* : a crystalline salt used as a fertilizer and in curing meat

sodium thiosulfate *n* : a hygroscopic crystalline salt used as a photographic fixing agent

sod·omy \'sä-də-mē\ *n* : anal or oral sexual intercourse with a member of the same or opposite sex; *also* : sexual intercourse with an animal — **sod·om·ize** \'sä-də-ˌmīz\ *vb*

so·ev·er \sō-'e-vər\ *adv* **1** : in any degree or manner ⟨how bad ∼⟩ **2** : at all : of any kind ⟨any help ∼⟩

so·fa \'sō-fə\ *n* [earlier, raised carpeted floor, fr. It *sofà,* fr. Turk *sofa,* fr. Ar *suffa* carpet, divan] : a couch usu. with upholstered back and arms

soft \'sòft\ *adj* **1** : not hard or rough : NONVIOLENT **2** : RESTFUL, GENTLE, SOOTHING **3** : emotionally susceptible **4** : not prepared to endure hardship **5** : not containing certain salts that prevent lathering ⟨∼ water⟩ **6** : occurring at such a speed as to avoid destructive impact ⟨∼ landing of a spacecraft on the moon⟩ **7** : BIODEGRADABLE ⟨a ∼ pesticide⟩ **8** : not alcoholic ⟨∼ drinks⟩ **9** : less detrimental than a hard narcotic ⟨∼ drugs⟩ — **soft·ly** adv — **soft·ness** n

soft·ball \'sȯft-ˌbȯl\ n : a game similar to baseball played with a ball larger and softer than a baseball; also : the ball used in this game

soft·bound \-ˌbau̇nd\ adj : not bound in hard covers ⟨∼ books⟩

soft coal n : BITUMINOUS COAL

soft·en \'sȯ-fən\ vb : to make or become soft — **soft·en·er** n

soft palate n : the fold at the back of the hard palate that partially separates the mouth from the pharynx

soft·ware \'sȯft-ˌwer\ n : the entire set of programs, procedures, and related documentation associated with a system; esp : computer programs

soft·wood \-ˌwu̇d\ n 1 : the wood of a coniferous tree as compared to that of a broad-leaved deciduous tree 2 : a tree yielding softwood — **softwood** adj

sog·gy \'sä-gē\ adj **sog·gi·er; -est** : heavy with water or moisture — **sog·gi·ly** \'sä-gə-lē\ adv — **sog·gi·ness** \-gē-nəs\ n

soi·gné or **soi·gnée** \swän-'yā\ adj : elegantly maintained; esp : WELL-GROOMED

¹**soil** \'sȯi(-ə)l\ vb 1 : CORRUPT, POLLUTE 2 : to make or become dirty 3 : STAIN, DISGRACE ⟨∼ed his reputation⟩

²**soil** n 1 : STAIN, DEFILEMENT 2 : EXCREMENT, WASTE

³**soil** n 1 : firm land : EARTH 2 : the upper layer of earth in which plants grow 3 : COUNTRY, REGION

soi·ree or **soi·rée** \swä-'rā\ n [F soirée evening period, evening party, fr. MF, fr. soir evening, fr. L sero at a late hour] : an evening party

so·journ \'sō-ˌjərn, sō-'jərn\ vb : to dwell in a place temporarily — **sojourn** n — **so·journ·er** n

¹**sol** \'säl, 'sȯl\ n — see MONEY table

²**sol** n : a fluid colloidal system

³**sol** abbr 1 solicitor 2 soluble 3 solution

Sol \'säl\ n : SUN

¹**sol·ace** \'sä-ləs\ n : COMFORT

²**solace** vb **so·laced; so·lac·ing** : to give solace to : CONSOLE

so·lar \'sō-lər\ adj 1 : of, derived from, or relating to the sun 2 : measured by the earth's course in relation to the sun ⟨the ∼ year⟩ 3 : operated by or using the sun's light or heat ⟨∼ energy⟩

solar cell n : a photoelectric cell used as a power source

solar collector n : a device for the absorption of solar radiation for the heating of water or buildings or the production of electricity

solar flare n : a sudden temporary outburst of energy from a small area of the sun's surface

so·lar·i·um \sō-'ler-ē-əm\ n, pl **-ia** \-ē-ə\ also **-i·ums** : a room exposed to the sun; esp : a room (as in a hospital) for exposure of the body to sunshine

solar mass n : a unit of mass equal to the mass of the sun or about 2×10^{30} kilograms

solar plexus n : the general area of the stomach below the sternum

solar system n : the sun together with the group of celestial bodies that revolve around it

solar wind n : plasma continuously ejected from the sun's surface

sold past and past part of SELL

sol·der \'sä-dər, 'sȯ-\ n : a metallic alloy used when melted to mend or join metallic surfaces — **solder** vb

soldering iron n : a metal device for applying heat in soldering

¹**sol·dier** \'sōl-jər\ n [ME soudeour, fr. AF, mercenary, fr. soudee shilling's worth, wage, fr. sou, soud shilling, fr. LL solidus a Roman coin, fr. L, solid] : a person in military service; esp : an enlisted man or woman — **sol·dier·ly** adj or adv

²**soldier** vb **sol·diered; sol·dier·ing** 1 : to serve as a soldier 2 : to pretend to work while actually doing nothing

soldier of fortune : ADVENTURER 2

sol·diery \'sōl-jə-rē\ n : a body of soldiers

¹**sole** \'sōl\ n : any of various flatfishes including some used for food

²**sole** n 1 : the undersurface of the foot 2 : the bottom of a shoe

³**sole** vb **soled; sol·ing** : to furnish (a shoe) with a sole

⁴**sole** adj : SINGLE, ONLY ⟨the ∼ survivor⟩ — **sole·ly** \'sōl-lē\ adv

so·le·cism \'sä-lə-ˌsi-zəm, 'sō-\ n 1 : a mistake in grammar 2 : a breach of etiquette

sol·emn \'sä-ləm\ adj 1 : marked by or observed with full religious ceremony ⟨a ∼ oath⟩ 2 : FORMAL, CEREMONIOUS 3 : highly serious : GRAVE ⟨a ∼ gathering⟩ 4 : SOMBER, GLOOMY ⟨a ∼ city⟩ — **so·lem·ni·ty** \sə-'lem-nə-tē\ n — **sol·emn·ly** \'sä-ləm-lē\ adv

sol·em·nize \'sä-ləm-ˌnīz\ vb **-nized; -niz·ing** 1 : to observe or honor with solemnity 2 : to celebrate (a marriage) with religious rites — **sol·em·ni·za·tion** \ˌsä-ləm-nə-'zā-shən\ n

so·le·noid \'sō-lə-ˌnȯid, 'sä-\ n : a coil of wire usu. in cylindrical form that when carrying a current acts like a magnet

so·lic·it \sə-'li-sət\ vb 1 : ENTREAT, BEG 2 : to approach with a request or plea 3 : TEMPT, LURE 4 : to try to obtain by request ⟨∼ donations⟩ — **so·lic·i·ta·tion** \-ˌli-sə-'tā-shən\ n

so·lic·i·tor \sə-'li-sə-tər\ n 1 : one that solicits 2 : LAWYER; esp : a legal official of a city or state

so·lic·i·tous \sə-'li-sə-təs\ adj 1 : WORRIED, CONCERNED 2 : EAGER, WILLING ♦ **Synonyms** AVID, IMPATIENT, KEEN, ANXIOUS — **so·lic·i·tous·ly** adv

so·lic·i·tude \sə-'li-sə-ˌtüd, -ˌtyüd\ n : CONCERN, ANXIETY

¹**sol·id** \'sä-ləd\ adj 1 : not hollow; also : written as one word without a hyphen ⟨a ∼ compound⟩ 2 : having, involving, or dealing with three dimensions or with solids ⟨∼ geometry⟩ 3 : not loose or spongy : COMPACT ⟨a ∼ mass of rock⟩; also : neither gaseous nor liquid : HARD, RIGID ⟨∼ ice⟩ 4 : of good substantial

quality or kind ⟨∼ comfort⟩ **5** : thoroughly dependable : RELIABLE ⟨a ∼ citizen⟩; *also* : serious in purpose or character ⟨∼ reading⟩ **6** : UNANIMOUS, UNITED ⟨∼ for pay increases⟩ **7** : of one substance or character — **solid** *adv* — **so·lid·i·ty** \sə-ˈli-də-tē\ *n* — **sol·id·ly** *adv* — **sol·id·ness** *n*

²**solid** *n* **1** : a geometrical figure (as a cube or sphere) having three dimensions **2** : a solid substance

sol·i·dar·i·ty \ˌsä-lə-ˈder-ə-tē\ *n* : unity based on shared interests, objectives, or standards

so·lid·i·fy \sə-ˈli-də-ˌfī\ *vb* **-fied; -fy·ing** : to make or become solid — **so·lid·i·fi·ca·tion** \-ˌli-də-fə-ˈkā-shən\ *n*

solid–state *adj* **1** : relating to the structure and properties of solid material **2** : using semiconductor devices rather than vacuum tubes

so·lil·o·quize \sə-ˈli-lə-ˌkwīz\ *vb* **-quized; -quiz·ing** : to talk to oneself : utter a soliloquy

so·lil·o·quy \sə-ˈli-lə-kwē\ *n, pl* **-quies** [LL *soliloquium,* fr. L *solus* alone + *loqui* to speak] **1** : the act of talking to oneself **2** : a dramatic monologue that represents unspoken reflections by a character

sol·i·taire \ˈsä-lə-ˌter\ *n* **1** : a single gem (as a diamond) set alone **2** : a card game for one person

sol·i·tary \ˈsä-lə-ˌter-ē\ *adj* **1** : being or living apart from others **2** : LONELY, SECLUDED **3** : SOLE, ONLY ⟨a ∼ example⟩

sol·i·tude \ˈsä-lə-ˌtüd, -ˌtyüd\ *n* **1** : the state of being alone : SECLUSION ⟨worked in ∼⟩ **2** : a lonely place

soln *abbr* solution

¹**so·lo** \ˈsō-lō\ *n, pl* **solos** [It, fr. *solo* alone, fr. L *solus*] **1** : a piece of music for a single voice or instrument with or without accompaniment **2** : an action in which there is only one performer — **solo** *adj or vb* — **so·lo·ist** *n*

²**solo** *adv* : without a companion : ALONE

so·lon \ˈsō-lən\ *n* **1** : a wise and skillful lawgiver **2** : a member of a legislative body

sol·stice \ˈsäl-stəs, ˈsōl-\ *n* [ME, fr. L *solstitium,* fr. *sol* sun + *-stit-, -stes* standing] : the time of the year when the sun is farthest north of the equator (**summer solstice**) about June 22 or farthest south (**winter solstice**) about Dec. 22 — **sol·sti·tial** \säl-ˈsti-shəl, sōl-\ *adj*

sol·u·ble \ˈsäl-yə-bəl\ *adj* **1** : capable of being dissolved in or as if in a liquid **2** : capable of being solved or explained — **sol·u·bil·i·ty** \ˌsäl-yə-ˈbi-lə-tē\ *n*

sol·ute \ˈsäl-ˌyüt\ *n* : a dissolved substance

so·lu·tion \sə-ˈlü-shən\ *n* **1** : an action or process of solving a problem; *also* : an answer to a problem **2** : an act or the process by which one substance is homogeneously mixed with another usu. liquid substance; *also* : a mixture thus formed

solve \ˈsälv\ *vb* **solved; solv·ing** : to find the answer to or a solution for — **solv·able** *adj*

sol·ven·cy \ˈsäl-vən-sē\ *n* : the condition of being solvent

¹**sol·vent** \-vənt\ *adj* **1** : able or sufficient to pay all legal debts **2** : dissolving or able to dissolve

²**solvent** *n* : a usu. liquid substance capable of dissolving or dispersing one or more other substances

som \ˈsôm\ *n* **1** *pl* **som** — see MONEY table **2** *or* **sum** *pl* **soms** *or* **sums** — see MONEY table

so·mat·ic \sō-ˈma-tik\ *adj* : of, relating to, or affecting the body in contrast to the mind or the sex cells and their precursors

som·ber *or* **som·bre** \ˈsäm-bər\ *adj* **1** : DARK, GLOOMY **2** : GRAVE, MELANCHOLY ⟨a ∼ mood⟩ — **som·ber·ly** *adv*

som·bre·ro \səm-ˈbrer-ō\ *n, pl* **-ros** [Sp, fr. *sombra* shade] : a broad-brimmed felt hat worn esp. in the Southwest and in Mexico

¹**some** \ˈsəm\ *adj* **1** : one unspecified ⟨∼ man called⟩ **2** : an unspecified or indefinite number of ⟨∼ berries are ripe⟩ **3** : at least a few or a little ⟨∼ years ago⟩

²**some** *pron* : a certain number or amount ⟨∼ of the berries are ripe⟩ ⟨∼ of it is missing⟩

¹**-some** \səm\ *adj suffix* : characterized by a (specified) thing, quality, state, or action ⟨awesome⟩ ⟨burdensome⟩

²**-some** *n suffix* : a group of (so many) members and esp. persons ⟨foursome⟩

¹**some·body** \ˈsəm-ˌbä-dē, -bə-\ *pron* : some person

²**somebody** *n* : a person of importance

some·day \ˈsəm-ˌdā\ *adv* : at some future time

some·how \-ˌhaú\ *adv* : by some means

some·one \-ˌ(ˌ)wən\ *pron* : some person

som·er·sault *also* **sum·mer·sault** \ˈsə-mər-ˌsólt\ *n* [MF *sombresaut* leap, ultim. fr. L *super* over + *saltus* leap, fr. *salire* to jump] : a leap or roll in which a person turns heels over head — **somersault** *vb*

som·er·set \-ˌset\ *n or vb* : SOMERSAULT

some·thing \ˈsəm-thiŋ\ *pron* : some undetermined or unspecified thing

some·time \-ˌtīm\ *adv* **1** : at a future time **2** : at an unknown or unnamed time

some·times \-ˌtīmz\ *adv* : OCCASIONALLY

¹**some·what** \-ˌhwät, -ˌhwət\ *pron* : SOMETHING

²**somewhat** *adv* : in some degree

some·where \-ˌhwer\ *adv* : in, at, or to an unknown or unnamed place

som·nam·bu·lism \säm-ˈnam-byə-ˌli-zəm\ *n* : performance of motor acts (as walking) during sleep; *also* : an abnormal condition of sleep characterized by this — **som·nam·bu·list** \-list\ *n*

som·no·lent \ˈsäm-nə-lənt\ *adj* : SLEEPY, DROWSY — **som·no·lence** \-ləns\ *n*

so·mo·ni \ˌsō-mō-ˈnē\ *n, pl* **somoni** — see MONEY table

son \ˈsən\ *n* **1** : a male offspring or descendant **2** *cap* : Jesus Christ **3** : a person deriving from a particular source (as a country, race, or school)

so·nar \ˈsō-ˌnär\ *n* [*so*und *na*vigation *r*anging] : a method or device for detecting and locating submerged objects (as submarines) by sound waves

so·na·ta \sə-ˈnä-tə\ n [It] : an instrumental composition with three or four movements differing in rhythm and mood but related in key

son·a·ti·na \ˌsä-nə-ˈtē-nə\ n [It, dim. of *sonata*] : a short usu. simplified sonata

song \ˈsȯŋ\ n 1 : vocal music; *also* : a short composition of words and music 2 : poetic composition 3 : a distinctive or characteristic sound (as of a bird) 4 : a small amount ⟨sold for a ∼⟩

song·bird \ˈsȯŋ-ˌbərd\ n : a bird that utters a series of musical tones

Song of Sol·o·mon \-ˈsä-lə-mən\ — see BIBLE table

Song of Songs — see BIBLE table

song·ster \ˈsȯŋ-stər\ n : one that sings

song·stress \-strəs\ n : a girl or woman who is a singer

son·ic \ˈsä-nik\ adj : of or relating to sound waves or the speed of sound

sonic boom n : an explosive sound produced by an aircraft traveling at supersonic speed

son–in–law \ˈsən-ən-ˌlȯ\ n, pl **sons–in–law** : the husband of one's daughter

son·net \ˈsä-nət\ n : a poem of 14 lines usu. in iambic pentameter with a definite rhyme scheme

son of a gun n, pl **sons of guns** : an offensive or disagreeable person

so·no·rous \sə-ˈnȯr-əs, ˈsä-nə-rəs\ adj 1 : giving out sound when struck 2 : loud, deep, or rich in sound : RESONANT ⟨a ∼ voice⟩ 3 : high-sounding : IMPRESSIVE — **so·nor·i·ty** \sə-ˈnȯr-ə-tē\ n

soon \ˈsün\ adv 1 : before long 2 : PROMPTLY, QUICKLY 3 archaic : EARLY 4 : WILLINGLY, READILY

soot \ˈsut, ˈsȯt, ˈsüt\ n : a fine black powder consisting chiefly of carbon that is formed when something burns and that colors smoke — **sooty** adj

sooth \ˈsüth\ n, archaic : TRUTH

soothe \ˈsüth\ vb **soothed; sooth·ing** 1 : to please by flattery or attention 2 : RELIEVE, ALLEVIATE ⟨∼ a burn⟩ 3 : to calm down : COMFORT ⟨∼ a child⟩ — **sooth·er** n — **sooth·ing·ly** adv

sooth·say·er \ˈsüth-ˌsā-ər\ n : one who foretells events — **sooth·say·ing** n

¹**sop** \ˈsäp\ n : a conciliatory bribe, gift, or concession

²**sop** vb **sopped; sop·ping** 1 : to steep or dip in or as if in a liquid 2 : to wet thoroughly : SOAK; *also* : to mop up (a liquid)

SOP abbr standard operating procedure; standing operating procedure

soph abbr sophomore

soph·ism \ˈsä-ˌfi-zəm\ n 1 : an argument correct in form but embodying a subtle fallacy 2 : SOPHISTRY

soph·ist \ˈsä-fist\ n : PHILOSOPHER; *esp* : a captious or fallacious reasoner

so·phis·tic \sä-ˈfis-tik, sə-\ *or* **so·phis·ti·cal** \-ti-kəl\ adj : of or characteristic of sophists or sophistry ♦ **Synonyms** FALLACIOUS, ILLOGICAL, UNREASONABLE, SPECIOUS

so·phis·ti·cat·ed \sə-ˈfis-tə-ˌkā-təd\ adj 1

: COMPLEX ⟨∼ instruments⟩ 2 : made worldly-wise by wide experience 3 : intellectually appealing ⟨a ∼ novel⟩ — **so·phis·ti·ca·tion** \-ˌfis-tə-ˈkā-shən\ n

soph·ist·ry \ˈsä-fə-strē\ n : subtly deceptive reasoning or argument

soph·o·more \ˈsäf-ˌmȯr, ˈsä-fə-\ n : a student in the second year of high school or college

soph·o·mor·ic \ˌsäf-ˈmȯr-ik, ˌsä-fə-\ adj 1 : being overconfident of knowledge but poorly informed and immature ⟨∼ reasoning⟩ 2 : of, relating to, or characteristic of a sophomore ⟨∼ humor⟩

So·pho·ni·as \ˌsä-fə-ˈnī-əs, ˌsō-\ n : ZEPHANIAH

sop·o·rif·ic \ˌsä-pə-ˈri-fik\ adj 1 : causing sleep or drowsiness 2 : LETHARGIC

so·pra·no \sə-ˈpra-nō, -ˈprä-\ n, pl **-nos** [It, fr. *sopra* above, fr. L *supra*] 1 : the highest singing voice; *also* : a singer with this voice 2 : the highest part in a 4-part chorus — **soprano** adj

sor·bet \sȯr-ˈbā\ n : a usu. fruit-flavored ice served for dessert or between courses as a palate refresher

sor·cery \ˈsȯr-sə-rē\ n [ME *sorcerie*, fr. AF, fr. *sorcier* sorcerer, fr. ML *sortiarius*, fr. L *sort-, sors* chance, lot] : the use of magic : WITCHCRAFT — **sor·cer·er** \-rər\ n — **sor·cer·ess** \-rəs\ n

sor·did \ˈsȯr-dəd\ adj 1 : marked by baseness or grossness : VILE 2 : DIRTY, SQUALID ⟨∼ living conditions⟩ — **sor·did·ly** adv — **sor·did·ness** n

¹**sore** \ˈsȯr\ adj **sor·er; sor·est** 1 : causing pain or distress ⟨a ∼ bruise⟩ 2 : painfully sensitive ⟨∼ muscles⟩ 3 : SEVERE, INTENSE 4 : IRRITATED, ANGRY — **sore·ly** adv — **sore·ness** n

²**sore** n 1 : a sore spot on the body; *esp* : one (as an ulcer) with the tissues broken and usu. infected 2 : a source of pain or vexation

sore·head \ˈsȯr-ˌhed\ n : a person easily angered or discontented

sore throat n : painful throat due to inflammation of the fauces and pharynx

sor·ghum \ˈsȯr-gəm\ n : a tall variable Old World tropical grass grown widely for its edible seed, for forage, or for its sweet juice which yields a syrup

so·ror·i·ty \sə-ˈrȯr-ə-tē\ n, pl **-ties** [ML *sororitas* sisterhood, fr. L *soror* sister] : a club or organization usu. of female students for social purposes

¹**sor·rel** \ˈsȯr-əl\ n : a brownish orange to light brown color; *also* : a sorrel-colored animal (as a horse)

²**sorrel** n : any of various herbs having a sour juice

sor·row \ˈsär-ō\ n 1 : deep distress, sadness, or regret; *also* : resultant unhappy or unpleasant state 2 : a cause of grief or sadness 3 : a display of grief or sadness — **sorrow** vb — **sor·row·ful** \-fəl\ adj — **sor·row·ful·ly** \-f(ə-)lē\ adv

sor·ry \ˈsär-ē\ adj **sor·ri·er; -est** 1 : feeling sorrow, regret, or penitence ⟨∼ for yelling at her⟩ 2 : MOURNFUL, SAD 3 : causing sorrow, pity, or scorn : PITIFUL ⟨a ∼ lot of ragamuffins⟩

¹sort \'sȯrt\ *n* **1** : a group of persons or things that have similar characteristics : CLASS **2** : QUALITY, NATURE **3** : an instance of sorting — **all sorts of** : many different — **out of sorts 1** : somewhat ill **2** : GROUCHY, IRRITABLE

²sort *vb* **1** : to put in a certain place according to kind, class, or nature **2** : to be in accord : AGREE **3** : SEARCH ⟨~ through this mess⟩ — **sort·er** *n*

sor·tie \'sȯr-tē, sȯr-'tē\ *n* **1** : a sudden issuing of troops from a defensive position against the enemy **2** : one mission or attack by one airplane

sort of *adv* : to a moderate degree

SOS \,es-(,)ō-'es\ *n* : a call or request for help or rescue

so–so \'sō-'sō\ *adv or adj* : PASSABLY

sot \'sät\ *n* : a habitual drunkard — **sot·tish** *adj* — **sot·tish·ly** *adv*

souf·flé \sü-'flā\ *n* [F, fr. *soufflé,* pp. of *souffler* to blow, puff up, fr. OF *sufler,* fr. L *sufflare,* fr. *sub-* up + *flare* to blow] : a spongy dish made light in baking by stiffly beaten egg whites

sough \'saů, 'sǝf\ *vb* : to make a moaning or sighing sound — **sough** *n*

sought *past and past part of* SEEK

¹soul \'sōl\ *n* **1** : the immaterial essence of an individual life **2** : the spiritual principle embodied in human beings or the universe **3** : an active or essential part **4** : the moral and emotional nature of human beings **5** : spiritual or moral force **6** : PERSON ⟨a kindly ~⟩ **7** : a strong, positive feeling (as of intense sensitivity and emotional fervor) conveyed esp. by African-American performers **8** : SOUL MUSIC — **souled** \'sōld\ *adj* — **soul·less** \'sōl-lǝs\ *adj*

²soul *adj* **1** : of, relating to, or characteristic of African-Americans or their culture ⟨~ food⟩ **2** : designed for or controlled by African-Americans ⟨~ radio stations⟩

soul brother *n* : an African-American male

soul·ful \'sōl-fǝl\ *adj* : full of or expressing deep feeling ⟨a ~ ballad⟩ — **soul·ful·ly** *adv*

soul music *n* : music that is closely related to rhythm and blues and characterized by intensity of feeling

¹sound \'saůnd\ *adj* **1** : not diseased or sickly **2** : free from flaw or defect ⟨a ~ structure⟩ **3** : FIRM, STRONG **4** : free from error or fallacy : RIGHT ⟨~ logic⟩ **5** : LEGAL, VALID **6** : THOROUGH **7** : UNDISTURBED ⟨~ sleep⟩ **8** : showing good judgment ⟨~ reasoning⟩ — **sound·ly** *adv* — **sound·ness** *n*

²sound *n* **1** : the sensation of hearing; *also* : mechanical energy transmitted by longitudinal pressure waves (**sound waves**) (as in air) that is the stimulus to hearing **2** : something heard : NOISE, TONE; *also* : hearing distance : EARSHOT **3** : a musical style ⟨the band's ~⟩ — **sound·less** *adj* — **sound·less·ly** *adv* — **sound·proof** \-,prüf\ *adj or vb*

³sound *vb* **1** : to make or cause to make a sound **2** : to order or proclaim by a

sound ⟨~ the alarm⟩ **3** : to convey a certain impression : SEEM ⟨that ~s like fun⟩ **4** : to examine the condition of by causing to give out sounds — **sound·able** \'saůn-dǝ-bǝl\ *adj*

⁴sound *n* : a long passage of water wider than a strait often connecting two larger bodies of water

⁵sound *vb* **1** : to measure the depth of (water) esp. by a weighted line dropped from the surface : FATHOM **2** : PROBE **3** : to dive down suddenly ⟨the hooked fish ~ed⟩ — **sound·ing** *n*

sound bite *n* : a brief recorded statement broadcast esp. on a news program — **sound–bite** *adj*

sound card *n* : a circuit board in a computer system designed to produce or reproduce sound

sound·er \'saůn-dǝr\ *n* : one that sounds; *esp* : a device for making soundings

sound·stage \'saůnd-,stāj\ *n* : the part of a motion-picture studio in which a production is filmed

sound·track \'saůn(d)-,trak\ *n* : music recorded to accompany a film or videotape

soup \'süp\ *n* **1** : a liquid food with stock as its base and often containing pieces of solid food **2** : something having the consistency of soup **3** : an unfortunate predicament ⟨in the ~⟩

soup·çon \süp-'sōⁿ\ *n* [F, lit., suspicion] : a little bit : ¹TRACE ⟨a ~ of garlic⟩

soup up *vb* : to increase the power of — **souped–up** \'süpt-'ǝp\ *adj*

soupy \'sü-pē\ *adj* **soup·i·er; -est 1** : having the consistency of soup **2** : densely foggy or cloudy

¹sour \'saů(-ǝ)r\ *adj* **1** : having an acid or tart taste ⟨~ as vinegar⟩ **2** : SPOILED, PUTRID ⟨a ~ odor⟩ **3** : UNPLEASANT, DISAGREEABLE ⟨~ disposition⟩ — **sour·ish** *adj* — **sour·ly** *adv* — **sour·ness** *n*

²sour *vb* : to become or make sour

source \'sȯrs\ *n* **1** : ORIGIN, BEGINNING **2** : a supplier of information **3** : the beginning of a stream of water

source code *n* : a computer program in its original programming language and before translation (as by a compiler)

¹souse \'saůs\ *vb* **soused; sous·ing 1** : PICKLE **2** : to plunge into a liquid **3** : DRENCH **4** : to make drunk

²souse *n* **1** : something (as pigs' feet) steeped in pickle **2** : a soaking in liquid **3** : DRUNKARD

¹south \'saůth\ *adv* : to or toward the south; *also* : into a state of decline

²south *adj* **1** : situated toward or at the south **2** : coming from the south

³south *n* **1** : the direction to the right of one facing east **2** : the compass point directly opposite to north **3** *cap* : regions or countries south of a specified or implied point; *esp* : the southeastern part of the U.S. — **south·er·ly** \'sǝ-thǝr-lē\ *adj or adv* — **south·ern** \'sǝ-thǝrn\ *adj* — **South·ern·er** *n* — **south·ern·most** \-,mōst\ *adj* — **south·ward** \'saůth-wərd\ *adv or adj* — **south·wards** \-wərdz\ *adv*

south·east \saù-'thēst, *naut* saù-'ēst\ *n* **1** : the general direction between south and east **2** : the compass point midway between south and east **3** *cap* : regions or countries southeast of a specified or implied point — **southeast** *adj or adv* — **south·east·er·ly** *adv or adj* — **south·east·ern** \-'ēs-tərn\ *adj*

south·paw \'saùth-,pó\ *n* : a left-handed person; *esp* : a left-handed baseball pitcher — **southpaw** *adj*

south pole *n, often cap S&P* : the southernmost point of the earth

south·west \saùth-'west, *naut* saù-'west\ *n* **1** : the general direction between south and west **2** : the compass point midway between south and west **3** *cap* : regions or countries southwest of a specified or implied point — **southwest** *adj or adv* — **south·west·er·ly** *adv or adj* — **south·west·ern** \-'wes-tərn\ *adj*

sou·ve·nir \,sü-və-'nir\ *n* [F] : something serving as a reminder

sou'·west·er \saù-'wes-tər\ *n* : a long waterproof coat worn at sea in stormy weather; *also* : a waterproof hat

¹sov·er·eign \'sä-vrən, -və-rən\ *n* **1** : one possessing the supreme power and authority in a state **2** : a gold coin of the United Kingdom

²sovereign *adj* **1** : EXCELLENT, FINE **2** : supreme in power or authority **3** : CHIEF, HIGHEST **4** : having independent authority ♦ **Synonyms** DOMINANT, PREDOMINANT, PARAMOUNT, PREPONDERANT

sov·er·eign·ty \-tē\ *n, pl* **-ties** **1** : supremacy in rule or power **2** : power to govern without external control **3** : the supreme political power in a state

so·vi·et \'sō-vē-,et, 'sä-, -ət\ *n* **1** : an elected governmental council in a Communist country **2** *pl, cap* : the people and esp. the leaders of the U.S.S.R. — **soviet** *adj, often cap* — **so·vi·et·ize** *vb, often cap*

¹sow \'saù\ *n* : an adult female swine

²sow \'sō\ *vb* **sowed**; **sown** \'sōn\ *or* **sowed**; **sow·ing** **1** : to plant seed for growing esp. by scattering **2** : to strew with seed **3** : to scatter abroad — **sow·er** \'sō-ər\ *n*

sow bug \'saù-\ *n* : WOOD LOUSE

sox *pl of* SOCK

soy \'sói\ *n* : a sauce made from soybeans fermented in brine

soy·bean \'sói-,bēn\ *n* : an Asian legume widely grown for forage and for its edible seeds that yield a valuable oil (**soybean oil**); *also* : its seed

sp *abbr* **1** special **2** species **3** specimen **4** spelling **5** spirit

Sp *abbr* Spain

SP *abbr* **1** shore patrol; shore patrolman **2** shore police **3** specialist

spa \'spä\ *n* [*Spa*, watering place in Belgium] **1** : a mineral spring; *also* : a resort with mineral springs **2** : a health and fitness facility **3** : a hot tub with a whirlpool device

¹space \'späs\ *n* **1** : a period of time **2**

: some small measurable distance, area, or volume **3** : the limitless area in which all things exist and move **4** : an empty place **5** : the region beyond the earth's atmosphere **6** : a definite place (as a seat on a train or ship) **7** : the distance from others that a person needs for comfort

²space *vb* **spaced**; **spac·ing** : to place at intervals — **spac·er** *n*

space-age \'späs-,āj\ *adj* : of or relating to the age of space exploration

space·craft \-,kraft\ *n* : a vehicle for travel beyond the earth's atmosphere

space·flight \-,flīt\ *n* : flight beyond the earth's atmosphere

space heater *n* : a usu. portable device for heating a relatively small area

space·man \'späs-,man, -mən\ *n* : one who travels outside the earth's atmosphere

space out *vb* : to become distracted or inattentive

space·ship \-,ship\ *n* : a vehicle used for space travel

space shuttle *n* : a reusable spacecraft designed to transport people and cargo between earth and space

space station *n* : a large artificial satellite serving as a base (as for scientific observation)

space suit *n* : a suit equipped to make life in space possible for its wearer

space walk *n* : a period of activity outside a spacecraft by an astronaut in space — **space·walk** \'späs-,wòk\ *vb* — **space·walk·er** *n*

spa·cious \'spä-shəs\ *adj* : very large in extent : ROOMY ♦ **Synonyms** COMMODIOUS, CAPACIOUS, AMPLE — **spa·cious·ly** *adv* — **spa·cious·ness** *n*

¹spade \'spād\ *n* : a shovel with a blade for digging — **spade·ful** *n*

²spade *vb* **spad·ed**; **spad·ing** : to dig with a spade — **spad·er** *n*

³spade *n* : any of a suit of playing cards marked with a black figure resembling an inverted heart with a short stem at the bottom

spa·dix \'spä-diks\ *n, pl* **spa·di·ces** \'spä-də-,sēz\ : a floral spike with a fleshy or succulent axis usu. enclosed in a spathe

spa·ghet·ti \spə-'ge-tē\ *n* [It, fr. pl. of *spaghetto*, dim. of *spago* cord, string] : pasta made in thin solid strings

spam \'spam\ *n* : unsolicited usu. commercial e-mail sent to a large number of addresses — **spam** *vb*

¹span \'span\ *n* **1** : an English unit of length equal to nine inches (about 23 centimeters) **2** : a limited portion of time **3** : the spread (as of an arch) from one support to another

²span *vb* **spanned**; **span·ning** **1** : MEASURE **2** : to extend across

³span *n* : a pair of animals (as mules) driven together

Span *abbr* Spanish

span·dex \'span-,deks\ *n* : any of various elastic synthetic textile fibers

span·gle \'span-gəl\ *n* : a small disk of shining metal or plastic used esp. on a dress for ornament — **spangle** *vb*

Span·glish \'spaŋ-glish\ n : Spanish with many English words included; *also* : a combination of Spanish and English

Span·iard \'span-yərd\ n : a native or inhabitant of Spain

span·iel \'span-yəl\ n [ME *spaynel, spaniell,* fr. AF *espainnel,* alter. of *espaignol,* Spaniard] : a dog of any of several breeds of mostly small and short-legged dogs usu. with long wavy hair and large drooping ears

Span·ish \'spa-nish\ n 1 : the chief language of Spain and of the countries colonized by the Spanish 2 **Spanish** *pl* : the people of Spain — **Spanish** *adj*

Spanish American n : a resident of the U.S. whose native language is Spanish; *also* : a native or inhabitant of one of the countries of America in which Spanish is the national language — **Spanish–American** *adj*

Spanish fly n : a toxic preparation of dried green European beetles that causes the skin to blister and is thought to be an aphrodisiac

Spanish moss n : a plant related to the pineapple that grows in pendent tufts of grayish green filaments on trees from the southern U.S. to Argentina

Spanish onion n : a large mild-flavored onion

spank \'spaŋk\ vb : to hit on the buttocks with the open hand — **spank** n

spank·ing \'spaŋ-kiŋ\ adj : BRISK, LIVELY ⟨~ breeze⟩ — **spanking** adv

¹spar \'spär\ n : a rounded wood or metal piece (as a mast, yard, boom, or gaff) for supporting sail rigging

²spar vb **sparred; spar·ring** : to box for practice without serious hitting; *also* : SKIRMISH, WRANGLE

¹spare \'sper\ vb **spared; spar·ing** 1 : to refrain from punishing or injuring : show mercy to 2 : to exempt from something 3 : to get along without ⟨can you ~ ten dollars?⟩ 4 : to use frugally or rarely

²spare adj **spar·er; spar·est** 1 : held in reserve 2 : SUPERFLUOUS 3 : not liberal or profuse 4 : LEAN, THIN 5 : SCANTY ♦ **Synonyms** MEAGER, SPARSE, SKIMPY, EXIGUOUS, SCANT — **spare·ness** n

³spare n 1 : a duplicate kept in reserve; *esp* : a spare tire 2 : the knocking down of all the bowling pins with the first two balls

sparing adj : SAVING, FRUGAL ♦ **Synonyms** THRIFTY, ECONOMICAL, PROVIDENT — **spar·ing·ly** adv

¹spark \'spärk\ n 1 : a small particle of a burning substance or a hot glowing particle struck from a mass (as by steel on flint) 2 : a short bright flash of electricity between two points 3 : SPARKLE 4 : a particle capable of being kindled or developed : GERM

²spark vb 1 : to emit or produce sparks 2 : to stir to activity : INCITE

³spark vb : WOO, COURT

¹spar·kle \'spär-kəl\ vb **spar·kled; spar·kling** 1 : FLASH, GLEAM 2 : to perform brilliantly 3 : EFFERVESCE ⟨*sparkling* wine⟩ — **spar·kler** n

²sparkle n 1 : GLEAM 2 : ANIMATION

spark plug n : a device that produces a spark to ignite the fuel mixture in an engine cylinder

spar·row \'spa-rō\ n : any of several small dull-colored singing birds

sparse \'spärs\ adj **spars·er; spars·est** : thinly scattered : SCANTY ⟨~ vegetation⟩ ♦ **Synonyms** MEAGER, SPARE, SKIMPY, EXIGUOUS, SCANT — **sparse·ly** adv — **sparse·ness** n

¹Spar·tan \'spär-t³n\ n 1 : a native or inhabitant of ancient Sparta 2 : a person of great courage and self-discipline

²Spartan adj 1 : of or relating to Sparta or Spartans 2 *often not cap* : marked by simplicity, frugality, or avoidance of luxury and comfort ⟨a ~ room⟩

spasm \'spa-zəm\ n 1 : an involuntary and abnormal muscular contraction 2 : a sudden, violent, and temporary effort, emotion, or sensation — **spas·mod·ic** \spaz-'mä-dik\ adj — **spas·mod·i·cal·ly** \-di-k(ə-)lē\ adv

spas·tic \'spas-tik\ adj : of, relating to, marked by, or affected with muscular spasm ⟨~ paralysis⟩ — **spastic** n

¹spat \'spat\ past and past part of SPIT

²spat n, pl **spat** or **spats** : a young bivalve mollusk (as an oyster)

³spat n : a gaiter covering instep and ankle

⁴spat n : a brief petty quarrel : DISPUTE

⁵spat vb **spat·ted; spat·ting** : to quarrel briefly

spate \'spāt\ n : a sudden outburst

spathe \'spāth\ n : a sheathing bract or pair of bracts enclosing an inflorescence (as of the calla lily) and esp. a spadix on the same axis

spa·tial \'spā-shəl\ adj : of or relating to space or to the facility to perceive objects in space — **spa·tial·ly** adv

spat·ter \'spa-tər\ vb 1 : to splash with drops of liquid ⟨clothes ~ed with paint⟩ 2 : to sprinkle around — **spatter** n

spat·u·la \'spa-chə-lə\ n : a flexible knifelike implement for scooping, spreading, or mixing soft substances

spav·in \'spa-vən\ n : a bony enlargement of the hock of a horse — **spav·ined** \-vənd\ adj

¹spawn \'spón\ vb [ME, fr. AF *espandre* to spread out, shed, scatter, spawn, fr. L *expandere,* fr. *ex-* out + *pandere* to spread] 1 : to produce eggs or offspring esp. in large numbers 2 : GENERATE ⟨~ed much protest⟩ — **spawn·er** n

²spawn n 1 : the eggs of water animals (as fishes or oysters) that lay many small eggs 2 : offspring esp. when produced in great numbers

spay \'spā\ vb **spayed; spay·ing** : to remove the ovaries of (a female animal)

SPCA abbr Society for the Prevention of Cruelty to Animals

SPCC abbr Society for the Prevention of Cruelty to Children

speak \'spēk\ vb **spoke** \'spōk\; **spo·ken** \'spō-kən\; **speak·ing** 1 : to utter words 2 : to express orally 3 : to mention in speech or writing 4 : to address an audience 5 : to use or be able to use (a language) in talking — **to speak of** : worthy of mention ⟨no progress *to speak of*⟩

speak·easy \'spēk-ˌē-zē\ *n, pl* **-eas·ies** : an illicit drinking place

speak·er \'spē-kər\ *n* **1** : one that speaks **2** : the presiding officer of a deliberative assembly **3** : LOUDSPEAKER

¹**spear** \'spir\ *n* **1** : a long-shafted weapon with a sharp point for thrusting or throwing **2** : a sharp-pointed instrument with barbs used in spearing fish — **spear·man** \-mən\ *n*

²**spear** *vb* : to strike or pierce with or as if with a spear — **spear·er** *n*

³**spear** *n* : a usu. young blade, shoot, or sprout (as of asparagus)

spear·head \-ˌhed\ *n* : a leading force, element, or influence — **spearhead** *vb*

spear·mint \-ˌmint\ *n* : a common highly aromatic garden mint

¹**spec** *abbr* **1** special; specialist **2** specifically

²**spec** \'spek\ *n* : SPECIFICATION 2 — usu. used in pl.

spe·cial \'spe-shəl\ *adj* **1** : UNCOMMON, NOTEWORTHY **2** : particularly favored **3** : INDIVIDUAL, UNIQUE **4** : EXTRA, ADDITIONAL **5** : confined to or designed for a definite field of action, purpose, or occasion ⟨a ~ assignment⟩ — **special** *n*

special delivery *n* : delivery of mail by messenger for an extra fee

special effects *n pl* : visual or sound effects introduced into a motion picture, video recording, or taped television production

Special Forces *n pl* : a branch of the army composed of soldiers specially trained in guerrilla warfare

spe·cial·ise *Brit var of* SPECIALIZE

spe·cial·ist \'spe-shə-list\ *n* **1** : a person who specializes in a particular branch of learning or activity **2** : a rank in the U.S. Army corresponding to that of corporal

spe·cial·ize \'spe-shə-ˌlīz\ *vb* **-ized; -iz·ing** : to concentrate one's efforts in a special activity or field; *also* : to change in an adaptive manner — **spe·cial·i·za·tion** \ˌspe-shə-lə-'zā-shən\ *n*

spe·cial·ly \'spe-shə-lē\ *adv* **1** : in a special manner **2** : for a special purpose : in particular

spe·cial·ty \'spe-shəl-tē\ *n, pl* **-ties** **1** : a particular quality or detail **2** : a product of a special kind or of special excellence **3** : a skill or discipline in which one specializes ⟨the doctor's ~ is dermatology⟩

spe·cie \'spē-shē, -sē\ *n* : money in coin

spe·cies \'spē-shēz, -sēz\ *n, pl* **spe·cies** [ME, fr. L, appearance, kind, species, fr. *specere* to look] **1** : SORT, KIND **2** : a category of biological classification ranking just below the genus or subgenus and comprising closely related organisms potentially able to breed with one another

specif *abbr* specific; specifically

¹**spe·cif·ic** \spi-'si-fik\ *adj* **1** : having a unique effect or influence or reacting in only one way or with only one thing ⟨~ antibodies⟩ ⟨~ enzymes⟩ **2** : DEFINITE, EXACT ⟨a ~ agreement⟩ **3** : of, relating to, or constituting a species — **spe·cif·i-**

cal·ly \-fi-k(ə-)lē\ *adv* — **spec·i·fic·i·ty** \ˌspe-sə-'fi-sə-tē\ *n*

²**specific** *n* : something specific : DETAIL, PARTICULAR — usu. used in pl.

spec·i·fi·ca·tion \ˌspe-sə-fə-'kā-shən\ *n* **1** : the act or process of specifying **2** : a description of work to be done and materials to be used (as in building) — usu. used in pl.

specific gravity *n* : the ratio of the density of a substance to the density of some substance (as water) taken as a standard when both densities are obtained by weighing in air

spec·i·fy \'spe-sə-ˌfī\ *vb* **-fied; -fy·ing** : to mention or name explicitly

spec·i·men \'spe-sə-mən\ *n* : an item or part typical of a group or whole

spe·cious \'spē-shəs\ *adj* : seeming to be genuine, correct, or beautiful but not really so ⟨~ reasoning⟩

speck \'spek\ *n* **1** : a small spot or blemish **2** : a small particle — **speck** *vb*

speck·le \'spe-kəl\ *n* : a little speck — **speckle** *vb*

specs \'speks\ *n pl* : GLASSES

spec·ta·cle \'spek-ti-kəl\ *n* **1** : an unusual or impressive public display **2** *pl* : GLASSES — **spec·ta·cled** \-kəld\ *adj*

spec·tac·u·lar \spek-'ta-kyə-lər\ *adj* : exciting to see : SENSATIONAL

spec·ta·tor \'spek-ˌtā-tər\ *n* : a person who looks on (as at a sports event)
♦ *Synonyms* OBSERVER, WITNESS, BYSTANDER, ONLOOKER, EYEWITNESS

spec·ter *or* **spec·tre** \'spek-tər\ *n* : a visible disembodied spirit : GHOST

spec·tral \'spek-trəl\ *adj* **1** : of, relating to, or resembling a specter **2** : of, relating to, or made by a spectrum

spec·tro·gram \'spek-trə-ˌgram\ *n* : a photograph, image, or diagram of a spectrum

spec·tro·graph \-ˌgraf\ *n* : an instrument for dispersing radiation into a spectrum and recording or mapping the spectrum — **spec·tro·graph·ic** \ˌspek-trə-'gra-fik\ *adj* — **spec·tro·graph·i·cal·ly** \-fi-k(ə-)lē\ *adv*

spec·trom·e·ter \spek-'trä-mə-tər\ *n* : an instrument for measuring spectra — **spec·tro·met·ric** \ˌspek-trə-'me-trik\ *adj* — **spec·trom·e·try** \spek-'trä-mə-trē\ *n*

spec·tro·scope \'spek-trə-ˌskōp\ *n* : an instrument that produces spectra esp. of visible electromagnetic radiation — **spec·tro·scop·ic** \ˌspek-trə-'skä-pik\ *adj* — **spec·tro·scop·i·cal·ly** \-pi-k(ə-)lē\ *adv* — **spec·tros·co·pist** \spek-'träs-kə-pist\ *n* — **spec·tros·co·py** \-pē\ *n*

spec·trum \'spek-trəm\ *n, pl* **spec·tra** \-trə\ *or* **spectrums** [NL, fr. L, appearance, fr. *specere* to look] **1** : a series of colors formed when a beam of white light is dispersed (as by a prism) so that its parts are arranged in the order of their wavelengths **2** : a series of radiations arranged in regular order **3** : a continuous sequence or range ⟨a wide ~ of political opinions⟩

spec·u·late \'spe-kyə-ˌlāt\ *vb* **-lat·ed; -lat·ing** [L *speculari* to spy out, examine, fr. *specula* lookout post, fr. *specere* to look, look at] **1** : to think or wonder about a subject **2** : to take a business risk in hope of gain ♦ *Synonyms* REASON, THINK, DELIBERATE, COGITATE — **spec·u·la·tion** \,spe-kyə-'lā-shən\ *n* — **spec·u·la·tive** \'spe-kyə-,lā-tiv\ *adj* — **spec·u·la·tive·ly** *adv* — **spec·u·la·tor** \-,lā-tər\ *n*

speech \'spēch\ *n* **1** : the act of speaking **2** : TALK, CONVERSATION **3** : a public talk or lecture **4** : LANGUAGE, DIALECT **5** : an individual manner of speaking **6** : the power of speaking — **speech·less** *adj*

¹speed \'spēd\ *n* **1** *archaic* : SUCCESS **2** : SWIFTNESS, RAPIDITY **3** : rate of motion or performance **4** : a transmission gear (as of a bicycle) **5** : METHAMPHETAMINE; *also* : a related drug ♦ *Synonyms* HASTE, HURRY, DISPATCH, CELERITY — **speed·i·ly** \'spē-də-lē\ *adv* — **speedy** *adj*

²speed *vb* **sped** \'sped\ *or* **speed·ed; speed·ing 1** *archaic* : PROSPER; *also* : GET ALONG, FARE **2** : to go fast; *esp* : to go at an excessive or illegal speed **3** : to cause to go faster — **speed·er** *n*

speed·boat \-,bōt\ *n* : a fast motorboat

speed bump *n* : a low raised ridge across a roadway (as in a parking lot) to limit vehicle speed

speed of light : a fundamental physical constant that is the speed of electromagnetic radiation propagation in a vacuum and has the value of 299,792,458 meters per second

speed·om·e·ter \spi-'dä-mə-tər\ *n* : an instrument for indicating speed

speed·up \'spēd-,əp\ *n* : ACCELERATION

speed·way \-,wā\ *n* : a racecourse for motor vehicles

speed·well \'spēd-,wel\ *n* : VERONICA

¹spell \'spel\ *vb* **spelled** \'speld, 'spelt\; **spell·ing** [ME, to signify, read by spelling out, fr. AF *espeleir*, of Gmc origin] **1** : to name, write, or print in order the letters of a word **2** : MEAN ⟨another drought may ~ famine⟩

²spell *n* [ME, talk, tale, fr. OE] **1** : a magic formula : INCANTATION **2** : a compelling influence ⟨under the ~ of a guru⟩

³spell *n* **1** : one's turn at work or duty **2** : a stretch of a specified kind of weather **3** : a period of bodily or mental distress or disorder : ATTACK ⟨a dizzy ~⟩

⁴spell *vb* **spelled** \'speld\; **spell·ing** : to take the place of for a time in work or duty : RELIEVE

spell·bind·er \-,bīn-dər\ *n* : a speaker of compelling eloquence; *also* : one that compels attention

spell·bound \-,baùnd\ *adj* : held by or as if by a spell : FASCINATED

spell–check·er \'spel-,che-kər\ *n* : a computer program that identifies possible misspellings in a block of text — **spell–check** \-,chek\ *vb*

spell·er \'spe-lər\ *n* **1** : one who spells words **2** : a book with exercises for teaching spelling

spelt \'spelt\ *chiefly Brit past and past part of* ¹SPELL

spe·lunk·er \spi-'ləŋ-kər, 'spē-,ləŋ-kər\ *n* [L *spelunca* cave, fr. Gk *spēlynx*] : one who makes a hobby of exploring caves — **spe·lunk·ing** *n*

spend \'spend\ *vb* **spent** \'spent\; **spend·ing 1** : to pay out : EXPEND **2** : WEAR OUT, EXHAUST; *also* : to consume wastefully **3** : to cause or permit to elapse : PASS — **spend·er** *n*

spend·thrift \'spend-,thrift\ *n* : one who spends wastefully or recklessly

spent \'spent\ *adj* : drained of energy

sperm \'spərm\ *n*, *pl* **sperm** *or* **sperms 1** : SEMEN **2** : a male gamete

sper·ma·to·zo·on \(,)spər-,ma-tə-'zō-,än, -zō-ən\ *n*, *pl* **-zoa** \-'zō-ə\ : a motile male gamete of an animal usu. with a rounded or elongated head and a long posterior flagellum

sperm cell *n* : SPERM 2

sper·mi·cide \'spər-mə-,sīd\ *n* : a preparation or substance used to kill sperm — **sper·mi·cid·al** \,spər-mə-'sī-dəl\ *adj*

sperm whale *n* : a large whale with a massive square-shaped head containing a fluid-filled cavity

spew \'spyü\ *vb* : VOMIT

SPF *abbr* sun protection factor

sp gr *abbr* specific gravity

sphag·num \'sfag-nəm\ *n* : any of a genus of atypical mosses that grow in wet acid areas where their remains become compacted with other plant debris to form peat; *also* : a mass of these mosses

sphere \'sfir\ *n* [ME *spere* globe, celestial sphere, fr. AF *espere*, fr. L *sphaera*, fr. Gk *sphaira*, lit., ball] **1** : a globe-shaped body : BALL **2** : a celestial body **3** : a solid figure so shaped that every point on its surface is an equal distance from the center **4** : range of action or influence — **spher·i·cal** \'sfir-i-kəl, 'sfer-\ *adj* — **spher·i·cal·ly** \-i-k(ə-)lē\ *adv*

spher·oid \'sfir-,óid, 'sfer-\ *n* : a figure similar to a sphere but not perfectly round — **sphe·roi·dal** \sfir-'ói-dəl\ *adj*

sphinc·ter \'sfiŋk-tər\ *n* : a muscular ring that closes a bodily opening

sphinx \'sfiŋks\ *n*, *pl* **sphinx·es** *or* **sphin·ges** \'sfin-,jēz\ **1** : a winged monster in Greek mythology having a woman's head and a lion's body and noted for killing anyone unable to answer its riddle **2** : an enigmatic or mysterious person **3** : an ancient Egyptian image having the body of a lion and the head of a man, ram, or hawk

spice \'spīs\ *n* **1** : any of various aromatic plant products (as pepper or nutmeg) used to season or flavor foods **2** : something that adds interest and relish — **spice** *vb* — **spicy** *adj*

spick–and–span *or* **spic–and–span** \,spik-ənd-'span\ *adj* : quite new; *also* : spotlessly clean

spic·ule \'spi-kyül\ *n* : a slender pointed body esp. of calcium or silica ⟨sponge ~s⟩

spi·der \'spī-dər\ *n* **1** : any of an order of arachnids that have a 2-part body, eight legs, and two or more pairs of abdominal organs for spinning threads of silk used esp. in making webs for catching prey **2** : a cast-iron frying pan — **spi·dery** *adj*

spider mite *n* : any of various small web-spinning mites that feed on and are pests of plants

spider plant *n* : a houseplant of the lily family having long green leaves usu. striped with white and producing tufts of small plants on long hanging stems

spi·der·web \'spī-dər-ˌweb\ *n* : the web spun by a spider

spiel \'spēl\ *vb* : to talk in a fast, smooth, and usu. colorful manner — **spiel** *n*

spig·ot \'spi-gət, -kət\ *n* : FAUCET

¹**spike** \'spīk\ *n* **1** : a very large nail **2** : any of various pointed projections (as on the sole of a shoe to prevent slipping) — **spiky** *adj*

²**spike** *vb* **spiked; spik·ing 1** : to fasten with spikes **2** : to put an end to : QUASH ⟨~ a rumor⟩ **3** : to pierce with or impale on a spike **4** : to add alcoholic liquor to (a drink)

³**spike** *n* **1** : an ear of grain **2** : a long cluster of usu. stemless flowers

¹**spill** \'spil\ *vb* **spilled** \'spild, 'spilt\ *also* **spilt** \'spilt\; **spill·ing 1** : to cause or allow to fall, flow, or run out esp. unintentionally **2** : to cause (blood) to be lost by wounding **3** : to run out or over with resulting loss or waste **4** : to let out : DIVULGE — **spill·able** *adj*

²**spill** *n* **1** : an act of spilling; *also* : a fall from a horse or vehicle or an erect position **2** : something spilled

spill·way \-ˌwā\ *n* : a passage for surplus water to run over or around an obstruction (as a dam)

¹**spin** \'spin\ *vb* **spun** \'spən\; **spin·ning 1** : to draw and twist into thread; *also* : to form (thread) by such means **2** : to form thread by extruding a sticky quickly hardening fluid; *also* : to construct from such thread ⟨spiders ~ their webs⟩ **3** : to produce slowly and by degrees ⟨~ a story⟩ **4** : TWIRL **5** : WHIRL ⟨my head is *spinning*⟩ **6** : to move rapidly along **7** : to present (as information) with a particular spin — **spin·ner** *n*

²**spin** *n* **1** : a rapid rotating motion **2** : an excursion in a wheeled vehicle **3** : a particular point of view, emphasis, or interpretation

spi·na bi·fi·da \ˌspī-nə-ˈbi-fə-də\ *n* : a birth defect in which the spinal column has a fissure

spin·ach \'spi-nich\ *n* : a dark green herb grown for its edible leaves

spi·nal \'spī-nᵊl\ *adj* : of or relating to the backbone or spinal cord — **spi·nal·ly** *adv*

spinal column *n* : BACKBONE 1

spinal cord *n* : the thick cord of nervous tissue that extends from the brain along the back in the cavity of the backbone and carries nerve impulses to and from the brain

spinal nerve *n* : any of the paired nerves which arise from the spinal cord and pass to various parts of the body and of which there are normally 31 pairs in human beings

spin control *n* : the act or practice of attempting to manipulate the way an event is interpreted

spin·dle \'spin-dᵊl\ *n* **1** : a round tapering stick or rod by which fibers are twisted in spinning **2** : a turned part of a piece of furniture ⟨the ~s of a chair⟩ **3** : a slender pin or rod which turns or on which something else turns

spin·dling \'spind-liŋ\ *adj* : SPINDLY

spin·dly \'spind-lē\ *adj* : being long or tall and thin and usu. weak

spin·drift \'spin-ˌdrift\ *n* : spray blown from waves

spine \'spīn\ *n* **1** : BACKBONE **2** : a stiff sharp process esp. on a plant or animal **3** : the part of a book where the pages are attached — **spiny** *adj*

spi·nel \spə-ˈnel\ *n* : a hard crystalline mineral of variable color used as a gem

spine·less \'spīn-ləs\ *adj* **1** : having no spines, thorns, or prickles **2** : lacking a backbone **3** : lacking courage or determination ⟨a ~ politician⟩

spin·et \'spi-nət\ *n* **1** : an early harpsichord having a single keyboard and only one string for each note **2** : a small upright piano

spin·na·ker \'spi-ni-kər\ *n* : a large triangular sail set on a long light pole

spinning jen·ny \-ˈje-nē\ *n* : an early multiple-spindle machine for spinning wool or cotton

spinning wheel *n* : a small machine for spinning thread or yarn in which a large wheel drives a single spindle

spin-off \'spin-ˌȯf\ *n* **1** : a usu. useful by-product **2** : something (as a TV show) derived from an earlier work — **spin off** *vb*

spin·ster \'spin-stər\ *n* : an unmarried woman past the common age for marrying — **spin·ster·hood** \-ˌhu̇d\ *n*

spiny lobster *n* : any of several edible crustaceans differing from the related lobsters in lacking the large front claws and in having a spiny carapace

¹**spi·ral** \'spī-rəl\ *adj* : winding or coiling around a center or axis and usu. getting closer to or farther away from it — **spi·ral·ly** *adv*

²**spiral** *n* **1** : something that has a spiral form; *also* : a single turn in a spiral object **2** : a continuously spreading and accelerating increase or decrease

³**spiral** *vb* **-raled** *or* **-ralled; -ral·ing** *or* **-ral·ling 1** : to move and esp. to rise or fall in a spiral course **2** : to form into a spiral

spi·rant \'spī-rənt\ *n* : a consonant (as \f\, \s\, \sh\) uttered with decided friction of the breath against some part of the oral passage — **spirant** *adj*

spire \'spī-(ə)r\ *n* **1** : a slender tapering stalk (as of grass) **2** : a pointed tip (as of an antler) **3** : STEEPLE — **spiry** *adj*

spi·rea *or* **spi·raea** \spī-ˈrē-ə\ *n* : any of a genus of shrubs related to the roses with dense clusters of small usu. white or pink flowers

¹**spir·it** \'spir-ət\ *n* [ME, fr. AF or L; AF, fr. L *spiritus*, lit., breath, fr. *spirare* to blow,

breathe] **1** : a life-giving force; *also* : the animating principle : SOUL **2** *cap* : HOLY SPIRIT **3** : SPECTER, GHOST **4** : PERSON ⟨a bold ∼⟩ **5** : DISPOSITION, MOOD ⟨in good ∼*s*⟩ **6** : VIVACITY, ARDOR **7** : essential or real meaning : INTENT **8** : distilled alcoholic liquor **9** : LOYALTY ⟨school ∼⟩ — **spir·it·less** *adj*

²**spirit** *vb* : to carry off secretly or mysteriously

spir·it·ed \'spir-ə-təd\ *adj* : full of energy, animation, or courage

¹**spir·i·tu·al** \'spir-i-chəl, -chə-wəl\ *adj* **1** : of, relating to, consisting of, or affecting the spirit : INCORPOREAL ⟨∼ needs⟩ **2** : of or relating to sacred matters **3** : ecclesiastical rather than lay or temporal — **spir·i·tu·al·i·ty** \ˌspir-i-chə-'wa-lə-tē\ *n* — **spir·i·tu·al·ize** \'spir-i-chə-ˌlīz, -chə-wə-\ *vb* — **spir·i·tu·al·ly** *adv*

²**spiritual** *n* : a religious song originating among African-Americans of the southern U.S.

spir·i·tu·al·ism \'spir-i-chə-ˌli-zəm, -chə-wə-\ *n* : a belief that spirits of the dead communicate with the living usu. through a medium — **spir·i·tu·al·ist** \-list\ *n, often cap* — **spir·i·tu·al·is·tic** \ˌspir-i-chə-'lis-tik, -chə-wə-\ *adj*

spir·i·tu·ous \'spir-i-chəs, -chə-wəs; 'spir-ə-təs\ *adj* : containing alcohol

spi·ro·chete *also* **spi·ro·chaete** \'spī-rə-ˌkēt\ *n* : any of an order of spirally undulating bacteria including those causing syphilis and Lyme disease

spirt *var of* SPURT

¹**spit** \'spit\ *n* **1** : a thin pointed rod for holding meat over a fire **2** : a point of land that runs out into the water

²**spit** *vb* **spit·ted**; **spit·ting** : to pierce with or as if with a spit

³**spit** *vb* **spit** *or* **spat** \'spat\; **spit·ting 1** : to eject (saliva) from the mouth **2** : to express by or as if by spitting **3** : to rain or snow lightly

⁴**spit** *n* **1** : SALIVA **2** : perfect likeness ⟨∼ and image of his father⟩

spit·ball \'spit-ˌbȯl\ *n* **1** : paper chewed and rolled into a ball to be thrown as a missile **2** : a baseball pitch delivered after the ball has been moistened with saliva or sweat

¹**spite** \'spīt\ *n* : ill will with a wish to annoy, anger, or frustrate : petty malice ◆ **Synonyms** MALIGNITY, SPLEEN, GRUDGE, MALEVOLENCE — **spite·ful** \-fəl\ *adj* — **spite·ful·ly** *adv* — **spite·ful·ness** *n* — **in spite of** : in defiance or contempt of : NOTWITHSTANDING

²**spite** *vb* **spit·ed**; **spit·ing** : to treat maliciously : ANNOY, OFFEND

spit·tle \'spi-tᵊl\ *n* : SALIVA

spit·tle·bug \-ˌbəg\ *n* : any of a family of leaping insects with froth-secreting larvae that are related to aphids

spit·toon \spi-'tün\ *n* : a receptacle for spit

splash \'splash\ *vb* **1** : to dash a liquid about **2** : to scatter a liquid on : SPATTER **3** : to fall or strike with a splashing noise ◆ **Synonyms** SPRINKLE, BESPATTER, DOUSE, SPLATTER — **splash** *n*

splash·down \'splash-ˌdau̇n\ *n* : the landing of a manned spacecraft in the ocean — **splash down** *vb*

splashy \'spla-shē\ *adj* **splash·i·er; -est** : conspicuously showy : OSTENTATIOUS

¹**splat·ter** \'spla-tər\ *vb* : SPATTER — **splatter** *n*

²**splatter** *adj* : extremely gory or violent ⟨a ∼ movie⟩

¹**splay** \'splā\ *vb* : to spread outward or apart ⟨∼ed out her fingers⟩ — **splay** *n*

²**splay** *adj* **1** : spread out : turned outward **2** : AWKWARD, CLUMSY

spleen \'splēn\ *n* **1** : a vascular organ located near the stomach in most vertebrates that is concerned esp. with the filtration and storage of blood, destruction of red blood cells, and production of lymphocytes **2** : SPITE, MALICE ◆ **Synonyms** MALIGNITY, GRUDGE, MALEVOLENCE, ILL WILL, SPITEFULNESS

splen·did \'splen-dəd\ *adj* [L *splendidus*, fr. *splendēre* to shine] **1** : SHINING, BRILLIANT **2** : SHOWY, GORGEOUS **3** : ILLUSTRIOUS **4** : EXCELLENT ⟨a ∼ opportunity⟩ ◆ **Synonyms** RESPLENDENT, GLORIOUS, SUBLIME, SUPERB — **splen·did·ly** *adv*

splen·dor \'splen-dər\ *n* **1** : BRILLIANCE ⟨the ∼ of the sun⟩ **2** : POMP, MAGNIFICENCE

splen·dour \'splen-dər\ *chiefly Brit var of* SPLENDOR

sple·net·ic \spli-'ne-tik\ *adj* : marked by bad temper or spite

splen·ic \'sple-nik\ *adj* : of, relating to, or located in the spleen

splice \'splīs\ *vb* **spliced; splic·ing 1** : to unite (as two ropes) by weaving the strands together **2** : to unite (as two lengths of film) by connecting the ends together — **splice** *n*

splint \'splint\ *n* **1** : a thin strip of wood interwoven with others to make something (as a basket) **2** : material or a device used to protect and keep in place an injured body part (as a broken arm)

¹**splin·ter** \'splin-tər\ *n* : a thin piece of something split off lengthwise : SLIVER

²**splinter** *vb* : to split into splinters

split \'split\ *vb* **split; split·ting 1** : to divide lengthwise or along a grain or seam **2** : to burst or break in pieces **3** : to divide into parts or sections **4** : LEAVE ⟨∼ the party⟩ ◆ **Synonyms** REND, CLEAVE, RIP, TEAR — **split** *n*

split–lev·el \'split-'le-vəl\ *n* : a house divided so that the floor in one part is about halfway between two floors in the other

split personality *n* : SCHIZOPHRENIA; *also* : MULTIPLE PERSONALITY DISORDER

split–sec·ond \'split-'se-kənd\ *adj* **1** : occurring in a very brief time **2** : extremely precise ⟨∼ timing⟩

split·ting *adj* : causing a piercing sensation ⟨a ∼ headache⟩

splotch \'spläch\ *n* : BLOTCH

splurge \'splərj\ *vb* **splurged; splurg·ing** : to spend more than usual esp. on oneself — **splurge** *n*

splut·ter \'splə-tər\ n : SPUTTER — **splutter** vb

¹**spoil** \'spȯi(-ə)l\ n : PLUNDER ⟨~s of war⟩

²**spoil** vb **spoiled** \'spȯi(-ə)ld, 'spȯi(-ə)lt\ or **spoilt** \'spȯi(-ə)lt\; **spoil·ing 1** : ROB, PILLAGE **2** : to damage seriously : RUIN **3** : to impair the quality or effect of **4** : to damage the disposition by pampering; also : INDULGE, CODDLE **5** : DECAY, ROT **6** : to have an eager desire ⟨~ing for a fight⟩ ♦ **Synonyms** INJURE, HARM, HURT, MAR — **spoil·age** \'spȯi-lij\ n

spoil·er \'spȯi-lər\ n **1** : one that spoils **2** : a device (as on an airplane or automobile) used to disrupt airflow and decrease lift **3** : information about a movie or TV plot that can spoil a viewer's sense of surprise or suspense

spoil·sport \'spȯi(-ə)l-ˌspȯrt\ n : one who spoils the fun of others

¹**spoke** \'spōk\ past & archaic past part of SPEAK

²**spoke** n : any of the rods extending from the hub of a wheel to the rim

spo·ken \'spō-kən\ past part of SPEAK

spokes·man \'spōks-mən\ n : a person who speaks as the representative of another or others

spokes·mod·el \-ˌmä-dᵊl\ n : a model who is a spokesman or spokeswoman

spokes·per·son \-ˌpər-sən\ n : SPOKESMAN

spokes·wom·an \-ˌwù-mən\ n : a woman who speaks as the representative of another or others

spo·li·a·tion \ˌspō-lē-'ā-shən\ n : the act of plundering : the state of being plundered

¹**sponge** \'spənj\ n **1** : an elastic porous water-absorbing mass of fibers that forms the skeleton of various primitive sea animals; also : any of a phylum of chiefly marine sea animals that are the source of natural sponges **2** : a spongelike or porous mass or material — **spongy** \'spən-jē\ adj

²**sponge** vb **sponged; spong·ing 1** : to bathe or wipe with a sponge **2** : to live at another's expense **3** : to gather sponges — **spong·er** n

sponge cake n : a light cake made without shortening

sponge rubber n : a cellular rubber resembling natural sponge

spon·sor \'spän-sər\ n [LL, fr. L, guarantor, surety, fr. spondēre to promise] **1** : one who takes the responsibility for some other person or thing : SURETY **2** : GODPARENT **3** : a business firm that pays the cost of a radio or television program usu. in return for advertising time during its course — **sponsor** vb — **spon·sor·ship** n

spon·ta·ne·ous \spän-'tā-nē-əs\ adj [LL spontaneus, fr. L sponte of one's free will, voluntarily] **1** : done or produced freely or naturally **2** : acting or taking place without external force or cause ♦ **Synonyms** IMPULSIVE, INSTINCTIVE, AUTOMATIC, UNPREMEDITATED — **sponta-**

ne·ity \ˌspän-tə-'nē-ə-tē, -'nā-\ n — **spon·ta·ne·ous·ly** adv

spontaneous combustion n : a bursting into flame of material through heat produced within itself by chemical action (as oxidation)

spoof \'spüf\ vb **1** : DECEIVE, HOAX **2** : to make good-natured fun of ⟨the movie ~s horror films⟩ — **spoof** n

¹**spook** \'spük\ n **1** : GHOST, APPARITION **2** : SPY 2 — **spooky** adj

²**spook** vb : FRIGHTEN

¹**spool** \'spül\ n : a cylinder on which flexible material (as thread) is wound

²**spool** vb **1** : to wind on a spool **2** : to regulate data flow by means of a spooler

spool·er \'spü-lər\ n : a computer program or routine for regulating data flow

spoon \'spün\ n [ME, fr. OE spōn splinter, chip] **1** : an eating or cooking implement consisting of a small shallow bowl with a handle **2** : a metal piece used on a fishing line as a lure — **spoon** vb — **spoon·ful** n

spoon·bill \'spün-ˌbil\ n : any of several wading birds related to the ibises that have a bill with a broad flat tip

spoon–feed \-ˌfēd\ vb **-fed** \-ˌfed\; **-feeding** : to feed by means of a spoon

spoor \'spùr, 'spȯr\ n, pl **spoor** or **spoors** : a track, a trail, a scent, or droppings esp. of a wild animal

spo·rad·ic \spə-'ra-dik\ adj : occurring now and then ⟨~ outbreaks of disease⟩ ♦ **Synonyms** OCCASIONAL, RARE, SCARCE, INFREQUENT, UNCOMMON — **spo·rad·i·cal·ly** \-di-k(ə-)lē\ adv

spore \'spȯr\ n : a primitive usu. one-celled often environmentally resistant dormant or reproductive body produced by plants, fungi, and some microorganisms

¹**sport** \'spȯrt\ vb [ME, to divert, amuse, short for disporten, fr. AF desporter, to carry away, comfort, entertain, fr. des- (fr. L dis- apart) + porter to carry, fr. L portare] **1** : to amuse oneself : FROLIC **2** : SHOW OFF 1 ⟨~ing new shoes⟩ — **sport·ive** adj

²**sport** n **1** : a source of diversion : PASTIME **2** : physical activity engaged in for pleasure **3** : JEST 4 : MOCKERY ⟨make ~ of his efforts⟩ **5** : BUTT, LAUGHING-STOCK **6** : one who accepts results cheerfully whether favorable or not **7** : an individual exhibiting marked deviation from its normal type esp. as a result of mutation ♦ **Synonyms** PLAY, FROLIC, FUN, RECREATION — **sporty** adj

³**sport** or **sports** adj : of, relating to, or suitable for sport or casual wear ⟨~ coats⟩

sport fish n : a fish noted for the sport it affords anglers

sports·cast \'spȯrts-ˌkast\ n : a broadcast dealing with sports events — **sports·cast·er** \-ˌkas-tər\ n

sports·man \'spȯrts-mən\ n **1** : a person who engages in sports (as in hunting or fishing) **2** : one who plays fairly and wins or loses gracefully — **sports·man·like** \-ˌlīk\ adj — **sports·man·ship** n

sports medicine *n* : a field of medicine dealing with the prevention and treatment of sports-related injuries

sports·wom·an \-ˌwu̇-mən\ *n* : a woman who engages in sports

sports·writ·er \-ˌrī-tər\ *n* : one who writes about sports esp. for a newspaper — **sports·writ·ing** *n*

sport–util·i·ty vehicle \ˈspȯrt-yü-ˈti-lə-tē-\ *n* : SUV

¹**spot** \ˈspät\ *n* **1** : STAIN, BLEMISH **2** : a small part different (as in color) from the main part **3** : LOCATION, SITE — **spot·less** *adj* — **spot·less·ly** *adv* — **on the spot 1** : at the place of action **2** : in difficulty or danger

²**spot** *vb* **spot·ted**; **spot·ting 1** : to mark or disfigure with spots **2** : to pick out : RECOGNIZE, IDENTIFY

³**spot** *adj* **1** : being, done, or originating on the spot ⟨a ~ broadcast⟩ **2** : paid upon delivery **3** : made at random or at a few key points ⟨a ~ check⟩

spot–check \ˈspät-ˌchek\ *vb* : to make a spot check of

spot·light \-ˌlīt\ *n* **1** : a circle of brilliant light projected upon a particular area, person, or object (as on a stage); *also* : the device that produces this light **2** : public notice — **spotlight** *vb*

spot–on \ˈspät-ˈän\ *adj* : exactly correct ⟨a ~ forecast⟩

spotted owl *n* : a rare large dark brown dark-eyed owl of humid old growth forests and thickly wooded canyons from British Columbia to southern California and central Mexico

spot·ter \ˈspä-tər\ *n* **1** : one that keeps watch : OBSERVER **2** : one that removes spots

spot·ty \ˈspä-tē\ *adj* **spot·ti·er**; **-est** : uneven in quality; *also* : sparsely distributed ⟨~ attendance⟩

spou·sal \ˈspau̇-zəl, -səl\ *n* : MARRIAGE 2, WEDDING — usu. used in pl.

spouse \ˈspau̇s\ *n* : one's husband or wife — **spou·sal** \ˈspau̇-zəl, -səl\ *adj*

¹**spout** \ˈspau̇t\ *vb* **1** : to eject or issue forth forcibly and freely ⟨wells ~ing oil⟩ **2** : to speak pompously

²**spout** *n* **1** : a pipe or hole through which liquid spouts **2** : a jet of liquid; *esp* : WATERSPOUT 2

spp *abbr* species (*pl*)

¹**sprain** \ˈsprān\ *n* : a sudden or severe twisting of a joint with stretching or tearing of ligaments; *also* : a sprained condition

²**sprain** *vb* : to subject to sprain

sprat \ˈsprat\ *n* : a small European fish related to the herring; *also* : SARDINE

sprawl \ˈsprȯl\ *vb* **1** : to lie or sit with limbs spread out awkwardly **2** : to spread out irregularly — **sprawl** *n*

¹**spray** \ˈsprā\ *n* : a usu. flowering branch; *also* : a decorative arrangement of flowers and foliage

²**spray** *n* **1** : liquid flying in small drops like water blown from a wave **2** : a jet of fine vapor (as from an atomizer) **3** : an instrument (as an atomizer) for scattering fine liquid

³**spray** *vb* **1** : to discharge spray on or into **2** : to scatter or let fall in a spray — **spray·er** *n*

spray can *n* : a pressurized container from which aerosols are sprayed

spray gun *n* : a device for spraying liquids (as paint or insecticide)

¹**spread** \ˈspred\ *vb* **spread**; **spread·ing 1** : to scatter over a surface **2** : to flatten out : open out **3** : to distribute over a period of time or among many persons **4** : to cover something with ⟨~ rugs on the floor⟩ **5** : to prepare for a meal ⟨~ a table⟩ **6** : to pass on from person to person **7** : to stretch, force, or push apart ⟨a bird ~ing its wings⟩ — **spread·er** *n*

²**spread** *n* **1** : the act or process of spreading **2** : EXPANSE, EXTENT **3** : a prominent display in a periodical **4** : a food to be spread on bread or crackers **5** : a cloth cover for a bed **6** : distance between two points : GAP

spread·sheet \ˈspred-ˌshēt\ *n* : an accounting program for a computer

spree \ˈsprē\ *n* : an unrestrained outburst ⟨buying ~⟩; *also* : a drinking bout

sprig \ˈsprig\ *n* : a small shoot or twig

spright·ly \ˈsprīt-lē\ *adj* **spright·li·er**; **-est** : LIVELY, SPIRITED ⟨a ~ musical⟩ ♦ *Synonyms* ANIMATED, VIVACIOUS, GAY — **spright·li·ness** *n*

¹**spring** \ˈspriŋ\ *vb* **sprang** \ˈspraŋ\ *or* **sprung** \ˈsprəŋ\; **sprung**; **spring·ing 1** : to move suddenly upward or forward **2** : to grow quickly ⟨weeds *sprang* up overnight⟩ **3** : to come from by birth or descent **4** : to move quickly by elastic force **5** : WARP **6** : to develop (a leak) through the seams **7** : to cause to close suddenly ⟨~ a trap⟩ **8** : to make known suddenly ⟨~ a surprise⟩ **9** : to make lame : STRAIN ⟨*sprang* a leg muscle⟩

²**spring** *n* **1** : a source of supply; *esp* : an issuing of water from the ground **2** : SOURCE, ORIGIN; *also* : MOTIVE **3** : the season between winter and summer **4** : an elastic body or device that recovers its original shape when it is released after being distorted **5** : the act or an instance of leaping up or forward **6** : RESILIENCE — **springy** *adj*

spring·board \ˈspriŋ-ˌbȯrd\ *n* : a springy board used in jumping or vaulting or for diving

spring fever *n* : a lazy or restless feeling often associated with the onset of spring

spring tide *n* : a tide of greater-than-average range that occurs at each new moon and full moon

spring·time \ˈspriŋ-ˌtīm\ *n* : the season of spring

¹**sprin·kle** \ˈspriŋ-kəl\ *vb* **sprin·kled**; **sprin·kling** : to scatter in small drops or particles — **sprin·kler** *n*

²**sprinkle** *n* : a light rainfall

sprin·kling *n* : SMATTERING

¹**sprint** \ˈsprint\ *vb* : to run at top speed esp. for a short distance — **sprint·er** *n*

²**sprint** *n* **1** : a short run at top speed **2** : a short distance race

sprite \ˈsprīt\ *n* **1** : GHOST, SPIRIT **2** : ELF, FAIRY

spritz \'sprits, 'shpritz\ *vb* : SPRAY ⟨~ the plants⟩ — **spritz** *n*

sprock·et \'sprä-kət\ *n* : a toothed wheel whose teeth engage the links of a chain

¹**sprout** \'sraút\ *vb* : to send out new growth ⟨~*ing* seeds⟩

²**sprout** *n* : a usu. young and growing plant shoot (as from a seed)

¹**spruce** \'sprüs\ *vb* **spruced; spruc·ing** : to make or become spruce

²**spruce** *adj* **spruc·er; spruc·est** : neat and smart in appearance ♦ *Synonyms* STYLISH, FASHIONABLE, MODISH, DAPPER, NATTY

³**spruce** *n, pl* **spruc·es** *also* **spruce** : any of a genus of evergreen pyramid-shaped trees related to the pines and having soft light wood; *also* : the wood of a spruce

sprung *past and past part of* SPRING

spry \'sprī\ *adj* **spri·er** *or* **spry·er** \'sprī-ər\; **spri·est** *or* **spry·est** \'sprī-əst\ : NIMBLE, ACTIVE ⟨a ~ 75-year-old⟩ ♦ *Synonyms* AGILE, BRISK, LIVELY, SPRIGHTLY

spud \'spəd\ *n* 1 : a sharp narrow spade 2 : POTATO

spume \'spyüm\ *n* : frothy matter on liquids : FOAM — **spumy** \'spyü-mē\ *adj*

spu·mo·ni *also* **spu·mo·ne** \spú-'mō-nē\ *n* [It *spumone*, fr. *spuma* foam] : ice cream in layers of different colors, flavors, and textures often with candied fruits and nuts

spun *past and past part of* SPIN

spun glass *n* : FIBERGLASS

spunk \'spəŋk\ *n* [fr. *spunk* tinder, fr. ScGael *sponge* sponge, tinder, fr. Middle Irish *spongc*, fr. L *spongia* sponge] : PLUCK, COURAGE — **spunky** *adj*

¹**spur** \'spər\ *n* 1 : a pointed device fastened to a rider's boot and used to urge on a horse 2 : something that urges to action 3 : a stiff sharp spine (as on the leg of a cock); *also* : a hollow projecting appendage of a flower (as a columbine) 4 : a ridge extending sideways from a mountain 5 : a branch of railroad track extending from the main line ♦ *Synonyms* GOAD, MOTIVE, IMPULSE, INCENTIVE, INDUCEMENT — **spurred** \'spərd\ *adj* — **on the spur of the moment** : on hasty impulse

²**spur** *vb* **spurred; spur·ring** 1 : to urge a horse on with spurs 2 : INCITE

spurge \'spərj\ *n* : any of a family of herbs and woody plants with a bitter milky juice

spu·ri·ous \'spyúr-ē-əs\ *adj* [LL *spurius* false, fr. L, *spurius*, n., son of an unknown father] : not genuine : FALSE ⟨~ eminence⟩

spurn \'spərn\ *vb* 1 : to kick away or trample on 2 : to reject with disdain

¹**spurt** \'spərt\ *vb* : to gush out : SPOUT

²**spurt** *n* : a sudden gushing or spouting

³**spurt** *n* 1 : a sudden brief burst of effort, speed, or development 2 : a sharp increase of activity ⟨~ in sales⟩

⁴**spurt** *vb* : to make a spurt

sput·ter \'spə-tər\ *vb* 1 : to spit small scattered particles : SPLUTTER 2 : to utter words hastily or explosively in excitement or confusion 3 : to make small popping sounds — **sputter** *n*

spu·tum \'spyü-təm\ *n, pl* **spu·ta** \-tə\ [L] : material (as phlegm) that is spit out or coughed up esp. during illness

¹**spy** \'spī\ *vb* **spied; spy·ing** 1 : to watch or search for information secretly : act as a spy 2 : to get a momentary or quick glimpse of : SEE

²**spy** *n, pl* **spies** 1 : one who secretly watches others 2 : a secret agent who tries to get information for one country in the territory of an enemy

spy·glass \'spī-ˌglas\ *n* : a small telescope

sq *abbr* 1 squadron 2 square

squab \'skwäb\ *n, pl* **squabs** *or* **squab** : a young bird and esp. a pigeon

squab·ble \'skwä-bəl\ *n* : a noisy altercation : WRANGLE ♦ *Synonyms* QUARREL, SPAT, ROW, TIFF — **squabble** *vb*

squad \'skwäd\ *n* 1 : a small organized group of military personnel 2 : a small group engaged in a common effort

squad car *n* : a police car connected with two-way radio with headquarters

squad·ron \'skwä-drən\ *n* : any of several units of military organization

squal·id \'skwä-ləd\ *adj* 1 : filthy or degraded through neglect or poverty 2 : SORDID, DEBASED ⟨a ~ political ploy⟩ ♦ *Synonyms* NASTY, FOUL, DIRTY, GRUBBY

squall \'skwȯl\ *n* : a sudden violent gust of wind often with rain or snow — **squally** *adj*

squa·lor \'skwä-lər\ *n* : the quality or state of being squalid

squa·mous cell \'skwä-məs-\ *n* : a scale-like cell of the outer layers of the skin from which a type of carcinoma arises

squan·der \'skwän-dər\ *vb* : to spend wastefully or foolishly

¹**square** \'skwer\ *n* 1 : an instrument used to lay out or test right angles 2 : a rectangle with all four sides equal 3 : something square 4 : the product of a number multiplied by itself 5 : an area bounded by four streets 6 : an open area in a city where streets meet 7 : a highly conventional person

²**square** *adj* **squar·er; squar·est** 1 : having four equal sides and four right angles 2 : forming a right angle ⟨cut a ~ corner⟩ 3 : multiplied by itself : SQUARED ⟨*x²* is the symbol for *x* ~⟩ 4 : being a unit of square measure equal to a square each side of which measures one unit ⟨a ~ foot⟩ 5 : being of a specified length in each of two dimensions ⟨an area 10 feet ~⟩ 6 : exactly adjusted 7 : JUST, FAIR ⟨a ~ deal⟩ 8 : leaving no balance ⟨make accounts ~⟩ 9 : SUBSTANTIAL ⟨a ~ meal⟩ 10 : highly conservative or conventional — **square·ly** *adv*

³**square** *vb* **squared; squar·ing** 1 : to form with four equal sides and right angles or with flat surfaces ⟨~ a timber⟩ 2 : to multiply (a number) by itself 3 : CONFORM, AGREE 4 : BALANCE, SETTLE ⟨~ an account⟩

square dance *n* : a dance for four couples arranged to form a square

square measure *n* : a unit or system of units for measuring area — see METRIC SYSTEM table, WEIGHT table

square–rigged \'skwer-'rigd\ *adj* : having the chief sails extended on yards that are fastened to the masts horizontally and at their center

square–rig·ger \-ˌri-gər\ *n* : a square-rigged craft

square root *n* : either of the two numbers whose squares are equal to a given number ⟨the *square root* of 9 is +3 or –3⟩

¹**squash** \'skwäsh, 'skwȯsh\ *vb* **1** : to beat or press into a pulp or flat mass **2** : QUASH, SUPPRESS ⟨~ a revolt⟩

²**squash** *n* **1** : the impact of something soft and heavy; *also* : the sound of such impact **2** : a crushed mass **3** : a game played on a 4-wall court with a racket and rubber ball

³**squash** *n, pl* **squash·es** *or* **squash** : any of various fruits of plants of the gourd family that are used esp. as vegetables; *also* : a plant and esp. a vine bearing squashes

squash racquets *n* : SQUASH 3

¹**squat** \'skwät\ *vb* **squat·ted; squat·ting** [ME *squatten* to crush, crouch in hiding, fr. MF (dial. of Picardy) *esquatir, escuater,* fr. OF *es-* ex- + *quatir* to hide, fr. VL **coactire* to squeeze, alter. of L *coactare* to compel, fr. *cogere* to compel] **1** : to sit down upon the hams or heels **2** : to settle on land without right or title; *also* : to settle on public land with a view to acquiring title — **squat·ter** *n*

²**squat** *adj* **squat·ter; squat·test** : low to the ground; *also* : short and thick in stature ♦ **Synonyms** THICKSET, STOCKY, HEAVYSET, STUBBY

³**squat** *n* : the act or posture of squatting

squawk \'skwȯk\ *n* : a harsh loud cry; *also* : a noisy protest — **squawk** *vb*

squeak \'skwēk\ *vb* **1** : to utter or speak in a weak shrill tone **2** : to make a thin high-pitched sound ⟨the door ~s⟩ — **squeak** *n* — **squeaky** *adj*

¹**squeal** \'skwēl\ *vb* **1** : to make a shrill sound or cry **2** : to betray a secret or turn informer **3** : COMPLAIN, PROTEST

²**squeal** *n* : a shrill sharp cry or noise

squea·mish \'skwē-mish\ *adj* **1** : easily nauseated; *also* : NAUSEATED **2** : easily disgusted ♦ **Synonyms** FUSSY, NICE, DAINTY, FASTIDIOUS, PERSNICKETY — **squea·mish·ness** *n*

squee·gee \'skwē-jē\ *n* : a blade set crosswise on a handle and used for spreading or wiping liquid on, across, or off a surface — **squeegee** *vb*

¹**squeeze** \'skwēz\ *vb* **squeezed; squeez·ing** **1** : to exert pressure on the opposite sides or parts of **2** : to obtain by pressure ⟨~ juice from a lemon⟩ **3** : to force or move into a small space ⟨*squeezed* into her jeans⟩ — **squeez·er** *n*

²**squeeze** *n* **1** : an act of squeezing **2** : a quantity squeezed out

squeeze bottle *n* : a flexible plastic bottle that dispenses its contents when it is squeezed

squelch \'skwelch\ *vb* **1** : to suppress

completely : CRUSH ⟨~ resistance⟩ **2** : to move in soft mud — **squelch** *n*

squib \'skwib\ *n* : a brief witty writing or speech

squid \'skwid\ *n, pl* **squid** *or* **squids** : any of an order of long-bodied sea mollusks having eight short arms and two longer tentacles and usu. a slender internal shell

squint \'skwint\ *vb* **1** : to look or aim obliquely **2** : to look or peer with the eyes partly closed ⟨~ing into the sun⟩ **3** : to be cross-eyed — **squint** *n or adj*

¹**squire** \'skwī(-ə)r\ *n* [ME *squier,* fr. AF *esquier,* fr. LL *scutarius,* fr. L *scutum* shield] **1** : an armor-bearer of a knight **2** : a man gallantly devoted to a lady **3** : a member of the British gentry ranking below a knight and above a gentleman; *also* : a prominent landowner **4** : a local magistrate

²**squire** *vb* **squired; squir·ing** : to attend as a squire or escort

squirm \'skwərm\ *vb* : to twist about like a worm : WRIGGLE

¹**squir·rel** \'skwər-əl\ *n, pl* **squirrels** *also* **squirrel** [ME *squirel,* fr. AF *escurel, esquirel,* fr. VL **scuriolus,* dim. of **scurius,* alter. of L *sciurus,* fr. Gk *skiouros,* prob. fr. *skia* shadow + *oura* tail] : any of various rodents usu. with a long bushy tail and strong hind legs; *also* : the fur of a squirrel

²**squirrel** *vb* **-reled** *or* **-relled; -rel·ing** *or* **-rel·ling** : to store up for future use

¹**squirt** \'skwərt\ *vb* : to eject liquid in a thin spurt

²**squirt** *n* **1** : an instrument (as a syringe) for squirting **2** : a small forcible jet of liquid

¹**Sr** *abbr* **1** senior **2** sister

²**Sr** *symbol* strontium

SR *abbr* seaman recruit

¹**SRO** \ˌes-(ˌ)är-'ō\ *n* [single-room occupancy] : a house or apartment building in which low-income tenants live in single rooms

²**SRO** *abbr* standing room only

SS *abbr* **1** saints **2** Social Security **3** steamship **4** sworn statement

SSA *abbr* Social Security Administration

SSE *abbr* south-southeast

SSG *or* **SSgt** *abbr* staff sergeant

SSI *abbr* supplemental security income

SSM *abbr* staff sergeant major

SSN *abbr* Social Security Number

ssp *abbr* subspecies

SSR *abbr* Soviet Socialist Republic

SSS *abbr* Selective Service System

SST \ˌes-(ˌ)es-'tē\ *n* [supersonic *t*ransport] : a supersonic passenger airplane

SSW *abbr* south-southwest

st *abbr* **1** stanza **2** state **3** stitch **4** stone **5** street

St *abbr* saint

ST *abbr* **1** short ton **2** standard time

-st — see -EST

sta *abbr* station; stationary

¹**stab** \'stab\ *n* **1** : a wound produced by a pointed weapon **2** : a quick thrust **3** : a brief attempt

²**stab** *vb* **stabbed; stab·bing** : to pierce or

wound with or as if with a pointed weapon; *also* : THRUST, DRIVE

sta·bile \'stā-ˌbēl\ *n* : an abstract sculpture or construction similar to a mobile but made to be stationary

sta·bi·lize \'stā-bə-ˌlīz\ *vb* **-lized; -liz·ing** **1** : to make stable **2** : to hold steady ⟨∼ prices⟩ — **sta·bi·li·za·tion** \ˌstā-bə-lə-'zā-shən\ *n* — **sta·bi·liz·er** \'stā-bə-ˌlī-zər\ *n*

¹sta·ble \'stā-bəl\ *n* : a building in which domestic animals are sheltered and fed — **sta·ble·man** \-mən, -ˌman\ *n*

²stable *vb* **sta·bled; sta·bling** : to put or keep in a stable

³stable *adj* **sta·bler; sta·blest** **1** : firmly established; *also* : mentally and emotionally healthy **2** : steady in purpose : CONSTANT **3** : DURABLE, ENDURING ⟨∼ civilizations⟩ **4** : resistant to chemical or physical change ♦ *Synonyms* LASTING, PERMANENT, PERPETUAL, PERDURABLE — **sta·bil·i·ty** \stə-'bi-lə-tē\ *n*

stac·ca·to \stə-'kä-tō\ *adj or adv* [It] : cut short so as not to sound connected ⟨∼ notes⟩

¹stack \'stak\ *n* **1** : a large pile (as of hay or grain) **2** : an orderly pile (as of poker chips) **3** : a large quantity **4** : a vertical pipe : SMOKESTACK **5** : a rack with shelves for storing books ⟨library ∼s⟩

²stack *vb* **1** : to pile up **2** : to arrange (cards) secretly for cheating

stack up *vb* : MEASURE UP ⟨how do they *stack up* against the competition?⟩

sta·di·um \'stā-dē-əm\ *n, pl* **-dia** \-dē-ə\ *or* **-di·ums** : a structure with tiers of seats for spectators built around a field for sports events

¹staff \'staf\ *n, pl* **staffs** \'stafs, 'stavz\ *or* **staves** \'stavz, 'stāvz\ **1** : a pole, stick, rod, or bar used for supporting, for measuring, or as a symbol of authority; *also* : CLUB, CUDGEL **2** : something that sustains ⟨bread is the ∼ of life⟩ **3** : the five horizontal lines on which music is written **4** : a body of assistants to an executive **5** : a group of officers holding no command but having duties concerned with planning and managing

²staff *vb* : to supply with a staff or with workers ⟨∼ a hotel⟩

staff·er \'sta-fər\ *n* : a member of a staff (as of a newspaper)

staff sergeant *n* : a noncommissioned officer ranking in the army next below a sergeant first class, in the air force next below a technical sergeant, in the marine corps next below a gunnery sergeant

¹stag \'stag\ *n, pl* **stags** *or* **stag** : an adult male of various large deer

²stag *adj* : restricted to or intended for men ⟨a ∼ party⟩ ⟨∼ movies⟩

³stag *adv* : unaccompanied by a date

¹stage \'stāj\ *n* [ME, fr. AF *estage* abode, story of a building, stage, fr. VL **staticum*, fr. L *stare* to stand] **1** : a raised platform on which an orator may speak or a play may be presented : THEATER **3** : the scene of a notable action or event **4** : a station or resting place on a traveled road **5** : STAGECOACH **6** : a degree of advance in an undertaking, process, or development **7** : a propulsion unit in a rocket — **stagy** \'stā-jē\ *adj*

²stage *vb* **staged; stag·ing** : to produce or perform on or as if on a stage ⟨∼ a play⟩ — **stage·able** *adj*

stage·coach \'stāj-ˌkōch\ *n* : a horse-drawn coach that runs regularly between stations

stage manager *n* : one who supervises the physical aspects of a stage production

stag·fla·tion \ˌstag-'flā-shən\ *n* : inflation with stagnant economic activity and high unemployment

¹stag·ger \'sta-gər\ *vb* **1** : to reel from side to side : TOTTER **2** : to begin to doubt : WAVER **3** : to cause to reel or waver **4** : to arrange in overlapping or alternating positions or times ⟨∼ working hours⟩ **5** : ASTONISH ⟨their indifference ∼s me⟩ — **stag·ger·ing·ly** *adv*

²stagger *n sing or pl* : an abnormal condition of domestic animals associated with damage to the central nervous system and marked by lack of coordination and a reeling unsteady gait **2** : a reeling or unsteady gait or stance

stag·ing \'stā-jiŋ\ *n* **1** : SCAFFOLDING **2** : the assembling of troops and matériel in transit in a particular place

staging post *n* : STOPOVER 2

stag·nant \'stag-nənt\ *adj* **1** : not flowing : MOTIONLESS ⟨∼ water in a pond⟩ **2** : DULL, INACTIVE ⟨∼ business⟩

stag·nate \'stag-ˌnāt\ *vb* **stag·nat·ed; stag·nat·ing** : to be or become stagnant — **stag·na·tion** \stag-'nā-shən\ *n*

staid \'stād\ *adj* **1** : SOBER, SEDATE ♦ *Synonyms* GRAVE, SERIOUS, EARNEST

¹stain \'stān\ *vb* **1** : DISCOLOR, SOIL **2** : TAINT, CORRUPT **3** : DISGRACE **4** : to color (as wood, paper, or cloth) by processes affecting the material itself

²stain *n* **1** : a small soiled or discolored area **2** : a taint of guilt : STIGMA **3** : a preparation (as a dye or pigment) used in staining — **stain·less** *adj*

stainless steel *n* : steel alloyed with chromium that is highly resistant to stain, rust, and corrosion

stair \'ster\ *n* **1** : a series of steps or flights of steps for passing from one level to another — often used in pl. **2** : one step of a stairway

stair·case \-ˌkās\ *n* : a flight of steps with their supporting framework, casing, and balusters

stair·way \-ˌwā\ *n* : one or more flights of stairs with connecting landings

stair·well \-ˌwel\ *n* : a vertical shaft in which stairs are located

¹stake \'stāk\ *n* **1** : a pointed piece of material (as of wood) driven into the ground as a marker or a support **2** : a post to which a person is bound for death by burning; *also* : execution by burning at the stake **3** : something that is staked for gain or loss **4** : the prize in a contest

²stake *vb* **staked; stak·ing** **1** : to mark the limits of by or as if by stakes **2** : to tie to a stake **3** : to support or secure with stakes **4** : BET, WAGER

stake-out \\'stāk-ˌaüt\\ *n* : a surveillance by police (as of a suspected criminal)

sta-lac-tite \\stə-'lak-ˌtīt\\ *n* [NL *stalactites,* fr. Gk *stalaktos* dripping, fr. *stalassein* to let drip] : an icicle-shaped deposit hanging from the roof or sides of a cavern

sta-lag-mite \\stə-'lag-ˌmīt\\ *n* [NL *stalagmites,* fr. Gk *stalagma* drop or *stalagmos* dripping, fr. *stalassein* to let drip] : a deposit resembling an inverted stalactite rising from the floor of a cavern

stale \\'stāl\\ *adj* **stal-er; stal-est 1** : having lost good taste and quality from age ⟨∼ bread⟩ **2** : used or heard so often as to be dull ⟨∼ news⟩ **3** : not as strong or effective as before ⟨∼ from lack of practice⟩ — **stale-ness** *n*

stale-mate \\'stāl-ˌmāt\\ *n* : a drawn contest : DEADLOCK — **stalemate** *vb*

¹**stalk** \\'stȯk\\ *n* : a plant stem; *also* : any slender usu. upright supporting or connecting part — **stalked** \\'stȯkt\\ *adj*

²**stalk** *vb* **1** : to pursue (game) stealthily **2** : to walk stiffly or haughtily **3** : to follow (a person) obsessively

¹**stall** \\'stȯl\\ *n* **1** : a compartment in a stable or barn for one animal **2** : a booth or counter where articles may be displayed for sale **3** : a seat in a church choir; *also* : a church pew **4** *chiefly Brit* : a front orchestra seat in a theater

²**stall** *vb* : to bring or come to a standstill unintentionally ⟨∼ an engine⟩

³**stall** *n* : the condition of an airfoil or aircraft in which lift is lost and the airfoil or aircraft tends to drop

⁴**stall** *n* [alter. of *stale* lure] : a ruse to deceive or delay

⁵**stall** *vb* : to hold off, divert, or delay by evasion or deception

stal-lion \\'stal-yən\\ *n* : a male horse

stal-wart \\'stȯl-wərt\\ *adj* : STOUT, STRONG; *also* : BRAVE, VALIANT

sta-men \\'stā-mən\\ *n* : an organ of a flower that produces pollen

stam-i-na \\'sta-mə-nə\\ *n* [L, pl. of *stamen* warp, thread of life spun by the Fates] : VIGOR, ENDURANCE ⟨had the ∼ to win⟩

sta-mi-nate \\'stā-mə-nət, 'sta-mə-, -ˌnāt\\ *adj* **1** : having or producing stamens **2** : having stamens but no pistils

stam-mer \\'sta-mər\\ *vb* : to hesitate or stumble in speaking — **stammer** *n* — **stam-mer-er** *n*

¹**stamp** \\'stamp; *for 2 also* 'stämp or 'stȯmp\\ *vb* **1** : to pound or crush with a heavy instrument **2** : to strike or beat with the bottom of the foot **3** : IMPRESS, IMPRINT ⟨∼ "paid" on the bill⟩ **4** : to cut out or indent with a stamp or die **5** : to attach a postage stamp to

²**stamp** *n* **1** : a device or instrument for stamping **2** : the mark made by stamping; *also* : a distinctive mark or quality **3** : the act of stamping **4** : a stamped or printed paper affixed to show that a charge has been paid ⟨postage ∼⟩ ⟨tax ∼⟩

¹**stam-pede** \\stam-'pēd\\ *n* : a wild headlong rush or flight esp. of frightened animals

²**stampede** *vb* **stam-ped-ed; stam-ped-ing 1** : to flee or cause to flee in panic **2** : to act or cause to act together suddenly and heedlessly

stance \\'stans\\ *n* : a way of standing

¹**stanch** \\'stȯnch, 'stänch, 'stanch\\ *or* **staunch** \\'stȯnch, 'stänch\\ *vb* : to check the flowing of (as blood); *also* : to cease flowing or bleeding

²**stanch** *var of* ²STAUNCH

stan-chion \\'stan-chən\\ *n* : an upright bar, post, or support

¹**stand** \\'stand\\ *vb* **stood** \\'stủd\\; **standing 1** : to take or be at rest in an upright or firm position **2** : to assume a specified position **3** : to remain stationary or unchanged **4** : to be steadfast **5** : to act in resistance ⟨∼ against a foe⟩ **6** : to maintain a relative position or rank **7** : to gather slowly and remain ⟨tears *stood* in her eyes⟩ **8** : to set upright **9** : ENDURE, TOLERATE ⟨I won't ∼ for that⟩ **10** : to submit to ⟨∼ trial⟩ — **stand pat** : to oppose or resist change

²**stand** *n* **1** : an act of standing, staying, or resisting **2** : a stop made to give a performance **3** : POSITION, VIEWPOINT **4** : a place taken by a witness to testify in court **5** *pl* : tiered seats for spectators **6** : a raised platform (as for speakers) **7** : a structure for a small retail business **8** : a structure for supporting or holding something upright ⟨music ∼⟩ **9** : a group of plants growing in a continuous area

stand–alone \\'stan-də-ˌlōn\\ *adj* : SELF-CONTAINED; *esp* : capable of operation independent of a computer system

¹**stan-dard** \\'stan-dərd\\ *n* **1** : a figure adopted as an emblem by a people **2** : the personal flag of a ruler; *also* : FLAG **3** : something set up as a rule for measuring or as a model to be followed **4** : an upright support ⟨lamp ∼⟩

²**standard** *adj* **1** : used as or meeting a standard established by law or custom **2** : regularly and widely used ⟨a ∼ practice⟩ **3** : well established by usage in speech or writing

stan-dard–bear-er \\-ˌber-ər\\ *n* : the leader of a cause

standard deviation *n* : a measure of dispersion in a set of data

stan-dard-ise *Brit var of* STANDARDIZE

stan-dard–is-sue \\'stan-dərd-'i-shü\\ *adj* : STANDARD, TYPICAL ⟨a ∼ blue suit⟩

stan-dard-ize \\'stan-dər-ˌdīz\\ *vb* **-ized; -iz-ing** : to make standard or uniform — **stan-dard-i-za-tion** \\ˌstan-dər-də-'zā-shən\\ *n*

standard of living : the necessities, comforts, and luxuries that a person or group is accustomed to

standard time *n* : the time established by law or by general usage over a region or country

¹**stand-by** \\'stand-ˌbī\\ *n, pl* **stand-bys** \\-ˌbīz\\ **1** : one that can be relied on **2** : a substitute in reserve — **on standby**

: ready or available for immediate action or use

²**standby** adj 1 : ready for use 2 : relating to airline travel in which the passenger must wait for an available unreserved seat — **standby** adv

stand-in \'stan-ˌdin\ n 1 : someone employed to occupy an actor's place while lights and camera are readied 2 : SUBSTITUTE

¹**stand-ing** \'stan-diŋ\ adj 1 : ERECT ⟨∼ timber⟩ 2 : not flowing : STAGNANT 3 : remaining at the same level or amount for an indefinite period ⟨∼ offer⟩ 4 : PERMANENT ⟨a ∼ army⟩ 5 : done from a standing position ⟨a ∼ jump⟩

²**standing** n 1 : length of service; also : relative position in society or in a profession : RANK 2 : DURATION ⟨a custom of long ∼⟩

stand-off \'stan-ˌdóf\ n : TIE, DRAW

stand-off-ish \ˌstan-'dó-fish\ adj : somewhat cold and reserved

stand-out \'stan-ˌdaút\ n : something conspicuously excellent

stand-pipe \'stan-ˌpīp\ n : a high vertical pipe or reservoir for water used to produce a uniform pressure

stand-point \-ˌpóint\ n : a position from which objects or principles are judged

stand-still \-ˌstil\ n : a state of rest

stand-up \'stan-ˌdəp\ adj : done or performing in a standing position ⟨a ∼ comic⟩ ⟨∼ comedy⟩

stank past of STINK

stan-za \'stan-zə\ n [It] : a group of lines forming a division of a poem

sta-pes \'stā-ˌpēz\ n, pl **stapes** or **sta-pe-des** \'stā-pə-ˌdēz\ : the innermost bone of the middle ear of mammals

staph \'staf\ n : STAPHYLOCOCCUS

staph-y-lo-coc-cus \ˌsta-fə-lō-'kä-kəs\ n, pl **-coc-ci** \-'kä-ˌkī, -'käk-ˌsī\ : any of a genus of spherical bacteria including some pathogens of skin and mucous membranes — **staph-y-lo-coc-cal** \-'kä-kəl\ adj

¹**sta-ple** \'stā-pəl\ n : a U-shaped piece of metal or wire with sharp points to be driven into a surface or through thin layers (as paper) for attaching or holding together — **staple** vb — **sta-pler** n

²**staple** n 1 : a chief commodity or product 2 : a chief part of something ⟨a ∼ of their diet⟩ 3 : unmanufactured or raw material 4 : a textile fiber suitable for spinning into yarn

³**staple** adj 1 : regularly produced in large quantities 2 : PRINCIPAL, MAIN ⟨the ∼ crop⟩

¹**star** \'stär\ n 1 : a celestial body that appears as a fixed point of light; esp : such a body that is gaseous, self-luminous, and of great mass 2 : a planet or configuration of planets that is held in astrology to influence one's fortune — usu. used in pl. 3 obs : DESTINY 4 : a conventional figure representing a star; esp : ASTERISK 5 : an actor or actress playing the leading role 6 : a superb performer — **star-dom** \'stär-dəm\ n — **star-less** adj — **star-like** adj — **star-ry** adj

²**star** vb **starred**; **star-ring** 1 : to adorn with stars 2 : to mark with an asterisk 3 : to play the leading role

star anise n : the small brown star-shaped fruit of an Asian tree used as a spice esp. in Chinese cooking

star-board \'stär-bərd\ n [ME sterbord, fr. OE stēorbord, fr. stēor- steering oar + bord ship's side] : the right side of a ship or airplane looking forward — **starboard** adj

star-burst \'stär-bərst\ n : a pattern that resembles diverging rays of light

¹**starch** \'stärch\ vb : to stiffen with or as if with starch

²**starch** n : a complex carbohydrate that is stored in plants, is an important foodstuff, and is used in adhesives and sizes, in laundering, and in pharmacy — **starchy** adj

stare \'ster\ vb **stared**; **star-ing** : to look fixedly with wide-open eyes ⟨stared in disbelief⟩ — **stare** n — **star-er** n

star-fish \'stär-ˌfish\ n : any of a class of echinoderms that have usu. five arms arranged around a central disk and feed largely on mollusks

star fruit n : CARAMBOLA 1

¹**stark** \'stärk\ adj 1 : rigid as if in death; also : STRICT 2 archaic : STRONG, ROBUST 3 : SHEER, UTTER ⟨∼ nonsense⟩ 4 : BARREN, DESOLATE ⟨∼ landscape⟩; also : UNADORNED ⟨∼ realism⟩ 5 : sharply delineated — **stark-ly** adv

²**stark** adv : WHOLLY, ABSOLUTELY ⟨∼ naked⟩

star-light \'stär-ˌlīt\ n : the light given by the stars

star-ling \'stär-liŋ\ n : a dark brown or in summer glossy greenish black European bird that is naturalized nearly worldwide and often considered a pest

¹**start** \'stärt\ vb 1 : to give an involuntary twitch or jerk (as from surprise) 2 : BEGIN, COMMENCE 3 : to set going ⟨an engine⟩ 4 : to enter or cause to enter a game or contest; also : to be in the starting lineup — **start-er** n

²**start** n 1 : a sudden involuntary motion : LEAP 2 : a spasmodic and brief effort or action 3 : BEGINNING; also : the place of beginning

start-er \'stär-tər\ adj : being an item acquired with the expectation that a more elaborate one will be acquired in the future ⟨a ∼ home⟩

star-tle \'stär-t³l\ vb **star-tled**; **star-tling** : to frighten or surprise suddenly : cause to start ⟨the noise startled the dog⟩

star-tling adj : causing sudden fear, surprise, or anxiety — **star-tling-ly** adv

starve \'stärv\ vb **starved**; **starv-ing** [ME sterven to die, fr. OE steorfan] 1 : to die or cause to die from hunger 2 : to suffer extreme hunger or deprivation ⟨starving for affection⟩ 3 : to subdue by famine — **star-va-tion** \stär-'vā-shən\ n

starve-ling \'stärv-liŋ\ n : one that is thin from lack of nourishment

stash \'stash\ vb : to store in a secret place for future use — **stash** n

sta-sis \'stā-səs, 'sta-\ n, pl **sta-ses** \'stä-

ˌsēz, ˈsta-\ 1 : a stoppage or slowing of the normal flow of a bodily fluid (as blood) 2 : a state of static balance : STAGNATION

¹**stat** \ˈstat\ adv [L statim] : without delay : IMMEDIATELY

²**stat** abbr statute

¹**state** \ˈstāt\ n [ME stat, fr. AF & L; AF estat, fr. L status, fr. stare to stand] 1 : mode or condition of being ⟨the four ∼s of matter⟩ 2 : condition of mind 3 : social position 4 : a body of people occupying a territory and organized under one government; also : the government of such a body of people 5 : one of the constituent units of a nation having a federal government — **state·hood** \-ˌhùd\ n

²**state** vb **stat·ed; stat·ing** 1 : to set by regulation or authority 2 : to express in words

state·craft \ˈstāt-ˌkraft\ n : the art of conducting state affairs

state·house \-ˌhaùs\ n : the building in which a state legislature meets

state·ly \ˈstāt-lē\ adj **state·li·er; -est** 1 : having lofty dignity : HAUGHTY 2 : IMPRESSIVE, MAJESTIC ⟨∼ homes⟩ ♦ **Synonyms** MAGNIFICENT, IMPOSING, AUGUST — **state·li·ness** n

state·ment \ˈstāt-mənt\ n 1 : the act or result of presenting in words 2 : a summary of a financial account

state·room \ˈstāt-ˌrüm, -ˌrûm\ n : a private room on a ship or railroad car

state·side \ˈstāt-ˌsīd\ adj : of or relating to the U.S. as regarded from outside its continental limits — **stateside** adv

states·man \ˈstāts-mən\ n : a person engaged in fixing the policies and conducting the affairs of a government; esp : one wise and skilled in such matters — **states·man·like** adj — **states·man·ship** n

¹**stat·ic** \ˈsta-tik\ adj 1 : acting by mere weight without motion ⟨∼ pressure⟩ 2 : relating to bodies at rest or forces in equilibrium 3 : showing little change 4 : not moving : not active 5 : of or relating to stationary charges of electricity 6 : of, relating to, or caused by radio static

²**static** n : noise produced in a radio or television receiver by atmospheric or other electrical disturbances

stat·in \ˈsta-t⁽ə⁾n\ n : any of a group of drugs that inhibit the synthesis of cholesterol

¹**sta·tion** \ˈstā-shən\ n 1 : the place where a person or thing stands or is assigned to remain 2 : a regular stopping place on a transportation route : DEPOT 3 : a place where a fleet is assigned for duty 4 : a stock farm or ranch esp. in Australia or New Zealand 5 : social standing 6 : a complete assemblage of radio or television equipment for sending or receiving

²**station** vb : to assign to a station

sta·tion·ary \ˈstā-shə-ˌner-ē\ adj 1 : fixed in a station, course, or mode 2 : unchanging in condition ⟨a ∼ population⟩

stationary front n : the boundary between two air masses neither of which is advancing

station break n : a pause in a radio or television broadcast to announce the identity of the network or station

sta·tio·ner \ˈstā-shə-nər\ n : one that sells stationery

sta·tio·nery \ˈstā-shə-ˌner-ē\ n : materials (as paper, pens, or ink) for writing; esp : letter paper with envelopes

station wagon n : an automobile having a long interior, one or more folding or removable rear seats, and usu. a door at the rear

sta·tis·tic \stə-ˈtis-tik\ n 1 : a single term or datum in a collection of statistics 2 : a quantity (as the mean) that is computed from a sample

sta·tis·tics \-tiks\ n sing or pl [G Statistik study of political facts and figures, fr. NL statisticus of politics, fr. L State state] : a branch of mathematics dealing with the collection, analysis, and interpretation of masses of numerical data; also : a collection of such numerical data — **sta·tis·ti·cal** \-ti-kəl\ adj — **sta·tis·ti·cal·ly** \-ti-k⁽ə⁾lē\ adv — **stat·is·ti·cian** \ˌsta-tə-ˈsti-shən\ n

stat·u·ary \ˈsta-chə-ˌwer-ē\ n, pl -ar·ies 1 : the art of making statues 2 : STATUES

stat·ue \ˈsta-chü\ n : a likeness (as of a person or animal) sculptured, modeled, or cast in a solid substance

stat·u·esque \ˌsta-chə-ˈwesk\ adj : tall and shapely

stat·u·ette \ˌsta-chə-ˈwet\ n : a small statue

stat·ure \ˈsta-chər\ n 1 : natural height (as of a person) 2 : quality or status gained (as by achievement)

sta·tus \ˈstā-təs, ˈsta-\ n 1 : the condition of a person in the eyes of others or of the law 2 : state or condition with respect to circumstances

sta·tus quo \-ˈkwō\ n [L, state in which] : the existing state of affairs

stat·ute \ˈsta-chüt\ n : a law enacted by a legislative body

stat·u·to·ry \ˈsta-chə-ˌtòr-ē\ adj : imposed by statute : LAWFUL

statutory rape n : sexual intercourse with a person who is below the statutory age of consent

¹**staunch** var of ¹STANCH

²**staunch** \ˈstònch, ˈstänch\ adj 1 : WATERTIGHT ⟨a ∼ ship⟩ 2 : FIRM, STRONG; also : STEADFAST, LOYAL ⟨a ∼ supporter⟩ ♦ **Synonyms** RESOLUTE, CONSTANT, TRUE, FAITHFUL — **staunch·ly** adv

¹**stave** \ˈstāv\ n 1 : CUDGEL, STAFF 2 : any of several narrow strips of wood placed edge to edge to make something (as a barrel) 3 : STANZA

²**stave** vb **staved** or **stove** \ˈstōv\; **stav·ing** 1 : to break in the staves of; also : to break a hole in 2 : to drive or thrust away ⟨∼ off hunger⟩

staves pl of STAFF

¹**stay** \ˈstā\ n 1 : a strong rope or wire used to support a mast 2 : ¹GUY

²**stay** vb **stayed** \ˈstād\ also **staid** \ˈstād\;

stay·ing 1 : PAUSE, WAIT 2 : REMAIN 3 : to stand firm 4 : LIVE, DWELL 5 : DELAY, POSTPONE 6 : to last out (as a race) 7 : STOP, CHECK 8 : to satisfy (as hunger) for a time ♦ *Synonyms* REMAIN, ABIDE, LINGER, TARRY

³**stay** n 1 : STOP, HALT 2 : a residence or sojourn in a place

⁴**stay** n 1 : PROP, SUPPORT 2 : CORSET — usu. used in pl.

⁵**stay** vb : to hold up : PROP

staying power n : STAMINA

stbd abbr starboard

std abbr standard

STD \ˌes-(ˌ)tē-ˈdē\ n : SEXUALLY TRANSMITTED DISEASE

Ste abbr [F sainte] saint (female)

stead \ˈsted\ n 1 : ADVANTAGE ⟨stood him in good ~⟩ 2 : the place or function ordinarily occupied or carried out by another ⟨acted in his brother's ~⟩

stead·fast \ˈsted-ˌfast\ adj 1 : firmly fixed in place 2 : not subject to change 3 : firm in belief, determination, or adherence : LOYAL ♦ *Synonyms* RESOLUTE, TRUE, FAITHFUL, STAUNCH — **stead·fast·ly** adv — **stead·fast·ness** n

¹**steady** \ˈste-dē\ adj **steadi·er; -est** 1 : direct or sure in movement; *also* : CALM 2 : FIRM, FIXED ⟨held the pole ~⟩ 3 : STABLE ⟨~ prices⟩ 4 : not easily disturbed 5 : RELIABLE ⟨~ friends⟩ 6 : temperate in character or demeanor ♦ *Synonyms* UNIFORM, EVEN — **steadi·ly** \ˈsted-ə-lē\ adv — **steadi·ness** \ˈsted-ē-nəs\ n — **steady** adv

²**steady** vb **stead·ied; steady·ing** : to make or become steady

steak \ˈstāk\ n : a slice of meat and esp. beef; *also* : a slice of a large fish

¹**steal** \ˈstēl\ vb **stole** \ˈstōl\; **sto·len** \ˈstō-lən\; **steal·ing** 1 : to take and carry away without right or permission 2 : to come or go secretly or gradually 3 : to get for oneself slyly or by skill and daring ⟨~ a kiss⟩ ⟨~ the ball in basketball⟩ 4 : to gain or attempt to gain a base in baseball by running without the aid of a hit or an error ♦ *Synonyms* PILFER, FILCH, PURLOIN, SWIPE

²**steal** n 1 : an act of stealing 2 : BARGAIN

¹**stealth** \ˈstelth\ n 1 : secret or unobtrusive procedure 2 : an aircraft design intended to produce a weak radar return

²**stealth** adj : STEALTHY ⟨a ~ campaign⟩

stealthy \ˈstel-thē\ adj **stealth·i·er; -est** : done by stealth : FURTIVE, SLY ⟨a ~ burglar⟩ ♦ *Synonyms* SECRET, COVERT, CLANDESTINE, SURREPTITIOUS, UNDERHANDED — **stealth·i·ly** \ˈstel-thə-lē\ adv

¹**steam** \ˈstēm\ n 1 : the vapor into which water is changed when heated to the boiling point 2 : water vapor when compressed so that it supplies heat and power 3 : POWER, FORCE, ENERGY — **steamy** adj

²**steam** vb 1 : to pass off as vapor 2 : to emit vapor 3 : to move by or as if by the agency of steam — **steam·er** n

steam·boat \ˈstēm-ˌbōt\ n : a boat driven by steam

steam engine n : a reciprocating engine having a piston driven by steam

steam·fit·ter \ˈstēm-ˌfi-tər\ n : a worker who puts in or repairs equipment (as steam pipes) for heating, ventilating, or refrigerating systems

steam·punk \ˈstēm-ˌpəŋk\ n : science fiction involving historical or imagined steam-powered technology

steam·roll·er \-ˌrō-lər\ n : a machine for compacting roads or pavements — **steam·roll·er** *also* **steam·roll** \-ˌrōl\ vb

steam·ship \-ˌship\ n : a ship driven by steam

steed \ˈstēd\ n : HORSE

¹**steel** \ˈstēl\ n 1 : iron treated with intense heat and mixed with carbon to make it hard and tough 2 : an article made of steel 3 : a quality (as hardness of mind) that suggests steel — **steel** adj — **steely** adj

²**steel** vb : to fill with courage or determination ⟨~ed himself for her rage⟩

steel wool n : long fine steel shavings used esp. for cleaning and polishing

¹**steep** \ˈstēp\ adj 1 : having a very sharp slope : PRECIPITOUS 2 : too high ⟨~ prices⟩ — **steep·ly** adv — **steep·ness** n

²**steep** n : a steep slope

³**steep** vb 1 : to soak in a liquid; *esp* : to extract the essence of by soaking ⟨~ tea⟩ 2 : SATURATE ⟨~ed in learning⟩

stee·ple \ˈstē-pəl\ n : a tall tapering structure built on top of a church tower; *also* : a church tower

stee·ple·chase \-ˌchās\ n [fr. the use of church steeples as landmarks to guide the riders] : a horse race across country; *also* : a race over a course obstructed by hurdles

¹**steer** \ˈstir\ n : a male bovine animal castrated before sexual maturity and usu. raised for beef

²**steer** vb 1 : to direct the course of (as by a rudder or wheel) 2 : GUIDE, CONTROL 3 : to pursue a course of action 4 : to be subject to guidance or direction — **steers·man** \ˈstirz-mən\ n

steer·age \ˈstir-ij\ n 1 : DIRECTION, GUIDANCE 2 : a section in a passenger ship for passengers paying the lowest fares

stego·sau·rus \ˌste-gə-ˈsȯr-əs\ n : any of a genus of plant-eating armored dinosaurs with a series of bony plates along the backbone

stein \ˈstīn\ n : an earthenware mug

stel·lar \ˈste-lər\ adj : of or relating to stars : resembling a star

¹**stem** \ˈstem\ n 1 : the main stalk of a plant; *also* : a plant part that supports another part (as a leaf or fruit) 2 : the bow of a ship 3 : a line of ancestry : STOCK 4 : that part of an inflected word which remains unchanged throughout a given inflection 5 : something resembling the stem of a plant — **stem·less** adj — **stemmed** \ˈstemd\ adj

²**stem** vb **stemmed; stem·ming** : to have a specified source : DERIVE

³**stem** vb **stemmed; stem·ming** : to make headway against ⟨~ the tide⟩

⁴stem *vb* **stemmed; stem·ming** : to stop or check by or as if by damming

STEM *abbr* science, technology, engineering, and math

stem cell *n* : an undifferentiated cell that may give rise to many different types of cells

stench \'stench\ *n* : STINK

sten·cil \'sten-səl\ *n* [prob. ultim. fr. ME *stanseld* brightly ornamented, fr. AF *estencelé* spangled, pp. of *estenceler* to sparkle, fr. *estencele* spark, fr. VL *stincilla, alter. of L *scintilla*] : an impervious material (as metal or paper) perforated with lettering or a design through which a substance (as ink or paint) is applied to a surface to be printed — **stencil** *vb*

ste·nog·ra·phy \stə-'nä-grə-fē\ *n* : the art or process of writing in shorthand — **ste·nog·ra·pher** \-fər\ *n* — **steno·graph·ic** \ˌste-nə-'gra-fik\ *adj*

ste·no·sis \stə-'nō-səs\ *n, pl* **-no·ses** \-ˌsēz\ : a narrowing of a bodily passage or orifice

stent \'stent\ *n* : a short narrow tube inserted into an anatomical vessel esp. to keep a passage open

sten·to·ri·an \sten-'tȯr-ē-ən\ *adj* : extremely loud ⟨~ tones⟩

¹step \'step\ *n* **1** : a rest for the foot in ascending or descending : STAIR **2** : an advance made by raising one foot and putting it down elsewhere **3** : manner of walking **4** : a small space or distance **5** : a degree, rank, or plane in a series **6** : a sequential measure leading to a result

²step *vb* **stepped; step·ping 1** : to advance or recede by steps **2** : to go on foot : WALK **3** : to move along briskly **4** : to press down with the foot **5** : to measure by steps **6** : to construct or arrange in or as if in steps

step aerobics *n sing or pl* : aerobics that involves repeatedly stepping on and off a raised platform

step aside *vb* : STEP DOWN 1

step-broth·er \'step-ˌbrə-thər\ *n* : the son of one's stepparent by a former marriage

step·child \-ˌchī(-ə)ld\ *n* : a child of one's husband or wife by a former marriage

step·daugh·ter \-ˌdȯ-tər\ *n* : a daughter of one's wife or husband by a former marriage

step down *vb* **1** : to give up a position : RETIRE, RESIGN **2** : to lower (a voltage) by means of a transformer

step·fa·ther \-ˌfä-thər\ *n* : the husband of one's mother when distinct from one's natural or legal father

step·lad·der \'step-ˌla-dər\ *n* : a light portable set of steps in a hinged frame

step·moth·er \-ˌmə-thər\ *n* : the wife of one's father when distinct from one's natural or legal mother

step·par·ent \-ˌper-ənt\ *n* : a person who is a stepfather or stepmother

steppe \'step\ *n* [Russ *step'*] : dry level grass-covered treeless land in regions of wide temperature range esp. in southeastern Europe and Asia

step·sis·ter \'step-ˌsis-tər\ *n* : the daughter of one's stepparent by a former marriage

step·son \-ˌsən\ *n* : a son of one's wife or husband by a former marriage

step up *vb* **1** : to increase (a voltage) by means of a transformer **2** : INCREASE, ACCELERATE **3** : to come forward — **step–up** \'step-ˌəp\ *n*

ster *abbr* sterling

ste·reo \'ster-ē-ˌō, 'stir-\ *n, pl* **ste·re·os** **1** : stereophonic reproduction **2** : a stereophonic sound system — **stereo** *adj*

ste·reo·phon·ic \ˌster-ē-ə-'fä-nik, ˌstir-\ *adj* : of or relating to sound reproduction designed to create the effect of listening to the original — **ste·reo·phon·i·cal·ly** \-'fä-ni-k(ə-)lē\ *adv*

ster·e·o·scope \'ster-ē-ə-ˌskōp, 'stir-\ *n* [Gk *stereos* solid + *-skopion* means for viewing] : an optical instrument that blends two slightly different pictures of the same subject to give the effect of depth

ste·reo·scop·ic \ˌster-ē-ə-'skä-pik, ˌstir-\ *adj* **1** : of or relating to the stereoscope **2** : characterized by the seeing of objects in three dimensions ⟨~ vision⟩ — **ste·reo·scop·i·cal·ly** \-'skä-pi-k(ə-)lē\ *adv* — **ste·re·os·co·py** \ˌster-ē-'äs-kə-pē, ˌstir-\ *n*

ste·reo·type \'ster-ē-ə-ˌtīp, 'stir-\ *n* **1** : a metal printing plate cast from a mold made from set type **2** : something agreeing with a pattern; *esp* : an idea that many people have about a thing or a group and that may often be untrue or only partly true — **stereotype** *vb* — **ste·reo·typ·i·cal** \ˌster-ē-ə-'ti-pi-kəl\ *adj* — **ste·reo·typ·i·cal·ly** \-pi-k(ə-)lē\ *adv*

ste·reo·typed \-ˌtīpt\ *adj* : lacking originality or individuality ♦ **Synonyms** TRITE, CLICHÉD, COMMONPLACE, HACKNEYED, STALE, THREADBARE

ster·ile \'ster-əl\ *adj* **1** : unable to bear fruit, crops, or offspring **2** : free from living things and esp. germs — **ste·ril·i·ty** \stə-'ri-lə-tē\ *n*

ster·il·ize \'ster-ə-ˌlīz\ *vb* **-ized; -iz·ing** : to make sterile; *esp* : to free from germs — **ster·il·i·za·tion** \ˌster-ə-lə-'zā-shən\ *n* — **ster·il·iz·er** \'ster-ə-ˌlī-zər\ *n*

¹ster·ling \'stər-liŋ\ *n* **1** : British money **2** : sterling silver

²sterling *adj* **1** : of, relating to, or calculated in terms of British sterling **2** : having a fixed standard of purity represented by an alloy of 925 parts of silver with 75 parts of copper **3** : made of sterling silver **4** : EXCELLENT ⟨a ~ record of achievement⟩

¹stern \'stərn\ *adj* **1** : SEVERE, AUSTERE ⟨~ taskmasters⟩ **2** : STOUT, STURDY ⟨~ resolve⟩ — **stern·ly** *adv* — **stern·ness** *n*

²stern *n* : the rear end of a boat

ster·num \'stər-nəm\ *n, pl* **sternums** or **ster·na** \-nə\ : a long flat bone or cartilage at the center front of the chest connecting the ribs of the two sides

ste·roid \'stir-ˌȯid, 'ster-\ *n* : any of various compounds including numerous hormones (as anabolic steroids) and sugar derivatives — **steroid** or **ste·roi·dal** \stə-'rȯi-d³l\ adj

stetho·scope \'ste-thə-ˌskōp\ n : an instrument used to detect and listen to sounds produced in the body

ste·ve·dore \'stē-və-ˌdȯr\ n [Sp estibador, fr. estibar to pack, fr. L stipare to press together] : one who works at loading and unloading ships

ste·via \'stē-vē-ə\ n [NL, plant from which it is derived, fr. Petrus Stevus †1555 Sp. botanist] : a plant-derived powder used as a noncaloric sweetener

¹**stew** \'stü, 'styü\ n 1 : a dish of stewed meat and vegetables served in gravy 2 : a state of agitation, worry, or resentment

²**stew** vb 1 : to boil slowly : SIMMER 2 : to be in a state of agitation, worry, or resentment ⟨~ed about her predicament⟩

stew·ard \'stü-ərd, 'styü-\ n [ME, fr. OE stīweard, fr. stī, stīg hall, sty + weard ward] 1 : one employed on a large estate to manage domestic concerns 2 : one who supervises the provision and distribution of food (as on a ship); also : an employee on a ship or airplane who serves passengers 3 : one actively concerned with the direction of the affairs of an organization — **stew·ard·ship** n

stew·ard·ess \'stü-ər-dəs, 'styü-\ n : a woman who is a steward esp. on an airplane

stg abbr sterling

¹**stick** \'stik\ n 1 : a cut or broken branch or twig; also : a long slender piece of wood : ROD, STAFF 3 : something resembling a stick 4 : a dull uninteresting person 5 pl : remote usu. rural areas

²**stick** vb stuck \'stək\; **stick·ing** 1 : STAB, PRICK 2 : IMPALE 3 : ATTACH, FASTEN 4 : to thrust or project in some direction or manner 5 : to be unable to proceed or move freely 6 : to hold fast by or as if by gluing : ADHERE 7 : to hold to something firmly or closely : CLING 8 : to become jammed or blocked ⟨the door always ~s⟩

stick·er \'sti-kər\ n : one that sticks (as a bur) or causes sticking (as glue); esp : an adhesive label

sticker shock n : astonishment and dismay on being informed of a product's unexpectedly high price

stick insect n : any of various usu. wingless insects with a long round body resembling a stick

stick·ler \'sti-klər, -kə-lər\ n : one who insists on exactness or completeness

stick shift n : a manually operated automobile gearshift usu. mounted on the floor

stick-to-it-ive·ness \stik-'tü-ə-tiv-nəs\ n : dogged perseverance : TENACITY

stick up vb : to rob at gunpoint — **stick-up** \'stik-ˌəp\ n

sticky \'sti-kē\ adj **stick·i·er; -est** 1 : ADHESIVE 2 : VISCOUS, GLUEY 3 : tending to stick ⟨~ valve⟩ 4 : DIFFICULT ⟨a ~ problem⟩

¹**stiff** \'stif\ adj 1 : not pliant : RIGID 2 : not limber ⟨~ joints⟩; also : TENSE, TAUT 3 : not flowing or working easily ⟨~ paste⟩ 4 : not natural and easy : FORMAL 5 : STRONG, FORCEFUL ⟨~ breeze⟩ 6 : HARSH, SEVERE ⟨a ~ penalty⟩ ♦ *Synonyms* INFLEXIBLE, INELASTIC — **stiff·ly** adv — **stiff·ness** n

²**stiff** vb : to refuse to pay or tip

stiff–arm \'stif-ˌärm\ vb : to treat with disdain or neglect ⟨~ed her advice⟩

stiff·en \'sti-fən\ vb : to make or become stiff — **stiff·en·er** n

stiff–necked \'stif-'nekt\ adj : STUBBORN, HAUGHTY ⟨too ~ to ask for help⟩

sti·fle \'stī-fəl\ vb **sti·fled; sti·fling** 1 : to kill by depriving of or die from lack of oxygen or air : SMOTHER 2 : to keep in check by effort : SUPPRESS ⟨~ a sneeze⟩ — **sti·fling·ly** adv

stig·ma \'stig-mə\ n, pl **stig·ma·ta** \stig-'mä-tə, 'stig-mə-tə\ or **stigmas** [L] 1 : a mark of disgrace or discredit 2 stigmata pl : bodily marks resembling the wounds of the crucified Jesus 3 : the upper part of the pistil of a flower that receives the pollen in fertilization — **stig·mat·ic** \stig-'ma-tik\ adj

stig·ma·tize \'stig-mə-ˌtīz\ vb **-tized; -tizing** 1 : to mark with a stigma 2 : to characterize as disgraceful ⟨was stigmatized by the scandal⟩

stile \'stī(-ə)l\ n : steps used for crossing a fence or wall

sti·let·to \stə-'le-tō\ n, pl **-tos** or **-toes** [It, dim. of stilo stylus, dagger] : a slender dagger

¹**still** \'stil\ adj 1 : MOTIONLESS 2 : making no sound : SILENT — **still·ness** n

²**still** vb : to make or become still

³**still** adv 1 : without motion ⟨sit ~⟩ 2 : up to and during this or that time 3 : in spite of that : NEVERTHELESS 4 : EVEN ⟨ran ~ faster⟩ 5 : YET ⟨has ~ to be recognized⟩

⁴**still** n 1 : STILLNESS, SILENCE 2 : a static photograph esp. from a motion picture

⁵**still** n 1 : DISTILLERY 2 : apparatus used in distillation

still·birth \'stil-ˌbərth\ n : the birth of a dead fetus

still·born \-'bȯrn\ adj : born dead

still life n, pl **still lifes** : a picture of inanimate objects

stilt \'stilt\ n : one of a pair of poles for walking with each having a step or loop for the foot to elevate the wearer above the ground; also : a polelike support of a structure above ground or water level

stilt·ed \'stil-təd\ adj : not easy and natural ⟨~ language⟩

Stil·ton \'stil-t³n\ n : a blue cheese of English origin

stim·u·lant \'sti-myə-lənt\ n 1 : an agent (as a drug) that temporarily increases the activity of an organism or any of its parts 2 : STIMULUS 3 : an alcoholic beverage — **stimulant** adj

stim·u·late \-ˌlāt\ vb **-lat·ed; -lat·ing** : to make active or more active : ANIMATE, AROUSE ⟨~ interest⟩ ♦ *Synonyms* EXCITE, PROVOKE, MOTIVATE, QUICKEN — **stim·u·la·tion** \ˌsti-myə-'lā-shən\ n — **stim·u·la·tive** \'sti-myə-ˌlā-tiv\ adj —

stim·u·la·tor \-ˌlā-tər\ n — **stim·u·la·to·ry** \-lə-ˌtȯr-ē\ adj

stim·u·lus \'sti-myə-ləs\ n, pl **-li** \-ˌlī\ [L] **1** : something that moves to activity **2** : an agent that directly influences the activity of a living organism or one of its parts

¹**sting** \'stiŋ\ vb **stung** \'stəŋ\; **sting·ing 1** : to prick painfully esp. with a sharp or poisonous process **2** : to cause to suffer acutely — **sting·er** n

²**sting** n **1** : an act of stinging; also : a resultant wound, sore, or pain **2** : a pointed often venom-bearing organ (as of a bee) : STINGER **3** : an elaborate confidence game; esp : one worked by undercover police to trap criminals

sting·ray \'stiŋ-ˌrā\ n : any of numerous rays with sharp stinging spines on a whiplike tail

stin·gy \'stin-jē\ adj **stin·gi·er; -est** : not generous : giving or spending as little as possible — **stin·gi·ness** n

stink \'stiŋk\ vb **stank** \'staŋk\ or **stunk** \'stəŋk\; **stunk; stink·ing** : to give forth a strong and offensive smell; also : to be extremely bad in quality or repute — **stink** n — **stink·er** n

stink·bug \'stiŋk-ˌbəg\ n : any of various true bugs that emit a disagreeable odor

¹**stint** \'stint\ vb **1** : to be sparing or frugal **2** : to cut short in amount

²**stint** n **1** : an assigned amount of work **2** : RESTRAINT, LIMITATION **3** : a period of time spent at a particular activity

sti·pend \'stī-ˌpend, -pənd\ n [ME, alter. of stipendy, fr. L stipendium, fr. stips gift + pendere to weigh, pay] : a fixed sum of money paid periodically for services or to defray expenses

stip·ple \'sti-pəl\ vb **stip·pled; stip·pling 1** : to engrave by means of dots and light strokes **2** : to apply (as paint or ink) with small short touches — **stipple** n

stip·u·late \'sti-pyə-ˌlāt\ vb **-lat·ed; -lat·ing** : to make an agreement; esp : to make a special demand for something as a condition in an agreement — **stip·u·la·tion** \ˌsti-pyə-'lā-shən\ n

¹**stir** \'stər\ vb **stirred; stir·ring 1** : to move slightly **2** : AROUSE, EXCITE **3** : to mix, dissolve, or make by continued circular movement ⟨~ eggs into cake batter⟩ **4** : to move to activity (as by pushing, beating, or prodding)

²**stir** n **1** : a state of agitation or activity **2** : an act of stirring

stir-fry \'stər-ˌfrī\ vb : to fry quickly over high heat while stirring continuously — **stir-fry** n

¹**stir·ring** \'stər-iŋ\ adj **1** : ACTIVE, BUSTLING **2** : ROUSING, INSPIRING ⟨a ~ speech⟩

²**stirring** n : a beginning of activity ⟨the first ~s of revolution⟩

stir·rup \'stər-əp\ n [ME stirop, fr. OE stigrāp, lit., mounting rope] **1** : a light frame hung from a saddle to support the rider's foot **2** : STAPES

¹**stitch** \'stich\ n **1** : a sudden sharp pain esp. in the side **2** : one of the series of

loops formed by or over a needle in sewing

²**stitch** vb **1** : to fasten or join with stitches **2** : to make (as a design) with stitches **3** : SEW

stk abbr stock

stoat \'stōt\ n, pl **stoats** also **stoat** : the common Old and New World ermine esp. in its brown summer coat

¹**stock** \'stäk\ n **1** archaic : a block of wood **2** : a stupid person **3** : a wooden part of a thing serving as its support, frame, or handle **4** pl : a device for publicly punishing offenders consisting of a wooden frame with holes in which the feet and hands can be locked **5** : the original from which others derive; also : a group having a common origin : FAMILY **6** : LIVESTOCK **7** : a supply of goods **8** : the ownership element in a corporation divided to give the owners an interest and usu. voting power **9** : a company of actors playing at a particular theater and presenting a series of plays **10** : liquid in which meat, fish, or vegetables have been simmered that is used as a basis for soup, gravy, or sauce

²**stock** vb : to provide with stock

³**stock** adj : kept regularly for sale or use; also : commonly used : STANDARD

stock·ade \stä-'kād\ n [Sp estacada, fr. estaca stake, pale, of Gmc origin] : an enclosure (as of posts and stakes) for defense or confinement

stock·bro·ker \-ˌbrō-kər\ n : one who executes orders to buy and sell securities

stock car n : a racing car that is similar to a regular car

stock exchange n : a place where the buying and selling of securities is conducted

stock·hold·er \'stäk-ˌhōl-dər\ n : one who owns corporate stock

stock·i·nette or **stock·i·net** \ˌstä-kə-'net\ n : an elastic knitted fabric used esp. for infants' wear and bandages

stock·ing \'stä-kiŋ\ n : a close-fitting knitted covering for the foot and leg

stock market n **1** : STOCK EXCHANGE **2** : a market for stocks

stock·pile \'stäk-ˌpī(-ə)l\ n : a reserve supply esp. of something essential — **stockpile** vb

stocky \'stä-kē\ adj **stock·i·er; -est** : being short and relatively thick : STURDY
♦ **Synonyms** THICKSET, SQUAT, HEAVYSET, STUBBY

stock·yard \'stäk-ˌyärd\ n : a yard for stock; esp : one for livestock about to be slaughtered or shipped

stodgy \'stä-jē\ adj **stodg·i·er; -est 1** : thick in texture : HEAVY ⟨~ bread⟩ **2** : not interesting : DULL ⟨a ~ accountant⟩ **3** : extremely old-fashioned

sto·ic \'stō-ik\ n [ME, fr. L stoicus, fr. Gk stōïkos, lit., of the portico, fr. Stoa (Poikilē) the Painted Portico, portico at Athens where the philosopher Zeno taught] : one who suffers without complaining

stoic or **sto·i·cal** \-i-kəl\ adj : not affected by passion or feeling; esp : showing indifference to pain ♦ **Synonyms**

IMPASSIVE, PHLEGMATIC, APATHETIC, STOLID — **sto·i·cal·ly** \-i-k(ə-)lē\ adv — **sto·i·cism** \'stō-ə-ˌsi zəm\ n

stoke \'stōk\ vb **stoked; stok·ing 1 :** to stir up a fire **2 :** to tend and supply fuel to a furnace — **stok·er** n

STOL abbr short takeoff and landing

¹stole past of STEAL

²stole \'stōl\ n **1 :** a long narrow band worn round the neck by some members of the clergy **2 :** a long wide scarf or similar covering worn by women

stolen past part of STEAL

stol·id \'stä-ləd\ adj **:** not easily aroused or excited **:** showing little or no emotion ⟨a ~ face⟩ ✦ Synonyms PHLEGMATIC, APATHETIC, IMPASSIVE, STOIC — **sto·lid·i·ty** \stä-'li-də-tē\ n — **stol·id·ly** adv

sto·lon \'stō-lən, -ˌlän\ n **:** RUNNER 6

¹stom·ach \'stə-mək\ n **1 :** a saclike digestive organ of a vertebrate into which food goes from the mouth by way of the throat and which opens below into the intestine **2 :** a cavity in an invertebrate animal that is analogous to a stomach **3 :** ABDOMEN **4 :** desire for food caused by hunger **:** APPETITE **5 :** INCLINATION, DESIRE ⟨had no ~ for an argument⟩

²stomach vb **:** to bear without open resentment **:** put up with

stom·ach·ache \-ˌāk\ n **:** pain in or in the region of the stomach

stom·ach·er \'stə-mi-kər, -chər\ n **:** the front of a bodice often appearing between the laces of an outer garment (as in 16th century costume)

stomp \'stämp, 'stómp\ vb **:** STAMP — **stomp** n

¹stone \'stōn\ n **1 :** hardened earth or mineral matter **:** ROCK **2 :** a small piece of rock **3 :** a precious stone **:** GEM **4 :** CALCULUS **3 5 :** a hard stony seed (as of a date) or one (as of a plum) with a stony covering **6** pl usu **stone :** a British unit of weight equal to 14 pounds — **stony** also **ston·ey** \'stō-nē\ adj

²stone vb **stoned; ston·ing 1 :** to pelt or kill with stones **2 :** to remove the stones of (a fruit)

Stone Age n **:** the first known period of prehistoric human culture characterized by the use of stone tools

stoned \'stōnd\ adj **1 :** DRUNK **2 :** being under the influence of a drug

stone·wall \'stōn-ˌwól\ vb **:** to refuse to comply or cooperate with

stone-washed \'stōn-ˌwósht, -ˌwäsht\ adj **:** having been washed with stones during manufacture to create a softer look ⟨~ jeans⟩

stood past and past part of STAND

stooge \'stüj\ n **1 :** a person who plays a subordinate or compliant role to a principal **2 :** STRAIGHT MAN

stool \'stül\ n **1 :** a seat usu. without back or arms **2 :** FOOTSTOOL **3 :** a seat used while urinating or defecating **4 :** a discharge of fecal matter

stool pigeon n **:** DECOY, INFORMER

¹stoop \'stüp\ vb **1 :** to bend forward and downward **2 :** CONDESCEND **3 :** to lower oneself morally ⟨~ to lying⟩

²stoop n **1 :** an act of bending forward **2 :** a bent position of head and shoulders

³stoop n [D stoep] **:** a porch, platform, or entrance stairway at a house door

¹stop \'stäp\ vb **stopped; stop·ping 1 :** to close (an opening) by filling or covering closely **2 :** BLOCK, HALT **3 :** to cease to go on **4 :** to bring activity or operation to an end **5 :** STAY, TARRY ✦ Synonyms QUIT, DISCONTINUE, DESIST, CEASE

²stop n **1 :** END, CESSATION **2 :** a set of organ pipes of one tone quality; also **:** a control knob for such a set **3 :** OBSTRUCTION **4 :** PLUG, STOPPER **5 :** an act of stopping **:** CHECK **6 :** a delay in a journey **:** STAY **7 :** a place for stopping **8** chiefly Brit **:** any of several punctuation marks **9 :** a function of an electronic device that stops a functioning

stop–ac·tion \'stäp-'ak-shən\ n **:** STOP-MOTION

stop·gap \'stäp-ˌgap\ n **:** something that serves as a temporary expedient

stop·light \-ˌlīt\ n **:** TRAFFIC LIGHT

stop-mo·tion \'stäp-'mō-shən\ n **:** a filming technique in which successive positions of objects are photographed to produce the appearance of movement

stop·over \'stäp-ˌō-vər\ n **1 :** a stop at an intermediate point in one's journey **2 :** a stopping place on a journey

stop·page \'stä-pij\ n **:** the act of stopping **:** the state of being stopped

stop·per \'stä-pər\ n **:** something (as a cork) for sealing an opening

stop·watch \'stäp-ˌwäch\ n **:** a watch that can be started or stopped at will for exact timing

stor·age \'stór-ij\ n **1 :** space for storing; also **:** cost of storing **2 :** MEMORY 6 **3 :** the act of storing; esp **:** the safekeeping of goods (as in a warehouse)

storage battery n **:** a group of connected rechargeable electrochemical cells used to provide electric current

¹store \'stór\ vb **stored; stor·ing 1 :** to place or leave in a safe location for preservation or future use **2 :** to provide esp. for a future need ⟨~ information⟩

²store n **1 :** something accumulated and kept for future use **2 :** a large or ample quantity **3 :** STOREHOUSE **4 :** a retail business establishment

store·house \-ˌhaús\ n **:** a building for storing goods or supplies; also **:** an abundant source or supply

store·keep·er \-ˌkē-pər\ n **:** one who operates a retail store

store·room \-ˌrüm, -ˌrùm\ n **:** a room for storing goods or supplies

sto·ried \'stór-ēd\ adj **:** celebrated in story or history ⟨a ~ career⟩

stork \'stórk\ n **:** any of various large stout-billed Old World wading birds related to the herons and ibises

¹storm \'stórm\ n **1 :** a heavy fall of rain, snow, or hail with high wind **2 :** a violent outbreak or disturbance **3 :** a mass attack on a defended position — **storm·i·ly** \'stór-mə-lē\ adv — **storm·i·ness** \-mē-nəs\ n — **stormy** adj

²storm vb **:** to blow with violence; also

: to rain, snow, or hail heavily **2** : to make a mass attack against **3** : to be violently angry : RAGE **4** : to rush along furiously ⟨*~ed* out of the room⟩

¹sto·ry \'stōr-ē\ *n, pl* **stories** **1** : NARRATIVE, ACCOUNT **2** : REPORT, STATEMENT **3** : ANECDOTE **4** : SHORT STORY **5** : LIE, FALSEHOOD **6** : a news article or broadcast ♦ *Synonyms* UNTRUTH, TALE, CANARD

²story *also* **sto·rey** \'stōr-ē\ *n, pl* **stories** *also* **storeys** : a floor of a building or the space between two adjacent floor levels

sto·ry·tell·er \-ˌte-lər\ *n* : a teller of stories

sto·tin \stō-ˈtēn\ *n, pl* **sto·ti·nov** \stō-ˈtē-ˌnóv\ : a monetary unit equal to ¹⁄₁₀₀ tolar formerly used in Slovenia

sto·tin·ka \stō-ˈtiŋ-kə\ *n, pl* **-tin·ki** \-kē\ — see *lev* at MONEY table

¹stout \'staút\ *adj* **1** : BRAVE **2** : FIRM ⟨a *~* refusal⟩ **3** : STURDY **4** : STAUNCH, ENDURING ⟨*~* loyalty⟩ **5** : SOLID **6** : FORCEFUL, VIOLENT ⟨a *~* attack⟩ ⟨a *~* wind⟩ **7** : BULKY, THICKSET ♦ *Synonyms* FLESHY, FAT, PORTLY, CORPULENT, OBESE, PLUMP — **stout·ly** *adv* — **stout·ness** *n*

²stout *n* : a dark heavy ale

¹stove \'stōv\ *n* : an apparatus that burns fuel or uses electricity to provide heat (as for cooking or heating)

²stove *past and past part of* STAVE

stow \'stō\ *vb* **1** : HIDE, STORE ⟨*~* baggage⟩ **2** : to pack in a compact mass

stow·away \'stō-ə-ˌwā\ *n* : one who hides on a vehicle to ride free

STP *abbr* standard temperature and pressure

strad·dle \'stra-d²l\ *vb* **strad·dled; strad·dling** **1** : to stand, sit, or walk with legs spread apart **2** : to favor or seem to favor two apparently opposite sides — **straddle** *n*

strafe \'strāf\ *vb* **strafed; straf·ing** [G *Gott strafe England* may God punish England, propaganda slogan during World War I] : to fire upon with machine guns from a low-flying airplane

strag·gle \'stra-gəl\ *vb* **strag·gled; straggling** **1** : to wander from the direct course : ROVE, STRAY **2** : to become separated from others of the same kind — **strag·gler** *n* — **strag·gly** \'stra-g(ə-)lē\ *adj*

¹straight \'strāt\ *adj* **1** : free from curves, bends, angles, or irregularities **2** : not wandering from the main point or proper course ⟨*~* thinking⟩ **3** : HONEST ⟨a *~* answer⟩ **4** : having the elements in correct order **5** : UNMIXED, UNDILUTED ⟨*~* whiskey⟩ **6** : CONVENTIONAL, SQUARE **7** : HETEROSEXUAL

²straight *adv* : in a straight manner

³straight *n* **1** : a straight line, course, or arrangement **2** : the part of a racetrack between the last turn and the finish **3** : a sequence of five cards in a poker hand

straight–arm \'strāt-ˌärm\ *n* : an act of warding off a person with the arm fully extended — **straight–arm** *vb*

straight·away \'strā-tə-ˌwā\ *n* : a straight stretch (as at a racetrack)

straight·edge \'strāt-ˌej\ *n* : a piece of material with a straight edge for testing straight lines and surfaces or for cutting along or drawing straight lines

straight·en \'strā-t²n\ *vb* : to make or become straight

straight flush *n* : a poker hand containing five cards of the same suit in sequence

straight·for·ward \strāt-ˈfór-wərd\ *adj* **1** : FRANK, CANDID, HONEST ⟨a *~* account⟩ **2** : proceeding in a straight course or manner

straight man *n* : an entertainer who feeds lines to a comedian who replies with usu. humorous quips

straight shooter *n* : a thoroughly upright straightforward person

straight·way \'strāt-ˈwā, -ˌwā\ *adv* : IMMEDIATELY ⟨get *~* to work⟩

¹strain \'strān\ *n* [ME *streen* progeny, lineage, fr. OE *strēon* gain, acquisition] **1** : LINEAGE, ANCESTRY **2** : a group (as of people or plants) of presumed common ancestry **3** : an inherited or inherent character or quality ⟨a *~* of madness in the family⟩ **4** : STREAK, TRACE ⟨a *~* of fanaticism⟩ **5** : MELODY **6** : the general style or tone

²strain *vb* [ME, fr. AF *estreindre*, fr. L *stringere* to bind or draw tight, press together] **1** : to draw taut **2** : to exert to the utmost **3** : to strive violently **4** : to injure by improper or excessive use **5** : to filter or remove by filtering **6** : to stretch beyond a proper limit — **strain·er** *n*

³strain *n* **1** : excessive tension or exertion (as of body or mind) **2** : bodily injury from excessive tension, effort, or use; *esp* : one in which muscles or ligaments are unduly stretched usu. from a wrench or twist **3** : deformation of a material body under the action of applied forces

¹strait \'strāt\ *adj* [ME, fr. AF *estreit*, fr. L *strictus* strait, strict, fr. pp. of *stringere*] **1** *archaic* : STRICT **2** *archaic* : NARROW **3** *archaic* : CONSTRICTED **4** : DIFFICULT, STRAITENED

²strait *n* **1** : a narrow channel connecting two bodies of water **2** *pl* : DISTRESS

strait·en \'strā-t²n\ *vb* **1** : to hem in : CONFINE **2** : to subject to distress or difficulty ⟨*~ed* by misfortune⟩

strait·jack·et *also* **straight·jack·et** \'strāt-ˌja-kət\ *n* : a cover or garment of strong material (as canvas) used to bind the body and esp. the arms closely in restraining a violent prisoner or patient — **straitjacket** *vb*

strait·laced *or* **straight·laced** \-'lāst\ *adj* : strict in manners, morals, or opinion

¹strand \'strand\ *n* : SHORE, BEACH

²strand *vb* **1** : to run, drift, or drive upon the shore ⟨a *~ed* ship⟩ **2** : to place or leave in a helpless position

³strand *n* **1** : one of the fibers twisted or plaited together into a cord, rope, or cable; *also* : a cord, rope, or cable made up of such fibers **2** : a twisted or plaited ropelike mass ⟨a ~ of pearls⟩ — **strand-ed** \'stran-dəd\ *adj*

¹**strange** \'strānj\ *adj* **strang·er; strang-est** [ME, fr. AF *estrange*, fr. L *extraneus*, lit., external, fr. *extra* outside] **1** : of external origin, kind, or character **2** : NEW, UNFAMILIAR ⟨moved to a ~ neighborhood⟩ **3** : DISTANT 6 **4** : UNACCUSTOMED, INEXPERIENCED ⟨she was ~ to his ways⟩ ♦ *Synonyms* SINGULAR, PECULIAR, ECCENTRIC, ERRATIC, ODD, QUEER, QUAINT, CURIOUS — **strange·ly** *adv* — **strange·ness** *n*

²**strange** *n* : a quark with a charge of $-\frac{1}{3}$ and a measured energy of approximately 150 million electron volts

strang·er \'strān-jər\ *n* **1** : FOREIGNER **2** : INTRUDER **3** : a person with whom one is unacquainted

stran·gle \'straŋ-gəl\ *vb* **stran·gled; stran·gling 1** : to choke to death : THROTTLE **2** : STIFLE, SUPPRESS ⟨repression ~s free speech⟩ — **stran·gler** *n*

strangler fig *n* : any of several figs that begin life atop a host tree and then send down roots that surround it

stran·gu·late \'straŋ-gyə-ˌlāt\ *vb* **-lat·ed; -lat·ing** : STRANGLE, CONSTRICT **2** : to become so constricted as to stop circulation

stran·gu·la·tion \ˌstraŋ-gyə-'lā-shən\ *n* : the act or process of strangling or strangulating; *also* : the state of being strangled or strangulated

¹**strap** \'strap\ *n* : a narrow strip of flexible material used esp. for fastening, holding together, or wrapping

²**strap** *vb* **strapped; strap·ping 1** : to secure with a strap **2** : BIND, CONSTRICT **3** : to flog with a strap **4** : STROP

strap·less \-ləs\ *adj* : having no straps; *esp* : having no shoulder straps

¹**strap·ping** *adj* : LARGE, STRONG, HUSKY

²**strapping** *n* : material for a strap

strat·a·gem \'stra-tə-jəm, -ˌjem\ *n* **1** : a trick to deceive or outwit the enemy; *also* : a deceptive scheme **2** : skill in deception

strat·e·gy \'stra-tə-jē\ *n, pl* **-gies** [Gk *stratēgia* generalship, fr. *stratēgos* general, fr. *stratos* camp, army + *agein* to lead] **1** : the science and art of military command aimed at meeting the enemy under conditions advantageous to one's own force **2** : a careful plan or method esp. for achieving an end — **stra·te·gic** \strə-'tē-jik\ *adj* — **strat·e·gist** \'stra-tə-jist\ *n*

strat·i·fy \'stra-tə-ˌfī\ *vb* **-fied; -fy·ing** : to form or arrange in layers — **strat·i·fi·ca·tion** \ˌstra-tə-fə-'kā-shən\ *n*

stra·tig·ra·phy \strə-'ti-grə-fē\ *n* : geology that deals with rock strata — **stratigraph·ic** \ˌstra-tə-'gra-fik\ *adj*

strato·sphere \'stra-tə-ˌsfir\ *n* : the part of the earth's atmosphere between about 7 miles (11 kilometers) and 31 miles (50 kilometers) above the earth — **strato-spher·ic** \ˌstra-tə-'sfir-ik, -'sfer-\ *adj*

stra·tum \'strā-təm, 'stra-\ *n, pl* **stra·ta** \'strā-tə, 'stra-\ [NL, fr. L, spread, bed, fr. neut. of *stratus*, pp. of *sternere* to spread out] **1** : a bed, layer, or sheetlike mass (as of one kind of rock lying between layers of other kinds of rock) **2** : a level of culture; *also* : a group of people representing one stage in cultural development

¹**straw** \'strȯ\ *n* **1** : stalks of grain left after threshing; *also* : a single coarse dry stem (as of a grass) **2** : a thing of small worth : TRIFLE **3** : a tube (as of paper or plastic) for sucking up a beverage

²**straw** *adj* **1** : made of straw **2** : having no real force or validity ⟨a ~ vote⟩

straw·ber·ry \'strȯ-ˌber-ē, -bə-rē\ *n* : an edible juicy usu. red pulpy fruit of any of several low herbs with white flowers and long slender runners; *also* : one of these herbs

straw boss *n* : a foreman of a small group of workers

straw·flow·er \'strȯ-ˌflaů(-ə)r\ *n* : any of several plants whose flowers can be dried with little loss of form or color

¹**stray** \'strā\ *n* **1** : a domestic animal wandering at large or lost **2** : WAIF

²**stray** *vb* **1** : to wander or roam without purpose **2** : DEVIATE ⟨~ed from the topic⟩

³**stray** *adj* **1** : having strayed : separated from the group or the main body **2** : occurring at random ⟨~ remarks⟩

¹**streak** \'strēk\ *n* **1** : a line or mark of a different color or texture from its background **2** : a narrow band of light; *also* : a lightning bolt **3** : a slight admixture : TRACE **4** : a brief run (as of luck); *also* : an unbroken series ⟨a winning ~⟩

²**streak** *vb* **1** : to form streaks in or on **2** : to move very swiftly

¹**stream** \'strēm\ *n* **1** : a body of water (as a river) flowing on the earth; *also* : any body of flowing fluid (as water or gas) **2** : a continuous procession ⟨a ~ of traffic⟩

²**stream** *vb* **1** : to flow in or as if in a stream **2** : to pour out streams of liquid **3** : to trail out in length **4** : to move forward in a steady stream

stream·bed \'strēm-ˌbed\ *n* : the channel occupied by a stream

stream·er \'strē-mər\ *n* **1** : a long narrow ribbonlike flag **2** : a long ribbon on a dress or hat **3** : a newspaper headline that runs across the entire sheet **4** *pl* : AURORA

stream·ing \'strē-miŋ\ *adj* : relating to or being the transfer of data (as music or videos) in a continuous stream esp. for immediate processing or playback

stream·let \'strēm-lət\ *n* : a small stream

stream·lined \-ˌlīnd\ *adj* **1** : made with contours to reduce resistance to motion through water or air **2** : SIMPLIFIED **3** : MODERNIZED — **stream·line** *vb*

street \'strēt\ *n* [ME *strete*, fr. OE *strǣt*, fr. LL *strata* paved road, fr. L, fem. of *stratus*, pp. of *sternere* to spread out] **1** : a thoroughfare esp. in a city, town, or village **2** : the occupants of the houses on a street ⟨the whole ~ objects to the proposal⟩

street·car \-ˌkär\ *n* : a passenger vehicle running on rails on city streets

street fighter *n* : a tough belligerent person

street hockey *n* : a game resembling ice hockey played on a hard surface with hockey sticks and a small ball

street railway *n* : a company operating streetcars or buses

street·walk·er \'strēt-ˌwȯ-kər\ *n* : PROSTITUTE

strength \'streŋth\ *n* **1** : the quality of being strong : ability to do or endure : POWER **2** : TOUGHNESS, SOLIDITY **3** : power to resist attack **4** : INTENSITY **5** : force as measured in numbers ⟨the ~ of an army⟩

strength·en \'streŋ-thən\ *vb* : to make or become stronger — **strength·en·er** *n*

stren·u·ous \'stren-yə-wəs\ *adj* **1** : VIGOROUS, ENERGETIC **2** : requiring energy or stamina — **stren·u·ous·ly** *adv*

strep \'strep\ *n* : STREPTOCOCCUS

strep throat *n* : an inflammatory sore throat caused by streptococci and marked by fever, prostration, and toxemia

strep·to·coc·cus \ˌstrep-tə-ˈkä-kəs\ *n, pl* **-coc·ci** \-ˈkä-ˌkī, -ˈkäk-ˌsī, -ˈkä-ˌkē, -ˈkäk-ˌsē\ : any of various spherical bacteria that usu. grow in chains and include some causing serious diseases — **strep·to·coc·cal** \-kəl\ *adj*

strep·to·my·cin \-ˈmī-sᵊn\ *n* : an antibiotic produced by soil bacteria and used esp. in treating tuberculosis

¹**stress** \'stres\ *n* **1** : PRESSURE, STRAIN; *esp* : a force that tends to distort a body **2** : a factor that induces bodily or mental tension; *also* : a state induced by such a stress **3** : EMPHASIS **4** : relative prominence of sound **5** : ACCENT; *also* : any syllable carrying the accent — **stress·ful** \'stres-fəl\ *adj*

²**stress** *vb* **1** : to put pressure or strain on **2** : to put emphasis on : ACCENT

¹**stretch** \'strech\ *vb* **1** : to spread or reach out : EXTEND ⟨~ed out her arm⟩ **2** : to draw out in length or breadth : EXPAND **3** : to make tense : STRAIN **4** : EXAGGERATE ⟨~ed the truth⟩ **5** : to become extended without breaking ⟨rubber ~es easily⟩ — **stretchy** \'stre-chē\ *adj*

²**stretch** *n* **1** : an act of extending or drawing out beyond ordinary or normal limits **2** : a continuous extent in length, area, or time **3** : the extent to which something may be stretched **4** : either of the straight sides of a racecourse

³**stretch** *adj* : easily stretched ⟨~ pants⟩

¹**stretch·er** \'stre-chər\ *n* **1** : one that stretches **2** : a device for carrying a sick, injured, or dead person

²**stretcher** *vb* : to carry or transport on a stretcher

stretch marks *n pl* : striae on the skin (as of the abdomen) due to excessive stretching and rupture of elastic fibers (as from pregnancy)

strew \'strü\ *vb* **strewed; strewed** *or* **strewn** \'strün\; **strew·ing 1** : to spread by scattering **2** : to cover by or as if by scattering something over or on ⟨a floor *strewn* with toys⟩ **3** : DISSEMINATE

stria \'strī-ə\ *n, pl* **stri·ae** \'strī-ˌē\ **1** : STRIATION **3 2** : a stripe or line (as in the skin)

stri·at·ed muscle \'strī-ˌā-təd-\ *n* : muscle tissue made up of long thin cells with many nuclei and alternate light and dark stripes that includes esp. the muscle of the heart and muscle that moves the vertebrate skeleton and is mostly under voluntary control

stri·a·tion \strī-ˈā-shən\ *n* **1** : the state of being marked with stripes or lines **2** : arrangement of striations or striae **3** : a minute groove, scratch, or channel esp. when one of a parallel series

strick·en \'stri-kən\ *adj* **1** : afflicted by or as if by disease, misfortune, or sorrow **2** : WOUNDED ⟨was ~ by an arrow⟩

strict \'strikt\ *adj* **1** : allowing no evasion or escape : RIGOROUS ⟨~ discipline⟩ **2** : ACCURATE, PRECISE ⟨the ~ sense of the word⟩ ♦ **Synonyms** STRINGENT, RIGID — **strict·ly** *adv* — **strict·ness** *n*

stric·ture \'strik-chər\ *n* **1** : an abnormal narrowing of a bodily passage; *also* : the narrowed part **2** : hostile criticism : a critical remark

¹**stride** \'strīd\ *vb* **strode** \'strōd\; **strid·den** \'stri-dᵊn\; **strid·ing** : to walk or run with long regular steps — **strid·er** *n*

²**stride** *n* **1** : a long step **2** : a stage of progress **3** : manner of striding : GAIT

stri·dent \'strī-dᵊnt\ *adj* : harsh sounding : GRATING, SHRILL ⟨a ~ voice⟩

strife \'strīf\ *n* : CONFLICT, FIGHT, STRUGGLE ♦ **Synonyms** DISCORD, CONTENTION, DISSENSION

¹**strike** \'strīk\ *vb* **struck** \'strək\; **struck** *also* **strick·en** \'stri-kən\; **strik·ing 1** : to take a course : GO ⟨*struck* off through the brush⟩ **2** : to touch or hit sharply; *also* : to deliver a blow **3** : to produce by or as if by a blow ⟨*struck* terror in the foe⟩ **4** : to lower (as a flag or sail) **5** : to collide with; *also* : to injure or destroy by collision **6** : DELETE, CANCEL **7** : to produce by impressing ⟨*struck* a medal⟩; *also* : COIN ⟨~ a new cent⟩ **8** : to cause to sound ⟨~ a bell⟩ **9** : to afflict suddenly : lay low ⟨*stricken* with a high fever⟩ **10** : to appear to; *also* : to appear to as remarkable : IMPRESS **11** : to reach by reckoning ⟨~ an average⟩ **12** : to stop work in order to obtain a change in conditions of employment **13** : to cause (a match) to ignite by rubbing **14** : to come upon ⟨~ gold⟩ **15** : TAKE ON, ASSUME ⟨~ a pose⟩ — **strik·er** *n*

²**strike** *n* **1** : an act or instance of striking **2** : a sudden discovery of rich ore or oil deposits **3** : a pitched baseball that is swung at but not hit **4** : the knocking down of all the bowling pins with the 1st ball **5** : a military attack

strike·break·er \-ˌbrā-kər\ *n* : a person hired to replace a striking worker

strike·out \-ˌaȯt\ *n* : an out in baseball as a result of a batter's being charged with three strikes

strike out *vb* **1** : to enter upon a course of action **2** : to start out vigorously **3** : to make an out in baseball by a strikeout

strike–slip \'strīk-ˌslip\ *n* : a fault about which movement is predominantly horizontal

strike up *vb* **1** : to begin or cause to begin to sing or play ⟨*strike up* the band⟩ **2** : BEGIN ⟨~ a conversation⟩

strike zone *n* : the area over home plate through which a pitched baseball must pass to be called a strike

striking *adj* : attracting attention : very noticeable ♦ *Synonyms* ARRESTING, SALIENT, CONSPICUOUS, OUTSTANDING, REMARKABLE, PROMINENT — **strik·ing·ly** *adv*

¹string \'striŋ\ *n* **1** : a line usu. composed of twisted threads **2** : a series of things arranged as if strung on a cord **3** : a plant fiber (as a leaf vein) **4** *pl* : the stringed instruments of an orchestra ♦ *Synonyms* SUCCESSION, PROGRESSION, SEQUENCE, CHAIN, TRAIN

²string *vb* **strung** \'strəŋ\; **string·ing 1** : to provide with strings ⟨~ a racket⟩ **2** : to make tense **3** : to thread on or as if on a string ⟨~ pearls⟩ **4** : to hang, tie, or fasten by a string **5** : to take the strings out of ⟨~ beans⟩ **6** : to extend like a string

string bean *n* : a bean of one of the older varieties of kidney bean that have stringy fibers on the lines of separation of the pods; *also* : SNAP BEAN

string bikini *n* : a scanty bikini

string cheese *n* : cheese that can be pulled apart in narrow strips

stringed \'striŋd\ *adj* **1** : having strings ⟨~ instruments⟩ **2** : produced by strings

strin·gen·cy \'strin-jən-sē\ *n* **1** : STRICTNESS, SEVERITY **2** : SCARCITY ⟨~ of money⟩ — **strin·gent** \-jənt\ *adj*

string·er \'striŋ-ər\ *n* **1** : a long horizontal member in a framed structure or a bridge **2** : a news correspondent paid by the amount of copy

stringy \'striŋ-ē\ *adj* **string·i·er; -est 1** : resembling string esp. in tough, fibrous, or disordered quality ⟨~ meat⟩ ⟨~ hair⟩ **2** : lean and sinewy in build

¹strip \'strip\ *vb* **stripped** \'stript\ *also* **stript; strip·ping 1** : to take the covering or clothing from **2** : to take off one's clothes **3** : to pull or tear off **4** : to make bare or clear (as by cutting or grazing) **5** : PLUNDER, PILLAGE ♦ *Synonyms* DIVEST, DENUDE, DEPRIVE, DISMANTLE — **strip·per** *n*

²strip *n* **1** : a long narrow flat piece **2** : AIRSTRIP

¹stripe \'strīp\ *vb* **striped** \'strīpt\; **strip·ing** : to make stripes on

²stripe *n* **1** : a line or long narrow division having a different color from the background **2** : a strip of braid (as on a sleeve) indicating military rank or length of service **3** : TYPE, CHARACTER — **striped** \'strīpt, 'strī-pəd\ *adj*

striped bass *n* : a large black-striped marine bony fish that occurs along the Atlantic and Pacific coasts of the U.S. and is an excellent food and sport fish

strip·ling \'stri-pliŋ\ *n* : YOUTH, LAD

strip mall *n* : a long building or group of buildings housing several retail stores or service establishments

strip mine *n* : a mine that is worked from the earth's surface by the stripping of the topsoil — **strip–mine** *vb*

strip–tease \'strip-ˌtēz\ *n* : a burlesque act in which a performer removes clothing piece by piece — **strip·teas·er** *n*

strive \'strīv\ *vb* **strove** \'strōv\ *also* **strived** \'strīvd\; **striv·en** \'stri-vən\ *or* **strived; striv·ing 1** : to make effort : labor hard **2** : to struggle in opposition : CONTEND ♦ *Synonyms* ENDEAVOR, ATTEMPT, TRY, ASSAY

strobe \'strōb\ *n* **1** : STROBOSCOPE **2** : a device for high-speed intermittent illumination (as in photography)

stro·bo·scope \'strō-bə-ˌskōp\ *n* : an instrument for studying rapid motion by means of a rapidly flashing light

strode *past of* STRIDE

¹stroke \'strōk\ *vb* **stroked; strok·ing 1** : to rub gently **2** : to flatter in a manner designed to persuade

²stroke *n* **1** : the act of striking : BLOW, KNOCK **2** : a sudden action or process producing an impact ⟨~ of lightning⟩; *also* : an unexpected result **3** : sudden weakening or loss of consciousness or the power to move or feel caused by rupture or obstruction (as by a clot) of a blood vessel of the brain **4** : one of a series of movements against air or water to get through or over it ⟨the ~ of a bird's wing⟩ **5** : a rower who sets the pace for a crew **6** : a vigorous effort **7** : the sound of striking (as of a clock) **8** : a single movement with or as if with a tool or implement (as a pen)

stroll \'strōl\ *vb* : to walk in a leisurely or idle manner — **stroll** *n* — **stroll·er** *n*

strong \'strȯŋ\ *adj* **stron·ger** \'strȯŋ-gər\; **stron·gest** \'strȯŋ-gəst\ **1** : POWERFUL, VIGOROUS **2** : HEALTHY, ROBUST **3** : of a specified number ⟨an army 10 thousand ~⟩ **4** : not mild or weak **5** : VIOLENT ⟨~ wind⟩ **6** : ZEALOUS ⟨a ~ supporter⟩ **7** : not easily broken **8** : FIRM, SOLID ⟨~ beliefs⟩ ♦ *Synonyms* STOUT, STURDY, STALWART, TOUGH — **strong·ly** *adv*

strong–arm \'strȯŋ-ˈärm\ *adj* : having or using undue force ⟨~ operatives⟩

strong force *n* : the physical force responsible for binding together nucleons in the atomic nucleus

strong·hold \-ˌhōld\ *n* : a fortified place : FORTRESS

strong·man \-ˌman\ *n* : one who leads or controls by force of will and character or by military strength

stron·tium \'strän-chē-əm, 'strän-tē-əm\ *n* : a soft malleable metallic chemical element

¹strop \'sträp\ *n* : STRAP; *esp* : one for sharpening a razor

²strop *vb* **stropped; strop·ping** : to sharpen a razor on a strop

stro·phe \'strō-fē\ *n* [Gk *strophē,* lit., act of turning] : a division of a poem — **stroph·ic** \'strä-fik\ *adj*

strove *past of* STRIVE

struck *past and past part of* STRIKE

¹**struc·ture** \'strək-chər\ *n* [ME, fr. L *structura*, fr. *structus*, pp. of *struere* to heap up, build] **1** : the action of building : CONSTRUCTION **2** : something built (as a house or a dam); *also* : something made up of interdependent parts in a definite pattern of organization **3** : arrangement or relationship of elements (as particles, parts, or organs) in a substance, body, or system — **struc·tur·al** *adj*

²**structure** *vb* **struc·tured; struc·tur·ing** : to make into a structure

stru·del \'strü-dᵊl, 'shtrü-\ *n* [G, lit., whirlpool] : a pastry made of a thin sheet of dough rolled up with filling and baked ⟨apple ∼⟩

¹**strug·gle** \'strə-gəl\ *vb* **strug·gled; strug·gling 1** : to make strenuous efforts against opposition : STRIVE **2** : to proceed with difficulty or with great effort ♦ **Synonyms** ENDEAVOR, ATTEMPT, TRY, ASSAY

²**struggle** *n* **1** : CONTEST, STRIFE **2** : a violent effort or exertion

strum \'strəm\ *vb* **strummed; strumming** : to play on a stringed instrument by brushing the strings with the fingers ⟨∼ a guitar⟩

strum·pet \'strəm-pət\ *n* : PROSTITUTE

strung \'strəŋ\ *past and past part of* STRING

¹**strut** \'strət\ *vb* **strut·ted; strut·ting** : to walk with an affectedly proud gait

²**strut** *n* **1** : a bar or rod for resisting lengthwise pressure **2** : a haughty or pompous gait

strych·nine \'strik-,nīn, -nən, -,nēn\ *n* : a bitter poisonous plant alkaloid used as a poison (as for rats) and medicinally as a stimulant of the central nervous system

¹**stub** \'stəb\ *n* **1** : STUMP **2** **2** : a short blunt end **3** : a small part of each leaf (as of a checkbook) kept as a memorandum of the items on the detached part

²**stub** *vb* **stubbed; stub·bing** : to strike (as one's toe) against something

stub·ble \'stə-bəl\ *n* **1** : the cut stem ends of herbs and esp. grasses left in the soil after harvest **2** : a rough surface or growth resembling stubble ⟨his face covered with ∼⟩ — **stub·bly** \-b(ə-)lē\ *adj*

stub·born \'stə-bərn\ *adj* **1** : FIRM, DETERMINED **2** : done or continued in a willful, unreasonable, or persistent manner **3** : not easily controlled or remedied ⟨a ∼ cold⟩ — **stub·born·ly** *adv* — **stub·born·ness** *n*

stub·by \'stə-bē\ *adj* : short, blunt, and thick like a stub ⟨∼ fingers⟩

stuc·co \'stə-kō\ *n, pl* **stuccos** *or* **stuccoes** [It] : plaster for coating exterior walls — **stuc·coed** \'stə-kōd\ *adj*

stuck *past and past part of* STICK

stuck–up \'stək-'əp\ *adj* : CONCEITED

¹**stud** \'stəd\ *n* : a male animal and esp. a horse (**stud·horse** \-,hȯrs\) kept for breeding

²**stud** *n* **1** : one of the smaller uprights in a building to which the wall materials are fastened **2** : a removable device like a button used as a fastener or ornament ⟨shirt ∼s⟩ **3** : a projecting nail, pin, or rod

³**stud** *vb* **stud·ded; stud·ding 1** : to supply with or adorn with studs **2** : DOT ⟨the sky was *studded* with stars⟩

⁴**stud** *abbr* student

stud·book \'stəd-,bük\ *n* : an official record of the pedigree of purebred animals (as horses or dogs)

studding *n* : the studs in a building or wall

stu·dent \'stü-dᵊnt, 'styü-\ *n* : SCHOLAR, PUPIL; *esp* : one who attends a school

stud·ied \'stə-dēd\ *adj* : INTENTIONAL ⟨a ∼ insult⟩ ♦ **Synonyms** DELIBERATE, CONSIDERED, PREMEDITATED, DESIGNED

stu·dio \'stü-dē-,ō, 'styü-\ *n, pl* **-dios 1** : a place where an artist works; *also* : a place for the study of an art **2** : a place where motion pictures are made **3** : a place equipped for the transmission of radio or television programs

stu·di·ous \'stü-dē-əs, 'styü-\ *adj* : devoted to study — **stu·di·ous·ly** *adv*

¹**study** \'stə-dē\ *n, pl* **stud·ies 1** : the use of the mind to gain knowledge **2** : the act or process of learning about something **3** : careful examination **4** : INTENT, PURPOSE **5** : a branch of learning **6** : a room esp. for reading and writing

²**study** *vb* **stud·ied; study·ing 1** : to engage in study or the study of **2** : to consider attentively or in detail ♦ **Synonyms** CONSIDER, CONTEMPLATE, WEIGH

¹**stuff** \'stəf\ *n* [ME, fr. AF *estuffes* goods, fr. *estuffer* to fill in (with rubble), furnish, equip, of Gmc origin] **1** : personal property **2** : raw material **3** : a finished textile fabric; *esp* : a worsted fabric **4** : writing, talk, or ideas of little or transitory worth **5** : an unspecified material substance or aggregate of matter **6** : fundamental material **7** : special knowledge or capability

²**stuff** *vb* **1** : to fill by packing things in : CRAM **2** : to eat greedily : GORGE **3** : to prepare (as meat) by filling with a stuffing **4** : to fill (as a cushion) with a soft material **5** : to stop up : PLUG

stuffed shirt \'stəft-\ *n* : a smug, conceited, and usu. pompous and inflexibly conservative person

stuff·ing *n* : material used to fill tightly; *esp* : a mixture of bread crumbs and spices used to stuff food

stuffy \'stə-fē\ *adj* **stuff·i·er; -est 1** : STODGY **2** : lacking fresh air : CLOSE; *also* : blocked up ⟨a ∼ nose⟩

stul·ti·fy \'stəl-tə-,fī\ *vb* **-fied; -fy·ing 1** : to cause to appear foolish or stupid **2** : to impair, invalidate, or make ineffective **3** : to have a dulling effect on — **stul·ti·fi·ca·tion** \,stəl-tə-fə-'kā-shən\ *n*

stum·ble \'stəm-bəl\ *vb* **stum·bled; stum·bling 1** : to blunder morally **2** : to trip in walking or running **3** : to walk unsteadily; *also* : to speak or act in a blundering or clumsy manner **4** : to happen by chance — **stumble** *n*

stumbling block *n* : an obstacle to belief, understanding, or progress

¹stump \'stəmp\ *n* **1** : the base of a bodily part (as a leg or tooth) left after the rest is removed **2** : the part of a plant and esp. a tree remaining with the root after the trunk is cut off **3** : a place or occasion for political public speaking — **stumpy** *adj*

²stump *vb* **1** : BAFFLE, PERPLEX **2** : to clear (land) of stumps **3** : to tour (a region) making political speeches **4** : to walk clumsily and heavily

stun \'stən\ *vb* **stunned; stun·ning 1** : to make senseless or dizzy by or as if by a blow **2** : BEWILDER, STUPEFY ⟨*stunned* by the news⟩

stung *past and past part of* STING

stunk *past and past part of* STINK

stun·ning *adj* **1** : causing astonishment or disbelief **2** : strikingly beautiful — **stun·ning·ly** *adv*

¹stunt \'stənt\ *vb* : to hinder the normal growth or progress of

²stunt *n* : an unusual or spectacular feat

stu·pe·fy \'stü-pə-ˌfī, 'styü-\ *vb* **-fied; -fy·ing 1** : to make stupid, groggy, or insensible **2** : ASTONISH — **stu·pe·fac·tion** \ˌstü-pə-'fak-shən, ˌstyü-\ *n*

stu·pen·dous \stü-'pen-dəs, styü-\ *adj* : causing astonishment esp. because of great size or height ♦ **Synonyms** TREMENDOUS, PRODIGIOUS, MONUMENTAL, MONSTROUS — **stu·pen·dous·ly** *adv*

stu·pid \'stü-pəd, 'styü-\ *adj* [MF *stupide*, fr. L *stupidus*, fr. *stupēre* to be numb, astonished] **1** : very dull in mind **2** : showing or resulting from dullness of mind — **stu·pid·i·ty** \stü-'pi-də-tē, styü-\ *n* — **stu·pid·ly** *adv*

stu·por \'stü-pər, 'styü-\ *n* **1** : a condition of greatly dulled or completely suspended sense or feeling **2** : a state of extreme apathy or torpor often following stress or shock — **stu·por·ous** *adj*

stur·dy \'stər-dē\ *adj* **stur·di·er; -est** [ME, brave, stubborn, fr. AF *esturdi* stunned, fr. pp. of *esturdir* to stun, fr. VL **exturdire*, fr. L *ex-* + VL **turdus* simpleton, fr. L *turdus* thrush] **1** : STRONG, ROBUST **2** : RESOLUTE, UNYIELDING ♦ **Synonyms** STOUT, STALWART, TOUGH, TENACIOUS — **stur·di·ly** \-də-lē\ *adv* — **stur·di·ness** \-dē-nəs\ *n*

stur·geon \'stər-jən\ *n* : any of a family of large bony fishes including some whose roe are made into caviar

stut·ter \'stə-tər\ *vb* : to speak with involuntary disruption or blocking of sounds — **stutter** *n* — **stut·ter·er** *n*

stutter step *n* : a move made by a runner (as in football) done to fake a defender out of position

¹sty \'stī\ *n, pl* **sties** : PIGPEN

²sty *or* **stye** *n, pl* **sties** *or* **styes** : an inflamed swelling of a skin gland on the edge of an eyelid

¹style \'stī(-ə)l\ *n* **1** : mode of address : TITLE **2** : a way of speaking or writing; *esp* : one characteristic of an individual,

period, school, or nation ⟨ornate ∼⟩ **3** : manner or method of acting, making, or performing; *also* : a distinctive or characteristic manner **4** : a slender pointed instrument or process; *esp* : STYLUS **5** : a fashionable manner or mode **6** : overall excellence, skill, or grace in performance, manner, or appearance **7** : the custom followed in spelling, capitalization, punctuation, and typography — **sty·lis·tic** \stī-'lis-tik\ *adj*

²style *vb* **styled; styl·ing 1** : NAME, DESIGNATE **2** : to make or design in accord with a prevailing mode ⟨∼ hair⟩

styling *n* : the way in which something is styled

styl·ise *Brit var of* STYLIZE

styl·ish \'stī-lish\ *adj* : conforming to current fashion ♦ **Synonyms** MODISH, SMART, CHIC — **styl·ish·ly** *adv* — **styl·ish·ness** *n*

styl·ist \'stī-list\ *n* **1** : one (as a writer) noted for a distinctive style **2** : a developer or designer of styles

styl·ize \'stī-ˌlīz, 'stī-ə-\ *vb* **styl·ized; styl·iz·ing** : to conform to a style; *esp* : to represent or design according to a pattern or style rather than according to nature or tradition ⟨*stylized* flower prints⟩ — **styl·i·za·tion** \ˌstī-lə-'zā-shən\ *n*

sty·lus \'stī-ləs\ *n, pl* **styl·li** \'stī-ˌlī\ *also* **sty·lus·es** \'stī-lə-səz\ [L *stylus, stilus* spike, stylus] **1** : a pointed implement used by the ancients for writing on wax **2** : a phonograph needle **3** : a pen-shaped pointing device for entering data into a computer

sty·mie \'stī-mē\ *vb* **sty·mied; sty·mie·ing** : BLOCK, FRUSTRATE ⟨managed to ∼ the opposition⟩

styp·tic \'stip-tik\ *adj* : tending to check bleeding — **styptic** *n*

suave \'swäv\ *adj* [F, fr. MF, pleasant, sweet, fr. L *suavis*] : persuasively pleasing : smoothly agreeable ♦ **Synonyms** URBANE, SMOOTH, BLAND — **suave·ly** *adv* — **sua·vi·ty** \'swä-və-tē\ *n*

¹sub \'səb\ *n* : SUBSTITUTE — **sub** *vb*

²sub *n* : SUBMARINE

³sub *abbr* **1** subtract **2** suburb

sub- \'səb\ *prefix* **1** : under : beneath **2** : subordinate : secondary **3** : subordinate portion of : subdivision of **4** : with repetition of a process described in a simple verb so as to form, stress, or deal with subordinate parts or relations **5** : somewhat **6** : falling nearly in the category of : bordering on

sub·al·pine \ˌsəb-'al-ˌpīn\ *adj* **1** : of or relating to the region about the foot and lower slopes of the Alps **2** : of, relating to, or inhabiting high upland slopes esp. just below the timberline

sub·al·tern \sə-'bȯl-tərn\ *n* : SUBORDINATE; *esp* : a junior officer (as in the British army)

sub·as·sem·bly \ˌsəb-ə-'sem-blē\ *n* : an

| subacute | subagent | subarctic | subarea |
| subagency | subaqueous | | |

assembled unit to be incorporated with other units in a finished product

sub·atom·ic \ˌsəb-ə-ˈtä-mik\ adj : of or relating to the inside of the atom or to particles smaller than atoms

sub·clin·i·cal \ˌsəb-ˈkli-nə-kəl\ adj : not detectable by the usual clinical tests ⟨a ~ infection⟩

sub·com·pact \ˈsəb-ˈkäm-ˌpakt\ n : an automobile smaller than a compact

¹**sub·con·scious** \ˌsəb-ˈkän-chəs, ˈsəb-\ adj : existing in the mind without entering conscious awareness — **sub·con·scious·ly** adv — **sub·con·scious·ness** n

²**subconscious** n : mental activities just below the threshold of consciousness

sub·con·ti·nent \ˌsəb-ˈkän-tə-nənt\ n : a major subdivision of a continent — **sub·con·ti·nen·tal** \ˌsəb-ˌkän-tə-ˈnen-tᵊl\ adj

sub·di·vide \ˌsəb-də-ˈvīd, ˈsəb-də-ˌvīd\ vb : to divide the parts of into more parts; esp : to divide (a tract of land) into building lots — **sub·di·vi·sion** \-ˈvi-zhən, -ˌvi-\ n

sub·duc·tion \səb-ˈdək-shən\ n : the descent of the edge of one crustal plate beneath the edge of an adjacent plate

sub·due \səb-ˈdü, -ˈdyü\ vb **sub·dued; sub·du·ing** 1 : to bring into subjection : VANQUISH 2 : to bring under control : CURB 3 : to reduce the intensity of

subj abbr 1 subject 2 subjunctive

¹**sub·ject** \ˈsəb-jikt\ n [ME suget, subget, fr. AF, fr. L subjectus one under authority & subjectum subject of a proposition, fr. subicere to subject, lit., to throw under, fr. sub- under + jacere to throw] 1 : a person under the authority of another 2 : a person subject to a sovereign 3 : an individual that is studied or experimented on 4 : the person or thing discussed or treated : TOPIC, THEME 5 : a word or word group denoting that of which something is predicated

²**subject** adj 1 : being under the power or rule of another 2 : LIABLE, EXPOSED ⟨~ to floods⟩ 3 : dependent on some act or condition ⟨appointment ~ to senate approval⟩ ♦ **Synonyms** SUBORDINATE, SECONDARY, TRIBUTARY, COLLATERAL, DEPENDENT

³**sub·ject** \səb-ˈjekt\ vb 1 : to bring under control : CONQUER 2 : to make liable 3 : to cause to undergo or endure — **sub·jec·tion** \-ˈjek-shən\ n

sub·jec·tive \(ˌ)səb-ˈjek-tiv\ adj 1 : of, relating to, or constituting a subject 2 : of, relating to, or arising within one's self or mind in contrast to what is outside : PERSONAL ⟨~ judgments⟩ ⟨a ~ sensation⟩ — **sub·jec·tive·ly** adv — **sub·jec·tiv·i·ty** \-ˌjek-ˈti-və-tē\ n

subject matter n : matter presented for consideration, discussion, or study

sub·join \(ˌ)səb-ˈjöin\ vb : APPEND ⟨~ed a statement of expenses to her report⟩

sub ju·di·ce \(ˌ)sùb-ˈyü-di-ˌkā, ˈsüb-jü-də-(ˌ)sē\ adv [L] : before a judge or court : not yet legally decided

sub·ju·gate \ˈsəb-ji-ˌgat\ vb **-gat·ed; -gat·ing** : CONQUER, SUBDUE; also : ENSLAVE ♦ **Synonyms** REDUCE, OVERCOME, OVERTHROW, VANQUISH, DEFEAT, BEAT — **sub·ju·ga·tion** \ˌsəb-ji-ˈgā-shən\ n

sub·junc·tive \səb-ˈjəŋk-tiv\ adj : of, relating to, or constituting a verb form that represents an act or state as contingent or possible or viewed emotionally (as with desire) ⟨the ~ mood⟩ — **subjunctive** n

sub·lease \ˈsəb-ˌlēs, -ˈlēs\ n : a lease by a lessee of part or all of leased premises to another person with the original lessee retaining some right under the original lease — **sublease** vb

¹**sub·let** \ˈsəb-ˈlet\ vb **-let; -let·ting** : to let all or a part of (a leased property) to another; also : to rent (a property) from a lessee

²**sublet** \-ˌlet\ n : property obtained by or available through a sublease

sub·li·mate \ˈsə-blə-ˌmāt\ vb **-mat·ed; -mat·ing** 1 : SUBLIME 2 : to direct the expression of (as a desire or impulse) from a primitive to a more socially and culturally acceptable form — **sub·li·ma·tion** \ˌsə-blə-ˈmā-shən\ n

¹**sub·lime** \sə-ˈblīm\ vb **sub·limed; sub·lim·ing** : to pass or cause to pass directly from the solid to the vapor state

²**sublime** adj 1 : EXALTED, NOBLE 2 : having awe-inspiring beauty or grandeur ♦ **Synonyms** GLORIOUS, SPLENDID, SUPERB, RESPLENDENT, GORGEOUS — **sub·lime·ly** adv — **sub·lim·i·ty** \-ˈbli-mə-tē\ n

sub·lim·i·nal \(ˌ)səb-ˈli-mə-nᵊl, ˈsəb-\ adj [sub- + L limin-, limen threshold] 1 : inadequate to produce a sensation or mental awareness ⟨~ stimuli⟩ 2 : existing or functioning below the threshold of consciousness ⟨the ~ mind⟩ ⟨~ advertising⟩

sub·ma·chine gun \ˌsəb-mə-ˈshēn-ˌgən\ n : an automatic firearm fired from the shoulder or hip

¹**sub·ma·rine** \ˈsəb-mə-ˌrēn, ˌsəb-mə-ˈrēn\ adj : UNDERWATER; esp : UNDERSEA

²**submarine** n 1 : a naval vessel designed to operate underwater 2 : a large sandwich made from a long split roll with any of a variety of fillings

sub·merge \səb-ˈmərj\ vb **sub·merged; sub·merg·ing** 1 : to put or plunge under the surface of water 2 : INUNDATE — **sub·mer·gence** \-ˈmər-jəns\ n

sub·merse \səb-ˈmərs\ vb **sub·mersed;**

---

subatmospheric	subclassify	subentry	subhead
subaverage	subcommittee	subfamily	subheading
subbasement	subcontract	subfield	subhuman
subcategory	subcontractor	subfreezing	subkingdom
subcellular	subculture	subgenre	sublethal
subchapter	subcutaneous	subgenus	subliterate
subclass	subdiscipline	subgroup	

sub·mers·ing : SUBMERGE — **sub·mersion** \-'mər-zhən\ *n*

¹sub·mers·ible \səb-'mər-sə-bəl\ *adj* : capable of being submerged

²submersible *n* : something that is submersible; *esp* : a small underwater craft used for deep-sea research

sub·mi·cro·scop·ic \ˌsəb-ˌmī-krə-'skäpik\ *adj* : too small to be seen in an ordinary light microscope

sub·min·ia·ture \ˌsəb-'mi-nē-ə-ˌchu̇r, 'səb-, -'mi-ni-ˌchu̇r, -chər\ *adj* : very small

sub·mit \səb-'mit\ *vb* **sub·mit·ted; sub·mit·ting 1** : to commit to the discretion or decision of another or of others **2** : YIELD, SURRENDER **3** : to put forward as an opinion — **sub·mis·sion** \-'mi-shən\ *n* — **sub·mis·sive** \-'mi-siv\ *adj*

sub·nor·mal \ˌsəb-'nȯr-məl\ *adj* : falling below what is normal; *also* : having less of something and esp. intelligence than is normal — **sub·nor·mal·i·ty** \ˌsəb-nȯr-'ma-lə-tē\ *n*

sub·or·bit·al \ˌsəb-'ȯr-bə-tᵊl, 'səb-\ *adj* : being or involving less than one orbit

¹sub·or·di·nate \sə-'bȯr-də-nət\ *adj* **1** : of lower class or rank ⟨a ~ officer⟩ **2** : INFERIOR **3** : submissive to authority **4** : subordinated to other elements in a sentence : DEPENDENT ⟨~ clause⟩ ♦ *Synonyms* SECONDARY, SUBJECT, TRIBUTARY, COLLATERAL

²subordinate *n* : one that is subordinate

³sub·or·di·nate \sə-'bȯr-də-ˌnāt\ *vb* **-nat·ed; -nat·ing 1** : SUBDUE **2** : to place in a lower rank or class — **sub·or·di·na·tion** \-ˌbȯr-də-'nā-shən\ *n*

sub·orn \sə-'bȯrn\ *vb* **1** : to induce secretly to do an unlawful thing **2** : to induce to commit perjury — **sub·or·na·tion** \ˌsə-ˌbȯr-'nā-shən\ *n*

¹sub·poe·na \sə-'pē-nə\ *n* [ME *suppena*, fr. L *sub poena* under penalty] : a writ commanding the person named in it to attend court under penalty for failure to do so

²subpoena *vb* **-naed; -na·ing** : to summon with a subpoena

sub-Sa·ha·ran \ˌsəb-sə-'her-ən\ *adj* : of, relating to, or being the part of Africa south of the Sahara

sub·scribe \səb-'skrīb\ *vb* **sub·scribed; sub·scrib·ing 1** : to sign one's name to a document **2** : to give consent to or as if by signing one's name **3** : to promise to contribute by signing one's name with the amount promised **4** : to place an order by signing **5** : to receive a periodical or service regularly on order **6** : FAVOR, APPROVE ⟨~ to the theory⟩ ♦ *Synonyms* AGREE, ACQUIESCE, ASSENT, ACCEDE — **sub·scrib·er** *n*

sub·script \'səb-ˌskript\ *n* : a symbol (as a letter and/or number) immediately below or below and to the right or left of another written character — **subscript** *adj*

sub·scrip·tion \səb-'skrip-shən\ *n* **1** : the act of subscribing : SIGNATURE **2** : a purchase by signed order

sub·se·quent \'səb-si-kwənt, -sə-ˌkwent\ *adj* : following after : SUCCEEDING ⟨~ events⟩ — **sub·se·quent·ly** *adv*

sub·ser·vi·ence \səb-'sər-vē-əns\ *n* **1** : a subordinate place or condition **2** : SERVILITY — **sub·ser·vi·en·cy** \-ən-sē\ *n* — **sub·ser·vi·ent** \-ənt\ *adj*

sub·set \'səb-ˌset\ *n* : a set each of whose elements is an element of an inclusive set

sub·side \səb-'sīd\ *vb* **sub·sid·ed; sub·sid·ing** [L *subsidere*, fr. *sub-* under + *sidere* to sit down, sink] **1** : to settle to the bottom of a liquid **2** : to tend downward : DESCEND **3** : SINK, SUBMERGE ⟨*subsided* into a chair⟩ **4** : to become quiet and tranquil ♦ *Synonyms* ABATE, WANE, MODERATE, SLACKEN — **sub·sid·ence** \səb-'sī-dᵊns, 'səb-sə-dəns\ *n*

¹sub·sid·iary \səb-'si-dē-ˌer-ē\ *adj* **1** : furnishing aid or support **2** : of secondary importance **3** : of or relating to a subsidy ♦ *Synonyms* AUXILIARY, CONTRIBUTORY, SUBSERVIENT, ACCESSORY

²subsidiary *n, pl* **-iar·ies** : one that is subsidiary; *esp* : a company controlled by another

sub·si·dise *Brit var of* SUBSIDIZE

sub·si·dize \'səb-sə-ˌdīz\ *vb* **-dized; -diz·ing** : to aid or furnish with a subsidy

sub·si·dy \'səb-sə-dē\ *n, pl* **-dies** [ME, *subsidie*, fr. AF, fr. L *subsidium* reserve troops, support, assistance, fr. *sub-* near + *sedēre* to sit] : a gift of public money to a private person or company or to another government

sub·sist \səb-'sist\ *vb* **1** : EXIST, PERSIST **2** : to have the means (as food and clothing) of maintaining life; *esp* : to nourish oneself

sub·sis·tence \səb-'sis-təns\ *n* **1** : EXISTENCE **2** : means of subsisting : the minimum (as of food and clothing) necessary to support life

sub·son·ic \ˌsəb-'sä-nik, 'səb-\ *adj* : being or relating to a speed less than that of sound; *also* : moving at such a speed

sub·species \'səb-ˌspē-shēz, -sēz\ *n* : a subdivision of a species; *esp* : a category in biological classification ranking just below a species that designates a geographic population genetically distinct from other such populations and potentially able to breed with them where its range overlaps theirs

sub·stance \'səb-stəns\ *n* **1** : essential nature : ESSENCE ⟨divine ~⟩; *also* : the fundamental or essential part or quality ⟨the ~ of the speech⟩ **2** : physical material from which something is made or which has discrete existence; *also* : matter of particular or definite chemical constitution **3** : something (as drugs or alcohol) deemed harmful and usu. subject to

---

legal restriction ⟨∼ abuse⟩ 4 : material possessions : PROPERTY, WEALTH

sub·stan·dard \ˌsəb-'stan-dərd\ adj : falling short of a standard or norm

sub·stan·tial \səb-'stan-chəl\ adj 1 : existing as or in substance : MATERIAL; also : not illusory : REAL 2 : IMPORTANT, ESSENTIAL ⟨a ∼ difference in the stories⟩ 3 : NOURISHING, SATISFYING ⟨∼ meal⟩ 4 : having means : WELL-TO-DO 5 : CONSIDERABLE ⟨∼ profit⟩ 6 : STRONG, FIRM — **sub·stan·tial·ly** adv

sub·stan·ti·ate \səb-'stan-chē-ˌāt\ vb **-at·ed; -at·ing** 1 : to give substance or body to 2 : VERIFY, PROVE ⟨a ∼ charge⟩ — **sub·stan·ti·a·tion** \-ˌstan-chē-'ā-shən\ n

¹**sub·stan·tive** \'səb-stən-tiv\ n : NOUN; also : a word or phrase used as a noun

²**substantive** adj : having substance : REAL ⟨∼ changes⟩

¹**sub·sti·tute** \'səb-stə-ˌtüt, -ˌtyüt\ n : a person or thing replacing another — **substitute** adj

²**substitute** vb **-tut·ed; -tut·ing** 1 : to put or use in the place of another 2 : to serve as a substitute — **sub·sti·tu·tion** \ˌsəb-stə-'tü-shən, -'tyü-\ n

sub·strate \'səb-ˌstrāt\ n 1 : the base on which a plant or animal lives 2 : a substance acted upon (as by an enzyme)

sub·stra·tum \'səb-ˌstrā-təm, -ˌstra-\ n, pl **-stra·ta** \-tə\ : the layer or structure (as subsoil) lying underneath

sub·struc·ture \'səb-ˌstrək-chər\ n : FOUNDATION, GROUNDWORK

sub·sume \səb-'süm\ vb **sub·sumed; sub·sum·ing** : to include or place within something larger or more comprehensive

sub·sur·face \'səb-ˌsər-fəs\ n : earth material near the surface of the ground — **subsurface** adj

sub·ter·fuge \'səb-tər-ˌfyüj\ n : a trick or device used in order to conceal, escape, or evade ♦ **Synonyms** FRAUD, DECEPTION, TRICKERY

sub·ter·ra·nean \ˌsəb-tə-'rā-nē-ən\ adj 1 : lying or being underground 2 : SECRET, HIDDEN ⟨a ∼ network of criminals⟩

sub·tile \'sə-t⁰l\ adj **sub·til·er** \'sə-t⁰l-ər\; **sub·til·est** \'sə-t⁰l-əst\ : SUBTLE ⟨a ∼ aroma⟩

sub·ti·tle \'səb-ˌtī-t⁰l\ n 1 : a secondary or explanatory title (as of a book) 2 : printed matter projected on a motion-picture screen during or between the scenes

sub·tle \'sə-t⁰l\ adj **sub·tler** \'sə-t⁰l-ər\; **sub·tlest** \'sə-t⁰l-əst\ 1 : hardly noticeable ⟨∼ differences⟩ 2 : SHREWD, PERCEPTIVE ⟨a ∼ mind⟩ 3 : CLEVER, SLY ⟨a ∼ rogue⟩ — **sub·tle·ty** \-tē\ n — **sub·tly** \'sə-t⁰l-ē\ adv

sub·tract \səb-'trakt\ vb : to take away (as one part or number) from another; also : to perform the operation of deducting one number from another — **sub·trac·tion** \-'trak-shən\ n

sub·tra·hend \'səb-trə-ˌhend\ n : a number that is to be subtracted from another

sub·trop·i·cal \ˌsəb-'trä-pi-kəl, 'səb-\ also **sub·trop·ic** \-pik\ adj : of, relating to, or being regions bordering on the tropical zone ⟨a ∼ environment⟩ — **sub·trop·ics** \-piks\ n pl

sub·urb \'sə-ˌbərb\ n 1 : an outlying part of a city; also : a small community adjacent to a city 2 pl : a residential area adjacent to a city — **sub·ur·ban** \sə-'bər-bən\ adj or n — **sub·ur·ban·ite** \sə-'bər-bə-ˌnīt\ n

sub·ur·bia \sə-'bər-bē-ə\ n 1 : SUBURBS 2 : suburban people or customs

sub·ven·tion \səb-'ven-chən\ n : SUBSIDY, ENDOWMENT

sub·vert \səb-'vərt\ vb 1 : OVERTHROW, RUIN 2 : CORRUPT ⟨∼ the rule of law⟩ — **sub·ver·sion** \-'vər-zhən\ n — **sub·ver·sive** \-'vər-siv\ adj

sub·way \'səb-ˌwā\ n : an underground way; esp : an underground electric railway

sub·woof·er \'səb-ˌwu̇-fər\ n : a loudspeaker responsive only to the lowest acoustic frequencies

suc·ceed \sək-'sēd\ vb 1 : to follow next in order or next after another; esp : to inherit sovereignty, rank, title, or property 2 : to attain a desired object or end : be successful

suc·cess \sək-'ses\ n 1 : favorable or desired outcome 2 : the gaining of wealth and fame 3 : one that succeeds — **suc·cess·ful** \-fəl\ adj — **suc·cess·ful·ly** adv

suc·ces·sion \sək-'se-shən\ n 1 : the order, act, or right of succeeding to a property, title, or throne 2 : the act or process of following in order 3 : a series of persons or things that follow one after another ♦ **Synonyms** PROGRESSION, SEQUENCE, CHAIN, TRAIN, STRING

suc·ces·sive \sək-'se-siv\ adj : following in order : CONSECUTIVE ⟨three ∼ days⟩ — **suc·ces·sive·ly** adv

suc·ces·sor \sək-'se-sər\ n : one that succeeds (as to a throne, title, estate, or office)

suc·cinct \(ˌ)sək-'siŋkt, sə-'siŋkt\ adj : BRIEF, CONCISE ⟨a ∼ description⟩ ♦ **Synonyms** TERSE, LACONIC, SUMMARY, CURT, SHORT — **suc·cinct·ly** adv — **suc·cinct·ness** n

suc·cor \'sə-kər\ n [ME socour, sucurs (taken as pl.), fr. AF sucur, sucors, fr. ML succursus, fr. L succurrere to run to the rescue, bring aid] : AID, HELP, RELIEF — **succor** vb

suc·co·tash \'sə-kə-ˌtash\ n [Narragansett msíckquatash boiled corn kernels] : beans and corn kernels cooked together

suc·cour chiefly Brit var of SUCCOR

¹**suc·cu·lent** \'sə-kyə-lənt\ adj : full of juice : JUICY; also : having fleshy tissues

substation	subthreshold	subtreasury	subvariety
subsystem	subtopic	subtype	subvisible
subteen	subtotal	subunit	subzero

that conserve moisture ⟨~ plants⟩ — **suc·cu·lence** \-ləns\ *n*

²**succulent** *n* : a succulent plant (as a cactus or an aloe)

suc·cumb \sə-'kəm\ *vb* **1** : to yield to superior strength or force or overpowering appeal or desire **2** : DIE ♦ **Synonyms** SUBMIT, CAPITULATE, RELENT, DEFER

¹**such** \'səch, 'sich\ *adj* **1** : of this or that kind **2** : having a quality just specified or to be specified

²**such** *pron* **1** : such a one or ones ⟨he's a star, and acted as ~⟩ **2** : that or those similar or related thereto ⟨boards and nails and ~⟩

³**such** *adv* : to that degree : so

such·like \'səch-,līk\ *adj* : SIMILAR

¹**suck** \'sək\ *vb* **1** : to draw in liquid and esp. mother's milk with the mouth **2** : to draw liquid from by action of the mouth ⟨~ an orange⟩ **3** : to take in or up or remove by or as if by suction **4** *slang* : to be objectionable

²**suck** *n* **1** : a sucking movement or force **2** : the act of sucking

suck·er \'sə-kər\ *n* **1** : one that sucks **2** : a part of an animal's body used for sucking or for clinging **3** : any of numerous freshwater fishes with thick soft lips for sucking in food **4** : a shoot from the roots or lower part of a plant **5** : a person easily deceived **6** — used as a generalized term of reference ⟨see if you can get that ~ working again⟩

suck·le \'sə-kəl\ *vb* **suck·led; suck·ling** : to give or draw milk from the breast or udder; *also* : NURTURE

suck·ling \'sə-kliŋ\ *n* : a young unweaned mammal

suck–up \'sək-,əp\ *n* : a person who seeks to gain favor by flattery ⟨a ~ to the teacher⟩

su·cre \'sü-(,)krā\ *n* : the basic monetary unit of Ecuador until 2000

su·crose \'sü-,krōs, -,krōz\ *n* : a sweet sugar obtained commercially esp. from sugarcane or sugar beets

suc·tion \'sək-shən\ *n* **1** : the act of sucking **2** : the act or process of drawing something (as liquid or dust) into a space (as in a vacuum cleaner or a pump) by partially exhausting the air in the space — **suc·tion·al** \-shə-nəl\ *adj*

suction cup *n* : a cup-shaped device in which a partial vacuum is produced when applied to a surface

sud·den \'sə-dᵊn\ *adj* [ME *sodain*, fr. AF *sudain*, fr. L *subitaneus*, fr. *subitus* sudden, fr. pp. of *subire* to come up] **1** : happening or coming unexpectedly ⟨~ shower⟩; *also* : changing angle or character all at once ⟨~ turn⟩ ⟨~ descent⟩ **2** : HASTY, RASH ⟨~ decision⟩ **3** : made or brought about in a short time : PROMPT ⟨~ cure⟩ ♦ **Synonyms** PRECIPITATE, HEADLONG, IMPETUOUS — **sud·den·ly** *adv* — **sud·den·ness** *n*

sudden infant death syndrome *n* : death due to unknown causes of an apparently healthy infant usu. before one year of age and esp. during sleep

su·do·ku \sü-'dō-kü\ *n* [Jp *sūdoku*, short

for *sūji wa dokushin ni kagiru* "the numerals must remain single"] : a puzzle in which several numbers are to be filled into a 9x9 grid of squares so that every row, every column, and every 3x3 box contains the numbers 1 through 9

suds \'sədz\ *n pl* : soapy water esp. when frothy — **sudsy** \'səd-zē\ *adj*

sue \'sü\ *vb* **sued; su·ing** [ME *sewen, siuen* to follow, strive for, petition, fr. AF *sivre, siure*, fr. VL **sequere*, fr. L *sequi* to follow] **1** : PETITION, SOLICIT ⟨sued for peace⟩ **2** : to seek justice or right by bringing legal action ⟨sued the company⟩

suede *also* **suède** \'swād\ *n* [F *gants de Suède* Swedish gloves] **1** : leather with a napped surface **2** : a fabric with a suede-like nap

su·et \'sü-ət\ *n* : the hard fat from beef and mutton that yields tallow

suff *abbr* **1** sufficient **2** suffix

suf·fer \'sə-fər\ *vb* **suf·fered; suf·fer·ing** **1** : to feel or endure pain **2** : EXPERIENCE, UNDERGO ⟨~ a defeat⟩ **3** : to bear loss, damage, or injury **4** : ALLOW, PERMIT ♦ **Synonyms** ENDURE, ABIDE, TOLERATE, STAND, BROOK, STOMACH — **suf·fer·able** \'sə-fə-rə-bəl\ *adj* — **suf·fer·er** *n*

suf·fer·ance \'sə-frəns, -fə-rəns\ *n* **1** : consent or approval implied by lack of interference or resistance **2** : ENDURANCE, PATIENCE

suf·fer·ing \'sə-friŋ, -fə-riŋ\ *n* : PAIN, MISERY, HARDSHIP ⟨human ~⟩

suf·fice \sə-'fīs\ *vb* **suf·ficed; suf·fic·ing** **1** : to satisfy a need : be sufficient **2** : to be capable or competent

suf·fi·cien·cy \sə-'fi-shən-sē\ *n* **1** : a sufficient quantity to meet one's needs **2** : ADEQUACY

suf·fi·cient \sə-'fi-shənt\ *adj* : adequate to accomplish a purpose or meet a need — **suf·fi·cient·ly** *adv*

¹**suf·fix** \'sə-,fiks\ *n* : an affix occurring at the end of a word

²**suf·fix** \'sə-,fiks, (,)sə-'fiks\ *vb* : to attach as a suffix — **suf·fix·ation** \,sə-,fik-'sā-shən\ *n*

suf·fo·cate \'sə-fə-,kāt\ *vb* **-cat·ed; -cat·ing** : STIFLE, SMOTHER, CHOKE — **suf·fo·cat·ing·ly** *adv* — **suf·fo·ca·tion** \,sə-fə-'kā-shən\ *n*

suf·fra·gan \'sə-fri-gən\ *n* : an assistant bishop; *esp* : one not having the right of succession — **suffragan** *adj*

suf·frage \'sə-frij\ *n* [L *suffragium*] **1** : VOTE **2** : the right to vote : FRANCHISE

suf·frag·ette \,sə-fri-'jet\ *n* : a woman who advocates suffrage for women

suf·frag·ist \'sə-fri-jist\ *n* : one who advocates extension of the suffrage esp. to women

suf·fuse \sə-'fyüz\ *vb* **suf·fused; suf·fus·ing** : to spread over or through in the manner of a fluid or light ♦ **Synonyms** INFUSE, IMBUE, INGRAIN, STEEP — **suf·fu·sion** \-'fyü-zhən\ *n*

¹**sug·ar** \'shu̇-gər\ *n* **1** : a sweet substance that is colorless or white when pure and is chiefly sucrose from sugarcane or sugar beets **2** : a water-soluble compound

(as glucose) similar to sucrose — **sug-ary** *adj*

²**sugar** *vb* **sug-ared; sug-ar-ing 1** : to mix, cover, or sprinkle with sugar **2** : SWEETEN ⟨∼ advice with flattery⟩ **3** : to form sugar ⟨a syrup that ∼*s*⟩ **4** : GRANULATE

sugar beet *n* : a large beet with a white root from which sugar is made

sug-ar-cane \'shu̇-gər-ˌkān\ *n* : a tall grass widely grown in warm regions for the sugar in its stalks

sugar daddy *n* **1** : a well-to-do usu. older man who supports or spends lavishly on a mistress or girlfriend **2** : a generous benefactor of a cause

sugar maple *n* : a maple with a sweet sap; *esp* : one of eastern No. America with sap that is the chief source of maple syrup and maple sugar

sugar pea *n* : SNOW PEA

sug-ar-plum \'shu̇-gər-ˌpləm\ *n* : a small ball of candy

sug-gest \səg-'jest, sə-\ *vb* **1** : to put (as a thought, plan, or desire) into a person's mind **2** : to remind or evoke by association of ideas ♦ **Synonyms** IMPLY, HINT, INTIMATE, INSINUATE, CONNOTE

sug-gest-ible \səg-'jes-tə-bəl, sə-\ *adj* : easily influenced by suggestion

sug-ges-tion \-'jes-chən\ *n* **1** : an act or instance of suggesting; *also* : something suggested **2** : a slight indication

sug-ges-tive \-'jes-tiv\ *adj* : tending to suggest something; *esp* : suggesting something improper or indecent — **sug-ges-tive-ly** *adv* — **sug-ges-tive-ness** *n*

¹**sui-cide** \'su̇-ə-ˌsīd\ *n* **1** : the act of killing oneself purposely **2** : one that commits or attempts suicide — **sui-cid-al** \ˌsu̇-ə-'sī-d°l\ *adj*

²**suicide** *adj* : being or performing a deliberate act resulting in the voluntary death of the person who does it ⟨a ∼ mission⟩ ⟨a ∼ bomber⟩

sui ge-ner-is \ˌsü-ˌī-'je-nə-rəs, ˌsu̇-ē-\ *adj* [L, of its own kind] : being in a class by itself : UNIQUE

¹**suit** \'süt\ *n* **1** : an action in court to recover a right or claim **2** : an act of suing or entreating; *esp* : COURTSHIP **3** : a number of things used together ⟨∼ of clothes⟩ **4** : all the playing cards in a pack bearing the same symbol

²**suit** *vb* **1** : to be appropriate or fitting **2** : to be becoming to **3** : to meet the needs or desires of : PLEASE

suit-able \'sü-tə-bəl\ *adj* : FITTING, PROPER, APPROPRIATE ⟨∼ dress⟩ ♦ **Synonyms** FIT, MEET, APT, HAPPY — **suit-abil-i-ty** \ˌsü-tə-'bi-lə-tē\ *n* — **suit-able-ness** \'sü-tə-bəl-nəs\ *n* — **suit-ably** \-tə-blē\ *adv*

suit-case \'süt-ˌkās\ *n* : a portable case designed to hold a traveler's clothing and personal articles

suite \'swēt, *for 4 also* 'süt\ *n* **1** : RETINUE **2** : a group of rooms occupied as a unit **3** : a modern instrumental composition in several movements of different character; *also* : a long orchestral concert arrangement in suite form of material

drawn from a longer work **4** : a set of matched furniture for a room

suit-ing \'sü-tiŋ\ *n* : fabric for suits of clothes

suit-or \'sü-tər\ *n* **1** : one who sues or petitions **2** : one who courts a woman or seeks to marry her

su-ki-ya-ki \skē-'yä-kē, ˌsu̇-kē-'yä-\ *n* : thin slices of meat, tofu, and vegetables cooked in soy sauce and sugar

sul-fa drug \'səl-fə-\ *n* : any of various synthetic organic bacteria-inhibiting drugs

sul-fate \'səl-ˌfāt\ *n* : a salt or ester of sulfuric acid

sul-fide \'səl-ˌfīd\ *n* : a compound of sulfur

sul-fur *also* **sul-phur** \'səl-fər\ *n* : a nonmetallic chemical element used esp. in the chemical and paper industries and in vulcanizing rubber

sulfur di-ox-ide \-dī-'äk-ˌsīd\ *n* : a heavy pungent toxic gas that is used esp. in bleaching, as a preservative, and as a refrigerant, and is a major air pollutant

sul-fu-ric \ˌsəl-'fyu̇r-ik\ *adj* : of, relating to, or containing sulfur

sulfuric acid *or* **sul-phu-ric acid** \ˌsəl-'fyu̇r-ik-\ *n* : a heavy corrosive oily strong acid

sul-fu-rous *also* **sul-phu-rous** \'səl-fə-rəs, -fyə-, *also esp for 1* ˌsəl-'fyu̇r-əs\ *adj* **1** : of, relating to, or containing sulfur **2** : of or relating to brimstone or the fire of hell : INFERNAL **3** : FIERY, INFLAMED ⟨∼ sermons⟩

¹**sulk** \'səlk\ *vb* : to be or become moodily silent or irritable

²**sulk** *n* : a sulky mood or spell

¹**sulky** \'səl-kē\ *adj* **sulk-i-er; -est** : inclined to sulk : MOROSE, MOODY ⟨a ∼ mood⟩ ♦ **Synonyms** SURLY, GLUM, SULLEN, GLOOMY — **sulk-i-ly** \'səl-kə-lē\ *adv* — **sulk-i-ness** \-kē-nəs\ *n*

²**sulky** *n, pl* **sulkies** : a light 2-wheeled horse-drawn vehicle with a seat for the driver and usu. no body

sul-len \'sə-lən\ *adj* **1** : gloomily silent : MOROSE **2** : DISMAL, GLOOMY ⟨a ∼ sky⟩ ♦ **Synonyms** GLUM, SURLY, DOUR, SATURNINE — **sul-len-ly** *adv* — **sul-len-ness** *n*

sul-ly \'sə-lē\ *vb* **sul-lied; sul-ly-ing** : SOIL, SMIRCH, DEFILE ⟨∼ his name⟩

sul-tan \'səl-t°n\ *n* : a sovereign esp. of a Muslim state — **sul-tan-ate** \-ˌāt\ *n*

sul-ta-na \ˌsəl-'ta-nə\ *n* **1** : a female member of a sultan's family **2** : a pale seedless grape; *also* : a raisin of this grape

sul-try \'səl-trē\ *adj* **sul-tri-er; -est** [obs. E *sulter* to swelter, alter. of E *swelter*] : very hot and moist : SWELTERING; *also* : exciting sexual desire ⟨a ∼ look⟩

¹**sum** \'səm\ *n* [ME *summe*, fr. AF *sume, somme*, fr. L *summa*, fr. fem. of *summus* highest] **1** : a quantity of money **2** : the whole amount **3** : GIST ⟨the ∼ of an argument⟩ **4** : the result obtained by adding numbers **5** : a problem in arithmetic

²**sum** *vb* **summed; sum-ming** : to find the sum of by adding or counting

³**sum** *n* : the som of Uzbekistan

su·mac *also* **su·mach** \'sü-ˌmak, 'shü-\ *n* : any of a genus of trees, shrubs, and woody vines having spikes or loose clusters of red or whitish berries

sum·ma·rise *Brit var of* SUMMARIZE

sum·ma·rize \'sə-mə-ˌrīz\ *vb* **-rized; -riz·ing** : to tell in a summary

¹**sum·ma·ry** \'sə-mə-rē\ *adj* **1** : covering the main points briefly : CONCISE **2** : done without delay or formality ⟨~ punishment⟩ ♦ **Synonyms** TERSE, SUCCINCT, LACONIC — **sum·mar·i·ly** \(ˌ)sə-'mer-ə-lē, 'sə-mə-rə-lē\ *adv*

²**summary** *n, pl* **-ries** : a concise statement of the main points

sum·ma·tion \(ˌ)sə-'mā-shən\ *n* : a summing up; *esp* : a speech in court summing up the arguments in a case

sum·mer \'sə-mər\ *n* : the season of the year in a region in which the sun shines most directly : the warmest period of the year — **sum·mery** *adj*

sum·mer·house \'sə-mər-ˌhaủs\ *n* : a covered structure in a garden or park to provide a shady retreat

summersault *var of* SOMERSAULT

summer squash *n* : any of various squashes (as zucchini) used as a vegetable while immature

sum·mit \'sə-mət\ *n* **1** : the highest point **2** : a conference of highest-level officials ⟨an economic ~⟩

sum·mon \'sə-mən\ *vb* [ME *somnen, somonen,* fr. AF *somondre,* fr. VL **summonere,* alter. of L *summonēre* to remind secretly] **1** : to call to a meeting : CONVOKE **2** : to send for; *also* : to order to appear in court **3** : to evoke esp. by an act of the will ⟨~ up courage⟩ — **sum·mon·er** *n*

sum·mons \'sə-mənz\ *n, pl* **sum·mons·es 1** : an authoritative call to appear at a designated place or to attend to a duty **2** : a warning or citation to appear in court at a specified time to answer charges

sump·tu·ous \'səmp-shə-wəs, -chə-\ *adj* : LAVISH, LUXURIOUS ⟨a ~ banquet⟩ ⟨a ~ residence⟩

sum up *vb* : SUMMARIZE

¹**sun** \'sən\ *n* **1** : the shining celestial body around which the earth and other planets revolve and from which they receive light and heat **2** : a celestial body like the sun **3** : SUNSHINE — **sun·less** *adj* — **sun·ny** *adj*

²**sun** *vb* **sunned; sun·ning 1** : to expose to or as if to the rays of the sun **2** : to sun oneself

Sun *abbr* Sunday

sun·bath \'sən-ˌbath, -ˌbäth\ *n* : an exposure to sunlight or a sunlamp — **sun·bathe** \-ˌbāth\ *vb*

sun·beam \-ˌbēm\ *n* : a ray of sunlight

sun·block \'sən-ˌbläk\ *n* : a preparation used on the skin to prevent sunburn (as by blocking ultraviolet radiation)

sun·bon·net \-ˌbä-nət\ *n* : a bonnet with a wide brim to shield the face and neck from the sun

¹**sun·burn** \-ˌbərn\ *vb* **-burned** \-ˌbərnd\ *or* **-burnt** \-ˌbərnt\; **-burn·ing** : to cause or become affected with sunburn

²**sunburn** *n* : a skin inflammation caused by overexposure to ultraviolet radiation esp. from sunshine

sun·dae \'sən-(ˌ)dā, -dē\ *n* : ice cream served with topping

Sun·day \'sən-dā, -dē\ *n* : the 1st day of the week : the Christian Sabbath

sun·der \'sən-dər\ *vb* : to force apart ⟨a family ~ed by scandal⟩ ♦ **Synonyms** SEVER, PART, DISJOIN, DISUNITE

sun·di·al \'sən-ˌdī(-ə)l\ *n* : a device for showing the time of day from the shadow cast on a plate by an object with a straight edge

sun·down \-ˌdaủn\ *n* : SUNSET 2

sun·dries \'sən-drēz\ *n pl* : various small articles or items

sun·dry \'sən-drē\ *adj* : SEVERAL, DIVERS, VARIOUS ⟨for ~ reasons⟩

sun·fish \'sən-ˌfish\ *n* **1** : a large marine fish with a deep flattened body **2** : any of numerous often brightly colored No. American freshwater fishes related to the perches and usu. having the body flattened from side to side

sun·flow·er \-ˌflaủ(-ə)r\ *n* : any of a genus of tall New World plants related to the daisies and often grown for the oil-rich seeds of their yellow-petaled dark-centered flower heads

sung *past and past part of* SING

sun·glasses \'sən-ˌgla-səz\ *n pl* : glasses to protect the eyes from the sun

sunk *past and past part of* SINK

sunk·en \'səŋ-kən\ *adj* **1** : SUBMERGED ⟨~ ships⟩ **2** : fallen in : HOLLOW ⟨~ cheeks⟩ **3** : lying in a depression ⟨~ garden⟩; *also* : constructed below the general floor level ⟨~ living room⟩

sun·lamp \'sən-ˌlamp\ *n* : an electric lamp designed to emit radiation of wavelengths from ultraviolet to infrared

sun·light \-ˌlīt\ *n* : SUNSHINE

sun·lit \-ˌlit\ *adj* : lighted by or as if by the sun

sun protection factor *n* : a number that is the factor by which the time required for unprotected skin to become sunburned is increased when a sunscreen is used

sun·rise \-ˌrīz\ *n* **1** : the apparent rising of the sun above the horizon **2** : the time at which the sun rises

sun·roof \-ˌrüf, -ˌrúf\ *n* : a panel in an automobile roof that can be opened

sun·screen \-ˌskrēn\ *n* : a preparation on the skin to prevent sunburn (as by absorbing ultraviolet radiation)

sun·set \-ˌset\ *n* **1** : the apparent descent of the sun below the horizon **2** : the time at which the sun sets

sun·shade \'sən-ˌshād\ *n* : something (as a parasol or awning) used as a protection from the sun's rays

sun·shine \-ˌshīn\ *n* : the direct light of the sun — **sun·shiny** *adj*

sun·spot \-ˌspät\ *n* : any of the dark spots that appear at times on the sun's surface

sun·stroke \-ˌstrōk\ *n* : heatstroke caused by direct exposure to the sun

sun·tan \-ˌtan\ *n* : a browning of the skin from exposure to the sun's rays

sun·up \-ˌəp\ *n* : SUNRISE 2

¹**sup** \ˈsəp\ *vb* **supped; sup·ping** : to take or drink in swallows or gulps

²**sup** *n* : a mouthful esp. of liquor or broth; *also* : a small quantity of liquid

³**sup** *vb* **supped; sup·ping** **1** : to eat the evening meal **2** : to make one's supper ⟨*supped* on roast beef⟩

⁴**sup** *abbr* **1** superior **2** supplement; supplementary **3** supply **4** supra

¹**su·per** \ˈsü-pər\ *adj* **1** : very fine : EXCELLENT **2** : EXTREME, EXCESSIVE ⟨∼ secrecy⟩

²**su·per** *n* : SUPERINTENDENT

super- \ˌsü-pər\ *prefix* **1** : over and above : higher in quantity, quality, or degree than : more than **2** : in addition : extra **3** : exceeding a norm **4** : in excessive degree or intensity **5** : surpassing all or most others of its kind **6** : situated above, on, or at the top of **7** : next above or higher **8** : more inclusive than **9** : superior in status or position

su·per·abun·dant \ˌsü-pər-ə-ˈbən-dənt\ *adj* : more than ample — **su·per·abun·dance** \-dəns\ *n*

su·per·an·nu·ate \ˌsü-pər-ˈan-yə-ˌwāt\ *vb* **-at·ed; -at·ing** **1** : to make out-of-date **2** : to retire and remove because of age or infirmity — **su·per·an·nu·at·ed** *adj*

su·perb \su̇-ˈpərb\ *adj* [L *superbus* excellent, proud, fr. *super* above] : marked to the highest degree by excellence, brilliance, or competence ♦ **Synonyms** RESPLENDENT, GLORIOUS, GORGEOUS, SUBLIME — **su·perb·ly** *adv*

su·per·charg·er \ˈsü-pər-ˌchär-jər\ *n* : a device for increasing the amount of air supplied to an internal combustion engine

su·per·cil·ious \ˌsü-pər-ˈsi-lē-əs\ *adj* [L *superciliosus*, fr. *supercilium* eyebrow, haughtiness] : haughtily contemptuous ♦ **Synonyms** DISDAINFUL, OVERBEARING, ARROGANT, LORDLY, SUPERIOR

su·per·com·put·er \ˈsü-pər-kəm-ˌpyü-tər\ *n* : a large very fast mainframe

su·per·con·duc·tiv·i·ty \ˌsü-pər-ˌkän-ˌdək-ˈti-və-tē\ *n* : a complete disappearance of electrical resistance in a substance esp. at very low temperatures — **su·per·con·duc·tive** \-kən-ˈdək-tiv\ *adj* — **su·per·con·duc·tor** \-ˈdək-tər\ *n*

su·per·con·ti·nent \ˈsü-pər-ˌkän-tə-nənt\ *n* : a former large continent from which other continents are held to have broken off and drifted away

su·per·ego \ˌsü-pər-ˈē-gō\ *n* : the one of the three divisions of the psyche in psychoanalytic theory that functions to reward and punish through a system of moral attitudes, conscience, and a sense of guilt

su·per·fi·cial \ˌsü-pər-ˈfi-shəl\ *adj* **1** : of or relating to the surface or appearance only **2** : not thorough : SHALLOW ⟨a ∼

analysis⟩ — **su·per·fi·ci·al·i·ty** \-ˌfi-shē-ˈa-lə-tē\ *n* — **su·per·fi·cial·ly** *adv*

su·per·flu·ous \su̇-ˈpər-flə-wəs\ *adj* : exceeding what is sufficient or necessary : SURPLUS ⟨∼ details⟩ ♦ **Synonyms** EXTRA, SPARE, SUPERNUMERARY — **su·per·flu·i·ty** \ˌsü-pər-ˈflü-ə-tē\ *n*

su·per·high·way \ˌsü-pər-ˈhī-ˌwā\ *n* : a broad highway designed for high-speed traffic

su·per·im·pose \-im-ˈpōz\ *vb* : to lay (one thing) over or above something else

su·per·in·tend \ˌsü-pə-rin-ˈtend\ *vb* : to have or exercise the charge and oversight of : DIRECT ⟨∼*ed* the school system⟩ — **su·per·in·ten·dence** \-ˈten-dəns\ *n* — **su·per·in·ten·den·cy** \-dən-sē\ *n* — **su·per·in·ten·dent** \-dənt\ *n*

¹**su·pe·ri·or** \su̇-ˈpir-ē-ər\ *adj* **1** : situated higher up, over, or near the top; *also* : higher in rank or numbers **2** : of greater value or importance **3** : courageously indifferent (as to pain or misfortune) **4** : better than most others of its kind **5** : ARROGANT, HAUGHTY — **su·pe·ri·or·i·ty** \-ˌpir-ē-ˈȯr-ə-tē\ *n*

²**superior** *n* **1** : one who is above another in rank, office, or station; *esp* : the head of a religious house or order **2** : one higher in quality or merit

¹**su·per·la·tive** \su̇-ˈpər-lə-tiv\ *adj* **1** : of, relating to, or constituting the degree of grammatical comparison that denotes an extreme or unsurpassed level or extent **2** : surpassing others : SUPREME ♦ **Synonyms** PEERLESS, INCOMPARABLE, SUPERB — **su·per·la·tive·ly** *adv*

²**superlative** *n* **1** : the superlative degree or a superlative form in a language **2** : the utmost degree : ACME

su·per·mar·ket \ˈsü-pər-ˌmär-kət\ *n* : a self-service retail market selling foods and household merchandise

su·per·mod·el \ˈsü-pər-ˌmä-dᵊl\ *n* : a famous and successful fashion model

su·per·mom \ˈsü-pər-ˌmäm\ *n* : an exemplary mother; *also* : a woman who performs the duties of housekeeping and raising children while also having a full-time job

su·per·nal \su̇-ˈpər-nəl\ *adj* **1** : being or coming from on high **2** : of heavenly or spiritual character

su·per·nat·u·ral \ˌsü-pər-ˈna-chə-rəl\ *adj* : of or relating to phenomena beyond or outside of nature; *esp* : relating to or attributed to a divinity, ghost, or devil — **su·per·nat·u·ral·ly** *adv*

su·per·no·va \ˌsü-pər-ˈnō-və\ *n* : the explosion of a very large star

¹**su·per·nu·mer·ary** \-ˈnü-mə-ˌrer-ē, -ˈnyü-\ *adj* : exceeding the usual or required number : EXTRA ♦ **Synonyms** SURPLUS, SUPERFLUOUS, SPARE

²**supernumerary** *n, pl* **-ar·ies** : an extra

---

superabsorbent	supercity	superheat	superindividual
superachiever	superclean	superheavy	superliner
superagency	superexpensive	superhero	superman
superblock	superfast	superhuman	supernormal
superbomb	superfine	superhumanly	

person or thing; *esp* : an actor hired for a nonspeaking part

su·per·pose \ˌsü·pər-ˈpōz\ *vb* **-posed; -pos·ing** : SUPERIMPOSE — **su·per·po·si·tion** \-pə-ˈzi-shən\ *n*

su·per·pow·er \ˈsü-pər-ˌpaü(-ə)r\ *n* **1** : excessive or superior power **2** : one of a few politically and militarily dominant nations

su·per·sat·u·rat·ed \-ˈsa-chə-ˌrā-təd\ *adj* : containing an amount of a substance greater than that required for saturation

su·per·scribe \ˈsü-pər-ˌskrīb, ˌsü-pər-ˈskrīb\ *vb* **-scribed; -scrib·ing** : to write on the top or outside : ADDRESS — **su·per·scrip·tion** \ˌsü-pər-ˈskrip-shən\ *n*

su·per·script \ˈsü-pər-ˌskript\ *n* : a symbol (as a numeral or letter) written immediately above or above and to one side of another character

su·per·sede \ˌsü-pər-ˈsēd\ *vb* **-sed·ed; -sed·ing** [ME (Sc) *superceden* to defer, fr. MF *superceder*, fr. L *supersedēre* to be superior to, refrain from, fr. *super-* above + *sedēre* to sit] : to take the place of : REPLACE ⟨this edition ~s the previous one⟩

su·per·son·ic \-ˈsä-nik\ *adj* **1** : ULTRASONIC **2** : being or relating to speeds from one to five times the speed of sound; *also* : capable of moving at such a speed ⟨a ~ airplane⟩

su·per·sti·tion \ˌsü-pər-ˈsti-shən\ *n* **1** : beliefs or practices resulting from ignorance, fear of the unknown, or trust in magic or chance **2** : an unreasoning fear of nature, the unknown, or God resulting from superstition — **su·per·sti·tious** \-shəs\ *adj*

su·per·struc·ture \ˈsü-pər-ˌstrək-chər\ *n* : something built on a base or as a vertical extension

su·per·ti·tle \ˈsü-pər-ˌtī-t⁹l\ *n* : a translation of foreign-language dialogue displayed above a screen or performance

su·per·vene \ˌsü-pər-ˈvēn\ *vb* **-vened; -ven·ing** : to occur as something additional or unexpected

su·per·vise \ˈsü-pər-ˌvīz\ *vb* **-vised; -vis·ing** : OVERSEE, SUPERINTEND — **su·per·vi·sion** \ˌsü-pər-ˈvi-zhən\ *n* — **su·per·vi·sor** \ˈsü-pər-ˌvī-zər\ *n* — **su·per·vi·so·ry** \ˌsü-pər-ˈvī-zə-rē\ *adj*

su·pine \sü-ˈpīn\ *adj* **1** : lying on the back or with the face upward **2** : LETHARGIC, SLUGGISH; *also* : ABJECT ⟨a ~ legislature⟩ ♦ **Synonyms** INACTIVE, INERT, PASSIVE, IDLE

supp *or* **suppl** *abbr* supplement; supplementary

sup·per \ˈsə-pər\ *n* : the evening meal esp. when dinner is taken at midday — **sup·per·time** \-ˌtīm\ *n*

sup·plant \sə-ˈplant\ *vb* **1** : to take the

place of (another) esp. by force or trickery **2** : REPLACE

sup·ple \ˈsə-pəl\ *adj* **sup·pler; sup·plest** **1** : COMPLIANT, ADAPTABLE **2** : capable of bending without breaking or creasing : LIMBER ♦ **Synonyms** RESILIENT, ELASTIC, FLEXIBLE

¹sup·ple·ment \ˈsə-plə-mənt\ *n* **1** : something that supplies a want or makes an addition **2** : DIETARY SUPPLEMENT **3** : a continuation (as of a book) containing corrections or additional material — **sup·ple·men·tal** \ˌsə-plə-ˈmen-t⁹l\ *adj* — **sup·ple·men·ta·ry** \ˌsə-plə-ˈmen-tə-rē\ *adj*

²sup·ple·ment \ˈsə-plə-ˌment\ *vb* : to fill up the deficiencies of : add to — **sup·ple·men·ta·tion** \ˌsə-plə-ˌmen-ˈtā-shən, -mən-\ *n*

sup·pli·ant \ˈsə-plē-ənt\ *n* : one who supplicates : PETITIONER, PLEADER

sup·pli·cant \ˈsə-pli-kənt\ *n* : SUPPLIANT

sup·pli·cate \ˈsə-plə-ˌkāt\ *vb* **-cat·ed; -cat·ing** **1** : to make a humble entreaty; *esp* : to pray to God **2** : to ask earnestly and humbly : BESEECH ♦ **Synonyms** IMPLORE, BEG, ENTREAT, PLEAD — **sup·pli·ca·tion** \ˌsə-plə-ˈkā-shən\ *n*

¹sup·ply \sə-ˈplī\ *vb* **sup·plied; sup·ply·ing** [ME *supplien*, to complete, compensate for, fr. MF *soupplier* fr. L *supplēre* to fill up, supplement, supply, fr. *sub-* under, up to + *plēre* to fill] **1** : to add as a supplement **2** : to satisfy the needs of **3** : FURNISH, PROVIDE — **sup·pli·er** *n*

²supply *n, pl* **supplies** **1** : the quantity or amount (as of a commodity) needed or available; *also* : PROVISIONS, STORES — usu. used in pl. **2** : the act or process of filling a want or need : PROVISION **3** : the quantities of goods or services offered for sale at a particular time or at one price

sup·ply-side \sə-ˈplī-ˌsīd\ *adj* : of, relating to, or being an economic theory that recommends the reduction of tax rates to expand economic activity

¹sup·port \sə-ˈpōrt\ *vb* **1** : BEAR, TOLERATE **2** : to take sides with : BACK, ASSIST **3** : to provide with food, clothing, and shelter **4** : to hold up or serve as a foundation for ♦ **Synonyms** UPHOLD, ADVOCATE, CHAMPION — **sup·port·able** *adj* — **sup·port·er** *n* — **sup·port·ive** \-ˈpōr-tiv\ *adj*

²support *n* **1** : the act of supporting : the state of being supported **2** : one that supports : PROP, BASE

support group *n* : a group of people with common experiences and concerns who provide emotional and moral support for one another

sup·pose \sə-ˈpōz\ *vb* **sup·posed; sup·pos·ing** **1** : to assume to be true (as for the sake of argument) **2** : EXPECT ⟨I am *supposed* to go⟩ **3** : to think probable ⟨I ~ so⟩ — **sup·pos·al** *n*

---

sup·posed \sə-'pōzd, -'pō-zəd\ *adj* : BE-LIEVED; *also* : mistakenly believed ⟨a ~ cure⟩ — **sup·pos·ed·ly** \-'pō-zəd-lē, -'pōzd-lē\ *adv*

sup·pos·ing *conj* : if by way of hypothesis : on the assumption that ⟨~ I did agree with you⟩

sup·po·si·tion \ˌsə-pə-'zi-shən\ *n* **1** : something that is supposed : HYPOTHESIS **2** : the act of supposing

sup·pos·i·to·ry \sə-'pä-zə-ˌtȯr-ē\ *n, pl* **-ries** [ME *suppositorie*, fr. AF, fr. ML *suppositorium*, fr. LL, neut. of *suppositorius* placed beneath] : a small easily melted mass of usu. medicated material for insertion (as into the rectum)

sup·press \sə-'pres\ *vb* **1** : to put down by authority or force : SUBDUE ⟨~ a revolt⟩ **2** : to keep from being known; *also* : to stop the publication or circulation of **3** : to hold back : REPRESS ⟨~ anger⟩ ⟨~ a cough⟩ — **sup·press·ible** \-'pre-sə-bəl\ *adj* — **sup·pres·sion** \-'pre-shən\ *n* — **sup·pres·sor** \-'pre-sər\ *n*

sup·pres·sant \sə-'pre-sᵊnt\ *n* : an agent (as a drug) suppressing rather than eliminating something ⟨a cough ~⟩

sup·pu·rate \'sə-pyə-ˌrāt\ *vb* **-rat·ed; -rat·ing** : to form or give off pus — **sup·pu·ra·tion** \ˌsə-pyə-'rā-shən\ *n*

su·pra \'sü-prə, -ˌprä\ *adv* : earlier in this writing : ABOVE

su·pra·na·tion·al \ˌsü-prə-'na-shə-nəl, -ˌprä-\ *adj* : going beyond national boundaries, authority, or interests ⟨~ organizations⟩

su·prem·a·cist \sù-'pre-mə-sist\ *n* : an advocate of group supremacy

su·prem·a·cy \sù-'pre-mə-sē\ *n, pl* **-cies** : supreme rank, power, or authority

su·preme \sù-'prēm\ *adj* [L *supremus*, superl. of *superus* upper, fr. *super* over, above] **1** : highest in rank or authority **2** : highest in degree or quality ⟨~ among poets⟩ **3** : ULTIMATE ⟨the ~ sacrifice⟩ ♦ **Synonyms** SUPERLATIVE, SURPASSING, PEERLESS, INCOMPARABLE — **su·preme·ly** *adv* — **su·preme·ness** *n*

Supreme Being *n* : GOD 1

supt *abbr* superintendent

sur·cease \'sər-ˌsēs\ *n* : CESSATION, RESPITE ⟨a ~ from pain⟩

¹sur·charge \'sər-ˌchärj\ *vb* **1** : to fill to excess : OVERLOAD **2** : to apply a surcharge to (postage stamps)

²surcharge *n* **1** : an extra fee or cost **2** : an excessive load or burden **3** : something officially printed on a postage stamp esp. to change its value

sur·cin·gle \'sər-ˌsiŋ-gəl\ *n* : a band put around a horse's body to make something (as a saddle) fast

¹sure \'shu̇r\ *adj* **sur·er; sur·est** [ME, *seur, sure,* fr. AF *seur,* fr. L *securus* secure] **1** : firmly established **2** : TRUSTWORTHY, RELIABLE ⟨a ~ friend⟩ **3** : CONFIDENT ⟨I'm ~ I'm right⟩ **4** : not to be disputed : UNDOUBTED **5** : bound to happen **6** : careful to remember or attend to something ⟨be ~ to lock the door⟩ ♦ **Synonyms** CERTAIN, COCKSURE, POSITIVE — **sure·ness** *n*

²sure *adv* : SURELY

sure-fire \'shu̇r-ˌfī(-ə)r\ *adj* : certain to get results : DEPENDABLE

sure·ly \'shu̇r-lē\ *adv* **1** : in a sure manner **2** : without doubt **3** : INDEED, REALLY ⟨~, you don't believe that⟩

sure·ty \'shu̇r-ə-tē\ *n, pl* **-ties** **1** : SURENESS, CERTAINTY **2** : something that makes sure : GUARANTEE **3** : one who is a guarantor for another person

¹surf \'sərf\ *n* : waves that break upon the shore; *also* : the sound or foam of breaking waves

²surf *vb* **1** : to ride the surf (as on a surfboard) **2** : to scan the offerings of (as television or the Internet) for something of interest — **surf·er** *n* — **surf·ing** *n*

¹sur·face \'sər-fəs\ *n* **1** : the outside of an object or body **2** : outward aspect or appearance — **surface** *adj*

²surface *vb* **sur·faced; sur·fac·ing** **1** : to give a surface to : make smooth **2** : to rise to the surface

surf·board \'sərf-ˌbȯrd\ *n* : a buoyant board used in surfing

¹sur·feit \'sər-fət\ *n* **1** : EXCESS, SUPERABUNDANCE **2** : excessive indulgence (as in food or drink) **3** : disgust caused by excess

²surfeit *vb* : to feed, supply, or indulge to the point of surfeit : CLOY

surg *abbr* surgeon; surgery; surgical

surge \'sərj\ *vb* **surged; surg·ing** **1** : to rise and fall actively : TOSS **2** : to move in waves **3** : to rise suddenly to an excessive or abnormal value

²surge *n* **1** : a sweeping onward like a wave of the sea ⟨a ~ of emotion⟩ **2** : a large billow **3** : a transient sudden increase of current or voltage in an electrical circuit

sur·geon \'sər-jən\ *n* : a physician who specializes in surgery

sur·gery \'sər-jə-rē\ *n, pl* **-ger·ies** [ME *surgerie*, fr. AF *cirurgerie, surgerie,* fr. L *chirurgia,* fr. Gk *cheirourgia,* fr. *cheirourgos* surgeon, fr. *cheirourgos* doing by hand, fr. *cheir* hand + *ergon* work] **1** : a branch of medicine concerned with the correction of physical defects, the repair of injuries, and the treatment of disease esp. by operations **2** : a room or area where surgery is performed **3** : the work done by a surgeon

sur·gi·cal \'sər-ji-kəl\ *adj* : of, relating to, or associated with surgeons or surgery — **sur·gi·cal·ly** \-k(ə-)lē\ *adv*

sur·ly \'sər-lē\ *adj* **sur·li·er; -est** [alter. of ME *serreli* lordly, imperious, prob. fr. *sire, ser* sire] : having a rude unfriendly disposition ⟨a ~ customer⟩ ♦ **Synonyms** MOROSE, GLUM, SULLEN, SULKY, GLOOMY — **sur·li·ness** \-lē-nəs\ *n*

sur·mise \sər-'mīz\ *vb* **sur·mised; sur·mis·ing** : to form a notion of from scanty evidence ♦ **Synonyms** CONJECTURE, PRESUME, SUPPOSE — **surmise** *n*

sur·mount \sər-'mau̇nt\ *vb* **1** : to prevail over : OVERCOME ⟨~ a problem⟩ **2** : to get to or lie at the top of

sur·name \'sər-ˌnām\ *n* **1** : NICKNAME **2**

: the name borne in common by members of a family

sur·pass \sər-ˈpas\ vb 1 : to be superior to in quality, degree, or performance : EXCEL 2 : to go beyond the reach or powers of ◆ **Synonyms** TRANSCEND, OUTDO, OUTSTRIP, EXCEED — **sur·pass·ing·ly** adv

sur·plice \ˈsər-pləs\ n : a loose white outer vestment usu. of knee length

sur·plus \ˈsər-(ˌ)pləs\ n 1 : quantity left over : EXCESS 2 : the excess of assets over liabilities ◆ **Synonyms** SUPERFLUITY, OVERABUNDANCE, SURFEIT

¹**sur·prise** \sər-ˈprīz\ n 1 : an attack made without warning 2 : a taking unawares 3 : something that surprises 4 : AMAZEMENT, ASTONISHMENT

²**surprise** vb **sur·prised; sur·pris·ing 1** : to come upon and attack unexpectedly **2** : to take unawares 3 ⟨his conduct *surprised* me⟩ **4** : to cause astonishment or surprise ⟨her success didn't ∼⟩ ◆ **Synonyms** ASTONISH, ASTOUND, DUMBFOUND — **sur·pris·ing** adj

sur·pris·ing·ly \-ˈprī-ziŋ-lē\ adv **1** : in a surprising manner or degree **2** : it is surprising that ⟨∼, voter turnout was high⟩

sur·re·al \sə-ˈrē-əl, -ˈrēl\ adj **1** : having the intense irrational reality of a dream **2** : of or relating to surrealism ⟨∼ art⟩ — **sur·re·al·ly** adv

sur·re·al·ism \sə-ˈrē-ə-ˌli-zəm\ n : art, literature, or theater characterized by fantastic or incongruous imagery or effects produced by unnatural juxtapositions and combinations — **sur·re·al·ist** \-list\ n or adj — **sur·re·al·is·tic** \sə-ˌrē-ə-ˈlis-tik\ adj — **sur·re·al·is·ti·cal·ly** \-ti-k(ə-)lē\ adv

¹**sur·ren·der** \sə-ˈren-dər\ vb **1** : to yield to the power of another : give up under compulsion **2** : RELINQUISH

²**surrender** n : the act of giving up or yielding oneself or the possession of something to another

sur·rep·ti·tious \ˌsər-əp-ˈti-shəs\ adj : done, made, or acquired by stealth : CLANDESTINE ⟨a ∼ relationship⟩ ◆ **Synonyms** UNDERHAND, COVERT, FURTIVE — **sur·rep·ti·tious·ly** adv

sur·rey \ˈsər-ē\ n, pl **surreys** : a 2-seated horse-drawn carriage

sur·ro·ga·cy \ˈsər-ə-gə-sē\ n : SURROGATE MOTHERHOOD

sur·ro·gate \ˈsər-ə-ˌgāt, -gət\ n **1** : DEPUTY, SUBSTITUTE **2** : a law officer in some states with authority in the probate of wills, the settlement of estates, and the appointment of guardians **3** : SURROGATE MOTHER

surrogate mother n : a woman who becomes pregnant (as by surgical implantation of a fertilized egg) in order to carry the fetus for another woman — **surrogate motherhood** n

sur·round \sə-ˈraủnd\ vb **1** : to enclose on all sides : ENCIRCLE **2** : to enclose so as to cut off retreat or escape

sur·round·ings \sə-ˈraủn-diŋz\ n pl : conditions by which one is surrounded

surround sound n : sound reproduction

that uses three or more transmission channels

sur·tax \ˈsər-ˌtaks\ n : an additional tax over and above a normal tax

sur·tout \(ˌ)sər-ˈtü\ n [F, fr. sur over + tout all] : a man's long close-fitting overcoat

surv abbr survey; surveying; surveyor

sur·veil·lance \sər-ˈvā-ləns\ n [F] : close watch; also : SUPERVISION

¹**sur·vey** \sər-ˈvā\ vb **sur·veyed; sur·vey·ing** [ME, fr. AF *surveer* to look over, fr. sur- over + veer to see, fr. L *vidēre*] **1** : to look over and examine closely **2** : to find and represent the contours, measurements, and position of a part of the earth's surface (as a tract of land) **3** : to view or study something as a whole ◆ **Synonyms** SCRUTINIZE, EXAMINE, INSPECT, STUDY — **sur·vey·or** \-ər\ n

²**sur·vey** \ˈsər-ˌvā\ n, pl **surveys** : the act or an instance of surveying; also : something that is surveyed

sur·viv·al·ism \sər-ˈvī-və-ˌli-zəm\ n : an attitude, policy, or practice based on the primacy of survival as a value — **sur·viv·al·ist** \-və-list\ n or adj

sur·vive \sər-ˈvīv\ vb **sur·vived; sur·viv·ing 1** : to remain alive or existent **2** : OUTLIVE, OUTLAST — **sur·viv·al** n — **sur·vi·vor** \-ˈvī-vər\ n

sus·cep·ti·ble \sə-ˈsep-tə-bəl\ adj **1** : of such a nature as to permit ⟨words ∼ of being misunderstood⟩ **2** : having little resistance to a stimulus or agency ⟨∼ to colds⟩ **3** : IMPRESSIONABLE, RESPONSIVE ⟨a ∼ mind⟩ ◆ **Synonyms** SENSITIVE, SUBJECT, EXPOSED, PRONE, LIABLE, OPEN — **sus·cep·ti·bil·i·ty** \-ˌsep-tə-ˈbi-lə-tē\ n

su·shi \ˈsü-shē\ n [Jp] : cold rice formed into various shapes and garnished esp. with bits of raw fish or seafood

¹**sus·pect** \ˈsəs-ˌpekt, sə-ˈspekt\ adj : regarded with suspicion; also : QUESTIONABLE ⟨his claim is ∼⟩

²**sus·pect** \ˈsəs-ˌpekt\ n : one who is suspected (as of a crime)

³**sus·pect** \sə-ˈspekt\ vb **1** : to have doubts of : MISTRUST **2** : to imagine to be guilty without proof **3** : SURMISE

sus·pend \sə-ˈspend\ vb **1** : to bar temporarily from a privilege, office, or function **2** : to stop temporarily : make inactive for a time **3** : to withhold (judgment) for a time **4** : HANG; esp : to hang so as to be free except at one point **5** : to put or hold in suspension **6** : to keep from falling or sinking by some invisible support

sus·pend·er \sə-ˈspen-dər\ n : one of two supporting straps which pass over the shoulders and to which the pants are fastened

sus·pense \sə-ˈspens\ n **1** : SUSPENSION **2** : mental uncertainty : ANXIETY **3** : excitement as to an outcome — **sus·pense·ful** adj

sus·pen·sion \sə-ˈspen-chən\ n **1** : the act of suspending : the state or period of being suspended **2** : the state of a substance when its particles are mixed with but undissolved in a fluid or solid; *also* : a substance in this state **3** : something suspended **4** : the system of devices supporting the upper part of a vehicle on the axles

sus·pen·so·ry \sə-'spen-sə-rē\ *adj* **1** : SUSPENDED; *also* : fitted or serving to suspend something **2** : temporarily leaving undetermined

sus·pi·cion \sə-'spi-shən\ *n* **1** : the act or an instance of suspecting something wrong without proof **2** : TRACE, SOUPÇON ⟨a ~ of garlic⟩ ♦ *Synonyms* MISTRUST, UNCERTAINTY, DOUBT, SKEPTICISM

sus·pi·cious \sə-'spi-shəs\ *adj* **1** : open to or arousing suspicion **2** : inclined to suspect **3** : showing suspicion ⟨is ~ of strangers⟩ — **sus·pi·cious·ly** *adv*

sus·tain \sə-'stān\ *vb* **1** : to provide with nourishment **2** : to keep going : PROLONG ⟨~ed effort⟩ **3** : to hold up : PROP **4** : to hold up under : ENDURE **5** : SUFFER ⟨~ a broken arm⟩ **6** : to support as true, legal, or valid ⟨the objection was ~ed⟩ **7** : PROVE, CORROBORATE — **sus·tain·able** \səs-'tā-nə-bəl\ *adj*

sus·te·nance \'səs-tə-nəns\ *n* **1** : FOOD, NOURISHMENT **2** : a supplying with the necessities of life **3** : something that sustains or supports

su·ture \'sü-chər\ *n* **1** : material or a stitch for sewing a wound together **2** : a seam or line along which two things or parts are joined by or as if by sewing

SUV \es-yü-'vē\ *n* [*sport-utility vehicle*] : a vehicle similar to a station wagon but built on a light-truck chassis

su·ze·rain \'sü-zə-rən, -ˌrān\ *n* [F] **1** : a feudal lord **2** : a nation that has political control over the foreign relations of another nation — **su·ze·rain·ty** \-tē\ *n*

svc *or* **svce** *abbr* service

svelte \'sfelt\ *adj* **svelt·er**; **svelt·est** [F, fr. It *svelto*, fr. pp. of *svellere* to pluck out, modif. of L *evellere*, fr. *e-* out + *vellere* to pluck] : SLENDER, LITHE ⟨a ~ figure⟩

svgs *abbr* savings

SW *abbr* **1** shortwave **2** southwest

¹**swab** \'swäb\ *n* **1** : MOP **2** : a wad of absorbent material esp. for applying medicine or for cleaning; *also* : a sample taken with a swab **3** : SAILOR

²**swab** *vb* **swabbed**; **swab·bing** : to use a swab on : MOP

swad·dle \'swä-d²l\ *vb* **swad·dled**; **swad·dling** **1** : to bind (an infant) in bands of cloth **2** : to wrap up : SWATHE

swaddling clothes *n pl* : bands of cloth wrapped around an infant

swag \'swag\ *n* : stolen goods : LOOT

swag·ger \'swa-gər\ *vb* **1** : to walk with a conceited swing or strut **2** : BOAST, BRAG — **swagger** *n*

Swa·hi·li \swä-'hē-lē\ *n* : a language that is a trade and governmental language over much of eastern Africa and the Congo region

swain \'swān\ *n* [ME *swein* boy, servant, fr. ON *sveinn*] **1** : RUSTIC; *esp* : SHEPHERD **2** : ADMIRER, SUITOR

SWAK *abbr* sealed with a kiss

¹**swal·low** \'swä-lō\ *n* : any of numerous small long-winged migratory birds that often have a deeply forked tail

²**swallow** *vb* **1** : to take into the stomach through the throat **2** : to envelop or take in as if by swallowing **3** : to accept or believe without question, protest, or anger

³**swallow** *n* **1** : an act of swallowing **2** : an amount that can be swallowed at one time

swal·low·tail \'swä-lō-ˌtāl\ *n* **1** : a deeply forked and tapering tail like that of a swallow **2** : TAILCOAT **3** : any of various large butterflies with the border of each hind wing usu. drawn out into a process resembling a tail — **swal·low–tailed** \-ˌtāld\ *adj*

swam *past of* SWIM

swa·mi \'swä-mē\ *n* [Hindi *svāmī*, fr. Skt *svāmin* owner, lord] : a Hindu ascetic or religious teacher

¹**swamp** \'swämp\ *n* : a spongy wetland — **swamp** *adj* — **swampy** *adj*

²**swamp** *vb* **1** : to fill or become filled with or as if with water **2** : OVERWHELM **3**

swamp·land \-ˌland\ *n* : SWAMP

swan \'swän\ *n, pl* **swans** *also* **swan** : any of various heavy-bodied long-necked mostly pure white swimming birds related to the geese

¹**swank** \'swaŋk\ *or* **swanky** \'swaŋ-kē\ *adj* **swank·er** *or* **swank·i·er**; **-est** : showily smart and dashing; *also* : fashionably elegant ⟨a ~ hotel⟩

²**swank** *n* **1** : PRETENTIOUSNESS **2** : ELEGANCE

swans·down \'swänz-ˌdaun\ *n* **1** : the very soft down of a swan used esp. for trimming **2** : a soft thick cotton flannel

swan song *n* : a farewell appearance, act, or pronouncement

swap \'swäp\ *vb* **swapped**; **swap·ping** : TRADE, EXCHANGE — **swap** *n*

sward \'sword\ *n* : the grassy surface of land

¹**swarm** \'sworm\ *n* **1** : a great number of honeybees leaving together from a hive with a queen to start a new colony; *also* : a hive of bees **2** : a large crowd

²**swarm** *vb* **1** : to form in a swarm and depart from a hive **2** : to throng together : gather in great numbers

swart \'swort\ *adj* : SWARTHY

swar·thy \'swor-thē, -thē\ *adj* **swar·thi·er**; **-est** : dark in color or complexion : dark-skinned

swash \'swäsh\ *vb* : to move about with a splashing sound — **swash** *n*

swash·buck·ler \-ˌbə-klər\ *n* : a swaggering or daring soldier or adventurer — **swash·buck·ling** *adj*

swas·ti·ka \'swäs-ti-kə\ *n* [Skt *svastika*, fr. *svasti* well-being, fr. *su-* well + *as-* to be] : a symbol or ornament in the form of a cross with the ends of the arms bent at right angles

swat \'swät\ *vb* **swat·ted**; **swat·ting** : to hit sharply ⟨~ a fly⟩ ⟨~ a ball⟩ — **swat** *n* — **swat·ter** *n*

SWAT *abbr* Special Weapons and Tactics

swatch \'swäch\ *n* : a sample piece (as of fabric) or a collection of samples

swath \'swäth, 'swòth\ *or* **swathe** \'swäth, 'swòth, 'swāth\ *n* [ME, fr. OE *swæth* footstep, trace] **1** : a row of cut grass or grain **2** : the sweep of a scythe or mowing machine or the path cut in mowing

swathe \'swäth, 'swòth, 'swāth\ *vb* **swathed; swath·ing** : to bind or wrap with or as if with a bandage

¹sway \'swā\ *n* **1** : a gentle swinging from side to side **2** : controlling influence or power : DOMINION

²sway *vb* **1** : to swing gently from side to side **2** : RULE, GOVERN **3** : to cause to swing from side to side **4** : BEND, SWERVE; *also* : INFLUENCE ⟨tried to ~ the jury⟩ ♦ **Synonyms** OSCILLATE, FLUCTUATE, VIBRATE, WAVER

sway-backed \'swā-ˌbakt\ *also* **sway-back** \-ˌbak\ *adj* : having an abnormally sagging back ⟨a ~ mare⟩ — **swayback** *n*

swear \'swer\ *vb* **swore** \'swòr\; **sworn** \'swòrn\; **swear·ing** **1** : to make a solemn statement or promise under oath **2** : to assert or promise emphatically or earnestly **3** : to administer an oath to **4** : to bind by or as if by an oath **5** : to use profane or obscene language — **swear·er** *n*

swear in *vb* : to induct into office by administration of an oath

sweat \'swet\ *vb* **sweat** *or* **sweat·ed; sweat·ing** **1** : to excrete salty moisture from glands of the skin : PERSPIRE **2** : to form drops of moisture on the surface **3** : to work so that one sweats : TOIL **4** : to cause to sweat **5** : to draw out or get rid of by or as if by sweating **6** : to make a person overwork — **sweat** *n* — **sweaty** *adj*

sweat·er \'swe-tər\ *n* **1** : one that sweats **2** : a knitted or crocheted jacket or pullover

sweat-shirt \'swet-ˌshərt\ *n* : a loose collarless pullover or jacket usu. of heavy cotton jersey

sweat-shop \'swet-ˌshäp\ *n* : a shop or factory in which workers are employed for long hours at low wages and under unhealthy conditions

Swed *abbr* Sweden

swede \'swēd\ *n* **1** *cap* : a native or inhabitant of Sweden **2** *chiefly Brit* : RUTABAGA

Swed·ish \'swē-dish\ *n* **1** : the language of Sweden **2 Swedish** *pl* : the people of Sweden — **Swedish** *adj*

¹sweep \'swēp\ *vb* **swept** \'swept\; **sweep·ing** **1** : to remove or clean by or as if by brushing **2** : to destroy completely; *also* : to remove or take with a single swift movement **3** : to remove from sight or consideration **4** : to move over with speed and force ⟨the tide *swept* over the shore⟩ **5** : to win in an overwhelming victory in; *also* : to win all the games or contests of **6** : to move or extend in a wide curve — **sweep·er** *n*

²sweep *n* **1** : something (as a long oar)

that operates with a sweeping motion **2** : a clearing off or away **3** : a winning of all the contests or prizes in a competition **4** : a sweeping movement **5** : CURVE, BEND **6** : RANGE, SCOPE

sweeping *adj* **1** : EXTENSIVE ⟨~ reforms⟩; *also* : indiscriminately inclusive ⟨~ generalities⟩

sweep·ings \'swē-piŋz\ *n pl* : things collected by sweeping

sweep–sec·ond hand \'swēp-ˌse-kənd-\ *n* : a hand marking seconds on a timepiece

sweep·stakes \'swēp-ˌstāks\ *also* **sweep·stake** \-ˌstāk\ *n, pl* **sweepstakes 1** : a race or contest in which the entire prize may go to the winner **2** : any of various lotteries

¹sweet \'swēt\ *adj* **1** : being or causing the one of the four basic taste sensations that is caused esp. by table sugar and is identified esp. by the taste buds at the front of the tongue; *also* : pleasing to the taste **2** : AGREEABLE ⟨how ~ it is⟩ **3** : pleasing to a sense other than taste ⟨a ~ smell⟩ ⟨~ music⟩ **4** : not stale or spoiled : WHOLESOME ⟨~ milk⟩ **5** : not salted ⟨~ butter⟩ — **sweet·ish** *adj* — **sweet·ly** *adv* — **sweet·ness** *n*

²sweet *n* **1** : something sweet : CANDY **2** : DARLING

sweet·bread \'swēt-ˌbred\ *n* : the pancreas or thymus of an animal (as a calf or lamb) used for food

sweet·bri·ar *or* **sweet·bri·er** \-ˌbrī-ər\ *n* : a thorny Old World rose with fragrant white to deep pink flowers

sweet clover *n* : any of a genus of erect legumes widely grown for soil improvement or hay

sweet corn *n* : corn of a variety having soft kernels containing a high percentage of sugar

sweet·en \'swē-tᵊn\ *vb* **sweet·ened; sweet·en·ing** : to make sweet — **sweet·en·er** *n* — **sweet·en·ing** *n*

sweet·heart \'swēt-ˌhärt\ *n* : one who is loved

sweet·meat \-ˌmēt\ *n* : CANDY 1

sweet pea *n* : a garden plant of the legume family with climbing stems and fragrant flowers of many colors; *also* : its flower

sweet pepper *n* : any of various large mild thick-walled fruits of a pepper; *also* : a plant bearing sweet peppers

sweet potato *n* : a tropical vine related to the morning glory; *also* : its large sweet edible root

sweet–talk \'swēt-ˌtòk\ *vb* : FLATTER, COAX — **sweet talk** *n*

sweet tooth *n* : a craving or fondness for sweet food

sweet wil·liam \ˌswēt-'wil-yəm\ *n, often cap W* : a widely cultivated Old World pink with small white to deep red or purple flowers often showily spotted, banded, or mottled

¹swell \'swel\ *vb* **swelled; swelled** *or* **swol·len** \'swō-lən\; **swell·ing 1** : to grow big or make bigger **2** : to expand or distend abnormally or excessively ⟨a *swollen* joint⟩; *also* : BULGE **3** : to fill or be filled with emotion (as pride) ♦ **Synonyms** EXPAND, AMPLIFY, DISTEND, INFLATE, DILATE — **swell·ing** *n*

²swell *n* **1** : a long crestless wave or series of waves in the open sea **2** : the condition of being protuberant **3** : a person dressed in the height of fashion; *also* : a person of high social position

³swell *adj* **1** : STYLISH; *also* : socially prominent **2** : EXCELLENT ⟨a ∼ party⟩

swelled head *n* : an exaggerated opinion of oneself : SELF-CONCEIT

swel·ter \'swel-tər\ *vb* [ME *sweltren*, fr. *swelten* to die, be overcome by heat, fr. OE *sweltan* to die] **1** : to be faint or oppressed with the heat **2** : to become exceedingly hot — **swel·ter·ing** \-tə-riŋ\ *adj*

swept *past and past part of* SWEEP

swerve \'swərv\ *vb* **swerved; swerv·ing** : to move abruptly aside from a straight line or course — **swerve** *n*

¹swift \'swift\ *adj* **1** : moving or capable of moving with great speed **2** : occurring suddenly **3** : READY, ALERT ⟨∼ for vengeance⟩ — **swift·ly** *adv* — **swift·ness** *n*

²swift *n* : any of numerous small insect-eating birds with long narrow wings

swig \'swig\ *vb* **swigged; swig·ging** : to drink in long drafts — **swig** *n*

¹swill \'swil\ *vb* **1** : to swallow greedily : GUZZLE **2** : to feed (as hogs) on swill

²swill *n* **1** : food for animals composed of edible refuse mixed with liquid **2** : GARBAGE

¹swim \'swim\ *vb* **swam** \'swam\; **swum** \'swəm\; **swim·ming** **1** : to propel oneself along in water by natural means (as by hands and legs, by tail, or by fins) **2** : to glide smoothly along **3** : FLOAT **4** : to be covered with or as if with a liquid **5** : to be dizzy ⟨his head *swam*⟩ **6** : to cross or go over by swimming ⟨*swam* the river⟩ — **swim·mer** *n*

²swim *n* **1** : an act of swimming **2** : the main current of activity ⟨in the ∼⟩

swim·ming *n* : the action, art, or sport of swimming and diving

swimming pool *n* : a tank (as of concrete or plastic) designed for swimming

swim·suit \'swim-ˌsüt\ *n* : a suit for swimming or bathing

swim·wear \'swim-ˌwer\ *n* : clothing for wear while swimming or bathing

swin·dle \'swin-dᵊl\ *vb* **swin·dled; swin·dling** [fr. *swindler*, fr. G *Schwindler* giddy person, fr. *schwindeln* to be dizzy] : CHEAT, DEFRAUD — **swindle** *n* — **swin·dler** *n*

swine \'swin\ *n, pl* **swine** **1** : any of a family of stout short-legged hoofed mammals with bristly skin and a long flexible snout; *esp* : one widely raised as a meat animal **2** : a contemptible person — **swin·ish** *adj*

¹swing \'swin\ *vb* **swung** \'swəŋ\; **swing·ing** **1** : to move or cause to move rapidly in an arc **2** : to sway or cause to sway back and forth **3** : to hang so as to move freely back and forth or in a curve **4** : to be executed by hanging **5** : to move or turn on a hinge or pivot **6** : to manage or handle successfully **7** : to march or walk with free swaying movements **8** : to have a steady pulsing rhythm; *also* : to play swing music **9** : to be lively and up-to-date; *also* : to engage freely in sex ♦ **Synonyms** WIELD, MANIPULATE, PLY, MANEUVER — **swing·er** *n* — **swing·ing** *adj*

²swing *n* **1** : the act of swinging **2** : a swinging blow, movement, or rhythm **3** : the distance through which something swings : FLUCTUATION **4** : progression of an activity or process ⟨in full ∼⟩ **5** : a seat suspended by a rope or chain for swinging back and forth for pleasure **6** : jazz music played esp. by a large band and marked by a steady lively rhythm, simple harmony, and a basic melody often submerged in improvisation

³swing *adj* **1** : of or relating to musical swing **2** : that may swing decisively either way (as on an issue) ⟨∼ voters⟩

¹swipe \'swip\ *n* : a strong sweeping blow

²swipe *vb* **swiped; swip·ing** **1** : to strike or wipe with a sweeping motion **2** : PILFER, SNATCH **3** : to slide (a card having a magnetic code) through a reading device

swirl \'swərl\ *vb* : to move or cause to move with a whirling motion — **swirl** *n* — **swirly** \'swər-lē\ *adj*

swish \'swish\ *n* **1** : a prolonged hissing sound **2** : a light sweeping or brushing sound — **swish** *vb*

Swiss \'swis\ *n* **1** *pl* **Swiss** : a native or inhabitant of Switzerland **2** : a hard cheese with large holes — **Swiss** *adj*

Swiss chard *n* : a beet having large leaves and succulent stalks often cooked as a vegetable

¹switch \'swich\ *n* **1** : a slender flexible whip, rod, or twig **2** : a blow with a switch **3** : a shift from one thing to another; *also* : change from the usual **4** : a device for adjusting the rails of a track so that a locomotive or train may be turned from one track to another; *also* : a railroad siding **5** : a device for making, breaking, or changing the connections in an electrical circuit **6** : a heavy strand of hair often used in addition to a person's own hair for some coiffures

²switch *vb* **1** : to punish or urge on with a switch **2** : WHISK ⟨a cow ∼*ing* her tail⟩ **3** : to shift or turn by operating a switch **4** : CHANGE, EXCHANGE

switch·back \'swich-ˌbak\ *n* : a zigzag road, trail, or section of railroad tracks for climbing a steep hill

switch·blade \-ˌblād\ *n* : a pocket-knife with a spring-operated blade

switch·board \-ˌbȯrd\ *n* : a panel for controlling the operation of a number of electric circuits; *esp* : one used to make and break telephone connections

switch-hit·ter \-'hi-tər\ *n* : a baseball player who bats either right-handed or left-handed — **switch-hit** \-'hit\ *vb*

switch·man \'swich-mən\ *n* : one who attends a railroad switch

Switz *abbr* Switzerland

¹**swiv·el** \'swi-vəl\ *n* : a device joining two parts so that one or both can turn freely

²**swivel** *vb* **-eled** *or* **-elled; -el·ing** *or* **-el·ling** : to swing or turn on or as if on a swivel

swiv·et \'swi-vət\ *n* : an agitated state

swiz·zle stick \'swi-zəl-\ *n* : a stick used to stir mixed drinks

swollen *past part of* SWELL

swoon \'swün\ *vb* — FAINT — **swoon** *n*

swoop \'swüp\ *vb* : to move with a sweep ⟨the eagle ∼*ed* down on its prey⟩ — **swoop** *n*

swoopy \'swü-pē\ *adj* : having lines that extend in a wide curve ⟨a ∼ silhouette⟩

swop *chiefly Brit var of* SWAP

sword \'sórd\ *n* **1** : a weapon with a long blade for cutting or thrusting **2** : the use of force

sword·fish \-ˌfish\ *n* : a very large ocean fish used for food that has the upper jaw prolonged into a long swordlike beak

sword·play \-ˌplā\ *n* : the art or skill of wielding a sword

swords·man \'sórdz-mən\ *n* : one skilled in swordplay; *esp* : FENCER

sword·tail \'sórd-ˌtāl\ *n* : a small brightly marked Central American fish often kept in aquariums

swore *past of* SWEAR

sworn *past part of* SWEAR

swum *past part of* SWIM

swung *past and past part of* SWING

syb·a·rite \'si-bə-ˌrīt\ *n* : a lover of luxury : VOLUPTUARY — **syb·a·rit·ic** \ˌsi-bə-'ri-tik\ *adj*

syc·a·more \'si-kə-ˌmór\ *n* : a large spreading tree chiefly of the eastern and central U.S. that has light brown flaky bark and small round fruits hanging on long stalks

sy·co·phant \'si-kə-fənt\ *n* : a servile flatterer — **sy·co·phan·cy** \'si-kə-fən-sē\ *n* — **sy·co·phan·tic** \ˌsi-kə-'fan-tik\ *adj*

syl *or* **syll** *abbr* syllable

syl·lab·i·ca·tion \sə-ˌla-bə-'kā-shən\ *n* : the division of words into syllables

syl·lab·i·fy \sə-'la-bə-ˌfī\ *vb* **-fied; -fy·ing** : to form or divide into syllables — **syl·lab·i·fi·ca·tion** \-ˌla-bə-fə-'kā-shən\ *n*

syl·la·ble \'si-lə-bəl\ *n* [ME, fr. AF *sillabe*, *silable*, fr. L *syllaba*, fr. Gk *syllabē*, fr. *syllambanein* to gather together, fr. *syn-* with + *lambanein* to take] : a unit of spoken language consisting of an uninterrupted utterance and forming either a whole word (as *cat*) or a commonly recognized division of a word (as *syl* in *syl-la-ble*); *also* : one or more letters representing such a unit — **syl·lab·ic** \sə-'la-bik\ *adj*

syl·la·bus \'si-lə-bəs\ *n, pl* **-bi** \-ˌbī\ *or* **-bus·es** : a summary containing the heads or main topics of a speech, book, or course of study

syl·lo·gism \'si-lə-ˌji-zəm\ *n* : a logical scheme of a formal argument consisting of a major and a minor premise and a conclusion which must logically be true if the premises are true — **syl·lo·gis·tic** \ˌsi-lə-'jis-tik\ *adj*

sylph \'silf\ *n* **1** : an imaginary being inhabiting the air **2** : a slender graceful woman

syl·van \'sil-vən\ *adj* **1** : living or located in a wooded area; *also* : of, relating to, or characteristic of forest **2** : abounding in woods or trees

sym *abbr* **1** symbol **2** symmetrical

sym·bi·o·sis \ˌsim-ˌbī-'ō-səs, -bē-\ *n, pl* **-o·ses** \-ˌsēz\ : the living together in close association of two dissimilar organisms esp. when mutually beneficial — **sym·bi·ot·ic** \-'ä-tik\ *adj*

sym·bol \'sim-bəl\ *n* **1** : something that stands for something else; *esp* : something concrete that represents or suggests another thing that cannot in itself be pictured ⟨the lion is a ∼ of bravery⟩ **2** : a letter, character, or sign used in writing or printing to represent operations, quantities, elements, sounds, or other ideas — **sym·bol·ic** \sim-'bä-lik\ *also* **sym·bol·i·cal** \-li-kəl\ *adj* — **sym·bol·i·cal·ly** \-k(ə-)lē\ *adv*

sym·bol·ise *Brit var of* SYMBOLIZE

sym·bol·ism \'sim-bə-ˌli-zəm\ *n* : representation of abstract or intangible things by means of symbols

sym·bol·ize \'sim-bə-ˌlīz\ *vb* **-ized; -iz·ing** **1** : to serve as a symbol of **2** : to represent by symbols — **sym·bol·i·za·tion** \ˌsim-bə-lə-'zā-shən\ *n*

sym·me·try \'si-mə-trē\ *n, pl* **-tries** **1** : an arrangement marked by regularity and balanced proportions **2** : correspondence in size, shape, and position of parts that are on opposite sides of a dividing line or center — **sym·met·ri·cal** \sə-'me-tri-kəl\ *or* **sym·met·ric** \sə-'me-trik\ *adj* — **sym·met·ri·cal·ly** \-k(ə-)lē\ *adv*

sympathetic nervous system *n* : the part of the autonomic nervous system that is concerned esp. with the body's response to stress and that tends to decrease the tone and contractility of smooth muscle and increase blood pressure and the activity of the heart

sym·pa·thise *chiefly Brit var of* SYMPATHIZE

sym·pa·thize \'sim-pə-ˌthīz\ *vb* **-thized; -thiz·ing** : to feel or show sympathy — **sym·pa·thiz·er** *n*

sym·pa·thy \'sim-pə-thē\ *n, pl* **-thies** **1** : a relationship between persons or things wherein whatever affects one similarly affects the other **2** : harmony of interests and aims **3** : FAVOR, SUPPORT **4** : the capacity for entering into and sharing the feelings or interests of another; *also* : COMPASSION, PITY **5** : an expression of sorrow for another's loss, grief, or misfortune — **sym·pa·thet·ic** \ˌsim-pə-'the-tik\ *adj* — **sym·pa·thet·i·cal·ly** \-ti-k(ə-)lē\ *adv*

sym·pho·ny \'sim-fə-nē\ *n, pl* **-nies** **1** : harmony of sounds **2** : a large and complex composition for a full orchestra **3** : a large orchestra of a kind that plays symphonies — **sym·phon·ic** \sim-'fä-nik\ *adj*

sym·po·sium \sim-'pō-zē-əm\ *n, pl* **-sia** \-zē-ə\ *or* **-siums** : a conference at which a particular topic is discussed by various speakers; *also* : a collection of opinions about a subject

symp·tom \'simp-təm\ *n* [LL *symptoma*, fr. Gk *symptōma* happening, attribute, symptom, fr. *sympiptein* to happen, fr *syn-* with + *piptein* to fall] **1** : something that indicates the presence of disease or abnormality; *esp* : something (as a headache) that can be sensed only by the individual affected **2** : SIGN, INDICATION ⟨~s of inner turmoil⟩ — **symp·tom·at·ic** \ˌsimp-tə-'ma-tik\ *adj*

syn *abbr* synonym; synonymous; synonymy

syn·a·gogue *also* **syn·a·gog** \'si-nə-ˌgäg\ *n* [ME *synagoge*, fr. AF, fr. LL *synagoga*, fr. Gk *synagōgē* assembly, synagogue, fr. *synagein* to bring together] **1** : a Jewish congregation **2** : the house of worship of a Jewish congregation

syn·apse \'si-ˌnaps, sə-'naps\ *n* : the point at which a nervous impulse passes from one neuron to another — **syn·ap·tic** \sə-'nap-tik\ *adj*

¹sync *also* **synch** \'siŋk\ *vb* **synced** *also* **synched** \'siŋkt\; **sync·ing** *also* **synch·ing** \'siŋ-kiŋ\ : SYNCHRONIZE

²sync *also* **synch** *n* : SYNCHRONIZATION, SYNCHRONISM — **sync** *adj*

syn·chro·ni·sa·tion, syn·chro·nise *Brit var of* SYNCHRONIZATION, SYNCHRONIZE

syn·chro·nize \'siŋ-krə-ˌnīz, 'sin-\ *vb* **-nized; -niz·ing 1** : to occur or cause to occur at the same instant **2** : to represent, arrange, or tabulate according to dates or time **3** : to cause to agree in time **4** : to make synchronous in operation — **syn·chro·nism** \-ˌni-zəm\ *n* — **syn·chro·ni·za·tion** \ˌsiŋ-krə-nə-'zā-shən, ˌsin-\ *n* — **syn·chro·niz·er** *n*

syn·chro·nous \'siŋ-krə-nəs, 'sin-\ *adj* **1** : happening at the same time : CONCURRENT **2** : working, moving, or occurring together at the same rate and at the proper time

syn·co·pa·tion \ˌsiŋ-kə-'pā-shən, ˌsin-\ *n* : a shifting of the regular musical accent : occurrence of accented notes on the weak beat — **syn·co·pate** \'siŋ-kə-ˌpāt, 'sin-\ *vb*

syn·co·pe \'siŋ-kə-(ˌ)pē, 'sin-\ *n* : the loss of one or more sounds or letters in the interior of a word (as in *fo'c'sle* for *forecastle*)

¹syn·di·cate \'sin-di-kət\ *n* **1** : a group of persons who combine to carry out a financial or industrial undertaking **2** : a loose association of racketeers **3** : a business concern that sells materials for publication in many newspapers and periodicals at the same time

²syn·di·cate \-də-ˌkāt\ *vb* **-cat·ed; -cat·ing 1** : to combine into or manage as a syndicate **2** : to publish through a syndicate — **syn·di·ca·tion** \ˌsin-də-'kā-shən\ *n*

syn·drome \'sin-ˌdrōm\ *n* : a group of signs and symptoms that occur together and characterize a particular abnormality or condition

syn·er·gism \'sin-ər-ˌji-zəm\ *n* : interac-

tion of discrete agencies (as industrial firms), agents (as drugs), or conditions such that the total effect is greater than the sum of the individual effects — **syn·er·gist** \-iist\ *n* — **syn·er·gis·tic** \ˌsi-nər-'jis-tik\ *adj* — **syn·er·gis·ti·cal·ly** \-ti-k(ə-)lē\ *adv*

syn·er·gy \'si-nər-jē\ *n, pl* **-gies** : SYNERGISM

syn·fuel \'sin-ˌfyül\ *n* [*synthetic*] : a fuel derived esp. from a fossil fuel

syn·od \'si-nəd\ *n* **1** : COUNCIL, ASSEMBLY; *esp* : a religious governing body — **syn·od·al** \-nə-dᵊl, -ˌnä-dᵊl\ *adj* — **syn·od·ic** \sə-'nä-dik\ *or* **syn·od·i·cal** \-di-kəl\ *adj*

syn·onym \'si-nə-ˌnim\ *n* : one of two or more words in the same language which have the same or very nearly the same meaning — **syn·on·y·mous** \sə-'nä-nə-məs\ *adj* — **syn·on·y·mous·ly** *adv* — **syn·on·y·my** \-mē\ *n*

syn·op·sis \sə-'näp-səs\ *n, pl* **-op·ses** \-ˌsēz\ : a condensed statement or outline (as of a treatise) : ABSTRACT

syn·op·tic \sə-'näp-tik\ *also* **syn·op·ti·cal** \-ti-kəl\ *adj* : characterized by or affording a comprehensive view

syn·tax \'sin-ˌtaks\ *n* : the way in which words are put together to form phrases, clauses, or sentences — **syn·tac·tic** \sin-'tak-tik\ *or* **syn·tac·ti·cal** \-ti-kəl\ *adj*

syn·the·sis \'sin-thə-səs\ *n, pl* **-the·ses** \-ˌsēz\ : the combination of parts or elements into a whole; *esp* : the production of a substance by union of chemically simpler substances — **syn·the·size** \-ˌsīz\ *vb* — **syn·the·siz·er** *n*

syn·thet·ic \sin-'the-tik\ *adj* : produced artificially esp. by chemical means; *also* : not genuine — **synthetic** *n* — **syn·thet·i·cal·ly** \-ti-k(ə-)lē\ *adv*

syph·i·lis \'si-fə-ləs\ *n* [NL, fr. *Syphilus*, hero of the poem *Syphilus sive Morbus Gallicus* (*Syphilis or the French disease*) (1530) by Girolamo Fracastoro †1553 Ital. physician] : an infectious usu. venereal disease caused by a spirochete — **syph·i·lit·ic** \ˌsi-fə-'li-tik\ *adj or n*

syphon *var of* SIPHON

Sy·rah \sē-'rä\ *n* : a red wine

¹sy·ringe \sə-'rinj\ *n* : a device used esp. for injecting liquids into or withdrawing them from the body

²syringe *vb* **sy·ringed; sy·ring·ing** : to flush or cleanse with or as if with a syringe

syr·up *also* **sir·up** \'sər-əp, 'sir-əp\ *n* **1** : a thick sticky solution of sugar and water often flavored or medicated **2** : the concentrated juice of a fruit or plant — **syr·upy** *adj*

syst *abbr* system

sys·tem \'sis-təm\ *n* **1** : a group of units so combined as to form a whole and to operate in unison **2** : the body as a functioning whole; *also* : a group of bodily organs (as the nervous system) that together carry on some vital function **3** : a definite scheme or method of procedure or classification **4** : regular method or order — **sys·tem·at·ic** \ˌsis-tə-'ma-tik\ — **sys·tem·at·i·cal·ly** \-ti-k(ə-)lē\ *adv*

sys·tem·a·tise *Brit var of* SYSTEMATIZE
sys·tem·a·tize \'sis-tə-mə-ˌtīz\ *vb* **-tized;**
-tiz·ing : to make into a system : arrange
methodically

¹**sys·tem·ic** \sis-'te-mik\ *adj* **1** : of, relating
to, or affecting the whole body ⟨∼ dis-
ease⟩ **2** : of, relating to, or being a pesticide that when absorbed into the sap or
bloodstream makes the entire plant or animal toxic to a pest (as an insect or fungus)
²**systemic** *n* : a systemic pesticide
systemic lupus er·y·the·ma·to·sus \ˌer-
ə-ˌthē-mə-'tō-səs\ *n* : a systemic disease
esp. of women characterized by fever,
skin rash, and arthritis, often by anemia,
by small hemorrhages of the skin and
mucous membranes, and in serious cases
by involvement of internal organs
sys·tem·ize \'sis-tə-ˌmīz\ *vb* **-ized;** **-iz-**
ing : SYSTEMATIZE
systems analyst *n* : a person who studies a procedure or business to determine
its goals or purposes and to discover the
best ways to accomplish them — **sys-**
tems analysis *n*
sys·to·le \'sis-tə-(ˌ)lē\ *n* : a rhythmically
recurrent contraction of the heart —
sys·tol·ic \sis-'tä-lik\ *adj*

¹**t** \'tē\ *n, pl* **t's** *or* **ts** \'tēz\ *often cap* : the
20th letter of the English alphabet
²**t** *abbr, often cap* **1** tablespoon **2** teaspoon
3 temperature **4** ton **5** transitive **6** troy
7 true
T *abbr* **1** toddler **2** T-shirt
Ta *symbol* tantalum
TA *abbr* teaching assistant
¹**tab** \'tab\ *n* **1** : a short projecting flap,
loop, or tag; *also* : a small insert or addition **2** : close surveillance : WATCH ⟨keep
∼s on him⟩ **3** : BILL, CHECK **4** : a key
on a keyboard esp. for putting data in
columns
²**tab** *vb* **tabbed; tab·bing** : DESIGNATE
tab·by \'ta-bē\ *n, pl* **tabbies** : a usu.
striped or mottled domestic cat; *also* : a
female domestic cat
tab·er·na·cle \'ta-bər-ˌna-kəl\ *n* [ME, fr.
AF, fr. LL *tabernaculum*, fr. L, tent, fr.
taberna hut] **1** *often cap* : a tent sanctu-
ary used by the Israelites during the Exodus **2** : a receptacle for the consecrated
elements of the Eucharist **3** : a house of
worship
¹**ta·ble** \'tā-bəl\ *n* **1** : TABLET **2** : a piece
of furniture consisting of a smooth flat
top fixed on legs **3** : a supply of food
: BOARD, FARE **4** : a group of people assembled at or as if at a table **5** : an orderly arrangement of data usu. in rows
and columns **6** : a short list ⟨∼ of con-
tents⟩ — **ta·ble·top** \-ˌtäp\ *n*
²**table** *vb* **ta·bled; ta·bling** **1** *Brit* : to place
on the agenda **2** : to remove (a parlia-
mentary motion) from consideration indefinitely
tab·leau \'ta-ˌblō\ *n, pl* **tab·leaux** \-ˌblōz\
also **tableaus** [F] : a scene or event usu.
presented on a stage by silent and motionless costumed participants
ta·ble·cloth \'tā-bəl-ˌklȯth\ *n* : a covering
spread over a dining table before the table is set
ta·ble d'hôte \ˌtä-bəl-'dōt\ *n* [F, lit., host's
table] : a complete meal of several courses offered at a fixed price
ta·ble·land \'tā-bəl-ˌland\ *n* : PLATEAU
ta·ble·spoon \-ˌspün\ *n* **1** : a large spoon
used esp. for serving **2** : a unit of measure equal to ½ fluid ounce (15 milliliters)
ta·ble·spoon·ful \-ˌfül\ *n, pl* **-spoonfuls**
\-ˌfülz\ *also* **-spoons·ful** \-ˌspünz-ˌfül\
: TABLESPOON **2**
tab·let \'ta-blət\ *n* **1** : a flat slab suited for
or bearing an inscription **2** : a collection
of sheets of paper glued together at one
edge **3** : a compressed or molded block
of material; *esp* : a usu. disk-shaped medicated mass
table tennis *n* : a game resembling tennis
played on a tabletop with wooden paddles and a small hollow plastic ball
ta·ble·ware \'tā-bəl-ˌwer\ *n* : utensils (as
of china or silver) for table use
¹**tab·loid** \'ta-ˌblȯid\ *adj* : condensed into
small scope
²**tabloid** *n* : a newspaper marked by small
pages, condensation of the news, and
usu. many photographs
¹**ta·boo** *also* **ta·bu** \tə-'bü, ta-\ *adj* [Tongan
(a Polynesian language) *tabu*] : prohibit-
ed by a taboo
²**taboo** *also* **tabu** *n, pl* **taboos** *also* **tabus**
1 : a prohibition against touching, saying,
or doing something for fear of immediate
harm from a supernatural force **2** : a
prohibition imposed by social custom
ta·bor *also* **ta·bour** \'tā-bər\ *n* : a small
drum used to accompany a pipe or fife
played by the same person
tab·u·lar \'ta-byə-lər\ *adj* **1** : having a flat
surface **2** : arranged in a table; *esp* : set
up in rows and columns **3** : computed by
means of a table
tab·u·late \-ˌlāt\ *vb* **-lat·ed; -lat·ing** : to
put into tabular form — **tab·u·la·tion**
\ˌta-byə-'lā-shən\ *n* — **tab·u·la·tor** \'ta-
byə-ˌlā-tər\ *n*
TAC \'tak\ *abbr* Tactical Air Command
tach \'tak\ *n* : TACHOMETER
ta·chom·e·ter \ta-'kä-mə-tər, tə-\ *n* [ul-
tim. fr. Gk *tachos* speed] : a device to indicate speed of rotation
tachy·car·dia \ˌta-ki-'kär-dē-ə\ *n* : relatively rapid heart action

tachy·on \'ta-kē-,än\ *n* : a hypothetical particle held to travel faster than light

tac·it \'ta-sət\ *adj* [F or L; F *tacite*, fr. L *tacitus* silent, fr. *tacēre* to be silent] **1** : expressed without words or speech **2** : implied or indicated but not actually expressed 〈~ consent〉 — **tac·it·ly** *adv* — **tac·it·ness** *n*

tac·i·turn \'ta-sə-,tərn\ *adj* : disinclined to talk ◆ **Synonyms** UNCOMMUNICATIVE, RESERVED, RETICENT, CLOSEMOUTHED — **tac·i·tur·ni·ty** \,ta-sə-'tər-nə-tē\ *n*

¹tack \'tak\ *vb* **1** : to fasten with tacks; *also* : to add on **2** : to change the direction of (a sailing ship) from one tack to another **3** : to follow a zigzag course

²tack *n* **1** : a small sharp nail with a broad flat head **2** : the direction toward the wind that a ship is sailing 〈starboard ~〉; *also* : the run of a ship on one tack **3** : a change of course from one tack to another **4** : a zigzag course **5** : a course of action

³tack *n* : gear for harnessing a horse

¹tack·le \'ta-kəl, *naut often* 'tā-\ *n* **1** : GEAR, APPARATUS, EQUIPMENT **2** : the rigging of a ship **3** : an arrangement of ropes and pulleys for hoisting or pulling heavy objects **4** : the act or an instance of tackling; *also* : a football lineman playing between guard and end

²tackle *vb* **tack·led; tack·ling 1** : to attach and secure with or as if with tackle **2** : to seize, grapple with, or throw down with the intention of subduing or stopping **3** : to set about dealing with 〈~ a problem〉 — **tack·ler** *n*

¹tacky \'ta-kē\ *adj* **tack·i·er; -est** : sticky to the touch

²tacky *adj* **tack·i·er; -est 1** : SHABBY, SEEDY **2** : marked by lack of style or good taste; *also* : cheaply showy 〈a ~ publicity stunt〉 〈a ~ outfit〉

ta·co \'tä-kō\ *n, pl* **tacos** \-kōz\ [MexSp] : a usu. fried tortilla rolled up with or folded over a filling

tact \'takt\ *n* [F, sense of touch, fr. L *tactus*, fr. *tangere* to touch] : a keen sense of what to do or say to keep good relations with others 〈a diplomat with ~〉 — **tact·ful** \-fəl\ *adj* — **tact·ful·ly** *adv* — **tact·less** *adj* — **tact·less·ly** *adv*

tac·tic \'tak-tik\ *n* : a planned action for accomplishing an end

tac·tics \'tak-tiks\ *n sing or pl* **1** : the science of maneuvering forces in combat **2** : the skill of using available means to accomplish an end — **tac·ti·cal** \-ti-kəl\ *adj* — **tac·ti·cian** \tak-'ti-shən\ *n*

tac·tile \'tak-t°l, 'tak-,tī(-ə)l\ *adj* : of, relating to, or perceptible through the sense of touch

tad·pole \'tad-,pōl\ *n* [ME *taddepol*, fr. *tode* toad + *polle* head] : an aquatic larva of a frog or toad that has a tail and gills

tae kwon do \'tī-'kwän-'dō\ *n* : a Korean martial art of self-defense

taf·fe·ta \'ta-fə-tə\ *n* : a crisp lustrous fabric (as of silk or rayon)

taff·rail \'taf-,rāl, -rəl\ *n* : the rail around a ship's stern

taf·fy \'ta-fē\ *n, pl* **taffies** : a candy usu. of molasses or brown sugar stretched until porous and light-colored

¹tag \'tag\ *n* **1** : a metal or plastic binding on an end of a shoelace **2** : a piece of hanging or attached material **3** : a hackneyed quotation or saying **4** : a descriptive or identifying epithet

²tag *vb* **tagged; tag·ging 1** : to provide or mark with or as if with a tag; *esp* : IDENTIFY **2** : to attach as an addition **3** : to follow closely and persistently 〈~s along everywhere we go〉 **4** : to hold responsible for something

³tag *n* : a game in which one player chases others and tries to touch one of them

⁴tag *vb* **tagged; tag·ging 1** : to touch in or as if in a game of tag **2** : SELECT

TAG *abbr* the adjutant general

tag sale *n* : GARAGE SALE

Ta·hi·tian \tə-'hē-shən\ *n* **1** : a native or inhabitant of Tahiti **2** : the Polynesian language of the Tahitians — **Tahitian** *adj*

tai·ga \'tī-gə\ *n* [Russ *taiga*] : a moist coniferous subarctic forest extending south from the tundra

¹tail \'tāl\ *n* **1** : the rear end or a process extending from the rear end of an animal **2** : something resembling an animal's tail **3** *pl* : full evening dress for men **4** : the back, last, lower, or inferior part of something; *esp* : the reverse of a coin — usu. used in pl. 〈~s, I win〉 **5** : one who follows or keeps watch on someone — **tailed** \'tāld\ *adj* — **tail·less** \'tāl-ləs\ *adj*

²tail *vb* : FOLLOW; *esp* : to follow for the purpose of surveillance

tail·coat \-'kōt\ *n* : a coat with tails; *esp* : a man's full-dress coat with two long tapering skirts at the back

¹tail·gate \-,gāt\ *n* : a board or gate at the back end of a vehicle that can be let down (as for loading)

²tailgate *vb* **tail·gat·ed; tail·gat·ing 1** : to drive dangerously close behind another vehicle **2** : to hold a tailgate picnic

³tailgate *adj* : relating to or being a picnic set up on a tailgate 〈a ~ party〉

tail·light \-,līt\ *n* : a usu. red warning light mounted at the rear of a vehicle

¹tai·lor \'tā-lər\ *n* [ME *taillour*, fr. AF *taillur*, fr. *tailler* to cut, fr. LL *taliare*, fr. L *talea* twig, cutting] : a person whose occupation is making or altering garments

²tailor *vb* **1** : to make or fashion as the work of a tailor **2** : to make or adapt to suit a special purpose

tail·pipe \'tāl-,pīp\ *n* : an outlet by which engine exhaust gases are expelled from a vehicle (as an automobile)

tail·spin \'tāl-,spin\ *n* : a rapid descent or downward spiral

tail·wind \'tāl-,wind\ *n* : a wind blowing in the same general direction as a course of movement (as of an aircraft)

¹taint \'tānt\ *vb* **1** : CORRUPT, CONTAMINATE **2** : to affect or become affected with something bad (as putrefaction)

²taint *n* : a contaminating mark or influence

ta·ka \'tä-kə\ *n* — see MONEY table

¹take \'tāk\ *vb* **took** \'tük\; **tak·en** \'tā-kən\; **tak·ing** [ME, fr. OE *tacan*, fr. ON *taka*] **1** : to get into one's hands or possession : GRASP, SEIZE **2** : CAPTURE; *also* : DEFEAT **3** : to obtain or secure for use **4** : to catch or attack through the effect of a sudden force or influence ⟨*taken* ill⟩ **5** : CAPTIVATE, DELIGHT **6** : to bring into a relation ⟨~ a wife⟩ **7** : REMOVE, SUBTRACT ⟨~ three from eight⟩ **8** : to pick out : CHOOSE **9** : ASSUME, UNDERTAKE **10** : RECEIVE, ACCEPT **11** : to use for transportation ⟨~ a bus⟩ **12** : to become impregnated with : ABSORB ⟨~ a dye⟩ **13** : to receive into one's body (as by swallowing) ⟨~ a pill⟩ **14** : ENDURE, UNDERGO ⟨~ a cut in pay⟩ **15** : to lead, carry, or cause to go along to another place **16** : NEED, REQUIRE ⟨~s a size nine shoe⟩ **17** : to obtain as the result of a special procedure ⟨~ a snapshot⟩ **18** : to undertake and do, make, or perform ⟨~ a walk⟩ **19** : to take effect : ACT, OPERATE ♦ *Synonyms* GRAB, CLUTCH, SNATCH, SEIZE, NAB, GRAPPLE — **tak·er** *n* — **take advantage of 1** : to profit by **2** : EXPLOIT — **take after** : RESEMBLE — **take care** : to be careful — **take care of** : to attend to — **take effect** : to become operative — **take exception** : OBJECT — **take for 1** : to suppose to be; *esp* : to mistake for — **take place** : HAPPEN — **take to 1** : to go to **2** : to apply or devote oneself to **3** : to conceive a liking for

²**take** *n* **1** : the number or quantity taken; *also* : PROCEEDS, RECEIPTS **2** : an act or the action of taking **3** : a television or movie scene filmed or taped at one time; *also* : a sound recording made at one time **4** : a distinct or personal point of view

take·off \'tāk-ˌȯf\ *n* **1** : IMITATION; *esp* : PARODY ⟨did a ~ of the president⟩ **2** : an act or instance of taking off

take off *vb* **1** : REMOVE **2** : DEDUCT **3** : to set out : go away **4** : to begin flight

take on *vb* **1** : to begin to perform or deal with; *also* : to contend with as an opponent **2** : ENGAGE, HIRE **3** : to assume or acquire as or as if one's own **4** : to make an unusual show of one's feelings esp. of grief or anger

take over *vb* : to assume control or possession of or responsibility for ⟨*took over* the company⟩ — **take·over** \'tāk-ˌō-vər\ *n*

take up *vb* **1** : PICK UP **2** : to begin to occupy (land) **3** : to absorb or incorporate into itself ⟨plants *taking up* nutrients⟩ **4** : to begin to engage in ⟨*took up* jogging⟩ **5** : to make tighter or shorter ⟨*take up* the slack⟩

tak·ings \'tā-kiŋz\ *n pl, chiefly Brit* : receipts esp. of money

ta·la \'tä-lə\ *n, pl* tala — see MONEY table

talc \'talk\ *n* : a soft mineral with a soapy feel used esp. in making a soothing powder (**tal·cum powder** \'tal-kəm-\) for the skin

tale \'tāl\ *n* **1** : a relation of a series of events **2** : a report of a confidential matter **3** : idle talk; *esp* : harmful gossip **4** : a usu. imaginative narrative **5** : FALSEHOOD **6** : COUNT, TALLY

tal·ent \'ta-lənt\ *n* **1** : an ancient unit of weight and value **2** : the natural endowments of a person **3** : a special often creative or artistic aptitude **4** : mental power : ABILITY **5** : a person of talent ♦ *Synonyms* GENIUS, GIFT, FACULTY, APTITUDE, KNACK — **tal·ent·ed** *adj*

ta·ler \'tä-lər\ *n* : any of numerous silver coins issued by German states from the 15th to the 19th centuries

tales·man \'tālz-mən\ *n* : a person summoned for jury duty

tal·is·man \'ta-ləs-mən, -ləz-\ *n, pl* **-mans** [F *talisman* or Sp *talismán* or It *talismano*, fr. Ar *ṭilsam*, fr. MGk *telesma*, fr. Gk, consecration, fr. *telein* to initiate into the mysteries, complete, fr. *telos* end] : an object thought to act as a charm

¹**talk** \'tȯk\ *vb* **1** : to express in speech : utter words : SPEAK **2** : DISCUSS ⟨~ business⟩ **3** : to influence or cause by talking ⟨~ed him into going⟩ **4** : to use (a language) for communicating **5** : CONVERSE **6** : to reveal confidential information; *also* : GOSSIP **7** : to give a talk : LECTURE — **talk·er** *n* — **talk back** : to answer impertinently

²**talk** *n* **1** : the act of talking **2** : a way of speaking **3** : a formal discussion **4** : REPORT, RUMOR **5** : the topic of comment or gossip ⟨the ~ of the town⟩ **6** : an informal address or lecture

talk·ative \'tȯ-kə-tiv\ *adj* : given to talking ♦ *Synonyms* LOQUACIOUS, CHATTY, GABBY, GARRULOUS — **talk·ative·ly** *adv* — **talk·ative·ness** *n*

talk·ing-to \'tȯ-kiŋ-ˌtü\ *n* : REPRIMAND, REPROOF

talk radio *n* : radio programming consisting of call-in shows

tall \'tȯl\ *adj* **1** : high in stature; *also* : of a specified height ⟨six feet ~⟩ **2** : LARGE, FORMIDABLE ⟨a ~ order⟩ **3** : UNBELIEVABLE, IMPROBABLE ⟨a ~ story⟩ — **tall·ness** *n*

tal·low \'ta-lō\ *n* : a hard white fat rendered usu. from cattle or sheep tissues and used esp. in candles

¹**tal·ly** \'ta-lē\ *n, pl* tallies **1** : a device for visibly recording or accounting esp. business transactions **2** : a recorded account **3** : a corresponding part; *also* : CORRESPONDENCE

²**tally** *vb* **tal·lied; tal·ly·ing 1** : to mark on or as if on a tally **2** : to make a count of : RECKON; *also* : SCORE **3** : CORRESPOND, MATCH ♦ *Synonyms* SQUARE, ACCORD, HARMONIZE, CONFORM, JIBE

tal·ly·ho \ˌta-lē-'hō\ *n, pl* **-hos** : a call of a huntsman at sight of the fox

Tal·mud \'täl-ˌmu̇d, 'tal-məd\ *n* [Late Heb *talmūdh*, lit., instruction] : the authoritative body of Jewish tradition — **Tal·mu·dic** \tal-'mü-dik, -'myü-, -'mə-; täl-'mu̇-\ *adj* — **Tal·mud·ist** \'täl-ˌmü-dist, 'tal-mə-\ *n*

tal·on \'ta-lən\ *n* : the claw of an animal and esp. of a bird of prey

ta·lus \'tā-ləs, 'ta-\ *n* : rock debris at the base of a cliff

tam \'tam\ *n* : TAM-O'-SHANTER

ta·ma·le \tə-'mä-lē\ *n* [MexSp *tamales*, pl. of *tamal*, fr. Nahuatl *tamalli* steamed cornmeal dough] : ground meat seasoned with chili, rolled in cornmeal dough, wrapped in corn husks, and steamed

tam·a·rack \'ta-mə-ˌrak\ *n* : a larch of northern No. America; *also* : its hard resinous wood

tam·a·rin \'ta-mə-rən\ *n* : any of several small So. American monkeys related to the marmosets

tam·a·rind \'ta-mə-rənd, -ˌrind\ *n* [Sp & Pg *tamarindo*, fr. Ar *tamr hindī*, lit., Indian date] : a tropical tree of the legume family with hard yellowish wood and feathery leaves; *also* : its acid fruit

tam·ba·la \täm-'bä-lə\ *n, pl* **-la** *or* **-las** — see *kwacha* at MONEY table

tam·bou·rine \ˌtam-bə-'rēn\ *n* : a small shallow drum with loose disks at the sides played by shaking or striking with the hand

¹**tame** \'tām\ *adj* **tam·er; tam·est** **1** : reduced from a state of native wildness esp. so as to be useful to humans : DOMESTICATED **2** : made docile : SUBDUED **3** : lacking spirit or interest : INSIPID ♦ *Synonyms* SUBMISSIVE, DOMESTIC, DOMESTICATED — **tame·ly** *adv* — **tame·ness** *n*

²**tame** *vb* **tamed; tam·ing** **1** : to make or become tame; *also* : to subject (land) to cultivation **2** : HUMBLE, SUBDUE — **tam·able** *or* **tame·able** \'tā-mə-bəl\ *adj* — **tame·less** *adj* — **tam·er** *n*

tam-o'-shan·ter \'ta-mə-ˌshan-tər\ *n* [fr. poem *Tam o' Shanter* (1790) by Robert Burns †1796 Scot. poet] : a Scottish woolen cap with a wide flat circular crown and usu. a pom-pom in the center

ta·mox·i·fen \tə-'mäk-sə-ˌfen\ *n* : a drug used esp. to treat breast cancer

tamp \'tamp\ *vb* : to drive down or in by a series of light blows

tam·per \'tam-pər\ *vb* **1** : to carry on underhand negotiations (as by bribery) ⟨~ with a witness⟩ **2** : to interfere so as to weaken or change for the worse ⟨~ with a document⟩ **3** : to try foolish or dangerous experiments

tam·pon \'tam-ˌpän\ *n* [F, lit., plug] : a plug (as of cotton) introduced into a body cavity usu. to absorb secretions (as from menstruation) or to arrest bleeding

¹**tan** \'tan\ *vb* **tanned; tan·ning** **1** : to change (hide) into leather esp. by soaking in a liquid containing tannin **2** : to make or become brown (as by exposure to the sun) **3** : WHIP, THRASH

²**tan** *n* **1** : a brown skin color induced by sun or weather **2** : a light yellowish brown color

³**tan** *abbr* tangent

tan·a·ger \'ta-ni-jər\ *n* : any of numerous American birds that are often brightly colored

tan·bark \'tan-ˌbärk\ *n* : bark (as of oak or sumac) that is rich in tannin and used in tanning

¹**tan·dem** \'tan-dəm\ *n* [L, at last, at length (taken to mean "lengthwise"), fr. *tam* so] **1** : a 2-seated carriage with horses hitched tandem; *also* : its team **2** : a bicycle for

two persons sitting one behind the other — **in tandem** : in a tandem arrangement

²**tandem** *adv* : one behind another

³**tandem** *adj* **1** : consisting of things arranged one behind the other **2** : working in conjunction with each other

tang \'taŋ\ *n* **1** : a part in a tool that connects the blade with the handle **2** : a sharp distinctive flavor; *also* : a pungent odor — **tangy** *adj*

¹**tan·gent** \'tan-jənt\ *adj* [L *tangent-, tangens*, prp. of *tangere* to touch] : TOUCHING; *esp* : touching a circle or sphere at only one point

²**tangent** *n* **1** : the trigonometric function that is the ratio between the side opposite and the side adjacent to an acute angle in a right triangle **2** : a tangent line, curve, or surface **3** : an abrupt change of course

tan·gen·tial \tan-'jen-chəl\ *adj* **1** : TANGENT **2** : touching lightly : INCIDENTAL ⟨~ involvement⟩ — **tan·gen·tial·ly** *adv*

tan·ger·ine \'tan-jə-ˌrēn, ˌtan-jə-'rēn\ *n* : a deep orange loose-skinned citrus fruit; *also* : a tree that bears tangerines

¹**tan·gi·ble** \'tan-jə-bəl\ *adj* **1** : perceptible esp. by the sense of touch : PALPABLE **2** : substantially real : MATERIAL ⟨~ rewards⟩ **3** : capable of being appraised ⟨~ assets⟩ ♦ *Synonyms* APPRECIABLE, PERCEPTIBLE, SENSIBLE, DISCERNIBLE — **tan·gi·bil·i·ty** \ˌtan-jə-'bi-lə-tē\ *n*

²**tangible** *n* : something tangible; *esp* : a tangible asset

¹**tan·gle** \'tan-gəl\ *vb* **tan·gled; tan·gling** **1** : to involve so as to hamper or embarrass; *also* : ENTRAP **2** : to unite or knit together in intricate confusion : ENTANGLE

²**tangle** *n* **1** : a tangled twisted mass **2** : a confusedly complicated state : MUDDLE

tan·go \'tan-gō\ *n, pl* **tangos** : a dance of Latin-American origin — **tango** *vb*

tank \'taŋk\ *n* **1** : a large artificial receptacle for liquids **2** : a heavily armed and armored combat vehicle that moves on tracks — **tank·ful** *n*

tan·kard \'tan-kərd\ *n* : a tall one-handled drinking vessel

tank·er \'tan-kər\ *n* : a vehicle equipped for transporting a liquid

tank top *n* : a sleeveless collarless pullover shirt with shoulder straps

tank town *n* : a small town

tan·ner \'ta-nər\ *n* : one that tans hides

tan·nery \'ta-nə-rē\ *n, pl* **-ner·ies** : a place where tanning is carried on

tan·nic acid \'ta-nik-\ *n* : TANNIN

tan·nin \'ta-nən\ *n* : any of various plant substances used esp. in tanning and dyeing, in inks, and as astringents

tan·sy \'tan-zē\ *n, pl* **tansies** : a common weedy herb related to the daisies with an aromatic odor and bitter-tasting finely divided leaves

tan·ta·lise *Brit var of* TANTALIZE

tan·ta·lize \'tan-tə-ˌlīz\ *vb* **-lized; -liz·ing** [fr. *Tantalus*, king of Greek myth punished in Hades by having to stand up to his chin in water that receded as he bent to drink] : to tease or torment by presenting something desirable but keeping it out of reach — **tan·ta·liz·er** *n* — **tan·ta·liz·ing·ly** *adv*

tan·ta·lum \'tan-tə-ləm\ *n* : a gray-white ductile metallic chemical element

tan·ta·mount \'tan-tə-ˌmaúnt\ *adj* : equivalent in value or meaning ⟨a relationship ~ to marriage⟩

tan·trum \'tan-trəm\ *n* : a fit of bad temper

Tao·ism \'taú-ˌi-zəm, 'daú-\ *n* : a Chinese mystical philosophy; *also* : a religion developed from Taoist philosophy and Buddhism — **Tao·ist** \-ist\ *adj or n*

¹tap \'tap\ *n* **1** : FAUCET, COCK **2** : liquor drawn through a tap **3** : the removing of fluid from a container or cavity by tapping **4** : a tool for forming an internal screw thread **5** : a point in an electric circuit where a connection may be made

²tap *vb* **tapped; tap·ping 1** : to release or cause to flow by piercing or by drawing a plug from a container or cavity **2** : to pierce so as to let out or draw off a fluid **3** : to draw from ⟨~ resources⟩ **4** : to cut in on (as a telephone signal) to get information **5** : to form an internal screw thread in by means of a tap **6** : to connect (as a gas or water main) with a local supply — **tap·per** *n*

³tap *vb* **tapped; tap·ping 1** : to rap lightly **2** : to bring about by repeated light blows **3** : SELECT; *esp* : to elect to membership

⁴tap *n* **1** : a light blow or stroke; *also* : its sound **2** : a small metal plate for the sole or heel of a shoe

ta·pa \'tä-pə, 'ta-\ *n* [Sp, lit., cover, lid] : an hors d'oeuvre served with drinks esp. in Spanish bars — usu. used in pl.

¹tape \'tāp\ *n* **1** : a narrow flexible band or strip (as of woven fabric) **2** : MAGNETIC TAPE; *also* : CASSETTE

²tape *vb* **taped; tap·ing 1** : to fasten or support with tape **2** : to record on magnetic tape

tape deck *n* : a device used to play back cassette tapes that usu. has to be connected to an audio system

tape measure *n* : a tape marked off in units (as inches) for measuring

¹ta·per \'tā-pər\ *n* **1** : a slender wax candle; *also* : a long waxed wick **2** : a gradual lessening of thickness or width in a long object

²taper *vb* **ta·pered; ta·per·ing 1** : to make or become gradually smaller toward one end **2** : to diminish gradually

tape–re·cord \ˌtāp-ri-'kórd\ *vb* : to make a recording of on magnetic tape — **tape recorder** *n* — **tape recording** *n*

tap·es·try \'ta-pə-strē\ *n, pl* **-tries** : a heavy reversible textile that has designs or pictures woven into it and is used esp. as a wall hanging

tape·worm \'tāp-ˌwərm\ *n* : any of a class of long flat segmented worms parasitic esp. in vertebrate intestines

tap·i·o·ca \ˌta-pē-'ō-kə\ *n* : a usu. granular preparation of cassava starch used esp. in puddings; *also* : a dish (as pudding) that contains tapioca

ta·pir \'tā-pər\ *n, pl* **tapirs** *also* **tapir** [Pg *tapir, tapira,* fr. Tupinambá (American Indian language of Brazil) *tapiʔtïra*] : any of a genus of large hoofed mammals of tropical America and southeastern Asia

tap·pet \'ta-pət\ *n* : a lever or projection moved by some other piece (as a cam) or intended to move something else

tap·room \'tap-ˌrüm, -ˌrúm\ *n* : BARROOM

tap·root \-ˌrüt, -ˌrút\ *n* : a large main root growing straight down and giving off small side roots

taps \'taps\ *n sing or pl* : the last bugle call at night blown as a signal that lights are to be put out; *also* : a similar call blown at military funerals and memorial services

tap·ster \'tap-stər\ *n* : BARTENDER

¹tar \'tär\ *n* **1** : a thick dark sticky liquid distilled from organic material (as wood or coal) **2** : SAILOR, SEAMAN

²tar *vb* **tarred; tar·ring** : to cover or smear with or as if with tar

tar·an·tel·la \ˌta-rən-'te-lə\ *n* : a lively folk dance of southern Italy in 6/8 time

ta·ran·tu·la \tə-'ran-chə-lə, -tə-lə\ *n, pl* **tarantulas** *also* **ta·ran·tu·lae** \-'ran-chə-ˌlē, -tə-ˌlē\ : any of a family of large hairy American spiders with a sharp bite that is not very poisonous to human beings

tar·dy \'tär-dē\ *adj* **tar·di·er; -est 1** : moving slowly : SLUGGISH **2** : LATE ⟨was ~ to work⟩ **♦ Synonyms** BEHINDHAND, OVERDUE, BELATED — **tar·di·ly** \-də-lē\ *adv* — **tar·di·ness** \-dē-nəs\

¹tare \'ter\ *n* : a weed of grain fields

²tare *n* : a deduction from the gross weight of a substance and its container made in allowance for the weight of the container — **tare** *vb*

¹tar·get \'tär-gət\ *n* [ME, fr. MF *targette,* dim. of *targe* light shield, of Gmc origin] **1** : a mark to shoot at **2** : an object of ridicule or criticism **3** : a goal to be achieved

²target *vb* : to make a target of

tar·iff \'ta-rəf\ *n* [It *tariffa,* fr. Ar *taʿrīf* notification] **1** : a schedule of duties imposed by a government esp. on imported goods; *also* : a duty or rate of duty imposed in such a schedule **2** : a schedule of rates or charges

tar·mac \'tär-ˌmak\ *n* : a surface paved with crushed stone covered with tar

tarn \'tärn\ *n* : a small mountain lake

tar·nish \'tär-nish\ *vb* : to make or become dull or discolored — **tarnish** *n*

ta·ro \'tär-ō, 'ter-\ *n, pl* **taros** : a largeleaved tropical plant related to the arums that is grown for its edible starchy corms; *also* : its corms

tar·ot \'ter-ō, 'ta-rō\ *n* : one of a set of usu. 78 playing cards used esp. for fortune-telling

tar·pau·lin \tär-'pó-lən, 'tär-pə-\ *n* : a piece of material (as durable plastic) used for protecting exposed objects

tar·pon \'tär-pən\ *n, pl* **tarpon** *or* **tarpons** : a large silvery bony fish often caught for sport in the warm coastal waters of the Atlantic esp. off Florida

tar·ra·gon \'ter-ə-gän\ [MF *targon*, ultim. fr. Ar *ṭarkhūn*] : a small widely cultivated perennial wormwood with aromatic leaves used as a seasoning; *also* : its leaves

¹tar·ry \'ta-rē\ *vb* **tar·ried; tar·ry·ing** 1 : to be tardy : DELAY; *esp* : to be slow in leaving 2 : to stay in or at a place : SOJOURN ♦ **Synonyms** REMAIN, WAIT, LINGER, ABIDE

²tar·ry \'tär-ē\ *adj* : of, resembling, or smeared with tar

tar sand *n* : sand or sandstone that is naturally soaked with the heavy sticky portions of petroleum

tar·sus \'tär-səs\ *n, pl* **tar·si** \-,sī\ [NL] : the part of a vertebrate foot between the metatarsus and the leg; *also* : the small bones that support this part — **tar·sal** \-səl\ *adj or n*

¹tart \'tärt\ *adj* 1 : agreeably sharp to the taste : PUNGENT 2 : BITING, CAUSTIC ⟨∼ comments⟩ — **tart·ly** *adv* — **tart·ness** *n*

²tart *n* 1 : a small pie or pastry shell containing jelly, custard, or fruit 2 : PROSTITUTE

tar·tan \'tärt-³n\ *n* : a plaid textile design of Scottish origin usu. distinctively patterned to designate a particular clan

tar·tar \'tär-tər\ *n* 1 : a substance in the juice of grapes deposited (as in wine casks) as a reddish crust or sediment 2 : a crust on the teeth formed from plaque hardened by calcium salts

tar·tar sauce *or* **tar·tare sauce** \'tär-tər-\ *n* : mayonnaise with chopped pickles, olives, or capers

¹task \'task\ *n* [ME *taske*, fr. MF dial. *tasque*, fr. ML *tasca* tax or service imposed by a feudal superior, fr. *taxare* to tax] : a piece of assigned work ♦ **Synonyms** JOB, DUTY, CHORE, STINT, ASSIGNMENT

²task *vb* : to oppress with great labor

task force *n* : a temporary grouping to accomplish a particular objective

task·mas·ter \'task-,mas-tər\ *n* : one that imposes a task or burdens another with labor

¹tas·sel \'ta-səl, 'tä-\ *n* 1 : a hanging ornament made of a bunch of cords of even length fastened at one end 2 : something suggesting a tassel; *esp* : a male flower cluster of corn

²tassel *vb* **-seled** *or* **-selled; -sel·ing** *or* **-sel·ling** : to adorn with or put forth tassels

¹taste \'tāst\ *vb* **tast·ed; tast·ing** 1 : EXPERIENCE, UNDERGO 2 : to try or determine the flavor of by taking a bit into the mouth 3 : to eat or drink esp. in small quantities : SAMPLE 4 : to have a specific flavor ⟨the milk ∼s sour⟩

²taste *n* 1 : a small amount tasted 2 : BIT; *esp* : a sample of experience 3 : the special sense that perceives and identifies sweet, sour, bitter, or salty qualities and is mediated by taste buds on the tongue 4 : a quality perceptible to the sense of taste; *also* : the sensation obtained from a substance in the mouth : FLAVOR 5 : individual preference 6 : critical judgment, discernment, or appreciation; *also* : aesthetic quality ♦ **Synonyms** TANG, RELISH, FLAVOR, SAVOR — **taste·ful** \-fəl\ *adj* — **taste·ful·ly** *adv* — **taste·less** *adj* — **taste·less·ly** *adv* — **tast·er** *n*

taste bud *n* : a sense organ mediating the sensation of taste

tasty \'tā-stē\ *adj* **tast·i·er; -est** : pleasing to the taste : SAVORY ⟨a very ∼ meal⟩ ♦ **Synonyms** PALATABLE, APPETIZING, TOOTHSOME, FLAVORSOME — **tast·i·ness** \'tā-stē-nəs\ *n*

tat \'tat\ *vb* **tat·ted; tat·ting** : to work at or make by tatting

¹tat·ter \'ta-tər\ *vb* : to make or become ragged

²tatter *n* 1 : a part torn and left hanging 2 *pl* : tattered clothing

tat·ter·de·ma·lion \,ta-tər-di-'māl-yən\ *n* : one that is ragged or disreputable

tat·ter·sall \'ta-tər-,sól, -səl\ *n* : a pattern of colored lines forming squares on solid background; *also* : a fabric in a tattersall pattern

tat·ting \'ta-tiŋ\ *n* : a delicate handmade lace formed usu. by looping and knotting with a single thread and a small shuttle; *also* : the act or process of making such lace

tat·tle \'ta-t³l\ *vb* **tat·tled; tat·tling** 1 : CHATTER, PRATE 2 : to tell secrets; *also* : to inform against another — **tat·tler** *n*

tat·tle·tale \'ta-t³l-,tāl\ *n* : one that tattles : INFORMER

¹tat·too \ta-'tü\ *n, pl* **tattoos** [alter. of earlier *taptoo*, fr. D *taptoe*, fr. the phrase *tap toe!* taps shut!] 1 : a call sounded before taps as notice to go to quarters 2 : a rapid rhythmic rapping

²tattoo *vb* : to mark (the skin) with tattoos

³tattoo *n, pl* **tattoos** [Tahitian *tatau*] : an indelible figure fixed upon the body esp. by insertion of pigment under the skin

tau \'taú, 'tó\ *n* : the 19th letter of the Greek alphabet — T or τ

taught *past and past part of* TEACH

¹taunt \'tónt\ *n* : a sarcastic challenge or insult

²taunt *vb* : to reproach or challenge in a mocking manner : jeer at ⟨the boys ∼ed each other⟩ ♦ **Synonyms** MOCK, DERIDE, RIDICULE, TWIT — **taunt·er** *n*

taupe \'tōp\ *n* : a brownish gray

Tau·rus \'tór-əs\ *n* [L, lit., bull] 1 : a zodiacal constellation between Aries and Gemini usu. pictured as a bull 2 : the 2d sign of the zodiac in astrology; *also* : one born under this sign

taut \'tót\ *adj* 1 : tightly drawn : not slack 2 : extremely nervous : TENSE 3 : TRIM, TIDY ⟨a ∼ ship⟩ — **taut·ly** *adv* — **taut·ness** *n*

tau·tol·o·gy \tó-'tä-lə-jē\ *n, pl* **-gies** : needless repetition of an idea, statement, or word; *also* : an instance of such repetition — **tau·to·log·i·cal** \,tó-tə-'läji-kəl\ *adj* — **tau·to·log·i·cal·ly** \-ji-k(ə-)lē\ *adv* — **tau·tol·o·gous** \tó-'tä-lə-gəs\ *adj* — **tau·tol·o·gous·ly** *adv*

tav·ern \'ta-vərn\ *n* [ME *taverne*, fr. AF, fr. L *taberna* hut, shop] 1 : an establishment where alcoholic liquors are sold to be drunk on the premises : INN

taw \'to\ *n* **1** : a marble used as a shooter **2** : the line from which players shoot at marbles

taw·dry \'to-drē\ *adj* **taw·dri·er; -est** [*tawdry lace* a tie of lace for the neck, fr. *St. Audrey* (St. Etheldreda) †679 queen of Northumbria] : cheap and gaudy in appearance and quality ⟨~ decorations⟩ ♦ *Synonyms* GARISH, FLASHY, CHINTZY, MERETRICIOUS — **taw·dri·ly** *adv*

taw·ny \'to-nē\ *adj* **taw·ni·er; -est** : of a brownish orange color

¹tax \'taks\ *vb* **1** : to levy a tax on **2** : CHARGE, ACCUSE **3** : to put under pressure — **tax·able** \'tak-sə-bəl\ *adj* — **tax·a·tion** \tak-'sā-shən\ *n*

²tax *n* **1** : a charge usu. of money imposed by authority on persons or property for public purposes **2** : a heavy charge : STRAIN

¹taxi \'tak-sē\ *n, pl* **tax·is** \-sēz\ *also* **tax·ies** : TAXICAB; *also* : a similarly operated boat or aircraft

²taxi *vb* **tax·ied; taxi·ing** *or* **taxy·ing; tax·is** *or* **tax·ies** **1** : to move along the ground or on the water under an aircraft's own power when starting or after a landing **2** : to go by taxicab

taxi·cab \'tak-sē-ˌkab\ *n* : an automobile that carries passengers for a fare usu. based on the distance traveled

taxi·der·my \'tak-sə-ˌdər-mē\ *n* : the skill or occupation of preparing, stuffing, and mounting skins of animals — **taxi·der·mist** \-mist\ *n*

tax·on \'tak-ˌsän\ *n, pl* **taxa** \-sə\; *also* **taxons** : a taxonomic group or entity

tax·on·o·my \tak-'sä-nə-mē\ *n* : classification esp. of animals or plants according to natural relationships — **tax·o·nom·ic** \ˌtak-sə-'nä-mik\ *adj* — **tax·on·o·mist** \tak-'sä-nə-mist\ *n*

tax·pay·er \'taks-ˌpā-ər\ *n* : one who pays or is liable for a tax — **tax·pay·ing** *adj*

Tay–Sachs disease \'tā-'saks-\ *n* : a hereditary disorder caused by the absence of an enzyme needed to break down fatty material, marked by buildup of lipids in nervous tissue, and causing death in childhood

tb *abbr* tablespoon; tablespoonful

Tb *symbol* terbium

TB \ˌtē-'bē\ *n* : TUBERCULOSIS

TBA *abbr, often not cap* to be announced

T–bar \'tē-ˌbär\ *n* : a ski lift with a series of T-shaped bars

tbs *or* **tbsp** *abbr* tablespoon; tablespoonful

Tc *symbol* technetium

TC *abbr* teachers college

T cell *n* : any of several lymphocytes (as a helper T cell) specialized esp. for activity in and control of immunity and the immune response

TCP/IP \ˌtē-(ˌ)sē-ˌpē-ˌī-'pē\ *n* [*transmission control protocol/Internet protocol*] : a set of communications protocols used over networks and esp. the Internet

TD *abbr* **1** touchdown **2** Treasury Department

TDD *abbr* telecommunications device for the deaf

TDY *abbr* temporary duty

Te *symbol* tellurium

tea \'tē\ *n* [Chin (dialect of Fujian province) *dē*] **1** : the cured leaves and leaf buds of a shrub grown chiefly in China, Japan, India, and Sri Lanka; *also* : this shrub **2** : a drink made by steeping tea in boiling water **3** : refreshments usu. including tea served in late afternoon; *also* : a reception at which tea is served

teach \'tēch\ *vb* **taught** \'tot\; **teach·ing** **1** : to cause to know something : act as a teacher **2** : to show how ⟨~ a child to swim⟩ **3** : to make to know the disagreeable consequences of an action **4** : to guide the studies of **5** : to impart the knowledge of ⟨~ algebra⟩ — **teach·able** *adj* — **teach·er** *n*

teach·ing *n* **1** : the act, practice, or profession of a teacher **2** : something taught; *esp* : DOCTRINE

tea·cup \'tē-ˌkəp\ *n* : a small cup used with a saucer for hot beverages

teak \'tēk\ *n* : the hard durable yellowish brown wood of a tall tropical Asian timber tree related to the vervains; *also* : this tree

tea·ket·tle \'tē-ˌke-t⁹l\ *n* : a covered kettle with a handle and spout for boiling water

teal \'tēl\ *n, pl* **teal** *or* **teals** **1** : any of various small short-necked wild ducks **2** : a dark greenish blue color

¹team \'tēm\ *n* [ME *teme*, fr. OE *tēam* offspring, lineage, group of draft animals] **1** : two or more draft animals harnessed to the same vehicle or implement **2** : a number of persons associated in work or activity; *esp* : a group on one side in a match

²team *adj* : of or performed by a team; *also* : marked by devotion to teamwork ⟨a ~ player⟩

³team *vb* **1** : to haul with or drive a team **2** : to form a team : join forces

team·mate \-ˌmāt\ *n* : a fellow member of a team

team·ster \'tēm-stər\ *n* : one who drives a team or truck

team·work \-ˌwərk\ *n* : the work or activity of a number of persons acting in close association as members of a unit

tea·pot \'tē-ˌpät\ *n* : a vessel with a spout for brewing and serving tea

¹tear \'tir\ *n* : a drop of the salty liquid that moistens the eye and inner side of the eyelids; *also, pl* : an act of weeping or grieving — **tear·ful** \-fəl\ *adj* — **tear·ful·ly** *adv* — **teary** \'tir-ē\ *adj*

²tear \'tir\ *vb* : to fill with or shed tears ⟨eyes ~ing in the wind⟩

³tear \'ter\ *vb* **tore** \'tor\; **torn** \'torn\; **tear·ing** **1** : to separate parts of or pull apart by force : REND **2** : LACERATE **3** : to disrupt by the pull of contrary forces **4** : to remove by force : WRENCH ⟨~ down a house⟩ **5** : to move or act with violence, haste, or force ♦ *Synonyms* RIP, SPLIT, CLEAVE, REND

⁴tear \'ter\ *n* **1** : the act of tearing **2** : a hole or flaw made by tearing : RENT

tear gas \'tir-\ *n* : a substance that on dispersion in the atmosphere blinds the eyes with tears — **tear gas** *vb*

tear-jerk-er \'tir-ˌjər-kər\ *n* : an extravagantly pathetic story, song, play, movie, or broadcast

¹**tease** \'tēz\ *vb* **teased; teas-ing 1** : to disentangle and lay parallel by combing or carding ⟨~ wool⟩ **2** : to scratch the surface of (cloth) so as to raise a nap **3** : to annoy persistently esp. in fun by goading, coaxing, or tantalizing ⟨stop *teasing* the dog⟩ **4** : to comb (hair) by taking a strand and pushing the short hairs toward the scalp with the comb
♦ *Synonyms* HARASS, WORRY, PESTER, ANNOY

²**tease** *n* **1** : the act of teasing or state of being teased **2** : one that teases

tea-sel \'tē-zəl\ *n* : a prickly herb or its flower head covered with stiff hooked bracts and used to raise the nap on cloth; *also* : an artificial device used for this purpose

tea-spoon \'tē-ˌspün\ *n* **1** : a small spoon suitable for stirring beverages **2** : a unit of measure equal to ⅙ fluid ounce (5 milliliters)

tea-spoon-ful \-ˌful\ *n, pl* **-spoonfuls** *also* **-spoons-ful** \-ˌspünz-ˌful\ : TEA-SPOON 2

teat \'tit, 'tēt\ *n* : the protuberance through which milk is drawn from an udder or breast

tech *abbr* **1** technical; technically; technician **2** technological; technology

tech-ne-tium \tek-'nē-shē-əm\ *n* : a radioactive metallic chemical element

tech-nic \'tek-nik, tek-'nēk\ *n* : TECHNIQUE 1

tech-ni-cal \'tek-ni-kəl\ *adj* [Gk *technikos* of art, skillful, fr. *technē* art, craft, skill] **1** : having special knowledge esp. of a mechanical or scientific subject ⟨~ experts⟩ **2** : of or relating to a particular and esp. a practical or scientific subject ⟨~ training⟩ **3** : according to a strict interpretation of the rules **4** : of or relating to technique — **tech-ni-cal-ly** \-k(ə-)lē\ *adv*

tech-ni-cal-i-ty \ˌtek-nə-'ka-lə-tē\ *n, pl* **-ties 1** : a detail meaningful only to a specialist **2** : the quality or state of being technical

technical sergeant *n* : a noncommissioned officer in the air force ranking next below a master sergeant

tech-ni-cian \tek-'ni-shən\ *n* : a person who has acquired the technique of a specialized skill or subject

tech-nique \tek-'nēk\ *n* [F] **1** : the manner in which technical details are treated or basic physical movements are used **2** : technical methods

tech-no \'tek-nō\ *n* : dance music featuring a fast beat and electronically created sounds usu. without vocals

tech-noc-ra-cy \tek-'nä-krə-sē\ *n* : management of society by technical experts — **tech-no-crat** \'tek-nə-ˌkrat\ *n* — **tech-no-crat-ic** \ˌtek-nə-'kra-tik\ *adj*

tech-nol-o-gy \tek-'nä-lə-jē\ *n, pl* **-gies** : ENGINEERING; *also* : a manner of accomplishing a task using technical methods or knowledge — **tech-no-log-i-cal** \ˌtek-nə-'lä-ji-kəl\ *adj*

tec-ton-ics \tek-'tä-niks\ *n sing or pl* **1** : geological structural features **2** : geology dealing esp. with the faulting and folding of a planet or moon — **tec-ton-ic** \-nik\ *adj*

ted-dy bear \'te-dē-ˌber\ *n* [*Teddy* Roosevelt; fr. a cartoon depicting the president sparing the life of a bear cub while hunting] : a stuffed toy bear

te-dious \'tē-dē-əs\ *adj* : tiresome because of length or dullness ⟨a ~ speech⟩
♦ *Synonyms* BORING, TIRING, IRKSOME — **te-dious-ly** *adv* — **te-dious-ness** *n*

te-di-um \'tē-dē-əm\ *n* : TEDIOUSNESS; *also* : BOREDOM

¹**tee** \'tē\ *n* : a small mound or peg on which a golf ball is placed to be hit at the beginning of play on a hole; *also* : the area from which the ball is hit to begin play

²**tee** *vb* **teed; tee-ing** : to place (a ball) on a tee

teem \'tēm\ *vb* : to become filled to overflowing : ABOUND ♦ *Synonyms* SWARM, CRAWL, FLOW

teen *adj* : TEENAGE

teen-age \'tē-ˌnāj\ *or* **teen-aged** \-ˌnājd\ *adj* : of, being, or relating to people in their teens — **teen-ag-er** \-ˌnā-jər\ *n*

teens \'tēnz\ *n pl* : the numbers 13 to 19 inclusive; *esp* : the years 13 to 19 in a person's life

tee-ny \'tē-nē\ *adj* **tee-ni-er; -est** : TINY

teepee *var of* TEPEE

tee shirt *var of* T-SHIRT

tee-ter \'tē-tər\ *vb* **1** : to move unsteadily **2** : SEESAW — **teeter** *n*

teeth *pl of* TOOTH

teethe \'tēth\ *vb* **teethed; teeth-ing** : to experience the rising of one's teeth through the gums : to grow teeth

teething *n* : growth of the first set of teeth through the gums with its accompanying phenomena

tee-to-tal-er *or* **tee-to-tal-ler** \'tē-'tō-tᵊl-ər\ *n* : a person who practices complete abstinence from alcoholic drinks — **tee-to-tal** \'tē-'tō-tᵊl, -ˌtō-\ *adj* — **tee-to-tal-ism** \-tᵊl-ˌi-zəm\ *n*

TEFL *abbr* teaching English as a foreign language

Te-ja-no \tā-'hä-(ˌ)nō\ *n, pl* **-nos** [Mex Sp, fr. *Tejas* Texas] : a Texan of Hispanic descent

tek-tite \'tek-ˌtīt\ *n* : a glassy body of probably meteoric origin

tel *abbr* **1** telegram **2** telegraph **3** telephone

tele-cast \'te-li-ˌkast\ *vb* **-cast** *also* **-cast-ed; -cast-ing** : to broadcast by television — **telecast** *n* — **tele-cast-er** *n*

tel-e-com \'te-li-ˌkäm\ *n* : TELECOMMUNICATION; *also* : the telecommunications industry

tele-com-mu-ni-ca-tion \ˌte-li-kə-ˌmyü-nə-'kā-shən\ *n* : communication at a distance (as by telephone or radio)

tele-com-mute \'te-li-kə-ˌmyüt\ *vb* : to

work at home by the use of an electronic linkup with a central office

tele·con·fer·ence \'te-li-ˌkän-fə-rəns\ *n* : a conference among people remote from one another held using telecommunications — **tele·con·fer·enc·ing** *n*

teleg *abbr* telegraphy

tele·gen·ic \ˌte-lə-'je-nik, -'jē-\ *adj* : markedly attractive to television viewers

tele·gram \'te-lə-ˌgram\ *n* : a message sent by telegraph

¹**tele·graph** \-ˌgraf\ *n* : an electric apparatus or system for sending messages by a code over wires — **tele·graph·ic** \ˌte-lə-'gra-fik\ *adj*

²**telegraph** *vb* : to send or communicate by or as if by telegraph — **te·leg·ra·pher** \tə-'le-grə-fər\ *n*

te·leg·ra·phy \tə-'le-grə-fē\ *n* : the use or operation of a telegraph apparatus or system

tele·mar·ket·ing \ˌte-lə-'mär-kə-tiŋ\ *n* : the marketing of goods or services by telephone — **tele·mar·ket·er** \-tər\ *n*

tele·med·i·cine \ˌte-lə-'me-də-sən\ *n* : the practice of medicine using two-way voice and visual communication

te·lem·e·try \tə-'le-mə-trē\ *n* : the transmission esp. by radio of measurements made by automatic instruments to a distant station — **tele·me·ter** \'te-lə-ˌmē-tər\ *n*

tel·e·no·vela \ˌte-lə-nō-'ve-lə\ *n* : a soap opera televised in or from many Latin-American countries

te·lep·a·thy \tə-'le-pə-thē\ *n* : apparent communication from one mind to another by extrasensory means — **tele·path·ic** \ˌte-lə-'pa-thik\ *adj* — **tele·path·i·cal·ly** \-thi-k(ə-)lē\ *adv*

¹**tele·phone** \'te-lə-ˌfōn\ *n* : an instrument for sending and receiving sounds over long distances by electricity

²**telephone** *vb* **-phoned; -phon·ing** **1** : to send or communicate by telephone **2** : to speak to (a person) by telephone — **tele·phon·er** *n*

te·le·pho·ny \tə-'le-fə-nē, 'te-lə-ˌfō-\ *n* : use or operation of an apparatus for transmission of sounds as electrical signals between distant points — **tele·phon·ic** \ˌte-lə-'fä-nik\ *adj*

tele·pho·to \ˌte-lə-'fō-tō\ *adj* : being a camera lens giving a large image of a distant object — **tele·pho·tog·ra·phy** \-fə-'tä-grə-fē\ *n*

tele·play \'te-li-ˌplā\ *n* : a story prepared for television production

tele·print·er \'te-lə-ˌprin-tər\ *n* : TELETYPEWRITER

tele·promp·ter \'te-lə-ˌprämp-tər\ *n* : a device for displaying prepared text to a speaker or performer

¹**tele·scope** \'te-lə-ˌskōp\ *n* **1** : a cylindrical instrument equipped with lenses or mirrors for viewing distant objects **2** : RADIO TELESCOPE

²**telescope** *vb* **-scoped; -scop·ing 1** : to slide or pass or cause to slide or pass one within another like the sections of a collapsible hand telescope **2** : COMPRESS, CONDENSE

tele·scop·ic \ˌte-lə-'skä-pik\ *adj* **1** : of or relating to a telescope **2** : seen only by a telescope **3** : able to discern objects at a distance **4** : having parts that telescope — **tele·scop·i·cal·ly** \-pi-k(ə-)lē\ *adv*

tele·text \'te-lə-ˌtekst\ *n* : a system for broadcasting text over a television signal and displaying it on a decoder-equipped television

tele·thon \'te-lə-ˌthän\ *n* : a long television program usu. to solicit funds for a charity

tele·type·writ·er \ˌte-lə-'tīp-ˌrī-tər\ *n* : a printing device resembling a typewriter used to send and receive signals over telephone lines

tele·vise \'te-lə-ˌvīz\ *vb* **-vised; -vis·ing** : to broadcast by television

tele·vi·sion \'te-lə-ˌvi-zhən\ *n* [F *télévision,* fr. Gk *tēle* far, at a distance + F *vision* vision] : a system for transmitting images and sound by converting them into electrical or radio waves which are converted back into images and sound by a receiver; *also* : a television receiving set

tell \'tel\ *vb* **told** \'tōld\; **tell·ing 1** : COUNT, ENUMERATE **2** : to relate in detail : NARRATE ⟨*told* us what happened⟩ **3** : SAY, UTTER **4** : to make known : REVEAL **5** : to report to : INFORM ⟨*told* me her name⟩ **6** : ORDER, DIRECT **7** : to find out by observing ⟨can ~ the difference⟩ **8** : to have a marked effect **9** : to serve as evidence **♦ Synonyms** DISCLOSE, DISCOVER, BETRAY

tell·er \'te-lər\ *n* **1** : one that relates : NARRATOR **2** : one that counts **3** : a bank employee handling money received or paid out

tell·ing \'te-liŋ\ *adj* : producing a marked effect : EFFECTIVE ⟨~ evidence⟩ **♦ Synonyms** COGENT, CONVINCING, SOUND

tell off *vb* : REPRIMAND, SCOLD

tell·tale \'tel-ˌtāl\ *n* **1** : INFORMER, TATTLETALE **2** : something that serves to disclose : INDICATION — **telltale** *adj*

tel·lu·ri·um \tə-'lùr-ē-əm\ *n* : a chemical element used esp. in alloys

tel·net \'tel-ˌnet\ *n* : a telecommunications protocol for accessing and using a remote computer via a local computer — **telnet** *vb*

tem·blor \'tem-blər\ *n* [Sp, lit., trembling] : EARTHQUAKE

te·mer·i·ty \tə-'mer-ə-tē\ *n, pl* **-ties** : rash or presumptuous daring : BOLDNESS **♦ Synonyms** AUDACITY, EFFRONTERY, GALL, NERVE, CHEEK

¹**temp** \'temp\ *n* **1** : TEMPERATURE **2** : a temporary worker

²**temp** *abbr* temporary

¹**tem·per** \'tem-pər\ *vb* **1** : to dilute or soften by the addition of something else ⟨~ justice with mercy⟩ **2** : to bring (as steel) to a desired hardness by reheating and cooling **3** : to toughen (glass) by gradual heating and cooling **4** : TOUGHEN **5** : TUNE

²**temper** *n* **1** : characteristic tone : TEN-

DENCY **2** : the hardness or toughness of a substance ⟨the ∼ of a knife blade⟩ **3** : a characteristic frame of mind : DISPOSITION **4** : calmness of mind : COMPOSURE **5** : state of feeling or frame of mind at a particular time **6** : heat of mind or emotion ♦ **Synonyms** TEMPERAMENT, CHARACTER, PERSONALITY, MAKEUP — **tem·pered** \'tem-pərd\ *adj*

tem·pe·ra \'tem-pə-rə\ *n* [It] : a painting process using an albuminous or colloidal medium as a vehicle; *also* : a painting done in tempera

tem·per·a·ment \'tem-prə-mənt, -pər-mənt\ *n* **1** : characteristic or habitual inclination or mode of emotional response : DISPOSITION ⟨nervous ∼⟩ **2** : excessive sensitiveness or irritability ♦ **Synonyms** CHARACTER, PERSONALITY, NATURE, MAKEUP — **tem·per·a·men·tal** \ˌtem-prə-'men-t²l, -pər-'ment-\ *adj*

tem·per·ance \'tem-prəns, -pə-rəns\ *n* : habitual moderation in the indulgence of the appetites or passions; *esp* : moderation in or abstinence from the use of alcoholic beverages

tem·per·ate \'tem-prət, -pə-rət\ *adj* **1** : not extreme or excessive : MILD **2** : moderate in indulgence of appetite or desire **3** : moderate in the use of alcoholic beverages **4** : having a moderate climate ♦ **Synonyms** SOBER, CONTINENT, ABSTEMIOUS

temperate zone *n, often cap T&Z* : the region between the Tropic of Cancer and the arctic circle or between the Tropic of Capricorn and the antarctic circle

tem·per·a·ture \'tem-pər-ˌchu̇r, -prə-ˌchu̇r, -chər\ *n* **1** : degree of hotness or coldness of something (as air, water, or the body) as shown by a thermometer **2** : FEVER 1

tem·pest \'tem-pəst\ *n* [ME *tempeste*, fr. AF, ultim. fr. L *tempestas* season, weather, storm, fr. *tempus* time] : a violent storm

tempest in a teapot : a great commotion over an unimportant matter

tem·pes·tu·ous \tem-'pes-chə-wəs\ *adj* : of, involving, or resembling a tempest : STORMY — **tem·pes·tu·ous·ly** *adv* — **tem·pes·tu·ous·ness** *n*

tem·plate \'tem-plət\ *n* : a gauge, mold, or pattern that functions as a guide to the form or structure of something being made

¹**tem·ple** \'tem-pəl\ *n* **1** : a building reserved for religious practice **2** : a place devoted to a special or exalted purpose ⟨a ∼ of cuisine⟩

²**temple** *n* : the flattened space on each side of the forehead esp. of humans

tem·po \'tem-pō\ *n, pl* **tem·pi** \-(ˌ)pē\ *or* **tempos** [It, lit., time] **1** : the rate of speed of a musical piece or passage **2** : rate of motion or activity : PACE

¹**tem·po·ral** \'tem-pə-rəl\ *adj* **1** : of, relating to, or limited by time ⟨∼ and spatial bounds⟩ **2** : of or relating to earthly life or secular concerns ⟨∼ power⟩

²**temporal** *adj* : of or relating to the temples or the sides of the skull

¹**tem·po·rary** \'tem-pə-ˌrer-ē\ *adj* : lasting for a time only : TRANSITORY ♦ **Synonyms** TRANSIENT, EPHEMERAL, MOMENTARY, IMPERMANENT — **tem·po·rar·i·ly** \ˌtem-pə-'rer-ə-lē\ *adv*

²**temporary** *n, pl* **-rar·ies** : one serving for a limited time

tem·po·rise *Brit var of* TEMPORIZE

tem·po·rize \'tem-pə-ˌrīz\ *vb* **-rized; -riz·ing** **1** : to adapt one's actions to the time or the dominant opinion : COMPROMISE **2** : to draw out matters so as to gain time — **tem·po·riz·er** *n*

tempt \'tempt\ *vb* **1** : to entice to do wrong by promise of pleasure or gain **2** : PROVOKE ⟨∼ fate⟩ **3** : to risk the dangers of **4** : to induce to do something : INCITE ♦ **Synonyms** INVEIGLE, DECOY, SEDUCE, LURE — **tempt·er** *n* — **tempt·ing·ly** *adv*

temp·ta·tion \temp-'tā-shən\ *n* **1** : the act of tempting : the state of being tempted **2** : something that tempts

tempt·ress \'temp-trəs\ *n* : a woman who tempts

ten \'ten\ *n* **1** : one more than nine **2** : the 10th in a set or series **3** : something having 10 units — **ten** *adj or pron* — **tenth** \'tenth\ *adj or adv or n*

ten·a·ble \'te-nə-bəl\ *adj* : capable of being held, maintained, or defended — **ten·a·bil·i·ty** \ˌte-nə-'bi-lə-tē\ *n*

te·na·cious \tə-'nā-shəs\ *adj* **1** : not easily pulled apart : COHESIVE, TOUGH ⟨a ∼ metal⟩ **2** : holding fast ⟨∼ of his rights⟩ **3** : RETENTIVE ⟨a ∼ memory⟩ — **te·na·cious·ly** *adv* — **te·nac·i·ty** \tə-'na-sə-tē\ *n*

ten·an·cy \'te-nən-sē\ *n, pl* **-cies** : the temporary possession or occupancy of something (as a house) that belongs to another; *also* : the period of a tenant's occupancy

ten·ant \'te-nənt\ *n* **1** : one who rents or leases (as a house) from a landlord **2** : DWELLER, OCCUPANT — **tenant** *vb* — **ten·ant·less** *adj*

tenant farmer *n* : a farmer who works land owned by another and pays rent either in cash or in shares of produce

ten·ant·ry \'te-nən-trē\ *n, pl* **-ries** : the body of tenants esp. on an estate

Ten Commandments *n pl* : the ten commandments of God given to Moses on Mount Sinai

¹**tend** \'tend\ *vb* **1** : to apply oneself ⟨∼ to your affairs⟩ **2** : to take care of ⟨∼ a plant⟩ **3** : to manage the operations of ⟨∼ a machine⟩

²**tend** *vb* **1** : to move or develop one's course in a particular direction **2** : to show an inclination or tendency

ten·den·cy \'ten-dən-sē\ *n, pl* **-cies** **1** : DRIFT, TREND **2** : a proneness to or readiness for a particular kind of thought or action : PROPENSITY ⟨a ∼ to overreact⟩ ♦ **Synonyms** BENT, LEANING, DISPOSITION, INCLINATION

ten·den·tious \ten-'den-chəs\ *adj* : marked by a tendency in favor of a particular point of view : BIASED ⟨∼ remarks⟩ — **ten·den·tious·ly** *adv* — **ten·den·tious·ness** *n*

¹**ten·der** \'ten-dər\ *adj* [ME, fr. AF *tendre*, fr. L *tener*] **1** : having a soft texture : easily broken, chewed, or cut **2** : physically weak : DELICATE; *also* : IMMATURE **3** : expressing or responsive to love or sympathy : LOVING, COMPASSIONATE ⟨a ∼ smile⟩ **4** : SENSITIVE, TOUCHY ⟨a ∼ ego⟩ ♦ **Synonyms** SYMPATHETIC, WARM, WARMHEARTED — **ten·der·ly** *adv* — **ten·der·ness** *n*

²**tender** *n* [AF *tendre*, fr. *tendre*, v., to stretch, hold out, offer, fr. L *tendere* to stretch, direct] **1** : an offer or proposal made for acceptance; *esp* : an offer of a bid for a contract **2** : something (as money) that may be offered in payment

³**tender** *vb* : to present for acceptance

⁴**tend·er** \'ten-dər\ *n* **1** : one that tends or takes care **2** : a boat carrying passengers and freight to a larger ship **3** : a car attached to a steam locomotive for carrying fuel and water

⁵**tender** *n* [prob. short for *tenderloin*] : a strip of meat (as chicken) often breaded

ten·der·foot \'ten-dər-ˌfût\ *n, pl* **-feet** \-ˌfēt\ *also* **-foots** \-ˌfûts\ **1** : one not hardened to frontier or rough outdoor life **2** : an inexperienced beginner

ten·der·heart·ed \ˌten-dər-'här-təd\ *adj* : easily moved to love, pity, or sorrow

ten·der·ize \'ten-də-ˌrīz\ *vb* **-ized; -iz·ing** : to make (meat) tender — **ten·der·iz·er** \'ten-də-ˌrī-zər\ *n*

ten·der·loin \'ten-dər-ˌlôin\ *n* **1** : a tender strip of meat of beef or pork from near the backbone **2** : a district of a city largely devoted to vice

ten·di·ni·tis *or* **ten·don·itis** \ˌten-də-'nī-təs\ *n* : inflammation of a tendon

ten·don \'ten-dən\ *n* : a tough cord of dense white fibrous tissue uniting a muscle with another part (as a bone) — **ten·di·nous** \-də-nəs\ *adj*

ten·dril \'ten-drəl\ *n* : a slender coiling organ by which some climbing plants attach themselves to a support

ten·e·brous \'te-nə-brəs\ *adj* : shut off from the light : GLOOMY, OBSCURE

ten·e·ment \'te-nə-mənt\ *n* **1** : a house used as a dwelling **2** : a building divided into apartments for rent to families; *esp* : one meeting only minimum standards of safety and comfort **3** : APARTMENT, FLAT

te·net \'te-nət\ *n* [L, he holds, fr. *tenēre* to hold] : one of the principles or doctrines held in common by members of a group (as a church or profession) ♦ **Synonyms** DOCTRINE, DOGMA, BELIEF

ten·fold \'ten-ˌfōld, -'fōld\ *adj* : being 10 times as great or as many — **ten·fold** \-'fōld\ *adv*

tenge \'ten-ˌgä\ *n, pl* **tenge** — see MONEY table

ten–gal·lon hat *n* : a wide-brimmed hat with a large soft crown

Tenn *abbr* Tennessee

ten·ne \'ten-ä\ *n*, *or* **ten·e·si** \'ten-ə-sē\ *or*

tenne *or* **ten·ne·si** \'ten-ə-sē\ — see *manat* at MONEY table

ten·nis \'te-nəs\ *n* : a game played with a ball and racket on a court divided by a net

ten·on \'te-nən\ *n* : a projecting part in a piece of material (as wood) for insertion into a mortise to make a joint

ten·or \'te-nər\ *n* **1** : the general drift of something spoken or written ⟨his speech had an angry ∼⟩ **2** : the highest natural adult male voice; *also* : a singer having this voice **3** : a continuing in a course, movement, or activity ⟨the ∼ of my life⟩

tenpenny nail *n* : a nail three inches (about 7.6 centimeters) long

ten·pin \'ten-ˌpin\ *n* : a bottle-shaped bowling pin set in groups of 10 and bowled at in a game (**tenpins**)

¹**tense** \'tens\ *n* [ME *tens* time, tense, fr. AF, fr. L *tempus*] : distinction of form of a verb to indicate the time of the action or state

²**tense** *adj* **tens·er; tens·est** [L *tensus*, fr. pp. of *tendere* to stretch] **1** : stretched tight : TAUT **2** : feeling or showing nervous tension ⟨a ∼ smile⟩ ♦ **Synonyms** STIFF, RIGID, INFLEXIBLE — **tense·ly** *adv* — **tense·ness** *n* — **ten·si·ty** \'ten-sə-tē\ *n*

³**tense** *vb* **tensed; tens·ing** : to make or become tense

ten·sile \'ten-səl, -ˌsī(-ə)l\ *adj* : of or relating to tension ⟨∼ strength⟩

ten·sion \'ten-chən\ *n* **1** : the act of straining or stretching; *also* : the condition of being strained or stretched **2** : a state of mental unrest often with signs of bodily stress **3** : a state of latent hostility or opposition

ten–speed \'ten-ˌspēd\ *n* : a bicycle with a derailleur having 10 possible combinations of gears

¹**tent** \'tent\ *n* **1** : a collapsible shelter of material stretched and supported by poles **2** : a canopy placed over the head and shoulders to retain vapors or oxygen given for medical reasons

²**tent** *vb* **1** : to lodge in tents **2** : to cover with or as if with a tent

ten·ta·cle \'ten-ti-kəl\ *n* : any of various long flexible projections about the head or mouth (as of an insect, mollusk, or fish) — **ten·ta·cled** \-kəld\ *adj* — **ten·tac·u·lar** \ten-'ta-kyə-lər\ *adj*

ten·ta·tive \'ten-tə-tiv\ *adj* **1** : not fully worked out or developed ⟨∼ plans⟩ **2** : HESITANT, UNCERTAIN ⟨a ∼ smile⟩ — **ten·ta·tive·ly** *adv* — **ten·ta·tive·ness** *n*

ten·u·ous \'ten-yə-wəs\ *adj* **1** : not dense : RARE ⟨a ∼ fluid⟩ **2** : not thick : SLENDER ⟨a ∼ rope⟩ **3** : having little substance : FLIMSY, WEAK ⟨∼ influences⟩ **4** : lacking stability : SHAKY ⟨∼ reasoning⟩ — **te·nu·i·ty** \te-'nü-ə-tē, tə-, -'nyü-\ *n* — **ten·u·ous·ly** *adv* — **ten·u·ous·ness** *n*

ten·ure \'ten-yər\ *n* : the act, right, manner, or period of holding something (as a landed property, an office, or a position)

ten·ured \'ten-yərd\ *adj* : having tenure ⟨∼ faculty members⟩

te·o·sin·te \ˌtā-ō-'sin-tē\ *n* : a tall annual

grass of Mexico that is closely related to and usu. considered ancestral to corn

te·pee *or* **tee·pee** \'tē-(ˌ)pē\ *n* [Dakota *thípi*, fr. *thi-* to dwell] : an American Indian conical tent usu. of skins

tep·id \'te-pəd\ *adj* 1 : moderately warm : LUKEWARM 2 : HALFHEARTED

te·qui·la \tə-'kē-lə, tā-\ *n* : a Mexican liquor distilled from an agave's sap

ter *abbr* 1 terrace 2 territory

tera·byte \'ter-ə-ˌbīt\ *n* [*tera-* trillion (10^12), fr. Gk *terat-, teras* monster] : 1024 gigabytes; *also* : one trillion bytes

ter·bi·um \'tər-bē-əm\ *n* : a metallic chemical element

ter·cen·te·na·ry \ˌtər-ˌsen-'te-nə-rē, tər-'sen-tə-ˌner-ē\ *n, pl* **-ries** : a 300th anniversary or its celebration — **tercentenary** *adj*

ter·cen·ten·ni·al \ˌtər-ˌsen-'te-ne-əl\ *adj or n* : TERCENTENARY

te·re·do \tə-'rē-dō, -'rā-\ *n, pl* **-dos** [L] : SHIPWORM

ter·i·ya·ki \ˌter-ē-'yä-kē\ *n* [Jp] : a Japanese dish of meat or fish soaked in a soy marinade and cooked

¹term \'tərm\ *n* 1 : END, TERMINATION 2 : DURATION; *esp* : a period of time fixed esp. by law or custom 3 : a mathematical expression connected with another by a plus or minus sign; *also* : an element (as a numerator) of a fraction or proportion 4 : a word or expression that has a precise meaning in some uses or is limited to a particular subject or field 5 *pl* : PROVISIONS, CONDITIONS ⟨∼s of a contract⟩ 6 *pl* : mutual relationship ⟨on good ∼s⟩ 7 : AGREEMENT, CONCORD 8 : a state of acceptance ⟨come to ∼s with his grief⟩

²term *vb* : to apply a term to : CALL

ter·ma·gant \'tər-mə-gənt\ *n* : an overbearing or nagging woman : SHREW

¹ter·mi·nal \'tər-mə-nᵊl\ *adj* 1 : of, relating to, or forming an end, limit, or terminus 2 : FATAL 2 ⟨∼ cancer⟩; *also* : being in or relating to the final stages of a fatal disease ⟨a ∼ patient⟩ ♦ *Synonyms* FINAL, CONCLUDING, LAST, LATEST — **ter·mi·nal·ly** *adv*

²terminal *n* 1 : EXTREMITY, END 2 : a device at the end of a wire or on electrical equipment for making a connection 3 : either end of a transportation line (as a railroad) with its offices and freight and passenger stations; *also* : a freight or passenger station 4 : a device (as in a computer system) for data entry and display

ter·mi·nate \'tər-mə-ˌnāt\ *vb* **-nat·ed; -nat·ing** : to bring or come to an end ♦ *Synonyms* CONCLUDE, FINISH, COMPLETE — **ter·mi·na·ble** \-nə-bəl\ *adj* — **ter·mi·na·tion** \ˌtər-mə-'nā-shən\ *n* — **ter·mi·na·tor** \'tər-mə-ˌnā-tər\ *n*

ter·mi·nol·o·gy \ˌtər-mə-'nä-lə-jē\ *n, pl* **-gies** : the technical or special terms used in a business, art, science, or special subject

ter·mi·nus \'tər-mə-nəs\ *n, pl* **-ni** \-ˌnī\ *or* **-nus·es** [L] 1 : final goal : END 2 : either end of a transportation line or travel route; *also* : the station or city at such a place

ter·mite \'tər-ˌmīt\ *n* : any of numerous pale soft-bodied social insects that feed on wood

tern \'tərn\ *n* : any of various chiefly marine birds with narrow wings and often a forked tail

ter·na·ry \'tər-nə-rē\ *adj* 1 : of, relating to, or proceeding by threes 2 : having three elements or parts

terr *abbr* territory

¹ter·race \'ter-əs\ *n* 1 : a flat roof or open platform 2 : a level area next to a building 3 : an embankment with level top 4 : a bank or ridge on a slope to conserve moisture and soil 5 : a row of houses on raised land; *also* : a street with such a row of houses 6 : a strip of park in the middle of a street

²terrace *vb* **ter·raced; ter·rac·ing** : to form into a terrace or supply with terraces

ter·ra-cot·ta \ˌter-ə-'kä-tə\ *n* [It *terra cotta*, lit., baked earth] : a reddish brown earthenware

terra fir·ma \-'fər-mə\ *n* [NL] : solid ground

ter·rain \tə-'rān\ *n* : the surface features of an area of land ⟨a rough ∼⟩

ter·ra in·cog·ni·ta \ˌter-ə-ˌin-ˌkäg-'nē-tə\ *n, pl* **ter·rae in·cog·ni·tae** \'ter-ˌī-ˌin-ˌkäg-'nē-tī\ [L] : an unexplored area or field of knowledge

ter·ra·pin \'ter-ə-pən\ *n* : any of various turtles of fresh or brackish water

ter·rar·i·um \tə-'rer-ē-əm\ *n, pl* **-ia** \-ē-ə\ *or* **-i·ums** : a usu. transparent enclosure for keeping or raising plants or small animals indoors

ter·res·tri·al \tə-'res-trē-əl\ *adj* 1 : of or relating to the earth or its inhabitants 2 : living or growing on land ⟨∼ plants⟩ ♦ *Synonyms* MUNDANE, EARTHLY, WORLDLY

ter·ri·ble \'ter-ə-bəl\ *adj* 1 : exciting terror : FEARFUL, DREADFUL ⟨∼ weapons⟩ 2 : hard to bear : DISTRESSING ⟨a ∼ situation⟩ 3 : extreme in degree : INTENSE ⟨∼ heat⟩ 4 : of very poor quality : AWFUL ⟨a ∼ play⟩ ♦ *Synonyms* FRIGHTFUL, HORRIBLE, SHOCKING, APPALLING — **ter·ri·bly** \-blē\ *adv*

ter·ri·er \'ter-ē-ər\ *n* [ME *terryer, terrer*, fr. AF (*chen*) *terrer*, lit., earth dog, fr. *terre* earth, fr. L *terra*] : any of various usu. small energetic dogs orig. used by hunters to drive small game animals from their holes

ter·rif·ic \tə-'ri-fik\ *adj* 1 : exciting terror ⟨a ∼ explosion⟩ 2 : EXTRAORDINARY, ASTOUNDING ⟨∼ speed⟩ 3 : MAGNIFICENT ⟨makes ∼ chili⟩

ter·ri·fy \'ter-ə-ˌfī\ *vb* **-fied; -fy·ing** : to fill with terror : FRIGHTEN ♦ *Synonyms* SCARE, TERRORIZE, STARTLE, ALARM — **ter·ri·fy·ing·ly** *adv*

ter·ri·to·ri·al·i·ty \ˌter-ə-ˌtȯr-ē-'a-lə-tē\ *n* : persistent attachment to a specific territory ⟨∼ in bears⟩

ter·ri·to·ry \'ter-ə-ˌtȯr-ē\ *n, pl* **-ries** 1 : a geographic area belonging to or under the jurisdiction of a governmental authority 2 : a part of the U.S. not included within any state but organized with a separate legislature **3** : REGION, DISTRICT; *also* : a region in which one feels at home **4** : a field of knowledge or interest **5** : an assigned area **6** : an area occupied and defended by one or a group of animals — **ter·ri·to·ri·al** \ˌter-ə-ˈtȯr-ē-əl\ *adj* — **go with the territory** *or* **come with the territory** : to accompany a situation naturally

ter·ror \ˈter-ər\ *n* **1** : a state of intense fear : FRIGHT **2** : one that inspires fear **3** : violent or destructive acts committed to intimidate a people or government ♦ *Synonyms* PANIC, CONSTERNATION, DREAD, ALARM, DISMAY, HORROR, TREPIDATION

ter·ror·ism \ˈter-ər-ˌi-zəm\ *n* : the systematic use of terror esp. as a means of coercion — **ter·ror·ist** \-ist\ *adj or n*

ter·ror·ize \ˈter-ər-ˌīz\ *vb* **-ized; -iz·ing 1** : to fill with terror : SCARE **2** : to coerce by threat or violence ♦ *Synonyms* TERRIFY, FRIGHTEN, ALARM, STARTLE

ter·ry \ˈter-ē\ *n, pl* **terries** : an absorbent fabric with a loose pile of uncut loops

terse \ˈtərs\ *adj* **ters·er; ters·est** [L *tersus* clean, neat, fr. pp. of *tergēre* to wipe off] : effectively brief : CONCISE — **terse·ly** *adv* — **terse·ness** *n*

ter·tia·ry \ˈtər-shē-ˌer-ē\ *adj* **1** : of third rank, importance, or value **2** *cap* : of, relating to, or being the earlier period of the Cenozoic era **3** : occurring in or being the third stage ⟨∼ medical care⟩
Tertiary *n* : the Tertiary period

TESL *abbr* teaching English as a second language

TESOL *abbr* Teachers of English to Speakers of Other Languages

¹**test** \ˈtest\ *n* [ME, vessel in which metals were assayed, potsherd, fr. AF, pot, fr. L *testum* earthen vessel] **1** : a critical examination or evaluation : TRIAL **2** : a means or result of testing

²**test** *vb* **1** : to put to test : TRY, EXAMINE **2** : to undergo or score on tests

³**test** *adj* : relating to or used in testing ⟨a ∼ group⟩

tes·ta·ment \ˈtes-tə-mənt\ *n* **1** *cap* : either of two main divisions of the Bible **2** : EVIDENCE, WITNESS **3** : CREED **4** : the legal instructions for the disposition of one's property after death : WILL — **tes·ta·men·ta·ry** \ˌtes-tə-ˈmen-tə-rē\ *adj*

tes·tate \ˈtes-ˌtāt, -tət\ *adj* : having left a valid will

tes·ta·tor \ˈtes-ˌtā-tər, tes-ˈtā-\ *n* : a person who dies leaving a valid will

tes·ta·trix \tes-ˈtā-triks\ *n* : a woman who is a testator

¹**tes·ter** \ˈtes-tər, ˈtes-\ *n* : a canopy over a bed, pulpit, or altar

²**test·er** \ˈtes-tər\ *n* : one that tests

tes·ti·cle \ˈtes-ti-kəl\ *n* : TESTIS; *esp* : one of a mammal usu. with its enclosing structures — **tes·tic·u·lar** *adj*

tes·ti·fy \ˈtes-tə-ˌfī\ *vb* **-fied; -fy·ing 1** : to make a statement based on personal knowledge or belief : bear witness **2** : to serve as evidence or proof

tes·ti·mo·ni·al \ˌtes-tə-ˈmō-nē-əl\ *n* **1** : a

statement testifying to benefits received; *also* : a character reference **2** : an expression of appreciation : TRIBUTE — **testimonial** *adj*

tes·ti·mo·ny \ˈtes-tə-ˌmō-nē\ *n, pl* **-nies 1** : evidence based on observation or knowledge **2** : an outward sign : SYMBOL **3** : a solemn declaration made by a witness under oath esp. in a court ♦ *Synonyms* EVIDENCE, CONFIRMATION, PROOF, TESTAMENT

tes·tis \ˈtes-təs\ *n, pl* **tes·tes** \ˈtes-ˌtēz\ [L, witness, testis] : a typically paired male reproductive gland that produces sperm and testosterone and that in most mammals is contained within the scrotum at sexual maturity

tes·tos·ter·one \te-ˈstäs-tə-ˌrōn\ *n* : a male sex hormone causing development of the male reproductive system and secondary sex characteristics

test-tube *adj* **1** : IN VITRO ⟨∼ experiments⟩ **2** : produced by in vitro fertilization ⟨∼ babies⟩

test tube *n* : a glass tube closed at one end and used esp. in chemistry and biology

tes·ty \ˈtes-tē\ *adj* **tes·ti·er; -est** [ME *testif*, fr. AF, headstrong, fr. *teste* head, fr. LL *testa* skull, fr. L, shell] : easily annoyed; *also* : marked by ill humor

tet·a·nus \ˈte-tə-nəs\ *n* : an infectious disease caused by bacterial poisons and marked by muscle stiffness and spasms esp. of the jaws — **tet·a·nal** \-əl\ *adj*

tetchy \ˈte-chē\ *adj* **tetchi·er; -est** : irritably or peevishly sensitive

¹**tête-à-tête** \ˌtāt-ə-ˈtāt\ *n* [F, lit., head to head] : a private conversation between two persons

²**tête-à-tête** \ˌtāt-ə-ˈtāt\ *adv* : in private

³**tête-à-tête** \ˈtāt-ə-ˌtāt\ *adj* : being face-to-face : PRIVATE

¹**teth·er** \ˈte-thər\ *n* **1** : something (as a rope) by which an animal is fastened **2** : the limit of one's strength or resources

²**tether** *vb* : to fasten or restrain by or as if by a tether

tet·ra·eth·yl lead \ˌte-trə-ˈe-thəl-\ *n* : a heavy oily poisonous liquid used esp. formerly as an antiknock agent in gasoline

tet·ra·he·dron \-ˈhē-drən\ *n, pl* **-drons** *or* **-dra** \-drə\ : a polyhedron that has four faces — **tet·ra·he·dral** \-drəl\ *adj*

tet·ra·hy·dro·can·nab·i·nol \-ˌhī-drə-kə-ˈna-bə-ˌnȯl, -ˌnōl\ *n* : THC

te·tram·e·ter \te-ˈtra-mə-tər\ *n* : a line of verse consisting of four metrical feet

tet·ri \ˈte-trē\ *n, pl* **tetri** — see *lari* at MONEY table

Teu·ton·ic \tü-ˈtä-nik, tyü-\ *adj* : GERMANIC

Tex *abbr* Texas

Tex-Mex \ˈteks-ˈmeks\ *adj* : characteristic of Mexican-American culture and esp. that of southern Texas

¹**text** \ˈtekst\ *n* **1** : the actual words of an author's work **2** : the main body of printed or written matter on a page **3** : a scriptural passage chosen as the subject esp. of a sermon **4** : THEME, TOPIC **5**

: TEXTBOOK **6** : TEXT MESSAGE — **tex·tu·al** \'teks-chə-wəl\ *adj*

²**text** *vb* : to send a text message from one cell phone to another

text·book \'tekst-ˌbùk\ *n* : a book used in the study of a subject

tex·tile \'tek-ˌstī(-ə)l, 'teks-t³l\ *n* : CLOTH; *esp* : a woven or knit cloth

text message *n* : a short message sent electronically to a cell phone or other device

tex·ture \'teks-chər\ *n* **1** : the visual or tactile surface characteristics of something ⟨a coarse ∼⟩ **2** : essential part **3** : basic scheme or structure : FABRIC **4** : overall structure — **tex·tur·al** \-chə-rəl\ *adj*

TGIF *abbr* thank God it's Friday

¹**Th** *abbr* Thursday

²**Th** *symbol* thorium

¹**-th** — see ¹-ETH

²**-th** *or* **-eth** *adj suffix* — used in forming ordinal numbers ⟨hundred*th*⟩

³**-th** *n suffix* **1** : act or process **2** : state or condition ⟨dear*th*⟩

Thai \'tī\ *n, pl* **Thai** *or* **Thais 1** : a native or inhabitant of Thailand **2** : the official language of Thailand — **Thai** *adj*

thal·a·mus \'tha-lə-məs\ *n, pl* **-mi** \-ˌmī\ [NL] : a subdivision of the brain that serves as a relay station to and from the cerebral cortex and functions in arousal and the integration of sensory information — **tha·lam·ic** \thə-'la-mik\ *adj*

thal·as·se·mia \ˌtha-lə-'sē-mē-ə\ *n* : any of a group of inherited disorders of hemoglobin synthesis

tha·las·so·ther·a·py \thə-ˌla-sō-'ther-ə-pē\ *n* [Gk *thalassa* sea] : the use of seawater or sea products (as seaweed) for the benefit of health or beauty

thal·li·um \'tha-lē-əm\ *n* : a poisonous metallic chemical element

¹**than** \'thən, 'than\ *conj* **1** — used after a comparative adjective or adverb to introduce the second part of a comparison expressing inequality ⟨older ∼ I am⟩ **2** — used after *other* or a word of similar meaning to express a difference of kind, manner, or identity ⟨adults other ∼ parents⟩

²**than** *prep* : in comparison with ⟨older ∼ me⟩

thane \'thān\ *n* **1** : a free retainer of an Anglo-Saxon lord **2** : a Scottish feudal lord

thank \'thaŋk\ *vb* : to express gratitude to ⟨∼*ed* them for the present⟩

thank·ful \'thaŋk-fəl\ *adj* **1** : conscious of benefit received **2** : expressive of thanks **3** : GLAD — **thank·ful·ness** *n*

thank·ful·ly \-fə-lē\ *adv* **1** : in a thankful manner **2** : as makes one thankful

thank·less \'thaŋ-kləs\ *adj* **1** : UNAPPRECIATED **2** : UNGRATEFUL

thanks \'thaŋks\ *n pl* : an expression of gratitude

thanks·giv·ing \thaŋks-'gi-viŋ\ *n* **1** : the act of giving thanks **2** : a prayer expressing gratitude **3** *cap* : the 4th Thursday in November observed as a legal holiday for giving thanks for divine goodness

¹**that** \'that, thət\ *pron, pl* **those** \'thōz\ **1** : the one indicated, mentioned, or understood ⟨∼ is my house⟩ **2** : the one farther away or first mentioned ⟨this is an elm, ∼'s a maple⟩ **3** : what has been indicated or mentioned ⟨after ∼, we left⟩ **4** : the one or ones : IT, THEY ⟨*those* who wish to leave may do so⟩

²**that** \that, 'that\ *conj* **1** : the following, namely ⟨he said — he would⟩; *also* : which is, namely ⟨there's a chance ∼ it may fail⟩ **2** : to this end or purpose ⟨shouted ∼ all might hear⟩ **3** : as to result in the following, namely ⟨so heavy ∼ it can't be moved⟩ **4** : for this reason, namely : BECAUSE ⟨we're glad ∼ you came⟩

³**that** *adj, pl* **those 1** : being the one mentioned, indicated, or understood ⟨∼ boy⟩ ⟨*those* people⟩ **2** : being the one farther away or less immediately under discussion ⟨this chair or ∼ one⟩

⁴**that** \that, 'that\ *pron* **1** : WHO, WHOM, WHICH ⟨the man ∼ saw you⟩ ⟨the man ∼ you saw⟩ ⟨the money ∼ was spent⟩ **2** : in, on, or at which ⟨the way ∼ he drives⟩ ⟨the day ∼ it rained⟩

⁵**that** \'that\ *adv* : to such an extent or degree ⟨I like it, but not ∼ much⟩

¹**thatch** \'thach\ *vb* : to cover with or as if with thatch — **thatch·er** *n*

²**thatch** *n* **1** : plant material (as straw) for use as roofing **2** : a mat of grass clippings accumulated next to the soil on a lawn **3** : a covering of or as if of thatch ⟨a ∼ of white hair⟩

thaw \'thò\ *vb* **1** : to melt or cause to melt **2** : to become so warm as to melt ice or snow **3** : to abandon aloofness or hostility — **thaw** *n*

THC \ˌtē-(ˌ)āch-'sē\ *n* [*tetrahydrocannabinol*] : a physiologically active chemical from hemp plant resin that is the chief intoxicant in marijuana

¹**the** \thə, *before vowel sounds usu* thē\ *definite article* **1** : that particular **2** — used before adjectives functioning as nouns ⟨a word to ∼ wise⟩

²**the** *adv* **1** : to what extent ⟨∼ sooner, the better⟩ **2** : to that extent ⟨the sooner, ∼ better⟩

theat *abbr* theater; theatrical

the·ater *or* **the·atre** \'thē-ə-tər\ *n* [ME *theatre*, fr. MF, fr. L *theatrum*, fr. Gk *theatron*, fr. *theasthai* to view, fr. *thea* act of seeing] **1** : a building or area for dramatic performances; *also* : a building or area for showing motion pictures **2** : a place of enactment of significant events ⟨∼ of war⟩ **3** : a place (as a lecture room) resembling a theater **4** : dramatic literature or performance

theater–in–the–round *n* : a theater with the stage in the center of the auditorium

the·at·ri·cal \thē-'a-tri-kəl\ *also* **the·at·ric** \-trik\ *adj* **1** : of or relating to the theater **2** : marked by artificiality of emotion : HISTRIONIC ⟨a ∼ gesture⟩ **3** : marked by extravagant display : SHOWY

the·at·ri·cals \-kəlz\ *n pl* : the performance of plays

the·at·rics \thē-'a-triks\ *n pl* 1 : THEAT-RICALS 2 : staged or contrived effects

the·be \'thā-bā\ *n, pl* **thebe** — see *pula* at MONEY table

thee \'thē\ *pron, archaic objective case of* THOU

theft \'theft\ *n* : the act of stealing

thegn \'thān\ *n* : THANE 1

their \thər, 'ther\ *adj* : of or relating to them or themselves

theirs \'therz\ *pron* : their one : their ones

the·ism \'thē-ˌi-zəm\ *n* : belief in the existence of a god or gods — **the·ist** \-ist\ *n or adj* — **the·is·tic** \thē-'is-tik\ *adj*

them \thəm, 'them\ *pron, objective case of* THEY

theme \'thēm\ *n* 1 : a subject or topic of discourse or of artistic representation 2 : a written exercise : COMPOSITION 3 : a melodic subject of a musical composition or movement — **the·mat·ic** \thi-'ma-tik\ *adj*

them·selves \thəm-'selvz, them-\ *pron pl* 1 : THEY, THEM — used reflexively, for emphasis, or in absolute constructions ⟨they govern ~⟩ ⟨they ~ came⟩ ⟨~ busy, they sent me⟩

¹**then** \'then\ *adv* 1 : at that time 2 : soon after that : NEXT 3 : in addition : BESIDES 4 : in that case 5 : CONSEQUENTLY

²**then** *n* : that time ⟨since ~⟩

³**then** *adj* : existing or acting at that time ⟨the ~ attorney general⟩

thence \'thens, 'thens\ *adv* 1 : from that place 2 *archaic* : THENCEFORTH 3 : from that fact : THEREFROM

thence·forth \-ˌfȯrth\ *adv* : from that time forward : THEREAFTER

thence·for·ward \thens-'fȯr-wərd, thens-\ *also* **thence·for·wards** \-wərdz\ *adv* : onward from that place or time

the·oc·ra·cy \thē-'ä-krə-sē\ *n, pl* **-cies** 1 : government by officials regarded as divinely inspired 2 : a state governed by a theocracy — **the·o·crat·ic** \ˌthē-ə-'kra-tik\ *adj*

theol *abbr* theological; theology

the·ol·o·gy \thē-'ä-lə-jē\ *n, pl* **-gies** 1 : the study of religious faith, practice, and experience; *esp* : the study of God and of God's relation to the world 2 : a theory or system of theology — **the·o·lo·gian** \ˌthē-ə-'lō-jən\ *n* — **the·o·log·i·cal** \-'lä-ji-kəl\ *adj*

the·o·rem \'thē-ə-rəm, 'thir-əm\ *n* 1 : a statement esp. in mathematics that has been or is to be proved 2 : an idea accepted or proposed as a demonstrable truth : PROPOSITION

the·o·ret·i·cal \ˌthē-ə-'re-ti-kəl\ *also* **the·o·ret·ic** \-tik\ *adj* 1 : relating to or having the character of theory 2 : existing only in theory : HYPOTHETICAL — **the·o·ret·i·cal·ly** \-ti-k(ə-)lē\ *adv*

the·o·rise *Brit var of* THEORIZE

the·o·rize \'thē-ə-ˌrīz\ *vb* **-rized; -riz·ing** : to form a theory : SPECULATE — **the·o·rist** \-rist\ *n*

the·o·ry \'thē-ə-rē, 'thir-ē\ *n, pl* **-ries** 1 : abstract thought 2 : the general principles of a subject 3 : a plausible or scien-tifically acceptable general principle offered to explain observed facts 4 : HYPOTHESIS, CONJECTURE

theory of games : GAME THEORY

the·os·o·phy \thē-'ä-sə-fē\ *n* : belief about God and the world held to be based on mystical insight — **theo·soph·i·cal** \ˌthē-ə-'sä-fi-kəl\ *adj* — **the·os·o·phist** \thē-'ä-sə-fist\ *n*

ther·a·peu·tic \ˌther-ə-'pyü-tik\ *adj* [Gk *therapeutikos*, fr. *therapeuein* to attend, treat, fr. *theraps* attendant] : of, relating to, or dealing with healing and esp. with remedies for diseases — **ther·a·peu·ti·cal·ly** \-ti-k(ə-)lē\ *adv*

ther·a·peu·tics \ˌther-ə-'pyü-tiks\ *n* : a branch of medical or dental science dealing with the use of remedies

ther·a·py \'ther-ə-pē\ *n, pl* **-pies** : treatment of bodily, mental, or behavioral disorders — **ther·a·pist** \-pist\ *n*

¹**there** \'ther\ *adv* 1 : in or at that place — often used interjectionally 2 : to or into that place ⟨went ~ after work⟩ 3 : in that matter or respect

²**there** \'ther, thər\ *pron* — used as a function word to introduce a sentence or clause ⟨~'s a pen here⟩

³**there** \'ther\ *n* 1 : that place ⟨get away from ~⟩ 2 : that point ⟨you take it from ~⟩

there·abouts \ˌthr-ə-'bau̇ts, 'ther-ə-ˌbau̇ts\ *or* **there·about** \-'bau̇t, -ˌbau̇t\ *adv* 1 : near that place or time 2 : near that number, degree, or quantity

there·af·ter \ther-'af-tər\ *adv* : after that : AFTERWARD

there·at \-'at\ *adv* 1 : at that place 2 : at that occurrence : on that account

there·by \ther-'bī, 'ther-ˌbī\ *adv* 1 : by that : by that means 2 : connected with or with reference to that

there·for \ther-'fȯr\ *adv* : for or in return for that ⟨wanted a refund ~⟩

there·fore \'ther-ˌfȯr\ *adv* : for that reason : CONSEQUENTLY

there·from \ther-'frəm\ *adv* : from that or it

there·in \ther-'in\ *adv* 1 : in or into that place, time, or thing 2 : in that respect

there·of \-'əv, -'äv\ *adv* 1 : of that or it 2 : from that : THEREFROM

there·on \-'ȯn, -'än\ *adv* 1 : on that 2 *archaic* : THEREUPON 3

there·to \ther-'tü\ *adv* : to that

there·un·to \ther-'ən-(ˌ)tü, ˌther-ən-'tü\ *adv, archaic* : THERETO

there·upon \'ther-ə-ˌpȯn, -ˌpän; ˌther-ə-'pȯn, -'pän\ *adv* 1 : on that matter 2 : THEREFORE 3 : immediately after that : at once

there·with \ther-'with\ *adv* 1 : with that 2 *archaic* : THEREUPON, FORTHWITH

there·with·al \'ther-wi-ˌthȯl, -ˌthȯl\ *adv* 1 *archaic* : BESIDES 2 : THEREWITH

therm *abbr* thermometer

ther·mal \'thər-məl\ *adj* 1 : of, relating to, or caused by heat 2 : designed to prevent the loss of body heat ⟨~ underwear⟩ — **ther·mal·ly** *adv*

thermal pollution *n* : the discharge of

heated liquid (as waste water from a factory) into natural waters at a temperature harmful to the environment

therm·is·tor \\'thər-ˌmis-tər\\ n : an electrical resistor whose resistance varies sharply with temperature

ther·mo·cline \\'thər-mə-ˌklīn\\ n : the region in a thermally stratified body of water that separates warmer surface water from cold deep water

ther·mo·cou·ple \\'thər-mə-ˌkə-pəl\\ n : a device for measuring temperature by measuring the temperature-dependent potential difference created at the junction of two dissimilar metals

ther·mo·dy·nam·ics \\ˌthər-mə-dī-'na-miks\\ n : physics that deals with the mechanical action or relations of heat — **ther·mo·dy·nam·ic** \\-mik\\ adj — **ther·mo·dy·nam·i·cal·ly** \\-mi-k(ə-)lē\\ adv

ther·mom·e·ter \\thər-'mä-mə-tər\\ n [F thermomètre, fr. Gk thermē heat + metron measure] : an instrument for measuring temperature typically by the rise or fall of a liquid (as mercury) in a thin glass tube — **ther·mo·met·ric** \\ˌthər-mə-'me-trik\\ adj — **ther·mo·met·ri·cal·ly** \\-tri-k(ə-)lē\\ adv

ther·mo·nu·cle·ar \\ˌthər-mō-'nü-klē-ər, -'nyü-\\ adj 1 : of or relating to changes in the nucleus of atoms of low atomic weight (as hydrogen) that require a very high temperature (as in the hydrogen bomb) 2 : utilizing or relating to a thermonuclear bomb ⟨~ war⟩

ther·mo·plas·tic \\ˌthər-mə-'plas-tik\\ adj : capable of softening when heated and of hardening again when cooled ⟨~ resins⟩ — **thermoplastic** n

ther·mos \\'thər-məs\\ n : a cylindrical container with a vacuum between an inner and an outer wall used to keep liquids hot or cold

ther·mo·sphere \\'thər-mə-ˌsfir\\ n : the part of the earth's atmosphere that lies above the mesosphere and that is characterized by steadily increasing temperature with height

ther·mo·stat \\'thər-mə-ˌstat\\ n : a device that automatically controls temperature — **ther·mo·stat·ic** \\ˌthər-mə-'sta-tik\\ adj — **ther·mo·stat·i·cal·ly** \\-ti-k(ə-)lē\\ adv

the·sau·rus \\thi-'sȯr-əs\\ n, pl **-sau·ri** \\-'sȯr-ˌī\\ or **-sau·rus·es** \\-'sȯr-ə-səz\\ [NL, fr. L, treasure, collection, fr. Gk thēsauros] : a book of words and their synonyms — **the·sau·ral** \\-'sȯr-əl\\ adj

these pl of THIS

the·sis \\'thē-səs\\ n, pl **the·ses** \\'thē-ˌsēz\\ 1 : a proposition that a person advances and offers to maintain by argument 2 : an essay embodying results of original research; esp : one written for an academic degree

¹thes·pi·an \\'thes-pē-ən\\ adj, often cap [fr. Thespis, 6th cent. B.C. Greek poet and reputed originator of tragedy] : relating to the drama : DRAMATIC

²thespian n : ACTOR

Thess abbr Thessalonians

Thes·sa·lo·nians \\ˌthe-sə-'lō-nyənz, -nē-ənz\\ n — see BIBLE table

the·ta \\'thā-tə\\ n : the 8th letter of the Greek alphabet — Θ or θ

thew \\'thü, 'thyü\\ n : MUSCLE, SINEW — usu. used in pl.

they \\'thā\\ pron 1 : those individuals under discussion : the ones previously mentioned or referred to 2 : unspecified persons : PEOPLE

thi·a·mine \\'thī-ə-mən, -ˌmēn\\ also **thi·a·min** \\-mən\\ n : a vitamin of the vitamin B complex essential to normal metabolism and nerve function

¹thick \\'thik\\ adj 1 : having relatively great depth or extent from one surface to its opposite ⟨a ~ plank⟩; also : heavily built : THICKSET 2 : densely massed : CROWDED; also : FREQUENT, NUMEROUS 3 : dense or viscous in consistency ⟨~ syrup⟩ 4 : marked by haze, fog, or mist ⟨~ weather⟩ 5 : measuring in thickness ⟨one meter ~⟩ 6 : imperfectly articulated : INDISTINCT ⟨~ speech⟩ 7 : STUPID, OBTUSE 8 : associated on close terms : INTIMATE 9 : EXCESSIVE ♦ *Synonyms* COMPACT, CLOSE, TIGHT — **thick·ly** adv

²thick n 1 : the most crowded or active part 2 : the part of greatest thickness

thick and thin n : every difficulty and obstacle ⟨was loyal through thick and thin⟩

thick·en \\'thi-kən\\ vb : to make or become thick — **thick·en·er** n

thick·et \\'thi-kət\\ n : a dense growth of bushes or small trees

thick·ness \\-nəs\\ n 1 : the smallest of three dimensions ⟨length, width, and ~⟩ 2 : the quality or state of being thick 3 : LAYER, SHEET ⟨a single ~ of canvas⟩

thick·set \\'thik-'set\\ adj 1 : closely placed or planted 2 : having a thick body : BURLY

thick–skinned \\-'skind\\ adj 1 : having a thick skin 2 : not easily bothered by criticism or insult ⟨a ~ politician⟩

thief \\'thēf\\ n, pl **thieves** \\'thēvz\\ : one that steals esp. secretly

thieve \\'thēv\\ vb **thieved**; **thiev·ing** : STEAL, ROB ♦ *Synonyms* FILCH, PILFER, PURLOIN, SWIPE

thiev·ery \\'thē-və-rē\\ n, pl **-er·ies** : the act of stealing : THEFT

thigh \\'thī\\ n : the part of the vertebrate hind or lower limb between the knee and the hip

thigh·bone \\'thī-ˌbōn\\ n : FEMUR

thim·ble \\'thim-bəl\\ n : a cap or guard worn on the finger to push the needle in sewing — **thim·ble·ful** n

¹thin \\'thin\\ adj **thin·ner**; **thin·nest** 1 : having little extent from one surface through to its opposite : not thick : SLENDER 2 : not closely set or placed : SPARSE ⟨~ hair⟩ 3 : not dense or not dense enough : more fluid or rarefied than normal ⟨~ air⟩ ⟨~ syrup⟩ 4 : lacking substance, fullness, or strength ⟨~ broth⟩ 5 : FLIMSY ⟨a ~ excuse⟩ — **thin·ly** adv — **thin·ness** n

²thin vb **thinned**; **thin·ning** : to make or become thin

thine \\'thīn\\ pron, archaic : one or the ones belonging to thee

thing \'thiŋ\ *n* **1** : a matter of concern : AFFAIR ⟨∼s to do⟩ **2** *pl* : state of affairs ⟨∼s are improving⟩ **3** : EVENT, CIRCUMSTANCE ⟨the crime was a terrible ∼⟩ **4** : DEED, ACT ⟨expected great ∼s of him⟩ **5** : a distinct entity : OBJECT **6** : an inanimate object distinguished from a living being **7** *pl* : POSSESSIONS, EFFECTS **8** : an article of clothing **9** : DETAIL, POINT ⟨checks every little ∼⟩ **10** : IDEA, NOTION ⟨says the first ∼ he thinks of⟩ **11** : something one likes to do : SPECIALTY ⟨doing her ∼⟩

think \'thiŋk\ *vb* **thought** \'thȯt\; **thinking 1** : to form or have in the mind **2** : to have as an opinion : BELIEVE **3** : to reflect on : PONDER **4** : to call to mind : REMEMBER **5** : REASON **6** : to form a mental picture of : IMAGINE **7** : to devise by thinking ⟨thought up a plan to escape⟩ ◆ **Synonyms** CONCEIVE, FANCY, REALIZE, ENVISAGE — **think·er** *n*

think tank *n* : an institute, corporation, or group organized for interdisciplinary research (as in technological or social problems)

thin·ner \'thi-nər\ *n* : a volatile liquid (as turpentine) used to thin paint

thin–skinned \'thin-'skind\ *adj* **1** : having a thin skin or rind **2** : extremely sensitive to criticism or insult

¹**third** \'thərd\ *adj* : next after the second — **third** *or* **third·ly** *adv*

²**third** *n* **1** : one of three equal parts of something **2** : one that is number three in a countable series **3** : the 3d forward gear in an automotive vehicle

third degree *n* : the subjection of a prisoner to mental or physical torture to force a confession

third dimension *n* **1** : thickness, depth, or apparent thickness or depth that confers solidity on an object **2** : a quality that confers reality — **third–dimensional** *adj*

third world *n*, *often cap* T&W : the aggregate of the underdeveloped nations of the world

¹**thirst** \'thərst\ *n* **1** : a feeling of dryness in the mouth and throat associated with a desire to drink; *also* : a bodily condition producing this **2** : an ardent desire : CRAVING ⟨a ∼ for knowledge⟩ — **thirsty** *adj*

²**thirst** *vb* **1** : to need drink : suffer thirst **2** : to have a strong desire : CRAVE

thir·teen \,thər-'tēn\ *n* : one more than 12 — **thirteen** *adj or pron* — **thir·teenth** \-'tēnth\ *adj or n*

thir·ty \'thər-tē\ *n, pl* **thirties** : three times 10 — **thir·ti·eth** \-tē-əth\ *adj or n* — **thirty** *adj or pron*

¹**this** \'this\ *pron, pl* **these** \'thēz\ **1** : the one close or closest in time or space ⟨∼ is your book⟩ **2** : what is in the present or under immediate observation or discussion ⟨∼ is a mess⟩; *also* : what is happening or being done now ⟨after ∼ we'll leave⟩

²**this** *adj, pl* **these 1** : being the one near, present, just mentioned, or more immediately under observation ⟨∼ book⟩ **2**

: constituting the immediate past or future ⟨friends all *these* years⟩

³**this** *adv* : to such an extent or degree ⟨didn't expect to wait ∼ long⟩

this·tle \'thi-səl\ *n* : any of various tall prickly composite plants with often showy heads of tightly packed tubular flowers

this·tle·down \-,daůn\ *n* : the down from the ripe flower head of a thistle

¹**thith·er** \'thi-thər\ *adv* : to that place

²**thither** *adj* : being on the farther side

thith·er·ward \-wərd\ *adv* : toward that place : THITHER

thong \'thȯŋ\ *n* **1** : a strip esp. of leather or hide **2** : a sandal held on the foot by a thong between the toes **3** : a narrow strip of swimwear or underwear that passes between the thighs

tho·rax \'thȯr-,aks\ *n, pl* **tho·rax·es** *or* **tho·ra·ces** \'thȯr-ə-,sēz\ **1** : the part of the body of a mammal between the neck and the abdomen; *also* : its cavity containing the heart and lungs **2** : the middle of the three main divisions of the body of an insect — **tho·rac·ic** \thə-'ra-sik\ *adj*

tho·ri·um \'thȯr-ē-əm\ *n* : a radioactive metallic chemical element

thorn \'thȯrn\ *n* **1** : a woody plant bearing sharp processes **2** : a sharp rigid plant process that is usu. a modified leafless branch **3** : something that causes distress — **thorny** *adj*

thor·ough \'thər-ō\ *adj* **1** : COMPLETE, EXHAUSTIVE ⟨a ∼ search⟩ **2** : very careful : PAINSTAKING ⟨a ∼ scholar⟩ **3** : having full mastery — **thor·ough·ly** *adv* — **thor·ough·ness** *n*

¹**thor·ough·bred** \'thər-ə-,bred\ *adj* **1** : bred from the best blood through a long line **2** *cap* : of or relating to the Thoroughbred breed of horses **3** : marked by high-spirited grace

²**thoroughbred** *n* **1** *cap* : any of an English breed of light speedy horses kept chiefly for racing **2** : one (as a pedigreed animal) of excellent quality

thor·ough·fare \-,fer\ *n* : a public road or street

thor·ough·go·ing \,thər-ə-'gō-iŋ\ *adj* : marked by thoroughness or zeal

thorp \'thȯrp\ *n, archaic* : VILLAGE

those *pl of* THAT

¹**thou** \'thaů\ *pron, archaic* : the person addressed

²**thou** \'thaů\ *n, pl* **thou** : a thousand of something (as dollars)

¹**though** \'thō\ *conj* **1** : despite the fact that ⟨∼ the odds are hopeless, they fight on⟩ **2** : granting that ⟨∼ it may look bad, still, all is not lost⟩

²**though** *adv* : HOWEVER, NEVERTHELESS ⟨not for long, ∼⟩

¹**thought** \'thȯt\ *past and past part of* THINK

²**thought** *n* **1** : the process of thinking **2** : serious consideration : REGARD **3** : reasoning power **4** : the power to imagine : CONCEPTION **5** : IDEA, NOTION **6** : OPINION, BELIEF ⟨spoke his ∼s freely⟩

thought·ful \'thȯt-fəl\ *adj* **1** : absorbed in thought **2** : marked by careful thinking

⟨a ∼ essay⟩ **3** : considerate of others ⟨a ∼ host⟩ — **thought·ful·ly** *adv* — **thought·ful·ness** *n*

thought·less \-ləs\ *adj* **1** : insufficiently alert : CARELESS ⟨a ∼ worker⟩ **2** : RECKLESS ⟨a ∼ act⟩ **3** : lacking concern for others : INCONSIDERATE ⟨∼ remarks⟩ — **thought·less·ly** *adv* — **thought·less·ness** *n*

thou·sand \'tha.u̇z-ᵊnd\ *n, pl* **thousands** *or* **thousand** : 10 times 100 — **thousand** *adj* — **thou·sandth** \-ᵊnth\ *adj or n*

thousands place *n* : the place four to the left of the decimal point in an Arabic number

thrall \'thrȯl\ *n* **1** : SLAVE, BONDMAN **2** : a state of servitude — **thrall·dom** *or* **thral·dom** \'thrȯl-dəm\ *n*

¹**thrash** \'thrash\ *vb* **1** : THRESH 1 **2** : BEAT, WHIP; *also* : DEFEAT **3** : to move about violently **4** : to go over again and again ⟨∼ over the matter⟩; *also* : to hammer out ⟨∼ out a plan⟩

²**thrash** *n* : rock music that is extremely fast and loud

¹**thrash·er** \'thra-shər\ *n* : one that thrashes or threshes

²**thrasher** *n* : any of various long-tailed American songbirds related to the mockingbird

¹**thread** \'thred\ *n* **1** : a thin continuous strand of spun and twisted textile fibers **2** : something resembling a textile thread **3** : the ridge or groove that winds around a screw **4** : a line of reasoning or train of thought **5** : a continuing element **6** : a tenuous or feeble support

²**thread** *vb* **1** : to pass a thread through the eye of (a needle) **2** : to pass (as film) through something **3** : to make one's way through or between **4** : to put together on a thread ⟨∼ beads⟩ **5** : to form a screw thread on or in

thread·bare \-ˌber\ *adj* **1** : having the nap worn off so that the thread shows : SHABBY **2** : TRITE ⟨∼ excuses⟩

thready \'thre-dē\ *adj* **1** : consisting of or bearing fibers of filaments ⟨a ∼ bark⟩ **2** : lacking in fullness, body, or vigor ⟨a ∼ voice⟩

threat \'thret\ *n* **1** : an expression of intent to do harm **2** : one that threatens

threat·en \'thre-tᵊn\ *vb* **1** : to utter threats against **2** : to give signs or warning of : PORTEND **3** : to hang over as a threat : MENACE **4** : to cause to feel insecure or anxious — **threat·en·ing·ly** *adv*

threat·ened \-tᵊnd\ *adj* : having an uncertain chance of continued survival; *esp* : likely to become an endangered species

three \'thrē\ *n* **1** : one more than two **2** : the 3d in a set or series **3** : something having three units — **three** *adj or pron*

3–D \'thrē-'dē\ *n* : a three-dimensional form or picture

three–dimensional *adj* **1** : relating to or having three dimensions **2** : giving the illusion of varying distances ⟨a ∼ picture⟩

three·fold \'thrē-ˌfōld, -'fōld\ *adj* **1** : having three parts : TRIPLE **2** : being three

times as great or as many — **three·fold** \-'fōld\ *adv*

three·pence \'thre-pəns, 'thri-, 'thrə-, *US also* 'thrē-pens\ *n* **1** *pl* **threepence** *or* **three·penc·es** : a coin worth three pennies **2** : the sum of three British pennies

three·score \'thrē-'skȯr\ *adj* : being three times twenty : SIXTY

three·some \'thrē-səm\ *n* : a group of three persons or things

thren·o·dy \'thre-nə-dē\ *n, pl* **-dies** : a song of lamentation : ELEGY

thresh \'thresh, 'thrash\ *vb* **1** : to separate (as grain from straw) mechanically **2** : THRASH — **thresh·er** *n*

thresh·old \'thresh-ˌhōld\ *n* **1** : the sill of a door **2** : a point or place of beginning or entering : OUTSET ⟨on the ∼ of a new era⟩ **3** : a point at which a physiological or psychological effect begins to be produced ⟨pain ∼s⟩

threw *past of* THROW

thrice \'thrīs\ *adv* **1** : three times **2** : in a threefold manner or degree

thrift \'thrift\ *n* [ME, fr. ON, prosperity, fr. *thrīfask* to thrive] : careful management esp. of money : FRUGALITY — **thrift·i·ly** \'thrif-tə-lē\ *adv* — **thrift·less** *adj* — **thrifty** *adj*

thrill \'thril\ *vb* [ME *thirlen, thrillen* to pierce, fr. OE *thyrlian*, fr. *thyrel* hole, fr. *thurh* through] **1** : to have or cause to have sudden sharp feeling of excitement ⟨was *thrilled* by their decision⟩; *also* : TINGLE, SHIVER **2** : TREMBLE, VIBRATE — **thrill** *n* — **thrill·er** *n* — **thrill·ing·ly** *adv*

thrips \'thrips\ *n, pl* **thrips** : any of an order of minute sucking insects including many plant-feeding pests

thrive \'thrīv\ *vb* **thrived** *or* **throve** \'thrōv\; **thrived** *also* **thriv·en** \'thri-vən\; **thriv·ing** **1** : to grow luxuriantly : FLOURISH **2** : to gain in wealth or possessions : PROSPER ⟨her business ∼s⟩

throat \'thrōt\ *n* : the part of the neck in front of the spinal column; *also* : the passage through it to the stomach and lungs — **throat·ed** *adj*

throaty \'thrō-tē\ *adj* **throat·i·er; -est** **1** : uttered or produced from low in the throat ⟨a ∼ voice⟩ **2** : heavy, thick, or deep as if from the throat ⟨∼ notes of a horn⟩ — **throat·i·ly** \-tə-lē\ *adv* — **throat·i·ness** \-tē-nəs\ *n*

¹**throb** \'thräb\ *vb* **throbbed; throb·bing** : to pulsate or pound esp. with abnormal force or rapidity : BEAT, VIBRATE

²**throb** *n* : BEAT, PULSE

throe \'thrō\ *n* **1** : PANG, SPASM ⟨death ∼s⟩ **2** *pl* : a hard or painful struggle

throm·bo·lyt·ic \ˌthräm-bə-'li-tik\ *adj* : destroying or breaking up a thrombus — **thrombolytic** *n*

throm·bo·sis \thräm-'bō-səs\ *n, pl* **-bo·ses** \-ˌsēz\ : the formation or presence of a clot in a blood vessel — **throm·bot·ic** \-'bä-tik\ *adj*

throm·bus \'thräm-bəs\ *n, pl* **throm·bi** \-ˌbī\ [NL, fr. Gk *thrombos* lump, clot] : a clot of blood formed within a blood vessel and remaining attached to its place of origin

throne \'thrōn\ *n* 1 : the chair of state of a sovereign or high dignitary 2 : royal power : SOVEREIGNTY

¹**throng** \'thròŋ\ *n* 1 : MULTITUDE 2 : a crowding together of many persons

²**throng** *vb* **thronged; throng·ing** : CROWD

¹**throt·tle** \'thrä-t°l\ *vb* **throt·tled; throt·tling** [ME *throtlen,* fr. *throte* throat] 1 : CHOKE, STRANGLE 2 : SUPPRESS ⟨policies that ∼ creativity⟩ 3 : to reduce the speed of (an engine) by closing the throttle — **throt·tler** *n*

²**throttle** *n* : a valve regulating the flow of steam or fuel to an engine; *also* : the lever controlling this valve

¹**through** \'thrü\ *prep* 1 : into at one side and out at the other side of ⟨go ∼ the door⟩ 2 : by way of ⟨entered ∼ a skylight⟩ 3 : in the midst of ⟨a path ∼ the trees⟩ 4 : by means of ⟨succeeded ∼ hard work⟩ 5 : over the whole of ⟨rumors swept ∼ the office⟩ 6 : during the whole of ⟨∼ the night⟩ 7 : to and including ⟨Monday ∼ Friday⟩

²**through** *adv* 1 : from one end or side to the other 2 : from beginning to end : to completion ⟨see it ∼⟩ 3 : to the core : THOROUGHLY ⟨he was wet ∼⟩ 4 : into the open : OUT ⟨break ∼⟩

³**through** *adj* 1 : permitting free passage ⟨a ∼ street⟩ 2 : going from point of origin to destination without change or transfer ⟨a ∼ train⟩ 3 : coming from or going to points outside a local area ⟨∼ traffic⟩ 4 : FINISHED ⟨∼ with the job⟩

¹**through·out** \thrü-'aut\ *adv* 1 : EVERYWHERE 2 : from beginning to end

²**throughout** *prep* 1 : in or to every part of 2 : during the whole period of

through·put \'thrü-,put\ *n* : OUTPUT, PRODUCTION ⟨the ∼ of a computer⟩

throve *past of* THRIVE

¹**throw** \'thrō\ *vb* **threw** \'thrü\; **thrown** \'thrōn\; **throw·ing** [ME, to cause to twist, throw, fr. OE *thrāwan* to cause to twist] 1 : to propel through the air esp. with a forward motion of the hand and arm ⟨∼ a ball⟩ 2 : to cause to fall or fall off 3 : to put suddenly in a certain position or condition ⟨∼ into panic⟩ 4 : to put on or take off hastily ⟨∼ on a coat⟩ 5 : to lose intentionally ⟨∼ a game⟩ 6 : to move (a lever) so as to connect or disconnect parts of something (as a clutch) 7 : to put (an automobile) into a different gear 8 : to act as host for ⟨∼ a party⟩ ♦ **Synonyms** TOSS, FLING, PITCH, SLING — **throw·er** *n*

²**throw** *n* 1 : an act of throwing, hurling, or flinging; *also* : CAST 2 : the distance a missile may be thrown 3 : a light coverlet 4 : a woman's scarf or light wrap

¹**throw·away** \'thrō-ə-,wā\ *n* : something that is or is designed to be thrown away esp. after one use

²**throwaway** *adj* : overly wasteful ⟨a ∼ society⟩

throw·back \-,bak\ *n* : reversion to an earlier type or phase; *also* : an instance or product of this

throw up *vb* 1 : to build hurriedly 2 : VOMIT

thrum \'thrəm\ *vb* **thrummed; thrum·ming** : to play or pluck a stringed instrument idly : STRUM

thrush \'thrəsh\ *n* : any of numerous small or medium-sized songbirds that are mostly of a plain color often with spotted underparts

¹**thrust** \'thrəst\ *vb* **thrust; thrust·ing** 1 : to push or drive with force : SHOVE 2 : STAB, PIERCE 3 : INTERJECT 4 : to press the acceptance of upon someone

²**thrust** *n* 1 : a lunge with a pointed weapon 2 : ATTACK 3 : the pressure of one part of a construction against another (as of an arch against an abutment) 4 : the force produced by a propeller or jet or rocket engine that drives a vehicle (as an aircraft) forward 5 : a violent push : SHOVE 6 : prominent or essential element ⟨the ∼ of the argument⟩

thrust·er *also* **thrust·or** \'thrəs-tər\ *n* : one that thrusts; *esp* : a rocket engine

thru·way \'thrü-,wā\ *n* : EXPRESSWAY

¹**thud** \'thəd\ *n* 1 : BLOW 2 : a dull sound

²**thud** *vb* **thud·ded; thud·ding** : to move or strike so as to make a thud

thug \'thəg\ *n* [Hindi & Urdu *thag,* lit., thief] : a brutal ruffian or assassin — **thug·gish** *adj*

thu·li·um \'thü-lē-əm, 'thyü-\ *n* : a rare metallic chemical element

¹**thumb** \'thəm\ *n* 1 : the short thick first digit of the human hand or a corresponding digit of a lower animal 2 : the part of a glove or mitten that covers the thumb

²**thumb** *vb* 1 : to leaf through (pages) with the thumb 2 : to wear or soil with the thumb by frequent handling 3 : to request or obtain (a ride) in a passing automobile by signaling with the thumb

¹**thumb·nail** \'thəm-,nāl\ *n* : the nail of the thumb

²**thumbnail** *adj* : BRIEF, CONCISE ⟨a ∼ description⟩ ⟨a ∼ picture⟩

thumb·print \-,print\ *n* : an impression made by the thumb

thumb·screw \-,skrü\ *n* 1 : a device of torture for squeezing the thumb 2 : a screw with a head that may be turned by the thumb and index finger

thumb·tack \-,tak\ *n* : a tack with a broad flat head for pressing with one's thumb into a board or wall

¹**thump** \'thəmp\ *vb* 1 : to strike with or as if with something thick or heavy so as to cause a dull sound 2 : POUND

²**thump** *n* : a blow with or as if with something blunt or heavy; *also* : the sound made by such a blow

¹**thun·der** \'thən-dər\ *n* 1 : the sound following a flash of lightning; *also* : a noise like such a sound 2 : a loud utterance or threat

²**thunder** *vb* 1 : to produce thunder 2 : ROAR, SHOUT ⟨jets ∼ed overhead⟩

thun·der·bolt \-,bōlt\ *n* : a flash of lightning with its accompanying thunder

thun·der·clap \-ˌklap\ *n* : a crash of thunder

thun·der·cloud \-ˌklau̇d\ *n* : a cloud charged with electricity and producing lightning and thunder

thun·der·head \-ˌhed\ *n* : a large cumulus or cumulonimbus cloud often appearing before a thunderstorm

thun·der·ous \ˈthən-də-rəs\ *adj* : producing thunder; *also* : making a noise like thunder — **thun·der·ous·ly** *adv*

thun·der·show·er \ˈthən-dər-ˌshau̇(-ə)r\ *n* : a shower accompanied by thunder and lightning

thun·der·storm \-ˌstȯrm\ *n* : a storm accompanied by thunder and lightning

thun·der·struck \-ˌstrək\ *adj* : stunned as if struck by a thunderbolt

Thurs *or* **Thu** *abbr* Thursday

Thurs·day \ˈthərz-ˌdā, -dē\ *n* [ME, fr. OE *thursdæg*, fr. ON *thōrsdagr*, lit., day of Thor (Norse god)] : the 5th day of the week

thus \ˈthəs\ *adv* **1** : in this or that manner **2** : to this degree or extent : SO **3** : because of this or that : HENCE

¹thwack \ˈthwak\ *vb* : to strike with or as if with something flat or heavy

²thwack *n* : a heavy blow : WHACK

¹thwart \ˈthwȯrt\ *vb* **1** : FOIL, BAFFLE **2** : BLOCK, DEFEAT ⟨~ed the attack⟩
♦ **Synonyms** BALK, OUTWIT, FRUSTRATE

²thwart \ˈthwȯrt, *naut often* ˈthȯrt\ *adv* : ATHWART

³thwart *adj* : situated or placed across something else

⁴thwart *n* : a seat extending across a boat

thy \ˈthī\ *adj, archaic* : of, relating to, or done by or to thee or thyself

thyme \ˈtīm, ˈthīm\ *n* [ME, fr. AF *time*, fr. L *thymum*, fr. Gk *thymon*, prob. fr. *thyein* to make a burnt offering, sacrifice] : a garden mint with small aromatic leaves used esp. in seasoning; *also* : its leaves so used

thy·mine \ˈthī-ˌmēn\ *n* : a pyrimidine base that is one of the four bases coding genetic information in the molecular chain of DNA

thy·mus \ˈthī-məs\ *n, pl* **thy·mus·es** : a glandular organ of the neck region that is composed largely of lymphoid tissue, functions esp. in the development of the immune system, and tends to atrophy in the adult

thy·ris·tor \thī-ˈris-tər\ *n* : a semiconductor device that acts as a switch, rectifier, or voltage regulator

thy·roid \ˈthī-ˌrȯid\ *n* [NL *thyroides*, fr. Gk *thyreoeidēs* shield-shaped, thyroid, fr. *thyreos* shield shaped like a door, fr. *thyra* door] : a large 2-lobed endocrine gland that lies at the base of the neck and produces several iodine-containing hormones that affect growth, development, and metabolism — **thyroid** *also* **thy·roi·dal** \thī-ˈrȯi-d°l\ *adj*

thy·rox·ine *or* **thy·rox·in** \thī-ˈräk-ˌsēn, -sən\ *n* : an iodine-containing hormone that is produced by the thyroid gland, in-

creases metabolic rate, and is used to treat thyroid disorders

thy·self \thī-ˈself\ *pron, archaic* : YOURSELF

Ti *symbol* titanium

ti·ara \tē-ˈer-ə, -ˈär-\ *n* **1** : a 3-tiered crown worn by the pope **2** : a decorative headband or semicircle for formal wear by women

Ti·bet·an \tə-ˈbe-t°n\ *n* **1** : the language of the Tibetan people **2** : a native or inhabitant of Tibet — **Tibetan** *adj*

tib·ia \ˈti-bē-ə\ *n, pl* **-i·ae** \-bē-ˌē\ *also* **-i·as** [L] : the inner of the two bones of the vertebrate hind or lower limb between the knee and the ankle

tic \ˈtik\ *n* : a local and habitual twitching of muscles esp. of the face

ti·cal \ti-ˈkäl, ˈti-kəl\ *n, pl* **ticals** *or* **tical** : BAHT

¹tick \ˈtik\ *n* : any of a large group of small bloodsucking arachnids

²tick *n* : the fabric case of a mattress or pillow; *also* : a mattress consisting of a tick and its filling

³tick *n* **1** : a light rhythmic audible tap or beat **2** : a small mark used to draw attention to or check something

⁴tick *vb* **1** : to make the sound of a tick or series of ticks **2** : to mark, count, or announce by or as if by ticking beats **3** : to mark or check with a tick **4** : to function as an operating mechanism : RUN

⁵tick *n, chiefly Brit* : CREDIT; *also* : a credit account

tick·er \ˈti-kər\ *n* **1** : something (as a watch) that ticks **2** : a telegraph instrument that prints information (as stock prices) on paper tape **3** *slang* : HEART

ticker tape *n* : the paper ribbon on which a telegraphic ticker prints

¹tick·et \ˈti-kət\ *n* [MF *etiquet, estiquette* notice attached to something, fr. MF dial. *estiquier* to attach, fr. MD *steken* to stick] **1** : CERTIFICATE, LICENSE, PERMIT; *esp* : a certificate or token showing that a fare or admission fee has been paid **2** : TAG, LABEL **3** : SLATE **4** : a summons issued to a traffic offender

²ticket *vb* **1** : to attach a ticket to **2** : to furnish or serve with a ticket

tick·ing \ˈti-kiŋ\ *n* : a strong fabric used in upholstering and as a mattress covering

tick·le \ˈti-kəl\ *vb* **tick·led; tick·ling 1** : to excite or stir up agreeably : PLEASE, AMUSE **2** : to have a tingling sensation **3** : to touch (as a body part) lightly so as to cause uneasiness, laughter, or spasmodic movements ⟨*tickled* her under the chin⟩ — **tickle** *n* — **tick·ler** *n*

tick·lish \-kə-lish\ *adj* **1** : OVERSENSITIVE, TOUCHY **2** : UNSTABLE ⟨a ~ foothold⟩ **3** : requiring delicate handling ⟨~ subject⟩ **4** : sensitive to tickling — **tick·lish·ly** *adv* — **tick·lish·ness** *n*

tidal wave *n* **1** : an unusually high sea wave that sometimes follows an earthquake **2** : an unusual rise of water alongshore due to strong winds

tid·bit \ˈtid-ˌbit\ *n* : a choice morsel

¹tide \ˈtīd\ *n* [ME, time, fr. OE *tīd*] **1** : the

alternate rising and falling of the surface of the ocean **2** : something that fluctuates like the tides of the sea ⟨the ～ of public opinion⟩ — **tid·al** \ˈtī-dᵊl\ adj

²**tide** vb **tid·ed; tid·ing** : to carry through or help along as if by the tide ⟨a loan to ～ us over⟩

tide·land \ˈtīd-ˌland, -lənd\ n **1** : land overflowed during flood tide **2** : land under the ocean within a nation's territorial waters — often used in pl.

tide·wa·ter \-ˌwȯ-tər, -ˌwä-\ n **1** : water overflowing land at flood tide **2** : low-lying coastal land

tid·ings \ˈtī-diŋz\ n pl : NEWS, MESSAGE

¹**ti·dy** \ˈtī-dē\ adj **ti·di·er; -est 1** : well ordered and cared for : NEAT **2** : LARGE, SUBSTANTIAL ⟨a ～ sum⟩ — **ti·di·ness** \ˈtī-dē-nəs\ n

²**tidy** vb **ti·died; ti·dy·ing 1** : to put in order **2** : to make things tidy

³**tidy** n, pl **tidies** : a decorated covering used to protect the back or arms of a chair from wear or soil

¹**tie** \ˈtī\ n **1** : a line, ribbon, or cord used for fastening, uniting, or closing **2** : a structural element (as a beam or rod) holding two pieces together **3** : one of the cross supports to which railroad rails are fastened **4** : a connecting link : BOND ⟨family ～s⟩ **5** : an equality in number (as of votes or scores); also : an undecided or deadlocked contest **6** : NECKTIE

²**tie** vb **tied; ty·ing** or **tie·ing 1** : to fasten, attach, or close by means of a tie **2** : to bring together firmly : UNITE **3** : to form a knot or bow in ⟨～ a scarf⟩ **4** : to restrain from freedom of action : CONSTRAIN **5** : to make or have an equal score with

tie·back \ˈtī-ˌbak\ n : a decorative strip for draping a curtain to the side of a window

tie-dye·ing \ˈtī-ˌdī-iŋ\ n : a method of producing patterns in textiles by tying parts of the fabric so that they will not absorb the dye — **tie-dyed** \-ˌdīd\ adj

tie-in \ˈtī-ˌin\ n : CONNECTION

tier \ˈtir\ n : ROW, LAYER; esp : one of two or more rows arranged one above another — **tiered** \ˈtird\ adj

tie-rod \ˈtī-ˌräd\ n : a rod used as a connecting member or brace

tie-up \-ˌəp\ n **1** : a slowing or stopping of traffic or business **2** : CONNECTION

tiff \ˈtif\ n : a petty quarrel — **tiff** vb

Tif·fa·ny \ˈti-fə-nē\ adj : made of pieces of stained glass ⟨a ～ lamp⟩

ti·ger \ˈtī-gər\ n : a very large tawny black-striped Asian cat — **ti·ger·ish** adj

¹**tight** \ˈtīt\ adj **1** : so close in structure as to prevent passage of a liquid or gas **2** : strongly fixed or held : SECURE **3** : TAUT **4** : fitting usu. too closely ⟨～ shoes⟩ **5** : set close together : COMPACT ⟨a ～ formation⟩ **6** : DIFFICULT, TRYING ⟨get in a ～ spot⟩ **7** : STINGY, MISERLY **8** : evenly contested : CLOSE **9** : INTOXICATED **10** : low in supply : hard to get ⟨money is ～⟩ — **tight·ly** adv — **tight·ness** n

²**tight** adv **1** : TIGHTLY, FIRMLY **2** : SOUNDLY ⟨sleep ～⟩

tight·en \ˈtī-tᵊn\ vb : to make or become tight

tight-fist·ed \ˈtīt-ˈfis-təd\ adj : STINGY

tight·rope \-ˌrōp\ n : a taut rope or wire for acrobats to perform on

tights \ˈtīts\ n pl : skintight garments covering the body esp. below the waist; also, Brit : PANTY HOSE

tight·wad \ˈtīt-ˌwäd\ n : a stingy person

ti·gress \ˈtī-grəs\ n : a female tiger

ti·la·pia \tə-ˈlä-pē-ə, -ˈlā-\ n, pl **tilapia** also **ti·la·pi·as** : any of numerous chiefly African freshwater fishes widely raised for food

til·de \ˈtil-də\ n [Sp, fr. ML titulus title] : a mark ˜ placed esp. over the letter n (as in Spanish señor sir) to denote the sound \nʸ\ or over vowels (as in Portuguese irmã sister) to indicate nasal quality

¹**tile** \ˈtī(-ə)l\ n **1** : a flat or curved piece of fired clay, stone, or concrete used for roofs, floors, or walls; also : a pipe of earthenware or concrete used for a drain **2** : a thin piece (as of linoleum) used for covering walls or floors — **til·ing** \ˈtī-liŋ\ n

²**tile** vb **tiled; til·ing** : to cover with tiles — **til·er** n

¹**till** \ˈtil\ prep or conj : UNTIL

²**till** vb : to work by plowing, sowing, and raising crops : CULTIVATE — **till·able** adj

³**till** n : DRAWER; esp : a money drawer in a store or bank

till·age \ˈti-lij\ n **1** : the work of tilling land **2** : cultivated land

¹**till·er** \ˈti-lər\ n [OE telgor, telgra twig, shoot] : a sprout or stalk esp. from the base or lower part of a plant

²**till·er** \ˈti-lər\ n : one that tills

³**till·er** \ˈti-lər\ n [ME tiler stock of a crossbow, tiller, fr. AF teiler stock of a crossbow] : a lever used for turning a boat's rudder from side to side

¹**tilt** \ˈtilt\ n **1** : a contest in which two combatants charging usu. with lances try to unhorse each other : JOUST; also : a tournament of tilts **2** : a verbal contest : DISPUTE **3** : a sloping surface : SLANT

²**tilt** vb **1** : to move or shift so as to incline : TIP **2** : to engage in or as if in combat with lances : JOUST, ATTACK

tilth \ˈtilth\ n **1** : TILLAGE **2 2** : the state of a soil esp. in relation to the suitability of its particle size and structure for growing crops

Tim abbr Timothy

tim·ber \ˈtim-bər\ n [ME, fr. OE, building, wood] **1** : growing trees or their wood — often used interjectionally to warn of a falling tree **2** : wood for use in making something **3** : a usu. large squared or dressed piece of wood

tim·bered \ˈtim-bərd\ adj : having walls framed by exposed timbers

tim·ber·land \ˈtim-bər-ˌland\ n : wooded land

tim·ber·line \ˈtim-bər-ˌlīn\ n : the upper limit of tree growth in mountains or high latitudes

timber rattlesnake *n* : a widely distributed rattlesnake of the eastern U.S.

timber wolf *n* : GRAY WOLF

tim·bre *also* **tim·ber** \'tam-bər, 'tim-\ *n* [F, fr. MF, bell struck by a hammer, fr. OF, drum, fr. MGk *tymbanon* kettledrum, fr. Gk *tympanon*] : the distinctive quality given to a sound by its overtones

tim·brel \'tim-brəl\ *n* : a small hand drum or tambourine

¹time \'tīm\ *n* **1** : a period during which an action, process, or condition exists or continues ⟨gone a long ∼⟩ **2** : LEISURE ⟨found ∼ to read⟩ **3** : a point or period when something occurs : OCCASION ⟨the last ∼ we met⟩ **4** : a set or customary moment or hour for something to occur ⟨arrived on ∼⟩ **5** : AGE, ERA **6** : state of affairs : CONDITIONS ⟨hard ∼s⟩ **7** : a rate of speed : TEMPO **8** : a moment, hour, day, or year as indicated by a clock or calendar ⟨what ∼ is it⟩ **9** : a system of reckoning time ⟨solar ∼⟩ **10** : one of a series of recurring instances; *also, pl* : added or accumulated quantities or examples ⟨five ∼s greater⟩ **11** : a person's experience during a particular period ⟨had a good ∼⟩ **12** : the hours or days of one's work; *also* : an hourly pay rate ⟨straight ∼⟩ **13** : TIME-OUT 1

²time *vb* **timed; tim·ing** **1** : to arrange or set the time of : SCHEDULE ⟨∼s his calls conveniently⟩ **2** : to set the tempo or duration of ⟨∼ a performance⟩ **3** : to cause to keep time with **4** : to determine or record the time, duration, or rate of ⟨∼ a sprinter⟩ — **tim·er** *n*

time bomb *n* **1** : a bomb so made as to explode at a predetermined time **2** : something with a potentially dangerous delayed reaction

time clock *n* : a clock that records the time workers arrive and depart

time frame *n* : a period of time esp. with respect to some action or project

time–hon·ored \'tīm-ˌä-nərd\ *adj* : honored because of age or long usage

time·keep·er \-ˌkē-pər\ *n* **1** : a clerk who keeps records of the time worked by employees **2** : one appointed to mark and announce the time in an athletic game or contest

time·less \-ləs\ *adj* **1** : ETERNAL **2** : not limited or affected by time ⟨∼ works of art⟩ — **time·less·ly** *adv* — **time·less·ness** *n*

time·ly \-lē\ *adj* **time·li·er; -est** **1** : coming early or at the right time ⟨a ∼ decision⟩ ⟨∼ payment⟩ **2** : appropriate to the time ⟨a ∼ book⟩ — **time·li·ness** *n*

time–out \'tīm-ˈaut\ *n* **1** : a brief suspension of activity esp. in an athletic game **2** : a quiet period used esp. as a disciplinary measure for a child

time·piece \-ˌpēs\ *n* : a device (as a clock) to show the passage of time

times \'tīmz\ *prep* : multiplied by ⟨2 ∼ 2 is 4⟩

time–shar·ing \'tīm-ˌsher-iŋ\ *n* **1** : simultaneous use of a computer by many users **2** *or* **time–share** \-ˌsher\ : joint ownership or rental of a vacation lodging by several persons with each taking turns using the place

times sign *n* : the symbol × used to indicate multiplication

time·ta·ble \'tīm-ˌtā-bəl\ *n* **1** : a table of the departure and arrival times (as of trains) **2** : a schedule showing a planned order or sequence

time warp *n* : an anomaly, discontinuity, or suspension held to occur in the progress of time

time·worn \-ˌwōrn\ *adj* **1** : worn by time **2** : HACKNEYED, STALE ⟨a ∼ joke⟩

tim·id \'ti-məd\ *adj* : lacking in courage or self-confidence : FEARFUL — **ti·mid·i·ty** \tə-'mi-də-tē\ *n* — **tim·id·ly** *adv*

tim·o·rous \'ti-mə-rəs\ *adj* : of a timid disposition : AFRAID ⟨a ∼ kitten⟩ — **tim·o·rous·ly** *adv* — **tim·o·rous·ness** *n*

tim·o·thy \'ti-mə-thē\ *n* : a perennial grass with long cylindrical spikes widely grown for hay in the U.S.

Tim·o·thy \'ti-mə-thē\ *n* — see BIBLE table

tim·pa·ni \'tim-pə-nē\ *n sing or pl* [It] : a set of kettledrums played by one performer in an orchestra — **tim·pa·nist** \-nist\ *n*

¹tin \'tin\ *n* **1** : a soft white crystalline metallic chemical element malleable at ordinary temperatures that is used esp. in solders and alloys **2** : a container (as a can) made of metal (as tinplate)

²tin *vb* **tinned; tin·ning** **1** : to cover or plate with tin **2** : to pack in tins

TIN *abbr* taxpayer identification number

tinct \'tiŋkt\ *n* : TINCTURE, TINGE

¹tinc·ture \'tiŋk-chər\ *n* **1** *archaic* : a substance that colors **2** : a slight admixture : TRACE **3** : an alcoholic solution of a medicinal substance ♦ *Synonyms* TOUCH, SUGGESTION, SUSPICION, TINGE

²tincture *vb* **tinc·tured; tinc·tur·ing** **1** : COLOR, TINGE **2** : AFFECT

tin·der \'tin-dər\ *n* **1** : a very flammable substance used as kindling **2** : something serving to incite or inflame

tin·der·box \'tin-dər-ˌbäks\ *n* **1** : a metal box for holding tinder and usu. flint and steel for striking a spark **2** : a highly flammable object or place

tine \'tīn\ *n* : a slender pointed part (as of a fork or an antler) : PRONG

tin·foil \'tin-ˌfȯi(-ə)l\ *n* : a thin metal sheeting usu. of aluminum or tin-lead alloy

¹tinge \'tinj\ *vb* **tinged; tinge·ing** *or* **ting·ing** **1** : to color slightly : TINT **2** : to affect or modify esp. with a slight odor or taste

²tinge *n* : a slight coloring, flavor, or quality : TRACE ⟨a ∼ of color⟩ ⟨a ∼ of regret⟩ ♦ *Synonyms* TOUCH, SUGGESTION, SUSPICION, SOUPÇON

tin·gle \'tiŋ-gəl\ *vb* **tin·gled; tin·gling** **1** : to feel a prickling or thrilling sensation **2** : TINKLE — **tingle** *n*

¹tin·ker \'tiŋ-kər\ *n* **1** : a usu. itinerant mender of household utensils **2** : an unskillful mender : BUNGLER

²tinker *vb* : to repair or adjust something

in an unskillful or experimental manner — **tin·ker·er** n

¹**tin·kle** \'tiŋ-kəl\ vb **tin·kled; tin·kling** : to make or cause to make a tinkle

²**tinkle** n : a series of short high ringing or clinking sounds

tin·ni·tus \'ti-nə-təs, tə-'nī-təs\ n : a sensation of noise (as ringing or roaring) in the ears

tin·ny \'ti-nē\ adj **tin·ni·er; -est** 1 : abounding in or yielding tin 2 : resembling tin; also : LIGHT, CHEAP 3 : thin in tone ⟨a ~ voice⟩ — **tin·ni·ly** \-nə-lē\ adv — **tin·ni·ness** \-nē-nəs\ n

tin·plate \'tin-'plāt\ n : thin sheet iron or steel coated with tin — **tin–plate** vb

tin·sel \'tin-səl\ n [ME tyneseyle cloth interwoven with metallic thread, prob. fr. AF tencelé, pp. of tenceler, estenceler to sparkle] 1 : threads, strips, or sheets of metal, paper, or plastic used to produce a glittering appearance 2 : something superficially attractive but of little worth

tin·smith \'tin-ˌsmith\ n : one that works with sheet metal (as tinplate)

¹**tint** \'tint\ n 1 : a slight or pale coloration : HUE 2 : any of various shades of a color

²**tint** vb : to impart a tint to : COLOR

tin·tin·nab·u·la·tion \ˌtin-tə-ˌna-byə-'lā-shən\ n 1 : the ringing of bells 2 : a tinkling or jingling sound as if of bells

tin·ware \'tin-ˌwer\ n : articles and esp. utensils made of tinplate

ti·ny \'tī-nē\ adj **ti·ni·er; -est** : very small : MINUTE ♦ *Synonyms* MINIATURE, DIMINUTIVE, WEE, LILLIPUTIAN

¹**tip** \'tip\ vb **tipped; tip·ping** 1 : OVERTURN, UPSET 2 : LEAN, SLANT; also : to raise and tilt forward ⟨tipped his hat⟩

²**tip** n : the act or an instance of tipping

³**tip** vb **tipped; tip·ping** 1 : to furnish with a tip 2 : to cover or adorn the tip of

⁴**tip** n 1 : the usu. pointed end of something 2 : a small piece or part serving as an end, cap, or point

⁵**tip** n : a light touch or blow

⁶**tip** vb **tipped; tip·ping** : to strike lightly : TAP

⁷**tip** n : a piece of advice or expert or confidential information : HINT

⁸**tip** vb **tipped; tip·ping** : to impart a piece of information about or to

⁹**tip** vb **tipped; tip·ping** : to give a gratuity to — **tip·per** n

¹⁰**tip** n : a gift or small sum given for a service performed or anticipated

tip–off \'tip-ˌȯf\ n : WARNING, TIP

tip·pet \'ti-pət\ n : a long scarf or shoulder cape

tipping point n : the critical point in a situation or process beyond which a significant effect takes place

tip·ple \'ti-pəl\ vb **tip·pled; tip·pling** : to drink intoxicating liquor esp. habitually or excessively — **tipple** n — **tip·pler** n

tip·ster \'tip-stər\ n : a person who gives or sells tips esp. for gambling

tip·sy \'tip-sē\ adj **tip·si·er; -est** : unsteady or foolish from the effects of alcohol — **tip·si·ly** \-sə-lē\ adv — **tip·si·ness** \-sē-nəs\ n

¹**tip·toe** \'tip-ˌtō\ n : the position of being

balanced on the balls of the feet and toes with the heels raised; also : the ends of the toes

²**tiptoe** adv or adj : on or as if on tiptoe

³**tiptoe** vb **tip·toed; tip·toe·ing** : to walk or proceed on or as if on tiptoe ⟨~ around the issue⟩

¹**tip–top** \'tip-'täp\ n : the highest point

²**tip–top** adj : EXCELLENT, FIRST-RATE

ti·rade \'tī-ˌrād\ n [F, shot, tirade, fr. MF, fr. It tirata, fr. tirare to draw, shoot] : a prolonged speech of abuse or condemnation

tir·a·mi·su \ˌtir-ə-'mē-sü, -mē-'sü\ n [It tiramisù] : a dessert made with ladyfingers, mascarpone, and espresso

¹**tire** \'tī(-ə)r\ vb **tired; tir·ing** 1 : to make or become weary : FATIGUE 2 : to wear out the patience of : BORE

²**tire** n 1 : a metal hoop that forms the tread of a wheel 2 : a rubber cushion usu. containing compressed air that encircles a wheel (as of a bike)

tired adj 1 : WEARY, FATIGUED 2 : HACKNEYED — **tired·ness** n

tire·less \'tī(-ə)r-ləs\ adj : not tiring : UNTIRING, INDEFATIGABLE ⟨~ workers⟩ — **tire·less·ly** adv — **tire·less·ness** n

tire·some \-səm\ adj : tending to bore : WEARISOME, TEDIOUS ⟨~ lectures⟩ — **tire·some·ly** adv — **tire·some·ness** n

ti·ro chiefly Brit var of TYRO

tis·sue \'ti-shü\ n [ME tysshewe, tyssew, a rich fabric, fr. AF, fr. tistre to weave, fr. L texere] 1 : a fine lightweight often sheer fabric 2 : NETWORK, WEB ⟨a ~ of lies⟩ 3 : a soft absorbent paper 4 : a mass or layer of cells forming a basic structural material of an animal or plant

¹**tit** \'tit\ n : TEAT

²**tit** n : any of various small plump Old World songbirds related to the titmice

Tit abbr Titus

ti·tan \'tī-t³n\ n 1 cap : one of a family of giants overthrown by the gods in Greek mythology 2 : one gigantic in size or power ⟨a media ~⟩

ti·tan·ic \tī-'ta-nik\ adj : enormous in size, force, or power ♦ *Synonyms* IMMENSE, GIGANTIC, GIANT, COLOSSAL, MAMMOTH

ti·ta·ni·um \tī-'tā-nē-əm\ n : a gray light strong metallic chemical element used esp. in alloys

titbit var of TIDBIT

tithe \'tīth\ n [ME, fr. OE teogotha tenth] : a 10th part paid or given esp. for the support of a church — **tithe** vb — **tith·er** n

tit·il·late \'ti-t³l-ˌāt\ vb **-lat·ed; -lat·ing** 1 : to excite pleasurably 2 : TICKLE 3 — **tit·il·la·tion** \ˌti-t³l-'ā-shən\ n

tit·i·vate or **tit·ti·vate** \'ti-tə-ˌvāt\ vb **-vat·ed; -vat·ing** : to dress up : spruce up — **tit·i·va·tion** \ˌti-tə-'vā-shən\ n

ti·tle \'tī-t³l\ n 1 : CLAIM, RIGHT; esp : a legal right to the ownership of property 2 : the distinguishing name of a written, filmed, or musical production or a work of art 3 : an appellation of honor, rank, or office 4 : CHAMPIONSHIP ♦ *Synonyms* DESIGNATION, DENOMINATION, APPELLATION

ti·tled \'tī-t⁹ld\ *adj* : having a title esp. of nobility

title page *n* : a page of a book bearing the title and usu. the names of the author and publisher

tit·mouse \'tit-ˌmaủs\ *n, pl* **tit·mice** \-ˌmīs\ : any of several small long-tailed No. American songbirds related to the chickadees

ti·tra·tion \tī-'trā-shən\ *n* : a process of finding the concentration of a solution (as of an acid) by adding small portions of a second solution of known concentration (as of a base) to a fixed amount of the first until an expected change (as in color) occurs

tit·ter \'ti-tər\ *vb* : to laugh in an affected or in a nervous or half-suppressed manner : GIGGLE — **titter** *n*

tit·tle \'ti-t⁹l\ *n* : a tiny part

tit·tle–tat·tle \'ti-t⁹l-ˌta-t⁹l\ *n* : idle talk : GOSSIP — **tittle–tattle** *vb*

tit·u·lar \'ti-chə-lər\ *adj* **1** : existing in title only : NOMINAL ⟨∼ ruler⟩ **2** : of, relating to, or bearing a title ⟨∼ role⟩

Ti·tus \'tī-təs\ *n* — see BIBLE table

ti·yin \'tē-ēn\ *n* **1** *pl* **ti·yins** — see *tenge* at MONEY table **2** *pl* **tiyin** *or* **tiyins** — see *som* at MONEY table

tiz·zy \'ti-zē\ *n, pl* **tizzies** : a highly excited and distracted state of mind

tk *abbr* **1** tank **2** truck

TKO \ˌtē-ˌkā-'ō\ *n* [*technical knockout*] : the termination of a boxing match when a boxer is declared unable to continue the fight

tkt *abbr* ticket

Tl *symbol* thallium

TLC *abbr* tender loving care

T lymphocyte *n* : T CELL

Tm *symbol* thulium

TM *abbr* trademark

T–man \'tē-ˌman\ *n* : a special agent of the U.S. Treasury Department

tn *abbr* **1** ton **2** town

TN *abbr* Tennessee

tng *abbr* training

tnpk *abbr* turnpike

TNT \ˌtē-(ˌ)en-'tē\ *n* : a flammable toxic compound used as a high explosive and in chemical synthesis

¹to \tə, 'tü\ *prep* **1** : in the direction of and reaching ⟨drove ∼ town⟩ **2** : in the direction of : TOWARD **3** : ON, AGAINST ⟨apply salve ∼ a burn⟩ **4** : as far as ⟨can pay up ∼ a dollar⟩ **5** : so as to become or bring about ⟨beaten ∼ death⟩ ⟨broken ∼ pieces⟩ **6** : BEFORE ⟨it's five minutes ∼ six⟩ **7** : UNTIL ⟨from May ∼ December⟩ **8** : fitting or being a part of : FOR ⟨key ∼ the lock⟩ **9** : with the accompaniment of ⟨sing ∼ the music⟩ **10** : in relation or comparison with ⟨similar ∼ that one⟩ ⟨won 10 ∼ 6⟩ **11** : in accordance with ⟨add salt ∼ taste⟩ **12** : within the range of ⟨∼ my knowledge⟩ **13** : contained, occurring, or included in ⟨two pints ∼ a quart⟩ **14** : as regards ⟨agreeable ∼ everyone⟩ **15** : affecting as the receiver or beneficiary ⟨whispered ∼ her⟩ ⟨gave it ∼ me⟩ **16** : for no one except ⟨a room ∼ myself⟩ **17** : into the

action of ⟨we got ∼ talking⟩ **18** — used for marking the following verb as an infinitive ⟨wants ∼ go⟩ and often used by itself at the end of a clause in place of an infinitive suggested by the preceding context ⟨goes to town whenever he wants ∼⟩ ⟨can leave if you'd like ∼⟩

²to \'tü\ *adv* **1** : in a direction toward ⟨run ∼ and fro⟩ **2** : into contact esp. with the frame of a door ⟨the door slammed ∼⟩ **3** : to the matter in hand ⟨fell ∼ and ate heartily⟩ **4** : to a state of consciousness or awareness ⟨came ∼ hours after the accident⟩

TO *abbr* turn over

toad \'tōd\ *n* : any of numerous tailless leaping amphibians differing typically from the related frogs in having a shorter stockier build, rough dry warty skin, and less aquatic habits

toad·stool \-ˌstül\ *n* : MUSHROOM; *esp* : one that is poisonous or inedible

toady \'tō-dē\ *n, pl* **toad·ies** : a person who flatters in the hope of gaining favors : SYCOPHANT — **toady** *vb*

to–and–fro \ˌtü-ən-'frō\ *adj* : forward and backward — **to–and–fro** *n*

¹toast \'tōst\ *vb* **1** : to warm thoroughly **2** : to make (as bread) crisp, hot, and brown by heat **3** : to become toasted

²toast *n* **1** : sliced toasted bread **2** : someone or something in whose honor persons drink **3** : an act of drinking in honor of a toast

³toast *vb* : to propose or drink to as a toast

toast·er \'tō-stər\ *n* : an electrical appliance for toasting

toaster oven *n* : a portable electrical appliance that bakes, broils, and toasts

toast·mas·ter \'tōst-ˌmas-tər\ *n* : a person who presides at a banquet and introduces the after-dinner speakers

toast·mis·tress \-ˌmis-trəs\ *n* : a woman who acts as toastmaster

toasty \'tō-stē\ *adj* **toast·i·er; -est** : pleasantly warm

Tob *abbr* Tobit

to·bac·co \tə-'ba-kō\ *n, pl* **-cos** [Sp *tabaco*] **1** : a tall broad-leaved herb related to the potato; *also* : its leaves prepared for smoking or chewing or as snuff **2** : manufactured tobacco products; *also* : smoking as a practice

to·bac·co·nist \tə-'ba-kə-nist\ *n* : a dealer in tobacco

To·bi·as \tō-'bī-əs\ *n* : TOBIT

To·bit \'tō-bət\ *n* — see BIBLE table

¹to·bog·gan \tə-'bä-gən\ *n* : a long flat-bottomed light sled made of thin boards curved up at one end

²toboggan *vb* **1** : to coast on or as if on a toboggan **2** : to decline suddenly (as in value) — **to·bog·gan·er** *n*

toc·sin \'täk-sən\ *n* **1** : an alarm bell **2** : a warning signal

¹to·day \tə-'dā\ *adv* **1** : on or for this day **2** : at the present time

²today *n* : the present day, time, or age

tod·dle \'täd-⁹l\ *vb* **tod·dled; tod·dling** : to walk with short tottering steps in the manner of a young child — **toddle** *n* — **tod·dler** *n*

tod·dy \'tä-dē\ *n, pl* **toddies** [Hindi & Urdu *tāṛī* juice of a palm, fr. *tāṛ* a palm, fr. Skt *tāla*] : a drink made of liquor, sugar, spices, and hot water

to–do \tə-'dü\ *n, pl* **to–dos** \-'düz\ : BUSTLE, STIR, FUSS

¹toe \'tō\ *n* **1** : one of the jointed parts of the front end of the vertebrate foot **2** : the front part of a foot or hoof

²toe *vb* **toed; toe·ing** : to touch, reach, or drive with the toes

toea \'tȯi-ə\ *n* — see *kina* at MONEY table

toe·hold \'tō-,hōld\ *n* **1** : a place of support for the toes **2** : a slight footing

toe·nail \'tō-,nāl\ *n* : a nail of a toe

tof·fee *or* **tof·fy** \'tȯ-fē, 'tä-\ *n, pl* **toffees** *or* **toffies** : candy of brittle but tender texture made by boiling sugar and butter together

to·fu \'tō-(,)fü\ *n* [Jp *tōfu*] : a soft white food product made from soybeans

tog \'täg, 'tȯg\ *vb* **togged; tog·ging** : to put togs on : DRESS

to·ga \'tō-gə\ *n* : the loose outer garment worn in public by citizens of ancient Rome — **to·gaed** \-gəd\ *adj*

¹to·geth·er \tə-'ge-thər\ *adv* **1** : in or into one place or group **2** : in or into contact or association ⟨mix ∼⟩ **3** : at one time : SIMULTANEOUSLY ⟨talk and work ∼⟩ **4** : in succession ⟨for days ∼⟩ **5** : in or into harmony or coherence ⟨get ∼ on a plan⟩ **6** : as a group : JOINTLY — **to·geth·er·ness** *n*

²together *adj* : composed of mind or manner

together with *prep* : in addition to : in association with

tog·gery \'tä-gə-rē, 'tȯ-\ *n* : CLOTHING

tog·gle \'tä-gəl\ *vb* : to switch between two options esp. of an electronic device

toggle switch *n* : an electric switch operated by pushing a projecting lever through a small arc

togs \'tägz, 'tȯgz\ *n pl* : CLOTHING; *esp* : clothes for a specified use ⟨riding ∼⟩

¹toil \'tȯi(-ə)l\ *n* **1** : laborious effort **2** : long fatiguing labor : DRUDGERY — **toil·ful** \-fəl\ *adj* — **toil·some** *adj*

²toil *vb* [ME, to argue, struggle, fr. AF *toiller* to make dirty, fight, wrangle, fr. L *tudiculare* to crush, grind, fr. *tudicula* machine for crushing olives, dim. of *tudes* hammer] **1** : to work hard and long **2** : to proceed with great effort : PLOD — **toil·er** *n*

³toil *n* [ME *toile* cloth, net, fr. OF *teile*, fr. L *tela* cloth on a loom] : NET, TRAP — usu. used in pl. ⟨caught in the ∼s of the law⟩

toi·let \'tȯi-lət\ *n* **1** : the act or process of dressing and grooming oneself **2** : BATHROOM **3** : a fixture for use in urinating and defecating; *esp* : one consisting essentially of a water-flushed bowl and seat — **toilet** *vb*

toi·let·ry \'tȯi-lə-trē\ *n, pl* **-ries** : an article or preparation used in cleaning or grooming oneself — usu. used in pl.

toi·lette \twä-'let\ *n* **1** : TOILET 1 **2** : formal attire; *also* : a particular costume

toilet training *n* : the process of training a child to control bladder and bowel movements and to use the toilet — **toilet train** *vb*

toil·worn \'tȯi(-ə)l-,wȯrn\ *adj* : showing the effects of toil

To·kay \tō-'kā\ *n* : naturally sweet wine from Hungary

toke \'tōk\ *n, slang* : a puff on a marijuana cigarette or pipe

¹to·ken \'tō-kən\ *n* **1** : an outward sign **2** : SYMBOL, EMBLEM **3** : SOUVENIR, KEEPSAKE **4** : a small part representing the whole **5** : a piece resembling a coin issued as money or for use by a particular group on specified terms

²token *adj* **1** : done or given as a token esp. in partial fulfillment of an obligation **2** : representing only a symbolic effort : MINIMAL, PERFUNCTORY

to·ken·ism \'tō-kə-,ni-zəm\ *n* : the policy or practice of making only a symbolic effort (as to desegregate)

tolar \'tō-lär\ *n, pl* **to·lar·ja** \'tō-lär-,yä\ *or* **to·lar·jev** \'tō-lär-,yev\ *or* **tolars** : the basic monetary unit of Slovenia from 1992 to 2007

told *past and past part of* TELL

tole \'tōl\ *n* : sheet metal and esp. tinplate for use in domestic and ornamental wares

tol·er·a·ble \'tä-lə-rə-bəl\ *adj* **1** : capable of being borne or endured **2** : moderately good : PASSABLE — **tol·er·a·bly** \-blē\ *adv*

tol·er·ance \'tä-lə-rəns\ *n* **1** : the act or practice of tolerating; *esp* : sympathy or indulgence for beliefs or practices differing from one's own **2** : the allowable deviation from a standard (as of size) **3** : the body's capacity to become less responsive over time to something (as a drug used repeatedly) — **tol·er·ant** *adj* — **tol·er·ant·ly** *adv*

tol·er·ate \'tä-lə-,rāt\ *vb* **-at·ed; -at·ing 1** : to exhibit physiological tolerance for (as a drug) **2** : to allow to be or to be done without hindrance ♦ *Synonyms* ABIDE, BEAR, SUFFER, STAND, BROOK — **tol·er·a·tion** \,tä-lə-'rā-shən\ *n*

¹toll \'tōl\ *n* **1** : a tax paid for a privilege (as for passing over a bridge) **2** : a charge for a service (as for a long-distance telephone call) **3** : the cost in life, health, loss, or suffering

²toll *vb* **1** : to cause the slow regular sounding of (a bell) esp. by pulling a rope **2** : to give signal of : SOUND **3** : to sound with slow measured strokes **4** : to announce by tolling

³toll *n* : the sound of a tolling bell

toll·booth \'tōl-,büth\ *n* : a booth where tolls are paid

toll·gate \-,gāt\ *n* : a point where vehicles stop to pay a toll

toll·house \-,haüs\ *n* : a house or booth where tolls are paid

tol·u·ene \'täl-yə-,wēn\ *n* : a liquid hydrocarbon used esp. as a solvent

tom \'täm\ *n* : the male of various animals (as a cat or turkey)

¹tom·a·hawk \'tä-mə-,hȯk\ *n* : a light ax

used as a missile and as a hand weapon esp. by No. American Indians

²**tomahawk** *vb* : to strike or kill with a tomahawk

to·ma·til·lo \ˌtō-mə-ˈtē-(ˌ)yō\ *n, pl* **-los** : a small round usu. pale green edible fruit of a Mexican herb related to the tomato; *also* : this herb

to·ma·to \tə-ˈmā-tō, -ˈmä-\ *n, pl* **-toes** [alter. of earlier *tomate*, fr. Sp, fr. Nahuatl *tomatl*] : a usu. large, rounded, and red or yellow pulpy edible berry of a widely grown tropical herb related to the potato; *also* : this herb

tomb \ˈtüm\ *n* 1 : a place of burial : GRAVE 2 : a house, chamber, or vault for the dead — **tomb** *vb*

tom·boy \ˈtäm-ˌbȯi\ *n* : a girl who behaves in a manner usu. considered boyish — **tom·boy·ish** *adj*

tomb·stone \ˈtüm-ˌstōn\ *n* : a stone marking a grave

tom·cat \ˈtäm-ˌkat\ *n* : a male domestic cat

Tom Col·lins \ˈtäm-ˈkä-lənz\ *n* : a tall iced drink with a base of gin

tome \ˈtōm\ *n* : BOOK; *esp* : a large or weighty one

tom·fool·ery \täm-ˈfü-lə-rē\ *n* : playful or foolish behavior

tom·my gun \ˈtä-mē-ˌgən\ *n* : SUBMACHINE GUN — **tommy–gun** *vb*

to·mog·ra·phy \tō-ˈmä-grə-fē\ *n* : a method of producing a three-dimensional image of the internal structures of a solid object (as the human body or the earth) — **to·mo·graph·ic** \ˌtō-mə-ˈgra-fik\ *adj*

to·mor·row \tə-ˈmär-ō\ *adv* : on or for the day after today — **tomorrow** *n*

tom–tom \ˈtäm-ˌtäm\ *n* : a small-headed drum beaten with the hands

ton \ˈtən\ *n, pl* **tons** *also* **ton** 1 — see WEIGHT table 2 : a unit equal to the volume of a long ton weight of seawater used in reckoning the displacement of ships and equal to 35 cubic feet

to·nal·i·ty \tō-ˈna-lə-tē\ *n, pl* **-ties** : tonal quality

¹**tone** \ˈtōn\ *n* [ME, fr. L *tonus* tension, tone, fr. Gk *tonos*, lit., act of stretching; fr. the dependence of the pitch of a musical string on its tension] 1 : vocal or musical sound; *esp* : sound quality 2 : a sound of definite pitch 3 : WHOLE STEP 4 : accent or inflection expressive of an emotion 5 : the pitch of a word often used to express differences of meaning 6 : style or manner of expression 7 : color quality; *also* : SHADE, TINT 8 : the effect in painting of light and shade together with color 9 : healthy and vigorous condition of a living body or bodily part; *also* : the state of partial contraction characteristic of normal muscle 10 : general character, quality, or trend ♦ *Synonyms* ATMOSPHERE, FEELING, MOOD, VEIN — **ton·al** \ˈtōn-ᵊl\ *adj*

²**tone** *vb* **toned; ton·ing** 1 : to give a particular intonation or inflection to 2 : to impart tone to 3 : SOFTEN, MELLOW ⟨~ down your language⟩ 4 : to harmonize in color : BLEND

tone·arm *n* : the movable part of a record player that carries the pickup and the needle

toney *var of* TONY

tong \ˈtäŋ, ˈtȯŋ\ *n* : a Chinese secret society in the U.S.

tongs \ˈtäŋz, ˈtȯŋz\ *n pl* : a grasping device consisting of two pieces joined at one end by a pivot or hinged like scissors — **tong** *vb*

¹**tongue** \ˈtəŋ\ *n* 1 : a fleshy movable process of the floor of the mouth used in tasting and in taking and swallowing food and in humans as a speech organ 2 : the flesh of a tongue (as of the ox) used as food 3 : the power of communication 4 : LANGUAGE 1 5 : manner or quality of utterance; *also* : intended meaning 6 : ecstatic usu. unintelligible utterance accompanying religious excitation — usu. used in pl. 7 : something resembling an animal's tongue esp. in being elongated and fastened at one end only — **tongued** \ˈtəŋd\ *adj* — **tongue·less** *adj*

²**tongue** *vb* **tongued; tongu·ing** 1 : to touch or lick with the tongue 2 : to articulate notes on a wind instrument

tongue–in–cheek *adj* : characterized by insincerity, irony, or whimsical exaggeration — **tongue in cheek** *adv*

tongue–lash \ˈtəŋ-ˌlash\ *vb* : CHIDE, REPROVE — **tongue–lash·ing** \-iŋ\ *n*

tongue–tied \-ˌtīd\ *adj* : unable or disinclined to speak clearly or freely (as from shyness or a tongue impairment)

tongue twister *n* : an utterance that is difficult to articulate because of a succession of similar consonants

¹**ton·ic** \ˈtä-nik\ *adj* 1 : of, relating to, or producing a healthy physical or mental condition : INVIGORATING 2 : relating to or based on the 1st tone of a scale — **to·nic·i·ty** \tō-ˈni-sə-tē\ *n*

²**tonic** *n* 1 : the 1st degree of a musical scale 2 : something that invigorates, restores, or refreshes

tonic water *n* : a carbonated beverage flavored with a bit of quinine, lemon, and lime

¹**to·night** \tə-ˈnīt\ *adv* : on this present night or the coming night

²**tonight** *n* : the present or the coming night

ton·nage \ˈtə-nij\ *n* 1 : a duty on ships based on tons carried 2 : ships in terms of the number of tons registered or carried 3 : total weight in tons shipped, carried, or mined

ton·sil \ˈtän-səl\ *n* : either of a pair of oval masses of lymphoid tissue that lie one on each side of the throat at the back of the mouth

ton·sil·lec·to·my \ˌtän-sə-ˈlek-tə-mē\ *n, pl* **-mies** : the surgical removal of the tonsils

ton·sil·li·tis \-ˈlī-təs\ *n* : inflammation of the tonsils

ton·so·ri·al \tän-ˈsȯr-ē-əl\ *adj* : of or relating to a barber or a barber's work

ton·sure \ˈtän-chər\ *n* [ME, fr. AF, ML *tonsura*, fr. L, act of shearing, fr. *tonsus*, pp. of *tondēre* to shear] 1 : the rite of admission to the clerical state by the clipping or shaving of the head **2** : the shaven crown or patch worn by clerics (as monks) — **tonsure** *vb*

tony *also* **ton·ey** \'tō-nē\ *adj* **ton·i·er; -est** : marked by an aristocratic manner or style

too \'tü\ *adv* **1** : in addition : ALSO **2** : EXCESSIVELY ⟨the music is ~ loud⟩ **3** : to such a degree as to be regrettable **4** : VERY ⟨didn't seem ~ interested⟩

took *past of* TAKE

¹tool \'tül\ *n* **1** : a hand instrument that aids in accomplishing a task **2** : the cutting or shaping part in a machine; *also* : a machine for shaping metal in any way **3** : something used in doing a job ⟨a scholar's books are his ~s⟩; *also* : a means to an end **4** : a person used by another : DUPE **5** *pl* : natural ability

²tool *vb* **1** : to shape, form, or finish with a tool; *esp* : to letter or decorate (as a book cover) by means of hand tools **2** : to equip a plant or industry with machines and tools for production **3** : DRIVE, RIDE ⟨~*ing* along at 60 miles per hour⟩

tool bar *n* : a strip of icons on a computer display providing quick access to the pictured functions

¹toot \'tüt\ *vb* **1** : to sound or cause to sound in short blasts **2** : to blow an instrument (as a horn) — **toot·er** *n*

²toot *n* : a short blast (as on a horn)

tooth \'tüth\ *n, pl* **teeth** \'tēth\ **1** : one of the hard bony structures borne esp. on the jaws of vertebrates and used for seizing and chewing food and as weapons; *also* : a hard sharp structure esp. around the mouth of an invertebrate **2** : something resembling an animal's tooth **3** : any of the projections on the edge of a wheel that fits into corresponding projections on another wheel **4** *pl* : effective means of enforcement — **toothed** \'tütht\ *adj* — **tooth·less** *adj*

tooth·ache \'tüth-ˌāk\ *n* : pain in or about a tooth

tooth·brush \-ˌbrəsh\ *n* : a brush for cleaning the teeth

tooth·paste \-ˌpāst\ *n* : a paste for cleaning the teeth

tooth·pick \-ˌpik\ *n* : a pointed instrument for removing food particles caught between the teeth

tooth powder *n* : a powder for cleaning the teeth

tooth·some \'tüth-səm\ *adj* **1** : AGREEABLE, ATTRACTIVE **2** : pleasing to the taste : DELICIOUS ♦ *Synonyms* PALATABLE, APPETIZING, SAVORY, TASTY

toothy \'tü-thē\ *adj* **tooth·i·er; -est** : having or showing prominent teeth

¹top \'täp\ *n* **1** : the highest part, point, or level of something **2** : the part of a plant with edible roots lying above the ground ⟨beet ~s⟩ **3** : the upper end, edge, or surface ⟨the ~ of a page⟩ **4** : an upper piece, lid, or covering **5** : the highest degree, pitch, or rank **6** : a quark with a charge of +⅔ and a measured energy of approximately 175 billion electron volts

²top *vb* **topped; top·ping** **1** : to remove or trim the top of : PRUNE ⟨~ a tree⟩ **2** : to cover with a top or on the top : CROWN, CAP **3** : to be superior to : EXCEL, SURPASS **4** : to go over the top of **5** : to strike (a ball) above the center **6** : to make an end or conclusion ⟨~ off a meal with coffee⟩

³top *adj* **1** : of, relating to, or being at the top : HIGHEST ⟨is ~ in her class⟩ **2** : CHIEF

⁴top *n* : a toy that has a tapering point on which it is made to spin

to·paz \'tō-ˌpaz\ *n* : a hard silicate of aluminum; *esp* : a yellow transparent topaz used as a gem

top·coat \'täp-ˌkōt\ *n* **1** : a lightweight overcoat **2** : a protective coating (as of paint)

top dollar *n* : the highest amount being paid for a commodity or service

top–dress \-ˌdres\ *vb* : to apply material to (as land) without working it in; *esp* : to scatter fertilizer over

top–dress·ing \-ˌdre-siŋ\ *n* : a material used to top-dress soil

top–end \'täp-'end\ *adj* : TOPFLIGHT

top–flight \'täp-'flīt\ *adj* : of, relating to, or being the highest level of excellence or rank ⟨a ~ staff⟩ — **top flight** *n*

top hat *n* : a tall-crowned hat usu. of beaver or silk

top–heavy \'täp-ˌhe-vē\ *adj* : having the top part too heavy for the lower part

to·pi·ary \'tō-pē-ˌer-ē\ *n, pl* **-ar·ies** : the art of training and trimming trees or shrubs with decorative shapes — **topiary** *adj*

top·ic \'tä-pik\ *n* **1** : a heading in an outlined argument **2** : the subject of a discourse or a section of it : THEME

top·i·cal \-pi-kəl\ *adj* **1** : of, relating to, or arranged by topics ⟨a ~ outline⟩ **2** : relating to current or local events **3** : designed to be applied to or to work on a part (as of the body) — **top·i·cal·ly** \-k(ə-)lē\ *adv*

top·knot \'täp-ˌnät\ *n* **1** : an ornament (as a knot of ribbons) forming a headdress **2** : a crest of feathers or tuft of hair on the top of the head

top·less \-ləs\ *adj* **1** : wearing no clothing on the upper body **2** : featuring topless waitresses or entertainers

top·mast \'täp-ˌmast, -məst\ *n* : the 2d mast above a ship's deck

top·most \'täp-ˌmōst\ *adj* : highest of all : UPPERMOST

top–notch \-'näch\ *adj* : of the highest quality : FIRST-RATE

top–of–the–line *adj* : being or belonging to the highest or most expensive class

to·pog·ra·phy \tə-'pä-grə-fē\ *n* **1** : the art of showing in detail on a map or chart the physical features of a place or region **2** : the outline of the form of a place showing its relief and the position of features (as rivers, roads, or cities) — **to·pog·ra·pher** \-fər\ *n* — **top·o·graph·ic** \ˌtä-pə-'gra-fik\ *or* **top·o·graph·i·cal** \-fi-kəl\ *adj*

topping *n* : a food served on top of another to make it look or taste better

top·ple \'tä-pəl\ *vb* **top·pled; top·pling** **1** : to fall from or as if from being topheavy **2** : to push over : OVERTURN; *also* : OVERTHROW ⟨*toppled* the dictator⟩

¹tops \'täps\ *adj* : topmost in quality or importance ⟨∼ in his field⟩

²tops *adv* : at the very most

top·sail \'täp-ˌsāl, -səl\ *also* **top·s'l** \-səl\ *n* : the sail next above the lowest sail on a mast in a square-rigged ship

top secret *adj* : demanding complete secrecy among those concerned

top·side \'täp-'sīd\ *adv or adj* **1** : to or on the top or surface **2** : on deck

top·sides \-'sīdz\ *n pl* : the top portion of the outer surface of a ship on each side above the waterline

top·soil \'täp-ˌsȯi(-ə)l\ *n* : surface soil usu. including the organic layer in which plants have most of their roots

top·sy–tur·vy \ˌtäp-sē-'tər-vē\ *adv* **1** : in utter confusion **2** : UPSIDE DOWN — **topsy-turvy** *adj*

toque \'tōk\ *n* : a woman's small hat without a brim

tor \'tȯr\ *n* : a high craggy hill

To·rah \'tȯr-ə\ *n* **1** : a scroll of the first five books of the Old Testament used in a synagogue; *also* : these five books **2** : the body of divine knowledge and law found in the Jewish scriptures and tradition

¹torch \'tȯrch\ *n* **1** : a flaming light made of something that burns brightly and usu. carried in the hand **2** : something that resembles a torch in giving light, heat, or guidance **3** : a portable burner for producing a hot flame **4** *chiefly Brit* : FLASHLIGHT

²torch *vb* : to set fire to

torch·bear·er \'tȯrch-ˌber-ər\ *n* **1** : a person who carries a torch **2** : one in the forefront (as of a political campaign)

torch·light \-ˌlīt\ *n* : light given by torches

torch song *n* : a popular sentimental song of unrequited love

tore *past of* TEAR

to·re·ador \'tȯr-ē-ə-ˌdȯr\ *n* : BULLFIGHTER

to·re·ro \tə-'rer-ō\ *n, pl* **-ros** [Sp] : BULLFIGHTER

¹tor·ment \'tȯr-ˌment\ *n* **1** : extreme pain or anguish of body or mind **2** : a source of vexation or pain

²tor·ment \tȯr-'ment\ *vb* **1** : to cause severe suffering of body or mind to **2** : DISTORT, TWIST ♦ *Synonyms* RACK, AFFLICT, TRY, TORTURE — **tor·men·tor** \-'men-tər\ *n*

torn *past part of* TEAR

tor·na·do \tȯr-'nā-dō\ *n, pl* **-does** *or* **-dos** [modif of Sp *tronada* thunderstorm, fr. *tronar* to thunder, fr. L *tonare*] : a violent destructive whirling wind accompanied by a funnel-shaped cloud that moves over a narrow path

¹tor·pe·do \tȯr-'pē-dō\ *n, pl* **-does** : a thin cylindrical self-propelled underwater weapon

²torpedo *vb* **tor·pe·doed; tor·pe·do·ing**

: to hit or destroy with or as if with a torpedo

torpedo boat *n* : a small very fast boat for firing torpedoes

tor·pid \'tȯr-pəd\ *adj* **1** : having lost motion or the power of exertion : DORMANT **2** : SLUGGISH **3** : lacking vigor — **tor·pid·i·ty** \tȯr-'pi-də-tē\ *n*

tor·por \'tȯr-pər\ *n* **1** : DULLNESS, APATHY **2** : extreme sluggishness : STAGNATION ♦ *Synonyms* STUPOR, LETHARGY, LANGUOR, LASSITUDE

¹torque \'tȯrk\ *n* : a force that produces or tends to produce rotation or torsion

²torque *vb* **torqued; torqu·ing** : to impart torque to : cause to twist (as about an axis)

tor·rent \'tȯr-ənt\ *n* [F, fr. L *torrent-, torrens,* fr. *torrent-, torrens* boiling, seething, rushing, fr. prp. of *torrēre* to parch, burn] **1** : a tumultuous outburst **2** : a rushing stream (as of water)

tor·ren·tial \tȯ-'ren-chəl\ *adj* : relating to or resembling a torrent ⟨∼ rains⟩

tor·rid \'tȯr-əd\ *adj* **1** : parched with heat esp. of the sun : HOT **2** : ARDENT

torrid zone *n* : the region of the earth between the Tropic of Cancer and the Tropic of Capricorn

tor·sion \'tȯr-shən\ *n* **1** : a wrenching by which one part of a body is under pressure to turn about a longitudinal axis while the other part is held fast or is under pressure to turn in the opposite direction **2** : a twisting of a bodily organ or part on its own axis — **tor·sion·al** \'tȯr-shə-nəl\ *adj* — **tor·sion·al·ly** *adv*

tor·so \'tȯr-sō\ *n, pl* **torsos** *or* **tor·si** \'tȯr-ˌsē\ [It, lit., stalk] : the trunk of the human body

tort \'tȯrt\ *n* : a wrongful act which does not involve a breach of contract and for which the injured party can recover damages in a civil action

tor·ti·lla \tȯr-'tē-ə\ *n* : a round thin cake of unleavened cornmeal or wheat flour bread

tor·toise \'tȯr-təs\ *n* : TURTLE; *esp* : any of a family of land turtles

tor·toise·shell \-ˌshel\ *n* : the mottled horny substance of the shell of some turtles used in inlaying and in making various ornamental articles — **tortoiseshell** *adj*

tor·to·ni \tȯr-'tō-nē\ *n* : rich ice cream often made with minced almonds and chopped cherries and flavored with rum

tor·tu·ous \'tȯr-chə-wəs\ *adj* **1** : marked by twists or turns : WINDING ⟨a ∼ path⟩ **2** : DEVIOUS, TRICKY

¹tor·ture \'tȯr-chər\ *n* **1** : anguish of body or mind **2** : the infliction of severe pain esp. to punish or coerce — **tor·tur·ous** \'tȯrch-rəs, 'tȯr-chə-\ *adj*

²torture *vb* **tor·tured; tor·tur·ing** **1** : to cause intense suffering to : TORMENT **2** : to punish or coerce by inflicting severe pain **3** : TWIST, DISTORT ♦ *Synonyms* RACK, HARROW, AFFLICT, TRY — **tor·tur·er** *n*

To·ry \'tȯr-ē\ *n, pl* **Tories** **1** : a member of a chiefly 18th century British party upholding the established church and the traditional political structure **2** : an American supporter of the British during the American Revolution **3** *often not cap* : an extreme conservative — **Tory** *adj*

¹toss \'tös, 'täs\ *vb* **1** : to fling to and fro or up and down **2** : to throw with a quick light motion; *also* : BANDY **3** : to fling or lift with a sudden motion ⟨∼*ed* her head angrily⟩ **4** : to move restlessly or turbulently ⟨∼*es* on the waves⟩ **5** : to twist and turn repeatedly **6** : FLOUNCE **7** : to accomplish readily ⟨∼ off an article⟩ **8** : to decide an issue by flipping a coin

²toss *n* : an act or instance of tossing; *esp* : TOSS-UP 1

toss–up \-‚əp\ *n* **1** : a deciding by flipping a coin **2** : an even chance **3** : something that offers no clear basis for choice

¹tot \'tät\ *n* **1** : a small child **2** : a small drink of alcoholic liquor : SHOT

²tot *vb* **tot·ted; tot·ting** : to add up

³tot *abbr* total

¹to·tal \'tō-t³l\ *adj* **1** : making up a whole : ENTIRE ⟨∼ amount⟩ **2** : COMPLETE, UTTER ⟨a ∼ failure⟩ ⟨a ∼ stranger⟩ **3** : involving a complete and unified effort esp. to achieve a desired effect — **to·tal·ly** *adv*

²total *n* **1** : SUM 4 **2** : the entire amount ♦ *Synonyms* AGGREGATE, WHOLE, GROSS, TOTALITY

³total *vb* **to·taled** or **to·talled; to·tal·ing** or **to·tal·ling** **1** : to add up : COMPUTE **2** : to amount to : NUMBER **3** : to make a total wreck of (a car)

to·tal·i·tar·i·an \tō-‚ta-lə-'ter-ē-ən\ *adj* : of, relating to, or advocating a political regime based on subordination of the individual to the state and strict control of all aspects of life esp. by coercive measures — **totalitarian** *n* — **to·tal·i·tar·i·an·ism** \-ē-ə-‚ni-zəm\ *n*

to·tal·i·ty \tō-'ta-lə-tē\ *n, pl* **-ties** **1** : an aggregate amount : SUM, WHOLE **2** : ENTIRETY, WHOLENESS

to·tal·iza·tor or **to·tal·isa·tor** \'tō-t³l-ə-‚zā-tər\ *n* : a machine for registering and indicating the number of bets and the odds on a horse or dog race

¹tote \'tōt\ *vb* **tot·ed; tot·ing** : CARRY

²tote *vb* **tot·ed; tot·ing** : ADD, TOTAL — usu. used with *up*

to·tem \'tō-təm\ *n* [Ojibwa *oto·te·man* his totem] : an object (as an animal or plant) serving as the emblem of a family or clan and often as a reminder of its ancestry; *also* : something usu. carved or painted to represent such an object

totem pole *n* : a pole that is carved with a series of totems and is erected before the houses of some northwest American Indians

tot·ter \'tä-tər\ *vb* **1** : to tremble or rock as if about to fall : SWAY **2** : to move unsteadily : STAGGER

tou·can \'tü-‚kan\ *n* [F, fr. Pg *tucano*, fr. Tupinambá (American Indian language of Brazil) *tukána*] : any of a family of chiefly fruit-eating birds of tropical America with brilliant coloring and a very large bill

¹touch \'təch\ *vb* **1** : to bring a bodily part (as the hand) into contact with so as to feel **2** : to be or cause to be in contact **3** : to strike or push lightly esp. with the hand or foot **4** : DISTURB, HARM **5** : to make use of ⟨never ∼*es* alcohol⟩ **6** : to induce to give or lend **7** : to get to : REACH **8** : to refer to in passing : MENTION **9** : to affect the interest of : CONCERN **10** : to leave a mark on; *also* : BLEMISH **11** : to move to sympathetic feeling **12** : to come close : VERGE **13** : to have a bearing : RELATE **14** : to make a usu. brief or incidental stop in port ♦ *Synonyms* AFFECT, INFLUENCE, IMPRESS, STRIKE, SWAY

²touch *n* **1** : a light stroke or tap **2** : the act or fact of touching or being touched **3** : the sense by which pressure or traction on the skin or mucous membrane is perceived; *also* : a particular sensation conveyed by this sense **4** : mental or moral sensitiveness : TACT **5** : a small quantity : HINT ⟨a ∼ of spring in the air⟩ **6** : a manner of striking or touching esp. the keys of a keyboard instrument **7** : an improving detail ⟨add a few ∼*es* to the painting⟩ **8** : distinctive manner or skill ⟨the ∼ of a master⟩ **9** : the state of being in contact ⟨keep in ∼⟩ ♦ *Synonyms* SUGGESTION, SUSPICION, TINCTURE, TINGE

touch·down \'təch-‚daůn\ *n* : the act of scoring six points in American football by being lawfully in possession of the ball on, above, or behind an opponent's goal line

tou·ché \tü-'shā\ *interj* [F] — used to acknowledge a hit in fencing or the success of an argument, an accusation, or a witty point

touch football *n* : football in which touching is substituted for tackling

touch·ing \'tə-chiŋ\ *adj* : capable of stirring emotions ♦ *Synonyms* MOVING, IMPRESSIVE, POIGNANT, AFFECTING

touch off *vb* **1** : to describe with precision **2** : to start by or as if by touching with fire ⟨*touched off* a riot⟩

touch·stone \'təch-‚stōn\ *n* : a test or criterion of genuineness or quality ♦ *Synonyms* STANDARD, GAUGE, BENCHMARK, YARDSTICK

touch–tone \'təch-'tōn\ *adj* : of, relating to, or being a telephone having push buttons that produce tones corresponding to numbers

touch up *vb* : to improve or perfect by small additional strokes or alterations ⟨*touch up* a photo⟩ — **touch–up** \'təch-‚əp\ *n*

touchy \'tə-chē\ *adj* **touch·i·er; -est** **1** : easily offended : PEEVISH **2** : calling for tact in treatment ⟨a ∼ subject⟩ ♦ *Synonyms* IRASCIBLE, CRANKY, CROSS, TETCHY, TESTY

¹tough \'təf\ *adj* **1** : strong or firm in texture but flexible and not brittle **2** : not easily chewed **3** : characterized by severity and determination ⟨a ∼ policy⟩ **4** : capable of enduring strain or hardship : ROBUST **5** : hard to influence : STUB-

BORN **6** : difficult to accomplish, resolve, or cope with ⟨a ~ problem⟩ **7** : ROWDYISH ♦ *Synonyms* TENACIOUS, STOUT, STURDY, STALWART — **tough·ly** *adv* — **tough·ness** *n*

²**tough** *n* : a tough person : ROWDY

tough·en \'tə-fən\ *vb* **tough·ened**; **tough·en·ing** : to make or become tough ⟨*training camp* ~*ed* him up⟩

tou·pee \tü-'pā\ *n* [F *toupet* forelock] : a small wig for a bald spot

¹**tour** \'tùr, *1 is also* 'taù(-ə)r\ *n* **1** : one's turn : SHIFT **2** : a journey in which one returns to the starting point

²**tour** *vb* : to make a tour

tour de force \ˌtùr-də-'fòrs\ *n, pl* **tours de force** *same*\ [F] : a feat or display of strength, skill, or ingenuity

Tou·rette's syndrome \tù-'rets-\ *n* : a familial neurological disorder marked by recurrent involuntary tics and vocal sounds

tour·ism \'tùr-ˌi-zəm\ *n* **1** : the practice of traveling for recreation **2** : promotion of touring **3** : accommodation of tourists — **tour·ist** \-ist\ *n*

tourist class *n* : economy accommodations (as on a ship)

tour·ma·line \'tùr-mə-lən, -ˌlēn\ *n* : a mineral that when transparent is valued as a gem

tour·na·ment \'tùr-nə-mənt, 'tər-\ *n* **1** : a medieval sport in which mounted armored knights contended with blunted lances or swords **2** : a championship series of games or athletic contests

tour·ney \-nē\ *n, pl* **tourneys** : TOURNAMENT

tour·ni·quet \'tùr-ni-kət, 'tər-\ *n* : a device (as a tight bandage) to check bleeding or blood flow

tou·sle \'taù-zəl\ *vb* **tou·sled**; **tou·sling** : to disorder by rough handling : DISHEVEL, MUSS ⟨*tousled* his hair⟩

tout \'taùt, *2 is also* 'tüt\ *vb* **1** : to give a tip or solicit bets on a racehorse **2** : to praise or publicize loudly — **tout** *n*

¹**tow** \'tō\ *vb* : to draw or pull along behind

²**tow** *n* **1** : an act of towing or condition of being towed **2** : something (as a barge) that is towed

³**tow** *n* : short or broken fiber (as of flax or hemp) used esp. for yarn, twine, or stuffing

to·ward \'tòrd, 'tō-ərd, tə-'wòrd\ *or* **to·wards** \'tòrdz, 'tō-ərdz, tə-'wòrdz\ *prep* **1** : in the direction of ⟨heading ~ the river⟩ **2** : along a course leading to ⟨efforts ~ reconciliation⟩ **3** : in regard to ⟨tolerance ~ minorities⟩ **4** : so as to face ⟨turn the chair ~ the window⟩ **5** : close upon ⟨it was getting along ~ sundown⟩ **6** : for part payment of ⟨here's $100 ~ your tuition⟩

tow·boat \'tō-ˌbōt\ *n* : TUGBOAT

tow·el \'taù(-ə)l\ *n* : an absorbent cloth or paper for wiping or drying

tow·el·ing *or* **tow·el·ling** *n* : a cotton or linen fabric for making towels

¹**tow·er** \'taù(-ə)r\ *n* **1** : a tall structure either isolated or built upon a larger structure ⟨an observation ~⟩ **2** : a towering citadel **3** : a personal computer case that stands in an upright position — **tow·ered** *adj*

²**tower** *vb* : to reach or rise to a great height

tow·er·ing \'taù(-ə)r-iŋ\ *adj* **1** : LOFTY ⟨~ pines⟩ **2** : reaching high intensity ⟨a ~ rage⟩ **3** : EXCESSIVE ⟨~ ambition⟩

tow·head \'tō-ˌhed\ *n* : a person having whitish blond hair — **tow·head·ed** \-ˌhe-dəd\ *adj*

to·whee \'tō-ˌhē, 'tō-(ˌ)ē, tō-'hē\ *n* : a common finch of eastern No. America having the male black, white, and reddish; *also* : any of several closely related finches

to wit *adv* : NAMELY

town \'taùn\ *n* **1** : a compactly settled area usu. larger than a village but smaller than a city **2** : CITY **3** : the inhabitants of a town **4** : a New England territorial and political unit usu. containing both rural and urban areas; *also* : a New England community in which matters of local government are decided by a general assembly (**town meeting**) of qualified voters

town house *n* **1** : the city residence of a person having a country home **2** : a single-family house of two or sometimes three stories connected to another house by a common wall

town·ie *or* **towny** \'taù-nē\ *n, pl* **townies** : a permanent resident of a town as distinguished from a member of another group

towns·folk \'taùnz-ˌfōk\ *n pl* : TOWNSPEOPLE

town·ship \'taùn-ˌship\ *n* **1** : TOWN 4 **2** : a unit of local government in some states **3** : an unorganized subdivision of a county **4** : a division of territory in surveys of U.S. public land containing 36 square miles **5** : an area in the Republic of South Africa segregated for occupation by persons of non-European descent

towns·man \'taùnz-mən\ *n* **1** : a native or resident of a town or city **2** : a fellow citizen of a town

towns·peo·ple \-ˌpē-pəl\ *n pl* **1** : the inhabitants of a town or city **2** : town-bred persons

towns·wom·an \-ˌwù-mən\ *n* **1** : a woman who is a native or resident of a town or city **2** : a woman who is a fellow citizen of a town

tow·path \'tō-ˌpath, -ˌpàth\ *n* : a path (as along a canal) traveled esp. by draft animals towing boats

tow truck *n* : a truck equipped for towing vehicles

tox·emia \täk-'sē-mē-ə\ *n* : a bodily disorder associated with the presence of toxic substances in the blood

tox·ic \'täk-sik\ *adj* [LL *toxicus*, fr. L *toxicum* poison, fr. Gk *toxikon* arrow poison, fr. neut. of *toxikos* of a bow, fr. *toxon* bow, arrow] : of, relating to, or caused by poison or a toxin : POISONOUS — **tox·ic·i·ty** \täk-'si-sə-tē\ *n*

tox·i·col·o·gy \ˌtäk-si-'kä-lə-jē\ *n* : a science that deals with poisons and esp. with problems of their use and control — **tox·i·co·log·i·cal** \-kə-'lä-ji-kəl\ *also* **tox·i·co·log·ic** \-kə-'lä-jik\ *adj* — **tox·i·col·o·gist** \-'kä-lə-jist\ *n*

toxic shock syndrome *n* : an acute disease associated with the presence of a bacterium that is characterized by fever, diarrhea, nausea, diffuse erythema, and shock and occurs esp. in menstruating females using tampons

tox·in \'täk-sən\ *n* : a poisonous substance produced by metabolic activities of a living organism that is usu. unstable, very toxic when introduced into the tissues, and usu. capable of inducing antibodies

¹**toy** \'tòi\ *n* **1** : something trifling **2** : a small ornament : BAUBLE **3** : something for a child to play with

²**toy** *vb* **1** : to deal with something lightly : TRIFLE **2** : FLIRT **3** : to amuse oneself as if with a plaything

³**toy** *adj* **1** : DIMINUTIVE ⟨a ~ dog⟩ **2** : designed for use as a toy

tp *abbr* **1** title page **2** township

tpk *or* **tpke** *abbr* turnpike

tr *abbr* **1** translated; translation; translator **2** transpose **3** troop

¹**trace** \'trās\ *n* **1** : a mark (as a footprint or track) left by something that has passed **2** : a minute or barely detectable amount ⟨disappeared without a ~⟩

²**trace** *vb* **traced; trac·ing 1** : to mark out : SKETCH **2** : to form (as letters) carefully **3** : to copy (a drawing) by marking lines on transparent paper laid over the drawing to be copied **4** : to follow the trail of : track down **5** : to study out and follow the development of ⟨~ed his family's history⟩ — **trace·able** *adj*

³**trace** *n* : either of two lines of a harness for fastening a draft animal to a vehicle

trac·er \'trā-sər\ *n* **1** : one that traces **2** : ammunition containing a chemical to mark the flight of projectiles by a trail of smoke or light

trac·ery \'trā-sə-rē\ *n, pl* **-er·ies** : ornamental work having a design with branching or interlacing lines

tra·chea \'trā-kē-ə\ *n, pl* **-che·ae** \-kē-ˌē\ *also* **-che·as** *or* **-chea** : the main tube by which air passes from the larynx to the lungs of vertebrates — **tra·che·al** \-kē-əl\ *adj*

tra·che·ot·o·my \ˌtrā-kē-'ä-tə-mē\ *n, pl* **-mies** : the surgical operation of cutting into the trachea esp. through the skin

tracing \'trā-siŋ\ *n* **1** : the act of one that traces **2** : something that is traced **3** : a graphic record made by an instrument for measuring vibrations or pulsations

¹**track** \'trak\ *n* **1** : a mark left in passing **2** : PATH, ROUTE, TRAIL **3** : a course laid out for racing; *also* : track-and-field sports **4** : one of a series of paths along which material (as music) is recorded (as on a CD or magnetic tape) **5** : the course along which something moves; *esp* : a way made by two parallel lines of metal rails **6** : awareness of a fact or progression ⟨lost ~ of time⟩ **7** : either of two

endless metal belts on which a vehicle (as a bulldozer) travels

²**track** *vb* **1** : to follow the tracks or traces of : TRAIL **2** : to observe the moving path of (as a missile) **3** : to make tracks on **4** : to carry (as mud) on the feet and deposit — **track·er** *n*

track·age \'tra-kij\ *n* : lines of railway track

track–and–field *adj* : of or relating to athletic contests held on a running track or on the adjacent field

¹**tract** \'trakt\ *n* **1** : an area without precise boundaries ⟨huge ~s of land⟩ **2** : a defined area of land **3** : a system of body parts or organs that act together to perform some function ⟨the digestive ~⟩

²**tract** *n* : a pamphlet of political or religious propaganda

trac·ta·ble \'trak-tə-bəl\ *adj* : easily controlled : DOCILE ♦ **Synonyms** AMENABLE, OBEDIENT, BIDDABLE

tract house *n* : any of many similar houses built on a tract of land

trac·tion \'trak-shən\ *n* **1** : the act of drawing : the state of being drawn **2** : the drawing of a vehicle by motive power; *also* : the particular form of motive power used **3** : the adhesive friction of a body on a surface on which it moves **4** : a pulling force applied to a skeletal structure (as a broken bone) by means of a special device; *also* : a state of tension created by such a pulling force ⟨a leg in ~⟩ — **trac·tion·al** \-shə-nəl\ *adj* — **trac·tive** \'trak-tiv\ *adj*

trac·tor \'trak-tər\ *n* **1** : an automotive vehicle used esp. for drawing farm equipment **2** : a truck for hauling a trailer

¹**trade** \'trād\ *n* **1** : one's regular business or work : OCCUPATION **2** : an occupation requiring manual or mechanical skill **3** : the persons engaged in a business or industry **4** : the business of buying and selling or bartering commodities **5** : an act of trading : TRANSACTION

²**trade** *vb* **trad·ed; trad·ing 1** : to give in exchange for another commodity : BARTER **2** : to engage in the exchange, purchase, or sale of goods **3** : to deal regularly as a customer — **trade on** : EXPLOIT ⟨*trades on* his family name⟩

trade–in \'trād-ˌin\ *n* : an item of merchandise traded in

trade in *vb* : to turn in as part payment for a purchase

¹**trade·mark** \'trād-ˌmärk\ *n* : a device (as a word or mark) that points distinctly to the origin or ownership of merchandise to which it is applied and that is legally reserved for the exclusive use of the owner; *also* : something that identifies a person or thing

²**trademark** *vb* : to secure the trademark rights for ⟨that name is ~ed⟩

trade name *n* : a name that is given by a manufacturer or merchant to a product to distinguish it as made or sold by him and that may be used and protected as a trademark

trad·er \'trā-dər\ *n* **1** : a person whose

business is buying or selling **2** : a ship engaged in trade

trades·man \'trādz-mən\ *n* **1** : one who runs a retail store : SHOPKEEPER **2** : CRAFTSMAN

trades·peo·ple \-ˌpē-pəl\ *n pl* : people engaged in trade

trade union *n* : LABOR UNION

trade wind *n* : a wind blowing almost constantly in one direction

trading stamp *n* : a printed stamp given as a premium to a retail customer that when accumulated may be redeemed for merchandise

tra·di·tion \trə-'di-shən\ *n* **1** : an inherited, established, or customary pattern of thought or action **2** : the handing down of beliefs and customs by word of mouth or by example without written instruction; *also* : a belief or custom thus handed down — **tra·di·tion·al** \-ˌdi-shə-nəl\ *adj* — **tra·di·tion·al·ly** *adv*

tra·duce \trə-'düs, -'dyüs\ *vb* **tra·duced; tra·duc·ing** : to lower the reputation of : DEFAME, SLANDER ⟨he was *traduced* in the past⟩ ♦ *Synonyms* MALIGN, LIBEL, CALUMNIATE — **tra·duc·er** *n*

¹traf·fic \'tra-fik\ *n* **1** : the business of bartering or buying and selling **2** : communication or dealings between individuals or groups **3** : the movement (as of vehicles) along a route; *also* : the vehicles, people, ships, or planes moving along a route **4** : the passengers or cargo carried by a transportation system

²traffic *vb* **traf·ficked; traf·fick·ing 1** : to carry on business dealings **2** : DEAL, TRADE ⟨*trafficked* in illegal drugs⟩ — **traf·fick·er** *n*

traffic circle *n* : ROTARY 2

traffic light *n* : a visual signal (as a system of lights) for controlling traffic

tra·ge·di·an \trə-'jē-dē-ən\ *n* **1** : a writer of tragedies **2** : an actor who plays tragic roles

tra·ge·di·enne \trə-ˌjē-dē-'en\ *n* [F] : an actress who plays tragic roles

trag·e·dy \'tra-jə-dē\ *n, pl* **-dies** [ME *tragedie,* fr. MF, fr. L *tragoedia,* fr. Gk *tragōidia,* fr. *tragos* goat + *aeidein* to sing] **1** : a serious drama with a sorrowful or disastrous conclusion **2** : a disastrous event : CALAMITY; *also* : MISFORTUNE **3** : tragic quality or element ⟨the ∼ of life⟩

trag·ic \'tra-jik\ *also* **trag·i·cal** \-ji-kəl\ *adj* **1** : of, relating to, or expressive of tragedy **2** : appropriate to tragedy : LAMENTABLE, UNFORTUNATE ⟨a ∼ mistake⟩ — **trag·i·cal·ly** \-ji-k(ə-)lē\ *adv*

¹trail \'trāl\ *vb* **1** : to hang down so as to drag along or sweep the ground **2** : to draw or drag along behind **3** : to extend over a surface in a straggling manner **4** : to lag behind **5** : to follow the track of : PURSUE **6** : DWINDLE ⟨her voice ∼*ed* off⟩

²trail *n* **1** : something that trails or is trailed ⟨a ∼ of smoke⟩ **2** : a trace or mark left by something that has passed or been drawn along : SCENT, TRACK ⟨a ∼ of blood⟩ **3** : a beaten path; *also* : a marked path through woods

trail bike *n* : a small motorcycle for off-road use

trail·blaz·er \-ˌblā-zər\ *n* : PATHFINDER, PIONEER — **trail·blaz·ing** *adj or n*

trail·er \'trā-lər\ *n* **1** : one that trails; *esp* : a creeping plant (as an ivy) **2** : a vehicle that is hauled by another (as a tractor) **3** : a vehicle equipped to serve wherever parked as a dwelling or place of business **4** : PREVIEW 3

trailer park *n* : a site equipped to accommodate mobile homes

trailing arbutus *n* : a creeping spring-flowering plant of the heath family with fragrant pink or white flowers

¹train \'trān\ *n* [ME, fr. AF, fr. *trainer* to draw, drag] **1** : a part of a gown that trails behind the wearer **2** : RETINUE **3** : a moving file of persons, vehicles, or animals **4** : a connected series ⟨a ∼ of thought⟩ **5** : AFTERMATH **6** : a connected line of railroad cars usu. hauled by a locomotive ♦ *Synonyms* SUCCESSION, SEQUENCE, PROCESSION, CHAIN

²train *vb* [ME, to trail, drag, train, fr. AF *trainer*] **1** : to cause to grow as desired ⟨∼ a vine on a trellis⟩ **2** : to form by instruction, discipline, or drill **3** : to make or become prepared (as by exercise) for a test of skill **4** : to aim or point at an object ⟨∼ guns on a fort⟩ ♦ *Synonyms* DISCIPLINE, SCHOOL, EDUCATE, INSTRUCT — **train·er** *n*

train·ee \trā-'nē\ *n* : one who is being trained esp. for a job

train·ing \'trā-niŋ\ *n* **1** : the act, process, or method of one who trains **2** : the skill, knowledge, or experience gained by one who trains

train·man \-mən\ *n* : a member of a train crew

traipse \'trāps\ *vb* **traipsed; traips·ing** : TRAMP, WALK ⟨∼ the countryside⟩

trait \'trāt\ *n* **1** : a distinguishing quality (as of personality) **2** : an inherited characteristic

trai·tor \'trā-tər\ *n* [ME *traytour,* fr. AF *traitre,* fr. L *traditor,* fr. *tradere* to hand over, deliver, betray, fr. *trans-* across + *dare* to give] **1** : one who betrays another's trust or is false to an obligation **2** : one who commits treason — **trai·tor·ous** *adj*

tra·jec·to·ry \trə-'jek-tə-rē\ *n, pl* **-ries** : the curve that a body (as a planet in its orbit) describes in space

tram \'tram\ *n* **1** : a boxlike car running on rails (as in a mine) **2** *chiefly Brit* : STREETCAR **3** : an overhead cable car

¹tram·mel \'tra-məl\ *n* [ME *tramayle,* a kind of net, fr. OF *tramail,* fr. LL *tremaculum,* fr. L *tres* three + *macula* mesh, spot] : something impeding activity, progress, or freedom — usu. used in pl.

²trammel *vb* **-meled** *or* **-melled; -mel·ing** *or* **-mel·ling 1** : to catch and hold in or as if in a net **2** : HAMPER ♦ *Synonyms* CLOG, FETTER, SHACKLE, HOBBLE

¹tramp \'tramp, *1 & 3 are also* 'trämp, 'trȯmp\ *vb* **1** : to walk, tread, or step heavily **2** : to walk about or through;

also : HIKE ⟨∼ed through the woods⟩ **3**
: to tread on forcibly and repeatedly
²tramp \'tramp, *5 is also* 'trämp, 'trömp\ *n*
1 : a begging or thieving vagrant **2** : a
foot traveler **3** : an immoral woman; *esp*
: PROSTITUTE **4** : a walking trip : HIKE **5**
: the succession of sounds made by the
beating of feet on a road **6** : a ship that
does not follow a regular course but
takes cargo to any port — **trampy**
\'tram-pē\ *adj*
tram·ple \'tram-pəl\ *vb* **tram·pled; tram·**
pling 1 : to tread heavily so as to bruise,
crush, or injure **2** : to inflict injury or
destruction **3** : to press down or crush by
or as if by treading — **trample** *n* —
tram·pler *n*
tram·po·line \ˌtram-pə-'lēn, 'tram-pə-
ˌlēn\ *n* [It *trampolino* springboard] : a resilient sheet or web (as of nylon) supported by springs in a metal frame and
used as a springboard in tumbling —
tram·po·lin·ist \-'lē-nist, -ˌlē-\ *n*
trance \'trans\ *n* [ME, fr. AF *transe*,
death, coma, rapture, fr. *transir* to depart, die, fr. L *transire* to cross, pass by,
fr. *trans-* across + *ire* to go] **1** : STUPOR,
DAZE **2** : a sleeplike state of altered consciousness (as of deep hypnosis) **3** : a
state of very deep absorption — **trance-**
like \-ˌlīk\ *adj*
tran·quil \'traŋ-kwəl, 'tran-\ *adj* : free
from agitation or disturbance : QUIET
♦ **Synonyms** SERENE, PLACID, PEACE-
FUL — **tran·quil·li·ty** *or* **tran·quil·i·ty**
\traŋ-'kwi-lə-tē, tran-\ *n* — **tran·quil·ly**
adv
tran·quil·ize *also* **tran·quil·lize** \'traŋ-
kwə-ˌlīz, 'tran-\ *vb* **-ized** *also* **-lized; -iz-**
ing *also* **-liz·ing** : to make or become
tranquil; *esp* : to relieve of mental tension
and anxiety by means of drugs
tran·quil·iz·er *also* **tran·quil·liz·er** \-ˌlī-
zər\ *n* : a drug used to relieve mental disturbance (as tension and anxiety)
¹trans \'tranz\ *adj* : TRANSGENDER,
TRANSSEXUAL
²trans *abbr* **1** transaction **2** transitive **3**
translated; translation; translator **4**
transmission **5** transportation **6** transverse
trans·act \tran-'zakt, -'sakt\ *vb* : CARRY
OUT, PERFORM; *also* : CONDUCT
trans·ac·tion \-'zak-shən, -'sak-\ *n* **1**
: something transacted; *esp* : a business
deal **2** : an act or process of transacting
3 *pl* : the records of the proceedings of a
society or organization — **trans·ac·tion-**
al \-shnəl, -shə-nᵊl\ *adj*
trans·at·lan·tic \ˌtrans-ət-'lan-tik, ˌtranz-\
adj : crossing or extending across or situated beyond the Atlantic Ocean ⟨a ∼
flight⟩
trans·ax·le \trans-'ak-səl\ *n* : a unit combining the transmission and differential
gear of a front-wheel-drive automobile
trans·ceiv·er \tran-'sē-vər\ *n* : a radio
transmitter-receiver that uses many of
the same components for both transmission and reception
tran·scend \tran-'send\ *vb* **1** : to rise
above the limits of ⟨music that ∼s cul-

tural boundaries⟩ **2** : SURPASS ♦ **Syn-**
onyms EXCEED, OUTDO, OUTSHINE,
OUTSTRIP
tran·scen·dent \-'sen-dənt\ *adj* **1** : exceeding usual limits : SURPASSING **2**
: transcending material existence ♦ **Syn-**
onyms SUPERLATIVE, SUPREME, PEER-
LESS, INCOMPARABLE
tran·scen·den·tal \ˌtran-ˌsen-'den-tᵊl,
-sən-\ *adj* **1** : TRANSCENDENT **2** **2** : of,
relating to, or characteristic of transcen-
dentalism; *also* : ABSTRUSE
tran·scen·den·tal·ism \-tə-ˌli-zəm\ *n* : a
philosophy holding that ultimate reality
is unknowable or asserting the primacy
of the spiritual over the material and empirical — **tran·scen·den·tal·ist** \-tə-list\
adj or n
trans·con·ti·nen·tal \ˌtrans-ˌkän-tə-'nen-
tᵊl\ *adj* : extending or going across a continent ⟨a ∼ railroad⟩
tran·scribe \tran-'skrīb\ *vb* **tran-**
scribed; tran·scrib·ing 1 : to write a
copy of **2** : to make a copy of (dictated
or recorded matter) in longhand or on a
typewriter **3** : to represent (speech
sounds) by means of phonetic symbols;
also : to make a musical transcription of
tran·script \'tran-ˌskript\ *n* **1** : a written,
printed, or typed copy **2** : an official
copy esp. of a student's educational record
tran·scrip·tion \tran-'skrip-shən\ *n* **1**
: an act or process of transcribing **2**
: COPY, TRANSCRIPT **3** : an arrangement
of a musical composition for some instrument or voice other than the original
4 : the process of constructing a messenger RNA molecule using a DNA molecule as a template
tran·scrip·tion·ist \-shə-nist\ *n* : one that
transcribes; *esp* : a typist who transcribes
medical reports
trans·der·mal \trans-'dər-məl, 'tranz-\
adj : relating to, being, or supplying a
medication in a form for absorption
through the skin ⟨∼ nicotine patch⟩
trans·duc·er \trans-'dü-sər, tranz-,
-'dyü-\ *n* : a device that is actuated by
power from one system and supplies
power usu. in another form to a second
system
tran·sept \'tran-ˌsept\ *n* : the part of a
cruciform church that crosses at right
angles to the greatest length; *also* : either
of the projecting ends
trans fat \'tran(t)s-, 'tranz-\ *n* : a fat containing unsaturated fatty acids (**trans-**
fatty acids) that have been linked to an
increase in blood cholesterol
¹trans·fer \trans-'fər, 'trans-ˌfər\ *vb* **trans-**
ferred; trans·fer·ring 1 : to pass or
cause to pass from one person, place, or
situation to another : MOVE, TRANSMIT **2**
: to make over the possession of : CON-
VEY **3** : to print or copy from one surface
to another by contact **4** : to change from
one vehicle or transportation line to another — **trans·fer·able** \trans-'fər-ə-bəl\
adj — **trans·fer·al** \-'əl\ *n*
²trans·fer \'trans-ˌfər\ *n* **1** : conveyance of
right, title, or interest in property from

one person to another **2** : an act or process of transferring **3** : one that transfers or is transferring **4** : a ticket entitling a passenger to continue a trip on another route

trans·fer·ence \trans-'fər-əns\ *n* : an act, process, or instance of transferring

trans·fig·ure \trans-'fi-gyər\ *vb* **-ured; -ur·ing 1** : to change the form or appearance of **2** : EXALT, GLORIFY — **trans·fig·u·ra·tion** \,trans-,fi-gyə-'rā-shən, -gə-\ *n*

trans·fix \trans-'fiks\ *vb* **1** : to pierce through with or as if with a pointed weapon **2** : to hold motionless by or as if by piercing ⟨stood ∼ed by her gaze⟩

trans·form \trans-'fȯrm\ *vb* : to change in structure, appearance, or character ♦ *Synonyms* TRANSMUTE, TRANSFIGURE, TRANSMOGRIFY — **trans·for·ma·tion** \,trans-fər-'mā-shən\ *n* — **trans·for·ma·tive** \trans-'fȯr-mə-tiv\ *adj*

trans·form·er \trans-'fȯr-mər\ *n* : one that transforms; *esp* : a device for converting variations of current in one circuit into variations of voltage and current in another circuit

trans·fuse \trans-'fyüz\ *vb* **trans·fused; trans·fus·ing 1** : to cause to pass from one to another **2** : to diffuse into or through **3** : to transfer (as blood) into a vein or an artery of a person or animal — **trans·fu·sion** \-'fyü-zhən\ *n*

trans·gen·der \tranz-'jen-dər\ *or* **trans·gen·dered** \-dərd\ *adj* : having physical or behavioral characteristics transcending traditional gender boundaries ⟨a ∼ person⟩

trans·gen·ic \tran(t)s-'je-nik\ *adj* : being or used to produce an organism or cell with genes introduced from another species of organism ⟨∼ crops⟩

trans·gress \trans-'gres, tranz-\ *vb* [ME, fr. MF *transgresser*, fr. L *transgressus*, pp. of *transgredi* to step beyond or across, fr. *trans-* across + *gradi* to step] **1** : to go beyond the limits set by ⟨∼ the divine law⟩ **2** : to go beyond : EXCEED **3** : SIN — **trans·gres·sion** \-'gre-shən\ *n* — **trans·gres·sor** \-'gre-sər\ *n*

¹tran·sient \'tran-shənt; -sē-ənt, -shē-, -zē-\ *adj* **1** : not lasting long : SHORT-LIVED ⟨∼ optimism⟩ **2** : passing through a place with only a brief stay ⟨∼visitors⟩ ♦ *Synonyms* TRANSITORY, PASSING, MOMENTARY, FLEETING — **tran·sient·ly** *adv*

²transient *n* : one that is transient; *esp* : a transient guest

tran·sis·tor \tran-'zis-tər, -'sis-\ *n* [*transfer* + *resistor;* fr. its transferring an electrical signal across a resistor] **1** : a small electronic semiconductor device used in electronic equipment **2** : a radio having transistors

tran·sis·tor·ized \-tə-,rīzd\ *adj* : having or using transistors

tran·sit \'tran-sət, -zət\ *n* **1** : a passing through, across, or over : PASSAGE **2** : conveyance of persons or things from one place to another **3** : usu. local transportation esp. of people by public con-

veyance **4** : a surveyor's instrument for measuring angles

tran·si·tion \tran-'si-shən, -'zi-\ *n* : passage from one state, place, stage, or subject to another : CHANGE — **tran·si·tion·al** \-'si-shə-nəl, 'zi-\ *adj*

tran·si·tive \'tran-sə-tiv, -zə-\ *adj* **1** : having or containing an object required to complete the meaning ⟨a ∼ verb⟩ **2** : TRANSITIONAL — **tran·si·tive·ly** *adv* — **tran·si·tive·ness** *n* — **tran·si·tiv·i·ty** \,tran-sə-'ti-və-tē, -zə-\ *n*

tran·si·to·ry \'tran-sə-,tȯr-ē, -zə-\ *adj* : of brief duration : SHORT-LIVED, TEMPORARY ♦ *Synonyms* TRANSIENT, PASSING, MOMENTARY, FLEETING

transl *abbr* translated; translation

trans·late \trans-'lāt, tranz-\ *vb* **trans·lat·ed; trans·lat·ing 1** : to change from one place, state, or form to another **2** : to convey to heaven without death **3** : to turn into one's own or another language — **trans·lat·able** *adj* — **trans·la·tor** \-'lā-tər\ *n*

trans·la·tion \tran(t)s-'lā-shən, tranz-\ *n* **1** : an act, process, or instance of translating **2** : the process of forming a protein molecule from information in messenger RNA — **trans·la·tion·al** \-shnəl, -shə-nᵊl\ *adj*

trans·lit·er·ate \trans-'li-tə-,rāt, tranz-\ *vb* **-at·ed; -at·ing** : to represent or spell in the characters of another alphabet — **trans·lit·er·a·tion** \,trans-,li-tə-'rā-shən, ,tranz-\ *n*

trans·lu·cent \trans-'lü-sᵊnt, tranz-\ *adj* : not transparent but clear enough to allow light to pass through — **trans·lu·cence** \-sᵊns\ *n* — **trans·lu·cen·cy** \-sᵊn-sē\ *n* — **trans·lu·cent·ly** *adv*

trans·mi·grate \-'mī-,grāt\ *vb* : to pass at death from one body or being to another — **trans·mi·gra·tion** \,trans-mī-'grā-shən, ,tranz-\ *n* — **trans·mi·gra·to·ry** \trans-'mī-grə-,tȯr-ē\ *adj*

trans·mis·sion \-'mi-shən\ *n* **1** : an act or process of transmitting **2** : the passage of radio waves between transmitting stations and receiving stations **3** : the gears by which power is transmitted from the engine of an automobile to the axle that propels the vehicle **4** : something transmitted

trans·mit \-'mit\ *vb* **trans·mit·ted; trans·mit·ting 1** : to transfer from one person or place to another : FORWARD **2** : to pass on by or as if by inheritance **3** : to cause or allow to spread abroad or to another ⟨∼ a disease⟩ **4** : to cause (as light, electricity, or force) to pass through space or a medium **5** : to send out (radio or television signals) ♦ *Synonyms* CONVEY, COMMUNICATE, IMPART — **trans·mis·si·ble** \-'mi-sə-bəl\ *adj* — **trans·mit·ta·ble** \-'mi-tə-bəl\ *adj* — **trans·mit·tal** \-'mit-ᵊl\ *n*

trans·mit·ter \-'mi-tər\ *n* : one that transmits; *esp* : an apparatus for transmitting telegraph, radio, or television signals

trans·mog·ri·fy \trans-'mä-grə-,fī, tranz-\ *vb* **-fied; -fy·ing** : to change or alter often with grotesque or humorous effect —

trans·mog·ri·fi·ca·tion \-ˌmä-grə-fə-ˈkā-shən\ *n*

trans·mute \-ˈmyüt\ *vb* **trans·muted; trans·mut·ing** : to change or alter in form, appearance, or nature ♦ *Synonyms* TRANSFORM, CONVERT, TRANSFIGURE, METAMORPHOSE — **trans·mu·ta·tion** \ˌtrans-myü-ˈtā-shən, ˌtranz-\ *n*

trans·na·tion·al \-ˈna-shə-nəl\ *adj* : extending beyond national boundaries

trans·oce·an·ic \ˌtrans-ˌō-shē-ˈa-nik, ˌtranz-\ *adj* **1** : lying or dwelling beyond the ocean **2** : crossing or extending across the ocean

tran·som \ˈtran-səm\ *n* **1** : a piece (as a crossbar in the frame of a window or door) that lies crosswise in a structure **2** : a window above an opening (as a door) built on and often hinged to a horizontal crossbar

tran·son·ic *also* **trans–son·ic** \trans-ˈsä-nik\ *adj* : being or relating to speeds near that of sound in air or about 741 miles (1185 kilometers) per hour

trans·pa·cif·ic \ˌtrans-pə-ˈsi-fik\ *adj* : crossing, extending across, or situated beyond the Pacific Ocean

trans·par·ent \trans-ˈper-ənt\ *adj* **1** : clear enough to be seen through **2** : SHEER, DIAPHANOUS ⟨a ~ fabric⟩ **3** : readily understood : CLEAR; *also* : easily detected ⟨a ~ lie⟩ ♦ *Synonyms* LUCID, TRANSLUCENT, LUCENT — **trans·par·en·cy** \-ən-sē\ *n* — **trans·par·ent·ly** *adv*

tran·spire \trans-ˈpī-(ə)r\ *vb* **tran·spired; tran·spir·ing** [MF *transpirer*, fr. ML *transpirare*, fr. L *trans-* across + *spirare* to breathe] **1** : to pass or give off (as water vapor) through pores or a membrane **2** : to become known **3** : to take place : HAPPEN — **tran·spi·ra·tion** \ˌtrans-pə-ˈrā-shən\ *n*

¹trans·plant \trans-ˈplant\ *vb* **1** : to dig up and plant elsewhere **2** : to remove from one place and settle or introduce elsewhere : TRANSPORT **3** : to transfer (an organ or tissue) from one part or individual to another — **trans·plan·ta·tion** \ˌtrans-ˌplan-ˈtā-shən\ *n*

²trans·plant \ˈtrans-ˌplant\ *n* **1** : a person or thing transplanted **2** : the act or process of transplanting

trans·po·lar \trans-ˈpō-lər\ *adj* : going or extending across either of the polar regions

tran·spon·der \tran-ˈspän-dər\ *n* [*transmitter* + *responder*] : a radio or radar set that upon receiving a certain signal emits a radio signal and that is used to locate and identify objects and in satellites to relay communications signals

¹trans·port \trans-ˈpȯrt\ *vb* **1** : to convey from one place to another : CARRY **2** : to carry away by strong emotion : ENRAPTURE **3** : to send to a penal colony overseas ♦ *Synonyms* BEAR, FERRY — **trans·por·ta·tion** \ˌtrans-pər-ˈtā-shən\ *n* — **trans·port·er** *n*

²trans·port \ˈtrans-ˌpȯrt\ *n* **1** : an act of transporting **2** : strong or intensely pleasurable emotion ⟨~s of joy⟩ **3** : a ship used in transporting troops or supplies;

also : a vehicle (as a truck or plane) used to transport persons or goods

trans·pose \trans-ˈpōz\ *vb* **trans·posed; trans·pos·ing 1** : to change the position or sequence of ⟨~ the letters in a word⟩ **2** : to write or perform (a musical composition) in a different key — **trans·po·si·tion** \ˌtrans-pə-ˈzi-shən\ *n*

trans·sex·u·al \(ˌ)trans-ˈsek-shə-wəl\ *n* : a person who psychologically identifies with the opposite sex and may seek to live as a member of this sex esp. by undergoing surgery to modify the external sex organs

trans·ship \tran-ˈship, trans-\ *vb* : to transfer for further transportation from one ship or conveyance to another — **trans·ship·ment** *n*

tran·sub·stan·ti·a·tion \ˌtran-səb-ˌstan-chē-ˈā-shən\ *n* : the change in the eucharistic elements from the substance of bread and wine to the substance of the body of Christ with only the appearances of bread and wine remaining

trans·verse \trans-ˈvərs, tranz-\ *adj* : lying across : set crosswise — **transverse** \ˈtrans-ˌvərs, ˈtranz-\ *n* — **trans·verse·ly** *adv*

trans·ves·tite \trans-ˈves-ˌtīt, tranz-\ *n* : a person and esp. a male who adopts the dress and often the behavior of the opposite sex — **transvestite** *adj* — **trans·ves·tism** \-ˌti-zəm\ *n*

¹trap \ˈtrap\ *n* **1** : a device for catching animals **2** : something by which one is caught unawares; *also* : a situation from which escape is difficult or impossible **3** : a machine for throwing clay pigeons into the air; *also* : SAND TRAP **4** : a light one-horse carriage on springs **5** : a device to allow some one thing to pass through while keeping other things out ⟨a ~ in a drainpipe⟩ **6** *pl* : a group of percussion instruments (as in a dance orchestra)

²trap *vb* **trapped; trap·ping 1** : to catch in or as if in a trap; *also* : CONFINE **2** : to provide or set (a place) with traps **3** : to set traps for animals esp. as a business ♦ *Synonyms* SNARE, ENTRAP, ENSNARE, BAG, LURE, DECOY — **trap·per** *n*

trap·door \ˈtrap-ˈdȯr\ *n* : a lifting or sliding door covering an opening in a floor or roof

tra·peze \tra-ˈpēz\ *n* : a gymnastic apparatus consisting of a horizontal bar suspended by two parallel ropes

trap·e·zoid \ˈtra-pə-ˌzȯid\ *n* [NL *trapezoides*, fr. Gk *trapezoeidēs* trapezoidal, fr. *trapeza* table, fr. *tra-* four + *peza* foot] : a 4-sided polygon with exactly two sides parallel — **trap·e·zoi·dal** \ˌtra-pə-ˈzȯi-d°l\ *adj*

trap·pings \ˈtra-piŋz\ *n pl* **1** : CAPARISON 1 **2** : outward decoration or dress; *also* : outward sign ⟨~ of success⟩

traps \ˈtraps\ *n pl* : personal belongings : LUGGAGE

trap·shoot·ing \ˈtrap-ˌshü-tiŋ\ *n* : shooting at clay pigeons sprung from a trap into the air away from the shooter

¹trash \ˈtrash\ *n* **1** : something of little

worth : RUBBISH **2** : empty or disparaging talk **3** : a worthless person; *also* : such persons as a group : RIFFRAFF — **trashy** *adj*

²**trash** *vb* **1** : to dispose of : DISCARD ⟨~*ed* the plans⟩ **2** : VANDALIZE, DESTROY **3** : ATTACK **4** : SPOIL, RUIN **5** : to criticize or disparage harshly

trau·ma \'trau̇-mə, 'trȯ-\ *n, pl* **traumas** *also* **trau·ma·ta** \-mə-tə\ [Gk, wound] : a bodily or mental injury esp. caused by an external agent; *also* : a cause of trauma — **trau·mat·ic** \trə-'ma-tik, trȯ-, trau̇-\ *adj*

trau·ma·tize \-ˌtīz\ *vb* **-tized; -tiz·ing** : to inflict trauma upon

¹**tra·vail** \trə-'vāl, 'tra-ˌvāl\ *n* **1** : painful work or exertion : TOIL **2** : AGONY, TORMENT **3** : CHILDBIRTH, LABOR

²**travail** *vb* : to labor hard : TOIL

¹**trav·el** \'tra-vəl\ *vb* **-eled** *or* **-elled; -el·ing** *or* **-el·ling** [ME *travailen* to torment, labor, journey, fr. AF *travailler* strive, fr. VL **trepaliare* to torture, fr. LL *trepalium* instrument of torture] **1** : to go on or as if on a trip or tour : JOURNEY **2** : to move as if by traveling ⟨news ~*s* fast⟩ **3** : ASSOCIATE **4** : to go from place to place as a sales representative **5** : to move from point to point ⟨light waves ~ very fast⟩ **6** : to journey over or through ⟨~*ing* the highways⟩ **7** : to take excessive steps while holding a basketball — **trav·el·er** *or* **trav·el·ler** *n*

²**travel** *n* **1** : the act of traveling : PASSAGE **2** : JOURNEY, TRIP — often used in pl. **3** : the number traveling : TRAFFIC **4** : the motion of a piece of machinery and esp. when to and fro

traveler's check *n* : a check paid for in advance that is signed when bought and signed again when cashed

traveling bag *n* : SUITCASE

trav·el·ogue *or* **trav·el·og** \'tra-və-ˌlȯg, -ˌläg\ *n* : a usu. illustrated lecture on travel

¹**tra·verse** \'tra-vərs\ *n* : something that crosses or lies across

²**tra·verse** \trə-'vərs, 'tra-vərs *or* 'tra-vərs\ *vb* **tra·versed; tra·vers·ing** **1** : to go or travel across or over **2** : to move or pass along or through **3** : to extend over **4** : SWIVEL

³**tra·verse** \'tra-vərs\ *adj* : TRANSVERSE

trav·er·tine \'tra-vər-ˌtēn, -tən\ *n* : a crystalline mineral formed by deposition from spring waters

¹**trav·es·ty** \'tra-və-stē\ *vb* **-tied; -ty·ing** : to make a travesty of

²**travesty** *n, pl* **-ties** [obs. E *travesty* disguised, parodied, fr. F *travesti*, pp. of *travestir* to disguise, fr. It *travestire*, fr. *tra-* across (fr. L *trans-*) + *vestire* to dress] : an imitation that makes crude fun of something; *also* : an inferior imitation

¹**trawl** \'trȯl\ *vb* : to fish or catch with a trawl — **trawl·er** *n*

²**trawl** *n* **1** : a large conical net dragged along the sea bottom in fishing **2** : a long heavy fishing line equipped with many hooks in series

tray \'trā\ *n* : an open receptacle with flat bottom and low rim for holding, carrying, or exhibiting articles

treach·er·ous \'tre-chə-rəs\ *adj* **1** : characterized by treachery **2** : UNTRUSTWORTHY, UNRELIABLE ⟨a ~ coworker⟩ **3** : providing insecure footing or support ⟨a ~ slope⟩ ♦ *Synonyms* TRAITOROUS, FAITHLESS, FALSE, DISLOYAL — **treach·er·ous·ly** *adv*

treach·ery \'tre-chə-rē\ *n, pl* **-er·ies** : violation of allegiance or trust

trea·cle \'trē-kəl\ *n* [ME *triacle* a medicinal compound, fr. AF, fr. L *theriaca*, fr. Gk *thēriakē* antidote against a poisonous bite, fr. *thērion* wild animal] *chiefly Brit* : MOLASSES — **trea·cly** \-k(ə-)lē\ *adj*

¹**tread** \'tred\ *vb* **trod** \'träd\; **trod·den** \'trä-dᵊn\ *or* **trod; tread·ing** **1** : to step or walk on or over **2** : to move on foot : WALK; *also* : DANCE **3** : to beat or press with the feet — **tread water** : to stay afloat and upright in water by sustaining a walking motion

²**tread** *n* **1** : a mark made by or as if by treading **2** : the manner or sound of stepping **3** : the part of a wheel that makes contact with a road **4** : the horizontal part of a step

trea·dle \'tre-dᵊl\ *n* : a lever device pressed by the foot to drive a machine — **treadle** *vb*

tread·mill \'tred-ˌmil\ *n* **1** : a mill worked by persons who tread on steps around the edge of a wheel or by animals that walk on an endless belt **2** : a device with an endless belt on which a person walks or runs in place **3** : a wearisome routine

treas *abbr* treasurer; treasury

trea·son \'trē-zᵊn\ *n* : the offense of attempting to overthrow the government of one's country or of assisting its enemies in war — **trea·son·able** \-zᵊn-ə-bəl\ *adj* — **trea·son·ous** \-zᵊn-əs\ *adj*

¹**trea·sure** \'tre-zhər, 'trā-\ *n* [ME *tresor*, fr. AF, fr. L *thesaurus*, fr. Gk *thēsauros*] **1** : wealth stored up or held in reserve **2** : something of great value

²**treasure** *vb* **trea·sured; trea·sur·ing** **1** : HOARD **2** : to keep as precious : CHERISH ♦ *Synonyms* PRIZE, VALUE, APPRECIATE, ESTEEM

trea·sur·er \'tre-zhə-rər, 'trā-\ *n* : an officer of a club, business, or government who has charge of money taken in and paid out

treasure trove \-ˌtrōv\ *n* **1** : treasure of unknown ownership found buried or hidden **2** : a valuable discovery

trea·sury \'tre-zhə-rē, 'trā-\ *n, pl* **-sur·ies** **1** : a place in which stores of wealth are kept **2** : the place where collected funds are stored and paid out **3** *cap* : a governmental department in charge of finances

¹**treat** \'trēt\ *vb* **1** : NEGOTIATE **2** : to deal with esp. in writing; *also* : HANDLE **3** : to pay for the food or entertainment of **4** : to behave or act toward ⟨~ them well⟩ **5** : to regard in a specified manner ⟨~ as inferiors⟩ **6** : to give medical or surgical care to **7** : to subject to some action ⟨~ soil with lime⟩

²**treat** *n* **1** : an entertainment given free to

those invited; *also* : food, drink, or entertainment provided at another's expense **2** : a source of joy or amusement

trea·tise \'trē-təs\ *n* : a systematic written exposition or argument

treat·ment \'trēt-mənt\ *n* : the act or manner or an instance of treating someone or something; *also* : a substance or method used in treating

trea·ty \'trē-tē\ *n, pl* **treaties** : an agreement made by negotiation or diplomacy esp. between two or more states or governments

¹**tre·ble** \'tre-bəl\ *n* **1** : the highest of the four voice parts in vocal music : SOPRANO **2** : a high-pitched or shrill voice or sound **3** : the upper half of the musical pitch range

²**treble** *adj* **1** : triple in number or amount **2** : relating to or having the range of a musical treble **3** : high-pitched : SHRILL — **tre·bly** *adv*

³**treble** *vb* **tre·bled; tre·bling** : to make or become three times the size, amount, or number

tree \'trē\ *n* **1** : a woody perennial plant usu. with a single main stem and a head of branches and leaves at the top **2** : a piece of wood adapted to a particular use ⟨a shoe ~⟩ **3** : something resembling a tree ⟨a genealogical ~⟩ — **tree·less** *adj*

²**tree** *vb* **treed; tree·ing** : to drive to or up a tree ⟨~ a raccoon⟩

tree farm *n* : an area of forest land managed to ensure continuous commercial production

tree frog *n* : any of numerous small usu. tree-dwelling amphibians with adhesive disks on the toes

tree line *n* : TIMBERLINE

tree of heaven : a Chinese ailanthus widely grown as an ornamental tree

tree surgery *n* : operative treatment of diseased trees esp. for control of decay — **tree surgeon** *n*

tre·foil \'trē-ˌfȯi(-ə)l, 'tre-\ *n* **1** : an herb (as a clover) with leaves that have three leaflets **2** : a decorative design with three leaflike parts

¹**trek** \'trek\ *vb* **trekked; trek·king 1** *chiefly southern Africa* : to travel or migrate by ox wagon **2** : to make one's way arduously

²**trek** *n* **1** *chiefly southern Africa* : a migration esp. of settlers by ox wagon **2** : a slow or difficult journey

¹**trel·lis** \'tre-ləs\ *n* [ME *trelis*, fr. AF *treleis*, fr. OF *treille* arbor, fr. L *trichila* summerhouse] : a frame of latticework used esp. to support climbing plants

²**trellis** *vb* : to provide with a trellis; *esp* : to train (as a vine) on a trellis

trem·a·tode \'tre-mə-ˌtōd\ *n* : any of a class of parasitic worms

¹**trem·ble** \'trem-bəl\ *vb* **trem·bled; trembling 1** : to shake involuntarily (as with fear or cold) : SHIVER **2** : to move, sound, pass, or come to pass as if shaken or tremulous or to be affected with fear or doubt

²**tremble** *n* : a spell of shaking or quivering

tre·men·dous \tri-'men-dəs\ *adj* **1** : causing dread, awe, or terror : TERRIFYING **2** : unusually large, powerful, great, or excellent ⟨~ strength⟩ ♦ **Synonyms** STUPENDOUS, MONUMENTAL, MONSTROUS — **tre·men·dous·ly** *adv*

trem·o·lo \'tre-mə-ˌlō\ *n, pl* **-los** [It] : a rapid fluttering of a tone or alternating tones

trem·or \'tre-mər\ *n* **1** : a trembling or shaking esp. from weakness, emotional stress, or disease **2** : a quivering motion of the earth (as during an earthquake)

trem·u·lous \'trem-yə-ləs\ *adj* : marked by trembling or tremors : QUIVERING ⟨~ hands⟩ **2** : TIMOROUS, TIMID — **trem·u·lous·ly** *adv*

¹**trench** \'trench\ *n* [ME *trenche* track cut through a wood, fr. AF, act of cutting, fr. *trencher* to cut, prob. fr. VL *trinicare* to cut in three, fr. L *trini* three each] **1** : a long narrow cut in the ground : DITCH; *esp* : a ditch protected by banks of earth and used to shelter soldiers **2** *pl* : a place or situation likened to warfare conducted from trenches **3** : a long narrow steep-sided depression in the ocean floor

²**trench** *vb* **1** : to cut or dig trenches in **2** : to protect (troops) with trenches **3** : to come close : VERGE

tren·chant \'tren-chənt\ *adj* **1** : vigorously effective; *also* : CAUSTIC ⟨~ comments⟩ **2** : sharply perceptive : KEEN ⟨a ~ wit⟩ **3** : CLEAR-CUT, DISTINCT

tren·cher \'tren-chər\ *n* : a wooden platter for serving food

tren·cher·man \'tren-chər-mən\ *n* : a hearty eater

trench foot *n* : a painful foot disorder resembling frostbite and resulting from exposure to cold and wet

trench mouth *n* : a progressive painful bacterial infection of the mouth and adjacent parts marked by ulceration, bleeding gums, and foul breath

¹**trend** \'trend\ *vb* **1** : to have or take a general direction : TEND **2** : to show a tendency : INCLINE

²**trend** *n* **1** : a general direction taken (as by a stream or mountain range) : DRIFT **2** : a prevailing tendency **3** : a current style or preference : VOGUE

trendy \'tren-dē\ *adj* **trend·i·er; -est** : very fashionable; *also* : marked by superficial or faddish appeal or taste

trep·i·da·tion \ˌtre-pə-'dā-shən\ *n* : nervous agitation : APPREHENSION ♦ **Synonyms** HORROR, TERROR, PANIC, CONSTERNATION, DREAD, FRIGHT, DISMAY

¹**tres·pass** \'tres-pəs, -ˌpas\ *n* **1** : SIN, OFFENSE **2** : unlawful entry on someone else's land ♦ **Synonyms** TRANSGRESSION, VIOLATION, INFRACTION, INFRINGEMENT

²**trespass** *vb* **1** : to commit an offense : ERR, SIN **2** : INTRUDE, ENCROACH; *esp* : to enter unlawfully upon the land of another — **tres·pass·er** *n*

tress \'tres\ *n* : a long lock of hair — usu. used in pl.

tres·tle *also* **tres·sel** \'tre-səl\ *n* **1** : a supporting framework consisting usu. of a horizontal piece with spreading legs at each end **2** : a braced framework of timbers, piles, or steel for carrying a road or railroad over a depression

T. rex \'tē-'reks\ n : TYRANNOSAUR

trey \'trā\ n, pl **treys** : a card or the side of a die with three spots

tri·ad \'trī-ˌad, -əd\ n : a union or group of three usu. closely related persons or things

tri·age \trē-'äzh, 'trē-ˌäzh\ n [F, sorting] : the sorting of and allocation of treatment to patients and esp. battle or disaster victims according to a system of priorities designed to maximize the number of survivors

tri·al \'trī-əl\ n **1** : the action or process of trying or putting to the proof : TEST **2** : the hearing and judgment of a matter in issue before a competent tribunal **3** : a source of vexation or annoyance **4** : an experiment to test quality, value, or usefulness **5** : EFFORT, ATTEMPT ♦ **Synonyms** CROSS, ORDEAL, TRIBULATION, AFFLICTION — **trial** adj

tri·an·gle \'trī-ˌaŋ-gəl\ n **1** : a polygon that has three sides **2** : something shaped like a triangle — **tri·an·gu·lar** \trī-'aŋ-gyə-lər\ adj — **tri·an·gu·lar·ly** adv

tri·an·gu·la·tion \(ˌ)trī-ˌaŋ-gyə-'lā-shən\ n : a method using trigonometry to find the location of a point using bearings from two fixed points a known distance apart — **tri·an·gu·late** \trī-'aŋ-gyə-ˌlāt\ vb

Tri·as·sic \trī-'a-sik\ adj : of, relating to, or being the earliest period of the Mesozoic era marked by the first appearance of the dinosaurs — **Triassic** n

tri·ath·lon \trī-'ath-lən, -ˌlän\ n : an athletic contest consisting of three phases (as swimming, bicycling, and running)

trib abbr tributary

tribe \'trīb\ n **1** : a social group comprising numerous families, clans, or generations **2** : a group of persons having a common character, occupation, or interest **3** : a group of related plants or animals ⟨the cat ∼⟩ — **trib·al** \'trī-bəl\ adj

tribes·man \'trībz-mən\ n : a member of a tribe

trib·u·la·tion \ˌtri-byə-'lā-shən\ n [ME tribulacion, fr. AF, fr. L tribulatio, fr. tribulare to press, oppress, fr. tribulum drag used in threshing] : distress or suffering resulting from oppression or persecution; also : a trying experience ♦ **Synonyms** TRIAL, AFFLICTION, CROSS, ORDEAL

tri·bu·nal \trī-'byü-nᵊl, tri-\ n **1** : the seat of a judge **2** : a court of justice **3** : something that decides or determines ⟨the ∼ of public opinion⟩

tri·bune \'tri-ˌbyün, tri-'byün\ n **1** : an official in ancient Rome with the function of protecting the interests of plebeian citizens from the patricians **2** : a defender of the people

¹**trib·u·tary** \'tri-byə-ˌter-ē\ adj **1** : paying tribute : SUBJECT **2** : flowing into a larger stream or a lake ♦ **Synonyms** SUBORDINATE, SECONDARY, DEPENDENT

²**tributary** n, pl **-tar·ies 1** : a ruler or state that pays tribute **2** : a tributary stream

trib·ute \'tri-(ˌ)byüt, -byət\ n **1** : a payment by one ruler or nation to another as an act of submission or price of protection **2** : a usu. excessive tax, rental, or levy exacted by a sovereign or superior **3** : a gift or service showing respect, gratitude, or affection; also : PRAISE ♦ **Synonyms** EULOGY, CITATION, ENCOMIUM, PANEGYRIC

trice \'trīs\ n : INSTANT, MOMENT

tri·ceps \'trī-ˌseps\ n, pl **triceps** : a large muscle along the back of the upper arm that is attached at its upper end by three main parts and acts to extend the forearm at the elbow joint

tri·cer·a·tops \(ˌ)trī-'ser-ə-ˌtäps\ n, pl **-tops** also **-tops·es** [NL, fr. Gk tri- three + kerat-, keras horn + ōps face] : any of a genus of large plant-eating Cretaceous dinosaurs with three horns, a bony crest on the neck, and hoofed toes

tri·chi·na \tri-'kī-nə\ n, pl **-nae** \-(ˌ)nē\ also **-nas** : a small slender nematode worm that in the larval state is parasitic in the striated muscles of flesh-eating mammals (as humans)

trich·i·no·sis \ˌtri-kə-'nō-səs\ n : infestation with or disease caused by trichinae and marked esp. by muscular pain, fever, and swelling

¹**trick** \'trik\ n **1** : a crafty procedure meant to deceive **2** : a mischievous action : PRANK **3** : a childish action **4** : a deceptive or ingenious feat designed to puzzle or amuse **5** : PECULIARITY, MANNERISM **6** : a quick or artful way of getting a result : KNACK ⟨∼s of the trade⟩ **7** : the cards played in one round of a card game **8** : a tour of duty : SHIFT ♦ **Synonyms** RUSE, MANEUVER, ARTIFICE, WILE, FEINT

²**trick** vb **1** : to deceive by cunning or artifice : CHEAT **2** : to dress ornately

trick·ery \'tri-kə-rē\ n : deception by tricks and stratagems

trick·le \'tri-kəl\ vb **trick·led; trick·ling 1** : to run or fall in drops **2** : to flow in a thin gentle stream — **trickle** n

trick·ster \'trik-stər\ n : one who tricks or cheats

tricky \'tri-kē\ adj **trick·i·er; -est 1** : inclined to trickery **2** : requiring skill or caution ⟨a ∼ situation to handle⟩ **3** : UNRELIABLE ⟨a ∼ lock⟩

tri·col·or \'trī-ˌkə-lər\ n : a flag of three colors ⟨the French ∼⟩

tri·cy·cle \'trī-(ˌ)si-kəl\ n : a 3-wheeled vehicle usu. propelled by pedals

tri·dent \'trī-dᵊnt\ n [L trident-, tridens, fr. tri- three + dent-, dens tooth] : a 3-pronged spear

tried \'trīd\ adj **1** : found trustworthy through testing **2** : subjected to trials

tri·en·ni·al \trī-'e-nē-əl\ adj **1** : occurring or being done every three years **2** : lasting for three years — **triennial** n

¹**tri·fle** \'trī-fəl\ n **1** : something of little value or importance **2** : a dessert of cake soaked with liqueur and served with toppings (as fruit or cream)

²**trifle** vb **tri·fled; tri·fling 1** : to talk in a jesting or mocking manner **2** : to treat

someone or something as unimportant **3**
: DALLY, FLIRT **4** : to handle idly : TOY
— **tri·fler** *n*

tri·fling \'trī-fliŋ\ *adj* **1** : FRIVOLOUS **2**
: TRIVIAL, INSIGNIFICANT ⟨~ details⟩
♦ **Synonyms** PETTY, PALTRY, MEASLY,
INCONSEQUENTIAL

tri·fo·cals \trī-'fō-kəlz\ *n pl* : eyeglasses
with lenses having one part for close focus, one for intermediate focus, and one
for distant focus

tri·fo·li·ate \trī-'fō-lē-ət\ *adj* : having
three leaves or leaflets

¹trig \'trig\ *adj* : stylishly trim : SMART

²trig *n* : TRIGONOMETRY

¹trig·ger \'tri-gər\ *n* [alter. of earlier *trick-
er*, fr. D *trekker*, fr. MD *trecker* one that
pulls, fr. *trecken* to pull] : a movable lever
that activates a device when it is
squeezed; *esp* : the part of a firearm lock
moved by the finger to fire a gun — **trigger** *adj* — **trig·gered** *adj*

²trigger *vb* **1** : to fire by pulling a trigger
2 : to initiate, actuate, or set off as if by a
trigger ⟨remarks that ~ed a fight⟩

tri·glyc·er·ide \trī-'gli-sə-,rīd\ *n* : any of a
group of lipids that are formed from
glycerol and fatty acids and are widespread in animal tissue

trig·o·nom·e·try \,tri-gə-'nä-mə-trē\ *n*
: the branch of mathematics dealing with
the properties of triangles and esp. with
finding unknown angles or sides given
the size or length of some angles or sides
— **trig·o·no·met·ric** \-nə-'me-trik\ *also*
trig·o·no·met·ri·cal \-tri-kəl\ *adj*

trike \'trīk\ *n* : TRICYCLE

¹trill \'tril\ *n* **1** : the alternation of two musical tones a scale degree apart **2** : WAR-
BLE **3** : the rapid vibration of one speech
organ against another (as of the tip of the
tongue against the teeth)

²trill *vb* : to utter as or with a trill

tril·lion \'tril-yən\ *n* **1** : a thousand billions **2** *Brit* : a million billions — **trillion**
adj — **tril·lionth** \-yənth\ *adj or n*

tril·li·um \'tri-lē-əm\ *n* : any of a genus of
spring-blooming herbs that are related to
the lilies and have an erect stem bearing
a whorl of three leaves and a solitary
flower

tril·o·gy \'tri-lə-jē\ *n, pl* **-gies** : a series of
three dramas or literary or musical compositions that are closely related and develop one theme

¹trim \'trim\ *vb* **trimmed; trim·ming** [OE
trymian, trymman to strengthen, arrange,
fr. *trum* strong, firm] **1** : to put ornaments on : ADORN **2** : to defeat esp. re-
soundingly **3** : to make trim, neat, regular, or less bulky by or as if by cutting
⟨~ a beard⟩ ⟨~ a budget⟩ **4** : to cause
(a boat) to assume a desired position in
the water by arrangement of the load;
also : to adjust (as a submarine or airplane) for horizontal motion **5** : to
adjust (a sail) to a desired position **6** : to
change one's views for safety or expediency — **trim·ly** *adv* — **trim·mer** *n* —
trim·ness *n*

²trim *adj* **trim·mer; trim·mest** : showing
neatness, good order, or compactness ⟨a

~ figure⟩ ♦ **Synonyms** TIDY, TRIG,
SMART, SPRUCE, SHIPSHAPE

³trim *n* **1** : good condition : FITNESS **2**
: material used for ornament or trim-
ming; *esp* : the woodwork in the finish of
a house esp. around doors and windows
3 : the position of a ship or boat esp. with
reference to the horizontal; *also* : the relation between the plane of a sail and the
direction of a ship **4** : the position of an
airplane at which it will continue in level
flight with no adjustments to the controls
5 : something that is trimmed off

tri·ma·ran \'trī-mə-,ran, ,trī-mə-'ran\ *n* : a
sailboat with three hulls

tri·mes·ter \trī-'mes-tər, 'trī-,mes-tər\ *n* **1**
: a period of three or about three months
(as in pregnancy) **2** : one of three terms
into which an academic year is sometimes divided

trim·e·ter \'tri-mə-tər\ *n* : a line of verse
consisting of three metrical feet

trim·ming \'tri-miŋ\ *n* **1** : DEFEAT **2** : the
action of one that trims **3** : something
that trims, ornaments, or completes

tri·month·ly \trī-'mənth-lē\ *adj* : occurring every three months

trine \'trīn\ *adj* : THREEFOLD, TRIPLE

Trin·i·da·di·an \,tri-nə-'dä-dē-ən, -'dā-\ *n*
: a native or inhabitant of the island of
Trinidad — **Trinidadian** *adj*

Trin·i·tar·i·an \,tri-nə-'ter-ē-ən\ *n* : a believer in the doctrine of the Trinity —
Trin·i·tar·i·an·ism \-ē-ə-,ni-zəm\ *n*

Trin·i·ty \'tri-nə-tē\ *n* **1** : the unity of Father, Son, and Holy Spirit as three per-
sons in one Godhead **2** *not cap* : TRIAD

trin·ket \'triŋ-kət\ *n* **1** : a small ornament
(as a jewel or ring) **2** : TRIFLE 1

trio \'trē-ō\ *n, pl* **tri·os 1** : a musical composition for three voices or three instruments **2** : the performers of a trio **3** : a
group or set of three

¹trip \'trip\ *vb* **tripped; trip·ping 1** : to
move with light quick steps **2** : to catch
the foot against something so as to stumble or cause to stumble **3** : to make a
mistake : SLIP; *also* : to detect in a mis-
step **4** : EXPOSE **4** : to release (as a spring
or switch) by moving a catch; *also* : ACTI-
VATE ⟨~ an alarm⟩ **5** : to get high on a
usu. hallucinatory drug

²trip *n* **1** : JOURNEY, VOYAGE **2** : a quick
light step **3** : a false step : STUMBLE; *also*
: ERROR **4** : the action of tripping mechanically; *also* : a device for tripping **5**
: an intense experience; *esp* : one trig-
gered by a hallucinatory drug **6** : absorption in an attitude or state of mind ⟨an
ego ~⟩

tri·par·tite \trī-'pär-,tīt\ *adj* **1** : divided
into three parts **2** : having three corresponding parts or copies **3** : made between three parties ⟨a ~ treaty⟩

tripe \'trīp\ *n* **1** : stomach tissue esp. of a
ruminant (as an ox) used as food **2**
: something poor, worthless, or offensive
: TRASH

¹tri·ple \'tri-pəl\ *vb* **tri·pled; tri·pling 1**
: to make or become three times as great
or as many **2** : to hit a triple

²triple *n* **1** : a triple quantity **2** : a group

of three **3** : a hit in baseball that lets the batter reach third base

³triple *adj* **1** : being three times as great or as many **2** : having three units or members **3** : repeated three times

triple bond *n* : a chemical bond in which three pairs of electrons are shared by two atoms in a molecule

triple point *n* : the condition of temperature and pressure under which the gaseous, liquid, and solid forms of a substance can exist in equilibrium

trip·let \'tri-plət\ *n* **1** : a unit of three lines of verse **2** : a group of three of a kind **3** : one of three offspring born at one birth

tri·plex \'tri-ˌpleks, 'trī-\ *adj* : THREEFOLD, TRIPLE

¹trip·li·cate \'tri-pli-kət\ *adj* : made in three identical copies

²trip·li·cate \-plə-ˌkāt\ *vb* **-cat·ed; -cat·ing 1** : TRIPLE **2** : to provide three copies of ⟨~ a document⟩

³trip·li·cate \-pli-kət\ *n* : three copies all alike — used with *in* ⟨typed in ~⟩

tri·ply \'tri-plē, 'tri-pə-lē\ *adv* : in a triple degree, amount, or manner

tri·pod \'trī-ˌpäd\ *n* : something (as a caldron, stool, or camera stand) that rests on three legs — **tripod** *or* **tri·po·dal** \'trī-pə-dˀl, 'trī-ˌpä-\ *adj*

trip·tych \'trip-tik\ *n* : a picture or carving in three panels side by side

tri·reme \'trī-ˌrēm\ *n* : an ancient galley having three banks of oars

tri·sect \'trī-ˌsekt, trī-'sekt\ *vb* : to divide into three usu. equal parts — **tri·sec·tion** \'trī-sek-shən\ *n*

trite \'trīt\ *adj* **trit·er; trit·est** [L *tritus*, fr. pp. of *terere* to rub, wear away] : used so commonly that the novelty is worn off : STALE ♦ *Synonyms* HACKNEYED, STEREOTYPED, COMMONPLACE, CLICHÉD

tri·ti·um \'tri-tē-əm, 'tri-shē-\ *n* : a radioactive form of hydrogen with one proton and two neutrons in its nucleus and three times the mass of ordinary hydrogen

tri·ton \'trī-tˀn\ *n* : any of various large marine gastropod mollusks with a heavy elongated conical shell; *also* : the shell of a triton

trit·u·rate \'tri-chə-ˌrāt\ *vb* **-rat·ed; -rat·ing** : to rub or grind to a fine powder

¹tri·umph \'trī-əmf\ *n* **1** : the joy or exultation of victory or success **2** : VICTORY, CONQUEST — **tri·um·phal** \trī-'əm-fəl\ *adj*

²triumph *vb* **1** : to obtain victory : PREVAIL **2** : to celebrate victory or success exultantly — **tri·um·phant** \trī-'əm-fənt\ *adj* — **tri·um·phant·ly** *adv*

tri·um·vir \trī-'əm-vər\ *n, pl* **-virs** *also* **-vi·ri** \-və-ˌrī\ : a member of a triumvirate

tri·um·vi·rate \-və-rət\ *n* : a ruling body of three persons

tri·une \'trī-ˌün, -ˌyün\ *adj* : being three in one ⟨the ~ God⟩

triv·et \'tri-vət\ *n* **1** : a 3-legged stand : TRIPOD **2** : a usu. metal stand with short feet for use under a hot dish

triv·ia \'tri-vē-ə\ *n sing or pl* : unimportant

matters : obscure facts or details ⟨movie ~⟩

triv·i·al \'tri-vē-əl\ *adj* [L *trivialis* found everywhere, commonplace, fr. *trivium* crossroads, fr. *tri-* three + *via* way] : of little importance — **triv·i·al·i·ty** \ˌtri-vē-'a-lə-tē\ *n*

triv·i·um \'tri-vē-əm\ *n, pl* **triv·ia** \-vē-ə\ : the three liberal arts of grammar, rhetoric, and logic in a medieval university

tri·week·ly \trī-'wē-klē\ *adj* **1** : occurring or appearing three times a week **2** : occurring or appearing every three weeks — **triweekly** *adv*

tro·che \'trō-kē\ *n* : LOZENGE 2

tro·chee \'trō-(ˌ)kē\ *n* : a metrical foot of one accented syllable followed by one unaccented syllable — **tro·cha·ic** \trō-'kā-ik\ *adj*

trod *past and past part of* TREAD

trodden *past part of* TREAD

troi·ka \'trȯi-kə\ *n* [Russ *troĭka*, fr. *troe* three] : a group of three; *esp* : an administrative or ruling body of three

¹troll \'trōl\ *vb* **1** : to sing the parts of (a song) in succession **2** : to fish by trailing a lure or baited hook from a moving boat **3** : to sing or play jovially

²troll *n* : a lure used in trolling; *also* : the line with its lure

³troll *n* : a dwarf or giant in Scandinavian folklore inhabiting caves or hills

trol·ley *also* **trol·ly** \'trä-lē\ *n, pl* **trolleys** *also* **trollies 1** : a device (as a grooved wheel on the end of a pole) to carry current from a wire to an electrically driven vehicle **2** : a streetcar powered electrically by overhead wires **3** : a wheeled carriage running on an overhead rail or track

trol·ley·bus \'trä-lē-ˌbəs\ *n* : a bus powered electrically by overhead wires

trolley car *n* : TROLLEY 2

trol·lop \'trä-ləp\ *n* : a disreputable woman; *esp* : one who engages in sex promiscuously

trom·bone \träm-'bōn, 'träm-ˌbōn\ *n* [It, fr. *tromba* trumpet] : a brass wind instrument that consists of a long metal tube with two turns and a flaring end and that usu. has a movable slide to vary the pitch — **trom·bon·ist** \-'bō-nist, -ˌbō-\ *n*

tromp \'trämp, 'trȯmp\ *vb* **1** : TRAMP, MARCH **2** : to stamp with the foot **3** : to defeat decisively

trompe l'oeil \(ˌ)trȯmp-'lə-ē, trō⁰p-'lœi\ *n* [F *trompe-l'oeil*, lit., deceives the eye] : a style of painting in which objects are depicted with photographic detail

¹troop \'trüp\ *n* **1** : a cavalry unit corresponding to an infantry company **2** *pl* : armed forces : SOLDIERS **3** : a collection of people, animals, or things **4** : a unit of Girl Scouts or Boy Scouts under an adult leader

²troop *vb* : to move or gather in crowds

troop·er \'trü-pər\ *n* **1** : an enlisted cavalryman; *also* : a cavalry horse **2** : a mounted or state police officer

troop·ship \'trüp-ˌship\ *n* : a ship or aircraft for carrying troops

trope \\'trōp\ *n* : a word or expression used in a figurative sense

tro·phic \\'trō-fik\ *adj* : of or relating to nutrition

tro·phy \\'trō-fē\ *n, pl* **trophies** : something gained or given in conquest or victory esp. when preserved or mounted as a memorial

trop·ic \\'trä-pik\ *n* [ME *tropik*, fr. L *tropicus* of the solstice, fr. Gk *tropikos*, fr. *tropē* turn] **1** : either of the two parallels of latitude approximately 23½ degrees north (**Tropic of Can·cer**) or south (**Tropic of Cap·ri·corn**) of the equator where the sun is directly overhead when it reaches its most northerly or southerly point in the sky **2** *pl, often cap* : the region lying between the tropics — **trop·i·cal** \\-pi-kəl\ *or* **tropic** *adj*

tro·pism \\'trō-,pi-zəm\ *n* : an automatic movement by an organism in response to a source of stimulation; *also* : a reflex reaction involving this

tro·po·sphere \\'trō-pə-,sfir, 'trä-\ *n* : the part of the atmosphere between the earth's surface and the stratosphere in which most weather changes occur — **tro·po·spher·ic** \,trō-pə-'sfir-ik, ,trä-, -'sfer-\ *adj*

¹trot \\'trät\ *n* **1** : a moderately fast gait of a 4-footed animal (as a horse) in which the legs move in diagonal pairs **2** : a human jogging gait between a walk and a run

²trot *vb* **trot·ted; trot·ting 1** : to ride, drive, or go at a trot **2** : to proceed briskly : HURRY — **trot·ter** *n*

troth \\'träth, 'trȯth, 'trōth\ *n* **1** : pledged faithfulness **2** : one's pledged word; *also* : BETROTHAL

trou·ba·dour \\'trü-bə-,dȯr\ *n* [F, fr. Old Occitan *trobador*, fr. *trobar* to compose] : any of a class of poet-musicians flourishing esp. in southern France and northern Italy during the 11th, 12th, and 13th centuries

¹trou·ble \\'trə-bəl\ *vb* **trou·bled; trou·bling 1** : to agitate mentally or spiritually : DISTURB, WORRY **2** : to produce physical disorder in : AFFLICT **3** : to put to inconvenience **4** : RUFFLE ⟨~ the waters⟩ **5** : to make an effort ♦ **Synonyms** DISTRESS, AIL, UPSET — **trou·ble·some** *adj* — **trou·ble·some·ly** *adv* — **trou·blous** \\-bə-ləs\ *adj*

²trouble *n* **1** : the quality or state of being troubled esp. mentally **2** : an instance of distress or annoyance **3** : DISEASE, AILMENT ⟨heart ~⟩ **4** : EXERTION, PAINS ⟨took the ~ to phone⟩ **5** : a cause of disturbance or distress

trou·ble·mak·er \\-,mā-kər\ *n* : a person who causes trouble

trou·ble·shoot·er \\-,shü-tər\ *n* **1** : a worker employed to locate trouble and make repairs in equipment **2** : an expert in resolving disputes or problems — **trou·ble·shoot** *vb*

trough \\'trȯf, 'trȯth\ *n, pl* **troughs** \\'trȯfs, 'trȯvz; 'trȯths, 'trȯthz\ **1** : a long shallow open boxlike container esp. for water or feed for livestock **2** : a gutter along the eaves of a house **3** : a long channel or depression (as between waves or hills) **4** : an elongated area of low barometric pressure

trounce \\'traůns\ *vb* **trounced; trouncing 1** : to thrash or punish severely **2** : to defeat decisively

troupe \\'trüp\ *n* : COMPANY; *esp* : a group of performers on the stage — **troup·er** *n*

trou·sers \\'traů-zərz\ *n pl* [alter. of earlier *trouse*, fr. ScGael *triubhas*] : PANTS — **trouser** *adj*

trous·seau \\'trü-sō, trü-'sō\ *n, pl* **trousseaux** \\-sōz, -'sōz\ *or* **trous·seaus** [F] : the personal outfit of a bride

trout \\'traůt\ *n, pl* **trout** *also* **trouts** [ME, fr. OE *trūht*, fr. LL *tructa*, a fish with sharp teeth, fr. Gk *trōktēs*, lit., gnawer] : any of various mostly freshwater food and game fishes usu. smaller than the related salmons

trow \\'trō\ *vb, archaic* : THINK, SUPPOSE

trow·el \\'traů-(ə)l\ *n* **1** : a hand tool used for spreading, shaping, or smoothing loose or plastic material (as mortar or plaster) **2** : a scoop-shaped tool used in gardening — **trowel** *vb*

troy \\'trȯi\ *adj* : expressed in troy weight ⟨~ ounce⟩

troy weight *n* : a system of weights based on a pound of 12 ounces and an ounce of 480 grains (31 grams) — see WEIGHT table

tru·ant \\'trü-ənt\ *n* [ME, vagabond, idler, fr. AF, of Celt origin] : a student who stays out of school without permission — **tru·an·cy** \\-ən-sē\ *n* — **truant** *adj*

truce \\'trüs\ *n* **1** : ARMISTICE **2** : a respite esp. from something unpleasant

¹truck \\'trək\ *vb* **1** : EXCHANGE, BARTER **2** : to have dealings : TRAFFIC

²truck *n* **1** : BARTER **2** : DEALINGS **3** : small goods or merchandise; *esp* : vegetables grown for market

³truck *n* **1** : a wheeled vehicle (as a strong heavy automobile) designed for carrying heavy articles or hauling a trailer **2** : a swiveling frame with springs and one or more pairs of wheels used to carry and guide one end of a locomotive or railroad car

⁴truck *vb* **1** : to transport on a truck ⟨~s vegetables⟩ **2** : to be employed in driving a truck — **truck·er** *n*

truck farm *n* : a farm growing vegetables for market — **truck farmer** *n*

truck·le \\'trə-kəl\ *vb* **truck·led; truck·ling** : to yield slavishly to the will of another : SUBMIT ♦ **Synonyms** FAWN, TOADY, CRINGE, COWER

truc·u·lent \\'trə-kyə-lənt\ *adj* **1** : feeling or showing ferocity : SAVAGE **2** : aggressively self-assertive : BELLIGERENT — **truc·u·lence** \\-ləns\ *n* — **truc·u·len·cy** \\-lən-sē\ *n* — **truc·u·lent·ly** *adv*

trudge \\'trəj\ *vb* **trudged; trudg·ing** : to walk or march steadily and usu. laboriously ⟨*trudged* through the snow⟩

true \\'trü\ *adj* **tru·er; tru·est 1** : STEADFAST, LOYAL **2** : agreeing with facts or reality ⟨a ~ description⟩ **3** : CONSISTENT ⟨~ to expectations⟩ **4** : properly so called ⟨∼ love⟩   5 : RIGHTFUL ⟨∼ and lawful king⟩   6 : conformable to a standard or pattern; *also* : placed or formed accurately   ♦ **Synonyms** CONSTANT, STAUNCH, RESOLUTE, STEADFAST

²**true** *adv* 1 : TRUTHFULLY 2 : ACCURATELY ⟨the bullet flew straight and ∼⟩ *also* : without variation from type ⟨breed ∼⟩

³**true** *n* 1 : TRUTH, REALITY — usu. used with *the* 2 : the state of being accurate (as in alignment) ⟨out of ∼⟩

⁴**true** *vb* **trued; tru·ing** *also* **true·ing** : to bring or restore to a desired precision

true–blue *adj* : marked by unswerving loyalty ⟨a ∼ patriot⟩

true bug *n* : BUG 2

true-heart·ed \'trü-'här-təd\ *adj* : FAITHFUL, LOYAL ⟨a ∼ soldier⟩

truf·fle \'trə-fəl, 'trü-\ *n* 1 : the dark or light edible spore-bearing organ of any of several European fungi that grow underground; *also* : one of these fungi 2 : a candy made of chocolate, butter, and sugar shaped into balls and coated with cocoa

tru·ism \'trü-ˌi-zəm\ *n* : an undoubted or self-evident truth   ♦ **Synonyms** COMMONPLACE, PLATITUDE, CLICH

tru·ly \'trü-lē\ *adv* 1 : in all sincerity ⟨is ∼ sorry⟩ 2 : in agreement with fact ⟨report it ∼⟩ 3 : ACCURATELY 4 : in a proper or suitable manner

¹**trump** \'trəmp\ *n* : TRUMPET

²**trump** *n* : a card of a designated suit any of whose cards will win over a card that is not of this suit; *also* : the suit itself — often used in pl.

³**trump** *vb* : to take with a trump

trumped–up \'trəmpt-'əp\ *adj* : fraudulently concocted : SPURIOUS ⟨∼ charges⟩

trum·pery \'trəm-pə-rē\ *n* 1 : NONSENSE 2 : trivial articles : JUNK

¹**trum·pet** \'trəm-pət\ *n* 1 : a wind instrument consisting of a long curved metal tube flaring at one end and with a cup-shaped mouthpiece at the other 2 : something that resembles a trumpet or its tonal quality 3 : a funnel-shaped instrument for collecting, directing, or intensifying sound

²**trumpet** *vb* 1 : to blow a trumpet 2 : to proclaim on or as if on a trumpet ⟨∼ the news⟩ — **trum·pet·er** *n*

¹**trun·cate** \'trəŋ-ˌkāt, 'trən-\ *adj* : having the end square or blunt

²**truncate** *vb* **trun·cat·ed; trun·cat·ing** : to shorten by or as if by cutting : LOP — **trun·ca·tion** \ˌtrəŋ-'kā-shən\ *n*

trun·cheon \'trən-chən\ *n* : a police officer's billy club

trun·dle \'trən-dᵊl\ *vb* **trun·dled; trun·dling** : to roll along : WHEEL

trundle bed *n* : a low bed that can be stored under a higher bed

trunk \'trəŋk\ *n* 1 : the main stem of a tree 2 : the body of a person or animal apart from the head and limbs 3 : the main or central part of something 4 : a box or chest used to hold usu. clothes or personal effects (as of a traveler); *also* : the enclosed luggage space in the rear of

an automobile 5 : the long muscular nose of an elephant 6 *pl* : men's shorts worn chiefly for sports ⟨swimming ∼s⟩ 7 : a usu. major channel or passage

trunk line *n* : a transportation system handling long-distance through traffic

¹**truss** \'trəs\ *vb* 1 : to secure tightly : BIND 2 : to arrange for cooking by binding close the wings or legs of (a fowl) 3 : to support, strengthen, or stiffen by or as if by a truss

²**truss** *n* 1 : a collection of structural parts (as beams) forming a rigid framework (as in bridge or building construction) 2 : a device worn to reduce a hernia by pressure

¹**trust** \'trəst\ *n* 1 : assured reliance on the character, strength, or truth of someone or something 2 : a basis of reliance, faith, or hope 3 : confident hope 4 : financial credit 5 : a property interest held by one person for the benefit of another 6 : a combination of firms formed by a legal agreement; *esp* : one that reduces competition 7 : something entrusted to one to be cared for in the interest of another 8 : CARE, CUSTODY   ♦ **Synonyms** CONFIDENCE, DEPENDENCE, FAITH, RELIANCE

²**trust** *vb* 1 : to place confidence : DEPEND 2 : to be confident : HOPE 3 : ENTRUST 4 : to permit to stay or go or to do something without fear or misgiving 5 : to rely on or on the truth of : BELIEVE 6 : to extend credit to

trust·ee \ˌtrəs-'tē\ *n* 1 : a person to whom property is legally committed in trust 2 : a country charged with the supervision of a trust territory

trust·ee·ship \ˌtrəs-'tē-ˌship\ *n* 1 : the office or function of a trustee 2 : supervisory control by one or more nations over a trust territory

trust·ful \'trəst-fəl\ *adj* : full of trust : CONFIDING — **trust·ful·ly** *adv* — **trust·ful·ness** *n*

trust territory *n* : a non-self-governing territory placed under a supervisory authority by the Trusteeship Council of the United Nations

trust·wor·thy \-ˌwər-thē\ *adj* : worthy of confidence : DEPENDABLE ⟨a ∼ assistant⟩   ♦ **Synonyms** TRUSTY, TRIED, RELIABLE — **trust·wor·thi·ness** *n*

¹**trusty** \'trəs-tē\ *adj* **trust·i·er; -est** : TRUSTWORTHY, DEPENDABLE ⟨a ∼ friend⟩

²**trusty** \'trəs-tē, ˌtrəs-'tē\ *n, pl* **trust·ies** : a trusted person; *esp* : a convict considered trustworthy and allowed special privileges

truth \'trüth\ *n, pl* **truths** \'trüthz, 'trüths\ 1 : TRUTHFULNESS, HONESTY 2 : the real state of things : FACT 3 : the body of real events or facts : ACTUALITY 4 : a true or accepted statement or proposition ⟨the ∼s of science⟩ 5 : agreement with fact or reality : CORRECTNESS   ♦ **Synonyms** VERACITY, VERITY

truth·ful \'trüth-fəl\ *adj* : telling or disposed to tell the truth — **truth·ful·ly** *adv* — **truth·ful·ness** *n*

truth serum *n* : a drug held to induce a subject under questioning to talk freely

¹**try** \'trī\ *vb* **tried; try·ing** [ME *trien,* fr. AF *trier* to select, sort, examine, prob. fr. LL *tritare* to grind] **1** : to examine or investigate judicially **2** : to conduct the trial of **3** : to put to test or trial **4** : to subject to strain, affliction, or annoyance **5** : to extract or clarify (as lard) by melting **6** : to make an effort to do something : ATTEMPT, ENDEAVOR ♦ **Synonyms** ESSAY, ASSAY, STRIVE, STRUGGLE

²**try** *n, pl* **tries** : an experimental trial

try·ing *adj* : severely straining the powers of endurance

try on *vb* : to put on (a garment) to test the fit and looks

try out *vb* : to participate in competition esp. for a position on an athletic team or a part in a play — **try·out** \'trī-,au̇t\ *n*

tryp·to·phan \'trip-tə-,fan\ *n* : a crystalline essential amino acid that is widely distributed in proteins

tryst \'trist\ *n* **1** : an agreement (as between lovers) to meet **2** : an appointed meeting or meeting place — **tryst** *vb* — **tryst·er** *n*

TSA *abbr* Transportation Security Administration

tsar, tsarist *var of* CZAR, CZARIST

tsarina *var of* CZARINA

tset·se fly \'tset-sē-, 'tsēt-, 'tet-, 'tēt-, 'set-, 'sēt-\ *n* : any of several sub-Saharan African dipteran flies including the vector of sleeping sickness

TSgt *abbr* technical sergeant

T-shirt \'tē-,shərt\ *n* : a collarless short-sleeved or sleeveless cotton undershirt; *also* : an outer shirt of similar design — **T-shirt·ed** \-,shər-təd\ *adj*

tsk *a click; often read as* 'tisk\ *interj* — used to express disapproval

tsp *abbr* teaspoon; teaspoonful

T square *n* : a ruler with a crosspiece at one end for making parallel lines

tsu·na·mi \su̇-'nä-mē, tsu̇-\ *n* [Jp] : a tidal wave caused esp. by an underwater earthquake or volcanic eruption

TT *abbr* Trust Territories

TTY *abbr* teletypewriter

Tu *abbr* Tuesday

tub \'təb\ *n* **1** : a wide low bucketlike vessel **2** : BATHTUB; *also* : BATH **3** : the amount that a tub will hold

tu·ba \'tü-bə, 'tyü-\ *n* : a large low-pitched brass wind instrument

tub·al \'tü-bəl, 'tyü-\ *adj* : of, relating to, or involving a tube and esp. a fallopian tube (~ infection)

tube \'tüb, 'tyüb\ *n* **1** : any of various usu. cylindrical structures or devices; *esp* : one to convey fluids **2** : a slender hollow anatomical part (as a fallopian tube) functioning as a channel in a plant or animal body : DUCT **3** : a soft round container from which a paste is squeezed **4** : a tunnel for vehicular or rail travel **5** *Brit* : SUBWAY **6** : INNER TUBE **7** : ELECTRON TUBE **8** : TELEVISION — **tubed** \'tübd, 'tyübd\ *adj* — **tube·less** *adj* — **tube·like** \'tüb-,līk, 'tyüb-\ *adj*

tu·ber \'tü-bər, 'tyü-\ *n* : a short fleshy usu. underground stem (as of a potato plant) bearing minute scalelike leaves each with a bud at its base

tu·ber·cle \'tü-bər-kəl, 'tyü-\ *n* **1** : a small knobby prominence or outgrowth esp. on an animal or plant **2** : a small abnormal lump in an organ or on the skin; *esp* : one caused by tuberculosis

tubercle bacillus *n* : a bacterium that is the cause of tuberculosis

tu·ber·cu·lar \tu̇-'bər-kyə-lər, tyu̇-\ *adj* **1** : TUBERCULOUS **2** : of, resembling, or being a tubercle

tu·ber·cu·lin \tu̇-'bər-kyə-lən, tyu̇-\ *n* : a sterile liquid extracted from the tubercle bacillus and used in the diagnosis of tuberculosis esp. in children and cattle

tu·ber·cu·lo·sis \tu̇-,bər-kyə-'lō-səs, tyu̇-\ *n, pl* **-lo·ses** \-,sēz\ : a communicable bacterial disease that affects esp. the lungs and is typically marked by fever, cough, difficulty in breathing, and formation of tubercles — **tu·ber·cu·lous** \-'bər-kyə-ləs\ *adj*

tube·rose \'tüb-,rōz, 'tyüb-\ *n* : a bulbous herb related to the agaves and often grown for its spike of fragrant waxy-white flowers

tu·ber·ous \'tü-bə-rəs, 'tyü-\ *adj* : of, resembling, or being a tuber

tub·ing \'tü-biŋ, 'tyü-\ *n* **1** : material in the form of a tube; *also* : a length of tube **2** : a series or system of tubes

tu·bu·lar \'tü-byə-lər, 'tyü-\ *adj* : having the form of or consisting of a tube; *also* : made with tubes

tu·bule \'tü-byül, 'tyü-\ *n* : a small tube

¹**tuck** \'tək\ *vb* **1** : to pull up into a fold (~ed up her skirt) **2** : to make tucks in **3** : to put into a snug often concealing place (~ a book under the arm) **4** : to secure in place by pushing the edges under (~ in a blanket) **5** : to cover by tucking in bedclothes

²**tuck** *n* **1** : a fold stitched into cloth to shorten, decorate, or control fullness **2** : a cosmetic surgical operation for the removal of excess skin or fat (a tummy ~)

tuck·er \'tə-kər\ *vb* **tuck·ered; tuck·er·ing** : EXHAUST, FATIGUE (was ~ed out after a long day's work)

Tues *or* **Tue** *abbr* Tuesday

Tues·day \'tüz-dē, 'tyüz-, -dā\ *n* : the 3d day of the week

tu·fa \'tü-fə, 'tyü-\ *n* : a porous rock (as travertine) formed as a deposit from springs or streams

tuff \'təf\ *n* : a rock composed of volcanic detritus

¹**tuft** \'təft\ *n* **1** : a small cluster of long flexible outgrowths (as hairs); *also* : a bunch of soft fluffy threads cut off short and used as ornament **2** : CLUMP, CLUSTER — **tuft·ed** *adj*

²**tuft** *vb* **1** : to provide or adorn with a tuft **2** : to make (as a mattress) firm by stitching at intervals and sewing on tufts — **tuft·er** *n*

¹**tug** \'təg\ *vb* **tugged; tug·ging** **1** : to pull hard **2** : to struggle in opposition : CON-

TEND **3** : to move by pulling hard : HAUL **4** : to tow with a tugboat

²**tug** *n* **1** : a harness trace **2** : an act of tugging : PULL **3** : a straining effort **4** : a struggle between opposing people or forces **5** : TUGBOAT

tug·boat \-ˌbōt\ *n* : a strongly built boat used for towing or pushing

tug–of–war \ˌtəg-əv-ˈwȯr\ *n, pl* **tugs–of–war 1** : a struggle for supremacy **2** : an athletic contest in which two teams pull against each other at opposite ends of a rope

tu·grik *or* **tu·ghrik** \ˈtü-grik\ *n* — see MONEY table

tu·ition \tu̇-ˈi-shən, tyu̇-\ *n* : money paid for instruction ⟨college ∼⟩

tu·la·re·mia \ˌtü-lə-ˈrē-mē-ə, ˌtyu̇-\ *n* : an infectious bacterial disease esp. of wild rabbits, rodents, humans, and some domestic animals that in humans is marked by symptoms (as fever) similar to those of influenza

tu·lip \ˈtü-ləp, ˈtyu̇-\ *n* [NL *tulipa*, fr. Turk *tülbent* turban] : any of a genus of Eurasian bulbous herbs related to the lilies and grown for their large showy erect cup-shaped flowers; *also* : a flower or bulb of a tulip

tulip tree *n* : a tall No. American timber tree that is related to the magnolias and has greenish tulip-shaped flowers and soft white wood

tulle \ˈtül\ *n* : a sheer often stiffened silk, rayon, or nylon net ⟨a veil of ∼⟩

¹**tum·ble** \ˈtəm-bəl\ *vb* **tum·bled; tum·bling** [ME, fr. *tumben* to dance, fr. OE *tumbian*] **1** : to fall or cause to fall suddenly and helplessly **2** : to fall into ruin **3** : to perform gymnastic feats of rolling and turning **4** : to roll over and over : TOSS **5** : to issue forth hurriedly and confusedly **6** : to come to understand **7** : to throw together in a confused mass

²**tumble** *n* **1** : a disorderly state **2** : an act or instance of tumbling

tum·ble·down \ˈtəm-bəl-ˈdȧu̇n\ *adj* : DILAPIDATED, RAMSHACKLE ⟨a ∼ shack⟩

tum·bler \ˈtəm-blər\ *n* **1** : one that tumbles; *esp* : ACROBAT **2** : a drinking glass without foot or stem **3** : a movable obstruction in a lock that must be adjusted to a particular position (as by a key) before the bolt can be thrown

tum·ble·weed \ˈtəm-bəl-ˌwēd\ *n* : a plant that breaks away from its roots in autumn and is driven about by the wind

tum·brel *or* **tum·bril** \ˈtəm-brəl\ *n* **1** : CART **2** : a vehicle carrying condemned persons (as during the French Revolution) to a place of execution

tu·mid \ˈtü-məd, ˈtyu̇-\ *adj* **1** : SWOLLEN, DISTENDED **2** : BOMBASTIC, TURGID

tum·my \ˈtə-mē\ *n, pl* **tummies** : BELLY, ABDOMEN, STOMACH

tu·mor \ˈtü-mər, ˈtyu̇-\ *n* : an abnormal and functionless new growth of tissue that arises from uncontrolled cellular proliferation — **tu·mor·ous** *adj*

tu·mour *chiefly Brit var of* TUMOR

tu·mult \ˈtü-ˌməlt, ˈtyu̇-\ *n* **1** : UPROAR **2** : violent agitation of mind or feelings

tu·mul·tu·ous \tu̇-ˈməl-chə-wəs, tyu̇-, -chəs\ *adj* **1** : marked by tumult ⟨∼ applause⟩ **2** : tending to incite a tumult **3** : marked by violent upheaval ⟨∼ war years⟩

tun \ˈtən\ *n* : a large cask

tu·na \ˈtü-nə, ˈtyu̇-\ *n, pl* **tuna** *or* **tunas** : any of several mostly large marine fishes related to the mackerels and caught for food and sport; *also* : the flesh of a tuna

tun·able \ˈtü-nə-bəl, ˈtyu̇-\ *adj* : capable of being tuned — **tun·abil·i·ty** \ˌtü-nə-ˈbi-lə-tē, ˌtyu̇-\ *n*

tun·dra \ˈtən-drə\ *n* [Russ] : a treeless plain of arctic and subarctic regions

¹**tune** \ˈtün, ˈtyün\ *n* **1** : a succession of pleasing musical tones : MELODY **2** : correct musical pitch **3** : harmonious relationship : AGREEMENT ⟨in ∼ with the times⟩ **4** : general attitude ⟨changed his ∼⟩ **5** : AMOUNT, EXTENT ⟨in debt to the ∼ of millions⟩

²**tune** *vb* **tuned; tun·ing 1** : to adjust in musical pitch **2** : to bring or come into harmony : ATTUNE **3** : to put in good working order **4** : to adjust a radio or television receiver so as to receive a broadcast **5** : to adjust the frequency of the output of (a device) to a chosen frequency — **tun·er** *n*

tune·ful \-fəl\ *adj* : MELODIOUS, MUSICAL ⟨a ∼ ballad⟩ — **tune·ful·ly** *adv* — **tune·ful·ness** *n*

tune·less \-ləs\ *adj* **1** : UNMELODIOUS **2** : not producing music — **tune·less·ly** *adv*

tune–up \ˈtün-ˌəp, ˈtyün-\ *n* : an adjustment to ensure efficient functioning ⟨an engine ∼⟩

tung·sten \ˈtəŋ-stən\ *n* [Sw, fr. *tung* heavy + *sten* stone] : a gray-white hard heavy ductile metallic chemical element used esp. in carbide materials, electrical components, and alloys

tu·nic \ˈtü-nik, ˈtyu̇-\ *n* **1** : a usu. knee-length belted garment worn by ancient Greeks and Romans **2** : a hip-length or longer blouse or jacket

tuning fork *n* : a 2-pronged metal implement that gives a fixed tone when struck and is useful for tuning musical instruments

¹**tun·nel** \ˈtə-nᵊl\ *n* : an enclosed passage (as a tube or conduit); *esp* : one underground (as in a mine)

²**tunnel** *vb* **-neled** *or* **-nelled; -nel·ing** *or* **-nel·ling** : to make a tunnel through or under — **tun·nel·er** \ˈtə-nə-lər, ˈtə-nᵊl-ər\ *n*

tun·ny \ˈtə-nē\ *n, pl* **tunnies** *also* **tunny** : TUNA

tuque \ˈtük, ˈtyük\ *n* [CanF] : a warm knitted cone-shaped cap

tur·ban \ˈtər-bən\ *n* **1** : a headdress worn esp. by Muslims and made of a cap around which is wound a long cloth **2** : a headdress resembling a turban; *esp* : a woman's close-fitting hat without a brim

tur·bid \ˈtər-bəd\ *adj* [L *turbidus* confused, turbid, fr. *turba* confusion, crowd] **1** : cloudy or discolored by suspended particles ⟨a ∼ stream⟩ **2** : CONFUSED,

MUDDLED — **tur·bid·i·ty** \ˌtər-ˈbi-də-tē\ n

tur·bine \ˈtər-bən, -ˌbīn\ n [F, fr. L *turbin-, turbo* top, whirlwind, whirl] : an engine whose central driveshaft is fitted with curved vanes spun by the pressure of water, steam, or gas

tur·bo·fan \ˈtər-bō-ˌfan\ n : a jet engine having a fan driven by a turbine for supplying air for combustion

tur·bo·jet \-ˌjet\ n : an airplane powered by a jet engine (**turbojet engine**) having a turbine-driven air compressor supplying compressed air to the combustion chamber

tur·bo·prop \-ˌpräp\ n : an airplane powered by a jet engine (**turboprop engine**) having a turbine-driven propeller

tur·bot \ˈtər-bət\ n, pl **turbot** also **turbots** : a European flatfish that is a popular food fish; also : any of several similar flatfishes

tur·bu·lence \ˈtər-byə-ləns\ n : the quality or state of being turbulent

tur·bu·lent \-lənt\ adj 1 : causing violence or disturbance 2 : marked by agitation or tumult : TEMPESTUOUS ⟨a ~ marriage⟩ — **tur·bu·lent·ly** adv

tu·reen \tə-ˈrēn, tyu̇-\ n [F *terrine,* fr. MF, fr. fem. of *terrin* of earth] : a deep bowl from which foods (as soup) are served at the table

¹**turf** \ˈtərf\ n, pl **turfs** \ˈtərfs\ also **turves** \ˈtərvz\ 1 : the upper layer of soil bound by grass and roots into a close mat; also : a piece of this 2 : an artificial substitute for turf (as on a playing field) 3 : a piece of peat dried for fuel 4 : a track or course for horse racing; also : horse racing as a sport or business

²**turf** vb : to cover with turf

tur·gid \ˈtər-jəd\ adj 1 : being in a swollen state 2 : excessively embellished in style or language : BOMBASTIC ⟨~ writing⟩ — **tur·gid·i·ty** \ˌtər-ˈji-də-tē\ n

tur·key \ˈtər-kē\ n, pl **turkeys** [*Turkey,* country in western Asia and southeastern Europe; fr. confusion with the guinea fowl, supposed to be imported from Turkish territory] : a large No. American bird related to the domestic chicken and widely raised for food

turkey buzzard n : TURKEY VULTURE

turkey vulture n : an American vulture with a red head and whitish bill

Turk·ish \ˈtər-kish\ n : the language of Turkey — **Turkish** adj

tur·mer·ic \ˈtər-mə-rik\ n : a spice or dyestuff obtained from the large aromatic deep-yellow rhizome of an Indian perennial herb related to the ginger; also : this herb

tur·moil \ˈtər-ˌmȯi(-ə)l\ n : an extremely confused or agitated condition

¹**turn** \ˈtərn\ vb 1 : to move or cause to move around an axis or center : ROTATE, REVOLVE ⟨~ a wheel⟩ 2 : to effect a desired end by turning something ⟨~ the oven on⟩ 3 : WRENCH ⟨~ an ankle⟩ 4 : to change or cause to change position by moving through an arc of a circle ⟨~ed her chair to the fire⟩ 5 : to cause

to move around a center so as to show another side of ⟨~ a page⟩ 6 : to revolve mentally : PONDER 7 : to become dizzy : REEL 8 : to reverse the sides or surfaces of ⟨~ a pancake⟩ 9 : UPSET, DISORDER ⟨things were ~ed topsy-turvy⟩ 10 : to set in another esp. contrary direction 11 : to change one's course or direction 12 : to go around ⟨~ a corner⟩ 13 : BECOME ⟨my hair ~ed gray⟩ ⟨~ed twenty-one⟩ 14 : to direct toward or away from something; also : DEVOTE, APPLY 15 : to have recourse 16 : to become or make hostile 17 : to cause to become of a specified nature or appearance ⟨~s the leaves yellow⟩ 18 : to make or become spoiled : SOUR 19 : to pass from one state to another ⟨water ~s to ice⟩ 20 : CONVERT, TRANSFORM 21 : TRANSLATE, PARAPHRASE 22 : to give a rounded form to; esp : to shape by means of a lathe 23 : to gain by passing in trade ⟨~ a quick profit⟩ — **turn·able** \ˈtər-nə-bəl\ adj — **turn color** 1 : BLUSH 2 : to become pale — **turn loose** : to set free

²**turn** n 1 : a turning about a center or axis : REVOLUTION, ROTATION 2 : the action or an act of giving or taking a different direction ⟨make a left ~⟩ 3 : a change of course or of tendency ⟨a ~ for the better⟩ 4 : a place at which something turns : BEND, CURVE 5 : a short walk or trip round about ⟨take a ~ around the block⟩ 6 : an act affecting another ⟨did him a good ~⟩ 7 : a place, time, or opportunity accorded in a scheduled order ⟨waited his ~ in line⟩ 8 : a period of duty : SHIFT 9 : a short act esp. in a variety show 10 : a special purpose or requirement ⟨the job serves his ~⟩ 11 : a skillful fashioning ⟨neat ~ of phrase⟩ 12 : a single round (as of rope passed around an object) 13 : natural or special aptitude 14 : a usu. sudden and brief disorder of body or spirits; esp : a spell of nervous shock or faintness

turn·about \ˈtərn-ə-ˌbau̇t\ n 1 : a reversal of direction, trend, or policy 2 : RETALIATION

turn·buck·le \ˈtərn-ˌbə-kəl\ n : a link with a screw thread at one or both ends for tightening a rod or stay

turn·coat \-ˌkōt\ n : one who switches to an opposing side or party : TRAITOR

turn down vb : to decline to accept : REJECT — **turn·down** \ˈtərn-ˌdau̇n\ n

turn·er \ˈtər-nər\ n 1 : one that turns or is used for turning 2 : one that forms articles with a lathe

turn·ery \ˈtər-nə-rē\ n, pl **-er·ies** : the work, products, or shop of a turner

turn in vb 1 : to deliver up 2 : to inform on 3 : to acquit oneself of ⟨turn in a good job⟩ 4 : to go to bed

turn·ing \ˈtər-niŋ\ n 1 : the act or course of one that turns 2 : a place of a change of direction

tur·nip \ˈtər-nəp\ n 1 : a garden herb related to the cabbage with a thick edible usu. white root 2 : RUTABAGA 3 : the root of a turnip

turn·key \'tərn-ˌkē\ n, pl **turnkeys** : one who has charge of a prison's keys

turn-off \'tərn-ˌȯf\ n : a place for turning off esp. from an expressway

turn off vb **1** : to deviate from a straight course or a main road **2** : to stop the functioning or flow of **3** : to cause to lose interest; also : to evoke a negative feeling in ⟨violence on TV *turns* her *off*⟩

turn on vb **1** : to cause to flow, function, or operate **2** : to get high or cause to get high as a result of using a drug (as marijuana) **3** : EXCITE, STIMULATE

turn-out \'tərn-ˌaut\ n **1** : an act of turning out **2** : the number of people who participate or attend an event **3** : a widened place in a highway for vehicles to pass or park **4** : manner of dress **5** : net yield : OUTPUT

turn out vb **1** : EXPEL, EVICT **2** : PRODUCE **3** : to cause to stop functioning by turning a switch **4** : to come forth and assemble **5** : to get out of bed **6** : to prove to be in the end

¹turn·over \'tərn-ˌō-vər\ n **1** : UPSET **2** : SHIFT, REVERSAL **3** : a filled pastry made by turning half of the crust over the other half **4** : the volume of business done **5** : movement (as of goods or people) into, through, and out of a place **6** : the number of persons hired within a period to replace those leaving or dropped **7** : an instance of a team's losing possession of the ball esp. through error

²turnover adj : capable of being turned over

turn over vb : TRANSFER ⟨*turn* the job *over* to her⟩

turn·pike \'tərn-ˌpīk\ n [ME *turnepike* revolving frame bearing spikes and serving as a barrier, fr. *turnen* to turn + *pike*] **1** : TOLLGATE; also : an expressway on which tolls are charged **2** : a main road

turn·stile \-ˌstī(-ə)l\ n : a post with arms pivoted on the top set in a passageway so that persons can pass through only on foot one by one

turn·ta·ble \-ˌtā-bəl\ n : a circular platform that revolves (as for turning a locomotive or a phonograph record)

turn to vb : to apply oneself to work

turn up vb **1** : to come to light or bring to light : DISCOVER, APPEAR **2** : to raise or increase by or as if by turning a control **3** : to arrive at an appointed time or place **4** : to happen unexpectedly

tur·pen·tine \'tər-pən-ˌtīn\ n **1** : a mixture of oil and resin obtained from various cone-bearing trees (as pines) **2** : an oil distilled from turpentine or pine wood and used as a solvent and paint thinner

tur·pi·tude \'tər-pə-ˌtüd, -ˌtyüd\ n : inherent baseness : DEPRAVITY

tur·quoise also **tur·quois** \'tər-ˌkȯiz, -ˌkwȯiz\ n [ME *turkeis*, fr. AF *turkeise*, fr. fem. of *turkeis* Turkish, fr. *Turc* Turk] **1** : a blue, bluish green, or greenish gray mineral that is valued as a gem **2** : a light greenish blue color

tur·ret \'tər-ət\ n **1** : a little ornamental tower often at a corner of a building **2** : a

low usu. revolving structure (as on a tank or warship) in which one or more guns are mounted — **tur·ret·ed** \'tər-ə-təd\ adj

¹tur·tle \'tər-t³l\ n, archaic : TURTLEDOVE

²turtle n, pl **turtles** also **turtle** : any of an order of horny-beaked land, freshwater, or sea reptiles with the trunk enclosed in a bony shell

tur·tle·dove \'tər-t³l-ˌdəv\ n : any of several small pigeons noted for plaintive cooing

tur·tle·neck \-ˌnek\ n : a high close-fitting turnover collar (as on a sweater); also : a sweater or shirt with a turtleneck — **tur·tle·necked** \-ˌnekt\ adj

turves pl of TURF

Tus·ca·ro·ra \ˌtəs-kə-'rȯr-ə\ n, pl **Tuscarora** or **Tuscaroras** : a member of an American Indian people of No. Carolina and later of New York and Ontario

tusk \'təsk\ n : a long enlarged protruding tooth (as of an elephant, walrus, or boar) used esp. to dig up food or as a weapon — **tusked** \'təskt\ adj

tusk·er \'təs-kər\ n : an animal with tusks; esp : a male elephant with two normally developed tusks

¹tus·sle \'tə-səl\ n **1** : a physical struggle : SCUFFLE **2** : an intense argument, controversy, or struggle

²tussle vb **tus·sled; tus·sling** : to struggle roughly ⟨players *tussled* for the ball⟩

tus·sock \'tə-sək\ n : a dense tuft esp. of grass or sedge; also : a hummock in a marsh or bog bound together by roots — **tus·socky** adj

tu·te·lage \'tü-t³l-ij, 'tyü-\ n **1** : an act of guarding or protecting **2** : the state of being under a guardian or tutor **3** : instruction esp. of an individual

tu·te·lary \'tü-tə-ˌler-ē, 'tyü-\ adj : acting as a guardian ⟨~ deity⟩

¹tu·tor \'tü-tər, 'tyü-\ n **1** : a person charged with the instruction and guidance of another **2** : a private teacher

²tutor vb **1** : to have the guardianship of **2** : to teach or guide individually : COACH ⟨~ed her in Latin⟩ **3** : to receive instruction esp. privately

tu·to·ri·al \tü-'tȯr-ē-əl, tyü-\ n : a class conducted by a tutor for one student or a small number of students

tut·ti \'tü-tē, 'tü-, -ˌtē\ adj or adv [It, pl. of *tutto* all] : with all voices and instruments playing together — used as a direction in music

tut·ti-frut·ti \ˌtü-ti-'frü-tē, ˌtü-\ n [It, lit., all fruits] : a confection or ice cream containing chopped usu. candied fruits

tu·tu \'tü-(ˌ)tü\ n [F] : a short projecting skirt worn by a ballerina

tux·e·do \ˌtək-'sē-dō\ n, pl **-dos** or **-does** [*Tuxedo* Park, N.Y.] **1** : a usu. black or blackish blue jacket **2** : a semiformal evening suit for men

TV \'tē-'vē\ n : TELEVISION

TVA abbr Tennessee Valley Authority

TV dinner n : a frozen packaged dinner that needs only heating before serving

twad·dle \'twä-d³l\ n : silly idle talk : DRIVEL — **twaddle** vb

twain \'twān\ *n* **1** : TWO **2** : PAIR

¹twang \'twaŋ\ *n* **1** : a harsh quick ringing sound like that of a plucked bowstring **2** : nasal speech or resonance **3** : the characteristic speech of a region

²twang *vb* **twanged; twang·ing 1** : to sound or cause to sound with a twang **2** : to speak with a nasal twang

tweak \'twēk\ *vb* **1** : to pinch and pull with a sudden jerk and twitch **2** : to make small adjustments to — **tweak** *n*

tweed \'twēd\ *n* **1** : a rough woolen fabric made usu. in twill weaves **2** *pl* : tweed clothing; *esp* : a tweed suit

tweedy \'twē-dē\ *adj* **tweed·i·er; -est 1** : of or resembling tweed **2** : given to wearing tweeds **3** : suggestive of the outdoors in taste or habits **4** : ACADEMIC, SCHOLARLY

tween \'twēn\ *prep* : BETWEEN

¹tweet \'twēt\ *n* **1** : a chirping note **2** : a short message posted on the Twitter online service

²tweet *vb* **1** : to make a chirping sound **2** : to post a tweet

tweet·er \'twē-tər\ *n* : a small loudspeaker that reproduces sounds of high pitch

twee·zers \'twē-zərz\ *n pl* [obs. E *tweeze*, n., case for small implements, short for obs. E *etweese*, fr. pl. of obs. E *etwee*, fr. F *étui*] : a small pincerlike implement usu. held between the thumb and index finger and used for grasping something

twelve \'twelv\ *n* **1** : one more than 11 **2** : the 12th in a set or series **3** : something having 12 units — **twelfth** \'twelfth\ *adj or n* — **twelve** *adj or pron*

twelve·month \-,mənth\ *n* : YEAR

12–step \'twelv-,step\ *adj* : of, relating to, or being a program designed esp. to help someone overcome a problem (as an addiction) by following 12 tenets

twen·ty \'twen-tē\ *n, pl* **twenties** : two times ten — **twen·ti·eth** \-tē-əth\ *adj or n* — **twenty** *adj or pron*

twenty–twenty *or* **20/20** \,twen-tē-'twen-tē\ *adj* : characterized by a visual capacity for seeing detail that is normal for the human eye ⟨~ vision⟩

twice \'twīs\ *adv* **1** : on two occasions **2** : two times ⟨~ two is four⟩

¹twid·dle \'twi-dᵊl\ *vb* **twid·dled; twid·dling 1** : to be busy with trifles; *also* : to play idly with something **2** : to rotate lightly or idly

²twiddle *n* : TURN, TWIST

twig \'twig\ *n* : a small branch — **twig·gy** *adj*

twi·light \'twī-,līt\ *n* **1** : the light from the sky between full night and sunrise or between sunset and full night **2** : a state of imperfect clarity **3** : a period of decline

twilight zone *n* **1** : an area just beyond ordinary legal or ethical limits **2** : TWILIGHT **3** : a world of fantasy or unreality

twill \'twil\ *n* [ME *twyll*, fr. OE *twilic* having a double thread, part trans. of L *bilic-, bilix*, fr. *bi-* two + *licium* thread] **1** : a fabric with a twill weave **2** : a textile weave that gives an appearance of diagonal lines

twilled \'twild\ *adj* : made with a twill weave

¹twin \'twin\ *n* **1** : either of two offspring produced at a birth **2** : one of two persons or things closely related to or resembling each other

²twin *vb* **twinned; twin·ning 1** : to be coupled with another **2** : to bring forth twins

³twin *adj* **1** : born with one other or as a pair at one birth ⟨~ brother⟩ ⟨~ girls⟩ **2** : made up of two similar or related members or parts **3** : being one of a pair ⟨~ city⟩

¹twine \'twīn\ *n* **1** : a strong thread of two or three strands twisted together **2** : an act of entwining or interlacing — **twiny** *adj*

²twine *vb* **twined; twin·ing 1** : to twist together; *also* : to form by twisting **2** : INTERLACE, WEAVE **3** : to coil about a support **4** : to stretch or move in a sinuous manner — **twin·er** *n*

¹twinge \'twinj\ *vb* **twinged; twing·ing** *or* **twinge·ing** : to affect with or feel a sharp sudden pain

²twinge *n* : a sudden sharp stab (as of pain or distress)

¹twin·kle \'twiŋ-kəl\ *vb* **twin·kled; twin·kling 1** : to shine or cause to shine with a flickering or sparkling light **2** : to appear bright with merriment **3** : to flutter or flit rapidly — **twin·kler** *n*

²twinkle *n* **1** : a wink of the eyelids; *also* : the duration of a wink **2** : an intermittent radiance **3** : a rapid flashing motion — **twin·kly** \'twiŋ-klē\ *adj*

twin·kling \'twiŋ-kliŋ\ *n* : the time required for a wink : INSTANT

¹twirl \'twərl\ *vb* : to turn or cause to turn rapidly ⟨~ a baton⟩ ♦ **Synonyms** REVOLVE, ROTATE, CIRCLE, SPIN, SWIRL, PIROUETTE — **twirl·er** *n*

²twirl *n* **1** : an act of twirling **2** : COIL, WHORL — **twirly** \'twər-lē\ *adj*

¹twist \'twist\ *vb* **1** : to unite by winding one thread or strand round another **2** : WREATHE, TWINE **3** : to turn so as to hurt : SPRAIN ⟨~ed my ankle⟩ **4** : to twirl into spiral shape **5** : to subject (as a shaft) to torsion **6** : to turn from the true form or meaning **7** : to pull off or break by torsion **8** : to follow a winding course **9** : to turn around

²twist *n* **1** : something formed by twisting or winding **2** : an act of twisting : the state of being twisted **3** : a spiral turn or curve; *also* : SPIN **4** : a turning aside **5** : ECCENTRICITY **6** : a distortion of meaning **7** : an unexpected turn or development **8** : DEVICE, TRICK **9** : a variant approach or method

twist·er \'twis-tər\ *n* **1** : one that twists; *esp* : a ball with a forward and spinning motion **2** : TORNADO; *also* : WATERSPOUT **2**

¹twit \'twit\ *n* : a silly or foolish person

²twit *vb* **twit·ted; twit·ting** : to ridicule as a fault; *also* : TAUNT ♦ **Synonyms** DERIDE, MOCK, RAZZ

¹twitch \'twich\ *vb* **1** : to move or pull

with a sudden motion : JERK 2 : to move jerkily : QUIVER 3 : to have a twitch

²**twitch** *n* 1 : an act or movement of twitching 2 : a brief spasmodic contraction of muscle fibers

¹**twit·ter** \'twi-tər\ *vb* 1 : to make a succession of chirping noises 2 : to talk in a chattering fashion 3 : to tremble with agitation : FLUTTER

²**twitter** *n* 1 : a slight agitation of the nerves 2 : a small tremulous intermittent noise (as made by a swallow) 3 : a light chattering

twixt \'twikst\ *prep* : BETWEEN ⟨∼ the two extremes⟩

two \'tü\ *n, pl* **twos** 1 : one more than one 2 : the second in a set or series 3 : something having two units — **two** *adj or pron*

two cents *n* 1 *or* **two cents' worth** : an opinion offered on a topic under discussion 2 : a sum or object of very small value

two–faced \'tü-'fāst\ *adj* 1 : DOUBLE-DEALING, FALSE 2 : having two faces

two·fold \'tü-,fōld, -'fōld\ *adj* 1 : having two units or members 2 : being twice as much or as many — **twofold** \-'fōld\ *adv*

2,4–D \,tü-,fōr-'dē\ *n* : an irritant compound used esp. as a weed killer

2,4,5–T \-,fīv-'tē\ *n* : an irritant compound used esp. as an herbicide and defoliant

two·pence \'tə-pəns, *US also* 'tü-,pens\ *n* : the sum of two pence

two·pen·ny \'tə-pə-nē, *US also* 'tü-,pe-nē\ *adj* : of the value of or costing twopence

two–ply \'tü-'plī\ *adj* 1 : woven as a double cloth 2 : consisting of two strands or thicknesses ⟨∼ toilet paper⟩

two·some \'tü-səm\ *n* 1 : a group of two persons or things : COUPLE 2 : a golf match between two players

two–step \'tü-,step\ *n* : a ballroom dance performed with a sliding step in march or polka time; *also* : a piece of music for this dance — **two–step** *vb*

two–time \'tü-,tīm\ *vb* : to betray (a spouse or lover) by secret lovemaking with another — **two–tim·er** *n*

two–way *adj* : involving two elements or allowing movement or use in two directions or manners

2WD *abbr* two-wheel drive

twp *abbr* township

TWX *abbr* teletypewriter exchange

TX *abbr* Texas

ty·coon \tī-'kün\ *n* [Jp *taikun* feudal lord] 1 : a masterful leader (as in politics) 2 : a powerful businessman or industrialist

tying *pres part of* TIE

ty·iyn \tē-'en\ *n, pl* **tyiyn** — see *som* at MONEY table

tyke \'tīk\ *n* : a small child

tym·pan·ic membrane \tim-'pa-nik-\ *n* : EARDRUM

tym·pa·num \'tim-pə-nəm\ *n, pl* **-na** \-nə\ *also* **-nums** : EARDRUM; *also* : MIDDLE EAR — **tym·pan·ic** \tim-'pa-nik\ *adj*

¹**type** \'tīp\ *n* [ME, fr. LL *typus*, fr. L & Gk; L *typus* image, fr. Gk *typos* blow, impression, model, fr. *typtein* to strike, beat] 1

: a person, thing, or event that foreshadows another to come : TOKEN, SYMBOL 2 : MODEL, EXAMPLE 3 : a distinctive stamp, mark, or sign : EMBLEM 4 : rectangular blocks usu. of metal each having a face so shaped as to produce a character when printed 5 : the letters or characters printed from or as if from type 6 : general character or form common to a number of individuals and setting them off as a distinguishable class ⟨horses of draft ∼⟩ 7 : a class, kind, or group set apart by common characteristics ⟨a seedless ∼ of orange⟩; *also* : something distinguishable as a variety ⟨reactions of this ∼⟩ ♦ *Synonyms* SORT, NATURE, CHARACTER, DESCRIPTION

²**type** *vb* **typed; typ·ing** 1 : to represent beforehand as a type 2 : to produce a copy of; *also* : REPRESENT, TYPIFY 3 : to write with a typewriter or computer keyboard 4 : to identify as belonging to a type 5 : TYPECAST

type A *adj* : relating to, having, or being a personality marked esp. by impatience and aggressiveness

type·cast \-,kast\ *vb* **-cast; -cast·ing** 1 : to cast (an actor) in a part calling for characteristics possessed by the actor 2 : to cast repeatedly in the same type of role

type·face \-,fās\ *n* : all type of a single design

type 1 diabetes \'tīp-'wən-\ *n* : a form of diabetes mellitus usu. developing before adulthood and marked by severe insulin deficiency

type·script \'tīp-,skript\ *n* : typewritten matter

type·set \-,set\ *vb* **-set; -set·ting** : to set in type : COMPOSE — **type·set·ter** *n*

type 2 diabetes \-'tü-\ *n* : a form of diabetes mellitus developing esp. in adults and usu. in obese individuals and marked by excess sugar in the blood

type·write \-,rīt\ *vb* **-wrote** \-,rōt\; **-writ·ten** \-,ri-t³n\ : TYPE 3

type·writ·er \-,rī-tər\ *n* 1 : a machine for writing in characters similar to those produced by printers' type by means of types striking a ribbon to transfer ink or carbon impressions onto paper 2 : TYPIST

type·writ·ing \-,rī-tiŋ\ *n* : the use of a typewriter ⟨teach ∼⟩; *also* : writing produced with a typewriter

¹**ty·phoid** \'tī-,fȯid, tī-'fȯid\ *adj* : of, relating to, or being a communicable bacterial disease **(typhoid fever)** marked by fever, diarrhea, prostration, and intestinal inflammation

²**typhoid** *n* : TYPHOID FEVER

ty·phoon \tī-'fün\ *n* : a hurricane occurring esp. in the region of the Philippines or the China sea

ty·phus \'tī-fəs\ *n* : a severe infectious disease transmitted esp. by body lice, caused by a rickettsia, and marked by high fever, stupor and delirium, intense headache, and a dark red rash

typ·i·cal \'ti-pi-kəl\ *adj* 1 : being or having the nature of a type 2 : exhibiting the essential characteristics of a group 3

: conforming to a type — **typ·i·cal·i·ty** \ˌti-pə-'ka-lə-tē\ *n* — **typ·i·cal·ness** *n*

typ·i·cal·ly \-pi-k(ə-)lē\ *adv* **1** : in a typical manner **2** : in typical circumstances

typ·i·fy \'ti-pə-ˌfī\ *vb* **-fied; -fy·ing 1** : to represent by an image, form, model, or resemblance **2** : to embody the essential or common characteristics of

typ·ist \'tī-pist\ *n* : a person who types esp. as a job

ty·po \'tī-pō\ *n, pl* **typos** : an error (as of spelling) in typed or typeset material

ty·pog·ra·pher \tī-'pä-grə-fər\ *n* : one who designs or arranges printing

ty·pog·ra·phy \tī-'pä-grə-fē\ *n* : the art of printing with type; *also* : the style, arrangement, or appearance of printed matter — **ty·po·graph·ic** \ˌtī-pə-'gra-fik\ *or* **ty·po·graph·i·cal** \-fi-kəl\ *adj* — **ty·po·graph·i·cal·ly** *adv*

ty·ran·ni·cal \tə-'ra-ni-kəl, tī-\ *also* **ty·ran·nic** \-nik\ *adj* : of or relating to a tyrant : DESPOTIC **♦ Synonyms** ARBITRARY, ABSOLUTE, AUTOCRATIC — **ty·ran·ni·cal·ly** \-ni-k(ə-)lē\ *adv*

tyr·an·nise *Brit var of* TYRANNIZE

tyr·an·nize \'tir-ə-ˌnīz\ *vb* **-nized; -niz·ing** : to act as a tyrant : rule with unjust severity — **tyr·an·niz·er** *n*

ty·ran·no·saur \tə-'ra-nə-ˌsȯr\ *n* : a massive American flesh-eating dinosaur of the Cretaceous that had small forelegs and walked on its hind legs

ty·ran·no·sau·rus \tə-ˌra-nə-'sȯr-əs\ *n* : TYRANNOSAUR

tyr·an·nous \'tir-ə-nəs\ *adj* : unjustly severe — **tyr·an·nous·ly** *adv*

tyr·an·ny \'tir-ə-nē\ *n, pl* **-nies 1** : oppressive power **2** : the rule or authority of a tyrant : government in which absolute power is vested in a single ruler **3** : a tyrannical act

ty·rant \'tī-rənt\ *n* **1** : an absolute ruler : DESPOT **2** : a ruler who governs oppressively or brutally **3** : one who uses authority or power harshly

tyre *chiefly Brit var of* ²TIRE

ty·ro \'tī-rō\ *n, pl* **tyros** [ML, fr. L *tiro* young soldier, tyro] : a beginner in learning : NOVICE

tzar, tzarist *var of* CZAR, CZARIST

---

¹u \'yü\ *n, pl* **u's** *or* **us** \'yüz\ *often cap* : the 21st letter of the English alphabet

²u *abbr, often cap* unit

¹U \'yü\ *adj* : characteristic of the upper classes

²U \'yü\ *abbr* **1** [abbr. of *Union of Orthodox Hebrew Congregations*] kosher certification — often enclosed in a circle **2** university **3** unsatisfactory

³U *symbol* uranium

UAE *abbr* United Arab Emirates

UAR *abbr* United Arab Republic

UAW *abbr* United Automobile Workers

ubiq·ui·tous \yü-'bi-kwə-təs\ *adj* : existing or being everywhere at the same time : OMNIPRESENT — **ubiq·ui·tous·ly** *adv* — **ubiq·ui·ty** \-kwə-tē\ *n*

U–boat \'yü-ˌbōt\ *n* [trans. of G *U-boot*, short for *Unterseeboot*, lit., undersea boat] : a German submarine

UC *abbr* uppercase

ud·der \'ə-dər\ *n* : an organ (as of a cow) consisting of two or more milk glands enclosed in a large hanging sac and each provided with a nipple

UFO \ˌyü-(ˌ)ef-'ō\ *n, pl* **UFO's** *or* **UFOs** \-'ōz\ : an unidentified flying object; *esp* : FLYING SAUCER

ug·ly \'ə-glē\ *adj* **ug·li·er; -est** [ME, fr. ON *uggligr*, fr. *uggr* fear] **1** : FRIGHTFUL, DIRE **2** : offensive to the sight : HIDEOUS **3** : offensive or unpleasant to any sense **4** : morally objectionable : REPULSIVE **5** : likely to cause inconvenience or discomfort **6** : SURLY, QUARRELSOME ⟨an ∼ disposition⟩ — **ug·li·ness** \-glē-nəs\ *n*

UHF *abbr* ultrahigh frequency

UK *abbr* United Kingdom

ukase \yü-'kās, -'kāz\ *n* [F & Russ; F, fr. Russ *ukaz*, fr. *ukazat'* to show, order] : an edict esp. of a Russian emperor or government

Ukrai·ni·an \yü-'krā-nē-ən\ *n* **1** : a native or inhabitant of Ukraine **2** : a Slavic language of the Ukrainian people — **Ukrainian** *adj*

uku·le·le *also* **uke·le·le** \ˌyü-kə-'lā-lē\ *n* [Hawaiian *'ukulele*, fr. *'uku* flea + *lele* jumping] : a small usu. 4-stringed guitar popularized in Hawaii

ul·cer \'əl-sər\ *n* **1** : an open eroded sore of skin or mucous membrane often discharging pus **2** : something that festers and corrupts like an open sore — **ul·cer·ous** *adj*

ul·cer·ate \'əl-sə-ˌrāt\ *vb* **-at·ed; -at·ing** : to become affected with an ulcer — **ul·cer·a·tive** \'əl-sə-ˌrā-tiv\ *adj*

ul·cer·a·tion \ˌəl-sə-'rā-shən\ *n* **1** : the process of forming or state of having an ulcer **2** : ULCER 1

ul·na \'əl-nə\ *n* : the bone on the little-finger side of the human forearm; *also* : a corresponding bone of the forelimb of vertebrates above fishes

ul·ster \'əl-stər\ *n* : a long loose overcoat

ult *abbr* **1** ultimate **2** ultimo

ul·te·ri·or \ˌəl-'tir-ē-ər\ *adj* **1** : lying farther away : more remote **2** : situated beyond or on the farther side **3** : going beyond what is openly said or shown : HIDDEN ⟨∼ motives⟩

¹ul·ti·mate \'əl-tə-mət\ adj 1 : most remote in space or time : FARTHEST 2 : last in a progression : FINAL 3 : the best or most extreme of its kind 4 : arrived at as the last resort 5 : FUNDAMENTAL, ABSOLUTE, SUPREME ⟨∼ reality⟩ 6 : incapable of further analysis or division : ELEMENTAL 7 : MAXIMUM ♦ Synonyms CONCLUDING, EVENTUAL, LATEST, TERMINAL — ul·ti·mate·ly adv

²ultimate n : something ultimate

ul·ti·ma·tum \,əl-tə-'mā-təm, -'mä-\ n, pl -tums or -ta \-tə\ : a final condition or demand whose rejection will bring about a resort to forceful action

ul·ti·mo \'əl-tə-,mō\ adj [L ultimo mense in the last month] : of or occurring in the month preceding the present

¹ul·tra \'əl-trə\ adj : going beyond others or beyond due limits : EXTREME

²ultra n : EXTREMIST

ul·tra·con·ser·va·tive \,əl-kən-'sər-və-tiv\ adj : extremely conservative

ul·tra·high frequency \-'hī-\ n : a radio frequency between 300 and 3000 megahertz

¹ul·tra·light \'əl-trə-,līt\ adj : extremely light esp. in weight

²ultralight n : a very light recreational aircraft typically carrying only one person

ul·tra·ma·rine \,əl-trə-mə-'rēn\ n 1 : a deep blue pigment 2 : a very bright deep blue color

ul·tra·mi·cro·scop·ic \-,mī-krə-'skä-pik\ adj : too small to be seen with an ordinary microscope

ul·tra·mod·ern \-'mä-dərn\ adj : extremely or excessively modern in idea, style, or tendency

ul·tra·mon·tane \-'män-,tān, -,män-'tān\ adj 1 : of or relating to countries or peoples beyond the mountains (as the Alps) 2 : favoring greater or absolute supremacy of papal over national or diocesan authority in the Roman Catholic Church — ultramontane n, often cap — ul·tra·mon·tan·ism \-'män-tə-,ni-zəm\ n

ul·tra·pure \-'pyu̇r\ adj : of the utmost purity

ul·tra·short \-'shȯrt\ adj 1 : having a wavelength below 10 meters 2 : very short in duration

ul·tra·son·ic \,əl-trə-'sä-nik\ adj : having a frequency too high to be heard by the human ear — ul·tra·son·i·cal·ly \-ni-k(ə-)lē\ adv

ul·tra·son·ics \-'sä-niks\ n sing or pl 1 : ultrasonic vibrations 2 : the science of ultrasonic phenomena

ul·tra·sound \-,sau̇nd\ n 1 : ultrasonic vibrations 2 : the diagnostic or therapeutic use of ultrasound and esp. a technique involving the formation of a two-dimensional image of internal body structures 3 : a diagnostic examination using ultrasound

ul·tra·vi·o·let \-'vī-ə-lət\ adj : having a wavelength shorter than those of visible light and longer than those of X-rays ⟨∼ radiation⟩; also : producing or employing ultraviolet radiation — ultraviolet n

ul·tra vi·res \'əl-trə-'vī-rēz\ adv or adj [NL, lit., beyond power] : beyond the scope of legal power or authority

ul·u·late \'əl-yə-,lāt\ vb -lat·ed; -lat·ing : HOWL, WAIL

uma·mi \u̇-'mä-mē\ n [Jp, flavor] : a meaty or savory taste sensation produced esp. by monosodium glutamate

um·bel \'əm-bəl\ n : a flat-topped or rounded flower cluster in which the individual flower stalks all arise near one point on the main stem

um·ber \'əm-bər\ n : a brown earthy substance valued as a pigment either in its raw state or burnt — umber adj

umbilical cord n : a cord containing blood vessels that connects the navel of a fetus with the placenta of its mother

um·bi·li·cus \,əm-'bi-li-kəs, ,əm-bə-'lī-\ n, pl um·bi·li·ci \,əm-'bi-lə-,kī; ,əm-bə-'lī-,kī, -,sī\ or um·bi·li·cus·es : NAVEL — um·bil·i·cal \,əm-'bi-li-kəl\ adj

um·bra \'əm-brə\ n, pl umbras or umbrae \-(,)brē, -,brī\ 1 : SHADE, SHADOW 2 : the conical part of the shadow of a celestial body from which the sun's light is completely blocked

um·brage \'əm-brij\ n 1 : SHADE; also : FOLIAGE 2 : RESENTMENT, OFFENSE ⟨take ∼ at a remark⟩

um·brel·la \,əm-'bre-lə\ n 1 : a collapsible shade for protection against weather consisting of fabric stretched over hinged ribs radiating from a center pole 2 : something that provides protection 3 : something that covers a range of elements

umi·ak \'ü-mē-,ak\ n : an open Inuit boat made of a wooden frame covered with skins

ump \'əmp\ n : UMPIRE

um·pire \'əm-,pī(-ə)r\ n [ME oumpere, alter. of noumpere (the phrase a noumpere being understood as an oumpere), fr. AF nounpier single, odd, fr. non not + per equal, fr. L par] 1 : one having authority to decide finally a controversy or question between parties 2 : an official in a sport who rules on plays — umpire vb

ump·teen \'əmp-,tēn\ adj : very many : indefinitely numerous — ump·teenth \-,tēnth\ adj

UN abbr United Nations

un- \,ən, 'ən\ prefix 1 : not : IN-, NON- 2 : opposite of : contrary to

un·able \,ən-'ā-bəl\ adj 1 : not able 2 : UNQUALIFIED, INCOMPETENT

un·abridged \,ən-ə-'brijd\ adj 1 : not abridged ⟨an ∼ edition of Shakespeare⟩ 2 : complete of its class : not based on one larger ⟨an ∼ dictionary⟩

un·ac·com·pa·nied \,ən-ə-'kəm-pə-nēd\

unabashed	unabsorbent	unaccented	unacclimatized
unabated	unacademic	unacceptable	unaccommodating
unabsorbed			

adj : not accompanied; *esp* : being without instrumental accompaniment

un·ac·count·able \ˌən-ə-ˈkau̇n-tə-bəl\ *adj* **1** : not to be accounted for : INEXPLICABLE **2** : not responsible — **un·ac·count·ably** \-blē\ *adv*

un·ac·count·ed \-ˈkau̇n-təd\ *adj* : not accounted ⟨the loss was ∼ for⟩

un·ac·cus·tomed \ˌən-ə-ˈkəs-təmd\ *adj* **1** : not customary : not usual or common **2** : not accustomed or habituated ⟨∼ to noise⟩

un·adul·ter·at·ed \ˌən-ə-ˈdəl-tə-ˌrā-təd\ *adj* : PURE, UNMIXED ⟨∼ meat⟩ ♦ *Synonyms* ABSOLUTE, SHEER, SIMPLE, UNALLOYED, UNDILUTED, UNMITIGATED

un·af·fect·ed \ˌən-ə-ˈfek-təd\ *adj* **1** : not influenced or changed mentally, physically, or chemically **2** : free from affectation : NATURAL, GENUINE — **un·af·fect·ed·ly** *adv*

un·alien·able \-ˈāl-yə-nə-bəl, -ˈā-lē-ə-\ *adj* : INALIENABLE

un·aligned \ˌən-ə-ˈlīnd\ *adj* : not associated with any one of competing international blocs ⟨∼ nations⟩

un·al·loyed \ˌən-ə-ˈlȯid\ *adj* : UNMIXED, UNQUALIFIED, PURE ⟨∼ happiness⟩

un·al·ter·able \ˌən-ˈȯl-tə-rə-bəl\ *adj* : not capable of being altered or changed ⟨a ∼ rule⟩ — **un·al·ter·ably** \-blē\ *adv*

un–Amer·i·can \ˌən-ə-ˈmer-ə-kən\ *adj* : not characteristic of or consistent with American customs or principles

unan·i·mous \yu̇-ˈna-nə-məs\ *adj* [L *unanimus*, fr. *unus* one + *animus* mind] **1** : being of one mind : AGREEING **2** : formed with or indicating the agreement of all — **una·nim·i·ty** \ˌyü-nə-ˈni-mə-tē\ *n* — **unan·i·mous·ly** *adv*

un·arm \ˌən-ˈärm\ *vb* : DISARM

un·armed \-ˈärmd\ *adj* : not armed or armored ⟨∼ civilians⟩

un·as·sail·able \ˌən-ə-ˈsā-lə-bəl\ *adj* : not liable to doubt, attack, or question ⟨an ∼ argument⟩

un·as·sum·ing \ˌən-ə-ˈsü-miŋ\ *adj* : MODEST ⟨an ∼ librarian⟩ ⟨an ∼ manner⟩ ⟨an ∼ neighborhood⟩ ♦ *Synonyms* HUMBLE, LOWLY, MEEK

un·at·tached \ˌən-ə-ˈtacht\ *adj* **1** : not married or engaged **2** : not joined or united

un·avail·ing \ˌən-ə-ˈvā-liŋ\ *adj* : being of no avail — **un·avail·ing·ly** *adv*

un·avoid·able \ˌən-ə-ˈvȯi-də-bəl\ *adj* : not avoidable : INEVITABLE ⟨an ∼ fact⟩

♦ *Synonyms* CERTAIN, INELUCTABLE, INESCAPABLE, NECESSARY — **un·avoid·ably** \-blē\ *adv*

¹un·aware \ˌən-ə-ˈwer\ *adv* : UNAWARES

²unaware *adj* : not aware : IGNORANT ⟨∼ of the danger⟩ — **un·aware·ness** *n*

un·awares \-ˈwerz\ *adv* **1** : without knowing : UNINTENTIONALLY **2** : without warning : by surprise ⟨taken ∼⟩

un·bal·anced \ˌən-ˈba-lənst\ *adj* **1** : not in a state of balance **2** : mentally disordered **3** : not adjusted so as to make credits equal to debits

un·bar \-ˈbär\ *vb* : UNBOLT, OPEN

un·bear·able \ˌən-ˈber-ə-bəl\ *adj* : greater than can be borne ⟨∼ pain⟩ ♦ *Synonyms* INSUFFERABLE, INSUPPORTABLE, INTOLERABLE, UNENDURABLE, UNSUPPORTABLE — **un·bear·ably** \-blē\ *adv*

un·beat·able \-ˈbē-tə-bəl\ *adj* : not capable of being defeated ♦ *Synonyms* INDOMITABLE, INVINCIBLE, INVULNERABLE, UNCONQUERABLE

un·beat·en \-ˈbē-tᵊn\ *adj* **1** : not pounded, beaten, or whipped **2** : UNTRODDEN **3** : UNDEFEATED

un·be·com·ing \ˌən-bi-ˈkə-miŋ\ *adj* : not becoming : UNSUITABLE, IMPROPER ⟨conduct ∼ an officer⟩ ♦ *Synonyms* INDECOROUS, INDECENT, INDELICATE, UNSEEMLY — **un·be·com·ing·ly** *adv*

un·be·knownst \ˌən-bi-ˈnōnst\ *also* **un·be·known** \-ˈnōn\ *adj* : happening or existing without one's knowledge

un·be·lief \ˌən-bə-ˈlēf\ *n* : the withholding or absence of belief : DOUBT — **un·be·liev·ing** \-ˈlē-viŋ\ *adj*

un·be·liev·able \-ˈlē-və-bəl\ *adj* : too improbable for belief; *also* : of such a superlative degree as to be hard to believe ⟨a ∼ catch for a touchdown⟩ ♦ *Synonyms* INCONCEIVABLE, UNIMAGINABLE, UNTHINKABLE — **un·be·liev·ably** \-blē\ *adv*

un·be·liev·er \-ˈlē-vər\ *n* **1** : INFIDEL **2** : DOUBTER

un·bend \-ˈbend\ *vb* **-bent** \-ˈbent\; **-bend·ing** **1** : to free from being bent : make or become straight **2** : UNTIE **3** : to make or become less stiff or more affable : RELAX

un·bend·ing *adj* : formal and distant in manner : INFLEXIBLE

un·bi·ased \ˌən-ˈbī-əst\ *adj* : free from bias; *esp* : UNPREJUDICED ⟨an ∼ opinion⟩ ♦ *Synonyms* DISINTERESTED, DIS-

unaccredited	unaltered	unappreciated	unattainable
unacknowledged	unambiguous	unappreciative	unattended
unacquainted	unambiguously	unapproachable	unattested
unadapted	unambitious	unappropriated	unattractive
unadjusted	unanchored	unapproved	unauthentic
unadorned	unannounced	unarguable	unauthorized
unadventurous	unanswerable	unarguably	unavailable
unadvertised	unanswered	unarmored	unavowed
unaesthetic	unanticipated	unartistic	unawakened
unaffiliated	unapologetic	unashamed	unbaked
unafraid	unapparent	unasked	unbaptized
unaggressive	unappealing	unassertive	unbeloved
unaided	unappeased	unassisted	
unalike	unappetizing	unathletic	

PASSIONATE, IMPARTIAL, NONDISCRIMINATORY, NONPARTISAN, OBJECTIVE, UNCOLORED

un·bid·den \-'bi-dⁿn\ *also* **un·bid** \-'bid\ *adj* : not bidden : UNASKED

un·bind \-'bīnd\ *vb* **-bound** \-'baúnd\; **-bind·ing 1** : to remove bindings from : UNTIE **2** : RELEASE

un·blessed *also* **un·blest** \ˌən-'blest\ *adj* **1** : not blessed **2** : EVIL

un·block \-'bläk\ *vb* : to free from being blocked

un·blush·ing \-'blə-shiŋ\ *adj* **1** : not blushing : SHAMELESS ⟨~ greed⟩ — **un·blush·ing·ly** *adv*

un·bod·ied \-'bä-dēd\ *adj* **1** : having no body; *also* : DISEMBODIED **2** : FORMLESS

un·bolt \ˌən-'bōlt\ *vb* : to open or unfasten by withdrawing a bolt

un·bolt·ed \-'bōl-təd\ *adj* : not fastened by bolts

un·born \-'bórn\ *adj* : not yet born

un·bos·om \-'bù-zəm, -'bü-\ *vb* **1** : DISCLOSE, REVEAL **2** : to disclose the thoughts or feelings of oneself

un·bound·ed \-'baún-dəd\ *adj* : having no bounds or limits ⟨~ enthusiasm⟩ ♦ **Synonyms** BOUNDLESS, ENDLESS, IMMEASURABLE, LIMITLESS, MEASURELESS, UNLIMITED

un·bowed \ˌən-'baúd\ *adj* **1** : not bowed down **2** : UNSUBDUED ⟨~ by failure⟩

un·bri·dled \-'brī-dⁿld\ *adj* **1** : UNRESTRAINED ⟨~ enthusiasm⟩ **2** : not confined by a bridle

un·bro·ken \-'brō-kən\ *adj* **1** : not damaged **2** : not subdued or tamed **3** : not interrupted : CONTINUOUS

un·buck·le \-'bə-kəl\ *vb* : to loose the buckle of : UNFASTEN ⟨~ a belt⟩

un·bur·den \-'bər-dⁿn\ *vb* **1** : to free or relieve from a burden **2** : to relieve oneself of (as cares or worries)

un·but·ton \-'bə-tⁿn\ *vb* : to unfasten the buttons of ⟨~ your coat⟩

un·called–for \ˌən-'kóld-ˌfór\ *adj* : not called for, needed, or wanted

un·can·ny \-'ka-nē\ *adj* **1** : GHOSTLY, MYSTERIOUS, EERIE **2** : suggesting superhuman or supernatural powers ♦ **Synonyms** SPOOKY, UNEARTHLY, WEIRD — **un·can·ni·ly** \-'ka-nə-lē\ *adv*

un·ceas·ing \-'sē-siŋ\ *adj* : never ceasing ♦ **Synonyms** CEASELESS, CONTINUOUS, ENDLESS, INTERMINABLE, UNENDING, UNREMITTING — **un·ceas·ing·ly** *adv*

un·cer·e·mo·ni·ous \ˌən-ˌser-ə-'mō-nē-əs\ *adj* : acting without or lacking ordinary courtesy : ABRUPT ⟨his ~ dismissal⟩ — **un·cer·e·mo·ni·ous·ly** *adv*

un·cer·tain \ˌən-'sər-tⁿn\ *adj* **1** : not determined or fixed ⟨an ~ quantity⟩ **2** : subject to chance or change : not dependable ⟨~ weather⟩ **3** : not definitely known **4** : not sure ⟨~ of the truth⟩ — **un·cer·tain·ly** *adv*

un·cer·tain·ty \-tⁿn-tē\ *n* **1** : lack of certainty : DOUBT **2** : something that is uncertain ♦ **Synonyms** CONCERN, DOUBT, DUBIETY, INCERTITUDE, SKEPTICISM, SUSPICION

un·chain \ˌən-'chān\ *vb* : to free by or as if by removing a chain

un·charged \ˌən-'chärjd\ *adj* : having no electrical charge

un·char·i·ta·ble \-'cha-rə-tə-bəl\ *adj* : not charitable; *esp* : severe in judging others — **un·char·i·ta·ble·ness** *n* — **un·char·i·ta·bly** \-blē\ *adv*

un·chart·ed \-'chär-təd\ *adj* **1** : not recorded on a map, chart, or plan **2** : UNKNOWN ⟨discussion moving into ~ territory⟩

un·chris·tian \-'kris-chən\ *adj* **1** : not of the Christian faith **2** : contrary to the Christian spirit

un·churched \-'chərcht\ *adj* : not belonging to or connected with a church

un·cial \'ən-shəl, -chəl; 'ən-sē-əl\ *adj* : relating to or written in a form of script with rounded letters used esp. in early Greek and Latin manuscripts — **uncial** *n*

un·cir·cu·lat·ed \ˌən-'sər-kyə-ˌlā-təd\ *adj* : issued for use as money but kept out of circulation

un·cir·cum·cised \ˌən-'sər-kəm-ˌsīzd\ *adj* **1** : not circumcised **2** : HEATHEN

un·civ·il \ˌən-'si-vəl\ *adj* **1** : not civilized : BARBAROUS **2** : DISCOURTEOUS, ILL-MANNERED, IMPOLITE ⟨~ remarks⟩

un·civ·i·lized \-'si-və-ˌlīzd\ *adj* **1** : not civilized : BARBAROUS **2** : remote from civilization : WILD

un·clasp \-'klasp\ *vb* : to open by or as if by loosing the clasp

un·cle \'əŋ-kəl\ *n* [ME, fr. AF, fr. L *avunculus* mother's brother] **1** : the brother of one's father or mother **2** : the husband of one's aunt

un·clean \ˌən-'klēn\ *adj* **1** : morally or spiritually impure **2** : prohibited by ritual law for use or contact **3** : DIRTY, SOILED — **un·clean·li·ness** \-'klē-nəs\ *n* — **un·clean·ly** *adj* — **un·clean·ness** *n*

un·clench \-'klench\ *vb* : to open from a clenched position : RELAX

Uncle Tom \-'täm\ *n* [fr. *Uncle Tom*, faithful slave in Harriet Beecher Stowe's novel *Uncle Tom's Cabin* (1851-52)] : a black

unbleached	unburied	unchallenged	unchivalrous
unblemished	unburned	unchangeable	unchristened
unblinking	uncanceled	unchanged	unclad
unbound	uncanonical	unchanging	unclaimed
unbranched	uncap	unchaperoned	unclassified
unbranded	uncapitalized	uncharacteristic	uncleaned
unbreakable	uncared–for	unchaste	unclear
unbridgeable	uncataloged	unchastely	uncleared
unbruised	uncaught	unchasteness	
unbrushed	uncensored	unchastity	
unbudging	uncensured	unchecked	

who is eager to win the approval of whites

un·cloak \ˌən-ˈklōk\ *vb* **1** : to remove a cloak or cover from **2** : UNMASK, REVEAL ⟨~ an impostor⟩

un·clog \-ˈkläg\ *vb* : to remove an obstruction from

un·close \-ˈklōz\ *vb* : OPEN — **un·closed** \-ˈklōzd\ *adj*

un·clothe \-ˈklōth̯\ *vb* : to strip of clothes or a covering — **un·clothed** \-ˈklōthd\ *adj*

un·coil \ˌən-ˈkȯi(-ə)l\ *vb* : to release or become released from a coiled state

un·com·fort·able \ˌən-ˈkəmf-tə-bəl, -ˈkəm-fər-tə-\ *adj* **1** : causing discomfort **2** : feeling discomfort — **un·com·fort·ably** \-blē\ *adv*

un·com·mit·ted \ˌən-kə-ˈmi-təd\ *adj* : not committed; *esp* : not pledged to a particular belief, allegiance, or program ⟨~ voters⟩

un·com·mon \ˌən-ˈkä-mən\ *adj* **1** : not ordinarily encountered : UNUSUAL, RARE **2** : REMARKABLE, EXCEPTIONAL ⟨a soldier of ~ courage⟩ ♦ *Synonyms* EXTRAORDINARY, PHENOMENAL, SINGULAR, UNIQUE — **un·com·mon·ly** *adv*

un·com·mu·ni·ca·tive \ˌən-kə-ˈmyü-nə-ˌkā-tiv, -ni-kə-\ *adj* : not inclined to talk or impart information : RESERVED ♦ *Synonyms* CLOSEMOUTHED, RETICENT, SILENT, TACITURN

un·com·pro·mis·ing \ˌən-ˈkäm-prə-ˌmīzin\ *adj* : not making or accepting a compromise : UNYIELDING ♦ *Synonyms* ADAMANT, INFLEXIBLE, OBDURATE, RIGID, UNBENDING

un·con·cern \ˌən-kən-ˈsərn\ *n* **1** : lack of care or interest : INDIFFERENCE **2** : freedom from excessive concern

un·con·cerned \-ˈsərnd\ *adj* **1** : not having any part or interest **2** : not anxious or upset : free of worry ♦ *Synonyms* ALOOF, DETACHED, INCURIOUS, REMOTE, UNCURIOUS, UNINTERESTED — **un·con·cern·ed·ly** \-ˈsər-nəd-lē\ *adv*

un·con·di·tion·al \ˌən-kən-ˈdi-shə-nəl\ *adj* : not limited in any way ⟨~ surrender⟩ — **un·con·di·tion·al·ly** *adv*

un·con·di·tioned \-ˈdi-shənd\ *adj* **1** : not subject to conditions **2** : not acquired or learned : NATURAL ⟨~ responses⟩ **3** : producing an unconditioned response ⟨~ stimuli⟩

un·con·quer·able \ˌən-ˈkäŋ-kə-rə-bəl\ *adj* : incapable of being conquered or overcome : INDOMITABLE

un·con·scio·na·ble \-ˈkän-shə-nə-bəl\ *adj* **1** : not guided or controlled by conscience **2** : not in accordance with what is right or just ⟨~ sales practices⟩ ♦ *Synonyms* UNREASONABLE, UNDUE, UNJUSTIFIABLE, UNWARRANTABLE, UNWARRANTED — **un·con·scio·na·bly** \-blē\ *adv*

¹un·con·scious \ˌən-ˈkän-chəs, -shəs\ *adj* **1** : not knowing or perceiving : not aware **2** : not done consciously or on purpose **3** : having lost consciousness **4** : of or relating to the unconscious — **un·con·scious·ly** *adv* — **un·con·scious·ness** *n*

²unconscious *n* : the part of one's mental life of which one is not ordinarily aware but which is often a powerful force in influencing behavior

un·con·sti·tu·tion·al \ˌən-ˌkän-stə-ˈtü-shə-nəl, -ˈtyü-\ *adj* : not according to or consistent with the constitution of a state or society — **un·con·sti·tu·tion·al·i·ty** \-ˌtü-shə-ˈna-lə-tē, -ˌtyü-\ *n* — **un·con·sti·tu·tion·al·ly** \-ˈtü-shə-nə-lē, -ˈtyü-\ *adv*

un·con·trol·la·ble \ˌən-kən-ˈtrō-lə-bəl\ *adj* : incapable of being controlled : UNGOVERNABLE — **un·con·trol·la·bly** \-blē\ *adv*

un·con·ven·tion·al \-ˈven-chə-nəl\ *adj* : not conventional : being out of the ordinary — **un·con·ven·tion·al·i·ty** \-ˌven-chə-ˈna-lə-tē\ *n* — **un·con·ven·tion·al·ly** \-ˈven-chə-nə-lē\ *adv*

un·cork \ˌən-ˈkȯrk\ *vb* **1** : to draw a cork from **2** : to release from a sealed or pent-up state; *also* : to let go

un·count·ed \-ˈkau̇n-təd\ *adj* **1** : not counted **2** : INNUMERABLE

un·cou·ple \-ˈkə-pəl\ *vb* : DISCONNECT ⟨~ railroad cars⟩

un·couth \-ˈküth\ *adj* [ME, unfamiliar, fr. OE *uncūth*, fr. *un-* + *cūth* known] **1** : strange, awkward, and clumsy in shape or appearance **2** : vulgar in conduct or speech : RUDE ♦ *Synonyms* DISCOURTEOUS, ILL-MANNERED, IMPOLITE, UNGRACIOUS, UNMANNERED, UNMANNERLY

un·cov·er \-ˈkə-vər\ *vb* **1** : to make known : DISCLOSE, REVEAL **2** : to expose to view by removing some covering **3** : to take the cover from **4** : to remove the hat from; *also* : to take off the hat as a token of respect — **un·cov·ered** *adj*

un·crit·i·cal \ˌən-ˈkri-ti-kəl\ *adj* **1** : not critical : lacking in discrimination **2** : showing lack or improper use of critical standards or procedures — **un·crit·i·cal·ly** \-k(ə-)lē\ *adv*

un·cross \-ˈkrȯs\ *vb* : to change from a crossed position ⟨~ed his legs⟩

---

unclouded	uncompleted	unconsecrated	uncooked
uncluttered	uncomplicated	unconsidered	uncooperative
uncoated	uncomplimentary	unconsolidated	uncoordinated
uncollected	uncompounded	unconstrained	uncorrected
uncolored	uncomprehending	unconsumed	uncorroborated
uncombed	unconcealed	unconsummated	uncountable
uncombined	unconfined	uncontaminated	uncreative
uncomely	unconfirmed	uncontested	uncredited
uncomic	unconformable	uncontrolled	uncropped
uncommercial	uncongenial	uncontroversial	uncrowded
uncompensated	unconnected	unconverted	uncrowned
uncomplaining	unconquered	unconvincing	uncrystallized

unc·tion \'əŋk-shən\ n **1** : the act of anointing as a rite of consecration or healing **2** : exaggerated or insincere earnestness of language or manner

unc·tu·ous \'əŋk-chə-wəs\ adj [ME, fr. MF or ML; MF unctueus, fr. ML unctuosus, fr. L unctus act of anointing, fr. unguere to anoint] **1** : FATTY, OILY **2** : insincerely smooth in speech and manner ⟨an ~ politician⟩ — **unc·tu·ous·ly** adv

un·curl \ˌən-'kərl\ vb : to make or become straightened out from a curled or coiled position

un·cut \ˌən-'kət\ adj **1** : not cut down or into **2** : not shaped by cutting ⟨an ~ diamond⟩ **3** : not having the folds of the leaves slit ⟨an ~ book⟩ **4** : not abridged or curtailed ⟨the ~ version of the film⟩ **5** : not diluted ⟨~ heroin⟩

un·daunt·ed \-'dȯn-təd\ adj : not daunted : not discouraged or dismayed ♦ **Synonyms** BOLD, BRAVE, DAUNTLESS, FEARLESS, INTREPID, VALIANT — **un·daunt·ed·ly** adv

un·de·ceive \ˌən-di-'sēv\ vb : to free from deception, illusion, or error

un·de·mon·stra·tive \ˌən-di-'män-strə-tiv\ adj : restrained in expression of feeling : RESERVED

un·de·ni·able \ˌən-di-'nī-ə-bəl\ adj **1** : plainly true : INCONTESTABLE **2** : unquestionably excellent or genuine ♦ **Synonyms** INCONTROVERTIBLE, INDISPUTABLE, INDUBITABLE, UNQUESTIONABLE — **un·de·ni·ably** \-blē\ adv

¹un·der \'ən-dər\ adv **1** : in or into a position below or beneath something **2** : below some quantity, level, or limit ⟨$10 or ~⟩ **3** : in or into a condition of subjection, subordination, or unconsciousness ⟨the ether put him ~⟩

²un·der \ˌən-dər, 'ən-\ prep **1** : lower than and overhung, surmounted, or sheltered by ⟨~ a tree⟩ **2** : subject to the authority or guidance of ⟨served ~ him⟩ ⟨was ~ contract⟩ **3** : subject to the action or effect of ⟨~ the influence of alcohol⟩ **4** : within the division or grouping of ⟨items ~ this heading⟩ **5** : less or lower than (as in size, amount, or rank) ⟨earns ~ $5000⟩

³under \'ən-dər\ adj **1** : lying below, beneath, or on the ventral side **2** : facing or protruding downward **3** : SUBORDINATE **4** : lower than usual, proper, or desired in amount, quality, or degree

un·der·achiev·er \ˌən-dər-ə-'chē-vər\ n : one (as a student) who performs below an expected level of proficiency

un·der·act \-'akt\ vb : to perform feebly or with restraint

un·der·ac·tive \-'ak-tiv\ adj : characterized by abnormally low activity ⟨an ~ thyroid gland⟩ — **un·der·ac·tiv·i·ty** \-ˌak-'ti-və-tē\ n

un·der·age \-'āj\ adj : of less than mature or legal age

un·der·arm \-'ärm\ adj **1** : UNDERHAND **2** ⟨an ~ throw⟩ **2** : placed under or on the underside of the arms ⟨~ seams⟩ — **underarm** adv or n

un·der·bel·ly \'ən-dər-ˌbe-lē\ n **1** : a vulnerable area **2** : the underside of a body or mass

un·der·bid \ˌən-dər-'bid\ vb **-bid; -bidding 1** : to bid less than another **2** : to bid too low

un·der·body \'ən-dər-ˌbä-dē\ n : the lower parts of the body of a vehicle

un·der·bred \ˌən-dər-'bred\ adj : marked by lack of good breeding

un·der·brush \'ən-dər-ˌbrəsh\ n : shrubs, bushes, or small trees growing beneath large trees

un·der·car·riage \-ˌka-rij\ n **1** : a supporting framework or underside (as of an automobile) **2** : the landing gear of an airplane

un·der·charge \ˌən-dər-'chärj\ vb : to charge (as a person) too little — **undercharge** \'ən-dər-ˌchärj\ n

un·der·class \'ən-dər-ˌklas\ n : LOWER CLASS

un·der·class·man \ˌən-dər-'klas-mən\ n : a member of the freshman or sophomore class

un·der·clothes \'ən-dər-ˌklōthz\ n pl : UNDERWEAR

un·der·cloth·ing \-ˌklō-thiŋ\ n : UNDERWEAR

un·der·coat \-ˌkōt\ n **1** : a coat worn under another **2** : a growth of short hair or fur partly concealed by the longer and usu. coarser hairs of a mammal **3** : a coat of paint under another

un·der·coat·ing \-ˌkō-tiŋ\ n : a special waterproof coating applied to the underside of a vehicle

un·der·cov·er \ˌən-dər-'kə-vər\ adj : acting or executed in secret; esp : employed or engaged in secret investigation ⟨an ~ agent⟩

un·der·croft \'ən-dər-ˌkrȯft\ n [ME, fr. under + crofte crypt, fr. MD, fr. ML crupta, fr. L crypta] : a vaulted chamber under a church

un·der·cur·rent \-ˌkər-ənt\ n **1** : a current below the surface **2** : a hidden tendency of feeling or opinion ⟨an ~ of dread⟩

un·der·cut \ˌən-dər-'kət\ vb **-cut; -cutting 1** : to cut away the underpart of **2** : to offer to sell or to work at a lower rate than **3** : to strike (the ball) obliquely downward so as to give a backward spin or elevation to the shot — **un·der·cut** \'ən-dər-ˌkət\ n

un·der·de·vel·oped \ˌən-dər-di-'ve-ləpt\ adj **1** : not normally or adequately developed ⟨~ muscles⟩ **2** : having a relatively

uncultivated	undamaged	undecorated	undemanding
uncultured	undamped	undefeated	undemocratic
uncured	undated	undefended	undenominational
uncurious	undecided	undefiled	undependable
uncurtained	undecipherable	undefinable	
uncustomary	undeclared	undefined	

low level of economic development ⟨the ~ nations⟩

un·der·dog \'ən-dər-ˌdȯg\ n : the loser or predicted loser in a struggle

un·der·done \ˌən-dər-'dən\ adj : not thoroughly done or cooked : RARE

un·der·draw·ers \ˌən-dər-ˌdrȯrz, -ˌdrȯ-ərz\ n pl : UNDERPANTS

un·der·draw·ing \'ən-dər-ˌdrȯ-iŋ\ n : a preliminary sketch made prior to painting

un·der·em·pha·size \ˌən-dər-'em-fə-ˌsīz\ vb : to emphasize inadequately — **un·der·em·pha·sis** \-ˌsəs\ n

un·der·em·ployed \ˌən-im-'plȯid\ adj : having less than full-time or adequate employment

un·der·es·ti·mate \-'es-tə-ˌmāt\ vb : to set too low a value on

un·der·ex·pose \-ik-'spōz\ vb : to expose (a photographic plate or film) for less time than is needed — **un·der·ex·po·sure** \-'spō-zhər\ n

un·der·feed \ˌən-dər-'fēd\ vb **-fed** \-'fed\; **-feed·ing** : to feed with too little food

un·der·foot \-'fu̇t\ adv **1** : under the feet ⟨flowers trampled ~⟩ **2** : close about one's feet : in the way

un·der·fur \'ən-dər-ˌfər\ n : an undercoat of fur esp. when thick and soft

un·der·gar·ment \-ˌgär-mənt\ n : a garment to be worn under another

un·der·gird \ˌən-dər-'gərd\ vb : to brace up : STRENGTHEN

un·der·go \ˌən-dər-'gō\ vb **-went** \-'went\; **-gone** \-'gȯn, -'gän\; **-go·ing 1** : to submit to : ENDURE **2** : to go through : EXPERIENCE ⟨~ a change⟩

un·der·grad \'ən-dər-ˌgrad\ n : UNDERGRADUATE

un·der·grad·u·ate \ˌən-dər-'gra-jə-wət, -jə-ˌwāt\ n : a student at a university or college who has not received a first degree

¹un·der·ground \ˌən-dər-'grau̇nd\ adv **1** : beneath the surface of the earth **2** : in or into hiding or secret operation

²un·der·ground \'ən-dər-ˌgrau̇nd\ n **1** : a space under the surface of the ground; esp : SUBWAY **2** : a secret political movement or group; esp : an organized body working in secret to overthrow a government or an occupying power **3** : an avant-garde group or movement that operates outside the establishment

³underground \'ən-dər-ˌgrau̇nd\ adj **1** : being, growing, operating, or located below the surface of the ground ⟨~ stems⟩ **2** : conducted by secret means **3** : produced or published by the underground ⟨~ publications⟩; also : of or relating to the avant-garde underground

un·der·growth \'ən-dər-ˌgrōth\ n : low growth (as of herbs and shrubs) on the floor of a forest

¹un·der·hand \'ən-dər-ˌhand\ adv **1** : in an underhanded or secret manner **2** : with an underhand motion

²underhand adj **1** : UNDERHANDED **2** : made with the hand kept below the level of the shoulder ⟨an ~ pitch⟩

¹un·der·hand·ed \ˌən-dər-'han-dəd\ adv : UNDERHAND

²underhanded adj : marked by secrecy and

deception ⟨~ tactics⟩ — **un·der·hand·ed·ly** adv — **un·der·hand·ed·ness** n

un·der·lie \-'lī\ vb **-lay** \-'lā\; **-lain** \-'lān\; **-ly·ing** \-'lī-iŋ\ **1** : to lie or be situated under **2** : to be at the basis of : form the foundation of : SUPPORT

un·der·line \'ən-dər-ˌlīn\ vb **1** : to draw a line under **2** : EMPHASIZE, STRESS — **underline** n

un·der·ling \'ən-dər-liŋ\ n : SUBORDINATE, INFERIOR

un·der·lip \ˌən-dər-'lip\ n : the lower lip

un·der·ly·ing \ˌən-dər-'lī-iŋ\ adj **1** : lying under or below **2** : FUNDAMENTAL, BASIC ⟨~ principles⟩

un·der·mine \-'mīn\ vb **1** : to excavate beneath **2** : to weaken or wear away secretly or gradually ⟨~ authority⟩

un·der·most \'ən-dər-ˌmōst\ adj : lowest in relative position — **undermost** adv

¹un·der·neath \ˌən-dər-'nēth\ prep **1** : directly under **2** : under subjection to

²underneath adv **1** : below a surface or object : BENEATH **2** : on the lower side

un·der·nour·ished \ˌən-dər-'nər-isht\ adj : supplied with insufficient nourishment — **un·der·nour·ish·ment** \-'nər-ish-mənt\ n

un·der·pants \'ən-dər-ˌpants\ n pl : a usu. short undergarment for the lower trunk : DRAWERS

un·der·part \-ˌpärt\ n : a part lying on the lower side (as of a bird or mammal)

un·der·pass \-ˌpas\ n : a crossing of a highway and another way (as a road) at different levels; also : the lower level

un·der·pay \ˌən-dər-'pā\ vb : to pay less than what is normal or required

un·der·pin·ning \'ən-dər-ˌpi-niŋ\ n : the material and construction (as a foundation) used for support of a structure — **un·der·pin** \ˌən-dər-'pin\ vb

un·der·play \ˌən-dər-'plā\ vb : to treat or handle with restraint; esp : to play a role with subdued force

un·der·pop·u·lat·ed \ˌən-dər-'pä-pyə-ˌlā-təd\ adj : having a lower than normal or desirable density of population

un·der·priv·i·leged \-'priv-lijd, -'pri-və-lijd\ adj : having fewer esp. economic and social privileges than others

un·der·pro·duc·tion \ˌən-dər-prə-'dək-shən\ n : the production of less than enough to satisfy the demand or of less than the usual supply

un·der·rate \-'rāt\ vb : to rate or value too low

un·der·rep·re·sent·ed \-ˌre-pri-'zen-təd\ adj : inadequately represented

un·der·score \'ən-dər-ˌskȯr\ vb **1** : to draw a line under : UNDERLINE **2** : EMPHASIZE — **underscore** n

¹un·der·sea \ˌən-dər-'sē\ adj : being, carried on, or used beneath the surface of the sea

²undersea or **un·der·seas** \-'sēz\ adv : beneath the surface of the sea

un·der·sec·re·tary \ˌən-dər-'se-krə-ˌter-ē\ n : a secretary immediately subordinate to a principal secretary ⟨~ of state⟩

un·der·sell \-'sel\ vb **-sold** \-'sōld\; **-selling** : to sell articles cheaper than

un·der·sexed \-'sekst\ *adj* : deficient in sexual desire

un·der·shirt \'ən-dər-ˌshərt\ *n* : a collarless undergarment with or without sleeves

un·der·shoot \ˌən-dər-'shüt\ *vb* **-shot** \-'shät\; **-shoot·ing** 1 : to shoot short of or below (a target) 2 : to fall short of (a runway) in landing an airplane

un·der·shorts \'ən-dər-ˌshorts\ *n pl* : underpants for men or boys

un·der·shot \'ən-dər-ˌshät\ *adj* 1 : moved by water passing beneath ⟨an ~ waterwheel⟩ 2 : having the lower front teeth projecting beyond the upper when the mouth is closed

un·der·side \'ən-dər-ˌsīd, ˌən-dər-'sīd\ *n* : the side or surface lying underneath

un·der·signed \'ən-dər-ˌsīnd\ *n, pl* **undersigned** : one whose name is signed at the end of a document

un·der·sized \ˌən-dər-'sīzd\ *also* **un·der·size** \-'sīz\ *adj* : of a size less than is common, proper, or normal

un·der·skirt \'ən-dər-ˌskərt\ *n* : a skirt worn under an outer skirt; *esp* : PETTICOAT

un·der·staffed \ˌən-dər-'staft\ *adj* : inadequately staffed

un·der·stand \ˌən-dər-'stand\ *vb* **-stood** \-'stůd\; **-stand·ing** 1 : to grasp the meaning of : COMPREHEND 2 : to have thorough or technical acquaintance with or expertness in ⟨~ finance⟩ 3 : to have reason to believe ⟨I ~ you are leaving tomorrow⟩ 4 : INTERPRET ⟨we ~ this to be a refusal⟩ 5 : to have a sympathetic attitude 6 : to accept as settled ⟨it is *understood* that he will pay the expenses⟩ — **un·der·stand·able** \-'stan-də-bəl\ *adj*

un·der·stand·ably \-blē\ *adv* : as can be easily understood

¹**un·der·stand·ing** \ˌən-dər-'stan-diŋ\ *n* 1 : knowledge and ability to judge : INTELLIGENCE ⟨a person of ~⟩ 2 : agreement of opinion or feeling 3 : a mutual agreement informally or tacitly entered into

²**understanding** *adj* : endowed with understanding : TOLERANT, SYMPATHETIC

un·der·state \ˌən-dər-'stāt\ *vb* 1 : to represent as less than is the case 2 : to state with restraint esp. for effect — **un·der·state·ment** *n*

un·der·stood \ˌən-dər-'stůd\ *adj* 1 : agreed upon 2 : IMPLICIT

un·der·sto·ry \'ən-dər-ˌstōr-ē\ *n* : the vegetative layer between the top layer of a forest and the ground cover

un·der·study \'ən-dər-ˌstə-dē\ *n* : one who is prepared to act another's part or take over another's duties — **understudy** \'ən-dər-ˌstə-dē, ˌən-dər-'stə-dē\ *vb*

un·der·sur·face \'ən-dər-ˌsər-fəs\ *n* : UNDERSIDE

un·der·take \ˌən-dər-'tāk\ *vb* **-took** \-'tůk\; **-tak·en** \-'tā-kən\; **-tak·ing** 1 : to take upon oneself : set about ⟨~ a task⟩ 2 : to put oneself under obligation 3 : GUARANTEE, PROMISE

un·der·tak·er \'ən-dər-ˌtā-kər\ *n* : one whose business is to prepare the dead for burial and to arrange and manage funerals

un·der·tak·ing \'ən-dər-ˌtā-kiŋ, ˌən-dər-'tā-kiŋ; *2 is* 'ən-dər-ˌtā-kiŋ *only*\ *n* 1 : the act of one who undertakes or engages in any project 2 : the business of an undertaker 3 : something undertaken 4 : PROMISE, GUARANTEE

under–the–counter *adj* : UNLAWFUL, ILLICIT ⟨~ sale of drugs⟩

un·der·tone \'ən-dər-ˌtōn\ *n* 1 : a low or subdued tone or utterance 2 : a subdued color (as seen through and modifying another color)

un·der·tow \-ˌtō\ *n* : the current beneath the surface that flows seaward when waves are breaking upon the shore

un·der·val·ue \ˌən-dər-'val-yü\ *vb* 1 : to value or estimate below the real worth 2 : to esteem lightly

un·der·wa·ter \ˌən-dər-'wȯ-tər, -'wä-\ *adj* : lying, growing, worn, or operating below the surface of the water ⟨an ~ camera⟩ — **un·der·wa·ter** *adv*

under way \-'wā\ *adv* 1 : into motion from a standstill 2 : in progress

un·der·wear \'ən-dər-ˌwer\ *n* : clothing or a garment worn next to the skin and under other clothing

un·der·weight \ˌən-dər-'wāt\ *adj* : weighing below what is normal, average, or necessary — **underweight** *n*

un·der·wire \'ən-dər-ˌwī(-ə)r\ *n* : a wire running through the bottom of a brassiere to aid in support

un·der·world \'ən-dər-ˌwərld\ *n* 1 : the place of departed souls : HADES 2 : the side of the world opposite to one 3 : the world of organized crime

un·der·write \'ən-dər-ˌrīt, ˌən-dər-'rīt\ *vb* **-wrote** \-ˌrōt, -'rōt\; **-writ·ten** \-ˌri-t°n, -ˌri-t°n\; **-writ·ing** 1 : to write under or at the end of something else 2 : to set one's name to an insurance policy and thereby become answerable for a designated loss or damage 3 : to subscribe to : agree to 4 : to guarantee financial support of — **un·der·writ·er** *n*

un·de·sign·ing \ˌən-di-'zī-niŋ\ *adj* : having no artful, ulterior, or fraudulent purpose : SINCERE

un·de·sir·able \-'zī-rə-bəl\ *adj* : not desirable — **undesirable** *n*

un·de·vi·at·ing \ˌən-'dē-vē-ˌā-tiŋ\ *adj* : keeping a true course

un·dies \'ən-dēz\ *n pl* : UNDERWEAR; *esp* : women's underwear

undeserved	undifferentiated	undirected	undisputed
undeserving	undigested	undisciplined	undissolved
undesired	undignified	undisclosed	undistinguished
undetected	undiluted	undiscovered	undistributed
undetermined	undiminished	undiscriminating	undisturbed
undeterred	undimmed	undisguised	undivided
undeveloped	undiplomatic	undismayed	

un·do \ˌən-ˈdü\ *vb* **-did** \-ˈdid\; **-done** \-ˈdən\; **-do·ing** 1 : to make or become unfastened or loosened : OPEN 2 : to make null or as if not done : REVERSE 3 : to bring to ruin; *also* : UPSET

un·doc·u·ment·ed \ˌən-ˈdä-kyə-ˌmen-təd\ *adj* 1 : not supported by documentary evidence 2 : lacking documents required for legal immigration

un·do·ing *n* : a cause of ruin

un·doubt·ed \-ˈdaù-təd\ *adj* : not doubted or called into question : CERTAIN — **un·doubt·ed·ly** *adv*

¹un·dress \ˌən-ˈdres\ *vb* : to remove the clothes or covering of : STRIP, DISROBE

²undress *n* 1 : informal dress; *esp* : a loose robe or dressing gown 2 : ordinary dress : NUDITY

un·due \-ˈdü, -ˈdyü\ *adj* 1 : not due 2 : exceeding or violating propriety or fitness : EXCESSIVE ⟨~ force⟩

un·du·lant \ˈən-jə-lənt, ˈən-də-, -dyə-\ *adj* : rising and falling in waves ⟨~ hills⟩

undulant fever *n* : a human disease caused by bacteria from infected domestic animals or their products and marked by intermittent fever, chills, headache, weakness, and weight loss

un·du·late \-ˌlāt\ *vb* **-lat·ed; -lat·ing** [LL *undula* small wave, fr. L *unda* wave] 1 : to have a wavelike motion or appearance 2 : to rise and fall in pitch or volume ⟨*undulating* music⟩

un·du·la·tion \ˌən-jə-ˈlā-shən, ˌən-də-, -dyə-\ *n* 1 : wavy or wavelike motion 2 : pulsation of sound 3 : a wavy appearance or outline — **un·du·la·to·ry** \ˈən-jə-lə-ˌtȯr-ē, ˈən-də-, -dyə-\ *adj*

un·du·ly \ˌən-ˈdü-lē, ˈən-, -ˈdyü-\ *adv* : in an undue manner : EXCESSIVELY

un·dy·ing \-ˈdī-iŋ\ *adj* : not dying : IMMORTAL, PERPETUAL

un·earned \-ˈərnd\ *adj* : not earned by labor, service, or skill ⟨~ income⟩

un·earth \ˌən-ˈərth\ *vb* 1 : to dig up out of or as if out of the earth ⟨~ buried treasure⟩ 2 : to bring to light : DISCOVER ⟨~ a secret⟩

un·earth·ly \-lē\ *adj* 1 : not of or belonging to the earth 2 : SUPERNATURAL, WEIRD; *also* : ABSURD

un·easy \ˌən-ˈē-zē\ *adj* 1 : AWKWARD, EMBARRASSED ⟨~ among strangers⟩ 2 : disturbed by pain or worry; *also* : RESTLESS 3 : UNSTABLE ⟨an ~ truce⟩ — **un·eas·i·ly** \-ˈē-zə-lē\ *adv* — **un·eas·i·ness** \-ˈē-zē-nəs\ *n*

un·em·ployed \ˌən-im-ˈplȯid\ *adj* : not being used; *also* : having no job

un·em·ploy·ment \-ˈplȯi-mənt\ *n* 1 : lack of employment 2 : money paid at regular intervals (as by a government agency) to an unemployed person

un·end·ing \ˌən-ˈen-diŋ\ *adj* : having no ending : ENDLESS

un·equal \ˌən-ˈē-kwəl\ *adj* 1 : not alike (as in size, amount, number, or value) 2 : not uniform : VARIABLE 3 : badly balanced or matched 4 : INADEQUATE, INSUFFICIENT ⟨~ to the task⟩ — **un·equal·ly** *adv*

un·equaled *or* **un·equalled** \-kwəld\ *adj* : not equaled : UNPARALLELED ⟨an artist of ~ talent⟩

un·equiv·o·cal \ˌən-i-ˈkwi-və-kəl\ *adj* : leaving no doubt : CLEAR — **un·equiv·o·cal·ly** *adv*

un·err·ing \ˌən-ˈer-iŋ, ˌən-ˈər-\ *adj* : making no errors : CERTAIN, UNFAILING ⟨~ accuracy⟩ — **un·err·ing·ly** *adv*

UNES·CO \yü-ˈnes-kō\ *abbr* United Nations Educational, Scientific, and Cultural Organization

un·even \ˌən-ˈē-vən\ *adj* 1 : ODD 3 2 : not even : not level or smooth : RUGGED, RAGGED 3 : IRREGULAR; *also* : varying in quality — **un·even·ly** *adv* — **un·even·ness** *n*

un·event·ful \ˌən-i-ˈvent-fəl\ *adj* : lacking interesting or noteworthy incidents — **un·event·ful·ly** *adv*

un·evolved \ˌən-i-ˈvälvd\ *adj* 1 : not fully developed ⟨an ~ wine⟩ 2 : lacking cultural refinement

un·ex·am·pled \ˌən-ig-ˈzam-pəld\ *adj* : UNPRECEDENTED, UNPARALLELED ⟨fought with ~ passion⟩

un·ex·cep·tion·able \ˌən-ik-ˈsep-shə-nə-bəl\ *adj* : not open to exception or objection : beyond reproach

un·ex·pect·ed \ˌən-ik-ˈspek-təd\ *adj* : not expected : UNFORESEEN — **un·ex·pect·ed·ly** *adv*

un·fail·ing \ˌən-ˈfā-liŋ\ *adj* 1 : not failing, flagging, or waning : CONSTANT 2 : INEXHAUSTIBLE ⟨a subject of ~ interest⟩ 3 : INFALLIBLE, SURE ⟨an ~ test⟩ — **un·fail·ing·ly** *adv*

un·fair \-ˈfer\ *adj* 1 : marked by injustice, partiality, or deception : UNJUST 2 : not equitable in business dealings — **un·fair·ly** *adv* — **un·fair·ness** *n*

un·faith·ful \ˌən-ˈfāth-fəl\ *adj* 1 : not observant of vows, allegiance, or duty : DISLOYAL 2 : INACCURATE, UNTRUST-

undogmatic	uneatable	unenforceable	unexciting
undomesticated	uneaten	unenforced	unexpired
undone	uneconomic	unenlightened	unexplained
undoubled	uneconomical	unenterprising	unexploded
undramatic	unedifying	unenthusiastic	unexplored
undraped	unedited	unenviable	unexposed
undreamed	uneducated	unequipped	unexpressed
undressed	unembarrassed	unessential	unexpurgated
undrinkable	unemotional	unethical	unfading
undulled	unemphatic	unexamined	unfaltering
undutiful	unenclosed	unexcelled	
undyed	unencumbered	unexceptional	
uneager	unendurable	unexcited	

WORTHY ⟨an ∼ copy of a document⟩ —
un·faith·ful·ly \adv — **un·faith·ful·ness**
n

un·fa·mil·iar \ˌən-fə-ˈmil-yər\ adj 1 : not
well-known : STRANGE ⟨an ∼ place⟩ 2
: not well acquainted ⟨∼ with the sub-
ject⟩ — **un·fa·mil·iar·i·ty** \-ˌmi-lē-ˈer-,
-ˈyer-\ n

un·fas·ten \ˌən-ˈfa-sᵊn\ vb : to make or
become loose : UNDO, DETACH

un·feel·ing \-ˈfē-liŋ\ adj 1 : lacking feeling : INSENSATE 2 : HARDHEARTED,
CRUEL — **un·feel·ing·ly** adv

un·feigned \-ˈfānd\ adj : not feigned : not
hypocritical

un·fet·ter \-ˈfe-tər\ vb 1 : to free from
fetters 2 : LIBERATE

un·fil·ial \ˌən-ˈfi-lē-əl, -ˈfil-yəl\ adj : not
observing the obligations of a child to a
parent : UNDUTIFUL

un·fin·ished \ˌən-ˈfi-nisht\ adj 1 : not
brought to an end 2 : being in a rough or
unpolished state

¹**un·fit** \-ˈfit\ adj : not fit or suitable; esp
: physically or mentally unsound ⟨∼ for
army service⟩ — **un·fit·ness** n

²**unfit** vb : to make unfit : DISQUALIFY

un·fix \-ˈfiks\ vb 1 : to loosen from a fastening : DETACH 2 : UNSETTLE

un·flap·pa·ble \-ˈfla-pə-bəl\ adj : not easily upset or panicked — **un·flap·pa·bly**
adv

un·fledged \ˌən-ˈflejd\ adj 1 : not feathered
or ready for flight; also : IMMATURE,
CALLOW

un·flinch·ing \-ˈflin-chiŋ\ adj : not flinch-
ing or shrinking : STEADFAST — **un-
flinch·ing·ly** adv

un·fold \-ˈfōld\ vb 1 : to open the folds of
: open up 2 : to lay open to view : DIS-
CLOSE 3 : BLOSSOM, DEVELOP

un·for·get·ta·ble \ˌən-fər-ˈge-tə-bəl\ adj
: incapable of being forgotten ⟨an ∼
event⟩ — **un·for·get·ta·bly** \-blē\ adv

un·formed \-ˈfórmd\ adj : not regularly
formed or ordered : UNDEVELOPED

un·for·tu·nate \-ˈfór-chə-nət\ adj 1 : not
fortunate : UNLUCKY 2 : attended with
misfortune 3 : UNSUITABLE ⟨an ∼
choice of words⟩ — **unfortunate** n

un·for·tu·nate·ly \-nət-lē\ adv 1 : in an
unfortunate manner 2 : it is unfortunate

un·found·ed \ˌən-ˈfaún-dəd\ adj : lacking
a sound basis : GROUNDLESS

un·freeze \-ˈfrēz\ vb **-froze** \-ˈfrōz\; **-fro-
zen** \-ˈfrō-zᵊn\; **-freez·ing** 1 : to cause to
thaw 2 : to remove from a freeze ⟨∼
prices⟩

un·fre·quent·ed \ˌən-frē-ˈkwen-təd; ˌən-

¹**frē-kwən-\ adj : seldom visited or traveled over

un·friend·ly \ˌən-ˈfrend-lē\ adj 1 : not
friendly or kind : HOSTILE 2 : UNFAVOR-
ABLE ⟨∼ to new business⟩ — **un·friend-
li·ness** \-lē-nəs\ n

un·frock \-ˈfräk\ vb : DEFROCK

un·fruit·ful \-ˈfrüt-fəl\ adj 1 : not producing fruit or offspring : BARREN 2 : yielding no valuable result : UNPROFITABLE
— **un·fruit·ful·ness** n

un·furl \-ˈfərl\ vb : to loose from a furled
state : UNFOLD

un·gain·ly \-ˈgān-lē\ adj [un- + obs. gainly
proper, becoming, fr. gain direct, handy,
fr. ME geyn, fr. OE gēn, fr. ON gegn
against] : CLUMSY, AWKWARD — **un-
gain·li·ness** \-lē-nəs\ n

un·gen·er·ous \ˌən-ˈje-nə-rəs\ adj : not
generous or liberal : STINGY

un·glued \ˌən-ˈglüd\ adj : UPSET, DISOR-
DERED ⟨became ∼ when she was re-
fused⟩

un·god·ly \ˌən-ˈgäd-lē, -ˈgòd-\ adj 1 : IM-
PIOUS, IRRELIGIOUS 2 : SINFUL, WICKED
3 : OUTRAGEOUS ⟨an ∼ hour⟩ — **un-
god·li·ness** \-lē-nəs\ n

un·gov·ern·able \-ˈgə-vər-nə-bəl\ adj
: not capable of being governed, guided,
or restrained : UNRULY

un·gra·cious \-ˈgrā-shəs\ adj 1 : not
courteous : RUDE 2 : not pleasing : DIS-
AGREEABLE ⟨an ∼ task⟩

un·grate·ful \ˌən-ˈgrāt-fəl\ adj 1 : not
thankful for favors 2 : DISAGREEABLE;
also : THANKLESS — **un·grate·ful·ly** adv
— **un·grate·ful·ness** n

un·guard·ed \-ˈgär-dəd\ adj 1 : UNPRO-
TECTED 2 : DIRECT, INCAUTIOUS ⟨∼
remarks⟩

un·guent \ˈəŋ-gwənt, ˈən-\ n : a soothing
or healing salve : OINTMENT

¹**un·gu·late** \ˈəŋ-gyə-lət, ˈən-, -ˌlāt\ adj [LL
ungulatus, fr. L ungula hoof, fr. unguis
nail, hoof] : having hoofs

²**ungulate** n : a hoofed mammal (as a cow,
horse, or rhinoceros)

un·hal·lowed \ˌən-ˈha-lōd\ adj 1 : not
consecrated : UNHOLY 2 : IMPIOUS, PRO-
FANE 3 : contrary to accepted standards
: IMMORAL

un·hand \ˌən-ˈhand\ vb : to remove the
hand from : let go

un·hand·some \-ˈhan-səm\ adj 1 : not
beautiful or handsome : HOMELY 2 : UN-
BECOMING 3 : DISCOURTEOUS, RUDE

un·handy \-ˈhan-dē\ adj : INCONVE-
NIENT; also : AWKWARD

un·hap·py \-ˈha-pē\ adj 1 : UNLUCKY,

UNFORTUNATE ⟨an ∼ coincidence⟩ **2** : SAD, MISERABLE **3** : INAPPROPRIATE ⟨an ∼ choice⟩ — **un·hap·pi·ly** \-'ha-pə-lē\ adv — **un·hap·pi·ness** \-pē-nəs\ n

un·har·ness \-'här-nəs\ vb : to remove the harness from (as a horse)

un·healthy \-'hel-thē\ adj **1** : not conducive to health : UNWHOLESOME ⟨∼ foods⟩ **2** : SICKLY, DISEASED

un·heard \-'hərd\ adj **1** : not heard **2** : not granted a hearing

unheard–of adj : previously unknown; esp : UNPRECEDENTED ⟨moving at ∼ speeds⟩

un·hinge \ˌən-'hinj\ vb **1** : to make unstable esp. mentally ⟨∼ by grief⟩ **2** : to take from the hinges

un·hitch \-'hich\ vb : UNFASTEN, LOOSE

un·ho·ly \-'hō-lē\ adj **1** : not holy : PROFANE, WICKED **2** : very unpleasant ⟨an ∼ mess⟩ — **un·ho·li·ness** \-lē-nəs\ n

un·hook \-'hůk\ vb : to loose from a hook

un·horse \-'hórs\ vb : to dislodge from or as if from a horse

uni·cam·er·al \ˌyü-ni-'ka-mə-rəl\ adj : having a single legislative house or chamber

UNI·CEF \'yü-nə-ˌsef\ abbr [United Nations International Children's Emergency Fund, its former name] United Nations Children's Fund

uni·cel·lu·lar \ˌyü-ni-'sel-yə-lər\ adj : having or consisting of a single cell

uni·corn \'yü-nə-ˌkórn\ n [ME unicorne, fr. AF, fr. LL unicornis, fr. L, having one horn, fr. unus one + cornu horn] : a mythical animal with one horn in the middle of the forehead

uni·cy·cle \'yü-ni-ˌsī-kəl\ n : a vehicle that has a single wheel and is usu. propelled by pedals

uni·di·rec·tion·al \ˌyü-ni-də-'rek-shə-nəl, -dī-\ adj : having, moving in, or responsive in a single direction

uni·fi·ca·tion \ˌyü-nə-fə-'kā-shən\ n : the act, process, or result of unifying : the state of being unified

¹**uni·form** \'yü-nə-ˌfórm\ adj **1** : not varying ⟨∼ procedures⟩ **2** : of the same form with others — **uni·form·ly** adv

²**uniform** vb : to clothe with a uniform

³**uniform** n : distinctive dress worn by members of a particular group (as an army or a police force)

uni·for·mi·ty \ˌyü-nə-'fór-mə-tē\ n, pl -ties : the state of being uniform

uni·fy \'yü-nə-ˌfī\ vb -fied; -fy·ing : to make into a coherent whole : UNITE

uni·lat·er·al \ˌyü-nə-'la-tə-rəl\ adj : of, having, affecting, or done by one side only — **uni·lat·er·al·ly** adv

un·im·peach·able \ˌən-im-'pē-chə-bəl\ adj : not liable to accusation : IRREPROACHABLE ⟨an ∼ reputation⟩

un·in·hib·it·ed \ˌən-in-'hi-bə-təd\ adj : free from inhibition; also : boisterously informal — **un·in·hib·it·ed·ly** adv

un·in·stall \ˌən-in-'stól\ vb : to remove (software) from a computer system

un·in·tel·li·gent \-'te-lə-jənt\ adj : lacking intelligence

un·in·tel·li·gi·ble \-jə-bəl\ adj : not intelligible : OBSCURE ⟨an ∼ voice mail⟩ — **un·in·tel·li·gi·bly** \-blē\ adv

un·in·ter·est·ed \ˌən-'in-trəs-təd, -'in-tə-rəs-, -tə-ˌres-\ adj : not interested : not having the mind or feelings engaged or aroused

un·in·ter·rupt·ed \ˌən-ˌin-tə-'rəp-təd\ adj : not interrupted : CONTINUOUS

union \'yün-yən\ n **1** : an act or instance of uniting two or more things into one : the state of being so united : COMBINATION, JUNCTION **2** : a uniting in marriage **3** : something formed by a combining of parts or members; esp : a confederation of independent individuals (as nations or persons) for some common purpose **4** : an organization of workers (as a labor union or a trade union) formed to advance its members' interests esp. in respect to wages and working conditions **5** : a device emblematic of union used on or as a national flag; also : the upper inner corner of a flag **6** : a device for connecting parts (as of a machine); esp : a coupling for pipes

union·ise Brit var of UNIONIZE

union·ism \'yün-yə-ˌni-zəm\ n **1** : the principle or policy of forming or adhering to a union; esp, cap : adherence to the policy of a firm federal union before or during the U.S. Civil War **2** : the principles or system of trade unions — **union·ist** n

union·ize \'yün-yə-ˌnīz\ vb -ized; -iz·ing : to form into or cause to join a labor union — **union·i·za·tion** \ˌyün-yə-nə-'zā-shən\ n

union jack n **1** : a flag consisting of the part of a national flag that signifies union **2** cap U&J : the national flag of the United Kingdom

unique \yů-'nēk\ adj **1** : being the only one of its kind : SINGLE, SOLE ⟨each snow-

unhardened	unhonored	unimposing	uninstructed
unharmed	unhoused	unimpressed	uninstructive
unharvested	unhurried	unimpressive	uninsured
unhatched	unhurt	unimproved	unintelligent
unhealed	unhygienic	unincorporated	unintelligible
unhealthful	unidentifiable	uninfected	unintelligibly
unheated	unidentified	uninfluenced	unintended
unheeded	unidiomatic	uninformative	unintentional
unhelpful	unimaginable	uninformed	unintentionally
unheralded	unimaginative	uninhabitable	uninteresting
unheroic	unimpaired	uninhabited	uninterrupted
unhesitating	unimpassioned	uninitiated	uninvited
unhindered	unimpeded	uninjured	uninviting
unhistorical	unimportant	uninspired	

flake is ~〉 2 : very unusual : NOTABLE — **unique·ly** adv — **unique·ness** n

uni·sex \'yü-nə-ˌseks\ adj : not distinguishable as male or female; also : suitable or designed for both males and females 〈~ clothing〉 — **unisex** n

uni·sex·u·al \ˌyü-nə-'sek-shə-wəl\ adj 1 : having only male or only female sex organs 2 : UNISEX

uni·son \'yü-nə-sən, -zən\ n [ME unisoun, fr. MF unisson, fr. ML unisonus having the same sound, fr. L unus one + sonus sound] 1 : sameness or identity in musical pitch 2 : the condition of being tuned or sounded at the same pitch or in octaves 〈sing in ~〉 3 : harmonious agreement or union : ACCORD

unit \'yü-nət\ n 1 : the smallest whole number greater than zero : ONE 2 : a definite amount or quantity used as a standard of measurement 3 : a single thing, person, or group that is a constituent of a whole; also : a part of a military establishment that has a prescribed organization — **unit** adj

Uni·tar·i·an \ˌyü-nə-'ter-ē-ən\ n : a member of a religious denomination stressing individual freedom of belief — **Uni·tar·i·an·ism** n

uni·tary \'yü-nə-ˌter-ē\ adj 1 : of or relating to a unit 2 : not divided — **uni·tar·i·ly** \ˌyü-nə-'ter-ə-lē\ adv

unite \yu̇-'nīt\ vb **unit·ed**; **unit·ing** 1 : to put or join together so as to make one : COMBINE, COALESCE 2 : to join by a legal or moral bond; also : to join in interest or fellowship 3 : AMALGAMATE, CONSOLIDATE 4 : to act in concert

unit·ed \yu̇-'nī-təd\ adj 1 : made one : COMBINED 2 : relating to or produced by joint action 3 : being in agreement : HARMONIOUS

unit·ize \'yü-nə-ˌtīz\ vb **-ized**; **-iz·ing** 1 : to form or convert into a unit 2 : to divide into units

uni·ty \'yü-nə-tē\ n, pl **-ties** 1 : the quality or state of being or being made one : ONENESS 2 : a definite quantity or combination of quantities taken as one or for which 1 is made to stand in calculation 3 : CONCORD, ACCORD, HARMONY 4 : continuity without change 〈~ of purpose〉 5 : reference of all the parts of a literary or artistic composition to a single main idea 6 : totality of related parts ◆ **Synonyms** SOLIDARITY, UNION, INTEGRITY

univ abbr 1 universal 2 university

uni·valve \'yü-ni-ˌvalv\ n : a mollusk having a shell with only one piece; esp : GASTROPOD — **univalve** adj

uni·ver·sal \ˌyü-nə-'vər-səl\ adj 1 : including, covering, or affecting the whole without limit or exception : available or applying to everyone 〈~ privileges〉 〈a ~ rule〉 2 : present or occurring everywhere : used for or use among all 〈a ~ language〉 4 : adaptable for various purposes 〈a ~ remote control〉 — **uni·ver·sal·ly** adv

uni·ver·sal·i·ty \-ˌvər-'sa-lə-tē\ n : the quality or state of being universal

uni·ver·sal·ize \-'vər-sə-ˌlīz\ vb **-ized**; **-iz·ing** : to make universal : GENERALIZE 〈would ~ equal rights〉 — **uni·ver·sal·i·za·tion** \-ˌvər-sə-lə-'zā-shən\ n

universal joint n : a shaft coupling for transmitting rotation from one axis to another not in a straight line with it

Universal Product Code n : a combination of a bar code and numbers by which a scanner can identify a product and usu. assign a price

uni·verse \'yü-nə-ˌvərs\ n [ME, fr. L universum, fr. neut. of universus entire, whole, fr. unus one + versus turned toward, fr. pp. of vertere to turn] : the whole body of things observed or assumed : COSMOS

uni·ver·si·ty \ˌyü-nə-'vər-sə-tē\ n, pl **-ties** : an institution of higher learning authorized to confer degrees in various special fields (as theology, law, and medicine) as well as in the arts and sciences generally

un·just \ˌən-'jəst\ adj : characterized by injustice — **un·just·ly** adv

un·kempt \-'kempt\ adj 1 : lacking order or neatness; also : ROUGH, UNPOLISHED 2 : not combed : DISHEVELED

un·kind \-'kīnd\ adj : not kind or sympathetic 〈an ~ remark〉 — **un·kind·ly** adv — **un·kind·ness** n

un·kind·ly \-'kīnd-lē\ adj : UNKIND — **un·kind·li·ness** n

un·know·ing \ˌən-'nō-iŋ\ adj : not knowing — **un·know·ing·ly** adv

un·known \-'nōn\ adj : not known or not well-known — **unknown** n

un·lace \ˌən-'lās\ vb : to loose by undoing a lace

un·lade \-'lād\ vb **-lad·ed**; **-lad·ed** or **-lad·en** \-'lā-dᵊn\; **-lad·ing** : to take the load or cargo from : UNLOAD

un·latch \-'lach\ vb 1 : to open or loose by lifting the latch 2 : to become loosed or opened

un·law·ful \ˌən-'lȯ-fəl\ adj 1 : not lawful : ILLEGAL 2 : ILLEGITIMATE — **un·law·ful·ly** adv

un·lead·ed \-'le-dəd\ adj : not treated or mixed with lead or lead compounds

un·learn \-'lərn\ vb : to put out of one's knowledge or memory; also : to discard the habit of

un·learned \-'lər-nəd for 1; -'lərnd for 2\ adj 1 : UNEDUCATED, ILLITERATE 2 : not gained by study or training

un·leash \-'lēsh\ vb : to free from or as if from a leash : let loose

un·less \ən-'les, 'ən-ˌles\ conj : except on condition that 〈won't go ~ you do〉

un·let·tered \ˌən-'le-tərd\ adj : not educated : ILLITERATE

¹**un·like** \-'līk\ adj 1 : not like : DISSIMI-

unjointed	unknowable	unladylike	unlicensed
unjustifiable	unknowledgeable	unlamented	unlighted
unjustified	unlabeled	unleavened	unlikable
unkept			

unlike • unparliamentary

LAR, DIFFERENT 2 : UNEQUAL — **un·like·ness** n

²**unlike** prep 1 : different from ⟨she's quite ~ her sister⟩ 2 : unusual for ⟨it's ~ you to be late⟩ 3 : differently from ⟨behaves ~ his brother⟩

un·like·li·hood \ˌən-ˈlī-klē-ˌhu̇d\ n : IMPROBABILITY

un·like·ly \-ˈlī-klē\ adj 1 : not likely : IMPROBABLE 2 : likely to fail

un·lim·ber \ˌən-ˈlim-bər\ vb : to get ready for action

un·list·ed \ˌən-ˈlis-təd\ adj 1 : not appearing on a list; esp : not appearing in a telephone book 2 : not listed on a stock exchange

un·load \-ˈlōd\ vb 1 : to take away or off : REMOVE ⟨~ cargo from a hold⟩; also : to get rid of 2 : to take a load from ⟨~ the ship⟩; also : to relieve or set free : UNBURDEN ⟨~ one's mind of worries⟩ 3 : to draw the charge from ⟨~ed the gun⟩ 4 : to sell in volume

un·lock \-ˈläk\ vb 1 : to open or unfasten through release of a lock 2 : RELEASE ⟨~ a flood of emotions⟩ 3 : DISCLOSE, REVEAL ⟨~ nature's secrets⟩

un·looked–for \-ˈlu̇kt-ˌfȯr\ adj : UNEXPECTED

un·loose \ˌən-ˈlüs\ vb 1 : to relax the strain of : set free; also : UNTIE

un·loos·en \-ˈlü-sᵊn\ vb : UNLOOSE

un·love·ly \-ˈləv-lē\ adj : having no charm or appeal : not amiable

un·luck·i·ly \-ˈlə-kə-lē\ adv : UNFORTUNATELY

un·lucky \-ˈlə-kē\ adj 1 : UNFORTUNATE, ILL-FATED 2 : likely to bring misfortune : INAUSPICIOUS 3 : REGRETTABLE

un·man \ˌən-ˈman\ vb 1 : to deprive of manly courage : CASTRATE

un·man·ly \-ˈman-lē\ adj : not manly : COWARDLY; also : EFFEMINATE

un·man·ner·ly \-ˈma-nər-lē\ adj : RUDE, IMPOLITE — **unmannerly** adv

un·mask \ˌən-ˈmask\ vb 1 : to strip of a mask or a disguise : EXPOSE 2 : to remove one's mask

un·mean·ing \-ˈmē-niŋ\ adj : having no meaning : SENSELESS

un·me·di·at·ed \ˌən-ˈmē-dē-ˌā-təd\ adj : not mediated : not communicated or transformed by an intervening agency

un·meet \-ˈmēt\ adj : not meet or fit : UNSUITABLE, IMPROPER

un·men·tion·able \-ˈmen-chə-nə-bəl\ adj : not fit or proper to be talked about ⟨an ~ topic⟩

un·mer·ci·ful \-ˈmər-si-fəl\ adj : not merciful : CRUEL, MERCILESS — **un·mer·ci·ful·ly** adv

un·mind·ful \-ˈmīnd-fəl\ adj : not mindful : CARELESS, UNAWARE

un·mis·tak·able \ˌən-mə-ˈstā-kə-bəl\ adj : not capable of being mistaken or misunderstood : CLEAR, OBVIOUS — **un·mis·tak·ably** \-blē\ adv

un·mit·i·gat·ed \ˌən-ˈmi-tə-ˌgā-təd\ adj 1 : not softened or lessened 2 : ABSOLUTE, DOWNRIGHT ⟨an ~ liar⟩

un·moor \-ˈmu̇r\ vb : to loose from or as if from moorings

un·mor·al \-ˈmȯr-əl\ adj : having no moral perception or quality : AMORAL — **un·mo·ral·i·ty** \ˌən-mə-ˈra-lə-tē\ n

un·muz·zle \-ˈmə-zəl\ vb : to remove a muzzle from

un·nat·u·ral \ˌən-ˈna-chə-rəl\ adj : contrary to or acting contrary to nature or natural instincts; also : ABNORMAL — **un·nat·u·ral·ly** adv — **un·nat·u·ral·ness** n

un·nec·es·sar·i·ly \ˌən-ˌne-sə-ˈser-ə-lē\ adv 1 : not by necessity 2 : to an unnecessary degree ⟨~ harsh⟩

un·nerve \ˌən-ˈnərv\ vb : to deprive of courage, strength, or steadiness ⟨fear unnerved them⟩; also : UPSET

un·num·bered \ˌən-ˈnəm-bərd\ adj : not numbered or counted : INNUMERABLE

un·ob·tru·sive \ˌən-əb-ˈtrü-siv\ adj : not obtrusive or forward : not bold : INCONSPICUOUS — **un·ob·tru·sive·ly** adv

un·oc·cu·pied \ˌən-ˈä-kyə-ˌpīd\ adj 1 : not busy : UNEMPLOYED 2 : not occupied : EMPTY, VACANT

un·or·ga·nized \-ˈȯr-gə-ˌnīzd\ adj 1 : not formed or brought into an integrated or ordered whole 2 : not organized into unions ⟨~ labor⟩

un·pack \ˌən-ˈpak\ vb 1 : to separate and remove things packed 2 : to open and remove the contents of

un·par·al·leled \ˌən-ˈpa-rə-ˌleld\ adj : having no parallel; esp : having no equal or match ⟨an ~ achievement⟩

un·par·lia·men·ta·ry \ˌən-ˌpär-lə-ˈmen-tə-rē\ adj : contrary to parliamentary practice

unlimited	unmasculine	unmoved	unopened
unlined	unmatched	unmusical	unopposed
unlit	unmeant	unnameable	unoriginal
unliterary	unmeasurable	unnamed	unorthodox
unlivable	unmeasured	unnecessary	unorthodoxy
unlovable	unmelodious	unneeded	unostentatious
unloved	unmentioned	unnewsworthy	unowned
unloving	unmerited	unnoticeable	unpaged
unmade	unmilitary	unnoticed	unpaid
unmalicious	unmilled	unobjectionable	unpainted
unmanageable	unmixed	unobservant	unpaired
unmanned	unmodified	unobserved	unpalatable
unmapped	unmolested	unobstructed	unpardonable
unmarked	unmotivated	unobtainable	unpasteurized
unmarketable	unmounted	unofficial	unpatriotic
unmarred	unmovable	unofficially	unpaved
unmarried			

un·peg \ˌən-ˈpeg\ vb **1** : to remove a peg from **2** : to unfasten by or as if by removing a peg

un·per·son \ˈən-ˌpər-sᵊn, -ˌpər-\ n : a person who usu. for political or ideological reasons is removed from recognition or consideration

un·pile \ˌən-ˈp(-ə)l\ vb : to take or disentangle from a pile

un·pin \-ˈpin\ vb : to remove a pin from : UNFASTEN

un·pleas·ant \-ˈple-zᵊnt\ adj : not pleasant : DISAGREEABLE — **un·pleas·ant·ly** adv — **un·pleas·ant·ness** n

un·plug \ˌən-ˈpləg\ vb **1** : UNCLOG **2** : to remove (a plug) from a receptacle; also : to disconnect from an electric circuit by removing a plug

un·plumbed \-ˈpləmd\ adj **1** : not tested or measured with a plumb line **2** : not thoroughly explored

un·pop·u·lar \ˌən-ˈpä-pyə-lər\ adj : not popular : looked upon or received unfavorably — **un·pop·u·lar·i·ty** \ˌən-ˌpä-pyə-ˈla-rə-tē\ n

un·prec·e·dent·ed \ˌən-ˈpre-sə-ˌden-təd\ adj : having no precedent : NOVEL

un·pre·ten·tious \ˌən-pri-ˈten-chəs\ adj : not pretentious : MODEST

un·prin·ci·pled \ˌən-ˈprin-sə-pəld\ adj : lacking sound or honorable principles : UNSCRUPULOUS ⟨an ~ criminal⟩

un·print·able \-ˈprin-tə-bəl\ adj : unfit or too offensive to be printed ⟨~ remarks⟩

un·prof·it·able \ˌən-ˈprä-fə-tə-bəl\ adj : not profitable : USELESS, VAIN

un·pro·tect·ed \ˌən-prə-ˈtek-təd\ adj **1** : lacking protection **2** : performed without measures to prevent pregnancy or sexually transmitted disease ⟨~ sex⟩

un·qual·i·fied \ˌən-ˈkwä-lə-ˌfīd\ adj **1** : not having requisite qualifications **2** : not modified or restricted by reservations : COMPLETE — **un·qual·i·fied·ly** \-ˌfī-əd-lē\ adv

un·ques·tion·able \-ˈkwes-chə-nə-bəl\ adj : not questionable : INDISPUTABLE — **un·ques·tion·ably** \-blē\ adv

un·ques·tion·ing \-chə-niŋ\ adj : not questioning : accepting without examina-

tion or hesitation ⟨~ obedience⟩ — **un·ques·tion·ing·ly** adv

un·qui·et \-ˈkwī-ət\ adj **1** : not quiet : AGITATED, DISTURBED **2** : physically, emotionally, or mentally restless : UNEASY

un·quote \ˈən-ˌkwōt\ n — used orally to indicate the end of a direct quotation

un·rav·el \ˌən-ˈra-vəl\ vb **1** : to separate the threads of **2** : SOLVE ⟨~ a mystery⟩ **3** : to become unraveled

un·read \-ˈred\ adj **1** : not read; also : left unexamined **2** : lacking the benefits or the experience of reading

un·re·al \-ˈrēl\ adj : lacking in reality, substance, or genuineness — **un·re·al·i·ty** \ˌən-rē-ˈa-lə-tē\ n

un·rea·son·able \-ˈrē-zᵊn-ə-bəl\ adj **1** : not governed by or acting according to reason; also : not conformable to reason : ABSURD **2** : exceeding the bounds of reason or moderation — **un·rea·son·able·ness** n — **un·rea·son·ably** adv

un·rea·soned \-ˈrē-zᵊnd\ adj : not based on reason or reasoning ⟨~ fears⟩

un·rea·son·ing \-ˈrē-zᵊn-iŋ\ adj : not using or showing the use of reason as a guide or control

un·re·con·struct·ed \ˌən-ˌrē-kən-ˈstrak-təd\ adj : not reconciled to some political, economic, or social change; esp : holding stubbornly to a particular belief, view, place, or style

un·reel \ˌən-ˈrēl\ vb **1** : to unwind from or as if from a reel **2** : to perform successfully

un·re·gen·er·ate \ˌən-ri-ˈje-nə-rət\ adj : not regenerated or reformed

un·re·lent·ing \-ˈlen-tiŋ\ adj **1** : not yielding in determination : STERN ⟨~ leader⟩ **2** : not letting up or weakening in vigor or pace : CONSTANT — **un·re·lent·ing·ly** adv

un·re·mit·ting \-ˈmi-tiŋ\ adj : CONSTANT, INCESSANT ⟨~ pain⟩ — **un·re·mit·ting·ly** adv

un·re·quit·ed \ˌən-ri-ˈkwī-təd\ adj : not requited : not reciprocated or returned in kind ⟨~ love⟩

un·re·served \-ˈzərvd\ adj **1** : not limited or partial ⟨~ enthusiasm⟩ **2** : not cautious or reticent : FRANK, OPEN **3** : not set aside for special use — **un·re·serv·ed·ly** \-ˈzər-vəd-lē\ adv

unpeeled	unpremeditated	unprovoked	unreflective
unperceived	unprepared	unpublished	unregistered
unperceptive	unpreparedness	unpunished	unregulated
unperformed	unprepossessing	unquenchable	unrehearsed
unpersuaded	unpressed	unquestioned	unrelated
unpersuasive	unpretending	unraised	unreliable
unperturbed	unpretty	unrated	unrelieved
unplanned	unprivileged	unratified	unremarkable
unplanted	unprocessed	unreachable	unremembered
unpleasing	unproductive	unreadable	unremovable
unplowed	unprofessed	unready	unrepentant
unpoetic	unprofessional	unrealistic	unreported
unpolished	unprogrammed	unrealized	unrepresentative
unpolitical	unprogressive	unrecognizable	unrepresented
unpolluted	unpromising	unrecognized	unrepressed
unposed	unprompted	unrecorded	unresistant
unpractical	unpronounceable	unrecoverable	unresisting
unpredictability	unpropitious	unredeemable	unresolved
unpredictable	unproven	unrefined	unresponsive
unprejudiced	unprovided	unreflecting	unresponsiveness

un·rest \ˌən-ˈrest\ n : a disturbed or uneasy state : TURMOIL

un·re·strained \ˌən-ri-ˈstrānd\ adj 1 : IMMODERATE, UNCONTROLLED ⟨~ anger⟩ 2 : SPONTANEOUS

un·re·straint \-ri-ˈstrānt\ n : lack of restraint

un·rid·dle \ˌən-ˈri-dᵊl\ vb : to find the explanation of : SOLVE

un·righ·teous \-ˈrī-chəs\ adj 1 : SINFUL, WICKED 2 : UNJUST — **un·righ·teous·ness** n

un·ripe \-ˈrīp\ adj : not ripe : IMMATURE

un·ri·valed or **un·ri·valled** \ˌən-ˈrī-vəld\ adj : having no rival : SUPREME

un·robe \-ˈrōb\ vb : DISROBE, UNDRESS

un·roll \-ˈrōl\ vb 1 : to unwind a roll of : open out 2 : DISPLAY, DISCLOSE 3 : to become unrolled or spread out

un·roof \-ˈrüf, -ˈrùf\ vb : to strip off the roof or covering of

un·ruf·fled \ˌən-ˈrə-fəld\ adj 1 : not agitated or upset 2 : not ruffled : SMOOTH ⟨~ water⟩

un·ruly \-ˈrü-lē\ adj [ME unreuly, fr. un- + reuly disciplined, fr. reule rule, fr. AF, fr. L regula straightedge, rule, fr. regere to direct] : not submissive to rule or restraint : TURBULENT ⟨~ passions⟩ — **un·rul·i·ness** \-ˈrü-lē-nəs\ n

un·sad·dle \ˌən-ˈsa-dᵊl\ vb 1 : to remove the saddle from a horse 2 : UNHORSE

un·sat·u·rat·ed \-ˈsa-chə-ˌrā-təd\ adj 1 : capable of absorbing or dissolving more of something 2 : containing double or triple bonds between carbon atoms ⟨~ fat⟩ — **un·sat·u·rate** \-rət\ n

un·saved \ˌən-ˈsāvd\ adj : not saved; esp : not rescued from eternal punishment

un·sa·vory \-ˈsā-və-rē\ adj 1 : TASTELESS 2 : unpleasant to taste or smell 3 : morally offensive ⟨~ characters⟩

un·say \-ˈsā\ vb **-said** \-ˈsed\; **-say·ing** : to take back (something said) : RETRACT, WITHDRAW

un·scathed \-ˈskāt͟hd\ adj : wholly unharmed : not injured

un·schooled \-ˈsküld\ adj : not schooled : UNTAUGHT, UNTRAINED

un·sci·en·tif·ic \ˌən-ˌsī-ən-ˈti-fik\ adj : not scientific : not in accord with the principles and methods of science

un·scram·ble \ˌən-ˈskram-bəl\ vb 1 : RESOLVE, CLARIFY 2 : to restore (as a radio message) to intelligible form

un·screw \-ˈskrü\ vb 1 : to draw the screws from or loosen by turning 2 : to loosen by turning

un·scru·pu·lous \-ˈskrü-pyə-ləs\ adj : not scrupulous : UNPRINCIPLED — **un-**

scru·pu·lous·ly adv — **un·scru·pu·lous·ness** n

un·seal \-ˈsēl\ vb : to break or remove the seal of : OPEN

un·search·able \-ˈsər-chə-bəl\ adj : not capable of being searched or explored ⟨~ forests⟩

un·sea·son·able \-ˈsē-zᵊn-ə-bəl\ adj : not seasonable : happening or coming at the wrong time : UNTIMELY — **un·sea·son·ably** \-blē\ adv

un·seat \-ˈsēt\ vb 1 : to throw from one's seat esp. on horseback 2 : to remove from political office

un·seem·ly \-ˈsēm-lē\ adj : not according with established standards of good form or taste ⟨~ behavior⟩; also : not suitable — **un·seem·li·ness** n

un·seen \-ˈsēn\ adj : not seen : INVISIBLE ⟨~ dangers⟩

un·seg·re·gat·ed \-ˈse-gri-ˌgā-təd\ adj : not segregated; esp : free from racial segregation

un·self·ish \-ˈsel-fish\ adj : not selfish : GENEROUS — **un·self·ish·ly** adv — **un·self·ish·ness** n

un·set·tle \ˌən-ˈse-tᵊl\ vb : to move or loosen from a settled position : DISPLACE, DISTURB

un·set·tled \-ˈse-tᵊld\ adj 1 : not settled : not fixed (as in position or character) 2 : not calm : DISTURBED 3 : not decided in mind : UNRESOLVED 4 : not paid ⟨~ accounts⟩ 5 : not occupied by settlers

un·shack·le \-ˈsha-kəl\ vb : to free from shackles

un·shaped \-ˈshāpt\ adj : not shaped; esp : not being in finished, final, or perfect form ⟨~ ideas⟩ ⟨~ timber⟩

un·sheathe \ˌən-ˈshēt͟h\ vb : to draw from or as if from a sheath

un·ship \-ˈship\ vb 1 : to remove from a ship 2 : to remove or become removed from position ⟨~ an oar⟩

un·shod \ˌən-ˈshäd\ adj : not wearing or provided with shoes

un·sight·ly \ˌən-ˈsīt-lē\ adj : unpleasant to the sight : UGLY ⟨an ~ mess⟩

un·skilled \-ˈskild\ adj 1 : not skilled; esp : not skilled in a specified branch of work 2 : not requiring skill

un·skill·ful \-ˈskil-fəl\ adj : lacking in skill or proficiency — **un·skill·ful·ly** adv

un·sling \-ˈsliŋ\ vb **-slung** \-ˈsləŋ\; **-sling·ing** : to remove from being slung

un·snap \-ˈsnap\ vb : to loosen or free by or as if by undoing a snap

un·snarl \-ˈsnärl\ vb : to remove snarls from : UNTANGLE

---

unrestful	unsalted	unself–conscious	unshorn
unrestricted	unsanctioned	unself–consciously	unsifted
unreturnable	unsanitary	unsensational	unsigned
unrewarding	unsatisfactory	unsentimental	unsinkable
unrhymed	unsatisfied	unserious	unsmiling
unrhythmic	unscented	unserviceable	unsociable
unripened	unscheduled	unsexual	unsoiled
unromantic	unscholarly	unshaded	unsold
unromantically	unsealed	unshakable	unsoldierly
unsafe	unseasoned	unshaken	unsolicited
unsaid	unseaworthy	unshapely	unsolvable
unsalable	unsegmented	unshaven	unsolved

un·so·phis·ti·cat·ed \ˌən-sə-ˈfis-tə-ˌkā-təd\ *adj* **1** : not worldly-wise : lacking sophistication **2** : SIMPLE ⟨~ designs⟩

un·sought \ˌən-ˈsòt\ *adj* : not sought : not searched for or asked for : not obtained by effort ⟨~ honors⟩

un·sound \-ˈsaùnd\ *adj* **1** : not healthy or whole; *also* : not mentally normal ⟨of ~ mind⟩ **2** : not valid **3** : not firmly made or fixed ⟨structurally ~⟩ — **un·sound·ly** *adv* — **un·sound·ness** *n*

un·spar·ing \-ˈsper-iŋ\ *adj* **1** : HARD, RUTHLESS ⟨~ criticism⟩ **2** : not frugal : LIBERAL, PROFUSE ⟨~ generosity⟩

un·speak·able \-ˈspē-kə-bəl\ *adj* **1** : impossible to express in words **2** : extremely bad ⟨~ offenses⟩ — **un·speak·ably** \-blē\ *adv*

un·spool \-ˈspül\ *vb* **1** : to unwind from a spool **2** : to present artfully ⟨~ a new film⟩

un·spot·ted \-ˈspä-təd\ *adj* : not spotted or stained; *esp* : free from moral stain

un·sprung \-ˈsprəŋ\ *adj* : not sprung; *esp* : not equipped with springs

un·sta·ble \ˌən-ˈstä-bəl\ *adj* **1** : not stable **2** : FICKLE, VACILLATING; *also* : lacking effective emotional control **3** : readily changing (as by decomposing) in chemical or physical composition or in biological activity ⟨an ~ atomic nucleus⟩

un·steady \ˌən-ˈste-dē\ *adj* : not steady : UNSTABLE — **un·stead·i·ly** \-ˈste-də-lē\ *adv* — **un·stead·i·ness** \-ˈste-dē-nəs\ *n*

un·stint·ing \-ˈstin-tiŋ\ *adj* **1** : not restricting or holding back **2** : giving or being given freely or generously ⟨~ praise⟩

un·stop \-ˈstäp\ *vb* **1** : UNCLOG **2** : to remove a stopper from

un·stop·pa·ble \ˌən-ˈstä-pə-bəl\ *adj* : incapable of being stopped

un·strap \-ˈstrap\ *vb* : to remove or loose a strap from

un·stressed \ˌən-ˈstrest\ *adj* : not stressed; *esp* : not bearing a stress or accent ⟨~ syllables⟩

un·strung \-ˈstrəŋ\ *adj* **1** : having the strings loose or detached **2** : made weak, disordered, or unstable

un·stud·ied \-ˈstə-dēd\ *adj* **1** : not acquired by study **2** : NATURAL, UNFORCED ⟨moved with ~ grace⟩

un·sub·stan·tial \ˌən-səb-ˈstan-chəl\ *adj* : INSUBSTANTIAL

un·sung \ˌən-ˈsəŋ\ *adj* **1** : not sung **2** : not celebrated in song or verse ⟨~ heroes⟩

un·swerv·ing \ˌən-ˈswər-viŋ\ *adj* **1** : not swerving or turning aside **2** : STEADY

un·tan·gle \-ˈtaŋ-gəl\ *vb* **1** : DISENTANGLE **2** : to straighten out : RESOLVE ⟨~ a problem⟩

un·taught \-ˈtòt\ *adj* **1** : not instructed or taught : IGNORANT **2** : NATURAL, SPONTANEOUS ⟨~ kindness⟩

un·think·able \-ˈthiŋ-kə-bəl\ *adj* : not to be thought of or considered as possible ⟨~ cruelty⟩

un·think·ing \ˌən-ˈthiŋ-kiŋ\ *adj* : not thinking; *esp* : THOUGHTLESS, HEEDLESS ⟨~ remarks⟩ — **un·think·ing·ly** *adv*

un·thought \ˌən-ˈthòt\ *adj* : not anticipated : UNEXPECTED — often used with *of* ⟨*unthought*-of development⟩

un·tie \-ˈtī\ *vb* **-tied; -ty·ing** *or* **-tie·ing 1** : to free from something that ties, fastens, or restrains : UNBIND **2** : DISENTANGLE, RESOLVE **3** : to become loosened or unbound

¹un·til \ˌən-ˈtil\ *prep* : up to the time of ⟨worked ~ 5 o'clock⟩

²until *conj* **1** : up to the time that ⟨wait ~ he calls⟩ **2** : to the point or degree that ⟨ran ~ she was breathless⟩

¹un·time·ly \ˌən-ˈtīm-lē\ *adv* : at an inopportune time : UNSEASONABLY; *also* : PREMATURELY

²untimely *adj* : PREMATURE ⟨~ death⟩; *also* : INOPPORTUNE, UNSEASONABLE

un·tir·ing \ˌən-ˈtī-riŋ\ *adj* : not becoming tired : INDEFATIGABLE ⟨an ~ worker⟩ — **un·tir·ing·ly** *adv*

un·to \ˈən-ˌtü\ *prep* : TO

un·told \ˌən-ˈtōld\ *adj* **1** : too great or numerous to count **2** : not told : not revealed

¹un·touch·able \ˌən-ˈtə-chə-bəl\ *adj* : forbidden to the touch

²untouchable *n* : a member of the lowest social class in India having in traditional Hindu belief the quality of defiling by contact a member of a higher caste

un·touched \ˌən-ˈtəcht\ *adj* **1** : not subjected to touching **2** : not described or dealt with **3** : not tasted **4** : being in a primeval state or condition **5** : UNAFFECTED ⟨~ by scandals⟩

un·to·ward \ˌən-ˈtòrd, -ˈtō-ərd; ˌən-tə-ˈwòrd\ *adj* **1** : difficult to manage : STUBBORN, WILLFUL ⟨an ~ child⟩ **2** : INCONVENIENT, TROUBLESOME ⟨an ~ encounter⟩

---

unsorted	unsuccessful	unsweetened	untended
unspecified	unsuccessfully	unsymmetrical	untested
unspectacular	unsuitable	unsympathetic	unthrifty
unspent	unsuited	unsystematic	untidy
unspiritual	unsullied	untactful	untilled
unspoiled	unsupervised	untainted	untitled
unspoken	unsupportable	untalented	untraceable
unsportsmanlike	unsupported	untamed	untraditional
unstained	unsure	untanned	untrained
unstated	unsurpassed	untapped	untrammeled
unsterile	unsurprising	untarnished	untranslatable
unstructured	unsurprisingly	untaxed	untranslated
unstylish	unsuspected	unteachable	untraveled
unsubdued	unsuspecting	untenable	untraversed
unsubstantiated	unsuspicious	untenanted	untreated
unsubtle			

un·tried \,ən-'trīd\ *adj* : not tested or proved by experience or trial; *also* : not tried in court

un·true \-'trü\ *adj* **1** : not faithful : DISLOYAL **2** : not according with a standard of correctness **3** : FALSE

un·truth \,ən-'trüth, 'ən-,trüth\ *n* **1** : lack of truthfulness **2** : FALSEHOOD

un·tune \-'tün, -'tyün\ *vb* **1** : to put out of tune **2** : DISARRANGE, DISCOMPOSE

un·tu·tored \-'tü-tərd, -'tyü-\ *adj* : UNTAUGHT, UNLEARNED, IGNORANT

un·twine \-'twīn\ *vb* : UNWIND, DISENTANGLE

un·twist \,ən-'twist\ *vb* **1** : to separate the twisted parts of : UNTWINE **2** : to become untwined

un·used \-'yüst, -'yüzd *for 1;* -'yüzd *for 2*\ *adj* **1** : UNACCUSTOMED ⟨~ to such treatment⟩ **2** : not used

un·usu·al \-'yü-zhə-wəl\ *adj* : not usual : UNCOMMON, RARE — **un·usu·al·ly** *adv*

un·ut·ter·able \,ən-'ə-tə-rə-bəl\ *adj* : being beyond the powers of description : INEXPRESSIBLE ⟨~ shame⟩ — **un·ut·ter·ably** \-blē\ *adv*

un·var·nished \-'vär-nisht\ *adj* **1** : not varnished **2** : not embellished : PLAIN ⟨the ~ truth⟩

un·veil \,ən-'vāl\ *vb* **1** : to remove a veil or covering from : DISCLOSE **2** : to remove a veil : reveal oneself

un·voiced \-'vȯist\ *adj* **1** : not verbally expressed : UNSPOKEN **2** : VOICELESS 2

un·war·rant·able \-'wȯr-ən-tə-bəl\ *adj* : not justifiable : INEXCUSABLE — **un·war·rant·ably** \-blē\ *adv*

un·weave \-'wēv\ *vb* **-wove** \-'wōv\; **-woven** \-'wō-vən\; **-weav·ing** : DISENTANGLE, RAVEL

un·well \,ən-'wel\ *adj* : SICK, AILING

un·whole·some \-'hōl-səm\ *adj* **1** : harmful to physical, mental, or moral well-being ⟨~ food⟩ **2** : CORRUPT, UNSOUND ⟨~ deals⟩; *also* : offensive to the senses : LOATHSOME ⟨an ~ stench⟩

un·wieldy \-'wēl-dē\ *adj* : not easily managed, handled, or used (as because of bulk, weight, or complexity) : AWKWARD ⟨an ~ tool⟩

un·wind \-'wīnd\ *vb* **-wound** \-'waȯnd\; **-wind·ing** **1** : to undo something that is wound : loose from coils **2** : to become unwound : be capable of being unwound **3** : RELAX ⟨~ after work⟩

un·wise \,ən-'wīz\ *adj* : not wise : FOOLISH — **un·wise·ly** *adv*

un·wit·ting \-'wi-tiŋ\ *adj* **1** : not knowing : UNAWARE **2** : not intended : INADVERTENT ⟨~ mistake⟩ — **un·wit·ting·ly** *adv*

un·wont·ed \-'wȯn-təd, -'wōn-\ *adj* **1** : RARE, UNUSUAL **2** : not accustomed by experience — **un·wont·ed·ly** *adv*

un·world·ly \-'wərld-lē\ *adj* **1** : not of this world; *esp* : SPIRITUAL **2** : NAIVE **3** : not swayed by worldly considerations — **un·world·li·ness** \-lē-nəs\ *n*

un·wor·thy \,ən-'wər-thē\ *adj* **1** : BASE, DISHONORABLE **2** : not meritorious : not worthy : UNDESERVING **3** : not deserved : UNMERITED ⟨~ treatment⟩ — **un·wor·thi·ly** \-thə-lē\ *adv* — **un·wor·thi·ness** \-thē-nəs\ *n*

un·wrap \-'rap\ *vb* : to remove the wrapping from : DISCLOSE

un·writ·ten \-'ri-tᵊn\ *adj* **1** : not in writing : ORAL, TRADITIONAL ⟨an ~ law⟩ **2** : containing no writing : BLANK

un·yield·ing \,ən-'yēl-diŋ\ *adj* **1** : characterized by lack of softness or flexibility **2** : characterized by firmness or obduracy ⟨~ opposition⟩

un·yoke \-'yōk\ *vb* : to remove a yoke from; *also* : SEPARATE, DISCONNECT

un·zip \-'zip\ *vb* : to zip open : open by means of a zipper

¹up \'əp\ *adv* **1** : in or to a higher position or level; *esp* : away from the center of the earth **2** : from beneath a surface (as ground or water) **3** : from below the horizon **4** : in or into an upright position; *esp* : out of bed **5** : with greater intensity ⟨speak ~⟩ **6** : to or at a greater rate or amount ⟨prices went ~⟩ **7** : in or into a better or more advanced state or a state of greater intensity or activity ⟨stir ~ a fire⟩ **8** : into existence, evidence, or knowledge ⟨the missing book turned ~⟩ **9** : into consideration ⟨brought the matter ~⟩ **10** : to or at bat **11** : into possession or custody ⟨gave himself ~⟩ **12** : ENTIRELY, COMPLETELY ⟨eat it ~⟩ **13** — used for emphasis ⟨clean ~ a room⟩ **14** : ASIDE, BY ⟨lay ~ supplies⟩ **15** : so as to arrive or approach ⟨ran ~ the path⟩ **16** : in a direction opposite to down **17** : in or into parts ⟨tear ~ paper⟩ **18** : to a stop ⟨pull ~ at the curb⟩ **19** : for each side ⟨the score was 15 ~⟩

²up *adj* **1** : risen above the horizon ⟨the sun is ~⟩ **2** : being out of bed ⟨~ by 6 o'clock⟩ **3** : relatively high ⟨prices are ~⟩ **4** : RAISED, LIFTED ⟨windows are ~⟩ **5** : BUILT, CONSTRUCTED ⟨the house is ~⟩ **6** : grown above a surface ⟨the corn is ~⟩ **7** : moving, inclining, or directed upward **8** : marked by agitation, excitement, or activity **9** : READY; *esp* : highly prepared **10** : going on : taking place ⟨find out what is ~⟩ **11** : EXPIRED, ENDED ⟨the time is ~⟩ **12** : extensively aware or informed ⟨~ on the news⟩ **13** : being ahead or in advance of

untrimmed / untrod / untrodden / untroubled / untrustworthy / untruthful / untypical / unusable / unvaried

unvarying / unventilated / unverifiable / unverified / unversed / unvisited / unwanted / unwarranted / unwary

unwashed / unwavering / unweaned / unwearable / unwearied / unweathered / unwed / unwelcome / unwilling

unwillingly / unwillingness / unwomanly / unworkable / unworn / unworried / unwounded / unwoven an opponent ⟨one hole ∼ in a match⟩ **14** : presented for or being under consideration ⟨∼ for promotion⟩ **15** : charged before a court ⟨∼ for robbery⟩

³**up** *prep* **1** : to, toward, or at a higher point of ⟨∼ a ladder⟩ **2** : to or toward the source of ⟨∼ the river⟩ **3** : to or toward the northern part of ⟨∼ the coast⟩ **4** : to or toward the interior of ⟨traveling ∼ the country⟩ **5** : ALONG ⟨walk ∼ the street⟩

⁴**up** *n* **1** : an upward course or slope **2** : a period or state of prosperity or success ⟨he had his ∼s and downs⟩ **3** : a quark with a charge of +⅔ that is one of the constituents of the proton and neutron

⁵**up** *vb* **upped** \'əpt\ *or in* 2 **up; upped; up·ping; ups** *or in* 2 **up 1** : to rise from a lying or sitting position **2** : to act abruptly or surprisingly ⟨she *upped* and left home⟩ **3** : to move or cause to move upward ⟨*upped* the prices⟩

Upa·ni·shad \ü-'pän-i-ˌshäd\ *n* : one of a set of Vedic philosophical treatises

¹**up·beat** \'əp-ˌbēt\ *n* : an unaccented beat in a musical measure; *esp* : the last beat of the measure

²**upbeat** *adj* : OPTIMISTIC, CHEERFUL

up·braid \ˌəp-'brād\ *vb* : to criticize, reproach, or scold severely

up·bring·ing \'əp-ˌbriŋ-iŋ\ *n* : the process of bringing up and training

UPC *abbr* Universal Product Code

up·chuck \'əp-ˌchək\ *vb* : VOMIT

up·com·ing \'əp-ˌkə-miŋ\ *adj* : FORTHCOMING, APPROACHING ⟨the ∼ election⟩

¹**up·coun·try** \'əp-ˌkən-trē\ *adj* : of or relating to the interior of a country or a region — **up·country** \ˌəp-'kən-\ *adv*

up·date \ˌəp-'dāt\ *vb* : to bring up to date — **update** \'əp-ˌdāt\ *n*

up·draft \'əp-ˌdraft, -ˌdraft\ *n* : an upward movement of gas (as air)

up·end \ˌəp-'end\ *vb* : to set, stand, or rise on end; *also* : OVERTURN

up-front \'əp-ˌfrənt, ˌəp-'frənt\ *adj* **1** : HONEST, CANDID ⟨an ∼ answer⟩ **2** : ADVANCE ⟨∼ payment⟩

up front *adv* : in advance ⟨paid *up front*⟩

¹**up·grade** \'əp-ˌgrād\ *n* **1** : an upward grade or slope **2** : INCREASE, RISE

²**up·grade** \'əp-ˌgrād, ˌəp-'grād\ *vb* **1** : to raise to a higher grade or position; *also* : to advance to a job requiring a higher level of skill **2** : to improve or replace (as software or a device) for increased usefulness

up·growth \'əp-ˌgrōth\ *n* : the process of growing upward : DEVELOPMENT; *also* : a product or result of this

up·heav·al \ˌəp-'hē-vəl\ *n* **1** : the action or an instance of uplifting esp. of part of the earth's crust **2** : a violent agitation or change

¹**up·hill** \'əp-'hil\ *adv* : upward on a hill or incline; *also* : against difficulties

²**up·hill** \-ˌhil\ *adj* **1** : situated on elevated ground **2** : ASCENDING **3** : DIFFICULT, LABORIOUS ⟨an ∼ struggle⟩

up·hold \ˌəp-'hōld\ *vb* **-held** \-'held\; **-hold·ing 1** : to give support to ⟨∼ the

law⟩ **2** : to support against an opponent **3** : to keep elevated — **up·hold·er** *n*

up·hol·ster \ˌəp-'hōl-stər\ *vb* : to furnish with or as if with upholstery — **up·hol·ster·er** *n*

up·hol·stery \-stə-rē\ *n, pl* **-ster·ies** [ME *upholdester* upholsterer, fr. *upholden* to uphold, fr. *up* + *holden* to hold] : materials (as fabrics, padding, and springs) used to make a soft covering esp. for a seat

UPI *abbr* United Press International

up·keep \'əp-ˌkēp\ *n* : the act or cost of keeping up or maintaining; *also* : the state of being maintained

up·land \'əp-lənd, -ˌland\ *n* : high land esp. at some distance from the sea — **upland** *adj*

¹**up·lift** \ˌəp-'lift\ *vb* **1** : to lift or raise up : ELEVATE **2** : to improve the condition of esp. morally, socially, or intellectually

²**up·lift** \'əp-ˌlift\ *n* **1** : a lifting up; esp : an upheaval of the earth's surface **2** : moral or social improvement ⟨spiritual ∼⟩; *also* : a movement to make such improvement

up·mar·ket \ˌəp-'mär-kət\ *adj* : appealing to wealthy consumers

up·most \'əp-ˌmōst\ *adj* : UPPERMOST

up·on \ə-'pón, -'pän\ *prep* : ON

¹**up·per** \'ə-pər\ *adj* **1** : higher in physical position, rank, or order ⟨∼ management⟩ **2** : constituting the smaller and more restricted branch of a bicameral legislature **3** *cap* : being a later part or formation of a specific geological period **4** : being toward the interior ⟨the ∼ Amazon⟩ **5** : NORTHERN ⟨∼ Minnesota⟩

²**upper** *n* : one that is upper; *esp* : the parts of a shoe or boot above the sole

up·per·case \ˌə-pər-'kās\ *adj* : CAPITAL 1 — **uppercase** *n*

upper class *n* : a social class occupying a position above the middle class and having the highest status in a society — **up·per-class** *adj*

up·per·class·man \ˌə-pər-'klas-mən\ *n* : a junior or senior in a college or high school

upper crust *n* : the highest social class or group; *esp* : the highest circle of the upper class

up·per·cut \'ə-pər-ˌkət\ *n* : a short swinging punch delivered (as in boxing) in an upward direction usu. with a bent arm

upper hand *n* : MASTERY, ADVANTAGE

up·per·most \'ə-pər-ˌmōst\ *adv* : in or into the highest or most prominent position — **uppermost** *adj*

up·pish \'ə-pish\ *adj* : UPPITY

up·pi·ty \'ə-pə-tē\ *adj* : ARROGANT, PRESUMPTUOUS ⟨an ∼ sales clerk⟩

up·raise \ˌəp-'rāz\ *vb* : to lift up : ELEVATE

¹**up·right** \'əp-ˌrīt\ *adj* **1** : PERPENDICULAR, VERTICAL **2** : erect in carriage or posture **3** : morally correct : JUST ⟨an ∼ family man⟩ — **upright** *adv* — **up·right·ly** *adv* — **up·right·ness** *n*

²**upright** *n* **1** : the state of being upright : a vertical position **2** : something that stands upright

upright piano *n* : a piano whose strings run vertically

up·ris·ing \'əp-ˌrī-ziŋ\ *n* : INSURRECTION, REVOLT, REBELLION

up·riv·er \'əp-'ri-vər\ *adv or adj* : toward or at a point nearer the source of a river

up·roar \'əp-ˌrȯr\ *n* [D *oproer*, fr. MD, fr. *op* up + *roer* motion] : a state of commotion, excitement, or violent disturbance

up·roar·i·ous \ˌəp-'rȯr-ē-əs\ *adj* 1 : marked by uproar 2 : extremely funny — **up·roar·i·ous·ly** *adv*

up·root \ˌəp-'rüt, -'rut\ *vb* 1 : to remove by or as if by pulling up by the roots 2 : DISPLACE 1 ⟨families were ~ed⟩

¹**up·set** \ˌəp-'set\ *vb* **-set; -set·ting** 1 : to force or be forced out of the usual upright, level, or proper position 2 : to disturb emotionally : WORRY; *also* : to make somewhat ill 3 : UNSETTLE, DISARRANGE 4 : to defeat unexpectedly

²**up·set** \'əp-ˌset\ *n* 1 : an upsetting or being upset; *esp* : a minor illness 2 : a derangement of plans or ideas 3 : an unexpected defeat

³**up·set** \(ˌ)əp-'set\ *adj* : emotionally disturbed or agitated ⟨~ about the divorce⟩

up·shot \'əp-ˌshät\ *n* : the final result

¹**up·side** \'əp-ˌsīd\ *n* 1 : the upper side 2 : a positive aspect 3 : PROMISE ⟨rookies with much ~⟩

²**up·side** \ˌəp-'sīd\ *prep* : up on or against the side of ⟨knocked him ~ the head⟩

up·side down \ˌəp-ˌsīd-'daun\ *adv* 1 : with the upper and the lower parts reversed in position 2 : in or into confusion or disorder — **upside-down** *adj*

up·si·lon \'üp-sə-ˌlän, 'yüp-, 'əp-\ *n* : the 20th letter of the Greek alphabet — Υ or υ

¹**up·stage** \'əp-'stāj\ *adv or adj* : toward or at the rear of a theatrical stage

²**up·stage** \ˌəp-'stāj\ *vb* : to draw attention away from (as an actor)

¹**up·stairs** \ˌəp-'sterz\ *adv* 1 : up the stairs : to or on a higher floor 2 : to or at a higher position

²**up·stairs** \'əp-'sterz\ *adj* : situated above the stairs esp. on an upper floor ⟨~ bedroom⟩

³**up·stairs** \'əp-ˌsterz, 'əp-ˌsterz\ *n sing or pl* : the part of a building above the ground floor

up·stand·ing \ˌəp-'stan-diŋ, 'əp-\ *adj* 1 : ERECT 2 : STRAIGHTFORWARD, HONEST ⟨~ citizens⟩

¹**up·start** \ˌəp-'stärt\ *vb* : to jump up suddenly

²**up·start** \'əp-ˌstärt\ *n* : one that has risen suddenly; *esp* : one that claims more personal importance than is warranted — **up·start** \-'stärt\ *adj*

up·state \'əp-'stāt\ *adj* : of, relating to, or characteristic of a part of a state away from a large city and esp. to the north — **upstate** *adv* — **upstate** *n*

up·stream \'əp-'strēm\ *adv* : at or toward the source of a stream — **upstream** *adj*

up·stroke \'əp-ˌstrōk\ *n* : an upward stroke (as of a pen)

up·surge \ˌ-'sərj\ *n* : a rapid or sudden rise ⟨an ~ in interest⟩

up·swept \'əp-ˌswept\ *adj* : swept upward ⟨~ hairdo⟩

up·swing \'əp-ˌswiŋ\ *n* : an upward swing; *esp* : a marked increase or rise (as in activity)

up·take \'əp-ˌtāk\ *n* 1 : UNDERSTANDING, COMPREHENSION ⟨quick on the ~⟩ 2 : an act or instance of absorbing and incorporating esp. into a living organism, tissue, or cell

up·thrust \'əp-ˌthrəst\ *n* : an upward thrust (as of the earth's crust) — **upthrust** *vb*

up·tight \'əp-'tīt\ *adj* 1 : TENSE, NERVOUS, UNEASY; *also* : ANGRY, INDIGNANT 2 : rigidly conventional

up-to-date *adj* 1 : extending up to the present time 2 : abreast of the times : MODERN — **up-to-date·ness** *n*

up·town \'əp-ˌtaun\ *n* : the upper part of a town or city; *esp* : the residential district — **up·town** \'əp-'taun\ *adj or adv*

¹**up·turn** \'əp-ˌtərn, ˌəp-'tərn\ *vb* 1 : to turn (as earth) up or over 2 : to turn or direct upward

²**up·turn** \'əp-ˌtərn\ *n* : an upward turn esp. toward better conditions or higher prices

¹**up·ward** \'əp-wərd\ *or* **up·wards** \-wərdz\ *adv* 1 : in a direction from lower to higher 2 : toward a higher or better condition 3 : toward a greater amount or higher number, degree, or rate

²**upward** *adj* : directed or moving toward or situated in a higher place or level : ASCENDING — **up·ward·ly** *adv*

upwards *also* **upward** *of adv* : more than : in excess of ⟨they cost *upwards* of $25 each⟩

up·well \ˌəp-'wel\ *vb* : to move or flow upward

up·well·ing \-'we-liŋ\ *n* : a rising or an appearance of rising to the surface and flowing outward; *esp* : the movement of deep cold usu. nutrient-rich ocean water to the surface

up·wind \'əp-'wind\ *adv or adj* : in the direction from which the wind is blowing

ura·cil \'yur-ə-ˌsil\ *n* : a pyrimidine base that is one of the four bases coding genetic information in the molecular chain of RNA

ura·ni·um \yu-'rā-nē-əm\ *n* : a silvery heavy radioactive metallic chemical element used as a source of atomic energy

Ura·nus \'yur-ə-nəs, yu-'rā-\ *n* [LL, the sky personified as a god, fr. Gk *Ouranos*, fr. *ouranos* sky, heaven] : the planet 7th in order from the sun

ur·ban \'ər-bən\ *adj* : of, relating to, characteristic of, or constituting a city

ur·bane \ˌər-'bān\ *adj* [L *urbanus* urban, urbane, fr. *urbs* city] : very polite and polished in manner : SUAVE

ur·ban·ite \'ər-bə-ˌnīt\ *n* : a person who lives in a city

ur·ban·i·ty \ˌər-'ba-nə-tē\ *n, pl* **-ties** : the quality or state of being urbane

ur·ban·ize \'ər-bə-ˌnīz\ *vb* **-ized; -iz·ing** : to cause to take on urban characteristics — **ur·ban·i·za·tion** \ˌər-bə-nə-'zā-shən\ *n*

ur·chin \'ər-chən\ n [ME, hedgehog, fr. AF *heriçun, hirechoun*, ultim. fr. L *ericius*] : a pert or mischievous youngster

Ur·du \'ur-dü, 'ər-\ n [Hindi & Urdu *urdū*, fr. Pers *zabān-e-urdū-e-muallā* language of the Exalted Comp (the imperial bazaar in Delhi)] : an Indo-Aryan language that is the official language of Pakistan and that is widely used by Muslims in urban areas of India

urea \yu̇-'rē-ə\ n : a soluble nitrogenous compound that is the chief solid constituent of mammalian urine

ure·mia \yu̇-'rē-mē-ə\ n : accumulation in the blood of materials normally passed off in the urine resulting in a poisoned condition — **ure·mic** \-mik\ adj

ure·ter \'yu̇r-ə-tər\ n : a duct that carries the urine from a kidney to the bladder

ure·thra \yu̇-'rē-thrə\ n, pl **-thras** or **-thrae** \-(,)thrē\ : the canal that in most mammals carries off the urine from the bladder and in the male also serves to carry semen from the body — **ure·thral** \-thrəl\ adj

ure·thri·tis \,yu̇r-i-'thrī-təs\ n : inflammation of the urethra

¹urge \'ərj\ vb **urged; urg·ing 1** : to present, advocate, or demand earnestly **2** : to try to persuade or sway ⟨~ a guest to stay⟩ **3** : to serve as a motive or reason for **4** : to impress or impel to some course or activity ⟨the dog *urged* the sheep onward⟩

²urge n **1** : the act or process of urging **2** : a force or impulse that urges or drives

ur·gent \'ər-jənt\ adj **1** : calling for immediate attention : PRESSING **2** : urging insistently — **ur·gen·cy** \-jən-sē\ n — **ur·gent·ly** adv

uric \'yu̇r-ik\ adj : of, relating to, or found in urine

uric acid n : a nearly insoluble acid that is the chief nitrogenous excretory product of birds but is present in only small amounts in mammalian urine

uri·nal \'yu̇r-ə-n⁰l\ n **1** : a receptacle for urine **2** : a place for urinating

uri·nal·y·sis \,yu̇r-ə-'na-lə-səs\ n : chemical analysis of urine

uri·nary \'yu̇r-ə-,ner-ē\ adj **1** : relating to, occurring in, or being organs for the formation and discharge of urine **2** : of, relating to, or for urine

urinary bladder n : a membranous sac in many vertebrates that serves for the temporary retention of urine and discharges by the urethra

uri·nate \'yu̇r-ə-,nāt\ vb **-nat·ed; -nat·ing** : to release or give off urine — **uri·na·tion** \,yu̇r-ə-'nā-shən\ n

urine \'yu̇r-ən\ n : a waste material from the kidneys that is usu. a yellowish watery liquid in mammals but is semisolid in birds and reptiles

URL \,yü-(,)är-'el, 'ər-(ə)l\ n [*uniform (or universal) resource locator*] : a series of usu. alphanumeric characters that specifies the storage location of a resource on the Internet

urn \'ərn\ n **1** : a vessel that typically has the form of a vase on a pedestal and often

is used to hold the ashes of the dead **2** : a closed vessel usu. with a spout for serving a hot beverage

uro·gen·i·tal \,yu̇r-ō-'je-nə-t⁰l\ adj : of, relating to, or being the excretory and reproductive organs or functions

urol·o·gy \yu̇-'rä-lə-jē\ n : a branch of medical science dealing with the urinary or urogenital tract and its disorders — **uro·log·i·cal** \,yu̇r-ə-'lä-ji-kəl\ also **uro·log·ic** \-jik\ adj — **urol·o·gist** \yu̇-'rä-lə-jist\ n

Ur·sa Ma·jor \,ər-sə-'mā-jər\ n [L, lit., greater bear] : the northern constellation that contains the stars which form the Big Dipper

Ursa Mi·nor \-'mī-nər\ n [L, lit., lesser bear] : the constellation including the north pole of the heavens and the stars that form the Little Dipper with the North Star at the tip of the handle

ur·sine \'ər-,sīn\ adj : of, relating to, or resembling a bear

ur·ti·car·ia \,ər-tə-'ker-ē-ə\ n [NL, fr. L *urtica* nettle] : HIVES

us \'əs\ pron, objective case of WE

US abbr United States

USA abbr **1** United States Army **2** United States of America

us·able also **use·able** \'yü-zə-bəl\ adj : suitable or fit for use — **us·abil·i·ty** \,yü-zə-'bi-lə-tē\ n

USAF abbr United States Air Force

us·age \'yü-sij, -zij\ n **1** : habitual or customary practice or procedure **2** : the way in which words and phrases are actually used **3** : the action or mode of using **4** : manner of treating

USB \,yü-(,)es-'bē\ n [*universal serial bus*] : a standardized computer interface for attaching peripherals

USCG abbr United States Coast Guard

USDA abbr United States Department of Agriculture

¹use \'yüs\ n **1** : the act or practice of using or employing something : EMPLOYMENT, APPLICATION **2** : the fact or state of being used **3** : the way of using **4** : USAGE, CUSTOM **5** : the privilege or benefit of using something **6** : the ability or power to use something (as a limb) **7** : the legal enjoyment of property that consists in its employment, occupation, or exercise; also : the benefit or profit esp. from property held in trust **8** : USEFULNESS, UTILITY; also : the end served : OBJECT, FUNCTION **9** : something useful or beneficial ⟨it's no ~ arguing⟩ **10** : the occasion or need to employ ⟨he had no more ~ for it⟩ **11** : ESTEEM, LIKING ⟨had no ~ for modern art⟩

²use \'yüz\ vb **used** \'yüzd; "used to" usu 'yüs-tə\; **us·ing 1** : to put into action or service : EMPLOY **2** : to consume or take (as drugs) regularly **3** : UTILIZE ⟨~ tact⟩; also : MANIPULATE ⟨used his friends to get ahead⟩ **4** : to expend or consume by putting to use **5** : to behave toward : TREAT ⟨used the horse cruelly⟩ **6** : to benefit from ⟨house could ~ a coat of paint⟩ **7** — used in the past with to to indicate a former practice, fact, or state ⟨we *used* to work harder⟩ — **us·er** *n*

used \'yüzd\ *adj* **1** : having been used by another : SECONDHAND ⟨∼ cars⟩ **2** : ACCUSTOMED, HABITUATED ⟨∼ to the heat⟩

use·ful \'yüs-fəl\ *adj* : capable of being put to use : ADVANTAGEOUS; *esp* : serviceable for a beneficial end — **use·ful·ly** *adv* — **use·ful·ness** *n*

use·less \-ləs\ *adj* : having or being of no use : WORTHLESS, INEFFECTUAL — **use·less·ly** *adv* — **use·less·ness** *n*

USES *abbr* United States Employment Service

use up *vb* : to consume completely

¹**ush·er** \'ə-shər\ *n* [ME *usshere*, fr. AF *ussier, usscher*, fr. VL **ustiarius* doorkeeper, fr. L *ostium, ustium* door, mouth of a river] **1** : an officer who walks before a person of rank **2** : one who escorts people to their seats (as in a church or theater)

²**usher** *vb* **1** : to conduct to a place **2** : to precede as an usher, forerunner, or harbinger **3** : INAUGURATE, INTRODUCE ⟨∼ in a new era⟩

ush·er·ette \ˌə-shə-'ret\ *n* : a girl or woman who is an usher (as in a theater)

USIA *abbr* United States Information Agency

USMC *abbr* United States Marine Corps

USN *abbr* United States Navy

USO *abbr* United Service Organizations

USP *abbr* United States Pharmacopeia

USPS *abbr* United States Postal Service

USS *abbr* United States ship

USSR *abbr* Union of Soviet Socialist Republics

usu *abbr* usual; usually

usu·al \'yü-zhə-wəl\ *adj* **1** : accordant with usage, custom, or habit : NORMAL **2** : commonly or ordinarily used **3** : ORDINARY ♦ *Synonyms* CUSTOMARY, HABITUAL, ACCUSTOMED, ROUTINE — **usu·al·ly** \'yü-zhə-wə-lē, 'yü-zhə-lē\ *adv*

usu·fruct \'yü-zə-ˌfrəkt\ *n* [L *ususfructus*, fr. *usus et fructus* use and enjoyment] : the legal right to use and enjoy the benefits and profits of something belonging to another

usu·rer \'yü-zhər-ər\ *n* : one that lends money esp. at an exorbitant rate

usu·ri·ous \yü-'zhùr-ē-əs\ *adj* : practicing, involving, or constituting usury ⟨a ∼ rate of interest⟩

usurp \yü-'sərp, -'zərp\ *vb* [ME, fr. AF *usorper*, fr. L *usurpare*, to take possession of without legal claim, fr. *usu* (abl. of *usus* use) + *rapere* to seize] : to seize and hold by force or without right ⟨∼ a throne⟩ — **usur·pa·tion** \ˌyü-sər-'pā-shən, -zər-\ *n* — **usurp·er** \yü-'sər-pər, -'zər-\ *n*

usu·ry \'yü-zhə-rē\ *n, pl* **-ries** **1** : the lending of money with an interest charge for its use **2** : an excessive rate or amount of interest charged; *esp* : interest above an established legal rate

UT *abbr* Utah

Ute \'yüt\ *n, pl* **Ute** *or* **Utes** : a member of an American Indian people orig. ranging

through Utah, Colorado, Arizona, and New Mexico

uten·sil \yü-'ten-səl\ *n* [ME, vessels for domestic use, fr. MF *utensile*, fr. L *uten-silia*, fr. neut. pl. of *utensilis* useful, fr. *uti* to use] **1** : an instrument or vessel used in a household and esp. a kitchen **2** : a useful tool

uter·us \'yü-tə-rəs\ *n, pl* **uter·us·es** *or* **uteri** \'yü-tə-ˌrī\ : the muscular organ of a female mammal in which the young develop before birth — **uter·ine** \-ˌrīn, -rən\ *adj*

utile \'yüt-ᵊl, 'yü-ˌtī(-ə)l\ *adj* : USEFUL

uti·lise *Brit var of* UTILIZE

util·i·tar·i·an \yü-ˌti-lə-'ter-ē-ən\ *n* : a person who believes in utilitarianism

²**utilitarian** *adj* **1** : of or relating to utilitarianism **2** : of or relating to utility : aiming at usefulness rather than beauty; *also* : serving a useful purpose

util·i·tar·i·an·ism \yü-ˌti-lə-'ter-ē-ə-ˌni-zəm\ *n* : a theory that the greatest good for the greatest number should be the main consideration in making a choice of actions

¹**util·i·ty** \yü-'ti-lə-tē\ *n, pl* **-ties** **1** : USEFULNESS **2** : something useful or designed for use **3** : a business organization performing a public service and subject to special governmental regulation **4** : a public service or a commodity (as electricity or water) provided by a public utility; *also* : equipment to provide such or a similar service

²**utility** *adj* **1** : capable of serving esp. as a substitute in various uses or positions ⟨a ∼ outfielder⟩ ⟨a ∼ cord⟩ **2** : being of a usable but poor quality ⟨∼ beef⟩

utility knife *n* : a knife designed for general use; *esp* : one with a retractable blade

uti·lize \'yü-tə-ˌlīz\ *vb* **-lized; -liz·ing** : to make use of : turn to profitable account or use — **uti·li·za·tion** \ˌyü-tə-lə-'zā-shən\ *n*

ut·most \'ət-ˌmōst\ *adj* **1** : situated at the farthest or most distant point : EXTREME **2** : of the greatest or highest degree, quantity, number, or amount — **utmost** *n*

uto·pia \yù-'tō-pē-ə\ *n* [*Utopia*, imaginary island described in Sir Thomas More's *Utopia*, fr. Gk *ou* not, no + *topos* place] **1** *often cap* : a place of ideal perfection esp. in laws, government, and social conditions **2** : an impractical scheme for social improvement

¹**uto·pi·an** \-pē-ən\ *adj, often cap* **1** : of, relating to, or resembling a utopia **2** : proposing ideal social and political schemes that are impractical **3** : VISIONARY

²**utopian** *n* **1** : a believer in the perfectibility of human society **2** : one who proposes or advocates utopian schemes

¹**ut·ter** \'ə-tər\ *adj* [ME, remote, fr. OE *ūtera* outer, compar. adj. fr. *ūt* out, adv.] : ABSOLUTE, TOTAL ⟨∼ ruin⟩ — **ut·ter·ly** *adv*

²**utter** *vb* [ME *uttren*, fr. *utter* outside, adv., fr. OE *ūtor*, compar. of *ūt* out] **1** : to send forth as a sound : express in usu. spoken

words : PRONOUNCE, SPEAK **2** : to put (as currency) into circulation — **ut·ter·er** *n*

ut·ter·ance \'ə-tə-rəns\ *n* **1** : something uttered; *esp* : an oral or written statement **2** : the action of uttering with the voice : SPEECH **3** : power, style, or manner of speaking

ut·ter·most \'ə-tər-ˌmōst\ *adj* : EXTREME, UTMOST ⟨the ~ parts of the earth⟩ — **uttermost** *n*

U–turn \'yü-ˌtərn\ *n* : a turn resembling the letter U; *esp* : a 180-degree turn made by a vehicle in a road

UV *abbr* ultraviolet

uvu·la \'yü-vyə-lə\ *n, pl* **-las** *or* **-lae** \-ˌlē, -ˌlī\ : the fleshy lobe hanging at the back of the roof of the mouth — **uvu·lar** \-lər\ *adj*

UW *abbr* underwriter

ux·o·ri·ous \ˌək-'sȯr-ē-əs, ˌəg-'zȯr-\ *adj* : excessively devoted or submissive to a wife

---

¹v \'vē\ *n, pl* **v's** *or* **vs** \'vēz\ *often cap* : the 22d letter of the English alphabet

²v *abbr, often cap* **1** vector **2** velocity **3** verb **4** verse **5** versus **6** very **7** victory **8** vide **9** voice **10** voltage **11** volume **12** vowel

V *symbol* **1** vanadium **2** volt

Va *abbr* Virginia

VA *abbr* **1** Veterans Administration **2** vice admiral **3** Virginia

va·can·cy \'vā-kən-sē\ *n, pl* **-cies** **1** : a vacating esp. of an office, position, or piece of property **2** : a vacant office, position, or tenancy; *also* : the period during which it stands vacant **3** : empty space : VOID **4** : the state of being vacant

va·cant \'vā-kənt\ *adj* **1** : not occupied ⟨~ seat⟩ ⟨~ room⟩ **2** : EMPTY ⟨~ space⟩ **3** : free from business or care ⟨a few ~ hours⟩ **4** : devoid of thought, reflection, or expression ⟨a ~ smile⟩ — **va·cant·ly** *adv*

va·cate \'vā-ˌkāt\ *vb* **va·cat·ed; va·cat·ing** **1** : to make void : ANNUL **2** : to make vacant (as an office or house); *also* : to give up the occupancy of

¹va·ca·tion \vā-'kā-shən, və-\ *n* : a period of rest from work : HOLIDAY

²vacation *vb* : to take or spend a vacation — **va·ca·tion·er** *n*

va·ca·tion·ist \-shə-nist\ *n* : a person taking a vacation

va·ca·tion·land \-shən-ˌland\ *n* : an area with recreational attractions and facilities for vacationists

vac·ci·nate \'vak-sə-ˌnāt\ *vb* **-nat·ed; -nat·ing** : to administer a vaccine to usu. by injection

vac·ci·na·tion \ˌvak-sə-'nā-shən\ *n* **1** : the act of vaccinating **2** : the scar left by vaccinating

vac·cine \vak-'sēn, 'vak-ˌsēn\ *n* [F *vaccin*, fr. *vaccine* cowpox, fr. NL *vaccina* (in *variolae vaccinae* cowpox), fr. L, fem. of *vaccinus* of or from cows, fr. *vacca* cow] : a preparation of material (as of killed or weakened viruses or bacteria) used in vaccinating to produce or increase immunity to a disease

vac·cin·ia \vak-'si-nē-ə\ *n* : COWPOX

vac·il·late \'va-sə-ˌlāt\ *vb* **-lat·ed; -lat·ing** **1** : SWAY, TOTTER; *also* : FLUCTUATE **2**

: to incline first to one course or opinion and then to another : WAVER — **vac·il·la·tion** \ˌva-sə-'lā-shən\ *n*

va·cu·ity \va-'kyü-ə-tē\ *n, pl* **-ities** **1** : an empty space **2** : the state, fact, or quality of being vacuous **3** : something that is vacuous

vac·u·ole \'va-kyə-ˌwōl\ *n* : a usu. fluid-filled cavity esp. in the cytoplasm of an individual cell — **vac·u·o·lar** \ˌva-kyə-'wō-lər, -ˌlär\ *adj*

vac·u·ous \'va-kyə-wəs\ *adj* **1** : EMPTY, VACANT, BLANK **2** : DULL, STUPID, INANE ⟨~ movies⟩ — **vac·u·ous·ly** *adv* — **vac·u·ous·ness** *n*

¹vac·u·um \'va-(ˌ)kyüm, -kyəm\ *n, pl* **vac·uums** *or* **vac·ua** \-kyə-wə\ [L, fr. neut. of *vacuus* empty] **1** : a space entirely empty of matter **2** : a space from which most of the air has been removed (as by a pump) **3** : VOID, GAP **4** : VACUUM CLEANER — **vacuum** *adj*

²vacuum *vb* : to use a vacuum device (as a vacuum cleaner) on ⟨~ the den⟩

vacuum bottle *n* : THERMOS

vacuum cleaner *n* : a household appliance for cleaning (as floors or rugs) by suction

vacuum-packed *adj* : having much of the air removed before being hermetically sealed ⟨~ fish⟩

vacuum tube *n* : an electron tube from which most of the air has been removed

va·de me·cum \ˌvā-dē-'mē-kəm, ˌvä-dē-'mä-\ *n, pl* **vade mecums** [L, go with me] : something (as a handbook or manual) regularly carried about

VADM *abbr* vice admiral

¹vag·a·bond \'va-gə-ˌbänd\ *adj* **1** : WANDERING, HOMELESS **2** : of, characteristic of, or leading the life of a vagrant or tramp **3** : leading an unsettled or irresponsible life

²vagabond *n* : one leading a vagabond life; *esp* : VAGRANT, TRAMP

va·gar·i·ous \vā-'ger-ē-əs\ *adj* : marked by vagaries : CAPRICIOUS ⟨~ leadership⟩ — **va·gar·i·ous·ly** *adv*

va·ga·ry \'vā-gə-rē, və-'ger-ē\ *n, pl* **-ries** : an odd or eccentric idea or action : WHIM, CAPRICE ⟨*vagaries* of the weather⟩

va·gi·na \və-'jī-nə\ *n, pl* **-nae** \-(ˌ)nē\ *or* **-nas** [L., lit., sheath] : a canal that leads from the uterus to the external opening of the female sex organs — **vag·i·nal** \'va-jə-n³l\ *adj* — **vag·i·nal·ly** \-n³l-ē\ *adv*

vag·i·ni·tis \ˌva-jə-'nī-təs\ *n* : inflammation of the vagina

va·gran·cy \'vā-grən-sē\ *n, pl* **-cies** 1 : the quality or state of being vagrant; *also* : a vagrant act or notion 2 : the offense of being a vagrant

¹**va·grant** \'vā-grənt\ *n* : a person who has no job and wanders from place to place

²**vagrant** *adj* 1 : of, relating to, or characteristic of a vagrant 2 : following no fixed course : RANDOM, CAPRICIOUS ⟨~ thoughts⟩ — **va·grant·ly** *adv*

vague \'vāg\ *adj* **vagu·er; vagu·est** [MF, fr. L *vagus*, lit., wandering] 1 : not clear, definite, or distinct ⟨a ~ plan⟩ — **silhouettes**⟩ 2 : not clearly felt or analyzed ⟨a ~ unrest⟩ ♦ *Synonyms* OBSCURE, DARK, ENIGMATIC, AMBIGUOUS, EQUIVOCAL — **vague·ly** *adv* — **vague·ness** *n*

vain \'vān\ *adj* [ME, fr. AF, empty, futile, fr. L *vanus*] 1 : of no real value : IDLE, WORTHLESS 2 : FUTILE, UNSUCCESSFUL 3 : proud of one's looks or abilities ♦ *Synonyms* CONCEITED, NARCISSISTIC, VAINGLORIOUS — **vain·ly** *adv* — **in vain** 1 : without success ⟨her efforts were *in vain*⟩ 2 : in a blasphemous manner ⟨took the Lord's name *in vain*⟩

vain·glo·ri·ous \ˌvān-'glōr-ē-əs\ *adj* : marked by vainglory : BOASTFUL

vain·glo·ry \'vān-ˌglōr-ē\ *n* 1 : excessive or ostentatious pride esp. in one's own achievements 2 : vain display : VANITY

val *abbr* valued

va·lance \'va-ləns, 'vā-\ *n* 1 : drapery hanging from an edge (as of an altar, table, or bed) 2 : a drapery or a decorative frame across the top of a window

vale \'vāl\ *n* : VALLEY, DALE

vale·dic·tion \ˌva-lə-'dik-shən\ *n* [L *valedicere* to say farewell, fr. *vale* farewell + *dicere* to say] : an act or utterance of leave-taking : FAREWELL

vale·dic·to·ri·an \-ˌdik-'tòr-ē-ən\ *n* : the student usu. of the highest rank in a graduating class who delivers the valedictory address at commencement

vale·dic·to·ry \-'dik-tə-rē\ *adj* : bidding farewell : delivered as a valediction ⟨a ~ address⟩ — **valedictory** *n*

va·lence \'vā-ləns\ *n* [LL *valentia* power, capacity, fr. L *valēre* to be strong] : the combining power of an atom as shown by the number of its electrons that are lost, gained, or shared in the formation of chemical bonds

Va·len·ci·ennes \və-ˌlen-sē-'en, ˌva-lən-sē-, -'enz\ *n* : a fine handmade lace

val·en·tine \'va-lən-ˌtīn\ *n* : a sweetheart chosen or complimented on Valentine's Day; *also* : a gift or greeting given on this day

Valentine's Day *also* **Valentine Day** *n* : February 14 observed in honor of St. Valentine and as a time for exchanging valentines

¹**va·let** \'va-lət, -(ˌ)lā; va-'lā\ *n* 1 : a male servant who takes care of a man's clothes and performs personal services 2 : an attendant in a hotel or restaurant who performs personal services (as parking cars) for customers

²**valet** *vb* : to serve as a valet

val·e·tu·di·nar·i·an \ˌva-lə-ˌtü-də-'ner-ē-ən, -ˌtyü-\ *n* : a person of a weak or sickly constitution; *esp* : one whose chief concern is his or her ill health — **val·e·tu·di·nar·i·an·ism** \-ē-ə-ˌni-zəm\ *n*

val·iant \'val-yənt\ *adj* : having or showing valor : BRAVE, HEROIC ♦ *Synonyms* VALOROUS, DOUGHTY, COURAGEOUS, BOLD, AUDACIOUS, DAUNTLESS, UNDAUNTED, INTREPID — **val·iant·ly** *adv*

val·id \'va-ləd\ *adj* 1 : having legal force ⟨a ~ contract⟩ 2 : founded on truth or fact : capable of being justified or defended : SOUND ⟨a ~ argument⟩ ⟨~ reasons⟩ — **va·lid·i·ty** \və-'li-də-tē\ *n* — **val·id·ly** *adv*

val·i·date \'va-lə-ˌdāt\ *vb* **-dat·ed; -dat·ing** 1 : to make legally valid 2 : to confirm the validity of 3 : VERIFY — **val·i·da·tion** \ˌva-lə-'dā-shən\ *n*

va·lise \və-'lēs\ *n* [F] : SUITCASE

val·ley \'va-lē\ *n, pl* **valleys** : a long depression between ranges of hills or mountains

val·or \'va-lər\ *n* [ME *valour*, worth, worthiness, bravery, fr. AF, fr. ML *valor*, fr. L *valēre* to be strong] : personal bravery ♦ *Synonyms* HEROISM, PROWESS, GALLANTRY — **val·or·ous** \'va-lə-rəs\ *adj*

val·o·ri·za·tion \ˌva-lə-rə-'zā-shən\ *n* : the support of commodity prices by any of various forms of government subsidy — **val·o·rize** \'va-lə-ˌrīz\ *vb*

val·our *chiefly Brit var of* VALOR

¹**valu·able** \'val-yə-bəl, -yə-wə-bəl\ *adj* 1 : having money value 2 : having great money value 3 : of great use or service ♦ *Synonyms* INVALUABLE, PRICELESS, COSTLY, EXPENSIVE, DEAR, PRECIOUS

²**valuable** *n* : a usu. personal possession of considerable value ⟨their ~s were stolen⟩

val·u·ate \'val-yə-ˌwāt\ *vb* **-at·ed; -at·ing** : to place a value on : APPRAISE — **val·u·a·tor** \-ˌwā-tər\ *n*

val·u·a·tion \ˌval-yə-'wā-shən\ *n* 1 : the act or process of valuing; *esp* : appraisal of property 2 : the estimated or determined market value of a thing

¹**val·ue** \'val-yü\ *n* 1 : a fair return or equivalent in money, goods, or services for something exchanged 2 : the monetary worth of a thing; *also* : relative worth, utility, or importance ⟨nothing of ~ to say⟩ 3 : an assigned or computed numerical quantity ⟨the ~ of *x* in an equation⟩ 4 : relative lightness or darkness of a color : LUMINOSITY 5 : the relative length of a tone or note 6 : something (as a principle or ideal) intrinsically valuable or desirable ⟨human rather than material ~s⟩ — **val·ue·less** *adj*

²**value** *vb* **val·ued; valu·ing** 1 : to estimate the monetary worth of : APPRAISE

2 : to rate in usefulness, importance, or general worth 3 : to consider or rate highly : PRIZE, ESTEEM ⟨*valued* your opinions⟩ — **val·u·er** *n*

val·ue–add·ed tax *n* : an incremental excise tax that is levied on the value added at each stage of the processing of a raw material or the production and distribution of a commodity

valve \'valv\ *n* 1 : a structure (as in a vein) that temporarily closes a passage or that permits movement in one direction only 2 : a device by which the flow of a fluid material may be regulated by a movable part; *also* : the movable part of such a device 3 : a device in a brass wind instrument for quickly varying the tube length in order to change the fundamental tone by some definite interval 4 : one of the separate usu. hinged pieces of which the shell of some animals and esp. bivalve mollusks consists 5 : one of the pieces into which a ripe seed capsule or pod separates — **valved** \'valvd\ *adj* — **valve·less** *adj*

val·vu·lar \'val-vyə-lər\ *adj* : of, relating to, or affecting a valve esp. of the heart ⟨~ heart disease⟩

va·moose \və-'müs, va-\ *vb* **va·moosed**; **va·moos·ing** [Sp *vamos* let us go] : to leave or go away quickly

¹vamp *n* 1 : the part of a boot or shoe upper covering esp. the front part of the foot 2 : a short introductory musical passage often repeated

²vamp \'vamp\ *vb* 1 : to provide with a new vamp 2 : to patch up with a new part 3 : INVENT, IMPROVISE ⟨~ up an excuse⟩

³vamp *n* : a woman who uses her charm or wiles to seduce and exploit men

⁴vamp *vb* : to practice seductive wiles on : to act like a vamp

vam·pire \'vam-ˌpī(-ə)r\ *n* [F, fr. G *Vampir*, fr. Serbian *vampir*] 1 : a reanimated corpse of folklore that bites and sucks the blood of the living 2 : a person who preys on other people; *esp* : a woman who exploits and ruins her lover 3 : VAMPIRE BAT

vampire bat *n* : any of various bats of Central and South America that feed on the blood of animals; *also* : any of several other bats that do not feed on blood but are sometimes reputed to do so

¹van \'van\ *n* : VANGUARD

²van *n* : a usu. enclosed wagon or motortruck for moving goods or animals; *also* : a versatile enclosed box-like motor vehicle

va·na·di·um \və-'nā-dē-əm\ *n* : a soft grayish ductile metallic chemical element used esp. to form alloys

Van Al·len belt \van-'a-lən-\ *n* : a belt of intense radiation in the magnetosphere composed of charged particles trapped by earth's magnetic field

van·co·my·cin \ˌvan-kə-'mī-sᵊn\ *n* : an antibiotic used esp. against staphylococci

van·dal \'van-dᵊl\ *n* 1 *cap* : a member of a Germanic people who sacked Rome in A.D. 455 2 : a person who willfully mars or destroys property

van·dal·ise *Brit var of* VANDALIZE

van·dal·ism \'van-də-ˌli-zəm\ *n* : willful or malicious destruction or defacement of public or private property

van·dal·ize \-ˌīz\ *vb* **-ized**; **-iz·ing** : to subject to vandalism : DAMAGE

Van·dyke \van-'dīk\ *n* : a trim pointed beard

vane \'vān\ *n* [ME, fr. OE *fana* banner] 1 : a movable device attached to a high object for showing wind direction 2 : a thin flat or curved object that is rotated about an axis by a flow of fluid or that rotates to cause a fluid to flow or that redirects a flow of fluid ⟨the ~s of a windmill⟩ 3 : a feather fastened near the back end of an arrow for stability in flight

van·guard \'van-ˌgärd\ *n* 1 : the troops moving at the front of an army 2 : the forefront of an action or movement

va·nil·la \və-'ni-lə\ *n* [NL, genus name, fr. Sp *vainilla* vanilla (plant and fruit), dim. of *vaina* sheath, fr. L *vagina*] : a flavoring extract made synthetically or obtained from the long beanlike pods (**vanilla beans**) of a tropical American climbing orchid; *also* : this orchid

van·ish \'va-nish\ *vb* : to pass from sight or existence : disappear completely — **van·ish·er** *n*

van·i·ty \'va-nə-tē\ *n, pl* **-ties** 1 : something that is vain, empty, or useless 2 : the quality or fact of being vain or futile : FUTILITY 3 : undue pride in oneself or one's appearance : CONCEIT 4 : a small case for cosmetics : COMPACT

vanity plate *n* : an automobile license plate bearing distinctive letters or numbers designated by the owner

van·quish \'vaŋ-kwish, 'van-\ *vb* 1 : to overcome in battle or in a contest 2 : to gain mastery over (as an emotion)

van·tage \'van-tij\ *n* 1 : superiority in a contest 2 : a position giving a strategic advantage or a commanding perspective

va·pid \'va-pəd, 'vā-\ *adj* : lacking spirit, liveliness, or zest : FLAT, INSIPID ⟨~ gossip⟩ — **va·pid·i·ty** \va-'pi-də-tē\ *n* — **vap·id·ly** *adv* — **vap·id·ness** *n*

va·por \'vā-pər\ *n* 1 : fine separated particles (as fog or smoke) floating in the air and clouding it 2 : a substance in the gaseous state; *esp* : one that is liquid under ordinary conditions 3 : something insubstantial or fleeting 4 *pl* : a depressed or hysterical nervous condition

va·por·ing \'vā-pə-riŋ\ *n* : an idle, boastful, or high-flown expression or speech — usu. used in pl. ⟨political ~s⟩

va·por·ise *Brit var of* VAPORIZE

va·por·ize \'vā-pə-ˌrīz\ *vb* **-ized**; **-iz·ing** 1 : to convert into vapor 2 : to destroy as if by converting to vapor ⟨*vaporized* enemy tanks⟩ — **va·por·i·za·tion** \ˌvā-pə-rə-'zā-shən\ *n*

va·por·iz·er \-ˌrī-zər\ *n* : a device that vaporizes something (as a medicated liquid)

vapor lock *n* : an interruption of flow of a fluid (as fuel in an engine) caused by

vaporous • vasoconstrictor

the formation of vapor in the feeding system

va·por·ous \'vā-pə-rəs\ *adj* **1** : full of vapors : FOGGY, MISTY **2** : UNSUBSTANTIAL, VAGUE ⟨~ speculations⟩ — **va·por·ous·ly** *adv* — **va·por·ous·ness** *n*

va·po·ry \'vā-pə-rē\ *adj* : MISTY

va·pour *chiefly Brit var of* VAPOR

va·que·ro \vä-'ker-ō\ *n, pl* **-ros** [Sp, fr. *vaca* cow, fr. L *vacca*] : a ranch hand : COWBOY

var *abbr* **1** variable **2** variant; variation **3** variety **4** various

¹var·i·able \'ver-ē-ə-bəl\ *adj* **1** : able or apt to vary : CHANGEABLE **2** : FICKLE **3** : not true to type : ABERRANT ⟨a ~ wheat⟩ — **var·i·abil·i·ty** \,ver-ē-ə-'bi-lə-tē, ,var-\ *n* — **var·i·ably** \-blē\ *adv*

²variable *n* **1** : a quantity that may take on any of a set of values; *also* : a mathematical symbol representing a variable **2** : something that is variable

vari·ance \'ver-ē-ons\ *n* **1** : variation or a degree of variation : DEVIATION **2** : DISAGREEMENT, DISPUTE **3** : a license to do something contrary to the usual rule ⟨a zoning ~⟩ **4** : the square of the standard deviation ♦ *Synonyms* DISCORD, CONTENTION, DISSENSION, STRIFE, CONFLICT

¹vari·ant \'ver-ē-ənt\ *adj* **1** : differing from others of its kind or class **2** : varying usu. slightly from the standard or type

²variant *n* **1** : one that exhibits variation from a type or norm **2** : one of two or more different spellings or pronunciations of a word

vari·a·tion \,ver-ē-'ā-shən\ *n* **1** : the act, process, or an instance of varying : a change in form, position, or condition : MODIFICATION, ALTERATION **2** : extent of change or difference **3** : divergence in the characteristics of an organism from those typical or usual for its group; *also* : one exhibiting such variation **4** : repetition of a musical theme with modifications in rhythm, tune, harmony, or key

vari·col·ored \'ver-i-,kə-lərd\ *adj* : having various colors : VARIEGATED

vari·cose \'va-rə-,kōs\ *adj* : abnormally swollen and dilated ⟨~ veins⟩ — **var·i·cos·i·ty** \,va-rə-'kä-sə-tē\ *n*

var·ied \'ver-ēd\ *adj* **1** : having many forms or types : DIVERSE ⟨~ interests⟩ **2** : VARIEGATED — **var·ied·ly** *adv*

vari·e·gat·ed \'ver-ē-ə-,gā-təd\ *adj* **1** : having patches, stripes, or marks of different colors ⟨~ flowers⟩ **2** : VARIED **1** — **vari·e·gate** \-,gāt\ *vb* — **vari·e·ga·tion** \,ver-ē-ə-'gā-shən\ *n*

¹va·ri·etal \və-'rī-ə-tᵊl\ *adj* : of or relating to a variety; *esp* : of, relating to, or producing a varietal

²varietal *n* : a wine bearing the name of the principal grape from which it is made

va·ri·ety \və-'rī-ə-tē\ *n, pl* **-et·ies** **1** : the state of being varied or various : DIVERSITY **2** : a collection of different things : ASSORTMENT **3** : something varying from others of the same general kind **4** : any of various groups of plants or animals within a species distinguished by characteristics insufficient to separate species : SUBSPECIES **5** : entertainment such as is given in a stage presentation comprising a series of performances (as songs, dances, or acrobatic acts)

var·i·o·rum \,ver-ē-'ōr-əm\ *n* : an edition or text of a work containing notes by various persons or variant readings of the text

var·i·ous \'ver-ē-əs\ *adj* **1** : VARICOLORED **2** : of differing kinds : MULTIFARIOUS **3** : UNLIKE ⟨animals as ~ as the jaguar and the sloth⟩ **4** : having a number of different aspects **5** : NUMEROUS, MANY **6** : INDIVIDUAL, SEPARATE ♦ *Synonyms* DIVERGENT, DISPARATE, DIFFERENT, DISSIMILAR, DIVERSE, UNALIKE — **var·i·ous·ly** *adv*

var·let \'vär-lət\ *n* **1** : ATTENDANT **2** : SCOUNDREL, KNAVE

var·mint \'vär-mənt\ *n* [alter. of *vermin*] **1** : an animal considered a pest; *esp* : one classed as vermin and unprotected by game law **2** : a contemptible person : RASCAL

¹var·nish \'vär-nish\ *n* **1** : a liquid preparation that is applied to a surface and dries into a hard glossy coating; *also* : the glaze of this coating **2** : something suggesting varnish by its gloss **3** : outside show : deceptive or superficial appearance

²varnish *vb* **1** : to cover with varnish **2** : to cover or conceal with something that gives a fair appearance : GLOSS

var·si·ty \'vär-sə-tē\ *n, pl* **-ties** [by shortening & alter. fr. *university*] **1** *Brit* : UNIVERSITY **2** : the principal team representing a college, school, or club

vary \'ver-ē\ *vb* **var·ied; vary·ing 1** : ALTER, CHANGE **2** : to make or be of different kinds : introduce or have variety : DIVERSIFY, DIFFER **3** : DEVIATE, SWERVE **4** : to change in bodily structure or function away from what is usual for members of a group

vas·cu·lar \'vas-kyə-lər\ *adj* [NL *vascularis*, fr. L *vasculum* small vessel, dim. of *vas* vase, vessel] : of or relating to a channel or system of channels for the conveyance of a body fluid (as blood or sap); *also* : supplied with or containing such vessels and esp. blood vessels ⟨the ~ system⟩

vascular plant *n* : a plant having a specialized system for carrying fluids that includes xylem and phloem

vas def·er·ens \'vas-'de-fə-rənz\ *n, pl* **va·sa def·er·en·tia** \'vā-zə-,de-fə-'ren-shē-ə\ : a sperm-carrying duct of the testis

vase \'vās, 'vāz\ *n* : a usu. round vessel of greater depth than width used chiefly for ornament or for flowers

va·sec·to·my \va-'sek-tə-mē, vā-'zek-\ *n, pl* **-mies** : surgical excision of all or part of the vas deferens usu. to induce sterility

va·so·con·stric·tion \,vā-zō-kən-'strik-shən\ *n* : narrowing of the interior diameter of blood vessels

va·so·con·stric·tor \-tər\ *n* : an agent (as

a nerve fiber or a drug) that initiates or induces vasoconstriction

vas·sal \'va-səl\ *n* **1** : a person under the protection of a feudal lord to whom he owes homage and loyalty : a feudal tenant **2** : one occupying a dependent or subordinate position — **vassal** *adj*

vas·sal·age \-sə-lij\ *n* **1** : the state of being a vassal **2** : the homage and loyalty due from a vassal **3** : SERVITUDE, SUBJECTION

¹vast \'vast\ *adj* : very great in size, amount, degree, intensity, or esp. extent ⟨∼ plains⟩ ⟨∼ knowledge⟩ ♦ *Synonyms* ENORMOUS, HUGE, GIGANTIC, COLOSSAL, MAMMOTH — **vast·ly** *adv* — **vast·ness** *n*

²vast *n* : a great expanse : IMMENSITY

vasty \'vas-tē\ *adj* : VAST, IMMENSE

vat \'vat\ *n* : a large vessel (as a tub or barrel) esp. for holding liquids in manufacturing processes

VAT *abbr* value-added tax

vat·ic \'va-tik\ *adj* : PROPHETIC, ORACULAR ⟨∼ pronouncements⟩

Vat·i·can \'va-ti-kən\ *n* **1** : the papal headquarters in Rome **2** : the papal government

va·tu \'vä-,tü\ *n, pl* **vatu** — see MONEY table

vaude·ville \'vod-vəl, 'väd-, 'vōd-, -,vil\ *n* [F, fr. MF, satirical song, alter. of *vaudevire*, fr. *vau-de-Vire* valley of Vire, town in northwest France where such songs were composed] : a stage entertainment consisting of unrelated acts (as of acrobats, comedians, dancers, or singers)

¹vault \'vȯlt\ *n* **1** : an arched masonry structure usu. forming a ceiling or roof; *also* : something (as the sky) resembling a vault **2** : a room or space covered by a vault esp. when underground **3** : a room or compartment for the safekeeping of valuables **4** : a burial chamber; *also* : a usu. metal or concrete case in which a casket is enclosed at burial — **vaulty** *adj*

²vault *vb* : to form or cover with a vault

³vault *vb* : to leap vigorously esp. by aid of the hands or a pole — **vault·er** *n*

⁴vault *n* : an act of vaulting : LEAP

vault·ed \'vȯl-təd\ *adj* **1** : built in the form of a vault : ARCHED **2** : covered with a vault

vault·ing \-tiŋ\ *adj* : reaching for the heights ⟨∼ ambition⟩

vaunt \'vȯnt\ *vb* [ME, fr. AF *vanter*, fr. LL *vanitare*, ultim. fr. L *vanus* vain] : to boast of ⟨∼*s* his successes⟩ — **vaunt** *n*

vaunt·ed \'vȯn-təd\ *adj* : much praised or boasted of

vb *abbr* verb; verbal

V–chip \'vē-,chip\ *n* : a computer chip in a television set used to block based on content the viewing of certain programs

VCR \,vē-(,)sē-'är\ *n* [*videocassette recorder*] : a device that records and plays back videotapes

VD *abbr* venereal disease

VDT *abbr* video display terminal

veal \'vēl\ *n* : the flesh of a young calf

vec·tor \'vek-tər\ *n* **1** : a quantity that has magnitude and direction **2** : an organism (as a fly or tick) that transmits a pathogen

Ve·da \'vā-də\ *n* [Skt, lit., knowledge] : any of a class of Hindu sacred writings — **Ve·dic** \'vā-dik\ *adj*

Ve·dan·ta \vā-'dän-tə, və-, -'dan-\ *n* : an orthodox Hindu philosophy based on the Upanishads

vee·jay \'vē-,jā\ *n* : an announcer of a program featuring music videos

veep \'vēp\ *n* : VICE PRESIDENT

veer \'vir\ *vb* : to shift from one direction or course to another ♦ *Synonyms* TURN, AVERT, DEFLECT, DIVERT — **veer** *n*

veg·an \'vē-gən, 'vā-; 'vē-jən, -,jan\ *n* : a strict vegetarian who consumes no animal food or dairy products — **veg·an·ism** \'vē-gə-,ni-zəm, 'vā-; 'vē-jə-\ *n*

¹veg·e·ta·ble \'vej-tə-bəl, 've-jə-\ *adj* [ME, fr. ML *vegetabilis* vegetative, fr. *vegetare* to grow, fr. L, to animate, fr. *vegetus* lively, fr. *vegēre* to enliven] **1** : of, relating to, or growing like plants ⟨the ∼ kingdom⟩ **2** : made from, obtained from, or containing plants or plant products ⟨∼ oils⟩ **3** : suggesting that of a plant (as in inertness) ⟨a ∼ existence⟩

²vegetable *n* **1** : PLANT 1 **2** : a usu. herbaceous plant grown for an edible part that is usu. eaten as part of a meal; *also* : such an edible part

veg·e·tal \'ve-jə-t³l\ *adj* **1** : VEGETABLE **2** : VEGETATIVE

veg·e·tar·i·an \,ve-jə-'ter-ē-ən\ *n* : one that believes in or practices living on a diet of vegetables, fruits, grains, nuts, and sometimes animal products (as milk and cheese) — **vegetarian** *adj* — **veg·e·tar·i·an·ism** \-ē-ə-,ni-zəm\ *n*

veg·e·tate \'ve-jə-,tāt\ *vb* **-tat·ed; -tat·ing** : to live or grow in the manner of a plant; *esp* : to lead a dull inert life

veg·e·ta·tion \,ve-jə-'tā-shən\ *n* **1** : the act or process of vegetating; *also* : inert existence **2** : plant life or cover (as of an area) — **veg·e·ta·tion·al** \-shə-nəl\ *adj*

veg·e·ta·tive \'ve-jə-,tā-tiv\ *adj* **1** : of or relating to nutrition and growth esp. as contrasted with reproduction **2** : of, relating to, or composed of vegetation ⟨∼ cover⟩ **3** : VEGETABLE 3

veg out \'vej-\ *vb* **vegged out; vegging out** [short for *vegetate*] : to spend time idly or passively

ve·he·ment \'vē-ə-mənt\ *adj* **1** : marked by great force or energy **2** : marked by strong feeling or expression : PASSIONATE, FERVID ⟨∼ opposition⟩ — **ve·he·mence** \-məns\ *n* — **ve·he·ment·ly** *adv*

ve·hi·cle \'vē-ə-kəl, 'vē-,hi-\ *n* **1** : a medium by which a thing is applied or administered ⟨linseed oil is a ∼ for pigments⟩ **2** : a medium through or by means of which something is conveyed or expressed **3** : a means of transporting persons or goods ♦ *Synonyms* INSTRUMENT, AGENT, AGENCY, ORGAN, CHANNEL — **ve·hic·u·lar** \vē-'hi-kyə-lər\ *adj*

¹veil \'vāl\ *n* **1** : a piece of often sheer or diaphanous material used to screen or curtain something or to cover the head or face **2** : the life of a nun ⟨take the ~⟩ **3** : something that hides or obscures like a veil ⟨a ~ of secrecy⟩

²**veil** vb : to cover with or as if with a veil : wear a veil

¹**vein** \'vān\ n **1** : a fissure in rock filled with mineral matter; also : a bed of useful mineral matter **2** : any of the tubular branching vessels that carry blood from the capillaries toward the heart **3** : any of the bundles of vascular vessels forming the framework of a leaf **4** : any of the thickened ribs that stiffen the wings of an insect **5** : something (as a wavy variegation in marble) suggesting veins **6** : a distinctive style of expression **7** : a distinctive element or quality : STRAIN **8** : MOOD, HUMOR — **veined** \'vānd\ adj

²**vein** vb : to pattern with or as if with veins — **vein·ing** n

vel abbr velocity

ve·lar \'vē-lər\ adj : of or relating to a velum and esp. that of the soft palate

veld or **veldt** \'velt, 'felt\ n [Afrikaans veld, fr. D. field] : an open grassland esp. in southern Africa usu. with scattered shrubs or trees

vel·lum \'ve-ləm\ n [ME velym, fr. AF velim, veeslin, fr. *veelin, adj., of a calf, fr. veel calf] **1** : a fine-grained lambskin, kidskin, or calfskin prepared for writing on or for binding books **2** : a strong cream-colored paper — **vellum** adj

ve·loc·i·pede \və-'lä-sə-ˌpēd\ n : an early bicycle

ve·loc·i·rap·tor \və-'lä-sə-ˌrap-tər\ n : any of a genus of agile flesh-eating bipedal dinosaurs of the Cretaceous having a sickle-shaped claw on each foot

ve·loc·i·ty \və-'lä-sə-tē\ n, pl **-ties** : quickness of motion : SPEED ⟨the ~ of light⟩

ve·lour or **ve·lours** \və-'lu̇r\ n, pl **velours** \-'lu̇rz\ : any of various textile fabrics with pile like that of velvet

ve·lum \'vē-ləm\ n, pl **ve·la** \-lə\ : a membranous body part (as the soft palate) resembling a veil

vel·vet \'vel-vət\ n [ME veluet, velvet, fr. AF, fr. velu shaggy, ultim. fr. L villus shaggy hair] **1** : a fabric having a short soft dense warp pile **2** : something resembling or suggesting velvet (as in softness or luster) **3** : the soft skin covering the growing antlers of deer — **velvet** adj — **velvety** adj

vel·vet·een \ˌvel-və-'tēn\ n **1** : a fabric woven usu. of cotton in imitation of velvet **2** pl : clothes made of velveteen

Ven abbr venerable

ve·nal \'vē-nᵊl\ adj : capable of being bought or bribed : MERCENARY, CORRUPT ⟨~ legislators⟩ — **ve·nal·i·ty** \vi-'na-lə-tē\ n — **ve·nal·ly** \'vē-nᵊl-ē\ adv

ve·na·tion \ve-'nā-shən, vē-\ n : an arrangement or system of veins ⟨the ~ of the hand⟩ ⟨leaf ~⟩

vend \'vend\ vb : SELL; esp : to sell as a hawker or peddler — **vend·ible** adj

vend·ee \ven-'dē\ n : one to whom a thing is sold : BUYER

ven·det·ta \ven-'de-tə\ n : a feud marked by acts of revenge

vending machine n : a coin-operated machine for selling merchandise

ven·dor \'ven-dər, for 1 also ven-'do̊r\ n **1** : one that vends : SELLER **2** : VENDING MACHINE

¹**ve·neer** \və-'nir\ n [G Furnier, fr. furnieren to veneer, fr. F fournir to furnish] **1** : a thin usu. superficial layer of material ⟨brick ~⟩; esp : a thin layer of fine wood glued over a cheaper wood **2** : superficial display : GLOSS

²**veneer** vb : to overlay with a veneer

ven·er·a·ble \'ve-nə-rə-bəl\ adj **1** : deserving to be venerated — often used as a religious title **2** : made sacred by association

ven·er·ate \'ve-nə-ˌrāt\ vb **-at·ed; -at·ing** : to regard with reverential respect
♦ *Synonyms* ADORE, REVERE, REVERENCE, WORSHIP — **ven·er·a·tion** \ˌve-nə-'rā-shən\ n

ve·ne·re·al \və-'nir-ē-əl\ adj : of or relating to sexual intercourse or to diseases transmitted by it ⟨a ~ infection⟩

venereal disease n : a contagious disease (as gonorrhea or syphilis) usu. acquired by having sexual intercourse with someone who already has it

ve·ne·tian blind \və-ˌnē-shən-\ n : a blind having thin horizontal parallel slats that can be adjusted to admit a desired amount of light

ven·geance \'ven-jəns\ n : punishment inflicted in retaliation for an injury or offense : REVENGE

venge·ful \'venj-fəl\ adj : filled with a desire for revenge : VINDICTIVE ⟨a ~ former employee⟩ — **venge·ful·ly** adv

ve·nial \'vē-nē-əl\ adj : capable of being forgiven : EXCUSABLE ⟨~ sin⟩

ve·ni·re \və-'nī-rē\ n : a panel from which a jury is drawn

ve·ni·re fa·ci·as \-'fā-shē-əs\ n [ME, fr. ML, you should cause to come] : a writ summoning persons to appear in court to serve as jurors

ve·ni·re·man \və-'nī-rē-mən, -'nir-ē-\ n : a member of a venire

ven·i·son \'ve-nə-sən, -zən\ n, pl **venisons** also **venison** [ME, fr. AF veneisun game, venison, fr. L venatio, fr. venari to hunt, pursue] : the edible flesh of a deer

ven·om \'ve-nəm\ n [ME venim, fr. AF, ultim. fr. L venenum magic charm, drug, poison] **1** : poisonous material secreted by some animals (as snakes, spiders, or bees) and transmitted usu. by biting or stinging **2** : ILL WILL, MALEVOLENCE

ven·om·ous \'ve-nə-məs\ adj **1** : full of venom : POISONOUS **2** : SPITEFUL, MALEVOLENT ⟨~ comments⟩ **3** : secreting and using venom ⟨~ snakes⟩ — **ven·om·ous·ly** adv

ve·nous \'vē-nəs\ adj **1** : of, relating to, or full of veins **2** : being purplish red oxygen-deficient blood rich in carbon dioxide that is present in most veins

¹**vent** \'vent\ vb **1** : to provide with a vent **2** : to serve as a vent for **3** : EXPEL, DISCHARGE **4** : to relieve oneself by vigorous or emotional expression

²**vent** n **1** : an opportunity or way of es-

cape or passage : OUTLET **2** : an opening for the escape of a gas or liquid or for the relief of pressure

³**vent** *n* : a slit in a garment esp. in the lower part of a seam (as of a jacket or skirt)

ven·ti·late \'ven-tə-ˌlāt\ *vb* **-lat·ed; -lat·ing 1** : to discuss freely and openly ⟨~ a question⟩ **2** : to give vent to ⟨~ one's grievances⟩ **3** : to cause fresh air to circulate through (as a room or mine) so as to replace foul air **4** : to provide with a vent or outlet ♦ *Synonyms* EXPRESS, VENT, AIR, UTTER, VOICE, BROACH — **ven·ti·la·tor** \-lā-tər\ *n*

ven·ti·la·tion \ˌven-tə-ˈlā-shən\ *n* **1** : the act or process of ventilating **2** : circulation of air (as in a room) **3** : a system or means of providing fresh air

ven·tral \'ven-trəl\ *adj* **1** : of or relating to the belly : ABDOMINAL **2** : of, relating to, or located on or near the surface of the body that in humans is the front but in most other animals is the lower surface — **ven·tral·ly** *adv*

ven·tri·cle \'ven-tri-kəl\ *n* **1** : a chamber of the heart that receives blood from the atrium of the same side and pumps it into the arteries **2** : any of the communicating cavities of the brain that are continuous with the central canal of the spinal cord — **ven·tric·u·lar** \ven-ˈtri-kyə-lər\ *adj*

ven·tril·o·quism \ven-ˈtri-lə-ˌkwi-zəm\ *n* [LL *ventriloquus* ventriloquist, fr. L *venter* belly + *loqui* to speak; fr. the belief that the voice is produced from the ventriloquist's stomach] : the production of the voice in such a manner that the sound appears to come from a source other than the speaker — **ven·tril·o·quist** \-kwist\ *n*

ven·tril·o·quy \-kwē\ *n* : VENTRILOQUISM

¹**ven·ture** \'ven-chər\ *vb* **ven·tured; ven·tur·ing 1** : to expose to hazard : RISK **2** : to undertake the risks of : BRAVE **3** : to offer at the risk of rebuff, rejection, or censure ⟨~ an opinion⟩ **4** : to proceed despite danger : DARE

²**venture** *n* **1** : an undertaking involving chance or risk; *esp* : a speculative business enterprise **2** : something risked in a speculative venture : STAKE

ven·ture·some \'ven-chər-səm\ *adj* **1** : involving risk : DANGEROUS, HAZARDOUS **2** : inclined to venture : BOLD, DARING ♦ *Synonyms* ADVENTUROUS, VENTUROUS, RASH, RECKLESS, FOOLHARDY — **ven·ture·some·ly** *adv* — **ven·ture·some·ness** *n*

ven·tur·ous \'ven-chə-rəs\ *adj* : VENTURESOME — **ven·tur·ous·ly** *adv* — **ven·tur·ous·ness** *n*

ven·ue \'ven-yü\ *n* [AF, alter. of *vinné, visné*, lit., neighborhood, neighbors, ultim. fr. L *vicinitas* vicinity] **1** : the place from which the jury is taken and where the trial is held **2** : the place in which the alleged events from which a legal action arises took place **3** : a place where events are held ⟨music ~s⟩

Ve·nus \'vē-nəs\ *n* : the planet 2d in order from the sun

Venus fly·trap *or* **Ve·nus's–fly·trap** \'vē-nə-səz-ˈflī-ˌtrap\ *n* : an insect-eating plant of the Carolina coast that has the leaf tip modified into an insect trap

Ve·nu·sian \vi-ˈnü-zhən, -ˈnyü-\ *adj* : of or relating to the planet Venus

ve·ra·cious \və-ˈrā-shəs\ *adj* **1** : TRUTHFUL, HONEST **2** : TRUE, ACCURATE ⟨~ details⟩ — **ve·ra·cious·ly** *adv*

ve·rac·i·ty \və-ˈra-sə-tē\ *n, pl* **-ties 1** : devotion to truth : TRUTHFULNESS **2** : conformity with fact : ACCURACY **3** : something true

ve·ran·da *or* **ve·ran·dah** \və-ˈran-də\ *n* : a long open usu. roofed porch

verb \'vərb\ *n* : a word that is the grammatical center of a predicate and expresses an act, occurrence, or mode of being

¹**ver·bal** \'vər-bəl\ *adj* **1** : of, relating to, or consisting of words; *esp* : having to do with words rather than with the ideas to be conveyed **2** : expressed in usu. spoken words : not written : ORAL ⟨a ~ contract⟩ **3** : of, relating to, or formed from a verb ⟨a ~ adjective⟩ **4** : LITERAL, VERBATIM — **ver·bal·ly** *adv*

²**verbal** *n* : a word that combines characteristics of a verb with those of a noun or adjective

verbal auxiliary *n* : an auxiliary verb

ver·bal·ize \'vər-bə-ˌlīz\ *vb* **-ized; -iz·ing 1** : to speak or write in wordy or empty fashion **2** : to express something in words ⟨verbalized her feelings⟩ **3** : to convert into a verb — **ver·bal·i·za·tion** \ˌvər-bə-lə-ˈzā-shən\ *n*

verbal noun *n* : a noun derived directly from a verb or verb stem and in some uses having the sense and constructions of a verb

ver·ba·tim \(ˌ)vər-ˈbā-təm\ *adv or adj* : in the same words : word for word

ver·be·na \(ˌ)vər-ˈbē-nə\ *n* : VERVAIN; *esp* : any of several garden vervains of hybrid origin with showy spikes of bright often fragrant flowers

ver·biage \'vər-bē-ij, -bij\ *n* **1** : superfluity of words usu. of little or obscure content **2** : DICTION, WORDING

ver·bose \(ˌ)vər-ˈbōs\ *adj* : using more words than are needed : WORDY ♦ *Synonyms* PROLIX, DIFFUSE, REDUNDANT, WINDY — **ver·bos·i·ty** \-ˈbä-sə-tē\ *n*

ver·bo·ten \vər-ˈbō-tᵊn, fər-\ *adj* [G] : forbidden usu. by dictate

ver·dant \'vər-dᵊnt\ *adj* : green with growing plants — **ver·dant·ly** *adv*

ver·dict \'vər-(ˌ)dikt\ *n* [ME *verdit, verdict,* fr. AF *veirdit,* fr. *veir* true (fr. L *verus*) + *dit* saying, dictum, fr. L *dictum,* fr. *dicere* to say] **1** : the finding or decision of a jury **2** : DECISION, JUDGMENT

ver·di·gris \'vər-də-ˌgrēs, -ˌgris\ *n* : a green or bluish deposit that forms on copper, brass, or bronze surfaces

ver·dure \'vər-jər\ *n* : the greenness of growing vegetation; *also* : such vegetation

¹**verge** \'vərj\ *n* [ME, rod, measuring rod, margin, fr. AF, rod, area of jurisdiction,

fr. L *virga* twig, rod, line] **1** : a staff carried as an emblem of authority or office **2** : something that borders or bounds : EDGE, MARGIN **3** : BRINK, THRESHOLD ⟨on the ~ of collapse⟩

²**verge** *vb* **verged; verg·ing 1** : to be contiguous **2** : to be on the verge

³**verge** *vb* **verged; verg·ing 1** : to move or extend in some direction or toward some condition : INCLINE **2** : to be in transition or change

verg·er \'vər-jər\ *n* **1** *chiefly Brit* : an attendant who carries a verge (as before a bishop) **2** : SEXTON

ve·rid·i·cal \və-'ri-di-kəl\ *adj* **1** : TRUTHFUL **2** : not illusory : GENUINE

ver·i·fy \'ver-ə-ˌfī\ *vb* **-fied; -fy·ing 1** : to confirm in law by oath **2** : to establish the truth, accuracy, or reality of ⟨~ the claim⟩ ◆ **Synonyms** AUTHENTICATE, CORROBORATE, SUBSTANTIATE, VALIDATE — **ver·i·fi·able** *adj* — **ver·i·fi·ca·tion** \ˌver-ə-fə-'kā-shən\ *n*

ver·i·ly \'ver-ə-lē\ *adv* **1** : in very truth : CERTAINLY **2** : TRULY, CONFIDENTLY

veri·si·mil·i·tude \ˌver-ə-sə-'mi-lə-ˌtüd, -ˌtyüd\ *n* : the quality or state of appearing to be true or real

ver·i·ta·ble \'ver-ə-tə-bəl\ *adj* : ACTUAL, GENUINE, TRUE — **ver·i·ta·bly** *adv*

ver·i·ty \'ver-ə-tē\ *n, pl* **-ties 1** : the quality or state of being true or real : TRUTH, REALITY **2** : something (as a statement) that is true **3** : HONESTY, VERACITY

ver·meil 1 [MF] **1** \'vər-məl, -ˌmāl\ : VERMILION **2** \ver-'mā\ : gilded silver

ver·mi·cel·li \ˌvər-mə-'che-lē, -'se-\ *n* [It, fr. pl. of *vermicello*, dim. of *verme* worm] : a pasta made in thinner strings than spaghetti

ver·mic·u·lite \vər-'mi-kyə-ˌlīt\ *n* : any of various lightweight water-absorbent minerals derived from mica

ver·mi·form appendix \'vər-mə-ˌform-\ *n* : APPENDIX 2

ver·mil·ion *also* **ver·mil·lion** \vər-'mil-yən\ *n* : a bright reddish orange color; *also* : any of various red pigments

ver·min \'vər-mən\ *n, pl* **vermin 1** : small common harmful or objectionable animals (as lice or mice) that are difficult to get rid of **2** : birds and mammals that prey on game — **ver·min·ous** *adj*

ver·mouth \vər-'müth\ *n* [F *vermout*, fr. G *Wermut* wormwood] : a dry or sweet wine flavored with herbs and often used in mixed drinks

¹**ver·nac·u·lar** \vər-'na-kyə-lər\ *adj* [L *vernaculus* native, fr. *verna* slave born in the master's house, native] **1** : of, relating to, or being a language or dialect native to a region or country rather than a literary, cultured, or foreign language **2** : of, relating to, or being the normal spoken form of a language **3** : applied to a plant or animal in common speech as distinguished from biological nomenclature ⟨~ names⟩

²**vernacular** *n* **1** : a vernacular language **2** : the mode of expression of a group or class **3** : a vernacular name of a plant or animal

ver·nal \'vər-nᵊl\ *adj* : of, relating to, or occurring in the spring ⟨~ equinox⟩

ver·ni·er \'vər-nē-ər\ *n* : a short scale made to slide along the divisions of a graduated instrument to indicate parts of divisions

ve·ron·i·ca \və-'rä-ni-kə\ *n* : any of a genus of herbs related to the snapdragons that have small usu. bluish flowers

ver·sa·tile \'vər-sə-tᵊl\ *adj* : turning with ease from one thing or position to another; *esp* : having many aptitudes — **ver·sa·til·i·ty** \ˌvər-sə-'ti-lə-tē\ *n*

¹**verse** \'vərs\ *n* **1** : a line of poetry; *also* : STANZA **2** : metrical writing distinguished from poetry esp. by its lower level of intensity : POETRY **4** : POEM **5** : one of the short divisions of a chapter in the Bible

²**verse** *vb* **versed; vers·ing** : to familiarize by experience, study, or practice ⟨well *versed* in the theater⟩

ver·si·cle \'vər-si-kəl\ *n* : a verse or sentence said or sung by a leader in public worship and followed by a response from the people

ver·si·fi·ca·tion \ˌvər-sə-fə-'kā-shən\ *n* **1** : the making of verses **2** : metrical structure

ver·si·fy \'vər-sə-ˌfī\ *vb* **-fied; -fy·ing 1** : to write verse **2** : to turn into verse — **ver·si·fi·er** \-ˌfī-ər\ *n*

ver·sion \'vər-zhən\ *n* **1** : TRANSLATION; *esp* : a translation of the Bible **2** : an account or description from a particular point of view esp. as contrasted with another **3** : a form or variant of a type or original

vers li·bre \ˌver-'lēbrᵊ\ *n, pl* **vers li·bres** *same*\ [F] : FREE VERSE

ver·so \'vər-sō\ *n, pl* **versos** : a left-hand page

ver·sus \'vər-səs\ *prep* **1** : AGAINST 1 ⟨the champion ~ the challenger⟩ **2** : in contrast to or as an alternative to ⟨free trade ~ protection⟩

vert *abbr* vertical

ver·te·bra \'vər-tə-brə\ *n, pl* **-brae** \-ˌbrā, -(ˌ)brē\ *or* **-bras** [L] : one of the segments of bone or cartilage making up the backbone

ver·te·bral \(ˌ)vər-'tē-brəl, 'vər-tə-\ *adj* : of, relating to, or made up of vertebrae : SPINAL

vertebral column *n* : BACKBONE 1

¹**ver·te·brate** \'vər-tə-brət, -ˌbrāt\ *adj* **1** : having a backbone **2** : of or relating to the vertebrates

²**vertebrate** *n* : any of a large group of animals (as mammals, birds, reptiles, amphibians, or fishes) that have a backbone or in some primitive forms (as a lamprey) a flexible rod of cells and that have a tubular nervous system arranged along the back and divided into a brain and spinal cord

ver·tex \'vər-ˌteks\ *n, pl* **ver·ti·ces** \'vər-tə-ˌsēz\ *also* **ver·tex·es** [ME, top of the head, fr. L *vertex, vortex* whirl, whirlpool, top of the head, summit, fr. *vertere* to turn] **1** : the point opposite to and farthest from the base of a geometrical figure **2** : the point where the sides of an angle or three or more edges of a polyhedron (as a cube) meet **3** : the highest point : TOP, SUMMIT

ver·ti·cal \'vər-ti-kəl\ *adj* **1** : of, relating to, or located at the vertex : directly overhead **2** : rising perpendicularly from a level surface : UPRIGHT — **vertical** *n* — **ver·ti·cal·i·ty** \ˌvər-tə-'ka-lə-tē\ *n* — **ver·ti·cal·ly** \-k(ə-)lē\ *adv*

ver·tig·i·nous \(ˌ)vər-'ti-jə-nəs\ *adj* : marked by, affected with, or tending to cause dizziness

ver·ti·go \'vər-ti-ˌgō\ *n, pl* **-goes** *or* **-gos** : DIZZINESS, GIDDINESS

vertu *var of* VIRTU

ver·vain \'vər-ˌvān\ *n* : any of a genus of chiefly American herbs or low woody plants with often showy heads or spikes of tubular flowers

verve \'vərv\ *n* : liveliness of imagination; *also* : VIVACITY

¹**very** \'ver-ē\ *adj* **veri·er; -est** [ME *verray, verry,* fr. AF *verai,* ultim. fr. L *verax* truthful, fr. *verus* true] **1** : EXACT, PRECISE ⟨the ∼ heart of the city⟩ **2** : exactly suitable ⟨the ∼ tool for the job⟩ **3** : ABSOLUTE, UTTER ⟨the *veriest* nonsense⟩ **4** — used as an intensive esp. to emphasize identity ⟨before my ∼ eyes⟩ **5** : MERE, BARE ⟨the ∼ idea scared him⟩ **6** : SELFSAME, IDENTICAL ⟨the ∼ man I saw⟩

²**very** *adv* **1** : in actual fact : TRULY **2** : to a high degree : EXTREMELY

very high frequency *n* : a radio frequency of between 30 and 300 megahertz

ves·i·cant \'ve-si-kənt\ *n* : an agent that causes blistering — **vesicant** *adj*

ves·i·cle \'ve-si-kəl\ *n* : a membranous and usu. fluid-filled cavity in a plant or animal; *also* : BLISTER — **ve·sic·u·lar** \və-'si-kyə-lər\ *adj*

¹**ves·per** \'ves-pər\ *n* **1** *cap, archaic* : EVENING STAR **2** : a vesper bell **3** *archaic* : EVENING, EVENTIDE

²**vesper** *adj* : of or relating to vespers or the evening ⟨a ∼ service⟩

ves·pers \-pərz\ *n pl, often cap* : a late afternoon or evening worship service

ves·sel \'ve-səl\ *n* **1** : a container (as a barrel, bottle, bowl, or cup) for holding something **2** : a person held to be the recipient of a quality (as grace) **3** : a craft bigger than a rowboat **4** : a tube in which a body fluid (as blood or sap) is contained and circulated

¹**vest** \'vest\ *vb* **1** : to place or give into the possession or discretion of some person or authority **2** : to grant or endow with a particular authority, right, or property **3** : to become legally vested **4** : to clothe with or as if with a garment; *esp* : to garb in ecclesiastical vestments

²**vest** *n* **1** : a sleeveless garment for the upper body usu. worn over a shirt **2** *chiefly Brit* : a man's sleeveless undershirt **3** : a front piece of a dress resembling the front of a vest

¹**ves·tal** \'ves-t³l\ *adj* : CHASTE

²**vestal** *n* : VESTAL VIRGIN

vestal virgin *n* **1** : a virgin consecrated to the Roman goddess Vesta and to the ser-

vice of watching the sacred fire perpetually kept burning on her altar **2** : a chaste woman

vest·ed \'ves-təd\ *adj* : fully and unconditionally guaranteed as a legal right, benefit, or privilege

vested interest *n* : an interest (as in an existing political, economic, or social arrangement) to which the holder has a strong commitment; *also* : one (as a corporation) having a vested interest

ves·ti·bule \'ves-tə-ˌbyül\ *n* **1** : a passage or room between the outer door and the interior of a building **2** : any of various bodily cavities forming or suggesting an entrance to some other cavity or space — **ves·tib·u·lar** \ve-'sti-byə-lər\ *adj*

ves·tige \'ves-tij\ *n* [F, fr. L *vestigium* footprint, track, vestige] : a trace or visible sign left by something lost or vanished; *also* : a minute remaining amount — **ves·ti·gial** \ve-'sti-jē-əl, -jəl\ *adj* — **ves·ti·gial·ly** *adv*

vest·ing \'ves-tiŋ\ *n* : the conveying to an employee of inalienable rights to share in a pension fund; *also* : the right so conveyed

vest·ment \'vest-mənt\ *n* **1** : an outer garment; *esp* : a ceremonial or official robe **2** *pl* : CLOTHING, GARB **3** : a garment or insignia worn by a cleric when officiating or assisting at a religious service

vest–pocket *adj* : very small ⟨a ∼ park⟩

ves·try \'ves-trē\ *n, pl* **vestries** **1** : a room in a church for vestments, altar linens, and sacred vessels **2** : a room used for church meetings and classes **3** : a body administering the temporal affairs of an Episcopal parish

ves·try·man \-mən\ *n* : a member of a vestry

ves·ture \'ves-chər\ *n* **1** : a covering garment **2** : CLOTHING, APPAREL

¹**vet** \'vet\ *n* : VETERINARIAN

²**vet** *adj or n* : VETERAN

³**vet** *vb* : to evaluate for appraisal or acceptance ⟨∼ a manuscript⟩

vetch \'vech\ *n* : any of a genus of twining leguminous herbs including some grown for fodder and green manure

vet·er·an \'ve-trən, -tə-rən\ *n* [L *veteranus,* fr. *veteranus* old, of long experience, fr. *veter-, vetus* old] **1** : an old soldier of long service **2** : a former member of the armed forces **3** : a person of long experience usu. in an occupation or skill — **veteran** *adj*

Veterans Day *n* : November 11 observed as a legal holiday in commemoration of the end of hostilities in 1918 and 1945

vet·er·i·nar·i·an \ˌve-trə-'ner-ē-ən, ˌve-tə-rə-\ *n* : one qualified and authorized to practice veterinary medicine

¹**vet·er·i·nary** \'ve-trə-ˌner-ē, 've-tə-rə-\ *adj* : of, relating to, or being the medical care of animals and esp. domestic animals

²**veterinary** *n, pl* **-nar·ies** : VETERINARIAN

¹**ve·to** \'vē-tō\ *n, pl* **vetoes** [L, I forbid] **1** : an authoritative prohibition **2** : a power of one part of a government to forbid the

carrying out of projects attempted by another part; *esp* : a power vested in a chief executive to prevent the carrying out of measures adopted by a legislature 3 : the exercise of the power of veto

²**veto** \'vē-tō\ *vb* 1 : FORBID, PROHIBIT 2 : to refuse assent to (a legislative bill) so as to prevent enactment or cause reconsideration — **ve·to·er** *n*

vex \'veks\ *vb* **vexed** *also* **vext**; **vex·ing** 1 : to bring trouble, distress, or agitation to ⟨a ~*ing* problem⟩ 2 : to annoy continually with little irritations

vex·a·tion \vek-'sā-shən\ *n* 1 : the act of vexing 2 : the quality or state of being vexed : IRRITATION 3 : a cause of trouble or annoyance

vex·a·tious \-shəs\ *adj* 1 : causing vexation : ANNOYING 2 : full of distress or annoyance : TROUBLED — **vex·a·tious·ly** *adv* — **vex·a·tious·ness** *n*

vexed \'vekst\ *adj* : fully debated or discussed ⟨a ~ question⟩

VF *abbr* 1 video frequency 2 visual field

VFD *abbr* volunteer fire department

VFW *abbr* Veterans of Foreign Wars

VG *abbr* 1 very good 2 vicar-general

VHF *abbr* very high frequency

VI *abbr* Virgin Islands

via \'vī-ə, 'vē-ə\ *prep* 1 : by way of 2 : by means of

vi·a·ble \'vī-ə-bəl\ *adj* 1 : capable of living; *esp* : sufficiently developed as to be capable of surviving outside the mother's womb ⟨a ~ fetus⟩ 2 : capable of growing and developing ⟨~ seeds⟩ 3 : capable of being put into practice : WORKABLE 4 : having a reasonable chance of succeeding ⟨a ~ candidate⟩ — **vi·a·bil·i·ty** \,vī-ə-'bi-lə-tē\ *n* — **vi·a·bly** \'vī-ə-blē\ *adv*

via·duct \'vī-ə-,dəkt\ *n* : a long elevated roadway usu. consisting of a series of short spans supported on arches, piers, or columns

vi·al \'vī-əl\ *n* : a small vessel for liquids

vi·and \'vī-ənd\ *n* : an article of food

vi·at·i·cum \vī-'a-ti-kəm, vē-\ *n, pl* **-cums** *or* **-ca** \-kə\ 1 : the Christian Eucharist given to a person in danger of death 2 : an allowance esp. in money for traveling needs and expenses

vibes \'vībz\ *n pl* 1 : VIBRAPHONE 2 : VIBRATIONS

vi·brant \'vī-brənt\ *adj* 1 : VIBRATING, PULSATING 2 : pulsating with vigor or activity ⟨a ~ personality⟩ 3 : readily set in vibration : RESPONSIVE 4 : sounding from vibration 5 : BRIGHT ⟨~ colors⟩ — **vi·bran·cy** \-brən-sē\ *n*

vi·bra·phone \'vī-brə-,fōn\ *n* : a percussion instrument like the xylophone but with metal bars and motor-driven resonators

vi·brate \'vī-,brāt\ *vb* **vi·brat·ed**; **vi·brat·ing** 1 : OSCILLATE 2 : to set in vibration 3 : to be in vibration 4 : WAVER, FLUCTUATE 5 : to respond sympathetically : THRILL

vi·bra·tion \vī-'brā-shən\ *n* 1 : a rapid to-and-fro motion of the particles of an elastic body or medium (as a stretched cord)

that produces sound 2 : an act of vibrating : a state of being vibrated : OSCILLATION 3 : a trembling motion 4 : VACILLATION 5 : a feeling or impression that someone or something gives off — usu. used in pl. ⟨good ~s⟩ — **vi·bra·tion·al** \-shə-nəl\ *adj*

vi·bra·to \vi-'brä-tō\ *n, pl* **-tos** [It] : a slightly tremulous effect imparted to vocal or instrumental music

vi·bra·tor \'vī-,brā-tər\ *n* : one that vibrates or causes vibration; *esp* : a vibrating electrical device used in massage or for sexual stimulation

vi·bra·to·ry \'vī-brə-,tōr-ē\ *adj* : consisting of, capable of, or causing vibration

vi·bur·num \vī-'bər-nəm\ *n* : any of a genus of widely distributed shrubs or small trees related to the honeysuckle and bearing small usu. white flowers in broad clusters

vic *abbr* vicinity

Vic *abbr* Victoria

vic·ar \'vi-kər\ *n* 1 : an administrative deputy 2 : a minister in charge of a church who serves under the authority of another minister — **vi·car·i·ate** \vī-'ker-ē-ət\ *n*

vic·ar·age \'vi-kə-rij\ *n* : a vicar's home

vicar–general *n, pl* **vicars–general** : an administrative deputy (as of a Roman Catholic or Anglican bishop)

vi·car·i·ous \vī-'ker-ē-əs\ *adj* [L *vicarius*, fr. *vicis* change, alternation, stead] 1 : acting for another 2 : done or suffered by one person on behalf of another or others ⟨a ~ sacrifice⟩ 3 : sharing in someone else's experience through the use of the imagination or sympathetic feelings ⟨~ thrills⟩ — **vi·car·i·ous·ly** *adv* — **vi·car·i·ous·ness** *n*

¹**vice** \'vīs\ *n* 1 : DEPRAVITY, WICKEDNESS 2 : a moral fault or failing 3 : a habitual usu. trivial fault 4 : an undesirable behavior pattern in a domestic animal

²**vice** *chiefly Brit var of* VISE

³**vi·ce** \'vī-sē\ *prep* : in the place of; *also* : rather than

vice admiral *n* : a commissioned officer in the navy or coast guard ranking above a rear admiral

vice·ge·rent \'vīs-'jir-ənt\ *n* : an administrative deputy of a king or magistrate — **vice·ge·ren·cy** \-ən-sē\ *n*

vi·cen·ni·al \vī-'se-nē-əl\ *adj* : occurring once every 20 years

vice presidency *n* : the office of vice president

vice president *n* 1 : an officer ranking next to a president and usu. empowered to act for the president during an absence or disability 2 : any of several of a president's deputies

vice·re·gal \'vīs-'rē-gəl\ *adj* : of or relating to a viceroy

vice·roy \'vīs-,rói\ *n* : the governor of a country or province who rules as representative of the sovereign — **vice·roy·al·ty** \-əl-tē\ *n*

vice ver·sa \,vī-si-'vər-sə, 'vīs-'vər-\ *adv* : with the order reversed

vi·chys·soise \,vi-shē-'swäz, ,vē-\ *n* [F]

: a soup made esp. from leeks or onions and potatoes, cream, and chicken stock and usu. served cold

vic·i·nage \'vi-sə-nij\ *n* : a neighboring or surrounding district : VICINITY

vi·cin·i·ty \və-'si-nə-tē\ *n, pl* **-ties** [MF *vicinité*, fr. L *vicinitas*, fr. *vicinus* neighboring, fr. *vicus* row of houses, village] **1** : NEARNESS, PROXIMITY **2** : a surrounding area : NEIGHBORHOOD

vi·cious \'vi-shəs\ *adj* **1** : having the quality of vice : WICKED, DEPRAVED **2** : DEFECTIVE, FAULTY; *also* : INVALID **3** : IMPURE, FOUL **4** : having a savage disposition; *also* : marked by violence or ferocity ⟨a ~ attack⟩ **5** : MALICIOUS, SPITEFUL ⟨~ gossip⟩ **6** : worsened by internal causes that augment each other ⟨~ wage-price spiral⟩ — **vi·cious·ly** *adv* — **vi·cious·ness** *n*

vi·cis·si·tude \və-'si-sə-,tüd, vī-, -,tyüd\ *n* : an irregular, unexpected, or surprising change ⟨the ~s of business⟩

vic·tim \'vik-təm\ *n* **1** : a living being offered as a sacrifice in a religious rite **2** : an individual injured or killed (as by disease or accident) **3** : a person cheated, fooled, or injured ⟨a ~ of circumstances⟩

vic·tim·ise *Brit var of* VICTIMIZE

vic·tim·ize \'vik-tə-,mīz\ *vb* **-ized; -iz·ing** : to make a victim of — **vic·tim·i·za·tion** \,vik-tə-mə-'zā-shən\ *n* — **vic·tim·iz·er** \'vik-tə-,mī-zər\ *n*

vic·tim·less \'vik-təm-ləs\ *adj* : having no victim ⟨considered gambling to be a ~ crime⟩

vic·tor \'vik-tər\ *n* : WINNER, CONQUEROR

vic·to·ria \vik-'tȯr-ē-ə\ *n* : a low 4-wheeled carriage with a folding top and a raised driver's seat in front

¹Vic·to·ri·an \vik-'tȯr-ē-ən\ *adj* **1** : of or relating to the reign of Queen Victoria of England or the art, letters, or tastes of her time **2** : typical of the standards, attitudes, or conduct of the age of Victoria esp. when considered prudish or narrow

²Victorian *n* **1** : a person and esp. an author of the Victorian period **2** : a typically large ornate house built during Queen Victoria's reign

vic·to·ri·ous \vik-'tȯr-ē-əs\ *adj* **1** : having won a victory **2** : of, relating to, or characteristic of victory ⟨~ exuberance⟩ — **vic·to·ri·ous·ly** *adv*

vic·to·ry \'vik-tə-rē\ *n, pl* **-ries** **1** : the overcoming of an enemy or an antagonist **2** : achievement of mastery or success in a struggle or endeavor

¹vict·ual \'vi-t²l\ *n* [ME *vitaille, victuayle*, fr. AF, fr. LL *victualia*, pl., provisions, food, fr. neut. pl. of *victualis* of nourishment, fr. L *victus* nourishment, way of living, fr. *vivere* to live] **1** : food fit for humans **2** *pl* : food supplies

²victual *vb* **-ualed** *or* **-ualled; -ual·ing** *or* **-ual·ling** **1** : to supply with food **2** : to store up provisions

vict·ual·ler *or* **vict·ual·er** \'vi-t²l-ər\ *n* : one that supplies provisions (as to an army or a ship)

vi·cu·ña *or* **vi·cu·na** \vi-'kün-yə, vī-; 'kü-nə, -'kyü-\ *n* : a So. American wild mammal related to the llama and alpaca; *also* : its wool **2** : a soft fabric woven from the wool of the vicuña; *also* : a sheep's wool imitation of this

vi·de \'vī-dē, 'vē-,dā\ *vb imper* [L] : SEE — used to direct a reader to another item

vi·de·li·cet \və-'de-lə-,set, vī-; vi-'dā-li-,ket\ *adv* [ME, fr. L, fr. *vidēre* to see + *licet* it is permitted] : that is to say : NAMELY

¹vid·eo \'vi-dē-,ō\ *n* **1** : TELEVISION **2** : VIDEOTAPE; *also* : a recording similar to a videotape but stored in digital form **3** : a videotaped performance ⟨music ~s⟩

²video *adj* **1** : relating to or used in transmission or reception of the television image **2** : relating to or being images on a television screen or computer display ⟨a ~ terminal⟩

video camera *n* : a camera that records visual images and usu. sound; *esp* : CAMCORDER

vid·eo·cas·sette \,vi-dē-ō-kə-'set\ *n* **1** : a case containing videotape for use with a VCR **2** : a recording (as of a movie) on a videocassette

videocassette recorder *n* : VCR

vid·eo·disc *or* **vid·eo·disk** \'vi-dē-ō-,disk\ *n* **1** : OPTICAL DISK **2** : a recording (as of a movie) on a videodisc

video game *n* : an electronic game played on a video screen

vid·e·o·gen·ic \,vi-dē-ō-'je-nik\ *adj* : TELEGENIC

vid·eo·phone \'vid-ē-ə-,fōn\ *n* : a telephone for transmitting both audio and video signals

¹vid·eo·tape \'vid-ē-ō-,tāp\ *n* : a recording of visual images and sound made on magnetic tape; *also* : the magnetic tape used for such a recording

²videotape *vb* : to make a videotape of

videotape recorder *n* : a device for recording and playing back videotapes

vie \'vī\ *vb* **vied; vy·ing** \'vī-iŋ\ : to compete for superiority : CONTEND — **vi·er** \'vī-ər\ *n*

Viet·cong \vē-'et-'käŋ, ,vē-ət-, -'kȯŋ\ *n, pl* **Vietcong** : a guerrilla member of the Vietnamese communist movement

¹view \'vyü\ *n* **1** : the act of seeing or examining : INSPECTION; *also* : SURVEY **2** : a way of looking at or regarding something **3** : ESTIMATE, JUDGMENT ⟨stated his ~s⟩ **4** : a sight (as of a landscape) regarded for its pictorial quality **5** : extent or range of vision ⟨within ~⟩ **6** : OBJECT, PURPOSE ⟨done with a ~ to promotion⟩ **7** : a picture of a scene

²view *vb* **1** : to look at attentively : EXAMINE **2** : SEE, WATCH ⟨~ a film⟩ **3** : to examine mentally : CONSIDER ⟨~ a problem⟩ — **view·er** *n*

view·er·ship \'vyü-ər-,ship\ *n* : a television audience esp. with respect to size or makeup

view·find·er \'vyü-,fīn-dər\ *n* : a device on a camera for showing the view to be included in the picture

view·point \-ˌpȯint\ *n* : POINT OF VIEW, STANDPOINT

vi·ges·i·mal \vī-ˈje-sə-məl\ *adj* : based on the number 20

vig·il \ˈvi-jəl\ *n* **1** : a religious observance formerly held on the night before a religious feast **2** : the day before a religious feast observed as a day of spiritual preparation **3** : evening or nocturnal devotions or prayers — usu. used in pl. **4** : an act or a time of keeping awake when sleep is customary; *esp* : WATCH 1

vigilance committee *n* : a committee of vigilantes

vig·i·lant \ˈvi-jə-lənt\ *adj* : alertly watchful esp. to avoid danger — **vig·i·lance** \-ləns\ *n* — **vig·i·lant·ly** *adv*

vig·i·lan·te \ˌvi-jə-ˈlan-tē\ *n* : a member of a volunteer committee organized to suppress and punish crime summarily (as when the processes of law are viewed as inadequate); *also* : a self-appointed doer of justice — **vig·i·lan·tism** \-ˈlan-ˌti-zəm\ *n*

¹vi·gnette \vin-ˈyet\ *n* [F, fr. MF *vignete*, fr. dim. of *vigne* vine] **1** : a small decorative design **2** : a picture (as an engraving or a photograph) that shades off gradually into the surrounding ground **3** : a short descriptive literary sketch

²vignette *vb* **vi·gnett·ed; vi·gnett·ing 1** : to finish (as a photograph) like a vignette **2** : to describe briefly

vig·or \ˈvi-gər\ *n* **1** : active strength or energy of body or mind **2** : INTENSITY, FORCE ⟨the ~ of their quarrel⟩

vig·or·ous \ˈvi-gə-rəs\ *adj* **1** : having vigor : ROBUST **2** : done with force and energy ⟨a ~ debate⟩ — **vig·or·ous·ly** *adv* — **vig·or·ous·ness** *n*

vig·our *chiefly Brit var of* VIGOR

Vi·king \ˈvī-kiŋ\ *n* [ON *vikingr*] : any of the pirate Norsemen who raided or invaded the coasts of Europe in the 8th to 10th centuries

vile \ˈvī(-ə)l\ *adj* **vil·er; vil·est 1** : morally despicable **2** : physically repulsive : FOUL **3** : of little worth **4** : DEGRADING, IGNOMINIOUS **5** : utterly bad or contemptible ⟨~ weather⟩ — **vile·ly** \ˈvī(-əl)-lē\ *adv* — **vile·ness** *n*

vil·i·fy \ˈvi-lə-ˌfī\ *vb* **-fied; -fy·ing** : to blacken the character of with abusive language : DEFAME ♦ **Synonyms** MALIGN, CALUMNIATE, SLANDER, LIBEL, TRADUCE — **vil·i·fi·ca·tion** \ˌvi-lə-fə-ˈkā-shən\ *n* — **vil·i·fi·er** \ˈvi-lə-ˌfī-ər\ *n*

vil·la \ˈvi-lə\ *n* **1** : a country estate **2** : the rural or suburban residence of a wealthy person

vil·lage \ˈvi-lij\ *n* [ME, fr. AF *vilage*, fr. *vile* manorial estate, farmstead, fr. L *villa*] **1** : a settlement usu. larger than a hamlet and smaller than a town **2** : an incorporated minor municipality **3** : the people of a village

vil·lag·er \ˈvi-li-jər\ *n* : an inhabitant of a village

vil·lain \ˈvi-lən\ *n* **1** : VILLEIN **2** : an evil person : SCOUNDREL

vil·lain·ess \-lə-nəs\ *n* : a woman who is a villain

vil·lain·ous \-lə-nəs\ *adj* **1** : befitting a villain : WICKED, EVIL **2** : highly objectionable : DETESTABLE ♦ **Synonyms** VICIOUS, INIQUITOUS, NEFARIOUS, INFAMOUS, CORRUPT, DEGENERATE — **vil·lain·ous·ly** *adv* — **vil·lain·ous·ness** *n*

vil·lainy \-lə-nē\ *n, pl* **-lain·ies 1** : villainous conduct; *also* : a villainous act **2** : villainous character or nature

vil·lein \ˈvi-lən, -ˌlān\ *n* **1** : a free villager of Anglo-Saxon times **2** : an unfree peasant having the status of a slave to a feudal lord

vil·len·age \ˈvil-ə-nij\ *n* **1** : the holding of land at the will of a feudal lord **2** : the status of a villein

vil·lous \ˈvi-ləs\ *adj* : covered with fine hairs or villi

vil·lus \ˈvi-ləs\ *n, pl* **vil·li** \-ˌlī, -(ˌ)lē\ : a slender usu. vascular process; *esp* : one of the tiny projections of the mucous membrane of the small intestine that function in the absorption of food

vim \ˈvim\ *n* : robust energy and enthusiasm : VITALITY

VIN *abbr* vehicle identification number

vin·ai·grette \ˌvi-ni-ˈgret\ *n* [F] : a sauce made typically of oil, vinegar, and seasonings

vin·ci·ble \ˈvin-sə-bəl\ *adj* : capable of being overcome or subdued

vin·di·cate \ˈvin-də-ˌkāt\ *vb* **-cat·ed; -cat·ing 1** : AVENGE **2** : EXONERATE, ABSOLVE **3** : CONFIRM, SUBSTANTIATE **4** : to provide defense for : JUSTIFY **5** : to maintain a right to : ASSERT — **vin·di·ca·tor** \-ˌkā-tər\ *n*

vin·di·ca·tion \ˌvin-də-ˈkā-shən\ *n* : the act of vindicating or the state of being vindicated; *esp* : justification against denial or censure : DEFENSE

vin·dic·tive \vin-ˈdik-tiv\ *adj* : disposed to revenge : intended for or involving revenge ⟨~ punishment⟩ **2** : VICIOUS, SPITEFUL — **vin·dic·tive·ly** *adv* — **vin·dic·tive·ness** *n*

vine \ˈvīn\ *n* [ME, fr. AF *vigne*, fr. L *vinea* vine, vineyard, fr. fem. of *vineus* of wine, fr. *vinum* wine] **1** : GRAPE **2 a** : a plant whose stem requires support and which climbs (as by tendrils) or trails along the ground; *also* : the stem of such a plant

vin·e·gar \ˈvi-ni-gər\ *n* [ME *vinegre*, fr. AF *vin egre*, lit., sour wine] : a sour liquid obtained by fermentation (as of cider, wine, or malt) and used to flavor or preserve foods

vin·e·gary \-gə-rē\ *adj* **1** : resembling vinegar : SOUR **2** : disagreeable in manner or disposition : CRABBED

vine·yard \ˈvin-yərd\ *n* **1** : a field of grapevines esp. to produce grapes for wine production **2** : a sphere of activity : field of endeavor

vi·nous \ˈvī-nəs\ *adj* **1** : of, relating to, or made with wine ⟨~ medications⟩ **2** : showing the effects of the use of wine ⟨~ bloodshot eyes⟩

¹vin·tage \ˈvin-tij\ *n* **1** : a season's yield of grapes or wine **2** : WINE; *esp* : a usu. superior wine which comes from a single year **3** : the act or period of gathering grapes or making wine **4** : a period of origin 〈clothes of the 1890 ~〉

²vintage *adj* **1** : of, relating to, or produced in a particular vintage **2** : of old, recognized, and enduring interest, importance, or quality : CLASSIC 〈~ cars〉 **3** : of the best and most characteristic — used with a proper noun

vint·ner \'vint-nər\ *n* : a dealer in wines

vi·nyl \'vī-n°l\ *n* **1** : a chemical derived from ethylene by the removal of one hydrogen atom **2** : a polymer of a vinyl compound or a product (as a textile fiber) made from one

vinyl chloride *n* : a flammable gaseous carcinogenic compound used esp. to make vinyl resins

vi·ol \'vī-əl\ *n* : a bowed stringed instrument chiefly of the 16th and 17th centuries having a fretted neck and usu. six strings

¹vi·o·la \vī-'ō-lə, 'vī-ə-lə\ *n* : VIOLET 1; *esp* : any of various hybrid garden plants with white, yellow, purple, or variously colored flowers that resemble but are smaller than those of the related pansies

²vi·o·la \vē-'ō-lə\ *n* : an instrument of the violin family slightly larger and tuned lower than a violin — **vi·o·list** \-list\ *n*

vi·o·la·ble \'vī-ə-lə-bəl\ *adj* : capable of being violated 〈~ boundaries〉

vi·o·late \'vī-ə-ˌlāt\ *vb* **-lat·ed; -lat·ing** **1** : BREAK, DISREGARD 〈~ a law〉 〈~ a frontier〉 **2** : RAPE **3** : PROFANE, DESECRATE **4** : INTERRUPT, DISTURB 〈*violated* his privacy〉 — **vi·o·la·tor** \-ˌlā-tər\ *n*

vi·o·la·tion \ˌvī-ə-'lā-shən\ *n* : an act or instance of violating : the state of being violated ♦ *Synonyms* BREACH, INFRACTION, TRESPASS, INFRINGEMENT, TRANSGRESSION

vi·o·lence \'vī-ləns, 'vī-ə-\ *n* **1** : exertion of physical force so as to injure or abuse **2** : injury by or as if by infringement or profanation **3** : intense or furious often destructive action or force **4** : vehement feeling or expression : INTENSITY **5** : jarring quality : DISCORDANCE ♦ *Synonyms* COMPULSION, COERCION, DURESS, CONSTRAINT

vi·o·lent \-lənt\ *adj* **1** : marked by extreme force or sudden intense activity **2** : caused by or showing strong feeling 〈~ words〉 **3** : EXTREME, INTENSE 〈~ pain〉 〈~ colors〉 **4** : emotionally agitated to the point of loss of self-control **5** : caused by force : not natural 〈~ death〉 — **vi·o·lent·ly** *adv*

vi·o·let \'vī-ə-lət\ *n* **1** : any of a genus of herbs or small shrubs usu. with heart-shaped leaves and both aerial and underground flowers; *esp* : one with small usu. solid-colored flowers **2** : a reddish blue color

vi·o·lin \ˌvī-ə-'lin\ *n* : a bowed stringed instrument with four strings that has a shallow body, a fingerboard without frets, and a curved bridge — **vi·o·lin·ist** \-'li-nist\ *n*

vi·o·lon·cel·lo \ˌvī-ə-lən-'che-lō\ *n* [It] : CELLO — **vi·o·lon·cel·list** \-list\ *n*

VIP \ˌvē-ˌī-'pē\ *n, pl* **VIPs** \-'pēz\ [*very im*-

portant *p*erson] : a person of great influence or prestige; *esp* : a high official with special privileges

vi·per \'vī-pər\ *n* **1** : a common stout-bodied Eurasian venomous snake having a bite only rarely fatal to humans; *also* : any snake (as a pit viper) of the same family as the viper **2** : any venomous or reputedly venomous snake **3** : a vicious or treacherous person — **vi·per·ine** \-pə-ˌrīn\ *adj*

vi·ra·go \və-'rä-gō, -'rā-\ *n, pl* **-goes** or **-gos** [ME, fr. L, strong or heroic woman, fr. *vir* man] **1** : a loud overbearing woman **2** : a woman of great strength and courage

vi·ral \'vī-rəl\ *adj* : of, relating to, or caused by a virus 〈a ~ infection〉 — **vi·ral·ly** *adv*

vi·reo \'vir-ē-ˌō\ *n, pl* **-e·os** [L, a small bird, fr. *virēre* to be green] : any of various small insect-eating American songbirds mostly olive green and grayish in color

¹vir·gin \'vər-jən\ *n* **1** : an unmarried woman devoted to religion **2** : an unmarried girl or woman **3** *cap* : the mother of Jesus **4** : a person who has not had sexual intercourse

²virgin *adj* **1** : free from stain : PURE, SPOTLESS **2** : CHASTE **3** : befitting a virgin : MODEST **4** : FRESH, UNSPOILED; *esp* : not altered by human activity 〈~ forest〉 **5** : INITIAL, FIRST

¹vir·gin·al \'vər-jə-n°l\ *adj* : of, relating to, or characteristic of a virgin or virginity 〈~ innocence〉 — **vir·gin·al·ly** *adv*

²virginal *n* : a small rectangular spinet without legs popular in the 16th and 17th centuries

Vir·gin·ia creeper \vər-'jin-yə-\ *n* : a No. American vine related to the grapes that has leaves with five leaflets and bluish-black berries

Virginia reel *n* : an American country-dance

vir·gin·i·ty \vər-'ji-nə-tē\ *n, pl* **-ties** **1** : the quality or state of being virgin; *esp* : MAIDENHOOD **2** : the unmarried life : CELIBACY

Vir·go \'vər-ˌgō\ *n* [L, lit., virgin] **1** : a zodiacal constellation between Leo and Libra usu. pictured as a young woman **2** : the 6th sign of the zodiac in astrology; *also* : one born under this sign

vir·gule \'vər-gyül\ *n* : ²SLASH 3

vir·i·des·cent \ˌvir-ə-'de-s°nt\ *adj* : slightly green : GREENISH

vir·ile \'vir-əl\ *adj* **1** : having the nature, powers, or qualities of a man **2** : MASCULINE, MALE **3** : MASTERFUL, FORCEFUL — **vi·ril·i·ty** \və-'ri-lə-tē\ *n*

vi·ri·on \'vī-rē-ˌän, 'vir-ē-\ *n* : a complete virus particle consisting of an RNA or DNA core with a protein coat

vi·rol·o·gy \vī-'rä-lə-jē\ *n* : a branch of science that deals with viruses and viral diseases — **vi·rol·o·gist** \-jist\ *n*

vir·tu \ˌvər-'tü, ˌvir-\ or **ver·tu** \ˌvər-, ˌver-\ *n* [It *virtù*, lit., virtue] **1** : a love of or taste for objects of art **2** : objects of art (as curios and antiques)

vir·tu·al \'vər-chə-wəl\ *adj* **1** : being in essence or in effect though not formally recognized or admitted ⟨a ~ dictator⟩ **2** : being on or simulated on a computer or computer network ⟨~ shopping⟩

vir·tu·al·ly \'vər-chə-wə-lē\ *adv* **1** : almost entirely : NEARLY **2** : for all practical purposes ⟨~ unknown⟩

virtual reality *n* : an artificial environment that is experienced through sensory stimuli (as sights and sounds) provided by an interactive computer program; *also* : the technology used to create or access a virtual reality

vir·tue \'vər-chü\ *n* [ME *vertu*, fr. AF, fr. L *virtus* strength, manliness, virtue, fr. *vir* man] **1** : conformity to a standard of right : MORALITY **2** : a particular moral excellence **3** : manly strength or courage : VALOR **4** : a commendable quality : MERIT **5** : active power to accomplish a given effect : POTENCY, EFFICACY **6** : chastity esp. in a woman

vir·tu·os·i·ty \,vər-chə-'wä-sə-tē\ *n, pl* **-ties** : great technical skill in the practice of a fine art

vir·tu·o·so \,vər-chə-'wō-sō, -zō\ *n, pl* **-sos** *or* **-si** \-sē, -zē\ [It] **1** : one skilled in or having a taste for the fine arts **2** : one who excels in the technique of an art; *esp* : a highly skilled musical performer ♦ **Synonyms** EXPERT, ADEPT, ARTIST, DOYEN, MASTER — **virtuoso** *adj*

vir·tu·ous \'vər-chə-wəs\ *adj* **1** : having or showing virtue and esp. moral virtue **2** : CHASTE — **vir·tu·ous·ly** *adv*

vir·u·lent \'vir-ə-lənt, 'vir-yə-\ *adj* **1** : highly infectious ⟨a ~ germ⟩; *also* : marked by a rapid, severe, and often deadly course ⟨a ~ disease⟩ **2** : extremely poisonous or venomous : NOXIOUS **3** : full of malice : MALIGNANT — **vir·u·lence** \-ləns\ *n* — **vir·u·lent·ly** *adv*

vi·rus \'vī-rəs\ *n, pl* **vi·rus·es** [L, venom, poisonous emanation] **1** : any of a large group of submicroscopic infectious agents that have an outside coat of protein around a core of RNA or DNA, that can grow and multiply only in living cells, and that cause important diseases in human beings, lower animals, and plants; *also* : a disease caused by a virus **2** : something (as a corrupting influence) that poisons the mind or spirit **3** : a computer program that is usu. hidden within another program and that reproduces itself and inserts the copies into other programs and usu. performs a malicious action (as destroying data)

vis *abbr* **1** visibility **2** visual

¹vi·sa \'vē-zə, -sə\ *n* [F] **1** : an endorsement by the proper authorities on a passport to show that it has been examined and the bearer may proceed **2** : a signature by a superior official signifying approval of a document

²visa *vb* **vi·saed** \-zəd, -səd\; **vi·sa·ing** \-zə-iŋ, -sə-\ : to give a visa to (a passport)

vis·age \'vi-zij\ *n* : the face or countenance of a person or sometimes an animal; *also* : LOOK, APPEARANCE

¹vis–à–vis \,vēz-ə-'vē, ,vēs-\ *prep* [F, lit., face-to-face] **1** : face-to-face with : OPPOSITE **2** : in relation to **3** : as compared with

²vis–à–vis *n, pl* **vis–à–vis** *same or* -'vēz\ **1** : one that is face-to-face with another **2** : ESCORT **3** : COUNTERPART **4** : TÊTE-À-TÊTE

³vis–à–vis *adv* : in company : TOGETHER

viscera *pl of* VISCUS

vis·cer·al \'vi-sə-rəl\ *adj* **1** : felt in or as if in the viscera **2** : not intellectual : INSTINCTIVE **3** : of or relating to the viscera — **vis·cer·al·ly** *adv*

vis·cid \'vi-səd\ *adj* : VISCOUS — **vis·cid·i·ty** \vi-'si-də-tē\ *n*

vis·cos·i·ty \vis-'kä-sə-tē\ *n, pl* **-ties** : the quality of being viscous; *esp* : the property of resistance to flow in a fluid

vis·count \'vī-,kaůnt\ *n* : a member of the British peerage ranking below an earl and above a baron

vis·count·ess \-,kaůn-təs\ *n* **1** : the wife or widow of a viscount **2** : a woman who holds the rank of viscount in her own right

vis·cous \'vis-kəs\ *adj* [ME *viscouse*, fr. AF *viscos*, fr. LL *viscosus* full of birdlime, viscous, fr. L *viscum* mistletoe, birdlime] **1** : having the sticky consistency of glue **2** : having or characterized by viscosity

vis·cus \'vis-kəs\ *n, pl* **vis·cera** \'vi-sə-rə\ : an internal organ of the body; *esp* : one (as the heart or liver) located in the cavity of the trunk

vise \'vīs\ *n* [ME *vys, vice* screw, fr. AF *vyz*, fr. L *vitis* vine] : a tool with two jaws for holding work that typically close by a screw or lever

vis·i·bil·i·ty \,vi-zə-'bi-lə-tē\ *n, pl* **-ties** **1** : the quality, condition, or degree of being visible **2** : the degree of clearness of the atmosphere

vis·i·ble \'vi-zə-bəl\ *adj* : capable of being seen ⟨~ stars⟩; *also* : MANIFEST, APPARENT ⟨has no ~ means of support⟩ — **vis·i·bly** \-blē\ *adv*

¹vi·sion \'vi-zhən\ *n* **1** : something seen otherwise than by ordinary sight (as in a dream or trance) **2** : a vivid picture created by the imagination ⟨~s of fame and fortune⟩ **3** : the act or power of imagination **4** : unusual wisdom in foreseeing what is going to happen **5** : the act or power of seeing : SIGHT **6** : something seen; *esp* : a lovely sight

²vision *vb* : IMAGINE, ENVISION

¹vi·sion·ary \'vi-zhə-,ner-ē\ *adj* **1** : of the nature of a vision : ILLUSORY, UNREAL **2** : not practical : UTOPIAN **3** : seeing or likely to see visions : given to dreaming or imagining ♦ **Synonyms** IMAGINARY, FANTASTIC, CHIMERICAL, QUIXOTIC

²visionary *n, pl* **-ar·ies** **1** : one whose ideas or projects are impractical : DREAMER **2** : one who sees visions

¹vis·it \'vi-zət\ *vb* **1** : to go to see in order to comfort or help **2** : to call on either as an act of courtesy or friendship **3** : to dwell with for a time as a guest **4** : to come to or upon as a reward, affliction, or punishment **5** : INFLICT ⟨~ed his wrath upon them⟩ **6** : to make a visit or regular or frequent visits **7** : CHAT, CONVERSE ⟨enjoys ~*ing* with the neighbors⟩ — **vis·it·able** *adj*

²**visit** *n* **1** : a short stay : CALL **2** : a brief residence as a guest **3** : a journey to and stay at a place **4** : a formal or professional call (as by a doctor)

vis·i·tant \'vi-zə-tənt\ *n* : VISITOR

vis·i·ta·tion \ˌvi-zə-'tā-shən\ *n* **1** : VISIT; *esp* : an official visit **2** : a special dispensation of divine favor or wrath; *also* : a severe trial

visiting nurse *n* : a nurse employed to visit sick persons or perform public health services in a community

vis·i·tor \'vi-zə-tər\ *n* : one that visits

vi·sor \'vī-zər\ *n* **1** : the front piece of a helmet; *esp* : a movable upper piece **2** : VIZARD **3** : a projecting part (as on a cap) to shade the eyes — **vi·sored** \-zərd\ *adj*

vis·ta \'vis-tə\ *n* **1** : a distant view through or along an avenue or opening **2** : an extensive mental view over a series of years or events

VISTA *abbr* Volunteers in Service to America

¹**vi·su·al** \'vi-zhə-wəl\ *adj* **1** : of, relating to, or used in vision ⟨~ organs⟩ **2** : perceived by vision ⟨a ~ impression⟩ **3** : VISIBLE ⟨~ objects⟩ **4** : done by sight only ⟨~ navigation⟩ **5** : of or relating to instruction by means of sight ⟨~ aids⟩ — **vi·su·al·ly** *adv*

²**visual** *n* : something (as a graphic) that appeals to the sight and is used for illustration, demonstration, or promotion — usu. used in pl.

vi·su·al·ize \'vi-zhə-wə-ˌlīz\ *vb* **-ized; -iz·ing** : to make visible; *esp* : to form a mental image of — **vi·su·al·i·za·tion** \ˌvi-zhə-wə-lə-'zā-shən\ *n* — **vi·su·al·iz·er** *n*

vi·ta \'vē-tə, 'vī-\ *n, pl* **vi·tae** \'vē-ˌtī, 'vī-tē\ [L, lit., life] : a brief autobiographical sketch

vi·tal \'vī-t³l\ *adj* **1** : concerned with or necessary to the maintenance of life ⟨~ organs⟩ **2** : full of life and vigor : ANIMATED **3** : of, relating to, or characteristic of life or living beings **4** : FATAL, MORTAL ⟨~ wound⟩ **5** : FUNDAMENTAL, INDISPENSABLE — **vi·tal·ly** *adv*

vi·tal·i·ty \vī-'ta-lə-tē\ *n, pl* **-ties 1** : the property distinguishing the living from the nonliving **2** : mental and physical vigor **3** : enduring quality **4** : ANIMATION, LIVELINESS ⟨the ~ of youth⟩

vi·tal·ize \'vī-tə-ˌlīz\ *vb* **-ized; -iz·ing** : to impart life or vigor to : ANIMATE — **vi·tal·i·za·tion** \ˌvī-tə-lə-'zā-shən\ *n*

vi·tals \'vī-t³lz\ *n pl* **1** : vital organs (as the heart and brain) **2** : essential parts

vital signs *n pl* : the pulse rate, respiratory rate, body temperature, and often blood pressure of a person

vital statistics *n pl* : statistics dealing with births, deaths, marriages, health, and disease

vi·ta·min \'vī-tə-mən\ *n* : any of various organic substances that are essential in tiny amounts to the nutrition of most

animals and some plants and are mostly obtained from foods

vitamin A *n* : any of several vitamins (as from egg yolk or fish-liver oils) required esp. for good vision

vitamin B *n* **1** : VITAMIN B COMPLEX **2** *or* **vitamin B₁** : THIAMINE

vitamin B complex *n* : a group of vitamins that are found widely in foods and are essential for normal function of certain enzymes and for growth

vitamin B₆ \-'bē-'siks\ *n* : any of several compounds that are considered essential to vertebrate nutrition

vitamin B₁₂ \-'bē-'twelv\ *n* : a complex cobalt-containing compound that occurs esp. in liver and is essential to normal blood formation, neural function, and growth; *also* : any of several compounds of similar action

vitamin C *n* : a vitamin found esp. in fruits and vegetables that is needed by the body to prevent scurvy

vitamin D *n* : any or all of several vitamins that are needed for normal bone and tooth structure and are found esp. in fish-liver oils, egg yolk, and milk or are produced by the body in response to ultraviolet light

vitamin E *n* : any of various oily fat-soluble liquid vitamins whose absence in the body is associated with such ailments as infertility, the breakdown of muscles, and vascular problems and which are found esp. in leaves and in seed germ oils

vitamin K *n* : any of several vitamins needed for blood to clot properly

vi·ti·ate \'vi-shē-ˌāt\ *vb* **-at·ed; -at·ing 1** : CONTAMINATE, POLLUTE; *also* : DEBASE, PERVERT **2** : to make legally ineffective : INVALIDATE ⟨~ a contract⟩ — **vi·ti·a·tion** \ˌvi-shē-'ā-shən\ *n* — **vi·ti·a·tor** \'vi-shē-ˌā-tər\ *n*

vi·ti·cul·ture \'vi-tə-ˌkəl-chər\ *n* : the growing of grapes — **vi·ti·cul·tur·al** \ˌvi-tə-'kəl-chə-rəl\ *adj* — **vi·ti·cul·tur·ist** \-rist\ *n*

vit·re·ous \'vi-trē-əs\ *adj* **1** : of, relating to, or resembling glass : GLASSY ⟨~ rocks⟩ **2** : of, relating to, or being the clear colorless transparent jelly (**vitreous humor**) behind the lens in the eyeball

vit·ri·ol \'vi-trē-əl\ *n* : something resembling acid in being caustic, corrosive, or biting — **vit·ri·ol·ic** \ˌvi-trē-'ä-lik\ *adj*

vit·tles \'vi-t³lz\ *n pl* : VICTUALS

vi·tu·per·ate \vī-'tü-pə-ˌrāt, və-, -'tyü-\ *vb* **-at·ed; -at·ing** : to abuse in words : SCOLD ♦ *Synonyms* REVILE, BERATE, RATE, UPBRAID, RAIL, LASH — **vi·tu·per·a·tive** \-'tü-pə-rə-tiv, -'tyü-, -ˌrā-\ *adj* — **vi·tu·per·a·tive·ly** *adv*

vi·tu·per·a·tion \(ˌ)vī-ˌtü-pə-'rā-shən, və-, -ˌtyü-\ *n* : lengthy harsh criticism or abuse

vi·va \'vē-və\ *interj* [It & Sp, long live] — used to express goodwill or approval

vi·va·ce \vē-'vä-chā\ *adv or adj* [It] : in a brisk spirited manner — used as a direction in music

vi·va·cious \və-'vā-shəs, vī-\ *adj* : lively in temper, conduct, or spirit : SPRIGHTLY ⟨a

~ personality) — **vi·va·cious·ly** *adv* — **vi·va·cious·ness** *n*

vi·vac·i·ty \-'va-sə-tē\ *n* : the quality or state of being vivacious

vi·va vo·ce \ˌvī-və-'vō-sē, ˌvē-və-'vō-ˌchā\ *adj* [ML, with the living voice] : expressed or conducted by word of mouth : ORAL — **viva voce** *adv*

viv·id \'vi-vəd\ *adj* **1** : BRILLIANT, INTENSE ⟨a ~ red⟩ **2** : having the appearance of vigorous life **3** : producing a strong impression on the senses; *esp* : producing distinct mental pictures ⟨a ~ description⟩ — **viv·id·ly** *adv* — **viv·id·ness** *n*

viv·i·fy \'vi-və-ˌfī\ *vb* **-fied; -fy·ing 1** : to put life into : ANIMATE ⟨details that ~ a story⟩ **2** : to make vivid — **viv·i·fi·ca·tion** \ˌvi-və-fə-'kā-shən\ *n* — **viv·i·fi·er** *n*

vi·vip·a·rous \vī-'vi-pə-rəs, və-\ *adj* : producing living young from within the body rather than from eggs — **vi·vi·par·i·ty** \ˌvī-və-'pa-rə-tē, ˌvi-\ *n*

viv·i·sec·tion \ˌvi-və-'sek-shən, 'vi-və-ˌsek-\ *n* : the cutting of or operation on a living animal; *also* : animal experimentation esp. if causing distress to the subject

vix·en \'vik-sən\ *n* **1** : an ill-tempered scolding woman **2** : a female fox

viz *abbr* videlicet

viz·ard \'vi-zərd\ *n* : a mask for disguise or protection

vi·zier \və-'zir\ *n* : a high executive officer of many Muslim countries

VJ *abbr* veejay

vlog \'vlóg, 'vläg\ *n* [*video* + b*log*] : a blog that contains video material — **vlog** *vb* — **vlog·ger** *n*

VOA *abbr* Voice of America

voc *abbr* **1** vocational **2** vocative

vocab *abbr* vocabulary

vo·ca·ble \'vō-kə-bəl\ *n* : TERM, NAME; *esp* : a word as such without regard to its meaning

vo·cab·u·lary \vō-'ka-byə-ˌler-ē\ *n, pl* **-lar·ies 1** : a list or collection of words usu. alphabetically arranged and defined or explained : LEXICON **2** : a stock of words in a language used by a class or individual or in relation to a subject

vocabulary entry *n* : a word (as the noun *book*), hyphened or open compound (as the verb *cross-refer* or the noun *boric acid*), word element (as the affix *-an*), abbreviation (as *agt*), verbalized symbol (as *Na*), or term (as *master of ceremonies*) entered alphabetically in a dictionary for the purpose of definition or identification or expressly included as an inflected form (as the noun *mice* or the verb *saw*) or as a derived form (as the noun *godlessness* or the adverb *globally*) or related phrase (as *in spite of*) run on at its base word and usu. set in a type (as boldface) readily distinguishable from that of the lightface running text which defines, explains, or identifies the entry

¹vo·cal \'vō-kəl\ *adj* **1** : uttered by the voice : ORAL **2** : relating to, composed or arranged for, or sung by the human voice ⟨~ music⟩ **3** : given to expressing oneself freely or insistently : OUTSPOKEN ⟨a ~ critic⟩ **4** : of or relating to the voice

²vocal *n* **1** : a vocal sound **2** : a vocal composition or its performance

vocal cords *n pl* : either of two pairs of elastic folds of mucous membrane that project into the cavity of the larynx and function in the production of vocal sounds

vo·cal·ic \vō-'ka-lik\ *adj* : of, relating to, or functioning as a vowel

vo·cal·ise *Brit var of* VOCALIZE

vo·cal·ist \'vō-kə-list\ *n* : SINGER

vo·cal·ize \-ˌlīz\ *vb* **-ized; -iz·ing 1** : to give vocal expression to : UTTER; *esp* : SING **2** : to make voiced rather than voiceless — **vo·cal·iz·er** *n*

vo·ca·tion \vō-'kā-shən\ *n* **1** : a summons or strong inclination to a particular state or course of action ⟨religious ~⟩ **2** : regular employment : OCCUPATION, PROFESSION — **vo·ca·tion·al** \-shə-nəl\ *adj*

vo·ca·tion·al·ism \-shə-nə-ˌli-zəm\ *n* : emphasis on vocational training in education

voc·a·tive \'vä-kə-tiv\ *adj* : of, relating to, or constituting a grammatical case marking the one addressed — **vocative** *n*

vo·cif·er·ate \vō-'si-fə-ˌrāt\ *vb* **-at·ed; -at·ing** [L *vociferari*, fr. *voc-, vox* voice + *ferre* to bear] : to cry out loudly : CLAMOR, SHOUT — **vo·cif·er·a·tion** \-ˌsi-fə-'rā-shən\ *n*

vo·cif·er·ous \vō-'si-fə-rəs\ *adj* : making or given to loud outcry — **vo·cif·er·ous·ly** *adv* — **vo·cif·er·ous·ness** *n*

vod·ka \'väd-kə\ *n* [Russ, fr. *voda* water] : a colorless liquor distilled from a mash (as of rye or wheat)

vogue \'vōg\ *n* [MF, action of rowing, course, fashion, fr. *voguer* to sail, fr. OF, fr. OIt *vogare* to row] **1** : popular acceptance or favor : POPULARITY **2** : a period of popularity **3** : one that is in fashion at a particular time ♦ *Synonyms* MODE, FAD, RAGE, CRAZE, TREND, FASHION

vogu·ish \'vō-gish\ *adj* **1** : FASHIONABLE, SMART **2** : suddenly or temporarily popular ⟨~ expressions⟩

¹voice \'vȯis\ *n* **1** : sound produced through the mouth by vertebrates and esp. by human beings (as in speaking or singing) **2** : musical sound produced by the vocal cords : the power to produce such sound; *also* : one of the melodic parts in a vocal or instrumental composition **3** : the vocal organs as a means of tone production ⟨train the ~⟩ **4** : sound produced by vibration of the vocal cords as heard in vowels and some consonants **5** : the power of speaking **6** : a sound suggesting a voice ⟨the ~ of the sea⟩ **7** : an instrument or medium of expression **8** : a choice, opinion, or wish openly expressed; *also* : right of expression **9** : distinction of form of a verb to indicate the relation of the subject to the action expressed by the verb

²voice *vb* **voiced; voic·ing** : to give voice or expression to : UTTER ⟨~ a complaint⟩　♦ *Synonyms* EXPRESS, VENT, AIR, VENTILATE

voice box *n* : LARYNX

voiced \'vȯist\ *adj* 1 : having a voice ⟨soft-*voiced*⟩ 2 : uttered with voice ⟨a ~ consonant⟩ — **voiced·ness** \'vȯist-nəs, 'vȯi-səd-nəs\ *n*

voice·less \'vȯis-ləs\ *adj* 1 : having no voice 2 : not pronounced with voice — **voice·less·ly** *adv* — **voice·less·ness** *n*

voice mail *n* : an electronic communication system in which spoken messages are recorded for later playback to the intended recipient; *also* : such a message

voice–over *n* : the voice in a film or television program of a person who is heard but not seen or not seen talking

voice·print \'vȯis-ˌprint\ *n* : an individually distinctive pattern of voice characteristics that is spectrographically produced

¹**void** \'vȯid\ *adj* 1 : UNOCCUPIED, VACANT ⟨a ~ bishopric⟩ 2 : containing nothing : EMPTY 3 : LACKING, DEVOID ⟨proposals ~ of sense⟩ 4 : VAIN, USELESS 5 : of no legal force or effect : NULL

²**void** *n* 1 : empty space : EMPTINESS, VACUUM 2 : a feeling of want or hollowness

³**void** *vb* 1 : to make or leave empty; *also* : VACATE, LEAVE 2 : DISCHARGE, EMIT ⟨~ urine⟩ 3 : to render void : ANNUL, NULLIFY ⟨~ a contract⟩ — **void·able** *adj* — **void·er** *n*

voi·là \vwä-'lä\ *interj* [F] — used to call attention to or express satisfaction or approval

voile \'vȯi(-ə)l\ *n* : a sheer fabric used for women's clothing and curtains

vol *abbr* 1 volume 2 volunteer

vol·a·tile \'vä-lə-t³l\ *adj* 1 : readily becoming a vapor at a relatively low temperature ⟨a ~ liquid⟩ 2 : tending to erupt into violence 3 : likely to change suddenly — **vol·a·til·i·ty** \ˌvä-lə-'ti-lə-tē\ *n* — **vol·a·til·ize** \'vä-lə-tə-ˌlīz\ *vb*

vol·ca·nic \väl-'ka-nik\ *adj* 1 : of, relating to, or produced by a volcano 2 : explosively violent ⟨~ emotions⟩

vol·ca·nism \'väl-kə-ˌni-zəm\ *n* : volcanic action or activity

vol·ca·no \väl-'kā-nō\ *n, pl* **-noes** *or* **-nos** [It or Sp; It *vulcano*, fr. Sp *vulcán*, ultim. fr. L *Volcanus*, Roman god of fire and metalworking] : an opening in the crust of the earth, a planet, or a moon from which molten rock and steam issue; *also* : a hill or mountain composed of the ejected material

vol·ca·nol·o·gy \ˌväl-kə-'nä-lə-jē\ *n* : a branch of geology that deals with volcanic phenomena — **vol·ca·nol·o·gist** \-kə-'nä-lə-jist\ *n*

vole \'vōl\ *n* : any of various small rodents that are closely related to the lemmings and muskrats

vo·li·tion \vō-'li-shən\ *n* 1 : the act or the power of making a choice or decision : WILL 2 : a choice or decision made — **vo·li·tion·al** \-'li-shə-nəl\ *adj*

¹**vol·ley** \'vä-lē\ *n, pl* **volleys** 1 : a flight of missiles (as arrows) 2 : simultaneous discharge of a number of missile weapons 3 : an act of volleying 4 : a burst of many things at once ⟨a ~ of angry letters⟩

²**volley** *vb* **vol·leyed; vol·ley·ing** 1 : to discharge or become discharged in or as if in a volley 2 : to hit an object of play (as a ball) in the air before it touches the ground

vol·ley·ball \-ˌbȯl\ *n* : a game played by volleying an inflated ball over a net; *also* : the ball used in this game

volt \'vōlt\ *n* : the meter-kilogram-second unit of electrical potential difference and electromotive force equal to the difference in potential between two points in a wire carrying a constant current of one ampere when the power dissipated between the points is equal to one watt

volt·age \'vōl-tij\ *n* : potential difference measured in volts

vol·ta·ic \väl-'tā-ik, vōl-\ *adj* : of, relating to, or producing direct electric current by chemical action

volte–face \ˌvȯlt-'fäs, ˌvȯl-tə-\ *n* : a reversal in policy : ABOUT-FACE

volt·me·ter \'vōlt-ˌmē-tər\ *n* : an instrument for measuring in volts the difference in potential between different points of an electrical circuit

vol·u·ble \'väl-yə-bəl\ *adj* : fluent and smooth in speech : GLIB　♦ *Synonyms* GARRULOUS, LOQUACIOUS, TALKATIVE — **vol·u·bil·i·ty** \ˌväl-yə-'bi-lə-tē\ *n* — **vol·u·bly** \'väl-yə-blē\ *adv*

vol·ume \'väl-yəm, -(ˌ)yüm\ *n* [ME, fr. AF, fr. L *volumen* roll, scroll, fr. *volvere* to roll] 1 : a series of printed sheets bound typically in book form; *also* : an arbitrary number of issues of a periodical 2 : space occupied as measured by cubic units ⟨the ~ of a cylinder⟩ 3 : sufficient matter to fill a book ⟨her glance spoke ~s⟩ 4 : AMOUNT ⟨increasing ~ of business⟩ 5 : the degree of loudness of a sound　♦ *Synonyms* BODY, BULK, MASS

vo·lu·mi·nous \və-'lü-mə-nəs\ *adj* : having or marked by great volume or bulk : LARGE — **vo·lu·mi·nous·ly** *adv* — **vo·lu·mi·nous·ness** *n*

¹**vol·un·tary** \'vä-lən-ˌter-ē\ *adj* 1 : done, made, or given freely and without compulsion ⟨a ~ sacrifice⟩ 2 : done on purpose : INTENTIONAL ⟨~ manslaughter⟩ 3 : of, relating to, or regulated by the will ⟨~ behavior⟩ 4 : having power of free choice 5 : provided or supported by voluntary action ⟨a ~ organization⟩　♦ *Synonyms* DELIBERATE, WILLFUL, WILLING, WITTING — **vol·un·tar·i·ly** \ˌvä-lən-'ter-ə-lē\ *adv*

²**voluntary** *n, pl* **-tar·ies** : an organ solo played in a religious service

voluntary muscle *n* : muscle (as most striated muscle) under voluntary control

¹**vol·un·teer** \ˌvä-lən-'tir\ *n* 1 : a person who voluntarily undertakes a service or duty 2 : a plant growing spontaneously esp. from seeds lost from a previous crop

²**volunteer** *vb* 1 : to offer or give voluntarily 2 : to offer oneself as a volunteer

vo·lup·tu·ary \və-'ləp-chə-ˌwer-ē\ *n, pl*

-ar·ies : a person whose chief interest in life is the indulgence of sensual appetites

vo·lup·tu·ous \-chə-wəs\ *adj* 1 : giving sensual gratification 2 : given to or spent in enjoyment of luxury or pleasure ♦ *Synonyms* LUXURIOUS, EPICUREAN, SENSUOUS — **vo·lup·tu·ous·ly** *adv* — **vo·lup·tu·ous·ness** *n*

vo·lute \və-ˈlüt\ *n* : a spiral or scroll-shaped decoration

¹**vom·it** \ˈvä-mət\ *n* : an act or instance of throwing up the contents of the stomach through the mouth; *also* : the matter thrown up

²**vomit** *vb* 1 : to throw up the contents of the stomach through the mouth 2 : to belch forth : GUSH

voo·doo \ˈvü-dü\ *n, pl* **voodoos** 1 : a religion that is derived from African polytheism and is practiced chiefly in Haiti 2 : a person who deals in spells and necromancy 3 : a charm used in voodoo; *also* : ²SPELL 1 — **voodoo** *adj*

voo·doo·ism \-ˌi-zəm\ *n* 1 : VOODOO 1 2 : the practice of witchcraft

vo·ra·cious \vȯ-ˈrā-shəs, və-\ *adj* 1 : having a huge appetite : RAVENOUS 2 : very eager ⟨a ~ reader⟩ ♦ *Synonyms* GLUTTONOUS, RAVENING, RAPACIOUS — **vo·ra·cious·ly** *adv* — **vo·ra·cious·ness** *n* — **vo·rac·i·ty** \-ˈra-sə-tē\ *n*

vor·tex \ˈvȯr-ˌteks\ *n, pl* **vor·ti·ces** \ˈvȯr-tə-ˌsēz\ *also* **vor·tex·es** \ˈvȯr-ˌtek-səz\ : WHIRLPOOL; *also* : something resembling a whirlpool

vo·ta·ry \ˈvō-tə-rē\ *n, pl* **-ries** 1 : ENTHUSIAST, DEVOTEE; *also* : a devoted adherent or admirer 2 : a devout or zealous worshiper

¹**vote** \ˈvōt\ *n* [ME (Sc), fr. L *votum* vow, wish, fr. *vovēre* to vow] 1 : a choice or opinion of a person or body of persons expressed usu. by a ballot, spoken word, or raised hand; *also* : the ballot, word, or gesture used to express a choice or opinion 2 : the decision reached by voting 3 : the right of suffrage 4 : a group of voters with some common characteristics ⟨the big city ~⟩ — **vote·less** *adj*

²**vote** *vb* **vot·ed; vot·ing** 1 : to cast a vote 2 : to elect, decide, pass, defeat, grant, or make legal by a vote 3 : to declare by general agreement 4 : to offer as a suggestion : PROPOSE 5 : to cause to vote esp. in a given way — **vot·er** *n*

vo·tive \ˈvō-tiv\ *adj* : consisting of or expressing a vow, wish, or desire

vou *abbr* voucher

vouch \ˈvau̇ch\ *vb* 1 : PROVE, SUBSTANTIATE 2 : to verify by examining documentary evidence 3 : to give a guarantee 4 : to supply supporting evidence or testimony; *also* : to give personal assurance

vouch·er \ˈvau̇-chər\ *n* 1 : an act of vouching 2 : one that vouches for another 3 : a documentary record of a business transaction 4 : a written affidavit or authorization 5 : a form indicating a credit against future purchases or expenditures

vouch·safe \vau̇ch-ˈsāf\ *vb* **vouch-**

safed; **vouch·saf·ing** : to grant or give as or as if a privilege or a special favor

¹**vow** \ˈvau̇\ *n* : a solemn promise or statement; *esp* : one by which a person is bound to an act, service, or condition ⟨marriage ~s⟩

²**vow** *vb* 1 : to make a vow or as a vow 2 : to bind or commit by a vow — **vow·er** *n*

vow·el \ˈvau̇-(ə)l\ *n* 1 : a speech sound produced without obstruction or friction in the mouth 2 : a letter representing such a sound

vox po·pu·li \ˈväks-ˈpä-pyə-ˌlī\ *n* [L, voice of the people] : popular sentiment

¹**voy·age** \ˈvȯi-ij\ *n* [ME, *viage, veyage*, fr. AF *veiage*, fr. LL *viaticum*, fr. L, traveling money, fr. neut. of *viaticus* of a journey, fr. *via* way] : a journey esp. by water from one place or country to another

²**voyage** *vb* **voy·aged; voy·ag·ing** : to take or make a voyage — **voy·ag·er** *n*

voya·geur \ˌvȯi-ə-ˈzhər, ˌvwä-yä-\ *n* [CanF] : a person employed by a fur company to transport goods to and from remote stations esp. in the Canadian Northwest

voy·eur \vwä-ˈyər, vȯi-ˈər\ *n* 1 : one who obtains sexual pleasure from viewing esp. covertly the nudity or sexual activity of others 2 : an observer of the sordid — **voy·eur·ism** \-ˌi-zəm\ *n* — **voy·eur·is·tic** \ˌvwä-(ˌ)yər-ˈis-tik, ˌvȯi-ər-\ *adj*

VP *abbr* 1 verb phrase 2 vice president

vs *abbr* 1 verse 2 versus

vss *abbr* 1 verses 2 versions

V/STOL *abbr* vertical or short takeoff and landing

Vt *or* **VT** *abbr* Vermont

VTOL *abbr* vertical takeoff and landing

VTR *abbr* videotape recorder

vul·ca·nize \ˈvəl-kə-ˌnīz\ *vb* **-nized; -niz·ing** : to treat rubber or rubberlike material chemically to give useful properties (as elasticity and strength)

Vulg *abbr* Vulgate

vul·gar \ˈvəl-gər\ *adj* [ME, fr. L *vulgaris* of the mob, vulgar, fr. *vulgus* mob, common people] 1 : VERNACULAR ⟨the ~ tongue⟩ 2 : of or relating to the common people : GENERAL, COMMON 3 : lacking cultivation or refinement : BOORISH; *also* : offensive to good taste or refined feelings ⟨~ language⟩ ♦ *Synonyms* GROSS, OBSCENE, RIBALD, DIRTY, INDECENT, PROFANE — **vul·gar·ly** *adv*

vul·gar·i·an \ˌvəl-ˈger-ē-ən\ *n* : a vulgar person

vul·gar·ism \ˈvəl-gə-ˌri-zəm\ *n* 1 : VULGARITY 2 : a word or expression originated or used chiefly by illiterate persons 3 : a coarse expression : OBSCENITY

vul·gar·i·ty \ˌvəl-ˈga-rə-tē\ *n, pl* **-ties** 1 : something vulgar 2 : the quality or state of being vulgar

vul·gar·ize \ˈvəl-gə-ˌrīz\ *vb* **-ized; -iz·ing** : to make vulgar — **vul·gar·i·za·tion** \ˌvəl-gə-rə-ˈzā-shən\ *n* — **vul·gar·iz·er** \ˈvəl-gə-ˌrī-zər\ *n*

Vul·gate \ˈvəl-ˌgāt\ *n* [ML *vulgata*, fr. LL *vulgata editio* edition in general circulation] : a Latin version of the Bible used by the Roman Catholic Church

vul·ner·a·ble \'vəl-nə-rə-bəl\ *adj* **1** : capable of being wounded : susceptible to wounds **2** : open to attack **3** : liable to increased penalties in contract bridge — **vul·ner·a·bil·i·ty** \,vəl-nə-rə-'bi-lə-tē\ *n* — **vul·ner·a·bly** \'vəl-nə-rə-blē\ *adv*

vul·pine \'vəl-,pīn\ *adj* : of, relating to, or resembling a fox esp. in cunning ⟨~ charms⟩

vul·ture \'vəl-chər\ *n* **1** : any of various large birds (as a turkey vulture) related to the hawks, eagles, and falcons but having weaker claws and the head usu. naked and living chiefly on carrion **2** : a rapacious person

vul·va \'vəl-və\ *n, pl* **vul·vae** \-,vē\ [ME, fr. ML, fr. L *volva, vulva* womb, female genitals] : the external parts of the female genital organs — **vul·val** \'vəl-vəl\ *or* **vul·var** \-vər, -,vär\ *adj*

vv *abbr* **1** verses **2** vice versa

VX \'vē-'eks\ *n* : an extremely toxic chemical weapon

vying *pres part of* VIE

¹w \'də-bəl-(,)yü\ *n, pl* **w's** *or* **ws** *often cap* : the 23d letter of the English alphabet

²w *abbr, often cap* **1** water **2** watt **3** week **4** weight **5** west; western **6** wide; width **7** wife **8** with

W *symbol* [G *Wolfram*] tungsten

WA *abbr* **1** Washington **2** Western Australia

wacky \'wa-kē\ *adj* **wack·i·er; -est** : ECCENTRIC, CRAZY

¹wad \'wäd\ *n* **1** : a little mass, bundle, or tuft ⟨~s of clay⟩ **2** : a soft mass of usu. light fibrous material **3** : a pliable plug (as of felt) used to retain a powder charge (as in a cartridge) **4** : a considerable amount (as of money) **5** : a roll of paper money

²wad *vb* **wad·ded; wad·ding 1** : to push a wad into ⟨~ a gun⟩ **2** : to form into a wad **3** : to hold in by a wad ⟨~ a bullet in a gun⟩ **4** : to stuff or line with a wad : PAD

wad·ding \'wä-diŋ\ *n* **1** : WADS; *also* : material for making wads **2** : a soft mass or sheet of short loose fibers used for stuffing or padding

wad·dle \'wä-dᵊl\ *vb* **wad·dled; wad·dling** : to walk with short steps swaying from side to side like a duck — **waddle** *n*

wade \'wād\ *vb* **wad·ed; wad·ing 1** : to step in or through a medium (as water) more resistant than air **2** : to move or go with difficulty or labor and often with determination ⟨~ through a dull book⟩ — **wad·able** *or* **wade·able** \'wā-də-bəl\ *adj* — **wade** *n*

wad·er \'wā-dər\ *n* **1** : one that wades **2** : SHOREBIRD; *also* : WADING BIRD **3** *pl* : a waterproof garment consisting of pants with attached boots for wading

wa·di \'wä-dē\ *n* [Ar *wādī*] : a streambed of southwest Asia and northern Africa that is dry except in the rainy season

wading bird *n* : any of an order of long-legged birds (as sandpipers, cranes, or herons) that wade in water in search of food

wa·fer \'wā-fər\ *n* **1** : a thin crisp cake or cracker **2** : a thin round piece of unleav-ened bread used in the Eucharist **3** : something (as a piece of candy) that resembles a wafer

¹waf·fle \'wä-fəl\ *n* : a soft but crisped cake of batter cooked in a special hinged metal utensil (**waffle iron**)

²waffle *vb* **waf·fled; waf·fling** \-f(ə)liŋ\ : to speak or write in a vague or evasive manner ⟨*waffled* on important issues⟩

¹waft \'wäft, 'waft\ *vb* : to cause to move or go lightly by or as if by the impulse of wind or waves

²waft *n* **1** : a slight breeze : PUFF **2** : the act of waving

¹wag \'wag\ *vb* **wagged; wag·ging 1** : to sway or swing shortly from side to side or to-and-fro ⟨the dog *wagged* his tail⟩ **2** : to move in chatter or gossip ⟨scandal caused tongues to ~⟩

²wag *n* : an act of wagging : a wagging movement

³wag *n* : WIT, JOKER

¹wage \'wäj\ *n* **1** : payment for labor or services usu. according to contract **2** *pl* : RECOMPENSE, REWARD

²wage *vb* **waged; wag·ing 1** : to engage in : CARRY ON ⟨~ a war⟩ **2** : to be in process of being waged

¹wa·ger \'wā-jər\ *n* **1** : BET, STAKE **2** : something on which bets are laid : GAMBLE

²wager *vb* : BET — **wa·ger·er** *n*

wag·gery \'wa-gə-rē\ *n, pl* **-ger·ies 1** : mischievous merriment : PLEASANTRY **2** : JEST, TRICK

wag·gish \'wa-gish\ *adj* **1** : resembling or characteristic of a wag : MISCHIEVOUS **2** : SPORTIVE, HUMOROUS

wag·gle \'wa-gəl\ *vb* **wag·gled; wag·gling** : to move backward and forward or from side to side : WAG — **waggle** *n*

wag·gon *chiefly Brit var of* WAGON

wag·on \'wa-gən\ *n* **1** : a 4-wheeled vehicle; *esp* : one drawn by animals and used for freight or merchandise **2** : PADDY WAGON **3** : a child's 4-wheeled cart **4** : STATION WAGON

wag·on·er \'wa-gə-nər\ *n* : the driver of a wagon

wagonette • walking papers

814

wag·on·ette \ˌwa-gə-ˈnet\ *n* : a light wagon with two facing seats along the sides behind a cross seat in front

wa·gon-lit \vä-gōⁿ-ˈlē\ *n, pl* **wagons–lits** *or* **wagon–lits** *same or* -ˈlēz\ [F, fr. *wagon* railroad car + *lit* bed] : a railroad sleeping car

wagon train *n* : a column of wagons traveling overland

wag·tail \ˈwag-ˌtāl\ *n* : any of various slender-bodied mostly Old World birds with a long tail that jerks up and down

wa·hi·ne \wä-ˈhē-nē, -ˌnä\ *n* **1** : a Polynesian woman **2** : a female surfer

wa·hoo \ˈwä-ˌhü\ *n, pl* **wahoos** : a large vigorous food and sport fish related to the mackerel and found in warm seas

waif \ˈwāf\ *n* **1** : something found without an owner and esp. by chance **2** : a stray person or animal; *esp* : a homeless child

wail \ˈwāl\ *vb* **1** : LAMENT, WEEP **2** : to make a sound suggestive of a mournful cry **3** : COMPLAIN — **wail** *n*

wail·ful \-fəl\ *adj* : SORROWFUL, MOURNFUL ♦ **Synonyms** MELANCHOLY, DOLEFUL, LUGUBRIOUS, LAMENTABLE, PLAINTIVE, WOEFUL — **wail·ful·ly** *adv*

wain \ˈwān\ *n* : a usu. large heavy farm wagon

wain·scot \ˈwān-skət, -ˌskōt, -ˌskät\ *n* **1** : a usu. paneled wooden lining of an interior wall of a room **2** : the lower part of an interior wall when finished differently from the rest — **wainscot** *vb*

wain·scot·ing *or* **wain·scot·ting** \-ˌskō-tiŋ, -ˌskä-, -skə-\ *n* : material for a wainscot; *also* : WAINSCOT

waist \ˈwāst\ *n* **1** : the narrowed part of the body between the chest and hips **2** : a part resembling the human waist esp. in narrowness or central position ⟨the ∼ of a ship⟩ **3** : a garment or part of a garment (as a blouse or bodice) for the upper part of the body

waist·band \-ˌband\ *n* : a band (as on pants or a skirt) that fits around the waist

waist·coat \ˈwes-kət, ˈwāst-ˌkōt\ *n, chiefly Brit* : VEST 1

waist·line \ˈwāst-ˌlīn\ *n* **1** : a line around the waist at its narrowest part; *also* : the length of this **2** : the line at which the bodice and skirt of a dress meet

¹wait \ˈwāt\ *vb* **1** : to remain inactive in readiness or expectation : AWAIT ⟨∼ for orders⟩ **2** : to delay serving (a meal) **3** : to act as attendant or servant ⟨∼ on customers⟩ **4** : to attend as a waiter : SERVE ⟨∼ tables⟩ ⟨∼ at a banquet⟩ **5** : to be ready ⟨a letter ∼*ing* for you⟩

²wait *n* **1** : a position of concealment usu. with intent to attack or surprise ⟨lie in ∼⟩ **2** : an act or period of waiting

wait·er \ˈwā-tər\ *n* **1** : one that waits on another; *esp* : a person who waits tables **2** : TRAY

waiting game *n* : a strategy in which one or more participants withhold action in the hope of an opportunity for more effective action later

waiting room *n* : a room (as at a doctor's office) for the use of persons who are waiting

wait·per·son \ˈwāt-ˌpər-sən\ *n* : a waiter or waitress

wait·ress \ˈwā-trəs\ *n* : a woman who waits tables

waive \ˈwāv\ *vb* **waived; waiv·ing** [ME *weiven* to decline, reject, give up, fr. AF *waiver, gaiver*, fr. *waif* lost, stray] **1** : to give up claim to ⟨*waived* his right to a trial⟩ **2** : POSTPONE

waiv·er \ˈwā-vər\ *n* : the act of waiving right, claim, or privilege; *also* : a document containing a declaration of such an act

¹wake \ˈwāk\ *vb* **woke** \ˈwōk\ *also* **waked** \ˈwākt\; **wo·ken** \ˈwō-kən\ *also* **waked** *or* **woke; wak·ing 1** : to be or remain awake; *esp* : to keep watch (as over a corpse) **2** : AWAKE, AWAKEN ⟨the baby *woke* up early⟩

²wake *n* **1** : the state of being awake **2** : a watch held over the body of a dead person prior to burial

³wake *n* : the track left by a ship in the water; *also* : a track left behind

wake·board \ˈwāk-ˌbȯrd\ *n* : a short board with foot bindings on which its rider is towed by a motorboat across its wake — **wake·board·er** *n* — **wake·board·ing** *n*

wake·ful \ˈwāk-fəl\ *adj* : not sleeping or able to sleep : SLEEPLESS, ALERT — **wake·ful·ness** *n*

wak·en \ˈwā-kən\ *vb* : WAKE

wake-rob·in \ˈwāk-ˌrä-bən\ *n* : TRILLIUM

wak·ing \ˈwā-kiŋ\ *adj* : passed in a conscious or alert state ⟨every ∼ hour⟩

wale \ˈwāl\ *n* : a ridge esp. on cloth; *also* : the texture esp. of a fabric

¹walk \ˈwȯk\ *vb* [partly fr. ME *walken*, fr. OE *wealcan* to roll, toss and partly fr. ME *walkien*, fr. OE *wealcian* to roll up, muffle up] **1** : to move or cause to move on foot usu. at a natural unhurried gait ⟨∼ to town⟩ ⟨∼ a horse⟩ **2** : to pass over, through, or along by walking ⟨∼ the streets⟩ **3** : to perform or accomplish by walking ⟨∼ guard⟩ **4** : to follow a course of action or way of life ⟨∼ humbly in the sight of God⟩ **5** : WALK OUT **6** : to receive a base on balls; *also* : to give a base on balls to — **walk·er** *n*

²walk *n* **1** : a going on foot ⟨go for a ∼⟩ **2** : a place, path, or course for walking **3** : distance to be walked ⟨a quarter-mile ∼ from here⟩ **4** : manner of living : CONDUCT, BEHAVIOR **5** : social or economic status ⟨various ∼*s* of life⟩ **6** : manner of walking : GAIT; *esp* : a slow 4-beat gait of a horse **7** : BASE ON BALLS

walk·away \ˈwȯ-kə-ˌwā\ *n* : an easily won contest

walk·ie-talk·ie \ˌwȯ-kē-ˈtȯ-kē\ *n* : a small portable radio transmitting and receiving set

¹walk-in \ˈwȯk-ˌin\ *adj* : large enough to be walked into ⟨a ∼ refrigerator⟩

²walk-in *n* **1** : an easy election victory **2** : one that walks in

walking papers *n pl* : DISMISSAL, DISCHARGE

walking stick *n* **1** : a stick used in walking **2** : STICK INSECT; *esp* : one of the U.S. and Canada

walk–on \'wȯk-ˌȯn, -ˌän\ *n* : a small part in a dramatic production

walk·out \-ˌaut\ *n* **1** : a labor strike **2** : the action of leaving a meeting or organization as an expression of disapproval

walk out *vb* **1** : to leave suddenly often as an expression of disapproval **2** : to go on strike

walk·over \-ˌō-vər\ *n* : a one-sided contest : an easy victory

walk–up \'wȯk-ˌəp\ *n* : a building or apartment house without an elevator — **walk–up** *adj*

walk·way \-ˌwā\ *n* : a passage for walking

¹**wall** \'wȯl\ *n* [ME, fr. OE *weall*, fr. L *vallum* rampart, fr. *vallus* stake, palisade] **1** : a structure (as of stone or brick) intended for defense or security or for enclosing something **2** : one of the upright enclosing parts of a building or room **3** : the inside surface of a cavity or container ⟨the ~ of a boiler⟩ **4** : something like a wall in appearance, function, or effect ⟨a tariff ~⟩ — **walled** \'wȯld\ *adj*

²**wall** *vb* **1** : to provide, separate, or surround with or as if with a wall ⟨~ in a garden⟩ **2** : to close (an opening) with or as if with a wall ⟨~ up a door⟩

wal·la·by \'wä-lə-bē\ *n, pl* **wallabies** *also* **wallaby** : any of various small or medium-sized kangaroos

wall·board \'wȯl-ˌbȯrd\ *n* : a structural material (as of wood pulp or plaster) made in large sheets and used for sheathing interior walls and ceilings

wal·let \'wä-lət\ *n* **1** : a bag or sack for carrying things on a journey **2** : a pocketbook with compartments (as for personal papers and usu. unfolded money) : BILLFOLD

wall·eye \'wȯl-ˌī\ *n* **1** : an eye with a whitish iris or an opaque white cornea **2** : a large vigorous No. American food and sport fish related to the perches — **wall·eyed** \-ˌlīd\ *adj*

wall·flow·er \'wȯl-ˌflaù-(-ə)r\ *n* **1** : any of several Old World herbs related to the mustards; *esp* : one with showy fragrant flowers **2** : a person who usu. from shyness or unpopularity remains alone (as at a dance)

Wal·loon \wä-'lün\ *n* : a member of a people of southern and southeastern Belgium and adjacent parts of France — **Walloon** *adj*

¹**wal·lop** \'wä-ləp\ *vb* **1** : to beat soundly : TROUNCE **2** : to hit hard : SOCK ♦ **Synonyms** BATTER, BEAT, LAMBASTE, POUND, PUMMEL, THRASH

²**wallop** *n* **1** : a powerful blow or impact **2** : the ability to hit hard **3** : emotional, sensory, or psychological force : IMPACT ⟨a story with a ~⟩

wal·lop·ing \'wä-lə-piŋ\ *adj* **1** : LARGE, WHOPPING ⟨a ~ storm⟩ **2** : exceptionally fine or impressive ⟨a ~ fun party⟩

¹**wal·low** \'wä-lō\ *vb* **1** : to roll oneself about sluggishly in or as if in deep mud ⟨hogs ~ing in the mire⟩ **2** : to indulge oneself excessively ⟨~ in luxury⟩ **3** : to become or remain helpless ⟨~ in ignorance⟩ ♦ **Synonyms** BASK, INDULGE, LUXURIATE, REVEL, WELTER

²**wallow** *n* : a muddy or dust-filled area where animals wallow

wall·pa·per \'wȯl-ˌpā-pər\ *n* : decorative paper for the walls of a room — **wallpaper** *vb*

wall–to–wall *adj* **1** : covering the entire floor ⟨*wall-to-wall* carpeting⟩ **2** : covering or filling one entire space or time ⟨crowds of *wall-to-wall* people⟩

wal·nut \'wȯl-(ˌ)nət\ *n* [ME *walnot*, fr. OE *wealhhnutu*, lit., foreign nut, fr. *Wealh* Welshman, foreigner + *hnutu* nut] **1** : a nut with a furrowed usu. rough shell and an adherent husk from any of a genus of trees related to the hickories; *esp* : the large edible nut of a Eurasian tree **2** : a tree that bears walnuts **3** : the usu. reddish to dark brown wood of a walnut used esp. in cabinetwork and veneers

wal·rus \'wȯl-rəs, 'wäl-\ *n, pl* **walrus** *or* **wal·rus·es** : a large mammal of arctic waters that is related to the seals and has long ivory tusks

¹**waltz** \'wȯlts\ *n* [G *Walzer*, fr. *walzen* to roll, dance] **1** : a gliding dance done to music having three beats to the measure **2** : music for or suitable for waltzing

²**waltz** *vb* **1** : to dance a waltz **2** : to move or advance easily, successfully, or conspicuously ⟨he ~ed off with the championship⟩ — **waltz·er** *n*

wam·ble \'wäm-bəl\ *vb* **wam·bled; wambling** : to progress unsteadily or with a lurching shambling gait

Wam·pa·no·ag \ˌwäm-pə-'nō-(ˌ)ag; ˌwȯm-\ *n, pl* **Wampanoag** *or* **Wampanoags** [Narragansett, lit., easterners] : a member of an American Indian people of parts of Rhode Island and Massachusetts

wam·pum \'wäm-pəm\ *n* [short for *wampumpeag*, fr. Massachuset (an Algonquian Indian language) *wampompeag*, fr. *wampan* white + *api* string + *-ag*, pl. suffix] **1** : beads made of shells strung in strands, belts, or sashes and used by No. American Indians as money and ornaments **2** *slang* : MONEY

wan \'wän\ *adj* **wan·ner; wan·nest 1** : SICKLY, PALLID; *also* : FEEBLE **2** : DIM, FAINT **3** : LANGUID ⟨a ~ smile⟩ ♦ **Synonyms** ASHEN, BLANCHED, DOUGHY, LIVID, PALE, WAXEN — **wan·ly** *adv* — **wan·ness** *n*

wand \'wänd\ *n* **1** : a slender staff carried in a procession **2** : the staff of a fairy, diviner, or magician

wan·der \'wän-dər\ *vb* **1** : to move about aimlessly or without a fixed course or goal : RAMBLE **2** : to go astray in conduct or thought; *esp* : to become delirious ♦ **Synonyms** GAD, GALLIVANT, MEANDER, RANGE, ROAM, ROVE — **wan·der·er** *n*

wandering Jew *n* : either of two trailing or creeping plants cultivated for their showy and often white-striped foliage

wan·der·lust \'wän-dər-ˌləst\ *n* : strong longing for or impulse toward wandering

¹**wane** \'wān\ *vb* **waned; wan·ing** **1** : to grow gradually smaller or less ⟨the full moon ~*s* to new⟩ ⟨his strength *waned*⟩ **2** : to lose power, prosperity, or influence **3** : to draw near an end ⟨summer is *waning*⟩ ♦ *Synonyms* ABATE, EBB, MODERATE, RELENT, REQUIRE, SLACKEN, SUBSIDE

²**wane** *n* : a waning (as in size or power); *also* : a period in which something is waning

wan·gle \'waŋ-gəl\ *vb* **wan·gled; wan·gling** **1** : to obtain by sly or devious means; *also* : to use trickery or questionable means to achieve an end **2** : MANIPULATE; *also* : FINAGLE

wan·na·be *also* **wan·na·bee** \'wä-nə-ˌbē\ *n* : a person who wants or aspires to be someone or something else or who tries to look or act like someone else

¹**want** \'wȯnt, 'wänt\ *vb* **1** : to fail to possess : LACK ⟨they ~ the necessities of life⟩ **2** : to feel or suffer the need of **3** : NEED, REQUIRE ⟨the house ~*s* painting⟩ **4** : to desire earnestly : WISH

²**want** *n* **1** : a lack of a required or usual amount : SHORTAGE **2** : dire need : DESTITUTION **3** : something wanted : DESIRE **4** : personal defect : FAULT

want·ing \'wȯn-tiŋ, 'wän-\ *adj* **1** : not present or in evidence : ABSENT **2** : falling below standards or expectations **3** : lacking in ability or capacity : DEFICIENT ⟨~ in common sense⟩

²**wanting** *prep* **1** : LESS, MINUS ⟨a month ~ two days⟩ **2** : WITHOUT ⟨a book ~ a cover⟩

¹**wan·ton** \'wȯn-tᵊn, 'wän-\ *adj* [ME, undisciplined, fr. *wan-* deficient, wrong + *towen,* pp. of *teen* to draw, train, discipline] **1** : UNCHASTE, LEWD, LUSTFUL; *also* : SENSUAL **2** : having no regard for justice or for other persons' feelings, rights, or safety : MERCILESS, INHUMANE ⟨~ cruelty⟩ **3** : having no just cause ⟨a ~ attack⟩ — **wan·ton·ly** *adv* — **wan·ton·ness** *n*

²**wanton** *n* : a wanton individual; *esp* : a lewd or immoral person

³**wanton** *vb* **1** : to be wanton : act wantonly **2** : to pass or waste wantonly

wa·pi·ti \'wä-pə-tē\ *n, pl* **wapiti** *or* **wapitis** : ELK **2**

¹**war** \'wȯr\ *n* **1** : a state or period of usu. open and declared armed fighting between states or nations **2** : the art or science of warfare **3** : a state of hostility, conflict, or antagonism **4** : a struggle between opposing forces or for a particular end ⟨~ against disease⟩ — **war·less** \-ləs\ *adj*

²**war** *vb* **warred; war·ring** : to engage in warfare : be in conflict

³**war** *abbr* warrant

¹**war·ble** \'wȯr-bəl\ *n* **1** : a melodious succession of low pleasing sounds **2** : a musical trill

²**warble** *vb* **war·bled; war·bling** **1** : to sing or utter in a trilling manner or with variations **2** : to express by or as if by warbling

³**warble** *n* : a swelling under the skin esp. of the back of cattle, horses, and wild mammals caused by the maggot of a fly (**warble fly**); *also* : its maggot

war·bler \'wȯr-blər\ *n* **1** : SONGSTER **2** : any of various small slender-billed chiefly Old World songbirds related to the thrushes and noted for their singing **3** : any of numerous small bright-colored insect-eating American birds with a usu. weak and unmusical song

war·bon·net \'wȯr-ˌbä-nət\ *n* : a feathered American Indian ceremonial headdress

war crime *n* : a crime (as genocide) committed during or in connection with war

war cry *n* **1** : a cry used by fighters in war **2** : a slogan used esp. to rally people to a cause

¹**ward** \'wȯrd\ *n* **1** : a guarding or being under guard or guardianship; *esp* : CUSTODY **2** : a body of guards **3** : a division of a prison **4** : a division in a hospital **5** : a division of a city for electoral or administrative purposes **6** : a person (as a child) under the protection of a guardian or a law court **7** : a person or body of persons under the protection or tutelage of a government **8** : a means of defense : PROTECTION

²**ward** *vb* : to turn aside : DEFLECT — usu. used with *off* ⟨~ off a blow⟩

¹**-ward** *also* **-wards** *adj suffix* **1** : that moves, tends, faces, or is directed toward ⟨wind*ward*⟩ **2** : that occurs or is situated in the direction of ⟨sea*ward*⟩

²**-ward** *or* **-wards** *adv suffix* **1** : in a (specified) direction ⟨up*wards*⟩ ⟨after*ward*⟩ **2** : toward a (specified) point, position, or area ⟨sky*ward*⟩

war dance *n* : a dance performed (as by American Indians) before going to war or in celebration of victory

war·den \'wȯr-dᵊn\ *n* **1** : GUARDIAN, KEEPER **2** : the governor of a town, district, or fortress **3** : an official charged with special supervisory or enforcement duties ⟨game ~⟩ ⟨air raid ~⟩ **4** : an official in charge of the operation of a prison **5** : one of two ranking lay officers of an Episcopal parish **6** : any of various British college officials

ward·er \'wȯr-dər\ *n* : WATCHMAN, WARDEN

ward heel·er \-ˌhē-lər\ *n* : a local worker for a political boss

ward·robe \'wȯr-ˌdrōb\ *n* [ME *warderobe,* fr. AF *warderobe, garderobe,* fr. *warder, garder* to guard + *robe* robe] **1** : a room or closet where clothes are kept; *also* : CLOTHESPRESS **2** : a collection of wearing apparel ⟨his summer ~⟩

ward·room \-ˌdrüm, -ˌdrum\ *n* : the dining area for officers aboard a warship

ward·ship \'wȯrd-ˌship\ *n* **1** : GUARDIANSHIP **2** : the state of being under care of a guardian

ware \'wer\ *n* **1** : manufactured articles or products of art or craft : GOODS ⟨glass*ware*⟩ **2** : an article of merchandise ⟨a peddler hawking his ~*s*⟩ **3** : items (as dishes) of fired clay : POTTERY

ware·house \-ˌhau̇s\ *n* : a place for the storage of merchandise or commodities

: STOREHOUSE — **warehouse** *vb* — **ware·house·man** \-mən\ *n* — **ware·hous·er** \-₁hau̇-zər, -sər\ *n*

ware·room \'wer-₁rüm, -₁ru̇m\ *n* : a room in which goods are exhibited for sale

war·fare \'wȯr-₁fer\ *n* 1 : military operations between enemies : WAR; *also* : an activity undertaken by one country to weaken or destroy another ⟨economic ~⟩ 2 : STRUGGLE, CONFLICT

war·fa·rin \'wȯr-fə-rən\ *n* : an anticoagulant compound used as a rodent poison and in medicine

war·head \'wȯr-₁hed\ *n* : the section of a missile containing the charge

war·horse \-₁hȯrs\ *n* 1 : a horse for use in war 2 : a veteran soldier or public person (as a politician) 3 : a musical composition that is often performed

war·like \-₁līk\ *adj* 1 : fond of war ⟨~ peoples⟩ 2 : of, relating to, or useful in war : MILITARY, MARTIAL ⟨~ supplies⟩ 3 : befitting or characteristic of war or of soldiers ⟨~ attitudes⟩

war·lock \-₁läk\ *n* [ME *warloghe,* fr. OE *wǣrloga* one that breaks faith, the Devil, fr. *wǣr* faith, troth + *-loga* (fr. *lēogan* to lie)] : SORCERER, WIZARD

war·lord \-₁lȯrd\ *n* 1 : a high military leader 2 : a military commander exercising local civil power by force ⟨former Chinese ~s⟩

¹**warm** \'wȯrm\ *adj* 1 : having or giving out heat to a moderate or adequate degree ⟨~ milk⟩ ⟨a ~ stove⟩ 2 : serving to retain heat ⟨~ clothes⟩ 3 : feeling or inducing sensations of heat ⟨~ from exercise⟩ ⟨a ~ climb⟩ 4 : showing or marked by strong feeling : ARDENT ⟨~ support⟩ 5 : marked by tense excitement or hot anger ⟨a ~ campaign⟩ 6 : giving a pleasant impression of warmth, cheerfulness, or friendliness ⟨~ colors⟩ ⟨a ~ tone of voice⟩ 7 : marked by or tending toward injury, distress, or pain ⟨made things ~ for the enemy⟩ 8 : newly made : FRESH ⟨a ~ scent⟩ 9 : near to a goal ⟨getting ~ in a search⟩ — **warm·ly** *adv*

²**warm** *vb* 1 : to make or become warm 2 : to give a feeling of warmth or vitality to 3 : to experience feelings of affection or pleasure ⟨she ~ed to her guest⟩ 4 : to reheat for eating ⟨~ed over the roast⟩ 5 : to make ready for operation or performance by preliminary exercise or operation ⟨~ up the motor⟩ 6 : to become increasingly ardent, interested, or competent ⟨the speaker ~ed to his topic⟩ — **warm·er** *n*

warm–blood·ed \-'blə-dəd\ *adj* : able to maintain a relatively high and constant body temperature relatively independent of that of the surroundings

warmed–over \'wȯrmd-'ō-vər\ *adj* 1 : REHEATED ⟨~ cabbage⟩ 2 : not fresh or new ⟨~ ideas⟩

warm front *n* : an advancing edge of a warm air mass

warm·heart·ed \'wȯrm-'här-təd\ *adj* : marked by warmth of feeling : CORDIAL — **warm·heart·ed·ness** *n*

warming pan *n* : a long-handled covered pan filled with live coals and formerly used to warm a bed

war·mon·ger \'wȯr-₁məŋ-gər, -₁mäŋ-\ *n* : one who urges or attempts to stir up war — **war·mon·ger·ing** \-g(ə-)riŋ\ *n*

warmth \'wȯrmth\ *n* 1 : the quality or state of being warm 2 : ZEAL, ARDOR, FERVOR

warm up *vb* : to engage in exercise or practice esp. before entering a game or contest — **warm–up** \'wȯrm-₁əp\ *n*

warn \'wȯrn\ *vb* 1 : to put on guard : CAUTION; *also* : ADMONISH, COUNSEL 2 : to notify esp. in advance : INFORM 3 : to order to go or keep away

¹**warn·ing** \'wȯr-niŋ\ *n* 1 : the act of warning : the state of being warned 2 : something that warns or serves to warn ⟨a tornado ~⟩

²**warning** *adj* : serving as an alarm, signal, summons, or admonition ⟨a ~ bell⟩ — **warn·ing·ly** *adv*

¹**warp** \'wȯrp\ *n* 1 : the lengthwise threads on a loom or in a woven fabric 2 : a twist out of a true plane or straight line ⟨a ~ in a board⟩

²**warp** *vb* [ME, fr. OE *weorpan* to throw] 1 : to turn or twist out of shape; *also* : to become so twisted 2 : to lead astray : PERVERT; *also* : FALSIFY, DISTORT

war paint *n* : paint put on the face and body by American Indians as a sign of going to war

war·path \'wȯr-₁path, -₁päth\ *n* : the course taken by a party of American Indians going on a hostile expedition — **on the warpath** : ready to fight or argue

war·plane \-₁plān\ *n* : a military airplane; *esp* : one armed for combat

warp speed *n* : the highest possible speed

¹**war·rant** \'wȯr-ənt, 'wär-\ *n* 1 : AUTHORIZATION; *also* : JUSTIFICATION, GROUND 2 : evidence (as a document) of authorization; *esp* : a legal writ authorizing an officer to take action (as in making an arrest, seizure, or search) 3 : a certificate of appointment issued to an officer of lower rank than a commissioned officer

²**warrant** *vb* 1 : to guarantee security or immunity to : SECURE 2 : to declare or maintain positively ⟨I ~ this is so⟩ 3 : to assure (a person) of the truth of what is said 4 : to guarantee to be as it appears or as it is represented ⟨~ goods as of the first quality⟩ 5 : SANCTION, AUTHORIZE 6 : to give proof of : ATTEST; *also* : GUARANTEE 7 : JUSTIFY ⟨his need ~s the expenditure⟩

warrant officer *n* 1 : an officer in the armed forces ranking next below a commissioned officer 2 : a commissioned officer ranking below an ensign in the navy or coast guard and below a second lieutenant in the marine corps

war·ran·ty \'wȯr-ən-tē, 'wär-\ *n, pl* **-ties** : an expressed or implied statement that some situation or thing is as it appears to be or is represented to be; *esp* : a usu. written guarantee of the integrity of a product and of the maker's responsibility for the repair or replacement of defective parts

war·ren \ˈwȯr-ən, ˈwär-\ n **1** : an area where rabbits breed; *also* : a structure where rabbits are bred or kept **2** : a crowded tenement or district

war·rior \ˈwȯr-yər, ˈwȯr-ē-ər, ˈwär-\ n : a man engaged or experienced in warfare

war·ship \ˈwȯr-ˌship\ n : a naval vessel

wart \ˈwȯrt\ n **1** : a small usu. horny projecting growth on the skin; *esp* : one caused by a virus **2** : a protuberance resembling a wart (as on a plant) — **warty** adj

wart·hog \ˈwȯrt-ˌhȯg, -ˌhäg\ n : a wild African hog that has large tusks and in the male two pairs of rough warty protuberances below the eyes

war·time \ˈwȯr-ˌtīm\ n : a period during which a war is in progress

wary \ˈwer-ē\ adj **war·i·er; -est** : very cautious; *esp* : careful in guarding against danger or deception — **war·i·ly** \ˈwer-ə-lē\ adv — **war·i·ness** \ˈwer-ē-nəs\ n

was past 1st & 3d sing of BE

wa·sa·bi \ˈwä-sə-bē; wä-ˈsä-\ n [Jp] : a condiment prepared from the ground greenish root of an Asian herb and similar in flavor and use to horseradish; *also* : the herb or its root

¹**wash** \ˈwȯsh, ˈwäsh\ vb **1** : to clean with water and usu. soap or detergent ⟨~ clothes⟩ ⟨~ your hands⟩ **2** : to wet thoroughly : DRENCH **3** : to flow along the border of ⟨waves ~ the shore⟩ **4** : to pour or flow in a stream or current **5** : to move or remove by or as if by the action of water **6** : to cover or daub lightly with a liquid (as whitewash) **7** : to run water over (as gravel or ore) in order to separate valuable matter from refuse ⟨~ sand for gold⟩ **8** : to undergo laundering ⟨a dress that doesn't ~ well⟩ **9** : to stand a test ⟨that story will not ~⟩ **10** : to be worn away by water

²**wash** n **1** : the act or process or an instance of washing or being washed **2** : articles to be washed or being washed **3** : a thin coat of paint (as watercolor) **4** : the flow or action of a mass of water (as a wave) **5** : worthless esp. liquid waste : REFUSE, SWILL **6** : erosion by waves (as of the sea) **7** : a disturbance in a fluid (as water or the air) caused by the passage of a wing or propeller **8** West : the dry bed of a stream

³**wash** adj : WASHABLE

Wash abbr Washington

wash·able \ˈwȯsh-ə-bəl, ˈwäsh-\ adj : capable of being washed without damage — **wash·abil·i·ty** \ˌwȯ-shə-ˈbi-lə-tē, ˌwä-\ n

wash-and-wear adj : of, relating to, or being a fabric or garment that needs little or no ironing after washing

wash·ba·sin \ˈwȯsh-ˌbā-sᵊn, ˈwäsh-\ n : WASHBOWL

wash·board \-ˌbȯrd\ n : a grooved board to scrub clothes on

wash·bowl \-ˌbōl\ n : a large bowl for water for washing hands and face

wash·cloth \-ˌklȯth\ n : a cloth used for washing one's face and body

washed-out \ˈwȯsht-ˈaut, ˈwäsht-\ adj **1** : faded in color **2** : EXHAUSTED ⟨felt ~ after working all night⟩

washed-up \-ˈəp\ adj : no longer successful, popular, skillful, or needed

wash·er \ˈwȯ-shər, ˈwä-\ n **1** : a ring or perforated plate used around a bolt or screw to ensure tightness or relieve friction **2** : one that washes; *esp* : a machine for washing

wash·er·wom·an \-ˌwu̇-mən\ n : a woman whose occupation is washing clothes

wash·ing \ˈwȯ-shiŋ, ˈwä-\ n **1** : material obtained by washing **2** : articles washed or to be washed

washing soda n : SODIUM CARBONATE

Wash·ing·ton's Birthday \ˈwȯ-shiŋ-tənz-, ˈwä-\ n : the 3d Monday in February observed as a legal holiday

wash·out \ˈwȯsh-ˌau̇t, ˈwäsh-\ n **1** : the washing away of earth (as from a road); *also* : a place where earth is washed away **2** : a complete failure

wash·room \-ˌrüm, -ˌru̇m\ n : BATHROOM

wash·stand \-ˌstand\ n **1** : a stand holding articles needed for washing face and hands **2** : LAVATORY 1

wash·tub \-ˌtəb\ n : a tub for washing or soaking clothes

wash·wom·an \ˈwȯsh-ˌwu̇-mən, ˈwäsh-\ n : WASHERWOMAN

washy \ˈwȯ-shē, ˈwä-\ adj **wash·i·er; -est 1** : WEAK, WATERY **2** : PALLID ⟨a ~ yellow⟩ **3** : lacking in vigor, individuality, or definiteness

wasp \ˈwäsp, ˈwȯsp\ n : any of numerous social or solitary winged insects related to the bees and ants with biting mouthparts and in females and workers an often formidable sting

WASP or **Wasp** n [white Anglo-Saxon Protestant] : an American of northern European and esp. British ancestry and of Protestant background

wasp·ish \ˈwäs-pish, ˈwȯs-\ adj **1** : SNAPPISH, IRRITABLE ⟨a ~ temper⟩ **2** : resembling a wasp in form; *esp* : slightly built ♦ **Synonyms** FRACTIOUS, FRETFUL, HUFFY, PEEVISH, PETULANT, QUERULOUS

wasp waist n : a very slender waist

¹**was·sail** \ˈwä-səl, wä-ˈsāl\ n [ME wæs hæil, washayl, fr. ON ves heill be well] **1** : an early English toast to someone's health **2** : a hot drink made with wine, beer, or cider, spices, sugar, and usu. baked apples and traditionally served at Christmas **3** : riotous drinking : REVELRY

²**wassail** vb **1** : CAROUSE **2** : to drink to the health of — **was·sail·er** n

Was·ser·mann test \ˈwä-sər-mən-, ˈvä-\ n : a blood test for the detection of syphilis

wast·age \ˈwā-stij\ n : WASTE 3

¹**waste** \ˈwāst\ n **1** : a sparsely settled or barren region : DESERT; *also* : uncultivated land **2** : the act or an instance of wasting : the state of being wasted **3** : gradual loss or decrease by use, wear, or decay **4** : material left over, rejected, or thrown away; *also* : an unwanted byproduct of a manufacturing or chemical

process **5** : refuse (as garbage) that accumulates about habitations **6** : material (as feces) produced but not used by a living organism — **waste·ful** \-fəl\ adj — **waste·ful·ly** adv — **waste·ful·ness** n

²**waste** vb **wast·ed**; **wast·ing** **1** : DEVASTATE **2** : to wear away or diminish gradually : CONSUME **3** : to spend or use carelessly or uselessly : SQUANDER **4** : to lose or cause to lose weight, strength, or energy ⟨*wasting* away from fever⟩ **5** : to become diminished in bulk or substance : DWINDLE ♦ *Synonyms* DEPREDATE, DESOLATE, DESPOIL, RAVAGE, SPOIL, STRIP — **wast·er** n

³**waste** adj **1** : being wild and uninhabited : BARREN, DESOLATE; *also* : UNCULTIVATED **2** : being in a ruined condition **3** : discarded as worthless after being used ⟨~ water⟩ **4** : excreted from or stored in inert form in a living organism as a byproduct of vital activity ⟨~ matter from birds⟩

waste·bas·ket \'wāst-,bas-kət\ n : a receptacle for refuse

waste·land \-,land, -lənd\ n : land that is barren or unfit for cultivation

waste·pa·per \-'pā-pər\ n : paper thrown away as used, not needed, or not fit for use

wast·rel \'wā-strəl\ n : a person who wastes resources : SPENDTHRIFT

¹**watch** \'wäch, 'wȯch\ vb **1** : to be or stay awake intentionally : keep vigil ⟨~ed by the patient's bedside⟩ ⟨~ and pray⟩ **2** : to be on the lookout for danger : be on one's guard **3** : to keep guard ⟨~ outside the door⟩ **4** : OBSERVE ⟨~ a game⟩ **5** : to keep in view so as to prevent harm or warn of danger ⟨~ a brush fire carefully⟩ **6** : to keep oneself informed about ⟨~ his progress⟩ **7** : to lie in wait for esp. so as to take advantage of ⟨~ed her opportunity⟩ — **watch·er** n

²**watch** n **1** : the act of keeping awake to guard, protect, or attend; *also* : a state of alert and continuous attention **2** : a public weather alert ⟨a winter storm ~⟩ **3** : close observation **4** : LOOKOUT, WATCHMAN, GUARD **5** : a period during which a part of a ship's crew is on duty; *also* : the part of a crew on duty during a watch **6** : a portable timepiece carried on the person

watch·band \'wäch-,band, 'wȯch-\ n : the bracelet or strap of a wristwatch

watch·dog \-,dȯg\ n **1** : a dog kept to guard property **2** : one that guards or protects

watch·ful \-fəl\ adj : steadily attentive and alert esp. to danger : VIGILANT — **watch·ful·ly** adv — **watch·ful·ness** n

watch·mak·er \-,mā-kər\ n : a person who makes or repairs watches — **watch·mak·ing** \-,mā-kiŋ\ n

watch·man \-mən\ n : a person assigned to watch : GUARD

watch night n : a devotional service lasting until after midnight esp. on New Year's Eve

watch·tow·er \'wäch-,tau̇(-ə)r, 'wȯch-\ n : a tower for a lookout

watch·word \-,wərd\ n **1** : a secret word used as a signal or sign of recognition **2** : a word or motto used as a slogan or rallying cry

¹**wa·ter** \'wȯ-tər, 'wä-\ n **1** : the liquid that descends as rain and forms rivers, lakes, and seas **2** : a natural mineral water — usu. used in pl. **3** pl : the water occupying or flowing in a particular bed; *also* : a band of seawater bordering on and under the control of a country **4** : any of various liquids containing or resembling water; *esp* : a watery fluid (as tears, urine, or sap) formed or circulating in a living organism **5** : a specified degree of thoroughness or completeness ⟨a scoundrel of the first ~⟩

²**water** vb **1** : to supply with or get or take water ⟨~ horses⟩ ⟨the ship ~ed at each port⟩ **2** : to treat (as cloth) so as to give a lustrous appearance in wavy lines **3** : to dilute by or as if by adding water to **4** : to form or secrete water or watery matter ⟨her eyes ~ed⟩ ⟨my mouth ~ed⟩

water bed n : a bed whose mattress is a watertight bag filled with water

wa·ter·borne \-,bȯrn\ adj : supported, carried, or transmitted by water

water buffalo n : a common oxlike often domesticated Asian bovine

water chestnut n : a whitish crunchy vegetable used esp. in Chinese cooking that is the peeled tuber of a widely cultivated Asian sedge; *also* : the tuber or the sedge itself

water closet n : a compartment or room with a toilet bowl : BATHROOM; *also* : a toilet bowl along with its accessories

wa·ter·col·or \'wȯ-tər-,kə-lər, 'wä-\ n **1** : a paint whose liquid part is water **2** : the art of painting with watercolors **3** : a picture made with watercolors

wa·ter·course \-,kȯrs\ n : a stream of water; *also* : the bed of a stream

wa·ter·craft \-,kraft\ n : a craft for water transport : SHIP, BOAT

wa·ter·cress \-,kres\ n : an aquatic perennial Eurasian cress that is naturalized in the U.S. and has edible leaves used esp. in salads

wa·ter·fall \-,fȯl\ n : a very steep descent of the water of a stream

wa·ter·fowl \'wȯ-tər-,fau̇(-ə)l, 'wä-\ n, pl **-fowl** also **-fowls** : a bird that frequents water; *esp* : a swimming bird (as a duck) hunted as game

wa·ter·front \-,frənt\ n : land or a section of a town fronting or abutting on a body of water

water gap n : a pass in a mountain ridge through which a stream runs

water glass n : a drinking glass

water hyacinth n : a showy floating aquatic plant of tropical America that often clogs waterways (as in the southern U.S.)

watering hole n : a place (as a bar) where people gather socially

watering place n : a resort that features mineral springs or bathing

water lily n : any of various aquatic plants

with floating roundish leaves and showy solitary flowers

wa·ter·line \'wȯ-tər-,līn, 'wä-\ n : a line that marks the level of the surface of water on something (as a ship or the shore)

wa·ter·logged \-,lȯgd, -,lägd\ adj : so filled or soaked with water as to be heavy or unmanageable ⟨a ∼ boat⟩

wa·ter·loo \,wȯ-tər-'lü, ,wä-\ n, pl **-loos** [*Waterloo*, Belgium, scene of Napoleon's defeat in 1815] : a decisive or final defeat or setback

¹**wa·ter·mark** \'wȯ-tər-,märk, 'wä-\ n 1 : a mark indicating height to which water has risen 2 : a marking in paper visible when the paper is held up to the light

²**watermark** vb : to mark (paper) with a watermark

wa·ter·mel·on \-,me-lən\ n : a large roundish or oblong fruit with sweet juicy usu. red pulp; *also* : a widely grown African vine related to the squashes that produces watermelons

water moccasin n : a venomous pit viper chiefly of the southeastern U.S. that is related to the copperhead

water ou·zel \-'ü-zəl\ n : DIPPER 1

water park n : an amusement park with a pool and wetted slides

water pill n : DIURETIC

water pipe n : a pipe for smoking that has a long flexible tube whereby the smoke is cooled by passing through water

water pistol n : a toy pistol for squirting a jet of liquid

water polo n : a team game played in a swimming pool with a ball resembling a soccer ball

wa·ter·pow·er \'wȯ-tər-,paú(-ə)r, 'wä-\ n : the power of moving water used to run machinery

¹**wa·ter·proof** \'wȯ-tər-,prüf, 'wä-\ adj : not letting water through; *esp* : covered or treated with a material to prevent permeation by water — **wa·ter·proof·ing** n

²**waterproof** n 1 : a waterproof fabric 2 *chiefly Brit* : RAINCOAT

³**waterproof** vb : to make waterproof

wa·ter–re·pel·lent \,wȯ-tər-ri-'pe-lənt, ,wä-\ adj : treated with a finish that is resistant to water penetration

wa·ter–re·sis·tant \-ri-'zis-tənt\ adj : WATER-REPELLENT

wa·ter·shed \'wȯ-tər-,shed, 'wä-\ n 1 : a dividing ridge between two drainage areas 2 : the region or area drained by a particular body of water

wa·ter·side \-,sīd\ n : the land bordering a body of water

water ski n : a ski used on water when the wearer is towed — **wa·ter·ski** vb — **wa·ter–ski·er** \-,skē-ər\ n

water snake n : any of various snakes found in or near freshwater and feeding largely on aquatic animals

wa·ter·spout \'wȯ-tər-,spaút, 'wä-\ n 1 : a pipe for carrying water from a roof 2 : a funnel-shaped cloud extending from a cloud down to a spray torn up by whirling winds from an ocean or lake

water strider n : any of various long-legged bugs that move about swiftly on the surface of water

water table n : the upper limit of the portion of the ground wholly saturated with water

wa·ter·tight \,wȯ-tər-'tīt, ,wä-\ adj 1 : constructed so as to keep water out 2 : allowing no possibility for doubt or uncertainty ⟨a ∼ case against the accused⟩

wa·ter·way \'wȯ-tər-,wā, 'wä-\ n : a navigable body of water

wa·ter·wheel \-,hwēl, -,wēl\ n : a wheel made to turn by water flowing against it

water wings n pl : an air-filled device to give support to a person's body esp. when learning to swim

wa·ter·works \'wȯ-tər-,wərks, 'wä-\ n pl : a system for supplying water (as to a city)

wa·tery \'wȯ-tə-rē, 'wä-\ adj 1 : containing, full of, or giving out water ⟨∼ clouds⟩ 2 : being like water : THIN, WEAK ⟨∼ lemonade⟩; *also* : being soft and soggy ⟨∼ turnips⟩

WATS \'wäts\ abbr Wide-Area Telecommunications Service

watt \'wät\ n [James *Watt* †1819 Scottish engineer and inventor] : the metric unit of power equal to the work done at the rate of one joule per second or to the power produced by a current of one ampere across a potential difference of one volt

watt·age \'wä-tij\ n : amount of power expressed in watts

wat·tle \'wä-t°l\ n 1 : a framework of rods with flexible branches or reeds interlaced used esp. formerly in building; *also* : material for this framework 2 : a naked fleshy process hanging usu. from the head or neck (as of a bird) — **wat·tled** \-t°ld\ adj

W Aust abbr Western Australia

¹**wave** \'wāv\ vb **waved**; **wav·ing** 1 : FLUTTER ⟨flags *waving* in the breeze⟩ 2 : to motion with the hands or with something held in them in signal or salute 3 : to become moved or brandished to-and-fro; *also* : BRANDISH, FLOURISH ⟨∼ a sword⟩ 4 : to move before the wind with a wavelike motion ⟨fields of *waving* grain⟩ 5 : to curve up and down like a wave : UNDULATE

²**wave** n 1 : a moving ridge or swell on the surface of water 2 : a wavelike formation or shape ⟨a ∼ in the hair⟩ 3 : the action or process of making wavy or curly 4 : a waving motion; *esp* : a signal made by waving something 5 : FLOW, GUSH ⟨a ∼ of anger swept over her⟩ 6 : a peak of activity ⟨a ∼ of selling⟩ 7 : a disturbance that transfers energy progressively from point to point in a medium ⟨light travels in ∼s⟩ ⟨a sound ∼⟩ 8 : a period of hot or cold weather — **wave·like** adj

wave·length \'wāv-,leŋth\ n 1 : the distance in the line of advance of a wave from any one point (as a crest) to the next corresponding point 2 : a line of thought that reveals a common understanding

wave·let \-lət\ n : a little wave : RIPPLE

wa·ver \'wā-vər\ vb **1** : to fluctuate in opinion, allegiance, or direction **2** : REEL, TOTTER; also : QUIVER, FLICKER ⟨~ing flames⟩ **3** : FALTER **4** : to give an unsteady sound : QUAVER ♦ **Synonyms** FALTER, HESITATE, SHILLY-SHALLY, VACILLATE — waver n — wa·ver·er n — wa·ver·ing·ly adv

wavy \'wā-vē\ adj wav·i·er; -est : having waves : moving in waves

¹wax \'waks\ n **1** : a yellowish plastic substance secreted by bees for constructing the honeycomb **2** : any of various substances like beeswax

²wax vb : to treat or rub with wax — **wax·er** n

³wax vb **1** : to increase in size, numbers, strength, volume, or duration **2** : to increase in apparent size ⟨the moon ~es toward the full⟩ **3** : to take on a quality or state : BECOME ⟨~ed indignant⟩ ⟨the party ~ed merry⟩

wax bean n : a kidney bean with pods that turn creamy yellow to bright yellow when mature enough to use as snap beans

wax·en \'wak-sən\ adj **1** : made of or covered with wax **2** : resembling wax (as in color or consistency)

wax museum n : a place where wax effigies are exhibited

wax myrtle n : any of a genus of shrubs or trees with aromatic leaves; esp : an evergreen shrub or small tree of the eastern U.S. that produces small hard berries with a thick coating of bluish-white wax used for candles

wax·wing \'waks-,wiŋ\ n : any of a genus of chiefly brown to gray singing birds with a showy crest and red waxy material on the tips of some wing feathers

wax·work \-,wərk\ n **1** : an effigy usu. of a person in wax **2** pl : an exhibition of wax figures

waxy \'wak-sē\ adj wax·i·er; -est **1** : made of or full of wax **2** : WAXEN 2

way \'wā\ n **1** : a thoroughfare for travel or passage : ROAD, PATH, STREET **2** : ROUTE ⟨knew the ~ home⟩ **3** : a course of action ⟨chose the easy ~⟩; also : opportunity, capability, or fact of doing as one pleases ⟨always had your own ~⟩ **4** : a possible course : POSSIBILITY ⟨no two ~s about it⟩ **5** : METHOD, MODE ⟨this ~ of thinking⟩ ⟨a new ~ of painting⟩ **6** : FEATURE, RESPECT ⟨a good worker in many ~s⟩ **7** : the usual or characteristic state of affairs ⟨as is the ~ with old people⟩; also : individual characteristic or peculiarity ⟨used to her ~s⟩ **8** : DISTANCE ⟨a short ~ from here⟩ ⟨a long ~ from success⟩ **9** : progress along a course ⟨working my ~ through college⟩ **10** : something having direction : LOCALITY ⟨out our ~⟩ **11** : STATE, CONDITION ⟨the ~ things are⟩ **12** pl : an inclined structure upon which a ship is built or is supported in launching **13** : CATEGORY, KIND ⟨get what you need in the ~ of supplies⟩ **14** : motion or speed of a boat through the water — **by the way** : by way of interjection or digression

— by way of 1 : for the purpose of ⟨by way of illustration⟩ **2** : by the route through : VIA **— out of the way 1** : WRONG, IMPROPER **2** : SECLUDED, REMOTE

way·bill \'wā-,bil\ n : a paper that accompanies a freight shipment and gives details of goods, route, and charges

way·far·er \'wā-,fer-ər\ n : a traveler esp. on foot — **way·far·ing** \-,fer-iŋ\ adj

way·lay \'wā-,lā\ vb **-laid** \-,lād\; **-lay·ing** : to lie in wait for or attack from ambush

way–out \'wā-'aut\ adj : FAR-OUT

-ways adv suffix : in (such) a way, course, direction, or manner ⟨sideways⟩

ways and means n pl : methods and resources esp. for raising revenues needed by a state; also : a legislative committee concerned with this function

way·side \'wā-,sīd\ n : the side of or land adjacent to a road or path

way station n : an intermediate station on a line of travel (as a railroad)

way·ward \'wā-wərd\ adj [ME, short for awayward turned away, fr. away, adv. + -ward directed toward] **1** : following one's own capricious or wanton inclinations ⟨~ children⟩ **2** : UNPREDICTABLE, IRREGULAR ⟨a ~ act⟩

WBC abbr white blood cells

WC 1 water closet **2** without charge

WCTU abbr Women's Christian Temperance Union

we \'wē\ pron **1** — used of a group that includes the speaker or writer **2** — used for the singular I by a monarch, editor, or writer

weak \'wēk\ adj **1** : lacking strength or vigor : FEEBLE **2** : not able to sustain or resist much weight, pressure, or strain **3** : deficient in vigor of mind or character; also : resulting from or indicative of such deficiency ⟨a ~ policy⟩ ⟨a ~ will⟩ **4** : not supported by truth or logic ⟨a ~ argument⟩ **5** : lacking skill or proficiency; also : indicative of a lack of skill or aptitude **6** : lacking vigor of expression or effect **7** : of less than usual strength ⟨~ tea⟩ **8** : not having or exerting authority ⟨~ government⟩; also : INEFFECTIVE, IMPOTENT ⟨~ measures to control crime⟩ **9** : of, relating to, or constituting a verb or verb conjugation that forms the past tense and past participle by adding -ed or -d or -t — **weak·ly** adv

weak·en \'wē-kən\ vb : to make or become weak ⟨bodies ~ed by hunger⟩ ♦ **Synonyms** ENFEEBLE, DEBILITATE, UNDERMINE, SAP, CRIPPLE

weak·fish \'wēk-,fish\ n [obs. D weekvis, fr. D week soft + vis fish] : a common marine fish of the Atlantic coast of the U.S. caught for food and sport; also : any of several related food fishes

weak force n : the physical force responsible for particle decay processes in radioactivity

weak–kneed \'wēk-'nēd\ adj : lacking willpower or resolution ⟨~ appeasers⟩

weak·ling \'wē-kliŋ\ n : a person who is physically, mentally, or morally weak

weak·ly \'wē-klē\ adj : FEEBLE, WEAK

weakness • weave

weak·ness \'wēk-nəs\ *n* **1** : the quality or state of being weak; *also* : an instance or period of being weak ⟨in a moment of ~ he agreed to go⟩ **2** : FAULT, DEFECT **3** : an object of special desire or fondness ⟨chocolate is her ~⟩

¹weal \'wēl\ *n* : WELL-BEING, PROSPERITY

²weal *n* : WELT

weald \'wēld\ *n* [The *Weald*, wooded district in England, fr. ME *Weeld*, fr. OE *weald* forest] **1** : FOREST **2** : WOLD

wealth \'welth\ *n* [ME *welthe* welfare, prosperity, fr. *wele* weal] **1** : abundance of possessions or resources : AFFLUENCE, RICHES **2** : abundant supply : PROFUSION ⟨a ~ of detail⟩ **3** : all property that has a money or an exchange value; *also* : all objects or resources that have economic value ♦ *Synonyms* FORTUNE, PROPERTY, SUBSTANCE, WORTH

wealthy \'wel-thē\ *adj* **wealth·i·er; -est** : having wealth : RICH

wean \'wēn\ *vb* **1** : to accustom (a young mammal) to take food by means other than nursing **2** : to free from a source of dependence; *also* : to free from a usu. unwholesome habit or interest

weap·on \'we-pən\ *n* **1** : something (as a gun, knife, or club) used to injure, defeat, or destroy **2** : a means of contending against another ⟨a ~ against cancer⟩ — **weap·on·less** \-ləs\ *adj*

weap·on·ry \-rē\ *n* : WEAPONS

¹wear \'wear\ *vb* **wore** \'wȯr\; **worn** \'wȯrn\; **wear·ing** **1** : to use as an article of clothing or adornment ⟨~ a coat⟩ ⟨~s earrings⟩; *also* : to carry on the person ⟨~ a gun⟩ **2** : EXHIBIT, PRESENT ⟨~ a smile⟩ **3** : to impair, diminish, or decay by use or by scraping or rubbing ⟨clothes *worn* to shreds⟩; *also* : to produce gradually by friction, rubbing, or wasting away ⟨~ a hole in the rug⟩ **4** : to exhaust or lessen the strength of : WEARY, FATIGUE ⟨*worn* by care and toil⟩ **5** : to endure use : last under use or the passage of time ⟨this cloth ~s well⟩ **6** : to diminish or fail with the passage of time ⟨the day ~s on⟩ ⟨the effect of the drug *wore* off⟩ **7** : to grow or become by attrition, use, or age ⟨the coin was *worn* thin⟩ — **wear·able** \'wer-ə-bəl\ *adj* — **wear·er** *n*

²wear *n* **1** : the act of wearing : the state of being worn ⟨clothes for everyday ~⟩ **2** : clothing usu. of a particular kind or for a special occasion or use ⟨children's ~⟩ **3** : wearing or lasting quality ⟨the coat still has lots of ~ in it⟩ **4** : the result of wearing or use : impairment due to use ⟨the suit shows ~⟩

wear and tear *n* : the loss, injury, or stress to which something is subjected in the course of use; *esp* : normal depreciation

wear down *vb* : to weary and overcome by persistent resistance or pressure

wea·ri·some \'wir-ē-səm\ *adj* : causing weariness : TIRESOME — **wea·ri·some·ly** *adv* — **wea·ri·some·ness** *n*

wear out *vb* **1** : TIRE **2** : to make or become useless by wear

¹wea·ry \'wir-ē\ *adj* **wea·ri·er; -est** **1** : worn out in strength, energy, or freshness **2** : expressing or characteristic of weariness ⟨a ~ sigh⟩ **3** : having one's patience, tolerance, or pleasure exhausted ⟨~ of war⟩ — **wea·ri·ly** \'wir-ə-lē\ *adv* — **wea·ri·ness** \-ē-nəs\ *n*

²weary *vb* **wea·ried; wea·ry·ing** : to become or make weary : TIRE

wea·sel \'wē-zəl\ *n, pl* **weasels** : any of various small slender flesh-eating mammals related to the minks — **wea·sel·ly** *also* **wea·sely** \'wēz-lē, 'wē-zə-lē\ *adj*

²weasel *vb* **wea·seled; wea·sel·ing** **1** : to use weasel words : EQUIVOCATE **2** : to escape from or evade a situation or obligation — often used with *out*

weasel word *n* [fr. the weasel's reputed habit of sucking the contents out of an egg while leaving the shell intact] : a word used to avoid a direct or forthright statement or position

¹weath·er \'we-thər\ *n* **1** : the state of the atmosphere with respect to heat or cold, wetness or dryness, calm or storm, clearness or cloudiness **2** : a particular and esp. a disagreeable atmospheric state : RAIN, STORM

²weather *vb* **1** : to expose to or endure the action of weather; *also* : to alter (as in color or texture) by such exposure **2** : to bear up against successfully ⟨~ a storm⟩ ⟨~ troubles⟩

³weather *adj* : WINDWARD

weath·er-beat·en \'we-thər-,bē-t²n\ *adj* : worn or damaged by exposure to the weather; *also* : toughened or tanned by the weather ⟨~ face⟩

weath·er·cock \-,käk\ *n* : a weather vane shaped like a rooster

weath·er·ing \'we-thə-riŋ\ *n* : the action of the weather in altering the color, texture, composition, or form of exposed objects; *also* : alteration thus effected

weath·er·ize \'we-thə-,rīz\ *vb* **-ized; -iz·ing** : to make (as a house) better protected against winter weather (as by adding insulation)

weath·er·man \-,man\ *n* : one who reports and forecasts the weather : METEOROLOGIST

weath·er·per·son \-,pər-sən\ *n* : a person who reports and forecasts the weather : METEOROLOGIST

weath·er·proof \'we-thər-,prüf\ *adj* : able to withstand exposure to weather — **weatherproof** *vb*

weath·er·strip·ping \'we-thər-,stri-piŋ\ *n* : material used to seal a door or window at the edges — **weath·er-strip** *vb* — **weather strip** *n*

weather vane *n* : VANE 1

weath·er·worn \'we-thər-,wȯrn\ *adj* : worn by exposure to the weather

¹weave \'wēv\ *vb* **wove** \'wōv\ *or* **weaved**; **wo·ven** \'wō-vən\ *or* **weaved**; **weav·ing** **1** : to form by interlacing strands of material; *esp* : to make on a loom by interlacing warp and filling threads ⟨~ cloth⟩ **2** : to interlace (as threads) into a fabric and esp. cloth **3** : SPIN 2 **4** : to make as if by weaving together parts **5** : to insert as a part : work in **6** : to move in a winding or zigzag course esp. to avoid obstacles ⟨we *wove* our way through the crowd⟩ — **weav·er** *n*

²**weave** *n* : something woven; *also* : a pattern or method of weaving ⟨a loose ∼⟩

¹**web** \'web\ *n* **1** : a fabric on a loom or coming from a loom **2** : COBWEB; *also* : SNARE, ENTANGLEMENT ⟨caught in a ∼ of deceit⟩ **3** : an animal or plant membrane; *esp* : one uniting the toes (as in many birds) **4** : NETWORK ⟨a ∼ of highways⟩ **5** : the series of barbs on each side of the shaft of a feather **6** : WORLD WIDE WEB — **webbed** \'webd\ *adj*

²**web** *vb* **webbed; web·bing 1** : to make a web **2** : to cover or provide with webs or a network **3** : ENTANGLE, ENSNARE

web·bing \'we-biŋ\ *n* : a strong closely woven tape designed for bearing weight and used esp. for straps, harness, or upholstery

web·cam \'web-,kam\ *n* : a camera used in transmitting live images over the World Wide Web

web·cast \'web-,kast\ *n* : a transmission of sound and images via the World Wide Web — **webcast** *vb*

web-foot·ed \'web-'fu̇-təd\ *adj* : having webbed feet

web·log \'web-,lȯg, -,läg\ *n* : BLOG

web·mas·ter \'web-,mas-tər\ *n, often cap* : a person responsible for the creation or maintenance of a website

web·site *or* **Web site** \'web-,sīt\ *n* : a group of World Wide Web pages made available online (as by an individual or business)

wed \'wed\ *vb* **wed·ded** *also* **wed; wed·ding 1** : to take, give, enter into, or join in marriage : MARRY **2** : to unite firmly

Wed *abbr* Wednesday

wed·ding \'we-diŋ\ *n* **1** : a marriage ceremony usu. with accompanying festivities : NUPTIALS **2** : a joining in close association **3** : a wedding anniversary or its celebration

¹**wedge** \'wej\ *n* **1** : a piece of wood or metal that tapers to a thin edge and is used to split logs or rocks or to raise heavy weights **2** : something (as an action or policy) that serves to open up a way for a breach, change, or intrusion **3** : a wedge-shaped object or part ⟨a ∼ of pie⟩

²**wedge** *vb* **wedged; wedg·ing 1** : to hold firm by or as if by driving in a wedge **2** : to force (something) into a narrow space

wed·lock \'wed-,läk\ *n* [ME *wedlok*, fr. OE *wedlāc* marriage bond, fr. *wedd* pledge + *-lāc*, suffix denoting activity] : the state of being married : MARRIAGE, MATRIMONY

Wednes·day \'wenz-(,)dā, -dē\ *n* [ME, fr. OE *wōdnsdæg*, lit., day of Woden (supreme god of the pagan Anglo-Saxons)] : the 4th day of the week

wee \'wē\ *adj* [ME (Sc) *we*, fr. *we*, n., little bit, fr. OE *wǣge* weight] **1** : very small : TINY **2** : very early ⟨∼ hours of the morning⟩

¹**weed** \'wēd\ *n* **1** : a plant that tends to grow thickly where it is not wanted and to choke out more desirable plants **2** : MARIJUANA

²**weed** *vb* **1** : to clear of or remove weeds or something harmful, inferior, or superfluous ⟨∼ a garden⟩ **2** : to get rid of ⟨∼ out the troublemakers⟩ — **weed·er** *n*

³**weed** *n* : mourning clothes — usu. used in pl. ⟨widow's ∼s⟩

weedy \'wē-dē\ *adj* **1** : full of weeds **2** : resembling a weed esp. in vigor of growth or spread **3** : noticeably lean and scrawny : LANKY ⟨a ∼ little man⟩

week \'wēk\ *n* **1** : seven successive days; *esp* : a calendar period of seven days beginning with Sunday and ending with Saturday **2** : the working or school days of the calendar week

week·day \'wēk-,dā\ *n* : a day of the week except Sunday or sometimes except Saturday and Sunday

¹**week·end** \-,end\ *n* : the period between the close of one working or business or school week and the beginning of the next

²**weekend** *vb* : to spend the weekend

¹**week·ly** \'wē-klē\ *adj* **1** : occurring, appearing, or done every week **2** : computed in terms of one week ⟨∼ rental rates⟩ — **weekly** *adv*

²**weekly** *n, pl* **weeklies** : a weekly publication

ween \'wēn\ *vb, archaic* : SUPPOSE 3

wee·ny \'wē-nē\ *also* **ween·sy** \'wēn-sē\ *adj* : exceptionally small

weep \'wēp\ *vb* **wept** \'wept\; **weep·ing 1** : to express emotion and esp. sorrow by shedding tears : BEWAIL, CRY **2** : to give off fluid slowly : OOZE — **weep·er** *n*

weeping *adj* **1** : TEARFUL ⟨∼ gratitude⟩ **2** : having slender drooping branches

weeping willow *n* : a willow with slender drooping branches

weepy \'wē-pē\ *adj* : inclined to weep

wee·vil \'wē-vəl\ *n* : any of a large group of beetles having a long head usu. curved into a snout and including many whose larvae are destructive plant-feeding pests — **wee·vily** *or* **wee·vil·ly** \'wē-və-lē\ *adj*

weft \'weft\ *n* **1** : a filling thread or yarn in weaving **2** : WEB, FABRIC; *also* : something woven

¹**weigh** \'wā\ *vb* [ME *weyen*, fr. OE *wegan* to move, carry, weigh] **1** : to find the heaviness of **2** : to have weight or a specified weight **3** : to consider carefully : PONDER **4** : to merit consideration as important : COUNT ⟨evidence ∼*ing* against him⟩ **5** : to raise before sailing ⟨∼ anchor⟩ **6** : to press down with or as if with a heavy weight

²**weigh** *n* [alter. of *way*] : WAY — used in the phrase *under weigh*

¹**weight** \'wāt\ *n* **1** : the amount that something weighs; *also* : the standard amount that something should weigh **2** : a quantity or object weighing a usu. specified amount **3** : a unit (as a pound or kilogram) of weight or mass; *also* : a system of such units **4** : a heavy object for holding or pressing something down;

U.S. WEIGHTS AND MEASURES

LENGTH

UNIT	SYMBOL	U.S. EQUIVALENT	METRIC EQUIVALENT
mile	mi	5280 feet, 1760 yards	1.609 kilometers
rod	rd	5.50 yards, 16.5 feet	5.029 meters
yard	yd	3 feet, 36 inches	0.9144 meter
foot	ft *or* '	12 inches, 0.333 yard	30.48 centimeters
inch	in *or* "	0.083 foot, 0.028 yard	2.54 centimeters

AREA

UNIT	SYMBOL	U.S. EQUIVALENT	METRIC EQUIVALENT
square mile	sq mi *or* mi^2	640 acres	2.590 square kilometers
acre	ac	4840 square yards, 43,560 square feet	4047 square meters
square rod	sq rd *or* rd^2	30.25 square yards	25.293 square meters
square yard	sq yd *or* yd^2	9 square feet	0.836 square meter
square foot	sq ft *or* ft^2	144 square inches	0.093 square meter
square inch	sq in *or* in^2	0.0069 square foot	6.452 square centimeter

VOLUME

UNIT	SYMBOL	U.S. EQUIVALENT	METRIC EQUIVALENT
cubic yard	cu yd *or* yd^3	27 cubic feet	0.765 cubic meter
cubic foot	cu ft *or* ft^3	1728 cubic inches	0.028 cubic meter
cubic inch	cu in *or* in^3	0.00058 cubic foot	16.387 cubic centimeters

WEIGHT—AVOIRDUPOIS

UNIT	SYMBOL	U.S. EQUIVALENT	METRIC EQUIVALENT
ton			
short ton		2000 pounds	0.907 metric ton
long ton		2240 pounds	1.016 metric tons
hundredweight	cwt		
short hundredweight		100 pounds	45.359 kilograms
long hundredweight		112 pounds	50.802 kilograms
pound	lb *also* #	16 ounces	0.454 kilogram
ounce	oz	16 drams, 437.5 grains	28.350 grams
dram	dr	27.344 grains	1.772 grams
grain	gr	0.037 dram	0.0648 gram

CAPACITY

UNIT	SYMBOL	U.S. EQUIVALENT	METRIC EQUIVALENT
		LIQUID MEASURE	
gallon	gal	4 quarts	3.785 liters
quart	qt	2 pints	0.946 liter
pint	pt	4 gills	473.176 milliliters
gill	gi	4 fluid ounces	118.294 milliliters
fluid ounce	fl oz *or* f℥	8 fluid drams	29.573 milliliters
fluid dram	fl dr *or* f℈	60 minims	3.697 milliliters
minim	min *or* ♍	⅟₆₀ fluid dram	0.061610 milliliter
		DRY MEASURE	
bushel	bu	4 pecks	35.239 liters
peck	pk	8 quarts	8.810 liters
quart	qt	2 pints	1.101 liters
pint	pt	½ quart	0.551 liter

also : a heavy object for throwing or lifting in an athletic contest **5** : a mental or emotional burden **6** : IMPORTANCE; *also* : INFLUENCE ⟨threw his ∼ around⟩ **7** : overpowering force **8** : relative thickness (as of a textile) ⟨summer-*weight* clothes⟩ ♦ **Synonyms** SIGNIFICANCE, MOMENT, CONSEQUENCE, IMPORT, AUTHORITY, PRESTIGE, CREDIT

²**weight** *vb* **1** : to oppress with a burden ⟨∼*ed* down with cares⟩ **2** : to load with or as if with a weight

weight·less \'wāt-ləs\ *adj* : having little weight : lacking apparent gravitational pull ⟨a ∼ environment⟩ — **weight·less·ly** *adv* — **weight·less·ness** *n*

weighty \'wā-tē\ *adj* **weight·i·er; -est 1** : of much importance or consequence : MOMENTOUS, SERIOUS ⟨∼ problems⟩ **2** : SOLEMN ⟨a ∼ manner⟩ **3** : HEAVY **4** : POWERFUL, TELLING ⟨∼ arguments⟩

weiner *var of* WIENER

weir \'wer, 'wir\ *n* **1** : a fence set in a waterway for catching fish **2** : a dam in a stream to raise the water level or divert its flow

weird \'wird\ *adj* [ME *wird, werd* fate, destiny, fr. OE *wyrd*] **1** : MAGICAL **2** : ODD, UNUSUAL ⟨∼ noises⟩ ♦ **Synonyms** EERIE, UNCANNY, SPOOKY — **weird·ly** *adv* — **weird·ness** *n*

weirdo \'wir-(,)dō\ *n, pl* **weird·os** : a person who is extraordinarily strange or eccentric

Welch *var of* WELSH

¹**wel·come** \'wel-kəm\ *vb* **wel·comed; wel·com·ing 1** : to greet cordially or courteously **2** : to accept, meet, or face with pleasure ⟨he ∼s criticism⟩

²**welcome** *adj* **1** : received gladly into one's presence ⟨a ∼ visitor⟩ **2** : giving pleasure : PLEASING ⟨∼ news⟩ **3** : willingly permitted or admitted ⟨all are ∼ to use the books⟩ **4** — used in the phrase "You're welcome" as a reply to an expression of thanks

³**welcome** *n* **1** : a cordial greeting or reception **2** : the state of being welcome ⟨overstayed their ∼⟩

¹**weld** \'weld\ *vb* **1** : to unite (metal or plastic parts) either by heating and allowing the parts to flow together or by hammering or pressing together **2** : to unite closely or intimately ⟨∼*ed* together in friendship⟩ — **weld·er** *n*

²**weld** *n* **1** : a welded joint **2** : union by welding

wel·fare \'wel-,fer\ *n* **1** : the state of doing well esp. in respect to happiness, well-being, or prosperity **2** : aid in the form of money or necessities for those in need; *also* : the agency through which the aid is given

welfare state *n* : a nation or state that assumes primary responsibility for the individual and social welfare of its citizens

wel·kin \'wel-kən\ *n* : SKY; *also* : AIR

¹**well** \'wel\ *n* **1** : a spring with its pool : FOUNTAIN; *also* : a source of supply ⟨a ∼ of information⟩ **2** : a hole sunk in the earth to obtain a natural deposit (as of water, oil, or gas) **3** : an open space (as for a staircase) extending vertically through floors of a structure **4** : something suggesting a well

²**well** *vb* : to rise up and flow out

³**well** *adv* **bet·ter** \'be-tər\; **best** \'best\ **1** : in a good or proper manner : RIGHTLY; *also* : EXCELLENTLY, SKILLFULLY **2** : SATISFACTORILY, FORTUNATELY ⟨the party turned out ∼⟩ **3** : ABUNDANTLY ⟨eat ∼⟩ **4** : with reason or courtesy : PROPERLY ⟨I cannot ∼ refuse⟩ **5** : COMPLETELY, FULLY, QUITE ⟨∼ worth the price⟩ ⟨*well*-hidden⟩ **6** : INTIMATELY, CLOSELY ⟨I know him ∼⟩ **7** : CONSIDERABLY, FAR ⟨∼ over a million⟩ ⟨∼ ahead⟩ **8** : without trouble or difficulty ⟨we could ∼ have gone⟩ **9** : EXACTLY, DEFINITELY ⟨remember it ∼⟩

⁴**well** *adj* **1** : PROSPEROUS; *also* : being in satisfactory condition or circumstances **2** : SATISFACTORY, PLEASING ⟨all is ∼⟩ **3** : ADVISABLE, DESIRABLE ⟨it is not ∼ to anger him⟩ **4** : free or recovered from ill health : HEALTHY **5** : FORTUNATE ⟨it is ∼ that this has happened⟩

well–ad·just·ed \,wel-ə-'jəs-təd\ *adj* : WELL-BALANCED

well–ad·vised \-əd-'vīzd\ *adj* **1** : PRUDENT ⟨∼ restraint⟩ **2** : resulting from, based on, or showing careful deliberation or wise counsel ⟨∼ plans⟩

well–ap·point·ed \-ə-'póin-təd\ *adj* : properly fitted out ⟨a ∼ house⟩

well–ba·lanced \'wel-'ba-lənst\ *adj* **1** : nicely or evenly balanced or arranged ⟨a ∼ meal⟩ **2** : emotionally or psychologically untroubled

well–be·ing \-'bē-iŋ\ *n* : the state of being happy, healthy, or prosperous

well–born \-'bórn\ *adj* : born of noble or wealthy lineage

well–bred \-'bred\ *adj* : having or indicating good breeding : REFINED

well–de·fined \-di-'fīnd\ *adj* : having clearly distinguishable limits or boundaries

well–dis·posed \-di-'spōzd\ *adj* : disposed to be friendly, favorable, or sympathetic ⟨∼ to the idea⟩

well–done \'wel-'dən\ *adj* **1** : rightly or properly performed **2** : cooked thoroughly

well–en·dowed \'wel-in-'daud\ *adj* **1** : having plenty of money or property **2** : having large breasts **3** : having a large penis

well–fa·vored \-'fā-vərd\ *adj* : GOOD-LOOKING, HANDSOME ⟨a ∼ face⟩

well–fixed \-'fikst\ *adj* : WELL-HEELED

well–found·ed \-'faun-dəd\ *adj* : based on good reasons

well–groomed \-'grümd, -'grumd\ *adj* : neatly dressed or cared for

well–ground·ed \-'graun-dəd\ *adj* **1** : having a firm foundation **2** : WELL-FOUNDED

well·head \-,hed\ *n* **1** : the source of a spring or a stream **2** : principal source **3** : the top of or a structure built over a well

well-heeled \-'hēld\ *adj* : financially well-off

well-known \-'nōn\ *adj* : fully or widely known

well-mean·ing \-'mē-niŋ\ *adj* : having or based on good intentions

well·ness \-nəs\ *n* : good health esp. as an actively sought goal ⟨∼ clinics⟩ ⟨lifestyles that promote ∼⟩

well-nigh \-'nī\ *adv* : ALMOST, NEARLY ⟨∼ impossible⟩

well-off \-'óf\ *adj* : being in good condition or circumstances; *esp* : WELL-TO-DO

well-or·dered \-'ór-dərd\ *adj* : having an orderly procedure or arrangement

well-placed \-'plāst\ *adj* : appropriately or advantageously directed or positioned

well-read \-'red\ *adj* : well informed through reading

well-round·ed \-'raún-dəd\ *adj* 1 : broadly trained, educated, and experienced 2 : COMPREHENSIVE ⟨a ∼ program of activities⟩

well-spo·ken \'wel-'spō-kən\ *adj* 1 : speaking well and esp. courteously 2 : spoken with propriety ⟨∼ words⟩

well·spring \-,spriŋ\ *n* : a source of continuous supply ⟨a ∼ of information⟩

well-timed \-'tīmd\ *adj* : TIMELY ⟨a ∼ announcement⟩

well-to-do \,wel-tə-'dü\ *adj* : having more than adequate financial resources : PROSPEROUS

well-turned \'wel-'tərnd\ *adj* 1 : pleasingly shaped ⟨a ∼ ankle⟩ 2 : pleasingly expressed ⟨a ∼ phrase⟩

well-wish·er \'wel-,wi-shər\ *n* : an admiring supporter or fan — **well-wish·ing** *adj or n*

welsh \'welsh, 'welch\ *vb* 1 : to avoid payment 2 : to break one's word ⟨∼ed on his promises⟩

Welsh \'welsh\ *also* **Welch** \'welch\ *n* [ME *walisch, welisch,* adj., Welsh, fr. OE *wælisc* foreign, British, Welsh, fr. *Wealh* foreigner, Briton, Welshman] **1 Welsh** *pl* : the people of Wales 2 : the Celtic language of Wales — **Welsh** *adj* — **Welsh·man** \-mən\ *n*

Welsh cor·gi \-'kór-gē\ *n* [W *corgi,* fr. *cor* dwarf + *ci* dog] : a short-legged longbacked dog with foxy head of either of two breeds of Welsh origin

Welsh rabbit *n* : melted often seasoned cheese served over toast or crackers

Welsh rare·bit \-'rer-bət\ *n* : WELSH RABBIT

¹welt \'welt\ *n* 1 : the narrow strip of leather between a shoe upper and sole to which other parts are stitched 2 : a doubled edge, strip, insert, or seam for ornament or reinforcement 3 : a ridge or lump raised on the skin usu. by a blow; *also* : a heavy blow

²welt *vb* 1 : to furnish (as a shoe) with a welt 2 : to hit hard

¹wel·ter \'wel-tər\ *vb* 1 : WRITHE, TOSS; *also* : WALLOW 2 : to rise and fall or toss about in or with waves 3 : to become deeply sunk, soaked, or involved 4 : to be in turmoil

²welter *n* 1 : TURMOIL 2 : a chaotic mass or jumble ⟨a ∼ of data⟩

wel·ter·weight \'wel-tər-,wāt\ *n* : a boxer weighing more than 135 but not over 147 pounds

wen \'wen\ *n* : an abnormal growth or a cyst protruding from a surface esp. of the skin

wench \'wench\ *n* [ME *wenche,* short for *wenchel* child, fr. OE *wencel*] 1 : a young woman 2 : a female servant

wend \'wend\ *vb* : to direct one's course : proceed on (one's way)

went *past of* GO

wept *past and past part of* WEEP

were *past 2d sing, past pl, or past subjunctive of* BE

were-wolf \'wer-,wúlf, 'wir-, 'wər-\ *n, pl* **were-wolves** \-,wúlvz\ [ME, fr. OE *wer-wulf,* fr. *wer* man + *wulf* wolf] : a person who in stories is transformed into a wolf or is capable of assuming a wolf's form

wes·kit \'wes-kət\ *n* : VEST 1

¹west \'west\ *adv* : to or toward the west

²west *adj* 1 : situated toward or at the west 2 : coming from the west

³west *n* 1 : the general direction of sunset 2 : the compass point directly opposite to east 3 *cap* : regions or countries west of a specified or implied point 4 *cap* : Europe and the Americas — **west·er·ly** \'wes-tər-lē\ *adv or adj* — **west·ward** *adv or adj* — **west·wards** *adv*

¹west·ern \'wes-tərn\ *adj* 1 : lying toward or coming from the west 2 *cap* : of, relating to, or characteristic of a region conventionally designated West 3 *cap* : of or relating to the Roman Catholic or Protestant segment of Christianity — **West·ern·er** *n*

²western *n, often cap* : a novel, story, film, or radio or television show about life in the western U.S. during the latter half of the 19th century

west·ern·ize \'wes-tər-,nīz\ *vb* **-ized; -iz·ing** : to give western characteristics to ⟨wanted to ∼ the country⟩ — **west·ern·i·za·tion** \,wes-tər-nə-'zā-shən\ *n*

West Nile virus \-'nī(-ə)l-\ *n* [*West Nile* province of Uganda] : a virus that is transmitted to humans by mosquitoes and causes an illness marked by fever, headache, muscle ache, and sometimes encephalitis or meningitis; *also* : this illness

¹wet \'wet\ *adj* **wet·ter; wet·test** 1 : consisting of or covered or soaked with liquid (as water) 2 : RAINY ⟨∼ days⟩ 3 : not dry ⟨∼ paint⟩ 4 : permitting or advocating the manufacture and sale of alcoholic beverages ⟨a ∼ town⟩ ⟨a ∼ candidate⟩ ♦ **Synonyms** DAMP, DANK, MOIST, HUMID — **wet·ly** *adv* — **wet·ness** *n*

²wet *n* 1 : WATER; *also* : WETNESS, MOISTURE 2 : rainy weather : RAIN 3 : an advocate of a wet liquor policy

³wet *vb* **wet** *or* **wet·ted; wet·ting** : to make or become wet

wet blanket *n* : one that quenches or dampens enthusiasm or pleasure

weth·er \'we-<u>th</u>ər\ *n* : a castrated male sheep or goat

wet·land \'wet-,land, -lənd\ *n* : land or areas (as swamps) containing much soil moisture — usu. used in pl.

wet nurse *n* : a woman who cares for and suckles children not her own

wet suit *n* : a rubber suit for swimmers that acts to retain body heat by keeping a layer of water against the body as insulation

wh *abbr* **1** which **2** white

¹**whack** \'hwak\ *vb* **1** : to strike with a smart or resounding blow **2** : to cut with or as if with a whack

²**whack** *n* **1** : a smart or resounding blow; *also* : the sound of such a blow **2** : POR-TION, SHARE 〈must each pay our ~〉 **3** : CONDITION, STATE 〈the machine is out of ~〉 **4** : an opportunity or occasion to do something : CHANCE **5** : a single action or occasion 〈made three pies at a ~〉

¹**whale** \'hwāl\ *n, pl* **whales 1** *or pl* **whale** : CETACEAN; *esp* : one (as a sperm whale or killer whale) of large size **2** : a person or thing impressive in size or quality 〈a ~ of a story〉

²**whale** *vb* **whaled; whal·ing** : to fish or hunt for whales

³**whale** *vb* **whaled; whal·ing 1** : THRASH **2** : to strike or hit vigorously

whale·boat \-,bōt\ *n* : a long narrow rowboat originally used by whalers

whale·bone \-,bōn\ *n* : BALEEN

whal·er \'hwā-lər\ *n* **1** : a person or ship that hunts whales **2** : WHALEBOAT

whale shark *n* : a shark of warm waters that is the largest known fish

wham·my \'hwa-mē\ *n, pl* **wham·mies** : JINX, HEX 〈put the ~ on him〉

wharf \'hwȯrf\ *n, pl* **wharves** \'hwȯrvz\ *also* **wharfs** : a structure alongside which ships lie to load and unload

¹**what** \'hwät, 'hwət\ *pron* **1** — used to inquire about the identity or nature of a being, an object, or some matter or situation 〈~ is he, a salesman〉 〈~'s that〉 〈~ happened〉 **2** : that which 〈I know ~ you want〉 **3** : WHATEVER 1 〈take ~ you want〉

²**what** *adv* **1** : in what respect : HOW 〈~ does he care〉 **2** — used with *with* to introduce a prepositional phrase that expresses cause 〈kept busy ~ with school and work〉

³**what** *adj* **1** — used to inquire about the identity or nature of a person, object, or matter 〈~ books do you read〉 **2** : how remarkable or surprising 〈~ an idea〉 **3** : WHATEVER

¹**what·ev·er** \hwät-'e-vər, hwət-\ *pron* **1** : anything or everything 〈does ~ he wants to〉 **2** : no matter what 〈~ you do, don't cheat〉 **3** : WHAT 1 — used as an intensive 〈~ do you mean〉

²**whatever** *adj* : of any kind at all 〈food ~〉

³**whatever** *adv* : in any case : whatever the case may be — often used to suggest the unimportance of an issue or choice 〈see a movie, watch TV,—~〉

¹**what·not** \'hwät-,nät, 'hwət-\ *pron* : any of various other things that might also be mentioned 〈needles, pins, and ~〉

²**whatnot** *n* : a light open set of shelves for small ornaments

what·so·ev·er \,hwät-sō-'e-vər, ,hwət-\ *pron or adj* : WHATEVER

wheal \'hwēl\ *n* : a rapidly formed flat slightly raised itching or burning patch on the skin; *also* : WELT

wheat \'hwēt\ *n* : a cereal grain that yields a fine white flour used chiefly in breads, baked goods, and pastas; *also* : any of several widely grown grasses yielding wheat — **wheat·en** *adj*

wheat germ *n* : the vitamin-rich wheat embryo separated in milling

whee·dle \'hwē-dᵊl\ *vb* **whee·dled; whee·dling 1** : to entice by flattery **2** : to gain or get by wheedling

¹**wheel** \'hwēl\ *n* **1** : a disk or circular frame that turns on a central axis **2** : a device whose main part is a wheel **3** : something resembling a wheel in shape or motion **4** : a curving or circular movement **5** : machinery that imparts motion : moving power 〈the ~s of government〉 **6** : a person of importance **7** *pl, slang* : AUTOMOBILE — **wheeled** \'hwēld\ *adj* — **wheel·less** *adj*

²**wheel** *vb* **1** : ROTATE, REVOLVE **2** : to change direction as if turning on a pivot **3** : to convey or move on wheels or in a vehicle

wheel·bar·row \-,ber-ō\ *n* : a vehicle with handles and usu. one wheel for carrying small loads

wheel·base \-,bās\ *n* : the distance in inches between the front and rear axles of an automotive vehicle

wheel·chair \-,cher\ *n* : a chair mounted on wheels esp. for the use of disabled persons

wheel·er \'hwē-lər\ *n* **1** : one that wheels **2** : WHEELHORSE **3** : something that has wheels — used in combination 〈a side= *wheeler*〉

wheel·er–deal·er \,hwē-lər-'dē-lər\ *n* : a shrewd operator esp. in business or politics

wheel·horse \'hwēl-,hȯrs\ *n* **1** : a horse in a position nearest the front wheels of a wagon **2** : a steady and effective worker esp. in a political body

wheel·house \-,haůs\ *n* : PILOTHOUSE

wheel–thrown \'hwēl-,thrōn\ *adj* : made on a potter's wheel

wheel·wright \-,rīt\ *n* : a maker and repairer of wheels and wheeled vehicles

¹**wheeze** \'hwēz\ *vb* **wheezed; wheez·ing** : to breathe with difficulty usu. with a whistling sound

²**wheeze** *n* **1** : a sound of wheezing 〈the ~ of an engine〉 **2** : an often repeated and well-known joke **3** : a trite saying

wheezy \'hwē-zē\ *adj* **wheez·i·er; -est 1** : inclined to wheeze **2** : having a wheezing sound — **wheez·i·ly** \-zə-lē\ *adv* — **wheez·i·ness** \-zē-nəs\ *n*

whelk \'hwelk\ *n* : a large sea snail; *esp* : one much used as food in Europe

whelm \\'hwelm\ *vb* : to overcome or engulf completely : OVERWHELM

¹whelp \\'hwelp\ *n* : any of the young of various carnivorous mammals (as a dog)

²whelp *vb* : to give birth to (whelps); *also* : bring forth young

¹when \\'hwen\ *adv* **1** : at what time ⟨~ will you return⟩ **2** : at or during which time ⟨a time ~ things were better⟩

²when *conj* **1** : at or during the time that ⟨leave ~ I do⟩ **2** : every time that ⟨they all clapped ~ he sang⟩ **3** : in the event that : IF ⟨disqualified ~ you cheat⟩ **4** : ALTHOUGH ⟨quit politics ~ he might have had a great career in it⟩

³when *pron* : what or which time ⟨since ~ have you been the boss⟩

⁴when *n* : the time of a happening

whence \\'hwens\ *adv or conj* : from what place, source, or cause

when·ev·er \hwe-'ne-vər, hwə-\ *conj or adv* : at whatever time

when·so·ev·er \\'hwen-sō-,e-vər\ *conj* : at any or every time that

¹where \\'hwer\ *adv* **1** : at, in, or to what place ⟨~ is it⟩ ⟨~ will we go⟩ **2** : at, in, or to what situation, position, direction, circumstances, or respect ⟨~ does this road lead⟩

²where *conj* **1** : at, in, or to what place ⟨knows ~ the house is⟩ **2** : at, in, or to what situation, position, direction, circumstances, or respect ⟨shows ~ the road leads⟩ **3** : WHEREVER ⟨goes ~ she likes⟩ **4** : at, in, or to which place ⟨the town ~ we live⟩ **5** : at, in, or to the place at, in, or to which ⟨stay ~ you are⟩ **6** : in a case, situation, or respect in which ⟨outstanding ~ endurance is called for⟩

³where *n* : PLACE, LOCATION ⟨the ~ and how of the accident⟩

¹where·abouts \-ə-,baůts\ *also* **whereabout** \-,baůt\ *adv* : about where : near what place ⟨~ does he live⟩

²whereabouts *n sing or pl* : the place where a person or thing is ⟨his present ~ are unknown⟩

where·as \hwer-'az\ *conj* **1** : while on the contrary; *also* : ALTHOUGH **2** : in view of the fact that : SINCE

where·at \-'at\ *conj* **1** : at or toward which **2** : in consequence of which : WHEREUPON

where·by \-'bī\ *conj* : by, through, or in accordance with which ⟨the means ~ we achieved our goals⟩

¹where·fore \\'hwer-,fȯr\ *adv* **1** : for what reason or purpose : WHY **2** : THEREFORE

²wherefore *n* : an answer or statement giving an explanation : REASON

¹where·in \hwer-'in\ *adv* : in what : in what respect ⟨~ was I wrong⟩

²wherein *conj* **1** : in which : WHERE ⟨the city ~ we live⟩ **2** : during which **3** : in what way : HOW ⟨showed me ~ I was wrong⟩

where·of \-'əv, -'äv\ *conj* **1** : of what ⟨knows ~ he speaks⟩ **2** : of which or whom ⟨books ~ the best are lost⟩

where·on \-'ȯn, -'än\ *conj* : on which ⟨the base ~ it rests⟩

where·so·ev·er \\'hwer-sō-,e-vər\ *conj* : WHEREVER

where·to \\'hwer-,tü\ *conj* : to which

where·up·on \\'hwer-ə-,pȯn, -,pän\ *conj* **1** : on which **2** : closely following and in consequence of which

¹wher·ev·er \hwer-'e-vər\ *adv* : where in the world ⟨~ did he get that tie⟩

²wherever *conj* **1** : at, in, or to whatever place ⟨thrives ~ he goes⟩ **2** : in any circumstance in which

where·with \\'hwer-,with, -,with\ *conj* : with or by means of which ⟨lack the tools ~ to repair the damage⟩

where·with·al \\'hwer-wi-,thȯl, -,thȯl\ *n* : MEANS, RESOURCES; *esp* : MONEY

wher·ry \\'hwer-ē\ *n, pl* **wherries** : a long light rowboat sharp at both ends

whet \\'hwet\ *vb* **whet·ted; whet·ting** **1** : to sharpen by rubbing on or with something abrasive (as a whetstone) **2** : to make keen : STIMULATE ⟨~ the appetite⟩

wheth·er \\'hwe-thər\ *conj* **1** : if it is or was true that ⟨ask ~ he is going⟩ **2** : if it is or was better ⟨uncertain ~ to go or stay⟩ **3** : whichever is or was the case, namely that ⟨~ we succeed or fail, we must try⟩ **4** : EITHER ⟨turned out well ~ by accident or design⟩

whet·stone \\'hwet-,stōn\ *n* : a stone for sharpening blades

whey \\'hwā\ *n* : the watery part of milk that separates after the milk sours and thickens

¹which \\'hwich\ *adj* **1** : being what one or ones out of a group ⟨~ shirt should I wear⟩ **2** : WHICHEVER

²which *pron* **1** : which one or ones ⟨~ is yours⟩ ⟨~ are his⟩ ⟨it's in May or June, I'm not sure ~⟩ **2** : WHICHEVER ⟨we have all kinds; take ~ you like⟩ **3** — used to introduce a relative clause and to serve as a substitute therein for the noun modified by the clause ⟨the money ~ is coming to me⟩

¹which·ev·er \hwich-'e-vər\ *adj* : no matter which ⟨~ way you go⟩

²whichever *pron* : whatever one or ones

which·so·ev·er \,hwich-sō-'e-vər\ *pron or adj, archaic* : WHICHEVER

whick·er \\'hwi-kər\ *vb* : NEIGH, WHINNY — **whicker** *n*

¹whiff \\'hwif\ *n* **1** : a quick puff or slight gust (as of air) **2** : an inhalation of odor, gas, or smoke **3** : a slight trace ⟨a ~ of scandal⟩ **4** : STRIKEOUT

²whiff *vb* **1** : to expel, puff out, or blow away in or as if in whiffs **2** : to inhale an odor **3** : STRIKE OUT 3

Whig \\'hwig\ *n* [short for *Whiggamore*, member of a Scottish group that marched to Edinburgh in 1648 to oppose the court party] **1** : a member or supporter of a British political group of the late 17th through early 19th centuries seeking to limit royal authority and increase parliamentary power **2** : an American favoring independence from Great Britain during the American Revolution **3** : a member or supporter of an American political party formed about 1834 to oppose the Democrats

¹while \'hwī-(ə)l\ *n* **1** : a period of time ⟨stay a ∼⟩ **2** : the time and effort used : TROUBLE ⟨worth your ∼⟩

²while *conj* **1** : during the time that ⟨she called ∼ you were out⟩ **2** : AS LONG AS ⟨∼ there's life there's hope⟩ **3** : ALTHOUGH ⟨∼ he's respected, he's not liked⟩

³while *vb* **whiled; whil·ing** : to cause to pass esp. pleasantly ⟨∼ away an hour⟩

¹whi·lom \'hwī-ləm\ *adv* [ME, lit., at times, fr. OE *hwīlum*, dat. pl. of *hwīl* time, while] *archaic* : FORMERLY

²whilom *adj* : FORMER ⟨his ∼ friends⟩

whilst \'hwīlst\ *conj, chiefly Brit* : WHILE

whim \'hwim\ *n* : a sudden wish, desire, or change of mind

whim·per \'hwim-pər\ *vb* : to make a low whining plaintive or broken sound — **whimper** *n*

whim·si·cal \'hwim-zi-kəl\ *adj* **1** : full of whims : CAPRICIOUS **2** : resulting from or characterized by whim or caprice : ERRATIC ⟨∼ notions⟩ — **whim·si·cal·i·ty** \ₕwim-zə-ˈka-lə-tē\ *n* — **whim·si·cal·ly** \'hwim-zi-k(ə-)lē\ *adv*

whim·sy *also* **whim·sey** \'hwim-zē\ *n, pl* **whimsies** *also* **whimseys 1** : WHIM, CAPRICE **2** : a fanciful or fantastic device, object, or creation esp. in writing or art ⟨decorative ∼⟩

whine \'hwīn\ *vb* **whined; whin·ing** [ME, fr. OE *hwīnan* to whiz] **1** : to utter a usu. high-pitched plaintive or distressed cry; *also* : to make a sound similar to such a cry **2** : to complain with or as if with a whine — **whine** *n* — **whin·er** *n* — **whiny** *also* **whin·ey** \'hwī-nē\ *adj*

¹whin·ny \'hwi-nē\ *vb* **whin·nied; whin·ny·ing** : to neigh usu. in a low or gentle manner

²whinny *n, pl* **whinnies** : NEIGH

¹whip \'hwip\ *vb* **whipped; whip·ping 1** : to move, snatch, or jerk quickly or forcefully ⟨∼ out a gun⟩ **2** : to strike with a slender lithe implement (as a lash) esp. as a punishment; *also* : SPANK **3** : to drive or urge on by or as if by using a whip **4** : to bind or wrap (as a rope or rod) with cord in order to protect and strengthen; *also* : to wind or wrap around something **5** : DEFEAT **6** : to stir up : INCITE ⟨∼ up enthusiasm⟩ **7** : to produce in a hurry ⟨∼ up a meal⟩ **8** : to beat (as eggs or cream) into a froth **9** : to proceed nimbly or briskly; *also* : to flap about forcefully ⟨flags *whipping* in the wind⟩ — **whip·per** *n* — **whip into shape** : to bring forcefully to a desired state or condition

²whip *n* **1** : a flexible instrument used for whipping **2** : a stroke or cut with or as if with a whip **3** : a dessert made by whipping a portion of the ingredients ⟨prune ∼⟩ **4** : a person who handles a whip **5** : a member of a legislative body appointed by a party to enforce party discipline **6** : a whipping or thrashing motion

whip·cord \-ₖȯrd\ *n* **1** : a thin tough

braided cord **2** : a strong cloth with fine diagonal cords or ribs

whip hand *n* : positive control : ADVANTAGE

whip·lash \'hwip-ˌlash\ *n* **1** : the lash of a whip **2** : injury resulting from a sudden sharp movement of the neck and head (as of a person in a vehicle that is struck from the rear)

whip·per·snap·per \'hwi-pər-ˌsna-pər\ *n* : a small, insignificant, or presumptuous person

whip·pet \'hwi-pət\ *n* : any of a breed of small swift slender dogs that are used for racing

whipping boy *n* : SCAPEGOAT

whip–poor–will \'hwi-pər-ˌwil\ *n* : an American insect-eating bird with dull variegated plumage whose call at nightfall and just before dawn is suggestive of its name

whip·saw \'hwip-ˌsȯ\ *vb* : to beset with two or more adverse conditions or situations at once

¹whir *also* **whirr** \'hwər\ *vb* **whirred; whir·ring** : to move, fly, or revolve with a whir

²whir *also* **whirr** *n* : a continuous fluttering or vibratory sound made by something in rapid motion

¹whirl \'hwərl\ *vb* **1** : to move or drive in a circle or curve esp. with force or speed **2** : to turn or cause to turn rapidly in circles **3** : to turn abruptly : WHEEL **4** : to move or go quickly **5** : to become dizzy or giddy : REEL

²whirl *n* **1** : a rapid rotating or circling movement; *also* : something whirling **2** : COMMOTION, BUSTLE ⟨the social ∼⟩ **3** : a state of mental confusion **4** : TRY ⟨gave it a ∼⟩

whirl·i·gig \'hwər-li-ˌgig\ *n* [ME *whirle-gigg*, fr. *whirlen* to whirl + *gigg* top] **1** : a child's toy having a whirling motion **2** : something that continuously whirls or changes

whirl·pool \'hwərl-ˌpül\ *n* : water moving rapidly in a circle so as to produce a depression in the center into which floating objects may be drawn

whirl·wind \-ˌwind\ *n* **1** : a small whirling windstorm **2** : a confused rush **3** : a violent or destructive force

whirly·bird \'hwər-lē-ˌbərd\ *n* : HELICOPTER

¹whish \'hwish\ *vb* : to move with a whish or swishing sound

²whish *n* : a rushing sound : SWISH

¹whisk \'hwisk\ *n* **1** : a quick light sweeping or brushing motion **2** : a usu. wire kitchen implement for beating food by hand **3** : WHISK BROOM

²whisk *vb* **1** : to move nimbly and quickly **2** : to move or convey briskly ⟨∼ed the children off to bed⟩ **3** : to beat or whip lightly ⟨∼ eggs⟩ **4** : to brush or wipe off lightly ⟨∼ a coat⟩

whisk broom *n* : a small broom with a short handle used esp. as a clothes brush

whis·ker \'hwis-kər\ *n* **1** : one hair of the beard **2** *pl* : the part of the beard that grows on the sides of the face or on the chin **3** : one of the long bristles or hairs

growing near the mouth of an animal (as
a cat or mouse) — **whis·kered** \-kərd\
adj

whis·key *or* **whis·ky** \'hwis-kē\ *n, pl*
whiskeys *or* **whiskies** [Ir *uisce beatha* &
ScGael *uisge beatha,* lit., water of life] : a
liquor distilled from fermented wort (as
that obtained from rye, corn, or barley
mash)

¹whis·per \'hwis-pər\ *vb* **1** : to speak very
low or under the breath; *also* : to tell or
utter by whispering ⟨∼ a secret⟩ **2** : to
make a low rustling sound — **whis·per·**
er \-pər-ər\ *n*

²whisper *n* **1** : something communicated
by or as if by whispering : HINT, RUMOR
2 : an act or instance of whispering

whist \'hwist\ *n* : a card game played by
four players in two partnerships with a
deck of 52 cards

¹whis·tle \'hwis-səl\ *n* **1** : a device by which
a shrill sound is produced ⟨steam ∼⟩
⟨tin ∼⟩ **2** : a shrill clear sound made by
forcing breath out or air in through the
puckered lips **3** : the sound or signal produced by a whistle or as if by whistling **4**
: the shrill clear note of an animal (as a
bird)

²whistle *vb* **whis·tled; whis·tling 1** : to
utter a shrill clear sound by blowing or
drawing air through the puckered lips **2**
: to utter a shrill note or call resembling a
whistle **3** : to make a shrill clear sound
esp. by rapid movements ⟨the wind *whis-*
tled⟩ **4** : to blow or sound a whistle **5** : to
signal or call by a whistle **6** : to produce,
utter, or express by whistling ⟨∼ a tune⟩
— **whis·tler** *n*

whis·tle–blow·er \'hwi-səl-ˌblō-ər\ *n* : IN-
FORMER

whis·tle–stop \-ˌstäp\ *n* : a brief personal
appearance by a political candidate esp.
on the rear platform of a touring train

whit \'hwit\ *n* [prob. alter. of ME *wiht,*
wight creature, thing, fr. OE *wiht*] : the
smallest part or particle : BIT

¹white \'hwīt\ *adj* **whit·er; whit·est 1**
: free from color **2** : of the color of new
snow or milk; *esp* : of the color white **3**
: light or pallid in color ⟨lips ∼ with
fear⟩ **4** : SILVERY; *also* : made of silver **5**
: of, relating to, or being a member of a
group or race characterized by light-colored skin **6** : free from spot or blemish
: PURE, INNOCENT **7** : BLANK **2** ⟨∼ space
in printed matter⟩ **8** : not intended to
cause harm ⟨a ∼ lie⟩ **9** : wearing white
⟨∼ friars⟩ **10** : marked by snow ⟨∼
Christmas⟩ **11** : consisting of a wide
range of frequencies ⟨∼ light⟩ — **white·**
ness \-nəs\ *n* — **whit·ish** \'hwī-tish\ *adj*

²white *n* **1** : the color of maximal lightness
that characterizes objects which both reflect and transmit light : the opposite of
black **2** : a white or light-colored part or
thing ⟨the ∼ of an egg⟩; *also, pl* : white
garments **3** : the light-colored pieces in a
2-player board game; *also* : the person by
whom these are played **4** : one that is or
approaches the color white **5** : a person
of a light-skinned race

white ant *n* : TERMITE

white blood cell *n* : any of the colorless
blood cells (as lymphocytes) that do not
contain hemoglobin but do have a nucleus

white–bread \'hwīt-'bred\ *adj* : being,
typical of, or having qualities (as bland-
ness) associated with the white middle
class ⟨∼ values⟩

white·cap \'hwīt-ˌkap\ *n* : a wave crest
breaking into white foam

white chocolate *n* : a whitish confection
chiefly of cocoa butter, milk, and sugar

white–col·lar \'hwīt-'kä-lər\ *adj* : of, relating to, or constituting the class of sala-
ried workers whose duties do not require
the wearing of work clothes or protective
clothing ⟨∼ jobs⟩

white dwarf *n* : a small very dense whitish
star of low luminosity

white elephant *n* **1** : an Indian elephant
of a pale color that is sometimes venerated in India, Sri Lanka, Thailand, and
Myanmar **2** : something requiring much
care and expense and giving little profit
or enjoyment

white feather *n* [fr. the superstition that a
white feather in the plumage of a game-
cock is a mark of a poor fighter] : a mark
or symbol of cowardice

white·fish \'hwīt-ˌfish\ *n* : any of various
freshwater food fishes related to the
salmons and trouts

white flag *n* : a flag of pure white used to
signify truce or surrender

white gold *n* : a pale alloy of gold resembling platinum in appearance

white goods *n pl* : white fabrics or articles (as sheets or towels) typically made
of cotton or linen

White·hall \'hwīt-ˌhȯl\ *n* : the British government

white hat *n* **1** : an admirable and honorable person **2** : a mark or symbol of
goodness

white·head \-ˌhed\ *n* : a small whitish
lump in the skin due to retention of secretion in an oil gland duct

white heat *n* : a temperature higher than
red heat at which a body becomes brightly incandescent

white–hot *adj* **1** : being at or radiating
white heat **2** : FERVID ⟨∼ enthusiasm⟩

White House \-ˌhau̇s\ *n* **1** : a residence of
the president of the U.S. **2** : the executive department of the U.S. government

white lead *n* : a heavy white poisonous
carbonate of lead used esp. formerly as a
pigment in exterior paints

white matter *n* : whitish nerve tissue esp.
of the brain and spinal cord that consists
largely of neuron processes enclosed in a
fatty material and that typically lies under the cortical gray matter

whit·en \'hwī-tᵊn\ *vb* : to make or become
white ♦ **Synonyms** BLANCH, BLEACH
— **whit·en·er** *n*

white oak *n* : any of various oaks with
acorns that take one year to mature; *also*
: its hard durable wood

white pepper *n* : a spice that consists of
the berry of a pepper plant ground after
removal of its black husk

white pine *n* : a tall-growing pine of eastern No. America with needles in clusters of five; *also* : its wood

white sale *n* : a sale on white goods

white shark *n* : GREAT WHITE SHARK

white slave *n* : a woman or girl held unwillingly for purposes of prostitution — **white slavery** *n*

white·tail \'hwīt-,tāl\ *n* : WHITE-TAILED DEER

white–tailed deer *n* : a No. American deer with a rather long tail white on the underside and the males of which have forward-arching antlers

white–tie \-tī\ *adj* : characterized by or requiring formal evening clothes consisting of usu. white tie and tailcoat for men and a formal gown for women

white–wall \'hwīt-,wȯl\ *n* : an automobile tire having a white band on the sidewall

¹**white·wash** \-,wȯsh, -,wäsh\ *vb* **1** : to whiten with whitewash **2** : to clear of a charge of wrongdoing by offering excuses, hiding facts, or conducting a perfunctory investigation **3** : SHUT OUT 2

²**whitewash** *n* **1** : a liquid mixture (as of lime and water) for whitening a surface **2** : a clearing of wrongdoing by whitewashing

white water *n* : frothy water (as in breakers, rapids, or falls)

white·wood \-,wu̇d\ *n* : any of various trees esp. a tulip tree having light-colored wood; *also* : such wood

¹**whith·er** \'hwi-thər\ *adv* **1** : to what place **2** : to what situation, position, degree, or end ⟨~ will this drive him⟩

²**whither** *conj* **1** : to the place at, in, or to which; *also* : to which place **2** : to whatever place

whith·er·so·ev·er \,hwi-thər-sō-'e-vər\ *conj* : to whatever place

¹**whit·ing** \'hwī-tiŋ\ *n, pl* **whiting** *also* **whit·ings** : any of several usu. light or silvery food fishes (as a hake) found mostly near seacoasts

²**whiting** *n* : calcium carbonate in powdered form used esp. as a pigment and in putty

whit·low \'hwit-,lō\ *n* : a deep inflammation of a finger or toe with pus formation

Whit·sun·day \'hwit-'sən-dē, -sən-,dā\ *n* [ME *Whitsonday*, fr. OE *hwīta sunnandæg*, lit., white Sunday; prob. fr. the custom of wearing white robes by those newly baptized at this season] : PENTECOST

whit·tle \'hwi-t³l\ *vb* **whit·tled; whit·tling** **1** : to pare or cut off chips from the surface of (wood) with a knife; *also* : to cut or shape by such paring **2** : to reduce as if by paring down ⟨~ down expenses⟩

¹**whiz** *or* **whizz** \'hwiz\ *vb* **whizzed; whiz·zing** : to hum, whir, or hiss like a speeding object (as an arrow or ball) passing through air

²**whiz** *or* **whizz** *n, pl* **whiz·zes** : a hissing, buzzing, or whizzing sound

³**whiz** *n, pl* **whiz·zes** : WIZARD 2

who \'hü\ *pron* **1** : what or which person or persons ⟨~ did it⟩ ⟨~ is he⟩ ⟨~ are they⟩ **2** : the person or persons that ⟨knows ~ did it⟩ **3** — used to introduce a relative clause and to serve as a substitute therein for the substantive modified by the clause ⟨the person ~ lives there is rich⟩

WHO *abbr* World Health Organization

whoa \'wō, 'hwō, 'hō\ *vb imper* **1** — a command to an animal to stand still **2** : cease or slow a course of action or a line of thought

who·dun·it *also* **who·dun·nit** \hü-'də-nət\ *n* : a detective or mystery story

who·ev·er \hü-'e-vər\ *pron* : whatever person : no matter who

¹**whole** \'hōl\ *adj* [ME *hool* healthy, unhurt, entire, fr. OE *hāl*] **1** : being in healthy or sound condition : free from defect or damage **2** : having all its proper parts or elements ⟨~ milk⟩ **3** : constituting the total sum of : ENTIRE ⟨owns the ~ island⟩ **4** : each or all of the ⟨the ~ family⟩ **5** : not scattered or divided : CONCENTRATED ⟨gave me his ~ attention⟩ **6** : seemingly complete or total ⟨the ~ idea is to help, not hinder⟩ ♦ **Synonyms** PERFECT, INTACT, SOUND — **whole·ness** *n*

²**whole** *n* **1** : a complete amount or sum **2** : something whole or entire — **on the whole 1** : in view of all the circumstances or conditions **2** : in general

³**whole** *adv* : COMPLETELY, WHOLLY, ENTIRELY ⟨a ~ new term⟩

whole food *n* : food eaten in its natural state with little or no artificial additives

whole·heart·ed \'hōl-'här-təd\ *adj* : undivided in purpose, enthusiasm, will, or commitment

whole hog *adv* : to the fullest extent : COMPLETELY ⟨accepted the proposals *whole hog*⟩

whole note *n* : a musical note equal to one measure of four beats

whole number *n* : any of the set of nonnegative integers; *also* : INTEGER

¹**whole·sale** \'hōl-,sāl\ *n* : the sale of goods in quantity usu. for resale by a retail merchant

²**wholesale** *adj* **1** : performed on a large scale without discrimination ⟨~ slaughter⟩ **2** : of, relating to, or engaged in wholesaling — **wholesale** *adv*

³**wholesale** *vb* **whole·saled; whole·sal·ing** : to sell at wholesale — **whole·sal·er** *n*

whole·some \'hōl-səm\ *adj* **1** : promoting mental, spiritual, or bodily health or well-being ⟨a ~ environment⟩ **2** : sound in body, mind, or morals : HEALTHY **3** : PRUDENT ⟨~ respect for the law⟩ — **whole·some·ness** *n*

whole step *n* : a musical interval comprising two half steps (as C–D or F#–G#)

whole wheat *adj* : made of ground entire wheat kernels

whol·ly \'hōl-lē\ *adv* **1** : COMPLETELY, TOTALLY **2** : SOLELY, EXCLUSIVELY

whom \'hüm\ *pron, objective case of* WHO

whom·ev·er \hü-'me-vər\ *pron, objective case of* WHOEVER

whom·so·ev·er \,hüm-sō-'e-vər\ *pron, objective case of* WHOSOEVER

¹whoop \'hwu̇p, 'hwu̇p, 'hu̇p, 'hu̇p\ *vb* **1** : to shout or call loudly and vigorously **2** : to make the characteristic whoop of whooping cough **3** : to go or pass with a loud noise **4** : to utter or express with a whoop; *also* : to urge, drive, or cheer with a whoop

²whoop *n* **1** : a whooping sound or utterance : SHOUT, HOOT **2** : a crowing intake of breath after a fit of coughing in whooping cough

whoop·ee \'hwu̇-(,)pē, 'hwu̇-\ *interj* — used to express exuberance

²whoopee *n* **1** : boisterous fun **2** : sexual play — usu. used with *make*

whooping cough *n* : an infectious bacterial disease esp. of children marked by convulsive coughing fits often followed by a shrill gasping intake of breath

whooping crane *n* : a large white nearly extinct No. American crane noted for its loud whooping call

whoop·la \'hwu̇p-,lä, 'hwu̇p-\ *n* **1** : HOOPLA **2** : boisterous merrymaking

whop·per \'hwä-pər\ *n* : something unusually large or extreme of its kind; *esp* : a monstrous lie

whop·ping \'hwä-piŋ\ *adj* : extremely large ⟨a ~ increase⟩

whore \'hȯr\ *n* : PROSTITUTE

whorl \'hwȯrl, 'hwərl\ *n* **1** : a group of parts (as leaves or petals) encircling an axis and esp. a plant stem **2** : something that whirls or coils around a center : COIL, SPIRAL **3** : one of the turns of a snail shell

whorled \'hwȯrld, 'hwərld\ *adj* : having or arranged in whorls

¹whose \'hüz\ *adj* : of or relating to whom or which esp. as possessor or possessors, agent or agents, or object or objects of an action ⟨asked ~ bag it was⟩

²whose *pron* : whose one or ones ⟨~ is this car⟩ ⟨~ are those books⟩

who·so \'hü-,sō\ *pron* : WHOEVER

who·so·ev·er \,hü-sō-'e-vər\ *pron* : WHOEVER

whs *or* **whse** *abbr* warehouse

whsle *abbr* wholesale

¹why \'hwī\ *adv* : for what reason, cause, or purpose ⟨~ did you do it⟩

²why *conj* **1** : the cause, reason, or purpose for which ⟨that is ~ you did it⟩ **2** : for which : on account of which ⟨knows the reason ~ you did it⟩

³why *n, pl* **whys** : REASON, CAUSE ⟨the ~s of racial prejudice⟩

⁴why \'wī, 'hwī\ *interj* — used to express surprise, hesitation, approval, disapproval, or impatience ⟨~, here's what I was looking for⟩

WI *abbr* **1** West Indies **2** Wisconsin

WIA *abbr* wounded in action

Wic·ca \'wi-kə\ *n* [prob. fr. OE *wicca* wizard] : a religion that affirms the existence of supernatural power (as magic) and of deities who inhere in nature and that ritually observes seasonal and life cycles

wick \'wik\ *n* : a loosely bound bundle of soft fibers that draws up oil, tallow, or wax to be burned in a candle, oil lamp, or stove

wick·ed \'wi-kəd\ *adj* **1** : morally bad : EVIL, SINFUL **2** : FIERCE, VICIOUS **3** : ROGUISH ⟨a ~ glance⟩ **4** : REPUGNANT, VILE ⟨a ~ odor⟩ **5** : HARMFUL, DANGEROUS ⟨a ~ attack⟩ **6** : impressively excellent ⟨throws a ~ fastball⟩ — **wick·ed·ly** *adv* — **wick·ed·ness** *n*

wick·er \'wi-kər\ *n* **1** : a small pliant branch (as an osier or a withe) **2** : WICKERWORK — **wicker** *adj*

wick·er·work \-,wərk\ *n* : work made of osiers, twigs, or rods : BASKETRY

wick·et \'wi-kət\ *n* **1** : a small gate or door; *esp* : one forming a part of or placed near a larger one **2** : a window-like opening usu. with a grille or grate (as at a ticket office) **3** : a set of three upright rods topped by two crosspieces bowled at in cricket **4** : an arch or hoop in croquet

wick·i·up \'wi-kē-,əp\ *n* : a hut used by nomadic Indians of the western and southwestern U.S. with a usu. oval base and a rough frame covered with reed mats, grass, or brushwood

wid *abbr* widow, widower

¹wide \'wīd\ *adj* **wider; wid·est 1** : covering a vast area **2** : measured across or at right angles to the length **3** : not narrow : BROAD; *also* : ROOMY **4** : opened to full width ⟨eyes ~ with wonder⟩ **5** : not limited : EXTENSIVE ⟨~ experience⟩ **6** : far from the goal, mark, or truth ⟨was ~ of the truth⟩ — **wide·ly** *adv*

²wide *adv* **wid·er; wid·est 1** : over a great distance or extent : WIDELY ⟨searched far and ~⟩ **2** : over a specified distance, area, or extent **3** : so as to leave a wide space between ⟨~ apart⟩ **4** : so as to clear by a considerable distance ⟨ran ~ around left end⟩ **5** : COMPLETELY, FULLY ⟨opened her eyes ~⟩

wide area network *n* : a computer network (as the Internet) over a large area (as a country or the globe) for sharing resources or exchanging data

wide-awake \,wīd-ə-'wāk\ *adj* : fully awake; *also* : KNOWING, ALERT

wide-body \'wīd-,bä-dē\ *n* : a large jet aircraft having a wide cabin

wide-eyed \'wīd-'īd\ *adj* **1** : having the eyes wide open esp. with wonder or astonishment **2** : NAIVE ⟨~ innocence⟩

wide-mouthed \-'mau̇thd, -'mau̇tht\ *adj* **1** : having one's mouth opened wide (as in awe) **2** : having a wide mouth ⟨~ jars⟩

wid·en \'wī-dᵊn\ *vb* : to increase in width, scope, or extent

wide·spread \'wīd-'spred\ *adj* **1** : widely scattered or prevalent **2** : widely extended or spread out ⟨~ wings⟩

widgeon *var of* WIGEON

¹wid·ow \'wi-dō\ *n* : a woman who has lost her husband by death and has not married again — **wid·ow·hood** *n*

²widow *vb* : to cause to become a widow or widower

wid·ow·er \'wi-də-wər\ *n* : a man who has lost his wife by death and has not married again

width \'width\ *n* **1** : a distance from side

to side : the measurement taken at right angles to the length : BREADTH **2** : largeness of extent or scope; *also* : FULLNESS **3** : a measured and cut piece of material ⟨a ∼ of calico⟩

wield \\'wēld\ *vb* **1** : to use or handle esp. effectively ⟨∼ a broom⟩ **2** : to exert authority by means of : EMPLOY ⟨∼ influence⟩ — **wield·er** *n*

wie·ner *also* **wei·ner** \\'wē-nər\ *n* [short for *wienerwurst*, fr. G, lit., Vienna sausage] : FRANKFURTER

wife \\'wīf\ *n, pl* **wives** \\'wīvz\ **1** *dial* : WOMAN **2** : a woman acting in a specified capacity — used in combination ⟨fish*wife*⟩ **3** : a female partner in a marriage — **wife·hood** *n* — **wife·less** *adj* — **wife·ly** *adj*

wig \\'wig\ *n* [short for *periwig*, modif. of MF *perruque*, fr. It *parrucca, perrucca* hair, wig] : a manufactured covering of natural or synthetic hair for the head; *also* : TOUPEE

wi·geon *or* **wid·geon** \\'wi-jən\ *n, pl* **wigeon** *or* **wigeons** *or* **widgeon** *or* **widgeons** : any of several medium-sized freshwater ducks

wig·gle \\'wi-gəl\ *vb* **wig·gled; wig·gling 1** : to move to and fro with quick jerky or shaking movements : JIGGLE ⟨wiggled his toes⟩ **2** : WRIGGLE — **wiggle** *n*

wig·gler \\'wi-glər, -gə-lər\ *n* **1** : a larva or pupa of a mosquito **2** : one that wiggles

wig·gly \\'wi-glē, -gə-lē\ *adj* **1** : tending to wiggle ⟨a ∼ worm⟩ **2** : WAVY ⟨∼ lines⟩

wight \\'wīt\ *n* : a living being : CREATURE

wig·let \\'wi-glət\ *n* : a small wig used esp. to enhance a hairstyle

¹wig·wag \\'wig-,wag\ *vb* **1** : to signal by or as if by a flag or light waved according to a code **2** : to make or cause to make a signal (as with the hand or arm)

²wigwag *n* : the art or practice of wigwagging

wig·wam \\'wig-,wäm\ *n* : a hut of the Indians of the eastern U.S. having typically an arched framework of poles overlaid with bark, rush mats, or hides

¹wild \\'wī(-ə)ld\ *adj* **1** : living in a state of nature and not ordinarily tamed ⟨∼ ducks⟩ **2** : growing or produced without human aid or care ⟨∼ honey⟩ ⟨∼ plants⟩ **3** : WASTE, DESOLATE ⟨∼ country⟩ **4** : UNCONTROLLED, UNRESTRAINED, UNRULY ⟨∼ passions⟩ ⟨a ∼ young stallion⟩ **5** : TURBULENT, STORMY ⟨a ∼ night⟩ **6** : EXTRAVAGANT, FANTASTIC, CRAZY ⟨∼ ideas⟩ **7** : indicative of strong passion, desire, or emotion ⟨a ∼ stare⟩ **8** : UNCIVILIZED, SAVAGE **9** : deviating from the natural or expected course : ERRATIC ⟨a ∼ throw⟩ **10** : able to represent any playing card designated by the holder ⟨deuces ∼⟩ — **wild·ly** *adv* — **wild·ness** *n*

²wild *adv* **1** : WILDLY **2** : without regulation or control ⟨running ∼⟩

³wild *n* **1** : WILDERNESS **2** : a natural or undomesticated state or existence

wild boar *n* : an Old World wild hog from which most domestic swine have been derived

wild card *n* **1** : an unknown or unpredictable factor **2** : one picked to fill a leftover play-off or tournament position **3** *usu* **wild-card** : a symbol (as ? or *) used in a keyword search to represent the presence of unspecified characters

wild carrot *n* : QUEEN ANNE'S LACE

¹wild·cat \\'wī(-ə)ld-,kat\ *n, pl* **wildcats 1** : any of various small or medium-sized cats (as a lynx or ocelot) **2** : a quicktempered hard-fighting person

²wildcat *adj* **1** : not sound or safe ⟨∼ schemes⟩ **2** : initiated by a group of workers without formal union approval ⟨∼ strike⟩

³wildcat *vb* **wild·cat·ted; wild·cat·ting** : to drill an oil or gas well in a region not known to be productive

wil·de·beest \\'wil-də-,bēst\ *n, pl* **wildebeests** *also* **wildebeest** [Afrikaans *wildebees*, fr. *wilde* wild + *bees* ox] : either of two large African antelopes with an oxlike head and horns and a horselike mane and tail

wil·der·ness \\'wil-dər-nəs\ *n* [ME, fr. *wildern* wild, fr. OE *wilddēoren* of wild beasts] : an uncultivated and uninhabited region

wild·fire \\'wī(-ə)ld-,fī(-ə)r\ *n* : an uncontrollable fire — **like wildfire** : very rapidly

wild·flow·er \\-,flaü(-ə)r\ *n* : the flower of a wild or uncultivated plant or the plant bearing it

wild·fowl \\-,faü(-ə)l\ *n* : a bird and esp. a waterfowl hunted as game

wild–goose chase *n* : the pursuit of something unattainable

wild·life \\'wī(-ə)ld-,līf\ *n* : nonhuman living things and esp. wild animals living in their natural environment

wild oat *n* **1** : any of several Old World wild grasses **2** *pl* : offenses and indiscretions attributed to youthful exuberance — usu. used in the phrase *sow one's wild oats*

wild rice *n* : a No. American aquatic grass; *also* : its edible seed

wild type *n* : a gene or trait that is typical of a natural population of organisms in contrast to that of mutant forms; *also* : an organism with such a gene or trait

wild·wood \\'wī(-ə)ld-,wùd\ *n* : a wood unaltered or unfrequented by humans

¹wile \\'wī(-ə)l\ *n* : a trick or stratagem intended to ensnare or deceive; *also* : a playful trick **2** : TRICKERY, GUILE

²wile *vb* **wiled; wil·ing** : LURE, ENTICE

¹will \\'wil\ *vb, past* **would** \\'wùd\ *pres sing & pl* **will 1** : WISH, DESIRE ⟨call it what you ∼⟩ **2** — used as an auxiliary verb to express (1) desire, willingness, or in negative constructions refusal ⟨∼ you have another⟩ ⟨he *won't* do it⟩, (2) customary or habitual action ⟨∼ get angry over nothing⟩, (3) simple futurity ⟨tomorrow we ∼ go shopping⟩, (4) capability or sufficiency ⟨the back seat ∼ hold three⟩, (5) determination or willfulness ⟨I ∼ go despite them⟩, (6) probability ⟨that ∼ be the mailman⟩, (7) inevitability ⟨accidents

~ happen⟩, or (8) a command ⟨you ~ do as I say⟩

²will *n* **1** : wish or desire often combined with determination ⟨the ~ to win⟩ **2** : something desired; *esp* : a choice or determination of one having authority or power **3** : the act, process, or experience of willing : VOLITION **4** : the mental powers manifested as wishing, choosing, desiring, or intending **5** : a disposition to act according to principles or ends **6** : power of controlling one's own actions or emotions ⟨a leader of iron ~⟩ **7** : a legal document in which a person declares to whom his or her possessions are to go after death

³will *vb* **1** : to dispose of by or as if by a will : BEQUEATH **2** : to determine by an act of choice; *also* : DECREE, ORDAIN **3** : INTEND, PURPOSE; *also* : CHOOSE

will·ful *or* **wil·ful** \'wil-fəl\ *adj* **1** : governed by will without regard to reason : OBSTINATE **2** : INTENTIONAL ⟨~ murder⟩ — **will·ful·ly** *adv*

wil·lies \'wi-lēz\ *n pl* : a fit of nervousness : JITTERS — used with *the*

will·ing \'wi-liŋ\ *adj* **1** : inclined or favorably disposed in mind : READY ⟨~ to go⟩ **2** : prompt to act or respond ⟨~ workers⟩ **3** : done, borne, or accepted voluntarily or without reluctance **4** : of or relating to the will : VOLITIONAL — **will·ing·ly** *adv* — **will·ing·ness** *n*

wil·li·waw \'wi-lē-ˌwȯ\ *n* : a sudden violent gust of cold land air common along mountainous coasts of high latitudes

will-o'-the-wisp \ˌwil-ə-thə-'wisp\ *n* **1** : a light that appears at night over marshy grounds **2** : a misleading or elusive goal or hope

wil·low \'wi-lō\ *n* **1** : any of a genus of quick-growing shrubs and trees with tough pliable shoots **2** : an object made of willow wood

wil·low·ware \-ˌwer\ *n* : dinnerware that is usu. blue and white and that is decorated with a story-telling design featuring a large willow tree by a little bridge

wil·lowy \'wi-lə-wē\ *adj* : PLIANT; *also* : gracefully tall and slender

will·pow·er \'wil-ˌpau̇-(ə)r\ *n* : energetic determination : RESOLUTENESS

wil·ly-nil·ly \ˌwi-lē-'ni-lē\ *adv or adj* [alter. of *will I nill I* or *will ye nill ye* or *will he nill he*; *nill* fr. archaic *nill* to be unwilling, fr. ME *nilen*, fr. OE *nyllan*, fr. *ne* not + *wyllan* to wish] : without regard for one's choice ⟨they rushed us along ~⟩

¹wilt \'wilt\ *vb* **1** : to lose or cause to lose freshness and become limp esp. from lack of water : DROOP ⟨the roses were ~ing⟩ **2** : to grow weak or faint : LANGUISH

²wilt *n* : any of various plant disorders marked by wilting and often shriveling

wily \'wī-lē\ *adj* **wil·i·er; -est** : full of guile : TRICKY — **wil·i·ness** \-lē-nəs\ *n*

wimp \'wimp\ *n* : a weak, cowardly, or ineffectual person — **wimpy** \'wim-pē\ *adj*

¹wim·ple \'wim-pəl\ *n* : a cloth covering

worn over the head and around the neck and chin by women esp. in the late medieval period and by some nuns

²wimple *vb* **wim·pled; wim·pling 1** : to cover with or as if with a wimple **2** : to ripple or cause to ripple

¹win \'win\ *vb* **won** \'wən\; **win·ning** [ME *winnen*, fr. OE *winnan* to struggle] **1** : to get possession of esp. by effort : GAIN; *also* : to obtain by work : EARN **2** : to gain in or as if in battle or contest; *also* : to be the victor in ⟨*won* the war⟩ **3** : to solicit and gain the favor of; *esp* : to induce to accept oneself in marriage

²win *n* : VICTORY; *esp* : 1st place at the finish (as of a horse race)

wince \'wins\ *vb* **winced; winc·ing** : to shrink back involuntarily (as from pain) : FLINCH — **wince** *n*

winch \'winch\ *n* : a machine that has a drum on which is wound a rope or cable for hauling or hoisting — **winch** *vb*

¹wind \'wind\ *n* **1** : a movement of the air **2** : a prevailing force or influence : TENDENCY, TREND **3** : BREATH ⟨he had the ~ knocked out of him⟩ **4** : gas produced in the stomach or intestines **5** : something insubstantial; *esp* : idle words **6** : air carrying a scent (as of game) **7** : INTIMATION ⟨they got ~ of our plans⟩ **8** : WIND INSTRUMENTS; *also, pl* : players of wind instruments

²wind *vb* **1** : to get a scent of ⟨the dogs ~*ed* the game⟩ **2** : to cause to be out of breath ⟨he was ~*ed* from the climb⟩ **3** : to allow (as a horse) to rest so as to recover breath

³wind \'wīnd, 'wind\ *vb* **wind·ed** \'wīn-dəd, 'win-\ *or* **wound** \'waund\; **wind·ing** : to sound by blowing ⟨~ a horn⟩

⁴wind \'wīnd\ *vb* **wound** \'waund\ *also* **wind·ed; wind·ing 1** : ENTANGLE, INVOLVE **2** : to introduce stealthily : INSINUATE **3** : to encircle or cover with something pliable : WRAP, COIL, TWINE ⟨~ a bobbin⟩ **4** : to hoist or haul by a rope or chain and a winch **5** : to tighten the spring of; *also* : CRANK **6** : to raise to a high level (as of excitement) **7** : to cause to move in a curving line or path **8** : to have a curving course or shape ⟨a river ~*ing* through the valley⟩ **9** : to move or lie so as to encircle

⁵wind \'wīnd\ *n* : COIL, TURN

wind·age \'win-dij\ *n* : the influence of the wind in deflecting the course of a projectile through the air; *also* : the amount of such deflection

wind·bag \'wind-ˌbag\ *n* : an overly talkative person

wind·blown \-ˌblōn\ *adj* : blown by the wind; *also* : having the appearance of being blown by the wind ⟨~ hair⟩

wind·break \-ˌbrāk\ *n* : a growth of trees or shrubs serving to break the force of the wind; *also* : a shelter from the wind

wind·burned \-ˌbərnd\ *adj* : irritated and inflamed by exposure to the wind — **wind·burn** \-ˌbərn\ *n*

wind·chill \-ˌchil\ *n* : a still-air temperature that would have the same cooling effect on exposed human skin as a given combination of temperature and wind speed

windchill factor *n* : WINDCHILL

wind down *vb* **1** : to draw toward an end **2** : RELAX, UNWIND

wind·er \'wīn-dər\ *n* : one that winds

wind·fall \'wind-ˌfȯl\ *n* **1** : something (as a tree or fruit) blown down by the wind **2** : an unexpected or sudden gift, gain, or advantage ⟨won a ~ from the lottery⟩

wind-flow·er \-ˌflau̇-(ə)r\ *n* : ANEMONE

¹wind·ing \'wīn-diŋ\ *n* : material (as wire) wound or coiled about an object

²winding *adj* **1** : having a pronounced curve or spiral ⟨~ stairs⟩ **2** : having a course that winds ⟨a ~ road⟩

wind·ing–sheet \-ˌshēt\ *n* : SHROUD

wind instrument *n* : a musical instrument (as a flute or horn) sounded by wind and esp. by the breath

wind·jam·mer \'wind-ˌja-mər\ *n* : a sailing ship; *also* : one of its crew

wind·lass \'wind-ləs\ *n* [ME *wyndlas*, alter. of *wyndase*, fr. OF *guindas, windas*, fr. ON *vindāss*, fr. *vinda* to wind + *āss* pole] : a winch used esp. on ships for hoisting or hauling

wind·mill \'wind-ˌmil\ *n* : a mill or machine worked by the wind turning sails or vanes that radiate from a central shaft

win·dow \'win-dō\ *n* [ME *windowe*, fr. ON *vindauga*, fr. *vindr* wind + *auga* eye] **1** : an opening in the wall of a building to let in light and air; *also* : the framework with fittings that closes such an opening **2** : WINDOWPANE **3** : an opening resembling or suggesting that of a window in a building **4** : an interval of time during which certain conditions or an opportunity exists **5** : a rectangular box appearing on a computer screen on which information (as files or program output) is displayed — **win·dow·less** *adj*

window box *n* : a box for growing plants in or by a window

window dressing *n* **1** : display of merchandise in a store window **2** : a showing made to create a deceptively favorable impression

win·dow·pane \'win-dō-ˌpān\ *n* : a pane in a window

win·dow–shop \-ˌshäp\ *vb* : to look at the displays in store windows without going inside the stores to make purchases — **win·dow–shop·per** *n*

win·dow·sill \-ˌsil\ *n* : the horizontal member at the bottom of a window

wind·pipe \'wind-ˌpīp\ *n* : TRACHEA

wind·proof \-'prüf\ *adj* : impervious to wind ⟨a ~ jacket⟩

wind·row \'wind-ˌrō\ *n* **1** : hay raked up into a row to dry **2** : a row of something (as dry leaves) swept up by or as if by the wind

wind shear *n* : a radical shift in wind speed and direction that occurs over a very short distance

wind·shield \'wind-ˌshēld\ *n* : a transparent screen (as of glass) in front of the occupants of a vehicle

wind sock *n* : an open-ended truncated cloth cone mounted in an elevated position to indicate wind direction

wind·storm \-ˌstȯrm\ *n* : a storm with high wind and little or no rain

wind·surf·ing \-ˌsər-fiŋ\ *n* : the sport or activity of riding a sailboard — **wind·surf** \-ˌsərf\ *vb* — **wind·surf·er** *n*

wind·swept \'wind-ˌswept\ *adj* : swept by or as if by wind ⟨~ plains⟩

wind tunnel *n* : an enclosed passage through which air is blown to investigate air flow around an object

wind·up \'wīn-ˌdəp\ *n* **1** : CONCLUSION, FINISH **2** : a series of regular and distinctive motions made by a pitcher preliminary to delivering a pitch

wind up *vb* **1** : to bring or come to a conclusion : END ⟨*wind up* the meeting⟩ **2** : to put in order for the purpose of bringing to an end **3** : to arrive in a place, situation, or condition at the end or as a result of a course of action ⟨*wound up* as paupers⟩ **4** : to make a pitching windup

¹wind·ward \'win-dwərd\ *n* : the side or direction from which the wind is blowing

²windward *adj* : being in or facing the direction from which the wind is blowing

windy \'win-dē\ *adj* **wind·i·er; -est 1** : having wind : exposed to winds ⟨a ~ day⟩ ⟨a ~ prairie⟩ **2** : STORMY **3** : FLATULENT **4** : indulging in or characterized by useless talk : VERBOSE

¹wine \'wīn\ *n* [ME *win*, fr. OE *wīn*, ultim. fr. L *vinum*] **1** : fermented grape juice used as a beverage **2** : the usu. fermented juice of a plant product (as fruit) used as a beverage ⟨rice ~⟩

²wine *vb* **wined; win·ing** : to treat to or drink wine

wine cellar *n* : a room for storing wines; *also* : a stock of wines

wine·grow·er \-ˌgrō-ər\ *n* : one that cultivates a vineyard and makes wine

wine·press \-ˌpres\ *n* : a vat in which juice is pressed from grapes

win·ery \'wī-nə-rē, 'wīn-rē\ *n, pl* **-eries** : a wine-making establishment

¹wing \'wiŋ\ *n* **1** : one of the movable feathered or membranous paired appendages by means of which a bird, bat, or insect flies **2** : something suggesting a wing; *esp* : an airfoil that develops the lift which supports an aircraft in flight **3** : a plant or animal appendage or part likened to a wing **4** : a turned-back or extended edge on an article of clothing **5** : a means of flight or rapid progress **6** : the act or manner of flying : FLIGHT **7** *pl* : the area at the side of the stage out of sight **8** : one of the positions or players on either side of a center position or line **9** : either of two opposing groups within an organization : FACTION **10** : a unit in military aviation consisting of two or more squadrons — **wing·less** *adj* — **wing·like** \-ˌlīk\ *adj* — **on the wing** : in flight : FLYING — **under one's wing** : in one's charge or care

²wing *vb* **1** : to fit with wings; *also* : to enable to fly easily **2** : to pass through in flight : FLY ⟨~ the air⟩ ⟨swallows ~*ing* southward⟩ **3** : to let fly : DISPATCH **4**

: to wound in the wing ⟨~ a bird⟩; *also* : to wound without killing **5** : to perform without preparation : IMPROVISE ⟨~*ing* it⟩

wing·ding \'wiŋ-ˌdiŋ\ *n* : a wild, lively, or lavish party

winged \'wiŋd, 'wiŋ-əd, *in compounds* 'wiŋd\ *adj* **1** : having wings esp. of a specified character **2** : soaring with or as if with wings : ELEVATED **3** : SWIFT, RAPID

wing nut *n* : a nut with winglike extensions that can be gripped with the thumb and finger

wing·span \'wiŋ-ˌspan\ *n* : the distance between the tips of a pair of wings

wing·spread \-ˌspred\ *n* : the spread of the wings; *esp* : the distance between the tips of the fully extended wings of a winged animal

¹**wink** \'wiŋk\ *vb* **1** : to close and open one eye quickly as a signal or hint **2** : to close and open the eyes quickly : BLINK **3** : to avoid seeing or noticing something ⟨~ at a traffic violation⟩ **4** : TWINKLE, FLICKER — **wink·er** \'wiŋ-kər\ *n*

²**wink** *n* **1** : a brief period of sleep : NAP **2** : an act of winking; *esp* : a hint or sign given by winking **3** : INSTANT ⟨dries in a ~⟩

win·ner \'wi-nər\ *n* : one that wins

¹**win·ning** \'wi-niŋ\ *n* **1** : VICTORY **2** : something won; *esp* : money won at gambling ⟨large ~s⟩

²**winning** *adj* **1** : successful esp. in competition **2** : ATTRACTIVE, CHARMING

win·now \'wi-nō\ *vb* **1** : to remove (as chaff) by a current of air; *also* : to free (as grain) from waste in this manner **2** : to sort or separate as if by winnowing

wino \'wī-nō\ *n, pl* **win·os** : one who is addicted to drinking wine

win·some \'win-səm\ *adj* [ME *winsum*, fr. OE *wynsum*, fr. *wynn* joy] **1** : generally pleasing and engaging ⟨a ~ smile⟩ **2** : CHEERFUL, GAY — **win·some·ly** *adv* — **win·some·ness** *n*

¹**win·ter** \'win-tər\ *n* : the season of the year in any region in which the noonday sun shines most obliquely : the coldest period of the year

²**winter** *vb* **1** : to pass the winter ⟨~*ed* in Florida⟩ **2** : to feed or find food during the winter ⟨~*ed* on hay⟩

³**winter** *adj* : sown in autumn for harvesting in the following spring or summer ⟨~ wheat⟩

win·ter·green \'win-tər-ˌgrēn\ *n* **1** : a low evergreen plant of the heath family with white bell-shaped flowers and spicy red berries **2** : an aromatic oil or its flavor from the wintergreen

win·ter·ize \'win-tə-ˌrīz\ *vb* **-ized; -iz·ing** : to make ready for winter

win·ter-kill \'win-tər-ˌkil\ *vb* : to kill or die by exposure to winter weather

winter squash *n* : any of various hard-shelled squashes that keep well in storage

win·ter·tide \-ˌtīd\ *n* : WINTER

win·ter·time \-ˌtīm\ *n* : WINTER

win·try \'win-trē\ *also* **win·tery** \'win-tə-rē\ *adj* **win·tri·er; -est 1** : of, relating to,

or characteristic of winter ⟨~ weather⟩ **2** : CHILLING, CHEERLESS ⟨a ~ welcome⟩

wipe \'wīp\ *vb* **wiped; wip·ing 1** : to clean or dry by rubbing ⟨~ dishes⟩ **2** : to remove by or as if by rubbing ⟨~ away tears⟩ **3** : to erase completely : OBLITERATE **4** : to pass or draw over a surface ⟨wiped his hand across his face⟩ — **wip·er** *n*

wipe *n* **1** : an act or instance of wiping; *also* : BLOW, STRIKE, SWIPE **2** : something used for wiping ⟨disposable ~s⟩

wipe out *vb* : to destroy completely

¹**wire** \'wī(-ə)r\ *n* **1** : metal in the form of a thread or slender rod; *also* : a thread or rod of metal **2** : hidden or secret influences controlling the action of a person or organization — usu. used in pl. ⟨pull ~s⟩ **3** : a line of wire for conducting electric current **4** : a telegraph or telephone wire or system **5** : TELEGRAM, CABLEGRAM **6** : the finish line of a race

²**wire** *vb* **wired; wir·ing 1** : to provide or equip with wire ⟨~ a house⟩ **2** : to bind, string, or mount with wire **3** : to send or send word to by telegraph

wired *adj* **1** : furnished with wires **2** : connected to the Internet **3** : feverishly excited ⟨~ fans⟩

wire·hair \'wī(-ə)r-ˌher\ *n* : a wirehaired dog or cat

wire·haired \-'herd\ *adj* : having a stiff wiry outer coat of hair

¹**wire·less** \-ləs\ *adj* **1** : having no wire or wires **2** : RADIO **3** : of or relating to data communications using radio waves

²**wireless** *n* **1** : telecommunication involving signals transmitted by radio waves; *also* : the technology used in radio telecommunication **2** *chiefly Brit* : RADIO

wire–pull·er \-ˌpu̇-lər\ *n* : one who uses secret or underhanded means to influence the acts of a person or organization — **wire–pull·ing** *n*

wire service *n* : a news agency that sends out syndicated news copy to subscribers by wire or satellite

wire·tap \-ˌtap\ *n* : the act or an instance of tapping a telephone or telegraph wire to get information; *also* : an electrical connection used for such tapping — **wiretap** *vb* — **wire·tap·per** \-ˌta-pər\ *n*

wire·worm \-ˌwərm\ *n* : any of various slender hard-coated beetle larvae esp. destructive to plant roots

wir·ing \'wī(-ə)r-iŋ\ *n* : a system of wires

wiry \'wī(-ə)r-ē\ *adj* **wir·i·er** \'wī-rē-ər\; **-est 1** : made of or resembling wire **2** : slender yet strong and sinewy ⟨~ arms⟩ — **wir·i·ness** \'wī-rē-nəs\ *n*

Wis *or* **Wisc** *abbr* Wisconsin

Wisd *abbr* Wisdom

wis·dom \'wiz-dəm\ *n* [ME, fr. OE *wīsdom*, fr. *wīs* wise] **1** : accumulated philosophic or scientific learning : KNOWLEDGE; *also* : INSIGHT **2** : good sense : JUDGMENT **3** : a wise attitude or course of action

Wisdom *n* — see BIBLE table

Wisdom of Sol·o·mon \-'sä-lə-mən\ — see BIBLE table

wisdom tooth *n* : the last tooth of the full set on each side of the upper and lower jaws of humans

¹**wise** \'wīz\ *n* : WAY, MANNER, FASHION ⟨in no ∼⟩ ⟨in this ∼⟩

²**wise** *adj* **wis·er; wis·est 1** : having wisdom : SAGE **2** : having or showing good sense or good judgment **3** : aware of what is going on : KNOWING ⟨got ∼ to his secrets⟩; *also* : CRAFTY, SHREWD **4** : possessing inside information **5** : INSOLENT, FRESH ⟨a ∼ retort⟩ — **wise·ly** *adv*

-wise \₁wīz\ *adv comb form* : in the manner or direction of ⟨slant*wise*⟩

wise·acre \'wīz-₁ā-kər\ *n* [MD *wijssegger* soothsayer] : SMART ALECK

¹**wise·crack** \'wīz-₁krak\ *n* : a clever, smart, or flippant remark

²**wisecrack** *vb* : to make a wisecrack

wise guy *n* : SMART ALECK

¹**wish** \'wish\ *vb* **1** : to have a desire : long for ⟨∼ you were here⟩ ⟨∼ for a puppy⟩ **2** : to form or express a wish concerning ⟨∼ed him a happy birthday⟩ **3** : BID ⟨he ∼ed me good morning⟩ **4** : to request by expressing a desire ⟨I ∼ you to go now⟩

²**wish** *n* **1** : an act or instance of wishing or desire : WANT; *also* : GOAL **2** : an expressed wish or desire

wish·bone \₁₋bōn\ *n* : a forked bone in front of the breastbone in most birds

wish·ful \'wish-fəl\ *adj* **1** : expressive of a wish; *also* : having a wish **2** : according with wishes rather than fact ⟨∼ thinking⟩

wishy–washy \'wi-shē-₁wȯ-shē, -₁wä-\ *adj* : WEAK, INSIPID; *also* : morally feeble

wisp \'wisp\ *n* **1** : a small handful (as of hay or straw) **2** : a thin strand, strip, or fragment ⟨a ∼ of hair⟩; *also* : a thready streak ⟨a ∼ of smoke⟩ **3** : something frail, slight, or fleeting ⟨a ∼ of a smile⟩ — **wispy** *adj*

wis·te·ria \wis-'tir-ē-ə\ *also* **wis·tar·ia** \-'tir-ē-ə *also* -'ter-\ *n* : any of a genus of chiefly Asian mostly woody vines related to the peas and widely grown for their long showy clusters of blue, white, purple, or rose flowers

wist·ful \'wist-fəl\ *adj* : feeling or showing a timid desire ⟨∼ memories⟩ — **wist·ful·ly** *adv* — **wist·ful·ness** *n*

wit \'wit\ *n* **1** : reasoning power : INTELLIGENCE **2** : mental soundness : SANITY — usu. used in pl. **3** : RESOURCEFULNESS, INGENUITY; *esp* : quickness and cleverness in handling words and ideas **4** : a talent for making clever remarks; *also* : a person noted for making witty remarks — **wit·ted** \'wi-təd\ *adj* — **at one's wit's end** : at a loss for a means of solving a problem

¹**witch** \'wich\ *n* **1** : a person believed to have magic power; *esp* : SORCERESS **2** : an ugly old woman : HAG **3** : a charming or alluring girl or woman

²**witch** *vb* : BEWITCH

witch·craft \'wich-₁kraft\ *n* : the power or practices of a witch : SORCERY

witch doctor *n* : a person in a primitive society who uses magic to treat sickness and to fight off evil spirits

witch·ery \'wi-chə-rē\ *n, pl* **-er·ies 1** : SORCERY **2** : FASCINATION, CHARM

witch·grass \'wich-₁gras\ *n* : any of several grasses that are weeds in cultivated areas

witch ha·zel \'wich-₁hā-zəl\ *n* **1** : a shrub of eastern No. America bearing small yellow flowers in the fall **2** : a soothing alcoholic lotion made from witch hazel bark

witch–hunt \'wich-₁hənt\ *n* **1** : a searching out and persecution of persons accused of witchcraft **2** : the searching out and deliberate harassment esp. of political opponents

witch·ing \'wi-chiŋ\ *adj* : of, relating to, or suitable for sorcery or supernatural occurrences

with \'with, 'with\ *prep* **1** : AGAINST ⟨a fight ∼ his brother⟩ **2** : FROM ⟨parting ∼ friends⟩ **3** : in mutual relation to ⟨talk ∼ a friend⟩ **4** : in the company of ⟨went there ∼ her⟩ **5** : AS REGARDS, TOWARD ⟨is patient ∼ children⟩ **6** : compared to ⟨on equal terms ∼ another⟩ **7** : in support of ⟨I'm ∼ you all the way⟩ **8** : in the presence of : CONTAINING ⟨tea ∼ sugar⟩ **9** : in the opinion of : as judged by ⟨their arguments had weight ∼ her⟩ **10** : BECAUSE OF, THROUGH ⟨pale ∼ anger⟩; *also* : by means of ⟨hit him ∼ a club⟩ **11** : in a manner indicating ⟨work ∼ a will⟩ **12** : GIVEN, GRANTED ⟨∼ your permission I'll leave⟩ **13** : HAVING ⟨came ∼ good news⟩ ⟨stood there ∼ his mouth open⟩ **14** : characterized by ⟨boys ∼ good morals⟩ **15** : at the time of : right after ⟨∼ that we left⟩ **16** : DESPITE ⟨∼ all her cleverness, she failed⟩ **17** : in the direction of ⟨swim ∼ the tide⟩

with·al \wi-'thȯl, -'thäl\ *adv* **1** : together with this : BESIDES **2** : on the other hand : NEVERTHELESS

with·draw \with-'drȯ, with-\ *vb* **-drew** \-'drü\; **-drawn** \-'drȯn\; **-draw·ing** \-'drȯ-iŋ\ **1** : to take back or away : REMOVE **2** : to call back (as from consideration); *also* : RETRACT **3** : to go away : RETREAT, LEAVE **4** : to terminate one's participation in or use of something

with·draw·al \-'drȯ-əl\ *n* **1** : an act or instance of withdrawing **2** : the discontinuance of the use or administration of a drug and esp. an addicting drug; *also* : the period following such discontinuance marked by often painful physiological and psychological symptoms **3** : a pathological retreat from the real world (as in some schizophrenic states)

with·drawn \with-'drȯn\ *adj* **1** : ISOLATED, SECLUDED **2** : socially detached and unresponsive ⟨became depressed and ∼⟩

withe \'with\ *n* : a slender flexible twig or branch

with·er \'wi-thər\ *vb* **1** : to shrivel from or as if from loss of bodily moisture and esp. sap **2** : to lose or cause to lose vitality, force, or freshness ⟨their enthusiasm ∼ed⟩ **3** : to cause to feel shriveled ⟨∼ him with a glance⟩

with·ers \'wi-thərz\ *n pl* : the ridge between the shoulder bones of a horse; *also* : the corresponding part in other 4-footed animals

with·hold \with-'hōld, with-\ *vb* **-held** \-'held\; **-hold·ing** 1 : to hold back : RESTRAIN; *also* : RETAIN 2 : to refrain from granting, giving, or allowing ⟨~ permission⟩ ⟨~ names⟩

withholding tax *n* : a tax on income withheld at the source

¹with·in \wi-'thin, -'thin-\ *adv* 1 : in or into the interior : INSIDE 2 : inside oneself : INWARDLY

²within *prep* 1 : inside the limits or influence of ⟨~ call⟩ 2 : in the limits or compass of ⟨~ a mile⟩ 3 : in or to the inner part of ⟨~ the room⟩

with·it \'wi-thət, -thət\ *adj* : socially or culturally up-to-date

¹with·out \wi-'thaut, -'thaut\ *prep* 1 : OUTSIDE 2 : LACKING ⟨~ hope⟩; *also* : not accompanied by or showing ⟨spoke ~ thinking⟩

²without *adv* 1 : on the outside : EXTERNALLY 2 : with something lacking or absent ⟨has learned to do ~⟩

with·stand \with-'stand, with-\ *vb* **-stood** \-'stud\; **-stand·ing** : to stand against : RESIST; *esp* : to oppose (as an attack) successfully

wit·less \'wit-ləs\ *adj* : lacking wit or understanding : FOOLISH — **wit·less·ly** *adv* — **wit·less·ness** *n*

¹wit·ness \'wit-nəs\ *n* [ME *witnesse*, fr. OE *witnes* knowledge, testimony, witness, fr. *wit* mind, intelligence] 1 : TESTIMONY ⟨bear ~ to the fact⟩ 2 : one that gives evidence; *esp* : one who testifies in a cause or before a court 3 : one present at a transaction so as to be able to testify that it has taken place 4 : one who has personal knowledge or experience of something 5 : something serving as evidence or proof : SIGN

²witness *vb* 1 : to bear witness : TESTIFY 2 : to act as legal witness of 3 : to furnish proof of : BETOKEN 4 : to be a witness of 5 : to be the scene of ⟨this region has ~ed many wars⟩

wit·ti·cism \'wi-tə-ˌsi-zəm\ *n* : a witty saying or phrase

wit·ting \'wi-tiŋ\ *adj* : done knowingly : INTENTIONAL — **wit·ting·ly** *adv*

wit·ty \'wi-tē\ *adj* **wit·ti·er**; **-est** : marked by or full of wit : AMUSING ⟨a ~ writer⟩ ⟨a ~ remark⟩ ♦ *Synonyms* HUMOROUS, FACETIOUS, JOCULAR, JOCOSE — **wit·ti·ly** \-tə-lē\ *adv* — **wit·ti·ness** \-tē-nəs\ *n*

wive \'wīv\ *vb* **wived**; **wiv·ing** : to take a wife

wives *pl of* WIFE

wiz·ard \'wi-zərd\ *n* [ME *wysard* wise man, fr. *wys* wise] 1 : MAGICIAN, SORCERER 2 : a very clever or skillful person ⟨a ~ at chess⟩

wiz·ard·ry \'wi-zər-drē\ *n, pl* **-ries** 1 : magic skill : SORCERY 2 : great skill or cleverness in an activity

wiz·en \'wi-zⁿn, 'wē-\ *vb* : to become or

cause to become dry, shrunken, or wrinkled ⟨a face ~ed by age⟩

wk *abbr* 1 week 2 work

WL *abbr* wavelength

wmk *abbr* watermark

WNW *abbr* west-northwest

WO *abbr* warrant officer

w/o *abbr* without

woad \'wōd\ *n* : a European herb related to the mustards; *also* : a blue dyestuff made from its leaves

wob·ble \'wä-bəl\ *vb* **wob·bled**; **wob·bling** 1 : to move or cause to move with an irregular rocking or side-to-side motion 2 : TREMBLE, QUAVER 3 : WAVER, VACILLATE — **wobble** *n* — **wob·bly** \-bə-lē\ *adj*

woe \'wō\ *n* 1 : deep suffering from misfortune, affliction, or grief 2 : TROUBLE, MISFORTUNE ⟨economic ~s⟩

woe·be·gone \'wō-bi-ˌgón\ *adj* : exhibiting woe, sorrow, or misery ⟨~ faces⟩; *also* : being in a sorry condition

woe·ful *also* **wo·ful** \'wō-fəl\ *adj* 1 : full of woe : AFFLICTED 2 : involving, bringing, or relating to woe ⟨~ stories⟩ 3 : DEPLORABLE ⟨~ test scores⟩ — **woe·ful·ly** *adv*

wok \'wäk\ *n* [Chin (Guangzhou & Hong Kong dial.) *wohk*] : a bowl-shaped cooking utensil used esp. in stir-frying

woke *past and past part of* WAKE

woken *past part of* WAKE

wold \'wōld\ *n* : an upland plain or stretch of rolling land without woods

¹wolf \'wulf\ *n, pl* **wolves** \'wulvz\ 1 : any of several large erect-eared bushy-tailed doglike predatory mammals that live and hunt in packs; *esp* : GRAY WOLF 2 : a fierce or destructive person — **wolf·ish** *adj* — **wolf in sheep's clothing** : one who hides a hostile intention with a friendly manner

²wolf *vb* : to eat greedily : DEVOUR

wolf·hound \-ˌhaund\ *n* : any of several large dogs orig. used in hunting wolves

wol·fram \'wul-frəm\ *n* : TUNGSTEN

wol·ver·ine \ˌwul-və-'rēn\ *n, pl* **wolverines** *also* **wolverine** : a dark shaggy-coated flesh-eating mammal of northern forests and associated tundra that is related to the weasels

wom·an \'wu-mən\ *n, pl* **wom·en** \'wi-mən\ [ME, fr. OE *wīfman*, fr. *wīf* woman, wife + *man* human being, man] 1 : an adult female person 2 : WOMANKIND 3 : feminine nature : WOMANLINESS 4 : a female servant or attendant

wom·an·hood \'wu-mən-ˌhud\ *n* 1 : the state of being a woman : the distinguishing qualities of a woman or of womankind 2 : WOMEN, WOMANKIND

wom·an·ish \'wu-mə-nish\ *adj* 1 : associated with or characteristic of women rather than men 2 : suggestive of a weak character : EFFEMINATE ⟨a ~ voice⟩

wom·an·ize \'wu-mə-ˌnīz\ *vb* : to pursue casual sexual relationships with numerous women — **wom·an·iz·er** *n*

wom·an·kind \'wu-mən-ˌkīnd\ *n* : the females of the human race : WOMEN

wom·an·like \-ˌlīk\ *adj* : WOMANLY

wom·an·ly \-lē\ *adj* : having qualities characteristic of a woman — **wom·an·li·ness** \-lē-nəs\ *n*

woman suffrage *n* : possession and exercise of suffrage by women

womb \'wüm\ *n* **1** : UTERUS **2** : a place where something is generated

wom·bat \'wäm-,bat\ *n* : any of several stocky burrowing Australian marsupials that resemble small bears

wom·en·folk \'wi-mən-,fōk\ *also* **wom·en·folks** \-,fōks\ *n pl* : WOMEN

¹won \'wən\ *past and past part of* WIN

²won \'wòn\ *n, pl* **won** — see MONEY table

¹won·der \'wən-dər\ *n* **1** : a cause of astonishment or surprise : MARVEL; *also* : MIRACLE **2** : the quality of exciting wonder ⟨the charm and ∼ of the scene⟩ **3** : a feeling (as of awed astonishment or uncertainty) aroused by something extraordinary or affecting

²wonder *vb* **1** : to feel surprise or amazement **2** : to feel curiosity or doubt ⟨∼ about the future⟩

wonder drug *n* : MIRACLE DRUG

won·der·ful \'wən-dər-fəl\ *adj* **1** : exciting wonder : MARVELOUS, ASTONISHING **2** : unusually good : ADMIRABLE ⟨did a ∼ job⟩ — **won·der·ful·ly** \-f(ə-)lē\ *adv* — **won·der·ful·ness** *n*

won·der·land \-,land, -lənd\ *n* **1** : an imaginary place of delicate beauty or magical charm **2** : a place that excites admiration or wonder ⟨a scenic ∼⟩

won·der·ment \-mənt\ *n* **1** : ASTONISHMENT, SURPRISE **2** : a cause of or occasion for wonder **3** : curiosity about something

won·drous \'wən-drəs\ *adj* : WONDERFUL, MARVELOUS ⟨a ∼ feat⟩ — **won·drous·ly** *adv* — **won·drous·ness** *n*

wonk \'wäŋk, 'wòŋk\ *n* : one who works in a specialized usu. intellectual field ⟨computer ∼s⟩

¹wont \'wònt, 'wōnt\ *adj* [ME *woned, wont,* fr. pp. of *wonen* to dwell, be used to, fr. OE *wunian*] **1** : ACCUSTOMED, USED ⟨as we are ∼ to do⟩ **2** : INCLINED, APT

²wont *n* : CUSTOM, USAGE, HABIT ⟨according to her ∼⟩

won't \'wōnt\ : will not

wont·ed \'wòn-təd, 'wōn-\ *adj* : ACCUSTOMED, CUSTOMARY ⟨his ∼ courtesy⟩

woo \'wü\ *vb* **1** : to try to gain the love of : COURT **2** : SOLICIT, ENTREAT **3** : to try to gain or bring about ⟨∼ public favor⟩ — **woo·er** *n*

¹wood \'wüd\ *n* **1** : a dense growth of trees usu. larger than a grove and smaller than a forest — often used in pl. **2** : a hard fibrous substance that is basically xylem and forms the bulk of trees and shrubs beneath the bark; *also* : this material fit for use or prepared for some use (as burning or building) **3** : something made of wood

²wood *adj* **1** : WOODEN **2** : suitable for holding, cutting, or working with wood **3** *or* **woods** \'wüdz\ : living or growing in the woods

³wood *vb* **1** : to supply or load with wood esp. for fuel **2** : to cover with a growth of trees

wood alcohol *n* : METHANOL

wood·bine \'wüd-,bīn\ *n* : any of several honeysuckles; *also* : VIRGINIA CREEPER

wood·block \-,bläk\ *n* : WOODCUT

wood·chop·per \-,chä-pər\ *n* : one engaged esp. in chopping down trees

wood·chuck \-,chək\ *n* : a thickset grizzled marmot of Alaska, Canada, and the northeastern U.S.

wood·cock \'wüd-,käk\ *n, pl* **wood·cocks** : a brown eastern No. American game bird with a short neck and long bill that is related to the snipe; *also* : a related and similar Old World bird

wood·craft \-,kraft\ *n* **1** : skill and practice in matters relating to the woods and esp. in how to take care of oneself in them **2** : skill in shaping or constructing articles from wood

wood·cut \-,kət\ *n* **1** : a relief printing surface engraved on a block of wood **2** : a print from a woodcut

wood·cut·ter \-,kə-tər\ *n* : a person who cuts wood

wood duck *n* : a showy crested American duck of which the male has iridescent multicolored plumage

wood·ed \'wu-dəd\ *adj* : covered with woods or trees ⟨∼ slopes⟩

wood·en \'wù-dᵊn\ *adj* **1** : made of wood **2** : lacking flexibility : awkwardly stiff ⟨∼ acting⟩ — **wood·en·ly** *adv* — **wood·en·ness** *n*

wood·en·ware \'wù-dᵊn-,wer\ *n* : articles made of wood for domestic use

wood·land \'wùd-lənd, -,land\ *n* : land covered with trees : FOREST — **woodland** *adj*

wood·lot \'wùd-,lät\ *n* : a restricted area of woodland usu. privately kept to meet fuel and timber needs

wood louse *n* : any of various small flat crustaceans that live esp. in ground litter and under stones and bark

wood·man \'wùd-mən\ *n* : WOODSMAN

wood·note \-,nōt\ *n* : verbal expression that is natural and artless

wood nymph *n* : a nymph living in the woods

wood·peck·er \'wùd-,pe-kər\ *n* : any of numerous usu. brightly marked climbing birds with stiff spiny tail feathers and a chisellike bill used to drill into trees for insects

wood·pile \-,pī(-ə)l\ *n* : a pile of wood and esp. firewood

wood rat *n* : PACK RAT

wood·shed \-,shed\ *n* : a shed for storing wood and esp. firewood

woods·man \'wùdz-mən\ *n* : a person who frequents or works in the woods; *esp* : one skilled in woodcraft

woodsy \'wùd-zē\ *adj* **woods·i·er; -est** : relating to or suggestive of woods ⟨a ∼ odor⟩

wood·wind \'wùd-,wind\ *n* : one of a group of wind instruments including flutes, clarinets, oboes, bassoons, and sometimes saxophones

wood·work \-,wərk\ *n* : work made of wood; *esp* : interior fittings (as moldings or stairways) of wood

woody \ˈwu̇-dē\ *adj* **wood·i·er; -est 1**
: abounding or overgrown with woods ⟨a ~ trail⟩ **2** : of or containing wood or wood fibers ⟨~ plants⟩ **3** : characteristic or suggestive of wood ⟨a ~ flavor⟩ — **wood·i·ness** \ˈwu̇-dē-nəs\ *n*

woof \ˈwu̇f\ *n* [alter. of ME *oof*, fr. OE *ōwef*, fr. ō- (fr. on on) + *wefan* to weave] **1** : WEFT 1 **2** : a woven fabric; *also* : its texture

woof·er \ˈwu̇-fər\ *n* : a loudspeaker that reproduces sounds of low pitch

wool \ˈwu̇l\ *n* **1** : the soft wavy or curly hair of some mammals and esp. the domestic sheep; *also* : something (as a textile or garment) made of wool **2** : material that resembles a mass of wool — **wooled** \ˈwu̇ld\ *adj*

¹**wool·en** *or* **wool·len** \ˈwu̇-lən\ *adj* **1** : made of wool **2** : of or relating to the manufacture or sale of woolen products ⟨~ mills⟩

²**woolen** *or* **woollen** *n* **1** : a fabric made of wool **2** : garments of woolen fabric — usu. used in pl.

wool·gath·er·ing \-ˌga-thə-riŋ\ *n* : idle daydreaming

¹**wool·ly** *also* **wooly** \ˈwu̇-lē\ *adj* **wool·li·er; -est 1** : of, relating to, or bearing wool **2** : consisting of or resembling wool **3** : mentally confused ⟨~ thinking⟩ **4** : marked by a lack of order or restraint ⟨the wild and ~ West⟩

²**wool·ly** *also* **wool·ie** *or* **wooly** \ˈwu̇-lē\ *n, pl* **wool·lies** : a garment made from wool; *esp* : underclothing of knitted wool — usu. used in pl.

woolly adel·gid \-ə-ˈdel-jəd\ *n* : either of two aphids accidentally introduced into No. America where they are serious pests of firs and hemlocks

woolly bear *n* : any of numerous very hairy moth caterpillars

woolly mammoth *n* : a heavy-coated mammoth formerly inhabiting colder parts of the northern hemisphere

woo·zy \ˈwu̇-zē\ *adj* **woo·zi·er; -est 1** : BEFUDDLED **2** : somewhat dizzy, nauseated, or weak ⟨~ from fatigue⟩ **3** : somewhat indistinct or unfocused : FUZZY — **woo·zi·ness** \ˈwu̇-zē-nəs\ *n*

¹**word** \ˈwərd\ *n* **1** : something that is said; *esp* : a brief remark **2** : a speech sound or series of speech sounds that communicates a meaning; *also* : a graphic representation of such a sound or series of sounds **3** : ORDER, COMMAND **4** *often cap* : the 2d person of the Trinity; *also* : GOSPEL **5** : NEWS, INFORMATION **6** : PROMISE **7** *pl* : QUARREL, DISPUTE **8** : a verbal signal : PASSWORD — **word·less** *adj*

²**word** *vb* : to express in words : PHRASE

word·age \ˈwər-dij\ *n* **1** : WORDS **2** : number of words **3** : WORDING

word·book \ˈwərd-ˌbu̇k\ *n* : VOCABULARY, DICTIONARY

word·ing \ˈwər-diŋ\ *n* : verbal expression : PHRASEOLOGY

word of mouth : oral communication

word·play \ˈwərd-ˌplā\ *n* : playful use of words

word processing *n* : the production of typewritten documents with automated and usu. computerized text-editing equipment — **word process** *vb*

word processor *n* : a keyboard-operated terminal for use in word processing; *also* : software to perform word processing

wordy \ˈwər-dē\ *adj* **word·i·er; -est** : using or having too many words ⟨~ sentences⟩ ♦ **Synonyms** PROLIX, DIFFUSE, REDUNDANT — **word·i·ness** \-dē-nəs\ *n*

wore *past of* WEAR

¹**work** \ˈwərk\ *n* **1** : TOIL, LABOR; *also* : EMPLOYMENT ⟨out of ~⟩ **2** : TASK, JOB ⟨have ~ to do⟩ **3** : the energy used when a force is applied over a given distance **4** : DEED, ACHIEVEMENT **5** : a fortified structure **6** *pl* : engineering structures **7** *pl* : a place where industrial labor is done : PLANT, FACTORY **8** *pl* : the moving parts of a mechanism **9** : something produced by mental effort or physical labor; *esp* : an artistic production (as a book or needlework) **10** : WORKMANSHIP ⟨careless ~⟩ **11** : material in the process of manufacture **12** *pl* : everything possessed, available, or belonging ⟨the whole ~s went overboard⟩; *also* : drastic treatment ⟨gave him the ~s⟩ ♦ **Synonyms** OCCUPATION, EMPLOYMENT, BUSINESS, PURSUIT, CALLING — **in the works** : in process of preparation

²**work** *adj* **1** : used for work ⟨~ elephants⟩ **2** : suitable or styled for wear while working ⟨~ clothes⟩

³**work** *vb* **worked** \ˈwərkt\ *or* **wrought** \ˈrȯt\; **work·ing 1** : to bring to pass : EFFECT **2** : to fashion or create a useful or desired product through labor or exertion **3** : to prepare for use (as by kneading) **4** : to bring into a desired form by a manufacturing process ⟨~ cold steel⟩ **5** : to set or keep in operation : OPERATE ⟨a pump ~ed by hand⟩ **6** : to solve by reasoning or calculation ⟨~ out a problem⟩ **7** : to cause to toil or labor ⟨~ed the men hard⟩; *also* : to make use of ⟨~ a mine⟩ **8** : to pay for with labor or service ⟨~ off a debt⟩ **9** : to bring or get into some position or condition by stages ⟨the stream ~ed itself clear⟩ ⟨the knot ~ed loose⟩ **10** : CONTRIVE, ARRANGE ⟨~ it so you can leave early⟩ **11** : to practice trickery or cajolery on ⟨~ed the management for a free ticket⟩ **12** : EXCITE, PROVOKE ⟨~ed himself into a rage⟩ **13** : to exert oneself physically or mentally; *esp* : to perform work regularly for wages **14** : to function according to plan or design **15** : to produce a desired effect : SUCCEED ⟨the plan ~ed⟩ **16** : to make way slowly and with difficulty ⟨he ~ed forward through the crowd⟩ **17** : to permit of being worked ⟨this wood ~s easily⟩ **18** : to be in restless motion; *also* : FERMENT 1 — **work on 1** : AFFECT **2** : to try to influence or persuade — **work upon** : to have effect upon : operate on : INFLUENCE

work·able \ˈwər-kə-bəl\ *adj* **1** : capable of being worked ⟨~ clay⟩ **2** : PRACTICABLE, FEASIBLE — **work·able·ness** *n*

work·a·day \\'wər-kə-ˌdā\ *adj* **1** : relating to or suited for working days **2** : PROSAIC, ORDINARY ⟨∼ chores⟩

work·a·hol·ic \ˌwər-kə-'hȯ-lik, -'hä-\ *n* : a compulsive worker

work·bench \-ˌbench\ *n* : a bench on which work esp. of mechanics, machinists, and carpenters is performed

work·book \-ˌbu̇k\ *n* **1** : a worker's manual **2** : a student's book of problems to be answered directly on the pages

work·day \\'wərk-ˌdā\ *n* **1** : a day on which work is done as distinguished from a day off **2** : the period of time in a day when work is performed

work·er \\'wər-kər\ *n* **1** : one that works; *esp* : a person who works for wages **2** : any of the sexually undeveloped individuals of a colony of social insects (as bees, ants, or termites) that perform the work of the community

workers' compensation *n* : a system of insurance that reimburses an employer for damages paid to an employee who was injured while working

work ethic *n* : belief in work as a moral good

work farm *n* : a farm on which persons guilty of minor law violations are confined

work·horse \\'wərk-ˌhȯrs\ *n* **1** : a horse used for hard work **2** : a person who does most of the work of a group task **3** : something that is useful, durable, or dependable

work·house \-ˌhau̇s\ *n* **1** *Brit* : POORHOUSE **2** : a house of correction for persons guilty of minor law violations

¹work·ing \\'wər-kiŋ\ *n* **1** : manner of functioning — usu. used in pl. **2** *pl* : an excavation made in mining or tunneling

²working *adj* **1** : engaged in work ⟨a ∼ journalist⟩ **2** : adequate to allow work to be done ⟨a ∼ majority⟩ ⟨a ∼ knowledge of French⟩ **3** : adopted or assumed to help further work or activity ⟨a ∼ draft⟩ **4** : spent at work ⟨∼ life⟩

work·ing·man \\'wər-kiŋ-ˌman\ *n* : WORKER 1

work·man \\'wərk-mən\ *n* **1** : WORKER 1 **2** : ARTISAN, CRAFTSMAN

work·man·like \-ˌlīk\ *adj* : worthy of a good workman : SKILLFUL

work·man·ship \-ˌship\ *n* : the art or skill of a workman : CRAFTSMANSHIP; *also* : the quality of a piece of work ⟨a vase of exquisite ∼⟩

work·out \\'wərk-ˌau̇t\ *n* **1** : a practice or exercise to test or improve one's fitness, ability, or performance **2** : a test or trial to determine ability or capacity or suitability

work out *vb* **1** : to bring about esp. by resolving difficulties **2** : DEVELOP, ELABORATE **3** : to prove effective, practicable, or suitable ⟨our plan didn't *work out*⟩ **4** : to amount to a total or calculated figure — used with *at* **5** : to engage in a workout

work·place \\'wərk-ˌplās\ *n* : a place (as an office) where work is done

work·room \\'wərk-ˌrüm, -ˌru̇m\ *n* : a room used for work

work·shop \-ˌshäp\ *n* **1** : a shop where manufacturing or handicrafts are carried on **2** : a seminar emphasizing exchange of ideas and practical methods

work·sta·tion \-ˌstā-shən\ *n* : an area with equipment for the performance of a specialized task; *also* : a personal computer usu. connected to a computer network

world \\'wərld\ *n* [ME, fr. OE *woruld* human existence, this world, age, fr. a prehistoric compound whose first constituent is represented by OE *wer* man and whose second constituent is akin to OE *eald* old] **1** : the earth with its inhabitants and all things upon it **2** : people in general : MANKIND **3** : human affairs ⟨withdraw from the ∼⟩ **4** : UNIVERSE, CREATION **5** : a state of existence : scene of life and action ⟨the ∼ of the future⟩ **6** : a distinctive class of persons or their sphere of interest ⟨the musical ∼⟩ **7** : a part or section of the earth or its inhabitants by itself **8** : a great number or quantity ⟨a ∼ of troubles⟩ **9** : a celestial body

world–beat·er \-ˌbē-tər\ *n* : one that excels all others of its kind : CHAMPION

world–class *adj* : of the highest caliber in the world ⟨a ∼ athlete⟩

world·ling \-liŋ\ *n* : a person absorbed in the concerns of the present world

world·ly \-lē\ *adj* **1** : of, relating to, or devoted to this world and its pursuits rather than to religion or spiritual affairs ⟨∼ pleasures⟩ **2** : WORLDLY-WISE, SOPHISTICATED — **world·li·ness** \-lē-nəs\ *n*

world·ly–wise \-ˌwīz\ *adj* : possessing a practical and often shrewd understanding of human affairs

world·wide \\'wərld-'wīd\ *adj* : extended throughout the entire world ⟨attracted ∼ attention⟩ — **worldwide** *adv*

World Wide Web *n* : a part of the Internet usu. accessed through a browser and containing files connected by hyperlinks

¹worm \\'wərm\ *n* **1** : any of various small long usu. naked and soft-bodied round or flat invertebrate animals (as an earthworm, nematode, tapeworm, or maggot) **2** : a human being who is an object of contempt, loathing, or pity : WRETCH **3** : something that inwardly torments or devours **4** *pl* : infestation with or disease caused by parasitic worms **5** : a spiral or wormlike thing (as the thread of a screw) — **worm·like** \-ˌlīk\ *adj* — **wormy** *adj*

²worm *vb* **1** : to move or cause to move or proceed slowly and deviously **2** : to insinuate or introduce (oneself) by devious or subtle means **3** : to obtain or extract by artful or insidious pleading, asking, or persuading ⟨∼ed the truth out of him⟩ **4** : to treat (an animal) with a drug to destroy or expel parasitic worms

worm–eat·en \\'wərm-ˌē-tᵊn\ *adj* : eaten or burrowed by worms

worm gear *n* : a mechanical linkage consisting of a short rotating screw whose threads mesh with the teeth of a gear wheel

worm·hole \'wərm-ˌhōl\ *n* : a hole or passage burrowed by a worm

worm·wood \-ˌwu̇d\ *n* 1 : any of a genus of aromatic woody plants (as a sagebrush); *esp* : one of Europe used in absinthe 2 : something bitter or grievous : BITTERNESS

worn *past part of* WEAR

worn–out \'wȯrn-ˈau̇t\ *adj* : exhausted or used up by or as if by wear

wor·ri·some \'wər-ē-səm\ *adj* 1 : causing distress or worry ⟨~ news⟩ 2 : inclined to worry or fret ⟨a ~ mother⟩

¹**wor·ry** \'wər-ē\ *vb* **wor·ried; wor·ry·ing** 1 : to shake and mangle with the teeth ⟨a terrier ~*ing* a rat⟩ 2 : to make anxious or upset ⟨her poor health *worries* me⟩ 3 : to feel or express great care or anxiety : FRET ⟨~*ing* about his health⟩ — **wor·ri·er** *n*

²**worry** *n*, *pl* **worries** 1 : ANXIETY 2 : a cause of anxiety : TROUBLE

wor·ry·wart \'wər-ē-ˌwȯrt\ *n* : one who is inclined to worry unduly

¹**worse** \'wərs\ *adj*, *comparative of* BAD *or of* ILL 1 : bad or evil in a greater degree : less good 2 : more unfavorable, unpleasant, or painful; *also* : SICKER

²**worse** *n* 1 : one that is worse 2 : a greater degree of ill or badness ⟨a turn for the ~⟩

³**worse** *adv*, *comparative of* BAD *or of* ILL : in a worse manner : to a worse extent or degree ⟨you drive ~ than he does⟩

wors·en \'wər-sᵊn\ *vb* : to make or become worse ⟨the rash ~ed⟩

¹**wor·ship** \'wər-shəp\ *n* [ME *worshipe* worthiness, respect, reverence paid to a divine being, fr. OE *weorthscipe* worthiness, respect, fr. *weorth* worthy, worth + *-scipe* -ship, suffix denoting quality or condition] 1 *chiefly Brit* : a person of importance — used as a title for officials 2 : reverence toward a divine being or supernatural power; *also* : the expression of such reverence 3 : extravagant respect or admiration or devotion ⟨~ of the dollar⟩

²**worship** *vb* **-shipped** *also* **-shiped; -ship·ping** *also* **-ship·ing** 1 : to honor or reverence as a divine being or supernatural power 2 : IDOLIZE ⟨~s his brother⟩ 3 : to perform or take part in worship — **wor·ship·er** *or* **wor·ship·per** *n*

wor·ship·ful \'wər-shəp-fəl\ *adj* 1 *archaic* : NOTABLE, DISTINGUISHED 2 *chiefly Brit* — used as a title for various persons or groups of rank or distinction 3 : VENERATING, WORSHIPING ⟨~ fans⟩

¹**worst** \'wərst\ *adj*, *superlative of* BAD *or of* ILL 1 : most bad, evil, ill, or corrupt ⟨the ~ criminals⟩ 2 : most unfavorable, unpleasant, or painful ⟨the ~ scenario⟩; *also* : most unsuitable, faulty, or unattractive 3 : least skillful or efficient ⟨her ~ students⟩

²**worst** *adv*, *superlative of* ILL *or of* BAD *or* BADLY 1 : to the extreme degree of badness or inferiority ⟨the ~ dressed person⟩ : in the worst manner 2 : MOST ⟨those who need help ~⟩

³**worst** *n* : one that is worst

⁴**worst** *vb* : DEFEAT

wor·sted \'wu̇s-təd, 'wər-stəd\ *n* [ME, fr. *Worsted* (now *Worstead*), England] 1 : a smooth compact yarn from long wool fibers; *also* : a fabric made from such yarn

wort \'wərt, 'wȯrt\ *n* : a sweet liquid drained from mash and fermented to form beer and whiskey

¹**worth** \'wərth\ *n* 1 : monetary value; *also* : the equivalent of a specified amount or figure ⟨$5 ~ of gas⟩ 2 : the value of something measured by its qualities 3 : MERIT, EXCELLENCE

²**worth** *prep* 1 : equal in value to; *also* : having possessions or income equal to 2 : deserving of ⟨well ~ the effort⟩

worth·less \'wərth-ləs\ *adj* 1 : lacking worth : VALUELESS; *also* : USELESS 2 : LOW, DESPICABLE ⟨a ~ coward⟩ — **worth·less·ness** *n*

worth·while \'wərth-'hwī(-ə)l\ *adj* : being worth the time or effort spent

¹**wor·thy** \'wər-thē\ *adj* **wor·thi·er; -est** 1 : having worth or value : ESTIMABLE ⟨a ~ cause⟩ 2 : HONORABLE, MERITORIOUS ⟨my ~ opponent⟩ 3 : having sufficient worth ⟨~ of the honor⟩ — **wor·thi·ly** \'wər-thə-lē\ *adv* — **wor·thi·ness** \-thē-nəs\ *n*

²**worthy** *n*, *pl* **worthies** : a worthy person

would \'wu̇d\ *past of* WILL 1 *archaic* : wish for : WANT 2 : strongly desire : WISH ⟨I ~ I were young again⟩ 3 — used as an auxiliary to express (1) preference ⟨~ rather run than fight⟩, (2) wish, desire, or intent ⟨those who ~ forbid gambling⟩, (3) habitual action ⟨we ~ meet often for lunch⟩, (4) a contingency or possibility ⟨if he were coming, he ~ be here by now⟩, (5) probability ⟨~ have won if he hadn't tripped⟩, or (6) a request ⟨~ you help us⟩ 4 : COULD 5 : SHOULD

would–be \'wu̇d-ˈbē\ *adj* : desiring or pretending to be ⟨a ~ artist⟩

¹**wound** \'wu̇nd\ *n* 1 : an injury involving cutting or breaking of bodily tissue (as by violence, accident, or surgery) 2 : an injury or hurt to feelings or reputation

²**wound** *vb* : to inflict a wound to or in

³**wound** \'wau̇nd\ *past and past part of* WIND

wove *past of* WEAVE

woven *past part of* WEAVE

¹**wow** \'wau̇\ *n* : a striking success : HIT

²**wow** *vb* : to arouse enthusiastic approval ⟨~ed the critics⟩

WP *abbr* word processing; word processor

WPM *abbr* words per minute

wpn *abbr* weapon

wrack \'rak\ *n* [ME, fr. OE *wræc* misery, punishment, something driven by the sea] : violent or total destruction

wraith \'rāth\ *n*, *pl* **wraiths** \'rāths, 'rāthz\ 1 : GHOST, SPECTER 2 : an insubstantial appearance : SHADOW

¹**wran·gle** \'raŋ-gəl\ *vb* **wran·gled; wran·gling** 1 : to quarrel angrily or peevishly : BICKER 2 : ARGUE ⟨they *wrangled* about money⟩ 3 : to obtain by persistent arguing 4 : to herd and care for (livestock) on the range — **wran·gler** *n*

²**wrangle** n : an angry, noisy, or prolonged dispute; *also* : CONTROVERSY

¹**wrap** \'rap\ vb **wrapped; wrap·ping 1** : to cover esp. by winding or folding **2** : to envelop and secure for transportation or storage **3** : to enclose wholly : ENFOLD **4** : to coil, fold, draw, or twine about something **5** : SURROUND, ENVELOP ⟨*wrapped* in mystery⟩ **6** : INVOLVE, ENGROSS ⟨*wrapped* up in a hobby⟩ **7** : to complete filming or recording

²**wrap** n **1** : WRAPPER, WRAPPING **2** : an article of clothing that may be wrapped around a person **3** pl : SECRECY ⟨kept under ∼s⟩ **4** : completion of filming or recording **5** : a thin piece of bread that is rolled around a filling

wrap·around \'ra-pə-ˌraùnd\ n : a garment (as a dress) adjusted to the figure by wrapping around

wrap·per \'ra-pər\ n **1** : that in which something is wrapped **2** : one that wraps **3** : an article of clothing worn wrapped around the body

wrap·ping \'ra-pin\ n : something used to wrap an object : WRAPPER

wrap—up \'rap-ˌəp\ n : SUMMARY

wrap up vb **1** : SUMMARIZE, SUM UP **2** : to bring to a usu. successful conclusion

wrasse \'ras\ n : any of a large family of usu. brightly colored marine fishes including many food fishes

wrath \'rath\ n **1** : violent anger : RAGE **2** : divine punishment ♦ *Synonyms* INDIGNATION, IRE, FURY, ANGER

wrath·ful \-fəl\ adj **1** : filled with wrath : very angry **2** : showing, marked by, or arising from wrath ⟨a ∼ assault⟩ — **wrath·ful·ly** adv — **wrath·ful·ness** n

wreak \'rēk\ vb [ME *wreken*, fr. OE *wrecan* to drive, punish, avenge] **1** : to exact as a punishment : INFLICT ⟨∼ vengeance on an enemy⟩ **2** : to give free scope or rein to ⟨∼ed his wrath⟩ **3** : BRING ABOUT, CAUSE ⟨∼ havoc⟩

wreath \'rēth\ n, pl **wreaths** \'rēthz, 'rēths\ : a circular band of flowers or leaves usu. for decoration; *also* : something having a circular or coiling form ⟨a ∼ of smoke⟩

wreathe \'rēth\ vb **wreathed; wreath·ing 1** : to shape or take on the shape of a wreath **2** : to crown, decorate, or cover with or as if with a wreath ⟨a face *wreathed* in smiles⟩

¹**wreck** \'rek\ n **1** : something (as goods) cast upon the land by the sea after a shipwreck **2** : SHIPWRECK **3** : a destructive crash ⟨a car ∼⟩ **4** : the action or process of breaking up or destroying something **5** : broken remains (as of a vehicle after a crash) **6** : something disabled or in a state of ruin; *also* : an individual broken in health or strength, or spirits ⟨he's a nervous ∼⟩

²**wreck** vb **1** : SHIPWRECK **2** : to ruin or damage by breaking up ⟨∼ed his marriage⟩ : involve in disaster or ruin

wreck·age \'re-kij\ n **1** : the act of wrecking : the state of being wrecked : RUIN **2** : the remains of a wreck

wreck·er \'re-kər\ n **1** : one that searches for or works upon the wrecks of ships **2** : TOW TRUCK **3** : one that wrecks; *esp* : one whose work is the demolition of buildings

wren \'ren\ n : any of a family of small mostly brown singing birds with short wings and often a tail that points upward

¹**wrench** \'rench\ vb **1** : to move with a violent twist **2** : to pull, strain, or tighten with violent twisting or force **3** : to injure or disable by a violent twisting or straining ⟨∼ed her back⟩ **4** : to snatch forcibly : WREST

²**wrench** n **1** : a forcible twisting; *also* : an injury (as to one's ankle) by twisting **2** : a tool for holding, twisting, or turning (as nuts or bolts)

¹**wrest** \'rest\ vb **1** : to pull or move by a forcible twisting movement **2** : to gain with difficulty by or as if by force or violence ⟨∼ control of the government from the dictator⟩

²**wrest** n : a forcible twist : WRENCH

¹**wres·tle** \'re-səl, 'ra-\ vb **wres·tled; wres·tling 1** : to grapple with and try to throw down an opponent **2** : to compete against in wrestling **3** : to struggle for control (as of something difficult) ⟨∼ with a problem⟩ — **wres·tler** \'res-lər, 'ras-\ n

²**wrestle** n : the action or an instance of wrestling : STRUGGLE

wres·tling \'res-lin\ n : the sport in which two opponents wrestle each other

wretch \'rech\ n [ME *wrecche*, fr. OE *wrecca* outcast, exile] **1** : a miserable unhappy person **2** : a base, despicable, or vile person

wretch·ed \'re-chəd\ adj **1** : deeply afflicted, dejected, or distressed : MISERABLE **2** : WOEFUL, GRIEVOUS ⟨a ∼ accident⟩ **3** : DESPICABLE ⟨a ∼ trick⟩ **4** : poor in quality or ability : INFERIOR ⟨∼ workmanship⟩ — **wretch·ed·ly** adv — **wretch·ed·ness** n

wrig·gle \'ri-gəl\ vb **wrig·gled; wrig·gling 1** : to twist or move to and fro like a worm : SQUIRM ⟨*wriggled* in his chair⟩ ⟨∼ your toes⟩; *also* : to move along by twisting and turning ⟨a snake *wriggled* along the path⟩ **2** : to extricate oneself as if by wriggling ⟨∼ out of difficulty⟩ — **wriggle** n

wrig·gler n **1** : one that wriggles **2** : WIGGLER 1

wring \'rin\ vb **wrung** \'rən\; **wring·ing** \'rin-in\ **1** : to squeeze or twist esp. so as to make dry or to extract moisture or liquid ⟨∼ wet clothes⟩ **2** : to get by or as if by twisting or pressing ⟨∼ the truth out of him⟩ **3** : to twist so as to strain or sprain : CONTORT ⟨∼ his neck⟩ **4** : to twist together as a sign of anguish ⟨*wrung* her hands⟩ **5** : to affect painfully as if by wringing : TORMENT ⟨her plight *wrung* my heart⟩

wring·er \'rin-ər\ n : one that wrings; *esp* : a device for squeezing out liquid or moisture ⟨clothes ∼⟩

¹**wrin·kle** \'rin-kəl\ n **1** : a crease or small fold on a smooth surface (as in the skin

or in cloth) **2** : a clever or new method, trick, or idea — **wrin·kly** \-k(ə-)lē\ *adj*

²**wrinkle** *vb* **wrin·kled; wrin·kling** : to develop or cause to develop wrinkles

wrist \'rist\ *n* : the joint or region between the hand and the arm; *also* : a corresponding part in a lower animal

wrist·band \-ˌband\ *n* : a band or the part of a sleeve encircling the wrist

wrist·let \-lət\ *n* : WRISTBAND; *esp* : a close-fitting knitted band attached to the top of a glove or the end of a sleeve

wrist·watch \-ˌwäch\ *n* : a small watch attached to a bracelet or strap to fasten about the wrist

writ \'rit\ *n* **1** : something written **2** : a written legal order signed by a court officer

writ·able \'rī-tə-bəl\ *adj* : being an electronic storage medium on which it is possible to introduce new data ⟨a ~ DVD⟩

write \'rīt\ *vb* **wrote** \'rōt\; **writ·ten** \'ri-t³n\ *also* **writ** \'rit\; **writ·ing** \'rī-tiŋ\ [ME, fr. OE *wrītan* to scratch, draw, inscribe] **1** : to form characters, letters, or words on a surface ⟨learn to read and ~⟩ **2** : to form the letters or the words of ⟨~ your name⟩ ⟨~ a check⟩ **3** : to put down on paper : express in writing **4** : to make up and set down for others to read ⟨~ a book⟩ ⟨~ music⟩ **5** : to write a letter to **6** : to communicate by letter : CORRESPOND

write–in \'rīt-ˌin\ *n* : a vote cast by writing in the name of a candidate; *also* : a candidate whose name is written in

write in *vb* : to insert (a name not listed on a ballot) in an appropriate space; *also* : to cast (a vote) in this manner

write off *vb* : to eliminate (an asset) from a bookkeeping record : enter as a loss or expense

writ·er \'rī-tər\ *n* : one that writes esp. as a business or occupation : AUTHOR

writer's cramp *n* : a painful spasmodic contraction of muscles of the hand or fingers brought on by excessive writing

write–up \'rīt-ˌəp\ *n* : a written account (as in a newspaper); *esp* : a flattering article

writhe \'rīth\ *vb* **writhed; writh·ing** **1** : to twist and turn this way and that ⟨~ in pain⟩ **2** : to suffer with shame or confusion

writing *n* **1** : the act of one that writes; *also* : HANDWRITING **2** : something that is written or printed **3** : a style or form of composition **4** : the occupation of a writer

Writings \'rī-tiŋz\ *n pl* : the third part of the Jewish scriptures

wrnt *abbr* warrant

¹**wrong** \'rȯŋ\ *n* **1** : an injurious, unfair, or unjust act **2** : a violation of the legal rights of another person **3** : something that is wrong : wrong principles, practices, or conduct ⟨know right from ~⟩ **4** : the state, position, or fact of being wrong ⟨was in the ~⟩

²**wrong** *adj* **wrong·er** \'rȯŋ-ər\; **wrong·est** \'rȯŋ-əst\ **1** : SINFUL, IMMORAL **2** : not right according to a standard or code : IMPROPER **3** : INCORRECT ⟨a ~ solution⟩ **4** : UNSATISFACTORY **5** : UNSUITABLE, INAPPROPRIATE **6** : constituting a surface that is considered the back, bottom, inside, or reverse of something ⟨iron only on the ~ side of the fabric⟩ **♦ Synonyms** FALSE, ERRONEOUS, INCORRECT, INACCURATE, UNTRUE — **wrong·ly** *adv*

³**wrong** *adv* **1** : INCORRECTLY **2** : in a wrong direction, manner, or relation

⁴**wrong** *vb* **wronged; wrong·ing** \'rȯŋ-iŋ\ **1** : to do wrong to : INJURE, HARM **2** : to treat unjustly : DISHONOR, MALIGN **♦ Synonyms** OPPRESS, PERSECUTE, AGGRIEVE

wrong·do·er \'rȯŋ-ˌdü-ər\ *n* : a person who does wrong and esp. moral wrong — **wrong·do·ing** \-ˌdü-iŋ\ *n*

wrong·ful \'rȯŋ-fəl\ *adj* **1** : WRONG, UNJUST **2** : UNLAWFUL ⟨~ conduct⟩ — **wrong·ful·ly** *adv* — **wrong·ful·ness** *n*

wrong·head·ed \-'he-dəd\ *adj* : stubborn in clinging to wrong opinion or principles — **wrong·head·ed·ly** *adv* — **wrong·head·ed·ness** *n*

wrote *past of* WRITE

wroth \'rȯth, 'rōth\ *adj* : filled with wrath : ANGRY

wrought \'rȯt\ *adj* [ME, fr. pp. of *worken* to work] **1** : FASHIONED, FORMED ⟨carefully ~ essays⟩ **2** : ORNAMENTED **3** : beaten into shape by tools : HAMMERED ⟨~ metals⟩ **4** : deeply stirred : EXCITED ⟨gets easily ~ up⟩

wrung *past and past part of* WRING

wry \'rī\ *adj* **wry·er** \'rī-ər\; **wry·est** \'rī-əst\ **1** : having a bent or twisted shape ⟨a ~ smile⟩; *also* : turned abnormally to one side : CONTORTED ⟨a ~ neck⟩ **2** : cleverly and often ironically humorous — **wry·ly** *adv* — **wry·ness** *n*

wry·neck \'rī-ˌnek\ *n* **1** : either of two Old World woodpeckers that differ from typical woodpeckers in having a peculiar manner of twisting the head and neck **2** : an abnormal twisting of the neck and head to one side caused by muscle spasms

WSW *abbr* west-southwest

wt *abbr* weight

wurst \'wərst, 'wu̇rst\ *n* : SAUSAGE

wu·shu \'wü-'shü\ *n* [Chin (Beijing) *wǔshù*, fr. *wǔ* martial + *shù* art] : Chinese martial arts

wuss \'wu̇s\ *n* : WIMP — **wussy** \'wu̇-sē\ *adj*

WV *or* **W Va** *abbr* West Virginia

WW *abbr* World War

w/w *abbr* wall-to-wall

WY *or* **Wyo** *abbr* Wyoming

WYS·I·WYG \'wi-zē-ˌwig\ *adj* [*what you see is what you get*] : of, relating to, or being a computer display that shows a document exactly as it will appear when printed out

¹x \'eks\ *n, pl* **x's** *or* **xs** \'ek-səz\ *often cap*
  1 : the 24th letter of the English alphabet
  2 : an unknown quantity
²x *vb* **x-ed** *also* **x'd** *or* **xed** \'ekst\; **x-ing** *or*
  x'ing \'ek-siŋ\ : to cancel or obliterate
  with a series of *x*'s — usu. used with *out*
³x *abbr* **1** ex **2** experimental **3** extra
⁴x *symbol* **1** times ⟨3 x 2 is 6⟩ **2** by ⟨a 3 x
  5 index card⟩ **3** *often cap* power of magnification
Xan·a·du \'za-nə-ˌdü, -ˌdyü\ *n* [fr. *Xanadu*,
  locality in *Kubla Khan* (1798), poem by
  Eng. poet Samuel Taylor Coleridge †1834]
  : an idyllic, exotic, or luxurious place
Xan·thip·pe \zan-'thi-pē, -'ti-\ *or* **Xan·tip·pe**
  \-'ti-pē\ *n* [Gk *Xanthippē*, shrewish
  wife of Socrates] : an ill-tempered woman
x–ax·is \'eks-ˌak-səs\ *n* : the axis of a graph
  or of a system of coordinates in a plane
  parallel to which abscissas are measured
X–C *abbr* cross-country
X chromosome *n* : a sex chromosome
  that usu. occurs paired in each female
  cell and single in each male cell in organisms
  (as humans) in which the male normally
  has two unlike sex chromosomes
Xe *symbol* xenon
xe·non \'zē-ˌnän, 'ze-\ *n* [Gk, neut. of *xenos*
  strange] : a heavy gaseous chemical element
  occurring in minute quantities in air
xe·no·pho·bia \ˌze-nə-'fō-bē-ə, ˌzē-\ *n*
  : fear and hatred of strangers or foreigners
  or of what is strange or foreign — **xe·no·phobe**
  \'ze-nə-ˌfōb, 'zē-\ *n* — **xe·no·pho·bic** \ˌze-nə-'fō-bik, ˌzē-\ *adj*
xe·ric \'zir-ik, 'zer-\ *adj* : characterized by
  or requiring only a small amount of
  moisture ⟨a ~ habitat⟩
xeri·scape \'zir-ə-ˌskāp, 'zer-\ *n, often
  cap* : a landscaping method utilizing water-conserving
  techniques
xe·rog·ra·phy \zə-'rä-grə-fē\ *n* : a process
  for copying printed matter by the action
  of light on an electrically charged surface
  in which the latent image is developed
  with a powder — **xe·ro·graph·ic** \ˌzir-ə-'gra-fik\ *adj*
xe·ro·phyte \'zir-ə-ˌfīt\ *n* : a plant adapted
  for growth with a limited water supply
  — **xe·ro·phyt·ic** \ˌzir-ə-'fi-tik\ *adj*
xi \'zī, 'ksī\ *n* : the 14th letter of the Greek
  alphabet — Ξ or ξ
XL *abbr* **1** extra large **2** extra long
Xmas \'kris-məs *also* 'eks-məs\ *n* [*X* (symbol
  for *Christ*, fr. the Gk letter chi (X),
  initial of *Christos* Christ) + *-mas* (in
  Christmas)] : CHRISTMAS
XML \ˌeks-(ˌ)em-'el\ *n* : a markup language
  that indicates the structural type
  of data
XO *abbr* executive officer
x–ra·di·a·tion \ˌeks-ˌrā-dē-'ā-shən\ *n, often
  cap* **1** : exposure to X-rays **2** : radiation
  consisting of X-rays
x–ray \'eks-ˌrā\ *vb, often cap* : to examine,
  treat, or photograph with X-rays
X–ray \'eks-ˌrā\ *n* **1** : a radiation with an
  extremely short wavelength of less than
  100 angstroms that is able to penetrate
  through various thicknesses of solids and
  to act on photographic film **2** : a photograph
  taken with X-rays — **X–ray** *adj*
XS *abbr* extra small
xu \'sü\ *n, pl* **xu** — see *dong* at MONEY
  table
xy·lem \'zī-ləm, -ˌlem\ *n* : a woody tissue
  of vascular plants that transports water
  and dissolved materials upward, functions
  in support and storage, and lies central
  to the phloem
xy·lo·phone \'zī-lə-ˌfōn\ *n* [Gk *xylon*
  wood + *phōnē* voice, sound] : a musical
  instrument consisting of a series of wooden
  bars graduated in length to produce
  the musical scale, supported on belts of
  straw or felt, and sounded by striking
  with two small wooden hammers — **xy·lo·phon·ist** \-ˌfō-nist\ *n*

¹y \'wī\ *n, pl* **y's** *or* **ys** \'wīz\ *often cap* : the
  25th letter of the English alphabet
²y *abbr* **1** yard **2** year
¹Y \'wī\ *n* : YMCA, YWCA
²Y *symbol* yttrium
¹-y *also* **-ey** \ē\ *adj suffix* **1** : characterized
  by : full of ⟨dirt*y*⟩ ⟨clay*ey*⟩ **2** : having the
  character of : composed of ⟨ic*y*⟩ **3** : like
  : like that of ⟨hom*ey*⟩ ⟨wintr*y*⟩ ⟨stag*y*⟩
  4 : tending or inclined to ⟨sleep*y*⟩ ⟨chatt*y*⟩
  5 : giving occasion for (specified) action
  ⟨tear*y*⟩ **6** : performing (specified) action
  ⟨curl*y*⟩
²-y \ē\ *n suffix, pl* **-ies** **1** : state : condition
  : quality ⟨beggar*y*⟩ **2** : activity, place of
  business, or goods dealt with ⟨laundr*y*⟩ **3**
  : whole body or group ⟨soldier*y*⟩
³-y *n suffix, pl* **-ies** : instance of a (specified)
  action ⟨entreat*y*⟩ ⟨inquir*y*⟩
YA *abbr* young adult
¹yacht \'yät\ *n* [obs. D *jaght*, fr. Middle
  Low German *jacht*, short for *jachtschip*,
  lit., hunting ship] : a usu. large recreational
  watercraft
²yacht *vb* : to race or cruise in a yacht

yacht·ing \'yä-tiŋ\ n : the sport of racing or cruising in a yacht

yachts·man \'yäts-mən\ n : a person who owns or sails a yacht

ya·hoo \'yä-hü, 'yä-\ n, pl **yahoos** [fr. *Yahoo*, one of a race of brutes having the form of men in Jonathan Swift's *Gulliver's Travels*] : a boorish, crass, or stupid person

Yah·weh \'yä-,wā\ also **Yah·veh** \-,vā\ n : GOD 1 — used esp. by the Hebrews

¹**yak** \'yak\ n, pl **yaks** also **yak** : a large long-haired wild or domesticated ox of Tibet and adjacent Asian uplands

²**yak** also **yack** \'yak\ n : persistent or voluble talk — **yak** also **yack** vb

yam \'yam\ n 1 : the edible starchy root of various twining plants used as a staple food in tropical areas; also : a plant that produces yams 2 : a usu. deep orange sweet potato

yam·mer \'ya-mər\ vb [ME *yameren*, alter. of *yomeren* to murmur, be sad, fr. OE *gēomrian*] 1 : WHIMPER 2 : CHATTER — **yammer** n

¹**yank** \'yaŋk\ vb : to pull with a quick vigorous movement

²**yank** n : a strong sudden pull : JERK

Yank \'yaŋk\ n : YANKEE

Yan·kee \'yaŋ-kē\ n 1 : a native or inhabitant of New England; also : a native or inhabitant of the northern U.S. 2 : AMERICAN

yan·qui \'yäŋ-kē\ n, often cap [Sp] : a citizen of the U.S. as distinguished from a Latin American

¹**yap** \'yap\ vb **yapped**; **yap·ping** 1 : BARK, YELP 2 : GAB

²**yap** n 1 : a quick sharp bark 2 : CHATTER

¹**yard** \'yärd\ n [ME, fr. OE *geard* enclosure, yard] 1 : a small enclosed area open to the sky and adjacent to a building 2 : the grounds of a building 3 : the grounds surrounding a house usu. covered with grass 4 : an enclosure for livestock 5 : an area set aside for a particular business or activity 6 : a system of railroad tracks for storing cars and making up trains

²**yard** n [ME *yarde*, fr. OE *gierd* twig, measure, yard] 1 — see WEIGHT table 2 : a long spar tapered toward the ends that supports and spreads the head of a sail — **the whole nine yards** : all of a set of circumstances, conditions, or details

yard·age \'yär-dij\ n : an aggregate number of yards; also : the length, extent, or volume of something as measured in yards

yard·arm \'yärd-,ärm\ n : either end of the yard of a square-rigged ship

yard·man \-mən, -,man\ n : a person employed in or about a yard

yard·mas·ter \-,mas-tər\ n : the person in charge of a railroad yard

yard·stick \-,stik\ n 1 : a graduated measuring stick three feet long 2 : a standard for making a critical judgment : CRITERION ♦ *Synonyms* GAUGE, TOUCHSTONE, BENCHMARK, MEASURE

yar·mul·ke \'yä-mə-kə, 'yär-, -məl-\ n [Yiddish *yarmlke*] : a skullcap worn esp.

by Jewish males in the synagogue and the home

yarn \'yärn\ n 1 : a continuous often plied strand composed of fibers or filaments and used in weaving and knitting to form cloth 2 : STORY; esp : a tall tale

yar·row \'ya-rō\ n : a strong-scented herb related to the daisies that has white or pink flowers in flat clusters

yaw \'yó\ vb : to deviate erratically from a course ⟨the ship ∼ed in the heavy seas⟩ — **yaw** n

yawl \'yól\ n : a 2-masted sailboat with the shorter mast aft of the rudder

¹**yawn** \'yón\ vb : to open wide; esp : to open the mouth wide and take a deep breath usu. as an involuntary reaction to fatigue or boredom — **yawn·er** n

²**yawn** n : the act of yawning

yawp or **yaup** \'yóp\ vb 1 : to make a raucous noise : SQUAWK 2 : CLAMOR, COMPLAIN — **yawp·er** n

yaws \'yóz\ n pl : a contagious tropical disease caused by a spirochete closely resembling the causative agent of syphilis and marked by skin lesions

y-ax·is \'wī-,ak-səs\ n : the axis of a graph or of a system of coordinates in a plane parallel to which the ordinates are measured

Yb symbol ytterbium

YB abbr yearbook

Y chromosome n : a sex chromosome that is characteristic of male cells in organisms (as humans) in which the male typically has two unlike sex chromosomes

yd abbr yard

¹**ye** \'yē\ pron : YOU 1

²**ye** \yē, yə, originally same as THE\ *definite article, archaic* : THE — used by early printers to represent the manuscript word þe (the)

¹**yea** \'yā\ adv 1 : YES — used in oral voting 2 : INDEED, TRULY

²**yea** n : an affirmative vote; also : a person casting such a vote

yeah \'yeə, 'yaə\ adv : YES

year \'yir\ n 1 : the period of about 365¼ solar days required for one revolution of the earth around the sun; also : the time in which a planet completes a revolution about the sun 2 : a cycle of 365 or 366 days beginning with January 1; also : a calendar year specified usu. by a number 3 pl : a time of special significance ⟨their glory ∼s⟩ 4 pl : AGE ⟨advanced in ∼s⟩ 5 : a period of time other than a calendar year ⟨the school ∼⟩

year·book \-,búk\ n 1 : a book published annually esp. as a report 2 : a school publication recording the history and activities of a graduating class

year·ling \'yir-liŋ, 'yir-lən\ n 1 : one that is a year old 2 : a racehorse between January of the year after the year in which it was born and the next January

year·long \'yir-'lóŋ\ adj : lasting through a year

¹**year·ly** \'yir-lē\ adj : ANNUAL

²**yearly** adv : every year

yearn \'yərn\ vb 1 : to feel a longing or

craving ⟨~*ing* for freedom⟩ **2** : to feel tenderness or compassion ♦ *Synonyms* LONG, PINE, HANKER, HUNGER, THIRST

yearn·ing *n* : a tender or urgent longing

year–round \'yir-'raund\ *adj* : effective, employed, or operating for the full year : not seasonal ⟨a ~ resort⟩

yeast \'yēst\ *n* **1** : a surface froth or a sediment in sugary liquids (as fruit juices) that consists largely of cells of a tiny fungus and is used in making alcoholic liquors and as a leaven in baking **2** : a commercial product containing yeast fungi in a moist or dry medium **3** : a minute one-celled fungus present and functionally active in yeast that reproduces by budding; *also* : any of several similar fungi **4** *archaic* : the foam of waves : SPUME **5** : something that causes ferment or activity

yeast infection *n* : infection of the vagina with an excess growth of a normally present fungus that resembles a yeast

yeasty \'yē-stē\ *adj* **yeast·i·er; -est 1** : of, relating to, or resembling yeast **2** : UNSETTLED **3** : full of vitality ⟨~ youths⟩; *also* : FRIVOLOUS

yegg \'yeg\ *n* : one that breaks open safes to steal; *also* : ROBBER

¹yell \'yel\ *vb* : to utter a loud cry or scream : SHOUT — **yell·er** *n*

²yell *n* **1** : SHOUT **2** : a cheer used esp. to encourage an athletic team (as at a college)

¹yel·low \'ye-lō\ *adj* **1** : of the color yellow **2** : having a yellow complexion or skin **3** : SENSATIONAL ⟨~ journalism⟩ **4** : COWARDLY ⟨was too ~ to fight⟩ — **yel·low·ish** \'ye-lə-wish\ *adj*

²yellow *n* **1** : a color between green and orange in the spectrum : the color of ripe lemons or sunflowers **2** : something yellow; *esp* : the yolk of an egg **3** *pl* : any of several plant diseases marked by stunted growth and yellowing of foliage

³yellow *vb* : to make or turn yellow

yellow birch *n* : a No. American birch with thin lustrous gray or yellow bark; *also* : its strong hard wood

yellow fever *n* : an acute infectious viral disease marked by prostration, jaundice, fever, and often hemorrhage and transmitted by a mosquito

yellow jack *n* : YELLOW FEVER

yellow jacket *n* : any of various small social wasps having the body barred with bright yellow

yel·low·tail \'ye-lō-ˌtāl\ *n* : any of various fishes with a yellow or yellowish tail including several valuable food fishes

yelp \'yelp\ *vb* [ME, to boast, cry out, fr. OE *gielpan* to boast, exult] : to utter a sharp quick shrill cry — **yelp** *n*

Ye·me·ni \'ye-mə-nē\ *n* : YEMENITE — **Yemeni** *adj*

Ye·men·ite \'ye-mə-ˌnīt\ *n* : a native or inhabitant of Yemen — **Yemenite** *adj*

¹yen \'yen\ *n, pl* **yen** — see MONEY table

²yen *n* [obs. E argot *yen-yen* craving for opium, fr. Chin (Guangdong dial.) *yīn-yáhn*, fr. *yīn* opium + *yáhn* craving] : a strong desire : LONGING ⟨a ~ to travel⟩

yeo·man \'yō-mən\ *n* **1** : an attendant or officer in a royal or noble household **2** : a naval petty officer who performs clerical duties **3** : a person who owns and cultivates a small farm; *esp* : one of a class of English freeholders below the gentry — **yeo·man·ly** \-lē\ *adj*

yeo·man·ry \-rē\ *n* : the body of yeomen and esp. of small landed proprietors

-yer — see -ER

¹yes \'yes\ *adv* — used as a function word esp. to express assent or agreement or to introduce a more emphatic or explicit phrase

²yes *n* : an affirmative reply

ye·shi·va *also* **ye·shi·vah** \yə-'shē-və\ *n, pl* **yeshivas** *or* **ye·shi·voth** \-ˌshē-'vōt, -'vōth\ : a Jewish school esp. for religious instruction

yes–man \'yes-ˌman\ *n* : a person who endorses uncritically every opinion or proposal of a superior

¹yes·ter·day \'yes-tər-dē, -ˌdā\ *adv* **1** : on the day preceding today **2** : only a short time ago

²yesterday *n* **1** : the day last past **2** : time not long past

yes·ter·year \'yes-tər-ˌyir\ *n* **1** : last year **2** : the recent past

¹yet \'yet\ *adv* **1** : in addition : BESIDES; *also* : EVEN **2** : up to now; *also* : STILL **3** : so soon as now ⟨not time to go ~⟩ **4** : EVENTUALLY **5** : NEVERTHELESS, HOWEVER

²yet *conj* : but nevertheless : BUT

ye·ti \'ye-tē, 'yā-\ *n* : ABOMINABLE SNOWMAN

yew \'yü\ *n* **1** : any of a genus of evergreen trees and shrubs with dark stiff poisonous needles and fleshy fruits **2** : the wood of a yew; *esp* : that of an Old World yew

Yid·dish \'yi-dish\ *n* [Yiddish *yidish*, short for *yidish daytsh*, lit., Jewish German] : a language derived from medieval German and spoken by Jews esp. of eastern European origin — **Yiddish** *adj*

¹yield \'yēld\ *vb* **1** : to give as fitting, owed, or required **2** : GIVE UP; *esp* : to give up possession of on claim or demand **3** : to bear as a natural product **4** : PRODUCE, SUPPLY **5** : to bring in : RETURN **6** : to give way (as to force or influence) **7** : to give place ♦ *Synonyms* RELINQUISH, CEDE, WAIVE, SURRENDER

²yield *n* : something yielded; *esp* : the amount or quantity produced or returned

yield·ing \'yēl-diŋ\ *adj* **1** : not rigid or stiff : FLEXIBLE **2** : SUBMISSIVE, COMPLIANT

yikes \'yīks\ *interj* — used to express fear or astonishment

yip \'yip\ *vb* **yipped; yip·ping** : YAP

YK *abbr* Yukon Territory

YMCA \ˌwī-ˌem-(ˌ)sē-'ā\ *n* : Young Men's Christian Association

YMHA \ˌwī-ˌem-ˌāch-'ā\ *n* : Young Men's Hebrew Association

yo \'yō\ *interj* — used to call attention, indicate attentiveness, or express affirmation

YOB *abbr* year of birth

yo·del \'yō-dᵊl\ *vb* **yo·deled** *or* **yo·delled; yo·del·ing** *or* **yo·del·ling** : to sing by suddenly changing from chest voice to falsetto and back; *also* : to shout or call in this manner — **yodel** *n* — **yo·del·er** *n*

yo·ga \'yō-gə\ n [Skt., lit., yoking, fr. *yunakti* he yokes] **1** cap : a Hindu theistic philosophy teaching the suppression of all activity of body, mind, and will in order that the self may realize its distinction from them and attain liberation **2** : a system of exercises for attaining bodily or mental control and well-being — **yo·gic** \-gik\ adj, often cap

yo·gi \'yō-gē\ also **yo·gin** \-gən, -ˌgin\ n **1** : a person who practices yoga **2** cap : an adherent of Yoga philosophy

yo·gurt also **yo·ghurt** \'yō-gərt\ n [Turk *yoğurt*] : a soured slightly acid often flavored semisolid food made of milk and milk solids to which cultures of bacteria have been added

¹**yoke** \'yōk\ n, pl **yokes 1** : a wooden bar or frame by which two draft animals (as oxen) are coupled at the heads or necks for working together; also : a frame fitted to a person's shoulders to carry a load in two equal portions **2** : a clamp that embraces two parts to hold or unite them in position **3** pl usu **yoke** : two animals yoked together **4** : SERVITUDE, BONDAGE **5** : TIE, LINK ⟨the ~ of matrimony⟩ **6** : a fitted or shaped piece esp. at the shoulder of a garment ♦ **Synonyms** COUPLE, PAIR, BRACE

²**yoke** vb **yoked; yok·ing 1** : to put a yoke on : couple with a yoke **2** : to attach a draft animal to ⟨~ a plow⟩ **3** : JOIN; esp : MARRY

yo·kel \'yō-kəl\ n : a naive or gullible country person

yolk \'yōk\ n **1** : the yellow rounded inner mass of the egg of a bird or reptile **2** : the stored food material of an egg that supplies nutrients (as proteins and cholesterol) to the developing embryo — **yolked** \'yōkt\ adj

Yom Kip·pur \'yōm-ki-ˈpu̇r, ˌyäm-, -ˈkipər\ n [Heb *yōm kippūr*, lit., day of atonement] : a Jewish holiday observed in September or October with fasting and prayer as a day of atonement

¹**yon** \'yän\ adj : YONDER

²**yon** adv **1** : YONDER **2** : THITHER ⟨ran hither and ~⟩

¹**yon·der** \'yän-dər\ adv : at or to that place

²**yonder** adj **1** : more distant ⟨the ~ side of the river⟩ **2** : being at a distance within view ⟨~ hills⟩

yore \'yȯr\ n [ME, fr. *yore*, adv., long ago, fr. OE *geāra*, fr. *gēar* year] : time long past ⟨in days of ~⟩

York·ie \'yȯr-kē\ n : YORKSHIRE TERRIER

York·shire terrier \'yȯrk-ˌshir-, -shər-\ n : any of a breed of compact toy terriers with long straight silky hair

you \'yü\ pron **1** : the person or persons addressed ⟨~ are a nice person⟩ ⟨~ are nice people⟩ **2** : ONE 2 ⟨~ turn this knob to open it⟩

¹**young** \'yəŋ\ adj **youn·ger** \'yəŋ-gər\; **youn·gest** \'yəŋ-gəst\ **1** : being in the first or an early stage of life, growth, or development **2** : having little experience **3** : recently come into being **4** : YOUTHFUL **5** cap : belonging to or representing a new or revived usu. political group or movement — **young·ish** \'yəŋ-ish\ adj

²**young** n, pl **young** : young persons; also : young animals

young·ling \'yəŋ-liŋ\ n : one that is young — **youngling** adj

young·ster \-stər\ n **1** : a young person **2** : CHILD

your \'yu̇r, 'yȯr, yər\ adj : of or relating to you or yourself

yours \'yu̇rz, 'yȯrz\ pron : one or the ones belonging to you

your·self \yər-ˈself\ pron, pl **yourselves** \-ˈselvz\ : YOU — used reflexively, for emphasis, or in absolute constructions ⟨you'll hurt ~⟩ ⟨do it ~⟩

youth \'yüth\ n, pl **youths** \'yüthz, 'yüths\ **1** : the period of life between childhood and maturity **2** : a young man; also : young persons **3** : YOUTHFULNESS

youth·ful \'yüth-fəl\ adj **1** : of, relating to, or appropriate to youth **2** : being young and not yet mature **3** : FRESH, VIGOROUS ⟨~ fervor⟩ — **youth·ful·ly** adv — **youth·ful·ness** n

youth hostel n : HOSTEL 2

yowl \'yau̇(-ə)l\ vb : to utter a loud long mournful cry : WAIL — **yowl** n

yo–yo \'yō-(ˌ)yō\ n, pl **yo–yos** [prob. fr. Ilocano (a Philippine language) *yóyó*] : a thick grooved double disk with a string attached to its center that is made to fall and rise to the hand by unwinding and rewinding on the string — **yo–yo** vb

yr abbr **1** year **2** your

yrbk abbr yearbook

YT abbr Yukon Territory

yt·ter·bi·um \i-ˈtər-bē-əm\ n : a rare metallic chemical element

yt·tri·um \'i-trē-əm\ n : a rare metallic chemical element

yu·an \'yü-ən, yü-ˈän\ n, pl **yuan 1** — see MONEY table **2** : the dollar of the Republic of China (Taiwan)

yuc·ca \'yə-kə\ n : any of a genus of plants related to the agaves that grow esp. in warm dry regions and bear large clusters of white cup-shaped flowers atop a long stiff stalk

yuck also **yuk** \'yək\ interj — used to express rejection or disgust

yule \'yül\ n, often cap : CHRISTMAS

Yule log n : a large log formerly put on the hearth on Christmas Eve as the foundation of the fire

yule·tide \'yül-ˌtīd\ n, often cap : CHRISTMASTIDE

yum·my \'yə-mē\ adj **yum·mi·er; -est** : highly attractive or pleasing

yup·pie \'yə-pē\ n [prob. fr. *y*oung *u*rban *p*rofessional + *-ie* (as in hippi*e*)] : a young college-educated adult employed in a well-paying profession and living and working in or near a large city — **yup·pie·dom** \-dəm\ n

yurt \'yu̇rt\ n : a light round tent of skins or felt stretched over a lattice framework used by pastoral peoples of inner Asia

YWCA \ˌwī-ˌdə-bəl-yü-(ˌ)sē-ˈā\ n : Young Women's Christian Association

YWHA \-ˌāch-ˈā\ n : Young Women's Hebrew Association

¹z \'zē\ *n, pl* z's *or* zs \'zēz\ *often cap* : the 26th letter of the English alphabet

²z *abbr* 1 zero 2 zone

Z *symbol* atomic number

Zach *abbr* Zacharias

Zach·a·ri·as \ˌza-kə-'rī-əs\ *n* : ZECHARI-AH

¹za·ny \'zā-nē\ *n, pl* zanies [It *zanni*, a traditional masked clown, fr. It dial. *Zanni*, nickname for It *Giovanni* John] 1 : CLOWN, BUFFOON 2 : a silly or foolish person

²zany *adj* za·ni·er; -est 1 : characteristic of a zany 2 : CRAZY, FOOLISH ⟨a ~ movie⟩ — za·ni·ly \'zā-nə-lē\ *adv* — za·ni·ness \'zā-nē-nəs\ *n*

zap \'zap\ *vb* zapped; zap·ping 1 : DE-STROY, KILL 2 : to heat or cook in a microwave oven ⟨*zapped* the soup⟩

zeal \'zēl\ *n* : eager and ardent interest in the pursuit of something : FERVOR
♦ **Synonyms** ENTHUSIASM, PASSION, ARDOR

zeal·ot \'ze-lət\ *n* : a zealous person; *esp* : a fanatical partisan ⟨a religious ~⟩
♦ **Synonyms** ENTHUSIAST, BIGOT

zeal·ous \'ze-ləs\ *adj* : filled with, characterized by, or due to zeal — zeal·ous·ly *adv* — zeal·ous·ness *n*

ze·bra \'zē-brə\ *n, pl* zebras *also* zebra : any of several African mammals related to the horse but conspicuously striped with black or dark brown and white or buff

zebra mussel *n* : a freshwater Eurasian mollusk introduced into U.S. waterways where it colonizes and clogs water intake pipes

ze·bu \'zē-bü, -byü\ *n* : any of various breeds of domestic oxen developed in India that have a large fleshy hump over the shoulders, a dewlap, drooping ears, and marked resistance to heat and to insect attack

Zech *abbr* Zechariah

Zech·a·ri·ah \ˌze-kə-'rī-ə\ *n* — see BIBLE table

zed \'zed\ *n, chiefly Brit* : the letter z

zeit·geist \'tsīt-ˌgīst, 'zīt-\ *n* [G, fr. *Zeit* time + *Geist* spirit] : the general intellectual, moral, and cultural state of an era

Zen \'zen\ *n* : a Japanese Buddhist sect that teaches self-discipline, meditation, and attainment of enlightenment through direct intuitive insight

ze·na·na \zə-'nä-nə\ *n* : HAREM

ze·nith \'zē-nəth\ *n* 1 : the point in the heavens directly overhead 2 : the highest point : ACME ⟨the ~ of her career⟩
♦ **Synonyms** CULMINATION, PINNACLE, APEX

ze·o·lite \'zē-ə-ˌlīt\ *n* : any of various feldsparlike silicates used esp. as water softeners

Zeph *abbr* Zephaniah

Zeph·a·ni·ah \ˌze-fə-'nī-ə\ *n* — see BIBLE table

zeph·yr \'ze-fər\ *n* : a breeze from the west; *also* : a gentle breeze

zep·pe·lin \'ze-plən, -pə-lən\ *n* [Count Ferdinand von *Zeppelin* †1917 Ger. airship manufacturer] : a cylindrical rigid blimplike airship

¹ze·ro \'zē-rō, 'zir-ō\ *n, pl* zeros *also* ze·roes [ultim. fr. Ar *ṣifr*] 1 : the numerical symbol 0 2 : the number represented by the symbol 0 3 : the point at which the graduated degrees or measurements on a scale (as of a thermometer) begin 4 : the lowest point

²zero *adj* 1 : of, relating to, or being a zero 2 : having no magnitude or quantity 3 : ABSENT, LACKING; *esp* : having no modified inflectional form

³zero *vb* : to adjust the sights of a firearm to hit the point aimed at — usu. used with *in*

zero hour *n* : the time at which an event (as a military operation) is scheduled to begin

zest \'zest\ *n* 1 : a quality of enhancing enjoyment : PIQUANCY 2 : keen enjoyment : GUSTO ⟨a ~ for life⟩ — zest·ful \-fəl\ *adj* — zest·ful·ly *adv* — zest·ful·ness *n* — zesty \'zes-tē\ *adj*

ze·ta \'zā-tə, 'zē-\ *n* : the 6th letter of the Greek alphabet — Z or ζ

zi·do·vu·dine \zi-'dō-vyü-ˌdēn\ *n* : AZT

¹zig·zag \'zig-ˌzag\ *n* : one of a series of short sharp turns, angles, or alterations in a course; *also* : something marked by such a series

²zigzag *adv* : in or by a zigzag path

³zigzag *adj* : having short sharp turns or angles

⁴zigzag *vb* zig·zagged; zig·zag·ging : to form into or proceed along a zigzag

zil·lion \'zil-yən\ *n* : a large indeterminate number

zinc \'zink\ *n* : a bluish-white metallic chemical element that is commonly found in minerals and is used esp. in alloys and as a protective coating for iron and steel

zinc oxide *n* : a white solid used esp. as a pigment, in compounding rubber, and in ointments and sunblocks

zine \'zēn\ *n* : a noncommercial publication usu. devoted to specialized subject matter

zin·fan·del \'zin-fən-ˌdel\ *n, often cap* : a dry red table wine made chiefly in California

zing \'zin\ *n* 1 : a shrill humming noise 2 : VITALITY 4 — zing *vb*

zing·er \'zin-ər\ *n* : a pointed witty remark or retort

zin·nia \'zi-nē-ə, 'zēn-yə\ *n* : any of a genus of tropical American herbs or low shrubs related to the daisies and widely grown for their showy long-lasting flowers

Zi·on \'zī-ən\ *n* 1 : the Jewish people 2 : the Jewish homeland as a symbol of Judaism or of Jewish national aspiration 3 : HEAVEN 4 : UTOPIA

Zi·on·ism \'zī-ə-,ni-zəm\ *n* : an international movement orig. for the establishment of a Jewish national or religious community in Palestine and later for the support of modern Israel — **Zi·on·ist** \-nist\ *adj or n*

¹**zip** \'zip\ *vb* **zipped; zip·ping** : to move, act, or function with speed or vigor

²**zip** *n* 1 : a sudden sharp hissing sound 2 : ENERGY, VIM ⟨the performance lacked ∼⟩

³**zip** *n* : NOTHING, ZERO ⟨the score was 27 to ∼⟩

⁴**zip** *vb* **zipped; zip·ping** : to close or open with a zipper

zip code *n, often cap Z&I&P* [*zone improvement plan*] : a number that identifies each postal delivery area in the U.S.

zip line *n* : a cable suspended usu. over an incline to which a rider is harnessed

zip·per \'zi-pər\ *n* : a fastener consisting of two rows of metal or plastic teeth on strips of tape and a sliding piece that closes an opening by drawing the teeth together

zip·py \'zi-pē\ *adj* **zip·pi·er; -est** 1 : very speedy ⟨a ∼ car⟩ 2 : strikingly appealing ⟨∼ clothes⟩

zir·con \'zər-,kän\ *n* : a zirconium-containing mineral transparent varieties of which are used as gems

zir·co·ni·um \,zər-'kō-nē-əm\ *n* : a gray corrosion-resistant metallic chemical element used esp. in alloys and ceramics

zit \'zit\ *n* : PIMPLE

zith·er \'zi-thər, -thər\ *n* : a musical instrument having 30 to 40 strings played with plectrum and fingers

zi·ti \'zē-tē\ *n, pl* **ziti** [It] : medium-size tubular pasta

zlo·ty \'zlȯ-tē\ *n, pl* **zlo·tys** \-tēz\ *or* **zloty** — see MONEY table

Zn *symbol* zinc

zo·di·ac \'zō-dē-,ak\ *n* [ME, fr. AF, fr. L *zodiacus*, fr. Gk *zōidiakos*, fr. *zōidion* carved figure, sign of the zodiac, fr. dim. of *zōion* living being, figure] 1 : an imaginary belt in the heavens that encompasses the paths of most of the planets and that is divided into 12 constellations or signs 2 : a figure representing the signs of the zodiac and their symbols — **zo·di·a·cal** \zō-'dī-ə-kəl\ *adj*

zom·bie *also* **zom·bi** \'zäm-bē\ *n* : a person who is believed to have died and been brought back to life without speech or free will

zon·al \'zō-nᵊl\ *adj* : of, relating to, or having the form of a zone — **zon·al·ly** *adv*

¹**zone** \'zōn\ *n* [ME, fr. AF, fr. L *zona* belt, zone, fr. Gk *zōnē*] 1 : any of five great divisions of the earth's surface made according to latitude and temperature including the torrid zone, two temperate zones, and two frigid zones 2 : something that forms an encircling band ⟨a ∼ of tissue⟩ 3 : a region or area set off as distinct from surrounding parts ⟨business ∼⟩ ⟨postal ∼⟩

²**zone** *vb* **zoned; zon·ing** 1 : ENCIRCLE 2 : to arrange in or mark off into zones; *esp* : to divide (as a city) into sections reserved for different purposes

zonked \'zäŋkt\ *adj* : being or acting as if under the influence of alcohol or a drug : HIGH

zoo \'zü\ *n, pl* **zoos** : a park where wild animals are kept for exhibition

zoo·ge·og·ra·phy \,zō-ə-jē-'ä-grə-fē\ *n* : a branch of biogeography concerned with the geographical distribution of animals — **zoo·ge·og·ra·pher** \-fər\ *n* — **zoo·geo·graph·ic** \-jē-ə-'gra-fik\ *also* **zoo·geo·graph·i·cal** \-fi-kəl\ *adj*

zoo·keep·er \'zü-,kē-pər\ *n* : a person who cares for animals in a zoo

zool *abbr* zoological; zoology

zoological garden *n* : ZOO

zo·ol·o·gy \zō-'ä-lə-jē\ *n* : a branch of biology that deals with the classification and the properties and vital phenomena of animals — **zo·o·log·i·cal** \,zō-ə-'lä-ji-kəl\ *adj* — **zo·ol·o·gist** \zō-'ä-lə-jist\ *n*

zoom \'züm\ *vb* 1 : to move with a loud hum or buzz 2 : to gain altitude quickly 3 : to focus a camera or microscope using a special lens that permits the apparent distance of the object to be varied — **zoom** *n*

zoom lens *n* : a camera lens in which the image size can be varied continuously while the image remains in focus

zoo·mor·phic \,zō-ə-'mȯr-fik\ *adj* 1 : having the form of an animal 2 : of, relating to, or being the representation of a deity in the form or with the attributes of an animal

zoo·plank·ton \,zō-ə-'plaŋk-tən, -,tän\ *n* : plankton composed of animals

zoo·spore \'zō-ə-,spȯr\ *n* : a motile spore

zoot suit \'züt-\ *n* : a flashy suit of extreme cut typically consisting of a thigh-length jacket with wide padded shoulders and pants that are wide at the top and narrow at the bottom — **zoot-suit·er** \-,sü-tər\ *n*

Zo·ro·as·tri·an·ism \,zȯr-ə-'was-trē-ə-,ni-zəm\ *n* : a religion founded by the Persian prophet Zoroaster — **Zo·ro·as·tri·an** \-trē-ən\ *adj or n*

zounds \'zaundz\ *interj* [euphemism for *God's wounds*] — used as a mild oath

zoy·sia \'zȯi-shə, -zhə, -sē-ə, -zē-ə\ *n* : any of a genus of creeping perennial grasses having fine wiry leaves and including some used as lawn grasses

ZPG *abbr* zero population growth

Zr *symbol* zirconium

zuc·chet·to \zü-'ke-tō, tsü-\ *n, pl* **-tos** [It] : a small round skullcap worn by Roman Catholic ecclesiastics

zuc·chi·ni \zü-'kē-nē\ *n, pl* **-ni** *or* **-nis** [It] : a smooth cylindrical usu. dark green summer squash; *also* : a plant that bears zucchini

Zu·lu \'zü-,lü\ *n, pl* **Zulu** *or* **Zulus** : a member of a Bantu-speaking people of

South Africa; *also* : the Bantu language of the Zulus

Zu·ni \'zü-nē\ *or* **Zu·ñi** \-nyē\ *n, pl* **Zuni** *or* **Zunis** *or* **Zuñi** *or* **Zuñis** : a member of an American Indian people of western New Mexico; *also* : the language of the Zuni people

zwie·back \'swē-,bak, 'swī-, 'zwē-, 'zwī-, -,bäk\ *n* [G, lit., twice baked, fr. *zwie-* twice + *backen* to bake] : a usu. sweetened bread that is baked and then sliced and toasted until dry and crisp

Zwing·li·an \'zwiŋ-glē-ən, 'swiŋ-, -lē-; 'tsfiŋ-lē-\ *adj* : of or relating to the Swiss religious reformer Ulrich Zwingli or his teachings — **Zwinglian** *n*

zy·de·co \'zī-də-,kō\ *n* : popular music of southern Louisiana that combines tunes of French origin with elements of Caribbean music and the blues

zy·gote \'zī-,gōt\ *n* : a cell formed by the union of two sexual cells; *also* : the developing individual produced from such a cell — **zy·got·ic** \zī-'gä-tik\ *adj*

Foreign Words & Phrases

Biographical Names

Geographical Names

FOREIGN WORDS & PHRASES

These words and phrases occur frequently enough in English context to be included in a general English dictionary, but they merit a special section because they have not become a part of the English vocabulary.

---

ab·eunt stu·dia in mo·res \'ä-be-,únt-'stü-dē-,ä-,in-'mō-,rās\ [L] : practices zealously pursued pass into habits

à bien·tôt \ä-byaⁿ-tō\ [F] : so long

ab in·cu·na·bu·lis \,äb-,in-kú-'nä-bú-,lēs\ [L] : from the cradle : from infancy

à bon chat, bon rat \ä-bōⁿ-'shä bōⁿ-'rä\ [F] : to a good cat, a good rat : retaliation in kind

à bouche ou·verte \ä-bü-shü-vert\ [F] : with open mouth : eagerly : uncritically

ab ovo us·que ad ma·la \,äb-'ō-vō-,üs-kwe-,äd-'mä-lä\ [L] : from egg to apples : from soup to nuts : from beginning to end

à bras ou·verts \ä-brä-zü-ver\ [F] : with open arms : cordially

ab·sit in·vi·dia \'äb-,sit-in-'wi-dē-,ä\ [L] : let there be no envy or ill will

ab uno dis·ce om·nes \,äb-'ü-nō-,dis-ke-'ōm-,nās\ [L] : from one learn to know all

ab ur·be con·di·ta \,äb-'ür-be-'kón-di-,tä\ [L] : from the founding of the city (Rome, founded 753 B.C.) — used by the Romans in reckoning dates

ab·usus non tol·lit usum \'ä-,bü-sús-,nōn-,tó-lit-'ü-süm\ [L] : abuse does not take away use, i.e., is not an argument against proper use

à compte \ä-'kōⁿt\ [F] : on account

à coup sûr \ä-kü-suer\ [F] : with sure stroke : surely

acte gra·tuit \äk-tə-grä-twē\ [F] : gratuitous impulsive act

ad ar·bi·tri·um \,ad-är-'bi-trē-úm\ [L] : at will : arbitrarily

ad as·tra per as·pe·ra \ad-'as-trə-,pər-'as-pə-rä\ [L] : to the stars by hard ways — motto of Kansas

ad ex·tre·mum \,äd-ek-'strä-,mùm, ,ad-ik-'strē-məm\ [L] : to the extreme : at last

ad ma·jo·rem Dei glo·ri·am \äd-mä-'yór-,em-'de-,ē-'glór-ē-,äm\ [L] : to the greater glory of God — motto of the Society of Jesus

ad pa·tres \äd-'pä-,trās\ [L] : (gathered) to his fathers : deceased

ad re·fe·ren·dum \,äd-,re-fe-'ren-dúm\ [L] : for reference : for further consideration by one having the authority to make a final decision

à droite \ä-drwät\ [F] : to or on the right hand

ad utrum·que pa·ra·tus \,äd-ù-'trùm-kwe-pä-'rä-tús\ [L] : prepared for either (event)

ad vi·vum \äd-'wē-,wùm\ [L] : to the life

ae·gri som·nia \,ī-grē-'sòm-nē-,ä\ [L] : a sick man's dreams

ae·quam ser·va·re men·tem \'ī-,kwäm-ser-,wä-rä-'men-,tem\ [L] : to preserve a calm mind

ae·quo ani·mo \,ī-,kwō-'ä-ni-,mō\ [L] : with even mind : calmly

à gauche \ä-gōsh\ [F] : to or on the left hand

age quod agis \'ä-ge-,kwòd-'ä-,gis\ [L] : do what you are doing : to the business at hand

à grands frais \ä-gräⁿ-fre\ [F] : at great expense

à huis clos \ä-w^yē-klō\ [F] : with closed doors : behind closed doors

aide-toi, le ciel t'ai·dera \ed-twä lə-'syel-te-drä\ [F] : help yourself (and) heaven will help you

aî·né \e-nā\ [F] : elder : senior (masc.)

aî·née \e-nā\ [F] : elder : senior (fem.)

à l'aban·don \ä-lä-bäⁿ-dōⁿ\ [F] : carelessly : in disorder

à la belle étoile \ä-lä-bel-ā-twäl\ [F] : under the beautiful star : in the open air at night

à la bonne heure \ä-lä-bò-nœr\ [F] : at a good time : well and good : all right

à la fran·çaise \ä-lä-fräⁿ-sez\ [F] : in the French manner

à l'amé·ri·caine \ä-lä-mä-rē-ken\ [F] : in the American manner : of the American kind

à l'an·glaise \ä-läⁿ-glez\ [F] : in the English manner

à la page \ä-lä-päzh\ [F] : at the page : up-to-the-minute

à la russe \ä-lä-rœs\ [F] : in the Russian manner

alea jac·ta est \'ä-lē-,ä-,yäk-tä-'est\ [L] : the die is cast

à l'im·pro·viste \ä-laⁿ-prò-vēst\ [F] : unexpectedly

alis vo·lat pro·pri·is \'ä-,lēs-'wò-,lät-'prō-prē-,ēs\ [L] : she flies with her own wings — motto of Oregon

al·ki \'al-,kī, -kē\ [Chinook Jargon] : by and by — motto of Washington

alo·ha oe \ä-,lō-hä-'òi, -'ō-ē\ [Hawaiian] : love to you : greetings : farewell

al·ter idem \,òl-tər-'ī-,dem, ,äl-ter-'ē-\ [L] : second self

à mer·veille \ä-mer-vā\ [F] : marvelously : wonderfully

ami·cus hu·ma·ni ge·ne·ris \ä-'mē-kùs-hü-,mä-nē-'ge-ne-ris\ [L] : friend of the human race

ami·cus us·que ad aras \-,ùs-kwe-,äd-'är-,äs\ [L] : a friend as far as to the altars, i.e., except in what is contrary to one's religion; *also* : a friend to the last extremity

ami de cour \ä-,mē-də-'kúr\ [F] : court friend : insincere friend

amor pa·tri·ae \'ä-,mór-'pä-trē-,ī\ [L] : love of one's country

amor vin·cit om·nia \'ä-,mór-,wiŋ-kit-'óm-nē-ä\ [L] : love conquers all things

an·guis in her·ba \'äŋ-gwis-in-'her-,bä\ [L] : snake in the grass

ani·mal bi·pes im·plu·me \'ä-ni-,mäl-,bi-,päs-im-'plü-me\ [L] : two-legged animal without feathers (i.e., the human race)

ani·mis opi·bus·que pa·ra·ti \'ä-ni-,mēs-,ó-pi-'bùs-kwe-pä-'rä-tē\ [L] : prepared in mind and resources — one of the mottoes of South Carolina

an·no ae·ta·tis su·ae \'ä-nō-ī-,tä-tis-'sü-,ī\ [L] : in the (specified) year of his (or her) age

an·no mun·di \,ä-nō-'mùn-dē\ [L] : in the year of the world — used in reckoning dates from the supposed period of the creation of the world, esp. as fixed by James Ussher at 4004 B.C. or by the Jews at 3761 B.C.

an·no ur·bis con·di·tae \,ä-nō-,ùr-bis-'kón-di-,tī\ [L] : in the year of the founded city : in the year that the city was founded (Rome, founded 753 B.C.)

an·nu·it coep·tis \,ä-nü-,it-'kóip-,tēs\ [L] : He (God) has approved our beginnings — motto on the reverse of the Great Seal of the United States

à peu près \ä-pœ-pre\ [F] : nearly : approximately

à pied \ä-pyä\ [F] : on foot

à point \ä-pwaⁿ\ [F] : at the right time

après moi le dé·luge \ä-pre-mwä-lə-dä-luezh\ *or* **après nous le déluge** \-ä-pre-nü-\ [F] : after me the deluge — attributed to Louis XV

à pro·pos de rien \-'ryaⁿ\ [F] : apropos of nothing

aqua et ig·ni in·ter·dic·tus \,ä-kwä-et-'ig-nē-,in-ter-'dik-tùs\ [L] : forbidden to be furnished with water and fire : outlawed

Ar·ca·des am·bo \'är-kä-,des-'äm-bō\ [L] : both Arcadians : two persons of like occupations or tastes; *also* : two rascals

ar·rec·tis au·ri·bus \ä-'rek-,tēs-'aú-ri-,bús\ [L] : with ears pricked up : attentively

ar·ri·ve·der·ci \,är-ē-vä-'der-chē\ [It] : till we meet again : farewell

ars lon·ga, vi·ta bre·vis \ärs-'lòŋ-,gä ,wē-,tä-'bre-vis\ [L] : art is long, life is short

: human life span limits all that might be accomplished

as·sa·laam alai·kum \əs-sə-'läm-ə-'li-kúm\ [Ar *as-salāmu 'alaykum*] : peace to you — used as a traditional greeting among Muslims

a ter·go \ä-'ter-(,)gō\ [L] : from behind

à tort et à tra·vers \ä-tór-ä-ä-trä-ver\ [F] : wrong and crosswise : at random : without rhyme or reason

au bout de son la·tin \ō-büd-sōⁿ-lä-taⁿ, -bü-də-\ [F] : at the end of one's Latin : at the end of one's mental resources

au con·traire \ō-kōⁿ-trer\ [F] : on the contrary

au·de·mus ju·ra nos·tra de·fen·de·re \aù-'dā-mùs-,yùr-ä-'nò-strä-dā-'fen-de-rä\ [L] : we dare defend our rights — motto of Alabama

au·den·tes for·tu·na ju·vat \aù-'den-,tās-fòr-,tü-nä-'yù-,wät\ [L] : fortune favors the bold

au·di al·te·ram par·tem \'aù-dē-,äl-te-,räm-'pär-,tem\ [L] : hear the other side

au fait \ō-fet, -fe\ [F] : to the point : fully competent : fully informed : socially correct

au fond \ō-fōⁿ\ [F] : at bottom : fundamentally

au grand sé·rieux \ō-gräⁿ-sä-ryœ\ [F] : in all seriousness

au mieux \ō-myœ\ [F] : on the best terms : on intimate terms

au pays des aveugles les borgnes sont rois \ō-pā-ē-dä-zä-vœglⁿ-lā-bórnⁿ-ə-sōⁿ-rwä\ [F] : in the country of the blind the one-eyed men are kings

au·rea me·di·o·cri·tas \'aù-rē-ä-,me-dē-'ó-kri-,täs\ [L] : the golden mean

au reste \ō-rest\ [F] : for the rest : besides

au sé·rieux \ō-sä-ryœ\ [F] : seriously

aus·si·tôt dit, aus·si·tôt fait \ō-sē-tō-dē ō-sē-tō-fe\ [F] : no sooner said than done

aut Cae·sar aut ni·hil \aùt-'kī-sär-,aùt-'ni-,hil\ [L] : either a Caesar or nothing

au·tres temps, au·tres mœurs \ō-trə-täⁿ ō-trə-mœrs\ [F] : other times, other customs

aut vin·ce·re aut mo·ri \aùt-'wiŋ-ke-rä-,aùt-'mò-,rē\ [L] : either to conquer or to die

aux armes \ō-zärm\ [F] : to arms

avant la lettre \ä-väⁿ-lä-letrⁿ\ [F] : before the letter : before a (specified) name or entity existed

ave at·que va·le \'ä-,wä-,ät-kwe-'wä-,lā\ [L] : hail and farewell

à vo·tre san·té \ä-vót-säⁿ-tä, -vó-trə-\ [F] : to your health — used as a toast

ax·is mun·di \'ak-səs-'mùn-dē\ [L] : turning point of the world : line through the earth's center around which the universe revolves

bel·la fi·gu·ra \'bel-lə-fē-'gü-rä\ [It] : fine appearance or impression

bel·lum om·ni·um con·tra om·nes \'be-

lùm-'ȯm-nē-ùm-ˌkȯn-trä-'ȯm-ˌnäs\   [L]
: war of all against all

bien en·ten·du \byaⁿ-ˌnäⁿ-täⁿ-dœ\   [F]
: well understood : of course

bien–pen·sant \byaⁿ-pä-säⁿ\ [F] : right=
minded : one who holds orthodox views

bis dat qui ci·to dat \'bis-ˌdät-kwē-'ki-tō-
ˌdät\ [L] : he gives twice who gives
promptly

bon ap·pé·tit \bȯ-nä-pā-tē\ [F] : good appetite : enjoy your meal

bon gré, mal gré \'bōⁿ-ˌgrä 'mäl-ˌgrä\ [F]
: whether with good grace or bad : willy-
nilly

bon·jour \bōⁿ-zhür\ [F] : good day : good
morning

bonne foi \bȯn-fwä\ [F] : good faith

bon·soir \bōⁿ-swär\ [F] : good evening

bru·tum ful·men \ˌbrü-tùm-'fùl-men\ [L]
: insensible thunderbolt : a futile threat
or display of force

ca·dit quae·stio \ˌkä-dit-'kwī-stē-ˌō\ [L]
: the question drops : the argument collapses

carte d'iden·ti·té \kärt-dē-däⁿ-tē-tā\ [F]
: identity card

cau·sa si·ne qua non \'kaȯ-ˌsä-ˌsi-nä-
kwä-'nōn\ [L] : an indispensable cause or
condition

ca·ve ca·nem \ˌkä-wä-'kä-ˌnem\ [L] : beware the dog

ce·dant ar·ma to·gae \'kā-ˌdänt-ˌär-mə-
'tō-ˌgī\ [L] : let arms yield to the toga : let
military power give way to civil power —
motto of Wyoming

ce n'est que le pre·mier pas qui coûte
\snek-lə-prə-myä-pä-kē-küt\ [F] : it is
only the first step that costs

c'est-à-dire \se-tä-dir\ [F] : that is to say
: namely

c'est au·tre chose \se-tōt-shōz, -tō-trə-\
[F] : that's a different thing

c'est la guerre \se-lä-ger\ [F] : that's war
: it cannot be helped

c'est la vie \se-lä-vē\ [F] : that's life
: that's how things happen

c'est plus qu'un crime, c'est une faute
\se-plue-kœⁿ-krēm se-tœn-fōt\ [F] : it is
worse than a crime, it is a blunder

ce·te·ra de·sunt \ˌkā-te-ˌrä-'dā-ˌsùnt\ [L]
: the rest is missing

cha·cun à son goût \shä-kœⁿ-nä-sōⁿ-gü\
[F] : everyone to his taste

châ·teau en Es·pagne \shä-tō-äⁿ-nes-
pänʸ\ [F] : castle in Spain : a visionary
project

cher·chez la femme \sher-shä-lä-fäm\
[F] : look for the woman

che sa·rà, sa·rà \ˌkä-sä-ˌrä sä-'rä\ [It]
: what will be, will be

che·val de ba·taille \shə-väl-də-bä-täʸ\
[F] : warhorse : argument constantly relied on : favorite subject

co·gi·to, er·go sum \'kō-gi-ˌtō ˌer-gō-
'sùm\ [L] : I think, therefore I exist

co·mé·die hu·maine \kȯ-mä-dē-œ-men\
[F] : human comedy : the whole variety
of human life

comme ci, comme ça \kȯm-sē kȯm-sä\
[F] : so-so

com·pa·gnon de voy·age \kōⁿ-pä-nyōⁿ-
də-vwä-yäzh\ [F] : traveling companion

compte ren·du \kōⁿt-rän-dœ\ [F] : report
(as of proceedings in an investigation)

con·cor·dia dis·cors \kȯn-'kȯr-dē-ä-'dis-
ˌkȯrs\ [L] : discordant harmony

con·fes·sio fi·dei \kȯn-'fe-sē-ō-'fi-dē-ˌē\
[L] : confession of faith

cor·rup·tio op·ti·mi pes·si·ma \kȯ-'rùp-
tē-ˌō-'äp-ti-ˌmē-'pe-si-ˌmä\ [L] : the corruption of the best is the worst of all

coup de maî·tre \küd-metrᵊ, kü-də-\ [F]
: masterstroke

coup d'es·sai \kü-dä-se\ [F] : experiment : trial

coûte que coûte \küt-kə-küt\ [F] : cost
what it may

cre·do quia ab·sur·dum est \ˌkrä-dō-
'kwē-ä-äp-ˌsùr-dùm-'est\ [L] : I believe it
because it is absurd

cres·cit eun·do \ˌkres-kit-'eùn-dō\ [L] : it
grows as it goes — motto of New Mexico

crise de nerfs *or* **crise des nerfs** \krēz-
də-ner\ [F] : crisis of nerves : nervous collapse : hysterical fit

cuj·us re·gio, ej·us re·li·gio \kü-yùs-'re-
gē-ˌō ˌe-yùs-re-'li-gē-ˌō\ [L] : whose region, his or her religion : subjects are to
accept the religion of their ruler

cum gra·no sa·lis \kùm-ˌgrä-nō-'sä-lis\
[L] : with a grain of salt

cus·tos mo·rum \ˌkùs-tōs-'mȯr-ùm\ [L]
: guardian of manners or morals : censor

d'ac·cord \dä-kȯr\ [F] : in accord : agreed

dame d'hon·neur \däm-dȯ-nœr\ [F] : la-
dy-in-waiting

dam·nant quod non in·tel·li·gunt
\'däm-ˌnänt-ˌkwȯd-ˌnōn-in-'te-li-ˌgùnt\
[L] : they condemn what they do not understand

de bonne grâce \də-bȯn-gräs\ [F] : with
good grace : willingly

de gus·ti·bus non est dis·pu·tan·dum
\dä-'gùs-tə-ˌbùs-ˌnōn-ˌest-ˌdis-pù-'tän-
ˌdùm\ [L] : there is no disputing about
tastes

Dei gra·tia \ˌde-ˌē-'grä-tē-ˌä\ [L] : by the
grace of God

de in·te·gro \dā-'in-te-ˌgrō\ [L] : anew
: afresh

de·len·da est Car·tha·go \dā-'len-dä-
ˌest-kär-'tä-gō\ [L] : Carthage must be
destroyed

de mal en pis \də-mä-läⁿ-pē\ [F] : from
bad to worse

de mi·ni·mis non cu·rat lex \dā-'mi-ni-
ˌmēs-ˌnōn-ˌkü-ˌrät-'leks\ [L] : the law
takes no account of trifles

de mor·tu·is nil ni·si bo·num \dā-'mȯr-tu̇·ēs·ˌnēl·ˌni-sē-'bȯ·ˌnu̇m\ [L] : of the dead (say) nothing but good

de nos jours \də-nō-zhu̇r\ [F] : of our time : contemporary — used postpositively esp. after a proper name

Deo fa·ven·te \ˌdā-ō-fä-'ven-tā\ [L] : with God's favor

Deo gra·ti·as \ˌdā-ō-'grä-tē-ˌäs\ [L] : thanks (be) to God

de pro·fun·dis \ˌdā-prō-'fu̇n-dēs\ [L] : out of the depths

de·si·pe·re in lo·co \dā-'si·pe-rā-in-'lō-kō\ [L] : to indulge in trifling at the proper time

de te fa·bu·la nar·ra·tur \ˌdā-ˌtā-'fä-bu̇-lä-nä-'rä-ˌtu̇r\ [L] : the story applies to you

De·us ab·scon·di·tus \ˌdā-u̇s-ˌäp-'skōn-di-ˌtu̇s\ [L] : hidden God : God unknowable by the human mind

De·us vult \ˌdā-u̇s-'wu̇lt\ [L] : God wills it — rallying cry of the First Crusade

di·es fau·stus \ˌdē-ˌäs-'fau̇-stu̇s\ [L] : lucky day

dies in·fau·stus \-'in-ˌfau̇-stu̇s\ [L] : unlucky day

dies irae \-'ē-ˌrī, -ˌrä\ [L] : day of wrath — used of the Judgment Day

Dieu et mon droit \dyœ-ā-móⁿ-drwä\ [F] : God and my right — motto on the British royal arms

Dieu vous garde \dyœ-vü-gärd\ [F] : God keep you

di·ri·go \'dē-ri-ˌgō\ [L] : I direct — motto of Maine

dis ali·ter vi·sum \ˌdēs-ˌä-li-ter-'wē-ˌsu̇m\ [L] : the Gods decreed otherwise

di·tat De·us \ˌdē-ˌtät-'dā-ˌu̇s\ [L] : God enriches — motto of Arizona

di·vi·de et im·pe·ra \'dē-wi-ˌde-ˌet-'im-pe-ˌrä\ [L] : divide and rule

do·cen·do dis·ci·mus \dȯ-ˌken-dō-'dis-ki-ˌmu̇s\ [L] : we learn by teaching

Do·mi·ne, di·ri·ge nos \'dō-mi-ˌne 'dē-ri-ˌge-'nōs\ [L] : Lord, direct us — motto of the City of London

Do·mi·nus vo·bis·cum \ˌdō-mi-ˌnu̇s-wō-'bēs-ˌku̇m\ [L] : the Lord be with you

dul·ce et de·co·rum est pro pa·tria mo·ri \ˌdu̇l-ˌke-et-de-'kōr-u̇m-ˌest-prō-ˌpä-trē-ˌä-'mō-ˌrē\ [L] : it is sweet and seemly to die for one's country

dum spi·ro, spe·ro \ˌdu̇m-'spē-rō 'spä-rō\ [L] : while I breathe, I hope — one of the mottoes of South Carolina

dum vi·vi·mus vi·va·mus \ˌdu̇m-'wē-wē-ˌmu̇s-wē-'wä-mu̇s\ [L] : while we live, let us live

d'un cer·tain âge \dœⁿ-ser-te-näzh\ [F] : of a certain age : no longer young

dux fe·mi·na fac·ti \ˌdu̇ks-ˌfä-mi-nä-'fäk-ˌtē\ [L] : a woman was leader of the exploit

ec·ce sig·num \ˌe-ke-'sig-ˌnu̇m\ [L] : behold the sign : look at the proof

e con·tra·rio \ˌā-kón-'trär-ē-ˌō\ [L] : on the contrary

écra·sez l'in·fâme \ā-krä-zä-laⁿ-fäm\ [F] : crush the infamous thing

eheu fu·ga·ces la·bun·tur an·ni \ˌā-ˌheu̇-fu̇-'gä-ˌkäs-lä-'bu̇n-ˌtu̇r-'ä-ˌnē\ [L] : alas! the fleeting years glide on

ein' fes·te Burg ist un·ser Gott \īn-ˌfes-tə-'bu̇rk-ist-ˌu̇n-zər-'gót\ [G] : a mighty fortress is our God

em·bar·ras de choix \äⁿ-bä-rä-də-shwä\ or **embarras du choix** \-du̇-shwä\ [F] : embarrassing variety of choice

em·bar·ras de ri·chesses or **embarras de ri·chesse** \äⁿ-bä-räd-rē-shes, -rä-də-\ [F] : embarrassing surplus of riches : confusing abundance

en ami \äⁿ-nä-mē\ [F] : as a friend

en ef·fet \äⁿ-nä-fe\ [F] : in fact : indeed

en fa·mille \äⁿ-fä-mē\ [F] : in or with one's family : at home : informally

en·fant ché·ri \äⁿ-fäⁿ-shä-rē\ [F] : loved or pampered child : one that is highly favored

en·fant gâ·té \äⁿ-fäⁿ-gä-tā\ [F] : spoiled child

en·fants per·dus \äⁿ-fäⁿ-per-du̇\ [F] : lost children : soldiers sent to a dangerous post

en·fin \äⁿ-faⁿ\ [F] : in conclusion : in a word

en gar·çon \äⁿ-gär-sōⁿ\ [F] : as or like a bachelor

en garde \äⁿ-gärd\ [F] : on guard

en plein air \äⁿ-ple-ner\ [F] : in the open air

en plein jour \äⁿ-plaⁿ-zhu̇r\ [F] : in broad day

en règle \äⁿ-regl^ə\ [F] : in order : in due form

en re·tard \äⁿr-(ə)tär\ [F] : behind time : late

en re·traite \äⁿr-(ə)tret\ [F] : in retreat : in retirement

en re·vanche \äⁿr-(ə)väⁿsh\ [F] : in return : in compensation

en·se pe·tit pla·ci·dam sub li·ber·ta·te qui·e·tem \ˌen-se-ˌpe-tit-'plä-ki-ˌdäm-ˌsu̇b-ˌlē-ber-ˌtä-te-kwē-'ä-ˌtem\ [L] : with the sword she seeks calm repose under liberty : by the sword we seek peace, but peace only under liberty — motto of Massachusetts

eo ip·so \ˌā-ō-'ip-(ˌ)sō\ [L] : by that itself : by that fact alone

épa·ter le bour·geois \ā-pä-tä-lə-bür-zhwä\ or **épater les bour·geois** \-lā-bür-\ [F] : to shock the middle classes

e plu·ri·bus unum \ˌē-ˌplu̇r-ə-bəs-'(y)ü-nəm, ˌā-ˌplu̇r-i-bu̇s-'ü-nu̇m\ [L] : one out of many — used on the Great Seal of the U.S. and on several U.S. coins

ep·pur si muo·ve \ä-ˌpu̇r-sē-'mwȯ-vä\ [It] : and yet it does move — attributed to Galileo after recanting his assertion of the earth's motion

Erin go bragh \ˌer-ən-gə-'brȯ, -gō-'brä\ [Ir *go brách* or *go bráth*, lit., till doomsday] : Ireland forever

er·ra·re hu·ma·num est \e-'rär-ä-hü-ˌmä-nùm-'est\ [L] : to err is human

es·prit de l'es·ca·lier \es-prēd-les-kä-lyä\ or **es·prit d'es·ca·lier** \-prē-des-\ [F] : wit of the staircase : repartee thought of only too late

es·se quam vi·de·ri \'e-sā-ˌkwäm-wi-'dā-rē\ [L] : to be rather than to seem — motto of North Carolina

est mo·dus in re·bus \est-'mȯ-ˌdùs-in-'rā-ˌbùs\ [L] : there is a proper measure in things, i.e., the golden mean should always be observed

es·to per·pe·tua \'es-ˌtō-per-'pe-tù-ˌä\ [L] : may she endure forever — motto of Idaho

et hoc ge·nus om·ne \et-ˌhōk-ˌge-nùs-'ȯm-ne\ *or* **et id genus omne** \et-ˌid-\ [L] : and everything of this kind

et sic de si·mi·li·bus \et-ˌsēk-dā-si-'mi-li-ˌbùs\ [L] : and so of like things

et tu Bru·te \et-'tü-'brü-te\ [L] : thou too, Brutus — exclamation attributed to Julius Caesar on seeing his friend Brutus among his assassins

eu·re·ka \yù-'rē-kä\ [Gk] : I have found it — motto of California

Ewig–Weib·li·che \ˌä-vik-'vīp-li-kə\ [G] : eternal feminine

ex·al·té \eg-zäl-tä\ [F] : emotionally excited or elated : fanatic

ex ani·mo \eks-'ä-ni-ˌmō\ [L] : from the heart : sincerely

ex·cel·si·or \ik-'sel-sē-ər, eks-'kel-sē-ˌȯr\ [L] : still higher — motto of New York

ex·cep·tio pro·bat re·gu·lam de re·bus non ex·cep·tis \eks-'kep-tē-ˌō-ˌprō-bät-'rā-gù-ˌläm-dā-'rā-ˌbùs-ˌnōn-eks-'kep-ˌtēs\ [L] : an exception establishes the rule as to things not excepted

ex·cep·tis ex·ci·pi·en·dis \eks-'kep-ˌtēs-eks-ˌki-pē-'en-ˌdēs\ [L] : with the proper or necessary exceptions

ex·i·tus ac·ta pro·bat \'ek-si-ˌtùs-ˌäk-tä-'prȯ-ˌbät\ [L] : the outcome justifies the deed

ex li·bris \eks-'lē-bris\ [L] : from the books of — used on bookplates

ex me·ro mo·tu \ˌeks-ˌmer-ō-'mō-tü\ [L] : out of mere impulse : of one's own accord

ex ne·ces·si·ta·te rei \ˌeks-ne-ˌke-si-'tä-te-'rā(ˌē)\ [L] : from the necessity of the case

ex ni·hi·lo ni·hil fit \eks-'ni-hi-ˌlō-ˌni-ˌhil-'fit\ [L] : from nothing nothing is produced

ex pe·de Her·cu·lem \eks-ˌpe-de-'her-kù-ˌlem\ [L] : from the foot (we may judge of the size of) Hercules : from a part we may judge of the whole

ex·per·to cre·de \eks-ˌper-tō-'krä-de\ or

experto cre·di·te \-'krā-di-ˌte\ [L] : believe one who has had experience

ex un·gue le·o·nem \eks-'ùṇ-gwe-le-'ō-ˌnem\ [L] : from the claw (we may judge of) the lion : from a part we may judge of the whole

ex vi ter·mi·ni \eks-ˌwē-'ter-mə-ˌnē\ [L] : from the force of the term

fa·ci·le prin·ceps \ˌfä-ki-le-'priṇ-ˌkeps\ [L] : easily first

fa·ci·lis de·scen·sus Aver·no \'fä-ki-ˌlis-dä-ˌskän-ˌsùs-ä-'wer-nō\ *or* **facilis descensus Aver·ni** \-(ˌ)nē\ [L] : the descent to Avernus is easy : the road to evil is easy

fa·çon de par·ler \fä-sōⁿ-də-pär-lā\ [F] : manner of speaking : figurative or conventional expression

fas est et ab ho·ste do·ce·ri \fäs-'est-et-äb-'hȯ-ste-dȯ-'kä-(ˌ)rē\ [L] : it is right to learn even from an enemy

Fa·ta vi·am in·ve·ni·ent \ˌfä-tä-'wē-ˌäm-in-'we-nē-ˌent\ [L] : the Fates will find a way

fat·ti mas·chii, pa·ro·le fe·mi·ne \ˌfät-tē-'mäs-ˌkē pä-ˌrō-lā-'fā-mē-ˌnä\ [It] : deeds are males, words are females : deeds are more effective than words — motto of Maryland, where it is generally interpreted as meaning "manly deeds, womanly words"

faux bon·homme \fō-bȯ-nȯm\ [F] : pretended good fellow

faux–naïf \fȯe-nä-ēf\ [F] : spuriously or affectedly childlike : artfully simple

fe·lix cul·pa \'fā-liks-'kùl-pä\ [L] : fortunate fault — used esp. of original sin in relation to the consequent coming of Christ

femme de cham·bre \fäm-də-shäⁿbrᵃ\ [F] : chambermaid : lady's maid

fe·sti·na len·te \fe-ˌstē-nä-'len-ˌtä\ [L] : make haste slowly

feux d'ar·ti·fice \fȯe-där-tē-fēs\ [F] : fireworks : display of wit

fi·at ju·sti·tia, ru·at cae·lum \ˌfē-ˌät-yùs-'ti-tē-ä ˌrü-ˌät-'kī-ˌlùm\ [L] : let justice be done though the heavens fall

fi·at lux \ˌfē-ˌät-'lùks\ [L] : let there be light

Fi·dei De·fen·sor \ˌfi-de-ˌē-dä-'fän-ˌsȯr\ [L] : Defender of the Faith — a title of the sovereigns of England

fille de cham·bre \fē-də-shäⁿbrᵃ\ [F] : lady's maid

fille d'hon·neur \fē-dȯ-nœr\ [F] : maid of honor

fi·nem re·spi·ce \ˌfē-ˌnem-'rä-spi-ˌke\ [L] : consider the end

fi·nis co·ro·nat opus \ˌfē-nis-kȯ-ˌrō-ˌnät-'ō-ˌpùs\ [L] : the end crowns the work

flo·re·at \'flō-re-ˌät\ [L] : may (he, she, or it) flourish — usu. followed by a name

fluc·tu·at nec mer·gi·tur \'flùk-tù-ˌät-ˌnek-'mer-gi-ˌtùr\ [L] : it is tossed by the waves but does not sink — motto of Paris

fo·lie de gran·deur *or* **fo·lie des gran·deurs** \fȯ-lē-də-gräⁿ-dœr\ [F] : delusion of greatness : megalomania

force de frappe \fȯrs-də-fráp\ [F] : a force equipped to deal a retaliatory blow

fors·an et haec olim me·mi·nis·se ju·va·bit \fȯr-sän-et-'hīk-ō-lim-me-mi-'ni-se-yù-'wä-bit\ [L] : perhaps this too will be a pleasure to look back on one day

for·tes for·tu·na ju·vat \'fȯr-tās-fȯr-tü-nä-'yù-wät\ [L] : fortune favors the brave

fron·ti nul·la fi·des \'frȯn-tē-nú-lä-fi-dās\ [L] : no reliance can be placed on appearance

fu·it Ili·um \'fú-it-'i-lē-ùm\ [L] : Troy has been (i.e., is no more)

fu·ror lo·quen·di \fùr-ȯr-lò-'kwen-(,)dē\ [L] : rage for speaking

furor po·e·ti·cus \-pò-'ā-ti-kùs\ [L] : poetic frenzy

furor scri·ben·di \-skrē-'ben-(,)dē\ [L] : rage for writing

Gal·li·ce \'gä-li-,ke\ [L] : in French : after the French manner

gar·çon d'hon·neur \gär-söⁿ-dò-nœr\ [F] : bridegroom's attendant

garde du corps \gärd-dœ-kȯr\ [F] : bodyguard

gar·dez la foi \gär-dā-lä-fwä\ [F] : keep faith

gau·de·a·mus igi·tur \gaù-dē-'ä-mús-'i-gi-,tùr\ [L] : let us then be merry

gens d'é·glise \zhäⁿ-dā-glēz\ [F] : church people : clergy

gens de guerre \zhäⁿ-də-ger\ [F] : military people : soldiery

gens du monde \zhäⁿ-dœ-mōⁿd\ [F] : people of the world : fashionable people

gno·thi se·au·ton \'gnō-thē-,se-aù-'tón\ [Gk] : know thyself

goût de ter·roir \gü-də-te-rwär\ [F] : taste of the earth

grand monde \gräⁿ-mōⁿd\ [F] : great world : high society

gros·so mo·do \'grò s-(,)sō-'mō-(,)dō\ [It] : roughly

guerre à ou·trance \ger-ä-ü-träⁿs\ [F] : war to the uttermost

gu·ten Tag \,gü-tən-'täk\ [G] : good day

has·ta la vis·ta \,äs-tə-lä-'vēs-tə\ [Sp] : good-bye

haute vul·ga·ri·sa·tion \ōt-vœl-gä-rē-zä-syōⁿ\ [F] : high popularization : effective presentation of a difficult subject to a general audience

hic et nunc \'hēk-et-'nùŋk\ [L] : here and now

hic et ubi·que \,hēk-et-ú-'bē-kwe\ [L] : here and everywhere

hic ja·cet \'hik-'jä-sət, hēk-'yä-ket\ [L] : here lies — used preceding a name on a tombstone

hinc il·lae la·cri·mae \,hiŋk-,i-,lī-'lä-kri-,mī\ [L] : hence those tears

hoc age \'hōk-'ä-ge\ [L] : do this : apply yourself to what you are about

homme d'af·faires \òm-dä-fer\ [F] : man of business : business agent

homme d'es·prit \òm-des-prē\ [F] : man of wit

homme moyen sen·suel \òm-mwä-yaⁿ-säⁿ-sw^yel\ [F] : the average nonintellectual man

ho·mo sum: hu·ma·ni nil a me ali·e·num pu·to \'hò-mō-,sùm hü-,mä-nē-'nēl-ä-,mā-,ä-lē-'ä-nùm-'pù-tò\ [L] : I am a human being: I regard nothing of human concern as foreign to my interests

ho·ni soit qui mal y pense \ò-nē-swä-kē-mäl-ē-päⁿs\ [F] : shamed be he who thinks evil of it — motto of the Order of the Garter

hu·ma·num est er·ra·re \hü-,mä-nùm-,est-e-'rär-ā\ [L] : to err is human

ich dien \ik-'dēn\ [G] : I serve — motto of the Prince of Wales

ici on parle fran·çais \ē-sē-ōⁿ-pärl-fräⁿ-se\ [F] : French is spoken here

idées re·çues \ē-dār-(ə-)sœ\ [F] : received ideas : conventional opinions

id est \id-'est\ [L] : that is

ig·no·ran·tia ju·ris ne·mi·nem ex·cu·sat \ig-nō-,rän-tē-ä-'yùr-is-'nä-mi-,nem-eks-'kü-,sät\ [L] : ignorance of the law excuses no one

ig·no·tum per ig·no·ti·us \ig-'nō-tùm-,per-ig-'nō-tē-,ùs\ [L] : (explaining) the unknown by means of the more unknown

il faut cul·ti·ver no·tre jar·din \ēl-fō-kuel-tē-vā-nȯt-zhär-daⁿ, -nó-trə-zhär-\ [F] : we must cultivate our garden : we must tend to our own affairs

in ae·ter·num \,in-ī-'ter-,nùm\ [L] : forever

in du·bio \in-'dú-bē-,ō\ [L] : in doubt : undetermined

in fu·tu·ro \,in-fù-'tùr-ō\ [L] : in the future

in hoc sig·no vin·ces \in-hōk-'sig-nō-'wiŋ-,kās\ [L] : by this sign (the Cross) you will conquer

in li·mi·ne \in-'lē-mi-,ne\ [L] : on the threshold : at the beginning

in om·nia pa·ra·tus \in-'òm-nē-ä-pä-'rä-,tùs\ [L] : ready for all things

in par·ti·bus in·fi·de·li·um \in-'pär-ti-,bùs-,in-fi-'dā-lē-,ùm\ [L] : in the regions of the infidels — used of a titular bishop having no diocesan jurisdiction, usu. in non-Christian countries

in prae·sen·ti \,in-prī-'sen-,tē\ [L] : at the present time

in sae·cu·la sae·cu·lo·rum \in-'sī-kù-,lä-,sī-kù-'lȯr-ùm, -'sā-kù-,lä-,sä-\ [L] : for ages of ages : forever and ever

in·shal·lah \,in-shä-'lä\ [Ar *in shā' Allāh*] : if Allah wills : God willing

in·te·ger vi·tae sce·le·ris·que pu·rus \ˌin-te-ˌger-ˈwē-ˌtī-ˌske-le-ˈris-kwe-ˈpü-rüs\ [L] : upright of life and free from wickedness

in·ter nos \ˌin-ter-ˈnōs\ [L] : between ourselves

in·tra mu·ros \ˌin-trä-ˈmü-ˌrōs\ [L] : within the walls

in utrum·que pa·ra·tus \ˌin-ü-ˈtrùm-kwe-pä-ˈrä-ˌtús\ [L] : prepared for either (event)

in·ve·nit \in-ˈwā-nit\ [L] : he or she devised it

in vi·no ve·ri·tas \in-wē-nō-ˈwā-ri-ˌtäs\ [L] : there is truth in wine

ip·sis·si·ma ver·ba \ip-ˈsi-si-ˌmä-ˈwer-ˌbä\ [L] : the very words

ira fu·ror bre·vis est \ˌē-rä-ˈfùr-ˌòr-ˈbre-wis-ˌest\ [L] : anger is a brief madness

j'ac·cuse \zhä-kœz\ [F] : I accuse : bitter denunciation

jac·ta alea est \ˈyäk-ˌtä-ˌä-lē-ˌä-ˈest\ [L] : the die is cast

j'adoube \zhä-düb\ [F] : I adjust — used in chess when touching a piece without intending to move it

ja·nu·is clau·sis \ˌyä-nù-ˌēs-ˈklaù-ˌsēs\ [L] : behind closed doors

je main·tien·drai \zhə-maⁿ-ˈtyaⁿ-drā\ [F] : I will maintain — motto of the Netherlands

jeu de mots \zhœd-mō, zhœ-də-\ [F] : play on words : pun

Jo·an·nes est no·men eius \yō-ˈä-näs-est-ˌnō-men-ˈā-yús\ [L] : John is his name — motto of Puerto Rico

jour·nal in·time \zhür-näl-aⁿ-tēm\ [F] : intimate journal : private diary

jus di·vi·num \ˌyüs-di-ˈwē-ˌnùm\ [L] : divine law

jus·ti·tia om·ni·bus \yús-ˌti-tē-ˌä-ˈòm-ni-ˌbús\ [L] : justice for all — motto of the District of Columbia

j'y suis, j'y reste \zhē-swᵛē zhē-rest\ [F] : here I am, here I remain

Kin·der, Kir·che, Küche \ˈkin-dər ˈkir-kə ˈkœ-kə\ [G] : children, church, kitchen

la belle dame sans mer·ci \lä-bel-däm-säⁿ-mer-sē\ [F] : the beautiful lady without mercy

la·bo·ra·re est ora·re \ˈlä-bō-ˌrär-ä-ˌest-ˈō-ˌrär-ä\ [L] : to work is to pray

la·bor om·nia vin·cit \ˈlä-ˌbòr-ˌòm-nē-ˌä-ˈwin-kit\ [L] : labor conquers all things — motto of Oklahoma

la·cri·mae re·rum \ˈlä-kri-ˌmī-ˈrä-ˌrúm\ [L] : tears for things : pity for misfortune; *also* : tears in things : tragedy of life

lais·sez—al·ler *or* **lais·ser—al·ler** \le-sä-ä-lā\ [F] : letting go : lack of restraint

lap·sus ca·la·mi \ˌläp-sùs-ˈkä-lä-ˌmē\ [L] : slip of the pen

lap·sus lin·guae \ˌ-ˈliŋ-ˌgwī\ [L] : slip of the tongue

la reine le veut \lä-ren-lə-vœ\ [F] : the queen wills it

la·scia·te ogni spe·ran·za, voi ch'en·tra·te \läsh-ˈshä-tä-ˌō-nᵛē-spä-ˈrän-tsä ˌvō-ē-kän-ˈträ-tä\ [It] : abandon all hope, ye who enter

lau·da·tor tem·po·ris ac·ti \laù-ˈdä-ˌtòr-ˌtem-pò-ris-ˈäk-ˌtē\ [L] : one who praises past times

laus Deo \laùs-ˈdā-ō\ [L] : praise (be) to God

Le·bens·welt \ˈlā-bəns-ˌvelt\ [G] : life world : world of lived experience

le cœur a ses rai·sons que la rai·son ne con·naît point \lə-kœr-ä-sä-re-zōⁿk-lä-re-zōⁿn-kò-ne-pwaⁿ\ [F] : the heart has its reasons that reason knows nothing of

le roi est mort, vive le roi \lə-rwä-e-mòr vēv-lə-rwä\ [F] : the king is dead, long live the king

le roi le veut \lə-rwä-lə-vœ\ [F] : the king wills it

le style, c'est l'homme \lə-stēl se-lòm\ [F] : the style is the man

l'état, c'est moi \lä-tä se-mwä\ [F] : the state, it is I

l'étoile du nord \lā-twäl-dœ-nòr\ [F] : the star of the north — motto of Minnesota

Lie·der·kranz \ˈlē-dər-ˌkränts\ [G] : wreath of songs : German singing society

lit·tera scrip·ta ma·net \ˌli-te-ˌrä-ˌskrip-tä-ˈmä-net\ [L] : the written letter abides

lo·cus in quo \ˌlō-kùs-in-ˈkwō\ [L] : place in which

l'union fait la force \lœ-nyōⁿ-fe-lä-fòrs\ [F] : union makes strength — motto of Belgium

lu·sus na·tu·rae \lü-sùs-nä-ˈtùr-ē, -ˈtùr-ˌī\ [L] : freak of nature

ma foi \mä-fwä\ [F] : my faith! : indeed

mag·na est ve·ri·tas et prae·va·le·bit \ˌmäg-nä-ˌest-ˈwä-ri-ˌtäs-et-ˌprī-wä-ˈlä-bit\ [L] : truth is mighty and will prevail

ma·ha·lo \ˈmä-hä-lō\ [Hawaiian] : thank you

ma·lade ima·gi·naire \mä-läd-ē-mä-zhē-ner\ [F] : imaginary invalid : hypochondriac

mal de siècle \mäl-də-syeklᵉ\ [F] : illness from worldly concerns : world-weariness

ma·lis avi·bus \ˌmä-ˌlēs-ˈä-wi-ˌbùs\ [L] : under evil auspices

man spricht Deutsch \män-shprikt-ˈdòich\ [G] : German spoken

ma·riage de con·ve·nance \mä-ryäzh-də-kōⁿv-näⁿs\ [F] : marriage of convenience

ma·ri com·plai·sant \mä-rē-kōⁿ-ple-zäⁿ\ [F] : complaisant husband : cuckold who accepts his wife's infidelity

mau·vaise honte \mò-vez-ōⁿt\ [F] : bad shame : bashfulness

mau·vais quart d'heure \mò-ve-kär-dœr\ [F] : bad quarter hour : an uncomfortable though brief experience

me·dio tu·tis·si·mus ibis \ˈme-dē-ˌō-tü-

ˌti-si-ˈmús-ˈē-bis\ [L] : you will go most safely by the middle course

me ju·di·ce \mä-ˈyü-di-ke\ [L] : I being judge : in my judgment

mens sa·na in cor·po·re sa·no \mäns-ˈsä-nä-in-ˌkòr-pò-re-ˈsä-nō\ [L] : a sound mind in a sound body

me·um et tu·um \ˌmē-əm-ˌet-ˈtü-əm, ˌme-ùm-ˌet-ˈtü-ùm\ [L] : mine and thine : distinction of private property

mi·ra·bi·le vi·su \mi-ˌrä-bi-lā-ˈwē-sü\ [L] : wonderful to behold

mi·ra·bi·lia \ˌmir-ə-ˈbi-lē-ˌä\ [L] : wonders : miracles

mœurs \mœr(s)\ [F] : mores : attitudes, customs, and manners of a society

mo·le ru·it sua \ˈmō-le-ˈrü-it-ˌsü-ä\ [L] : it collapses from its own bigness

monde \mōⁿd\ [F] : world : fashionable world : society

mon·ta·ni sem·per li·be·ri \mòn-ˈtä-nē-ˌsem-per-ˈlē-be-ˌrē\ [L] : mountaineers are always free — motto of West Virginia

mo·nu·men·tum ae·re per·en·ni·us \ˌmò-nü-ˈmen-tùm-ˌī-re-pe-ˈre-nē-ùs\ [L] : a monument more lasting than bronze — used of an immortal work of art or literature

mo·re suo \ˌmòr-ä-ˈsü-ō\ [L] : in his (or her) own manner

mo·ri·tu·ri te sa·lu·ta·mus \ˌmòr-i-ˈtùr-ē-ˌtä-ˌsä-lü-ˈtä-mùs, *or* mo·ri·tu·ri te sa·lu·tant \-ˈsä-lü-ˌtänt\ [L] : we (or those) who are about to die salute thee

mul·tum in par·vo \ˌmùl-tùm-in-ˈpär-vō, -ˈpär-wō\ [L] : much in little

mu·ta·to no·mi·ne de te fa·bu·la nar·ra·tur \mü-ˌtä-tō-ˈnò-mi-ne-ˌdā-ˌtä-ˈfä-bù-lä-ˈnä-ˈrä-ˌtùr\ [L] : with the name changed the story applies to you

my·ste·ri·um tre·men·dum \mi-ˈster-ē-ˌùm-tre-ˈmen-dùm\ [L] : overwhelming mystery

na·tu·ram ex·pel·las fur·ca, ta·men us·que re·cur·ret \nä-ˈtü- räm-ek-ˌspe-läs-ˈfùr-ˌkä, ˌtä-men-ˈùs-kwe-re-ˈkúr-et\ [L] : you may drive nature out with a pitchfork, but she will keep coming back

na·tu·ra non fa·cit sal·tum \nä-ˈtü-rä-ˌnōn-ˌfä-kit-ˈsäl-ˌtùm\ [L] : nature makes no leap

ne ce·de ma·lis \nä-ˌkä-de-ˈmä-ˌlēs\ [L] : yield not to misfortunes

ne·mo me im·pu·ne la·ces·sit \ˈnä-mō-ˈmä-im-ˌpü-nä-lä-ˈke-sit\ [L] : no one attacks me with impunity — motto of Scotland and of the Order of the Thistle

ne quid ni·mis \ˌnä-ˌkwid-ˈni-mis\ [L] : not anything in excess

n'est–ce pas? \nes-ˈpä\ [F] : isn't it so?

nicht wahr? \nikt-ˈvär\ [G] : not true? : isn't it so?

nil ad·mi·ra·ri \ˈnēl-ˌäd-mi-ˈrär-ē\ [L] : to be excited by nothing : equanimity

nil de·spe·ran·dum \ˈnēl-ˌdä-spä-ˈrän-dùm\ [L] : never despair

nil si·ne nu·mi·ne \ˈnēl-ˌsi-nä-ˈnü-mi-ne\ [L] : nothing without the divine will — motto of Colorado

n'im·porte \naⁿ-ˈpórt\ [F] : it's no matter

no·lens vo·lens \ˌnò-ˌlenz-ˈvò-ˌlenz\ [L] : unwilling (or) willing : willy-nilly

non om·nia pos·su·mus om·nes \nōn-ˈóm-nē-ä-ˌpò-sù-mùs-ˈóm-ˌnäs\ [L] : we can't all (do) all things

non sans droict \nōⁿ-sä ⁿ-drwä\ [OF] : not without right — motto on Shakespeare's coat of arms

non sum qua·lis eram \nōn-ˌsùm-ˌkwä-lis-ˈer-ˌäm\ [L] : I am not what I used to be

nos·ce te ip·sum \ˌnós-ke-ˌtä-ˈip-ˌsùm\ [L] : know thyself

nos·tal·gie de la boue \nòs-täl-zhēd-lä-bü-, -zhē-də-\ [F] : yearning for the mud : attraction to what is unworthy, crude, or degrading

nous avons chan·gé tout ce·la \nü-zä-vōⁿ-shä ⁿ-zhä-tü-sə-lä\ [F] : we have changed all that

nous ver·rons ce que nous ver·rons \nü-ve-rōⁿs-kə-nü-ve-rōⁿ, -rōⁿ-sə-kə-\ [F] : we shall see what we shall see

no·vus ho·mo \ˌnó-wùs-ˈhò-mō\ [L] : new man : man newly ennobled : upstart

novus or·do se·clo·rum \-ˈòr-ˌdō-sä-ˈklór-ùm\ [L] : a new cycle of the ages — motto on the reverse of the Great Seal of the United States

nu·gae \ˈnü-ˌgī\ [L] : trifles

nuit blanche \nwē-blä ⁿsh\ [F] : white night : a sleepless night

nyet \ˈnyet\ [Russ] : no

ob·iit \ˈò-bē-ˌit\ [L] : he or she died

ob·scu·rum per ob·scu·ri·us \òb-ˈskyúr-ùm-ˌper-òb-ˈskyúr-ē-ùs\ [L] : (explaining) the obscure by means of the more obscure

ode·rint dum me·tu·ant \ˈō-de-ˌrint-ˌdùm-me-tú-ˌänt\ [L] : let them hate, so long as they fear

odi et amo \ˈò-ˌdē-et-ˈä-(ˌ)mō\ [L] : I hate and I love

omer·tà \ò-ˈmer-tä\ [It] : conspiracy of silence

om·ne ig·no·tum pro mag·ni·fi·co \ˌòm-ne-ig-ˈnò-ˌtùm-prō-mäg-ˈni-fi-ˌkō\ [L] : everything unknown (is taken) as grand : the unknown tends to be exaggerated in importance or difficulty

om·nia mu·tan·tur, nos et mu·ta·mur in il·lis \ˌóm-nē-ä-mü-ˈtän-ˌtùr, ˌnòs-ˌet-mü-ˌtä-mùr-in-ˈil-ˌlis\ [L] : all things are changing, and we are changing with them

om·nia vin·cit amor \ˈóm-nē-ä-ˈwiŋ-kit-ˈä-ˌmòr\ [L] : love conquers all

onus pro·ban·di \ˌò-nùs-prō-ˈban-ˌdī, -dē\ [L] : burden of proof

ora pro no·bis \ˌō-rä-prō-ˈnò-ˌbēs\ [L] : pray for us

ore ro·tun·do \ˌ ̄or-ē-rō-'tən-dō\ [L] : with round mouth : eloquently

oro y pla·ta \ˌ ̄or-ō-ē-'plä-tə\ [Sp] : gold and silver — motto of Montana

o tem·po·ra! o mo·res! \ō-'tem-pȯ-rä ō-'mō-ˌrās\ [L] : oh the times! oh the manners!

oti·um cum dig·ni·ta·te \'ō-tē-ˌúm-kúm-ˌdig-ni-'tä-te\ [L] : leisure with dignity

où sont les neiges d'an·tan? \ü-sȯⁿ-lā-nezh-däⁿ-'täⁿ\ [F] : where are the snows of yesteryear?

outre—mer \ütr³-mer\ [F] : overseas : distant lands

pal·li·da Mors \ˌpa-li-dä-'mȯrz\ [L] : pale Death

pa·nem et cir·cen·ses \'pä-ˌnem-et-kir-'kän-ˌsās\ [L] : bread and circuses : provision of the means of life and recreation by government to appease discontent

pan·ta rhei \ˌpän-ˌtä-'rä\ [Gk] : all things are in flux

par avance \pär-ä-väⁿs\ [F] : in advance : by anticipation

par avion \pär-ä-vyōⁿ\ [F] : by airplane — used on airmail

par ex·em·ple \pär-äg-zäⁿpl³\ [F] : for example

pars pro to·to \'pärs-(ˌ)prō-'tō-(ˌ)tō\ [L] : part (taken) for the whole

par·tu·ri·unt mon·tes, nas·ce·tur ri·di·cu·lus mus \pär-'túr-ē-ˌúnt-'mȯn-ˌtās näs-'kä-ˌtúr-ri-ˌdi-kù-lùs-'müs\ [L] : the mountains are in labor, and a ridiculous mouse will be brought forth

pa·ter pa·tri·ae \'pä-ˌter-'pä-trē-ˌī\ [L] : father of his country

pau·cis ver·bis \ˌpaú-ˌkēs-'wer-ˌbēs\ [L] : in a few words

pax vo·bis·cum \ˌpäks-vō-'bēs-ˌkúm\ [L] : peace (be) with you

peine forte et dure \pen-fȯr-tā-dųer\ [F] : strong and hard punishment : torture

per an·gus·ta ad au·gus·ta \per-'än-ˌgús-tä-äd-'aú-ˌgús-tä\ [L] : through difficulties to honors

per·fide Al·bion \per-fēd-äl-byōⁿ\ [F] : perfidious Albion (England)

peu à peu \pœ-ä-pœ\ [F] : little by little

peu de chose \pœd-shōz, pœ-də-\ [F] : a trifle

pinx·it \'piŋk-sit\ [L] : he or she painted it

place aux dames \pläs-ō-däm\ [F] : (make) room for the ladies

ple·no ju·re \ˌplä-nō-'yúr-e\ [L] : with full right

plus ça change, plus c'est la même chose \plœ-sä-shäⁿzh plœ-se-lä-mem-shōz\ [F] : the more that changes, the more it's the same thing — often shortened to *plus ça change*

plus roy·a·liste que le roi \plœ-rwä-yä-lēst-kəl-rwä\ [F] : more royalist than the king

po·cas pa·la·bras \ˌpō-käs-pä-'lä-vräs\ [Sp] : few words

po·eta nas·ci·tur, non fit \pȯ-ˌā-tä-'näs-ki-ˌtúr nōn-'fit\ [L] : a poet is born, not made

po·ète mau·dit \pȯ-et-mō-dē\ [F] : accursed poet : a writer dogged by misfortune and lack of recognition

pol·li·ce ver·so \ˌpȯ-li-ke-'wer-sō\ [L] : with thumb turned : with a gesture or expression of condemnation

post hoc, er·go prop·ter hoc \'pȯst-ˌhōk ˌer-gō-'prȯp-ter-ˌhōk\ [L] : after this, therefore on account of it (a fallacy of argument)

post ob·itum \ˌpȯst-'ȯ-bi-ˌtúm\ [L] : after death

pour en·cou·ra·ger les autres \pür-äⁿ-kü-rä-zhä-lā-zōtr³\ [F] : in order to encourage the others — said ironically of an action (as an execution) carried out in order to compel others to obey

pri·mum non no·ce·re \ˌprē-múm-ˌnōn-nȯ-'kä-rä\ [L] : the first thing (is) to do no harm

pro bo·no pu·bli·co \prō-ˌbó-nō-'pü-bli-ˌkō\ [L] : for the public good

pro hac vi·ce \prō-ˌhäk-'wi-ke\ [L] : for this occasion

pro pa·tria \prō-'pä-trē-ˌä\ [L] : for one's country

pro re·ge, le·ge, et gre·ge \prō-'rä-ˌge 'lä-ˌge et-'gre-ˌge\ [L] : for the king, the law, and the people

pro re na·ta \ˌprō-ˌrä-'nä-tä\ [L] : for an occasion that has arisen : as needed — used in medical prescriptions

quand même \käⁿ-mem\ [F] : even so : all the same

quan·tum mu·ta·tus ab il·lo \ˌkwän-tùm-mü-'tä-tús-äb-'i-lō\ [L] : how changed from what he once was

quan·tum suf·fi·cit \ˌkwän-təm-'sə-fə-ˌkit\ [L] : as much as suffices : a sufficient quantity — used chiefly in medical prescriptions

¿quién sa·be? \kyän-'sä-vä\ [Sp] : who knows?

qui fa·cit per ali·um fa·cit per se \kwē-ˌfä-kit-per-'ä-lē-ˌúm-ˌfä-kit-ˌper-'sä\ [L] : he who does (something) through another does it through himself

quis cus·to·di·et ip·sos cus·to·des? \ˌkwis-kùs-'tō-dē-ˌet-ˌip-ˌsōs-kùs-'tō-ˌdäs\ [L] : who will keep the keepers themselves?

qui s'ex·cuse s'ac·cuse \kē-'sek-ˌskūez-'sä-ˌkūez\ [F] : he who excuses himself accuses himself

quis se·pa·ra·bit? \ˌkwis-ˌsä-pə-'rä-bit\ [L] : who shall separate (us)? — motto of the Order of St. Patrick

qui trans·tu·lit sus·ti·net \kwē-'träns-tù-ˌlit-'sùs-ti-ˌnet\ [L] : He who transplanted sustains (us) — motto of Connecticut

qui va là? \kē-vä-lä\ [F] : who goes there?

quo·ad hoc \ˌkwȯ-äd-'hōk\ [L] : as far as this : to this extent

quod erat de·mon·stran·dum \ˌkwȯd-
ˈer-ˌät-ˌde-mən-ˈstran-dəm, -ˌdä-ˈmȯn-
ˈsträn-ˌdùm\ [L] : which was to be demonstrated

quod erat fa·ci·en·dum \-ˌfä-kē-ˈen-
ˌdùm\ [L] : which was to be done

**quod sem·per, quod ubi·que, quod ab
om·ni·bus** \kwȯd-ˈsem-ˌper kwȯd-ˈù-bi-
ˌkwä ˌkwȯd-äb-ˈȯm-ni-ˌbùs, -ˌkwȯd-ù-ˈbē-
(ˌ)kwä-\ [L] : what (has been held) always, everywhere, by everybody

quod vi·de \kwȯd-ˈwi-ˌde\ [L] : which see

quo·rum pars mag·na fui \ˈkwȯr-ùm-
ˌpärs-ˌmäg-nä-ˈfù-ē\ [L] : in which I played a great part

quos de·us vult per·de·re pri·us de·men·tat \kwȯs-ˈdā-ùs-ˌwùlt-ˈper-de-ˌrä-
ˌpri-ùs-dā-ˈmen-ˌtät\ [L] : those whom a god wishes to destroy he first drives mad

quot ho·mi·nes, tot sen·ten·ti·ae \ˈkwȯt-
ˈhȯ-mi-ˌnäs ˌtȯt-sen-ˈten-tē-ˌi\ [L] : there are as many opinions as there are men

quo va·dis? \kwō-ˈwä-dis, -ˈvä-dəs\ [L] : whither are you going?

rai·son d'état \re-zōⁿ-dä-tä\ [F] : reason of state

reg·nat po·pu·lus \ˌreg-ˌnät-ˈpȯ-pù-ˌlùs\ [L] : the people rule — motto of Arkansas

re in·fec·ta \ˌrä-in-ˈfek-ˌtä\ [L] : the business being unfinished : without accomplishing one's purpose

re·li·gio lo·ci \re-ˈli-gē-ˌō-ˈlȯ-ˌkē\ [L] : religious sanctity of a place

rem acu te·ti·gis·ti \ˈrem-ˈä-ˌkü-te-ti-ˈgis-
tē\ [L] : you have touched the point with a needle : you have hit the nail on the head

ré·pon·dez s'il vous plaît \rā-pōⁿ-dā-sēl-
vü-ple\ [F] : reply, if you please

re·qui·es·cat in pa·ce \ˌre-kwē-ˈes-ˌkät-
in-ˈpä-ˌke, ˌrā-kwē-ˈes-ˌkät-in-ˈpä-ˌchä\ [L] : may he or she rest in peace — used on tombstones

re·spi·ce fi·nem \ˌrā-spi-ˌke-ˈfē-ˌnem\ [L] : look to the end : consider the outcome

re·sur·gam \re-ˈsùr-ˌgäm\ [L] : I shall rise again

re·te·nue \rət-nœ\ [F] : self-restraint : reserve

re·ve·nons à nos mou·tons \rəv-nōⁿ-ä-
nō-mü-tōⁿ\ [F] : let us return to our sheep : let us get back to the subject

ruse de guerre \rœz-də-ger\ [F] : war stratagem

rus in ur·be \ˌrüs-in-ˈùr-ˌbe\ [L] : country in the city

sae·va in·dig·na·tio \ˌsī-wä-ˌin-dig-ˈnä-
tē-ō\ [L] : fierce indignation

salle à man·ger \säl-ä-mäⁿ-zhä\ [F] : dining room

sa·lus po·pu·li su·pre·ma lex es·to \ˌsä-
ˌlùs-ˈpȯ-pù-ˌlē-sù-ˌprä-mä-ˌleks-ˈes-tō\ [L] : let the welfare of the people be the supreme law — motto of Missouri

sanc·ta sim·pli·ci·tas \ˌsäŋk-tä-sim-ˈpli-
ki-ˌtäs\ [L] : holy simplicity — often used

ironically in reference to another's naïveté

sans doute \säⁿ-düt\ [F] : without doubt

sans gêne \säⁿ-zhen\ [F] : without embarrassment or constraint

sans peur et sans re·proche \säⁿ-pœr-
ä-säⁿ-rə-ˈprȯsh\ [F] : without fear and without reproach

sans sou·ci \säⁿ-sü-sē\ [F] : without worry

sa·yo·na·ra \ˌsī-ə-ˈnär-ə, ˌsä-yə-\ [Jp] : good-bye

sculp·sit \ˈskəlp-sət, ˈskúlp-sit\ [L] : he or she carved it

scu·to bo·nae vo·lun·ta·tis tu·ae co·ro·nas·ti nos \ˈskü-ˌtō-ˈbȯ-ˌnī-ˌvȯ-lùn-ˌtä-
tis-ˈtù-ˌī-ˈkȯr-ȯ-ˌnäs-tē-ˈnōs\ [L] : Thou hast crowned us with the shield of Thy good will — a motto on the Great Seal of Maryland

se·cun·dum ar·tem \se-ˌkún-dùm-ˈär-
ˌtem\ [L] : according to the art : according to the accepted practice of a profession or trade

secundum na·tu·ram \-nä-ˈtü-ˌräm\ [L] : according to nature : naturally

se de·fen·den·do \ˈsä-dä-fen-ˈden-dō\ [L] : in self-defense

se ha·bla es·pa·ñol \sä-ˌäv-lä-ˌäs-pä-
ˈnyȯl\ [Sp] : Spanish spoken

sem·per ea·dem \ˌsem-ˌper-ˈe-ä-ˌdem\ [L] : always the same (fem.) — motto of Queen Elizabeth I

sem·per fi·de·lis \ˌsem-pər-fə-ˈdä-ləs\ [L] : always faithful — motto of the U.S. Marine Corps

sem·per idem \ˌsem-ˌper-ˈē-ˌdem\ [L] : always the same (masc.)

sem·per pa·ra·tus \ˌsem-pər-pə-ˈrä-təs\ [L] : always prepared — motto of the U.S. Coast Guard

se non è ve·ro, è ben tro·va·to \sä-ˌnōn-
e-ˈvä-rō e-ˌben-trō-ˈvä-tō\ [It] : even if it is not true, it is well conceived

sha·lom alei·chem \shȯ-ˌläm-ə-ˈlā-kəm,
ˌshō-, -ˌkəm\ [Heb *shālōm 'alēkhem*] : peace to you — used as a traditional Jewish greeting

sic itur ad as·tra \sēk-ˈi-ˌtùr-ˌäd-ˈäs-trə\ [L] : thus one goes to the stars : such is the way to immortality

sic sem·per ty·ran·nis \ˌsik-ˌsem-pər-tə-
ˈra-nəs\ [L] : thus ever to tyrants — motto of Virginia

sic trans·it glo·ria mun·di \sēk-ˈträn-sit-
ˌglȯr-ē-ä-ˈmùn-dē\ [L] : so passes away the glory of the world

si jeu·nesse sa·vait, si vieil·lesse pou·vait! \sē-ˈzhœ-nes-ˈsä-ve sē-ˈvye-yes-ˈpü-
ve\ [F] : if youth only knew, if age only could!

si·lent le·ges in·ter ar·ma \ˌsi-ˌlent-ˈlā-
ˌges-ˌin-tēr-ˈär-mä\ [L] : the laws are silent in the midst of arms (i.e., in time of war)

s'il vous plaît \sēl-vü-ple\ [F] : if you please

si·mi·lia si·mi·li·bus cu·ran·tur \si-'mi-lē-ä-si-'mi-li-bùs-kü-'rän-,túr\ [L] : like is cured by like

si·mi·lis si·mi·li gau·det \'si-mi-lis-'si-mi-lē-'gaù-,det\ [L] : like takes pleasure in like

si mo·nu·men·tum re·qui·ris, cir·cum·spi·ce \sē-,mò-nù-,men-tùm-re-'kwē-ris kir-'kùm-spi-ke\ [L] : if you seek his monument, look around — epitaph of Sir Christopher Wren in St. Paul's, London, of which he was architect

sim·pliste \san-'plēst\ [F] : simplistic : overly simple or naïve

si quae·ris pen·in·su·lam amoe·nam, cir·cum·spi·ce \sē-'kwi-ris-pā-'nin-sə-,läm-ä-'mòi-,näm kir-'kùm-spi-ke\ [L] : if you seek a beautiful peninsula, look around — motto of Michigan

sis·te vi·a·tor \sis-te-wē-'ä-,tòr\ [L] : stop, traveler — used on Roman roadside tombs

si vis pa·cem, pa·ra bel·lum \sē-'wēs-'pä-,kem 'pä-rä-'be-,lùm\ [L] : if you wish peace, prepare for war

sol·vi·tur am·bu·lan·do \'sól-wi-,tùr-,äm-bù-'län-dò\ [L] : it is solved by walking : the problem is solved by a practical experiment

spo·lia opi·ma \,spò-lē-ä-ò-'pē-mä\ [L] : rich spoils : the arms taken by the victorious from the vanquished general

sta·tus quo an·te bel·lum \'stä-tús-kwò-,än-te-'be-lùm\ [L] : the state existing before the war

sua·vi·ter in mo·do, for·ti·ter in re \'swä-wi-,ter-in-'mò-dō 'fòr-ti-,ter-in-'rä\ [L] : gently in manner, strongly in deed

sub ver·bo \sùb-'wer-bò, ,sab-'vər-bò\ or **sub vo·ce** \,sùb-'wō-ke, ,sab-'vō-sē\ [L] : under the word — introducing a cross-reference in a dictionary or index

sunt la·cri·mae re·rum \sùnt-,lä-kri-,mī-'rä-rùm\ [L] : there are tears for things : tears attend trials

suo ju·re \,sù-ō-'yùr-e\ [L] : in his or her own right

suo lo·co \-'lò-kò\ [L] : in its proper place

suo Mar·te \-'mär-te\ [L] : by one's own exertions

su·um cui·que \,sù-ùm-'kwi-kwe\ [L] : to each his own

tant mieux \tän-myœ\ [F] : so much the better

tant pis \-pē\ [F] : so much the worse : too bad

tem·po·ra mu·tan·tur, nos et mu·ta·mur in il·lis \,tem-pò-rä-mü-'tän-,tùr ,nōs-,et-mü-,tä-mùr-in-'i-,lēs\ [L] : the times are changing, and we are changing with them

tem·pus edax re·rum \'tem-pùs-,e-,däks-'rä-rùm\ [L] : time, that devours all things

tem·pus fu·git \,tem-pəs-'fyü-jət, ,tem-pùs-'fü-git\ [L] : time flies

ti·meo Da·na·os et do·na fe·ren·tes \,ti-mē-,ō-'dä-nä-,ōs-,et-,dò-nä-fe-'ren-,täs\ [L] : I fear the Greeks even when they bring gifts

to·ti·dem ver·bis \,tò-ti-,dem-'wer-,bēs\ [L] : in so many words

to·tis vi·ri·bus \,tō-,tēs-'wē-ri-,bùs\ [L] : with all one's might

to·to cae·lo \,tō-tō-'kī-lō\ or **toto coe·lo** \-'kòi-lō\ [L] : by the whole extent of the heavens : diametrically

tou·jours per·drix \tü-zhür-per-drē\ [F] : always partridge : too much of a good thing

tour d'ho·ri·zon \tür-dò-rē-zōⁿ\ [F] : circuit of the horizon : general survey

tous frais faits \tü-fre-fe\ [F] : all expenses defrayed

tout à fait \tü-tä-fe\ [F] : altogether : quite

tout au con·traire \tü-tō-kōⁿ-trer\ [F] : quite the contrary

tout à vous \tü-tä-vü\ [F] : wholly yours : at your service

tout bien ou rien \tü-'byaⁿ-nü-'ryaⁿ\ [F] : everything well (done) or nothing (attempted)

tout com·pren·dre c'est tout par·don·ner \'tü-kōⁿ-präⁿ-drə-se-'tü-pär-dò-nä\ [F] : to understand all is to forgive all

tout court \tü-kür\ [F] : quite short : and nothing else : simply : just; also : brusquely

tout de même \tüt-mem\ [F] : all the same : nevertheless

tout de suite \tüt-swᵉēt\ [F] : immediately; also : all at once : consecutively

tout en·sem·ble \tü-täⁿ-säⁿblᵃ\ [F] : all together : general effect

tout est per·du fors l'hon·neur \tü-te-per-dᵫ-fòr-lò-nœr\ or **tout est perdu hors l'honneur** \-dᵫ-òr-\ [F] : all is lost save honor

tout le monde \tü-lə-mōⁿd\ [F] : all the world : everybody

tra·hi·son des clercs \trä-ē-zōⁿ-dä-klerk\ [F] : treason of the intellectuals

tranche de vie \tränsh-də-'vē\ [F] : slice of life

trist·esse \trē-stes\ [F] : melancholy

tu·e·bor \tü-'ä-,bòr\ [L] : I will defend — a motto on the Great Seal of Michigan

ua mau ke ea o ka ai·na i ka po·no \,ù-ä-'mä-ù-kā-'ä-ä-ō-kä-'ī-ē-nä-,ē-kä-'pō-nō\ [Hawaiian] : the life of the land is perpetuated in righteousness — motto of Hawaii

über al·les \ᵫe-ber-'ä-les\ [G] : above everything else

Über·mensch \ᵫe-bər-,mench\ [G] : superman

ul·ti·ma ra·tio re·gum \'ùl-ti-mä-,rä-tē-ō-'rä-gùm\ [L] : the final argument of kings, i.e., war

und so wei·ter \ùnt-zō-'vī-tər\ [G] : and so on

uno ani·mo \\,ü-nō-'ä-ni-,mō\\ [L] : with one mind : unanimously

ur·bi et or·bi \\,úr-bē-,et-'ór-bē\\ [L] : to the city (Rome) and the world : to everyone

uti·le dul·ci \\,ü-ti-le-'dúl-,kē\\ [L] : the useful with the agreeable

ut in·fra \\ùt-'in-frä\\ [L] : as below

ut su·pra \\ùt-'sü-prä\\ [L] : as above

va·de re·tro me, Sa·ta·na \\,wä-de-'rä-trō-,mä 'sä-tä-,nä\\ [L] : get thee behind me, Satan

vae vic·tis \\wī-'wik-,tēs\\ [L] : woe to the vanquished

va·ri·um et mu·ta·bi·le sem·per fe·mi·na \\,wär-ē-ùm-,et-,mü-'tä-bi-le-,sem-,per-'fä-mi-nä\\ [L] : woman is ever a fickle and changeable thing

ve·di Na·po·li e poi mo·ri \\,vä-dē-'nä-pō-lē-ä-,pò-ē-'mò-rē\\ [It] : see Naples and then die

ve·ni, vi·di, vi·ci \\wā-nē 'wē-dē 'wē-kē, ,vä-nē ,vē-dē 'vē-chē\\ [L] : I came, I saw, I conquered

ven·tre à terre \\vänⁿ-trä-ter\\ [F] : belly to the ground : at very great speed

ver·ba·tim ac lit·te·ra·tim \\wer-'bä-tim-,äk-,li-te-'rä-tim\\ [L] : word for word and letter for letter

ver·bum sat sa·pi·en·ti est \\,wer-búm-'sät-,sä-pē-'en-tē,est\\ [L] : a word to the wise is sufficient

via cru·cis \\wē-ä-'krü-sis\\ [L] : Way of the Cross : path of suffering

vieux jeu \\vyœ-zhœ\\ [F] : old game : old hat

vin·cit om·nia ve·ri·tas \\,win-kit-'òm-nē-ä-'wä-ri-,täs\\ [L] : truth conquers all things

vin·cu·lum ma·tri·mo·nii \\,win-kù-lùm-,mä-tri-'mō-nē-,ē\\ [L] : bond of marriage

vin du pays \\vanⁿ-due-pä-ē\\ *or* **vin de pays** \\vanⁿ-də-\\ [F] : wine of the locality

vir·gi·ni·bus pu·e·ris·que \\wir-'gi-ni-bús-,pù-e-'rēs-kwe\\ [L] : for girls and boys

vir·go in·tac·ta \\'vir-,gō-in-'täk-tä\\ [L] : untouched virgin

vir·tu·te et ar·mis \\wir-'tü-te-,et-'är-mēs\\ [L] : by valor and arms — motto of Mississippi

vis me·di·ca·trix na·tu·rae \\'wēs-,me-di-'kä-triks-nä-'tü-,rī\\ [L] : the healing power of nature

vive la dif·fé·rence \\vēv-lä-dē-fä-räⁿs\\ [F] : long live the difference (between the sexes)

vive la reine \\vēv-lä-ren\\ [F] : long live the queen

vive le roi \\vēv-lə-rwä\\ [F] : long live the king

vogue la ga·lère \\vòg-lä-gä-ler\\ [F] : let the galley be kept rowing : keep on, whatever may happen

voi·là tout \\vwä-lä-tü\\ [F] : that's all

vox et prae·te·rea ni·hil \\'wōks-et-prī-'ter-e-ä-'ni,hil\\ [L] : voice and nothing more

vox po·pu·li vox Dei \\wōks-'pò-pù-,lē-,wōks-'dā-ē\\ [L] : the voice of the people is the voice of God

Wan·der·jahr \\'vän-dər-,yär\\ [G] : year of wandering

wie geht's? \\vē-'gäts\\ [G] : how goes it? : how is it going? — used as a greeting

wun·der·bar \\'vún-dər-,bär\\ [G] : wonderful

BIOGRAPHICAL NAMES

This section gives basic information on many notable figures from contemporary culture, history, legend, mythology, and biblical tradition. Figures from the Bible, myth, and legend are clearly identified as such.

In cases where individuals have alternate names, they are entered under the name by which they are best known. Names are generally alphabetized by the main element of the surname, without regard for connectives such as *da, de, van,* or *von* (as **Gama**... Vasco da). Names appearing in the entry in italics are original names, maiden names, or nicknames.

The first dates given in the entry are birth/death dates; other dates refer to terms in office, reigns, achievements, or honors. Abbreviations used here are listed in the front section Abbreviations in This Work.

Aar·on \'er-ən\ brother of Moses and 1st high priest of the Hebrews in the Bible

Aaron Hank 1934–   *Henry Louis Aaron* Amer. baseball player

Abel \'ā-bəl\ son of Adam and Eve and brother of Cain in the Bible

Abra·ham \'ā-brə-,ham\ patriarch and founder of the Hebrew people in the Bible; also revered by Muslims

Achil·les \ə-'ki-lēz\ hero of the Trojan War in Greek mythology

Ad·am \'a-dəm\ the 1st man in biblical tradition

Ad·ams \'a-dəmz\ Abigail 1744–1818 née *Smith* Amer. writer; wife of John Adams

Adams Ansel Easton 1902–1984 Amer. photographer

Adams John 1735–1826 2d pres. of the U.S. (1797–1801)

Adams John Quin·cy \'kwin-zē, -sē\ 1767–1848 6th pres. of the U.S. (1825–29); son of John and Abigail Adams

Adams Samuel 1722–1803 patriot in the Amer. Revolution

Ad·dams \'a-dəmz\ Jane 1860–1935 Amer. social worker; Nobel Prize winner (1931)

Ado·nis \ə-'dä-nəs, -'dō-\ youth in Greek mythology loved by Aphrodite

Ae·ne·as \i-'nē-əs\ Trojan hero in Greek and Roman mythology

Ae·o·lus \'ē-ə-ləs\ god of the winds in Greek mythology

Aes·chy·lus \'es-kə-ləs, 'ēs-\ 525–456 B.C. Greek dramatist

Aes·cu·la·pi·us \,es-k(y)ə-'lā-pē-əs\ god of medicine in Roman mythology — compare ASCLEPIUS

Ae·sop \'ē-,säp, -səp\ legendary Greek writer of fables

Ag·a·mem·non \,a-gə-'mem-,nän, -nən\ leader of the Greeks during the Trojan War in Greek mythology

Ag·nes \'ag-nəs\ Saint *died* 304 A.D. Christian martyr

Ahab \'ā-,hab\ king of Israel in the 9th cent. B.C. and husband of Jezebel

Ajax \'ā-,jaks\ hero in Greek mythology who kills himself because the armor of Achilles is awarded to Odysseus during the Trojan War

Alad·din \ə-'la-d°n\ youth in the *Arabian Nights' Entertainments* who acquires a magic lamp

Al·bee \'ól-(,)bē, 'al-\ Edward Franklin 1928–   Amer. dramatist

Al·bright \'ól-,brīt\ Madeleine 1937–   née *Korbel* Amer. (Czech-born) diplomat; U.S. secretary of state (1997–2001)

Al·cott \'ól-kət, 'al-, -,kät\ Louisa May 1832–1888 Amer. author

Al·ex·an·der \,a-lig-'zan-dər, ,e-\ name of eight popes: esp. **VI** 1431–1503 (pope 1492–1503)

Alexander the Great 356–323 B.C. *Alexander III* king of Macedonia (336–323)

Al·fred \'al-frəd, -fərd\ 849–899 *Alfred the Great* king of the West Saxons (871–899)

Ali \ä-'lē\ Muhammad 1942–   orig. *Cassius Clay* Amer. boxer

Ali Ba·ba \,a-lē-'bä-bə, ,ä-lē-\ woodcutter in the *Arabian Nights' Entertainments* who enters the cave of the Forty Thieves by using the password *Sesame*

Al·len \'a-lən\ Ethan 1738–1789 Amer. Revolutionary soldier

Al·va·rez \'al-və-,rez\ Luis 1911–1988 Amer. physicist

Amerigo Vespucci — see VESPUCCI

Am·herst \'a-(,)mərst\ Jeffery 1717–1797 Baron *Amherst* Brit. general in America

Amund·sen \'ä-mən-sən\ Roald 1872–1928 Norwegian explorer

An·a·ni·as \,a-nə-'nī-əs\ early Christian in the Bible struck dead for lying

An·der·sen \'an-dər-sən\ Hans Christian 1805–1875 Danish writer of fairy tales

An·der·son \\'an-dər-sən\\ Marian 1897–1993 Amer. contralto

An·ge·lou \\'an-jə-(,)lō, *commonly* -,lü\\ Maya 1928–2014 orig. *Marguerite Johnson* Amer. author

Anne \\'an\\ 1665–1714 queen of Great Britain (1702–14)

An·tho·ny \\'an(t)-thə-nē\\ Susan Brownell 1820–1906 Amer. suffragist

An·tig·o·ne \\an-'ti-gə-(,)nē\\ daughter of Oedipus and Jocasta in Greek mythology

An·to·ny \\'an-tə-nē\\ Mark *ca* 82–30 B.C. *Marc Anthony; Marcus An·to·ni·us* \\an-'tō-nē-əs\\ Roman general and triumvir (43–30)

Aph·ro·di·te \\,a-frə-'dī-tē\\ goddess of love and beauty in Greek mythology — compare VENUS

Apol·lo \\ə-'pä-(,)lō\\ god of sunlight, prophecy, music, and poetry in Greek and Roman mythology

Ap·ple·seed \\'ap-əl-,sēd\\ Johnny 1774–1845 orig. *John Chapman* Amer. pioneer

Aqui·nas \\ə-'kwī-nəs\\ Saint Thomas 1224/25–1274 Ital. theologian

Ar·chi·me·des \\,är-kə-'mē-dēz\\ *ca* 287–212 B.C. Greek mathematician and inventor

Ares \\'a-(,)rēz, 'er-(,)ēz\\ god of war in Greek mythology — compare MARS

Ar·is·toph·a·nes \\,a-rə-'stä-fə-,nēz\\ *ca* 450–*ca* 388 B.C. Greek playwright

Ar·is·tot·le \\'a-rə-,stä-tᵊl\\ 384–322 B.C. Greek philosopher

Arm·strong \\'ärm-,strȯŋ\\ Lance 1971– Amer. cyclist

Armstrong Louis 1901–1971 *Satch·mo* \\'sach-,mō\\ Amer. jazz musician

Armstrong Neil Alden 1930–2012 Amer. astronaut; 1st man on the moon (1969)

Ar·nold \\'är-nᵊld\\ Benedict 1741–1801 Amer. Revolutionary general and traitor

Ar·te·mis \\'är-tə-məs\\ goddess of the moon, wild animals, and hunting in Greek mythology — compare DIANA

Ar·thur \\'är-thər\\ legendary king of the Britons whose story is based on traditions of a 6th-century military leader — *Ar·thu·ri·an* \\är-'thùr-ē-ən, -'thyùr-\\ *adj*

Arthur Chester Alan 1829–1886 21st pres. of the U.S. (1881–85)

As·cle·pi·us \\ə-'sklē-pē-əs\\ god of medicine in Greek mythology — compare AESCULAPIUS

Astaire \\ə-'ster\\ Fred 1899–1987 orig. *Frederick Austerlitz* Amer. dancer and actor

As·tor \\'as-tər\\ John Jacob 1763–1848 Amer. (Ger.-born) fur trader and capitalist

Athe·na \\ə-'thē-nə\\ *or* **Athe·ne** \\-nē\\ goddess of wisdom in Greek mythology — compare MINERVA

At·las \\'at-ləs\\ Titan in Greek mythology forced to bear the heavens on his shoulders

At·ti·la \\'a-tə-lə, ə-'ti-lə\\ 406?–453 A.D. king of the Huns

At·tucks \\'a-təks\\ Crispus 1723?–1770 Amer. patriot

At·wood \\'at-,wùd\\ Margaret 1939– Canad. author

Au·den \\'ȯ-dᵊn\\ Wystan Hugh 1907–1973 Amer. (Eng.-born) poet

Au·du·bon \\'ȯ-də-bən, -,bän\\ John James 1785–1851 Amer. (Haitian-born) artist and naturalist

Au·gus·tine \\'ȯ-gə-,stēn; ȯ-'gəs-tən, ə-\\ Saint 354–430 A.D. church father; bishop of Hippo (396–430)

Au·gus·tus \\ȯ-'gəs-təs, ə-\\ *or* **Caesar Augustus** *or* **Oc·ta·vi·an** \\äk-'tā-vē-ən\\ 63 B.C.–14 A.D. 1st Roman emperor (27 B.C.–14 A.D.)

Aus·ten \\'ȯs-tən, 'äs-\\ Jane 1775–1817 Eng. author

Bab·bage \\'ba-bij\\ Charles 1791–1871 Eng. mathematician and inventor

Bac·chus \\'ba-kəs, 'bä-\\ — see DIONYSUS

Bach \\'bäk, 'bäk\\ Johann Sebastian 1685–1750 Ger. composer

Ba·con \\'bā-kən\\ Francis 1561–1626 Eng. philosopher and author

Ba·den–Pow·ell \\'bā-dᵊn-'pō-əl\\ Robert Stephenson Smyth 1857–1941 Baron *Baden-Powell* Brit. general and founder of Boy Scout movement

Baf·fin \\'ba-fən\\ William *ca* 1584–1622 Eng. navigator

Bal·an·chine \\,ba-lən-'shēn\\ George 1904–1983 orig. *Georgy Melitonovich Balanchivadze* Amer. (Russ.-born) choreographer

Bal·boa \\bal-'bō-ə\\ Vasco Núñez de 1475–1519 Span. explorer

Bal·zac \\'bȯl-,zak, 'bal-\\ Honoré de 1799–1850 French author

Ba·rab·bas \\bə-'ra-bəs\\ prisoner in the Bible released in preference to Jesus at the demand of the multitude

Bar·num \\'bär-nəm\\ P. T. 1810–1891 *Phineas Taylor Barnum* Amer. showman

Bar·rie \\'ba-rē\\ Sir James Matthew 1860–1937 Scot. author

Bar·thol·di \\bär-'täl-dē, -'tȯl-, -'thäl-, -'thȯl-\\ Frédéric-Auguste 1834–1904 French sculptor of the Statue of Liberty

Bar·tók \\'bär-,täk\\ Béla 1881–1945 Hung. composer

Bar·ton \\'bär-tᵊn\\ Clara 1821–1912 founder of American Red Cross

Beau·re·gard \\'bȯr-ə-,gärd\\ Pierre Gustave Toutant 1818–1893 Amer. Confederate general

Beck·et \\'be-kət\\ Saint Thomas *ca* 1118–1170 *Thomas à Becket* archbishop of Canterbury (1162–70)

Beck·ett \\'be-kət\\ Samuel 1906–1989 Irish playwright in France; Nobel Prize winner (1969)

Bee·tho·ven \\'bā-,tō-vən\\ Ludwig van 1770–1827 Ger. composer

Bell \'bel\ Alexander Graham 1847–1922 Amer. (Scot.-born) inventor of the telephone

Bel·low \'be-(ˌ)lō\ Saul 1915–2005 Amer. (Canad.-born) author

Ben·e·dict \'be-nə-ˌdikt\ name of 16 popes: esp. **XIV** 1675–1758 (pope 1740–58); **XV** 1854–1922 (pope 1914–22); **XVI** 1927– (pope 2005–13)

Be·nét \bə-'nā\ Stephen Vincent 1898–1943 Amer. author

Ben·ja·min \'ben-jə-mən\ youngest son of Jacob and ancestor of one of the 12 tribes of Israel in the Bible

Ben·ton \'ben-tᵊn\ Thomas Hart 1889–1975 Amer. painter

Be·o·wulf \'bā-ə-ˌwulf\ legendary warrior and hero of the Old Eng. poem *Beowulf*

Berg·man \'bərg-mən\ Ingmar 1918–2007 Swed. film director

Be·ring \'ber-iŋ, 'bir-\ Vitus 1681–1741 Danish navigator and explorer for Russia

Ber·lin \(ˌ)bər-'lin\ Irving 1888–1989 Amer. (Russ.-born) composer

Ber·ners–Lee \'bər-nərz-'lē\ Sir Timothy John 1955– Brit. inventor

Ber·ni·ni \ber-'nē-nē\ Gian Lorenzo 1598–1680 Ital. sculptor, architect, and painter

Bern·stein \'bərn-ˌstīn, -ˌstēn\ Leonard 1918–1990 Amer. conductor and composer

Bes·se·mer \'be-sə-mər\ Sir Henry 1813–1898 Eng. engineer and inventor

Bi·den \'bī-dᵊn\ Joseph Robinette, Jr. 1942– vice pres. of the U.S. (2009–)

Bish·op \'bi-shəp\ Elizabeth 1911–1979 Amer. poet

Bi·zet \bē-'zā\ Georges 1838–1875 French composer

Black Hawk \'blak-ˌhòk\ 1767–1838 Amer. Indian chief

Black·well \'blak-ˌwel, -wəl\ Elizabeth 1821–1910 Amer. (Eng.-born) physician

Blair \'bler\ Tony 1953– *Anthony Charles Lynton Blair* Brit. prime minister (1997–2007)

Blake \'blāk\ William 1757–1827 Eng. poet and artist

Bloom·er \'blü-mər\ Amelia 1818–1894 née *Jenks* Amer. social reformer

Boc·cac·cio \bō-'kä-ch(ē-ˌ)ō\ Giovanni 1313–1375 Ital. author

Bohr \'bòr\ Niels 1885–1962 Danish physicist; Nobel Prize winner (1922)

Bo·leyn \bù-'lin, -'lēn\ Anne 1507?–1536 2d wife of Henry VIII and mother of Elizabeth I of England

Bo·li·var \bə-'lē-ˌvär; 'bä-lə-ˌvär, -vər\ Simón \sē-ˌmōn, ˌsī-mən\ 1783–1830 South Amer. liberator

Bon·i·face \'bä-nə-fəs, -ˌfās\ name of 9 popes: esp. **VIII** *ca* 1235 (or 1240)–1303 (pope 1294–1303)

Boone \'bün\ Daniel 1734–1820 Amer. pioneer

Booth \'büth\ John Wilkes 1838–1865 Amer. actor; assassin of Abraham Lincoln

Bo·re·as \'bòr-ē-əs\ god of the north wind in Greek mythology

Bosch \'bäsh, 'bòsh\ Hieronymus *ca* 1450–*ca* 1516 Dutch painter

Bot·ti·cel·li \ˌbä-tə-'che-lē\ Sandro 1445–1510 Ital. painter

Bow·ie \'bü-ē, 'bō-\ Jim 1796–1836 *James Bowie* Amer. hero of the Texas revolution

Boyle \'bòi(-ə)l\ Robert 1627–1691 Eng. physicist and chemist

Brad·bury \'brad-ˌber-ē, -b(ə-)rē\ Ray Douglas 1920–2012 Amer. author

Brad·dock \'bra-dək\ Edward 1695–1755 Brit. general in America

Brad·ford \'brad-fərd\ William 1590–1657 Pilgrim leader

Brad·street \'brad-ˌstrēt\ Anne *ca* 1612–1672 Amer. poet

Bra·dy \'brā-dē\ Mathew B. 1823?–1896 Amer. photographer

Brahe \'brä; 'brä-hē, -hə\ Tycho 1546–1601 Danish astronomer

Brah·ma \'brä-mə\ creator god of the Hindu sacred triad — compare SHIVA, VISHNU

Brahms \'brämz\ Johannes 1833–1897 Ger. composer

Braille \'brāl, 'brī\ Louis 1809–1852 French blind teacher of the blind

Bran·deis \'bran-ˌdīs, -ˌdīz\ Louis Dembitz 1856–1941 Amer. jurist

Brant \'brant\ Joseph 1742–1807 *Thayendanegea* Mohawk Indian chief

Brant Mary 1736?–1796 *Molly Brant* Mohawk Indian leader; sister of Joseph Brant

Braun \'braun\ Wernher von 1912–1977 Amer. (Ger.-born) rocket engineer

Brezh·nev \'brezh-ˌnef\ Leonid Ilich 1906–1982 Soviet leader of the Communist Party (1964–82); pres. of the U.S.S.R. (1960–64; 1977–82)

Brit·ten \'bri-tᵊn\ Edward Benjamin 1913–1976 *Baron Britten of Aldeburgh* Eng. composer

Bron·të \'brän-tē, -(ˌ)tā\ family of Eng. writers: Charlotte 1816–1855 and her sisters Emily 1818–1848 and Anne 1820–1849

Brooks \'brúks\ Gwendolyn Elizabeth 1917–2000 Amer. poet

Brown \'braun\ John 1800–1859 Amer. abolitionist

Brown James Gordon 1951– Brit. prime minister (2007–10)

Brown·ing \'brau-niŋ\ Elizabeth Barrett 1806–1861 Eng. poet

Browning Robert 1812–1889 Eng. poet; husband of the preceding

Brue·ghel \'brü-gəl, 'bròi-\ Pieter *ca*

Biographical Names

1525–1569 known as *Pieter Brughel the Elder* Flemish painter

Bru·tus \'brü-təs\ Marcus Junius 85–42 B.C. Roman politician; one of Julius Caesar's assassins

Bry·an \'brī-ən\ William Jennings 1860–1925 Amer. lawyer and politician

Bu·chan·an \byü-'ka-nən, bə-\ James 1791–1868 15th pres. of the U.S. (1857–61)

Buck \'bək\ Pearl S. 1892–1973 née *Sydenstricker* Amer. author; Nobel Prize winner (1938)

Bud·dha \'bü-də, 'bü-\ *ca* 563–*ca* 483 B.C. orig. *Siddhartha Gautama* Indian founder of Buddhism

Buffalo Bill — see W. F. CODY

Bun·yan \'bən-yən\ John 1628–1688 Eng. preacher and author

Bunyan Paul — see PAUL BUNYAN

Bur·bank \'bər-ˌbaŋk\ Luther 1849–1926 Amer. horticulturist

Bur·goyne \(ˌ)bər-'gȯin, 'bər-ˌ\ John 1722–1792 Brit. general in America

Burns \'bərnz\ Robert 1759–1796 Scot. poet

Burn·side \'bərn-ˌsīd\ Ambrose Everett 1824–1881 Amer. general

Burr \'bər\ Aaron 1756–1836 vice pres. of the U.S. (1801–5)

Bush \'bu̇sh\ George (Herbert Walker) 1924–   41st pres. of the U.S. (1989–93)

Bush George W. 1946–   *George Walker Bush* 43rd pres. of the U.S. (2001–09); son of the preceding

By·ron \'bī-rən\ Lord 1788–1824 *George Gordon Byron*, 6th Baron *Byron* Eng. poet

Cab·ot \'ka-bət\ John *ca* 1450–*ca* 1499 orig. *Giovanni Ca·bo·to* \kä-'bō-tō\ Ital. navigator; explorer for England

Cabot Sebastian 1476?–1557 Eng. navigator; son of J. Cabot

Ca·bri·ni \kə-'brē-nē\ Saint Frances Xavier 1850–1917 *Mother Cabrini* 1st Amer. (Ital.-born) saint (1946)

Cae·sar \'sē-zər\ (Gaius) Julius 100?–44 B.C. Roman general, political leader, and writer

Cain \'kān\ son of Adam and Eve and brother of Abel in the Bible

Calamity Jane \kə-'la-mə-tē-\ 1852?–1903 *Martha Jane Burk* \'bərk\ née *Cannary* \'ka-nə-rē\ Amer. frontier figure

Cal·houn \kal-'hün\ John Caldwell 1782–1850 vice pres. of the U.S. (1825–32)

Ca·lig·u·la \kə-'li-gyə-lə\ 12–41 A.D. Roman emperor (37–41)

Cal·li·ope \kə-'lī-ə-(ˌ)pē\ muse of heroic poetry in Greek mythology

Cal·vert \'kal-vərt\ George 1580?–1632 Baron *Baltimore* Eng. colonist in America

Cal·vin \'kal-vən\ John 1509–1564 *Jean Calvin* or *Cau·vin* \kō-'vaⁿ\ French theologian and reformer

Ca·mus \kä-'mᵫ\ Albert 1913–1960 French author; Nobel Prize winner (1957)

Ca·nute \kə-'nüt, -'nyüt\ *died* 1035 *Canute the Great* Danish king of England (1016–35); of Denmark (1018–35); of Norway (1028–35)

Ca·ra·vag·gio \ˌka-rə-'vä-j(ē-)ˌō\ Michelangelo da 1571–1610 orig. *Michelangelo Merisi* Ital. painter

Car·ne·gie \kär-'ne-gē, 'kär-nə-gē\ Andrew 1835–1919 Amer. (Scot.-born) industrialist and philanthropist

Car·roll \'ka-rəl\ Lewis 1832–1898 pseud. of *Charles Lutwidge Dodgson* Eng. author and mathematician

Car·son \'kär-sᵊn\ Kit 1809–1868 *Christopher Carson* Amer. frontiersman and guide

Carson Rachel Louise 1907–1964 Amer. scientist and writer

Car·ter \'kär-tər\ Jimmy 1924–   orig. *James Earl Carter, Jr.* 39th pres. of the U.S. (1977–81); Nobel Prize winner (2002)

Car·tier \kär-'tyā, 'kär-tē-ˌā\ Jacques 1491–1557 French explorer

Ca·ru·so \kə-'rü-(ˌ)sō, -(ˌ)zō\ En·ri·co \en-'rē-kō\ 1873–1921 Ital. tenor

Car·ver \'kär-vər\ George Washington 1861?–1943 Amer. agricultural chemist and agronomist

Ca·sa·no·va \ˌka-zə-'nō-və, ˌka-sə-\ Giovanni Giacomo 1725–1798 Ital. adventurer

Cas·san·dra \kə-'san-drə, -'sän-\ daughter of Priam in Greek mythology who is endowed with the gift of prophecy but fated never to be believed

Cas·satt \kə-'sat\ Mary 1845–1926 Amer. painter

Cas·tro \'käs-(ˌ)trō\ **(Ruz)** \'rüs\ Fidel 1926–   Cuban leader (1959–2008)

Cath·er \'ka-thər\ Willa 1873–1947 Amer. author

Cath·er·ine \'ka-th(ə-)rən\ name of 1st, 5th, and 6th wives of Henry VIII of England: Catherine of Aragon 1485–1536; Catherine Howard 1520?–1542; Catherine Parr 1512–1548

Catherine I 1684–1727 wife of Peter the Great; empress of Russia (1725–27)

Catherine II 1729–1796 *Catherine the Great* empress of Russia (1762–96)

Catherine de Mé·di·cis \-də-ˌmā-dē-'sēs, -'me-də-(ˌ)chē\ 1519–1589 Ital. *Ca·te·ri·na de' Me·di·ci* \ˌkä-tä-'rē-nä-dā-'me-dē-(ˌ)chē\ queen consort of Henry II of France (1547–59) and regent of France (1560–74)

Cav·en·dish \'ka-vən-(ˌ)dish\ Henry 1731–1810 Eng. scientist

Ce·ci·lia \sə-'sēl-yə, -'sil-\ Saint *fl.* 3d cent. A.D. Christian martyr; patron saint of music

Ce·res \'sir-(ˌ)ēz\ goddess of agriculture

in Roman mythology — compare DEME-TER

Cer·van·tes \sər-'van-,tēz, -'vän-,täs\ Miguel de 1547–1616 Span. author

Cé·zanne \sā-'zan\ Paul 1839–1906 French painter

Cha·gall \shə-'gäl, -'gal\ Marc 1887–1985 Russ. painter in France

Cham·plain \sham-'plān, shäⁿ-'plaⁿ\ Samuel de 1567–1635 French explorer in America

Chap·lin \'cha-plən\ Charlie 1889–1977 Sir *Charles Spencer Chaplin* Brit. actor and producer

Chapman \'chap-mən\ John — see John-ny APPLESEED

Char·le·magne \'shär-lə-,mān\ 742–814 A.D. *Charles the Great* or *Charles I* Frank-ish king (768–814); Holy Roman emperor (800–814)

Charles \'chär(-ə)lz\ name of 10 kings of France: esp. II 823–877 A.D. *Charles the Bald* (r. 840–77); Holy Roman emperor (875–77); IV 1294–1328 *Charles the Fair* (r. 1322–28); V 1337–1380 *Charles the Wise* (r. 1364–80); VI 1368–1422 *Charles the Mad* (or *the Beloved*) (r. 1380–1422); VII 1403–1461 *Charles the Well-Served* or *the Victorious* (r. 1422–61); IX 1550–1574 (r. 1560–74); X 1757–1836 (r. 1824–30)

Charles name of 2 kings of Great Britain: I 1600–1649 (r. 1625–49); II 1630–1685 (r. 1660–85); son of Charles I

Charles V 1500–1558 Holy Roman em-peror (1519–56); king of Spain as *Charles I* (1516–56)

Charles Edward Stuart — see Charles Edward STUART

Charles Mar·tel \-mär-'tel\ *ca* 688–741 A.D. Frankish ruler (719–41); grandfather of Charlemagne

Cha·ryb·dis \kə-'rib-dəs\ whirlpool off the coast of Sicily personified in Greek mythology as a female monster

Chau·cer \'chȯ-sər\ Geoffrey *ca* 1342–1400 Eng. poet

Cha·vez \'chä-vəs, -,vez\ Cesar Estrada 1927–1993 Amer. labor leader

Che·khov \'che-,kȯf, -,kȯv\ Anton Pav-lovich 1860–1904 Russ. author

Che·ney \'chē-nē, *commonly* 'chā-\ Rich-ard Bruce 1941–   vice pres. of the U.S. (2001–2009)

Cheops — see KHUFU

Ches·ter·ton \'ches-tər-tən\ G. K. 1874–1936 *Gilbert Keith Chesterton* Eng. author

Chiang Kai–shek \jē-'äŋ-'kī-'shek, 'chaŋ-\ 1887–1975 Chinese general and politician; president of China (1948–1949; Taiwan, 1950–1975)

Cho·pin \'shō-,pan, -,paⁿ\ Frédéric François 1810–1849 Polish composer

Chou En–lai *or* **Zhou Enlai** \'jō-'en-'lī\ 1898–1976 Chinese Communist politi-cian; premier (1949–76)

Chré·tien \krā-'tyaⁿ\ Jean 1934–   Ca-nad. prime minister (1993–2003)

Christ Jesus — see JESUS

Chris·tie \'kris-tē\ Dame Agatha 1890–1976 née *Miller* Eng. author

Chur·chill \'chər-,chil, 'chȯrch-,hil\ Sir Winston Leonard Spencer 1874–1965 Brit. prime minister (1940–45; 1951–55) Nobel Prize winner (1953)

Cic·ero \'si-sə-,rō\ Marcus Tullius 106–43 B.C. Roman statesman, orator, and au-thor

Clark \'klärk\ George Rogers 1752–1818 Amer. soldier and frontiersman

Clark William 1770–1838 Amer. explorer (with Meriwether Lewis)

Clay \'klā\ Henry 1777–1852 Amer. poli-tician and orator

Clem·ens \'kle-mənz\ Samuel Langhorne — see Mark TWAIN

Cle·o·pa·tra \,klē-ə-'pa-trə, -'pä-\ 69–30 B.C. queen of Egypt (51–30)

Cleve·land \'klēv-lənd\ (Stephen) Grover 1837–1908 22nd and 24th pres. of the U.S. (1885–89; 1893–97)

Clin·ton \'klin-tⁿn\ Hillary Rodham née *Rodham* 1947–   Amer. politician; U.S. secretary of state (2009–13); wife of W.J. Clinton

Clinton William Jefferson 1946–   *Bill Clinton* 42nd pres. of the U.S. (1993–2001)

Cly·tem·nes·tra \,klī-təm-'nes-trə\ wife of Agamemnon in Greek mythology

Cobb \'käb\ Ty 1886–1961 *Tyrus Ray-mond Cobb* Amer. baseball player

Co·chise \kō-'chēs\ 1812?–1874 Apache Indian chief

Co·dy \'kō-dē\ William Frederick 1846–1917 *Buffalo Bill* Amer. hunter, guide, and showman

Co·han \'kō-,han\ George Michael 1878–1942 Amer. composer

Cole·ridge \'kōl-rij, 'kō-lə-rij\ Samuel Taylor 1772–1834 Eng. poet

Co·lette \kō-'let\ 1873–1954 orig. *Sido-nie-Gabrielle Colette* French author

Co·lum·bus \kə-'ləm-bəs\ Christopher 1451–1506 Ital. navigator and explorer for Spain

Con·fu·cius \kən-'fyü-shəs\ 551–479 B.C. Chinese philosopher

Con·rad \'kän-,rad\ Joseph 1857–1924 Brit. (Polish-born) author

Con·sta·ble \'kən(t)-stə-bəl, 'kän(t)-\ John 1776–1837 Eng. painter

Con·stan·tine I \'kän(t)-stən-,tēn, -,tīn\ *after* 280–337 A.D. *Constantine the Great* Roman emperor (306–37)

Cook \'kuk\ Captain James 1728–1779 Eng. navigator

Coo·lidge \'kü-lij\ (John) Calvin 1872–1933 30th pres. of the U.S. (1923–29)

Coo·per \'kü-pər, 'ku-\ James Fenimore 1789–1851 Amer. author

Biographical Names

Co·per·ni·cus \kō-ˈpər-ni-kəs\ Nicolaus 1473–1543 Polish astronomer

Cop·land \ˈkō-plənd\ Aaron 1900–1990 Amer. composer

Cop·ley \ˈkä-plē\ John Singleton 1738–1815 Amer. painter

Corn·wal·lis \kȯrn-ˈwä-ləs\ Charles 1738–1805 1st Marquess *Cornwallis* Brit. general in America

Co·ro·na·do \ˌkȯr-ə-ˈnä-(ˌ)dō, ˌkär-\ Francisco Vásquez de *ca* 1510–1554 Span. explorer of southwestern U.S.

Cor·tés \kȯr-ˈtez, ˈkȯr-ˌ\ Hernán *or* Hernando 1485–1547 Span. conqueror of Mexico

Cous·teau \kü-ˈstō\ Jacques-Yves 1910–1997 French marine explorer

Crane \ˈkrān\ Stephen 1871–1900 Amer. author

Crazy Horse \ˈkrā-zē-ˌhȯrs\ 1842?–1877 *Ta-sunko-witko* Sioux Indian chief

Crock·ett \ˈkrä-kət\ *Davy* 1786–1836 *David Crockett* Amer. frontiersman

Crom·well \ˈkräm-ˌwel, ˈkrȯm-, -wəl\ Oliver 1599–1658 Eng. general; lord protector of England (1653–58)

Cro·nus \ˈkrō-nəs, ˈkrä-\ Titan in Greek mythology overthrown by his son Zeus

Cum·mings \ˈkə-minz\ Edward Estlin 1894–1962 known as *e. e. cummings* Amer. poet

Cu·pid \ˈkyü-pəd\ god of love in Roman mythology — compare EROS

Cu·rie \kyu̇-ˈrē, ˈkyu̇r-(ˌ)ē\ Marie 1867–1934 née *Sklo·dow·ska* \sklə-ˈdȯf-skə\ French (Polish-born) chemist; Nobel Prize winner (1903, 1911)

Curie Pierre 1859–1906 French chemist; husband of M. Curie; Nobel Prize winner (1903)

Cus·ter \ˈkəs-tər\ George Armstrong 1839–1876 Amer. general

Cy·ra·no de Ber·ge·rac \ˈsir-ə-ˌnō-də-ˈber-zhə-ˌrak\ Savinien 1619–1655 French playwright

Cy·rus II \ˈsī-rəs\ *ca* 585–*ca* 529 B.C. *Cyrus the Great* king of Persia (*ca* 550–529)

Dae·da·lus \ˈde-də-ləs, ˈdē-\ builder in Greek mythology of the Cretan labyrinth and inventor of wings by which he and his son Icarus escape imprisonment

Da·lí \ˈdä-lē, *by himself* dä-ˈlē\ Salvador 1904–1989 Span. painter

Dal·ton \ˈdȯl-tᵊn\ John 1766–1844 Eng. chemist and physicist

Dan·iel \ˈdan-yəl\ prophet in the Bible who is held captive in Babylon and delivered from a den of lions

Dan·te \ˈdän-(ˌ)tā, ˈdan-, -(ˌ)tē\ 1265–1321 *Dante Ali·ghie·ri* \ˌa-lə-ˈgyer-ē\ Ital. poet

Da·ri·us I \də-ˈrī-əs\ 550–486 B.C. *Darius the Great* king of Persia (522–486)

Dar·row \ˈda-(ˌ)rō\ Clarence Seward 1857–1938 Amer. lawyer

Dar·win \ˈdär-wən\ Charles Robert 1809–1882 Eng. naturalist

Da·vid \ˈdā-vəd\ a youth in the Bible who slays Goliath and succeeds Saul as king of Israel

Da·vis \ˈdā-vəs\ Jefferson 1808–1889 pres. of the Confederate States of America (1861–65)

Davis Miles 1926–1991 Amer. jazz musician

Debs \ˈdebz\ Eugene Victor 1855–1926 Amer. socialist and labor organizer

De·bus·sy \ˌde-byü-ˈsē, ˌdā-\ Claude 1862–1918 French composer

De·ca·tur \di-ˈkā-tər\ Stephen 1779–1820 Amer. naval officer

De·foe \di-ˈfō\ Daniel 1660–1731 Eng. author

De·gas \də-ˈgä\ Edgar 1834–1917 French painter

de Gaulle \di-ˈgōl, -ˈgȯl\ Charles 1890–1970 French general; pres. of Fifth Republic (1958–69)

De·li·lah \di-ˈlī-lə\ mistress and betrayer of Samson in the Bible

De·me·ter \di-ˈmē-tər\ goddess of agriculture in Greek mythology — compare CERES

de Mille \də-ˈmil\ Agnes 1905–1993 Amer. dancer and choreographer

De·mos·the·nes \di-ˈmäs-thə-ˌnēz\ 384–322 B.C. Athenian orator and statesman

Demp·sey \ˈdem(p)-sē\ Jack 1895–1983 orig. *William Harrison Dempsey* Amer. boxer

Des·cartes \dā-ˈkärt\ René 1596–1650 French mathematician and philosopher

de So·to \thä-ˈsō-(ˌ)tō, di-\ Hernando *ca* 1496–1542 Span. explorer

Dew·ey \ˈdü-ē, ˈdyü-\ George 1837–1917 Amer. admiral

Dewey John 1859–1952 Amer. philosopher and educator

Di·ana \dī-ˈa-nə\ ancient Ital. goddess of the forest and of childbirth who was identified with Artemis by the Romans

Dick·ens \ˈdi-kənz\ Charles 1812–1870 pseud. *Boz* \ˈbäz, ˈbōz\ Eng. author

Dick·in·son \ˈdi-kən-sən\ Emily Elizabeth 1830–1886 Amer. poet

Di·do \ˈdī-(ˌ)dō\ legendary queen of Carthage who falls in love with Aeneas and kills herself when he leaves her

Di·Mag·gio \də-ˈmä-zhē-(ˌ)ō, -ˈma-jē-(ˌ)ō\ Joe 1914–1999 *Joseph Paul DiMaggio* Amer. baseball player

Di·o·ny·sus \ˌdī-ə-ˈnī-səs, -ˈnē-\ god of wine and ecstasy in classical mythology

Dis·ney \ˈdiz-nē\ Walt 1901–1966 *Walter Elias Disney* Amer. film producer and cartoonist

Dis·rae·li \diz-ˈrā-lē\ Benjamin 1804–1881 Earl of *Beaconsfield* Brit. prime minister (1868; 1874–80)

Dix \ˈdiks\ Dorothea Lynde 1802–1887 Amer. social reformer

Dodg·son \'däd-sən, 'däj-\ Charles Lutwidge — see Lewis CARROLL

Donne \'dən\ John 1572–1631 Eng. poet and clergyman

Don Qui·xote \ˌdän-kē-'(h)ō-tē, ˌdän-\ hero of Cervantes' *Don Quixote*

Dos·to·yev·sky \ˌdäs-tə-'yef-skē, -'yev-\ Fyodor Mikhaylovich 1821–1881 Russ. novelist

Doug·las \'də-gləs\ Stephen Arnold 1813–1861 Amer. politician

Doug·lass \'də-gləs\ Frederick 1817–1895 Amer. abolitionist

Doyle \'dȯi(-ə)l\ Sir Arthur Conan 1859–1930 Brit. physician and author

Drake \'drāk\ Sir Francis *ca* 1540–1596 Eng. navigator, explorer, and admiral

Drei·ser \'drī-sər, -zər\ Theodore 1871–1945 Amer. author

DuBois \dü-'bȯis, dyü-\ William Edward Burghardt 1868–1963 Amer. educator and writer

Du·mas \dü-'mä, dyü-\ Alexandre 1802–1870 *Dumas père* \'per\ French author

Dun·can \'dən-kən\ Isadora 1877–1927 Amer. dancer

Dü·rer \'dủr-ər, 'dyủr-, 'dủer-\ Albrecht 1471–1528 Ger. painter and engraver

Dy·lan \'di-lən\ Bob 1941– orig. *Robert Allen Zimmerman* Amer. singer and songwriter

Ea·kins \'ā-kənz\ Thomas 1844–1916 Amer. artist

Ear·hart \'er-ˌhärt, 'ir-\ Amelia 1897–1937 Amer. aviator

Earp \'ərp\ Wyatt 1848–1929 Amer. frontiersman and lawman

Ed·dy \'e-dē\ Mary Baker 1821–1910 Amer. founder of Christian Science

Ed·i·son \'e-də-sən\ Thomas Alva 1847–1931 Amer. inventor

Ed·ward \'ed-wərd\ name of 8 post-Norman kings of England: **I** 1239–1307 *Edward Longshanks* (r. 1272–1307); **II** 1284–1327 (r. 1307–27); **III** 1312–1377 (r. 1327–77); **IV** 1442–1483 (r. 1461–70; 1471–83); **V** 1470–1483 (r. 1483); **VI** 1537–1553 (r. 1547–53); son of Henry VIII and Jane Seymour; **VII** 1841–1910 (r. 1901–10); son of Queen Victoria; **VIII** 1894–1972 (r. 1936; abdicated) *Duke of Windsor*; son of George V

Ein·stein \'īn-ˌstīn\ Albert 1879–1955 Amer. (Ger.-born) physicist; Nobel Prize winner (1921)

Ei·sen·how·er \'ī-zᵊn-ˌhaủ(-ə)r\ Dwight David 1890–1969 Amer. general; 34th pres. of the U.S. (1953–61)

Elec·tra \i-'lek-trə\ sister of Orestes in Greek mythology who aids him in avenging their father's murder

Eli·jah \i-'lī-jə\ Hebrew prophet of the 9th cent. B.C.

El·i·on \'e-lē-ən\ Gertrude Belle 1918–1999 Amer. pharmacologist; Nobel Prize winner (1988)

El·iot \'e-lē-ət, 'el-yət\ George 1819–1880 pseud. of *Mary Ann Evans* Eng. author

Eliot T. S. 1888–1965 *Thomas Stearns Eliot* Brit. (Amer.-born) poet; Nobel Prize winner (1948)

Eliz·a·beth I \i-'li-zə-bəth\ 1533–1603 queen of England (1558–1603); daughter of Henry VIII and Anne Boleyn

Elizabeth II 1926– queen of the United Kingdom (1952–); daughter of George VI

El·ling·ton \'e-liŋ-tən\ Duke 1899–1974 *Edward Kennedy Ellington* Amer. bandleader and composer

Em·er·son \'e-mər-sən\ Ralph Waldo 1803–1882 Amer. essayist and poet

En·dym·i·on \en-'di-mē-ən\ beautiful youth in Greek mythology loved by the goddess of the moon

Ep·i·cu·rus \ˌe-pi-'kyủr-əs\ 341–270 B.C. Greek philosopher

Er·ik the Red \'er-ik\ *fl.* 10th cent. orig. *Erik Thorvaldson* Norwegian explorer; father of Leif Eriksson

Eriksson Leif — see LEIF ERIKSSON

Eros \'er-ˌäs, 'ir-\ god of love in Greek mythology — compare CUPID

Esau \'ē-(ˌ)sȯ\ son of Isaac and Rebekah and elder twin brother of Jacob in the Bible

Es·ther \'es-tər\ Hebrew woman in the Bible who as the queen of Persia delivers her people from destruction

Eu·clid \'yü-kləd\ *fl. ca.* 300 B.C. Greek mathematician

Eu·rip·i·des \yủ-'ri-pə-ˌdēz\ *ca* 484–406 B.C. Greek playwright

Eu·ro·pa \yủ-'rō-pə\ princess in Greek mythology who was carried off by Zeus disguised as a white bull

Eu·ryd·i·ce \yủ-'ri-də-(ˌ)sē\ wife of Orpheus in Greek mythology

Eve \'ēv\ the 1st woman in biblical tradition; wife of Adam

Eze·kiel \i-'zē-kyəl, -kē-əl\ Hebrew prophet of the 6th cent. B.C.

Fahr·en·heit \'fa-rən-ˌhīt, 'fär-ən-\ Daniel Gabriel 1686–1736 Ger. physicist

Far·a·day \'fa-rə-ˌdā, -dē\ Michael 1791–1867 Eng. chemist and physicist

Far·ra·gut \'fa-rə-gət\ David Glasgow 1801–1870 Amer. admiral

Faulk·ner \'fȯk-nər\ William 1897–1962 Amer. author; Nobel Prize winner (1949)

Faust \'faủst\ *or* **Fau·stus** \'faủ-stəs, 'fȯ-\ magician in Ger. legend who sells his soul to the devil for knowledge and power

Fawkes \'fȯks\ Guy 1570–1606 Eng. conspirator

Fel·li·ni \fə-'lē-nē\ Federico 1920–1993 Ital. film director

Fer·di·nand \'fər-də-ˌnand\ **V** of Castile *or* **II** of Aragon 1452–1516 *Ferdinand the Catholic* king of Castile (1474–1504), of Aragon (1479–1516), of Naples (1504–16); husband of Isabella I

Fer·mi \'fer-(ˌ)mē\ Enrico 1901–1954 Amer. (Ital.-born) physicist; Nobel Prize winner (1938)

Field·ing \'fēl-diŋ\ Henry 1707–1754 Eng. author

Fill·more \'fil-ˌmȯr\ Millard 1800–1874 13th pres. of the U.S. (1850–53)

Fitz·ger·ald \fits-'jer-əld\ Ella 1917–1996 Amer. singer

Fitzgerald F. Scott 1896–1940 *Francis Scott Key Fitzgerald* Amer. author

Flem·ing \'fle-miŋ\ Sir Alexander 1881–1955 Brit. bacteriologist; Nobel Prize winner (1945)

Flying Dutchman legendary Dutch mariner condemned to sail the seas until Judgment Day

Ford \'fȯrd\ Gerald Rudolph 1913–2007 38th pres. of the U.S. (1974–77)

Ford Henry 1863–1947 Amer. automobile manufacturer

Fos·sey \'fȯ-sē, 'fä-\ Dian 1932–1985 Amer. zoologist

Fos·ter \'fȯs-tər, 'fäs-\ Stephen Collins 1826–1864 Amer. songwriter

Fran·cis \'fran(t)-səs\ 1936– pope (2013–)

Francis of As·si·si \-əv-ə-'si-sē, -'sē-\ Saint 1181/1182–1226 Ital. friar; founder of Franciscan order

Fran·co \'frän-(ˌ)kō, 'fraŋ-\ Francisco 1892–1975 Span. general, dictator, and head of Span. state (1936–75)

Frank \'fraŋk, 'fräŋk\ Anne 1929–1945 Ger.-born diarist during the Holocaust

Frank·lin \'fraŋ-klən\ Benjamin 1706–1790 Amer. patriot, author, and inventor

Fred·er·ick I \'fre-d(ə-)rik\ *ca* 1123–1190 *Frederick Barbarossa* Holy Roman emperor (1152–90)

Frederick II 1712–1786 *Frederick the Great* king of Prussia (1740–86)

Fré·mont \'frē-ˌmänt\ John Charles 1813–1890 Amer. general and explorer

French \'french\ Daniel Chester 1850–1931 Amer. sculptor

Freud \'frȯid\ Sigmund 1856–1939 Austrian neurologist; founder of psychoanalysis

Fried·man \'frēd-mən\ Milton 1912–2006 Amer. economist

Frig·ga \'fri-gə\ wife of Odin and goddess of married love and the hearth in Norse mythology

Frost \'frȯst\ Robert Lee 1874–1963 Amer. poet

Ful·ler \'fu̇-lər\ (Richard) Buckminster 1895–1983 Amer. engineer and architect

Fuller (Sarah) Margaret 1810–1850 Amer. author and reformer

Ful·ton \'fu̇l-tᵊn\ Robert 1765–1815 Amer. inventor

Ga·bri·el \'gā-brē-əl\ archangel named in Hebrew tradition — compare MICHAEL, RAPHAEL, URIEL

Ga·ga·rin \gə-'gär-ən\ Yury Alekseyevich 1934–1968 Russ. astronaut; 1st man in space (1961)

Gage \'gāj\ Thomas 1721–1787 Brit. general in America

Gal·a·had \'ga-lə-ˌhad\ knight of the Round Table in medieval legend who finds the Holy Grail

Gal·a·tea \ˌga-lə-'tē-ə\ female figure sculpted by Pygmalion in Greek mythology and given life by Aphrodite in answer to the sculptor's prayer

Ga·len \'gā-lən\ 129–*ca* 216 A.D. Greek physician and writer

Ga·li·leo \ˌga-lə-'lē-(ˌ)ō, -'lā-\ 1564–1642 *Galileo Galilei* Ital. astronomer and physicist

Gall \'gȯl\ 1840?–1894 Sioux Indian leader

Ga·ma \'ga-mə, 'gä-\ Vasco da *ca* 1460–1524 Portuguese navigator and explorer

Gan·dhi \'gän-dē, 'gan-\ Indira 1917–1984 Indian prime minister (1966–77; 1980–84); daughter of Jawaharlal Nehru

Gandhi Mohandas Karamchand 1869–1948 *Ma·hat·ma* \mə-'hät-mə, -'hat-\ *Gandi* Indian leader

Gar·cía Már·quez \gär-'sē-ə-'mär-ˌkäs\ Gabriel 1928–2014 Colombian author; Nobel Prize winner (1982)

Gar·field \'gär-ˌfēld\ James Abram 1831–1881 20th pres. of the U.S. (1881)

Gar·i·bal·di \ˌga-rə-'bȯl-dē\ Giuseppe 1807–1882 Ital. patriot

Gar·ri·son \'ga-rə-sən\ William Lloyd 1805–1879 Amer. abolitionist

Gates \'gāts\ Bill 1955– *William Henry Gates III* Amer. computer software manufacturer

Gau·guin \gō-'gaⁿ\ Paul 1848–1903 French painter

Geh·rig \'ger-ig\ Lou 1903–1941 *Henry Louis Gehrig* Amer. baseball player

Gehry \'ger-ē\ Frank Owen 1929– orig. *Ephraim Owen Goldberg* Amer. (Canad.-born) architect

Gei·sel \'gī-zəl\ Theodor Seuss 1904–1991 pseud. *Dr. Seuss* \'süs\ Amer. author and illustrator

Gen·ghis Khan \ˌjeŋ-gəs-'kän, ˌgeŋ-\ *ca* 1162–1227 Mongol conqueror

George \'jȯrj\ name of 6 kings of Great Britain: I 1660–1727 (r. 1714–27); II 1683–1760 (r. 1727–60); III 1738–1820 (r. 1760–1820); IV 1762–1830 (r. 1820–30); V 1865–1936 (r. 1910–36); VI 1895–1952 (r. 1936–52); father of Elizabeth II

Ge·ron·i·mo \jə-'rä-nə-ˌmō\ 1829–1909 Apache Indian leader

Gersh·win \'gər-shwən\ George 1898–1937 Amer. composer

Gil·bert \'gil-bərt\ Sir William Schwenck 1836–1911 Eng. librettist and poet; collaborator with Sir Arthur Sullivan

Gins·burg \'ginz-ˌbərg\ Ruth Bader 1933– Amer. jurist

Glad·stone \'glad-ˌstōn, *chiefly Brit* -stən\

William Ewart 1809–1898 Brit. prime minister (1868–74; 1880–85; 1886; 1892–94)

Glenn \\'glen\ John Herschel 1921– Amer. astronaut and politician; 1st Amer. to orbit the earth (1962)

Go·di·va \gə-'dī-və\ an Eng. gentlewoman who in legend rode naked through Coventry to save its citizens from a tax

Goe·thals \\'gō-thəlz\ George Washington 1858–1928 Amer. engineer who directed the building of the Panama Canal

Goe·the \\'gə(r)-tə, 'gœ-tə\ Johann Wolfgang von 1749–1832 Ger. author

Gogh, van \van-'gō, -'gäk\ Vincent Willem 1853–1890 Dutch painter

Gol·ding \\'gōl-diŋ\ William Gerald 1911–1993 Eng. author; Nobel Prize winner (1983)

Go·li·ath \gə-'lī-əth\ Philistine giant who is killed by David in the Bible

Gom·pers \\'gäm-pərz\ Samuel 1850–1924 Amer. (Brit.-born) labor leader

Goo·dall \\'gu̇-(ₗ)dȯl, -(ₗ)däl\ Jane 1934– Brit. zoologist

Good·year \\'gu̇d-ₗyir\ Charles 1800–1860 Amer. inventor

Gor·ba·chev \ₗgȯr-bə-'chȯf, -'chef\ Mikhail Sergeyevich 1931– Soviet leader of Communist party (1985–91); pres. of U.S.S.R. (1990–91); Nobel Prize winner (1990)

Gore \\'gȯr\ Albert, Jr. 1948– vice pres. of the U.S. (1993–2001); Nobel Prize winner (2007)

Gor·gas \\'gȯr-gəs\ William Crawford 1854–1920 Amer. army surgeon

Go·ya (y Lu·cien·tes) \\'gȯi-ə-(ₗ)ē-,lü-sē-'en-ₗtäs\ Francisco José de 1746–1828 Span. painter

Gra·ham \\'grā-əm, 'gra(-ə)m\ Martha 1893–1991 Amer. dancer and choreographer

Grant \\'grant\ Ulysses S. 1822–1885 orig. *Hiram Ulysses Grant* Amer. general; 18th pres. of the U.S. (1869–77)

Gre·co, El \el-'gre-(ₗ)kō\ 1541–1614 *Doménikos Theotokópoulos* Span. (Cretan-born) painter

Gree·ley \\'grē-lē\ Horace 1811–1872 Amer. journalist and politician

Greene \\'grēn\ (Henry) Graham 1904–1991 Brit. author

Greene Nathanael 1742–1786 Amer. Revolutionary general

Greg·o·ry \\'gre-g(ə-)rē\ name of 16 popes: esp. I Saint *ca* 540–604 A.D. *Gregory the Great* (pope 590–604); VII Saint *ca* 1020–1085 (pope 1073–85); XIII 1502–1585 (pope 1572–85)

Grey \\'grā\ Lady Jane 1537–1554 queen of England for 9 days (1553)

Grey Zane 1872–1939 Amer. author

Grieg \\'grēg\ Edward Hagerup 1843–1907 Norwegian composer

Grimm \\'grim\ Jacob 1785–1863 and his

brother Wilhelm 1786–1859 Ger. philologists and folklorists

Gro·pi·us \\'grō-pē-əs\ Walter 1883–1969 Amer. (Ger.-born) architect

Gue·va·ra \ge-'vär-ə, gā-\ Che 1928–1967 orig. *Ernesto* Cuban (Arg.-born) revolutionary

Guin·e·vere \\'gwi-nə-ₗvir\ legendary wife of King Arthur and lover of Lancelot

Gu·ten·berg \\'gü-t⁰n-ₗbərg\ Johannes *ca* 1400–1468 Ger. inventor of printing method from movable type

Ha·des \\'hā-(ₗ)dēz\ — see PLUTO

Ha·dri·an \\'hā-drē-ən\ 76–138 A.D. Roman emperor (117–138)

Hai·le Se·las·sie \\'hī-lē-sə-'la-sē, -'lä-\ 1892–1975 emperor of Ethiopia (1930–36; 1941–74)

Hale \\'hāl\ Edward Everett 1822–1909 Amer. minister and author

Hale Nathan 1755–1776 Amer. Revolutionary hero

Hal·ley \\'ha-lē\ Edmond *or* Edmund 1656–1742 Eng. astronomer and mathematician

Hal·sey \\'hȯl-sē, -zē\ William Frederick 1882–1959 Amer. admiral

Ham·il·ton \\'ha-məl-tən\ Alexander 1755–1804 Amer. political leader

Ham·mu·ra·bi \ₗha-mə-'rä-bē\ *died ca* 1750 B.C. king of Babylon (*ca* 1792–50)

Han·cock \\'han-ₗkäk\ John 1737–1793 Amer. Revolutionary patriot

Han·del \\'han-d⁰l\ George Frideric 1685–1759 Brit. (Ger.-born) composer

Han·dy \\'han-dē\ W. C. 1873–1958 *William Christopher Handy* Amer. blues musician and composer

Han·ni·bal \\'ha-nə-bəl\ 247–183? B.C. Carthaginian general

Har·ding \\'här-diŋ\ Warren Gamaliel 1865–1923 29th pres. of the U.S. (1921–23)

Har·dy \\'här-dē\ Thomas 1840–1928 Eng. author

Har·per \\'här-pər\ Stephen 1959– Canad. prime minister (2006–)

Har·ri·son \\'ha-rə-sən\ Benjamin 1833–1901 23rd pres. of the U.S. (1889–93); grandson of W. H. Harrison

Harrison William Henry 1773–1841 Amer. general; 9th pres. of the U.S. (1841)

Harte \\'härt\ Bret 1836–1902 orig. *Francis Brett Harte* Amer. author

Har·vey \\'här-vē\ William 1578–1657 Eng. physician and anatomist

Haw·king \\'hȯ-kiŋ\ Stephen William 1942– Brit. physicist

Haw·thorne \\'hȯ-ₗthȯrn\ Nathaniel 1804–1864 Amer. author

Haydn \\'hī-d⁰n\ Franz Joseph 1732–1809 Austrian composer

Hayes \\'hāz\ Rutherford Birchard 1822–1893 19th pres. of the U.S. (1877–81)

Hearst \'hərst\ William Randolph 1863–1951 Amer. newspaper publisher

Hec·tor \'hek-tər\ son of Priam and Hecuba; Trojan hero slain by Achilles in Greek mythology

Hec·u·ba \'he-kyə-bə\ wife of Priam in Greek mythology

He·gel \'hā-gəl\ Georg Wilhelm Friedrich 1770–1831 Ger. philosopher

Hei·sen·berg \'hī-zᵊn-bərg, -ˌberk\ Werner Karl 1901–1976 Ger. physicist

Hel·en of Troy \ˌhe-lən-əv-'trȯi\ wife of Menelaus whose abduction by Paris in Greek mythology causes the Trojan War

He·li·os \'hē-lē-əs, -ˌ)ȯs\ god of the sun in Greek mythology — compare SOL

Hem·ing·way \'he-miŋ-ˌwā\ Ernest Miller 1899–1961 Amer. author; Nobel Prize winner (1954)

Hen·ry \'hen-rē\ name of 8 kings of England: **I** 1068–1135 (r. 1100–35); **II** 1133–1189 (r. 1154–89); **III** 1207–1272 (r. 1216–72); **IV** 1366–1413 (r. 1399–1413); **V** 1387–1422 (r. 1413–22); **VI** 1421–1471 (r. 1422–61; 1470–71); **VII** 1457–1509 (r. 1485–1509); **VIII** 1491–1547 (r. 1509–47)

Henry name of 4 kings of France: **I** *ca* 1008–1060 (r. 1031–60); **II** 1519–1559 (r. 1547–59); **III** 1551–1589 (r, 1574–89); **IV** 1553–1610 *Henry of Navarre* (r. 1589–1610)

Henry O. 1862–1910 pseud. of *William Sydney Porter* Amer. author

Henry Patrick 1736–1799 Amer. patriot and orator

Hen·son \'hen(t)-sən\ Matthew Alexander 1866–1955 Amer. arctic explorer

He·phaes·tus \hi-'fes-təs, -'fēs-\ god of fire and of metalworking in Greek mythology — compare VULCAN

He·ra \'hir-ə, 'he-rə, 'her-ə\ sister and wife of Zeus and goddess of women and marriage in Greek mythology — compare JUNO

Her·cu·les \'hər-kyə-ˌlēz\ *or* **Her·a·cles** \'her-ə-ˌklēz-, 'he-rə-\ hero in Greek mythology noted for his strength

Her·mes \'hər-(ˌ)mēz\ god of commerce, eloquence, invention, travel, and theft who serves as herald and messenger of the other gods in Greek mythology — compare MERCURY

Her·od \'her-əd\ 73–4 B.C. *Herod the Great* Roman king of Judea (37–4)

Herod An·ti·pas \'an-tə-pəs, -ˌpas\ 21 B.C.–39 A.D. Roman governor of Galilee (4 B.C.–39 A.D.); son of Herod the Great

Her·schel \'hər-shəl\ Sir William 1738–1822 Eng. astronomer

Hes·se \'he-sə\ Hermann 1877–1962 Ger. author; Nobel Prize winner (1946)

Hey·er·dahl \'hā-ər-ˌdäl\ Thor 1914–2002 Norwegian explorer and author

Hi·a·wa·tha \ˌhī-ə-'wȯ-thə, ˌhē-ə-, -'wä-\ legendary Iroquois Indian chief

Hick·ok \'hi-ˌkäk\ Wild Bill 1837–1876 orig. *James Butler Hickok* Amer. frontiersman and U.S. marshal

Hi·dal·go (y Cos·ti·lla) \ē-'thäl-gō-ē-kȯ-'stē-yä\ Miguel 1753–1811 Mex. priest and revolutionary leader

Hil·ton \'hil-tᵊn\ James 1900–1954 Eng. novelist

Hip·poc·ra·tes \hi-'pä-krə-ˌtēz\ *ca* 460–*ca* 377 B.C. Greek physician

Hi·ro·hi·to \ˌhir-ō-'hē-(ˌ)tō\ 1901–1989 emperor of Japan (1926–89)

Hitch·cock \'hich-ˌkäk\ Sir Alfred Joseph 1899–1980 Eng. film director

Hit·ler \'hit-lər\ Adolf 1889–1945 Ger. (Austrian-born) chancellor and dictator (1933–45)

Hodg·kin \'häj-kin\ Dorothy Mary 1910–1994 née *Crowfoot* Brit. physicist; Nobel Prize winner (1964)

Hol·i·day \'hä-lə-ˌdā\ Billie 1915–1959 orig. *Eleanora Fagan* Amer. jazz singer

Holmes \'hōmz, 'hōlmz\ Oliver Wendell 1809–1894 Amer. physician and author

Holmes Oliver Wendell, Jr. 1841–1935 Amer. jurist; son of the preceding

Ho·mer \'hō-mər\ *fl.* 9th *or* 8th cent. B.C. Greek epic poet

Homer Winslow 1836–1910 Amer. painter

Hooke \'hu̇k\ Robert 1635–1703 Eng. scientist

Hook·er \'hu̇-kər\ Thomas 1586?–1647 Eng. colonist; a founder of Connecticut

Hoo·ver \'hü-vər\ Herbert Clark 1874–1964 31st pres. of the U.S. (1929–33)

Hoover John Edgar 1895–1972 Amer. director of the Federal Bureau of Investigation (1924–72)

Hop·per \'hä-pər\ Edward 1882–1967 Amer. painter

Hopper Grace 1906–1992 née *Murray* Amer. admiral, mathematician, and computer scientist

Hou·di·ni \hü-'dē-nē\ Harry 1874–1926 orig. *Erik Weisz* Amer. magician

Hous·ton \'hyü-stən, 'yü-\ Sam 1793–1863 *Samuel Houston* Amer. politician; pres. of the Republic of Texas (1836–38; 1841–44)

Howe \'haū\ Elias 1819–1867 Amer. inventor

Howe Julia 1819–1910 née *Ward* Amer. suffragist and reformer

Hub·ble \'hə-bəl\ Edwin Powell 1889–1953 Amer. astronomer

Hud·son \'həd-sən\ Henry *ca* 1565–1611 Eng. explorer

Hughes \'hyüz\ Charles Evans 1862–1948 Amer. jurist; chief justice U.S. Supreme Court (1930–1941)

Hughes (James) Langston 1902–1967 Amer. author

Hugo \'hyü-(ˌ)gō, 'yü-\ Victor 1802–1885 French author

Hus·sein I \hü-'sān\ 1935–1999 king of Jordan (1952–99)

Hussein Saddam 1937–2006 pres. of Iraq (1979–2003)

Hutch·in·son \\'hə-chə(n)-sən\\ Anne 1591–1643 née *Marbury* Eng. colonist and religious leader in America

Hutchinson Thomas 1711–1780 Amer. colonial administrator

Hux·ley \\'həks-lē\\ Aldous Leonard 1894–1963 Eng. author

Hy·men \\'hī-mən\\ god of marriage in Greek mythology

Ib·sen \\'ib-sən, 'ip-\\ Henrik 1828–1906 Norwegian playwright

Ic·a·rus \\'i-kə-rəs\\ son of Daedalus who in Greek mythology falls into the sea when the wax of his artificial wings melts as he flies too near the sun

Ig·na·tius \\ig-'nā-sh(ē-)əs\\ Saint 1491–1556 *Ignatius of Loyola* Span. priest; founder of Society of Jesus (Jesuits)

In·no·cent \\'i-nə-sənt\\ name of 13 popes: esp. **III** 1160/61–1216 (pope 1198–1216); **IV** *died* 1254 (pope 1243–54)

Ir·ving \\'ər-viŋ\\ Washington 1783–1859 Amer. author

Isaac \\'ī-zik, -zək\\ son of Abraham and father of Jacob in the Bible

Is·a·bel·la \\,i-zə-'be-lə\\ 1451–1504 queen of Castile (1474–1504) and of Aragon (1479–1504); wife of Ferdinand V

Isa·iah \\ī-'zā-ə, *chiefly Brit* -'zī-\\ Hebrew prophet of the 8th cent. B.C.

Ish·ma·el \\'ish-(,)mā-əl, -mē-\\ outcast son of Abraham and Hagar in the Bible

Ives \\'īvz\\ Charles Edward 1874–1954 Amer. composer

Jack·son \\'jak-sən\\ Andrew 1767–1845 Amer. general; 7th pres. of the U.S. (1829–37)

Jackson Thomas Jonathan 1824–1863 *Stonewall Jackson* Amer. Confederate general

Ja·cob \\'jā-kəb\\ son of Isaac and Rebekah and younger twin brother of Esau in the Bible

James \\'jāmz\\ one of the 12 apostles in the Bible

James *the Less* one of the 12 apostles in the Bible

James name of 2 kings of Great Britain: **I** 1566–1625 (r. 1603–25); king of Scotland as *James VI* (r. 1567–1625); **II** 1633–1701 (r. 1685–88)

James Henry 1843–1916 Brit. (Amer.-born) author

Ja·nus \\'jā-nəs\\ god of gates and doors and of all beginnings in Roman mythology and that is pictured with two opposite faces

Ja·son \\'jā-sᵊn\\ hero in Greek mythology noted for his successful quest of the Golden Fleece

Jay \\'jā\\ John 1745–1829 Amer. jurist and statesman; 1st chief justice of the U.S. Supreme Court (1789–95)

Jef·fer·son \\'je-fər-sən\\ Thomas 1743–1826 3d pres. of the U.S. (1801–09)

Jer·e·mi·ah \\,jer-ə-'mī-ə\\ Hebrew prophet of the 7th–6th cent. B.C.

Je·sus \\'jē-zəs, -zəz\\ *or* **Jesus Christ** *ca* 6 B.C.–*ca* 30 A.D. source of the Christian religion and Savior in the Christian faith

Jez·e·bel \\'je-zə-,bel\\ queen of Israel and wife of Ahab who is noted for her wickedness in the Bible

Joan of Arc \\,jōn-əv-'ärk\\ Saint *ca* 1412–1431 *the Maid of Orléans* French national heroine

Job \\'jōb\\ man in the Bible who has many sufferings but keeps his faith

Jobs \\'jäbz\\ Steven Paul 1955–2011 Amer. computer entrepreneur

Jo·cas·ta \\jō-'kas-tə\\ queen of Thebes in Greek mythology who unknowingly marries her son Oedipus

John \\'jän\\ one of the 12 apostles believed to be the author of the 4th Gospel, three Epistles, and the Book of Revelation

John name of 21 popes: esp. **XXIII** 1881–1963 (pope 1958–63)

John 1167–1216 *John Lackland* king of England (1199–1216)

John Paul \\'pȯl\\ name of 2 popes; esp. **II** 1920–2005 (pope 1978–2005)

John·son \\'jän(t)-sən\\ Andrew 1808–1875 17th pres. of the U.S. (1865–69)

Johnson Lyndon Baines 1908–1973 36th pres. of the U.S. (1963–69)

Johnson Samuel 1709–1784 *Dr. Johnson* Eng. lexicographer and author

John the Baptist Saint, 1st cent. A.D. prophet and baptizer of Jesus in the Bible

Jol·liet *or* **Jo·liet** \\zhȯl-'yā\\ Louis 1645–1700 French-Canad. explorer

Jo·nah \\'jō-nə\\ Hebrew prophet who in the Bible spends three days in the belly of a great fish

Jones \\'jōnz\\ John Paul 1747–1792 Amer. (Scot.-born) naval officer

Jop·lin \\'jä-plən\\ Scott 1868–1917 Amer. pianist and composer

Jor·dan \\'jȯr-dᵊn\\ Michael 1963– Amer. basketball player

Jo·seph \\'jō-zəf\\ son of Jacob in the Bible who rises to high office in Egypt after being sold into slavery by his brothers

Joseph Chief *ca* 1840–1904 Nez Percé Indian chief

Joseph Saint, husband of Mary, the mother of Jesus, in the Bible

Josh·ua \\'jä-sh(ə-)wə\\ Hebrew leader in the Bible who succeeds Moses during the settlement of the Israelites in Canaan

Joyce \\'jȯis\\ James Augustine 1882–1941 Irish author

Juan Car·los \\'(h)wän-'kär-,lōs\\ 1938– king of Spain (1975–2014)

Juá·rez \\'(h)wär-əs\\ Benito Pablo 1806–1872 president of Mexico (1861–65; 1867–72)

Biographical Names

Ju·dah \'jü-də\ son of Jacob and ancestor of one of the 12 tribes of Israel in the Bible

Ju·das \'jü-dəs\ *or* **Judas Is·car·i·ot** \-is-'ka-rē-ət\ one of the 12 apostles and the betrayer of Jesus in the Bible

Jung \'yùŋ\ Carl Gustav 1875–1961 Swiss psychologist

Ju·no \'jü-(,)nō\ queen of heaven, wife of Jupiter, and goddess of light, birth, women, and marriage in Roman mythology — compare HERA

Ju·pi·ter \'jü-pə-tər\ chief god and god of light, of the sky and weather, and of the state in Roman mythology — compare ZEUS

Kaf·ka \'käf-kə, 'kaf-\ Franz 1883–1924 Czech author

Kalb \'kälp, 'kalb\ Johann 1721–1780 Baron *de Kalb* \di-'kalb\ Ger. general in Amer. Revolutionary army

Ka·me·ha·me·ha I \kə-,mā-ə-'mā-(,)hä\ 1758?–1819 orig. *Paiea* Hawaiian king (1795–1819)

Kant \'kant, 'känt\ Immanuel 1724–1804 Ger. philosopher

Keats \'kēts\ John 1795–1821 Eng. poet

Kel·ler \'ke-lər\ Helen Adams 1880–1968 Amer. deaf and blind lecturer and author

Kel·vin \'kel-vən\ 1st Baron 1824–1907 *William Thomson* Brit. mathematician and physicist

Ken·ne·dy \'ke-nə-dē\ John Fitzgerald 1917–1963 35th pres. of the U.S. (1961–63)

Kennedy Robert Francis 1925–1968 attorney general of the U.S. (1961–64); brother of the preceding

Ke·o·kuk \'kē-ə-,kək\ 1780?–1848 Amer. Indian chief

Kep·ler \'ke-plər\ Johannes 1571–1630 Ger. astronomer

Key \'kē\ Francis Scott 1779–1843 Amer. lawyer; author of "The Star-Spangled Banner"

Keynes \'kānz\ John Maynard 1883–1946 Eng. economist

Khayyám Omar — see OMAR KHAYYÁM

Khru·shchev \krush-'chóf, -'chòv\ Nikita Sergeyevich 1894–1971 premier of U.S.S.R. (1958–64)

Khu·fu \'kü-(,)fü\ *or Greek* **Che·ops** \'kē-,äps\ *fl.* 25th cent. B.C. king of Egypt and pyramid builder

Kidd \'kid\ William *ca* 1645–1701 *Captain Kidd* Scot. pirate

Kier·ka·gaard \'kir-kə-,gär(d), -,gòr\ Søren 1813–1855 Danish philosopher

King \'kiŋ\ Billie Jean 1943–   Amer. tennis player

King Martin Luther, Jr. 1929–1968 Amer. minister and civil rights leader; Nobel Prize winner (1964)

Kip·ling \'kip-liŋ\ Rudyard 1865–1936 Eng. author; Nobel Prize winner (1907)

Kis·sin·ger \'ki-sᵊn-jər\ Henry Alfred 1923–   Amer. (Ger.-born) government official; U.S. secretary of state (1973–77); Nobel Prize winner (1973)

Knox \'näks\ John *ca* 1514–1572 Scot. religious reformer

Koch \'kók, 'kókʹ, 'kōk, 'kōkʹ\ Robert 1843–1910 Ger. bacteriologist; Nobel Prize winner (1905)

Koś·ciusz·ko \kòsh-'chùsh-(,)kō, ,kä-sē-'əs-,kō\ Tadeusz 1746–1817 Polish patriot and general in Amer. Revolutionary army

Krish·na \'krish-nə, 'krēsh-\ god worshipped in later Hinduism

Ku·blai Khan \'kü-,blə-'kän, -,blī-\ 1215–1294 Mongol leader; grandson of Genghis Khan

La·fa·yette \,lä-fē-'et, ,la-\ Marquis de 1757–1834 French general in Amer. Revolutionary army

La·ius \'lā-əs, 'lī-əs\ king of Thebes who in Greek mythology is killed by his son Oedipus

Lan·ce·lot \'lan(t)-sə-,lät, 'län(t)-, -s(ə-)lət\ legendary knight of the Round Table and lover of Queen Guinevere

Lange \'laŋ\ Dorothea 1895–1965 Amer. photographer

Lao-tzu \'laúd-'zə\ *fl.* 6th cent. B.C. Chinese philosopher

La Salle \lə-'sal\ Sieur de 1643–1687 *René-Robert Cavelier* French explorer

La·voi·sier \ləv-'wä-zē-,ā\ Antoine-Laurent 1743–1794 French chemist

Law·rence \'lór-ən(t)s, 'lär-\ D. H. 1885–1930 *David Herbert Lawrence* Eng. author

Lawrence Thomas Edward 1888–1935 *Lawrence of Arabia* Brit. soldier and author

Laz·a·rus \'laz-rəs, 'la-zə-\ brother of Mary and Martha who in the Bible is raised by Jesus from the dead

Lazarus beggar in the biblical parable of the rich man and the beggar

Le·da \'lē-də\ Spartan princess in Greek mythology who is courted by Zeus in the form of a swan

Lee \'lē\ Ann 1736–1784 Eng. mystic; founder of Shaker society in the U.S.

Lee Robert Edward 1807–1870 Amer. Confederate general

Leeu·wen·hoek \'lā-vən-,húk\ Antonie van 1632–1723 Dutch naturalist

Leib·niz \'līb-nəts\ Gottfried Wilhelm 1646–1716 Ger. philosopher and mathematician

Leif Er·iks·son *or* **Er·ics·son** \,läv-'er-ik-sən, ,lēf-\ *fl.* 1000 Norwegian explorer; son of Erik the Red

Le·nin \'le-nən\ 1870–1924 orig. *Vladimir Ilyich Ul·ya·nov* \ül-'yän-əf, -,óf, -,óv\ Russ. Communist leader

Leo \'lē-(,)ō\ name of 13 popes: esp. **I** Saint *died* 461 A.D. *Leo the Great* (pope 440–61); **III** Saint *died* 816 (pope 795–816); **XIII** 1810–1903 (pope 1878–1903)

Le·o·nar·do da Vin·ci \lē-ə-'när-(ˌ)dō-də-'vin-chē, ˌlā-, -'vēn-\ 1452–1519 Ital. painter, sculptor, architect, and engineer

Lew·is \'lü-əs\ C. S. 1898–1963 *Clive Staples Lewis* Brit. author

Lewis John Llewellyn 1880–1969 Amer. labor leader

Lewis Meriwether 1774–1809 Amer. explorer (with William Clark)

Lewis Sinclair 1885–1951 Amer. author; Nobel Prize winner (1930)

Lin·coln \'liŋ-kən\ Abraham 1809–1865 16th pres. of the U.S. (1861–65)

Lind·bergh \'lin(d)-ˌbərg\ Charles Augustus 1902–1974 Amer. aviator

Lin·nae·us \lə-'nē-əs, -'nā-\ Carolus 1707–1778 *Carl von Linné* Swedish botanist

Lis·ter \'lis-tər\ Joseph 1827–1912 Eng. surgeon and medical scientist

Liszt \'list\ Franz 1811–1886 Hungarian pianist and composer

Liv·ing·stone \'li-viŋ-stən\ David 1813–1873 Scot. missionary in Africa

Locke \'läk\ John 1632–1704 Eng. philosopher

Lon·don \'lən-dən\ Jack 1876–1916 *John Griffith London* Amer. author

Long·fel·low \'lȯŋ-ˌfe-(ˌ)lō\ Henry Wadsworth 1807–1882 Amer. poet

Lou·is \'lü-ē, lü-'ē\ name of 18 kings of France: esp. **IX** Saint 1214–1270 (r. 1226–70); **XI** 1423–1483 (r. 1461–83); **XII** 1462–1515 (r. 1498–1515); **XIII** 1601–1643 (r. 1610–43); **XIV** 1638–1715 (r. 1643–1715); **XV** 1710–1774 (r. 1715–74); **XVI** 1754–1793 (r. 1774–92; guillotined); **XVII** 1785–1795 (r. in name 1793–95); **XVIII** 1755–1824 (r. 1814–15; 1815–24)

Lou·is \'lü-əs\ Joe 1914–1981 orig. *Joseph Louis Barrow* Amer. boxer

Low \'lō\ Juliette 1860–1927 née *Gordon* Amer. founder of the Girl Scouts

Low·ell \'lō-əl\ Amy 1874–1925 Amer. poet

Lowell James Russell 1819–1891 Amer. author

Luke \'lük\ physician and companion of the apostle Paul believed to be the author of the 3d Gospel and the Book of Acts

Lu·ther \'lü-thər\ Martin 1483–1546 Ger. Reformation leader

Ly·on \'lī-ən\ Mary 1797–1849 Amer. educator

Mac·Ar·thur \mə-'kär-thər\ Douglas 1880–1964 Amer. general

Mac·don·ald \mək-'dä-nᵊld\ Sir John Alexander 1815–1891 first prime minister of Canada (1867–1873; 1878–1891)

Ma·chi·a·vel·li \ˌmä-kē-ə-'ve-lē\ Niccolò 1469–1527 Ital. political philosopher

Mad·i·son \'ma-də-sən\ James 1751–1836 4th pres. of the U.S. (1809–17)

Ma·gel·lan \mə-'je-lən, *chiefly Brit* -'ge-\ Ferdinand *ca* 1480–1521 Portuguese navigator and explorer

Mah·ler \'mä-lər\ Gustav 1860–1911 Austrian composer

Mal·colm X \'mal-kəm-'eks\ *Malcolm Little* 1925–1965 Amer. civil rights leader

Man·dela \man-'de-lə\ Nelson Rolihlahla 1918–2013 pres. of South Africa (1994–99); Nobel Prize winner (1993)

Ma·net \ma-'nā, mä-\ Édouard 1832–1883 French painter

Mann \'man\ Horace 1796–1859 Amer. educator

Mao Tse–tung *or* **Mao Zedong** \'maȯ-(ˈ)(d)zə-'dùŋ, -(ˈ)tsə-\ 1893–1976 leader of People's Republic of China (1949–76)

Mar·co·ni \mär-'kō-nē\ Guglielmo 1874–1937 Ital. physicist and inventor; Nobel Prize winner (1909)

Marco Polo — see POLO

Ma·rie An·toi·nette \ˌan-twə-'net, -tə-\ 1755–1793 wife of Louis XVI of France

Mar·i·on \'mer-ē-ən\ Francis 1732?–1795 *the Swamp Fox* Amer. commander in Revolution

Mark \'märk\ evangelist believed to be the author of the 2d Gospel

Mark Antony — see ANTONY

Mar·quette \mär-'ket\ Jacques 1637–1675 *Père Marquette* French-born Jesuit missionary and explorer in America

Mars \'märz\ god of war in Roman mythology — compare ARES

Mar·shall \'mär-shəl\ George Catlett 1880–1959 Amer. general and diplomat; Nobel Prize winner (1953)

Marshall John 1755–1835 Amer. jurist; chief justice of the U.S. Supreme Court (1801–35)

Marshall Thurgood 1908–1993 Amer. jurist

Mar·tha \'mär-thə\ sister of Lazarus and Mary and friend of Jesus in the Bible

Mar·tin \'mär-tᵊn, mär-'taⁿ\ Saint 316–397 *Martin of Tours* \-'tùr\ patron saint of France

Mar·tin \'mär-tᵊn\ Paul (Edgar Phillipe) 1938– Canad. prime minister (2003–06)

Marx \'märks\ Karl 1818–1883 Ger. political philosopher and socialist

Mary \'mer-ē, 'ma-rē, 'mā-rē\ *Saint Mary*; *Virgin Mary* mother of Jesus

Mary sister of Lazarus and Martha in the Bible

Mary I 1516–1558 *Mary Tudor*; *Bloody Mary* queen of England (1553–58)

Mary II 1662–1694 joint Brit. sovereign with William III (1689–94)

Mary Mag·da·lene \'mag-də-lən, -ˌlēn\ woman in the Bible who sees the risen Christ

Mary, Queen of Scots 1542–1587 *Mary Stuart* queen of Scotland (1542–67)

Mas·sa·soit \ˌma-sə-'sȯit\ *died* 1661 Amer. Indian chief

Math·er \'ma-thər, -thər\ Cotton 1663–1728 Amer. religious leader and author

Mather Increase 1639–1723 Amer. minister and author; father of Cotton Mather

Ma·tisse \ma-'tēs, mə-\ Henri 1869–1954 French painter

Mat·thew \'ma-(ˌ)thyü\ apostle believed to be the author of the 1st Gospel

Mau·pas·sant \ˌmō-pə-'säⁿ\ Guy de 1850–1893 French author

Max·well \'maks-ˌwel, -ˌwəl\ James Clerk 1831–1879 Scot. physicist

Mays \'māz\ Willie Howard 1931– Amer. baseball player

Mc·Au·liffe \mə-'kól-əf\ Christa 1948–1986 Amer. teacher; 1st private citizen in space (1986)

Mc·Car·thy \mə-'kär-thē\ Joseph Raymond 1908–1957 Amer. politician

Mc·Clel·lan \mə-'kle-lən\ George Brinton 1826–1885 Amer. general

Mc·Clin·tock \mə-'klin-tək\ Barbara 1902–1992 Amer. botanist; Nobel Prize winner (1983)

Mc·Cor·mick \mə-'kór-mik\ Cyrus Hall 1809–1884 Amer. inventor

Mc·Kin·ley \mə-'kin-lē\ William 1843–1901 25th pres. of the U.S. (1897–1901)

Mead \'mēd\ Margaret 1901–1978 Amer. anthropologist

Meade \'mēd\ George Gordon 1815–1872 Amer. Civil War general

Mea·ny \'mē-nē\ George 1894–1980 Amer. labor leader

Me·dea \mə-'dē-ə\ woman with magic powers in Greek mythology who helps Jason to win the Golden Fleece and who kills her children when he leaves her

Medici Catherine de' — see CATHERINE DE MÉDICIS

Me·di·ci \'me-də-chē\ Lorenzo de' 1449–1492 *Lorenzo the Magnificent* Florentine statesman, ruler, and patron of the arts

Me·du·sa \mi-'dü-sə, -'dyü-, -zə\ Gorgon in Greek mythology slain by Perseus

Me·ir \mā-'ir\ Golda 1898–1978 prime minister of Israel (1969–74)

Mel·ville \'mel-ˌvil\ Herman 1819–1891 Amer. author

Men·del \'men-dᵊl\ Gregor Johann 1822–1884 Austrian botanist

Men·dels·sohn (**–Bar·thol·dy**) \'men-dᵊl-sən(-bär-'tól-dē, -'thól-)\ Felix 1809–1847 Ger. composer

Men·e·la·us \ˌme-nə-'lā-əs\ king of Sparta, brother of Agamemnon, and husband of Helen of Troy in Greek mythology

Meph·is·toph·e·les \ˌmc-fə-'stä-fə-ˌlēz\ chief devil in the Faust legend

Mer·ca·tor \(ˌ)mər-'kā-tər\ Gerardus 1512–1594 orig. *Gerhard Kremer* Flemish cartographer

Mer·cu·ry \'mər-kyə-rē, -k(ə-)rē\ god of commerce, eloquence, travel, and theft who serves as messenger of the other gods in Roman mythology — compare HERMES

Mer·lin \'mər-lən\ prophet and magician in the legend of King Arthur

Met·a·com \'me-tə-ˌkäm\ *or* **King Philip** *ca* 1638–1676 *Met·a·com·et* \ˌme-tə-'käm-ət\ Amer. Indian chief; son of Massasoit

Mi·chael \'mī-kəl\ archangel named in Hebrew tradition — compare GABRIEL, RAPHAEL, URIEL

Mi·chel·an·ge·lo \ˌmī-kə-'lan-jə-ˌlō, ˌmi-, ˌmē-kə-'län-\ 1475–1564 Ital. sculptor, painter, architect, and poet

Mi·das \'mī-dəs\ legendary king having the power to turn everything he touched into gold

Mil·lay \mi-'lā\ Edna St. Vincent 1892–1950 Amer. poet

Mil·ler \'mi-lər\ Arthur 1915–2005 Amer. playwright

Milne \'mil(n)\ A. A. 1882–1956 *Alan Alexander Milne* Eng. author

Mil·ton \'mil-tᵊn\ John 1608–1674 Eng. poet

Mi·ner·va \mə-'nər-və\ goddess of wisdom in Roman mythology — compare ATHENA

Mi·no·taur \'mi-nə-ˌtór, 'mī-\ monster in Greek mythology shaped half like a man and half like a bull

Min·u·it \'min-yə-wət\ Peter *ca* 1580–1638 Dutch colonial administrator in America

Mitch·ell \'mi-chəl\ Maria 1818–1889 Amer. astronomer

Mo·lière \mōl-'yer, 'mōl-ˌ\ 1622–1673 orig. *Jean-Baptiste Poquelin* French actor and playwright

Mo·net \mō-'nā\ Claude 1840–1926 French painter

Mon·roe \mən-'rō\ James 1758–1831 5th pres. of the U.S. (1817–25)

Mont·calm \mänt-'kälm-, -'käm-\ Marquis de 1712–1759 *Louis-Joseph de Montcalm-Grozon* French field marshal in Canada

Mon·tes·so·ri \ˌmän-tə-'sór-ē\ Maria 1870–1952 Ital. educator

Mon·te·ver·di \ˌmän-tə-'ver-dē, -'vər-\ Claudio 1567–1643 Ital. composer

Mon·te·zu·ma II \ˌmän-tə-'zü-mə\ 1466–1520 last Aztec emperor of Mexico (1502–20)

Moore \'mór, 'mùr\ Marianne 1887–1972 Amer. poet

More \'mór\ Sir Thomas 1478–1535 *Saint Thomas More* Eng. public official and author

Mor·gan \'mór-gən\ J. P. 1837–1913 *John Pierpont Morgan* Amer. financier

Mor·ri·son \'mór-ə-sən, 'mär-\ Toni 1931– orig. *Chloe Anthony Wofford* Amer. author; Nobel Prize winner (1993)

Morse \'mórs\ Samuel Finley Breese 1791–1872 Amer. artist and inventor

Mo·ses \'mō-zəz\ Hebrew prophet and lawgiver in the Bible

Moses Grandma 1860–1961 *Anna Mary Moses* née *Robertson* Amer. painter

Mott \'mät\ Lucretia 1793–1880 Amer. reformer

Mo·zart \'mōt-,särt\ Wolfgang Amadeus 1756–1791 Austrian composer

Mu·ham·mad \mō-'ha-məd, -'hä-\ *ca* 570–632 A.D. Arab prophet and founder of Islam

Mun·ro \(,)mən-'rō\ Alice 1931–   née *Laidlaw* Canadian writer; Nobel Prize Winner (2013)

Mur·row \'mər-(,)ō, 'mə-(,)rō\ Edward Roscoe 1908–1965 Amer. journalist

Mus·so·li·ni \,mü-sə-'lē-nē, ,mú-\ Be·ni·to \bə-'nēt-ō\ 1883–1945 *Il Du·ce* \ēl-'dü-chä\ Ital. fascist premier (1922–43)

Na·bo·kov \nə-'bò-kəf\ Vladimir 1899–1977 Amer. (Russ.-born) author

Na·po·leon \nə-'pōl-yən, -'pō-lē-ən\ *or* **Napoleon Bo·na·parte** \'bō-nə-,pärt\ 1769–1821 French general and emperor of the French (1804–15)

Nar·cis·sus \när-'si-səs\ beautiful youth in Greek mythology who pines away for love of his own reflection and is then turned into the narcissus flower

Nash \'nash\ Ogden 1902–1971 Amer. poet

Na·tion \'nā-shən\ Car·ry \'kar-ē\ Amelia 1846–1911 née *Moore* Amer. temperance agitator

Nav·ra·ti·lo·va \,nav-rə-tə-'lō-və\ Martina 1956–   Amer. (Czech-born) tennis player

Neb·u·cha·drez·zar II \,ne-byə-kə-'dre-zər, -bə-\ *or* **Neb·u·chad·nez·zar** \-kəd-'ne-\ *ca* 630—*ca* 561 B.C. Chaldean king of Babylon (605–562)

Neh·ru \'ner-(,)ü, 'nā-(,)rü\ Ja·wa·har·lal \jə-'wä-hər-,läl\ 1889–1964 1st prime minister of Republic of India (1947–64)

Nel·son \'nel-sən\ Horatio 1758–1805 Viscount *Nelson* Brit. admiral

Nem·e·sis \'ne-mə-səs\ goddess of reward and punishment in Greek mythology

Nep·tune \'nep-,tün, -,tyün\ god of the sea in Roman mythology — compare POSEIDON

Ne·ro \'nē-(,)rō, 'nir-(,)ō\ 37–68 A.D. Roman emperor (54–68)

Ne·ru·da \nā-'rü-də, -(,)thä\ Pablo 1904–1973 orig. *Neftalí Ricardo Reyes Basoalto* Chilean poet

Nev·el·son \'ne-vəl-sən\ Louise 1900?–1988 Amer. sculptor

New·ton \'nüt-ᵊn, 'nyü-\ Sir Isaac 1642–1727 Eng. mathematician and physicist

Nich·o·las \'ni-k(ə-)ləs\ Saint *fl.* 4th cent. A.D. Christian bishop

Nicholas I 1796–1855 czar of Russia (1825–55)

Nicholas II 1868–1918 last czar of Russia (1894–1917)

Nietz·sche \'nē-chə, -chē\ Friedrich Wilhelm 1844–1900 Ger. philosopher

Night·in·gale \'nī-tᵊn-,gāl, -tiŋ-\ Florence 1820–1910 *Lady of the Lamp* Eng. nurse and philanthropist

Ni·ke \'nī-kē\ goddess of victory in Greek mythology

Ni·o·be \'nī-ə-bē\ bereaved mother in Greek mythology who while weeping for her slain children is turned into a stone from which her tears continue to flow

Nix·on \'nik-sən\ Richard Milhous 1913–1994 37th pres. of the U.S. (1969–74)

No·ah \'nō-ə\ biblical builder of the ark in which he, his family, and living creatures of every kind survive the biblical Flood

No·bel \nō-'bel\ Alfred Bernhard 1833–1896 Swedish manufacturer, inventor, and philanthropist

Oak·ley \'ōk-lē\ Annie 1860–1926 orig. *Phoebe Anne Oakley Moses* Amer. sharpshooter

Oba·ma \ō-'bä-mə\ **Ba·rack** \bə-'räk\ Hussein, Jr. 1961–   44th pres. of the U.S. (2009–); Nobel Prize winner (2009)

Oce·anus \ō-'sē-ə-nəs\ Titan who rules over a great river encircling the earth in Greek mythology

O'·Con·nor \ō-'kä-nər\ (Mary) Flannery 1925–1964 Amer. author

O'Connor Sandra Day 1930–   Amer. jurist

Odin \'ō-dᵊn\ *or* **Wo·den** \'wō-dᵊn\ chief god, god of war, and patron of heroes in Norse mythology

Odys·seus \ō-'di-sē-əs, -'dis-yəs, -'di-shəs, -'di-,shüs\ *or* **Ulys·ses** \yù-'li-(,)sēz\ king of Ithaca and hero in Greek mythology

Oe·di·pus \'e-də-pəs, 'ē-\ son of Laius and Jocasta who in Greek mythology kills his father and marries his mother not knowing their identity

Ogle·thorpe \'ō-gəl-,thórp\ James Edward 1696–1785 Eng. general and founder of Georgia

O'·Keeffe \ō-'kēf\ Georgia 1887–1986 Amer. painter

Olaf V \'ō-ləf, -läf, -laf; 'ü-läf\ 1903–1991 king of Norway (1957–91)

Omar Khay·yám \,ō-,mär-,kī-'yäm, ,ō-mər-, -'yam\ 1048–1131 Persian poet and astronomer

O'·Neill \ō-'nēl\ Eugene Gladstone 1888–1953 Amer. playwright; Nobel Prize winner (1936)

Or·pheus \'ór-,fyüs, -fē-əs\ poet and musician in Greek mythology

Or·well \'ór-,wel, -wəl\ George 1903–1950 pseud. of *Eric Arthur Blair* Eng. author

Osce·o·la \,ä-sē-'ō-lə, ,ō-\ *ca* 1804–1838 Seminole Indian chief

Otis \\'ō-təs\ James 1725–1783 Amer. Revolutionary patriot

Ov·id \\'ä-vəd\ 43 B.C.–17 A.D.? Roman poet

Ow·en \\'ō-ən\ Robert 1771–1858 Welsh social reformer

Ow·ens \\'ō-ənz\ Jesse 1913–1980 orig. *James Cleveland Owens* Amer. track-and-field athlete

Paine \\'pān\ Thomas 1737–1809 Amer. (Eng.-born) political philosopher and author

Pan \\'pan\ god of pastures, flocks, and shepherds in Greek mythology who is usu. represented as having the legs, ears, and horns of a goat

Pan·do·ra \pan-'dȯr-ə\ woman in Greek mythology who out of curiosity opens a box and lets loose all of the evils that trouble humans

Pank·hurst \\'paŋk-ˌhərst\ Emmeline 1858–1928 née *Goulden* Eng. suffragist

Par·is \\'pa-rəs\ son of Priam whose abduction of Helen of Troy in Greek mythology leads to the Trojan War

Park·man \\'pärk-mən\ Francis 1823–1893 Amer. historian

Parks \\'pärks\ Rosa 1913–2005 née *McCauley* Amer. civil rights activist

Pas·cal \pa-'skal, päs-'käl\ Blaise 1623–1662 French mathematician and philosopher

Pas·ter·nak \\'pas-tər-ˌnak\ Boris Leonidovich 1890–1960 Russ. author; Nobel Prize winner (1958)

Pas·teur \pas-'tər\ Louis 1822–1895 French chemist and microbiologist

Pat·rick \\'pa-trik\ Saint *fl.* 5th cent. A.D. apostle and patron saint of Ireland

Pat·ton \\'pa-tⁿn\ George Smith 1885–1945 Amer. general

Paul \\'pȯl\ Saint *died ca.* 67 A.D. Christian missionary and author of several New Testament epistles

Paul name of 6 popes: esp. III 1468–1549 (pope 1534–49); V 1552–1621 (pope 1605–21); VI 1897–1978 (pope 1963–78)

Paul Bun·yan \\'bən-yən\ giant lumberjack in Amer. folklore

Paul·ing \\'pȯ-liŋ\ Linus Carl 1901–1994 Amer. chemist; Nobel Prize winner (1954, 1962)

Pav·lov \\'päv-ˌlȯf, 'pav-, -ˌlȯv\ Ivan Petrovich 1849–1936 Russ. physiologist; Nobel Prize winner (1904)

Pa·vlo·va \\'päv-lə-və, pav-'lō-\ Anna 1881–1931 Russ. ballerina

Pea·ry \\'pir-ē\ Robert Edwin 1856–1920 Amer. arctic explorer

Peg·a·sus \\'pe-gə-səs\ winged horse in Greek mythology

Pei \\'pā\ Ieoh Ming 1917–   Amer. (Chinese-born) architect

Penn \\'pen\ William 1644–1718 Eng. Quaker leader and founder of Pennsylvania

Per·i·cles \\'per-ə-ˌklēz\ *ca* 495–429 B.C. Athenian political leader

Per·ry \\'per-ē\ Matthew Calbraith 1794–1858 Amer. commodore

Perry Oliver Hazard 1785–1819 Amer. naval officer; brother of the preceding

Per·seph·o·ne \pər-'se-fə-nē\ daughter of Zeus and Demeter who in Greek mythology is abducted by Pluto to rule with him over the underworld

Per·shing \\'pər-shiŋ, -zhiŋ\ John Joseph 1860–1948 Amer. general

Pe·ter \\'pē-tər\ Saint *died ca.* 64 A.D. orig. *Si·mon* \\'sī-mən-\ one of the 12 apostles in the Bible

Peter I 1672–1725 *Peter the Great* czar of Russia (1682–1725)

Phil·ip \\'fi-ləp\ Saint, one of the 12 apostles in the Bible

Philip King — see METACOM

Philip name of 6 kings of France: esp. II *or* Philip Augustus 1165–1223 (r. 1179–1223); IV 1268–1314 *Philip the Fair* (r. 1285–1314); VI 1293–1350 (r. 1328–50)

Philip name of 5 kings of Spain: esp. II 1527–1598 (r. 1556–98); V 1683–1746 (r. 1700–46)

Philip II 382–336 B.C. king of Macedon (359–336); father of Alexander the Great

Pi·cas·so \pi-'kä-(ˌ)sō, -'kä-\ Pablo 1881–1973 Span. painter and sculptor in France

Pic·card \pi-'kär, -'kärd\ Auguste 1884–1962 and his son Jacques 1922–2008 Swiss scientists and developers of the bathyscaphe

Pick·ett \\'pi-kət\ George Edward 1825–1875 Amer. Confederate general

Pierce \\'pirs\ Franklin 1804–1869 14th pres. of the U.S. (1853–57)

Pi·late \\'pī-lət\ Pon·tius \\'pän-chəs, 'pən-chəs\ *died after* 36 A.D. Roman governor of Judea (26–36)

Pinkerton \\'piŋ-kər-tⁿn\ Allan 1819–1884 Amer. (Scot.-born) detective

Pis·sar·ro \pə-'sär-(ˌ)ō\ Camille 1830–1903 French (West Indian-born) painter

Pitt \\'pit\ William 1759–1806 *the Younger Pitt* Eng. prime minister (1783–1801; 1804–6)

Pi·us \\'pī-əs\ name of 12 popes: esp. VII 1742–1823 (pope 1800–23); IX 1792–1878 (pope 1846–78); X Saint 1835–1914 (pope 1903–14); XI 1857–1939 (pope 1922–39); XII 1876–1958 (pope 1939–58)

Pi·zar·ro \pə-'zär-(ˌ)ō\ Francisco *ca* 1475–1541 Span. conqueror of Peru

Planck \\'pläŋk\ Max Karl Ernst Ludwig 1858–1947 Ger. physicist

Pla·to \\'plā-(ˌ)tō\ *ca* 428–348 (*or* 347) B.C. Greek philosopher

Plu·to \\'plü-(ˌ)tō\ god of the underworld in Greek mythology

Po·ca·hon·tas \ˌpō-kə-'hän-təs\ *ca* 1595–1617 Amer. Indian friend of the colonists at Jamestown; daughter of Powhatan

Poe \'pō\ Edgar Allan 1809–1849 Amer. author

Polk \'pōk\ James Knox 1795–1849 11th pres. of the U.S. (1845–49)

Pol·lock \'pä-lək\ (Paul) Jackson 1912–1956 Amer. painter

Po·lo \'pō-(ˌ)lō\ Marco ca 1254–1324 Venetian merchant and traveler

Poly·phe·mus \ˌpä-lə-'fē-məs\ a one-eyed creature in Greek mythology that is blinded by Odysseus

Ponce de Le·ón \ˌpän(t)-sə-ˌdā-lē-'ōn, ˌpänts-də-, -'lē-ən\ Juan 1460–1521 Span. explorer

Pon·ti·ac \'pän-tē-ˌak\ ca 1720–1769 Ottawa Indian chief

Por·ter \'pȯr-tər\ Cole Albert 1891–1964 Amer. composer

Porter Katherine Anne 1890–1980 Amer. author

Porter William Sydney — see O. HENRY

Po·sei·don \pə-'sī-dᵊn\ god of the sea in Greek mythology — compare NEPTUNE

Pot·ter \'pä-tər\ (Helen) Beatrix 1866–1943 Brit. author and illustrator

Pound \'paund\ Ezra Loomis 1885–1972 Amer. poet

Pound·mak·er \'paund-ˌmā-kər\ 1826–1886 Cree Indian chief

Pow·ell \'pau̇(-ə)l\ Colin Luther 1937– Amer. general; U.S. secretary of state (2001–05)

Pow·ha·tan \ˌpau̇-ə-'tan, pau̇-'ha-tᵊn\ 1550?–1618 Amer. Indian chief of a confederacy of Algonquian-speaking tribes; father of Pocahontas

Pres·ley \'pres-lē, 'prez-\ Elvis Aaron 1935–1977 Amer. popular singer

Pri·am \'prī-əm, -ˌam\ king of Troy during the Trojan War in Greek mythology

Price \'prīs\ (Mary) Leontyne 1927– Amer. soprano

Pro·me·theus \prə-'mē-thē-əs, -ˌthyüs\ Titan in Greek mythology who is punished by Zeus for stealing fire from heaven and giving it to humans

Pro·teus \'prō-tyüs, -tē-əs\ sea god in Greek mythology who is capable of assuming different forms

Proust \'prüst\ Marcel 1871–1922 French novelist

Ptol·e·my \'tä-lə-mē\ fl. 2d cent. A.D. Greco-Egyptian astronomer, geographer, and mathematician in Alexandria

Puc·ci·ni \pü-'chē-nē\ Giacomo 1858–1924 Ital. composer

Pu·las·ki \pə-'las-kē, pyü-\ Kazimierz 1747–1779 Polish soldier in Amer. Revolutionary army

Pu·lit·zer \'pu̇-lət-sər (*family's pron*), 'pyü-\ Joseph 1847–1911 Amer. (Hungarian-born) journalist

Pu·tin \'pü-tin\ Vladimir Vladimirovich 1952–   pres. of Russia (2000–08; 2012–   )

Pyg·ma·lion \pig-'māl-yən, -'mā-lē-ən\ sculptor in Greek mythology who creates Galatea

Py·thag·o·ras \pə-'tha-gə-rəs, pī-\ ca 580–ca 500 B.C. Greek philosopher and mathematician

Ra \'rä\ god of the sun and chief deity of ancient Egypt

Ra·leigh or **Ra·legh** \'rȯ-lē, 'rä- also 'ra-\ Sir Walter 1554?–1618 Eng. navigator and writer

Ram·ses \'ram-ˌsēz\ or **Ram·e·ses** \'ra-mə-ˌsēz\ name of 12 kings of Egypt: esp. **II** (r. 1279–1213 B.C.); **III** (r. 1187–1156 B.C.)

Ran·dolph \'ran-ˌdälf\ Asa Philip 1889–1979 Amer. labor and civil rights leader

Ra·pha·el \'ra-fē-əl, 'rä-, -ˌel\ archangel named in Hebrew tradition — compare GABRIEL, MICHAEL, URIEL

Ra·pha·el \'ra-fē-əl, 'rä-, 'rä-\ 1483–1520 orig. *Raffaello Sanzio* or *Santi* Ital. painter

Ras·pu·tin \ra-'spyü-tᵊn, -'spü-, -'spu̇-\ Grigory Yefimovich 1872–1916 Russ. mystic

Ra·vel \rə-'vel, ra-\ Joseph Maurice 1875–1937 French composer

Rea·gan \'rā-gən\ Ronald Wilson 1911–2004 40th pres. of the U.S. (1981–89)

Re·bek·ah \ri-'be-kə\ wife of Isaac and mother of Jacob in the Bible

Red Cloud \'red-ˌklau̇d\ 1822–1909 Sioux Indian chief

Red Jack·et \'red-ja-kət\ 1758?–1830 *Sa·go·ye·wa·tha* \ˌsä-ˌgȯi-(y)ə-'wä-thə\ Seneca Indian chief

Reed \'rēd\ Walter 1851–1902 Amer. army surgeon

Rehn·quist \'ren-ˌkwist, 'reŋ-kwəst\ William Hubbs 1924–2005 Amer. jurist; chief justice of the U.S. Supreme Court (1986–2005)

Rem·brandt \'rem-ˌbrant also -ˌbränt\ 1606–1669 *Rembrandt (Harmenszoon) van Rijn* Dutch painter

Rem·ing·ton \'re-miŋ-tən\ Frederic 1861–1909 Amer. painter and sculptor

Re·mus \'rē-məs\ son of Mars who in Roman mythology is killed by his twin brother Romulus

Re·noir \'ren-ˌwär, rən-'\ (Pierre-) Auguste 1841–1919 French painter

Re·vere \ri-'vir\ Paul 1735–1818 Amer. patriot and silversmith

Rich·ard \'ri-chərd\ name of 3 kings of England: **I** 1157–1199 *Richard the Lion-Hearted* (r. 1189–99); **II** 1367–1400 (r. 1377–99); **III** 1452–1485 (r. 1483–85)

Ride \'rīd\ Sally Kristen 1951–2012 Amer. astronaut; 1st Amer. woman in space (1983)

Rob·erts \'rä-bərts\ John Glover Jr. 1995–   Amer. jurist; chief justice of the U.S. Supreme Court (2005–   )

Rob·in Good·fel·low \ˌrä-bən-'gu̇d-ˌfe-(ˌ)lō\ mischievous elf in Eng. folklore

Robin Hood \‚hůd\ legendary Eng. outlaw who gave to the poor what he stole from the rich

Rob·in·son \'rä-bən-sən\ Edwin Arlington 1869–1935 Amer. poet

Robinson Jackie 1919–1972 *Jack Roosevelt Robinson* Amer. baseball player

Rob·in·son Cru·soe \'rä-bə(n)-sən-'krü-(‚)sō\ shipwrecked sailor in Daniel Defoe's *Robinson Crusoe* who lives for many years on a desert island

Ro·cham·beau \‚rō-‚sham-'bō\ Comte de 1725–1807 French general in Amer. Revolution

Rocke·fel·ler \'rä-ki-‚fe-lər\ John Davison 1839–1937 and his son John Davison, Jr. 1874–1960 Amer. oil magnates and philanthropists

Ro·din \rō-‚daⁿ(n)\ François-Auguste-René 1840–1917 French sculptor

Ro·ma·nov \rō-'mä-nəf, 'rō-mə-‚näf\ Michael 1596–1645 1st czar (1613–45) of Russ. Romanov dynasty (1613–1917)

Rom·u·lus \'räm-yə-ləs\ son of Mars in Roman mythology who is the twin brother of Remus and the founder of Rome

Rönt·gen *or* **Roent·gen** \'rent-gən, 'rənt-, -jən\ Wilhelm Conrad 1845–1923 Ger. physicist; Nobel Prize winner (1901)

Roo·se·velt \'rō-zə-vəlt, -‚velt\ (Anna) Eleanor 1884–1962 Amer. lecturer and writer; wife of F. D. Roosevelt

Roosevelt Franklin Delano 1882–1945 32nd pres. of the U.S. (1933–45)

Roosevelt Theodore 1858–1919 26th pres. of the U.S. (1901–09); Nobel Prize winner (1906)

Ross \'ròs\ Betsy 1752–1836 née *Griscom* reputed maker of 1st Amer. flag

Ros·si·ni \rò-'sē-nē, rə-\ Gioacchino Antonio 1792–1868 Ital. composer

Roth \'ròth\ Philip Milton 1933–   Amer. author

Rous·seau \rù-'sō, 'rü-\ Jean-Jacques 1712–1778 French (Swiss-born) philosopher and writer

Row·ling \'rō-liŋ\ J. K. 1965–   *Joanne Kathleen Rowling* Brit. author

Ru·bens \'rü-bənz\ Peter Paul 1577–1640 Flemish painter

Ru·dolph \'rü-‚dòlf, -‚dälf\ Wilma Glodean 1940–1994 Amer. athlete

Rus·sell \'rə-səl\ Bertrand Arthur William 1872–1970 3d Earl *Russell* Eng. mathematician and philosopher; Nobel Prize winner (1950)

Ruth \'rüth\ woman in the Bible who was one of the ancestors of King David

Ruth Babe 1895–1948 *George Herman Ruth* Amer. baseball player

Ruth·er·ford \'rə-thə(r)-fərd, -thə(r)-\ Ernest 1871–1937 Baron *Rutherford* Brit. physicist; Nobel Prize winner (1908)

Sa·bin \'sā-bin\ Albert Bruce 1906–1993 Amer. (Polish-born) physician and microbiologist

Sac·a·ga·wea \‚sa-kə-jə-'wē-ə\ 1786?–1812 Shoshone Indian guide to Lewis and Clark

Sa·dat \sə-'dat, -'dät\ Anwar el- 1918–1981 pres. of Egypt (1970–81); Nobel Prize winner (1978)

Sa·gan \'sā-gən\ Carl Edward 1934–1996 Amer. astronomer and science writer

Saint Nicholas — see Saint NICHOLAS, SANTA CLAUS

Sal·a·din \'sa-lə-‚dēn, -dən\ 1137 (or 1138)–1193 Kurdish general; sultan of Egypt and Syria

Sal·in·ger \'sa-lən-jər\ J. D. 1919–2010 *Jerome David Salinger* Amer. author

Salk \'sò(l)k\ Jonas Edward 1914–1995 Amer. physician and medical researcher

Sa·lo·me \sə-'lō-mē, 'sa-lə-(‚)mā\ niece of Herod Antipas who in the Bible is given the head of John the Baptist as a reward for her dancing

Sa·mo·set \'sa-mə-‚set, sə-'mä-sət\ *died ca.* 1653 Amer. Indian leader

Sam·son \'sam(p)-sən\ powerful Hebrew hero in the Bible who fights against the Philistines but is betrayed by Delilah

Sam·u·el \'sam-yə-wəl, -yəl\ Hebrew judge in the Bible who appoints Saul and then David king

Sand·burg \'san(d)-‚bərg\ Carl 1878–1967 Amer. author

Sang·er \'saŋ-ər\ Margaret 1883–1966 née *Higgins* Amer. birth-control activist

San·ta Claus \'san-tə-‚klòz\ plump white-bearded and red-suited old man in modern folklore who delivers presents to good children at Christmastime

Sap·pho \'sa-(‚)fō\ *fl. ca* 610–*ca* 580 B.C. Greek poet

Sa·rah \'ser-ə, 'sä-rə\ wife of Abraham and mother of Isaac in the Bible

Sar·gent \'sär-jənt\ John Singer 1856–1925 Amer. painter

Sar·tre \'särtr³\ Jean-Paul 1905–1980 French philosopher and author

Sat·urn \'sa-tərn\ god of agriculture in Roman mythology

Saul \'sòl, 'säl\ 1st king of Israel in the Bible

Saul *or* **Saul of Tarsus** the apostle Paul in the Bible

Sche·her·a·zade \shə-‚her-ə-'zäd\ fictional wife of a sultan and narrator of the tales in the *Arabian Nights' Entertainments*

Schin·dler \'shind-lər\ Oskar 1908–1974 Ger. humanitarian during the Holocaust

Schoen·berg \'shə(r)n-‚bərg, 'shoen-‚berk\ Arnold Franz Walter 1874–1951 Amer. (Austrian-born) composer

Schu·bert \'shü-bərt, -‚bert\ Franz Peter 1797–1828 Austrian composer

Schu·mann \'shü-‚män, -mən\ Clara 1819–1896 née *Wieck* \'vēk\ Ger. pianist; wife of R. Schumann

Schumann Robert Alexander 1810–1856 Ger. composer

Schweit·zer \\'shwīt-sər, 'shvīt-, 'swīt-\\ Albert 1875–1965 French theologian, philosopher, physician, and music scholar; Nobel Prize winner (1952)

Scott \\'skät\\ Dred \\'dred\\ 1795?–1858 Amer. slave

Scott Robert Falcon 1868–1912 Brit. polar explorer

Scott Sir Walter 1771–1832 Scot. author

Scott Winfield 1786–1866 Amer. general

Scyl·la \\'si-lə\\ nymph in Greek mythology who is changed into a monster and inhabits a cave opposite the whirlpool Charybdis off the coast of Sicily

Se·at·tle \\sē-'a-tʰl\\ 1786?–1866 Amer. Indian chief

Se·le·ne \\sə-'lē-nē\\ goddess of the moon in classical mythology

Se·quoy·ah or **Se·quoia** \\si-'kwòi-ə\\ ca 1760–1843 *George Guess* Cherokee Indian scholar

Ser·ra \\'ser-ə\\ Junípero 1713–1784 Span. missionary in Mexico and California

Se·ton \\'sē-tʰn\\ Saint Elizabeth Ann 1774–1821 *Mother Seton* née *Bayley* Amer. religious leader

Seu·rat \\sə-'rä\\ Georges 1859–1891 French painter

Seuss Dr. — see GEISEL, THEODOR SEUSS

Sew·ard \\'sü-ərd, 'sürd\\ William Henry 1801–1872 Amer. politician; U.S. secretary of state (1861–69)

Shack·le·ton \\'sha-kəl-tən\\ Sir Ernest Henry 1874–1922 Brit. polar explorer

Shake·speare \\'shāk-,spir\\ William 1564–1616 Eng. playwright and poet

Shaw \\'shò\\ George Bernard 1856–1950 Brit. playwright; Nobel Prize winner (1925)

Shaw Robert Gould 1837–1863 Amer. soldier

Shel·ley \\'she-lē\\ Mary Wollstonecraft 1797–1851 née *Godwin* Eng. author; wife of P. B. Shelley

Shelley Percy Bysshe \\'bish\\ 1792–1822 Eng. poet

Shep·ard \\'she-pərd\\ Alan Bartlett, Jr. 1923–1998 Amer. astronaut; 1st Amer. in space (1961)

Sher·i·dan \\'sher-ə-dən\\ Philip Henry 1831–1888 Amer. general

Sher·lock Holmes \\'shər-,läk-'hōmz, -'hōlmz\\ detective in stories by Sir Arthur Conan Doyle

Sher·man \\'shər-mən\\ John 1823–1900 Amer. statesman; brother of W. T. Sherman

Sherman William Tecumseh 1820–1891 Amer. general

Shi·va \\'shi-və, 'shē-\\ or **Si·va** \\'si-və, 'shi-, 'sē-, 'shē-\\ god of destruction and regeneration in the Hindu sacred triad — compare BRAHMA, VISHNU

Sieg·fried \\'sig-,frēd, 'sēg-\\ hero in Germanic legend who kills a dragon guarding a gold hoard

Si·mon \\'sī-mən\\ or **Simon the Zealot** one of the 12 apostles in the Bible

Si·na·tra \\sə-'nä-trə\\ Frank 1915–1998 *Francis Albert Sinatra* Amer. singer and actor

Sind·bad the Sailor \\'sin-,bad\\ citizen of Baghdad whose adventures are narrated in the *Arabian Nights' Entertainments*

Sis·y·phus \\'si-sə-fəs\\ king of Corinth who in Greek mythology is condemned to roll a heavy stone up a hill in Hades only to have it roll down again as it nears the top

Sit·ting Bull \\,si-tiŋ-'bùl\\ ca 1831–1890 Sioux Indian chief

Siva — see SHIVA

Smith \\'smith\\ Adam 1723–1790 Scot. economist

Smith Bessie 1894?–1937 Amer. blues singer

Smith John ca 1580–1631 Eng. colonist in America

Smith Joseph 1805–1844 Amer. founder of the Mormon Church

Soc·ra·tes \\'sä-krə-,tēz\\ ca 470–399 B.C. Greek philosopher

Sol \\'säl\\ god of the sun in Roman mythology — see HELIOS

Sol·o·mon \\'sä-lə-mən\\ 10th-century B.C. king of Israel noted for his wisdom

Sond·heim \\'sänd-(,)hīm\\ Stephen Joshua 1930– Amer. composer and songwriter

Soph·o·cles \\'sä-fə-,klēz\\ ca 496–406 B.C. Greek playwright

Sou·sa \\'sü-zə, 'sü-sə\\ John Philip 1854–1932 Amer. bandmaster and composer

Spar·ta·cus \\'spär-tə-kəs\\ died 71 B.C. Roman slave and gladiator

Sphinx \\'sfiŋ(k)s\\ monster in Greek mythology having a lion's body, wings, and the head and bust of a woman

Spiel·berg \\'spēl-,bərg\\ Steven 1947– Amer. filmmaker

Spi·no·za \\spi-'nō-zə\\ Benedict de 1632–1677 Hebrew *Baruch Spinoza* Dutch philosopher

Squan·to \\'skwän-tō\\ died 1622 Amer. Indian friend of the Pilgrims

Sta·lin \\'stä-lən, 'sta-, -,lēn\\ Joseph 1879–1953 Soviet Communist party leader (1922–53), premier (1941–53), and dictator

Stan·dish \\'stan-dish\\ Myles or Miles 1584?–1656 Amer. colonist

Stan·ley \\'stan-lē\\ Sir Henry Morton 1841–1904 Brit. explorer in Africa

Stan·ton \\'stan-tʰn\\ Elizabeth Cady 1815–1902 Amer. suffragist

Stein \\'stīn\\ Gertrude 1874–1946 Amer. author

Stein·beck \\'stīn-,bek\\ John Ernst 1902–

1968 Amer. author; Nobel Prize winner (1962)

Steu·ben \'stü-bən, 'styü-, 'shtói-\ Friedrich Wilhelm von 1730–1794 Prussian-born general in Amer. Revolution

Ste·vens \'stē-vənz\ Wallace 1879–1955 Amer. poet

Ste·ven·son \'stē-vən-sən\ Adlai Ewing 1900–1965 Amer. politician

Stevenson Robert Louis 1850–1894 Scot. author

Sto·ker \'stō-kər\ Bram 1847–1912 *Abraham Stoker* Irish author

Stowe \'stō\ Harriet Beecher 1811–1896 Amer. author

Stra·di·va·ri \ˌstra-də-'vär-ē, -'ver-\ Antonio 1644?–1737 Ital. violin maker

Strauss \'shtraús, 'straús\ Johann 1804–1849 and his sons Johann, Jr. 1825–1899 and Josef 1827–1870 Austrian composers

Strauss Richard 1864–1949 Ger. composer

Stra·vin·sky \strə-'vin(t)-skē\ Igor 1882–1971 Amer. (Russ.-born) composer

Stu·art \'stü-ərt, 'styü-; 'st(y)úrt\ Charles Edward 1720–1788 *the Young Pretender; Bonnie Prince Charlie* claimant to the Brit. throne

Stuart Gilbert Charles 1755–1828 Amer. painter

Stuart Jeb 1833–1864 *James Ewell Brown Stuart* Amer. Confederate general

Stuy·ve·sant \'stī-və-sənt\ Peter *ca* 1610–1672 Dutch colonial administrator in America

Sul·li·van \'sə-lə-vən\ Sir Arthur Seymour 1842–1900 Eng. composer; collaborator with Sir William Gilbert

Sullivan Louis Henri 1856–1924 Amer. architect

Sum·ner \'səm-nər\ Charles 1811–1874 Amer. politician

Sun Yat-sen \'sùn-'yät-'sen\ 1866–1925 Chinese statesman

Sut·ter \'sə-tər, 'sü-\ John Augustus 1803–1880 Amer. (Ger.-born) pioneer in California

Swift \'swift\ Jonathan 1667–1745 Eng. (Irish-born) author

Synge \'sin\ John Millington 1871–1909 Irish playwright

Taft \'taft\ William Howard 1857–1930 27th pres. of the U.S. (1909–13); chief justice of the U.S. Supreme Court (1921–30)

Ta·gore \tə-'gór\ Ra·bin·dra·nath \rə-'bin-drə-ˌnät\ 1861–1941 Indian poet; Nobel Prize winner (1913)

Tall·chief \'tól-ˌchēf\ Maria 1925–2013 Amer. dancer

Tan \'tan\ Amy 1952–   Amer. author

Ta·ney \'tó-nē\ Roger Brooke 1777–1864 Amer. jurist; chief justice of the U.S. Supreme Court (1836–64)

Tan·ta·lus \'tan-tə-ləs\ king in Greek mythology who is condemned to stand up to his chin in a pool of water in Hades and beneath fruit-laden boughs only to have the water or fruit go out of reach at each attempt to drink or eat

Tay·lor \'tā-lor\ Zachary 1784–1850 Amer. general; 12th pres. of the U.S. (1849–50)

Tchai·kov·sky \chī-'kóf-skē, chə-, -'kóv-\ Pyotr Ilich 1840–1893 Russ. composer

Te·cum·seh \tə-'kəm(p)-sə, -sē\ 1768–1813 Shawnee Indian chief

Tek·a·kwitha \ˌte-kə-'kwi-thə\ Kateri 1656–1680 *Lily of the Mohawks* canonized Mohawk Indian religious

Ten·ny·son \'te-nə-sən\ Alfred 1809–1892 Baron *Tennyson* known as *Alfred, Lord Tennyson* Eng. poet

Te·re·sa \tə-'rā-zə, -'rē-sə\ Mother 1910–1997 beatified Albanian religious in India; Nobel Prize winner (1979)

Teresa of Ávi·la \'ä-vi-lə\ Saint 1515–1582 Span. nun and mystic

Tes·la \'tes-lə\ Nikola 1856–1943 Amer. (Croatian-born) electrical engineer and inventor

Thatch·er \'tha-chər\ Margaret Hilda 1925–2013 Baroness *Thatcher of Kesteven* née *Roberts* Brit. prime minister (1979–90)

The·seus \'thē-ˌsüs, -sē-əs\ hero in Greek mythology who kills the Minotaur and conquers the Amazons

Thom·as \'tä-məs\ apostle in the Bible who demanded proof of Jesus' resurrection

Thomas à Becket — see Saint Thomas BECKET

Thomas Aquinas Saint — see AQUINAS

Thor \'thór\ god of thunder, weather, and crops in Norse mythology

Tho·reau \thə-'rō, thó-\ Henry David 1817–1862 Amer. author

Thorpe \'thórp\ Jim 1888–1953 *James Francis Thorpe* Amer. athlete

Thur·ber \'thər-bər\ James Grover 1894–1961 Amer. author

Ti·be·ri·us \tī-'bir-ē-əs\ 42 B.C.–37 A.D. Roman emperor (14–37)

Ti·tian \'ti-shən\ *ca* 1488–1576 orig. *Tiziano Vecellio* Ital. painter

Tocque·ville \'tōk-ˌvil, 'tók-, 'täk-, -ˌvēl, -vəl\ Alexis de 1805–1859 French politician and author

Tol·kien \'tól-ˌkēn\ J. R. R. 1892–1973 *John Ronald Reuel Tolkien* Brit. author

Tol·stoy \tól-'stói, tōl-', täl-', 'tól-ˌ, 'tōl-ˌ, 'täl-ˌ\ Leo 1828–1910 Count *Lev Nikolayevich Tolstoy* Russ. author

Tou·louse–Lau·trec \tü-ˌlüz-lō-'trek\ Henri de 1864–1901 French painter

Tri·ton \'trī-t°n\ sea god in Greek mythology who is half man and half fish

Trots·ky \'trät-skē\ Leon 1879–1940 orig. *Lev Davidovich Bronstein* Russ. Communist leader

Tru·deau \'trü-(ˌ)dō, trü-'\ Pierre Elliott

1919–2000 Canad. prime minister (1968–79, 1980–84)

Tru·man \'trü-mən\ Harry S. 1884–1972 33rd pres. of the U.S. (1945–53)

Truth \'trüth\ Sojourner 1797?–1883 Amer. abolitionist

Tub·man \'təb-mən\ Harriet *ca* 1820–1913 Amer. abolitionist

Tu·ring \'tùr-iŋ\ Alan Mathison 1912–1954 Eng. mathematician and logician

Tur·ner \'tər-nər\ Joseph Mallord William 1775–1851 Eng. painter

Tut·ankh·a·men \ˌtü-ˌtaŋ-'kä-mən, -ˌtäŋ-\ originally *Tut·ankh·a·ten* \-'k-tə²n\ *ca* 1370–1352 B.C. king of Egypt (1361–1352 B.C.)

Twain \'twän\ Mark 1835–1910 pseud. of *Samuel Langhorne Clem·ens* \'klem-ənz\ Amer. author

Tweed \'twēd\ William Marcy 1823–1878 *Boss Tweed* Amer. politician

Ty·ler \'tī-lər\ John 1790–1862 10th pres. of the U.S. (1841–45)

Ulysses — see ODYSSEUS

Up·dike \'əp-ˌdīk\ John 1932–2009 Amer. author

Ura·nus \'yùr-ə-nəs, yù-'rā-\ the sky personified as a god and father of the Titans in Greek mythology

Ur·ban \'ər-bən\ name of eight popes: esp. II *ca* 1035–1099 (pope 1088–99)

Uri·el \'yùr-ē-əl\ archangel named in Hebrew tradition — compare GABRIEL, MICHAEL, RAPHAEL

Val·en·tine \'va-lən-ˌtīn\ Saint, 3d cent. Christian martyr

Van Bu·ren \va-lən-'byùr-ən, vən-\ Martin 1782–1862 8th pres. of the U.S. (1837–41)

Van Dyck *or* **Van·dyke** \van-'dīk, vən-\ Sir Anthony 1599–1641 Flemish painter

van Gogh Vincent — see GOGH, VAN

Ve·láz·quez \və-'las-kəs, -'läs-, -kwiz, -(ˌ)käs\ Diego 1599–1660 Span. painter

Ve·nus \'vē-nəs\ goddess of love and beauty in Roman mythology — compare APHRODITE

Ver·di \'ver-dē\ Giuseppe 1813–1901 Ital. composer

Ver·meer \vər-'mer, -'mir\ Jan *or* Johannes 1632–1675 Dutch painter

Verne \'vərn, 'vern\ Jules \'jülz\ 1828–1905 French author

Ves·puc·ci \ve-'spü-chē, -'spyü-\ Amerigo \ə-'mer-i-ˌgō\ 1454–1512 Latin *Americus Ves·pu·cius* \ə-'mer-ə-kəs,-ves-'pyü-sh(ē-)əs\ Ital. navigator for Spain and namesake of America

Vic·to·ria \vik-'tòr-ē-ə\ 1819–1901 *Alexandrina Victoria* queen of the United Kingdom (1837–1901)

Vinci, da Leonardo — see LEONARDO DA VINCI

Vir·gil *also* **Ver·gil** \'vər-jəl\ 70–19 B.C. Roman poet

Vish·nu \'vish-(ˌ)nü\ god of preservation

in the Hindu sacred triad — compare BRAHMA, SHIVA

Vi·val·di \vi-'väl-dē, -'vòl\ Antonio Lucio 1678–1741 Ital. composer

Vol·ta \vōl-'tar, väl-, vòl-, -'ter\ Alessandro 1745–1827 Ital. physicist

Vol·taire \vōl-'tar, väl-, vòl-, -'ter\ 1694–1778 orig. *François-Marie Arouet* French author

Vul·can \'vəl-kən\ god of fire and metalworking in Roman mythology — compare HEPHAESTUS

Wag·ner \'väg-nər\ Ri·chard \'ri-ˌkärt, -ˌkärt\ 1813–1883 Ger. composer

Walk·er \'wò-kər\ Alice Malsenior 1944– Amer. writer

Wal·lace \'wä-ləs\ Alfred Russel 1823–1913 Eng. naturalist

Wal·len·berg \'wä-lən-ˌbərg\ Raoul 1912–1947? Swedish diplomat and hero of the Holocaust

War·hol \'wär-ˌhòl, -ˌhōl\ Andy 1928–1987 orig. *Andrew Warhola* Amer. artist and filmmaker

War·ren \'wòr-ən, 'wär-\ Earl 1891–1974 Amer. jurist; chief justice of the U.S. Supreme Court (1953–69)

Wash·ing·ton \'wò-shiŋ-tən, 'wä-\ Booker Tal·ia·ferro \'tä-lə-vər\ 1856–1915 Amer. educator

Washington George 1732–1799 Amer. general; 1st pres. of the U.S. (1789–97)

Watt \'wät\ James 1736–1819 Scot. inventor

Wayne \'wän\ Anthony 1745–1796 *Mad Anthony* Amer. general

Web·ster \'web-stər\ Daniel 1782–1852 Amer. politician

Webster Noah 1758–1843 Amer. lexicographer

Wel·ling·ton \'we-liŋ-tən\ Duke of 1769–1852 *Arthur Wellesley; the Iron Duke* Brit. general and statesman

Wells \'welz\ H. G. 1866–1946 *Herbert George Wells* Eng. author and historian

Wel·ty \'wel-tē\ Eudora 1909–2001 Amer. author

Wes·ley \'wes-lē, 'wez-\ John 1703–1791 Eng. founder of Methodism

Wes·ting·house \'wes-tiŋ-ˌhaùs\ George 1846–1914 Amer. inventor and industrialist

Whar·ton \'hwòr-t²n, 'wòr-\ Edith 1862–1937 née *Jones* Amer. author

Whis·tler \'hwis-lər, 'wis-\ James (Abbott) McNeill 1834–1903 Amer. artist

Whit·man \'hwit-mən, 'wit-\ Walt 1819–1892 Amer. poet

Whit·ney \'hwit-nē, 'wit-\ Eli 1765–1825 Amer. inventor

Whit·ti·er \'hwi-tē-ər, 'wit-\ John Greenleaf 1807–1892 Amer. poet

Wie·sel \vē-'zel, wē-\ Elie 1928– Amer. (Romanian-born) author; Nobel Prize winner (1986)

Wilde \'wī(-ə)ld\ Oscar 1854–1900 Irish author

Wil·der \'wī(-ə)l-dər\ Thornton Niven 1897–1975 Amer. author

Wil·liam \'wil-yəm\ name of 4 kings of England: **I** *ca* 1028–1087 *William the Conqueror* (r. 1066–87); **II** *ca* 1056–1100 *William Rufus* \'rü-fəs\ (r. 1087–1100); **III** 1650–1702 (r. 1689–1702); **IV** 1765–1837 (r. 1830–37)

Wil·liam Tell \,wil-yəm-'tel\ legendary Swiss patriot commanded to shoot an apple off his son's head

Wil·liams \'wil-yəmz\ Roger 1603?–1683 Eng. colonist

Williams Ted 1918–2002 *Theodore Samuel Williams* Amer. baseball player

Williams Tennessee 1911–1983 orig. *Thomas Lanier Williams* Amer. playwright

Williams Venus 1980–   and her sister Serena 1981–   Amer. tennis players

Wil·son \'wil-sən\ August 1945–2005 orig. *Frederick August Kittel* Amer. playwright

Wilson Edward Osborne 1929–   Amer. biologist

Wilson (Thomas) Woodrow 1856–1924 28th pres. of the U.S. (1913–21); Nobel Prize winner (1919)

Win·throp \'win(t)-thrəp\ John 1588–1649 1st governor of Massachusetts Bay Colony

Witt·gen·stein \'vit-gən-,shtīn, -,stīn\ Ludwig Josef Johan 1889–1951 Eng. (Austrian-born) philosopher

Woden — see ODIN

Woll·stone·craft \'wul-stən-,kraft\ Mary 1759–1797 Eng. feminist and writer

Woods \'wudz\ Tiger 1975–   *Eldrick Woods* Amer. golfer

Woolf \'wulf\ Virginia 1882–1941 Eng. author

Words·worth \'wərdz-(,)wərth\ William 1770–1850 Eng. poet

Wo·vo·ka \wō-'vō-kə\ 1858?–1932 *Jack Wilson* Paiute Indian mystic

Wren \'ren\ Sir Christopher 1632–1723 Eng. architect

Wright \'rīt\ Frank Lloyd 1867–1959 Amer. architect

Wright Orville 1871–1948 and his brother Wilbur 1867–1912 Amer. pioneers in aviation

Wright Richard 1908–1960 Amer. author

Wy·eth \'wī-əth\ Andrew Newell 1917–2009 Amer. painter

Xi Jin·ping \'shē-'jin-'piŋ\ 1953–   general secretary of Chinese Communist Party (2012–); president of China (2013–)

Yeats \'yāts\ William Butler 1865–1939 Irish author

Yel·tsin \'yelt-sən, 'yel-sin\ Boris Nikolayevich 1931–2007 pres. of Russia (1990–99)

York \'york\ Alvin Cullum 1887–1964 Amer. hero in World War I

Young \'yəŋ\ Brig·ham \'brig-əm\ 1801–1877 Amer. Mormon leader

Za·har·i·as \zə-'ha-rē-əs\ Babe Didrikson 1914–1956 *Mildred Ella Zaharias* née *Didrikson* Amer. athlete

Za·pa·ta \sä-'pä-tä\ Emiliano 1879–1919 Mex. revolutionary

Zech·a·ri·ah \,ze-kə-'rī-ə\ Hebrew prophet of the 6th cent. B.C.

Zeng·er \'zeŋ-gər, -ər\ John Peter 1697–1746 Amer. (Ger.-born) journalist and printer

Zeph·y·rus \'ze-fə-rəs\ god of the west wind in Greek mythology

Zeus \'züs\ chief god and ruler of the sky and weather in Greek mythology — compare JUPITER

GEOGRAPHICAL NAMES

This section gives basic information about the world's countries, regions, cities, and major physical features. The latest population figures are given for nations, cities, and some regions. For many of these entries, derived nouns and adjectives are also listed (as **Iceland . . . Icelander . . . n**). Other derived words not shown here have been separately entered in the main A-Z section, because of the presence of additional senses (as **Chinese**).

Abbreviations used here are listed in the front section Abbreviations in This Work. The capital letters N, E, S, and W, used singly or in combination and without a period, indicate direction. For example, "N India" means "northern India." Where direction is a part of the name, the word is spelled out.

The symbol ✳ denotes a capital. Sizes are given in conventional U.S. units, with metric equivalents following.

Ab·er·deen \\ˌa-bər-'dēn\\ city NE Scotland; *pop* 223,000 — **Ab·er·do·ni·an** \\ˌa-bər-'dō-nē-ən\\ *adj or n*

Ab·i·djan \\ˌä-bē-'jän, ˌa-bi-\\ city, seat of government of Cote d'Ivoire; *pop* 1,934,342

Ab·i·lene \\'a-bə-ˌlēn\\ city NW *cen* Texas; *pop* 117,063

Abu Dha·bi \\ˌä-bü-'dä-bē, -'thä-\\ city, ✳ of United Arab Emirates; *pop* 2,394,000

Abu·ja \\ä-'bü-jä\\ city *cen* Nigeria; its ✳; *pop* 1,144,000

Ab·ys·sin·ia \\ˌa-bə-'si-nē-ə, -nyə\\ — see ETHIOPIA — **Ab·ys·sin·i·an** \\-nē-ən, -nyən\\ *adj or n*

Aca·dia \\ə-'kā-dē-ə\\ *or French* **Aca·die** \\ä-kä-'dē\\ NOVA SCOTIA — an early name — **Aca·di·an** \\-ē-ən\\ *adj or n*

Aca·pul·co \\ˌä-kä-'pül-(ˌ)kō, ˌa-\\ city & port S Mexico on the Pacific; *pop* 789,971

Ac·cra \\'ä-krə, 'a-; ə-'krä\\ city & port, ✳ of Ghana; *pop* 1,849,000

Acon·ca·gua \\ˌä-kōn-'kä-gwä\\ mountain 22,834 ft. (6960 m.) W Argentina; highest in the Andes & in Western Hemisphere

Ad·dis Aba·ba \\'ä-dis-'ä-bä-ˌbä, ˌa-dəs-'a-bə-bə\\ city, ✳ of Ethiopia; *pop* 2,740,000

Ad·e·laide \\'a-də-ˌlād\\ city S Australia, ✳ of South Australia; *pop* 1,103,979

Aden \\'ä-dən, 'ā-\\ city & port S Yemen; *pop* 240,370

Aden, Gulf of arm of Indian Ocean between Yemen (Arabia) & Somalia (Africa)

Ad·i·ron·dack \\ˌa-də-'rän-ˌdak\\ mountains NE New York; highest Mount Marcy 5344 ft. (1629 m.)

Admiralty \\'ad-m(ə-)rəl-tē\\ **1** island SE Alaska **2** islands W Pacific N of New Guinea; part of Papua New Guinea

Adri·at·ic Sea \\ˌā-drē-'a-tik, ˌa-\\ arm of Mediterranean between Italy & Balkan Peninsula

Ae·ge·an Sea \\i-'jē-ən\\ arm of Mediterranean between Asia Minor & Greece

Af·ghan·i·stan \\af-'ga-nə-ˌstan, -'gä-nə-ˌstän\\ country W Asia E of Iran; ✳, Kabul; *pop* 22,576,000

Af·ri·ca \\'a-fri-kə\\ continent S of the Mediterranean

Agana — see HAGÅTÑA

Agra \\'ä-grə, 'ä-\\ city N India SSE of Delhi; *pop* 1,585,704

Aguas·ca·lien·tes \\ˌä-gwäs-ˌkäl-'yen-ˌtäs\\ city *cen* Mexico NE of Guadalajara; *pop* 797,010

Agul·has, Cape \\ə-'gə-ləs\\ cape Republic of South Africa; most southerly point of Africa, at 34° 52′ S latitude

Ahag·gar \\ə-'hä-gər, ˌä-hə-'gär\\ mountains S Algeria in W *cen* Sahara

Ah·mad·abad \\'ä-mə-də-ˌbäd, -ˌbad\\ city W India N of Bombay; *pop* 5,577,940

Ak·ron \\'a-krən\\ city NE Ohio; *pop* 199,110

Al·a·bama \\ˌa-lə-'ba-mə\\ state SE U.S.; ✳, Montgomery; *pop* 4,779,736 — **Al·a·bam·i·an** \\-'ba-mē-ən\\ *or* **Al·a·bam·an** \\-'ba-mən\\ *adj or n*

Alas·ka \\ə-'las-kə\\ **1** peninsula SW Alaska SW of Cook Inlet **2** state of U.S. in NW North America; ✳, Juneau; *pop* 710,231 **3** mountain range S Alaska extending from Alaska Peninsula to Yukon boundary — **Alas·kan** \\-kən\\ *adj or n*

Alaska, Gulf of inlet of Pacific off S Alaska between Alaska Peninsula on W & Alexander Archipelago on E

Al·ba·nia \\al-'bā-nē-ə, -nyə\\ country S Europe in Balkan Peninsula on Adriatic; ✳, Tirane; *pop* 3,823,000

Al·ba·ny \\'ol-bə-nē\\ city, ✳ of New York; *pop* 97,856

Albemarle Sound \\'al-bə-ˌmärl\\ inlet of the Atlantic in NE North Carolina

Albert, Lake \\'al-bərt\\ lake E Africa between Uganda & Democratic Republic of the Congo in course of the Nile

Al·ber·ta \\al-'bər-tə\\ province W Canada;

*, Edmonton; *pop* 3,290,350 — **Al·ber·tan** \-'bər-t°n\ *adj or n*

Al·bu·quer·que \'al-bə-ˌkər-kē\ city *cen* New Mexico; *pop* 545,852

Al·ca·traz \'al-kə-ˌtraz\ island California in San Francisco Bay

Al·da·bra \äl-'dä-brə\ island NW Indian Ocean N of Madagascar; belongs to Seychelles

Al·der·ney \'ôl-dər-nē\ — see CHANNEL

Alep·po \ə-'le-(ˌ)pō\ city N Syria; *pop* 1,445,000

Aleu·tian \ə-'lü-shən\ islands SW Alaska extending 1700 mi. (2735 km.) W from Alaska Peninsula

Al·ex·an·der \ˌal-ig-'zan-dər, ˌel-\ archipelago SE Alaska

Al·ex·an·dria \ˌa-lig-'zan-drē-ə, ˌe-\ 1 city N Virginia S of District of Columbia; *pop* 139,966 2 city N Egypt on the Mediterranean; *pop* 4,123,869 — **Al·ex·an·dri·an** \-drē-ən\ *adj or n*

Al·ge·ria \al-'jir-ē-ə\ country NW Africa on Mediterranean; *, Algiers; *pop* 34,200,000 — **Al·ge·ri·an** \-ē-ən\ *adj or n*

Al·giers \al-'jirz\ city, * of Algeria; *pop* 2,364,230 — **Al·ge·rine** \ˌal-jə-'rēn\ *adj or n*

Al·lah·a·bad \'ä-lä-hä-ˌbäd, 'a-lə-hə-ˌbad\ city N India on the Ganges; *pop* 1,212,395

Al·le·ghe·ny \ˌa-lə-'gā-nē\ 1 river 325 mi. (523 km.) long W Pennsylvania & SW New York 2 mountains of Appalachian system E U.S. in Pennsylvania, Maryland, Virginia, & West Virginia

Al·len·town \'a-lən-ˌtaůn\ city E Pennsylvania; *pop* 118,032

Al·maty \əl-'mä-tē\ *or* **Al·ma–Ata** \əl-'mä-ə-'tä; ˌal-mə-'ä-tə, -ə-'tä\ city, former * of Kazakhstan; *pop* 1,365,632

Alps \'alps\ mountain system *cen* Europe — see MONT BLANC

Al·tai *or* **Al·tay** \al-'tī\ mountain system *cen* Asia between Mongolia & W China & between Kazakhstan & Russia

Ama·ga·sa·ki \ˌä-mä-gä-'sä-kē\ city Japan in W *cen* Honshu; *pop* 453,748

Am·a·ril·lo \ˌa-mə-'ri-(ˌ)lō, -lə\ city NW Texas; *pop* 190,695

Am·a·zon \'a-mə-ˌzän, -zən\ river 3900 mi. (6436 km.) long N South America flowing from Peruvian Andes into Atlantic in N Brazil

Amer·i·ca \ə-'mer-ə-kə, -'me-rə-\ 1 either continent (**North America** *or* **South America**) of Western Hemisphere 2 *or* **the Amer·i·cas** \-kəz\ lands of Western Hemisphere including North, Central, & South America & West Indies 3 UNITED STATES OF AMERICA — **American** *adj or n*

American Falls — see NIAGARA FALLS

American Samoa *or* **Eastern Samoa** islands SW *cen* Pacific; U.S. territory; *, Pago Pago (on Tutuila Island); *pop* 55,519

Am·man \ä-'män, a-, -'man\ city, * of Jordan; *pop* 627,505

Am·ster·dam \'am(p)-stər-ˌdam, ˌam(p)-stər-ˌdäm\ city, official * of the Netherlands; *pop* 810,767

Amur \ä-'můr\ river 1780 mi. (2784 km.) long E Asia flowing into the Pacific & forming part of boundary between China & Russia

An·a·heim \'a-nə-ˌhīm\ city SW California E of Long Beach; *pop* 336,265

An·a·to·lia \ˌa-nə-'tō-lē-ə, -'tōl-yə\ — see ASIA MINOR — **An·a·to·li·an** \-'tō-lē-ən, -'tōl-yən\ *adj or n*

An·chor·age \'aŋ-k(ə-)rij\ city S *cen* Alaska; *pop* 291,826

An·da·man \'an-də-mən, -ˌman\ 1 islands India in Bay of Bengal S of Myanmar & N of Nicobar Islands 2 sea, arm of Bay of Bengal S of Myanmar — **An·da·man·ese** \ˌan-də-mə-'nēz, -'nēs\ *adj or n*

An·des \'an-(ˌ)dēz\ mountain system W South America extending from Panama to Tierra del Fuego — see ACONCAGUA — **An·de·an** \'an-(ˌ)dē-ən, an-'\ *adj* — **An·dine** \'an-ˌdēn, -ˌdīn\ *adj*

An·dor·ra \an-'dôr-ə, -'där-ə\ country SW Europe in E Pyrenees between France & Spain; *, Andorra la Vella; *pop* 76,100 — **An·dor·ran** \an-'dôr-ən\ *adj or n*

Andorra la Vel·la \lä-'vel-yä\ town, * of Andorra; *pop* 21,513

An·dros \'an-drəs\ island, largest of Bahamas

An·gel Falls \'än-jəl\ waterfall 3212 ft. (979 m.) SE Venezuela; world's highest waterfall

Ang·kor \'aŋ-ˌkôr\ ruins of ancient city NW Cambodia

An·gle·sey \'aŋ-gəl-sē\ island NW Wales

An·go·la \aŋ-'gō-lə, an-\ country SW Africa S of mouth of Congo River; *, Luanda; *pop* 24,383,000 — **An·go·lan** \-lən\ *adj or n*

An·i·ak·chak Crater \ˌa-nē-'ak-ˌchak\ volcanic crater SW Alaska on Alaska Peninsula; 6 mi. (10 km.) in diameter

An·ka·ra \'aŋ-kə-rə, 'äŋ-\ city, * of Turkey in N *cen* Anatolia; *pop* 4,609,000

An·nap·o·lis \ə-'na-pə-lis\ city, * of Maryland; *pop* 38,394

Ann Ar·bor \(ˌ)an-'är-bər\ city SE Michigan; *pop* 113,934

An·shan \'än-'shän\ city NE China; *pop* 1,203,986

An·ta·nan·a·ri·vo \ˌän-tä-ˌnä-nä-'rē-(ˌ)vō\ city, * of Madagascar; *pop* 958,929

Ant·arc·ti·ca \ant-'ärk-ti-kə, -'är-ti-\ body of land around the South Pole; plateau covered by great ice cap

An·ti·gua \an-'tē-gə, -gwä\ island West Indies in the Leewards; with Barbuda forms independent **Antigua and Barbuda**; *, Saint John's; *pop* 83,700

An·til·les \an-'ti-lēz\ the West Indies except for the Bahamas — see GREATER ANTILLES, LESSER ANTILLES — **An·til·le·an** \-lē-ən\ adj

An·trim \'an-trəm\ district E Northern Ireland; pop 54,000

Ant·werp \'ant-,wərp, 'an-,twərp\ city N Belgium; pop 509,200

Aomen — see MACAO

Aoraki — see COOK, MOUNT

Ap·en·nines \'a-pə-,nīnz\ mountain chain Italy extending length of the peninsula; highest peak Monte Corno (NE of Rome) 9560 ft. (2897 m.) — **Ap·en·nine** \'a-pə-,nīn\ adj

Apia \ä-'pē-ä\ town, ✳ of Samoa; pop 36,735

Apo, Mount \'ä-(,)pō\ volcano Philippines in SE Mindanao 9692 ft. (2954 m.); highest peak in the Philippines

Ap·pa·la·chia \,a-pə-'lä-chə, -'la-chə, -'lä-shə\ region E U.S. including Appalachian Mountains from S cen New York to cen Alabama

Ap·pa·la·chian Mountains \,a-pə-'lä-ch(ē-)ən, -sh(ē-)ən\ mountain system E North America extending from S Quebec to cen Alabama — see MITCHELL, MOUNT

Aqa·ba, Gulf of \'ä-kä-bə\ arm of Red Sea E of Sinai Peninsula

Aquid·neck \ə-'kwid-,nek\ or **Rhode** island SE Rhode Island in Narragansett Bay

Ara·bia \ə-'rā-bē-ə\ peninsula of SW Asia including Saudi Arabia, Yemen, Oman, & Persian Gulf States

Ara·bi·an Sea \ə-'rä-bē-ən\ NW section of Indian Ocean between Arabia & India

Ara·fu·ra \,ä-rä-'fü-rä\ sea between N Australia & W New Guinea

Ar·al Sea \'a-rəl\ formerly **Lake Aral** formerly large lake W Asia which has shrunk into sections some of which are now entirely in Kazakhstan and others between Kazakhstan & Uzbekistan

Ar·a·rat \'a-rə-,rat\ mountain 16,946 ft. (5165 m.) E Turkey near border of Iran

Arc·tic \'ärk-tik, 'är-tik\ 1 ocean N of Arctic Circle 2 Arctic regions 3 archipelago N Canada in Nunavut & Northwest Territories

Ar·da·bil or **Ar·de·bil** \,är-də-'bēl\ city NW Iran; pop 418,000

Ards \'ärdz\ district E Northern Ireland; pop 78,000

Are·ci·bo \,ä-rä-'sē-(,)bō\ city & port N Puerto Rico; pop 96,440

Ar·gen·ti·na \,är-jən-'tē-nə\ country S South America between the Andes & the Atlantic; ✳, Buenos Aires; pop 40,117,000 — **Ar·gen·tine** \'är-jən-,tīn, -,tēn\ adj or n — **Ar·gen·tin·ean** or **Ar·gen·tin·i·an** \,är-jən-'ti-nē-ən\ adj or n

Ar·gos \'är-gəs, -gäs, -gəs\ ancient Greek city-state S Greece

Ar·i·zo·na \,a-rə-'zō-nə\ state SW U.S.; ✳,

Phoenix; pop 6,392,017 — **Ar·i·zo·nan** \-nən\ or **Ar·i·zo·nian** \-nē-ən, -nyən\ adj or n

Ar·kan·sas \'är-kən-,sò\ 1 river 1450 mi. (2334 km.) long SW cen U.S. flowing SE into the Mississippi 2 state S cen U.S.; ✳, Little Rock; pop 2,915,918 — **Ar·kan·san** \är-'kan-zən\ adj or n

Ar·ling·ton \'är-liŋ-tən\ city N Texas; pop 365,438

Ar·magh \är-'mä, 'är-,\ 1 district S Northern Ireland; pop 59,000 2 town cen Armagh district; pop 14,265

Ar·me·nia \är-'mē-nē-ə, -nyə\ 1 region W Asia in mountainous area SE of Black Sea & SW of Caspian Sea divided between Iran, Turkey, & Armenia (country) 2 country W Asia; ✳, Yerevan; pop 3,018,854

Arn·hem Land \'är-nəm\ region N Australia on N coast of Northern Territory

Ar·no \'är-(,)nō\ river 150 mi. (241 km.) long cen Italy flowing through Florence

Aru·ba \ə-'rü-bə\ Dutch island in Caribbean Sea off coast of NW Venezuela; pop 101,484

Ar·va·da \är-'va-də\ city N cen Colorado NW of Denver; pop 106,433

Ash·ga·bat \'äsh-gə-,bät\ or **Ashkh·a·bad** \'äsh-kə-,bad, -,bäd\ city, ✳ of Turkmenistan; pop 412,200

Asia \'ā-zhə, -shə\ continent of Eastern Hemisphere N of the Equator — see EURASIA

Asia Mi·nor \-'mī-nər\ or **An·a·to·lia** \,a-nə-'tō-lē-ə, -'tōl-yə\ peninsula in modern Turkey between Black Sea on N & the Mediterranean on S

As·ma·ra \az-'mä-rə, -'ma-rə\ city, ✳ of Eritrea; pop 342,706

As·syr·ia \ə-'sir-ē-ə\ ancient empire W Asia extending along the middle Tigris & over foothills to the E — **As·syr·i·an** \-ən\ adj or n

As·ta·na \ä-stä-'nä\ city, ✳ of Kazakhstan; pop 814,400

Asun·ción \ä-sün-'syōn\ city, ✳ of Paraguay; pop 502,426

As·wân \ä-'swän, ä-\ city S Egypt on the Nile near site of **Aswân High Dam**; pop 265,500

Ata·ca·ma \,ä-tä-'kä-mä\ desert N Chile

Atchaf·a·laya \(ə-),cha-fə-'lī-ə\ river 225 mi. (362 km.) long S Louisiana flowing S into Gulf of Mexico

Ath·a·bas·ca \,a-thə-'bas-kə, ,ä-\ river 765 mi. (1231 km.) long NE Alberta flowing into **Lake Athabasca** on Alberta–Saskatchewan border

Ath·ens \'a-thənz\ 1 city NE Georgia; pop 115,452 2 city, ✳ of Greece; pop 664,046 — **Athe·nian** \ə-'thē-nē-ən, -nyən\ adj or n

At·lan·ta \ət-'lan-tə, at-\ city, ✳ of Georgia; pop 420,003

At·lan·tic \ət-'lan-tik, at-\ ocean separat-

ing North America & South America
from Europe & Africa; often divided into
North Atlantic and **South Atlantic** —
Atlantic *adj*

At·las \'at-ləs\ mountains NW Africa extending from SW Morocco to N Tunisia

At·ti·ca \'a-ti-kə\ ancient state E Greece; chief city Athens — **At·tic** \'at-ik\ *adj*

Auck·land \'ò-klənd\ city N New Zealand on NW North Island; *pop* 404,658

Au·gus·ta \ò-'gəs-tə, ə-\ **1** city E Georgia; *pop* 195,844 **2** city, ✻ of Maine; *pop* 19,136

Au·ro·ra \ə-'ròr-ə, ò-\ **1** city NE *cen* Colorado; *pop* 325,078 **2** city NE Illinois; *pop* 197,899

Auschwitz — see OSWIECIM

Aus·tin \'òs-tən, 'äs-\ city, ✻ of Texas; *pop* 790,390

Aus·tral·asia \,òs-trə-'lā-zhə, ,äs-, -'lā-shə\ Australia, Tasmania, New Zealand, & Melanesia — **Aus·tral·asian** \-zhən, -shən\ *adj or n*

Aus·tra·lia \ò-'strāl-yə, ä-, ə-\ **1** continent of Eastern Hemisphere SE of Asia **2** country including continent of Australia & island of Tasmania; ✻, Canberra; *pop* 21,508,000 — **Aus·tra·lian** \-yən\ *adj or n*

Australian Alps mountain range SE Australia in E Victoria & SE New South Wales; part of Great Dividing Range

Australian Capital Territory district SE Australia including two areas, one containing Canberra (✻ of Australia) & the other on Jervis Bay (inlet of the South Pacific); surrounded by New South Wales

Aus·tria \'òs-trē-ə, 'äs-\ country *cen* Europe; ✻, Vienna; *pop* 8,402,000 — **Aus·tri·an** \-ən\ *adj or n*

Aus·tria–Hun·ga·ry \-'həŋ-gə-rē\ country 1867–1918 *cen* Europe including Bohemia, Moravia, Transylvania, Galicia, and what are now Austria, Hungary, Slovenia, Croatia, & part of NE Italy — **Aus·tro–Hun·gar·i·an** \'òs-(,)trō-,həŋ-'ger-ē-ən, 'äs-\ *adj or n*

Aus·tro·ne·sia \,òs-trə-'nē-zhə, ,äs-, -'nē-shə\ **1** islands of the South Pacific **2** area extending from Madagascar through Malay Peninsula & Malay Archipelago to Hawaii & Easter Island — **Aus·tro·ne·sian** \-zhən, -shən\ *adj or n*

Avon \'ā-vən, 'a-\ river 96 mi. (154 km.) long *cen* England flowing WSW into the Severn

Ayers Rock — see ULURU

Ayles·bury \'ālz-b(ə-)rē\ town SE *cen* England; *pop* 41,288

Ayr \'er\ *or* **Ayr·shire** \-,shir, -shər\ former county SW Scotland

Azer·bai·jan \,a-zər-,bī-'jän, ,ä-\ country W Asia & SE Europe bordering on Caspian Sea; ✻, Baku; *pop* 9,477,000 — **Azer·bai·ja·ni** \,a-zər-,bī-'jä-nē, ,ä-\ *adj or n*

Azores \'ā-,zòrz, ə-'\ islands Portugal in North Atlantic lying 800 mi. (1287 km.) W of Portuguese coast; *pop* 246,800 — **Azor·e·an** \ā-'zòr-ē-ən, ə-\ *adj or n*

Bab·y·lon \'ba-bə-lən, -,län\ ancient city, ✻ of Babylonia; site 55 mi. (89 km.) S of Baghdad near the Euphrates — **Bab·y·lo·nian** \,ba-bə-'lō-nyən, -nē-ən\ *adj or n*

Bab·y·lo·nia \,ba-bə-'lō-nyə, -nē-ə\ ancient country W Asia in valley of lower Euphrates and Tigris rivers

Bac·tria \'bak-trē-ə\ ancient country W Asia in present NE Afghanistan — **Bac·tri·an** \'bak-trē-ən\ *adj or n*

Bad·lands barren region SW South Dakota & NW Nebraska

Baf·fin \'ba-fən\ **1** bay of the Atlantic between W Greenland & E Baffin Island **2** island NE Canada in Arctic Archipelago N of Hudson Strait

Bagh·dad \'bag-,dad, bäg-'däd\ city, ✻ of Iraq on the Tigris; *pop* (est.) 3,841,000

Ba·guio \,bä-gē-'ō\ city, former summer ✻ of the Philippines in NW *cen* Luzon; *pop* 318,676

Ba·ha·mas \bə-'hä-məz\ islands in N Atlantic SE of Florida; ✻, Nassau; *pop* 367,000 — **Ba·ha·mi·an** \bə-'hä-mē-ən, -'hä-\ *or* **Ba·ha·man** \-'hä-mən, -'häm-ən\ *adj or n*

Bahia — see SALVADOR

Bah·rain \bä-'rān\ islands in Persian Gulf off coast of Arabia; country; ✻, Manama; *pop* 651,000 — **Bah·raini** \-'rā-nē\ *adj or n*

Bai·kal, Lake *or* **Lake Bay·kal** \bī-'käl, -'kal\ lake Russia, in mountains N of Mongolia

Ba·ja California \'bä-(,)hä\ peninsula NW Mexico W of Gulf of California

Ba·kers·field \'bā-kərz-,fēld\ city S California; *pop* 347,483

Ba·ku \bä-'kü\ city, ✻ of Azerbaijan on W coast of Caspian Sea; area *pop* 2,046,000

Bal·a·ton \'ba-lə-,tän, 'bò-lò-,tōn\ lake W Hungary

Bal·boa Heights \(,)bal-'bō-ə\ town Panama; formerly the center of administration for Canal Zone

Bal·e·ar·ic Islands \,ba-lē-'a-rik\ islands E Spain in the W Mediterranean

Ba·li \'bä-lē, 'ba-\ island Indonesia off E end of Java; *pop* 3,891,000 — **Ba·li·nese** \,bäl-i-nēz, ,bal-, -'nēs\ *adj or n*

Bal·kans \'bòl-kənz\ **1** *or* **Balkan Mountains** mountains N Bulgaria extending from Serbia border to Black Sea; highest 7793 ft. (2375 m.) **2** *or* **Balkan Peninsula** peninsula SE Europe between Adriatic & Ionian seas on the W & Aegean & Black seas on the E **3** *or* **Balkan States** countries occupying the Balkan Peninsula: Slovenia, Croatia, Bosnia and Herzegovina, Macedonia, Kosovo, Serbia,

Montenegro, Romania, Bulgaria, Albania, Greece, Turkey (in Europe)

Bal·ly·me·na \ˌba-lē-ˈmē-nə\ district NE *cen* Northern Ireland; *pop* 64,000

Bal·ly·mon·ey \ˌba-lē-ˈmə-nē\ district N *cen* Northern Ireland; *pop* 31,000

Bal·tic Sea \ˈbȯl-tik\ arm of the Atlantic N Europe E of Scandinavian Peninsula

Bal·ti·more \ˈbȯl-tə-ˌmȯr, -mər\ city N *cen* Maryland; *pop* 620,961

Ba·ma·ko \ˈbä-mä-ˌkō\ city, ✲ of Mali on the Niger; *pop* 1,016,000

Ban·bridge \ban-ˈbrij\ district SE *cen* Northern Ireland; *pop* 48,000

Ban·dar Se·ri Be·ga·wan \ˌbən-dər-ˌser-ē-bə-ˈgä-wän\ town, ✲ of Brunei; *pop* 27,285

Ban·dung \ˈbän-ˌdu̇ŋ\ city Indonesia in W Java SE of Jakarta; *pop* 2,394,873

Ban·ga·lore \ˈbaŋ-gə-ˌlȯr\ city S India W of Madras; *pop* 8,482,000

Bang·kok \ˈbaŋ-ˌkäk, baŋ-ˈ\ city, ✲ of Thailand; *pop* 6,160,000

Ban·gla·desh \ˌbäŋ-glə-ˈdesh, ˌbaŋ-, ˌbəŋ-, -ˈdäsh\ country S Asia E of India; ✲, Dhaka; *pop* 149,772,000 — see EAST PAKISTAN — **Ban·gla·deshi** \-ˈde-shē, -ˈdä-\ *adj or n*

Ban·gor \ˈbaŋ-ˌgȯr, ˈban-ˌgȯr\ town E Northern Ireland; *pop* 46,585

Ban·gui \bäŋ-ˈgē\ city, ✲ of Central African Republic; *pop* 532,000

Ban·jul \ˈbän-ˌjül\ *formerly* **Bath·urst** \ˈbath-(ˌ)ərst\ city & port, ✲ of Gambia; *pop* 44,188

Bao·tou *or* **Pao·t'ou** \ˈbau̇-ˈtō\ city N China; *pop* 1,999,000

Bar·ba·dos \bär-ˈbā-(ˌ)dōs, -dəs, -(ˌ)dōz\ island West Indies in Lesser Antilles E of Windward Islands; country, ✲, Bridgetown; *pop* 277,821 — **Bar·ba·di·an** \-ˈbä-dē-ən\ *adj or n*

Bar·bu·da \bär-ˈbü-də\ island West Indies; part of independent Antigua and Barbuda; *pop* 1600

Bar·ce·lo·na \ˌbär-sə-ˈlō-nə\ city NE Spain on the Mediterranean; chief city of Catalonia; *pop* 1,611,013

Bar·king and Dag·en·ham \ˈbär-kiŋ-ən(d)-ˈda-gə-nəm\ borough of E Greater London, England; *pop* 186,000

Bar·na·ul \ˌbär-nə-ˈül\ city S Russia; *pop* 612,000

Bar·net \ˈbär-nət\ borough of N Greater London, England; *pop* 356,000

Bar·ran·qui·lla \ˌbär-än-ˈkē-yä\ city N Colombia; *pop* 1,142,000

Barren Grounds treeless plains N Canada W of Hudson Bay

Bar·row, Point \ˈba-(ˌ)rō\ most northerly point of Alaska & of U.S. at about 71°25′ N latitude

Ba·si·lan \bä-ˈsē-ˌlän\ island S Philippines SW of Mindanao

Bas·il·don \ˈba-zəl-dən\ town SE England; *pop* 157,500

Bass \ˈbas\ strait separating Tasmania & continent of Australia

Basse·terre \bas-ˈter, bäs-\ seaport Saint Kitts, ✲ of Saint Kitts and Nevis; *pop* 14,725

Basutoland — see LESOTHO

Bathurst — see BANJUL

Bat·on Rouge \ˌba-tᵊn-ˈrüzh\ city, ✲ of Louisiana; *pop* 229,493

Ba·var·ia \bə-ˈver-ē-ə\ *or German* **Bay·ern** \ˈbī-ərn\ state SE Germany bordering on Czech Republic & Austria; *pop* 12,397,614 — **Ba·var·i·an** \bə-ˈver-ē-ən, -ˈvar-\ *adj or n*

Ba·ya·mon \ˌbī-ä-ˈmōn\ city NE *cen* Puerto Rico; *pop* 208,116

Beau·fort \ˈbō-fərt\ sea consisting of part of Arctic Ocean NE of Alaska & NW of Canada

Beau·mont \ˈbō-ˌmänt, bō-ˈ\ city SE Texas; *pop* 118,296

Bech·u·a·na·land \ˌbech-ˈwä-nə-ˌland, ˌbe-chə-\ **1** region S Africa N of Orange River **2** — see BOTSWANA — **Bech·u·a·na** \ˌbech-ˈwä-nə, ˌbe-chə-\ *adj or n*

Bed·ford·shire \ˈbed-fərd-ˌshir, -shər\ *or* **Bedford** county SE England

Bedloe's — see LIBERTY

Bei·jing \ˈbā-ˈjiŋ\ *or* **Pe·king** \ˈpē-ˈkiŋ, ˈpā-\ city, ✲ of China; *pop* 10,819,407

Bei·rut \bā-ˈrüt\ city, ✲ of Lebanon; urban area *pop* 1,100,000

Be·la·rus \ˌbē-lə-ˈrüs, ˌbye-lə-\ country *cen* Europe; ✲, Minsk; *pop* 9,503,807 — **Be·la·ru·si·an** \-ˈrü-sē-ən, -ˈrə-shən\ *or* **Be·la·rus·sian** \-ˈrə-shən\ *adj or n*

Belau — see PALAU

Be·lém \be-ˈlem\ city N Brazil; *pop* 1,393,399

Bel·fast \ˈbel-ˌfast, bel-ˈ\ city, ✲ of Northern Ireland; *pop* 281,000

Bel·gium \ˈbel-jəm\ *or French* **Bel·gique** \bel-ˈzhēk\ *or Flemish* **Bel·gië** \ˈbel-kē-ə\ country W Europe; ✲, Brussels; *pop* 11,125,500 — **Bel·gian** \ˈbel-jən\ *adj or n*

Bel·grade \ˈbel-ˌgrād, -ˌgräd, -ˌgrad, bel-ˈ\ *or* **Beo·grad** \bā-ˈȯ-ˌgräd\ city, ✲ of Serbia on the Danube; *pop* 1,120,000

Be·lize \bə-ˈlēz\ *formerly* **British Honduras** country Central America on the Caribbean; ✲, Belmopan; *pop* 324,500 — **Be·liz·ean** *adj or n*

Belize City seaport E Belize; *pop* 55,400

Belle·vue \ˈbel-ˌvyü\ city W Washington E of Seattle; *pop* 122,363

Bel·mo·pan \ˌbel-mō-ˈpän\ city, ✲ of Belize; *pop* 13,800

Be·lo Ho·ri·zon·te \ˈbä-lō-ˌȯr-ē-ˈzȯn-tē\ city E Brazil N of Rio de Janeiro; *pop* 2,375,151

Be·lo·rus·sia \ˌbe-lō-ˈrə-shə, ˌbye-lō-\ *or* **Bye·lo·rus·sia** \ˌbē-ˌe-lō-, ˌbye-lō-\ former republic of U.S.S.R.; became independent Belarus in 1991 — **Belo·rus·sian** \ˌbe-lō-ˈrə-shən, ˌbye-\ *adj or n*

Ben·gal \ben-ˈgȯl, beŋ-, -ˈgäl\ region S

Asia including delta of Ganges & Brahmaputra rivers; divided between Bangladesh & India — **Ben·gal·ese** \ˌbeŋ-gə-ˈlēz, ˌben-, -ˈlēs\ *adj or n*

Bengal, Bay of arm of Indian Ocean between India & Myanmar

Be·nin \bə-ˈnēn, -ˈnin; ˈbe-nin\ *formerly* **Da·ho·mey** \də-ˈhō-mē\ country W Africa on Gulf of Guinea; ✻, Porto-Novo; *pop* 9,984,000 — **Ben·i·nese** \bə-ˌni-ˈnēz, -ˌnē-, -ˈnēs; ˌbe-ni-ˈnēz, -ˈnēs\ *adj or n*

Ben Nev·is \ben-ˈne-vəs\ mountain 4406 ft. (1343 m.) in the Grampians; highest in Great Britain

Beograd — see BELGRADE

Ber·gen \ˈbər-gən, ˈber-\ city & port SW Norway; *pop* 271,949

Be·ring \ˈbir-iŋ, ˈber-\ **1** sea, arm of the North Pacific between Alaska & NE Siberia **2** strait at narrowest point 53 mi. (85 km.) wide between North America (Alaska) and Asia (Russia)

Berke·ley \ˈbər-klē\ city W California on San Francisco Bay N of Oakland; *pop* 112,580

Berk·shire \ˈbərk-ˌshir, -shər\ hills W Massachusetts; highest point Mount Greylock 3491 ft. (1064 m.)

Ber·lin \(ˌ)bər-ˈlin, *G* ber-ˈlēn\ city, ✻ of Germany; divided 1945–90 into **East Berlin** (✻ of East Germany) & **West Berlin** (city of West Germany lying within East Germany); *pop* 3,292,365 — **Ber·lin·er** \(ˌ)bər-ˈli-nər\ *n*

Ber·mu·da \(ˌ)bər-ˈmyü-də\ islands W Atlantic ESE of Cape Hatteras; a British colony; ✻, Hamilton; *pop* 71,000 — **Ber·mu·dan** \-dᵊn\ *or* **Ber·mu·di·an** \-dē-ən\ *adj or n*

Bern \ˈbərn, ˈbern\ city, ✻ of Switzerland; *pop* 128,848 — **Ber·nese** \(ˌ)bər-ˈnēz, -ˈnēs\ *adj or n*

Bes·sa·ra·bia \ˌbe-sə-ˈrā-bē-ə\ region SE Europe now chiefly in Moldova — **Bes·sa·ra·bi·an** \-bē-ən\ *adj or n*

Beth·le·hem \ˈbeth-li-ˌhem, -lē-həm, -lēəm\ town of ancient Palestine in Judaea; the present-day town is SW of Jerusalem in the West Bank; *pop* 30,200

Bev·er·ly Hills \ˈbe-vər-lē\ city SW California within Los Angeles; *pop* 34,109

Bex·ley \ˈbek-slē\ borough of E Greater London, England; *pop* 211,200

Bho·pal \bō-ˈpäl\ city N *cen* India; *pop* 1,886,100

Bhu·tan \bü-ˈtän, -ˈtan\ country S Asia in the Himalayas on NE border of India; ✻, Thimphu; *pop* 753,000 — **Bhu·ta·nese** \ˌbüt-ᵊn-ˈēz, -ˈēs\ *adj or n*

Bi·ki·ni \bi-ˈkē-nē\ atoll W Pacific in Marshall Islands

Bil·lings \ˈbi-liŋz\ city S *cen* Montana; largest in state; *pop* 104,170

Bi·lox·i \bə-ˈlək-sē, -ˈläk-\ city & port SE Mississippi on Gulf of Mexico; *pop* 44,054

Bi·o·ko \bē-ˈō-(ˌ)kō\ *formerly* **Fer·nan·do Póo** \fer-ˈnän-(ˌ)dō-ˈpō\ island portion of Equatorial Guinea in Gulf of Guinea

Bir·ken·head \ˈbər-kən-ˌhed, ˌbər-kən-ˈ\ borough NW England on the Mersey opposite Liverpool; *pop* 123,907

Bir·ming·ham \ˈbər-miŋ-ˌham\ **1** city N *cen* Alabama; *pop* 212,237 **2** city W *cen* England; *pop* 1,086,000

Bis·cay, Bay of \ˈbis-ˌkā, -kē\ inlet of the Atlantic between W coast of France & N coast of Spain

Bish·kek \bish-ˈkek\ *formerly 1926–91* **Frun·ze** \ˈfrün-zi\ city, ✻ of Kyrgyzstan; *pop* 794,000

Bis·marck \ˈbiz-ˌmärk\ **1** city, ✻ of North Dakota; *pop* 61,272 **2** archipelago W Pacific N of E end of New Guinea

Bis·sau \bi-ˈsau̇\ city, ✻ of Guinea-Bissau; *pop* 386,500

Bi·thyn·ia \bə-ˈthi-nē-ə\ ancient country NW Asia Minor bordering on Sea of Marmara and Black Sea — **Bi·thyn·i·an** \-nēən\ *adj or n*

Bit·ter·root \ˈbi-tə(r)-ˌrüt, -ˌru̇t\ range of the Rockies along Idaho–Montana boundary

Black·burn \ˈblak-(ˌ)bərn\ town NW England; *pop* 132,800

Black Forest forested mountain region Germany along E bank of the upper Rhine

Black Hills mountains W South Dakota & NE Wyoming

Black·pool \ˈblak-ˌpül\ town NW England on Irish Sea; *pop* 144,500

Black Sea sea between Europe & Asia connected with Aegean Sea through the Bosporus, Sea of Marmara, & Dardanelles

Blanc, Mont — see MONT BLANC

Blan·tyre \ˈblan-ˌtī(-ə)r\ city S Malawi; *pop* 661,000

Bloem·fon·tein \ˈblüm-fən-ˌtān, -ˌfän-\ city Republic of South Africa, judicial ✻ of the country; *pop* 149,836

Blue Ridge E range of the Applachians E U.S. extending from S Pennsylvania to N Georgia

Bodh Gaya \ˈbōd-ˈgī-ä\ village NE India; one of the holiest sites of Buddhism

Boe·o·tia \bē-ˈō-sh(ē-)ə\ ancient state E *cen* Greece NW of Attica; chief ancient city, Thebes — **Boe·o·tian** \bē-ˈō-shən\ *adj or n*

Bo·go·tá \ˌbō-gō-ˈtä, ˈtō, ˈbō-gə-ˌ\ city, ✻ of Colombia; *pop* 6,850,500

Bo Hai *or* **Po Hai** \ˈbō-ˈhī\ *or* **Gulf of Chih·li** \ˈchē-ˈlē, ˈjir-\ arm of Yellow Sea NE China

Bo·he·mia \bō-ˈhē-mē-ə\ region W Czech Republic; chief city, Prague

Bo·hol \bō-ˈhól\ island S *cen* Philippines

Boi·se \ˈbói-sē, -zē\ city, ✻ of Idaho; *pop* 205,761

Bo·liv·ia \bə-ˈli-vē-ə\ country W *cen* South America; administrative ✻, La Paz;

constitutional ✳, Sucre; *pop* 10,044,000 — **Bo·liv·i·an** \-vē-ən\ *adj or n*

Bo·lo·gna \bō-'lō-nyä\ city N Italy; *pop* 371,000

Bol·ton \'bōl-t⁸n\ town NW England; *pop* 253,300

Bom·bay \bäm-'bā\ *or* **Mum·bai** \'məm-₁bī\ city & port W India; area *pop* 12,442,373

Bonn \'bän, 'bȯn\ city Germany on the Rhine SSE of Cologne, formerly (1949–99) ✳ of West Germany; *pop* 305,765

Boo·thia \'bü-thē-ə\ peninsula N Canada W of Baffin Island; its N tip is most northerly point in mainland North America

Bor·ders \'bȯr-dərz\ former administrative region SE Scotland

Bor·neo \'bȯr-nē-₁ō\ island Malay Archipelago SW of the Philippines; divided between Brunei, Indonesia, and Malaysia

Bos·nia \'bäz-nē-ə\ region S Europe; with Herzegovina forms independent **Bosnia and Her·ze·go·vi·na** \₁hert-sə-gō-'vē-nə, ₁hərt-, -'gō-və-nə\ ; ✳, Sarajevo; *pop* 3,832,000 — **Bos·ni·an** \-nē-ən\ *adj or n*

Bos·po·rus \'bäs-p(ə-)rəs\ strait 18 mi. (29 km.) long between Turkey in Europe & Turkey in Asia connecting Sea of Marmara & Black Sea

Bos·ton \'bȯs-tən\ city, ✳ of Massachusetts; *pop* 617,594 — **Bos·to·nian** \bȯ-'stō-nē-ən, -nyən\ *adj or n*

Bot·a·ny Bay \'bä-tə-nē\ inlet of South Pacific SE Australia in New South Wales S of Sydney

Both·nia, Gulf of \'bäth-nē-ə\ arm of Baltic Sea between Sweden & Finland

Bo·tswa·na \bät-'swä-nə\ *formerly* **Bech·u·a·na·land** \₁bech-'wä-nə-land\ country S Africa; ✳, Gaborone; *pop* 2,032,000

Boul·der \'bōl-dər\ city N *cen* Colorado; *pop* 97,385

Boulder Dam — see HOOVER DAM

Bourne·mouth \'bȯrn-məth, 'bu̇rn-\ town S England on English Channel; *pop* 154,400

Brad·ford \'brad-fərd\ city N England; *pop* 350,000

Brah·ma·pu·tra \₁brä-mə-'pü-trə\ river about 1800 mi. (2900 km.) long S Asia flowing from the Himalayas in Tibet to Ganges Delta

Bra·sí·lia \brə-'zil-yə\ city, ✳ of Brazil; *pop* 2,570,160

Bra·ti·sla·va \₁bra-tə-'slä-və, ₁brä-\ city on the Danube; ✳ of Slovakia; *pop* 411,000

Bra·zil \brə-'zil\ country E & *cen* South America; ✳, Brasília; *pop* 190,733,000 — **Bra·zil·ian** \brə-'zil-yən\ *adj or n*

Braz·za·ville \'bra-zə-₁vil, 'brä-zə-₁vēl\ city, ✳ of Republic of the Congo on W bank of lower Congo River; *pop* 1,373,000

Bre·men \'bre-mən, 'brā-\ city & port NW Germany; *pop* 542,707

Bren·ner \'bre-nər\ pass 4495 ft. (1370 m.) high in the Alps between Austria & Italy

Brent \'brent\ borough of W Greater London, England; *pop* 311,200

Bret·on, Cape \kăp-'bre-t⁸n, kə-'bre-, -'bri-\ cape Canada; most easterly point of Cape Breton Island & of Nova Scotia

Bridge·port \'brij-₁pȯrt\ city SW Connecticut on Long Island Sound; *pop* 144,229

Bridge·town \'brij-₁tau̇n\ city, ✳ of Barbados; *pop* 5996

Brigh·ton \'brī-t⁸n\ town S England on English Channel; *pop* 133,400

Bris·bane \'briz-bən, -₁bān\ city & port E Australia; ✳ of Queensland; *pop* 1,874,427

Bris·tol \'bris-t⁸l\ **1** city & port SW England; *pop* 536,000 **2** channel between S Wales & SW England

Brit·ain \'bri-t⁸n\ **1** the island of Great Britain **2** UNITED KINGDOM

British Columbia province W Canada on Pacific coast; ✳, Victoria; *pop* 4,113,487

British Commonwealth — see COMMONWEALTH, THE

British Empire former empire consisting of Great Britain & the British dominions & dependencies

British Guiana — see GUYANA

British Honduras — see BELIZE

British India the part of India formerly under direct British administration

British Indian Ocean Territory British colony in Indian Ocean consisting of Chagos Archipelago

British Isles island group W Europe consisting of Great Britain, Ireland, & nearby islands

British Virgin Islands E islands of Virgin Islands; a British possession; *pop* 14,786

British West Indies islands of the West Indies including Jamaica, Trinidad and Tobago, & the Bahama & Cayman islands, Windward Islands, Leeward Islands, & British Virgin Islands

Brit·ta·ny \'bri-tə-nē\ region NW France SW of Normandy

Brom·ley \'bräm-lē\ borough of SE Greater London, England; *pop* 309,000

Bronx \'bräŋks\ *or* **The Bronx** borough of New York City NE of Manhattan; *pop* 1,385,108

Brook·lyn \'bru̇k-lən\ borough of New York City at SW end of Long Island; *pop* 2,504,700

Brooks Range \'bru̇ks\ mountains N Alaska

Browns·ville \'brau̇nz-₁vil, -vəl\ city S Texas on the Rio Grande; *pop* 175,023

Bru·nei \bru̇-'nī, 'brü-₁nī\ country NE Borneo; ✳, Bandar Seri Begawan; *pop* 406,200 — **Bru·nei·an** \bru̇-'nī-ən\ *adj or n*

Brus·sels \'brə-səlz\ city, ✳ of Belgium; *pop* 163,000

Bu·cha·rest \'bü-kə-ˌrest, 'byü-\ city, ✳ of Romania; *pop* 1,926,000

Buck·ing·ham·shire \'bə-kiŋ-əm-ˌshir\ *or* **Buckingham** county SE *cen* England

Bu·da·pest \'bü-də-ˌpest\ city, ✳ of Hungary; *pop* 1,729,040

Bue·nos Ai·res \ˌbwā-nəs-'a-rēz, *Sp* ˌbwā-nōs-'ī-rās\ city, ✳ of Argentina; *pop* 2,960,976

Buf·fa·lo \'bə-fə-ˌlō\ city W New York on Lake Erie; *pop* 261,310

Bu·jum·bu·ra \ˌbü-jəm-'bur-ə\ city, ✳ of Burundi; *pop* 497,166

Bu·ko·vi·na \ˌbü-kō-'vē-nə\ region E *cen* Europe in foothills of E Carpathians

Bul·gar·ia \ˌbəl-'ger-ē-ə, bul-\ country SE Europe on Black Sea; ✳, Sofia; *pop* 7,246,000 — **Bul·gar·i·an** \ˌbəl-'ger-ē-ən, bul-\ *adj or n*

Bull Run \'bul-'rən\ stream NE Virginia

Bun·ker Hill \'bəŋ-kər\ height in Boston, Massachusetts

Bur·bank \'bər-ˌbaŋk\ city SW California; *pop* 103,340

Bur·gun·dy \'bər-gən-dē\ region E France — **Bur·gun·di·an** \(ˌ)bər-'gən-dē-ən\ *adj or n*

Bur·ki·na Fa·so \bur-'kē-nə-'fä-sō, bər-\ *formerly* **Upper Vol·ta** \'vōl-tə, 'väl-\ country W Africa N of Cote d'Ivoire, Ghana, & Togo; ✳, Ouagadougou; *pop* 14,017,000

Bur·ling·ton \'bər-liŋ-tən\ city NW Vermont; largest in state; *pop* 42,417

Bur·ma \'bər-mə\ — see MYANMAR — **Bur·mese** \ˌbər-'mēz, -'mēs\ *adj or n*

Bu·run·di \bu-'rün-dē, -'rün-\ country E *cen* Africa; ✳, Bujumbura; *pop* 8,300,000 — **Bu·run·di·an** \-dē-ən\ *adj or n*

Busan — see PUSAN

Bute \'byüt\ island SW Scotland in Firth of Clyde

Butte \'byüt\ city SW Montana; county *pop* 32,996

Byelorussia — see BELORUSSIA

By·zan·tine Empire \'bi-zⁿn-ˌtēn, 'bī-, -ˌtīn; bə-'zan-ˌtēn, -tīn, bī-\ empire of SE & S Europe and W Asia from 4th to 15th century

By·zan·ti·um \bə-'zan-sh(ē-)əm, -'zant-ē-əm\ ancient city on site of modern Istanbul

Cabo Verde — see CAPE VERDE

Caer·nar·von \kär-'när-vən, kə(r)-\ town & seaport NW Wales; *pop* 9506

Ca·guas \'kä-ˌgwäs\ town E *cen* Puerto Rico; *pop* 142,893

Cai·ro \'kī-(ˌ)rō\ city, ✳ of Egypt; *pop* 7,787,000 — **Cai·rene** \kī-'rēn\ *adj or n*

Ca·la·bria \kə-'lä-brē-ə, -'lä-\ district of ancient Italy consisting of area forming heel of Italian Peninsula — **Ca·la·bri·an** \kə-'lä-brē-ən, -'lä-\ *adj or n*

Cal·cut·ta \kal-'kə-tə\ *or* **Kol·ka·ta** \kōl-'kä-tä\ city E India on Hugli River; *pop* 4,496,694 — **Cal·cut·tan** \-'kə-tⁿn\ *adj or n*

Cal·e·do·nia \ˌka-lə-'dō-nyə, -nē-ə\ — see SCOTLAND — **Cal·e·do·nian** \-nyən, -nē-ə\ *adj or n*

Cal·ga·ry \'kal-gə-rē\ city SW Alberta, Canada; *pop* 1,096,833

Ca·li \'kä-lē\ city W Colombia; *pop* 2,326,500

Cal·i·for·nia \ˌka-lə-'fȯr-nyə\ state SW U.S.; ✳, Sacramento; *pop* 37,253,956 — **Cal·i·for·nian** \-nyən\ *adj or n*

California, Gulf of arm of the Pacific NW Mexico

Cal·va·ry \'kal-v(ə-)rē\ place outside ancient Jerusalem where Jesus was crucified

Cambay, Gulf of — see KHAMBHAT (Gulf of)

Cam·bo·dia \kam-'bō-dē-ə\ *or* **Kam·pu·chea** \ˌkam-pu-'chē-ə\ country SE Asia in S Indochina; ✳, Phnom Penh; *pop* 13,396,000 — **Cam·bo·di·an** \kam-'bō-dē-ən\ *adj or n*

Cam·bria \'kam-brē-ə\ WALES — an old name

Cam·bridge \'kām-brij\ **1** city E Massachusetts W of Boston; *pop* 105,162 **2** city E England; *pop* 92,772

Cam·bridge·shire \'kām-brij-ˌshir, -shər\ *or* **Cambridge** county E England

Cam·den \'kam-dən\ borough of N Greater London, England; *pop* 220,000

Cam·er·oon *or* **French Cam·er·oun** \ˌka-mə-'rün\ country W Africa; ✳, Yaoundé; *pop* 17,464,000 — **Cam·er·oo·nian** \-'rü-nē-ən, -'nyən\ *adj or n*

Ca·mi·guin \ˌkä-mē-'gēn\ island Philippines, off N coast of Mindanao

Ca·naan \'kā-nən\ the part of ancient Palestine between Jordan River & Mediterranean Sea; sometimes used to refer to all of ancient Palestine — **Ca·naan·ite** \'kā-nə-ˌnīt\ *adj or n*

Can·a·da \'ka-nə-də\ country N North America; ✳, Ottawa; *pop* 33,476,688 — **Ca·na·di·an** \kə-'nā-dē-ən\ *adj or n*

Canadian Falls — see NIAGARA FALLS

Canadian Shield *or* **Lau·ren·tian Pla·teau** \lȯ-'ren(t)-shən\ plateau region E Canada & NE U.S. extending from Mackenzie River basin E to Davis Strait & S to S Quebec, S *cen* Ontario, NE Minnesota, N Wisconsin, NW Michigan, and NE New York including the Adirondacks

Canal Zone *or* **Panama Canal Zone** strip of territory Panama leased to U.S. (until 1979) for Panama Canal

Ca·nary \kə-'ner-ē\ islands Spain in the Atlantic off NW coast of Africa; *pop* 2,118,679

Ca·nav·er·al, Cape \kə-'nav-rəl, -'na-və-\ *or 1963–73* **Cape Ken·ne·dy** \-'ken-ə-dē\

cape E Florida in the Atlantic on **Canaveral Peninsula** E of Indian River

Can·ber·ra \'kan-b(ə-)rə, -ˌber-ə\ city, ✻ of Australia in Australian Capital Territory; *pop* 355,596

Cannes \'kan, 'kän\ port SE France; *pop* 73,671

Can·ter·bury \'kan-tə(r)-ˌber-ē, -b(ə-)rē\ city SE England; *pop* 34,404

Canton — see GUANGZHOU

Cape Bret·on Island \kăp-'bret-t³n, kə-'bre-, -'bri-\ island NE Nova Scotia

Cape Coral city SW Florida; *pop* 154,305

Cape Horn — see HORN, CAPE

Cape of Good Hope — see GOOD HOPE, CAPE OF

Cape Province *or* **Cape of Good Hope** *or before 1910* **Cape Colony** former province S Republic of South Africa

Cape Town \'kăp-ˌtaůn\ city, legislative ✻ of Republic of South Africa and formerly ✻ of Cape Province; *pop* 3,740,026

Cape Verde \'vərd\ *or* **Ca·bo Ver·de** \ˌkä-bü-'ver-də\ islands in the North Atlantic off W Africa; country; ✻, Praia; *pop* 491,875 — **Cape Verd·ean** \'vər-dē-ən\ *adj or n*

Cape York Peninsula \'yórk\ peninsula NE Australia in N Queensland

Ca·pri \kä-'prē, kə-; 'kä-(ˌ)prē, 'kä-\ island Italy S of Bay of Naples; *pop* 7270

Ca·ra·cas \kə-'rä-käs\ city, ✻ of Venezuela;*pop* 1,836,000

Car·diff \'kär-dif\ city, ✻ of Wales; *pop* 335,000

Ca·rib·be·an Sea \ˌka-rə-'bē-ən, kə-'ri-bē-\ arm of the Atlantic; on N & E are the West Indies, on S is South America, & on W is Central America — **Caribbean** *adj*

Car·lisle \kär-'lī(-ə)l, kər-, 'kär-ˌ\ city NW England; *pop* 99,800

Carls·bad Caverns \'kär(-ə)lz-ˌbad\ series of caves SE New Mexico

Car·mar·then \kär-'mär-thən, kə(r)-\ port S Wales; *pop* 54,800

Car·o·li·na \ˌka-rə-'lī-nə\ English colony on E coast of North America founded 1663 & divided 1729 into North Carolina & South Carolina (the **Carolinas**) — **Car·o·lin·i·an** \ˌka-rə-'li-nē-ən, -nyən\ *adj or n*

Ca·ro·li·na \ˌkä-rō-'lē-nä\ city NE Puerto Rico; *pop* 176,762

Car·o·line \'ka-rə-ˌlīn, -lən\ islands W Pacific E of S Philippines; comprising Palau & the Federated States of Micronesia

Car·pa·thi·an \kär-'pä-thē-ən\ mountains E cen Europe along boundary between Slovakia & Poland & in N & cen Romania; highest Gerlachovsky 8711 ft. (2655 m.)

Car·pen·tar·ia, Gulf of \ˌkär-pən-'ter-ē-ə\ inlet of Arafura Sea N of Australia

Car·rick·fer·gus \ˌka-rik-'fər-gəs\ district E Northern Ireland; *pop* 39,000

Car·roll·ton \'ka-rəl-tən\ city N Texas; *pop* 119,097

Car·son City \'kär-s³n\ city, ✻ of Nevada; *pop* 55,274

Car·thage \'kär-thij\ ancient city N Africa NE of modern Tunis; ✻ of an empire that once included much of NW Africa, E Spain, & Sicily — **Car·tha·gin·ian** \ˌkär-thə-'ji-nyən, -nē-ən\ *adj or n*

Ca·sa·blan·ca \ˌka-sə-'blaŋ-kə, ˌkä-sə-'bläŋ-, -zə-\ city W Morocco on the Atlantic; *pop* 3,102,000

Cas·cade Range \(ˌ)kas-'kād\ mountains NW U.S. in Washington, Oregon, & N California — see RAINIER, MOUNT

Cas·per \'kas-pər\ city *cen* Wyoming; *pop* 55,316

Cas·pi·an Sea \'kas-pē-ən\ salt lake between Europe and Asia about 90 ft. (27 m.) below sea level

Cas·tile \ka-'stēl\ *or in full* **Cas·ti·lla** \kä-'stēl-yä, -'stē-yä\ region & ancient kingdom *cen* & N Spain

Cast·le·reagh \'ka-səl-(ˌ)rā\ district E Northern Ireland; *pop* 67,000

Cas·tries \'kas-ˌtrēz, -ˌtrēs\ seaport, ✻ of Saint Lucia; *pop* 11,900

Cat·a·lo·nia \ˌka-tə-'lō-nyə, -nē-ə\ region NE Spain bordering on France & the Mediterranean; chief city, Barcelona; *pop* 7,519,843 — **Cat·a·lo·nian** \-'ō-nyən, -nē-ən\ *adj or n*

Ca·thay \ka-'thā\ an old name for China

Cats·kill \'kat-ˌskil\ mountains in Appalachian system SE New York W of the Hudson

Cau·ca·sus \'kó-kə-səs\ mountain system SE Europe between Black & Caspian seas in Russia, Georgia, Azerbaijan, & Armenia

Cay·enne \kī-'en, kā-\ city, ✻ of French Guiana; *pop* 37,097

Cay·man \(ˌ)kā-'man, *attributively* 'kā-mən\ islands West Indies NW of Jamaica; a British colony; *pop* 56,700

Ce·bu \sā-'bü\ island E *cen* Philippines

Ce·dar Rapids \'sē-dər\ city E Iowa; *pop* 126,326

Cel·tic Sea \'kel-tik, 'sel-\ inlet of the Atlantic in British Isles SE of Ireland, SW of Wales, & W of SW England

Central African Republic country N *cen* Africa; ✻, Bangui; *pop* 2,998,000

Central America narrow portion of North America from S border of Mexico to South America — **Central American** *adj or n*

Central Valley valley of Sacramento & San Joaquin rivers in California between Sierra Nevada & Coast Ranges

Cey·lon \si-'län, sā-\ **1** island in Indian Ocean off S India **2** — see SRI LANKA — **Cey·lon·ese** \ˌsä-lə-'nēz, ˌsē-, ˌse-, -'nēs\ *adj or n*

Chad \'chad\ country N *cen* Africa; ✻,

N'Djamena; *pop* 9,253,000 — **Chad·ian** \'cha-dē-ən\ *adj or n*

Chad, Lake shallow lake N *cen* Africa at junction of boundaries of Chad, Niger, & Nigeria

Cha·gos Archipelago \'chä-gəs\ island group cen Indian Ocean; forms British Indian Ocean Territory — see DIEGO GARCIA

Chal·dea \kal-'dē-ə\ ancient region SW Asia on Euphrates River & Persian Gulf — **Chal·de·an** \-'dē-ən\ *adj or n* — **Chal·dee** \'kal-ˌdē\ *n*

Cham·pagne \sham-'pān\ region NE France

Cham·plain, Lake \sham-'plān\ lake between New York & Vermont extending N into Quebec

Chan·di·garh \'chən-dē-gər\ city N India N of Delhi; *pop* 809,000

Chan·dler \'chan(d)-lər\ city SW *cen* Arizona; *pop* 236,123

Chang \'chän\ *or traditionally* **Yang·tze** \'yaŋ-'sē, 'yaŋ(k)t-'sē; 'yän-'tsə\ river 3434 mi. (5525 km.) long *cen* China flowing into East China Sea

Chang·chun \'chäŋ-'chún\ city NE China; *pop* 3,802,000

Chang·sha \'chäŋ-'shä\ city SE *cen* China; *pop* 3,094,000

Channel islands in English Channel including Jersey, Guernsey, & Alderney & belonging to United Kingdom; *pop* 135,694

Charles \'chär(-ə)lz\ river 47 mi. (76 km.) long E Massachusetts flowing into Boston harbor

Charles, Cape cape E Virginia N of entrance to Chesapeake Bay

Charles·ton \'chär(-ə)l-stən\ **1** seaport SE South Carolina; *pop* 120,083 **2** city, ✳ of West Virginia; *pop* 51,400

Char·lotte \'shär-lət\ city S North Carolina; *pop* 731,424

Charlotte Ama·lie \ə-'mäl-yə, 'a,mə-lē\ city, ✳ of Virgin Islands of the U.S.; on island of Saint Thomas; *pop* 11,004

Char·lottes·ville \'shär-ləts-ˌvil, -vəl\ city *cen* Virginia; *pop* 43,475

Char·lotte·town \'shär-lət-ˌtaún\ city, ✳ of Prince Edward Island, Canada; *pop* 32,174

Chat·ta·noo·ga \ˌcha-tə-'nü-gə\ city SE Tennessee; *pop* 167,674

Chech·nya \chech-'nyä, 'chech-nyə\ republic of SE Russia in Europe; ✳, Grozny

Chelms·ford \'chemz-fərd\ town SE England; *pop* 150,000

Che·lya·binsk \chel-'yä-bən(t)sk\ city W Russia; *pop* 1,130,000

Cheng–chou — see ZHENGZHOU

Cheng·du *or* **Ch'eng–tu** \'chəŋ-'dü\ city SW *cen* China; *pop* 7,416,000

Chennai — see MADRAS

Cher·no·byl \chər-'nō-bəl, (ˌ)cher-\ site N Ukraine of town abandoned after 1986 nuclear accident

Ches·a·peake \'che-sə-ˌpēk, 'ches-ˌpēk\ city SE Virginia; *pop* 222,209

Chesapeake Bay inlet of the Atlantic in Virginia & Maryland

Chesh·ire \'che-shər, -ˌshir\ *or* **Ches·ter** \'ches-tər\ former county W England bordering on Wales

Chester \'ches-tər\ city NW England; *pop* 58,436

Chev·i·ot \'chē-vē-ət, 'che-\ hills along English–Scottish border

Chey·enne \shī-'an, -'en\ city, ✳ of Wyoming; *pop* 59,466

Chi·ba \'chē-bä\ city E Japan in Honshu on Tokyo Bay E of Tokyo; *pop* 961,749

Chi·ca·go \shə-'kä-(ˌ)gō, -'kò-, -gə\ city & port NE Illinois on Lake Michigan; *pop* 2,695,598 — **Chi·ca·go·an** \-'kä-gō-ən, -'kò-\ *n*

Chi·chén It·zá \chē-ˌchen-ēt-'sä, -'ēt-sə\ ruined Mayan city SE Mexico in Yucatán Peninsula

Chich·es·ter \'chi-chəs-tər\ city S England; *pop* 24,189

Ch'i–ch'i–ha–erh — see QIQIHAR

Chihli, Gulf of — see BO HAI

Chile \'chi-lē, 'chē-(ˌ)lä\ country SW South America; ✳, Santiago; *pop* 16,341,929 — **Chil·ean** \'chi-lē-ən, chə-'lā-ən\ *adj or n*

Chim·bo·ra·zo \ˌchēm-bō-'rä-(ˌ)zō\ mountain 20,561 ft. (6267 m.) W *cen* Ecuador

Chi·na \'chī-nə\ **1** country E Asia; ✳, Beijing; *pop* 1,335,000,000 — see TAIWAN **2** sea section of the W Pacific; divided into East China & South China seas

Chin–chou *or* **Chinchow** — see JINZHOU

Chi·și·nău \ˌkē-shē-'naú\ *or* **Ki·shi·nev** \ˌki-shi-'nyóf; 'ki-shə-ˌnef, -ˌnev\ city *cen* Moldova; its ✳; *pop* 669,000

Chit·ta·gong \'chi-tə-ˌgäŋ, -ˌgòŋ\ city SE Bangladesh on Bay of Bengal; *pop* 7,616,000

Chong·qing *or* **Ch'ung–ch'ing** \'chùŋ-'chiŋ\ *or* **Chung·king** \'chúŋ-'kiŋ\ city SW *cen* China; *pop* 6,861,000

Christ·church \'krīs(t)-ˌchərch\ city New Zealand on E coast of South Island; urban area *pop* 341,469

Christ·mas \'kris-məs\ island E Indian Ocean SW of Java; governed by Australia; *pop* 1000

Chu·la Vis·ta \ˌchü-lə-'vis-tə\ city SW California S of San Diego; *pop* 243,916

Chuuk \'chúk\ *or* **Truk** \'trək, 'trúk\ islands *cen* Carolines, part of Federated States of Micronesia; *pop* 53,300

Cin·cin·na·ti \ˌsin(t)-sə-'na-tē, -'na-tə\ city SW Ohio; *pop* 296,943

Ciu·dad Juá·rez \syü-'thäth-'hwär-es, ˌwär-; ˌsē-ù-'dad-\ city Mexico on Texas border; *pop* 1,332,131

Ciudad Trujillo — see SANTO DOMINGO

Clarks·ville \'klärks-,vil, -vǝl\ city N Tennessee NW of Nashville; *pop* 132,929

Clear·wa·ter \'klir-,wò-tǝr, -,wä-\ city W Florida NW of St. Petersburg; *pop* 107,685

Cleve·land \'klēv-lǝnd\ city & port NE Ohio on Lake Erie; *pop* 396,815

Clyde \'klīd\ river 106 mi. (171 km.) long SW Scotland flowing into **Firth of Clyde** (estuary)

Coast Mountains mountain range W British Columbia, Canada; the N continuation of Cascade Range

Coast Ranges chain of mountain ranges W North America extending along Pacific coast W of Sierra Nevada & Cascade Range & through Vancouver Island into S Alaska to Kenai Peninsula & Kodiak Island

Cod, Cape \-'käd\ peninsula SE Massachusetts

Coim·ba·tore \,kòim-bǝ-'tór\ city S India; *pop* 1,050,721

Cole·raine \kōl-'rān, 'kōl-,\ 1 district N Northern Ireland; *pop* 59,000 2 port in Coleraine district

Co·logne \kǝ-'lōn\ city W Germany on the Rhine; *pop* 1,005,775

Co·lom·bia \kǝ-'lǝm-bē-ǝ\ country NW South America; *, Bogotá; *pop* 41,468,000 — **Co·lom·bi·an** \-bē-ǝn\ *adj or n*

Co·lom·bo \kǝ-'lǝm-(,)bō\ city, * of Sri Lanka; *pop* 647,100

Col·o·ra·do \,kä-lǝ-'ra-(,)dō\ 1 river 1450 mi. (2334 km.) long SW U.S. & NW Mexico flowing from N Colorado into Gulf of California 2 desert SE California 3 plateau region SW U.S. W of Rocky Mountains 4 state W U.S.; *, Denver; *pop* 5,029,196 — **Col·o·rad·an** \-'ra-dⁿn, -'rä-\ *or* **Co·lo·ra·do·an** \-'ra-dō-ǝn, -'rä-\ *adj or n*

Colorado Springs city *cen* Colorado E of Pikes Peak; *pop* 416,427

Co·lum·bia \kǝ-'lǝm-bē-ǝ\ 1 river 1214 mi. (1953 km.) long SW Canada & NW U.S. flowing S & W from SE British Columbia into the Pacific 2 plateau in Columbia River basin in E Washington, E Oregon, & SW Idaho 3 city, * of South Carolina; *pop* 129,272

Co·lum·bus \kǝ-'lǝm-bǝs\ 1 city W Georgia; *pop* 189,885 2 city, * of Ohio; *pop* 787,033

Com·mon·wealth, the \'käm-ǝn-,wel(t)th\ *or* **Commonwealth of Nations** *formerly* **British Commonwealth** the United Kingdom & most of the countries formerly dependent on it

Com·o·ros \'kä-mǝ-,rōz\ islands off SE Africa NW of Madagascar; country (except for Mayotte Island); *, Moroni; *pop* 752,000

Con·a·kry \'kä-nǝ-krē\ city, * of Guinea; *pop* 1,668,000

Con·cord \'kän-,kòrd, 'kän-\ 1 city W California; *pop* 122,067 2 town E Massachusetts NW of Boston; *pop* 17,668 3 city, * of New Hampshire; *pop* 42,695

Con·go \'kän-(,)gō\ 1 *or* **Zaire** \zä-'ir\ river over 2700 mi. (4344 km.) long W Africa flowing into the Atlantic 2 *officially* **Democratic Republic of the Congo** *formerly 1971–97* **Zaire** country *cen* Africa consisting of most of Congo River basin E of lower Congo River; *, Kinshasa; *pop* 67,800,000 3 *or officially* **Republic of the Congo** country W *cen* Africa W of lower Congo River; *, Brazzaville; *pop* 3,697,000 — **Con·go·lese** \,kän-gǝ-'lēz, -'lēs\ *adj or n*

Con·nacht \'kä-,nòt\ province W Ireland; *pop* 464,296

Con·nect·i·cut \kǝ-'ne-ti-kǝt\ 1 river 407 mi. (655 km.) long NE U.S. flowing S from N New Hampshire into Long Island Sound 2 state NE U.S.; *, Hartford; *pop* 3,574,097

Constantinople — see ISTANBUL

Continental Divide line of highest points of land separating the waters flowing W from those flowing N or E and extending SSE from NW Canada across W U.S. through Mexico & Central America to South America where it joins the Andes Mountains

Cook \'kúk\ 1 inlet of the Pacific S Alaska W of Kenai Peninsula 2 islands South Pacific SW of Society Islands belonging to New Zealand; *pop* 19,600 3 strait New Zealand between North Island & South Island

Cook, Mount *or* **Ao·ra·ki** \aú-'rä-kē\ mountain 12,349 ft. (3764 m.) New Zealand in W *cen* South Island in Southern Alps; highest in New Zealand

Cooks·town \'kúks-,taún\ district *cen* Northern Ireland; *pop* 37,000

Co·pen·ha·gen \,kō-pǝn-'hä-gǝn, -'hā-\ city, * of Denmark; *pop* 579,513

Cor·al Sea \'kòr-ǝl, 'kär-\ arm of the W Pacific NE of Australia

Coral Springs city SE Florida; *pop* 121,096

Cór·do·ba \'kòr-dǝ-bǝ, 'kòr-thō-,vä\ city N *cen* Argentina; *pop* 1,293,000

Cor·inth \'kòr-ǝn(t)th, 'kär-\ 1 region of ancient Greece 2 ancient city; site SW of present city of Corinth — **Co·rin·thi·an** \kǝ-'rin(t)-thē-ǝn\ *adj or n*

Corinth, Gulf of inlet of Ionian Sea *cen* Greece N of the Peloponnese

Cork \'kòrk\ city S Ireland; *pop* 198,582

Corn·wall \'kòrn-,wòl, -wǝl\ *or* **1974–2009 Cornwall and Isles of Scilly** \'si-lē\ former county SW England

Co·ro·na \kǝ-'rō-nǝ\ city SW California E of Los Angeles; *pop* 152,374

Cor·pus Chris·ti \,kòr-pǝs-'kris-tē\ city & port S Texas; *pop* 305,215

Cor·reg·i·dor \kə-'re-gə-ˌdȯr\ island Philippines at entrance to Manila Bay

Cor·si·ca \'kȯr-si-kə\ island France in the Mediterranean N of Sardinia; *pop* 309,693 — **Cor·si·can** \'kȯr-si-kən\ *adj or n*

Cos·ta Me·sa \ˌkȯs-tə-'mā-sə\ city SW California; *pop* 109,960

Costa Ri·ca \-'rē-kə\ country Central America between Nicaragua & Panama; ✻, San José; *pop* 4,301,712 — **Cos·ta Ri·can** \-kən\ *adj or n*

Côte d'Ivoire \ˌkōt-dē-'vwär\ *or English* **Ivory Coast** country W Africa on Gulf of Guinea; official ✻, Yamoussoukro; seat of government, Abidjan; *pop* 22,650,000

Cots·wold \'kät-ˌswōld, -swəld\ hills SW *cen* England

Cov·en·try \'kə-vən-trē\ city *cen* England; *pop* 326,000

Craig·av·on \krā-'ga-vən\ district *cen* Northern Ireland; *pop* 93,000

Cra·ter \'krā-tər\ lake 1932 ft. (589 m.) deep SW Oregon in Cascade Range

Crete \'krēt\ island Greece in E Mediterranean; *pop* 623,065 — **Cre·tan** \'krē-t³n\ *adj or n*

Cri·mea \krī-'mē-ə, krə-\ peninsula SE Europe extending into Black Sea — **Cri·me·an** \krī-'mē-ən, krə-\ *adj*

Cro·atia \krō-'ā-sh(ē-)ə\ country SE Europe; ✻, Zagreb; *pop* 4,288,000 — **Croat** \'krō-ˌat\ *n*

Croy·don \'krȯi-d³n\ borough of S Greater London, England; *pop* 363,000

Cu·ba \'kyü-bə, 'kü-vä\ island in the West Indies; country; ✻, Havana; *pop* 11,167,000 — **Cu·ban** \'kyü-bən\ *adj or n*

Cum·ber·land \'kəm-bər-lənd\ river 687 mi. (1106 km.) long S Kentucky & N Tennessee

Cumberland Gap pass through Cumberland Plateau NE Tennessee

Cumberland Plateau mountain region E U.S.; part of S Appalachian Mountains extending from S West Virginia to NE Alabama

Cum·bria \'kəm-brē-ə\ county NW England; *pop* 499,858

Cum·bri·an \'kəm-brē-ən\ mountains NW England chiefly in Cumbria county

Cu·par \'kü-pər\ town E Scotland; *pop* 6642

Cu·ri·ti·ba \ˌkùr-ə-'tē-bə\ city S Brazil SW of São Paulo; *pop* 1,751,907

Cush \'kəsh, 'küsh\ ancient country NE Africa in upper Nile valley S of Egypt — **Cush·ite** \'kə-ˌshīt, 'kü-\ *n* — **Cush·it·ic** \kə-'shi-tik, kü-\ *adj*

Cuz·co \'küs-(ˌ)kō\ city S *cen* Peru; *pop* 348,935

Cymru — see WALES

Cy·prus \'sī-prəs\ island E Mediterranean S of Turkey; country; ✻, Nicosia; *pop* 1,100,000 — **Cyp·ri·ot** \'si-prē-ət, -ˌät\ *or* **Cyp·ri·ote** \-ˌōt, -ət\ *adj or n*

Cy·re·na·ica \ˌsir-ə-'nā-ə-kə, ˌsī-rə-\ ancient region N Africa on coast W of Egypt — **Cy·re·na·i·can** \-'nā-ə-kən\ *adj or n*

Czecho·slo·va·kia \ˌche-kə-slō-'vä-kē-ə, -slə-, -'va-\ former country *cen* Europe divided into the independent states of the Czech Republic & Slovakia — **Czecho·slo·vak** \-'slō-ˌväk, -ˌvak\ *adj or n* — **Czecho·slo·va·ki·an** \-slō-'vä-kē-ən, -slə-, -'va-\ *adj or n*

Czech Republic country *cen* Europe; ✻, Prague; *pop* 10,332,000

Daegu — see TAEGU

Daejeon — see TAEJON

Dahomey — see BENIN

Dairen — see DALIAN

Da·kar \'da-ˌkär, də-'kär\ city, ✻ of Senegal; *pop* 2,200,000

Da·ko·ta 1 *or* **James** river 710 mi. (1143 km.) long North Dakota & South Dakota flowing S into the Missouri **2** territory 1861–89 NW U.S. divided 1889 into states of North Dakota & South Dakota (the **Dakotas** \-təz\)

Da·lian *or* **Ta·lien** \'dä-'lyen\ *or* **Lü·da** *or* **Lü–ta** \'lü-'dä\ *or* **Dai·ren** \'dī-'ren\ city NE China; *pop* 3,995,000

Dal·las \'da-ləs, -lis\ city NE Texas; *pop* 1,197,816

Dal·ma·tia \dal-'mā-sh(ē-)ə\ region W Balkan Peninsula on the Adriatic — **Dal·ma·tian** \-shən\ *adj or n*

Da·ly City \'dā-lē\ city W California S of San Francisco; *pop* 101,123

Da·mas·cus \də-'mas-kəs\ city, ✻ of Syria; *pop* 1,451,000

Dan·ube \'dan-(ˌ)yüb\ river 1771 mi. (2850 km.) long S Europe flowing from SW Germany into Black Sea — **Da·nu·bi·an** \də-'nü-bē-ən, da-, -'nyü-\ *adj*

Dar·da·nelles \ˌdär-də-'nelz\ *or* **Hel·les·pont** \'he-lə-ˌspänt\ strait NW Turkey connecting Sea of Marmara & the Aegean

Dar es Sa·laam \ˌdär-ˌe(s)-sə-'läm\ city, historic ✻ of Tanzania; *pop* 4,365,000

Dar·ling \'där-liŋ\ river about 1700 mi. (2735 km.) long SE Australia in Queensland & New South Wales flowing SW into the Murray

Dar·win \'där-wən\ city Australia, ✻ of Northern Territory; *pop* 103,016

Da·vao \'dä-ˌvaù, dä-'vaù\ city S Philippines in E Mindanao on Davao Gulf; *pop* 1,313,000

Dav·en·port \'da-vən-ˌpȯrt\ city E Iowa; *pop* 99,685

Da·vis \'dā-vəs\ strait between SW Greenland & E Baffin Island connecting Baffin Bay & the Atlantic

Day·ton \'dā-t³n\ city SW Ohio; *pop* 141,527

Dead Sea salt lake between Israel & Jordan; 1312 ft. (400 m.) below sea level

Death Valley dry valley E California & S

Nevada containing lowest point in U.S. (282 ft. *or* 86 m. below sea level)

Dec·can \'de-kən, -ˌkan\ plateau region S India

Del·a·ware \'de-lə-ˌwer, -wər\ **1** river 296 mi. (476 km.) long E U.S. flowing S from S New York into Delaware Bay **2** state E U.S.; *, Dover; *pop* 897,934 — **Del·a·war·ean** *or* **Del·a·war·ian** \ˌde-lə-'wer-ē-ən\ *adj or n*

Delaware Bay inlet of the Atlantic between SW New Jersey & E Delaware

Del·hi \'de-lē\ city N India; *pop* 11,034,555 — see NEW DELHI

De·los \'dē-ˌläs\ island Greece — **De·lian** \'dē-lē-ən, 'dēl-yən\ *adj or n*

Del·phi \'del-ˌfī\ ancient town *cen* Greece on S slope of Mt. Parnassus

Democratic Republic of the Congo — see CONGO 2

Denali — see MCKINLEY, MOUNT

Den·mark \'den-ˌmärk\ country N Europe occupying most of Jutland & neighboring islands; *, Copenhagen; *pop* 5,604,000

Den·ver \'den-vər\ city, * of Colorado; *pop* 600,158

Der·by \'där-bē\ city N *cen* England; *pop* 214,000

Der·by·shire \'där-bē-ˌshir, -shər\ *or* **Derby** county N *cen* England

Der·ry \'der-ē\ *or* **Lon·don·der·ry** \ˌlən-dən-'der-ē\ city & port NW Northern Ireland; *pop* 83,000

Des Moines \di-'mòin\ city, * of Iowa; *pop* 203,433

De·troit \di-'tròit\ **1** river 31 mi. (50 km.) long between SE Michigan & Ontario connecting Lake Saint Clair & Lake Erie **2** city SE Michigan; *pop* 713,777

Dev·on \'de-vən\ *or* **De·von·shire** \'de-vən-ˌshir, -shər\ county SW England

Dha·ka \'dä-kə\ city, * of Bangladesh; *pop* 7,033,000

Die·go Gar·cia \dē-ˌā-gō-ˌgär-'sē-ə\ island in Indian Ocean; chief island of Chagos Archipelago

Di·li *also* **Dil·li** \'di-lē\ city & port N Timor, * of East Timor; *pop* 193,000

Di·nar·ic Alps \də-'na-rik\ range of the E Alps in W Slovenia, N Croatia, Bosnia and Herzegovina, & Montenegro

District of Co·lum·bia \kə-'ləm-bē-ə\ federal district E U.S. coextensive with city of Washington; *pop* 601,723

Djakarta — see JAKARTA

Dji·bou·ti \jə-'bü-tē\ **1** country E Africa on Gulf of Aden; *pop* 818,000 **2** city, its *; *pop* 339,500

Dni·pro·pe·trovs'k *or* **Dne·pro·pe·trovsk** \də-ˌnye-prə-pə-'tròfsk\ city E *cen* Ukraine; *pop* 996,500

Dodge City \'däj\ city S Kansas on Arkansas River; *pop* 27,340

Do·do·ma \dō-'dō-(ˌ)mä\ city, legislative * of Tanzania; *pop* 312,500

Do·ha \'dō-(ˌ)hä\ city & port, * of Qatar on Persian Gulf; *pop* 521,000

Dom·i·ni·ca \ˌdä-mə-'nē-kə\ island West Indies in the Leeward Islands; country; *, Roseau; *pop* 71,300

Do·min·i·can Republic \də-'mi-ni-kən\ country West Indies in E Hispaniola; *, Santo Domingo; *pop* 9,445,000 — **Dominican** *adj or n*

Don \'dän\ river 1224 mi. (1969 km.) long SW Russia

Do·nets'k \də-'nyetsk\ city E Ukraine; *pop* 952,500

Dor·ches·ter \'dòr-chəs-tər, -ˌches-\ town S England; *pop* 14,049

Dor·set \'dòr-sət\ *or* **Dor·set·shire** \-ˌshir, -shər\ county S England on English Channel

Dort·mund \'dòrt-ˌmùnt, -mənd\ city W Germany in the Ruhr; *pop* 571,143

Dou·a·la \dü-'ä-lä\ seaport W Cameroon; *pop* 1,900,000

Dou·ro \'dòr-(ˌ)ü\ *or Spanish* **Due·ro** \'dwe(ə)r-ō\ river 556 mi. (895 km.) long N Spain & N Portugal flowing into the Atlantic

Do·ver \'dō-vər\ city, * of Delaware; *pop* 36,047

Dover, Strait of channel between SE England & N France; the most easterly section of English Channel

Down \'daùn\ district SE Northern Ireland; *pop* 67,000

Dow·ney \'daù-nē\ city SW California SE of Los Angeles; *pop* 111,772

Down·pat·rick \daùn-'pa-trik\ town E Northern Ireland; *pop* 8245

Dra·kens·berg \'drä-kənz-ˌbərg\ mountain range E Republic of South Africa & Lesotho; highest peak Thabana Ntlenyana 11,425 ft. (3482 m.)

Dres·den \'drez-dən\ city E Germany; *pop* 512,354

Dub·lin \'də-blən\ city, * of Ireland; *pop* 527,612

Dud·ley \'dəd-lē\ town W *cen* England; *pop* 300,000

Duis·burg \'dü-əs-ˌbərg, 'düz-ˌ, 'dyüz-ˌ\ city W Germany at junction of Rhine & Ruhr rivers; *pop* 488,468

Du·luth \də-'lüth\ city & port NE Minnesota at W end of Lake Superior; *pop* 86,265

Dum·fries \ˌdəm-'frēs, -'frēz\ burgh S Scotland; *pop* 32,084

Dumfries and Gal·lo·way \'ga-lə-ˌwā\ administrative subdivision of S Scotland

Dun·dee \ˌdən-'dē\ city E Scotland; *pop* 147,000

Dun·gan·non \ˌdən-'ga-nən\ district W Northern Ireland; *pop* 53,000

Dur·ban \'dər-bən\ city and seaport E Republic of South Africa; *pop* 736,852

Dur·ham \'dər-əm, 'də-rəm, 'dùr-əm\ city N *cen* North Carolina; *pop* 228,330

Du·shan·be \dü-'sham-bə, dyü-, -'shäm-,

'dyü-,; ,dyü-shäm-'bä\ city, ✳ of Tajikistan; *pop* 749,500

Düs·sel·dorf \'dü-səl-,dȯrf, 'dyü-, 'dᵫ-\ city W Germany on the Rhine; *pop* 586,291

Ea·ling \'ē-liŋ\ borough of W Greater London, England; *pop* 338,000

East An·glia \'aŋ-glē-ə\ region E England; *pop* 1,366,300

East China Sea — see CHINA

Eas·ter \'ē-stər\ island Chile SE Pacific about 2000 mi. (3200 km.) W of Chilean coast

Eastern Cape province SE Republic of South Africa; *pop* 6,562,053

Eastern Desert desert E Egypt between the Nile & the Red Sea

Eastern Ghats \'gäts, 'gȯts, 'gạts\ chain of low mountains SE India along coast

Eastern Hemisphere the half of the earth E of the Atlantic Ocean including Europe, Asia, Australia, and Africa

Eastern Roman Empire the Byzantine Empire from 395 to 474

Eastern Samoa — see AMERICAN SAMOA

East Germany — see GERMANY

East Indies the Malay Archipelago — **East Indian** *adj or n*

East London city S Republic of South Africa; *pop* 296,000

East Pakistan the former E division of Pakistan consisting of E portion of Bengal; now Bangladesh

East River strait SE New York connecting upper New York Bay & Long Island Sound and separating Manhattan & Long Island

East Sea — see JAPAN, SEA OF

East Sus·sex \'sə-siks\ county SE England; *pop* 526,671

East Timor *or* **Ti·mor–Les·te** \'tē-mȯr-'lesh-,tā\ country SE Asia on E Timor; ✳, Dili; *pop* 1,066,000

Ebro \'ā-(,)brō\ river 565 mi. (909 km.) long NE Spain flowing into the Mediterranean

Ec·ua·dor \'e-kwə-,dȯr, ,e-kwä-'thȯr\ country W South America; ✳, Quito; *pop* 14,483,000 — **Ec·ua·dor·an** \,e-kwə-'dȯr-ən\ *or* **Ec·ua·dor·ean** *or* **Ec·ua·dor·ian** \-ē-ən\ *adj or n*

Ed·in·burgh \'e-dᵊn-,bər-ə\ city, ✳ of Scotland; *pop* 459,000

Ed·mon·ton \'ed-mən-tən\ city, ✳ of Alberta, Canada; *pop* 812,201

Edom \'ē-dəm\ ancient country SW Asia S of Judaea & Dead Sea — **Edom·ite** \'ēd-ə-,mīt\ *n*

Egypt \'ē-jipt\ country NE Africa & Sinai Peninsula of SW Asia bordering on Mediterranean & Red seas; ✳, Cairo; *pop* 72,798,000

Eire — see IRELAND

Elam \'ē-ləm\ ancient country SW Asia at head of Persian Gulf E of Babylonia — **Elam·ite** \'ē-lə-,mīt\ *n*

Elbe \'el-bə, 'elb\ river 720 mi. (1159 km.) long N Czech Republic & NE Germany flowing NW into North Sea

El·bert, Mount \'el-bərt\ mountain 14,433 ft. (4399 m.) W *cen* Colorado; highest in Colorado & the Rocky Mountains

El·brus, Mount \el-'brüz, -'brüs\ mountain 18,510 ft. (5642 m.) Russia; highest in the Caucasus & in Europe

El·burz \el-'bùrz\ mountains N Iran

Eliz·a·beth \i-'li-zə-bəth\ city NE New Jersey; *pop* 124,969

Elles·mere \'elz-,mir\ island N Canada in Nunavut

Ellice — see TUVALU

El·lis Island \'e-ləs\ island SE New York S of Manhattan; served as immigration station 1892–1954

El Mon·te \el-'män-tē\ city SW California E of Los Angeles; *pop* 113,475

El Paso \el-'pa-(,)sō\ city W Texas on Rio Grande; *pop* 649,121

El Sal·va·dor \el-'sal-və-,dȯr, -,sal-və-'\ ,el-,säl-vä-'thȯr\ country Central America bordering on the Pacific; ✳, San Salvador; *pop* 5,744,113

Ely, Isle of \'ē-lē\ area of high ground amid marshes in East Anglia, England

En·field \'en-,fēld\ borough of N Greater London, England; *pop* 312,000

En·gland \'iŋ-glənd, 'iŋ-lənd\ country S Great Britain; a division of United Kingdom; ✳, London; *pop* 53,012,456

English Channel arm of the Atlantic between S England & N France

En·nis·kil·len \,e-nə-'ski-lən\ town SW Northern Ireland in Fermanagh district

Ephra·im \'ē-frē-əm\ **1** hilly region N Jordan E of Jordan River **2** — see ISRAEL — **Ephra·im·ite** \'ē-frē-ə-,mīt\ *n*

Equatorial Guinea *formerly* **Spanish Guinea** country W Africa including Mbini & Bioko; ✳, Malabo; *pop* 722,000

Erie \'ir-ē\ **1** city & port NW Pennsylvania; *pop* 101,786 **2** canal New York between Hudson River at Albany & Lake Erie at Buffalo; now superseded by New York State Barge Canal

Erie, Lake lake E *cen* North America in U.S. & Canada; one of the Great Lakes

Er·in \'er-ən\ poetic name of Ireland

Er·i·trea \,er-ə-'trē-ə, -'trā-\ country NE Africa; ✳, Asmara; *pop* 4,252,000 — **Er·i·tre·an** \-ən\ *adj or n*

Es·con·di·do \,es-kən-'dē-(,)dō\ city SW California N of San Diego; *pop* 143,911

Es·fa·han \,es-fə-'hän, -'han\ *or* **Is·fa·han** \,is-\ city W *cen* Iran; *pop* 1,756,126

Española — see HISPANIOLA

Es·sen \'e-s²n\ city W Germany in the Ruhr; *pop* 566,201

Es·sex \'e-siks\ county SE England on North Sea; *pop* 1,393,587

Es·to·nia \e-'stō-nē-ə, -nyə\ country E Europe on Baltic Sea; ✳, Tallinn; *pop* 1,294,000 — **Es·to·nian** \e-'stō-nē-ən, -nyən\ *adj or n*

Ethi·o·pia \ē-thē-'ō-pē-ə\ *historically* **Ab·ys·sin·ia** \ab-ə-'si-nē-ə, -nyə\ country E Africa; ✳, Addis Ababa; *pop* 73,835,000 — **Ethi·o·pi·an** \-pē-ən\ *adj or n*

Et·na, Mount \'et-nə\ volcano 10,902 ft. (3323 m.) Italy in NE Sicily

Eto·bi·coke \e-'tō-bi-ˌkō\ former city Canada in SE Ontario; now part of Toronto

Etru·ria \i-'trür-ē-ə\ ancient country *cen* peninsula of Italy

Eu·gene \yü-'jēn\ city W Oregon; *pop* 156,185

Eu·phra·tes \yù-'frā-(ˌ)tēz\ river 1700 mi. (2736 km.) long SW Asia flowing from E Turkey & uniting with the Tigris to form the Shatt al Arab

Eur·asia \yù-'rā-zhə, -shə\ landmass consisting of Europe & Asia — **Eur·asian** \-zhən, -shən\ *adj or n*

Eu·rope \'yùr-əp\ continent of the Eastern Hemisphere between Asia & the Atlantic

European Union economic, scientific, & political organization consisting of Belgium, France, Italy, Luxembourg, Netherlands, Germany, Denmark, Greece, Ireland, United Kingdom, Spain, Portugal, Austria, Finland, Sweden, Cyprus, Czech Republic, Estonia, Hungary, Latvia, Lithuania, Malta, Poland, Slovakia, Slovenia, Bulgaria, Romania, & Croatia

Ev·ans·ville \'e-vənz-ˌvil\ city SW Indiana; *pop* 117,429

Ev·er·est, Mount \'ev-rəst, 'e-və-rəst\ mountain 29,035 ft. (8850 m.) S Asia in the Himalayas on border between Nepal & Tibet; highest in the world

Ev·er·glades \'e-vər-ˌglādz\ swamp region S Florida now partly drained

Ex·e·ter \'ek-sə-tər\ city SW England; *pop* 101,100

Faer·oe or **Far·oe** \'fer-(ˌ)ō\ islands NE Atlantic NW of the Shetlands belonging to Denmark; *pop* 48,250 — **Faer·oe·se** \ˌfar-ə-'wēz, ˌfer-, -'wēs\ *adj or n*

Fair·banks \'fer-ˌbaŋks\ city E *cen* Alaska; *pop* 31,535

Fai·sa·la·bad \ˌfī-ˌsä-lə-'bäd, -ˌsa-lə-'bad\ *formerly* **Ly·all·pur** \lē-ˌäl-'pùr\ city NE Pakistan W of Lahore; *pop* 2,008,861

Falk·land Islands \'fȯ-klənd, 'fȯl-\ or *Spanish* **Is·las Mal·vi·nas** \ˌēs-läs-mäl-'vē-näs\ island group SW Atlantic E of S end of Argentina; a British colony; ✳, Stanley; *pop* 2700

Far East the countries of E Asia & the Malay Archipelago — usually thought to consist of the Asian countries bordering on the Pacific but sometimes including also India, Sri Lanka, Bangladesh, Tibet, & Myanmar — **Far Eastern** *adj*

Far·go \'fär-(ˌ)gō\ city E North Dakota; largest in state; *pop* 105,549

Faroe — see FAEROE

Fay·ette·ville \'fā-ət-ˌvil, -vəl\ city SE *cen* North Carolina; *pop* 200,564

Fear, Cape \'fir\ cape SE North Carolina

Fer·man·agh \fər-'ma-nə\ district SW Northern Ireland; *pop* 62,000

Fernando Póo — see BIOKO

Fes \'fes\ city N *cen* Morocco; *pop* 947,000

Fife \'fīf\ administrative subdivision of E Scotland; *pop* 365,198

Fi·ji \'fē-(ˌ)jē\ islands SW Pacific; country; ✳, Suva; *pop* 837,000 — **Fi·ji·an** \'fē-(ˌ)jē-ən, fi-'\ *adj or n*

Fin·land \'fin-lənd\ country NE Europe; ✳, Helsinki; *pop* 5,453,000 — **Fin·land·er** *n*

Flan·ders \'flan-dərz\ **1** region W Belgium & N France on North Sea **2** semi-autonomous region W Belgium; *pop* 6,396,000

Flat·tery, Cape \'fla-tə-rē\ cape NW Washington at entrance to Strait of Juan de Fuca

Flint \'flint\ city SE Michigan; *pop* 102,434

Flor·ence \'flȯr-ən(t)s, 'flär-\ or *Italian* **Fi·ren·ze** \fē-'rent-sä\ city *cen* Italy; *pop* 358,079 — **Flor·en·tine** \'flȯr-ən-ˌtēn, 'flär-, -ˌtīn\ *adj or n*

Flor·i·da \'flȯr-ə-də, 'flär-\ state SE U.S.; ✳, Tallahassee; *pop* 18,801,310 — **Flo·rid·i·an** \flə-'ri-dē-ən\ or **Flor·i·dan** \'flȯr-ə-dən, 'flär-\ *adj or n*

Florida, Straits of channel between Florida Keys on NW & Cuba & Bahamas on S & E connecting Gulf of Mexico & the Atlantic

Florida Keys chain of islands off S tip of Florida

Foochow — see FUZHOU

For·a·ker, Mount \'fȯr-i-kər, 'fär-\ mountain 17,400 ft. (5304 m.) S *cen* Alaska in Alaska Range

For·mo·sa \fȯr-'mō-sə, fər-, -zə\ — see TAIWAN — **For·mo·san** \fȯr-'mō-sᵊn, fər-, -zᵊn\ *adj or n*

For·ta·le·za \ˌfȯr-tə-'lā-zə\ city & port NE Brazil on the Atlantic; *pop* 2,452,185

Fort Col·lins \'kä-lənz\ city N Colorado; *pop* 143,986

Fort–de–France \ˌfȯr-də-'frä°s\ city West Indies, ✳ of Martinique on W coast; *pop* 87,216

Forth \'fȯrth\ river 116 mi. (187 km.) long S *cen* Scotland flowing E into North Sea through **Firth of Forth**

Fort Knox \'näks\ military reservation N *cen* Kentucky SSW of Louisville; location of U.S. Gold Bullion Depository

Fort Lau·der·dale \'lȯ-dər-ˌdāl\ city SE Florida; *pop* 165,521

Fort Wayne \'wān\ city NE Indiana; *pop* 253,691

Fort Worth \'wərth\ city NE Texas; *pop* 741,206

Fox \'fäks\ islands SW Alaska in the E Aleutians

Foxe Basin \'fäks\ inlet of the Atlantic N Canada in E Nunavut W of Baffin Island

France \'fran(t)s, 'frän^s\ country W Europe between the English Channel & the Mediterranean; *, Paris; *pop* 64,613,000

Frank·fort \'fraŋk-fərt\ city, * of Kentucky; *pop* 25,527

Frank·furt \'fraŋk-fərt, 'fräŋk-,fúrt\ *or in full* **Frankfurt am Main** \(,)äm-'mīn\ city W Germany on Main River; *pop* 667,925

Frank·lin \'fraŋk-klən\ former district N Canada in Northwest Territories including Arctic Archipelago & Boothia & Melville peninsulas

Fra·ser \'frā-zər, -zhər\ river 850 mi. (1368 km.) long Canada in S *cen* British Columbia flowing into the Pacific

Fred·er·ic·ton \'fre-drik-tən, 'fre-də-rik-\ city, * of New Brunswick, Canada; *pop* 50,535

Free State *formerly* **Or·ange Free State** \'òr-inj, 'är-, -ənj\ province E *cen* Republic of South Africa; *pop* 2,745,590

Free·town \'frē-,taún\ city, * of Sierra Leone; *pop* 178,600

Fre·mont \'frē-,mänt\ city W California; *pop* 214,089

French Guiana country N South America on the Atlantic; an overseas division of France; *, Cayenne; *pop* 239,849

French Indochina — see INDOCHINA

Fres·no \'frez-(,)nō\ city S *cen* California SE of San Francisco; *pop* 494,665

Frunze — see BISHKEK

Fu·ji, Mount \'fü-jē\ *or* **Fu·ji·ya·ma** \,fü-jē-'yä-mä\ mountain 12,388 ft. (3776 m.) Japan in S *cen* Honshu; highest in Japan

Fu·ku·o·ka \,fü-kü-'ō-kä\ city Japan in N Kyushu; *pop* 1,463,743

Ful·ler·ton \'frē-lər-tən\ city SW California; *pop* 135,161

Fu·na·fu·ti \,fü-nä-'fü-tē\ city, * of Tuvalu; *pop* 1328

Fun·dy, Bay of \'fən-dē\ inlet of the Atlantic SE Canada between New Brunswick & Nova Scotia

Fu·shun \'fü-'shún\ city NE China E of Shenyang; *pop* 1,319,000

Fu·zhou \'fü-'jō\ *or* **Foo·chow** \'fü-'jō, -'chaú\ city & port SE China; *pop* 2,873,000

Ga·bon \gä-'bō^n\ country W Africa on the Equator; *, Libreville; *pop* 1,600,000 — **Gab·o·nese** \,ga-bə-'nēz, -'nēs\ *adj or n*

Ga·bo·rone \,gä-bō-'rō-(,)nä, ,kä-\ city, * of Botswana; *pop* 229,500

Gads·den Purchase \'gadz-dən\ area of land S of Gila River in present Arizona & New Mexico purchased 1853 by the U.S. from Mexico

Ga·la·pa·gos Islands \gə-'lä-pə-gəs, -'lä-, -,gōs\ island group Ecuador in the Pacific 600 mi. (965 km.) W of South America; *pop* 25,000

Ga·la·tia \gə-'lā-sh(ē-)ə\ ancient country *cen* Asia Minor in region around modern Ankara, Turkey — **Ga·la·tian** \-shən\ *adj or n*

Ga·li·cia \gə-'li-sh(ē-)ə\ **1** region E *cen* Europe now divided between Poland & Ukraine **2** region NW Spain on the Atlantic — **Ga·li·cian** \-'li-shən\ *adj or n*

Gal·i·lee \'ga-lə-,lē\ hilly region N Israel — **Gal·i·le·an** \,ga-lə-'lē-ən\ *adj or n*

Galilee, Sea of *or modern* **Lake Ti·be·ri·as** \tī-'bir-ē-əs\ lake N Israel on Syrian border; crossed by Jordan River

Gal·lo·way \'ga-lə-,wā\ former administrative district of SW Scotland — see DUMFRIES AND GALLOWAY

Gam·bia \'gam-bē-ə, 'gäm-\ country W Africa; *, Banjul; *pop* 1,882,000 — **Gam·bi·an** \-bē-ən\ *adj or n*

Gan·ges \'gan-jēz\ river 1550 mi. (2494 km.) long N India flowing from the Himalayas SE & E to unite with the Brahmaputra and empty into Bay of Bengal through a vast delta — **Gan·get·ic** \gan-'je-tik\ *adj*

Gao·xiong \'gaú-'shyúŋ\ *or* **Kao–hsiung** \'kaú-'shyúŋ, 'gaú-\ city & port SW Taiwan; *pop* 2,780,000

Garden Grove city SW California; *pop* 170,883

Gar·land \'gär-lənd\ city NE Texas NNE of Dallas; *pop* 226,876

Ga·ronne \gə-'rän, gä-'rón\ river 355 mi. (571 km.) long SE France flowing NW

Gary \'ger-ē\ city NW Indiana on Lake Michigan; *pop* 80,294

Gas·co·ny \'gas-kə-nē\ region SW France — **Gas·con** \'gas-kən\ *adj or n*

Gas·pé \ga-'spā, 'ga-,\ peninsula SE Quebec E of mouth of the Saint Lawrence — **Gas·pe·sian** \ga-'spē-zhən\ *adj or n*

Gaul \'gòl\ *or Latin* **Gal·lia** \'ga-lē-ə\ ancient country W Europe chiefly consisting of region occupied by modern France & Belgium

Gau·teng \'gaú-,teŋ\ province *cen* NE Republic of South Africa; *pop* 12,272,000

Ga·za Strip \'gä-zə, 'ga-\ district NE Sinai Peninsula on the Mediterranean

Ge·ne·va \jə-'nē-və\ city SW Switzerland on Lake Geneva; *pop* 187,000 — **Ge·ne·van** \-vən\ *adj or n* — **Gen·e·vese** \,je-nə-'vēz, -'vēs\ *adj or n*

Geneva, Lake lake on border between SW Switzerland & E France

Gen·oa \'je-nō-ə\ *or Italian* **Ge·no·va** \'je-nō-(,)vä\ city & port NW Italy; *pop* 586,180 — **Gen·o·ese** \,je-nō-'ēz, -'ēs\ *or* **Gen·o·vese** \-nə-'vēz, -'vēs\ *adj or n*

George·town \'jòrj-,taún\ **1** a W section of Washington, District of Columbia **2** city & port, * of Guyana; *pop* 162,000

Geor·gia \'jòr-jə\ **1** state SE U.S.; *, Atlanta; *pop* 9,687,653 **2** *or* **Republic of Georgia** country SW Asia on Black Sea S of Caucasus Mountains; ✳, Tbilisi; *pop* 4,630,000 — **Geor·gian** \'jȯr-jən\ *adj or n*

Georgia, Strait of channel Canada & U.S. between Vancouver Island & main part of British Columbia NW of Puget Sound

Georgian Bay inlet of Lake Huron in S Ontario

Ger·man·town \'jər-mən-ˌtaůn\ a NW section of Philadelphia, Pennsylvania

Ger·ma·ny \'jər-mə-nē\ country *cen* Europe bordering on North & Baltic seas; ✳, Berlin; divided 1946–90 into two independent states: the **Federal Republic of Germany** (West Germany; ✳, Bonn) & the **German Democratic Republic** (East Germany; ✳, East Berlin); *pop* 80,219,695

Get·tys·burg \'ge-tēz-ˌbərg\ town S Pennsylvania; *pop* 7620

Gha·na \'gä-nə, 'ga-\ *formerly* **Gold Coast** country W Africa on Gulf of Guinea; ✳, Accra; *pop* 24,659,000 — **Gha·na·ian** \gä-'nä-ən, ga-, -'nī-ən\ *or* **Gha·ni·an** \'gä-nē-ən, 'ga-, -nyən\ *adj or n*

Ghats \'gȯts\ two mountain chains S India consisting of **Eastern Ghats** & **Western Ghats**

Ghent \'gent\ city NW *cen* Belgium; *pop* 250,000

Gi·bral·tar \jə-'brȯl-tər\ British colony on S coast of Spain including Rock of Gibraltar; *pop* 31,000

Gibraltar, Rock of cape on S coast of Spain in Gibraltar at E end of Strait of Gibraltar; highest point 1396 ft. (426 m.)

Gibraltar, Strait of passage between Europe & Africa connecting the Atlantic & the Mediterranean

Gi·la \'hē-lə\ river 630 mi. (1014 km.) long SW New Mexico and S Arizona flowing W into the Colorado

Gil·bert \'gil-bərt\ town SW *cen* Arizona; *pop* 208,453

Gilbert and El·lice Islands \'e-lis\ island group W Pacific; divided into Kiribati and Tuvalu

Gil·e·ad \'gi-lē-əd\ mountain region of NE ancient Palestine E of Jordan River; now in NW Jordan — **Gil·e·ad·ite** \-lē-ə-ˌdīt\ *n*

Gi·za \'gē-zə\ city N Egypt on the Nile SW of Cairo; *pop* 2,865,000

Gla·cier Bay \'glā-shər\ inlet SE Alaska at S end of Saint Elias Range

Glas·gow \'glas-(ˌ)kō, 'glas-(ˌ)gō, 'glaz-(ˌ)gō\ city S *cen* Scotland on the Clyde; *pop* 586,000 — **Glas·we·gian** \gla-'swē-jən, glaz-\ *adj or n*

Glen·dale \'glen-ˌdāl\ **1** city *cen* Arizona NW of Phoenix; *pop* 226,721 **2** city S California NE of Los Angeles; *pop* 191,719

Glouces·ter \'gläs-tər, 'glȯs-\ town SW *cen* England; *pop* 91,800

Glouces·ter·shire \'gläs-tər-ˌshir, -shər, 'glȯs-\ *or* **Gloucester** county SW *cen* England; *pop* 596,984

Goa \'gō-ə\ state W India on Malabar coast; *pop* 1,458,545

Goat Island island W New York in Niagara River — see NIAGARA FALLS

Go·bi \'gō-(ˌ)bē\ desert E *cen* Asia in Mongolia & N China

Godthab — see NUUK

Godwin Austen — see K2

Go·lan Heights \'gō-ˌlän, -lən\ hilly region NE of Sea of Galilee

Gol·con·da \gäl-'kän-də\ ruined city *cen* India W of Hyderabad

Gold Coast 1 — see GHANA **2** coast region W Africa on N shore of Gulf of Guinea E of Côte d'Ivoire

Golden Gate strait W California connecting San Francisco Bay with Pacific Ocean

Good Hope, Cape of \ˌgůd-'hōp\ cape S Republic of South Africa on SW coast of Western Cape province

Gorki — see NIZHNIY NOVGOROD

Gö·te·borg \ˌyœ-tə-'bȯr-ē\ city & port SW Sweden; *pop* 538,000

Gram·pi·an \'gram-pē-ən\ hills N *cen* Scotland

Grand Banks shallow area in the W North Atlantic SE of Newfoundland

Grand Canyon gorge of Colorado River NW Arizona

Grand Canyon of the Snake — see HELLS CANYON

Grande, Rio — see RIO GRANDE

Grand Prairie city NE *cen* Texas W of Dallas; *pop* 175,396

Grand Rapids city SW Michigan; *pop* 188,040

Graz \'gräts\ city S Austria; *pop* 253,000

Great Australian Bight wide bay on S coast of Australia

Great Barrier Reef coral reef Australia off NE coast of Queensland

Great Basin region W U.S. between Sierra Nevada & Wasatch Range including most of Nevada & parts of California, Idaho, Utah, Wyoming, & Oregon; has no drainage to ocean

Great Bear lake Canada in Northwest Territories draining through Great Bear River into Mackenzie River

Great Brit·ain \'bri-tᵊn\ **1** island W Europe NW of France consisting of England, Scotland, & Wales; *pop* 61,371,000 **2** UNITED KINGDOM

Great Dividing Range mountain system E Australia extending S from Cape York Peninsula into Tasmania — see KOSCIUSKO, MOUNT

Greater Antilles group of islands of the West Indies including Cuba, Hispaniola,

Jamaica, & Puerto Rico — see LESSER ANTILLES

Greater London metropolitan county SE England consisting of City of London & 32 surrounding boroughs

Greater Manchester metropolitan county NW England including city of Manchester

Greater Sudbury — see SUDBURY, GREATER

Great Lakes chain of five lakes (Superior, Michigan, Huron, Erie, & Ontario) *cen* North America in U.S. & Canada

Great Plains elevated plains region W *cen* U.S. & W Canada E of the Rockies; extending from W Texas to NE British Columbia & NW Alberta

Great Rift Valley basin SW Asia & E Africa extending with several breaks from valley of the Jordan S to *cen* Mozambique

Great Salt Lake lake N Utah having salty water & no outlet

Great Slave Lake lake NW Canada in S Northwest Territories drained by Mackenzie River

Great Smoky mountains between W North Carolina & E Tennessee

Greece \'grēs\ country S Europe at S end of Balkan Peninsula; ✳, Athens; *pop* 10,816,286

Green \'grēn\ **1** mountains E North America in the Appalachians extending from S Quebec S through Vermont into W Massachusetts **2** river 730 mi. (1175 km.) long W U.S. flowing from W Wyoming S into the Colorado in SE Utah

Green Bay 1 inlet of NW Lake Michigan 120 mi. (193 km.) long in NW Michigan & NE Wisconsin **2** city NE Wisconsin on Green Bay; *pop* 104,057

Green·land \'grēn-lənd, -ˌland\ island in the North Atlantic off NE North America belonging to Denmark; ✳, Nuuk; *pop* 56,300

Greens·boro \'grēnz-ˌbər-ō\ city N *cen* North Carolina; *pop* 296,666

Green·wich \'gre-nich, 'grēn-ˌwich, 'grin-ˌwich\ borough SE Greater London, England; *pop* 200,800

Green·wich Village \'gre-nich\ section of New York City in W Manhattan

Gre·na·da \grə-'nā-də\ island West Indies in S Windward Islands; independent country; ✳, Saint George's; *pop* 102,632

Gren·a·dines, the \ˌgre-nə-'dēnz, 'gre-nə-ˌ\ islands West Indies in *cen* Windward Islands; N islands part of Saint Vincent and the Grenadines; S islands dependency of Grenada

Groz·ny \'gróz-nē, 'gräz-\ city S Russia in Europe; ✳ of Chechnya; *pop* 272,000

Gua·da·la·ja·ra \ˌgwä-də-lə-'här-ə, ˌgwä-thä-lä-'hä-rä\ city W *cen* Mexico; *pop* 1,495,189

Gua·dal·ca·nal \ˌgwä-dʳl-kə-'nal, ˌgwä-

də-kə-\ island W Pacific in the SE Solomons; *pop* 93,600

Gua·dal·qui·vir \ˌgwä-dʳl-ki-'vir, -'kwi-vər\ river 408 mi. (656 km.) long S Spain flowing into the Atlantic

Gua·de·loupe \'gwä-də-ˌlüp\ two islands separated by a narrow channel in West Indies in *cen* Leeward Islands; an overseas division of France; *pop* 403,400

Gua·lla·ti·ri \ˌgwä-yə-'tir-ē, ˌgwī-ä-\ volcano 19,882 ft. (6060 m.) high N Chile

Guam \'gwäm\ island W Pacific in S Marianas belonging to U.S.; ✳, Hagåtña; *pop* 159,400 — **Gua·ma·ni·an** \gwä-'mä-nē-ən\ *adj or n*

Gua·na·ba·ra Bay \ˌgwä-nä-'bär-ə\ inlet of the Atlantic SE Brazil on which city of Rio de Janeiro is located

Guang·dong \'gwäŋ-'dùŋ\ *or* **Kwang·tung** \'gwäŋ-'dùŋ, 'kwäŋ-, -'tùŋ\ province SE China bordering on South China Sea & Gulf of Tonkin; ✳, Guangzhou; *pop* 104,320,459

Guang·zhou \'gwäŋ-'jō\ *or* **Can·ton** \'kan-ˌtän, kan-'\ city & port SE China; *pop* 11,000,000

Guan·tá·na·mo Bay \gwän-'tä-nä-ˌmō\ inlet of the Caribbean in SE Cuba; site of U.S. naval station

Gua·te·ma·la \ˌgwä-tə-'mä-lə, -tä-'mä-lä\ **1** country Central America; *pop* 15,073,000 **2** *or* **Guatemala City** city, its ✳; *pop* 942,000 — **Gua·te·ma·lan** \-'mä-lən\ *adj or n*

Gua·ya·quil \ˌgwī-ə-'kēl, -'kil\ city & port W Ecuador; *pop* 2,285,000

Guay·na·bo \gwī-'nä-(ˌ)bō, -(ˌ)vō\ city NE *cen* Puerto Rico; *pop* 97,924

Guern·sey \'gərn-zē\ — see CHANNEL

Gui·a·na \gē-'a-nə, -'ä-nə; gī-'a-nə\ region N South America on the Atlantic; includes Guyana, French Guiana, Suriname, & nearby parts of Brazil & Venezuela — **Gui·a·nan** \-nən\ *adj or n*

Guin·ea \'gi-nē\ **1** region W Africa on the Atlantic extending along coast from Gambia to Angola **2** country W Africa N of Sierra Leone & Liberia; ✳, Conakry; *pop* 10,629,000 — **Guin·ean** \'gi-nē-ən\ *adj or n*

Guinea, Gulf of arm of the Atlantic W *cen* Africa

Guin·ea–Bis·sau \ˌgi-nē-bi-'saù\ country W Africa; ✳, Bissau; *pop* 1,521,000

Gui·yang \'gwä-'yäŋ\ *or* **Kuei–yang** \'gwä-'yäŋ\ city S China; *pop* 2,750,000

Gulf States states of U.S. bordering on Gulf of Mexico: Florida, Alabama, Mississippi, Louisiana, and Texas

Gulf Stream warm current of the Atlantic Ocean flowing from Gulf of Mexico NE along coast of U.S. to Nantucket Island and from there eastward

Guy·ana \gī-'an-ə\ *formerly* **British Guiana** country N South America on the

Atlantic; ✳, Georgetown; *pop* 748,000 — **Guy·a·nese** \ˌgī-ə-'nēz, -'nēs\ *adj or n*

Gwangju — see KWANGJU

Gwent \'gwent\ former county SE Wales

Gwyn·edd \'gwi-neth\ former county NW Wales

Hack·ney \'hak-nē\ borough of N Greater London, England; *pop* 246,000

Ha·gåt·ña \hə-'gät-nyə\ *formerly* **Aga·na** \ä-'gä-nyä\ town, ✳ of Guam; *pop* 1051

Hague, The \the̱-'häg\ city, seat of government of Netherlands; *pop* 825,018

Hai·kou \'hī-'kō\ city & port SE China; *pop* 1,517,000

Hai·phong \'hī-'fȯŋ, -'fäŋ\ city & port N Vietnam; *pop* 808,000

Hai·ti \'hā-tē\ country West Indies in W Hispaniola; ✳, Port-au-Prince; *pop* 9,923,000 — **Hai·tian** \'hā-shən\ *adj or n*

Ha·le·a·ka·la Crater \ˌhä-lā-,ä-kä-'lä\ crater over 2500 ft. (762 m.) deep Hawaii in E Maui

Hal·i·fax \'ha-lə-ˌfaks\ municipality & port, ✳ of Nova Scotia, Canada; *pop* 390,096

Ham·burg \'ham-ˌbərg; 'häm-ˌbu̇rg, -ˌbu̇rk\ city N Germany on the Elbe; *pop* 1,706,696 — **Ham·burg·er** \-ˌbər-gər, -ˌbu̇r-\ *n*

Ham·hung *or* **Ham·heung** \'häm-ˌhu̇ŋ\ city E *cen* North Korea; *pop* 704,000

Ham·il·ton \'ha-məl-tən\ **1** town, ✳ of Bermuda; *pop* 1010 **2** city & port, S Ontario, Canada on Lake Ontario; *pop* 519,949

Ham·mer·smith and Ful·ham \'ha-mər-ˌsmith-ənd-'fu̇l-əm\ borough of SW Greater London, England; *pop* 182,000

Hamp·shire \'hamp-ˌshir, -shər\ county S England on English Channel

Hamp·ton \'hamp-tən\ city SE Virginia; *pop* 137,436

Hampton Roads channel SE Virginia through which James River flows into Chesapeake Bay

Hang·zhou \'häŋ-'jō\ *or* **Hang·chow** \'haŋ-'chau̇, 'häŋ-'jō\ *or* **Hang·chou** \-'jō\ city E China; *pop* 5,700,000

Han·ni·bal \'ha-nə-bəl\ city NE Missouri on the Mississippi River; *pop* 17,916

Han·no·ver *or* **Han·o·ver** \'ha-ˌnō-vər, -nə-vər, *G* hä-'nō-fər\ city N *cen* Germany; *pop* 506,416

Ha·noi \ha-'nȯi, hə-, hä-\ city, ✳ of Vietnam; *pop* 2,481,000

Hao·ra \'hau̇-rə\ city E India on Hugli River opposite Calcutta; *pop* 1,077,000

Ha·ra·re \hə-'rä-(ˌ)rä\ *formerly* **Salis·bury** \'sȯlz-ˌber-ē, -b(ə-)rē\ city, ✳ of Zimbabwe; *pop* 1,485,000

Har·bin \'här-bən, här-'bin\ *or* **Ha·erh–pin** \'hä-'ər-'bin\ city NE China; *pop* 5,237,000

Har·in·gey \'ha-riŋ-ˌgā\ borough of N Greater London, England; *pop* 255,000

Har·lem \'här-ləm\ section of New York City in N Manhattan

Har·ris·burg \'ha-rəs-ˌbərg\ city, ✳ of Pennsylvania; *pop* 49,528

Har·row \'ha-(ˌ)rō\ borough of NW Greater London, England; *pop* 239,000

Hart·ford \'härt-fərd\ city, ✳ of Connecticut; *pop* 124,775

Hat·ter·as, Cape \'ha-tə-rəs\ cape North Carolina on **Hatteras Island**

Ha·vana \hə-'va-nə\ city, ✳ of Cuba; *pop* 2,106,000

Hav·ant \'ha-vənt\ town S England; *pop* 117,400

Ha·ver·ing \'häv-riŋ, 'hā-və-riŋ\ borough of NE Greater London, England; *pop* 237,000

Ha·waii \hə-'wä-yē, -'wä-ˌē\ **1** *or* **Ha·wai·ian Islands** *formerly* **Sand·wich Islands** \ˌsan-(d)wich\ group of islands *cen* Pacific belonging to U.S. **2** island, largest of the group **3** state of U.S., ✳, Honolulu; *pop* 1,360,301

Hay·ward \'hā-wərd\ city W California SE of Oakland; *pop* 144,186

Heb·ri·des \'he-brə-ˌdēz\ islands W Scotland in the North Atlantic consisting of **Outer Hebrides** (to W) and **Inner Hebrides** (to E); *pop* 30,660 — **Heb·ri·de·an** \ˌhe-brə-'dē-ən\ *adj or n*

Hel·e·na \'he-lə-nə\ city, ✳ of Montana; *pop* 28,190

Hellespont — see DARDANELLES

Hells Canyon \'helz\ canyon of Snake River on Idaho–Oregon boundary

Hel·sin·ki \'hel-ˌsiŋ-kē, hel-'\ city, ✳ of Finland; *pop* 612,664

Hen·der·son \'hen-dər-sən\ city S Nevada; *pop* 257,729

Hen·ry, Cape \'hen-rē\ cape E Virginia S of entrance to Chesapeake Bay

Her·e·ford and Wor·ces·ter \'her-ə-fərd-ən-'wu̇s-tər\ former county W England

Hert·ford·shire \'här-fərd-ˌshir, 'härt-, -shər\ *or* **Hertford** county SE England

Her·ze·go·vi·na \ˌhert-sə-gō-'vē-nə, ˌhərt-, -'gō-və-nə\ *or Serb* **Her·ce·go·vi·na** \ˌkert-sə-gō-vē-nä\ region S Europe; with Bosnia to the N forms Bosnia and Herzegovina — **Her·ze·go·vi·nian** \ˌhert-sə-gō-'vē-nē-ən, ˌhərt-, -nyən\ *n*

Hi·a·le·ah \ˌhī-ə-'lē-ə\ city SE Florida; *pop* 224,669

Hi·ber·nia \hī-'bər-nē-ə\ — see IRELAND — **Hi·ber·ni·an** \-ən\ *adj or n*

Hi·ga·shi·ōsa·ka \hē-ˌgä-shē-'ō-sä-kä\ city Japan in S Honshu E of Osaka; *pop* 509,533

High·land \'hī-lənd\ administrative subdivision of NW Scotland; *pop* 232,132

High·lands \'hī-ləndz\ the mountainous N part of Scotland lying N & W of the Lowlands

High Plains the Great Plains esp. from Nebraska southward

Hil·ling·don \'hi-liŋ-dən\ borough of W Greater London, England; *pop* 274,000

Hi·ma·la·yas, the \,hi-mə-'lā-əz\ *or* the **Himalaya** mountain system S Asia on border between India & Tibet and in Kashmir, Nepal, & Bhutan — see EVEREST, MOUNT — **Hi·ma·la·yan** \,him-ə-'lā-ən, hə-'mäl-(ə-)yən\ *adj*

Hin·du Kush \'hin-(,)dü-'kush, -'kəsh\ mountain range *cen* Asia SW of the Pamirs on border of Kashmir and in Afghanistan

Hin·du·stan \,hin-(,)dü-'stan, -də-, -'stän\ **1** a name for N India **2** the subcontinent of India **3** the country of India

Hi·ro·shi·ma \,hir-ə-'shē-mə, hə-'rō-shə-mə\ city Japan in SW Honshu on Inland Sea; *pop* 1,173,843

His·pan·io·la \,his-pə-'nyō-lə\ *or Spanish* **Es·pa·ño·la** \,es-,pä-'nyō-lä\ island West Indies in Greater Antilles; divided between Haiti on W & Dominican Republic on E

Ho·bart \'hō-bərt\ city Australia, ✻ of Tasmania; *pop* 170,975

Ho Chi Minh City \'hō-,chē-'min\ *formerly* **Sai·gon** \sī-'gän, 'sī-,\ city S Vietnam; *pop* 5,950,000

Hoh·hot \'hō-'hōt\ *or* **Hu·he·hot** \'hü-(,)hä-'hōt\ city N China, ✻ of Inner Mongolia; *pop* 1,497,000

Hok·kai·do \hò-'kī-(,)dō\ island N Japan N of Honshu; *pop* 5,506,419

Hol·land \'hä-lənd\ **1** county of Holy Roman Empire bordering on North Sea & consisting of area now forming part of W Netherlands **2** — see NETHERLANDS — **Hol·land·er** \-lən-dər\ *n*

Hol·ly·wood \'hä-lē-,wüd\ **1** section of Los Angeles, California, NW of downtown district **2** city SE Florida; *pop* 140,768

Holy Roman Empire empire consisting mainly of German & Italian territories & existing from 9th or 10th century to 1806

Hon·du·ras \hän-'dúr-əs, -'dyúr-; ón-'dü-räs\ country Central America; ✻, Tegucigalpa; *pop* 8,100,000 — **Hon·du·ran** \-ən\ *adj or n*

Hong Kong \'häŋ-,käŋ, -'käŋ\ *or Chinese* **Xiang·gang** \'shyäŋ-,gäŋ\ special administrative region China on SE coast including Hong Kong Island & Jiulong Peninsula; chief city Victoria; *pop* 7,072,000

Ho·ni·a·ra \,hō-nē-'är-ə\ town, ✻ of Solomon Islands; *pop* 49,107

Ho·no·lu·lu \,hä-nə-'lü-(,)lü, ,hō-nə-\ city, ✻ of Hawaii on Oahu; *pop* 337,256

Hon·shu \'hän-(,)shü, 'hón-\ island Japan; largest of the four chief islands; *pop* 100,254,208

Hood, Mount \'húd\ mountain 11,235 ft. (3424 m.) NW Oregon in Cascade Range

Hoo·ver Dam \'hü-vər\ *or* **Boul·der Dam** \'bōl-dər\ dam 726 ft. (221 m.) high in Colorado River between Arizona & Nevada — see MEAD, LAKE

Hor·muz, Strait of \'(h)òr-,məz, (h)òr-'müz\ strait connecting Persian Gulf & Gulf of Oman

Horn, Cape \'hórn\ cape S Chile on an island in Tierra del Fuego; the most southerly point of South America at 56° S latitude

Horn of Africa the easternmost projection of Africa; variously used to refer to Somalia, SE or all of Ethiopia, often Djibouti, & sometimes Eritrea, Sudan, & Kenya

Horseshoe Falls — see NIAGARA FALLS

Houns·low \'haúnz-(,)lō\ borough of SW Greater London, England; *pop* 254,000

Hous·ton \'hyüs-tən, 'yüs-\ city SE Texas; *pop* 2,096,798

Hsi·an — see XI'AN

Huang *or* **Hwang** \'hwäŋ\ *or* **Yellow** river about 3396 mi. (5464 km.) long N China flowing into Bo Hai

Hud·ders·field \'hə-dərz-,fēld\ town N England NE of Manchester; *pop* 123,888

Hud·son \'həd-sən\ **1** river 306 mi. (492 km.) long E New York flowing S **2** bay, inlet of the Atlantic in N Canada **3** strait NE Canada connecting Hudson Bay & the Atlantic

Hu·gli *or* **Hoo·ghly** \'hü-glē\ river 120 mi. (193 km.) long E India flowing S into Bay of Bengal

Huhehot — see HOHHOT

Hull \'həl\ *or* **Kings·ton upon Hull** \'kiŋ-stən\ city & port N England; *pop* 284,000

Hun·ga·ry \'həŋ-gə-rē\ country *cen* Europe; ✻, Budapest; *pop* 9,937,628

Hun·ting·ton Beach \'hən-tiŋ-tən\ city SW California; *pop* 189,992

Hunts·ville \'hənts-,vil, -vəl\ city N Alabama; *pop* 180,105

Hu·ron, Lake \'hyúr-,än, 'yúr-\ lake E *cen* North America in U.S. & Canada; one of the Great Lakes

Hy·der·abad \'hī-d(ə-)rə-,bad, -,bäd\ **1** city S *cen* India; *pop* 7,204,000 **2** city SE Pakistan on the Indus; *pop* 1,166,894

Iba·dan \i-'bä-d∘n, -'ba-\ city SW Nigeria; *pop* 2,600,000

Ibe·ri·an \ī-'bir-ē-ən\ peninsula SW Europe occupied by Spain & Portugal

Ice·land \'īs-lənd, 'īs-,land\ island SE of Greenland between Arctic & Atlantic oceans; country; ✻, Reykjavik; *pop* 315,600 — **Ice·land·er** \'īs-,lan-dər, 'īs-lən-\ *n*

Ida·ho \'ī-də-,hō\ state NW U.S.; ✻, Boise; *pop* 1,567,582 — **Ida·ho·an** \,ī-də-'hō-ən\ *adj or n*

Igua·çú *or* **Igua·zú** \,ē-gwə-'sü\ river 745 mi. (1199 km.) long S Brazil flowing W

IJs·sel *or* **Ijs·sel** \'ī-səl, 'ā-\ river 70 mi. (113 km.) long E Netherlands flowing out of Rhine N into IJsselmeer

IJs·sel·meer \'ī-səl-,mer, 'ā-\ *or* **Lake Ijs-**

sel freshwater lake N Netherlands separated from North Sea by a dike; part of former Zuider Zee (inlet of North Sea)

Ilium — see TROY

Il·li·nois \ˌi-lə-ˈnȯi\ state N *cen* U.S.; ✳, Springfield; *pop* 12,830,632 — **Il·li·nois·an** \ˌi-lə-ˈnȯi-ən\ *adj or n*

Il·lyr·ia \i-ˈlir-ē-ə\ ancient country S Europe and Balkan Peninsula on the Adriatic — **Il·lyr·i·an** \-ē-ən\ *adj or n*

Im·pe·ri·al Valley \im-ˈpir-ē-əl\ valley SE corner of California & partly in NE Baja California, Mexico

In·chon *or* **In·cheon** \ˈin-ˌchən\ city South Korea on Yellow Sea; *pop* 2,650,000

In·de·pen·dence \ˌin-də-ˈpen-dən(t)s\ city W Missouri E of Kansas City; *pop* 116,830

In·dia \ˈin-dē-ə\ **1** subcontinent S Asia S of the Himalayas between Bay of Bengal & Arabian Sea **2** country consisting of major portion of the subcontinent; ✳, New Delhi; *pop* 1,210,855,000 **3** *or* **Indian Empire** before 1947 those parts of the subcontinent of India under British rule or protection

In·di·an \ˈin-dē-ən\ ocean E of Africa, S of Asia, W of Australia, & N of Antarctica

In·di·ana \ˌin-dē-ˈa-nə\ state E *cen* U.S.; ✳, Indianapolis; *pop* 6,483,802 — **In·di·an·an** \-ˈa-nən\ *or* **In·di·an·i·an** \-ˈa-nē-ən\ *adj or n*

In·di·a·nap·o·lis \ˌin-dē-ə-ˈna-pə-lis\ city, ✳ of Indiana; *pop* 820,445

Indian River lagoon 165 mi. (266 km.) long E Florida between main part of the state & coastal islands

Indian Territory former territory S U.S. in present state of Oklahoma

In·dies \ˈin-(ˌ)dēz\ **1** EAST INDIES **2** WEST INDIES

In·do·chi·na \ˌin-(ˌ)dō-ˈchī-nə\ **1** peninsula SE Asia including Myanmar, Malay Peninsula, Thailand, Cambodia, Laos, & Vietnam **2** *or* **French Indochina** former country SE Asia consisting of area now forming Cambodia, Laos, & Vietnam — **In·do–Chi·nese** \-chī-ˈnēz, -ˈnēs\ *adj or n*

In·do·ne·sia \ˌin-də-ˈnē-zhə, -shə\ country SE Asia in Malay Archipelago consisting of Sumatra, Java, S & E Borneo, Sulawesi, W New Guinea, & many smaller islands; ✳, Jakarta; *pop* 237,641,000 — **In·do·ne·sian** \-zhən, -shən\ *adj or n*

In·dore \in-ˈdȯr\ city W *cen* India; *pop* 2,067,000

In·dus \ˈin-dəs\ river 1800 mi. (2897 km.) long S Asia flowing from Tibet NW & SSW through Pakistan into Arabian Sea

In·land Sea \ˈin-ˌland, -lənd\ inlet of the Pacific in SW Japan between Honshu on N and Shikoku and Kyushu on S

Inner Hebrides — see HEBRIDES

Inner Mon·go·lia \män-ˈgōl-yə, män-, -ˈgō-lē-ə\ *or* **Nei Mong·gol** \ˈnā-ˈmän-ˌgōl, -ˈmän-\ region N China; *pop* 24,706,291

Inside Passage protected shipping route between Puget Sound, Washington, & the lower part of Alaska

In·ver·ness \ˌin-vər-ˈnes\ town NW Scotland; *pop* 48,000

Io·ni·an \ī-ˈō-nē-ən\ sea, arm of the Mediterranean between SE Italy & W Greece

Io To — see IWO JIMA

Io·wa \ˈī-ə-wə\ state N *cen* U.S.; ✳, Des Moines; *pop* 3,046,355 — **Io·wan** \-wən\ *adj or n*

Ips·wich \ˈip-(ˌ)swich\ town SE England; *pop* 145,000

Iqa·lu·it \ē-ˈka-lü-ət\ town Canada, ✳ of Nunavut on Baffin Island; *pop* 6699

Iran \i-ˈrän, -ˈran\ *formerly by outsiders* **Per·sia** \ˈpər-zhə\ country SW Asia; ✳, Tehran; *pop* 75,150,000 — **Irani** \-ˈrä-nē, -ˈra-\ *adj or n* — **Ira·nian** \i-ˈrä-nē-ən, -ˈran-ē-, -ˈrän-ē-\ *adj or n*

Iraq \i-ˈräk, -ˈrak\ country SW Asia in Mesopotamia; ✳, Baghdad; *pop* (est.) 34,500,000 — **Iraqi** \-ˈräk-ē, -ˈrak-\ *adj or n*

Ire·land \ˈī(-ə)r-lənd\ **1** *or Latin* **Hi·ber·nia** \hī-ˈbər-nē-ə\ island W Europe in the North Atlantic; one of the British Isles **2** *or* **Eire** \ˈer-ə\ country occupying major portion of Ireland (island); ✳, Dublin; *pop* 4,588,000

Irish Sea arm of the North Atlantic between Great Britain & Ireland

Ir·kutsk \ir-ˈkütsk, ˌər-\ city S Russia near Lake Baikal; *pop* 587,500

Ir·ra·wad·dy \ˌir-ə-ˈwä-dē\ river 1300 mi. (2092 km.) long Myanmar flowing S into Bay of Bengal

Ir·tysh \ir-ˈtish, ˌər-\ river over 2600 mi. (4180 km.) long *cen* Asia flowing NW & N from Altay Mountains in China, through Kazakhstan, & into W *cen* Russia

Ir·vine \ˈər-ˌvīn\ city SW California; *pop* 212,375

Ir·ving \ˈər-viŋ\ city NE Texas NW of Dallas; *pop* 216,290

Isfahan — see ESFAHAN

Is·lam·abad \is-ˈlä-mə-ˌbäd, iz-, -ˈla-mə-ˌbad\ city, ✳ of Pakistan; *pop* 529,180

Islas Malvinas — see FALKLAND ISLANDS

Isle of Man — see MAN, ISLE OF

Isle of Wight \ˈwīt\ island England in English Channel

Isle Roy·ale \ˈī(-ə)l-ˈrȯi(-ə)l\ island Michigan in Lake Superior

Isles of Scilly 1 — see CORNWALL AND ISLES OF SCILLY **2** — see SCILLY

Is·ling·ton \ˈiz-liŋ-tən\ borough of N Greater London, England; *pop* 206,000

Ispahan — see ESFAHAN

Is·ra·el \ˈiz-rē(-ə)l, -(ˌ)rā(-ə)l\ **1** kingdom in ancient Palestine consisting of lands occupied by the Hebrew people **2** or **Ephra·im** \ˈē-frē-əm\ the N part of the Hebrew kingdom after about 933 B.C. **3** country SW Asia; ✳, Jerusalem; pop 7,412,000 — **Is·rae·li** \iz-ˈrā-lē\ adj or n

Is·tan·bul \ˌis-tən-ˈbül, -ˌtan-, -ˌtän-, -ˈbül, ˈis-tən-ˌ, or with m for n\ formerly **Con·stan·ti·no·ple** \ˌkän-ˌstan-tə-ˈnō-pəl\ city NW Turkey on the Bosporus & Sea of Marmara; pop 12,500,000

Is·tria \ˈis-trē-ə\ peninsula in Croatia & Slovenia extending into the N Adriatic — **Is·tri·an** \-trē-ən\ adj or n

It·a·ly \ˈi-tə-lē\ country S Europe including a boot-shaped peninsula & the islands of Sicily & Sardinia; ✳, Rome; pop 59,434,000

Itas·ca, Lake \ī-ˈtas-kə\ lake NW cen Minnesota; source of the Mississippi

Ivory Coast — see CÔTE D'IVOIRE — **Ivor·i·an** \(ˌ)ī-ˈvȯr-ē-ən\ adj or n — **Ivory Coast·er** \ˈkō-stər\ n

Iwo Ji·ma \ˌē-(ˌ)wō-ˈjē-mə\ or **Io To** \ˈē-(ˌ)ō-ˈtō\ island Japan in W Pacific SSE of Tokyo

Izhevsk \ˈē-ˌzhefsk\ or 1985–87 **Usti·nov** \ˈüs-ti-ˌnof, -ˌnȯv\ city W Russia; pop 628,000

Iz·mir \iz-ˈmir\ formerly **Smyr·na** \ˈsmər-nə\ city W Turkey; pop 1,757,414

Jack·son \ˈjak-sən\ city, ✳ of Mississippi; pop 173,514

Jack·son·ville \ˈjak-sən-ˌvil\ city NE Florida; pop 821,784

Jai·pur \ˈjī-ˌpu̇r\ city NW India; pop 3,046,000

Ja·kar·ta also **Dja·kar·ta** \jə-ˈkär-tə\ city, ✳ of Indonesia in NW Java; pop 9,608,000

Ja·mai·ca \jə-ˈmā-kə\ island West Indies in Greater Antilles; country; ✳, Kingston; pop 2,698,000 — **Ja·mai·can** \-kən\ adj or n

James \ˈjāmz\ **1** — see DAKOTA **2** river 340 mi. (547 km.) long Virginia flowing E into Chesapeake Bay

James Bay the S extension of Hudson Bay between NE Ontario & W Quebec

James·town \ˈjāmz-ˌtau̇n\ ruined village E Virginia on James River; first permanent English settlement in America (1607)

Jam·shed·pur \ˈjäm-ˌshed-ˌpu̇r\ city E India; pop 570,349

Ja·pan \jə-ˈpan, ja-\ country E Asia consisting of Honshu, Hokkaido, Kyushu, Shikoku, & other islands in the W Pacific; ✳, Tokyo; pop 128,057,000

Japan, Sea of also **East Sea** arm of the Pacific between Japan & Korea

Ja·va \ˈjä-və, ˈja-\ island Indonesia SW of Borneo; chief city, Jakarta; pop 107,581,306 — **Ja·va·nese** \ˌja-və-ˈnēz, jä-, -ˈnēs\ n

Jef·fer·son City \ˈje-fər-sən\ city, ✳ of Missouri; pop 43,079

Jer·sey \ˈjər-zē\ — see CHANNEL

Jersey City city NE New Jersey on Hudson River; pop 247,597

Je·ru·sa·lem \jə-ˈrü-s(ə-)ləm, -ˈrü-z(ə-)ləm\ city NW of Dead Sea, ✳ of Israel; pop 765,000

Jid·da or **Jid·dah** \ˈji-də\ or **Jed·da** or **Jed·dah** \ˈje-də\ city W Saudi Arabia on Red Sea; pop 561,104

Ji·lin \ˈjē-ˈlin\ or **Ki·rin** \ˈkē-ˈrin\ city NE China; pop 1,470,000

Ji·nan or **Tsi·nan** \ˈjē-ˈnän\ city E China; pop 3,932,000

Jin·zhou or **Chin–chou** or **Chin·chow** \ˈjin-ˈjō\ city NE China; pop 946,000

Jiu·long \ˈjü-ˈlȯŋ\ or **Kow·loon** \ˈkau̇-ˈlün\ **1** peninsula SE China in Hong Kong opposite Hong Kong Island **2** city on Jiulong Peninsula; pop 1,975,265

Jo·han·nes·burg \jō-ˈhä-nəs-ˌbərg, -ˈha-\ city NE Republic of South Africa; pop 4,434,827

Jo·li·et \ˌjō-lē-ˈet\ city NE Illinois; pop 147,433

Jor·dan \ˈjȯr-dᵊn\ **1** river 200 mi. (322 km.) long Israel & Jordan flowing S from Syria into Dead Sea **2** country SW Asia in NW Arabia; ✳, Amman; pop 6,350,000 — **Jor·da·ni·an** \jȯr-ˈdā-nē-ən\ adj or n

Juan de Fu·ca, Strait of \ˌwän-də-ˈfyü-kə, -hwän-\ strait 100 mi. (161 km.) long between Vancouver Island, British Columbia, & Olympic Peninsula, Washington

Ju·ba \ˈjü-bə, -ˌbä\ town, ✳ of South Sudan

Ju·daea or **Ju·dea** \jü-ˈdē-ə, -ˈdā-\ region of ancient Palestine forming its S division under Persian, Greek, & Roman rule — **Ju·dae·an** or **Ju·dean** \-ən\ adj or n

Ju·neau \ˈjü-(ˌ)nō, jü-ˈ\ city, ✳ of Alaska; pop 31,275

Ju·ra \ˈju̇r-ə\ mountain range extending along boundary between France & Switzerland N of Lake of Geneva

Jut·land \ˈjət-lənd\ **1** peninsula N Europe extending into North Sea and consisting of main part of Denmark & N portion of Germany **2** the main part of Denmark

Ka·bul \ˈkä-bəl, -ˌbül; kə-ˈbül\ city, ✳ of Afghanistan; pop 1,424,000

Ka Lae \kä-ˈlä-ä\ or **South Cape** or **South Point** most southerly point of Hawaii & of U.S.

Kal·a·ha·ri \ˌka-lə-ˈhär-ē, ˌkä-\ desert region S Africa N of Orange River in S Botswana & NW Republic of South Africa

Kalgan — see ZHANGJIAKOU

Ka·li·man·tan \ˌka-lə-ˈman-ˌtan, ˌkä-lē-ˈmän-ˌtän\ **1** BORNEO — its Indonesian name **2** the S & E portion of Borneo belonging to Indonesia

Ka·li·nin·grad \kə-'lē-nən-ˌgrad, -nyən-, -ˌgrät\ *formerly* **Kö·nigs·berg** \'kā-nigz-ˌbərg\ city & port W Russia; *pop* 431,500

Kam·chat·ka \kam-'chat-kə, -'chät-\ peninsula 750 mi. (1207 km.) long E Russia

Kam·pa·la \käm-'pä-lä, kam-\ city, ✳ of Uganda; *pop* 1,516,000

Kampuchea — see CAMBODIA

Kan·da·har \'kən-də-ˌhär\ city SE Afghanistan; *pop* 130,200

Ka·no \'kä-(ˌ)nō\ city N cen Nigeria; *pop* 3,000,000

Kan·pur \'kän-ˌpu̇r\ city N India on the Ganges; *pop* 2,900,000

Kan·sas \'kan-zəs\ state W cen U.S.; ✳, Topeka; *pop* 2,853,118 — **Kan·san** \'kan-zən\ adj or n

Kansas City 1 city NE Kansas bordering on Kansas City, Missouri; *pop* 145,786 **2** city W Missouri; *pop* 459,787

Kao–hsiung — see GAOXIONG

Ka·ra·chi \kə-'rä-chē\ city S Pakistan on Arabian Sea; *pop* 12,100,000

Ka·ra·gan·da \ˌkär-ə-'gän-də\ or **Qa·ra·ghan·dy** \-dē\ city cen Kazakhstan *pop* 460,000

Kar·a·ko·ram Pass \ˌkär-ə-'kȯr-əm\ mountain pass NE Kashmir in **Karakoram Range** (system connecting the Himalayas with the Pamirs)

Ka·re·lia \kə-'rē-lē-ə, -'rēl-yə\ region NE Europe in Finland & Russia; *pop* 643,548 — **Ka·re·lian** \kə-'rē-lē-ən, -'rēl-yən\ adj or n

Ka·roo or **Kar·roo** \kə-'rü\ plateau region W Republic of South Africa W of Drakensberg Mountains

Kash·mir \'kash-ˌmir, 'kazh-, kash-', kazh-'\ disputed territory N subcontinent of India; claimed by India & Pakistan — **Kash·miri** \kash-'mi(ə)r-ē, kazh-\ adj or n

Ka·thi·a·war \ˌkä-tē-ə-'wär\ peninsula W India N of Gulf of Khambhat

Kath·man·du or **Kat·man·du** \ˌkat-ˌman-'dü, ˌkät-ˌmän-\ city, ✳ of Nepal; *pop* 1,003,000

Kat·mai, Mount \'kat-ˌmī\ volcano 6715 ft. (2047 m.) S Alaska on Alaska Peninsula

Kat·te·gat \'ka-ti-ˌgat\ arm of North Sea between Sweden & E coast of Jutland Peninsula of Denmark

Kau·ai \kä-'wä-ē\ island Hawaii NW of Oahu; *pop* 67,091

Kau·nas \'kau̇-nəs, -ˌnäs\ city cen Lithuania; *pop* 315,993

Ka·wa·sa·ki \ˌkä-wä-'sä-kē\ city Japan in E Honshu S of Tokyo; *pop* 1,425,512

Ka·zakh·stan also **Ka·zak·stan** \ˌka-(ˌ)zak-'stan\ country NW cen Asia; ✳, Astana; *pop* 16,010,000 — **Ka·zakh** also **Ka·zak** \kə-'zak, -'zäk\ n

Ka·zan \kə-'zan\ city W Russia; *pop* 1,144,000

Kee·wa·tin \kē-'wä-tⁿn, -'wä-\ former district N Canada in E Northwest Territories NW of Hudson Bay; area now part of Nunavut

Ke·me·ro·vo \'kye-mə-rə-və\ city S cen Russia; *pop* 533,000

Ke·nai \'kē-ˌnī\ peninsula S Alaska E of Cook Inlet

Kennedy, Cape — see CANAVERAL, CAPE

Ken·sing·ton and Chel·sea \'ken-ziŋ-tən-ənd-'chel-sē, 'ken(t)-siŋ-\ borough of W Greater London, England; *pop* 158,500

Kent \'kent\ county SE England; *pop* 1,463,740 — **Kent·ish** \'ken-tish\ adj

Ken·tucky \kən-'tə-kē\ state E cen U.S.; ✳, Frankfort; *pop* 4,339,367 — **Ken·tuck·i·an** \-kē-ən\ adj or n

Ken·ya \'ke-nyə, 'kē-\ **1** mountain 17,058 ft. (5199 m.) cen Kenya **2** country E Africa S of Ethiopia; ✳, Nairobi; *pop* 38,610,000 — **Ken·yan** \-nyən\ adj or n

Key West \'west\ city SW Florida on Key West (island); *pop* 24,649

Kha·ba·rovsk \kə-'bär-əfsk, k̲ə-\ city SE Russia; *pop* 577,500

Kham·bhat, Gulf of \'kəm-bət\ or **Gulf of Cam·bay** \kam-'bā\ inlet of Arabian Sea in India N of Bombay

Khar·kiv \'kär-kəf, 'kär-\ or **Khar·kov** \'kär-ˌkȯf, 'kär-, -ˌkȯv, -kəf\ city NE Ukraine; *pop* 1,446,000

Khar·toum \kär-'tüm\ city, ✳ of Sudan; *pop* 1,950,000

Khy·ber \'kī-bər\ pass 33 mi. (53 km.) long on border between Afghanistan & Pakistan

Ki·bo \'kē-(ˌ)bō\ mountain peak 19,340 ft. (5895 m.) NE Tanzania; highest peak of Kilimanjaro & highest point in Africa

Kiel \'kēl\ — see NORD-OSTSEE

Ki·ev \'kē-ˌef, -ˌev, -if\ or Ukrainian **Kyiv** \'kyē-ü\ city, ✳ of Ukraine; *pop* 2,800,000

Ki·ga·li \kē-'gä-lē\ city, ✳ of Rwanda; *pop* 859,000

Ki·lau·ea \ˌkē-ˌlä-'wä-ä\ volcanic crater Hawaii on Hawaii Island on E slope of Mauna Loa

Kil·i·man·ja·ro \ˌki-lə-mən-'jär-(ˌ)ō, -'ja-(ˌ)rō\ mountain NE Tanzania; highest in Africa — see KIBO

Kil·lar·ney, Lakes of \ki-'lär-nē\ three lakes SW Ireland

Kings·ton \'kiŋ-stən\ city & port, ✳ of Jamaica; *pop* 103,771

Kingston upon Hull — see HULL

Kingston upon Thames borough of SW Greater London, England; *pop* 160,000

Kings·town \'kiŋz-ˌtau̇n\ seaport, ✳ of Saint Vincent and the Grenadines; *pop* 12,900

Kin·sha·sa \kin-'shä-sə\ city, ✳ of Democratic Republic of the Congo; *pop* 3,804,000

Ki·ri·bati \\'kir-ə-,bas\ island group W Pacific; country; ✳, Tarawa; *pop* 103,000

Kirin — see JILIN

Kirk·wall \\'kər-,kwȯl\ town and port N Scotland, ✳ of Orkney Islands; *pop* 5947

Kishinev — see CHIȘINĂU

Ki·ta·kyu·shu \kē-,tä-'kyü-(,)shü\ city Japan in N Kyushu; *pop* 976,846

Kitch·e·ner \\'kich-nər, 'ki-chə-\ city SE Ontario, Canada; *pop* 219,153

Kit·ty Hawk \\'kit-ē-,hȯk\ town E North Carolina; *pop* 3272

Klon·dike \\'klän-,dīk\ region NW Canada in *cen* Yukon in valley of Klondike River

Knox·ville \\'näks-,vil, -vəl\ city E Tennessee; *pop* 178,874

Ko·be \\'kō-bē, -,bā\ city Japan in S Honshu; *pop* 1,544,200

Ko·di·ak \\'kō-dē-,ak\ island S Alaska E of Alaska Peninsula

Ko·la \\'kō-lə\ peninsula NW Russia bordering on Finland

Ko·rea \kə-'rē-ə\ peninsula E Asia between Yellow Sea & East Sea (Sea of Japan); divided 1948 into independent countries of North Korea & South Korea — **Ko·re·an** \kə-'rē-ən\ *adj or n*

Ko·ror \\'kȯr-,ȯr\ town, former ✳ of Palau; *pop* 13,303

Kos·ci·us·ko, Mount \,kä-zē-'əs-(,)kō, ,kä-sē-\ mountain 7310 ft. (2228 m.) SE Australia in SE New South Wales; highest in Great Dividing Range & in Australia

Ko·so·vo \\'kȯ-sȯ-,vō, 'kä-\ country S Europe in the Balkans; *pop* 1,757,000

Kowloon — see JIULONG

Krak·a·tau \,kra-kə-'taů\ *or* **Krak·a·toa** \-'tō-ə\ island & volcano Indonesia between Sumatra & Java

Kra·kow \\'krä-,kaů, 'kra-, 'krä-, -(,)kō, *Pol* 'krä-,küf\ city S Poland; *pop* 758,000

Kras·no·dar \,kräs-nə-'där\ city SW Russia; *pop* 745,000

Kras·no·yarsk \,kräs-nə-'yärsk\ city S *cen* Russia; *pop* 973,850

Kry·vyy Rih \kri-'vē-'rik\ *or* **Kri·voy Rog** \,kri-,vȯi-'rȯg, -'rȯk\ city SE *cen* Ukraine; *pop* 675,000

K2 \,kā-'tü\ *or* **God·win Aus·ten** \,gäd-dwən-'ȯs-tən, ,gȯ-, -'äs-\ mountain 28,250 ft. (8611 m.) N Kashmir in Karakoram Range; second highest in the world

Kua·la Lum·pur \,kwä-lə-'lům-,půr, -'ləm-, -,lům-'\ city, ✳ of Malaysia; *pop* 1,145,075

Kuei-yang — see GUIYANG

Kun·lun \\'kůn-'lůn\ mountain system W China extending E from the Pamirs; highest peak Muztag 25,340 ft. (7724 m.)

Kun·ming \\'kůn-'miŋ\ city S China; *pop* 3,567,000

Kur·di·stan \,kůr-də-'stan, ,kər-, -'stän; 'kər-də-,\ region SW Asia chiefly in E Turkey, NW Iran, & N Iraq — **Kurd** \'kůrd, 'kərd\ *n* — **Kurd·ish** \'kůr-dish, 'kər-\ *adj*

Ku·ril *or* **Ku·rile** \'kyůr-,ēl, 'kůr-; kyů-'rēl, ků-\ islands Russia in W Pacific between Kamchatka Peninsula & Hokkaido Island

Ku·wait \ků-'wāt\ **1** country SW Asia in Arabia at head of Persian Gulf; *pop* 3,986,000 **2** city, its ✳; *pop* 28,859 — **Ku·waiti** \-'wā-tē\ *adj or n*

Kuybyshev — see SAMARA

Kuz·netsk Basin \kůz-'netsk\ *or* **Kuz·bas** *or* **Kuz·bass** \'kůz-,bas\ basin S *cen* Russia

Kwa·ja·lein \'kwä-jə-lən, -,lān\ island W Pacific in Marshall Islands

Kwang·ju *or* **Gwang·ju** \'gwäŋ-(,)jü\ city SW South Korea; *pop* 1,472,000

Kwa·Zu·lu–Na·tal \kwä-'zü-(,)lü-nə-'täl\ province E Republic of South Africa; *pop* 10,267,300

Kyo·to \kē-'ōt-ō\ city Japan in W *cen* Honshu; *pop* 1,474,015

Kyr·gyz·stan \,kir-gi-'stan, -'stän\ country W *cen* Asia; ✳, Bishkek; *pop* 5,234,000

Kyu·shu \'kyü-(,)shü\ island Japan S of W end of Honshu; *pop* 13,445,561

Lab·ra·dor \'la-brə-,dȯr\ **1** peninsula E Canada between Hudson Bay & the Atlantic divided between the provinces of Quebec & Newfoundland and Labrador **2** the part of the peninsula belonging to the province of Newfoundland and Labrador — **Lab·ra·dor·ean** *or* **Lab·ra·dor·ian** \,la-brə-'dȯr-ē-ən\ *adj or n*

Lac·ca·dive \'la-kə-,dēv, -,dīv, -div\ islands India in Arabian Sea N of Maldive Islands

La·co·nia \lə-'kō-nē-ə, -nyə\ ancient country S Greece in SE Peloponnese; ✳, Sparta — **La·co·nian** \-nē-ən, -nyən\ *adj or n*

La·fay·ette \,la-fē-'et, ,lä-\ city S Louisiana; *pop* 120,623

La·gos \'lä-,gäs, -,gōs\ city, former ✳ (1960–91) of Nigeria; *area pop* 9,114,000

La·hore \lə-'hȯr\ city E Pakistan; *pop* 5,143,495

Lake District region NW England containing many lakes & mountains

Lake·hurst \'läk-(,)hərst\ borough E New Jersey; *pop* 2654

Lake·wood \'läk-,wůd\ city *cen* Colorado; *pop* 142,980

Lam·beth \'lam-bəth, -,beth\ borough of S Greater London, England; *pop* 303,000

La·nai \lə-'nī, lä-\ island Hawaii W of Maui

Lan·ca·shire \'laŋ-kə-,shir, -shər\ *or* **Lan·cas·ter** \'laŋ-kəs-tər\ county NW England — **Lan·cas·tri·an** \laŋ-'kas-trē-ən, lan-\ *adj or n*

Lan·cas·ter \'laŋ-kəs-tər, 'lan-,kas-tər\ city NW England; *pop* 125,600

Land's End \'landz-'end\ cape SW England; most westerly point of England

Lan·sing \'lan-siŋ\ city, ✱ of Michigan; *pop* 114,297

Lan·zhou *or* **Lan–chou** \'län-'jō\ city W China; *pop* 2,533,000

Laos \'laus, 'lä-(,)ōs, 'lä-,äs\ country SE Asia in Indochina NE of Thailand; ✱, Vientiane; *pop* 6,514,000 — **Lao·tian** \lä-'ō-shən, 'lau-shən\ *adj or n*

La Paz \lä-'päz, -'päs\ city, administrative ✱ of Bolivia; *pop* 762,000

Lap·land \'lap-,land, -lənd\ region in N Europe above the Arctic Circle in N Norway, N Sweden, N Finland, & Kola Peninsula of Russia — **Lap·land·er** \-,lan-dər, -lən-\ *n*

La·re·do \lə-'rā-(,)dō\ city S Texas on the Rio Grande; *pop* 236,091

Larne \'lärn\ district NE Northern Ireland; *pop* 32,000

Las·sen Peak \'la-sᵊn\ volcano 10,457 ft. (3187 m.) N California at S end of Cascade Range

Las Ve·gas \läs-'vā-gəs\ city SE Nevada; *pop* 583,756

Latin America 1 Spanish America and Brazil 2 all of the Americas S of the U.S. — **Latin–American** *adj* — **Latin American** *n*

Latin Quarter section of Paris, France S of the Seine

Lat·via \'lat-vē-ə\ country E Europe on Baltic Sea; ✱, Riga; *pop* 2,070,000

Lau·ren·tian Mountains \lȯ-'ren(t)-shən\ hills E Canada in S Quebec N of the Saint Lawrence on S edge of Canadian Shield

Laurentian Plateau — see CANADIAN SHIELD

La·val \lə-'val\ city S Quebec NW of Montreal; *pop* 401,553

Law·rence \'lȯr-ən(t)s, 'lär-\ 1 city NE Kansas *pop* 87,643 2 city NE corner of Massachusetts; *pop* 76,377

League of Nations political organization established at the end of World War I; replaced by United Nations 1946

Leb·a·non \'le-bə-nən\ 1 mountains Lebanon (country) running parallel to coast 2 country SW Asia on the Mediterranean; ✱, Beirut; *pop* 4,100,000 — **Leb·a·nese** \,le-bə-'nēz, -'nēs\ *adj or n*

Leeds \'lēdz\ city N England; *pop* 475,000

Lee·ward Islands \'lē-wərd, 'lü-ərd\ 1 islands Hawaii extending WNW from main islands of the group 2 islands South Pacific in W Society Islands 3 islands West Indies in N Lesser Antilles extending from Virgin Islands (on N) to Dominica (on S)

Le Ha·vre \lə-'hävrᵊ, -'häv\ city N France on English Channel; *pop* 175,497

Leh·man Caves \'lē-mən\ limestone caverns E Nevada

Leices·ter \'les-tər\ city *cen* England ENE of Birmingham; *pop* 444,000

Leices·ter·shire \'les-tər-,shir, -shər\ *or* **Leicester** county *cen* England

Lein·ster \'len(t)-stər\ province E Ireland; *pop* 2,504,814

Leip·zig \'līp-sig, -sik\ city E Germany; *pop* 502,979

Le·na \'lē-nə, 'lā-\ river about 2700 mi. (4345 km.) long E Russia, flowing NE & N from mountains W of Lake Baikal into Arctic Ocean

Leningrad — see SAINT PETERSBURG

Le·ón \lā-'ōn\ city *cen* Mexico; *pop* 1,436,000

Ler·wick \'lər-(,)wik, 'ler-\ town and port N Scotland in the Shetlands; *pop* 7223

Le·so·tho \lə-'sō-(,)tō, -'sü-(,)tü\ *formerly* **Ba·su·to·land** \bə-'sü-tō-,land\ country S Africa surrounded by Republic of South Africa; ✱, Maseru; *pop* 1,877,000

Lesser Antilles islands in the West Indies including Virgin Islands, Leeward Islands, & Windward Islands, Barbados, Trinidad, Tobago, & islands in the S Caribbean N of Venezuela — see GREATER ANTILLES

Le·vant \lə-'vant\ the countries bordering on the E Mediterranean — **Lev·an·tine** \'lev-ən-,tīn, -,tēn, lə-'van-\ *adj or n*

Lew·es \'lü-əs\ town S England

Lew·i·sham \'lü-ə-shəm\ borough of SE Greater London, England; *pop* 276,000

Lewis with Harris \'lü-əs-with-'ha-rəs, -with-\ island NW Scotland in Outer Hebrides

Lex·ing·ton \'lek-siŋ-tən\ 1 city NE *cen* Kentucky; area *pop* 295,803 2 town NE Massachusetts; *pop* 31,394

Ley·te \'lā-tē\ island Philippines S of Samar

Lha·sa \'lä-sə, 'la-\ city SW China, ✱ of Tibet; *pop* 199,000

Li·be·ria \lī-'bir-ē-ə\ country W Africa on the North Atlantic; ✱, Monrovia; *pop* 3,477,000 — **Li·be·ri·an** \-ē-ən\ *adj or n*

Lib·er·ty \'li-bər-tē\ *formerly* **Bed·loe's** \'bed-,lōz\ island SE New York; site of the Statue of Liberty

Li·bre·ville \'lē-brə-,vil, -,vēl\ city, ✱ of Gabon; *pop* 419,596

Lib·ya \'li-bē-ə\ country N Africa on the Mediterranean W of Egypt; ✱, Tripoli; *pop* 5,658,000 — **Lib·y·an** \'li-bē-ən\ *adj or n*

Libyan desert N Africa W of the Nile in Libya, Egypt, & Sudan

Liech·ten·stein \'lik-tən-,stīn, 'lik-tən-,shtīn\ country W Europe between Austria & Switzerland; ✱, Vaduz; *pop* 36,000 — **Liech·ten·stein·er** \-,stī-nər, -,shtī-\ *n*

Lif·fey \'li-fē\ river 50 mi. (80 km.) long E Ireland

Li·gu·ria \lə-'gyur-ē-ə\ region NW Italy on Ligurian Sea — **Li·gu·ri·an** \-ē-ən\ *adj or n*

Ligurian Sea arm of the Mediterranean N of Corsica

Li·lon·gwe \li-'lȯṅ-(ˌ)gwā\ city, * of Malawi; *pop* 674,448

Li·ma \'lē-mə\ city, * of Peru; *pop* 8,039,000

Lim·a·vady \ˌli-mə-'va-dē\ district NW Northern Ireland; *pop* 34,000

Lim·po·po \lim-'pō-(ˌ)pō\ river 1000 mi. (1609 km.) long Africa flowing from Republic of South Africa into Indian Ocean in Mozambique

Lin·coln \'liṅ-kən\ **1** city, * of Nebraska; *pop* 258,379 **2** city E England; *pop* 81,900

Lin·coln·shire \'liṅ-kən-ˌshir, -shər\ *or* **Lincoln** county E England

Line \'līn\ islands Kiribati S of Hawaii; *pop* 4782

Lis·bon \'liz-bən\ *or Portuguese* **Lis·boa** \lēzh-'vō-ə\ city, * of Portugal; *pop* 547,733

Lis·burn \'liz-(ˌ)bərn\ district E Northern Ireland; *pop* 120,000

Lith·u·a·nia \ˌli-thə-'wā-nē-ə, ˌli-thyə-, -nyə\ country E Europe; *, Vilnius; *pop* 3,043,000

Lit·tle Rock \'li-t⁰l-ˌräk\ city, * of Arkansas; *pop* 193,524

Liv·er·pool \'li-vər-ˌpül\ city NW England; *pop* 552,000

Li·vo·nia \lə-'vō-nē-ə, -nyə\ city SE Michigan; *pop* 96,942

Lju·blja·na \lē-ˌü-blē-'ä-nə\ city, * of Slovenia; *pop* 272,000

Lla·no Es·ta·ca·do \'la-(ˌ)nō-ˌes-tə-'kä-(ˌ)dō, 'lä-, 'yä-\ *or* **Staked Plain** \'stāk(t)-\ plateau region SE New Mexico & NW Texas

Lo·bam·ba \lō-'bäm-bə\ town, legislative * of Swaziland; *pop* (est.) 10,000

Lodz \'lüj, 'lädz\ city *cen* Poland WSW of Warsaw; *pop* 729,000

Lo·fo·ten \lō-ˌfō-t⁰n\ islands NW Norway

Lo·gan, Mount \'lō-gən\ mountain 19,551 ft. (5959 m.) NW Canada in Saint Elias Range; highest in Canada & second highest in North America

Loire \lə-'wär, 'lwär\ river 634 mi. (1020 km.) long *cen* France flowing NW & W into Bay of Biscay

Lo·mé \lō-'mā\ city, * of Togo; *pop* 838,550

Lo·mond, Loch \'lō-mənd\ lake S *cen* Scotland

Lon·don \'lən-dən\ **1** city SE Ontario, Canada; *pop* 366,151 **2** city, * of England & of United Kingdom on the Thames; consists of **City of London** & **Greater London** metropolitan county; *pop* 8,174,000 — **Lon·don·er** \-də-nər\ *n*

Londonderry — see DERRY

Long Beach city SW California S of Los Angeles; *pop* 462,257

Long Island island 118 mi. (190 km.) long SE New York S of Connecticut

Long Island Sound inlet of the Atlantic between Connecticut & Long Island, New York

Lon·gueuil \lȯṅ-'gäl\ city Canada in S Quebec E of Montreal; *pop* 231,409

Lor·raine \lə-'rān, lȯ-\ region NE France

Los An·ge·les \lȯs-'an-jə-ləs\ city SW California; *pop* 3,792,621

Lou·ise, Lake \lü-'ēz\ lake SW Alberta, Canada

Lou·i·si·ana \lü-ˌē-zē-'a-nə, ˌlü-ə-zē-, ˌlü-zē-\ state S U.S.; *, Baton Rouge; *pop* 4,533,372 — **Lou·i·si·an·ian** \-'a-nē-ən, -'a-nyən\ *or* **Lou·i·si·an·an** \-'a-nən\ *adj or n*

Louisiana Purchase area W *cen* U.S. between Rocky Mountains & the Mississippi purchased 1803 from France

Lou·is·ville \'lü-i-ˌvil, -vəl\ city N Kentucky on the Ohio River; *pop* 597,337

Low Countries region W Europe consisting of modern Belgium, Luxembourg, & the Netherlands

Low·ell \'lō-əl\ city NE Massachusetts NW of Boston; *pop* 106,519

Lower 48 the continental states of the U.S. excluding Alaska

Low·lands \'lō-ləndz, -ˌlandz\ the *cen* & E part of Scotland

Lu·an·da \lü-'än-də\ city, * of Angola; *pop* 2,600,000

Lub·bock \'lə-bək\ city NW Texas; *pop* 229,573

Lu·bum·ba·shi \ˌlü-büm-'bä-shē\ city SE Democratic Republic of the Congo; *pop* 739,000

Luck·now \'lək-ˌnaủ\ city N India ESE of Delhi; *pop* 2,817,105

Lüda *or* **Lü·ta** — see DALIAN

Lu·ray Caverns \'lü-ˌrā, lü-'\ series of caves N Virginia

Lu·sa·ka \lü-'sä-kä\ city, * of Zambia; *pop* 1,747,000

Lü·shun \'lü-'shủn, 'lуе-\ *or* **Port Ar·thur** \-'är-thər\ seaport NE China; part of greater Dalian

Lu·ton \'lü-t⁰n\ town SE *cen* England; *pop* 211,000

Lux·em·bourg *or* **Lux·em·burg** \'lək-səm-ˌbərg, 'lúk-səm-ˌbủrk\ **1** country W Europe bordered by Belgium, France, & Germany; *pop* 512,000 **2** city, its *; *pop* 95,000 — **Lux·em·bourg·er** \-ˌbər-gər, -ˌbùr-\ *n* — **Lux·em·bourg·ian** \ˌlək-səm-'bər-gē-ən, ˌlúk-səm-'bủr-\ *adj*

Lu·zon \lü-'zän\ island N Philippines; *pop* 42,784,360

L'viv \lə-'vē-ü, -'vēf\ *or* **L'vov** \lə-'vȯf, -'vȯv\ *or Polish* **Lwów** \lə-'vüf, -'vüv\ city W Ukraine; *pop* 729,400

Lyallpur — see FAISALABAD

Lyd·ia \'li-dē-ə\ ancient country W Asia Minor on the Aegean — **Lyd·i·an** \-ē-ən\ *adj or n*

Lyon \'lyō͞ⁿ\ *or* **Lyons** \lē-'ō͞ⁿ, 'li-ənz\ city SE *cen* France; *pop* 505,094

Ma·cao *or Portuguese* **Ma·cau** \mə-'kaủ\ *or Chinese* **Ao·men** \'aủ-'mən\ **1** special administrative region on coast of SE

China W of Hong Kong; *pop* 553,000 **2** city, its ✳; *pop* 469,000 — **Mac·a·nese** \ˌmä-kə-ˈnēz, -ˈnēs\ *n*

Mac·e·do·nia \ˌma-sə-ˈdō-nē-ə, -nyə\ **1** region S Europe in Balkan Peninsula in NE Greece, the former Yugoslav section & now independent country of Macedonia, & SW Bulgaria including territory of ancient kingdom of Macedonia (**Mac·e·don** \ˈmas-ə-dən, -ə-ˌdän\ ) **2** country S *cen* Balkan Peninsula; ✳, Skopje; a former republic of Yugoslavia; *pop* 2,063,000 — **Mac·e·do·nian** \ˌmas-ə-ˈdō-nyən, -nē-ən\ *adj or n*

Mac·gil·li·cud·dy's Reeks \mə-ˈgi-lə-ˌkə-dēz-ˈrēks\ mountains SW Ireland; highest Carrantuohill 3414 ft. (1041 m.)

Ma·chu Pic·chu \ˌmä-(ˌ)chü-ˈpē-(ˌ)chü, -ˈpēk-\ site SE Peru of ancient Inca city

Mac·ken·zie \mə-ˈken-zē\ river 1120 mi. (1802 km.) long NW Canada flowing from Great Slave Lake NW into Beaufort Sea

Mack·i·nac, Straits of \ˈma-kə-ˌnô, -ˌnak\ channel N Michigan connecting Lake Huron & Lake Michigan

Ma·con \ˈmā-kən\ city *cen* Georgia; *pop* 91,351

Mad·a·gas·car \ˌma-də-ˈgas-kər, -kär\ *formerly* **Mal·a·gasy Re·pub·lic** \ˌma-lə-ˈga-sē\ island country W Indian Ocean off SE Africa; ✳, Antananarivo; *pop* 21,842,000 — **Mad·a·gas·can** \ˌma-də-ˈgas-kən\ *adj or n*

Ma·dei·ra \mə-ˈdir-ə, -ˈder-ə\ **1** river 2013 mi. (3239 km.) long W Brazil flowing NE into the Amazon **2** islands Portugal in the North Atlantic N of the Canary Islands; *pop* 261,313 **3** island; chief of the Madeira group — **Ma·dei·ran** \-ˈdir-ən, -ˈder-\ *adj or n*

Ma·di·nat ash Sha'b \mə-ˈdē-ˌnə-tash-ˈshab\ city S Yemen

Mad·i·son \ˈma-də-sən\ city, ✳ of Wisconsin; *pop* 233,209

Ma·dras \mə-ˈdras, -ˈdräs\ *or* **Chen·nai** \ˈche-ˌnī\ city SE India; *pop* 4,646,732

Ma·drid \mə-ˈdrid\ city, ✳ of Spain; *pop* 3,198,645

Ma·du·rai \ˌmä-də-ˈrī\ city S India; *pop* 1,241,000

Mag·da·len Islands \ˈmag-də-lən\ *or F* **Îles de la Ma·de·leine** \ˌēl-də-lä-mäd-ˈlen, -mä-də-ˈlen\ islands Canada in Gulf of Saint Lawrence between Newfoundland & Prince Edward Island

Ma·gel·lan, Strait of \mə-ˈje-lən, *chiefly Brit* -ˈge-\ strait at S end of South America between mainland & Tierra del Fuego

Magh·er·a·felt \ˈmär-ə-ˌfelt, ˈma-kə-rə-ˌfelt\ district *cen* Northern Ireland; *pop* 45,000

Maid·stone \ˈmād-stən, -ˌstōn\ town SE England; *pop* 108,000

Main \ˈmīn, ˈmän\ river 325 mi. (523 km.) long S *cen* Germany flowing W into the Rhine

Maine \ˈmān\ state NE U.S.; ✳, Augusta; *pop* 1,328,361 — **Main·er** \ˈmā-nər\ *n*

Ma·jor·ca \mə-ˈjȯr-kə, mə-, -ˈyȯr-\ *or Spanish* **Ma·llor·ca** \mä-ˈyȯr-kä\ island Spain in W Mediterranean — **Ma·jor·can** \-ˈjȯr-kən, -ˈyȯr\ *adj or n*

Ma·ju·ro \mə-ˈjür-(ˌ)ō\ atoll that contains ✳ of Marshall Islands; *pop* 23,700

Mal·a·bar Coast \ˈma-lə-ˌbär\ region SW India on Arabian Sea

Ma·la·bo \mä-ˈlä-(ˌ)bō\ city, ✳ of Equatorial Guinea; *pop* 134,400

Ma·lac·ca, Strait of \mə-ˈla-kə, -ˈlä-\ channel between S Malay Peninsula & island of Sumatra

Ma·la·wi \mə-ˈlä-wē\ *formerly* **Ny·asa·land** \nī-ˈa-sə-ˌland, nē-\ country SE Africa on Lake Nyasa; ✳, Lilongwe; *pop* 13,077,000 — **Ma·la·wi·an** \-ən\ *adj or n*

Ma·lay \mə-ˈlā, ˈmā-(ˌ)lā\ **1** archipelago SE Asia including Sumatra, Java, Borneo, Sulawesi, Moluccas, & Timor; usu. thought to include the Philippines & sometimes New Guinea **2** peninsula SE Asia divided between Thailand & Malaysia (country)

Ma·laya \mə-ˈlā-ə, mā-\ **1** the Malay Peninsula **2** former country SE Asia on Malay Peninsula; now part of Malaysia

Ma·lay·sia \mə-ˈlā-zh(ē-)ə, -sh(ē-)ə\ **1** the Malay Archipelago **2** the Malay Peninsula & Malay Archipelago **3** country SE Asia; ✳, Kuala Lumpur; *pop* 27,566,000 — **Ma·lay·sian** \mə-ˈlā-zhən, -shən\ *adj or n*

Mal·dives \ˈmȯl-ˌdēvz, -ˌdīvz\ islands in Indian Ocean SW of Sri Lanka; country; ✳, Male Atoll; *pop* 299,000 — **Mal·div·i·an** \mȯl-ˈdi-vē-ən, mal-\ *adj or n*

Ma·le \ˈmä-lē\ atoll containing national ✳ of Maldives; *pop* 103,693

Ma·li \ˈmä-lē, ˈma-\ country W Africa; ✳, Bamako; *pop* 14,500,000 — **Ma·li·an** \-lē-ən\ *adj or n*

Mal·ta \ˈmȯl-tə\ islands in the Mediterranean S of Sicily; country since 1964; ✳, Valletta; *pop* 417,000 — **Mal·tese** \mȯl-ˈtēz, -ˈtēs\ *adj or n*

Malvinas, Islas — see FALKLAND ISLANDS

Mam·moth Cave \ˈma-məth\ limestone caverns SW *cen* Kentucky

Man, Isle of \ˈman\ island British Isles in Irish Sea; has own legislature & laws; *pop* 60,496

Ma·na·gua \mä-ˈnä-gwä\ city, ✳ of Nicaragua; *pop* 1,007,000

Ma·na·ma \mä-ˈna-mə\ city, ✳ of Bahrain; *pop* 143,045

Man·ches·ter \ˈman-ˌches-tər, -chəs-tər\ **1** city S *cen* New Hampshire; *pop* 109,565 **2** city NW England; *pop* 503,000

Man·chu·ria \man-ˈchur-ē-ə\ region NE

China S of the Amur — **Man·chu·ri·an** \-ē-ən\ *adj or n*

Man·hat·tan \man-'ha-t³n, mən-\ **1** island SE New York in New York City **2** borough of New York City consisting chiefly of Manhattan Island; *pop* 1,585,873

Ma·nila \mə-'ni-lə\ city, ✱ of Philippines in W Luzon; *pop* 1,661,000

Man·i·to·ba \ma-nə-'tō-bə\ province *cen* Canada; ✱, Winnipeg; *pop* 1,208,268 — **Man·i·to·ban** \-bən\ *adj or n*

Man·i·tou·lin \ma-nə-'tü-lən\ island 80 mi. (129 km.) long S Ontario in Lake Huron

Ma·pu·to \mä-'pü-(,)tō, -(,)tü\ city, ✱ of Mozambique; *pop* 1,094,628

Mar·a·cai·bo \ma-rə-'kī-(,)bō, mär-ä-\ city NW Venezuela; *pop* 1,207,513

Maracaibo, Lake extension of a gulf of the Caribbean NW Venezuela

Mar·a·thon \'ma-rə-,thän\ plain E Greece NE of Athens

Mar·i·ana \mer-ē-'a-nə\ islands W Pacific N of Caroline Islands; comprise Commonwealth of Northern Mariana Islands & Guam

Mariana Trench ocean trench W Pacific extending from SE of Guam to NW of Mariana Islands; deepest in world

Ma·rin·du·que \ma-rən-'dü-(,)kā, mär-ēn-\ island *cen* Philippines; *pop* 173,715

Maritime Provinces the Canadian provinces of New Brunswick, Nova Scotia, & Prince Edward Island & formerly thought by some to include Newfoundland and Labrador

Ma·ri·u·pol \ma-rē-'ü-,pól, -pəl\ *or 1949–89* **Zhda·nov** \zhə-'dä-nəf\ city E Ukraine; *pop* 461,000

Mar·ma·ra, Sea of \'mär-mə-rə\ sea NW Turkey connected with Black Sea by the Bosporus & with Aegean Sea by the Dardanelles

Marne \'märn\ river 325 mi. (523 km.) long NE France flowing W into the Seine

Mar·que·sas \mär-'kā-zəz, -zəs, -səz, -səs\ islands South Pacific; belonging to France; *pop* 7358 — **Mar·que·san** \-zən, -sən\ *adj or n*

Mar·ra·kech \ma-rə-'kesh, 'ma-rə-, mə-'rä-kish\ city *cen* Morocco; *pop* 823,154

Mar·seille \mär-'sā\ *or* **Mar·seilles** \mär-'sā, -'sālz\ city SE France; *pop* 850,726

Marshall Islands \'mär-shəl\ islands W Pacific E of the Carolines; republic, in association with U.S.; ✱, Majuro; *pop* 53,200

Mar·tha's Vineyard \'mär-thəz\ island SE Massachusetts off SW coast of Cape Cod WNW of Nantucket

Mar·ti·nique \mär-tə-'nēk\ island West Indies in the Windward Islands; an overseas division of France; ✱, Fort-de-France; *pop* 394,173

Mary·land \'mer-ə-lənd\ state E U.S.; ✱, Annapolis; *pop* 5,773,552 — **Mary·land·er** \-lən-dər, -,lan-\ *n*

Mas·ba·te \mäz-'bä-tē, mäs-\ island *cen* Philippines

Mas·e·ru \'ma-sə-,rü, -zə-\ city, ✱ of Lesotho; *pop* 227,880

Mash·had \mə-'shad\ city NE Iran; *pop* 2,749,374

Ma·son–Dix·on Line \'mā-s³n-'dik-sən\ boundary between Maryland & Pennsylvania; often considered the boundary between N & S states

Masqat — see MUSCAT

Mas·sa·chu·setts \ma-sə-'chü-səts, -zəts\ state NE U.S.; ✱, Boston; *pop* 6,547,629

Mat·a·be·le·land \ma-tə-'bē-lē-,land, mä-tä-'bā-lä-\ region SW Zimbabwe

Mat·lock \'mat-,läk\ town N England; *pop* 20,610

Mat·ter·horn \'ma-tər-,hórn, 'mä-\ mountain 14,691 ft. (4478 m.) on border between Switzerland & Italy

Maui \'maù-ē\ island Hawaii NW of Hawaii Island; *pop* 154,834

Mau·na Kea \maù-nä-'kā-ä, mò-\ extinct volcano 13,796 ft. (4205 m.) Hawaii in N *cen* Hawaii Island

Mau·na Loa \-'lō-ə\ volcano 13,680 ft. (4170 m.) Hawaii in S *cen* Hawaii Island

Mau·re·ta·nia *or* **Mau·ri·ta·nia** \mór-ə-'tā-nē-ə, mär-, -nyə\ ancient country NW Africa in modern Morocco & W Algeria — **Mau·re·ta·ni·an** *or* **Mau·ri·ta·ni·an** \-nē-ən, -nyən\ *adj or n*

Mauritania country NW Africa on the Atlantic N of Senegal River; ✱, Nouakchott; *pop* 3,537,000 — **Mauritanian** *adj or n*

Mau·ri·tius \mò-'ri-sh(ē-)əs\ island in Indian Ocean E of Madagascar; country; ✱, Port Louis; *pop* 1,237,091 — **Mau·ri·tian** \-'ri-shən\ *adj or n*

May, Cape \'mā\ cape S New Jersey at entrance to Delaware Bay

Ma·yon, Mount \mä-'yón\ volcano 8077 ft. (2462 m.) Philippines in SE Luzon

Ma·yotte \mä-'yät, -'yòt\ island Comoros group; French dependency; *pop* 213,000 — see COMOROS

Ma·za·ma, Mount \mə-'zäm-ə\ prehistoric mountain SW Oregon the collapse of whose top formed Crater Lake

Mba·bane \əm-bä-'bä-nä\ city, ✱ of Swaziland; *pop* 57,992

Mbi·ni \em-'bē-nē\ *formerly* **Río Mu·ni** \rē-ō-'mü-nē\ mainland portion of Equatorial Guinea; *pop* 750,000

Mc·Al·len \mə-'ka-lən\ city S Texas; *pop* 129,877

Mc·Kin·ley, Mount \mə-'kin-lē\ *or* **De·na·li** \də-'nä-lē\ mountain 20,320 ft. (6194 m.) S *cen* Alaska in Alaska Range; highest in U.S. & North America

Mead, Lake \'mēd\ reservoir NW Arizona

& SE Nevada formed by Hoover Dam in Colorado River

Mec·ca \'me-kə\ city W Saudi Arabia; contains Islam's Great Mosque; *pop* 1,294,106

Me·dan \mā-'dän\ city Indonesia, in N Sumatra; *pop* 2,097,610

Me·de·llín \ˌme-də-'lēn, ˌmā-thā-'yēn\ city NW Colombia; *pop* 2,400,000

Me·di·na \mə-'dī-nə\ city W Saudi Arabia; *pop* 1,100,000

Med·i·ter·ra·nean \ˌme-də-tə-'rā-nē-ən, -nyən\ sea 2300 mi. (3700 km.) long between Europe & Africa connecting with the Atlantic through Strait of Gibraltar

Me·kong \'mā-'koŋ, -'käŋ; 'mā-, 'mā-\ river 2600 mi. (4184 km.) long SE Asia flowing from E Tibet S & SE into South China Sea in S Vietnam

Mel·a·ne·sia \ˌme-lə-'nē-zhə, -shə\ islands of the Pacific NE of Australia & S of Micronesia including Bismarck, the Solomons, Vanuatu, New Caledonia, & the Fijis

Mel·bourne \'mel-bərn\ city SE Australia, ✱ of Victoria; metropolitan area *pop* 3,708,000

Mel·e·ke·ok \'me-lə-ˌkā-ˌȯk\ town, ✱ of Palau

Melos — see MILOS

Mel·ville \'mel-ˌvil\ 1 island N Canada, split between Northwest Territories & Nunavut 2 peninsula Canada in Nunavut

Mem·phis \'mem(p)-fəs\ 1 city SW Tennessee; *pop* 646,889 2 ancient city N Egypt S of modern Cairo

Mem·phre·ma·gog, Lake \ˌmem(p)-fri-'mā-ˌgäg\ lake on border between Canada (Quebec) & United States (Vermont)

Men·do·ci·no, Cape \ˌmen-də-'sē-(ˌ)nō\ cape NW California

Mer·cia \'mər-sh(ē-)ə\ ancient Anglo-Saxon kingdom *cen* England — **Mer·cian** \'mər-shən\ *adj or n*

Mer·sey \'mər-zē\ river 70 mi. (113 km.) long NW England flowing NW & W into Irish Sea

Mer·sey·side \'mər-zē-ˌsīd\ metropolitan county NW England; includes Liverpool

Mer·ton \'mər-tᵊn\ borough of SW Greater London, England; *pop* 200,000

Me·sa \'mā-sə\ city S *cen* Arizona; *pop* 439,041

Me·sa·bi Range \mə-'sä-bē\ region NE Minnesota that contains iron ore

Mes·o·po·ta·mia \ˌme-s(ə-)pə-'tā-mē-ə, -myə\ 1 region SW Asia between Euphrates & Tigris rivers 2 the entire Tigris–Euphrates valley — **Mes·o·po·ta·mian** \-mē-ən, -myən\ *adj or n*

Mes·quite \mə-ˈskēt, me-\ city NE Texas E of Dallas; *pop* 139,824

Meuse \'myūz, 'mə(r)z, 'mœz\ river 580 mi. (933 km.) long W Europe flowing from NE France into North Sea in the Netherlands

Mex·i·co \'mek-si-ˌkō\ 1 country S North America; *pop* 112,337,000 2 or **Mexico City** city, its ✱; *pop* 8,851,000 — **Mex·i·can** \'mek-si-kən\ *adj or n*

Mexico, Gulf of inlet of the Atlantic SE North America

Mi·ami \mī-'a-mē\ city & port SE Florida; *pop* 399,457

Miami Beach city SE Florida; *pop* 87,779

Mich·i·gan \'mi-shi-gən\ state N *cen* U.S.; ✱, Lansing; *pop* 9,883,640 — **Mich·i·gan·der** \ˌmi-shi-'gan-dər\ *n* — **Mich·i·ga·ni·an** \ˌmi-shə-'gā-nē-ən, -'ga-\ *n* — **Mich·i·gan·ite** \'mi-shi-gə-ˌnīt\ *n*

Michigan, Lake lake N *cen* U.S.; one of the Great Lakes

Mi·cro·ne·sia \ˌmī-krə-'nē-zhə, -shə\ islands of the W Pacific E of the Philippines & N of Melanesia including Caroline, Kiribati, Mariana, & Marshall groups — **Mi·cro·ne·sian** \-zhən, -shən\ *adj or n*

Micronesia, Federated States of islands W Pacific in the Carolines; country in association with U.S.; ✱, Palikir; *pop* 103,000

Middle East the countries of SW Asia & N Africa — usually thought to include the countries extending from Libya on the W to Afghanistan on the E — **Middle Eastern** *adj*

Mid·dles·brough \'mi-dᵊlz-brə\ town N England; *pop* 175,000

Middle West — see MIDWEST

Mid Gla·mor·gan \'mid-glə-'mȯr-gən\ former county SE Wales

Mid·i·an \'mi-dē-ən\ ancient region NW Arabia E of Gulf of Aqaba — **Mid·i·an·ite** \-ē-ə-ˌnīt\ *n*

Mid·lands \'mid-ləndz\ the *cen* counties of England

Mid·way \'mid-ˌwā\ islands *cen* Pacific 1300 mi. (2092 km.) WNW of Honolulu belonging to U.S.

Mid·west \'mid-'west\ or **Middle West** region N *cen* U.S. including area around Great Lakes & in upper Mississippi valley from Ohio on the E to North Dakota, South Dakota, Nebraska, & Kansas on the W — **Mid·west·ern** \ˌmid-'wes-tərn\ or **Middle Western** *adj* — **Mid·west·ern·er** \ˌmid-'wes-tə(r)-nər\ or **Middle Westerner** *n*

Mi·lan \mə-'lan, -'län\ or *Italian* **Mi·la·no** \mē-'lä-(ˌ)nō\ city NW Italy; *pop* 1,242,123 — **Mil·a·nese** \ˌmi-lə-'nēz, -'nēs\ *adj or n*

Mí·los or **Me·los** \'mē-ˌlȯs\ island Greece

Mil·wau·kee \mil-'wȯ-kē\ city SE Wisconsin on Lake Michigan; *pop* 594,833

Mi·nas Basin \'mī-nəs\ bay *cen* Nova Scotia; NE extension of Bay of Fundy

Min·da·nao \ˌmin-də-'nä-ˌō, -'naù\ island S Philippines; *pop* 13,966,000

Min·do·ro \min-'dȯr-(ˌ)ō\ island *cen* Philippines; *pop* 473,940

Min·ne·ap·o·lis \ˌmi-nē-'a-pə-lis\ city SE Minnesota; *pop* 383,578

Min·ne·so·ta \ˌmi-nə-'sō-tə\ state N *cen* U.S.; ✻, Saint Paul; *pop* 5,303,925 — **Min·ne·so·tan** \-'sō-tᵊn\ *adj or n*

Mi·nor·ca \mə-'nór-kə\ island Spain in W Mediterranean — **Mi·nor·can** \mə-'nór-kən\ *adj or n*

Minsk \'min(t)sk\ city, ✻ of Belarus; *pop* 1,836,808

Mis·sis·sau·ga \ˌmi-sə-'só-gə\ city Canada in S Ontario; *pop* 713,443

Mis·sis·sip·pi \ˌmi-sə-'si-pē\ **1** river 2340 mi. (3765 km.) long *cen* U.S. flowing into Gulf of Mexico — see ITASCA, LAKE **2** state S U.S.; ✻, Jackson; *pop* 2,967,297

Mis·sou·ri \mə-'zúr-ē\ **1** river 2466 mi. (3968 km.) long W U.S. flowing from SW Montana to the Mississippi in E Missouri (state) **2** state *cen* U.S.; ✻, Jefferson City; *pop* 5,988,927 — **Mis·sou·ri·an** \-'zúr-ē-ən\ *adj or n*

Mitch·ell, Mount \'mi-chəl\ mountain 6684 ft. (2037 m.) N North Carolina in the Appalachians; highest in U.S. E of the Mississippi

Mo·bile \mō-'bēl, 'mō-ˌbēl\ city SW Alabama on **Mobile Bay** (inlet of Gulf of Mexico); *pop* 195,111

Mo·des·to \mə-'des-(ˌ)tō\ city *cen* California; *pop* 201,165

Mog·a·di·shu \ˌmä-gə-'di-(ˌ)shü, ˌmō-, -'dē-\ *or* **Mog·a·di·scio** \-(ˌ)shō\ city, ✻ of Somalia; *pop* 349,245

Mo·hawk \'mō-ˌhók\ river E *cen* New York flowing into the Hudson

Mo·hen·jo Da·ro \mō-'hen-(ˌ)jō-'där-(ˌ)ō\ prehistoric city in valley of the Indus NE of modern Karachi, Pakistan

Mo·ja·ve *or* **Mo·ha·ve** \mə-'hä-vē, mō-\ desert S California SE of S end of Sierra Nevada

Mol·da·via \mäl-'dā-vē-ə, -vyə\ region E Europe in NE Romania & Moldova — **Mol·da·vian** \-vē-ən, -vyən\ *adj or n*

Mol·do·va \mäl-'dō-və, mòl-\ country E Europe in E Moldavia region; ✻, Chişinău; *pop* 3,785,000 — **Mol·do·van** \-vən\ *adj or n*

Mol·o·kai \ˌmä-lə-'kī, ˌmō-lō-'kä-ē\ island Hawaii ESE of Oahu

Mo·luc·cas \mə-'lə-kəz\ islands Indonesia E of Sulawesi; *pop* 2,300,000 — **Mo·luc·ca** \mə-'lə-kə\ *adj* — **Mo·luc·can** \-kən\ *adj or n*

Mom·ba·sa city & port S Kenya; *pop* 926,000

Mo·na·co \'mä-nə-ˌkō\ country W Europe on Mediterranean coast of France; ✻, Monaco; *pop* 31,100 — **Mo·na·can** \'mä-nə-kən, mə-'nä-kən\ *adj or n* — **Mon·e·gasque** \ˌmä-ni-'gask\ *n*

Mon·go·lia \män-'gōl-yə, mäŋ-, -'gō-lē-ə\ **1** region E Asia E of Altay Mountains; includes Gobi Desert **2** country E Asia consisting of major portion of Mongolia region; ✻, Ulaanbaatar; *pop* 2,701,000

Mo·non·ga·he·la \mə-ˌnän-gə-'hē-lə, -ˌnäŋ-gə-, -ˌhā-lə\ river N West Virginia & SW Pennsylvania

Mon·ro·via \(ˌ)mən-'rō-vē-ə\ city, ✻ of Liberia; *pop* 1,016,500

Mon·tana \män-'ta-nə\ state NW U.S.; ✻, Helena; *pop* 989,415 — **Mon·tan·an** \-nən\ *adj or n*

Mont Blanc \ˌmōⁿ-'bläⁿ\ mountain 15,771 ft. (4807 m.) SE France on Italian border; highest in the Alps

Mon·te·go Bay \män-'tē-(ˌ)gō\ city & port NW Jamaica on **Montego Bay** (inlet of the Caribbean); *pop* 110,115

Mon·te·ne·gro \ˌmän-tə-'nē-(ˌ)grō, -'nā-, -'ne\ country S Europe on the Adriatic Sea; ✻, Podgorica; *pop* 620,029

Mon·ter·rey \ˌmän-tə-'rā\ city NE Mexico; *pop* 1,135,550

Mon·te·vi·deo \ˌmän-tə-və-'dā-(ˌ)ō, -'vi-dē-ˌō; ˌmón-tā-vē-'thā-ō\ city, ✻ of Uruguay; *pop* 1,312,000

Mont·gom·ery \(ˌ)mən(t)-'gə-mə-rē, män(t)-, -'gä-; -'gəm-rē, -'gäm-\ city, ✻ of Alabama; *pop* 205,764

Mont·pe·lier \mänt-'pēl-yər, -'pil-\ city, ✻ of Vermont; *pop* 8,035

Mon·tre·al \ˌmän-trē-'ól, ˌmən-\ city S Quebec, Canada on **Montreal Island** in the Saint Lawrence; *pop* 1,649,519

Mont·ser·rat \ˌmän(t)-sə-'rat\ island British West Indies in the Leeward Islands; *pop* 4922

Mo·ra·via \mə-'rā-vē-ə\ region E Czech Republic — **Mo·ra·vi·an** \mə-'rā-vē-ən\ *adj or n*

Mo·re·no Valley \mə-'rē-(ˌ)nō\ city S California; *pop* 193,365

Mo·roc·co \mə-'rä-(ˌ)kō\ country NW Africa; ✻, Rabat; *pop* 31,900,000 — **Mo·roc·can** \-kən\ *adj or n*

Mo·ro·ni \mō-'rō-nē\ city, ✻ of Comoros; *pop* 41,500

Mos·cow \'mäs-(ˌ)kō, -ˌkaú\ *or Russian* **Mos·kva** \mäsk-'vä\ city, ✻ of Russia; *pop* 11,563,000

Mo·selle \mō-'zel\ river about 340 mi. (545 km.) long E France & W Germany

Moyle \'mói(-ə)l\ district N Northern Ireland; *pop* 17,000

Mo·zam·bique \ˌmō-zəm-'bēk\ **1** channel SE Africa between Mozambique (country) & Madagascar **2** country SE Africa; ✻, Maputo; *pop* 20,252,000 — **Mo·zam·bi·can** \ˌmō-zəm-'bē-kən\ *adj or n*

Mpu·ma·lan·ga \ˌəm-ˌpü-mä-'läŋ-gä\ province NE Republic of South Africa; *pop* 4,040,000

Mukden — see SHENYANG

Mul·tan \mul-'tän\ city NE Pakistan SW of Lahore; *pop* 1,197,384

Mumbai — see BOMBAY

Mu·nich \'myü-nik\ *or German* **Mün-**

chen \'mʉɛn-kən\ city S Germany in Bavaria; *pop* 1,348,335

Mun·ster \'mən(t)-stər\ province S Ireland; *pop* 1,246,000

Mur·cia \'mər-sh(ē-)ə\ region & ancient kingdom SE Spain

Mur·ray \'mər-ē, 'mə-rē\ river over 1560 mi. (2510 km.) long SE Australia flowing W from E Victoria into Indian Ocean in South Australia

Mur·rum·bidg·ee \,mər-əm-'bi-jē, ,mərəm-\ river almost 1000 mi. (1609 km.) long SE Australia in New South Wales flowing W into the Murray

Mus·cat \'məs-,kät, -,kat, -kət\ *or* **Mas·qat** \'məs-,kät\ town E Arabia; * of Oman *pop* 24, 893

Muz·tag \müs-'täg, məz-\ mountain 25,340 ft. (7724 m.) W China; highest in Kunlun Mountains

Myan·mar \'myän-,mär\ *or unofficially* **Bur·ma** \'bər-mə\ country SE Asia; *, Nay Pyi Taw; *pop* 51,419,000

My·ce·nae \mī-'sē-(,)nē\ ancient city S Greece in NE Peloponnese

Myr·tle Beach \'mər-t²l\ city E South Carolina on the Atlantic; *pop* 27,109

My·sore \mī-'sȯr\ city S India; *pop* 991,000

Nab·a·taea *or* **Nab·a·tea** \,na-bə-'tē-ə\ ancient Arab kingdom SE of Palestine — **Nab·a·tae·an** *or* **Nab·a·te·an** \-'tē-ən\ *adj or n*

Na·goya \nə-'gȯi-ə, 'nä-gȯ-(,)yä\ city Japan in S *cen* Honshu; *pop* 2,263,894

Nag·pur \'näg-,pu̇r\ city E *cen* India; *pop* 2,452,000

Nai·ro·bi \nī-'rō-bē\ city, * of Kenya; *pop* 3,133,518

Na·mib·ia \nə-'mi-bē-ə\ *formerly* **South-West Africa** country SW Africa on the Atlantic; *, Windhoek; *pop* 2,113,000 — **Na·mib·ian** \-bē-ən, -byən\ *adj or n*

Nan·chang \'nän-'chäŋ\ city SE China; *pop* 2,291,000

Nan·jing \'nän-'jiŋ\ *or* **Nan·king** \'nan-'kiŋ, 'nän-\ city E China; *pop* 6,496,000

Nan·tuck·et \nan-'tə-kət\ island SE Massachusetts S of Cape Cod; *pop* 7446

Na·per·ville \'nā-pər-,vil\ city NE Illinois W of Chicago; *pop* 141,853

Na·ples \'nā-pəlz\ *or Italian* **Na·po·li** \'nä-pō-lē\ *ancient* **Ne·ap·o·lis** \nē-'a-pə-ləs\ city S Italy on Bay of Naples; *pop* 962,003 — **Ne·a·pol·i·tan** \,nē-ə-'päl-ə-tən\ *adj or n*

Nar·ra·gan·sett Bay \,na-rə-'gan(t)-sət\ inlet of the Atlantic SE Rhode Island

Nash·ville \'nash-,vil, -vəl\ city, * of Tennessee; *pop* 601,222

Nas·sau \'na-,sȯ\ city, * of Bahamas on New Providence Island; *pop* 246,329

Na·tal \nə-'tal, -'täl\ former province E Republic of South Africa

Na·u·ru \nä-'ü-(,)rü\ island W South Pacific; country; *, Yaren; *pop* 10,065 — **Na·u·ru·an** \-'ü-rə-wən\ *adj or n*

Nay Pyi Taw *or* **Nay·pyi·daw** \'nē-pyē-,dȯ\ site of * of Myanmar

Naz·a·reth \'na-zə-rəth\ town of ancient Palestine in *cen* Galilee; now a city of N Israel; *pop* 72,000

N'Dja·me·na \ən-jä-'mä-nä, -'mē-\ city, * of Chad; *pop* 951,000

Neagh, Lough \,läk-'nä\ lake Northern Ireland; largest in British Isles

Near East the countries of NE Africa & SW Asia — **Near Eastern** *adj*

Ne·bras·ka \nə-'bras-kə\ state *cen* U.S.; *, Lincoln; *pop* 1,826,341 — **Ne·bras·kan** \-kən\ *adj or n*

Neg·ev \'ne-,gev\ desert region S Israel

Ne·gro \'nä-(,)grō, 'ne-\ river 1400 mi. (2253 km.) long in E Colombia & N Brazil flowing into the Amazon

Ne·gros \'nä-(,)grōs, 'ne-\ island *cen* Philippines

Nei Monggol — see INNER MONGOLIA

Ne·pal \nə-'pȯl, nä-\ country Asia on NE border of India in the Himalayas; *, Kathmandu; *pop* 26,495,000 — **Nep·a·lese** \,ne-pə-'lēz, -'lēs\ *adj or n* — **Ne·pali** \nə-'pȯl-ē, -'päl-, -'pal-\ *adj or n*

Ness, Loch \'nes\ lake NW Scotland

Neth·er·lands \'ne-thər-ləndz\ **1** *or Dutch* **Ne·der·land** \'nād-ər-,länt\ *also* **Holland** country NW Europe on North Sea; *, Amsterdam; seat of the government, The Hague; *pop* 16,829,000 **2** LOW COUNTRIES — an historical usage — **Neth·er·land** \'ne-thər-lənd\ *adj* — **Neth·er·land·er** \-,lan-dər, -lən-\ *n* — **Neth·er·land·ish** \-,lan-dish, -lən-\ *adj*

Netherlands Antilles islands of the West Indies, formerly an overseas territory of the Netherlands; *, Willemstad

Ne·va \'nē-və, 'nä-, nye-'vä\ river 40 mi. (64 km.) long W Russia; flows through Saint Petersburg

Ne·vada \nə-'va-də\ state W U.S.; *, Carson City; *pop* 2,700,551 — **Ne·vad·an** \-'va-d²n, -'vä-\ *or* **Ne·vad·i·an** \-'va-dē-ən, -'vä-\ *adj or n*

Ne·vis \'nē-vəs\ island West Indies in the Leeward Islands — see SAINT KITTS

New Amsterdam town founded 1625 on island of Manhattan by the Dutch; renamed New York 1664 by the British

New·ark \'nü-ərk, 'nyu̇-\ city NE New Jersey; *pop* 277,140

New Britain island W Pacific in Bismarck group; *pop* 263,500

New Bruns·wick \-'brənz-(,)wik\ province SE Canada; *, Fredericton; *pop* 751,171

New Caledonia island SW Pacific SW of Vanuatu; an overseas department of France; *, Nouméa; *pop* 245,600

New·cas·tle \'nü-,ka-səl, 'nyu̇-\ city SE Australia in E New South Wales; metropolitan area *pop* 308,308

Newcastle *or* **Newcastle upon Tyne** \'tīn\ city N England; *pop* 268,000

New Delhi city, ✳ of India S of Delhi; *pop* 294,783

New England section of NE U.S. consisting of states of Maine, New Hampshire, Vermont, Massachusetts, Rhode Island, & Connecticut — **New En·gland·er** \'iŋ-glən-dər\ *n*

New·found·land \'nü-fən(d)-lənd, 'nyü-, -ˌland; ˌnü-fən(d)-'land, ˌnyü-\ island Canada in the Atlantic — **New·found·land·er** \-ˌlən-dər, -ˌlan-\ *n*

Newfoundland and Labrador province E Canada consisting of Newfoundland Island and Labrador; ✳, Saint John's; *pop* 514,536

New France the possessions of France in North America before 1763

New Guinea 1 island W Pacific N of E Australia; divided between West Papua, Indonesia & independent Papua New Guinea **2** the NE portion of the island of New Guinea together with some nearby islands; now part of Papua New Guinea — **New Guinean** *adj or n*

New·ham \'nü-əm, 'nyü-\ borough of E Greater London, England; *pop* 308,000

New Hamp·shire \'hamp-shər, -ˌshir\ state NE U.S.; ✳, Concord; *pop* 1,316,470 — **New Hamp·shire·man** \-mən\ *n* — **New Hamp·shir·ite** \-ˌīt\ *n*

New Ha·ven \'hā-vən\ city S Connecticut; *pop* 129,779

New Hebrides — see VANUATU

New Jersey state E U.S.; ✳, Trenton; *pop* 8,791,894 — **New Jer·sey·an** \-ən\ *n* — **New Jer·sey·ite** \-ˌīt\ *n*

New Mex·i·co \'mek-si-ˌkō\ state SW U.S.; ✳, Santa Fe; *pop* 2,059,179 — **New Mex·i·can** \-si-kən\ *adj or n*

New Neth·er·land \'ne-thər-lənd\ former Dutch colony (1613–64) North America along Hudson & lower Delaware rivers

New Or·leans \'ȯr-lē-ənz, 'ȯr-lənz, 'ȯrl-yənz, (ˌ)ȯr-'lēnz\ city SE Louisiana; *pop* 343,829

New·port \'nü-ˌpȯrt, 'nyü-, -ˌpȯrt\ **1** town S England in Isle of Wight; *pop* 25,000 **2** city SE Wales; *pop* 128,000

Newport News \'nü-ˌpȯrt-'nüz, 'nyü-ˌpȯrt-'nyüz, -pərt-\ city SE Virginia; *pop* 180,719

New Providence island NW *cen* Bahamas; chief town, Nassau; *pop* 247,500

New·ry and Mourne \'n(y)u̇(ə)-rē-ən(d)-'mȯrn\ district S Northern Ireland; *pop* 99,000

New South Wales state SE Australia; ✳, Sydney; *pop* 6,917,658

New Spain former Spanish possessions in North America, Central America, West Indies, & the Philippines

New Sweden former Swedish colony (1638–55) North America on W bank of Delaware River

New·town·ab·bey \ˌnü-tᵊn-'a-bē, ˌnyü-\ district E Northern Ireland; *pop* 85,000

Newtown Saint Bos·wells \'nü-ˌtau̇n-sənt-'bäz-wəlz, 'nyü-, -ˌsänt-\ village S Scotland

New World the Western Hemisphere including North America and South America

New York 1 state NE U.S.; ✳, Albany; *pop* 19,378,102 **2** *or* **New York City** city SE New York (state); *pop* 8,175,133 — **New York·er** \'yȯr-kər\ *n*

New York State Barge Canal — see ERIE

New Zea·land \'zē-lənd\ country SW Pacific ESE of Australia; ✳, Wellington; *pop* 4,242,000 — **New Zea·land·er** \-lən-dər\ *n*

Ni·ag·a·ra Falls \(ˌ)nī-'a-g(ə-)rə\ falls New York & Ontario in **Niagara River** (flowing N from Lake Erie into Lake Ontario); divided by Goat Island into Horseshoe Falls, or Canadian Falls (158 ft. or 48 m. high) & American Falls (167 ft. or 51 m. high)

Nia·mey \nē-'ä-(ˌ)mā, nyä-'mä\ city, ✳ of Niger; *pop* 1,026,848

Ni·caea \nī-'sē-ə\ *or* **Nice** \'nīs\ ancient city W Bithynia; site at modern village in NW Turkey — **Ni·cae·an** \nī-'sē-ən\ *adj or n* — **Ni·cene** \'nī-ˌsēn, nī-'sēn\ *adj*

Ni·ca·ra·gua \ˌni-kə-'rä-gwə, -kē-\ **1** lake about 100 mi. (160 km.) long S Nicaragua **2** country Central America; ✳, Managua; *pop* 5,142,000 — **Ni·ca·ra·guan** \-'rä-gwən\ *adj or n*

Nice \'nēs\ city & port SE France on the Mediterranean; *pop* 343,304

Nic·o·bar \'ni-kə-ˌbär\ islands India in Bay of Bengal S of the Andamans; *pop* 14,563

Nic·o·sia \ˌni-kə-'sē-ə\ city, ✳ of Cyprus; *pop* 55,014

Ni·ger \'nī-jər, nē-'zher\ **1** river 2600 mi. (4184 km.) long W Africa flowing into Gulf of Guinea **2** country W Africa N of Nigeria; ✳, Niamey; *pop* 17,139,000 — **Ni·ger·ien** \ˌnī-ˌjir-ē-'en, nē-'zher-ē-ən\ *adj or n* — **Ni·ger·ois** \ˌnē-zhər-'wä, -zher-\ *n*

Ni·ge·ria \nī-'jir-ē-ə\ country W Africa on Gulf of Guinea; ✳, Abuja; *pop* 140,432,000 — **Ni·ge·ri·an** \-ē-ən\ *adj or n*

Nii·hau \'nē-ˌhau̇\ island Hawaii WSW of Kauai

Nile \'nī(-ə)l\ river 4160 mi. (6693 km.) long E Africa flowing from Lake Victoria in Uganda N into the Mediterranean in Egypt

Nil·gi·ri \'nil-gə-rē\ hills S India

Nin·e·veh \'ni-nə-və\ ancient city, ✳ of Assyria; ruins in Iraq on the Tigris

Nip·i·gon, Lake \'ni-pə-ˌgän\ lake Canada in W Ontario N of Lake Superior

Nizh·niy Nov·go·rod \'nizh-nē-'näv-gə-

‚räd, -ˈnȯv-gə-rət\ *formerly 1932–89* **Gor-ki** \ˈgȯr-kē\ city W Russia; *pop* 1,250,600

Nord–Ost-see \ˈnȯrt-ˈȯst-ˈzā\ *or* **Kiel** \ˈkēl\ canal 61 mi. (98 km.) long N Germany across base of Jutland Peninsula connecting Báltic Sea & North Sea

Nor-folk \ˈnȯr-fək\ city & port SE Virginia; *pop* 242,803

Nor-man-dy \ˈnȯr-mən-dē\ region NW France NE of Brittany

North **1** river estuary of the Hudson between NE New Jersey & SE New York **2** sea, arm of the Atlantic E of Great Britain **3** island N New Zealand; *pop* 3,237,048

North-al-ler-ton \nȯr-ˈtha-lər-tən\ town N England; *pop* 9556

North America continent of Western Hemisphere NW of South America & N of the Equator — **North American** *adj or n*

North-amp-ton \nȯr-ˈtham(p)-tən, nȯrth-ˈham(p)-\ town *cen* England; *pop* 215,000

North-amp-ton-shire \-ˌshir, -shər\ *or* **Northampton** county *cen* England

North Cape cape New Zealand at N end of North Island

North Car-o-li-na \ˌker(-ə)-ˈlī-nə, ˌka-rə-\ state E U.S.; ✻, Raleigh; *pop* 9,535,483 — **North Car-o-lin-ian** \-ˈli-nē-ən, -ˈli-nyən\ *adj or n*

North Da-ko-ta \də-ˈkō-tə\ state N U.S.; ✻, Bismarck; *pop* 672,591 — **North Da-ko-tan** \-ˈkō-tᵊn\ *adj or n*

North Down district E Northern Ireland; *pop* 79,000

Northern Cape province W Republic of South Africa; *pop* 1,145,861

Northern Cook islands S *cen* Pacific N of Cook Islands

Northern Hemisphere the half of the earth that lies N of the Equator

Northern Ireland region N Ireland comprising 26 districts of Ulster; a division of United Kingdom; ✻, Belfast; *pop* 1,810,900

Northern Mar-i-ana Islands \ˌmer-ē-ˈa-nə\ islands W Pacific; commonwealth in association with U.S.; seat of the government on Saipan; *pop* 53,900

Northern Rhodesia — see ZAMBIA

Northern Territory territory N & *cen* Australia; ✻, Darwin; *pop* 211,945

North Korea *or* **Democratic People's Republic of Korea** country N half of Korean Peninsula in E Asia; ✻, Pyongyang; *pop* 24,700,000

North Las Vegas city SE Nevada; *pop* 216,061

North Slope region N Alaska between Brooks Range & Arctic Ocean

North-um-ber-land \nȯr-ˈthəm-bər-lənd\ county N England

North-um-bria \nȯr-ˈthəm-brē-ə\ ancient country Great Britain in what is now N England and S Scotland — **North-um-bri-an** \-brē-ən\ *adj or n*

North Vietnam — see VIETNAM

North West province N Republic of South Africa; *pop* 3,509,953

Northwest Passage sea passage between the Atlantic and the Pacific along the N coast of North America

Northwest Territories territory NW Canada consisting of the area of the mainland north of 60° between Yukon (territory) & Nunavut; ✻, Yellowknife; *pop* 41,462

North York former city Canada in SE Ontario; now part of Toronto

North Yorkshire county N England

Nor-walk \ˈnȯr-ˌwȯk\ city SW California SE of Los Angeles; *pop* 105,549

Nor-way \ˈnȯr-ˌwā\ country N Europe in Scandinavia; ✻, Oslo; *pop* 5,156,000

Nor-wich \ˈnȯr-(ˌ)wich\ city E England; *pop* 187,000

Not-ting-ham \ˈnä-tiŋ-əm\ city N *cen* England; *pop* 289,000

Not-ting-ham-shire \ˈnä-tiŋ-əm-ˌshir, -shər\ *or* **Nottingham** county N *cen* England; *pop* 692,000

Nouak-chott \nu̇-ˈäk-ˌshät\ city, ✻ of Mauritania; *pop* 958,399

Nou-méa \nü-ˈmā-ə\ city, ✻ of New Caledonia; *pop* 76,293

No-va Sco-tia \ˌnō-və-ˈskō-shə\ province SE Canada; ✻, Halifax; *pop* 921,727 — **No-va Sco-tian** \-shən\ *adj or n*

No-vo-kuz-netsk \ˌnō-(ˌ)vō-ku̇z-ˈnetsk, ˌnȯ-və-ku̇z-ˈnyetsk\ city S Russia in Asia; *pop* 548,000

No-vo-si-birsk \ˌnō-(ˌ)vō-sə-ˈbirsk, ˌnȯ-və-\ city S Russia in Asia; *pop* 1,474,000

Nu-bia \ˈnü-bē-ə, ˈnyü-\ region NE Africa in Nile valley in S Egypt & N Sudan — **Nu-bi-an** \ˈnü-bē-ən, ˈnyü-\ *adj or n*

Nu-ku-a-lo-fa \ˌnü-kü-ä-ˈlō-fä\ seaport, ✻ of Tonga; *pop* 24,000

Nu-mid-ia \nü-ˈmi-dē-ə, nyü-\ ancient country N Africa E of Mauretania in modern Algeria — **Nu-mid-i-an** \-dē-ən\ *adj or n*

Nu-na-vut \ˈnü-nə-ˌvu̇t\ semiautonomous territory NE Canada; ✻, Iqaluit; *pop* 31,906

Nu-rem-berg \ˈnu̇r-əm-ˌbərg, ˈnyu̇r-\ *or German* **Nürn-berg** \ˈnu̇rn-ˌberk\ city S Germany; *pop* 486,314

Nuuk \ˈnük\ *or Danish* **Godt-håb** \ˈgȯt-ˌhȯp\ town, ✻ of Greenland on SW coast; *pop* 15,000

Ny-asa, Lake \nī-ˈas-ə, nē-\ lake SE Africa in Malawi, Mozambique, & Tanzania

Nyasaland — see MALAWI

Oa-hu \ō-ˈä-(ˌ)hü\ island Hawaii; site of Honolulu

Oak-land \ˈō-klənd\ city W California on San Francisco Bay E of San Francisco; *pop* 390,724

Ob \'äb, 'ôb\ river over 2250 mi. (3620 km.) long W Russia in Asia flowing NW & N into Arctic Ocean

Oce·a·nia \ˌō-shē-'a-nē-ə, -'ä-\ lands of the *cen* & S Pacific: Micronesia, Melanesia, Polynesia including New Zealand, & by some thought to include Australia & Malay Archipelago

Ocean·side \'ō-shən-ˌsīd\ city SW California NNW of San Diego; *pop* 167,086

Oder \'ō-dər\ *or* **Odra** \'ō-drə\ river about 565 mi. (909 km.) long *cen* Europe flowing from Silesia NW into Baltic Sea; forms part of boundary between Poland & Germany

Odes·sa \ō-'de-sə\ city & port S Ukraine on Black Sea; *pop* 1,012,500

Ohio \ō-'hī-(ˌ)ō, ə-, -ə\ **1** river about 981 mi. (1578 km.) long E U.S. flowing from W Pennsylvania into the Mississippi **2** state E *cen* U.S.; *, Columbus; *pop* 11,536,504 — **Ohio·an** \-'hī-ō-ən\ *adj or n*

Oka·ya·ma \ˌō-kä-'yä-mä\ city Japan in W Honshu on Inland Sea; *pop* 709,584

Okee·cho·bee, Lake \ˌō-kə-'chō-bē\ lake S *cen* Florida

Oke·fe·no·kee \ˌō-kə-fə-'nō-kē, ˌō-kē-\ swamp SE Georgia & NE Florida

Okhotsk, Sea of \ō-'kätsk, ə-'ḵotsk\ inlet of the North Pacific E Russia in Asia

Oki·na·wa \ˌō-kə-'nä-wə, -'naù-ə\ **1** islands Japan in *cen* Ryukyus **2** island, chief of group — **Oki·na·wan** \-'nä-wən, -'naù-ən\ *adj or n*

Okla·ho·ma \ˌō-klə-'hō-mə\ state S *cen* U.S.; *, Oklahoma City; *pop* 3,751,351 — **Okla·ho·man** \-mən\ *adj or n*

Oklahoma City city, * of Oklahoma; *pop* 579,999

Old·ham \'ōl-dəm\ city NW England; *pop* 97,000

Old Point Comfort cape SE Virginia N of entrance to Hampton Roads

Ol·du·vai Gorge \'ōl-də-ˌvī\ canyon N Tanzania SE of Serengeti Plain; site of fossil beds

Old World the half of the earth to the E of the Atlantic Ocean including Europe, Asia, and Africa & esp. the continent of Europe

Olym·pia \ə-'lim-pē-ə, ō-\ **1** city, * of Washington; *pop* 46,478 **2** plain S Greece in NW Peloponnese

Olym·pic \-pik\ mountains NW Washington on Olympic Peninsula; highest Mt. Olympus 7965 ft. (2428 m.)

Olym·pus \ə-'lim-pəs, ō-\ mountains NE Greece

Omagh \'ō-mə, -(ˌ)mä\ **1** district W Northern Ireland; *pop* 51,000 **2** town in Omagh district; *pop* 19,000

Oma·ha \'ō-mə-ˌhò, -ˌhä\ **1** beach NW France in Normandy **2** city E Nebraska on Missouri River; *pop* 408,958

Oman \ō-'män, -'man\ country SW Asia in SE Arabia; *, Muscat; *pop* 2,773,479 — **Omani** \ō-'mä-nē, -'ma-\ *adj or n*

Oman, Gulf of arm of Arabian Sea between Oman & SE Iran

Omsk \'óm(p)sk, 'äm(p)sk\ city SW Russia in Asia; *pop* 1,154,000

On·tar·io \än-'ter-ē-ˌō\ **1** city SW California; *pop* 163,924 **2** province E Canada; *, Toronto; *pop* 12,851,821 — **On·tar·i·an** \-ē-ən\ *adj or n*

Ontario, Lake lake E *cen* North America in U.S. & Canada; one of the Great Lakes

Oran \ō-'rän\ city & port NW Algeria; *pop* 803,329

Or·ange \'är-inj, 'är-(ə)nj, 'ór-inj, 'ór(-ə)nj\ **1** city SW California; *pop* 136,416 **2** river 1300 mi. (2092 km.) long S Africa flowing W from Drakensberg Mountains into the Atlantic

Orange Free State — see FREE STATE

Or·e·gon \'ór-i-gən, 'är-\ state NW U.S.; *, Salem; *pop* 3,831,074 — **Or·e·go·nian** \ˌór-i-'gō-nē-ən, ˌär-, -nyən\ *adj or n*

Oregon Trail pioneer route to the NW U.S. about 2000 mi. (3220 km.) long from Missouri to Washington

Ori·no·co \ˌór-ē-'nō-(ˌ)kō\ river 1336 mi. (2150 km.) long Venezuela flowing into the Atlantic

Ork·ney \'órk-nē\ islands N Scotland; *pop* 19,570

Or·lan·do \ór-'lan-(ˌ)dō\ city *cen* Florida; *pop* 238,300

Osa·ka \ō-'sä-kä, 'ō-sä-ˌkä\ city Japan in S Honshu; *pop* 2,665,314

Osh·a·wa \'ä-shə-wə, -ˌwä, -ˌwó\ city SE Ontario, Canada on Lake Ontario ENE of Toronto; *pop* 149,607

Os·lo \'äz-(ˌ)lō, 'äs-\ city, * of Norway; *pop* 636,000

Oś·wię·cim \ˌósh-'fyen-chēm\ *or German* **Ausch·witz** \'aùsh-ˌvits\ town S Poland W of Krakow; *pop* 45,282

Ot·ta·wa \'ä-tə-wə, -ˌwä, -ˌwó\ **1** river 696 mi. (1120 km.) E Canada in SE Ontario & S Quebec flowing E into the Saint Lawrence **2** city, * of Canada in SE Ontario on Ottawa River; *pop* 883,391

Ot·to·man Empire \'ä-tə-mən\ former Turkish sultanate in SE Europe, W Asia, & N Africa

Oua·ga·dou·gou \ˌwä-gä-'dü-(ˌ)gü\ city, * of Burkina Faso; *pop* 1,475,223

Outer Hebrides — see HEBRIDES

Over·land Park \'ō-vər-lənd\ city NE Kansas; *pop* 173,372

Ox·ford \'äks-fərd\ city *cen* England; *pop* 160,000

Ox·ford·shire \'äks-fərd-ˌshir, -shər\ *or* **Oxford** county *cen* England

Ox·nard \'äks-ˌnärd\ city SW California; *pop* 197,899

Ozark Plateau \'ō-ˌzärk\ *or* **Ozark Mountains** eroded plateau N Arkansas, S Missouri, & NE Oklahoma with E extension into S Illinois

Pa·cif·ic \pə-'si-fik\ ocean extending from Arctic Circle to the Equator (**North Pacific**) and from the Equator to the Antarctic regions (**South Pacific**) & from W North America & W South America to E Asia & Australia — **Pacific** *adj*

Pacific Islands, Trust Territory of the grouping of islands in W Pacific formerly under U.S. administration: the Carolines & the Marshalls

Pacific Rim the countries bordering on or located in the Pacific Ocean — used esp. of Asian countries on the Pacific

Pa·dang \'pä-,däŋ\ city Indonesia in W Sumatra; *pop* 834,000

Pa·dre \'pä-drē, -drā\ island 113 mi. (182 km.) long S Texas in Gulf of Mexico

Pa·go Pa·go \,pä-(,)gō-'pä-(,)gō, ,päŋ-(,)ō-'päŋ-(,)ō\ town, ✳ of American Samoa on Tutuila Island; *pop* 3656

Painted Desert region N *cen* Arizona

Pak·i·stan \'pa-ki-,stan, ,pä-ki-'stän\ country S Asia NW of India; ✳, Islamabad; *pop* 193,240,000 — see EAST PAKISTAN — **Pak·i·stani** \,pa-ki-'sta-nē, ,pä-ki-'stä-\ *adj or n*

Pa·lau \pə-'laû\ *or* **Be·lau** \bə-\ island group W Pacific in the W Carolines; country in association with U.S.; ✳, Melekeok; *pop* 17,501 — **Pa·lau·an** \pə-'laû-ən\ *n*

Pa·la·wan \pə-'lä-wən, -,wän\ island W Philippines between South China & Sulu seas; *pop* 528,287

Pa·lem·bang \,pä-ləm-'bäŋ\ city Indonesia in SE Sumatra; *pop* 1,455,000

Pa·ler·mo \pə-'lər-(,)mō, pä-'ler-\ city Italy, ✳ of Sicily; *pop* 657,561

Pal·es·tine \'pa-lə-,stīn\ region SW Asia dating back to ancient times with unofficial, disputed, & fluctuating boundaries, but extending from E coast of Mediterranean Sea up to or beyond Jordan River — **Pal·es·tin·ian** \,pa-lə-'sti-nē-ən, -nyən\ *adj or n*

Pa·li·kir \'pä-lē-'kir\ town, ✳ of Federated States of Micronesia on Pohnpei Island; *pop* 6227

Pal·i·sades \,pa-lə-'sādz\ line of high cliffs 15 mi. (24 km.) long on W bank of the Hudson in SE New York & NE New Jersey

Palm·dale \'päm-,dāl, 'pälm-\ city SW California NE of Los Angeles; *pop* 152,750

Pa·mirs \pə-'mirz\ elevated mountainous region *cen* Asia in E Tajikistan & on borders of China, India, Pakistan, & Afghanistan; many peaks over 20,000 ft. (6096 m.)

Pam·li·co Sound \'pam-li-,kō\ inlet of the North Atlantic E North Carolina between main part of the state & offshore islands

Pam·pa \'pam-pə\ city NW Texas; *pop* 17,994

Pan·a·ma \'pan-ə-,mä, -,mò; ,pan-ə-'mä, -'mò\ **1** country S Central America; *pop* 3,406,000 **2** *or* **Panama City** city, its ✳ on the Pacific; *pop* 411,549 **3** canal 40 mi. (64 km.) long Panama connecting Atlantic & Pacific oceans — **Pan·a·ma·ni·an** \,pan-ə-'mä-nē-ən\ *adj or n*

Panama, Isthmus of *formerly* **Isthmus of Dar·i·en** \,der-ē-'en\ strip of land *cen* Panama connecting North America & South America

Panama Canal Zone — see CANAL ZONE

Pa·nay \pə-'nī\ island *cen* Philippines in the Visayas

Pan·gaea \pan-'jē-ə\ land area believed to have once connected the landmasses of the Southern Hemisphere with those of the Northern Hemisphere

Pan·mun·jom *or* **Pan·mun·jeom** \,pän-,mùn-'jəm\ village on North Korea–South Korea border

Pao–t'ou — see BAOTOU

Pap·ua, Territory of \'pa-pyü-wə, 'pä-pù-wə\ former British territory consisting of SE New Guinea & offshore islands; now part of Papua New Guinea

Papua New Guinea country SW Pacific; ✳, Port Moresby; *pop* 7,275,000

Par·a·guay \'pa-rə-,gwī, -,gwä\ **1** river 1584 mi. (2549 km.) long *cen* South America flowing from Brazil S into the Paraná in Paraguay **2** country *cen* South America; ✳, Asunción; *pop* 6,600,000 — **Par·a·guay·an** \,pa-rə-'gwī-ən, -'gwä-\ *adj or n*

Par·a·mar·i·bo \,pa-rə-'ma-rə-,bō\ city, ✳ of Suriname; *pop* 240,924

Pa·ra·ná \,pär-ə-'nä\ river about 2500 mi. (4022 km.) long *cen* South America flowing S from Brazil into Argentina

Pa·ri·cu·tin \pä-,rē-kü-'tēn\ volcano Mexico on site of a former village

Par·is \'pa-rəs\ city, ✳ of France; *pop* 2,243,833 — **Pa·ri·sian** \pə-'ri-zhən, -'rē-\ *adj or n*

Par·nas·sus \pär-'na-səs\ mountain *cen* Greece

Par·os \'pär-,òs\ island Greece — **Par·i·an** \'par-ē-ən, 'per-\ *adj*

Par·ra·mat·ta \,pa-rə-'ma-tə\ city SE Australia in New South Wales; *pop* 166,858

Par·thia \'pär-thē-ə\ ancient country SW Asia in NE modern Iran — **Par·thi·an** \-thē-ən\ *adj or n*

Pas·a·de·na \,pa-sə-'dē-nə\ **1** city SW California E of Glendale; *pop* 137,122 **2** city SE Texas; *pop* 149,043

Pat·a·go·nia \,pa-tə-'gō-nyə, -nē-ə\ region South America S of about 40° S latitude in S Argentina & S tip of Chile; sometimes thought to include Tierra del Fuego — **Pat·a·go·nian** \-nyən, -nē-ən\ *adj or n*

Pat·er·son \'pa-tər-sən\ city NE New Jersey; *pop* 146,199

Pat·mos \'pat-məs\ island Greece SSW of Samos

Pat·na \'pət-nə\ city NE India on the Ganges; *pop* 1,866,500

Pearl Harbor inlet Hawaii on S coast of Oahu W of Honolulu

Peking — see BEIJING

Pe·li·on \'pē-lē-ən\ mountain 5089 ft. (1551 m.) NE Greece

Pel·o·pon·nese \'pe-lə-pə-,nēz, -,nēs\ *or* **Pel·o·pon·ni·sos** \,pe-lə-pə-'nē-səs\ peninsula forming S part of mainland of Greece

Pem·broke Pines \'pem-,brōk\ city SE Florida; *pop* 154,750

Pen·nine Chain \'pe-,nīn\ mountains N England; highest Cross Fell 2930 ft. (893 m.)

Penn·syl·va·nia \,pen(t)-səl-'vā-nyə, -nē-ə\ state E U.S.; ✳, Harrisburg; *pop* 12,702,379

Pe·o·ria \pē-'ȯr-ē-ə\ **1** town SW *cen* Arizona; *pop* 154,065 **2** city N *cen* Illinois; *pop* 115,007

Per·ga·mum \'pər-gə-məm\ *or* **Per·ga·mus** \-məs\ ancient Greek kingdom including most of Asia Minor

Perm \'pərm, 'perm\ city E Russia in Europe; *pop* 991,300

Pernambuco — see RECIFE

Persia — see IRAN

Per·sian Gulf \'pər-zhən\ arm of Arabian Sea between Iran & Arabia

Perth \'pərth\ city, ✳ of Western Australia; area *pop* 1,728,867

Pe·ru \pə-'rü, pā-\ country W South America; ✳, Lima; *pop* 27,412,000 — **Pe·ru·vi·an** \-'rü-vē-ən\ *adj or n*

Pe·tra \'pē-trə, 'pe-\ ancient city NW Arabia; site in SW Jordan

Petrograd — see SAINT PETERSBURG

Phil·a·del·phia \,fi-lə-'del-fyə, -fē-ə\ city SE Pennsylvania; *pop* 1,526,006 — **Phil·a·del·phian** \-fyən, -fē-ən\ *adj or n*

Phil·ip·pines \,fi-lə-'pēnz, 'fi-lə-,pēnz\ island group approximately 500 mi. (805 km.) off SE coast of Asia; country; ✳, Manila; *pop* 92,338,000 — **Phil·ip·pine** \,fi-lə-'pēn, 'fi-lə-,\ *adj*

Phnom Penh \(pə-)'näm-'pen, (pə-)'nóm-\ city, ✳ of Cambodia; *pop* 1,200,000

Phoe·ni·cia \fi-'ni-sh(ē-)ə, -'nē-\ ancient country SW Asia on the Mediterranean in modern Syria & Lebanon

Phoe·nix \'fē-niks\ city, ✳ of Arizona; *pop* 1,445,632

Phry·gia \'fri-j(ē-)ə\ ancient country W *cen* Asia Minor

Pic·ar·dy \'pi-kər-dē\ *or F* **Pi·car·die** \pē-kär-'dē\ region & former province N France bordering on English Channel N of Normandy — **Pi·card** \'pi-,kärd, -,kərd\ *adj or n*

Pied·mont \'pēd-,mänt\ plateau region E U.S. E of the Appalachians between SE New York & NE Alabama

Pierre \'pir\ city, ✳ of South Dakota; *pop* 13,646

Pie·ter·mar·itz·burg \,pē-tər-'ma-rəts-,bərg\ city E Republic of South Africa; *pop* 475,000

Pigs, Bay of \'pigz\ *or* **Ba·hía de Co·chi·nos** \bä-'ē-ä-thä-kō-'chē-nōs\ bay W Cuba on S coast

Pikes Peak \'pīks\ mountain 14,110 ft. (4301 m.) E *cen* Colorado in a range of the Rockies

Pin·dus \'pin-dəs\ mountains W Greece; highest point 8136 ft. (2480 m.)

Pi·sa \'pē-zə, *It* -sä\ city W *cen* Italy W of Florence; *pop* 85,900

Pit·cairn \'pit-,kern\ island South Pacific; a British colony; *pop* 62

Pitts·burgh \'pits-,bərg\ city SW Pennsylvania; *pop* 305,704

Plac·id, Lake \'pla-səd\ lake NE New York

Pla·no \'plā-(,)nō\ city NE Texas N of Dallas; *pop* 259,841

Plov·div \'plȯv-,dif, -,div\ city S Bulgaria; *pop* 335,000

Plym·outh \'pli-məth\ **1** town SE Massachusetts; *pop* 56,468 **2** city & port SW England; *pop* 235,000

Po \'pō\ river 405 mi. (652 km.) N Italy flowing into the Adriatic

Pod·go·ri·ca \'pȯd-,gȯr-ēt-sä\ city ✳ of Montenegro; *pop* 150,977

Po Hai — see BO HAI

Pohn·pei \'pȯn-,pā\ island W Pacific in the E Carolines; part of Federated States of Micronesia

Po·land \'pō-lənd\ country *cen* Europe on Baltic Sea; ✳, Warsaw; *pop* 38,512,000 — **Pole** *n*

Pol·y·ne·sia \,pä-lə-'nē-zhə, -shə\ islands of the *cen* & S Pacific including Hawaii, the Line, Tonga, Cook, & Samoa islands, & often New Zealand among others

Pom·er·a·nia \,pä-mə-'rā-nē-ə, -nyə\ region N Europe on Baltic Sea; formerly in Germany, now mostly in Poland

Po·mo·na \pə-'mō-nə\ city SW California E of Los Angeles; *pop* 149,058

Pom·peii \päm-'pā, -'pā,ē\ ancient city S Italy SE of Naples destroyed 79 A.D. by eruption of Vesuvius — **Pom·pe·ian** \-'pā-ən\ *adj or n*

Pon·ce \'pȯn(t)-(,)sä\ city S Puerto Rico; *pop* 166,327

Pon·do·land \'pän-(,)dō-,land\ region S Republic of South Africa

Pon·ta Del·ga·da \,pȯn-tə-del-'gä-də\ city & port Portugal, largest in the Azores; *pop* 41,000

Pont·char·train, Lake \'pänt-shər-,trān, ,pänt-shər-'\ lake SE Louisiana E of the Mississippi & N of New Orleans

Pon·tus \'pän-təs\ ancient country NE Asia Minor — **Pon·tic** \'pänt-ik\ *adj or n*

Poole \'pül\ town S England on English Channel; *pop* 155,000

Po·po·ca·te·petl \,pō-pə-'ka-tə-,pe-t⁹l, -,ka-tə-'\ volcano 17,887 ft. (5452 m.) SE *cen* Mexico

Port Arthur — see LÜSHUN

Port—au—Prince \,pȯrt-ō-'prin(t)s, ,pȯr-(t)ō-'praⁿs\ city, ✳ of Haiti; *pop* 875,978

Port Jack·son \'jak-sən\ inlet of South Pacific SE Australia in New South Wales; harbor of Sydney

Port·land \'pȯrt-lənd\ **1** city SW Maine; largest in state; *pop* 66,194 **2** city NW Oregon; *pop* 583,776

Port Lou·is \'lü-əs, 'lü-ē\ city, ✳ of Mauritius; *pop* 146,876

Port Mores·by \'mȯrz-bē\ city, ✳ of Papua New Guinea; *pop* 341,000

Por·tq \'pȯr-(,)tü\ city & port NW Portugal; *pop* 327,368

Por·to Ale·gre \'pȯr-(,)tü-ä-'lä-grē\ city & port S Brazil; *pop* 1,409,351

Port of Spain city NW Trinidad, ✳ of Trinidad and Tobago; *pop* 37,074

Por·to—No·vo \,pȯr-tō-'nō-(,)vō\ city, ✳ of Benin; *pop* 263,600

Port Phil·lip Bay \'fil-əp\ inlet of South Pacific SE Australia in Victoria; harbor of Melbourne

Port Said \sä-'ēd, 'sīd\ city & port NE Egypt on the Mediterranean at N end of the Suez Canal; *pop* 571,000

Ports·mouth \'pȯrts-məth\ **1** city SE Virginia; *pop* 95,535 **2** city S England; *pop* 238,000

Por·tu·gal \'pȯr-chi-gəl, ,pür-tü-'gäl\ country SW Europe; ✳, Lisbon; *pop* 10,562,178

Portuguese India former Portuguese possession on W coast of India; became part of India 1962

Port—Vi·la \,pȯrt-'vē-lə\ or **Vila** city, ✳ of Vanuatu; *pop* 44,040

Po·to·mac \pə-'tō-mək, -mik\ river 287 mi. (462 km.) long flowing from West Virginia into Chesapeake Bay and forming boundary between Maryland & Virginia

Pough·keep·sie \pə-'kip-sē, pō-\ city & river port SE New York on the Hudson; *pop* 32,736

Po·wys \'pō-əs\ administrative subdivision E *cen* Wales; *pop* 132,976

Prague \'präg\ or *Czech* **Pra·ha** \'prä-(,)hä\ city, ✳ of Czech Republic; *pop* 1,169,106

Praia \'prī-ə\ town, ✳ of Cape Verde; *pop* 132,000

Prairie Provinces the Canadian provinces of Alberta, Manitoba, & Saskatchewan

Pres·ton \'pres-tən\ town NW England; *pop* 98,000

Pre·to·ria \pri-'tȯr-ē-ə\ city Republic of South Africa in the municipality of Tshwane, administrative ✳ of the country; *pop* 742,000

Prib·i·lof \'pri-bə-,lȯf\ islands Alaska in Bering Sea

Prince Ed·ward Island \'ed-wərd\ island SE Canada in Gulf of Saint Lawrence; a province; ✳, Charlottetown; *pop* 140,204

Prince Ru·pert's Land \'rü-pərts\ historical region N & W Canada consisting of drainage basin of Hudson Bay

Prince·ton \'prin(t)-stən\ borough W *cen* New Jersey; *pop* 12,307

Prín·ci·pe \'prin(t)-si-pē\ island W Africa in Gulf of Guinea; *pop* 7450 — see SÃO TOMÉ AND PRÍNCIPE

Pro·vence \prə-'vän(t)s, prō-'väⁿs\ region SE France on the Mediterranean

Prov·i·dence \'prä-və-dən(t)s, -,den(t)s\ city, ✳ of Rhode Island; *pop* 178,042

Pro·vo \'prō-(,)vō\ city N *cen* Utah; *pop* 112,488

Prud·hoe Bay \'prü-(,)dō, 'prə-\ inlet of Beaufort Sea N Alaska

Prus·sia \'prə-shə\ former kingdom, & later, state Germany — **Prus·sian** \'prə-shən\ *adj or n*

Pueb·lo \'pwe-,blō\ city SE *cen* Colorado SSE of Colorado Springs; *pop* 106,595

Puer·to Ri·co \,pȯr-tə-'rē-(,)kō, ,pwer-tō-\ island West Indies E of Hispaniola; a self-governing commonwealth associated with U.S.; ✳, San Juan; *pop* 3,725,789 — **Puer·to Ri·can** \'rē-kən\ *adj or n*

Pu·get Sound \'pyü-jət\ arm of the North Pacific W Washington

Pu·ne \'pü-nə\ city W India, ESE of Bombay; *pop* 5,057,709

Pun·jab \,pən-'jäb, -'jab, 'pən-,\ region in Pakistan & NW India in valley of the Indus

Pu·san \'pü-,sän, 'bü-\ or **Bu·san** \'bü-\ city SE South Korea; *pop* 3,403,000

Pyong·yang or **Pyeong·yang** \'pyȯŋ-'yaŋ, 'pyəŋ-, -'yäŋ\ city, ✳ of North Korea; *pop* 2,581,076

Pyr·e·nees \'pir-ə-,nēz\ mountains on French–Spanish border extending from Bay of Biscay to the Mediterranean

Qaraghandy — see KARAGANDA

Qa·tar \'kä-tər, 'gä-, 'gə-; kə-'tär\ country E Arabia on peninsula extending into Persian Gulf; ✳, Doha; *pop* 1,699,000 — **Qa·tari** \kə-'tär-ē, gə-\ *adj or n*

Qing·dao \'chiŋ-'daú\ or **Tsing·tao** \'chiŋ-'daú, '(t)siŋ-'daú\ city & port E China; *pop* 3,719,000

Qi·qi·har \'chē-'chē-'här\ or **Ch'i-ch'i-ha-erh** \'chē-'chē-'hä-'ər\ city NE China; *pop* 1,315,000

Que·bec \kwi-'bek, ki-\ or *French* **Qué·bec** \kā-'bek\ **1** province E Canada; *pop* 7,903,001 **2** city, its ✳, on the Saint Lawrence; *pop* 516,622

Queens \'kwēnz\ borough of New York City on Long Island E of Brooklyn; *pop* 2,230,722

Geographical Names

Queens·land \'kwēnz-ˌland, -lənd\ state NE Australia; ✳, Brisbane; *pop* 4,332,739 — **Queens·land·er** \-ˌlan-dər, -lən-\ *n*

Que·zon City \'kā-ˌsȯn\ city Philippines in Luzon; formerly ✳ of the country; *pop* 2,761,720

Qui·to \'kē-(ˌ)tō\ city, ✳ of Ecuador; *pop* 1,607,734

Ra·bat \rə-'bät\ city, ✳ of Morocco; *pop* 621,480

Rai·nier, Mount \rə-'nir, rā-\ mountain 14,410 ft. (4392 m.) W *cen* Washington; highest in Cascade Range

Raj·pu·ta·na \ˌräj-pə-'tä-nə\ *or* **Ra·ja·sthan** \'räj-ə-ˌstän\ region NW India S of Punjab

Ra·leigh \'rȯ-lē, 'rä-lē\ city, ✳ of North Carolina; *pop* 403,892

Ran·cho Cu·ca·mon·ga \'ran-(ˌ)chō-ˌkü-kə-'mäŋ-gə, ˌrän-, -'mäŋ-\ city SW California; *pop* 165,269

Rand·wick \'ran-(ˌ)dwik\ municipality SE Australia in E New South Wales; *pop* 128,989

Rangoon — see YANGON

Ra·wal·pin·di \ˌrä-wəl-'pin-dē, raúl-', rȯl-'\ city NE Pakistan NNW of Lahore; *pop* 1,409,768

Read·ing \'re-diŋ\ town S England; *pop* 219,000

Re·ci·fe \ri-'sē-fē\ *formerly* **Per·nam·bu·co** \ˌpər-nəm-'bü-(ˌ)kō, -'byü-\ city NE Brazil; *pop* 1,537,704

Red \'red\ **1** river 1018 mi. (1638 km.) long flowing E on Oklahoma–Texas boundary and into the Atchafalaya & the Mississippi in Louisiana **2** sea between Arabia & NE Africa

Red·bridge \'red-(ˌ)brij\ borough of NE Greater London, England; *pop* 279,000

Re·gi·na \ri-'jī-nə\ city, ✳ of Saskatchewan, Canada; *pop* 193,100

Re·no \'rē-(ˌ)nō\ city NW Nevada; *pop* 225,221

Republic of the Congo — see CONGO 3

Ré·union \rē-'yü-nyən, ˌrā-ue-'nyō{n}\ island W Indian Ocean; an overseas division of France; ✳, Saint-Denis; *pop* 834,000

Reyk·ja·vik \'rā-kyə-ˌvik, -ˌvēk\ city, ✳ of Iceland; *pop* 117,976

Rhine \'rīn\ river 820 mi. (1320 km.) long W Europe flowing from SE Switzerland to North Sea in the Netherlands — **Rhen·ish** \'re-nish, 'rē-\ *adj*

Rhine·land \'rīn-ˌland, -lənd\ *or German* **Rhein·land** \'rīn-ˌlänt\ the part of Germany W of the Rhine — **Rhine·land·er** \'rīn-ˌlan-dər, -lən-\ *n*

Rhode Is·land \rōd-'ī-lənd\ **1** *or officially* **Rhode Island and Providence Plantations** state NE U.S.; ✳, Providence; *pop* 1,052,567 **2** — see AQUIDNECK — **Rhode Is·land·er** \-lən-dər\ *n*

Rhodes \'rōdz\ island Greece in the SE Aegean

Rho·de·sia \rō-'dē-zh(ē-)ə\ — see ZIMBABWE — **Rho·de·sian** \-zh(ē-)ən\ *adj or n*

Rhone *or French* **Rhône** \'rōn\ river 505 mi. (813 km.) long Switzerland & SE France

Rich·mond \'rich-mənd\ **1** — see STATEN ISLAND **2** city, ✳ of Virginia; *pop* 204,214

Richmond upon Thames borough of SW Greater London, England; *pop* 187,000

Ri·ga \'rē-gə\ city, ✳ of Latvia; *pop* 658,640

Rio de Ja·nei·ro \'rē-(ˌ)ō-dā-zhə-'ner-(ˌ)ō, -dē-\ city SE Brazil on Guanabara Bay; *pop* 6,320,446

Rio Grande \ˌrē-(ˌ)ō-'grand, -'gran-dē\ *or Mexican* **Rio Bra·vo** \ˌrē-(ˌ)ō-'brä-(ˌ)vō\ river 1885 mi. (3034 km.) long SW U.S., forming part of U.S.–Mexico boundary, and flowing into Gulf of Mexico

Río Muni — see MBINI

Riv·er·side \'ri-vər-ˌsīd\ city S California; *pop* 303,871

Riv·i·era \ˌri-vē-'er-ə\ coast region SE France & NW Italy

Ri·yadh \rē-'yäd\ city, ✳ of Saudi Arabia; *pop* 4,700,000

Ro·a·noke \'rō-(ə-)ˌnōk\ city W Virginia; *pop* 97,032

Roanoke Island island North Carolina S of entrance to Albemarle Sound

Rob·son, Mount \'räb-sən\ mountain 12,972 ft. (3954 m.) W Canada in E British Columbia; highest in the Canadian Rockies

Roch·es·ter \'rä-chəs-tər, -ˌches-tər\ city W New York; *pop* 210,565

Rock·ford \'räk-fərd\ city N Illinois; *pop* 152,871

Rocky Mountains *or* **Rock·ies** \'rä-kēz\ mountains W North America extending SE from N Alaska to *cen* New Mexico

Roman Empire the empire of ancient Rome

Ro·ma·nia \rü-'mā-nē-ə, rō-, -nyə\ *or* **Ru·ma·nia** \rü-\ country SE Europe on Black Sea; ✳, Bucharest; *pop* 20,122,000

Rom·blon \räm-'blön\ island group *cen* Philippines

Rome \'rōm\ *or Italian* **Ro·ma** \'rō-mä\ city, ✳ of Italy; *pop* 2,617,175

Ro·sa·rio \ro-'zär-e-ˌo, -'sär-\ city E *cen* Argentina on the Paraná; *pop* 1,236,000

Ro·seau \rō-'zō\ seaport, ✳ of Dominica; *pop* 14,725

Ros·tov–on–Don \rə-'stȯf-ˌän-'dän, -'stȯv, -ˌȯn-\ city S Russia in Europe; *pop* 1,090,000

Ros·well \'räz-ˌwel, -wəl\ city SE New Mexico; *pop* 48,366

Ro·ta \'rō-tə\ island W Pacific in the Marianas

Rot·ter·dam \'rä-tər-ˌdam, -ˌdäm\ city & port SW Netherlands; *pop* 618,357

Ru·an·da–Urun·di \rü-ˌän-dä-ü-'rün-dē\

former trust territory E *cen* Africa bordering on Lake Tanganyika; now divided into Burundi & Rwanda

Rudolf, Lake — see TURKANA, LAKE

Ruhr \'rur\ **1** river 146 mi. (235 km.) long W Germany flowing NW & W to the Rhine **2** industrial district W Germany E of the Rhine in valley of Ruhr River

Rumania — see ROMANIA

Rupert's Land PRINCE RUPERT'S LAND

Rush·more, Mount \'rəsh-,mór\ mountain 5600 ft. (1707 m.) W South Dakota in Black Hills

Rus·sia \'rə-shə\ **1** former empire largely having the same boundaries as U.S.S.R. **2** UNION OF SOVIET SOCIALIST REPUBLICS **3** country E Europe & N Asia; ✳, Moscow; *pop* 143,300,000

Ru·the·nia \rü-'thē-nyə, -nē-ə\ region W Ukraine W of the N Carpathians — **Ru·the·nian** \-'thē-nyən, -nē-ən\ *adj or n*

Ru·wen·zo·ri \,rü-ən-'zór-ē\ mountain group E *cen* Africa between Uganda & Democratic Republic of the Congo; highest Mount Margherita 16,763 ft. (5109 m.)

Rwan·da *formerly* **Ru·an·da** \rü-'än-dä\ country E *cen* Africa; ✳, Kigali; *pop* 10,516,000 — **Rwan·dan** \-dən\ *adj or n*

Ryu·kyu \rē-'yü-(,)kyü, -(,)kü\ islands Japan extending in an arc from S Japan, to N tip of Taiwan; *pop* 1,222,458 — **Ryu·kyu·an** \-,kyü-ən, -,kü-\ *adj or n*

Saar \'sär, 'zär\ **1** river about 150 mi. (241 km.) long Europe flowing from E France to W Germany **2** *or* **Saar·land** \'sär-,land, 'zär-\ region W Europe in valley of Saar River between France & Germany

Sac·ra·men·to \,sa-krə-'men-(,)tō\ **1** river 382 mi. (615 km.) long N California flowing S into Suisun Bay **2** city, ✳ of California; *pop* 466,488

Sag·ue·nay \'sa-gə-,nā, ,sa-gə-'\ **1** river 105 mi. (169 km.) long Canada in S Quebec flowing E into the Saint Lawrence **2** city Canada in S Quebec; *pop* 144,746

Sa·ha·ra \sə-'her-ə, -'här-\ desert region N Africa extending from Atlantic coast to Red Sea — **Sa·ha·ran** \-ən\ *adj*

Sa·hel \'sa-hil, sə-'hil\ the S fringe of the Sahara

Saigon — see HO CHI MINH CITY

Saint Al·bans \'ól-bənz\ city SE England; *pop* 82,000

Saint Cath·a·rines \'ka-th(ə-)rənz\ city Canada in SE Ontario; *pop* 131,400

Saint Christopher — see SAINT KITTS

Saint Clair, Lake \'kler\ lake SE Michigan & SE Ontario connected by **Saint Clair River** (40 mi. or 64 km. long) with Lake Huron & draining by Detroit River into Lake Erie

Saint Croix \sänt-'krói, sənt-\ **1** river 129 mi. (208 km.) long Canada & U.S. on border between New Brunswick &

Maine **2** island West Indies; largest of Virgin Islands of the U.S.; *pop* 50,601

Saint Eli·as, Mount \i-'lī-əs\ mountain 18,008 ft. (5489 m.) on Alaska–Canada boundary in **Saint Elias Range**

Saint George's \'jór-jəz\ town, ✳ of Grenada; *pop* 4000

Saint George's Channel channel British Isles between SW Wales & Ireland

Saint Gott·hard \sänt-'gä-tərd, sənt-, 'gät-hərd\ pass S *cen* Switzerland in Saint Gotthard Range of the Alps

Saint He·le·na \,sänt-ə-'lē-nə, ,sänt-hə-'lē-nə\ island South Atlantic; a British colony; *pop* 4100

Saint Hel·ens, Mount \sänt-'he-lənz, sənt-\ volcano S Washington

Saint John \sänt-'jän, sənt-\ city & port Canada in New Brunswick; *pop* 70,063

Saint John's \sänt-'jänz, sənt-\ **1** city, ✳ of Antigua and Barbuda; *pop* 23,000 **2** city, ✳ of Newfoundland and Labrador, Canada; *pop* 106,172

Saint Kitts \'kits\ *or* **Saint Chris·to·pher** \'kris-tə-fər\ island West Indies in the Leeward Islands; with Nevis forms independent **Saint Kitts and Nevis**; ✳, Basseterre (on Saint Kitts); *pop* 51,000

Saint Law·rence \sänt-'lór-ən(t)s, sənt-, -'lär-\ **1** river 760 mi. (1223 km.) long E Canada in Ontario & Quebec bordering on U.S. in New York and flowing from Lake Ontario NE into the **Gulf of Saint Lawrence** (inlet of the Atlantic) **2** seaway Canada & U.S. in and along the Saint Lawrence between Lake Ontario & Montreal

Saint Lou·is \sänt-'lü-əs, sənt-\ city E Missouri on the Mississippi; *pop* 319,294

Saint Lu·cia \sänt-'lü-shə, sənt-\ island West Indies in the Windwards S of Martinique; country; ✳, Castries; *pop* 166,500

Saint Mo·ritz \sänt-mə-'rits, sənt-\ *or* **G Sankt Mo·ritz** \,zäŋkt-mə-'rits\ town E Switzerland; *pop* 5900

Saint Paul \'pòl\ city, ✳ of Minnesota; *pop* 285,068

Saint Pe·ters·burg \'pē-tərz-,bərg\ **1** city W Florida; *pop* 244,769 **2** *or* 1914–24 **Pet·ro·grad** \'pe-trə-,grad, -,grät\ *or* 1924–91 **Le·nin·grad** \'le-nən-,grad, -,grät\ city W Russia in Europe; *pop* 4,864,500

Saint Thom·as \'tä-məs\ island West Indies, one of Virgin Islands of the U.S.; chief town, Charlotte Amalie

Saint Vin·cent \sänt-'vin(t)-sənt, sənt-\ island West Indies in the *cen* Windward Islands; with N Grenadines forms independent **Saint Vincent and the Grenadines**; ✳, Kingstown (on Saint Vincent); *pop* 110,000

Sai·pan \sī-'pan, -'pän, 'sī-,\ island W Pacific in S *cen* Marianas; *pop* 48,220

Sa·kai \(,)sä-'kī\ city Japan in S Honshu; *pop* 841,966

Sa·kha·lin \\'sa-kə-ˌlēn, -lən; ˌsä-kä-'lēn\ island SE Russia in W Pacific N of Hokkaido, Japan

Sal·a·mis \\'sa-lə-məs\ ancient city Cyprus on E coast

Sa·lem \\'sā-ləm\ city, ✷ of Oregon; *pop* 154,637

Sa·li·nas \sə-'lē-nəs\ city W California; *pop* 150,441

Salisbury — see HARARE

Salisbury Plain plateau S England; site of Stonehenge

Salop — see SHROPSHIRE

Salt Lake City city, ✷ of Utah; *pop* 186,440

Sal·ton Sea \\'sȯl-tᵊn\ saline lake about 235 ft. (72 m.) below sea level SE California; formed by diversion of water from Colorado River

Sal·va·dor \\'sal-və-ˌdȯr, ˌsal-və-'\ *or* Ba·hia \bä-'ē-ə\ city NE Brazil on the Atlantic; *pop* 2,675,656 — **Sal·va·dor·an** \ˌsal-və-'dȯr-ən\ *or* **Sal·va·dor·ean** *or* **Sal·va·dor·ian** \-ē-ən\ *adj or n*

Sal·ween \\'sal-ˌwēn\ river about 1500 mi. (2415 km.) long SE Asia flowing from Tibet S into Bay of Bengal in Myanmar

Sa·mar \\'sä-ˌmär\ island *cen* Philippines

Sa·ma·ra \sə-'mär-ə\ *or 1935–91* **Kuy·by·shev** \\'kwē-bə-ˌshef, 'kü-ē-bə-, -ˌshev\ city W Russia, on the Volga; *pop* 1,165,000

Sa·mar·ia \sə-'mer-ē-ə\ district of ancient Palestine W of the Jordan between Galilee & Judaea

Sam·ar·qand *or* **Sam·ar·kand** \\'sa-mərˌkand\ city E Uzbekistan; *pop* 370,500

Sam·ni·um \\'sam-nē-əm\ ancient country S *cen* Italy — **Sam·nite** \\'sam-ˌnīt\ *adj or n*

Sa·moa \sə-'mō-ə\ **1** islands SW *cen* Pacific N of Tonga; divided at longitude 171° W into American Samoa (or Eastern Samoa) & independent Samoa **2** *formerly* **Western Samoa** islands Samoa W of 171° W; country; ✷ Apia; *pop* 187,800 — **Sa·mo·an** \sə-'mō-ən\ *adj or n*

Sa·mos \\'sā-ˌmäs, 'sä-ˌmós\ island Greece in the Aegean off coast of Turkey

San·aa *or* **Sana** \sa-'nä, 'sa-ˌnä\ city SW Arabia, ✷ of Yemen; *pop* 1,700,000

San An·dre·as Fault \ˌsan-an-'drā-əs\ zone of faults in California extending from N coast toward head of Gulf of California

San An·to·nio \ˌsan-ən-'tō-nē-ˌō\ city S Texas; *pop* 1,327,407

San Ber·nar·di·no \ˌsan-ˌbər-nə(r)-'dē-(ˌ)nō\ city S California; *pop* 209,924

San Di·ego \ˌsan-dē-'ā-(ˌ)gō\ coastal city SW California; *pop* 1,307,402

San·i·bel Island \\'sa-nə-bəl, -ˌbel\ island SW Florida

Sand·wich \\'san(d)-(ˌ)wich\ town SE England; *pop* 4227

Sandwich Islands — see HAWAII

San Fran·cis·co \ˌsan-frən-'sis-(ˌ)kō\ city W California on San Francisco Bay & Pacific Ocean; *pop* 805,235

San Joa·quin \ˌsan-wä-'kēn, -wȯ-\ river 350 mi. (563 km.) long *cen* California flowing NW into the Sacramento

San Jo·se \ˌsan-(h)ō-'zā\ city W California SE of San Francisco; *pop* 945,942

San Jo·sé \ˌsän-hō-'sā, ˌsan-(h)ō-'zā\ city, ✷ of Costa Rica; *pop* 330,529

San Juan \san-'wän, ˌsän-'hwän\ city, ✷ of Puerto Rico; *pop* 395,326

San Ma·ri·no \ˌsan-mə-'rē-(ˌ)nō\ **1** small country S Europe surrounded by Italy ENE of Florence near Adriatic Sea; *pop* 32,500 **2** town, its ✷; *pop* 4100 — **Sam·mar·i·nese** \ˌsa(m)-ˌma-rə-'nēz, -'nēs\ *n* — **San Mar·i·nese** \ˌsan-ˌma-\ *adj or n*

San Pe·dro Su·la \ˌsän-ˌpā-(ˌ)thrō-'sü-lä\ city NW Honduras; *pop* 300,400

San Sal·va·dor \san-'sal-və-ˌdȯr, ˌsän-'säl-vä-ˌthȯr\ **1** island *cen* Bahamas **2** city, ✷ of El Salvador; *pop* 316,090

San·ta Ana \ˌsan-tə-'a-nə, ˌsän-tä-'ä-nä\ city SW California ESE of Long Beach; *pop* 324,528

San·ta Bar·ba·ra \'bär-b(ə-)rə\ *or* **Channel** islands California off SW coast in the North Pacific

Santa Clara \'kler-ə\ city W California NW of San Jose; *pop* 116,468

Santa Cla·ri·ta \klə-'rē-tə\ city S California N of Los Angeles; *pop* 176,320

San·ta Fe \ˌsan-tə-'fā\ city, ✷ of New Mexico; *pop* 67,947

Santa Fe Trail pioneer route to the SW U.S. about 1200 mi. (1930 km.) long used esp. 1821–80 from vicinity of Kansas City, Missouri, to Santa Fe, New Mexico

San·ta Ro·sa \ˌsan-tə-'rō-zə\ city W California N of San Francisco; *pop* 167,815

San·ti·a·go \ˌsan-tē-'ä-(ˌ)gō, ˌsän-\ city, ✷ of Chile; metropolitan area *pop* 4,668,500

San·to Do·min·go \ˌsan-tə-dō-'min̄-(ˌ)gō\ *formerly* **Tru·ji·llo** \trü-'hē-(ˌ)yō\ city, ✷ of Dominican Republic; *pop* 1,971,000

São Pau·lo \saů̇-'paů̇-(ˌ)lü, -(ˌ)lō\ city SE Brazil; *pop* 11,253,503

São To·mé \saů̇-tə-'mā\ town, ✷ of São Tomé and Príncipe; *pop* 43,420

São Tomé and Príncipe country W Africa; ✷ São Tomé; *pop* 192,000

Sap·po·ro \\'sä-pō-ˌrō; sä-'pȯr-(ˌ)ō\ city Japan on W Hokkaido; *pop* 1,913,545

Sa·ra·je·vo \ˌsa-rə-'yä-(ˌ)vō, ˌsär-ə-\ city SE *cen* Bosnia and Herzegovina, its ✷; *pop* 330,500

Sa·ra·tov \sə-'rä-təf\ city W Russia, on the Volga; *pop* 838,000

Sar·din·ia \sär-'di-nē-ə, -'di-nyə\ island Italy in the Mediterranean S of Corsica; *pop* 1,639,362 — **Sar·din·ian** \sär-'di-nē-ən, -'din-yən\ *adj or n*

Sar·gas·so Sea \sär-'ga-(ˌ)sō\ area of nearly still water in the North Atlantic lying chiefly between 20° & 35° N latitude & 30° & 70° W longitude

Sas·katch·e·wan \sə-'ska-chə-wən, sa-, -ˌwän\ province W Canada; ✳, Regina; *pop* 1,033,381

Sas·ka·toon \ˌsas-kə-'tün\ city *cen* Saskatchewan, Canada; *pop* 222,189

Sau·di Ara·bia \'saů-dē, 'sȯ-dē, sä-'ü-dē\ country SW Asia occupying largest part of Arabian Peninsula; ✳, Riyadh; *pop* 27,000,000 — **Saudi** *adj or n* — **Saudi Arabian** *adj or n*

Sault Sainte Ma·rie Canals \'sü-(ˌ)sānt-mə-'rē\ *or* **Soo Canals** \ˌsü\ three ship canals, two in U.S. (Michigan) & one in Canada (Ontario), at rapids in river connecting Lake Superior & Lake Huron

Sa·vaii \sə-'vī-ˌē\ island, largest in independent Samoa

Sa·van·nah \sə-'va-nə\ city & port E Georgia; *pop* 136,286

Sa·voy \sə-'vȯi\ *or French* **Sa·voie** \sä-'vwä\ region SE France SW of Switzerland bordering on Italy — **Sa·voy·ard** \sə-'vȯi-ˌärd, ˌsa-ˌvȯi-'ärd, ˌsa-ˌvwä-'yär(d)\ *adj or n*

Sca·fell Pike \ˌskȯ-'fel\ mountain 3210 ft. (978 m.) NW England; highest in Cumbrian Mountains & in England

Scan·di·na·via \ˌskan-də-'nā-vē-ə, -vyə\ **1** peninsula N Europe occupied by Norway & Sweden **2** Denmark, Norway, Sweden, & as used by some also Iceland & Finland — **Scan·di·na·vian** \ˌskandə-'nā-vē-ən, -vyən\ *adj or n*

Scar·bor·ough \'skär-ˌbər-ō\ former city Canada in SE Ontario; now part of Toronto

Schel·de \'skel-də\ *or* **Scheldt** \'skelt\ river 270 mi. (434 km.) long W Europe flowing from N France through Belgium into North Sea in Netherlands

Schuyl·kill \'skü-k²l, 'skül-ˌkil\ river 131 mi. (211 km.) long SE Pennsylvania flowing SE into the Delaware River at Philadelphia

Scil·ly, Isles of \'si-lē\ island group SW England off Land's End; *pop* 2900

Sco·tia \'skō-shə\ SCOTLAND — the Medieval Latin name

Scot·land \'skät-lənd\ *or Latin* **Cal·e·do·nia** \ˌka-lə-'dō-nyə, -nē-ə\ country N Great Britain; a division of United Kingdom; ✳, Edinburgh; *pop* 5,295,000

Scotts·dale \'skäts-ˌdāl\ city SW *cen* Arizona E of Phoenix; *pop* 217,385

Scyth·ia \'si-thē-ə, -thē-\ *ancient* area of Europe & Asia N & NE of Black Sea & E of Aral Sea — **Scyth·i·an** \'si-thē-ən, -thē-\ *adj or n*

Se·at·tle \sē-'a-t²l\ city & port W Washington; *pop* 608,660

Seine \'sān, 'sen\ river 480 mi. (772 km.) long N France flowing NW into English Channel

Sel·kirk \'sel-ˌkərk\ range of the Rocky Mountains SE British Columbia, Canada; highest peak, 11,555 ft. (3522 m.)

Se·ma·rang \sə-'mär-ˌäŋ\ city Indonesia in *cen* Java; *pop* 1,556,000

Sen·dai \(ˌ)sen-'dī\ city Japan in NE Honshu; *pop* 1,045,986

Sen·e·ca Falls \'se-ni-kə\ village W *cen* New York; *pop* 6681

Sen·e·gal \ˌse-ni-'gȯl, -'gäl, 'se-ni-ˌ\ **1** river 1015 mi. (1633 km.) long W Africa flowing W into the North Atlantic **2** country W Africa; ✳, Dakar; *pop* 13,509,000 — **Sen·e·ga·lese** \ˌse-ni-gə-'lēz, -'lēs\ *adj or n*

Seoul \'sōl\ city, ✳ of South Korea; *pop* 9,750,000

Ser·bia \'sər-bē-ə\ country S Europe in the Balkans; ✳ Belgrade; *pop* 7,150,000

Serbia and Montenegro *or 1992–2003* **Yugoslavia** former country S Europe on Balkan Peninsula

Ser·en·ge·ti Plain \ˌser-ən-'ge-tē\ area N Tanzania

Seven Hills the seven hills upon and about which was built the city of Rome, Italy

Sev·ern \'se-vərn\ river 210 mi. (338 km.) long Wales & England flowing from E *cen* Wales into Bristol Channel

Se·ville \sə-'vil\ *or Spanish* **Se·vi·lla** \sā-'vē-(ˌ)yä\ city SW Spain; *pop* 700,169

Sew·ard Peninsula \'sü-ərd\ peninsula 180 mi. (290 km.) long W Alaska projecting into Bering Sea

Sey·chelles \sā-'shel(z)\ islands W Indian Ocean NE of Madagascar; country; ✳, Victoria; *pop* 90,900 — **Sey·chel·lois** \ˌsā-shəl-'wä, -ˌshel-\ *n*

Shang·hai \ˌshaŋ-'hī\ city & port E China; *pop* 12,693,000

Shan·non \'sha-nən\ river 230 mi. (370 km.) long W Ireland flowing S & W into the North Atlantic

Shar·on, Plain of \'sher-ən\ region Israel on the coast

Shas·ta, Mount \'shas-tə\ mountain 14,162 ft. (4316 m.) N California in Cascade Range

Shatt al Ar·ab \ˌshat-al-'a-rəb\ river 120 mi. (193 km.) long SE Iraq formed by flowing together of Euphrates & Tigris rivers and flowing SE into Persian Gulf

Shef·field \'she-ˌfēld\ city N England; *pop* 518,000

Shen·an·do·ah \ˌshe-nən-'dō-ə, ˌsha-nə-'dō-ə\ valley Virginia between the Allegheny & Blue Ridge mountains

Shen·yang \'shən-'yäŋ\ *or traditionally* **Muk·den** \'mük-dən, 'mək-; ˌmük-'den\ city NE China; chief city of Manchuria; *pop* 5,987,000

Sher·brooke \'shər-ˌbrůk\ city Quebec, Canada E of Montreal; *pop* 154,601

Sher·wood Forest \'shər-ˌwůd\ ancient royal forest *cen* England

Shet·land \'shet-lənd\ islands N Scotland NE of the Orkneys; *pop* 21,960

Shi·jia·zhuang *or* **Shih–chia–chuang** \'shir-'jyä-'jwäŋ, 'shē-\ city NE China; *pop* 2,802,500

Shi·ko·ku \shē-'kō-(ˌ)kü\ island S Japan E of Kyushu; *pop* 4,154,039

Shi·raz \shi-'räz, -'raz\ city SW *cen* Iran; *pop* 1,460,665

Shreve·port \'shrēv-ˌpȯrt\ city NW Louisiana on Red River; *pop* 199,311

Shrews·bury \'sh(r)üz-ˌber-ē, -b(ə-)rē\ town W England; *pop* 31,640

Shrop·shire \'shräp-shər, -ˌshir\ *or 1974–80* **Sal·op** \'sal-əp\ county W England bordering on Wales; *pop* 306,000

Shu·ma·gin \'shü-mə-gən\ islands SW Alaska S of Alaska Peninsula

Siam — see THAILAND

Siam, Gulf of — see THAILAND, GULF OF

Si·be·ria \sī-'bir-ē-ə\ region N Asia in Russia between the Urals & the North Pacific — **Si·be·ri·an** \-ən\ *adj or n*

Sic·i·ly \'si-s(ə-)lē\ *or Italian* **Si·ci·lia** \sē-'chēl-yä\ island S Italy SW of toe of peninsula of Italy; ✻, Palermo; *pop* 5,002,904 — **Si·cil·ian** \sə-'sil-yən\ *adj or n*

Si·er·ra Le·one \sē-ˌer-ə-lē-'ōn, ˌsir-ə-, -lē-'ōnē\ country W Africa on the North Atlantic; ✻, Freetown; *pop* 4,491,000 — **Si·er·ra Le·on·ean** \-'ō-nē-ən\ *adj or n*

Si·er·ra Ma·dre \sē-ˌer-ə-'mä-drä, 'syer-ä-'mä-thrä\ mountain system Mexico including **Sierra Madre Oc·ci·den·tal** \ˌäk-sə-ˌden-'täl, ˌȯk-sē-ˌthen-'täl\ range W of the *cen* plateau, **Sierra Madre Ori·en·tal** \ˌȯr-ē-ˌen-'täl\ range E of the plateau, & **Sierra Madre del Sur** \'sür, 'sùr\ range to the S

Sierra Ne·va·da \nə-'va-də, -'vä-\ **1** mountain range E California & W Nevada — see WHITNEY, MOUNT **2** mountain range S Spain

Sik·kim \'si-kəm, -ˌkim\ former country SE Asia on S slope of the Himalayas between Nepal & Bhutan; state of India since 1975; *pop* 610,577

Si·le·sia \sī-'lē-zh(ē-)ə, sə-, -sh(ē-)ə\ region E *cen* Europe in valley of the upper Oder; formerly chiefly in Germany now chiefly in E Czech Republic & SW Poland — **Si·le·sian** \-zh(ē-)ən, -sh(ē-)ən\ *adj or n*

Silk Road *or* **Silk Route** ancient trade route that extended from China to the Mediterranean

Sim·coe, Lake \'sim-(ˌ)kō\ lake Canada in SE Ontario

Si·mi Valley \sē-'mē\ city SW California W of Los Angeles; *pop* 124,237

Sim·plon Pass \'sim-ˌplän\ mountain pass 6590 ft. (2009 m.) between Switzerland & Italy

Si·nai \'sī-ˌnī\ **1** mountain on Sinai Peninsula where according to the Bible the Law was given to Moses **2** peninsula extension of continent of Asia NE Egypt between Red Sea & the Mediterranean

Sin·ga·pore \'siŋ-ə-ˌpȯr\ **1** island off S end of Malay Peninsula; country; *pop* 5,077,000 **2** city, its ✻; *pop* 206,500 — **Sin·ga·por·ean** \ˌsiŋ-ə-'pȯr-ē-ən\ *adj or n*

Sinkiang Uighur — see XINJIANG UYGUR

Sioux Falls \'sü\ city SE South Dakota; largest in state; *pop* 153,888

Skag·ge·rak \'ska-gə-ˌrak\ arm of North Sea between S Norway & N Denmark

Skop·je \'skȯ-pye, -pyə\ city, ✻ of independent Macedonia; *pop* 487,000

Sla·vo·nia \slə-'vō-nē-ə, -nyə\ region E Croatia; *pop* 78,000 — **Sla·vo·ni·an** \-nē-ən, -nyən\ *adj or n*

Slo·va·kia \slō-'vä-kē-ə, -'va-\ country *cen* Europe; ✻, Bratislava; *pop* 5,397,036

Slo·ve·nia \slō-'vē-nē-ə, -nyə\ country S Europe; ✻, Ljubljana; *pop* 2,050,000

Smyrna — see IZMIR

Snake \'snāk\ river NW U.S. flowing from NW Wyoming into the Columbia in SE Washington

Snow·don \'snō-dᵊn\ massif 3560 ft. (1085 m.) in **Snow·do·nia** \snō-'dō-nē-ə, -nyə\ (mountainous district) NW Wales; highest point in Wales

So·ci·ety \sə-'sī-ə-tē\ islands South Pacific; belonging to France; chief island, Tahiti; *pop* 162,573

So·fia \'sō-fē-ə, 'sȯ-, sō-'\ city, ✻ of Bulgaria; *pop* 1,291,600

So·ho \'sō-ˌhō\ district of *cen* London, England

So·li·hull \ˌsō-li-'həl\ city *cen* England; *pop* 123,000

Sol·o·mon \'sä-lə-mən\ **1** islands W Pacific E of New Guinea divided between Papua New Guinea & independent Solomon Islands **2** sea, arm of Coral Sea W of the Solomons

Solomon Islands country, SW Pacific E of New Guinea; ✻, Honiara (on Guadalcanal); *pop* 516,000

So·ma·lia \sō-'mä-lē-ə, sə-, -'mäl-yə\ country E Africa on Gulf of Aden & Indian Ocean; ✻, Mogadishu; *pop* 10,250,000 — **So·ma·li·an** \-'mä-lē-ən, -'mäl-yən\ *adj or n*

So·ma·li·land \sō-'mä-lē-ˌland, sə-\ historical region E Africa consisting of Somalia, Djibouti, & part of E Ethiopia — **So·ma·li** \sō-'mä-lē, sə-\ *n*

Som·er·set \'sə-mər-ˌset, -sət\ *or* **Som·er·set·shire** \-ˌshir, -shər\ county SW England

So·nor·an \sə-'nȯr-ən\ *or* **So·no·ra** \sə-'nȯr-ə\ desert SW U.S. & NW Mexico

Soo Canals — see SAULT SAINTE MARIE CANALS

South island S New Zealand; *pop* 906,756

South Africa, Republic of *formerly* **Union of South Africa** country S Africa; administrative ✻, Pretoria; legislative

∗, Cape Town; judicial ∗, Bloemfontein; *pop* 51,771,000 — **South African** *adj or n*

South America continent of Western Hemisphere SE of North America and chiefly S of the Equator — **South American** *adj or n*

South·amp·ton \saù-'tham(p)-tən, saùth-'ham(p)-\ city S England; *pop* 254,000

South Australia state S Australia; ∗, Adelaide; *pop* 1,596,572 — **South Australian** *adj or n*

South Bend \'bend\ city N Indiana; *pop* 101,168

South Cape *or* **South Point** — see KA LAE

South Car·o·li·na \,ker(-ə)-'lī-nə, ,ka-rə-\ state SE U.S.; ∗, Columbia; *pop* 4,625,364 — **South Car·o·lin·i·an** \-'li-nē-ən, -'li-nyən\ *adj or n*

South China Sea — see CHINA

South Da·ko·ta \də-'kō-tə\ state NW *cen* U.S.; ∗, Pierre; *pop* 814,180 — **South Da·ko·tan** \-'kō-t°n\ *adj or n*

South·end–on–Sea \,saù-,thend-,òn-'sē, -,än-\ seaside resort SE England E of London; *pop* 176,000

Southern Alps mountain range New Zealand in W South Island extending almost the length of the island

Southern Hemisphere the half of the earth that lies S of the Equator

South Georgia island S Atlantic E of Tierra del Fuego; administered by United Kingdom

South Korea *or* **Republic of Korea** country S half of Korean Peninsula in E Asia; ∗, Seoul; *pop* 48,400,000

South Seas the areas of the Atlantic, Indian, & Pacific oceans in the Southern Hemisphere

South Shields \'shēldz\ seaport N England; *pop* 75,000

South Sudan country E Africa formed 2011 from the S part of Sudan; ∗, Juba; *pop* 8,260,500

South Vietnam — see VIETNAM

South·wark \'sə-thərk, 'saùth-wərk\ borough of S Greater London, England; *pop* 288,000

South–West Africa — see NAMIBIA

South Yorkshire metropolitan county N England; *pop* 1,343,600

Soviet Central Asia portion of *cen* & SW Asia formerly belonging to U.S.S.R. and including the former soviet socialist republics of present-day Kyrgyzstan, Tajikistan, Turkmenistan, Uzbekistan & by some thought also to include Kazakhstan

Soviet Union — see UNION OF SOVIET SOCIALIST REPUBLICS

So·we·to \sō-'wā-tō, -'we-, -tü\ residential area NE Republic of South Africa adjoining SW Johannesburg

Spain \'spān\ country SW Europe on Iberian Peninsula; ∗, Madrid; *pop* 46,816,000

Spanish America **1** the Spanish-speaking countries of America **2** the parts of America settled and formerly governed by the Spanish

Spanish Guinea — see EQUATORIAL GUINEA

Spanish Sahara — see WESTERN SAHARA

Spar·ta \'spär-tə\ ancient city S Greece in Peloponnese; ∗ of Laconia

Spo·kane \spō-'kan\ city E Washington; *pop* 208,916

Spring·field \'sprin-,fēld\ **1** city, ∗ of Illinois; *pop* 116,250 **2** city SW Massachusetts; *pop* 153,060 **3** city SW Missouri; *pop* 159,498

Sri Lan·ka \(,)srē-'län-kə, (,)shrē-, -'lan-\ *formerly* **Cey·lon** \si-'län, sā-\ country having the same boundaries as island of Ceylon; ∗, Colombo; *pop* 20,300,000 — **Sri Lan·kan** \-'län-kən, -'lan-\ *adj or n*

Sri·na·gar \srē-'nə-gər\ city N India; *pop* 1,222,500

Staf·ford \'sta-fərd\ town W *cen* England; *pop* 68,000

Staf·ford·shire \'sta-fərd-,shir, -shər\ *or* **Stafford** county W *cen* England

Staked Plain — see LLANO ESTACADO

Stam·ford \'stam-fərd\ city SW Connecticut; *pop* 122,643

Stan·ley \'stan-lē\ town, ∗ of Falkland Islands; *pop* 1559

Stat·en Island \'sta-t°n\ **1** island SE New York SW of mouth of the Hudson **2** *formerly* **Rich·mond** \'rich-mənd\ borough of New York City including Staten Island; *pop* 468,730

Ster·ling Heights \'stər-lin\ city SE Michigan; *pop* 129,699

Stir·ling \'stər-lin\ town *cen* Scotland; *pop* 36,000

Stock·holm \'stäk-,hō(l)m\ city, ∗ of Sweden; *pop* 758,148

Stock·port \'stäk-,pórt\ town NW England; *pop* 106,000

Stock·ton \'stäk-tən\ city *cen* California; *pop* 291,707

Stoke–on–Trent \'stōk-,än-'trent, -,òn-\ city *cen* England; *pop* 271,000

Stone·henge \'stōn-,henj, (,)stōn-'\ prehistoric assemblage of megaliths S England in Wiltshire on Salisbury Plain

Stone Mountain mountain 1686 ft. (514 m.) NW Georgia E of Atlanta

Stor·no·way \'stór-nə-,wā\ seaport NW Scotland; chief town of Lewis with Harris Island; *pop* 8660

Stra·bane \strə-'ban\ district W Northern Ireland; *pop* 39,843

Strath·clyde \strath-'klīd\ former region SW Scotland; included Glasgow

Strom·bo·li \'sträm-bō-(,)lē\ volcano 2500 ft. (758 m.) Italy on **Stromboli Island** in Tyrrhenian Sea

Stutt·gart \'shtút-,gärt, 'stút-, 'stət-\ city SW Germany; *pop* 585,890

Styx \'stiks\ chief river of the underworld in Greek mythology

Süchow — see XUZHOU

Su·cre \'sü-(,)krā\ city, constitutional ✳ of Bolivia; *pop* 244,000

Su·dan \sü-'dan, -'dän\ 1 region N Africa S of the Sahara between the Atlantic & the upper Nile 2 country NE Africa S of Egypt; ✳, Khartoum; *pop* 30,900,000 — **Su·da·nese** \,sü-də-'nēz, -'nēs\ *adj or n*

Sud·bury, Greater \'səd,ber-ē, -b(ə)rē\ city SE Ontario, Canada; *pop* 160,274

Su·ez, Gulf of \sü-'ez, 'sü-,ez\ arm of Red Sea

Suez, Isthmus of isthmus NE Egypt between Mediterranean & Red seas connecting Africa & Asia

Suez Canal canal 100 mi. (161 km.) long NE Egypt across the Isthmus of Suez

Suf·folk \'sə-fək\ county E England on North Sea; *pop* 728,163

Sui·sun Bay \sə-'sün\ inlet of San Francisco Bay, W *cen* California

Su·la·we·si \,sü-lä-'wä-sē\ island Indonesia E of Borneo; *pop* 12,520,711

Su·lu \'sü-(,)lü\ 1 archipelago SW Philippines SW of Mindanao 2 sea W Philippines

Su·ma·tra \sù-'mä-trə\ island W Indonesia S of Malay Peninsula — **Su·ma·tran** \-trən\ *adj or n*

Su·mer \'sü-mər\ the S division of ancient Babylonia — **Su·me·ri·an** \sü-'mer-ē-ən, -'mir-\ *adj or n*

Sun·belt \'sən-,belt\ region S & SW U.S.

Sun·da \'sün-də, 'sən-\ strait between Java & Sumatra

Sun·der·land \'sən-dər-lənd\ seaport N England; *pop* 174,000

Sun·ny·vale \'sə-nē-,vāl\ city W California; *pop* 140,081

Sun Valley resort center *cen* Idaho

Su·pe·ri·or, Lake \sù-'pir-ē-ər\ lake E North America in U.S. & Canada; largest of the Great Lakes

Su·ra·ba·ya \,sùr-ə-'bī-ə\ city Indonesia in NE Java; *pop* 2,765,000

Su·ri·na·me \,sùr-ə-'nä-mə\ country N South America between Guyana & French Guiana; ✳, Paramaribo; *pop* 542,000 — **Su·ri·nam·er** \'sùr-ə-,nä-mər, ,sùr-ə-'nä-\ *n* — **Su·ri·nam·ese** \,sùr-ə-nə-'mēz, -'mēs\ *adj or n*

Sur·rey \'sər-ē, 'sə-rē\ city Canada in SW British Columbia; *pop* 468,251

Sut·ton \'sə-t³n\ borough of S Greater London, England; *pop* 190,000

Su·va \'sü-və\ city & port, ✳ of Fiji on Viti Levu Island; *pop* 86,178

Su·wan·nee \sə-'wä-nē, 'swä-\ river 250 mi. (400 km.) long SE U.S. flowing SW into Gulf of Mexico

Sverdlovsk — see YEKATERINBURG

Swan·sea \'swän-zē\ city & port SE Wales; *pop* 179,000

Swa·zi·land \'swä-zē-,land\ country SE Africa between Republic of South Africa & Mozambique; ✳, Mbabane; *pop* 1,018,000 — **Swa·zi** \'swä-zē\ *adj or n*

Swe·den \'swē-d³n\ country N Europe on Scandinavia (peninsula) bordering on Baltic Sea; ✳, Stockholm; *pop* 8,016,000

Swit·zer·land \'swit-sər-lənd\ country W Europe in the Alps; ✳, Bern; *pop* 7,800,000

Syd·ney \'sid-nē\ city SE Australia, ✳ of New South Wales; *pop* 3,908,642

Syr·a·cuse \'sir-ə-,kyüs, -,kyüz\ city *cen* New York; *pop* 145,170

Syr·ia \'sir-ē-ə\ 1 ancient region SW Asia bordering on the Mediterranean 2 country S of Turkey; ✳, Damascus; *pop* 17,952,000 — **Syr·i·an** \'sir-ē-ən\ *adj or n*

Syrian Desert desert region between Mediterranean coast & the Euphrates in N Saudi Arabia, SE Syria, W Iraq, & NE Jordan

Table Bay harbor of Cape Town, Republic of South Africa

Ta·briz \tə-'brēz\ city NW Iran; *pop* 1,494,998

Ta·co·ma \tə-'kō-mə\ city & port W Washington S of Seattle; *pop* 198,397

Tae·gu \'tā-gü, 'dä-\ *or* **Dae·gu** \'dä-\ city SE South Korea; *pop* 2,444,000

Tae·jon \'tā-jən, 'dä-\ *or* **Dae·jeon** \'dä-\ city *cen* South Korea NW of Taegu; *pop* 1,495,000

Ta·gus \'tā-gəs\ *or Spanish* **Ta·jo** \'tä-(,)hō\ *or Portuguese* **Te·jo** \'tä-(,)zhü\ river 626 mi. (1007 km.) long Spain & Portugal flowing W into the North Atlantic

Ta·hi·ti \tə-'hē-tē\ island South Pacific in Society Islands; *pop* 131,309

Tai·bei \'tī-'bā\ *or* **Tai·pei** \'tī-'pā, -'bā\ city, ✳ of (Nationalist) China in N Taiwan; *pop* 2,700,000

T'ai·nan \'tī-'nän\ city SW Taiwan; *pop* 1,883,000

Tai·wan \'tī-'wän\ *formerly* **For·mo·sa** \fòr-'mō-sə, fər-, -zə\ 1 island China off SE coast of mainland; seat of government of (Nationalist) Republic of China; ✳, Taibei; *pop* 23,340,000 2 strait between Taiwan & mainland of China connecting East China & South China seas — **Tai·wan·ese** \,tī-wə-'nēz, -'nēs\ *adj or n*

Tai·yuan \'tī-'ywen, -'ywän\ city N China; *pop* 3,290,500

Tai·zhong \'tī-'jùŋ\ *or* **Tai·chung** \'tī-'chùŋ\ city W Taiwan; *pop* 1,004,400

Ta·jik·i·stan \tä-,ji-ki-'stan, tə-, -,jē-, -'stän\ country W *cen* Asia bordering on China & Afghanistan; ✳, Dushanbe; *pop* 7,564,500

Ta·kli·ma·kan *or* **Ta·kla Ma·kan** \,tä-klə-mə-'kän\ desert W China

Ta·lien — see DALIAN

Tal·la·has·see \,ta-lə-'ha-sē\ city, ✳ of Florida; *pop* 181,376

Tal·linn \'ta-lən, 'tä-\ city, * of Estonia; *pop* 405,000

Tam·pa \'tam-pə\ city W Florida on **Tampa Bay** (inlet of Gulf of Mexico); *pop* 335,709

Tan·gan·yi·ka \ˌtan-gə-'nyē-kə, ˌtaŋ-gə-, -'nē-\ former country E Africa S of Kenya; now part of Tanzania

Tanganyika, Lake lake E Africa between Tanzania & Democratic Republic of the Congo

Tang·shan \'däŋ-'shän, 'täŋ-\ city NE China; *pop* 2,750,000

Tan·za·nia \ˌtan-zə-'nē-ə, ˌtän-\ country E Africa on Indian Ocean, including Zanzibar; legislative *, Dodoma; historic *, Dar es Salaam; *pop* 44,929,000 — **Tan·za·ni·an** \-'nē-ən\ *adj or n*

Ta·ra·wa \tə-'rä-wə, 'ta-rə-ˌwä\ island *cen* Pacific, contains * of Kiribati; *pop* 41,194

Tar·ry·town \'ta-rē-ˌtaún\ village SE New York; *pop* 11,277

Tar·sus \'tär-səs\ ancient city of S Asia Minor; now a city in S Turkey

Tash·kent \tash-'kent, täsh-\ city, * of Uzbekistan; *pop* 2,200,000

Tas·ma·nia \taz-'mā-nē-ə, -nyə\ *or earlier* **Van Die·men's Land** \van-'dē-mənz\ island SE Australia S of Victoria; a state; *, Hobart; *pop* 495,354 — **Tas·ma·nian** \taz-'mā-nē-ən, -nyən\ *adj or n*

Tas·man Sea \'taz-mən\ the part of the South Pacific between SE Australia & New Zealand

Ta·try \'tä-trē\ *or* **Ta·tra** \'tä-trə\ mountains N Slovakia & S Poland in *cen* Carpathian Mountains

Taun·ton \'tón-tᵊn, 'tän-\ town SW England; *pop* 60,000

Tbi·li·si \tə-ˌbē-lə-sē, tə-bə-'lē-sē\ *or* **Tiflis** \'ti-fləs, tə-'flēs\ city, * of Republic of Georgia; *pop* 1,106,500

Te·gu·ci·gal·pa \tə-ˌgü-sə-'gal-pə, tä-ˌgü-sē-'gäl-pä\ city, * of Honduras; *pop* 879,000

Teh·ran \ˌtā-(ə-)'ran, te-'ran, -'rän\ city, * of Iran; at foot of S slope of Elburz Mountains; *pop* 8,154,051

Tel Aviv \ˌtel-ə-'vēv\ *or officially* **Tel Aviv-Ya·fo** \-'yä-fō\ city W Israel on the Mediterranean; *pop* 410,000

Tem·pe \tem-'pē\ city S *cen* Arizona; *pop* 161,719

Ten·nes·see \ˌte-nə-'sē, 'te-nə-ˌ\ **1** river 652 mi. (1049 km.) long in Tennessee, N Alabama, & W Kentucky **2** state E *cen* U.S.; *, Nashville; *pop* 6,346,105 — **Ten·nes·se·an** *or* **Ten·nes·see·an** \ˌte-nə-'sē-ən\ *adj or n*

Te·noch·ti·tlan \tä-ˌnóch-tēt-'län\ ancient name of Mexico City

Tex·as \'tek-səs, -siz\ state S U.S.; *, Austin; *pop* 25,145,561 — **Tex·an** \-sən\ *adj or n*

Texas Panhandle the NW projection of land in Texas

Thai·land \'tī-ˌland, -lənd\ *formerly* **Si·am** \sī-'am\ country SE Asia on Gulf of Thailand; *, Bangkok; *pop* 65,982,000 — **Thai·land·er** \-ˌlan-dər, -lən-\ *n*

Thailand, Gulf of *formerly* **Gulf of Siam** arm of South China Sea between Indochina & Malay Peninsula

Thames \'temz\ river over 200 mi. (322 km.) long S England flowing E from the Cotswolds into the North Sea

Thar \'tär\ desert E Pakistan & NW India (country) E of Indus River

Thebes \'thēbz\ **1** *or* **The·bae** \'thē-(ˌ)bē\ ancient city S Egypt on the Nile **2** ancient city E Greece NNW of Athens — **The·ban** \'thē-bən\ *adj or n*

Thes·sa·lo·ni·ki \ˌthe-sä-lō-'nē-kē\ city N Greece; *pop* 325,000

Thim·phu \tim-'pü\ city, * of Bhutan; *pop* 79,185

Thi·ru·van·an·tha·pur·am \ˌtir-ü-və-ˌnən-tə-'pür-əm\ city S India; *pop* 744,700

Thousand Islands island group Canada & U.S. in the Saint Lawrence River in Ontario & New York

Thousand Oaks city SW California W of Los Angeles; *pop* 126,683

Thrace \'thrās\ *or ancient* **Thra·cia** \'thrā-sh(ē-)ə\ region SE Europe in Balkan Peninsula N of the Aegean now divided between Greece & Turkey; in ancient times extended N to the Danube — **Thra·cian** \'thrā-shən\ *adj or n*

Thunder Bay city SW Ontario, Canada on Lake Superior; *pop* 108,359

Tian·jin \'tyän-'jin\ *or* **Tien·tsin** \'tyen-'tsin, 'tin-\ city NE China SE of Beijing; *pop* 10,190,000

Tian Shan *or* **Tien Shan** \'tyen-'shän, -'shän\ mountain system *cen* Asia extending NE from Pamirs

Ti·ber \'tī-bər\ *or Italian* **Te·ve·re** \'tä-vä-rä\ river 252 mi. (405 km.) long *cen* Italy flowing through Rome into Tyrrhenian Sea

Tiberias, Lake — see GALILEE, SEA OF

Ti·bes·ti \tə-'bes-tē\ mountains N *cen* Africa in *cen* Sahara in NW Chad; highest 11,204 ft. (3415 m.)

Ti·bet \tə-'bet\ *or* **Xi·zang** \'shēd-'zäŋ\ region SW China on high plateau at average altitude 16,000 ft. (4877 m.) N of the Himalayas; *, Lhasa; *pop* 3,002,165

Tier·ra del Fue·go \tē-'er-ə-(ˌ)del-fü-'ā-(ˌ)gō, 'tyer-ä-(ˌ)thel-'fwä-gō\ **1** island group off S South America **2** chief island of the group; divided between Argentina & Chile

Tiflis — see TBILISI

Ti·gris \'tī-grəs\ river 1180 mi. (1899 km.) long Turkey & Iraq flowing SSE and uniting with the Euphrates to form the Shatt al Arab

Ti·jua·na \ˌtē-ə-'wä-nə, tē-'hwä-nä\ city NW Mexico on the U.S. border; *pop* 1,559,683

Tim·buk·tu \ˌtim-ˌbək-ˈtü, tim-ˈbək-(ˌ)tü\ or **Tom·bouc·tou** \tōⁿ-bük-ˈtü\ town Mali near Niger River; *pop* 31,925

Ti·mor \ˈtē-ˌmȯr, tē-ˈ\ island S Malay Archipelago SE of Sulawesi; W half part of Indonesia, E half independent East Timor

Timor–Leste — see EAST TIMOR

Ti·ra·ne *or* **Ti·ra·na** \ti-ˈrä-nə, tē-\ city, ✳ of Albania; *pop* 418,495

Ti·rol *or* **Ty·rol** \tə-ˈrōl\ *or Italian* **Ti·ro·lo** \tē-ˈrȯ-(ˌ)lō\ region in E Alps in W Austria & NE Italy — **Ti·ro·le·an** \tə-ˈrō-lē-ən, tī-\ *or* **Ti·ro·lese** \ˌtir-ə-ˈlēz, ˌtī-rə-, -ˈlēs\ *adj or n*

Ti·ti·ca·ca, Lake \ˌti-ti-ˈkä-kä, ˌtē-tē-\ lake on Bolivia–Peru boundary at altitude of 12,500 ft. (3810 m.)

To·ba·go \tə-ˈbā-(ˌ)gō\ island West Indies NE of Trinidad; part of independent Trinidad and Tobago; *pop* 60,874 — **To·ba·go·ni·an** \ˌtō-bə-ˈgō-nē-ən, -nyən\ *n*

To·go \ˈtō-(ˌ)gō\ country W Africa on Gulf of Guinea; ✳, Lomé; *pop* 6,191,000 — **To·go·lese** \ˌtō-gə-ˈlēz, -ˈlēs\ *adj or n*

To·kyo \ˈtō-kē-ˌō, -ˌkyō\ city, ✳ of Japan in SE Honshu on Tokyo Bay; *pop* 8,945,695 — **To·kyo·ite** \ˈtō-kē-(ˌ)ō-ˌīt\ *n*

To·le·do \tə-ˈlē-(ˌ)dō, -ˈlē-də\ city NW Ohio; *pop* 287,208

Tol'·yat·ti \tȯl-ˈyä-tē\ city W Russia; NW of Samara; *pop* 720,000

Ton·ga \ˈtäŋ-gə, ˈtäŋ-ə, ˈtȯŋ-ä\ islands SW Pacific E of Fiji Islands; country; ✳, Nukualofa; *pop* 103,300 — **Ton·gan** \-(g)ən\ *adj or n*

Ton·kin, Gulf of \ˈtäŋ-kən\ arm of South China Sea E of N Vietnam

To·pe·ka \tə-ˈpē-kə\ city, ✳ of Kansas; *pop* 127,473

Tor·bay \(ˌ)tȯr-ˈbā\ district SW England; *pop* 131,000

To·ron·to \tə-ˈrän-(ˌ)tō, -ˈrän-tə\ city, ✳ of Ontario, Canada; *pop* 2,615,060

Tor·rance \ˈtȯr-ən(t)s, ˈtär-\ city SW California; *pop* 145,438

Tor·res \ˈtȯr-əs\ strait between New Guinea & Cape York Peninsula, Australia

Tou·louse \tü-ˈlüz\ city SW France; *pop* 441,802

Tower Hamlets borough of E Greater London, England; *pop* 254,000

Trans·vaal \tran(t)s-ˈväl, tranz-\ former province NE Republic of South Africa

Tran·syl·va·nia \ˌtran(t)-səl-ˈvā-nyə, -nē-ə\ region W Romania — **Tran·syl·va·nian** \-nyən, -nē-ən\ *adj or n*

Transylvanian Alps a S extension of Carpathian Mountains in *cen* Romania

Tren·ton \ˈtren-tᵊn\ city, ✳ of New Jersey; *pop* 84,913

Trin·i·dad \ˈtri-nə-ˌdad\ island West Indies off NE coast of Venezuela; with Tobago forms the independent country of **Trinidad and Tobago**; ✳, Port of Spain;

pop 1,328,000 — **Trin·i·da·di·an** \ˌtri-nə-ˈdä-dē-ən, -ˈda-\ *adj or n*

Trip·o·li \ˈtri-pə-lē\ **1** city & port NW Lebanon; *pop* 127,611 **2** city & port, ✳ of Libya; *pop* 591,062

Tris·tan da Cu·nha \ˌtris-tən-də-ˈkü-nə, -nyə\ island South Atlantic, chief of the Tristan da Cunha Islands (part of British colony of Saint Helena); *pop* 274

Tro·bri·and \ˈtrō-brē-ˌänd, -ˌand\ islands SW Pacific in Solomon Sea belonging to Papua New Guinea

Trond·heim \ˈträn-ˌhām\ city & port *cen* Norway; *pop* 182,035

Trow·bridge \ˈtrō-(ˌ)brij\ town S England; *pop* 39,000

Troy \ˈtrȯi\ *or* **Il·i·um** \ˈi-lē-əm\ *or* **Tro·ja** \ˈtrō-jə, -yə\ ancient city NW Asia Minor SW of the Dardanelles

Truk — see CHUUK

Tru·ro \ˈtrür-(ˌ)ō\ city SW England; *pop* 20,000

Tshwa·ne \ˈchwä-nä\ municipality Republic of South Africa which includes city of Pretoria; *pop* 2,921,488

Tsinan — see JINAN

Tsingtao — see QINGDAO

Tuc·son \ˈtü-ˌsän\ city SE Arizona; *pop* 520,116

Tu·la \ˈtü-lä\ city W Russia S of Moscow; *pop* 501,000

Tul·sa \ˈtəl-sə\ city NE Oklahoma; *pop* 391,906

Tu·nis \ˈtü-nəs, ˈtyü-\ city, ✳ of Tunisia; *pop* 674,100

Tu·ni·sia \tü-ˈnē-zh(ē-)ə, tyü-, -ˈni-\ country N Africa on the Mediterranean E of Algeria; ✳, Tunis; *pop* 10,983,000 — **Tu·ni·sian** \-zh(ē-)ən\ *adj or n*

Tu·rin \ˈtür-ən, ˈtyür-\ city NW Italy on the Po; *pop* 872,367

Tur·ka·na, Lake \tər-ˈka-nə\ *or* **Lake Ru·dolf** \ˈrü-ˌdȯlf, -ˌdälf\ lake N Kenya in Great Rift Valley

Tur·key \ˈtər-kē\ country W Asia & SE Europe between Mediterranean & Black seas; ✳, Ankara; *pop* 73,085,000 — **Turk** \ˈtərk\ *n*

Turk·men·i·stan \(ˌ)tərk-ˌme-nə-ˈstan, -ˈstän\ country *cen* Asia; ✳, Ashkhabad; *pop* 5,479,000 — **Turk·me·ni·an** \ˌtərk-ˈmē-nē-ən\ *adj*

Turks and Cai·cos \ˈtərks-ənd-ˈkā-kəs, -ˌkōs\ two groups of islands West Indies at SE end of the Bahamas; a British colony; *pop* 31,458

Tu·tu·i·la \ˌtü-tü-ˈwē-lä\ island South Pacific, chief of American Samoa group

Tu·va·lu \tü-ˈvä-(ˌ)lü, -ˈvär-(ˌ)ü\ *formerly* **El·lice** \ˈe-lis\ islands W Pacific N of Fiji; country; ✳, Funafuti; *pop* 11,000 — see GILBERT AND ELLICE ISLANDS

Tyne and Wear \ˈtīn-ənd-ˈwir\ metropolitan county N England; *pop* 1,105,000

Tyre \ˈtī(-ə)r\ ancient city, ✳ of Phoenicia; now a town of S Lebanon — **Tyr·i-an** \'tir-ē-ən\ *adj or n*

Tyrol — see TIROL — **Ty·ro·le·an** \tə-'rō-lē-ən, tī-\ *adj or n* — **Ty·ro·lese** \,tir-ə-'lēz, ,tī-rə-, -'lēs\ *adj or n*

Tyr·rhe·ni·an Sea \tə-'rē-nē-ən\ the part of the Mediterranean SW of Italy, N of Sicily, & E of Sardinia & Corsica

Ufa \ü-'fä\ city W Russia NE of Samara; *pop* 1,062,000

Ugan·da \ü-'gän-də, yü-, -'gan-\ country E Africa N of Lake Victoria; ✳, Kampala; *pop* 34,857,000 — **Ugan·dan** \-dən\ *adj or n*

Ukraine \yü-'krän, 'yü-,\ country E Europe on N coast of Black Sea; ✳, Kiev; *pop* 45,500,000 — **Ukrai·ni·an** \yü-'krä-nē-ən\ *adj or n*

Ulaan·baa·tar or **Ulan Ba·tor** \ü-,län-'bä-,tór\ city, ✳ of Mongolia; *pop* 1,088,000

Ul·san \'ül-'sän\ city SE South Korea; *pop* 1,130,500

Ul·ster \'əl-stər\ 1 region N Ireland (island) consisting of Northern Ireland & N Ireland (country) 2 province N Ireland (country); *pop* 295,000 3 NORTHERN IRELAND

Ulu·ru \ü-'lü-rü\ or **Ayers Rock** \'erz\ outcrop *cen* Australia in SW Northern Territory

Um·bria \'əm-brē-ə\ region *cen* Italy in the Apennines; *pop* 884,268

Un·ga·va \,ən-'ga-və\ 1 bay, inlet of Hudson Strait NE Canada 2 peninsula region NE Canada in N Quebec

Union of South Africa — see SOUTH AFRICA, REPUBLIC OF

Union of Soviet Socialist Republics or **U.S.S.R.** or **Soviet Union** country 1922–91 E Europe & N Asia; former union of 15 republics comprising present-day countries of Armenia, Azerbaijan, Belarus, Estonia, Georgia, Kazakhstan, Krygyzstan, Latvia, Lithuania, Moldova, Russia, Tajikistan, Turkmenistan, Ukraine, & Uzbekistan

United Arab Emir·ates \'e-mə-rəts, -,rāts\ country E Arabia on Persian Gulf; composed of seven emirates; ✳, Abu Dhabi; *pop* 4,105,000

United Kingdom or in full **United Kingdom of Great Britain and Northern Ireland** country W Europe in British Isles consisting of England, Scotland, Wales, Northern Ireland, Channel Islands, & Isle of Man; ✳, London; *pop* 63,182,000

United Nations political organization established in 1945 with headquarters in international territory in New York City

United States of America or **United States** country North America bordering on Atlantic, Pacific, & Arctic oceans & including Hawaii; ✳, Washington; *pop* 308,745,538

Upper Volta — see BURKINA FASO —
Upper Vol·tan \'väl-t°n, 'vōl-, 'vòl-\ *adj or n*

Ural \'yùr-əl\ 1 mountains Russia & Kazakhstan extending about 1640 mi. (2640 km.); usually thought of as dividing line between Europe & Asia; highest about 6214 ft. (1894 m.) 2 river over 1500 mi. (2414 km.) long Russia & Kazakhstan flowing from S end of Ural Mountains into Caspian Sea

Uru·guay \'ùr-ə-,gwī, 'yùr-\ 1 river about 1000 mi. (1609 km.) long SE South America 2 country SE South America; ✳, Montevideo; *pop* 3,286,314 — **Uru·guay·an** \,ùr-ə-'gwī-ən, ,yùr-\ *adj or n*

Ürüm·qi \'ue-'rəm-'chē\ or **Urum·chi** \ù-'rùm-chē, ,ùr-əm-'\ city NW China; *pop* 2,941,000

Us·pa·lla·ta \,üs-pä-'yä-tä, -'zhä-\ mountain pass S South America in the Andes between Argentina & Chile

Ustinov — see IZHEVSK

Utah \'yü-,tò, -,tä\ state W U.S.; ✳, Salt Lake City; *pop* 2,763,885 — **Utah·an** \-,tò(-ə)n, -,tä(-ə)n\ *adj or n* — **Utahn** \-,tò(-ə)n, -,tä(-ə)n\ *n*

Uz·bek·i·stan \(,)ùz-,be-ki-'stan, ,əz-, -'stän\ country W *cen* Asia between Aral Sea & Afghanistan; ✳, Tashkent; *pop* 30,000,000

Va·duz \vä-'düts\ town, ✳ of Liechtenstein; *pop* 5400

Val·dez \val-'dēz\ city & port S Alaska; *pop* 4949

Va·len·cia \və-'len(t)-sh(ē-)ə, -sē-ə\ 1 region & ancient kingdom E Spain 2 city, its ✳, on the Mediterranean; *pop* 792,000

Val·le·jo \və-'lā-(,)ō\ city W California; *pop* 115,942

Valley Forge locality SE Pennsylvania

Val·let·ta \və-'le-tə\ city, ✳ of Malta; *pop* 5760

Van·cou·ver \van-'kü-vər\ 1 city SW Washington on Columbia River opposite Portland, Oregon; *pop* 161,791 2 island W Canada in SW British Columbia 3 city & port SW British Columbia, Canada; *pop* 603,502

Van Diemen's Land — see TASMANIA

Van·u·atu \,van-,wä-'tü, ,vän-\ *formerly* **New Heb·ri·des** \'he-brə-,dēz\ islands SW Pacific W of Fiji; country; ✳, Port=Vila; *pop* 234,000

Va·ra·na·si \və-'rä-nə-sē\ city N India; *pop* 1,432,280

Vat·i·can City \'va-ti-kən\ independent state within Rome, Italy; *pop* 800

Ven·e·zu·e·la \,ve-nə-'zwā-lə, -zə-'wā-; ,bä-nä-'swä-lä\ country N South America; ✳, Caracas; *pop* 29,000,000 — **Ven·e·zu·e·lan** \-lən\ *adj or n*

Ven·ice \'ve-nəs\ or *Italian* **Ve·ne·zia** \ve-'net-sē-ä\ city N Italy on islands in Lagoon of Venice; *pop* 261,362 — **Ve·ne·tian** \və-'nē-shən\ *adj or n*

Ven·tu·ra \ven-'tūr-ə, -'tyūr-\ city & port SW California; *pop* 106,433

Ve·ra·cruz \ˌver-ə-'krüz, -'krüs\ city E Mexico; *pop* 552,156

Ver·mont \vər-'mänt\ state NE U.S.; *, Montpelier; *pop* 625,741 — **Ver·mont·er** \-'män-tər\ *n*

Ve·ro·na \ve-'rō-nä\ city N Italy W of Venice; *pop* 252,520

Ver·sailles \(ˌ)vər-'sī, ver-\ city N France, WSW suburb of Paris; *pop* 86,110

Ve·su·vi·us \və-'sü-vē-əs\ volcano about 4190 ft. (1277 m.) S Italy near Bay of Naples

Vicks·burg \'viks-ˌbərg\ city W Mississippi; *pop* 23,856

Vic·to·ria \vik-'tōr-ē-ə\ **1** city, * of British Columbia, Canada on Vancouver Island; *pop* 80,017 **2** island N Canada in Arctic Archipelago **3** state SE Australia; *, Melbourne; *pop* 5,354,042 **4** city & port, Hong Kong; *pop* 1,035,000 **5** seaport, * of Seychelles; *pop* 26,000 — **Vic·to·ri·an** \vik-'tōr-ē-ən\ *adj or n*

Victoria, Lake lake E Africa in Tanzania, Kenya, & Uganda

Victoria Falls waterfall 355 ft. (108 m.) S Africa in the Zambezi on border between Zambia & Zimbabwe

Vi·en·na \vē-'e-nə\ *or German* **Wien** \'vēn\ city, * of Austria on the Danube; *pop* 1,700,000 — **Vi·en·nese** \ˌvē-ə-'nēz, -'nēs\ *adj or n*

Vien·tiane \(ˌ)vyen-'tyän\ city, * of Laos; *pop* 200,000

Vie·ques \vē-'ā-kās\ island Puerto Rico off E end of main island; *pop* 9301

Viet·nam \vē-'et-'näm, vyet-, ˌvē-ət-, vēt-, -'nam\ country SE Asia in Indochina; *, Hanoi; *pop* 85,847,000 ; divided 1954–75 into the independent states of **North Vietnam** (*, Hanoi) & **South Vietnam** (*, Saigon) — **Viet·nam·ese** \vē-ˌet-nə-'mēz, ˌvyet-, ˌvē-ət-, ˌvēt-, -na-, -nä-, -'mēs\ *adj or n*

Vila — see PORT-VILA

Vi·la No·va de Ga·ia \'vē-lə-'nō-və-də-'gī-ə\ city NW Portugal; *pop* 302,295

Vil·ni·us \'vil-nē-əs\ city, * of Lithuania; *pop* 524,000

Vin·land \'vin-lənd\ a portion of the coast of North America visited & so called by Norse voyagers about 1000 A.D.; thought to be located along the North Atlantic in what is now E or NE Canada

Vir·gin·ia \vər-'ji-nyə, -'ji-nē-ə\ state E U.S.; *, Richmond; *pop* 8,001,024 — **Vir·gin·ian** \-nyən, -nē-ən\ *adj or n*

Virginia Beach city SE Virginia; *pop* 437,994

Virginia City locality W Nevada; *pop* 855

Virgin Islands island group West Indies E of Puerto Rico — see BRITISH VIRGIN ISLANDS, VIRGIN ISLANDS OF THE UNITED STATES

Virgin Islands of the United States the W islands of the Virgin Islands; U.S. territory; *, Charlotte Amalie (on Saint Thomas); *pop* 106,405

Vi·sa·yan \və-'sī-ən\ islands *cen* Philippines

Vish·a·kha·pat·nam \vi-ˌshä-kə-'pət-nəm\ *or* **Vis·a·kha·pat·nam** \vi-ˌsä-\ city E India; *pop* 1,728,128

Vis·tu·la \'vis-chə-lə, 'vish-chə-, 'vis-tə-\ river over 660 mi. (1062 km.) long Poland flowing N from the Carpathians

Vi·ti Le·vu \ˌvē-tē-'le-(ˌ)vü\ island SW Pacific; largest of the Fiji group

Vlad·i·vos·tok \ˌvla-də-və-'stäk, -'väs-ˌtäk\ city & port SE Russia on an inlet of Sea of Japan; *pop* 592,000

Vol·ga \'väl-gə, 'vol-, 'vōl-\ river about 2300 mi. (3700 km.) long W Russia; longest river in Europe

Vol·go·grad \'väl-gə-ˌgrad, 'vol-, 'vōl-, -ˌgrät\ city S Russia in Europe, on the Volga; *pop* 1,021,000

Vol·ta \'väl-tə, 'vōl-, 'vol-\ river about 300 mi. (485 km.) long Ghana flowing from **Lake Volta** (reservoir) into Gulf of Guinea

Vo·ro·nezh \və-'rō-nish\ city S *cen* Russia in Europe; *pop* 932,500

Vosges \'vōzh\ mountains NE France on W side of Rhine valley

Wa·co \'wā-(ˌ)kō\ city *cen* Texas; *pop* 124,805

Wad·den·zee \ˌvä-dᵊn-'zā\ inlet of the North Sea N Netherlands

Wake \'wāk\ island North Pacific N of Marshall Islands; U.S. territory

Wake·field \'wāk-ˌfēld\ city N England; *pop* 99,000

Wa·la·chia *or* **Wal·la·chia** \wä-'lä-kē-ə\ region S Romania between Transylvanian Alps & the Danube

Wales \'wālz\ *or Welsh* **Cym·ru** \'kəm-ˌrē\ principality SW Great Britain; a division of United Kingdom; *, Cardiff; *pop* 3,063,456

Wal·lo·nia \wä-'lō-nē-ə\ semiautonomous region S Belgium; *pop* 3,600,000

Wal·sall \'wol-ˌsol, -səl\ town W *cen* England; *pop* 68,000

Wal·tham Forest \'wol-thəm\ borough of NE Greater London, England; *pop* 258,000

Wal·vis Bay \'wol-vəs\ town & port W Namibia on Walvis Bay (inlet of the Atlantic); formerly administered by Republic of South Africa; *pop* 61,700

Wands·worth \'wän(d)z-(ˌ)wərth\ borough of SW Greater London, England; *pop* 307,000

War·ren \'wor-ən, 'wär-\ city SE Michigan; *pop* 134,056

War·saw \'wor-ˌso\ *or Polish* **War·sza·wa**

\vär-'shä-vä\ city, ✳ of Poland; *pop* 1,700,000

War·wick \'wär-ik\ town *cen* England; *pop* 31,000

War·wick·shire \'wär-ik-,shir, -shər\ *or* **Warwick** county *cen* England

Wa·satch \'wȯ-,sach\ range of the Rockies SE Idaho & N *cen* Utah; highest Mount Timpanogos 12,008 ft. (3660 m.), in Utah

Wash·ing·ton \'wȯ-shiŋ-tən, 'wä-\ **1** state NW U.S.; ✳, Olympia; *pop* 6,724,540 **2** city, ✳ of U.S.; having the same boundaries as District of Columbia; *pop* 601,723 — **Wash·ing·to·nian** \,wȯ-shiŋ-'tō-nē-ən, ,wä-, -nyən\ *adj or n*

Washington, Mount mountain 6288 ft. (1916 m.) N New Hampshire; highest in White Mountains

Wa·ter·bury \'wȯ-tə(r)-,ber-ē, 'wä-\ city W *cen* Connecticut; *pop* 110,366

Wei·mar Republic \'vī-,mär, 'wī-\ the German republic 1919–33

Wel·land \'we-lənd\ canal 27 mi. (44 km.) long SE Ontario connecting Lake Erie & Lake Ontario

Wel·ling·ton \'we-liŋ-tən\ city, ✳ of New Zealand; *pop* 179,466

Wes·sex \'we-siks\ ancient kingdom S England

West Bank area Middle East W of Jordan River; occupied by Israel since 1967 with parts having been transferred to Palestinian administration since 1993

West Brom·wich \'brä-mich\ town W *cen* England; *pop* 73,000

West Co·vi·na \kō-'vē-nə\ city SW California; *pop* 106,098

Western Australia state W Australia; ✳, Perth; *pop* 2,239,170 — **Western Australian** *adj or n*

Western Cape province SW Republic of South Africa; *pop* 5,822,734

Western Ghats — see GHATS

Western Hemisphere the half of the earth lying W of the Atlantic Ocean & comprising North America, South America, & surrounding waters

Western Isles former administrative area of W Scotland consisting of the Outer Hebrides

Western Sahara *formerly* **Spanish Sahara** territory NW Africa; occupied by Morocco; *pop* 522,000

Western Samoa — see SAMOA

West Germany — see GERMANY

West Indies islands lying between SE North America & N South America & consisting of the Greater Antilles, Lesser Antilles, & Bahamas — **West Indian** *adj or n*

West Midlands metropolitan county W *cen* England; includes Birmingham

West·min·ster \'wes(t)-,min(t)-stər\ city N *cen* Colorado NW of Denver; *pop* 106,114

West Pakistan the former W division of Pakistan now having the same boundaries as Pakistan

West·pha·lia \west-'fāl-yə, -'fā-lē-ə\ region W Germany E of the Rhine — **West·pha·lian** \west-'fāl-yən, -'fā-lē-ən\ *adj or n*

West Point site SE New York of United States Military Academy on W bank of Hudson River N of New York City

West Quod·dy Head \'kwä-dē\ cape; most easterly point of Maine & of the Lower 48

West Sus·sex \'sə-siks\ county SE England; *pop* 806,892

West Valley City city N Utah S of Salt Lake City; *pop* 129,480

West Virginia state E U.S.; ✳, Charleston; *pop* 1,852,994 — **West Virginian** *adj or n*

West York·shire metropolitan county NW England; includes Wakefield

White sea NW Russia in Europe

White·horse \'hwīt-,hȯrs, 'wīt-\ city, ✳ of Yukon, Canada; *pop* 23,276

White Mountains mountains N New Hampshire in the Appalachians — see WASHINGTON, MOUNT

Whit·ney, Mount \'hwit-nē, 'wit-\ mountain 14,495 ft. (4418 m.) SE *cen* California in Sierra Nevada; highest in U.S. outside of Alaska

Wich·i·ta \'wi-chə-,tȯ\ city S Kansas; *pop* 382,368

Wichita Falls city N Texas; *pop* 104,553

Wien — see VIENNA

Wight, Isle of — see ISLE OF WIGHT

Wil·lem·stad \'vi-ləm-,stät\ city, formerly ✳ of Netherlands Antilles; *pop* 93,600

Wil·liams·burg \'wil-yəmz-,bərg\ city SE Virginia; *pop* 14,068

Wil·ming·ton \'wil-miŋ-tən\ city N Delaware; largest in state; *pop* 70,851

Wilt·shire \'wilt-,shir, -shər\ county S England; *pop* 470,981

Win·ches·ter \'win-,ches-tər, -chəs-tər\ city S England; *pop* 45,000

Win·der·mere \'win-də(r)-,mir\ lake NW England in Lake District

Wind·hoek \'vint-,húk\ city, ✳ of Namibia; *pop* 233,529

Wind·sor \'win-zər\ city S Ontario, Canada on Detroit River; *pop* 210,891

Wind·ward Islands \'wind-wərd\ islands West Indies in the S Lesser Antilles extending S from Martinique but not including Barbados, Tobago, or Trinidad

Win·ni·peg \'wi-nə-,peg\ city, ✳ of Manitoba, Canada; *pop* 663,617

Winnipeg, Lake lake S *cen* Manitoba, Canada

Win·ni·pe·sau·kee, Lake \,wi-nə-pə-'sȯ-kē\ lake *cen* New Hampshire

Win·ston–Sa·lem \,win(t)-stən-'sā-ləm\ city N *cen* North Carolina; *pop* 229,617

Geographical Names

938

Wis·con·sin \wi-'skän(t)-sən\ state N cen U.S.; ✻, Madison; *pop* 5,686,986 — **Wis·con·sin·ite** \-sə-ˌnīt\ *n*

Wit·wa·ters·rand \'wit-ˌwȯ-tərz-ˌrand, -ˌwä-, -ˌränd, -ˌränt\ ridge of gold-bearing rock NE Republic of South Africa

Wol·lon·gong \'wu̇-lən-ˌgäŋ, -ˌgȯŋ\ city SE Australia in E New South Wales S of Sydney; *pop* 245,942

Wol·ver·hamp·ton \ˌwu̇l-vər-'ham(p)-tən\ town W cen England NW of Birmingham; *pop* 210,000

Worces·ter \'wu̇s-tər\ city E cen Massachusetts; *pop* 181,045

Wran·gell, Mount \'raŋ-gəl\ volcano 14,163 ft. (4317 m.) S Alaska in **Wrangell Mountains**

Wro·claw \'vrȯt-ˌswäf, -ˌsläv\ city SW Poland in Silesia; *pop* 630,500

Wu·han \'wü-'hän\ city E cen China; *pop* 8,663,500

Wu·xi or **Wu–hsi** \'wü-'shē\ city E China; *pop* 3,151,000

Wy·o·ming \wī-'ō-miŋ\ state NW U.S.; ✻, Cheyenne; *pop* 563,626 — **Wy·o·ming·ite** \-miŋ-ˌīt\ *n*

Xi'·an or **Hsi–an** \'shē-'än\ city E cen China; *pop* 5,853,500

Xianggang — see HONG KONG

Xin·jiang Uy·gur or **Sin·kiang Ui·ghur** \'shin-'jyän-'wē-gər\ region W China between the Kunlun & Altai mountains; *pop* 21,815,815

Xizang — see TIBET

Xu·zhou \'shü-'jō\ or **Sü·chow** \'shü-'jō, 'sü-\ city E China; *pop* 2,634,500

Yak·i·ma \'ya-kə-ˌmȯ\ city S cen Washington; *pop* 91,067

Ya·lu \'yä-(ˌ)lü\ river 500 mi. (804 km.) long SE Manchuria & North Korea

Ya·mous·sou·kro \ˌyä-mə-'sü-krō\ town, official ✻ of Cote d'Ivoire; *pop* 207,412

Yan·gon \ˌyän-'gȯn\ formerly **Ran·goon** \ran-'gün, raŋ-\ city, former ✻ of Myanmar; *pop* 4,477,600

Yangtze — see CHANG

Yaoun·dé \yaün-'dā\ city, ✻ of Cameroon; *pop* 1,817,524

Yap \'yap, 'yäp\ island W Pacific in the W Carolines; *pop* 11,377

Ya·ren \'yä-ˌrən\ district containing ✻ of Nauru; *pop* 747

Ya·ro·slavl \ˌyär-ə-'slä-vᵊl\ city cen Russia in Europe, NE of Moscow; *pop* 591,486

Yaz·oo \ya-'zü, 'ya-(ˌ)zü\ river W cen Mississippi

Ye·ka·te·rin·burg \yi-ˌka-tə-rən-ˌbȯrg, yi-ˌka-ti-rēm-'bu̇rk\ formerly **Sverd·lovsk** \sverd-'lȯfsk\ city W Russia, in cen Ural Mountains; *pop* 1,350,000

Yellow 1 — see HUANG **2** sea, section of East China Sea between N China, North Korea, & South Korea

Yel·low·knife \'ye-lō-ˌnīf\ town, ✻ of Northwest Territories, Canada; *pop* 19,234

Ye·men \'ye-mən\ country S Arabia bordering on Red Sea & Gulf of Aden; ✻, Sanaa; *pop* 24,500,000 — **Ye·me·ni** \'ye-mə-nē\ *adj* or *n* — **Ye·men·ite** \-mə-ˌnīt\ *adj* or *n*

Ye·ni·sey or **Ye·ni·sei** \ˌyi-ni-'sā\ river over 2500 mi. (4022 km.) long cen Russia, flowing N into Arctic Ocean

Ye·re·van \ˌyer-ə-'vän\ city, ✻ of Armenia; *pop* 1,100,000

Yo·ko·ha·ma \ˌyō-kō-'hä-mä\ city Japan in SE Honshu on Tokyo Bay S of Tokyo; *pop* 3,688,773

Yon·kers \'yäŋ-kərz\ city SE New York N of New York City; *pop* 195,976

York \'yȯrk\ city N England; *pop* 153,000

York, Cape cape NE Australia in Queensland at N tip of Cape York Peninsula

York·shire \-ˌshir, -shər\ former county N England

Yo·sem·i·te Falls \yō-'se-mə-tē\ waterfall E California in Yosemite Valley; includes two falls, the upper 1430 ft. (436 m.) & the lower 320 ft. (98 m.)

Youngs·town \'yəŋz-ˌtau̇n\ city NE Ohio; *pop* 66,982

Yu·ca·tan \ˌyü-kə-'tan, -kä-'tän\ peninsula SE Mexico & N Central America including Belize & N Guatemala

Yu·go·sla·via \ˌyü-gō-'slä-vē-ə, ˌyü-gə-\ **1** former country S Europe including Serbia, Montenegro, Slovenia, Croatia, Bosnia and Herzegovina, & Macedonia; ✻, Belgrade **2** — see SERBIA AND MONTENEGRO — **Yu·go·slav** \ˌyü-gō-'släv, -'slav; 'yü-gō-ˌ\ or **Yu·go·sla·vi·an** \ˌyü-gō-'slä-vē-ən, -gə-\ *adj* or *n*

Yu·kon \'yü-ˌkän\ **1** river 1979 mi. (3185 km.) long NW Canada & Alaska flowing into Bering Sea **2** or formerly **Yukon Territory** territory NW Canada; ✻, Whitehorse; *pop* 33,897

Yu·ma \'yü-mə\ city SW corner of Arizona on the Colorado; *pop* 93,064

Za·greb \'zä-ˌgreb\ city, ✻ of Croatia; *pop* 687,000

Zaire \zä-'ir\ **1** river in Africa — see CONGO 1 **2** country in Africa — see CONGO 2 — **Zair·ean** or **Zair·ian** \zä-'ir-ē-ən\ *adj* or *n*

Zam·be·zi or **Zam·be·si** \zam-'bē-zē, zäm-'bä-zē\ river about 1700 mi. (2735 km.) long SE Africa flowing from NW Zambia into Mozambique Channel

Zam·bia \'zam-bē-ə\ formerly **Northern Rhodesia** country S Africa N of the Zambezi; ✻, Lusaka; *pop* 13,200,000 — **Zam·bi·an** \'zam-bē-ən\ *adj* or *n*

Zan·zi·bar \'zan-zə-ˌbär\ island Tanzania off NE Tanganyika coast; united 1964 with Tanganyika forming Tanzania

Za·po·rizh·zhya or **Za·po·ro·zh'ye** \ˌzäpə-ʹrēzh-zhyə\ city SE Ukraine; *pop* 815,000

Zhang·jia·kou \ʹjäŋ-ʹjyä-ʹkō\ *or* **Kal·gan** \ʹkal-ʹgan\ city NE China NW of Beijing; *pop* 925,000

Zhdanov — see MARIUPOL

Zheng·zhou *or* **Cheng–chou** \ʹjəŋ-ʹjō\ city NE *cen* China; *pop* 3,965,500

Zim·ba·bwe \zim-ʹbä-bwē, -(ˌ)bwä\ *for-* merly **Rhodesia** country S Africa S of Zambezi River; ✳, Harare; *pop* 13,061,000 — **Zim·ba·bwe·an** \-ən\ *adj or n*

Zui·der Zee \ˌzī-dər-ʹzā, -ʹzē\ — see IJS-SELMEER

Zu·lu·land \ʹzü-(ˌ)lü-ˌland\ territory E Republic of South Africa on Indian Ocean

Zu·rich \ʹzur-ik\ city N Switzerland; *pop* 363,300